This Book
was donated to the
Richmond Public Library
By

THE FRIENDS OF THE RICHMOND
PUBLIC LIBRARY

AFRICANA

THE ENCYCLOPEDIA OF THE AFRICAN AND AFRICAN AMERICAN EXPERIENCE

SECOND EDITION

ADVISORY BOARD

Wole Soyinka, *Chairman*
1986 Nobel Laureate in Literature;
Robert W. Woodruff Professor of the Arts, Emory University

Kofi Agawu
Princeton University

Sara S. Berry
Johns Hopkins University

Suzanne Preston Blier
Harvard University

Lawrence Bobo
Harvard University

Frederick Cooper
New York University

Moore Crossey
Yale University

Selwyn R. Cudjoe
Wellesley College

Jacques d'Adesky
Centros de Estudos das Américas

Howard Dodson
Schomburg Center for Research in Black Culture

Anani Dzidzienyo
Brown University

David Eltis
Emory University

Paul Gilroy
Yale University

Jane Guyer
Johns Hopkins University

Martin Hall
University of Cape Town

Stuart Hall
The Open University, United Kingdom

Evelyn Brooks Higginbotham
Harvard University

Paulin J. Hountondji
African Institute for Advanced Study at Porto Novo, Benin

John Hunwick
Northwestern University

Abiola Irele
Harvard University

Miriam Jiménez-Roman
Columbia University

Randall Kennedy
Harvard University

Jamaica Kincaid
Harvard University

Marvín Lewis
University of Missouri at Columbia

J. Lorand Matory
Harvard University

Ali A. Mazrui
State University of New York at Binghamton

Lucia Nagib
Pontificia Universidade Católica de São Paulo

Nell Irvin Painter
Princeton University

Hans Panofsky
Northwestern University

Orlando Patterson
Harvard University

Arnold Rampersad
Stanford University

Thomas E. Skidmore
Brown University

Werner Sollors
Harvard University

Doris Sommer
Harvard University

Claude Steele
Stanford University

Cornel West
Princeton University

William Julius Wilson
Harvard University

AFRICANA

The Encyclopedia of the African and African American Experience

SECOND EDITION

Editors

Kwame Anthony Appiah
Laurance S. Rockefeller University Professor of Philosophy and the University Center for Human Values, Princeton University

Henry Louis Gates, Jr.
W. E. B. Du Bois Professor of the Humanities Chair of the Department of African and African American Studies, Harvard University

VOLUME 4
Michael–Sobukwe

2005

OXFORD
UNIVERSITY PRESS

Oxford University Press, Inc., publishes works that further
Oxford University's objective of excellence
in research, scholarship, and education.

Oxford   New York
Auckland   Cape Town   Dar es Salaam   Hong Kong   Karachi
Kuala Lumpur   Madrid   Melbourne   Mexico City   Nairobi
New Delhi   Shanghai   Taipei   Toronto

With offices in
Argentina   Austria   Brazil   Chile   Czech Republic   France   Greece
Guatemala   Hungary   Italy   Japan   Poland   Portugal   Singapore
South Korea   Switzerland   Thailand   Turkey   Ukraine   Vietnam

Copyright © 2005 by Oxford University Press, Inc.

Published by Oxford University Press, Inc.
198 Madison Avenue, New York, New York, 10016
http://www.oup.com/us

Oxford is a registered trademark of Oxford University Press

All rights reserved. No part of this publication may be reproduced,
stored in a retrieval system, or transmitted, in any form or by any means,
electronic, mechanical, photocopying, recording, or otherwise,
without the prior permission of Oxford University Press.

Library of Congress Cataloging-in-Publication Data

Africana : the encyclopedia of the African and African American experience / editors,
Kwame Anthony Appiah, Henry Louis Gates, Jr.—2nd ed.
v. cm.
Includes bibliographical references and index.
ISBN-13: 978-0-19-517055-9 (set)   ISBN-10: 0-19-517055-5 (set)
ISBN-13: 978-0-19-522325-5 (v. 1 : alk. paper) ISBN-10: 0-19-522325-X (v. 1 : alk. paper)
ISBN-13: 978-0-19-522326-2 (v. 2 : alk. paper) ISBN-10: 0-19-522326-8 (v. 2 : alk. paper)
ISBN-13: 978-0-19-522327-9 (v. 3 : alk. paper) ISBN-10: 0-19-522327-6 (v. 3 : alk. paper)
ISBN-13: 978-0-19-522328-6 (v. 4 : alk. paper) ISBN-10: 0-19-522328-4 (v. 4 : alk. paper)
ISBN-13: 978-0-19-522329-3 (v. 5 : alk. paper) ISBN-10: 0-19-522329-2 (v. 5 : alk. paper)
1. Africa—Civilization—Encyclopedias. 2. Blacks—Encyclopedias. 3. African diaspora—Encyclopedias.
4. African Americans—Encyclopedias. I. Title: Encyclopedia of the African and African American experience.
II. Appiah, Anthony. III. Gates, Henry Louis.
DT14.A37435 2005
960'.03—dc22
2004020222

Printed in China

M
(continued)

Michael, Theodor

1925?–

African German editor, civil servant, and theater artist who survived Nazi oppression.

Theodor Michael grew up in Germany, in one of only about sixty black families living there in the early twentieth-century. His father, Theophilus Wonja Michael, had emigrated from CAMEROON in the late 1800s, after studying theology at Oxford University and deciding against a career as a pastor in Cameroon. He settled in the German capital of Berlin and married a white German woman with whom he had four children. Although black families were rare in Germany at that time, Theodor Michael has stated that his early years were free from racial discrimination. When the Nazi Party came to power in the 1930s, however, the government instituted new policies based on the assumption of "Aryan" racial superiority. These policies deemed blacks to be intellectually inferior to whites and incapable of receiving training for any profession. Nazi laws forbade Michael and other blacks from attending school. His siblings managed to escape to France, but Michael was unable to leave Germany. The Nazis declared him stateless and sent him, at the age of eighteen, to a forced labor camp where he remained for the duration of World War II.

Michael's strong evangelical faith helped him to survive the camp's horrific conditions, including twelve-hour workdays and insufficient food. When the war ended, Michael enrolled in the University of Bayreuth, where he studied political science and obtained a degree. After a job as editor of the Deutsche Welle program *African Bulletin,* he began a thirty-year career in the civil service. He also acted on the stage, appearing in several plays.

Michael grew up surrounded by German cultural influences and considers himself "a real Prussian" yet also notes that he has "a very deep African root". Michael developed an interest in African subjects at an early age, and after the war he was able to learn more about black cultural expressions, such as classical JAZZ, which had been vilified by the Nazis and for which he has developed a deep appreciation. He has also spoken out on the subject of racial discrimination in Germany, which has attracted a growing number of African immigrants in recent years. African communities in Germany still lack legal protection from race-based discrimination, which stems, Michael believes, from competition for jobs. Although African immigrants face difficulties in present-day Germany, Michael believes that they should remain in the country, adapting in some ways to European customs while at the same time fighting for full legal rights.

In his later years, Michael has become more active in the theater. His recent stage projects include a tour of Germany with the play *I Have a Dream,* based on the life and work of MARTIN LUTHER KING JR. As Michael remarked in an interview in the *African Courier,* "What connects all of us is our skin colour, and it should be a source of our solidarity. We should all struggle and fight against injustice anywhere and against any human being."

Elizabeth Shostak

Michaux, Lightfoot Solomon

1884–1968

African American radio evangelist.

Lightfoot Solomon Michaux was born in Newport News, Virginia, the son of John Michaux, a fish peddler and grocer, and May Blanche. Lightfoot, whose ancestry was African, Indian, and French-Jewish, spent his formative years in Newport News among Jewish and white gentile merchants on Jefferson Avenue, the main commercial street where the Michauxs lived in quarters above the family's store. He attended the Twenty-second Street School, quitting after the fourth grade to become a seafood peddler. Impressed with the town's commercial atmosphere, he aspired to be a successful businessman. While engaged in one business venture, he met Mary Eliza Pauline, a mulatto orphan. They married in 1906; the couple had no children of their own but helped raise Michaux's two young sisters.

During WORLD WAR I, Michaux obtained government contracts to furnish food to defense establishments. With the profits from his enterprises he moved his business to Hopewell, Virginia, in 1917. Finding no churches in that wartime boomtown, he and his wife joined with a Filipino evangelist to found a church there. Michaux's wife subsequently convinced him to accept the call to preach, and in 1918 he was licensed and ordained in the Church of Christ (Holiness) U.S.A. He returned to Newport News in 1919, went into business with his father, and launched a tent revival. The first 150 of Michaux's converts formed a congregation within the Church of Christ denomination. In 1921 the Michaux congregation seceded from the Church of Christ to establish an independent church, calling it the Church of God. This church, along with its other related operations, was incorporated under an umbrella grouping known as the Gospel Spreading Tabernacle Association. In 1922 Michaux and several of his members were arrested for singing on the streets of Newport News during early morning hours while inviting townsfolk to join the church. When Michaux was fined, he unsuccessfully appealed to the Virginia Supreme Court, contending that his actions were based on a directive from God. In 1924 he began to establish branch churches in cities along the East Coast as he followed members who had migrated north to find jobs during the postwar recession.

Michaux began his radio ministry in 1929 at station WJSV in WASHINGTON, D.C., and became famous as a radio evangelist. The broadcast moved to the Columbia Broadcasting System (CBS) in 1932, the eve of radio's golden era. As a result of the radio program's syncopated signature song, "Happy Am I," Michaux became known from coast to coast and overseas as the "'Happy Am I' Preacher." His aphorisms and fundamentalist-like sermons of hope and good neighborliness caught the attention of millions. His wife, an exhorter and the premiere broadcast soloist, was a regular on the radio program. Michaux's radio program was so popular that American and foreign dignitaries flocked to his live, theatrically staged radio broadcasts. The British Broadcasting Corporation contracted with him for two broadcasts in the British Empire, in 1936 and 1938. Booking agents and moviemakers offered him contracts. In 1942 he collaborated with Jack Goldberg to make one commercial film, *We've Come a Long, Long Way*.

During the GREAT DEPRESSION, Michaux used his radio pulpit to offer free housing and employment services to the black and white indigent, and he invited the hungry to sell copies of the church's *Happy News* paper in exchange for meals in the Happy News Cafe. After President Herbert Hoover evicted the Bonus Army (15,000 unemployed World War I veterans and their families who converged on the capital in 1932 to demand immediate payment of bonuses that were not due until 1945), for which Michaux had been holding worship services, Michaux used his radio pulpit to campaign for Franklin Delano Roosevelt in 1932, 1936, and 1940. For this reason, observers credit Michaux with influencing the first African Americans to leave the REPUBLICAN PARTY and enter the DEMOCRATIC fold in 1932. Political observers were baffled therefore when, in 1952, Michaux campaigned as vigorously for Republican candidate Dwight Eisenhower as he had for Roosevelt and Harry Truman.

Crowds attended Michaux's annual baptisms, which he moved from the Potomac River bank in 1938 and held in Griffith Stadium until 1961. These patriotically festooned stadium services were full of pageantry, fireworks, and enthralling precision drills and choral singing from the 156-voice Cross Choir. Vocal renditions were supported by the syncopated instrumentation of the church band, while hundreds were baptized annually in a canvas-covered tank at center field. About Michaux and his baptismal services, Bill Sunday quipped that "any man who had to hire a national baseball park, seating 35,000 to hold . . . meetings is the man to preach the gospel."

One reporter observed that Michaux should "not be passed off as just another gospel spreader . . . but should be regarded as a shrewd businessman." He had made lucrative deals in real estate, such as the 1934 purchase of 1,800 acres of land along the beachfront in Jamestown, Virginia, where he intended to develop a National Memorial to the Progress of the Colored Race of America. His plans for selling investment shares fell through when lawsuits that alleged mismanagement of monies were filed against him. Around 1940 he purchased the old Benning Race Track in Washington and received $3.5 million from the Reconstruction Finance Corporation to construct Mayfair Mansions, a 594-unit housing development, which was completed in 1946. Despite allegations on Capitol Hill in the 1950s of favoritism from federal lending agencies, in 1964 he acquired $6 million in FHA loans to build Paradise Manor, a 617-apartment complex adjacent to Mayfair Mansions. These successes were due in part to his friendship with prominent Washingtonians, some of whom were honorary members of the "Radio Church."

While Michaux initially espoused race consciousness and proclaimed the brotherhood of all races, he became increasingly conservative in his later years. In the 1960s he criticized the CIVIL RIGHTS and BLACK NATIONALISM movements and alleged that the activities of ELIJAH MUHAMMAD and MARTIN LUTHER KING JR. were contributing to racial polarization.

Because of his successful radio ministry in the nation's capital, Michaux had moved the church's headquarters there in 1929 and had renamed and reincorporated it several times. During the forty-nine years of his career he established seven churches and several branches and attracted a membership that numbered in the thousands. He amassed and bequeathed to the church an estate, consisting of temples, apartment dwellings, cafés, tracts of land, and private residences in several cities, that was estimated to be in excess of $20 million in 1968. When Michaux died in Washington, D.C., his radio program was estimated to be the longest continuous broadcast in radio annals.

Continuing to operate under the name Church of God, the institution founded by Michaux had 3,000 members and 11 churches by the mid-1990s. Michaux's most significant contribution was in religious broadcasting, where he pioneered in the use of electronic and print media for worldwide evangelism.

Bibliography

The bulk of material on Michaux is located in the Church of God's headquarters in Washington, D.C. Additional correspondence is located in the Franklin D. Roosevelt, Harry Truman, and Dwight D. Eisenhower Papers and in Department of the Interior Correspondence in the National Archives. Sound recordings from Michaux's radio ministry are at the Library of Congress.

Lark, Pauline, ed. *Sparks from the Anvil of Elder Michaux.* 1950.

Obituaries: *Washington Post* and *New York Times,* October 21, 1968.

Webb, Lillian Ashcraft. *About My Father's Business: The Life of Elder Michaux.* 1981.

From *American National Biography*. John A. Garraty and Mark C. Carnes, eds. Oxford University Press, 1999. Reprinted by permission of the American Council of Learned Societies.

Lillian Ashcraft-Eason

Micheaux, Oscar

1884–1951

American filmmaker, novelist, businessman, and pioneer best known for his dramatic films about African American life.

Oscar Micheaux was born near Murphysboro, Illinois, the fifth of thirteen children. He went to Chicago at the age of seventeen, where he worked as a shoeshine boy and Pullman porter. In 1904 he used his savings to buy a homestead in South Dakota on land newly opened to settlement. Micheaux's experiences as an African American settler in the rough-and-tumble environment of the South Dakota frontier provided him with material for several of his most important books and movies.

Micheaux's first creative work was the 1913 novel *The Conquest: The Story of a Negro Pioneer.* This novel followed the adventures of a self-made black settler caught between love for a white woman and the perceived demands of his racial identity. A similar plot defined Micheaux's longer novel *The Homesteader* (1917). Micheaux used the proceeds from *The Conquest* to start a Sioux City business, the Western Book and Supply Company, which published several of his novels.

When black filmmakers George and Noble Johnson negotiated unsuccessfully with Micheaux to film *The Homesteader* in 1919, the writer's interest turned to making movies. He filmed *The Homesteader* himself and subsequently renamed his business the Micheaux Book and Film Company. Micheaux went on to produce, write, and direct more than thirty films—the exact number remains unclear—over the next three decades. The first African American feature-length sound movie, *The Exile* (1931), was a Micheaux creation. Another Micheaux film, *Body and Soul* (1924), featured singer and actor PAUL ROBESON in his first American appearance on screen.

The budgets for Micheaux's many films came from the director's own entrepreneurial efforts. He personally transported prints from town to town, sometimes for a single showing, and edited his movies on the road. To raise money from theater-owners, Micheaux asked his actors to give private performances of scenes from upcoming productions. At the height of his success, branch offices of Micheaux's film company opened in NEW YORK and CHICAGO.

Many of Micheaux's films have been lost. Those that survive today include *Within Our Gates* (1919), *Body and Soul,* and *God's Stepchildren* (1937). Micheaux's works dramatized individual characters' struggles against prejudice within the black community as well as in opposition to outer racism. BOOKER T. WASHINGTON's doctrines of industry, self-sufficiency, and accommodation to whites profoundly influenced Micheaux's worldview and art.

African American critics in Micheaux's own time sometimes criticized his films for their perpetuation of negative stereotypes, idealization of interracial relationships, and blindness to the problems of a black lower class. Recent scholars such as BELL HOOKS and Joseph Young have defended Micheaux's portrayals of black women and a black middle class as subversive antidotes to racial myths of Micheaux's era.

Micheaux returned to writing novels in the last decade of his life. Another retelling of his pioneer memories appeared in 1944 as *The Wind from Nowhere.* Three more books followed. Micheaux continued to address African American concerns while framing them within the familiar narratives of white mainstream writing. The three-hour epic *The Betrayal*, his final film, failed commercially when it was released in 1948.

See also Accomodationism in the United States; Film, Blacks in American.

Micombero, Michel

1940–1983

Burundian army captain and president of Burundi (1966–1976).

Born in the southern Burundian province of Buriri, Michel Micombero attended a local Catholic school before entering the military in 1960. In 1962 the newly independent government of BURUNDI recalled Micombero from the École Royale military academy in Brussels to head the gendarmerie. In 1965 the constitutional monarch King MWAMBUTSA put Micombero in control after a coup attempt left the serving prime minister hospitalized. A year later the king was ousted by his teenage son, Prince Ndizeye, who asked Micombero to form a new cabinet. After appointing a cabinet that included five army officers, in November 1966 Micombero, age twenty-seven, effectively carried out a bloodless coup d'état—he deposed both the young king and the official prime minister and proclaimed a republic with himself as president.

Micombero changed the political dynamics of ethnic identity in Burundi. A socially low-standing Tutsi-Hima of mixed Tutsi-Hutu parentage from the south, he did not participate in the clan conflicts between the northern Bezi and Batare that had long dominated Burundian politics. Once in office, Micombero surrounded himself with family members and others from Buriri, appointing them to top positions in the government, judicial system, army, and state-run businesses. He also used the sole legal party, the Union for National Progress (UPRONA), as a base of support for the military as well as a tool for promoting "Micombérisme," a vague ideology advocating revolutionary socialism, democratic centralism, and hard work. By supporting fellow Tutsi southerners who lambasted northern "moderate" Tutsi and warned of a Hutu peril, Micombero heightened tensions between the HUTU AND TUTSI.

In 1972 Micombero sent troops to quell an attempted Hutu uprising, resulting from what the Hutu considered to be ongoing discrimination and repression. But the Tutsi-dominated army became an errant force, influenced by extremist politicians and fears of a replay of the Rwandan revolution where the Hutu overthrew the Tutsi; and between April and September, 100,000 to 200,000 Burundians died, most of whom were Hutu. Although the extent of Micombero's personal involvement in the killing is debated, he did nothing to stop it. In 1976 a member of his "family corporation," Colonel JEAN-BAPTISTE BAGAZA, overthrew Micombero in another bloodless coup. Micombero sought asylum in Somalia, where he later graduated from the university with a degree in economics. He died of a heart attack in 1983.

Eric Young

Middle Congo

Former name of the Republic of the Congo.

See also Congo, Republic of the.

Middle East

Region comprising the present-day countries of Israel, Jordan, Lebanon, Syria, Iraq, Iran, and the Arabian Peninsula that has imported slaves and drawn migrants from Africa since ancient times.

Because the Mediterranean Sea, the Red Sea, and the Indian Ocean have always been active trading zones between AFRICA and the Middle East, an African presence has existed in the Arabian Peninsula, the Persian Gulf, and other parts of the Middle East since ancient times. Even before the emergence of Islam in the seventh century C.E., Arabs had contact with the Africans of "Habash," a term used to refer to ETHIOPIA and the Horn of Africa. After the early Islamic jihads, or holy wars, brought them into contact with larger areas of Africa, Arabs referred to the entire region west of Ethiopia and south of the SAHARA as "al-Sudan," meaning the land of the blacks. They referred to the East African coast and its people as Zanj. Poets and leaders of African descent were famous in the Middle East from pre-Islamic times, and Africans numbered among the prophet Muhammad's companions. Many Africans ended up in the Middle East as a result of the slave trade across the Red Sea and the Indian Ocean. Most of these slaves were concubines, domestics, or eunuchs, although some labored as agricultural workers. Unlike in the Americas, these slaves did not leave distinct communities of descendants. Most scholars believe that the peoples of the Middle East gradually accepted the slaves' descendants into their communities through intermarriage. The expansion of Islam continues to bring many Muslims from Africa and the African diaspora to the Middle East in the twentieth century.

Africans in the Middle East from Antiquity to the Early Islamic Period

Even in pre-Roman times, Ethiopians journeyed to the Arabian Peninsula and the Persian Gulf for trade. According to the anonymous writer of *Periplus of the Erythraean Sea,* which dates from the first century C.E., African merchants, sailors, and adventurers had already established these routes to trade ivory, rhinoceros horn, tortoise shell, and slaves for lances, hatchets, swords, and many kinds of small glass objects. Some scholars suggest that in pre-Islamic times there was a large African population in the Hijaz (the area of Mecca and Medina). They claim that this accounts for the "green" Hijazis—recognized as darker than most Arabs—many of whom gained fame as tribal leaders, entertainers, and poets.

Warfare also brought many Africans to the Arabian Peninsula in ancient times. The Byzantines enlisted Ethiopian Christians to defend Yemen from Persian invaders during the sixth century C.E. Ethiopian deserters from these wars anointed their own king, Abraha. Abraha may have led a failed attempt to capture the trading post of Mecca. In 570 Persians conquered this region, but many Ethiopians remained.

Arab men held Ethiopian women as concubines in the Middle East. In pre-Islamic times, children born of a slave mother and an Arab father generally remained slaves, though the father could manumit and recognize the child as part of his family. During pre-Islamic and early Islamic times, several well-known poets of African slave origin came to be known collectively as *Aghribat al-Arab,* meaning Crows of the Arabs. The famous pre-Islamic poet and warrior Antara was born of an Ethiopian slave mother named Zabiba and an Arab father from the Abs ethnic group. After valiantly defending his father's people in battle, Antara was recognized by his father as a legitimate son. Other recognized sons of slaves also became leaders. A contemporary of the prophet Muhammad, Khufaf ibn Nadba, was born to a black slave mother, yet he became the chief of his Arab father's ethnic group.

Since many Arabs identified blackness with slave status, Africans faced widespread prejudice, which they often internalized. Troubled by his color, Antara wrote, "Enemies revile me for the blackness of my skin, but the whiteness of my character effaces the blackness." Like Antara, many of the poets wrote of blackness as an affliction. A black slave named Suhaym (d. 660), meaning "little black man," wrote, "the lord has marred me with blackness." The slaves were equally disturbed by their lack of Arab lineage. Abu Dulama (d. 776?), a black jester for the early Abassid caliphs whose name means "father of blackness," claimed of the Crows: "We are alike in color; our faces are black and ugly, our names shameful." However, the black poet Nusayb ibn Raba (d. 726), recognized as one of the most gifted of this group, celebrated his own victory over racist limitations:

> Blackness does not diminish me, as long as I have this tongue and this stout heart.
> Some are raised up by means of their lineage; the verses of my poems are my lineage!
> How much better a keen-minded, clear-spoken black than a mute white!

Other African poets of the era included a slave, al-Hayqutan, who lived during the Umayyid caliphs' reign (661–750); Nusayb al-Ashgar the Younger (d. 791), who was a poet of the Caliph Harun al-Rashid's court; and Daud ibn Salm (d. 750?). A black singer, Said ibn Misja (d. 705?), was considered the greatest musician of his time. For unknown reasons, historians record few black poets and entertainers in the Middle East after the tenth century.

Africans were known to be among the prophet Muhammad's companions; thus, they hold an honorable status in Islamic history. The Ethiopian Bilal ibn Raba was a freed slave who fought on behalf of Muhammad in Arabia, Pakistan, and India; he was the first muezzin, the chanter of the Islamic call to prayer. Another companion of the Prophet was Abu Bakra, an Ethiopian slave who joined the Muslims when they came to the oasis town of Taif. He converted to Islam and was manumitted by the Prophet himself; later, he settled in Basra, where he died in 672. The Prophet is known to have had close relations with Africans in Ethiopia as well; when early Muslims were persecuted in Mecca, he sent them to find refuge in that country. Many of the early leaders of Islam had African heritage. For instance, an Ethiopian concubine was the paternal grandmother of Umar, the second caliph of the Islamic community, who reigned from 634 to 644.

African Slaves and Freed Africans in the Muslim Middle East from the Eighth to Nineteenth Centuries

For centuries in the Middle East and North Africa, peoples defeated in battle had to send slaves as a tribute or payment to the victors. In 652 C.E. a pact between Muslims and NUBIANS required an annual levy of 360 black slaves in exchange for peace. The Arab Islamic conquest of much of northern Africa beginning in the late seventh century seems to have expanded the slave trade and brought more African slaves to the Middle East. According to Islamic jurists, however, slaves could not be taken from Dar al-Islam, or, the Land of Islam, but only from Dar al-Harb, the Land of War. It became commonly accepted that this land of war was all non-Islamic lands, where indiscriminate raiding could occur, under the assumption that these were jihads or holy wars. The purchasing of slaves from non-Muslim lands, where no official agreement existed, could occur legally. In practice, raids often occurred in lands where an agreement did exist and sometimes on Muslim peoples. However, as Africans converted to Islam in the tenth century, the supply of slaves decreased, because Islam prohibits the enslaving of fellow Muslims (although if a slave converts to Islam, a master is under no obligation to free him or her). Despite this, the slave trade continued well into the nineteenth century.

Slaves were brought to the Middle East mostly from East Africa. Traders transported them down the NILE to EGYPT, where they crossed the Red Sea. Or the traders led them to ports on the Indian Ocean, from which ships carried them to the Arabian Peninsula, Iraq, or Persia. Slave traders also led some slaves across the Sahara to North African ports, then shipped them across the Mediterranean Sea. It is said that certain African Muslims would purchase slaves to sell on their way to Mecca, to pay for their pilgrimage to the Holy Land.

These slaves were often sold to work in Arabia, the lands of the Persian Gulf, or later, the Ottoman Empire (present-day Turkey) and other parts of the Middle East. Some slaves were taken through the Middle East en route to other parts of Asia, such as India or even China. Both Jews and Christians in the Middle East could hold slaves according to Islamic law, as long as the slaves were not Muslim.

The majority of African slaves brought to the Middle East were females sold for domestic use or concubinage. According to Islamic law, when a concubine had a child by her master, the child was a free person who took on his father's name and status; the mother could not be sold by her master and would be manumitted upon his death. No doubt, many African women and their children in the Middle East became free in this manner. Most African female slaves were taken as concubines, but if taken as a legal wife (as was the case with many Ethiopians), they and their descendants were free.

African male slaves were purchased by the upper, and sometimes middle, classes to serve in the households. African men also served rulers as bodyguards or palace staff and, less often, as soldiers. Slaves taken from Central Asia and the Caucasus generally served as slave-soldiers, or mamluks, while African, Armenian, Greek, and other Christian slaves, called *abd*, mostly fulfilled domestic or commercial purposes. African slaves sometimes labored as construction workers in cities or as agricultural workers, miners, and pearl fishers. In the ninth century, a large number of black slaves were put to work in southern Iraq to collect salt from coastal flats. At the same time, east African slaves worked in western Persia producing SUGAR. These Africans united in a force of 15,000 men, led by rebel leader Ali b. Muhammad, and revolted against the ruling Abassids around 869. The Zanj Revolt, as it is called, briefly established an independent African-ruled state called Dawlat al-Zanj. Arabs dissolved this threat to their dominance in 883.

Many male African slaves suffered castration so that they could be sold in the Middle East as eunuchs. Eunuchs were needed as custodians at holy sites, such as the Kaaba in Mecca, or to guard tombs; they were also used as confidential servants and palace staff. Most of the time, they were bought to guard the harems of the sultan and of the elite. The black eunuchs of the Ottoman palace in Istanbul were powerful and wealthy. The chief black eunuch, or *kizlar agasi,* meaning "chief of the girls," was entitled to own slaves himself (including concubines) and was entrusted with financial tasks. He alone had unencumbered access to the sultan at all times and served as the confidential messenger between the sultan and the vizier. Eunuchs who were dismissed or retired became free members of society. One eunuch became a tax collector for the port of Jiddah; another became the governor of Aden. Still others were able to purchase their freedom and go on to study, travel, donate to public works, and even marry.

Muslim law did not make racial distinctions among slaves. However, as the white slave supply dwindled beginning in the sixteenth century and became practically nonexistent in the nineteenth century, Middle Easterners became so dependent on Africa for slaves that *abd* came to mean black man in many Arabic dialects. Slavery persisted in the Middle East through the nineteenth century; it was increasingly a racial institution, imposed exclusively on people of African origin. Africans continued to serve as slaves in parts of the Middle East into the twentieth century, when slavery was banned.

Generally, manumitted slaves became "clients" of their former masters; often, even if not related, they would take the names of their masters and acquire the status of their lineages. There is some evidence that communities of African people emerged in Arabian and Persian cities such as Jiddah, Mecca, and Aden in the Red Sea area; Muscat, Basra, Bushire, and Bandar Abbas in the Persian Gulf; and inland at Shiraz. People of African origin worked as merchants, dock workers, clerks, agricultural laborers, shopkeepers, and civil servants. In the 1860s and 1870s European travelers to Arabia remarked on the communities of Arabized Africans. English traveler William Palgrave noted that the Wahabi ruler, Faisal, employed an African freedman as his treasurer. Palgrave also wrote of a community of mixed African and Middle Eastern background, called *khudayriyya,* meaning "little green ones," who worked in and around Riyadh. He claimed that these communities held equal rights with the Arab populations.

But generally most scholars note the lack of a visible African community in the Middle East. They speculate that many slaves died as a result of disease and, in Iran, as a result of the high altitudes. Some scholars note that the lack of a black community may be the result of the Africans' dispersal and confinement to remote places and their marginalized status as former slaves or descendants of slaves. The most compelling thesis seems to be that no large community exists because most slaves were concubines or eunuchs, and as a result the black population could not replenish itself. With high rates of manumission and subsequent intermarriage with Arab populations, children of freed slaves often became indistinguishable members of society.

In the late nineteenth century European colonial powers occupied Africa and forced the Ottoman Empire to suppress the slave trade to the Middle East. Subsequently, the Ottomans attempted to ban slavery within the empire. The Hijaz rebelled against the Ottoman attempts at abolition. Citing the fact that the Qur'an recognized slavery, they declared a holy war against their Ottoman rulers in 1855. This rebellion was defeated in 1856, but the Hijaz population was exempted from the Ottoman abolition decree in 1857. Abolition was completed in the Middle East in the 1920s under League of Nations mandates, though it was only when nations emerged in the region, mostly after World War II, that they enacted individual decrees outlawing slavery.

Africans and African Americans in the Middle East in the Postcolonial Era

In the twentieth century Africans have continued to come to the Middle East, most visibly as pilgrims making the hajj to Mecca. Many Africans have also sought refuge in the Middle East. IDI AMIN lived in Saudi Arabia after fleeing Uganda in 1979. Writers have also traveled there; JAMES BALDWIN, for example, spent many years in Istanbul, Turkey, in the 1960s. While an Ethiopian Orthodox Christian presence has existed in Jerusalem for centuries, a large-scale migration of ETHIOPIAN JEWS to Israel fleeing discrimination in Ethiopia began in 1984 and continued in the early 1990s. In 2003 Israel allowed another 20,000 Ethiopian Jews to join the 80,000 already living in the country. This Ethiopian population, however, has faced poverty and persisting discrimination since immigrating to Israel.

In recent decades Africans from SUDAN, Ethiopia, ERITREA, NIGERIA, and other countries have remained in Saudi Arabia after completing their pilgrimage. Many have traveled from there to other parts of the Arab Middle East to search for work in the oil fields, in the region's wealthy cities, or as domestic servants for the elite. Even though most of these Africans are Muslim, government authorities generally have not welcomed these "overstayers," as they are called. In 1996 the Saudi government forced the return of all illegal foreign workers to their countries of origin. It is unlikely that the Saudi government can entirely stop the movement of African workers to the Arabian Peninsula until the demand for cheap labor subsides.

High-profile visits by African Americans to the Middle East have impacted U.S. politics, particularly since the 1960s. The emergence and popularity of the NATION OF ISLAM created a community of Black Muslims in the United States and stimulated an interest in Islam among African Americans. After MALCOLM X went on a pilgrimage to Mecca in 1964, he disassociated himself with the Nation's brand of Islam and converted to orthodox Islam, changing his name to an Islamic one: El-Hajj Malik El-Shabazz. In 1979 the U.S. ambassador to the United Nations, ANDREW YOUNG, was forced to resign after it became known that he had held secret meetings with the Palestine Liberation Organization (PLO). When other black leaders, including the

Reverend JESSE JACKSON, showed their support for Young in the Middle East that same year and met with Yasser Arafat, the leader of the PLO, they faced the criticism that these meetings demonstrated anti-Semitism.

Perhaps because of their shared history as victims of slavery and colonialism, Africans and African Americans have been able to bridge the gulf between Western powers and the Arab world and to act as mediators in regional crises. In 1983 Jesse Jackson successfully negotiated the release of an African American hostage in Syria. In 1998 United Nations Secretary General KOFI ANNAN negotiated an agreement with Iraq's Saddam Hussein that averted the threat of war between Iraq and the United States. Blacks from Africa, the Americas, and other parts of the world continue to travel to the Middle East, as Muslims for the pilgrimage, or as tourists and visitors. Thus, the ancient connection between people of African origin and the peoples of the Middle East continues today.

See also Diaspora and Displacement; Ethiopian Orthodox Church; Indian Ocean Slave Trade; Islam and African Americans; Islam in Africa; Ivory Trade; South Asia, Africans in; Trans-Saharan and Red Sea Slave Trade.

Bibliography

Hunwick, J. O. "African Slaves in the Mediterranean World: A Neglected Aspect of the African Diaspora." In *Global Dimensions of the African Diaspora*. Edited by Joseph Harris. Howard University Press, 1993.

Lewis, Bernard. *Race and Slavery in the Middle East: An Historical Enquiry*. Oxford University Press, 1990.

Leyla Keough

Middle Passage, The

Term used to describe the transatlantic slave voyages between Africa and the Americas that claimed the lives of nearly two million slaves over a period of about 350 years.

The "Middle Passage" was a physical and psychological nightmare for an estimated twelve million slaves who were packed like animals aboard slave vessels. This middle, or second, leg of the TRANSATLANTIC SLAVE TRADE marked the beginning of a terrifying experience. OLAUDAH EQUIANO, a former slave turned antislavery activist, captured his experience aboard a slave vessel in his autobiography. He wrote, "When I looked round the ship . . . and saw . . . a multitude of black people of every description chained together, every one of their countenances expressing dejection and sorrow, I no longer doubted my fate; and, quite overpowered with horror and anguish, I fell motionless on the deck and fainted."

Typically, slaves were shackled in pairs, the right arm and leg of one chained to the left arm and leg of the other. Men were separated from women, but all were confined below deck and packed into slave quarters throughout the ship's belly. These quarters were no more than 1.8 meter (6 foot) long and not high enough to allow an individual to sit upright. Conditions were miserable. Slaves were forced to lie naked on wooden planks, and many developed bruises and open sores. The human waste and vomit produced an overpowering stench in the unbearable heat below deck. The unsanitary conditions were breeding grounds for diseases such as dysentery, smallpox, and measles. Close to 5 percent of the slaves aboard these vessels died from disease and many more from malnutrition. Slaves were fed twice-a-day rations of fish, beans, or yams that were prepared in large copper vats below deck. Those who refused to eat, hoping to starve themselves to death, were force-fed.

Slaves were sometimes allowed, in small groups, to come on deck for exercise. Women and children were often permitted to roam freely, a practice that opened opportunities for the ship's crew to abuse and rape them. Occasionally some slaves managed to break free from their shackles and organize mutinies. Over 250 cases of rebellion at sea are documented, including the AMISTAD MUTINY, an unsuccessful revolt that was the subject of a film by director Steven Spielberg in the fall of 1997.

Resistance was not limited to mutiny. Instances of Africans in war canoes attacking slave vessels near the African coast are known. Eyewitness reports tell of slaves hanging or starving themselves to death during the Middle Passage. Some captives jumped overboard to escape slavery.

Millions of Africans were forced to endure the dehumanizing Middle Passage as they were transported into slavery in the Americas. Of these millions Toni Morrison wrote: "Nobody knows their names, and nobody thinks about them. In addition to that, they never survived in the lore; there are no songs or dances or tales of these people. The people who arrived—there is lore about them. But nothing survives about—*that*."

See also Transatlantic Slave Trade Database.

Bibliography

Klein, Herbert S. *The Middle Passage*. Princeton University Press, 1978.

Alonford James Robinson

Mighty Sparrow

1935–

Grenadian musician, one of Trinidad's most popular calypso singers.

According to Caribbean scholar Peter Manuel, Mighty Sparrow is "[one of the] two most important figures in modern Trinidadian culture," rivaled only by the late ERIC WILLIAMS, the longtime head of the People's National Movement and a popular prime minister. Born in GRENADA as Francisco Slinger, the singer made his name in Trinidad's Carnival, the long celebration ending with Lent for which most CALYPSO music is produced.

Mighty Sparrow has a strong voice and is an effective performer. He is also a capable songwriter. He has won more of the island's prestigious calypso competitions—the National Calypso Monarchy (for the best performer of the year) and Road March (for the most popular party song)—than any other performer. His first popular success was "Jean and Dinah" (1956). In 1957 he paid tribute to the wild Carnival spirit: The biggest bacchanal is in Trinidad Carnival,

> Regardless of color, creed, or race,
> Jump up and shake your waist.
> So jump as you mad, this is Trinidad;
> We don't care who say we bad.

The lyrics are vintage Mighty Sparrow, verbally playful and incorporating less social commentary than ribald humor.

Manuel noted that Mighty Sparrow's lyrics are "consistently clever, pithy, and catchy." For example, his song warning of the dangers of cocaine abuse is titled "Coke Is Not It." Although not a profound social critic, Mighty Sparrow has repeatedly distilled the mood of the nation in his topical songs. One of the most highly regarded of his many albums is *King of the World* (1984). A winner of numerous awards, he received the Order of the Caribbean Community in 2001 and the Marcus Garvey Lifetime Achievement Award at the 2002 Jamerican Film and Music Festival. Mighty Sparrow continues to record new music and perform on stage.

See also Carnivals in Latin America and the Caribbean; Music, Caribbean; Trinidad and Tobago.

James Sellman

Migrancy and African Literature

Many writers from parts of the world that have been colonized leave home and migrate to Europe and North America, including a number from Africa. They come from all over the continent. Some went into exile involuntarily, some emigrated by choice. Others move between continents. Few of the well-known and widely published writers remain permanently in Africa, without spending time in Europe or North America. To take just a very few examples, there is Jamal Mahjoub from the SUDAN, who lives in Spain, having spent some years in Denmark; there is Leila Aboulela, also from the Sudan, who now lives in Scotland. From KENYA there is the renowned NGUGI WA THIONG'O, who lives in the United States. M. G. Vassanji migrated from TANZANIA to Toronto and Abdulrazak Gurnah from ZANZIBAR to Britain. BUCHI EMECHETA and BEN OKRI, both from NIGERIA have for many years lived in Britain, where Okri recently won the coveted Booker Prize for his novel, *The Famished Road*.

Globalization

These connections across the world are often referred to as the process of *globalization*. The traffic between worlds is beginning to amount to a jam with borders under seige in all directions. This has enormous consequences for the ways in which writers see and represent themselves and others in their fictions. Globalization challenges boundaries and confronts and transforms the old divide between colonizer and colonized, white and black. European capitals have been transformed culturally, politically, and economically by immigrants from areas of the world it once colonized. Anthony Giddens in *The Consequences of Modernity* defines globalization as "the intensification of worldwide social relations which link distant localities in such a way that local happenings are shaped by events occurring many miles away and vice versa."

This "brain drain" has affected Africa very radically, given the extent of the migration of its writers and intellectuals, scholars and artists away from the continent. The Nigerian poet Pius Adesanmi, in his paper "Europhonism, Universities, and Other Stories," says he belongs to "an emergent generation of writers that became very visible in the nineties." He outlines how, as "everywhere on the continent, bloodthirsty tyrants shot their way into the corridors of power" and as the infrastructure decayed and the universities were increasingly underfunded, there has been "an unprecedented emigration of African intellectuals," and "European and North American universities played host to an ever expanding army of African intellectual refugees."

Diaspora

The concept of "diaspora" has been reincarnated in this context. African communities in the West develop ties with other black communities from other once-colonized places, such as India or Latin America. At the same time, they link up in some or other way with host communities and weave these new networks into their roots back home. With each new generation the "woof and weave" of these networks develop and change in texture, color, and style. As new generations grow up and are born in northern climates, so questions of the past, of identity, of roots become more complex. For the first time in her fiction, for example, Buchi Emecheta focuses on *The New Tribe*, as she titles her novel. These are children of Nigerian background, born and bred in England. This new tribe of black British have different agendas and alliances in their attempts to stake a place in the country in which they were born and yet where racism continues to fissure the land. Paul Gilroy looks at "the syncretic cultures of black Britain" in his book *There Ain't No Black in the Union Jack*. He explains that "black British cultures have been created from diverse and contradictory elements apprehended through discontinuous histories."

Third Space and Hybridity

While "back home" transforms through the lens of memory and the distortions of nostalgia, new homes are not very easily established. In fact, these travelers from places in Africa, who migrate to places in the United States or the United Kingdom, have been characterized by Homi Bhahba in *The Location of Culture* as occupying a kind of "third space." These newcomers to London or Aberdeen from LAGOS or KHARTOUM occupy an ambiguous, hybrid, and changing site, neither fully on one continent or the other. This space is sometimes productive and fertile and at other times lonely and rootless.

More than a place, however, the third space is a mental and emotional construct, a way of being in the world, a search for a new identity. Postcolonial migrants rely on the books that they write in order to assist them with a ritual of relocation, one that is a painful, labored struggle for reemergence into sociality.

Conceptualizing this third space is made even more challenging by the fact that "here" and "there" are not themselves homogenous places. It makes a big difference whether the writer ends up in London or Aberdeen, Amsterdam or the West Coast of America. Africa, moreover, is a highly heterogeneous continent, and writers coming from West, East, or North Africa have had profoundly different experiences from one another.

There are a number of other variables. Are these writers Muslim, Christian, or "traditional" or any combination and mixture of belief? Do their ancestors include migrants to East Africa long ago from the Middle or Far East? The terrible history of persecution of Africans of Asian descent has profoundly affected such writers as Abdulrazak Gurnah and M. G. Vassanji, whose emigration from East Africa was not entirely voluntary and whose stories entwine uneasy citizenship in Africa with all the difficulties of settling in new countries. In other words, their third space is a palimpsest of yet other places and histories, across the centuries. May Joseph, herself an East African Asian migrant from Tanzania to New York, in her *Nomadic Identities*, outlines her encounters with "dispersed communities of East African Asians in India, the Gulf states, Britain, Canada and the United States." She describes crossing paths "with these enclaves of displaced East African Asians through the years, in Bangalore, Trivandrum, Doha, London, New York, Los Angeles."

African Novels in the Third Space

This strange thirdness takes many different forms in different writers, who have come from different African countries and arrived at different European or North American cities. It could be captured by the fantastic, as in B. Kojo Laing's magical interplays between two fictional towns, Tukwan in GHANA and Levensvale in Scotland in his *Woman of the Aeroplanes*. It might be that perch in Amsterdam, where Moses Isegawa's protagonist eventually lands up in *Abyssinian Chronicles*. This African trickster on Dutch soil will continue to buck the system and live in the cracks, as successfully in Amsterdam as he did in Kampala.

It could be the seedy flat in Toronto occupied by the Lalani family in M. G. Vassanji's *No New Land*. This family, like many others, fled DAR ES SALAAM and an East Africa dominated by the anti-Asian sentiments fueled by IDI AMIN, only to find life in Toronto hard and hostile. Or it could be prosaically named and identified as Brixton High Street in Biyi Bandele's *The Street*. Bandele's Brixton is a weird and wonderful amalgam of Nigeria and Britain, the living and the dead, the real and the imagined, the dream and the reality. It is a new Britain in which the formerly colonized have come to stay and to transform local and national realities, even while these African men and women are themselves transformed. These are all third spaces.

Gender

Men and women also experience uprooting quite differently. Men have more mobility and opportunities of new jobs and economic empowerment in new places, however difficult these moves are for all postcolonial travelers. Ama Darko's *Beyond the Horizon* enacts the particular horror of a naive woman from the village being sold into prostitution by conniving Ghanaian men in Germany. By contrast, however, in *Yoruba Girl Dancing*, Simi Bedford portrays an equally naive Nigerian girl, who quickly learns the ropes in her English public school and capitalizes on her differences from her female classmates in her determination to stay on top, rather than becoming a victim. Ama Ata Aidoo, the well-known Ghanaian writer, captures some of the particular paradoxes and perplexities of the professional African woman traveler in her story "Some Global News" from her collection suggestively entitled *The Girl Who Can and Other Stories*. The story focuses on etiquette around dress codes, which carries loaded cultural and gendered meaning.

Language

From stranger to citizen, from foreign alien to new community, from visitor to resident, characters hold onto their possessions, the things, which anchor them in the potential abyss of "in-betweenness." Pointing, then, in many directions, in both time and space, the objects that these travelers gather, store, pack, and bring speak in tongues and tell new stories. Migrant writers tend to use European languages to tell their stories. However, they explore ways of possessing the language and making it their own, much like the possessions they and their characters bring from home and the new objects they furnish their lives with when they arrive. If English is a forked tongue for the once-colonized, then it is doubly so for migrants arriving in England or Amsterdam, who lose their sense of place in the world, their words, their selves. African writers, who are foreigners, make new languages out of English. This they do as a means of forging new metaphors, meanings, and images. According to Bill Ashcroft, in his *Post-Colonial Transformation*, they may include some of the indigenous language from where they came, in order to install their difference from colonial culture and language. They change the rhyme, rhythm, and texture of the language. The new English language that is acquired is, of course, also a blended one.

Conclusion

Useful terms and concepts like *migration, globalization, diaspora, hybridity,* and *third space* come alive in the plots, themes, devices, humor, conundrums, and everyday occurrences of African fictional tales. African writers use the landscapes and stories of where they were born and where they now live. They borrow from other African places and people, from the cultures of India and Latin America, where they identify with those who have also been colonized, albeit in different ways and at different times. They express themselves in European languages and inherit European traditions. Out of this patchwork they construct visions that are uniquely linked to their own lives, their countries of origin, their generation, the privileged perch from which they view the world, and their individual talents and idiosyncrasies.

Bibliography

Adesanmi, Pius. "Europhonism, Universities, and Other Stories: How Not to Speak for the Future of African Literature?" *Palavers of African Literature: Essays in Honor of Bernth Lindfors.* Vol. 1. Edited by Totin Falola and Barbara Harlow. Africa World Press, 2002.

Ashcroft, Bill. *Post-Colonial Transformation.* Routledge, 2001.

Bhabha, Homi. *The Location of Culture.* Routledge, 1994.

Giddens, Anthony. *The Consequences of Modernity.* Polity Press, 1990.

Gilroy, Paul. *"There Ain't No Black in the Union Jack."* University of Chicago Press, 1991.

Joseph, May. *Nomadic Identities: The Performance of Citizenship.* University of Minnesota Press, 1999.

Brenda Cooper

Migration, Black, in the United States

See Great Migration.

Migration in African History

See How Africa Became Black: An Interpretation.

Mijikenda

Ethnic group of Kenya.

The Mijikenda primarily inhabit coastal southeastern KENYA. Others live in TANZANIA. They speak a Bantu language and are comprised of several subgroups, including the GIRIYAMA, the DURUMA, and the DIGO of Tanzania. Approximately one million people consider themselves Mijikenda.

See also Bantu: Dispersion and Settlement.

Milanés, Pablo

1943–

Afro-Cuban protest singer and representative of the Nueva Trova (New Song) Movement of the 1960s and 1970s.

Pablo Milanés was born in Bayamo, a historically important town in the eastern part of CUBA, to a poor mulatto family. When he was only five years old his mother took him to amateur contests on radio programs, where he sang boleros (a Cuban genre of romantic ballads) and *rancheras* (a style of Mexican song). His family moved to HAVANA in 1949, where he began to play the guitar, taking lessons sporadically at the Havana Municipal Conservatory. Working in menial jobs and studying at night, he began playing in 1959 in the Del Rey Quartet, which specialized in American hymns of African American influence. He wrote his first songs in 1963. In 1964 he switched to the Los Bucaneros Quartet, which had a broader repertoire. He also sang as a soloist, collaborating with composers of the "feeling" movement (romantic ballads of the 1950s and 1960s) or sometimes joining singers such as Omara Portuondo. His first hit song, written in 1965, was "Mis 22 años" (My 22 years).

In 1966 he was obligated to serve in the UMAP centers (Unidad Militar de Ayuda a la Producción, or Military Unit of Production Assistance), a forced labor system created by the Cuban government to rehabilitate and reeducate those alienated from the revolution, such as homosexuals and hippies. In 1967 he was transferred to perform his required military service. That same year he wrote his first politically motivated song, "Yo vi la sangre de un niño brotar" (I saw a child's blood running). Through Omara Portuondo he met Silvio Rodríguez, another luminary of the Nueva Trova Movement, with whom he established a solid friendship that continues to the present. They realized that they had many similar ideas about the future of the new Cuban song. In February 1968 they appeared together, along with Noel Nicola, in the first concert of the Protest Song Center.

His compositions continued to reflect everyday life as well as political concerns. "Yo no te pido" (I don't ask you) and "Para vivir" (To live) are examples of the former; songs reflecting a political content include "Si el poeta eres tu" (If you are the poet), composed after Cuban revolutionary hero Ernesto "Che" Guevara's death, with lyrics by author Miguel Barnet, and "Su nombre puede ponerse en verso" (His name can be written in verse), dedicated to Ho Chi Minh.

Unlike most singers in the Nueva Trova, Milanés frequently ventured into other musical styles, both in concerts and recordings. His talents extend to singing the Cuban SON, old trova songs, and "feeling," a Cuban musical style influenced by JAZZ.

Milanés draws more upon Cuba's traditional musical styles, such as son, *guaguancó* (RUMBA), *guajira*, and bolero than does Silvio Rodriguez or other representatives of the genre. Of the leading figures of the Nueva Trova, he is the only nonwhite;

he specifically addresses issues of race in some of his songs, including, "NELSON MANDELA: sus dos amores" (Nelson Mandela: His two loves) and "Háblame de colores" (speak to me of colors). He has recorded more than forty LPs and CDs, and his songs have been interpreted and recorded by more leading figures of other countries than those of any other Nueva Trova singer. Though now in his sixties, Milanés's music career shows little sign of slowing down.

See also Music, Afro-Caribbean Secular.

Cristobal Diaz-Ayala

Miley, James Wesley ("Bubber")

1903–1932

African American trumpeter who was one of the first great soloists in jazz music.

Along with LOUIS ARMSTRONG, SIDNEY BECHET, and Bix Beiderbecke, Bubber Miley was one of the great JAZZ soloists of the 1920s. Miley's career, like that of Bechet, also demonstrates the importance of professionalism in securing long-term success in jazz, something that Armstrong and DUKE ELLINGTON, each in his own way, clearly understood. Ironically, however, much of Ellington's early renown as a composer and bandleader was a direct product of Miley's contributions to the Ellington orchestra. As a member of the band, Miley was largely responsible for the early "jungle" sound of jazz.

Born in Aiken, South Carolina, Miley moved with his family to NEW YORK CITY in 1909. He began playing music in public school, initially trombone, then cornet. During 1918 he joined the navy and served for eighteen months, including the final months of WORLD WAR I. In 1920, after his discharge from the navy, Miley began playing professionally. The following year he joined the Jazz Hounds, the group that had accompanied BLUES singer MAMIE SMITH on many of her recordings, including "Crazy Blues" (1920), the song that initiated the blues craze of the 1920s. In the fall of 1923 Miley joined banjo player Elmer Snowden's Washingtonians, which soon came under the leadership of its pianist, Duke Ellington.

The addition of Miley transformed the Washingtonians, giving them an instantly recognizable sound. Prior to Miley's arrival, the group had often played "sweet" dance music. Ellington recalled, "Our band changed character when Bubber came in. He used to growl all night long, playing gutbucket on his horn. That was when we decided to forget all about the sweet music." In particular, Miley's playing reflected the influence of the great NEW ORLEANS cornet player JOE "KING" OLIVER. Oliver's playing was suffused with a deep blues feeling. He combined his gift for melody with the use of a plunger mute: by variously positioning the rubber cup of a toilet plunger over the bell of his instrument, he could alter the sounds and produce vocal-like growling effects.

Miley adopted this technique—combining the plunger mute with a straight mute inserted directly into the cornet's bell—and raised it to an expressive art. Most importantly, he did not use the plunger mute strictly for novelty effects; he made it an expressive element of the music, intrinsic to the emotional content of the melody. Miley became the most prominently featured soloist in the early Ellington band. He also taught trombone player Joe "Tricky Sam" Nanton everything that he knew about mutes. During the mid- to late 1920s the two provided a distinctive tonal quality, commonly referred to as the "jungle-music sound," for which the early Ellington band became well known.

Miley and Nanton's musical influence is particularly evident in many of Ellington's recordings between 1926 and 1928—for example, the various renditions of the slow-tempo "Black and Tan Fantasy" (1927), particularly the Victor Records version, on which Miley played what may be his greatest recorded solo. He opened on a keening high b-flat, which he held for four long measures before tumbling downward in a brilliant, bluesy cascade of plunger-muted notes. "It is also a highly dramatic solo," musicologist Gunthar Schuller concluded, "equal to anything achieved up to that time by the New Orleans trumpet men. And perhaps none of them ever achieved the extraordinary contrast produced by the intense stillness of the four-bar-long high b-flat, suddenly erupting, as if unable to contain itself any longer, into a magnificently structured melodic creation."

Miley's superb improvisation may even have influenced the great Louis Armstrong. Eight months after Miley recorded this solo on "Black and Tan Fantasy," Armstrong took a strikingly similar approach in his classic improvisation on "West End Blues" (1928), entering on a high b-flat that he held for four tension-building measures before falling away in a cascade of notes. Armstrong did not directly copy Miley's solo; after the first four measures, their note choices, phrasing, and rhythms were quite different, and Armstrong's bravura open horn sounded completely different from Miley's plunger-muted growl. Yet the two solos share a remarkable similarity in their ways of building and releasing dramatic tension.

Miley also created some of the Ellington band's most memorable melodies. It is difficult to determine who was responsible for many pieces in the band's early repertoire. However, Schuller and Ellington scholar John Edward Hasse agree in assigning Miley a key role in creating some of the group's signature pieces, including "Black and Tan Fantasy," "East St. Louis Toodle-Oo" (1926), "Creole Love Call" (1927), and "The Mooche" (1928). Late in 1927 the Ellington band secured a long-term gig at the COTTON CLUB, New York City's most prestigious nightclub, and by the following year emerged as the nation's foremost jazz ensemble.

But early in 1929 Ellington forced Miley, his most celebrated soloist, out of the band. Miley's heavy drinking and increasing unpredictability had at last exhausted Ellington's patience. Hasse wrote that on occasion Miley did "not show up for several days," missing performances and recording sessions. As his replacement, trumpeter Charles "Cootie" Williams, explained, "[E]very time some big shot come up [to the Cotton Club] to listen to the band, there wasn't no Bubber Miley, and [Ellington] had the whole band built around Bubber Miley."

After leaving Ellington, Miley joined the NOBLE SISSLE band on a 1929 trip to Paris. During the early 1930s he played with several other ensembles and briefly led his own group before succumbing to tuberculosis, aggravated by alcoholism, in the spring of 1932. He was twenty-nine years old.

Miley left an enduring legacy within the Ellington band. Many of his compositions remained an active part of the band's repertoire, and Tricky Sam Nanton showed Cootie Williams the secrets of Miley's plunger-mute technique. Through the years, Ellington brass players passed on this knowledge to succeeding generations of musicians, maintaining a living link to the band's first famous soloist.

James Sellman

Military, Blacks in the American

African Americans serving in various branches of the United States armed services and in every military conflict entered by the United States, often in the face of white resistance.

In 1948, as a result of President Harry S. Truman's Executive Order 9981, the military became the first major American institution to undertake racial integration. Although the military did not welcome the change, over the years it made great strides toward eliminating racial segregation and discrimination. Today large numbers of African Americans serve in the armed forces because—to a much greater extent than the larger society—the various branches of service reward ability regardless of race or class. For much of American history, however, white Americans resisted the admission of blacks to the military. Like other parts of the African American past, the story of blacks in the American military is closely entwined with the historical American realities of slavery and racism.

African Americans in the armed forces have faced conditions that varied widely over the years and from branch to branch within the services. Their story encompasses three major themes: first, black efforts to gain the right to serve and their changing reception within the various services; second, the service records and combat experiences of African American soldiers; and third, the complex impact of black military service on other aspects of American society and African American life. For African Americans, the most significant American military conflicts were the AMERICAN REVOLUTION (1775–1783), the CIVIL WAR (1861–1865), World War I (1914–1918), World War II (1939–1945), and the VIETNAM WAR (1959–1975). Each of these wars had a profound impact on African American life as well as on the nation as a whole, and each involved significant numbers of black soldiers. African Americans, largely unsung, have played a part in every military conflict in American history.

Role of African Americans in Colonial Militias

In the early seventeenth century, British colonists—conscious of their vulnerability—welcomed slaves and free blacks into the provincial militias that defended their settlements from NATIVE AMERICAN, French, or Spanish attack. But as white colonists came to fear slave rebellions more than foreign aggression, they began to exclude African Americans from military service. Virginia passed such a law in 1639; Massachusetts in 1656; and Connecticut followed five years later, after a joint rebellion of Native Americans and slaves near Hartford. In wartime, however, whites were receptive to black volunteers. Black militiamen fought and died in King William's War (1689–1697), Queen Anne's War (1702–1713), and the French and Indian War (1754–1763) as well as in countless skirmishes with Native Americans.

Slaves who distinguished themselves in battle were often granted their freedom, but most did not escape bondage in this manner because they had few opportunities to demonstrate their heroism. In what would be an enduring pattern, white commanders relegated black soldiers to support positions such as laborers and teamsters. As Lieutenant Colonel (Ret.) Michael Lee Lanning observed in *The African-American Soldier* (1997), it was only when whites felt immediately "threatened by outside enemies" that they welcomed blacks in "armed positions," and black soldiers consistently found themselves "fighting and dying for a culture which did not recognize them as equals."

At sea, on the other hand, African Americans experienced much greater acceptance. Because of intolerable living conditions aboard ships, many white seamen deserted. Free blacks and runaway slaves, however, welcomed the comparative freedom and relative equality of pay, and they were therefore willing to endure the hardships faced by American merchantmen, whalers, and privateers. Although few blacks served as officers or ship captains—the most notable exception being black Massachusetts captain and ship owner PAUL CUFFE—black seamen served in racially integrated crews. A similar tradition of racial openness would continue in the U.S. Navy until the late nineteenth century.

African Americans in the American Revolution

Black soldiers also played their part in the American Revolution, although the role of CRISPUS ATTUCKS, the most celebrated black revolutionary hero, has been misunderstood. In 1770, when Attucks and four whites were killed in the Boston Massacre, they did not die in the cause of American independence—a political goal that would not emerge until several years later. Rather, they were involved in a labor struggle. Attucks's role in leading a mob against British soldiers reflected rising anger at soldiers who were taking jobs in their off-duty hours and augmenting their pay at the expense of Boston workingmen. It would thus be more accurate to view Attucks as an early martyr in the American labor movement.

African Americans—especially those who were slaves—faced a difficult choice between siding with the patriots, whose leaders included prominent slaveholders such as George Washington and Thomas Jefferson, or with the British Loyalists. Late in 1775 Virginia's royal governor John Murray, the earl of Dunmore, tried to take advantage of implicit racial divisions by offering freedom to any slave who joined the Loyalist forces. Although Lord Dunmore organized one black regiment, a surprisingly small number of slaves answered his call—probably 2,000, although higher figures have been reported.

But the threat of a wholesale slave exodus to the British led patriot leaders to reconsider their original policy of excluding black soldiers. Ultimately, some 5,000 African Americans—both free blacks and slaves—joined the Continental Army, and many others served in local militias. Most of those who were slaves won their freedom in the process. These black soldiers proved their courage under fire, and many died in the struggle for American independence, beginning with Prince Estabrook, a black militiaman killed at Lexington Green on April 19, 1775.

In 1775, after the Battle of Bunker Hill, the Massachusetts legislature particularly commended African American militiaman Salem Poor, declaring that "in the person of this said Negro centers a brave and gallant soldier." Black sailors in the fledgling American navy also saw extensive action, including service aboard John Paul Jones's *Bonhomme Richard* in its 1778 victory over the British *Serapis*. LEMUEL HAYNES, a black soldier from Connecticut and later a Congregational minister, dramatically broadened the patriots' own logic of liberty and inalienable rights in "Liberty Further Extended." This essay, written around 1776 though long unpublished, offers an early natural-rights argument against slavery.

Gains and Losses from the Revolution to the Civil War

Revolutionary ideals gave impetus to the abolition of slavery in the North—beginning with Vermont in 1777 and concluding with a plan for gradual emancipation that New Jersey ratified in 1804—certainly the most significant consequence of the Revolutionary War for African Americans. At the same time, however, Southern slavery became more entrenched and the military more firmly whites-only. The Militia Act, passed by Congress in 1792, was restrictively understood to limit militia service to "able-bodied white male citizen between the ages of 18 and 45." In 1798, in the act that formally organized the U.S. Marine Corps, Congress expressly excluded "Negroes, mulattos (of African and European descent), and Indians" from serving. The Marines remained lily-white until the manpower crisis of World War II.

African Americans encountered a very different reception in the army and the navy, the nation's principal military branches. The navy remained a bastion of opportunity for African Americans, in large part because it had to compete with the expanding fleet of American merchant vessels and fishing and whaling ships. Thus many blacks fought as sailors against the Barbary States (1801–1805) and in the WAR OF 1812 (1812–1815); at the end of the latter, fully 10 percent of the U.S. Navy was black. On land, however, blacks had a far less prominent role, although black explorers did play an important part in westward expansion. The Lewis and Clark Expedition (1804–1805) included one African American, Captain William

Henry O. Flipper was the first African America to graduate from the U.S. Military Academy at West Point. *CORBIS/Bettmann*

Clark's slave, York. Black MOUNTAIN MEN and fur trappers—such as JIM BECKWOURTH and Pierre Bonga—gained extensive knowledge of the mountainous West and later served as scouts and guides for the military.

In peacetime, the services once again sought to exclude African Americans. In 1820 the U.S. Army ordered that no blacks be accepted as recruits, and in 1839 the navy ordered that African Americans not exceed a maximum of 5 percent of total naval manpower, a policy that was often ignored yet unambiguously revealed the beginning of racial discrimination at sea. During these years at least some blacks thought it better to oppose the United States and its military. In the First Seminole War (1816–1818) and Second Seminole War (1835–1842), the Native American forces included many escaped slaves, maroons who had taken refuge with Florida Seminoles and who fought courageously against a numerically superior U.S. Army. During the MEXICAN WAR (1846–1848), however, just a handful of African Americans served in the U.S. Army, principally as servants to white officers or in support roles.

Military Role in the Civil War

The Civil War offered significant numbers of African Americans the chance to prove themselves in combat. At the outset, however, the war gave every appearance of being strictly a white man's fight. President ABRAHAM LINCOLN specifically refused to accept black recruits for the Union army. "Colored men were good enough to fight under Washington," remarked a frustrated FREDERICK DOUGLASS, "but they are not good enough to fight under McClellan." However, Union forces advancing through the slave states attracted large numbers of blacks who sought freedom and refuge and who confronted Union commanders with a significant tactical, legal, and moral problem. Southern slaveholders who were noncombatants regularly appealed to Union commanders demanding the return of their slave property. Army commanders faced with such pleas discovered that no set policy or precedent existed to guide them.

General Benjamin Butler, a Massachusetts abolitionist and political appointee, argued that if Southerners chose to regard runaway slaves as property, those slaves should be considered "contrabands of war" and, in light of their obvious strategic value, should not be returned. Soon these "contrabands" were put to work in support roles, and eventually some were outfitted with discarded Union equipment to serve as sentries to protect other African Americans. On the Sea Islands off the coast of Georgia, General David C. Hunter began organizing contrabands into military units as early as May 1862. That August, General Hunter's successor, General Rufus Saxton, received authorization from the War Department to recruit, arm, and train 5,000 African American volunteers under the leadership of white officers. That unit, named the First South Carolina Colored Volunteers, was the first African American regiment organized in the war, although it was not called into active duty until January 31, 1863.

In 1863—through the diligent efforts of Northern black leaders, most notably Frederick Douglass, and because of a growing manpower shortage in the North—President Abraham Lincoln issued the Emancipation Proclamation, which set the Union on the path to dismantling slavery and authorized African American military recruitment. This change in policy did not alter the profound racial hostility of many Northern whites, evidenced in the Draft Riots of 1863 that erupted in various Northern cities, most seriously in NEW YORK City, where a massive race riot by whites against blacks resulted in as many as 1,200 fatalities.

Nonetheless, Douglass, MARTIN R. DELANY, the Reverend HENRY HIGHLAND GARNET, and other African American leaders enthusiastically engaged in recruiting black volunteers. Black leaders even accepted that the new black regiments were to be commanded by white officers, although eventually Delany—commissioned a major in 1865—became the nation's first African American field officer. The most celebrated black regiment was the Fifty-Fourth Massachusetts Volunteers, subject of the 1989 film *Glory*. Like their white counterparts, African American women also took part in the Civil War, although mostly in support roles. The nation's two most prominent black women were actively involved in the struggle: SOJOURNER TRUTH worked as a nurse in a field hospital, and HARRIET TUBMAN performed valuable service as a scout and Union spy.

As historian Eric Foner pointed out, African American soldiers "played a crucial role not only in winning the Civil War, but also in defining the war's consequences." Even more important, they helped to transform the black community. In the course of military service, many former slaves learned to read and write, and a considerable number of black soldiers acquired the fundamentals of leadership, including, during RECONSTRUCTION, sixty state legislators, forty-one delegates to state constitutional conventions, three lieutenant governors, and four congressmen. For African Americans as a group, the war instilled a new confidence. Thus in 1865 black troops of the Fifty-Fourth Massachusetts marched into CHARLESTON, SOUTH CAROLINA—that city of planter-aristocrats and secessionist "fire-eaters" that had started the war—singing "John Brown's Body."

Reconstruction and the Late 1800s

Black soldiers were prominent in the U.S. military forces that occupied the defeated South during the early years of Reconstruction, at least until 1867 when complaints by Southerners led President Andrew Johnson to phase most of them out. Moreover, the contributions of the 180,000 black Union army volunteers—accounting for 9 to 10 percent of the total Union army enrollment—provided a compelling case not only for emancipation, accomplished by the Thirteenth Amendment (1865), but for granting African Americans citizenship through the FOURTEENTH AMENDMENT (1868) and for extending the suffrage to black males through the FIFTEENTH AMENDMENT (1870). Indeed, when President Abraham Lincoln cautiously endorsed the idea of black suffrage, he proposed a limited extension to "the very intelligent" and to "those who serve our cause as soldiers."

The late nineteenth century was a time of heightened racial animus on the part of white America, marked by a sharp increase in the LYNCHING of African Americans and the development of JIM CROW social segregation and black disfranchisement throughout the South. Black wartime contributions faded quickly from white memories. White harassment cut short the military careers of James Webster Smith and Henry O. Flipper, the first two African American cadets at the U.S. Military Academy at West Point, New York. Smith was dismissed before graduating; Flipper graduated in 1877, earning a commission as a lieutenant, but four years later was court-martialed and dishonorably discharged. Nearly a century passed before the army exonerated him and made his discharge honorable.

Peacetime reductions in defense spending after the Civil War resulted in the disbandment of almost all of the army's black regiments. But unlike peacetime contractions in years past, the U.S. Army did not wholly abandon African American soldiers. Until World War I it maintained four black units, the Twenty-Fourth and Twenty-Fifth Infantry and the Ninth and Tenth Cavalry Regiments. These regiments served mainly in the Far West and became known by Native Americans as BUFFALO SOLDIERS.

Spanish-American War and Philippines Insurrection

All four African American units played a prominent role in the Spanish-American War of 1898. The regimental quartermaster for the Tenth Cavalry was young Captain John J. Pershing, whose nickname Black Jack derived from his service with African American troops. The Tenth fought gallantly at the Battle of San Juan Hill, and in a speech several months later Pershing declared, "We officers of the Tenth Cavalry could have taken our black heroes into our arms. They had fought their way into our affections as they have fought their way into the hearts of the American people."

After the war, the army's four permanent black regiments—later augmented by two regiments of black volunteers—were ordered to the Philippines (1899–1902) to join in the jungle fighting between U.S. troops and Filipino freedom fighters that had erupted shortly after the Spanish capitulation. The so-called Philippines Insurrection, an undeclared and unpopular jungle war fought against an elusive enemy, had much in common with the later conflict in Vietnam. It was also potentially divisive for African Americans, since the Filipino freedom fighters were dark-skinned people seeking freedom from oppression. Moreover, white American troops in the Philippines consistently referred to the Filipino nationalists as "niggers."

In the United States, some black newspapers emphasized the similarities between the Filipinos and African Americans. The *Colored American* of Washington, D.C., observed that both groups were "struggling for the right of liberty and the pursuit of happiness." However, most African Americans stood by their country. When white newspapers questioned the ability of blacks to fight their racial "brothers," African American soldiers were adamant in their patriotism. "We are American citizens," one man in the Twenty-Fourth Infantry declared, "and we have at heart the interests of our native land in the same manner as do all Americans."

In late November and December 1899 on the island of Luzon, some 350 men of the Twenty-Fourth Infantry participated in one of the most successful operations of the war. After marching more than 480 kilometers (300 miles) through uncharted jungle, they captured rebel commander Daniel Tirona and his 1,000-man force. General Elwell S. Otis commended the Twenty-Fourth for its accomplishments despite "the difficulties encountered and the discomfort suffered by the troops."

In the U.S. Navy, however, conditions for African Americans deteriorated significantly by the turn of the twentieth century. The navy, once the most receptive branch of the military to African Americans, deliberately acted to reduce the number of black sailors. Service heads and ship captains justified the new policies as inevitable, given the navy's shift from sailing vessels that required a large and relatively unspecialized crew of common seamen, to steamships that relied on more highly trained engineers, gunners, and other specialists. Naval officers argued that blacks lacked the intellectual or technical capabilities to master the high technology of steam engines, and black sailors found themselves increasingly confined to work as stewards or messmen in ships' galleys. After the war in the Philippines, even those positions became fewer. Around the time of World War I, the navy began recruiting allegedly more tractable Filipino messmen.

Early 1900s and World War I

Thus the United States entered the twentieth century with a whites-only Marine Corps, a largely white navy, and a segregated army. After returning from duty in the Philippines, the nation's four black army regiments resumed their isolated postings in the West. The Tenth Cavalry served with distinction in General "Black Jack" Pershing's Punitive Expedition (1916–1917) against Mexican revolutionary leader Pancho Villa, riding 1,210 kilometers (750 miles) in the first four weeks of the ten-month operation. On January 9, 1918, members of the Tenth made the last cavalry charge against Native Americans in the history of the American West.

In general, however, African Americans learned to expect little in the way of recognition or justice from any branch of the armed forces. In the Southwest, the buffalo soldiers encountered steady racial harassment and intimidation—including lynching—yet no white citizen was ever punished for engaging in such assaults. In the 1906 BROWNSVILLE AFFAIR, President Theodore Roosevelt ordered the discharge without honor of 167 black enlisted men after a Texas shooting incident in which the men quite likely had no part. The men—of Companies B, C, and D of the Twenty-fifth Infantry—had served with distinction in CUBA and the Philippines, yet their exemplary record counted for little.

However, African Americans found greater opportunities as the nation mobilized for its 1917 entry into World War I, an ongoing conflict in EUROPE since August 1914. Ultimately, 200,000 black soldiers would be deployed to Europe, some serving with the American Expeditionary Force and others detailed to the French army. But almost 90 percent of those troops were relegated to service and labor battalions far behind the lines. Curiously, the War Department did not order its four black regiments—the U.S. Army's most experienced soldiers—to Europe; they remained at their posts along the Mexican border. The army did organize two black combat divisions, the Ninety-Second and Ninety-third Divisions, but when the Ninety-Third arrived in FRANCE, General Pershing, the supreme American commander, turned it over to the French army. As Colonel William Hayward, commander of the 369th Infantry Regiment and part of the 93rd Division wrote, "Our great American general simply put the black orphan in a basket, set it on the doorstep of the French, pulled the bell, and went away."

Both the Ninety-Third Division and the French inadvertently benefited from white Americans' unwillingness to serve with blacks. With the French, the Ninety-Third experienced far greater acceptance and more equal treatment than the U.S. Army then provided. The unit served heroically throughout the remainder of the war, suffering a casualty rate of 35 percent. The 369th Infantry Regiment spent 191 days on the front lines—longer than any other American unit, during which time it neither gave up an inch of Allied territory nor lost a single soldier through capture. Although no black soldiers were awarded a Medal of Honor during the war, in the 369th alone, 171 officers and men received either the Croix de Guerre or the Legion of Merit from the French government. The 369th included Lieutenant James Reese Europe, the black society musician from New York City who organized the regimental band. Lieutenant Europe was the first black officer to lead troops into combat in World War I, and he and his band also introduced the French to African American music, catalyzing a lasting French fascination with JAZZ.

Colored Officers Training Camp and the Houston Mutiny

African American leaders faced great difficulties in gaining recognition for black soldiers. In light of the service academies' hostility to black cadets, the NATIONAL ASSOCIATION FOR THE ADVANCEMENT OF COLORED PEOPLE (NAACP) pressed for the establishment of a training school for black officers. Joel E. Spingarn, a white member of the NAACP board of directors, coordinated the effort that established the Colored Officers' Training Camp at Fort Dodge in Des Moines, Iowa. Over the course of the war, Fort Dodge trained and commissioned 639 African American officers. However important the achievement of these officers was in symbolic terms, it did little to alter the reality of racial imbalance. During the war, African Americans comprised 13 percent of active-duty military manpower but a mere seven-tenths of 1 percent of the officer corps.

Black aspirations were dealt a further setback when members of the Third Battalion of the Twenty-Fourth Infantry took part in the Houston Mutiny of August 23, 1917—the first race riot in American history in which more whites than blacks died. The violence left sixteen whites and four black soldiers dead. After hasty courts-martial, nineteen more African American soldiers were executed for their part in the mutiny, and numerous others received lengthy jail sentences. Ironically, Lieutenant Colonel (Ret.) Michael Lee Lanning, author of *The African-American Soldier*, concluded that a key factor in the riot was the previous transfer of twenty-five of the battalion's most senior sergeants to Des Moines to attend the Colored Officers Training Camp, leaving only one experienced company first sergeant and seriously undermining battalion discipline. In the years to come, this incident effectively undermined any proposal to increase the role of black troops.

World War II

During World War I, challenges to racial injustice were fitful and fruitless, but in World War II, the nation faced a crisis of such magnitude that it swept away much of the rationale for exclusion and segregation. At the outset, however, African Americans encountered an all-too-familiar resistance from the white majority. In 1941, as the United States began to mobilize for war, there were few opportunities for African Americans in the booming defense industry. In response, black labor leader and civil rights activist A. PHILIP RANDOLPH organized a massive March on Washington Movement, and President Franklin D. Roosevelt, who was eager to head off the protest, signed EXECUTIVE ORDER 8802, banning racial discrimination in hiring for jobs in the defense industry and the federal government. Executive Order 8802 also established the FAIR EMPLOYMENT PRACTICES COMMITTEE to implement and oversee the new policy. Randolph's victory would be the first of many during the war years.

Throughout the war, the NAACP stressed the need for a Double-V campaign, meaning victory over fascism overseas and over racism at home. In fact, World War II set in motion a process of change that would not only integrate the armed services, it would transform the whole of African American life and remake the nation. Above all, World War II greatly accelerated the GREAT MIGRATION that first began in the early decades of the twentieth century. Between the 1940s and the 1960s, millions upon millions of African Americans would leave the South for newly opened high-paying factory jobs in urban areas in the North and West.

Within the armed services, World War II offers a long list of firsts, advancements, and breakthroughs. Initially, however, the opportunities for blacks remained few. The army's mobilization plan on the eve of World War II would have allowed African Americans to contribute only 6 percent of total army manpower. And few African American soldiers were given combat assignments. For example, DORIE MILLER, who shot down two enemy aircraft—and possibly downed two more—during the Japanese attack on Pearl Harbor, Hawaii, was a messman ineligible for military training. Moreover, he was ignored for months after the battle; only after concerted protests in the African American press did Miller receive a Navy Cross and an invitation to speak to the 1942 graduating class at the Great Lakes Naval Training Center. Miller was then assigned to the aircraft carrier *Liscome Bay*, but a year later, when a Japanese submarine sank the ship, the black hero of Pearl Harbor died as a messman.

Throughout the war, the official American policy was "not to intermingle colored and white enlisted personnel in the same regimental organizations." On the other hand, in 1940 President Franklin D. Roosevelt did commit the nation to establishing combatant and noncombatant black units in each branch of the armed forces. A year later the army activated the first black tank battalion, the 758th Tank Battalion. On March 7, 1942, the U.S. Army Air Corps commissioned its first black pilots, part of the all-black Ninety-Ninth Pursuit Squadron—the famed TUSKEGEE AIRMEN—that Colonel BENJAMIN O. DAVIS, JR., would command. On June 1st, the U.S. Marine Corps admitted African Americans for the first time in its 144-year history, taking as its first recruit a former Nashville, Tennessee, dogcatcher named George Thompson. A month later, the army accepted the first black women for the Women's Auxiliary Army Corps (WAAC), later simplified to the Women's Army Corps (WAC). Nonetheless, African American soldiers never accounted for more than 8.7 percent of army manpower, and only 15 percent of that number received combat assignments.

The U.S. Navy, in contrast to its record in the late eighteenth and early nineteenth centuries, remained the service most obdurate on racial issues. Secretary of the Navy Frank Knox and senior naval officers resisted assigning African American sailors to any but the most menial shipboard duties, as servants to officers, in construction battalions, or as messmen or stewards in ships' galleys. The navy did not commission its first group of black officers, known as the Golden Thirteen, until March 17, 1944. Three days later, it finally commissioned the USS *Mason,* an antisubmarine ship and the first navy vessel manned by black sailors under the command of white officers, at last providing African Americans with an official opportunity for naval combat. The navy would not order the desegregation of its shore facilities until after the end of the KOREAN WAR (1950–1953). Understandably, therefore, during World War II, African Americans represented only 5 percent of the navy's total manpower.

Integrating the Military

In contrast, the U.S. Army began to take steps to challenge the assumptions of Jim Crow segregation. In 1941 it began integrating its officers' candidate schools. In July 1944 the War Department prohibited discrimination in transportation and recreational facilities on all army bases. On a Texas military base not long after this directive was issued, Lieutenant JACKIE ROBINSON—who would soon become the first African American to break the long-standing color bar in major league baseball—refused to go to the back of a bus, resulting in his court-martial and complete vindication. Lieutenant Robinson's refusal to abide Southern Jim Crow practices was by no means an isolated example. Indeed, the pride and confidence of African American military veterans and their unwillingness to endure further discrimination would help provide the impetus for the CIVIL RIGHTS MOVEMENT of the 1950s and 1960s.

On December 26, 1944, during the worst days of the Battle of the Bulge, the army issued a directive requesting African American volunteers to be integrated into white combat units, a request that clearly marked the beginning of the end for the Jim Crow army. But no service branch welcomed the prospect of integration. The persistent delaying tactics of the various service heads outraged African Americans, whose pressure in 1948 moved President Harry S. Truman to order the integration of America's armed forces and to establish the President's Committee on Equality of Treatment and Opportunity in the Armed Services.

During the Korean War, the first integrated American combat units saw action, and they proved that racial prejudices and enmities fall away quickly under the pressure of battle. By the war's end, over 90 percent of black troops were serving in integrated units. The only regrets that African Americans expressed about this process were at the disbandment of the four historic black regiments, which closed a part of black history reaching back to the end of the Civil War. Above all, the Korean War transformed the U.S. Marine Corps. At the start of that conflict, African Americans made up only 1,075 of the nation's 74,279 marines, and of that 1,075, nearly half (427) were stewards. In the space of two years, the corps changed from the most segregated branch of the armed forces to one approaching complete integration. The United States disbanded its last segregated unit in 1954, the year in which the Supreme Court of the United States issued its pivotal decision in BROWN V. BOARD OF EDUCATION. Thus when the nation had scarcely begun its effort to end segregation in public schools, racial integration was nearly an accomplished fact in the armed forces.

Integration proceeded, not always smoothly, through the 1950s and 1960s. The military made great strides toward integrating its rank and file, but progress was much slower in the officer corps, although undeniable gains were made there as well. Moreover, during the Vietnam War, African American soldiers faced a new problem—rather than being excluded from combat, they now found themselves almost inevitably condemned to it. African Americans, as military historian Colonel Lanning observed, were "13.5 percent of the military-age population [and] 10.6 percent of the total force in the war zone," but accounted for "20 percent of U.S. battlefield casualties." It was, as one black soldier remarked, "the kind of integration that could kill you."

The Vietnam War was the first war in which African American leaders gradually turned against the federal government—which they had long regarded as African Americans' best ally. Paradoxically, as Colonel Lanning noted, the first black leaders to come out against the war were not, generally speaking, those who advocated nonviolence. Thus the militant and often bellicose MALCOLM X spoke out against the war as early as 1964; the Reverend MARTIN LUTHER KING, JR., on the other hand, did not voice his opposition until 1967.

Far more quickly than most civil rights activists, African American soldiers in Vietnam came to doubt the wisdom of their political and military leaders. Black soldiers—along with Mexican Americans and working-class whites—faced the most dangerous and thankless combat assignments. Regardless of race, these combat troops came in many ways to share a common outlook. They questioned military discipline, sometimes challenged orders, and generally developed a cynical attitude toward military authority and political leaders. On the other hand, soldiers in the field learned that they needed to count on one another, regardless of race. Indeed, in a war where the difficulty in knowing the enemy and the obduracy of the high command were equally legendary, they discovered that they could not really count on anyone else.

African Americans in the All-Volunteer Army

During the war, Americans black and white came to mistrust the draft, which had been established by the Selective Service Act of 1948. In response, President Richard M. Nixon approved a proposal for an all-volunteer military, and the army inducted its last draftees in mid-1973. The new policy resulted in a sharp increase in the proportion of African Americans in military service. Many blacks joined the military because it offered jobs, training, and educational and other benefits, while in the larger

In 1848 President Harry Truman issued an executive order ending segregation in the United States armed forces. The first integrated combat units saw action in Korea in the 1950s.
CORBIS

society African Americans faced an unemployment rate significantly higher than that of the white majority. But critics argued that the phrase *all-volunteer* misrepresented what was in fact an economic draft, in which the lack of alternatives forced a disproportionate number of blacks into military service. Thus in 1972 about 17 percent of the army was African American, but by 1981 that figure had nearly doubled to one-third. The navy continued to be the least congenial service for blacks; nonetheless, the proportion of black sailors also essentially doubled from 6.4 to 12 percent. Only the U.S. Air Force lagged in its ability to attract African Americans, posting a much smaller increase from 12.6 to 16.5 percent.

At the same time, the military did not measure its success in achieving racial integration in merely quantitative terms. It also confronted much thornier problems of prejudice and discriminatory attitudes, and it made an unprecedented effort to redress past injustices. Since the 1970s, military historical commissions have reexamined the records of various courts-martial, disciplinary hearings, and recommendations for service awards in which the original decisions may have been tainted by racial prejudice and discrimination.

In 1972 the army exonerated the 167 black soldiers punished in the 1906 Brownsville Affair. Four years later it provided an honorable discharge for Lieutenant HENRY O. FLIPPER, and in 1977, the 100th anniversary of Lieutenant Flipper's graduation from West Point, the military academy unveiled a bust in his honor. In 1991 President George Bush presented family members of Corporal Freddie Stowers with a "long overdue" Medal of Honor for his heroism on September 28, 1918, while serving in the Ninety-Third Infantry Division in France, making Corporal Stowers the first black soldier granted a Medal of Honor for service in World War I.

In 1996 the Department of Defense decided to honor seven African Americans with Medals of Honor for their heroism during World War II. During the war itself not one African American soldier was judged worthy of the nation's highest military honor. In a White House ceremony on January 13, 1997, President Bill Clinton presented the Medal of Honor to the only survivor among the seven recipients, Lieutenant Vernon J. Baker. On April 5, 1945, Lieutenant Baker had led his twenty-five-man platoon against heavily fortified German positions. He killed two Germans in an observation post and led his men on to destroy six German machine gun nests and kill twenty-six German soldiers. Only Lieutenant Baker and six of his men survived the assault. In presenting the medal, President Clinton declared: "History has been made whole again, and our nation is bestowing honor on those who have long deserved it. They were denied their nation's highest honor, but their deeds could not be denied, and they cleared the way to a better world." When journalists asked Lieutenant Baker how he had felt about defending his country in a Jim Crow army, he replied, "I was an angry young man. We were all angry. But we had a job to do, and we did it."

Persian Gulf War and After

The PERSIAN GULF WAR (1991) was the first war in the nation's history in which the top military commander, General COLIN POWELL, chairman of the Joint Chiefs of Staff, was black. Moreover, General Cal Waller, an African American, was second-in-command to General Norman Schwarzkopf in Operation Desert Storm, as the Pentagon designated the Allied war effort. African Americans were also heavily overrepresented in U.S. forces in the war zone. Although only 12 percent of the military-age population, African Americans accounted for 26 percent of the troops in the Gulf. This trend continued in the Iraq War twelve years later. More than sixty black U.S. military personnel had died in that conflict by December 2003.

Between the early 1980s and the early 2000s, the proportion of African Americans in the military has remained relatively constant. In 1996 African Americans comprised about 21.9 percent of the total enlisted forces—30.2 of the army, 18.5 percent of the navy, 17.1 percent of the Marines, and 16.8 percent of the air force—all well above the proportion of African Americans in the total population. In 2003 blacks continued to represent about one-fifth of all military personnel. There is an obvious reason for the prevalence of blacks in the military. As Colin Powell, who became secretary of state in 2001, observed: "The army was living the democratic idea ahead of the rest of America. Beginning in the fifties, less discrimination, a truer merit system, and leveler playing fields existed inside the gates of our military posts than in any Southern city hall or Northern corporation."

Although some problems remain—particularly the relative shortage of blacks within the officer corps—in the early twenty-first century, African Americans have achieved a level of equality in the armed forces that the larger society cannot yet approach.

See also Abolitionism in the United States; Emancipation Proclamation and the Thirteenth Amendment; Fifty-Fourth Massachusetts Volunteer Infantry Regiment; Free Blacks in the United States; Integration, An Interpretation; March on Washington, 1941; Maroonage in the Americas; New York City Draft Riot of 1863; Runaway Slaves in the United States; Segregation in the United States; Seminole Wars; Slavery in the United States; Spanish-American War, African Americans in the; World War I and African Americans; World War II and African Americans.

James Sellman

Millender-McDonald, Juanita

1938–

Democratic member of the United States House of Representatives from California since 1996.

Born in BIRMINGHAM, ALABAMA, Juanita Millender-McDonald earned a bachelor's degree from the University of Redlands and a master's degree from California State University, LOS ANGELES. She taught in the Los Angeles School District and received national recognition when she served on the National Commission on Teaching and America's Future. In 1990 Millender-McDonald became the first black elected to the Carson City Council. During her second year on the council, she was elected mayor pro tem for Carson. In 1992 she won a seat in the California State Assembly.

After Representative Walter R. Tucker III resigned as U.S. representative for California's Thirty-Seventh Congressional District, Millender-McDonald announced her candidacy for the vacant seat. She defeated eight other candidates in the March 1996 Democratic primary. In the general election, she ran unopposed. She was sworn into office in April 1996 and has been reelected in subsequent elections. She is a member of the CONGRESSIONAL BLACK CAUCUS and currently serves on the Committee on House Administration, the House Committee on Small Business, and the House Committee on Transportation and Infrastructure. *Ebony* magazine has named her as one of the 100 Most Influential Black Americans.

See also Democratic Party; United States House of Representatives, African Americans in.

Miller, Cheryl

1964–

African American basketball player, one of the greatest female players ever.

Born in Riverside, California, Cheryl Miller was a four-time All-American in high school and scored 105 points in a single high school BASKETBALL game in 1982. Her high school team won 132 games and lost only four during her four years there. In 1982 Miller enrolled at the University of Southern California (USC), where she became a four-time collegiate All-American. For three consecutive years she also won the Naismith Award as the nation's outstanding female basketball player (1984–1986). In 1983 and in 1984 Miller led USC to the National Collegiate Athletic Association (NCAA) women's basketball championship, and was named most valuable player of the tournament both years. She finished her collegiate career with averages of 23.6 points per game and twelve rebounds per game, and in her four years USC's win-loss record was 112-20. She was the first basketball player at USC—male or female—to have a jersey number retired (an honor whereby future players do not wear the number).

Miller also starred on the United States national basketball teams that won gold medals at the 1983 Pan-American Games in Caracas, Venezuela; the 1984 Olympic Games in LOS ANGELES; and the 1986 Goodwill Games in Moscow. After graduating from USC in 1986, she was drafted by several professional basketball leagues, including the United States Basketball League, a men's league. In the late 1980s, however, Miller suffered knee injuries that prevented her from continuing her playing career. From 1986 to 1991 she worked as an assistant coach at USC and as a television sports commentator. She became the head coach of the USC women's basketball team in 1993 but after two seasons she left to resume her broadcasting career. In 1995 Miller was inducted into the Basketball Hall of Fame. In 1997 she was hired as head coach of the Phoenix Mercury of the Women's National Basketball Association (WNBA). She coached the Mercury to the 1998 WNBA Finals, where her team lost, then resigned after the 2000 season, citing fatigue. Miller is currently a sideline reporter, studio analyst, and announcer for Turner Sports.

See also Olympics, African Americans and the; Sports and African Americans; Television and African Americans.

Miller, Dorie

1919–1943

African American war hero.

Dorie Miller was born Doris Miller in Waco, Texas, the son of Conery Miller and Henrietta (maiden name unknown), sharecroppers. Miller attended Waco's segregated Moore High School and became the school's 200-pound star fullback. As the third of four sons in a family engaged in subsistence farming, however, he was forced to drop out of school to find work. In September 1939 he joined the navy as a mess attendant.

The navy was then rigidly segregated. Except for a small group of black sailors in the general service, survivors of the mostly integrated pre–WORLD WAR I fleet, blacks were restricted to the steward's branch, where they wore distinctive uniforms and insignia. Even chief stewards could not exercise authority over men with lower ratings in the general service. Stewards manned the officers' mess, maintained the officers' billets aboard ship, and, in some instances, took care of the quarters of high officials ashore. Despite the fact that their enlistment contracts restricted their training and duties, stewards, like everyone aboard ship, were assigned battle stations, including positions at the guns and on the bridge. Miller received the standard eight-week training course given mess attendants at the Naval Receiving Station, Norfolk, Virginia, and, after a brief stint on an ammunition ship, was assigned to the battleship *West Virginia*.

In the early hours of December 7, 1941, the *West Virginia* was at its berth in Pearl Harbor, Hawaii, and Miller was going about his daily chore of collecting officers' laundry when the call to battle stations sounded. Miller arrived at his station in the antiaircraft battery magazine amidships to find it in flames, a victim of the initial Japanese torpedo attack. Hurrying topside, he followed his supervisory officer to the bridge where, despite enemy strafing and in the face of a serious fire, the powerful young sailor carried the ship's mortally wounded captain to a safer place.

The officer then loaded the two 50-mm bridge guns and ordered the untrained Miller to man one of them. Asked later about his subsequent actions, Miller said, "It wasn't hard. I just pulled the trigger and she worked fine. I'd watched others use those guns. I guess I fired her for about fifteen minutes. I think I got one of those Jap planes. They were diving pretty close to us." In fact Miller continued firing at the enemy planes until ordered to abandon the burning bridge.

In the confused aftermath of Pearl Harbor, Miller's feat, although noted in naval dispatches, went unheralded. Rumors continued to circulate, however, and on March 14, 1942, the *Pittsburgh Courier*, a widely read black newspaper, broke the story, demanding official public recognition of Miller's heroism. Secretary of the Navy Frank Knox, an ardent defender of the navy's racial exclusion policy, reacted belatedly by writing Miller a letter of commendation, but this only fueled the growing demand for public honors. Edgar Brown, representing the National Negro Council, urged congressmen to pass a bill introduced by Senator James M. Mead of New York and others to award Miller the Medal of Honor, and Wendell Willkie, the REPUBLICAN PARTY leader, called on President Franklin D. Roosevelt to intervene.

Knox argued that his letter of commendation and Miller's anticipated promotion to mess attendant, first class, provided sufficient recognition, but the president, no doubt reacting to widespread charges of racism in the navy, overruled Knox. In an extraordinary move, President Roosevelt personally ordered Miller awarded the Navy Cross. On May 27, 1942, the commander of the Pacific fleet, Admiral Chester W. Nimitz, bestowed the navy's second-highest award on Miller with due ceremony.

Despite Knox's intransigence, the position of blacks in the navy had changed considerably by mid-1942. Forced to open its general service to African Americans and now dependent exclusively on the Selective Service with its 10 percent black quota for manpower, the navy witnessed a dramatic increase in the number of black sailors in all jobs and ratings. The Bureau of Naval Personnel faced the daunting task of training and assigning thousands of minority members while maintaining their morale in a segregated environment. Civil rights leaders deftly connected recognition of Miller's heroism to the growing aspirations of the new black sailors and the black public at large, and the bureau readily endorsed the *Courier*'s suggestion that Miller come home to speak to the young black draftees.

Miller, the high school dropout, proved surprisingly effective at his public affairs assignments, speaking before large audiences throughout the United States. In due course, however, he was promoted to petty officer rank (cook, third class) in the general service and was reassigned to sea. He returned to the fleet in time to participate in the battle for Tarawa, but on November 24, 1943, he was among the 644 men lost when the escort carrier *Liscome Bay* sank during the battle for Makin.

Almost thirty years after Miller's death a more racially enlightened navy, desiring to honor the exploits of its minority heroes, named the Service School Command barracks at Great Lakes Naval Station, Illinois, in Miller's honor, and in June 1973 his mother christened the USS *Miller*, a Knox-class destroyer escort. But again such honors were controversial because they followed closely another effort to use the memory of Miller's experience to advance the general civil rights agenda. The navy opposed an effort, this time led by Senator Edward M. Kennedy, among others, to award Miller the Medal of Honor posthumously. The chief of naval operations, Admiral Elmo M. Zumwalt, himself an ardent champion of minority rights in the navy, rejected the request on the grounds that, in the absence of new evidence, the Navy Cross had been the appropriate award and that naming a ship and barracks in Miller's honor constituted sufficient recognition. In the late 1980s Representative Joe DioGuardi of New York, chagrined that no black serviceman was awarded the Medal of Honor in either world war, again nominated Miller for the nation's highest decoration as representative of all the black heroes of WORLD WAR II, but to no avail.

Ironically, this son of humble sharecroppers, who during his short life knew nothing but segregation and discrimination, was transformed by an extraordinary act of personal heroism into an enduring symbol of the struggle of African Americans for equal treatment and opportunity.

Bibliography

Materials about Dorie Miller are in the Operational Archives Branch, U.S. Naval Historical Center.

Foner, Jack D. *Blacks and the Military in American History*. 1974.

MacGregor, Morris J. *Integration of the Armed Forces*. 1981.

Nalty, Bernard C. *Strength for the Fight: A History of Black Americans in the Military*. 1986.

Prange, Gordon W., with Donald M. Goldstein and Katherine V. Dillon. *At Dawn We Slept: The Untold Story of Pearl Harbor*. 1978.

From *American National Biography*. John A. Garraty and Mark C. Carnes, eds. Oxford University Press, 1999. Reprinted by permission of the American Council of Learned Societies.

Morris J. MacGregor

Miller, Kelly

1863–1939

African American educator and scholar who sought to achieve a middle ground between the conservatism of Booker T. Washington and the radicalism of W. E. B. Du Bois.

Kelly Miller was the sixth of ten children of a slave woman and a freedman who served the Confederate army during the AMERICAN CIVIL WAR. He was educated at missionary schools and in his mid-teens was admitted to the Fairfield Institute, a preparatory school in Winnsboro, South Carolina. Earning a scholarship to HOWARD UNIVERSITY in WASHINGTON, D.C., Miller finished his preparatory education there and entered Howard's bachelor's program while working as a clerk for the federal government. He graduated in 1886 and continued to work as a clerk. In addition, Miller studied privately with a mathematician at the U.S. Naval Observatory.

On the strength of this relationship, in 1887 Miller became the first African American admitted to Johns Hopkins University in BALTIMORE, MARYLAND. A tuition increase in 1889 prevented him from completing his graduate studies, but after a short stint as a high school teacher in Washington, D.C., he was appointed professor of mathematics at Howard. In 1894 he married Annie May Butler, a Baltimore teacher, with whom he had five children.

Miller soon became interested in the emerging field of sociology and its application to the study of race relations. By the mid-1890s he had relegated his mathematical pursuits to a secondary status and published extensively on the current and future state of African Americans. His writings earned him a joint appointment as professor of mathematics and sociology. At the time, Booker T. Washington's philosophy—that blacks should receive an industrial rather than a liberal education and seek accomodation rather than confrontation with whites—had achieved widespread acceptance among whites and many blacks.

Although Miller praised Washington for encouraging blacks to apply themselves where and when they could, he criticized Washington for denigrating higher education. When W. E. B. Du Bois and other black scholars founded the NIAGARA MOVEMENT in opposition to Washington, Miller appraised the movement equally sharply, saying that the radicals were right for trying to return higher education to greater esteem, but that they went too far in their condemnations of industrial schooling. In one of his many articles Miller wrote that "the subject of industrial and higher education is merely one of ratio and proportion, and not one of fundamental controversy." Because of his importance as a centrist, Miller was courted by both camps; neither, however, completely trusted him.

In 1907 Miller became dean of Howard University's College of Arts and Sciences. In the hope of enrolling more students, he oversaw a controversial addition of sciences—including applied (industrial) sciences—to the mostly classical curriculum. He traveled widely and recruited students throughout the country; as a result Howard's enrollment increased dramatically. He also oversaw the donation of Howard alumnus JESSE E. MOORLAND's private library to the school, forming the core of what would become the MOORLAND-SPINGARN RESEARCH COLLECTION. Miller was prominent in prodding Howard's board of directors to allow blacks to govern the school. (Since its founding, Howard had always had a white president.) On many occasions Miller himself was mentioned as a potential candidate for the post, and so influential was he at Howard that the school was sometimes called "Kelly Miller's University." When an African American, MORDECAI W. JOHNSON, was finally appointed to the presidency in 1926, however, Miller was overlooked, perhaps because of his stinging criticism of incompetent and racist white university presidents. J. Stanley Durkee, the last of these presidents, demoted Miller, who never completely recovered his lost power.

Miller wrote and published his opinions on a variety of issues. He refuted the argument that blacks' problems were caused by genetic inferiority; he critiqued and then opposed the migration of blacks from rural areas to highly competitive cities; and he condemned the racial discrimination of white LABOR UNIONS (his antiunion stance grew to include opposition to black unions as well). He also published a weekly column in the 1920s and 1930s in more than one hundred newspapers. At its peak the column reached as many as half a million readers. In his later years he was disturbed by the large number of radicals appointed at Howard and urged a government investigation on the teaching of communism there. He was rebuked by Mordecai W. Johnson, Howard's first black president, for attempting to restrict freedom of speech. Miller retired from Howard in 1934 and died of a heart attack in 1939.

Miller, Thomas Ezekiel

1849–1938

African American political leader and educator.

Thomas Ezekiel Miller was born in Ferrebeeville, South Carolina, the son of Richard Miller and Mary Ferrebee, occupations unknown. Miller's race was a source of periodic concern and speculation. Although he always considered himself to be black, Miller's very fair complexion led to allegations during his political career that he was white, the abandoned child of an unmarried white couple.

Miller moved to CHARLESTON with his parents in the early 1850s, where he attended schools for free black children. His mother died when he was nine. As a youngster he distributed the *Charleston Mercury* to local hotels, and during the CIVIL WAR he worked aboard South Carolina railroad trains delivering newspapers between Charleston and Savannah. When the Confederate government seized the railroads, Miller found himself in the service and in the uniform of the Confederacy. Union forces captured him as they advanced into South Carolina in January 1865 and confined him for two weeks in a Union stockade.

Following the war Miller accompanied Union troops to Long Island, New York, and then pursued his education at Hudson School, north of NEW YORK CITY. After graduation from Pennsylvania's LINCOLN UNIVERSITY in 1872, he returned to South Carolina and enrolled at South Carolina College (now the University of South Carolina), where he took at least one law course. He read law with both state solicitor P. L. Wiggins and state supreme court chief justice Franklin J. Moses, Sr., and was admitted to the South Carolina bar in 1875, moving to the city of Beaufort to set up practice. Miller had married Anna M. Hume, probably in 1874; they had nine children, seven of whom survived him.

Miller spent most of the next two decades active in politics and the REPUBLICAN PARTY. He was elected to the Beaufort County School Commission in 1872, and he represented Beaufort in the state house of representatives from 1874 to 1880. Elected to the state senate in 1880, Miller resigned two years later. He lost a bid for a seat in the U.S. House of Representatives in 1886, but in 1888 he challenged William Elliott's election to the U.S. House, and following a protracted House investigation, Miller was seated. He represented South Carolina's Seventh District from September 1890 to March 1891. In reaction to white Southern DEMOCRATIC attacks on the Lodge Federal Elections bill (also known as the "Force Bill"), a proposal created to protect the voting rights of Southern black men, Miller passionately defended the progress made by blacks since emancipation. He also condemned white landowners for exploiting black farmers, charging that they negotiated unfair contracts and paid blacks in often worthless scrip. Miller defeated Elliott again in the 1890 congressional election but lost the subsequent challenge in the South Carolina Supreme Court when the justices ruled that though Miller's ballots were printed on the required white paper, it was "white paper of a distinctly yellow tinge." The 1892 congressional election went to black candidate GEORGE W. MURRAY when Miller's too-light coloring became an issue in the campaign. Miller returned to the South Carolina house in 1894 to serve until 1896. When not in public office, Miller returned to his position as an attorney on the payroll of Beaufort merchant D. H. Wall, an association he maintained for fifty years until Wall's death in 1935.

Miller was one of six black men elected to the 1895 state constitutional convention called expressly for the purpose of disfranchising black voters. Tenaciously and eloquently he defended black voting rights, rejecting claims that black political leaders had proven more corrupt and dishonest than white politicians. He challenged the convention's presiding officer, U.S. senator Benjamin R. Tillman, to recognize the contributions and sacrifices made by black Americans to the nation:

> Mr. President, this country and its institutions are as much the common birthright and heritage of the American negro as it is the possession of you and yours. We have fought in every Indian war, in every foreign war, in every domestic struggle by the side of the white soldiers from Boston commons and Lake Erie to the Mississippi Valley and the banks of the Rio Grande.

He tried to reassure whites by insisting that black people neither sought political control nor opposed segregation: "The negroes do not want to dominate. They do not want and would not have social equality, but they do want to cast a ballot for the men who make their laws and administer the laws. Is there anything new in this plaintive appeal to the nation[?]" He concluded by "pleading for justice to a people whose rights are about to be taken away with one fell swoop." Most of the 154 white delegates were unmoved. Urged on by Tillman, they fabricated an array of disfranchisement measures—the principal one of which required potential voters to demonstrate an understanding of the state constitution—allowing election officials to exclude black voters at will. Miller and the other five black delegates refused to sign the new constitution.

Miller was more successful in demanding the establishment of a black college. Beginning in 1872 most of the state's federal land-grant funds were appropriated to State A&M College, an institution operated by Claflin University in Orangeburg. Claflin, a Methodist school for freedmen that opened in 1869, was run by Northern white teachers and administrators. Miller and other black leaders wanted the land-grant monies allocated to an autonomous black institution. Miller convinced Tillman and his lieutenants to support legislation creating the Colored Normal, Industrial, Agricultural, and Mechanical College of South Carolina (currently South Carolina State University) by severing the State A&M College's ties with Claflin. By law, the awkwardly named new institution could admit and employ only blacks. Miller later exclaimed, "Thank God the College is in the hands of Negroes."

Four days after the legislation creating the college passed, Miller resigned his house seat, and a few weeks later Governor John Gary Evans and the all-white board of trustees selected Miller as the institution's first president. The new college became a training school modeled after Hampton Institute and BOOKER T. WASHINGTON'S TUSKEGEE INSTITUTE. Opened in 1896, it did not grant four-year bachelor's degrees until 1925. In an 1897 speech Miller explained the purpose of the new institution: "The work of our college is along the industrial line. We are making educated and worthy school teachers, educated and reliable mechanics, educated, reliable and frugal farmers."

In 1910 Miller publicly opposed the election as governor of Coleman Blease, a demagogue devoted to white supremacy. Following Blease's victory, the new governor demanded and received Miller's resignation as president of the college. Miller moved to Charleston, where he retired but remained active in community affairs. He enthusiastically supported U.S. entry into WORLD WAR I and offered to help recruit 30,000 black men. When an all-white state committee on civic preparedness decided to appoint a black subcommittee to aid the war effort, Miller agreed to serve on it. He was a prominent figure in the successful effort in 1919 to replace white teachers with black teachers in Charleston's black public schools. In 1923 Miller moved to PHILADELPHIA but returned in 1934 to Charleston, where he died.

Deeply devoted to American ideals, Thomas E. Miller fervently believed black people should enjoy every right and privilege accorded whites. He defiantly opposed efforts to disfranchise black men. He endorsed hard work, frugality, and industrial training as means to success. While he accepted segregation, he sought to turn it to the advantage of black people through establishing a black college and by insisting that black teachers have the opportunity to teach in black schools. The inscription on his tombstone reads: "Not having loved the white man less, but having felt the Negro needed me more."

Bibliography

Some information on Miller is located in the Carter G. Woodson Papers in the Library of Congress. For his speech on the Lodge Federal Elections bill, see the Congressional Record 22 (1891): 2691–96.

Drago, Edmund L. *Initiative, Paternalism, and Race Relations: Charleston's Avery Normal Institute.* 1990.
Holt, Thomas. *Black over White: Negro Political Leadership in South Carolina during Reconstruction.* 1977.
Newby, I. A. *Black Carolinians: A History of Blacks in South Carolina from 1895 to 1968.* 1973.
Obituary, *(Charleston) News & Observer,* April 9, 1938.
Obituary, *Journal of Negro History,* July 1938.
Rawick, George P., ed. *The American Slave: A Composite Autobiography,* 392–96. Supp., ser. 2. Vol. 1. 1979.

The Suffrage: Speeches by Negroes in the Constitutional Convention. c. 1896.
Tindall, George B. *South Carolina Negroes 1877–1900.* 1952.

From *American National Biography*. John A. Garraty and Mark C. Carnes, eds. Oxford University Press, 1999. Reprinted by permission of the American Council of Learned Societies.

William C. Hine

Millet

Variety of grass that is a staple crop throughout much of Africa.

The term *millet* is used to describe several species of the *Poaceae* (grass) family, which people first began cultivating in Africa approximately 4,000 years ago. Millet plants produce flowers called racemes, which yield small edible seeds. Generally the seeds are hulled, and cereals are then made from them. Millet plants range in height from 0.3 to 1.3 m (about 1 to 4 ft), except for pearl millet (*Pennisetum americanum*), the tallest of all the millet species, which can produce stalks ranging from 1.5 to 3 m (about 5 to 10 ft) and yields the largest seeds.

Several kinds of millet are cultivated in Africa, among them pearl and finger millet (*Eleusine coracana*). It is a particularly valued grain crop in arid regions because it grows relatively quickly (in approximately 60 to 80 days) and can tolerate both drought and poor soil. It is also higher in protein than most of Africa's other staple starch crops such as rice, maize, and cassava, and its bland taste combines well with other foods and spices. Porridge made from boiled millet flour (once ground primarily by women by hand, though now increasingly machine-milled) is the core of many traditional African dishes, typically accompanied by spicy sauces made from a combination of vegetables and fish, meat, or peanuts. Millet can also be used to brew beer.

Bibliography

Hulse, Joseph H. *Sorghum and the Millets: Their Composition and Nutritive Value.* Academic Press, 1980.
Rachie, Kenneth O. *The Millets: Importance, Utilization, and Outlook.* International Crops Research Institute for the Semi-Arid Tropics, 1975.

Robert Fay

Million Man March

Rally organized in 1995 by Nation of Islam minister Louis Farrakhan and Benjamin Chavis to draw attention to the social conditions of African Americans and to urge black men to assume control over their lives.

The Million Man March emerged from a call by NATION OF ISLAM minister LOUIS FARRAKHAN for a Day of Atonement that would draw attention to the social and economic problems plaguing African American males. On October 16, 1995, approximately 900,000 black men congregated in WASHINGTON, D.C., to hear speeches from black luminaries such as ROSA PARKS, JESSE JACKSON, and MAYA ANGELOU. Farrakhan provided the keynote address. He asked black men to assume responsibility for themselves, their families, their communities, and America as a whole, instead of placing the blame for their conditions on outside forces. Primarily organized by BENJAMIN CHAVIS, the former executive director of the NATIONAL ASSOCIATION FOR THE ADVANCEMENT OF COLORED PEOPLE (NAACP), the Million Man March was the largest gathering of African Americans in history, surpassing in size the 1963 MARCH ON WASHINGTON.

Despite the numbers, from its inception the march drew severe criticism. It was denounced on the basis of Farrakhan's reputation as an anti-Semitic firebrand. Both men and women within the black community criticized the males-only policy and the undue emphasis placed on males as leaders within the African American community. (This eventually led to a MILLION WOMAN MARCH in PHILADELPHIA, PENNSYLVANIA, on October 25, 1997.) Others scorned the Nation of Islam's brand of black capitalism. And with its emphasis on individual responsibility as the means of racial uplift, it was charged with overlooking the systemic problem of racism within American social, economic, and political institutions.

While the long-term effects of the march have yet to be determined, it reinvigorated African American grassroots activism. It was also seen as an attempt by Farrakhan to move the Nation of Islam into the mainstream of American politics through development of a secular, coalition-based movement inclusive of the broad spectrum of African American political thought.

Peter Hudson

Million Woman March

Rally of more than one million African American women seeking to build coalitions within the black community.

Asia Coney and Phile Chionesu do not command the same attention on the American political scene as LOUIS FARRAKHAN, minister of the NATION OF ISLAM, or BENJAMIN CHAVIS, former chairman of the NATIONAL ASSOCIATION FOR THE ADVANCEMENT OF COLORED PEOPLE (NAACP). Yet the two African American women organized a march in PHILADELPHIA, PENNSYLVANIA, the size of which eclipsed that of the much publicized MILLION MAN MARCH, organized by Farrakhan and Chavis two years earlier. On October 25, 1997, an estimated 1.5 million women congregated along Philadelphia's Benjamin Franklin Parkway for the Million Woman March. Under the slogan "Repentance, Resurrection, and Restoration," the march aimed to forge black economic, social, and political coalitions that could rebuild an African American community that was quickly losing the gains made during the CIVIL RIGHTS MOVEMENT.

Although the Nation of Islam endorsed the march, traditional African American political institutions, such as the NAACP, were not involved in its organization. Organizers relied instead on grassroots activist networks, independent black media, and the Internet. Keynote speeches were delivered by United States Representative MAXINE WATERS, South African activist WINNIE MADIKIZELA-MANDELA, and Tynnetta Muhammad, the widow of the Nation of Islam's founder, ELIJAH MUHAMMAD. Waters drew the loudest cheers for a statement that summed up the significance of the event. "America, be placed on notice," she proclaimed. "We know who we are. We understand our collective power. Following today, we will act on that power."

Despite such bold pronouncements, the immediate impact of the march was unclear. Its major accomplishments may have been to draw attention to the declining social conditions of African Americans in the post–Civil Rights era and to demonstrate solidarity among black women. In 2000 Louis Farrakhan organized a Million Family March that took place on the fifth anniversary of the Million Man March.

Peter Hudson

Mills Brothers

African American pop vocal quartet that became famous in the 1930s for the ability to imitate jazz instruments.

The four Mills brothers were born to a musical family in Piqua, Ohio. Their paternal grandfather had sung with the Sourbeck Jubilee Singers, and as children John Jr., Herbert, Harry, and Donald performed professionally at local social events. In 1925 the boys—then between the ages of ten and fifteen—auditioned to appear on CINCINNATI radio station WLW and won a prolonged broadcasting contract.

During the next few years they became station regulars and adopted stage-names in accord with station sponsors—the Tasty Yeast Jesters (Tasty Yeast) and the Steamboat Four (Sohio Motor Oil)—but also achieved renown as Four Boys and a Guitar. Their success caught the attention of talent scouts from NEW YORK CITY, and in 1930 they signed a three-year contract with CBS Records, at the time an unusually long contract for African American musicians. The Mills Brothers' debut album in 1931 won them instant acclaim. Their single "Tiger Rag" sold a million copies, and in 1932 they performed with Bing Crosby in *The Big Broadcast*, the first of the numerous films in which the quartet appeared.

Much of the Mills Brothers' popularity originated from arrangements in which they simulated a full instrumental ensemble by singing as horns. The only accompaniment came from John Jr.'s guitar playing; the rest of their rich sound comprised saxophone, trumpet, and tuba imitations as well as tight, sweet, four-part harmonies. Throughout the 1930s they scored hit after hit with this formula, including "You Rascal You," "Good-Bye Blues," and "Swing It Sister." In the 1940s the quartet adopted conventional pop arrangements yet maintained their popularity—their 1942 hit, "Paper Doll," sold six million copies. Meanwhile they undertook collaborations with some of the era's top African American musicians, such as DUKE ELLINGTON, CAB CALLOWAY, and ELLA FITZGERALD.

The group remained together until 1982, although with changes in their roster. The oldest brother, John Jr., died in 1935, after which his father filled his role as bass vocalist and ex-bandleader Bernard Addison played guitar. At times the three remaining brothers performed as a trio. By the end, the group had recorded almost 2,500 songs.

The Mills Brothers' legacy involved social as well as musical accomplishments. Their vocal styles were a historical first, as were the terms under which they recorded them for white record companies. Their popularity among audiences of different races was unprecedented and influenced the formation—and mainstream acceptance—of doo-wop and RHYTHM AND BLUES groups in the 1950s.

Bibliography
Shaw, Arnold. *Honkers and Shouters: The Golden Years of Rhythm and Blues.* Macmillan, 1978.

Eric Bennett

Mills, Florence

1896–1927

African American musical comedy singer and dancer, one of the most celebrated black entertainers of the Jazz Age and the Harlem Renaissance.

Florence Mills, who rose to stardom in the early 1920s, combined performing with a crusade for racial justice. She expressed a profound race consciousness and a conviction that her career could advance the status of African Americans. "The stage is the quickest way to get to the people," she said in an interview in London's *Daily Express* in 1927. "My own success makes people think better of other colored folk."

Rejecting an offer to join the *Ziegfeld Follies,* America's leading white musical revue, she helped create a rival all-black musical revue in the heart of Broadway. She also broke through Broadway's racial barriers, performing in some of NEW YORK CITY's leading white vaudeville theaters, including the Palace Theater, where she was the first black ever to headline. Her principal goal, however, was to foster opportunities for black entertainers and to remain true in her art to her black roots. "Harlem loves Florence Mills," wrote journalist Dudley Nichols in 1926. "She is the melodious, impish spirit of the Afro-American embodied piquantly."

The youngest of three daughters of John and Nellie (Simon) Winfrey, Mills was born in WASHINGTON, D.C., and grew up in that city's poverty-stricken Goat Alley. Her mother and father, former slaves and tobacco workers from Virginia, worked as a laundry worker and a day laborer to make ends meet. It was the golden age of vaudeville, and Mills, a child prodigy, began singing and dancing at local black theaters at the age of three.

In 1903, under the guidance of RAGTIME singer AIDA OVERTON WALKER, Mills sang "Miss Hannah from Savannah" in a touring production of Bert Williams and George Walker's musical *Sons of Ham.* Although her talent won her recognition and much-needed family income, she suffered racial exploitation performing as a pickaninny with a white vaudeville team. In 1910 she began touring the East Coast with her two sisters and faced the difficult travel conditions imposed on blacks by segregation. Eventually she found herself in CHICAGO, ILLINOIS, where gangster-controlled cabarets welcomed black clientele and the new jazz music. She sang with Cora Green and ADA "BRICKTOP" SMITH at the Panama Cafe, a notorious cabaret in the city's red-light district. She also met and married the dancer "Slow Kid" Thompson, with whom she shared a devoted and lifelong relationship.

Mills's career took off in 1921 when she replaced Gertrude Sanders in the black musical comedy *Shuffle Along,* by NOBLE SISSLE and EUBIE BLAKE. Performed on Broadway, the musical introduced white audiences to the ebullient, fast-paced rhythms of authentic black song and dance and heralded the beginning of the HARLEM RENAISSANCE.

Dainty and elfin, Mills dazzled listeners and critics with her flutelike voice and quick, frolicking dance steps. Impressed by Mills's talent, the white promoter Lew Leslie hired her as a nightly performer at the Plantation Club (so named to inform would-be patrons that its entertainers were black). The club drew a variety of famed black performers, including WILL VODERY and his orchestra, and in 1922 Leslie turned his nightclub show into a Broadway musical group called the Plantation Review. Mills starred in the show and received effusive praise from New York critics.

In 1923 the Plantation Review cast performed in the musical *Dover Street to Dixie* at the Pavilion in London. Hostile to the visiting black Americans, British entertainers threatened to demonstrate in the theater on opening night. However, Mills's poignant rendition of "The Sleeping Hills of Tennessee" left the British audience enchanted; their opposition to the review immediately subsided. For many British critics, the review's performance was nothing short of high art. American Alexander Wollcott described Mills as "a slender streak of genius five feet tall." Another reviewer wrote that she was "by far the most artistic person London had ever had the good fortune to see."

When Mills returned to London in 1926, this time in the widely acclaimed musical *Blackbirds of 1926,* she became the toast of British society. The Prince of Wales saw the revue more than a dozen times, and many artists and intellectuals of the period mentioned Mills in their writings and personal diaries. "Anything she did was super," wrote one critic, "whether spotlighted solo singing . . . or high-stepping in a smashing full-dress suit, her top hat at a rakish angle, jauntily swinging a malacca cane."

For Mills the London visit proved an auspicious time to voice openly her feelings about racial prejudice. British journalist Hannen Swaffer, who heard a speech Mills gave in the Picadilly Cabaret, wrote that "her eloquent plea for tolerance made an impression on many minds." Her title song "I'm a Little Blackbird, Looking for a Bluebird," which for Mills contained a message about the quest for racial equality, became a hit with

British and American audiences alike. "Few realized it, but the number was a protest song," noted black American journalist Alvin White. "There were no hidden meanings, no dramatic phrases, just simple words that told of the poignant yearnings of black women everywhere."

Throughout her short life Mills worked relentlessly; eventually she became seriously ill. Unable to continue her British tour, she sailed back to New York where she died on November 1, 1927, following an operation for appendicitis. Her funeral on November 6 was an elaborately planned public event. Over 5,000 people filled the Mother African Methodist Episcopal Zion Church in Harlem, New York, while 150,000 more lined the streets to witness the funeral cortege and pay homage to the beloved "blackbird" who had never forgotten her heritage.

Bibliography

Johnson, James Weldon. *Black Manhattan.* Knopf, 1930.

Roanne Edwards

Milner, Ronald

1938–

American playwright and producer prominent in the Black Theater Movement of the 1970s.

With training from Harvey Swando's writing workshop at Columbia University, plus a wealth of creative material from his childhood in inner-city DETROIT, MICHIGAN, Ronald Milner produced his first play, *Who's Got His Own,* off-Broadway in 1966. Three years later, as one of four African American playwrights in the production *A Black Quartet,* Milner helped inaugurate the Black Theater Movement. With connections to the Black Power Movement, the Black Theater Movement promoted plays allowing African Americans to represent their lives on stage.

With *What the Wine-Sellers Buy* (1973), Milner achieved national recognition and followed with *Jazz Set* (1980), *Checkmates* (1987), and *Don't Get God Started* (1987). He worked closely with fellow playwright Woodie King Jr., cofounding the theater company Concept-East in 1962 and coediting the *Black Drama Anthology* in 1971. In 2001 Wayne State University Press published a collection of Milner's works, *What the Wine-Sellers Buy Plus Three,* including *Checkmates, Jazz-Set,* and *Urban Transition* along with the title play.

See also Black Power in the United States.

Marian Aguiar

Mina

Ethnic group of West Africa; also known as the Popo.

The Mina primarily inhabit southern TOGO and southern BENIN. They speak a dialect of EWE, a Niger-Congo language, and are sometimes considered an Ewe subgroup. The Mina are the descendants of GA and FANTE migrants. Approximately 400,000 people consider themselves Mina.

See also Languages, African: An Overview.

Minas Gerais

State in southeastern Brazil whose extensive gold and diamond deposits resulted in an influx of slave labor during the eighteenth century.

Minas Gerais was a densely forested region sparsely inhabited by Tupi and Guarani Indians before the arrival of Europeans in the seventeenth century. At that time explorers and *bandeirantes* (slave raiders) moved inland from São Paulo in search of Indian slaves as well as precious stones and metals.

Discovery of Gold

In the early 1690s they discovered large deposits of gold in the mountainous region in the central-western part of the state, near the present-day city of Belo Horizonte. During the gold rush that ensued, the population boomed from only a few inhabitants in the 1690s to 30,000 by 1709 and 500,000 by the end of the century.

Competition over mining sites became fierce, sometimes resulting in violent conflicts. This led the Portuguese Crown to establish the *capitania* of Minas Gerais (Portuguese for "general mines") in 1720 and to create an administrative headquarters in Vila Rica (est. 1711), now known as Ouro Preto. About this time two civilian rebellions occurred in protest of having to pay *quintos,* a royal tax of 20 percent: the Revolta de Pitangui (1719) and the Revolta de Felipe dos Santos (1720). In 1729 diamonds were discovered in the region surrounding the city of Tejuco (present-day Diamantina), to the north of the gold-mining region. The wealth generated by gold and diamonds during the eighteenth century (more than two million pounds of gold and three million carats of diamonds) enabled miners in Minas Gerais to finance the construction of churches, homes, and public buildings in the rococo and baroque styles popular at the time.

By the 1770s the production of gold began to decrease and numerous mining ventures fell into debt. Many smuggled their finds to avoid having to pay taxes to the Crown and faced harassment and tightening restrictions from government officials. The colonizers' frustration culminated in the Inconfidência Mineira in 1788–1789. This was an independence movement launched by members of the elite class in Ouro Preto who, influenced by the ideas of the European Enlightenment, were discontented with the colonial status of Minas Gerais. Provincial authorities exposed the conspiracy against the Portuguese Crown and executed its leader, Joaquim José "Tiradentes" (Toothpuller) da Silva Xavier, who became a symbol of the nationalist spirit.

After a period of stagnation, the economy of Minas Gerais recovered in the mid–nineteenth century with the cultivation of coffee in the southern part of the state and the growth of cattle ranching and dairy farming in its central, southern, and western areas. Since then, Minas Gerais, along with Rio de Janeiro and São Paulo, has been one of the nation's three most economically and politically powerful states. Today Minas Gerais accounts for nearly one-half of Brazil's coffee production and, with the country's largest cattle population, almost one-third of the nation's milk production. Faithful to its name, mining and the processing of metals such as iron ore and steel continue to be a major part of the economy of Minas Gerais.

Arrival of Slaves

The state of Minas Gerais is the one exception to the generalization that Africans were only concentrated and exerted an influence in the coastal regions of Brazil. Gold and diamond prospectors brought large numbers of African slaves to Minas Gerais during the eighteenth century to work in the mines. While prospectors arriving from Portugal brought slaves from Africa with them for this purpose, those already living in Brazil tended to rely more heavily on Indian slaves. In 1708 these two groups clashed in the interior of Minas Gerais in the Guerra dos Emboabas, Emboaba being the term used by Brazilian-born prospectors to refer to the Portuguese. With the help of free and enslaved black soldiers, the Portuguese prospectors defeated the Brazilians the following year, thus also largely ending the use of Indian slaves.

While some slaves came with prospectors from other parts of the colony, especially Bahia and Pernambuco via the San Francisco River, many were imported directly from Africa for the explicit purpose of mining. Between one-fourth and one-third of all the slaves entering Brazil in the eighteenth century were destined for Minas Gerais. Slave traders categorized slaves according to their *nações* (nations), which referred to the part of Africa from which they embarked (and not necessarily the diverse regions from which different slaves came). The Minas, slaves that embarked from the Gold Coast (including Ghana, Benin, and Dahomey), tended to be experienced in and knowledgeable about mining (unlike the prospectors) and made up the bulk of the slave population in Minas Gerais. After the Minas slaves, the predominant "nations" included Congos, Cabindas/Benguelas, and Angolas, among others. The prevalent ethnic groups in this diverse body of slaves were Sudanese during the first part of the eighteenth century and Bantu during the second part of the eighteenth century. At the end of the eighteenth century the number of Bantu imports was more than double the number of Sudanese imports.

By the second decade of the eighteenth century African slaves constituted the majority of the population of Minas Gerais. This population increased quickly, and by the last quarter of the eighteenth century the population of African descent in Minas Gerais, including free and enslaved blacks, was more than three times the size of the white population. Although the free black population increased steadily over time, slaves continued to constitute the majority of the black population through the end of the eighteenth century. Miscegenation had occurred since the beginning of slavery in Minas Gerais and resulted in a mulatto population that, by the early nineteenth century, was more numerous than the African-born population.

During the later colonial period and the early years of the empire, which was created in 1822, some free members of the growing mulatto population in Minas Gerais gained social prominence. This small group of mulattoes owned slaves, helped fund the construction and decoration of churches, and participated in the artistic life of their towns, distinguishing themselves as musicians, composers, and artists. For example, Ouro Preto was home to the famous mulatto sculptor Antônio Francisco Lisboa (1730–1814), known as "Aleijadinho" (Portuguese for "the little cripple"), whose religious sculptures adorn the city's historic churches. Despite their successes, the mulatto population was often accused of engaging in contraband commerce, harboring runaways, and providing escaped slave communities with supplies and information. Notwithstanding the inaccuracy of many of these claims in relation to mulattos, black brotherhoods such as those of Nossa Senhora do Rosário had a close relationship with escaped slaves, to whom they offered help and protection.

Toward Freedom

Although slaves were concentrated in the mining regions for much of the eighteenth century, over the course of the century they became increasingly involved in other economic activities in order to acquire their freedom. The calendar year included a month's worth of holidays, most of them Catholic, on which slaves could work to earn money to purchase their *cartas de alforria* (manumission documents). To this end some slaves grew their own crops or raised livestock. Many male slaves intermittently worked as carpenters, blacksmiths, barbers, cooks, and tailors. Records from this era in Minas Gerais also mention the prevalence of *negras de tabuleiro,* black female street vendors who moved between a village and its surrounding plantations and/or mines selling food products.

There were also opportunities to win free time and even freedom while working in the mines. Some prospectors allowed their slaves to take the remainder of the day off after finding a certain amount of gold. In the diamond fields some prospectors gave freedom to those slaves who found diamonds of a certain size (of twenty carats, according to a 1734 law). In evasion of end-of-the-day inspections, some slaves smuggled small quantities of gold or diamonds away from mining sites by concealing these goods between their toes, in their ears, or in their mouths. Others hid gold or diamonds while on the job and later returned to collect it. The slaves then sold the gold and diamonds to contraband dealers in the hope of eventually accumulating enough money to purchase their freedom. Their success at achieving manumission is reflected in the fact that the provincial government attempted to restrict the granting of cartas de alforria out of the fear that the growing number of free blacks and mulattos would take over the province.

Although slavery in Minas Gerais was no more benign than in any other part of the colony, it was easier to achieve manumission in that province than, for example, on the sugar plantations in the northeast. Manumission was, however, still a long and arduous process that lasted an average of four to six years. Nor was it equally available to all who sought it; both in Minas Gerais and in Brazil as a whole, Brazilian-born slaves were favored over African-born slaves for manumission, and female slaves tended to win or be granted their freedom more easily than male slaves. In the city of Diamantina, the famous slave woman XICA DA SILVA not only won her freedom, but through her personal charm attained, however briefly, a position of social prestige.

Quilombos and Slave Revolts

Although manumission had become commonplace by the end of the 1720s, many slaves simply escaped. The diamond-mining region and the region surrounding the cities of Vila Rica and Araxá were both major refuges for escaped slaves, who as early as 1711 organized themselves into communities known as *quilombos*. In the eighteenth century alone there were more than 125 documented quilombos in Minas Gerais. The most famous one was Quilombo do Ambrósio (named after its leader), also known as Quilombo do Campo Grande, which emerged sometime in the mid-1720s. It was located near the present-day city of Cristais and was unsuccessfully attacked twice (in 1741 and in 1743) before being overthrown in 1746. It then relocated to the region surrounding the present-day city of Ibiá, where it was finally destroyed in 1759. This quilombo contained some 10,000 members and lasted for nearly thirty-five years.

Quilombos comprised a diverse group of slaves of various origins: some mulatto slaves, some free blacks, and in a few cases, Indians and poor whites. They usually acquired what they needed by raiding nearby towns or plantations. These raids inspired great and widespread fear in the colonizing population. In Minas Gerais, however, some escaped slaves subsisted by collecting gold in hidden streams or abandoned mining sites and using it to purchase food, arms, and other goods. Some slaves, such as the legendary CHICO REI, mined gold on their own in order to purchase the freedom of enslaved family members and friends.

Escaped slave communities posed the greatest threat to the colonial social order in Minas Gerais, not only because of their raids and attacks on colonial society, but because they provided a compelling impetus for the enslaved to escape. These communities were repeatedly attacked by *capitães do mato* (bush captains), government-sponsored slave-catching regiments that were first formed in Minas Gerais in 1715. While the prospectors in Minas Gerais viewed the Indians as an obstacle to their lucrative plans, capitães do mato often employed Indians to help them track down escaped slaves and attack quilombos because of their familiarity with the land. Blacks and mulattos also worked as capitães do mato.

Though escaping and forming quilombos was the most common form of slave resistance in Minas Gerais, the state did experience a few slave revolts during and after the gold rush. One of the earliest slave risings in Minas Gerais occurred 1719 and was known as the Inconfidência Quilombola. On the night of March 30, taking advantage of the fact that most of their owners and their owners' families were at church, the rebelling slaves looted houses for firearms. Colonial officials discovered the plot and prepared defenses around the churches. When the revolting blacks arrived at the churches, the colonial regiments were able to defeat them. Two other significant rebellions occurred in Catas Altas, in 1735, and in Ouro Preto, in 1821. Both of these resulted in several deaths and the executions of their black leaders.

Transition to Freedom

Although the neighboring states of São Paulo and Rio de Janeiro were leading abolitionist centers, Minas Gerais did not become extensively involved in the abolition movement during the 1870s and 1880s. In Ouro Preto, then the capital, students from the Escola de Minas and the Escola de Farmácia founded an emancipation society in 1882 called the Sociedade Abolicionista Ouropretana. Their primary activity was the production of antislavery propaganda. In provincial assembly meetings, politicians Theodomiro Alves Pereira and Ignacio Antonio de Assis Martins advocated the emancipation of the slaves in Minas Gerais. Prominent religious figures, such as Bishop Antonio Maria Corrêa de Sá e Benevides and his successor Dom Silverio Gomes Pimenta, both from the city of Mariana, frequently condemned slavery. Small-scale abolitionist activism occurred in several cities in Minas Gerais, including Barbacena, Cataguases, and Guanhães.

Following abolition in 1888 the freedpeople demanded food and clothing from their former owners, who refused their requests. Anticipating a violent outburst from the slaves, the colonial government quickly organized the recently freed blacks into military defense units known as the *guarda-negras* (black guards). Later that year, in order to diminish the number of unemployed blacks in the cities, the colonial government made military service an obligation for all able-bodied former slaves. However, these were preventive measures against Afro-Brazilian rioting, rather than preparatory measures for Afro-Brazilian integration.

The Brazilian government did little to facilitate former slaves' transition to freedom. Lacking the means to compete effectively with whites, Afro-Brazilians were forced into menial and often dangerous jobs. Because of their debased socioeconomic status, they were denied access to medical care, education, and decent housing. In the 1930s and 1940s, during the Getúlio Vargas era, low-income housing became available and enabled a number of black families residing in shacks on the outskirts of urban centers in Minas Gerais to live in healthier and more centrally located homes. Toward the middle of the twentieth century, however, inflation kept many black families from being able to continue living in these homes. Black communities in Minas Gerais still contend with illiteracy as well as poor health, which is reflected in high infant mortality rates and a shorter life expectancy than for Brazilians of European descent.

Despite these problems, blacks in Minas Gerais have found an inspirational figure in Milton Nascimento. Hailing from Minas Gerais, Nascimento has become one of the most famous musician/singers in contemporary MPB (Música Popular Brasileira). Black heritage, unity, and liberation are recurring themes in his songs. Nascimento's most complete expression of these themes was his *Missa dos Quilombos* (Mass of the Quilombos, 1982), written with Dom Pedro Casadáliga and Pedro Tierra, prominent figures in the Brazilian church's Liberation Theology movement. The album synthesizes Afro-Brazilian rhythms with Catholic hymns in commemoration of the suffering and resistance of African slaves in Brazil. In the song "Em Nome de Deus" (In the Name of God), Nascimento invokes the power of the African deity Xangô:

> To liberate Quilombos Palmares.
> In the name of a people continually dragged into
> Suppressive exile over the ocean.
> Who established its own palm groves
> Its free republic
> Of runaway slaves.

By celebrating Afro-Brazilian history and calling for political change, Milton Nascimento's music has become a source of pride and hope for blacks in Minas Gerais and throughout Brazil.

See also Maroonage in the Americas; Mining in Latin America and the Caribbean; Slave Rebellions in Latin America and the Caribbean; Sudan.

Bibliography

Paiva, Eduardo Franca. *Escravos e libertos nas Minas Gerais do século XVIII: Estratégias de resistência através dos testamentos.* Annablume, 1995.

Scarano, Julita. *Cotidiano e solidariedade: Vida diária da gente de cor nas Minas Gerais, século XVIII.* Editora Brasiliense, 1994.

Aaron Myers

Minerals and Mining in Africa

Overview of the mining industry and resource distribution in Africa.

The exploitation of minerals found on or under the ground has long been a major aspect of how Africans have learned to master their natural environment. The Iron Age had begun in sub-Saharan Africa by 500 b.c.e., and the use of iron spread rapidly, with an attested site within modern South Africa by the third century c.e. Iron was crucial in the improvement of agricultural tools and weapons. The processes Africans developed for refining metal, either through invention or imitation, were also applied to other mineral substances such as gold, copper, and tin. Gold from Africa found its way far outside the continent. Gold mines located in what became Ghana and Guinea were linked to the Middle East by trade routes over the Sahara, while gold in what is now Zimbabwe provided wealth for the coastal sultanate of Kilwa (in present-day Tanzania) and was shipped across the Indian Ocean. In south-central Ghana, probably the most important African producer of gold, gold dust was used as a form of currency, and gold was fashioned into distinctive and beautiful ornaments.

Precolonial Mining in Africa

Mining in the precolonial African context was quite different from the forms that it would take under the impulse of the Industrial Revolution. Although ingenious, African methods of underground mining allowed only relatively shallow access to deposits. Furthermore, there were no means for emptying water out of flooded mines. Mines had to be abandoned when the limits of the technical means for retrieving ore were reached. Most labor was performed in the dry season, much of it by women, so that it had a subsidiary character to core household accumulation processes. Culturally the practice of mining was shot through with ritual ceremony and taboos and had a semisacral character; in western Africa, smiths were often a caste set apart from the population at large.

Links to growing Western markets often exhausted African mining activities. Mines ran out of workable ore, while imported metal products replaced local raw materials. The fabled gold mines of south central Africa lured the Portuguese up the Zambezi Valley and onto the central plateau of modern Zimbabwe, but they never succeeded in organizing any effective mineral production. As the slave trade expanded to new levels in the eighteenth century, the Gold Coast (later Ghana) exported slaves instead of gold, and the slave traders purchased men and women with imported gold. Nonetheless, the mining activities of the colonial period depended heavily on the relocation of sites of production that had long been known and worked by Africans. This was true of major copper sources such as Tsumeb in Namibia, Phalaborwa in South Africa, and the extraordinarily rich deposits of the Copperbelt lying in the Democratic Republic of the Congo (DRC) and Zambia as well as the gold of Ghana or the tin of the Jos Plateau region of Nigeria.

Mining and Modern South Africa. The development and export of mineral resources played a central part in the development of capitalism in colonial Africa from early days. By contrast to the difficulties inherent in creating new systems of agriculture and the slowness with which modern industry developed, mineral development proceeded successfully and profitably in many colonies. The most successful mineral development of all occurred in what is now South Africa. It began with the exploitation of Namaqualand copper in 1854 and reached a turning point with the discovery of the rich diamond deposits around Kimberley after 1867. Within a few years Kimberley rivaled Cape Town in size, and unprecedented amounts of capital and labor poured into the diamond fields. In the early years mining was dominated by small diggers, mainly but not exclusively white. Labor was expensive, and the profits in large part accrued to speculators, illegal diamond buyers, and the purveyors of goods and services to the mining camp population. By 1888, however, a process of amalgamation had been completed, and the entire industry became dominated by one firm, De Beers, associated with CECIL RHODES. Amalgamation allowed for the rational recovery of ore from the ground and the hoarding of diamonds at times of glut. With it went the transformation of the labor force; by the 1880s a reduced number of white skilled workers, who lived in family suburbs, were employed together with black migrants who received lower wages and lived in closed compounds under constant surveillance for theft.

Developments from 1886 on the Witwatersrand followed from those in Kimberley in terms of labor control, race relations, and the organization of capital. The gold mines of the TRANSVAAL contained reliable, if not especially rich, shafts of gold-bearing ore at great distances from the ground. With technical difficulties overcome, the field could be developed only through harnessing capital and labor on a larger scale than anywhere else in world mining. The Rand gold mines attracted the majority of all capital invested in Africa up to WORLD WAR II (1939–1945). Within South Africa the impact was convulsive. A complex series of events relates the discoveries to the political crisis that doomed the Boer republics and led to the formation of the Union of South Africa. The country's urban infrastructure and agriculture had to be transformed to make the mining industry viable. Between 1907 and 1922 a series of major strikes, mainly on the part of white workers, challenged the industry at a time when accident and disease rates were terrifying. In order to obtain a sufficient labor force the gold mines created a subcontinental recruitment system, with the majority of workers in most of the twentieth century coming from outside the borders of South Africa itself.

Gold mining formed the base of a new era of capitalist accumulation in South Africa. For one thing, the mines spawned the creation of secondary industry in sectors such as metals, timber, and chemicals. For a second, the state succeeded in harnessing the revenues derived from mine taxes to create a modern infrastructure and put resources into other sectors of the economy. The means by which labor was recruited and controlled were widely imitated not only in other mining industries in the region but also in other sectors of the economy. These means included settlement in compounds; the pass system, which controlled the free movement of prospective workers; and the deferred forms of payment and down payment systems. The once-turbulent white mining community was transformed into a small class of supervisory and skilled labor. It accounted for less than one-tenth of the total yet at a peak in the early 1970s absorbed two-thirds of the wage bill.

By contrast with Kimberley, a single firm never monopolized the gold mines. Instead, from an early date they were dominated by a small number of mining finance houses whose investments interpenetrated to a significant extent. These houses, of which the most important from the 1920s was the Anglo-American Corporation, were increasingly South African in character. When the state fiscal regime for developmental and security reasons made it difficult for South African investments to go outside the country, mining-based investment flowed into property, agriculture, and industry.

Despite the continued preeminence of gold and diamonds, from the late nineteenth to the late twentieth centuries a major feature of mining in South Africa was coal and base metals, including asbestos, antimony, chrome, tin, copper, and iron ore. In certain phases such as the 1960s, good demand for base metals allowed these mining activities to take up the slack in the export economy when the price of gold lowered prices in the South African gold mines.

Colonialism and the Mining Economy. The great economic significance of South African mining to twentieth century capitalism should not take away from the large-scale development of mining elsewhere in colonial Africa. A second great mining complex in south-central Africa included the Copperbelt of NORTHERN RHODESIA (now Zambia) and Katanga (now Shaba) Province in the BELGIAN CONGO (now DRC). This set of mines was a major world producer of copper, and those on the DRC side of the frontier also came to yield uranium and cobalt in important quantities. Elsewhere in the region, copper also proved the salvation of German colonialism in South-West Africa (now Namibia) and, from the eve of WORLD WAR I (1914–1918) up to the late twentieth century, the Namibian economy has depended on mineral exports. SOUTHERN RHODESIA (now Zimbabwe) never witnessed the development of a "second Rand," as its conquerors had hoped, but scattered coal, gold, tin, asbestos, chrome, and other deposits were a very important part of its economy. The Belgian Congo was a mineral-rich colony that exported gold, tin, and other ores. In western Africa mining was also a major economic activity. Especially notable were the diamond mines of the Gold Coast and SIERRA LEONE, the tin mines in northern Nigeria, the coal mines in eastern Nigeria, and underground gold mining in the Gold Coast. In TANGANYIKA, commercial gold and diamond mining played an important part in the economy.

Mines sustained many African colonial economies. In contrast with South Africa, however, these economies were classics of the enclave type of development excoriated by radical dependency theorists. Investment was confined fairly narrowly to the mining industry, with few linkages beyond the necessary transport and other infrastructural developments. The mine owners remained overwhelmingly based in the metropolitan countries, where profits reverted, and had little stake in African society.

In some cases even tighter controls over mine workers were maintained than in South Africa. However, this was not the general pattern. In the Copperbelt workers were encouraged from an early date to bring their families to the mining towns. To take an extreme example, in the Nigerian tin-mining camps employers had little control over the lives of workers, and hiring remained largely in the hands of Nigerian labor contractors. The large workforce was characterized by massive turnover as tens of thousands of short-term migrants arrived during the course of the year. While African workers in colonies such as the Congo and the Gold Coast did increasingly include a significant skilled stratum, the mass of workers did not easily become transformed into an urban proletariat, and the retention of rural roots and affinities was everywhere important.

Mining since 1960. The early years of independence saw a further increase in mining development in many African countries, typically with single Western investors giving way to consortia. Examples would include the diamond mines of Botswana, iron-ore mining in Mauritania, bauxite mining in Guinea, and uranium mining in Niger. Often the newly independent African state got a share of ownership in addition to tax revenues from mining operations. In countries such as Tanzania, Ghana, and Nigeria, miner insurgency in the late colonial period had played an important part in a growing challenge to colonial hegemony on which national movements had battened. With independence, the unions' wings were clipped since the new states were responsible for enforcing a profitable order on the mines. A striking feature in the postcolonial era was the growing importance of industrial as opposed to precious minerals, partly linked to the Cold War arms buildup.

It was a natural temptation for new states to contemplate nationalization of the mines. The Convention People's Party government of Kwame Nkrumah in Ghana, the United National Independence Party government in Zambia, and Mobutu Sese Seko's regime in Zaire (now the DRC) were among those that actually took this step with regard to major mining property. The results proved disastrous. Continued dependence on foreign expertise and management proved inevitable. As mining suffered increasing economic setbacks from the 1970s, it proved very difficult for the state to rein in expenses and maintain equipment. Also, it has not proven very easy for independent African governments to find a discipline in the labor process to replace the harsh controls of the colonial era. With the growing pressure from the World Bank and other Western agencies to impose structural adjustment on state budgets in Africa, the nationalization movement went into reverse, and in the 1990s African governments were in the process of trying to privatize the mines they had taken over.

A key part of the background to this ebb and flow has been the faltering position of mining in the world economy. Change in industrial processes has greatly reduced the once-increasing demand for metals such as copper and iron ore, virtually eliminating new mining developments in Africa since the beginning of the 1980s. Questions about nuclear power have cut back uranium mining. While gold and diamond mining have better survived, they have had an erratic prosperity. Much production today comes from petty entrepreneurs, often evading state controls, who shoulder their own risks. Big international mining houses tend to cold-shoulder Africa, preferring to build up their investments in more stable and conservative political environments. Even South Africa is an important case in point. Since the mid-1980s a majority of gold miners have joined a militant trade union, a fact linked to the declining share of workers coming from outside the country. Perhaps even more important than the struggles within the industry, the entire national economy suffers from the stagnation in the mining sector. After a remarkable boom from 1979 to 1982, the price of gold fell dramatically, and gold no longer provided a fiscal base for economic activity on the part of the South African state. South Africa has continued to depend on minerals as its core export and must make a difficult adjustment in its trade economy. There and in the majority of African states the heritage of mining is inseparable from the colonial economy, with its characteristic forms of control and extraction. This heritage is increasingly problematic from the point of view of both economic and social development today.

Resource Distribution

Africa is resource-rich, but mineral and metal deposits, as well as the benefits from this wealth, are unevenly distributed. Sub-Saharan Africa accounts for 4 percent of the world's total export of nonfuel minerals. If petroleum is included, the production value is more than $36 billion. Not all sub-Saharan countries, however, benefit substantially from mineral wealth, and even those that do have sizable mineral and metal deposits do not always obtain the benefits of these riches. Sub-Saharan countries with mineral exports accounting for more than one-half of total earnings are Angola, Botswana, DRC, Gabon, Guinea, Namibia, Niger, Nigeria, and Zambia; in Ghana and South Africa minerals account for between one-third and one-half of earnings.

Distribution. The basis for Africa's mineral wealth is the geology of sub-Saharan Africa. The foundation of Africa is a core of stable, continental crust composed of Precambrian rocks. This is the craton, composed mainly of granite, gneiss, and greenstones. In terms of mineral and metal deposits, greenstones are the most favorable rocks for gold and other mineral deposits. Such areas include the principal goldfields of Ghana (Ashanti), Ethiopia (Adola), Zimbabwe (Midlands), and the border between Swaziland and South Africa (Barberton Belt). In addition to these known gold deposits, there are undeveloped greenstone belts in Burkina Faso (Boromo, Aribinda, and Dori-Assakan), northwestern Tanzania, and northern DRC (Kilo, Moto, Nagayu, and Isiro). Minerals and metals are also found in depositional basins. Examples are the goldfields of the Witwatersrand in South Africa, Tarkwa in Ghana, and the Copperbelt that runs through Zambia and the DRC. Mineral and metal deposits are associated with crustal movements that have led to the formation of sedimentary basins. The Karoo sequence, which holds most of Africa's coal, is a large sedimentary deposit located in Mozambique, Malawi, South Africa, Tanzania, and Zimbabwe.

Furthermore, minerals and metal resources are associated with areas where the crust has fragmented, allowing magma to well up and form what are called kimberlite intrusives. These are the source of diamond deposits in Angola, Guinea, Botswana, South Africa, Tanzania, and the DRC. Mineral and metal deposits are also found in areas where the crustal plates are diverging. One such area is the RIFT VALLEY, which runs through eastern Africa. This geological activity has led to the formation of nonmetallic minerals such as kaolin clay, bentonite, pozzolana, and fluorite as well as of salt lakes, which contain valuable minerals, including salt, soda ash, and potash.

Mineral and metal deposits are also associated with volcanic activity, which formed the South African Bushveld Complex and the Great Dyke of Zimbabwe. These areas contain chromium and platinum. Younger volcanic areas contain phosphates (Angola, UGANDA, Tanzania) and, under some circumstances, copper (South Africa), gold, and nickel. Mineral deposits are also created by erosional processes and chemical weathering, as is the case with bauxite in Guinea; rutile in MADAGASCAR, Mozambique, and Sierra Leone; alluvial gold deposits in southern Ethiopia and northern DRC; and alluvial diamonds in Namibia.

As a result of its geological past, Africa is well-endowed in bauxite, copper, cobalt, diamonds, manganese, rutile, uranium, iron, and petroleum. Mines in Africa produce much of the world's platinum (81 percent), chromite (49 percent), diamonds (48 percent), and cobalt (42 percent). African mines also produce a large share of the world's manganese (28 percent), rutile (27 percent), and uranium (20 percent) and supply an important part of its bauxite (14 percent), copper (5 percent), iron ore (5 percent), petroleum (5 percent), and phosphates (2 percent).

The distribution of mineral wealth is, however, highly uneven. Nineteen countries benefit from commercial-scale mining, but out of these countries only two, South Africa (gold and diamonds) and Nigeria (petroleum), account for more than half the total mineral production. Five other countries—Zambia (copper and cobalt), the DRC (copper and cobalt), Botswana (diamonds), Angola (petroleum), and Gabon (petroleum, manganese, and uranium)—are major producers of minerals. Some African countries are important because they are world leaders in the production of strategic minerals and metals. Zambia and the DRC produce 37 percent of the world's cobalt. Guinea is the world's second-largest bauxite producer; Zimbabwe is the fifth-largest producer of asbestos; South Africa is the second- and Gabon the fifth-largest manganese producer. Gabon, Namibia, and Niger together produce 16 percent of the world's uranium.

In spite of Africa's mineral wealth, only South Africa has become wealthy as a result of its mineral deposits. This is because most of Africa's mineral wealth is controlled by transnational corporations or parastatal companies. In addition, the majority of minerals and metals are exported as raw ore. While some of this production is exported as finished metals, none of the ore is used to make manufactured products. As a result, the jobs generated by mining are, for the most part, unskilled or semiskilled, and in several areas, notably South Africa, migrant labor is dominant. Another important reason why Africa's mineral wealth has failed to generate real wealth for Africa's nations is that mining operations are enclaves to the rest of the economy. They have strong links to the export market but few links to the local economy. Thus wealth is siphoned off rather than put back into local economies.

History of Exploitation. The history of mineral development in Africa provides clues to the current state of mineral production and the reasons behind the uneven distribution of mineral wealth. Mining has always been an important economic activity in Africa. Gold panned from alluvial deposits and riverbeds was the mainstay of trade in the West African kingdoms of Ghana, MALI, and SONGHAI. Copper was found in the watersheds of the Congo and ZAMBEZI rivers in central Africa and mined in Katanga (Shaba) long before the arrival of Europeans. Iron was worked in the ancient civilization of Meroië, which straddled the banks of the upper reaches of the NILE. Ironworking technology spread slowly south, and Africans closely guarded its secrets from Europeans.

Until the middle of the nineteenth century Africans maintained control over their mineral resources, but this declined as the slave trade caused social upheaval and the presence of Europeans on the continent increased. The discovery of diamonds in South Africa, at Kimberley in 1867, marked the beginnings of the transfer of Africa's mineral wealth to Europeans. GREAT BRITAIN annexed the Kimberley area in 1871 from the Griqua ethnic group and the South African Republic. And while the British controlled the production, African miners were the basis of the fortunes made by the likes of Cecil Rhodes. Rhodes, along with European financiers, bought up the claims of individual miners and formed mineral giants such as De Beers, which today controls the production and marketing of diamonds throughout the world.

Other mineral discoveries soon followed. Gold was discovered in the Witwatersrand in the 1880s. From the 1880s to the 1930s prospectors and financiers from Germany, the United States, Belgium, FRANCE, South Africa, and Britain established mines throughout the mineral-rich areas of the continent, including Angola, the Belgian Congo (present-day DRC), Southern Rhodesia (present-day Zimbabwe), Northern Rhodesia (present-day Zambia), Nigeria, and Sierra Leone. Mineral production increased dramatically during the twentieth century, displacing agricultural products, and led to the transformation of trading routes. Prior to mining, trading routes ran across the continent to the Indian Ocean, where traders plied between Arabia, INDIA, and China. But new mining trade routes were designed simply to bring the minerals to waiting ships that took them to Europe and the Americas. Railways were built, but they did not connect centers of population. For instance, the route from the Katanga copper mines in the Belgian Congo ran through Angola, not the Congo, so this railway provided little economic stimulus to the area. The mines operated as enclave economies until the 1960s.

Independence brought a wave of nationalization to Africa, and mines in Zambia, Sierra Leone, Uganda, Ghana, Tanzania, the DRC, TOGO, and Mauritania were nationalized following independence. As a result, African mining enterprises are now roughly split between privately owned and state-owned mines. The private mines are owned by transnational corporations or are jointly owned by private companies and the state. The rest are controlled by parastatal mining companies run by national governments. The lock, however, that transnational corporations have historically had on African mineral production means that there are few small-scale mining operations. Technology drives this as well. Mining has become more mechanized and larger scale. In addition, with marketing and production of key minerals in some cases controlled by a single company, as is the case with De Beers, it is hard for small companies to compete. Mining does occur, however, on a small, noncommercial scale in more than thirty African countries. Artisanal mining generates an estimated $800 million a year and employs more than 1 million workers.

Africa's share of the world mineral production has slipped since independence. Private companies, wary of political instability and the threat of nationalization, have invested elsewhere, notably Latin America and Asia. As a result, sub-Saharan Africa's share of the world mineral production has fallen since 1960 and is stagnant with a growth rate of 1 to 2 percent a year. The irony behind this decline is that Africa still contains vast mineral wealth, but much of it has not been tapped or investments in new mining projects have been curtailed or halted. For example, new deposits have been discovered but have yet to be developed. These include the Fungerume copper deposits in the DRC and the Adola gold belt in Ethiopia.

As a result of Africa's history and the way in which its minerals and metals are controlled by a few large companies, Africa's mineral wealth is largely a source of *potential* wealth for much of Africa. Without more refining of ore and the creation of finished products, better linkages to local economies, and indigenous capital for investment in new exploration, Africa's mineral wealth will continue to be unevenly distributed and underdeveloped.

"Minerals and Metals: Mining Industries" by Bill Freund and "Minerals and Metals: Resource Distribution" by David Smethurst. Used by permission of Charles Scribner's Sons, an imprint of Macmillan Library Reference USA, from *Encyclopedia of Africa South of the Sahara*. John Middleton, editor in chief. Vol. 3, pp. 159–65. Copyright 1997, Charles Scribner's Sons. Updated by *Encarta Africana* staff by permission of Charles Scribner's Sons.

Bibliography

Crush, Jonathan S., Alan Jeeves, and David Yudelman. *South Africa's Labor Empire: A History of Black Migrancy to the Gold Mines.* Westview, 1991.

Ferguson, James. "Mobile Workers, Modernist Narratives: A Critique of the Historiography of Transition on the Zambian Copperbelt." *Journal of Southern African Studies* 16 (1990): 385–412, 603–21.

Freund, Bill. *Capital and Labour in the Nigerian Tin Mines.* Humanities Press, 1981.

James, Wilmot C. *Our Precious Metal: African Labour in South Africa's Gold Industry, 1970–1990.* Indiana University Press, 1992.

Lanning, Greg, and Marti Mueller. *Africa Undermined: Mining Companies and the Underdevelopment of Africa.* Penguin, 1979.

Turrell, Robert Vicat. *Capital and Labour on the Kimberley Diamond Fields, 1871–1890.* Cambridge University Press, 1987.

Van Onselen, Charles. *Chibaro: African Mine Labour in Southern Rhodesia, 1900–1933.* Pluto, 1976.

Yachir, Faysal. *Mining in Africa Today: Strategies and Prospects.* Zed, 1988.

Mingus, Charles, Jr.

1922–1979

African American bassist, bandleader, and composer who foreshadowed free jazz but grounded his music in the black gospel and blues tradition.

Charles Mingus was a temperamental iconoclast, a virtuoso bassist, and a man who protested racial injustice through his music. Mingus's compositions reveal his deep involvement in the musical experimentation of the 1940s known as BEBOP, in which young black musicians significantly expanded the harmonic boundaries of JAZZ. He also drew from the legacy of older jazz styles and the rich African American traditions of blues and gospel music, but he created a jazz world uniquely his own. Few jazz musicians gain renown for their compositions. Apart from Mingus, critics identify only three great jazz composers: JELLY ROLL MORTON, DUKE ELLINGTON, and THELONIOUS MONK. Of these, Mingus is the most contemporary and the least appreciated. His intensely personal music seemed to look both backward and forward. He invoked the origin of jazz by grounding his compositions in the blues—the music from which jazz emerged. He also made extensive use of collective improvisation, a playing style that was characteristic of New Orleans jazz of the early 1900s but that had virtually disappeared from jazz by the middle of the century. On the other hand, Mingus looked forward to the dissonance and openness of the free jazz that appeared in the 1960s.

The titles of Mingus's compositions are some of the most striking in jazz. He repeatedly addressed issues of racial injustice, as in "Haitian Fight Song" (1955), "Prayer for Passive Resistance" (1960), and "Remember Rockefeller at Attica" (1974). He also revealed a lively humor—as in his take on Oscar Hammerstein II and Jerome Kern's "All the Things You Are," which he titled "All the Things You Could Be By Now if Sigmund Freud's Wife Were Your Mother" (1960).

Mingus was born in Nogales, Arizona. Shortly after his birth, his family moved to Watts, the principal black neighborhood of Los Angeles. His mother died when he was six months old, and his father remarried. His stepmother introduced him to the fervent gospel music of the Holiness Church. Such Mingus compositions as "Wednesday Night Prayer Meeting" (1959) and "Better Git It in Your Soul" (1959) reveal the continuing influence of the religious music that he had heard as a child, not only in the titles but also in their ecstatic, bluesy quality.

In grade school Mingus began playing the trombone, then the cello, and finally the bass. Hearing Duke Ellington in a late-night radio broadcast was what inspired his interest in jazz. In 1939 he began taking lessons from jazz bassist Red Callender (1916–1992), and later he studied with ex–New York Philharmonic bassist Herman Rheinshagen. As a teenager, Mingus was part of the jazz scene that flourished along Los Angeles's Central Avenue, along with such aspiring musicians as tenor saxophonist DEXTER GORDON and drummer Chico Hamilton. But like other young musicians of the 1940s, Mingus found it difficult to gain a foothold in jazz.

In 1942 Mingus played with clarinetist Barney Bigard (1906–1980), and in 1943 he toured with trumpeter LOUIS ARMSTRONG's big band. The changing musical tastes of the latter half of the 1940s, however, put an end to the big bands that had provided work for many young musicians. In 1946 Mingus made his recording debut with an octet playing several of his early, Ellington-influenced compositions. Still, that year he took a more secure job with the U.S. post office. In 1947 he toured with LIONEL HAMPTON's big band, but during 1948–1950 he returned to post office work, playing jazz and RHYTHM AND BLUES gigs freelance.

Mingus's breakthrough came with a 1950–1951 stint with the Red Norvo Trio, composed of white vibraphonist Norvo, white guitarist Tal Farlow, and Mingus. The small group offered a showcase for his early playing style, which combined the virtuosity of style-setting jazz bassist Jimmy Blanton (1918–1942) and the harmonic sophistication of bop. As he recounted in his searing autobiographical novel *Beneath the Underdog* (1971), the months of touring with the interracial trio brought Mingus face-to-face with the harsh realities of racial discrimination. He left the group after an incident in which a white bass player temporarily took his place for a television broadcast in NEW YORK CITY.

Despite that unpleasant racial incident, Mingus decided to relocate to New York City in 1951. There he played with such jazz musicians as alto saxophonist and bop innovator CHARLIE PARKER, swing piano master ART TATUM, and white pianist Lennie Tristano, a cool jazz pioneer. But in 1952 Mingus returned to working at the post office. In that year, with drummer MAX ROACH, he founded Debut Records (1952–1957), his first of many attempts to exert greater control over the business side of music. The label's crowning achievement lay in recording a 1953 concert at Toronto's Massey Hall that featured the finest bop group ever assembled: Parker, trumpeter DIZZY GILLESPIE, pianist BUD POWELL, Roach, and Mingus.

Mingus contributed numerous compositions to the Jazz Composers Workshop during 1953–1955 and in 1955 founded his own repertory group, the Jazz Workshop. During this period he moved beyond his bop-based approach and reached his mature playing style. Earlier he had played steady, harmonically complex single-note lines and had soloed with horn-like virtuosity; now he simplified his approach. He played more slowly, using varied rhythms that were less metronomic. He emphasized simpler, more basic harmonies and made effective use of pedal points, in which the bass plays a single note for an extended period. His compositional style simplified as well, moving away from the rapid chord changes of bebop and harking back to the basic essence of the blues—as can be heard on such albums as *Blues and Roots* (1959).

From 1955 to 1960 Mingus perfected a unique approach to composition. In the interest of spontaneity, he largely abandoned standard musical notation. He introduced new compositions by playing them at the piano and then singing the various parts to his sidemen. He preferred emotional immediacy to precision ensemble playing, and he introduced a degree of dissonance that foreshadowed the free jazz of alto saxophonist ORNETTE COLEMAN, pianist CECIL TAYLOR, and, after 1965, tenor saxophonist JOHN COLTRANE. An important early example of his new style is found in *Weary Blues* (1957), a collaboration with poet LANGSTON HUGHES.

Like Ellington, Mingus composed works with specific musicians in mind, and he encouraged his sidemen to find their own styles rather than copy someone else's. From the 1950s to the 1970s his ensembles provided a training ground for such key musicians as multi-instrumentalists ERIC DOLPHY (1928–1964) and RAHSAAN ROLAND KIRK (1935–1977), alto saxophonist Jackie McLean, tenor saxophonist Booker Ervin (1930–1970), pianist Roland Hanna, and drummer Dannie Richmond (1935–1988).

Mingus's most productive period was in 1959–1960, during which he recorded such important albums as *Blues and Roots, Mingus Ah Um* (1959), *Mingus Dynasty* (1959), and *Mingus Presents Mingus* (1960). During the 1960s Mingus continued to try to wrest control of jazz from record companies and concert producers. He protested the conservative booking policies of the Newport Jazz Festival by organizing a counter-festival that featured swing trumpeter ROY ELDRIDGE (1911–1989), free jazz saxophonist Ornette Coleman, and Max Roach. This effort led to the formation of the Jazz Artists Guild, which sought to give musicians greater artistic control, but the organization disbanded in rancor after a 1962 concert in New York City's Town Hall turned into a costly failure. Mingus then formed Charles Mingus Records (1964–1965), but when it failed, he left jazz for three years.

Mingus resumed his musical career in 1969 and in the mid-1970s recorded two notable albums, *Changes One* (1974) and *Changes Two* (1975). In 1977 he was diagnosed with amyotrophic lateral sclerosis (Lou Gehrig's disease) and within a year was confined to a wheelchair. Although he could no longer play the bass, he continued to compose music. In the last year of his life, Mingus collaborated with white pop singer Joni Mitchell on the album *Mingus* (1979). President Jimmy Carter honored him along with other leading jazz musicians at a 1978 White House reception.

Since his death, Mingus's legacy has endured through the efforts of his former sidemen, jazz scholars, such as Gunther Schuller, and above all his widow, Sue Mingus. Mingus's large-scale composition *Epitaph*, which had never been performed during his lifetime, had its premiere in 1989 and appeared on compact disc the following year. Former Mingus sidemen in the George Adams–Don Pullen Quartet, the Mingus Dynasty Band, and the Mingus Big Band have kept alive Mingus's musical spirit and repertory. In 1993 Mingus became the first African American composer to have his papers preserved by the Library of Congress. The library acquired an extensive collection of his musical and literary writings, including the 1,000-page manuscript of *Beneath the Underdog.* In 2003 Sue Mingus published her autobiographical memoir, *Tonight at Noon: A Love Story,* which tells of her fifteen tumultuous years with Mingus, from 1964 to the time of his death.

See also Attica Uprising.

Bibliography

Mingus, Charles. *Beneath the Underdog: His World as Composed by Mingus.* Edited by Nel King. Random House, 1971.

Priestley, Brian. *Mingus: A Critical Biography.* Da Capo Press, 1984.

Coleman, Janet, and Al Young. *Mingus/Mingus: Two Memoirs.* Creative Arts, 1989.

James Sellman

Minianka

Ethnic group of West Africa.

The Minianka primarily inhabit northeastern Côte d'Ivoire and southern Mali. They speak Senufo, a Niger-Congo language, and are generally considered a Senufo subgroup. Approximately 400,000 people consider themselves Minianka.

See also Languages, African: An Overview.

Mini-Jazz

Form of popular music in Haiti that was based on compas music and was also heavily influenced by American rock and jazz.

In the 1960s middle-class Haitian youth began listening to rock and roll music broadcast on American radio stations. France, seeking to open up the Haitian buying market, inundated the island with records, and subsequently a rock craze was born among the well-off youth. The term *yeye* came to describe the young rock bands formed at that time. Taken from the Beatles' lyric "she loves you, yeah, yeah, yeah," yeye embraced an unexpected middle-class optimism in the early years of dictator François Duvalier's reign.

In 1963 U.S. president John Kennedy decreased American government aid to Haiti, seeking to persuade Duvalier to leave office. As a result, tourism slowed to a trickle, and the emergent Haitian nationalism rejected foreign cultural influences. Yeye responded to the aggressive cultural climate by incorporating native compas. The setup of yeye bands included electric guitars and bass, drums, and a horn section. American pop songs were played alongside Haitian classics, but the main emphasis was on teenage themes of sports, dancing, and lighthearted romance. The small size of yeye bands drastically altered the compas sound, as compas was traditionally played in orchestras or large ensembles. The fusion led to a distinct new sound that was called *mini-jazz.* The versatility of mini-jazz's small bands brought live compas to school events, house parties, and other small social events. "Mini" referred to the miniskirt fad and associated the sound with stylistic newness rather than diminutive size.

When Duvalier declared himself president-for-life in 1964, the unprecedented optimism of yeye deepened with mini-jazz. Political terror escalated, while the bands continued producing what was essentially teenage dance music. Avoiding political suspicion was crucial to survival during the height of François Duvalier's reign. This could be seen directly in Haitian popular music, as many bands sought to avoid any form of confrontation. The mini-jazz ensemble Shleu-Shleu, for example, popularized the use of nonsense names, and within months numerous bands had sprung up bearing nonsense syllables in lieu of an actual title.

Jean-Claude Duvalier, François Duvalier's son and 1971 successor, heavily patronized the mini-jazz ensemble Bossa Combo. During the mid-1970s the band used its favor with the dictator to develop mini-jazz into a critical form: they incorporated lyrics with mild, often allusive elements of social critique and precipitated an interest in Haitian musical history. A period of stylistic experimentation followed. Tabou Combo, the most famous mini-jazz band, now performs an international mix, with heavy influences from zouk, American rap, and funk and a lead vocalist who sings in French, Spanish, English, and Haitian Creole. Founded in 1968 as Los Incognitos, the band soon opted for a more Haitian-sounding name. The success of their 1974 hit single "Haiti" brought compas mini-jazz into the international spotlight. With a drummer incorporating rock and Brazilian samba beats and an all-American horn section, Tabou Combo crossed over into a number of markets, as did many of the mini-jazz bands of the 1980s. Like many other Haitian artists, activists, intellectuals, and musicians, Tabou Combo immigrated to New York to escape Duvalier's repressive regime.

Today Coupé Coupé is one of the few bands continuing to produce traditional compas mini-jazz—a choice influenced by their residence in Haiti. Haitians living outside of the country have incorporated more non-Haitian influences, partly because they have had easy access to synthesizers and other electronic instruments. The New York All-Stars is a Tabou Combo side project that combines rap with Haitian ra-ra, or Carnival music; the Brooklyn-based Ra-Ra Machine employs a similar fusion.

See also Nationalist Movements and Blacks in Latin America and the Caribbean.

Jace Clayton

Mining in Latin America and the Caribbean

Extraction of minerals, chiefly silver, gold, and diamonds; European colonists depended primarily on Native Americans and to a lesser degree on Africans for mining labor.

From the earliest days of slavery in the New World, Africans were sent from Europe and, later, directly from Africa to toil in mines. Spanish governor Nicolás Ovando arrived on the Caribbean island of Hispaniola (shared today by the DOMINICAN REPUBLIC and HAITI) in 1502, accompanied by domestic slaves. Ovando soon requested King Ferdinand of SPAIN to bolster his labor force with Africans to work in Hispaniola's mines. Lured by the promise of what looked like infinite amounts of GOLD, the monarchs of Spain obliged and set in motion the infrastructure of an extractive economy-based empire. For the next two centuries, both Spanish and Portuguese settlers introduced shackled Africans to mine silver in the shafts of Zacatecas and Durango in MEXICO; gold and diamonds in the fields of interior BRAZIL; gold from Honduran hillsides and the river valleys of COLOMBIA and VENEZUELA; and silver, mercury, and gold from the Andes in PERU, BOLIVIA, and CHILE. Africans, however, never made up the majority of miners in the Americas, except in Brazil, because Europeans were able to rely on the labor of indigenous peoples.

Mining in Brazil

The discovery of gold in the 1690s in the mountainous interior of the Brazilian southeast triggered the second in the colonies' great economic cycles, displacing the declining sugar-based economy of the northeast. The thickly forested basin of the Rio das Velhas lay a month's journey from the coastal settlements of RIO DE JANEIRO and São Paulo. The distance, nonetheless, did not deter thousands of settlers from streaming into the area, quickly driving away the indigenous peoples from their land or killing them through war or the effects of disease. The few remaining Native Americans were put to work mining, but their supply of labor soon proved insufficient to the task—especially after diamonds were also discovered in the region. The Portuguese settlers filled the shortage with African slaves who had accompanied the earliest settlers to the gold region. As mining grew in importance, more slaves were shipped to the area. In 1720 Portugal established the captaincy of MINAS GERAIS (General Mines). By 1750 it was the most populated captaincy in Brazil, with a majority population of Afro-Brazilians. Other important mining captaincies such as Goiás and Mato Grosso were also heavily populated with Africans.

Gold was procured by panning streams. Occasionally miners diverted rivers over hillsides and valleys to strip the surface and reach the minerals buried just beneath. Work for the (mostly male) African slaves, while exhausting, was not as typically brutal as labor in the deep-shaft mines of Spanish Mexico and Peru. Although a few Afro-Brazilian women worked in mines, most female slaves were used for domestic work in mining towns or as cooks and laundresses for mining camps.

The impact of the mining boom on colonial Brazil cannot be overstated. It opened the country's interior to large-scale colonization. It contributed to the shift of the colony's economic center from the declining sugar plantations in the northeast to the increasingly prosperous southern region, leading to the transferal of the colonial capital in 1763 from Salvador, BAHIA, to Rio de Janeiro. By the end of the eighteenth century the gold boom had drawn to a close, but Brazil remained one of the world's largest producers of diamonds until the end of the nineteenth century—an industry driven by black labor.

Mining in Spanish America

Most of colonial Spain's efforts in mining focused on the silver in Mexico and the silver, gold, and mercury in the Andean highlands of Peru, western BOLIVIA, and northern CHILE. Copper, iron, and mercury were also mined throughout Spanish America, but because many such materials could be found at a lesser cost in Spain, large operations rarely developed around these minerals. While Brazilian deposits were mined at or just beneath the surface, minerals in Mexico and the Andes typically lay in deep veins in mountainous regions. The vast majority of laborers in the deep-shaft mines were the Native Americans who inhabited these regions. Some were free workers, but others were "drafted" into periods of forced labor at nominal wages through systems known as the *repartimiento* in Mexico and *mita* in the colonial Andes. Africans nonetheless arrived at mining camps as servants of European masters. They performed skilled and unskilled labor as carpenters, blacksmiths, and cooks and occasionally worked in the mines.

By the start of the seventeenth century the total number of workers in Mexico's silver mines was slightly fewer than 10,000, roughly 85 percent of whom received some form of wages (though in the case of indigenous peoples "drafted" into forced labor, the wages were unconscionably low); the remaining 15 percent of miners were Afro-Mexican slaves. The percentage of Africans working in Andean mines is believed to have been significantly lower than in Mexico's, probably due to the prevailing belief that Africans did not fare well in the cool, high Andean mines. Ample evidence indicates that many African miners died of diseases. As the seventeenth century progressed and mining increased in scale, Spanish mine owners repeatedly sought to supplement their drafts of Native American miners with greater imports of African slave miners; however, because of the high cost of slave importation and the harsh conditions of living and working, which reduced the chances of survival for those slaves, mining in the Andes continued to be an industry dominated by indigenous peoples. Bolivia's small black population is nonetheless believed to have been largely derived from those early arrivals.

In the lowlands of the Pacific and Chocó region of New Granada (present-day Colombia), however, Spanish colonizers depended on African slave labor to mine gold. Gold deposits in the region were discovered in the sixteenth century; but large-scale mining did not begin until the late seventeenth century as the indigenous Cuna and Chocó peoples who inhabited the area resisted the European incursions. By the late eighteenth century well over half the population was of African descent. As elsewhere in Latin America, slave resistance included sabotage and work slowdowns. The BLACK CODES formalizing the system of slavery, furthermore, allowed slaves some time to work for themselves and self-purchase. Mining thus provided one important path to manumission. Mining continues to be Chocó's most important industry.

See also Slave Laws in Colonial Spanish America.

Minstrelsy

Nineteenth-century American vernacular entertainment, featuring white performers mimicking blacks, that reinforced negative stereotypes of African Americans yet also preserved aspects of black humor and performance style.

During the Middle Ages, minstrels were servant-performers who entertained their patrons by playing music, singing, telling stories, juggling, or performing comic antics and buffoonery. In the antebellum United States, the term referred to comic performers, almost always white, who wore blackface makeup—generally burnt cork—and mimicked African Americans. The most popular entertainment of the nineteenth century, minstrel shows had a powerful impact on American culture; in particular, they served to "codify the public image of blacks as the prototypical Fool or Sambo," as Mel Watkins observed in his *On the Real Side: Laughing, Lying, and Signifying—The Underground Tradition of African-American Humor.*

During the decades before the CIVIL WAR, minstrel companies found great success in GREAT BRITAIN, Australia, and elsewhere in the English-speaking world. Minstrelsy helped to create misleading and highly demeaning stereotypes of African Americans. Yet it also captured something of the distinctive qualities of African American humor and song, especially during the late nineteenth century, when a number of African American minstrel troupes appeared. Although black minstrel companies were largely trapped by the stereotypes of white minstrelsy, they nonetheless provided an important showcase for black performing talent and served as a springboard for black participation in the twentieth-century entertainment industry.

In the 1820s a number of white actors began to include brief sketches of Southern blacks as part of their acts. In Cincinnati, Edwin Forrest—who became one of America's most prominent actors—made himself up as a black man and portrayed a plantation slave on stage. During two tours of the United States, the well-known British actor and comedian Charles James Mathews collected characteristic American types that he later presented in *A Trip to America,* a one-man show that included a blackface rendition of what became a popular minstrel song, "Possum up a Gum Tree."

The career of Thomas D. "Daddy" Rice marked the true beginnings of American minstrelsy. In about 1828 Rice began impersonating a black man during the intermissions in a minor drama of the period. His act featured a song and dance that became known as "Jim Crow." Rice claimed that he based his sketch on a song and dance he had seen performed—in the words of Mel Watkins—by a "crippled and deformed black hostler or stable groom." The chorus of the song was simple:

Wheel about an' turn about an' do jes so,
An' eb'ry time I wheel about, I jump Jim Crow.

Rice dressed his "Jim Crow" character in the long blue coat and striped pants associated with another popular stereotype, the stage Yankee. Rice's sketch won him such acclaim that he quickly added additional blackface characters and music to his performances. Another African American source for Rice's minstrel act was the black street vendor and singer known as "Signor Cornmeali," or "Old Corn Meal." Signor Cornmeali traveled about NEW ORLEANS with horse and cart, selling cornmeal and singing such songs as "Rosin up the Bow" and his own "Fresh Corn Meal" in a rich baritone alternating with a resonant falsetto. Thomas "Daddy" Rice heard Cornmeali in 1837 and soon added a sketch titled "Corn Meal" to his minstrel act.

The notion of a minstrel troupe emerged as a response to a severe depression that began in 1837, an economic downturn that continued into the early 1840s and hit theatrical performers particularly hard. In 1842 four out-of-work white minstrels—Frank Brower, Dan Emmett, Frank Pelham, and Billy Whitlock—met in a NEW YORK CITY hotel and decided to work together as the Virginia Minstrels, the nation's first true minstrel troupe. The company concentrated exclusively on blackface comedy. From their first performance in 1843 the Virginia Minstrels were a sensation and within a year had begun a well-received tour of England. However, despite its great success, while still touring abroad the troupe broke up as a result of personal disagreements.

With the demise of the Virginia Minstrels, the Ethiopian Serenaders emerged as the nation's foremost minstrel company. In 1848 the Ethiopian Serenaders hired an African American dancer, William Henry Lane, known as "Master Juba." Apart from Lane, Thomas Dilward was the only other African American known to have worked as a minstrel before the Civil War. Dilward was a singer and dancer, but his chief attraction lay in his diminutive height; he was reportedly about three feet tall. Lane, on the other hand, was widely recognized as a gifted dancer. English author Charles Dickens declared unequivocally that Lane was the "greatest dancer known" and in his *American Notes* described the black dancer in action:

"Single shuffle, double shuffle, cut and cross-out: snapping his fingers, rolling his eyes, turning in his knees, presenting the backs of his legs in front, spinning about on his toes and heels . . . all sorts of legs and no legs—what is this to him?"

Lane's performances, by all accounts, represented the first time many whites had seen authentic African American dance.

Besides being a master of the Irish jig, Lane incorporated distinctly African American elements in his performances, including what would later be known as TAP DANCING and the hand jive. Indeed, Lane is commonly regarded as the father of tap dancing. He also utilized the dance style known as "patting juba," in which a dancer sets complex rhythms through hand clapping, foot stomping, and striking his hands against different portions of his body. (Juba was a title or nickname commonly conferred on slaves who showed talent in music or dancing and derived from the African *Gioube,* an intricate step dance with many variations.) Lane first began performing professionally with white minstrels in 1845 and appeared with several companies before joining the Ethiopian Serenaders for their 1848 tour of England. At the end of this tour Lane elected to remain in England, where he died in 1852 at the age of twenty-seven.

The troupe that had the most enduring legacy and the greatest impact on the conventions of minstrel performance was Christy's Original Band of Virginia Minstrels founded in 1843 by Edwin P. Christy. In 1847 this company began a ten-year run in New York City and soon became as popular in the city as P. T. Barnum's Museum. Christy's Minstrels introduced many "Ethiopian songs" that mimicked or evoked an African American style, especially the compositions of Stephen C. Foster, including "Old Folks at Home," "Massa's in de Cold, Cold Ground," and "My Old Kentucky Home"—the type of songs for which Foster is best remembered. Ironically, in 1851 Foster asked that his name be removed as the composer of "Old Folks at Home" because he feared that being associated with such a song might injure his reputation as a serious songwriter. But a year later he had a change of heart. Insisting on his responsibility for popularizing such music, Foster announced that he would "establish [his] name as the best Ethiopian songwriter" in the country.

In addition to popularizing many of Stephen Foster's most memorable songs, Christy's Minstrels also established minstrelsy's standard three-act format. The first act opened with a general walkabout of the costumed minstrels or with a CAKEWALK—a traditional African American dance that stressed flamboyant improvisation. Then came a long routine in which the minstrels sat in a semicircle and engaged in a rapid-fire comic exchange interspersed with popular dances and love songs. The key figures in this part of the show were the interlocutor, the most proper and sophisticated character, who acted as the master of ceremonies and straight man, and two outrageously costumed endmen, who served as the focal points of mischief and mayhem. The second set, known as the olio, employed a variety show format, presenting a mix of music, dance, and novelty numbers highlighted by a farcical "stump speech." The final act was a theatrical—originally a freewheeling plantation skit but, after the mid-1850s, typically a send-up of some serious drama—marked by broad slapstick and innumerable pratfalls. During the 1850s most other minstrel companies adopted the Christy Minstrels' program.

In performance, minstrels exuded an energy bordering on the manic, as Robert C. Toll vividly recounted in *Blacking Up: The Minstrel Show in Nineteenth Century America*:

> They burst on stage in makeup [that] gave the impression of huge eyes and gaping mouths. They dressed in ill-fitting, patchwork clothes, and spoke in heavy "nigger" dialects. Once on stage, they could not stay still for an instant. Even while sitting, they contorted their bodies, cocked their heads . . . and twisted their outstretched legs. . . . [T]heir . . . seemingly compulsive movements charged the entire performance with excitement.

In *Black Literature in White America*, Berndt Ostendorf argued that despite its reliance on demeaning caricature, minstrelsy introduced white Americans—if only indirectly—to the "influence and influx of black American culture." Perhaps more immediately important, minstrelsy was a response to profound strains within white society.

During the 1840s and 1850s the United States received its first massive influx of European immigrants. To many native-born Anglo-Americans, these newcomers seemed frighteningly alien. At the same time American society had clearly acquired the beginnings of a working class; although the permanence of its membership was a matter of debate, it was without question growing. Profound economic dislocations accompanied America's Industrial Revolution, as seen in national depressions during the late 1830s and early 1840s and the mid- to late 1850s and in the strikes and conflicts of the early labor movement. And the ever-present and highly divisive political issue of slavery threatened to set white Americans against one another.

In an atmosphere marked by political acrimony and social tension, minstrelsy had a vital unifying function for white Americans. By constructing an image of happy-go-lucky plantation slaves and irresponsible free black dandies, minstrel shows made light of slavery and emancipation as political issues and denied the human suffering that the institution exacted daily. In addition—much like their medieval counterparts—antebellum minstrels and their absurd antics served not only to entertain, but also to reassure their patrons of their own superiority. By defining blackness so ludicrously, antebellum minstrels constructed a cultural "other" over whom all whites—whether immigrant or native-born, urban or rural, working class or well-to-do—could feel superior. Thus minstrelsy provided indirect but not inconsequential grounds for white social and political unity—at the expense of African Americans.

Although a greater number of African Americans took part in minstrelsy during the Civil War, the first influential black minstrel troupes appeared during the RECONSTRUCTION era. In 1865–1866 an African American company known as Brooker and Clayton's Georgia Minstrels toured in the Northeast, billing itself as "the Only Simon Pure Negro Troupe in the World." From 1866 to 1872 British minstrel dancer Sam Hague toured England with a troupe of black minstrels—billed as Sam Hague's Slave Troupe of Georgia Minstrels. A short time later,

African American minstrel performer Charles Hicks organized yet another company of "Georgia Minstrels." As black minstrel troupes proved their popularity and profitability, their ownership and management generally fell into the hands of whites. By the mid-1870s the most successful black minstrel troupes were all owned by whites.

These prestigious companies toured throughout the United States and in CANADA, the British Isles, GERMANY, Australia, New Zealand, and Java. They typically featured large casts and played in prominent venues and major cities, often traveling in their own railroad cars. Although there were a number of less prestigious black-owned minstrel troupes, these were generally smaller and less likely to travel in such comfort. Black-owned companies tended to appear in less desirable venues and in the smaller towns and cities of America's hinterland. Notable black-owned troupes included Johnson's Plantation Minstrels, which also appeared as the Black Baby Boy Minstrels or as Lew Johnson's Original Tennessee Jubilee Singers, and companies organized by prominent black minstrels such as Billy Kersands, Bob Height, and James Bland. Below these professional troupes were many amateur minstrels.

Minstrelsy provided invaluable experience for countless African American composers, comedians, and musicians. W. C. HANDY, who later gained fame as the composer of "St. Louis Blues," worked for many years as a cornet player and bandleader with Mahara's Minstrels. James Bland—best remembered for composing "Carry Me Back to Old Virginny" and "Oh, Dem Golden Slippers"—was a particularly prolific minstrel composer. The talented African American minstrel and dramatic actor Sam Lucas also composed numerous minstrel songs, of which "Grandfather's Clock" remains the best known.

Numerous twentieth-century black performers also had experience with minstrelsy. Vaudeville comedians BERT WILLIAMS and Ernest Hogan got their start by serving as endmen in minstrel troupes. BLUES singer GERTRUDE "MA" RAINEY was a featured performer with the Rabbit's Foot Minstrels, a company that also included a young dancer who would one day be recognized as the greatest of all female blues singers, BESSIE SMITH. New Orleans JAZZ musicians such as pianist FERDINAND "JELLY ROLL" MORTON and trumpeter Bunk Johnson did stints playing in minstrel companies. And modern jazz trumpeter DIZZY GILLESPIE made his first public performance in 1929 playing in the pit band for a minstrel show put on by his elementary school.

Although black performers found opportunities in minstrelsy, they also found themselves trapped by its restrictive racial conventions. However, as author Mel Watkins cautioned, if African Americans adopted "many of the epithets and referents of minstrel humor, they did not necessarily accept [its] general racist connotations." In *On with the Show: The First Century of Show Business in America,* Robert C. Toll noted that "most early black minstrels did not wear burnt cork, although the endmen used blackface as a comic mask." In a sense, blackface was like the exaggerated facial makeup of the circus clown—with the obvious difference that minstrelsy created a comic mask that ridiculed an entire race.

During the late nineteenth century, as racial hostilities sharpened throughout the United States, white audiences came to expect that all minstrels, black as well as white, should appear in blackface, and the practice became general among black troupes. Although some black performers may have resisted using blackface, the great African American dancer and comedian Bert Williams found it liberated him as a comedian. Recalling his first experience in blackface, Williams said, "Then I began to find myself. It was not until I was able to see myself as another person that my sense of humor developed."

By the turn of the century, professional minstrelsy was in decline. Vaudeville—its generally accepted advent being B. F. Keith's opening of the nation's first vaudeville theater in BOSTON in 1882—gradually supplanted minstrel shows as America's foremost entertainment. George M. Cohan and Sam Harris's Minstrels, the last full-fledged minstrel company to appear on Broadway, had brief runs in 1908 and 1909. Minstrelsy, however, did not simply disappear. Even today its legacy remains extensive and complex. Long after vaudeville became the principal popular entertainment in major cities of the Northeast, minstrel companies continued to tour the small towns of that region and widely through the South and Midwest. Amateur minstrel performances, black as well as white, continued well into the twentieth century.

Many have criticized minstrelsy for its demeaning stereotypes and its nostalgia for plantation slavery. But the minstrel legacy was not wholly negative. Minstrelsy had a powerful impact on vaudeville. Many early vaudeville performers had their first professional experience in minstrel companies. The routines of many black vaudeville comedians—including STEPIN FETCHIT, JACKIE "MOMS" MABLEY, DEWEY "PIGMEAT" MARKHAM, Mantan Moreland, and Bert Williams—clearly reflected the influence of minstrelsy.

Minstrelsy helped transform American humor and, to a lesser extent, African American popular music. Minstrels' energy and verbal inventiveness—including fast-paced repartee, puns, double entendres, and assorted malapropisms—had a major impact on an emerging American comic tradition, as can be seen not only in such vaudeville comedians as Williams and Mabley but also in literature, above all in the humor of Mark Twain. Evan Esar's *The Comic Encyclopedia* observed that minstrelsy's endmen, the most popular minstrel characters, were "chiefly responsible for turning riddle wit in America into gags." During the twentieth century their comic legacy would help shape not just vaudeville but also American musical theater, motion pictures, RADIO, and TELEVISION.

The musical legacy of minstrelsy is less obvious, but also important. Admittedly, the songs of black minstrels—no less than those of their white counterparts—perpetuated extreme stereotypes of African Americans. Minstrel song lyrics featured degrading heavy dialects, and they tended to invoke a warm nostalgia for the bygone days of plantation slavery. But the key musical contribution of black minstrels lay not as much in their compositions as in their overall performance style. Like the dancing of William Henry Lane, the musical performances of black minstrels introduced a measure of authentic African American culture to a wider audience.

Black minstrel companies often featured renditions, in harmony, of SPIRITUALS, jubilee songs, and sentimental ballads. The singing of such professional entertainers—along with performances by college-trained choirs, such as the FISK JUBILEE SINGERS—had a profound influence on subsequent vocal harmony groups, evident in secular singing no less than in GOSPEL QUARTETS. Professional minstrels and college choral groups offered slick versions of African American music, but they nonetheless provided an eye-opening experience for white audiences, and they inspired countless young African American singers and performers. At age fifteen W. C. Handy played his first amateur minstrel show in Florence, Alabama—his hometown—as first tenor in a vocal quartet. In his autobiography, *Father of the Blues,* Handy recalled how professional minstrels served as models for his own group of amateurs:

> We had seen the famous Georgia Minstrels in Florence. . . . We were all acquainted with Billy Kersands, the man who could "make a mule laugh." . . . We had seen Sam Lucas and Tom McIntosh walking at the head of the parade in high silk hats and long-tailed coats. We had an idea of how the thing should be done, but I suppose our trouble was lack of experience.

The passage of more than fifty years had not dimmed Handy's awareness of the importance of black minstrelsy. "All the best black talent," he recalled, "the composers, the singers, the musicians, the speakers, the stage performers—the Minstrel Show got them all."

See also Labor Unions in the United States.

James Sellman

Miracles, The

See Robinson, William ("Smokey").

Miscegenation

From the Latin words *miscere* (to mix) and *genus* (race); referred to sexual relations across racial lines and is no longer in use because of its racist implications.

The word *miscegenation* was coined by two Democrats during the presidential election campaign of 1864 in an attempt to embarrass and discredit Abraham Lincoln, the Republican incumbent running for reelection. In an anonymous pamphlet that appeared in December 1863 entitled *Miscegenation: The Theory of the Blending of the Races Applied to the American White Man and Negro,* the authors played on white fears of interracial sex by pretending to issue a Republican-sponsored booklet advocating racial mixing and amalgamation. The real authors were David Goodman Croly, managing editor of the *New York World,* a staunchly Democratic paper, and George Wakeman, a *World* reporter.

Sex across the color line was an obsession of white America, particularly the stereotype of black men's alleged craving for white women, along with believers in Anglo-Saxon "racial" superiority who feared that "mongrelization" was degenerative. In fact, black-white sex existed from the beginning of the slave trade in the sixteenth century, virtually always on the initiative of Europeans who held Africans in their total power. During the notorious MIDDLE PASSAGE between Africa and the New World, for example, black women and children were allowed mobility on board ship so that white sailors could have unlimited sexual access to them.

Sex played a role in the gradual differentiation of Africans from other indentured servants in Virginia, a process that culminated around 1700 in the unique North American phenomenon of chattel slavery, by which people were legally defined as property. The very first case in this chain was a sexual one: in 1630 Hugh Davis was sentenced by the Virginia court to a whipping "for defiling his body in lying with a Negro." Even though it was a white man who was convicted and punished for the act, the case shows the early eroticization of racial differences.

The interracial sexual pattern in the antebellum South is clear: Because slaves were property, like animals or objects, they had no rights, and all black women were sexually available to all white men. In addition, African American marriage and parenthood were not recognized in law, and there was no recourse for sexual abuse in the courts, government, church, or press. Virtually every plantation produced children of mixed race; the 1860 federal census classified 588,532 persons as mulattos. A minuscule number of white fathers recognized their children and provided for them; some parents encouraged the fairest skinned to run away and hide their racial identity by passing for white. Most mixed-blood slave children were simply worked and sold like all other slaves.

The white South combined the permissive sexual exploitation of black women by white men with a fanatic "protection" of white women from black men. In both cases, the ideology was that people of African descent were closer to nature and savagery, but the real reason was probably economic: Legally, a child was slave or free depending on the status of the mother. All white women were free and nearly all black women were slaves.

The uniqueness of chattel slavery prohibited in North America (except for NEW ORLEANS) the emergence of mulattos as a distinct third group between black and white, as existed in the WEST INDIES, LATIN AMERICA, and SOUTH AFRICA. American slavery was race- and color-based, but it would have become weakened ideologically and economically if it had allowed any deviation from the one-drop rule, that is the belief that any black ancestry made one black.

Miscegenation was about marriage as well as sex, since sexual relationships were legitimized by marriage. Therefore, interracial marriage was prohibited, upheld by the U.S. Supreme Court in *Pace v. Alabama* (1883). That decision was not overturned until well after the modern CIVIL RIGHTS MOVEMENT had begun, in *Loving v. Virginia* (1967), when sixteen states still had laws prohibiting interracial marriage. Civil rights and voting rights were extended to African Americans before the right was granted both to whites and blacks to marry (and have legitimate sexual relationships) across the color line.

Richard Newman

Misik Raisin

Haitian Creole for "roots music," a highly political Haitian musical movement spearheaded by the group Boukman Eksperyans.

Misik raisin appeared on HAITI's music scene in the late 1970s. The Jamaican-based philosophy of Rastafarianism and roots REGGAE had a profound impact on a new generation of middle-class Haitian musicians. Reggae musician BOB MARLEY's stirring message of Afrocentrism, black cultural autonomy, and strong political commitment inspired Haitians to seek out their own version of roots music. The roots musicians used traditional Haitian VODOU as a common national heritage to engender community against dictatorship and imperial control. The up-tempo dance music of the *ra-ra* festival (second in size only to Haiti's Carnival) also became part of misik raisin's repertoire.

The band BOUKMAN EKSPERYANS is the most well known of the Haitian roots reinterpreters. BOUKMAN was a slave leader and Vodou priest active in Haiti during the late eighteenth century. Boukman led a successful slave insurrection that relied on Vodou's power to unify slaves of various African ethnicities. Boukman Eksperyans titled their 1991 album *Vodou Adjae* (Concerned Vodou). It abandoned the all-popular compas sound in favor of Vodou drumming and the rhythms of ra-ra music. The title track, "Se Kreyo'l Nou Ye" (We Speak Creole), came into usage as an anthem of Creole/Haitian pride. The government harassed performers of misik raisin for their aggressively political lyrics accompanied by Vodou rhythms.

The music of Boukman Eksperyans played a role in the ousting of President General Prospère Avril in 1990. Their song for Carnival that year, "Kè m pa sote" (My heart doesn't leap / I'm not afraid) caused great commotions whenever it was played. Their popularity prevented the government from forbidding them access to Carnival performances; their oblique lyrics promoted fearlessness against an unnamed enemy, and the military government was thus unsure how to respond. The song won Carnival awards, and countless other misik raisin and ra-ra bands incorporated it as a kind of populist national anthem. A week after Carnival, "Kè m pa sote" was sung in support of a strike protesting the unprovoked murder of a young girl by Avril's military. The government publicly labeled Boukman Eksperyans "a band of paranoid frauds and idiots," which only gave the strikers added determination. The grassroots strike swelled into a large-scale uprising that ended with Avril's ousting.

Thus, out of the political noninvolvement of compas came misik raisin, a powerful new movement inextricably tied to the political developments in Haiti. Boukman Eksperyans sang songs in support of democratically elected president JEAN-BERTRAND ARISTIDE, as did many of their fellow musicians. Aristide's overthrow by military coup led to renewed efforts to quell misik raisin. Because of the international fame they gained after the release of their 1991 album *Vodou Adjae*, Boukman Eksperyans was essentially safe from physical harm, although the government tormented members with surveillance, harassment, and edicts of silence. The military threw tear gas at a 1993 Boukman Eksperyans concert. Audiences worldwide loved the African-influenced drumming of misik raisin, and bands such as Boukman Eksperyans received greater recognition than their less "ethnic"-sounding compas predecessors. The group's 1992 album *Kalfou Danjere* (Dangerous Crossroads) topped world music sales charts.

See also Afrocentricity; Carnivals in Latin America and the Caribbean; Haitian Revolution; Rastafarians.

Jace Clayton

Mississippi Freedom Democratic Party

Political organization, primarily African American, formed to protest racial exclusion by the all-white Mississippi Democratic Party at the Democratic National Convention in 1964.

At an April 1964 meeting the COUNCIL OF FEDERATED ORGANIZATIONS (COFO), an umbrella group that sought to unite all civil rights organizations working in Mississippi, formed the Mississippi Freedom Democratic Party (MFDP). MFDP organizers realized that registering voters would have no lasting impact in Mississippi unless blacks could also participate within the state party, which the all-white membership made impossible. The Mississippi Democratic Party refused to endorse either the Civil Rights Act of 1964, the national party's pro–civil rights position, or its presidential candidate, incumbent Lyndon B. Johnson. In light of these exclusions and refusals, the MFDP hoped the DEMOCRATIC PARTY would declare the MFDP its legitimate Mississippi representative at the 1964 national convention in Atlantic City, New Jersey.

To prove that the regular Mississippi party blocked black participation, the MFDP sent members to the regular Democratic precinct, county, district, and state conventions, at which the party chose its convention delegates. At the various conventions, blacks found that whites attempted to prevent their access in many ways, such as changing the location or time of a convention, denying blacks entry to the convention halls or, when they were present, denying them opportunities to speak or vote. In addition to proving that the regular party excluded blacks, MFDP organizers believed they needed to demonstrate that the MFDP had widespread support among Mississippi residents. Thus, in the face of white violence and intimidation, organizers tried to recruit blacks to register to vote and join the MFDP.

The MFDP selected forty-four delegates and twenty-two alternates to attend the Democratic National Convention. To be recognized as the official Mississippi delegation, the MFDP needed approval from the credentials committee. Although the delegation believed that it would receive the support it needed to unseat the regular Democratic delegation, Democratic nominee President Lyndon B. Johnson, fearing a general walkout by Southern Democrats, opposed seating the MFDP. Johnson went so far as to enlist the Federal Bureau of Investigation to gather information about MFDP strategy through wiretapping, posing as NBC reporters (with NBC's cooperation), and sending informants to infiltrate MFDP meetings.

The most dramatic scenes at the convention occurred during the nationally televised credentials committee meeting, which featured MFDP testimony, most memorably that of FANNIE LOU HAMER, who movingly described her life as a former sharecropper and her eviction for registering to vote. Johnson, afraid that Hamer's testimony would inspire support for the MFDP, gave a live address on television during her testimony. His address interrupted the television broadcast of Hamer's testimony. He then mobilized Minnesota senator Hubert H. Humphrey, his prospective running mate, who was told that to retain the vice presidential nomination, he had to neutralize the MFDP. After a series of meetings, Humphrey offered a compromise: two "at large" seats, with the rest of the delegation designated "honored guests." The MFDP ultimately refused, and Johnson then sought to quash remaining MFDP support by cajoling and threatening MFDP supporters, including one credentials committee member who, Johnson warned, would lose a judgeship if he continued supporting the MFDP. In large part because of Johnson's powerful influence, the credentials committee denied the MFDP any seats, although the national party stated that it would no longer allow segregated delegations.

MFDP delegates staged a sit-in on the convention floor, but security guards quickly removed them, and they left the convention feeling betrayed. Prior to the convention, many MFDP members believed they were working within the Democratic Party, but as Student Nonviolent Coordinating Committee activist and MFDP organizer ROBERT MOSES said, the convention proved that Democratic support of blacks was merely "puddle-deep." In 1968 the MFDP merged with other Mississippi civil rights groups to form the Mississippi Loyal Democrats, which, with Democratic National Committee support, successfully deposed the Mississippi Democratic delegation to the convention in 1968.

Robert Fay

Missouri Compromise

Legislative measure, enacted by the U.S. Congress in 1820, that regulated the extension of slavery in the United States for three decades.

When Missouri, a territory settled mainly by migrants from the slaveholding South, applied for statehood in 1818, the long-standing balance of free and slave states (at eleven each) was jeopardized. A Northern-sponsored amendment was then attached to the bill authorizing statehood in 1819; it prohibited the entry of slaves into Missouri and provided for the gradual emancipation of those already there. A proslavery faction was unable to prevent the bill's passage by the House of Representatives, where free states held a majority, but Southern strength in the Senate defeated the bill.

Maine, then a part of Massachusetts, also applied for statehood in 1819. Speaker of the House Henry Clay of Kentucky warned Northern congressmen that unless they changed their position on Missouri the Southerners would reject Maine's petition. To please the South the slavery restrictions for Missouri were then removed, and to satisfy the North, Senator Jesse B. Thomas of Illinois introduced in February 1920 a proviso by which slavery would be prohibited forever from territories north of the 36°30' latitudinal line acquired under the Louisiana Purchase. Southern extremists opposed any limit on the extension of slavery, but Clay maneuvered the measure through the House by a three-vote majority. Missouri and Maine were to enter statehood simultaneously to preserve sectional equality in the Senate. In 1821, when Northern congressmen balked over antiblack clauses in Missouri's constitution, Clay again adjusted differences, and Missouri's admission was ensured.

The compromise became the precedent for settling subsequent North-South disagreements over slavery and tariff issues, and it remained in effect until repealed by the Kansas-Nebraska Act of 1854, which left the choice of slavery in the new states of Kansas and Nebraska (both of which were above the 36°30' line) to the voters of each state. In 1857, in the *Dred Scott v. Sandford* decision, proslavery Chief Justice Roger B. Taney of the Supreme Court of the United States declared that the Missouri Compromise had been unconstitutional, because, he claimed, the Constitution did not give Congress the right to regulate the Louisiana Purchase territories.

Mitchell, Clarence Maurice, Jr.

1911–1984

Congressional lobbyist for the National Association for the Advancement of Colored People (NAACP).

Less visible than many of his NAACP colleagues, Clarence Mitchell nonetheless had a major impact on the lives of African Americans. Known as the 101st senator, the longtime NAACP lobbyist was instrumental in the passage of both the Civil Rights Act of 1964 and the VOTING RIGHTS ACT OF 1965, the two most significant successes of the CIVIL RIGHTS MOVEMENT. Mitchell was a 1932 graduate of LINCOLN UNIVERSITY in Pennsylvania and the husband of JUANITA JACKSON MITCHELL, an NAACP official. He joined the NAACP staff following his work with the NATIONAL URBAN LEAGUE and the FAIR EMPLOYMENT PRACTICES COMMITTEE (FEPC).

The FEPC was formed in 1941 to eliminate employment discrimination and was dissolved in 1946. While acting as the NAACP's labor secretary, Mitchell continued to fight for economic fair play, founding the National Council for a Permanent FEPC in 1949 and participating the following year in the Leadership Conference on Civil Rights, a group with representatives from more than fifty civil rights organizations. Mitchell began his legislative work as part of this struggle and quickly became the association's chief lobbyist, a position he held until he retired in 1978. The veteran lobbyist became a lawyer himself in 1962 after completing four years of nightly study at the University of Maryland Law School. In 1969 the NAACP awarded Mitchell the Spingarn Medal, and in 1980 he was honored with the Presidential Medal of Freedom, the nation's highest nonmilitary decoration. After his death in 1984 his hometown of BALTIMORE, MARYLAND, renamed its courthouse after him.

Kate Tuttle

Mitchell, Juanita Jackson

1913–1992

Civil rights lawyer, first African American woman admitted to the Maryland bar, and first National Youth Director of the National Association for the Advancement of Colored People (NAACP).

By the time Juanita J. Mitchell had received her law degree in 1950, she had already spent nearly twenty years working for civil rights on the local and national levels. Born to racially conscious parents—her mother, LILLIE MAE CARROLL JACKSON, was president of the state conference of NAACP branches—Mitchell earned a degree in education from the University of Pennsylvania in 1931. Upon graduation she returned to her native BALTIMORE to help African Americans struggling with both the economic devastation of the GREAT DEPRESSION and the persistence of LYNCHING and other racist violence. Hoping to alleviate some of their suffering, Mitchell founded the City-Wide Young People's Forum of Baltimore in 1931 and served as its president until 1934. In 1935 WALTER WHITE, then executive secretary of the NAACP, recruited Jackson to head that organization's newly created youth program, a position she held until her 1938 marriage to CLARENCE M. MITCHELL, JR.

After the births of four sons, Mitchell entered law school at the University of Maryland, from which she graduated in 1950. That same year she became the first African American woman to be admitted to the bar in her state. As a lawyer Mitchell continued the work she had begun as an organizer: improving the lives of African Americans. She filed lawsuits that helped integrate public beaches and schools, represented students arrested during SIT-INS in the 1960s, and continued to direct voter registration drives. By the time she died in 1992 at the age of seventy-nine, Mitchell had been recognized by the NAACP's Youth/College Division, the Maryland Women's Hall of Fame, and the NATIONAL COUNCIL OF NEGRO WOMEN—which she had helped found with MARY MCLEOD BETHUNE.

Bibliography

McNeil, Glenna Rae. *Groundwork: Charles Hamilton Houston and the Struggle for Civil Rights.* University of Pennsylvania Press, 1983.

Kate Tuttle

Mitchell, Loften

1919–2001

African American playwright and novelist.

Born in Columbia, North Carolina, Loften Mitchell grew up in HARLEM, NEW YORK, where as a young man he began working in theater with the Rose McClendon Players. In 1943 he completed an A.B. at Talladega College in Alabama and studied playwriting with John Glassner at Columbia University.

Mitchell's play *A Land beyond the River* is based on a court case, involving Joseph DeLaine, a South Carolina pastor and schoolteacher, that ended school segregation. The play received critical acclaim when it was produced in 1957. He continued to write prolifically. His later works include *The Photographer* (1962), *Ballad of Bimshire* (1963), *Ballad for the Winter Soldiers* (1964), *Tell Pharaoh* (1967), and the successful musical co-written with ROSETTA LENOIRE, *Bubbling Brown Sugar* (1975).

Mitchell also taught at the State University of New York at Binghamton, published the novel *The Stubborn Old Lady Who Resisted Change* (1973), and wrote two histories of drama, *Black Drama: The Story of the American Negro in the Theatre* (1967) and *Voices of the Black Theatre* (1975).

Marian Aguiar

Mittelhölzer, Edgar Austin

1909–1965

Afro-Guyanese novelist who lived and died in exile but used Caribbean and Creole history and themes in his work.

Edgar Mittelhölzer has been called the father of the novel in the English-speaking Caribbean. He was the first Caribbean author to make a living entirely by his writing, and he remains the most prolific Caribbean novelist to date, even though his career was cut short by his suicide at age fifty-five.

Mittelhölzer was born into a mixed-race middle-class family in Guyana and had Swiss, German, French, English, and African heritage—although his father's resentment of their black blood shaped his childhood. He attended the well-known Barbice High School, and by the time he was nineteen his love for movies, detective fiction, and the Buffalo Bill stories had convinced him that he "had to be a writer."

For his first decade as a writer he received mainly rejection slips, but he supported himself by menial jobs and continued writing until his first novel, *Corentyne Thunder,* was published in 1941. Shortly after that he moved to TRINIDAD, where he lived for several years before deciding that he needed to leave the Caribbean to achieve true success as a writer. In 1947 Mittelhölzer emigrated to London and so became one of the first of many Caribbean writers who have gone to London to find success "in exile."

Mittelhölzer's success was represented in his brisk publishing pace. *A Morning at the Office,* his second novel, was published in 1950, and he went on to publish at least one novel each year until his death. In 1952 he began writing full-time, and that year he moved to CANADA on a Guggenheim Fellowship. Mittelhölzer spent the next three years in BARBADOS before returning to England in May 1956. By that time his books included the first two volumes of his Kaywana trilogy, which is often his most celebrated work.

The Kaywana books trace the saga of one Guyanese family from the colonial period to the mid-twentieth century, and they have been praised for their elegant interweaving of Guyana's history into the family's story. While several of his books are set abroad, many others also treat Caribbean themes—and particularly the tangled connections between races and classes in West Indian society.

Mittelhölzer himself, however, said that his two main themes were "sex and religion," and the adultery, rape, incest, and other recurring sexual themes in his work led one book (*The Piling Clouds*) to be initially rejected as pornography. But Mittelhölzer's works also included many characters who were in psychological torment or suicidal, a tragic reflection of his own life, and he attempted suicide twice before setting himself on fire in his Surrey home in May 1965.

See also Great Britain; Literature, English-Language, in the Caribbean.

Lisa Clayton Robinson

Mkapa, Benjamin

1938–

President of Tanzania since 1995.

Born in Ndanda in the Masasi District of southeastern TANZANIA, the last of four children, Benjamin Mkapa attended local schools before completing a bachelor's degree at Makerere University in UGANDA in 1962. He worked as a district administrative officer in Dodoma and DAR ES SALAAM for one year before joining the foreign service in 1963. Having joined the ruling party, the Tanganyika African National Union (TANU), Mkapa was appointed managing editor of the party's newspaper in May 1966. In July 1974 he was promoted to press secretary for President JULIUS NYERERE. Mkapa served briefly as the first director of Shihata, the Tanzanian news agency, in 1974 before becoming high commissioner to NIGERIA (1976–1977). In a series of rapid promotions and reassignments resulting from cabinet reshuffles, Mkapa held a succession of important government posts in the late 1970s and 1980s. Initially appointed to parliament in 1977, Mkapa was elected to represent the Masasi District in 1985. He was elected to the central committee of TANU's successor, the Revolutionary Party of Tanzania (Chama Cha Mapinduzi, or CCM), in 1987 and received the party's nomination for president in July 1995. In October 1995 he took 62 percent of the vote in Tanzania's first multiparty elections and began his five-year term as president in November 1995. Mkapa was reelected in October 2000 with more than 70 percent of the vote. His current challenges include how to alleviate poverty in one of the world's poorest countries.

Mobeur

Ethnic group of West Africa; also known as Mavar and Mober.

The Mobeur inhabit primarily southeastern NIGER and northeastern NIGERIA. They speak an Afro-Asiatic language in the Chadic group and are closely related to the KANURI people. Approximately 400,000 people consider themselves Mobeur.

See also Languages, African: An Overview.

Mobutu Sese Seko

1930–1997

Former president and long-term dictator of Zaire (now the Democratic Republic of the Congo).

Once the personification of the African autocrat and shrewd Cold War politician, Mobutu Sese Seko fled KINSHASA, Zaire's capital, on May 16, 1997, after three decades in power. Known as a corrupt and brutal dictator for most of his reign, Mobutu abdicated power after rebels conquered Zaire within a span of six months. Dying of cancer and politically unpopular, Mobutu lacked the support necessary to maintain control.

Mobutu was born in Lisala, in what was then the BELGIAN CONGO, and was educated by Belgian missionaries. In 1950 he joined the colonial army, the Force Publique, and within six years rose to the rank of sergeant. He left the army in 1956 and became a columnist for the Léopoldville (now Kinshasa) newspaper, *L'Avenir.* Three years later he received a fellowship from the colonial administration to study at the Institute of Journalism and Social Sciences in Brussels, Belgium. Because of his studies, Mobutu missed most of the independence movement in the Belgian Congo, but he did attend the 1960 Round Table Conference in Brussels, at which the Belgian government negotiated the terms of decolonization for Zaire. It is widely believed that while at the conference Mobutu spied on fellow Congolese for the Belgian government. He returned to the Belgian Congo before independence and was appointed army chief of staff by the new prime minister, PATRICE LUMUMBA.

Shortly afterward he took advantage of a rift between President JOSEPH KASAVUBU and Lumumba to make his own bid for power. With support from the United States Central Intelligence Agency (CIA), he helped overthrow and track down Lumumba.

It is believed that Mobutu ordered Lumumba's murder in January 1961.

Mobutu returned Kasavubu to power in February 1961 and for the next four years led military operations against regional rebellions. Not content to stay behind the scenes, however, he staged another coup d'état and on November 25, 1965, seized permanent control of the government.

Mobutu ruled for the next thirty-two years. Spending the first five years centralizing authority, Mobutu held and easily won presidential elections in 1970. After these elections, however, Mobutu created an autocratic state maintained by an elaborate system of terror and corruption coupled with unpredictable generosity. At times Mobutu would force political opponents into exile, only to invite them back later to be pardoned. In some instances his opponents would be publicly executed; in others, they would be won over and brought into the president's inner circle of well-paid advisers.

Mobutu justified his dictatorial power, as well as all his economic and social policies, by referring to an ideology he called *authenticité* and others called Mobutuism. Exalting the superiority of African "authentic" traditions, he portrayed himself as a traditional chief. He changed his name to Mobutu Sese Seko Kuku Ngbendu waza Banga, which means "the all-powerful warrior who, because of his endurance and inflexible will to win, will go from conquest to conquest leaving fire in his wake." He adopted his trademark leopard skin cap and wooden walking stick topped with an eagle, a symbol of power that allegedly took the strength of eight normal men to carry. He ordered all citizens to adopt African names and dress and renamed the country Zaire. In 1973 Mobutu undertook the "Zaireanization" of the economy, in which he nationalized foreign businesses, including the valuable copper and diamond mines. Much of the revenue from these enterprises financed Mobutu's luxurious lifestyle (including villas on the French Riviera, yachts, and limousines) and accumulated in his private bank account (once estimated at $5 billion).

Despite his infamous corruption and brutality, Mobutu received generous financial and military support from Western powers, especially FRANCE and the United States, who were eager to maintain a barrier to the "communist threat" in Central Africa. Western banks and construction companies were equally eager to help Mobutu realize his elaborate development plans, such as the Inga dam, which was projected to generate one-third of the world's hydroelectricity. The dam and many other projects failed as Mobutu and his friends pocketed the funds.

During the 1980s mounting debts and a drop in world copper prices plunged Zaire into economic crisis. Food shortages, unpaid government salaries, and a decaying infrastructure all contributed to popular discontent. After a 1990 massacre of students at a prodemocracy rally at the University of Lubumbashi, France and the United States—no longer so inclined to support Mobutu once the Cold War was over—demanded political reforms. Mobutu agreed to create a multiparty state and national assembly but repeatedly undermined efforts to carry out these reforms. In 1991 Etienne Tshisekedi was named prime minister, and although dismissed shortly afterward, he was reinstated in 1992. For the next two years Mobutu, angered by Tshisekedi's popularity, avoided the capital and spent his time in his various homes in AFRICA and Europe. Mobutu did resume a more active role in 1994 when Kengo wa Dondo, a close associate of the president, was appointed prime minister. In addition, civil conflict in neighboring RWANDA returned international attention to Mobutu. This renewed authority, however, was to be short-lived.

In October 1996 the Alliance of Democratic Forces for the Liberation of Congo-Zaire, led by LAURENT-DÉSIRÉ KABILA, began an offensive that conquered virtually the entire country within six months. Already sick with prostate cancer, Mobutu was also politically weak and thus unable to rally support from treatment centers in Europe. Despite some external aid, Mobutu's demoralized forces melted away, and he returned to Zaire too late to reverse the situation. Nevertheless, Mobutu refused to accept defeat until Kabila's army threatened to take over Kinshasa in May, and he fled the capital with his family. Refused entrance in France and TOGO, Mobutu finally found refuge in MOROCCO, where he died on September 7, 1997.

Bibliography

Schatzberg, Michael. *The Dialectics of Oppression in Zaire.* University of Indiana Press, 1988.

Schatzberg, Michael. *Mobutu or Chaos? The United States and Zaire, 1960–1990.* University Press of America, 1991.

Elizabeth Heath

Modernism from Afro-America: An Interpretation of Wifredo Lam's Paintings

The history of art has, to a large extent, been a Eurocentric story, a Western construction that has excluded, diminished, and decontextualized a good part of the aesthetic production of the world. It is becoming increasingly urgent—especially for Latin Americans—to deconstruct it in search of more decentralized, integrative, contextualized, and multidisciplinary discourses. Some time ago the literary critic Etiemble invalidated "any theory which is based exclusively on European phenomena," and his remark has a tinge of urgency in our field.

This article analyzes the work of the Afro-Cuban painter and sculptor WIFREDO LAM (1902–1982), a paradigmatic figure in Latin American modernism and the first artist for whom African culture appears in its own right as a decisive factor of expression. Lam's work will be discussed not, as many critics have done, as a product of surrealism, primitivism, or cubism but rather as a pioneering expression of Afro-Cuban and Afro-Caribbean culture and a means by which this culture came to influence and infiltrate European avant-garde art. This is what Lam must have meant when he said that he was a "Trojan horse." This new approach to Lam does not imply nonrecognition of his academic training, the influence of Picasso and surrealism, nor his status as a participant in the European avant-garde movement. He himself once surprised me during an interview when he showed me a picture of a work, which was African in appearance, and commented: "You need to have seen a lot of Poussin to do this."

The perspective in this article also implies recognition of Western culture as characteristic of the world today, as a result of the global expansion of industrial capitalism, which for the first time integrated the world into a global system centered in Europe. Many elements of Western culture have ceased to be "ethnic" and have become internationalized as intrinsic elements of a world shaped by the development of the West. The very idea of "art" as a self-sufficient activity based on aesthetics, a definition dating from no earlier than the end of the eighteenth century, is also a product of Western culture. The traditional art of other cultures, as well as that of the West from earlier epochs, was a different type of creation, determined by functions of a religious, representational, or commemorative nature.

The difficulties of deconstructing Eurocentrism are many. Even though much of postmodernism introduces a diversification in the center-periphery and hegemony-subordination oppositions, it is itself a Western mode of thought imposed by the "center" and thereby reproduces Western domination. The center, disguised as relativism, "threatens to supplant the periphery in its alternative role," as scholar Nelly Richard has pointed out, and to deprive it of oppositional force by integration. Much of contemporary interest in difference is itself Eurocentric, a move from the dominator toward the dominated: in this equation the "other" is always us. In all events, subordinate cultures must exploit for themselves the opportunities offered by this new situation and by the rhetoric of decentralization. One of the unavoidable challenges is to transform the dominant culture to their advantage, de-Eurocentralizing it without depriving it of its contemporary relevance, introducing into it new discourses based on hybridization and transformation.

The intercultural dialogue implicit in Lam's work is an example of the cultural diversity inherent in the Caribbean nationalities. These nationalities are part of the Western trunk, and European culture lies at their origins, although they are modulated from within by very active non-Western ingredients. Western culture is not foreign to the Caribbean, unlike African or Asian countries, which to a certain extent are divided between their traditional cultures and Western culture imposed by colonialism. Thus, for Lam, the academic, cubist, or surrealist poetics were part of a familiar tradition. His contribution was to make a qualitative turn and base his art on those elements of African heritage that are alive in Cuban culture. In this sense his work reproduces the plurality characteristic of the Caribbean, centering it on the African component, which indeed determines the profile of the region.

The son of a Cantonese immigrant and a mulatta (of African and European descent), Lam was raised in Sagua la Grande, CUBA. His godmother was a priestess in the chapter of Santa Barbara (Changó), and he grew up in a region strongly marked by Afro-Cuban traditions such as SANTERÍA and *palo monte*, although he was never formally initiated into any such traditions. He left Cuba in 1923, heading first to Spain, where he acquired a classical artistic training and earned a living by painting portraits. Toward the end of the 1920s Lam produced some works in the style of Spanish surrealism tinged with academicism. In Paris, however, where he settled in 1938, he consolidated himself as a late modernist, with the support of Picasso. His painting from 1938 to 1940, although based to a large extent on African MASKS and geometry, was reminiscent of Picasso and in general of the School of Paris. At that time Lam also began to develop a passion for the traditional art of Africa and became a permanent collector of such pieces.

The features that most attracted Lam to Picasso—the African element and certain surrealist-like expressive deformation—would subsequently become decisive in his own painting. Picasso was interested in African art in terms of geometry, as a constructive synthesis of the human image. The Spanish painter's most expressive paintings or surrealist works were based less directly on African geometry, which inspired colder and more abstract pieces. Lam managed to link both sides, a process that would engender the personal style that was to characterize his subsequent work. He developed this process in France in works dating from 1940, such as *Portrait*, *Homme-Femme*, and *Symbiosis*; and from 1941, for example, in his illustrations for Breton's *Fata Morgana*. At the same time, Lam was becoming powerfully influenced by surrealism. Although he never actually joined the surrealist movement, he used surrealistic features, such as double eyes, in his paintings and began to depict mythological, fantastic, and more carnal figures than his earlier schematized characters from African geometry.

Lam returned to Cuba in 1942. The cultural mood introduced by surrealism had encouraged him to express his own world, the world of his culture, in an exercise of modernity. His arrival in Cuba marked his encounter with that world in reality. This arrival did not produce any sense of astonishment but a feeling of belonging. It was the confirmation of, and final encounter with, his own space. It was a *"retour au pays natal,"* in the sense of the moving poem by Martinican poet and intellectual AIMÉ CÉSAIRE. Indeed, back in Cuba, Lam found his cultural universe as a personal artistic universe. The return occurred at the right moment: fascinated by African and what was then called "primitive" elements thanks to modern art, he had begun to give outward expression to those aspects of himself. This came about through his direct contact with Afro-Cuban traditions, greatly facilitated by the Cuban folklore specialist LYDIA CABRERA, who helped familiarize Lam with the myths, liturgies, and representations of that world. As FERNANDO ORTIZ writes, "The Afroid world is in Lam and in all his environment"; it is not some diffuse feeling, a dream, a sense of longing, or something in a museum. While "ethnographic" artists such as Joseph Beuys looked to Africa to obtain a distance from their own cultures in order to transform them, Lam's approach aimed at moving more deeply into Cuban culture, thus reaffirming it. Unlike many ethnologists who engage in "participant observation," Lam emerged from his immersion in

Afro-Cuban folklore as an "observant participant" whose ethnographic material became a subject with which he established a relationship from within the very culture itself.

From 1942 Lam's works became the vehicle for his own, definitive kind of expression, the first vision ever of modern art from the standpoint of Africa. His art became dominated by a figuration that, although indebted to cubism, distanced itself from the analytical breaking down of forms and moved toward invention, with the object of communicating, rather than strictly representing, a mythology of the Caribbean. There is a baroque gathering of natural and fantastic elements in these works whose message is, as Desiderio Navarro writes, the unity of life, a vision characteristic of Afro-Cuban traditions, where everything is interconnected because everything—gods, energies, human beings, animals, plants, minerals—is full of mystical force and depends and acts on everything else. This message questions and ultimately deconstructs standard Western oppositions between beauty and ugliness, good and bad, life and death, creation and destruction. As Cuban writer ALEJO CARPENTIER wrote, Lam had come from the "fixed" world of the West to another kind of world, "one of symbiosis, metamorphosis, confusion, vegetable and telluric transformations."

A major element in Lam's works is the god Eleguá, the only god whose basic image was used by Lam in nearly all his pictures. Eleguá is the trickster, the principle of uncertainty, who stands in opposition to Orula-Ifa, the principle of structure and accumulated wisdom. He is the master of doors and crossroads, he opens and closes everything but is unpredictable and mischievous. Similarly, in Lam's works everything seems to change into something unexpected; his art is a metamorphosis, "a praise of osmosis," as he entitled one of his paintings. Eleguá's influence is also apparent in the displacement of vision in Lam's art and in its representation and embodiment of a cultural crossroads.

Thus Lam had come a long way from pure cubism. Picasso and other modern artists had sought inspiration in African masks and statues essentially to achieve a formal renovation of Western art. They remained unaware of the context of these objects and their religious meanings and functions. In his "Picasso period" of 1938 to 1940, Lam emulated this geometric interpretation of African art. However, under the influence of surrealism, his own personal world became activated in a way that was to foster a more internal manipulation of those forms. As a modern artist, Lam displaced the focus from forms to meanings in a coherent, natural, and spontaneous manner. He was attempting to create for himself, and within the context of a more personal imagery, that which the creators of the masks themselves had sought: the construction of something both fantastic and natural. Lam's art was an abstract approximation, through the necessarily different resources and functions of easel painting and modern Western art, to the mystical sense expressed in the masks.

Despite the fact that Lam's painting is often described as a set of symbols, there is no precise or direct encoding of Afro-Cuban religious elements, which are always referred to indirectly. As Lam himself said, "I do not tend to use an exact symbology." Given the degree of decomposition, mixing, and processing of the sources, there is no strict quotation of specific kinds of masks (although some, such as the *gbon*, can still be recognized). A stricter symbolic codification appears only in a few large oil works from the second half of the 1940s such as *Eternal Presence, The Wedding, Belial,* and *Annunciation,* which are also characterized by a greater figurative naturalism and by their expressionist aggression.

The displacements that occur in Lam's work were often proclaimed in a polemical manner. His art, like that of many surrealist painters, is often very challenging to bourgeois good taste, as he himself admitted when he said he wanted to create "hallucinating figures that can cause surprise and trouble the minds of the exploiters." Such an ingenuous program can only be understood in a figurative sense, as poetics. Lam had a preference for certain aggressive forms such as thorns, horns, and teeth (which sometimes filled an entire picture, as in *Escolopendras*), grotesque shapes alluding to repulsive animals, snakelike forms, and deformities. He viewed this attempt to shock as a Third World offensive against established taste and, in the final analysis, against what he called the "aristocratic" Western aesthetic. Lam, however, acted from within the context of modernity and even classicism, which he never abandoned but rather reoriented. Lam created a non-Western space within the Western tradition, decentralizing, transforming, and de-Europeanizing it. The irony of the fact that the cultured "exploiters" now hang Lam's pictures in their drawing rooms is rather like the problem posed by the glass that is "half full" or "half empty." Such ambivalence and contradictions are part of the postcolonial culture games, particularly those of the immigrant in the power centers, who is absorbed by the center and at the same time infiltrates and transforms from within.

The polemical synthesis characteristic of Lam's art is evident in the very concept of certain of his works; for example, in those dated between 1949 and 1961 that show women sitting in poses reminiscent of academic paintings, with their hands arranged in a conventional expression of "good manners." But these elegant ladies are endowed with a most "savage" mixture of masks, tails, horns, manes, and thorns, with all those kinds of animal and plant references that enabled Lam to create his mythological figures. These pieces can be seen almost as an allegory of Lam's work and of his aesthetic stand.

Just like Eleguá, Lam's work is at the crossroads. His work not only infiltrates modernism, it participates in it. More accurate than Lam's view of himself as a Trojan horse is the metaphor of the horse of Santería, CANDOMBLÉ, VODOU, and other Afro-American religions. The horse is the name given to the initiated, "ridden" by a deity, who appropriates the body, voice, and whole being of the initiated in order to manifest himself or herself in a possession trance that is the major liturgical event in these religions. Lam became an orisha riding the horse of modernism and making it utter new words. By using the artistic language of modernism, Lam's voice became legitimized by the centers of power, and it communicated from them.

Syncretism, to a greater or lesser extent, has always been a path to resistance and affirmation on the part of subordinates.

A historical example of syncretism, comparable to Lam's achievement, was the identification of African gods with Catholic saints by slaves in Latin America who were forced to become Christians, a strategy that combined resistance and appropriation. In this way the adoption of Christianity was like pushing a door that was already open and that led to Africa. Similar to Lam, although the slaves worshipped their own deities in the shape of Catholic figures, they also incorporated the Catholic religion into an inclusive system in which Santería and Candomblé practitioners worship all gods and saints simultaneously. Syncretism, in both examples, is a strategy of participation, a resignification and pluralization against hegemony, although the fact that Lam used the language of modernism limits his audience to those familiar with elite Western art. Lam's modernism even inclined him toward a view of himself and Afro-Cuban culture as primitive and exotic. However, this in no way diminishes his achievement.

See also Art in Latin America and the Caribbean; Catholic Church in Latin America and the Caribbean; Orishas.

Gerardo Mosquera

Modern Jazz Quartet

American quartet that was one of the first and most important ensembles to combine group jazz improvisation with elements of classical music.

The Modern Jazz Quartet, also known as MJQ, came together in 1952, consisting of John Lewis, piano and director; Milt Jackson, vibraphone; Percy Heath, double bass; and Kenny Clarke, drums. The group had evolved from the Milt Jackson Quartet, which included Lewis, Clarke, and bassist Ray Brown, veterans of the 1946 big-band of trumpeter DIZZY GILLESPIE. Drummer Connie Kay replaced Clarke in 1955. The quartet's refined ensemble sound, closely aligned with the style known as cool jazz, eventually came to be known as third-stream music, a fusion of classical music and jazz.

Lewis's compositions featured his own understated, melodic playing layered against Jackson's freer, more rhythmically complex solos. The group recorded many of Lewis's compositions, including "Versailles" (1956), "Three Windows" (1957), and "England's Carol" (1960), as well as pieces by American composer Gunther Schuller and French composer André Hodeir. Playing together for more than twenty years, the group disbanded annually, during the summer, giving members the opportunity to play in other ensembles. Formally dissolved in July 1974, MJQ reunited for a concert in November of that year and in later years for occasional tours.

In 1981, the group reunited permanently. Connie Kay died in 1994 and was succeeded by drummer Albert "Tootie" Heath, brother of Percy Heath. The group continued touring for several more years. Milt Jackson died in 1999, and John Lewis, the guiding genius behind the ensemble, died in 2001. It was Lewis, committed to the notion that jazz was a serious musical art form, who decided that the group should wear tuxedos when performing. He also sought to secure many bookings in concert halls rather than in nightclubs. MJQ's albums include *Fontessa* (1956), *The Modern Jazz Quartet* (1957), *The Modern Jazz Quartet and Orchestra* (1960), *The Last Concert* (1974), and *Together Again!* (1982).

Bibliography

Bourne, M. "Bob, Baroque, the Blues: Modern Jazz Quartet." *Down Beat* 59, no.1 (Jan. 1992): 24(4).

Mogadishu, Somalia

Capital city of Somalia.

To most outside SOMALIA, Mogadishu is known as a city wracked by civil war. For centuries, however, it was a prosperous port and market town. Mogadishu was founded on the Benadir coast of modern-day Somalia by Arab and Persian settlers in the tenth century. It was one of many port towns in that region that participated in the trade between East Africa, Arabia, the Indian subcontinent, China, and Southeast Asia. Like LAMU, MOMBASA, KENYA, ZANZIBAR, and other East African coastal cities, Mogadishu became influenced by Swahili culture, traces of which are still apparent in the city's language.

Mogadishu, also called Hammawein or Xamar Weyne, was at first governed by a loose federation of families, mostly of Arab and Persian origin but later including Arab-influenced Somali clans such as the Hawiye. Although Islam arrived in Somalia around the seventh century, the ruling families of the tenth century were responsible for widespread conversion.

By the thirteenth century, the GOLD TRADE with southern Africa had made Mogadishu a prosperous city, and political power had been consolidated under the rule of the Fakhr al-Din Sultanate. Once primarily an entrepôt for coastal commerce, Mogadishu now also traded in goods from the hinterlands, such as livestock, leather, ivory, and slaves. Famed traveler IBN BATTUTAH visited the city in the fourteenth century.

The Muzaffar dynasty ruled Mogadishu in the late fifteenth and early sixteenth centuries. The city fought off the Portuguese, who were expanding their sphere of influence all along the SWAHILI COAST, but by the end of the seventeenth century it had been taken over by another foreign power, the sultan of Oman. Mogadishu, following the lead of Mombasa to the south, attempted to throw off the yoke of Omani rule in 1825. But unlike Mombasa, Mogadishu refused offers of British protection and in 1828 faced Omani reprisals alone. SAYYID SA'ID IBN SULTAN of Zanzibar then had jurisdiction over the city.

In 1892 Said agreed to lease the port of Mogadishu to Italy for twenty-five years, in return for an annual rent of 160,000 rupees. In a later treaty, the Italians bought the city outright, and Mogadishu became the administrative capital for their colony in southern Somalia. They built the city's cathedral as well as a government school.

Mogadishu became a center of the nationalist activities of the Somali Youth League (SYL), founded in 1943. During a

1947 SYL demonstration, Italian police opened fire and launched grenades into the crowd, provoking a riot and killing several demonstrators. In the violence that ensued, fifty-one Italians were killed.

Mogadishu became the capital of independent Somalia, despite efforts by groups from northern Somalia to have the capital located in a northern political center such as Hargeysa. Already a major port and Somalia's largest city, Mogadishu grew rapidly through the 1960s and 1970s. Although much of the urban economy centered on the export of primary commodities such as fruit, meat, and animal hides, the city developed a number of light industries, including milk processing, soft-drink bottling, and textile production.

By the 1980s, political instability under the military dictatorship of Major General MOHAMED SIAD BARRE was beginning to consume Mogadishu. In 1989 his troops bombarded Mogadishu for four weeks, leaving more than 50,000 dead and three-quarters of the city in ruins, and massacring 50 youths of the Issaq clan.

Siad Barre fled Mogadishu in early 1991, but he left a violent legacy. Soon after his overthrow, a schism in the opposition group known the United Somali Congress (USC) led to a three-month battle between faction leaders General MOHAMED FARAH AIDID and Ali Mahdi Mohamed. Following a devastating famine in 1992, United Nations (UN) troops occupied the city in order to prevent armed factions from interfering with the distribution of relief aid. After what many considered an unsuccessful mission, the UN pulled out in 1994. Though the Transitional National Government (TNG), an interim government led by president Abdiqassim Salad Hassan, is centered in Mogadishu, it has not succeeded in reestablishing law and order in the city. Kidnappings for ransom have become prevalent; after a UN employee was kidnapped at gunpoint in the city in 2002, the UN suspended all operations in Mogadishu.

Since the early 1990s, more than more than 12,000 have been killed and 40,000 injured from violence in Mogadishu, and 400,000 have fled the city. Although Mogadishu's markets are once again busy, much of its infrastructure is in ruins, and the city, which by 2003 numbered about 1,208,800, remains largely ungoverned. The conflicts during the early 1980s left a generation of orphans, many of whom have joined violent gangs. Even in the midst of this violence, however, many in Mogadishu continue to struggle to maintain a peaceful existence. One such person, the charismatic Elman Ali Ahmed, ran the Mogadishu-based Gunman Project from the early stages of the conflict until his death in 1996, giving hundreds of the city's youths choices outside of war by teaching them the technical skills necessary to build the city's future.

See also Islam in Africa; Swahili Civilization.

Bibliography

Adam, Hussein M., and Richard Ford. *Mending Rips in the Sky: Options for Somali Communities in the 21st Century.* Red Sea Press, 1997.

Afrah, Mohamoud M. *Mogadishu: A Hell on Earth.* Copos Ltd., 1993.

Lewis, I. M. *A Modern History of Somalia: Nation and State in the Horn of Africa.* Westview Press, 1988.

Marian Aguiar

Moi, Daniel arap

1924–

Second president of Kenya, one of the last of a generation of postcolonial African "big men," authoritarian rulers notorious for their human rights abuses.

Daniel arap Moi was born in Karing'wo village in the Baringo Rift Valley District of KENYA. He is a member of the Tugen, a subgroup of the KALENJIN, a relatively small ethnic group famous for producing many of Kenya's champion long-distance runners. Moi has displayed a different kind of stamina. President from 1978 to 2002, he was also a longtime legislator in Kenya, joining the Legislative Council (now the National Assembly) in 1955 and retaining his seat two years later in Kenya's first elections. Previously, Moi worked as a schoolteacher, rising to become headmaster of the Kabarnet Intermediate School in 1948, where he taught many current members of the National Assembly.

In 1960 Moi was one of the Kenyan representatives to the Lancaster House Conference in London, where the terms of Kenyan independence were negotiated. Shortly afterward he became the national chairman for the Kenya African Democratic Union (KADU), a rival political party to the party of then-president JOMO KENYATTA, the Kenya African National Union (KANU). KADU dissolved in 1964, and Kenyatta recruited Moi into his cabinet of ministers.

Moi began as Kenyatta's minister of education but quickly widened his influence. He became minister of local government, then minister for home affairs, taking responsibility for internal security, police, and immigration. In 1967 he became Kenya's vice president, following the ouster of OGINGA ODINGA.

As Kenyatta's health declined during the 1970s, Moi began overseeing day-to-day government operations. When Kenyatta died on August 22, 1978, Moi succeeded him, despite opposition from many KIKUYU in the Kenyatta administration. On assuming the presidency, Moi, who lacked Kenyatta's charisma and broad-based support, outlined a policy for his government. He called it *Nyayo*, or "footsteps," implying his intention to continue Kenyatta's policies. These included an emphasis on national unity as opposed to tribalism; the gradual "Kenyanization" of the economy, which consisted of replacing noncitizen officials with Kenyans; a market economy; close economic ties with the West, especially with GREAT BRITAIN; and political nonalignment. But after this program failed to address high unemployment, inflation, and constant political infighting, members of the Kenyan air force attempted a coup in 1982. Loyal soldiers defeated the rebels, but only after a bloody battle and extensive property damage. Moi immediately sought to tighten control over the government and to eliminate opposition—real or imagined.

Moi replaced high-ranking Kikuyus in government and in various industries. Claiming that ethnic conflicts caused much of the political instability in Kenya, Moi outlawed ethnically based political organizations. A series of parliamentary measures in the mid-1980s further consolidated Moi's power over the civil service and the judiciary. Taking advantage of colonial-era laws that limited press, speech, and political freedoms, Moi censored the press and jailed editors and activists who criticized him or his policies. Allegations of torture and illegal imprisonment, combined with a recession in the late 1980s, contributed to Moi's declining popularity.

By the early 1990s student groups and churches were holding demonstrations calling for increased freedom of speech and a multiparty political system. Security forces often met such protests with violence. In response many Western aid donors, who had overlooked Moi's repressive tactics during the COLD WAR, began to demand political reforms and respect for human rights as a condition of continued aid. Although Moi habitually criticized the foreign media and organizations for "meddling" in Kenya's internal affairs, he succumbed to international pressure in 1992, authorizing multiparty elections and restoring partial judicial independence.

Due in part to a highly fragmented political opposition, Moi managed to win the 1993 presidential election with a mere 36 percent of the popular vote. During the next few years, his political legitimacy further deteriorated, especially after a series of mass killings in areas of concentrated political opposition raised suspicions of government-sponsored terrorism.

Moi held presidential elections in late December 1997. While Kenyans of every political stripe had become fed up with his regime, Moi's tactics of divide and rule among ethnic groups helped him win a fifth term as president. Kenya's constitution barred him from running for another term as president in the 2002 election. Moi then backed Uhuru Kenyatta as the KANU party candidate for president. Kenyan voters, however, overwhelming chose Mwai Kibaki as their new leader, sweeping the ruling party from power. Moi stepped down peacefully after the election results were confirmed. In September 2003 he retired from his position as head of the KANU party.

See also Cold War and Africa; Human Rights in Africa; Political Movements in Africa.

Robert Fay

Molineaux, Tom

1784–1818

African American boxer who was the first American to fight in an international bout.

Tom Molineaux was born a slave, probably in Georgetown, District of Columbia, on March 23, 1784. Molineaux was the name of the slave-owner family that owned Tom, his parents, and his four brothers. Strongly influenced by his father, Zachary, who is credited as the founder of boxing in the United States, Tom took up the sport at an early age. After his father died, fourteen-year-old Tom took his place as chief handyman around his master's estate. Several years later, his owner promised him the sum of $100 and his freedom if he were successful in defeating the slave of a neighboring planter in a boxing match. Intent on winning his freedom, Molineaux accepted the match and won.

With the prize money and his newly gained freedom, Molineaux headed for London, England, where, he had been told, fame and fortune were to be won in boxing. Arriving in London at the age of twenty-four, Molineaux fought several matches and earned the distinction of being the first American to fight in an international bout. With strength, confidence, and determination as his chief assets, he soon became known to boxing enthusiasts as the "Negro challenger to British heavyweight supremacy."

The highlight of Molineaux's ring career came in his two matches with Tom Cribbs, the British champion. The first match took place on December 18, 1810, on Copthall Commons, near East Grimstead. Cribbs held little respect for Molineaux, boasting that he would roundly beat him so that Molineaux would never again challenge an Englishman. The fight was hard-fought and appeared to be an even match, until Molineaux accidentally fell and badly injured himself in the last round. He attempted to rise, but his legs gave way, and he signaled to the referee that he could not go on. The victory went to Cribbs, who retained his title. Molineaux was granted a rematch in 1811, but this time he proved to be no match for the British champion, and Cribbs easily defeated him.

Molineaux's ring career plunged steadily following his second defeat by Cribbs. Engaging in street brawls, drinking beyond his capacity, and failing to keep in proper fighting condition, Molineaux quickly lost the bulk of his ring earnings. Hoping to regain his financial status, he decided to take another boxing tour of England. Because he had twice fought Cribbs, his reputation made him a favorite. He knew how to wrestle well, and when he struck a spot where wrestling was more lucrative than boxing, he engaged in active competition. However, as a top-flight wrestler, he failed miserably.

During the tour, Molineaux drank excessively and soon found himself in deplorable physical condition. He was still able to defeat several mediocre opponents. Because he had won these bouts, a match was set up for him with George Cooper, a famous British boxer. They met on March 11, 1815, at Corset Hill, Lanarkshire, Scotland. It took less than twenty minutes for Molineaux to lose his last big fight.

After the Cooper bout, Molineaux embarked on a tour through Ireland. At the end of 1817 he was teaching the art of boxing as he watched his savings dwindle until he was poverty-stricken. The sun of the once-great fighter's prosperity had set. During the last ten months of his life, he depended on others for food, banking on the sympathy of his black friends in the 77th Regiment, which was stationed in Galway. He died in the band room of that regiment on August 4, 1818, a wasted skeleton, a penniless beggar, a shell of his former self.

Mainly because Molineaux was illiterate, he was victimized throughout his career by dishonest managers, trainers, and promoters. His chief weakness was his habit of giving away money with such generosity that he could never shake hangers-on. However, in spite of his handicaps, he holds the distinction of being America's first great boxer.

An early reference is R. K. Fox's *Black Champions of the Prize Ring from Molineaux to Jackson* (1890). Later accounts, based in large part on Fox, are in the standard books: Edwin Bancroft Henderson's *Negro in Sports* (1949) and N. S. Fleischer's *Black Dynamite: The Story of the Negro in the Prize Ring from 1782 to 1938* (1938).

From *Dictionary of American Negro Biography* by Rayford W. Logan and Michael R. Winston, editors. Copyright © 1982 by Rayford W. Logan and Michael R. Winston. Reprinted by permission of W. W. Norton & Company, Inc.

Al-Tony Gilmore

Mombasa, Kenya

Second largest city of Kenya and main port of East Africa.

Mombasa, with a population estimated at 712,600 in 2003, is the largest port city in East Africa and the second largest city in KENYA. Located on a bay of the Indian Ocean, it serves Kenya, northeastern TANZANIA, UGANDA, RWANDA, and BURUNDI. Originally founded on the island of Mombasa, the city now sprawls across the neighboring mainland, which is connected to the island by a causeway, a bridge, and ferries. Mombasa's modern deep-water port, Kilindini, handles transoceanic shipping, while smaller vessels, including wooden dhows engaged in coastal trade and fishing, use the Old Mombasa Harbor. Mombasa also has a sizable industrial zone, with SUGAR and oil refineries and other factories.

Mombasa was founded in the eleventh century by Arabs who exchanged cloth, beads, metal goods, silks, and porcelain for gold, ivory, and salves from the African interior. By the fifteenth century it had become the primary trading center in East Africa. Transplanted Arabs mixed with the Bantu-speaking African inhabitants, eventually creating the SWAHILI PEOPLE, with their distinctive culture and language. Architecture in Mombasa shows Arab influences in its narrow streets, tall houses, and mosques.

In 1498 Portuguese explorer VASCO DA GAMA became the first European to visit Mombasa. Six years later the Portuguese, seeking greater control over the profitable Indian Ocean trade, captured the city. But the Portuguese were never able to establish steady control of the city. Constant challenges from the rulers of Oman in the Arabian Peninsula led them to build Fort Jesus in 1593. Today the fort is a historic landmark and tourist stop.

In 1740 a local Swahili clan, the Mazrui, captured Mombasa; they lost it to the Omani sultan of ZANZIBAR in 1832. Even after the British established COLONIAL RULE over Kenya in 1887, the sultan remained in formal control of the city. The British linked Mombasa to LAKE VICTORIA with the Uganda Railway, completed in 1902. During the 1950s, Mombasa became a favorite vacation destination for European settlers from ZIMBABWE (then called Rhodesia) and SOUTH AFRICA. Tourism became a vital part of Mombasa's economy in the 1970s and 1980s, when the city attracted more than 250,000 visitors annually. But ethnic violence in Mombasa beginning in 1997 quickly diminished the number of tourists. This followed a general decline of tourism nationwide, which many experts blamed on disintegrating infrastructure, increased ethnic violence, and the declining quality of services. Soon hundreds of workers in the tourist industry were being laid off each week. Despite the ups and downs of the tourism industry, however, Mombasa will likely hold onto its position as East Africa's most important port well into the twenty-first century.

See also Bantu: Dispersion and Settlement; Gold Trade; Ivory Trade; Transatlantic Slave Trade.

Robert Fay

Mongoose

Common name for several small carnivores found in many countries of Africa and in Asia.

The mongoose is 23 to 65 centimeters (9 to 26 inches) long, excluding the tail. Grayish or brownish in color, it has a tapered head, a long tail, and short feet. The female has one to four young in each litter. The animals subsist on rodents and snakes. They are renowned for attacking even the largest and most poisonous of snakes—to whose poison they are not immune—by avoiding their strikes with agility. Mongooses live about seven to twelve years in the wild, but in captivity they may live more than twenty years. They have been introduced to many areas of the world in order to control rodents and snakes, but importation of mongooses into the United States is prohibited because they also destroy many other animals.

The best-known species is the Egyptian mongoose, the *ichneumon*. Ancient Egyptians worshipped the ichneumon, and today the species is found in many parts of Africa. There are several other mongoose species, and these are found in a wide range of African countries, including ANGOLA, the CENTRAL AFRICAN REPUBLIC, ETHIOPIA, DEMOCRATIC REPUBLIC OF CONGO, GUINEA-BISSAU, KENYA, LIBERIA, NIGERIA, UGANDA, SOMALIA, SOUTH AFRICA, and SUDAN. A related animal from southern Africa, the suricate, sometimes called the slender-tailed meerkat, is easy to tame.

Scientific classification: The mongoose belongs to the family Herpestidae. The Egyptian species ichneumon is classified as *Herpestes ichneumon* and the suricate as *Suricata suricatta*.

Monk, Thelonious Sphere

1917–1982

African American jazz pianist and composer noted for his angular and rhythmic style of playing and his highly individual compositions.

Thelonious Monk was one of the great iconoclasts of JAZZ. Monk has long been classed among the main creators of BEBOP or modern jazz in the 1940s, along with alto sax player CHARLIE PARKER, trumpeter DIZZY GILLESPIE, drummer Kenny Clarke, and guitarist CHARLIE CHRISTIAN. Many also emphasize Monk's importance as a precursor of free jazz; jazz scholar Joachim Berendt noted that "what leads to ORNETTE COLEMAN, JOHN COLTRANE, ERIC DOLPHY, and all the other avant-gardists of jazz was heard for the first time in his music." Although Monk had some formal instruction, he was essentially self-taught and never really fit within any larger movement or style. Still, in going his own way, he ultimately took much of the jazz world with him.

Monk was born in Rocky Mount, North Carolina, but moved with his family to NEW YORK CITY when he was an infant. He first became interested in playing piano when he was five or six years old. Growing up he lived near the great HARLEM stride pianist JAMES P. JOHNSON, and Monk himself initially played in the stride style. In effect, the stride piano style divides the piano keyboard into three ranges. The pianist's left hand covers the two lower ranges, alternating single bass notes at the bottom with chord clusters struck higher up. The term "stride" comes from the characteristic bouncing "oom-pah, oom-pah" of the pianist's "striding" left hand. While the left hand sets up a propulsive beat and outlines the tune's harmonic structure, the pianist's right hand plays the melody, adds ornamentation, and improvises solo lines.

Throughout his performing career Monk continued to display hints of the stride piano style of his youth. But he soon began moving further, not just away from the stride style, but beyond the conventions of swing jazz in general. His explorations coincided with the experiments of a generation of young jazz players who were in the process of creating bebop or modern jazz. Monk himself became a part of these efforts during his 1940–1943 stint in the house band of Minton's, a New York City jazz club and bop incubator. There he played with Charlie Christian, Dizzy Gillespie, and Don Byas, among others. Impromptu recordings made at Minton's reveal a pianist strongly influenced by the stripped-down melodic swing of Teddy Wilson. These early recordings also capture some of the irregular rhythms and jarring harmonies that would characterize Monk's mature playing.

Monk played briefly with Lucky Millinder in 1942 and two years later joined Cootie Williams's short-lived big-band, which had recorded two Monk compositions, "Epistrophy" and his most famous piece, "'Round Midnight." Monk enjoyed much wider recognition—and had his recording debut—after joining tenor saxophonist COLEMAN HAWKINS, who consistently supported creative younger players. Nonetheless, during a period when other bop musicians found growing acceptance—in fact, near pop-culture celebrity during the short-lived bebop craze of the late 1940s—Monk continued to play in obscurity.

In certain respects his compositions and solos are forbidding. The chord progressions are unexpected and sometimes jarring, the melodies often agitated and edgy. In an era in which jazz soloists strove to play more and more notes at ever-faster tempos, Monk's lines were spare, with open space between the notes and phrases. And the tempos he played in were often remarkably slow. Between 1947 and 1952 Monk recorded several sessions for Blue Note that were later acclaimed by jazz musicians and listeners alike—featuring such classic Monk compositions as "Ruby My Dear," "Well You Needn't," "'Round Midnight," and "Straight No Chaser"—but he remained too "far out" for widespread acceptance until the latter half of the 1950s.

Monk did not alter his style between 1947 and the end of his life. But after 1955, when he began recording for Riverside Records with jazz producer Orrin Keepnews, jazz at last caught up with him. In 1956 Monk recorded his outstanding *Brilliant Corners* album, praised in *Downbeat* magazine by jazz critic Nat Henthoff. Monk's talent was finally recognized 1957 when he played an extended gig at the Five Spot, then one of New York City's premiere jazz clubs. At the Five Spot, Monk performed with a quartet that featured tenor saxophonist John Coltrane. Under the pianist's tutelage Coltrane began his own rapid growth toward musical greatness.

Pianist Thelonius Monk performs at the Newport Jazz Festival in 1959. *Ted Williams/CORBIS*

During the 1960s Monk established a longstanding quartet, featuring Charlie Rouse on tenor saxophone, which recorded regularly for Columbia Records. In his later years Monk suffered psychiatric problems that led to his effective retirement in 1973, though he made occasional appearances to the end of the decade. Since his death jazz musicians have continued to embrace his music. It has become almost de rigueur for jazz players to include at least one Monk tune in their recording sessions and nightclub sets.

Bibliography

Collier, James Lincoln. *The Making of Jazz: A Comprehensive History.* Delta Books, 1978.

De Wilde, Laurent. *Monk.* Marlowe, 1997.

James Sellman

Monrovia, Liberia

Capital of the West African nation of Liberia.

In 1821 the first African American settlers in the area that would become the Republic of LIBERIA purchased land from King Peter, an indigenous leader, to establish a settlement at Mesurado Bay. They called the small town, set on a rocky hilltop on the banks of the Mesurado River, Christopolis, "the City of Christ." Three years later they renamed it Monrovia, after James Monroe, who was then president of the United States. Monrovia grew quickly. Settlers with adequate means built houses with columns and verandas that echoed the architecture of the American South, from which many of them had come.

Traditionally the home of AMERICO-LIBERIANS, through the years Monrovia became an important center of both commerce and government as well as the home of the University of Liberia and the presidential palace. In contrast to the Liberian countryside, where indigenous languages and religious beliefs prevail, Monrovia has long had a largely Christian population. But following the outbreak of civil war in Liberia in December 1989, the capital became a magnet for refugees fleeing violence in the countryside. Analysts estimate that about 100,000 rural Liberians sought refuge in the capital during the early 1990s. Beginning in the late 1990s, fighting between the forces of President CHARLES TAYLOR and various rebel groups spilled into Monrovia, causing severe damage as well as many civilian casualties. The arrival of international peacekeeping forces and Taylor's resignation in 2003 brought the hope of peace and eventual rebuilding to the distressed capital, whose population is estimated at about 557,500.

Kate Tuttle

Montego Bay, Jamaica

City in northwestern Jamiaca.

Montego Bay is the administrative center of Saint James Parish, Cornwall County, in the Caribbean island nation of JAMAICA. The city is located on Montego Bay at the mouth of the Montego River, on the island's northwestern coast. Chrisopher Columbus visited a village of the Native American Arawak people on the site in 1494. The settlement that arose later was called Manteca Bay.

Montego Bay's population is around 93,500 (2003 estimate). The city is an important port and railway center that ships SUGAR, BANANAS, coffee, rum, ginger, dyewood, and hides. The area also has sugar-milling and liqueur-processing industries and produces shoes, ice, and aerated water. Marine gardens with oyster beds are nearby in the offshore Bogue Islands. In addition, Montego Bay is a major tourist resort and the heart of Jamaica's so-called Gold Coast, with fine beaches, golf courses, yacht basins, and other sports facilities. Tourism developed around the beginning of the twentieth century, and soon nearby Doctor's Cave and White Sands became centers for winter visitors.

Montejo, Esteban

1860-1973

Runaway Cuban slave whose life story was recorded by author Miguel Barnet.

As a child, Esteban Montejo escaped a sugar plantation to live as a maroon until the abolition of slavery in 1885. His memories were published by the Cuban writer Miguel Barnet in *Maroon's Biography* (1966), considered a pioneering work of the Latin American testimonial genre. The first part of the book is one of the most detailed descriptions of the harsh working and living conditions of slaves on the sugar plantations. Montejo's account of his survival as a solitary runaway affirms that hunger and lack of shelter were preferable to living the life of a slave.

In the last part of the book Montejo narrates his experience in the Cuban Liberation Army during the CUBAN WAR OF INDEPENDENCE (1895-1898). His account underscores the important role played by the Afro-Cuban officials and soldiers, particularly of ANTONIO MACEO. This section of the book also describes the racial discrimination within the Cuban army, which anticipated the racial disputes among Cuban political parties in the early twentieth century. Montejo's life in the nineteenth century is presented as an allegory of Cuban liberation from Spain and the socialist revolution, though this is attributed to Barnet's mediation in compiling the narrative.

See also Maroonage in the Americas; Partido Independiente de Color.

Juan Otero-Garabis

Monte y Aponte, Domingo del

1804-1853

White Cuban intellectual and patron to the principal antislavery writers of the period, such as Anselmo

Suárez Romero, Cirilo Villaverde, and the black poet Juan Francisco Manzano.

See also Abolitionist Novels in Cuba: An Interpretation.

Montgomery Bus Boycott

Year-long protest in Alabama that galvanized the American Civil Rights Movement and led to a 1956 decision by the U.S. Supreme Court declaring segregated seating on buses unconstitutional.

In December 1955, around 42,000 black residents of Montgomery, Alabama, began a year-long boycott of city buses to protest racially segregated seating. After 381 days of taking taxis, carpooling, and walking the hostile streets of Montgomery, African Americans eventually won their fight to desegregate seating on public buses, not only in Montgomery but throughout the United States.

The protest was first organized by the Women's Political Council as a one-day boycott to coincide with the trial of ROSA PARKS, who had been arrested on December 1, 1955, for refusing to give up her seat to a white man on a segregated Montgomery bus. By the next morning, the council, led by JOANN ROBINSON, had printed 52,000 fliers asking Montgomery blacks to stay off public buses on December 5, the day of the trial. Meanwhile, labor activist E. D. NIXON, who had bailed Parks out of jail, notified RALPH ABERNATHY, minister of the First Baptist Church, and MARTIN LUTHER KING, JR., the new minister at Dexter Avenue Baptist Church, of Parks's arrest. A group of about fifty black leaders and one white minister, Robert Graetz, gathered in the basement of King's church to endorse the boycott and begin planning a massive rally for the evening of the trial. Graetz offered his support from the pulpit of his predominantly white Lutheran church. The Montgomery Chapter of the NATIONAL ASSOCIATION FOR THE ADVANCEMENT OF COLORED PEOPLE (NAACP), which had been looking for a test case for segregation, began preparing for the legal challenge.

The issue of segregated seating had long been a source of resentment in Montgomery's black community. African Americans were forced to pay their fares at the front then reboard the bus at the back. They faced systematic harassment from white drivers, who sometimes pulled away before black passengers could reboard. On the bus, blacks sat behind a mobile barrier dividing the races, and as the bus filled, the barrier was pushed back to make room for white passengers. No black person could sit in the same row as a white, and whites had priority in this middle "no-man's land."

On the morning of Parks's trial, buses rumbled nearly empty through the streets of Montgomery. Police officers with shotguns roamed in search of imaginary "Negro goon squads," which they believed were forcing blacks to stay off the buses. After Parks lost her case and was convicted of violating the segregated seating laws, black leaders met again to organize an extension of the bus boycott. To this end, they formed the MONTGOMERY IMPROVEMENT ASSOCIATION (MIA) and elected King as its president. That evening 7,000 blacks crowded into Holt Street Baptist Church, where King inspired the audience with his words: "There comes a time when people get tired of being trampled over by the iron feet of oppression."

With this speech King was able to spark the black residents' collective outrage into a grassroots movement that would sustain the boycott. The Montgomery Bus Boycott followed King's credo of nonviolent resistance, even in the face of a police crackdown and attempts by white supremacists to undermine the protest. Montgomery police threatened to arrest taxi drivers giving discount rates to the black riders, and when the MIA arranged carpools, the police systematically harassed drivers, arresting them for allegedly going too fast or too slow. Meanwhile, the boycott leaders squared off at the bargaining table with the local officials. The MIA presented its modest demands for bus seating by race, with no mobile area, and "Negro routes" with black drivers. They were met with unconditional refusal.

Many white supremacists joined the White Citizens Council, one of many racist citizens' organizations that gained power throughout the South in the 1960s. Convinced that there was an outside mastermind of the movement, they focused their attention on terrorizing boycott leaders. Vigilante groups set off bombs at black homes and churches. In addition there were several police sweeps, and twice King joined the other black protesters in Montgomery's crowded jails. In one attempt to sabotage the boycott, the *Montgomery Advertiser,* a white newspaper, planned to put out a false story that the boycott had ended. King and other leaders, warned in advance of the story, traveled late that night to the rural jook joints where black workers went to dance and relax. Thus forewarned, African Americans continued to stay off the local buses. Shortly after,

Rosa Parks, accompanied by her lawyer, Charles Langford (right), is on her way to jail after being arrested for violating the city's segregation laws. *Bettmann/CORBIS*

the *Advertiser* announced that Montgomery was on the verge of a "full scale racial war."

Even as the protesters and black leaders were confronted with escalating violence, they maintained both nonviolent resistance and their exhausting day-to-day schedule without public transportation. At the same time the MIA moved ahead on the legal front. On February 1, 1956, shortly after a bomb went off in King's home, the MIA filed a federal suit against bus segregation in the names of four black women.

In the spring, protesters led by Nixon turned the tables on the local government and caught the attention of the national press. Indicted under a statute that prohibited boycotts "without just cause or legal excuse," leaders presented themselves at the courthouse rather than waiting to be arrested. The national press came down to cover the scene of black leaders marching into the courthouse while hundreds cheered them on. As protesters walked to work through the summer of 1956, the issue of civil rights took center stage in the national consciousness. After the March trial of the MIA, King appeared on the cover of *Time* magazine and the *New York Times Magazine*.

In June a federal court ruled segregated seating unconstitutional, and the case went on appeal to the U.S. Supreme Court. Meanwhile, King and the MIA leadership went to the Montgomery court to try to stave off an injunction against the carpools. They were in court when they were handed a notice from the Associated Press wire announcing the Supreme Court decision that ruled segregated seating on public buses unconstitutional. King addressed a euphoric crowd that night, and over the next week celebrities, such as singer MAHALIA JACKSON and New York minister GARDNER C. TAYLOR, came to Montgomery to celebrate. On December 20, 1956, when the federal ruling took effect, an integrated group of boycott supporters, including King, Abernathy, Fred Gray, and Glenn Smiley, rode the city buses.

The Montgomery Bus Boycott had implications that reached far beyond the desegregation of public buses. The protest propelled the Civil Rights Movement into national consciousness and Martin Luther King Jr. into the public eye. In the words of King: "We have gained a new sense of dignity and destiny. We have discovered a new and powerful weapon—nonviolent resistance."

Marian Aguiar

Montgomery Improvement Association

Group formed by African American leaders in 1955 to organize and sponsor the Montgomery Bus Boycott.

In 1955, following the arrest of ROSA PARKS for refusing to give up her bus seat to a white man, black leaders in Montgomery formed the Montgomery Improvement Association (MIA) to sustain a bus boycott. The MONTGOMERY BUS BOYCOTT was organized by the Women's Political Council as a one-day protest, but the MIA and its leader MARTIN LUTHER KING, JR., rallied African American support in the city to keep the boycott going for almost a year. The boycott gained national attention for the CIVIL RIGHTS MOVEMENT and helped create the favorable political climate in which the U.S. Supreme Court ruled against segregated seating on public buses in 1956.

On December 5, 1955, as blacks in Montgomery stayed off the buses for a day, Rosa Parks was convicted of violating Montgomery's segregation laws. A group of Montgomery's black leaders met that afternoon and formed the Montgomery Improvement Association (MIA), electing Martin Luther King, Jr., the new pastor at Dexter Avenue Baptist Church, as the organization's president. Their evening rally at the Holt Street Baptist Church drew over 5,000 people, and King inspired the audience to continue the boycott. Several other activists played key roles in the MIA boycott, including labor activist E. D. NIXON, the Reverend RALPH D. ABERNATHY, and the Reverend Robert Graetz, the only white member.

While the Montgomery Improvement Association attempted to negotiate modest changes in the segregated seating policies of public buses, black workers took taxis, carpooled, and walked to and from work. MIA member Rufus Lewis organized a carpool, finding Montgomery residents (mostly whites) who were willing to lend their cars and drivers to take the protesters to and from work. Later, the Reverend B. J. Simms ran the carpool. African Americans donated portions of their meager earnings to keep the organization running.

On February 1, Fred Gray, the association's attorney, filed a petition in federal court to declare segregated seating unconstitutional. This led in November 1956 to the Supreme Court decision outlawing segregated seating on public buses.

The association went on to become one of the founders of the Southern Christian Leadership Conference (SCLC). Although the MIA lost momentum after King moved to Atlanta in 1960, the group continued its civil rights efforts in Montgomery, including a voter-registration drive and a failed attempt to integrate the city's parks. In 1962 the MIA achieved one of its early goals when the Montgomery bus company finally hired black drivers. Under the leadership of longtime president Johnnie Carr, the MIA has also worked for the integration of local schools.

Marian Aguiar

Montgomery, Isaiah Thornton

1847–1924

African American planter and founder of Mound Bayou, Mississippi.

Isaiah Thornton Montgomery was born on the "Hurricane" plantation of Joseph Davis at Davis Bend, Mississippi, the son of Benjamin Montgomery, the plantation business manager and later a planter and owner of a mercantile store, and Mary Lewis. As a result of his father's prominent position among the slaves, Montgomery was chosen at the age of nine or ten to serve as

Davis's personal secretary and office attendant. Davis, the older brother of Confederate president Jefferson Davis, granted Montgomery full access to all the books, newspapers, and periodicals within his home, enabling Montgomery to continue the education begun first by his father and later continued by another slave. Following the CIVIL WAR, in November 1866, Davis sold his two plantations to the Montgomery family. During the next fifteen years, the Montgomerys struggled and ultimately failed to make the plantations profitable, yet they still succeeded in garnering numerous prizes for the quality of their cotton and consistently high ratings from national credit firms. The Montgomery family lost both plantations in 1881. In 1871 Montgomery married Martha Robb; they had twelve children, only four of whom survived to adulthood.

In 1877 Montgomery embarked on his most successful venture, the founding of the all-black town of MOUND BAYOU in the Yazoo-Mississippi Delta. The Louisville, New Orleans, and Texas Railroad, which actively sought farmers to settle the land alongside the newly laid tracks between NEW ORLEANS and MEMPHIS, hired Montgomery as a land agent with the understanding that he would choose an area of land within the delta for exclusive purchase by blacks. Montgomery enlisted the support of family and friends, especially former residents of Davis Bend, in purchasing the plots, and the group quickly cleared and settled the heavily overgrown land. During the early years, Montgomery and his cousin Benjamin Green, the town's generally acknowledged cofounder, established several joint ventures, including the town's first cotton gin, mercantile firm, and post office.

In 1890 Montgomery was the only African American delegate elected to the Mississippi constitutional convention. The convention delegates drafted a constitution that effectively disfranchised African American Mississippians. During the proceedings, Montgomery gave a speech supporting disfranchisement. He described his support as "a fearful sacrifice laid upon the burning altar of liberty." In an interview published in the *New York World* (October 3, 1890), he explained that the temporary disfranchisement of blacks would hopefully signal "the beginning of the end of the great race question," allowing political division along lines other than race. Montgomery mistakenly believed that as African Americans became better educated, white Mississippians would allow them to vote and integrated parties would be formed based on political beliefs, not race. Not surprisingly, most white leaders, including former president Grover Cleveland, applauded Montgomery's position, while most black leaders initially expressed surprise and then dismay. According to FREDERICK DOUGLASS: "We may denounce his policy, but must spare the man . . . . He has made peace with the lion by allowing himself to be swallowed." In many ways, Montgomery's stance foreshadowed BOOKER T. WASHINGTON's infamous ATLANTA COMPROMISE of 1895. Washington and Montgomery maintained a correspondence throughout their lives, and Washington often pointed to Mound Bayou as a model African American community. Later in his life, Montgomery privately lamented the impact of the disfranchisement proposals, expressing frustration with the racist application of the law. Publicly, he never rescinded his initial stance.

In 1898, following the incorporation of Mound Bayou, Montgomery was elected the town's first mayor. He held that office until 1902, when President Theodore Roosevelt, under guidance from Washington, appointed him as receiver of public monies in Jackson, Mississippi. The honor proved short-lived, however, as Montgomery was forced to resign in 1903 amidst controversy over the alleged placement of $5,000 in government funds in his personal account. While he never held another elective or appointive office, Montgomery maintained an active role in both the Mississippi REPUBLICAN PARTY and local politics throughout the remainder of his life.

Montgomery's political ambitions, however, remained secondary to his efforts on behalf of Mound Bayou. In a letter to the director of the U.S. Land Office in Mississippi upon acceptance of his position as receiver of public monies, Montgomery noted that in the previous fourteen years he had expended his "best energies" to ensure the "advancement materially, morally, and socially" of his community and thus he was "loath to turn aside for political preferment." During his lifetime, Montgomery had a hand in almost every project that concerned Mound Bayou. He played a key role in the founding and improvement of the town's educational institutions, joined with his son-in-law E. P. Booze to establish the Farmer's Cooperative Mercantile Company in 1909, and helped with the development of the Mound Bayou Oil Mill & Manufacturing Company between 1911 and 1913. Montgomery's importance to the town was suggested by Charles Banks, a banker and community leader, who insisted in a letter to Washington's secretary that "no work or statement on Mound Bayou, however brief, should be without [Montgomery's] name." Montgomery died in Mound Bayou.

Montgomery's historical significance derives from his role as an African American accommodationist and entrepreneur. Through his 1890 address and his activities on behalf of Mound Bayou, he displayed a consistent belief that educational and economic advancement, not political activity, offered the best means for African Americans to improve their plight. He closely monitored his own actions and those of his fellow Mound Bayou citizens to ensure the continual support of the white community. As a result, he earned nearly universal acclaim from white Mississippians, and upon his death, local whites purchased a lavish headstone. In contrast, the reaction among the African American community was decidedly mixed and increasingly hostile after his death. The African American Mississippi politician Sidney Redmond declared fifty years after Montgomery's speech that Montgomery would always be remembered as "the Judas of his people." Montgomery's actions, however, highlight the horrific conditions for African Americans in Mississippi at the turn of the century and demonstrate the pragmatic philosophy that was necessary for survival and limited success.

Bibliography

Montgomery's papers are in several collections, including the Benjamin Montgomery Family Papers and the Booker T. Washington Papers at the Library of Congress. The Mississippi Department of Archives and History in Jackson contains a substantial collection of material on Mound Bayou.

Crockett, Norman L. *The Black Towns.* 1979.
Hamilton, Kenneth Marvin. *Black Towns and Profit: Promotion and Development in the Trans-Appalachian West, 1877–1915.* 1991.
Hermann, Janet Sharp. *The Pursuit of a Dream.* 1981.
———. "Isaiah T. Montgomery's Balancing Act." In *Black Leaders of the Nineteenth Century,* edited by Leon Litwack and August Meier. 1988.
McMillen, Neil R. *Dark Journey: Black Mississippians in the Age of Jim Crow.* 1989.
Obituary, *Vicksburg Evening Post,* March 24, 1985.

From *American National Biography.* John A. Garraty and Mark C. Carnes, eds. Oxford University Press, 1999. Reprinted by permission of the American Council of Learned Societies.

David Mark Silver

Montgomery, Wes

1923–1968

African American jazz guitarist, one of the most distinctive soloists in the bebop style.

Wes Montgomery was born John Leslie Montgomery in Indianapolis, Indiana. Almost entirely self-taught, Montgomery began playing the four-string tenor guitar at age twelve, the six-string guitar at about age eighteen. He began learning solos by pioneering electric guitarist CHARLIE CHRISTIAN from recordings, and by age twenty he was skilled enough to work regularly in Indianapolis clubs. From 1948 to 1950 he toured with the big band led by vibist LIONEL HAMPTON, but he tired of life on the road and returned home to work. In the late 1950s and early 1960s he and his brothers, vibraphonist Buddy Montgomery and bassist Monk Montgomery, performed and recorded together intermittently. He also performed or recorded with cornetist Nat Adderley, saxophonist JOHN COLTRANE, vibraharpist Milt Jackson, and others. In 1965 he recorded the album *Goin' out of My Head* with a large ensemble; it won a Grammy Award the following year and provided him with a new level of economic security. During the remaining years of his life he enjoyed continued success with his recordings and performances.

Unlike his colleagues, Montgomery plucked the strings of his Gibson guitar with his left thumb (nicknamed "the golden thumb") rather than with a pick, thus achieving a softened attack on each note. He had an impeccable sense of swing and an ability to construct lengthy solos that were continuously exciting. Often he would begin a solo with single-note melodies, then switch into melodies in octaves played with great dexterity, and end with block chords (harmonized melodies). The thumbed-octave sound became the most instantly recognizable feature of his style and dominates his last recordings almost entirely. Though his late records were his most popular, his best solos occur on earlier recordings that he made with small groups. Among the latter recordings are *Montgomeryland* (1958–1959), *The Incredible Jazz Guitar of Wes Montgomery* (1960), *Full House* (1962), and Wynton Kelly's *Smokin' at the Half Note* (1965). His best-known compositions include "Bumpin' on Sunset," "Four on Six," and "West Coast Blues."

Bibliography

Ingram, Adrian. *Wes Montgomery.* Leonard, 1993.

Montserrat

British dependent territory in the Caribbean Sea, southeast of Puerto Rico and about halfway between Guadeloupe and Saint Kitts and Nevis.

A nineteenth-century visitor to Montserrat wrote in a letter home that "no island in these seas is bolder in its general aspect, more picturesque, more beautiful in the details of its scenery . . . it has the fatal gifts of beauty." The island's beauty earned it its reputation as the "Emerald Isle" of the Caribbean.

Montserrat's earliest residents were most likely Ciboney Amerindians who arrived on the island between 500 B.C.E. and 500 C.E. after migrating north from VENEZUELA. They were later succeeded by Taíno Arawak Amerindians, and the Taíno were followed by the Carib, who named the island Alliouagana, or "Land of the Prickly Bush." On November 11, 1493, Christopher Columbus and his crew were the first Europeans to see the island during their second voyage to the Caribbean. Columbus immediately renamed the mountainous island Santa Maria de Monserrate, after a Spanish abbey set in the mountains outside Barcelona.

The first permanent European settlers on Montserrat were English settlers who migrated from nearby Saint Kitts and Nevis in 1632. Within months, they were followed by a group of Irish Catholic colonists who had recently fled the British settlement in Virginia because of religious persecution. Montserrat soon became known as a safe haven for those seeking religious freedom; Irish Catholic settlers from other British colonies began to settle there. At the same time, however, it also became a common destination for many Irish Catholics who did not come voluntarily but were forced into indentured servitude and exile by British rulers at home.

The Irish laborers were forced to work on the island's small farms and plantations, growing tobacco, cotton, and indigo. But when sugarcane was found to be a profitable crop in the 1650s, there were not enough Irish workers to fill the demand for sugar plantations. British Montserratians turned to the same labor force that was being exploited by colonists across the Americas: African slaves. The first black slaves probably arrived in Montserrat in 1651. Within twenty years there were 1,000 black slaves on the island, and by 1729 that number had grown to 5,858, with blacks outnumbering whites by five to one.

Rumors of planned slave uprisings roused fear among Montserratian whites in 1768 and 1770—each supposedly intended to coincide with St. Patrick's Day, a holiday when many

Montserrat (At a Glance)

AREA: 102 sq km (39 sq mi)

LOCATION: Island in the Caribbean Sea, southeast of Puerto Rico

CAPITAL: Plymouth (evacuated in 1995 because of volcanic activity)

POPULATION: 8,995 (2003 estimate)

POPULATION BELOW AGE 15: 23.4 percent (male 1,062; female 1,041; 2003 estimates)

POPULATION GROWTH RATE: 4.5 percent (2003 estimate)

TOTAL FERTILITY RATE: 1.8 children born per woman (2003 estimate)

LIFE EXPECTANCY AT BIRTH: Total population: 78.36 years (male 76.24 years; female 80.59 years; 2003 estimates)

INFANT MORTALITY RATE: 7.77 deaths per 1,000 live births (2003 estimate)

LITERACY RATE (AGE 15 AND OVER WHO HAS EVER ATTENDED SCHOOL): Total population: 97 percent (male 97 percent; female 97 percent; 2003 estimates)

EDUCATION: Education is compulsory and free for children between the ages of five and fourteen. Because of volcanic eruptions in the region, the schools and library had to be moved north of Plymouth.

LANGUAGES: English

ETHNIC GROUPS: Black and white

RELIGIONS: Anglican, Methodist, Roman Catholic, Pentecostal, Seventh-Day Adventist, and other Christian denominations

CLIMATE: Tropical, with an average temperature that varies from a low of 70–76°F (21–24°C) to a high of 80–86°F (27–30°C). About 57 inches (1,448 mm) of rain falls annually, and Montserrat is subject to hurricanes.

LAND, PLANTS, AND ANIMALS: Montserrat has three forested, mountainous regions known as the Silver Hills, Centre Hills, and Soufrière Hills. In the mid-1990s volcanic eruptions killed 19 people in the Soufrière Hills and destroyed 2.7 sq mi (7 sq km) of farmland, forests, and villages. The volcanic sand on Montserrat's beaches is gray or brown, with only Rendezvous Bay, in the north, having a white-sand beach. Animals on Montserrat include lizards, orioles, and edible frogs (called "mountain chickens").

NATURAL RESOURCES: Montserrat has negligible natural resources.

CURRENCY: East Caribbean dollar (XCD)

GROSS DOMESTIC PRODUCT (GDP): $29 million (2002 estimate)

GDP PER CAPITA: $3,400 (2002 estimate)

GDP REAL GROWTH RATE: −1 percent (2002 estimate)

PRIMARY ECONOMIC ACTIVITIES: Agriculture, industry, and services

PRIMARY CROPS: Cabbages, carrots, cucumbers, tomatoes, onions, peppers, and livestock products

INDUSTRIES: Tourism, rum, textiles, and electronic appliances

PRIMARY EXPORTS: Electronic components, plastic bags, apparel, hot peppers, live plants, and cattle

PRIMARY IMPORTS: Machinery and transportation equipment, foodstuffs, manufactured goods, fuels, lubricants, and related materials

PRIMARY TRADE PARTNERS: United States, Antigua and Barbuda, United Kingdom, Trinidad and Tobago, Japan, and Canada

GOVERNMENT: Montserrat is an overseas territory of the United Kingdom. The chief of state is Queen Elizabeth II, represented by Governor Anthony Longrigg (since May 2001; appointed by the monarch). The head of government is Chief Minister John Osborne (since April 2001; the leader of the majority party usually becomes chief minister after legislative elections). The legislative branch is the unicameral eleven-member Legislative Council (nine members are popularly elected to five-year terms). The judicial branch is the Eastern Caribbean Supreme Court. Political parties include the National Progressive Party (NPP) and the New People's Liberation Movement (NPLM).

Shelle Sumners

---

whites would have been caught off guard. Neither uprising actually took place, but it was not surprising that Montserrat slaves wanted their freedom. Montserrat laws forbade slaves from becoming coopers, smiths, tailors, sawyers, masons, or shinglers, and while they were allowed to keep small gardens for their own use, they were forbidden from planting indigo, ginger, coffee, cotton, and COCOA. Their exclusion from the most profitable trades and crops ensured that few slaves were able to make extra money that might have allowed them to purchase their freedom. It also meant that most Montserratian blacks were relegated to laboring in the SUGAR fields, a condition that remained constant even after slavery was finally abolished in 1834.

By the late nineteenth century it became clear that Montserrat's economy could not depend on sugar alone. In 1897 three-fifths of the island's cultivated land was still planted in sugarcane, but because the industry was no longer profitable, planters began experimenting with such crops as limes, coffee, tomatoes, silkworms, and cotton. Limes and cotton were the most successful, and for the first few decades of the twentieth century, they formed the backbone of Montserrat's economy. But the change in crops did not change the fact that the majority of Montserratians worked as poorly paid field laborers on white-owned estates. Black workers were understandably frustrated by this status quo, and in the 1930s laborers in Montserrat, like laborers throughout the Caribbean, began unionizing.

As the unions became more powerful, union members were able to fight for political changes. For most of the nineteenth century and the beginning of the twentieth century Montserrat's governing council was entirely appointed. This factor had allowed the white minority to retain political power, but by the 1940s Montserrat's black majority began insisting on change. In 1951 elections were held under universal adult suffrage for the first time. Union leader W. H. Bramble was elected to the council and became Montserrat's first chief minister.

Montserrat is one of several British colonies that have not pushed for increased independence. Montserrat's culture, while not necessarily British, is an unusual mix of African and Irish elements. Citizens celebrate Carnival and St. Patrick's Day, and while CALYPSO and other Afro-Caribbean musical forms are extremely popular, Montserratian folk music and dance also have roots in Irish step dances and bodhrans. For a time, Montserratians enjoyed the increased financial stability associated with being a British dependency. The island was a popular vacation destination for both British and American tourists, and British stars such as Elton John, the Rolling Stones, and Sting recorded at a famous studio on the island. Tourism was the island's most important economic sector.

The late twentieth century, however, brought disaster to the island. Montserratians rebuilt their island after Hurricane Hugo struck in 1989, only to be faced with an even more devastating disaster in the 1990s: the eruption of the Soufrière Hills volcano. The Soufrière Hills eruptions began in 1995 and reached their worst level in the summer of 1997. Between June and August of that year twenty people were killed, thousands more evacuated, and much of the southern two-thirds of the island was destroyed, including the capital, Plymouth. The volcano continued to erupt through 2002. Though some of the 8,000 Montserratians who fled their homes have returned, half of the island will be uninhabitable for another decade.

The volcanic eruptions have cast uncertainty on all aspects of Montserratian life, including the country's relationship with GREAT BRITAIN. Many critics claimed that the British government should have done more to relocate residents before the eruptions and provided more help in their aftermath. In 2003 the British government approved a three-year $122.8 million aid program to help the people on the island start rebuilding their homes and their economy. It remains to be seen how Montserrat will be able to recover from this difficult chapter in its national history.

See also Carnivals in Latin America and the Caribbean; Independence Movements in the British Caribbean; Latin America and the Caribbean, Blacks in; Music, Afro-Caribbean Secular; Slavery in Latin America and the Caribbean.

Lisa Clayton Robinson

Moody, Anne

1940–

African American civil rights activist and writer.

The daughter of sharecroppers, Anne Moody was educated in the segregated schools of rural Mississippi and began her college career at Natchez Junior College on a BASKETBALL scholarship. She later transferred to Tougaloo College in Jackson, Mississippi, where she became active in the CIVIL RIGHTS MOVEMENT.

From 1961 to 1963 Moody served as an organizer for the CONGRESS OF RACIAL EQUALITY (CORE) in Mississippi, then considered to be the state with the most violent and dangerous white resistance to civil rights activities in the South. She participated in direct action protests, including the first SIT-IN demonstration at a Woolworth's lunch counter in Jackson, Mississippi. In 1964, the same year she graduated from Tougaloo, Moody began fund-raising for CORE. From 1964 to 1965 she also worked for Cornell University as its civil rights project coordinator. Her civil rights activities soon cooled, however, because of her frustration with the changing nature of the movement, in particular its shift toward Black Nationalism.

But Moody is best known for her autobiography *Coming of Age in Mississippi* (1968), which received the Best Book of the Year Award from the National Library Association in 1969. One of the most widely read works to come out of the Civil Rights Movement, this moving book traces her life from the poverty and racism of the rural Mississippi Delta, through her educational struggles and civil rights activities, up to the March on Washington in 1963. In 1975 Moody published *Mr. Death,* a book of short stories. She currently works as a counselor for the New York City Poverty Program.

See also Black Nationalism in the United States; March on Washington, 1963.

Robert Fay

Moore, Audley ("Queen Mother")

1898–1997

American black nationalist and Harlem civil rights leader.

Born in rural Louisiana, Audley Moore and her family experienced the terror of racism in its most brutal form with the LYNCHING of her paternal grandfather. Her parents died when Moore was in the fourth grade, and by the time she was fifteen she had to raise and support herself and her two sisters by working as a hairdresser.

Her family's suffering and the racism she faced pushed Moore to political activism. In NEW ORLEANS she joined MARCUS GARVEY's militant UNIVERSAL NEGRO IMPROVEMENT ASSOCIATION, inspired by Garvey's Black Nationalism and pride in blacks' African heritage. Part of the great migration from rural South to urban North, Moore and her sisters moved to HARLEM in the 1920s. Moore became a prominent organizer for the Communist Party, particularly in defense of the Scottsboro Boys, eight young men in Alabama who were wrongly convicted of rape and sentenced to death. Through the party she fought on behalf of black tenants and for black political representation, but because of the racism she encountered within the party, she eventually resigned.

Moore continued her political activity by fighting for education for the poor and becoming a leader in the movement demanding REPARATIONS from the federal government for the labor of blacks under slavery. She stated:

> Ever since 1950, I've been on the trail fighting for reparations. They owe us more than they could ever pay. They stole our language, they stole our culture. They stole us from our mothers and fathers and took away our names from us. They worked us free of charge 18 hours a day, 7 days a week, under the lash, for centuries.

Moore promoted PAN-AFRICANISM and was one of the founders of the Universal Association of Ethiopian Women. In 1972, on one of her many visits to Africa, she was honored by the the ASANTE people of GHANA as "Queen Mother." In 1989 Moore was among the black women honored at the Corcoran Gallery of Art, where "I Have A Dream," an exhibition of one of these prominent women, was on display. Moore participated in the MILLION MAN MARCH in 1995.

In a life that spanned some six decades of activism, Moore exemplified South African leader Nelson Mandela's dictum, which she often referred to: "The struggle is my life."

See also Scottsboro Case.

Leyla Keough

Moore, Frederick Randolph

1857–1943

African American journalist and politician.

Frederick Randolph Moore was born in Prince William County, Virginia, the son of Eugene Moore and Evelina Diggs. Information concerning the parents' occupations is unavailable. Having left Virginia in early childhood, Fred Moore grew up in WASHINGTON, D.C., where he attended public schools and sold newspapers to help support himself and his family. At eighteen, he began work as a messenger for the U.S. Treasury Department and became personal messenger a few years later for the secretary of the treasury. He worked under six successive secretaries and traveled to Europe in 1887 with Secretary Daniel Manning. That same year Moore resigned from the Treasury Department and moved to NEW YORK CITY, where he became a clerk at the Western National Bank, which later merged with the National Bank of Commerce, a position he held for eighteen years.

Moore began his journalistic career in New York City as general manager and then editor and publisher in 1904 of the *Colored American Magazine*. Originating in Boston in 1900, the magazine changed, under Moore's editorship, from a mainly literary magazine into one that primarily stressed black economic advancement. Moore's purchase of the magazine and its removal to New York were aided by the secret financial support of influential black educator BOOKER T. WASHINGTON. Washington wanted a publication that promoted his philosophy of black economic development, and he supported editors who accepted his conservative position on black political and civil rights. Washington also intended to silence opponents, such as W. E. B. DU BOIS and WILLIAM MONROE TROTTER, who condemned him repeatedly for emphasizing vocational training rather than challenging LYNCHING, disfranchisement, and JIM CROW legislation. Moore shared Washington's belief in cultivating economic development in the black community as a means for gaining political equality. Black unity was key to Moore's political and economic philosophy. He believed African Americans should own their own homes and businesses in their communities. Black success in this endeavor, Moore thought, would mean political and economic equality.

Consequently, as editor of the *Colored American Magazine*, Moore explained that the new focus of the periodical was to illustrate "the successes of our people as a whole and as individuals." In this way, the editor hoped that the magazine would reach "the masses of the people," not merely "those who are highly educated and cultured." The *Colored American Magazine* became a didactic tool that encouraged African Americans to become entrepreneurs and, equally important, to patronize black businesses. The majority of black Americans needed, Moore argued, "information of the doings of the members of the race rather [than] the writing of dreamers or theorists." Yet, Moore did not ignore political issues. He consistently published articles and wrote editorials that condemned disfranchisement and lynching. At the same time, Washington's public policy of accommodationism and gradualism regarding Southern black political and legal rights was promoted through articles by Washington and pro-Washington writers. Also, Tuskegee Institute, Washington's agricultural and vocational training school in Alabama, received extensive coverage. Most important, there were no longer attacks on Washington in the *Colored American Magazine* as there had been before Moore became editor.

In 1907 Moore again advanced through Washington's clandestine maneuvering and financial support by becoming editor and publisher of the *New York Age*. Published under various names and editors, the weekly newspaper had become the most prominent black paper in the country under the editorship of TIMOTHY THOMAS FORTUNE. Fortune supported Washington's goals but not his accommodationist strategy or his loyalty to the REPUBLICAN PARTY. Under Moore's editorship the *Age* became a much more partisan paper. However, even though he was a devoted Republican, Moore did not endorse Washington or Republican Party policies completely; in fact, he challenged them on the editorial pages of the *Age*, condemning Republican quiescence on lynching and disfranchisement and criticizing white Southern political inequities and brutality.

Moore redirected the *Age* toward his own interest in black business development and highlighted such activities. Numerous articles featured the successes of black businessmen and women, stressing not only their achievements but also a work ethic of industry, frugality, and sobriety. Moreover, Moore almost entirely ignored black radicals like Du Bois, Trotter, and MARCUS GARVEY. And, as he had done with the *Colored Ameri-*

can Magazine, which died under new editorship in 1909, Moore increased the circulation (to about 27,000 in 1937) and the volume of the *New York Age* and added special features.

After Washington's death in 1915, Moore was more outspoken in his support for southern black migration and political protest, two activities Washington had decried. After a trip to the South, Moore in 1917 urged Southern blacks to agitate for fair treatment: "Now is the time for the Negroes of the South to speak out for their rights—not offensively but frankly." He began publishing speeches by selected liberals like ADAM CLAYTON POWELL, SR., who called in 1917 for blacks to take advantage of the nation's need for manpower and wage a "bloodless war" for constitutional rights. By 1924 the *Age* focused extensively on HARLEM, where Moore had moved, and revealed his concern for social issues, including medical services for Harlem residents. In the 1920s and 1930s, the pages of the *Age* supported boycotts of white Harlem merchants who refused to employ blacks in their stores and advocated city government investment in the rehabilitation of substandard housing for the poor. Moore's last contributions to the *Age* were during the early years of U.S. involvement in World War II when he supported A. PHILIP RANDOLPH's March on Washington movement, which demanded fair employment practices in the defense industry. Still, Moore's firm belief in black economic development and black patronage of black business remained a prominent theme in the newspaper.

Moore's career in journalism coexisted with the development of his own business interests. Consistent with his philosophy of racial solidarity and black economic development, in 1893 he helped establish the Afro-American Investment and Building Company, which bought New Jersey and New York property and sold it to blacks-at reasonable interest rates. By late 1904 Moore was owner of the Moore Publishing and Printing Company, which published both the *Colored American Magazine* and the *New York Age*. Moore noted with pride that the company was black owned and "that all of the mechanical work of construction connected with publishing the magazine has been done by members of the race exclusively." Also in 1904, he was organizer and in the following year general secretary of the National Negro Business League, an organization Washington created to promote black business. Moore was secretary and treasurer in 1904 of an investment company, the Afro-American Realty Company, which purchased Harlem property to sell or rent to New York City blacks in need of decent housing. Although the company failed in 1908, Afro-American Realty played a significant role in creating a predominantly black Harlem community.

Moore was also a politician and community activist. Always a faithful Republican, he began his political career as district captain in his Brooklyn community. In 1904 he was appointed deputy collector of internal revenue but resigned within a few months to become organizer of the National Negro Business League. Moore also acted as a delegate or alternate delegate to several Republican National Conventions and served on the National Negro Republican Committee from 1908 to 1920. Although he quit after three months and did not actually leave the United States, Moore was appointed minister of Liberia by President William Howard Taft in 1912. After moving to Harlem, Moore joined the New York City Board of Aldermen for the Nineteenth District in 1927, replacing a white incumbent. He was reelected to this position in 1929.

Moore's community activism continued until his death, at eighty-five, when he was serving as president of the Parent Teacher's Association for the local public school in his neighborhood. More important, Moore helped found the NATIONAL URBAN LEAGUE in 1911. The Urban League grew out of several interracial Northern urban service organizations established to help the great wave of black migrants from the South. Moore had served on the board of several of these groups and was founder and chairman of the New York Association for the Protection of Colored Women in 1905, an organization created to protect Southern black women migrants from labor exploitation in the North. He was also active in the National League for the Protection of Colored Women founded the following year.

Moore married Ida Lawrence, a Washington, D.C., native, 1879. The Moores had eighteen children, six of whom lived to adulthood. Actively involved with the *Age* until 1942, Moore died in New York City.

As editor and publisher of one of the nation's major black newspapers, Moore both reported on and influenced black public opinion during a critical period of African-American life. His career reveals the complexity and diversity of black thought, particularly conservative philosophy, and shows that at specific times and under certain circumstances black conservatism in his era was often liberal and militant.

Bibliography

Moore's editorials are available in numerous issues of the *Colored American Magazine* and in the *New York Age*.
Bardolph, Richard. *The Negro Vanguard*. 1959.
Harlan, Louis R. *Booker T. Washington: The Wizard of Tuskegee, 1901–1915*. 1983.
Lewinson, Edwin R. *Black Politics in New York City*. 1974
Osofsky, Gilbert. *Harlem: The Making of a Ghetto*. 1963.
Parris, Guichard, and Lester Brooks. *Blacks in the City: A History of the National Urban League*. 1971.
Scheiner, Seth M. *Negro Mecca: A History of the Negro in New York City, 1865–1920*. 1965.

From *American National Biography*. John A. Garraty and Mark C. Carnes, eds. Oxford University Press, 1999. Reprinted by permission of the American Council of Learned Societies.

Rita Roberts

Moore, Harry Tyson

1905–1951

Teacher, political activist, and Florida state coordinator of the National Association for the Advancement of Colored People (NAACP) whose murder was never solved.

The victim of a bombing on Christmas night, Harry Tyson Moore was only forty-six when he died, but in his short life he accomplished much. Trained as a schoolteacher, Moore worked for the Brevard County, Florida, school system from 1925 until 1946, when his NAACP–supported campaign to secure equal pay for African American teachers cost him his position as superintendent of the area's Negro high school. Following the loss of his job, Moore continued to work for the state branch of the NAACP, focusing not only on economic and educational equality but also on voter registration and the fair enforcement of laws. When in November 1951 a white sheriff shot two black handcuffed defendants, killing one, Moore demanded that he be indicted for murder.

On December 25 of that year a bomb exploded under the bedroom of Moore's house, killing him instantly (his wife, Harriet, died a few days later). Neither local law enforcement nor the Federal Bureau of Investigation (FBI) was able to solve Moore's murder. Documents unveiled when Florida's governor reopened the case in 1991 reveal that the FBI's initial investigation focused solely on African American suspects, including all six hundred people who attended Moore's funeral. At present, no one has been charged with the crime, which a 1952 editorial in *The Nation* described as "part of a clear pattern of open force directed against the struggle of racial minorities to win full rights as citizens."

Kate Tuttle

Moore, Richard Benjamin

1893–1978

Activist and intellectual who was a leading figure in black socialism and labor politics in the United States.

Richard Moore became a political activist when he immigrated to NEW YORK in 1901. He joined the Socialist Party in 1918 and also became a member of the AFRICAN BLOOD BROTHERHOOD (ABB), a secret organization with ties both to BLACK NATIONALISM and the Communist Party U.S.A.

In 1921 Moore left the Socialist Party because of its indifference to African American concerns and soon after joined the Workers Party, the HARLEM branch of the Communist Party. In 1925 he was elected to the executive board and council of directors of the American Negro Labor Congress (ANLC), a national organization of black radicals, and became a contributing editor to the ANLC's the *Negro Champion*. In 1931 Moore became vice president of the International Labor Defense (ILD), which was formed to resolve legal problems caused by labor disputes and racism. Moore and the ILD became well known for defending the SCOTTSBORO CASE, in which nine black boys were sent to prison for raping two white girls, although doctors determined that no rape had taken place.

Moore founded the Pathway Press and the Frederick Douglass Historical and Cultural League in 1940. In 1942 he established the Frederick Douglass Book Center, an Afro-American and Caribbean bookstore, which was a well-known intellectual center in Harlem until it was burned in 1968. The Communist Party expelled him in 1942 for his "Negro Nationalist way of thinking."

Throughout his life Moore was dedicated to the independence of Caribbean nations and was invited by BARBADOS to participate in its independence celebration in 1966.

Moore fought ceaselessly to end racism and published in 1960 *The Name "Negro"—Its Origin and Evil Use*. He strongly promoted the term *Afro-American*, which, he felt, "proclaims at once our past continental heritage and our present national status."

Moorhead, Scipio

fl. 1773

American slave and artist primarily known for painting of Phillis Wheatley.

Despite Scipio Moorhead's position as a slave in the home of John Moorhead, a Presbyterian minister in Boston, he managed to develop his artistic talent. Sarah Moorhead, a painter who was the wife of the minister, probably provided some instruction.

The painting of African-American poet PHILLIS WHEATLEY that inspired the engraved frontispiece of her book of poetry is attributed to Moorhead. The volume, *Poems on Various Subjects, Religious and Moral*, was published in London in 1773 and created public debate concerning the intellectual abilities of those of African descent.

Unfortunately no signed works by Moorhead are known to exist. It is believed that it is Moorhead whom Wheatley immortalized with her 1773 poem, *To S. M., A Young African Painter, on Seeing His Work*. The poem is thought to be inspired by Scipio Moorhead and describes two paintings presumably by Moorhead, *Aurora* and *Damon and Pythia*.

Moorish Science Temple

See Ali, Noble Drew.

Moorland, Jesse Edward

1863–1939

American minister and leader in the Young Men's Christian Association (YMCA).

After attending Northwestern Normal University in Ada, Ohio, Jesse Edward Moorland enrolled in the theology department of HOWARD UNIVERSITY. Moorland graduated from Howard with a master's degree in 1891 and was ordained a minister in the Congregational Church. In that year he also became secretary of the Colored Branch of the YMCA in WASHINGTON, D.C. He moved to Nashville, Tennessee, in 1893 to become pastor of Howard Church. In 1896 he became pastor of Cleveland's

Mount Zion Congregational Church. He struggled to make Congregationalism a "practical, muscular Christianity" that directly addressed social needs.

Returning to the YMCA in 1898, Moorland served as administrator and fund-raiser for their Colored Men's Department in Washington, D.C. He raised over $2 million for twenty-nine new YMCA buildings for black communities throughout America. In 1914 Moorland became senior secretary of the YMCA's Colored Men's Department. Under his leadership, the department expanded significantly its number of college student chapters and city associations. He retired in 1923.

Moorland collected a substantial library of books by and about people of African descent. His collection, the largest of its time, went to Howard University and formed the basis of the MOORLAND-SPINGARN RESEARCH COLLECTION.

Moorland continued his efforts with black social organizations such as the National Health Circle for Colored People. In 1907 he joined the executive committee of Howard University's board of trustees, which he chaired in the 1930s.

Moorland-Spingarn Research Collection

Comprehensive collection of scholarly materials by and about people of African descent, located at Howard University.

The Moorland-Spingarn Research Center (MSRC) is a research facility located in Founder Library at HOWARD UNIVERSITY in WASHINGTON, D.C. It aims to collect, organize, preserve, and make available valuable resources on the history and culture of Africans and people of African descent. The MSRC's holdings chronicle the experiences of people of African descent in AFRICA, the Americas, and other parts of the world from the sixteenth century through the present.

The MSRC is composed of two divisions: Library and Manuscript. The Library Division houses more than 175,000 books, periodicals, and microforms in numerous languages. This body of literature includes rare works by early black writers such as DAVID WALKER, PHILLIS WHEATLEY, and FREDERICK DOUGLASS and first edition works by twentieth-century black authors including W. E. B. DU BOIS, RICHARD WRIGHT, and ALICE WALKER. The Library Division also features special resources such as theses on black subjects by students from other colleges and a vertical file collection covering an array of people and events.

The Manuscript Division is a collection of primary source materials divided into four departments: manuscripts, music, oral history, and prints and photographs. The manuscript department contains the correspondences, writings, and memorabilia of more than 160 African American people and organizations. The music department's collection covers more than 400 black composers, starting in the eighteenth century. Its sheet music, songbooks, and recordings span all musical genres, including classical, spiritual, and jazz. The oral history department brings together over 700 transcripts of the speeches made by participants in the CIVIL RIGHTS MOVEMENT. The prints and photographs department houses over 50,000 images dating from the 1800s to the present.

The MSRC is named for its two benefactors, JESSE E. MOORLAND (1863–1939) and Arthur B. Spingarn (1878–1971). Moorland was a minister, YMCA executive, and collector of materials about African American culture and history, with an emphasis on the history of slavery. After inheriting a book collection from an uncle, he began collecting black-related books, pamphlets, and manuscripts as well as portraits and engravings. As a member of the board of trustees at Howard University, he advocated the establishment of an African American research library. In 1914 Moorland decided to donate his private library of over 3,000 items to Howard. At that time, it was regarded as the most extensive collection of materials in the world by and about people of African descent. The collection became known as the Moorland Foundation, a Library of Negro Life, and established Howard University as the center of black scholarship.

Arthur B. Spingarn was a lawyer, an officer of the NATIONAL ASSOCIATION FOR THE ADVANCEMENT OF COLORED PEOPLE (NAACP), and a collector of books by black authors. A European American, he began collecting books by black authors in response to white scholars' claim that people of African descent would continue to be viewed as inferior until the day a black man could read a book by a black author. The books he accumulated explored topics in every academic field of study and were written in all major African and European languages. In 1946 Spingarn donated his eclectic collection to Howard University. From then until his death, Spingarn sent Howard a copy of every book by a black author he could find.

While Moorland and Spingarn laid the foundation for the research library, scholar-librarian DOROTHY PORTER WESLEY (1905–1995) reorganized and expanded its holdings through her own collecting efforts. For patrons of the library, she was an invaluable resource with a profound knowledge of black history and culture. In 1973 associate Letitia Woods Brown said Porter Wesley "has the broadest understanding of Black bibliography of anyone living. If it has been written or even spoken about, Dorothy Porter knows." The same year, another associate, Benjamin Quarles, stated that "without exaggeration, there hasn't been a major history book in the last thirty years in which the author hasn't acknowledged Mrs. Porter's help."

After serving as the director of the Moorland Foundation for forty-three years, Porter Wesley retired in 1973 and the library's name changed to the Moorland-Spingarn Research Center. Largely through the efforts of Porter Wesley, the Moorland-Spingarn Research Center has become one of the most valuable resources for the study of the black experience.

Aaron Myers

Morales, José María

1818–1894

One of the highest-ranking Afro-Argentine military leaders and a musician, poet, and politician.

José María Morales was the son of a military man who fought in the Battle of the Patricios in 1807 against the British forces. His father's continued participation in ARGENTINA's independence and civil wars forced Morales to leave school early and work as a tinsmith. In 1838 Morales followed his father's example, setting out for Montevideo to fight with the Unitarians (who envisioned a centralized political system based in Buenos Aires) in exile against the Argentine leader Juan Manuel Rosas. Rosas enjoyed widespread support in the black community—including DOMINGO SOSA, another rising Afro-Argentine military figure and contemporary of Morales—in part because his opposition to Buenos Aires's white Creole elite allowed for a more socially diverse society. Rosas's highly authoritarian government sparked opposition, however, especially among some middle-class blacks, including Morales. Argentina's civil war lasted until 1852, when the Unitarians finally marched triumphantly into Buenos Aires, and Rosas went into exile in England. The Unitarians assumed control of the city and province of Buenos Aires, establishing it as the seat of a highly centralized national government at the expense of the political power of the other provinces.

The future colonel Morales continued to serve in many battles, including the war against PARAGUAY (1865–1870), and the so-called Conquest of the Desert, the war against the Indians who lived in the southern plains of the country (1879–1880). Having held a variety of military posts as a gunrunner, battlefield soldier, commander, and military strategist, he went on to become chief of conscription. In 1874 Morales became a regional representative in the Buenos Aires legislature during the presidency of Nicolás Avellaneda (1874–1880), serving for three terms. He took part in the convention to reform the Constitution of Buenos Aires in the late 1870s and later participated in yet another revolution, this time against President Miguel Juárez Celman in 1890. Shortly before his death he was named head of the National Penitentiary by President Carlos Pellegrini (1890–1892).

Despite his many accomplishments and the fact that he became a hero within Afro-Argentine communities, literary critic Marvin Lewis points out that today Morales appears more frequently in the often ignored Afro-Argentine sources than in military history books. Historian George Reid Andrews explains that mythologizing black patriot martyrs was a convenient way of writing them out of the history that followed the wars:

> By claiming an almost complete destruction of the black male population through military service, the nation's historians were able to ignore the fact that many of those soldiers returned alive from the wars to contribute to Buenos Aires's cultural, social, and demographic development.

HORACIO MENDIZÁBAL, perhaps the most famous Afro-Argentine poet, dedicated two poems to Morales in *First Verses,* "¡Alerta!" and "Conmemoración de la Batalla de Cepeda." Another compatriot, Jorge Miguel Ford, in his biographical volume, *Beneméritos de mi estirpe* (Outstanding Members of My Race), includes Morales as one of a number of prominent Afro-Argentine military figures, writers, composers, and intellectuals.

Joy Elizondo

Morant Bay Rebellion

Black uprising against racial injustice in Jamaica in 1865.

The Morant Bay Rebellion erupted on October 11, 1865, when several hundred men and women, mostly black peasants or workers on plantations, marched into Morant Bay, the capital of the predominately sugar-growing parish of Saint Thomas, in southeastern JAMAICA. They pillaged the police station, seized weapons, and then confronted the volunteer militia that had been called in to protect the meeting of the vestry, the political body that administered the parish. Fighting erupted between the militia and the crowd. By the end of the day, twenty-five people were dead (including seven of the protestors), and numerous others were injured. Two additional casualties occurred in the days that immediately followed.

PAUL BOGLE, the leader of the rebellion, was a farmer and Native Baptist deacon from the district of Stony Gut. He and his associates planned the uprising in secretly held meetings, during which they enlisted volunteers in expectation of a violent confrontation at Morant Bay. The conspirators met in the chapels or meetinghouses of the Native Baptist Church, a black-led independent church that provided a religious and political counterweight to the prevailing white norms of the colonial society.

The reasons for the rebellion were numerous. Blacks were bitter about the continued political, social, and economic domination by whites, despite the abolition of slavery in 1834. Among other things, this domination meant an unfair judicial structure that consistently favored planters' interests and meted out excessive punishment for petty offences committed by the poor. Another grievance had to do with land rights. Access to land was a symbol of freedom for former slaves, and they were opposed to paying rent for their homes and garden plots. In addition, they received extremely low wages on the plantations that were often the sole opportunity for employment. By 1865 the conditions for the island's poor had worsened due to droughts, poor crops, and food shortages resulting from the AMERICAN CIVIL WAR.

The precipitating factor for the Morant Bay Rebellion was an altercation that erupted in the Magistrates Court on October 7 between police and a group of more than one hundred people. Bogle was among the crowd, having arrived to support a man charged with trespassing on a plantation. On October 10 police arrived at Stony Gut to arrest Bogle and several others for rioting, but their plans were foiled when a crowd of about 300 gathered to defend Bogle. The crowd captured and briefly held some police officers. Bogle then drafted a petition to the governor requesting his protection from local administrators, and the following day the rebellion broke out in Morant Bay.

The Jamaican authorities responded swiftly and brutally. They mobilized all of the armed forces at their disposal—some British troops, the Jamaican militiamen, and the maroons (former runaway slaves who had established their autonomy before abolition, in part by agreeing to aid the colonial troops)—to put down the rebellion. In the process, nearly 500 people were killed and hundreds of others were severely wounded. During the crackdown GEORGE GORDON, a person of mixed African and European descent who was an elected member of the Jamaican legislature's House of Assembly, was arrested on the orders of Governor Edward John Eyre. A close associate of Bogle and a religious and political radical, Gordon was found guilty of treason by a court-martial and hanged at Morant Bay. Bogle, too, was executed.

The nature of the suppression led to demands in Britain for an official inquiry, and a royal commission was sent to Jamaica to gather evidence on the rebellion and its suppression. After nearly three months of investigation, the commission drew a conclusion that was critical of Governor Eyre and of the harsh measures he ordered in the wake of the rebellion. As a result the governor was dismissed, and more importantly, the political structure of the colony was transformed. Its system of representative self-rule, in place since 1662, was abolished, and GREAT BRITAIN began to rule Jamaica more directly, establishing a crown colony government that remained in place until 1944. There were also attempts in Britain to put Eyre on trial for his role in the suppression; although these failed, the events at Morant Bay were widely debated throughout Britain.

See also Protestant Church in Latin America and the Caribbean.

Bibliography

Heuman, Gad. *The Killing Time: The Morant Bay Rebellion in Jamaica.* University of Tennessee Press, 1994.

Heuman, Gad. "Post-Emancipation Protest in Jamaica: The Morant Bay Rebellion." In *From Chattel Slaves to Wage Slaves: The Dynamics of Labour Bargaining in the Americas.* Edited by Mary Turner. Indiana University Press, 1995.

Holt, Thomas. *The Problem of Freedom: Race, Labor, and Politics in Jamaica and Britain, 1832–1938.* Johns Hopkins University Press, 1992.

Semmel, Bernard. *The Governor Eyre Controversy.* Mac Gibbon & Kee, 1962.

Stewart, Robert J. *Religion and Society in Post-Emancipation Jamaica.* University of Tennessee Press, 1992.

Moré, Beny

1919–1963

Afro-Cuban singer and bandleader regarded by many critics as one of the greatest popular singers Cuba has ever produced.

Beny Moré was one of CUBA's greatest singers and entertainers. Cuba's musical culture draws upon the dual legacy of AFRICA and Europe. Moré was not only a talented vocalist, he was a master of both the Afro-Cuban and the more European-derived musical traditions. He was a superb interpreter of a wide range of musical styles, including the SON, the MAMBO, the RUMBA, the BOLERO, and the Spanish-derived rural music known as *guajiro*. Early in his career he sang both up-tempo songs and ballads, but by the 1950s he was concentrating primarily on ballads, especially boleros and slow-tempo son. In *Salsa!,* Hernando Calvo Ospina wrote that Moré was "the greatest *son* musician of all time." Music writer Spencer Harrington observed that in the three decades since his death, no Cuban singer has been able to replace him.

As a teenager, Bartolome Maximiliano Moré moved to HAVANA, where he performed as a street singer, making ends meet by taking various odd jobs. In 1945 he toured MEXICO with the band of Miguel Matamoro and remained behind when the band returned to Cuba. Before leaving, Matamoro advised Moré to change his name: *bartolo* meant donkey in Mexican slang. Moré took the name Beny. Two years later he was given a contract by RCA-Victor Mexico. RCA paired Moré with a number of large orchestras, notably that of fellow Cuban expatriate DÁMASO PÉREZ PRADO. In these early recordings Moré showed himself to be a mature vocalist. Harrington noted that Moré's "signature vocal technique" was an impressive upward glissando in which he "would hold a note, then slide up the scale to a higher note and hold it" in turn.

After a series of influential and popular recordings in Mexico, in 1953 Moré returned to Cuba where he assembled his own big-band, featuring musicians like trumpeter ALFREDO "CHOCOLATE" ARMENTEROS and trombonist and arranger Generoso "El Tojo" Jimenez. Although Moré could not read music, he composed two of his most popular songs, which others then transcribed into musical notation: "*Bonito y sabroso*" and "*Que bueno baila usted.*" His orchestra established itself as Cuba's quintessential big band, and for the rest of his life he toured the country with it. Moré remained in Cuba after the Cuban Revolution and died of cirrhosis of the liver six months short of his forty-fourth birthday.

James Sellman

Morehouse College

America's only historically black, all male, liberal arts college.

Morehouse College, located in ATLANTA, GEORGIA, has conferred bachelor's degrees on more African American men than any other private college in the nation. Each year nearly 3,000 students from more than forty states and eighteen foreign countries are educated at Morehouse. It provides a balanced liberal arts education in social sciences, mathematics, natural sciences, arts, humanities, and business. But Morehouse is perhaps best known for the achievements of its distinguished alumni, in-

Professor Frederick Mapp, a specialist in freshwater biology, examines a transparency in his laboratory at Morehouse College. CORBIS/Krist

cluding MARTIN LUTHER KING JR., Olympian Edwin Moses, filmmaker SPIKE LEE, former mayor of Atlanta MAYNARD JACKSON, activist JULIAN BOND, and several United States congressmen.

The college was founded in 1867 as the Augusta Institute to train blacks for professions in teaching and ministry. Three ministers, William Jefferson White, Richard C. Coulter, and Edmund Turney, organized the institute. They conducted its first classes in the basement of Springfield Baptist Church, which today ranks as the oldest independent African American church in the country. Twelve years later the institute moved to the basement of Friendship Baptist Church in Atlanta and changed its name to the Atlanta Baptist Seminary.

In 1906 JOHN HOPE became the first African American president of the college. Hope, a Phi Beta Kappa graduate of Brown University, led the college during an era of unprecedented growth. Under his leadership the college was renamed Morehouse in 1913, in honor of Henry L. Morehouse, the white secretary of the Northern Baptist Home Mission Society.

Morehouse College gained an international reputation for excellence in 1940 when another African American, BENJAMIN MAYS, assumed its presidency. Mays, considered by many the father of the CIVIL RIGHTS MOVEMENT, was a mentor and friend to Martin Luther King Jr. While Mays was president from 1940 until 1967, the number of faculty members grew, and the percentage with doctoral degrees tripled.

During Mays's tenure the term "Morehouse Man" came to symbolize an elite group of young men—confident, intelligent, and honest leaders. Morehouse men were the best-educated and often the most prominent African American men in the country. The image that many refer to as the Morehouse mystique has brought criticism that the college is an elitist institution catering exclusively to the black middle class. Despite this criticism, Morehouse has consistently provided a high-quality education for students from all backgrounds.

As one of 109 historically black colleges and universities (HBCUs) in the United States, Morehouse continues to contribute to the education and empowerment of the entire African American community. Morehouse is a member of the Atlanta University Center (AUC), the oldest and largest consortium of historically black private institutions of higher education in the world. The AUC is located in downtown Atlanta and comprises six interlinked campuses represented by six independent black institutions: Clark Atlanta University; the INTERDENOMINATIONAL THEOLOGICAL CENTER; the Morehouse School of Medicine; Morehouse College; Morris Brown College; and SPELMAN COLLEGE.

See also Colleges and Universities, Historically Black, in the United States.

Bibliography
Brawley, Benjamin G. *History of Morehouse College.* McGrath, 1970.

Alonford James Robinson

Moreira, Airto, and Flora Purim

Two leading figures in Brazilian jazz who made their mark in fusion music of the 1970s—Moreira by expanding the role of jazz percussion, Purim as a vocalist with an astonishing range.

Over the last quarter-century, few have done more than Flora Purim and her husband, Airto Moreira, to popularize Afro-Brazilian jazz. The two met through Brazilian musician Hermeto Pascoal. In the early 1960s Purim studied voice with Pascoal, who was coleader, along with Moreira, of the Quarteto Novo. The Quarteto Novo was known in BRAZIL for combining jazz with lyrics protesting the repressive regime of the time. Moreira and Purim met in 1963 and were soon inseparable. But their beginnings were dissimilar.

Generally known by his first name, Airto was born in 1941 in Itaiopolis, a small village in southern Brazil. When he began playing rhythms with his fists before he could walk, his mother feared that he might have a developmental disorder. But his family soon recognized his musical talent. He performed on the radio at the age of seven, and at sixteen moved to São Paulo, where he began playing professionally. During the 1960s he collected and studied over 120 traditional Brazilian percussion instruments.

Flora Purim (1942–) grew up in RIO DE JANEIRO, and her parents—who were professional musicians—gave her an early introduction to music. Her father, a Jewish émigré from the Ukraine, played first violin with the Rio Symphony Orchestra; her Brazilian mother played classical piano. Studying voice enabled Purim to increase her range to six octaves. She also gained a reputation for her unique wordless style of singing and for her voice—described variously as ethereal, sensual, soothing, and haunting.

Following the 1967 military coup, the couple emigrated to the United States. They made their mark in fusion music or jazz-rock, pioneered by MILES DAVIS, in which the musicians play jazz improvisations over rock-style rhythms. Davis asked Moreira to join his band (1969–1970), and in 1971 he appeared on the first recording of Weather Report, another innovative fusion band. Purim worked with pianist Duke Pearson and then with white arranger Gil Evans. In the early 1970s she joined Moreira in the original lineup of Chick Corea's popular Return to Forever, recording two classic albums, *Return to Forever* (1972) and *Light as a Feather* (1972), and the two worked together consistently thereafter.

Since the early 1970s Purim and Moreira have been less visible. Purim was convicted on a charge of cocaine possession and spent time in prison during 1974 and 1975. During the late 1970s and 1980s the recordings of the two were more light pop music than jazz, but they have repeatedly returned to their Brazilian jazz origins. In the late 1980s Purim toured with DIZZY GILLESPIE's United Nation Orchestra, an ensemble of African American and Latin American jazz musicians. Although she never enjoyed a hit to rival Astrud Gilberto's "The Girl from Ipanema" (1963), Purim remains a gifted singer with superb timing and a memorable voice.

Moreira, even in settings that seem quite alien to Afro-Brazilian rhythms, has raised interest in his many Brazilian percussion instruments. His greatest musical contribution remains his creation of the role of percussionist—as distinguished from role of the traditional jazz drummer. Although Moreira plays the drums, his distinctive approach is to assemble a vast array of small instruments—including many that are improvised, such as metal refrigerator racks and wooden shoes—and to use them for adding rhythms and textures to the music. In their performances together Moreira and Purim remain Brazil's best-known jazz ambassadors.

James Sellman

Moreira, Juliano

1873–1933

Pioneering Afro-Brazilian scholar in the field of psychiatry.

Juliano Moreira spoke out for blacks and *mestiços* (Brazilian term for people of mixed race) by challenging racial prejudices in Brazilian society, such as the then-prevalent belief in the negative impact of racial mixing. In his article "Assistance to the Alienated," published in 1905, he affirmed that "the bad elements that constitute our nationality are due our ample physical, moral and social degradation, and have been unfairly attributed solely to fact of *mestiçagem* [racial mixing]." Moreira believed that descendents of the mixture of natives, Africans, and Europeans were in every social class in BRAZIL, a Brazilian social phenomenon that he considered important.

Moreira was born in Salvador, BAHIA, Brazil. He was admitted to the Medical School of Bahia in 1891, where he dedicated his studies to psychiatry. His academic career began when he was accepted as an assistant professor of psychiatry at the Medical School of Bahia in 1896. He was the first Brazilian delegate to represent Brazil at an international medical congress in Paris, FRANCE, in 1900. Moreira published his first important essay, called "Klinotherapy," in 1901. After moving to Rio de Janiero, Brazil, in 1903, he continued to represent Brazil in successive international congresses, such as those held at Lisbon, PORTUGAL, in 1906; Amsterdam, THE NETHERLANDS, in 1907; and London, England, and Brussels, Belgium, in 1913.

Moreira became highly respected at national and international levels for his knowledge in the field of mental diseases. He was given the title of Honorary President of the Fourth Congress of Mental Diseases, in Berlin, GERMANY, the first time that such a title was given to a foreign scientist. In Brazil he founded the Medical Society of Bahia and advanced both psychiatric and forensic medical studies.

Morejón, Nancy

1944–

Afro-Cuban poet, historian, translator, and literary critic; the best-known black woman poet in Spanish America.

Born in HAVANA, CUBA, Nancy Morejón grew up in a working-class district of the city known as Los Sitios. As a young child Morejón was discouraged by her parents from observing the SANTERÍA religion (a traditional Yoruban-based Cuban faith). Nevertheless she absorbed Santería's musical rites, including performances of neighborhood RUMBA bands, through members of her extended family. (Rumba is an Afro-Cuban song and dance form that synthesizes Bantu-derived rituals and rhythms. It was later modified into a ballroom dance.) She is particularly interested in Afro-Cuban religious forms as modes of cultural expression. In her article "Las poéticas de Nancy Morejón," she explains that she incorporates Santería themes and motifs in her literary work. References to YORUBA deities such as Eleguá and OSHÚN are abundant in her poetry (ORISHAS).

Morejón's parents, though not formally educated, emphasized her education from an early age and instilled in her a love for reading. She first read poetry in her father's collection of books by Cuba's national poet, NICOLÁS GUILLÉN. As a consequence she developed an early appreciation for poetry and languages. By the age of thirteen she had mastered English, translating for her family during her cousin's wedding to a Protestant North American minister. Taking advantage of the free education available as a result of the Cuban Revolution, she went on to study French language and literature at the University of Havana. In an interview with Lucía Suárez, Morejón highlights the importance of knowing several languages, saying, "[it] gives you the opportunity to see other literary worlds and compare different methods of doing literature."

In 1962 Morejón published her first collection of poems titled *Mutismos* (Silences). These poems illustrated her fundamental poetic concerns and provided her with the foundation and the aesthetic framework for decades to come: a kind of self-examination of her role as a black woman and as a young writer against the backdrop of the climactic changes of the Cuban Revolution. Literary critic William Luis notes that these early poems are marked by intimate self-examination as well as Morejón's proud assertion of her Afro-Cuban roots. In 1964 she published *Amor, ciudad atribuida* (Love, Attributed City) and in 1967 another poetry collection entitled *Richard trajo su flauta* (Richard Brought his Flute). During the late 1960s Morejón began to experiment with the more conversational and less abstract style that characterizes many of the works of other revolutionary poets. In addition, she focused on collective political and historical themes as manifested through race, gender, and Afro-Cuban religions in her personal experience, as literary critic Miriam DeCosta Willis points out.

In 1979 Morejón published *Parajes de una época* (Places of an Era), which renews her commitment to the revolution while placing less emphasis on racial pride and Afro-Cuban themes. Luis attributes this shift in the author's writing to growing nationalist tendencies in Cuba at that time, in part exacerbated by the intensification of the conflict with the United States. In 1982 Morejón published *Cuadernos de Granada* (Grenada Notebook) and in 1984 *Piedra pulida* (On Polished Stone).

From a critical standpoint Morejón's 1993 collection, *Paisaje célebre* (Famous Landscape) (a finalist in the international poetry competition of Pérez Bonalde), represents the most recent stage of the author's poetry and a relative break with her previous work. As Luis writes, *Paisaje célebre* "underscores a coming to terms with a struggle within, regarding her poetry and position in the revolution." With this book, Morejón emerges as an independent Cuban writer whose poetry is informed but not dominated by race and revolutionary politics.

In addition to poetry Morejón has also written important works of literary criticism, including a crucial study on the poetry of Guillén titled *Nación y mestizaje en Nicolás Guillén* (Nation and Racial Mixture in Nicolás Guillén, 1982). Until 1995 she directed the editorial house, Ediciones PM, of the Pablo Milanés Foundation, a multimedia, nonprofit center for the promotion and support of all artistic expression that "contributes to the preservation of the cultural identity of the Cuban nation." She currently directs the Caribbean Studies Center at Casa de las Américas at Havana, the epicenter of Cuban and Latin American intelligentsia.

Morejón's received the 2001 National Prize for Literature, becoming the first black woman to win Cuba's most prestigious literary prize. She continues to write poetry and literary criticism while residing in Havana. Morejón often travels to Europe, Latin America, Africa, the Caribbean, and the United States. Her poetry has been translated into many languages.

See also Afrocubanismo; Cuba; Poetry, Caribbean; Women Writers, Black, in Spanish America.

Joy Elizondo

Morel Campos, Juan

1857–1896

Afro–Puerto Rican composer and musician, critical figure in the development of the *danza,* a musical style that incorporates Afro-Caribbean and European elements.

Juan Morel Campos was born in the city of Ponce, the main cultural center of PUERTO RICO during the nineteenth century. He studied music and composition with Manuel G. Tavárez, the most acclaimed Puerto Rican composer of his time. His musical production was varied and rich, including *zarzuelas* (Spanish light opera), masses, symphonies, waltzes, marches, and *danzas*. In the latter, Morel Campos made his most important and lasting contribution to classical music in Latin America. Of the 550 works attributed to him, approximately half of them are danzas for piano, including *No me toques, El torbellino, Felices dias,* and *Vano empeño*.

Morel Campos created a distinct national style by modifying the classic European molds. For his creative compositions he is considered the father of the *danza puertorriqueña*. Like other composers in CUBA, MEXICO, and BRAZIL, he transformed classical styles by incorporating Afro-Caribbean styles and folk-rhythmic formulas in his compositions.

In 1882 Morel Campos founded the firemen's band of Ponce, one of the first bands in Puerto Rico. He conducted many concerts in Ponce and in various towns around the island, at a time of national awakening and cultural enthusiasm. Morel Campos also toured South America with a company of zarzuelas.

Unfortunately Morel Campos's production ended prematurely when he suffered a stroke while conducting the overture of an opera in Ponce. He died a few days later, before reaching the age of forty.

See also Music, Classical, in Latin America and the Caribbean.

Carlos Dalmau

Morelos y Pavón, José María

1765–1815

Mulatto leader of the Mexican wars of independence (1810–1821).

José María Morelos y Pavón was born in Valladolid, New Spain—what is now the city of Morelia in the Mexican state of Michoacán (the city was named in his honor). Educated there, Morelos worked as a scribe and accountant from 1770 to 1790, when he began studies for the priesthood. The CATHOLIC CHURCH

A former priest who played a major role in winning Mexican independence, Morelos y Pavón practiced progressive racial policies in his military command. *Oronoz*

had long forbidden blacks, mulattos, and *zambos* (Afro-Indians) from becoming priests. Morelos's baptismal record, however, had been tampered with—he was originally designated a mulatto, but the record later indicated he was white—and throughout his life the leader maintained that he was of Spanish (white) descent. In all likelihood his parents paid the local priest to make the change in his baptismal record so he would receive more favorable treatment in New Spain's rigid caste system.

Morelos's studies took him to the College of San Nicolás, where he met Miguel Hidalgo y Costilla (1753–1811), future leader of the Mexican independence movement. On completing his religious education in 1796, Morelos became an auxiliary priest; in 1799 he was ordained as a full priest. For the next decade he was parish priest in a string of towns in present-day Michoacán: Churumuco, La Huacana, Carácuaro, and Nocupétaro.

In September 1810 Hidalgo initiated the Mexican struggle for independence with a call to Indians, mestizos (persons of indigenous and European descent), and Afro-Mexicans to overthrow Spanish rule and the white-dominated caste system. Morelos soon joined Hidalgo, who charged the former with raising troops in southern MEXICO. Morelos spent the latter part of 1810 mustering men and weapons. While in this position of authority he encouraged social change within the movement. He abolished slavery and the caste system in his ranks and prohibited his followers from describing themselves with racial terms like *mulatto* or *Indian*. Racial conflict nonetheless stirred among his men. When two officers tried to incite blacks to slaughter whites in the army, Morelos had the instigators shot.

In 1810 and 1811 Morelos entered the first of his conflicts against the Spanish royalist army, which included a long-running siege of the port town ACAPULCO. Although Acapulco would not succumb to his troops for two more years, Morelos achieved far-reaching victories throughout the rest of south-central Mexico. By the time Hidalgo was executed by a Spanish firing squad in midsummer of 1811, Morelos was the clear heir apparent of the revolt.

Morelos's successes in south-central Mexico continued through 1813, and at the end of the year he convened a supreme congress that vested him with executive power for the insurgent provinces. In short order, however, he suffered a series of battlefield defeats, including significant setbacks in his hometown of Valladolid in December 1813, in Puruarán in January 1814, and in Tlacotepec in February 1814. Morelos spent much of the last two years of his life protecting the rebel congress as it fled from one town to the next in the face of royalist advances.

On November 5, 1815, at Temalaca in what is now the state of Guerrero, Morelos was captured during one such protective run. He was immediately taken to Mexico City, tried, found guilty, and condemned to death. His execution on December 22 marked the end, for several years, of the organized rebellion. His legacy to Afro-Latin Americans remains complex. Morelos is largely heralded for his progressive social policies, for his martyrdom, and for taking difficult positions (such as denying his black heritage) in order to advance worthy anti-caste positions. However, some latter-day critics have argued that his attempts to abolish slavery and the caste system were little more than gambits to win support for his anti-Spanish army; they also question whether Morelos would have made such bold moves if he had won control of all of Mexico.

See also Colonial Latin America and the Caribbean; Struggles for Independence in Latin America, Racial Questions during the.

Morgan, Clement Garnett

1859–1929

African Amerian attorney and civil rights leader.

Clement Garnett Morgan was born in Stafford County, Virginia, the son of slaves. After being emancipated during the CIVIL WAR, the family moved to WASHINGTON, D.C., where Morgan attended the well-regarded Preparatory High School for Colored Youth. He left school and worked briefly as a barber in Washington before moving to St. Louis, Missouri, where he worked as a teacher for four years.

In 1885 Morgan moved to BOSTON to attend the Boston Latin School. After graduating in 1886, he enrolled in Harvard College, where he and W. E. B. DU BOIS were then the only African American students. While at Harvard, Morgan supported himself by working as a barber and by giving readings and speeches at summer resorts. Sizable scholarships for academic excellence took care of most of his tuition costs. In 1889 he won the Boylston Prize for oratory (Du Bois finished second). In his senior year Morgan was named class orator. After graduating from college in 1890, Morgan entered Harvard Law School, receiving his LL.B. in 1893. That year he passed the bar and established a law office in Cambridge.

In addition to his law practice, Morgan developed a career in local electoral politics. Running as a REPUBLICAN in 1895, he became the first African American elected from predominately white Ward Two to the Common Council of Cambridge. In 1898, after serving the two-year term on the common council, he successfully ran for a two-year term as alderman. He then ran unsuccessfully for the state legislature in 1899, 1900, and 1908. In 1897 Morgan married Gertrude Wright.

In the late 1890s Morgan became a part of the so-called "Negro Radicals," a group of prominent African American intellectuals, attorneys, and activists that included Butler R. Wilson, ARCHIBALD H. GRIMKÉ, George Forbes, and most notably, WILLIAM MONROE TROTTER. This group, which advocated agitation for full civil rights, led the opposition to BOOKER T. WASHINGTON's politics of accommodation for African Americans. Morgan served as an attorney for Trotter when the latter was charged with inciting what came to be known as the "Boston Riot" of 1903, when several of the Radicals disrupted a speech being given by Washington.

In 1904 Morgan helped form the Committee of Twelve for the Advancement of the Interests of the Negro Race, a short-lived coalition of Radicals and Washington's followers that attempted to reconcile the two factions. In 1905, after the Committee of Twelve fell apart, Morgan joined the NIAGARA MOVEMENT, an organization founded by Du Bois that split sharply from Washington in its strident denunciations of JIM CROW laws and militant advocacy for African American rights. Morgan was named as the head of the Massachusetts branch of the new organization.

Morgan soon became involved in factional disputes that ultimately led to the demise of the Niagara Movement. He feuded with Trotter over support for Massachusetts governor Curtis Guild's reelection. In exchange for supporting Guild, Morgan had been nominated for the state legislature by the Republicans. Trotter opposed the governor on the grounds that Guild had approved of giving state funds to Jamestown, Virginia, for the town's segregated tricentennial exposition. In 1907 Morgan excluded Trotter from the planning of a Niagara fundraising event in Boston. The Niagara Executive Committee sided with Trotter and voted to remove Morgan from his position as president of the Massachusetts branch. Du Bois then interceded and convinced the executive committee to retain Morgan. A subsequent split developed between Du Bois and Trotter over another Boston event in which Morgan was involved, leading to the virtual disintegration of the Niagara Movement by 1909.

In 1910 Morgan and Du Bois joined the newly formed NATIONAL ASSOCIATION FOR THE ADVANCEMENT OF COLORED PEOPLE (NAACP). From 1912 to 1914 Morgan served on the executive committee of the Boston branch of the NAACP. In the last years of his life he continued his law practice in Cambridge and remained active in local civil rights work. He was a leading organizer of the campaigns to stop the showing of the film *The Birth of a Nation* in Boston in 1915 and 1921. Morgan died in Cambridge.

Bibliography

Fox, Stephen R. *The Guardian of Boston: William Monroe Trotter.* 1970.

Lewis, David Levering. *W. E. B. Du Bois: Biography of a Race, 1868–1919.* 1993.

Obituary, *Boston Globe,* June 3, 1929.

Obituary, *New York Age,* June 8, 1929.

Rudwick, Elliott M. *W. E. B. Du Bois: Propagandist of the Negro Protest.* 1969.

From *American National Biography.* John A. Garraty and Mark C. Carnes, eds. Oxford University Press, 1999. Reprinted by permission of the American Council of Learned Societies.

Thaddeus Russell

Morgan, Garrett Augustus

1875–1963

Inventor and community leader who invented the gas mask and the automatic traffic signal.

Born in Paris, Kentucky, Garrett Augustus Morgan moved to Cincinnati, Ohio, at the age of fourteen and became a handyman. In 1895 he moved to Cleveland where he worked as a sewing machine repairman. In Cleveland, Morgan developed several successful enterprises: a sewing machine repair service in 1907, a tailor shop in 1909, and a hair-straightening company in 1913. The most important of his various inventions was a "breathing device" that served as the prototype for the modern gas mask. In 1914 the National Safety Device Company awarded the Morgan Safety Hood First Grand Prize.

On July 25, 1916, Morgan himself demonstrated the use of his invention by wearing it as he, along with others, rescued twenty-four trapped workers from a smoke-filled tunnel beneath Lake Erie. The city of Cleveland awarded Morgan a gold medal for his heroism, which also led to a contract from the U.S. Navy to develop his hood for combat use. It was used in World War I and by fire departments throughout the country, although some canceled their orders when they discovered the inventor was black.

In 1922 Morgan patented the three-way automatic traffic signal. Before this time, traffic signals had no yellow caution light. Morgan's signal gave drivers warning to slow down before a red stop light. Noting the marked improvement in traffic safety, the General Electric Company bought the rights to his invention in 1923 for $40,000 and developed today's standard three-way traffic light.

In addition to his work on safety devices, Morgan also was involved in civil rights work. He published from 1920 to 1923 the African American newspaper *Cleveland Call* and was a long-standing member of the Cleveland branch of the NATIONAL ASSOCIATION FOR THE ADVANCEMENT OF COLORED PEOPLE (NAACP).

Morgan, Sister Gertrude

1900–1980

American artist and preacher whose religious folk art and colorful personality made an invaluable contribution to New Orleans' street culture.

Born in Lafayette, Alabama, Sister Gertrude Morgan became an evangelist and moved to NEW ORLEANS, LOUISIANA, in 1939. She took the title "Sister" in the 1950s when, with two other street missionaries, she founded a church and an orphanage.

Morgan began painting in 1956, concentrating primarily on religious visions and biblical scenes. She believed that she was mystically married to Jesus Christ, which she symbolized by dressing entirely in white. Her paintings frequently depicted her with Jesus as bride and groom, often with herself in black before and in white after the marriage. As a street preacher, Morgan eschewed the formal art world, preferring to make folk art with any material at hand, including Styrofoam, cardboard, lamp shades, and jelly jars. Her work frequently includes calligraphy, which communicates a spiritual message or a biblical verse. All her inspiration, she felt, came from God, saying: "He moves my hand. Do you think I would ever know how to do a picture like this by myself?"

Among her most famous works is a series of illustrated scenes from the Book of Revelations, which she called "charters." She also made fans that she distributed during her prayer meetings. In 1971 her original prayer compositions were set to music and were released as an album, *Let's Make a Record*.

Bibliography

Livingston, Jane. *Black Folk Art in America, 1930–1980*. Corcoran Gallery of Art, 1982.

Morganfield, McKinley

See Waters, Muddy.

Mormons

American religious group with an ambivalent history regarding people of African descent.

The recent rapid growth of the Church of Jesus Christ of Latter-day Saints, commonly known Mormons, among the black populations of Africa, the Caribbean, and BRAZIL has reversed a long-standing trend within the church. Mormons traditionally have refused to ordain people of African descent to the priesthood—a status conferred on all adult males. Indeed, when Mormon missionaries tried to settle in NIGERIA in the 1960s—in itself a radical departure from the usual practice of avoiding missionary work in predominantly black communities—they were denied residency visas by the Nigerian government because of their discriminatory policies.

Founded in 1830, the Mormon Church adopted an explicitly racist doctrine that claimed the skin tones of black people were the sign of a curse that God placed on the descendants of Cain and Ham for refusing to follow his will. The Mormons believed that as punishment for this wickedness, people of African descent were condemned to perpetual servitude. In the first decade after the church was organized few blacks joined, and those who did are remembered more for being expelled from the church than for their work within it. While Elijah Abel became a respected elder, others such Black Peter and William McLary were expelled for having revelations that competed with the church leaders.

After the Mormons established themselves in Utah in 1847, church leader Brigham Young further affirmed a ban on black ordination and approved "An Act in Relation to Service" reversing their surprising abolitionist stance and legalizing black slavery—making Utah the only slave state in the American West. After emancipation, the subordinate status of people of African descent within the church remained unchanged, but the Mormon position on race was confused as missionaries ventured into the wide world. A black man thought to be native Hawaiian was ordained by mistake, as were two elders later revealed to have African ancestry.

Only during the CIVIL RIGHTS MOVEMENT did the church become more flexible, primarily through the work of outsiders. Although Mormon elders were resistant, in 1963 the small but active Utah chapter of the NATIONAL ASSOCIATION FOR THE ADVANCEMENT OF COLORED PEOPLE pressured the church into issuing a proclamation in support of civil rights. Two years later, the Mormon-dominated Utah legislature enacted a number of acts favoring nondiscriminatory treatment in housing and employment. In 1971, three black people were allowed positions within the famous Mormon Tabernacle Choir, and the Mormons' Brigham Young University began recruiting black students, although largely for its athletic teams. Although in 1978 the Mormons finally lifted their ban on ordaining black males, the church remains mostly white.

Peter Hudson

Morocco

Hereditary monarchy in the northwest of Africa bounded on the north by the Mediterranean Sea, on the east and southeast by Algeria, on the south by Western Sahara, and on the west by the Atlantic Ocean. The southeastern boundary, in the Sahara, is not precisely defined.

Though it has an area of 453,730 square kilometers (175,186 square miles), Morocco is a nation known by its cities. MARRAKECH, RABAT, FÈS, CASABLANCA, and TANGIER all played crucial roles in the nation's dynastic history, serving as political, economic, and cultural capitals of the kingdoms that mapped what is now Moroccan territory. For centuries these cities also provided vital centers for the commerce in goods and ideas that came from the Islamic world and Christian EUROPE as well as sub-Saharan AFRICA. In the nineteenth century, as European investment poured in, Morocco's cities held perhaps too much appeal: the gravitation of people and resources toward urban areas, especially on the coast, sapped the vitality of the rural agricultural economy on which urban prosperity had always depended. After becoming perilously indebted to Europe, Morocco fell under French control in the early twentieth century. Even as French colonial planners attempted to impose functionality and racial segregation on Morocco's cities, European and American artists, writers, and wanderers were drawn by a vision of the "exotic" beauty of Morocco. Today, Morocco's economy still depends largely on agriculture, but its cities remain dynamic commercial centers as well as destinations for migrants seeking a better life and travelers in search of legends.

History

The BERBER people have lived in the region of present-day Morocco since about the second millennium B.C.E. Although a number of dynasties flourished on Moroccan soil, they were all influenced by Berber political traditions, such as decentralized rule by confederacies. Berber confederacies sometimes helped to direct the course of Moroccan history, as strong Berber rulers mounted religious or political reform movements. At the same time, the Berber identity itself was shaped by migrations and invasions from Romans, Arabs, Europeans, and Africans of the SAHARA.

When the Romans came to northern Africa in the second century B.C.E., they sought control of the region they called Mauretania Tingitana through alliances with Berber confederacies. By the first century B.C.E., Roman cultural influences were felt mostly in the cities, where immigrants from the larger Roman world brought to North Africa the religions of CHRISTIANITY and Judaism. After the Vandals, a Germanic tribe, conquered Roman holdings to the east (in what is now ALGERIA and TUNISIA), the Berbers resumed control of the Moroccan region.

Although Arab raiders had first passed into the coastal plains beyond the Taza Gap of the Atlas Mountains in 683 C.E., most Berbers did not convert to Islam until Musa ibn Nusayr pushed west the border of the region the Arabs called Ifriqiya. Morocco then fell under political and religious leadership of the Umayyad dynasty, which was based in Damascus. As the Berbers converted to Islam and intermarried with Arabs, they became an important military force for Islamic incursions into southern SPAIN.

IDRIS was one of the strongest Berber rulers, bringing the region under definitive Islamic rule. According to one legend, he founded twin Arab and Berber cities at Fès; another legend credits Idris with founding one city and his son, Idris II, with founding its twin. With the opening of al Qarawîyîn University in 859, the city of Fès flourished as a center for learning, attracting Muslims from southern Spain and Ifriquiya. Some historians credit the Idris dynasty with creating around Fès the first Moroccan state, but it did not control the entire area comprising modern-day Morocco: some territory remained under the control of Umayyad emirs in southern Spain or the Fatimid empire in eastern Ifriquiya, and several Berber confederacies maintained autonomous rule in neighboring territories. During the ninth century, Idris's kingdom fragmented as Idris II followed the Berber tradition of succession, dividing the kingdom among seven sons rather than passing it on whole.

Two hundred years later, a religious reformation generated another empire and metropolis. The ALMORAVIDS began as a confederacy of religious warriors, Berbers who founded a brotherhood in secluded fortified retreats. They secured their economic prosperity by exerting control over portions of the trans-Saharan trade routes. In 1062 the Almoravids founded the city of Marrakech as their capital, and by the end of the century they had pushed the borders of their empire east to ALGIERS, south to the SENEGAL RIVER, and north to the Ebro River in Spain.

During the next century, however, the Almoravids' political power waned. In 1146 the ALMOHADS massacred the inhabitants of Marrakech and seized control of the region. Although the Almohads ruled through a centralized Islamic theocracy, they incorporated Berber traditions of rule, such as representative government and tribal councils. They also sponsored an intellectual renaissance, and even after the Almohads moved their throne to Andalusian Spain, philosophers and scientists such as Ibn Bajja (Avempace), Ibn Tufayl, Ibn Rushd (AVERROËS), and the great explorer IBN BATTUTAH came to live in Morocco. At the same time that Morocco's cities became centers of Islamic scholarship, the face of the countryside was also changing as the Hilalian, originally Bedouin Arabs, settled the Maghreb, bringing with them Arabic culture and language.

In 1212 the Almohads were defeated on European soil by the Spanish, who were engaged in a Christian reconquest of Spain, and by the Marinids, a dynasty rising from the Zenata Berber confederacy in northwestern Africa. For fifty years the region was engaged in war, in part over the trans-Saharan gold and salt trades with the western SUDAN. The Spanish and Portuguese took advantage of the instability to capture coastal enclaves such as Tétouan and Ceuta, which were seen as key locations to the reconquest of Granada. A branch of the Marinids, the Wattasids, held onto Tangier, and as when Granada fell in 1492, they received thousands of fleeing Spanish Muslims and Jews.

This period marked the rise of the mystical MARABOUT tradition. Begun as a philosophic tradition perpetuated by wandering Sufi mystics, the marabouts gained a populist foothold in Morocco during the period of Marinid decline. During the fifteenth and sixteenth centuries, these "men of the soil" became the political leaders of small republics in Morocco.

In the late sixteenth century, another power rose in the south and became a major trade empire along the trans-Saharan trade route. The Sa'dians, originally Arab nomads, took Marrakech and Fès, defeating the Wattasids as they waged a holy war against Christians. Once established, the Sa'dians resisted the incursions of both the Ottomans, who held North Africa to the east, and the Portuguese. In 1591 one of the strongest Sa'dian rulers, Ahmed al-Mansur (1578–1603) conquered a portion of the gold-rich SONGHAI empire, including Gao and TOMBOUCTOU. Although after the initial looting Ahmed al-Mansur did not find as much gold as he had anticipated, he nevertheless took Songhai captives for his army. Moroccan rule in the Sahara never went uncontested, but Ahmed al-Mansur's leadership unified Morocco as a political entity. With wealth acquired in military campaigns, Ahmed al-Mansur sponsored a golden age of cultural revival.

For a short period after the death of Ahmed al-Mansur, the state was divided under the rule of rival sultanates until Mawlay al-Rashid and his successor Mawlay Isma'il founded the Alawid dynasty. They raised their grand palace in Meknès and filled the ranks of the 150,000-strong professional army with slaves captured in the western Sudan as well as Berber, European, and Turkish mercenaries. Although confederacies beyond the Atlas mountains paid tribute, the Alawids directly controlled and taxed only the coastal areas near Fès and Marrakesh.

After the death of Mawlay Isma'il in 1727, political control was wielded by the elite personal guard of his former army through a series of puppet sultans. Beginning in the early nineteenth century, a new European influence spread in Morocco: speculation and investment. FRANCE, GREAT BRITAIN, GERMANY, and Spain—nations whose influences were previously contained—benefited from a series of trade agreements with Morocco. France became Morocco's major creditor; Great Britain built railroads; and Germany acquired the largest amount of foreign-held property. Spain, meanwhile, held several coastal regions, including Ceuta, which it had acquired from the Portuguese in 1580, and a portion of western Sahara that had been placed under Spanish protectorate in 1884. Relations with Europe were often tense. After France invaded neighboring Algeria in 1830, resistance leader ABD AL-QADIR used Morocco as a base for anticolonial activities, prompting skirmishes on the border and, finally, French bombardment of Tangier and Essaouira. The sultan clashed with Spain over the borders of Ceuta, and following a threat of war, Morocco was forced to cede the enclave of Ifni.

Morocco's internal economy was transformed at this time. As agricultural exports to Europe boomed during the AMERICAN CIVIL WAR, Morocco increased European imports such as textiles and leather, displacing the traditional markets for goods produced locally. When European demand for grain declined, a trade imbalance developed, and Morocco's rural economy stagnated. Migrants flocked to the port cities looking for work, thus further undermining the once-dynamic relationship between the cities, with their craft industries, and the rural areas, which had provided raw materials as well as markets for urban goods. Meanwhile, a small, elite Moroccan population benefited from trade with the Europeans and emerged as a powerful bourgeois class.

As Morocco's economy increasingly fell under foreign control, Sultan Mawlay Hassan I took steps to maintain sovereignty. He reorganized the Moroccan army, enacted a series of modernizing reforms, and even secured European guarantees for Morocco's independence at the Madrid Conference of 1880. His son and successor Abd al-Aziz attempted to Europeanize the court and introduced an unpopular land taxation. But the monarchy fragmented in the face of regional rebellions, rival court systems, and popular discontent. European creditors stepped in to enact a series of trade agreements that, among other stipulations, allowed foreigners to hold property and exempted them from local taxes.

Fortresses, or casbahs, made from earthern bricks cover a hillside in the old town of Ait Benhaddou. *CORBIS*

Morocco

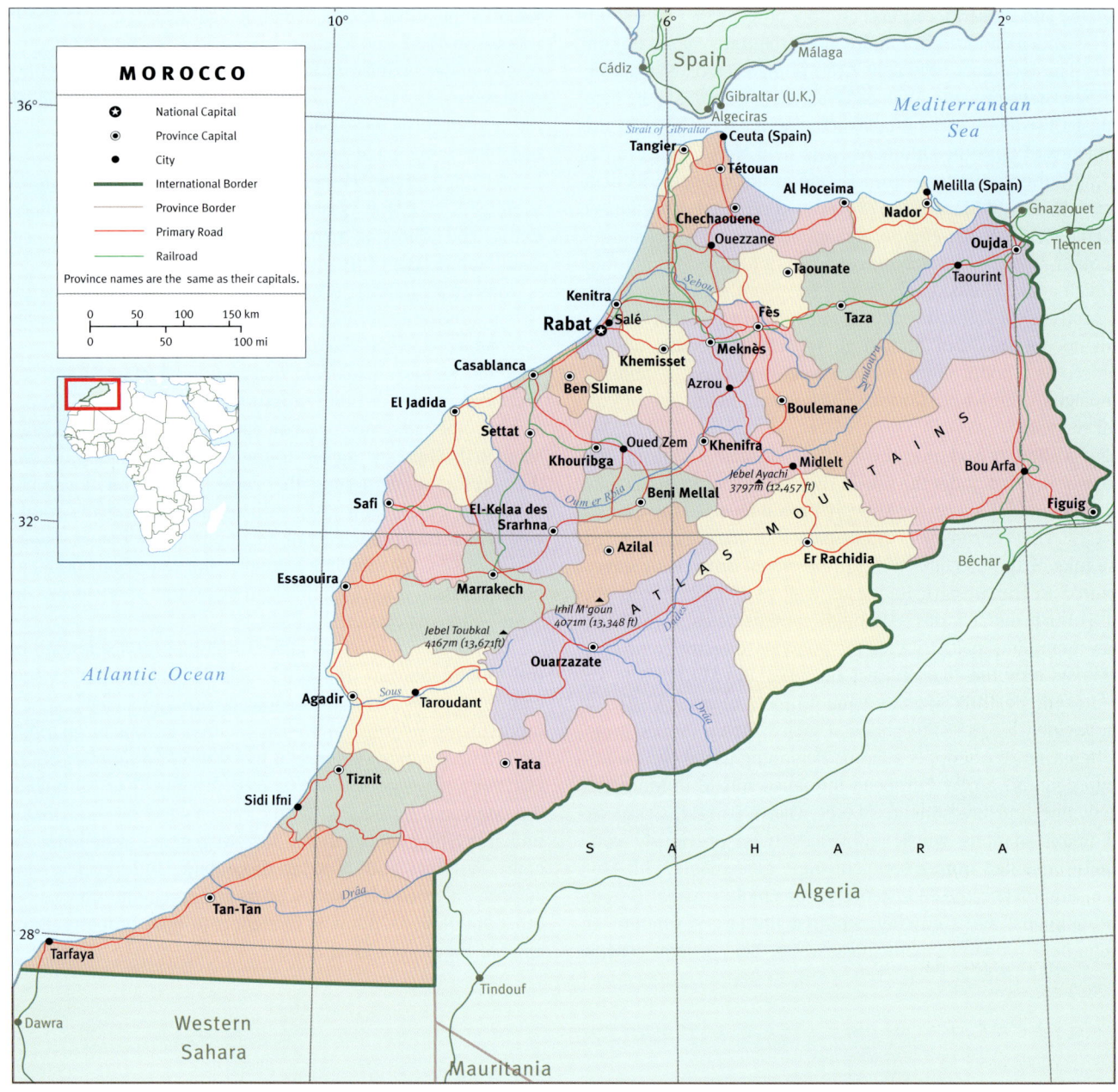

France moved to occupy Morocco in 1904, after ceding its claims on EGYPT to Britain, its claims on LIBYA to Italy, and granting some Moroccan territory to Spain. The Germans, ignored in this divvying up of North Africa, sought to undermine French authority by encouraging nationalist resistance, which nearly led to war in 1904 and again in 1911. After negotiations, the Germans agreed to a French protectorate in Morocco. With little alternative, the sultan of Morocco acquiesced, signing the Treaty of Fès in 1912.

French Rule and Moroccan Resistance

The treaty gave France control of Morocco's foreign relations, police powers, and finances. Although it stripped the sultan of most of his powers, it did grant him the right to veto protectorate legislation, a right that would become critical during the nationalist struggle. The treaty left about a tenth of the country under Spanish control, including parts of present-day WESTERN SAHARA, and granted Tangier special status as an international zone. Some parts of the south were also left under semi-independent Berber control, but France moved quickly to suppress dissident groups, particularly marabout rulers in the Atlas Mountains.

Industrialization and modernization in early twentieth-century Morocco brought more railroads, electricity, and irrigation. Most of these benefits were enjoyed primarily by the protectorate's European population, who appropriated the richest agricultural land and established elite, European-only neigh-

Morocco (At a Glance)

OFFICIAL NAME: Kingdom of Morocco

AREA: 446,550 sq km (about 172,413 sq mi); the southeastern boundary, in the Sahara, is contested; within Morocco are the Spanish exclaves of Ceuta and Melilla.

LOCATION: Northern Africa; borders the Mediterranean Sea, Algeria, Western Sahara, and the Atlantic Ocean

CAPITAL: Rabat (population 1,636,600; 2003 estimate)

OTHER MAJOR CITIES: Casablanca (3,397,000), the country's largest city and main seaport; Marrakech (755,200) and Fès (941,800), both important trade centers; and Tangier (604,000), a seaport on a bay of the Strait of Gibraltar (2003 estimates)

POPULATION: 31,689,265 (2003 estimate)

POPULATION DENSITY: 71 persons per sq km (about 181 persons per sq mi); the population has almost an equal number of urban and rural dwellers. Most Moroccans inhabit the Atlantic coastal plain.

POPULATION BELOW AGE 15: 33.2 percent (male 5,360,666; female 5,162,168; 2003 estimates)

POPULATION GROWTH RATE: 1.64 percent (2003 estimate)

TOTAL FERTILITY RATE: 2.89 children born per woman (2003 estimate)

LIFE EXPECTANCY AT BIRTH: Total population: 70.04 years (male 67.77 years; female 72.41 years; 2003 estimates)

INFANT MORTALITY RATE: 44.87 deaths per 1,000 live births (2003 estimate)

LITERACY RATE (AGE 15 AND OVER WHO CAN READ AND WRITE): Total population: 51.7 percent (male 64.1 percent; female 39.4 percent; 2003 estimates)

EDUCATION: Schooling is compulsory in Morocco for children between ages 7 and 13. In 2000 primary schools enrolled 78 percent of eligible children, but significantly fewer girls than boys attend classes, and only about 30 percent of secondary-school-age Moroccans actually attend secondary school. Arabic is the main language of instruction, and French is also used in secondary schools. Traditional higher education is centered in Fès at al Qarawîyîn University, and modern higher education is offered at Mohammed V University, Mohammed Ben Abdellah University, Cadi Ayyad University, Hassan II University, and Mohammed I University.

LANGUAGES: Arabic is the official language. Berber languages, French, and Spanish are also spoken.

ETHNIC GROUPS: Arab-Berber, 99.1 percent; European (mostly French), 0.7 percent; Jewish, 0.2 percent

RELIGIONS: Islam is the established state religion of Morocco. Almost the entire population is Sunni Muslim. The monarch is the supreme Muslim authority in the country. About 1 percent of the population is Christian, and less than 0.2 percent is Jewish.

CLIMATE: Along the Mediterranean, Morocco has a subtropical climate, tempered by oceanic influences that give the coastal cities moderate temperatures averaging about 16.4°C (61.5°F) in January and 22.5°C (72.5°F) in August. Toward the interior, the mean temperature is 10°C (50°F) in January and 26.9°C (80.5°F) in August. At high altitudes temperatures of less than −17.8°C (0°F) are not uncommon. Rain falls mainly during the winter months, with precipitation heaviest in the northwest: about 955 mm (about 37.5 in) in Tangier and less than 102 mm (4 in) in the Sahara.

LAND, PLANTS, AND ANIMALS: Morocco has an area of highlands, called Er Rif, that parallels the Mediterranean coast. The Atlas Mountains extend across the country in a southwestern to northeastern direction, while a region of broad coastal plains stretches along the Atlantic Ocean. South of the Atlas Mountains, plains and valleys merge with the Sahara along the southeastern borders of the country. Morocco has many rivers, including the Moulouya and the Sebou.

The mountainous regions of Morocco contain extensive forests, including large stands of cork oak, evergreen oak, juniper, cedar, fir, and pine. Moroccan wildlife includes the gazelle, wild boar, panther, baboon, wild goat, fox, rabbit, otter, squirrel, and horned viper.

NATURAL RESOURCES: Morocco's resources are primarily agricultural, but mineral resources are also significant. Among the latter the most important is phosphate rock; other minerals include coal, iron, lead, manganese, petroleum, silver, tin, and zinc. Cork is a major forest product of Morocco.

CURRENCY: The Moroccan dirham

GROSS DOMESTIC PRODUCT (GDP): $115 billion (2002 estimate)

GDP PER CAPITA: $3,900 (2002 estimate)

GDP REAL GROWTH RATE: 3.2 percent (2002 estimate)

PRIMARY ECONOMIC ACTIVITIES: Morocco is primarily an agricultural country but is also a leading producer of phosphate rock.

PRIMARY CROPS: The principal crops of Morocco are cereals, particularly wheat and barley, plus potatoes, tomatoes, melons, olives, grapes, pulses, dates, sugarcane, and sugar beets. Livestock includes sheep, goats, and cattle; fishing yields pilchard, tuna, mackerel, anchovies, and shellfish.

INDUSTRIES: Phosphate rock mining and processing, food processing, leather goods, textiles, construction, and tourism

PRIMARY EXPORTS: Food and beverages, semiprocessed goods, consumer goods, and phosphates

PRIMARY IMPORTS: Capital goods, semiprocessed goods, raw materials, fuel and lubricants, food and beverages, and consumer goods

PRIMARY TRADE PARTNERS: European Union, United States, Libya, India, and Saudi Arabia

GOVERNMENT: Morocco is a hereditary monarchy governed by a king, currently Mohammed VI, who appoints the prime minister, currently Driss Jettou, and cabinet. A 1996 ammendment to Morocco's 1972 constitution created a bicameral legislature consisting of a 270-member upper house, the Chamber of Counselors, and a 325-member lower house, the Chamber of Representatives. The major political parties are the Istiqlal (Independence Party), the Socialist Union of Popular Forces, the National Rally of Independents, and the Constitutional Union. The king has the power to call for a reconsideration of legislative measures and to dissolve the legislature. Morocco's provinces are administered by governors who are appointed by the king. Each province is divided into *cercles,* which are subdivided into *circonscriptions* (constituencies).

Marian Aguiar

borhoods in the cities and towns, including the commercial port of Casablanca. Protectorate administration was based in Rabat.

Abd el-Krim led the first major anticolonial revolt in the Spanish-held northern coastal area, where he founded the RIF REPUBLIC. In the French territory, two separate movements merged by 1930: the Salafiya religious reform movement and the secret reformist organizations led by French-educated students in Rabat and Fès. Protonationalists harnessed the popular resentment provoked by French attempts to divide Berbers and Arabs and in 1934 founded the reformist Comité d'Action Marocaine (CAM; Moroccan Action Committee). Three years later, Moroccans in Meknès rioted when town water was diverted to irrigate settler land. The French responded swiftly, exiling nationalist leader Muhammad 'Allal al-Fasi.

A berber bride wears a ceremonial robe and jewelry at an engagement festival in Imilchil, Morocco. *CORBIS/Nik Wheeler*

Internal tension was diverted during World War II (1939–1945), when more than 40,000 Moroccans served in the French army. The sultan, who called for full support for the French at the start of the war, refused to approve the subsequent French Vichy government's anti-Jewish measures. In 1942 American troops occupied the country, using it as a supply base for the Allied forces.

In 1944 the Hizb al-Istiqlal (Independence Party), known as Istiqlal, drafted a manifesto of independence. The French responded by arresting the leaders on accusations of Nazi collaboration. After French troops fired on crowds demonstrating in Fès, the French government, hoping to appease the outraged Moroccan populace, gave Sultan Sidi Muhammad permission to make his first visit to the Spanish Zone and Tangier. The sultan took the opportunity of a public appearance in Tangier to emphasize Morocco's ties to the rest of the Arab world rather than to France. Later, the sultan used his veto power to halt the resident general's decrees that granted France more power. French troops, with the help of some Berber opposition factions, surrounded Fès and Rabat in 1951, forcing the sultan into temporary submission. Two years later they again surrounded Rabat, this time forcing the sultan out of office.

Opposition to French rule increased rapidly during the early 1950s, especially after a trade union protest in Casablanca over the allegedly French-planned assassination of a union leader led to hundreds of arrests in 1952. By this time, Istiqlal had more than 80,000 members and several hundred thousand sympathizers, including many from Berber communities. The French government, meanwhile, was increasingly preoccupied with civil unrest in colonial Algeria.

The 1955 French-Moroccan Agreement gave Morocco independence from the French, although the Spanish areas were ceded later—Tarfaya in 1958 and Ifni in 1969. In March 1956 the sultan became the king of independent Morocco, presiding over an appointed legislature, the Consultative Assembly.

Independent Morocco

Four years later, the political alliance that won independence fragmented, as Istiqlal broke into conservative and socialist factions. Hassan II ascended to the throne amid growing antimonarchist sentiment and dissolved Parliament. After two un-

Dressed in traditional garments, a Berber bridegroom awaits his wedding. CORBIS/Robert van der Hilst

successful military coups against him, Hassan II revived popular support through his aggressive tactics to claim contested territories.

The territories at stake included coastal enclaves and the SPANISH SAHARA. Although it had ceded the enclaves of Tarfaya and Ifni following Morocco's independence, Spain had held onto Ceuta and Melilla as well as phosphate-rich territory in the Sahara. Until 1970 Hassan II refused to recognize MAURITANIA, claiming the iron-ore rich region as a sphere of influence. He waged a war against Spain for Western Sahara, and in 1975, after the United Nations declared that the territory should be self-determined, he organized the Green March that sent 350,000 unarmed people across the border to occupy the land and effectively claim it for Morocco. But even after Spain ceded Spanish Sahara to a joint Moroccan-Mauritanian administration the next year, King Hassan was still faced with the liberation group POLISARIO FRONT, who waged a guerrilla campaign for an independent state, the SAHRAWI Arab Democratic Republic. The leaders of the independence movement won the support of Algeria, Libya, and later, a number of foreign governments.

In the early 1980s the Kingdom of Morocco undertook a program of structural adjustment in response to the International Monetary Fund's demands to improve the balance of foreign debt. As a result, basic food prices skyrocketed, workers declared a general strike, and a series of riots swept through the cities of Morocco, killing an estimated 200 people and injuring 5,000 others. Human rights observers both inside and outside of Morocco accused King Hassan at this time and later of using brutal methods, such as torture and detention without trial, to quash antimonarchist sentiment from socialist and Islamist groups as well as dissent from separatist Shrawi, or Western Sahara, groups. On this latter issue, the United Nations (UN) has planned for more than a decade to hold a referendum for self-determination for Western Sahara, which is currently occupied by UN peacekeeping forces. Morocco continues to assert its claim to the area.

Morocco approved a new constitution in 1992 and held a parliamentary election the following year. Despite the initial victory of the left-wing Socialist Union of Populist Forces, accusations of election fraud arose, and loyalist parties ultimately carried the day. King Hassan died in 1999, and his son, Crown Prince Sidi Mohammed (now King Mohammed VI), replaced him as the leader of one of the world's oldest monarchies. In the late 1990s Morocco was once again attracting foreign investment in areas such as phosphate mining, export agriculture, and tourism. However, a decline in agricultural production accompanied droughts and internal unrest over the issue of the Western Sahara. Beneficial rainfalls led to good harvests and economic growth in 2001 and 2002. As it continues to develop, Morocco faces the formidable long-term challenges of servicing its external debt and lowering its unemployment rate.

See also Gold Trade; Islam in Africa; Judaism in North Africa; Nationalism in Africa; North Africa, Roman Rule of; Roman Africa; An Interpretation; Salt Trade; Structural Adjustment in Africa; Sufism; United Nations in Africa; Urbanism and Urbanization in Africa.

Bibliography

Abu-Lughod, Janet L. *Rabat: Urban Apartheid in Morocco.* Princeton University Press, 1980.
Findlay, A. M. *Morocco.* Clio Press, 1994.
Porch, Douglas. *The Conquest of Morocco.* Knopf, 1983.
Zartman, I. William, ed. *The Political Economy of Morocco.* Praeger, 1987.

Marian Aguiar

Morris, Robert

1823–1882

African American lawyer.

Robert Morris was born in Salem, Massachusetts, the son of York Morris, a waiter, and Nancy Morris, both free blacks. He came of age at a time of strident antiblack prejudice. Although Massachusetts had abolished slavery and had indeed even proclaimed that blacks and whites were equal before the law, vigorous social and economic discrimination ensured that few blacks could aspire to any but the most menial of occupations.

Morris was educated in the common schools of Salem. At the age of fifteen he left his parents' household to become the servant of Ellis Gray Loring, a BOSTON attorney and abolitionist. Loring quickly became impressed with young Morris and allowed him to read his law books in his spare time. Soon Morris became Loring's law clerk, formally studying law through apprenticeship, the principal route to the legal profession in nineteenth-century America.

Admitted to the (Massachusetts) Suffolk County bar in February 1847, Morris quickly began a busy practice. His first case, in which he successfully represented a black man in a labor dispute, was the first occasion in which a black lawyer represented a client in an American court. That action ensured Morris's fame and brought him to the attention of abolitionists and CIVIL RIGHTS activists in antebellum Boston as well as to the city's black community.

Morris's first effort at civil rights litigation would prove to have a long-reaching effect on the jurisprudence of race in the United States. At the request of black activist Benjamin Roberts, Morris brought suit against the Boston School Committee for requiring that Roberts's daughter attend the segregated "colored school" instead of the common school closer to her home, which was reserved for white students. Morris lost the case at the 1848 trial and later joined Charles Sumner in appealing it to the Massachusetts Supreme Judicial Court. Although the claim brought by Morris and Sumner that segregation was inherently stigmatizing and thus violated the free and equal provision of the Massachusetts Constitution was rejected in an opinion written in 1849 by Chief Justice Lemuel Shaw, the argument would nonetheless have an important life in American jurisprudence. The equation of legal segregation with stigmatization would later be considered and rejected by the U.S. Supreme Court in *Plessy v. Ferguson*. That claim would finally be adopted by the Court in the school desegregation case *Brown v. Board of Education* decided in 1954, more than a century after the argument was first made by Morris and Sumner.

Like many in Boston's antebellum black community, Morris actively opposed the federal Fugitive Slave Act of 1851. Involved in many of the famous fugitive slave cases of the era, including the cases of ANTHONY BURNS and Thomas Sims, Morris was best known in this regard for aiding one fugitive slave, Frederick Wilkens—also known as "Shadrack." Morris represented Wilkens in court and later aided his escape from the courtroom. For this Morris and other antislavery activists, including Charles Sumner and Richard Henry Dana, were tried and acquitted on criminal charges.

In addition to his prominence as a civil rights activist, Morris had a strong reputation as a trial attorney. His clientele was evenly divided between blacks and whites, the latter group mainly consisting of poor Irish immigrants. He was able to build up a fairly lucrative legal practice. Due to his prominence, he was appointed as a magistrate in Massachusetts in 1852, one of the earliest judicial appointments of a black man, albeit a minor appointment, in the United States. In 1866 Morris unsuccessfully ran for mayor of Chelsea, Massachusetts.

Morris had married Catherine Mason in 1844, and the couple had one child, Robert Morris Jr. Morris sent his son to FRANCE and England to be educated, partly to shield him from the social prejudices of the day. His son was admitted to the Massachusetts bar in 1874. Morris died in Boston.

Morris, the second American of African descent to be admitted to the practice of law in the United States, had a professional career that spanned some thirty-five years. During that time he was a pioneer civil rights litigator, prominently involved in fugitive slave cases, efforts to desegregate Boston's public schools, and cases involving discrimination in public accommodations. Morris was also a highly successful trial attorney in a variety of criminal and civil cases.

Bibliography

Baltimore, Roderick T., and Robert F. Williams. "The State Constitutional Roots of the 'Separate but Equal' Doctrine: *Roberts v. City of Boston*." *Rutgers Law Journal* 17 (1986): 537–52.

Hopkins, Pauline E. "Robert Morris." *Colored American Magazine*, September 1901.

Obituary, *Boston Evening Transcript*, December 13, 1882.

Oliver, James, and Lois E. Horton. *Black Bostonians: Family Life and Community Struggle in the Antebellum North*. 1979.

Smith, J. Clay. *Emancipation: The Making of the Black Lawyer, 1844–1944*. 1993.

From *American National Biography*. John A. Garraty and Mark C. Carnes, eds. Oxford University Press, 1999. Reprinted by permission of the American Council of Learned Societies.

Robert J. Cottrol

Morrison, Toni

1931–

African American writer; one of the most celebrated twentieth-century American writers, and the first black woman and first African American to receive the Nobel Prize in Literature.

> I'm interested in how men are educated, how women relate to each other, how we are able to love, how we balance political and personal forces, who survives in certain situations and who doesn't and, specifically, how these and other universal issues relate to African Americans. The search for love and identity runs through most everything I write.

In this comment from a 1992 interview, Toni Morrison gives one description of the complex range of issues she explores in her work. Morrison is widely recognized as one of the most influential American writers, and her novels are taught in literature, history, women's studies, and African American studies courses across the United States and around the world. She has received numerous honorary degrees, prizes, and awards, including the Nobel Prize in Literature. Above all, Morrison is known for her rich, lyrical prose, which fuses the rhythms and imagery of African American speech and music with other literary influences to create a discourse of its own. In a 1977 interview, she said that it "seemed to [her] Black people's grace has been what they do with language." Morrison is unparalleled in her ability to capture that grace on the page.

Toni Morrison was born Chloe Anthony Wofford in Lorain, Ohio, a small, racially mixed steel town. Her grandparents were

A jubilant Toni Morrison reacts to the news that she has been awarded the 1993 Nobel Prize for Literature. *Hoffman Danny/Corbis Sygma*

all originally from the South, and Morrison credits her family with giving her a rich foundation in the language and rhythms of African American culture. She has said she was born into a family of storytellers and considers her father's folktales and her mother's singing as examples of the uniquely black language she absorbed as a child. After graduating with honors from Lorain public schools, Morrison received a bachelor's degree from HOWARD UNIVERSITY in 1953. In 1955 she earned a master's degree in English from Cornell University, where she wrote her thesis on alienation in the works of William Faulkner and Virginia Woolf. She taught at Texas Southern University for two years before accepting a teaching position at Howard.

While teaching at Howard, she married Jamaican architect Harold Morrison and gave birth to two sons. She later said it was the "powerlessness" she felt during her years as a wife and a mother of small children that led her to begin writing. In 1964 Morrison and her husband divorced, and she took a job in Syracuse, New York, as a textbook editor for Random House. In 1968 she moved to Random House's trade division in Manhattan, becoming their first black woman senior editor. There, she focused on black authors and edited books by ANGELA DAVIS, TONI CADE BAMBARA, GAYL JONES, and MUHAMMAD ALI. Morrison also continued writing her own fiction at night, after her sons were asleep, and in 1970 published her first novel, *The Bluest Eye*.

The Bluest Eye tells the story of a nine-year-old black girl in a 1940s Ohio town who prays for blue eyes, thinking that will stop the emotional, physical, and sexual abuse she receives from her peers and the adults around her. Morrison became part of a new generation of black women writers, including Jones, Bambara, and ALICE WALKER, who were interested in telling black women's stories, and stories set wholly within the black community. *The Bluest Eye* received critical praise, and Morrison became sought-after for book reviews and articles on black literature and culture. Her next novel, *Sula* (1973), was nominated for the 1975 National Book Award in fiction. Set in another Ohio town, *Sula* is a novel about the classic forces of good and evil, placed within the context of a friendship between two black women and the community that surrounds them. Morrison truly rose to prominence as a novelist, however, with her third book, *Song of Solomon* (1977).

Like both of her earlier novels, *Song of Solomon* is set mainly in a Midwestern town, one of Morrison's innovations in African American fiction, which is traditionally set in either the urban North or the rural South. But unlike the others, *Song of Solomon*'s main character is male, and the book has been described as incorporating more traditionally Western and male themes of flight, journey, and violence into its narrative of a particular black community and a particular black family. *Song of Solomon* was chosen a Book-of-the-Month Club selection, the first novel by a black author to be so honored since *Native Son* (1940), by RICHARD WRIGHT. It also won Morrison the National Book Critics Circle Award and appointment to the American Academy of Arts and Letters and the National Council of the Arts. Twenty years after its publication, the book was again featured as a national book club selection—this time, for the popular television feature *Oprah's Book Club* on *The Oprah Winfrey Show*.

Morrison's next novel, *Tar Baby* (1981), received similar acclaim. It was the first of her novels to be set primarily outside of the United States (on a Caribbean island), and in the historical present, and to feature several white main characters. *Tar Baby* was also a best seller. But Morrison's fifth novel, *Beloved* (1987), is her most celebrated work to date. *Beloved* is loosely based on a news clipping that Morrison read years earlier while editing a book on black history. The clipping told the true story of Margaret Garner, a slave who ran away with her four children, and when captured, tried to slit their throats—succeeding with one child—rather than see them returned to slavery. In its fullness, *Beloved* becomes a novel about slavery, about history, about community, about possession—and ultimately, about love. *Beloved* was another national best seller, was internationally reviewed, and won the Pulitzer Prize for fiction in 1988.

Morrison has said that *Beloved* is the first novel in a trilogy about love. The second novel in that trilogy, *Jazz*, was published in 1992. Set in New York during the HARLEM RENAISSANCE, the novel pieces together the story of a love triangle in a narrative form that imitates the rhythms of JAZZ music. The third novel, *Paradise,* was published in 1998. It portrays the lives of the townspeople of Ruby, Oklahoma, who believe their community is "the one all-black town worth the pain," and the women who inhabit the abandoned convent just outside town, whom the townspeople wish to exclude from their Eden. In 1993 Morrison received the Nobel Prize in Literature for her six novels to that date. She was the first African American and the first black woman of any nationality ever to receive that prize.

Morrison has taught at several universities and in 1989 was named the Robert F. Goheen Professor in the Council of the Humanities at Princeton University. Her reputation as one of the most influential American writers rests not only on her fiction but also on her work as a literary and cultural critic. Her essays and speeches have been included in numerous journals and books, and in 1992 she published her first volume of literary criticism, *Playing in the Dark: Whiteness and the Literary Imagination*. That same year she also edited *Race-ing Justice, En-Gendering Power*, a collection of essays on the HILL-THOMAS HEARINGS. In 1996 she coedited a second essay collection, *Birth of a Nation'hood: Gaze, Script, and Spectacle in the O. J. Simpson Case*, about the former professional athlete who was tried for murder in a highly publicized case. Morrison has also written a play, *Dreaming Emmett*, first produced in New York in 1986. In 2002 she and her son Slade Morrison, along with illustrator Pascal Lemaitre, published the children's book *The Book of Mean People*, based on Aesop's fables. A year later the trio continued their collaboration with *Who's Got Game?: The Ant or the Grasshopper?* and *The Lion or the Mouse?* In 2003 Morrison published her eighth novel, *Love*. She is currently the Andrew D. White Professor-at-Large at Cornell University.

Through all of her works Morrison has had a tremendous impact on the American and the African American literary landscapes. Her novels are widely accessible to readers and internationally praised for the quality of their prose, yet they remain dedicated to exploring nuances of African American culture and language. In *Black Women Writers*, a 1984 book by poet Mari Evans, Morrison states that to her the best art "is unquestionably political and irrevocably beautiful at the same time," a standard many readers believe she has met in all of her work.

See also Literature, African American; Women Writers, Black, in the United States.

Bibliography

Gates, Henry Louis, Jr., and K. A. Appiah, eds. *Toni Morrison: Critical Perspectives Past and Present*. Amistad, 1993.

Harris, Trudier. *Fiction and Folklore in the Novels of Toni Morrison*. University of Tennessee Press, 1991.

McKay, Nellie. *Critical Essays on Toni Morrison*. G. K. Hall, 1988.

Lisa Clayton Robinson

Morrow, Everett Frederick

1909–

Republican business leader who was the first African American appointed to a White House staff position.

Everett Frederick Morrow was born in Hackensack, New Jersey. He graduated from Bowdoin College in 1930 and then worked as a field secretary for the NATIONAL ASSOCIATION FOR THE ADVANCEMENT OF COLORED PEOPLE (NAACP).

In 1952 Morrow became a consultant to Dwight D. Eisenhower's Republican presidential campaign and in 1955 became the first African American White House staff member when Eisenhower appointed him administrative officer for the Special Projects group, a position with little real responsibility. Morrow tried to use his position to turn Eisenhower's attention to civil rights matters, but he was largely frustrated in these efforts. He later campaigned for Richard Nixon's unsuccessful 1960 election bid. In 1964 Morrow became the first African American to work as a corporate executive for Bank of America.

See also Republican Party.

Morrow, Tracey

See Ice-T.

Morton, Ferdinand Joseph ("Jelly Roll")

1890–1941

Early jazz pianist and composer who, since his death, has risen to the highest tier of critical acclaim for his mastery of the piano.

Jelly Roll Morton was born Ferdinand Joseph La Menthe to fair-skinned Creole parents in NEW ORLEANS, LOUISIANA, and all his life he considered himself more white than black. His father, who left the family when Morton was young, played trombone, as did Morton's stepfather, Ed Morton. Morton received guitar lessons by the age of six but soon abandoned guitar for piano. At the age of twelve he began playing piano in the bordellos of New Orleans's Storyville district, and as a teenager he traveled the Gulf Coast, mingling with famous regional musicians, including RAGTIME pianist Tony Jackson. Morton also received some formal musical training at Saint Joseph Seminary College in Saint Benedict, Louisiana.

Beginning with his trip to the St. Louis World's Fair in 1904, Morton embarked on a decade of itinerant music making that carried him throughout the South and to New York City and CHICAGO, ILLINOIS. Morton played with vaudeville troupes and minstrel shows, supplementing his income with profits from pool hustling, card playing, and pimping. Indeed, his notoriety as a swindler, braggart, and womanizer often preceded his reputation as a musician.

Morton settled in Chicago from around 1911 until 1915, playing music with a small ensemble. He published "Jelly Roll Blues" in 1915, an accomplishment that set him apart from other JAZZ pianists of the time. While his performances evinced high passion and spontaneity, Morton made music with a composer's fastidious mind. Even when fast and improvised, Mor-

Composer and pianist Jelly Roll Morton is shown in 1938 when he traveled to Washington, D.C., to record for Library of Congress archivist Alan Lomax. *AP/Library of Congress*

ton's playing reflected rational, intentional calculations. In 1915 Morton uprooted once more, traveling up and down the West Coast until he resettled in Chicago in 1923.

In Chicago, Morton observed the new and thriving recording industry and decided to cut his own takes. In 1923 and 1924 he recorded as a solo pianist, and from 1926 to 1930 he led the ensemble Red Hot Peppers, which featured legendary players such as clarinetist Johnny Dodds and trombonist EDWARD ("KID") ORY. With this group Morton recorded some of his most famous compositions, including "Kansas City Stomps" and "Smokehouse Blues." Critics often describe Morton's style in these recordings as orchestral; instead of backing the melody with the chords and steady rhythm in the bass, he created one or two lines of counterpoint in which his left hand emulated a trombone for the cornet of his right.

Morton moved to New York in 1928 and began running an all-girl revue that doubled as a prostitution racket. He continued to record, but both the advent of big-band music and the onset of the GREAT DEPRESSION diminished his popularity. Morton moved to WASHINGTON, D.C., in 1935, managed a nightclub, and eventually worked with folklorist Alan Lomax on a set of recordings for the Library of Congress. In the hours of collected footage, Morton expounds upon his playing style and reconstructs a history of jazz. Although many of Morton's observations have historical and musicological value, his arrogance and hyperbole limit the recording's veracity. Morton claims he "invented jazz in 1902," the year he turned twelve.

Morton moved to LOS ANGELES, CALIFORNIA, at the end of his life and died in 1941, with the bulk of his popularity seeming to have passed. Throughout his life Morton had managed his career poorly, often spoiling business relationships with displays of arrogance and pomp. He is now recognized as a musical genius, however, and jazz pianists today cite his direct influence on style, approach, and repertoire.

Bibliography

Lomax, Alan. *Mister Jelly Roll.* University of California Press, 1973.

Eric Bennett

Morúa Delgado, Martín

1856–1910

Afro-Cuban author, journalist, activist, and statesman.

Poverty and racism forced Martín Morúa Delgado, born in HAVANA, CUBA, to a Spanish immigrant father and an ex-slave mother, to leave school at an early age and find work. He managed to educate himself, often by purchasing books with part of his salary. His experiences working in a barrel factory led him to become a labor activist. Besides organizing workers in several Cuban cities, Morúa made speeches and wrote newspaper and magazine articles on workers' rights, thus launching his career as a political leader and a journalist.

In the nineteenth century, paid readers read books aloud to factory workers while they engaged in nonmechanical tasks like rolling cigars. Even before slavery had been abolished, Morúa was the first man of African descent to become a professional reader in CUBA. He also became the first reader of color in NEW YORK, NEW YORK, when he worked in a tobacco factory there years later.

Besides defending workers' rights, Morúa dedicated himself to the struggle for Cuban independence and the abolition of slavery. His labor and political activities displeased the Spanish colonial government that ruled Cuba at the time. He was arrested and held briefly as a political prisoner in 1881. Soon afterward, he left the country.

He continued his political activism as he traveled through PANAMA, MEXICO, JAMAICA, and the United States. He worked as a journalist and learned French, English, and other languages. Part of his exile was spent in New York, where he developed the skill of translating into English.

Upon returning to Cuba in 1890, Morúa deepened his commitment to political struggle through the written word. He soon founded the newspaper *El Tribuno.* (He had already started a journal in MATANZAS, CUBA, in 1879 and a magazine in Key West, Florida, during the 1880s.) He also established the magazine *La Nueva Era* to deal with the new social situation created by the 1886 abolition of slavery. He expressed dissatisfaction with Cuban antislavery novels, especially the most famous one, *Cecilia Valdés* (1882), by Cirilo Villaverde. To stress the need for racial equality, Morúa wrote two novels about slavery and racism: *Sofía* (1891) and *La familia Unzúazu* (1901). He also translated a biography of FRANÇOIS DOMINIQUE TOUSSAINT LOUVERTURE, hero of the HAITIAN REVOLUTION.

In 1898 Morúa joined the Cuban revolutionaries in their war against Spain. Two years later he helped to set up the Cuban Republican Party and was elected to serve as a delegate to the constitutional convention. Morúa was later appointed the founding secretary of the municipality of Palmira. Eventually he became a senator and advanced to the post of president of the senate. In 1909 the president of Cuba appointed him the minister of agriculture, commerce, and labor. As architect and advocate of the Ley Morúa—a law that discouraged the organization of political parties along racial lines—he argued staunchly for integrationism, which caused considerable controversy. Still, Morúa was such a respected citizen and important historical figure that in 1956 Cuba celebrated the centennial of his birth.

See also Colonial Latin America and the Caribbean; Slavery in Latin America and the Caribbean.

Marveta Ryan

Moseley-Braun, Carol

1947–

African American lawyer and public official, first black woman to serve as a United States senator.

Carol Moseley-Braun, the oldest of four children, was born in CHICAGO, ILLINOIS. Her mother, Edna Moseley, was a medical technician, and her father, Joseph Moseley, was a police officer. Reared a Roman Catholic on Chicago's South Side, Moseley-Braun graduated from the University of Illinois at Chicago in 1969 with a B.A. degree in political science, and three years later, she finished a J.D. at the University of Chicago Law School. While in law school, she met and eventually married Michael Braun, also a lawyer. Moseley-Braun gave birth to her only child, Matthew, in 1977, and in 1986 she and her husband divorced.

Moseley-Braun served in the Illinois State Legislature from 1978 to 1987, and she was the first African American to serve as that body's assistant majority leader. In 1992 Moseley-Braun ran for the U.S. Senate against two-term incumbent Alan Dixon, who had voted to confirm the nomination of CLARENCE THOMAS to the Supreme Court. She won the Democratic primary in March 1992 and went on to win the election in November over Republican candidate Richard S. Williamson. Moseley-Braun's victory made her the fourth African American and the first African American woman to serve in the U.S. Senate. Sworn in to the 103rd Congress in January 1993, she was one of six women who served in the U.S. Senate during that session.

Throughout her career, Moseley-Braun commanded attention for her legislative leadership in sponsoring progressive bills on education and for her ability to build successful coalitions. In 1998 she lost her bid for reelection to Republican Peter Fitzgerald. The following year Moseley-Braun was named U.S. ambassador to New Zealand, a position she held until 2001. After returning from her ambassadorial posting, she taught law and political science at DePaul University and Morris Brown College. She also had a business law practice and business consultancy in Chicago. In 2003 Moseley-Braun announced that she was seeking the Democratic Party nomination for president in the 2004 election.

See also Democratic Party; United States Senate, African Americans in the.

Moses, Edwin Corley

1955–

African American hurdler and Olympic athlete.

Edwin Corley Moses, who won two Olympic gold medals and achieved the world record for the most consecutive victories in the history of track and field sports, was born in 1955, in Dayton, Ohio, to Irving and Gladys Moses. His parents were educators, and they encouraged Moses and his two brothers to strive for educational excellence. Moses committed himself to learning from an early age. He was an excellent student at Dayton Fairview High School, where he was named a National Merit Scholar. Although Moses was also active in sports, including basketball, football, and track, he never distinguished himself in high school athletics. Indeed, he was cut from the basketball team and never qualified to compete in Ohio's Track and Field Championships. His strength was academics.

For his academic achievements, Moses received a scholarship from MOREHOUSE COLLEGE, a historically black school in ATLANTA, GEORGIA, known for its high academic standards. Moses majored in physics and engineering. Although he competed on the track team, he spent the first two years at Morehouse directing most of his energy toward his studies. During his junior year, the track coach encouraged him to train for the 1976 Olympics. Inspired, Moses committed himself to track the way he had committed himself to academic achievement. He also used his knowledge of physics—especially friction, energy, and motion—to improve his training and his running technique. His great success was as a hurdler, who must race along a track, jumping barriers called hurdles at regular intervals. Track and field experts claim that much of his success came from developing a stride that many had thought impossible. Hurdlers usually took fourteen or fifteen steps between each hurdle, but Moses took only thirteen. His training breakthroughs produced immediate results. By March of 1976 he had raced in only one 400-meter hurdles event, but his qualifying times were good enough for him to compete in the Summer Olympics in Montreal, Canada.

On the eve of the Olympics, twenty-year-old Edwin Moses was relatively unknown. Unlike his competitors, he had never competed in an international meet, but his limited experience did not hinder him. Moses set a world record of 47.64 seconds, eclipsing the previous mark of 47.82, and defeated the second-place runner by 1.05 seconds, the largest winning margin ever in the Olympic event.

After his success at the Olympics, Moses returned to Morehouse, where he again worked on ways to improve his technique. In 1977 his efforts resulted in a 47.45 world-record performance. But defeat, not victory, set the stage for Moses to accomplish perhaps his greatest track and field achievement. On August 26, 1977, Moses lost to Harald Schmid of West Germany in Berlin. Just one week later Moses beat Schmid by fifteen yards. He did not lose another 400-meter high hurdle race for nine years, nine months, and nine days. By the time Moses was defeated by fellow American Danny Harris in Madrid, Spain, in 1987, he had won 122 consecutive races.

During the winning streak, Moses' accomplishments continued on and off the track. In 1978 Moses received his B.S. degree from Morehouse. In 1980 he set his third world record with a winning time of 47.13. He also qualified to compete on the United States Olympic team at the 1980 Olympic Games in Moscow, but he missed the chance to compete for a gold medal after the United States boycotted the games in protest against the Soviet invasion of Afghanistan. In 1983 Moses set his fourth world record, winning in 47.02, his best time ever. He also won the James E. Sullivan award, which goes to the best U.S. amateur athlete. The following year, Moses won his second gold medal at the 1984 Olympic Games in Los Angeles with a time of 47.75. He was selected Sportsman of the Year by the United States Olympic Committee and *Sports Illustrated* in 1984.

In 1988, at the age of thirty-three, Moses tried to win his third gold medal in Seoul, South Korea. Instead he won a bronze medal, finishing third. Moses retired from track and field a short time later. Because of his numerous track and field accomplishments and the way he changed training for and racing 400-meter hurdle events, many consider Moses the greatest hurdler in history. Moses earned his M.A. degree from Pepperdine University in 1994. Later he moved to Atlanta to work as a financial consultant. In 2000 he became a founding member of the World Sports Academy, a group of outstanding athletes from many nations who volunteer their time to programs that promote the concept of sports as a positive force in individual lives, in communities, and in the world.

See also Olympics, African Americans and the.

Moses, Robert Parris

1935–

Civil rights activist and a leading Student Nonviolent Coordinating Committee (SNCC) worker in Mississippi.

Inspired by student sit-ins in 1960, twenty-five-year-old Harvard Ph.D. candidate and middle-school teacher Robert Parris Moses left his New York teaching job to join the CIVIL RIGHTS MOVEMENT. He led the effort of the STUDENT NONVIOLENT COORDINATING COMMITTEE to register black voters in Mississippi. Many civil rights workers had believed that Mississippi was too dangerous a place to attempt to organize. His courage and stoicism made Moses an almost mythical figure to other civil rights workers. They stood amazed by stories such as the one in which a bloodied Moses accompanied prospective black registrants to the county courthouse just minutes after being beaten by whites.

Disturbed by competition between SNCC and other civil rights organizations in Mississippi, Moses helped found the COUNCIL OF FEDERATED ORGANIZATIONS (COFO), an umbrella organization that coordinated all of Mississippi's civil rights organizations. As COFO's project director in September 1963 he developed the Freedom Vote, a mock gubernatorial election in which 80,000 blacks voted to protest their disfranchisement. Encouraged by the turnout, COFO launched FREEDOM SUMMER the following year, a massive voter registration and education project. Later in 1964 Moses helped establish the MISSISSIPPI FREEDOM DEMOCRATIC PARTY, which challenged the all-white Mississippi Democratic delegation to the Democratic National Convention.

Moses believed that math literacy was the key to modern citizenship just as literacy and voter registration had been the keys to citizenship in the 1960s. In 1982 Moses founded the Algebra Project, a program in which students use concrete examples from their lives to master abstract algebraic concepts. He brought the Algebra Project to the Mississippi Delta in 1992, thereby helping to empower a new generation of Mississippi blacks.

Moses has been the subject of several written works, including *And Gently He Shall Lead Them: Robert Parris Moses and Civil Rights in Mississippi* (1994) by Eric Burner, and the children's biography, *Robert Moses* (2004), by Bianca Dumas. His numerous awards include a MacArthur Fellowship, a Heinze Award, and the inaugural Puffin/Nation Prize. Moses currently teaches mathematics in NEW YORK CITY.

Robert Fay

Moshoeshoe

1786?–1870

Founder and first king of the Basotho nation.

Born in Menkwaneng, the son of a SOTHO leader, Moshoeshoe began to gather together refugees from the upheaval in southeastern Africa known as the MFECANE in the early 1820s. Retiring to an impregnable mountaintop known as Thaba Bosiu (Sotho for "Mountain of the Night"), he fought off several attacks but more often used his formidable diplomatic skills to defend his growing number of Basotho people. In the early 1830s, French missionaries arrived in the region. While continuing to support the traditional customs and religion of the Sotho, Moshoeshoe welcomed the missionaries and sought their advice in dealing with the British and the AFRIKANER groups, or

Boers, who were seeking to colonize southern Africa. Fearing Afrikaner settlement on his lands, he asked for British protection, but an alliance with the government of the CAPE COLONY was not enough to prevent armed incursions by settlers into Basotho territory. Fighting between the Basotho and the Afrikaners continued until the 1860s, resulting in the loss of some Basotho land. In 1868 Moshoeshoe arranged for BASUTOLAND to become a British protectorate, thereby saving it from the Afrikaners and other European settlers. When Moshoeshoe died in 1870, he ruled roughly 150,000 people in what was essentially a federal state. Basutoland eventually became the independent nation of LESOTHO.

Moshoeshoe II

?–1996

Paramount chief of Basutoland and king of Lesotho.

Born in Mokhotlong, LESOTHO, the eldest son of Paramount Chief Seeiso Griffith, Moshoeshoe II was a direct descendent of MOSHOESHOE, the nineteenth-century founder of the Basotho nation. He studied politics, philosophy, economics, and law at Corpus Christi College, University of Oxford. Moshoeshoe II returned home before completing his studies to be throned paramount chief of Basutoland in March 1960. When Basutoland became independent as Lesotho in 1966, he was declared king. After Chief Joseph Leabua Jonathan was elected prime minister in 1965, conflict developed over the extent of the king's power. In 1967 Moshoeshoe agreed to abide by the constitution, which vested executive authority in the prime minister. In the January 1970 general elections, Jonathan recognized his party would be voted out so he nullified the elections and suspended the constitution. Moshoeshoe was arrested and then exiled in March. After agreeing to avoid political activity, Moshoeshoe returned from the NETHERLANDS in December 1970 as a ceremonial head of state, subject to the rule of Jonathan's military government. However, he was exiled a second time in March 1990 when he refused to endorse the orders of Major-General Justin Lekhanya, Jonathan's successor.

On November 6, 1990, Lekhanya dethroned Moshoeshoe, after the monarch rebuffed an offer to return from exile and demanded the reinstitution of constitutional government and the end of military rule. The king's eldest son was crowned King Letsie III two days later. Moshoeshoe resettled in London, where he cofounded the International Institute for the Promotion of Human Rights and Democracy in Africa. In August 1994 Letsie attempted a royal coup, dismissing the government and suspending sections of the constitution. The ensuing internal unrest, along with international condemnation and sanctions, led to the return of democratic rule and the restoration, on January 25, 1995, of Moshoeshoe II to the throne. The constitutional provision prohibiting political activity by the monarch remained in effect. Moshoeshoe II was killed in a car accident in Lesotho on January 15, 1996.

Mosley, Walter

1952–

African American novelist known for his detective fiction.

Walter Mosley was born to an African American father and a Jewish mother in south central LOS ANGELES, where he lived until he left for college in Vermont. After college, Mosley worked a series of jobs, including caterer, potter, and computer programmer. In 1981 he moved to New York and began taking graduate writing courses at the City College of New York. There he completed *Gone Fishin'* and *Devil in a Blue Dress*, two novels that centered on the same Los Angeles protagonist, a working-class African American named Easy Rawlins.

Although *Gone Fishin'* did not sell, the rights to *Devil in a Blue Dress* were soon purchased by Norton, which published the book in 1990. *Devil* portrayed the Easy Rawlins character as a private investigator, and Mosley seemed to have found a strong voice as an author of detective fiction. After *Devil* he published four more Easy Rawlins books: *A Red Death* (1991), *White Butterfly* (1992), *Black Betty* (1994), and *A Little Yellow Dog* (1996).

Although Mosley's fiction falls into a category that many consider subliterary—detective fiction—his depth of character, researched historical details, and realistic dialogue transcend the clichés of the genre. He portrays the complexity of the Los Angeles African American community between the late 1940s and mid-1960s and does so with nuance and at times painful realism. Mosley's novel outside the series, *R. L.'s Dream* (1995), evinces a similar level of sophistication in its speculative portrayal of bluesman ROBERT JOHNSON.

Mosley's books experienced a boom in sales during the 1992 presidential campaign, when Bill Clinton cited them as among his favorites. Mosley has been included in the *Norton Anthology of African American Literature*, compared to renowned detective novelist Raymond Chandler, and praised as a superior writer of his generation. A film version of *Devil in a Blue Dress*, directed by Jonathan Demme and starring DENZEL WASHINGTON, was released in 1998. Mosely has also written several works of short fiction. His recent books include *Bad Boy Brawly Brown* (2002), marking the return of Easy Rawlins, along with the novels *Fearless Jones* (2001) and *Fear Itself* (2003), which are part of a new mystery series set in 1950s Los Angeles. Mosley lives in New York and serves on the board of directors for the National Book Awards and the Poetry Society of America.

See also Literature, African American.

Eric Bennett

Mossell, Gertrude E. H. Bustill

1855–1948

African American teacher, journalist, and author.

Gertrude Mossell was born on July 3, 1855, in PHILADELPHIA, PENNSYLVANIA, the daughter of Charles H. and Emily (Robinson) Bustill of Philadelphia, originally members of the Society of Friends (also known as QUAKERS) who later joined the Old School Presbyterian Church. Mossell was educated in the public elementary schools of Philadelphia, the Institute for Colored Youth, and the Robert Vaux Consolidated Grammar School. Her writing ability was developed with care during her years at Vaux Grammar School. As a graduating student she delivered the class oration, "Influence," which brought her to the attention of Bishop HENRY McNEAL TURNER, editor of the *Christian Recorder*. He secured the essay for publication in the magazine and invited the young writer to contribute future articles; several articles appeared in the *Recorder* and the *Standard Echo*. For seven years Mossell taught in the public schools of Camden, New Jersey; Philadelphia; and Frankfort, Kentucky. From 1880 to 1887 she wrote for the *Philadelphia Press, Times,* and *Inquirer*.

In 1893 she married NATHANIEL FRANCIS MOSSELL of Lockport, New York. A leading physician in Philadelphia, Mossell was the founder of the Frederick Douglass Memorial Hospital and Training School in Philadelphia. Marriage and the birth of two children curtailed her dual careers as teacher and journalist for a time.

In 1891 Gertrude Mossell was on the staff of the *Indianapolis Freeman, Richmond Rankin Institute,* and *Our Women and Children*. Two articles of particular interest to the reading public of the 1890s were "Power of the Press" and "Women in Journalism." Throughout Mossell's career she urged the expansion in black newspapers of all news pertinent to blacks. These papers had a special mission, she stated, which called for diligence and constant struggle to excel in news reporting. In a letter to the editor of the *New York Age,* Mossell suggested that the papers had not done all they could to become known or to use other means of distribution, such as sales by youth. She noted, "I have never yet seen a colored newspaper sold on the streets by a newsboy." She further suggested the use of other means than subscriptions, such as news dealers and agents.

Mossell's writing career continued with syndicated columns and articles in leading Philadelphia newspapers—the *Philadelphia Echo,* the *Philadelphia Times,* the *Independent,* and the *Press Republican*—on issues of "race literature and women's questions." She edited the Women's Department of the *New York Age,* the *Indianapolis World,* and the *New York Freeman,* assisted in editing the *Lincoln Alumni Magazine,* and contributed to the *A.M.E. Church Review* and other journals.

Mossell was the author of two books: *Little Dansie's One Day at Sabbath School* (1902) and *The Work of the Afro-American Women* (1894). *The Work* related the story of the rise of African American women during the nineteenth century, which she called the "Women's Century." It witnessed abolitionist and temperance movements, the emergence of coeducational institutions of higher learning, the struggle for suffrage, and women's place in the world of journalism, literature, medicine and science, business, scientific inventions, and education. The intelligence and diligence of black women made them a valuable asset in securing rights and privileges for black people. While half the book presented African American women in historical perspective, most of the other half presented poems written by women writers like PHILLIS WHEATLEY, Sarah Forten, FRANCES ELLEN WATKINS HARPER, and Josephine Heard. Black institutions such as Livingstone College, Tuskegee Institute (now TUSKEGEE UNIVERSITY), and HOWARD UNIVERSITY were briefly discussed.

Mossell engaged in many social welfare activities. After 1895 she was collector for the charity fund of the Frederick Douglass Hospital; she organized a fund-raising project of $30,000 for the hospital building and served as president of its Social Service Auxiliary. She published two postcards, "Emancipation" and "Dear Old Philadelphia," founded the Bustill Family Association, and organized the Philadelphia branch of the National Afro-American Council.

Mossell died on January 21, 1948, at the Frederick Douglass Memorial Hospital at the age of ninety-two, after an illness of about three months. Private funeral services were held at the Morris Funeral Home, and she was buried in Eden Cemetery. She was survived by two daughters, four grandchildren, a niece, and two nephews (PAUL ROBESON and Benjamin O. Robeson).

Monroe A. Majors's *Noted Negro Women: Their Triumphs and Activities* (1971 reprint) is an important source. See *The Black Press, 1827–1890: The Quest for National Identity* (1971), edited by Martin Dann. Mossell's *Work of the Afro-American Women* (1894) reveals her civil rights activism and feminist leanings. Her obituary appeared in the *Philadelphia Tribune* (January 24, 1948, pp. 1, 2).

From *Dictionary of American Negro Biography* by Rayford W. Logan and Michael R. Winston, editors. Copyright © 1982 by Rayford W. Logan and Michael R. Winston. Reprinted by permission of W. W. Norton & Company, Inc.

Claudette Brown

Mossell, Nathan Francis

1856–1946

African American physician, hospital founder, and administrator.

Nathan Francis Mossell was born in Hamilton, Ontario, CANADA, the son of Aaron Mossell, a brick manufacturer, and Eliza Bowers; both parents were freeborn African Americans from BALTIMORE, MARYLAND, who had moved to Canada to escape racial discrimination. When the CIVIL WAR ended and slavery was abolished, Aaron Mossell moved his family back to the United States. In 1865 they settled in Lockport, New York, a small town near Rochester.

In Lockport the Mossell children were assigned to a separate all-black school. Mossell's father successfully petitioned the Lockport Board of Education to close the all-black school, and Nathan and the other black children were allowed to attend integrated schools. The Mossell family's home life was highly religious: his father donated the bricks for the first AFRICAN METHODIST EPISCOPAL ZION CHURCH in Lockport.

After graduation from high school in Lockport in 1873, Nathan Mossell moved to PHILADELPHIA, where he worked to acquire funds for college. He enrolled at LINCOLN UNIVERSITY in Lincoln, Pennsylvania, in 1875 and graduated in 1879 with a B.A. degree. During his four years at Lincoln University he taught Sunday school at the Bethel A.M.E. Zion Church in Wilmington, Delaware.

In 1879 Mossell gained admission to the Medical School of the University of Pennsylvania, from which he graduated with high honors in 1882. He was the first African American to apply to the university's medical program and the first to graduate. In the year before his medical school graduation he married Gertrude Bustill; they had two daughters.

After medical school Mossell worked in the outpatient clinic of the University Hospital. Because of racial attitudes, he was reluctantly given this position only through the influence of his former professors. Concurrently he completed a postgraduate course at the Philadelphia Polyclinic. He was refused membership, again because of his race, in the Philadelphia County Medical Society. After a bitter struggle and with letters of support from his former professors, he was accepted into the society in 1888, the first African American member.

In 1885 Mossell went to Europe for advanced medical training. He studied surgery at Guy's Hospital and St. Thomas Hospital in London, England. Back in Philadelphia, however, he was unable to gain a hospital staff appointment. Furthermore, he was disturbed that none of the more than twenty-four hospitals in the Philadelphia area would admit African American medical graduates to internships or African American women into their nurse training programs. Mossell was convinced of the necessity of better hospital care for African Americans and of training opportunities for black doctors and nurses. Several medical colleges in Philadelphia offered to assist him in establishing a hospital if he would agree that it would be segregated. Mossell and other black leaders refused this offensive condition.

Mossell was against hospitals exclusively for black people, which he thought were a wasteful duplication of effort and perpetuation of a caste system. However, the great needs of Philadelphia's African American community and discrimination at other hospitals forced him to act against his philosophy. In June 1895 Mossell convened other doctors to lay plans for establishing a hospital for patients of all races; it would provide a place for black physicians to treat their patients and to gain professional development and for African American interns and nurses to acquire training. With public fund-raising, church donations, and the work of African American women volunteers led by Gertrude Mossell, a three-story building was leased at 1512 Lombard Street and outfitted as a fifteen-bed facility. Frederick Douglass Memorial Hospital and Training School opened on October 31, 1895. Eighty-six percent of the funds needed to open the hospital and to operate it during the first year were raised in the African American community. Some blacks, however, criticized Mossell for conceding to race prejudice; some whites argued that there were already enough charitable hospitals.

Each year during its first decade Douglass Hospital's outpatient and inpatient censuses increased. Some of the first patients were veterans of the SPANISH-AMERICAN WAR. Beginning in 1905 annual state funding of $6,000 was gained in recognition of the number of poor patients being served. From the founding of Douglass Hospital until early 1931, Mossell served as both superintendent and medical director. The administrative and professional duties were separated in 1931, and he retained the post of medical director.

In early 1905 Mossell faced opposition from a segment of Douglass's professional staff. The board of directors requested his resignation. Some physicians had accused Mossell of retarding the professional growth of younger physicians by limiting their assignments to perform operations. Others faulted him for what they judged to be a turning of the hospital from a quasi-public institution to a more private one. Mossell overcame the attacks on him during 1905 with strong community support. In late 1905 a dissident group of doctors failed to get the board of managers to reorganize the hospital to free it from all appearances of being a private institution. They ended their affiliation with Douglass and established Mercy Hospital, which opened in 1907. The split between the supporters of Douglass and Mercy hospitals continued until the mid-1940s, when a merger was proposed. Mossell felt that a single hospital would better serve the growing African American population of Philadelphia and provided strong leadership toward the eventual merger forming Mercy-Douglass Hospital, which was not realized until two years after his death.

Mossell was a leading organizer of African American medical affairs and politics. In 1895 he was a founder of the National Medical Association (NMA), established by African American physicians because they were barred from the American Medical Association and its local chapters. In 1900 he helped to establish the Philadelphia Academy of Medical and Allied Sciences, an NMA chapter. In 1907 he served as the eighth president of the NMA.

Medicine was not the only field in which Mossell combated racial discrimination and championed CIVIL RIGHTS. In 1905 he joined the NIAGARA MOVEMENT, organized by W.E. B. DU BOIS, which called for immediate and full civil rights for African Americans. The Niagara Movement led to the founding of the NATIONAL ASSOCIATION FOR THE ADVANCEMENT OF COLORED PEOPLE (NAACP) in 1910. Mossell spearheaded protests in Philadelphia against the antiblack novel, *The Clansmen,* and a Hollywood film, *Birth of a Nation,* based on the novel. He led a fight in Philadelphia in 1944 to have African American youth admitted to Girard College, a privately funded but publicly administered institution.

Mossell died at his home in Philadelphia. For more than forty years he was a pioneering hospital developer and a forceful advocate for black-controlled hospitals, essential during a time when medical training and hospital practice for African American physicians and nurses were severely limited in the United States.

Bibliography

Cobb, William Montague. "Nathan Francis Mossell, 1856–1946." *Journal of the National Medical Association* 46 (March 1954): 118–30.

Gamble, Vanessa S. *Making a Place for Ourselves: The Black Hospital Movement 1920–1945*, 19–21, 26–28, 32. 1995.

Obituaries: *Philadelphia Inquirer* and *Philadelphia Evening Bulletin*, both October 28, 1946, and *Pittsburgh Courier*, November 2, 1946.

From *American National Biography*. John A. Garraty and Mark C. Carnes, eds. Oxford University Press, 1999. Reprinted by permission of the American Council of Learned Societies.

Robert C. Hayden

Mossi

Kingdom and the largest ethnic group in Burkina Faso; members also live in Côte d'Ivoire, Ghana, Togo, and Benin.

Although the origin of Mossi society is debated, oral tradition claims that the kingdom was founded by Ouédraogo, the son of a Mamprusi princess from Gambaga (in present-day GHANA), and a MANDE hunter. Ouédraogo (meaning "stallion," after the horse that his mother rode to find her husband) migrated north as a young man with a group of DAGOMBA followers and founded the village of Tenkodogo, site of the first Mossi kingdom. Ouédraogo later sent three of his sons and a cavalry to acquire new territory in the Volta River basin region; by the fifteenth century his descendants had established over twenty kingdoms and had assimilated numerous peoples, including the Nioniosse, Ninsi, Gurunis, DOGON, and BISA. The most important dynasty was founded in OUAGADOUGOU, BURKINA FASO, in 1495 by Ouédraogo's grandson, Oubry, who called himself the *mogho naaba*, "king of the world," a title that was adopted by subsequent Ouagadougou kings.

Mossi expansion into the SAHEL met challenges from the SONGHAI EMPIRE, led first by SUNNI ALI and then his successor, Askiya Muhammad. Askiya's jihad against the Mossi, who observed a form of ancestor worship, failed to win Mossi conversion to Islam. Although many Mossi traders did convert later, even today BURKINA FASO remains less Islamized than its Sahelian neighbors.

By the eighteenth century the Mossi had developed a complex hierarchy, ruled by the nobles, or *nakombse*, who claimed direct patrilineal descent from Ouédraogo. The ruler of Ouagadougou exercised loose authority over the kings *(naaba)* of the four other largest kingdoms—Tenkodogo, Yatenga, Boussouma, and Gurma—who in turn collected tribute from smaller kingdoms. Mossi society also distinguished between the *talse* (commoners) and *yemse* (slaves). Among the *talse*, those lineages who claimed descent from the original settlers were known as the *tengabiise* (children of the earth); this indigenous status gave them privileged claims to land as well as responsibility for harvest rites.

Most Mossi kingdoms supplemented agricultural production with trade. Caravans brought gold and KOLA from the south and salt and livestock from the north. The region's predominant traders were the *yarse*, assimilated Mande Muslims who paid the naaba annual tributes in return for market space in Mossi towns and safe passage through the region. In the late eighteenth century some Mossi kingdoms also participated in the TRANSATLANTIC SLAVE TRADE, but many slaves were diverted to the royal court in Ouagadougou after the European abolition of the trade.

In the late nineteenth century the mogho naaba repeatedly rebuffed French efforts to establish a protectorate over the Mossi region, but these kings finally fled the French conquest of Ouagadougou in 1896. Within the colony of UPPER VOLTA (present-day Burkina Faso), the Mossi royal hierarchy was used by the French to administer colonial rule. Where necessary, the French replaced recalcitrant naaba with more willing collaborators, thus undermining—though never destroying—the basis of nakombse authority.

In 1932 the French dismantled the bankrupt Upper Volta and annexed much of the Mossi region to CÔTE D'IVOIRE, thereby facilitating the flow of labor to the southern colony's plantations. After thousands of Mossi volunteered to fight in World War II, Mossi chiefs convinced FRANCE to reunite Upper Volta—a move that increased their own political clout as independence approached. After independence in 1960, the Mossi were crucial in the election of Burkina Faso's first president, Maurice Yaméogo. The current mogho naaba remains a respected figure in contemporary Ouagadougou society. Today the Mossi constitute over half the population of Burkina Faso. Known for their traditions of migration, hundreds of thousands of the approximately 5.5 million Mossi move seasonally for farming work in neighboring countries, especially Côte d'Ivoire.

See also Togo; Benin; Islam in Africa.

Bibliography

Englebert, P. *Burkina Faso: Unsteady Statehood in West Africa*. Westview Press, 1996.

Skinner, E. P. *The Mossi of Burkina Faso: Chiefs, Politicians, and Soldiers*. Waveland Press, 1989.

Elizabeth Heath

Moten, Benjamin (Bennie)

1894–1935

American jazz bandleader, who popularized the "Kansas City" sound in big-band jazz.

In his youth, Benjamin Moten played baritone saxophone in brass bands in his native Kansas City, Missouri. Switching to the piano, he studied ragtime with two of SCOTT JOPLIN's students. In 1918, he formed the RAGTIME trio B.B.&D. Moten's band toured the Midwest through the 1920s, settling in NEW YORK, NEW YORK, near the end of the decade. By the beginning of the 1930s, Moten's group included a roster of intensely talented musicians and arrangers. Those who later acquired fame as independent artists included singer JIMMY RUSHING, tenor saxophonist Ben Webster, trumpeter Oran "Hot Lips" Page, and pianist and bandleader WILLIAM JAMES ("COUNT") BASIE.

Key early Moten recordings such as "Elephant's Wobble" and "Crawdad Blues" (1923) showcased his band's tight ensemble playing and heavy, percussive beat. The band's characteristic sound wed stellar solo passages and instrumental riffs to a distinctive, underlying flow. Important later recordings included "Moten Stomp" (1927), "Kansas City Breakdown" (1928), "Lafayette" (1932), and "Prince of Wails" (1932).

Moten died in 1935 during an operation to remove his tonsils. Members of his band reformed as the Count Basie Orchestra in 1936.

Bibliography
Russell, Ross. *Jazz Style in Kansas City and the Southwest.* University of California Press, 1971.

Moten, Lucy Ellen

1851–1933

African American educator.

Lucy Ellen Moten was born in Fauquier County, Virginia, near White Sulphur Springs, the daughter of Benjamin Moten, a U.S. Patent Office clerk, and Julia Withers. Taking advantage of their status as free blacks, the Motens moved to the District of Columbia when Lucy was only a child to secure the best possible education for their precocious daughter. Lucy attended Washington's pay schools until 1862, when she was admitted to the district's first public schools for African Americans. After attending the preparatory and normal departments of HOWARD UNIVERSITY, Lucy Moten began teaching in the primary grades of the local public schools and taught there continuously, except for a two-year interruption, from 1870 until 1883. In 1873 Moten moved to Salem, Massachusetts, to attend the State Normal School, from which she graduated in 1875.

In 1883 FREDERICK DOUGLASS recommended that Moten be appointed to fill the vacant principalship of the Miner Normal School, a public teacher training institution for black primary teachers in the District of Columbia. Although impressed with her experience and academic credentials, the members of the Board of Trustees of the Miner School were concerned that Moten's youth and physical attractiveness made her unsuited for such a responsible position. Only after she assured the trustees that she would refrain from theatergoing, cardplaying, and dancing were they convinced that she was the right person for the job.

From 1883 to 1920 Moten ran the Miner Normal School with an iron hand. She was a strict taskmaster who demanded that her students maintain the highest personal and professional standards. She never challenged them, however, to do anything that she was unwilling to do herself and over time won their universal respect. Moten strongly urged the students with whom she worked to continue to educate themselves. She maintained a high standard in this regard by spending much of her spare time away from Miner furthering her own professional development. The same year she assumed the principalship at Miner, she graduated from the Spencerian Business College with honors. She worked closely with Alfred Townsend, a well-known elocution teacher, to sharpen her public speaking abilities.

Moten participated in countless professional conferences to increase her stock of pedagogical knowledge. She believed that all teachers should know something about health, physiology, and anatomy and attended medical school at Howard University to master these subjects, earning her M.D. in 1897. She employed the medical knowledge she had accumulated by initiating a series of lectures at Miner on health and hygiene. She spent many of her summers in the South teaching in vacation schools for veteran teachers and also found time to continue graduate work in education at New York University.

Moten's energy and enthusiasm for teaching were legendary and inspired at least two generations of African American educators in the District of Columbia. During the thirty-seven years that she was the principal of Miner Normal School, Moten took an active part in preparing most of the black primary teachers subsequently employed in the Washington Public Schools. She became so successful, in fact, in furnishing African American teachers for the District of Columbia that by 1890 the local school board was recommending that prospective teachers from around the country enroll at Miner to benefit from her outstanding leadership. To maintain the highest educational standards, Moten worked unceasingly for more rigorous admissions standards, smaller class sizes, and a larger, better trained, and better compensated faculty. Most of all she sought to make the Miner curriculum more demanding and relevant. In 1896 she successfully expanded the school's program from one to two years, and by the end of her tenure she had laid the foundation for extending the program to a full four years.

Moten probably worked hardest to ensure that the teachers with whom she worked were as committed to character development as they were to fostering academic success. This meant that she expected them to maintain habits of strict integrity and intellectual honesty, to be models of self-control and patience, to remain sympathetic and cheerful at all times, and to cultivate a refined aesthetic taste. To Moten, manners, morals, and intellect were all equally important, especially for teachers preparing to instruct the very young. Her dignity, grace, and decency remained the moral standard by which her students proudly gauged their own contributions to the profession of teaching.

In 1914 Miner Normal School opened a new building modeled on a design suggested by Moten. An avid traveler and Anglophile, she had long admired the architecture of Christ's College at Cambridge University and urged the architects who planned the new Miner facility to base their design on this well-known English college. She also insisted, often over the objections of the board of education, which worried about the added expense, that the classrooms and hallways be well ventilated and well lighted and that in general the new building reflect the latest technology regarding the conditions most conducive to good education.

After Moten retired from Miner she lived most of the rest of her life in NEW YORK CITY and never married. She died tragically in 1933 when a taxicab struck her in New York's Times Square. Even in death her contributions to education continued. She left $51,000 to Howard University, requesting that the money be made available to students wishing to visit and study abroad. Finally, in recognition of Moten's important impact on primary education in the District of Columbia, a Washington elementary school was named for her in 1954.

Bibliography

The annual reports that Moten wrote for Miner Normal School can be found in the annual reports of the District of Columbia Public Schools.

Boyd, Norma, and Julia Hamilton Smith, *Black Women Oral History Project*. 10 vols. 1992.

Carothers, Thomasine. "Lucy Ellen Moten, 1851–1933." *Journal of Negro History* 19 (January 19, 1934): 102–106.

Hatter, Henrietta. "History of Miner Teachers College." Master's thesis, Howard University, 1939.

Obituary, *Washington Post*, March 8, 1934.

From *American National Biography*. John A. Garraty and Mark C. Carnes, eds. Oxford University Press, 1999. Reprinted by permission of the American Council of Learned Societies.

Stephen Preskill

Motion Pictures

Visual and audio communications medium in which Africans and people of African descent have been both creators and subjects.

For information on

American films: *See* Birth of a Nation, The; Blaxploitation Films, *Eyes on the Prize*; Film, Blacks in American; *Green Pastures, The*; Representations of Afro-Diasporic Religions in Cinema.

European films: *See* Black and White; *Toxi*.

Films of Hispanic America and Brazil: *See* Cinema, Black, in Brazil; Cinema Novo; Cinema, Black, in Spanish America; Representations of Afro-Diasporic Religions in Cinema; Third Cinema.

African films: *See* Cinema, African; Fédération Panafricaine des Cinéastes; Groupe Africaine du Cinéma, Le.

British colonial film projects in Africa: *See* Bantu Educational Cinema Experiment.

Motion Pictures, African

See Cinema, African.

Motion Pictures, American, African Americans in

See Film, Blacks in American.

Motion Pictures, Black, in Brazil

See Cinema, Black, in Brazil.

Motion Pictures, Black, in Spanish America

See Cinema, Black, in Spanish America.

Motion Pictures, Caribbean

See Cinema, Black, in Spanish America.

Moton, Robert Russa

1867–1940

American educator and lawyer who succeeded Booker T. Washington as president of Tuskegee Institute.

The son of Book and Emily (Brown) Moton, Robert Moton enrolled in the HAMPTON INSTITUTE in 1885. After his junior year, he taught in Cottontown, Cumberland County, and subsequently obtained a license to practice law. He returned to Hampton in 1889, and finished his senior year to become assistant commandant in charge of the male student cadet corps. He was appointed "major" commandant, a position he retained for twenty-five years. In 1900, Moton was elected president of the National Negro Business League and was reelected for the next twenty years.

Moton's first wife, Elizabeth Hunt Harris, died in 1906, only one year after their marriage. He had four children with his second wife, Jennie Dee Booth.

Moton's working relationship with BOOKER TALIAFERRO WASHINGTON began in 1908, the year of his second marriage, when he accompanied Washington on several tours through the Southern states to promote the Hampton-Tuskegee model of racial advancement through vocational education and interracial cooperation. Their routine consisted of singing "Negro melodies" led by Moton, followed by a speech from Washington.

When Washington died in 1915, Moton assumed many of Washington's roles as race leader, advising the federal government on racial policies and Negro appointments, consulting philanthropists in the distribution of educational funds, and steering organizations serving the cause of racial advancement.

As president of TUSKEGEE INSTITUTE from 1915 until 1930, Moton increased Tuskegee's endowment from $2.3 million to $7.77 million, introduced college-level coursework, improved the administrative structure, and managed to insure that Tuskegee's vocational curriculum kept up with the changing employment world.

Moton received honorary degrees from several colleges and universities including Oberlin, Williams, Harvard, Virginia Union, WILBERFORCE UNIVERSITY and HOWARD UNIVERSITY. In 1930, he won the Harmon Award for contributions to better race relations, and in 1932 the NATIONAL ASSOCIATION FOR THE ADVANCEMENT OF COLORED PEOPLE honored him with the Spingarn medal for distinguished service.

Motown

Black-owned record company, most commercially successful and culturally influential record company of the 1960s, which produced a distinct musical style that appealed to audiences across racial boundaries.

Some of Motown's leading popular acts were THE SUPREMES, THE TEMPTATIONS, THE FOUR TOPS, SMOKEY ROBINSON and THE MIRACLES, MARTHA AND THE VANDELLAS, the Contours, and the Jackson Five as well as solo artists Mary Wells, MARVIN GAYE, and STEVIE WONDER. This collection of musical talent produced scores of hits, including "My Girl," "Stop! In the Name of Love," "Shop Around," "I Heard It through the Grapevine," "Baby, I Need Your Loving," and "Dancing in the Street." These songs captured the spirit of an era and became, as the company motto promised, the "Sound of Young America."

Berry Gordy Jr. founded the company in DETROIT, MICHIGAN, in 1959 with the support of a family loan of $800. Gordy, who worked briefly at the Ford Motor Company, named the company Motown after Detroit's "Motor Town" nickname. Gordy believed that the efficiency of the automobile assembly line could be applied to the music industry.

He designed his "hit factory" in a modest two-story home on West Grand Boulevard in Detroit. Gordy's concept involved finding young talent from local neighborhoods and transforming these amateur musicians and singers into professional artists. Gordy set up a separate artist development department, which was often referred to as the company charm school, to teach performers how to sing, dance, and comport themselves in the public spotlight. Legendary bandleader Maurice King led the musical instruction. CHOLLY ATKINS, a veteran choreographer, taught the synchronized black dance steps that became an integral part of Motown's signature style. Maxine Powell instructed performers on the etiquette of celebrity life, including how to dress, greet dignitaries, and behave on stage. With this schooling, Gordy's young artists, many of whom were just out of high school, exuded the confidence of seasoned entertainers.

The "Motown Sound" has always been difficult to define yet easy to recognize. Motown songs often combine strong bass lines and a gritty back beat with call and response vocals and clever lyrics about the trials and joys of teenage romance. The music's magic resulted from the combined efforts of skilled songwriters, producers, and musicians. Gordy, a talented songwriter, gained early fame writing songs for Jackie Wilson, including, "Reet Petite" (1957) and "Lonely Teardrops" (1958). He mentored other Motown writers and producers in the art of romantic storytelling through popular song.

In 1959 Gordy signed a new group, the Miracles, to the label. In February 1961 their song "Shop Around" became the company's first million seller. Smokey Robinson, the lead singer, quickly became one of Motown's most prolific songwriters. He composed several top hits, including "My Girl," "The Way You Do the Things You Do," and "You've Really Got a Hold on Me." Motown's innovative studio musicians, also known as the Funk Brothers, created the company's unique "sound." The original members of the Funk Brothers included James Jamerson on bass, Earl Van Dyke on keyboards, Benny "Papa Zita" Benjamin on drums, Robert White on guitar, and Thomas "Beans" Bowles on saxophone.

With such a powerful array of creative talent, the Motown recording studio soon lived up to its ambitious nickname, Hitsville, U.S.A. Early hits included Barrett Strong's "Money (That's What I Want)" (1959) and the Marvelettes' "Please Mr. Postman" (1961). In 1962 Motown developed enough new acts to send its own road show, the Motortown Revue, on a national tour. The tour, the first sponsored solely by a black-owned record company, was a music industry first. The Revue's roster, which included Mary Wells, the Contours, Martha and the Vandellas, the Supremes, the Miracles, Little Stevie Wonder, Marvin Gaye, and the Marvelettes, testified to the company's rich potential. From 1961 to 1972 Motown performers sent over 100 songs to the Top Ten of the popular music charts, including 31 number-one hits.

The key to Motown's success was the company's ability to produce music that appealed to audiences across racial boundaries. No Motown group exemplified this skill more than the Supremes, the company's most commercially successful group. The Supremes first reached number one on the pop charts with their song "Where Did Our Love Go?" in the summer of 1964. A string of hits followed, including "Baby Love," "Come See about Me," "Stop! In the Name of Love," and "I Hear a Symphony." The songwriting team of Eddie Holland, Lamont Dozier, and Brian Holland, known as Holland-Dozier-Holland, masterminded the Supremes' unique sound. DIANA ROSS, Florence Ballard, and Mary Wilson became international celebrities through national television appearances and world tours. Ross left the group in 1970 to pursue a solo singing career and film acting.

By the late 1960s and early 1970s Motown music had moved beyond carefree teenage themes to address the political and social struggles of the CIVIL RIGHTS MOVEMENT and the VIETNAM WAR (1959–1975). Stevie Wonder was the first Motown artist to address social issues through song in 1966, when he recorded a cover version of Bob Dylan's song "Blowin' in the Wind." Wonder's moving interpretation spoke to the challenges of the civil rights campaign. The Supremes recorded "Love Child" (1968) and "I'm Livin' in Shame" (1969), both of which depicted the problems of urban ghetto life. The Temptations also recorded a series of "message" songs, including "Ball of Confusion (That's What the World Is Today)" (1970) and "Papa was a Rollin' Stone" (1972). Edwin Starr's song "War!" (1970) became one of the strongest anti–Vietnam War anthems on the airwaves.

In 1971 Marvin Gaye produced his groundbreaking album *What's Going On,* which commented not only on the Vietnam War but also on ecology, racism, and urban violence. Motown Records also founded the Black Forum label, which produced spoken-word recordings on political and literary subjects. Black Forum releases included *Free Huey!* (1970), *Writers of the Revolution* (1970), *The Congressional Black Caucus* (1972), and MARTIN LUTHER KING JR.'s speech *Why I Oppose the War in Vietnam,* which won a Grammy Award in 1970 for Best Spoken-Word Recording.

In 1972 the Motown Record Company announced its plans to relocate its headquarters from Detroit to LOS ANGELES, CALIFORNIA. Gordy wanted to expand into filmmaking as well as record producing. Motown's first feature film was *Lady Sings the Blues* (1973), starring Diana Ross. Ross's moving portrayal of BILLIE HOLIDAY earned her an Academy Award nomination for Best Actress. Other Motown feature films include *Mahogany* (1975) and *The Bingo Long and the Traveling All-Star and Motor Kings* (1976). In the early 1980s Motown produced television specials, including "Motown 25: Yesterday, Today, Forever" (1983), which first featured Michael Jackson's famous moonwalk dance. In 1988 Gordy sold Motown to MCA for $61.9 million. In the 1990s the Motown label was owned by Polygram Records and featured groups such as Boyz II Men. Recently acquired by Universal Music Group, the label is now called Universal Motown Records. Its current roster includes the artists Nelly, Nick Lachey, and 3 Doors Down.

See also Film, Blacks in American; Jackson, Michael, and the Jackson Family; Music, African American.

Suzanne Smith

Motta, Zezé

1944–

Afro-Brazilian actor.

One of the best-known modern Afro-Brazilian actors, Zezé Motta starred as the cunning and powerful slave Xica in the film *Xica da Silva* (1976) by director CARLOS DIEGUES. She also performed the role of the spiritual force and warrior Dandara in *Quilombo* (1984) by the same director. In 1987 Motta appeared in Wilson Barros's *Anjos da noite* (Angels of the Night), and seven years later she played the wife of nineteenth-century black Brazilian poet João de Cruz e Sousa in Maria Emília de Azeredo's *Ava Paixão.*

During the 1990s Motta appeared in the Brazilian *telenovela,* or televised soap opera, *Xica da Silva,* based on the Diegues movie in which she had starred years earlier. This time around, Motta played the heroine's mother. She worked again with Diegues in the film *Orfeo* (2000), a remake of the classic 1959 movie BLACK ORPHEUS. In addition to her acting career, Motta has long been a political activist in Brazil, working to overcome racial prejudice by encouraging and promoting young black actors and directors.

See also Cinema, Black, in Brazil.

Mound Bayou

Planned community in the Mississippi wetlands that demonstrated, at its height of prosperity, the possibilities of black self-help.

By applying the philosophy of BOOKER TALIAFERRO WASHINGTON, ISAIAH THORNTON MONTGOMERY gained national attention for the success of his experiment at Mound Bayou. He founded Mound Bayou with fellow freedman Ben Green in 1888 on the rich alluvial land halfway between MEMPHIS, TENNESSEE, and Vicksburg, Mississippi. The site flanked a new railroad line and cost little because of its swampy ground and thick underbrush. Green and Montgomery intended the settlement to be a refuge from discrimination and a place where freedpeople could live independent and self-sustaining lives.

Mound Bayou grew quickly; by 1907 around 400 families, totaling about 8,000 residents, populated the town. Mound Bayou townsfolk earned money by clearing and selling swampland hardwood and by cultivating cotton on the fertile soil. This capital, in turn, fostered a dozen businesses, a newspaper, two private schools, ten churches, a bank, and a cottonseed oil mill. The Mound Bayou community governed itself through town-hall meetings and, by means of effective local democracy, enforced prohibition, outlawed premarital cohabitation, banned prostitution, and dealt with a negligible crime rate.

Although Isaiah Montgomery played an instrumental role in these successes, his interests extended beyond the settlement. He won an office in the state government by adopting a position of accommodation from which he advocated the temporary disfranchisement of African Americans for the sake of later gains. Sympathetic with Montgomery's rhetoric, Booker T. Washington became his friend, and President Theodore Roosevelt appointed him to a position collecting monies in Mississippi for the federal government.

Montgomery, however, continued to devote most of his attention to Mound Bayou. When hard times hit in the 1910s, Montgomery's connections with the white establishment proved a mixed blessing. White philanthropists, including Andrew Carnegie and Julius Rosenwald, subsidized the town's bank and cottonseed oil mill, which had faltered from the economic shifts induced by World War I. Since the citizens of Mound Bayou prided themselves on their success in maintaining self-help and economic independence, the subsidies undermined the town's founding philosophy.

Despite perennial attempts to reinvigorate the economy, Mound Bayou struggled through the rest of the twentieth century but failed to regain the prosperity of its first twenty-five years. The Mound Bayou experiment exemplified both the possibilities and limits of self-help, both the pride of black independence and the inescapable burden of economic dependency.

See also Free Blacks in the United States.

Eric Bennett

Mountain Men

Fur trappers, Indian interpreters, and trailblazers who became mythical emblems of the American frontier.

According to the historian Kenneth W. Porter, any account of the early-nineteenth-century fur trade that left out African Americans would be "so incomplete as to give a false impression." Sadly, such false impressions have run rampant. When Hollywood filmed the life of the famous black trapper JAMES PIERSON BECKWOURTH, a white man played the lead.

Mountain men, who trapped animals for their valuable fur, roamed the mythic American West, stock characters representing independence, courage, and self-reliance. They were, in many cases, the first non–NATIVE AMERICANS to explore the vast territory unsettled by Europeans. Starting in the early 1800s, several fur companies sought men to travel into the upper Midwest and the Rocky Mountains. Beckwourth and Edward Rose were two of the black men who went. Although most were porters and trappers, George Bonga, descended from African slaves and Chippewa Indians, became an important fur trader in his own right during the 1830s.

Bears, wolves, and snakes made the work treacherous, and many mountain men died of exposure to the harsh western winters. Many Native Americans fought to defend their land against the interlopers who sought to profit from it. But the fur trade offered some of the black men more freedom and independence than they found in more-settled parts of the country, and their experience with Indian cultures was not always antagonistic. Some black mountain men, like Beckwourth and Bonga, married Native American women.

Changing fashions doomed the fur trade. But the mountain men remained, putting their skills to use as interpreters, Indian agents, guides, army scouts, and soldiers. The African Americans among them became some of the first blacks in the American frontier West.

Bibliography
Vestal, Stanley. *Mountain Men.* Houghton Mifflin Company, 1937.

Kate Tuttle

Mount Kenya

Second-highest mountain in Africa; also known by its Swahili name *Kirinyaga,* which means "mountain of whiteness."

An extinct volcano located in central KENYA, Mount Kenya reaches 5,199 meters (17,057 feet) at its summit. The mountain features several different vegetative zones and is surrounded by forest up to about 3,200 meters (10,500 feet). The KIKUYU and the Embu and Meru peoples have traditionally inhabited the area, farming the fertile lower slopes. Now part of Mount Kenya National Park, the mountain has become a popular destination for both recreational climbing and wildlife viewing and a valuable source of revenue for the Kenyan government.

See also Tourism in Africa.

Bibliography
Kenyatta, Jomo. *Facing Mount Kenya: The Tribal Life of the Gikuyu.* AMS Press, 1978.

Robert Fay

MOVE

Counterculture organization founded in Philadelphia, Pennsylvania; its activities led to two controversial clashes with police in 1978 and 1985 resulting in the imprisonment or death of over two dozen members.

MOVE was founded in 1972 by Vincent Leaphart, an African American handyman. Leaphart believed that various problems plaguing American society such as crime, substance abuse, and violence grew out of humanity's growing alienation from the natural world through technology and various social institutions. He advocated a lifestyle based on the "principle of natural law," which included certain observances that included eating only uncooked, unprocessed foods, living without electric heat, letting one's hair grow naturally, and rejecting "man's [corrupt] laws." Donald Glassey, a white leftist graduate student at the University of Pennsylvania, befriended Leaphart—who began calling himself John Africa—and collected Leaphart's ideas into a manuscript called *The Guidelines.*

The Guidelines circulated throughout the Powelton Village section of PHILADELPHIA, PENNSYLVANIA, attracting a small number of disciples—mostly students from surrounding universities, relatives of John Africa's, working-class folk from the community, and veterans of various radical groups, including the BLACK PANTHER PARTY. Although the group's membership was predominantly African American and its activities often focused on racially charged issues such as police brutality against blacks, a few sympathizers and members like Glassey were white. All followers, emulating their leader, took "Africa" as their surname. The group was first named the Christian Movement for Life; John Africa eventually shortened the name of his new "family" to MOVE. Glassey purchased a house on North Thirty-third Street. Although not all members lived there, the house became MOVE's communal residence.

MOVE's early activities included protests against city and school board policies, police brutality (rampant under law-and-order Mayor Frank Rizzo, 1971–1979), pollution, and other environmental abuses. They picketed the Philadelphia Zoo, comparing the caging of animals to the Jewish Holocaust and the treatment of blacks during times of slavery. Meanwhile, MOVE's neighbors on North Thirty-third Street had their own complaints: rats, rotting garbage, fecal odor, unclothed children, the fifty to sixty stray animals adopted by the "family," and increasingly violent arguments with group members (with MOVE usually gaining the upper hand). The complaints finally led to a court-ordered inspection that Rizzo hesitated to enforce, especially after he received reports that the organization was stockpiling food and weapons at the house in anticipation of an invasion.

After a politically embarrassing ten-month delay, Rizzo had a four-block area surrounding the MOVE house blockaded by police, cutting off all food, water, and supplies to the house. Supporters somehow smuggled provisions to the group. Three months later, on August 8, 1978, Rizzo sanctioned a police raid, during which five police officers and firefighters were wounded and one police officer was killed. Police beat one MOVE member, Delbert Africa, while he was trying to escape (local television news crews captured this beating on videotape). After the house was evacuated, it was immediately seized, condemned, and razed by the city. Rizzo blamed the group and a hostile media presence for the violence. The group briefly dispersed, with some members going underground to avoid various weapons and conspiracy charges, while others remained to work toward the release of members who had been detained after the 1978 showdown.

In 1980, after a controversial trial in which compelling evidence suggested that "friendly fire" may have been the cause of the officer's death, nine MOVE members (including Delbert Africa) were convicted of manslaughter charges stemming from the confrontation and were sentenced to terms of thirty to one hundred years. The three police officers charged with beating Delbert Africa were acquitted in 1981 by a judge, before the case could go to a jury trial.

That same year, John Africa returned to Philadelphia to face weapons and conspiracy charges and was acquitted. Soon after, the family regrouped and moved into a house at 6221 Osage Avenue. Nearly two years passed before problems with neighbors arose again. A community delegation appealed to the new city administration, now led by Philadelphia's first black mayor, Wilson Goode, who had been elected in November 1983. Goode, fearful of another deadly showdown, avoided any direct action against the group and even delayed the arrests of several MOVE members for outstanding warrants. But Goode was eventually forced into action because of political pressure from the community and the media and because of reports that bunker-like additions were being built around the house. He authorized a hastily planned raid of the MOVE house on May 13, 1985.

The police attempted to break into 6221 Osage Avenue from neighboring houses but failed. Then they dropped a bomb on the house from a helicopter, presumably in an effort to make an opening in the roof for tear gas. A fire started, but police intentionally allowed it to burn, hoping to disable the rooftop bunkers. The blaze soon grew wildly out of control, spreading to neighboring houses and adjoining city blocks. In the end, the fire consumed sixty-one homes and killed eleven MOVE members, including John Africa and five children. Only two of the members in the house escaped the blaze: Ramona Africa, who was eventually imprisoned for seven years on conspiracy and riot charges, and Birdie Africa, a thirteen-year-old boy.

Two grand jury investigations—city-commissioned and independent—found that the decision to drop the bomb had been "unconscionable," and they exposed a police cover-up concerning the use of "C-4," a military-grade explosive, in the bomb. But no criminal charges were ever filed against Goode, the other city officials, or any of the police officers involved.

Wrongful death lawsuits by relatives and surviving MOVE members (including Ramona Africa, released in 1992) against the city have already led to nearly $5 million in damages, with more suits pending. Several active MOVE members are either still in prison or living in the Philadelphia area.

Bibliography

Anderson, John, and Hilary Hevenor. *Burning Down the House: MOVE and the Tragedy of Philadelphia.* Norton, 1987.

Boyette, Michael, and Randi Boyette. *Let It Burn: The Philadelphia Tragedy.* Contemporary Books, 1989.

Marc Mazique

Movimento Negro Unificado

Organization created in the 1970s to fight racial discrimination against blacks in Brazil.

The Movimento Negro Unificado (Unified Black Movement), or MNU, was created on June 18, 1978, in São Paulo, BRAZIL, by a group of Afro-Brazilians, among whom were political activists, journalists, artists, and athletes. The MNU was conceived during a phase when Brazil's military regime, which took power in a 1964 coup, was conducting a transition to democracy. The military government was therefore allowing political organizations and social movements to freely organize. It is likely that international decolonization and independence movements, especially in Africa, and the CIVIL RIGHTS MOVEMENT in the United States influenced the upsurge of a black movement in Brazil.

In a context where routine police violence against blacks was one of the public faces of racial discrimination, the torture and assassination of a black taxi driver, Robson Luz, is considered to be the decisive impulse for the creation of the MNU. Flavio Carranca, Hamilton Cardoso, Vanderlei José Maria, and ABDIAS DO NASCIMENTO were some of the leaders of the MNU at the time of its creation. On July 7, 1978, the MNU organized its first public act, bringing together some 2,000 participants in downtown São Paulo.

The MNU is a national organization, bringing together associates from all over Brazil. Approximately 300 people participated in the MNU's first national assembly, which took place in Rio de Janeiro on September 10, 1978. The MNU is made up of several independent bodies, including action groups, municipal coordinating committees, state coordinating committees, the National Executive Commission, and a National Congress. Each body has a certain amount of autonomous power, and decisions are necessarily taken only with the agreement of all the members of the groups, instead of just the national coordination committee. It is a decentralized structure that reserves to the activists the power to decide over the programs that will be developed by the MNU. The National Congress has limited power to interfere on the other bodies, and it is only responsible for defining the MNU's general policy.

The MNU was preceded by a number of Afro-Brazilian groups, newspapers, and events during the 1970s. These included groups such as Grupo Evolução, the Center for Black Culture and Art, and QUILOMBHOJE; events like the First Meeting of Black Entities of São Paulo, the First Week of Black Art and Culture; and publications such as *Jornegro* and *Cadernos Negros*. In *Orpheus and Power* (1994) scholar Michael Hanchard comments on the significance of the MNU: "For the first time in Brazil, the advocacy of a race-class position was not marginalized by the Afro-Brazilian intelligentsia, and in fact had come to supplant accommodationist, assimilationist paradigms as the dominant position of the black movement. What was missing, by the later part of the 1970s, were events to propel these intellectual and political positions into forms of praxis."

The organization holds a comprehensive view of the problem of racial discrimination in Brazil. Unlike the FRENTE NEGRA BRASILEIRA (Black Brazilian Front) of the 1930s, TEATRO EXPERIMENTAL DO NEGRO (Black Experimental Theater), which was active from 1944 to 1968, and other precursors, the MNU deals with the racial question in all its aspects: political, social, cultural, and economic. Therefore, the MNU combines a broad range of activities in order to carry on its political project, ranging from grassroots rights education to public campaigns. For instance, the MNU participated in the 1979 campaign for amnesty of political prisoners in Brazil. In this case, the MNU made a statement protesting the exclusionary social-economic process that particularly victimizes the black population and in part explains the disproportionate number of Afro-Brazilians in the country's penal system. The MNU's concerns embraced topics as diverse as police violence, job opportunities for blacks, agrarian reform, education, health, and housing.

It also embraced questions related to black women and homosexuals. The MNU women, for instance, carried out educational programs in BAHIA. Furthermore, the MNU supported individual candidates in electoral campaigns, such as BENEDITA DA SILVA, who in 1982 was elected as a city councilor in RIO DE JANEIRO and then in 1986 became the first black woman elected to the National Congress.

After its birth and ascendance during the late 1970s and the early 1980s, the MNU began to decline. The MNU's reduced impact on the national political arena is in part attributed to poor material resources and to the proliferation of competing groups. The MNU was never financially self-sufficient and relied on donations in order to carry out its activities. The MNU's organizational diversity, which made unity difficult to achieve, was another factor relevant to the progressive decrease in the MNU's action: the independence of the MNU's action groups often generated internal conflict.

Nevertheless, among the groups that have been responsible for building the black movement in Brazil, the MNU is the organization that came the closest to the mass-based claims and aspirations of its proponents and represents a rupture in the history of Brazil's black movements. It moved away from an elitist and academic approach to the racial question and instead took a more pragmatic and cross-class approach. The coalitions that the MNU created with political parties contributed to career politicians' acceptance of the racial question. From the end of the 1970s on, all the leftist political parties included special policies directed to the black population in their platforms, and many were in fact implemented. When Leonel Brizola was elected governor of the state of Rio de Janeiro in 1982, he nominated several activists of the black movement as heads of some governmental secretariats during his mandate. For instance, Carlos Alberto Cão was appointed secretary of labor, Edialeda Salgado Nascimento was the minister of social promotion, and Carlos Magno Nazareth headed the military police. The MNU was fundamental in introducing new challenges to racial discrimination and inequality in Brazil.

See also Black Consciousness in Brazil; Gay and Lesbian Movements in Latin America and the Caribbean.

Michelle Gueraldi

Movimento Popular de Libertação de Angola

See Popular Movement for the Liberation of Angola.

Mozambican National Resistance

Mozambican opposition movement and later political party.

The Resistência Nacional Moçambicana, or Mozambican National Resistance (RENAMO), emerged in the late 1970s as the Mozambican National Resistance (MNR) and in 1980 became a South African instrument to destabilize MOZAMBIQUE. The movement was organized by Rhodesian security forces and Portuguese Mozambicans who recruited disaffected Mozambicans, many of whom were former African members of the Portuguese colonial armed forces. Its initial objective was to undermine the Mozambican-based Zimbabwean freedom fighters, but when ZIMBABWE became independent in 1980, the South African government transferred the MNR to SOUTH AFRICA. The South African government viewed the fall of white-ruled colonial regimes in ANGOLA, Mozambique, and Zimbabwe, combined with rising internal unrest, as the beginning of a "total onslaught" on the

APARTHEID regime and saw the MNR as an instrument to keep the Mozambican government weak and dependent.

Under South African instruction, RENAMO set out to destroy the Mozambican economy, targeting railways, health centers, schools, bridges, administrative posts, roads, and other infrastructure projects. RENAMO initially relied on violent coercion to recruit new members, but over time many rural people voluntarily joined or provided other forms of support, due to their disaffection with the ruling party FRONT FOR THE LIBERATION OF MOZAMBIQUE (FRELIMO)'s socialist policies. Despite waning South African support (due to international pressure and domestic reform), by the late 1980s RENAMO numbered between 15,000 and 20,000 troops and had brought the Mozambican government to its knees. Negotiations concluded with a 1992 ceasefire and demobilization, and by the national elections in 1994 RENAMO had transformed itself into a political party and the primary opposition in Mozambique's new multiparty political system. As a political party, RENAMO continued to lack a coherent ideology other than very superficial calls for democracy, a free market economy, individual freedoms, and the reinstatement of traditional authorities. It later formed a multiparty coalition with the Electoral Union. In the 1999 elections, REMAMO-EU won 117 of the 250 parliamentary seats. It remains the chief opposition to the governing Frelimo Party in Mozambique.

See also Political Movements in Africa.

Bibliography

Vines, Alex. *Renamo: Terrorism in Mozambique.* Centre for Southern African Studies, 1991.

Minter, William. *Apartheid's Contras: An Inquiry into the Roots of War in Angola and Mozambique.* Witwatersrand University Press, 1994.

Eric Young

Mozambique

Country on the east coast of southern Africa bounded on the north by Tanzania, on the east by the Mozambique Channel of the Indian Ocean, on the south and southwest by South Africa and Swaziland, and on the west by Zimbabwe, Zambia, and Malawi.

Much of Mozambique's history has been marked by strife. Conflicts between the numerous indigenous societies were exacerbated by the initial expansion of regional kingdoms in the eighth century and then by Portuguese imperialism beginning in the sixteenth century. Eventually, Mozambicans turned against the Portuguese in a long and bloody war for independence. PORTUGAL relinquished control of its African colonies in 1975, but independence did not bring lasting peace. In the late 1970s the Mozambican government fought a costly war against the MOZAMBICAN NATIONAL RESISTANCE (Portuguese acronym, RENAMO), a force backed by RHODESIA (now ZIMBABWE) and SOUTH AFRICA. The war with RENAMO devastated Mozambique's economy and left thousands dead. Although peace came to Mozambique in the mid-1990s, the country remains one of the poorest in Africa and is deeply dependent on foreign aid.

Early History

In the third century C.E., as Bantu-speaking people migrated to the area now known as Mozambique, they displaced descendants of the KHOIKHOI of southwestern Africa. The character of the societies that emerged was defined largely by geography. In the south, the Chopi, Tonga, and TSONGA ethnic groups, all descendants of larger groups from southeastern Africa, were typically organized into village-sized political units. In the central regions, around the ZAMBEZI RIVER, lived the Barue, Maravi, Macua-Lomue, SHONA, and Tonga (to be distinguished from the southern ethnic group of the same name). These groups, however, were not internally homogeneous and relied on a variety of forms of social organization. The Maravi, for example, were composed of a series of decentralized kingdoms, which included the subgroups CHEWA, Nyanja, Chipeta, Zimba, Nsenga, and Nyassa. The Macua-Lomue, in contrast, were organized around clans, which often made alliances against invading Maravi peoples. Further north were the MAKONDE and YAO, living in isolation among the hills of the Mueda Plateau, about sixty kilometers (about forty miles) south of what is now TANZANIA.

Arab traders began coming to what is now Mozambique as early as the eighth century. The early trade focused on northern regions and along the Zambezi River. The Arab traders brought beads, ceramics, cloth, glass, salt, and metal goods to trade for gold, ivory, palm oil, and rhinoceros horn. This trade expanded with the cooperation of local African leaders, and by the fifteenth century the Arabs had established several trading stations along the Zambezi. Not long after the Arab traders established themselves, the Shona of present-day Zimbabwe became a major influence in central Mozambique. Before the eleventh century, Shona influence was negligible, but the Shona presence increased after the ascendance of the Karanga subgroup. The Karanga leader Nyatsimba Mutota, who became known as the *Monomotapa* (the Pillager), tried to conquer the Zambezi Valley in the latter half of the fifteenth century. Although Mutota was unsuccessful, his son carried on the war, which eventually destroyed many small kingdoms. The war also disrupted many local political entities and dislocated people throughout southern Mozambique.

Early Arab and Portuguese Influence in Mozambique

After Portuguese explorer VASCO DA GAMA arrived in 1498, the Portuguese colonizers who followed soon challenged the Arabs' economic preeminence and the Shona's military dominance. The Portuguese initially confined their activities to trading for supplies along the coast while en route to India. Soon, however, they ventured inland as part of the GOLD TRADE and the

Mozambican voters cast their ballots in 1999, in the country's second multiparty elections. The first multiparty elections were held in 1994. *Associated Press.*

IVORY TRADE. Jesuit priests brought CHRISTIANITY, and some African leaders proved amenable to the demands of the Portuguese, who had taken over much of the domestic and international trade. The Portuguese gradually fragmented and dismantled the Monomotapa kingdom through material enticement and force. More importantly, using land ceded to them by local rulers in 1629, the Portuguese introduced settlers to Mozambique and the system of *prazos,* or leaseholds. The prazos were a semifeudal system of land tenure in which the land remained the property of the Portuguese Crown, but settlers could lease it for a fixed time, usually three lifetimes. With the proceeds from the land, which included the right to compel local inhabitants to provide labor, the leaseholders were expected to provide for their own defense.

The prazos system was an affordable way for Portugal, the poorest European imperial power, to expand its influence, but the system also gave wide-ranging autonomy to the leaseholders, the *prazeros*. The prazeros adopted many indigenous practices and eventually used their land rights to build kingdoms modeled on indigenous political units. These hybrid colonial kingdoms were ruled by families of mixed African and Portuguese descent and depended on slave armies for defense. The prazeros and their African collaborators also played a prominent role in sustaining the INDIAN OCEAN SLAVE TRADE, which reached its height in the 1820s and 1830s after Britain banned slave trading in British colonies. The booming slave trade provided about 15,000 slaves annually to BRAZIL, which amounted to about 10 percent of the annual trade across the Atlantic at the time. During the middle of the nineteenth century, the area of Mozambique south of the Zambezi River effectively came under the control of the NGUNI leader Soshangane and his Gaza empire. With their authority threatened by the independence of the prazeros in the Zambezi Valley and by Soshangane's de facto control of southern Mozambique, the Portuguese changed tactics to save their "overseas province." Portugal feared that the British and the Germans would challenge Portuguese claims to Mozambique when the European SCRAMBLE FOR AFRICA began in earnest in the 1880s. To deter such a challenge, Portuguese troops swept through the interior and occupied much of the colony. Having conquered the land, colonial authorities then gave large concessions to charter companies to occupy it. After the BERLIN CONFERENCE OF 1884–1885, at which the European powers divided Africa among themselves, Portuguese colonial forces maintained at least a minimal presence in most of what is today Mozambique. Although some indigenous groups surrendered to Portuguese colonial rule, many others fought extended wars of resistance, particularly in the Zambezi Valley and on the Mueda Plateau.

Portuguese Colonialism

Violence and neglect characterized Portuguese COLONIAL RULE in Mozambique. The Portuguese dictator Antonio de Oliveira Salazar, who ruled Portugal from 1932 to 1968, centralized administrative control over the territory for the first time and instituted a system of forced labor on the indigenous people. The forced labor could be avoided only by the few who could find employment outside the colony or by those who owned land and obtained a Portuguese education, thus earning *assimilado* (assimilated) status. To avoid forced labor, thousands of people migrated to South Africa to work in gold and diamond mines. Thousands of others who did not leave the country were forced to work on large plantations harvesting SUGAR, tea, and other agricultural products.

Few Africans in Mozambique gained the status of assimilado, which meant embracing Salazar's concept of "Lusotropicalism." This theory claimed that Portugal was uniquely capable of creating a nonracial society. However, the theory was little more than a myth created to persuade the Portuguese people to support their country's colonial presence in Mozambique and other parts of Africa. In addition, although Salazar's rhetoric was race-neutral on the surface, in reality his colonial policies blatantly discriminated against Africans. Salazar's policies did little to improve Mozambique. When Marcello Caetano replaced Salazar as Portugal's prime minister in 1968, Africans in Mozambique had few opportunities for education, health care, or skilled employment, and violent repression was commonplace.

Struggle for Independence

Organized opposition to Portuguese colonialism was initially fragmented. Colonial authorities suppressed expressions of discontent in virtually all urban and rural areas of Mozambique.

Instead, opposition groups formed among students in Lisbon, Portugal, and in Paris, FRANCE, and among exiles in SOUTHERN RHODESIA, NYASALAND (now MALAWI), and Tanzania. In 1962 the fragmented opposition united to form the FRONT FOR THE LIBERATION OF MOZAMBIQUE (Portuguese acronym, Frelimo) under the leadership of Eduardo Mondlane. Mondlane and Frelimo used nationalist appeals to unite opposition groups against the injustices of Portuguese colonialism. Frelimo leaders soon concluded that independence could be won only through armed struggle because the Portuguese denied even basic rights to Africans. In 1964 the war for independence began in northern Mozambique.

Relying on bases in Tanzania, Frelimo's Chinese-trained troops faced little Portuguese resistance and quickly asserted control over much of northern Mozambique. Frelimo's initial successes were soon rebuffed, however, by stiffening Portuguese resistance and by a civilian resettlement program that denied Frelimo much-needed local support. Frelimo responded by opening a second front in the northwestern Tete Province, catching the Portuguese off guard. By the late 1960s, however, Frelimo faced a series of devastating setbacks. In 1969 Portugal's colonial secret police assassinated Mondlane, and many Frelimo bases were destroyed in a major Portuguese offensive. Portuguese authorities also stepped up their resettlement program, and construction of the Cabora Bassa Dam on the Zambezi River blocked some of Frelimo's transport routes into the south. Odds against Frelimo worsened further as the colonial armed forces increased African recruitment, siphoning off potential rebel recruits and swelling the ranks of Portugal's colonial army.

Under the leadership of SAMORA MACHEL, Frelimo survived the Portuguese counteroffensive and moved into the Zambezi Valley. By the early 1970s, Frelimo claimed "liberated zones" in approximately one-fourth of the country. As the war turned against Portugal, many in the Portuguese military became increasingly frustrated because their forces were spread thin fighting counterinsurgency wars in the Portuguese colonies of ANGOLA and GUINEA-BISSAU. Military officers in Portugal overthrew the Caetano government in April 1974, and the new military government soon ended the war in Mozambique and agreed to a transition to independence.

A Luta Continua (The Struggle Continues)

The coup d'état in Lisbon did not bring peace to Mozambique. Soon after independence in June 1975, Mozambique closed its border with Rhodesia and began supporting rebel forces of the Zimbabwe African National Union (ZANU) in their war against white minority rule in Rhodesia. In response, the Rhodesian regime attacked refugee camps and military training bases inside Mozambique and created the Mozambican National Resistance (Portuguese acronym, RENAMO) to destabilize Mozambique. Even as it battled RENAMO, the Frelimo government sought to implement wide-ranging socialist policies and to consolidate its power throughout the country. Frelimo thus conceived of the battle as one with two fronts: one was a defensive strategy to protect itself from Rhodesian, South African, and international imperialism; the second was an offensive for the creation of a new socialist society. *A Luta Continua!* ("The struggle continues!") became a popular slogan with dual meaning.

Rhodesia won its independence in 1980 and was renamed Zimbabwe. Control of RENAMO was then transferred to South Africa. The apartheid government in South Africa used RENAMO to continue destabilizing Mozambique and to pressure the Frelimio government to stop supporting the antiapartheid AFRICAN NATIONAL CONGRESS (ANC). In the early 1980s RENAMO became little more than a proxy force for South Africa. Under South African command, RENAMO attacked administrative buildings, health centers, schools, rural villages, and infrastructure projects throughout central Mozambique. RENAMO boosted its numbers through forced recruitment, but it also attracted some support from rural Mozambicans who were alienated by Frelimo's socialist policies. Support for Frelimo had faltered after the government failed in its effort to mechanize agriculture production on state-run collective farms. Agricultural production was further devastated by a cycle of severe floods and droughts in the late 1970s and early 1980s. Many rural Mozambicans also resented Frelimo's opposition to traditional leaders and traditional religious practices.

Despite receiving substantial military aid from the Union of Soviet Socialist Republics (USSR) and from Malawi, Tanzania, and Zimbabwe, Frelimo was unable to gain the upper hand in the war against RENAMO. In 1984 Mozambique and South Africa signed a mutual nonaggression pact, but South Africa ignored the agreement and continued to orchestrate RENAMO attacks. In 1986 President Machel was killed in a mysterious plane crash in South Africa. Evidence that surfaced in the late 1990s indicates that the South African military may have downed the aircraft, although some blamed the crash on errors made by the Soviet pilots. (Machel was survived by his wife, GRAÇA MACHEL, a prominent human rights advocate who married NELSON MANDELA in 1998.) With Machel dead and RENAMO attacks continuing to wreak havoc on the economy, Mozambique was on the brink of disintegration. Frelimo's socialist economic policies failed as well, in part because Frelimo was unable to defend Mozambique against South African aggression.

Structural Adjustment and Peace

Mozambique's minister of foreign affairs JOAQUIM CHISSANO took Machel's place as president and soon began working to guide the country out of its economic and military crisis. Chissano gradually backed away from the socialist economic policies of his predecessors, but RENAMO attacks continued. After the USSR began to collapse in 1989, Britain, Portugal, and the United States became the primary supporters of the beleaguered Frelimo government. Support did not come without conditions, particularly from the International Monetary Fund and World Bank, which tied the financing of Mozambique's economic program to political liberalization. At Frelimo's Fifth Congress in July 1989, the party dropped its Marxist-Leninist ideology and

Mozambique (At a Glance)

OFFICIAL NAME: Republic of Mozambique

AREA: 801,590 sq km (309,494 sq mi)

LOCATION: Southern Africa, bounded on the north by Tanzania; on the east by the Mozambique Channel of the Indian Ocean; on the south and southwest by South Africa and Swaziland; and on the west by Zimbabwe, Zambia, and Malawi

CAPITAL: Maputo (population 1,114,000; 2003 estimate)

OTHER MAJOR CITIES: Beira (population 458,200) and Nampula (349,800) (2003 estimates)

POPULATION: 17,479,266 (2003 estimate)

POPULATION DENSITY: 22 persons per sq km (65 persons per sq mi)

POPULATION BELOW AGE 15: 42.1 percent (male 3,634,173; female 3,725,396; 2003 estimates)

POPULATION GROWTH RATE: .82 percent (2003 estimate)

TOTAL FERTILITY RATE: 4.87 children born per woman (2003 estimate)

LIFE EXPECTANCY AT BIRTH: Total population: 31.3 years (male 30.98 years; female 31.63 years; 2003 estimates)

INFANT MORTALITY RATE: 199 deaths per 1,000 live births (2003 estimate)

LITERACY RATE (AGE 15 AND OVER WHO CAN READ AND WRITE): Total population: 47.8 percent (male 63.5 percent; female 32.7 percent; 2003 estimates)

EDUCATION: Due to civil instability and the limited number of trained teachers, in the early 1990s only about 1.2 million pupils attended primary schools and just over 150,000 students went to secondary schools. In 2000 only 54 percent of primary-school-age children attended primary schools. Secondary schools enrolled less than 10 percent of eligible children.

LANGUAGES: Portuguese is the official language, though Swahili and various Bantu languages are spoken commonly.

ETHNIC GROUPS: Mozambique has ten major ethnic groups, including the Makua-Lomwe (which accounts for nearly 50 percent of the northern population), Tsonga, Malawi, Shona, and Yao.

RELIGIONS: Indigenous beliefs, 50 percent; Christian, 30 percent; Muslim, 20 percent

CLIMATE: Mozambique has tropical savanna with a dry season lasting from April to October. July (winter) temperatures range from an average of 21°C (70°F) in the north to 18°C (65°F) in the south. January (summer) temperatures average about 27°C (80°F). Although rainfall can be irregular, the northern regions receive around 1,500 mm (about 60 in) annually, as opposed to 750 mm (about 30 in) in the south.

LAND, PLANTS, AND ANIMALS: Two-fifths of Mozambique is coastal lowland. Inland the land rises to the western low hills and plateaus to the far western mountains, including Mount Binga's 2,436 m (7,992 ft) peak. Northwest Mozambique's Angonia Plateau lies in the Great Rift Valley. Flowing from the western highlands to the Mozambique Channel are several rivers, including the Zambezi; other major rivers include the Ruvuma, Save, and Limpopo. With landscapes ranging from grassland to tropical rain forest, Mozambique is home to many species, including zebra, buffalo, rhinoceros, giraffe, lion, and elephant.

NATURAL RESOURCES: Mineral resources include coal, iron, salt, tantalite, diamonds, asbestos, bauxite, copper, manganese, titanium, natural gas, and soil.

CURRENCY: The metical (Mt)

GROSS DOMESTIC PRODUCT (GDP): $19.2 billion (2002 estimate)

GDP PER CAPITA: $1,000 (2002 estimate)

GDP REAL GROWTH RATE: 8 percent (2002 estimate)

PRIMARY ECONOMIC ACTIVITIES: Agriculture, industry, and services

PRIMARY CROPS: Cotton, cashew nuts, sugarcane, tea, cassava, corn, rice, and tropical fruits

INDUSTRIES: Food, beverages, chemicals (fertilizer, soap, paints), petroleum products, textiles, cement, glass, asbestos, and tobacco

PRIMARY EXPORTS: Aluminum, cashews, cotton, and sugar

PRIMARY IMPORTS: Food, clothing, farm equipment, and petroleum

PRIMARY TRADE PARTNERS: South Africa, United Kingdom, Zimbabwe, Japan, and Portugal

GOVERNMENT: Following a new constitution in 1990, a multiparty republic was instituted. In the executive branch, the prime minister, currently Pascal Mocumbi, is head of government, while the president, currently Joaquim Chissano, is chief of state. The Assembly of the Republic, a unicameral national legislature with 250 members, is directly elected. In the 1999 elections, the Front for the Liberation of Mozambique (FRELIMO) won 133 seats; the main opposition party, the Mozambique National Resistance-Electoral Union (RENAMO-UE), claimed 117 seats.

Kate Tuttle

---

opened party membership to business and religious leaders. Later that year the president submitted a new constitution to the Popular Assembly. The new constitution included provisions for multiparty elections.

The government also entered negotiations with RENAMO. In 1992, after protracted negotiations monitored by the United Nations (UN), both parties signed the General Peace Agreement. The agreement called for an immediate cease-fire, the demobilization of the militaries and the creation of a new national military, and democratic elections in 1994. In the 1994 UN–monitored elections, Chissano won reelection as president, and Frelimo won control of the legislature. RENAMO became the official opposition. In December 1999 presidential elections Chissano defeated RENAMO leader Afonso Dhlakama. Legislative elections held at the same time renewed Frelimo's hold on the Assembly of the Republic. Dhlakama and RENAMO claimed that electoral fraud had tainted the results of both elections, but the Supreme Court of Mozambique disagreed and certified the elections in January 2000. In the November 2003 municipal elections, Frelimo dealt RENAMO another blow by capturing twenty-nine out of thirty-three municipalities.

The end of the war in 1992 did not end all of Mozambique's problems. The war left thousands of guns throughout the country, feeding an increase in crime. In addition, Mozambique became a major shipment point for drugs to South Africa. Both crime and corruption hobbled the country's attempts to rebuild the economy. However, from its low point during the 1980s, the economy grew at a healthy overall rate throughout the 1990s; inflation dropped to single digits. But heavy floods in 1999 and 2000 displaced more than one million people and disrupted the economy again; the inflation rate returned to double digits. Though two-thirds of its population remains in poverty, Mozambique has recently increased export revenues through aluminum production. The tourism industry, which seeks to attract visitors to Mozambique's beaches and to Gorongosa National Park, is also growing.

See also African Socialism; Bantu Migrations in Sub-Saharan Africa; Nationalism in Africa; Structural Adjustment in Africa; United Nations in Africa.

Bibliography

Hall, Margaret, and Tom Young. *Confronting Leviathan: Mozambique since Independence.* Ohio University Press, 1997.

Isaacman, Allen. *Mozambique: From Colonialism to Revolution, 1900–1982.* Westview Press, 1983.

Newitt, Malyn. *A History of Mozambique.* Hurst & Co., 1995.

Eric Young

Mozambique, Luis de

Panamanian slave who led a maroon settlement, located in the San Blas Mountains, in the mid-sixteenth century.

See also Panama.

Mphahlele, Es'kia

1919–

South African writer best known for his autobiography *Down Second Avenue*, which portrays his early life as a black South African.

Born Ezekiel Mphahlele (in 1977 he changed his first name to Es'kia) in Marabastad Township, PRETORIA, Mphahlele was educated at Adams Teaching Training College. He became a teacher, but in the early 1950s he was banned from teaching because of his opposition to the Bantu Education Act of 1953, which created an inferior educational system for blacks. In the mid-1950s he worked as an editor for the literary journal *Drum*, and in 1956 he obtained a master's degree from the University of South Africa. Mphahlele went into exile from SOUTH AFRICA in 1957. He subsequently lived in NIGERIA, where he was an editor for the periodical *Black Orpheus*; in KENYA; in ZAMBIA; and in the United States, where he attended the University of Denver and taught at the University of Pennsylvania. He returned to South Africa in 1977 and later became a professor at the University of Witwatersrand. In 1987 he retired from his position at the university.

Mphahlele's first book, *Man Must Live* (1947), is a collection of short stories about black life in South Africa. *Down Second Avenue* (1959), his second and most famous work, achieved great critical and popular success and is considered a classic of South African literature. *The Wanderers* (1971) is an autobiographical novel dealing with themes of exile. His novel *Chirundu* (1979) focuses on the conflicts felt by a fictional African politician. *Afrika My Music* (1984) is another autobiographical work, describing Mphahlele's exile and return to South Africa. His novel *Father Come Home* (1984) is concerned with the suffering caused by the Natives Land Act of 1913, which restricted blacks from residing in certain areas in South Africa. The characters in Mphahlele's fictional works are drawn with vivid realism and are portrayed not as victims but as survivors who overcome the harshness of their lives.

Mphahlele's other books include the critical works *The African Image* (1962) and *Voices in the Whirlwind, and Other Essays* (1972). A collection of his letters, *Bury Me at the Marketplace*, was published in 1984. In 1999 Ruth Obee published the literary study *Es'kia Mphahlele: Themes of Alienation and African Humanism* (1999).

See also Fiction, English-Language, in Africa.

Mpondo

Ethnic group of South Africa; also known as the Amapondo and the Pondo.

The Mpondo primarily inhabit Eastern Cape Province, SOUTH AFRICA. They speak XHOSA, a Bantu language in the NGUNI group. Approximately 2 million people consider themselves Mpondo.

See also Bantu: Dispersion and Settlement.

Mpongwe

Ethnic group of northwestern Gabon.

Some historians believe that the Mpongwe migrated to the northwest coast of present-day GABON from the interior around 2,000 years ago, while others contend that they migrated during the tenth century C.E. The Mpongwe's own legends hold that their ancestors emerged spontaneously from the ground.

The Mpongwe and the neighboring ORUNGU share many ethnolinguistic similarities. Their languages both belong to the Myènè group, whose speakers say *myènè,* "I say that," to initiate conversation. As a result of migrations throughout the centuries, the Mpongwe formed numerous clans, each headed by an *oga,* or chief. According to tradition, the Ndiwa were the first of the clans to reach the coast. The clans of the Mpongwe traded extensively among themselves and probably with the Loango kingdom to the south. The Mpongwe fished, hunted, and grew yams and other crops. Each settlement included a few artisans who made utensils and religious paraphernalia. The Mpongwe were also accomplished sailors who traveled in dugout canoes along the coast as far north as the Cameroon River.

In the sixteenth century, as competition for trade with European ships increased, the interior Orungu forced many of the Mpongwe clans toward the Estuary of Gabon. Slaveholders themselves, the Mpongwe became extensively involved as middlemen in the transatlantic trade in slaves and other commodities. The incursions of the Orungu and a Dutch massacre of the Ndiwa clan in 1698 began to undermine Mpongwe hegemony in the estuary region. Mpongwe dominance was further eroded in the early nineteenth century, when the FANG migrated to the region and a subsequent low birthrate and smallpox epidemic cut the Mpongwe population by between one-third and one-half. But as traders and entrepreneurs, the Mpongwe prospered. Their access to mission schools earned them an elite status within the French colonial bureaucracy; this in turn permitted them to become an instrumental part of the Gabonese nationalist movement. Since independence, the Mpongwe have continued to play a preeminent role in the country's political and economic life. Today the Mpongwe number around 60,000.

See also Languages, African: An Overview; Loango, Transatlantic Slave Trade.

Eric Young

Mpumalanga

Province in northeastern South Africa bounded on the east by Mozambique and Swaziland, on the south by the province of KwaZulu-Natal, on the north by Northern Province, and on the west by Gauteng and Free State provinces.

Created in 1994, Mpumalanga, formerly Eastern Transvaal, covers 79,490 sq km (30,691 sq mi) and includes part of TRANSVAAL, one of the four former South African provinces, and the three former Bantustans (or black homelands) of KaNgwane, KwaNdebele, and Lebowa. The name *Mpumalanga* means "the place where the sun rises."

Most of Mpumalanga consists of grassy plains. The western part of the province is situated on the High Veld, a large plateau that covers much of central SOUTH AFRICA. The Drakensberg Mountains rise in the northeastern region of Mpumalanga, an area that also features deep gorges. The highest peaks are Die Berg, Mount Anderson, and Mauchsberg. Extensive commercial forests and timber mills are located in the northeastern region. In the eastern part of the province the land drops abruptly to the Low Veld, an area of lower elevation, which has subtropical vegetation. The Olifants, Blyde, and Krokodil rivers flow through the province. Temperatures range from 18° to 29°C (64° to 84°F) in the summer and from 6° to 27°C (43° to 80°F) in the winter. Annual rainfall totals about 430 mm (about 17 in), with most of the rain falling in the summer months, from November to March.

In 1999 the population of Mpumalanga was three million. Black Africans make up the majority of the population. The two primary languages spoken are siSwati and Zulu; Afrikaans and English are also spoken. The province's capital at Nelspruit serves as an administrative and commercial hub. Other important cities include Witbank, a major center for the coal industry; Secunda, the site of a large coal-to-oil conversion plant; Lydenburg; Heidelberg; and Ermelo. Important historical sites in the province include Barberton, Pilgrim's Rest, and Sabie, three gold rush towns from the late nineteenth century; and Fort Merensky, built near Middelburg by Sotho and a German missionary during the nineteenth century.

Mpumalanga has a varied economy built around timber, coal, agriculture, and tourism. Chief agricultural products include maize (corn), sugarcane, and citrus fruits; farmers also raise sheep and dairy cattle. Nature reserves such as Kruger National Park, one of the world's largest national parks, attract many tourists. The park is situated along the Mozambique border, and the northern section extends into neighboring Northern Province.

Mpumalanga's provincial government consists of a premier, an executive council of ten ministers, and a legislature. The provincial assembly and premier are elected for five-year terms or until the next national election. Political parties are awarded assembly seats based on the percentage of votes each party receives in the province during the national elections. The assembly elects a premier, who then appoints the members of the executive council.

See also Free State; Gauteng; KwaZulu-Natal; Mozambique; Swaziland.

Msiri

African trader who was founder and ruler of the Yeke (Garenganze) kingdom located in southern Central Africa; also known as Mwanda, Msidi, or Moshidi.

Born with the name of Ngelengwa in TANZANIA, Msiri was the son of a SUMBWA chief and trader. Msiri started his career on the trade routes forged by his father between East and Central Africa. In 1856 he negotiated with Mwata Kazembe, chief of the LUNDA empire, for the right to settle and trade in south Katanga.

There Msiri used alliances with local ruling families and firearms acquired from traders to build his own empire, the Yeke or Garenganze. By 1870 Msiri's empire extended throughout Katanga. He also built his trade networks by forging ties with TIPPU TIP, a trader of the SWAHILI PEOPLE. He forged ties with many other East African merchants as well. With these traders he exported slaves and copper, also working in the IVORY TRADE, in return for cloth and firearms.

In 1880, after the death of his father, Msiri proclaimed himself *mwami,* or king, of the region. For the next six years he was the most powerful ruler in what is now the southern DEMOCRATIC REPUBLIC OF THE CONGO. His empire extended over former LUBA and Lunda states, including areas formerly controlled by Mwata Kazembe, the salt springs of Mwashya and the Lualaba River. The stability of this empire, however, was short-lived. Revolts in newly acquired territories coupled with colonial advances weakened Msiri's control. Msiri tried to deter the Europeans, but they were intent on acquiring the mineral-rich land. In 1891 he was shot by a Belgian soldier after refusing to negotiate with representatives of the CONGO FREE STATE, declaring, "I am the master here, and so long as I live, the Kingdom of Garenganze shall have no other."

See also Slavery in Africa.

Bibliography

Verbeken, Auguste. *Msiri: Roi du Garenganze.* L. Cuypers, 1956.

Elizabeth Heath

Mswati III

1968–

***Ngwenyama* (chief or king) of Swaziland.**

The second youngest of at least sixty-seven sons of King SOBHUZA II, Makhosetive was only fifteen years old when chosen by his ailing father to succeed him to the throne. According to tradition, he was not to be crowned king until he turned twenty-one, and royal duties would be attended to by a regent, one of Sobhuza's wives. In 1983 Makhosetive was called away from his studies at Sherborne, England, to quell unrest generated by the removal of Queen Mother Dzeliwe as regent and the installation of Queen Ntombi. Further disputes between royal factions led to his coronation as King Mswati III, in April 1986, three years earlier than expected. In May 1986 Mswati dismissed the Liqoqo, the traditional advisory council to regents, which had assumed greater powers than were customary. In July 1986 he dismissed and charged with treason Prime Minister Prince Bhekimpi and several government officials for their role in the ejection of Queen Regent Dzeliwe, though he eventually pardoned those who were convicted. Following the confirmation of his kingship when he turned twenty-one, Mswati faced increasing demands by opposition leaders for transition to a multiparty democratic state in which the monarchy only serves a ceremonial function. Mswati refused these demands and again dismissed his prime minister. Swaziland's economy suffers from the withdrawal of large multinational corporations, which had considered the small nation a safe investment in the midst of the political volatility in neighboring SOUTH AFRICA and MOZAMBIQUE during the 1980s. In addition, criticism of the royal family with its monopoly on agricultural lands and its lavish spending on luxuries has intensified. A January 1996 eight-day prodemocracy strike by timber and sugar workers prompted Mswati to agree to hold forums on the future of the monarchy, but he insisted that he would not be forced to cede power.

Mubarak, Haji

1833–c.1873

Participant in many of the foundational events in Babi and Baha'i history.

Usually referred to as the "Ethiopian servant" of the Bab (Sayyid 'Ali-Muhammad Shirazi, founder of Babism), Haji Mubarak is celebrated in Baha'i literature for his saintliness and loyalty. Mubarak (which means "blessed" in Arabic) was a slave sold to the Bab's uncle, Haji Mirza Abu'l-Qasim, at the age of five and educated within the uncle's household. He was fully literate and astute at business affairs.

In 1842, the Bab—returning to Shiraz after a six-year absence—purchased Mubarak from his uncle for fourteen *tumans* (about $28). Mubarak served the Bab and his family for the rest of his life. He witnessed the sacred events surrounding the founding of the Babi religion, being present (in an adjoining room) on May 22, 1844, when the Bab first declared his mission. Members of the Baha'i faith recognize this event as the beginning of their religious history.

Shortly after that event, the Bab chose only two of his followers to accompany him on a pilgrimage to Mecca, Quddus (Mirza Muhammad 'Ali Barfarushi, the first in rank of the Bab's disciples) and Mubarak, who is known to have protected and defended his master faithfully. The Bab is recorded to have sacrificed, in accordance with the customs of Islamic pilgrimage, nineteen lambs in Mecca—nine in his own name, seven for Quddus, and three for Mubarak, securing for the latter the full rites of the hajj, and entitling him to the honorific title *Haji.*

When the Bab was arrested and exiled to Isfahan because of his heretical teachings, Mubarak remained in the Bab's house in Shiraz to serve the leader's wife (Khadijih Bagum) and mother. After the Bab's execution in 1850, his mother and his grandmother were forced to move to Karbala in Iraq. Mubarak accompanied them and died there, in their service, at about the age of forty.

To salvage their respectability, members of the Bab's family maintained in public that the Bab had not been executed but was still alive and on an extended business trip to India. Haji Mubarak helped to preserve this polite fiction by vowing to sweep the courtyard around the tomb of the Imam Husayn in Karbala every day until his master returned. He performed this pious duty every morning until his death.

Bibliography

Afnan, Abu'l-Qasim. *Black Pearls: Servants in the Households of the Bab and Baha'u'llah.* Kalimat Press, 1988.

Balyuzi, H. M. *The Bab: The Herald of the Day of Days.* George Ronald, 1973.

Nabil-i 'Azam (Muhammad-i Zarandi). *The Dawn-Breakers: Nabil's Narrative of the Early Days of the Baha'i Revelation.* Baha'i Publishing Trust, 1932.

Anthony A. Lee

Mubarak, Hosni

1928–

President of Egypt.

Hosni Mubarak's life largely parallels that of his predecessor and mentor, ANWAR AL-SADAT. Both were sons of minor government officials, and both were born in the NILE Delta region of EGYPT. Both pursued careers in the military, which seized political control of Egypt from the royal family in a 1952 coup. Each was considered weak and politically vulnerable when he assumed the presidency, and each emerged as a strong leader who solidified his hold on power. Yet Mubarak's career also differed from Sadat's in several important ways.

Mubarak graduated from the Cairo Military Academy in 1949. He then attended Egypt's air force academy and received advanced flight and bomber training at the Frunze General Staff Academy in the Soviet Union. Mubarak rose to prominence after the purge of air force leadership that followed its ignominious defeat in the 1967 Six-Day War with Israel. During this period he served as director of the Egyptian Air Force Academy. In 1971 Sadat named Mubarak air force commander. Many credit Mubarak with rebuilding the air force in the wake of the Six-Day War. He also received much of the credit for the air force's strong performance in the Yom Kippur War of 1973, when combined Egyptian and Syrian forces launched a surprise attack against Israel. Sadat promoted Mubarak to the rank of air marshal in 1974 and to vice president in 1975, a position he held until Sadat's assassination in October 1981.

After assuming office, Mubarak pursued a course of moderation. He upheld the Camp David Accords, the 1979 peace treaty between Egypt and Israel that stated that Israel would return portions of the Sinai Peninsula to Egypt in April 1982. Israel's invasion of Lebanon later that year, however, strained relations with Egypt. Meanwhile, Mubarak worked to improve Egypt's relationship with other Arab states—conditions had deteriorated in the wake of the accords. He also sought to reclaim Egypt's prominence among Arab nations by mediating between Arab states and Israel and by brokering Arab League support for military action against Iraq after its 1990 invasion of Kuwait. Mubarak sent approximately 40,000 Egyptian troops to support the anti-Iraq coalition during the 1991 PERSIAN GULF WAR. Mubarak also figured prominently in the 1993 deal between Israel and the Palestinian Liberation Organization.

Though Mubarak won reelection in 1987, 1993, and 1999, he has also faced a series of crises, including an assassination attempt in 1995, from which he emerged unharmed. In addition, Mubarak faces threats from radical Islamic opposition groups, most notably the Muslim Brotherhood and the Islamic Group. Just before parliamentary elections in 1995, Mubarak arrested several leaders of the Muslim Brotherhood, including some who were candidates in the election. He has also imposed martial law in Egypt and resorted to repression to quell violence by Islamic fundamentalists, though with little lasting effect. In late 1997 in the VALLEY OF THE KINGS in Luxor, members of the Islamic Group attacked and killed dozens of foreign tourists. The attack crippled Egypt's tourism industry, which attracts more than $3 billion per year in foreign currency. The Mubarak government currently wrestles with Egypt's high unemployment, widespread corruption, and determining who will succeed the man who is already the longest-serving leader in the nation's modern history.

See also Islam in Africa; Islamic Fundamentalism: An Interpretation; Tourism in Africa; Political Movements in Africa.

Bibliography

McDermott, Anthony. *Egypt from Nasser to Mubarak: A Flawed Revolution.* Croom Helm, 1988.

Tripp, Charles, and Roger Owen, eds. *Egypt under Mubarak.* Routledge, 1989.

Robert Fay

Mugabe, Robert

1924–

Revolutionary leader and president of Zimbabwe.

A teacher by training and a politician by practice, Robert Mugabe has been the preeminent political leader in ZIMBABWE for more than two decades. Born, raised, and trained as a teacher at Kutama Mission in Zvimba in what is now northwestern Zimbabwe, Mugabe taught at the mission school between 1941

Robert Mugabe leaves a polling station after casting his vote in the 2002 election. Reuters/CORBIS

and 1943. After several other brief teaching jobs around Zimbabwe (then Southern Rhodesia), Mugabe won a scholarship to the University of Fort Hare College in SOUTH AFRICA. There he was introduced to literature on communism, Marxism, and Gandhian passive resistance. After completing his bachelor's degree, he returned to Zimbabwe to teach. He later taught in Northern Rhodesia (now ZAMBIA) and GHANA.

In 1960 Mugabe returned home to enter politics. He first joined the nationalist group the Zimbabwe African People's Union (ZAPU), but in 1964, after several arrests and a falling-out with its leadership, Mugabe went to TANZANIA and joined the newly formed Zimbabwe African National Union (ZANU). ZANU inaugurated the war for independence that same year.

On returning to Southern Rhodesia, Mugabe was again arrested and spent most of the next decade in prison, earning bachelor degrees in law and administration while incarcerated. In prison, ZANU members elected Mugabe to replace Ndabaningi Sithole as party head. His position as party head was contested until 1976, when the military wing of ZANU recognized him as leader. After four more years of war, Mugabe and ZAPU leader JOSHUA NKOMO entered negotiations with the Rhodesians, concluding with Zimbabwe's independence in April 1980. In elections just before independence, Mugabe and ZANU won by a landslide, and he became prime minister.

In the early years of his regime, Mugabe proved to be a highly pragmatic leader. After the war he called for reconciliation and took care not to offend Western governments or the white community of Zimbabwe, whose skills and wealth the country needed. Although he has often espoused socialism, he has maintained an essentially free-market economy. At the same time, Mugabe has consolidated his power. He put considerable pressure on Nkomo and the ZAPU party until 1987, when they agreed to join ZANU, creating the ZANU–Patriotic Front (ZANU-PF). With the creation of an executive presidency the same year, opposition, official or otherwise, effectively ended. In elections in 1990 Mugabe won 78 percent of the popular vote. ZANU-PF remained the de facto ruling party, typically winning all but a handful of parliamentary seats.

Elitism and cronyism have become the norm in Mugabe's government. The Zimbabwean parliament has served as little more than a rubber stamp, and the president and his few advisers retain a tight grip on the most powerful ministries, such as defense, home affairs, and justice. In several corruption scandals Mugabe has intervened to halt the prosecution of close associates and family members. For many years, few within or outside government dared to oppose Mugabe, in the face of the bureaucracy's powerful patronage system.

Mugabe's policies in the early 2000s stirred greater domestic unrest and international condemnation. His disastrous land redistribution campaign drove white farmers out of the country, caused widespread shortages, and wrecked the economy. Increasingly unpopular, Mugabe fixed the 2002 presidential election to ensure his victory while his security forces repressed any opposition to the government. In 2003 labor groups and activists organized strikes and demonstrations to pressure Mugabe to step down. The president responded by arresting union activists and protesters. International leaders have become more outspoken in their opposition to Mugabe, accusing him of using murder, torture, and violence to remain in power. Meanwhile, his nation remains in crisis, facing runaway inflation, famine, poverty, and an AIDS pandemic.

See also Acquired Immunodeficiency Syndrome in Africa: An Interpretation; African Socialism; Political Movements in Africa.

Eric Young

Muhammad, Elijah

1897–1975

Black separatist leader of the Nation of Islam.

Elijah Muhammad was born Elijah Poole in Sandersville, Georgia, the sixth of seven children of William and Mariah Poole. He was favored by his siblings, parents, and grandfather and was perceived by them as destined for greatness. It was his grandfather who named him after the biblical Elijah, and throughout his childhood he was teasingly referred to as "the Prophet."

Aside from sharecropping and working at a sawmill, William Poole also pastored at two Baptist churches. Young Elijah was exposed to the ministry from a tender age. He took an avid interest in Christian theology, but his father's fire and brimstone sermons caused him to question what seemed like a dour interpretation of spirituality. It was many years before he would break away from Christianity completely, and ironically it was William Poole who first introduced him to the NATION OF ISLAM.

When he was around ten years old, he left school out of economic necessity and began chopping firewood with his sister. Up until this point he had lived in relative shelter from the brutal racist practices of the region. This ended when he witnessed, as an adolescent, the lynching of an eighteen-year-old acquaintance. On another occasion, walking home from work, a white man taunted him with the severed ears of a black person. The horror of these two incidents, he later recounted, made him ripe for black separatist ideology: "I had seen enough of the white man's brutality in Georgia to last me 26,000 years."

Elijah's youth and early adulthood were marked by a pattern of floating jobs and long periods of unemployment. In 1923, married with two children, he migrated to industrial Detroit. But even in the years before the Depression there was an economic downturn in many large cities. With the pressure of three more children to support and little prospect for work, Elijah went through a period of listlessness and heavy drinking.

It was at this time that his father, on a spiritual quest of his own, started speaking to Elijah and his brothers about the Islamic movement. In 1931, Elijah attended his first Islamic meeting and met its leader WALLACE D. FARD (pronounced Far-rood). He became fully immersed in the movement, abandoning his "slave owner" surname. He was initially called Karriem, and then later Muhammad. Within the year he became Fard's top assistant. As the Muslim movement grew more prominent in the black community it became a target for government investigation, and Fard's leadership began to suffer. In 1933, in an attempt to remove himself from the negative spotlight, Fard named Muhammad supreme minister, and when Fard disappeared the following year Muhammad succeeded him as head of the Nation of Islam.

Despite continual police hostility and subsequent relocation to CHICAGO, ILLINOIS, the Nation of Islam under Muhammad prospered and evolved. Rather than shunning the technology of Western culture, as Fard had encouraged, Muhammad invested in radios and modern farm equipment. In order for black separatism to succeed, he believed, total economic independence was crucial. In 1945 the Nation purchased 140 acres of farmland in Michigan. Two years later, a Nation-owned grocery store, restaurant, and bakery opened in Chicago.

As the Nation's influence spread throughout various black communities around the United States, Muhammad began to live a more luxurious lifestyle that seemingly contradicted the Muslim creed of stringency and humility. He purchased cars and real estate and apparently had sexual liaisons with a number of young women in the movement. When MALCOLM X was murdered after leaving the movement, there were many who believed that Muhammad's violent denunciation of his onetime protégé instigated the assassination.

As a leader in the quest for black nationalism, Muhammad was, for a long time, considered a hostile force by the United States government. He served a jail sentence for draft evasion during World War II and was wired by the FBI for over two decades. Nevertheless, by the time of his death in 1975, his conservative approach made him seem moderate compared to other radical groups of the Civil Rights era. His emphasis on black self-sufficiency rather than overthrow of the government made him an appealing ally to such local officials as Mayor Richard Daley of Chicago. In 1974 he was commemorated by Daley who declared March 29th as "Honorable Elijah Muhammad Day" in Chicago.

See also Baptists; Civil Rights Movement.

Suzanne Albulak

Muhammad Idris

See Idris I.

Mukomberanwa, Nicholas

1940–2002

Zimbabwean sculptor.

Nicholas Mukomberanwa was one of Africa's most internationally successful sculptors. He grew up in the countryside outside HARARE (formerly known as Salisbury) and attended the Serima Mission School, where he was encouraged to experiment with woodcarving. During his school years, he also became familiar with representations of Christian and African religion. In 1965, while working as a police officer, Mukomberanwa began studying at Salisbury's Rhodes National Gallery. The new director, critic, and curator Frank McEwan had just established a workshop at the gallery to encourage local artists to pursue their talents. The workshop supplied artists with materials and some instruction and exposed the artists to some Western European art, particularly the work of the modernists.

While some of Mukomberanwa's sculpture can be likened to the work of European artists like Picasso and Brancusi, Mukomberanwa's work draws directly on his SHONA cultural heritage. Observers of Shona sculptors like Mukomberanwa, Tapfuma Gusta, and HENRY MUNYARADZI have described how they begin each work with a large piece of stone, typically serpentine or soapstone, but make no preliminary sketches. After a long meditation with the stone, the artist perceives what spirit lies within the rock and begins carving in order to bring it out. Mukomberanwa's sculptures are highly stylized and often use abstract, anthropomorphic forms. Generally, his pieces explore the complex relationships between humans and nature. Mukomberanwa's 1995 sculpture *Rainmaker* depicts a personification of the Shona rain spirit, and *Man and His Half-Shadow* (1995) contrasts two elongated heads of different colored stone, exploring the contrasts between earthly and spiritual life.

Mukomberanwa achieved tremendous international commercial success. His work was featured in the prestigious

Venice Biennale exhibition as well as the Africa Art Festival in London. He received numerous awards, and his work was acclaimed by many international art publications. At the time of his death in November 2002, a one-man exhibition of his sculptures was being planned at the Reece Gallery in New York for 2003.

See also Art and Architecture, African; African Religions: An Interpretation; Christianity; Zimbabwe.

Christopher Tiné

Muluzi, Bakili

1943–

President of Malawi since 1994.

Bakili Muluzi was born in Machinga in southern MALAWI (called Nyasaland at the time) and was educated in GREAT BRITAIN and Denmark. He entered parliament in 1975 after rising through the ranks of the ruling Malawi Congress Party (MCP) and held posts as the minister of education and party secretary general during the next several years. In 1982 Muluzi, having recently been demoted to a less prestigious post at the ministry of transport and communications and fearing that President HASTINGS KAMUZU BANDA might have him killed because he was gaining power in the party, left the MCP for private business. He served for several years as deputy head of the national chamber of commerce, slowly gathering his forces until 1992, when he founded the United Democratic Front (UDF), the first political alternative under Banda's dictatorship. Banda was forced to hold a referendum on one-party rule in June 1993 following widespread protests and a 1992 decision by Western donors to suspend their support of Malawi's repressive regime and its poor human rights record.

A majority of the voters approved of reform, and a new constitution providing for a multiparty system was adopted in May 1994. Muluzi defeated Banda in the country's first multiparty elections held that month. Muluzi's stated aims for his administration were to combat poverty and corruption, liberalize the economy, and improve Malawi's human rights situation. He immediately freed political prisoners and shut down three prisons that were reportedly the sites of many tortures. In the 1999 elections, Muluzi won a second five-year term while his party, the UDF, failed to capture a majority in parliament. He is currently working with other Southern African leaders to end the conflict between the ruling and opposition parties in ZIMBABWE. Economic and political unrest in Zimbabwe, one of Malawi's biggest trading partners, has had a disruptive effect on the economies of several Southern African nations.

See also Human Rights in Africa; Political Movements in Africa.

Mumuye

Ethnic group of Nigeria.

The Mumuye primarily inhabit Taraba State in eastern NIGERIA. They speak a Niger-Congo language. Approximately 400,000 people consider themselves Mumuye.

See also Languges, African: An Overview.

Mundang

Ethnic group of West Africa; also known as the Moundang.

The Mundang primarily inhabit northern CAMEROON, southwestern CHAD, and northeastern NIGERIA. They speak a Niger-Congo language and are closely related to the SARA people. Over 100,000 people consider themselves Mundang.

See also Languages, African: An Overview.

Muñequitos de Matanzas, Los

Family-based Cuban musical group founded in Matanzas in 1952 and renowned for its folkloric presentations of Afro-Cuban music and dance, especially the rumba.

For more than four decades, Los Muñequitos de Matanzas has sought to preserve and strengthen traditional Afro-Cuban song and dance. Founded in 1952 as Guanguanco Matancero, the group adopted its current name—which in English means "The Little Dolls of Matanzas"—a year later, after recording a hit song by that name. The group's music is highly percussive, with layers of complex rhythms played on congas, maracas, wooden box drums, and cylindrical wooden claves. Over the percussion, vocalists perform call-and-response choruses that alternate with the lead singer's improvisations. Beyond drawing attention to Cuba's rich legacy of folk music and dance, the troupe was also an important influence on the rise of SALSA MUSIC in the 1960s. With the growing popularity of world music during the 1980s and 1990s, the troupe has gained a much larger, international following.

Los Muñequitos de Matanzas is a family-based musical troupe, and many of its members have remained together for decades. The group is currently in its third generation. Los Muñequitos's original dancer, Diosdado Ramos, is its current director. His son also danced with the group, and his grandson, Luis Deyvis Ramos, has recently emerged as a crowd-pleasing dancer in his own right. Musical director Jesus Alfonso Miro and his son Ivan Miro are both drummers in the group. Los Muñequitos also features the father-and-son vocalists Israel Berriel Gonzalez and Israel Berriel Jimenez.

As its name implies, Los Muñequitos de Matanzas has its roots in Matanzas, a musically influential city located in western Cuba, which has an extensive African legacy. In its role as cultural conservator, the group performs music and dances that reflect various African religious traditions and rituals. But the RUMBA and its variants continue to be the group's trademark.

See also Dance in Latin America and the Caribbean; Matanzas, Cuba; Percussion Instruments of the Caribbean.

James Sellman

Munyaradzi, Henry

1931–1998

Zimbabwean sculptor.

Henry Munyaradzi of ZIMBABWE, a country famous for ancient stone monuments and carvings, created stone sculptures that have been exhibited in North America, Europe, Australia, and Africa.

Born in Guruve, Rhodesia (present-day Zimbabwe), Munyaradzi received little formal education as a child and worked primarily as a farm hand in his natal village. In 1968 the international community stopped doing business with Rhodesia to protest the policies of the country's white minority government. Munyaradzi, then thirty-seven, was one of the many workers laid off by hard-hit tobacco farms. With free time on his hands, Munyaradzi was drawn to an artist's community known as Tengenenge, set up in 1966 by a white tobacco farmer. Although most of its members, like Munyaradzi, had little or no formal artistic training, they later achieved significant international attention.

Munyaradzi was immediately drawn to sculpting. Hard stones such as serpentine and granite, as well as carving tools and supplies, were supplied by Frank McEwan, the newly appointed director of the National Gallery of HARARE (then called Salisbury), who hoped to strengthen the gallery's weak collection of modern art by supporting local artists. Munyaradzi, who lived and worked in Runa, Zimbabwe, was the most famous of the artists to come out of Tengenenge. He works has been widely collected and displayed in galleries and art exhibitions New York, London, Paris, and Venice, Italy. In his sculptures Munyaradzi sought to release the spirit and forms that he felt were "imprisoned" in the stone. He cut very few lines and made his cuts strong and deep, intending to release the spirit while keeping the stone massive. Muntaradzi died in 1998 on his farm.

Murphy, Carl

1889–1967

Publisher of the influential *Baltimore Afro-American*.

Carl Murphy was born in BALTIMORE, MARYLAND, where his father, John Henry, began publishing the *Baltimore Afro-American* in 1892. Murphy graduated from HOWARD UNIVERSITY in 1911 and then attended Harvard, where he received an M.A. in German in 1913.

After working at Howard as a teacher of German, Murphy resigned in 1918 to work for his father's newspaper. He assumed leadership of the newspaper when his father died in 1922, a position which he retained until 1961. When he retired, the paper's circulation had risen to 200,000, and his company owned newspapers in several other cities.

Murphy served on the Board of Directors of the NATIONAL ASSOCIATION FOR THE ADVANCEMENT OF COLORED PEOPLE (NAACP) in 1931. In 1955, he received the Spingarn Medal for his dedication to civil rights and education.

Murphy, Eddie

1961–

African American comedian and actor.

Born in Brooklyn, New York, Eddie Murphy first attracted attention in 1980, as a featured performer on the popular television show *Saturday Night Live (SNL)*, at the age of nineteen. Already a veteran of comedy clubs, where he had been performing since age fifteen, *SNL*'s sketch comedy format proved the perfect vehicle for Murphy's hard-edged comedic characterizations and, at times, unflattering celebrity impersonations. Murphy became *SNL*'s biggest star.

In 1982 Murphy released *Eddie Murphy,* an album of his stand-up material, which earned a Grammy nomination. Murphy capitalized on his popularity, taking his first film role later that year in *48 Hours*, which was well received, both critically and commercially. The success of *48 Hours* led to a costarring role with former *SNL* cast member Dan Ackroyd in *Trading Places*, which was among the top ten earning films of 1983. *Eddie Murphy: Comedian*, another comedy album, won a Grammy. By 1984, when he left *SNL* to pursue a film career full-time, Murphy was considered one of Hollywood's leading box-office attractions.

Murphy's films had uneven success—he sometimes achieved box-office triumph at the expense of critical acclaim. *Beverly Hills Cop* (1984) broke box-office records, which prompted Paramount Pictures to sign him to a $25 million contract for six-films. Sequels to *48 Hours* and *Beverly Hills Cop*, on the other hand, were poorly received critically and enjoyed only modest commercial success. Critics panned Murphy's first attempt at writing and directing, *Harlem Nights* (1989). In addition, the success of *Coming to America* (1988) was diminished when, in 1990, writer Art Buchwald successfully sued Murphy and Paramount Pictures for stealing his idea for the screenplay. Murphy's career rebounded in the 1990s, with the success of such films as *Boomerang* (1992), a remake of *The Nutty Professor* (1996), and *Doctor Dolittle* (1998), all of which earned Murphy critical and popular acclaim.

In 1998 Murphy branched out into animation by providing the voice of Mushu for the Disney animated film, *Mulan*. The next year he originated and produced the first stop-animation series to appear on prime-time television. The series, entitled *The PJ's,* chronicled life in a community of blacks living in a low-income housing project, with Murphy providing the voice of the lead character, Superintendent Thurgoode Orenthal Stubbs. In 2001 Murphy provided the voice for the mischievous, but charming, donkey in the animated blockbuster *Shrek.*

Murphy was in front of the camera again for the comedy films *Showtime* (2002) and *Daddy Day Care* (2003). His popularity and success has translated into some hefty paychecks. He received $20 million for each of the films *Nutty Professor II* (2000), *Dr. Dolittle 2* (2002), and *The Adventures of Pluto Nash* (2002) and picked up another $10 million to again be the voice of the donkey in *Shrek 2* (2004). Despite the occasional bomb, Murphy remains one of Hollywood's top stars.

See also Film, Blacks in American; Television and African Americans.

Murphy, Isaac

1861–1896

African American jockey.

Isaac Murphy was born Isaac Burns on a farm near Frankfort, Kentucky, the son of James Burns, a bricklayer, and a mother (name unknown) who worked as a laundrywoman. During the CIVIL WAR his father, a free black, joined the Union army and died in a Confederate prisoner-of-war camp. Upon the death of his father, his widowed mother moved with her family to Lexington, Kentucky, to live with her father, Green Murphy, a bell ringer and auction crier. Accompanying his mother to work at the Richard and Owings Racing Stable, the diminutive Isaac was noticed by the black trainer Eli Jordan, who had him suited up for his first race at age fourteen. His first winning race was aboard the two-year-old filly Glentina on September 15, 1875, at the Lexington Crab Orchard. Standing five feet tall and weighing only seventy-four pounds, Murphy had by the end of 1876 ridden eleven horses to victory at Lexington's Kentucky Association track.

Since colonial times, African Americans had been involved in the care and training of horses, particularly on antebellum and post–CIVIL WAR farms and plantations in the South. They had also ridden them as jockeys, an occupation once considered beneath the dignity of white men. At the inaugural Kentucky Derby in 1875, fourteen of the fifteen jockeys were black. Blacks triumphed in fifteen of the first twenty-eight derbies. In his first Kentucky Derby in 1877, Murphy (who had adopted his grandfather's surname as a tribute) placed fourth aboard Vera Cruz. He later rode the same horse to victory in another major stakes race and tallied nineteen first-place finishes that year. Two years later, Murphy signed with J. W. Hunt Reynolds and came in second in the Kentucky Derby with the moneymaker Falsetto. Among Murphy's numerous victories between 1879 and 1884 (the year he signed with Ed Corrigan of New York) were the Clark Handicap in LOUISVILLE, KENTUCKY; the Distillers Stakes in Lexington, Kentucky; the Saratoga Cup in New York; the Brewers Cup in St. Louis, Missouri; and the first American Derby in CHICAGO, ILLINOIS. Incredibly, he posted wins in forty-nine of the fifty-one races he entered at Saratoga in 1882. His first Kentucky Derby win at Churchill Downs, on May 27, 1884, aboard Modesty, was clocked at 2 minutes, 40.25 seconds, two lengths ahead of his nearest rival. It was the first of three such conquests there; the other two occurred successively in 1890 and 1891, with the mounts Riley and Kingman, respectively.

Renowned for his adept manipulation of his mounts via intuitive, precise pacing, Murphy rarely used stirrups or the whip, except to please the crowd, and his trademark come-from-behind finishes became known as "Murfinishes." It was his habit to lay on the horse's neck to coax it to the finish line. At a time when jockeys customarily wagered on the outcome of races, Murphy, a devout BAPTIST, enjoyed a reputation for scrupulous honesty and integrity. A mild-mannered, gracious man who never swore, he married Lucy Osborn in 1882; they had no children. Murphy and his wife resided in a mansion at 143 North Eastern Avenue in Lexington, overlooking the backstretch of a nearby racetrack. At the peek of his career, his yearly salary ranged from $10,000 to $20,000 excluding bonuses, making him the highest-paid jockey in the nation. His income befitted a man who rode nearly every premier horse of the era to victory at all the major racing events except the Futurity. It is believed that Murphy was the first black American to own a racehorse—he owned several, in fact—and he invested his winnings in racehorses and real estate. He spent extravagantly on clothes and soirees at his home and was attended to at the track by his personal valet.

Several writers have asserted that Murphy's most memorable and exciting race occurred at Sheepshead Bay in New York on June 25, 1890. It matched him against the heralded white jockey Ed "Snapper" Garrison and attempted to settle the long-standing debate as to who was the better professional. The event had pronounced racial overtones that in certain respects prefigured the Jack Johnson versus Jim Jeffries boxing match twenty years later. Murphy, riding Salvador, edged out Garrison, aboard Tenny, by half a head in one of the most publicized races of the century.

Ironically, just two months later Murphy's popularity was tarnished and his career began to unravel when he fell off of his mount at the end of the running of the Monmouth Handicap. He maintained that he suffered from chronic dieting and that he may even have been drugged. Nonetheless, he was charged with drunkenness and suspended. The press, including the *New York Times* (August 27, 1890), was quite baffled by such uncharacteristic behavior from the gentlemanly Murphy and roundly chastised him. Although he continued to rack up victories at the track the following year (1891), his penchant for champagne and the struggle to hold down his weight, which had risen to 140 pounds, eventually took their toll. In 1892 he won six races, the next year four races, and in 1894, the year he was suspended for a second time for being drunk at the track, he failed to win a race. Retirement was forced upon him in November 1895. Within three months Murphy died in Lexington, the ravages of alcohol and dieting having weakened his resistance to pneumonia. He left $30,000 to his wife, but this sum was hardly enough to satisfy his creditors, and she died a pauper.

Murphy, arguably the most influential and widely respected African American athlete of the nineteenth century, was curiously ignored for many years by historians and journalists. Half a century after his death, an article filled with anecdotes and quotations pertaining to his career appeared in the *Negro Digest* (November 1950). Its title bemoaned, "No Memorial for Isaac Murphy." In 1967, through the efforts of Lexington sportswriter Frank Borries Jr., Murphy's remains were transported from their ignominious location in the city's decrepit No. 2 Cemetery and reinterred in Man o' War Park. In 1977 the remains of both the jockey and the famed thoroughbred (whom Murphy never rode) were moved to hallowed ground near one another at the Kentucky Horse Park outside of Lexington. In 1955 he was the first jockey inducted into the National Museum of Racing Hall of Fame, and in 1956 he was also enshrined in the National Jockey's Hall of Fame at Pimlico, Maryland.

Murphy's three Kentucky Derby wins were later exceeded by Eddie Arcaro (five), Bill Hartack (five), and Bill Shoemaker (four); his back-to-back Kentucky Derby wins were later equaled by African American Jimmy Winkfield (1901 and 1902), Ron Tucotte (1972 and 1973), and Eddie Delahoussaye (1982 and 1983). To his recollection, he was victorious in 44 percent of his contests, winning 628 of 1,412 mounts; but according to other sources, Murphy's winning percentage was closer to 33 percent. In any event, 33 percent represented the best winning record of any jockey in American turf history. The annual Isaac Murphy Award was established in 1993 by the National Turf Writers' Association to honor the jockey with the best win-loss record. The Isaac Murphy Stakes (formerly the American Derby, which Murphy won on four occasions) was initiated in 1997 at Chicago's Arlington International Racecourse.

Bibliography

Ashe, Arthur R. *A Hard Road to Glory: A History of the African American Athlete, 1619–1918.* 1988.

Bolus, Jim. "Honest Isaac's Legacy." *Sports Illustrated,* April 29, 1996.

Borries, Betty. *Isaac Murphy: Kentucky's Record Jockey.* 1988.

Cushing, Rick. "Isaac Murphy: A Pioneer Who's Had Few Followers." *Louisville Courier-Journal,* April 30, 1990.

Phelps, Frank T. "The Nearest Perfect Jockey." *Thoroughbred Record,* May 13, 1967, pp. 1245–48.

Savage, Stephen P. "Isaac Murphy: Black Hero in Nineteenth Century American Sport, 1861–1896." *Canadian Journal of History and Physical Education* 10 (1979): 15–32.

Tarelton, L. P. "A Memorial." *Thoroughbred Record,* March 21, 1896, p. 136.

From *American National Biography.* John A. Garraty and Mark C. Carnes, eds. Oxford University Press, 1999. Reprinted by permission of the American Council of Learned Societies.

Robert Fikes

Murphy, John Henry, Sr.

1840–1922

African American newspaper publisher.

John Henry Murphy, Sr., was born in BALTIMORE, MARYLAND, the only son of Benjamin Murphy, Jr., a whitewasher, and Susan Coby. Murphy was born a slave. The *Baltimore Afro-American,* the newspaper he would guide to prominence during the first two decades of the twentieth century, described Murphy's educational attainment as "limited." A short man, he walked with a limp, the result of a childhood horseback riding incident that left one leg longer than the other. Freedom for the Murphys came via the Maryland Emancipation Act of 1863.

Despite his limp, Murphy answered ABRAHAM LINCOLN's call for troops and joined the Union army during the CIVIL WAR. He enlisted as a private in Company G of the mostly black Thirtieth Regiment of the Maryland Volunteers—an infantry unit—on March 18, 1864. During his twenty-one months in uniform he served under General Ulysses S. Grant in Virginia and General William T. Sherman in North Carolina. He left the army in December 1865 as a sergeant.

After his discharge, Murphy returned to Baltimore. On his first day back home he met Martha Elizabeth Howard, daughter of a wealthy Montgomery County, Maryland, farmer. Howard's family had been born slaves, but her father, Enoch George Howard, had purchased his freedom and later that of his wife and children and eventually even bought his former master's property. It took two years for Murphy to convince Howard's father that he was sincere about marriage. The couple married in 1868 and eventually had eleven children.

To support his growing clan, Murphy worked at various jobs over the next twenty years. He followed his father as a whitewasher for a time, until the use of wallpaper became widespread. Murphy later used his veteran's status to get a political patronage job with the U.S. Post Office, but he lost that when the Democrats came to power with the 1884 election of Grover Cleveland as president. Subsequent jobs included being a porter, a janitor, and a feed store manager. (Neither Murphy nor others who have written about him cite dates or lengths of time that he stayed at his various jobs.)

Murphy was in his forties when he decided to become a printer, as he described himself. Active in local organizations, particularly the AFRICAN METHODIST EPISCOPAL CHURCH (AME), in the 1880s Murphy became superintendent of Sunday schools for the Hagerstown (Md.) AME Church District. For years Murphy had wanted to structure black church schools into some type of organization, and he saw a newspaper as a means of achieving this goal. His initial publication, designed to generate more community interest in Sunday school work, was the

Sunday School Helper, which he began in the late 1880s in the basement of his home. Murphy's competition came from publications started by other local black church groups. The *Afro-American,* which, under the leadership of the Reverend William Alexander, carried a combination of church and community news, was the Baptists' publication. The *Ledger,* edited by the Reverend GEORGE F. BRAGG, was allied with the EPISCOPAL CHURCH. (Initial publication dates have yet to be established for any of these weekly publications.)

The *Afro-American*'s parent company was the Northwestern Family Supply Company, a Reverend Alexander enterprise that operated a dry goods store. When Alexander's larger business failed and was auctioned off, in 1896 Murphy acquired, with $200 borrowed from his wife, the *Afro-American,* then a one-page weekly with a circulation of 250. Murphy merged the two publications and dropped the *Sunday School Helper* name but retained the church and community news content. As time passed, Murphy brought his children into the enterprise by assigning them various editorial, printing, and circulation tasks. Between 1900 and 1901 the *Afro-American* merged with the *Ledger* and was known for a time as the *Afro-American Ledger* (1901–1916), when it was published semiweekly. Under this arrangement, Murphy became the publisher, and Bragg became the editor. Murphy eventually obtained control and returned the newspaper to its former—and current—name, the *Afro-American.* During the last three decades of his life, Murphy guided the operation as it became one of the premier black newspapers of all time. In the process he not only achieved success, fame, and financial reward, he laid the foundation for a venerable publishing concern that would be headed by generations of Murphys for nearly a century.

Murphy said he wanted to publish a newspaper that would "render service to the whole community." Like many of his black newspaper executive contemporaries he was a REPUBLICAN, but he vowed not to let the *Afro-American* be a newspaper "tied to the apron strings of any political party, fraternal organization or religious denomination." He established the paper's motto of "Independent in All Things, Neutral in Nothing." Murphy credited two characteristics for his success: faith and industry. He said he had "faith in the ability of the black man to succeed in this civilization, faith in myself and faith in God. Then, too, I believe in just plain, everyday, hard work."

Murphy had hoped to live to be one hundred years old and on his eightieth birthday wrote a letter to be opened on Christmas Day 1940. A reflection on his life and a statement of the philosophy that made him one of the most respected "race" men of his time, the letter reads in part:

> I measure a newspaper not in buildings, equipment and employees—those are trimmings. A newspaper succeeds because its management believes in itself, in God and in the present generation. It must always ask itself whether it has kept faith with the common people; whether it has no other goal except to see that their liberties are preserved and their future assured; whether it is fighting to get rid of slums, to provide jobs for everybody; whether it stays out of politics except to expose corruption and condemn injustice, race prejudice or the cowardice of compromise . . . . [The *Afro-American*] has always had a loyal constituency who believed it honest, decent and progressive. It is that kind of newspaper now and I hope it never changes.

Murphy remained active until shortly before his death in Baltimore. Tributes poured in. The one from the Negro (later National) Newspaper Publishers Association (NNPA), the black newspaper publishers trade organization, was a fitting epitaph. To his peers, it said, Murphy was "a noble Roman of the fourth estate and . . . an inspiration to future generations of black men."

By the time he died, Murphy had managed to establish a newspaper with an extensive readership outside the city that was once called "the graveyard of black newspapers." The *Afro-American*'s circulation of 14,000 at the time of his death made it one of the ten largest black newspapers in the United States. As the number of black newspapers grew with the migration of blacks to the North, the *Afro-American* became one of the "Big Five" black newspapers of the first half of the twentieth century. Although Murphy did not start the *Afro-American,* he was the driving force that transformed the publication from a local newspaper into one of the most significant and influential black journals in the nation. John Henry Murphy was a man of perseverance and vision, and his life indicates that one is never too old to succeed.

Bibliography

The *Afro-American* Archives are located at Bowie State College, Bowie, Md. An additional primary source is a letter by John H. Murphy, "Sergeant Murphy: Story of a Civil War Veteran," dated December 25, 1920, Schomburg Center for the Study of Black Culture Clipping File 3003, 362–61.

"John Henry Murphy, Sr., 1840–1922." *Afro-American* (magazine section), January 9, 1957.
"Letters and Telegrams Eulogize John H. Murphy." *Afro-American,*" April 14, 1922, p. 7.
Obituary, *Afro-American,* April 7, 1922.
Wolseley, Roland E. *The Black Press: U.S.A.* 2d ed. 1990.

From *American National Biography.* John A. Garraty and Mark C. Carnes, eds. Oxford University Press, 1999. Reprinted by permission of the American Council of Learned Societies.

James Phillip Jeter

Murray, Albert L.

1916–

African American writer whose work depicts the history of blues music in language that intertwines rhythm and the vernacular.

Albert L. Murray was born in Nokomis, Alabama, and adopted by Albert Lee Murray and his wife, Mattie James Murray. He grew up in Magazine Point, outside of Mobile. Often characterized as a member of the "Talented Tenth," Murray excelled academically and won a scholarship to TUSKEGEE INSTITUTE in 1935. Following his graduate study at the University of Michigan, he returned to Tuskegee to teach English and theater. In 1943 he enlisted in the U.S. Air Force and served until 1962, when he retired as a major. During his retirement, Murray has lived mostly in NEW YORK CITY but has been a visiting professor in various schools, including Colgate, Barnard, Columbia, Emory, the University of Massachusetts, and Washington and Lee.

Like his friend and Tuskegee classmate, RALPH ELLISON, Murray is interested in the cultural complexity of America, especially for African Americans. He strongly contends that African culture permeates American life. Murray's first published work, *The Omni-Americans* (1970), is a compilation of essays in which he presents himself as an ardent critic of theories that contend that African Americans are subservient to white social infrastructures. Murray views African American culture as an advantageous extension of the American self.

In his second work, *South to a Very Old Place* (1971), Murray offers autobiographical appeal to his social theory. The book guides the reader through the South from New York to Mobile with Murray as mediator. *South to a Very Old Place* centers around balancing and understanding the relationship between black and white, oral tradition and journalism, past and present. Other works include a collection of public lectures given at the University of Missouri, titled *The Hero and the Blues* (1973), emphasizing the natural synthesis of BLUES ballads and prose.

Train Whistle Guitar (1974) was the first of a fiction trilogy, followed by *The Spyglass Tree* (1991) and *Seven League Boots*. These novels trace the life of a bright young man named Scooter, Murray's fictional alter ego. *Train Whistle Guitar* won the Lillian Smith Award for Southern Fiction; its intertwining of rhythm and use of vernacular is attributed to the author's passion for the blues and his efforts to place them on the page. *Stomping the Blues* (1976) pays homage to Murray's tenet of the "vernacular imperative," transcending everyday life into aesthetic. Within this framework, Murray transforms the rhythmic, improvisational, style of JAZZ and the blues into prose.

Good Morning Blues (1985), the autobiography of COUNT BASIE as narrated by Murray, is his ultimate tribute to the aesthetic, stepping into the shoes of a black jazz artist. In *The Blue Devils of Nada* (1996), Murray presents essays analyzing some of his favorite artists (Ellington, Hemingway, Bearden), using tenets of both blues and prose in American culture. His recent works include *Conjugations and Reiterations* (2001), his first book of poetry, and *From the Briarpatch File* (2001), a collection of essays, reviews, and interviews about music, social conditions, and intellectual life in America. In 1997 Murray received the Anisfield-Wolf Lifetime Achievement Award.

See also Literature, African American; Music, African American.

Bibliography
Gates, Henry Louis, Jr. *Thirteen Ways of Looking at a Black Man*. Random House, 1997.

Eva Stahl Brown

Murray, Daniel (Alexander Payne)
1852–1925

African American librarian, bibliographer, and biographical researcher.

The youngest child of George and Eliza Murray, Daniel Murray was born on March 3, 1852, in BALTIMORE, MARYLAND. He was named after Daniel Alexander Payne, the African Methodist Episcopal (AME) bishop who pastored Baltimore's Bethel Church from 1845 to 1850. Shortly after 1861, Murray left home for WASHINGTON, D.C., where his brother managed the restaurant in the United States Senate. In 1871 he became a personal assistant to the librarian of Congress, Ainsworth R. Spofford. Under Spofford's tutelage Murray broadened his knowledge, became proficient in several foreign languages, and acquired invaluable research skills. In 1879 he married Anna Evans, a graduate of Oberlin College in Ohio. Her uncle, Lewis Sheridan Leary, and cousin, John Anthony Copeland Jr., had participated in John Brown's antislavery raid on Harpers Ferry, Virginia (now West Virginia). Advancing to assistant librarian in 1881, Murray held this position until his retirement from the Library of Congress in 1923, after fifty-two years of service. In 1899 he was asked to prepare a special display on "Negro Literature" for the American Exhibit at the 1900 Paris Exposition in France. The search for materials by black authors and the drive to document their lives absorbed Murray in a lifelong project.

Murray's work on the Negro Literature display for the Paris Exposition helped to establish him as an authority on black bibliography. Because he planned to secure as many volumes as possible for the Paris exhibit and future preservation in the Library of Congress, he sought the title of every book and pamphlet written by persons of African ancestry. In January 1900 he published an eight-page preliminary list of 270 titles, with an appeal for additional citations. Responses to this list led to identification of 1,100 works, 500 of which became the Negro Literature display. Seven years later he catalogued 5,000 titles for the Jamestown, Virginia, Tercentenary and assembled a list of more than 12,000 books and pamphlets by black authors. Murray developed a personal library of 1,488 volumes, which he bequeathed to the Library of Congress. Together with the works shown in Paris, this material for some time constituted the Library of Congress's Colored Author Collection.

As he accumulated more titles, Murray felt compelled to document the authors' lives. Working to authenticate their ancestry, he began to write his *Bibliographia-Africania* to include all known literature by black writers, with biographical data about them. Convinced that the record of black progress and achievement was in black literature, he designed his book to dispel notions of racial inferiority and to prove that color was not an impediment to intellectual accomplishment.

Murray published some of his research in a column for the black journal *Voice of the Negro*. Because of his bibliographic knowledge and background in the Library of Congress, he was frequently called on to give information on black history and literature, to lecture before historical and literary societies, and to give testimony before the United States Congress. At the Library of Congress he had developed a reputation for his remarkable memory. Without consulting the serial lists, he often directed patrons to the precise location for the books they requested. Among his chief concerns were civil rights and a rigorous education for black youth. He often testified before Congress against segregation laws. He believed that African Americans, even with equal opportunity, could achieve only limited success in life if their education did not prepare them for industrial employment. Despite his endorsement of industrial education, Murray maintained the need for quality instruction in all subjects, whether vocational or academic.

Murray was one of the first among African Americans seeking knowledge about their past. The rich vein of material that he unearthed, as well as the desire to provide positive images for black children, influenced Murray in 1910 to expand his efforts into a "Historical and Biographical Encyclopedia of the Colored Race Throughout the World." For this project he solicited some of the most prominent and knowledgeable blacks in Africa, America, and the Caribbean to serve as assistant editors. Among those who consented were historians JOHN E. BRUCE, JOHN W. CROMWELL, WILLIAM S. SCARBOROUGH, ARTHUR A. SCHOMBURG, and Richard R. Wright, Jr. Murray was disturbed by the fact that sources used to vindicate black people were in large measure written solely by whites. What would have been the nature of history for Greek posterity, he mused, if it had been written exclusively by Romans? His six-volume encyclopedia composed by blacks would survey the "Colored Race's Progress and Achievements" from antiquity to the twentieth century.

Murray found it difficult to secure a publisher for his encyclopedia, discovering that several firms would print the work but none would market it. He soon devised a plan of advance subscriptions similar to the *Jewish Cyclopedia*, which had been published with a guarantee of 8,000 subscribers. Receiving an enthusiastic but limited response, Murray continued his quest for a publisher. When he died, he left a book-length manuscript, "Bibliography of Negro Literature and Historical Sketch of Negro Authors and Authorship," almost 500 biographical portraits of black historical figures, and more than 250,000 index cards with book titles, background material, and information on events significant to black people worldwide. He bequeathed the manuscripts to the State Historical Society, Madison, Wisconsin.

Murray was a member of Philadelphia's American Negro Historical Society, of which his cousin, William Carl Bolivar, was a founding member in 1897. He was also a member of the Bethel Literary and Historical Society and of the Benjamin Banneker Association, both in Washington. He was a corresponding member of the Negro Library Association of New York City, of which Schomburg, Bruce, and writer JAMES WELDON JOHNSON were also members. Murray wrote several articles for *Voice of the Negro* between September 1904 and July 1906.

Daniel Murray's vision of a black encyclopedia was similar to those of black leader W. E. B. DU BOIS and historian CARTER G. WOODSON, who also made ill-fated attempts to produce a multivolume reference work on the heritage of blacks. Although his prodigious research was never published, his role as a bibliographer of black literature makes him a pioneer in the black history movement.

Murray died of natural causes at his residence, 924 S Street NW, Washington, D.C., and was buried in Woodlawn Cemetery, Washington. He was survived by his widow Anna and seven children.

There are brief references to Murray in Frank L. Mather's *Who's Who of the Colored Race* (1915, pp. 203–4) and *History of the American Negro*, edited by Arthur Bunyan Caldwell (1922, 6: 25–27). Brief references are also found in *The Negro in the United States: A Selected Bibliography*, compiled by Dorothy B. Porter (1970, pp. v–vi), and Wallace Van Jackson's piece, "Some Pioneer Negro Library Workers," (*Library Journal*, March 15, 1939, pp. 215–217). An obituary appeared in *The Crisis*, June 1926. There are pictures of Murray in the *Library Journal* and *The Crisis*. Pictures of his wife and most of their children are in *Negro History Bulletin*, November 1946. Information about his testimony before Congress is in *How to Solve the Race Problem: The Proceedings of the Washington Conference on the Race Problem in the United States*, edited by James Lawson (1904), and in the Murray papers. Information on other aspects of Murray's life are in these papers, most of them in the State Historical Society, Madison, Wisconsin; and a few in the Moorland-Spingarn Research Center, Howard University, and the Manuscript Division, Library of Congress. See the piece by Robert L. Harris, Jr., titled "Daniel Murray and the Encyclopedia of the Colored Race," *Phylon*, September 1976, pp. 270–282.

From *Dictionary of American Negro Biography* by Rayford W. Logan and Michael R. Winston, editors. Copyright © 1982 by Rayford W. Logan and Michael R. Winston. Reprinted by permission of W. W. Norton & Company, Inc.

Robert L. Harris, Jr.

Murray, George Washington

1853–1926

African American agricultural inventor and Republican congressman.

Murray was born a slave in Sumter County near Rembert, South Carolina, on September 24, 1853. He attended the University of South Carolina from 1874 to 1876, after it had been opened to black students by the Republican state government. From 1876 to 1890 Murray taught in the public schools and operated a small farm in Sumter County. In February 1890 he was appointed inspector of customs in the Charleston Customs House.

Although he was active in local politics prior to his custom house appointment, Murray's political ambitions appear to have been focused on the national stage by this politically important position. A few months after his appointment, he became a candidate for the REPUBLICAN PARTY nomination to the United States Congress. Running against the veteran politician Thomas E. Miller and the white collector of internal revenue E. M. Brayton, Murray failed to get the nomination. However, his visibility as a prominent candidate and as chairman of the state Republican convention may have helped him win the nomination two years later. Again he was pitted against Miller and Brayton, but this time Murray won as a compromise candidate on the fourth ballot. After a closely contested general election, he defeated the Democrat E. W. Moise by fifty votes after the Democratic State Returning Board decided several key precincts in his favor. The board's surprising decision was probably the result of internal divisions between competing Democratic factions.

Although he was officially elected to two terms in Congress (1893–1895 and 1895–1897), Murray actually spent little time in his seat. During the second and third sessions of his first term (August 7, 1893, to March 3, 1895) he was absent for extended periods. Apparently defeated by Democrat William Elliott in his campaign for reelection in 1894, Murray successfully contested Elliott's election and won back his seat. However, the final vote on the contest did not come until June 1896, during the last months of the Fifty-fourth Congress. Murray won the Republican nomination again, but he lost to William Elliott by more than 2,000 votes in the 1896 campaign. His second challenge failed, and he retired to his real estate enterprises in Sumter County.

Murray's independence of thought and action were perhaps his most striking features as a congressman. He demonstrated supreme self-confidence and oratorical ability when, as a freshman congressman, he rose to speak on the deeply divisive free-silver coinage issue. After the elimination of the silver dollar in 1873, the expanded production of silver in the West caused the value of silver to drop, until some favored free coinage of silver to improve the economy. Murray won loud applause from free-silver advocates when he drew a witty and deft analogy between the condition of the devalued silver certificates and the discrimination and prejudices against blacks. He noted playfully that the usual order of things was reversed with metals in that the "little yellow, gold man" was considered superior to the "white man" silver. Refusing to play the usual role of the reticent freshman member, he spoke in vain against the repeal of the last provisions of the RECONSTRUCTION Acts, which provided basic civil rights to freed slaves and to enfranchised blacks. He introduced, again in vain, bills to establish normal and industrial schools, to exempt the Young Men's Christian Association (YMCA) from taxes, and to provide funds for aged and needy blacks. In addition, he highlighted black achievements by reading a list of black inventors who held patents. His own name was among them, as he had received numerous patents for inventing improved farm implements. During his second term (June 4, 1896, to March 3, 1897), he repeatedly and unsuccessfully called for an investigation of fraud and intimidation in South Carolina. He frequently engaged in floor debates and heckled opposition speakers with sharp questions.

Murray was not only an excellent debater but also a resourceful leader. To help counter Democratic attempts to disenfranchise blacks by imposing property requirements for voting, he purchased 4,000 hectares (10,000 acres) of land, subdivided it into tracts of 10, 20, and 40 hectares (25, 50, and 100 acres), and resold them to blacks. A dark-horse victor for the congressional nomination in 1892, he was practically cut off financially by major Republican contributors. Yet he managed a successful congressional campaign after several years of political drought for Republicans. When he ran for reelection in 1896, he found the party split between so-called "Black and Tan" and "Lily White" Republican factions. Murray joined the Lily Whites and worked toward a reunification of the two groups. The party names were actually misnomers, for prominent blacks and white Republicans participated in both factions, and both conventions nominated all-white state tickets for the 1896 elections. The reunification efforts failed, and the Republican Party went down to defeat, ending Murray's political career.

In 1905 Murray moved to Chicago, Illinois, where he wrote two rather turgid books on race relations that were privately printed: *Race Ideals* (1914) and *Light in Dark Places* (1925). He remained an active platform speaker and political figure until his death on April 21, 1926. He was buried in Lincoln Cemetery in Chicago after a large, well-attended funeral service at which politician and lawyer JOHN ROY LYNCH was the principal speaker. Murray was survived by his wife, Cornelia, and two children.

A major source for Murray's life is his own account in *The Biographical Directory of the American Congress* (1971). The sketch in Samuel Denny Smith's work *The Negro in Congress, 1870–1901* (1940) relies largely on racially and politically biased sources. Maurine Christopher's *America's Black Congressmen* (1971) adds new information but fails to document its sources. The best secondary source is George B. Tindall's *South Carolina Negroes, 1877–1900* (1952).

From *Dictionary of American Negro Biography* by Rayford W. Logan and Michael R. Winston, editors. Copyright © 1982 by Rayford W. Logan and Michael R. Winston. Reprinted by permission of W. W. Norton & Company, Inc.

Thomas Holt

Murray, Pauli

1910–1985

African American lawyer, teacher, poet, women's rights advocate, and the first African American female Episcopal priest.

A pioneer in fields previously inaccessible to women and African Americans, Pauli Murray was the first African American to be awarded a doctor of judicial science degree from Yale University. A freedom rider in the 1940s who later led student SIT-IN demonstrations in Washington, D.C., restaurants, Murray graduated at the top of her class at HOWARD UNIVERSITY. Nominated by the NATIONAL COUNCIL OF NEGRO WOMEN as one of the twelve outstanding women in Negro life in 1945, Murray was the recipient of many honorary degrees and was a founding member of the National Organization for Women. In 1977 she was the first African American woman ordained as a priest of the EPISCOPAL CHURCH.

The daughter of a racially mixed middle-class family, Murray was born in BALTIMORE, MARYLAND, the fourth of Agnes Georgianna Fitzgerald Murray and William Henry Murray's six children. When Pauli Murray was three years old, her mother died from a cerebral hemorrhage. Three years later, while she and her siblings were in the care of their aunt, their father was committed to a mental institution, where he died in 1923.

In 1933 Murray finished a bachelor's degree at Hunter College, where she was one of four black students in a class of 247 women. She was unsuccessful in breaking the color line at the University of North Carolina at Chapel Hill, although that institution later awarded her an honorary degree and honored her with a scholarship in her name. She was accepted at the Howard University Law School, where she was the only female in the class of 1944. Murray completed a master of laws degree at the University of California at Berkeley in 1945, after she was denied entrance to the all-male Harvard Law School. She received her doctor of juridical science degree from Yale in 1966. In 1976 Murray graduated from the General Theological Seminary with a master of divinity degree.

A writer since her early adolescence, Murray documented her interracial family history in *Proud Shoes: The Story of an American Family* (1956). Her collection of poetry, *Dark Testament and Other Poems,* appeared in 1970.

While teaching in ACCRA, GHANA, she coauthored the first textbook on law in Africa, titled *The Constitution and Government in Africa.* THURGOOD MARSHALL lauded her book *States' Law on Race and Color* (1951) as a bible for lawyers battling segregation.

Murray's autobiography, *Song in a Weary Throat: An American Pilgrimage,* appeared posthumously in 1987 and received both the Robert F. Kennedy Book Award and the Christopher Award.

Bibliography

Murray, Pauli. *Dark Testament and Other Poems.* Silvermine Publishers, 1970.
Murray, Pauli. *Proud Shoes: The Story of an American Family.* Harper and Row, 1956.
Murray, Pauli. *Song in a Weary Throat: An American Pilgrimage.* Harper, 1987.

Murray, Peter Marshall

1888–1969

African American physician.

Peter Marshall Murray was born in Houma, Louisiana, the son of John L. Murray, a longshoreman, and Louvinia Smith, a laundress and practical nurse. Murray received his B.A. from Dillard University in 1910. His medical degree, awarded by HOWARD UNIVERSITY in 1914, was one early sign of his drive and talent, bolstered by solid preparation. Like many Howard students, he financed his medical education by working a full-time government job, in his case a clerical post in the census bureau. But his responsibilities went beyond his own wants. His ailing mother in Louisiana also needed help, so he took a second job, a night watchman position; its sole advantage was that it gave him some time for study. After receiving his degree he remained in WASHINGTON, first as an intern at FREEDMEN'S HOSPITAL and then as a Howard instructor in surgery. In 1917 he married Charlotte Wallace, the daughter of a Colored Methodist Episcopal minister; the couple had one child.

By 1920, his preparation over, Murray was ready to make his own way. The path he took was that of hundreds of talented young blacks. Their destination was NEW YORK CITY and HARLEM, and the influence Murray would exert—in the 1920s and until his death there a half-century later—in opening medicine and surgery to blacks made him as much a part of the HARLEM RENAISSANCE as JEAN TOOMER or LANGSTON HUGHES. By the mid-1920s he had performed surgery and won staff privileges in a number of New York and New Jersey hospitals, whose staffs were previously all white, including in 1928 the prestigious Harlem Hospital (where Murray was the second black physician admitted to practice and where he served until his retirement in 1953). In 1930 he was the first black physician to be board-certified in gynecology. In 1949, as a member of the Medical Society of the County of New York, the nation's largest affiliate of the American Medical Association, Murray became the first black to gain a seat in the AMA House of Delegates. From that position he pushed the AMA to officially repudiate the segregation practices of southern medical societies. Though the AMA took no action that year, Murray sensed a growing readiness, and in 1950, aided by pressure from the NATIONAL ASSOCIATION FOR THE ADVANCEMENT OF COLORED PEOPLE (NAACP) and from National Medical Association editor MONTAGUE COBB (who like Murray had been battling AMA exclusion for years), Murray won the passage of an AMA resolution urging segregated affiliates to eliminate racial restrictions. Leaving the pace of change up to the Southern societies, the AMA appeal brought no immediate change, but it did put segregation under a cloud. By the mid-1950s, owing to pushing by black doctors at the local level, every Southern state organization but two had integrated. Now, the way lay open for black doctors not just to mingle professionally with white physicians but also—and more important—to gain staff privileges at Southern hospitals. In addition they were able to become part of the medical referral system and win appointment to state and local boards of health—all relevant to professional success and all contingent on membership in local AMA affiliates. In 1954, in recognition of Murray's achievements, his New York medical society elected him its first black president.

Murray's success in breaching white barriers was draped in irony, however. He built it not by militantly challenging white discrimination but by going along with medical segregation, to the extent of publicly acknowledging white medical superiority and black professional dependence. Had BOOKER T. WASHINGTON been alive in the pre–WORLD WAR II era, he surely would have applauded Murray's strategy, for it seemed to bear out his own faith that the route to black inclusion in white society lay in hard work and accommodation to segregation.

One memorial to Murray's racial conservatism was his long campaign as leader of the all-black National Medical Association (which he served as president-elect in 1931, president in 1932, and chairman of its publications committee from 1943 to 1957) to improve black hospitals—a crusade that aimed to improve opportunities for black physicians and patients alike. That campaign also exposed the sharp division within the black medical community between those who, like Murray, supported accommodation and a minority that insisted on integration as the only moral course.

In 1932, for example, spokesmen for the latter strategy—a group led by a combative New York doctor, Louis Wright—strongly opposed the creation of a new, all-black Veterans Administration (VA) hospital in the city on the ground that it would transplant segregation to a region where it had not yet taken root. To Murray, who favored the VA facility, Wright's position was not only misguided but also demagogic. Admittedly, he told the National Medical Association (in his 1932 presidential address), demanding "our full rights" instead of half a loaf "might send a thrill down your spines." But when the issues were the welfare of thousands of black veterans and the professional needs of hundreds of black doctors, Murray felt, as did one professional correspondent, that "we must look to practical results rather than resort to cowardly cant." Discrimination was objectionable, but "we must not be so everlastingly afraid of so-called segregation that we rule ourselves out of . . . opportunities. It is not the ideal America that we are dealing with. . . . It is a prejudiced America."

Although the VA hospital project collapsed, Murray persevered in what he saw as the more realistic approach to "prejudiced America." One critical need of black Americans was better hospital care. Not only were available facilities shockingly deficient, but their physicians were poorly prepared and professionally torpid. To Murray the surest way to address those problems was by improving black hospitals. Usually that meant providing white directors; blacks, he lamented in 1932, simply were not capable of running their own facilities.

But black physicians would ultimately benefit. One defect of black medical education was a lack of accredited internships (a shortfall of about twenty per year). Although 1,400 approved posts went unfilled in white hospitals each year, Murray's preferred solution was not to try to open any of them to blacks but to create accredited internships by making black hospitals better. Although his foes protested, Murray's segregationist strategy usually prevailed in the councils of white foundations (such as the Duke Endowment and the Rosenwald Fund) because they found it philosophically preferable to integration. Probably Murray owed his own rise in establishment medicine to the same cause: whites liked him because he was safe, a man unlikely to make an issue of segregation.

To his credit, however, once he was inside white gates, Murray tried to push them open to other blacks—witness his effort against AMA segregation. Moreover, where black professional gains clearly depended on forcing open the doors of white institutions, Murray did not hang back. Thus, early on he lined up the NMA behind the desegregation of health department staffs, medical schools, and internships in tax-supported hospitals. Integrationists like Louis Wright might have finally won the day, but until desegregation occurred, conservative realists like Murray pushed black medicine steadily ahead via the segregated road.

In the annals of African-American history, the career of Peter Marshall Murray is in a way comparable to those of PHILLIS WHEATLEY, MATTHEW HENSON, JULIAN BOND, and EDWARD BROOKE. Just as those individuals registered important "firsts"—the first black published poet, polar explorer, major party vice presidential nominee, and modern U.S. senator—Murray, too, was a breaker of color bars, in medicine and public health. He died in New York City.

Bibliography

Murray's papers are in the Moorland-Spingarn Research Collection at Howard University.

Beardsley, E. H. *A History of Neglect: Health Care for Blacks and Mill Workers in the Twentieth Century South.* 1987.

Logan, Rayford W. *Howard University: The First 100 Years, 1867–1967.* 1969.

Murray, Peter. "Presidential Address." *Journal of the NMA* 24 (November 1932): 1–8.

Obituary, *New York Times,* December 21, 1969.

From *American National Biography*. John A. Garraty and Mark C. Carnes, eds. Oxford University Press, 1999. Reprinted by permission of the American Council of Learned Societies.

E. H. Beardsley

Musa

d. 1337

Ruler of Mali, whose wealth was legendary throughout the Middle East and Europe; also known as Mansa (meaning "king") Musa.

A grandson or grandnephew of the warrior king SUNDIATA KEITA, who first established MALI as a major empire in the thirteenth century, Musa extended it still further and ruled it at the height of its extent and power. The pivotal event in Musa's reign was his famous pilgrimage to Mecca (1324–1325). It involved a retinue of thousands, including 500 slaves bearing golden staffs and 100 camels, each loaded with 300 pounds of gold; and such lavish spending in CAIRO, EGYPT, that the price of gold plummeted and took a dozen years to recover. On his return Musa brought with him numerous Muslim scholars and artisans. With their help, he attempted a systematic conversion to Islam of the sub-Saharan population, built splendid mosques, introducing Asian architecture, and spread Islamic law and civilization. During Musa's reign (1312–1337) TOMBOUCTOU became the unquestioned cultural center and commercial metropolis of western Africa.

See also Islam in Africa.

Museum Collection Practices in Africa

See Commodification of African Art: An Interpretation.

Museveni, Yoweri

1944–

Revolutionary military leader and president of Uganda.

Many modern African leaders have come to power through military force. Few, however, have gone on to win as much international praise for their diplomacy and good governing as Yoweri Museveni, president of UGANDA since 1986.

Museveni's political career began when he was a student helping country people from RWANDA who were living in Uganda to organize against forced relocation. In 1967 Museveni entered Dar es Salaam University in TANZANIA. He became president of the University Students' African Revolutionary Front (USARF) and befriended many future African leaders. Later Museveni traveled to recently liberated areas in northern MOZAMBIQUE, gaining firsthand experience in guerrilla warfare with the FRONT FOR THE LIBERATION OF MOZAMBIQUE (FRELIMO). Later he returned to Uganda and worked in the administration of MILTON OBOTE. When IDI AMIN overthrew the Obote government, Museveni fled to Tanzania and formed a guerrilla group called the Front for National Salvation (FRONASA). Museveni joined the Tanzanian forces when they invaded Uganda and expelled Amin in 1979.

After serving in two short-lived governments, Museveni ran for president in 1980, but Obote won the election by a wide margin. Claiming that the elections were fraudulent, Museveni helped form the National Resistance Movement/Army (NRM/A). Disillusioned by Obote's thirst for power above all else, the NRM/A launched a campaign to undermine the Obote regime, particularly through the sabotage of transportation and communication. To conserve his limited troops, Museveni tried to avoid direct confrontations with Obote's soldiers. By the beginning of 1983 the NRM/A controlled a large area outside the capital city of KAMPALA, and its ranks swelled to several thousand volunteers.

In 1985 Obote fled when one of his generals, Tito Lutwa Okello, marched on Kampala. Okello remained in power only a short while, however. NRM/A troops began an offensive against his supporters. Fighting continued until NRM/A troops finally invaded Kampala in January 1986.

Museveni became president in 1986 and immediately outlawed opposition parties. In 2002 the country's parliament passed a law that allowed other parties to operate within Uganda, but only his own party is allowed to sponsor candidates for election. Called the Movement, it is descended from the NRM, and Museveni is its chairman. He has denied accusations that Uganda has become a one-party state. Instead, he says, he has created a "no-party" state in which candidates may run for office as individuals. His approach to leadership stresses democratic processes and respect for human rights, but it allows no multiparty politics. Arguing that Western-style political parties in Africa only foster ethnic and religious conflict, he has instead focused on decentralizing and democratizing the structure of Uganda's government, creating village-level councils for a degree of grassroots participation. To promote national unity, Museveni has also restored Uganda's traditional monarchies, although each king has ceremonial powers only.

Museveni came to power as a believer in the economic theories of SOCIALISM, but he has closely followed the market reforms called for by international financial institutions. Although many Ugandans remain extremely poor, the country's rapid economic growth in the 1990s earned Museveni's practical economic policies high praise from the World Bank and other international donors. In addition, many Asians expelled by Idi Amin have accepted Museveni's invitation to return to Uganda and reclaim their properties, restoring energy to the country's manufacturing, trade, and commercial farming. Museveni has also received praise from the international community for his administration's highly successful campaign against ACQUIRED IMMUNODEFICIENCY SYNDROME (AIDS), which has reduced the rate of infection by two-thirds.

Ugandans reelected Museveni to the presidency in 1996 and again in 2001. The relative peace under Museveni's leadership has won him broad support from Ugandans, even if his human rights record is still criticized by international organizations such as Amnesty International. He also faces ongoing challenges from rebel groups, particularly in the poorer northern and eastern regions of Uganda. So, like Ugandan presidents before him, Museveni has relied on his military force to remain in power. In addition, although he has reduced the size of the armed forces, he has given military support to regional allies. Although Museveni's willingness to use military force has raised concern in the international community, it has earned him considerable respect within Africa, where he has already once chaired the ORGANIZATION OF AFRICAN UNITY. Museveni has written several books, including an autobiography and compilations of his presidential speeches and essays on obstacles to African development.

See also Structural Adjustment in Africa.

Ari Nave

Musgu

Ethnic group of West Africa; also known as Mousgoum and Musgum.

The Musgu primarily inhabit northern CAMEROON, southwestern CHAD, and northeastern NIGERIA. They speak an Afro-Asiatic language in the Chadic group. Over 100,000 people consider themselves Musgu.

See also Languages, African: An Overview.

Music, African

Musical practices and traditions of African peoples who live south of the Sahara.

In most parts of Africa, music is more than simply recreation or entertainment. It is also closely intertwined with every aspect of daily life and is seen as an integral part of important rituals, such as births, coming-of-age ceremonies, marriages, and funerals. In addition to its importance in African societies, African music has had a strong impact on music in other parts of the world, particularly in the United States, Latin America, and the Caribbean.

African music from south of the SAHARA is distinct from NORTH AFRICAN MUSIC. During antiquity the musical styles of the Sahara and what is now North Africa were much less separate from the rest of Africa. But although sub-Saharan music has a limited influence on the present-day music of North African countries such as MOROCCO and SUDAN, experts consider most styles of North African music to be closer to those of the Eurasian area.

African music is both a timeless and ancient art. As with music everywhere, it changes constantly. Numerous sources, including ancient documents written in Arabic, indicate that many of the musical instruments that are now considered part of an ancient heritage originated, in fact, only several hundred years ago. One such instrument, the kora, a string instrument often found with the itinerant *jali* (West African bards), developed in the seventeenth and eighteenth centuries in MALI and GUINEA. Other instruments associated with the Islamic kingdoms of West Africa were introduced to the area from North Africa by the sixteenth century. These include the *algaita,* a cone-shaped, collapsible oboe, and the *kakaki,* a slender tin trumpet that is sometimes as long as 3 meters (9 feet).

A few African musical instruments, however, have endured for thousands of years. Rock paintings discovered in the Sahara, for example, show that as early as 700 B.C.E. a six-string harp was common in the entire region, although by the twentieth century a similar type of instrument survived only in MAURITANIA. Similarly, archaeological findings in western NIGERIA suggest that some types of drums and bells still used in modern YORUBA culture date back as far as the eleventh century, but the better-known hourglass-shaped *dóndún* drum (often called talking drum) dates from a much later period. Although diverse, the musical styles of Africa share a broad range of traits relating to three fundamental aspects of musical performance: the organization of movement, time, and tone.

Movement and Timbre

In most African societies music and dance form an indivisible whole. In the large area inhabited by Bantu-speaking peoples, for instance, the term *ngoma* means both song and dance. Sound production, therefore, can never be considered in isolation from bodily movement. The basis of African music is not, as is commonly believed, rhythm. Instead, one of the most important stylistic traits of African music is the interaction between language-related patterns of movement and timbre (the distinctive tonal quality of a voice or musical instrument). Thus some instrumental styles cannot be understood without prior knowledge of how the musicians perform them. For example, the *amadinda* xylophone of the Buganda in UGANDA is played by three players facing one another across the xylophone. The resulting sound is a dense succession of as many as 600 beats per minute, composed of the interplay of different kinetic patterns.

Tempo

The second set of stylistic traits common to musical styles across the entire African continent relates to the organization and tempo—the lengths of notes and rests in music. These features sharply distinguish African musical styles from European and North American music and have often led to much confusion about the fundamental principles of African music making. The first of these distinctively African time-related features has been called "metronome sense" or "elementary pulsation." This refers to the strikingly infallible ability of African musicians to keep musical time even when the most complex rhythmic patterns are being interwoven with each other. Although it is not always sounded, the elementary pulsation is the smallest rhythmic unit in a piece of music, suggesting uninterrupted flow and serving as a reference grid that keeps performers together.

Another feature of timing in African music is the beat. The beat is often misunderstood outside of Africa as a specific rhythmic pattern associated with certain kinds of dances or musical genres. Instead, the beat is an equally spaced series of reference points. African music is unlike some Western forms of music in which some of these points may be stressed, creating the impression of "strong" and "weak" parts. In African music the beat is rarely played and is not in any way accentuated.

Another distinctive aspect of timing in African music is its reliance on cyclic form. Cycles vary in length, with cycles of twelve or twenty-four pulses being the most common. This repetitiveness of African music does not, as has often been as-

A Gwi man plays the mbira, sometimes called a thumb piano, in Botswana. CORBIS/Peter Johnson

sumed, reflect a lower stage of development but is an essential component of musical composition that enables listeners and performers to become intensely immersed and to participate communally. Finally, the timing in African music is distinctive because of its use of the time-line, a short pattern of several, asymmetrically spaced strokes on an iron bell, the rim of a drum, or a glass bottle. Encountered primarily on the coast of West Africa, central Africa, and in parts of Southeast Africa, time-line patterns, like the elementary pulses, orient the musicians.

Variations of Tone

The third fundamental stylistic trait of African music is the organization of tones. Tones—sounds with specific pitch and duration—are the basic unit of musical organization. According to musicologist Gerhard Kubik, African music has three basic tonal families. The first includes systems derived from the natural harmonic series. (Natural harmonics are those tones created by plucking an open string in such a way that they produce partials—subsidiary overtones produced by primary tones. Together the natural harmonic and its partials constitute a natural harmonic series.) Much of the music in southern Africa, for example, is based on the partials obtained from two or three fundamental tones. The second tonal family consists of systems based on tonal languages in which relative pitch levels in spoken speech determine the melodic contour of a song (the rise and fall in the sound of the melody). The third tonal family consists of systems that include some idea of musical "temperature"—a layout of the tonal material in equidistant intervals. (Intervals are the distance in pitch—the highness or lowness of a tone—between tones.) These three families do not necessarily overlap with other criteria, such as regional styles, and often even intermingle with one another in one area.

With the exception of some areas in West and East Africa influenced by Arabic musical styles, most African music consists of multiple parts, in which performers assume distinct roles. Distribution across the continent of different styles of multipart singing is somewhat uneven. The most common type of multipart singing is the call-and-response interaction between a soloist and a choir, in which the lead singer's line (call) partly overlaps with that of the chorus (response).

Musical styles are often linked to a group's spoken language. Among people who speak tone-based languages, such as the Yoruba of Nigeria, musical style tends to follow the spoken emphasis on the use of tone to convey meaning. Among such ethnic groups, the different vocal parts tend to move together in parallel. In addition, music is commonly used as a sort of surrogate speech. African people who speak tone-based languages also tend to create polyphonic music, in which two or more independent melodic lines are sounded together. In contrast, groups that speak languages that are not tone-based generally have musical traditions that accommodate contrary movement of vocal parts.

Regional Styles

Despite the homogeneity of music south of the Sahara, several major stylistic regions of African music can be distinguished. The bases for these regional differences are not defined by political boundaries of countries, nor are they necessarily tied to geographical divisions such as central, east, west, and southern Africa. Musical styles do not always coincide with the ethnic identity of the musicians and their audiences. A simple differentiation along ethnic lines often ignores existing internal subdivisions within these groups as well as the extensive diffusion of certain musical features or musical instruments among several groups who often live at considerable distances from one another. Far more reliable than geography or ethnicity are the correspondences between the major language families and musical areas. Alternatively, it is possible to find patterns of musical styles that are linked to historical contacts between different groups.

The *likembe,* for example, is a type of lamellaphone—a small instrument with hand-plucked metal strips that is often mistakenly called a thumb piano. The likembe emerged during the nineteenth century in the area of the lower Congo River. But toward the early part of the twentieth century Lingala-speaking colonial agents and railway workers carried the instrument to areas in the northwestern Belgian Congo (now the DEMOCRATIC REPUBLIC OF THE CONGO, or DRC) and the CENTRAL AFRICAN REPUBLIC, where it was adopted by the NGBANDI and Gbaya peoples. They also carried the likembe to Uganda, where ACHOLI, ALUR, and Busoga musicians adapted their traditional xylophone music to the new instrument.

Most musicologists divide Africa into seven major musical stylistic regions. The first is the Sahara and SAHEL zone, which includes countries such as CHAD, THE GAMBIA, Mali, Mauritania, NIGER, and SENEGAL. This stylistic region also includes the northern parts of BENIN, CÔTE D'IVOIRE, GHANA, Nigeria, and TOGO. Arabic culture and Islam have strongly influenced this area since as early as the ninth century. Many musical instruments, such as the *goge (goje)*, a one-string fiddle, and the algaita oboe, were adopted from North Africa and the Middle East. Highly ornamented, monophonic music (music with a single line of melody) dominates the region. Music in this region tends to rely less on the complex interlocking rhythmic techniques that are common in other parts of Africa.

The second area, the West African coast, comprises parts of Benin, Côte d'Ivoire, Ghana, Guinea, LIBERIA, Nigeria, SIERRA LEONE, and Togo. It also includes the coastal areas of CAMEROON, GABON, and the REPUBLIC OF THE CONGO. Trading and migration have been particularly strong and enduring along the West African coast, resulting in a rich but unified musical heritage. Most prominent among the stylistic features of this area are polyphonic singing and complex interlocking rhythms. The complex rhythms are used primarily by drumming ensembles but are sometimes used by other types of instrumental groups.

The central Africa music region consists of the eastern parts of Cameroon, Central African Republic, and Gabon, southern parts of Chad, and western parts of the Republic of the Congo and the DRC. It shares many of the features of the West African coast but also includes the musically distinct enclave of the so-called PYGMY peoples, whose style is characterized by yodeling and complex polyphonic singing.

The fourth music region includes ETHIOPIA and parts of other countries in the eastern part of what is known as the Horn of Africa, specifically DJIBOUTI and SOMALIA. As in the Sahara and Sahel zone, Arabic and Islamic influence is intense in this region, especially along the coastal areas. In the highlands of Ethiopia the music of the Coptic Church (a major Christian church) forms a distinct style of music, emphasizing strong vocals and the use of cymbals and triangles.

The stylistic region of east Africa covers BURUNDI, RWANDA, and Uganda, and includes parts of the DRC, KENYA, TANZANIA, and the northern parts of MOZAMBIQUE. The music of this region has been subject to some Islamic influence along the coasts of Kenya, Tanzania, and Mozambique. The musical styles of the inland areas, however, feature a variety of lyre and xylophone styles with complex interlocking performance techniques.

The south central Africa music region comprises eastern parts of ANGOLA and ZAMBIA and southern Mozambique. It shares many of the features of the central Africa region, including the prominent use of plucked lamellaphones such as the likembe.

The seventh area, southern Africa, includes BOTSWANA, SOUTH AFRICA, SWAZILAND, and ZIMBABWE. Music in this area is known for musical systems based on the series of natural harmonics. Music in this region is also distinctive for its use of a large number of musical bows (bow-shaped instruments with one string), complex vocal polyphony, and a general tendency not to use "hot" drumming. The origin of some of these features is the music of KHOISAN-speaking peoples (often known as the SAN, or derogatorily, Bushmen).

Wearing robes and head wraps designed to echo the South African flag, this choir sings at Nelson Mandela's inauguration in 1994. *CORBIS/PeterTurnley*

Music in Society

A vital means of communication and cultural expression, music in sub-Saharan Africa plays an important role in society. Music is a social practice filled with meaning and linked to economic life, religion, politics, and the arts.

In many parts of Africa, the influences of Christianity and Islam have led to new forms of religious music. In Sudan the *zikr* ceremonies of the Ahmadiyya Sufi order blend Islamic and African musical elements. Spirit possession cults, such as the bori among the HAUSA of northern Nigeria, combine North African vocal styles with dance styles of the Sahel zone. New Christian churches in southern Africa use Western harmony and hymn tunes but sing these in a distinctly African vocal style. Many societies, however, do not maintain a strict division between sacred and secular uses of music. Among the Hausa, goge fiddle players perform for bori rituals and prostitutes alike.

Music is an integral component of political life in Africa. In many African societies special kinds of musical instruments are used as insignia of power. In highly stratified societies, such as the Hausa city-states of West Africa, each craft group was associated with its own set of musical genres, instruments, and professional musicians. Nevertheless, musical styles associated with institutions of power, such as chiefs, kings, and religious leaders, rarely form a separate realm of elite tastes as they often do in other parts of the world. Instead, in most parts of Africa the rich and powerful enjoy the same types of music that are favored by farmers, factory workers, and people in other sectors of society.

African music also takes up political themes, sometimes in overt ways. Song lyrics may attack or ridicule irresponsible political leaders. In other cases music supports national liberation movements, as did the CHIMURENGA MUSIC in Zimbabwe during the struggle against white-minority rule. Conversely, many African governments have sought to shape their country's musical landscape by attempting to control the influx of foreign music, as in Tanzania. In other countries the governments suppress the music of communities that oppose the dominant political or ethnic group. In still other cases, African governments attempt to shape their national musical culture by vigorously supporting the traditional arts, as was the case in Zaire (now Democratic Republic of the Congo).

African musicians often occupy low social positions, although their art is generally highly appreciated. In the savanna region of West Africa, professional musicians often attached themselves to rulers or important families, singing their praises and chronicling their family or clan histories. Often misnamed griots, these bards have become important symbols in modern African and African American attempts to reclaim their cultural heritage. But not all professional musicians in West Africa are griots, nor are all griots necessarily storytellers.

Distinctions between traditional and popular music styles in Africa are often problematic. The problem arises because the musical styles that emerged during the twentieth century, which tended to be heavily influenced by Western popular music, were also deeply rooted in precolonial indigenous traditions.

Two general trends were crucial in shaping African popular music. The first was a general modernization of African societies; the second was a number of significant developments in local musical practices. The modernization of African societies entailed a rapid process of urbanization and industrialization in South Africa, the DRC, Zambia, the West African coast, and parts of East Africa. Along with urbanization and industrialization, most governments also adopted Western-style bureaucracies. New modes of transport and increased mobility

A Bobo man in Burkina Faso plays the *balo,* a xylophone-like instrument made from gourds and wooden keys. *CORBIS/Charles & Josette Lenars*

favored the expansion of a variety of languages as lingua franca (common language), such as Swahili in East Africa and Lingala in Central Africa. Even more important was the growth of the mass media and the rise of an African music industry.

The first radio stations in Africa were established in South Africa, Kenya, and Nigeria in the 1920s. Most African countries, however, did not introduce nationwide radio broadcasting networks until after World War II (1939–1945) and television until the 1960s and 1970s. These new media brought a wide range of African and foreign musical styles to virtually every corner of the continent. In many countries the media also have continued to provide the most powerful and often the only existing infrastructure for the production and mass distribution of popular music. Record production began in South Africa in 1908, but the majority of African countries lacked production facilities such as studios and pressing plants, even as late as the 1990s. With the bursting onto the scene in the 1970s of cheap audiocassettes and given the absence of strict copyright legislation in most countries, it became impossible for African music companies to prevent counterfeiting of their music. Problems with counterfeiting meant that what little was left of the African music industry in the late 1970s had practically ceased to exist by the 1980s.

Styles of Popular Music

Several factors account for the emergence of distinct popular music styles in Africa. The first of these and possibly the most important was the European Christian missions. In many countries, missionaries spread hymns and other religious practices that were then combined with local musical styles. The influence of missionaries varied from region to region, with the oldest and probably the deepest impact in South Africa. In South Africa, ancient traditions of polyphonic singing favored the adoption of Western church hymns and resulted in a style known as *makwaya* (ZULU for "choir").

Colonialism also left its mark on African music in another major way: through military bands. European military bands and brass band music attracted many young musicians and led to a variety of local styles. In Ghana, for example, musicians combined Western-style brass band music and guitars with local styles to create highlife music. In East Africa a number of performance genres emerged in the late nineteenth and early twentieth century. These include *beni, malipenga,* and *mganda.* In each of these genres European brass instruments were gradually indigenized (adapted to local use) and replaced with gourd trumpets and *mirlitons* (a kazoolike wind instrument).

A third influence on African popular music, African American music from the Americas, began to have a crucial effect as early as the 1920s. African American performers such as Orpheus McAdoo's Virginia Jubilee Singers toured South Africa as early as the 1890s. But it was on the West African coast and in the Belgian Congo that African American and Caribbean seamen and West African KRU sailors intermingled and blended local traditions with African American–derived genres such as RAGTIME. In Ghana, African American vaudeville comedians Glass and Grant blended elements of the (white) minstrel stage with key figures of local lore, such as the spider Ananse. The result was the concert party, one of the country's most lively forms of popular entertainment. In Central Africa, Afro-Caribbean musical forms, such as rumba, merengue, and chachachá, were instrumental in shaping early Congolese *maringa* music. In South Africa, finally, African American JAZZ influenced a variety of styles, especially the kwela pennywhistle music of the 1950s and 1960s.

The fourth factor contributing to the rise of popular music was the spread of musical instruments of Western manufacture. Of these, the guitar proved the most popular, although accordions also found widespread acceptance. Yet in many cases, the music that is being played on these Western instruments is rooted in local tradition. Zulu *maskanda* guitar music, for example, is played using the two-finger picking technique—a technique popular throughout Africa and much more widespread than strumming—that was based primarily on the *umakweyana* style of bow music popular with young girls.

Due to the strong impact of these factors, and despite some minor local variations, only five major stylistic regions of popular African music can be distinguished. The first of these is in the Sahel zone, where a number of distinct styles have emerged in more recent years, such as the *mbalax* in Senegambia and in Mali. Mbalax music transfers parts normally played by traditional drums to electric guitars and keyboards. The influence of Manding (or MANDE, a linguistic group in West Africa) music is particularly strong in the music of Malian singer and songwriter Salif Keita. WOLOF traditions have shaped the music of Senegalese stars YOUSSOU N'DOUR, who plays a modern version of mbalax. Fulbe traditions have inspired the music of Baaba Mal and Malian diva OUMOU SANGARÉ. Sangaré's music uses instruments typical of Wassoulou music—guitar, *kamelen ngoni* (a small, harplike stringed instrument), and a variety of percussion instruments—but she adds lyrics with modern themes.

The second area, Sudan and the East African coast, also has a distinctive sound. In this area Egyptian popular music has been important for decades. But performers have added local African elements such as call-and-response structures. In this way Sudanese musicians have created a distinctly Sudanese style of accordion and string ensembles. Their Swahili and Zanzibari counterparts are known for the related *taarab* style of music, a style of sung Swahili poetry.

In the third region, the West African coast, popular music styles date from the turn of the twentieth century. These include the Ghanaian highlife style and the JUJU and *fuji* styles of the Yoruba in Nigeria. Other West African styles dating from the early twentieth century include *bikutsi* in Cameroon, the soul-influenced AFRO-BEAT of Nigerian FELA ANIKULAPO KUTI, and the *makossa* style of Cameroonian saxophonist Manu Dibango. All of these styles draw on a complex mix of local musical traditions, African American music, rock and roll, and Islamic or Christian religious elements.

The fourth and possibly largest area is Central Africa, centered in what is now the Democratic Republic of Congo and the Republic of Congo. Soon after World War II the Belgian colonial administration and foreign capital in the area combined to create one of the continent's most thriving national music industries. The basis of the guitar band music that is today known as SOUKOUS at first consisted of a number of Afro-Caribbean styles and only later incorporated more traditional material derived from the likembe. Soukous and its numerous predecessors and offshoots were made popular by musicians such as Franco and O.K. JAZZ, Rochereau, Mbilia Bel, Papa Wemba, and Kanda Bongo Man.

Soukous and its related styles are no longer confined to the Democratic Republic of the Congo alone. They also displaced an older Congolese guitar style (sometimes called Katanga guitar style) that was equally important during the 1950s and whose main proponents include Jean Mwenda Bosco, Losta Abelo, and Edouard Masengo. Traces of this earlier style survive in the popular music of Kenya and Tanzania, where the Katangan guitar technique merged with the older lyre traditions of the Luo people to form BENGA.

The fifth stylistic region of popular music is southern Africa. As elsewhere, strong local styles exist, and some have even attracted international attention, such as the chimurenga music of THOMAS MAPFUMO in Zimbabwe and the *isicathamiya* a cappella music of LADYSMITH BLACK MAMBAZO of South Africa. By far the most important popular style, however, is *mbaqanga*. This electric guitar–based style influenced the *kalindula* of Zambia, *jit* of Zimbabwe, and *simanje-manje* of MALAWI. This style is sometimes also called jive and draws heavily on jazz of the SWING era. Despite the jazz influence, leading mbaqanga performers such as Phuz'shukela and Mahlathini and the Mahotella Queens drew partly on Zulu guitar music to reintroduce shorter, more cyclic patterns than are common in jazz.

Despite their diversity, all these styles of African popular music have a number of things in common. They address many of the issues confronting Africans living in the modern world, issues such as chronic poverty, the changed role of the individual in the vastly restructured social landscape, and many others. A great deal of African popular music expresses a yearning for the precolonial past, often couching this desire in a nostalgia for a lost Africa of stability and ethnic identity. This longing for the past within the modern context is often expressed through performances that are neotraditional (new variations on traditional styles). The desire to restore some parts of the past stems from the fact that the colonial powers and, in their aftermath, the independent nation-states failed to deliver on the promises they had made. Zulu migrant workers, for example, living under the dehumanizing conditions of industrial South Africa, invoke symbols of the past in their dances.

The prevalence of neotraditional themes is also evident in REGGAE. Although reggae originated on the Caribbean island of JAMAICA, it is probably the most important style popular throughout Africa, with Alpha Blondy of Côte d'Ivoire and Lucky Dube of South Africa as its most successful stars. Reggae in Africa expresses Africans' search for an identity in a medium that is both modern and committed to core African social values. The key difference between reggae and other forms of neotraditional popular music is that reggae appeals to ideologies of PAN-AFRICANISM, rather than to more narrowly defined ethnic or national identity.

Influence from Abroad

African musicians absorbed and reinterpreted European and Asian musical styles for centuries before the modern era. But the strongest international effect of African music has been on the Americas. This impact was primarily a by-product of the slave trade. The wealth of black musical traditions in the United States, the Caribbean, and BRAZIL can be directly traced to various parts of Africa. The West African Sahel zone, for example, influenced the development of American BLUES. The West African coast shaped Afro-Caribbean music styles such as the Cuban RUMBA, and the sources of much of Brazilian music lie in Angola.

As a result of the decline of the African music industry and the growing role of African popular music in world beat—a broad category of non-Western pop music that gained popularity in the 1980s—numerous African musicians have taken up residence in Paris, France. Access to Western recording companies and audiences enabled performers such as Guinean-born kora player Mory Kanté and Youssou N'Dour to top sales charts in Europe and the United States. Ladysmith Black Mambazo achieved another notable international success in 1986 when the group teamed up with American pop star Paul Simon in the Grammy Award–winning album *Graceland*. A year later they became the first African musicians to receive a Grammy Award, for their album *Shaka Zulu*.

See also Christianity: Missionaries in Africa; Dance in Sub-Saharan Africa; Griot; Islam in Africa; Music, African American; Music, Caribbean; Radio, African; World Music, World Beat, and the Re-Africanization of Latin American Popular Music.

Kofi Agawu

Music, African American

Wide-ranging musical traditions of African Americans, which have played a dominant role in American music and represent one of the most significant expressions of African American culture.

Early African American music in the United States joined African musical practices with the vocabulary and structures of European-American music. Comprising work songs, calls, field and street cries, hollers, rhyme songs, and spirituals, this music provided slaves with a means of effectively pacing their work, a form of sung prayer and praise, a means of surreptitious communication, and psychic relief from the degradation of bondage. Many of the work songs used the African call-and-response form: a lead singer gave the line of melody and the others joined in for the refrain. This pattern, as well as a number of actual African tunes, also influenced the AFRICAN AMERICAN SPIRITUALS. Both the spirituals and, later, the BLUES—a form of secular solo folk song—incorporated the African freedom to improvise variations in the melodic line. Also derived from African heritage was polyrhythmic drumming, simultaneously combining several different rhythmic patterns of different meters. The interplay of contrasting rhythms was eventually carried over into a later African American musical style, JAZZ.

Although sacred music such as the spirituals was the most common African American music in the early nineteenth century, secular music also existed. Like the spirituals, the work songs, calls, and cries were performed a cappella (without instrumental accompaniment); some of the other secular songs were accompanied by instruments. The earliest slave instruments included drums and an African transplant, the BANJO; later, the flute, violin, and guitar were also used. Guitar, violin, and banjo frequently constituted the string bands that provided music for the American social dances of the nineteenth century—jigs, reels, the buck-and-wing, cotillions, and quadrilles. Makeshift instruments such as quills, gutbuckets (bass fiddles made from washtubs), and jugs were also employed in string bands.

Following the AMERICAN CIVIL WAR (1861–1865), rhyme songs and ballads became plentiful, and the blues began to take on its modern forms. The music of black minstrel shows, string bands, brass bands, and honky-tonk pianos became increasingly influential, and such genres as RAGTIME gradually emerged. Having originated in the southern and midwestern United States, ragtime reached its classic form in the 1890s in the St. Louis, Missouri, school of ragtime pianists led by SCOTT JOPLIN. In the first decade of the twentieth century, the musical practices of black Americans formed a new American music called jazz. Jazz first flourished in NEW ORLEANS, LOUISIANA, then spread to cities all across the country. Among the most important jazz innovators in the first half of the twentieth century were LOUIS ("SATCHMO") ARMSTRONG, FLETCHER HAMILTON HENDERSON JR., BILLIE HOLIDAY, EDWARD KENNEDY ("DUKE") ELLINGTON, and DIZZY GILLESPIE.

In the 1940s RHYTHM AND BLUES (R&B) music emerged as a combined product of rural blues and black-oriented, big-band swing music, performed by small ensembles with a lead vocalist or instrumentalist and rhythm and backup sections. The pioneers and popularizers of R&B included AARON ("T-BONE") WALKER, Little Walter, Louis Jordan, FATS DOMINO, JAMES BROWN, RAY CHARLES, and RUTH BROWN. Since the 1950s R&B has been the generic source of black pop music as well as American pop music in general.

SOUL MUSIC was a further development of R&B. Essentially, soul combines the R&B sound of the 1950s with techniques, effects, and performance practices borrowed from black GOSPEL MUSIC. It has two main substyles: the polished, sophisticated Detroit style associated with Motown Records, featuring such artists as STEVIE WONDER, THE SUPREMES, and THE TEMPTATIONS; and the earthier, more gospel-oriented Memphis, Tennessee, style of STAX RECORDS, exemplified by OTIS REDDING and Booker T. and the MGs.

The black gospel movement had its beginnings in the early performance practices of the black Holiness and Pentecostal churches and in the published songs of the Philadelphia minister CHARLES ALBERT TINDLEY in the early twentieth century. Using the resources of work songs, hollers, cries, spirituals, blues, and jazz, black gospel music was fully developed by the composer THOMAS ANDREW DORSEY and the singer Roberta Martin, gradually becoming an important part of black worship among some denominations. Famous performers of gospel music include MAHALIA JACKSON, the Mighty Clouds of Joy, JAMES EDWARD CLEVELAND, and Andrae Crouch and the Disciples.

In the 1970s a new musical form called RAP arose on the streets of NEW YORK, NEW YORK. The Sugar Hill Gang's *Rapper's Delight* (1979) was the first rap hit record. Using bits of FUNK and hard-rock records and a miscellany of other sounds as background, rap performers chanted rhyming couplets, generally about ghetto life. In the 1980s the music spread across the United States as young audiences responded to the rap performers' angry words about social injustice, racism, and drug abuse.

The relationship of Latin American music to black music in the United States is most evident in the offbeat accents that are common in both. Between 1900 and 1940, Latin American dances—the TANGO (Argentina), the RUMBA (Cuba), and the merengue (Dominican Republic)—were all introduced into the United States. In the 1940s a fusion of Latin and jazz elements began, stimulated at first by the Afro-Cuban MAMBO and later on by the Brazilian bossa nova. The late 1960s brought a mingling of Latin and soul music—notably by RAMÓN ("MONGO") SANTAMARIA and Willie Bobo—and the recognition of the Cuban-Puerto Rican SALSA MUSIC as an important genre. Reversing the direction of influence, African American music of the United States also affected musical fusions in the Caribbean, Latin America, and Africa, giving rise to Jamaican REGGAE and its predecessors—SKA, ROCK STEADY, and African highlife.

See also Merengue: Music, Race, and Nation in the Dominican Republic; Minstrelsy; Motown; Music, African; Pentecostalism.

Music, Afro-Caribbean Religious

Music performed within a religious context.

Afro-Caribbean religious music exhibits extraordinary diversity and richness, which are made all the more conspicuous by the adverse conditions under which they were created. As in traditional music cultures in Africa, distinctions between sacred and secular genres are often ambiguous, and performance of explicitly devotional music may serve an important role as social recreation. In many respects, however, Afro-Caribbean religious music genres constitute a relatively discrete category, spanning a continuum from Creole styles, which include overtly Westernized genres, to those that bear no evident Euro-American influence.

Many of the most significant and distinctive types of Afro-Caribbean sacred music are associated with syncretic religions such as SANTERÍA and VODOU, which clearly reflect their African roots. Typically, such religions combine European and African elements, identifying African deities (ORISHAS) with Christian saints and reflecting other superficial aspects of Christian worship. Music genres associated with these religions, however, often exhibit no Western influence either in style or content; indeed, it is in such music that the greatest influence of African music is to be found. This influence is reflected in the use of call-and-response vocal style, the emphasis on rhythm, the use of percussion-based ensembles (typically featuring two or three drums), the fondness for syncopation and polyrhythm, and the tendency for pieces to be structured on repetition of short, rhythmically complex ostinatos. At the same time, such music genres seldom correspond directly to modern counterparts in Africa, because they are products of transculturation processes involving slaves and free Afro-Caribbeans of different African ethnic backgrounds and because they have been creatively rearticulated and modified by generations of performers, although on primarily African-derived aesthetic lines. While such neo-African music styles have been of particular interest to scholars, much research relating them to their African sources remains to be done.

Neo-African religious music genres are particularly prominent and diverse in CUBA, where their survival was facilitated by various factors, including the late importation of slaves (continuing until the 1860s) and relatively lenient Spanish manumission laws. From early in the colonial period, such policies led to the presence of a substantial free black population, many of whose members formed ethnically based societies called *cabildos*, in which they were able, despite intermittent repression, to practice their traditional religions, together with their associated music and dance. The most widespread of these religions is Santería (also called *Lucumí*), which can be seen as a particularly dynamic efflorescence of the international phenomenon of YORUBA-derived religion. Santería worship centers around ceremonies in which songs and dances are used to honor the deities and, ideally, induce spirit possession. Typically, three instrumentalists play relatively standardized rhythms on hourglass-shaped *batá* drums, while a vocalist leads devotees in responsorial singing. The rhythms, dances, and lyrics (sung in a somewhat garbled, archaic Yoruba dialect) are all associated with particular spirits (orishas) in the Yoruba pantheon. A more festive kind of Santería event is the *bembé*, whose distinctive music features improvised solos played on the single-headed drum of the same name. Yoruba-derived religious music also includes that of the *iyesá cabildos*, deriving from a related West African regional tradition.

Congolese-derived religious practices have also flourished in Cuba, where they are sometimes grouped under the name *Palo*. Although Palo is in many respects less formalized as a religion than Santería, its repertoire of songs and dances is prodigious and may have been influential in the evolution of the secular Afro-Cuban music and dance form RUMBA. Another Afro-Cuban religious sect with a distinctive music tradition is *arará*, which, like the Rada traditions of HAITI and TRINIDAD, evidently derives from the old Dahomean port town of Alada. Also still vital is the music tradition of the ABAKUÁS, secret societies whose songs and dances reenact Carabali-derived mythology (of the IGBO ethnic group). Starting with the monumental works of Cuban anthropologist FERNANDO ORTIZ (1881–1969), such Afro-Cuban religious music genres have received a fair amount of scholarly attention and continue to be actively performed by devotees and folkloric groups, both in Cuba and in places like New York City. In Cuba today, Santería flourishes with great vigor and has been essentially tolerated by the Communist government.

Haiti is another stronghold of neo-African religious music, especially that associated with the complex known to outsiders as Vodou, which syncretizes Congolese and Yoruba traditions with those of Benin/Dahomey. Since the HAITIAN REVOLUTION (ending around 1804), such religions and associated music styles have resiliently withstood repression by the Catholic Church and the mulatto elite, although their practice in many communities has been curtailed in recent decades by American-based Protestant evangelism. Despite the negative publicity associated with Vodou, its associated music, dance, and mythology traditions are comparable in richness to those of Santería, with which it shares many features. Vodou music thrives in a variety of regional forms, many of which have yet to be documented. The religion and its music are also perpetuated by ethnic Haitians in the neighboring DOMINICAN REPUBLIC, alongside a less standardized set of neo-African religious music that reflect Congolese influence. These Dominican traditions, however, are considerably weaker than in Haiti and Cuba and occupy little legitimacy in the more Afro-phobic national ideology.

Neo-African religions and their music are somewhat less prominent in the English-speaking Caribbean, due to such factors as the earlier cessation of slave imports (in 1807), the limited numbers of free blacks during the slave period (ending 1838), the more intensive presence of Protestant churches in sociocultural life, and perhaps, the greater intolerance of pagan and syncretic practices on the part of missionaries and colonial authorities. Nevertheless, several neo-African religious traditions did survive and were reinforced in the mid-nineteenth century by the immigration of African indentured workers, particularly Yorubans. Such workers were the evident source for the Afro-Trinidadian sect known as SHANGO or orisha worship, whose songs, dances, instruments, and practices, although of evident Yoruba derivation, differ substantially from those of Santería. Similarly, Congolese indentured immigrants appear to have contributed to the *kumina* sect in JAMAICA, which survives in eastern parts of that island. By contrast, the Jamaican religious tradition of *kromanti* appears to derive from the older practices established by maroons (escaped slaves). The most extensive and culturally autonomous maroon societies of the Caribbean Basin are those of the former Dutch colony of SURINAME, where neo-African music styles of the Kwinti, Njuka, Saramaka, and other groups have flourished unimpeded by legal or Christian repression. However diverse, all these traditions, like Santería and Vodou, center around performance of songs and dances in neo-African style, with texts abundant with African words used to invoke spirit possession. Other neo-African West Indian music genres, such as Guyanese *cumfa* and *kwe-kwe* (queh-queh) and the "big drum dance" from Carriocou (an island of GRENADA) do not involve possession trance but honor spirits of departed ancestors. Aside from Surinamese maroon religions, most of these West Indian neo-African sects were repressed, with varying degrees of vigor, until around the 1960s; British authorities also attempted to ban all drumming in most of their West Indian colonies. While such persecution no longer occurs, neo-African religions and music genres in independent West Indian countries have, on the whole, found relatively little public recognition, whether among state culture ministries or popular opinion, where more "Creole" notions of cultural identity tend to dominate.

In the English-speaking Caribbean, more widespread than neo-African religions are acculturated, Creole Protestant sects whose theologies and devotional practices reflect a more Western orientation. Accordingly, their associated music styles lie somewhere closer to the middle of the African-versus-European spectrum. In this category would fall the Jamaican pocomania (pukimina) and Revival Zion sects, and the Trinidadian Spiritual Baptists (Shouters). The music styles of these sects, which bear certain affinities to American GOSPEL MUSIC, typically consist of English-language Protestant hymns rendered in a vigorously rhythmic style, often accompanied by animated clapping and drumming. Spirit possession may occur, although the trance is less likely to be associated with African deities. With colonial repression over, the neo-African features of such sects, along with the popularity of faiths like Santería, appear in many respects to be increasing rather than declining.

See also Catholic Church in Latin America and the Caribbean; Dahomey, Early Kingdom of; Music, Afro-Caribbean Secular; Maroonage in the Americas; Music, Afro-Cuban; Protestant Church in Latin America and the Caribbean.

Peter Manuel

Music, Afro-Caribbean Secular

The Caribbean Basin has proved to be an extraordinarily fertile site for musical creation, with several forms of modern Caribbean popular music coming to enjoy global renown and appeal. These musics can be regarded as "Creole" products in the sense that they are uniquely Caribbean idioms distinct from Old World predecessors. Most can be characterized as Afro-Caribbean in the sense that their most distinctive features derive from African influences. More specifically, they are products of syncretic transculturation involving African- and European-derived features and can be seen as occupying various points on a stylistic continuum ranging from neo-African genres on one end to more purely European-derived idioms on the other.

Although the Caribbean is perhaps best known for its commercial popular musics, the field of Afro-Caribbean secular music has comprised a considerably broader range of expressive idioms. Various forms of work songs, although less often heard today, flourished throughout the region and constituted one of the most common forms of creolized musical expression. Some of these, such as Haitian *combite* (*konbit*) songs chanted responsorially by communal work teams, retain a strong neo-African flavor and are still performed today. Another traditional category of Afro-Caribbean secular music comprises the diverse processional music associated with Carnival festivities, most of which commenced as European pre-Lenten occasions but came to be dominated by Afro-Caribbean celebrants. While some of these musics, such as Trinidadian *camboulay*, have died out,

The music of Afro-Caribbean steel bands—immensely popular throughout the world—is performed in Louisiana by the Rising Stars Youth Steel Orchestra of St. Thomas, Virgin Islands. *CORBIS/Bob Krist*

others, such as the Cuban conga, still survive. The conga (as distinct from the drum of the same name) consists of a processional dance, accompanied by animated Afro-Cuban drumming and singing, performed by costumed participants in *comparsa* processions during that island's Carnival (now held in July). Another vibrant Carnival music is Haitian rara (and the derivative Dominican *gaga*), comprising processional groups based around players of bamboo tubes called *vaksin*, which are blown in hocket technique to produce complex interlocking melodies, in a manner closely related to similar contemporary practices in West Africa. English-speaking West Indian islands have their own Carnival tradition musics, some of which, like the "mummies" of SAINT KITTS AND NEVIS, include fife-and-drum music that appears to blend European military drumming and African flute-and-drum traditions.

While such occasion-specific musics are of considerable interest and originality, it is in the realm of recreational social dance music that the greatest richness and diversity of Caribbean music are to be found. As with AFRO-CARIBBEAN RELIGIOUS MUSIC, many of these genres, such as Cuban RUMBA and Puerto Rican bomba, are free from any particular European stylistic influence, deriving overwhelmingly from African sources (although their lyrics tend to be in European or local Creole languages rather than the African languages encountered in SANTERÍA or VODOU musics, for example). At the same time, they differ from their African counterparts in having evolved through centuries of interethnic syncretism among Africans of different regions and through being creatively transformed by generations of Afro-Caribbean musicians. In that sense such musics are best regarded as "neo-African." They tend to reflect with particular clarity the quintessential features of African music, including call-and-response singing, reliance on repetition and ostinato, and an emphasis on rhythm, including offbeat phrasing and, often, polyrhythm. Aside from still-vital genres like Cuban rumba, colonial accounts attest to a wide variety of such musics flourishing in the past throughout the Caribbean, including now-obscure forms like *bamboula* and *calinda*.

Most traditional Afro-Caribbean dance musics, however, reflect some degree of stylistic syncretism with European influences. In many cases, these have involved rendering European-style melodies, whether vocally or on instruments like violin or guitar, with a more syncopated and animated rhythmic accompaniment provided on percussion instruments. When black musicians were hired to play European quadroons, waltzes, jigs, and other genres, the resultant music often acquired a distinctive Afro-Caribbean flavor, still manifest in genres like Trinidadian "heel-and-toe."

One prominent set of Creole social dance musics emerging from the early nineteenth century was that comprising the local varieties of contredanse, *contradanza, danza*, and related idioms. The nucleus of this cluster appears to have been the Franco-Haitian contredanse, which formed the basis for the subsequent Haitian *méringue*, the early Dominican merengue, the Cuban contradanza (known elsewhere as the habanera) and the subsequent *danzón*, and the derivative but distinctive Puerto Rican danza. Most of these idioms could be rendered either in refined parlor styles for white elites or in more vigorous and rhythmic styles by dance bands typically consisting of black or mixed-race musicians. These genres were significant both for their subdued but insistent Afro-Caribbean lilt and their gradual transition from line dances to ballroom-style couple dances. As such, they were vehicles both for the Afro-Caribbeanization and the choreographic liberalization of Creole music culture—features that made genres like the habanera popular in nineteenth-century Europe as well.

With the spread of recording technology around 1900, Afro-Caribbean popular musics rapidly evolved into a set of unique and dynamic genres. Most of these styles were products of creative cross-fertilization, at once borrowing features from one another and from European and especially American popular music, while influencing these latter musics in their turn. Almost all of these music genres have derived their most distinctive features from Afro-Caribbean sources and have been created and performed largely by black or mixed-race artists. Most, from rumba to REGGAE, encountered vigorous opposition from negrophobic, Eurocentric elites. Several, however, eventually came to be accepted as national musics, thus playing crucial roles in the emergence of Creole national and cultural identities and legitimizing the Afro-Caribbean presence therein.

CUBA has been the most musically influential island in the region, both by virtue of its relative size and, perhaps, the particularly balanced and felicitous nature of its syntheses of Afro-Caribbean and European-derived elements. By the nineteenth century, Cuba hosted a thriving Creole music culture comprising neo-African genres like rumba as well as more Europeanized styles like the contradanza (habanera). The development of the more syncopated and rhythmic danzón out of the contradanza typified the gradual, if then controversial, Afro-Cubanization of the island's popular musics. Such tendencies became more pronounced in the early twentieth century with the emergence of the SON, which synthesized Spanish-derived chordal harmonies and instruments (especially the guitar and guitar-like tres) with Afro-Cuban features, including the use of the clave rhythmic cell, the progression to an extended call-and-response section (the *montuno*), and the use of the bongo and the *marimbula*, an enlarged bass version of African lamellaphones like the mbira. By the 1920s, the son, although played primarily by black musicians, was increasingly accepted as the nation's most popular dance music. In subsequent decades the son became in some respects more Westernized, adopting JAZZ harmonies and larger ensembles including piano and additional brass instruments; at the same time it also acquired a more Afro-Cuban flavor through the use of faster tempi and a generally more percussive flavor reminiscent of the rumba. Such tendencies were epitomized in the MAMBO, which emerged in the 1950s as a largely instrumental adaptation of up-tempo Cuban rhythms to jazz big-band format. In the 1940s and 1950s, the innovations of ARSENIO RODRÍGUEZ, the Conjunto Casino, Félix Chapotin, and others established the essential form of the modern son, which remains the stylistic basis for what is now called "SALSA MUSIC." By this time Cuban genres like the son, the mambo, and the chachachá had become thoroughly international, flourishing among Latino communities in New York and elsewhere, and throughout much of urban Africa. Dance music based on the modern son has continued to flourish in Cuba since the 1950s, and it took on a new life in New York and elsewhere from the 1960s under the new label "salsa," especially as linked to the sharpened sociopolitical consciousness of Caribbean Basin Latinos during the 1960s and 1970s.

By the late nineteenth century, Cuba's sister Spanish colony of PUERTO RICO had developed its own thriving Creole music culture, encompassing both neo-African forms like bomba as well as the more Europeanized danza, which, however, retained a subtle Afro-Caribbean syncopation. In the early twentieth century, Cuban popular musics, especially the son and BOLERO, took root in Puerto Rico, especially as performed and composed by black and mulatto artists. Meanwhile, the plena had emerged as a lively, syncopated, informal topical song genre, rooted in lower-class social life. The 1940s saw the adaptation of big-band format to somewhat diluted versions of the plena, but the genre regained its proletarian, Afro-Caribbean flavor in the 1950s in the music of bandleaders RAFAEL CORTIJO and Mon Rivera. Since then, however, salsa and merengue have dominated the Puerto Rican popular music scene. For its part, the Dominican merengue has become similarly international, while retaining some Afro-Caribbean flavor in its animated rhythms and its frequent use of a call-and-response second section. As merengue and salsa become increasingly popular among all social classes and are increasingly performed by white and mixed-race musicians, salsa, son, and merengue have come to be less exclusively regarded as Afro-Latin, although their Afro-Caribbean characteristics and origins remain clear.

By the 1950s distinctive forms of Afro-Caribbean popular music had also emerged in the French Caribbean. The creolized biguine of MARTINIQUE enjoyed some international popularity, although the Haitian compas bands of Jean Baptiste Nemours and Wéber Sicot had larger local constituencies. These bands laid the foundation for the emergence of modern Haitian compas, as well as the electric guitar- and brass-dominated "mini-jazz" groups that emerged in the 1960s and 1970s. Haitian popular musics, as well as the ZOUK emerging in the 1980s from Martinique and GUADELOUPE, retain a strong Afro-Caribbean flavor in their rhythms, their use of creole patois and local proverbs and expressions, and, in some cases, specific melodies, rhythms, and other features derived from local neo-African musics such as Guadeloupian *gwo-ka* drumming.

Neo-African musics in the English-speaking WEST INDIES have been somewhat less resilient than those in the French and Spanish Caribbean, such that the urban popular musics emerging in these areas have reflected somewhat less overt Afro-Caribbean character. Trinidadian CALYPSO evolved from around 1900 as a Creole urban folk idiom whose style reflected only a subtle Afro-Caribbean rhythmic flavor. Nevertheless, it has been performed largely by black musicians and is regarded by some as a perpetuation of African-derived satirical or topical song traditions; further, SOCA, which emerged in the latter 1970s as a dance-oriented variant of calypso, has a more animated rhythmic character, reflecting both Afro-Caribbean as well as East Indian inspiration. For its part, the popular music that evolved in JAMAICA in the 1950s and 1960s as SKA was informed less by local Creole or neo-African musics than by American RHYTHM AND BLUES. With the evolution of REGGAE around 1970, however, Jamaican popular music became at once more indigenous and more distinctively Afro-Caribbean, both in style and in lyric content. DUB and dance hall, which largely replaced "classic" reggae by the mid-1980s, illustrate even more clearly how a regional popular music can become more distinctively Afro-Caribbean by evolving in a new direction rather than by returning to local neo-African roots. In this sense, as well as in stylistic parameters, dance hall's development has paralleled that of Afro-American HIP-HOP music. As the Caribbean region and its emigrant communities increasingly become involved in the globalization of world culture, many Afro-Caribbean musics at once cross-fertilize and modernize while continuing to regenerate themselves through inspirations from traditional neo-African musics.

See also Carnivals in Latin America and the Caribbean; Merengue: Music, Race, and Nation in the Dominican Republic; Percussion Instruments of the Caribbean.

Peter Manuel

Music, Afro-Cuban

Music developed and produced in Cuba, recognized around the world for its strongly syncopated rhythms. Afro-Cuban musicians have also gained renown for their contributions to musical styles not originating in Cuba, such as classical music and jazz.

For information on

Afro-Cuban musical styles: *See* Mambo; Rumba; Salsa Music; Son.

Afro-Cuban musicians and groups: *See* Armenteros, Alfredo "Chocolate;" Bauzá, Mario; Bola de Nieve; Brindis de Salas, Claudio; Cruz, Celia; Irakere; López, Israel ("Cachao"); Machito; Moré, Beny; Muñequitos de Matanzas, Los; Rodríguez, Arsenio; Roldán, Amadeo; Ros, Lázaro.

Afro-Cubans and classical music: *See* Lecuona, Ernesto; León, Tania J.; Music, Classical, in Latin America and the Caribbean.

Music, Caribbean

Music that derives from or depends on the rhythms and melodies of music from the islands of the Caribbean.

For information on

Types of music in the Caribbean islands: *See* Afrocubanismo; Carnivals in Latin America and the Caribbean; Creolized

Musical Instruments of the Caribbean; Music, Afro-Caribbean Religious; Music, Afro-Caribbean Secular; Percussion Instruments of the Caribbean; Reggae.

Expressions of Caribbean music outside the Caribbean: See Caribana; Fania Records; Jazz, Afro-Latin; Lovers' Rock; Musicians, Black, in Great Britain and the Age of Jazz; Notting Hill Carnival; World Music, World Beat, and the Re-Africanization of Latin American Popular Music.

Some Caribbean musicians who made careers outside the Caribbean: See Bauzá, Mario; Belafonte, Harold George (Harry); Cliff, Jimmy; Colón, Willie; Cruz, Celia; Lecuona, Ernesto; Machito; Marley, Bob; Pacheco, Johnny; Pérez Prado, Dámaso; Puente, Ernesto Antonio (Tito); Pozo y Gonzáles, Luciano (Chano); Rodríguez, Arsenio; Santamaría, Ramón ("Mongo"); Scott, Hazel.

Caribbean bands and bandleaders: See Armenteros, Alfredo "Chocolate;" Bauzá, Mario; Paquito D'Rivera, Paquito; Boukman Eksperyans; Irakere; Machito; Los Muñequitos de Mantanzas; Moré, Beny; Nemours, Jean Baptiste and Sicot, Wéber; Rodríguez, Arsenio; Santamaría, Ramón ("Mongo").

Music, Classical, in Latin America and the Caribbean

Influence of African musical traditions and artists of African descent on Latin American classical music.

The African presence in LATIN AMERICA has had a significant effect on the development of its classical or art music. During the colonial period (early 1500s to 1820s), as SPAIN and PORTUGAL imported African slaves into the region, African idioms, folk traditions, and musical instruments came to form an integral part of Latin American popular music. In addition, as historian Darién J. Davis has noted, "contact among Europeans, aborigines, and Africans created a mixed people—Afro-Creoles—and facilitated a distinct New World culture through *mestizaje*, or the combining of elements of distinct cultures." In some countries of the New World, composers and musicians of African descent were at times able to pursue musical careers within the military or the church—institutions that provided a means of social mobility to nonwhites. Nowhere is this more evident than in BRAZIL, where composers of African descent dominated the country's musical life during the eighteenth century and part of the nineteenth century.

Between 1810 and 1830, Latin America was beginning to free itself from the political dominance of Spain and Portugal. This development considerably influenced musical composition and performance in the emerging nations and culminated, during the late nineteenth century, in musical nationalism. Latin American composers consciously sought to differentiate their music from classical European styles by incorporating local folk idioms into their works. By the 1860s, Latin America had all but abolished the institution of slavery. Only Brazil, PUERTO RICO, and CUBA continued to receive African slaves until the late 1880s, thus reinforcing the African influences in their music. By the turn of the century, many blacks were able to participate more fully in the musical life of Latin American societies.

In countries with a substantial African presence, such as Brazil, Cuba, and other Caribbean countries, composers, black and white, liberally incorporated the rhythms, folklore, and popular music of their countries' Afro-Creole heritage. For some prominent composers, such as AMADEO ROLDÁN (Cuba) and Heitor Villa-Lobos (Brazil), Afro-Creole traditions were the principal source of inspiration and thus a significant component in the expression and affirmation of their countries' national identities. As musicologist Nicolas Slonimsky notes, "The creative musician occupies an exalted place in the social fabric of the Latin-American countries. He is the pride of the nation . . . [and] serves his country by enhancing its cultural prestige."

Afro-Creole Musicians and Musical Traditions in the Colonial Era

In colonial Latin America and the Caribbean, the African presence in classical music dates from the sixteenth century, when Spanish and Portuguese colonists introduced African slaves into the region. Although Latin American slavery was no less brutal than its counterpart in the United States, Spanish and Portuguese rulers did institute laws of manumission that eventually enabled a sizable number of black slaves to buy their freedom. In colonial Brazil and VENEZUELA, composers of African descent had a highly influential role in their country's musical life. In other countries, such as MEXICO, the African presence made itself felt mainly through the works of important artists of Spanish descent. For example, composers Gaspar Fernandes and Gutiérrez de Padilla and the poet Sor Juana Inés de la Cruz all drew from Afro-Hispanic musical traditions for their religious *villancicos* (settings for voice and instrumental accompaniment, written for church festivals).

In Brazil, as early as 1610, Portuguese noblemen and church conductors began to organize both black slaves and freedpeople into choral and instrumental groups. According to music scholar Claver Filho, such "musical groups from the townships and sugar estates were numerous . . . not only in the first two centuries of the Colony but later also." The Portuguese colonizers also provided musical instruction in the form of such Jesuit-run schools as the Conservatorio dos Negros. These schools greatly benefited composers of African descent, a significant number of whom flourished as professional musicians in Pernambuco, Minas Gerais, and RIO DE JANEIRO. Although these composers did contend with racial discrimination, their profession gave them a measure of status in Brazilian colonial society. As Filho said, "It was above all the mulattoes (of African and European descent) who best produced theatrical matter, composed military music and especially religious music, in a display of serious-minded professionalism."

Luiz Álvares Pinto, José Joaquim Emerico Lobo de Mesquita, and JOSÉ MAURÍCIO NUNES GARCIA had outstanding careers as composers of church music, the predominant musical genre of the colonial era. Garcia, the most distinguished eighteenth-century Brazilian composer, is considered the "father of Brazilian music." As chapelmaster of Rio de Janeiro Cathedral from 1798 to 1808, he produced a wealth of liturgical music, influenced by the late baroque and classical Viennese styles. During the early nineteenth century he was appointed chapelmaster of the royal chapel of Dom João VI and became famous for his improvisational skills at the keyboard. He also taught some of Brazil's leading young musicians, including Francisco Manuel da Silva, composer of the Brazilian national anthem—a work later orchestrated by the noted Afro-Brazilian composer Antonio de Assis Republicano.

Musicians of African descent also pursued successful careers in Venezuela. Like Brazil, colonial society in Venezuela was divided into whites (in this case of Spanish descent), people of mixed Afro-European descent, slaves, and Indians. During the latter half of the eighteenth century, a group of Venezuela's most significant church music composers formed around the composer Juan Manuel Olivares at the Academia de Música. According to musicologist Gerard Béhague, the majority of the younger composers of the [group] Escuela de Chacao were "free mulattoes, since the circumstance of exercising the music profession put them in a privileged social position." Prominent Escuela members of African descent included José Francisco Velásquez, José Antonio Caro de Boesi, Juan José Landaeta, and Lino Gallardo.

Postcolonial Latin America and the Roots of Musical Nationalism

Toward the end of the colonial period, as Latin America's classical music left the confines of the church, professional composers began to focus on secular forms of music. Some colonial-era composers had already written secular villancicos and OPERAS, the first of which was produced in 1701 in Lima, Peru. With Latin America on its way to political independence, new foreign influences entered the region, particularly that of the European Romantic tradition. While composers of instrumental music looked to Liszt, Chopin, and other European virtuosos, opera composers sought inspiration in such Italian masters as Rossini, Bellini, and Verdi.

For much of the nineteenth century, Latin American art music was judged according to the stylistic conventions of European music. National conservatories and theaters for opera performance were established, but they were mostly dominated by foreign music professionals and visiting celebrities. By the 1860s, however, Latin American composers began to reveal elements of a national musical style. Like their European counterparts, they sought inspiration in folk and popular music, some of which was derived from African traditions.

Ignacio Cervantes was Cuba's most important nineteenth-century composer. He transcended the regnant conventions of European classical music that had inspired a plethora of superficial salon pieces throughout Latin America. He wrote works centered on the rhythmic patterns of the *contradanza*, a popular Cuban dance based on African-derived syncopations.

Similar innovations were employed by Mexican Ernesto Elorduy, Puerto Rican JUAN MOREL CAMPOS, Mexican Felipe Villanueva, and Brazilian Alberto Nepomuceno.

The reigning master of Brazilian opera, ANTÔNIO CARLOS GOMES, who was of African descent, also found inspiration in indigenous material. He achieved world renown in 1870 when his opera *Il guarany* premiered at La Scala in Milan, ITALY. Gomes gave *Il guarany* a Brazilian subject and setting, and a later opera, *Lo schiavo* (1888), was inspired by the liberation struggle of black slaves in Brazil. Although Gomes's works reflect a European style, Claver Filho considers his piano piece *A caiumba* (1857), a dance based on the African *congada*, "the first composition that ushered in Brazilian pre-nationalism."

Musicians of African descent were among the region's leading instrumentalists, particularly violinists, including Brazilian José Pedro de Santana Gomes and Cubans CLAUDIO J. D. BRINDIS DE SALAS and JOSÉ SILVESTRE WHITE. White gained world fame as a violinist and composer after the American pianist Louis Moreau Gottschalk, impressed with White's talent, persuaded his family to send him to Paris for musical studies. In 1856 White won the Prix de Rome and began touring widely in Europe, South America, and the Caribbean. In 1875 he debuted with the New York Philharmonic, reputedly the first black to perform with an American orchestra. He had not come to the United States intending to perform. Rather, he had been expelled from Cuba by the government after his performance of "La bella cubana"—his own composition written in support of the Cuban insurgents during the Ten Years' War (1868–1878) against Spain—incited the HAVANA audience to protest Spanish domination.

African Traditions in Latin American Musical Nationalism

During the late nineteenth and early twentieth centuries, Latin American musical nationalism developed in full force—a movement that emerged contemporaneously with similar trends in Russia and various central European countries. Nationalist composers, like many writers and thinkers of the time, looked to their countries' historical roots in order to create a distinctly national form of expression in art music. In many Latin American countries, musical nationalism was also a reaction to centuries of colonial domination in the arts.

Peter Wade, author of *Race and Ethnicity in Latin America*, notes that Brazil and Cuba, with their large black populations, were the Latin American countries most inclined to see blacks "as symbols of a glorious heritage." Indeed, many composers of nationalist art music in Brazil and Cuba were inspired first and foremost by their countries' African heritage. In countries where mestizo (mixed European and Indian descent) or Indian folk traditions were most prevalent—ECUADOR, PERU, BOLIVIA, CHILE, and URUGUAY—these traditions became the principal basis for art music. Yet even countries with relatively small black communities have evinced an African influence in some of their classical music. In ARGENTINA, for example, the TANGO inspired the classical works of the composer Astor Piazzolla.

Mestizo musical traditions strongly influenced the nationalist composers of Mexico, Colombia, Venezuela, and Panama, but several of these composers also deliberately sought material from African sources. Panamanian Roque Cordero, who is of African descent, based some of his early works on Afro-Panamanian folklore; José Rozo Contreras found inspiration in the Afro-Colombian folk music of the Pacific and Atlantic coastal areas—enclaves of black and Caribbean cultures. In Venezuela, the Afro-Caribbean musical tradition served as source material for the nationalist composer Juan Bautista Plaza, while in Mexico, Silvestre Revueltas based songs and an orchestral piece, *Sensemayá* (1938), on the rhythms of verse by the renowned Afro-Cuban poet Nicolás Guillén.

Among countries of the Caribbean Basin, Cuba was at the forefront of musical nationalism with the founders of its modern school of composition, Amadeo Roldán and Alejandro García Caturla. In the 1920s, Roldán and Caturla became the principal musical exponents of Afrocubanismo, an artistic and literary movement that looked to Cuba's urban black culture as a basis for new musical and literary forms. Roldán and Caturla also played a central role in the expression of Cuban nationalism in the arts. According to music scholar Peter Manuel, this assertion was a response to "the late persistence of Spanish rule, its replacement in 1902 by a thinly disguised North American domination, and above all, the ambivalence toward nationalistic struggles on the part of the Cuban bourgeoisie."

Both Roldán and Caturla used Afro-Cuban folk rhythms and dance music, such as the rumba, conga, *danzon*, and son, as their principal source materials. They endeavored to give stature to the popular urban music often denigrated by Cuban elites and distorted in American commercial music. Roldán, who was of African descent, was particularly inspired by Afro-Cuban ritual music, as reflected in his string quartet *Poema negro* (1930) and ballet *La rebambaramba*—a work in which he collaborated with the eminent Cuban ethnomusicologist Alejo Carpentier. Roldán's orchestral piece *Rítmica V* is quintessential African-derived art music. Describing the work, music critic Octavio Roca wrote, "Never before or since Roldán's day have Afro-Cuban rhythms been so exuberantly integrated into the fabric of a symphony orchestra."

Though Caturla was of Spanish descent, he devoted himself to researching and incorporating Cuba's black cultural traditions into his works. As well as using Afro-Cuban rhythms, he attempted to synthesize white and black elements of Cuban folk music. In his *Berceuse campesina* for piano, for example, he employed African-based rhythms in the left hand with *guajiro* (Hispanic peasant) melodies in the right. His most important work, *Yamba-O*, is a symphonic poem based on African-derived ritual music.

Composers in other Caribbean countries also produced works inspired by African musical traditions. Haitian composer Justin Elie wrote several pieces that reflect the ceremonial music of the Vodou ritual, while Ludovic Lamothe, called "the black Chopin," delved into Haitian folklore for some of his piano compositions.

It was in Brazil that African-derived musical traditions were most widely explored in the creation of art music. Among Brazil's many composers who saw Afro-Brazilian folk traditions as essential to their musical roots were Heitor Villa-Lobos, Oscar Lorenzo Fernândez, Francisco Mignone, Camargo Guarnieri, and José Siqueira. In their compositions, all five employed the varied and complex rhythms of Afro-Brazilian dances, such as the *batuque, congada, jongo,* and samba and, in this respect, they contributed to preserving these rhythms in musical literature. According to musicologist Slonimsky, "[Guarnieri] and other Brazilian composers have elevated the *samba* to an art form, as distinctive as any of the European dance forms used in classical music."

Villa-Lobos, Brazil's most celebrated composer, traveled throughout Brazil researching and collecting Afro-Brazilian folk songs. Later trained in the European classical tradition, he made it his foremost goal to shape Afro-Brazilian folklore into a classical art form. In his works, he used elements of popular song as well as complex rhythmic patterns and a variety of percussion instruments traditional in Afro-Brazilian ritual music. His experimental piece *Bachianas brasileiras,* in which he applied Bach's contrapuntal technique to Afro-Brazilian folk melodies, was cited by music critic Mark Holston as "one of the most successful marriages of indigenous idioms and the European classical tradition ever accomplished."

African Influences in Contemporary Latin American Art Music

Latin American musical nationalism continued until the 1950s, outlasting its European counterpart by more than twenty years. It compelled the region's composers to reflect deeply on what distinguished their nations' musical idioms from the European idiom and to adapt Western musical forms to their own cultural setting, language, and temperament. At the same time, some composers, taking the lead from such European neoclassicist composers as Stravinsky and Schoenberg, returned to the classical ideal in music, which strictly separated classical music from popular and folk genres. Thus, by the mid–twentieth century, a strong countercurrent to musical nationalism had developed in Latin America and the Caribbean, where many composers once again cultivated a predominantly European musical language.

Yet the late twentieth century witnessed the revival of a more eclectic approach to classical music among some Latin American composers. For example, the Afro-Cuban composer Tania León and the Cuban jazz trumpeter Arturo Sandoval created classical compositions that fuse elements of several musical genres, including Afro-Latin jazz and folk music. This trend has continued in the early twenty-first century, as evidenced by the works of versatile musicians such as Paquito D'Rivera. "Nothing is as special as the immense task of creating," noted the contemporary Afro-Peruvian composer and vocalist Susana Baca. "In other words, to take, transforming with illusion, the old towards the new, the forgotten towards the dreamed."

See also Afro-Creole Music in Central America; Latin America and the Caribbean, Blacks in; Nationalism in Latin America and the Caribbean; Slavery in Latin America and the Caribbean.

Roanne Edwards

Music, North African

Music produced in the countries of North Africa.

North African culture is the product of several great traditions, reaching back to ancient Egypt. The five countries of the region—Morocco, Algeria, Tunisia, Libya, and Egypt—are clearly a part of the African continent, but they also border on the Mediterranean Sea and connect directly to West Asia over the land bridge of the Sinai Peninsula. Despite the formidable desert barrier of the Sahara, the peoples of North Africa have been in contact with the rest of the continent throughout history. At the same time, North Africans have influenced and been influenced by European culture since the time of the Greeks and Romans. Beginning in about 650 C.E. and continuing for several centuries, a series of Arab invasions transformed the culture of North Africa, spreading Islam and the Arabic language among the indigenous Berber peoples. Finally, from the early nineteenth century to the middle of the twentieth century, North Africa came under European colonial domination. Each of these cultures influenced the music of the region.

Sounds of Islam

Today the great majority of North Africans are Muslim, and the sounds of prayer and devotion, which some believers are reluctant to call "music," can be heard throughout the day. The call to prayer (*adhan*) is announced five times daily from the minarets (towers) of nearly every neighborhood mosque, and is broadcast on radio and television. The Qur'an (Koran), the Holy Book of Islam, is frequently recited at important events like weddings and funerals or simply as a demonstration of faith. The call to prayer (and, in many cases, the Qur'an) is performed by a soloist, who may recite the words in a simple, straightforward manner or chant them to a highly ornamented melody with no fixed rhythm. Some Muslims also belong to mystical associations that venerate and celebrate saints and spirits. Their ceremonies, which may be used to cure illnesses, often consist of hymns and group chanting of prayers and invocations. Some groups also dance to the accompaniment of an instrumental ensemble, which may include a long flute (*qasba*) and round frame drum *(bendir),* or an oboelike reed instrument (*mizmar* or *ghaita*) and double-headed side drums *(tabal).* North African Arabs often use the same instruments to mark secular celebrations.

Berber Music

The first known inhabitants of western North Africa were the Berbers, who were already present along the southern coast of the Mediterranean when the Phoenicians established trading settlements there 2,500 years ago. The Berbers have their own languages, which are still widely spoken in Algeria and Morocco. In addition to work songs, lullabies, and other functional genres, traditional Berber music can be divided into two broad categories—communal and professional. In communal music, two choruses (which may include more than 100 singers and dancers) alternate singing in a call-and-response pattern, usually to the accompaniment of round frame drums. Communal performances (known as *ahidus* in the Middle Atlas Mountains of Morocco) take place during agricultural festivals, religious or national holidays, and life-cycle celebrations such as weddings. In most instances, the event brings together groups from different factions or villages and may provide the opportunity to debate local politics and family disputes through the medium of improvised poetry.

While communal music is closely tied to a specific village or mountain valley, professional musicians usually travel alone or in small groups, not only through the countryside but also to the big cities of North Africa and Europe, wherever there are communities of Berber merchants and workers. These musicians are both entertainers and social critics; the topics of their songs range from love and the praise of nature to interpretations of the Qur'an and commentaries on modern life. Professional bards usually accompany their singing with stringed instruments, bowed or plucked. For example, those from the High Atlas Mountains of Morocco play the *ribab*, a single-string fiddle, and the *lotar,* a four-stringed lute, both of which combine traits of Middle Eastern and West African instruments.

Arab Music

Arabic speakers in North Africa have their own communal music performances, but they tend to be smaller in scale, less thoroughly organized, and more spontaneous than their Berber counterparts. Arabs have an important bardic tradition as well, especially in Egypt, where singers recite the epic of the Banu Hilal invasions and their hero, Abu Zeyd. The best-known forms of Arab music, however, are part of a sophisticated urban tradition originally developed under royal and aristocratic patronage. Closely related styles exist in Turkey, Iran, and central Asia.

Traditionally, North African art music, like music in the Middle East, has been performed by small ensembles of four to five performers, although much larger orchestras are now common. Many aspects of Middle Eastern music may sound unusual to Western listeners, but the basic design of the instruments, at least, should be familiar. In fact, many instruments came to Europe (and later the United States) from the Middle East and North Africa. For example, the lute, a popular instrument in Renaissance Europe, took both its name and its pear-shaped design from *al-'ud,* an instrument still widely used in the Middle East today. Other traditional instruments in common use include the *nai*, an end-blown reed flute; the *qanun*, a plucked zither distantly related to the piano; the *riqq* or *tar*, a small tambourine; and the *darabuka*, a goblet-shaped drum.

A variety of traditional fiddles exist as well, but they have largely been replaced in art ensembles by the Western violin or viola.

Art music is organized in a suite form, in which a series of vocal and instrumental pieces are linked to one another through the use of a principal *maqam*, or melodic mode. The scale tones of a given maqam are selected from a background scale with seventeen or more pitches to the octave (rather than the twelve tones used in most music derived from Western Europe). The microtonal division of the octave permits a greater diversity of scales and a far subtler gradation of pitch than is possible in the Western system. There is, however, no harmony (the simultaneous sounding of different notes); instead, all members in a group play the same basic melody, but individual musicians embellish it according to their own tastes and the technical possibilities of their instruments.

The art music of the MAGHREB (the area west of Libya) is known as *andalusi*, because it first developed in southern SPAIN, where Muslims ruled from the eighth to the fifteenth century. The musical system is said to be based on principles laid down by Ziryab, a ninth-century refugee from Baghdad who was not only a virtuoso musician but also an excellent chef and an arbiter of fashion. The song texts, on the other hand, were a product of the ecumenical spirit of the Muslim courts of the period. Texts in Romance (the language of medieval Spanish Roman Catholics) were used as models by Muslim and Jewish poets, who in turn created an entirely new form of Arabic poetry. After the Muslims and Jews were expelled from Spain in 1492, refugees brought this musical and poetic tradition to North Africa, where it developed into separate but closely related styles in Morocco, Algeria, and Tunisia.

Sub-Saharan Connection

North Africa and sub-Saharan Africa have always been in contact with one another. In the east, the NILE RIVER has provided a thoroughfare from the Mediterranean deep into what is now SUDAN, and the Red Sea has accommodated ship traffic along the coast. In Egypt, especially along the Red Sea and in Sinai, the most prominent evidence of sub-Saharan influence is the *simsimiyya*, a lyre. Although the lyre itself can be traced to ancient Egypt and Babylon, the use of the instrument in healing ceremonies, called *zar*, is clearly derived from practices developed in Sudan and East Africa.

In the Maghreb, on the other hand, sub-Saharan influence has come primarily from the HAUSA, FULANI, WOLOF, and other groups in the central and western SAHEL. West African style is most clearly evident in the music of certain religious groups. Although the participants are Muslims, their healing rituals incorporate worship of different families of spirits, which resemble sub-Saharan deities for water, sky, earth, and so forth.

These groups make use of double-headed side drums (*tbel*, pl. *tbola*) for both entertainment and ceremonial purposes. Similar drums can be found in northern GHANA and elsewhere in West Africa, but they probably came originally from the Middle East; the curved, knobbed drumsticks, on the other hand, are clearly of sub-Saharan origin, as are the barbell-shaped castanets (*qarqabou* or *qaraqeb*) that accompany the music. The principal ritual instrument is usually a single-string fiddle (in Tunisia) or a three-stringed lute. The Gnawa of Morocco, for example, play the *guimbri*, a lute with a skin-covered body, sliding leather tuning rings, and at the end of the neck, a small rattle made of a thin sheet of metal surrounded by dangling metal rings. Instruments of identical construction have been found in Egyptian tombs and illustrated on temple walls. The structure and playing technique also have clear connections to West African instruments like the *khalam* as well as to the American BANJO. Indeed, there are many parallels between the Gnawa and AFRICAN AMERICAN MUSIC: The responsory singing and the interlocking clapping patterns have the spiritual attraction and propulsive drive of good GOSPEL MUSIC, while the pentatonic riffs and deep percussive sound of the guimbri remind some listeners of a bass laying down the harmonic and rhythmic foundation in a JAZZ or rock group.

Popular Music

Egyptian popular music has dominated the recording and broadcast industries of North Africa (and much of the Arab world) throughout most of the twentieth century. The great innovator of this period, Mohammed Abdelwahhab, used a large ensemble consisting of traditional Arab instruments, Western orchestral instruments such as violins and cellos, and more modern Western instruments like the electic guitar and organ. The leading performer of this style, UMM KULTHUM, was one of the world's most popular singers, admired for the power of her voice, the inventiveness of her melodic variations, and the deep emotion conveyed in her enunciation of the poetic text. More than a million people filled the streets of CAIRO, EGYPT, to watch her funeral procession in 1975.

For nearly fifty years, popular singers in North Africa and the Middle East imitated the style created by Abdelwahhab and Umm Kulthum, and this imitation continues to some extent even today. In the early 1970s, however, a new popular style emerged in Morocco. The musicians drew on elements of traditional music—Arab, Berber, and West African—but mixed them together in ways that they had never been used before. In its use of traditional materials, and in the widespread participation of young urban people who had lost touch with their roots, the new style resembled the folk revival that took place in the United States and Europe around the same time. A few years later, popular musicians began to shift from acoustic instruments to electric while still drawing on traditional forms of music. One of the resulting styles, *Rai*, first appeared in western Algeria and soon became popular not only throughout North Africa, but in Europe and the United States as well.

See also Banu Hilal and Banu Sulaim; Egypt, Ancient Kingdom of; Islam in Africa.

Philip Schuyler

Musical Theater in the United States

Popular theatrical performances that depend on music, singing, and dancing for their effect.

For information on
Shuffle Along: *See* Blake, James Hubert ("Eubie"); Dance, African American; Lyles, Aubrey; *Shuffle Along*; Sissle, Noble; Vodery, Will (Henry Bennett); Walker, George.
Performers in *Shuffle Along*: *See* Baker, Josephine; Cole, Nat "King;" Harrington, Hamtree; Mills, Florence; Robeson, Paul; Still, William Grant.
Porgy and Bess: *See* Angelou, Maya; Bailey, Pearl; Barnett, Etta Moten; Brown, Anne Wiggins; Buck and Bubbles; Calloway, Cabell ("Cab"); Carroll, Diahann; Dandridge, Dorothy; Davis, Sammy, Jr.; Duncan, Todd; Jessye, Eva; McClendon, Rose; Nugent, Richard Bruce; Poitier, Sidney; *Porgy and Bess*.
Some other composers and performers in musical theater: *See* Brown, Ruth; Cole, Bob; Cook, Will Marion; Du Bois, Shirley Graham; Dudley, Sherman H.; Gonzaga, Chiquinha; Hogan, Ernest; Johnson, James Weldon; Johnson, John Rosamond; Jones, M. Sissieretta ("Black Patti"); Walker, George; Williams, Bert.
Popular musical entertainment based on stereotypes of African Americans: *See* Minstrelsy.
Dance in musical theater: *See* Dance, African American; Tap Dance.

Musicians, Black, in Great Britain and the Age of Jazz

Music or musical styles performed or developed by Africans and people of African descent in Great Britain.

Instrumentalists, singers, and dancers of Africa and African descent have played an important role in British social and cultural life since the eighteenth century and possibly before, although little recorded evidence is available for earlier periods. Although most black musicians have remained anonymous or have received little recognition, the steady growth in black migration and settlement in GREAT BRITAIN since World War II (1939–1945) has established black music and its originators as dominant forces in the nation's music scene.

First Black Musicians

The presence of black musicians in the British Isles predates the birth of Christ. The invading Roman Imperial Army (55 B.C.E. and 44 B.C.E.) included African soldiers and servants, and musicians would have been among them. Court records from the sixteenth century show that black musicians were performing for British royalty. James IV of Scotland employed a black drummer who had his family with him in Edinburgh in 1505. Around the same time, a black trumpeter named John Blanke played for the English kings Henry VII and Henry VIII. During the reign of Henry VIII's daughter, Elizabeth I, from 1558 to 1603, the black population had grown sufficiently to be used as scapegoats for the social and economic ills of the white majority. In 1596 the queen ordered the expulsion of black itinerants, musicians, and entertainers; the order was ignored. She issued another edict in 1601, but black Britons stayed put. History does not record the queen's reaction, although she was known to be proud of the troupe of "Ethiopian" drummers she kept at court.

With the growth of the TRANSATLANTIC SLAVE TRADE, Africans and people of African descent were brought to Great Britain for domestic and other labor; by the late eighteenth century they numbered between 15,000 and 20,000. The musicians among them—drummers, fiddlers, and horn and fife players—played mainly for their own entertainment; stylish blacks-only balls were held in the center of London.

Black professional musicians, however, were associated with the Janissary (or Turkish) band music that was in vogue in the late eighteenth century. Modeled after Turkish martial music, this style, with its shrill use of flutes and its jangling percussion section, appealed to the contemporary taste for the exotic among the European nobility. The use of black musicians heightened the exotic appeal of this style. The augmented percussion section of these bands included an instrument known as the Turkish crescent, or "Jingling Johnny," composed of a staff mounted with bells and clanging bits of metal, often mounted on a metal crescent. Black flutists and fife players were members of navy bands, too, and continuing an African-inspired tradition, army bass drummers wore animal skins over their uniforms.

IGNATIUS SANCHO (1729–1780) was among the eighteenth-century black Britons who studied French horn, violin, oboe, and fife and learned musical theory. Born in 1729 on a slave ship en route to present-day COLOMBIA, Sancho became a London shopkeeper, a friend of intellectuals, and a prolific correspondent. He wrote a theory of music and published volumes of musical compositions, including vocal pieces, orchestrated country dances, minuets, and miniature works, or brief, ornamental compositions for the harpsichord.

Only a few black instrumentalists broke through the barriers of prejudice to perform professionally. Among them was violinist GEORGE FREDERICK POLGREEN BRIDGETOWER (1779–1860), born to a Barbadian father and a German Polish mother. Bridgetower earned a music degree at Cambridge University and formed a friendship with Ludwig van Beethoven, who accompanied the young black violinist in concert and dedicated one of his sonatas to him. (The dedication, however, was withdrawn following a disagreement.)

Throughout the nineteenth century, itinerant black musicians performed in the streets and hostelries of major cities. In *The Uncommercial Traveller* (1861), the campaigning novelist Charles Dickens recalled the black fiddlers and tambourine players he heard while visiting a Liverpool tavern. Other observers wrote of impromptu dockside sessions in London, the center of the seafaring world, where black seamen often played for their own entertainment. Other black musicians earned a livelihood on fairgrounds and in markets and circuses, which provided employment into modern times.

The fashion for black performers grew with the widespread popularity of MINSTRELSY performed by white entertainers in "blackface"; increasingly, the theater introduced shows featuring authentic black artists. The arrival of the FISK JUBILEE SINGERS from Tennessee in 1873 marked the beginning of Great Britain's fascination with AFRICAN AMERICAN SPIRITUALS. Queen Victoria was among the thousands who heard and were moved by the group, several of whom had been born into slavery. The African American spiritual soon became a staple in the repertoire of British concert parties and community singing. The influence of the Fisk Jubilee Singers is still apparent, for example at Rugby football matches, where the singing of the preemancipation spiritual "Swing Low, Sweet Chariot" has become a tradition.

Before the dawn of the Jazz Age, SAMUEL COLERIDGE-TAYLOR was among the most famous composers of his time. Born in 1875 to a father from SIERRA LEONE and an English mother in London, he was a prolific composer who introduced African and African American influences to Western classical music. He was best known for his cantata *Hiawatha's Wedding Feast* (1898); among his other works, he set the poetry of PAUL LAURENCE DUNBAR to music. But it was Coleridge-Taylor's theatrical production *In Dahomey* (1903) that made the CAKEWALK a social fad and introduced a variety of vernacular African American music. *In Dahomey* was the forerunner of many similar African American musical productions in the following decades, most notably *Blackbirds*. The popularity of such shows provided an important source of work for members of the British black community at a time when discrimination severely restricted their employment opportunities.

Beginnings of the Jazz Age

During the 1910s, black bands and orchestras began to travel to Europe from the United States. A black vocal-instrumental trio called the Versatile Three (later Four) was among the black groups that entertained British high society during World War I (1914–1918). Jamaican-born pianist Daniel Kildare led a black band that was introduced by the prestigious London nightclub Ciro's in 1915.

Before World War I, most theatergoers had been members of the upper and upper-middle classes. After the war a general public weary of world conflict and thirsty for change welcomed the opportunity to become acquainted with black American performance. In 1919 the Southern Syncopated Orchestra arrived in Great Britain and began to play for working-class audiences as well as royalty. Conducted by Will Marion Cook, its thirty black musicians included the young virtuoso clarinetist SIDNEY JOSEPH BECHET, a key figure in the history of JAZZ, and several female instrumentalists, including one who played double bass. The Southern Syncopated Orchestra performed light orchestral works, minstrelsy, and RAGTIME, spiced with the popular songs of the day. Africans and West Indians from Great Britain swelled the ranks of the orchestra, absorbing African American influences. Most important, the virtuoso drumming of Buddy Gilmore brought modern syncopated percussion to Europe.

In 1922, under the leadership of (the probably Dutch) violinist Victor Vorzanger, the Southern Syncopated Orchestra provided three members of the first racially mixed group recorded in Britain. Then, with a range of opportunities pulling them in other directions, the orchestra broke up into smaller ensembles.

The Original Dixieland Jazz Band was a white group generally credited with being the first jazz band to record. Appearing in Great Britain around the time that the Southern Syncopated Orchestra arrived, the Dixieland band played a caricatured version of the black NEW ORLEANS, LOUISIANA, ensemble that influenced the first local attempts to play "hot" music, using loud, clumsy percussion, rather than authentic black music. At the start of the Jazz Age, white Britons embraced their "hot" style and liked their funny hats.

The black musician and composer NOBLE SISSLE had sung in France with Lieutenant Jim Europe's black Hell-Fighters band during World War I. When Sissle brought an orchestra to London, his patrons included members of the royal family. The New Jersey–born Ellis Jackson was in Sissle's trombone section. Jackson had come to England in a minstrel show with his parents at the turn of the twentieth century and achieved fame in the dance-band world.

Despite the success of the Southern Syncopated Orchestra and other black groups, ragtime remained little known outside society circles. Then, in the 1920s, the arrival in Great Britain of two new dances, the Charleston and "the blues" (not to be confused with the musical form the BLUES), further popularized African American music. American musicians were imported to modernize British dance bands, but most of the musicians were white. One well-known exception was the South Carolina–born saxophonist and composer Edmund Thornton Jenkins, who worked with Jack Hylton's orchestra.

As gramophone recordings became more popular, more Britons could listen to jazz, and it became more accessible to listeners' musical sensibilities. The first jazz recordings by American artists, which appeared in Britain in 1927, featured many white artists. By the early 1930s, however, serious enthusiasts, clamoring for recordings made solely by black musicians, formed record appreciation societies in order to listen to and analyze black music.

Musicians steeped in the "classical" Western tradition, among them two notable black figures, were still influential in dance-music circles. One was pianist-composer Reginald Foresythe; the other was clarinetist Rudolph Dunbar.

Foresythe was born in London in 1907 to a West African father and an English mother. During a three-year sojourn in the United States, he wrote for many bandleaders, including pianist EARL KENNETH ("FATHA") HINES. Sheet music still sold better than records, and Foresythe's "Serenade for a Wealthy Widow" became the best-selling nonvocal number in Great Britain in 1934. Inspired by composers Stravinsky and Delius, Foresythe sought to blend African American and Western elements in a dance-band setting. In his New Music ensemble, woodwind instruments replaced the conventional brass. Foresythe briefly shattered the status quo with his innovations, but his experiments were too avant-garde to provide him with a steady income, and he returned to more commercial fare.

Guyanese clarinetist Rudolph Dunbar had studied music in New York, given clarinet recitals, and worked with black jazz and dance-band musicians. He opened a clarinet school, made recordings with his African Polyphony band, and became a journalist, but his main interest lay in conducting the symphony orchestra.

The first British jazz band of any musical interest was the recording band of the Irish-born bass player Spike Hughes, who greatly admired the work of EDWARD KENNEDY ("DUKE") ELLINGTON. Hughes employed an African American singer, and Jamaican Leslie Thompson was the band's lead trumpeter. In 1933 Hughes went to the United States to record with an African American band that featured trumpeter Henry "Red" Allen and saxophonists COLEMAN RANDOLPH HAWKINS and BENNETT LESTER (BENNY) CARTER. Carter then moved to England to work as staff arranger for the BBC radio dance orchestra. During his three-year sojourn he made several clandestine appearances—his work permit did not allow him to work as an instrumentalist—and hired British-based Caribbean musicians for his band on the Continent.

A number of renowned African American singers made Britain their home, PAUL ROBESON, Adelaide Hall, Elizabeth Welch, and pianist Turner Layton, who composed several standards, including "After You've Gone." When Layton teamed up with Clarence "Tandy" Johnstone, they became two of the highest-paid performers in British show business. Like Leslie "Hutch" Hutchinson from GRENADA, who had once played dynamic jazz piano in HARLEM, NEW YORK, these were society entertainers who did not feature vernacular black music. It was not until the 1930s, when LOUIS ("SATCHMO") ARMSTRONG, Duke Ellington, Coleman Hawkins, CABELL (CAB) CALLOWAY, and THOMAS WRIGHT ("FATS") WALLER played variety (the British vaudeville), that audiences could listen to the newest jazz styles, enjoy improvisations at special concerts, and attend impromptu nightclub sessions given by the visiting black artists.

Inspired by these Americans, local black dance bands were formed. In 1936 Thompson, who had worked with Spike Hughes and Benny Carter, formed a twelve-piece black band, the Emperors of Jazz, to accompany Guyanese dancer Ken "Snake Hips" Johnson. Among the band members were two well-known Jamaican musicians, trumpeter Leslie (later "Jiver") Hutchinson and saxophonist Bertie King, along with the lyrical Barbadian trumpeter Dave Wilkins. In 1937 Ken Johnson became the group's new leader and turned the Emperors of Jazz into the first established black British band. They recorded, appeared on television when it was a new medium, and assumed a prestigious nightclub residency. Changing their name to the West Indian Dance Orchestra, they broadcast frequently from London's Café de Paris. Many listeners were thus able to hear the first British band to absorb the African American aesthetic and vernacular "swing." Johnson was killed when a German bomb fell on the nightclub at the height of the World War II air raids on the British capital.

The war years saw the emergence of two other important black instrumentalists. Cuban-born Don Marino Barretto, a virtuoso pianist who had lived in Europe since 1926, was probably the initiator of authentic Afro-Cuban—or, as they were then known, Latin American—rhythms in Britain. Lauderic Caton (born in TRINIDAD in 1910) was a guitar soloist, renowned for his rhythm and driving energy, who helped establish the electric guitar as a popular instrument. It was during Caton's tenure as leader of the band at Jigs', an after-hours club, that general audiences were first introduced to an amplified guitar. Live recordings made at Jigs' and released under the name of trumpeter Cyril Blake captured a rare milieu in which white jazz lovers and musicians mixed with black musician colleagues and other black people.

Hutchinson tried to assume Johnson's mantle, but the fortunes of his all-black group fell as white musicians returned from wartime placements expecting their old jobs back. Still, Hutchinson helped raise the profile of black musicians and became one of the few black instrumentalists, apart from Thompson, to break into session work, which he used to subsidize the band. Another Johnson alumnus, Carl Barritteau (born in Trinidad in 1914), was consistently voted Great Britain's leading clarinetist. However, Barritteau led an all-white group. Like many other black artists, he found that he had to perform as an entertainer rather than play uncompromising jazz. But the music world was changing.

Emergence of a Postwar Jazz Scene

A new generation of British musicians was beginning to embrace bop, the revolutionary form of jazz that relied on chordal rather than melodic improvisation. The black population was growing as West African and West Indian seamen and World War II West Indian aircrew and munitions workers settled in Great Britain and persuaded others to join them. By 1950 Caribbean musicians were performing in all the major cities of Great Britain. Among this rich mix of calypsonians and instrumentalists schooled in marching and dance bands appeared the brilliant trumpeter Alphonso "Dizzy" Reece (born in JAMAICA in 1931).

The black community continued to expand in the 1950s, and jazz in Great Britain grew more sophisticated. All-around entertainers like the Trinidadian pianist Winifred Atwell remained popular, but serious jazz lovers continued their quest for authenticity. The Nigerian guitarist Ambrose Campbell and his percussion-dominated West African Rhythm Brothers gave performances highlighting the music's African origins, and white jazz musicians, notably the drummer Phil Seamen, frequented the clubs where they played. In 1951 the alto saxophonist Joe Harriott, known for his robust sound and spontaneity, arrived from Jamaica. With Dizzy Reece, he experimented with unusual time signatures and began laying the groundwork for an innovative approach to form. Harriott developed his "free form" concept around 1960 in a band that included seaman and Saint Vincent–born Ellsworth "Shake" Keane, the most accomplished trumpeter of his generation playing in Europe.

In contrast to the situation in other European countries, a disagreement between the British and American musicians' unions prevented all but a handful of American performers from working in Britain for over two decades. When the ban was lifted in 1956, Louis Armstrong played in London. Then such artists as Duke Ellington became regular visitors, along with the MODERN JAZZ QUARTET, JOHN WILLIAM COLTRANE, MILES DAVIS, DIZZY GILLESPIE, and THELONIOUS SPHERE MONK. Blues and folk performers had not been affected by the prohibitions, so in the 1950s, jazz enthusiasts had been entertained by visiting guitarists Lonnie Johnson and Josh White and the duo of Brownie McGhee and Sonny Terry. In 1958 the Mississippi guitarist MUDDY WATERS introduced modern electric blues to British audiences. With the addition of GOSPEL MUSIC singers like "SISTER" ROSETTA THARPE and other artists who appeared in LANGSTON HUGHES's play *Black Nativity*, jazz audiences in Great Britain had become accustomed to authentic black performance styles.

In 1965 the Blue Notes arrived from SOUTH AFRICA, with white pianist Chris McGregor and four Africans: trumpeter Mongezi Feza, alto saxophonist Dudu Pukwana, bassist Johnny Dyani, and drummer Louis Moholo. The Blue Notes combined a South African township aesthetic with traditional jazz values and rhythmic enterprise. Inspired by the unshackled musical freedom promoted by American saxophonist ORNETTE COLEMAN, they found kindred freethinking spirits, black and white, and completed the musical-social revolution begun by the Fisk Jubilee Singers, *In Dahomey,* and the Southern Syncopated Orchestra.

New Generation of Black Music

In Caribbean settler households the traditional calypso of community spokesmen such as Lord Kitchener was replaced by SKA, a new music that combined traditional forms with a RHYTHM AND BLUES shuffle rhythm. Ska's derivatives, bluebeat and ROCK STEADY, later helped shape REGGAE. The character of Great Britain changed as Trinidadian steel bands replaced traditional British fare in school and as blacks and whites alike embraced American SOUL MUSIC. By 1966 the first pop band with a black British identity was formed: the Equals.

For the new generation of black Britons, reggae, DUB, and soul music were powerful vehicles for self-expression. Then in 1986, the emergence of the Jazz Warriors rekindled an interest in earlier forms of jazz. With the Jazz Warriors, for the first time since Ken "Snake Hips" Johnson had held center stage, there was a serious black big-band in Britain. It would take a while before young jazz players found their individual voices, but by the beginning of the 1990s, South African trumpeter Claude Deppa and British saxophonists Steve Williamson and Courtney Pine were among the outstanding contemporary black British performers.

By the early 2000s, black music in Britain had incorporated influences from American RAP and HIP-HOP. Emerging musicians such as songwriter and singer Craig David, whose genre is known as "UK garage," and rapper Dizzee Rascal are among those who have attracted international audiences and critical acclaim.

Val Wilmer

Muslim Uprisings in Bahia

Series of rebellions against slavery that took place during the early nineteenth century in Brazil.

Most African Muslims who arrived in BRAZIL did so during the first half of the nineteenth century. Primarily HAUSA and YORUBA, and less frequently Bornu, NUPE, and FULANI, they were brought to work on the sugar plantations of the northeastern state of BAHIA and its capital, Salvador. Bahia practically monopolized the Brazilian slave trade from the BIGHT OF BENIN ports, where most Muslims embarked. At least 354,100 slaves, including a significant number of Muslims, were imported from that area between 1791 and 1850. Most had been made prisoners during political and religious conflicts within present-day NIGERIA, mainly successive revolts leading to the demise of the Yoruba empire of Oyo and the jihad (Muslim holy war) begun by USUMAN DAN FODIO in Hausaland, in 1804.

In Brazil, Muslim slaves were known as *malê*, from the Yoruba *imale*, because Yorubas predominated in the Muslim community in the 1820s and 1830s. There is evidence that Muslims in Bahia may have forged at least two rebellions and two important conspiracies and that they may have been involved in other revolts and conspiracies, more than twenty of which happened during the first half of the nineteenth century in the region.

In May 1807 an extensive Hausa conspiracy was uncovered before the planned rebellion could occur. Organized under a complex hierarchy of leaders, the rebels planned to surround the city of Salvador and seal it to food provisions, conquer the hungry city, make contact with Muslim slaves in the northern province of Pernambuco, and establish a kingdom in the country's backlands. In the city itself, Roman Catholic churches would be stormed, and the images of saints gathered in a public square and burned. Whites would be massacred and black Creoles and mulattos enslaved.

In 1814 slave fishermen revolted with the help of runaway urban slaves and freedpeople. More than 200 men put fire to fishing nets and warehouses, attacked a village near the capital, and tried to reach the plantation area, killing more than 50 people before being overpowered by troops. Rebel ranks were again overwhelmingly Hausa but included a few Nupe, Bornu, and Yoruba. Their principal leader was described as a *malomi,* or priest, the term malomi certainly being a variation of *malam,* a Hausa word for Muslim preacher. That Muslims contributed to the episode is confirmed by confiscated papers written in Arabic. Three months later the Hausa were again conspiring in Salvador and surrounding runaway communities. Their leader was the same malomi who had led the previous rebellion. Besides the Hausa, other African "nations" and even Indians were said to have been involved, but the scheme was discovered and dismantled by the government.

A more serious movement, which came to be known as the Malê rebellion, took place ten years later. On January 25, 1835, some 600 rebels fought for nearly four hours in the streets of Salvador, and at least 70 died, while 9 were killed in the opposing camp.

Some have suggested that this movement, which was led by Muslim preachers, was a continuation in Bahia of the Fulani jihads, or holy wars. This interpretation overemphasizes the continuity of African traditions to the exclusion of the Bahian context. Jihadic ideology may have inspired some of its leaders, but this does not make the movement itself a jihad, much less a continuation of the Fulani jihad. Of the very few Fulani among the Bahian slaves, none were involved in this movement. Most Muslims in Bahia in 1835, including their leaders, were Yoruba and secondarily Hausa. In contrast to the conspiracy uncovered in 1807, nothing in the records of the trials of the leaders indicates a particularly violent opposition to Roman Catholicism and its symbols. During the uprising, the Africans, among whom there were non-Muslims, did not attack any of the large number of churches of Salvador. There is no reason to believe that the rebels sought to establish an Islamic state or saw the movement as a jihad of the sword; at the same time, the uprising did not lack a religious, even ritualistic, dimension. A strong process of conversion to Islam was under way at the time of the rebellion, particularly among the more numerous Yoruba slaves and freedpeople. And the rebellion was planned to begin at the end of the Islamic festival of Ramadan, probably after the Lailat al-Qadr festival of 1250 A.H. (January 25, 1835).

The repression that followed disrupted and dispersed the Muslim community. Four rebels were executed, hundreds whipped and imprisoned, the freedpeople deported back to Africa, and numerous slaves sold outside Bahia. Anywhere in Brazil, and particularly in Bahia, blacks found with Muslim writings were immediately viewed as suspect. The Malê rebellion had a tremendous repercussion throughout Brazil: local and federal laws were passed to improve slave control, including the death penalty for slaves accused of killing masters, overseers, or members of their families. The repression against Muslims and the hardening of slave laws were mild when compared to other countries and colonies in the Americas, and these events occurred at a time when a liberal discourse, including some steps toward abolitionism, were prevailing in Brazilian society and government.

See also African Ethnic Groups in Latin America and the Caribbean; Oyo, Early Kingdom of; Transatlantic Slave Trade.

João José Reis

Musoke, Theresa

See Women Artists, African: An Interpretation.

Mutabaruka

1952–

Jamaican poet and producer best known for recording his poetry influenced by Rastafarian and Black Power ideologies to reggae rhythm tracks.

Born Allan Hope in KINGSTON, JAMAICA, Mutabaruka began his literary and musical career when he became affiliated with Rastafarianism in the 1970s. He published three poetry collections during that decade, all marked by his imaginative handling of Jamaican colloquial speech patterns, his praise of Africanisms in Jamaican culture, and his fiery condemnations of Western politics and materialism. The release of his first recordings in 1982 signaled the start of a new career as a so-called dub poet (a poet writing and performing poetry within the context of reggae instrumental music). Inspired by the example of poet LINTON KWESI JOHNSON, Mutabaruka sought to arouse his audiences to take political action to counter what he perceived as the destructive actions of hypocritical authorities. But his recording of "Revolutionary Poets" revealed a self-critical examination of that stance ("revolutionary poets / have all gone to the / creative art centre / to watch/the sufferin / of the people"), and although sympathetic to Rastafarianism, he has emphasized feminist themes and produced recordings of feminist dub poets antagonistic to Rastafarianism's traditional patriarchalism.

His albums blend a "back-to-Africa" vision with a pantheistic "back-to-nature" sensibility; his reggae-anchored poems attack aspects of Western civilization, such as processed foods and other things that are antithetical to what in his perception belong to ancient and indigenous African civilization. A comprehensive overview of his recording career is offered on a compact disc titled *Mutabaruka: The Ultimate Collection* (Shanachie Records).

Norman Weinstein

Mutesa I

1838?–1884

Kabaka or king of the Buganda kingdom.

When the Bugandan king Suna II died in 1856, his son Mutesa I (Mutesa Walugembe Mukaabya) ascended to the throne—over more senior and apparently competent brothers—with the help of prominent Bugandan chiefs who hoped to become more powerful under a weak monarchy. Initially unpopular, Mutesa quickly consolidated his authority, partly through a brutal campaign of executions that continued throughout his reign. Many of his political rivals were burned alive.

Mutesa presided over Buganda during a period of increasing contact with Arab-Swahili merchants from ZANZIBAR and European explorers in search of the NILE RIVER. Threatened by an expansionist EGYPT to the north, Mutesa actively sought diplomatic relations with potential allies. He sent an envoy to meet the Sultan of Zanzibar and invited English missionaries to his court; he also adopted the Muslim faith and learned to speak Arabic. He declined circumcision, however, as Bugandan culture opposed body modification. Furthermore, when some 200 men refused to eat meat killed by Mutesa's butcher on the grounds that it had not been ritually cleansed according to Muslim law, he had them executed.

Depicted as an aggressive and witty strategist, Mutesa used cunning political maneuvers to avoid annexation by Egypt. In 1873 the Egyptian khedive, Isma'il Paha, hired the British general Charles George Gordon to take control of the regions to the south of Egypt. When Gordon made plans to establish a fort in Mutesa's territory, the *kabaka* invited the troops to visit his capital. An army of some 150 soldiers was greeted by an enormous gathering of Bugandans, recruited and armed by Mutesa. Once the army was settled in the capital, Mutesa arranged for their porters to leave. Immobilized, the troops found themselves essentially captured by Mutesa. Ultimately, Gordon abandoned plans to conquer Buganda and instead recognized the kabaka's sovereignty.

Toward the end of his reign Mutesa became ill. Because his own sons had died of disease and his brother had been killed, he began maneuvers to ensure that his prime minister, Prince Mwanga, would succeed him. Despite the administration of an unknown pharmaceutical by Arabs at the court, Mutesa died. He was buried in a makeshift lead coffin at Muzibuazaalapanga palace in Buganda.

See also Buganda, Early Kingdom of; Islam in Africa.

Ari Nave

Mutual Benefit Societies

Black American organizations that have provided financial and social support otherwise denied to African Americans, especially during the nineteenth century.

First formed near the end of the eighteenth century, mutual benefit societies represent one of the oldest and most durable kinds of African American self-help organizations. The earliest known mutual benefit society, the Union Society of Newport, Rhode Island, was founded in 1780. Blacks soon founded similar societies in BOSTON, MASSACHUSETTS, and PHILADELPHIA, PENNSYLVANIA.

Most mutual benefit societies formed to provide financial assistance for members who were unable to work because of illness, funeral and burial expenses, pensions for widows and orphans, and low-interest loans. In addition to financial aid, many societies attempted to provide social uplift, encouraging temperance and discouraging fighting and profanity and expelling members convicted of a crime. One organization in CHARLESTON, SOUTH CAROLINA, however, realizing that blacks were often jailed unfairly, established extended benefits for those members. By the 1820s most organizations had similar membership requirements.

Blacks originally formed their own societies because organizations founded by whites excluded them, although some black societies also restricted membership based on color and gender. The BROWN FELLOWSHIP SOCIETY of Charleston admitted only light-skinned members, forcing the excluded members to form the Free Dark Men of Color. Similarly, women frequently founded their own societies when men excluded them from their societies or when mixed societies denied women equal rights.

Mutual benefit societies became one of the most popular forms of organization for free blacks during the nineteenth century. By 1848 Philadelphia contained 106 mutual aid societies with nearly 8,000 members—half of Philadelphia's black population. Societies also organized in several Southern cities, including BALTIMORE, MARYLAND, WASHINGTON, D.C., RICHMOND, VIRGINIA, Charleston, and NEW ORLEANS, LOUISIANA, although Southern societies were less common than their Northern counterparts because of restrictions local Southern governments imposed on free blacks. Slaves were categorically forbidden by whites from joining, although some joined despite the laws, notably the slave FREDERICK DOUGLASS. Evidence also suggests that slaves themselves formed such societies for mutual benefit and burial.

Mutual benefit societies flourished after the AMERICAN CIVIL WAR, especially in the South, to provide social welfare services for black Americans. Newly freed blacks were particularly vulnerable to economic hardship because the federal government offered few social welfare programs and excluded African Americans from programs that were available. In 1910 mutual benefit societies in Mississippi had a combined membership of 80,000, almost equaling the number of black church members in the state.

Southern whites criticized mutual benefit societies, believing that such organizations—especially those that met secretly—were plotting the overthrow of the JIM CROW South. Many black ministers also objected to the growing influence exercised by mutual benefit societies, though many societies were affiliated with churches, because they believed that societies were drawing members from the churches. Black leaders, such as W(ILLIAM) E(DWARD) B(URGHARDT) DU BOIS and BOOKER TALIAFERRO WASHINGTON, however, praised these organizations, citing the value of the services they provided.

Mutual benefit societies, especially small ones, declined in importance after the GREAT DEPRESSION. During the Depression, with largely aged memberships, societies began losing money by paying an increasing amount of benefits with no corresponding rise in income, as younger members could no longer afford the dues. In addition, the social welfare programs developed during the New Deal eliminated much of the need for mutual benefit societies. Even as they have declined, many mutual benefit societies remain active in the early twenty-first century, providing support for blacks living in the rural South and within immigrant groups.

See also Free Blacks in the United States.

Robert Fay

Mwambutsa IV

1912–1977

King of Burundi from 1913 to 1966; cooperated with and then outlasted Belgian colonial rule but also helped set the country on a path toward violence.

A heavy-drinking womanizer and a poorly educated monarch, King Mwambutsa, born Mwambutsa Bangiricenge, was described by the Belgian governor of colonial Burundi as leading a "dissolute life." Many Burundians considered him to be a puppet of the Belgian colonial regime. He began his long reign at the age of two, at the time of his father's unexpected and mysterious death. While his supporters came to see Mwambutsa as a "just king," a victim of an unholy alliance between powerful members of his own clan and the colonial administration, other Burundians came to resent Mwambutsa's unwillingness to enlist Belgian support for their own interclan political struggles. The king played little part in the nationalist movement of the 1950s, but the court retained its popular prestige, and many royal family members became nationalist leaders.

In 1962 Burundi became an independent constitutional monarchy, granting the king official control over the military and provincial governors. Mwambutsa quickly began consolidating his power by reducing the number of elected commune leaders and appointing Tutsi to prime posts. Although the monarchy had been preserved partly as a symbol of national unity, in 1965 the king angered HUTU citizens by appointing a Tutsi prime minister over the Hutu candidate in a Hutu-majority parliament. The resulting hostilities culminated in the 1972 Burundian genocide. As one historian writes, "By making a parody of the constitution and concentrating even more power around the throne, the *mwami* (king) thoroughly exasperated the Hutu elite." After surviving a coup attempt that same year, Mwambutsa fled to Europe after conferring substantial power to his son Charles Ndizeye and appointing MICHEL MICOMBERO prime minister. While Mwambutsa was in Switzerland, his son usurped the kingship but was soon deposed by Micombero, who proclaimed a republic after a bloodless coup. After 1972 Mwambutsa offered to return, hoping to bring stability and national reconciliation to Burundi, but Micombero refused the offer.

See also Rwagasore, Prince Louis.

Eric Young

Mwere

Ethnic group of southeastern Africa; also known as the Mwera.

The Mwere primarily inhabit TANZANIA. Others live in MALAWI and MOZAMBIQUE. They speak a Bantu language and are closely related to the YAO people. Approximately 400,000 people consider themselves Mwere.

See also Bantu: Dispersion and Settlement.

Mwezi II

1845–1908

King of Burundi who used collaboration with the Germans to solidify his rule; also known as Gisabo, Kisabo, or Kissabo.

Born Gisabo, Mwezi II Gisabo became the king, or *mwami*, of BURUNDI in 1860 upon the death of his father NTARE II. Although tradition dictated that the king had near absolute power, several of Ntare II's sons had actively rebelled, sparking dynastic feuds over succession and territory that continued throughout Gisabo's reign. Explorer SIR RICHARD BURTON observed that Gisabo could "gather in a short time a large host of warriors who are the terror of the neighboring tribes"; but still the king was constantly frustrated in his attempts to consolidate authority.

Gisabo welcomed the arrival of German troops in Burundi in the late 1890s, hoping that GERMANY would help him vanquish his opponents and control his unruly chiefs. This strategy proved only partially successful. Convinced Gisabo was a threat to German interests, Captain von Beringe led a military campaign against him, which the governor of GERMAN EAST AFRICA opposed. The governor ordered that all chiefs in Burundi be treated as subordinate to Gisabo as long as he recognized German authority; thus Gisabo's original aspirations were fulfilled. In response, the chiefs revolted against both the Germans and Gisabo. With considerable German assistance, Gisabo brought them under control, satisfying German hopes of establishing "indirect rule" in the colony. But Gisabo died in 1908, and his son Mutanga II proved much less useful to the Germans, as he was unable to prevent rebellion among his subordinates.

Bibliography

Lemarchand, René. *Rwanda and Burundi.* Praeger Publishers, 1970.

Burton, Sir Richard Francis. *The Source of the Nile.* Folio Society, 1993.

Eric Young

Mwinyi, Ali Hassan

1925–

President of Tanzania from 1985 to 1995; initiated the country's transition to a multiparty system.

Born in DAR ES SALAAM (in what was then TANGANYIKA), Ali Hassan Mwinyi spent his youth on the island of ZANZIBAR, his parents' birthplace. He attended local schools before earning a degree from the University of Durham in England in 1956. Mwinyi was an early member of the Afro-Shirazi Party (ASP), the nationalist party that led Zanzibar to independence in 1963 and cooperated with the Tanganyika African National Union (TANU) after the 1964 federation of Zanzibar and Tanganyika into TANZANIA. Mwinyi left his job as a schoolteacher and administrator in 1964 and served in a number of Zanzibari and Tanzanian ministerial positions. In 1977 he resigned from his post as Tanzanian minister of home affairs as a matter of principle after several deaths resulted from the unauthorized conduct of junior security officers under his charge. After serving as ambassador to EGYPT from 1977 to 1982, he returned to the Tanzanian cabinet, first as minister of natural resources and tourism (1982–1983), then as minister of state in the administration of Aboud Jumbe. Mwinyi succeeded Jumbe as both vice president of Tanzania and president of Zanzibar in 1984.

Mwinyi was elected president of Tanzania in November 1985 and reelected to another five-year term in 1990. He succeeded JULIUS K. NYERERE, who had been president of Tanzania since 1963. Nyerere implemented a form of collectivized self-help SOCIALISM, *Ujamaa,* in the hopes that Tanzania could build a productive economy through the energies and skills of its people rather than through foreign aid. Nyerere's experiments largely failed, however, and as a result, Mwinyi inherited a huge national debt and an economy in shambles. During his first term, Mwinyi focused on converting Tanzania to a free-market economy and on privatizing state companies. In addition, he adopted International Monetary Fund (IMF) reforms in exchange for new grants, despite resistance within the Socialist Revolutionary Party of Tanzania (Chama Cha Mapinduzi, or CCM). Although Mwinyi's austerity measures were successful in his first term, he lost control of government spending in his second term and broke with the IMF in 1994.

During his second term, Mwinyi targeted corruption and inefficiency. He dismissed many government officials, but in 1994 a tax-evasion scandal involving many government officials demonstrated that his anticorruption efforts had not succeeded. He also initiated a transition to a multiparty state. Under the terms of Tanzania's constitution, Mwinyi was barred from seeking a third term. He completed his term in 1995 after the election of Augustine Mvema, the leader of the National Convention for Construction and Reform (NCCR).

Mwinyi continues to attend public functions and has supported the multinational efforts to help children in Africa affected by HIV and AIDS. His son, Dr. Hussein Ali Mwinyi, served as the deputy minister for health in Tanzania.

See also Acquired Immunodeficiency Syndrome in Africa: An Interpretation; Nationalism in Africa; Political Movements in Africa.

Elizabeth Heath

Myers, George A.

1859–1930

Barber, civic leader, and political adviser who organized some of the most astute Republican campaign strategies and played a major role in getting African Americans appointed to key political posts in the early twentieth century.

Born in BALTIMORE, MARYLAND, on March 5, 1859, George A. Myers was the eldest of ISAAC MYERS and Emma V. Myers's three children. In May 1868 his mother died. Two years later Myers enrolled in the preparatory department of LINCOLN UNIVERSITY in Chester County, Pennsylvania. After his father married Sarah E. Deaver, he returned to Baltimore, where he graduated from the city's first grammar school for African American children. Because of the racial practices in that city, however, Myers was denied admission to Baltimore City College.

Myers left Baltimore in 1875 and worked as an apprentice to Thomas James, a veteran painter in WASHINGTON, D.C. Not liking the trade, he returned to Baltimore and studied the barber trade under Thomas Gamble and George S. Ridgeway. He pursued this trade against the will of his father, who had wanted him to enroll in Cornell Medical School. In 1879 Myers settled in Cleveland, Ohio, and served for nine years as the foreman for James E. Benson's Waddell House Barber Shop. Because he was an affable person, he made many friends and later opened the famous Hollenden Barber Shop at the Hollenden Hotel in 1888. Elbert Hubbard, author of *A Message to Garcia* (1962), styled his shop as "the best barber shop in America." With such a reputation, Myers's shop became a recruiting station for African American political leaders.

Myers's father, an influential labor leader who fought for equal rights, influenced his son's career. Although his father urged him to stay out of politics, Myers's environment and background led him to it. His contacts with famous politicians and the wide acquaintance he developed within his race motivated his decision. Myers first sprang into political prominence when he served as a delegate to the Republican National Convention at Minneapolis, Minnesota, in 1892. It was his vote that elected William M. Hahn national committeeman from Ohio and brought "the McKinley-Hanna Organization into being." Later McKinley and Hanna played important roles in supporting Myers's political endorsements.

During the campaign of 1896 Hanna chose Myers to organize the African American delegates from Ohio. He not only organized these delegates but also had almost the entire control of McKinley's interests in Louisiana and Mississippi. Before the convention in St. Louis, Myers informed the delegates of their specific duties and procured the money for their expenditures. After the convention McKinley personally thanked Myers for his aid and promised him a political appointment in the event of his election. Myers refused to accept any office. But through his recommendations, Major William T. Anderson served as chaplain of the 10th U.S. Cavalry, JOHN ROY LYNCH became paymaster in the U.S. Army, and BLANCHE KELSO BRUCE was appointed register of the U.S. Treasury. Later Myers secured the appointment of Charles A. Cottrell as collector of internal revenue at Honolulu, Hawaii. Moreover, Myers served as Hanna's personal representative on the Republican State Executive Committee from 1897 to 1898. The committee eventually proved to be the most important state committee in the history of the Republican Party of Ohio.

The men Myers recommended were usually representative African Americans, because if Myers found a person unworthy of serving, he refused to grant his endorsement. To Myers, a man evinced his importance as "a race man" by having a profound interest in his people, by helping the members of his race whenever possible, and by defending them against unjust accusations.

In 1900 the Republican State Convention elected Myers its alternate delegate-at-large to the Republican National Convention in PHILADELPHIA, PENNSYLVANIA. Through his efforts, Senator Matthew S. Quay's resolution to reduce Southern representation, which Hanna controlled, was defeated. After serving three terms as a member of the Republican State Executive Committee, and after the deaths of President McKinley and Senator Hanna, Myers retired from politics and devoted his entire time to his family, business, and civic activities. In 1896 Myers took as his second wife Maude E. Stewart.

In 1912, through the recommendation of BOOKER TALIAFERRO WASHINGTON, Myers was offered the management of the entire Republican organization among African American voters of the country by Charles D. Hilles, chairman of the Republican National Committee. Again, because of his family and business, he refused to accept the offer. This was the first time that conducting a national campaign among African Americans was offered to a single individual.

Although conservative in politics, in any matter that concerned African Americans, Myers was "an uncompromising reformer." For example, despite his friendship with historiographer James Ford Rhodes, he had no qualms questioning and criticizing the treatment in Rhodes's historical accounts of the so-called black control of the Reconstruction governments following the Emancipation Proclamation. According to Myers, Rhodes made his mistake when he did not talk "with prominent Negro participants." He expected Rhodes, whom he felt was fair and free of anti–African American prejudice, to aid in dissipating "this damnable prejudice . . . that we as people have to contend with." In Myers's view African Americans desired only basic political and civil rights.

Because he was respected in Cleveland, Myers was able to do much to alleviate anti–African American prejudice in that city. He called to the attention of Elliot H. Baker, editor of the *Plain Dealer,* the objectionable use of the terms *negroes* (in lowercase) and *darky* in that paper. A few years later, when the *Plain Dealer* reverted in this matter, he obtained from editor Paul Bellamy a clear-cut promise that these terms would not be used again. He also had two African American policemen placed in the area around the Woodlawn Hill municipal swimming pool to prevent threatened trouble over its use by African Americans.

In the last few years of his life Myers did not change his philosophy. He continued to manage his shop and maintained his interest in civic matters. After serving almost half a century as a barber, he was financially secure and ready to retire. After years of hard work, he had developed a chronic heart condition. Nevertheless, when the management of the hotel informed him that after his retirement his thirty African American employees would be replaced by white manicurists and barbers, he chose to sacrifice his health and kept working at the shop.

He died on January 17, 1930, at the New York Central ticket office in Cleveland, just after purchasing transportation to Hot Springs, Arkansas, where he intended to spend a month improving his heart condition. His funeral was held at his home in Cleveland on January 21, and he was buried in Lake View Cemetery. He was survived by his first wife, Sarah E. Myers of Baltimore; their son Herbert D.; his widow, Maude; and their daughter Dorothy Virginia. Both children taught in the Cleveland public schools (*Cleveland Gazette,* January 25, 1930, p. 1).

John A. Garraty's introduction to the *Correspondence of George A. Myers and James Ford Rhodes, 1910–1923* (1965) contains valuable information. Russell H. Davis's *Black Americans in Cleveland* (1972) is a convenient source. Felix James's article "The Civil and Political Activities of George A. Myers," *JNH*, April 1973, pp. 166–78, is a brief summary, based in large measure on the George A. Myers Papers in the Ohio Historical Society and the John P. Green Papers in the Western Reserve Historical Society.

From *Dictionary of American Negro Biography* by Rayford W. Logan and Michael R. Winston, editors. Copyright © 1982 by Rayford W. Logan and Michael R. Winston. Reprinted by permission of W. W. Norton & Company, Inc.

See also Republican Party.

Felix James

Myers, Isaac

1835–1891

African American labor leader.

Isaac Myers was born in BALTIMORE, MARYLAND, the son of free African American parents, whose names and occupations are unknown. Myers was barred from public education, but he did attend a private day school run by a local clergyman. Leaving school at sixteen, he served an apprenticeship with a leading black ship caulker and then entered the trade himself, becoming by the age of twenty a supervisor, responsible for caulking some of Baltimore's largest clipper ships. During this period he married Emma V.; neither the precise year nor her full maiden name is known. They had three children, the first born in 1859.

Myers worked as a porter and shipping clerk for a wholesale grocer from 1860 to 1864, ran his own store for a year, and then went back to ship caulking. Soon after he returned to this trade, however, the city's white caulkers went on strike, demanding that all black caulkers be fired. With the support of the city government and the police, more than 1,000 black workers were driven from their jobs. In response, Myers proposed that the ousted men establish their own shipyard. Canvassing the local black churches, he managed to raise $10,000 in $5 shares. With another $30,000 borrowed from a ship captain, the group bought a shipyard and railway and in the winter of 1866 established the Chesapeake Marine Railway and Dry Dock Company. Within six months the firm was providing work for more than 250 African Americans. The business grew rapidly, virtually dominating the local shipbuilding industry and winning a major government contract against the bids of shipbuilders in several cities. Soon whites too joined the workforce, while the mortgage—scheduled to run six years—was paid off in five.

Myers's first wife having died in 1868, he married Sarah E. Deaver; they had no children. The following year Myers helped organize a statewide union of "colored mechanics," with representatives from every trade. About the same time, he was elected head of Baltimore's Colored Caulkers' Trades Union Society. Segregation was still the rule in the labor movement, but the relatively harmonious cooperation between these black unions and their white counterparts led Myers to think that it might be possible to achieve the same kind of relationship on a larger scale—a national union of African Americans working in tandem with the leading white labor organizations.

White leaders were having similar thoughts, and in August 1869 the National Labor Union (NLU) for the first time opened its convention to African Americans and women. Myers, who attended with nine other blacks (four from Maryland), galvanized the convention with a speech hailing biracial cooperation. "Silent, but powerful and far-reaching," he said, "is the revolution inaugurated by your act in taking the colored laborer by the hand and telling him that his interest is common with yours." The speech was warmly received, and although little integration occurred within individual unions, the convention did agree to admit black unions as affiliates.

At their own national labor convention that December, 214 African American delegates from eighteen states established the Colored National Labor Union (CNLU), with Myers as president. A few months later he set out on a nationwide tour, promoting the CNLU gospel of public education, apprentice training, unionism, and cooperative business ventures. Speaking to audiences of both black and white workers, Myers reiterated that they must work together, but he stressed that black unity was the necessary first step. Unions and cooperative associations were the key to black prosperity.

By this time, Myers had left the shipyard to become a messenger to the collector of customs in Baltimore, a position that made him only the second African American in Maryland history to receive a federal appointment. In 1870, with support from both white and black Republicans, Myers became a special agent of the Post Office Department. Returning to the NLU that summer (this time as one of five black delegates), Myers found his political loyalties put to the test, since many of those present had decided that labor should abandon the Republicans and form a new party dedicated to labor reform. The black delegates strongly disagreed. Though acknowledging the Republicans' flaws, they felt it would be foolish to abandon the party that had emancipated their race for an untested alliance with the white workers, who had so often excluded them in the past. When Myers urged the convention to stick with the Republicans, he aroused such intense hostility that he was almost assaulted. The Labor Reform Party was endorsed in a landslide vote, and black delegates attended no more NLU conventions.

Five months later, Myers ended his presidential term at the Colored National Labor Union. Progress had been made in organizing black workers, he reported, but not as much as had been hoped, and the union faced severe financial difficulties. Calling for the creation of more black unions, Myers urged members to avoid politics and concentrate on "the business interests of the people." He closed by stressing again the need for solidarity among black workers as a necessary prelude to cooperation among workers of all races. The CNLU survived only one more year, disbanding soon after its third and final convention in 1871.

Myers worked as a detective in the Post Office Department from 1872 until his retirement in 1879, after which he operated a coal yard in Baltimore and then held another federal appointment as a gauger (1882–1887). He organized and directed the Maryland Colored State Industrial Fair Association in 1888, founded the Colored Business Men's Association of Baltimore and the Colored Building and Loan Association, and was an active member of the AFRICAN METHODIST EPISCOPAL CHURCH. He died from paralysis at his home in Baltimore.

"If American citizenship means anything at all," Myers told the NLU convention in 1869, "it means the freedom of labor, as broad and universal as the freedom of the ballot." While the larger institutions with which Myers worked—the white labor movement and the Republican Party—proved less staunch than he had hoped in defending those two freedoms, he held to his conviction that black workers could, by their own energy and talent, achieve the status they sought. Although he suffered many disappointments in pursuing that vision, his career represents an important milestone in the history of the African American labor movement.

Bibliography

Foner, Philip S. *History of the Labor Movement in the United States.* Vol. 1. 1947.

———. *Organized Labor and the Black Worker, 1679–1973.* 1974.

Foner, Philip S., and Ronald L. Lewis. *The Black Worker: A Documentary History.* Vol. 1. 1978.

James, Felix. "The Civil and Political Activities of George A. Myers." *Journal of Negro History* 58 (April 1973): 166–78.

Laurie, Bruce. *Artisans into Workers: Labor in Nineteenth-Century America.* 1989.

Montgomery, David. "William H. Sylvis and the Search for Working-Class Citizenship." In *Labor Leaders in*

America, edited by Melvyn Dubofsky and Warren Van Tine. 1987.

From *American National Biography.* John A. Garraty and Mark C. Carnes, eds. Oxford University Press, 1999. Reprinted by permission of the American Council of Learned Societies.

Sandra Opdycke

Myers, Walter Dean

1937–

Poet, editor, and novelist.

A versatile and prolific writer, Walter Dean Myers has published short fiction, essays, and poetry in such disparate periodicals as the *Liberator, Negro Digest, McCall's, Essence, Espionage,* and Alfred Hitchcock's *Mystery Magazine.* In 1968 he wrote his first children's book as an entry to a contest sponsored by the Council on Interracial Books on Children. He won, *Where Does the Day Go?* was published by Parent's Magazine Press, and thus began his career as a writer of children's and young adult literature. To date, Myers has published more than forty books, many of which have earned awards and citations such as the American Library Association Best Book for Young Adults, the Newbery Honor Book, the Boston Globe/Horn Book Honor Book, and the Coretta Scott King Award.

Myers writes fantasy with black characters (*The Golden Serpent,* 1980, and *The Legend of Tarik,* 1981). He retells his father's and grandfather's ghost stories and legends (*The Black Pearl and the Ghost,* 1980, and *Mr. Monkey and the Gotcha Bird,* 1984). His adventure tales take black adolescents to Peruvian jungles and Hong Kong temples (*The Nicholas Factor,* 1983, and *The Hidden Shrine,* 1985). His nonfiction is often innovative in form and subject matter. In *Sweet Illusions* (1987), Myers examines pregnancy through the stories of fourteen teenage mothers, fathers, and their friends and relatives. Each chapter ends with blank pages for readers to complete the ending. His biography of MALCOLM X (1994) uses actual photographs and inserts from newspapers, interviews, and magazines to create an inspirational and provocative book. Myers pairs poems and commentary to turn-of-the-century photographs of African American children in *Brown Angels* (1993) and JACOB LAWRENCE's pictures in *The Great Migration* (1994).

Walter Dean Myers is best known, however, for his young adult novels about Harlem residents. Like many black writers, Myers loved to read but rarely encountered books about people like him or his friends and family. This desire to fill a void, to create for other youth that which had been lacking in his own adolescence, was further motivated by his displeasure with the prevalent images of African Americans as exotics, misfits, criminals, victims, and "unserious" people. Having grown up in Harlem, he was particularly upset by the negative and monolithic portrayals of that community. Myers's stories usually take place within a Harlem community of diverse people who love, laugh, work, and dream as much as any other people in the world. Though praised for his natural dialogues, his optimistic endings, and his eccentric but loveable characters, Myers does not romanticize. Drugs and violence, loneliness and indifference, sex, religion, economics, and other oppressive and challenging agencies figure into his plots. In *It Ain't All for Nothin'* (1978), Tippy's grandmother is put into a nursing home, and his ex-convict father involves him in a robbery. Steve's parents in *Won't Know Till I Get There* (1982) try to rehabilitate a troubled teen only to have their middle-class child and his friends end up in juvenile court. Lonnie Jackson escapes Harlem with an athletic scholarship, but the predominantly white midwestern college presents a new set of problems in *The Outside Shot* (1984). Richie Perry's escape, on the other hand, moves him from the frying pan of Harlem to the fire of Vietnam in *Fallen Angels* (1989). Myers tends to focus upon male relationships, but his female protagonists are neither stereotypical nor predictable. *Crystal* (1987) presents a sixteen-year-old fashion model and actress whose meteoric rise does not satisfy her. In *Motown and Didi: A Love Story* (1984) a disciplined and intelligent student's college career is jeopardized by her brother's drug addiction and her mother's mental instability. Each individual works out her or his own destiny, but each comes to recognize and value supportive relationships.

As a member of JOHN O. KILLENS's writers workshop, Walter Dean Myers practiced his craft with Wesley Brown, George Davis, and Askia M. Touré. When he became an editor at Bobbs-Merrill in 1970, Myers learned not only the business of publishing that helped his own career, but he published fellow writers NIKKI GIOVANNI, Ann Allen Shockley, and Richard Perry. Among the African American writers who served as his literary models, Myers names Frank Yerby and his Harlem neighbor and fellow children's book writer, Langston Hughes. Today, Walter Dean Myers ranks as one of the foremost writers of children's and young adult literature.

Bibliography

Bishop, Rudine Sims. *Presenting Walter Dean Myers,* 1990.

Senick, Gerald J., ed. *Children's Literature Review,* vol. 16, 1989, pp. 134–44.

Telgen, Diane, ed. *Something about the Author,* vol. 71, 1993, pp. 133–37.

Frances Smith Foster

Myth of Racial Democracy in Latin America and the Caribbean

"There's no racism in BRAZIL!" Manuel declared with a dismissive wave of his glass. "Here we're all equal! How could there be racism when people of all colors intermarry and have children?" We were leaning against the counter in a small bar in a working-class town on the outskirts of Rio de Janeiro. Pointing to his brown skin and short frizzy hair, he said, "I have the blood of all races in me—white, black, Indian. How could we be racists?"

Litanies about "racial democracy" can be heard throughout Latin America. The key, racial democrats argue, is that, in contrast to North America's pattern of categorizing people as either black or white, in much of Latin America people fall somewhere in between these extremes, along a broad color spectrum. Venezuelans, for example, often say theirs is a *café con leche* country: 70 percent of all Venezuelans are *pardos*, of mixed African and non-African origin, descended from the hundred thousand slaves forced to work on coastal cacao plantations before the nineteenth century. About 40 percent of all Brazilians are mulattos, that is, people with some degree of descent from the more than 3.5 million slaves who once sweated in that country's SUGAR and coffee plantations and gold fields; and at least a quarter of all Colombians are partially descended from the 200,000 slaves brought to toil in the cane fields and pan for gold in New Granada, the former Spanish colony composed of present-day COLOMBIA, VENEZUELA, and ECUADOR. Even in the Andean country of Ecuador, up to a tenth of the population is descended from the hundred thousand slaves sent there centuries ago. According to racial democrats, the presence of so many mixed-bloods promotes fraternal race relations.

The reality is less sanguine. People on the lighter end of the color-race continuum hold strong prejudices against those toward the darker end. Mulattos, anxious to maximize their distance from people darker than themselves, can be as racist as whites. One Brazilian mulatta recalls her childhood in this way: "I didn't know my place, but I knew I wasn't black. Blacks were dirty, and I was clean; blacks were stupid, and I was intelligent; blacks lived in the slum and I did not; and above all, blacks had thick noses and lips, and I didn't. I was a mulatta; I still had hopes of being saved."

Such attitudes have direct consequences for blacks' life chances. In Colombia virtually no graduate from middle-class secondary or law schools is black, while two-thirds of the slum dwellers near CARTAGENA DE INDIAS are. In Venezuela most dark-skinned people work in the lowest-paying jobs, such as domestic service, informal labor, stevedoring, and sharecropping. In Brazil blacks are concentrated in the low-paying service sector, working as janitors, porters, laundresses, day laborers, domestic servants, and at other, similar positions. Jobs asking for applicants of a "good appearance" (read, "of light complexion"), such as receptionist, secretary, bank teller, or low-level federal employee, are effectively closed to blacks.

So strong is antiblack sentiment in Latin America that for much of the region's history, those toward the lighter end of the color spectrum have sought to "bleach" blacks right out of existence. If, as Richard Jackson has put it, whites in the United States tried to get rid of blacks "through extermination," in Latin America they attempted to do so "through amalgamation." As early as 1835, Cuban historian José Antonio Saco was already proclaiming that "the only remedy for making us respectable is whitening." "WHITENING" meant eliminating Africa's racial heritage by means of MISCEGENATION. In practical terms, this required the importation of Europeans and restrictions on the immigration of blacks. Throughout the twentieth century, the governments of Colombia, Venezuela, ARGENTINA, Ecuador, and GUATEMALA, among others, passed such racist, antiblack immigration legislation.

COSTA RICA, for example, refused citizenship in the 1930s to the West Indians who came to work on its railroads and banana plantations and denied them the right to live outside certain provinces. In PANAMA racism was intensified during the construction of the Panama Canal, because U.S. supervisors treated West Indian workers the same as lighter-skinned Panamanians. This enraged the latter, who proceeded between 1920 and 1940 to ban any further black immigration, refuse blacks citizenship, and threaten to expel them. In the early twentieth century Brazilian newspapers were up in arms at the suggestion that North American blacks be encouraged to migrate to their country. Such immigration, the editor of the *Getulino* wrote, would "be the death blow to the mathematical process of the disappearance of the black race of Brazil."

If racial democracy has any meaning at all, it refers to the fact that Latin American societies make some provision for better treatment of people of visibly mixed ancestry. Mulattos usually enjoy at least some advantages over blacks, but their status varies greatly throughout the hemisphere. Shunted aside from the most respectable professions, such as medicine, law, academia, upper-level government, and the officer and diplomatic corps, Brazilian mulattos are still able to enter a secondary occupational tier as schoolteachers, journalists, artists, clerks, and low-level officials in municipal government and tax offices. Mulattos get promoted more easily and earn more than their black counterparts. Marriages between whites and mulattos are less stigmatized than those between whites and blacks.

In contrast, for much of the last 200 years in CUBA—at least until the Cuban Revolution in 1959 and, some say, even afterward—only the smallest minority of the lightest-skinned mulattos have been able to attain positions of prestige; most have faced the same sort of discrimination as darker-skinned Cubans. In the nineteenth century, rural mulattos and blacks were mainly agricultural laborers, while their urban counterparts were prevented from entering the navy, air force, and various food-handling occupations. The segregation introduced by U.S. occupation early this century, affecting mulattos and blacks equally, dovetailed neatly with white attitudes; so that even after the United States no longer directly implemented segregationist rules, whites continued to keep many of them in force. Ten years before the 1959 revolution, mulatto workers were still primarily "hewers of wood and drawers of water." Whether such patterns have survived in revolutionary Cuba is open to furious debate. Official sources and some observers claim that racism has been eradicated, but contrary claims made by black nationalists ELDRIDGE LEROY CLEAVER, ROBERT FRANKLIN WILLIAMS, and Carlos Moore have become virtually legendary. Most observers of revolutionary Cuba concur that there is essentially no difference in status between blacks and mulattos.

Two societies, two patterns of mixed-blood status. Any explanation of the difference should take into account the experiences of free mulattos in Brazil and Cuba during the long night of slavery. In Brazil, free mulattos remained so economically vital throughout the slave era that the white ruling class had little choice but to concede some social mobility to them. This concession nurtured among Brazilian mulattos a willingness after the abolition of slavery to play the role of buffer between whites and blacks.

In Cuba, by contrast, a small, economically marginal, politically vulnerable free mulatto population found itself the victim, in the nineteenth century, of harsh repression at the hands of a jittery slaveholding elite. This experience forged among many Cuban mulattos a deep-seated resentment against whites and a willingness to fight on the side of the slaves for abolition. This, in turn, reinforced whites' hostility toward the mulattos and rendered unworkable a Brazilian-style white-mulatto alliance after slavery was ended.

Marvin Harris has argued that at the very inception of the Brazilian colony, planters needed free mulattos as overseers, slave catchers, foot soldiers and gunmen, cattle hands and subsistence farmers. Slaves could not be used for these functions, and a labor shortage in PORTUGAL meant that not enough whites were available either. (The rate of white immigration remained static throughout the entire colonial period.) Slaveholders manumitted mulattos in such numbers that by the late eighteenth and early nineteenth centuries, free people of color represented, in virtually every province of the country, between half and two times the size of the white population.

Many of these mulattos were employed in militias to protect the property of white slaveholders. By distinguishing themselves in this service, mulattos found ample opportunity for promotion through the ranks. Mulatto farmers also had a stake in slave society. Many of them worked small parcels of land to supply nearby sugar plantations with food. A surprisingly large number of these poor farmers, up to 77 percent of them in one locality, owned one or two slaves. Add to this that most of them depended on large slaveholders for land rights, credit, and protection, and it is not hard to see why rural mulattos identified with the slave system and were unwilling to fight against it.

By the eighteenth century, many mulattos had migrated to the burgeoning cities of Salvador, São Luis, and RIO DE JANEIRO, where they found opportunities as self-employed artisans and petty merchants. On the eve of abolition, mulattos outnumbered free blacks in urban artisanal occupations by more than four to one and, not surprisingly, feared that the end of slavery would threaten their position in the labor market.

From such favored positions in urban areas, Brazilian mulattos readily advanced into the arts, letters, and liberal professions, including medicine. While slavery was still in force, free mulattos could become engineers, civil servants, and lawyers. And at the culmination of their careers, they could buy a certificate of whiteness.

A historical bargain had been struck: in exchange for at least some social recognition and advancement, mulattos threw in their lot with the white elite against the blackest members of society. As early as the seventeenth century, mulattos helped Portuguese slaveholders expel Dutch invaders. During the Pernambucan independence rebellion of 1817–1823, mulatto leaders proclaimed support for slavery. And during every major slave revolt of the nineteenth century, mulattos sided with the whites. So reliable were mulattos, in fact, that at the height of the sugar boom, the rate of manumission increased steadily and free mulattos played an important role in local militias.

Support for slavery is most striking in the period leading up to abolition in 1888. Though a few prominent mulattos, like ANDRÉ REBOUÇAS and LUÍS GONZAGA PINTO DA GAMA, were abolitionists, most of the mulatto political elite studiously refrained from taking a stand, while others, such as the Baron of Cotegipe, were strongly antiabolitionist. Only the combination of international pressure, the growing expense of slaveholding in many regions of the country, and massive slave rebellion finally broke the back of Brazilian slavery.

That mulattos "sat out" the abolition of slavery entered, it seems, into the popular consciousness of many working-class blacks. The elderly black men and women I spoke with in 1988 found no place for mulattos in their recounting of the story of abolition, even those who believed that abolition was a gift from the white masters. As one told me, "The mulattos were sitting pretty up on high. They never cared for the slave, even if they shared his blood. They wanted only to forget him."

The process of abolition thus strengthened ties between whites and mulattos and allowed whites to continue counting on mulatto support in efforts to exclude blacks from social power. As long as dark-skinned blacks were forced to remain in the lowest-paying jobs, mulattos would gladly take up the slack in the skilled trades, petty commerce, and the professions. In exchange, mulattos pledged allegiance to white values, modes of behavior, and physical aesthetics. "Let us not seek to perpetuate our race," wrote a Brazilian mulatto leader in the 1920s, "but, yes, to infiltrate ourselves into the bosom of the privileged race, the white race."

Cuba's was a different story. An economic backwater of the Spanish Empire until the late eighteenth century, its inhabitants occupied themselves primarily with cattle raising and producing food to provision the Spanish ships and troops passing through the port of HAVANA. Until the sugar boom of the eighteenth and nineteenth centuries, slavery was a fairly minor institution on the island.

Mulattos never established themselves as key actors in the Cuban economy. The Cuban mulatto population grew not from the slaveholders' economic needs but from the desire of the Spanish Crown to people the colony as thickly as possible in order to ward off the territorial pretensions of the French and British. Only a small though visible percentage of mulattos migrated to Havana, where limited opportunities as artisans and small merchants awaited them.

The absolute number of Cuban mulattos always remained relatively small. Unlike Portugal, which was hard-pressed to send migrants to Brazil, SPAIN provided a small but steady flow of settlers to Cuba before 1800. By the end of the eighteenth century, free nonwhites accounted for only about 20 percent of Cuba's population. Numbering far fewer than whites and lacking a sizable, skilled, literate urban contingent, Cuban mulattos remained vulnerable both socially and politically.

Immediately after the HAITIAN REVOLUTION of 1791–1804, Cuba's sugar industry began to prosper, requiring hundreds of thousands of slaves. By mid-century, free nonwhites, mainly mulattos, numbered just over 200,000, only half the number of slaves on the island and a quarter of the whites. These ratios spelled political trouble for the mulattos. The sudden influx of slaves at the very moment that slavery was being abolished in much of the hemisphere—as well as Cuba's geographic proximity to HAITI—made Cuban slaveholders more than a little nervous.

The planters were haunted by the specter not just of a slave revolution but of a mulatto-led slave revolution. As far as the Cuban elite were concerned, the events in Haiti were the handiwork of mixed-bloods who had been coddled by the decadent French. In 1845 Vicente Queipo, attorney general of Cuba, declared in no uncertain terms that Cuba's leaders had learned "the severe lesson of the neighboring island of SANTO DOMINGO, whose loss depended a great deal on the close intimacy in which the white inhabitants of the French part lived with their slaves, and the numerous colored population resulting from this foreboding association."

Regardless of the accuracy of this perception of Haitian history, it led to a full-scale attack on the rights of mulattos. An 1809 decree banned freedpeople and mulattos from teaching at or attending Cuban schools, followed soon after by laws prohibiting them from owning land, serving in the militia, and traveling without special passes. The most dramatic change, and undoubtedly the cruelest blow, was the government's reclassification of mulattos after 1841 as belonging to the same category as blacks: *gente de color*. This act accelerated other laws restricting interracial marriage, so that by the 1860s all interracial marriages were prohibited.

Such antimulatto legislation and color classifications left an indelible mark on the consciousness of the mixed-blood population. In the Cespedes Rebellion of 1868, which called for the end of Spanish rule and freedom for the slaves, one observer estimated that two-thirds of the fighting men were "of color other than black, all shades of brown predominating." These were men of little means, who, in contrast to the mulattos of Brazil, owned no slaves. Ten years later, in yet another revolt that included the call for abolition, the so-called Guerra Chiquita (Little War), mulattos again figured prominently.

The end of slavery in 1886, however, did not bring about an improvement in the condition of mulattos. Throughout the 1890s, in Havana and the sugar-producing areas, mulattos continued to be victims of the same racism as blacks.

In Brazil throughout much of the twentieth century, mulattos identified their ultimate interest as incorporation into, rather than rejection of, the established system of race relations. This identification did not prevent many of them from keenly resenting their exclusion from the highest echelons of power, a resentment periodically translated into mulatto-based social and political organizations. Such groups, however, have characteristically avoided calling for a distinct black identity, aiming instead to improve chances for assimilation. The Brazilian Negro Front of the 1930s insisted in one of its publications that "the problem of the Brazilian Negro is that of definitive, total integration of the Negro in all aspects of Brazilian life."

Brazilian mulattos often redirected their resentment away from dominant whites and toward other vulnerable groups, a tendency reinforced by job competition with foreign immigrants. In the 1930s mulatto newspapers adopted a virulently antiforeign, anti-immigrant stance, as when *O Clarim da Alvorada* denounced "the colonies of foreigners, who organize themselves and discriminate." Nearly all of the limited number of mulatto politicians active in the last generation adopted similar postures, doing their best to blend into mainstream party politics and avoid being pulled into the political orbit of the small but growing Black Consciousness Movement.

By contrast, a strong mulatto and black political movement emerged in Cuba at the beginning of the twentieth century. The PARTIDO INDEPENDIENTE DE COLOR (Independent party of Color; PIC) was founded in 1908. Unlike the Black Brazilian Front, the PIC demonstrated sensitivity to the concerns of rural dark-skinned blacks by calling for land distribution to poor tenants in the densely black province of Oriente. In 1912 PIC leaders led rural blacks in a revolt against the white oligarchy. In the hysterical repression that followed, more than 3,000 blacks and mulattos lost their lives. The slaughter seared the consciousness of Cuban mulattos in ways entirely unknown to people of color in Brazil. The memory of the massacre was still alive in small villages in Oriente Province as recently as 1968.

In the aftermath of the bloodshed, urban blacks and mulattos limited their demands to the urban area, yet they continued to work together toward achieving common objectives. The Organización Celular Asteria, formed in the 1930s, argued that "since half of all Cubans were Negroid, the same percentage of government jobs must be held by Afro-Cubans." Also in the 1930s, the Committee for the Rights of the Negro brought blacks and mulattos together to fight racist employment policies and to demonstrate against segregation at public beaches and parks. Given such a strong nonassimilationist political tradition, it is not surprising that in the 1950s blacks and mulattos joined the Communist Party in droves.

The jury is still out on the impact of the Cuban Revolution on race relations in that country. The revolution did eliminate the visible, legal pillars of racism, and it seems to have enjoyed the support of poor blacks and mulattos. Declaring its own version of racial democracy, the government has made race and racism taboo subjects, and no race-based political movements (or any other for that matter) have been allowed to emerge.

Brazil, on the other hand, has witnessed the emergence of an entirely new kind of black movement over the past two decades. Though still largely middle-class, intellectual, and mulatto-based, the Black Consciousness Movement no longer calls for assimilation but rather black pride and power. Buried in Brazilian whites' strategy of selective privilege—generally successful in dividing mulattos from blacks, thereby conquering them both—lies the seed of its own destruction. Put simply, while white society holds out the promise of acceptance to mulattos, it fails to fulfill it.

My barroom companion Manuel once told me, "There is a saying in Brazil: If you're not white, you're black. That's not really true, you know. Here you can be other things. Like me. I'm a *moreno* [brown]. But to a white man, I'm a *moreno* only if he likes me. If he doesn't like me, I'm a mulatto, or I'm even a *preto* [black]. They play a game, you know? I guess the real saying should be, If you're not white, you lose." Herein lies a glimmer of the consciousness that has led an entire generation of mulattos to become activists in black consciousness movements, a process that has begun to undermine the hold of the myth of racial democracy.

From *NACLA Report on the Americas* 25, no. 4 (February 1992): 40–45. Copyright 1997 by the North American Congress on Latin America, 475 Riverside Dr., #454, New York, NY 10115-0122. Used with permission.

See also Bahia; Black Consciousness in Brazil; Slavery in Latin America and the Caribbean; Ten Years' War.

John Burdick

N

NAACP Legal Defense and Educational Fund

Major organization by which African Americans have, through law, achieved advances in civil rights in the twentieth century.

Created in 1939 by the NATIONAL ASSOCIATION FOR THE ADVANCEMENT OF COLORED PEOPLE (NAACP), the NAACP Legal Defense and Educational Fund (LDF) pioneered the field of public interest law, using the courts to gain and expand civil rights for African Americans when other avenues were blocked. The LDF was most visible during the 1940s, when its first director, future Supreme Court justice THURGOOD MARSHALL, led it in the fight against legal segregation in the South. Its victories laid the groundwork for, and inspired participants in, the CIVIL RIGHTS MOVEMENT. After overcoming legalized segregation in the courts, the LDF fought against the backlash of angry Southern state governments, several of which attempted to challenge the LDF's right to practice in their states. It also worked to strengthen and protect civil rights through the courts, by lobbying and providing scholarships to help African Americans attend law schools.

The LDF is most famous for arguing before the Supreme Court in 1954's landmark case BROWN V. BOARD OF EDUCATION, which ended legal segregation in public education in the United States. *Brown* marked the culmination of a long-term strategy to desegregate public education. Since shortly after the end of RECONSTRUCTION (about 1877), the South had been a one-party region, dominated by the DEMOCRATIC PARTY and its white supremacist policies. Southern states were able to retain their segregationist policies because voters reelected the same representatives, who gained seniority and influence in both houses of Congress and blocked any federal civil rights legislation proposed. In response, the head of the NAACP's legal department, CHARLES HAMILTON HOUSTON, called the Moses of the Civil Rights Movement, developed a strategy in the mid-1930s that gained civil rights for blacks through the courts by indirectly attacking segregated public education. Houston believed that suing for greater African American participation in graduate schools would be less incendiary to segregationist whites than directly attacking public schools because the number of people attending graduate programs at that time was low.

Houston aimed to force Southern states to strengthen black public schools or eliminate them by underscoring the high cost of maintaining two "separate but equal" school systems. The strategy proved effective as early as 1938 when the NAACP's legal department successfully argued *Missouri ex rel. Gaines v. Canada*. The Court determined in *Gaines* that Missouri's proposal to provide financial aid so that Lloyd Gaines could attend an out-of-state law school while denying him admission to an in-state whites-only law school was not equal treatment under the Constitution, violating the FOURTEENTH AMENDMENT.

The NAACP, because it lobbied and issued propaganda, was ineligible for nonprofit status. Thus, its contributors could not deduct donations to the NAACP on their tax returns. In 1939 NAACP secretary WALTER WHITE attempted to attract contributors by creating a separate organization to administer the NAACP's charitable activities. On March 20, 1940, the NAACP created the LDF. Although the LDF was independent of the NAACP, the boards of directors for each organization were interlocked, and the LDF was largely guided by the same principles as the NAACP. Director-counsel Marshall, an NAACP lawyer who was a former student of Houston's, continued the NAACP legal department's strategy at the LDF. With Marshall executing Houston's strategy, the LDF won a number of graduate school desegregation cases, including *Sipuel v. Board of Regents of the University of Oklahoma* (1948), *McLaurin v. Oklahoma State Regents* (1950), and SWEATT V. PAINTER (1950), all of which contributed to the final assault on segregated education, *Brown*.

Supreme Court justice Earl Warren, writing for the Court in *Brown*, worded the decision ambiguously, directing schools to desegregate "with all deliberate speed." Many Southern states emphasized the "deliberate" rather than the "speed," maneuvering to slow integration. The LDF, therefore, began concentrating on ensuring that states complied with *Brown*, as in *Cooper v. Aaron* (1958), in which the Court ordered the desegregation of Central High School in Little Rock, Arkansas. The Supreme Court did not order complete school desegregation, however, until *Green v. County School Board of New Kent County* in 1968.

Brown ended one era for the LDF and it began another era, as African Americans began to demand equal access to all public facilities and equal treatment before the law, and the protest moved from the courthouses to the streets. The LDF, which had set the agenda in the fight against legal segregation, now yielded to civil rights activists and organizations, representing their members when they were arrested for participating in SIT-INS, protest marches, and rallies.

In addition to attempting to block integration, Southern governments reacted to *Brown* by attacking the NAACP and the LDF, which it saw as the catalysts of all the activism and protest. According to Jack Greenberg, an LDF lawyer who became the organization's director after Thurgood Marshall left in 1961, almost every Southern state "passed laws and started legislative investigations . . . to put the NAACP and the LDF out of business." South Carolina's legislature prohibited schools from hiring NAACP members. Arkansas, Florida, Georgia, Louisiana, North Carolina, Tennessee, Texas, and Virginia all followed suit. Virginia's attempt to outlaw the NAACP ended in *NAACP v. Button*, in which the Supreme Court ruled that the NAACP had a First Amendment right to pursue public interest law.

Although the LDF, which fully separated from the NAACP because of threats to its tax-exempt status, is best known for its fight against school segregation, it also sought changes in other areas. In its earliest days, despite a small budget and the threat of violence posed by angry whites, LDF lawyers often traveled to small Southern towns to represent accused African Americans and to make certain they received fair trials. Many of those local cases became Supreme Court cases, such as *Shepherd and Irvin v. Florida* (1950), in which the LDF successfully argued that a defendant must be tried in a bias-free venue. In *Smith v. Allwright* (1944), the Supreme Court ruled that primary elections excluding blacks were unconstitutional. *Morgan v. the Commonwealth of Virginia* outlawed segregated accommodations on interstate buses. In *Shelley v. Kraemer* (1948), the Court ruled that covenants prohibiting blacks from purchasing homes were unconstitutional.

In recent decades the LDF's efforts continued in the courtroom and beyond. In court, it worked to end discrimination in employment, education, and in the criminal justice system. Among the issues it championed were fair employment practices, AFFIRMATIVE ACTION in employment and education, and an end to the death penalty, which its studies indicated was applied disproportionately to black defendants. It has also formed and strengthened coalitions of civil rights groups to monitor the enforcement of civil rights laws, to report civil rights abuses, and to inform the American public about areas of need. The LDF, with its lasting and profound influence, has successfully pioneered a style of civil rights law that numerous agencies have emulated, as seen in agencies with the phrase "legal defense fund" in their titles.

See also Desegregation in the United States; National Association for the Advancement of Colored People; Segregation in the United States.

Bibliography
Greenberg, Jack. *Crusaders in the Courts: How a Dedicated Band of Lawyers Fought for the Civil Rights Movement.* BasicBooks, 1994.

Robert Fay

Nabrit, James Madison
1900–1997

American civil rights attorney and university president who became the first African American United States Delegate to the United Nations.

James Madison Nabrit was born in WASHINGTON, D.C., to the Reverend James Madison and Gertrude Nabrit. He graduated from MOREHOUSE COLLEGE in 1923 and from Northwestern University Law School in 1927. In 1930 Nabrit moved to Houston, where he worked as a civil rights lawyer. Nabrit joined the faculty of HOWARD UNIVERSITY Law School in 1936, where in 1938 he taught the first formal civil rights course in any law school in the United States. While a teacher and administrator at Howard from 1936 to 1960, Nabrit was involved in numerous civil rights cases including *Bolling v. Sharpe*, in which he and attorney George E. C. Hayes challenged segregation in the public schools of the District of Columbia. *Bolling* was ruled upon by the Supreme Court in conjunction with *BROWN V. BOARD OF EDUCATION*, wherein the court found segregation to be unconstitutional. In 1960 Nabrit became the president of Howard University, a post he retired from in 1969. He took a leave of absence from 1965 to 1967 to serve on the U.S. delegation to the United Nations. In 1966 President Lyndon Johnson appointed Nabrit to the second-highest post in the U.S. mission, deputy to the chief delegate.

Bibliography
Logan, Rayford. *Howard University: The First Hundred Years.* New York University Press, 1969.

Nabuco, Joaquim
1849–1910

Brazilian politician, author, and abolitionist whose 1883 book *O abolicionismo*, one of the most influential abolitionist works of its time, catalyzed Brazil's abolition movement.

Born in Recife, BRAZIL, into an aristocratic and politically active family, Joaquim Nabuco spent the first eight years of his life on his family's large SUGAR plantation in the northeastern province of Pernambuco. He later moved with his parents to RIO DE JANEIRO, then attended the prestigious law academies of São Paulo and Recife. At the former he met ANTÔNIO DE CASTRO ALVES, "the Poet of the Slaves," and the abolitionist RUI BARBOSA. Between 1873 and 1876 he made several trips to Europe and the United States, where he learned about abolitionists such as WILLIAM LLOYD GARRISON, in the process strengthening his belief in abolition.

Nabuco opposed slavery for moral reasons. At the age of eight he became aware of the cruelties of slavery when a slave from a nearby plantation approached him and begged to be purchased by Nabuco's family, explaining that his master often punished him. When Nabuco was twenty he returned to the plantation where he had grown up, and reflected: "The sacrifice of the poor blacks who had incorporated their lives into the future of that property no longer existed except perhaps in my own memory." Nabuco recalled that it was then that he "resolved to devote my life, if it was given to do so, to [this] generous race."

Nabuco had become familiar with abolitionist activities at a young age. His father, José Tomás Nabuco de Araújo, a prominent politician and advocate of gradual emancipation, was instrumental in passing the so-called FREE WOMB LAWS which freed all children born to slave women. While in law school Nabuco composed his own abolition treatise and, in a case in which he eloquently critiqued slavery and capital punishment, saved from the death penalty a young black man accused of murdering several people.

Following the death of his father in 1878, Nabuco was elected to the Brazilian Parliament and initiated his abolitionist campaign by introducing bills providing for a gradual end to slavery. After their rejection, in 1880 Nabuco founded the *Sociedade Brasileira contra a escravidão* (Brazilian Antislavery Society) and the monthly bulletin *O abolicionista* (*The Abolitionist*). The organization's manifesto declared: "Slavery has been for [Brazil] only an impediment to progress; it is a tree whose roots sterilize the physical and moral soil wherever they extend." The *Sociedade Brasileira contra a escravidão* used propaganda to fight slavery, attacking the government and appealing to the patriotic sentiments of the people.

Nabuco was defeated in the 1881 parliamentary elections and spent the next three years in London writing his book *O abolicionismo* (1883), a comprehensive analysis of the slave trade, slavery, and the abolition movement in Brazil. The publication of this book renewed the antislavery movement in Brazil, sparking emancipation movements in the provinces of Amazonas and Rio Grande do Sul.

Nabuco returned to Brazil in 1884 and resumed his abolition campaign. He was elected to the Brazilian Parliament in 1885. That year he became an outspoken critic of the Saraiva-Cotegipe, or Sexagenarian Law, which freed slaves aged sixty-five and older. Although this law liberated the oldest slaves—and, not coincidentally, the least economically valuable—Nabuco feared that plantation owners would use it to abandon the old and infirm, and argued that the nation was in need of more radical reforms.

Nabuco lost the 1886 elections, but an article he had written, about the death of two slaves who had been sentenced to 300 lashes, inspired a bill to outlaw corporal punishment of slaves. The bill became a law later that year and, with the threat of whipping removed, slaves abandoned plantations in large numbers. The military soon complained about having to pursue runaway slaves, and was absolved of this responsibility. Responding to these and other pressures, Princess Isabela freed Brazil's slaves on May 13, 1888, by signing the *Lei Áurea* (Golden Law). Nabuco remained active in politics and died in 1910, after five years of service as an ambassador in the United States.

Aaron Myers

Nachtigal, Gustav

1834–1885

German explorer who made treaties establishing German colonies in Africa.

Born in Eichstedt, GERMANY, Gustav Nachtigal earned his medical degree after attending several German universities. He practiced as a military surgeon until 1863 when health concerns forced his move to ALGERIA. He then moved to TUNIS, TUNISIA, where he served as a physician for the bey of Tunis, learned Arabic, and traveled often to the Saharan interior. Aborting a planned return to Germany, he began a journey in 1869 to bring gifts to the sultan of Bornu on behalf of Wilhelm I, King of Prussia. He traveled through territories presently known as CHAD and SUDAN, visited TOMBOUCTOU, MALI, and was the first known European to visit the Tibesti region or to make the journey from Chad to the NILE RIVER. He faced hardships, delays, and imprisonment before reaching CAIRO, EGYPT in November 1874.

The expertise Nachtigal gained on these journeys led to his appointment as German consul to Tunis. In Tunis he received a telegram in May 1884 from Otto von Bismarck, the German chancellor, who sent him on a publicly declared mission to secure trade agreements with West African rulers. His true directive, however, was to establish German colonies. This he accomplished by means of threats and political maneuvering, which resulted in the July 1884 treaties signed in TOGO with Mlapa III, the chief of Togoville, and in CAMEROON with the DUALA people. In September 1884 Nachtigal also signed treaties that provided the basis for an additional colony in South-West Africa (present-day NAMIBIA). Nachtigal died aboard the ship that was returning him to Germany in 1885.

Bibliography

Nachtigal, Gustav. *Sahara and Sudan*. Translated from the original German by Allan G. B. Fisher and Humphrey J. Fisher with Rex S. O'Fahey. University of California Press, 1971.

Robert Fay

Nago

Ethnic group of Benin; also known as the Nagot.

The Nago primarily inhabit southern BENIN. They speak YORUBA, a Niger-Congo language, and are one of the Yoruba peoples, although they have increasingly assimilated to the surrounding GOUIN people. Approximately 200,000 people consider themselves Nago.

See also Languages, African: An Overview.

Nagô

Term often applied to slaves and freed blacks in Brazil who originally came from the Yoruba-controlled parts of present-day Nigeria.

See African Ethnic Groups in Latin America and the Caribbean.

Naguib, Muhammad

1901–1984

Egyptian revolutionary who served as the first titular head of the republic of Egypt.

Born in KHARTOUM, SUDAN, and educated at the Royal Military Academy in CAIRO, EGYPT, Muhammad Naguib became a general in the Egyptian army and was hailed as a national hero of EGYPT's 1948 war with Israel. In July 1952 he and a group of fellow officers seized control of the government and forced King Faruk I to abdicate. Although the real leader of the coup was GAMAL ABDEL NASSER, the popular Naguib at first emerged as commander in chief of the army and spokesman for the military junta; he was made premier in September. Supreme authority was vested in a thirteen-member revolutionary council, which in June 1953 proclaimed Egypt a republic and Naguib its first president. When he endorsed a return to parliamentary rule, which the council opposed, he was forced out of office. Naguib was put under house arrest and held until freed by ANWAR AL-SADAT in 1971. He died in Cairo on August 28, 1984.

Nail, John E.

1883–1947

African American real estate entrepreneur.

John E. Nail was born in New London, Connecticut, the son of John Bennett Nail, a businessman, and Elizabeth (maiden name unknown). Nail was raised in NEW YORK CITY and graduated from a New York City public high school. His father was the role model on which he based his own business career. The elder Nail was an entrepreneur who prospered from the growth of HARLEM and its inflated real estate market. He was one of several blacks who prior to the turn of the century recognized the potential of Harlem's housing market and profited from his prescience. Nail, known to friends and family as Jack, worked for a time in his father's business, where he first entered into the real estate profession in the 1900s. After a brief stint as a self-employed real estate agent in his own Bronx office, Nail accepted employment with Philip A. Payton, Jr., whose Afro-American Realty Company was one of the most successful black-owned real estate firms in New York at the time.

Payton, a real estate trailblazer like Nail's father, had also seized on the opportunity to invest in the Harlem real estate market. Between 1890 and 1914 Southern blacks flooded into New York City in pursuit of social and economic betterment. Many gravitated to Harlem, where a sizable black settlement had taken shape as a result of earlier migration. By 1910 there were 91,709 blacks living in New York City, 60,534 of whom were Southern-born. This mass migration of blacks placed an unforeseen pressure on the city. Racial antagonism and violence intensified, as did social and residential segregation. Areas formerly open to blacks became restricted, and blacks found themselves relegated to an increasingly crowded Harlem. Nail saw his opportunity in this evolving situation. Following Payton's example he educated himself on the intricacies of New York City's segregated housing market. In 1907, when Payton's company suffered financial setbacks (it went bankrupt in 1908), Nail and a colleague, Henry C. Parker, resigned their sales positions and founded the real estate firm of Nail & Parker, Inc. In 1910 Nail married Grace Fairfax; they had no children.

Nail was the moving force in Nail & Parker. He served as president, and Parker acted as secretary-treasurer. The firm had modest beginnings that, with the implementation of an aggressive advertising campaign, developed into a full-service company that offered mortgages to blacks, bought, sold, managed, and appraised properties, and collected rents. Nail recognized the need for black property ownership as a way to counter the discriminatory real estate practices of white lending institutions and white landlords. He urged blacks to invest in Harlem property to secure the future of the black community there. The firm engineered a significant coup when it successfully broke the deeply entrenched unwritten "covenant" that maintained that certain Harlem blocks were to remain white; blacks could neither own nor rent property in these areas. Furthermore, the covenant established restrictions in an attempt to prevent black real estate agents from controlling the Harlem housing market. It was a difficult battle to combat, but ultimately Nail & Parker were victorious in their efforts to dismantle the system.

In 1911 Nail & Parker, Inc., negotiated a million-dollar deal. Working as agents for St. Philip's Episcopal Church, of which Nail was a member, the real estate firm figured prominently in the transaction in which the church purchased several properties in Harlem for $1,070,000. The annual rents collected on these investments amounted to $25,000. The church, the real estate agents, and the black community all benefited from this transaction. Nail & Parker aggressively pursued other Harlem properties not only to increase the company's revenues but also to provide housing and stability for the community. The firm also sold a $200,000 property to MADAME C. J. WALKER, who had amassed a fortune developing hair-care products. In 1929 the firm was granted management responsibilities of the largest and finest apartment building in Harlem, which was owned by the Metropolitan Life Insurance Company. As their client list expanded and their transactions multiplied, Parker and Nail established respectable reputations both for themselves and for their business. Nail, particularly, earned respect from members of the white and black communities alike, and emerged as an authority on property condemnation. Even the City of New York sought his expertise.

Despite his status, black tenants claimed that Nail was an exploitive landlord who overcharged his renters. The threat of a mass exodus from Harlem during the 1920s and early 1930s in response to exceedingly high rentals was quelled when the company reluctantly reduced some rents. In his own defense, Nail cited the high rents elsewhere in the city. Nail's philosophy reflected that of BOOKER T. WASHINGTON, who emphasized the importance of establishing an economic foundation on which blacks could build a stronger and more stable community and compete more directly with the white power structure.

Although Nail & Parker temporarily weathered the depression, the firm collapsed in 1933, at which time Parker and Nail divided forty-five shares of the company apiece, and the remaining ten shares were apportioned to Isador D. Brokow, their silent white partner. Parker and Nail parted company, and that same year Nail established a new real estate venture, the John E. Nail Company, Inc., with Nail as president and David B. Peskin, a white real estate agent, as secretary and treasurer. The firm was active in several large real estate transactions, including as broker in a deal whereby St. Philip's Church leased to Louis B. Lipman ten six-story apartment houses for an aggregate rental of $1 million.

Nail's reputation earned him a place as the first black member of the Real Estate Board of New York, and he became the only black member of the Housing Committee of New York and was a member of the Harlem Board of Commerce. News of his accomplishments extended beyond New York's boundaries; he acted as consultant for President Herbert Hoover's Committee on Housing during the depression.

Nail's interests were not confined to housing. He and a coterie of influential cohorts, including ROBERT ABBOTT, publisher of the *Chicago Defender,* and HARRY PACE, a respected entrepreneur, engineered a campaign to discredit race leader MARCUS GARVEY. Garvey's rise to prominence threatened this elite core group who accused Garvey and his black nationalism philosophy of inciting hatred between the races. Nail and this selfstyled Committee of Eight had nurtured a careful relationship with the white community, and they believed Garvey's rhetoric undermined their efforts to balance race relations. The battle between Garvey, who charged his attackers with being "Uncle Tom Negroes," and the members of the committee represented a broader split between an elite group of blacks and the masses of lower-income blacks who supported Garvey's celebration of African culture and his philosophy of self-help. Ironically, the two opposing factions shared a belief in the importance of economic development.

Nail's deep commitment to the black community is reflected in his role in the development of the Colored Merchant's Association, created to advance race solidarity and economic stability. Unfortunately, the first Harlem CMA cooperative, established in 1930, failed to attract black consumers, who complained of high prices during a time when survival was their chief concern. Nail was also concerned with the overall plight of urban blacks and held the position of vice president of the New York Urban League for a time. He was chair of the Finance Committee of the 135th Street Branch of the YMCA, which was located in the heart of Harlem, and was involved with the NATIONAL ASSOCIATION FOR THE ADVANCEMENT OF COLORED PEOPLE (NAACP). Nail died in New York City.

Bibliography

The John E. Nail Scrapbook is included in the papers of his brother-in-law, James Weldon Johnson, at Yale University's Beinecke Rare Book and Manuscript Library.

Ingham, John N., and Lynne B. Feldman. *African American Business Leaders: A Biographical Dictionary.* 1994.

Osofsky, Gilbert. *Harlem: The Making of a Ghetto.* 1966.

From *American National Biography.* John A. Garraty and Mark C. Carnes, eds. Oxford University Press, 1999. Reprinted by permission of the American Council of Learned Societies.

Lynne B. Feldman

Naipaul, V. S.

1932–

Trinidadian expatriate novelist and essayist, known especially for works that explore the experience of South Asians in the Caribbean.

When Vidiadhar Surajprasad Naipaul was asked by a Jamaican newspaper interviewer whether he considered himself British or Trinidadian, his answer was "[n]ot Trinidadian . . . One was born there, but there's no importance in that. They don't understand literature there." Because of statements like that one, and because he has spent his entire adult life living in England, some have criticized Naipaul for becoming alienated from his West Indian roots. He has also been accused of similar insensitivity in his essays on India, his parents' homeland, and on other Asian and African countries. But despite these ideological criticisms of his work, Naipaul is acknowledged as one of the best writers of his generation, and a good part of this reputation is based on his books about the Caribbean.

Naipaul is unusual among contemporary Caribbean writers, however, in that his work is not centered on the black Caribbean experience. Instead, it focuses on the South Asian and Caribbean culture that he himself came from, but he is quick to point out the common effects of colonization on both communities. Naipaul was born in Chaguanas, a small sugarcane-growing village, and moved to Port of Spain at the age of six. After graduating from Queens Royal College in 1949,

Naipaul won a scholarship to attend University College, Oxford. The opportunity to go to England was "a dream come true" for him, and he never returned home.

One of his first jobs after leaving Oxford was writing and editing for the British Broadcasting Corporation's *Caribbean Voices*, which was already an outlet for such emerging Caribbean writers as EDWARD KAMAU BRATHWAITE and GEORGE LAMMING. Naipaul published his first novel in 1957, and within five years he had completed five books, including the novels *Miguel Street* (1959) and *A House for Mr. Biswas* (1961), and the essay collection *The Middle Passage* (1962). These three books established his position as a chronicler of the West Indian experience.

In *A House for Mr. Biswas,* widely considered his masterpiece, Naipaul chronicles a South Asian Trinidadian man's struggle to own a home. In the process, he also outlined the existing social and economic conditions on the island that made that struggle so difficult. A year after its publication, the government of Trinidad and Tobago awarded Naipaul a scholarship to spend seven months studying Caribbean culture and history. The result was *The Middle Passage,* a combination of historical narrative and travel narrative covering five Caribbean countries. Naipaul's criticisms of Trinidad as "unimportant, uncreative, cynical" and the entire Caribbean as "the Third World's third world" are often repeated as proof of his unwillingness to understand the Caribbean. However, he has also been praised for creating a valuable collection of insights into the WEST INDIES from an insider's perspective.

The Mimic Men (1967) and *Guerrillas* (1975) presented similarly cynical fictional accounts of the Caribbean independence and BLACK POWER MOVEMENT of the 1960s. As his career progressed, Naipaul traveled farther abroad for his novels and travel books, setting them in England, India, Africa, and even the United States. Such books as *India: A Wounded Civilization* (1977) and *A Bend in the River* (1979) solidified his reputation, and the author has won numerous honors and awards for his work, including the Nobel Prize for Literature in 2001. For all the pessimism Naipaul continues to display toward his homeland, it is undeniable that he writes about the Caribbean honestly and with a wealth of observed detail and insight that many consider unparalleled. Anthologies and critical studies of West Indian literature acknowledge Naipaul as one of the region's most important writers.

See also East Indian Communities in the Caribbean; Literature, English Language, in the Caribbean.

Lisa Clayton Robinson

Nairobi, Kenya

Capital and largest city of Kenya.

Nairobi, capital of KENYA, is the largest city between CAIRO, EGYPT and JOHANNESBURG, SOUTH AFRICA, with a population estimated at 2.4 million in 2003. Nairobi sits in the highlands of southern Kenya. It was founded in 1899 by the British, at the 317th-mile mark of the railroad they were constructing between the Indian Ocean port of MOMBASA and LAKE VICTORIA in the interior. Named for a nearby MAASAI watering hole, Enkare Nairobi (cold water), the settlement became a stopping point for the railway's 32,000 workers, many of whom were from India. It eventually grew into a small town, and in 1905 the British made it the capital of the British East African Protectorate, later to become the nation of Kenya.

Around 1900, Indian merchants in Nairobi established a small bazaar, which soon became the main marketplace for nearby KIKUYU farmers to sell their produce. European settlers, drawn by the fertile farmlands and temperate climate, also came to Nairobi, as did big game hunters. In 1919 Nairobi was declared a municipality; it earned city status in 1954. By that time it was the center of Kenya's growing food-processing industries and had developed large working-class neighborhoods. Kikuyu migrants, many of whom had been educated at mission schools and held municipal jobs, began to organize politically in the city in the 1920s. During the 1950s Kikuyu protest solidified into a nationalist movement across all ethnic groups, centered in Nairobi. When the government declared a state of emergency during the MAU MAU REBELLION, approximately 15,000 Africans were arrested in Nairobi and sent to detention camps.

When Kenya gained its independence from GREAT BRITAIN in December of 1963, Nairobi became the national capital. Under President JOMO KENYATTA the city's economy flourished. The urban population grew rapidly as Kenyans migrated to the city from rural areas. Shantytowns sprang up and were periodically bulldozed. Although the capital city offers educational opportunities including many secondary schools and the University of Nairobi, employment has grown increasingly scarce for its educated youth. In the mid-1990s Nairobi was shaken repeatedly by protests against the authoritarian regime of President DANIEL ARAP MOI. Since that time, political unrest—including a bombing of the U.S. Embassy in Nairobi in 1998—has damaged Kenya's tourist industry, one of the country's major sources of foreign exchange. Still, Nairobi remains a prime destination for tourists to East Africa. They are attracted by the city's abundance of modern conveniences, including cafés, bars, bookstores, and museums, as well as by the many nearby game parks, such as Amboseli, Tsavo, and Maasai Mara. Nairobi is also Kenya's most industrialized city. Its skyscrapers house the headquarters of many foreign corporations. Major industries include food processing and the manufacturing of cigarettes and plastics.

Robert Fay

Nalu

Ethnic group of West Africa; also known as the Nalou.

The Nalu primarily inhabit GUINEA, GUINEA-BISSAU, SENEGAL, and THE GAMBIA. They speak a Niger-Congo language and are closely related to the neighboring JOLA people. About 200,000 people consider themselves Nalu.

See also Languages, African: An Overview.

Nama

Ethnic group of southern Africa; also known as the Namakwa.

The Nama primarily inhabit western BOTSWANA and southern NAMIBIA. They speak a KHOISAN language and are considered part of the KHOIKHOI group of peoples, pejoratively known as the HOTTENTOT peoples. Approximately 100,000 people consider themselves Nama.

See also Languages, African: An Overview.

Namib Desert

World's oldest desert and the only true African desert south of the equator.

Lying along Africa's west coast, the Namib Desert stretches from Namibe in ANGOLA south through NAMIBIA to the Olifants River in Cape Province, SOUTH AFRICA, extending some 1,500 km from north to south (about 930 mi). The Namib reaches eastward about 130 to 160 km (about 80 to 100 mi) from the Atlantic Ocean to the foot of the GREAT ESCARPMENT of southern Africa. The Benguela Current, which carries icy Atlantic water from Antarctica to the African coast, helps to cool the desert. The collision of cold water with warm air creates a dense fog that causes a hazard to ships in the area now known as the Skeleton Coast. The current also provides moisture for the coastal region of the desert, supplementing the scant 50 mm (2 in) of rain it averages yearly.

Though many describe the landscape as barren, the Namib in fact supports a variety of vegetation, including Tumboa (*Welwitschia mirablisis*). Numerous forms of wildlife also inhabit the desert, including the ANTELOPE, the OSTRICH, the ZEBRA, the jackal, and large flocks of birds along the coast. Several indigenous groups practice PASTORALISM, including the Ovahimba and Obatjimba HERERO, who herd goats between waterholes in the north, and Topnaar Nama (KHOIKHOI), who graze sheep and cattle along the Kuiseb River in the central Namib region. In addition, the desert is the largest source of diamonds in the world.

Some parts of the Namib Desert are spectacularly scenic. The Sossusvlei region, located in the Namib-Naukluft National Park, is known for its huge sand dunes, some of which rise as much as 60 to 240 m high (about 200 to 800 ft) and span 16 to 32 km long (about 10 to 20 mi). The Namib-Naukluft National Park is also home to the Naukluft Mountains and Sesriem Canyon.

Robert Fay

Namibia

Country on the southwest coast of Africa.

The history of Namibia, one of Africa's newest independent countries, has long been shaped by its geography. For centuries few African populations inhabited its two vast deserts, the NAMIB and the KALAHARI, while European vessels avoided its rough coastline. The region was still sparsely populated when missionaries and, later, traders finally arrived in the eighteenth century, but its inhabitants fiercely resisted German settlement and colonization, resulting in one of Africa's bloodiest colonial wars of suppression. SOUTH AFRICA wrested control of mineral-rich SOUTH-WEST AFRICA from GERMANY in 1915, but its occupation proved no less repressive and discriminatory than European colonialism had been. Land and labor policies aimed at creating a cheap migrant labor supply for the region's diamond and gold mines fostered nationalist sentiment and, ultimately, armed struggle. The war between South Africa and nationalist forces, fueled by international Cold War rivalries, finally ended with Namibian independence in 1990. Today, land distribution in Namibia is still highly stratified, and labor unions remain a powerful political force. In addition, the government's efforts to harness the natural resources necessary for supporting Namibia's growing population and economy have met with protests from its neighbors and international groups.

Precolonial History

Despite the challenges of the harsh climate, the SAN people were living in the arid region of present-day Namibia as early as 8000 B.C.E. Often referred to as "BUSHMEN," they were a nomadic, foraging people living in small communities on the central plateau. They gradually assimilated with their southern neighbors, the Khoi, to become the KHOIKHOI people. Between the ninth and fourteenth centuries C.E., Bantu-speakers migrated to the region. Armed with iron tools and weapons, they began pushing the Khoikhoi into the Kalahari and established sedentary societies based on a combination of agriculture, PASTORALISM, and mining. Some were small and decentralized chieftainships, such as the Masubia and Mafue of the Caprivi. In the north of the country, however, the OVAMBO and the KAVANGO built small, loosely federated kingdoms in which each clan had a centralized authority and hereditary system of succession. They traded copper, iron ore, salt, and agricultural products, and controlled trade routes throughout southwest Africa. Reaching the height of their power during the seventeenth and eighteenth centuries, the eight Ovambo clans engaged in mutual cattle raids as well as periodic skirmishes over land and water sources. Meanwhile, the cattle-raising HERERO migrated further south on the central plateau, where they established a centralized state. Typically residing in self-sufficient homesteads, the Herero needed great tracts of land to graze their large herds, occasionally bringing them into conflict with neighboring groups, including the Ovambo and Khoikhoi.

156 Namibia

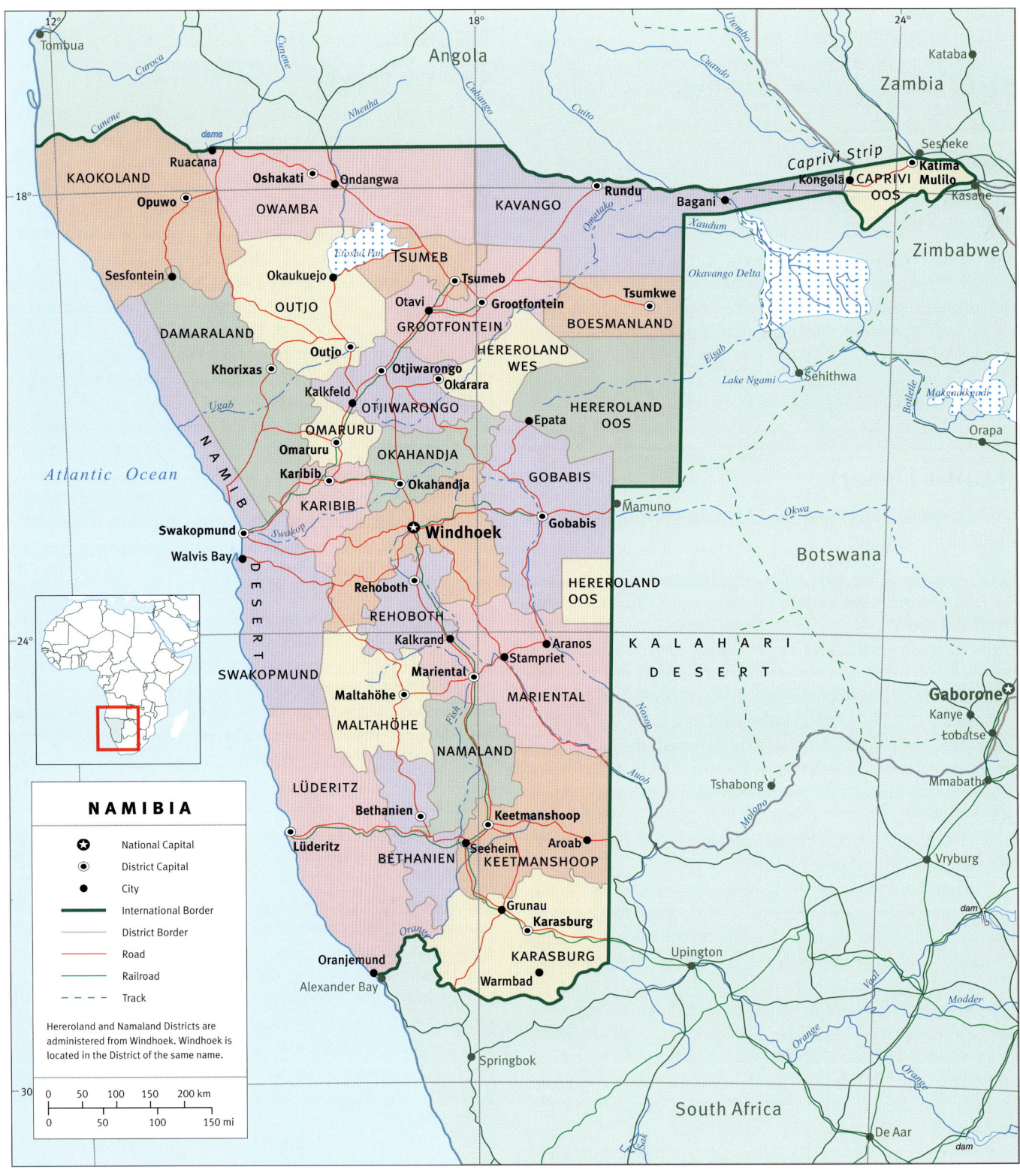

Although Portuguese sailors erected a stone cross on the coast of Namibia in 1484, few Europeans ventured much further inland until the Dutch East Indies Company conducted a brief exploration of the region in the 1650s. The greatest natural barrier to European intrusion was the rough, inaccessible coastline, much of which became known as the Skeleton Coast because of the number of vessels that shipwrecked on the rocks. Although American, British, Dutch, and French sealing and whaling ships frequented the Namibian coast in the 1700s, only a few Europeans actually settled there, most of them traders who took up residence among the Khoi people in present-day southern Namibia. Seeking ivory, the merchants brought

Diamonds have long been one of Namibia's most valuable natural resources and remain an important source of export revenue. *Jason Laure*

firearms, which the Ovambo and Herero clans used in their struggles for regional domination and to defend their herds. Over time, communities of mixed Khoi and European descent, particularly the Oorlams and Rehoboth, also established a prominent presence. They traded firearms for cattle with the Nama, whom they soon came to dominate.

In the early 1800s British, American, Finnish, and German missionaries stepped up their activities in Namibia. With their own rifle factory at the Otijibingue mission trading post, the missionaries quickly came to dominate regional commerce, trading firearms and luxury items for cattle and ivory. As roads were constructed further inland, missionaries also settled in WINDHOEK, at that time a kingdom composed of AFRIKANERS, Nama, and Herero. By the 1850s the discovery of diamonds in the southern Namib Desert was luring increasing numbers of European miners and traders, including Portuguese from nearby ANGOLA.

To meet the booming demand for slaves, ivory, and cattle, the Ovambo raided their neighbors and nearly wiped out the region's elephant populations. At the same time, however, these lucrative trading activities were undermining the Ovambo's economic independence. To satisfy their desires for European goods, Ovambo leaders raised taxes among their people, forcing thousands of young men to migrate to diamond-mine operations in the south. Ovambo leaders were often able to exploit the tensions between Portuguese, German, and British South African commercial interests in Namibia, until European powers came together at the BERLIN CONFERENCE OF 1884–1885. There they drew the borders of present-day Namibia and declared it a German colony.

German Colonization and Genocide

Due to their isolation and diplomatic skills, the Ovambo avoided falling under direct European rule until after WORLD WAR I. But floods, drought, locusts, and a rinderpest epidemic in the 1890s did create severe hardship, and pushed even more Ovambo away from their homeland in search of paid employment. By the 1910s, as many as 10,000 Ovambo and Kavango migrated south annually, and another 2,000 went north each year to work on plantations in Angola.

Meanwhile, expanding European settlement in the southern part of the colony began pushing the Nama into Herero territory, leading to wars between the two groups. The German colonial administration also introduced a system of private land ownership, initially setting aside 25 percent of the colony's land for Africans. But even this portion was gradually eroded as concession companies, the German Crown, and settlers acquired more property from local Africans through direct purchases, treaties, and the extension of credit. Sporadic resistance to German COLONIAL RULE mounted until 1904, when the Herero, led by Chief SAMUEL MAHARERO and supported by the Nama and Damara, attacked German towns as well as the colonial headquarters at Okahandja. After negotiations, the Germans initially appeared willing to accept the Herero's surrender in 1904, but they soon turned to a strategy of tacit annihilation. Over the next four years they engaged in the most genocidal war in Africa's colonial history: nearly 80 percent of the Herero and more than half the Nama and Damara died at the hands of the German colonial forces.

The annihilation led to a severe labor shortage in the mines and on ranches. The owners of both turned to recruiting contract workers, those tied to their employer through a strict contract which the state enforced, among the Ovambo and Kavango, who had not been involved in the war as the Germans were selective in their genocide. After the war, the colonial administration created more African "reserves" and instituted a South African form of geographic segregation known as the "Red Line." This divided the country between the south, a "white area" where rights to live and work were determined by the administration through PASS LAWS, and the north, where local African leaders were permitted a degree of autonomy, as long as they completed the required labor.

South African Occupation

In 1915, after war broke out in Europe, South Africa quickly overran German South-West Africa. Five years later it assumed a mandate for South-West Africa under the League of Nations, effectively annexing the territory. Afrikaners replaced German settlers, and the new administration maintained its predecessor's repressive policies. The Ovambo, the Bondelswaart, and

Namibia (At a Glance)

OFFICIAL NAME: Republic of Namibia

FORMER NAME: South-West Africa

AREA: 825,418 sq km (about 318,694 sq mi)

LOCATION: Southwestern Africa; borders Angola, Zambia, Botswana, South Africa, and the Atlantic Ocean

CAPITAL: Windhoek (population 216,000; 2002 estimate)

POPULATION: 1,927,447 (2003 estimate)

POPULATION DENSITY: 2 persons per sq km (about 6 persons per sq mi)

POPULATION BELOW AGE 15: 42.5 percent (male 414,559; female 404,346; 2003 estimate)

POPULATION GROWTH RATE: 1.49 percent (2003 estimate)

TOTAL FERTILITY RATE: 4.71 children born per woman (2003 estimate)

LIFE EXPECTANCY AT BIRTH: Total population: 42.77 years (male 44.27 years; female 41.22 years; 2003 estimate)

INFANT MORTALITY RATE: 68.44 deaths per 1000 live births (2003 estimate)

LITERACY RATE (AGE 15 AND OVER WHO CAN READ AND WRITE): Total population: 84 percent (male 84.4 percent; female 83.7 percent; 2003 estimate)

EDUCATION: Officially compulsory for children ages 6–16; in the early 1990s about 349,200 students attended primary schools and 84,600 attended secondary schools. In 2000 primary schools enrolled 82 percent of eligible children, while 38 percent of secondary-school-age children attended secondary schools.

LANGUAGES: English is the official language though Afrikaans is the most widely spoken. About one third of the white population speaks German. Indigenous languages include Oshivambo, Herero, and Nama.

ETHNIC GROUPS: About 50 percent of the population belong to the Ovambo cultural group. Other principal ethnic groups include the Kavango, the Herero, the Damara, the Khoikhoi, and the San.

RELIGIONS: About 80 to 90 percent of the population are Christian (mainly Lutheran), and about 10 to 20 percent adhere to indigenous beliefs.

CLIMATE: Namibia has a hot, dry, desert climate. Average rainfall ranges from 50 mm (about 2 in) in the Namib Desert along the coast to about 560 mm (about 22 in) in the north. Average temperatures in Windhoek vary from 17° C (63° F) in January to 6° C (43° F) in July.

LAND, PLANTS, AND ANIMALS: Namibia is located mostly on a high plateau, with the Namib Desert along the coast and the Kalahari Desert in the east; its highest point is about 2,606 m (8,550 ft) in elevation. Vegetation is sparse in both deserts. A woodland savanna is found in the central plateau, and forests in the northeast. Animals include elephants, rhinoceroses, lions, giraffes, zebras, and hartebeests.

NATURAL RESOURCES: Diamonds, copper, uranium, zinc, lead, gold, tin, lithium, cadmium, salt, vanadium, suspected deposits of natural gas, oil, coal, and iron ore; Namibia's waters also have over a million metric tons of fish.

CURRENCY: Namibian dollar; South African rand

GROSS DOMESTIC PRODUCT (GDP): $12.6 billion (2002 estimate)

GDP PER CAPITA: $6,900 (2002 estimate)

GDP REAL GROWTH RATE: 3.2 percent (2002 estimate)

PRIMARY ECONOMIC ACTIVITIES: Livestock raising and subsistence agriculture (47 percent of employment), mining (20 percent of GDP), industry and commerce

PRIMARY CROPS: Millet, sorghum, peanuts, and livestock

INDUSTRIES: Meat packing, fish processing, dairy products, and mining

PRIMARY EXPORTS: Diamonds, copper, gold, zinc, lead, uranium, cattle, processed fish, and karakul skins

PRIMARY IMPORTS: Food, petroleum, machinery, and equipment

PRIMARY TRADE PARTNERS: South Africa, Germany, Switzerland, United Kingdom, and United States

GOVERNMENT: Namibia is a constitutional republic. The executive branch is led by President Sam Nujoma. The bicameral legislative branch consists of the 26-member National Council and the 72-member National Assembly, both currently dominated by President Nujoma's party, the South West Africa People's Organization (SWAPO).

Lisa Clayton Robinson

Rehobothers all encountered violent police retribution after unsuccessful revolts in the 1920s and 1930s. The administration also imported South Africa's policies of racial discrimination, with slight local modifications.

After World War II the United Nations changed the status of the colony from a mandate to a trust territory, thereby making South Africa responsible for preparing for its independence. But South Africa had other plans. The colonial administration established a democratic system for the territory's white community but remained in control of defense, foreign affairs, "native policy," and the infrastructure, including the mining industry, harbors, and railways.

It also called upon the German, Finnish, British, and South African missions—which had always maintained close ties to the colonial government—to help instill subservience. Through their schools and sermons, churches promoted the separation of white from black, master from servant, and Christian from pagan. They also confiscated African land for private farming and ranching, and used African contract laborers on church estates.

The colonial economy rested on commercial farming, fisheries, and mining. On the central plateau, large white-owned farms depended on African labor to raise cattle, grains, and horticultural products. In WALVIS BAY, the fishing industry's catches (primarily pilchard and mackerel) accounted for approximately one-quarter of South-West Africa's income. South African and Western multinationals controlled the mining industry, extracting large quantities of diamonds from the restricted-access Diamond Area in the southwest as well as uranium, copper, lead, and zinc from other parts of the territory. Despite its mineral wealth and nearly total integration into the South African economy, South-West Africa itself remained underdeveloped, and most of its African population poor. Productivity in the countryside was limited by the contract labor system, which bound a large proportion of the working-age Ovambo male population to jobs in the mines and on the plantations. Living in overcrowded compounds and earning only 5 percent of the average white worker's wages, contract laborers were typically granted only two weeks of home leave annually.

South African rule increasingly divided the African population. Employing the 1923 Group Areas Act, the government pushed Africans onto reserves, ultimately creating ten "homelands" for the "indigenous peoples" based upon the blueprint provided by APARTHEID. Although South African capital flowed into the colony, Africans' economic status deteriorated as they were pushed onto less productive land. Ultimately, 93 percent of the colony's population inhabited 40 percent of the land, while white settlers (who comprised only 7 percent of the population) and the white-ruled government controlled the remainder.

Nationalism and the Struggle for Independence

Resistance to South African race-based policies emerged in the 1950s. After 1948, when the first blacks graduated from secondary school, youths began protesting the government's discriminatory educational policies. Churches such as the AFRICAN METHODIST EPISCOPAL CHURCH (AME), no longer as willing to help the government carry out these policies, backed the students as well as workers' growing demands for labor policy reforms. In the early 1950s, newly-formed mineworkers' unions staged strikes in Luderitz, led by the Ovamboland People's Organization (OPO) and its founder, ANDIMBA TOIVO JA TOIVO.

Three main anticolonial movements had emerged by the late 1950s: the OPO; the student-based South-West African National Union, or SWANU; and the Herero Council, an elite, relatively conservative association of Herero leaders. These and many smaller groups staged numerous protests against South African rule, often employing Gandhian methods of passive resistance. The largest demonstration occurred when the authorities sought to relocate Africans living in the Old Location quarter of Windhoek to an area known as Katutura, or "the place where no one lives." Eleven African demonstrators were killed by the police, and the Windhoek Shooting, as the event became known, both radicalized the Namibian population and provoked international outcry.

In 1959, in an attempt to create a truly nationalist political party, leaders of the OPO created the SOUTH WEST AFRICA PEOPLE'S ORGANIZATION, or SWAPO, led by SAMUEL NUJOMA. In the early 1960s SWAPO and SWANU joined forces, but SWANU continued to identify SWAPO with the Ovambo and, fearing Ovambo dominance, broke from the coalition. SWAPO also petitioned the United Nations and ORGANIZATION OF AFRICAN UNITY for recognition as the sole representative of the people of South-West Africa, recognition it won in 1962. In 1966, however, the International Court of Justice reversed the decision and refused to denounce South African occupation.

That same year SWAPO's small military wing, the People's Liberation Army of Namibia, or PLAN, started the war for independence. Although PLAN enjoyed great popular support, the insurgents were at a disadvantage fighting on flat, open ground against the large and well-armed South African army. South Africa also used laws such as the Terrorism Act of 1967 to suppress African resistance and put many SWAPO leaders in prison. In 1969 the UN declared that the territory would henceforth be referred to as Namibia, from the Nama word *namib*, or shield, coined by the nationalist leader Mburumba Kerina some years before.

In 1971 the International Court of Justice declared South African occupation illegal, requested withdrawal, and called upon the international community to impose sanctions on South Africa for its conduct. The UN also once again recognized SWAPO as the sole representative of the Namibian people. While South Africa began a dialogue with the United Nations, it also began to seek an "internal settlement." In 1975 and 1976 the South African government brought eleven leaders of the African homelands, though not SWAPO or other nationalist groups, to the Turnhalle Conference. There it proposed a political system for an independent Namibia that would provide the white community, considered an ethnic group, with veto power over national decisions as well as continued control over most of the economy.

South Africa's proposals satisfied neither the international community nor most Namibians. The late 1970s saw increasing confrontation between South Africa and PLAN, which had received arms and training from the Eastern Bloc, China, and North Korea. During this time South Africa established military checkpoints and a restrictive curfew in the northern "war zone" of Ovamboland, Caprivi, and Okavango, increased African conscription into the army, attempted to co-opt many traditional chiefs by expanding their authority, and undertook development projects aimed at winning popular support.

Meanwhile, SWAPO pushed the international community, in particular the so-called Contact—GREAT BRITAIN, CANADA, FRANCE, the United States, and West Germany—to pressure South Africa to abide by UN resolutions 385 (of 1976), which called for a ceasefire and withdrawal, and 435 (of 1978), which called for elections and independence. But recently elected conservative governments in the United States and Great Britain showed little interest. Instead, South Africa held internal elections that ensured the victory of the Democratic Turnhalle Alliance, or DTA, an alliance of minor ethnic-based parties led by the white community.

Fighting continued between South Africa and PLAN and its supporters during the mid-1980s. Not until 1987, when Angolan and Cuban forces defeated South Africa at the battle of Cuito Cuanavale, was South Africa finally forced back to the negotiating table. SWAPO meanwhile toned down its rhetoric advocating "scientific socialism," aiming to calm international and especially South African fears that independence would bring a Marxist takeover and economic nationalization. Indeed, during much of the struggle the exiled SWAPO leadership had increasingly advocated development policies and political solutions acceptable to the international community, forcing these ideas upon the more radical PLAN leadership and the labor unions that remained inside Namibia.

In 1988 the Contact Group successfully linked the withdrawal of Cuban military forces from Angola with the South African withdrawal from Namibia. In 1989 South Africa agreed to implement UN resolutions 385 and 435, and set elections for the following year. In November 1989 SWAPO won a majority of the seats to the assembly charged with writing a constitution for an independent Namibia.

Politics and the Economy in Independent Namibia

Namibia became independent on March 21, 1990. SAM NUJOMA became president and immediately began promoting private-sector growth and foreign investment. The International Monetary Fund (IMF) and World Bank provided substantial loans for a wide range of development projects, while foreign firms stepped up investment in diamond and uranium mining in the southern Namib. In other ways, however, Namibia's economy changed little. It continued to export much of its beef, fish, and agricultural produce to South Africa, and the Namibian dollar was tied to the South African rand. Although some assembly ministers pushed the government to follow up on SWAPO's wartime promises of land reform, most large cattle ranches remained in the hands of a small minority of whites, and 5 percent of the population still controlled over 70 percent of the GDP. The average white person earned fourteen times that of the average black person.

In 1994 elections SWAPO increased its representation in the assembly, at the expense of the opposition party DTA. But dissatisfaction with SWAPO and Nujoma mounted. International donors criticized Nujoma's plans to run for a third term as president (which the constitution does not permit) as well as his government's lavish spending on limousines, helicopters, and presidential jets. While the public criticized the elite privileges extended to members of parliament, strong labor unions prevented significant cuts in the large state bureaucracy. Nujoma won a third presidential term in Namibia's December 1999 elections, defeating former SWAPO member Ben Ulenga of the Congress of Democrats (COD). SWAPO dominated the concurrent elections to the National Assembly, winning fifty-five seats. The COD and DTA each won seven seats, with the remainder divided among smaller parties.

Some of Namibia's greatest economic and political challenges lie in the realm of natural resource management. In an effort to compensate for perennially uneven rainfall patterns, the government began steps in the late 1990s to siphon river water from the Okavango and to provide residents of Walvis Bay with desalinated seawater. It even discussed a pipeline from the CONGO RIVER. Meanwhile a government plan to build the highest hydroelectric dam in Africa on the Kunene river threatened to displace the Himba people, who voiced strong opposition to the project.

Livestock and wildlife issues have also generated domestic and international controversy. Neighboring BOTSWANA's 140-kilometer-long Northern Buffalo Fence, which runs partially along the Namibian border, was built to prevent the cross-border transmission of cattle-lung disease. But this fence—like many private fences built by ranchers—has created a barrier to wildlife in search of water, and large numbers of animal deaths have provoked outcries from wildlife conservationists. International animal-rights groups have also pushed the Namibian government to stop RHINOCEROS-culling as well as the annual killing of thousands of seals, practices that produce significant revenue for the government.

Several other issues have recently created unrest and controversy in Namibia. In 1999 fighting broke out between Namibian troops and separatists who want independence for the CAPRIVI STRIP. The UN recently estimated that about 20 percent of the adult population in Namibia has HIV or AIDS. In 2001 Nujoma launched a campaign to remove homosexuals from Namibia through imprisonment or deportation. In 2003 the government appealed to the United States for relief after a severe drought deprived several hundred thousand Namibians of food and water.

See also Acquired Immunodeficiency Syndrome in Africa: An Interpretation; Bantu: Dispersion and Settlement; Christianity: Missionaries in Africa; Cold War and Africa; Colonial Rule; Drought and Desertification; Minerals and Mining in Africa; Nationalism in Africa; Salt Trade; Slavery in Africa; United Nations in Africa; Wildlife Management in Africa.

Eric Young

Nandi

Ethnic group of Kenya.

The Nandi primarily inhabit the highlands of western KENYA. They speak a Nilo-Saharan language and are one of the KALENJIN peoples. Over 400,000 people consider themselves Nandi.

See also Languages, African: An Overview.

Nanny

?–1733

Legendary Jamaican maroon and a leader of the Windward Maroons, who lived in the Blue Mountains.

Nanny was said to have used supernatural powers in battles against the British. She was killed by a slave named Cuffe in 1733.

See also Jamaica; Maroonage in the Americas; Nanny Town.

Nanny Town

Former maroon community in the Blue Mountains of Jamaica that was destroyed by colonial officials in 1734 and is now a symbol of slave resistance.

Nanny Town, which is now known as Mooretown, was one of five major eighteenth-century maroon communities in JAMAICA. Located in the inaccessible Blue Mountain range of Portland parish, Nanny Town was home to the Windward or Eastern maroons. The town and its destruction by the British in 1734 have become a powerful symbol of slave resistance. The town's legendary leader was an African chief named NANNY, and her mysterious life and death have become an integral part of Jamaican history.

According to legend, Nanny was the wife or sister of the legendary maroon CUDJOE. She is described in myths as possessing impressive magical powers. Local oral tradition recalls how she was able to repel bullets fired from European guns, and how she could capture colonial soldiers in her boiling cauldron.

Colonial militias attacked the town named in Nanny's honor several times. It fell victim to a massive European offensive in 1734. That year, according to colonial history, Captain Stoddart led a small army by night into the maroon community and set up portable swivel guns high above the town's sleeping residents. Firing down upon the unsuspecting maroons, Stoddart killed most of them before they could mount an organized resistance. According to colonial history, Nanny Town was sacked and many of its survivors chose to commit suicide rather than suffer the humiliation of defeat.

The maroons have their own version of the events at Nanny Town. According to maroon legend, lookouts spotted Stoddart and his army as they approached. The town was evacuated and maroon fighters hid themselves along the path to the town, lying in wait as the white soldiers passed. When they reached Nanny Town they found an empty village. Disappointed and tired, they chose to set up camp and sleep throughout the night. Once the soldiers were asleep the maroons set upon the town, throwing burning candles onto the tents and setting the town afire. The terrified soldiers chose not to fight and instead leapt over the surrounding cliffs to their death. Historians currently believe that the truth lies somewhere in between these two accounts.

Nanny Town was never resettled after the confrontation in 1734. The maroons who survived the attack fled into the mountains, and many joined forces with Cudjoe and his army. Some believe that ghosts haunted Nanny Town. The legend of the place, and the controversy surrounding its demise, continue to add fuel to the powerful tales of slave resistance in Jamaica.

See also Maroonage in the Americas.

Alonford James Robinson

Napier, James Carroll

1845–1940

African American politician, attorney, and businessman.

James Carroll Napier was born on the western outskirts of Nashville, Tennessee. His parents, William C. Napier and Jane E., were slaves at the time of his birth but were freed in 1848. After manumission and a brief residency in Ohio, William Napier moved his family to Nashville, where he established a livery stable business. James attended the black elementary and secondary schools of Nashville before entering WILBERFORCE UNIVERSITY (1864–1866) and Oberlin College (1866–1868), both in Ohio.

James Napier began his career as a race leader and politician during the RECONSTRUCTION era in Tennessee as Davidson County commissioner of refugees and abandoned lands in the Freedmen's Bureau. In 1870 he led a delegation of black Tennesseans to petition President Ulysses S. Grant and Congress for relief from politically motivated violence aimed at nullifying black voting strength, for removal of the state's conservative government, and for rejection of the state's 1870 constitution. Unsuccessful in this effort, Napier and his delegation urged the president and Congress to establish a national school system and to enforce the FIFTEENTH AMENDMENT in their home state. Napier subsequently received a position as a Treasury Department clerk in WASHINGTON, D.C., possibly the first African American to hold such a post. Under the tutelage of JOHN MERCER LANGSTON, the prominent black politician and acting president of HOWARD UNIVERSITY, Napier entered the institution's law school in the District of Columbia. After obtaining a law degree in 1872, he returned to Nashville to begin a practice and in 1878 married Langston's only surviving daughter, Nettie Langston. Theirs was a childless union that lasted sixty years.

Under Presidents Rutherford B. Hayes, James A. Garfield, and Chester A. Arthur, Napier held patronage appointments in the Nashville offices of the Internal Revenue Service, serving as a gauger (1879–1881), clerk (1883–1884), and deputy collector (1885). Owing to his business, legal, and political acumen, Napier emerged as the ranking African American politician in Tennessee in the two decades after the CIVIL WAR. He served on the Nashville City Council from 1878 to 1889 and the state REPUBLICAN PARTY executive committee, was a delegate to six Republican national conventions, and made an unsuccessful bid for election to the Fifth District congressional seat in 1898. As a city councilman Napier led successful efforts for the hiring of the first African American schoolteachers in Nashville, the establishment of the city's first modern schools (including high school training) for black Americans, and the employment of the city's first black firefighters. In the 1890s, however, the rise to power of the "lily whites," dedicated to the removal of blacks from political participation in the South, and the emergence of more outspoken, younger African American leaders such as ROBERT R. CHURCH, JR., of MEMPHIS curtailed Napier's influence in state and local politics.

Napier still remained a force to be reckoned with, however, due to his dignified manner, political connections, and behind-the-scenes approach to getting things done. His friendship and alliance with the educator BOOKER T. WASHINGTON in 1891 kept him in the inner circles of federal politics. He became a member of the so-called "black cabinet" that advised Republican presidents. Offered positions as consul to BAHIA, BRAZIL, and as consul-general for LIBERIA in 1906 and 1910, respectively, Napier refused both appointments. A recommendation from Washington led to Napier's appointment in 1911 as register of the U.S. Treasury, the most prestigious and highest federal position then available to an African American. Napier acquitted himself well in this position. Presiding over a staff of seventy-three, in addition to his official duties accounting for the receipt and expenditure of all public money, Napier found time to press for the continued development of the African American community. He testified before Congress in 1912 for passage of the Page Bill for equitable distribution of funds (set aside in the Morrill Acts of 1863 and 1890) for African American land-grant southern colleges. Napier's efforts were to no avail. He resigned from his post two years later to protest President Woodrow Wilson's sanctioning of segregation in federal office facilities. After 1913 Napier retreated from involvement in national politics to focus more exclusively on economic self-help in the black community.

Napier used his influence as lawyer, lecturer, businessman, head of the Nashville Board of Trade, and organizer of a branch of the National Negro Business League (NNBL) to promote economic and educational development among African Americans. Aware of the collapse of the FREEDMEN'S BANK and the resulting economic dislocation in the African American community during Reconstruction, Napier entered the banking business to provide saving, credit, and investment opportunities to blacks and to demonstrate the advantages, both personal and collective, of entrepreneurial endeavors. He utilized his own estate as collateral for funds to underwrite the first year's operation of the Nashville One-Cent Savings Bank in 1903. He went without salary as the cashier of the bank to ensure its success and development. He and RICHARD HENRY BOYD, the founding president of the enterprise (later renamed the Citizens Savings Bank) steered it toward ultraconservative fiscal policies in lending and investment to guarantee the bank's financial success so that it might serve as a model for other black businessmen and bankers. The bank was founded to inspire "systematic saving among our people," according to Napier. From its opening on January 6, 1904 (with deposits of $6,392 from 145 individuals), deposits of the Citizens Savings Bank reached a high of $209,942 within thirty-five years.

Napier supported larger cooperative black capitalist endeavors by joining Booker T. Washington's NNBL, which first convened in Boston in 1900. This organization was designed to bring black businessmen from around the nation to annual meetings to discuss entrepreneurship as a means to individual and collective uplift in the black community. The 1903 annual NNBL meeting was held in Nashville, under the aegis of Napier, one of the vice presidents of the organization. Napier inherited and held the NNBL presidential mantle after Washington's death in 1915, serving until 1919. He attended the upstate New York AMENIA CONFERENCE OF 1916 and was one of the ranking Bookerites to effect a successful but short-lived modus vivendi between the Washington and W. E. B. DU BOIS-NAACP factions vying for controlling leadership of the black community.

Napier continued to promote the idea of industrial development and training as an economic strategy to provide jobs and entrepreneurial opportunities for blacks as one of the founders of Nashville's Tennessee Agricultural and Industrial State Normal School for Negroes (now Tennessee State University). Serving as a trustee of Meharry Medical College, FISK UNIVERSITY, and HOWARD UNIVERSITY, Napier also took a keen interest in higher education and publicly extolled the virtues of both higher and industrial education in preparing African Americans for "all the duties and responsibilities of life." As trustee of the Anna T. Jeanes Fund, which supported educational opportunities for black southerners, Napier was instrumental in obtaining more than $75,965 between 1909 and 1926 for Tennessee and establishing the organization's presence in twenty-eight counties in the state. Napier lectured frequently on medical jurisprudence at Meharry. In the 1920s he served as a member of the southern regional Commission on Interracial Cooperation established to prevent violence and conflict between blacks and whites. Two years before his death in Nashville, Napier was appointed to the city's housing authority at age ninety-three. He was reported shortly after 1900 to have amassed personal wealth of more than $100,000; the value of his real estate was assessed at $43,016 at the time of his death.

Napier eschewed confrontational politics in favor of cooperative efforts to further African American organizational and institutional development within a segregated society. He was clearly in the cadre of elite African American leaders in the first half of the twentieth century.

Bibliography

Atlanta University's Woodruff Library, Special Collections, has a vertical file of clippings on Napier. A collection of Napier papers is at Fisk University.

Clark, Herbert L. "James Carroll Napier: National Negro Leader." *Tennessee Historical Quarterly* 49 (1990): 243–52.

Harlan, Louis. *The Booker T. Washington Papers*. Vol. 4, pp. 453–54. 1975.

Lamon, Lester Crawford. *Black Tennesseans, 1900–1930*. 1977.

———. *Blacks in Tennessee, 1791–1970*. 1981.

Obituary, *Journal of Negro History* (July 1940): 400–401.

Obituary, *Nashville Banner*, 23 Apr. 1940.

From *American National Biography*. John A. Garraty and Mark C. Carnes, eds. Oxford University Press, 1999. Reprinted by permission of the American Council of Learned Societies.

Maceo Crenshaw Dailey

Nascimento, Abdias do

1914–

Afro-Brazilian playwright, poet, educator, artist, and political activist; one of the leading figures of Brazil's black movement.

Abdias do Nascimento grew up in Franca, São Paulo, BRAZIL, where his father was a shoemaker and his mother worked as a sweetmaker, cook, and seamstress. Very early he distinguished himself as an excellent student, and by the age of thirteen he was teaching primary school and working as an accountant for local farmers. Nascimento served in the army from 1930 to 1936, during the dictatorship of Getúlio Vargas. At this time Nascimento began his career as a black activist by joining the FRENTE NEGRA BRASILEIRA (United Black Front). In 1937, when Vargas established the Estado Novo dictatorship, the Frente Negra was shut down, along with all other political organizations.

Nascimento's first major Afro-Brazilian project was the theater group TEATRO EXPERIMENTAL DO NEGRO (TEN), which he founded in 1944. For the next twenty-four years he worked as its director and as a playwright. Nascimento created TEN in order to redefine the role of blacks in Brazilian theater. TEN trained the first generation of Afro-Brazilian actors and actresses and won critical acclaim for its productions of Eugene O'Neill's *Emperor Jones* and Nascimento's *Sortilégio (Black Mystery)*.

TEN also served as a vehicle for Nascimento's political activism. From 1949 to 1951 TEN published *Quilombo: Black Life, Problems, and Aspirations*, a journal promoting the Afro-Brazilian freedom struggle through various Afro-Brazilian–centered articles, biographies, and illustrations. As an extension of TEN, Nascimento convened the Comité Democrático Afro–Brasileiro (Afro-Brazilian Democratic Committee) in 1945 in order to lobby the Brazilian Congress to enact anti-discrimination legislation. He was the President of the 1945 and 1946 National Convention of Blacks, held in São Paulo and RIO DE JANEIRO, respectively, which drafted a bill defining and urging the banning of racial discrimination. With the help of TEN, Nascimento also organized the Primero Congreso Negro Brasileiro (First National Congress of Brazilian Blacks) in 1950. These conferences paved the way for the passing of the Afonso Arinos Law of 1951, which outlawed racial discrimination, classifying it as a misdemeanor rather than a crime.

In 1968, four years after a military dictatorship suspended many individual and collective rights, Nascimento sought exile in the United States. There he traveled and lectured extensively, gaining recognition for his role in the black movement in Brazil. He was a lecturer at the Yale School of Dramatic Arts in 1969 and was a visiting scholar at Wesleyan University from 1969–1970. From 1976–1981, he was a member of the faculty of the State University of New York, Buffalo, where he created the chair of African Culture in the New World and taught at the Puerto Rican Studies and Research Center. In 1976 and 1977, he taught at the Department of African Languages and Literatures at the University of Ife (later renamed Obafemi Awolowo University) in Ife, NIGERIA. He returned to Brazil in 1981 and was named the professor of black studies at the Pontifical Catholic University in São Paulo, where he founded the Afro-Brazilian Studies and Research Institute (IPEAFRO).

In addition to his work as a scholar, Nascimento devoted himself to painting while in exile. Just before his departure from Brazil, he founded the Black Arts Museum in Rio de Janeiro in 1968 and began to create his own artwork. Nascimento uses bold, unmodulated colors and geometric forms in his paintings to depict scenes from African and Afro-Brazilian mythology. The inspiration for many of his works is the Afro-Brazilian religion of CANDOMBLÉ. Nascimento's wife Elisa Larkin Nascimento, who has collaborated with him on many publications, said that her husband's painting "expresses, in artistic terms, his role of adding to Afro-Brazilian human rights demands, and develops . . . the dimension of African cultural heritage vital to rescuing and recovering Afro-Brazilian identity and human dignity."

While in exile, Nascimento also participated in and helped organize many Pan-African conferences. These include the Sixth Pan-African Congress (Dar es Salaam, Tanzania; 1974), the Encounter for African World Alternatives (Dakar, Senegal; 1976), and the Second World Festival of Black and African Arts and Culture (Lagos, Nigeria; 1977). He also played a major role in all three of the Congresses of Black Culture in the Americas (held in Cali, Colombia, 1977; Panama in 1980; and São Paulo, Brazil, in 1982).

Nascimento has also been deeply involved in electoral politics, mainly though the Partido Democrático Trabalhista [PDT], led by Leonel Brizola. In the 1940s Nascimento, along with Brizola, co-founded the Brazilian Labor Party (PTB) and helped create a black caucus within the party to work for Afro-Brazilian interests. During Nascimento's exile, the PTB was reorganized and renamed the Partido Democrático Trabalhista (PDT). At this point the party identified the issue of racial discrimination as one of its major priorities. In 1981 the PDT founded the National Secrtetariat of the Black Movement, making it the first political party in the country with a committee dedicated to fighting racism and addressing the needs of the Afro-Brazilian community.

Nascimento, Milton

1942–

Afro-Brazilian vocalist and composer who achieved international success and critical acclaim for his otherworldly fusions of jazz, rock, and classical music with the popular traditions of Minas Gerais, his home state in the interior of Brazil.

Born in RIO DE JANEIRO, BRAZIL, Milton Nascimento is noted for his extraordinary vocal range and rich timbre. Caetano Veloso has written that "Milton Nascimento's falsetto is one of the most beautiful sounds produced today by the human species." Elis Regina, the legendary vocalist who recorded several of his songs, simply remarked: "If God sang, it would be with the voice of Milton."

He was adopted as an infant by a family in Rio de Janeiro who had employed his deceased mother. The family later moved to Três Pontas, a small town in the mountainous interior of MINAS GERAIS. Like most musicians of his generation, Nascimento was deeply inspired by the emergence of BOSSA NOVA in the late 1950s. In 1963 he moved to the state capital, Belo Horizonte, where he met future collaborators Márcio and Lô Borges, who turned him on to the Beatles.

In 1967 Nascimento gained national attention at the Second International Song Festival in Rio de Janeiro. He was selected best performer of the festival and his song "Travessia" received second prize. Nascimento was subsequently invited to tour the United States, where he released an album, *Courage,* featuring HERBIE HANCOCK on keyboards and AIRTO MOREIRA on percussion. In 1975 he returned to the United States to record a landmark fusion album, *Native Dancer,* with saxophonist Wayne Shorter. In the meantime, a cohort of musicians known as the *clube da esquina* (corner club) had coalesced around him. This group, which included Wagner Tiso, Toninho Horta, Fernando Brant, and the Borges brothers, produced two beautiful and eclectic double albums in the 1970s.

Throughout this period Nascimento recorded Spanish-American songs of the *Nueva Canción* movement and explored Afro-Catholic traditions of Minas Gerais, such as the *reisada do congo.* In 1982 he composed and produced the *Missa dos Quilombos,* a choral work celebrating the legacy of black resistance to slavery and racial oppression, which combines Afro-Brazilian rhythms and Catholic hymns. Remarking on the melancholic and introspective nature of his region's musical traditions compared to upbeat Afro-Bahian music of the coast, Nascimento cites the history of gold and diamond mining dating to the eighteenth century, "The blacks who came from Africa to BAHIA worked on the land, while those who went to Minas Gerais worked *inside* the land."

Following a long journey up the Juruá River, Nascimento became sensitized to the plight of indigenous peoples of the Amazonian rain forest whose lives are disrupted and threatened by deforestation. His 1990 recording, *Txai,* features clips

Nascimento's academic, artistic, and political experiences while in exile prepared him for increased political activism upon his return to Brazil in 1981. The centrality of Afro-Brazilian concerns in his political agenda was evident during his first campaign for office in 1962, when he unsuccessfully ran for Rio de Janeiro's City Council using the slogan "Don't vote white (a phrase in Portuguese that also means "don't cast a blank ballot"), vote black—Abdias." In 1982 Nascimento was elected to the House of Deputies and became the first federal congressman to systematically defend the civil rights of Afro-Brazilians. In a 1983 bill he encouraged the House of Deputies to create a Committee on African Brazilians. He advocated that November 20, the anniversary of the death of ZUMBI, the leader of the famous *quilombo* PALMARES, be declared National Black Consciousness Day and proposed that racial discrimination be declared a crime against humanity. He also pressed the issue of affirmative action as compensation for centuries of persecution and discrimination. In terms of employment, Nascimento's bill proposed setting 20 percent hiring quotas for Afro-Brazilian men and women and offering incentives to private businesses to eliminate racial discrimination. The bill also called for the creation of scholarships for Afro-Brazilian students and the inclusion of African and Afro-Brazilian histories in school textbooks.

In the years leading up to the 1988 constitutional assembly, Nascimento stressed that racism and racial discrimination were not merely black communal concerns, but issues of national significance. Largely as a result of his efforts, the 1988 constitution included provisions that recognized the multiethnic character of Brazilian society, that defined racism as an "imprescriptable and non-bondable crime," and that determined the boundaries of lands that were formerly quilombos.

In 1990 Nascimento was elected to the Senate as a delegate from Rio de Janeiro; soon thereafter he became a member of the Rio de Janeiro State Council of Culture. The following year the Governor of Rio de Janeiro created the Secretariat for the Defense and Promotion of Afro-Brazilian Peoples (SEAFRO), the first state agency of its sort, and appointed Nascimento as its state secretary.

In February 1997 Nascimento was reelected to represent Rio de Janeiro in the Senate. As a Congressman, Nascimento has addressed not only Afro-Brazilian issues, but also international issues concerning Africans. He has addressed relations between SOUTH AFRICA and Brazil and defended efforts of Portuguese-speaking countries in Africa to achieve national liberation. In addition to his political accomplishments, Nascimento has written or edited more than twenty books, plays, and collections of essays on Afro-Brazilian culture and politics. Nascimento's achievements in such diverse fields have led some scholars to call him the twentieth century's most complete African intellectual.

See also Art in Latin America and the Caribbean.

Aaron Myers

of indigenous music with poignant songs about the destruction of the rain forest and the cultural identities it sustains. Nascimento has continued to record with international musical luminaries such as Pat Metheny, Paul Simon, QUINCY JONES, Peter Gabriel, and James Taylor. In 1997, after a life-threatening bout with diabetes, he released a triumphant comeback recording, *Nascimento,* which received a Grammy Award for the Best World Music album.

He has followed this recording with several newer releases, including *Crooner* (1999), in which he covers Brazilian and U.S. pop hits; *Musica Do Mundo* (2000); and *Pieta* (2003). After more than thirty years of performing, Nascimento is still drawing rave reviews for the quality of his vocals.

See also Slave Rebellions in Latin America and the Caribbean.

Christopher Dunn

Nash, Diane Bevel

1938–

American civil rights activist, a founder of the Student Nonviolent Coordinating Committee, and one of the few female leaders of the Civil Rights Movement.

Diane Nash, a native of CHICAGO, ILLINOIS, attended HOWARD UNIVERSITY and then transferred to FISK UNIVERSITY in Nashville. In Nashville she confronted Southern racial segregation, and became active in the young CIVIL RIGHTS MOVEMENT. She cofounded the STUDENT NONVIOLENT COORDINATING COMMITTEE (SNCC) in Raleigh, N.C., in April 1960. In February 1961 in Rock Hill, S.C., she was a member of the first group arrested for civil rights protest, who refused to pay bail and remained in prison as a symbol of the plight of blacks in America.

Nash soon became the SNCC's head of direct action. After marrying fellow civil rights activist James Bevel, taking his last name as her middle name, Nash moved to Georgia in 1962. There she worked with the SOUTHERN CHRISTIAN LEADERSHIP CONFERENCE (SCLC), a civil rights organization led by MARTIN LUTHER KING, JR., which coordinated civil rights activities. SCLC awarded Bevel and Nash the ROSA PARKS Award in 1965.

Later in her career Nash moved back to Chicago. She completed her studies there and became an educator. Divorced from Bevel, she remains active in organizations that promote peace and justice.

Bibliography

Powledge, Fred. *Free at Last? The Civil Rights Movement and the People Who Made It.* Little, Brown, 1991.

Nassau, The Bahamas

Capital and chief port of the Commonwealth of the Bahamas.

The site of the city of Nassau was discovered in 1492 by Christopher Columbus and settled in 1656 as Charles Towne (named for King Charles II of England). It was attacked and destroyed by SPAIN in 1694 for harboring pirates and was rebuilt in 1695 as Nassau (for the family name of William III of England). American revolutionaries held it briefly in 1776, and during the American CIVIL WAR (1861–1865) it served as a supply base for Confederate blockade runners.

Nassau is a world-famous tourist center, known for its fine beaches, colorful tropical vegetation, and the resort community of Paradise Island across the harbor. In 2002 the city hosted the first World Music and Jazz Festival, and the following year the National Art Gallery of the Bahamas opened in Nassau's historic Villa Doyle. Among the landmarks of the city are the Parliament Building and Court House; Government House (1801), the official residence of the governor-general; and Christ Church Cathedral. Nearby attractions include marine gardens at the eastern end of the harbor; Fort Charlotte (1787–1789); Fort Fincastle (1793); Ardastra Gardens, with many tropical and subtropical plants; and Jumbey Village, a reproduction of an eighteenth-century Bahamian community. The College of the Bahamas is also located here. The population is approximately 210,832 (2000 estimate).

Nasser, Gamal Abdel

1918–1970

Former prime minister and president of Egypt and a leading proponent of Third World and pan-Arab unity.

Gamal Abdel Nasser is widely considered one of Africa's greatest modern leaders. Although his leadership style was highly authoritarian and some of his foreign policy decisions had disastrous consequences, he was lauded not only for ending British COLONIAL RULE and implementing ambitious social reforms in EGYPT, but also for his support for Third World independence movements worldwide.

Nasser was born in ALEXANDRIA, EGYPT. He went to primary school in the village where his father, a postman, worked, then attended secondary school in CAIRO, where he participated in street protests against the British. He briefly attended law school before entering the Royal Military Academy, graduating in 1938, and receiving a commission as a second lieutenant.

While serving in the SUDAN, Nasser and three other officers formed the Free Officers, a secret organization that aimed to overthrow the British as well as the Egyptian monarch, Farouk I. In July 1952 the Free Officers deposed King Farouk and installed the Revolutionary Command Council, led by Nasser. He initially kept a low profile, naming the older and more experienced Major General MUHAMMAD NAGUIB head of state. In the spring of 1954, however, Nasser deposed Naguib and declared himself prime minister.

Nasser's first major accomplishment was the 1954 Anglo-Egyptian treaty, which provided for the gradual British pullout of troops from the SUEZ CANAL Zone. Later that year he survived an assassination attempt by a member of the Muslim Brotherhood who disapproved of the treaty's terms; Nasser responded with a harsh crackdown on the group. Throughout his career he would repeatedly use this tactic to block opposition.

Nasser won international renown at the 1955 Bandung Conference in Indonesia, where, along with other African and Asian leaders, he called for Third World decolonization and solidarity within the Non-Aligned Movement. Nasser first demonstrated his nonalignment to the West in September 1955, when he announced an arms purchase agreement with Czechoslovakia. The following year, a month after Nasser was elected president, the United States withdrew its offer of $270 million to subsidize construction of the ASWAN HIGH DAM; Nasser responded by nationalizing the Suez Canal. When Israel attacked Egypt in October 1956, British and French forces joined in and ultimately crippled the Egyptian air force. Nasser ordered the sinking of forty vessels, rendering the canal impassable. The United Nations, with the support of both the United States and the Soviet Union, subsequently arranged for the withdrawal of the British, French, and Israeli forces and undertook repairs to the canal, now an acknowledged Egyptian possession.

The Suez Crisis, as it came to be called, enormously increased Nasser's popularity among Arab countries. Although in his *Philosophy of the Revolution* (1954), he wrote of wishing to lead all the world's Arabs, Africans, and followers of Islam, he was best known for his efforts to achieve Arab unity, creating the United Arab Republic, a union of Syria and Egypt, in 1958. Syria, however, split from the union in 1961.

Within Egypt, Nasser's regime brought a true revolution. The Free Officers ousted the landholding elites who, along with Europeans, had traditionally dominated the government, and nationalized their land. Nasser's land policies prohibited any individual from owning more than 100 *feddans* (104 acres). Crucial to his vision for improving the lives of Egyptians was the Aswan High Dam, completed in 1968, which provided for irrigation of the fertile Nile Delta as well as inexpensive hydroelectric power. Egypt's industries, educational programs, and medical services all expanded during the Nasser era, and women gained more civil rights.

Yet Nasser increasingly depended on repressive tactics, such as the prohibition of political parties, censorship, and detention of political enemies. Furthermore, the birth rate in Egypt remained high, thwarting the efforts to create a higher standard of living.

Throughout the first half of the 1960s, Egypt disguised its moderate stance toward Israel with belligerent public rhetoric, though among Arab leaders Nasser urged restraint. By 1966, however, Palestinian raiders were launching attacks in Israel from bases in Jordan, Syria, and Lebanon. On November 13, 1966, Israel struck a Palestinian base in Jordan, killing eighteen and wounding fifty-four. Nasser, under pressure from his fellow Arabs, requested the removal of UN troops, which had been stationed in the Sinai Peninsula since the Suez Crisis, and Egypt closed the Gulf of Aqaba to Israeli shipping. On June 6, 1967, Israel launched a simultaneous strike at Jordan and Egypt in what would be called the Six-Day War, crippling Egypt's air forces on the ground and routing its army. Nasser resigned, only to return at the urging of the Egyptian people, who took to the streets in a show of support. He never reclaimed the luster of his early years, however, and he began a conservative shift that his successor, ANWAR AL-SADAT, continued.

See also Islam in Africa; Nile River.

Bibliography

Baker, Raymond William. *Egypt's Uncertain Revolution Under Nasser and Sadat*. Harvard University Press, 1978.

Robbe, Martin, and Jurgen Hosel, eds. *Egypt: the Revolution of July 1952 and Gamal Abdel Nasser*. Akademie-Verlag, 1989.

Robert Fay

Natera, Ramón

?–1923

Leading guerrilla general during the Dominican Republic's war against United States occupation forces.

Motivated by both economic and strategic military interests, the United States in 1916 initiated an eight-year occupation of the DOMINICAN REPUBLIC. From 1916 to 1920 the United States introduced a number of reforms and programs meant to change the Dominican political, economic, and social structure. While some members of Dominican society cooperated with the United States, others resisted. In the eastern part of the country, opposition to the U.S. presence led to a five-year war between hundreds of guerrilla soldiers and U.S. Marines. General Ramón Natera emerged as the most important leader of the guerrilla troops, which consisted primarily of peasants and SUGAR workers who had been displaced from their homes or jobs as a result of the U.S. occupation.

Little is known about Natera's life before the U.S occupation. He was briefly captured by U.S. Marine forces in 1918 while attempting to seize the town of Hato Mayor, but escaped the following day when a band of guerrilla soldiers attacked the Marines guarding him. Other American attempts to capture or kill Natera failed. He eluded the larger and better equipped U.S. forces by staying in an undisclosed location apart from his soldiers and because civilians kept him informed of American plans and troop movements.

One of Natera's boldest actions came in September 1921, when he and his soldiers abducted the British manager of the *La Angelina* sugar estate, Thomas J. Steele. They released Steele two days later after he agreed to their demand to make clear to U.S officials in Washington the political goals of the guerrillas—that the United States end its occupation of the country. The United States responded by increasing troops in the region.

Despite increased military activity by the U.S Marines, Natera's revolutionary campaign continued. He gained support from the elite *Congreso Nacionalista del Seibo* (National Congress of Seibo), which issued a public statement in November 1921 arguing that the insurgents in the east were merely acting in response to the harsh treatment they received from the U.S Marines. As a result, the United States reversed its policy and began to arrange for amnesty to those revolutionary insurgents who surrendered, and many did. In the beginning of May 1922, U.S. District Commander Lyman and Natera met and arranged a cease-fire. On May 5, 1922, Natera surrendered; he brought his troops in three days later. In November 1923 he was shot to death during a dispute with a *guarda campestre* (rural guard), ending a life dedicated to restoring the Dominican Republic's independence.

Aaron Myers

National Association for the Advancement of Colored People

Interracial organization devoted to civil rights and racial justice.

The National Association for the Advancement of Colored People (NAACP) has been instrumental in improving the legal, educational, and economic lives of African Americans. Combining the white philanthropic support that characterized BOOKER T. WASHINGTON's accommodationist organizations with the call for racial justice delivered by W. E. B. DU BOIS's militant NIAGARA MOVEMENT, the NAACP forged a middle road of interracial cooperation. Throughout its existence it has worked primarily through the American legal system to fulfill its goals of full suffrage and other civil rights, and an end to segregation and racial violence. Since the end of the CIVIL RIGHTS MOVEMENT of the 1950s and 1960s, however, the influence of the NAACP has waned, and it has suffered declining membership and a series of internal scandals.

The NAACP was formed in response to the 1908 race riot in Springfield, capital of Illinois and birthplace of President Abraham Lincoln. Appalled at the violence that was committed against blacks, a group of white liberals that included Mary White Ovington and Oswald Garrison Villard, both the descendants of abolitionists, issued a call for a meeting to discuss racial justice. Some sixty people, only seven of whom were African American (including W. E. B. Du Bois, IDA B. WELLS-BARNETT, and MARY CHURCH TERRELL), signed the call, which was released on the centennial of Lincoln's birth. Echoing the focus of Du Bois's militant all-black Niagara Movement, the NAACP's stated goal was to secure for all people the rights guaranteed in the Thirteenth, FOURTEENTH, and FIFTEENTH AMENDMENTS to the United States Constitution, which promised an end to slavery, the equal protection of the law, and universal adult male suffrage, respectively.

The NAACP established its national office in NEW YORK City and named a board of directors as well as a president, Moorfield Storey, a white constitutional lawyer and former president of the American Bar Association. The only African American among the organization's executives, Du Bois was made director of publications and research and in 1910 he established the official journal of the NAACP, *THE CRISIS*. With a strong emphasis on local organizing, by 1913 the NAACP had established branch offices in such cities as BOSTON, MASSACHUSETTS; KANSAS CITY, MISSOURI; WASHINGTON, D.C.; DETROIT, MICHIGAN; and St. Louis, Missouri.

By the late 1940s, when this poster urged African Americans to join the NAACP, the organization had a membership of half a million. *Library of Congress*

The NAACP joined with civic and religious groups to organize the 1917 silent protest parade in Harlem. About 8,000 African American men, women, and children marched down Fifth Avenue, silently bearing signs protesting the racist violence of the recent East St. Louis riot and the continuing scourge of lynching. Marchers questioned as well the bitter irony of the United States' entrance into World War I—a war meant to "make the world safe for democracy"—while the government continued to tolerate racial injustice at home. *CORBIS/Bettmann*

A series of early court battles, including a victory against a discriminatory Oklahoma law that regulated voting by means of a grandfather clause (*Guinn v. United States,* 1910), helped establish the NAACP's importance as a legal advocate, a role it would play with overwhelming success. The fledgling organization also learned to harness the power of publicity through its 1915 battle against D. W. Griffith's inflammatory BIRTH OF A NATION, a motion picture that perpetuated demeaning stereotypes of African Americans and glorified the KU KLUX KLAN.

Its membership grew rapidly, from around 9,000 in 1917 to around 90,000 in 1919, with more than 300 local branches. The writer and diplomat JAMES WELDON JOHNSON became the association's first black secretary in 1920, and LOUIS T. WRIGHT, a surgeon, was named the first black chairman of its board of directors in 1934; neither position was ever again held by a white person. Meanwhile, *The Crisis* became a voice of the HARLEM RENAISSANCE, as Du Bois published works by LANGSTON HUGHES, COUNTEE CULLEN, and other African American literary figures.

Throughout the 1920s the fight against LYNCHING was among the association's top priorities. After early worries about its constitutionality, the NAACP strongly supported the federal DYER BILL, which would have punished those who participated in or failed to prosecute lynch mobs. Though the U.S. Congress never passed the bill, or any other antilynching legislation, many credit the resulting public debate—fueled by the NAACP's report, *Thirty Years of Lynching in the United States, 1889–1919*—with drastically decreasing the incidence of lynching.

Johnson stepped down as secretary in 1930 and was succeeded by WALTER F. WHITE. White was instrumental not only in his research on lynching (in part because, as a very fair-skinned African American, he had been able to infiltrate white groups), but also in his successful block of segregationist Judge John J. Parker's nomination by President Herbert Hoover to the Supreme Court of the United States. Though some historians blame Du Bois's 1934 resignation from *The Crisis* on White, the new secretary presided over the NAACP's most productive period of legal advocacy. In 1930 the association commissioned the Margold Report, which became the basis for its successful reversal of the separate-but-equal doctrine that had governed public facilities since 1896's PLESSY V. FERGUSON. In 1935 White recruited CHARLES H. HOUSTON as NAACP chief counsel. Houston was the HOWARD UNIVERSITY law school dean whose strategy on school-segregation cases paved the way for his protégé THURGOOD MARSHALL to prevail in 1954's BROWN V. BOARD OF EDUCATION, the decision that overturned Plessy.

During the GREAT DEPRESSION of the 1930s, which was disproportionately disastrous for African Americans, the NAACP began to focus on economic justice. After years of tension with white labor unions, the association cooperated with the newly formed Congress of Industrial Organizations (CIO) in an effort to win jobs for black Americans. Walter White, a friend and adviser to First Lady Eleanor Roosevelt, who was sympathetic to civil rights, met with her often in attempts to convince President Franklin D. Roosevelt to outlaw job discrimination in the armed forces, defense industries (which were booming in anticipation of U.S. entry into WORLD WAR II), and the agencies spawned by Roosevelt's NEW DEAL legislation. Though not initially successful, Roosevelt agreed to open thousands of jobs to black workers when the NAACP supported labor leader A. PHILIP RANDOLPH and his March on Washington movement in 1941. Roosevelt also agreed to set up a FAIR EMPLOYMENT PRACTICES COMMITTEE (FEPC) to ensure compliance.

Throughout the 1940s the NAACP saw enormous growth in its membership, claiming nearly 500,000 members by 1946. It continued to act as a legislative and legal advocate, pushing (albeit unsuccessfully) for a federal antilynching law and for an end to state-mandated segregation. By the 1950s the NAACP's LEGAL DEFENSE AND EDUCATIONAL FUND, headed by Marshall, secured the last of these goals through *Brown v. Board of Education* (1954), which outlawed segregation in public schools. The NAACP's Washington, D.C., bureau, led by lobbyist CLARENCE M. MITCHELL, JR., helped advance not only integration of the armed forces in 1948 but also passage of the Civil Rights Acts of 1957, 1964, and 1968, as well as the VOTING RIGHTS ACT OF 1965.

Despite such dramatic courtroom and congressional victories, the implementation of civil rights was a slow, painful, and sometimes violent process. The unsolved 1951 murder of HARRY T. MOORE, an NAACP field secretary in Florida whose home was bombed on Christmas night, was just one of many crimes of retribution against the NAACP and its staff and members during the 1950s. Violence also met black children attempting to enter previously segregated schools in Little Rock, Arkansas, and other Southern cities, and throughout the South many African Americans were still denied the right to register and vote.

The Civil Rights Movement of the 1950s and 1960s echoed the NAACP's moderate, integrationist goals, but leaders such as MARTIN LUTHER KING, JR., of the SOUTHERN CHRISTIAN LEADERSHIP CONFERENCE (SCLC), felt that direct action was needed to obtain them. Though the NAACP was opposed to extralegal popular actions, many of its members, such as Mississippi field secretary MEDGAR EVERS, participated in nonviolent demonstrations such as SIT-INS to protest the persistence of JIM CROW segregation throughout the South. Although it was criticized for working exclusively within the system by pursuing legislative and judicial solutions, the NAACP did provide legal representation and aid to members of more militant protest groups.

Led by ROY WILKINS, who had succeeded Walter White as secretary in 1955, the NAACP cooperated with organizers A. Philip Randolph and BAYARD RUSTIN in planning the 1963 MARCH ON WASHINGTON. With the passage of civil rights legislation the following year, the association had finally accomplished much of its historic legislative agenda. In the following years, the NAACP began to diversify its goals and, in the opinion of many, to lose its focus. Millions of African Americans continued to be afflicted as urban poverty and crime increased, *de facto* racial segregation remained, and job discrimination lingered throughout the United States. With its traditional interracial, integrationist approach, the NAACP found itself attracting fewer members as many African Americans became sympathetic to more militant, even separatist, philosophies, such as that espoused by the Black Power Movement.

Wilkins retired as executive director in 1977 and was replaced by BENJAMIN L. HOOKS, whose tenure included the Bakke case (1978), in which a California court outlawed several aspects of AFFIRMATIVE ACTION. At around the same time tensions between the executive director and the board of directors, tensions that had existed since the association's founding, escalated into open hostility that threatened to weaken the organization. With the 1993 selection of BENJAMIN F. CHAVIS (now Chavis Muhammad) as director, more controversies arose. In an attempt to take the NAACP in new directions, Chavis offended many liberals by reaching out to NATION OF ISLAM leader LOUIS FARRAKHAN. After using NAACP funds to settle a sexual harassment lawsuit, Chavis was forced to resign in 1995 and subsequently joined the Nation of Islam.

In the twenty-first century the NAACP has focused on economic development and educational programs for youth, while also continuing its role as legal advocate for civil rights issues. KWEISI MFUME, former congressman and head of the CONGRESSIONAL BLACK CAUCUS, is president and chief executive officer, and JULIAN BOND is chairman of the board. The organization currently has more than 500,000 members.

See also Antilynching Movement; Black Power in the United States; Desegregation in the United States; Labor Unions in the United States; March on Washington, 1941; NAACP Legal Defense and Educational Fund; Segregation in the United States; Slavery in the United States.

Bibliography

Kluger, Richard. *Simple Justice.* Knopf, 1976.

McNeil, Genna Rae. *Groundwork: Charles Hamilton Houston and the Struggle for Civil Rights.* University of Pennsylvania Press, 1983.

Watson, Denton L. *Lion in the Lobby: Clarence Mitchell, Jr.'s Struggle for the Passage of Civil Rights Laws.* Morrow, 1990.

Kate Tuttle

National Association of Black Journalists

American organization, founded in 1975, of black reporters, editors, and managers of media outlets.

Based in WASHINGTON, D.C., the National Association of Black Journalists (NABJ) encourages black employment in journalism and fair reporting about blacks. The group has used its monthly *NABJ Journal* and its regular conferences to increase communication between black journalists; to monitor and publicize institutionalized racism; and to advocate an increase in the number of blacks who manage newspapers, magazines, and television and radio networks and stations. The NABJ also offers scholarships to young blacks interested in journalism and finances exchanges between African and African American journalists. In 2003 the NABJ had 3,300 members.

See also News Magazines and African Americans; Radio and African Americans; Television and African Americans.

National Association of Colored Women

Organization to advance the cause of African American women.

The familiar slogan of the National Association of Colored Women (NACW), "Lifting As We Climb," sums up its century-long commitment to service, uplift, and advancement in the African American community. The NACW grew out of the network of local black women's clubs and organizations that began to develop in the United States in the late nineteenth century to promote racial progress by providing necessary social services in black communities. These clubs were formed by women who firmly believed that improving conditions in individual black homes would have positive effects on the social, educational, and economic advancement of the entire African American community.

In 1895 a widely reprinted editorial by a white Southerner, which accused black women of being dishonest and immoral, led club leaders across the country to realize that they needed to work together in their efforts to protect and advance the race and the cause of black womanhood. In July of that year, one hundred women from organizations in ten states met in BOSTON to begin planning a national coalition of black women. One year later, the NACW was officially formed. Within a few years the NACW had 5,000 members; by 1916 it had grown to 50,000 members and over 1,000 local clubs.

The slogan "Lifting As We Climb" was coined by the NACW's first president, MARY CHURCH TERRELL, who explained that "self-preservation demands that [black women] go among the lowly to whom they are bound by ties of race and sex," and that NACW members had "determined to come into the closest possible touch with the masses of our women, through whom the womanhood of our people is always judged." This statement points out a key feature of the original black women's club movement: the NACW's members were overwhelmingly middle-class, educated women, and thus in a class and social situation different from many of the women and families for whom their programs were designed to help.

They planned to solve this division by raising as many women as they could to their own level of relative material comfort. Teaching middle-class values became one of their early priorities, and the NACW's first programs included temperance societies and classes on housekeeping and child-rearing. Club members were also dedicated to protecting the most vulnerable members of their communities, the very young and the very old. By the turn of the century, clubs all over the country had begun establishing kindergartens and homes for the aged. These facilities were generally staffed by NACW volunteers, and members held fund-raisers to gain additional money for their projects.

While NACW members believed that the progress of the race could and should begin in the home, they were also fully aware of the constant outside injustices faced daily by black women and men. Club members supported the passage of the Nineteenth Amendment, which gave women the right to vote, and they played a key role in the antilynching campaign of the 1920s. Individual branches also led boycotts of segregated facilities and expressed other protests against racial injustices. By the time prominent activist MARY MCLEOD BETHUNE became president of the NACW in 1924, the organization had grown to 100,000 members, who were involved in social reform programs across the country.

In the next few decades, however, the NACW began to decline in influence. During the GREAT DEPRESSION, the government finally began providing many of the services the black community had received from the NACW. And after Bethune founded the NATIONAL COUNCIL OF NEGRO WOMEN in 1935, the NACW was no longer the only national black women's association. In 1957 the NACW changed its name to the National Association of Colored Women's Clubs (NACWC), and narrowed its focus to educational and social services, such as providing college scholarships for young black women. The NACWC celebrated its centennial in 1996, with approximately 40,000 members in 1,500 clubs, retaining its original commitment to uplifting the black community. It remains the oldest national African American secular organization in existence today.

See also Antilynching Movement; Black Women's Club Movement; Women's Organizations, Early African American.

Lisa Clayton Robinson

National Council of Negro Women

Influential African American women's organization founded by Mary McLeod Bethune.

The National Council of Negro Women (NCNW), one of the largest and most prominent black women's groups of the twentieth century, was the inspiration of civil rights and women's rights leader MARY MCLEOD BETHUNE. In 1924, after almost two decades of activism in clubs and organizations dedicated to black women's issues, Bethune became president of the NATIONAL ASSOCIATION OF COLORED WOMEN (NACW), then the country's leading association of African American women. But five years later, she was announcing her dream of creating a larger coalition of black women's groups, modeled after the mainstream National Council of Women. As Bethune wrote in a letter to her friend MARY CHURCH TERRELL, "Such an organization will, I believe, make for unity of opinion among Negro women who must do some thinking on public questions; it will ensure greater cooperation among women in varied lines of endeavor: and it will lift the ideals not only of the individual organizations, but of the organizations as a group."

After almost six years of planning, Bethune's vision was realized when the NCNW held its founding meeting in HARLEM on December 5, 1935. Several groups were initially hesitant about joining the NCNW, including Bethune's former organization, the NACW, because of fears that it might detract from the prestige or power of individual groups. But representatives from twenty-nine groups, including religious, political, and professional organizations, sororities, and even the NACW, ultimately attended the founding meeting.

Members of the NCNW quickly began to speak out on issues they felt were important to African Americans in general and black women in particular. Their documentation of discriminatory hiring practices in government factories during WORLD WAR II helped lead to the establishment of the national FAIR EMPLOYMENT PRACTICES COMMITTEE. They also fought for the integration of the military and the desegregation of schools and other public facilities. In addition to their work for racial and social equality at home, the NCNW spoke out on international affairs. NCNW delegates were present at the founding of the United Nations, and have since attended all United Nations proceedings as official observers. By the mid-1950s the council's eleven national departments included Archives and Museum, Citizenship Education, Education, Fine Arts, Human Relations, International Relations, Labor and Industry, Public Relations, Religious Education, Social Welfare, and Youth Conservation.

In 1957 DOROTHY HEIGHT became the fourth president of the NCNW. Height has continued to hold that post for more than four decades, and under her administration the NCNW became a nonprofit organization, allowing it to receive grants from such sources as the Ford Foundation and the U.S. Department of Health, Education and Welfare. During the last thirty years the NCNW has sponsored such programs as Operation Sisters United, Youth Career Development, the FANNIE LOU HAMER Day Care Centers, Project Woman Power, the NCNW Leadership Development Project, and the national Black Family Reunion celebrations. In 1975 a grant from the Agency for International Development enabled the NCNW to establish an international department, making it possible for African American women to coordinate their efforts with those of black women across the diaspora. The NCNW was instrumental in the founding of the National Archives for Black Women's History, and in 1974 Height and the NCNW were able to oversee the unveiling of the Bethune Memorial Statue in WASHINGTON, D.C., a long-overdue tribute to the organization's extraordinary founder. In 2003 the NCNW had an outreach to nearly four million women through its thirty-eight national affiliate organizations and 200-plus community based sections.

See also Desegregation in the United States; Women's Organizations, Early African American.

Bibliography

Collier-Thomas, Bettye. *N.C.N.W., 1935–1980*. Holt, Rackham, 1984.

Giddings, Paula. *When and Where I Enter: The Impact of Black Women on Race and Sex in America*. William Morris, 1984.

Lisa Clayton Robinson

National Federation of Afro-American Women

Early African American women's organization that became part of the National Association of Colored Women.

The National Federation of Afro-American Women was an early attempt to unite some of the many black women's organizations that had formed throughout the United States during the nineteenth century. In many cities black women had formed clubs and associations to provide social services for the elderly, young, and poor in their communities. At the same time, black women's clubs worked to uplift the public image of African American womanhood, since black women had long been portrayed as oversexed, unintelligent creatures. In July 1895, after a white editor published a letter in a Missouri newspaper that he then forwarded to papers in the United States and England accusing "all Afro-American women of having no sense of virtue and of being altogether without character," one hundred black women activists from across the country came together for a conference in BOSTON, MASSACHUSETTS to strategize about coordinating their efforts.

The National Federation of Afro-American Women was formed at that meeting. MARGARET MURRAY WASHINGTON, the "lady principal" of TUSKEGEE INSTITUTE and wife of educator BOOKER TALIAFERRO WASHINGTON, became its first president, and thirty-six clubs from twelve states joined the federation. But even as the federation was beginning its work, the National League of Colored Women (NLCW), a similar organization, was founded in WASHINGTON, D.C. In an effort to return to the goal of national cooperation, in 1896 the National Federation of Afro-American Women and the NLCW merged to form the National Association of Colored Women (NACW), which remains active today.

See also Black Women's Club Movement.

Lisa Clayton Robinson

Nationalism in Africa

Efforts toward establishing national sovereignties in Africa unfettered by colonial rule.

Between 1951 and 1980 nationalist movements toppled European colonial governments throughout AFRICA. The names of these movements' leaders are legendary: KWAME NKRUMAH in GHANA, GAMAL ABDEL NASSER in EGYPT, JOMO KENYATTA in KENYA, Léopold Senghor in SENEGAL, JULIUS NYERERE in TANZANIA, AMÍLCAR CABRAL in GUINEA-BISSAU, and NELSON MANDELA in SOUTH AFRICA. More recently, in 1993 ERITREA won a decades-long struggle for independence from ETHIOPIA, arguably showing that nationhood is still a viable goal for African regions seeking political autonomy.

African nationalism was born out of opposition to the injustices of COLONIAL RULE and thus was inseparable from the struggle for decolonization. Since race had provided European powers with a rationale for colonial domination, racial identification was one important source of anticolonial solidarity and nation building—but it was certainly not the only source. Participants in independence struggles sought to reclaim appropriated lands, rid themselves of poverty and burdensome taxation, and gain the civil liberties enjoyed by citizens of the colonizing countries themselves—England, FRANCE, PORTUGAL, Belgium, ITALY, and (on much smaller scales) GERMANY and SPAIN.

The advantages of national sovereignty were debated among African leaders, particularly in France's colonies in West and Central Africa. There leaders such as Léopold Senghor of Senegal and FÉLIX HOUPHOUËT-BOIGNY of the CÔTE D'IVOIRE advocated not complete independence but rather "association" with France (a comparable option was not given to the English colonies). These leaders had enjoyed the privileges accorded to *assimilés* (French-speaking Africans whose education qualified them for French citizenship) and believed their countries would benefit both economically and strategically from continued close ties with France and neighboring Francophone territories. In 1958 French President Charles de Gaulle allowed France's African colonies to vote on their proposed membership in an international French community of semi-autonomous countries; all but GUINEA voted in favor of the revised political alliance.

Although Guinea's 1958 vote was anomalous—and owed much to the charisma and organizing talents of labor activist and political leader SÉKOU TOURÉ—the aspirations of the colony's people to achieve independence were not unique. The motivation for decolonization was in part economic: Touré's movement depended on convincing Guinea's peasants, market women, wageworkers, and youth—all citizens who had never enjoyed opulence under colonial rule anyway—that they could only ultimately escape poverty if their colony achieved independence. But when Touré proclaimed, "We prefer poverty in freedom to opulence in slavery," he underscored the fact that it was the desire for autonomy that ultimately propelled nationalist movements throughout Africa.

Nationalism in Africa

Scholars have long debated the meaning of African nationalism. For many years the dominant view was that nationalism was a European political ideal promoted by Africa's westernized, educated elite. According to the dominant view, this elite used the European concept of the nation to forge unity among disparate African groups and thereby build a cohesive resistance to colonialism. This analysis is certainly well founded. Nineteenth-century African social reformers such as James Africanus Horton in SIERRA LEONE and EDWARD WILMOT BLYDEN in LIBERIA as well as twentieth-century political theorists like ALBERT MEMMI, FRANTZ FANON, and Amílcar Cabral were educated in Europe or at least studied European texts. Colonialism introduced to Africa European versions of CHRISTIANITY, modernity, SOCIALISM, democracy, and citizenship. It also brought irreversible changes: borders partitioned the continent into distinct colonial states; mining, plantation agriculture, and urbanization transformed the landscape; and new communication and transportation systems brought together once-distant communities. Unable to reverse the changes brought by colonial rule, Africans sought a new model for the organization of their society, one that would be recognized in the international arena that colonization had introduced. The nation provided that.

But clearly, Western-educated elite were not the only participants in nationalist movements. To understand nationalism in Africa, we must examine the forms of mass mobilization behind the political motivations and parties—the movements that stood behind the famous names. Two strains of grassroots resistance stand out in Africa's history of nationalist struggle. The first type of resistance drew its inspiration from identities forged before and during the colonial period—identities based on ethnicity, religion, and language in particular. This resistance mobilized to reclaim or reinstate places or institutions considered crucial to those identities, such as sacred homelands or preexisting forms of political and spiritual authority. The second type of resistance came out of the labor movements, whose members included railroad workers, miners, civil servants, and dockworkers as well as agricultural workers. These movements mobilized to claim the rights demanded by workers worldwide, such as fair wages, pensions, and equal employment opportunities. The different kinds of resistance movements sometimes clashed over methods and goals, but moments of unity—or at least collaboration—between them convinced the European powers that decolonization was inevitable.

Identity and Nationalism in Libya and Kenya

The history of LIBYA provides a clear example of a struggle for independent statehood that drew its power from traditional identity, in this case the religious identity of Islam. Libyan nationalism was expressed in three arenas. There was an urban-based movement in the city of TRIPOLI and an Egyptian-based

Kenya's prime minister Jomo Kenyatta is shown here with former Mau Mau field marshall Mwariama on the eve of independence in 1963. *CORBIS/Bettmann*

pan-Arab movement, which by 1950 was attracting support in several parts of North Africa. But the Islamic brotherhood of the Sanusi order arguably provided the most important foundation for anticolonial resistance. Founded in the nineteenth century, prior to colonization, the brotherhood constructed lodges and schools throughout the Cyrenaica region that became gathering places for residents and long-distance caravan traders alike. The gathering places were much more than simply meeting points, and the social and political structure they provided helped create a cohesive regional identity that would later prove a persistent source of resistance to Italian colonial control.

Nationalists in the city of Tripoli had lived under a European-controlled economy and held a more secular, republican ideal of the nation than did the leaders of the Sanusi order. Nevertheless, the Tripolitanians saw the advantage of cooperation with the powerful Sanusi, and so in 1922 they appointed the head of the order, IDRIS I, as the leader of their collective nationalist movement.

After independence in 1951 Idris assumed the throne of the United Kingdom of Libya, but the idea of a republic was not forgotten. The successful challenge to the monarchy came from a coup led by MUAMMAR AL-QADDAFI that drew upon pan-Arab sentiments generated by Gamal Abdel Nasser's revolution in neighboring Egypt. Thus in Libya two traditional political and cultural movements identified with Islam played dominant roles in both the anticolonial struggle and the establishment of a republic.

In Kenya, as in Libya, the nationalist movement was not homogeneous. But cultural identity played a crucial role in the KIKUYU people's anticolonial struggle, which culminated in an event the British referred to as the MAU MAU REBELLION. Beginning in the late 1940s the Kikuyu guerrilla movement began with uprisings on Kikuyu reservations around the country and sporadic violence against white settlers' plantations that had appropriated prime Kikuyu farmland. The group's goals were expanded, however, and they began to fight for an end to British colonial rule. The colonial government responded with a declaration of emergency, mass arrests, and military force. Over 80,000 people were detained and 11,000 killed in the conflict, among them only about one hundred Europeans.

The Kikuyu movement used oaths, songs, and prayers to unite and mobilize its members in a culturally meaningful way. To the British colonial government, however, the oath-taking simply proved that Mau Mau adherents were barbaric, and that their violence represented an atavistic protest against progress. Not all Kikuyu supported Mau Mau; indeed, those Kikuyu who had benefited themselves by taking on colonial administration duties under British rule (known as Loyalists) were among the guerrillas' main victims.

It is important to realize that the Kikuyu-dominated Mau Mau uprising was not the only expression of anticolonialism in Kenya. Other regional rural rebellions, moderate urban-based political associations, and labor unions also contributed to the anticolonial cause. Yet as historian Frederick Cooper has observed, even the groups that sought a constitution based on a Western model invoked the "discipline and patience of the Kikuyu elder" as model qualities for political activism. Thus the parallel movements retained, or at least acknowledged, the traditional Kikuyu principles—in this case following the wisdom of respected elders. The man who finally took up the nationalist banner, Jomo Kenyatta, was himself a Kikuyu but headed a multiethnic political party, the Kenya Africa Union, and considered himself a Pan-Africanist. Yet Kenyatta's own scholarly work on the history and culture of the Kikuyu, published in his 1938 monograph, *Facing Mount Kenya*, provided early evidence of how important ethnic identity was to Kenyans' perspectives on their new nation-state.

Labor and Nationalist Movements

The rise of labor movements as vehicles of nationalist mobilization corresponded with the rapid expansion of both colonial bureaucracies and import/export infrastructures during and after WORLD WAR II. Workers protested both colonial labor policies and broader economic conditions. During the war workers found themselves caught between shortages of imported goods and high inflation on the one hand and an acceleration of export production on the other; profits derived from the increased production benefited only the colonizers and a small group of indigenous elite. As a result, a wave of strikes swept through many colonies. Wartime labor protests included major strikes by miners and industrial workers in the British Copperbelt colonies. For example, in 1935 a wave of strikes spread through the mines in NORTHERN RHODESIA.

Soon after World War II the labor movements gained momentum, fueled both by the rising expectations of mission-educated, urban-based civil servants and the challenging idealism of veterans returned from service abroad. The year 1945 saw a large-scale strike in DAKAR, SENEGAL, and a colony-wide strike of government and railway workers that paralyzed NIGERIA for a month. Two years later, railway workers organized a massive transnational strike in FRENCH WEST AFRICA, a protest immortalized by OUSMANE SEMBÈNE's novel *God's Bits of Wood*. In the same period a wave of strikes swept through East Africa's port cities, including MOMBASA, KENYA (1947); DAR ES SALAAM, TANZANIA (1947); and ZANZIBAR (1948).

Although these strikes were prompted by immediate economic concerns, they also challenged the fundamental terms of colonial labor policies and, by extension, colonial rule itself. For example, as Cooper points out, negotiations regarding a minimum wage in Dakar brought into question the different standards of living available to Africans and Europeans. This forced the French to face the inherent contradiction between their racially stratified colonial labor policies and their rhetoric of assimilation. As one African labor negotiator in Saint-Louis put it, "Your goal is to elevate us to your level; without the means, we will never succeed."

Although most union leaders were educated, male, and often from relatively elite backgrounds, their movements needed—and found—community support. According to Cooper, "Each of these strike movements took place in a particular milieu, and it was the ability of workers to draw on the resources and solidarity of communities that made them so effective." Social connections provided an important basis for the organization of these strikes; the early protests, such as the one in RHODESIA in 1935, were organized through social connections and religious organizations rather than trade unions. In the 1947 Mombasa strike, for example, word of protests spread through the Swahili-speaking area where most of the workers lived. Tapping into local channels of communication, such as meetings in homes and dance societies, the labor struggle spread as a truly grass-roots movement. Later these channels were formalized, with mass assemblies called to organize the protests.

The history of nationalism in Ghana provides one of the best examples of the nexus between the labor movement and the nationalist movement. Between 1937 and 1947, Ghana, then called the GOLD COAST, witnessed a series of small strikes, most of which were led by former servicemen returned from service in World War II. The unrest culminated in 1947 with a wave of strikes involving over 46,000 workers from the railway, gold mines, and other industrial sectors. During the same period farmers protested government intervention in COCOA production. To protest goods shortages and high prices, Nii Kwabena Bonne II, a local chief turned businessman, organized a wide-scale, urban boycott of European- and Syrian-owned businesses in ACCRA, KUMASI, and other cities. At the same time leaders such as Kwame Nkrumah were going further and articulating nationalist agendas.

The British colonial governments, which had originally viewed African trade unions with suspicion, soon realized that organized unions with which they could negotiate presented a far less threatening possibility than mass mobilization for independence. As a result, by 1948 the British sought to invest official bargaining power in trade unions that did not espouse overtly political agendas. In some cases the British revised their opinions about unions previously considered hostile. The United Gold Coast Convention (UGCC), which distanced itself from more militant urban workers, was one such union to come into British favor.

As the labor movement split in the late 1940s between those in favor of labor reform and those who sought full decolonization, many of these militant urban workers ultimately threw their lot in with Nkrumah and the Convention People's Party (CPP). Railway union leaders Anthony Woode and Pobee Biney allied themselves with this group, helping to build massive popular support for the nationalist cause. Over the next ten years Nkrumah led the nationalist demonstrations and elections that dismantled the British colonial state in 1957.

In the Portuguese colonies large-scale labor movements developed in the 1950s. Responding to the fascist Portuguese ruler António Salazar's harsh colonial labor practices, including forced labor, labor organizers in Guinea-Bissau allied with the growing antifascist movement in Portugal itself, which included communist groups. Nationalists organized around labor struggles led by Amílcar Cabral's Partido Africano da Independencia da Guine e Cabo Verde (PAIGC) (1956), staging a series of general strikes. The PAIGC's size and militancy grew in 1959 after Portuguese troops massacred striking dockworkers in BISSAU. Four years later the PAIGC's guerrilla actions exploded into full-scale anticolonial war in Guinea-Bissau, with clandestine operations based on the islands. The PIAGC ultimately won independence in Guinea-Bissau in 1974, and in CAPE VERDE a year later.

Contemporary Nationalism

Once independence had been achieved, many of Africa's postcolonial governments invoked their national identities to justify their administration's agendas. Many of the changes were made in the name of economic development, with approaches varying from the socialism of Guinea and Tanzania to the free-market path of Côte d'Ivoire. All too often African bureaucratic or military elite leaders proved as despotic and unaccountable as the colonial administrations they replaced. Some postcolonial regimes outlawed the organizations that had helped win the nationalist struggles. In Libya, for example, the Sanusi order was outlawed under Qaddafi and its role suppressed in official history books. In Guinea, Touré had enormous popular support when he became the country's first president in 1958, but during the 1970s thousands fled the country in response to the police and army brutality of his paranoid, one-party regime. Although labor unions continued to exercise a degree of political clout in a number of countries—such as Ghana and its northern neighbor UPPER VOLTA (now BURKINA FASO)—economic stagnation in the years after independence highlighted the fact that the unions of urban wage- and salary workers represented only a fraction of the population in these countries. Many people lived in rural areas and did not benefit at all from policies aimed at pacifying the "labor elite." In Kenya, as in several other countries where ethnic identity had informed nationalist movements, postcolonial political groups were quickly divided along tribal lines.

In short, many of the ideals of the nationalist struggles proved more difficult to achieve than independence itself.

Since the end of the Cold War and the speedup of economic globalization, political turmoil both in Africa and elsewhere has led many to question the meaning of nationalism and the future of the nation-state. But these concepts have not lost relevance in Africa. In South Africa the AFRICAN NATIONAL CONGRESS finally achieved its long-standing goal: the transformation of the nation to one in which all races are afforded equal rights. In Central Africa LAURENT-DÉSIRÉ KABILA's 1997 overthrow of Zairean dictator MOBUTU SESE SEKO proved that an era of Cold War-enforced balances of power in the region had definitely ended. But one of Kabila's first actions as self-proclaimed president was to change the country's name from ZAIRE—a name associated with Mobutu since he chose it for the former Belgian colony in 1965—to the DEMOCRATIC REPUBLIC OF THE CONGO. Whether or not Kabila had any intention of establishing a democracy soon became questionable, but by changing the name of the entire country he demonstrated that the image of national liberator was still significant in contemporary Africa. Finally, when tensions over trade and a disputed border between Eritrea and Ethiopia erupted into a thirty-month armed conflict (1998–2000), the two countries—whose citizenries are linked by language, religion, and even family ties—justified their actions as the defense of national sovereignty. All these events demonstrate that national movements and national identity remain dynamic concepts in contemporary Africa.

See also Africa, Decolonization of; African Socialism; Decolonization in Africa: An Interpretation; Development in Africa: An Interpretation; Ethnicity and Identity in Africa: An Interpretation; Globalization and Africa: An Interpretation; Islam in Africa; Urbanism and Urbanization in Africa.

Marian Aguiar

Nationalism in Latin America and the Caribbean

See Nationalist Movements and Blacks in Latin America and the Caribbean.

Nationalist Movements and Blacks in Latin America and the Caribbean

Interaction between national identity and blackness in Latin America and the Caribbean, central to an understanding of the region's history.

As a result of the slave trade, in which millions of Africans were brought over to work on the plantations, blacks form a majority (or an important minority of over 10 percent of the population) in the following areas: virtually all of the Caribbean islands; the Central American countries of BELIZE, NICARAGUA, and PANAMA; and northeastern South America, including BRAZIL, COLOMBIA, VENEZUELA, GUYANA, SURINAME, FRENCH GUIANA, ECUADOR, and PERU.

In many of these countries, peoples of African descent have had a considerable role in forging, defining, and determining the goals of nationalist movements. While some movements have been openly political in their aims, others have distinguished themselves through predominantly cultural or religious modes of resistance. In most cases, these movements have had to contend with repressive colonial regimes and, later, repressive autocratic governments. Indeed, political leaders, threatened by burgeoning revolution or a challenge to their definition of national unity, have resorted to violence, ideological manipulation, and appropriation of black cultural forms to suit their own national agenda. As a result, the region's blacks and African-descended populations have had to struggle not only for social, political, and economic equality, but also for the preservation of their African-derived cultural and religious traditions.

This survey will consider three of the region's countries: BRAZIL, CUBA, and JAMAICA. Both Brazil and Cuba continued to receive African slaves until the late 1880s; this reinforced the African influences in these countries and left a profound imprint on the developing conception of the nation. Yet, despite the considerable presence of blacks in Brazil and Cuba, national identity in these countries has often been defined by white Creoles: people of European descent born in the Americas. In Jamaica the institution of slavery was abolished by the British colonizers in 1834. Yet Jamaica did not gain independence from GREAT BRITAIN until 1962—a reality that has had a marked and lasting influence on the formation of national identity. Although around 90 percent of the population is of African ancestry, many middle- and upper-class Jamaicans identify strongly with Great Britain as a source of cultural leadership, while they express a deep ambivalence toward their African heritage. Jamaica's black working class, on the other hand, played a major role in spawning the radical, militant, black nationalism that propelled Jamaica to the forefront of the black movement worldwide.

Brazil

In 1798 Brazilian blacks and mulattos instigated what is arguably one of the first pre-nationalist movements, aimed at freeing parts of Brazil from Portuguese rule. The "Tailors' Conspiracy" (1798) occurred in BAHIA, where two out of three residents were black or mulatto. It was led by the mulatto tailor João de Deus do Nascimento and involved merchants, soldiers, clerics, black slaves, and a large number of free mulattos. Indeed, the conspirators' manifesto claimed that the movement included more than 650 adherents. Inspired by the French Revolution, the Bahian plotters promised to end slavery and to establish a Bahian republic based on freedom, equality, and fraternity. The Portuguese authorities swiftly crushed the plot: thirty-three conspirators, including Nascimento, who was hanged and quartered, were executed or exiled to Africa. "The clear objective," noted scholar Dauril Alden, "was to convince persons of African origin of the futility of seeking to alter their status by radical means and to reassure the dominant white colonials that as long as they supported the existing regime, Brazil would not become another Saint-Domingue (present-day HAITI)." Nonetheless, the conspiracy instilled in the Brazilian elite a fear of burgeoning revolution, and thus contributed to paving the way for independence in 1822.

The conditions of black slaves changed little under monarchical rule (1809–1889). The half-hearted attempts by Emperor Pedro II to eradicate slavery were ineffective. Mass slave uprisings, such as the Cabanagem revolt (1834–1840) in Pará province, were violently repressed. Nonetheless, the monarchy, fearing a social revolution and reprisals by foreign governments and feeling the effects of the British-enforced ban on the TRANSATLANTIC SLAVE TRADE, finally abolished slavery in 1888. A year later the monarchy was replaced by a secular federal republic. Under the new federal system, the wealthier states located in the Center-South prospered, while the poorer regions, subjected to the arbitrary rule of local landowners, fell increasingly into decline.

It was in the impoverished backlands of Canudos, in northeastern Brazil, that the Roman Catholic lay preacher Antônio Conselheiro founded the holy settlement of Belo Monte. The settlement, made up of mud dwellings scattered throughout a mountain-ringed valley, included mainly peasants of mixed African, European, and Indian descent, who centered their lives around pastoral and religious activities. Although the settlement remained linked to the regional economy through trade, it became self-sufficient enough to free its inhabitants from exploitation by local landowners. Indeed, visiting journalists were astonished to see that Belo Monte had its own water cisterns, warehouses, schools, stockpiles of weapons, and churches. The settlement also provided a haven from police violence in the Brazilian backlands. By 1896 the community had grown to nearly 20,000 inhabitants.

Conselheiro, who was seen as a wise councilor by many northeastern peasants, had led the life of a nomadic preacher. His sermons, delivered in public squares, mainly addressed moral and work issues and were heavily laden with the millennialism that had often characterized folk Roman Catholicism in rural Brazil. He was also known for his scathing denunciations of slavery, his criticism of the new republic, and open advocacy of a return to monarchy. Yet local officials, fearful of Conselheiro's increasing influence in the region, portrayed him as a seditious anti-Republican and revolutionary fanatic. The Roman Catholic hierarchy, which disapproved of the independent initiatives of its priests, also sought to curtail his activities.

In November 1896 the Brazilian government began a series of military assaults on the Canudos settlement. Although the settlers fought to the very end, Belo Monte was eventually destroyed. A few thousand settlers died in the fighting, while many more managed to escape. The government justified its decision by stating that Belo Monte was an enclave of ethnically degenerate criminals and fanatics who posed a threat to the nation itself. Moreover, as scholar Robert M. Levine affirms in *Father of the Poor: Vargas and His Era* (1998), the settlement "affected two major elements of rural oligarchical power: the docile labor system and the 'herd vote' (*voto de cabresto*), the Old Republic's arrangement whereby rural bosses captured all of the votes under their control and delivered them in exchange for local power. Out migration from all parts of the backlands to Canudos posed an immediate, real threat to the system."

Levine has argued that "Canudos represented a trauma that raised far-reaching questions about Brazil's national identity and racial composition," particularly as the new republican government "rested on a national population 85 percent illiterate and mostly living in misery." Indeed, in 1902 Brazilian journalist Euclides da Cunha published a book on Canudos, *Os sertões* (Rebellion in the Backlands). The book became a widely influential interpretation of the rebellion during most of the twentieth century, and indeed a treatise on Brazilian national identity. While da Cunha lauded the peasants for their tenacity and individualism, he considered them racially degenerate and portrayed Canudos as "a clash between urban progress and rural backwardness in the early republican years." Da

Cunha's views, like those of the Brazilian elite generally during this time, were strongly influenced by the late nineteenth-century ideology of racial determinism that equated dark skin with degeneracy. One mulatto academic, RAIMUNDO NINA RODRIGUES, later claimed that Canudos was the product of "the fetishistic belief of the African deeply rooted in our population."

During the early twentieth century, the Brazilian elite continued to espouse the concept of racial determinism as a justification for virtually excluding blacks from the labor market. Despite the abolition of slavery, which freed a large pool of skilled Afro-Brazilian laborers, the Brazilian government encouraged a mass influx of European immigrants into Brazil. This policy was intended not only to marginalize blacks, who, emboldened by centuries of servitude, often refused the slave-like working conditions that their immigrant counterparts accepted, but also to diminish the African influence in Brazilian society through interracial marriage.

Nowhere was this policy more vigorously pursued than in São Paulo, Brazil's industrial capital, which was then the third-largest black population after RIO DE JANEIRO and MINAS GERAIS. Efforts by immigrant labor leaders to forge a unified labor movement that promoted racial equality among workers were swiftly counteracted by employers, who used the mass of unemployed blacks to break strikes, keep wages low, and undermine union activities. The gap between immigrant and Afro-Brazilian workers widened: by the early 1900s, European laborers virtually dominated São Paulo's labor market, while job opportunities for Afro-Brazilians continued to dwindle. As scholar George Reid Andrews noted, "blacks were almost completely barred from factory work, and black artisans had virtually disappeared from the city."

By the 1920s, however, European immigrant workers had begun collectively to bargain for better wages and working conditions, to the dismay of the Paulista elite. Afro-Brazilians once again found favor in the manual labor market—a development that led to greater economic mobility and thus increasing social differentiation within the black population. With the rise to power of President Getúlio Vargas in 1930, the position of urban-based Afro-Brazilians continued to improve. The Vargas regime briefly attempted to establish a representative democracy in Brazil, and in 1931 black professionals forged the FRENTE NEGRA BRAZILEIRA (Black Brazilian Front, or FNB). This political party developed into what Afro-Brazilian scholar and activist Lélia Gonzalez called "the greatest Black mass movement ever achieved in Brazil." Along with denouncing racial discrimination, the FNB sought to "develop 'buy black' campaigns, employment opportunities, schools, and political and even paramilitary organizations within Afro-Brazilian communities." However, Gonzalez also notes that the FNB leadership was authoritarian and paternalistic towards blacks. Limited in its overall perspective on the dynamics of race relations in Brazil, she argues, the FNB "failed to perceive the necessity of challenging the contradiction of the system itself . . . [and] did not fight for the inclusion of Blacks" into the labor market.

Following the establishment of the authoritarian "Estado Novo" dictatorship in 1937, the Vargas regime banned all opposition parties. The regime continued to formulate policies that reinforced racial discrimination while promoting the idea, developed by the sociologist GILBERTO FREYRE of Brazil, of a "racial democracy." Ideological manipulation, combined with the introduction of labor legislation favorable to blacks, allowed the regime to co-opt the black movement; indeed, many blacks transferred their allegiance from the defunct FNB to Vargas's newly created Brazilian Labor Party (PTB). Black opposition groups continued to exist, but, as scholar Michael George Hanchard affirmed, now "had to couch their language . . . in indirect, ambiguous and fragmented forms under the veil of cultural practice, and even then, according to state and elite definitions of what constituted Afro-Brazilian and Brazilian culture."

During the 1940s a new group of Afro-Brazilian professionals emerged in São Paulo and Rio de Janeiro, a development that contributed to further widening the gap between working-class and relatively well-to-do blacks. Brazilian intellectuals, both black and white, created Brazil's first institutes and centers for the study of Afro-Brazilian culture. Such institutions sought to propagate the "racial democracy" myth and integrate Afro-Brazilian cultural practices into Brazil's emergent national identity. They also served the political elite: while the Vargas regime selectively raised such Afro-Brazilian practices as the annual CARNIVAL celebration and SAMBA music to the level of a national institution, it suppressed others, such as Afro-Brazilian religions and institutions. Although some Afro-Brazilian artists and professionals created their own cultural organizations, the majority of them remained unconcerned about race and class issues in the labor market.

During the 1960s and early 1970s, cultural expression remained the central vehicle of protest for the majority of Afro-Brazilian activists. The Black Soul movement in Rio de Janeiro, for example, was inspired by the SOUL MUSIC of African Americans and the means of protest that accompanied it. While some scholars have minimized the importance of Black Soul in Brazil because of its origin in the United States, others have shown to what extent the movement significantly challenged the image of national unity propagated by the Brazilian elite. As Hanchard notes, "Because it was independent of white elite definitions of both national 'Brazlianness' and Afro-Brazilian cultural practice, as well as resistant to appropriations by white elites, Black Soul was subject to criticism and, ultimately, repressed." Gilberto Freyre, fearing that black soul might lead to a full-fledged Afro-Brazilian protest movement, considered it a threat to both national identity and security.

During the late 1970s the military government of Ernesto Geisel (1974–1979) initiated an *abertura democratica* (transition to democracy), seeking to gradually shift away from the military rule that was instituted in 1964 by the enacting measures to establish the "rule of law" and basic civil liberties. Press censorship was lifted, many political prisoners were granted amnesty, the officially sanctioned two-party system was replaced, and the judicial basis for Brazil's institutions of repression, namely the internal security police, was abolished. Some critics saw the abertura as simply another, more subtle, form of authoritarianism. Nonetheless, a black political movement began to reemerge and develop in response to such international developments as the American CIVIL RIGHTS MOVEMENT and the liberation of black Africa from colonial rule.

The MOVIMENTO NEGRO UNIFICADO (Unified Black Movement, MNU) became the dominant black political movement of the 1980s. The MNU was founded in June 1978 in São Paulo in direct response to the torture and murder in police custody of black worker Robson Silveira da Luz. What distinguished the MNU from its predecessors was its militant focus on issues of race, class, and gender within the black movement. MNU activists set up state coordinating committees throughout Brazil, established action groups in villages, prisons, FAVELAS (squatter settlements), and forged links with enterprises, and with CANDOMBLÉ and UMBANDA temples. MNU groupings were also created within the leftist Partido dos Trabalhadores (Workers Party, PT).

Although the MNU succeeded in pushing racial issues to the forefront of public debate in Brazil, it never attained the momentum of the U.S. Civil Rights Movement. The MNU had little effect on the outcome of elections in Brazil, as the majority of blacks had long been excluded from the country's political life. Moreover, a lack of financial resources, combined with the proliferation of competing Afro-Brazilian organizations, prevented the MNU from becoming the overarching leadership body it once aspired to be. Finally, the MNU's systematic efforts to counter the "racial democracy" myth left it mired in academic debates at the expense of grassroots activism.

Since the late 1980s an increasing number of grassroots Afro-Brazilian activists, such as PT congresswoman BENEDITA DA SILVA, have sought positions of authority within local and national government institutions. With direct access to state funding and the decision-making process, black politicians have been able to lobby on behalf of specific communities, such as the favelas of Rio de Janeiro. However, whether Afro-Brazilians will be able to create an integrated and sustainable mass black movement remains to be seen.

Cuba

The involvement of blacks in Cuba's independence movements has been central to the forging of a Cuban national identity, the earliest seeds of which can be found in black participation in such anticolonial rebellions as the CONSPIRACIÓN DE LA ESCALERA (Ladder Conspiracy) in 1843. The Ladder Conspiracy is particularly notable not only because of its magnitude and level of planning, but also because it incited leading members of Cuba's sugar plantation oligarchy—fearful of a replay of the HAITIAN REVOLUTION in Cuba—to call for the abolition of the slave trade. The conspiracy, plotted from a Matanzas plantation, allegedly included a large number of slaves, as well as whites and free blacks. Officials based their suspicion of the plot on the testimony of a female slave, and in 1844 the Cuban government arrested nearly 2,000 people, including the mulatto poet GABRIEL DE LA CONCEPCIÓN VALDÉS. While free persons were imprisoned or exiled, the slaves were executed or brutally flogged. Yet Matanzas' slaves continued to rebel against the landowners. In 1866 the government had to deploy troops to several Matanzas estates to force the slaves, who had refused to labor without pay, to return to work.

During that same year Cuban pro-independence activists initiated the Guerra de los Diez Años (THE TEN YEARS' WAR, 1868–1878). Early leaders of the independence movement included mainly small and middle-level landowners and professionals, many of whom fell under the conservative influence of disgruntled reformists—proslavery landowners who had failed to convince Spain to grant them greater social and economic autonomy. Annexationists, who had promoted the incorporation of Cuba into the United States as a means of preserving slavery, also joined the independence movement.

However, by 1871 the revolution had become decidedly pro-abolitionist—a development reflecting the overall makeup of the independence movement, whose rank-and-file included mainly slaves, laborers, and peasants, while more than 70 percent of the Independence Army consisted of blacks and mulattos. Indeed, the latter soon came to play a central role in the leadership of the movement. Such black and mulatto leaders as Vicente García, Antonio and José Maceo, Guillermón Moncada, and Quintin Bandera rose to the level of military chiefs. Yet the conservative wing of the movement opposed the growing ascendancy of blacks in the military—a reaction that contributed significantly to the failure of the war, which concluded in 1878 with the treaty Pacto del Zanjón.

During the early 1880s the Cuban elite introduced capitalist modes of economic development in the sugar industry that led to the abolition of slavery in 1886. The Cuban landowning class was progressively displaced by U.S. capital. Cuban blacks and mulattos, who in 1887 made up about 32 percent of the population, soon composed a substantial portion of the working class. Subjected to racial discrimination and segregation, as well as job competition from Spanish immigrants—imported by the Cuban government with the aim of "WHITENING" the population—Cuban blacks once again took up the struggle for equality.

Among the leading architects of the burgeoning independence movement was the radical thinker JOSÉ MARTÍ, exiled from Cuba for several decades for his political views. In 1892, while residing in New York, Martí drafted the first constitution of the Partido Revolucionario Cubano (Cuban Revolutionary Party, PRC). He collaborated with the PRC delegate in Cuba, JUAN GUALBERTO GÓMEZ, who was the son of slaves, to raise funds and garner support for the movement, organized around the sociedades de color (societies of colored people). With the onset of the War of Independence in 1895, Gómez, Martí, and Antonio Maceo, the hero of the Ten Years' War, took the lead. Maceo became the general of the Liberation Army, comprised mainly of blacks and mulattos, although he was apparently prevented from becoming the military leader of the movement because of his skin color.

Following the death of Martí and Maceo in battle, reformists and annexationists within the movement collaborated with the U.S. government to bring an abrupt end to the war. In 1898

U.S. troops entered Cuba. Cuban freedom fighters were swiftly forced into obscurity, while the sovereignty of Cuba was handed—via the Paris Treaty—from the Spanish to the Americans. In 1901 Cuba was turned into a protectorate of the United States, which allowed the latter considerable influence over domestic affairs. The U.S. presence also resulted in the establishment of a racist social order: the politics of whitening continued, while Cuban history was rewritten to avoid reference to Afro-Cuban leaders. Blacks were systematically excluded from positions of power as well as from artistic, literary, and musical life—spheres largely dominated by white middle-class artists, who looked down on black and working-class forms of expression. At the same time, selective Afro-Cuban cultural forms, such as the *danzon,* were appropriated and elevated by the elite to a national institution.

Yet Cuban blacks did not give up their struggle for a just society. A black movement developed in Cuba, culminating in 1908 in the founding of the PARTIDO INDEPENDIENTE DE COLOR (Party of Independent Colored People). Under the leadership of Evaristo Estenoz, the Independientes aimed to fulfill the republican aspirations of the 1895 revolutionaries. Barred from electoral politics, the Independientes staged an armed rebellion in 1912, which was brutally suppressed by the Cuban government—with the help of U.S. troops—and resulted in the death of more than 3,000 blacks and mulattos.

During the 1920s, increasing national tensions, due to a protracted economic crisis and a surge in political repression under the rule of Gerardo Machado (1924–1933), led to the creation of several prominent organizations aimed at protesting the established order as well as U.S. dominance in the region. Among these organizations was the Partido Comunista de Cuba (Cuban Communist Party), founded in 1925. Proclaiming itself the defender of the predominantly black and mulatto working class, the Partido Comunista took up many of the grievances expressed earlier by the Independientes de Color. According to scholars Gayle McGarrity and Osvaldo Cárdenas, it was the "only political grouping [of its time] in which black Cubans were present to a significant degree." In 1933 the Partido Comunista played a central role in the overthrow of the Machado dictatorship. Three of its members, the Cuban blacks Lázaro Peña, Jesús Menéndez, and Aracelio Iglesia, subsequently became the leaders of the trade union movement.

The 1920s and 1930s also saw the development of AFROCUBANISMO, an artistic and literary movement that looked to Cuba's urban black culture both as a basis for new art forms and as a symbol of Cuban national identity. The movement arose as a direct response to the persistent hegemony of the United States in the region. While some artists sought inspiration in Afro-Cuban musical forms, others focused on the social dimensions of the Cuban black. However, the popularity of Afro-Cuban cultural forms did not engender a social acceptance of Cuban blacks, who remained subject to widespread poverty, segregation, and exclusion from both the political sphere and skilled labor market. Indeed, it seemed to the vast majority of blacks that white Cubans were more interested in them as cultural symbols than as equal participants in Cuban society.

The success of the Cuban Revolution in 1959—a feat accomplished with the help of black and mulatto activists—brought with it deep changes in Cuba's social and economic order: for the first time the black men and women "gained access to most workplaces and to education, as well as to recreational institutions." Yet, although communist leaders effectively attacked the ideological foundation of racism in Cuba, their strivings for national unity later led them to suppress debate on race relations. A group of black professionals who endeavored to openly address racial issues in the late 1960s were branded as counter revolutionaries by the state, while black protest groups of the 1970s, such as the RASTAFARIANS, were at times subject to police repression.

McGarrity and Cárdenas have argued that "in Cuba there has been relatively little development of a progressive consciousness of racism and of anti-racist strategies, perhaps partly because of the island's relative isolation from the international BLACK POWER and BLACK CONSCIOUSNESS movements" of the 1960s and 1970s. As the Cuban state did not acknowledge the relevance of these movements to Cuba, those blacks—primarily intellectuals and professionals—who did have access to the movements' ideas were given little opportunity to debate them in public. Today, blacks continue to make up a substantial portion of Cuba's low-income class. Education and elite culture remain strongly influenced by European traditions, while Cubans who are socially defined as white continue to dominate the country's political life.

Jamaica

Contemporary nationalist movements in Jamaica reflect forms of resistance that date back to the maroon settlements—communities of African slaves, who, following the British defeat of the Spaniards in 1655, escaped to the mountains, where they waged guerrilla warfare against the British colonizers. Because the British troops could not easily penetrate the settlements that were surrounded by rugged terrain, the maroons were able to preserve a measure of autonomy within the plantation system. Yet following the first Maroon War (1729–1739), the British granted the Maroons a limited freedom: they were allowed their own lands and leaders, but they were also required to police the plantation slaves, a duty they accepted. To what extent the maroon movement was a form of resistance to slavery remains unclear. After 1739, however, the maroons appeared to accommodate the British—a development that cast a longstanding shadow of ambivalence over the movement. Henceforth, the freedom movement was taken over by the plantation slaves, for whom religion and resistance became inextricably intertwined.

According to scholar Richard D. E. Burton, the African-derived dance and masquerade Jonkonnu became a principal means of opposition among Jamaican slaves during the first quarter of the nineteenth century. At this time, Jonkonnu, initially practiced in isolation, became part of the Christmas celebrations on Jamaican estates. Dressed in animal hides and headdresses embellished with horns or tusks, the slaves assembled for the festivities in their master's house, along with other whites employed on the plantation. Here black and white dancers mingled together; some Jonkonnu dancers also enacted subtle effigies of the plantation hierarchy, thus symbolically appropriating the power of the ruling elite. While the slave masters recognized the subversive potential of Jonkonnu, they allowed it to flourish because they believed it to be a safe alternative to more violent forms of protest. Nonetheless, as Burton noted, "For the duration of the feast all the oppositions in colonial society . . . are both dramatically heightened and fictively resolved, creating as great a sense of social unity—perhaps even a sense of protonational identity—as was possible" in colonial society.

In 1831 the BAPTIST WAR (or Christmas Rebellion), led by the slave and Baptist religious leader SAMUEL SHARPE, brought religion-inspired opposition to the level of a concerted, mass movement, armed and prepared to overthrow the planters. According to Burton, the movement involved "one in five slaves in active roles in the west of the island, plus many thousands more giving sympathy and support." The rebellion was a direct response to the Jamaican Assembly's decision to reduce the number of free days granted to slaves at Christmas, but the underlying motive of the rebellion was the abolition of slavery. Like Sharpe, many Jamaican slaves believed that God was calling on them to fight for their freedom—a messianic vision partly influenced by Baptist and Methodist missionaries, who, during the mid-eighteenth century, established churches in Jamaica and contributed to the syncretism of Christianity and the island's African religions. Although the rebellion was violently suppressed by the British authorities in Jamaica, it was one of the main reasons why Britain abolished slavery with a law that went into effect on August 1, 1834.

In 1865 the Morant Bay Rebellion, another large-scale uprising of Jamaica's rural blacks against the colonial elite, forced political and economic reforms that diminished the power of Jamaica's white planter class. The British drew up a new constitution that removed direct rule from the hands of the local elite and gave decision-making power to an appointed British governor, who presided over a legislative council. Yet the reforms went only so far: the overwhelming majority of council members, nominated by the governor himself, were white, and the gulf that existed between Jamaica's poor blacks (a significant majority of the island's population) and middle-class whites and mulattos continued to widen.

During the early twentieth century, it was Jamaica's large working class, where blackness provided the sole source of self-worth in an environment of desperate poverty, that spawned the radical black nationalism that included, as a central goal, the overthrow of the colonial regime in all its manifestations. Abysmal working conditions led many blacks to seek employment abroad. One of these workers, MARCUS GARVEY, migrated to Great Britain and, later, the United States. While living abroad he formulated his Pan-Africanist philosophy, which established a sense of national identity based on race and instilled in many blacks worldwide the belief that their economic and political liberation could be found in a strong and unified Africa. In 1927 he returned to Jamaica, where he spread his political views among black workers and farmers.

Garvyism, combined with the 1930 crowning of Prince Tafari Makonnen as the new emperor of Ethiopia, HAILE SELASSIE I, led to the birth of Rastafarianism: as much an Afrocentric worldview and form of black nationalism as it was a new religion, inspired by the independent, anticolonial Christian tradition of the ETHIOPIAN ORTHODOX CHURCH. Indeed, although previous black movements in Jamaica had struggled against the status quo of the time, it was not until the 1930s that anticolonialism became the focus of mass resistance. Among the earliest preachers of the Rastafarian worldview was the Jamaican Leonard Howell. He asserted the idea of a black God, who physically lived on the earth; proclaimed that the African peoples shared in this divinity; and equated the liberation of blacks with their repatriation to Africa. According to scholar Robert Hill, "Rastafarian millenarian ideology . . . [was] an active catalyst in the developing popular consciousness that led to the labour uprisings of 1938."

As a result of Jamaica's protracted economic crisis, the Rastafarian movement became increasingly politicized during the 1940s and 1950s: leaders intensified their opposition to the colonial state by defying the police and organizing illegal street marches. One Rastafarian activist Claudius Henry even set up a guerrilla training camp in the hills around Kingston. At the same time, Labor Party leader ALEXANDER BUSTAMANTE managed to co-opt the support of much of the black population by portraying himself as a savior of the working class and appropriating the hymns and leadership style of Jamaican Revivalism, a popular form of Afro-Christianity.

During the late 1960s and 1970s, the majority of Jamaica's blacks, including many Rastafarians, turned to more peaceful means of protest—a development significantly influenced by the Civil Rights Movement in the United States and the visit of Haile Selassie to Jamaica in 1966. Indeed, MARTIN LUTHER KING, JR.'s philosophy of nonviolent protest had a powerful role in directing Jamaican workers' anger toward such measurable goals as increasing the number of blacks in positions of power.

More militant activists, however, looked to the Black Power philosophy of university lecturer WALTER RODNEY. Black Power was a call to blacks to overthrow the capitalist order that ensured white dominion, and to reconstruct their societies in the image of blacks. As historian Colin Palmer wrote, "It was Rodney's vision that a knowledge of African history coupled with the growth of a strong racial identity and an understanding of contemporary social, political, and economic realities would provide the motive force for a thorough restructuring of Jamaican society." Far from being a typical movement led by elite intellectuals and emphasizing cultural identity and political independence, the radical thrust of black nationalism terrified the Jamaican and the British elite. Demonstrations promoting Black Power were violently repressed by the Jamaican police and military, while Bustamante's crusade was taken up by MICHAEL MANLEY, leader of the People's National Party. Manley not only appealed to popular religious beliefs, but also enlisted leading Rastafarians, such as the reggae singers BOB MAR-

LEY and PETER TOSH, to promote his political campaign in 1972. Manley further boosted his popularity by traveling to ETHIOPIA to visit Haile Selassie, who gave Manley the gift of a carved ebony rod.

Since the 1980s the revolutionary edge of black nationalism has moderated, while many of its beliefs and cultural manifestations, such as REGGAE music, have permeated Jamaican society as a whole. Although the influence of Rastafarian ideology on urban youth has noticeably declined, the Rastafarian movement continues to retain considerable moral authority.

See also Afro-Brazilian Culture; Contemporary Afro-Brazilian Music; Maroonage in the Americas; Myth of Racial Democracy in Latin America and the Caribbean; Religions, African, in Brazil.

Roanne Edwards

National League for the Protection of Colored Women

Early twentieth-century organization designed to aid African American women; eventually became part of the National Urban League.

The National League for the Protection of Colored Women grew out of the Associations for the Protection of Negro Women, an organization founded by white social worker Frances Kellor in 1902 to help black women workers in NEW YORK, NEW YORK. By the turn of the century, many African Americans had started migrating to Northern cities from the South in search of economic opportunity, but 90 percent of urban black women found work only in low-paying domestic service jobs. Some agents had begun meeting black women travelers at train stations and docks and taking advantage of their precarious economic situation by coercing them into signing unfair contracts, or encouraging them into prostitution. The Associations for the Protection of Negro Women established travelers' aid networks in BALTIMORE, MARYLAND, WASHINGTON, D.C., RICHMOND, VIRGINIA, and Savannah, Georgia, to prepare women passing through those cities for what they might find in the North. The organization also set up employment agencies in black neighborhoods and worked with the White Rose Mission, the Young Women's Christian Association, and other agencies to provide safe lodging houses for African American women.

The first affiliated branch of the Associations for the Protection of Negro Women was located in PHILADELPHIA, PENNSYLVANIA and run by Mrs. S. W. Layten, a black activist. In 1906 the organization became the National League for the Protection of Colored Women, opening up additional branches in Baltimore, Washington, D.C., and CHICAGO, ILLINOIS, and extending its travelers' aid service to MEMPHIS, TENNESSEE and Norfolk. In October 1911 the National League for the Protection of Colored Women merged with several other African American social welfare organizations to form the National League on Urban Conditions Among Negroes, which in turn became the NATIONAL URBAN LEAGUE.

See also Great Migration.

Lisa Clayton Robinson

National Liberation Front

See Front de Libération Nationale.

National Movement of Street Children

Organization established in Brazil in 1985 to represent the interests of street children, many of whom are of African descent; called Movimento Nacional de Meninos e Meninas de Rua, or MNMMR, in Brazil.

See also Street Children in Brazil.

National Negro Labor Council

American organization formed in 1951 to promote the cause of black workers; labeled a "Communist-front organization" by the House Committee on Un-American Activities.

In 1951 the National Negro Labor Council (NNLC) was established to end discrimination against blacks in hiring, in promotions, and within labor unions themselves. Within five years, however, the organization had succumbed to attacks by the U.S. House Committee on Un-American Activities (HUAC). The collapse of the NNLC shows that Cold War anticommunist hysteria pervaded the ranks of organized labor in the United States and undercut the fledgling movement to advance the cause of the black worker.

In the late 1940s one of the most powerful American unions, the Congress of Industrial Organizations (CIO), had purged from its ranks a number of affiliate unions because of alleged Communist leanings. Several of these affiliates had been the leading advocates within the CIO for racial equality, and had histories of promoting job opportunities and increased union representation for black workers. The expulsion of these affiliates left a dearth of black proponents in the labor movement.

In 1950, 900 predominantly black labor delegates from various unions met in CHICAGO, ILLINOIS, to air the problems of African American workers, who faced discrimination not only on the job, in their own unions as well. The next year, twenty-three newly formed Negro Labor Councils, representing industrial centers around the county, forged a permanent vehicle of advocacy, the National Negro Labor Council.

Working under the guiding principle that "blacks would attain first-class citizenship only if black workers organized to fight for full economic opportunity," the NNLC also promised to fight police brutality and segregation of housing and public facilities. Local NLCs targeted large corporations such as the Ford Motor Company, Sears-Roebuck, and the Detroit Tigers to force fair hiring and promotion practices, while the national council pushed for fair employment practices clauses in union contracts. Throughout the 1950s the NNLC supported black workers in a number of important strikes, including those against International Harvester in Chicago (1952) and Louisiana sugarcane plantations (1953). In the well-orchestrated "Let Freedom Crash the Gateway to the South" campaign of 1954, the NNLC anticipated hiring discrimination at a new General Electric plant in Louisville, Kentucky, and organized an extensive workers' training program. When the plant opened, it attempted to exclude black workers for lack of training, a common tactic of employment discrimination. The workers, with certificates from night classes to prove their qualifications, forced General Electric to reconsider. Despite the relatively successful outcome of these efforts, there was still firm resistance to reform in many industries. American Airlines, for example, refused to hire black pilots and flight attendants in spite of the national attention the NNLC drew to its discriminatory practices.

The NNLC became a highly visible force in the labor movement and attracted support from the likes of PAUL ROBESON. One of the key features of the NNLC was its links to progressive unions, to black-worker bastions of mainstream unions, such as Detroit's UAW Local 600, and to the unions that had been expelled from the CIO. These associations led to charges that the NNLC was controlled by the Communist Party—accusations that came not only from organized labor, but from African-American organizations themselves, including the NATIONAL ASSOCIATION FOR THE ADVANCEMENT OF COLORED PEOPLE (NAACP) and the NATIONAL URBAN LEAGUE. In 1952 and again in 1956 the House Committee on Un-American Activities and Subversive Activities Control Board charged the NNLC with being "a Communist-front organization." Although the Communist Party may well have had some adherents within the ranks of the NNLC, the degree to which the party controlled the organization is open to debate. Unable to meet the legal costs of defending itself before HUAC, the organization voted to disband in 1956.

See also Labor Unions in the United States.

Marian Aguiar

National Party

South African political party known for its harsh apartheid policies.

Conservative AFRIKANERS, the descendants of Dutch colonial settlers to SOUTH AFRICA, founded the National Party (NP) in 1914, just four years after the birth of the Union of South Africa. The party, first led by General J. B. M. Hertzog, primarily sought to defend Afrikaner interests against British domination. In addition, the NP's founders were in favor of maintaining racial segregation laws that had prevailed in the Afrikaner republics, as opposed to the more liberal policies of the British.

In the beginning, though, the NP was not overtly racist. Indeed, the anti-segregationist AFRICAN NATIONAL CONGRESS (ANC) favored the NP over the more conservative South African Party in 1924 elections. But in 1934 a new leader, Dr. D. F. Malan, launched what he called the Purified National Party, from which today's party grew. The new NP came to power in 1948 and immediately instituted laws that formalized and extended the racial inequality traditional throughout most of the country. These included acts that restricted where black South Africans could live, denied their children an equal education, and prohibited interracial marriages. In addition, the NP rescinded voting rights for "coloured" (mixed race) citizens.

Although black South Africans had faced injustice for years, the new laws, commonly referred to by the Dutch word APARTHEID ("apartness"), represented a harsher, more systematic oppression. During the more than forty years the National Party held power, it continued to defend apartheid, at times violently, until growing internal dissent and international economic pressure forced President P. W. BOTHA to initiate minor reforms beginning in the late 1970s. His legalization of trade unions and mixed marriages outraged the party's right wing, which defected and formed the Conservative Party. Objections also came from South Africa's ANTIAPARTHEID MOVEMENT, which sought the complete dismantling of the system, not merely reforms.

F. W. DE KLERK, the NP member who had succeeded Botha as president in 1989, surprised many by freeing NELSON MANDELA, the ANC leader imprisoned for treason in 1962. In addition, de Klerk, who promised a "new South Africa," lifted the long ban on opposition parties, including the ANC, the PAN-AFRICANIST CONGRESS, and the SOUTH AFRICAN COMMUNIST PARTY, and began negotiating with these and other groups. The talks led to a new constitution and, in 1994, South Africa's first multiracial, democratic elections. With the white electorate now reduced to a mere 15 percent of the vote, the National Party lost its long hold on the presidency and the legislature. Under de Klerk, who has tried to shed the taint of apartheid, the National Party reached out to Indian and mixed-race South Africans, winning more than 60 percent of their votes in 1994. By the late 1990s, however, its support had dwindled drastically. In 1998 the party changed its name to the New National Party (NNP). The party won only twenty-eight seats in the June 1999 national elections, forcing it to cede the role of official opposition to the rival Democratic Party (DP). The two parties merged to form the Democratic Alliance, but the NNP split from the DP in 2001.

Kate Tuttle

National Socialist Sterilization Policies in Germany

Policies of "racial hygiene" implemented by the National Socialist (Nazi) government of Germany that involved the sterilization of black Germans.

The precise number of blacks in Germany when the Nazi government took power in 1933 is unknown. Probably a few hundred black citizens of former German colonies and black foreign nationals were present in the country. More significantly, however, the post–WORLD WAR I occupation of the German Rhineland by French troops, including black soldiers from the French colonies, had resulted in the birth of an estimated 500 to 800 children of mixed race (popularly referred to as "Rhineland bastards") to German women. In contrast to their policy toward Jews, the Nazis did not attempt to exterminate this small minority, though mixed-race Germans did suffer harassment and persecution in the Third Reich. The Nazis' main concern with regard to blacks, however, was racial mixing. They aimed to prevent this through a policy of sterilizing the Rhineland children.

The Nazis' EUGENIC theories (like similar theories popular throughout Europe and the United States in the early twentieth century) included ideas of racial purity and genetic "health," promoted through the sterilization of the supposedly unfit. Proponents of what the Nazis termed "racial hygiene" believed that mixing races created weak, genetically inferior offspring. German doctors "proved" the inferiority of biracial children in pseudo-scientific experiments. The Nazis' 1933 Law for the Prevention of Offspring with Hereditary Defects authorized forcible sterilization in certain cases. The sterilization of black Germans took place separately, however, under the aegis of "Special Commission 3," established in 1937 to implement the sterilization of black Germans. Though the policy supposedly required parental permission for the operations, the Nazis seem to have coerced most parents to comply. They carried out the entire program in secrecy, sterilizing some 385 of the Rhineland children. The 1986 book *FARBE BEKENNEN* (Showing our Colors, 1992) includes interviews with two survivors of the period.

Belinda Cooper

National Union for the Total Independence of Angola

Leading nationalist group, insurgency movement, and opposition party in Angola; called União Nacional para a Independência Total de Angola, in Angola.

After splitting with other nationalist parties over ideology and strategy, JONAS MALHEIRO SAVIMBI created the National Union for the Total Independence of Angola, or UNITA, in March 1966. With its base in the southern town of Jamba, in the south and east of Portuguese-ruled ANGOLA, UNITA gained most of its domestic support from the OVIMBUNDU ethnic group.

Although its ideology was often unclear, in general UNITA promoted democracy, capitalist development, and the recognition of African ethnic identities and customs. With military aid from SOUTH AFRICA, the United States, and several western European countries, the movement built one of the largest armies in Africa. In areas under its control, UNITA reinvigorated chieftainships, established a barter economy, mined diamonds for international export, and maintained strict army discipline.

During the war to overthrow Portuguese COLONIAL RULE, UNITA often fought the other two major nationalist parties, the POPULAR MOVEMENT FOR THE LIBERATION OF ANGOLA (MPLA), and the National Front for the Liberation of Angola. In 1974, when Angolan independence seemed inevitable, UNITA allied briefly with these groups. But the alliance soon fell apart and in 1975 South Africa supported UNITA in its drive to take the capital, LUANDA. The following year UNITA abandoned the cities and launched an insurgency war against the Marxist-Leninist MPLA government that lasted until 1992.

In the late 1980s, UNITA entered into negotiations to end the war. The negotiations resulted in elections in 1992, but when it became obvious Savimbi would lose, UNITA accused the government of electoral irregularities and attacks on demobilized UNITA soldiers, and again took up arms. In 1994 UNITA was forced by international pressure to negotiate, and it has since been slowly integrated into the government and military. In early 1997, seventy elected UNITA deputies and several ministers began serving in a government of national reconciliation, although sanctions remained on UNITA's activities.

In early 2002 Savimbi was killed by government troops, which prompted a cease-fire deal and plans for UNITA to disband. On August 2, 2002, UNITA's acting leader, Paulo Lukamba Gato, declared the war officially over.

Eric Young

National Urban League

Interracial social service organization that attempts to obtain full participation in American society for African Americans through lobbying, research, and direct social services.

Unlike organizations such as the NATIONAL ASSOCIATION FOR THE ADVANCEMENT OF COLORED PEOPLE (NAACP), which has been judged by how successfully it has fought for blacks' civil and political rights, the National Urban League (NUL) has pursued less measurable goals. Since its founding in 1911, the organization has used the tools of scientific social work to offer programs to help African Americans. NUL originally provided direct services to African Americans who migrated from the rural South to Northern cities. Later in the century, as social conditions changed, the organization increased its scope. It undertook sociological research that disputed commonly held misconceptions about African American inferiority; began to lobby businesses, labor unions, and the government; and embraced direct protest during the CIVIL RIGHTS MOVEMENT as a means of gaining greater social and economic participation for African Americans.

At its inception, NUL modeled its social services on white charitable organizations of the day, such as settlement houses, charitable agencies, and immigrant aid societies, and adapted them to blacks' needs. As many African Americans moved north during the GREAT MIGRATION, NUL worked through local affiliates to help them adjust to urban life. The affiliates taught basic skills such as behavior, dress, sanitation, health, and

Persons Living Below the Poverty Level 1959–2002

Year	Total (In Millions)	Percent	Blacks (In Millions)	Percent
1959	39.5	22.4	9.9	55.1
1970	25.4	12.6	7.5	33.5
1980	29.3	13.0	8.6	32.5
1990	33.6	13.5	9.8	31.9
2002	34.57	12.1	8.6	24.1

*Persons are classified as being above or below the poverty level using the poverty index, based on the Department of Agriculture's 1961 Economy Food Plan. Poverty thresholds are updated every year. In 1990 the weighted average poverty threshold for a family of four was $13,359.
Source: U.S. Census Bureau, 2002.

homemaking. NUL also sponsored community centers, clinics, kindergartens, day care, and summer camps. League workers provided individual care to African Americans in a range of areas, including juvenile delinquency, truancy, and marital adjustment.

The Great Migration increased demands on NUL, and the organization soon had affiliates in nearly every industrial city in the United States. NUL began offering vocational training to immigrants, urging businesses to hire blacks, and attempting to persuade unions such as the American Federation of Labor (AFL) to accept black members. NUL achieved its main aim of improving employment opportunities for blacks, but such gains were temporary. At the end of WORLD WAR I (1914–1918), returning soldiers put many blacks out of work again.

During the Great Depression of the 1930s, NUL broadened its scope still more under the leadership of LESTER B. GRANGER. While continuing to offer vocational training and social services to urban blacks, NUL sought to persuade the federal government to include blacks in President Franklin Roosevelt's New Deal programs. The organization lobbied the federal government to end discrimination in allocating government benefits. During WORLD WAR II (1939–1945), NUL fought to desegregate wartime employment and the armed forces, supporting a plan by labor leader A. PHILIP RANDOLPH for a march on Washington. In exchange for Randolph's calling off the march, Roosevelt issued Executive Order 8802, which barred discrimination in defense industries and in federal agencies, and established the FAIR EMPLOYMENT PRACTICES COMMITTEE.

NUL also sought to shape public and private opinion through its research. Its sociological studies—published independently and, from 1923 to 1949, in its journal, OPPORTUNITY—took an explicitly scientific approach to social problems. NUL leaders criticized the NAACP's journal, THE CRISIS, believing it to be too "subjective." Opportunity also published black writers and artists such as Gwendolyn Bennett, LANGSTON HUGHES, JAMES WELDON JOHNSON, and COUNTEE CULLEN.

In the 1960s, under WHITNEY M. YOUNG JR., NUL expanded its traditional social service approach by strengthening its commitment to civil rights. It embraced direct action, promoted community organization, and sponsored leadership development and voter education and registration projects. It helped organize two important events of the Civil Rights Movement: the MARCH ON WASHINGTON in 1963 and the POOR PEOPLE'S WASHINGTON CAMPAIGN in 1968. Toward the end of the 1960s, NUL attempted to revitalize ghettos by calling for a domestic Marshall Plan.

Following Young's death in 1971, VERNON JORDAN became president of NUL. Jordan helped begin programs in health, housing, education, and job training. In 1975 NUL began to publish a journal, *The Urban League Review,* and began issuing an annual report, *The State of Black America.* In 1982 Jordan was succeeded by John Jacobs.

When the federal government cut social programs in the 1980s, NUL responded by emphasizing self-help and seeking solutions to new and continuing problems for African Americans, including high rates of teen pregnancy, families headed by single women, declining quality of public schools, and crime. Under Hugh Price, who became NUL president in 1994, the Urban League tackled the consequences of welfare reform, the rollback of AFFIRMATIVE ACTION programs, and the persistence of racial discrimination and exclusion in the work place. Price, a communications veteran, was a strong national voice on behalf of economic opportunity and equality. In 2003, former New Orleans mayor Marc H. Morial became NUL president and CEO.

See also Desegregation in the United States; Labor Unions in the United States.

Bibliography

Weiss, Nancy J. *Whitney M. Young, Jr. and the Struggle for Civil Rights.* Princeton University Press, 1989.

Moore, Jesse. *A Search for Equality: The National Urban League, 1910–1961.* Pennsylvania State University Press, 1981.

Robert Fay

National Welfare Rights Organization

Coalition of poor Americans, mostly black and mostly women, who demanded better welfare assistance from state and federal governments in the late 1960s and early 1970s.

By the mid-1960s the CIVIL RIGHTS MOVEMENT in the United States had achieved several of its basic political goals: blacks could vote, eat at integrated lunch counters, and send their children to integrated schools. Many activists, however, believed such gains were of little value as long as most blacks lived in poverty. Among these activists were several black women in LOS ANGE-

LES, CALIFORNIA, NEW YORK, NEW YORK, and other cities who received Aid to Families with Dependent Children (AFDC, or welfare). Separately and somewhat spontaneously, they organized fellow welfare recipients to demand better benefits and treatment from welfare agencies.

To coordinate and spread their protests, George Wiley, a black chemistry professor and former worker for the CONGRESS OF RACIAL EQUALITY (CORE), created the Poverty Rights Action Center in 1966. The following year the office evolved into the National Welfare Rights Organization (NWRO), with headquarters in WASHINGTON, D.C. With help from the NWRO, women receiving welfare gathered by the dozens or hundreds, went to the local welfare office, and demanded money for basic needs—such as clothes for school—that were not being met by their welfare benefits. If refused, they held a SIT-IN. The strategy won better benefits for large numbers of women. The NWRO, in turn, received valuable publicity and thousands of dollars from the antipoverty agencies of President Lyndon Johnson's Great Society as well as from private donors.

In the late 1960s the NWRO held mass marches and rallies to publicize its demands, which by then included livable grants for all welfare recipients, access to day care, and programs for job training. Although these goals went mostly unmet, the NWRO did succeed in ending the intrusive investigations that were often a prerequisite for receiving benefits. Partly due to the NWRO and partly to the programs of the Great Society, many women previously reluctant to apply for welfare now did so, and were accepted. Others denied relief earlier were finally accepted. Welfare rolls, with about 750,000 participants in 1960, were at three million by 1972.

The NWRO had a peak membership of about 100,000. As such, it was one of the first large-scale attempts by poor black women to take control of their political and economic future. While the women on welfare exercised great power locally, however, NWRO's national staff, who were primarily white, male, and middle class, dominated many of NWRO's important decisions. By the early 1970s relations between national and local offices had grown increasingly strained over the question of how much autonomy to give locals. That question, though, was eclipsed by a broad public backlash against welfare programs that emerged at the end of the 1960s. After 1970 the NWRO had few important successes. By 1972 it was badly in debt, and by the mid-1970s was defunct.

Bibliography
Piven, Frances Fox, and Richard A. Cloward. *Poor People's Movements: Why They Succeed, How They Fail.* Pantheon Books, 1977.
West, Guida. *The National Welfare Rights Movement: The Social Protest of Poor Women.* Praeger, 1981.

Nation of Islam

Religious movement based on black separatism, founded in Detroit, Michigan, around 1930.

The Nation of Islam (NOI) was established in DETROIT, at the beginning of the GREAT DEPRESSION, by WALLACE D. FARD (pronounced Farood), a door-to-door silk salesman. In addition to selling his wares, he spread his message of salvation and self-determination throughout Detroit's black neighborhoods. He held the first meetings in people's homes, but the movement soon grew big and Fard rented halls for his gatherings. Far from adhering to strict Islamic law, the Nation under Fard was an eclectic mix of philosophy that borrowed from earlier black Muslim movements, Christian scripture (largely to debunk Christianity), and Fard's Afrocentric interpretation of the story of Origin. The organization attracted many followers because of its angry rejection of white society.

Fard wrote two manuals, *The Secret Ritual of the Nation of Islam,* which is still used as a blueprint for oral instruction, and *Teaching for a Lost-Found Nation of Islam in a Mathematical Way,* written in a coded language that a select few are able to decipher. He also established the University of Islam, the Muslim Girls Training Corps—an instruction center that trained females to follow the tenets of proper Muslim womanhood—and the Fruit of Islam, a militaristic unit that served as Fard's bodyguard faction and enforced the Nation's laws.

When word reached white authorities that Fard was preaching about the Western "blue-eyed devil" whose civilization would soon perish, the Nation was deemed subversive; the hostile relationship between the movement and law enforcement (including ultimately the FBI) would continue for the next several decades. In 1931 Fard was investigated and detained by the Detroit police department for endorsing a sacrificial killing performed by a fringe member of the movement. There is no evidence to indicate that Fard was involved in the murder. Despite the fact that the victim was black, the charge against Fard was exacerbated when authorities found a pamphlet calling for the annihilation of "white devils" in his possession. Fard apparently had the foresight to know that his presence in the Nation would potentially lead to its demise. In 1933, months before he was told to leave Detroit or face incarceration, Fard began preparing his young right-hand man, ELIJAH MUHAMMAD, for leadership. Fard's departure and his replacement with Muhammad led to internal strife within the movement. The Nation of Islam splintered and within a couple of years Muhammad's trusted circle, including his family, moved to CHICAGO. The Temple of Islam No. 2 was built and later became the national headquarters of the Nation.

Under Muhammad, the Nation was able to put into practice the concept of black economic self-sufficiency, a premise that Fard envisioned but never fully realized. Because of their highly disciplined lifestyle, Muslims were hired more readily than other blacks. A good portion of their salary went into the Nation's coffers. One decade later, in 1945, members had pooled enough earnings to invest in 140 acres of farmland in rural Michigan. In subsequent years, over one hundred temples flourished nationwide, and Muslim-owned bakeries, grocery stores, and other small businesses were opened in African American communities.

Elijah Muhammad speaks at a Nation of Islam convention in Chicago in 1966. CORBIS/Bettmann

During its early days, the Nation tended to attract Southerners who had migrated north and had little formal education. The appeal of the movement was not just self-sufficiency but the structured lifestyle, with its emphasis on marriage, family, strict diet, and hygiene. In particular, the image of womanhood in the Nation was acclaimed for "purity, domesticity, and piety." Muhammad carried on Fard's program of providing female members with an education that included nursing classes, gymnastics, cooking, sewing, child rearing, and the proper approach to gender relations. While its women seemed to be put on a pedestal, the Nation has nevertheless been criticized over the years for being ambiguously caught between glorification and objectification of females.

By the 1950s the Nation of Islam had begun to resemble a nation. Complete with its own national flag and anthem, militaristic marches and salutes, the movement was, in essence, a military theocracy. The structure and ritual, and the promise of salvation from the "grave," the soulless dog-eat-dog world outside the Nation, appealed to many poor blacks, particularly convicts in jail. One of those recruited from prison was a young man named Malcolm Little. Like all inductees into the movement, Little discarded his "slave" surname and became known as MALCOLM X. Recognized as a brilliant orator, Malcolm X quickly rose through the ranks of the Nation. He had arrived at an opportune time. The early rumblings of the CIVIL RIGHTS MOVEMENT were beginning as a result of the government's failure to satisfy African American demands for equality. The Nation would soon be competing with other black movements for members. Malcolm's charisma and the advent of television brought the movement greater visibility than ever before. The Nation actively began to recruit black, middle-class professionals. Not only was Muhammad interested in incorporating their skills for the betterment of the Nation, but he was also adamant that their expertise not be wasted in "the white man's world."

By the late 1950s the Nation's separatist beliefs stood in contrast to the growing Civil Rights Movement, which sought integration. The primary focus was on economic self-sufficiency and by the early 1960s some, including Malcolm X, criticized the interest in financial gain and the money-and-wealth fixation among the upper ranks of the movement. In 1964, discontented with Muhammad's political philosophy and allegations that the leader had fathered several illegitimate children, Malcolm broke away from the Nation to form his own religious organization. One year later he was assassinated. Critics of Muhammad claimed that his violent denunciation of Malcolm X in speeches and in the Nation's newspaper, *Muhammad Speaks,* incited the murder. The Nation has continued to prosper economically but there has not been another surge in membership since the 1960s. In 1975, after Elijah Muhammad's death, his son Wallace Deen Muhammad was named supreme minister. However, two months into his leadership he declared that whites were no longer viewed as evil and would be allowed into the movement. This shift, as well as a move toward the more orthodox Sunni Islam, shocked and alienated a large group of followers. The Nation splintered into several alliances and by 1978 national spokesman LOUIS FARRAKHAN led a group that resurrected the original Nation of Islam teachings of Black Nationalism and separatism.

Despite his controversial persona, Farrakhan in the 1990s has been credited with reaching out to non-Muslim black religious leaders and activists in order to effect positive change in inner cities. In 1995 he successfully orchestrated the MILLION MAN MARCH, an event that brought together many people and organizations of opposing political viewpoints.

Information on the size of the Nation's current membership has varied. Estimates range from 19,000 to 60,000 followers.

See also Black Nationalism in the United States; Islam and African Americans.

Suzanne Albulak

Native Americans

Indigenous peoples of North America, also known as American Indians, with whom African Americans have had a long history of contact, characterized by both cooperation and confrontation; many African Americans trace their lineage in part to Native American ancestors.

After arriving in the Americas, Europeans turned first to Native Americans as a source of forced labor. They introduced African slaves to the region only after calculating the difficulty of coercing large numbers of Native Americans into their labor systems. Africans who fled from slavery frequently mixed with Native Americans to avoid being captured. Native Americans who escaped from slavery could evade the colonists through their knowledge of the surrounding areas, and some of them returned to help free enslaved Africans.

Wherever they established slavery in the Americas, Europeans feared the revolutionary potential of alliances between Native Americans and Africans. The first slave rebellion on North American soil took place along the Carolina coast in 1526 and was organized and executed by a coalition of Africans and Native Americans. Europeans especially feared communities of escaped slaves, known as maroon societies or *quilombos,* that arose in frontier areas and that often allied with Native Americans. These communities established themselves outside the boundaries of European settlement, where they sometimes allied with local Native Americans.

Despite the limited number of these maroon communities, they provoked strong reactions among the Europeans, who sought to keep the African and Native American peoples separated and mutually hostile if possible. They taught Africans to fight Native Americans and bribed Native Americans to hunt escaped Africans. Further sowing division between the peoples, whites introduced African slavery into the Five Civilized Tribes, as the indigenous peoples of southeastern North America were known.

By the time of the Revolutionary War (1775–1783), the enslavement of Native Americans had been abolished. The U.S. government, however, still attempted to enlist Native Americans in enforcing the slavery of Africans. Until the onset of the AMERICAN CIVIL WAR in the early 1860s, the government negotiated treaties with indigenous peoples that included promises by the Native Americans to return escaped slaves. Such promises, however, were largely ignored, and Native Americans often harbored fugitives.

The most powerful alliance between Africans and Native Americans linked escaped Africans who had settled in the Spanish territory of Florida with the Seminole people (whose name, meaning "runaway" or "pioneer," is derived from the same Spanish root as *maroon*), who were an offshoot of the Creek federation to the north. The Africans taught the Native Americans how to cultivate rice, and the groups joined military forces. In 1816 a U.S. soldier reported that thriving plantations run by Seminole and Africans stretched for 80 km (50 mi) along the banks of the Apalachicola River. The African and Seminole forces resisted raids by slaveholders and soldiers from the United States. In 1819, in an attempt to eliminate Florida as a refuge for runaway slaves, the U.S. government purchased the territory from SPAIN. The Second Seminole War (1835–1842) finally drove most of the Seminole out of Florida. The war resulted in the deaths of 1,600 U.S. soldiers and several hundred Native Americans and cost the U.S. government an estimated $40 million.

Like the Seminole community, many Native American nations on the eastern seaboard of the United States became biracial communities. When these nations were removed in 1838 and 1839 to the Indian Territory in Oklahoma, on what was known as the Trail of Tears, African Americans were well represented among them. By 1860 the population of the Five Civilized Nations in the Indian Territory included 18 percent African Americans, and the Seminole there appointed six black Seminole as members of their governing council. The most significant African Native American was JOHN HORSE, a black Seminole chief who negotiated a treaty with the U.S. government in 1870.

Not all blacks were allied with the Native Americans, however. After the Civil War, organized units of African American U.S. Army troops known as BUFFALO SOLDIERS helped end native resistance to U.S. control. Beginning in the 1870s, government and missionary educators attempted to assimilate young Native Americans by placing them in boarding schools in the East that followed the model of the missionary schools for black freedpeople. In 1878 Hampton Normal and Agricultural Institute (now HAMPTON UNIVERSITY), a prominent black college, added a small program for these transplanted Native American students.

See also Maroonage in the Americas.

Bibliography
Forbes, Jack D. *Africans and Native Americans: The Language of Race and the Evolution of Red-Black Peoples.* University of Illinois Press, 1993.

Nat Turner's Rebellion

See Turner, Nat.

Natural Resources in Africa

Animals, minerals, water, and other resources in Africa that have economic potential.

For information on
Animals in modern trade and tourism: *See* Fisheries, African; Ivory Trade; Wildlife Management in Africa.
Distribution and management of natural resources: *See* Development in Africa: An Interpretation; Forestry, Participation, and Representation in Africa: An Interpretation; Gold Trade; Minerals and Mining in Africa.
Historic use of natural resources: *See* Development in Africa: An Interpretation; Gold Trade; Ivory Trade; Iron in Africa; Salt Trade.
Hydroelectric resources: *See* Aswan High Dam; Blue Nile; Cabora Bassa; Nile River; Volta, Lake; Zambezi River.

Naudeba

Ethnic group of West Africa.

The Naudeba primarily inhabit BURKINA FASO. They speak a Niger-Congo language and are related to the MOSSI people. Approximately 100,000 people consider themselves Naudeba.

See also Languages, African: An Overview.

Naude, Beyers

1915–2004

South African Afrikaner minister in the Dutch Reformed Church and opponent of apartheid, South Africa's rigid policy of racial segregation.

Born in Roodepoort-Maraisburg, near JOHANNESBURG, Beyers Naude was the son of a Dutch Reformed Church (DRC) minister whose family moved to Graaff-Reinet in southwestern SOUTH AFRICA in 1921. Naude obtained a master's degree in languages and a degree in theology from the University of Stellenbosch School of Theology in 1939. That same year he became an assistant minister at a DRC chapter in Wellington, Western Cape province. He married at this time and joined the Afrikaner Broederbond, a secret organization dedicated to the promotion of Afrikaner nationalism and white rule in South Africa. He remained an orthodox DRC minister and supporter of the NATIONAL PARTY, which promoted APARTHEID, for many years.

In 1960, however, the events of the SHARPEVILLE MASSACRE caused Naude to rethink his views. On March 21 of that year, sixty-nine blacks were killed by police during a demonstration against apartheid's PASS LAWS, which forced nonwhites to carry identity papers and restricted their movement. This event so horrified Naude that, after much reflection and Bible study, he began to preach that apartheid was unjust and immoral. As a result, he was strongly criticized by the DRC, and he resigned as moderator of his congregation (the highest local position) in 1963. Naude also left the Broederbond and founded the Christian Institute, which sought to unite all churches and languages in an effort to reconcile blacks and whites in South Africa. He edited the Institute's controversial publication *Pro Veritate*. In addition to opposing apartheid, Naude denounced the use of violence. For the rest of the 1960s he was bitterly attacked by right wing members of the DRC, and security police searched both his home and the Christian Institute.

In 1972 Naude traveled to Germany and GREAT BRITAIN, where he was asked to preach at Westminster Abbey; the following year his passport was withdrawn. In 1974 he was awarded an honorary doctorate of law by the University of the Witwatersrand in Johannesburg and received the Reinhold Niebuhr Award for "steadfast and self-sacrificing services in South Africa for justice and peace" (shared with Soviet dissident Andrei Sakharov). In 1975, after a three-year government investigation, the Christian Institute was deprived of its income from abroad and its activities greatly restricted. In 1977 Naude was banned for five years by the government, which meant he was confined to his home area, and prohibited from attending meetings or being quoted anywhere in South Africa. He was awarded the Swedish Free Church prize for reconciliation and development and another award by the Bruno Kreisky Foundation for "untiring work in race relations." In 1980 he broke away from the DRC to be admitted to the African Reformed Church, its separate black equivalent. In 1982 his banning order was renewed for a further three years but this was lifted in 1984. In November of that year he became secretary general of the South African Council of Churches and in that capacity traveled to Europe, the United States, and ZIMBABWE.

Naude retired in 1987 but served on the AFRICAN NATIONAL CONGRESS (ANC)'s negotiating team when it conducted talks with the government in 1992 on a new constitution. After the end of apartheid, Naude received many honors in South Africa, with many public spaces rededicated in his name. The Beyers Naude Centre for Public Theology at the University of Stellenbosch was established in his honor in 2002.

Navarro, Theodore "Fats"

1923–1950

American jazz trumpeter who helped pioneer the genre of jazz known as bebop during the 1940s.

Born in Key West, Florida, Theodore "Fats" Navarro was considered one of the foremost JAZZ trumpeters of the 1940s. He was one of the pioneers of BEBOP, which featured quick tempos and highly complex musical phrasing. Navarro, with the help of DIZZY GILLESPIE, toured with several famous musicians in his career, including WILLIAM CLARENCE (BILLY) ECKSTINE, LIONEL LEO HAMPTON, and COLEMAN RANDOLPH HAWKINS. Navarro was a big man who at one point weighed over 300 lbs., earning him the nickname "Fat Girl." Despite an addiction to heroin and a severe case of tuberculosis, Navarro continued to record until his death in 1950.

Naylor, Gloria

1950–

African American writer whose novels depict different African American communities and often incorporate elements of magical realism.

Gloria Naylor once recalled the influence that writer TONI MORRISON's work has had on her life. Naylor remembered discovering that for "a young black woman, struggling to find a mirror to her worth in this society, not only is your story worth telling but it can be told in words so painstakingly eloquent that it becomes a song." The realization was a turning point for Naylor, who at age twenty-seven began "gathering the authority within" to write her own stories.

Naylor's stories drew upon the legacy of her parents, former cotton sharecroppers in Mississippi who migrated north to NEW YORK CITY. Her father found a job as a transit worker and her mother as a telephone operator. Naylor was born in New York. After graduating from high school in 1968, Naylor traveled as a missionary for the Jehovah's Witnesses in New York,

North Carolina, and Florida. She returned to New York after seven years, completing a bachelor's degree in English at Brooklyn College in 1981 and a master's degree at Yale University in Afro-American studies in 1983.

While she was still an undergraduate student, Naylor began to write about the many black communities to which her parents' stories and her own travels had brought her. Her first short story, "A Life on Beekman Place," was published in ESSENCE magazine in 1980 and became a cornerstone for the novel she developed as her master's thesis, *The Women of Brewster Place* (1982). The novel portrays a disparate group of African American women who, having found themselves on a dead-end street in the inner city, explore their differences and draw upon their shared strength to survive. "All the good men are either dead or waiting to be born," one character comments. With an unswerving gaze, Naylor looks at the brutality of relationships forged in the wake of oppression. *The Women of Brewster Place* received the American Book Award for best first novel of 1983.

Naylor's next novel, *Linden Hills* (1985), also derives narrative from place, this time an affluent community set on a hillside. As two young men, Willie and Lester, explore the sloping spiral of streets descending from Linden Hills, Naylor uses the structure of Dante's *Inferno* to portray a middle-class community obsessed with material gain. Wealth flows toward the bottom of the hill, where undertaker Luther Nedeed has ruled for five generations. Naylor's novel is not only a critique of materialism but also a feminist story of women's unwritten history, as Nedeed's wife Willa, banished to the basement for producing a light-skinned son, garners strength from the dusty testimonies of her predecessors.

Naylor develops the theme of spirituality in her third novel, *Mama Day* (1988), which explores the composition of individual belief. Again, Naylor juxtaposes disparate African American experiences, as George travels with his wife Cocoa from New York to the island of Willow Springs, the home of healer Mama Day. Naylor relies on the legacy of African American healers and conjurers to create an ambiguous narrative in which characters and readers are left to grapple with the notions of the real, the magical, and the process of fiction itself.

Naylor's fourth novel, *Bailey's Café* (1992), brings magic to New York City, where it enters the lives of a group of people who gather in a café. With a narrative that resonates with the BLUES, Naylor depicts the hard lives of the café patrons. As in *Mama Day*, Naylor blurs the line between the real and the magical, placing a magical dock behind the real café.

In 1998 Naylor published *The Men of Brewster Place*, a novel focusing on the male characters who played peripheral roles in her debut novel. Critics welcomed the book for its much-needed perspective on African American male culture, though some reviewers found it less lyrical and complex than Naylor's previous works. *The Men of Brewster Place* won an American Book Award in 1998. Naylor received a Guggenheim Fellowship in 1988 and has taught at many universities, including George Washington, New York, Princeton, Cornell, and Boston Universities.

Bibliography
Gates, Henry Louis, Jr., and K. A. Appiah, eds. *Gloria Naylor: Critical Perspectives Past and Present.* Penguin USA, 1993.

Marian Aguiar

Nazi Party, Racial Policies of
See National Socialist Sterilization Policies in Germany.

Ndau
Ethnic group of southern Africa; also known as Buzi and Vandau.

The Ndau primarily inhabit southeastern ZIMBABWE and south-central MOZAMBIQUE. They speak a Bantu language and are closely related to the SHONA people. Over 100,000 people consider themselves Ndau.

See also Bantu: Dispersion and Settlement.

Ndebele
Ethnic group of Botswana, South Africa, and Zimbabwe.

The founder of the Ndebele was Mzilikazi, the head of the Khumalo Dynasty. His people spoke a NGUNI language like that of the ZULU. In 1838, under constant Zulu attack and after a falling-out with the Zulu leader SHAKA, Mzilikazi led his kinsmen to the area around present-day BULAWAYO, ZIMBABWE, in SHONA territory. The region became known as Matabeleland and ultimately comprised a kingdom of around 10,000 sq km as the Ndebele raided the Shona for cattle. The kingdom included both hereditary chieftainships, which were linked to the king through kin ties, and independent chieftainships, or *izinduna*, which maintained militias and paid allegiance to the king, first Mzilikazi and later his son Lobengula. Through intermarriage and the incorporation of Shona villages, the Ndebele adopted the Shona *Mwari* cult, in which the High God, or *Mwari*, speaks through oracles. Although the Ndebele built their capital at Bulawayo, most lived in villages, growing maize and other subsistence crops and herding cattle.

The Ndebele kingdom began to disintegrate in 1893 when a war broke out between King Lobengula and the British South African Company over Ndebele cattle raiding. In 1896 the two sides reached an uneasy peace after Lobengula burnt down Bulawayo and died without leaving a successor, but subsequent Ndebele leadership was divided and relatively weak. Under Rhodesian colonial rule the Ndebele were forced onto reserves, though the colonial administration considered the Ndebele able warriors and recruited many of them into the colonial army, the Rhodesian African Rifles. Although many of the early nationalist leaders were Ndebele, the war for independence was fought primarily by Shona-dominated opposition groups.

Today the Ndebele people number approximately two million and live in northern SOUTH AFRICA, eastern BOTSWANA, and ZIMBABWE. Although they are the second-largest ethnic group in Zimbabwe, they account for only around 15 percent of the total population and hold few senior political, military, or corporate posts. Many Zimbabwean Ndebele believe the Shona have tried to keep them poor and weak, despite evidence that development projects and assistance is equitably distributed to the Matabeleland provinces. Ndebele promote their interests through regional associations, although the Mwari cult is also an important part of Ndebele identity. The Ndebele have recently become renowned for their artwork, typically bright colored geometric patterns painted on the exterior walls of their houses.

Bibliography

Powell, Ivor. *Ndebele: A People and Their Art.* Struik Publishers, 1995.

Bozingwana, Wallace. *Ndebele Religion and Customs.* Mambo Press, 1983.

Eric Young

N'Djamena, Chad

Capital, largest city, and economic center of Chad.

N'Djamena lies at the confluence of the Logone and CHARI rivers close to CHAD's border with CAMEROON and 80 km (50 mi) southeast of LAKE CHAD. Known as Fort Lamy from its establishment until September 1973 when President FRANÇOIS TOMBALBAYE "Africanized" all French place names, N'Djamena acquired its present name from a small KOTOKO fishing village, Am-Djamena, founded on the site by the nineteenth century. In 1900 the French defeated and killed the Sudanese slaver RABIH AL-ZUBAYR at the Battle of Kousseri, across the Chari River from Am-Djamena. That same year, for strategic reasons, the French built fortifications on both sides of the river: Fort Kousseri at the battle site and Fort Lamy on the site of Am-Djamena. The latter was named after the French soldier Major Lamy, who had also died in the battle.

Fort Lamy became the colonial capital under French rule; it remained a small town, however, throughout the colonial period. Located at the center of cotton-growing, livestock-keeping, and fishing areas, it witnessed rapid growth after independence in 1960 as the national capital and an important market center. In 1958 Fort Lamy had a population of just 53,000, but by 1972 this had grown to 130,000. Chad's intermittent warfare during the 1970s and 1980s drove many refugees to seek security and economic opportunity in the capital. The city's population, which is 95 percent Muslim, was estimated at 601,500 (2000 estimate).

N'Djamena is Chad's main financial and industrial center. Meat processing is the most important single industry in the city. N'Djamena sits at the hub of Chad's road network, from which roads extend east into SUDAN and southwest into Cameroon and NIGERIA, whose ports handle Chad's seaborne trade. The city remains a major transit center on the east-west pilgrimage route to Mecca. The town is divided into two sections: a modern commercial center and a bustling African township. Much of N'Djamena's infrastructure was damaged as a result of faction fighting during Chad's long-running civil war. Although most of this damage had been repaired, some was still in evidence in the mid-1990s.

Andrew Burton

Ndongo

Kingdom founded in Angola in the early 1500s.

The kingdom of Ndongo was probably founded in the highlands that lay between the Kwanza and Lukala rivers in northern Angola in the early sixteenth century. Its earliest traditions maintain that it was founded from KONGO, its northern neighbor, and probably acknowledged some Kongo overlordship at the time. Kongo kings claimed Angola (which they called Ndongo) among their possessions in the 1530s. But Kongo had little real control over the country, and Ndongo's first king Ngola Kiluanje expanded the kingdom to the west, right up to the coast along the south bank of the Kwanza River and up to Kongo's own possessions in the vicinity of LUANDA. In the mid-sixteenth century, Ndongo focused its expansion to the south and southwest and into the east and southeast. Ndongo's kings ruled a central district called Kabasa directly though their own officials and shared power with the subordinate ruler of the greater of their provinces, whose leaders often rivaled the king in power and who frequently married into the royal line.

In 1518 Ndongo sought to establish direct contact with Portugal, which had been in diplomatic relations with Kongo since the late fifteenth century. Among the requests made was for missionaries to be sent in order to convert the king to Christianity. The first mission to Ndongo from Portugal, which commenced in 1520, failed because of rivalries among the Portuguese who lived in Ndongo. This led to fighting in which Kongo intervened to save the ambassadors. Attempts to reestablish contact in 1549 reached Portugal after long delays and resulted in the dispatch of Paulo Dias de Novais and some Jesuit priests to Ndongo. The second mission also failed, and although the new king, Ndambi a Ngola welcomed them, Dias de Novais was subsequently forced to return to Portugal leaving only one Jesuit priest behind.

While he was in Portugal, Dias de Novais obtained a royal grant to build a colony in Angola that was to include some Ndongo territory. When he returned to Africa in 1575, he established a settlement in Kongo territory at LUANDA and then offered his services as a mercenary to Ndongo. Ndongo's ruler relied on the Portuguese to assist him, and for four years Dias de Novais and his men served him in war, mostly against rebels on the western side of Ndongo's domains. In 1579, however, at the instigation of Francisco Barbuda, a Portuguese in Ndongo's service, the king decided to attack the Portuguese and drive them from his kingdom.

Although defeated, Dias de Novais was not driven from Africa. He retreated to positions near Luanda and with Kongo's aid, managed to hold on to some land along the Kwanza River. From this point he launched a counterattack against Ndongo, fomenting revolt among some of Ndongo's vassals along the Kwanza. Several wars fought between 1579 and 1589 resulted in the establishment of the Portuguese fort at Masangano, where the Kwanza and Lukala rivers meet, and the defection or defeat of most of Ndongo's positions west of the highlands. However, when Dias de Novais' successor, Luis Serrão, sought to invade Ndongo's heartland in 1589, he was severely defeated by Ndongo, which had formed a crucial alliance with MATAMBA, its eastern neighbor.

In the aftermath of the Portuguese defeat, Ndongo recovered some of its lost provinces, but not the post of Masangano. In the subsequent years Mbandi a Ngola Kiluanje took over as king, but faced serious opposition from factions in the country, which gave the Portuguese the opportunity to establish new posts at Cambambe (in 1602) and then at Hango (in 1611). Four years later, Portuguese governors established an alliance with the IMBANGALA, whose military support helped them to attack Ndongo again. The Portuguese-Imbangala alliance was strongest under the Portuguese governor Luis Mendes de Vasconcelos, who arrived in Angola as the new king, Ngola Mbandi (1617–1624), was installed. Mendes de Vasconcelos sacked Ndongo's capital and drove the king to seek refuge on the islands of Kindonga in the Kwanza River, at the eastern end of his realm. From there Ngola Mbandi sought peace with Portugal and the withdrawal of the Imbangala bands. Although they made promises of help, none of the Portuguese governors were willing or able to drive out the Imbangala or to restore the lands they had taken from Ngola Mbandi. The king, despondent over the destruction of so much of his kingdom, committed suicide in 1624, leaving only a minor son to succeed him. Ngola Mbandi's sister, NJINGA MBANDI, took over as regent after her brother's death and pressed harder for the Portuguese to fulfill their promises. The Portuguese government, however, demanded concessions of Njinga that she was unprepared to make and war broke out in 1626. In a series of wars and lesser engagements, the Portuguese drove Njinga from the old capital on the islands of Kindonga, and established Ngola Hari as a puppet king of Ndongo. Ngola Hari, who ruled from his capital in the rocky fortress of Mpungo a Ndongo, fought against Njinga and helped to force her from the country.

Njinga took the remnants of the army and fled into the lowlands east of Ndongo. There she made her own alliances with the Imbangala army of KASANJE and captured Matamba, making it her new base, around 1631. She reoccupied the Kindonga islands and in 1639 was prepared to make peace with Portugal.

When Dutch forces took Luanda in 1641 and drove the Portuguese to seek refuge at Masangano, Njinga led armies back to the west, reclaiming lands that had been lost to the Portuguese since the 1620s. In 1647 a combined Dutch-Ndongo force defeated the Portuguese and besieged Masangano, but a Portuguese relief expedition in 1648 forced them to abandon the siege and return to Matamba. In 1656 Njinga negotiated a new peace treaty with Portugal recognizing their possession of many of her lands and recognizing her as the queen of Matamba and a part of Ndongo. The treaty left the puppet kings of Mpungo a Ndongo without clear legal footing as rulers of Ndongo, leading them to revolt in 1670. After a long campaign, the Portuguese took Mpungu a Ndongo in 1671 and extinguished the last claims of that line to independence. After this point the history of Ndongo merges with that of Matamba.

Ndowe

Coastal people of Equatorial Guinea, Cameroon, and Gabon.

Ndowe is a name broadly given to the Bantu-speaking coastal people of EQUATORIAL GUINEA. The two primary ethnic groups who speak the Kombe language are the Boumba, including the Banga and Bapuku people, and Bongue, including the Kombe, Bomoudi, Asangon, Muiko, and others. The Spanish referred to them as *playeros*, or "beach dwellers."

Historians believe that these groups began arriving on the coast from the upper UBANGI RIVER between the twelfth and fourteenth centuries. Settling along the Mbini, or Muni, River and its affluents and the beaches, they fished, hunted, and grew cassava, malanga, and plantains. Living in scattered village communities linked by lineage and clans, they were increasingly dominated by the more politically centralized FANG and prevented from settling inland. Despite frequent conflicts, intermarriage between the Ndowe and the Fang was common, as it was between the Ndowe and the Bayele "PYGMY" peoples. The most unifying force among Ndowe communities was the transethnic BWITI, adopted at the end of the 1800s, which promotes "one-heartness" among its followers.

When European slave traders became increasingly active in the region during the late fifteenth century, the Ndowe first fled inland but later returned to act as middlemen between the Fang and Europeans. Foreign diseases and the return of the Fang following the end of the slave trade decimated the Ndowe. Under Spanish COLONIAL RULE in Equatorial Guinea, the Ndowe's subordinate position vis à vis the Fang was sustained, though they were also protected from Fang dominance. At the 1967 Constitutional Conference, the ethno-nationalist Ndowe Union advocated for Ndowe representation. But soon after independence the following year, the Ndowe became a subject of the Fang-dominated government's repression.

See also Cameroon; Gabon.

Eric Young

Neal, Larry

1937–1981

American poet, essayist, and editor who helped develop the aesthetic theory of the Black Arts Movement.

An important contributor to the development of the BLACK ARTS MOVEMENT, Larry Neal received his B.A. from LINCOLN UNIVERSITY and his M.A. from the University of Pennsylvania in 1963. He published two books of poetry using BEBOP and the BLUES as aesthetic references: *Black Boogaloo: Notes on Black Liberation* (1969) and *Hoodoo Hollerin' Bebop Ghosts* (1971). In addition to founding several journals, Neal, with AMIRI BARAKA, founded Harlem's Black Arts Repertory Theater and edited the seminal nationalist anthology, *Black Fire*. (1968).

Bibliography

Martin, Reginald. "Total Life Is What We Want: The Progressive Stages of the New Black Aesthetic in Literature." *South Atlantic Review*, Nov. 1988.

Peter Hudson

Nefertiti

Queen of ancient Egypt.

Nefertiti was one of the most powerful women in the history of Egypt. Scholars generally believe that she exercised priestly powers previously reserved for the pharaoh alone. However, our knowledge of Nefertiti comes almost exclusively from the archaeological record, which allows few firm conclusions and leaves much room for speculation.

Nefertiti's origins are uncertain, although many believe she was a princess from the MIDDLE EAST. She was the chief wife of the pharaoh Akhenaton, who reigned 1353–1335 B.C.E. Akhenaton's rule is famous because of the religious reforms that he and Nefertiti instituted. Some scholars believe that Nefertiti was primarily responsible for these reforms. The royal couple established monotheism in Egypt by abandoning the Egyptian pantheon and instituting the worship of the sun god Aton, and requiring all Egyptian people to do the same.

By all accounts Nefertiti believed devoutly in Aton, and some scholars believe that her devotion caused her demise. Such religious change was controversial in Egypt, which had a powerful priestly caste that pressured Akhenaton to revert to traditional religious beliefs. The woman with whom Akhenaton had six daughters and who, in Akhenaton's words, was "The Hereditary Princess, Great of Favor, Mistress of Happiness . . . Great and Beloved Wife of the King . . . Nefertiti," largely disappears from the historical record in the twelfth year of his reign. Many scholars believe she retired to the northern palace at Amarna after a confrontation with Akhenaton in which she proved unwilling to abandon exclusive worship of Aton. Nefertiti is perhaps best known from the painted limestone bust that was discovered at Tell el-Amarna, the ruins of the ancient capital, Akhetaton, from which she reigned until her fall from grace.

Robert Fay

Negrista Poets

Group of Latin American and Caribbean poets, mostly white and middle class, who incorporated black themes of folklore, religious practices, music, and dance in their work.

Negrista, or "blackish" poetry, also known as *poesía negroide* (negroid poetry) or *afroantillano* (afro-antillean, the term preferred by Palés Matos), should not be confused with *poesía negra*, or black poetry. Black poetry—also identified as *poesía mulata* (mulatto poetry, the term preferred by Afro-Cuban poet NICOLÁS GUILLÉN), *afrocubanista* (AFROCUBANISMO), or Afro-Hispanic—generally refers to poetry written mostly by black and mulatto authors that reflects a social and cultural investment in black communities. In contrast, negrista poets, or the negrismo movement more generally, refers to mostly white, middle-class writers whose poetry tended to objectify blacks and mulattoes as exotic. Both definitions represent an extreme; many poets fell somewhere in between on the spectrum.

In 1925 Puerto Rican poet LUIS PALÉS MATOS published the poem "Black Town," which in the view of some scholars initiated the negrista poetry movement. Others cite earlier poems published in the 1920s, such as "The African Dancer," by Ballagas, or "Black Man and Black Woman," by Llorens Torres. In any case, as literary critic Leslie Wilson notes, negrista poetry conjures racist stereotypes of "pseudo-African rhythms and expressions . . . grotesque gestures and simian capers for provoking white laughter . . . jiving, high-stepping Black carousers . . . and sinewy, vivacious, voluptuous, and carefree Black and mulatto women who light the lamps of love." Caricaturesque portrayals of blacks emerged in negrista poetry that were fashioned largely to satisfy a growing penchant for African themes in art and literature, sparked by nineteenth-century scholars who had written of their travels to Africa. Wilson explains that scholars like the German Leo Frobenius "thronged to Dark Africa to drink from its bountiful fountain of human knowledge and artistic inspiration." Ethnographic narratives about sub-Saharan Africa, and anthologies of oral literature of African kingdoms like BENIN, MALI, and SONGHAI compiled by European travelers captured the attention of artists and intellectuals both in Europe and in Latin America, resulting in a burgeoning audience for all things African. Negrista poetry exoticized black themes, incorporating them as curiosities for a largely white, elite audience. The thematic and formal characteristics of much of this poetry included the use of black musical forms as a basis for linguistic and literary experiments; onomatopoeic words; African words; allusions to a mythical Africa; oral histories; and religious practices, dances, and beliefs.

In contrast, black poetry generally resisted the folkloric in favor of a poetics that denoted a social and linguistic collective history. Thus, it was not a poetry that imitated or recreated superficial cultural expressions or racist stereotypes, but one that tried to invoke a social and cultural authenticity in relating everyday black and mulatto experiences. Still, such divisions between blackish and black poetry were not always well defined in the 1940s and 1950s. As Wilson observes, Guillén himself wrote folkloric poems at one point in his career, and one of the negrista poets, Emilio Ballagas, published a poem that advocated racial harmony and solidarity with his Afro-Cuban compatriots.

In the 1930s Cuban scholar FERNANDO ORTIZ's anthropological studies in Latin America, as well as the dominance of Afro-Cuban music throughout the world, contributed to the popularity of negrismo as an intellectual and artistic movement. Unlike NÉGRITUDE in the Francophone Caribbean, however, negrista poetry tended to essentialize black and mulatto stereotypes. While Négritude represented a key movement for black pride and political independence for MARTINIQUE and GUADELOUPE, negrismo's political implications are more ambiguous. Early on, in the 1920s, many negrista poets remained essentially aloof to everyday black and mulatto experiences, preferring to portray blacks with mythical or comical connotations. However, in CUBA, for example, when middle-class artists began to feel the pressure of the Gerardo Machado dictatorship in the 1930s, they ironically turned to Afro-Cubans, targets of much discrimination at the time, as models for forging a national identity. Influenced by afrocubanismo and by the HARLEM RENAISSANCE, some negrista poets, like Emilio Ballagas, would invoke mulatto nationalism. Still others, Palés Matos in particular, argued for a Pan-Caribbean or Antillean identity but remained focused on technical poetic innovation rather than the social status of Afro-Cubans. Thus some links between early blackish poets and black poets were established, though the two were distinct movements that implied very different sociocultural viewpoints. Negrista poets, by most scholars' accounts, stereotyped blacks in their writings. Such portrayals mostly affirmed elite ideas about blacks and the popular classes, yet they were influential in ushering Afro-Caribbean themes to the forefront of emerging national identities.

Joy Elizondo

Négritude

Neologism coined by Martinican poet and statesman Aimé Césaire in Paris in the 1930s in discussions with fellow students Léopold Sédar Senghor and Léon Gontran-Damas.

The concept of Négritude represents a historic development in the formulation of African diasporic identity and culture in this century. The term marks a revalorization of Africa on the part of New World blacks, affirming an overwhelming pride in black heritage and culture, and asserting, in MARCUS GARVEY's words, that blacks are "descendants of the greatest and proudest race who ever peopled the earth." The concept finds its roots in the thought of MARTIN DELANY, EDWARD WILMOT BLYDEN, and W. E. B. DU BOIS, each of whom sought to erase the stigma attached to the black world through their intellectual and political efforts on behalf of the African diaspora. Early in this century, French Caribbean politicians such as HÉGÉSIPPE LÉGITIMUS, René Boisneuf, and Gratien Candace affirmed the right and necessity of blacks to enter into the global community as equals, while historians such as Oruno Lara strove to "edify a more beautiful past, drawing upon our heritage of sacrifice and probity." The inspiration for AIMÉ CÉSAIRE's term comes most directly, however, from the example of the HARLEM RENAISSANCE, in which writers such as LANGSTON HUGHES and CLAUDE MCKAY explored and revendicated the richness of black culture. LÉOPOLD SÉDAR SENGHOR himself has referred to McKay as the "the true inventor of [the values of] Négritude. . . . Far from seeing in one's blackness an inferiority, one accepts it, one lays claim to it with pride, one cultivates it lovingly." Like the evolution of the term *black* in the United States, Négritude took a stigmatized term and turned it into a point of pride.

As a historical movement, Négritude received two competing interpretations. Césaire's original conception sees the specificity and unity of black existence as a historically developing phenomenon that arose through the highly contingent events of the African slave trade and the New World plantation system. This formulation was gradually displaced in intellectual debate by Senghor's essentialist interpretation of Négritude, which argues for an unchanging core or essence to black existence. As this later formulation gained currency, it was widely attacked, all the more so as Senghor, then president of an independent SENEGAL, came to use the term ideologically to justify his own political platform. Senghor's Négritude nonetheless served to reverse the system of values that had informed Western perception of blacks since the earliest voyages of discovery to Africa. Césaire's developmental model of Négritude, on the other hand, continues to offer a model for the ongoing project of black liberation in all its fullness, at once spiritual and political.

First used by Césaire in his 1939 poem "Cahier d'un retour au pays natal" (Notebook of a Return to My Native Land), Négritude refers to a collective identity of the African Diaspora born of a common historical and cultural experience of subjugation. Césaire writes, "Négritude, not a cephalic index, or a plasma, or a soma, but measured by the compass of suffering." Both the term and the subsequent literary and cultural movement that developed equally emphasized the possible negation of that subjugation via concerted actions of racial affirmation, of which the HAITIAN REVOLUTION (1791–1804) is the prototype. In succeeding decades the term became a focus for ideological disputes among the black intelligentsia of a Francophone world in the process of decolonization, and writers such as Léopold Sédar Senghor, FRANTZ FANON, and the Anglophone WOLE SOYINKA each weighed in with their own reformulations and critiques of Césaire's concept. Négritude as a concept encompassed and distilled a wide range of previous historical moments, in turn generating a diverse field of debate that has, in its use of the term, extended, and at times even contradicted, Césaire's original intervention.

Origins of Négritude

The historical origins of Négritude can be traced to the various forms of cultural expression in the French Caribbean that find their roots in the African continent, practices that were transmogrified by the experience of the MIDDLE PASSAGE and slavery. Like the North American spirituals first championed in W. E. B. Du Bois' *The Souls of Black Folk,* a variety of arts and practices served as refuges for Afro-Caribbean pride and African culture: the dances called *calenda, bamboula,* and *laghia;* the drumming and songs of the *bel-air, Gwoka,* and *léwoz;* Creole culinary arts; the *Kric-Krac* folktales; and the multitude of practices arising from Hatian VODOU. Forced underground by the violence and racism of slavery, this proto-Négritude manifested itself less as overt, self-proclaimed affirmation than through the concrete, positive production of cultural, religious, and aesthetic practices. In addition, black slaves at times responded to the threat of annihilation with self-affirmation in the form of overt resistance: feigned laziness, ignorance or incompetence, theft, poisoning of animals and burning of buildings, escape into maroon communities, and organized revolts.

The social dynamics of a Caribbean society created through the institution of slavery and its vehicle, the plantation (in its French variant, *l'habitation*), resulted in a powerful ideological valorization of and identification with a highly centralized metropolitan French culture. For commentators such as EDOUARD GLISSANT, this identification explains the success and longevity of a French colonial project that, in his estimation, continues to this day in the very MARTINIQUE that Aimé Césaire helped to integrate juridically in 1945. This overwhelming cultural identification points to the radicality of Césaire's revalorization of African, rather than French, culture. The Franco-centric cultural reference also explains why literary models for Négritude must be sought elsewhere in the African Diaspora. No equivalent of OLAUDAH EQUIANO's 1789 slave narrative, *Interesting Narrative of the Life of Olaudah Equiano,* or the various autobiographical narratives of Anglophone authors such as PHILLIS WHEATLEY, OTTOBAH CUGOANO, and FREDERICK DOUGLASS, appears to have survived in French Antillean letters. The French Code Noir of 1685 had forbidden blacks to read or write, and remained in effect through 1848. The authors PATRICK CHAMOISEAU and RAPHAËL CONFIANT have described how, in a century and a half of literary production preceding Césaire, Martinican writing was characterized by a triple rupture. "From oral to written [production], a rupture of enunciation; from the Creole language to French, a rupture of language; from the storyteller to the writer, a temporal-spatial rupture." The result was a literature entirely subordinated to a "French cultural superego," mimetically echoing succeeding French literary fashions (Romantic, Parnassian, then Symbolist poetry), mired in the tradition of literary exoticism (*doudouisme*).

Despite the fundamental importance of the German philosopher Georg Wilhelm Friedrich Hegel for both Césaire and subsequent participants in the Négritude debate such as Frantz Fanon, RICHARD WRIGHT, and Jean-Paul Sartre, an insidious aspect of Hegel's philosophy decisively marked the development of proto-Négritude thought in the nineteenth century. Hegel notoriously exempted blacks from the processes of historical development in his *Philosophy of History,* stating that their "condition is capable of no development of Culture, and as we see them at this day, such they have always been." Hegel's thesis participated in the development of a biological racism, whose main proponents in the French tradition were the doctor J. J. Virey, the biologist Georges Cuvier, and the writer Joseph-Artur de Gobineau. This field of thought articulated a belief in the inferiority of blacks based upon supposed physical and intellectual traits, furthermore presupposing the existence of discrete races that modern genetics has repeatedly disproved. In response, writers such as ALEXANDER CRUMMELL, Martin Robison Delany, and Edward Wilmot Blyden sought to rescue the image of Africa for New World blacks. Delany organized the first scientific expedition to Africa from the Western Hemisphere and is acknowledged as the founder of BLACK NATIONALISM in America, while Blyden undertook the revalorization of African history after Hegel's blanket condemnation, developing as well an early form of Pan-Africanist thought that prefigures the championing of African culture enacted in Césaire's Négritude. W. E. B. Du Bois continued this turn to Africa, and initiated reflection upon the formal continuities of African diasporic culture. The fruits of that more general reflection informed Du Bois's critique of North American racism in works such as *The Souls of Black Folk* in ways strikingly similar to Césaire's later critique of the specific forms of French racism as found in Martinique and Paris. Though not well known to Césaire in 1939, intellectual forerunners like Du Bois, Delany, and Blyden thus anticipated that aspect of Négritude that strives for the revalorization of Africa in French Caribbean culture.

Certain lone figures in the French Caribbean, however, also participated in the affirmation of black culture. The early years of the French Third Republic (1871–1940) witnessed profound changes in Martinican and Guadeloupean culture. Economies previously based on the production of sugarcane were thrown into a long decline that would continue into this century, after the introduction of cheaply produced sugar beets undercut global sugar prices, making competition impossible. This recession, combined with the presence of a black proletariat and nascent middle class following the abolition of slavery in the French colonies in 1848, paved the way for the novel success of black socialist politicians such as Hégésippe Légitimus of Guadeloupe. Martinican politics remained dominated through this period by members of the white land-owning béké class, such as Ernest Deproge and Osman Duquesnay. In contrast, a relatively small béké population in Guadeloupe led that island's elected positions to be filled by representatives of the mulatto bourgeoisie, such as Gerville-Réache, Sarlat, Auguste Isaac, and Emile Réaux. The electoral defeat of the mulatto Issac by Légitimus in 1898 signals the triumph of black electoral politics in the region, foreshadowing Césaire's fifty-year dominance of Martinican politics as both mayor of Fort-de-France and Martinican representative in the French General Assembly. If Légitimus's early affirmation of racial pride and solidarity predated the Négritude movement by three decades, his recourse to race baiting in electoral politics soon reduced him to inflammatory diatribes against mulatto politicians, whom he referred to as "parasites" and "yellow politicians." Other black Guadeloupean politicians, such as René Boisneuf and Gratien Candace, continued the processes initiated by Légitimus in the years before the emergence of Négritude. Candace, along with Césaire one of the leading black political figures in French politics of the twentieth century, was one of the first black colonial leaders to begin questioning French racial and colonial hegemony.

World War I (1914–1919) had brought blacks from the French Caribbean colonies of Martinique, Guadeloupe, and FRENCH GUIANA to Europe. Already benefiting from full French citizenship since 1848, they, along with Senegalese blacks, fought beside metropolitan and black American soldiers, and sent representatives to the French parliament following the war. BLAISE DIAGNE of Senegal and Gratien Candace organized the first PAN-AFRICAN CONGRESS with W. E. B. Du Bois in 1919, immediately following the armistice. Though only tentative steps were taken in condemning colonialism at the congress, it nonetheless marked the beginnings of a truly international solidarity among members of the African Diaspora.

In addition, a series of journals, publications, and organizations appeared that prefigure the Négritude of Aimé Césaire. In 1924 Kojo Tovalou Houénou of BENIN founded the *Ligue universelle de défense de la race noire,* which two years later would change its name to the *Comité de défense de la race nègre.* The league's journal, *La Voix des Nègres,* quotes Légitimus's revendication of black pride: "We honor and glorify ourselves in using the word *Black* [*Nègre*] with a capital B." In 1927 Lenis Blanche founded an *Association des étudiants guadeloupéens,* while the *Comité de défense* confusingly changes name again to become the *Ligue de défense de la race nègre,* arguing in its journal, *La Race Nègre,* for the collaboration between (Francophone) black intellectuals and workers, and calling for a student-led PAN-AFRICANISM. In 1928 the Internationale Syndicale Rouge published in Moscow *L'Ouvrier Nègre,* in defense of "the disinherited son of the proletarian family." In 1931 the Ligue split, and Tiémoko Garan Kouyaté founded, with the Martinican communist Trissot, the journal *Le Cri des Nègres.* This black communist journal vigorously defended Antillean workers, and its circulation was severely limited by the French authorities.

In the realm of black cultural production, *La Dépêche africaine,* published from 1928 to 1930 with the participation of RENÉ MARAN and the Nardal sisters, saw its mission as forming a "juncture between Negroes of the entire world" via the valorization of black aesthetic and intellectual production. In 1928 the publication of JEAN PRICE-MARS's *Ainsi parla l'oncle* (So Spoke the Uncle) was the first overt condemnation of the colonial identification with French culture, which had led, in Price-Mars's famous formulation, to a "collective boveryism" or romanticized yearning for French cultural products and the denigration of African-derived culture such as Haitian Vodou. In 1931 the *Revue du monde noir* valorized black cultural production, positioning itself as a moderate, pro-assimilationist voice. Far more radical, the revue *Légitime Défense,* founded in 1932 by the Martinican ETIENNE LÉRO, combined in its single published issue discourses of Surrealism, Hegelian Marxism, and Freudianism in its vehement condemnation of French colonialism, racism, and capitalist exploitation. Despite a certain lack of depth in its analysis and the immaturity of its poetic texts, it marked a fundamental step in the assertion of black identity in the Francophone world. In 1934 the twenty-one-year-old student Césaire, along with GILBERT GRATIANT, Léonard Sainville, Paulette Nardal, and Césaire's fellow student Léopold Sédar Senghor, founded the review *L'Etudiant Noir.* More moderate in tone than *Légitime Défense,* it nonetheless contains Césaire's first published text, the poem "Nègreries," in which he clearly prefigures Négritude in his forceful, affirmative use of the stigmatized term *nègre,* refusing the assimilation of blacks into French society in favor of "emancipation."

Throughout the 1920s the triumph of Russian Bolshevism was followed closely throughout the African Diaspora. Though the French Communist Party long regarded colonialism as strictly subsidiary to the triumph of European proletarian revolution, journals such as *Les Continents* (founded in 1924 by René Maran and Kodjo Touvalou) and, in particular, *L'Action coloniale* (founded in 1918 by Maurice Boursaud) were fundamental in articulating a preliminary Marxist condemnation of colonialism. An increasing social and juridical permeability between colonized and colonizer helped make possible the rapid changes in black consciousness that occurred through the 1920s and 1930s.

The Harlem Renaissance was also central to Césaire's concept of Négritude. Césaire wrote a dissertation on the movement in the 1930s, and Langston Hughes, Claude McKay, JAMES WELDON JOHNSON, JEAN TOOMER, and COUNTEE CULLEN were already well known among the Paris-based Antillean intelligentsia when Césaire arrived there in 1931. The Jamaican McKay in particular, in works such as *Banjo,* expressed a keen perception of the fractures dividing black cultures along lines of pigmentation and class. Indeed, Senghor has gone so far as to cite McKay as the spiritual founder of Négritude: "Claude McKay can rightfully be considered the true inventor of Négritude. I speak not of the word, but of the values of Négritude. . . . Far from seeing in one's blackness an inferiority, one accepts it, one lays claim to it with pride, one cultivates it lovingly." Léon Gontran Damas's 1930 collection of poems *Pigments* powerfully appropriated many of McKay's insights, its violent condemnation of racial division and colonialist assimilation serving as the most immediate spur to Césaire's invention of Négritude. In Haiti a similar renaissance occurred during the 1920s and 1930s, as journals like the *Revue indigène* and writers such as JACQUES ROUMAIN, Emile Roumer, and JACQUES STÉPHEN ALÉXIS developed the racial revendication articulated in Price-Mars's *Ainsi parla l'oncle.*

The work of another Caribbean, Marcus Garvey, though unknown to Césaire in 1939, anticipates the concept of Négritude in more than one respect. Garvey's critique of an assimilationist black middle class announces that of French Antilleans such as Léro and Césaire, while his revalorization of African culture is similar to both Césaire's and Senghor's subsequent development of Négritude. "Negroes," Garvey implored, "teach your children that they are direct descendants of the greatest and proudest race who ever peopled the earth." In 1933 the Jamaican LEONARD PERCIVAL HOWELL founded the Rastafarian movement, striving to "construct the black race economically, the better to serve God." Elsewhere in the Caribbean, Cuban poets allied with the *Revista de Estudios Afrocubanos,* and NICOLAS GUILLÉN in particular, along with the Cuban painter WIFREDO LAM, sought to explore and valorize their African heritage.

Certain European intellectuals were central to the elaboration of Négritude. The fashionable interest in African art and culture that arose in 1920s Paris in the work of Pablo Picasso, the writers Jean Cocteau, Blaise Cendrars, and André Gide, and the composer Darius Milhaud made reference to an often vague amalgam known as *l'art nègre*. Too often, little effort was made to differentiate between the cultural traditions of regions as diverse as DAKAR, SENEGAL, BAHIA, Brazil, and HARLEM, NEW YORK, in deference to a putative "black soul." Nonetheless, this movement created a climate of receptivity in which intellectuals such as André Breton and Sartre would quickly recognize the importance of Négritude in the 1940s. Anthropologists also turned to Africa and its diaspora in these years. Maurice Delafosse, in his 1927 work *Les Nègres,* applied to African culture the methods of ethnographic analysis. The German Leo Frobenius's *History of African Civilization* was translated into French in 1936 and avidly read by both Césaire and Senghor. "We knew by heart chapter II of the first book of the History," Senghor has written, "entitled 'What does Africa mean to us?' a chapter adorned with lapidary phrases such as this: 'The idea of the "barbarous Negro" is a European invention, which in turn dominated Europe until the beginning of this century.'" Frobenius's work, along with Oswald Spengler's *The Decline of the West* (1918), provided Césaire and Senghor with a conception of history in which a tired, defeated West might be replaced by more vital African diasporic cultures.

Césaire's revendication of the term *nègre,* though mirroring parallel processes occurring in the North American adoption first of *black,* then *African American* as self-designations, occurred in a specific historical and linguistic environment. In 1939, when Césaire's poem appeared, the term *noir* (black) roughly corresponded to the socially valorized North American *Negro.* The traditional French Caribbean identification with metropolitan French culture also meant, in the view of commentators like Frantz Fanon, that black Antilleans were largely alienated from their African roots. In Fanon's words, the Antillean black until 1939 conceived of Africa as "a country of savages, of barbarians, of natives, of 'boys.' . . . The African was a nigger ['nègre'] and the Antillean a European." In France during the 1920s and 1930s, *nègre,* particularly in its adjectival form, was used more or less interchangeably with *noir* (*l'art nègre, la musique nègre*). In Martinique, however, the term *nègre* shared a functional similarity with the racist North American epithet *nigger.* A. James Arnold credits Césaire with being the first black intellectual outside Africa to have taken the humiliating term *nigger* and boldly transformed it into the proud term *black.* The specificity of Césaire's intervention and affirmation arises from this highly specific historical conjuncture of self-alienation, in which, Fanon states, "haunted by impurity, overwhelmed by sin, ridden by guilt, [the Antillean] lives the drama of being neither white nor black ['nègre']."

In addition to its historical importance, Césaire's coining of the term *Négritude* possesses a philosophical dimension later developed in the work of Fanon (1952) and Sartre. Theoretically, and in contradistinction to the uses and abuses that the term would undergo in succeeding decades, Négritude in the "Cahier d'un retour au pays natal" possesses a decidedly objective status. That is to say, Césaire refuses to presuppose the existence of a self-identical, autonomous black subject, and instead describes a self-alienated subject that is forced to confront, as if in a mirror, its own "unfreedom" and predetermination within a racist society. Previous articulations of black identity in the Francophone world opted uniformly for the latter. Earlier in the century—to cite two relevant examples—Hégésippe Légitimus had affirmed with pride his status as *nègre,* while Oruno Lara in his 1921 *History of Guadeloupe* proclaimed his pride to be a "writer of the black race." Lara states that his book—a little-known precursor to Négritude—is "the image of the painful and formidable creation of an American continent wrought with African tears and blood," written to serve "our advancement." The first black historian of the region and author of the 1923 novel *Questions de couleur: Blanches et noires,* went on to affirm that "If, born yesterday, we seem to have neither a past, nor civil status, it was up to one of us to edify a more beautiful past, drawing upon our heritage of sacrifice and probity."

Césaire's concept of Négritude, in contrast to these and many other postulations of black identity that came before it, objectifies the self-alienation of colonized black subjects through an act of creation: the neologism. In Césaire's usage, an alienated black identity is forced to confront itself as a reified object:

ma négritude n'est pas une pierre, sa surdité ruée contre la clameur du jour
ma négritude n'est pas une taie d'eau morte sur l'œil mort de la terre
ma négritude n'est ni une tour ni une cathédrale
elle plonge dans la chair rouge du sol
elle plonge dans la chair ardente du ciel
elle troue l'accablement opaque de sa droite patience. (1994: 42)

(my Négritude is not a stone, its deafness dashed against the clamor of the day
my Négritude is not an opaque spot of dead water on the dead eye of the earth
my Négritude is neither a tower nor a cathedral
it plunges into the red flesh of the soil
it plunges into the ardent flesh of the sky
it pierces opaque prostration with its upright patience.)

This conception postulates Négritude as self-estrangement, a fact or quality that confronts the black subject as an object. Such a gesture initiates a movement in Césaire's poem toward a self-consciousness that breaks the bonds of subjugation through a grappling with negativity in the form of self-alienation. Négritude is not the lifeless object society has reduced it to (stone, spot, or even tower). Instead, it is active, creative, and liberatory (plunging, piercing through the world that had enchained it in subjection). Césaire applies to the realm of black subjectivity Hegel's insight that "alienation" is in fact a transformational process in which the individual's so-called "natural" existence—in this case the ideological subjugation of blacks—is concretely negated for an artificial, self-created one: "[The self's] actuality consists solely in the setting-aside of its natural self. . . . The self knows itself as actual only as a transcended self." Césaire's neologism is at once the naming and active instantiation of the very process it describes, tracing the liberation of black subjectivity through a confrontation with racism and colonialism. Négritude is thus for Césaire the self-created object that negates the very objectivity of black existence itself—where humans are reduced to pure animal-objects (slaves)—in a becoming-human. Humans, following Marx's articulation of Hegel, "distinguish themselves from animals as soon as they begin to produce . . ." In the concept of Négritude, Aimé Césaire produced the material, textual objectification of black self-consciousness, a program for self-understanding and liberation.

Growth of Négritude as a Movement

When Aimé Césaire returned to Martinique in 1939, the term *Négritude* was known and used only by the small circle of black intellectuals who had surrounded Césaire in Paris, in particular Senghor and Léon-Gantron Damas. Césaire's "Cahier" was itself virtually unknown, having appeared only in an obscure Parisian review, *Volontés*. During the occupation of Martinique by the Nazi-controlled Vichy government, Césaire, along with his wife, Suzanne, René Menil, and Aristide Maugée, edited from 1941 to 1945 the journal Tropiques. The journal enacted a profound refusal of white European cultural values and references in favor of those of the African diaspora. Unlike Césaire's earlier historicizing use of the term Négritude, articles such as "What Does Africa Mean to Us?" argued for a biologically based notion of black identity inherited from Frobenius, in which a black "biological reality" is invoked to account for black identity. During this period, as A. James Arnold has argued, both Césaire's and Senghor's uncritical reliance upon a sanguinary ideology of African "blood" resonates disturbingly with Fascist doctrine of the era. At the same time, *Tropiques* appealed non-dogmatically to a heterogeneous field of influences, invoking those elements of a European aesthetic heritage (surrealism, the French poets Rimbaud and Leautréamont) whose iconoclastic work could be appropriated as a tool in refashioning black Caribbean culture.

In 1947 Léon-Gontran Damas published an anthology of poetry from the French colonies, and in the following year Léopold Senghor published a similar collection, *Anthologie de la nouvelle poésie nègre et malgache de langue française*. In addition to Césaire, Damas, and Senghor, a number of black Francophone poets and writers produced works that participated indirectly in the project of Négritude, reflecting upon the vicissitudes of black existence. Paul Niger, David Diop, and Guy Tirollien all explored diasporic psyches damaged by colonialism and the contradictions of a dual African and European heritage. The novels of Cheikh Hamadou Kane (*L'Aventure ambiguée*), Mongo Beti (*Pauvre Christ de Bomba*), and Ousmane Sembène (*La Femme noire*) articulated the various forms of alienation encountered by colonized African subjects.

Senghor's 1948 anthology featured a preface by Jean-Paul Sartre, "Black Orpheus," that is largely responsible for establishing the concept of Négritude at the center of postwar Francophone debate regarding black identity. Sartre's position as the dominant postwar Francophone intellectual caused the Négritude debate to focus on his articulation of the concept, with subsequent participants often defining their use of the term in relation to Sartre's analysis. Sartre's text develops the Hegelian category of negativity in relation to black consciousness, building upon the Russian philosopher Alexandre Kojève's influential lectures on Hegel's master/slave dialectic. Sartre endorses the notion of a racial essence ("The black soul is an Africa from which the black ['nègre'] is exiled amidst the cold buildings of white culture and technology"), grounding this conception within the undeniable visibility of skin color: "A Jew, a white among whites, can deny that he is a Jew, declaring himself a man among men. The black cannot deny that he is black nor claim for himself an abstract, colorless humanity: he is black. Thus he is driven to authenticity: insulted, enslaved, he raises himself up. He picks up the word *black* [nègre] that they had thrown at him like a stone, he asserts his blackness, facing the white man, with pride." Frantz Fanon critiques Senghor's famous statement "Emotion is black as Reason is Hellenic," indicting Césaire and Senghor's glorification of the irrational as a "regressive process" in his 1952 study *Black Skin, White Masks*. He then proceeds to attack Sartre's interpretation of Négritude as what the latter termed an "antiracist racism." Fanon critiques Sartre's reduction of Négritude to "the weak pole (or antithesis) of a dialectical progression" from within the very Hegelian perspective Sartre invokes: "For once, this born Hegelian [Sartre] had forgotten that consciousness needs to lose itself in absolute night, this being the only requirement for the attainment of self-consciousness." Fanon violently refuses Sartre's vision of an instrumentalized black identity dissolved in the Hegelian *aufhebung* (sublation) of a "raceless society," asserting: "I am not a potentiality for something. I am fully that which I am."

In 1947 Alioune Diop of Senegal began in Paris the journal Présence Africaine with the backing of the Parisian and colonial intelligentsia, including André Gide, Jean-Paul Sartre, Albert Camus, Aimé Césaire, and many others. The journal was fundamental in articulating the parameters of African diasporic culture, addressing a global audience of English and French speakers in more than a half century of publication. In addition, *Présence Africaine* sponsored a series of celebrated conferences uniting black scholars of the world, at the Sorbonne in 1956 and in Rome in 1959. In 1966 *Présence Africaine* also sponsored the First World Festival of Negro Arts in Dakar, Senegal. By the time Senghor organized a Colloquium on Négritude in 1971, Négritude had itself become a highly contested term, whose interpretation had rigidified into a largely ideological concept.

During the postwar period, the concept of Négritude developed along two opposing lines of interpretation. The first sustains the notion as a cultural, historically developing process. This, we have seen, was implicit in Césaire's original conception of the term, and he increasingly abandoned any notion of Négritude as based upon a genetic or "blood" inheritance: "My Négritude has a ground. It is a fact that there is a black culture: it is historical, there is nothing biological about it." Similarly, recent interpretations of Fanon's work have underlined its historical dimensions; in this view, the author of *The Wretched of the Earth,* following Hegel's 1804 *Phenomenology of Spirit,* undertakes a veritable phenomenology of black consciousness as it moves from immersion in the immediacy of experience to self-consciousness and fully historical, human existence. In contrast, Léopold Senghor's notion of Négritude and the general reception and critique of the concept in West Africa following Senghor, focused on the putatively African characteristics of emotion, intuition, and artistic creativity as opposed to a Western, or Hellenic, rationality.

Senghor elaborates his conception of Négritude in various texts collected in the five-volume work *Liberté.* Dismissing without engaging the scientific invalidation of races, Senghor constructs a typology of an "eternal . . . black soul" based upon the categories of emotion, rhythmic attitude, humor, and "anthropopsychism." This last trait refers to the unmediated relation of the "black soul" to the phenomenological world, the "eternal . . . essential" trait, Senghor affirms, of the black soul. Though this early formulation dates from 1939, Senghor continued to defend and develop this conception of an "african personality" in the 1966 text "Négritude is a Humanism of the Twentieth Century," arguing tautologically for the objective existence of such a category (the "african personality"), since it had been accepted as a given over "60 years" of ethnological and sociological investigation. In this text, Senghor further elaborates his articulation of an immediate black apprehension of phenomena, invoking the philosophers Henri Bergson and Pierre Teilhard de Chardin. Senghor's Négritude is, to use his own term, an ontology, or study of the being of blacks in the world, a fundamentally ahistorical, transcultural determination of the constituents and commonalities of blackness in African diasporic societies. In 1969 he refers to it as a modification of the Hedeggerian Dasein, a "Neger-sein" or "black being." As Senghor himself points out in 1993, this ontological definition of Négritude has become the accepted one: in the standard French Robert dictionary, we find the definition "The ensemble of characteristics, of manners of thinking, of feeling, proper to the black race; belonging to the black race." There follows a quotation of Senghor. No mention is made of Césaire's act of neologism. Senghor's Négritude reverses the stigmatization of blacks derived from the nineteenth-century racialism of Gobineau, Lucien Lévy-Bruhl's concept of a prelogical "primitive mentality," and fictional works such as Paul Morand's stereotype-laden novel, *Magie noire* (1928). Senghor's postulation of an African ontology is echoed in works such as Placied Tempel's *La Philosophie bantoue* (1949). In turn, philosophers such as Marcien Towa (*Essai sur la problématique philosophique dans l'Afrique actuelle* [1971]) and Paulin Hountondji (*Sur la "Philosophie africain"* [1977]) have questioned whether traditional African philosophies can truly sustain such ontological interpretations.

Due to Senghor's overwhelming cultural and political influence in West Africa (he was president of Senegal from its independence in 1960 till 1981) it is precisely this ontological conception of Négritude that fueled attacks by writers such as Stanislas Adotevi. Adotevi's 1972 study *Négritude et négrologues* argues against a Senghorian racial explanation for African suffering in deference to a Marxist model of global capitalist exploitation. The Anglophone African nations received Négritude primarily as a politicized, ideological movement. Writers such as Es'kia Mphahlele, in *The African Image* (1962), and Wole Soyinka, in *Myth, Literature, and the African World* (1976), attacked a perceived cultural imperialism on the part of Francophone African intellectuals, the latter stating that "the tiger does not stalk about crying his tigritude." Senghor, responding to these attacks in 1969, points to the Anglophone historical derivation of Négritude from the African American writers of the Harlem Renaissance.

In the French Caribbean, Césaire's notion of Négritude has been developed and extended by another of his students, the writer Edouard Glissant. Glissant's notion of *antillanité,* developed in works such as the 1981 *Caribbean Discourse,* envisages an opening of black experience to the entirety of global culture. Like Césaire's earlier critique of cultural assimilation, Glissant argues against subsuming or dissolving an African and Creole Martinican identity in the economic and cultural imperialism of a North American-led "New World Order," without, on the other hand, limiting that region to a stifling provincialism. Other Antilleans have been more critical of aspects of Césaire's concept. The Guadeloupean author Maryse Condé critiques the notion of a return to Africa by black Antilleans in novels such as *Heremakonon* (1976). Her 1974 article "Négritude césairienne, Négritude senghorienne," while drawing attention to Césaire's neologism, offers a trenchant warning against the fetishization of blackness: "The Black ('Nègre') does not exist . . . [Négritude] is a sentimental and empty trap. Starting from an illusory 'racial' community founded upon a heritage of suffering, it obliterates the true problems that have always been of a political, social, and economic nature . . . Our liberation will come through the knowledge that there will never be any Blacks ('Nègres'). There has only ever been human exploitation." Condé's critique implies that Césaire's Négritude cannot remain a mere invocation to black identity politics; instead, the shock of its alienating gesture must serve to illuminate the very construction of blackness itself.

More recently, Jean Bernabé, Patrick Chamoiseau, and Raphaël Confiant attack what they see as the mythologization of Africa in Césaire's Négritude, affirming instead the heterogeneous status of Antillean culture, with its French, Hindu, Chinese, Amerindian, and African elements. This attack reaches its apex in Confiant's 1993 polemic against Césaire, *Une traversée paradoxale du siècle.*

The concept of Négritude represents a fundamental development in notions of African diasporic identity and culture in this century. The African and Antillean controversies around the term's reception and its rigidification into a politicized, ideological category initiated one of the fundamental debates in postwar global black thought, while Senghor's elaboration of the term itself constituted a radical reversal of dominant racialist discourse in the West. Finally, Césaire's historicizing phenomenological use of the term remains largely unexplored, implying for the black subject a developmental model of enlightenment that sustains and advances the transformational project of black liberation, pointing beyond the circularity of identity politics toward the elusive instantiation of a fully realized utopian freedom.

See also Afrocubanismo; Black Codes in Latin America; Dance in Latin America and the Caribbean; Literature, French-Language, in the Caribbean; Maroonage in the Americas; Music, Afro-Caribbean Secular; Slave Rebellions in Latin America and the Caribbean; Transatlantic Slave Trade; World War I and African Americans.

Bibliography
Arnold, A. James. *Modernism and Negritude.* Harvard University Press, 1981.
Césaire, Aimé. *La Poésie.* Editions du Seuil, 1994.
Sartre, Jean Paul. "Orphée Noire." *Situations III.* Gallimard, 1949.
Senghor, Léopold Sedar. *Liberté.* 5 vols. Editions du Seuil, 1964–1993.

Nick Nesbitt

Negro American Labor Council

Splinter group of the AFL-CIO, consisting of black workers who organized in 1960 to pressure the federation to end discrimination in its affiliate unions; became a driving force behind the 1963 March on Washington.

In May 1960, after the AMERICAN FEDERATION OF LABOR AND CONGRESS OF INDUSTRIAL ORGANIZATIONS (AFL-CIO) refused to impose sanctions against affiliate unions practicing discrimination, seventy-five African American trade unionists formed the Negro American Labor Council (NALC). Under the leadership of A. PHILIP RANDOLPH, president of the BROTHERHOOD OF SLEEPING CAR PORTERS, the new organization set out to accelerate the unionization of black workers and to put blacks into positions of union leadership. The broader aim of the group was to end discrimination against blacks in hiring and promotion.

By 1961 membership in the NALC had swelled to 10,000 across the nation. That year, Randolph presented a series of demands to the AFL-CIO Executive Council. Asserting that the status of black workers in the labor movement was that of "second class citizenship," he called on the federation to end discrimination within its ranks. This would require, he said, not only ending the color bar in affiliate unions and desegregating unions, but also placing African Americans on the AFL-CIO Executive Council and fighting to abolish barriers to employment training programs. The AFL-CIO's immediate response was to censure Randolph, and its officers charged that he himself had created the breach between blacks and labor with his accusations. At its fall convention the federation passed a series of civil rights resolutions that vowed an end to discrimination in the union. The AFL-CIO refused to meet the NALC demands fully, however, and left the decision to desegregate a voluntary one for the affiliates.

In one of the group's most important achievements, Randolph and the NALC first envisioned a massive march on Washington to demand jobs. The movement led to the 1963 March on Washington for Jobs and Freedom, where MARTIN LUTHER KING, JR., gave his famous "I have a dream" speech. The AFL-CIO refused to publicly support the march but other powerful unions, such as the United Auto Workers, did put their force behind it. The 1963 March on Washington solidified alliances between the leaders of the NALC and those of the CIVIL RIGHTS MOVEMENT that was expanding rapidly in the South.

See also Desegregation in the United States; March on Washington, 1963; Labor Leaders; Labor Unions in the United States.

Bibliography
Foner, Philip S. *Organized Labor and the Black Worker 1619–1973.* Praeger, 1974.

Marian Aguiar

Negro Ensemble Company

Longest-running black theater company in the United States.

The Negro Ensemble Company was founded in NEW YORK City in 1967 by actor-director-playwright Douglas Turner Ward, actor Robert Hooks, and white manager Gerald Krone. Their intent was to provide a space where black playwrights "could communicate with an audience of other Negroes, better informed through commonly shared experience to readily understand, confirm, or reject the truth or paucity of [their] creative explorations." This was during the height of the BLACK ARTS MOVEMENT, and many other companies shared this vision of creating theater by black people for black people. But while others were committed to theater with strong nationalistic and political messages, the Negro Ensemble Company produced a much wider spectrum of plays, including family dramas, folk musicals, and plays from African and Caribbean perspectives.

The Company was criticized by more militant artists for its less political messages, and for its early support from mainstream white sources such as the Ford Foundation. Its broader appeal, however, gave it staying power. In addition to producing plays, the company also offered actor training programs and playwrights' workshops. The Negro Ensemble Company's most successful productions included Joseph Walker's *The River Niger* (1972), which went to Broadway and won a Tony Award for best play of the year; Charles Fuller's Pulitzer-prize winning *A Soldier's Play* (1982); and Samm-Art Williams's *Home* (1979), which also became a Broadway success.

In 2003 the National Black Arts Festival honored the company for its contributions to American theater. Many current stage, movie, and television actors are Negro Ensemble Company alumni. The list includes Denzel Washington, Angela Bassett, Samuel L. Jackson, and Phylicia Rashad.

See also Black Arts Movement: An Interpretation; Drama.

Lisa Clayton Robinson

Negro History Week

See Black History Month.

Negro Leagues

All-black baseball leagues that formed in the United States in the 1880s and enjoyed popular success through the middle of the twentieth century, giving African American baseball players opportunities denied to them by the major leagues.

Baseball in the United States is said to be the national pastime, but only since the spring of 1947 can it be said to have become truly national. That year Jackie Robinson entered the Brooklyn Dodgers lineup, becoming the first African American to play major league baseball since Moses Fleetwood "Fleet" Walker and his brother Weldy played for Toledo, Ohio, in 1884. The exclusion of African Americans from major league baseball paralleled their treatment in other areas of American society. Negro baseball leagues, like other segregated African American institutions, recognized and developed the talent of black people in their full humanity.

Early Professional Teams

During the Jim Crow period, baseball became one of the most thriving institutions of African American life. Professional teams started forming in the 1880s, including the Philadelphia Orions (1882), the St. Louis Black Stockings (1882), and the Cuban Giants (1885). Under the management of S. K. Govern, the Cuban Giants were immensely successful, spawning many African American teams named the Giants, including the Columbia Page Fence Giants, the Chicago Leland Giants, the Brooklyn Royal Giants, even the Cuban X Giants. The genuine Cuban Giants competed in the predominantly white Middle States (Minor) League from 1889 to 1891, along with another African American team, the New York Gorhams (or Gothams). In 1886 and 1887 African American baseball leagues were formed but soon folded.

During the height of the Jim Crow period—from 1890 to 1920—successful African American baseball teams played outside of formal leagues, barnstorming the nation. Teams such as the Indianapolis ABCs and the Lincoln Giants traveled to any town or city that could field an opposing team and promise financial return. The major problem for barnstormers was dependence on white booking agents who controlled the sporting activities in major cities. Games between barnstorming teams were lucrative; they allowed fans to watch black teams face anyone who would play, including teams composed of white major and minor leaguers.

Negro Leagues

At the turn of the century, Rube Foster, a star pitcher for several African American teams, envisioned a baseball league for blacks that would rival the white major league, eventually forcing full recognition and inclusion of African American ballplayers. With partner John Schorling, Foster formed the Chicago American Giants in 1911, setting the foundation for the creation of a black baseball league. In February 1920, Foster founded the Negro National League (NNL) with the owners and representatives of the Indianapolis ABCs, the Chicago Giants, the Kansas City Monarchs (owned by white promoter J.L. Wilkinson), the St. Louis Giants, the Detroit Stars, and the Cuban Stars. As the first enduring professional sports league managed by African Americans, the NNL was widely successful. With players such as sluggers Oscar Charleston, John Henry Lloyd, and the great Smokey Joe Williams, the new, mostly Midwestern league garnered fanfare and popular support in African American communities. In 1923 the Eastern Colored League (ECL) was formed by white booking agent Nat Strong, leading to a feud with the NNL. Tensions were alleviated in 1924, however, when owners in each league agreed to a system based on the major league, with split schedules and the two best teams meeting for a black World Series. In the mid-1920s, league teams such as the Birmingham Black Barons and the Cuban Stars enjoyed success in league play and in the ever-fruitful barnstorming circuit.

Both leagues failed, however, soon after Foster's leadership was cut short by mental illness in 1926 and by his death in 1930. The ECL folded in 1928 and NNL followed in 1931. In 1932 black baseball thrived mainly in the Southern Negro League (which had been a lesser league prior to that year), and in Latin America, where great ballplayers were welcome, regardless of race.

In 1933 Pittsburgh, Pennsylvania, numbers banker Gus Greenlee and several other African American owners revived the NNL. Even though the Great Depression was a catastrophe for black communities, the wealth of Greenlee and other alleged gangsters allowed the league to flourish. Beginning with

Negro Baseball Leagues

Negro National League I

Team	Years	Team	Years	Team	Years
Birmingham Black Barons	1925, 1927–1930	Cleveland Elites	1926	Louisville White Sox	1931
Chicago American Giants	1920–1931	Cleveland Hornets	1927	Memphis Red Sox	1924–1925, 1927–1930
Chicago Giants	1920–1921	Cleveland Tate Stars	1922	Milwaukee Bears	1923
Columbus Buckeyes	1921	Dayton Marcos	1920, 1926	Nashville Elite Giants	1930
Cuban Stars	1920, 1922	Detroit Stars	1920–1931	Pittsburgh Keystones	1922
Cleveland Browns	1924	Indianapolis ABC's	1920–1926, 1931	St. Louis Giants	1920–1921
Cleveland Cubs	1931	Kansas City Monarchs	1920–1931	Toledo Tigers	1923

Negro National League II

Team	Years	Team	Years	Team	Years
Bacharach Giants (Atlantic City)	1934	Columbus Blue Birds	1933	New York Black Yankees	1936–1948
Baltimore Black Sox	1933–1934	Columbus Elite Giants	1935	New York Cubans	1935–1936, 1939–1948
Baltimore Elite Giants	1938–1948	Detroit Stars	1933		
Brooklyn Eagles	1935	Harrisburg-St. Louis Stars	1943	Philadelphia Stars	1934–1948
Cleveland Giants	1933	Homestead (Pa.) Grays	1935–1948	Pittsburgh Crawfords	1933–1938
Cleveland Red Sox	1934	Nashville Elite Giants	1933–1934	Washington Black Senators	1938
Cole's American Giants (Chicago)	1933–1935	Newark Dodgers	1934–1935		
		Newark Eagles	1936–1948	Washington Elite Giants	1936–1937

Eastern Colored League (American Negro League, 1929)

Team	Years	Team	Years	Team	Years
Bacharach Giants (Atlantic City)	1923–1929	Harrisburg (Pa.) Giants	1924–1927	Newark Stars	1926
Baltimore Black Sox	1923–1929	Hilldale (Philadelphia)	1923–1927, 1929	Philadelphia Tigers	1928
Brooklyn Royal Giants	1923–1927	Homestead (Pa.) Grays	1929	Washington Potomacs	1924
Cuban Stars East	1923–1929	Lincoln Giants (New York)	1923–1926, 1928–1929		

Negro Southern League

Team	Years	Team	Years	Team	Years
Cole's American Giants (Chicago)	1932	Indianapolis ABC's	1932	Monroe Monarchs	1932
		Louisville Black Caps	1932	Montgomery Grey Sox	1932
Columbus Turfs (Ohio)	1932	Memphis Red Sox	1932	Nashville Elite Giants	1932

East-West League

Team	Years	Team	Years	Team	Years
Baltimore Black Sox	Spring 1932	Cuban Stars	Spring 1932	Homestead (Pa.) Grays	Spring 1932
Cleveland Stars	Spring 1932	Hilldale (Philadelphia)	Spring 1932	Newark Browns	Spring 1932

Negro-American League

Team	Years	Team	Years	Team	Years
Atlantic Black Crackers	1938	Cleveland Bears	1939–1940	Kansas City Monarchs	1937–1950
Baltimore Elite Giants	1949–1950	Detroit Stars	1937	Louisville Buckeyes	1949
Birmingham Black Barons	1937–1938, 1940–1950	Houston Eagles	1949–1950	Memphis Red Sox	1937–1941, 1943–1950
		Indianapolis ABC's	1938–1939		
Chicago American Giants	1937–1950	Indianapolis Athletics	1937	New York Cubans	1949–1950
Cleveland Buckeyes	1943–1948, 1950	Indianapolis Clowns	1943–1950	Philadelphia Stars	1949–1950
Cincinnati Buckeyes	1942	Indianapolis Crawfords	1940	St. Louis Stars	1937, 1939, 1941
Cincinnati Tigers	1937	Jacksonville Red Caps	1938, 1941–1942	Toledo Crawfords	1939

six teams and later expanding to eight, the NNL boasted some of the best baseball talent to ever play the game. Greenlee's Pittsburgh Crawfords competed with the great Homestead Grays for the best local players. Often winning the battle, the Crawfords possessed five future Hall of Fame players at one time: Oscar Charleston, COOL PAPA BELL, JOSH GIBSON, JUDY JOHNSON, and SATCHEL PAIGE.

When Greenlee instituted an East-West All-Star game to be played each year in CHICAGO, ILLINOIS, the amassed talent drew from 30,000 to over 40,000 fans, becoming a major social event of the Jim Crow era. The enormous popularity of black baseball led white businessmen to form the Negro American League in 1937, which brought the ever-popular Kansas City Monarchs back into league play. That same year Dominican Republic president RAFAEL TRUJILLO brought Paige, Gibson, and Bell to play on his own team, but they returned to the Negro Leagues the following year.

During this period Latin America was an important arena for baseball, because in the winter the best Negro Leaguers played in such nations as CUBA, the DOMINICAN REPUBLIC, and MEXICO with stars of the major league. Black players excelled alongside and against white players, exposing the lie that African Americans were inferior baseball players. From Latin America, Negro Leaguers moved on to spring training, which was based in the American South. Steadily traveling northward, teams would barnstorm until they reached their home cities. On the way, they would often compete against barnstorming major leaguers. Researchers estimate that African American teams won 60 percent of these games.

Demise of the Negro Leagues

The NNL folded in 1948, due in great part to Jackie Robinson's integration of the major leagues. Although the Negro American League lasted until 1960, it failed to capture the imagination of black ticket buyers in later years. Those buyers were now watching former Negro Leaguers play in major league baseball. These players included Paige (NL: Philadelphia Stars, ML: Cleveland Indians); Monte Irvin (NL: Newark Eagles, ML: New York Giants); ROY CAMPANELLA (NL: Baltimore Elite Giants, ML: Brooklyn Dodgers); HANK AARON (NL: Indianapolis Clowns, ML: Milwaukee Braves); and WILLIE MAYS (NL: Birmingham Black Barons, ML: New York Giants).

African American baseball players have had a profound impact on major league baseball by bringing to center stage the showmanship and skill that characterized the Negro Leagues. The legacy of vision and excellence proffered by the Negro Leagues has been recognized recently by many Americans and has emerged as a source of great pride, as well as a necessary embarrassment to those who permitted the system of exclusion.

See also Baseball in Latin America and the Caribbean.

Negro National Anthem

African American national hymn.

"Lift Ev'ry Voice and Sing," popularly considered the Negro national anthem, was composed in 1900 at the Colored High School in Jacksonville, Florida, by JAMES WELDON JOHNSON and his brother, J. Rosamond Johnson. It is a thirty-four-line poem that expresses the difficulty African Americans have experienced in reaching the present, exemplified in the line "Stony the road we trod." Despite acknowledging the pain and disappointment faced by black Americans, the song is essentially a hymn of faith in God, to whom it says, "Thou has brought us thus far on the way;" and the Johnsons' lyrics express both hope for the future and American patriotism.

Richard Newman

Negro Writer's Vision of America Conference

See Harlem Writers Guild.

Nell, William Cooper

1816–1874

African American abolitionist and historian.

William Cooper Nell was born in BOSTON, MASSACHUSETTS, the son of William Guion Nell, a tailor, and Louisa (maiden name unknown). His father, a prominent figure in the small but influential African American community in Boston's West End during the 1820s, was a next-door neighbor and close associate of the controversial black abolitionist DAVID WALKER. Nell studied at the all-black Smith School, which met in the basement of Boston's African Meeting House. Although he was an excellent student, in 1829 he was denied honors given to outstanding pupils by the local school board because of his race. This and similar humiliations prompted him to dedicate his life to eliminating racial barriers. To better accomplish that task, Nell read law in the office of local abolitionist William I. Bowditch in the early 1830s. Although he never practiced, his legal skills and knowledge proved valuable in the antislavery and CIVIL RIGHTS struggles of his era.

Nell naturally gravitated toward the emerging abolitionist crusade. In 1831 he became an errand boy for THE LIBERATOR, the leading antislavery journal, beginning a long and close relationship with its editor, WILLIAM LLOYD GARRISON. His talents were quickly recognized, and he was soon made a printer's apprentice, then a clerk in the paper's operations. In the latter position, which he assumed in 1840, he wrote articles, supervised the paper's Negro Employment Office, arranged meetings, corresponded with other abolitionists, and represented Garrison at various antislavery functions. The pay was low, so he was forced to supplement his income by advertising his services as a bookkeeper and copyist. But he remained one of Garrison's most ardent supporters, even as the Boston abolitionist grew increasingly controversial because of his singular devotion to moral rather than political means and his embrace of a wide variety of reforms.

After the antislavery movement divided into two hostile camps in 1840 over questions of appropriate tactics and women's role, Nell vehemently criticized those black abolitionists who parted company with Garrison. He moved to Rochester, New York, in 1848 and helped FREDERICK DOUGLASS publish the *North Star*. But when growing conflict between Garrison and Douglass forced him to choose sides, he returned to Boston and *The Liberator*. In 1856 Nell traveled through lower Canada West (now Ontario) and the Midwest, visiting black communities, attending antislavery meetings, and submitting regular reports to *The Liberator*. His accounts of this journey are a useful record of African American life in those areas at the time.

Nell was perhaps the most outspoken and consistent advocate of racial integration in the antebellum United States. He worked closely with white reformers and regularly pressed other blacks to abandon "all separate action, and becom[e] part and parcel of the general community" (quoted in Smith, p. 184). Nell participated in a statewide campaign to end segregated "JIM CROW" cars on Massachusetts railroads in the early 1840s. He used the antislavery press as a vehicle to attack black exclusion from or segregation in churches, schools and colleges, restaurants, hotels, militia units, theaters, and other places of entertainment.

From 1840 to 1855 Nell led a successful petition campaign to integrate the public schools of Boston, which ended when the Massachusetts legislature outlawed racially separate education in the state. He even opposed the existence of voluntary separatism among African Americans. In 1843 he represented Boston at the National Convention of Colored Citizens in Buffalo and used that forum as a vehicle to speak out against exclusive black gatherings and activism. An outspoken critic of the black churches, he often attended the predominantly white Memorial Meeting House in West Roxbury.

But Nell supported separate black organizations when they met needs not performed by integrated ones. For example, in 1842 he helped establish the Freedom Association, a group of local blacks founded to aid and protect fugitive slaves. He remained active in this group for four years until the interracial Boston Vigilance Committee was founded for the same purpose. Although he established numerous cultural and literary societies—most notably the Adelphic Union and the Boston Young Men's Literary Society—among Boston blacks after 1830, these were always open to individuals of every race and class.

Nell tempered his opposition to politics and exclusive black activism in the early 1850s. He was nominated by the Free-Soil Party for the Massachusetts legislature in 1850. After the FUGITIVE SLAVE ACT of 1850 was passed, he stepped up his role in local underground railroad activities until illness forced his temporary retirement from the antislavery stage.

About this time Nell began extensive research on the African American experience in the United States. He perceived that black history and memory would help shape the identity of his race and advance the struggle against slavery and racial prejudice. His research resulted in the publication of *Services of Colored Americans in the Wars of 1776 and 1812* (1851), *Colored Patriots of the American Revolution* (1855), and dozens of articles and pamphlets. The careful scholarship and innovative use of oral sources in Nell's works, which were far broader than their titles suggest, made them the most useful and important histories of African Americans written in the CIVIL WAR era.

Nell's historical activism also took a more popular turn. In 1858 he organized the first of seven annual CRISPUS ATTUCKS Day celebrations in Boston to honor African American heroes of the American Revolution. Held the fifth day of every March in Faneuil Hall, the festivities consisted of speeches, martial music, displays of revolutionary war relics, and the recollections of aged black veterans. These gatherings symbolically rejected the decision of the U.S. Supreme Court in *Dred Scott v. Sandford* (1857), which unequivocally denied black claims to American citizenship. Nell also petitioned the Massachusetts state legislature on numerous occasions for an Attucks monument in Boston.

When the Civil War came, Nell embraced the Union cause, anticipating the end of slavery and racial inequality in American life. His hopes were buoyed in 1861, when he was employed as a postal clerk in the Boston post office. This made him the first African American appointed to a position in the U.S. government, and he held the job until his death. He was further encouraged by the EMANCIPATION PROCLAMATION and the decision to enlist black troops in the Union army.

The end of the war brought a series of personal changes for Nell. When *The Liberator* ceased operations in December 1865, it marked the denouement of Nell's lengthy career in reform journalism. But it did not mean the abandonment of activism; during the late 1860s he waged a successful campaign to end racial discrimination in theaters and other public places in Boston. Nell married Frances A. Amers of New Hampshire in 1869; they had two sons. He spent the remainder of his life completing a study of African American troops in the Civil War. It was apparently unfinished when he died in Boston of "paralysis of the brain."

Bibliography

Most of Nell's published letters and editorials can be found in *The Liberator* (Boston) and the *North Star* (Rochester). These and many manuscript letters are available in the microfilm edition of the *Black Abolitionist Papers* (1981).

Horton, James O. "Generations of Protest: Black Families and Social Reform in Ante-Bellum Boston." *New England Quarterly* 94 (1976): 242–256.

Horton, James O., and Lois E. Horton. *Black Bostonians: Family Life and Community Struggle in the Antebellum North*. 1979.

Obituary, *Pacific Appeal* (San Francisco), July 18, 1874.

Ripley, C. Peter, et al., eds. *The Black Abolitionist Papers*. Vol. 3. 1991.

Smith, Robert P. "William Cooper Nell: Crusading Black Abolitionist." *Journal of Negro History* 55 (1970): 182–199.

Wesley, Dorothy Porter. "Integration versus Separatism: William Cooper Nell's Role in the Struggle for Equality." In *Courage and Conscience: Black and White Abolitionists in Boston*, 207–224, edited by Donald M. Jacobs. 1993.

From *American National Biography*. John A. Garraty and Mark C. Carnes, eds. Oxford University Press, 1999. Reprinted by permission of the American Council of Learned Societies.

Roy E. Finkenbine

Nemours, Jean Baptiste and Sicot, Wéber

Haitian bandleader and musician, respectively, whose brief collaboration and later rivalry influenced the development of *compas*, Haiti's first national popular music.

During the summer of 1955, Haitian bandleader Jean Baptiste Nemours initiated a transformation of Haitian popular music by creating a new dance rhythm that he called the *compas-direct* (direct beat). At first, COMPAS sounded quite similar to the Dominican MERENGUE, which was enormously popular in HAITI at that time. Nevertheless, ethnomusicologist Gage Averill notes an important distinction between the repeated rhythmic pattern of the *tambora* (conga-like drum) in merengue, and that of its cousin, the *tanbou*, in compas music. He explains that the pattern on the tanbou is shifted forward one eighth note in compas, spilling over into each following measure. This shift creates even stronger forward propulsion in compas than is found in the Dominican merengue.

Nemours's composition "Tioule 3" (c. 1955) is generally accepted as the first fully developed example of compas music. The song's orchestration, (tanbou, saxophone, accordion, and bass), its rhythms and harmonies, and its use of ostinati and dialogue between instruments, all combine to create a form of Haitian popular music that was to endure for decades to come. One Haitian journalist describes Nemours's pioneer status in these terms: "Jean Bapiste Nemours was the first Haitian maestro to grasp the significance of show business. Producing an extremely commercial music, he succeeded in imposing his rhythm at the very outset."

Nemours, however, was not alone in his attempt to corner the market on Haitian music. He had many imitators and rivals, including former band mate, Wéber Sicot. Nemours and Sicot played together briefly in a band called Conjunto International, eventually splitting up in order to form their own groups. In 1958 relations between the two musicians became irreparably strained when Wéber Sicot coined a new dance rhythm that was almost indistinguishable from Nemours's compas-direct. He called his rhythm *kadans ranpa* (from *rempart*, meaning "defense" or "fortification"). From that point on, their relationship was strictly competitive, the two composers constantly striving to imitate and outdo the other. Occasionally, their rivalry resulted in the outright piracy of material. Wagmer Lalanne, Nemours's former keyboardist explains: "If we heard Sicot make a good song, we picked it up. So when we hear on the radio the Sicot song 'Cadence rampas numero un,' Nemours said, 'By God, that's a very good song. We'll pick up the same song and ours will beat it.'" Nemours's promise held true when his band scored the biggest hit in the country by stealing "Cadence rampas," changing only the lyrics and renaming it "Compas cabane choucune."

The *epòk polemik Nemou ak Siko* (period of controversy between Nemours and Sicot), as it is referred to in Haiti, was marked by a continuous argument between the two artists over whose band was superior. Sicot was widely considered the better musician, and often corroborated this opinion, lashing out at Nemours in his songs:

You have to stop trying to fool serious people
Because every Haitian knows good music.
From when you start until you finish, it's a single saxophone honk! . . .
You have no shame! You can't play a solo!
("Deux guidons")

Nemours, on the other hand, was considered to be the originator of compas and used this prestige to his advantage in his song "Rhythme commercial," which portrays Nemours as a productive, fruit-bearing mango tree at which others, namely Sicot, throw rocks out of jealousy. Nemours borrowed this image from the Haitian proverb, "One only throws rocks at mango trees that are full":

The tree that's bearing fruit
It's at him they're throwing rocks
But let's halt all this jealousy, truly!
Nemours is a mango tree
Defying time, always yielding fruit
They're throwing rocks all the time, at him!

In 1964 the rivalry between Sicot and Nemours culminated when the two bands resolved to play a soccer game in order to decide once and for all which group was better. The resulting match took place in March of that year and drew a crowd of over 35,000 people. It is perhaps fitting that the game ended in a draw (1–1). Today Nemours and Sicot are both considered important figures in the development of Haiti's first national pop music, compas.

Gordon Root

Netherlands Antilles

Part of the kingdom of the Netherlands consisting of five islands in the Caribbean Sea.

The present-day kingdom of THE NETHERLANDS consists of three separate states: the Netherlands, the Caribbean island of ARUBA, and the five Caribbean islands that together compose the Netherlands Antilles. Many European nations competed to be part of the fifteenth- and sixteenth-century European invasion of the Caribbean, and most of them were hoping to establish control of islands that contained either gold or fertile soils that would facilitate plantation farming. But the Dutch had a simple, unique need that led them to establish Caribbean colonies: salt. The herring industry was an important part of the Dutch economy, and salt was required to cure the fish. This salt had traditionally come from the Spanish Iberian Peninsula, but conflicts between the Netherlands and SPAIN in the 1500s led the Spanish to outlaw that trade. The Dutch needed to find a new region of the world that could furnish a suitable salt supply.

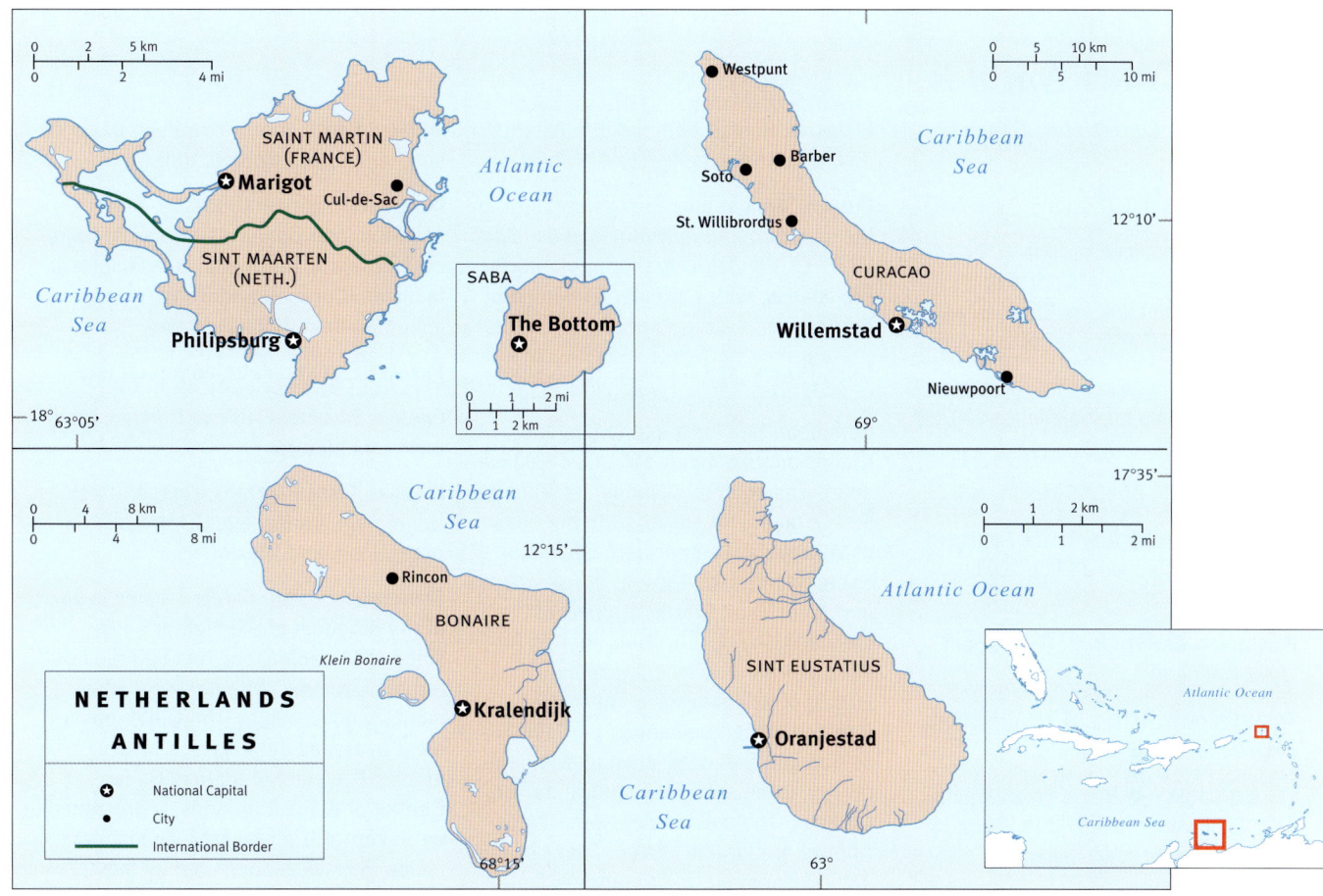

The result of their quest changed the kingdom and the six Caribbean islands that were destined to become part of it.

The six islands are geographically divided into two distinct groups. The first of these contains Aruba, BONAIRE, and CURAÇAO, all located forty miles off the coast of VENEZUELA. Although Aruba has been a separate state since 1986, it was a part of the Netherlands Antilles for 250 years before that. As a result Aruba shares many linguistic and cultural traditions with Bonaire and Curaçao, and the three islands are still often referred to collectively as the "ABC" islands. Saint Maarten, Saint Eustatius, and Saba, all about 500 miles northeast of the first group and east of the VIRGIN ISLANDS and PUERTO RICO, are often called the "three S's." The five islands that comprise the Netherlands Antilles do have significant differences as a result of their geographical separation. Many of the differences and similarities between them can be traced to the islands' pre-colonial and colonial histories.

Like most Caribbean islands, all five of the islands in the Netherlands Antilles had significant indigenous Amerindian populations for centuries before Christopher Columbus and other European explorers reached the region. At the time of Columbus's arrival in the Caribbean at the end of the fifteenth century, Aruba, Curaçao, and Bonaire were inhabited by Caiquetíos Arawak Indians, who were primarily peaceful farmers and fishermen. Saint Maarten, Saint Eustatius, and Saba were uninhabited when they were first discovered by Europeans, but there was evidence that they too had once been inhabited by the Arawaks. Most likely those Arawaks had been taken into slavery by the Caribs, a second Amerindian tribe, and the Arawaks who lived in the "ABC" islands would soon meet the same fate at the hands of the Spanish.

The soils in all of these islands were generally poor, and so the Spanish declared them *islas inutiles* (useless islands). The Spanish captured many of the Arawaks on Bonaire and Curaçao in order to bring them to work on Spanish plantations on more profitable islands; they chose to let Saint Maarten, Saint Eustatius, and Saba remain uninhabited. The abundant salt deposits off the coasts of Bonaire, Curaçao, and Saint Maarten made these islands quite appealing to the Dutch, who began eyeing them in the early seventeenth century.

The Dutch made their first move in 1631, sending a group of colonists to settle on Saint Maarten. In 1634 Dutch colonists occupied Curaçao, and after a brief battle with the small group of Spanish settlers already on the island they were granted control of Curaçao and Bonaire. Meanwhile, the Dutch settlers on Saint Maarten spread to Saint Eustatius in 1636, and from there to Saba in 1640. Although a conflict arose with FRANCE over the island of Saint Maarten in 1638, it was resolved amicably with each power agreeing to keep control of one side (with the French side changing its spelling to Saint Martin). With their

Netherlands Antilles (At a Glance)

Former Name: Curaçao and Dependencies

Area: 960 sq km (371 sq mi)

Location: Two island groups in the Caribbean Sea—one is north of Venezuela and includes Curaçao and Bonaire; the other is east of the Virgin Islands

Capital: Willemstad (population 130,000; 1993 estimate)

Population: 216,226 (2003 estimate)

Population Below Age 15: 24.7 percent (male 27,383; female 26,122; 2003 estimate)

Population Growth Rate: 0.9 percent (2003 estimate)

Total Fertility Rate: 2.04 children born per woman (2003 estimate)

Life Expectancy at Birth: Total population: 75.38 years (male 73.16 years; female 77.7 years; 2003 estimate)

Infant Mortality Rate: 10.71 deaths per 1,000 live births (2003 estimate)

Literacy Rate (age 15 and over who can read and write): Total population: 96.7 percent (male 96.7 percent; female 96.8 percent; 2003 estimate)

Education: Education in the Netherlands Antilles is not compulsory. About 88.4 percent of children are enrolled in primary school, and 64.6 percent of teens are enrolled in secondary school.

Languages: Dutch is the official language. Also spoken are Papiamento (a Spanish-Portuguese-Dutch-English dialect) English, and Spanish.

Ethnic Groups: 85 percent mixed black; also Carib Amerindian, white, and East Asian

Religions: Roman Catholic, Protestant, Jewish, and Seventh-Day Adventist

Climate: Annual average temperature in the southern and northern islands is 81° F (27° C). Rainfall is higher in the northern islands, with a greater likelihood of hurricanes.

Land, Plants, and Animals: The Netherlands Antilles are five islands in the Caribbean Sea, split into two island groups approximately 500 miles (800 km) apart. The southern islands are Bonaire and Curaçao, fifty miles from the coast of Venezuela. The northern islands of Saba, Saint Eustatius, and the southern portion of Saint Martin are part of the Leeward Islands. The Netherlands Antilles, surrounded by coral reefs, consist largely of volcanic rock. There are forested extinct volcanoes on Saint Eustatius and Saba. Willemstad, the capital city, is situated on a natural bay on Curaçao. The soils of the Netherlands Antilles are largely barren. There is little natural irrigation; seawater must be distilled for drinking. The sparse vegetation includes plants that thrive in drought conditions, such as the paddle cactus. Animals include wild donkeys, parrots, sea turtles, and flamingos.

Natural Resources: Phosphates (Curaçao) and salt (Bonaire)

Currency: Netherlands Antillean guilder (ANG)

Gross Domestic Product (GDP): $2.4 billion (2002 estimate)

GDP per Capita: $11,400 (2002 estimate)

GDP Real Growth Rate: 0 percent (2002 estimate)

Primary Economic Activities: Services, industry, and agriculture

Primary Crops: Aloes, sorghum, peanuts, vegetables, and tropical fruit

Industries: Tourism (Curaçao, Sint Maarten, and Bonaire), petroleum refining (Curaçao), petroleum transshipment facilities (Curaçao and Bonaire), and light manufacturing (Curaçao)

Primary Exports: Petroleum products

Primary Imports: Crude petroleum, food, and manufactures

Primary Trade Partners: United States, Guatemala, Venezuela, Guyana, Singapore, Cuba, and Mexico

Government: Netherlands Antilles is part of the Kingdom of the Netherlands; since 1954 each island has had full internal autonomy, with its own parliamentary government. The Dutch government oversees defense and foreign affairs. The chief of state is Queen Beatrix of the Netherlands, represented by Governor General Frits Goedgedrag (since July 2002; appointed by the monarch for a six-year term). The head of government is Prime Minister Mirna Louisa-Godett (since August 2003; the majority party leader is elected prime minister by the Staten). The legislative branch is the unicameral Staten (States), whose twenty-two members are elected by popular vote for four-year terms. The judicial branch is the Joint High Court of Justice.

Shelle Sumners

foothold in the Caribbean established, the Dutch immediately focused on the commodity they had come for—salt.

Salt mining, which involved long hours of standing in the ocean and manually sifting salt from the water, was extremely difficult work. There were not nearly enough Dutch colonists willing to do it, and so the Dutch turned to African slaves as a captive labor force. Slaves from Angola and Congo composed the first group of Africans in the Netherlands Antilles, arriving in Curaçao as early as 1639. The DUTCH WEST INDIA COMPANY, the Netherlands' slave-trading enterprise, grew so rapidly during that period that the Dutch became the second largest slave-trading power in the Atlantic by the 1640s.

Curaçao quickly became one of the Dutch West India Company's main bases of operation because of the valuable convenience of the island's natural deep-water harbor. Slaves arriving in Curaçao were brought to Venezuela and other parts of the South American mainland. Saint Eustatius provided a second port for shipments to that region of the Dutch Caribbean. The slave trade was ultimately more important to the economy of the Netherlands Antilles than slavery itself. In 1700 there were approximately 4,000 slaves on Curaçao and Bonaire, with another 250 on Saint Maarten and 750 on Saint Eustatius. One hundred years later there were 4,000 slaves on Saint Maarten, 5,000 on Saint Eustatius, and 750 on Saba, with similar gains on Curaçao and Bonaire. While these figures represent a dramatic increase, the numbers of slaves were still much smaller here than they were on many Caribbean islands.

The numbers stayed relatively low because none of the islands in the Netherlands Antilles had soil fertile enough for large-scale plantation farming. The Dutch added Aruba to their holdings in 1686 but chose to send very few settlers and almost no slaves to that island. As a consequence Aruba had virtually no slave or African presence at all. Slaves in the rest of the Netherlands Antilles worked primarily in the salt mines, as domestic servants, or as laborers on the small tobacco plantations that Dutch planters had been able to establish on Saint Maarten, Saint Eustatius, and Saba. Some historians have claimed that slavery was milder in Dutch colonies than in some others, but it is clear that Dutch slaves also resisted their captivity.

In 1750 a group of slaves on a Curaçao plantation led an armed revolt; the rebels burned several buildings and were about to march on the main settlement at WILLEMSTED when the colony's Dutch governor sent a military detachment of white soldiers and free blacks to recapture them. Several of the rebels drowned themselves to avoid being returned to slavery. A second revolt happened on Curaçao in 1795, when fifty slaves on one plantation decided to go on strike. Within days the rebellion, whose leaders were named Tula and Carpata, had grown to include over 1,000 slaves. This time it took several days before the militia was able to end the uprising. When the struggle was finally over, twenty-nine slaves were executed. While there were no more open slave rebellions after that one, slaves continued to use the limited legal opportunities they had to protest mistreatment by cruel masters and to express their unhappiness with their treatment.

The slaves' voices were often ignored by the Dutch, but outside influences gradually intervened. When the French freed their slaves on Saint Martin in 1848, the remaining slaves on the Dutch half of the island simply declared that they were free too; Dutch slaves on Saint Eustatius and Saba soon followed their lead. It was nearly impossible for the Dutch to do anything about the declarations since slaves from those islands could so easily escape to nearby free territories. The Dutch agreed to let these former slaves remain free and concentrated instead on maintaining slavery in the "ABC" islands. But abolitionist sentiment at home and from Roman Catholic missionaries who had come to the islands to work with the slaves made the Dutch goal difficult. In 1863 slavery was finally abolished in all of the Netherlands Antilles.

By the time of emancipation the salt industry on the islands was in decline, and so the newly free black majority in the Netherlands Antilles needed other methods of making a living. There were a few jobs on aloe and sisal plantations and at plants that produced sand for construction or fresh water for the island's dry interior areas. But the economic situation in the islands had grown so bleak by the turn of the century that many Antilleans began migrating to CUBA in search of jobs in the booming sugarcane fields. Just then, however, new developments completely changed of the economic structure of the Netherlands Antilles.

In 1907 oil was discovered in nearby Venezuela. Shell, a Dutch-British petroleum company, immediately began looking for suitable sites from which to refine and export the oil, and the Netherlands suggested Curaçao because of its excellent harbor. The first refinery on Curaçao was built in 1917. Within a few years refineries were sprinkled across Curaçao and Aruba, special tankers had been designed to carry thousands of tons of oil to the islands every day, and, above all, new workers were being recruited to fill the plentiful jobs. Oil jobs paid better than those in farming or fishing, and so Antilleans from all six islands arrived to work in the refineries. Even after this migration there were still more jobs to be filled, and so immigrants from other countries—especially GRENADA and other neighboring islands in the Anglophone Caribbean—began arriving to work in the Dutch refineries.

Oil brought increased prosperity to the majority of Antilleans, and with prosperity came increased demand for autonomy and political power. Throughout colonial history the Netherlands Antilles had been governed exclusively by appointed representatives of the Dutch crown, giving blacks no political voice at all. But in 1941, Dutch Queen Wilhelmina finally promised that the Dutch East and West Indies—an empire that at the time included the Netherlands Antilles, Indonesia, and SURINAME—would be granted self-government at the end of World War II. In 1948 the first important step towards political autonomy came when the appointed government of the Netherlands Antilles was replaced by a new government, called the Staten, elected through universal adult suffrage. In 1950 a new statute was introduced that granted the Netherlands, Suriname, and the Netherlands Antilles each equal status as separate partners in the kingdom of the Antilles. All three countries signed the statute in 1954.

Suriname declared full independence from the kingdom of the Netherlands in 1975, but the majority of the population of the Netherlands Antilles was content to stay under the Dutch crown. More pressing problems arose in governing and unifying the home state. In May 1969 labor tensions stemming from the oil refineries led to several days of rioting, burning, and looting in downtown Willemsted that eventually had to be subdued by Dutch marines. Unemployment figures for that year ran as high as 20 to 25 percent, a sign that the oil industry miracle was no longer working for all Antilleans.

Tourism had played a minor role in the country's economy since the 1920s, but from the 1960s on there was a serious attempt to expand that industry. This proved an excellent move when the worldwide collapse of oil prices in the 1980s put the refineries into jeopardy. By then, several of the Netherlands Antilles—most notably Aruba and Saint Maarten—already had well-established tourist industries that gave the country's economy a small buffer. But during the 1980s, Arubans became convinced that their island would be more successful without official ties to the other Netherlands Antilles. Aruba was granted its status as a separate state within the kingdom in 1986.

In the early 1990s there was discussion of dividing the remaining Netherlands Antilles into two more separate states—one composed of Bonaire and Curaçao and the other of Saint Maarten, Saint Eustatius, and Saba—a measure that made sense to many politicians and voters. The islands had developed very different cultures as a result of the hundreds of miles that separated them; they did not even share a common language. While Dutch is the official language across the Netherlands Antilles, people on Bonaire and Curaçao speak Papiamento and Spanish, and residents of the other island group speak English. The distribution of the country's population was also significant: in 1992, 155,000 of the Netherlands Antilles' 190,000 residents lived on Curaçao and Bonaire, and those islands' large, urban populations had some very specific needs. But a 1993 referendum on the question of political division was resoundingly defeated. This led to the resignation of the country's first female prime minister, Maria Liberia-Peters, who had supported the measure.

Separation reemerged as a dominant political issue in the Netherlands Antilles after the turn of the twenty-first century. In 2000 more than two-thirds of the population on Saint Maarten indicated their preference for independence from the Netherlands Antilles. A similar movement has since surfaced in Curaçao. On the other hand, unification has many determined supporters among the Netherlands Antilles' 216,000 residents. The five islands share a common history under the Dutch flag and some aspects of a common culture that mixes Dutch and African elements. Many Caribbean traditions, such as the Carnival celebration, are also a part of the Netherlands Antilles' culture. The warm Papiamento phrase *bon bini* (welcome) has been adopted as a general introduction to all of the Netherlands Antilles.

See also Carnivals in Latin America and the Caribbean; Colonial Rule; Mining in Latin America and the Caribbean; Salt Trade; Slave Rebellions in Latin America and the Caribbean; Slavery in Latin America and the Caribbean; Transatlantic Slave Trade.

Lisa Clayton Robinson

Netherlands, The

Western European country where blacks have had a presence for centuries.

As early as the sixteenth century, a small population of Africans and people of African descent resided in the Netherlands as servants and laborers, military servicemen, and intellectuals. Black military recruits served in the Dutch army in SURINAME and Indonesia, and fought for the Dutch in WORLD WAR II. Black Surinamese intellectuals, who have studied in the Netherlands, have challenged racism in Dutch society, the Dutch view of its colonies, and the tolerant and pluralist self-image that is prevalent among the Dutch.

However, a significant black presence in the Netherlands did not exist until the 1950s. With the arrival of blacks from former Dutch colonies, the Netherlands has faced the consequences of its past involvement in the slave trade and colonialism. In the 1960s, Moroccans and other North Africans entered the Netherlands to work in Dutch industry. When Suriname attained independence in 1975, many Surinamers migrated to the Netherlands to retain their Dutch citizenship. While the Netherlands is known as a country of refuge and home to one of the most comprehensive social benefits systems in EUROPE, the continued presence of these ethnic minorities has revealed the limits of Dutch tolerance. However, the Dutch government has attempted to accommodate these migrants by promoting multiculturalism and addressing issues of economic disparity and racial discrimination.

Slaves and Freedmen

The Dutch had little direct contact with Africans until they began trading slaves in the late sixteenth century. Before this, their ideas about blacks derived largely from SPAIN, which ruled the Netherlands until the Dutch revolted in the sixteenth century. Images of blacks appeared in Dutch heraldry as early as the thirteenth century. In the Saint Nicholas tradition of the Dutch, a black boy called *Zwarte Piet,* meaning Black Pete, accompanies Santa Claus on his nocturnal rounds. As the tale goes, it is Black Pete who slides down the chimney to give children candy if they are good, or to steal the children away if they are bad. This image of blacks was not controversial until large numbers of blacks immigrated to the Netherlands in the 1970s.

During the seventeenth century, the Dutch became the leading slave traders on the west coast of Africa. Over the course of their involvement in the slave trade, which peaked in the late seventeenth century and ended in the early nineteenth century, the Dutch transported several hundred thousand slaves to the Americas. Founded in 1602, the Dutch East India Company brought slaves from the Dutch holding in Elmina, in present-day GHANA, and several other Dutch posts on the west coast of Africa, to the Dutch holdings in the Cape Colony (today part of SOUTH AFRICA) and Indonesia. The DUTCH WEST INDIA COMPANY, founded in 1621, brought slaves from West Africa, mostly from Elmina, to Dutch colonies in BRAZIL (collectively called Dutch Brazil), Suriname, ARUBA, and the NETHERLANDS ANTILLES—a group of islands including Saint Maarten, Saint Eustatius, Saba, BONAIRE, and CURAÇAO.

The Dutch brought hundreds of blacks from AFRICA or the Caribbean to the Netherlands as slaves, servants, and students. A privateer carried the first known group of Africans to the Zeeland region of the Netherlands in the late sixteenth century. Local authorities ruled that these Africans, seized from a Portuguese slave ship, could not be kept as slaves in the Netherlands and must be freed. Though slavery was legal in the Dutch colonies, the Dutch did not condone it in the Netherlands proper. While some Dutch brought slaves to the Netherlands, courts often ruled in favor of those slaves who petitioned for freedom.

Church and city documents record manumissions, baptisms, and marriages of blacks as early as the sixteenth century. For instance, Jan Kompanie was the slave of Admiral de Ruiter in Zeeland for a few years during the early seventeenth century. The admiral then freed Kompanie, and the former slave returned to Africa. In many cases, freed blacks married white Dutch spouses. Tabo, a freed slave, opened a tobacco store and changed his name to Adriaan de Bruijn (the Brown). He later married a Dutch woman, Wolmetje Bakkers. Louis Alons, described as "a Negro from Curaçao" in the Sappemeer town marriage register, wedded a Dutch woman in 1779. Interestingly, documents do not mention his children's ethnicity.

Africans also worked in the Netherlands as servants. These blacks, in costumes with feathered turbans, appear in seventeenth- and eighteenth-century portraits of the royalty and upper classes. In the late eighteenth century, blacks served the bourgeoisie of Groningen. The Dutch in this region had connections with trading companies in the colonies.

During this period, children of white Dutch men and black Caribbean and Surinamese women often traveled to the Netherlands for schooling, as did other Surinamese blacks. For instance, in 1767 the Dutch Reformed Church in Paramaribo, the capital of Suriname, sent Jeboa, the son of a chief of the Aucaner people, for schooling in Amsterdam. The Aucaner were one of the communities of Maroons, or independent descendants of escaped slaves in the Dutch colonies.

By the eighteenth century the Dutch seafaring empire was in decline, and the British had come to dominate the TRANSATLANTIC SLAVE TRADE. Both the West India Company and the East India Company lost profits when the French and English gained hold of Dutch trade routes and colonies. The British abolished the slave trade in 1807, and the Netherlands followed suit in 1814. In reality, the Dutch slave trade had become unprofitable and was all but finished by the 1780s. In 1863 the Dutch outlawed slavery in their colonies.

Soldiers and Sailors

As early as the seventeenth century, the Dutch employed blacks in military roles, mainly in the colonies. The first blacks to be employed in the military were musicians—mainly drummers and buglers—as a sort of curiosity. The Dutch West Indian Army organized a contingent called the Black Rangers of Suriname in 1772 to fight Maroon revolts. After the abolition of the slave trade, many former slaves from Suriname traveled to the Netherlands for training as members of colonial armies. Blacks served in the East Indian Army in Indonesia from the early nineteenth to the twentieth century. Noting that these West Africans and West Indian blacks were Europeanized and Christianized, local Indonesians called them *Blanda Itam,* meaning Black Hollanders. In Dutch colonial societies, these black servicemen formed a community separate from both the white Dutch, who gave them lower pay and fewer benefits than white soldiers, and from the peoples whom they policed. Still, in Suriname and Indonesia, these soldiers often took local wives and settled after their retirement from service. Some Black Hollanders, and even some Black Rangers, fought for the Netherlands against Indonesian independence in 1949. In modern Indonesia, seventy-five families who are descended from the Black Hollanders hold annual reunions.

Jan Kooi, a West African, joined the Dutch East Indian Army in 1882 and became a corporal. Kooi suffered wounds while saving the lives of a commander and a lieutenant. At the age of thirty-three he became the first Black Hollander to be decorated by the Dutch authorities. Kooi returned to Holland after his service in Indonesia was complete. Blacks from Indonesia and Suriname also fought with the Dutch army against the Germans in World War II.

Intellectuals

Blacks from throughout the Dutch empire traveled to the Netherlands to acquire an education. Some became well-known intellectuals. For example, JACOBUS ELISA CAPITEIN studied at the University of Leiden. Although he believed in equality for blacks, he was acclaimed by Dutch colonists and slave traders because his dissertation condoned slavery as a means for Africans' conversion to Christianity. In 1742 Capitein became the first known black Protestant minister. He served as a missionary in the West Indies.

Another black man who impressed Europe with his intellectual abilities was ANTON WILHELM AMO. The West Indian Company brought Amo as a boy from the GOLD COAST (present-day Ghana) to the Netherlands during the early eighteenth century and presented him to the duke of Wolfenbüttel in GERMANY. The duke named him Anton Wilhelm and educated him. Amo knew at least six languages, earned a doctorate, and lectured in Europe on philosophy for a time, but he eventually returned to Africa. The sons of African kings also came to the Netherlands for education or other purposes. Aquasie Boachi, the son of King Kwaku Dua of ASANTE, entered the Dutch military during the early nineteenth century at the expense of the Dutch colonial ministry. He attended boarding school in the Netherlands, frequented the highest social circles, and befriended the crown prince Willem III of the Netherlands.

In the twentieth century, with the development of independence movements in the colonies, black intellectuals from

Suriname came to the Netherlands to attend university and often used their learning to challenge Dutch conceptions of Suriname. Anton de Kom, a Surinamer known as a radical socialist and anticolonial agitator, studied in Amsterdam and wrote *We, Slaves of Suriname* (1934), the first history of Suriname. De Kom married a Dutch woman and was forbidden to return to Suriname to settle because the Dutch feared he would start a revolt. More recently, Rudolf Asveer Jacob van Lier, a Surinamer of African and Jewish descent, attended the University of Leiden and the Sorbonne in Paris. After his studies, he became chair of the department of sociology at Leiden and wrote *Frontier Society* (1971), a classic sociological study of Suriname.

From 1900 to 1950, Surinamers and Antilleans who entered the Netherlands were mostly from the elite class. They came for an education and planned to return to Africa. Many of these people of African descent, however, remained and settled in the Netherlands.

Postwar Immigrants

It was not until after World War II and decolonization that substantial numbers of Africans and peoples of African descent migrated to the Netherlands. Two of the largest migrant groups were Moroccans and Surinamers. Each group arrived under different circumstances.

The Dutch recruited Moroccans, along with other peoples of the Mediterranean region, as "guest workers" to fill the postwar labor shortage in the 1960s. The government treated them as temporary inhabitants of the Netherlands and they acted as such; they did not invest in housing and worked only to save money to bring back to Morocco. As the labor shortage in the Netherlands disappeared, however, unemployment began to rise. In 1968 the government restricted labor migration and decided that migrants who returned home would lose their residence permits. Thus, in the 1970s, instead of returning to their native lands, many laborers remained in the Netherlands and, in the 1980s, brought their families to join them. By the turn of the century, Moroccans constituted one of the largest immigrant groups in the Netherlands, with 273,000 people living in the country in 2001.

Surinamers began coming to the Netherlands in significant numbers beginning in 1954 when they gained Dutch citizenship with the incorporation of Suriname into the kingdom of the Netherlands. The 1954 charter incorporated Aruba and the Dutch Antilles into the kingdom as well. All three colonies had internal self-rule. Many of the first Surinamers who arrived were elite, but as transportation costs dropped, laborers and others began to migrate. By 1973 the Surinamese and Antillean immigrant population in the Netherlands was approximately 40,000 to 45,000.

In 1973 Surinamers voted for independence from the Netherlands, to take effect in 1975. However, about 40 percent of Surinamers opposed independence, partly due to the advantages of Dutch citizenship. Beginning in 1974 many migrated to the Netherlands to retain Dutch citizenship. In order to discourage "last-minute" mass migration, the Dutch decided to allow a five-year transition period during which borders were open to Surinamers. But political instability in Suriname in the 1980s instigated more Surinamers to migrate to the Netherlands as political refugees. Within a few years, over 200,000 Surinamers, almost one-third of the entire population of Suriname, resided in the Netherlands. In the 1990s Surinamese migration steadied at about 6,000 immigrants yearly. In 2001 the Surinamese population of the Netherlands was 309,000, and is continuing to rise.

Emigration of people of African descent from the Dutch Antilles and Aruba largely depends on the economic situation on the islands, but it tends to be at a lesser rate than from Morocco or Suriname. Aruba gained its independence in 1986, but, initially, migration to the Netherlands increased little. The oil industry in Curaçao kept many Curaçaoans employed on the island. Since 1998, however, an economic downturn has caused about 5 percent of the islands' population to migrate to the Netherlands annually. In 2001 there were 117,000 people of Antillean origin in the Netherlands.

Other Africans have also migrated to the Netherlands since 1960. Tunisians and other North Africans migrated with the Moroccans as laborers in the 1960s. In the early 1970s about 300 Ugandans of Asian origin sought refuge in the Netherlands when dictator IDI AMIN exiled them. About 20,000 refugees from Ghana and CAPE VERDE migrated in the 1980s. Ethiopians have also sought refuge in the Netherlands.

The Surinamers and Moroccans were not the first postcolonial migrants to the Netherlands. After Indonesian independence in 1949, approximately 300,000 people migrated to the Netherlands from Indonesia; 180,000 were of mixed Dutch and Asian background. The Dutch government dealt with that population with a policy of assimilation.

This was not the case with the newcomers in the 1960s and 1970s. Because migrant workers and even Surinamese or Antillean migrants were originally considered temporary—they were there for an education, or to make money, and would then return to their homelands—the Dutch made little effort to assimilate them. Most immigrant children were educated in their own languages, under the assumption that they would return to their country of origin. It was not until the late 1970s that the Dutch government started to acknowledge that many of these newer immigrants were permanent residents.

The Dutch government has responded to these newcomers in a number of ways. The Netherlands is one of the world's most densely populated nations. It also has one of the world's most comprehensive social security systems. The government has tried to restrict immigration rather than extend all benefits to those who enter. Since the 1980s it has been increasingly difficult for Surinamers and North Africans to get entry visas. In addition, the Dutch have restricted economic and labor migration and tightened the criteria for asylum-seekers in order to make immigration unattractive.

Since the nineteenth century, the Dutch government has divided its population into "pillars" (*zuilen*) according to religious orientation. Traditionally, all Dutch have belonged to one of three pillars—Roman Catholic, Protestant (mostly Dutch Reformed Church), or nonreligious (humanist). Children attend schools according to their religious orientation. Though the pillar system has been in decline since the 1960s, the principle that each religious or cultural group should retain a distinct existence has remained the basic assumption of Dutch pluralism. However, the immigrant population of the Netherlands is so diverse that organization into one pillar or even separate pillars according to national origin has largely failed. For instance, the Surinamese population consists of peoples of African, South Asian, and Indonesian descent; longstanding conflicts exist among these peoples in Suriname. The biggest criticism of pillarization (*verzuiling*) is that it ignores racial discrimination and economic or educational disadvantage, and that it promotes segregation in instances such as school choice.

Government policy since the 1980s has attempted to address immigrants' economic disadvantages and has generally acknowledged immigrants as a permanent population—as "minority groups." Since the 1980s the government has developed a two-tiered strategy of socioeconomic integration and cultural pluralism. The state has extended social security benefits to legal foreign residents. Affirmative action policies have aimed to decrease socioeconomic disadvantages and institutional discrimination in housing, education, and employment. The government has begun to promote education in both the migrants' own languages and Dutch. At the same time, an integration course has encouraged assimilation. Heavily subsidized by the government, the 500-hour, eighteen-month course aims to teach Dutch ways to immigrants—from acceptable business attire to behavior on public transportation—in order to increase their chances of getting jobs and "fitting in." Some immigrants feel the course has benefited them, but few believe it should be made mandatory for all immigrants, as some government officials proposed in 1997.

The Netherlands has led the European Union (EU) in extending citizenship to immigrants. Many have gained Dutch citizenship without abandoning citizenship in their country of origin, and are thus dual citizens. This law also allows foreigners who are residents in the Netherlands for three years to vote and run for office in municipal elections. In the 1986 elections, these 330,000 new voters made a significant difference in election results and gave a boost to the socialist Labour Party.

Despite these government efforts, many immigrants face unemployment and poor living conditions. About 80 percent of the residents of the Amsterdam district of Bijlmermeer—known as "the biggest ghetto in Europe"—are minorities; most are Surinamers, Moroccans, or Turks. It is estimated that 10,000 illegal immigrants from Ghana also reside in the neighborhood. In the 1970s the government put up public housing in the area for incoming Surinamers, but now this housing development is old and dilapidated. Drugs, crime, and racial violence abound. Even so, some people insist that certain parts of the neighborhood are safe. They point out that the various cultural communities in Bijlmermeer coexist harmoniously.

Problems such as those in Bijlmermeer have led some people to oppose the government's liberal social benefits policies. As Dutch unemployment has increased since the 1970s, many Dutch have voiced resentment at the immigrants' demands for space and resources, and have viewed the immigrants as a burden. As a result, discrimination in employment, housing, education, and political life have become commonplace. In addition, some have blamed immigrants for the rise in crime and drug trafficking. Although fascist and racist groups have not taken hold in the Netherlands as they have in other European countries, far-right parties gained ground with promises to restrict immigration in 1994. Tolerance of immigrants seemed to be waning. That year the government gave police the right to stop and search people suspected of being illegal immigrants and implemented a stricter screening process for those seeking political asylum. Immigrants and liberals feared that these policies would lead to a police state in the Netherlands. In 2003 the Dutch foreign police intensified its campaign against illegal aliens and those who employ them.

Since 2002 the Dutch government, seeking to reduce the number of foreign youths immigrating to the Netherlands, has operated special camps for unaccompanied underage asylum seekers (AMAs). The camps, known for their tough regulations, have drastically reduced the number of AMAs traveling to the Netherlands. This success inspired the Dutch to finance a similar camp in ANGOLA to reduce AMA arrivals from that country.

Historically, the Dutch have taken pride in their tolerance of religious and cultural differences. But some Dutch have reacted to immigrants with racism and discrimination, forcing others to doubt the Dutch reputation as an unprejudiced society. Racist imagery, such as Santa Claus's helper, Black Pete, still lingers just barely out of sight, and racist ideas, though discouraged, are present. To be sure, the Dutch, more than most Europeans, have attempted to engender peaceful coexistence between peoples, and many immigrants have become Dutch citizens. The Dutch face a choice of whether to cling to the attitudes that supported the slave trade and colonialism, or to embrace people of African or Caribbean descent as fellow Dutch citizens in a peaceful, multicultural society.

See also Colonial Rule; Maroonage in the Americas.

Leyla Keough

Neto, Agostinho

1922–1979

Physician, poet, nationalist leader and president of Angola.

The son of a Methodist minister, António Agostinho Neto received his high school education in Luanda. In 1947, after spending three years in the government health service, Neto traveled to PORTUGAL to attend medical school on a Methodist church scholarship. While there he met his Portuguese wife, Maria Eugénia da Silva, and other students from Portuguese Africa, including future nationalist leaders AMÍLCAR CABRAL of GUINEA-BISSAU and Eduardo Mondlane of MOZAMBIQUE. He also became involved in the youth organization of the Portuguese opposition movement. Between 1952 and 1962, during various stays in prison for his political activity, Neto began writing poetry. The publication of his nationalist poetry and his subsequent detention delayed his graduation from medical school until 1958.

By mid-1957 he had joined the recently formed opposition group the POPULAR MOVEMENT FOR THE LIBERATION OF ANGOLA (MPLA). He fit in well with the MPLA's educated, middle-class leadership, which was dominated by Africans of the Kimbundu ethnic group, whites, and mestiços, or those of mixed race. Despite his religious upbringing, Neto soon adopted the movement's Marxist-Leninist and Stalinist rhetoric. After escaping from detention in Portugal, in 1962 Neto was elected MPLA president while in exile in the DEMOCRATIC REPUBLIC OF THE CONGO. Thereafter, Neto was consumed with trying to gain international support for the movement and its struggle, writing little poetry after the 1963 publication of the collection *Sacred Hope*.

In 1975, after Portugal withdrew from Angola, the MPLA succeeded in gaining control of the capital. Neto, after twenty years in exile, became president of independent ANGOLA. But ongoing conflict between the former nationalist movement NATIONAL UNION FOR THE TOTAL INDEPENDENCE OF ANGOLA (UNITA) and the MPLA quickly overshadowed Neto's political, organizational, and intellectual skills. A civil war soon consumed the country and an unsuccessful coup d'état in 1977 threatened Neto's leadership. Although Neto remained beholden to the Soviet Union and CUBA for both their military assistance and their aid for his socialist development policies, he also encouraged business ties with the West.

Neto's poetry, always more about nationalism and exile than about politics, often spoke of hope, and as such became part of modern Angola's political lexicon and literary canon. In 1979 Neto died of cancer in a Moscow hospital. He was succeeded as president by JOSÉ EDUARDO DOS SANTOS.

See also Nationalism in Africa; Socialism.

Bibliography

Neto, Agostino. *Sacred Hope.* Tanzania Publishing House, 1974.
Khazanov, A.M. *Agostino Neto.* Progress Publishers, 1986.

Eric Young

Newark, New Jersey

City in northeastern New Jersey, home to a large African American population.

Slavery was gradually abolished in New Jersey beginning in 1804, so that by the time Newark incorporated in 1836, a small, free black community had already formed. African Americans established the Clinton Memorial AFRICAN METHODIST EPISCOPAL CHURCH in 1822 and founded an auxiliary of the AMERICAN ANTI-SLAVERY SOCIETY in 1834. Four years later the Colored School (later renamed the Baxter School) was founded. The city remained ambivalent about its black community and its commitment to the Union cause in the CIVIL WAR. In 1863 the NEW YORK CITY DRAFT RIOT spread to Newark, where whites blamed blacks, and then attacked them, as the cause of their conscription into the Union Army.

After 1870 African Americans migrated to Newark from the South and worked as unskilled labor. Black leaders, such as James Baxter, fought to integrate schools well into the twentieth century, even though segregation had been outlawed in 1884 by a New Jersey Supreme Court decision. As Newark evolved into an industrial city with substantial immigrant populations, the African American community grew as well. By 1910 it had grown to around 10,000, five times larger than the total in 1870. African Americans could rarely get industrial jobs, except occasionally as strikebreakers. Because unions excluded them, African Americans began to organize their own labor actions, as Prosper Brewer did in 1917, when black dockworkers struck Port Newark.

The black community established its own institutions. Newark's first black newspaper, *The Appeal,* began publishing in 1902, and the Newark branch of the NATIONAL ASSOCIATION FOR THE ADVANCEMENT OF COLORED PEOPLE (NAACP) was established in 1914. Five years later a chapter of the URBAN LEAGUE developed from the Negro Welfare League of Newark. The Community Hospital of Newark was founded in 1927.

During WORLD WAR I the industrial job market opened to African Americans. Black migration to Newark increased significantly—nearly 22,000 blacks arrived between 1920 and 1930. Segregation in housing, which had begun in 1870, increased dramatically during the 1920s, leading to de facto segregation of schools and concentrating many African Americans in the Hill District, one of the poorest ghettos in the United States. A JAZZ scene developed around the Orpheum and Paramount theaters and the Kinney and Skateland nightclubs, where JIMMIE LUNCEFORD and ELLA FITZGERALD performed regularly.

During the GREAT DEPRESSION, the unemployment level among African Americans quickly reached twice that among whites. NEW DEAL programs instituted by the Roosevelt administration shifted black political allegiance to the DEMOCRATIC PARTY, resulting in Guy Moorehead's election as the first black Democrat to the state assembly in 1938. With the outbreak of WORLD WAR II in 1939, jobs in war-related industries opened to blacks, and the African American community began its most significant growth, tripling its population in the city by 1960—to 34 percent of the total. The resulting "white flight" to the suburbs led to a population decline, and by 1970 African Americans accounted for 54.2 percent of the population of Newark.

With the exception of city councilor and political boss Irvine Turner, Newark had little black political representation before the mid-1960s, and conditions in the city were extreme. Corrupt government, high unemployment, crime, and especially police brutality against African Americans were pervasive problems. The predominantly white school board resisted integration and failed to rescue an increasingly deteriorating school

Poet, playwright, and novelist Amiri Baraka, a Newark native, organized the Committee for a United Newark to aid the city's black community. *The Everett Collection*

system. In the early 1960s the black community became politically organized, more insistent on the need for change, and increasingly frustrated with each failure to improve conditions. The CONGRESS OF RACIAL EQUALITY (CORE) chapter fought housing discrimination and police brutality. The Newark Coordination Council attacked discrimination in city jobs and contracts. The more radical Newark Community Union Project used rent strikes and SIT-INS to push for enforcement of building codes. In 1966 playwright and black nationalist AMIRI BARAKA, a Newark native, organized the Committee for a United Newark to focus on education and other issues vital to the survival of the black community. A year later the first National Conference on Black Power convened in Newark.

Despite these efforts, by 1967 Newark had the highest percentage of substandard housing, and the second-highest crime and infant mortality rates in the country. In July of that year, frustration with poverty and racism erupted into one of the bloodiest and most devastating racial insurrections in recent U.S. history. Sparked by an incident of police brutality, four days of rioting left twenty-six people dead and more than $10 million in property damaged. A second riot followed the assassination of MARTIN LUTHER KING, JR., one year later.

Although reform-minded Kenneth Gibson was elected the first black mayor of Newark in 1970, the history of Newark from 1960 to 1980 is the history of one of the poorest urban black communities in the nation. Gibson further integrated the school board and secured some federal funding for building projects and jobs. Yet in 1983 nearly one-quarter of all black families in Newark still lived in poverty. The number has declined only slightly in the past fifteen years. Sharpe James defeated Gibson to become mayor in 1986, and DONALD PAYNE became the first black representative to the U.S. Congress from New Jersey in 1988. Still Newark remains a city with difficult and challenging problems in the areas of housing, crime, education, and unemployment.

Bibliography

Hayden, Tom. *Rebellion in Newark: Official Violence and Ghetto Response.* Random House, 1967.

Jackson, Kenneth T., and Barbara B. Jackson. "The Black Experience in Newark: The Growth of the Ghetto, 1870–1970." In *New Jersey Since 1860: New Findings and Interpretations.* Edited by William C. Wright. New Jersey Historical Commission, 1972.

Rich, Wilbur C. *Black Mayors and School Politics: The Failure of Reform in Detroit, Gary, and Newark.* Garland, 1996.

Wright, Giles R. *Afro-Americans in New Jersey: A Short History.* New Jersey Historical Commission, Dept. of State, 1988.

Jim Mendelsohn

Newby, Dangerfield

1815?–1859

African American who participated in John Brown's raid at Harpers Ferry.

Dangerfield Newby was born in Virginia. His mother was a slave, but his father, a Scotsman, granted freedom to his children when he died. Newby lived on a farm near Harpers Ferry, Virginia (now West Virginia). He was known as a quiet man, strong, sensible, and devoted to his wife and their seven children, all of whom were slaves. They lived near Warrenton, Virginia on their master's farm. His wife had written a letter to Newby saying that her master was planning to sell her "down river." Newby, willing to do anything he thought might help to free members of his family, participated in the raid led by JOHN BROWN on the government arsenal at Harpers Ferry. The raid was meant to spark a massive slave revolt.

John Brown arrived in Harpers Ferry six months before his planned attack. During that time, Newby served Brown as a spy in the community. He did not join Brown's group until the eve of the raid. He was first among them to die when the fighting started on October 16, 1859. After he was killed, angry citizens fired into his body repeatedly, and those without guns beat it with clubs. His ears were cut off as souvenirs. Later, hogs rooted and tugged at the torn body, consuming its parts.

Newby's remains were buried in a shallow grave at Harpers Ferry. In 1899 the body was disinterred and taken to North

Elba, New York, where it was laid in a grave near that of John Brown.

After the raid Newby's wife and children were sold to a trader who took them to the Deep South.

Osborne P. Anderson's *A Voice from Harper's Ferry* (1861) is the only eyewitness account by one of the participants. W. E. B. Du Bois's *John Brown* (1909) gives details about the raid. Jules Abels's *Man on Fire: John Brown and the Cause of Liberty* (1971) is the source for the reburial of Newby.

From *Dictionary of American Negro Biography* by Rayford W. Logan and Michael R. Winston, editors. Copyright © 1982 by Rayford W. Logan and Michael R. Winston. Reprinted by permission of W. W. Norton & Company, Inc.

Lorenz Graham

New Deal

President Franklin Delano Roosevelt's domestic reform program of 1933–1941, which, although inconsistent in its treatment of African Americans, greatly strengthened black hopes for racial justice.

The New Deal, a reform effort unparalleled in American history, took shape during the troubled times of the GREAT DEPRESSION. It gave substance to President Franklin Delano Roosevelt's vague campaign promises to restore hope and revive the U.S. economy. When he took office in March 1933, Americans had already endured more than three years of the worst depression in the nation's history. African Americans, in particular, had suffered the brunt of the hardship. In the early 1930s, nearly one-in-three African American families was receiving some form of public assistance, and roughly half the black workers in NEW YORK CITY, CHICAGO, PHILADELPHIA, and DETROIT were unemployed.

During his first hundred days in office, Roosevelt secured passage of a record number of programs, and he continued implementing domestic reforms until the onset of WORLD WAR II (1939–1945). Temporary initiatives included the WORKS PROGRESS ADMINISTRATION (WPA) and Public Works Administration (PWA), which created work projects for the unemployed, and the Federal Emergency Relief Administration (FERA), which offered federal assistance to individuals in need.

The New Deal also sought more far-reaching reforms. A wave of Great Depression-era bank failures led to the Federal Deposit Insurance Corporation (FDIC), which guaranteed bank deposits. The Securities Exchange Commission (SEC) was established to regulate the stock market, whose 1929 collapse had triggered the Great Depression. The Tennessee Valley Authority (TVA) and the Rural Electrification Authority (REA) were development projects aimed primarily at the South and the West. Roosevelt flirted briefly with national economic planning in the National Recovery Administration (NRA), but with the Social Security Administration (SSA) left a lasting mark.

Although their need was particularly great, African Americans found themselves shortchanged by Roosevelt's New Deal. The social security system, which excluded agricultural workers, had nothing to offer the South's black sharecroppers. Many southern landowners, rather than share Agricultural Adjustment Administration (AAA) subsidies with their sharecroppers as the enabling legislation intended, evicted their tenants and kept the entire payment for themselves. Overt racial discrimination was evident in the segregated camps of the Civilian Conservation Corps (CCC) and in the hiring and housing policies of the TVA. NRA guidelines permitted lower wages for blacks than for whites doing the same work. Although a 1935 executive order banned discrimination in WPA projects, a cut in the WPA budget in 1937 helped bring on a sharp economic downturn from 1937 to 1939, known as the "Roosevelt Recession," that jeopardized many black families.

In general, the Roosevelt administration recognized blacks in ways that were more symbolic than substantive. Yet Roosevelt appointed an unprecedented number of African American advisers. His Federal Council on Negro Affairs, known informally as the BLACK CABINET, included WILLIAM H. HASTIE, ROBERT C. WEAVER, and MARY MCLEOD BETHUNE. In 1939 First Lady Eleanor Roosevelt played a prominent role in arranging an Easter Sunday recital by famed black contralto MARIAN ANDERSON at Washington's Lincoln Memorial after the Daughters of the American Revolution refused to let Anderson perform at a concert hall owned by the organization.

Politically, the New Deal solidified Roosevelt's Democratic coalition into a force that dominated American politics for more than a generation, but for African Americans the political results were less clear. In northern cities, blacks achieved greater political influence. In the 1936 presidential election, they rallied around Roosevelt and the New Deal. Their support represented a political shift of historic proportions; northern black voters became a cornerstone of the liberal-labor coalition that challenged the dominance of southern conservatives in national politics. During the 1930s, however, most African Americans still lived in the South, where disfranchisement effectively deprived them of any political voice. Yet the New Deal had particularly important political consequences for southern blacks.

The New Deal encouraged political activism among African Americans in the South. In 1934, groups of black citizens organized in South Carolina and Georgia to try and vote in whites-only Democratic primaries. In Arkansas a number of black and white sharecroppers formed the Southern Tenant Farmers Union to press the federal government to enforce protections written into the Agricultural Adjustment Act of 1933. Student activism in the 1930s and the growth of the industrial labor movement frequently facilitated interracial alliances in support of economic reform. During the New Deal era, the NATIONAL ASSOCIATION FOR THE ADVANCEMENT OF COLORED PEOPLE (NAACP) undertook major organizing drives among southern blacks, building black membership, supporting voter registration efforts, and initiating the legal campaign against unequal education, which laid the groundwork for the 1954 *BROWN V. BOARD OF EDUCATION* decision.

New Deal programs and policies often accommodated the racial status quo. But African Americans responded to the democratic rhetoric of the New Deal, and the unprecedented expansion of federal power it envisioned, in ways that created an atmosphere conducive to organizing and mobilizing for full citizenship rights. Indeed, the roots of the modern CIVIL RIGHTS MOVEMENT can be traced to the black political activism of the New Deal era.

See also Voting Rights Act of 1965.

Bibliography

Bunche, Ralph. *The Political Status of the Negro in the Age of FDR.* University of Chicago Press, 1973.

Sitkoff, Harvard. *A New Deal for Blacks.* Oxford University Press, 1978.

Sullivan, Patricia. *Days of Hope: Race and Democracy in the New Deal Era.* University of North Carolina Press, 1996.

Weiss, Nancy. *Farewell to the Party of Lincoln: Black Politics in the Age of FDR* Princeton University Press, 1983.

James Sellman

New Negro, The

Term associated with the African American artistic and political activity of the 1920s—particularly the Harlem Renaissance—that was substantially defined by Alain Locke in the anthology *The New Negro*, which he edited.

See Harlem Renaissance; Locke, Alain Leroy.

New Orleans, Louisiana

Most European and African of North American cities, in which French, Spanish, Creole, African, and English cultures have blended to produce distinctive music, cuisine, and festivals.

New Orleans spent nearly a century under European rule before the United States purchased it. Jean-Baptiste Le Moyne, Sieur de Bienville, the governor of the French colony of Louisiana, founded the city in 1718. In 1767 it was ceded to Spain. France reclaimed sovereignty in 1800, and three years later Napoleon I sold all of the Louisiana Territory, including New Orleans, to the United States.

French Rule

From the first years of French rule, slaves labored in New Orleans and its surrounding plantations. In 1721 more black male slaves than free white men lived in the city, and, until the massive European immigration of the 1830s and 1840s, nonwhite residents formed the majority. A large number of slaves arrived in New Orleans between 1719 and 1731, most of them abducted directly from SENEGAL. The influence of African culture, therefore, was stronger in Louisiana than in the British colonies, where larger proportions of the slave population were not African-born.

Slavery in New Orleans also differed from the English model in other ways. Owners admitted to sexual liaisons with slaves, often taking financial responsibility for their mistresses and offspring. Unlike the English model, in which whites drew a firm line between the two races and considered all people of mixed race to be black, the New Orleans system produced a third caste, that of mixed-race CREOLES. (The term *Creole* has been used to describe a variety of types of people, and in Louisiana it has referred to whites and blacks with French or Spanish ancestry or culture as well as people of mixed race.) French and Spanish fathers treated their black Creole children equitably, often sending them to Europe for education and making them legal heirs. Although the French and Spanish governments attempted to limit this propagation of a privileged black Creole class with a series of *code noir* (black code) laws, citizens frequently ignored the legislation. By the time of the AMERICAN CIVIL WAR (1861–1865), New Orleans hosted a considerable black Creole population, some of whose members owned slaves themselves.

Antebellum Period

When the United States purchased New Orleans in 1803, it obtained a thriving and culturally distinct crossroads. Spanish and French sensibilities intermingled with African and Caribbean ones, producing a fusion of religions and a distinctive, innovative cuisine. Black Creoles and slaves, many of whom had immigrated to New Orleans from Haiti after the HAITIAN REVOLUTION (1791–1804), combined African beliefs, Haitian rituals, and Catholic pageantry into the religion of VODOU. New Orleans Catholics celebrated Mardi Gras by donning lavish costumes and feasting on spicy Creole food.

The upper-class black Creoles also flourished: NORBERT RILLIEUX invented a vacuum pump for refining sugar; VICTOR SÉJOUR wrote plays; Alexandre Chaumette, James Derham, and Charles Roundanez practiced medicine; EDMOND DÉDÉ composed and directed music; Eugene Warbourg sculpted. In 1850 nearly 85 percent of black Creoles possessed the skills to be classified as doctors, clerks, teachers, and skilled workers. Educated black Creoles proliferated as merchants and dominated the trades of cabinetmaking, carpentry, cigar manufacturing, masonry, and plastering. These middle-class blacks distanced themselves from the black African slave culture and founded Roman Catholic churches based on European models.

Despite the assimilation of the black Creole community, however, discrimination intensified toward the mid-nineteenth century. The decision of the Supreme Court of the United States in *DRED SCOTT V. SANDFORD* (1857) impinged on black freedom everywhere by ruling that neither free nor enslaved blacks had constitutional rights. By the start of the Civil War, new laws restricted the mobility of free blacks and limited the release of slaves from bondage. Hundreds of free blacks did, for a variety of reasons, volunteer for unarmed positions in the Confederate Army, but after the Union takeover of the city in 1862, the majority of black soldiers fought on the side of the North.

Reconstruction and Segregation

Although REPUBLICAN PARTY lawmakers enfranchised African Americans in New Orleans during RECONSTRUCTION (1865–1877), conservative whites soon voted these politicians out of office. The DEMOCRATIC PARTY won power in 1867, intent on "redeeming" the state by returning it to the social and political conditions of the pre-war period. New white leaders segregated accommodations and schools, and, after the U.S. Supreme Court decision in PLESSY V. FERGUSON (1896) allowed these "separate but equal" public facilities, whites pushed for the segregation of public transit. The historian Caryn Cossé Bell writes, "Radical Reconstruction's promise of freedom, opportunity, and equal citizenship had ended in a nightmare of semiservitude, JIM CROW laws, and disfranchisement." The growing tension led to the New Orleans riot of 1900, which was sparked by an instance of police harassment and marked by rampant violence of whites against blacks.

While Reconstruction-era politics strained relations between blacks and whites, it also upset relationships within the African American community. The educated black Creoles, whose racism often rivaled that of whites, suddenly found themselves grouped with black freedpeople. African American leaders had to contend with internal prejudice and resentment in governing this larger community.

Despite the growing discrimination, however, African American culture thrived. In the last quarter of the century, blacks created secret societies and social lodges, opened theaters, played baseball, and founded three colleges. Ensembles of children roamed the streets, improvising music in so-called SPASM BANDS, and BLUES, RAGTIME, and JAZZ music developed.

After the riot in 1900, which marked the height of the city's racial discord, blacks fought a slow battle for civil rights. A branch of the NATIONAL ASSOCIATION FOR THE ADVANCEMENT OF COLORED PEOPLE (NAACP) formed in the 1920s, under the leadership of A. P. Tureaud, a Creole activist. Over the following three decades, the chapter won gains in housing desegregation, salary equalization for teachers, expanded voting rights, and access to Louisiana State University.

Post–World War II

Police harassment of the kind that precipitated the riot of 1900 persisted through the 1950s, and city landlords continued to discriminate by color. Although a moderate mayor, deLesseps "Chep" Morrison, helped to curtail police racism, he opposed the desegregation of schools, transportation, and lunch counters. The NAACP, however, won these gains in the late 1950s and early 1960s. After the passage of the federal VOTING RIGHTS ACT OF 1965, political victories for African Americans became far more common, and New Orleans elected its first black mayor, Ernest "Dutch" Morial, in 1978.

These changes in the political sphere reflected the major demographic shift that came with the advent of the suburbs. New Orleans's location on the Mississippi River delta had restricted the city's growth for 200 years, because most of the surrounding land was useless swamp. Using modern technology, developers drained marshlands and built new neighborhoods, and white residents moved in as soon as they could. Between 1950 and 1975, the greater metropolitan area doubled in geographic size, and the white population within the city itself declined drastically.

New Orleans lost a good deal of its tax base as whites fled to the suburbs, yet the city did not die the death of many Northern industrial cities. Through the end of the twentieth century, the distinctive food, music, and annual Mardi Gras celebration attracted thousands of tourists. The historians Arnold R. Hirsh and Joseph Logsdon contend, "the delicate cultural amalgam that gave us jazz, a unique cuisine, and a love for public festivals is beleaguered but not yet obliterated."

Music

In the early 1800s, blacks were allowed to sing, dance, and play drums in accordance with their African traditions in Congo Square, in what is known today as the French Quarter. At these Sunday gatherings traditional African music could cross-pollinate with European musical traditions. African-styled instruments, made by slaves after they arrived in America, were commonly used in the festivities. European music and dances were also performed, and participating musicians added trumpets, clarinets, and even violins to their collections of African-styled instruments. Congo Square became a melting pot of music. By the late 1800s, New Orleans at large was filled with the shouts of black street vendors, the hallelujahs of Baptist church choirs, the strains of traditional Spanish dance music, the lilt of British folk songs, and the marching figures of brass bands modeled on French and Prussian ensembles.

New Orleans may not have been the sole birthplace of jazz, as is often claimed, but the city was a principal hub for the singular fusion of African and European musical elements into what became known as jazz music. The first documented jazz band, formed in 1895, was led by New Orleans cornet player CHARLES JOSEPH ("BUDDY") BOLDEN. Bolden's group played ragtime melodies, marches, quadrilles (a song form based on a European square dance), and the blues. A typical early New Orleans jazz ensemble consisted of three melody instruments (cornet, trombone, clarinet) and a rhythm section of BANJO or guitar, string bass or tuba, and drums.

A white New Orleans group, the Original Dixieland Jazz Band, is credited with making the first jazz recording. The term "Dixieland" came to refer both to jazz music played by white musicians of the early New Orleans school and to traditional New Orleans jazz.

Early New Orleans jazz developed at the same time as ragtime, principally a piano-based musical style, and ultimately the two styles merged. In the early decades of the twentieth century the new music flourished in Storyville, the city's red-light district. The most prominent jazz musicians of the era were trumpeters: Bolden, Freddie Keppard, JOSEPH ("KING") OLIVER, and Louis ("SATCHMO") ARMSTRONG. Armstrong is generally regarded as the first great improviser in jazz. Other significant musicians from the time included pianist FERDINAND

Joseph ("Jelly Roll") Morton; clarinetists Sidney Joseph Bechet, Barney Bigard, Johnny Dodds, Jimmie Noone, and George Lewis; drummer Baby Dodds; and trombonist and bandleader Edward ("Kid") Ory.

In the decade after World War I (1914–1918), nearly all of these musicians, with the exceptions of Bolden and Lewis, followed the Great Migration of blacks to Northern cities such as Chicago, Illinois, and New York, New York. Their performances and recordings in these cities helped to popularize New Orleans jazz throughout the country. In later decades, early New Orleans jazz came to be known as traditional jazz and enjoyed a revival in the 1940s. Beginning in the 1950s, many older Dixieland musicians were recorded under the auspices of the New Orleans Jazz Club.

Since the 1980s New Orleans has been a spawning ground for a new school of jazz players, among them trumpeter Wynton Marsalis and his brothers, saxophonist Branford Marsalis and trombonist Delfeayo Marsalis. Together with their father, pianist Ellis Marsalis, the Marsalis family has brought widespread attention to jazz and a new appreciation of the city and its jazz tradition. The city hosts the annual New Orleans Jazz and Heritage Festival, one of the largest jazz and blues festivals in the country.

Other musical genres also thrived in New Orleans. Mahalia Jackson, generally recognized as the greatest of gospel music singers, was influenced both by the hymns of her local Baptist churches and by the blues and jazz she heard while growing up in the city. In the late 1940s and 1950s, Professor Longhair and Fats Domino became heirs to Morton's legacy of New Orleans rhythm and blues piano playing. The four Neville brothers—Aaron, Art, Charles, and Cyril—introduced a decidedly New Orleans brand of pulsing funk music as leaders of bands such as the Meters and the Wild Tchoupitoulas in the 1970s. As the Neville Brothers they continued the family tradition of genre-crossing New Orleans music.

See also Black Codes in the United States; Free Blacks in the United States; Music, African; Redemption; Slavery in the United States.

Bibliography
Hirsh, Arnold R., and Joseph Logsdon. *Creole New Orleans: Race and Americanization.* Louisiana State University Press, 1992.

Rogers, Kim Lacy. *Righteous Lives: Narratives of the New Orleans Civil Rights Movement.* New York University Press, 1993.

Eric Bennett
Keith Raether

News Magazines and African Americans
Presence of African Americans in publishing, editing, and reporting for magazines and journals.

For information on

Magazines and journals founded and run by African Americans: *See* Crisis, The; *Ebony*; *Essence*; *Jet*; *Journal of Negro History, The*; *Messenger, The*; *Opportunity*; *Transition*.

Magazine editors and publishers: *See* Barber, Jesse Max; Bennett, Lerone, Jr.; Du Bois, W(illiam) E(dward) B(urghardt); Johnson Publishing Company; Owen, Chandler; Randolph, A(sa) Philip; Ruggles, David; West, Dorothy.

Magazine photographers: *See* Parks, Gordon, Sr.; Sleet, Moneta J., Jr.

Magazine writers: *See* Kincaid, Jamaica; Matthews, Victoria Earle.

Newton, Huey P.
1942–1989

African American political activist and cofounder of the Black Nationalist organization, the Black Panther Party.

Born in New Orleans, Louisiana, Huey Newton grew up in Oakland, California, a place that would become the West Coast center of the American Black Nationalist movement. While attending Merritt College in Oakland, he met Bobby Seale, and the two began to work together on a project to diversify the school's curriculum. Inspired by nationalist struggles in the Third World and revolutionaries such as Fidel Castro and Mao Zedong, Newton became critical of the racist oppression of blacks in the United States and the capitalist system he saw as underpinning that exploitation.

As a response to the condition of black America, Newton and Seale founded the Black Panther Party for Self-Defense, later simply called the Black Panther Party. "We want land, bread, housing, education, clothing, justice and peace," concluded the organization's ten-point program, which Newton coauthored. Patrolling black neighborhoods with shotguns, which were deemed legal as long as they were visible, the Panthers set themselves up as monitors of the police. These "justice patrols" sought to inform African Americans of their rights and counteract a history of police brutality against blacks. Not surprisingly, the Panthers developed a hostile relationship with the police, with Newton becoming a magnet for police antagonism.

On October 28, 1967, Newton was charged with murdering a police officer and wounding another. He pleaded innocent, and the trial provoked an intensive "Free Huey" campaign, drawing thousands to Black Panther rallies and rapidly boosting Panther membership and visibility. Viewed by many as a political prisoner, Newton continued to address political issues from prison.

In 1970, after his 1968 conviction was overturned because of procedural errors, Newton left prison to return to the Black Panther Party. He found the party weakened by regional conflict, in part because of disputes about the militant programs of ELDRIDGE CLEAVER, who influenced an East Coast-based movement. Leading a West Coast faction, Newton advocated political education and programs that he believed would link the Panthers to the broader African American community.

As his prominence in the Panthers declined, conflict with the law continued to trouble Newton. In 1974, he was accused of killing a woman and fled to CUBA. Three years later, he returned to face the murder charge of the woman victim, which after two hung juries, the state eventually dropped. He was retried and convicted for the 1967 murder of the policeman, but the conviction was later overturned.

In 1980, Newton received a Ph.D. in social philosophy from the University of California at Santa Cruz; he wrote a thesis on the "War Against the Panthers—A Study of Repression in America." Newton's life began a downward spiral after the Panthers were finally disbanded in 1982. Rumors about drug abuse surrounded him, and he was arrested in 1989 for embezzling funds from an Oakland children's nutritional program founded by the Panthers. He served six months of jail time. Later that year, he was killed in what was believed to be a drug-trade related incident.

See also Black Nationalism in the United States; Socialism.

Marian Aguiar

New York African Society for Mutual Relief

New York City's first African American mutual benefit society.

While some scholars believe that the New York African Society for Mutual Relief began meeting secretly in 1784, it was officially founded by Peter Williams Jr., a carpenter and talented public speaker, in 1808, the year of the society's first public meeting and the printing of its constitution. Its mission, like that of other MUTUAL BENEFIT SOCIETIES, was to provide a pool of resources from which members and their families could draw benefits otherwise denied to African Americans, such as burial insurance and financial aid in times of sickness. The society also provided financial assistance to widows, orphans, and the disabled. Its membership constituted a diverse segment of New York's African American community, but its leaders were mainly merchants and ministers. The society was formally incorporated on March 23, 1810, an event that was commemorated in an annual parade until around 1830.

An important safety net for many struggling African American families and small businessmen, the society quickly became a valuable source of financial aid for the needy, despite its own troubles. In 1812, for example, the society became financially strapped when one of its officers went bankrupt, but it was able to raise the additional funds necessary to save itself from ruin. By 1820 the society was financially stable enough to invest in real estate and to build a regular meeting house on Orange (now Baxter) Street, which also served as a school and a stop on the UNDERGROUND RAILROAD. The society also bought properties at 27 Greenwich Avenue and 41 West 66th Street, which it rented to raise money for its relief activities.

By the 1850s the society's importance had waned with the sudden proliferation of African American organizations and the lessening need for assistance among its sixty-five increasingly secure members. The society continued to raise money through its properties however, and after the NEW YORK DRAFT RIOT OF 1863, in which many African Americans were hard hit, the society's leader at the time, abolitionist Charles B. Ray, provided much needed financial assistance to many of the victims.

One of the first African American organizations of its kind, the New York African Society for Mutual Relief provided a blueprint for later African American civic organizations, including the Clarkson Society, the Dorcas Association, the Wilberforce Benevolent Society and the Phoenix Society. It also attracted many prominent black community leaders of the nineteenth century, including William Hamilton, believed to be a black descendant of Alexander Hamilton; Philip Bell, editor and publisher of *The Colored American*; Abraham Lawrence, president of the Harlem Railroad; and SAMUEL E. CORNISH, who with JOHN RUSSWURM founded *FREEDOM'S JOURNAL*, the first African American newspaper in the United States.

In the 1920s much of the society's work began to be shouldered by two related organizations, the William Hamilton Society and the Eato Aid Society, each named after past New York African Society presidents. Despite a diminishing role, the New York African Society for Mutual Relief remained active until the 1950s.

Bibliography

Harris, Robert. "Early Black Benevolent Societies, 1780–1830." *Massachusetts Review,* vol 20 (autumn 1979).

Robert Fay

New York City Draft Riot of 1863

Most violent urban insurrection during the Civil War, largely directed at black Americans.

In northern American cities like Toledo, CINCINNATI, Harrisburg, and DETROIT, the economic and social disruption caused by the CIVIL WAR (1861–1865) led to violence directed at free northern blacks, but the New York riot of 1863 was by far the most violent. Factors contributing to the New York City Draft Riot were labor unrest, unfair draft laws in an unpopular war, ethnic tensions, and disruptive street gangs. Before the 1840s, New York City's blacks held most of the city's jobs as longshoremen, hod carriers, brick makers, barbers, waiters, and domestic servants. Irish immigrants, particularly those arriving after 1846, competed with blacks for these unskilled jobs and eventually gained control of the occupations, leaving many blacks to work only as strike breakers.

The animosity between New York's whites and blacks was further intensified by the EMANCIPATION PROCLAMATION. Democratic politicians used it to their advantage by claiming, paradoxically, that Republicans would transport freed people to New York to replace white workers while lazy blacks lived on relief services provided by industrious whites. Shortly after President Abraham Lincoln issued the Emancipation Proclamation, Congress passed the Conscription Act, which had a provision allowing a draftee to decline service for a $300 fee. This financial arrangement widened class divisions.

The three-day riot began on July 13 as a protest against the Conscription Act. After the protesters, many of them Irish laborers, destroyed draft headquarters, they roamed the streets, at times razing entire city blocks, cutting telegraph lines, tearing up railroad tracks, and causing factories and shops to close. They assaulted the offices of the *New York Tribune*, trying to find the pro-Union editor Horace Greeley, and they attacked the home of the city's provost marshal.

The mob then split into groups. Some destroyed mansions; others attacked the mayor's house in a failed attempt to level it. Still others targeted New York's black residents with intense violence. They terrorized blacks, burned the Colored Orphan Asylum, and looted the Colored Seamen's Home. They raided and destroyed homes; they shot, stomped, clubbed, burned, and hanged black victims. Rioters killed eleven blacks. Most blacks fled the city, but a few desperately sought the sanctuary of police station jail cells. Union Army regiments—including some men returning from the battle at Gettysburg—finally restored order.

Although New York City merchants raised $50,000 to pay black victims and to rebuild the Colored Orphan Asylum, the psychic scars remained. By 1865 New York's black population had decreased by 20 percent, from 12,472 to 9,945, because of the fear resulting from the three nights of rioting.

Bibliography
Bernstein, Iver. *The New York City Draft Riots*. Oxford University Press, 1990.

Robert Fay

New York Manumission Society

Antislavery organization of white men who supported the gradual abolition of slavery and the betterment of African Americans.

MANUMISSION SOCIETIES emerged after the AMERICAN REVOLUTION to advocate the end of the TRANSATLANTIC SLAVE TRADE and the gradual abolition of slavery. Manumission, which entailed the formal and legal release of a slave, was the most common path to freedom. It could occur privately, by an individual slave owner, or officially, by state law. One of the most active and organized proponents was the New York Manumission Society, founded by QUAKERS on January 25, 1785, in lower Manhattan. Although many of its members were slaveholders, the New York Manumission Society actively pushed for better treatment of slaves and pursued legal action on behalf of slaves who had been mistreated or enslaved illegally.

Under the guidance of John Jay and Alexander Hamilton, the New York Manumission Society was a leader in the education of blacks in New York City for sixty-four years. In 1787 the Society established the AFRICAN FREE SCHOOL in New York City to provide primary education for free blacks. The school emphasized reading, writing, and arithmetic, and also provided specialized training in navigation to encourage seafaring as a potential career for blacks. In addition to teaching basic skills, the black faculty of the school provided moral and religious instruction to its students, some of whom became prominent in the black community. Among this influential group of teachers were James McCune Smith, IRA ALDRIDGE, PETER WILLIAMS, JR., and ALEXANDER CRUMMELL.

By 1909 the African Free School was the largest in the city, and by 1814 it had educated more than 2,300 black students. The Society closed its doors in 1849 and donated its financial resources to organizations in New York that were committed to the antislavery movement.

Alonford James Robinson

New York, New York

City in southeastern New York State, home to the largest black population in the United States.

The first Africans arrived in New York City (then known as New Amsterdam) in 1626, as slaves to the DUTCH WEST INDIA COMPANY. As early as 1630 the community had free blacks, and in 1644 a group of slaves were given conditional freedom. They settled in what is now Greenwich Village, which remained a black neighborhood for nearly 200 years.

In 1664 the English took over New Netherland and renamed it New York, instituting a still more severe form of slavery. Africans, however, began to organize and to protest their enslavement in the early eighteenth century. A slave rebellion in 1712 was brutally suppressed, as was another in 1741, when twenty-nine blacks were executed.

Abolitionist sentiment grew in the city, and in 1787 a law was passed to begin to abolish the practice. That same year free blacks founded the African Free School, which future black leaders HENRY HIGHLAND GARNET and ALEXANDER CRUMMELL attended. In 1800 the AFRICAN METHODIST EPISCOPAL ZION CHURCH (AME Zion) was founded, and in 1809 the Abyssinian Baptist Church was established. After 1820 many African Americans lived in the infamous Five Points slum in lower Manhattan, and in areas west of the Hudson River. In 1827 slavery was finally abolished, and the first black newspaper in the United States began, *Freedom's Journal*, edited by JOHN RUSSWURM and SAMUEL CORNISH. The abolitionist movement gained momentum in 1835, when DAVID RUGGLES organized the New York Committee of Vigilance.

Two African American workers tighten a rivet during construction of the Holland Tunnel into New York City in 1924. *CORBIS/Bettmann*

At the same time, immigrants from Europe pushed African Americans out of the skilled labor force and rioted against them in 1834 and 1835. The 1840s and 1850s were characterized by widespread discrimination against African Americans, and during the CIVIL WAR poor whites rebelled against conscription, venting their anger during the draft riot of 1863, in which eleven African Americans, including children, were murdered by marauding white mobs. The mob burned down the Colored Orphan Asylum, and many African Americans fled to Brooklyn.

Despite unfair treatment and outright persecution, the African American community grew and developed its own institutions, most notably the *New York Age,* a newspaper published by T. THOMAS FORTUNE, in 1870. But African Americans were excluded from most unions and hence from much of the growing industrial labor market. By 1890 the 33,000-person community lived in the old and new Tenderloin districts between 20th and 53rd Streets and eventually the San Juan Hill district between West 61st and West 63rd Streets (so named for its racial conflicts).

In 1898 New York consolidated five boroughs into a single municipality, including Brooklyn, the third largest city in the United States. By 1890 Brooklyn's black population was 10,287.

The collapse of the housing market in HARLEM in 1904 led many in the black community of Manhattan to relocate there. Philip Payton's Afro-Am Realty Company was instrumental in that resettlement, and a new migration of African Americans from the South and the Caribbean added to the growth of the Harlem community. From 1900 to 1920 the black population of New York nearly tripled, making New York the largest black community in the United States. Harlem quickly became the cultural and political epicenter of black America. The AME Zion, St. Philip's Protestant Episcopal, and Abyssinian Baptist churches relocated to Harlem. In 1919 the influential *Amsterdam News* was founded there. From Harlem, THE CRISIS and OPPORTUNITY magazines, established by the NATIONAL ASSOCIATION FOR THE ADVANCEMENT OF COLORED PEOPLE and the NATIONAL URBAN LEAGUE, respectively, published pioneering black literature and editorials. In the 1920s Harlem nurtured a socialist movement, led by H. H. Harrison, W. A. Domingo, and (later) A. PHILIP RANDOLPH, while the enormously popular UNIVERSAL NEGRO IMPROVEMENT ASSOCIATION of MARCUS GARVEY promoted not simply a back-to-Africa drive, but also the first black nationalist movement.

In 1925 ALAIN LOCKE edited an issue of *Survey Graphic* magazine, filling it with poetry, art, essays, fiction, and folklore, and declaring a "New Negro" renaissance. Through cultural expression, African Americans would be "a new figure on the national canvas and a new force in the foreground of affairs." The issue signaled a brief but intense interest in Harlem and African America, from nightclubs such as the COTTON CLUB to the literature of JESSIE FAUSET, JAMES WELDON JOHNSON, JEAN TOOMER, LANGSTON HUGHES, CLAUDE MCKAY, WALLACE THURMAN, NELLA LARSEN, COUNTEE CULLEN, ZORA NEALE HURSTON, and ARNA BONTEMPS. EUBIE BLAKE, FATS WALLER, and DUKE ELLINGTON developed a jazz tradition that over the decades brought CHARLIE PARKER, BUD POWELL, ORNETTE COLEMAN, and MILES DAVIS to New York. In politics, Charles Fillmore became the first black district leader in 1929.

The GREAT DEPRESSION brought much of the momentum to a halt. African Americans were thrown out of work in disproportionately larger numbers than white New Yorkers. Discrimination and segregation became more pronounced, leading to the HARLEM RIOT OF 1935, when thousands of frustrated Harlem residents destroyed more than $2 million of property. The disturbance led to greater black political organizing efforts. Four black district leaders were elected. In 1937 black leaders formed the Greater New York City Coordinating Committee for the Employment of Negroes, an activist organization that used boycotts to force hiring of African Americans.

In the 1940s African Americans from the South and the Caribbean poured into Harlem and Brooklyn, especially after A. Philip Randolph organized the MARCH ON WASHINGTON in 1941, which opened defense industry jobs to blacks. In 1943, however, frustration with racism led to another Harlem riot, in which six African Americans were killed and more than 180 injured. The event galvanized citywide efforts to improve race relations. One year later, ADAM CLAYTON POWELL, JR., was elected to the U.S. Congress and BENJAMIN DAVIS, SR., to the city council.

During the 1940s growth and consolidation turned Brooklyn's Bedford-Stuyvesant into the most populous black neighborhood in New York, but also into an impoverished ghetto that reached into the Crown Heights and Brownsville sections by 1960. Caribbean immigration shifted to Brooklyn until 40 percent of all African Americans in the city lived in Brooklyn by 1970. The population shift led to increased black political strength, and state assemblywoman SHIRLEY CHISHOLM was elected to the U.S. Congress in 1968.

Harlem developed as a political, religious, and literary mecca in the 1940s and 1950s. Hulan Jack became the first black Manhattan borough president in 1953. Around the same time MALCOLM X expanded the Harlem Mosque into one of the most dynamic centers of the NATION OF ISLAM and spearheaded a black nationalist movement aimed at defending black Americans with force against white racism and violence. Malcolm X was assassinated in 1965, however, and his death led to a call for still greater black power, as well as to the decline of his movement. From the 1940s through the 1970s, Harlem nurtured some of the most powerful and original literary voices in the United States, including those of RALPH ELLISON, JAMES BALDWIN, LORRAINE HANSBERRY, Leroy Jones (later AMIRI BARAKA and AUDRE LORDE. In the late 1970s, black New York also developed a vital, new musical style—rap—notably through such pioneer rappers as RUN-DMC, GRAND MASTER FLASH, and PUBLIC ENEMY.

In 1970 CHARLES RANGEL was elected to the congressional seat vacated by Adam Clayton Powell. PERCY SUTTON was Manhattan borough president for eleven years, beginning in 1966. But the African American community had not advanced into other citywide offices, and widespread unemployment and poverty once again increased frustrations. A power brownout in 1977 led to looting in Brooklyn that was reminiscent of the earlier Harlem riot.

In 1989 DAVID DINKINS was the first African American to be elected mayor of New York City. But Dinkins inherited serious problems, notably crime and a deteriorating school system. In 1993 Dinkins was defeated for reelection by Rudolph W. Giuliani in a city that was newly polarized along racial lines after an incident in Crown Heights, in which the accidental death of a black boy, killed by a Jewish driver, led to the murder of a rabbinical student by a black mob.

The administration of Mayor Giuliani was marked by a significant decrease in crime in New York, and by criticism, particularly from black leaders in the city, that his aggressive policing threatened civil liberties and was directed disproportionately at African Americans. This criticism reached a boiling point following two incidents in the late 1990s. In the first, Abner Louima, a Haitian immigrant, was tortured in a Brooklyn police station house in 1997, a crime to which a white police officer ultimately pleaded guilty. Then in 1999, Amadou Diallo, an unarmed immigrant from Guinea, was killed by a barrage of bullets from the guns of four white police officers. The Diallo killing led to widespread protests against police brutality in the city. As the city recovers from the terrorist attacks of September 11, 2001, when the World Trade Center was destroyed, race relations and other urban issues have taken a backseat as city officials work to rebuild the downtown area.

Bibliography

Bloch, Herman D. *The Circle of Discrimination: An Economic and Social Study of the Black Man in New York.* New York University Press, 1969.

Connolly, Harold X. *A Ghetto Grows in Brooklyn.* New York University Press, 1977.

Ottley, Roi, and William Weatherby, eds. *The Negro in New York: An Informal Social History.* New York Public Library, 1967.

Walker, George E. *The Afro-American in New York City, 1827–1860.* Garland Pub., 1993.

Jim Mendelsohn

New York Renaissance

One of the most successful all-black professional basketball teams in the 1920s and 1930s.

The New York Renaissance were created in 1922 by Robert L. Douglass, a native of the Caribbean island SAINT KITTS and a former professional BASKETBALL player with the New York Spartans. The team gained their name from their playing venue—the Renaissance Casino ballroom in HARLEM, NEW YORK—where they dazzled fans with their innovative style of play. The Rens, as they were called, were one of the few all-black, traveling professional basketball teams of that era. Formed five years before one of America's most famous all-black professional basketball teams, the HARLEM GLOBETROTTERS, the Rens provided African American men with the opportunity to compete against white athletes on an equal footing.

They toured the country competing against black and white teams, and in the process compiled one of the most impressive winning streaks in history. In 1934 the Rens won eighty-eight consecutive games, and between 1932 and 1936 they won 473 games and lost only forty-nine. Three years later they won the first World Basketball Tournament held in CHICAGO, ILLINOIS. In 1963 the entire team was inducted into the Professional Basketball Hall of Fame, including Charles T. "Tarzan" Cooper, John "Casey" Holt, Clarence "Fats" Jenkins, James "Pappy" Ricks, Eyre "Bruiser" Satch, William "Wee Willie" Smith, and William J. "Bill" Yancey.

New York Slave Conspiracy of 1741

Alleged insurrection planned by New York City's black slaves and white poor, which highlighted the fear whites had of violent slave rebellions and the punitive measures they employed to prevent them.

Between May 11 and August 29, 1741, following years of increasing paranoia among white New Yorkers, thirty blacks and four whites were executed for allegedly planning an insurrection against slaveholders. Scholars disagree about whether or not a conspiracy existed. The trial's record contains evidence of widespread dissatisfaction, unrest, and sporadic violence among blacks, but it provides no conclusive evidence of an actual insurrectionary plot. What seems clear is that the charges, and the executions that followed, grew out of New York whites' mounting fear of the city's blacks.

White New Yorkers' fear was fueled by a series of events. Two dozen slaves participated in the NEW YORK SLAVE REBELLION OF 1712, killing seven and wounding ten. Many whites believed rumors that slaves had poisoned the city's water supply in 1740. In response, they drank only bottled water for months. White New Yorkers also felt threatened by the relatively high concentration of slaves in the city. Blacks represented about 20 percent of the city's 11,000 residents. In the colonies, only CHARLESTON, SOUTH CAROLINA, had a higher proportion of blacks. In 1739 slaves in Charleston rebelled, and white New Yorkers associated that incident with Charleston's similarly high concentration of slaves. Further, many white men had left the city to fight in the "King's War" against Spain. Those who remained felt more vulnerable.

Widespread discontent that had existed among the black and white poor who were adversely affected by an economic depression throughout the colony increased during the winter of 1740–1741. More than ten feet of snow had fallen on the city, and over 60 miles of the Hudson River had frozen. Commerce in the city virtually stopped. Supplies dwindled, and merchants raised food and heating fuel prices beyond the reach of the poor. The wealthy passed the winter comfortably (as did their slaves), able to afford the price increases. Many of the poor long remembered the merchants who profited by the scarcity, and the uncharitable among the wealthy.

Finally, a series of fires from mid-March into April 1741 persuaded many whites that blacks were plotting an insurrection. First, Fort George, a government complex, burned to the ground. A week later, a resident's house caught fire. Eight more fires occurred by April 5, some of suspicious origin. No conclusive evidence tied blacks to the fires, but one resident claimed to have heard a slave repeating, "Fire, Fire, Scorch, Scorch, A LITTLE, damn it, BY-AND-BY," which she believed indicated that blacks were responsible for the fires.

One hundred and fifty slaves were charged with the capital crime of conspiracy. The subsequent trial was marred by coercion and bribes. When investigators could find no conclusive evidence that a conspiracy existed, they began seeking witnesses who could link the fires to a planned uprising. Many slaves confessed after being tortured or promised rewards. The most damaging testimony came from Mary Burton, a servant indentured to an innkeeper who had been granted immunity by prosecutor Daniel Horsmanden. Burton stated that several slaves had met frequently at her employer's house, and that she heard them "talk frequently of burning the fort and that they'd go down to the Fly and burn the whole town. My master and mistress (the innkeeper and his wife) said they'd aid and assist them as much as they could."

The Hughsons, two other whites, and 104 blacks were convicted. Of the thirty slaves executed, thirteen were burned to death and seventeen hanged. All four whites were hanged. Authorities pardoned thirty-three of the slaves, returning them to their owners. The remaining seventy-two slaves confessed, pleaded for mercy, and were pardoned and deported.

Bibliography

Davis, Thomas J. *A Rumor of Revolt: The "Great Negro Plot" in Colonial New York.* Free Press, 1985.

Robert Fay

New York Slave Rebellion of 1712

Slave rebellion against inhumane treatment that resulted in harsher slave codes in New York and ended the importation of slaves to Massachusetts and Pennsylvania.

On April 6, 1712, about twenty-five AMERICAN INDIAN and black slaves in colonial New York City retaliated against harsh treatment by their masters. They set fire to an outhouse and then lay in ambush, killing nine men and wounding seven others as they came to extinguish the fire. They then fled to the woods. Within two days more than forty had been arrested and six committed suicide before arrest rather than face what they knew would be harsh consequences.

Twenty-seven slaves were convicted of murder and sentenced to death, although much of the evidence used to convict them was suspect; eighteen were acquitted. Six, including a pregnant woman, were reprieved. Of the approximately twenty-one people executed, most were hanged, three were burned to death, one was hung in chains until he died, and one was broken on the wheel.

Shortly after the rebellion, New York's legislature toughened its slave codes. Slaves gathering in groups of three or more were subject to forty lashes, and such crimes as burning barns, outhouses, stables, and stacks of corn or hay were all made punishable by death. Wanting to avoid similar uprisings, the Massachusetts legislature passed a law forbidding slave importation, and the Pennsylvania legislature placed an import duty on blacks that effectively ended their importation.

See also Slave Rebellions in the United States.

Robert Fay

Ngala

Ethnic group of Democratic Republic of the Congo; also known as Bangala and Mangala.

The Ngala primarily inhabit northwestern Congo-Kinshasa and neighboring Congo-Brazzaville. Others live in ANGOLA. They speak a Bantu language, Lingala, which serves as a means of communication among different peoples in western Congo-Kinshasa. Approximately 400,000 people consider themselves Ngala.

See also Bantu: Dispersion and Settlement.

Ngandu

Ethnic group of the Democratic Republic of the Congo.

The Ngandu primarily inhabit central Congo-Kinshasa. They speak a Bantu language. Approximately 200,000 people consider themselves Ngandu.

See also Bantu: Dispersion and Settlement.

Ngbandi

Ethnic group of Central Africa.

The Ngbandi primarily inhabit the northwestern DEMOCRATIC REPUBLIC OF THE CONGO and the southern CENTRAL AFRICAN REPUBLIC. They speak a Niger-Congo language. Approximately 200,000 people consider themselves Ngbandi.

See also Languages, African: An Overview.

Ngindu

Ethnic group of Tanzania; also known as Ngindo.

The Ngindu primarily inhabit TANZANIA. They speak a Bantu language. Over 200,000 people consider themselves Ngindu.

See also Bantu: Dispersion and Settlement.

Ngombe

Ethnic group of the Democratic Republic of the Congo.

The Ngombe primarily inhabit northwestern Congo-Kinshasa along the CONGO RIVER. They speak a Bantu language. Approximately 200,000 people consider themselves Ngombe.

See also Bantu: Dispersion and Settlement.

Ngonde

Ethnic group of southeastern Africa.

The Ngonde inhabit primarily the Northern Province of MALAWI. Others live in eastern ZAMBIA and southwestern TANZANIA. They speak a Bantu language and are closely related to the NYASA people. Around 200,000 people consider themselves Ngonde.

See also Bantu: Dispersion and Settlement.

Ngoni

Ethnic group consisting of approximately twelve distinct peoples; also known as Angoni, Abangoni, Mangoni, and Wangoni.

The Ngoni are a BANTU-speaking NGUNI group who, before the nineteenth century, inhabited the area of modern-day Natal, in SOUTH AFRICA. Starting in 1818 the Ngoni began to flee north as Shaka Zulu's army undertook its campaign of expansion. Led by their chief, Zwangendaba, they traveled through present-day MOZAMBIQUE and crossed the ZAMBEZI RIVER in 1835. Traversing ZAMBIA, they settled on the southeastern shores of LAKE TANGANYIKA. Today, they live in Zambia, TANZANIA, and MALAWI.

Adopting the military strategies of the ZULU, the Ngoni dominated most of the groups they encountered while spreading northward in the wake of the Zulu expansion. Their large, compact villages, which, for defensive purposes, were inhabited by 2,000 to 3,000 adults, were strategically clustered and surrounded by a buffer zone. A centralized political hierarchy, led by a hereditary chief, also contributed to their military success. But the Ngoni could not conquer the BEMBA or Bisa, despite frequent raids. These groups, having acquired guns through the sale of ivory and slaves to Swahili and Arab merchants, were able to stand their ground.

When Zwangendaba fled in 1845, the Ngoni splintered and dispersed. Under the leadership of Zwangendaba's son, Mpezeni I, a large group migrated south and in 1880 subdued the CHEWA and Nsenga of southeastern Zambia and the adjacent areas of Malawi and Mozambique. Although these and other groups came under the political umbrella of the Ngoni, they retained their ethnic identity and much of their culture. The Ngoni themselves soon faced an overpowering military force of British colonial troops, who conquered the area in 1897 and banned slave trading. The colonial administration appointed the grandson of Mpezeni I to administer local government as the Ngoni Native Authority.

Today, three-quarters of the more than one million Ngoni live in Malawi. About 350,000 live in Zambia, another 170,000 inhabit Tanzania, and a small number live in northwestern Mozambique. Having been pacified by the British colonial authorities, Ngoni men married women from subjugated groups and the Ngoni gradually assimilated into the local culture. As a result, the Ngoni have almost lost their original language and primarily speak Nyanja except during religious ceremonies and royal praises. They have become matrilineal cultivators of maize and herders of cattle, and also maintain fenced vegetable gardens.

Ari Nave

Ngouabi, Marien

1938–1977

Congolese army officer and president of the Congo (1968–1977) who was assassinated by rivals.

Born into a chiefly lineage, Marien Ngouabi proved to be a popular political moderate during his term as president of the REPUBLIC OF THE CONGO. Ngouabi attended the Général Leclerc school for veterans' children in BRAZZAVILLE, hundreds of miles from his hometown of Ombélé in northeastern Congo (then the French colony of Moyen-Congo). Later he joined the French colonial military in Oubangui-Chari (present-day CENTRAL AFRICAN REPUBLIC), became a sergeant, served in suppressing the BAMILÉKÉ rebellion in CAMEROON, and received military training in FRANCE. He was arrested twice during his early years as an officer, first for criticizing French policies in Cameroon and later for joining riots in Brazzaville. Acceptance in the French officers' academy, St. Cyr, however, redeemed his military career.

In 1963 Ngouabi became commander of the parachute corps in the newly independent Republic of the Congo. As he became more active in the ruling party, then-president Alphonse Massemba-Debat began to fear the charismatic captain's popularity and influence, and so he demoted and later arrested Ngouabi. This arrest led to a mutiny, Massemba-Debat's resignation, and Ngouabi's release and takeover in 1968. To assuage the radical left and gain support among his MBOCHI ethnic kinsmen, Ngouabi established a vanguard party (the Congolese Workers Party, or PCT), proclaimed a people's republic, and adopted scientific SOCIALISM. In theory, socialism would be rationally planned and implemented thoroughly throughout the country.

Ngouabi increasingly employed the security apparatus to crush opposition, while he also attempted to broaden the government's popular appeal by reestablishing the national assembly. An ideological moderate in Congolese terms, Ngouabi tried to please all sides through a belated incorporation of southerners into his government. But this move alienated many radical northern military officers. A number of these officers, including current president DENIS SASSOU-NGUESSO, are alleged to have plotted the still-unsolved assassination of Ngouabi in March 1977. Brigadier General J. Yhombi-Opango succeeded Ngouabi.

Eric Young

Ngugi wa Thiong'o

1938–

Kenyan writer whose fictional work depicts events in colonial and postcolonial Kenya and whose essays emphasize the role of language and culture in the process of decolonization in Africa.

During a critical time in Kenyan history, Ngugi wa Thiong'o's fiction brought to life the struggle for independence and the task of nation-building. He integrated Marxist-Leninist beliefs into his writing, depicting the lives of Kenyan peasants and workers with an aesthetic finesse that for the most part avoided the doctrinaire, yet at times landed him in trouble with Kenyan authorities. His vivid characterizations of women illustrated the range of women's roles in national struggles. Yet, for many, what set Ngugi apart was his decision to radicalize his contribution to Kenyan culture by writing in his native language of KIKUYU rather than English, the colonial tongue.

James Ngugi was born into a polygamous family in a village near Limuru Town in Central Province, KENYA. While attending a prestigious British-sponsored high school, Ngugi witnessed the intensifying independence struggle of the Kenyan people against the British colonial government in a guerrilla war that became known as the MAU MAU REBELLION. The war came very close to home for Ngugi. His mother was arrested and tortured for his brother's involvement with the guerrillas, and his stepbrother, a deaf mute, was shot by soldiers simply because he did not hear their order to stop. Ngugi later incorporated many of these experiences into his fictional work.

After completing an undergraduate degree at Makerere University, Ngugi traveled to England to enroll at the University of Leeds. His first two novels were written there. *Weep Not Child* (1964) portrays a young Kenyan man who pursues a Western education while his village suffers the ravages of the war of independence. In this novel, Ngugi revealed how personal tragedy is interconnected with the larger tragedy of ancestral lands lost and resources plundered under COLONIAL RULE. Like many of Ngugi's later works, the novel draws on Kikuyu myth, most significantly the story of the creation, and emphasizes the connection between the people and the land of Kenya.

The River Between (1965), written first but published second, explores the conflict between traditional African beliefs and CHRISTIANITY. In this novel, a mission-educated character tries unsuccessfully to synthesize the Christian worldview with the Kikuyu, even as he comes to understand the ultimately destructive force Christianity will have on his own culture.

Ngugi did not complete his masters thesis, which focused on Caribbean Literature, because he refused to make the designated revisions. Instead, he spent his time studying Marxism and reading the works of national liberation writers such as FRANTZ FANON. When he returned to Kenya in 1967, he became the first black African member of the University of Nairobi English department. A year later, citing the need for the newly independent nation to develop a national culture, Ngugi coauthored a successful proposal to abolish the English department and replace it with a Department of Literature focusing primarily on national literature and indigenous ORAL TRADITION, with reference to other writings of Africa, the African DIASPORA, and the "Third World."

With his third and best-known novel *A Grain of Wheat* (1967), Ngugi revealed his sophistication as an artist. The novel portrays several characters in a village whose intertwined lives are transformed by the 1952–1960 Emergency in Kenya. As events unfold, compromises are forced, friendships are betrayed, and romantic loves are tested. The narrative of *A Grain of Wheat* is interwoven with myth as well as allusions to real-life leaders of the nationalist struggle, such as JOMO KENYATTA. Ngugi explored the psychology of his characters, yet employed a shifting narrative voice to evoke a strong sense of community. He also did not hesitate to portray harshly those Kenyans, specifically the Home Guard, who made compromises with the colonial government for their own personal gain.

In 1969, claiming lack of academic freedom, Ngugi resigned from his post in Nairobi. After two years teaching in the United States at Northwestern University, he returned to the department in Nairobi and published the collection *Homecoming: Essays on African and Caribbean Literature, Culture, and Politics* (1972). In one essay, Ngugi implicated the missionary church in bolstering colonial authority in Kenya, and shortly after he dropped the Christian name "James" in favor of the name Ngugi wa Thiong'o.

His next novel, *Petals of Blood* (1977), criticized the elite post-Independence leaders and the role capitalism had played in creating a Kenyan society increasingly polarized between rich and poor. Although *Petals of Blood* painted a harsh picture of the Kenyan government, it was Ngugi's work in popular theater that provoked the ire of Kenyan authorities and landed the writer in prison. During the 1960s and 1970s, Ngugi had written several plays, including *The Black Hermit* (1968; produced 1962), and cowritten others, including the critically acclaimed *The Trial of Dedan Kimathi* (1976; produced 1974), and the Kikuyu play *Ngaahika ndeenda* (1980; *I Will Marry When I Want*). When *Ngaahika ndeenda* was used as a call-to-arms to organize exploited Kenyan peasants, the government imprisoned Ngugi for a year in 1977–1978.

While in prison, Ngugi made the decision to write in Kikuyu. He explained his reasons in a later collection of essays, *Decolonising the Mind* (1983), in which he discussed how language carries ideology, and how national culture is endangered when the colonial language supplants the indigenous: "Language carries culture, and culture carries, particularly through orature and literature, the entire body of values by which we perceive ourselves and our place in the world . . . Language is thus inseparable from ourselves as a community of human beings with a specific form and character, a specific history, a specific relationship to the world."

Caitaani Mutharaba-ini (1980; *Devil on the Cross*), begun on a roll of toilet paper hidden from the guards in the prison, portrayed a gruesome contest between participants at the Devil's Feast, who compete for the title of greatest criminal. The party symbolizes a nation cannibalized by greedy individuals, both Kenyan and foreign. The heroes are the Kenyan peasants and workers, some of whom later heard the work read aloud in villages. Ngugi followed this book with another play, *Maitu njugira* (1981; *Mother, Sing for Me*), never officially performed but seen by many in public rehearsals, and the essay collection *Writers in Politics* (1981).

During a book tour in 1982, Ngugi was forced to remain in England after he learned that he would be arrested if he returned to Kenya. That year he wrote the novel *Matigari ma Mjiruumgi* (1986; *Matigari*), which quickly became an underground success in Kenya. By this time Ngugi's work had become so influential that the Kenyan government waged a campaign to route out the rebel leader "Matigari," a man said to be inciting revolutions throughout the Kenyan countryside, only to discover that he was merely a fictional character.

Ngugi, who joined the faculty of New York University in 1992, is now a Distinguished Professor of English and Comparative Literature and Director of the International Center for Writing and Translation at University of California-Irvine. In 2002 he received the Nonino Prize. Ngugi has designated the role of literature as a life force in the struggle for social justice: "The very act of writing is a social act: writing about somebody for somebody. Writing reflects a community wrestling with its environment to make it yield the means of life."

See also Christianity: Missionaries in Africa; Marriage, African Customs of; Nationalism in Africa; Theater, African.

Bibliography

Cook, David, and Michael Okenimpke. *Ngugi wa Thiong'o: An Explanation of His Writing.* Heinemann, 1982.

Ngugi wa Thiong'o. *Decolonising the Mind: The Politics of Language in African Literature.* Heinemann, 1986.

Ngugi wa Thiong'o. *Moving the Centre: The Struggle for Cultural Freedoms.* Heinemann, 1993.

Marian Aguiar

Nguni

Southern African ethnic groups that speak related Bantu languages and inhabit southeast Africa from Cape Province to southern Mozambique.

Historians believe that the ancestors of contemporary Nguni were the first Bantu speakers to arrive in southeastern Africa, some time after the second century C.E. Linguists point to the use of "clicks" in Nguni languages as evidence of not only the antiquity of the migration but also of the early migrants' likely assimilation of KHOISAN speakers, whose languages use similar phonemes. No other Bantu languages use "clicks." The large number of cognates between Nguni languages and Swahili also suggests that the Bantu migrants traveled south via Africa's east coast. Today most Nguni languages are not mutually intelligible. Some of the more prominent Nguni ethnic groups include the XHOSA and the ZULU of SOUTH AFRICA, the SWAZI of SWAZILAND, the NDEBELE of ZIMBABWE and the NGONI of MALAWI.

For centuries the Nguni peoples are thought to have lived in scattered patrilineal chiefdoms, cultivating cereal crops such as millet and raising cattle. The current geographic distribution of Nguni peoples largely reflects the turbulent political developments and population movements of the nineteenth century. In the 1820s the cattle-herding Zulu, led by their king SHAKA, embarked on an aggressive campaign of conquest and expansion known as the MFECANE. Shaka's large and well-armed armies conquered a number of neighboring peoples and sent others fleeing. Some Nguni groups adopted the Zulu's methods of warfare and used them to subjugate the peoples in whose territory they ultimately settled. The Ndebele of Zimbabwe are one such group; the Soshangane of MOZAMBIQUE are another. The Swazi kingdom was also established during this period.

Even before the *mfecane,* trade and colonialism made their mark on the regions inhabited by Nguni peoples. From the sixteenth century onwards, European merchant vessels frequented trading posts on the coast of present-day southern Mozambique, seeking goods such as gold, ivory, and slaves. The Portuguese, in particular, brought maize from the New World, which soon became a staple crop in much of southeastern Africa, and which some historians argue contributed to both population growth and the eventual rise of complex states in the region. Nguni cattle-herding groups such as the Xhosa also traded their livestock for the guns and tobacco of European settlers from the Cape Colony (in present-day South Africa).

During the nineteenth century, European expansionism brought the Xhosa and other Nguni groups into conflicts with both migrating AFRIKANERS and British troops. Many communities lost both land and cattle. The discovery of diamonds in the 1860s and gold in the 1880s provided an even greater motive for European conquest of Nguni-occupied lands. By the turn of the century, many men from Nguni communities were migrating to work in the gold mines near Witwatersrand.

In rural areas many Nguni peoples still herd cattle and cultivate cereal crops as well as a variety of cash crops. But a significant proportion of many Nguni groups' populations now either live in cities or depend upon earnings from seasonal migrant labor in the mines.

See also Bantu: Dispersion and Settlement; Gold Trade; Ivory Trade; Transatlantic Slave Trade.

Ari Nave

Nguru

Ethnic group of Tanzania; also known as Ngulu and Wanguru.

The Nguru primarily inhabit the coastal highlands of northeastern TANZANIA. They speak a Bantu language. Around 200,000 people consider themselves Nguru.

See also Bantu: Dispersion and Settlement.

Niagara Movement

African American political action organization founded by W. E. B. Du Bois and William Monroe Trotter.

At the start of the twentieth century, no African American voice carried such authority with both black and white audiences as that of BOOKER T. WASHINGTON. As the founder of Tuskegee Institute (later TUSKEGEE UNIVERSITY), Washington presided over a network of membership organizations, including the Afro-American Council and the National Negro Business League, which worked to promote racial uplift among black Americans. Some African Americans, however, were dissatisfied with Washington's message of ACCOMMODATIONISM, which counseled economic self-help and patience. Washington's critics demanded that black American citizens be granted the same civil rights enjoyed by whites. The militant Niagara Movement was a direct response to Washington's cautious approach to racial justice. Though short-lived, it was an important step in the formation of modern African American protest movements.

Both W. E. B. DU BOIS and WILLIAM MONROE TROTTER, the Niagara Movement's organizers, had long opposed Washington's philosophy. Trotter was the editor of the BOSTON, MASSACHUSETTS *Guardian,* an African American daily newspaper known for its militant editorials. Trotter had publicly rebuked Washington at a Boston meeting in 1903, after which he was jailed for allegedly trying to cause a riot. That same year Du Bois had published in his classic book *The Souls of Black Folk* an essay condemning Washington for his acceptance of lowered expectations for African Americans. In 1904 Du Bois had joined Washington on the Committee of Twelve, a coalition that met to discuss solutions to the problems facing black Americans. But the preponderance of Washington's allies on the committee and its general air of conservatism caused Du Bois to resign the following year.

Trotter and Du Bois first met in the spring of 1905, while Du Bois was investigating charges that Washington had been using financial pressure to control the mainstream black press in the United States. Trotter proposed that the two collaborate further, this time in creating, as he said, a "national 'strategy board' for defensive and offensive and constructive action." Together with C. E. Bentley and F. L. McGHEE, two Midwestern activists, Du Bois and Trotter planned a conference to be held in upstate New York later that year. Du Bois sent invitations to nearly sixty men whose anti-Washington feelings were known, asking them to join in "organized, determined and aggressive action on the part of men who believe in Negro freedom and growth."

Because they had difficulty finding hotel accommodations on the United States side of Niagara Falls, Du Bois, Trotter, and the twenty-seven other men who came met across the river in Canada. Du Bois was chosen as secretary and Trotter as chairman of the committee on press and public opinion. The group issued a "Declaration of Principles," which stated that the movement sought economic justice, educational equality, fully protected suffrage, and an end to racial segregation. They argued that "persistent manly agitation is the way to liberty." In advocating direct action for African American civil rights, the Niagara Movement placed itself in direct opposition to Booker T. Washington's cautious stance. Though never naming Washington, the declaration further said, "We refuse to allow the impression to remain that the Negro-American assents to inferiority, is submissive under oppression and apologetic before insults."

Even before the Niagara members met, spies from the Washington camp had tried to infiltrate the movement, though they were stymied by the change in location. After the first meeting, the black press, which typically championed Washington, kept mention of the Niagara Movement from its pages. Though the movement's membership grew to include 170 members in thirty-four states, it was already in trouble by 1906. Trotter and Du Bois clashed on the inclusion of women, which Trotter opposed, and feuds within Boston's black community further unbalanced the *Guardian* editor. In 1907 Trotter resigned his chairmanship of the press committee. The following year neither Du Bois nor Trotter attended the annual conference. In 1908 Trotter started his own group, the Negro-American Political League, and by 1909 Du Bois was asking remaining Niagara contacts to consider joining the newly formed NATIONAL ASSOCIATION FOR THE ADVANCEMENT OF COLORED PEOPLE (NAACP).

Historian Stephen R. Fox cites three reasons, in addition to the tensions between Du Bois and Trotter, for the collapse of the Niagara Movement: Washington's opposition; a persistent lack of money, stemming in part from the white philanthropic world's loyalty to Washington; and a racial message too militant for its own time. At its 1906 meeting in Harpers Ferry, Du Bois had written that the Niagara Movement claimed for black Americans "every single right that belongs to a freeborn American, political, civil, and social; and until we get these rights we will never cease to protest and assail the ears of America." The NAACP and other groups voiced this plea for racial justice. The plea also resonated through the CIVIL RIGHTS MOVEMENT of the 1960s, but in 1905 few Americans were ready to hear it.

See also Press, Black, in the United States.

Bibliography

Fox, Stephen R. *The Guardian of Boston: William Monroe Trotter.* Atheneum, 1970.

Tuttle, William M., Jr., ed. *W. E. B. Du Bois.* Prentice-Hall, 1973.

Kate Tuttle

Niamey, Niger

The capital and largest city of Niger.

The administrative, economic, and cultural capital of NIGER, Niamey is located on the left bank of the NIGER RIVER in the southwestern part of the country. The city's early history is subject to dispute. Some claim that it was originally a SONGHAI fishing village named after the local *Niami* tree, while others believe it was founded by a Djerma chief named Kouri Mali. Nevertheless, most historians agree that small groups of Djerma, HAUSA, and Wazi peoples coexisted in the Niamey area prior to European colonialism. In 1926 the French moved the capital of Niger from ZINDER to Niamey, in order to facilitate trade with other French colonies along the Niger River.

Since the colonial era Niamey has served as a crossroads, linking Niger's regional towns and farming areas such as AGADEZ and Zinder to West African cities such as ABIDJAN and LAGOS. Trade between the city and neighboring countries suffers, however, from the poor state of the region's roadways, which are often impassable during the rainy seasons. Although it is expected that Niamey will greatly profit from the trans-Saharan highway now under construction, many critics believe that the government should instead spend the money to construct a railway linking Niamey to the BURKINA FASO capital of OUAGADOUGOU, which is already connected to Abidjan by rail. Although the French had planned to construct such a railway during the colonial era, it was never completed.

Niamey is also home to several minor factories that manufacture bricks, textiles, and process grains, much of which is also exported. In 2003 the city had a population of 748,600.

See also Colonial Rule.

Elizabeth Heath

Nicaragua

Republic and largest nation in Central America.

Called "the land of lakes and volcanoes," Nicaragua contains regions of thick rain forests, rugged highlands, and fertile farming areas. The largest lakes in Central America and a chain of volcanic peaks dominate its western heartland, the center of its population and economy. Twice in the twentieth century severe earthquakes have destroyed Managua, its capital and largest city.

See also Central America.

Nicholas Brothers

Fayard, 1918– and Harold, 1924–2000

American tap dancers who performed in Hollywood musicals in the 1930s and 1940s.

Born in PHILADELPHIA, PENNSYLVANIA, Harold and Fayard Nicholas began dancing in that city in the 1930s. Rising to stardom as a TAP DANCING duo, they appeared in the musicals *Tin Pan Alley, Stormy Weather, Down Argentine Way* and *The Big Broadcast of 1936*. The pair performed with such contemporary stars as JOSEPHINE BAKER, LENA HORNE, Gene Kelly, BILL (BOJANGLES) ROBINSON and CAB CALLOWAY. In the late 1940s, with tap dance's popularity waning in the United States, the Nicholas Brothers moved to Europe. They gave a Royal Command Performance for the King of England in 1948 and performed at President Eisenhower's 1955 inauguration.

During the 1960s the brothers pursued solo careers, but reunited as an act in 1964 in the United States. They continued to perform together until the 1980s, when Fayard's declining health forced him to retire from dancing. Harold then continued as a solo performer, singing in touring productions and acting in several films, including *Uptown Saturday Night* (1974), *Tap* (1989), *The Five Heartbeats* (1991), and *Funny Bones* (1995). Fayard also appeared on screen in the drama *The Liberation of L.B. Jones* (1970). Fayard received a Tony Award in 1989 for choreography for the Broadway show *Black and Blue*.

The Nicholas brothers received Kennedy Center Honors in 1991, as well as a Carnegie Hall tribute in 1998. They have been inducted into the APOLLO THEATER Hall of Fame and the Black Filmmakers' Hall of Fame. Harold died in 2000; Fayard now lives in southern California.

Marian Aguiar

Nickens, James

?–1838?

African American seaman and soldier of the American Revolution.

James Nickens was a freeborn descendant of Edward Nickens, a well-to-do black landowner of Lancaster County, Virginia. Nickens, along with several brothers and cousins, fought against the British on land and at sea. He enlisted in the naval service in the early days of the AMERICAN REVOLUTION (1775–1783) for a period of three years. He served on three or four vessels, notably for two years and three months on the *Norfolk Revenge*, an armed galley propelled by sails. After his discharge from the U.S. Navy, he enlisted at the Lancaster Court House for land service until the end of the war in 1783. He joined troops under Baron von Steuben in Cumberland County, North Carolina, and served in an artillery regiment in South Carolina under General Nathaniel Greene. At the Battle of Eutaw Springs, near Eutawville, South Carolina, on September 8, 1781, officers reportedly prevented Nickens from fighting, stationing him in the rear to take charge of the baggage.

After three years of service in the army, Nickens returned to Virginia and in 1818 began to receive the regular veterans' federal pension of ninety-six dollars a year. His son, James Jr., received a grant of 80 hectares (200 acres) of land in Ohio from the state government for his father's service. Like many other Virginia veterans and their descendants, he sold his claim and perhaps purchased land in Virginia. As late as the 1940s, descendants of Nickens were well-known residents of Stafford, Fauquier, Culpepper, and Warren counties, Virginia.

This sketch is based on Luther Porter Jackson's work, *Virginia Negro Soldiers and Seamen in the Revolutionary War* (1944, pp. 24–8).

From *Dictionary of American Negro Biography* by Rayford W. Logan and Michael R. Winston, editors. Copyright © 1982 by Rayford W. Logan and Michael R. Winston. Reprinted by permission of W. W. Norton & Company, Inc.

Rayford W. Logan

Niger

West African country bordered by Burkina Faso, Benin, Nigeria, Chad, Libya, Algeria, and Mali.

Straddling the SAHARA and the SAHEL, the fragile environment of Niger has shaped the lives of its peoples from the earliest days to the present. Niger's early societies enabled their people to sustain themselves even in times of drought through such means as shifting cultivation and participation in trans-Saharan trade networks that supplemented local production. These practices preserved the fragile Sahel and buffered against famine. During the last century, however, French colonialism forced Nigeriens to abandon such centuries-old techniques in order to produce cash crops. This left Nigeriens more vulnerable to drought and dependent upon unreliable global commodity markets. French colonial neglect and the demands of the global market economy have perpetuated Nigerien poverty, ecological vulnerability, and political instability since independence. As a result, Nigeriens, like other peoples of the Sahel, struggle to meet their social and ecological needs amid the pressures of the global economy.

Early History

Thinly populated and peripheral to the major kingdoms of West Africa, Niger and its early history have frequently been ignored for that of the nearby great empires—MALI, GHANA, and SONGHAI. Niger has a rich history of its own, however. The human presence in the region dates back at least 60,000 years. Archaeology provides evidence that pastoralists settled in the north-central regions of the country during a time of frequent rainfall more than 7,000 years ago. These groups migrated southward and adopted settled agriculture, based on the cultivation of millet and sorghum, around 2500 B.C.E., when the the SAHARA region became more arid. By 1000 C.E. two empires had started to develop along the borders of present-day Niger—Songhai to the west and Kanem-Bornu to the east. Both empires periodically extended their rule over parts of present-day Niger. Nomadic TUAREG people controlled the northern two-thirds of Niger for much of this period.

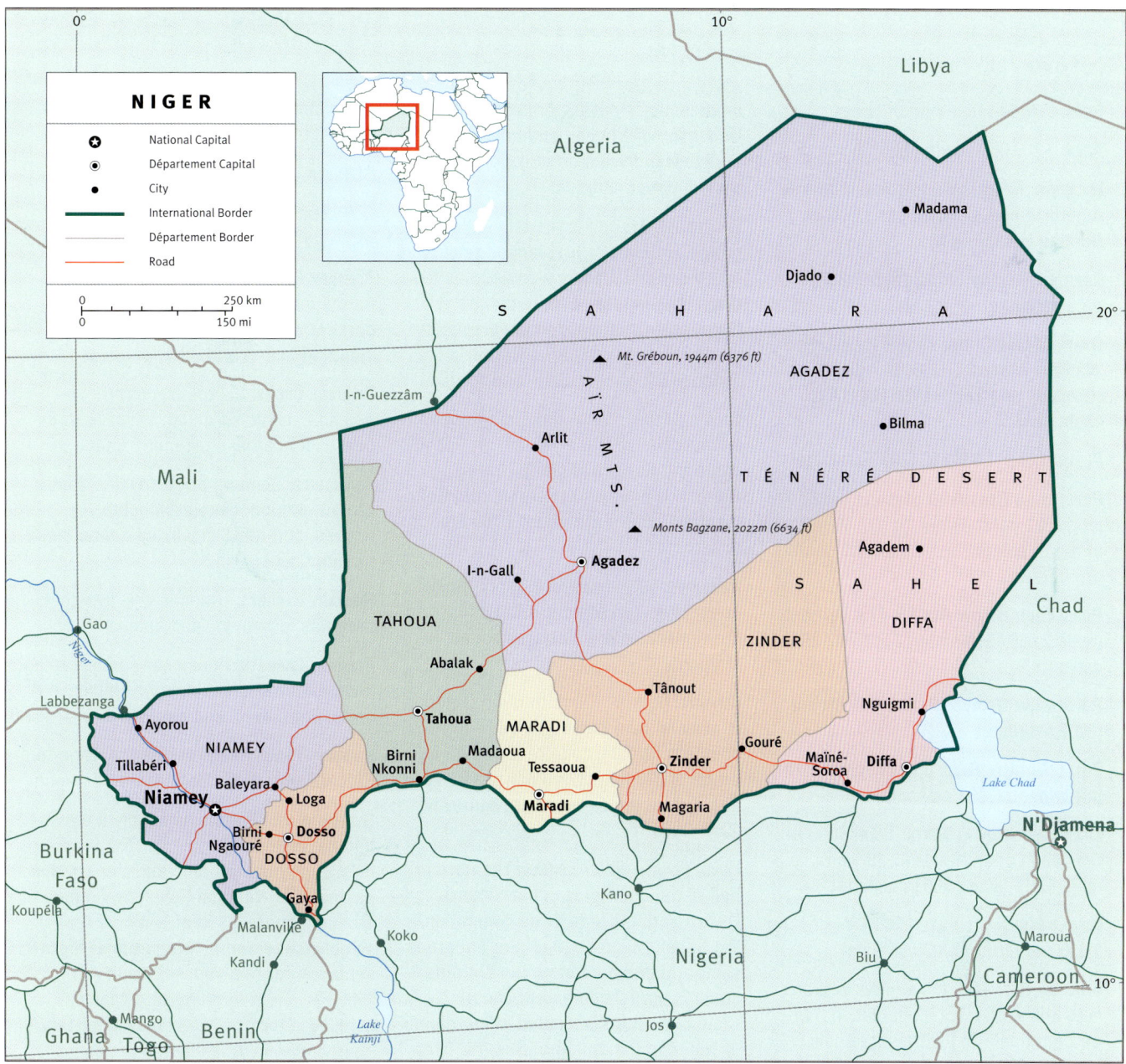

The strength and prosperity of these empires was based on their ability to control the lucrative trans-Saharan and trans-Sudanic trade in slaves, valuable metals, and salt. Their security depended on maintaining a successful symbiosis with the nomadic groups—Tuareg, TOUBOU, and FULANI—who led the caravans. Attacked by Moroccan invaders in 1591, the SONGHAI EMPIRE gradually disintegrated into separate city-states, many of them subject to Mali. Refugees from this invasion settled in present-day Niger. Kanem-Bornu, although weakened by a series of succession disputes, recovered sufficiently to remain an important player in the region for the next three centuries. Meanwhile, in Hausaland to the south, the expansion of trade had led to the rise of the HAUSA STATES as independent centers of power by the fifteenth century.

During the nineteenth century, external aggressors reconfigured the region's geopolitics. Fulani warriors launched jihads and began attacking the Hausa states in the early nineteenth century; they eventually conquered most of the northern states. This drove many HAUSA to flee northward into present-day Niger. The jihads produced a new state—the SOKOTO CALIPHATE—and attracted various adventurers who wanted to build their own empires from the remnants of disintegrating states or to conquer existing ones. Sokoto's attacks on Kanem-Bornu allowed Damagaram, initially a tributary to Kanem-Bornu, to establish autonomous power over much of central Niger. Allied with Tuareg traders, Damagaram took control of much of the trans-Saharan trade from its base at ZINDER, and by the late nineteenth century had declared its independence from Kanem-

Niger (At a Glance)

OFFICIAL NAME: Republic of Niger

AREA: 1,267,000 sq km (489,189 sq mi)

LOCATION: Inland West Africa; borders Algeria, Libya, Chad, Nigeria, Benin, Burkina Faso, and Mali

CAPITAL: Niamey (population 748,600; 2003 estimate)

OTHER MAJOR CITIES: Zinder (population 202,300), Maradi (189,000), Agadez (122,000), and Tahoua (95,900) (2003 estimates)

POPULATION: 11,058,590 (2003 estimate)

POPULATION DENSITY: 9 persons per sq km (about 22 persons per sq mi); 90 percent of the population lives near the southern border.

POPULATION BELOW AGE 15: 47.6 percent (male 2,686,169; female 2,581,785; 2003 estimate)

POPULATION GROWTH RATE: 2.71 percent (2003 estimate)

TOTAL FERTILITY RATE: 6.91 children born per woman (2003 estimate)

LIFE EXPECTANCY AT BIRTH: Total population: 42.21 years (male 42.29 years; female 42.12 years; 2003 estimate)

INFANT MORTALITY RATE: 123.64 deaths per 1,000 live births (2003 estimate)

LITERACY RATE (AGE 15 AND OVER WHO CAN READ AND WRITE): Total population: 17.6 percent (male 25.8 percent; female 9.7 percent; 2003 estimate)

EDUCATION: In the early 1990s Niger had some 368,700 pupils in primary schools, 74,300 in secondary schools, and 2,400 in vocational and teacher-training schools. In 2000 less than one-third of primary-school-aged children received an education. Secondary schools enrolled only 5 percent of eligible children that year. Drastic budget cuts have recently gutted Niger's educational system. Since 1998, 60 percent of the nation's teachers and professors have been laid off. In 2003, professors at the University of Niamey and teachers across Niger went on strike protesting the education cuts.

LANGUAGES: French is the official language. Hausa, the first language of over half the population, is also used as a trade language by a large number of Nigeriens. Other spoken languages include Temasheq (Tuareg Berber), Djerma (Songhai), Fulani, and Arabic.

ETHNIC GROUPS: More than half the population is Hausa. Other ethnic groups include the Songhai, Fulani, Tuareg, Beriberi (Kanuri), Arab, Tubu, and Gourmantche. There are about 1,200 French expatriates.

RELIGIONS: 80 percent are Sunni Muslims; fewer than 1 percent are Christian; and the remainder practice traditional religions.

CLIMATE: Rainfall (June through October) is minimal over most of Niger; the southern farming zone receives an average of 820 mm (32 in) per year. Average annual temperature at Niamey is 29.4° C (85° F).

LAND, PLANTS, AND ANIMALS: The northern half of the country is in the Sahara Desert and has little or no vegetation; the Sahel region south of the Sahara is semi-arid brush country; the extreme south is partially forested. The Air Mountain range is located in the center of Niger, in the southern Sahara. The Niger River flows through the western part of the country, and Lake Chad lies on the southeastern border. Wildlife on protected reserves include elephants, hippopotamuses, giraffes, and lions; gazelles, hyenas, and vipers are widespread, and monkeys are found in the Air Mountains.

NATURAL RESOURCES: Gold, uranium, coal, iron ore, tin, and phosphates

CURRENCY: The Communauté Financière Africaine (CFA) franc

GROSS DOMESTIC PRODUCT (GDP): $8.8 billion (2002 estimate)

GDP PER CAPITA: $830 (2002 estimate)

GDP REAL GROWTH RATE: 3 percent (2002 estimate)

PRIMARY ECONOMIC ACTIVITIES: Agriculture (farming and animal husbandry, 38.5 percent of GDP, 90 percent of employment), industry, and other services

PRIMARY CROPS: Cowpeas, cotton, peanuts, millet, sorghum, cassava (tapioca), rice; cattle, sheep, and goats

INDUSTRIES: Cement, brick, textiles, food processing, chemicals, slaughterhouses, and other small, light industries; uranium mining

PRIMARY EXPORTS: Uranium ore, livestock products, cowpeas, and onions

PRIMARY IMPORTS: Consumer goods, primary materials, machinery, vehicles and parts, petroleum, and cereals

PRIMARY TRADE PARTNERS: France, Nigeria, Côte d'Ivoire, Italy, Germany, and Japan

GOVERNMENT: Niger is nominally a constitutional multiparty republic. The president appoints the prime minister and his cabinet, the National Salvation Council. The unicameral 83-seat National Assembly is elected by proportional representation for five-year terms. In April 1999 President Ibrahim Bare Mainassara, who took power in a 1996 military coup and who was elected president later that same year, was assassinated. The army vested power in a National Reconciliation Council. Niger's constitution was revised and new presidential and legislative elections were held. Current president Tandja Mamdou won 60 percent of the vote and took office in December 1999.

Barbara Worley

The lifestyle of Niger nomads, such as the Tuareg and the Toubou, has been threatened by both colonial and postcolonial regimes, which have attempted to suppress the movements of the nomads in the Sahel. *CORBIS/Tiziana and Gianni B*

Bornu. During the 1890s RABIH AL-ZUBAYR, a slave trader, conquered Kanem-Bornu and Bagirmi, and merged the two to create his own empire, including parts of southeastern Niger. These new powers, however, proved short-lived. Both Damagaram and Rabih's empire soon succumbed to a new invader—the French.

French Colonialism

In the late nineteenth century the French began a frantic scramble (SCRAMBLE FOR AFRICA) to claim the West African interior before GREAT BRITAIN could. Having already established colonies on the coast, both European powers wished to extend their possessions inland. In particular the French sought this region to establish an empire extending from the Mediterranean to the REPUBLIC OF THE CONGO, and from the Red Sea to the Atlantic. In addition, both powers sought control of the valuable resources—gold, valuable minerals, and salt—carried by the lucrative trans-Saharan trade caravans that traversed the region. FRANCE dispatched several missions to the area to determine the extent of British influence in the region and seize control of any and all available land.

After securing treaties with several smaller groups, France launched the Mission Afrique Central in order to conquer most of southern Niger. As part of this operation, a military party led by Voulet and Chanoine seized food and supplies from drought-stricken local populations and responded to local resistance with a brutal scorched-earth policy that killed thousands. The French conquered Damagaram, seized Zinder, and defeated Rabih in 1900. The French concluded by claiming possession of the region.

It took the French another twenty-two years to assume complete control of the territory and declare it a colony. Although France controlled most of the sedentary groups by 1900, northern nomadic groups such as the Tuareg and Toubou successfully resisted France until 1922. French COLONIAL RULE, which attempted to control and regulate subject populations, threatened the lifestyle of the nomads, whose unrestricted movement was a clear threat to French hegemony.

Eventually France launched a military mission into the Sahara expressly to control and tax the trade caravans. Predictably, the Tuareg resisted for years. The two groups seized animals and supplies from one another, filled in wells, and destroyed crops. The French, however, had a larger army, aided by sedentary Tuareg, many of whom were servants of the Tuareg nomads. Eventually the French defeated the Tuareg, and many fled their devastated homeland for temporary exile in NIGERIA. Having subdued the Nigerien populations, France declared Niger a colony in 1922.

By this time, however, France's attempts to exploit the Nigerien colony had already destroyed much of the local economy. When the French first seized Niger, the majority of its "sedentary" farmers and herders actually engaged in seminomadic behavior; small family groups migrated every year (within a small area) in order to allow the fragile Sahel land to regain fertility for future use. The French considered these farming techniques disorderly, wasteful, and ill-suited to the export crops they hoped to cultivate in Niger.

As a result, the French blocked access to the land in order to prevent nomadic movement, forcing people to move to larger sedentary villages that were responsible for export crop production on nearby state-owned plantations. The French imposed taxes to force farmers to work on the plantations and instructed them to cultivate as much as possible and to leave no land fallow. In addition, the French, having already experienced drought in the Sahel, attempted to impose a strict storage program among the farmers. The program required farmers to allocate a percentage of their personal crops to regional storage bins; this created resentments and broke down the centuries-old technique for dealing with drought. Within twenty years these colonial policies had devastating effects: land had become sterile and arid, and thereafter farmers could grow little more than peanuts.

When the French finally imposed taxes and tariffs (payable in French currency) on the trans-Saharan trade caravans that passed through Niger, they undermined this ancient economic institution as well. Because there was a severe shortage of French currency in the colony, traders often could not pay the exact amount in the requisite currency. Consequently, the French forced the traders to overpay. To add insult to economic injury, the French army also seized goods and CAMELS, which were not only symbolic of traders' nomadic lifestyles, but integral to their economic prosperity. Furious with the policy, many traders abandoned the trans-Saharan routes and moved their business across the border to British-controlled Nigeria, whose ports offered easy access to world markets. Again, in an attempt to exploit the local economy, France had destroyed the prospect of future revenues.

Consequently, in 1922 when France formally declared Niger a colony, the colonial administration no longer saw much value in the economically ruined country. They invested very little in its social or infrastructural development. Underdeveloped and supported by a meager one-crop economy, Niger became an undesirable posting among the West African colonies. As a result, the colonial administration relied more heavily on indigenous rulers in Niger than they did in more profitable colonies. Because the French built only a few schools and provided little opportunity for Nigeriens to obtain a modern education, Niger lacked the sizable elite of indigenous but westernized *assimilés* that developed in many coastal colonies. Instead, in Niger the colonial government essentially left local administration to indigenous rulers who received little French scrutiny so long as they produced the required taxes and crops. This system encouraged authoritarian rulers who exploited their subjects. The French government did little to intervene, despite recurrent criticism.

At the Brazzaville Conference of 1944, France moved to give colonies more autonomy. The immediate beneficiaries of this new policy in Niger were its tiny percentage of educated elite. This clique, led by individuals like HAMANI DIORI, organized to promote its own political and economic interests and to protest French colonial neglect. In 1946 members of this circle founded the Parti Progressiste Nigérien (PPN), an affiliate of the RASSEMBLEMENT DÉMOCRATIQUE AFRICAIN (RDA). They were joined by small numbers of workers in the urban centers of NIAMEY and Zinder. By 1949, however, PPN's core elite had essentially marginalized the workers' concerns.

By 1956 two other political parties had formed in Niger: the Bloc Nigérien d'Action (BNA) and the Union Démocratique Nigérienne (UDN), later renamed Sawaba (or "Freedom"). Hamani Diori emerged victorious in the 1958 elections for president, and he retained this post when Niger gained independence in August 1960. Diori outlawed Sawaba, which drew its support largely from the Hausa, Niger's largest ethnic group. Diori and the mostly Djerma PPN elite would continue to dominate Nigerien politics until 1974.

Independence

During the first five years of independence, Diori concentrated on consolidating his own power. Faced with an attempted military coup in 1963 and attacks by members of Sawaba, Diori used French advisers and troops to repress opposition, despite student and union protests against French neocolonialism. Diori limited cabinet appointments to fellow Djerma, family members, and close friends. In addition, he acquired new powers by declaring himself the minister of foreign and defense affairs.

As internal affairs settled and Niger experienced a slight economic boom, Diori dismissed many of the government's French advisers—a move that both satisfied popular demands and further centralized government power in the presidency. Diori attempted to bypass the traditional elite with a rural development program aimed at collectivizing farms and introducing modern agricultural techniques, but the traditional elite undermined this effort. In 1971, a French firm began mining Niger's uranium deposits in the northern desert region. The exploitation of this valuable resource raised hopes for economic improvement.

But Diori faced a number of new problems that ultimately led to his downfall. His relationship with France suffered for the first time when his government voiced dissatisfaction with the level of investment in uranium production. Meanwhile the price for peanuts, Niger's main export crop, plummeted. Economic deterioration coincided with an increasingly severe drought during the early 1970s. These economic difficulties forced the government to reduce funding to schools, universities, and civil servants—moves which met with violent student and union protests.

Diori managed to maintain order until the devastating drought reached its peak in 1973. Popular unrest escalated into riots when evidence emerged that Diori and members of his administration were enriching themselves with diverted foreign food aid. The situation continued to worsen until April 1974, when a group of military leaders led by SEYNI KOUNTCHÉ toppled the government and imprisoned Diori, a move that won overwhelming popular support.

Kountché declared himself president of a transitional government and immediately provided relief to the drought-stricken areas. He distributed free seed and stopped black-market sales of food aid. In addition, he devised a new program—called Samariya—through which he attempted to revitalize the rural economy. Modeled on "traditional" Hausa youth groups, the program initiated new public works projects in the villages and attempted to increase food production through collectivized farms. Like Diori, Kountché bypassed the traditional elite and targeted rural development aid directly to the peasantry. But his programs had little success. Samariya failed to increase crop production, and the traditional elite again blocked attempts to undermine their power in rural areas. The program also ignored the nomadic Tuareg, whose pastoral economy had not recovered from the years of drought. Nonetheless, a rise in uranium prices in the wake of the 1973–1974 Arab oil embargo brought an economic recovery that bolstered Kountché's regime.

Over the course of his rule, Kountché confronted growing popular opposition and attempted coups with an increasingly authoritarian style. In an effort to maintain control, he dismissed most military advisers and replaced them with family members and friends, who in turn faced dismissal whenever Kountché suspected them of threatening his power. After 1979, uranium prices plummeted and Niger faced a fiscal crisis.

To conserve state resources, Kountché halted state development projects, including construction and mining projects that employed a large sector of the Nigerien population. Popular opposition increased as the economy declined, but Kountché put down expressions of dissent, such as a 1983 student strike. A new drought in 1984 intensified Niger's economic woes as uranium prices continued to decline. The return of normal rains in 1985 and an infusion of international assistance brought a slow economic recovery during the late 1980s.

Democracy or Military Rule?

In 1986 Kountché was diagnosed with a brain tumor; he spent the last year of his life in a Paris hospital. During this period Niger was governed by the chief of staff of the armed forces, Ali Saibou, who assumed the presidency upon Kountché's death in November 1987. Though he continued many of Kountché's policies, the more liberal Saibou took steps to introduce constitutional rule, and a referendum approved Saibou's proposed constitution in 1989. That year Saibou founded a ruling party, the Mouvement National de la Société de Développement (MNSD), and, in the wake of single-party elections, he declared himself the legitimate leader of Niger.

Like his predecessor, however, Saibou resorted to repression. Although he permitted greater personal freedom and public protest, he had inherited a national government that was teetering on bankruptcy. Beginning in 1990, foreign lenders forced Saibou to accept austerity measures and structural adjustment plans, including privatization of state enterprises and cuts in student scholarships and civil servant salaries. The cuts prompted student and union demonstrations; the military dispersed them by shooting into the crowds. Meanwhile the army suppressed a Tuareg rebellion in the northern countryside. A brutal military raid at AGADEZ in 1990 left hundreds of Tuaregs dead, including many innocent civilians.

In response to domestic and international pressures, Saibou declared a new multiparty system and invited both pro-government and opposition delegates to convene at a national conference in Niamey in 1991. Led by André Salifou, a prominent Nigerien scholar, the conference declared itself sovereign and it implemented massive reforms. Saibou subsequently renounced most of his political power, and the conference named Amadou Cheiffou prime minister of the new transitional government. Cheiffou assumed presidential duties. He helped orchestrate a new emergency grant from France that saved the government from bankruptcy and made possible the first multiparty presidential election in Nigerien history in 1993.

MAHAMANE OUSMANE won the presidency in this election, and Mahamadou Issoufou was elected prime minister. Within a year of his election, however, Issoufou resigned because differences with the president made it impossible for him to implement desired economic and social reforms. Ousmane held new parliamentary elections in December 1994, and opposition leader Hama Amadou was elected. For the next year, personal attacks between Ousmane and Amadou paralyzed government, while bankruptcy loomed and internal unrest mounted, particularly among students and northern Tuareg rebels. Consequently, in January 1996 Ousmane disbanded the general assembly and unconstitutionally designated a new prime minister.

In the midst of this crisis, Colonel Ibrahim Bare Mainassara staged a military coup. International donors responded by suspending foreign aid. Unable to pay civil servants, military troops, and government administrators, Mainassara appeased the international donors by promising elections. He introduced a new constitution and held presidential and parliamentary elections in 1996. Mainassara easily won the contested November presidential election and declared himself president of the Fourth Republic of Niger. The larger opposition parties boycotted the parliamentary elections, and many observers claimed that the elections had been rigged in Mainassara's favor.

After the elections, Mainassara promoted interregional cooperation and trade. He strongly supported the Economic Community of West African States (ECOWAS). In 1997 he co-founded a new organization to promote economic cooperation among states of the Sahara and Sahel. But Mainassara never managed to build a solid base of support at home, and his hold on power weakened. In April 1999 his own presidential guard assassinated him. He was replaced by Major Mallam Daouda Wanke, leader of the presidential guard. Facing close international scrutiny, Wanke and the other coup leaders drafted constitutional amendments that restored the constitutional balance between the executive and legislative branches and absolved the participants in both the 1996 and the 1999 coups. The revised constitution was approved by referendum, and presidential and legislative elections were held in October and November 1999. MNSD candidate Tandja Mamadou was elected president, and the MNSD again took the largest number of seats in the National Assembly.

In 2000 Niger received $73 million from the International Monetary Fund (IMF) for poverty reduction, and $115 million for debt relief under the Heavily Indebted Poor Countries (HIPC) initiative. The nation received more aid in 2002. To reverse its bleak economic situation, Niger hopes to develop its oil, gold, and coal resources in the coming years.

See also Drought and Desertification; Gold Trade; Islam in Africa; Minerals and Mining in Africa; Salt Trade; Structural Adjustment in Africa; Trans-Saharan and Red Sea Slave Trade.

Bibliography

Charlick, Robert. *Niger: Personal Rule and Survival in the Sahel.* Westview Press, 1991.

Decalo, Samuel. *Historical Dictionary of Niger.* Scarecrow Press, 1997.

Fugelstad, Finn. *A History of Niger, 1850–1960.* Cambridge University Press, 1983.

Elizabeth Heath

Nigeria

Country with the world's largest black population, located on the Atlantic coast of West Africa, sharing borders with Benin, Niger, Chad, and Cameroon.

The NIGER RIVER is Nigeria's most remarkable physical feature, as well as the source of its name. But AFRICA's most populous nation did not even have a name, nor for that matter a national identity, before the late nineteenth century. Rather, British colonization brought together three vast and culturally distinctive regions—north, southeast, and southwest—and at least 250 different language groups, more than any other African country. Generously endowed as well with natural resources such as crude oil, gas, coal, iron, limestone, columbite, and tin, Nigeria in its early postcolonial years was viewed as a potential middle-level economic power. Since independence in 1960, however, corrupt military rule has conspired with religious as well as ethnic fractiousness to all but dissipate the nation's early promise.

Following independence, Nigeria was rocked by political crises: disputed elections led to widespread violence, then to a coup and countercoup, then to ethnic tensions that exploded into the thirty-month Biafran War (1967–1970). Since the Biafran War, promised returns to democratic civilian rule have been repeatedly thwarted by military-sponsored coups, crackdowns on opposition groups, and electoral maneuverings. Many of Nigeria's most esteemed intellectuals have left the country, and others have faced severe state prosecution. By the late 1990s, however, many Nigerians held out new hope for democracy. In 1998 General SANI ABACHA, Nigeria's military head of state for five years, died suddenly. In his place, Nigeria's military government handed power to Major-General Abdulsalam Abubakar, who established a timetable for democratic elections in May 1999. Nigeria's onetime civilian president OLUSEGUN OBASANJO won the elections, marking the end of fifteen years of military rule.

Early Societies in Northern Nigeria

The best evidence of early civilizations in northern Nigeria is provided by the NOK terracotta heads, named after a village of the Jaba people in northern Nigeria. The highly stylized figurines, at least 2,500 years old, point to a thriving Iron Age culture in a wide swath of northern Nigeria.

Also important among the groups that established some of the northern region's largest and most enduring states were the HAUSA. During the first millennium C.E. they were village-dwelling cultivators and artisans, living on the belt of open woodland and grass savanna known as the SAHEL, on the southern edge of the SAHARA. After about 1000 C.E., the rise of Hausa statehood coincided with the building of walled cities known as birane. The kings who resided within the birane were charged with warding off external aggression, in return for which they collected taxes from commoners.

Economic and cultural life in the early Hausa states was deeply shaped by trade. Hausa farmers and artisans—weavers and dyers, smiths and leatherworkers—produced goods for local markets as well as long-distance caravans. From southern forested regions these caravans brought ivory, gold, and slaves. From the North they brought desert salt, goods from the Mediterranean and, beginning around the ninth century, Islam.

Only after the thirteenth century did Hausa rulers begin to convert to Islam. In the centuries following, cities such as KANO and Katsina became centers for Islamic scholarship as well as commerce, but many Hausa commoners were little affected by Islamic culture until the early nineteenth century, when a jihad, or crusade, led by the FULANI cleric USUMAN DAN FODIO created a vast Islamic empire with its headquarters in Sokoto. Triggered in 1804 by the attempts of King Yunfa of Gobir to stem the cleric's growing popularity, the jihad defeated most of the Hausa kings by 1810, putting Usuman dan Fodio and later his son MUHAMMAD BELLO in control of the largest state in nineteenth-century West Africa, spanning some 400,000 square kilometers. This period also marked the ascendancy of the Fulani, a numerical minority in the North.

Another important precolonial state in northern Nigeria was Kanem Borno (KANURI). Founded between 700 and 800 C.E., it went through periods of growth and contraction but at its peak, under the leadership of Idris Alooma (1571–1603), the ruling Sefawa Dynasty of Kanem Borno extended its control as far as the region of Fezzan, in modern LIBYA.

Northern Nigeria was also home to a multitude of other ethnic groups and cultures, including the TIV, Jukun, the IDOMA, the IGALA, the Igbira, and the NUPE. Some, such as the Jukun, developed centralized forms of government, while others—notably the Idoma—remained politically decentralized.

Early Societies in Southern Nigeria

The YORUBA peoples of southwestern Nigeria claim a common ancestry in Ife. The spiritual epicenter of the Yoruba is the home of one of the most magnificent traditions of bronze casting, dating back to the eleventh century. Among the several highly urbanized Yoruba kingdoms that arose beginning in the fourteenth century, Oyo, on the northern fringe of the forest, was best located for commerce both with Hausaland and with coastal traders, including, eventually, European slave ships. By the early eighteenth century the Oyo cavalry had conquered many neighboring kingdoms, including Dahomey (in modern-day BENIN).

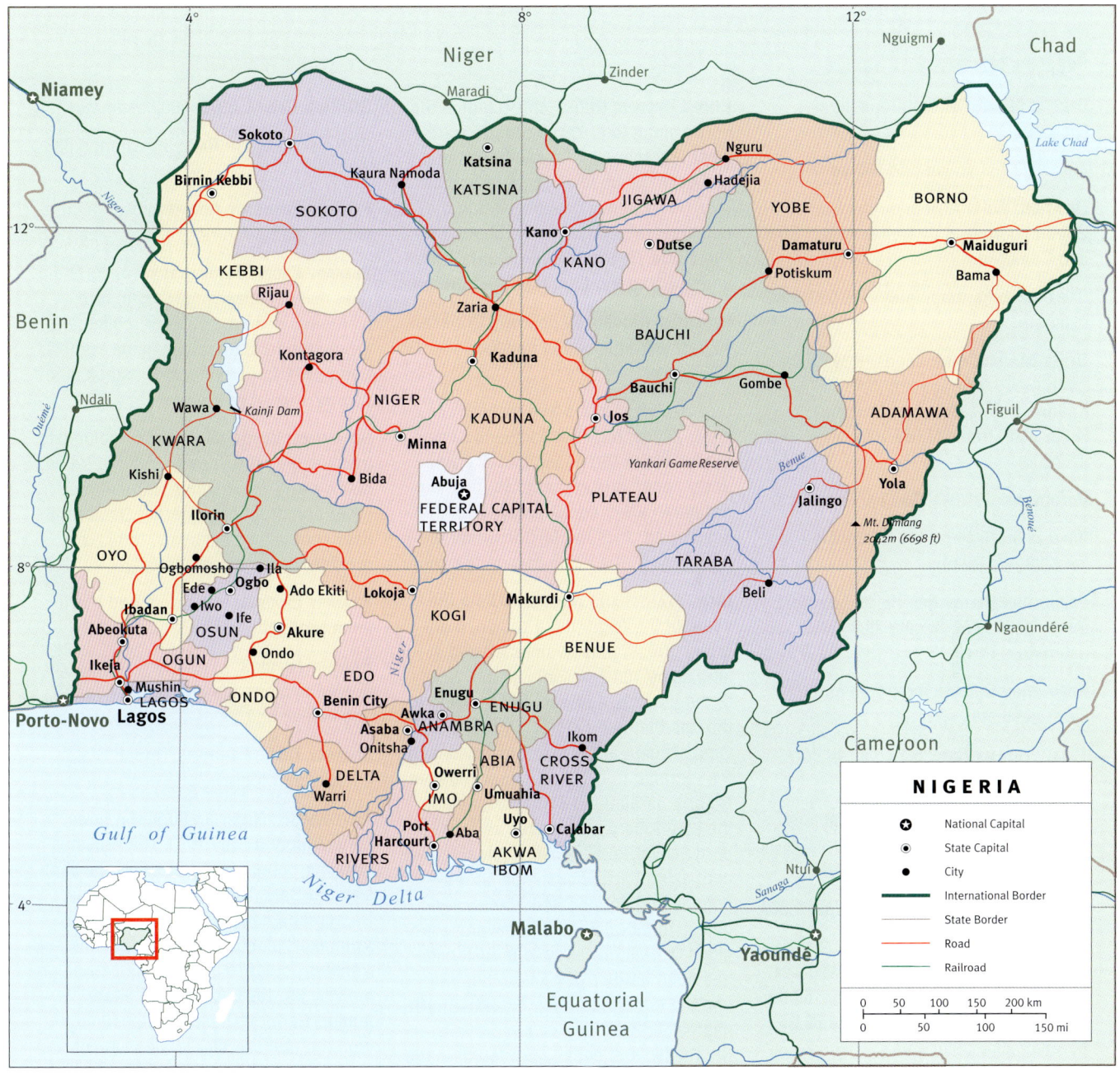

The ancient Benin empire of the EDO people, with its capital in a city of the same name, was already an extensive political and military force when Portuguese traders came ashore in the fifteenth century. Highly influenced by the artistic traditions of Ife, Benin architecture and court life deeply impressed fifteenth-century Dutch traders as well. The long tradition of internal slavery that evolved from the kingdom's formidable martial history enabled Benin to play an important role in the TRANSATLANTIC SLAVE TRADE.

In southeastern Nigeria, the IGBO maintained a largely decentralized and republican mode of political organization based on clan units. Apart from the Igbo's philosophical disposition against absolutist powers, the dense tropical swamp covering much of Igboland acted as a natural obstacle to expansionist schemes and the formation of centralized states. Instead, Igbo communities handled decision making and judicial matters at open village congresses attended by all eligible citizens. However politically decentralized, the Igbo were united in their reverence for the powerful oracle at Arochukwu, named the "Long Juju" by Europeans. This oracle once represented the final adjudicator of cases in Igboland.

The Igbo practiced both farming and trade, and by the fifteenth century, Igbo merchants were trading throughout southern Nigeria. Certain Igbo clans, such as the ARO, made a rep-

Nigeria (At a Glance)

OFFICIAL NAME: Federal Republic of Nigeria

AREA: 923,768 sq km (356,669 sq mi)

LOCATION: West Africa, on the Gulf of Guinea, bordered by Benin, Niger, Chad, and Cameroon

CAPITAL: Abuja (population 420,000; 2002 estimate)

OTHER MAJOR CITIES: Lagos (8,349,700), Kano (3,329,900), Ibadan (3,139,500), Kaduna (1,510,300), Port Harcourt (1,093,000), Benin (1,082,100), and Sokoto (512,800)

POPULATION: 133,881,793 (2003 estimate)

POPULATION DENSITY: 145 persons per sq km (369 per sq mi)

POPULATION BELOW AGE 15: 43.6 percent (male 29,322,774; female 28,990,702; 2003 estimate)

POPULATION GROWTH RATE: 2.53 percent (2003 estimate)

TOTAL FERTILITY RATE: 5.4 children born per woman (2003 estimate)

LIFE EXPECTANCY AT BIRTH: Total population: 51.01 years (male 50.89 years; female 51.14 years; 2003 estimate)

INFANT MORTALITY: 71.35 deaths per 1,000 live births (2003 estimate)

LITERACY RATE (AGE 15 AND OVER WHO CAN READ AND WRITE): Total population: 68 percent (male 75.7 percent; female 60.6 percent; 2003 estimate)

EDUCATION: In the early 1990s Nigeria had 14.8 million pupils enrolled in primary schools and more than 3.6 million in secondary schools. Education is free and compulsory for children ages 6–15. Institutions of higher education include the University of Ibadan, Ahmadu Bello University, the Obafemi Awolowo University, the University of Lagos, and the University of Nigeria.

LANGUAGES: English is the official language. Hausa, Yoruba, Igbo, and Fulani are also spoken.

ETHNIC GROUPS: Hausa and Fulani in the north, along with Yoruba in the southwest and Igbos in the southeast, together make up 68 percent of population. Other ethnic groups include the Edo, Ijaw, and Ibibio in the south, the Nupe and Tiv in the central part of the country, and the Kanuri in the northeast.

RELIGIONS: Muslim 50 percent; Christian 40 percent; indigenous beliefs 10 percent.

CLIMATE: Nigeria has two distinct climatic zones: high humidity and heavy rainfall along the coast, and dry and dusty conditions in the north. The temperature varies considerably with the season, as does rainfall, of which there is far less in the north than in the south.

LAND, PLANTS, AND ANIMALS: Along the coast of the Niger delta region, mangrove forests and swamps extend inland some 100 km (some 60 mi). North of the coast is a forested belt, rising to the Jos Plateau. Farther north is a savanna region and a semidesert zone in the extreme north. Vegetation zones in Nigeria parallel the climatic zones. In the south the well-watered zone is partly covered by dense tropical forests containing hardwoods such as mahogany and obeche and abundant oil palms. In the plateau and savanna regions forests give way to grasslands and such hardy trees as the baobab and the tamarind. In the extreme northeast semidesert vegetation prevails. Crocodiles and snakes are found in the swamps and rain forest zones. Most large animals have disappeared from heavily populated areas. Some antelope, camels, and hyenas live in the north.

NATURAL RESOURCES: Petroleum, tin, columbite, iron ore, coal, limestone, lead, zinc, and natural gas

CURRENCY: The naira

GROSS DOMESTIC PRODUCT (GDP): $113.5 billion (2002 estimate)

GDP PER CAPITA: $875 (2002 estimate)

GDP REAL GROWTH RATE: 3 percent (2002 estimate)

PRIMARY ECONOMIC ACTIVITIES: Agriculture, mining, manufacturing, and services

PRIMARY CROPS: Yams, cassava, sorghum, rice, millet, maize, sugar cane, taro, plantains, peanuts, palm oil, chiles and green peppers, tomatoes, palm kernels, cotton lint, cacao beans, livestock, and poultry

INDUSTRIES: Crude oil, coal, tin, columbite, palm oil, peanuts, cotton, rubber, wood, hides and skins, textiles, cement and other construction materials, food products, footwear, chemicals, fertilizer, printing, ceramics, and steel

PRIMARY EXPORTS: Petroleum and petroleum products, cocoa, and rubber

PRIMARY IMPORTS: Machinery, transportation equipment, manufactured goods, chemicals, and food

PRIMARY TRADE PARTNERS: United States, Europe, and India

GOVERNMENT: Nigeria adopted a new constitution in May 1999. The previous year the country's repressive president, General Sani Abacha, died suddenly. His replacement, General Abdulsalam Abubakar, pledged to hold elections and transfer power to a civilian government on May 29, 1999. A former military leader, General Olusegun Obasanjo, won the nationwide elections in February 1999 with 62 percent of the vote. He assumed the office of president in May 1999, returning civilian government to Nigeria for the first time in 15 years. Elections for the National Assembly, consisting of a 346-member House of Representatives and a 107-seat Senate, were last held in April 2003.

Barbara Worley

utation for themselves as fierce slave raiders. The Igbo were also known for their artisanry; bronze works unearthed at Igbo-Ukwu have been dated to the ninth century.

European Contact and Conquest

Although the Portuguese were the first Europeans to arrive in the region that is now Nigeria, it was the British—coming into the picture only in 1553—who were to play the starring role in the drama of colonization as well as Nigeria's birth as a modern nation-state. British merchants, initially interested in the region's gold, ivory, and pepper, soon shifted their attention to the slave trade and quickly became the dominant foreign commercial interest in Nigeria.

In the early part of the nineteenth century, as GREAT BRITAIN reaped the fruits of the Industrial Revolution, the need for African slaves became subordinate to the need for African markets and raw materials. After Great Britain outlawed the transatlantic slave trade in 1804—a decision driven less by humanitarian considerations than by economic logic—that need translated into a vague policy of territorial acquisition. For British merchants based around the Oil Rivers on the coast, the top priority was to penetrate the hinterlands and establish direct links with the primary producers of palm oil, thereby dispensing with coastal African middlemen. But they faced stiff challenges from both the threatened middlemen and from nature. King Ja Ja of Opobo, for example, deployed a number of strategic devices to beat back the British campaign, including direct shipment of his oil to Europe. In 1887, when Ja Ja was lured onto a British vessel "to talk," he was arrested, sent to the GOLD COAST (now GHANA) for trial, then sentenced to a five-year exile in the WEST INDIES, where he died.

MALARIA was the other formidable obstacle to Great Britain's exploration of the Nigerian interior. In 1830 the Lander brothers discovered that the Oil Rivers were in fact the mouth of the Niger River, thus the gateway to the interior. But the several expeditions that tried to ply this highway met with many fatalities. Macgregor Laird's 1832 expedition up the Niger claimed the lives of all but nine of the forty-eight Europeans. A major breakthrough came, however, in 1854, when W. B. Baikie's expedition into Fulani country in the North demonstrated the prophylactic effects of quinine; not a single person died. British trading companies began moving operations inland soon afterward.

In 1861 LAGOS became the first territory of modern-day Nigeria to be annexed by the British. Thenceforth, British colonial acquisitions followed two patterns—so-called "treaties of protection" signed between British officials (or merchants acting in that de facto capacity) and local rulers, or conquest. Violence and trickery were essential to both approaches, since many customary rulers were assured of tragic consequences if they refused to sign. Evidence abounds, too, that the British officials often misrepresented the letter and import of the treaties, while exaggerating reports about impending threats from neighboring communities.

Trading concerns played an extensive role in the formal colonial subjugation of Nigeria. Faced with strong French competition in the North in the 1870s, a number of British trading firms, under the leadership of George Taubman Goldie, merged in 1879 to form the United African Company. By 1882 the company had secured enough treaties of protection to reestablish British supremacy. Goldie subsequently attended the BERLIN CONFERENCE OF 1884–1885, where he argued for British control in northern Nigeria. In 1886 the English crown, reluctant to commit the resources needed to administer the vast region, gave a royal charter to Goldie's company. In return for shouldering the cost of running the territory, the company, now renamed the Royal Niger Company, was granted a trade monopoly. But as the cost of administration escalated—and in the face of renewed French designs on the territory—the company's charter was revoked in 1900. The company's FREDERICK LUGARD was then appointed high commissioner of the protectorate of Northern Nigeria.

That same year Great Britain formalized its control over most of what is modern Nigeria. But it continued to administer the area as two separate units, the colony and protectorate of Southern Nigeria (so named in 1906 after a merger of Lagos and southern Nigeria) and the protectorate of Northern Nigeria, until 1914, when they were joined. Lugard, who became the first governor-general of an amalgamated Nigeria, was the architect of indirect rule—the policy of ruling colonies through the structures of customary authority. Given Nigeria's vast size and malarial climate, indirect rule offered an innovative solution to a real problem, namely the dearth of colonial officers willing to serve there.

Lugard had applied indirect rule quite successfully in the North, where the Sokoto Caliphate, the century-old Fulani empire, had established a highly centralized, hierarchical administrative order. Indirect rule elsewhere in Nigeria, however, ran into formidable problems. Although the Yoruba recognized long-standing monarchies, they resisted turning their traditional administrative structures over to the goals of British colonialism. In Igboland, the absence of even rudimentary states led the British to the misadventure of appointing warrant chiefs. These "invented" chiefs, usually little respected within their communities, became power-drunk and corrupt, in turn provoking their subjects' revolt. One of the fiercest revolts was the Aba Women's tax riots of 1929. Responding to rumors that their commerce would be taxed, Igbo market women organized themselves and attacked both British officials and their appointed minions. The colonial police escalated the violence, killing fifty women and wounding many more.

The colonial government made an early decision to seclude the largely Islamic northern region from the influences of Western education and CHRISTIANITY. The logic was that Islam had established a stable system that was at once universal and—if provoked by proselytizers—capable of great violence. And while Islam had penetrated the southwestern region, it had not won over many converts among the Yoruba who, like the Igbo, adhered to a variety of traditional religions.

Pedestrians, cars, trucks, and buses crowd a street market in Lagos, Nigeria's capital.
CORBIS/Daniel Lainé

The preservation of the North's "cultural purity," however, deprived northerners of access to Western education—the key to employment in the colony's growing civil service. In addition, the North's isolation fostered a cultural and political divide that later shaped Nigerian nationalism. Some northern leaders, hardly enamored of the prospect of southern domination, found themselves in the odd position of advocating continued COLONIAL RULE.

Colonialism dramatically altered economic and social relations in Nigeria. The installation of an internal communication system and transportation grid facilitated trade and travel, and the expansion of the cash economy aided the emergence of a wider system of division of labor. As coal and tin mines, ports, and railways drew laborers from the countryside (sometimes through conscription), they fostered the development of urban working classes, whose mass strikes in the 1940s and 1950s would force the colonial government to grant wage increases. As the cities grew, they also became increasingly multiethnic.

In rural areas, the colonial administration promoted the production of crops needed by British industries. The decades of colonial rule saw a steady growth in the volume of export crops—palm oil and other palm produce from the Southeast, COCOA from the Southwest, and peanuts from the North. But customary land ownership patterns and farming methods did not change dramatically. This was in part because the British had no desire to alienate those who traditionally exercised control over land distribution—elders, lineage heads, chiefs—and partly because of the reluctance of banks and other financial institutions to invest in commercial farms or other indigenously run enterprises.

This reluctance to encourage Nigerian entrepreneurship was also apparent in commerce. Initially, British trade firms made use of Nigerian middlemen in the export trade, feeding the growth of an already vibrant class of indigenous businesspeople. But as these firms progressively marginalized Nigerian traders, they bred resentment and contributed to the deepening of nationalist sentiments in many parts of the colony.

The early stages of nationalist revolt against entrenched British rule took the form of localized skirmishes like the Aba Women's riots, provoked by specific grievances. But an embryonic nationalist movement began to emerge around World War I, bolstered by the first Pan-African Congress, convened by W. E. B. DU BOIS in Paris in 1918–1919 (PAN-AFRICAN CONGRESS OF 1919). In response to early nationalism, British officials either denied that the agitators for independence represented popular sentiments or, paradoxically, insisted—as did Sir Hugh Clifford, then governor of Nigeria—that the very idea of "nation" in the colonies was absurd.

The emergence in the 1930s of NNAMDI AZIKIWE, a charismatic American-educated newspaper editor, broadened and transformed the nationalist struggle. Azikiwe's publications made him a prominent advocate for independence, and the political party he founded in 1944, the National Council of Nigeria and the Cameroons (NCNC), became one of the largest nationalist organizations, albeit one supported primarily by fellow Igbo from the Southeast. In the Southwest, nationalist support rallied around OBAFEMI AWOLOWO and his party, the Action Group.

The British, meanwhile, oscillated between a policy of divide and rule—encouraging the divisions already apparent in the regionalist nature of early political parties, and playing especially on the North's fear of domination by southern civil servants and intellectuals—and a recognition of the need to prepare for inevitable decolonization. Reforms in the late 1940s through the 1950s allowed Nigerians limited political representation, but southerners pushed for full autonomy. Yet northern political leaders, under the auspices of the Northern People's Congress (NPC), opposed a motion calling for independence by 1956 and agreed to support self-rule only after constitutional concessions were made to the North. On October 1, 1960, after years of constitutional conferences, Great Britain lowered the Union Jack, ushering in Nigerian independence.

Early Independence and Civil War

Nigeria inherited the British-style parliamentary system, with Azikiwe as the first governor-general (and, from 1963, president); ABUBAKAR TAFAWA BALEWA of the NPC as the prime minister, exercising executive power; and Obafemi Awolowo as the opposition leader. The Northern, Western, and Eastern Regions constituted the country's tripartite structure, until the Mid-Western Region was created in 1963. Owing partly to the conservative nature of the coalition that formed the first national government, independent Nigeria proceeded cautiously. Professing nonalignment, it stayed close to Great Britain on a number of foreign policy issues, with the understandable exception of white rule in southern Africa. For a nation expected to assume the leadership of the black world, the rhetoric of its leaders was remarkably tame. In economic policy as well, the country continued to ply the route of a primary commodity export economy, ensuring that Great Britain remained an important trade partner as well as an aid donor.

Soon after independence, however, efforts by the government at modest industrial development were, like much else in the country, drowned in the din of raucous politics. The coalition government seemed racked by mutual incomprehension, and many politicians began using their offices to enrich themselves and their supporters. Massive electoral rigging, especially in the 1965 Western Region parliamentary elections, unleashed widespread violence, and paved the way for a military coup d'état on January 15, 1966. Prime Minister Balewa and several other politicians were killed, and army commander Johnson Aguiyi-Ironsi, from the Eastern Region, became head of state.

Six months later, northern army officers launched a countercoup, and installed YAKUBU GOWON as the country's new ruler. During Gowon's nine-year term, Nigeria was rocked by a series of tumultuous events, beginning almost immediately with the massacre of Igbo people throughout the Northern region. When the Igbo then began pushing for a separate state, Gowon announced instead the creation of a twelve-state structure, calculated to weaken the petroleum-rich eastern region. The governor of the Eastern Region declared its secession and created a new name, the Republic of Biafra; within weeks a civil war had begun.

The thirty-month-long Biafran War cost an estimated million lives—the majority of them civilians who died of famine in the blockaded East—and ended with Biafra's surrender in January 1970. Gowon then announced a policy of "reconciliation, reconstruction, and recovery," and plans for a gradual transition to civilian rule. He also opened the government's coffers—flush with money since crude oil exploitation began shortly before the war—to fund the reconstruction of the country's war-damaged infrastructure, as well as a number of new "white elephant" projects. The government almost entirely neglected the agricultural sector, however; so even as the economy enjoyed unprecedented growth, it grew increasingly dependent on imported food and capital goods, and foreign loans. Moreover, much of the new wealth was concentrated in relatively few hands, and much of the state funding for development projects was funneled toward the North. In years to come, this inequitable distribution of wealth would become a major grievance of Nigeria's smaller and less politically influential ethnic groups.

Shortly after Gowon declared that the 1976 date he set for elections was "unrealistic," he was removed in a coup on July 29, 1975, and replaced by Murtala Muhammad, another northern officer. Muhammad set out to stem corruption by dismissing several public servants and adopted a bold new foreign policy, mustering other African nations to back AGOSTINHO NETO's POPULAR MOVEMENT FOR THE LIBERATION OF ANGOLA (MPLA). After only months in office, the popular Muhammad was assassinated on February 13, 1976. Muhammad's chief of staff, Yoruba officer Olusegun Obasanjo, kept his predecessor's promise and handed over power to a democratically elected government on October 1, 1979.

Democracy Delayed

The new government, modeled after the U.S. presidential system, was headed by Shehu Shagari, another northerner. In December 1983, following national elections that the opposition charged were extensively rigged, he was overthrown and replaced by military officer Muhammadu Buhari, who was himself deposed two years later in a palace coup led by IBRAHIM BABANGIDA. By this time a worldwide recession had brought Nigeria's oil boom to a definitive end, and the country was deeply indebted. Babangida's adoption of World Bank–prescribed austerity measures forced communities and individuals to rely less on government handouts, but also caused great hardship. During the 1980s, urban streets and marketplaces grew increasingly crowded with hawkers and petty traders, many of them women, struggling to earn an income.

After several years of promising a transition to democratic rule, Babangida agreed to presidential elections in 1993, then promptly annulled the victory of the opposition candidate, wealthy businessman MOSHOOD ABIOLA. Babangida's hand-picked transition government was soon ousted by SANI ABACHA, his own defense minister. Even in the face of mounting international criticism, Abacha proved as repressive as any of his predecessors. He jailed the popular Abiola in 1994, and in 1995 his regime hanged the environmental and human rights activist KEN SARO-WIWA, along with eight Ogoni colleagues. They had been jailed on trumped-up murder charges, but it was widely recognized that the group's demands for Ogoni statehood and protests against Shell Oil's environmentally destructive practices in Ogoniland were the real reasons they were silenced.

Abacha announced an elaborate democratic transition program when he first took office, but repeatedly delayed elections. Many critics doubted his pledge to hand over power to an elected government by October 1998, especially after all five registered political parties invited Abacha to continue in office as their "consensus candidate." On June 7, 1998, death vetoed Abacha's self-succession bid. To the relief of many observers, Abacha's successor, General Abubakar, appeared determined to retrieve Nigeria from its status as an international pariah. Abubakar met with several opposition and foreign diplomats, promised to respect the election timetable, and released many political prisoners.

The announcement of the release of Moshood Abiola raised hopes across the country and prompted a meeting on July 7 between Abiola, Nigerian government officials, and U.S. State Department representatives. Abiola, who was known to be in poor health, fell gravely ill during the meeting. He died within hours—like Abacha, of apparent cardiac arrest. At least fifty people died in riots that occurred after his death. Although an autopsy conducted by an international team of pathologists confirmed that Abiola died of natural causes, many of his followers remained suspicious and bitter. In the tense climate following Abiola's funeral, opposition leaders urged Abubakar to transfer power to a transitional "national unity" government, led by eminent citizens from all regions. Instead, the military leader announced a new transition program calling for the military's withdrawal and democratic elections in 1999.

Many observers doubted that the military would give up power as promised. But the elections were held according to schedule, and in May 1999 Nigeria elected its first civilian government in fifteen years. Soon after Obasanjo took office, he announced an anti-corruption program and other badly needed reforms. In response to the end of military rule, the Commonwealth of Nations lifted its suspension of Nigeria's membership.

Difficult issues threaten the progress of twenty-first century Nigeria. The adoption of a strict Islamic law code by several of Nigeria's states has led to fighting between Muslims and Christians that claimed more than 1,600 lives between 2000 and 2002. The government also faces the daunting challenge of rebuilding its petroleum-based economy, which had been disrupted by corruption and mismanagement.

See also African Religions: An Interpretation; Dahomey, Early Kingdom of; Decolonization in Africa: An Interpretation; Environmental Movements in Africa; Gold Trade; Islam in Africa; Ivory Trade; Languages, African: An Overview; Nationalism in Africa; Oyo, Early Kingdom of; Slavery in Africa; Sokoto Caliphate.

Bibliography

Soyinka, Wole. *The Open Sore of a Continent: A Personal Narrative of the Nigerian Crisis.* Oxford University Press, 1996.

Okey Ndibe

Nigerian Super Eagles

First African soccer team to win an Olympic gold medal.

Shortly after gaining independence in 1960, NIGERIA joined other newly independent African nations in international soccer tournaments. With the largest population in Africa, Nigeria was expected by many observers to become an immediate soccer power. In fact it took the Super Eagles nearly twenty years to achieve star status, but they have since maintained it.

In 1961 the Super Eagles first participated in the AFRICAN CUP OF NATIONS, but more experienced African teams easily eliminated them. By 1976, when the team finished third in the African Cup, Nigeria had gained respect in African soccer circles. By 1980 the Super Eagles had emerged as one of Africa's perennial powers. They won the African Cup that year and again in 1994, and finished runner-up in 1988 and 1990.

Similar to its performance in the African Cup, Nigeria has made a slow climb in World Cup soccer. The Super Eagles began World Cup competition in 1962, but the team failed to push past the qualification rounds until the 1994 games in the United States.

The surest sign that Nigerian football was developing into a world-class operation came in 1985, when the Nigerians won the Federation Internationale de Football Association's World Sixteen-Under Championship in China, defeating West Germany in the final and signaling the wealth of talent that would soon join the senior ranks. The crowning success for the Super Eagles came at the 1996 Olympic games in ATLANTA, GEORGIA, where they took the gold medal by defeating ARGENTINA 3–2. Considered one of the most creative and athletic teams in competition, the Super Eagles were ranked among the contenders to win the 1998 World Cup in France. After advancing out of the first round, however, they were knocked out of the tournament by Denmark in a 4–1 match.

See also Olympics, Africans and the.

Robert Fay

Niger, Paul (Albert Beville)

1915–1962

One of the most powerful writers of the Négritude movement and an outspoken critic of French colonialism.

Born in Basse-Terre on the French Caribbean island of GUADELOUPE, Paul Niger completed his primary schooling at the lycée Carnot. He then traveled to Paris, France, where he studied at lycée Louis-le-Grand and the École Nationale de la France d'outre-mer. While in Paris, Niger frequented the milieu of black intellectuals like AIMÉ CÉSAIRE and LÉOPOLD SÉDAR SENGHOR before the war. He also fought for the French resistance following the installation of the Nazi-supported Vichy regime. Niger subsequently began a career as a colonial administrator in Dahomey (now BENIN), MALI, and NIGER in 1944. This experience led him to an increasingly violent condemnation of French Colonialism. In turn, he celebrated a somewhat mythical, essentialized Africa in poems such as "Or j'avais renoncé à proncer ton nom" (1959). Niger was a frequent contributor to the journal PRESENCE AFRICAINE in the postwar years. In 1954 he published a collection of poems entitled *Initiation*, in which his violent condemnation of colonialism announces the coming explosion of African independence of the late 1950s:

L'Afrique va parler,
J'entends chanter la sève au coeur du flamboyant
(Africa is going to speak,
I hear the sap sing from the heart of the flame tree)

Niger fought for the decolonization and independence of the French Overseas Departments (FRENCH GUIANA, MARTINIQUE, and Guadeloupe) during the late 1950s as part of the *Front des Antilles-Guyane* organization. France's De Gaulle government banned him from Guadeloupe in the early 1960s. Niger was one of the authors of the pro-independence text produced by the Congress for the Independence of the Antilles, held April 22 and 23, 1961. In 1962, while attempting to return to Guadeloupe clandestinely, Niger died in a plane crash in Sainte-Rose, Guadeloupe.

Niger's last writings (*Les puissants* [1956] and *Les Grenouilles du Mont Kimbo* [1964]) describe both his experience of colonialism and his vision of a future liberation from the domination of colonialist exploitation.

See also Colonial Rule.

Nick Nesbitt

Niger River

Third largest river in Africa.

The Niger River is located in western Africa, originating in GUINEA and running generally east through MALI, NIGER, and NIGERIA, where it discharges into the Gulf of Guinea in the Atlantic Ocean. The third largest river in Africa, it flows for 4,180 km (2,600 mi). Its chief tributary is the Lokoja River in Nigeria.

The Niger is an important travel artery in Mali, Niger, and Nigeria and is also a source of fish, including carp, Nile perch, and catfish. In Mali, the river's inland delta is the country's richest agricultural region. In Nigeria, the Niger River delta constitutes one of the world's largest wetlands and contains one of Africa's largest mangrove forests. It is also the location of some of Africa's largest petroleum and natural gas deposits, which are critical to the Nigerian economy. Pollution caused by the oil and natural gas industries has damaged farms, FISHERIES, and mangrove stands and provoked protests from local peoples such as the Ogoni. The Movement for the Survival of the Ogoni People, led by the late KEN SARO-WIWA until his death in 1995, has become one of the biggest ENVIRONMENTAL MOVEMENTS in Africa.

Robert Fay

Niggaz with Attitude

Los Angeles rap group that brought "gangsta rap" to a mass audience.

Niggaz with Attitude (N.W.A.) was formed in Compton, California, in 1987 and included Eazy-E (Eric Wright), MC Ren (Lorenzo Patterson), ICE CUBE (O'Shea Jackson), Dr. Dre (Andre Young), and Yella (Antoine Carraby). Recording for Eazy-E's own Ruthless Records, N.W.A made its debut with one of the most important albums in RAP history. *Straight Outta Compton* (1988) was powered by the innovative production of Dr. Dre, which emphasized the heavy, loping beats of 1970s SOUL and FUNK.

The group's rhymes, especially those of Ice Cube, helped reinvent rap lyrics through the unflinching portraits of gang life that they created. While rap lyrics had traditionally been built around ebullient (if violent) boasts, songs like "Dopeman" told graphic stories of drugs and gangs and "bitches and ho's" without apology. "F—- tha Police," a block party anthem during the summer of 1989, was condemned by law enforcement officials nationwide, including the Federal Bureau of Investigation. Despite receiving scant radio play, *Straight Outta Compton* sold over two million copies, and N.W.A's gangsta rap style made LOS ANGELES the capital of the hip-hop world for years to come.

Soon after the release of the band's debut album Ice Cube quit the group, and N.W.A became even more reliant on Dr. Dre's production skills. But despite being ignored by commercial radio and many critics, the band's next album, *Efil4zaggin* (1991)—the title is "Niggaz4life" written backwards—went immediately to the top of the album charts.

The "gangsta rap" group Niggaz with Attitude included (left to right) Eazy-E, Dr. Dre, MC Ren, and Yella. Ice Cube, not pictured, was an early member of the group before launching a solo career. *CORBIS*

After N.W.A disbanded in 1992 each of its members pursued solo careers. Despite several attempts, MC Ren and Yella never achieved much success on their own. But Eazy-E, embroiled in an explosive public feud with Dr. Dre, found success with an anti-Dre album entitled *It's On (Dr. Dre) 187um Killa* (1993). Eazy-E continued to release albums and run Ruthless Records (which found huge success with Cleveland's Bone Thugs-N-Harmony); he died of ACQUIRED IMMUNODEFICIENCY SYNDROME (AIDS) in 1995. Dr. Dre went on to cofound Death Row Records, where he released his wildly successful solo debut, *The Chronic* (1992); Dre's menacing yet accessible beats also powered the meteoric rise of Death Row's young stars TUPAC SHAKUR and SNOOP DOGGY DOGG. By the late 1990s Dre had achieved considerable success as a record producer, most notably for signing rapper Eminem. In 2001 he won a Grammy award for Producer of the Year; he also won for Best Rap Performance for a song he performed with Eminem, "Forget about Dre."

Ice Cube established himself as one of HIP-HOP's most important voices with *Amerikkka's Most Wanted* (1990); his success continued with solo and collaborative albums throughout the 1990s. He has acted as well, starring in John Singleton's *Boyz N the Hood* (1991) and F. Gary Gray's *Friday* (1995), for which he was also the screenwriter. *The Player's Club* (1998) was Cube's directorial debut. He went on to produce, write, and act in several major films, including *Next Friday* (2000), *All About the Benjamins* (2002), and *Barbershop* (2002).

Andrew Du Bois

Nile River

Longest river in the world and principal source of water for Egyptian agriculture.

From its source, LAKE VICTORIA in east Central Africa, the Nile flows generally north through UGANDA, SUDAN, and EGYPT to the Mediterranean Sea, stretching 5,584 km (3,470 mi). From its remotest headstream, the Ruvyironza River in BURUNDI, the river is 6,695 km (4,160 mi) long. The area of the river basin is more than 2.8 million sq km (1.1 million sq mi).

The Ruvyironza, regarded as the ultimate source of the Nile, is one of the upper branches of the Kagera River in TANZANIA. The Kagera follows the boundary of RWANDA northward, turns along the boundary of Uganda, and drains into Lake Victoria. The Nile leaves Lake Victoria at the site of the now-submerged Ripon Falls and rushes for 483 km (300 mi) between high rocky walls and over rapids and cataracts, running first northwest and then west, until it enters Lake Albert. The section between the two lakes is called the Victoria Nile.

The river leaves the northern end of Lake Albert as the Albert Nile, flows through northern Uganda, and becomes the Bahr al Jabal at the Sudan border. At its junction with the Bahr al Ghazal, the river becomes the Bahr al Abyad, or the White Nile. At KHARTOUM the White Nile is joined by the BLUE NILE, or Bahr al Azraq, so named because of the color of the water. The Blue Nile, 1,370 km (850 mi) long, gathers its volume mainly from Lake T'ana in the Ethiopian Highlands; it is known there as the Abbai. From Khartoum the Nile flows northeast; 322 km (200 mi) below that city, it is joined by the 'Atbarah River. During its course from the confluence of the 'Atbarah through the Nubian Desert, the river makes two deep bends. The Nile enters the Mediterranean Sea by a delta that separates into the Rosetta and Damietta distributaries. The Nile valley is home to a host of wildlife, including the Nile CROCODILE, HIPPOPOTAMUSES, more than 300 species of birds, and numerous fish species.

Europeans considered the source of the Nile one of the last great mysteries on earth until the mid-nineteenth century, when a series of expeditions brought British and German explorers into the Lake Victoria region for the first time. These explorers included the Englishmen JOHN HANNING SPEKE and Sir Samuel White Baker; a German, Georg August Schweinfurth; and a British-American, Sir HENRY MORTON STANLEY. Speke reached Lake Victoria in 1858 and Ripon Falls in 1862, and Baker sighted Lake Albert in 1864. Schweinfurth explored the western feeders of the White Nile from 1868 to 1871. In 1875 Stanley sailed around Lake Victoria, and in 1889 he traced the Semliki River and reached Lake Edward and the Ruwenzori Range.

For thousands of years the August rains in the Ethiopian highlands and the runoff from snowmelt in the Mountains of the Moon flooded the Nile delta in Egypt. When the floodwaters receded, a heavy layer of silt was left. The intensive irrigated agriculture in the fertile Nile valley supported one of the world's earliest civilizations and in more recent times earned Egypt the title "Breadbasket of the Middle East."

The first dam on the Nile, the High Dam, was built in 1902 and heightened in 1936. The Makwar Dam, now called the Sennar Dam, was built across the Blue Nile south of Khartoum following WORLD WAR I (1914–1918) to provide storage water for cotton plantations in the Sudan. A dam at Jabal Awliya was constructed on the White Nile south of Khartoum in 1937. But the ASWAN HIGH DAM, which opened in the early 1970s, most dramatically transformed the ecology and economic role of the Nile. It created one of the world's largest reservoirs, Lake Nasser, and allowed the Egyptian government to produce hydroelectric power, control flooding, and minimize droughts. On the other hand, the dam has severely reduced the sediment deposits that the floodwaters once brought to the delta and increased the river's salinity. Consequently, the Nile delta has become less fertile, forcing Egyptian farmers to increase use of chemical fertilizers.

The lack of sedimentation has had other harmful effects, such as erosion of the river's banks. The silt in the floodwaters also used to feed into the coastal waters of the Mediterranean Sea, nourishing the algae blooms and sea-bottom detritus that in turn fed sardines, shrimp, and other sea creatures. Since the opening of the Aswan High Dam, fish and shrimp catches in the Mediterranean have declined significantly.

Bibliography

Collins, Robert O. *The Waters of the Nile*. Oxford University Press, 1990.

Moorehead, Alan. *The White Nile.* Hamilton, 1971.

Robert Fay

Nilotes of Sudan

Ethnic group that originated over 2,000 years ago in the region that is present-day Sudan.

The East African Nilotic culture evolved 2,000 years ago in the Gezira, the land between the Blue and White Niles in present-day SUDAN. Over time the Nilotes migrated southward in clans and currently reside in southern Sudan, ETHIOPIA, UGANDA, KENYA and TANZANIA. They are linguistically divided into the Western, Eastern and Southern Nilotes.

The Western Nilotes, the greatest population of Nilotic peoples in Sudan, include the DINKA, SHILLUK, ANUAK, NUER, LUO, Atwot, ACHOLI, and Burun (and numerous smaller groups). The Burun remain in the Gezira and the others reside in southern Sudan or on the Sudanese/Ethiopian border (Anuak) and Ugandan/Sudanese border (Acholi). The Western Nilotic Luo, close relations of the Shilluk and Anuak, also reside in numerous discrete groups throughout southern Sudan, as well as in Kenya and Uganda. The Dinka are by far the largest of the Western Nilotes numbering three to five million.

The Eastern Nilotes reside in southern Sudan (the BARI, Mundari, Latuka and other smaller populations east and west of the Nile) and Kenya (the MAASAI of Southern Kenya and Northern Tanzania) as well as on the Sudanese/Kenyan border (the TURKANA and TOPOSA). The Southern Nilotes (KALENJIN, NANDI, SEBEI, Dorobo, and Omotik/Datoga) reside only in Kenya.

For centuries, the most numerous of the Western Nilotes, the Dinka, lived throughout the Gezira near the Blue and White Niles. With the fall of the thirteenth-century Nubian kingdom, Alwa, they forged south, pressured by slave raiders and severe droughts. From the sixteenth to the eighteenth centuries this culture found new homelands in central South Sudan. Simultaneously, many Luo, because of drought, migrated further south into the Great Lakes region of Uganda, as well as to Kenya and Tanzania. Many others remained in South Sudan as small discrete unintegrated groups.

At the same time Dinka ethnic expansion took place and these Nilotes absorbed numerous peoples on their inner and outer peripheries. Since the mid-eighteenth century, the Dinka dominated southern Sudan numerically. Eventually, ethnic conflict came to predominate among the Nilotes as pastoral systems commonly raided each other for animals and women. Thus the Dinka, Nuer, and Atwot have often been at war. Other Nilotes who were forced to convert to agro-pastoralism and fishing did not, however, engage in such high level warfare.

During the eighteenth century the Shilluk and Bari centralized into small states/kingdoms while simultaneously in 1770 slave raiders from the northwestern Islamic kingdoms of Wadai and Darfur forged southeast plundering the decentralized Dinka and Nuer communities. This era marked the beginning of centuries of slave raids and instability in the region, forcing the Nuer located on the periphery of the Dinka communities to move east in large numbers, and in the process, absorb numerous Dinka and Anyuak. By the twentieth century, former Dinka peoples accounted for 70 percent of the Nuer.

In 1821 Sudan came under the colonial control of Egyptian ruler Mohammed Ali, who needed new recruits to strengthen his armies. Slave raiding, on a scale hitherto unknown, occurred. The Dinka, as the most desirable slave soldiers, were most heavily raided and some estimates suggest that two million southern people died during the turbulent nineteenth century. Simultaneously the Dinka formed into a resistant confederation that eventually expelled the Egyptians in 1885. Violence increased when a northern Sudanese Muslim nationalist, known as the Mahdi, "liberated" all of Sudan in 1885 with the aid of the Dinka in the south, but then turned around and pillaged the Dinka for slaves. In 1898 the British overthrew the Mahdists creating the Anglo-Egyptian Condominium. The latter forcibly pacified the south and slave raids halted until independence in 1956. At that time the British hastily and unthinkingly bestowed political, military, and economic power over the entire Sudan on northern Sudanese Islamic elites in Khartoum, the old enemies of the south. Southerners, and particularly the Nilotes, were passionately unwilling to be governed by their former enemies.

Civil war erupted, and in the 1960s the Western Nilotes, particularly the Dinka, came to dominate the civil war movement. Peace prevailed for a decade during the 1970s, but war erupted once more in 1983. This time a new resistance force, the Sudan People's Liberation Movement and Army (SPLM/A), spearheaded by Dinka leader JOHN GARANG DE MABIOR, prepared to fight another long civil war. Although peace talks were underway in 2004, the SPLA continued to fight the fundamentalist northern Sudanese army. Islamic Baggara slave raiders have continued to plunder the northwestern Dinka territory for slaves.

See also Nile River.

Further Reading

Beswick, Stephanie. *Sudan's Blood Memory: The Legacy of War, Ethnicity and Slavery in Early South Sudan.* Rochester University Press, 2004.

Burton, John W. *A Nilotic World: The Atuot Speaking Peoples Of The Southern Sudan.* Greenwood Press, 1987.

Evans-Pritchard, E. E. *The Nuer.* Clarendon Press, 1940.

Hutchinson, Sharon. *Nuer Dilemmas.* University of California Press, 1996.

Stephanie Beswick

Nimeiry, Gaafar Muhammad al-

1930–

Military leader and former president of Sudan.

Gaafar Muhammad al-Nimeiry was born in 1930 in Wad Nubawi, in the Omdurman area of central SUDAN. Nimeiry attended the Sudan Military College and graduated in 1952, four years before Sudanese independence. After 1960 he belonged to a small group of politically active military officers who were strongly influenced by Pan-Arabist and socialist thought. In 1966 he graduated from the United States Army Command College at Fort Leavenworth, Kansas. On his return to Sudan, Nimeiry became director of the Gebeit military training school, where he had ready access to the newest members of the Sudanese officer corps.

In 1969 Nimeiry and five other officers overthrew the civilian government of Ismail al-Azhari. Nimeiry was promoted to major general and was chosen prime minister and chairman of the Revolutionary Command Council. This group included military officers and a number of civilians who favored a range of socialist, Communist, and Pan-Arabist political programs. Nimeiry's government nationalized banks and some industries, carried out limited land reform, and expanded the rights of organized labor. In 1970 Sadiq al-Mahdi, a conservative Muslim leader, substantial landholder, and direct descendant of the Mahdi, led an unsuccessful attempt to overthrow Nimeiry. In 1971 Communists briefly succeeded in removing him from office, but Nimeiry returned to power. Later that year he was elected president with over 98 percent of the vote.

Once securely in power Nimeiry established a political party, the Sudanese Socialist Union, and began negotiations to end the Sudanese civil war with the Anya-Nya guerrilla organization, which had been fighting for regional autonomy in the south. In 1972 Nimeiry concluded a peace settlement, the Addis Ababa Agreement. This granted regional autonomy to southern Sudan, which was predominantly non-Muslim. The agreement brought peace to southern Sudan for eleven years. Embittered by the role of Sudanese Communists in the 1971 coup, Nimeiry began to shift to a more market-oriented economic program and sought cordial relations with the United States and other Western powers. He denationalized the banks and developed economic policies that encouraged Western and Arab investment in Sudan, and he purged his government of leftists suspected of supporting the 1971 coup.

In 1976 another unsuccessful coup associated with al-Mahdi impressed Nimeiry with the power of Islamic opposition. In 1981 he formed an alliance with the Muslim Brotherhood and, in 1983, imposed Islamic law throughout the country. In direct violation of the Addis Ababa Agreement he dissolved the southern Sudanese government and divided the region into three provinces. This provoked a mutiny of southern Sudanese troops and led directly to the revival of the southern Sudanese secessionist movement. In 1985, while undergoing a medical examination in the United States, Nimeiry was overthrown in a bloodless military coup. He lived in exile in Cairo, Egypt, until 1999, when he returned to Sudan to help end the country's civil war. Despite criticism from Muslim groups, who accused Nimeiry of atrocities against them during his sixteen-year rule, the former president received a government amnesty.

See also Islam in Africa; Mahdist State.

Robert Baum

Nina Rodrigues, Raimundo

1862–1906

Brazilian physician, one of the first social scientists to study Afro-Brazilian culture and particularly Brazilian religious syncretism.

Raimundo Nina Rodrigues was born in Vargem Grande, Maranhão, Brazil. Trained as a medical doctor, he graduated from the medical school of BAHIA. He was also interested in the study of anthropology, sociology, and criminology. He became a professor of general pathology and forensic medicine at the medical school in the early 1890s and was a pioneer in Afro-Brazilian ethnology and forensic medicine. Rodrigues founded the *Forensic Medicine* magazine and was a member of the Forensic Medicine Society of New York and of the Société de Medico-Psychologique de Paris.

Rodrigues identified two distinct African "cults," which he termed the *Iorubanos* and the MALÊs. He devoted most of his attention to the Iorubano cults, which he felt were more strongly influenced by Catholicism. These originated from the CANDOMBLÉ *Gêgê-Nagô*, whereas the Malês were thought to be more associated with Islam.

Among his most important works were *O animismo fetichista dos negros da Bahianos* (The Fetishist Animism of Bahian Blacks, 1935), *Os Africanos no Brasil* (Africans in Brazil, a posthumous collection of his papers, 1932), and *Brasil* (The Human Races and Penal Responsibility in Brazil, 1958).

Rodrigues's works embraced theories of scientific racism and social Darwinism broadly held by the Brazilian intellectual elite of his time. He viewed racial mixing and the black presence in BRAZIL more generally as hindering the nation's progress. His views greatly influenced a national immigration policy that discriminated against Africans and Asians while encouraging European immigrants. Rodrigues also applied his theory of racial inferiority in the field of forensic medicine. In 1894 he published a book stating that the "degenerates," that is, the Negroes and Indians, should have only attenuated criminal responsibility, given the allegedly different capacities of what he believed to be inferior races. Rodrigues also influenced generations of students of Afro-Brazilian culture. Rodrigues died in 1906 while in Paris.

See also Whitening.

Nixon, Edgar Daniel

1899–1987

African American civil rights leader and organizer of the Montgomery Bus Boycott.

E. D. Nixon's struggle to organize African Americans in Montgomery, Alabama illustrated several sources of tension within the Civil Rights Movement: social class, the roles of the labor movement and the church, and older versus newer leadership. Born in Robinson Springs, Alabama, Nixon was the son of Wesley Nixon, a tenant farmer turned Primitive Baptist preacher, and Susan (Chappell) Nixon. Having little formal education, E. D. Nixon began to work fulltime at age thirteen and worked for forty-one years as a Pullman car porter.

A supporter of African American labor union leader A. Philip Randolph, Nixon became president of the Brotherhood of Sleeping Car Porters' Montgomery chapter in 1938. Despite white hostility, he also organized a registration drive for black voters in Montgomery.

When the middle–class Montgomery branch of the National Association for the Advancement of Colored People (NAACP) failed to actively support the 1943 voter registration drive, Nixon organized poorer African Americans to gain control of the local chapter; he was elected its president in 1945 and 1946. After he became president of the state NAACP in 1947, the national NAACP leadership, embarrassed by Nixon's homespun demeanor and sixth-grade education, orchestrated his 1949 re-election defeat. The following year Nixon was also ousted from the presidency of the NAACP Montgomery chapter.

Nixon spearheaded a plan to challenge Montgomery's segregated public transportation system, and when Montgomery NAACP secretary Rosa L. Parks was arrested for refusing to relinquish her bus seat to a white patron, it was Nixon who posted her bail and called for a Montgomery bus boycott. As treasurer of the Montgomery Improvement Association, organized to end discrimination on the buses, Nixon resented association president Martin Luther King, Jr. King was associated with Montgomery's African American middle class and, Nixon believed, did not properly credit him and the masses of poor African Americans for the boycott's ultimate success. Following a number of unsuccessful attempts to regain leadership roles, an embittered Nixon withdrew from public life.

Bibliography

Branch, Taylor. *Parting the Waters: America During the King Years, 1954–1963.* Simon & Schuster, 1988.

Garrow, David J. *Bearing the Cross: Martin Luther King, Jr., and the Southern Christian Leadership Conference.* W. Morrow, 1986.

Jalane Schmidt

Njinga Mbandi

Queen of Ndongo and Matamba in seventeenth-century Angola.

Njinga Mbandi was born around 1582, the eldest daughter of King Mbandi Ngola of Ndongo. He favored her above his other children, allowing her to sit in court sessions and to exercise with the army. Njinga Mbandi had unusual physical gifts and was skilled in military arts even in her old age. When Mbandi Ngola died, around 1617, his son, Njinga's brother Ngola Mbandi, became king. From 1619 to 1621, Portuguese-led forces from the colony of Angola, under Governor Luis Mendes de Vasconcelos, attacked Ndongo, destroying the capital city and forcing the king and his government to flee to the Kindonga Islands in the Kwanza River. Ngola Mbandi sought a peace agreement with the Portuguese government, and in 1622 dispatched Njinga Mbandi to Luanda to negotiate a treaty on his behalf. While in Luanda, Njinga was baptized, taking the Christian name of Ana de Sousa (the last name being that of the governor who stood as her godfather). Njinga's diplomatic efforts succeeded and the new governor, João Correa de Sousa, agreed to withdraw Portuguese forces from Ndongo's territory, return some servile populations to Ndongo's control, evacuate the fort of Ambaca, and assist Ngola Mbandi in eliminating some bands of Imbangala mercenary soldiers who were pillaging in Ndongo.

The Portuguese government, however, reneged on its promises, and in desperation, Ngola Mbandi committed suicide. He left a small child as his successor and Njinga as regent. Njinga Mbandi immediately entered into diplomatic relations with the new Angolan governor, Fernão de Sousa, but quickly faced an impasse in negotiations. De Sousa was interested in honoring the treaty only insofar as it made Ndongo a subordinate to Portugal. De Sousa sided with dissident nobles in Ndongo, most notably with Hari a Ngola, who denied Njinga's claim to the rule. When Njinga decided to rule on her own and killed Ngola Mbandi's son, de Sousa determined that she should be removed. These developments led to war, and in 1626 the first of several armed conflicts between Ndongo and Portugal erupted. Njinga was forced to flee the island of Kindonga in 1629, as Portuguese forces captured her sisters Barbara Kifunji and Graça Kambu. Njinga herself made a dramatic escape into the Baixa de Cassanje lowlands to the east, her troops having to descend the cliffs on rope. By the time she reached safety, she had only a few hundred followers left. Forced to throw herself on the mercy of Kasanje, an Imbangala leader, she was made to take a humiliating subordinate position.

Njinga recovered, however, due to the fact that she was still widely regarded as the legitimate leader of Ndongo by many people. She was generally able to retain effective control over the eastern part of the country and soon reoccupied Kindonga. From a position of strength she succeeded in conquering the neighboring kingdom of Matamba, and by 1635 she had transferred her capital to that country. In 1639 Njinga entered into negotiations with the Portuguese to recognize her claims. But because no governor was willing to accept her right to rule, she ultimately failed in her quest.

When the Dutch forces of the West India Company occupied Luanda in 1641, Njinga immediately sent emissaries to them, offering an alliance against the Portuguese. Njinga then moved her capital and army to Cavanga on the upper Dande River, close to the heart of the old capital of Ndongo and began to reassert her claims. Her old rival Hari a Ngola contested her move and threw his full weight behind Portugal in their war against her. Njinga received relatively little help from the Dutch during this period, although she managed to defeat one Portuguese army that attacked her capital in 1644, taking a number of important prisoners. The Portuguese, reinforced from Brazil, counterattacked in 1646 and won a shattering victory. Incriminating letters found in her camp caused them to condemn her sister Graça to death. For many years Graça had been sending Njinga intelligence about the Portuguese. Meanwhile, the Dutch began to take a more active role in Angola and in 1647 they joined forces with Njinga, winning a crushing victory over the Portuguese. By 1648 Portugal was narrowly holding on to their forts and the rest of the country was in Njinga's hands. Later that year Portuguese reinforcements recaptured Luanda, forcing the Dutch to surrender and causing Njinga to retreat from Cavanga to Matamba.

After protracted negotiations, the Portuguese eventually signed a peace treaty with Njinga, which was ratified in 1657. The treaty recognized Njinga's claim to rule as queen, defined her territory as that portion of Ndongo and Matamba that she held before the Dutch invasion, and also agreed to eliminate some Imbangala bands. Njinga also agreed to become Christian again and to allow missionaries into her country. Her later years were spent defending her territories, especially against the Imbangala of Kasanje, and arranging for her succession. Njinga was concerned that the throne would pass to Njinga Mona, her second in command and an Imbangala. She wanted the throne to remain in the hands of aristocratic families from Ndongo, and to this end she promoted the fortunes of Ngola Kanini, a man she hoped would marry her sister Dona Barbara and create a dynasty. This marriage failed, but Barbara succeeded to the throne when Njinga died on December 17, 1663.

John Thornton

Nkomo, Joshua

1917–1999

Nationalist leader and politician of Zimbabwe who helped lead the country's struggle for independence.

Joshua Nkomo was born in Matabeleland, Southern Rhodesia (now ZIMBABWE), the home of the NDEBELE ethnic group. After attending elementary school in Southern Rhodesia, Nkomo traveled to SOUTH AFRICA for high school in DURBAN and college in JOHANNESBURG. He returned to Rhodesia in 1947, becoming a social worker for the railways and later secretary of the Railway Worker's Association. An effective organizer, in 1952 Nkomo was elected president of the Southern Rhodesia AFRICAN NATIONAL CONGRESS (ANC), and represented African opinion in the Central African Federation.

After the ANC was banned, Nkomo, then in London, was elected president, *in absentia*, of the new Rhodesian National Democratic Party (NDP) in 1960. The NDP was also banned, re-forming as the increasingly militant Zimbabwe African People's Union (ZAPU), with Nkomo as president. Soon afterward many of his cohorts left ZAPU to form the Zimbabwe African National Union (ZANU). From 1964 to 1974, Nkomo remained either in confinement or restricted to certain areas, rarely appearing in public. Nevertheless, his stature grew as ZAPU built a conventional army and carried out attacks on the white minority establishment. After his release, Nkomo worked hard to negotiate a peaceful transition to independence, fought to retain his position in ZAPU in the face of opposition from younger, more militant members, and led ZAPU from Zambia in its fight against the Rhodesian regime.

In the transition to independence, ROBERT MUGABE and ZANU disavowed Nkomo, leading to ZAPU's electoral defeat in the 1980 elections. Nkomo became the minister of home affairs but was soon forced from office when Mugabe cracked down on opposition parties, particularly ZAPU. Outside of the government Nkomo retained a huge popular following among the Ndebele. In 1988, after the union of ZAPU and Mugabe's ZANU created the ZANU-Patriotic Front (ZANU-PF), Nkomo reentered the government as a senior minister and as one of two vice presidents. He transferred his allegiance to ZANU-PF and, although promoting development in Matabeleland, the Ndebele homeland, he remained strongly aligned with the policies of Mugabe and ZANU-PF. In late 1997 Nkomo stepped down from his government positions due to ill health, and he died two years later.

Eric Young

Nkrumah, Kwame

1909–1972

Leading nationalist and prime minister of the Gold Coast from 1952 until its independence in 1957; later became prime minister and then president of independent Ghana.

Leader of the first sub-Saharan African colony to gain independence, Kwame Nkrumah was a towering figure in the PAN-AFRICANISM movement and a tireless advocate of an independent African SOCIALISM. Nkrumah was born Francis Nwia Kofi Nkrumah into a Nzima family in Nkroful, in the southwestern Gold Coast (present-day GHANA). His father was a goldsmith and his mother a retail market trader. A baptized Roman Catholic, Nkrumah attended the Roman Catholic mission school in the nearby town of Half Assini and graduated from another Roman Catholic school in Sekondi. He studied teaching at Achimota College. After teaching in the early 1930s, Nkrumah considered becoming a Jesuit priest, but decided to study in the United States instead. He earned degrees from Lincoln University and the University of Pennsylvania. Nkrumah's political philosophy began to develop as he studied the international socialism of Marx and Lenin, the African nationalist writings of American leader MARCUS GARVEY, and the nonviolence of Mahatma Gandhi. He also met W. E. B. DU BOIS and GEORGE PADMORE, leading advocates of Pan-Africanism.

When he moved to England in 1945 to earn a doctorate degree from the London School of Economics, Nkrumah became secretary of the West African Students Union and helped organize the fifth Pan-African Congress in Manchester. He also wrote three pamphlets on fighting colonialism and met other future leaders, including JOMO KENYATTA of KENYA and KAMUZU BANDA of MALAWI. In 1947 Nkrumah returned to Africa to become secretary general of United Gold Coast Convention (UGCC), a party calling for self-government in the Gold Coast, at the invitation of its leaders, including JOSEPH B. DANQUAH. Membership in the party increased as Nkrumah toured the region, urging Africans to unite. In 1948 the British colonial governor, Gerald Creasy, blamed rioting and looting on the party's activities, and ordered the arrests of Danquah and Nkrumah. Police found a Communist Party membership card in Nkrumah's possession, but it was not signed and Nkrumah denied ever having joined the party, calling himself a Marxist-socialist and nondenominational Christian. Later that year he established the *Accra Evening News*. In 1949 Nkrumah broke with the UGCC because its middle-class leaders distrusted his more radical populism; he formed the Convention People's Party (CPP), which advocated mass action in the form of boycotts, strikes, and civil disobedience to gain independence.

This strategy led to Nkrumah's arrest and imprisonment on charges of "subversion" and "sedition," which won him widespread public sympathy. In February 1951 the CPP won thirty-four of the thirty-eight popularly contested seats in the Legislative Assembly. Consequently, the British administration released Nkrumah from jail. On the next day, Governor Charles Arden-Clarke summoned him to Christiansborg Castle in ACCRA and asked him to lead the new government in cooperation with the colonial administration. He took office as prime minister in 1952 and guided the country to independence on March 6, 1957, with the name Ghana. In 1960 a new constitution created Ghana into a republic, with Nkrumah as president.

At first the Nkrumah administration was widely popular. Nkrumah brought Africans into the government, offered free education, provided scholarships for study abroad, built hospitals, and paved roads. But the borrowing necessary to pay for domestic spending pushed Ghana into debt. In the face of mounting financial problems, Nkrumah's government abandoned its 1959 Development Plan two years later. Meanwhile, Nkrumah became increasingly autocratic. He introduced laws enabling the government to jail without trial people who were labeled security risks. In 1961 Nkrumah strengthened his grip on the CPP. Later that year he introduced a law under which anyone found guilty of insulting Nkrumah faced a three-year prison term. Economic troubles, worsened by falling COCOA prices, generated labor unrest and a general strike in 1961. Following the strike, Nkrumah assumed command of the armed forces and dismissed all foreign officers. In 1964 Nkrumah declared Ghana a one-party state, and his government tightened censorship. Several assassination attempts prompted Nkrumah's increasing isolation, a substantial increase in the internal security apparatus, and the number of political prisoners.

While the situation within Ghana continued to deteriorate, Nkrumah continued to advocate Pan-Africanism internationally. From 1960 to 1963, Ghanaian troops served with United Nations forces in Congo-Kinshasa. Ghana became a charter member of the ORGANIZATION OF AFRICAN UNITY in 1963. Also that year, Nkrumah published his book, *Why Africa Must Unite*. On February 24, 1966, while Nkrumah was visiting Beijing and Hanoi in an effort to end the Vietnam War, a military coup ousted him from office. He went into exile in GUINEA. He wrote *Handbook for Revolutionary Warfare* (1968) and *Class Struggle in Africa* (1970). Nkrumah died in 1972 while seeking cancer treatment in Romania.

See also Nationalism in Africa.

David P. Johnson, Jr.

Nkumbula, Harry Mwaanga

1916–1983

Prominent Zambian nationalist and leader of the African National Congress (ANC).

Harry Mwaanga Nkumbula is considered a father of Zambian NATIONALISM. He was born in Maala, Northern Rhodesia (present-day ZAMBIA). After working as a schoolteacher and being influenced by GEORGE PADMORE's *How Britain Rules Africa*, Nkumbula became the secretary of the Mufulira Welfare Association and later the cofounder of the Kitwe African Society. Welfare associations were precursors to formal political parties, and provided black Zambians with an opportunity to mobilize against colonial authorities. After studying in UGANDA, he moved to England and earned a degree from the London School of Economics. While he was in London, he associated with such African nationalist figures as KWAME NKRUMAH, JOMO KENYATTA, and HASTINGS BANDA, who were all to achieve political prominence in later years.

In 1951 Nkumbula returned to Northern Rhodesia and became president of the AFRICAN NATIONAL CONGRESS, or ANC (a separate entity from the South African organization of the same name). He led the moderate ANC campaign against the formation of the Central African Federation, the consolidation of Northern and Southern Rhodesia. When his ANC campaign failed and the Central African Federation was established in 1953, Nkumbula's prestige began to fade. In 1955 he and future Zambian president KENNETH KAUNDA were jailed for distributing ANC literature. Following his release Nkumbula campaigned for the adoption of a new constitution and universal adult suffrage.

In 1958 Nkumbula lost the support of his colleague Kaunda, who broke with the more moderate ANC to form the United National Independence Party (UNIP). In 1959 Nkumbula was elected to the legislative council. However, Nkumbula was clearly eclipsed by Kaunda by the time the two nationalists attended the 1961 London constitutional conference on the future of the Central African Federation.

The ANC lost much of its support to Kaunda's UNIP. But following the 1962 election, the ANC joined the ruling coalition with the UNIP, and Nkumbula received a ministerial appointment. He remained active in politics and joined the UNIP in 1973.

Ari Nave

Nobel Prize

Awards granted annually to persons or institutions for outstanding contributions made during the previous year in the fields of physics, chemistry, physiology or medicine, literature, international peace, and economic sciences.

Generally considered the world's most prestigious awards, Nobel Prizes come from a trust fund established by Swedish chemist, inventor, and philanthropist Alfred Bernhard Nobel. As designated in Nobel's will, the Royal Swedish Academy of Sciences awards prizes for physics and chemistry; the Nobel Assembly at the Karolinksa Institute awards prizes for physiological or medical works; the Swedish Academy awards prizes for literature; and the Norwegian Nobel Committee selects the winner of the peace prize. In 1968 a new prize for economics was established and endowed by the national bank of Sweden.

The first Nobel Prizes were awarded on December 10, 1901, but it was not until 1950 that a black person was a recipient. An American from DETROIT, RALPH J. BUNCHE was the first person of African descent to receive the distinguished prize for his work as a United Nations mediator; his efforts led to the 1949 Arab-Israeli armistice agreement. Since then a growing list of Africans or people of African descent have received a Nobel: MAX THEILER, 1951 Physiology or Medicine Prize; ALBERT JOHN LUTHULI, 1960 Peace Prize; MARTIN LUTHER KING, JR., 1964 Peace Prize; ANWAR AL-SADAT, 1978 Peace Prize; Sir William ARTHUR LEWIS, 1979 Economics Prize; Bishop DESMOND TUTU, 1984 Peace Prize; WOLE SOYINKA, 1986 Literature Prize; NAGUIB MAHFOUZ, 1988 Literature Prize; NADINE GORDIMER, 1991 Literature Prize; DEREK WALCOTT, 1992 Literature Prize; TONI MORRISON, 1993 Literature Prize; NELSON MANDELA and F. W. DE KLERK, 1993 Peace Prize; KOFI ANNAN, 2001 Peace Prize; J.M. COETZEE, 2003 Literature Prize. Nobel Prize winners receive a cash award, a gold medal, and a diploma.

See also Literature, African American.

Liliana Obregón

Nok

Ancient African culture.

The name Nok was given to the culture of a group of people who lived in what are now the northern and central parts of NIGERIA, in the area north of the confluence of the Niger and Benue rivers, from 900 B.C.E. to 200 C.E. Remains of this culture were first discovered in the area of the Jos Plateau, and similar artifacts have been found in the middle valley of the Benue River.

The Nok were also the earliest people yet known in this part of Africa who made IRON tools and weapons. They also produced very fine sculpture, usually of human forms, in terra cotta (baked clay). These magnificent pottery heads and figures are the earliest known African sculptures. It is believed that the Nok had a well-organized economy and administrative system, and that their culture influenced later peoples of the region.

Noone, Jimmie

1894–1944

American musician who was considered one of the great first-generation jazz clarinetists, influential in the development of swing music.

Born in NEW ORLEANS, LOUISIANA, Jimmie Noone began playing clarinet around 1910, taking lessons from Lorenzo Tio, Jr., and SIDNEY BECHET (who was himself only thirteen years old). In 1915 Noone got his first professional job, playing in Buddy Petit's Young Olympia Band. During his stint with Petit's band Noone befriended Freddie Keppard, whose band, the Original Creole Orchestra in CHICAGO, he joined in 1917. From 1920 to 1926 he played with Doc Cooke's Dreamland Orchestra, at the same time studying classical clarinet. Noone led his own bands in Chicago between 1927 and 1931, the most famous of which was Jimmie Noone's Apex Club Orchestra, which performed at the Apex Club on Chicago's South Side.

Noone's style differed from that of Johnny Dodds and Bechet, two other great New Orleans clarinetists, in that Noone's was smoother and more romantic. His style had a major influence on the swing music that was popular in the 1930s, in particular the music of fellow clarinetists Bennie Goodman and Jimmy Dorsey.

Between 1927 and 1931 Noone and his bands recorded many songs that are considered classic examples of Noone's clarinet virtuosity. Noone led several bands in Chicago throughout the 1930s. In the early 1940s he moved to southern California where he played on several famous radio programs, recordings of which are available. He was playing in a band led by "KID" ORY when he died of a heart attack.

Bibliography

Kenney, William Howland, III. "Jimmie Noone, Chicago's Classical Jazz Clarinetists." *American Music,* vol 4 (1986).

Robert Fay

Norman, Jessye

1945–

African American opera singer.

Jessye Norman is a dramatic soprano whose rich voice is recognized for its strength, warmth and intensity, dynamic coloration, affective depth and impressive range—from the E above high C to the E below middle C. Born in Augusta, Georgia, Norman is one of five children from an educated and musical family. Her mother Janie (King) is an amateur pianist. Her father Silas, an insurance broker, often sang in Augusta's Mount Calvary Baptist Church, the site of Norman's earliest singing performances.

Norman entered HOWARD UNIVERSITY in 1963 on a full-tuition scholarship to train under voice instructor Carolyn Grant and received her Bachelor of Music degree, cum laude, in 1967. The following year she won the International Music Competition in Munich, Germany. This showing won her in 1969 an operatic debut with the Deutsche Oper and many subsequent performances before German and Italian audiences. The glowing reviews from these European recitals, her 1972 appearances in the United States, and her recordings for Philips Records attracted a sellout crowd to her January 21, 1973, New York City debut in the Great Performers series at Lincoln Center.

As an internationally recognized OPERA star, Norman is considered to have excellent stylistic and linguistic command of the French, German and Italian compositions of the operatic canon. She has broadened her performance repertoire by reintroducing lesser-known works, including significant interpretations of theater songs and African American spirituals, to the appreciation of audiences and critics alike. In 1985, despite her disagreement with Republican politics, she sang the folk song "Simple Gifts" at the inauguration of President Ronald Reagan.

Norman continued performing and touring through the 1990s. In 1993 she appeared in the Metropolitan Opera's *Ariadne auf Naxsoin*, and in 1999 collaborated with choreographer BILL T. JONES on the project "How! Do! We! Do!" at the Lincoln Center. Norman released an album of songs, *I Was Born in Love*, in 2000, and the following year performed in a three-part concert series at Carnegie Hall. On March 11, 2002, Norman sang "America the Beautiful" at an on-site memorial service for victims of the World Trade Center terrorist attacks of September 11, 2001. In addition to performing as a recording artist, guest orchestral soloist, and recitalist, Norman also directs masters classes.

See also Spirituals, African American.

Bibliography

Ewen, David. "Jessye Norman." In *Musicians Since 1900: Performers in Concert and Opera.* H. W. Wilson Co., 1978.

Jalane Schmidt

North Africa, Roman Rule of

See Roman Africa: An Interpretation.

North Africa and the Greco-Roman World

See Alexandria and Grecian Africa: An Interpretation.

North Carolina Mutual Life Insurance Company

First black-controlled United States company to surpass the $1 billion mark.

Seven men founded the North Carolina Mutual Provident Association by investing fifty dollars each, founding what was later named the North Carolina Mutual Life Insurance Company on April 1, 1899. The founders intended for the Durham-based company to provide insurance for black people. The company initially offered mostly cheap industrial insurance. Workers could insure themselves against financial problems accompanying sickness and death for as little as three cents per week, a sum that yielded correspondingly small benefits.

By the summer of 1900, North Carolina Mutual faced the prospect of bankruptcy, leading five of the original seven investors to withdraw. The two remaining investors lent the company personal funds: they were businessman John Merrick, the president, and physician Aaron Moore, the secretary. They promoted entrepreneur CHARLES C. SPAULDING to general manager, and by the end of 1902 the company showed a profit. By 1906 the company had quadrupled its customer base, expanding within North Carolina and later into South Carolina. By 1913 it had successfully raised $100,000 to meet the requirement of a higher state deposit.

North Carolina Mutual's success drew national attention to the Durham area. The company's growing economic base enabled it to invest in many business ventures, like Merrick-Moore-Spaulding Land Company, dealing in real estate (1907), and Mechanics and Farmers Bank (1908), with a branch in Raleigh (1922). Other business ventures were Banker's Fire, a fire insurance company (1920); Mutual Building & Loan Association (1921); the National Negro Finance Corporation (1924); and the Mortgage Company of Durham (1929). All of these firms offered economic services to blacks and furthered economic development of Durham's black community.

In part because rising cotton prices led to black prosperity during WORLD WAR I (1914–1918), North Carolina Mutual's life insurance in force grew from $5 million to $26 million under Spaulding. Becoming president in 1918, Spaulding renamed it North Carolina Mutual Life Insurance Company the following year. By 1926, however, after expanding north to follow the MIGRATION of African Americans, Spaulding realized that new costs exceeded new revenue. He decided against further expansion until the company was once again secure. Mutual did not grow again until 1938.

Spaulding's retrenchment plan and North Carolina Mutual's conservative investments in real estate, government bonds, and mortgage loans protected the company. For example, in 1929 Mutual's life insurance in force reached $39 million and remained above $33 million during the GREAT DEPRESSION. The company was ready to take advantage of the wartime recovery during WORLD WAR II (1941–1945), during which time its life insurance in force jumped from $51 million to $100 million. This growth yielded dividends to its investors for the first time. It also allowed Mutual to compete with mainstream insurance companies, which were beginning to sell to blacks at standard rates, luring black customers from black-controlled companies. The movement toward racial solidarity in the 1960s brought many blacks back to Mutual from the white companies. This strengthened Mutual's position in the overall insurance market. Urban riots put pressure on white-controlled companies to invest in black businesses and communities. When these riots occurred, companies like General Motors, IBM, Procter and Gamble, Atlantic Richfield Company, Sun Oil, and Chrysler bought more than $400 million in insurance contracts from Mutual between 1969 and 1971, helping to make it the first black-controlled company to gross $1 billion. North Carolina Mutual continued its rise, growing tenfold between 1970 and 1990.

See also Business and African Americans.

Bibliography

Weare, Walter B. *Black Business in the New South: A Social History of the North Carolina Mutual Life Insurance Company.* University of Illinois Press, 1973.

Robert Fay

North Carolina Sea Islands

See Gullah.

Northern Cape

Province in northwestern South Africa.

Bounded on the north by Namibia and Botswana, on the west by the Atlantic Ocean, on the south by Western Cape, and on the east by Eastern Cape, Free State, and North-West Province, Northern Cape is South Africa's largest province, with an area of 361,830 sq km (139,703 sq mi). The province was created in 1994 from a section of Cape Province, one of the four former South African provinces. Most of Northern Cape is flat, rocky, and sparsely vegetated. The southern region is part of the Great Karroo (Karoo), a vast, arid plateau. In the north, the KALAHARI DESERT extends into SOUTH AFRICA from BOTSWANA. Along the Atlantic coast is Namaqualand, an area noted for its abundant minerals and for the profusion of wildflowers that bloom there in the spring. The Orange River and its major tributary, the Vaal River, converge in the province, and the Orange River then continues its course until it empties into the Atlantic Ocean. Near Upington on the Orange River is Augrabies Falls, one of Africa's tallest waterfalls. Rainfall in the province is normally limited to the summer months, from November to March, and amounts to only about 250 mm (about 10 in) annually. Average temperatures range from 17° to 32° C (62° to 90° F) in the summer and from 3° to 18° C (37° to 64° F) in the winter.

Although it ranks as South Africa's largest province in area, Northern Cape is the least densely populated. In 1999 its population was 875,222. People of mixed racial descent make up the majority of the population. The principal language of the province is Afrikaans; Setswana and XHOSA, two Bantu languages, are also widely spoken. The provincial capital and the province's only major city is Kimberley. Other towns include Upington, Victoria West, Kuruman, and De Aar. Important historical sites in Northern Cape include the Big Hole in Kimberley, a hole about 790 m (about 2600 ft) deep that was the site of a major diamond dig in the nineteenth century; Kuruman, where Robert Moffat, father-in-law of the Scottish explorer DAVID LIVINGSTONE, founded a mission station in 1824; and Griekwastad, a city founded by the Griqua, a people of mixed Khoikhoi and European descent, and the site of a famous mission station. Kimberley is the site of the McGregor Museum (founded in 1907), which specializes in natural history, and the Duggan Cronin Gallery (1938). The province is also known for its nature reserves, such as the Kalahari Gemsbok National Park.

Northern Cape's economy depends largely on agriculture and mining. The agricultural sector primarily centers on sheep farming and the production of wool and sheep pelts. Other products include wine, cotton, and fruit, which is grown along the Orange River valley. The principal minerals extracted are copper, iron ore, manganese, gypsum, asbestos, and gem stones, especially diamonds. Diamonds are mined around Kimberley, which is the headquarters of the diamond conglomerate De Beers Consolidated Mines, Ltd., and along the coast, especially around the mouth of the Orange River at the Atlantic Ocean. Two major airports serve the province at Kimberley and Upington.

Northern Cape's provincial government consists of a premier, an executive council of ten ministers, and a legislature. The provincial assembly and premier are elected for five-year terms, or until the next national election. The number of seats allocated to political parties in the provincial assembly is determined by the percentage of votes each party receives in the province during the national elections. The assembly elects a premier, who then appoints the members of the executive council.

Northern Province

Province in northern South Africa.

Northern Province is bounded on the north by the Limpopo River and Zimbabwe, on the east by Mozambique, on the west by Botswana, and on the south by North-West, Gauteng, and Mpumalanga provinces. Created in 1994, Northern Province covers 123,910 sq km (47,842 sq mi) and includes part of TRANS-

VAAL (one of the four former South African provinces) and two former bantustans (or black homelands), VENDA and Lebowa. Northern Province has several mountainous areas. The Waterberge, Strydpoortberge, and Drakensberg ranges are found in the south, and the Soutpansberg mountain range is located in the north. Savannas, or open grasslands, cover most of the western part of the province, while the north is a subtropical zone containing plains scattered with baobab trees. The average temperatures in Northern Province range from 17° to 27° C (62° to 81° F) in the summer and from 4° to 20° C (40° to 68° F) in the winter. Average annual rainfall totals about 300 mm (about 12 in), with most of it falling in the summer months, between November and March.

The population of Northern Province was 5.3 million in 1999. Black Africans make up the majority of the population. They speak a variety of languages, including Sesotho sa Leboa (also known as Northern Sotho or Pedi), Shangaan, Venda, Ndebele, siSwati, Zulu, and Tsonga. English and Afrikaans are also spoken. The provincial capital is Pietersburg. Other important towns include Louis Trichardt, Messina, Phalaborwa, Potgietersrus, and Warmbaths (noted for its mineral springs). The province has two universities, the University of the North (founded in 1959), near Pietersburg, and the University of Venda (1981).

Significant historical and cultural sites include: Mapungubwe, an early Iron Age settlement; the headquarters of the Zion Christian Church, a large African denomination, at Zion City in the town of Moria; Makapansgat and Moorddrif, sites of clashes between the Pedi people and AFRIKANER soldiers in 1854; the home of the Rain Queen, the queen of the Lovedu people, near Duiwelskloof; and the Bakone Malapa Open-Air Museum near Pietersburg. The northern section of Kruger National Park, one of the world's largest game reserves, lies along the border with MOZAMBIQUE in the eastern part of the province.

The mainstay of Northern Province's economy is agriculture. Plantation agriculture in the northern region produces oranges, bananas, avocados, mangoes, papaws, guavas, and litchi nuts. The area around Nylstroom and Warmbaths in the south produces table grapes, corn, cotton, peanuts, and sunflowers. The western region of the province is primarily used for cattle ranches. Northern Province is also rich in minerals, including copper, asbestos, phosphite, coal, iron ore, and platinum. Major copper mines operate in Messina and Phalaborwa.

The provincial government consists of a premier, an executive council of ten ministers, and a legislature. The provincial assembly and premier are elected for five-year terms, or until the next national election. Political parties are awarded assembly seats on the basis of the percentage of votes each party receives in the province during the national elections. The assembly elects a premier, who then appoints the members of the executive council.

Northern Rhodesia

Former name of Zambia.

See also Zambia.

Northrup, Solomon

1808?–1863?

Author of a best-selling book that chronicled his kidnapping and years of enslavement.

In 1841 Solomon Northrup, a free black, was kidnapped in NEW YORK and sold to slave traders. He spent the next twelve years as a slave in Louisiana. In 1852 Northrup met Samuel Bass, a Canadian carpenter, who informed the former owner of Northrup's father, who then traveled to Louisiana to gain Northrup's freedom. Inspired by UNCLE TOM'S CABIN, Northrup wrote the story of his enslavement with the help of David Wilson. Published in 1853, *Twelve Years a Slave: Narrative of Solomon Northrup* was an immediate success. The book described the daily acts of resistance that most slaves directed against their owners.

See also Free Blacks in the United States.

Bibliography

Northrup, Solomon. *Twelve Years a Slave: Narrative of Solomon Northrup.* 2nd ed. Louisiana State University, 1968.

North-West Province

Province in northern South Africa.

Bounded on the north by Botswana, on the south by the provinces of Free State and Northern Cape, and on the northeast and east by Northern Province and Gauteng, North-West Province covers 116,320 sq km (44,911 sq mi). It was created in 1994 by the merger of BOPHUTHATSWANA, one of the former *bantustans* (or black homelands), and the western part of TRANSVAAL, one of the four former South African provinces.

Much of the province consists of flat areas of scattered trees and grassland. The Magaliesberg mountain range in the northeast extends about 130 km (about 80 mi) from Pretoria to Rustenburg. The Vaal River flows along the southern border of the province. Temperatures range from 17° to 31° C (62° to 88° F) in the summer and from 3° to 21° C (37° to 70° F) in the winter. Annual rainfall totals about 360 mm (about 14 in), with almost all of it falling during the summer months, between October and April.

In 1999 the population of North-West Province was 3.6 million. The majority of the province's residents are Tswana, a black group that speaks Setswana. Smaller groups include AFRIKANERS, SOTHO, and XHOSA. English is spoken primarily as a second language. Most of the residents belong to Christian denominations. Mmabatho, formerly the capital of Bophuthatswana, serves as the provincial capital. Other significant towns include Brits, Klerksdorp, Lichtenburg, Mafikeng, Potchefstroom, Rustenburg, Sun City, and Vanderbijlpark. The province has two universities: the University of North-West, which was formerly called the University of Bophuthatswana (founded in 1979), in Mmabatho; and Potchefstroom University for Christian Higher Education (founded in 1869; became a constituent college of the University of South Africa in 1921 and an independent university in 1951).

Important historical sites in the province include Mafikeng, the traditional capital of the Barolong people, where a British garrison was placed under siege by Afrikaners during the Boer War (1899–1902); Lotlamoreng Cultural Village near Mafikeng, which recreates a traditional African village; and Boekenhoutfontein, the farm of Paul Kruger, who was the last president of the South African Republic (a state created by Afrikaners in what is now northeastern SOUTH AFRICA), from 1883 to 1902. The province has several national parks. The largest, Pilanesberg Game Reserve, is located in the crater of an extinct volcano.

The mainstay of the economy of North-West Province is mining, which generates more than half of the province's gross domestic product and provides jobs for a quarter of its work force. The chief minerals are gold, mined at Orkney and Klerksdorp; uranium, mined at Klerksdorp; platinum, mined at Rustenburg and Brits; and diamonds, mined at Lichtenburg, Christiana, and Bloemhof. The northern and western parts of the province have many sheep farms and cattle and game ranches. The eastern and southern parts are crop-growing regions that produce maize (corn), sunflowers, tobacco, cotton, and citrus fruits. An entertainment and casino complex at Sun City also contributes to the economy.

The provincial government consists of a premier, an executive council of ten ministers, and a legislature. The provincial assembly and premier are elected for five-year terms, or until the next national election. Political parties are awarded assembly seats based on the percentage of votes each party receives in the province during the national elections. The assembly elects a premier, who then appoints the members of the executive council.

Norton, Eleanor Holmes

1937–

District of Columbia delegate to U.S. House of Representatives and the first woman chair of the Equal Employment Opportunity Commission.

Eleanor Holmes Norton was born in WASHINGTON, D.C., and graduated from Yale University Law School. In the 1960s she became active in the CIVIL RIGHTS MOVEMENT, joining the STUDENT NONVIOLENT COORDINATING COMMITTEE (SNCC) and the MISSISSIPPI FREEDOM DEMOCRATIC PARTY. From 1965 to 1970 she was a highly visible lawyer for the American Civil Liberties Union in NEW YORK CITY, where she specialized in controversial free speech cases. She represented VIETNAM WAR protesters, KU KLUX KLAN members, and politicians, most notably Alabama's segregationist Governor George Wallace, then a presidential candidate who had been denied a permit to hold a rally.

Norton's activist credentials led to her appointment as chair of the New York City's Human Rights Commission (HRC) in 1970, an agency charged with ending discriminatory practices in the workplace and schools. Her seven-year HRC record, which ranged from reforming workmen's compensation laws to helping women sportswriters gain access to the press box at hockey games, prompted then-President Jimmy Carter to appoint her chair of the Equal Employment Opportunity Commission (EEOC) in 1977, a post she held until 1981. Norton emphasized bureaucratic reform during her tenure at EEOC, cutting a 130,000-case backlog in half.

In 1990 Norton was elected D.C. Delegate to the U.S. House of Representatives, where she waged an uphill battle to maintain the autonomy of the D.C. government. She was reelected to a seventh term in 2002.

Norton has devoted much of her professional life to defending human rights and combating racial and gender discrimination. She continues to teach at Georgetown University, where she is a tenured professor of law. She received a citation of merit as an Outstanding Alumna from Yale Law School, as well as the Yale Wilbur Cross Medal as Outstanding Alumna of the Yale Graduate School. She has also received more than fifty honorary degrees.

Bibliography

Feldman, Linda. "Norton Biography." In *Christian Science Monitor,* Mar. 31, 1992.

Robert Fay

Nossa Senhora Aparecida

Patron saint of Brazil, an invocation of the Virgin Mary who is represented as black.

The devotion to the Virgin Mary, the mother of Jesus Christ, has for centuries been common in Catholicism and arrived in Latin America with the first Portuguese and Spanish conquerors in the sixteenth century. An image of the Virgin Mary, Nossa Senhora da Esperança, was present in the ship that took Pedro Álvares Cabral and the first Europeans to BRAZIL in 1500. Another image popular in PORTUGAL, that of Nossa Senhora da Glória, is believed to have been taken to Brazil in 1503.

In the colonial period that followed, variations of the devotion to the Virgin Mary spread throughout Brazil. Slaves of African descent were particularly devoted to Our Lady of the Rosary and Our Lady of Lampadosa, while those of mixed blood preferred Our Lady of Mercy. In the state of BAHIA, where a majority of the population is of African descent and African religious practices have historically been strongest, the preference is for Our Lady of the Conception and Our Lady of Candeias. Both of these invocations of the Virgin Mary have been associated with certain *orixás* of the Afro-Brazilian religion of CANDOMBLÉ.

Although at first part of European colonialism, Catholicism was appropriated in different ways by the less powerful, and in the process was often transformed into a new practice that can only be called partially European. In sixteenth-century MEXICO, for instance, the devotion to Our Lady of Guadalupe combined Spanish Catholic practices with indigenous religious traditions. The Virgin of Guadalupe, who is believed to have appeared to the Indian Juan Diego in 1531, has since been represented with dark skin and indigenous features.

In Brazil, the lesser-known image of Our Lady of Brazil also has indigenous features. Yet in a country with such a significant population of African descent it should not come as a surprise that the patron saint would be represented with black skin. The invocation of Our Lady of Aparecida dates from the eighteenth century. In 1717, three fishermen, Domingos Garcia, João Alves, and Filipe Pedroso, were fishing in the Paraíba River near the town of Itaguaçu in the state of São Paulo. After little success, they threw their net into the river and upon withdrawing it found a sculpture of the Virgin Mary with its head missing. After a second attempt they found the image's head, and for the remainder of the day the fishermen caught an extraordinary number of fish.

The sculpture they found was a black image of the Virgin. It had most likely originally been painted in colors, but the time under water had caused its color to darken, an effect that would be enhanced by the smoke from candles in the first oratories where the image was housed.

More than ten years after its discovery, a small chapel was built for the image. Stories about extraordinary events involving the image circulated and drew increasingly larger crowds to pray at the site. A larger chapel was built in 1743, and in 1930 Pope Pius XI declared Our Lady of Aparecida the patron saint of Brazil. The image, and the church that houses it, are currently the objects of great devotion, and some seven million pilgrims visit the icon every year. The climax of these pilgrimages occurs on October 12, when more than 200,000 pilgrims descend on the city of Aparecida.

However, Our Lady of Aparecida is not the preferred object of devotion of black Brazilians. Historically, saints such as Saint Benedict, Saint Efigênia, Saint Onofre, Saint Gonçalo, and Saint Anthony of Catagerona, all of whom have been represented in traditional hagiography as black or of mixed race, have been more popular among Brazilians of African descent. Among the invocations of the Virgin, the white Our Lady of the Rosary has been preferred.

See also Religions, African, in Brazil.

Marcos Natalí

Nossa Senhora do Rosário

Catholic invocation of the Virgin Mary and the patron saint of Brazilian blacks.

The devotion to Nossa Senhora do Rosário (Our Lady of the Rosary) began in France in the thirteenth century, when Saint Dominick claimed the Virgin Mary had appeared to him and demonstrated a new form of prayer: the rosary. In the following centuries, the devotion gained popularity, especially in the Iberian Peninsula. A large number of *irmandades* (brotherhoods), Catholic associations providing various forms of support for its members and performing charitable deeds, were formed in connection to this invocation of the Virgin Mary.

African slaves taken to the Portuguese colony of BRAZIL worshiped a number of Catholic saints, with particular preference for saints of African origin such as Saint Benedict. There is disagreement, however, over the reasons for the special devotion of Africans in Brazil to Our Lady of the Rosary. The fact that many Africans from Angola and the Congo might have already been familiar with Our Lady of the Rosary from interactions with Portuguese missionaries in their homelands could have affected the rapid spread of the invocation among slaves in Brazil.

Since colonial times, people of African descent, whether slave or free, have used the brotherhoods devoted to Our Lady of the Rosary to form their own independent associations. These were some of the first collective black organizations in Brazil, some founded as early as 1522. The irmandades of Our Lady of the Rosary were usually comprised entirely of blacks, and most declared explicitly that the leader should be black as well. During slavery, they were the only legal black organizations.

The irmandades represented, in effect, a relatively autonomous religious sphere that unavoidably acquired political significance. In 1683 a group of these organizations asked the Portuguese king to grant the freedom of all slaves in Brazil. When the king did not meet the demand, many irmandades gathered funds to purchase the freedom of slaves and guaranteed a network of support for blacks. Although the adoption of Catholicism did imply a distancing, to different degrees, from African religions, which had by this time been prohibited, the irmandades also played a fundamental role in maintaining African traditions of music and dance. The yearly festivals held by the irmandades in honor of their patron saints have for centuries involved the staging of elaborate traditional black dances and processions known as *reisados* and *congadas*.

During the twentieth century, Our Lady of the Rosary became the patron saint of Afro-Brazilians. In 1980 more than 115 parishes were dedicated to her in Brazil, more than to the country's official patron saint. Among the most beautiful are those in the former mining town of Ouro Preto, in the state of MINAS GERAIS, and the church of Nossa Senhora do Rosário dos Homens Pretos do Alto da Cruz, an important center for Brazil's black irmandades.

See also Music, African; Religions, African, in Brazil.

Marcos Natalí

Notes on Africa in Greek Mythology

References to sub-Saharan Africans in ancient Greek mythology and literature.

In Greek mythology and literature the ancient Ethiopians figure prominently. The name *Ethiopian* comes from the Greek word *Aithiopes*, meaning "burnt-faced." Cepheus was the king of the Ethiopians, and Cassiopeia was his queen. She thought herself more beautiful than even the sea-nymphs, the Nereids. Andromeda, Cassiopeia's daughter, was chained to a rock to be eaten by a sea monster sent by the god Poseidon as a punishment for her mother's vanity. The hero Perseus rescued Andromeda and married her.

When Cassiopeia died, she was transformed into the constellation of the same name. The great English poet John Milton in the seventeenth century memorialized her in "Il Penseroso."

But hail thou Goddess, sage, and holy,
Hail divinest Melancholy,
Whose saintly visage is too bright
To hit the sense of human sight,
And therefore, to our weaker view,
O'er laid with black staid Wisdom's hue;
Black, but such as in esteem,
Prince Memnon's sister might beseem,
Or that starred Ethiop queen [Cassiopeia] that strove
To set her beauties praise above
The sea-nymphs and their powers offended.

Milton's poem alludes to Memnon, a king of Ethiopia who fought in the Trojan War. He was the son of Eos, the goddess of the dawn, and Tithonous, a son of Laomedon. Laomedon was the king of Troy, who was succeeded by his son Priam. Memnon brought his troops to aid his uncle, King Priam, in the war. The Greek warrior Achilles killed Memnon in battle. Memnon's brothers, the Winds, carried his body to the upper reaches of the Esepus River in Paphlagonia (in what is now Turkey). Thomas Bulfinch, in his book *Age of Fable,* recounts that "In the evening Aurora [Eos] came, accompanied by the Hours and the Pleiad[e]s, and wept and lamented for her son. Night spread the heaven with the clouds, all nature mourned for the offspring of the Dawn." Eos's tears over the death of her son are the morning dew. Phineus, Andromedas's original fiancé, was also Ethiopian. He was slain by Perseus. In the *Iliad* and the *Odyssey,* the ancient Greek poet Homer refers to the deep affection of most of the gods for the Ethiopians, the gods' admiration for the piety of the Ethiopians, and the quality of the sacrifices made by the Ethiopians.

Other references to Africans and Africa also appear in Greek mythology and literature. The Greeks thought that the Pygmies lived in Africa near the source of the NILE. The modern English word PYGMY comes from the Ancient Greek word *pygmaios,* which means "dwarf." In North Africa, Perseus used the severed head of Medusa to change Atlas, the Titan who held up the sky, into Mount Atlas.

Notorious B.I.G. ("Biggie Smalls")

1972–1997

African American rap artist.

Notorious B.I.G. was born Christopher Wallace in New York City. His debut album, *Ready to Die,* appeared on SEAN "P. DIDDY" COMBS's Bad Boy Entertainment music label in 1995. The record was a critical and commercial success, exhibiting the rapper's lyrical talents through a series of taut, first-person narratives chronicling life as a hustler on the streets of NEW YORK's Bedford-Stuyvesant neighborhood. The grim humor of B.I.G.'s lyrics emphasized the claustrophobia of his ghetto universe. On "Warning," he raps, "There's gonna be a lot of slow singing / and flower bringing / If my burglar alarm starts ringing." Songs like "Suicidal Thoughts" and "Things Done Changed" helped create one of "gangsta rap's" most sophisticated personas, a strange brew of subdued self-loathing and energetic violence. In B.I.G.'s world, the sexual boasting typical of RAP and HIP-HOP became an occasion for self-parody, as on "#!*@ Me (Interlude)," a skit describing a sexual encounter complicated by the rapper's prodigious girth.

Soon after the success of his debut album, B.I.G. found himself immersed in a simmering feud with LOS ANGELES gangsta rap label Death Row Records in a manifestation of hip-hop's growing coastal animosity. Death Row star TUPAC SHAKUR claimed that B.I.G. and Combs were behind a 1994 robbery in which Shakur was shot five times in the chest. The violent climate turned fatal in September 1996, when Shakur was murdered in a mysterious Las Vegas drive-by shooting; some suggested that the Bad Boy Entertainment crew was involved. Soon after, in March 1997, Notorious B.I.G. was gunned down while making an appearance in Los Angeles.

B.I.G.'s posthumously released double album, *Life After Death* (1997), topped the *Billboard* album charts and sold more than seven million copies, thanks to radio-friendly songs like "Mo Money Mo Problems" and "Hypnotize." Death has only enhanced B.I.G.'s legend: Sean "P. Diddy" Combs's "I'll Be Missing You," a tribute to his fallen friend, was one of the best-selling singles of 1997.

Andrew Du Bois

Nottingham and Notting Hill Riots of 1958

First riots involving white-on-black violence in Great Britain after large-scale immigration of West Indians to that nation began in 1948.

Between August 23 and September 2, 1958, after a summer of isolated, racially charged incidents between whites and blacks in GREAT BRITAIN's cities, whites attacked West Indians and their properties in the city of Nottingham in the English Midlands and in London's Notting Hill neighborhood. White working-class teenagers committed most of the violence in both riots. But a wider population was also involved, specifically, adult whites who lived at the edge of poverty and felt that West Indian immigrants threatened their jobs.

Beginning in 1948, the British government and various employers had welcomed West Indians to Great Britain as workers. As the number of immigrants grew, however, many white British, fearing for their own jobs, came to resent this new population. Some whites joined fascist and racist groups such as Oswald Moseley's Union Movement, which called for the deportation of West Indians. In this hostile environment, West Indians faced discrimination that left them unemployed, with inadequate or overcrowded housing, and without places to socialize.

Blacks complained of harassment in the St. Ann's district of Nottingham, especially during the summer of 1958. Late on Saturday, August 23, these tensions exploded. That night, a black man allegedly hassled a white woman in a pub. A fight broke out between whites and blacks and spilled into the street. After this altercation, more than 1,000 whites attacked blacks with sticks, bricks, and stones. Some blacks retaliated, but most, shocked and frightened, hid in their homes. Several people suffered serious injuries. Sporadic events occurred the next day; by Monday the riot had subsided.

The following weekend, whites gathered again to attack West Indians, but most blacks stayed indoors. The crowd turned on itself and on the police, whom many of these whites blamed for protecting the West Indians rather than "their own." The next weekend, on September 6, a crowd of 200 whites attacked the houses of blacks.

A parallel series of violent incidents occurred in London. On August 23, the same day that violence broke out in Nottingham, police apprehended nine white youths cruising the streets of London's Notting Hill neighborhood "nigger hunting," a practice in which whites, usually teenagers, would search for and attack individual blacks. In Notting Hill a week later, on August 30, an argument between a West Indian man and his white wife drew the attention of a group of white men, who proceeded to attack some of the man's friends. The next day these same white men assaulted the woman with milk bottles and other objects and called her a "nigger lover"; police intervened to protect her. But by this time, a white crowd was already rioting. The police responded by escorting most of the black residents out of the area. The next day, a group of one hundred white teenagers, who were soon joined by 300 others, gathered and attacked police officers and the few black individuals they could find.

The worst rioting in Notting Hill occurred on the following day, September 1. Although the previous conflict had remained local, news had since spread, and whites across London went to Notting Hill to "nigger hunt." Blacks also gathered to support their friends and relatives. Whites chased and attacked blacks, set their houses ablaze, and smashed store windows. Most blacks stayed indoors, but some organized to defend themselves. Collecting an arsenal of knives, bottles, glass, and other makeshift weapons, they retaliated against the whites. Police arrested three white men and eight black, including Baron Baker and Michael de Freitas, who went on to become activists for racial equality.

Police regained control the following day, and within a couple of weeks a tense calm had returned. Officers arrested more than one hundred people during the riots, over two-thirds of whom were white. Judges reprimanded them with fines or prison sentences. Despite the threat of punishment, isolated racial incidents continued to occur in London and other cities.

After the riots, conservative parliamentarian Cyril Osborne led a legal battle for restricted immigration. He and other lawmakers suggested the deportation of West Indians as the solution to racial violence. In 1962 the government passed the Immigration Act, which restricted West Indian immigration. Others called for campaigns to alleviate racism in British society, and in 1965 the government instituted a Race Relations Act to fight discrimination, though many liberals and blacks claim the act was largely ineffective.

Sadly, the events of 1958 were part of a long history of racial violence in Britain, and late into the twentieth century race riots continued to erupt in British cities.

See also Brixton Riots; Great Britain Riots of 1985.

Bibliography

Pilkington, Edward. *Beyond the Mother Country: West Indians and the Notting Hill White Riots.* Tauris & Co., 1988.

Wikendon, James. *Colour in Britain.* Oxford University Press, 1958.

Leyla Keough

Notting Hill Carnival

Annual outdoor celebration of British black culture that has grown to be one of the largest street festivals in all of Europe.

The Notting Hill Carnival is the largest and most prominent public event in GREAT BRITAIN organized by and primarily for the black community. The Carnival has grown from a small West Indian community event to a celebration of multicultural London.

The Notting Hill Carnival takes its inspiration from Carnival of TRINIDAD. Trinidadian immigrants began celebrating Carnival in London during the 1950s. In Notting Hill, the Carnival first took place as a summer street parade in 1965. In the following years, other West Indians joined Trinidadians in Notting Hill for one collective event. This neighborhood, home to many black Britons, was the site of the first widely publicized white-on-black violence in Great Britain in 1958, so the Carnival carried special significance as an effort to reclaim the streets of the neighborhood for a peaceful black celebration.

At the first official Carnival in 1965, one steel drum band played and 500 people attended. The festival grew in the late 1960s. With some government funding, participants were able to better organize the Carnival and offer prizes in band contests and costume competitions. The five official "disciplines" of Carnival are the steel drum bands, CALYPSO performers, mas (masquerade) bands, mobile sound systems, and static sound systems. Each mas band focuses on a specific theme, and preparations for costumes often begin months in advance. Sometimes the themes are political, at other times they reflect the West Indians' African heritage. Mas bands are usually led by mobile sound systems on trucks called "Soca [a fusion of Soul and Calypso] on the move." The static sound systems stay on the perimeter of the parade route and usually play reggae, techno, and jungle (drum and bass) music. Each discipline has a seat on the official Carnival board. The disciplines represent the basic elements of the Carnival, but the festival is far from formal.

In fact, the spontaneity that reigns during the festival has sometimes resulted in clashes when the police have attempted to restrain revelers and establish order, often with severe methods. In the 1970s, as tension between blacks and whites in Great Britain was on the rise, the Carnival became a site of confrontation. Riots occurred at the Carnivals of 1976, 1979, and 1989. Over-policing was a problem: in 1979, 10,000 police (half of the entire London police force) were present at the Carnival. Since one of the Carnival's purposes was to reclaim the streets for blacks, many participants resented heavy-handed and sometimes brutal efforts by police to assert control. After each Carnival during this era, delicate negotiations took place when police and some conservative white residents of Notting Hill asked that the Carnival be moved to another outdoor area, to an indoor arena, or cancelled altogether.

Despite these troubles, the Carnival has survived, and as it has won greater acceptance among British whites, the event has become less violent. What began as a West Indian event is now embraced by all of London. In 1997 close to two million people, including visitors from all over the world, crowded the streets for the celebration.

See also Carnivals in Latin America and the Caribbean; Music, Afro-Caribbean Secular; Nottingham and Notting Hill Riots of 1958.

Bibliography
Owusu, Kwesi, and Jacob Ross. *Behind the Masquerade: The Story of Notting Hill Carnival.* Arts Media Group, 1984.

Leyla Keough

Nouakchott, Mauritania

The largest city and capital of Mauritania.

Nouakchott is one of Africa's younger capital cities. Positioned halfway between St. Louis, in Senegal, and Nouadhibou, in northern Mauritania, Nouakchott sits slightly inland from the Atlantic coast. It was originally a small fishing village frequented by desert traders traveling northward from Dakar, and became the capital of Mauritania in 1959. Colonial Mauritania had previously been governed from St. Louis, and did not have a separate capital. As independence approached in the 1950s, however, French and Mauritanian officials debated which of the colony's few towns, most of which were located in the remote interior or along the Moor-dominated northern coast, would be a suitable national capital. After much deliberation, Mauritania's most prominent politician, Moktar Ould Daddah, and his advisers chose the centrally positioned Nouakchott, aiming to bridge the divide between the country's southern and northern regions. The city's construction, carefully planned to accommodate the national government and a population of 15,000, began in early 1958 and was completed by Mauritanian independence in November 1960.

During the first years of independence, Nouakchott remained a fairly small town, inhabited primarily by civil servants. But employment-seeking migrants soon flooded in, and by 1969 the city's population exceeded its expected size. High rates of urban migration continued throughout the 1970s, especially after a series of droughts forced thousands of farmers and nomads from the interior into Nouakchott, where they took up residence in makeshift shanties on the edge of town. Nouakchott had 661,400 residents in 2003, nearly one quarter of the country's population. Although the 1986 completion of the Friendship Port brought an influx of business, Nouakchott's infrastructure is sorely inadequate relative to the population's demand for water, housing, and other services. The city also faces the unusual problem of encroaching sand dunes. Construction is currently in progress on a Nouadhibou to Nouakchott road that will be part of a larger trans-Saharan highway stretching from Morocco to Lagos, Nigeria.

See also Drought and Desertification.

Bibliography
Pazzanita, Anthony. *Historical Dictionary of Mauritania.* Scarecrow Press, 1996.

Pitte, Jean-Robert. *Nouakchott, Capitale de la Mauritanie.* Universite de Paris-Sorbonne, 1977.

Elizabeth Heath

Ntare II

?–1852

Considered the first monarch of modern Burundi.

Although fifth in a line of Burundian kings, Ntare II is widely regarded as the first monarch of the nation, because it was during his reign that the kingdom expanded to the borders of present-day Burundi. Born Rugaamba, he ascended the throne upon the death of his father, Mwambutswa I, and took the name Ntare, meaning "skin of the lion."

Ntare II conquered outlying chieftainships until his own kingdom included parts of present-day Rwanda and Tanzania, establishing himself in history as one of Burundi's most powerful kings. Although the spoils of his victories went to his sons, several of them ultimately rebelled. The families of these rebellious sons became known as the Batare clan, and the family of Ntare II's successor son, Gisabo Mwezi IV, became known as the Bezi. Conflicts between the two clans influenced Burundian politics long before the conflicts between the Hutu and Tutsi.

Eric Young

Nuba

Ethnic group of south-central Sudan.

The Nuba, numbering somewhat over one million people, inhabit a mountainous area in the southern part of Kordofan Province in Sudan. They are distantly related to the peoples of southern Sudan, and they represent a minority in the predominantly Arab province of Kordofan. The languages of the Nuba belong to the Kordofanian group, a distant branch of the Niger-Congo family, though most Nuba also speak Arabic.

It appears that the Nuba retreated into the mountains to flee persistent slave raiding by Baggara and Kababish Arabs beginning in the sixteenth century. In their mountainous environment the Nuba practiced intensive agriculture, employing terraced fields, manure-based fertilizers, and irrigation systems in order to maximize their production of millet, sorghum, cotton, onions, sesame, and a variety of vegetables. During the period of the Anglo-Egyptian Condominium, they began growing peanuts, peppers, and corn.

Interesting conclusions may be drawn from an overview of gender and age distinctions in Nuba society. Both men and women do farm work, though men are responsible for clearing the land and herding livestock. Southern Nuba trace descent matrilineally, while central and northern Nuba families are patrilineal, perhaps as a result of their greater interaction with patrilineal Arab communities. Unlike neighboring groups the Nuba have never practiced either male or female circumcision. Traditionally, headmen and rain priests exercised relatively weak authority within Nuba communities. Age sets, cohorts of similar age who undergo initiation together and share an age-based status, were an important source of social authority.

Until the intensification of the Sudanese Civil War in the 1980s most Nuba lived in small, kin-related villages. During the war their minority status has made them especially vulnerable to attacks by the Sudanese military, and many Nuba have sought refuge in the Khartoum metropolitan area.

Robert Baum

Nubia

Historical region encompassing present-day southern Egypt and northern Sudan.

What was Nubia? This has always been a controversial question. The controversy stems from the difficulties determining the origin of the name Nubia, when Nubia first appeared in history, and its geographical limits. There is general agreement among most scholars that the name derives from *nob,* the Nubian word for gold, and is linked to the importance of gold to the Nubians.

However, recent research suggests other possibilities. The modern Nubian word *kiji* means "fertile land, dark gray mud, silt, or black land"; the sound of this word is near to the Egyptian name Kish or Kush, referring to the land south of Egypt. It is believed that the name Kush also meant "the land of dark silt" or "the black land." This was the Egyptian name for Nubia. But what did the Kushites call their land?

We know from modern and recent analogies that peoples do not always adopt the name attributed to them by others. Therefore it is likely that the Egyptian's Kushites had their own name for their home, which must have had the same meaning as Kush: the black land. It was Nubia, the black land, the Sudan of today, which is a straightforward Arabic translation: *sûd* is the plural form of *aswad,* meaning "black"; *ān* means "of the"; thus, Sudan means "of the blacks." In modern Nubian, *nugud* means "black." So do *nuger, nugur,* and *nub.* This suggests that Kush, Nubia, and Sudan all mean the same thing, the "black land" and/or the "land of the blacks."

It is evident, both historically and archaeologically, that Nubia's boundaries have fluctuated over time. In other words, there were times when Nubian rule and cultural influence were limited to lower and middle Nubia, in the Sudanese-Egyptian borderlands. At other times, Nubia covered all of present-day northern Sudan, while Nubian rule extended to even greater territory.

However, in modern times Nubia typically refers to the region along the Nile between the first cataract (just south of Aswân in Egypt) and present-day Ed Debba in Sudan, where Nubian speakers live today. The region borders the Nubian Desert to the east and Libyan Desert to the west. Land suitable for farming is confined to scattered plots along the riverbanks. Modern Nubians live in the region's many *irki* (villages or communities), which are distributed unevenly on both sides of the Nile and on islands within the course of the river wherever there is land suitable for cultivation.

From this description it is obvious that Nubia is not rich in resources. It is surprising then that, as a result of many factors, Nubia was subject to repeated raids and domination by its neighbors, especially Egypt to the north. First, Egypt tried to expand its authority over Nubia to secure its southern frontier. Second, Egyptians greatly desired Nubian natural resources, in the form of gold, copper, diorite stones used to build royal monuments, and African animal products. Third, the Egyptians sought African slaves for many purposes.

The trade in natural resources and slaves between Egypt and the African interior, together with the fertile riverine ecology of the Nile and its banks, encouraged settlement in Nubia from early times. And despite the scarcity of land for cultivation, agricultural activities were and still are the basis of the subsistence economy of most Nubians. To compensate for this limitation, the Nubians adopted intensive rather than extensive cultivation. Moreover, in recent years the Nubian economy has increasingly relied on income from Nubians working outside their country, particularly in the Middle East.

Nubia has never been the exclusive domain of any one group of people. Foreign conquerors, alien merchants and adventurers, and both friendly and hostile nomads have always interacted with and settled among the indigenous peasant population of Nubia and have contributed significantly to its cultural development. Hence the present population is the product of a long and fairly continuous mingling of the ancient inhabitants with newcomers from a variety of places.

In the seventh century, Arabs settled in Nubia and intermarried with the indigenous population. During the sixteenth century the Ottoman Sultan Salim sent garrisons into Nubia, comprised largely of soldiers from Bosnia, Circassia, Hungary, and the Kurdish region. They were stationed at Aswān, Gasr Ibrim, and Sai to protect Egypt's southern borders. Their descendants (known as *al-Kushaf*), born of Nubian women and speaking only the Nubian language, regarded themselves as Bosnians or Turks rather than Nubians and claimed special privileges on this basis as late as the nineteenth century. Consequently, one can say that Nubian society now consists of a mixture of indigenous as well as Arab and Turkish elements.

Other groups of non-Nubians inhabit the area. They are small in number and made up of descendants of slaves, nomadic, and semi-nomadic groups. Descendants of slaves who have been living with Nubians for generations and are accustomed to their ways of life can be regarded culturally as Nubians. They work mainly in domestic service and farming. Other non-Nubians in the region include Arab ethnic groups, mainly Bisharia and Gararish, who raise camels. They play an important role in the Nubian economy and society. During the nineteenth and early twentieth centuries Arab camel drivers provided the only means of transporting heavy loads, but during the late twentieth century the Arabs have been obliged to adopt a settled life beside the Nile and have begun to cultivate small plots leased from the Nubians. They have no land rights, and although they use the Nubian language to communicate with Nubians, they are linguistically and culturally distinct from them. This present-day ethnic diversity reflects Nubia's ancient history as a cultural crossroads.

See also Egypt, Ancient Kingdom of.

Ali Osman Mohammad Salih

Nubian

Primary ethnic group of the middle Nile Valley from Aswân in Egypt to the region of Dongola in northern Sudan.

Archaeological evidence suggests that hunters and gatherers occupied the middle NILE region by the Mesolithic period, over 10,000 years ago. Farming, both of Egyptian and Sudanic crops, became important in the region by 3000 B.C.E. When pharaonic EGYPT occupied NUBIA between 1970 and 1520 B.C.E., Egyptian culture increasingly influenced Nubia. Nubia regained its independence in the eleventh century B.C.E. A new Nubian kingdom, centered at Napata, adopted an Egyptian model of the monarchy, including royal brother-sister marriages. In 742 B.C.E. Pianchi, king of Napata, conquered Egypt and founded the Twenty-Fifth Dynasty, which ruled Egypt for nearly a century. Soon after the conquest, the Nubian capital shifted to Meroe. The Meroe kingdom developed its own form of writing as well as a technologically sophisticated IRON industry. Around 350 C.E., the Ethiopian kingdom of AKSUM invaded the Meroe and defeated its forces.

During a long period of political instability in Nubia, Coptic Christianity, similar to the Christianity practiced in Egypt and ETHIOPIA, became an important influence in the region. By the sixth century two small states, Makuria and Alwa, dominated the region. The Muslim conquest of Egypt in 639 C.E. isolated Christian Nubia from most of the Christian world, but the Nubian states were able to resist the Arab armies. Gradually, Islam became important and intermarriage between Nubians and Arabs became common. By the end of the fifteenth century an Arab confederacy had conquered the Nubian states, which thereafter remained overwhelmingly Muslim. However, unlike their neighbors in the Nile Valley to the south, the Nubians resisted complete Arabization and maintained their Nilo-Saharan languages and elements of their own culture. In the nineteenth century Ottoman-ruled Egypt conquered Nubia until the MAHDIST STATE assumed control during the 1880s. In 1898 southern Nubia became a part of the Anglo-Egyptian Sudan, while the north was incorporated into Egypt.

Beginning in 1897, successive dams built at Aswān by the British displaced Nubians from their homeland. Many relocated to Egyptian cities. During the 1960s, the construction of the new ASWAN HIGH DAM flooded a large part of the Nubian homeland and forced 100,000 Nubians to seek refuge around Aswân in Egypt and in the cities of Sudan, including KHARTOUM. The forced relocation of the Nubians to Arabic-speaking regions created a shared Nubian ethnic identity, whereas previously linguistic and regional distinctions had divided Nubians. On the other hand, relocation had led to the gradual disappearance of the ancient Nubian languages. Today, more and more Nubians communicate in Arabic. The Nubians number around one million people, with about half of them located in Egypt and the other half in Sudan.

See also Alexandria, Egypt; Egypt, Ancient Kingdom of; Ethiopian Orthodox Church.

Robert Baum

Nuer

Major ethnic group of southern Sudan.

Until the Sudanese Civil War intensified in the 1980s, most Nuer occupied an area of swamps and low-lying plains from the White NILE RIVER eastward to the Ethiopian escarpment, and relied on cattle keeping as their primary economic activity.

Before the colonial conquest, the Nuer did not form states or have recognized paramount chiefs. Instead, councils of village elders and religious specialists called leopard-skin priests exercised primary authority. Leopard-skin priests served as arbiters of feuds between Nuer clans and villages. Their homes served as a sanctuary for those fleeing possible retribution from rival clans. They had the power to curse those who refused to attempt to resolve a dispute in good faith. For ordinary decision-making, the Nuer convened community assemblies in order to reach a consensus. Under Anglo-Egyptian COLONIAL RULE (1898–1956), government officials appointed a series of local "chiefs," but the Nuer did not recognize their legitimacy.

Since they inhabited the Sudd, the largest swamp in the world, and the surrounding plains, the Nuer had to develop a complex mode of adaptation to a difficult environment. Before warfare and government population control interfered, Nuer inhabited small, kin-related villages along narrow ridges of high ground during the rainy season. After the rains ended, the Nuer left these settlements and moved with their herds across the rich pasturage land that emerged alongside the receding floodwaters. By the peak of the dry season, they arrived with their cattle to graze in the permanent river valleys of Nuerland. During the rainy season, women planted a crop of MILLET. Men hunted and fished and controlled cattle keeping, the dominant economic activity. Cattle provided most necessities of Nuer material culture. Not only did the Nuer rely on cattle as a source of meat and milk, but they also used the skin, bones, and internal organs of cattle for beds, tools, musical instruments, and weapons. They used cow dung for cooking fuel and for plastering their homes. The sacrifice of cattle played an important role in most Nuer rites of passage, birth, initiation, marriage, and death. During male initiation young men received an "ox-name" to mark their entrance into the ranks of cattle owners.

Nuer religion centered on a supreme being, known as Kwoth Nhial, who was the source of all life. The Nuer associated lesser spirits, also known as kwoth, with the celestial realm (spirits of the above) or with the earthly realm (spirits of the below). All the powers of lesser spirits originated with Kwoth Nhial. This religious category of lesser spirits became a major source of innovation in Nuer religion in the nineteenth and twentieth centuries. The Nuer assimilated lesser deities of the DINKA and other neighboring peoples, even the authority of the Mahdi (an Islamic reformer) and Jesus, into their religion as spirits of the above.

At the time that the Ottoman government of EGYPT (the Turkiyya) established its first contacts with the Nuer, in 1841, Dinka and AZANDE expansion was driving the Nuer eastward. The slave raiding and warfare of the mid- to late nineteenth century accelerated that process. It also produced a new type of Nuer leader, the prophet, who claimed direct revelation from spirits of the above. Prophets became important military and spiritual leaders at a time of endemic warfare. The most famous of these was Ngundeng. His son, Gwek, led Nuer opposition to the British in the early twentieth century. The Nuer resisted British occupation until the 1930s, when the British had to use airplanes and machine guns to subdue them. By 1956 the Nuer had joined the armed struggle for southern Sudanese autonomy, within a Sudanese federal state, or independence. They continue to participate in the Sudanese Civil War, both as a source of soldiers for the secessionist movement and as victims of raids by government forces. Large numbers of Nuer have been forced from their homelands to seek protection in the large refugee camps in the relatively peaceful areas surrounding the capital of KHARTOUM. The estimated population of the Nuer is approximately one million.

See also Hunting in Africa.

Robert Baum

Nuestra Raza

Longest running black Uruguayan newspaper; published from 1917 to 1948.

As the flagship of an active black Uruguayan press that began in the nineteenth century with such journals as *La Conservación* and *La Propaganda*, and continues today with *Mundo Afro*, *Nuestra Raza* provided an important outlet for social and cultural black organizations of the time. It published poetry, editorials, news by and about black Uruguayans, and expressed solidarity with international Pan-African movements. In addition, the journal supported black candidates for office, an art and culture program, and even called for a black university. Articles in *Nuestra Raza* tended to emphasize intellectual accomplishments and included frequent profiles of prominent national and international figures, such as Americans GEORGE WASHINGTON CARVER, LANGSTON HUGHES, BOOKER T. WASHINGTON, Cuban NICHOLÁS GUILLÉN, and Brazilian JOAQUIM MARIA MACHADO DE ASSIS.

Many of its editors and contributors, such as PILAR BARRIOS and his brother Ventura, were important coordinators of the first black political party in Uruguay, the *Partido Autóctono Negro*. Maruja Pereira, Pilar Barrios's wife, organized a sister group called the *Comité de Mujeres Negras por la paz y contra el fascismo*. Manuel Villa, another influential journalist, founded *Sociedad Amigos de Africa* (Association of Friends of Africa). Writer Elemo Cabral, also a contributor to *Nuestra Raza*, maintained an archive of his literary production, which his granddaughter, poet and essayist, Cristina Rodríguez Cabral, would later draw from to write a history of Afro-Uruguayan literature.

One of the key goals of *Nuestra Raza*, which becomes apparent in the social activism of its contributors, was to raise black consciousness and to encourage opposition to the ironic social double bind of discrimination and invisibility. Blacks were often conceptualized in the popular press as outsiders. *Nuestra Raza* decried "perpetual Africanization" by creating a public voice that was both black and Uruguayan. By publishing many of the first poems, stories and plays of Afro-Uruguayans, such as Pilar Barrios, VIRGINIA BRINDIS DE SALAS, and Juan Julio Arrascaeta, the editors hoped to foster lively intellectual and cultural debates within the community that would successfully counter racial stereotypes.

See also Black Journalism in Latin America and the Caribbean; Literature, Black, in Spanish America; Pan-Africanism and Afro-Latin Americans; Press, Black in Latin America and the Caribbean.

Bibliography

Jackson, Richard. *Black Writers in Latin America.* University of New Mexico Press, 1979.

Young, Caroll. "The New Voices of Afro-Uruguay." *Afro-Hispanic Review*, Spring 1995.

Nueva Trova

Cuban protest music of the 1960s and 1970s.

Almost all Cuban folkloric and popular music has components, particularly rhythmic ones, that were brought from Africa during the conquest of America, either directly or through SPAIN, which itself had been influenced by African culture. Of course, the extent of this presence varies, from strongly African genres such as RUMBA to genres with less apparent vestiges, like the Cuban *canción* (song). The Nueva Trova (the New Song) grows out of the canción tradition, drawing influence from Afro-Cuban music, jazz, rock, and the New Song Movement from the rest of Latin America.

The first Encuentro de la Canción Protesta (Meeting on the Protest Song) took place in Havana in 1967, hosted by the Casa de las Americas, a cultural institution created by the Cuban revolutionary government of 1959. Young musicians and singers from sixteen countries were present. Some of them were already known, such as Daniel Viqlietti from URUGUAY. Also attending were some young Cuban artists who had created songs in a style completely different from the one prevailing in Cuba at that time.

After the meeting, these young songwriters continued to meet and play at Casa de las Américas and at schools, work centers, and other meeting places. They made contact with other musicians throughout Cuba, not just Havana. In February 1968 they held their first concert at Casa de Las Américas, under the name Centro de la Canción Protesta (Protest Song Center). Leading figures were Silvio Rodríguez (b. 1946, San Antonio de los Baños), PABLO MILANÉS (b. 1943, Bayamo), and Noel Nicola (b. 1946, Havana). Soon other names began to emerge as well, such as Amaury Pérez (b. 1953, Havana) and Sara González (b. 1951, Havana). In 1969 they were all invited to join the Instituto Cubano de Arte e Industria Cinematográfica (Cuban Institute for Cinematic Arts and Industry, or ICAIC) to produce music for documentaries and films.

The young songwriters encountered opposition from traditional musicians and even from some sectors of the government. Their music was too new and too different. Fortunately, under the auspices of the Young Communists Union, the first meeting of Jóvenes Trovadores (Young Troubadours) took place in Manzanillo in November 1972. In the group's final declaration, they changed their name to Movimiento de la Nueva Trova (New Song Movement). They did this for two reasons. First, unlike protest song movements in other countries, which were directed to a great extent against their own governments, Cuba's movement stood against the United States and other developed countries. Moreover, its scope was broader, expressing new views about everyday life, mainly love. Second, these new singer-songwriters believed themselves to be the followers of and heirs to the original trova creators, who in the late nineteenth century, in Oriente province, developed the canción, the bolero, and other forms of Cuban music. The new name thus encompassed political songs, like "Si el poeta eres tú" (If you are the poet), dedicated to Che Guevara, and lyrical songs like "Unicornio azul" (The blue unicorn).

Initially, these artists used only a guitar accompaniment. The time spent at the ICAIC by some leaders of the movement, however, led to a more complex instrumentation, with keyboards, percussion, and other instruments. The emphasis on musical traditions varies within the group. Some figures, such as Silvio Rodríguez, have drawn on the whole gamut of modern pop music, including not only Cuban genres but also rock, ballads, and RHYTHM AND BLUES. Others, like Nicola and Milanés, are more centered on Afro-Cuban rhythms, such as SON, rumba, and *guaguancó*.

The Nueva Trova soon attracted other groups, such as Las Cañas, Moncada, and Manguaré, imparting a broader spectrum of musical styles and traditions. During the 1970s and 1980s, leading figures like Rodríguez, Milanés, González, Pérez, and a few others enjoyed success in Cuba, performed extensively throughout Europe and Latin America, and recorded dozens of albums. But the movement as such dwindled and almost disappeared. Although the major figures continued to dominate, a few newcomers were able to achieve moderate recognition.

Significantly, some of the new artists are much more critical of the Cuban Revolution. Two of them are Pedro Luis Ferrer, whose music is almost completely based on Afro-Cuban genres, and Carlos Varela. Both have been banned at times by the Cuban government.

Important artists have emerged from the Nueva Trova movement, such as the Gema and Pavel duet, who spend most of their time in Spain. Lost is the optimism of the first days of the Trova; the new troveros are pessimistic, almost neurotic, with great sensitivity and a yearning for the past. Gema and Pavel have helped a group of even younger *trovadores* who call themselves "La Habana Oculta" (Hidden Havana), a name that reflects their dissatisfaction with the situation in Cuba. All these new trovadores, including Gema and Pavel, tend to draw more on Afro-Cuban music than did their predecessors. There is also a *"Trova cubana en el exilio"* (Cuban *trova* in exile), largely in Miami, but with no great success.

The two superstars, Pablo Milanés and Silvio Rodríguez, were still able to attract large audiences in the 1990s, but the rest had almost disappeared. Meanwhile Cuban dance music by such new orchestras such as IRAKERE, Los VanVan, NG la Banda, Charanga Habanera and many others, all of them with a dominant Afro-Cuban sound, are gaining fans throughout the world.

In short, outside the rock and ballads that surged in the Cuban music scene of the early 1960s, the Nueva Trova may be less influenced by Afro-Cuban genres than any other style of Cuban music. Nonetheless, this influence remains a very important one. Standards like "Yolanda," "La muralla," and "De que callada manera," by Milanés, and "Son desangrado" by Rodríguez, will always speak to the Nueva Trova's Afro-Cubanism.

See also Salsa Music.

Nugent, Richard Bruce

1906–1987

American writer and artist of the Harlem Renaissance.

The son of Richard Henry and Pauline Minerva Nugent, Richard Bruce Nugent left WASHINGTON, D.C. with his recently widowed mother at the age of thirteen and moved to NEW YORK CITY, where he attended Dunbar High School. To support himself Nugent worked as an errand boy, bellhop, designer, and elevator operator, as well as a "secretary and a confidance man for a modiste."

Openly gay at the age of nineteen, Nugent went by the name Richard Bruce to protect his mother from public embarrassment about his homosexuality. Although his gay identity cost him some friendships, Nugent associated with gay and bisexual contemporaries LANGSTON HUGHES, Carl Van Vechten, E. M. Forster, and ALAIN LOCKE. His dramatic "ultimate bohemian" style was the basis for WALLACE THURMAN's character Paul Arbian in *Infants of the Spring* (1932), the roman-a-clef that satirized figures of the Harlem Renaissance. JESSIE FAUSET chaffed at Nugent's "rather too deliberate eccentricies."

Nugent's first published poem, "Shadows," appeared in OPPORTUNITY, the magazine of the NATIONAL URBAN LEAGUE, before COUNTEE CULLEN reprinted it in *Caroling Dusk: An Anthology of Verse by Negro Poets,* in 1927. Alain Locke published Nugent's short story "Sahdji" in *The New Negro* in 1925. Nugent later developed "Sadhji" into a play, published as *Sahdji—An African Ballet* in Locke's anthology *Plays of Negro Life* (1927) and produced in 1932.

Nugent published the first explicitly gay short story written by an African American entitled, "Smoke, Lilies, and Jade," in the sole issue of *Fire!!,* a controversial journal he founded with ZORA NEALE HURSTON, Hughes, Thurman, and AARON DOUGLAS. Two years later, Nugent and Thurman co-edited another journal, *Harlem.* Nugent's bold, often erotic illustrations were showcased in *Harlem* as they were in *Fire!!, Opportunity,* and *Crisis,* well-known publications of the period. His series *Drawing for Mulattoes* appeared in 1927. A talented illustrator and painter, Nugent had shows at the Harmon Foundation in 1931 and 1936. While Nugent's work was well received, Thurman characterized his drawings as "nothing but highly colored phalli."

In his later years, Nugent amassed a substantial collection of Afro-Americana. In the 1960s, he cofounded the Harlem Cultural Council with ROMARE BEARDEN. He appeared on stage in *Porgy,* and in 1984 (three years before his death) in the documentary film *Before Stonewall.* Director Isaac Julien celebrated the artistic contributions of Bruce Nugent and other African American gay men of the Harlem Renaissance in his 1992 film *Looking for Langston.*

Bibliography

Ruff, Shawn Stewart. *Go the Way Your Blood Beats: An Anthology of Lesbian and Gay Fiction by African-American Writers.* Henry Holt, 1996.

Smith, Charles Michael."Bruce Nugent: Bohemian of the Harlem Renaissance." In *In the Life: A Black Gay Anthology.* Edited by Joseph Beam. Alyson, 1986.

Nujoma, Samuel

1929–

Nationalist politician and first president of Namibia.

By the time NAMIBIA achieved independence in 1990, the nationalist leader Samuel "Sam" Nujoma, known for his fiery rhetoric, had matured into a seasoned and charismatic but not unanimously popular politician. Nujoma was born in Etunda, SOUTH-WEST AFRICA (present-day Namibia). As a young boy he attended the Finnish Mission Primary School while helping his father tend cattle around his home. As a teenager he traveled to WALVIS BAY and, later, WINDHOEK, where he lived with relatives and attended secondary school. In 1955 he began working for the South African Railways. Although he was later fired for participating in labor union activities, his job at the railway company enabled him to meet leading Namibian nationalists as well as to travel throughout southwestern Africa, where he witnessed the injustices of SOUTH AFRICAN control over the territory.

In 1959 Nujoma joined the Ovamboland People's Organization (OPO) and the South-West African National Union, both of which were active in the nationalist movement. His prominent role in boycotts against the forced removal of blacks and Coloureds (people of mixed African and European ancestry) from Windhoek suburbs quickly brought him to the forefront of the movement and made him vulnerable to government retribution. Also in 1959 Nujoma fled South-West Africa, remaining in exile for thirty years as president of the successor to the OPO, the SOUTH WEST AFRICA PEOPLES' ORGANIZATION, or SWAPO.

In his first decade as SWAPO president, Nujoma gained support for the movement and organized the nationalist leaders. When the armed struggle for independence began in 1966, Nujoma turned his attention to managing the guerrilla war, though he continued to travel extensively to African, Scandinavian, and Eastern bloc countries and to the United Nations. During the 1970s Nujoma, an increasingly shrewd politician, reorganized

SWAPO and its military to ensure his leadership. In the 1980s he intensified his international efforts to win independence for Namibia. To further the cause he toned down his socialist rhetoric and relaxed ties to the Eastern bloc, and when independence seemed inevitable, he emphasized the need for national reconciliation.

In 1989 Nujoma returned to Namibia a hero. Shortly thereafter, Namibians elected him to the National Assembly, a seat he relinquished in 1990 when the assembly unanimously elected him president. After independence, Nujoma and his SWAPO-dominated National Assembly upheld a policy of reconciliation, permitting white Namibians to control much of the economy. But a strong labor movement and high unemployment were persistent threats to Nujoma's leadership, and his lavish spending on presidential limousines, helicopters, and jets sparked criticism. The United States and other western donors condemned extravagant government spending and urged Nujoma to limit his time in office to two five-year terms, but he won a third presidential term in Namibia's December 1999 elections.

During the 1990s and early 2000s Nujoma's administration focused on economic growth and land redistribution, with Nujoma making a speech in 2001 accusing white farmers of "imperialist actions" in their claims to agricultural land in Namibia. Another challenge facing the country is its high incidence of ACQUIRED IMMUNODEFICIENCY SYNDROME (AIDS), estimated to affect about 25 percent of the adult population. Though Namibia generally pursues neutrality in international affairs, Nujoma sparked controversy in 1999 by sending military support to the DEMOCRATIC REPUBLIC OF CONGO and to the NATIONAL UNION FOR THE TOTAL INDEPENDENCE OF ANGOLA (UNITA). In 2001, Nujoma surprised his party by announcing that he would not seek a constitutional amendment to allow him to run for reelection in 2004.

See also Nationalism in Africa; Ovambo.

Eric Young

Numbers Games

Form of gambling that was widespread among inner city African Americans from the end of the nineteenth century until the 1970s, when state-run lotteries were established.

Also known as the "policy racket" or just "numbers," numbers games influenced the lives of many African Americans, as both an economic activity and a source of hope. Until the birth of state lotteries in the 1970s, "policy stations," where bets were made and winners awarded, usually appeared on every block of black neighborhoods in northern cities. Poet CLAUDE MCKAY called the numbers "the greatest industrial phenomenon in HARLEM." Indeed, by the 1960s numbers games comprised an estimated 60 percent of the neighborhood's financial transactions.

In numbers games, a player tries to guess the numbers of the day. Historically, the source of winning numbers has taken various forms. At the end of the nineteenth century, when numbers games first achieved widespread popularity, racketeers provided such numbers themselves, often drawing numbered balls from a drum-shaped container. As the policy racket became more established, however, and customers demanded fairness, managers began taking numbers from outside sources that could not be manipulated. Until the 1960s, Harlem bettors would wager on the last three numbers of the total volume of New York Stock Exchange trade. From the 1960s through the 1990s, bets were placed on harness racing numbers.

In some places, city governments attempted to curtail gambling by ordering that newspapers round off such numbers. In others, however, local officials accepted the existence of the games. In Kingston, New York, where bettors wagered on the U.S. Treasury Balance, the local newspaper printed the daily balance in its sports section.

The policy racket involved a constant exchange of money between bettors and a managerial hierarchy: runners, who took the bets; collectors, who oversaw the rackets' daily management; and bankers, who backed the operations. The policy rackets were profitable endeavors; lower managers generally took 10 percent on winnings, and bankers took 25 percent. Some policy bankers won esteem in the communities that supplied their wealth by investing in philanthropic programs.

In the 1920s, banker Casper Holstein was a sponsor of the HARLEM RENAISSANCE, supporting an Elks Lodge and contributing money to *Opportunity* magazine. Numbers games also supported the community simply by providing extra income to the businesses that fronted them. To avoid police crackdowns, many centers of operation were fronted by newsstands, barbershops, liquor stores, and other small businesses.

Bettors' techniques for choosing lucky numbers engendered much lore. The popular "dream books" assigned specific numbers to words and images, allowing gamblers to translate their thoughts and experiences into bets. Players also took numbers from the hymn boards in churches, the license plates of crashed cars, and the suggestions of children; they betted on the dates of births, deaths, and other significant events. Some male gamblers favored numbers that dream books assigned to sexual acts and parts, especially when attractive women took the bets.

What began in the early 1900s as locally-run operations had by mid-century been widely co-opted by white organized crime. Although the numbers continued to thrive, profits increasingly left the communities that generated them. In the 1970s and 1980s most policy racket activity was replaced by state-run lotteries. Through the end of the century, however, numbers games remained popular in urban centers as an unofficial form of betting.

Eric Bennett

Nunuma

Ethnic group of West Africa; also known as Nanoumba, Nibulu, Nouna, and Nounouma.

The Nunuma primarily inhabit the Northern Province of GHANA. Some also live in southern and west-central BURKINA FASO. They speak a Niger-Congo language and belong to the GRUSI cultural and linguistic group. Over 500,000 people consider themselves Nunuma.

See also Languages, African: An Overview.

Nupe

Ethnic group of Nigeria.

The Nupe primarily inhabit west-central NIGERIA, along the NIGER and Kaduna rivers. They speak a Niger-Congo language related to YORUBA and IGBO. Approximately one million people consider themselves Nupe.

See also Languages, African: An Overview.

Nurses, African American

African Americans who have worked or been trained as nurses; some have made important contributions to health care and the nursing profession, while others trained as nurses have gained fame in other fields.

For information on
Nineteenth century nurses with informal training: *See* Eldridge, Elleanor; Grimké, Charlotte L. Forten; Mason, Biddy Bridget; Taylor, Susie Baker King.
Nurses who became writers: *See* Larsen, Nella; Ogot, Grace.
Nurses who went on to political careers: *See* Johnson, Eddie Bernice; Shabazz, Hajj Bahiyah Betty; Wattleton, Faye.
Pioneers in nursing as a formally trained profession: *See* Mahoney, Mary (Eliza); Thoms, Adah B. Samuels.
Rap group of former nursing students: *See* Salt-N-Pepa.

Nuyorican Poets

New York poets, writers, and artists who are of Puerto Rican descent.

Poet and educator MIGUEL ALGARÍN was one of the most prolific writers in the Puerto Rican poetic movement that thrived in NEW YORK CITY during the 1960s and 1970s. Poets in this movement produced verse that combined English and Spanish vernacular, while exploring their own daily lives. In 1974 Algarín founded the Nuyorican Poets Café for poetry readings and other performances. The Café has been located at 236 East Third Street since 1980.

See also Pietri, Pedro Juan.

Nwapa, Flora

1931–1993

Nigerian author of children's books and novels dealing with the transformation of women's roles.

NIGERIA's best-known woman writer, Flora Nwapa was also a teacher, businesswoman, and government official. Her multiple careers echo the complicated lives of her fictional female characters: women who grow beyond the traditional ambitions of wife and motherhood to seek economic and personal independence. Nwapa changed her society through business as well as art, founding Tana Press Limited and Flora Nwapa Books. She was, in fact, the first African woman to own and operate a publishing house.

Florence Nwanzuruahu Nkiru Nwapa was born in Oguta, Nigeria, the eldest daughter in a large and relatively wealthy IGBO family. Her mother was a teacher and her father an agent with the British-owned United Africa Company in Nigeria. She attended Christian schools in Oguta and LAGOS, including Queen's College, from which she graduated in 1951. After teaching for a year, Nwapa studied briefly in London before entering University College in Idaban, Nigeria. She graduated in 1957 with a bachelor's degree in English, history, and geography. The following year she earned a diploma in education from the University of Edinburgh, Scotland. Back in Nigeria, then on the brink of independence, Nwapa worked for the next seven years as an education officer, college teacher, and university administrator.

After traveling to the United States for further study in 1965, Nwapa returned to Lagos where, with the help of novelist CHINUA ACHEBE, she found a publisher for her first novel, *Efuru* (1966). Nwapa, who later said that she never planned to become a writer, had begun the book while working as a teacher and quickly realized that she had "a good story to tell." Like many of her subsequent novels, *Efuru* was about a woman struggling with the traditional roles of wife and mother. Between the publication of *Efuru* and *Idu* (1970), Nwapa served as minister of Nigeria's East Central State during the turmoil of the Nigerian Civil War (also called the Biafran War). Her 1980 short story collection *Wives at War,* described the importance of women to the Biafran cause, both as family wage earners and as expert bargainers who negotiated with the enemy for needed supplies. She also married and had her second child (the first was born while Nwapa was single); a third was born in 1971, and shortly thereafter Nwapa, at the suggestion of writer CHRISTOPHER OKIGBO, began writing children's books.

Nwapa's government career continued after the war; she was appointed Commissioner for Health and Social Welfare in 1971 and later headed the commission for Lands, Survey, and Urban Development. Her belief that Nigerian women deserved a greater role in politics was inspired by both modern feminism and Igbo political traditions, in which priestesses held great power. Establishing her own publishing house in 1977, Nwapa took control of her literary career, which many critics believe reached its peak in the 1980s.

One Is Enough (1981) attacked multiple marriage, a widespread custom in Nigeria, and featured a heroine who chose single motherhood over subservience. *Women are Different* (1986) reasserted women's need for economic independence, as did Nwapa's *Wives at War* (1980), a collection of short stories that also dealt with the disintegration of traditional society following civil strife. After her death in 1993, Nwapa was remembered as a literary pioneer, giving eloquent voice to the lives of African women.

See also Feminism in Africa: An Interpretation.

Nyabinghi

Ceremonial music of the Rastafarian faith played at ritual meetings called *groundings* or *grounations*; nyabinghi is also often used to refer to ceremonies held to mark special occasions.

The birth of Rastafarianism in JAMAICA in the late 1930s brought with it the need for a liturgical music based on African sources, rather than the European-influenced Jamaican folk music. Dissatisfied with the revivalist Afro-European hymns rewritten with Rastafarian lyrics, Rastas turned to the drumming of the rural Burru men for inspiration. The Burrus originally worked on plantations but relocated to urban centers as agriculture work declined. Considered disreputable by mainstream Jamaicans, the Burrus found fraternity among the equally downtrodden RASTAFARIANS. The two groups shared close proximity while living in West KINGSTON ghettos. Burru music was performed at Christmas and to welcome released prisoners back into the community. Burru featured a West African rhythmic base with sung and chanted accompaniment. The predominantly African form fit perfectly into the Rastafarians' Afrocentric program. Rastas swiftly embraced Burru drumming as their own liturgical music. The Burrus in turn adopted Rastafarianism and with this exchange the two groups mixed into one.

Music of the neo-African Kumina cult also influenced the evolution of Rastafarian nyabinghi. Kumina drumming styles were closely related to Burru, although esoteric religious beliefs and ceremonies involving animal sacrifice greatly hindered Kumina's accessibility. Kumina differed enough from Burru so that when Burru evolved into nyabinghi, significant aspects of both forms had been altered in nyabinghi's distinct sound.

Nyabinghi uses three drums: the bass (used for timekeeping), the *funde* (used for syncopation), and the repeater (featured in improvisational solos). Religious nyabinghi is called *churchical* and employs slow, ponderous drumming. The secular version, known as *heartical*, relies on a lighter, faster sound. The term *nyabinghi* originally meant "death to the white oppressors and their black allies." Passage of time softened the definition into "death to evil forces." The music is played continually throughout Rastafarian grounation ceremonies, also often called *reasonings*, where believers discuss biblical scripture and philosophy, often sharing a chalice filled with ganja, or marijuana (considered a holy sacrament by many Rastafarians). Nyabinghi exerted a profound influence on REGGAE music. Renowned Rasta drummer COUNT OSSIE held lengthy open jams in Kingston during the late 1940s. The prolonged nature of nyabinghi gave musicians space and opportunity to explore the synthesis of American RHYTHM AND BLUES within nyabinghi's loping percussive framework. The founding members of the Skatalites, ska's seminal band, all developed their skills at Ossie's legendary sessions. In 1960 Count Ossie's nyabinghi drumming and melodic arrangements were used on the Folks Brothers' hit ska single "Oh Carolina." Ossie was happiest recording traditional nyabinghi and went on to produce several albums with his band, the Mystic Revelation of Rastafari. Ossie's prolific career ended with his death in 1976. By this time roots reggae's emphasis on Rastafarian beliefs fostered the development of nyabinghi groups Ras Michael and the Sons of Negus and Light of Saba. Roots reggae songs featuring nyabinghi influences surfaced regularly. BOB MARLEY's "Rastaman Chant" is an excellent example of the churchical style fused with reggae. Reciprocally, nyabinghi bands opened up to diverse influences. Ras Michael and the Sons of Negus successfully fused nyabinghi with commercial reggae, rock, and FUNK.

Jace Clayton

Nyakyusa

Ethnic group of Tanzania; also known as Niabiussa, Sochile, and Sokile.

The Nyakyusa primarily inhabit southwestern TANZANIA. They speak the same Bantu language as the NGONDE people of MALAWI and are closely related to the NYASA people. Approximately 600,000 people consider themselves Nyakyusa.

See also Bantu: Dispersion and Settlement.

Nyamwezi

One of the largest ethnic groups in Tanzania.

The ancestors of the Nyamwezi are believed to have first inhabited their current homeland in the Tabora region of western TANZANIA around the first millennium C.E., during the period of Bantu expansion. There they established more than thirty small, loosely linked chiefdoms but never unified into a centralized kingdom. Over several centuries the Nyamwezi established farming villages throughout the region and gradually assimilated neighboring peoples, such as the SUKUMA, into their chiefdoms. These people were apparently given land and political security by local chiefs in exchange for tribute and allegiance but were not required to adopt Nyamwezi religious customs, which centered on ancestor worship and divination.

By the eighteenth century, the Nyamwezi were taking part in trade between the African interior and the East African Coast. They carved out a trade route from the Great Lakes region of East Africa to Bagamoyo, a port on the mainland opposite the island of ZANZIBAR. They soon became one of the biggest suppliers of ivory, copper, and wax to coastal Arab-Swahili traders. When ivory became scarce during the late nineteenth century, the Nyamwezi used guns they had acquired through trade to conduct slave raids in the eastern CONGO RIVER basin and then sold their hostages into the INDIAN OCEAN SLAVE TRADE in Zanzibar. Some powerful Nyamwezi slave traders, such as MSIRI and Mirambo, even established their own trading empires deep within the Central African interior. For ordinary Nyamwezi, slave raiding raised the possibility of retaliation, and many moved from their scattered farms into walled villages. Nevertheless, the Nyamwezi remained active traders, and by the late nineteenth century it is estimated that more than 15,000 Nyamwezi traveled to the coast each year. The journey had become a rite of passage among young men, especially chiefs, who were expected to lead a caravan at least once before they could be considered adults in the chiefdoms.

In 1891 the German East Africa Company colonized the area now called Tanzania. The Germans restricted trade and forced Nyamwezi and other peoples to cultivate export crops such as tea, coffee, and cotton. Nyamwezi chiefs were made into local agents of the colonial administration, responsible for carrying out the COLONIAL RULE and colonial labor policies of the Germans and later the British, who named the colony Tanganyika. This role often cost the chiefs the respect of their followers. Many chiefs also became unpopular when they denounced the pro-independence Tanganyikan African National Unity party led by JULIUS K. NYERERE because they believed it threatened their power. After independence, the 1962 constitution abolished chiefdoms as a political office and few Nyamwezi disputed the edict.

Today most Nyamwezi in the Tabora region live in farming villages and raise cattle. Under Nyerere, many were forced into *ujamaa* (family hood) villages, but most maintained subsistence crops on their family farms, to which they returned in the early 1980s.

See also Ivory Trade.

Bibliography

Abrahams, R.G. *The Nyamwezi Today: A Tanzanian People in the 1970s.* Cambridge University Press, 1981.

Isichei, Elizabeth. *A History of African Societies to 1870.* University Press, 1997.

Roberts, A. "Nyamwezi Trade." In *Pre-colonial African Trade.* Edited by R. Gray and D. Birmingham. Oxford University Press, 1970.

Elizabeth Heath

Nyanhongo, Agnes

See Women Artists, African: An Interpretation.

Nyanja

Ethnic group of southern Africa.

The Nyanja comprise one of the largest ethnic groups in MALAWI, with an estimated population of 500,000. Hundreds of thousands more live in other countries, especially in ZAMBIA. The majority of them live near Lake Malawi and Lake Chilwa, although Nyanja people live in the Zomba and Blantyre districts of southern Malawi as well as in MOZAMBIQUE.

The Nyanja are closely associated with the CHEWA, and both ethnic groups descend from the Bantu-speaking peoples of the Maravi Confederacy. The Maravi groups are believed to have migrated from what is now the Democratic Republic of the Congo to their current locations in about the thirteenth century. By the eighteenth century the confederacy had dissolved, and the Nyanja had gravitated toward the lakes; the group's name means "lake people."

The Nyanja speak Chichewa, also called Chinyanja, a language they share with the Chewa. Most Nyanja practice Catholicism as a result of missionary activity. Their traditional social structures persist, which emphasize matrilineal kinship, or descent through the mother's line, and allow men to have several wives. Rural Nyanja continue to practice subsistence farming, cultivating rice, corn, and beans.

Nyankore

Ethnic group of Uganda; also known as Ankole, Banyankole, Nkole, and Nyankole.

The Nyankore primarily inhabit southwestern UGANDA. They speak a Bantu language. The Nyankore had formed a centralized kingdom, known as Ankole, before the British imposed COLONIAL RULE in 1901. The Nyankore comprise two main subgroups: the Iru are the majority and traditionally peasant farmers, while the Hima, a minority, are traditionally the pastoralist-ruling elite. Approximately one million people consider themselves Nyankore.

See also Bantu: Dispersion and Settlement; Pastoralism.

Nyasa

Ethnic group of Tanzania.

The Nyasa primarily inhabit southwestern TANZANIA. Some also live in northwestern MOZAMBIQUE. They speak a Bantu language. The term Nyasa is also sometimes used to refer to the inhabitants of MALAWI, particularly the NYANJA. Approximately 500,000 people consider themselves Nyasa.

See also Bantu: Dispersion and Settlement.

Nyasaland

Former name of Malawi.

See also Malawi.

Nyerere, Julius Kambarage

1922–1999

Socialist leader who led Tanganyika from colonial rule to independence as the United Republic of Tanzania and became its first president.

Called both father of the nation and *Mwalimu* (teacher), Julius Kambarage Nyerere is considered by many to be the founder of modern-day TANZANIA. The leader of one of the most unified nationalist movements in all of Africa, Nyerere guided Tanzania through a peaceful transition to independence and then pursued an ambitious plan to build a self-reliant socialist economy. Although lauded for his role in building a nation free of ethnic and civil conflict, his experimental socialist policies severely damaged Tanzania's economy. He stepped down from the presidency when it became clear that his policies had failed, but continued to be one of the most influential people in Tanzania and East Africa.

Nyerere was born in Butiama, TANGANYIKA (present-day Tanzania), the son of a minor chief of the Zanaki, one of the smallest ethnic groups in Tanzania. Nyerere excelled in primary school and studied at colonial Tanganyika's only secondary school, in the town of Tabora. He later received a scholarship and attended Makerere University in UGANDA. He graduated with a teaching degree in 1945 and taught for several years in the city of Makerere, where he helped organize a branch of the Tanganyikan African Association, a civic organization. In 1949 Nyerere left Africa to attend the University of Edinburgh in Scotland. After three years, he returned to Tanganyika with a degree in economics and history, ready to take a leading role in the emerging anticolonial movement.

In 1953 Nyerere became the president of the Tanganyikan African Association, and a year later transformed it into the more overtly political Tanganyika African National Union (TANU). TANU's goal, Nyerere announced, was to win full self-governance for Tanganyika, and to build a nation free of ethnic and racial divisions. He began traveling throughout the colony to encourage grassroots support for the movement. By 1957 TANU was the single largest organization in the country, and Nyerere had become the voice of Tanganyika's independence movement.

When in 1958 the British colonial government announced open elections for the Tanganyika Legislative Council, Nyerere protested electoral rules that reserved two-thirds of the seats for Europeans and Asians, restricted African voter registration, and effectively excluded TANU candidates from being elected to the Council. Britain responded by replacing the colonial governor and holding new elections in 1960. This time, TANU candidates won a majority and Nyerere was named chief minister. For the next year, Nyerere helped outline and implement the transition to independence, and on December 9, 1961, he was named prime minister of independent Tanganyika. Surprisingly, Nyerere stepped down after only a month to restructure TANU. But ten months later he was elected again, this time as president of Tanganyika.

During his first term as president, Nyerere sought to discard the divisive structures of COLONIAL RULE and to build a sense of national identity. He immediately declared SWAHILI the national language, making Tanganyika the only African nation with an official indigenous African language. He even translated William Shakespeare's plays *Julius Caesar* and *The Merchant of Venice* into Swahili. Shortly afterwards, he persuaded the neighboring and politically fragile island of ZANZIBAR to unify with Tanganyika; the agreement created the United Republic of Tanzania in 1964.

After the government reaffirmed confidence in Nyerere in 1965 and declared him the head of a one-party state, he began developing his vision of a uniquely AFRICAN SOCIALISM, combining Maoist principles with African values such as hard work, egalitarianism, and above all, *ujamaa*, or familyhood. In his famous February 7, 1967, Arusha Declaration, Nyerere described how socialism would create a self-reliant nation of peasants. He outlined a plan to resettle Tanzania's primarily rural population on large collectivized ujamaa villages where, Nyerere believed, their combined efforts would improve productivity and resource distribution. After few people moved voluntarily, the government became more forceful, and by 1977 over 80 percent of the population had been resettled.

Although the program did improve rural access to clean water, health care, and schools, it failed to produce sufficient food to feed the country's population, and the low state-mandated crop prices deepened rural poverty. By 1985 Nyerere had realized the necessity for reform. He took public responsibility for the economic failure, announcing, "I failed. Let's admit it." He stepped down to allow his successor, ALI HASSAN MWINYI to implement the reforms required by the International Monetary Fund and other international aid donors. Nevertheless, Nyerere remained the head of Chama Cha Mapinduzi (CCM, formerly TANU) until 1990, when he retired to his modest house in Butiama with his wife and seven children.

Although Nyerere slipped into the background of Tanzanian politics, he continued to play an active role in the country's diplomatic affairs. While president, Nyerere called for a new moral order in international politics. He supported nationalist movements in MOZAMBIQUE and ANGOLA, and was one of the first to lead an antiapartheid boycott of South Africa. In addition, he initiated the military overthrow of Ugandan dictator IDI AMIN in 1979, which returned to power the democratically elected MILTON OBOTE.

Nyerere also spoke out against STRUCTURAL ADJUSTMENT, in which economic reform programs are undertaken by countries in return for assistance from the World Bank and other international donor institutions. He believed structural adjustment compels developing nations to deprive children of food and education in order to pay off debts. He criticized the so-called new world order, which he said concentrates the world's wealth in the hands of a few. In 1995 Nyerere acted as the mediator of failed peace talks between Burundi's former democratic leader Sylvestre Ntibantunganya and rebel leader PIERRE BUYOYA. He also organized an East African trade embargo of Buyoya's military government. He remained a strong advocate of greater regional cooperation and spoke at times of the need for Tanzania and neighboring nations to unite and form an East African Federation.

Bibliography

Duggan, William, and John Civille. *Tanzania and Nyerere: A Study of Ujamma and Nationhood.* Orbis Books, 1976.

Legum, Colin, and Geoffrey Mmari. *Mwalimu: The Influence of Nyerere.* James Currey, 1995.

Nyerere, Julius K. *Arusha Declaration: Ten Years After.* Government Printer, 1977.

Nyerere, Julius K. *Freedom and Socialism.* Oxford University Press, 1973.

Nyerere, Julius K. *Ujamaa: Essays on Socialism.* Oxford University Press, 1968.

Elizabeth Heath

Nyoro

Ethnic group of Uganda; also known as Banyoro and Runyoro.

The Nyoro primarily inhabit western UGANDA. They speak a Bantu language and historically constituted the centralized kingdom of Bunyoro. More than 1.5 million people consider themselves Nyoro.

See also Bantu: Dispersion and Settlement.

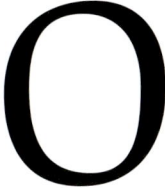

Obá

Yoruba deity, or orisha, who is the senior wife of Changó.

On the advice of Oshún, Changó's favorite, Obá cut off her ear to make Changó a soup that Oshún said would tie her husband to her forever. Changó was so disgusted with the ear soup that he repudiated Obá. Obá dances with her hand cupped over her missing ear.

See also Candomblé; Orishas; Religions, African, in Latin America and the Caribbean; Santería.

Obaluaiyé

Orisha, or Yoruba deity, of smallpox and infectious diseases; also known as Omolú in Brazil and as Obaluaiyé or Babaluaiyé in Cuba and the United States.

The Omolú always dances in BRAZIL covered from head to toe with raffia so as not to be seen, and his initiates are said to be people with unfortunate, difficult lives. He is thought to be very ugly, completely disfigured by disease. In all areas he is a feared orisha. In CUBA he is represented by San Lázaro, and his initiates wear burlap or purple.

See also Candomblé; Orishas; Religions, African, in Latin America and the Caribbean; Santería.

Obasanjo, Olusegun

1935–

Nigerian head of state and president.

Olusegun Obasanjo was born in Abeokuta, in Ogun State, NIGERIA, to a Christian YORUBA family that lacked the means to send him to college. He excelled at the provincial Abeokuta Baptist High School, however, and when he enlisted in the army in 1958, it was partly with an eye toward further schooling. During his tenure as a soldier, he studied in both India and England.

Obasanjo specialized as an engineer and rose through the ranks of Nigeria's Engineering Corps. Later, while serving as head of state, he credited this training for the systematic clarity of his thought. Between 1959 and 1976 Obasanjo advanced from second lieutenant to chief of staff, supreme headquarters. During this time he led Nigerian forces in the country's civil war (1969–1970), and he accepted the surrender of the Biafran troops in 1970.

Obasanjo was devoted to military service but appeared to have a limited appetite for power. He claimed that his ascendance to head of state after Murtala Muhammad's assassination in 1976 was "not my will." This reticence distinguished Obasanjo as the only Nigerian leader ever to relinquish power peacefully, which he did after three years in office.

Obasanjo's regime faced the task of preparing Nigeria for civilian rule. Obasanjo oversaw the Constituent Assembly that drafted the constitution, and ensured that the transition occurred according to the initial timetable. He also worked to integrate Nigeria's profusion of trade unions into the National Labor Congress. After the 1979 election, he duly handed over power to the elected government.

Obasanjo retired from the government and military service and took up farming in his home region. He made this move partly out of concern for the country's agricultural development, which suffered, in his view, from a lack of esteem for farming and farmers in Nigeria. He also continued his studies, at the University of Ibadan.

Although Obasanjo refrained from involvement in domestic politics, he wrote critical essays about subsequent Nigerian regimes and began involving himself with international affairs. In 1989 he published *Constitution for National Integration and Development*, a book advocating a one-party government rather than the multiparty system he himself had helped to install a decade before. That same year Obasanjo began publishing *Africa Forum*, a self-promotional magazine that was part of his failed campaign to become secretary general of the United Nations. In the late 1980s and early 1990s he served on the Commonwealth Eminent Person's Group, which pressed for justice in SOUTH AFRICA. In 1990 he won the Africa Prize for leadership for leading the search for a sustainable end to hunger.

Obasanjo, though not directly active in politics, remained a steady critic of Nigerian political life. As a consequence, the repressive Nigerian military government imprisoned him in 1995 under charges of "concealing treason." He was sentenced to death, but after international protest the sentence was commuted to fifteen years in prison. Obasanjo was released in June 1998 after the death of Nigerian leader SANI ABACHA. When democratic presidential elections were held in May 1999, Obasanjo was elected president, marking the end of fifteen years of military rule in the country.

During his first presidential term Obasanjo worked to improve Nigerians' sense of confidence in a government historically riddled with corruption. He also faced increasing tensions between the country's Muslim and Christian populations, with some regions imposing Islamic law in defiance of the national constitution. In addition, Obasanjo made efforts to increase foreign investment in Nigeria, and to unite African leaders around economic and policy reforms aimed at improving future economic aid. Obasanjo won a second term in a landslide victory in 2003, despite claims that the voting had been rigged.

Eric Bennett

Obeah

African-derived spiritual practice that involves conjuring and healing; found in parts of the English-speaking Caribbean.

Much confusion and mystery surround the practice of Obeah, and this itself is indicative of the situations under which it has been practiced. The term *Obeah* is used for the practice itself, for the men and women that perform it, and for the objects or charms that are used. In the broadest sense, Obeah is a spiritual practice designed to bring about some desired outcome; thus, it is a form of magic or sorcery. Obeah is not an organized religion; it has no recognized places of public worship, no organized community of worshippers, and no publicly recognized priests or priestesses. Instead, Obeah involves a private one-on-one meeting between an Obeahman or Obeahwoman and his or her client, who has a specific goal to reach or problem to be solved. Solutions may involve influencing the actions or feeling of a third person (as in encouraging a former lover to return, or influencing an employer to grant a promotion) or putting "fixes" on particular objects (so that, for example, a prized possession cannot be stolen). Most commonly, however, Obeah is associated with what is called black (or negative) magic: putting curses on people, or otherwise causing harm to one's enemies.

For several reasons, any discussion of Obeah must be treated with caution. Regardless of its actual origins or practices, *Obeah* became a term used by British colonists in the Caribbean in a derogatory and inaccurate manner to refer to all black traditional healers, as well as to the real or supposed magical practices of slaves. Obeah thus made its appearance in much British Romantic literature and drama at the end of the eighteenth century. Scholar Alan Richardson notes that in such plays as *Obi; or Three-Fingered Jack* (1800), an interest in Obeah reflected British fears and anxieties associated with changes in imperial power and the potential of slave rebellions more than the actual practice.

In addition, the lack of clarity about Obeah reflects the circumstances under which it has been developed, practiced, and often outlawed and persecuted. Although scholars debate the origins of the term *Obeah*, it appears to have its roots in either ASANTE or Twi words related to witchcraft. The most common etymologies trace it to either the Twi word *obeye* (which are spiritual beings believed to inhabit witches) or the Asante word *obayifo* (meaning "wizard" or "witch"). Regardless of its provenance, it was probably associated with people from the region that is present-day GHANA, who were brought against their will to British and Dutch colonies in the Caribbean during the TRANSATLANTIC SLAVE TRADE.

Due to the oppressive conditions of slavery, traditional African religious practices were often altered in the New World. Belief in magic—or the idea that certain powerful individuals can manipulate natural and supernatural forces in order to alter events—was common among many African groups. Unlike the Spaniards and Portuguese, British colonists were notoriously unwilling to Christianize the slaves that they brought to the Caribbean. In the harsh setting of plantation slavery, beliefs in magic could provide a form of resistance against slavery, as Obeah could be used to target slaveowners for revenge or could increase the powers of potential rebels. Scholar Orlando Patterson has argued, for example, that Obeahmen were "essential in administering oaths of secrecy" during slave revolts and sometimes distributed fetishes meant to "immunize the insurgents from the arms of the whites." In the 1770s, for example, the British traveler John Gabriel Stedman witnessed wars conducted by the Dutch colonial authorities against communities of maroons, or runaway slaves, in SURINAME. He reported that maroon fighters often wore amulets, which were called obeah, as a form of protection, believing that these made them bulletproof. Obeah could also serve as a means of enforcing order within slave communities and maintaining links with African customs.

Indeed, as in HAITI, where the initial uprising of slaves in 1791 that became the HAITIAN REVOLUTION was sparked by a VODOU ceremony presided over by the rebel and Vodou priest BOUKMAN, Obeah has been linked to slave uprisings in JAMAICA. Those involved in Tacky's Rebellion in 1760, for example, reportedly included Obeahmen who administered oaths of secrecy and promised to make participants in the rebellion invulnerable to European weapons. Reports from that period state that Tacky himself "caught all the bullets fired at him with his hand, and hurled them back with destruction upon his foes." Nanny, a legendary leader of Jamaican maroons, reportedly had similar supernatural powers, and was said to be able to catch bullets between her buttocks without injuring herself.

As a result of its role in promoting rebellion, Obeah was repeatedly outlawed in the British Caribbean—laws were passed against the practice in Jamaica in 1788, 1816, and 1826. People convicted of engaging in Obeah were severely punished, which served to drive the practice further underground. Repeated anti-Obeah campaigns in nineteenth century Jamaica indicate that belief in Obeah was hardly eradicated. As Barry Chevannes reveals, these campaigns were often associated with Myal, another African-derived religion in Jamaica, which was thought to be capable of counteracting Obeah. He states that in the Great Myal Procession of 1842, "groups led by Myal men would gather at night singing and dancing in circles and undergoing possession, and then would follow their leaders as they discovered and destroyed obeahs, or released the shadows of those thought to be bewitched."

Thus persecution drove Obeahmen and women underground. In addition, the very practices said to be characteristic of Obeah encourage its clandestine nature. Obeah flows from a belief that people have multiple souls—which is similar to YORUBA ideas about personhood, and has clear African origins. In Jamaica and TRINIDAD, for example, some believe that a person has a physically located soul and a twin noncorporeal, or shadow soul. Obeah can involve putting fixes or hexes on people by capturing their shadow souls, which are believed to wander freely in dreams. Obeah practitioners are said to use various means to put *duppies* (the shadow souls of the deceased, which linger on earth after death) on people. The belief that one has been a victim of such practices can cause extreme suffering and even death. For this reason, Obeah practitioners thought to be capable of such acts would, clearly, prefer not to make their practices publicly visible for fear of retaliation. On the other hand, being surrounded by such secrecy and mystery could promote the prestige of a particular Obeahman or Obeahwoman.

Although much attention has focused on Obeah's negative aspects, the practice seems to serve positive ends as well. Here Obeah merges with religions, such as Jamaica's Revivalism and Myalism and other proto-Christian religions that practice healing. For example, while Obeah practitioners are believed to have the ability to ensorcell, or bewitch, individuals at the request of their clients, they can also remove duppies from people who believe that they have been bewitched. Similarly, Obeahmen and -women can provide protection against curses and spells by using charms, amulets, and bottles filled with special substances, which are hung in the house. Obeahmen and Obeahwomen often provided the only medical treatment people of African descent received in Jamaica, Trinidad, and other parts of the British Caribbean

Although Obeah continues to be outlawed in the BAHAMAS and other parts of the British Caribbean, these regulations are usually not strictly enforced. Obeah thus remains a common, if misunderstood, practice and belief in Jamaica, the Bahamas, BARBADOS, GRENADA, and other parts of the Caribbean, as well as in Suriname.

See also Magic, Sorcery, and Witchcraft in the Americas; Maroonage in the Americas; Nanny; Nanny Town; Religions, African, in Latin America and the Caribbean.

Bibliography

Chevannes, Barry, ed. *Rastafari and other African-Caribbean Worldviews*. Rutgers University Press, 1998.

Hendrick, Basil C., and Jeanette E. Stephens. *It's a Natural Fact: Obeah in the Bahamas*. University of Northern Colorado, Museum of Anthropology, 1977.

Patterson, Orlando. *The Sociology of Slavery: An Analysis of the Origins, Development and Structure of Negro Slave Society in Jamaica*. MacGibbon & Kee, 1967.

Richardson, Alan. "Romantic Voodoo: Obeah and British Culture, 1797–1807." In *Sacred Possessions: Vodou, Santería, Obeah, and the Caribbean*, Margarite Fernández Olmos and Lizabeth Paravisini-Gebert (eds.). Rutgers University Press, 1997.

Simpson, George Eaton. *Black Religions in the New World*. Columbia University Press, 1978.

Obeso, Candelario
1849–1884

Afro-Colombian poet and writer, a precursor of black poetry in Colombia, and one of the first in Latin America to use nonstandard Spanish in his literary work.

Obeso was born three years before the Colombian government abolished slavery. The illegitimate son of a white lawyer and a mulatto laundrywoman, Obeso was raised by his mother in the small town of Mompós along the banks of the Magdalena River. At the age of seventeen he moved to Bogotá to study at a military academy. Just one year after his arrival, a military coup closed down the academy, and Obeso then entered the recently inaugurated National University. Even though Obeso never graduated, he received a teaching certificate and started writing his first poems.

In 1871 he released his first novel, *La familia Pygmalión* (The Pygmalion Family), in which he ridiculed a family that got him imprisoned for a love affair. Obeso then published articles and poems in Bogotá's most important newspapers and magazines; he gradually gained notoriety. The 1876 civil war interrupted his literary career. He enlisted as a government soldier and fought in the Battle of Garrapata, in which his brave efforts led to his appointment as lieutenant colonel.

The crowning of his literary career came in 1877 with the publication of *Cantos populares de mi tierra* (Popular Songs of My Land), a collection of sixteen poems that employed the linguistic particularities of blacks from the Atlantic coast to depict the daily activities of the Caribbean poor. Obeso initiated a literary tradition in which blacks spoke with their own voice about their struggles, ambiguities, and contradictions. He was one of the first poets to present blacks as fully human and in a positive light, challenging the racial, social, and cultural inequalities of his time.

Despite his artistic and military accomplishments—which landed him a diplomatic post in FRANCE and a high military position in PANAMA, both of which lasted just a few months—he faced many tribulations in his life in Bogotá. Being black, poor, and from the coastal lands, Obeso was often discriminated against in a city that prided itself on its white and European heritage. He aspired to join society's privileged ranks but met stark opposition that prevented him from improving socioeconomically. To make a living for his companion Zenaida and himself, he continued publishing his works, including the play *Secundino el zapatero* (Secundino, the Cobbler, 1880), and he used his remarkable polyglot ability to teach languages and to translate texts into Spanish.

Obeso died tragically at the age of thirty-five as a result of a self-inflicted gunshot wound. Even today it is uncertain if the wound was accidental. Some claim that a life mired by financial burdens and a feeling of despondency over the unrequited love for an upper-class woman led him to commit suicide. In any case, with his untimely death, Colombia lost one of its most original poets and its first major writer of African descent.

Alberto Arenas

Obiang Nguema Mbasogo, Teodoro

1942–

President of Equatorial Guinea.

Born to the Esangui (Fang) ethnic group in EQUATORIAL GUINEA, Teodoro Obiang Nguema Mbasogo attended secondary school in Bata and underwent military training at Saragossa Military Academy in Spain from 1963 to 1965. His uncle FRANCISCO MACÍAS NGUEMA was elected Equatorial Guinea's first president in 1968, and Obiang Nguema was appointed military governor of the island of Fernando Po. In 1975 he became the personal aide-de-camp (military assistant) to the tyrannical President Macías Nguema. Early in 1979 one of Obiang Nguema's brothers, who complained about not receiving the wages he was due, was executed on Macías Nguema's orders, and Obiang Nguema began plotting the overthrow of his uncle. In August 1979 Obiang Nguema (then a Lieutenant-Colonel) seized power with the support of the Supreme Military Council. Obiang Nguema proclaimed an amnesty for refugees overseas and released an estimated 5,000 political prisoners, but his close identification with the Macías Nguema regime (even after Macías Nguema's trial and execution) meant that most were still afraid to return home.

After being sworn in as president in October 1979, Obiang Nguema continued his uncle's policies of absolute personal control and extensive corruption. He took over companies he coveted, executed opponents, and ruled through a single-party state. A series of coup attempts were harshly subdued. A new constitution approved by 95 percent of the voters in 1982 provided for a return to civilian government after a seven-year transitional period, but it also gave him nearly total powers as president. In 1985 and 1986, the United Nations Human Rights Commission complained of flagrant and repeated violations of human rights in the country.

In 1987 Obiang Nguema ended his ban on formal political activity and announced the establishment of the official single legal party, the Democratic Party of Equatorial Guinea (Portuguese acronym, PDGE). In 1988 he began taking steps to consolidate his power by arresting opposition leadership. As the sole candidate in 1989, he was reconfirmed for another term. A new constitution legalized opposition political parties in 1991 and 1992, but Obiang Nguema placed restrictions that eliminated most of the opposition, at the time living in exile outside the country. By mid-1993, thirteen small opposition parties had been recognized, and a number of opposition leaders had received amnesty. Soon thereafter, however, Obiang Nguema again arrested many of the important leaders, postponed the elections, and enabled his party (the PDGE) to easily win sixty-eight out of the eighty seats, as the opposition boycotted the elections.

In January 1996 Obiang Nguema announced that the presidential election would be held in February of that year instead of June. Almost all of the opposition dropped out of the race, and Obiang Nguema won with 97.9 percent of the vote. In parliamentary elections in 1999, the first multiparty legislative elections in the country, thirteen parties fielded candidates but power was once again returned to the PDGE, which won seventy-five of eighty seats.

Obote, Milton

1924–

Prime minister and two-time president of Uganda.

Born in the LANGO district of UGANDA to a family of nine children, Apollo Milton Obote established a pattern of scholastic achievement at an early age. After attending Busoga College, Obote enrolled at Makerere University College. Although he was an excellent student, he was expelled in 1949 on the grounds that he had engaged in subversive political activities on campus. The British colonial administration subsequently prevented Obote from accepting scholarships offered to him by universities in the United States and Germany. Frustrated, he traveled to KENYA, where he worked odd jobs and became active in the Kenya African Union, a banned nationalist group. While Obote was suspected of having helped organize the Mau Mau resistance movement, IDI AMIN, who eventually succeeded him as leader of Uganda, had suppressed the Mau Mau movement as an officer in the British colonial force known as the King's African Rifles.

Shortly after returning to Uganda in 1957, Obote was elected to the Central Legislative Council for Lango District, where he established a reputation for outspoken opposition to colonial dictates. As president of the Uganda National Congress (UNC) he called for decolonization, despite fellow Langos' fears that an independent Uganda would be dominated by the more numerous BAGANDA ethnic group. After internal divisions led to the collapse of the UNC, Obote founded the Uganda People's

Congress (UPC), a party composed primarily of ethnic Lango and ACHOLI.

Soon after Obote was elected prime minister in 1962, Uganda gained independence. The federal constitution recognized the a priori territories associated with Uganda's major ethnic groups, including the ancient kingdom of BUGANDA. As the Baganda compose the single largest ethnic group and consequently held significant political sway, Obote formed a coalition with Mutesa II, the king of Buganda. Mutesa II was elected president while Obote retained the more powerful post of prime minister.

Obote's career as head of government was beset with difficulties from an early date. The Uganda Army mutinied in 1964, as did the armies of Kenya and TANZANIA. While the leadership in these other countries dealt harshly with the insubordination, Obote gave in to the demands of the military leadership, establishing a precedent for the armed forces to dictate political policy and ultimately leading to instability for years to come. In 1966 he was implicated in a gold and ivory smuggling scheme with General Idi Amin. It was discovered that Obote had ordered Amin to secretly provide support to Simba rebels in the Congo. Several ministers moved against Obote, ordering an investigation of Amin's activities. Obote preemptively eliminated the political challenge by ordering the arrest of the cabinet ministers who had initiated the investigation. He then implemented a new constitution to secure himself greater powers, and promoted Amin to the position of army chief of staff. He then declared himself executive president at the expense of Mutesa II. When Mutesa II subsequently ordered national government officials to leave Buganda, Obote instructed Amin to attack the Bugandan palace, forcing the king to flee to London. In 1967, Obote introduced yet another constitution which eliminated the sovereign status of Ugandan kingdoms, including Buganda.

With his political legitimacy weakened, in 1969 Obote finally began to outline a political platform, described as the "Move to the Left," where he proposed socialist reforms in hopes of cultivating a Ugandan nationalist identity and improving the economy. In 1969 Obote narrowly survived an assassination attempt, made while he was attending a UPC conference in KAMPALA. Several Baganda were arrested and convicted, although Obote declined to sign the execution orders. Meanwhile, relations were deteriorating between the president and Amin, and though Obote placed the general under house arrest (for misappropriating military funds) Obote returned from a summit in Singapore in 1971 to find that Amin had staged a coup d'état. Exiled to Tanzania, Obote attempted an unsuccessful counter-coup in September 1972.

Amin was eventually forced from office when Tanzania invaded Uganda in 1979. The following year, Obote regained the presidency in allegedly rigged elections. Although he was able to make some initial repairs to the gutted Ugandan economy with the support of foreign aid, the festering ethnic conflicts of Amin's rule continued, especially in the army. Nor did Obote's own government abstain from the violence. Faced with numerous insurgency groups, particularly YOWERI MUSEVENI's National Resistance Army/Movement, Obote responded with a harsh military campaign to suppress the rebellions, particularly in the Luwero Triangle. The human-rights group Amnesty International reported widespread use of torture against civilians, and the U.S. Congress received reports in 1984 that as many as 100,000 people had died since Obote took power for a second time.

In 1985, Obote was again ousted by his own army chief of staff, this time Tito Okello. He fled to ZAMBIA, where he remains in exile.

See also Mau Mau Rebellion; Nationalism in Africa.

Odinga, Oginga

1911?–1994

Kenyan nationalist and first vice president of Kenya.

After his death in 1994, Oginga Odinga was described by Kenyan President DANIEL ARAP MOI as a "patriotic citizen," ironic praise for a man who spent most of his career in opposition to the government. As Moi also noted, Odinga was a nationalist as well, a teacher who became a leading member of the independence struggle while president of the LUO Union from 1952 to 1957. In addition, he was one of the first Africans to be directly elected to the colonial government's legislative council.

In 1960 Odinga, with fellow Luo TOM MBOYA, founded the Kenya African National Union (KANU). After KENYA achieved independence in December 1963 he served briefly in JOMO KENYATTA's administration, first as minister for home affairs and then as vice president. But Odinga's political beliefs lay considerably to the left of Kenyatta's, and in 1966 he resigned to form the Kenya People's Union (KPU). In 1969 Kenyatta banned the KPU and placed Odinga in detention for two years. After his release, he was blocked from political office until Moi "rehabilitated" him in the early 1980s.

Odinga then became an outspoken critic of Moi and a leading agitator for multiparty elections, earning an expulsion from KANU in 1982. In 1988 he organized the Forum for Restoration of Democracy (FORD-Kenya), and in 1992 he was that party's candidate in Kenya's first multiparty presidential election in which he finished third. He was the official leader of the opposition in parliament until his death in 1994.

Robert Fay

Ogaden

Territory between Ethiopia and Somalia.

The Ogaden is a contested territory, currently under Ethiopian jurisdiction, but also claimed by SOMALIA. Since the sixteenth century, SOMALI nomadic pastoralists have grazed their herds annually on this plain. But the arid Ogaden has also long been a site of contestation, first between Christian ABYSSINIA and the first Muslim emirs, then between ETHIOPIA and European colonial states, and finally between Ethiopia and the Somalia nation.

The dispute over the Ogaden stretches back to the fifteenth and sixteenth century conflict between the Muslim city-state Ifat and the Abyssinian (Ethiopian) Christian empire. In the sixteenth century, Somali's legendary Ahmed ibn Ibrahim al Ghazi ("Ahmed the Left-handed") conquered the Ogaden as well as a large portion of Abyssinia, only to lose it again to the Portuguese-backed Abyssinians. During a period of relative peace, Somali herders migrated to the area in search of annual pasturage.

The 1891 and 1894 treaties between the British and Italian colonial powers gave the Ogaden to ITALY, while the neighboring Haud region went to GREAT BRITAIN. The British gained some support from Somali clans by promising protection from the well-armed Ethiopian army. After King MENELIK II of Ethiopia defeated Italy in the battle of Adwa, Italy was forced to cede territory in the Ogaden to Ethiopia. The British, uneasy about an Ethiopian military strength across the border, gave the Haud to Ethiopia in 1897, arguably reneging on promises of Somali protection for simply a promise of "good treatment" of the Somalis, who traditionally used the land for grazing. Shortly after, Italy and Ethiopia conducted secret negotiations of borders, drawing a later-disputed boundary for the Ogaden, KENYA, and Italian Somaliland.

Shortly before WORLD WAR II, Italy's Benito Mussolini offered to protect Somalis in the Ogaden from Ethiopian rule. A military skirmish between Italy and Ethiopia over the border prompted a 1935 declaration of war. After the Italians captured ADDIS ABABA, the Italians claimed the Ogaden as part of Italian Somaliland. Following the war, Great Britain returned the Ogaden to Ethiopia.

Repossession of the Ogaden remains a goal for the pan-Somali movement, which sought to unite all territories occupied by Somalis into one political state. Following Somali independence in 1960, the Somali Youth League party spent a large portion of the new nation's resources to pursue the dream of a Somali Ogaden.

No one leader devoted more resources to the Ogaden than MOHAMED SIAD BARRE. In 1977 he declared open war, sending 35,000 troops to join 15,000 guerrillas from the Western Somali Liberation Front (WSLF) to take the Ogaden. After the former Soviet Union switched its alliance to Ethiopia, Ethiopia reclaimed the territory. The violence sent over two million Somali refugees over the border into Somalia.

Since the fall of Siad Barre and the subsequent civil war throughout Somalia, the Ogaden has remained in Ethiopian hands. Oil has been discovered in the territory, adding to the desirability of the otherwise arid and mostly rural region. Tensions have remained high on the border in the twenty-first century. The Ogaden National Liberation Front (ONLF), in its continuing fight for Somali self-determination, has repeatedly clashed with the Ethiopian government. The human rights group Amnesty International has reported torture and extrajudicial executions by Ethiopian security forces in Somali regions where there is armed conflict.

See also Human Rights in Africa; Islam in Africa; Pastoralism.

Marian Aguiar

Ogé, James Vincent

1755–1791

Leader of uprising in Saint-Domingue.

Free mulatto (of mixed African and European descent) leader of an uprising against the French in the southern section of Saint-Domingue (now HAITI) in 1790. The rebellion was put down, and Ogé was captured. He died the following year from a punishment inflicted on him in prison.

Ogot, Grace

1930–

Kenyan author of short stories and novels, the first female writer from Kenya to win international attention, and one of the most widely read short-story writers from that country.

Born Grace Emily Akinyi in the village of Butere in western KENYA, Grace Ogot received her early education in local schools before training as a nurse in UGANDA and England. After working as a nurse in the 1950s in Kenya and Uganda, she pursued various career routes, although her writing continued to draw on her nursing experience.

Ogot worked as a broadcaster and scriptwriter for the British Broadcasting Corporation in London in 1959 and 1960 and later as an announcer on a weekly radio magazine program in the LUO and Kiswahili languages for the Voice of Kenya broadcasting company. Her career moved in a literary direction in the early 1960s, and she wrote most of her works in English. Her first novel, *The Promised Land* (1966), explores the issue of marriage in modern Kenya, especially a woman's relationship to her husband. It also considers the relation of past and present in traditional and modern medicine. In her work Ogot focuses on the preservation of family and on the sacrifices made to achieve that goal. She is also committed to showing the truths embodied in traditional law and folk wisdom. Both of these issues appear as themes in her short-story collections *Land without Thunder* (1968) and *The Other Woman* (1976).

In 1975 and 1976 Ogot lived in NEW YORK CITY, first as a delegate to the General Assembly of the United Nations (UN) and then as a member of the Kenya delegation to the United Nations Educational, Scientific and Cultural Organization (UNESCO). Her short-story collection *The Island of Tears* (1980) reflects her UN experiences as well as her interest in the common ancestry of African Americans and Africans. Ogot later became involved in politics and served in the National Assembly, the legislative branch of Kenya's government, from 1983 to 1992. Her other works include the novella *The Graduate* (1980) and the Luo-language novel *Miaha* (1983; translated as *The Strange Bride,* 1989).

Ogum

Orisha, or Yoruba deity, of iron, knives, the forge, and war; known as Ogum in Brazil and as Ogun in Cuba and the United States.

Ogum is the former lover of OSHÚN, has a terrible temper, and inhabits the forest where he can be alone. In BRAZIL his color is blue; in CUBA and the United States he wears green and black. Dogs and the truth are sacred to Ogum, and because he owns the knife he eats first in the sacrifice.

See also Candomblé; Orishas; Religions, African, in Latin America and the Caribbean; Santería.

O'Hara, James Edward

1844–1905

African American lawyer and politician.

James Edward O'Hara was born in NEW YORK CITY, the illegitimate son of an Irish merchant and a West Indian woman. Little is known of his early life, most of which he spent in the Danish WEST INDIES. He returned to the United States as a teenager, visiting Union-occupied eastern North Carolina for the first time in 1862. At nineteen he became a teacher and operated freedmen's primary schools in the eastern North Carolina towns of New Bern and Goldsboro. He married Ann Marie Harris in 1864, but they separated in 1866, when he accepted the teaching post in Goldsboro. They later divorced.

With the advent of congressional RECONSTRUCTION, O'Hara began to participate in politics, serving as engrossing clerk at the state constitutional convention of 1868 and the subsequent session of the legislature. In 1869 he married Elizabeth Eleanor Harris; they had one son. O'Hara had earlier fathered an illegitimate son. O'Hara spent about two years in WASHINGTON, D.C., working as a clerk in the Treasury Department and studying at HOWARD UNIVERSITY. Upon his return to North Carolina, he secured a license to practice law in 1873 and assumed a leading role in Republican politics. Hostile Democratic journalists soon noticed O'Hara, calling him "a bright mulatto, with cheek a plenty" and a man with "more than ordinary intelligence."

The young lawyer settled in Halifax County, one of the state's most important cotton-growing counties and the most populous county in the Second Congressional District, which had a strong black (and Republican) majority. Speaking at the Second District Republican Convention in 1874, O'Hara insisted to applause that "colored aspirants" should not be ruled out "on account of their color."

Though not nominated for Congress in 1874, O'Hara was elected to the Halifax County Board of Commissioners and served for the next four years as chairman of this powerful arm of local government. He was elected to the state constitutional convention in 1875. Nominated as a presidential elector in 1876, he withdrew after Democrats attempted to make an issue of his race.

It is difficult to assess O'Hara's tenure as county commissioner, especially in the light of repeated Democratic accusations that the board was corrupt and extravagant. The Republican commissioners were indeed indicted for malfeasance in office, although O'Hara claimed that the charges were politically motivated. The results of these court cases were inconclusive, and the state prosecutor dropped all charges after O'Hara and one associate pleaded nolo contendere and agreed to pay costs. The polemical language used by many of his opponents disguised their basic ideological difference with O'Hara about the role of local government in education and poor relief.

For five consecutive elections O'Hara pursued the Republican congressional nomination in the "Black Second." When he was first nominated to Congress in 1878, a host of enemies within the Republican party accused him of corruption and asserted that O'Hara, who had divorced his first wife a decade earlier, was actually guilty of bigamy. Three weeks before election day Republican leaders convened a new nominating convention and chose another candidate. Refusing to withdraw, O'Hara was victorious in the three-way general election until canvassing boards in three counties rejected hundreds of votes on flimsy technicalities and gave the victory to the Democratic nominee, William H. Kitchin. O'Hara contested the election but was unsuccessful.

O'Hara held no elective office between 1878 and 1883, though he was a significant leader in the statewide antiprohibition campaign of 1881, in the Liberal coalition between Republicans and dissident Democrats in 1882, and in organized black protests against Republican patronage policy. At another disorderly district convention in 1882 he claimed the Republican nomination for Congress and, after several months of conflict, secured the withdrawal of a competing Republican candidate, incumbent representative Orlando Hubbs. O'Hara easily won election and, backed by an unusually united party, won a second term two years later. He was then at the zenith of his political career, not only dominating his district but wielding considerable influence in the state and national party.

In 1886, however, O'Hara faced renewed opposition, as a divided Republican convention once again produced two "nominees." On election day O'Hara received three-quarters of the Republican votes, despite complaints that he had grown distant from his constituents, protests about the way he distributed patronage, and even negative comments about his complexion from an opponent proud to be "of unmixed African blood." But the election was lost to the youthful Democratic candidate, Furnifold Simmons.

During his four years in Congress, with the Republican Party in the minority, O'Hara found it difficult to shape significant legislation or influence debate. He proposed a constitutional amendment to fill the void left by the Supreme Court's nullification of the CIVIL RIGHTS Act of 1875, advocated reimbursement for depositors in the failed Freedman's Savings and Trust Company, and sought federal aid for education, but these bills were ignored by the Democratic majority. His only success was securing the passage of seven private, pension, or relief bills. He made no lengthy speeches on the floor of the House, preferring instead to offer brief comments.

O'Hara's only significant national attention came in December 1884, when he offered a controversial amendment to the Reagan Interstate Commerce Bill providing that all railway passengers should "receive the same treatment and be afforded equal facilities . . . as are furnished all other persons holding tickets of the same class without discrimination." Supported by racially moderate northern Democrats, the amendment passed, although, after considerable debate, southern Democrats succeeded in tacking on another amendment making the point that equal could be separate.

O'Hara never held public office again after 1887, though he remained active in the Republican Party into the twentieth century. He practiced law and briefly published a weekly newspaper, the *Enfield Progress*. He moved to New Bern, North Carolina, in 1890 and spent the last fifteen years of his life there.

Throughout his career O'Hara served as a convenient symbol for both friends and foes. For Republicans, this talented "carpetbagger" represented the aspirations of a small but increasing group of black professionals who demanded a greater voice in the party's awkward biracial alliance. For black voters, even impoverished landless laborers, he symbolized the hope that ex-slaves could participate in American democracy. For Democrats, especially the generation that ultimately chose to disfranchise blacks, O'Hara was a symbol of dangerous black assertiveness, though time and again they paid grudging compliments to his skill and resourcefulness.

Bibliography

The Regenstein Library, University of Chicago, has a small collection of O'Hara's papers that includes scrapbooks, photographs, and a significant biographical sketch by O'Hara's granddaughter, Vera Jean O'Hara Rivers.

Anderson, Eric. *Race and Politics in North Carolina, 1872–1901: The Black Second*. 1981.

———. "James O'Hara of North Carolina: Black Leadership and Local Government." In *Southern Black Leaders of the Reconstruction Era*, edited by Howard N. Rabinowitz. 1982.

From *American National Biography*. John A. Garraty and Mark C. Carnes, eds. Oxford University Press, 1999. Reprinted by permission of the American Council of Learned Societies.

Eric Anderson

Ojukwu, Emeka Odumegwu

1933–

Historian, Nigerian army officer, and ex-governor of eastern Nigeria; served as head of the secessionist Republic of Biafra from 1967 to 1970 and was a candidate for the presidency of Nigeria in 2003.

Although he was born in northern Nigeria, Emeka Odumegwu Ojukwu is an Igbo; he hails from Nnewi in Anambra State in eastern Nigeria. His father, a knight of the British empire, Sir Louis Philippe Odumegwu Ojukwu (1908–1966), was a multimillionaire and one of the richest African businessmen of his day, who sent his son to the best school in Nigeria, King's College, Lagos, and later sent him to Epson College in Surrey, England.

The young Ojukwu received his bachelor's and master's degrees from Oxford University. At the age of twenty-two, he returned to Nigeria. Contrary to his father's wish, he joined the colonial government service as a district admistrative officer in a rural Igbo village. In 1957 he joined the Nigerian army as a private. However, after attending the Officer Cadet School in England in 1958, he rose rapidly to higher military ranks: lieutenant in 1959, captain in 1960, major in 1961, and lieutenant colonel in 1963. He served in in the army in different capacities both at home and abroad. In 1963 he became the first Nigerian to hold the post of quartermaster general.

Following the failure of the military coup led by Major Chukwuma Kaduna Nzeogwu in Nigeria on January 15, 1966, Major-General Aguiyi-Ironsi, who assumed control of the country, appointed Ojukwu military governor of eastern Nigeria. General Ironsi was killed in the countercoup of July 29, 1966, which was followed by the killing of around 30,000 Nigerian eastern refugees, mainly Igbos, in northern Nigeria. Continued grievances associated with these killings, combined with other issues and with the influx and suffering of people in the east, resulted in approximately two million refugees fleeing from the region. On May 30, 1967, with a mandate of the Eastern Consultative Assembly, Ojukwu declared the secession and independence of eastern Nigeria, which he renamed the Republic of Biafra.

During the ensuing Nigeria-Biafra war, the Biafrans, under the leadership of Ojukwu, put up fierce resistance for nearly three years. At the beginning of 1970, when they were on the verge of being overrun by federal troops, Ojukwu conferred with his cabinet and escaped to Côte d'Ivoire, where he was granted political asylum. After nearly thirteen years in exile, the Nigerian president, Shehu Usman Shagari, granted him amnesty. On June 18, 1982, Ojukwu returned to Nigeria. Since then, he has been a strong advocate of Nigerian unity as well as a vehement critic of the marginalization of the Igbos in Nigeria.

Ojukwu has published several books, including *Biafra: Selected Speeches and Random Thoughts of C. Odumegwu Ojukwu, with Diaries of Events* (1969), *Principles of the Biafran Revolution: As Enunciated by General C. Odumegwu Ojukwu* (1969), and *Because I Am Involved* (1989). Actively involved in present-day politics, Ojukwu competed, although unsuccessfully, for the presidency of Nigeria during the election of 2003.

See also Colonial Rule.

Eddie Enyeobi Okafor

Okebu

Ethnic group of east-Central Africa; also known as Ndu.

The Okebu primarily inhabit northwestern UGANDA, northeastern Congo-Kinshasa, and southern SUDAN. They speak a Nilo-Saharan language. Approximately 300,000 people consider themselves Okebu.

See also Languages, African: An Overview.

Okigbo, Christopher

1932–1967

Nigerian poet.

Born in Ojoto, a small village in eastern NIGERIA, Christopher Okigbo was the fourth of five children of a Catholic school teacher of IGBO heritage. He attended Catholic schools, the Umuahia Government College (secondary school), and the University of Ibadan, receiving a degree in classics in 1956. He worked as a teacher, an editor, a librarian at the University of Nsukka, and as secretary to the Nigerian minister of research and information; he was also the West African editor of the journal TRANSITION.

Okigbo published two volumes of poetry during his lifetime—*Heavensgate* (1962) and *Limits* (1964)—as well as poems in the journals *Horn*, *Black Orpheus*, and *Transition*. His work shows the influence of Igbo mythology and the American modernists as well as his training in Greek and Latin. Offered the poetry prize at the 1966 Dakar Festival of Negro Arts, Okigbo declined it because he thought it racially exclusive to black writers. "There is no such thing as Negro art," he said. Deeply committed to political change, he resisted the 1930s neologism NÉGRITUDE, a concept introduced by AIMÉ CÉSAIRE and LÉOPOLD SENGHOR that describes a particular mode of black experience and artistic expression. He also showed little interest in the opinions of critics and literary theorists. He had begun a plan with Nigerian writer CHINUA ACHEBE to establish a publishing house when he was killed while fighting on the Biafran side during the Biafran war of independence from Nigeria. His collected poems were published as *Labyrinths with Path of Thunder* (1971). *Collected Poems* was published in 1986. Okigbo posthumously received the National Order of Merit of Biafra for his service to the cause of Biafran independence.

O.K. Jazz

An influential and popular musical group from Zaire (now the Democratic Republic of the Congo).

Begun on June 6, 1956, the high-energy ensemble O.K. Jazz was the creation of Franco Luambo Makiadi, known to most people simply as Franco. For thirty years, Franco led O.K. Jazz, recording more than 100 albums and touring widely.

Franco was a musical prodigy, having joined the band Watam when he was twelve years old. He was a talented guitarist; by the time he founded O.K. Jazz at the age of eighteen, other African musicians were imitating his powerful, Latin-influenced sound. The band's full name—Franco et le Tout Puissant O.K. Jazz (Franco and the all-powerful O.K. Jazz)—perfectly matched its confident, satirical tone. Franco's songs for O.K. Jazz frequently took on social themes familiar to average Zaireans; his early lyrics dealt with polygamy and government corruption, while he later penned songs about acquired immunodeficiency syndrome (AIDS) and African unity.

In its early years the band achieved great popularity in both KINSHASA, ZAIRE (present-day DEMOCRATIC REPUBLIC OF THE CONGO), and Lumumba, Congo, settling in Kinshasa only after MOBUTU SESE SEKO came to power in 1965. Despite their many songs that criticized the government, Franco and O.K. Jazz became great favorites of Mobutu, who awarded Franco the title "Le Grand Maitre" of Zairean music in 1980. By its 1978 African tour, O.K. Jazz had grown from its original ten members to a big band of twenty-three musicians and had become Africa's most popular group. When the band was on the verge of conquering the world market, Franco became ill and eventually died of AIDS in 1989. Mobutu declared four days of mourning after Franco's death. The band teamed up with former O.K. Jazz members to record a tribute album in Franco's honor. A few years later band members formed a new group, Bana OK, which has continued to record and tour, though not with O.K. Jazz's success.

See also Acquired Immunodeficiency Syndrome in Africa: An Interpretation; Music, African.

Bibliography

Ewens, Graeme. *Congo Colossus: The Life and Legacy of Franco & OK Jazz*. Buku Press, 1994.

Kate Tuttle

Okri, Ben

1959–

Prize-winning Nigerian-British author whose work incorporates elements of magical realism and social commentary.

Ben Okri, the son of a British-educated tenants' lawyer, was born in Minna, NIGERIA to parents of the Urhobo ethnic group. Through his father's work, he was exposed to the world of the dispossessed; through myths and folktales as well as Western classics, he discovered the landscape of the imagination. Okri finished school at the age of fourteen and went on to spend the next five years writing. His first publication was an article on a rent edict, but he soon turned to writing short stories for Nigerian women's journals and evening papers.

In 1978 Okri went to England to study philosophy and English at the University of Essex. Two years later he published his first novel, *Flowers and Shadows*. In chronicling a son's discovery of his businessman father's legacy of corruption, the story depicts the moral disintegration of contemporary Nigeria. His next work, *The Landscapes Within* (1981), was a novel Okri described as a "double mirror" of two realities: the psychic world of the artist and the chaos of daily life. Although *The Landscapes Within* gives an account of what Okri has called "the violent relations" of Nigeria, it marked a shift toward his growing preoccupation with the spiritual world.

During the next six years, Okri worked as a journalist for BBC Television's African department and as a poetry editor for *West Africa* magazine. His short stories and poetry received growing recognition and were published in prominent journals such as *Paris Review, New Statesman, Firebird*, and *PEN New Fiction*. In 1986 he published *Incidents at the Shrine*, a collection of short stories that won the *Paris Review* Aga Khan Prize for Fiction, and, the following year, the Commonwealth Writers Prize for Africa. Set in the seamy urban underworld of Nigeria and England, Okri blurs the boundaries between the "real world" and the world of the dream. In his next collection, *Stars of the New Curfew* (1988), Okri moved further into the literary realm known as magical realism.

Okri's Booker Prize-winning novel *The Famished Road* (1991) is told from the viewpoint of Azaro, who is an *abiku*, a child believed to be caught in a cycle of death and rebirth. Set in the squalor of the ghetto, the novel's experimental storyline, which Okri characterizes as "open toward infinity," mirrors the cyclical and eternal nature of the abiku cycle. Okri continued the story of Azaro in *Songs of Enchantment* (1993), setting even more of the narrative in the spiritual world.

The novel *Astonishing the Gods* (1995) recounts a man's transformative explorations of an enchanted island. Okri's most recent works are *Birds of Heaven* (1996), *Dangerous Love* (1996), *A Way of Being Free* (1997), *Infinite Riches* (1999), and *In Arcadia* (2002).

Marian Aguiar

Olajuwon, Hakeem

1963–

Nigerian-born basketball player.

One of the first African professional BASKETBALL players in the United States, Hakeem Olajuwon did not take up the game until age fifteen. Born in LAGOS, NIGERIA, Olajuwon was the third of six children and a standout high-school soccer player. The 2.06 m (6-ft, 9-in) teenager was discovered by the coach of the Nigerian national basketball team, and by the age of seventeen he was receiving recruitment offers from several United States colleges. Olajuwon chose the University of Houston, which he entered in 1981. Sitting out one year to gain weight and focus on the sport's fundamentals, Olajuwon, soon nicknamed "the Dream," was starting at center by his sophomore year. Twice he took his team to the Final Four of the National Collegiate Athletic Association (NCAA) basketball tournament. At the end of his junior year, Olajuwon entered the draft of the National Basketball Association (NBA).

Now 2.13 m (7 ft) tall and weighing 107 kg (235 lb), Olajuwon was the first player chosen in the 1984 NBA draft. As a rookie for the Houston Rockets he quickly established himself as one of the league's best players, averaging 20.6 points and 11.9 rebounds per game. Over the next decade, Olajuwon led the Rockets to two NBA titles (1993–94, 1994–95), winning most valuable player (MVP) awards for the regular season (1993–94) and for both championship finals. He also played in numerous All-Star games. In 1996 he was named one of the NBA's fifty greatest players of all time. That same year, he played on the U.S. "Dream Team" that won gold at the Olympic Games. He is one of only eight players in the history of the NBA to score more than 20,000 points in his career.

In 2001 Olajuwon joined the Toronto Raptors. Despite his brilliant athleticism and intelligent play, Olajuwon's criticism of management has earned him a mixed reputation, and his Nigerian accent has kept him from the lucrative endorsement contracts that lesser NBA stars enjoy.

Kate Tuttle

O'Leary, Hazel Rollins

1937–

American public official, first female secretary of energy.

Born in Newport News, Virginia, Hazel O'Leary was raised by her father, Russell E. Reid, a physician, and by her stepmother. She earned a B.A. degree from FISK UNIVERSITY in Nashville, Tennessee in 1959, and a J.D. degree from Rutgers University Law School in 1966.

From 1974 to 1980, O'Leary worked in the Federal Energy Administration (later part of the Department of Energy), reaching the position of chief of the Economic Regulatory Administration. She worked at her own energy consulting firm from 1980 to 1989. She was president of Northern States Power Company in 1993, when President Bill Clinton appointed her secretary of energy, a position she held until 1996.

In addition to her position as president of O'Leary and Associates, a consulting firm, O'Leary also serves as trustee on several boards, including those of Morehouse College, Africare, the AES Corporation, the Center for Democracy, the Keystone Center, and ICF Kaiser, Inc.

Robert Fay

Olinga, Enoch

1926–1979

Only African appointed to the position of a "Hand of the Cause of God" (a title of great distinction) in the Baha'i faith.

Enoch Olinga was born into a family of Christian (Anglican) converts among the Teso people in UGANDA. His father was a catechist and missionary for the church, and he was educated in missionary schools. During WORLD WAR II, he joined the British Army Education Corps and served in the East African King's Rifles Corps in South Asia: Burma, East Pakistan, Ceylon, and India. When he returned to Uganda in 1946, he was employed by the colonial Department of Public Relations and Welfare as a translator, eventually moving to Kampala. He produced two books in his own language, Ateso.

In 1951, fired from his job because of heavy drinking, Olinga began to study the Baha'i faith, recently introduced into Uganda by Ali and Violette Nakhjavani, a Baha'i couple from Iran. In February 1952, Olinga converted to the Baha'i religion. Almost immediately, he returned to his home village with Ali to convert his family. There he initiated a wave of conversions that represented the first substantial entry of sub-Saharan African peoples into the Baha'i faith.

In 1953, Olinga agreed to become the first Baha'i pioneer (missionary) to the British Cameroons. In West Africa, he was able to repeat his earlier success and became a catalyst for the conversion of large numbers of Christians (Basel Mission Presbyterians) and others into the Baha'i faith. He was invited by Shoghi Effendi Rabbani (1897–1957), then head of the religion, to make a pilgrimage to the Baha'i World Center in Israel, in February 1957. Olinga was the first black African Baha'i to make such a visit. Given the honorific title of Abu'l-Futuh (Arabic for "Father of Victories"), he shortly thereafter became one of the "Hands of the Cause of God," an office given to him by the Baha'i leader. At the age of thirty-one, he was the youngest Hand. When Shoghi Effendi died, in 1957, the Hands collectively assumed leadership of the religion until 1963, when the international Baha'i community elected its governing Universal House of Justice.

Olinga eventually returned from West Africa to live in his native Uganda. He traveled extensively as a Baha'i teacher and was especially beloved by Baha'i communities around the world. His journeys took him to all parts of Africa, to India, Southeast Asia, Australia, Japan, the Pacific Islands, North and South America, and Europe. When IDI AMIN banned the Baha'i faith in Uganda in 1977, Olinga remained in the country, caring for the (then closed) Baha'i Temple properties and encouraging the persecuted Baha'is.

In 1979, after the fall of Idi Amin's regime, but while Uganda was still in a state of near anarchy, armed gunmen attacked Olinga's house in Kampala. Their motives are unknown. Olinga, his wife, and three of his children were brutally murdered. Their bodies were interred near the Baha'i Temple in Kampala.

Bibliography

"Enoch Olinga: Knight of Baha'u'llah, Father of Victories, Hand of the Cause of God," Video. Olinga Productions Association, 2000.

Harper, Barron Deems. *Lights of Fortitude: Glimpses into the Lives of the Hands of the Cause of God*. George Ronald, 1997.

Rabbani, Ruhiyyih. "In Memorium: Enoch Olinga," in *The Baha'i World: An International Record,* Volume 18 (1979–1983).

Anthony A. Lee.

Olive

Common name for a plant family representative genus and for the fruit of the olive tree.

The family contains about 900 species, placed in twenty-four genera. The olive is in a small group of woody flowering plants of horticultural and economic importance. Other familiar members of the family include ash, lilac, privet, jasmine, forsythia, and the fringe tree.

Most members of this family of dicots are shrubs or small trees, although a few are climbers. Nearly all have opposite leaves, which may be simple, as in lilacs and forsythias, or compound (composed of several separate leaflets), as in ashes. Flower structure is rather uniform in the family, but some variation occurs. Typically, flowers have four sepals (outer floral whorls) and four petals (inner floral whorls), two stamens (male flower parts) attached to the inner surface of the petals, and a single ovary (female flower part), which is superior (borne above and free from other flower parts). The fruits, which develop from the ovary after fertilization, vary considerably but usually contain a single seed. Examples of distinctive fruits include those of the olive, which are technically drupes (hard seeds surrounded by fleshy material); those of the ashes, which are indehiscent (remain closed at maturity) and winged and are technically known as samaras; and those of the lilacs, which are dry and dehiscent (splitting at maturity).

The olive genus contains about twenty species. A few species produce good timber—for example, the black ironwood, of southern Africa. The hard, variegated wood of the cultivated olive is valued in cabinetry. The cultivated olive is originally native to the eastern Mediterranean region but now widely cultivated throughout that area and in other parts of the world that have Mediterranean-type climates. The olive is valued for its fruits, which yield edible oil and are also pickled for eating. Olive oil, which is derived from fresh, ripe fruits that contain about 20 percent oil, is used in cooking, in canning, and as table oil. Olives for eating are picked either when unripe or when ripe. Unripe olives are green and remain so during pickling. Ripe olives are dark bluish when fresh and turn blackish during pickling. The seed, or stone, of the olive is often removed and the cavity stuffed with spicy materials such as sweet red pepper.

Scientific classification: Olives make up the family Oleaceae. The representative genus is *Olea*. The black ironwood is classified as *Olea laurifolia* and the cultivated olive as *Olea europaea*.

Oliver, Joseph ("King")

1885–1938

American cornetist and bandleader who was a pioneering figure in New Orleans and Chicago-style jazz.

Joseph Oliver was born in Donaldsville, Louisiana. After his family moved to NEW ORLEANS, he learned to play the trombone from local street musicians. He soon switched to the cornet and trumpet, and by 1907 Oliver had begun to play professionally with various local brass bands.

From 1916 to 1919 Oliver played in EDWARD "KID" ORY's band. Ory gave him the moniker "King" because he was the best cornetist in the most popular JAZZ band in New Orleans. In 1918 Oliver was courted by bassist/banjoist Bill Johnson to join his band in CHICAGO, ILLINOIS. A year later, Oliver moved to Chicago, where he became first cornetist in the Johnson-led Creole Jazz Band. Oliver soon assumed the leadership of the band, taking them to California from 1920 to 1921.

Returning to Chicago, Oliver solidified the Creole Jazz Band with powerful new members, creating one of the most important ensembles in the history of jazz. From 1922 to 1924 the band included LOUIS ARMSTRONG on cornet, Honore Dutrey on trombone, Johnny Dodds on clarinet, his brother Baby Dodds on drums, LILLIAN HARDIN ARMSTRONG on piano, and Bill Johnson on bass and banjo. Featuring a "wa-wa" cornet sound and polyphonic four-to-the-beat rhythmic attack, such Oliver performances as "Dipper Mouth Blues," "Riverside Blues," and "Snake Rag" influenced a new generation of jazz musicians that included many aspiring white performers.

The Creole Jazz Band disbanded after Armstrong left. Oliver then recorded several duos with the great JELLY ROLL MORTON during 1924. From 1924 through 1927 Oliver led the Dixie Syncopators, made up of former Creole Jazz Band members, along with trombonist "Kid" Ory and clarinetist and saxophonist Barney Bigard. From 1930 until 1937 he led several bands on tours of the Midwest and the South but did not play after 1931 due to painful gum disease. Oliver retired from music in 1937.

Oller, Francisco

1833–1917

Afro–Puerto Rican painter.

Born in Bayamón, Puerto Rico, Francisco Oller traveled to Spain and France in the 1850s, where he was influenced by impressionist painting. Among his most noted paintings is *El Velorio*.

See also Art in Latin America and the Caribbean.

Olodum

Internationally acclaimed Afro-Brazilian Carnival association whose music celebrates black history and protests racial discrimination.

Olodum was founded in Salvador, BAHIA, BRAZIL, on April 25, 1979. That year marked the beginning of the *abertura* (opening), the gradual return to democracy after fifteen years of military rule in Brazil. Many rights were curtailed during this period and, as a result, Carnival became an increasingly important occasion for voicing political concerns and asserting cultural pride. The 1970s in Salvador, Bahia, witnessed the emergence of *blocos Indios* (Indian Carnival associations) and *blocos Afros* (African Carnival associations), whose presentations at the annual pre-Lent Carnival celebration revolved around indigenous and African themes. Olodum emerged out of this bloco Afro movement just as abertura was paving the way for increased social, political, and cultural activism. Olodum's name comes from Olodumaré, the name of the supreme YORUBA deity.

Drum, voice, and liberation ideology are the foundations of Olodum's music. Every February, Olodum brings together some 200 large *surdo* bass drums and smaller, high-pitched *repique* drums in a thunderous and irresistibly kinetic presentation. The group is at the center of a sea of some 4,000 elaborately costumed performers who accompany the booming percussion with short call-and-response phrases. The occasion is Carnival, and for Olodum, the most famous of Salvador's blocos Afros, the theme is black history.

Olodum's yearly Carnival themes focus on black history and contemporary black political movements in Africa and in the African diaspora. In 1981, for example, Olodum developed its music, lyrics, and costumes around the history of GUINEA-BISSAU and its revolutionary black leader during the 1970s, AMÍLCAR CABRAL. Then, in 1986, Olodum's parade celebrated the black culture and history of CUBA. Olodum has also frequently explored Afro-Brazilian heritage. In 1998, Olodum's Carnival theme was *A Revolta dos Búzios—A Rota da Liberdade,* in commemoration of the 200th anniversary of this slave revolt, the first of a string of slave rebellions in Bahia that lasted through the first part of the nineteenth century.

One of the masterminds behind Olodum is João Jorge Santos Rodrigues. He was a member of Ilê Aiyê, the first bloco Afro (est. 1974), before joining Olodum in 1983. He helped rescue Olodum from disorganization and debt and, as a scholar of African history, has provided much of the black historical information that has inspired Olodum's songs and Carnival presentations. In addition to serving as Olodum's president, Rodrigues has distinguished himself as one of the leading defenders of Afro-Brazilian interests. In the early 1990s, he established contacts with human rights organizations and universities in the United States to gain support for and to promote a broader understanding of the Afro-Brazilian struggle against racial discrimination.

Another creative force in Olodum was musical director Neguinho do Samba (Antonio Luis Alves de Souza). In the mid-1980s he mixed Afro-Caribbean rhythms, including Jamaican REGGAE, with Brazilian SAMBA to create a new genre of music known as *samba-reggae,* which quickly became the dominant musical form at Bahian Carnival. In 1995, after twelve years with Olodum, Neguinho do Samba left the group.

Olodum's success in Brazil caught the attention of American songwriter Paul Simon, who invited Olodum to collaborate on his 1991 album *The Rhythm of the Saints*. This union brought Olodum international recognition, which led to tours outside of Brazil and collaboration with other famous musicians, including JIMMY CLIFF and MICHAEL JACKSON. Some critics have lamented the elaboration of Olodum's percussion-and-voice formula to include horns, synthesizers, and longer singing arrangements. The message, however, remains centered on the black communities in Brazil and abroad.

Olodum's activities go well beyond Carnival and music. When not performing, Olodum has been the spearhead of black protests and demonstrations in the city of Salvador. Locally, the group has engaged in protests against police brutality targeting Salvador's black population. On the international front, Olodum spent over ten years calling for the release of NELSON MANDELA and an end to APARTHEID in SOUTH AFRICA. With the end of apartheid, Olodum raised concern over the internal strife in ANGOLA.

Over the years, Olodum has evolved into a community organization that serves the people in its immediate vicinity as well as the general black community in Salvador. It has launched several community uplift programs, including a health campaign to prevent the spread of diseases such as acquired immunodeficiency syndrome (AIDS) and cholera as well as an effective clean-up program in the neighborhoods of Maciel and Pelourinho. Olodum was instrumental in lobbying for a $12 million bill, which was passed in 1993, to restore some 450 historic buildings in Pelourinho. Olodum has also attempted to address the high level of unemployment in the Maciel-Pelourinho neighborhood, in part by creating a factory where instruments, clothing, and Olodum paraphernalia are manufactured (est. 1993). Olodum also runs a reggae bar and the Africa Bar, where the group performs regularly.

The profits from Olodum's factory and bars help to fund the Olodum Creative School, which was established to provide people of all ages with an education they might otherwise not be able to afford. The school's courses are designed to give students of African descent a greater sense of Afro-Brazilian history, which is largely omitted in the traditional Brazilian curriculum, and to equip them with the social and technical skills that will make them better job candidates. The school also develops the artistic talents of its students through courses in dance, music, and theater, and an extracurricular youth samba group called Banda Mirim (est. 1983). Olodum has taken hundreds of homeless children off of Salvador's streets, enrolled them in their school, and launched efforts to improve their self-esteem and prepare them for fuller participation in Brazilian society.

As an extension of these educational activities, Olodum organizes and participates in seminars, speeches, and conferences on various issues affecting the black community in Brazil and in other parts of the world. It also has its own publishing house (est. 1994) that prints books as well as a monthly journal called *Bantu Nagô*. Olodum is an outstanding example of how Carnival organizations, in particular blocos Afros, have become building blocks for black economic and political power.

See also Carnivals in Latin America and the Caribbean; Slave Rebellions in Latin America and the Caribbean.

Aaron Myers

Olorun

Supreme god of the Yoruba pantheon.

Olodumaré, also known as Olorun, is the sky god to whom all of the ORISHAS answer, and he is mentioned first in all prayers. He is somewhat remote because he is busy, which is why the orishas do most of the work dealing with human beings.

See also Candomblé; Religions, African, in Latin America and the Caribbean; Santería.

Oluwu, Elizabeth

See Women Artists, African: An Interpretation.

Olympics, African Americans and the

The international competition that has been the stage for numerous historic performances by African American athletes.

The Olympian Games, the forerunner of the Olympic Games, began in ancient Greece in 776 B.C.E. and were held regularly for over a millennium to celebrate physicality through competition and to honor the gods. In 1896 the Games were revived in their modern form by French educator Pierre de Coubertin. The Summer Games have been held every four years since then, with the exception of wartime cancellations in 1916, 1940, and 1944. The Winter Games were added in 1924. The modern Olympics have been recognized as the supreme athletic competition in the world, and African American athletes have consistently proven themselves in the Games to be among the best of the world's top athletes.

Track and Field

African Americans made their entrance into the Olympics in St. Louis, Missouri, in 1904 when George Poage became the first black to participate in the Games, winning the bronze medal for third place in the 400-meter hurdles. The first African American to win an Olympic gold medal was sprint sensation John Baxter Taylor, who ran the third leg on the United States 4 x 400-meter relay team at the 1908 Games in London, England. The first to win gold in an individual event was DeHart Hubbard in the long jump in 1924 in Paris, FRANCE. As the number of African American athletes participating in the Games increased, so did America's track and field medal count. In the 1936 Games in Berlin, GERMANY, JESSE OWENS set an incredible mark when he won four gold medals. Since that time, African American men have dominated the sprint and long jump events at the Games, but Owens's feat went unmatched for nearly fifty years until CARL LEWIS captured four gold medals in the 1984 Games in LOS ANGELES, CALIFORNIA. Other historic achievements have included Bob Beamon's record-shattering long jump in 1968 in Mexico City, Mexico, the double victories of MICHAEL JOHNSON in the 200- and 400-meter sprint events in 1996 (ATLANTA, GEORGIA), and the gold medals in the decathalon for Rafer Johnson in 1960 (Rome, ITALY) and Dan O'Brien in 1996. At the 2000 Games in Sydney, Australia, Johnson became the first man to win gold in the 400-meter race at consecutive Olympics. He picked up a second gold medal as a member of the U.S. 4 × 400 relay team. Maurice Greene also won two gold medals in Sidney.

African American women were not allowed on the U.S. Olympic team prior to 1936. Had the doors been open earlier, Louise Stokes, better known as the Malden Meteor, would have been a likely bet to bring home a medal. Although her superb times at the Olympic trials qualified her for the 1932 team in the 400-meter dash, the U.S. women's team coaches refused to accept any blacks on the squad. In 1948 Alice Coachman brought home the gold in the high jump from the Games in London, England. In the 1960 Rome Games, WILMA RUDOLPH electrified Olympic fans as no one had since Owens by winning three gold medals in track—in the 100- and 200-meter dashes, and the 4 x 400-meter relay. Since that time, African Americans WYOMIA TYUS, EVELYN ASHFORD, Valerie Brisco-Hooks, FLORENCE GRIFFITH JOYNER, JACKIE JOYNER-KERSEE, and Gail Devers have also won at least three gold medals in track and field. In 2000, Marion Jones became the first woman to win five track medals (three gold, two bronze) at one Olympiad.

Boxing and Basketball

African Americans in recent decades have constituted the majority of athletes on the U.S. BOXING team. Perhaps the most celebrated of those squads was the 1976 team, for which Sugar Ray Leonard, Michael and LEON SPINKS, Howard Davis, and Leo Randolph all brought home a gold medal from the Games in Montreal, Canada. The U.S. team has often taken the gold in its native sport of BASKETBALL as well. After international basketball authorities voted to allow professionals in the Olympics, the United States fielded perhaps the greatest basketball team ever assembled for the 1992 Games in Barcelona, Spain. The Dream Team, as it was known, included National Basketball Association stars such as MICHAEL JORDAN, KARL MALONE, Charles Barkley, and SCOTTIE PIPPEN, and swept all comers to take the gold medal. African Americans helped the U.S. men's basketball team win gold again in 1996 and 2000. Similarly, African American women were major contributors to the U.S. women's basketball team's gold medal performances in 1984, 1988, 1996, 2000, and 2004.

Other Summer Events

While African Americans continue to play major roles in track and field, basketball, and boxing, their presence has diversified into other Olympic events. In gymnastics Ron Galimore was arguably the country's best gymnast going into the 1980 Olympics in Moscow, Union of Soviet Socialist Republics, but was kept home by the American boycott of the Games that year. In 1996 Dominique Dawes earned a gold medal as part of the winning U.S. women's gymnastics team (and a bronze in the individual floor exercise), and Jair Lynch won a silver in the men's parallel bars. Nelson Vails took a silver medal in cycling and Peter Westbrook won a bronze in fencing at the 1984 Games in LOS ANGELES, CALIFORNIA. In tennis in 1988 in Seoul, South Korea, Zina Garrison captured a gold medal in women's doubles and a bronze in singles. In 2000, tennis star Venus Williams captured the gold in women's singles and in women's doubles with her sister Serena. Anthony Ervin won a gold medal in the men's 50-meter freestyle swimming competition at the 2000 Games. African Americans have made their presence felt in other events including wrestling, weightlifting, judo, field hockey, and volleyball.

Winter Games

Few African Americans have participated in the Winter Olympics. Willie Davenport, who had already won a gold and a bronze in the hurdles in the Summer Olympics, and Jeff Gadley became the first African Americans in the Winter Games when they competed in the bobsled event in Lake Placid, New York, in 1980. Eight years later Debi Thomas won the first Winter Games medal for an African American, a bronze in figure skating. In 2002 Vonetta Flowers, a member of the U.S. two-women bobsled team, became the first African American to win a gold medal at the Winter Olympics

Sports and Politics

The Olympics have been an international stage for politics as well as athletics, and African Americans have often been at the center of such events. Jesse Owens's heroic performance at the 1936 Games, as the world stood on the verge of war, was seen as a powerful symbolic triumph for American democracy over German Nazism. Mal Whitfield, holder of four Olympic medals in track, urged African Americans to boycott the 1964 Games in Tokyo, Japan, as a protest against racial discrimination in the United States, but no athletes joined the boycott. Another protest occurred when African nations called for a boycott of the 1968 Mexico City Games if the white-ruled countries of SOUTH AFRICA and RHODESIA were allowed to participate. The Olympic Project for Human Rights, orchestrated by African American professor Harry Edwards, urged support of the boycott to protest against racism not only in southern Africa but in the United States as well. The invitations to South Africa and Rhodesia were rescinded but some African Americans stayed home from the Games anyway. Some of those who did participate made their own protests, the most significant of which was that of sprinters Tommie Smith and John Carlos, who had won the gold and bronze medals in the 200 meters. Wearing black socks and one black glove each on the victory stand, Smith and Carlos bowed their heads and gave the Black Power salute of a raised fist during the playing of the national anthem. As a result they were later stripped of their medals and expelled from the Olympics. The vilification both athletes received for their nonviolent protest obscured Smith's remarkable performance in the 200 meters, which would stand as a world record for eleven years.

See also Black Power in the United States; Olympics, Africans and the; Sports and African Americans; Track and Field in the United States.

Bibliography

Ashe, Arthur R., Jr. *A Hard Road to Glory: A History of the African-American Athlete.* 3 vols. Amistad, 1993.

Davis, Michael D. *Black American Women in Olympic Track and Field.* McFarland, 1992.

Henderson, Edwin B. *The Negro in Sports.* Rev. ed. Associated Publishers, 1949.

Page, James A. *Black Olympian Medalists.* Libraries Unlimited, 1991.

Spivey, Donald. "Black Consciousness and Olympic Protest Movement, 1964–1980." In *Sport in America: New Historical Perspectives.* Edited by Donald Spivey. Greenwood, 1985.

Olympics, Africans and the

International sports competition.

At the 1996 Summer Olympic Games, held in ATLANTA, GEORGIA, African athletes brought home thirty-four medals, eleven of them gold. The continent, however, which sent teams from fifty-two nations to the Atlanta games, has had a shorter history of Olympic participation than EUROPE or the Americas, and one marked by exclusion alternating with triumph.

The first African country to claim a gold medal in the modern Olympic Games was SOUTH AFRICA, which won gold in 1908 for the 100-meter race. South African athletes—until 1992, only whites were permitted to participate—also won gold in cycling in 1912, TENNIS in 1912 and 1920, wrestling in 1928, and swimming in 1952. Gold medals for weightlifting went to the Egyptians in 1928, 1936, and 1948. In 1960 the barefoot Ethiopian marathoner ABEBE BIKILA became the first black sub-Saharan athlete to win a gold medal, and his victory began an era in which Africans dominated international long-distance running. A Moroccan, Abdesiam Rhadi, finished second. Also in 1960, Egyptians won medals in wrestling and BOXING, a Senegalese athlete running for FRANCE won the bronze in the 200-meter race, and Ghanaian welterweight Clement Quartey won a silver medal in boxing.

African nations, many of them recently freed from COLONIAL RULE, participated in great numbers in the 1964 and 1968 Summer Olympic Games, held in Tokyo and Mexico City, respectively. In Tokyo, not only did Bikila repeat his gold-medal performance, but Kenyan Wilson Kiprugut won a bronze in the 800-meter race, the first medal for his country, which has since become known for its middle- and long-distance runners. Boxers from NIGERIA and GHANA also collected bronze medals. In 1968, twenty-five newly independent African nations sent athletes to Mexico City, where high altitude proved treacherous for many world-class runners—but not those who had trained in the highlands of ETHIOPIA and KENYA. Kenyan Nafutali Temu won gold in the 10,000-meter race and bronze in the 5,000-meter race. His countrymen KIPCHOGO KEINO and Benjamin Jipcho finished first and second in the 1,500-meter event, and Africans also won the 3,000-meter steeplechase and finished second in the 800-meter and 4 × 400-meter relays. In addition, Africans won four medals in boxing.

It was also in the 1960s that African politics—and the worldwide Black Power Movement—first influenced the Olympic Games. After the International Olympic Committee (IOC) decided in 1968 to readmit South Africa, which had been excluded in 1964 for its APARTHEID policies, a group of thirty-two African nations planned a boycott of the Mexico City games. Several non-African nations, such as ITALY, Sweden, Denmark, and Norway, joined their protest. Kenya's Kip Keino, who won two medals in Mexico City, said before the games, "I'd prefer to give up all hope of a medal than have to run with South Africans, who regard my black brothers and colored brothers as second-class citizens." Finally the IOC decided to retain the ban against South Africa.

Again in 1972, it took the threat of boycott by not only African but African American athletes to force the IOC to keep similarly racist RHODESIA (now ZIMBABWE) from participating in the Olympic Games. On the field, the 1972 Munich games yielded medals for Kip Keino, fellow Kenyan Mike Boit (who won bronze in the 800-meter race), Ugandan John Akii-bua (who won gold in the 400-meter hurdles), and the Kenyan 4 x 400-meter relay team, which won gold. As in Mexico City, Africa's boxers did almost as well as its runners, winning seven medals. Africa has since continued to produce world-class track-and-field athletes, including women runners who won gold in 1984 and 1992. In 1988 Africans won five gold medals—with four going to Kenyan athletes and one to a Moroccan. The 1992 games, held in Barcelona, Spain, yielded five gold medals out of a total of twenty-five for African athletes, including Namibian sprinter FRANKIE FREDERICKS, who won two silver medals.

The 1996 Summer Olympic games saw Africa's best showing ever, with African nations taking home eleven gold medals. Perhaps most inspiring was the victory of Nigeria's SOCCER team in a sport long dominated by South America and Europe. Fredericks again won two silver medals, while Ethiopian HAILE GEBRSELASSIE won gold in the 10,000-meter race. Nigerian Chioma Ajunwa, gold medalist in the long jump, and Gatuma Roba, Ethiopian marathon winner, were two of the African

African Olympic Gold Medalists

Year	Name	Country	Event
Track and Field (Men)			
1908	Reginald Walker	South Africa	100m
1920	Bevil Rudd	South Africa	400m
1988	Paul Ereng	Kenya	800m
1992	William Tanui	Kenya	800m
1968	Kipchogo Keino	Kenya	1500m
1988	Peter Rono	Kenya	1500m
2000	Noah Ngeny	Kenya	1500m
1968	Mohamed Gammoudi	Tunisia	5000m
1980	Miruts Yifter	Ethiopia	5000m
1984	Said Aouita	Morocco	5000m
1988	John Ngugi	Kenya	5000m
1996	Venuste Niyongabo	Burundi	5000m
2000	Millon Wolde	Ethiopia	5000m
1968	Naftall Temu	Kenya	10,000m
1980	Miruts Yifter	Ethiopia	10,000m
1988	Brahim Boutaib	Morocco	10,000m
1992	Khalid Skah	Morocco	10,000m
1996	Haile Gebrselassie	Ethiopia	10,000m
2000	Haile Gebrselassie	Ethiopia	10,000m
1928	Sydney Atkinson	South Africa	110m Hurdles
1972	John Akii-Bua	Uganda	400m Hurdles
1968	Amos Biwott	Kenya	3000m Steeple Chase
1972	Kipchogo Keino	Kenya	3000m Steeple Chase
1984	Julius Korir	Kenya	3000m Steeple Chase
1988	Julius Karviki	Kenya	3000m Steeple Chase
1992	Matthew Birer	Kenya	3000m Steeple Chase
1996	Joseph Keter	Kenya	3000m Steeple Chase
2000	Reuben Kosgei	Kenya	3000m Steeple Chase
1912	Kenneth McArthur	South Africa	Marathon
1960	Abebe Bikila	Ethiopia	Marathon
1964	Abebe Bikila	Ethiopia	Marathon
1968	Mamo Wolde	Ethiopia	Marathon
1996	Josia Thugwane	South Africa	Marathon
2000	Gezahgne Abera	Ethiopia	Marathon
Track and Field (Women)			
2000	Maria Mutola	Mozambique	800m
1992	Hassiba Boulmerka	Algeria	1500m
2000	Nouria Benida Merah	Algeria	1500m
1992	Derartu Tulu	Ethiopia	10,000m
2000	Derartu Tulu	Ethiopia	10,000m
1984	Nawal el Moutawakel	Morocco	400m Hurdles
1996	Fatuma Roba	Ethiopia	Marathon
1952	Esther Brand	South Africa	High Jump
1996	Chioma Ajunwa	Nigeria	Long Jump
Swimming and Diving (Women)			
1996	Penny Heyns	South Africa	100m Breast Stroke
1996	Penny Heyns	South Africa	200m Breast Stroke
Boxing			**Weight Class**
1920	Clarence Walker	South Africa	Bantam Weight
1924	William Smith	South Africa	Bantam Weight
1932	Lawrence Stevens	South Africa	Lightweight
1948	Gerald Dreyer	South Africa	Lightweight
1996	Hocine Soltani	Algeria	Lightweight
1932	David Carstens	South Africa	Light Heavyweight
1948	George Hunter	South Africa	Light Heavyweight

women to shine in Atlanta. As one African sports fan told the *New York Times,* after decades of exclusion and controversy, 1996 was "the year of the black athlete."

African athletes continued to excel at the 2000 Olympics in Sydney, Australia, capturing thirty-five medals. An African nation once again won the gold medal in soccer, as CAMEROON defeated SPAIN in the final game in a shootout. Africans also continued their dominance in Olympic distance running, taking all three medals in the 1,500 meters, 5,000 meters, 10,000 meters, and the 3,000-meter steeplechase. Kenyans and Ethiopians were the best represented, with Gebrselassie successfully defending his 10,000-meter gold medal and other Ethiopian runners winning the 5,000 meters and the marathon.

See also Olympics, African Americans and the.

Kate Tuttle

Ometo

Ethnic group of Ethiopia.

The Ometo inhabit primarily southwestern ETHIOPIA. They speak an Afro-Asiatic language in the Cushitic group and are considered one of the SIDAMO peoples. Approximately one million people consider themselves Ometo.

See also Languages, African: An Overview.

Omotoso, Kole

1943–

Nigerian novelist, poet, and critic who has maintained a commitment to address the common people of Africa.

Kole Omotoso was born into a YORUBA family in the Akura, NIGERIA and received his early education in local schools. Inspired by his uncle, the author Olaiya Fagbamigbe, and by evenings spent listening to Yoruba folktales, Omotoso went on to publish stories while at King's College in LAGOS. He earned a bachelor of arts degree in French and Arabic from the University of IBADAN in 1968 and a docorate in modern Arabic literature from the University of Edinburgh in Scotland in 1972. He returned to Nigeria to write and teach, and took a post as professor at the University of Ibadan in 1976.

Influenced by the Nigerian writer WOLE SOYINKA, Omotoso's increasingly political writings have dealt with issues affecting Africa's future from the perspective of ordinary people. Omotoso believes in the power of the arts to bring social change. He contributes frequently to magazines and newspapers and has written novels, plays, short stories, essays, and literary criticism. Focusing on Nigeria and Africa, Omoto's works address interracial marriage, childhood poverty, communism, SOCIALISM, the Nigerian civil war, and criticisms of materialism and neocolonialism—especially the relationship of Africa's colonial past to its postcolonial economic problems and ethnic discord.

The tireless Omotoso was a founder of the Association of Nigerian Authors and served as its national secretary and its national president. He also helped to create the Union of Writers of the African Peoples in Accra, GHANA, and worked as an editor of both *Afriscope* and *Ch'Indaba Magazine.*

By the late 1980s and early 1990s Omotoso's work had become more directly critical of political and social problems in Nigeria. In 1991 he made a controversial decision to leave Nigeria for SOUTH AFRICA, which was then still a white-ruled APARTHEID state. He took a position as professor at the University of the Western Cape, and his writings after 1991 addressed the transition to majority rule in South Africa and the implications of the South African experience for the rest of the continent. His first book written in South Africa, *Season of Migration to the South,* was banned in Nigeria.

Bibliography

Balogun, F. Odun. "Populist Fiction: Omotoso's Novels." *African Literature Today,* no. 13 (1983): 98–121.

Robert Fay

Onchocerciasis

Parasitic disease most commonly found in Africa; also referred to as "oncho" and "the lion's stare."

According to the World Health Organization (WHO), river blindness, a disease caused by the parasitic nematode *Onchocerca volvulus,* is the second leading cause of infectious blindness. Of the approximately eighteen million people infected with the parasite, 99 percent live in Africa, principally the SAHEL region in West Africa.

Impact

More than six million people have serious skin problems as a result of river blindness, and another 270,000 are blind as a result of the disease. Fear of the disease has caused populations to abandon fertile river valleys where the Simulium fly is endemic, such as the Volta River Basin in BURKINA FASO and GHANA. The area affected is massive, covering hundreds of thousands of square kilometers of the fertile lands in the region. The economic loss is compounded by the large number of adults, often only in their thirties, who are disabled by disease and must be cared for by family.

Life Cycle

The parasite that causes river blindness is transmitted from person to person by a species of black fly, *Simulium damnosum,* which lays its eggs in oxygen-rich river water. Adult flies may travel hundreds of kilometers searching for a host to bite, but people living near affected rivers are the most likely victims. If the fly bites an individual infected with river blindness, they often ingest the microfilariae of *Onchocerca volvulus* along with the person's blood. These microfilariae develop into larvae that can be transmitted to the next person the fly bites. Symptoms of the disease appear approximately one to three years after initial infection, after the larvae have matured, mated, and produced millions of microfilariae, which migrate throughout the body and cause severe itching and dendritis. The deterioration of microfilariae killed by the immune system causes more severe pathologies, including loss of skin pigmentation, swelling, and lichenification (hardening and thickening of the skin due to continual scratching or other irritation). As the parasite load increases, the severity of the symptoms worsens, leading ultimately to blindness as disintegrating dead microfilariae in the cornea cause ocular lesions and cataracts.

Eradication

African governments have teamed up with WHO and the World Bank, as well as nongovernmental organizations such as the Carter Center and the African Programme for Onchocerciasis Control (APOC), to implement programs in eleven West African countries where the disease is endemic. In 1974 WHO began administering the World Bank–funded Onchocerciasis Control Programme (OCP) in an attempt to eradicate the disease by eliminating the vector, namely the Simulium fly. It was later discovered that ivermectin, an antiparisitic medicine developed to prevent heartworms in dogs, also helps prevent the transmission of microfilariae if administered annually. WHO considers the OCP program to be one of its greatest achievements, as it has virtually eliminated the disease within the program area, opening up land to support approximately seventeen million people. WHO predicts that river blindness can be effectively eliminated as a health problem in Africa within the next few decades, if current levels of support are maintained.

Bibliography

Kim, Aehyung, and Bruce Benton. *Cost-benefit Analysis of the Onchocerca Control Program (OCP)*. World Bank, 1995.

McMillan, Della E. *Sahel Visions: Planned Settlement and River Blindness Control in Burkina Faso*. University of Arizona Press, 1995.

Peters, Wallace, and Herbert M. Gilles. *Color Atlas of Tropical Medicine and Parasitology*. Mosby-Year Book, 1995.

Wigg, David. *And Then Forgot to Tell Us Why: A Look at the Campaign against River Blindness in West Africa*. World Bank, 1993.

Ari Nave

O'Neal, Shaquille

1972–

African American basketball player, one of the greatest players of the 1990s.

Born in Newark, New Jersey, Shaquille O'Neal attended high school in San Antonio, Texas, where he led the school BASKETBALL team to the state championship. O'Neal then entered Louisiana State University (LSU) in 1989. He quickly became a dominating player in college basketball, and he averaged 21.6 points and 13.5 rebounds per game over three seasons. In his last year at LSU he led the nation in blocked shots and was second in rebounding.

In 1992 O'Neal entered the National Basketball Association (NBA) draft and was the first player chosen, by the Orlando Magic, then a recent expansion team. Although his inexperience was evident in his first professional year, O'Neal's high level of play made him a nearly unanimous choice as rookie of the year for the 1992–1993 season. That year he led the season's rookies in points (23.4), rebounds (13.9), and blocked shots (3.53) per game, and he was second overall in the league in rebounds and eighth overall in scoring. During the 1993–1994 season O'Neal's play continued to improve. He led the NBA in field-goal percentage (.599) and finished second in points (29.3) and rebounds per game (13.2). In 1994 he was also a member of the United States national basketball team known as Dream Team II, which won the gold medal at the world basketball championships in Toronto, Ontario, in Canada.

In the 1994–1995 season O'Neal led the NBA in points per game (29.3) and finished second in field-goal percentage (.583) and third in rebounds per game (11.4). He also led the Magic to the NBA Finals, where the team lost to the Houston Rockets. O'Neal's success continued in the 1995–1996 season, when he was selected as an All-Star for the fourth consecutive year. After the season he played for the U.S. national basketball team at the 1996 Olympic Games in ATLANTA, GEORGIA. In July 1996 O'Neal signed with the Los Angeles Lakers; he powered the team to playoff appearances in 1997, 1998, and 1999. In 2000 he helped lead the Lakers to the NBA Finals, where they defeated the Indiana Pacers in six games. He was named NBA Most Valuable Player (MVP), and NBA Finals MVP, in 2000 and in 2001.

O'Neal also became popular as an entertainer. In 1993 *Shaq Diesel*, a best-selling RAP music album, was released. The following year he acted in the motion picture *Blue Chips*. In 1994 he also issued a second rap album, *Shaq Fu—Da Return*, and an action-oriented home video game, *Shaq-Fu*, which stars O'Neal as a kung fu warrior. Further entertainment projects included the albums *You Can't Stop the Reign* (1996), *The Best of Shaquille O'Neal* (1997), and *Shaquille O'Neal Presents His Superfriends* (2001), and a role in the 1997 movie *Steel*. He has also appeared in *He Got Game* (1998), *Freddy Got Fingered* (2001), and *The Brothers* (2001). O'Neal has also written an autobiography, *Shaq Attack* (1993), as well as the books *Shaq and the Beanstalk and Other Very Tall Tales* (1999) and *Shaq Talks Back* (2001).

O'Neale, Charles Duncan

1879–1936

Black activist in Barbados during the 1920s and 1930s.

Charles Duncan O'Neale was the initial leader of the Democratic League (DL), the first political party in BARBADOS, founded in 1924.

See also Barbados.

Opera

Musical drama that originated in 1600 in Italy; numerous African Americans have risen to prominence within the genre.

Early-nineteenth-century African American opera singers and performers were crossover artists. Barred from all major American stages, they transgressed the boundaries between high and low culture by playing the marginal American concert stages and opera houses that permitted them. They also performed in minstrel and vaudeville shows. Careers were short-lived, usually lasting only two or three years—the length of time it typically took for the novelty of seeing a black singer to wear off for white audiences. Europe often proved a more hospitable climate for African American artists.

Nonetheless, a number of black performers rose to prominence in the American opera scene. Elizabeth Taylor Greenfield, known as the Black Swan, toured North America and England with an African American troupe in the 1850s and 1860s. During the same period, the multitalented Luca family included opera in their performances, as did the Hyers Sisters, who were renowned for their renditions of the works of Verdi and Donizetti. SISSIERETTA JONES was the most celebrated opera performer of the time. Known as the Black Patti, after white soprano Adelina Patti, she gave a recital at the White House for President Benjamin Harrison. Jones outlasted her contemporaries, extending her career to fifteen years, by forming in 1896 the Black Patti Troubadours, which mixed opera with musical theatre and offered a vehicle to showcase her talents. Similarly, soprano Nellie Brown Mitchell's career lasted almost ten years, thanks to her creation of the Nellie Brown Mitchell Concert Company.

Until the color bar that prevented African Americans from performing on America's greatest stages was lifted, recitals were the quickest way to success for black performers. After years of dazzling audiences on recital stages, in 1955 contralto MARIAN ANDERSON became the first African American to perform at New York City's Metropolitan Opera, having won renown for her unmatched talent and the breadth of her repertoire. Anderson's performances, like those of her predecessor, tenor recitalist ROLAND HAYES, opened the stages for other opera singers. Anderson and Hayes incorporated the concert spiritual—an indigenous African American contribution that fused European art music with black SPIRITUALS—into their recitals.

Throughout the mid-twentieth century African Americans were usually cast in secondary roles, confined to playing marginal dark-skinned characters. This changed in 1966 when Mississippi-born soprano Leontyne Price prefigured the era of the African American diva by performing at the opening of the new Metropolitan Opera House at New York City's Lincoln Center. By the 1980s the African American diva was well represented by the glamorous sopranos JESSYE NORMAN and KATHLEEN BATTLE.

African American opera companies have developed alongside individual artists. Organizations such as the Colored American Opera Company and the Theodore Drury Opera Company staged productions in the early twentieth century. These were followed by productions by the Imperial Company, the National Negro Opera Company, the Dra-Mu Opera Company, and the Harlem Opera Company. With the establishment of Opera/South and the National Ebony Opera in the 1970s, black productions flourished. Their mandate was to create opportunities for African American professionals working in the field.

William Franklin and Lillian Evanti sing in the second act of *La Traviata,* produced by the National Negro Opera Company in 1944. *Library of Congress*

By the early 1990s mainstream American stages had reconsidered earlier compositions written by African Americans and staged productions that conveyed the tragedy and triumph of the black experience. DUKE ELLINGTON's *Queenie Pie* and Leroy Jenkins's *The Mother of Three Sons* were among the first works to take part in this mainstream revival. These compositions are part of a body of African American work that includes long-neglected pieces by composers such as Harry Laurence Freeman, writer of fourteen grand operas including *Octoroon* and the early JAZZ opera *The Flapper,* and RAGTIME innovator SCOTT JOPLIN, who created an indigenous African American opera with *Treemonisha.* Anthony Davis, founder of the instrumental group Episteme, is the dominant figure in late-twentieth-century African American composition. His *X: The Life and Times of Malcolm X, Under the Double Moon,* and *Amistad* have all reached well-known halls in the United States, bringing a contemporary flavor to traditional opera.

See also Music, African American.

Peter Hudson

Operation Breadbasket

Organization formed by the Southern Christian Leadership Conference and later led by Jesse Jackson that put pressure on corporations to hire blacks and support black businesses.

In 1962 the SOUTHERN CHRISTIAN LEADERSHIP CONFERENCE (SCLC) established Operation Breadbasket to put "bread, money, and income into the baskets of black and poor people." With the broad mandate of improving the economic conditions of African Americans, Operation Breadbasket organized black consumers to press for jobs and to encourage and expand black-owned businesses. In its first campaign in ATLANTA, GEORGIA, the organization won a commitment from local companies for 5,000 jobs over the next five years.

After establishing affiliates in several Southern states, the organization expanded north. In 1966 JESSE JACKSON, then a student at Chicago Theological Seminary, helped found the CHICAGO chapter, which directed protests at several dairy companies and supermarket chains to demand that they hire black workers and support black-owned businesses. Although the protesters were able to secure promises of employment for black workers from several major corporations, they had trouble ensuring compliance. The A&P supermarket, for example, promised 770 permanent jobs and 1,200 summer jobs in May 1967, but did not deliver until another protest was launched in 1970.

As Operation Breadbasket expanded across the country in 1967, MARTIN LUTHER KING JR. appointed Jackson to be its national director. From then on the group became increasingly identified with Jackson's high-profile leadership. Under Jackson, Operation Breadbasket took on a number of projects, among them a free breakfast program and the 1968 Poor People's Campaign in WASHINGTON, D.C. The organization also became a voice in local and national politics, opposing welfare cuts and supporting electoral candidates.

By 1971 the group had started to collapse under the weight of too many projects, too few resources, and charges of financial corruption. Some criticized Jackson for using Operation Breadbasket as his own personal power base in Chicago, Illinois, and faulted him for the failure of the group to act like a true national organization. The same year, Jackson left the SCLC, dissolving the Chicago chapter and forming OPERATION PUSH. Since then, Operation Breadbasket has continued as a subsidiary operation of the SCLC, but has never regained the momentum it had during the 1960s.

See also Poor People's Washington Campaign.

Marian Aguiar

Operation PUSH

Organization founded by Jesse Jackson in 1971 to promote economic security for black workers and businesses and to provide assistance to African American urban youth.

In 1971 JESSE JACKSON left OPERATION BREADBASKET, the economic arm of the SOUTHERN CHRISTIAN LEADERSHIP CONFERENCE, to found Operation People United to Save Humanity (PUSH). Like Operation Breadbasket, the new organization set its sights on strengthening the economic security of African Americans. Under Jackson's charismatic leadership, Operation PUSH organized boycotts for black consumers to press for minority employment and support for black-owned businesses.

Over the years Operation PUSH expanded its mission and focused on national issues like education and national politics. In the late 1970s Jackson brought national attention to the subject of minority education, and raised money for an elementary school education program called PUSH for Excellence, or PUSH/EXCEL. Despite substantial federal and private support, the education program foundered because of poor administration. Following accusations of shady business alliances and fund embezzlement, the organization scaled down, and, by the early 1980s, had reduced its agenda to consciousness raising.

Operation PUSH, which was largely dependent on Jackson's powerful personality for its success, lost momentum when he left to run in the 1984 presidential election primaries. Jackson remained a spokesperson for the organization through the 1980s, however, keeping Operation PUSH afloat through his fund-raising efforts. Returning to a more active role in 1991, Jackson turned the group toward the issues that had been a part of his election campaign, including the crises of acquired immunodeficiency syndrome (AIDS) and urban violence. In 1993 Operation PUSH began a program in CHICAGO to promote education and employment opportunities for minority youth. Three years later, Jackson merged Operation PUSH with the national Rainbow Coalition to form the Rainbow/PUSH Coalition.

See also Acquired Immunodeficiency Syndrome in the Untied States.

Bibliography

House, Ernest R. *Jesse Jackson and the Politics of Charisma: The Rise and Fall of the PUSH/Excel Program.* Westview Press, 1988.

Marian Aguiar

Opportunity

Early publication of the National Urban League, which documented the social and economic conditions of African Americans.

Founded in 1923, *Opportunity* provided a forum for young writers and artists, many of whom became famous during the Harlem Renaissance. Founding editor Charles Spurgeon Johnson intended *Opportunity* not only to publicize the National Urban League's (NUL) projects and staff, but also to provide information about and analysis of the social and economic conditions that faced blacks. The journal's scientific approach was meant in part to serve as a counterweight to the National Association for the Advancement of Colored People's publication The Crisis, which NUL leaders considered too subjective. Through articles addressing the migration of Southern blacks to the North, the intelligence of people of African descent, and the influence of Marcus Garvey, the magazine became one of the most respected black publications in the United States. During World War II (1939–1945), Johnson's successor, Elmer A. Carter, devoted significant space to discussions of the contradiction between, on the one hand, blacks fighting overseas in a war for democracy, and on the other, their exclusion from democracy at home.

Opportunity also published black authors who had difficulty selling their work to white publications, including such stars of the Harlem Renaissance as Langston Hughes, Countee Cullen, James Weldon Johnson, Claude McKay, Angelina Weld Grimké, and Sterling Brown. *Opportunity* also sponsored literary contests and organized social events that introduced these writers to editors and publishers.

Opportunity never earned enough to cover production costs. In 1923, the journal's first year of operation, circulation was only around 4,000. By 1927 it had peaked at 11,000. Although in 1949 circulation stood at approximately 10,000, *Opportunity*'s publishers ended the journal's production, citing persistent deficits and the availability of other journals to continue its work.

See also Magazines, Newspapers, and Journals.

Bibliography

Johnson, Abby Arthur, and Ronald Maberry Johnson. *Propaganda and Aesthetics: The Literary Politics of Afro-American Magazines in the Twentieth Century.* University of Massachusetts Press, 1979.

Robert Fay

Oral Traditions in Africa

Variety of oral forms that developed in Africa, including epics, tales, riddles, poetry, and proverbs.

The African oral tradition distills the essence of human experience. Performers of these oral forms take ancient images and shape them into spoken texts that influence audiences in contemporary societies. Some African performers have used the oral tradition to document centuries of history and to pass on cultural practices over several generations. "When those of us in my generation awakened to earliest consciousness," said Nongenile Masithathu Zenani, a contemporary Xhosa storyteller from South Africa, "we were born into a tradition that was already flourishing." Ikabbo, a San performer in South Africa in the nineteenth century, also recognized the long history of the oral tradition: "A story is like the wind: it comes from a distant place, and we feel it."

However, the African oral tradition is more than simply a means of recording history and maintaining cultural continuity. In these oral art forms, storytellers remember past experiences and the wisdom of ancient times; their stories, epics, and poems become an artistic medium that organizes, examines, and interprets an audience's experiences of the present.

Social Role

The African oral tradition is not simply a spoken art; it is also an event, a ritual, and a performance. Performers use metaphor to take an audience's routine experiences and link them to ancient, often fantastic, images from the artistic tradition. When the storytellers bring the two sets of images together, audiences are brought to see the connections between them. This enables the members of the audience to understand their daily experiences at the same time that they are rooted in history.

An important theme in some oral traditions is the connection between all living things. A tale from the Mbuti people of the Democratic Republic of the Congo identifies a splendid bird with a deformed child who is neglected by her family. By comparing the child and the bird, the storyteller reveals that, in the realm of nature, there is no distinction between the perfection of the bird and the seemingly flawed child. In nature, both are sacred.

This theme of interconnectedness is also revealed in the *Mwindo* epic of the Nyanga people of the Democratic Republic of the Congo. In this epic, the hero is taken by the gods into the heavens where he learns that all relationships in the universe are in harmony and that any tampering with that balance will result in disaster.

Many tales propose that the order of nature echoes the mythic harmonious era and thus provides a model for ordering the human world. Performers suggest that the age of the gods gave way to the age of the hero, who tries to restore order on the model of nature. The hero is a composite of all elements of nature and society. Both nature and society flow through the hero, and he comes to represent their interdependence. In virtually all such oral traditions, the hero transcends time, occupying the past, present, and future. In this way, the hero represents the people as a whole and their struggle with the world.

Varied Forms

The various oral forms, including riddles, proverbs, poems, and tales, are interwoven. They all rely heavily on metaphor, through which a word, phrase, or concept that normally has one meaning comes to represent another. By means of this new designation, which creates an implicit comparison, performers engage the audience and persuade its members to accept their explanation of paradoxes and conflicts.

The oral forms have a common internal structure, usually a rhythmical ordering of images and themes which establishes the connection between the artistic tradition and the real world. The metaphors and the rhythmic ordering link the oral tradition with the visual arts, such as painting, sculpture, and architecture, and with dance, mime, and music: All involve a poetic ordering of images. Each of the oral forms nourishes the others. The lyric poet uses riddles, the storyteller incorporates riddles and lyrics, and myths become the basis for epic tales. In these and other ways, each oral form builds on others.

Riddle

The riddle establishes a model for all African oral art. The relationship between images in a riddle always contains at least the potential for metaphor and complexity. When a Lingala riddler poses the riddle, "A chief who only sits among thorns," the answer, "The tongue," reveals a description not only of the tongue but also of the chief. The paradox of the riddle—in this case, how a chief can sit only among thorns—challenges the audience to solve the puzzle by relying on the intellect. Riddles also rely on the imagination: In this case, the audience imagines a tongue as a chief and teeth as thorns. This reliance on imagery encourages the members of the audience to use their imagination to find the answer. By engaging the audience in this way, the riddler brings the members of the audience into the center of the riddle, the metaphor that is at its core, allowing them to learn from it by becoming part of the process.

Lyric Poem

The lyric poem expresses an emotion or set of ideas. If a story is involved, it is hidden deep within the images of the poem or is present only in fragments. Lyric poetry is often more complex than the riddle because it contains a number of riddling connections. The lyric poem is further complicated because a single riddle may be introduced into the context of another, and yet another, and so on as the riddling images of the poem interact. Some lyric poems have several layers of related riddles, making them quite intricate and challenging.

A lyric poet uses a series of images to repeat a basic theme or to present an intense emotion. Each set of repetitions of the image is in itself a riddle. These repetitions become a kind of clue, moving the audience closer to an understanding of the poet's intent. "My heart is joyful," begins a Mbuti song from the Democratic Republic of the Congo, establishing the heart as a theme. The image is repeated concretely and metaphorically, "My heart flies away, singing." Then one image is followed by another: "Under the trees of the forest,/Forest our home and our mother." The poet contrasts herself with a bird and evokes the relationship between bird and forest. In that homely image and, in the idea of the forest as a mother, its suggestion of childbirth, the poet continues, "In my net I have caught/a little bird." The poet repeats the image yet again, but with a thematic change: "My heart is caught in the net,/In the net with the bird," tying the separate image strands of heart, bird, and net together. The lyric poet repeats the image, establishes the boundaries of the varieties of imagery that may be introduced into the poem, and creates the rhythmic structure. These elements ensure that members of the audience will experience the different sets of images in a similar way. In the Mbuti song, the singer unites the images of ensnared heart and trapped bird; when the audience learns that the poem is performed by a woman while giving birth, the images of joy, forest, and snaring achieve a metaphorical union, and the lyrical riddling ends.

Proverb

In proverbs, the performer uses metaphor to evoke a perception about everyday life or a universally recognized truth. "Can one mouth take meat from a lion?" asks the TUMBUKA sage, suggesting that, within the context of tradition, the opinions of a single person are useless. "Wisdom," says the Tumbuka wise man, "is like mushrooms that come in season when the porridge is finished," suggesting that judgment is valuable only when it can be immediately applied to a problem. The proverb establishes a metaphorical relationship, tying a well-known saying to a situation to which it may or may not be clearly applicable. In some cases, the power of a proverb lies in its ambiguity. A MENDE proverb, for example, contains many possible interpretations: "There is no mercy in the tomb." Some might argue that this means that all people face final judgment from a god after they die. But others might argue that it means that after one has died, one's friends and family will be ruthless in assessing one's actions. This ambiguity makes the proverb a constantly evolving form.

Tale

The tale is in narrative form and involves the movement of characters from a conflict to a resolution. In the tale, performers bring into connection realistic and fantastic images to tell the story. By doing so, they tie the members of the audience to their pasts. Metaphor is often used in the tale, but it is not always necessary to the sense of the story. When it does occur—when both narrative and metaphor are present—the tale assumes the form of the lyric poem.

In African trickster tales, the relationship is typically between the trickster and his dupe. The trickster creates a deceptive world to approximate the real world, taking advantage of the dupe. This link between the real world and the trickster's illusory world makes it possible for the performer to create a corresponding metaphorical relationship, a set of worlds controlled and manipulated by the trickster. In a TIGRE story from ETHIOPIA, for example, Beiho tricks his greedy uncles in a series of events. Because of their greed, the uncles move stupidly into the worlds of illusion created by Beiho and so are doomed.

In some tales, the metaphor is a crucial compositional device that holds the story together. In a Lamba story from ZAMBIA, two youths are going through their puberty ritual. The storyteller moves the characters through three distinct worlds as they journey toward the celestial realm. In the first world, the storyteller establishes a model set of experiences and events; these are then repeated with metaphorical depth in the second and third worlds. Each experience in the three worlds is at once the same yet more complex, as worlds two and three comment on the previous world. Through this device, the audience is moved to an emotional and subtle understanding of the significance of the ritual.

Heroic Poetry

In heroic poetry, the performer often focuses on a single hero and his or her struggle against adversity. Heroic poems are sometimes panegyric, offering praise for the hero's moral character and actions. TUAREG oral poets in northern and western AFRICA often sing of love. The female soloist plays a stringed instrument, singing of the virtues of a great warrior, an ideal man, a famous camel. In TOMBOUCTOU (Timbuktu), MALI, the words of SONGHAI poets accompany puberty rituals, singing the praises of the youths undergoing these transformations in their lives. Among the SONINKÉ of THE GAMBIA, MALI, and MAURITANIA, the *diare* (poet) accompanies men to battle, encourages them as they fight, praises their victories, and sings the stories of family and genealogy. He is the archivist of his master's family traditions.

Heroic poetry often relies on complex images, sometimes focusing on historical events. A heroic poem may describe the notable achievements of great cultural heroes, and it can also be used to praise a group. For example, the mabe, Songhai professional praise singers in Tombouctou, recount a person's family history and ancestors to the accompaniment of a drum and chanting. However, heroic poetry can also cast humans in a negative light. For example, a heroic poem might contrast a flawed contemporary leader with the great heroes of the past.

Epic

Fragmented history is also frequently a part of African epic. Typically, epics include both real and fictional characters. An epic affects the audience not necessarily because of its historical accuracy but because of the insight it brings to history and culture. As with other African oral traditions, the epic form relies heavily on metaphor. An epic often contains a number of smaller tales, and the metaphor ties these together. The central metaphor and the tales center on the character of the hero. The epic gradually reveals the hero's strengths and frailties, vision and uncertainties, and may portray the hero as a symbol of a group's culture and traditions. The epic is thus a complex reshaping of the tale. Epics also rely on heroic poetry to provide structure, helping to organize the narratives and narrative fragments into a large epic framework. Heroic poetry may also supply the specific historical and geographical data for epics.

The West African epic of *Sundiata* occurs within a network of praises. It is strongly tied to historical events and relies heavily on heroic poetry. The story itself is straightforward, with common themes from the African oral tradition. Women play a central role in the epic, as an extension of the hero. Sundiata goes through the several stages of life—miraculous birth, coming to manhood, and accomplishing impossible tasks that reveal him as a man destined for nobility. Sundiata struggles with the great enemy, Sumanguru; discovers Sumanguru's secret and destroys him; and becomes an important leader. The *Ozidi Saga* of the Ijo of NIGERIA also begins with a miraculous birth. The story describes the birth of Ozidi, the son of a murdered general; Ozidi's development as a ward of his supernatural grandmother; and the battle he fights to restore his family's greatness.

These and other epics have a grander sweep than either the tale or oral poetry. By combining the tale patterns with poetic rhythms, the epic transfers the imagery of those genres to historical figures and acts. The epic thus endows history with the cultural symbolism of the imaginative tradition. Heroes, whether or not they have existed in fact, become emblems of change.

Influence on Written Literature

African verbal art forms are closely tied to written genres, such as novels and poetry. The oral and written forms have long existed side by side. Egyptian scribes, HAUSA and Swahili copyists and memorizers, and contemporary writers of popular novellas have all based their work on the traditions of oral cultures. The early African literary traditions were beneficiaries of the oral genres; the oral epic and its hero are the predecessors of the African novel and its central characters. Literacy spread rapidly through Africa, especially in the nineteenth and twentieth centuries, but the oral tradition remains robust, retaining its strength alongside written forms.

Early African writers in the contemporary period were often a combination of copyist and oral storyteller. This is evident in popular literature, which usually takes the form of shorter works in both African and European languages. These written works often attempt to convey a warning or a moral lesson, and sometimes include extreme imagery. The strong interaction between the oral tradition and the growing literary tradition follows a pattern seen in ancient Egypt, where precisely the same transition from oral tradition to written literature occurred. Although the use of literary genres such as the novel may have been triggered by the Western schooling of Africans, African writers placed the forms into African oral contexts at once. In any case, the novel as a literary form is indigenous to Africa.

The oral tradition, then, has directly influenced the production of literary works. This influence is clear in some of the great literary works of Africa, from Tayeb Salih's Arabic-language *Mawsim al-hijrah ila al-Shamal* (1969, *Season of Migration to the North,* 1969) to A. C. Jordan's Xhosa-language *Ingqumbo yeminyanya* (1954, *The Wrath of the Ancestors,* 1980). The stories of A. Onwudiwe of Nigeria, Stephen Andrea Mpashi of Zambia, and Njogu Gitene of KENYA contain suggestions of themes and forms more fully developed in the novels of Nigerian author CHINUA ACHEBE, Cape Verdean Baltasar Lopes, and Thomas Mofolo of LESOTHO. These writers focus on the modern hero and his options, his agony, and his internal struggle. As the authors probe the hero's psyche, they deviate from the patterns of the oral tradition, replacing the cyclical romanticism of the ancient works with a realistic ambiguity.

Influence on Oral Traditions

African storytelling traditions have had a wide-ranging influence on other parts of the world. In the United States, African American oral traditions and storytelling dating from the slavery era have profoundly shaped American culture as a whole, an influence reflected in JAZZ, RAP, and ballads.

Outside the United States, the influence of African oral traditions is also apparent. A common African storytelling character, the trickster, is found in oral traditions in BRAZIL, HAITI, and JAMAICA—all countries with sizable populations of African descent. Of equal significance is the fact that the oral traditions of Africa find their counterparts in cultures around the world. The epic of Mwindo in Central Africa compares to the epic of Odysseus in Greece; the story of Sundiata in West Africa corresponds to the story of Ramayana in India; a tale depicting a child's puberty ritual in Gabon parallels one describing a child's transformation into adulthood in Japan. We tell the same stories, sing the same songs. Seen in the global context, Africa has a rich and enduring oral tradition.

See also Egypt, Ancient Kingdom of; Languages, African: An Overview; Poetry, African; Swahili Language.

Harold Scheub

Organization of African Unity

Organization of African nations created to promote continental peace, unity, and cooperation; it was replaced by the African Union in 2002.

The Organization of African Unity (OAU) was founded in ADDIS ABABA, ETHIOPIA on May 25, 1963. At that time, African leaders disagreed about what kind of organization the OAU should be. Some leaders pushed for the creation of a central government that would unite all of Africa under one authority. However, many of the nations had just recently gained independence from COLONIAL RULE and their leaders opposed the idea. The leaders eventually reached a compromise but in so doing created an organization that is controlled by its member nations, leaving it with little power to act on its own.

Structure

The OAU had three major governing bodies—the Assembly of the Heads of States and Governments, the Council of Ministers, and the General Secretariat. The Assembly consisted of a representative from each member nation. It met once a year to discuss policy and consider recommendations from the Council of Ministers. Each year a different African leader became chair of the OAU and handled disputes among member nations. The Council of Ministers was headed by the foreign ministers of each member nation. It met at least twice during the year to recommend policies and actions to the assembly. The General Secretariat ran the day-to-day operations of the organization. It was headed by a secretary general, who helped build consensus among member nations.

Problems in the OAU

Throughout its history, the OAU was troubled by disputes among its member nations. In 1975 the organization's members became divided over which side to support in the Angolan Civil War. In this conflict, rival factions fought for control of ANGOLA, which had won independence from Portugal in 1974. One faction, the POPULAR MOVEMENT FOR THE LIBERATION OF ANGOLA (officially known as Movimento Popular de Libertação de Angola-Partido de Trabalho, or MPLA), was backed by CUBA and the Soviet Union. The other two, the National Front for the Liberation of Angola (Frente Nacional de Libertação de Angola, or FNLA) and the National Union for the Total Independence of Angola (União Nacional para a Independência Total de Angola, or UNITA), were supported by the United States, its Western allies, and SOUTH AFRICA. In a December 1975 vote to decide which side to support, half of the nations chose one side, half the other.

The split in the OAU continued during a series of wars, including the 1977 and 1978 invasions of the Katanga Province in ZAIRE (now the DEMOCRATIC REPUBLIC OF THE CONGO) by Angolan-backed forces, SOMALIA's war with ETHIOPIA in 1978, and the conflict between UGANDA and TANZANIA in 1978 and 1979. In 1981 the same nations that had supported the MPLA government in Angola also recognized the WESTERN SAHARA as an independent state and admitted it into the OAU. Morocco and other states that had supported the UNITA/FNLA side of the Angolan conflict did not approve of this move and Morocco temporarily withdrew from the OAU. The OAU's strength was sapped further by an accelerating economic decline in Africa during the 1970s and 1980s.

Successes of the OAU

Despite these problems, the OAU scored a number of successes over the years. It mediated a border dispute between ALGERIA and Morocco in 1964 and 1965. It also mediated the border conflicts of Somalia with Ethiopia and KENYA from 1968 to 1970.

The OAU formed the African Liberation Committee in 1963 to channel financial support to movements trying to defeat Portuguese colonial rule in GUINEA-BISSAU, Angola, and MOZAMBIQUE. Those movements were victorious in 1974. It also supported movements against white minority rule in South Africa, ZIMBABWE, and NAMIBIA. South Africa was excluded from OAU membership until 1994, when white minority rule and APARTHEID (the policy of racial segregation) ended.

The organization sent an *observer mission* to the United Nations (UN) in 1963. An observer mission refers to the representatives sent by a nation or organization that is not a member of the UN, but wishes to participate in UN discussions. Observer missions cannot vote on UN actions. The OAU also coordinated collective action among African nations at the UN. It promoted decisions that led to South Africa being barred from participating in the UN's General Assembly in 1974, and to the admission of the People's Republic of China to the UN in 1971. In 1986 the OAU established the African Commission on Human and People's Rights to monitor human rights practices in member nations.

Recent Developments

In the 1990s the OAU experienced a revival, partly due to the election of Salim Ahmed Salim of TANZANIA as its secretary general in 1989 for a five-year term. Salim was one of Africa's most respected statesmen and brought increased authority and prestige to the post. Salim was reelected in 1993 and 1997.

Under Salim's leadership, the OAU established a new mechanism for conflict resolution and a peace fund in 1992 to deal with a growing number of conflicts. In 1993 the OAU sent peacekeepers to LIBERIA to support other peacekeeping missions trying to end a civil war. In 1994 African nations ratified an OAU initiative to establish an African Economic Community to promote trade between African nations and remove tariffs and other restrictions that hamper commercial exchange. The African Economic Community was also to work to establish a common currency in Africa. The OAU received another boost when South Africa became a member in 1994. South Africa has since been a major force for peace, democracy, and economic development in Africa.

During the 1990s, OAU continued to work to resolve conflicts between nations and to coordinate political, economic, cultural, scientific, medical, and defense policies. Critics, however, considered it to be little more than a "dictators' club." In 2002 the OAU disbanded and was relaunched as the AFRICAN UNION (AU). Similar to the OAU, the new organization has 53 members. But it is designed to be more people-oriented than the OAU. The AU's charter calls for the creation of a peacekeeping force, a central bank, and a court of justice. The founding document further authorizes the AU to intervene in member nations to stop war crimes, genocide, and human rights abuses. Following the OAU precedent, the AU is headquartered in Addis Ababa.

See also Cold War and Africa; Decolonization in Africa: An Interpretation; Human Rights in Africa; Nationalism in Africa; United Nations in Africa.

Orishas

Pantheon of deities in the traditional Yoruba religion of Nigeria and in Yoruba-derived religious traditions in the African Diaspora; the name for these deities is spelled differently depending on language and culture areas—*orisa* in Yoruba, *orixá* in Portuguese, and *orisha* in Spanish—and they are also often known colloquially as *santos*, or saints.

The orishas are not equal to the sky god (Olodumare) nor do they supplant him, but rather they are semi-independent divinities capable of working their own will with or without the propitiation (which often takes the form of the delivery of offerings to) or supplication of human beings. They are believed, however, to act in accordance with the wishes of Olodumare, but they often appear autonomous in their behavior and in how they are worshiped and propitiated. Although their names are the same in all areas, they are spelled differently. For reasons of consistency, this essay uses the most common Cuban-derived spelling, unless otherwise indicated.

The religion based on the worship of the orishas is known by several names. In urban BRAZIL, especially BAHIA, RIO DE JANEIRO, and São Paulo, one form is called CANDOMBLÉ and another UMBANDA. There is a significant difference between these two in that Umbanda incorporates a great deal of the spiritism, or European philosophy developed by the French writer known as Alan Kardec, with a complicated pantheon of spirits that are not orishas. Spiritism is a type of spiritual practice which originated in FRANCE in the mid-nineteenth century, and which combines the summoning of disincarnated spirits, healing, and the practice of charitable activities.

Further, in Umbanda, humans negotiate neither with God nor with the orishas, who are considered too remote, but rather with a cohort of lesser spirits. Farther north in Brazil, in Recife, the religion is known as XANGÔ, as in Trinidad, where the same term is spelled SHANGO. Both Xangô and Shango refer to a specific orisha, Changó (see below). In the United States and CUBA, the orisha religion is called SANTERÍA, which is a colonial term imposed by the Spanish and maintained in academic and journalistic literature. Terms more frequently used by practitioners in the United States and Cuba are *Regla de Ocha*, or *Ocha*, or simply, "the religion."

Divination forms one of two primary activities in the orisha religion. The divination system most frequently used is the sixteen-cowrie shell system (*dilogun*). It is through this system that the orishas speak and their will can be determined. Typically the diviner throws the cowrie shells onto a special tray.

Macumba worshipers prepare food for the orishas before a ceremony to induct a novice into the temple in Rio de Janeiro. CORBIS/Stephanie Maze

Then, depending upon their position and upon whether they land with the cowrie shell's opening up or down, he determines the significance of the toss. Each orisha corresponds to a specific number and sign, which is determined according to how the cowrie shells fall. In this way, the diviner ascertains the problem or situation facing the practitioner, what is causing the problem, and which orisha will help.

Another more complicated system of divination is called *IFA*, which is the tool of the high priests, the *babalawos*. Ifa divination contains 256 signs, or *odu*, and each sign contains hundreds of verses, each potentially pertaining to the individual's destiny. Here the position of the cowrie shells, or often the position of several necklaces tossed onto a sacred tray, determines which odu is to be interpreted and applied to the particular question or problem put to the babalawo. Ifa divination is consulted in all major life changes, such as birth, marriage, and death. Ifa divination can be used for everyday consultations, but also for determining the destiny of the person in a ritual called *Mano de Orúnmila* (Hand of Orúnmila) for men and *Kofa* for women. Ifa divination relays the words and advice of the orisha Orúnmila, who also is in charge of the sixteen cowries. Orúnmila never comes to earth, however, and speaks only through Ifa divination. Apparently, Orúnmila was insulted by the youngest of his sixteen sons, who refused to bow to his father (the appropriate greeting to a senior family member in YORUBA culture) and who believed himself as wise and talented as his elder. Orúnmila removed himself to heaven and refused to come back. After being entreated by his children to return to earth, Orúnmila sent instead sixteen palm nuts, which would speak in his absence. The palm nuts became the system of divination known as Ifa.

After finding out the origin of the petitioner's problem and which orisha to propitiate, through further divination the diviner determines what type of offering should be given to the orisha to ensure his or her help. An offering is called an *ebo*. This cycle of divination and ebo represents the fundamental, daily praxis of worship in the orisha religion. Since the orishas are manifestations of energy and the embodiment of the forces of nature, it is this energy that is harnessed through ebo to work on behalf of the practitioner.

The other major activity in the orisha religion is possession. Here, the orishas visit the earth and, to do so, they must borrow the body of a devotee who has been ritually prepared and trained to receive them. Mediums can enter a trance state and begin channeling the orisha at any time, whenever the orisha wants to come, but this activity mostly occurs within the context of a party for the orisha. At these parties, called *festas* in Brazil and *tambors* in the United States and Cuba, people gather to hear drumming and singing, and specific members of the group, or "house," dance.

In Brazil, festas are highly choreographed performances. The members of the house dance in a circle (*roda* or *roça*); the women wear fine traditional dress consisting of several heavily starched petticoats under a brightly colored, full skirt and a lace blouse. They are then wrapped with a large cloth (*pano da costa*), which extends from chest to knees, and finally the costume is tied just under the armpits and tightly across the breasts with a long strip of cloth. The head is always covered with a scarf, often made of lace.

The dancers dance in order of length of time initiated. Songs and dances specific to the orishas are performed in a predetermined order. Interestingly, the order corresponds to that of the Cuban tradition. After the songs have been performed to each orisha, and generally not before, the dancers begin falling into trance and become possessed by their orishas. In Brazil, most mediums present become possessed with their orishas.

At this point, the mediums are cared for by special priestesses called *ekedes*, whose role is to take care of the belongings of the persons in trance, to bring them out of trance when necessary or at the orders of the house leader, to wipe the

The African deities known as orishas have their own particular colors, symbols, and ritual garments. These two members of a Candomblé in Belém are dressed as Omolú (left) and Xangó. CORBIS/Barnabas Bosshart

sweat off their faces as they dance, and to adjust their clothing. Ekedes go through a similar initiation process as that of a medium, but unlike the medium their head is not shaved, as it was determined through divination that they were not destined to become possessed. There is no official position in the Cuban tradition analogous to the ekede, but frequently a medium brings trusted assistants who essentially perform the same function with him or her to tambors to watch out for the medium while he or she is in trance.

After the orishas appear and possess their mediums, they dance a little bit and then are taken away from the scene of the dancing and are dressed in ritual clothing specific to their attributes and colors. They are subsequently brought back out to dance and to dispense advice to those present. In the United States and Cuba, the orishas are allowed to remain as long as they wish at a tambor, and individual supplicants seek their advice. In Brazil, however, they speak much less to individual guests, and they are not accorded the freedom to come and go but are handled skillfully by the ekedes. Each orisha dances for a few songs only, and at the end of the performance they leave. In the Cuban tradition, generally only one or two orishas come and take possession of a medium at any one tambor, and they stay much longer, being the center of attention while they are at the tambor.

Each orisha has certain attributes corresponding to a natural phenomenon. Changó is represented by lightning and thunder; Oyá or Yansan by the wind; Orisha Oko by the farm or agriculture in Cuba and the United States and by the home in Brazil; Agayú by the volcano; Ochún by the river and sweet water; and Yemayá by the sea (in Trinidad, these aspects of Yemayá and Ochún are reversed). Many orishas live in the forest and can be worshiped in wooded areas or urban parks. These include Osain, the herbalist and doctor, and Ochosi, the hunter. Ogun, the solitary warrior, divinity of iron and the forge, can be found wherever transportation facilities are located, especially train tracks and stations, and in contemporary times is thought to inhabit airports. Eleguá, the trickster, is the lord of the crossroads. His offerings are frequently taken to a crossroads.

The warrior orishas include Eleguá, Ogun, and Ochosi. Members of the religion in the Cuban tradition who have not yet been initiated into the priesthood can be dedicated to, or "given to," these orishas, along with Osun, the guardian of one's destiny, in a ritual known as "giving the warriors." There does not appear to be an analogous initiation in Brazil. In fact, Eleguá in Brazil, where he is known as Exú, is treated completely differently than he is in Caribbean culture. This is one of the most interesting discrepancies in a comparative study. In the Cuban tradition, Eleguá is a trickster and causes many problems, such as car trouble or other problems in travel, or inexplicable confusions. He is the orisha of choices, and he must be propitiated first, before all other orishas, so that he is kept content and so that he does not play disruptive jokes. Although considered dangerous, he is something of a childlike orisha in that he likes toys and candy. He manifests in his devotees at tambors, is taken along on vacations, and is kept close to his keepers—inside the house behind the door to guard the home, where practitioners can ask him for protection before exiting.

In Brazil, however, Exú is thought of as quite maleficent. There, he also lives behind the door or preferably outside at the front gate. He is also propitiated first, but this is done in order to send him away so that he will not disrupt rituals and festas. He is sent away at least three hours before a festa begins: for example, the ceremony to propitiate Exú usually takes place at approximately five o'clock in the afternoon for a nine o'clock festa. In Brazil, Exú is regarded with absolute respect mixed with a little terror. The idea of giving him candy and toys and keeping him nearby is met with horrified looks. Speaking to him or propitiating him by spraying rum on him prior to leaving the home is considered disturbing him and thought to cause problems by "calling" him to accompany one.

The orishas all have their favorite foods, colors, and numbers. Offerings as well as material culture adhere to these specific preferences. A typical food offering for Changó might be okra cooked with cornmeal; for Oxun of Brazil one might cook a dish of black-eyed beans or for Ochun of Cuba, a pastry soaked in honey. The food and colors of Obatalá (Oxalá in Brazil) are all of the strictest purity and white, such as the whites of eggs and cocoa butter. Oyá or Yansan uses brown, and Babaluaié, the orisha of smallpox, uses purple and burlap in Cuba and the United States, and raffia in Brazil.

Material culture in the orisha religion is quite rich. Practitioners of Ocha, from the very earliest initiations, all wear strings of beads in the specific colors of the orishas. Generally, a newcomer starts with five necklaces, called *elekes,* which pertain to Obatalá (white), Changó (red and white), Ochún (yellows, gold, and coral with possibly a few single green and blue beads), Eleguá (black and red), and Yemayá (blue, crystal, and silver). Bead wearing in Brazil is at once more casual and more formal: casual wearing of the beads can be observed among nonmembers who simply are fond of the religion from the outside; and initiates wear long heavy strings, often of twenty-one strands held together at points by larger beads. The colors in the two areas are very similar; the notable exceptions are the beads for Ogun (green and black in the Cuban tradition and dark blue in Brazil). In Brazil, further, one does not wear beads for Exú.

Costumes for the orishas are very elaborate in both Brazil and in the Cuban tradition. In the Cuban initiation, the novice must have seven new white outfits, consisting of a full petticoat, an overskirt, and a lace blouse. During the party for the new initiate on the third day, he or she wears a very elaborate costume in the colors of the orisha to whom the initiate is dedicated. These clothes are usually in nineteenth-century colonial style, with long full skirts, puffed sleeves, and tight waists for the women; the men wear tunics with loose pants. The preferred fabric is heavy satin, and the costumes are decorated with sequins, lace, appliqués, and are often heavily and beautifully beaded. In Brazil, the preferred decoration is lace, as making lace is a skill that remains fairly common and available, although increasingly expensive, as are the fabrics. Clothing design in Brazil, as described above, is an intriguing combination of the colonial with the African: colonial skirts and blouse are worn below an African pano da costa, which is tied on top. In both traditions, covering the legs is very important for modesty.

The orishas each have Catholic saints to which they correspond as well. Changó, for example, corresponds to Saint Barbara in most areas. Other correspondences are not uniform and vary regionally, even within the same country. This phenomenon occurred from the first entry of the orisha religion to the diaspora. Most slave-receiving areas were Catholic, and slaves were required to embrace the faith of their masters. Since Catholicism already had an established cult of saints, it was easy for slaves to view the saints as manifestations of their orishas and worship them in this guise. The orishas, therefore, are also known from colonial times as the saints (*los santos* or *os santos*). This subterfuge has caused the religion in all areas, particularly Trinidad, often to be described in academic discourse as "syncretic," that is, a melding of two traditions.

The more research scholars do, however, the clearer it becomes that the two traditions are not melded at all but are kept very strictly apart. For example, in Ocha homes there may be an altar to the Catholic saints and family ancestors on which are placed glasses of water, crucifixes, images of saints and pictures of deceased relatives, candles, and flowers. In another space, on the floor, there may be a shrine to the *egun,* the ancestral African dead. For the egun, there may be candles, servings of food, coffee, rum, and cigars. But the two shrines are never under any circumstances combined. Also, at *missas,* or seances where non-orisha spirits are contacted, all manifestations of the orisha religion, such as the elekes, are removed.

In Brazil, Candomblé ceremonies have no Catholic saints represented whatsoever, although one might see an image or a lithograph of a saint corresponding to the orisha who rules the house. Special Catholic masses figure in Candomblé and Ocha ritual festivity, but these are always held in separate spaces. Masses on the first Friday of every month are held at the Church of Nosso Senhor do Bomfim in Bahia in honor of Oxalá, who corresponds loosely to Jesus Christ. However, it is unclear that the mass is being said for Christ, since it is Oxalá who is mentioned in the homily, and fireworks are set off (a common means in Brazil to attract the attention of the orishas). In the ritual context, however, no Catholic processes or imagery appear.

See also Catholic Church in Latin America and the Caribbean; Dance in Latin America and the Caribbean; Religions, African; Religions, African and Afro-Caribbean, in the United States; Religions, African, in Brazil; Religions, African, in Latin America and the Caribbean.

Kathleen O'Connor

Oromo

Ethnic group of Ethiopia and Kenya.

The Oromo, sometimes known as the Galla (a term they find insulting), speak a language that belongs to the Eastern Cushitic family of Afro-Asiatic languages, similar to SOMALI. They occupy an area from the southern highlands of ETHIOPIA in the north, to the OGADEN and SOMALIA in the east, to the SUDAN border in the west, and across the Kenyan border to the Tana River in the south. Although they are the largest single ethnic group in Ethiopia, their division along regional and religious lines has historically prevented them from uniting to block AMHARA domination in Ethiopia.

The Oromo originated in present-day southern Ethiopia. During the sixteenth century C.E., the then almost exclusively pastoralist Oromo began to expand northward into the Ethiopian highlands. After their migration to the relatively lush highlands, home to the agricultural Amhara and TIGRE people, many of the northern Oromo adopted agriculture. The main crops grown by the Oromo are wheat, barley, and teff.

The Oromo migration fostered regional differences that contributed to the development of sixteen subgroups. While the northern Oromo practice agriculture, the southern Oromo groups, including those in KENYA, generally practice PASTORALISM.

Over half of the Oromo are Sunni Muslims, while some practice CHRISTIANITY. Other Oromo still practice the traditional Oromo religion. Of the adherents to indigenous religion, members of the BORAN subgroup follow what many consider the prototypical traditional Cushitic religion. The Boran worship and offer sacrifices to Waqa, who created and sustains life. Priests called *qaallu*, who belong to a sacred lineage among the Boran, represent Waqa on earth.

During the twentieth century the Oromo subgroups began to unite behind a nationalist movement to resist Amhara dominance in Ethiopia, and many Oromo define themselves not as Ethiopians but as Oromo. After the overthrow of the regime of Emperor HAILE SELASSIE in 1974, the new Marxist government, led by MENGISTU HAILE MIRIAM, gave the Oromo more political prominence.

In 1991 a coalition led by the mostly Tigrean Ethiopian People's Revolutionary Democratic Front, which included organizations representing other ethnic groups, including the Oromo People's Democratic Organization, overthrew the Mengistu regime. However, the Oromo are divided into a number of factions. While the Oromo People's Democratic Organization belongs to the coalition government, other organizations, such as the Oromo Liberation Front and the United Oromo People's Liberation Front, have declared armed struggles seeking either independence from Ethiopia, or the imposition of Islamic law in Ethiopia.

See also Ethnicity and Identity in Africa: An Interpretation; Islam in Africa; Languages, African: An Overview; Nationalism in Africa; Religions, African.

Robert Fay

Oron

Ethnic group of Nigeria; also known as Oro.

The Oron primarily inhabit Cross River State, southeastern NIGERIA. They speak a Niger-Congo language and are closely related to the IBIBIO people. Over 100,000 people consider themselves Oron.

See also Ethnicity and Identity in Africa: An Interpretation; Languages, African: An Overview.

Orquesta Anacaona

One of the first all-female ensembles of Cuba; repertoire consisted heavily of Afro-Cuban rhythms.

Founded in 1932, Orquesta Anacaona, named after the famed Arawak princess *Anacaona*, who struggled against the Spaniards in the early sixteenth century, was initiated by eight multi-talented sisters who each played a different instrument: Ada (trumpet and violin), Argimira (drums), Caridad (string bass), Concepción (saxophone), Xiomara (trumpet), Olga (saxophone, clarinet, flute, and maracas), and Ondina (trumpet). Hortensia Palacios (piano) later joined along with Graciela Pérez, who became the lead singer of the band. The ensemble developed amidst the political shifts taking place in CUBA during the early twentieth century, particularly in 1932 when students led strikes against the dictatorship of MACHADO. The women were secondary students who attempted to pursue studies in music; because the school offered no music courses, they formed the *orquesta*. The band performed in a style called SON, a syncretic musical form combining African and Spanish musical structures and elements.

The orquesta became more visible through opportunities in television, radio, and cinema in the periods before and after WORLD WAR II; gender and social barriers in the music industry, where men had dominated, were dismantled. The ensemble traveled throughout Latin America, in COLOMBIA, VENEZUELA, MEXICO, PUERTO RICO, and PANAMA. The band also performed in the United States and FRANCE. After the revolution the Ministerio de Cultura in Cuba sponsored the group. Members of this assemblage of pioneering women were reportedly still performing in Havana in the mid-1980s.

Ortiz, Adalberto

1914–

Afro-Ecuadorian writer, painter, poet, teacher, and diplomat, one of the most recognized Afro–Spanish American writers.

When Adalberto Ortiz was only three months old, his mother and grandmother abruptly fled the city of ESMERALDAS with him to escape from the civil war launched by the Esmeraldian colonel Carlos Concha against the national government in Quito, ECUADOR. Leaving Ortiz's father behind, the family found refuge in the city of Guayaquil, where Ortiz's mother joined a convent and the boy grew up with his maternal grandmother. He discovered his father in Esmeraldas when he was eleven years old. Due to family financial constraints, Ortiz had to work at a young age. An assiduous reader, he soon developed a taste for literature. In 1928 he obtained a scholarship to study in the Colegio Normal Juan Montalvo in Quito, which was one of the most exclusive schools in the country. He spent most of his academic holidays in Esmeraldas. He obtained his diploma as a schoolteacher in 1937.

During a boat trip from Guayaquil to Esmeraldas in 1937, he had the opportunity to read Emilio Ballagas's *Antología de poesía Negra* (Anthology of Black Poetry). The reading of that text marked, in his own words, the awakening of his interest in writing *negrista* poetry, a genre that tries to "convey the rhythm and musicality" of black speech, which he did while teaching in various schools in Esmeraldas. Ortiz was greatly influenced by and participated actively in the so-called *Grupo de Guayaquil* or *Generación del 30* (Group of Guayaquil or Generation of the 1930s), which was a group of innovative writers residing in Guayaquil who had a great impact on modern Ecuadorian literature.

In 1939 Ortiz moved back to Guayaquil, taught in a correctional school, and wrote his first novel, which is also his most famous: *Juyungo: Historia de un negro, una isla y otros negros* (translated as *Juyungo: A Classic Afro-Hispanic Novel*, 1982). After many difficulties with Ecuadorian publishing companies, the first edition came out in MEXICO in 1943.

From 1944 on, with the first government of José María Velasco Ibarra, Ortiz began a diplomatic career. He was first sent to Mexico for more than three years as the secretary of the Ecuadorian embassy there. While in Mexico, he published *Tierra, son y tambor* (1944) and *Camino y puerto de la angustia* (1945), two collections of poems. His diplomatic career also brought him to PARAGUAY, ARGENTINA, and PANAMA.

Juyungo has been reedited numerous times in Spanish since 1943, and it has been translated into French, German, Russian, Croat, and English. The central themes Ortiz addresses in his work are those of black, Indian, and white interracial relations and processes of identity formation. While *Juyungo* expresses some Marxist views, over time Ortiz became less and less preoccupied with political engagement. In *El espejo y la ventana* (1967), he portrays the decadence of an Ecuadorian mulatto family that immigrated to the coastal city of Guayaquil. Here he explores the psychological dimensions of racial identity in an Ecuadorian social context. More recent publications include *La envoltura del sueño* (1982), *Niebla encendida* (1984), and *Poemas de Adalberto Ortiz* (1985). In 1995 he received a national literary prize, Premio Eugenio Espejo. For more than thirty years, Ortiz has also been a renowned painter, frequently exhibiting his work in Guayaquil and Quito.

See also Literature, Black, in Spanish America; Negrista Poets.

Jean Mutaba Rahier

Ortiz, Fernando

1881–1969

Cuban scholar, scientist, sociologist, musicologist, writer, linguist, ethnologist, social psychologist, journalist, anthropologist, legal expert, and criminologist.

Fernando Ortiz's intellectual legacy is one of astonishing breadth and erudition. Cuban scholar Juan Marinello has likened him to a third discoverer of CUBA, after Columbus and Humboldt. A Cuban-American critic has called him "Mr. Cuba." The claim is no exaggeration: he is one of a great line of Caribbean intellectual figures such as Eugenio María de Hostos, JOSÉ MARTÍ, Pedro Henríquez Ureña, FRANTZ FANON, and C. L. R. JAMES.

Along with the work of LYDIA CABRERA, Ortiz's seminal works deal with the African traditions that have uniquely shaped the identity of Cuban music, religion, society, and culture. His major theoretical contribution is in coining the concept of transculturation, a term used to describe the rich, textured, and sometimes bloody encounter between two or more cultures that mutually transforms them. It provides a refined framework for understanding the complexity and diversity of Caribbean culture, history, and identity.

While a meticulous social scientist, Ortiz created work that was unique in its creativity, expressiveness, and freedom of form. He wrote ingeniously about different themes, using a *contrapunteo*, or contrapuntal method, that allowed for solid research with immense literary flair. His method went beyond the interdisciplinary, creating a discourse that blurred boundaries between essay, history, and narrative.

Born in HAVANA of a Spanish father and Cuban mother, Ortiz spent most of his youth in Minorca (1882–1895), then returned to the island to study law at the University of Havana, eventually obtaining a degree in law from the University of Barcelona (1900), and a doctorate in law one year later from the University of Madrid.

In Madrid, he began his first criminological investigations, observing prisoners in jail using the positivist scientific theories of Lombroso and Ferri. This marked the beginning of Ortiz's interest in the social behavior of both individuals and groups, a lifelong pursuit that over time shifted from a more narrow scientific to a historical-humanistic methodology.

Ortiz held a wide variety of professional positions over the years. In 1902 he worked in the Cuban consulate in ITALY, where he met Lombroso and Ferri in person, as well as Marxist sociologist Alfonso Asturaro. From 1906 to 1908, Ortiz was a lawyer for the district court of Havana, and from 1908 to 1917 a professor in the School of Public Law at the University of Havana.

During this period, he wrote and edited a prolific body of work, often engaged with his political life. In 1910, along with Ramiro Guerra, Ortiz codirected (and later directed) the magazine *Revista Bimestre Cubana*, until it ceased publication in 1959. By 1915 he had joined the Liberal Party, and in 1917 he became the party's representative in the Chamber of Deputies. Five years later, disgusted with the corruption and the political chaos of the country, he retired from the Chamber but kept active politically. In 1924 he founded the Sociedad de Folklore Cubano, as well as the magazine *Archivos de Folklore Cubano* (1924–1929). By this time, the Machado dictatorship (1925–1933) was in power. Ortiz, who fervently opposed the regime, spent from 1931 to 1933 in WASHINGTON, D.C., involved in the anti-Machado struggle, returning to the island after the dictator fled. In 1936 Ortiz founded the Institución Hispanoamericana de Cultura and edited its magazine, *Ultra* (1936–1947). A year later, he founded the Sociedad de Estudios Afrocubanos, which also published a journal, *Estudios Afrocubanos* (1937–1940 and 1945–1946). Ortiz was also active during the 1940s in organizing intellectuals against fascism.

In 1942 he inaugurated an ethnographic seminar at the University of Havana and continued publishing as well as lecturing widely, penning four books in that period.

In the 1950s Ortiz published eight books, totaling over 3,500 pages, almost all related to the themes of AFRO-CUBAN MUSIC and culture; he continued to lecture internationally and was awarded honorary doctorates from many prestigious universities.

In 1961 he was designated a member of the National Commission of the Cuban Academy of Sciences and during the 1960s continued working on the third volume (*Los negros curros*) of his trilogy *Hampa afrocubana,* which remained unfinished at the time of his death.

Ortiz was influenced by positivism in the beginning of his career; he was concerned with the terrible problems that beset Cuba: poverty, unemployment, racism, crime, political corruption, and fragmentation. His intellectual formation was within a largely white and Hispanophile cultural elite, with little interest in or appreciation of the black population of the island and deeply influenced by the legal and criminological studies of the time.

When he wrote his first book, *Los negros brujos* (1906), a certain Eurocentric and white bias existed in the work as Ortiz saw blacks as "outside" of societal norms. And yet Ortiz admitted that without blacks there would be no Cuba, in the truest sense of the word. Speaking of the book some forty years after its publication, Ortiz said it was motivated by the absolute lack of sociological research on blacks in Cuba. It was also the first major book published on the island to use the term *Afro-Cuban*. Ortiz's discourse on identity began a major shift in white Cuban discourse on identity and race. Furthermore, the book, as well as his subsequent research, dispelled the notion of a monolithic black culture in Cuba. While the YORUBA influence is perhaps the strongest, there are Abakuá, Arará, Carabalí, Kongo, WOLOF, and Bantu influences that are by no means insignificant.

Aside from some legal writings, research on the indigenous roots of Cuban culture, and a long historical tome on the seventeenth century, the great bulk of Ortiz's writing focused on Cuba's African traditions. His research delved into linguistics (*Glosario de afronegrismos*), economics (*Contrapunteo cubano del tabaco y el azúcar*), racism (*El engaño de las razas*), history (*Los negros esclavos*), music (*Africanía de la música folklórica de Cuba*), and dance and theater (*Los bailes y el teatro de los negros en el folklore de Cuba*), to name only a few. Ortiz's work and pursuit of truth were a persistent reminder to whites in Cuba that the contribution of Afro-Cubans was not merely limited to providing cheap labor in a plantation economy but was essential to Cuba's identity in matters that ranged from cooking to speaking, and from how they socialized to areas of production, worship, and play.

Ortiz's best-known work is *Contrapunteo cubano del tabaco y azúcar* (1940; *Cuban Counterpoint: Tobacco and Sugar,* 1947, 1995), in which he elaborates the concept of transculturation, one of his most influential contributions.

But Ortiz's legacy is more than one of the devoted scholar doing meticulous research. He lectured widely, wrote about current affairs, and was very active in the fight to combat racism in Cuba. He belonged to a generation of reformist intellectuals that could be highly critical of Cuban society, including Carlos Loveira, Miguel de Carrión, Ramiro Guerra, and Medardo Vitier. The next generation would include such revolutionaries as Ruben Martínez Villena, Julio Antonio Mella, Juan Marinello, and NICOLÁS GUILLÉN, all of whom had close relations with Ortiz.

Ortiz's work has also illuminated complex issues of contemporary Caribbean culture in the work of scholars such as STUART HALL, EDOUARD GLISSANT, and Antonio Benítez-Rojo. In addition, his influence has reached beyond a geographical sphere to inflect the work of Latino/a writers in the United States like Guillermo Gómez-Peña, Juan Flores, and Gloria Anzaldúa, who struggle with the issues of border experiences, cultures, and migration.

See also Latin America and the Caribbean, Blacks in; Transculturation, Mestizaje, and the Cosmic Race: An Interpretation.

Alan West

Orungu

Ethnic group and historical kingdom of Gabon.

The Orungu developed a prosperous kingdom in the eighteenth century during the height of the TRANSATLANTIC SLAVE TRADE in the region. Scholars debate the exact origin of the Orungu, though most agree that they came from the south, probably as an offshoot of the Eshira, and migrated into the Ogooué River delta in the early seventeenth century.

Like the MPONGWE, the Orungu speak a Myènè language: they both say "*myènè*," or "I say that," to initiate conversation. They also share a number of cultural practices with the Mpongwe, including ironworking and boatbuilding. In the seventeenth century, in an attempt to dominate trade with Europeans, the Orungu drove many of the Mpongwe clans toward the Gabon Estuary. By 1700 they succeeded in gaining direct access to European traders. The Orungu clans at Cape Lopez organized a kingdom sustained by its control of trade through the mouth of the Ogooué River. There were approximately twenty Orungu clans; one of them held the line of succession to the kingship, and another exercised control over maritime commerce in such goods as ivory, beeswax, copal, dyewood, and ebony.

By the 1760s the Orungu were trading slaves. The Orungu monarchs grew rich and increasingly powerful through their taxation of the slave trade on the Nazareth and San Mexias rivers. In 1853 the Orungu monarchy under King Ombango-Rogombe agreed to abandon the slave trade, but in fact the Orungu moved their operations to more protected points upriver in an attempt to continue the trade clandestinely. This attempt failed, but most Orungu proved unwilling to return to the farming and fishing ways of their ancestors. The king, who had become dependent on the slave trade, was unable to maintain the tradition of royal patronage as the trade declined, and the kingdom subsequently disintegrated. In 1873 King Ntchengué signed a treaty granting the French a post on Orungu territory. Because of their hostility toward European missionaries in the nineteenth century, few Orungu obtained a Western education. This limited their influence in the colonial adminis-

Ory, Edward ("Kid")

1889-1973

American musician, jazz trombonist, and band leader, pioneer of New Orleans style jazz.

Born on a farm in St. John Baptist Parish near NEW ORLEANS, Edward "Kid" Ory arrived on the New Orleans music scene in 1917. Joining up with cornetist JOE "KING" OLIVER and clarinetist Johnny Dodds, he led several prominent bands in New Orleans. He carried the tradition of New Orleans style JAZZ to California in 1919, leading Kid Ory's Brownskinned Babies, and Kid Ory's Original Creole Jazz Band in the LOS ANGELES and San Francisco Bay Area.

Ory's Sunshine Orchestra recorded such hits as "Ory's Creole Trombone" and "Society Blues" under the Nordskog label in June 1922. With these recordings, Ory's band became the first African American group to make all-instrumental jazz records. Ory moved to CHICAGO in 1925, where he participated in some of the most significant sound recordings of the period, alongside LOUIS ARMSTRONG in "Muskrat Ramble" (1926), with "JELLY ROLL" MORTON in "Doctor Jazz" (1926), and with King Oliver in "Every Tub" (1927).

Ory's style was distinctive: expressive and highly rhythmic, incorporating glissando runs of the early tailgate trombone style. With his recorded compositions, including "Muskrat Ramble," he left the sounds of New Orleans style jazz band as his legacy to music history. In 1930, Ory left the music scene for ten years, returning to California to work on a poultry farm and in a railroad office. He managed to regain some prominence when he reappeared, performing on an Orson Welles radio broadcast in 1944. He toured with various musicians until 1966, when he retired to Hawaii.

See also Music, African American.

Bibliography

Williams, Martin. *Jazz Masters of New Orleans*. Da Capo Press, 1978.

Marian Aguiar

Osei Tutu

1650?-1717

Founder and first king of the Asante nation.

Osei Tutu followed a model established by the earlier AKAN military states of Denkyira and Akwamu. He forged ASANTE into a powerful state that dominated most of present-day GHANA for 200 years. Osei Tutu tripled the area under Asante control and gained the Asante access to, though not control of, the seacoast. There they could trade directly with the Europeans to exchange slaves and gold for firearms.

According to legend, Osei Tutu was named after the shrine of Otutu, where his mother had prayed for a child. Obiri Yeboa, Osei Tutu's uncle and ruler of the Asante chiefdom of Kwaman, sent the young man as his heir for training at the court of Denkyira, the state that then ruled over the Asante. A love affair with the Denkyira king's sister forced Osei Tutu to flee to Akwamu, a neighboring state to the east. There he met Okomfo Anokye, an Akwamu priest who became his lifelong friend and adviser. After observing the political institutions of the powerful kingdoms of Denkyira and Akwamu, Osei Tutu determined to unite the Asante into a single state. Succeeding his uncle, he ascended to the stool of Kwaman around 1670 and combined the various Asante chiefdoms into a military alliance under his leadership, though the other chiefs retained rights and privileges. From 1698 to 1701 Asante crushed Denkyira. In 1701 Asante won sovereignty over Elmina Castle, a Dutch trading post, which paid tribute to Asante and offered the nation access to the lucrative slave trade.

To unify the new nation, Osei Tutu and Anokye created a state structure that endured for 200 years. They made Kwaman, renamed KUMASI, the kingdom's capital. They borrowed the Denkyira concept of a sacred stool for the monarch: according to legend the Asante GOLDEN STOOL descended from heaven onto Osei Tutu's knees. The stool became a revered symbol of Asante nationhood. In addition, Osei Tutu established the Odwira Festival, in which the bones of enemies were displayed and Asante solidarity celebrated. He also created a bureaucracy to administer the newly conquered vassal states. Osei Tutu died in 1717 during a battle on the Pra River in which Akyem Kotoku defeated Asante.

See also Gold Trade; Transatlantic Slave Trade.

David P. Johnson, Jr.

Oshún

Riverine orisha (Yoruba deity) of beauty, feminine ways, and reproduction.

Oshún is also known as Ochún in CUBA and the United States and Oxum in BRAZIL. Women pray to Oshún when they want to bear children. She is vain and represents the spirit of happiness; she is fond of mirrors and perfume. The queen of sorceresses wears yellow and gold and is the youngest orisha as well as the favorite woman of XANGÔ.

See also Candomblé; Orishas; Religions, African, in Latin America and the Caribbean; Santería; Yoruba (religion).

Ossie, Count

1928–1976

Jamaican drummer, composer, leader of the Mystic Revelation of Rastafari band, best known for recordings combining Afro-Jamaican musical ritual rhythms.

Born Oswald Williams in St. Thomas Parish, JAMAICA, Count Ossie was drawn to hand-drumming accompanied by chanting as a young child. His impoverished family could not afford to buy him a drum. Ossie did his first drumming on discarded tin cans. Through informal contacts with Rastafarian drummers, Count Ossie began to gain enough proficiency on his instrument to start his own drumming band, the Count Ossie Group, in the 1950s. He would have been one of many obscure drummers using a "Back to Africa" concept if not for a historic recording studio collaboration with the singer/producer Prince Buster (Cecil Bustamante). The result was the recording of "Oh Carolina," the first Jamaican recording to combine SKA, REGGAE, and Rastafarian ritual music. Count Ossie's drum rhythms undergirding this pop music hit on several continents greatly influenced the evolution of ska and reggae, inspiring scores of musicians to incorporate these African-tinged sounds. Jam sessions organized by Count Ossie attracted major Jamaican pop and JAZZ musicians. Two album-length recordings by Count Ossie and his Mystic Revelation of Rastafari band in the 1970s, *Grounation* and *Tales of Mozambique,* combine chanting, spoken poetry, storytelling, jazz sax improvisations, and ritual drumming, telling tales to catalyze Afrocentric consciousness. After successfully touring the United States, Count Ossie was killed in a tragic accident at the National Arena, KINGSTON, at the age of forty-eight.

See also Music, Afro-Caribbean Religious; Rastafarians.

Norman Weinstein

Ostrich

Common name for a large, flightless bird, formerly found in the Middle East, now found in fragmented populations in East, West, and southern Africa.

The ostrich makes up the family Struthionidae in the order Struthioniformes and is classified as *Struthio camelus.* Ostriches are the largest and strongest of living birds, attaining a height from crown to foot of 2.4 meters (8 feet) and a weight of up to 136 kilograms (300 pounds). Male ostriches are black, with white wings and tail. The white feathers of the male, which are large and soft, are the ostrich plumes of commercial value. The female is a dull grayish brown.

Ostriches can run up to 65 kilometers per hour (40 miles per hour). The males are polygamous and travel about in hot, sandy areas with three or four females, or in groups of four or five males accompanied by mates and young. The females lay their yellowish-white eggs together in a single large depression in the sand. The eggs weigh 1.4 kilograms (3 pounds) each and have a volume of 1.4 liters (3 pints). The male sits on them at night, and the female incubates them by day.

Ostrich feathers have been exported from AFRICA for many centuries. Medieval caravan traders carried them across the SAHARA to sell in EUROPE, where knights wore the plumes in their helmets. In the nineteenth century, ostrich feathers adorned women's hats and dresses. Ostriches were bred and raised for their plumes in SOUTH AFRICA, ALGERIA, Australia, FRANCE, and the United States. As styles changed after WORLD WAR I and demand dropped, ostrich farms almost disappeared as well. In recent years, however, the introduction of ostrich hide as a luxury leather and the marketing of ostrich as an alternative meat source have renewed interest in ostrich farming.

See also Animals in Africa; Middle East.

Robert Fay

Ouagadougou, Burkina Faso

Capital and largest city of Burkina Faso.

The MOSSI people founded Ouagadougou in the early fourteenth century, at a time when Mossi warriors were expanding their control over the savanna region south of the NIGER RIVER. Located on a plateau irrigated by tributaries of the White Volta River, the site was suitable for agriculture. It would become an important market for caravans moving between the forests and the SAHARA. According to Mossi oral history, the settlement was originally called *Woge Zabra Soba Koumbemb' tenga,* or "Honored Chief Zabra Soba's Village." MANDE traders altered the name, using *Ouaga* for Woge, and *dougou,* their word for "village."

By the sixteenth century, Ouagadougou had become the capital of the most powerful of the Mossi states and home of the Mossi king whose title, the *Mogho Naaba*, meant "king of the world." Nevertheless, nineteenth-century European explorers were unimpressed by Ouagadougou's mud-brick, thatched-roof architecture. In 1888 Captain Louis Binger wrote, "I did not have to wait long to find out the true state of affairs . . . what was acknowledged as a palace and seraglio was nothing but a group of miserable huts surrounded by heaps of filth . . ."

As European powers raced to colonize Africa in the late nineteenth century, FRANCE made claims on the Mossi region. The Mogho Naaba Wobogo, however, refused French offers to make his kingdom a protectorate, so French troops took the city by force on September 5, 1896. When Ouagadougou's residents resisted, the French set the town afire. Wobogo fled, and the French later appointed his brother, Sighiri, as the new Mogho Naaba.

The French built a garrison for African soldiers at Ouagadougou, which was originally part of the larger French colony of Haut-Sénégal-Niger. Roman Catholic missionaries arrived soon afterward. By 1904 the town's population had swelled to 8,000, only twelve of whom were European. Unlike coastal cities such as DAKAR or ABIDJAN, the arid and remote town of Ouagadougou attracted few European settlers. During WORLD WAR I, however, the population skyrocketed to nearly 20,000. In 1919 the French declared Upper Volta a separate colony and made Ouagadougou its capital. Using some 2,000 Mossi laborers recruited by the Mogho Naaba, the French built a capital with wide, tree-lined streets, and they drained swamps to create a fresh water supply.

In 1932 Upper Volta was dissolved and administered from CÔTE D'IVOIRE. No longer a colonial capital, Ouagadougou's economy languished and its population declined. At the end of WORLD WAR II, however, Mossi chiefs successfully lobbied to have France reconstitute Upper Volta as a separate colony, and Ouagadougou once again became its capital. In 1955 the rail line from the port city of Abidjan, Côte D'Ivoire reached Ouagadougou, further reducing the city's isolation.

Ouagadougou remained the capital when Upper Volta, now BURKINA FASO, won independence in 1960. Over the next three decades the city was the site of frequent labor unrest and several coups d'état. Despite the political instability, Ouagadougou grew rapidly, attracting migrants from the countryside as well as from the neighboring countries. Ouagadougou now has an international airport, a university, and a two-story central market. Major industries include textiles, a brewery, and several agricultural products processing plants. Every other year, the city hosts the famous African film festival, FESPACO. The Mogho Naaba, now a ceremonial king, still lives in Ouagadougou. The weekly reenactment of the Mossi empire's founding, staged outside the Mogho Naaba's palace, is a popular tourist attraction. Population: 1,000,000 (2003 estimate).

See also Christianity: Missionaries in Africa; Cinema, African.

Bibliography

Skinner, E. P. *African Urban Life: The Transformation of Ouagadougou.* Princeton University Press, 1974.

David P. Johnson, Jr.

Oubangui-Chari

Former name of Central African Republic.

See also Central African Republic.

Ouédraogo, Idrissa

1954–

Burkinabé film director.

Idrissa Ouédraogo is widely considered one of the leading members of a new generation of African filmmakers. The son of a civil servant, Ouédraogo was born in Banfora, Upper Volta (now BURKINA FASO) and studied English at the University of OUAGADOUGOU. But forays into playwriting soon piqued his interest in film, and he enrolled in the Institut Africain d'Éducation Cinématographique de Ouagadougou, Burkina Faso's film institute. He later studied film at the Gorki Institute in the Soviet Union and at the Institut des Hautes Études Cinématographiques (IDHEC) in Paris. He graduated from the IDHEC in 1985 but remained in France to pursue a Ph.D. under the direction of anthropologist JEAN ROUCHE.

Ouédraogo has directed several widely acclaimed films and is considered one of the most technically accomplished film directors in Africa. His first film to receive international attention was *Yam Daabo,* which opened at the 1986 Cannes Film Festival in France. Other internationally recognized films by Ouédraogo include *Zan Boko* (1988), *Yaaba* (1989), *Tilaï* (1990), *Samba Traoré* (1992), *Afrique mon Afrique* (1994), and *Kini and Adams* (1997). The latter film—his first in English—was the opening feature at the 1997 Festival Panafricain du Cinéma (FESPACO) in Ougadougou.

Ouédraogo's fluid style and skillful film technique have prompted critics to compare him to the French film director Jean Renoir. Ouédraogo's films have also won praise for their sensitive portrayals and astute criticisms of Burkinabé society. Although many of his films take place in rural MOSSI villages, *Zan Boko* examines life in rapidly growing Ouagadougou, and *Kini and Adams* is shot in an industrializing region of southern Africa.

Among Ouédraogo's recent projects is *11'09"01: September 11* (2003), a film about the terrorist attacks on the World Trade Center on September 11, 2001. Several leading filmmakers from throughout the world contributed short pieces to this composite film. Ouédraogo's segment portrays a group of children in Ouagadougou who, believing that they have seen Osama bin Laden, decide to collect the $25,000 reward for his capture so that they can use the money to fund desperately needed health programs.

See also Cinema, African.

Elizabeth Heath

Ousmane, Mahamane

1950–

Former President of the Republic of Niger.

A statistician and economist by training, Mahamane Ousmane was not involved in NIGER's politics until he founded the Convention Démocratique et Sociale-Rhama (CDS) in Zinder. With the support of the town's wealthy HAUSA merchants, he was able to organize a coalition of opposition parties, the Alliance des Forces du Changement (AFC), and defeat the ruling the Mouvement National de la Société de Développement (MNSD) in 1993 presidential elections.

As president, Ousmane eventually alienated many of his allies because of his lack of political finesse and charisma. He also faced a number of problems familiar to his predecessors:

state bankruptcy, unrest among the TUAREG, labor protests, and severe droughts. In order to obtain vital funding from international donors, Ousmane was forced to enact structural adjustment austerity measures, which only increased popular discontent. Although his government both helped stabilize the economy and signed a peace treaty with Tuareg rebels, opposition to Ousmane's leadership only mounted. In the 1995 parliamentary elections, opposition candidates won a majority in the General Assembly and political rival Hama Amadou was elected prime minister. Fighting between the two leaders grew so fierce that government activities came to a virtual standstill and Ousmane contemplated dissolving the assembly and unconstitutionally nominating a new prime minister. The threat of this action, coupled with the decline in world prices for uranium, Niger's major export, prompted Colonel Ibrahim Bare Mainassara to overthrow the government in a military coup on January 27, 1996. Mainassara was assassinated in April 1999, and in December of that year Ousmane was elected to a five-year term as Speaker of the National Assembly.

See also Drought and Desertification; Structural Adjustment in Africa.

Elizabeth Heath

Ovambo

Largest ethnic group of Namibia and southern Angola.

The Bantu-speaking Ovambo (or Owambo) migrated from Central Africa in the seventeenth century, settling in an area that today spans northern NAMIBIA and southern ANGOLA. Organized into eight matrilineal clans, the Ovambo lived in small villages where extended families raised cattle and cultivated MILLET, sorghum, and beans. The Ovambo are closely related to the KAVANGO and possibly to the HERERO, as most share a belief in a supreme being, the Kalunga, and the tradition of a holy fire of ritual significance.

Highly productive farmland, the development of a flourishing metal-working industry, and participation in the long-distance caravan trade in salt, copper, and iron ore brought prosperity to the Ovambo. Over time the eight clans formed a loose federation of kingdoms, each with its own hereditary system of succession. Although European influence in Namibia grew during the 1800s, Ovamboland saw relatively few Europeans apart from the establishment of a Finnish mission. The region remained isolated during the brief era of German COLONIAL RULE, and in 1915, when SOUTH AFRICA occupied Namibia, Ovamboland became a self-governing "homeland."

During the 1930s Ovambo men began to migrate to work as contract laborers in the mines of southern Namibia and South Africa. Their experiences of unjust labor policies and racial discrimination helped build support for groups in the Namibian nationalist movement, particularly the Ovambo People's Organization, led by ANDIMBA TOIVO JA TOIVO, which later became the SOUTH WEST AFRICA PEOPLE'S ORGANIZATION, or SWAPO. At independence, SWAPO leader SAMUEL NUJOMA became the president of Namibia, and Ovambos have since come to dominate the national government. Today the Ovambo are the largest ethnic group in Namibia, numbering around 650,000, or approximately half the population. Many Ovambo men still earn their livelihoods as migrant mine laborers, and women continue to farm the land.

See also Bantu: Dispersion and Settlement; Ethnicity and Identity in Africa: An Interpretation; Iron in Africa; Minerals and Mining in Africa; Salt Trade.

Eric Young

Ovimbundu

Largest ethnic group of Angola.

The Ovimbundu, "people of the mist," are the largest ethnolinguistic group in ANGOLA, comprising approximately 40 percent of the national population. Although most of the 3.6 million Ovimbundu today speak umBundu, historically they separated themselves into regional-political subgroups, including the Bailundu, Bié, Dombe, Baganda, Huambo, Hanha, Caconda, Chiyaka, Sambu, and Sele. This was a result of migration patterns and the emergence of numerous kingdoms.

In the sixteenth and seventeenth centuries, peoples migrating to the Benguela plateau from the north and east settled in the fertile central highlands of Angola and forged a common Ovimbundu identity. After the introduction of maize as the staple crop in the seventeenth century, Ovimbundu women became the primary farmers while men engaged in hunting, trading, and raiding neighboring groups for cattle and women as slaves. By the late eighteenth century twenty-two centralized kingdoms had emerged among the Ovimbundu, dominated by the Bié, Bailundu, and Ciyaka. Many built forts in large granite and sandstone outcroppings scattered around the highlands. Although there was often a degree of popular democracy within the kingdoms, an Ovimbundu king played the role of lead hunter, senior diplomat, judge, diviner, and high priest of the warrior cult.

These kingdoms owed their wealth to commerce as well as to agriculture. They participated actively in the TRANSATLANTIC SLAVE TRADE and took advantage of Portuguese and Afro-Portuguese military expeditions between 1773 and 1775 to consolidate their power vis-à-vis their rivals. After slave trading was abolished they became involved in the caravan trade in ivory and wild rubber between the interior African kingdoms—among them the CHOKWE, LOZI, and LUNDA—and the Portuguese settlements.

Although politically not united, many Ovimbundu resisted the Portuguese colonial policies of taxation, forced labor, and land acquisition. In 1902 the Bailundu fought the Portuguese in the so-called Bailundu War, but the Portuguese successfully suppressed the revolt and other forms of resistance. Meanwhile, new rail and road systems marginalized the Ovimbundu. As their role as caravan traders waned, their dependency on the colonial administration and the cash economy grew, and many Ovimbundu men migrated to jobs on northern coffee plantations. Ovimbundu kings, deprived of their primary sources of wealth and authority, became little more than symbolic leaders.

When nationalism swept Angola in the 1960s, the Ovimbundu found a voice in the NATIONAL UNION FOR THE TOTAL INDEPENDENCE OF ANGOLA (UNITA) movement, which they dominated under the leadership of JONAS SAVIMBI. The movement operated from Huambo, the historical capital of the Bailundu. After Angolan independence was achieved in 1975, UNITA fought the government of Angola over the government's socialist policies, and because of what many Ovimbundu saw as ethnic discrimination within the MBUNDU-dominated Angolan government. As part of the peace effort to end the war in the early 1990s, the government appointed Ovimbundu politician Marcelino Moco as prime minister, though he was sacked four years later after UNITA had renewed the war. In February 2002 government forces killed Savimbi. Two months later UNITA agreed to end the fighting. The movement has since transformed itself into a legitimate political party that seeks to effect change through the ballot box. Nearly three decades of war, however, devastated the highlands of the Ovimbundu, which remain a site of poverty and massive popular dislocation.

See also Ethnicity and Identity in Africa: An Interpretation; Ivory Trade; Languages, African: An Overview; Nationalism in Africa; Slavery in Africa.

Eric Young

Owen, Chandler

1889–1967

Coeditor of the socialist magazine *The Messenger* and, later, Republican Party activist.

Chandler Owen was born in Warrenton, North Carolina. Graduating from RICHMOND's Virginia Union University in 1913, Chandler Owen left the South for NEW YORK CITY to become a fellow of the NATIONAL URBAN LEAGUE. He studied at the New York School of Philanthropy and then at Columbia University. During this time, he met another young migrant from the South, A. PHILIP RANDOLPH. Randolph exerted a great influence over Owen, convincing him to sever ties with the Urban League and, in 1916, join the Socialist Party.

The following year, Owen and Randolph coedited *The Hotel Messenger,* a newsletter of a local hotel and restaurant employees' union. A few months into their tenure, they criticized the union for overcharging its members for uniforms. Their reward was a swift dismissal, to which they responded by founding THE MESSENGER in late 1917.

In *The Messenger,* Owen and Randolph praised the Russian Revolution, opposed WORLD WAR I, advocated the more radical elements of unionization (as exemplified by the Industrial Workers of the World), and promoted the Socialist Party. Owen also played a large role in the magazine's effort to have MARCUS GARVEY, whose back-to-Africa views he opposed, deported to his native JAMAICA.

By 1923, however, Owen had grown disenchanted with radical SOCIALISM. He left *The Messenger,* settled in CHICAGO, and became managing editor of *The Chicago Bee,* a black newspaper. Though he continued to advocate unionism—through the *Bee* he supported Randolph's efforts to organize railroad porters—he became increasingly involved in Republican politics. In 1928 he ran unsuccessfully as a Republican for a seat in the U.S. House of Representatives.

Owen then became involved in public relations. Before and during WORLD WAR II, he wrote about black anti-Semitism for the Anti-Defamation League of B'nai B'rith. Although he had deep reservations about the civil rights record of President Franklin D. Roosevelt, he set them aside and wrote on race relations for the U.S. War Department. The department distributed millions of copies of his pamphlet *Negroes and the War* (1942), in which he reminded blacks of the liberties they would lose if Adolf Hitler won. Owen also stressed the gains blacks had made under Roosevelt's New Deal.

During and after the war, Owen continued to rise in the REPUBLICAN PARTY. In his later years he was an important speechwriter and campaigner for several Republican politicians, including presidential candidates Wendell Wilkie, Robert Taft, and Dwight Eisenhower, as well as Illinois governor William Stratton and U.S. Senator Everett Dirksen.

See also Labor Leaders; Magazines, Newspapers, and Journals; World War II and African Americans.

Bibliography

Korweibel, Theodore, Jr. *No Crystal Stair: Black Life and the "Messenger," 1917–1928.* Greenwood Press, 1975.

Owens, Dana

See Queen Latifah.

Owens, James Cleveland ("Jesse")

1913–1980

African American sprinter, winner of four gold medals in the 1936 Olympic Games, and in his time heralded as "the world's fastest human."

James Cleveland Owens was born in Oakville, Alabama, the tenth of eleven children of Henry and Emma Fitzgerald Owens, who earned their livelihood as sharecroppers. As a child Jesse Owens was chronically ill, probably because of poor diet, substandard housing, and inadequate clothing. During several winters he contracted pneumonia, which he was forced to endure since his family lacked money for a doctor or medicine. In the early 1920s the Owens family left the South as part of the GREAT

Jesse Owens, shown here at a 1937 track meet, was one of the greatest athletes of all time. His four gold medals at the 1936 Olympic Games embarrassed Nazi leader Adolf Hitler and stood as an unparalleled achievement for nearly fifty years. *CORBIS/Bettmann*

MIGRATION, and settled in Cleveland, Ohio, where Owens's father and three brothers found work in the steel mills. For the first time Owens attended school regularly.

In a racially integrated junior high school, a white physical education teacher named Charles Riley noticed Owens's athletic ability and began coaching him in track and field. After Owens entered a vocational high school, Riley continued to coach him. Owens's success was immediate: school records in the 220-yard and 100-yard sprints and the long jump fell to his smooth stride.

In 1932 he made an unsuccessful attempt for the United States Olympic team, but by 1933 his dominance of the sport was undeniable. At a high-school meet in May 1933, he set a world record in the long jump with a leap of 24 feet, 3-3/4 inches—an improvement of more than three inches on the old mark. A month later he helped his high school to a national track title with another world record in the long jump and 9.4-second 100-yard dash, which tied the world record. Cleveland welcomed him home with a celebratory parade.

Owens was the first member of his family to graduate from high school. Although by most accounts his educational preparation was minimal, he was recruited aggressively by colleges around the country because of his athletic prowess. Despite the fact that he was urged by the black press to choose a less discriminatory school, Owens chose to stay near home. He entered the Ohio State University in Columbus, where he was barred from living on the whites-only campus, and where he and other black athletes were forced to ride to meets in cars separate from their white teammates.

By the spring of 1934, Owens was on academic probation, which prompted his coach to set up public speaking engagements for him—perhaps to bolster his confidence, perhaps in the belief that an African American could not be helped academically. Whatever the motivation, the chance to develop and display his charisma and charm was fortuitous; it was a strength he would rely on the rest of his professional life. In May 1935 Owens broke five world records at a single meet, earning him the title among sportswriters as "the world's fastest human."

The 1936 Olympic Games in Berlin were embroiled in controversy long before the athletes arrived. The Amateur Athletic Union (AAU) threatened a U.S. boycott to protest the treatment of German Jews under Adolf Hitler, and black journalists were inflamed by Nazi claims of Aryan racial superiority. The U.S. Olympic Committee, however, overruled the AAU and sent athletes to the games. To many American blacks, Owens symbolized a rebuttal to Nazi racism, and he became a symbol that gained all the more importance after German boxer Max Schmeling delivered a surprising defeat to black American JOE LOUIS in early 1936.

Owens delivered an outstanding Olympic performance. He won gold medals for the 100-meter and 200-meter sprints, the 400-meter relay, and the long jump, in which he set a record lasting twenty-five years. When Hitler refused to invite Owens and other black victors to shake his hand (an invitation that had been extended to several German athletes), the press seized on the snub and the International Olympic Committee rebuked the German leader.

Owens was welcomed home to a series of triumphal parades, but before long he was again confronted with American racism—forced to enter through back doors and ride at the back of buses—and he found that no jobs were open to him. As he later told an interviewer, "I wasn't invited up to shake hands with Hitler, but I wasn't invited to the White House to shake hands with the president, either." He was initially given several offers for public appearances, but most opportunities dissolved or were bogus. Failing to graduate from Ohio State, Owens relied on low-income jobs and the few personal appearances he could muster for money—including Carnival races against horses.

He started a laundry business that failed, then returned to Ohio State. After four semesters, however, his grades were no better than they had been in his first effort and he withdrew. By the 1940s Owens was able to rely on public speaking for his income; he eventually opened his own public relations firm. In his later years Owens abstained from the CIVIL RIGHTS MOVEMENT. His conservative response to the black-power salute of Tommie Smith and John Carlos at the 1968 Olympic Games in Mexico City won him derision as an "Uncle Tom" by young black activists, but others continued to admire him for his entrepreneurial achievements.

See also Olympics, African Americans and the; Segregation in the United States; Sports and African Americans; Track and Field in the United States.

Owens, Major

1936–

Democratic member of the United States House of Representatives from New York.

Born in Memphis, Tennessee, Major Owens received a bachelor's degree from MOREHOUSE COLLEGE in 1956 and a master's degree in library science from Atlanta University in 1957. Before entering politics, he worked in NEW YORK at the Brooklyn Public Library and as director of the Community Media Library Program at Columbia University. From the mid-1960s through the early 1970s, Owens served in a number of community service posts, eventually leading up to a five-year stint as New York City community development commissioner. In 1974 Owens won a seat in the New York Senate. In 1982 he was elected to Congress to succeed Democrat SHIRLEY CHISHOLM as the U.S. representative from New York's eleventh Congressional District. He was reelected to his eleventh term in 2002.

See also Democratic Party.

Oxalá

White orisha (Yoruba deity), around which everything must be pure white.

Oxalá is known as *Obatalá* in CUBA and the United States, and known in BRAZIL as Oxalá or by other avatars, such as the youthful *Oxaguian* and the elderly *Oxalufon*. He had a role in creating the world, but drank too much palm wine, became drunk, and began making deformed people. All those with deformities are sacred to Oxalá, and his initiates do not drink alcohol or wear dark-colored clothing.

See also Candomblé; Orishas; Religions, African, in Latin America and the Caribbean; Santería; Yoruba (religion).

Oxóssi

Hunter orisha (Yoruba deity).

Oxóssi is known as *Oxosse* in BRAZIL, and as *Ochosi* in CUBA and United States. His assistance is sought in connection with any trouble with the law or the police.

See also Candomblé; Orishas; Religions, African, in Latin America and the Caribbean; Santería; Yoruba (religion).

Oxumaré

Orisha (Yoruba deity) of the rainbow; often represented with serpents.

Also known as *Oxunmaré*, Oxumaré is seen mostly in BRAZIL, and rarely in CUBA and the United States. Oxumaré is a hardworking and patient orisha who assists those who want to be rich.

See also Candomblé; Orishas; Religions, African, in Latin America and the Caribbean; Santería; Yoruba (religion).

Oyo, Early Kingdom of

Precolonial West African state.

Oyo was the most powerful of the Yoruba states during the peak of its power between roughly 1650 and 1750 C.E. Its capital, the town of Oyo, was situated slightly to the north of present-day Oyo in Nigeria. Legend has it that Oyo's first *alafin*, or ruler, was a son of Oduduwa, the mythical ancestor of the Yoruba people. In the sixteenth century, Oyo began its ascent to power under the *alafin* Orompoto, who established a cavalry and maintained a trained army. During the first half of the eighteenth century, Oyo subjugated the neighboring kingdom of Dahomey, but in 1818 Dahomey regained its independence from Oyo. Numerous internal disputes, war with Dahomey, and an invasion by the Fulani from the north contributed to the collapse of the empire soon afterward. In the mid-1830s the old town of Oyo was destroyed by a Fulani invasion, and the capital was subsequently relocated to its present site. In the treaty of 1888, after the Yoruba civil wars of the middle part of the century, Oyo, along with much of Yorubaland, was placed under British rule.

See also Dahomey, Early Kingdom of.

P–Q

Pace, Harry Hubert

1884–1943

Music publisher and founder of first African American recording company.

Harry Hubert Pace began his printing and business career in 1903, opening a company in MEMPHIS with his former teacher W. E. B. DU BOIS. Together, they produced *Moon Illustrated Weekly* (1905), the first illustrated African American journal. Pace met composer W. C. HANDY in 1908, and they formed one of the most enduring African American music companies, Pace and Handy Music Company (1909). Pace went on to establish Pace Phonograph Company, issuing records by such artists as ALBERTA HUNTER and ETHEL WATERS under the label of Black Swan. With the bankruptcy of the company in 1923, Pace returned to insurance work, expanding CHICAGO's Supreme Liberty Life Insurance Co. into the largest black-owned business in the North.

See also Magazines, Newspapers, and Journals; Music, African American.

Bibliography

Johnson, John H., and Lerone Bennett, Jr. *Succeeding Against the Odds.* Warner Books, 1989.

Marian Aguiar

Pacheco, Johnny

1935–

Afro-Dominican bandleader, composer, singer, flutist, and percussionist who played an important role in creating New York salsa music during the 1960s and 1970s; an important Latin music record producer and cofounder of Fania Records.

Johnny Pacheco made his mark during the 1960s and 1970s as part of NEW YORK CITY's Latin music scene. Pacheco was born in Santiago de los Caballeros, DOMINICAN REPUBLIC. His father, Rafael Azarías Pacheco, was a prominent clarinetist and conductor of the Orquestra Santa Cecilia, a leading Dominican orchestra. In the late 1940s his family moved to New York City. Johnny Pacheco learned to play saxophone, flute, and percussion in high school. In 1959 Pacheco joined the pianist Charlie Palmieri as the flutist in the newly formed group Charanga Duboney.

Charanga Duboney, featuring a Cuban-style *charanga* flute-and-violins front line, inspired an early 1960s charanga craze among Latino New Yorkers. In September of 1959 Pacheco left Palmieri to organize his own charanga. With the album *Pacheco y su Charanga* (1961) he introduced the *pachanga,* an energetic dance style that combined elements of the charanga and the *chachachá.*

During the mid-1960s, when the pachanga fell out of favor with the Latin music audience, Pacheco turned to the Cuban *conjunto,* a traditional ensemble that featured a two-trumpet front line, as a new formula for success. His group, Pacheco y su Nuevo Tumbao, was a Cuban-style conjunto that featured pianist Eddie Palmieri, the younger brother of Charlie Palmieri. The band renewed interest in traditional Cuban music among New York City's Latino population, spearheading what became known as the *típico* movement. More than a musical style, típico reflected, as John Storm Roberts wrote, a "prevailing rhetoric of roots, purity, and a concept (related to the growth of Latino political awareness) of 'community music.'"

Over the years, Pacheco continued to play traditional, Cuban-influenced music. At the same time, he was instrumental in broadening the Cuban musical legacy. In part, his success was a matter of historical timing. As a result of the successful revolution led by FIDEL CASTRO and a U.S. embargo on trade with CUBA, there were few new musical influences coming from the island, allowing Pacheco and other Latino musicians in New York City to develop their own sound.

In 1964 Pacheco turned his attention from musical performance to the recording business. He established his own record company, FANIA RECORDS. In partnership with Gerald "Jerry" Masucci, he helped shape a Latin music style that Fania Records marketed as SALSA MUSIC. At the outset, the company's prospects were hardly promising. The only group signed to the label was Pacheco's own, and the two partners delivered their records to music stores out of their car trunks. Although the company started with little money and few resources it quickly built a reputation for excellence among Latino listeners.

As Fania's musical director, Pacheco recorded many of the major talents in Latin music, including trombonist WILLIE COLÓN, percussionist Ray Barreto, singer/songwriter RUBÉN BLADES, and vocalists CELIA CRUZ, Hector Lavoe, and Pete "El Conde" Rodriguez. For several years, Pacheco led the Fania All Stars, before Willie Colón assumed the leadership. The Fania All Stars, with their irresistibly danceable, percussion-driven sound, epitomized salsa music. Blades, who sang with the Fania All Stars for six years before launching a solo career, brought an innovative social consciousness to his lyrics. Through the influence of Blades and other songwriters, salsa music came to closely reflect the realities of life in El Barrio, New York City's poor Latino community. During the 1970s, the salsa sound gained a following throughout Latin America and with a broad range of non-Latino listeners as well.

New York Times music critic Peter Watrous noted that for more than a decade Fania Records was "extraordinarily consistent, comparable to MOTOWN at its peak in popular music or the Blue Note label for JAZZ." Changing musical tastes brought hard times for the independent label, and Fania ceased operations in the 1980s. For some time Pacheco seemed to fall from sight as well. In 1992, however, the label was resurrected and reissued several albums under his leadership. Pacheco's legacy extends well beyond either his musical career or his entrepreneurial achievements. During the 1960s and 1970s, his music and the albums that he produced for Fania Records expressed a growing pride in Latino identity and were an important counterpart of other contemporaneous forms of Latino empowerment.

In addition to his career with Fania, Pacheco has also written music for feature films, including *Something Wild* (1986) and *The Mambo Kings* (1992).

See also Afro-Latino Cultures in the United States; Son.

James Sellman

Pacheco, Luís

1800–1895

African American slave and controversial figure during the Second Seminole War when the United States military detachment for which he was an interpreter was massacred by Seminoles and blacks.

Luis Pacheco owes his fame principally to Republican Joshua R. Giddings's semifictional antislavery work *The Exiles of Florida* (1858). Pacheco was born on December 26, 1800, in Spanish Florida, at New Switzerland, a plantation on the Saint Johns River. He was the slave of Francis Philip Fatio. His parents were "pureblooded negroes," and his father, Adam, was a "remarkably intelligent and ambitious negro," a "carpenter, boat-builder, and driver." Early on, Pacheco became acquainted with the neighboring Seminoles, among whom he had a sister. A brother had been captured as a child but had returned some twenty years later, and from him Pacheco "picked up a great deal of the language." During his boyhood, his master's daughter, Susan Philippa Fatio, taught him to read and write. "He was ambitious to learn, and of quick perception" and acquired "a good deal . . . of book learning." But he was also of "a roving disposition" and "hated restraint." His knowledge of the free-and-easy life of the Seminole Indians and the blacks who lived among them encouraged these tendencies, and as he grew older he occasionally ran away to live with the Seminoles. While he was still young, he married a female slave belonging to Ramón Sanchez of Saint Augustine. She later purchased her freedom, and the contrast between her position and his own probably contributed to his restlessness.

Pacheco's last flight from New Switzerland occurred shortly before Christmas 1824. He is said to have run away at that time to Saint Augustine to visit his wife and decided not to return. After several months he was located at the Spanish fisheries on the Gulf Coast and taken to Tampa where, at his own request, he was sold to Colonel George Mercer Brooke. Commanding the fort there, Colonel Brooke employed Pacheco as an interpreter, since he spoke four languages: English, Spanish, and probably the two Muskogean languages of the Seminole, Hitchiti and Muskogi. Pacheco was later sold from officer to officer until Major James McIntosh in 1830 sold him to Antonio Pacheco, a Cuban with a trading post in Sarasota. After Don Antonio's death, Pacheco continued in the service of his widow. During the decade after his last unauthorized departure from the Fatio plantation, Pacheco had shown none of his previous restlessness. His duties were not onerous, and his position as interpreter was one of responsibility and prestige.

However, on December 23, 1835, Pacheco was hired at $25 per month to accompany as guide and interpreter the command of Major F. L. Dade. Major Dade, in anticipation of the outbreak of war with the Seminoles, was being sent from Fort Brooke, Tampa Bay, to reinforce the garrison at Fort King in Ocala. En route, on December 28, the Seminoles and blacks attacked the detachment and killed the entire command except two, who escaped terribly wounded. Pacheco was assumed to have been among the slain. After the Treaty of Fort Dade on March 6, 1837, many Seminole chiefs began to gather with their people for shipment to the West. In April or May, Pacheco appeared in the entourage of Chief Jumper, who claimed to have saved his life and therefore to be "entitled to him."

Pacheco thereupon entered a twilight zone of controversy and legend. As a black survivor of a detachment of United States soldiers that had been annihilated by an enemy force in which blacks were particularly conspicuous, it was alleged, in finishing off the wounded, Pacheco was a convenient scapegoat. A widely circulated 1837 publication described him as a free black who had joined the enemy and read to them the papers found on the dead. Major General Thomas Sidney Jesup, commanding in Florida, later declared "the evidence . . . almost conclusive that he had been in constant communication with the Indians from the time the [Dade] command marched from Tampa Bay to that of its defeat." Jesup stated he also found "abundant evidence that he had, on several occasions . . . taken part with the hostiles in their depredations upon the frontier inhabitants of Florida." If the general had not been so busy "he would have had him tried upon a criminal charge" and probably executed. As an alternative, after keeping Pacheco under confinement at Tampa Bay until the spring of 1838, Jesup had him shipped to Fort Pike, Louisiana, en route to the Indian Territory (in present-day Oklahoma). But Jesup never presented any of this "abundant" and "almost conclusive" evidence, and not until many years later was Pacheco able to reply to these charges.

At Fort Pike a white slave trader claimed Pacheco and thirty-one other blacks. He asserted his right to them on the basis of claims, purchased from Creek mercenaries, to blacks the mercenaries had captured. Pacheco, whether legally slave or free—and he was listed as *Said to be Free*—had certainly not been captured by the Creeks, so the claimant probably singled him out because he looked valuable. However, after civil authorities had retained these blacks in New Orleans from May 21 to June 28, 1838, the courts refused to sustain the claim, and by September Pacheco had reached the Indian Territory—after which he vanished from more than local notice for well over half a century. However, during the next twenty years he gained, in his absence, a stature and notoriety—as a cause célèbre, a symbol, and a character in fictional history—that he never entirely lost.

Antonio Pacheco's widow had moved to Cuba not long after the destruction of Dade's command. A representative of the Pacheco estate had claimed Luís Pacheco as soon as he surrendered, only to have the claim rejected on the grounds that he was too dangerous to be left in or even near Florida. It is not known exactly what action was taken during the following decade, except that in January 1842 Major General Jesup defended his shipment of Pacheco to the West and that Captain John C. Casey, who had hired Pacheco as guide and interpreter, strongly supported the general's action. Although describing Pacheco as "very intelligent—speaking four languages . . . able to read and write . . . an able-bodied, likely negro, in the prime of life," he added that he "would be very valuable"—probably worth $1,000—"where [*sic*] he not as bad as he is bright. It would be far better to pay any price for such a man and leave him in Arkansas, or hang him, than to return him to his owners, and let him return to the borders of Florida."

In 1847 the representative of Antonio Pacheco's widow petitioned the United States Congress for compensation on the grounds that her slave, while in the service of the U.S., had been captured by Native Americans. When these Native Americans surrendered him, Major General Jesup, instead of returning him, had shipped him west, beyond her ability to recover him, as admitted in the general's own statement. A majority of the House Committee on Military Affairs agreed to recommend a bill for fair compensation, but four antislavery members drew up a minority report, opposing the bill on the grounds that it recognized slavery. After protracted discussion and parliamentary maneuvering, during which the bill was both narrowly passed and narrowly defeated, on January 19, 1849, it finally again passed the House but was never brought before the Senate. Antonio Pacheco's widow remained uncompensated, to the great satisfaction of Joshua R. Giddings of Ohio and other antislavery congressmen. Giddings was already aware of the Seminole Indians and their black allies, whose history about a decade later he treated so romantically and imaginatively. A more important result was that the Pacheco case was responsible for Giddings's decision to make Luís Pacheco a principal hero.

Giddings achieved this objective by accepting as valid Major General Jesup's most extreme charges regarding Pacheco's involvement in the Second Seminole War (1835–1842). Giddings, however, treated these accusations as greatly redounding to Pacheco's credit. Giddings elaborated considerably upon those accusations, even deliberately distorting well-known facts to produce a more dramatic and tightly knit narrative.

Pacheco's own story was that after being hired as guide and interpreter, he was sent after the Dade detachment and found it on the Little Hillsborough. At the time of the attack he was with the advance guard, in "perfectly open country, and . . . had just looked carefully for Indians," when he "heard a rifle shot, and looked back . . . just in time to see Major Dade fall . . . shot in the breast." The country, a little before apparently empty, was now filled with charging Indians. Pacheco, much frightened, threw down his gun and lay down behind a tree. As each Indian came up and leveled his gun at him, he pled for his life, saying that he was a slave who was only doing as he was bidden. Chief Jumper finally intervened to protect him, but the next day when he asked permission to go back to his people, since he was "Spanish property," the chief angrily refused. Pacheco consequently "remained with the Indians," although once he stole a canoe and, traveling by night, reached the mouth of Peace (Pease) Creek, only to be captured and returned. Eventually he came to Tampa with the Seminoles and at Major General Jesup's order was sent "in irons" to the Indian Territory near Fort Gibson, Oklahoma.

Pacheco's life thereafter was far less romantic than the one imagined by Giddings, and more tragic. After living for a decade with the Seminole people as a free man, he was in 1849 arbitrarily sold, along with about thirty other blacks, at $50 a head, to Marcellus DuVal, the corrupt Seminole subagent (probably by the new head chief Jim Jumper, Old Jumper's despicable son). Pacheco was put to work on the large DuVal farm south of Van Buren, Arkansas. In 1852 Pacheco and the other blacks were moved to the vicinity of Austin, Texas, where they were living in 1861.

In 1892 a silvery-bearded black man with deeply lined features appeared in Jacksonville, Florida, and identified himself so convincingly to Susan L'Engle (the former Susan Philippa Fatio) as her former pupil Luís, that she supported him during the remaining two years or so of his life. During this period his "thoughts were fixed on the beyond" and his time was largely devoted to church attendance. He said many times that he "did not care to live now as he had set himself right before the world" in an interview of October 1892. In that interview he presented one of the most vivid accounts on record of the destruction of Dade's command and exonerated himself, to general satisfaction, from the old charges of betrayal. He died on

January 5, 1895, and after a funeral "attended by many representatives of the old families of Jacksonville" was buried at his birthplace of New Switzerland.

Pacheco was a man of remarkable intelligence and energy who, in a free society, would probably have achieved distinction, but the frontier slave communities in which he spent his active life gave no proper scope for these qualities. His fate was to be remembered principally in the roles imposed on him from outside: as the scapegoat for the military in the Dade debacle and as the symbol of the rebellious, red-handed slave in Giddings's semifictitious *Exiles*.

Some important authorities for Pacheco's early life, prior to December 1835, and for his later life, after his arrival in the Indian Territory, are two interview statements and an obituary. "The Dade Massacre" (*Florida Times-Union* [Jacksonville], October 30, 1892) was called to public attention by Minnie Moore-Wilson in *The Seminoles of Florida* (1896); Kenneth Wiggins Porter used the work and an obituary published January 8, 1895, in "The Early Life of Luis Pacheco Né Fatio" (*Negro History Bulletin*, December 1943). Volume 2 of *Pioneer Florida* (1959), edited by D. B. McKay, brought to light a statement allegedly published in the *Austin* (Texas) *Commercial Journal* (August 1861), which agrees in many respects with the 1892 interview but adds important details. Unfortunately, however, the *Commercial Journal* was published only from 1877 to 1881, so that August 1861 could not have been the date of publication. Probably an interview of that date was published later, and a copy of the issue, whatever date it was, fell into the hands of McKay.

A congressional report is a principal authority for Pacheco's career, from the "Dade massacre" to his arrival in the Indian Territory. Refer to "Report of the Committee of Military Affairs on the Petition of Joseph Elzaurdi, the Legal Representative of Antonio Pacheco, Praying Compensation for a Slave" (*House Report*, 30th Cong., 1st sess. [1847–1848], vol. 1, no. 187, serial no. 524). The National Archives, Department of the Interior, Florida Emigration Files, May to July 1838, contains lists and letters mentioning Pacheco. See also John Lee Williams's work *The Territory of Florida* (1837).

Kirk Munroe's *Through Swamp and Glade: A Tale of the Seminole War* (1896), a "boys' novel," uses a character named Louis Pacheco who is a youthful person of mixed race rather than a mature black man. He is the companion of Wild Cat, a Seminole leader, and he has a sister Louisa, who is Wild Cat's lover.

From *Dictionary of American Negro Biography* by Rayford W. Logan and Michael R. Winston, editors. Copyright © 1982 by Rayford W. Logan and Michael R. Winston. Reprinted by permission of W. W. Norton & Company, Inc.

See also Seminole Wars; Slavery in the United States.

Kenneth Wiggins Porter

Pacific Coast of Colombia

Humid forested lowland, in the western portion of Colombia, between the Andes and the Pacific Ocean, where black culture is predominant.

Colombia's Pacific coast covers approximately 46,619 sq km (18,000 sq mi), and is one of the most biodiverse areas in the world. It is one of the rainiest places on earth, with a mean annual precipitation ranging from 2,000 mm (79.4 in) to almost 13,000 mm (516 in). It is also one of the most isolated and poorest areas of Colombia, with a relatively low population density and few major urban centers. According to the 1993 national census, the region had fewer than one million inhabitants—about 3 percent of Colombia's population. Although there is no official estimate of its ethnic composition, over 90 percent of the area's inhabitants are black and mulatto. Indians comprise about 5 percent and mestizos (people of Indian and European descent) a smaller percentage of the region's population.

Approximately half of the population lives in small towns and villages, and to a lesser extent in scattered dwellings, along the rivers, the coast, and the four roads that connect the lowlands with the Andes. The other half inhabits the region's three cities: Buenaventura, Quibdó, and Tumaco. Buenaventura is the largest of them, with about 200,000 inhabitants. Trade from the Panama Canal and coffee production hastened the growth of this port, through which most of Colombia's imports and exports pass. Quibdó is an inland city, located on the Atrato River. It is the capital of the department of Chocó, the only independent political entity that lies entirely in the lowlands. In the South, three departments—Valle, Cauca, and Nariño—extend into the lowlands, but all have their capital cities (Cali, Popayán, and Pasto) in the Andes.

Colonial History of the Region

Prior to the arrival of the Spanish conquerors, the area was inhabited by the Kuna and Embera peoples, among other indigenous groups. The Spanish conquest of this region was launched from the western Andean urban enclaves—among which Popayán was the most important—in an effort to seize the area's gold riches. Although military expeditions into the lowlands began in the sixteenth century, success was a long time in coming. The mines in the area of the Telembí River, centered around the town of Barbacoas, first yielded a steady supply of gold shortly after the mid-seventeenth century. Only at the very end of that century was gold production consolidated in the upper Atrato and San Juan river drainages (the present Chocó), with Novitá and Citará (now Quibdó) as its major centers. The mining frontier expanded throughout the eighteenth century, forming small and provisional settlements. In this way, small valuable areas were brought under Spanish dominion, while large territorial extensions were still uncontrolled by the Spanish Empire.

From the outset mining was carried out by slave labor. The fact that the Andean cities had developed a mining economy that had already begun to use African slaves favored the rapid spread of this form of labor. This subsequently fueled the TRANSATLANTIC SLAVE TRADE, especially in the early eighteenth century, when this commerce reached its height in the viceroyalty of New Granada, now COLOMBIA. The example of the region that now constitutes the department of Chocó illustrates this point: the number of slaves increased from 821 in 1717 to 4,000 by 1738. Until 1770 the increase in the lowland black population was due primarily to purchases, which by that time were mostly black CREOLES, or blacks born in the Americas. Slave women represented in this area a smaller proportion than men throughout the eighteenth century. Slaves were legally introduced through the city of CARTAGENA DE INDIAS and sold directly in the lowlands or in the market of Popayán. There was, however, an illegal trade that reached the region by the Atrato River and the Pacific Ocean, via PANAMA.

Mining labor was organized into slave gangs called *cuadrillas*, which consisted of anywhere from five or six slaves to more than one hundred. At the head of each labor gang was a slave captain who mediated the relations between the other slaves and the administrator. He helped organize work, distribute food, and gather the produce. Some of the slaves engaged in agriculture near the mining camps. However, most of the supplies needed to feed the gangs were brought from the highland farms owned by the same people who owned the mines. That landed elite benefited from the colonial economy and enjoyed the wealth produced by black slave labor. Popayán, one of the most important colonial cities of what is now Colombia, achieved its splendor based on a system that treated black people as commodities.

Nevertheless, slaves were a special type of commodity; they had limited rights. They could work on Saturdays for themselves, either producing food or mining for gold, and on Sundays they were allowed to rest. With the gold they saved from the weekend some were able to buy their freedom. Once free, many continued to work to liberate their families. Data collected to document how the *libres* from the Citará and Nóvita mining districts moved into the Baudó River valley indicate that the self-purchase process could have begun to gain momentum as early as 1720. In the south of Colombia, for instance, around the turn of the eighteenth century, over 40 percent of the black population was free. By the mid-nineteenth century the slave-based colonial gold mining industry had lost its force and importance.

Throughout the eighteenth and nineteenth centuries, free blacks looked for new places to live. Some stayed in the mining areas in the upper parts of the watersheds. Others went downstream and settled where the narrow alluvial terraces are wider and hence provide more space for agriculture. Plantain, corn, and sugarcane were among the most important crops, although the quantities produced—for subsistence or local markets—were small. Others went farther, to the coasts, both to the flat and marshy southern coastline and to the northern high and mountainous shore. Fishing and coconut groves contributed to develop a sustainable lifestyle by the sea. Their subsistence economy was complemented, in some localities and for certain periods of time, by the gathering of natural products to supply larger market networks. Small quantities of gold continued to be sold in the mining areas, and the bonanzas of products demanded in the international market, such as black rubber and tagua nuts, provided a source of income and encouraged the colonization of certain areas.

Ethnicity and Culture of the Region

Little by little, until the mid-twentieth century, descendants of African slaves occupied the region, forming a myriad of villages among the forests. Indians continued to live primarily in the headwaters of some rivers, as they had done since the Spanish arrival. During these years, black communities developed their own ways of organizing themselves and of understanding and using their environment. Their productive practices, based in part on those performed by Indians, are specific to local conditions. Communal labor forms reminiscent of the mining *cuadrilla* still exist today. The ways black people classify their environment and illnesses denote their peculiar way of making sense of the world they live in. The importance of extended family relations is another trait that distinguishes the inhabitants of the Pacific coast of Colombia. Religious practices, such as holding a wake for one week for adults and for one night for *pangels* (babies), are unique to this population. Music types, such as the *chirimía* in the north and the *currulao* in the south, are products of the particular histories of the lowland black people.

It would be misleading, however, to portray a single image of the Afro-Colombian groups that inhabit the Pacific coast. There are cultural differences between the north and the south, of which music is one example. Dissimilarities can also be seen between older and younger people, just as between genders, and between rural and urban people. In recent decades urbanization and migration have altered the region. Some towns have become small chaotic cities, and young black men and women have joined the cane plantation workers of the Cauca Valley, the construction workers of Medellín, and the domestic service of Andean cities. Changes in the lowland economy have also shaped the lives of these people. The development of palm oil plantations near ECUADOR, for example, has transformed many peasants into landless workers.

Coastal Region Today

A significant recent development may prove to have serious consequences for the future of AFRO-COLOMBIANS. The 1991 Constitution, and the following Law 70 of 1993, recognized collective land rights to territories occupied by black people and opened the possibility for communal titling. This law was the product of an emerging movement that was reinforced by the law itself, which based its claims in the argument that black people constitute an ethnic group. Community leader DIEGO CÓRDOBA and the Movimiento Nacional Cimarrón had previously fought for the rights of black people under the idea of equality. Despite these efforts, the recent "discovery" of the enormous wealth of natural resources in the region and of its strategic location for international trade has attracted government modernization projects and investors. Many armed groups seeking wealth and territorial control have also reached the area. In the Chocó, for instance, guerrilla groups arrived first, and then the armed forces and paramilitary organizations followed. The traditional inhabitants, both indigenous and black, have been caught in the crossfire and have become victims of summary executions, disappearances, forced displacement, and hunger. These pervasive violations were previously unknown in the Chocó, which, though poor, was one of the most peaceful regions of Colombia. Despite such terrible threats, by March 1998 the National Land Reform Institute (INCORA) entitled the first 670,000 hectares to community councils throughout the region. However, immediately thereafter the head of one of the councils was gunned down. Hopes for the future of the black communities of the Chocó lie in their continued struggle and resistance to save their culture, lands, and lives.

See also Black Codes in Latin America; Colonial Latin America and the Caribbean; Slavery in Latin America and the Caribbean

Claudia Leal

Padmore, George

1902–1959

Anticolonial activist, Communist, and Pan-Africanist whose career spanned the Americas, Europe, the Soviet Union, and Africa.

George Padmore dedicated his life to the black liberation movement in AFRICA. After Padmore died in 1959, Ghanaian leader KWAME NKRUMAH stated that "one day the whole of Africa will surely be free and united and when the final tale is told the significance of George Padmore's work will be revealed."

Padmore was born Malcolm Ivan Meredith Nurse in Tacarigua, Trinidad. He was the son of Anna Susanna Syminster and James Nurse, a senior agricultural instructor and the son of a former slave. After graduating from a Trinidadian private school in 1918, Padmore became a reporter for the *Weekly Guardian* newspaper. In 1924 he emigrated to the United States with the aim of obtaining a university medical education, and a year later enrolled at FISK UNIVERSITY in Nashville, Tennessee. He did not, however, complete his degree at Fisk, possibly because of KU KLUX KLAN threats, and in 1927 he transferred to HOWARD UNIVERSITY Law School, where he became known as an excellent public speaker and student leader. As his professor Metz Lochard recalled, Padmore "was admired immensely by both faculty and student body. . . . He was our favorite speaker." Padmore also organized protests on campus, including a demonstration against a visit to the university by British ambassador Sir Esme Howard.

By 1928 Padmore had joined the Communist Party, adopting the name he is now known by as a cover for his political work. A year later, he took up an invitation from the Moscow-based Communist International (Comintern) to visit the Soviet Union, which many black intellectuals at the time regarded as a haven of racial tolerance and a positive force for black emancipation worldwide. On receiving his tickets, he discovered that they were one-way, and that the Comintern expected him to stay abroad. Such was his enthusiasm for the Communist cause that he withdrew from Howard and emigrated to the Soviet Union. He never returned to the United States.

Once in Moscow, Padmore became secretary of the International Trade Union Committee of Negro Workers, the Soviet Union's agency for promoting revolution among black peoples worldwide. After a stint in Moscow, during which he had an office in the Kremlin, he was transferred to Vienna. From there he traveled widely, recruiting leaders for African liberation movements. In 1934 Soviet priorities shifted: wishing to align with GREAT BRITAIN and FRANCE in opposition to GERMANY, the Soviet Union decided to soften its anticolonialist policies, and Padmore was instructed to discontinue his work. He refused, and was expelled from the Comintern and the Communist Party. Padmore became a staunch critic of Stalin's policies, but retained his faith in the Soviet Union. In his 1947 book *How Russia Transformed her Colonial Empire: A Challenge to Imperialist Powers,* he wrote that "national and cultural independence and political unity among multi-racial and national groups is possible only along the lines of a socialized planned economy."

In 1935 Padmore moved permanently to London. Over the next twenty years, with the help of his typist and companion Dorothy Pizer, he established himself as a leading spokesman for anticolonialist sentiment in Africa and around the world. His numerous books on Africa's struggle for independence include *How Britain Rules Africa* (1936), *Africa and World Peace* (1937), *Africa: Britain's Third Empire* (1949), and *Pan-Africanism or Communism?* (1956). Shortly before World War II he established the International African Service Bureau, which in 1939 condemned all the European colonial powers, equating the Nazi takeover of EUROPE with the European colonization of Africa. That same year, he wrote an article humorously entitled "The British Empire is the Worst Racket Yet Invented by Man."

During the 1940s Padmore moved closer to PAN-AFRICANISM, advocating the unification of Africa into a single country. He was instrumental in founding the Pan-African Federation (PAF), which in 1945 organized the All-Colonial Peoples' Conference in Manchester, England. Among the attendees was Kwame Nkrumah, a radical Pan-Africanist leader from the British GOLD COAST (present-day GHANA). Padmore and Nkrumah became close friends. As Nkrumah later recalled, "there existed between us that rare affinity for which one searches for so long but seldom finds in another human being." Nkrumah's Convention People's Party came to power in 1956 and helped Ghana achieve independence the following year, and Padmore became Nkrumah's chief adviser on African affairs. He met with considerable opposition from Ghana's elite, who objected to his special privileges as an outsider. Illness and exhaustion forced Padmore to return to Great Britain in 1959, shortly before his death.

See also Cold War and Africa; Nationalism in Africa; Trinidad and Tobago.

Bibliography

Blakely, Allison. *Russia and the Negro: Blacks in Russian History and Thought.* Howard University Press, 1986.

Hooker, James R. *Black Revolutionary: George Padmore's Path From Communism to Pan-Africanism.* Praeger Publishers, 1967.

Jonathan Edwards

Pagode

Type of Brazilian samba music played at informal parties and social gatherings, and which was popularized in the 1980s by artists such as Grupo Fundo de Quintal, Zeca Pagodino, and Beth Carvalho.

See also Samba.

Paige, Leroy Robert ("Satchel")

1906–1982

American baseball player, the first African American pitcher in the American League, and the first representative of the Negro Leagues to be inducted into the Baseball Hall of Fame.

Born in Mobile, Alabama, to gardener John Paige and washerwoman Lulu Paige, Leroy Robert Paige earned his nickname as a boy who carried satchels, or suitcases, at the Mobile train station. After being accused of stealing toy rings, Paige was sent at a young age to reform school in Mount Meigs, Alabama. It was here that he began to play baseball, assuming a place on the pitcher's mound that he would hold for over forty years, becoming, according to American ballplayer Dizzy Dean, the greatest pitcher of all time.

Paige began his career with the semiprofessional Mobile Tigers in 1924. He played for several teams in the NEGRO LEAGUES, including the Birmingham Black Barons. Paige was the most widely known African American baseball player until JACKIE ROBINSON integrated the major leagues in the late 1940s. With a lanky 6-foot, 3-inch body and huge feet, Paige's characteristic stance was unmistakable on the mound as he uncoiled his long arms and let the ball fly. In the 1930s he drew huge crowds as he was pitted against major leaguers, including Dean. Throughout the 1930s he appeared regularly in the East-West All-Star games. Due in part to Paige's enormous popular following, this yearly event drew together unprecedented numbers of African Americans. The barnstorming tours of the Negro League were exhausting, as the teams traveled as many as 30,000 miles a year to play exhibition games. Paige once commented that, at times, it was only when he put on his uniform that he found the spark to continue. It is little wonder that Paige suffered from exhaustion: he once pitched twenty-nine consecutive games in twenty-nine days.

As a free agent, Paige played throughout North and South America, as well as in the Caribbean during winter seasons. He left the Pittsburgh Crawfords in 1937 to accept Dominican president RAFAEL TRUJILLO's invitation to play for the DOMINICAN REPUBLIC team Ciudad Trujillo. He returned to the United States several years later and pitched the Kansas City Monarchs to victory in the 1942 Negro League World Series.

Paige became the first African American pitcher in the American League when he joined the Cleveland Indians in 1948. With Paige on the pitcher's mound, the Indians won the 1948 World Series. By 1952 Paige was pitching on the American League All-Star squad. Paige, who kept fans guessing at his true age, was in his forties at the time. "Don't look back," the quick-witted Paige once advised, "something might be gaining on you."

By his own count, Paige threw fifty-five no-hitters and won over 2,000 of the 2,500 games he pitched. He pitched his last game for the Indianapolis Clowns in 1967. Four years later, long after the disbanding of the Negro League, he was the first member of that league to be inducted into the Baseball Hall of Fame. Paige continued to work as a pitching coach for the Atlanta Braves of the National League. Appropriately, his autobiography is titled *Maybe I'll Pitch Forever* (1961).

See also Baseball in Latin America and the Caribbean; Baseball in the United States; Sports and African Americans.

Bibliography

Holway, John B. *Josh and Satch: The Life and Times of Josh Gibson and Satchel Paige.* Meckler, 1991.

Paige, Leroy. *Pitchin' Man: Satchel Paige's Own Story.* Meckler, 1992.

Ribowsky, Mark. *Don't Look Back: Satchel Paige and the Shadows of Baseball.* Simon and Schuster, 1994.

Marian Aguiar

Painting, African American

African American painters and the artistic movements associated with their work.

For information on

Art movements and collections: *See* Art Collections in the United States; Art, African American; Artists, African American; Black Mural Movement, The; Graffiti Art; Graphic Arts and Printmaking, African Americans in; Harlem Renaissance: The Vogue of the New Negro; Wall of Respect, The.

Eighteenth- and nineteenth-century painters: *See* Bannister, Edward Mitchell; Duncanson, Robert S.; Johnston, Joshua; Moorhead, Scipio; Tanner, Henry Ossawa.

Twentieth-century painters through 1960: *See* Alston, Charles Henry; Biggers, John; Crite, Alan Rohan; Delaney, Beauford; Delaney, Joseph; Douglas, Aaron; Harleston, Edwin A(gustus); Hunter, Clementine Clemence Rubin; Johnson, William Henry; Jones, Lois Mailou; Morgan, Sister Gertrude; Nugent, Richard Bruce; Pippin, Horace; Porter, James Amos; Smith, Albert Alexander; Waring, Laura Wheeler; Woodruff, Hale Aspacio.

Twentieth-century painters since 1960: *See* Basquiat, Jean-Michel; Bearden, Romare; Colescott, Robert H.; Driskell, David; Lawrence, Jacob Armstead; Ringgold, Faith.

Pakistan, Blacks in

See South Asia, Africans in.

Palacios, Arnoldo

1924–

Afro-Colombian novelist, short-story writer, and collector of cultural artifacts from the Pacific Coast and the department of Chocó, a predominantly black region.

Little is known about the life of Arnoldo Palacios, an intensely private man. He grew up in his native Chocó, COLOMBIA and moved to Bogotá to continue his studies at the Universidad Nacional. Later, he left the country and lived in France and the Soviet Union. His reputation was established in 1949 with publication of the critically acclaimed novel *Las estrellas son negras* (The Stars Are Black). Set on the riverbank of the Atrato River, in the department of Chocó, it portrays the brutal impact of utter poverty and social marginalization on the region's black communities. In its detached and cold depiction of the cruelest aspects of poverty, the novel recalls other classics in the genre such as Knut Hamsun's *Hunger* (1890), RICHARD WRIGHT's *American Hunger* (1977), and CAROLINA MARIA DE JESUS's *Quarto de Despejo* (1962; Child of the Dark). As Richard Jackson points out, *Las estrellas son negras* illustrates "how black rage stemming from unemployment and gnawing hunger, two aspects of the black experience in Colombia, can drive a man to drastic acts."

Using a technique reminiscent of James Joyce's stream of consciousness, *Las estrellas son negras* follows the path of a man, Israel, for a whole day and records in its most minute details the hopelessness, terror, and humiliation brought about by constant pangs of hunger. Israel, or Irra (phonetically, "anger" in Spanish), as he is referred to throughout the novel, in the end realizes that his will to survive is greater than his desire for violent retaliation or self-destruction. Despite its fierce depiction of misery, the novel reaches a lyric beauty that has few precedents in black literature in Spanish America.

In 1958, in Moscow, Palacios published *La selva y la lluvia* (The Jungle and the Rain). Though it revisits many of the themes in his first novel, this one was not well received by critics, who deemed it too politically charged. More recently it has been hailed by some as a superb synthesis of the region's three cultural influences (African, Indian, and European), especially in its treatment of oral culture. Palacios has also published various books about the region's folklore and a survey of black literature in the Americas. Since 1974 he has lived in France.

See also Literature, Black, in Spanish America.

Francisco Ortega

Palenque de San Basilio

Colombian community descended from an encampment of fugitive African-born slaves who, rebelling against the Spanish colonial system of slavery, fled into swamps, marshes, and shrublands in search of liberty.

The settlement of some 3,000 inhabitants, in the foothills of the Sierra de María, is 70 kilometers (43.75 miles) from CARTAGENA DE INDIAS, which was the principal Caribbean port of the TRANSATLANTIC SLAVE TRADE from the sixteenth century to the beginning of the nineteenth century. In Cartagena de Indias, resistance to slavery was constant. Those who were able to escape were known as *cimarrones*, a word that in the Americas was applied to insurgent NATIVE AMERICANS, wild plants and fruits, escaped domesticated animals, and later, runaway African slaves. The slaves fled from the galleys of ships, from mining operations, from ranches, and from domestic service; after their escape, they often came together to form small bands. Many were able to settle in rough encampments protected by swamps and thick brush. To protect themselves from the weapons and dogs of the Spanish slave-hunting parties, these communities surrounded themselves with fences made of posts, branches, and thorns. Such encampments became known as *palenques*.

Armed with arrows, blunderbusses, and stones, the encamped CIMARRÓN communities fought furiously against colonial domination, and often went to battle with their faces painted red and white. They attacked local ranches, burned them, stole cattle, and at times raped indigenous and black women. Some palenques grew to comprise 600 men, organized in squads headed by a *capitán*, or captain, and a warlord. Spanish militias counterattacked by burning cassava, corn, bean, potato, and plantain patches maintained by the palenques, and by capturing indigenous and black women to obtain inside information about the encampments. The inhabitants of the palenque (the *palenqueros*) were often forced to flee deeper into the bush to seek new refuge or other palenques. The history of these rebellions in Colombia has been called the *Guerra de los cimarrones*, or the Cimarrón War

In 1603 clashes at the palenque of La Matuna between Spanish forces and groups of palenqueros headed by Domingo BENKOS BIOHÓ, known in traditional lore as the King of Matuna, brought about a peace settlement signed by the governor of Cartagena, Gerónimo Suazo. On August 23, 1691, the king of Spain issued a decree that granted liberty to palenqueros in the Sierra de María. The decree affirmed the urgency of a "comprehensive and absolute liberty, which unless unconditionally granted would never be accepted [by the palenqueros]."

Palenque de San Basilio is the result of a series of concessions agreed to by Spaniards and palenqueros in the Sierra de María in 1713. It was established as the outcome of a dispute, mediated by the bishop of Cartagena, Father Antonio María Casiani, concerning the recognition of land rights and the authority of a palenquero government that was led by a cimarrón capitán. The bishop gave the palenque the name San

Basilio. In 1774 San Basilio for the first time figured in the census of the Spanish colonial government

Palenquero, a Creole language still spoken by the inhabitants of San Basilio, is a living legacy of the Bantu KONGO and MBUNDU languages. Likewise, the day-to-day culture of this and other villages in the Colombian Caribbean bears the stamp of their African past, evident in musical rhythms, the particularity of gestures, funeral rites such as the *lumbalú*, modes of kinship and social organization, and a strong oral tradition

Representations of an early liberation movement and a history of resistance to colonial slavery in COLOMBIA and the Americas remain in the oral tradition of Domingo Benkos Biohó, the African leader of La Matuna, as well as in the modern-day Palenque de San Basilio, a community directly descending from the days of maroonage in Colombia.

See also Colonial Latin America and the Caribbean; Complexities of Ethnic and Racial Terminology in Latin America and the Caribbean; Creoles; Maroonage in the Americas; Slave Rebellions in Latin America and the Caribbean; Slavery in Latin America and the Caribbean.

Nina Friedemann

Palés Matos, Luis

1898–1959

Puerto Rican poet and novelist, whose writing explores the contributions of African culture to the Americas.

Although he was neither black nor mulatto (of African and European descent), Luis Palés Matos is one of the few non-Cuban poets from the Caribbean who has seriously represented blacks in his literary work. The Palés Matos family was very prominent in PUERTO RICO, and Luis probably received his first exposure to African culture from the black servants who lived in the family mansion and took care of him when he was a boy.

Palés Matos was born on March 20, 1898, in Guayama, Puerto Rico. He began his career writing modernist poems (his first book, *Azaleas,* was published in 1915) and acquired fame when he started publishing poems with a "Negro" theme. These poems include "Danzarina Africana" (1918) and "Pueblo Negro" (1925). His work picked up on the contemporary cultural interest in primitivism, African arts, and folklore. The "Negro" in Palés Matos's writing symbolizes a redemptive, primitive, sensual, revitalizing force that stands in antithesis to a desiccated Western civilization. The association of African cultural traditions with primitive animal sensuality, a hallmark of modernism, is apparent in Palés Matos's first collection with a black theme, *Tuntún de pasa y grifería* (1937). In this collection, Palés Matos evokes African rhythms, uses nonsense words meant to reference the sound of African languages, and comments on the vitality of African culture in Puerto Rico.

Most critics agree that Palés Matos's interest in African culture represents only one dimension of his idiosyncratic poetry. In the 1920s, while living and working in SAN JUAN, PUERTO RICO, Palés Matos engaged in modernist experiments with sound and onomatopoeia. This interest in sound may have led him to represent African speech in his later poetry. Palés Matos's interest in interpreting African culture in his poems abruptly stopped in the 1950s. He published a collection of his life's work in 1957, entitled *Poesías, 1915–1956*. He died in San Juan on February 23, 1959.

See also Poetry, Caribbean.

Palm

Common name for a family of woody flowering plants widespread in the tropics.

Palms are of great economic importance because of the food, fiber, and oil they provide, and because of their ornamental uses. The family is the only member of its order and contains about 2,600 species, making it the fourth largest among the monocots, after the grasses, lilies, and orchids.

Palms have a characteristic growth form: a single, unbranched trunk topped with a tuft of fanlike or featherlike leaves. The flowers are borne in axillary clusters (inflorescences), and a large, interwoven mass of roots occurs at the trunk base. The trunks of palms, like those of other monocots, have no secondary growth; thus, the diameter of the trunk does not increase with the age of the tree, as in dicots. The growing tip of the trunk instead is built up into a large mass in the seedling stage, and maintains that broad width as the trunk matures. Bundles of vascular tissue are scattered throughout the trunks. The leaves of palms, often large, are formed a few at a time at the stem tips. They have large, sheathing bases that may leave semicircular scars on the stems when they fall off. The leaf blades are folded in a distinctive fashion called plicate.

Flowers of palms are usually individually inconspicuous but are often borne in great masses, some containing as many as 250,000 flowers. Flower parts are in threes, with three sepals (outer floral whorls) and petals (inner floral whorls) and six stamens (male flower parts). The pistil (female flower part), which usually consists of three separate or fused carpels (egg-bearing structures), matures into a single-seeded fruit that may be either a berry (a seed surrounded by a fleshy covering) or a drupe (a seed with a stony layer surrounded by a fleshy covering).

Palms are overwhelmingly tropical in distribution. They occur there in habitats that range from lowland rain forests to high mountains, and from deserts to mangrove swamps. Their distribution in the tropical zones, however, is uneven. About 1,400 species occur in tropical Asia, whereas only about 120 occur in AFRICA. Another 130 species occur on MADAGASCAR and other nearby islands in the western Indian Ocean near Africa, and about 950 species occur in the American tropics.

Palms are important sources of foods such as dates, coconuts, and sago. Copra and coir, which are useful fibers, raffia, and rattan fiber also come from palms. The oil palm, native to West Africa but widely cultivated, has become a source of the vegetable oil used in making margarine and soap and in cooking. Palms are grown as ornamentals in tropical and subtropical regions, and many smaller species are used as houseplants.

Scientific classification: Palms make up the family Palmae. The oil palm is classified as *Elaeis guineensis*.

See also Date Palm; Plants in Africa.

Palmares: An African State in Brazil

History of an independent African state in seventeenth-century Brazil.

Without slaves from AFRICA, reported an early Portuguese source, "it is impossible to do anything in BRAZIL." Although prior arrivals are suspected, the first known landing of slaves from Africa on Brazilian soil occurred in 1552. In 1580, five years after the founding of Loanda (now Luanda) and on the eve of Brazil's SUGAR boom, there were no fewer than 10,000 Africans in Brazil. Fifty years later, Pernambuco alone imported 4,400 slaves annually from Africa. It also contained 150 *engenhos,* or a third of the total sugar mill and plantation complex in Brazil. In 1630 the DUTCH WEST INDIA COMPANY captured Pernambuco, and within a decade PORTUGAL had abandoned Brazil to the Dutch. It was ultimately the decision of local settlers, the *moradores,* to fight the West India Company that led to restoration of Portuguese control in 1654. The Dutch retreat from Brazil, however, was secured through a joint Afro-Portuguese effort, which gave the Black Regiment of HENRIQUE DIAS its colonial fame. If early settlement and a sugar-based economy could not have been sustained without the African laborer, neither could the Portuguese continue to hold Brazil without the African soldier. The subsequent evolution of Brazil is no less a story of Euro-African enterprise. Exploitation of gold and diamonds in the eighteenth century, pioneering shifts of population from the coast to the interior, dilution of monoculture, formation of mining states, or advent of an abolitionist movement in the nineteenth century were all dependent on the same combination. The blend of race, language, and culture in contemporary Brazil confirms this evolution.

Africa's impact on Brazil and, more generally, the role of the Negro in Brazilian history and society are subjects of an extensive literature. Its principal stress is on assimilation rather than divergence, and frequently the early colonial society has been postulated from descriptions left by European and North American travelers who visited Brazil much later. It is hence not surprising that active Negro resistance to slavery in Brazil has not received comparable attention and is consequently less known.

According to one working definition, there were three basic forms of active resistance: fugitive slave settlements called *quilombos;* attempts at seizure of power; and armed insurrections, which sought neither escape nor control but ameliora-

tion. The latter two prevailed in the first half of the nineteenth century, a period of political transition in Brazil and of accelerated slave trade with Africa. They encompass, for example, nine Bahian revolts between 1807 and 1835, which involved a number of HAUSA, YORUBA, and Kwa-speaking groups, as well as the Ogboni Society, Muslim *alufas,* and even a "BACK TO AFRICA MOVEMENT." The quilombos constitute a pre-nineteenth-century phenomenon and are of considerable interest to the African historian. They came closest to the idea of re-creating African societies in a new environment and against consistently heavier odds. Once formed, the quilombos were regarded as a threat to the Portuguese plantation, an inducement for escape from the slave hut. They were rarely, therefore, allowed to last a long time. Of the ten major quilombos in colonial Brazil, seven were destroyed within two years of being formed. Four fell in the state of BAHIA in 1632, 1636, 1646, and 1796. The other three met the same fate in Rio in 1650, Parahyba (now Paraíba) in 1731, and Piumhy (now Piauí) in 1758. One quilombo, in MINAS GERAIS, lasted from 1712 to 1719. Another, the "Carlota" of Mato Grosso, was wiped out after existing for twenty-five years, from 1770 to 1795.

Nothing, however, compares in the annals of Brazilian history with the "Negro Republic" of Palmares in Pernambuco. It spanned almost the entire seventeenth century. Between 1672 and 1694, it withstood, on the average, one Portuguese expedition every fifteen months. In the last *entrada* against Palmares, a force of 6,000 took part in forty-two days of siege. The Portuguese Crown sustained a cumulative loss of 400,000 *cruzados,* or roughly three times the total revenue lease of eight Brazilian captaincies in 1612. As Brazil's classic quilombo, Palmares gained two more distinctions. It opened the study of Negro history in modern Brazil. Minutes of the Brazilian Historical Institute reveal that Palmares was the subject of lively discussions in 1840, and that search for written materials relative to it began in 1851. Important gaps in knowledge persist, but enough primary sources have been found and published to trace the development of Palmares, to examine it as a society and government, and to suggest its significance to both Brazilian and African history.

Founders of Palmares

Early writers attributed the birth of Palmares to Portuguese-Dutch struggles for Pernambuco, from which slaves profited by escaping in groups. They made no reference to Palmares as a quilombo. Southey came across the term in a Minas Gerais decree of 1722. An official letter, sent from Pernambuco to Lisbon in 1692, contains the first and only definition of Palmares as a quilombo in primary sources. The point is worth stressing. The accepted definition of a quilombo as a fugitive slave settlement has been continuously applied to Palmares since the turn of the twentieth century, and the problem of interpretation has been more difficult as a result. An early-nineteenth-century historian, for example, could easily classify Palmares as the "unusual exception, a real government of escaped Blacks on Brazilian soil." But subsequent identification of the state, which was a major historical event with a mere colony of escaped slaves, could not provide a framework to fit the problem. *Ki-lombo,* according to Cavazzi, was a Jaga war camp, and there is no lack of sources that have translated it correctly as "arrayal." Could a historico-linguistic link between a Palmares in a formative stage and the Jaga *ki-lombo* perhaps be assumed?

Slaves who freed themselves by escaping into the bush became something of a problem several decades before the Dutch took Pernambuco. In 1597 a Jesuit Father, Pero Rodrigues, was able to write that the "foremost enemies of the colonizer are revolted Negroes from Guiné in some mountain areas, from where they raid and give much trouble, and the time may come when they will dare to attack and destroy farms as their relatives do on the island of São Thomé." Shortly after his arrival from Portugal, Governor Diogo Botelho (1602–1608) learned from an Amerindian chief named Zorobabé that there was a "*mocambo* . . . of Negroes from Guiné . . . in the *palmares* of river Itapicuru." Zorobabé was asked to destroy the mocambo and return with slaves, but "few were brought back since the Indians killed many and Zorobabé sold some along the way." If the Itapicuru mocambo went almost unnoticed by Portuguese authorities, this was not the case with a similar manifestation farther north. In the captaincy of Pernambuco, reported a high official in 1612, "some thirty leagues inland, there is a site between mountains called Palmares which harbours runaway slaves . . . whose attacks and raids force the whites into armed pursuits which amount to little for they return to raid again. . . . This makes it impossible to . . . end the transgressions which gave Palmares its reputation." Diogo Botelho, before he left Brazil, sent a punitive expedition to Palmares.

Clearly, *quilombo* does not appear in the vocabulary of early-seventeenth-century Brazil. Instead, the fugitive slave settlement is known as mocambo, an appropriate description since *mu-kambo* in Ambundu means a hideout. Around 1603 *palmares* was simply any area covered by palm trees. There was no connection between the Itapicuru mocambo south of Sergipe and the Palmares of Pernambuco. Palmares was not regarded as an ordinary mocambo. By 1612 it had a considerable reputation. It was an organization with which the moradores could not cope alone. The foundation of Palmares thus appears to have taken place in 1605–1606, possibly earlier, but certainly not later. As the report of 1612 indicates, the first Portuguese expedition against Palmares attained little by way of military victory. Nothing else, however, is heard of Palmares until the mid-1630s. Do Salvador's history of Brazil, written in 1629, and recently published official documents for the years 1607 to 1633 are equally silent on Palmares. In 1634 a Pernambucan morador described Palmares as a "great calamity." The Dutch viewed it as a "serious danger" in 1640. Increasing *palmarista* militancy after 1630 can safely be associated with slaves who took advantage of the Dutch presence to escape and who eventually found their way into Palmares. It is also certain that Palmares antedates the Dutch in Brazil by at least a quarter of a century. Given an earlier origin, and the absence of *quilombo* from the contemporary vocabulary, it is even less probable that Jagas were the founders of Palmares. It would be tempting to accept a recent claim that the Jagas gave Palmares its ruling dynasty, after being sent to Brazil in 1616 by the Angolan governor, Luis Mendes de Vasconcellos, who assumed office in August 1617 and fought against the Ngola *with* Jaga auxiliaries. A large contingent of Jagas was sold into slavery after a punitive expedition against Kasanje in 1624 and may have reached Brazil along with other prisoners from the *guerra preta.* But the account of Andrew Battell, who was with the Jagas until 1603, shows nothing to indicate that any of them could have landed in Pernambuco by 1605. There remains the alternative of "Negroes from Guiné."

"Negroes from Guiné" were mentioned long before 1597 in connection with attempted rebellion. Rocha Pitta, a contemporary of Palmares, held that it was founded by "forty Negroes from Guiné" who had abandoned plantations around Porto Calvo. But the "Guiné" of early Portuguese sources is not a useful geographical expression. It stood for nearly anything between a limited section of West Africa and the entire continent. "Slaves from Guiné," according to the 1612 report, "are bought dearly because of the gifts and duties which must be paid for them in ANGOLA." Henrique Dias wrote a letter—most likely in 1648—which stated that the Black Regiment was composed mainly of "Angolas" and *crioulos* with a sprinkling of "Minas" and "Ardras." With Loanda as the undisputed slave funnel from the 1580s until well into the seventeenth century, it is quite unlikely that more than a handful of palmaristas originated outside the Angola-Congo perimeter. Crioulos (or Brazil-born slaves)—in Pernambuco of 1605—could not have been numerous either. All of this leads to the only plausible hypothesis about the founders of Palmares. They must have been Bantu-speaking and could not have belonged exclusively to any subgroup. Palmares was a reaction to a slaveholding society entirely out of step with forms of bondage familiar to Africa. As such, it had to cut across ethnic lines and draw upon all those who managed to escape from various plantations and at different times. The Palmares that emerged out of this amalgam may be glimpsed in a little more detail during the second half of the seventeenth century.

Campaigns to Destroy Palmares

Dutch activities concerning Palmares, from 1640 until the Reijmbach expedition of 1645, are known mainly through Barleus and Nieuhof. They begin with a reconnaissance mission by Bartholomeus Lintz, a Dutch scout who brought back the first rudimentary information about Palmares. Lintz discovered that Palmares was not a single enclave, but a combination of many *kleine* (small) and two *groote* (large) units. The smaller ones were clustered on the left bank of the Gurungumba, six leagues from its confluence with the larger Paraiba and twenty leagues from Alagoas. They contained "about 6,000 Negroes living in numerous huts." The two large *palmares* were deeper inland, thirty leagues from Santo Amaro, in the mountain region of Barriga, and "harboured some 5,000 Negroes." In January 1643 the West India Company sent its Amerindian interpreter Roelox Baro with a force of Tapuyas (and several Dutch regulars) to "put the large Palmares through 'fire and sword,' devastate and plunder the small Palmares." Baro seems to have returned without his men to report that "100 Negroes of Palmares were killed as against one killed and four wounded Dutchmen, our force having captured 31 defenders, including 7 Indians and some mulatto children." The four Dutchmen and a handful of Tapuyas were found two months later. There was no one with them.

A second Dutch expedition left Selgado for Palmares on February 26, 1645. It was headed by Jürgens Reijmbach, an army lieutenant who kept a diary for thirty-six consecutive days. His task was to destroy the two *groote* Palmares. On March 18 Reijmbach reached the first and found that it had been abandoned months earlier. "When we arrived the bush growth was so thick that it took much doing to cut a path through." Three days later, his men located the second one. "Our Brasilenses managed to kill two or three Negroes in the bush but most of the people had vanished. Their kin"—the few captives told Reijmbach—"knew of the expedition for some time because he had been forewarned from Alagoas." This Palmares, reads the entry of March 21: "is equally half a mile long, its street six feet wide and running along a large swamp, tall trees alongside. . . . There are 220 *casas* [houses], amid them a church, four smithies and a huge *casa de conselho* [or counsel house]; all kinds of artifacts are to be seen. . . . (The) king rules . . . with iron justice, without permitting any *feticeiros* [sorcerers] among the inhabitants; when some Negroes attempt to flee, he sends *crioulos* after them and once retaken their death is swift and of the kind to instill fear, especially among the Angolan Negroes; the king also has another *casa*, some two miles away, with its own rich fields. . . . We asked the Negroes how many of them live (here) and were told some 500, and from what we saw around us as well we presumed that there were 1,500 inhabitants all told. . . . This is the Palmares *grandes* of which so much is heard in Brazil, with its well-kept lands, all kinds of cereals, beautifully irrigated with streamlets. In military terms, Reijmbach fared no better than his two predecessors, Bartolomeu Bezzerra and Roelox Baro. An undestroyed Palmares, of which "so much is heard in Brazil," remained free of further interference by Pernambucan authorities until 1672. The ensuing two decades can best be described as a period of sustained war, which ended in the complete destruction of Palmares in 1694. As is often the case, warfare and more intimate knowledge of the enemy went together, and the growing information about Palmares in the 1670s threw light on its evolution during the twenty-seven years of relative peace.

"Our campaigns," complained a group of Pernambucan moradores in 1681, "have not had the slightest effect on the Negroes of Palmares . . . who seem invincible." The claim was not altogether true. Of the eight expeditions between 1672 and 1680, two did hurt Palmares. They were led by *capitão-mor* Fernão Carrilho, who had distinguished "himself in the destruction of *mocambos* in the Captaincy of Sergipe del Rey." The Carrilho *entradas* of 1676–1677 produced the most extensive firsthand report ever found. The Palmares of 1677 encompassed over sixty leagues, and included several villages: In the northeast, *mocambo* of *Zambi*, located sixteen leagues from Porto Calvo; north of it, at five leagues' distance, mocambo of *Arotirene*; alongside it two others called *Tabocas*; northeast of these, at fourteen leagues, the one of *Dombabanga*; eight leagues north another, called *Subupuira*; another six leagues north, the royal enclave of *Macoco*; west of it, at five leagues, the mocambo of *Osenga*; at nine leagues from our Serinhaem, northwest, the enclave of *Amaro*; at twenty-five leagues from Alagoas, northwest, the palamar of *Andalaquituche*, brother of *Zambi*; and between all these, which are the largest and most fortified, there are others of lesser importance and with less people in them.

There was no doubt, went the report, that Palmares maintained its "real strength" by providing "food as well as security" for the inhabitants—largely tillers of land who planted "every kind of vegetables" and knew how to store them against "wartime and winter." All the inhabitants of Palmares considered themselves subjects of a king who is called *Ganga Zumba*, which means Great Lord. He is recognized as such both by those born in Palmares and by those who join them from outside; he has a palatial residence, *casas* for members of his family, and is assisted by guards and officials who have, by custom, *casas* which approach those of royalty. He is treated with all respect due a Monarch and all the honours due a Lord. Those who are in his presence kneel on the ground and strike palm leaves with their hands as sign of appreciation of His excellence. They address him as Majesty and obey him with reverence. He lives in the royal enclave, called *Macaco,* a name which was begotten from the death of an animal on the site. This is the capital of Palmares; it is fortified with parapets full of caltrops, a big danger even when detected. The enclave itself consists of some 1,500 *casas*. There are keepers of law (and) their office is duplicated elsewhere. And although these barbarians have all but forgotten their subjugation, they have not completely lost allegiance to the Church. There is a *capela* [chapel], to which they flock whenever time allows, and *imagens* [images] to which they direct their worship. . . . One of the most crafty, whom they venerate as *paroco*, baptizes and marries them. Baptismals are, however, not identical with the form determined by the Church and the marriage is singularly close to laws of nature. . . . The first has given him many sons, the other two none. All the foregoing applies to the *cidade principal* of Palmares and it is the king who rules it directly; other *cidades* are in the charge of potentates and major chiefs who govern in his name. The second *cidade* in importance is called *Subupuira* and is ruled by king's brother (Gana) *Zona*. . . . It has 800 *casas* and occupies a site one square league in size, right along the river *Cachingi*. It is here that Negroes are trained to fight our assaults (and weapons are forged there).

Nearly three decades of peace had a number of important results in the internal evolution of Palmares. Instead of the two major *palmars* of 1645, there were now ten. There was a very substantial element in the Macaco of those native to Palmares, people unfamiliar with engenho slavery. Afro-Brazilians continued to enjoy preferential status, but the distinction between crioulos and Angolas does not appear to have been as sharp as it was in 1645. There was a greater degree of religious acculturation. The reference to a population composed mainly of those born in Palmares and those who joined from outside suggests that slaves had become less numerous than free commoners. According to Pitta, the only slaves in Palmares were those captured in *razzias*. But they had the option of going out on raids to secure freedom by returning with a substitute. This is confirmed by Nieuhof, who wrote that the main "business" of palmaristas "is to rob the Portuguese of their slaves, who remain in slavery among them, until they have redeemed themselves by stealing another; but such slaves as run over to them, are as free as the rest."

Although slim and often corrupted, the linguistic evidence leads to two unavoidable conclusions. The king and most of the hierarchy at the head of individual mocambos were not crioulos. Macoco/Makoko points to Loango; Tabocas/Taboka to Ambundu; Andalaquituche/Ndala Kafuche to Kisama; Osenga/Osanga/Hosanga to Kwango; Subupuira/Subusupu hara vura and Zumba to Zande; Dombabanga/Ndombetbanga to a Benguella-Yombe composite. Arotirene appears to be Amerindian. Zambi/Nzambi and Ganga/Nganga, respectively "divinity" and "lord," are too widely used in Central Africa to be traced further. Given as "brother," Zona may be an extreme corruption of Mona, an equally common term. Amaro/Amargo derives from a very bitter kind of wild-growing tea shrub, chimarrão, which is close enough to *cimarrones,* as marooned slaves were called in the West Indies. The principle of *cujus regio ejus religio,* slightly bent to accommodate ethnic subgroups, cannot be deduced from this evidence. What it does affirm, however, is that Palmares did not spring from a single social structure. It was, rather, an African political system that came to govern a plural society and thus give continuity to what could have been at best a group of scattered hideouts.

The almost equally long years of peace and war between 1645 and 1694 point to Palmares as a fluctuating "peril." While this is not necessarily unfair to the merits of a particular event, the Portuguese took it for an article of faith that Palmares was an aggressor state. No written document originating within Palmares has come to light. It probably does not exist. The late Arthur Ramos made a search for oral traditions in the 1930s. It yielded only an annual stage play he was able to attend in the township of Pilar: The sensation of security (in Palmares) diminished after the first attacks of the colonists. The Palmares Negroes reacted by increasing their defenses . . . to maintain their little republic, the Negroes were forced to make sorties to the neighboring Indian villages and the towns of nearby valleys. This brought about (more) reprisals. . . . The play recalls this sequence of events as it persists in the memory of the people. However blurred by the passage of time, the play at least allows for aggression on each side. There is no need to depend, in this case, on collective memory to look for evidence with which both the specific and broad nature of the "peril" can be illustrated.

Pernambucan authorities did not view Palmares from the perspective of the moradores who were in contact with it. They were too far removed from the general area of Palmares. Reijmbach, for example, had to march at a fast clip for twenty days to reach it from the coast, which the Pernambucan governors—Dutch or Portuguese—seldom left. The governors did, however, respond to morador pressure. "Moradores of this Captaincy, Your Majesty, are not capable of doing much by themselves in this war. . . . At all hours they complain to me of tyrannies they must suffer from [the Negroes of Palmares]." Among the complaints most frequently heard were loss of field hands and domestic servants, loss of settler lives, kidnapping and rape of white women. Two of the common grievances do not stand up too well. Women were a rarity in Palmares and were actively sought during razzias. But female relatives of the morador did not constitute the main target, and those occasionally taken were returned unmolested for ransom. Checking the "rape of Sabines" tales, EDISON CARNEIRO discovered one exception to the ransom rule, reported by a Pernambucan soldier in 1682. Equally, close examination of documents in the Ennes and Camara de Alagoas collections—117 in all—failed to reveal a single substantiated case of a morador killed in palmarista raids. Settler lives appear to have been lost in the numerous and forever unrecorded "little" entradas into Palmares. They were carried out by small, private armies of plantation owners who sought to recapture lost hands or to acquire new ones without paying for them. Some of the moradores had secret commercial compacts with Palmares, usually exchanging firearms for gold and silver taken in the razzias. Evidence of this is not lacking. A gubernatorial proclamation of November 26, 1670 bitterly denounced "those who possess firearms" and pass them on to palmaristas "in disregard of God and local laws." In 1687 the state of Pernambuco empowered a Paulista Colonel-of-Foot to imprison moradores merely suspected of relations with Palmares, "irrespective of their station." Town merchants are also known to have carried on an active trade with Palmares, bartering utensils for agricultural produce. More than that, they "were most useful to the Negroes . . . by supplying advance information on expeditions prepared against them [and] for which the Negroes paid dearly." And Reijmbach's entry of March 21, 1645 makes it clear that this relationship was an old one.

Loss of plantation slaves, through raids as well as escape, emerges as the one solid reason behind the morador-palmarista conflict. The price of slaves is known to have increased considerably by the late 1660s. The very growth of Palmares served to increase its fame among the plantation slaves. "More and more Negroes from Angola," wrote a governor in 1671, "have now for some years fled on their own from the *rigor de cativeiro* in mills and plantations of this Captaincy." But its growth was not one-sided. Salients in the *morador* frontier, which had protruded from the littoral by the early 1640s, contracted between 1645 and 1654, a decade of Portuguese-Dutch struggle for Pernambuco. Contacts with Palmares were thus minimized until new bulges began to form. In a painstaking study of territorial expansion in Brazil, Felisbello Freire has shown that this movement away from the coast began in the late 1650s from Bahia, Sergipe, and Espírito Santo. It was retarded by no more than a few years for southern Pernambuco. The northern section merely took a little longer. "The Negroes," writes Carneiro, "had good relations with moradores, as long as the latter kept their slave huts and plantations away from the free lands of Palmares." But what looked like free lands to the Portuguese were not regarded in the same light by rulers of Palmares, and neither party understood the problem. There were, to be sure, no "great frontier" proportions in the inland movement of the concluding seventeenth-century decades. According to Basílio Magalhães, it was an "*expansão pequena,*" at fifty or so leagues inland. Palmares was, however, well within it. Toward the end of the seventeenth century its territorial domain was estimated at about 1,100 square leagues. "Those who live in a state of constant danger," reads another proclamation, "are people in the vicinity of the mocambos belonging to Palmares."

The hard-hitting Carrilho entradas of 1676–1677 evoked at least one response familiar to Palmares besides warfare. As he had done earlier, whenever a new governor came to Pernambuco, Ganga-Zumba sued for peace. The terms, however, were new and rather surprising. On June 18, 1678: The junior lieutenants whom don Pedro (de Almeida) had sent to Palmares returned with three of the king's sons and twelve more Negroes who prostrated themselves at the feet of don Pedro. . . .

They brought the king's request for fealty, asking for peace which was desired, stating that only peace could end the difficulties of Palmares, peace which so many governors and leaders had proffered but never stuck to; that they have come to ask for his good offices; that they have never desired war; that they only fought to save their own lives; that they were being left without *cidades,* without supplies, without wives. . . . The king had sent them to seek peace with no other desires but to trade with moradores, to have a treaty, to serve his Highness in whatever capacity; it is only the liberty of those born in Palmares that is now being sought while those who fled from our people will be returned; Palmares will be no more as long as a site is provided where they will be able to live, at his grace."

Three days after the embassy's arrival, the new governor, Aires de Souza Castro—replacing Almeida—called a council of state. He proposed that a draft treaty be sent to Ganga-Zumba extending peace, the requested liberties, and the release of palmarista women, who seem to have constituted by far the largest group of captives. The council agreed, and a *sargento-mor* who had served in the Black Regiment and knew how to read and write, was sent to the Macoco, "*para que lesse e declarasse ao rei e aos mais o tratado de paz*" ("in order to read and to declare to the King and others the peace treaty"). Ganga-Zumba was confirmed as supreme ruler over his people. The question of Palmares's territorial limits was not settled in any precise way. "The solemnity which surrounded all these acts," wrote Nina Rodrigues, "gave a real importance to the Negro State which now the Colony treated as one nation would another, (for) this was no mere pact of a strong party concluded with disorganized bands of fugitive Negroes."

On paper, the treaty seemed conclusive. But there were peculiarities in the immediate situation. A strong detachment, which had been attacking Palmares since 1677 or early 1678, was not demobilized, and a group of Alagoan moradores, led by a spokesman named João da Fonseca, made certain that it would remain there. The ink was hardly dry when Aires de Souza Castro began to distribute some 192 leagues of land to sixteen individuals who had taken part in wars against Palmares, Carrilho alone obtaining a twenty-league *sesmaria*. By 1679 a palmarista "captain named Zambi (whose uncle is Ganga-Zona) was in revolt (with João Mulato, Canhonga, Gaspar [and] Amaro), having done the person of Ganga-Zumba to death." By March 1680 Zambi was being called upon to surrender, without success. The war was on once more.

Reactions to the treaty, on both sides, are revealing. Ganga-Zumba's peace proposal contained two clauses that could not be fulfilled. To allow a sovereign, if vassal, state to exist in Pernambuco would have meant reversing a 150-year-old policy of exclusive Portuguese claim to Brazil. The Almeida–de Souza move, was, therefore, a tactical one. It was, as Ennes stated after careful study, "an easy way of postponing that question which already had, without any positive accomplishment, consumed infinite time." Conversely, to hand over to the Portuguese half or more of some 15,000 to 20,000 palmaristas—a difficult logistical problem in its own right—would have required the kind of obedience that only a modern totalitarian state can secure.

The native-newcomer ratio was not identical in every mocambo of Palmares. The Macoco, at forty-five leagues from Porto Calvo, must have had a far greater number of the native-born than did the mocambos of Zumbi, at sixteen leagues from Porto Calvo, and Amaro, at nine leagues from Serinhaem. Sociocultural differences, moreover, between crioulos and recent arrivals from Africa were not sufficiently great to challenge the unity of Palmares, which stood against the Portuguese economic and political order. The diplomacy of Ganga-Zumba, an elected ruler, might have worked had the promise to return those who found refuge in Palmares been observed. It might have worked if Palmares had been contiguous to other similar states facing an intrusive minority. Again, it might have worked if Palmares had been a homogeneous society with hereditary rulers. None of these conditions was present. In its time and place, Palmares had only two choices. It could continue to hold its ground as an independent state or suffer complete extinction. Zambi's palace revolt finally brought the unyielding palmarista and morador elements to full agreement.

Six expeditions went into Palmares between 1680 and 1686. Their total cost must have been large. In 1694 the Overseas Council in Lisbon was advised that Palmares caused a cumulative loss of not less than one million cruzados to the "people of Pernambuco." The estimate appears exaggerated unless the 400,000 cruzados contributed directly by the Crown were included. A single municipality did, however, spend 3,000 cruzados (109,800 reis) in the fiscal year 1679–1680 to cover the running cost of Palmares wars, and a tenfold figure for the local and state treasuries would seem modest for the six years. Casualties aside, the results did not justify the cost. Palmares stood undefeated at the end of 1686. It was apparent that the state of Pernambuco could not deal with Palmares out of its own resources. In March 1687 the new governor, Sotto-Maior, informed Lisbon that he had accepted the services of *bandeirantes* (or expedition leaders and slave-raiders) from São Paulo, "at small expense to the treasure of Your Majesty." The Paulistas of the time were Portuguese-Amerindian *metis* and transfrontiersmen, renowned in Brazil for special skills in jungle warfare. Their leader, Domingos Jorge Velho, had written to Sotto-Maior in 1685 asking "for commissions as commander-in-chief and captains in order to subdue . . . (Palmares)." Largely because Lisbon could not be convinced that their services would come cheap, the Paulistas did not reach Pernambuco until 1692. In crossing so great a distance, 192 lives were lost in the backlands of Brazil, and 200 men deserted the Paulista ranks, unable to face "hunger, thirst, and agony."

The story of Palmares's final destruction has been told in great detail. Two-thirds of the secondary works discuss the Paulistas and the 1690s, some sixty of the ninety-five documents in the Ennes collection refer to little else, and Ennes has published a useful summary in English. The Paulistas had to fight for two years to reduce Palmares to a single fortified site. After twenty days of siege by the Paulistas, the state of Pernambuco had to provide an additional 3,000 men to keep it going for another twenty-two days. The breakthrough occurred during the night of February 5–6, 1694. Some 200 palmaristas fell or hurled themselves—the point has been long debated—"from a rock so high that they were broken to pieces." Hand-to-hand combat took another 200 palmarista lives, and over 500 "of both sexes and all ages" were captured and sold outside Pernambuco. Zambi, taken alive and wounded, was decapitated on November 20, 1695. The head was exhibited in public "to kill the legend of his immortality."

Significance of Palmares

The service rendered by the destruction of Palmares, wrote one of Brazil's early Africanists, is beyond discussion. It removed, Nina Rodrigues stated, the "greatest threat to future evolution of the Brazilian people and civilization—a threat which this new HAITI, if victorious, would have planted (forever) in the heart of Brazil." Indeed, Palmares came quite close to altering the subsequent history of Brazil. Had they not experienced the threat of Palmares in the seventeenth century, the Portuguese might well have found themselves hugging the littoral and facing not one, but a number of independent African states dominating the backlands of eighteenth-century Brazil. In spite of hundreds of mocambos that tried to come together, Palmares was never duplicated on Brazilian soil. This is ample testimony of its impact on the Portuguese settler and official. They organized special units, under *capitães-do-mato*, or bush captains, to hunt for mocambos and nip them in the bud. And they sought to prevent, at ports of entry, an overconcentration of African slaves from the same ethnic group or ship. This policy was abandoned in the wake of the Napoleonic wars, and the immediate repercussion came by way of the nine Bahian revolts after 1807. The well-established thesis that uninhibited miscegenation and the corporate nature of the Portuguese society in Brazil produced a successful example of social engineering must also take into account the historical role of Palmares.

Palmares was a centralized kingdom with an elected ruler. Ganga-Zumba delegated territorial power and appointed to office. The most important ones went to his relatives. His nephew, Zambi, was the war chief. Ganga-Zona, the king's brother, was in charge of the arsenal. Interregnum problems do not seem to have troubled Palmares, the history of which spans about five generations of rulers. Zambi's palace revolt did not displace the ruling family. Assuming that Loanda was the main embarkation point for Pernambucan slaves, which is confirmed by the linguistic evidence, the model for Palmares could have come from nowhere else but Central Africa. Can it be pinpointed? Internal attitude toward slavery, prostrations before the king, site initiation with animal blood, the placing of the casa de conselho in the "main square," or the use of a high rock as part of a manmade fortress lead in no particular direction. The names of mocambo chiefs suggest a number of possible candidates. The most likely answer is that the political system did not derive from a particular Central African model, but from several. Only a far more detailed study of Palmares through additional sources in the archives of Angola and Torre do Tombo could refine the answer. Nonetheless, the most apparent significance of Palmares to African history is that an African political system could be transferred to a different continent; that it could come to govern not only individuals from a variety of ethnic groups in Africa but also those born in Brazil, pitch black or almost white, Latinized or close to Amerindian roots; and that it could endure for almost a full century against two European powers, the NETHERLANDS and Portugal. And this is no small tribute to the vitality of the traditional African art in governing men.

From "Palmares: An African State in Brazil," in *Maroon Societies: Rebel Slave Communities in the Americas,* third edition, ed. Richard Price, 170–188. Johns Hopkins University Press, 1996. Used with permission.

See also Afro-Brazilian Culture; Colonial Latin America and the Caribbean; Maroonage in the Americas; Mining in Latin America and the Caribbean; Muslim Uprisings in Bahia, Brazil; Slave Rebellions in Latin America and the Caribbean; Slavery in Latin America and the Caribbean.

R. K. Kent

Palma Sola

Town in the Dominican Republic and site of the massacre of a largely Afro-Dominican religious community by government forces.

The massacre of a largely black and mulatto (of African and European descent) group of Dominicans in the Palma Sola township in the province of San Juan de la Maguana in 1962 remains an unresolved historical incident with regard to its specific causes. The resulting death of hundreds of unarmed human beings, however, is clear.

Palma Sola was a small and somewhat isolated community near the Haitian-Dominican border. Its location is significant. Members of the Dominican elite have long held racist views toward neighboring HAITI, which they have associated with African culture and with barbarism. Dominican intellectuals have extended these same ascriptions to Dominicans living near the Haitian border, who they have seen as predisposed to involvement in Haitian VODOU, while denying the existence of a native Dominican Vodou.

There is some variation in historical accounts of the events leading to the massacre. The Palma Sola movement of the 1960s was considered a threat to the social, economic, and religious status quo. Essentially a religious community, it was led by the eleven-member Ventura Rodríguez family, referred to as *Los Mellizos,* meaning "the twins." (A family with a set of twins has great prestige in the Haitian/Dominican Vodou tradition. The Ventura Rodríguez family had a set of twins, León Remilgio and a sister who died at a young age, but the name Los Mellizos became generalized to refer to the entire family.)

The threat allegedly posed by the Palma Sola community was seen in its practice of Vodou, which was regarded as immoral and opposed to Christian values. Other activities were considered antiestablishment as well. For example, the community did not use money and prohibited the sale of food. Also, land distributions were made by the Ventura Rodríguez family. The members did not interact with the local or national government, but established their own laws and alternative form of government. While the residents of Palma Sola were never involved in physical attacks on people or property—in fact, they were not allowed to carry weapons—their activities were considered a major form of social protest, a quiet revolution in effect.

The province of San Juan de la Maguana has, in fact, served throughout Dominican history as the home of a people who challenged the system and prevailing ideologies. As early as 1543, it was the home of hundreds of Dominican runaway slaves. Some viewed the community in Palma Sola as a religious peasant movement reviving the cult of Liborio Mateo (Andrés Olivo Mateo), an Afro-Dominican who, at the turn of the century, was a messianic spiritual leader of a group of followers known as Liboristas. In 1922 Liborio was killed with the assistance of the U.S. military.

The provisional government of President Rafael Filberto Bonnelly (1961–1963), established after the assassination in 1961 of dictator RAFAEL TRUJILLO, determined that the religious activities and social protest of the inhabitants of Palma Sola were subverting "Christian values and morals" in the country. It ordered an attack on the residents of Palma on December 28, 1962. Allegedly, Miguel Rodríguez Reyes, inspector general of the armed forces, arrived at Palma Sola that day in the hope of negotiating an agreement with the Mellizos to avert the violence. According to accounts, he was extremely surprised to learn that he had been followed to the site by the chief of police, Francisco Camaño Denó, and about 600 soldiers. Confusion and shooting ensued, and General Rodríguez Reyes was accidentally killed.

What followed was the murder by gas and bullets of hundreds of innocent victims—adults and children. After the massacre, officers of the police and army burned the bodies or buried them in mass graves. The survivors were carried off to various jails throughout the region.

The move to extinguish the followers of Liborio Mateo, and the shootings and burnings at Palma Sola, recall the massacre of about 20,000 Haitians and Dominican-Haitians ordered by Trujillo in 1937. The genocide of Afro-Dominicans in Palma Sola should be seen, on one level, as a racist act to be added to the list of atrocities that have been committed against people of African descent in the Americas.

See also Dominican-Haitian Relations.

James Davis

Pan-African Congress of 1919

Major international gathering to promote worldwide black unity, held in Paris in 1919.

African American activist and writer W. E. B. DU BOIS organized the Pan-African Congress in order to bring together Africans and leaders of nations involved in the African diaspora, and to promote the cause of African independence. Du Bois insisted that the conference be held in Paris in 1919 during the proceedings of the Paris Peace Conference, soon after World War I. He wanted GERMANY's former colonies in eastern and southern Africa internationalized as the first step in gradual African self-determination. The Paris gathering followed a previous conference held in London in 1900, organized by Henry Sylvester Williams, a London barrister born in Trinidad.

The congress received considerable publicity, partly because of the cooperation of French Prime Minister Georges Clemenceau, who accepted its resolutions. The congress delegates did not advocate immediate independence for AFRICA. Instead, they called for greater African participation in the affairs of the colonies, and for the newly created League of Nations to undertake the protection and well-being of the African people. Individual resolutions called on the colonial powers to allow Africans to own land and participate in government, to tax and regulate companies operating in Africa in the interests of Africans' welfare, to ban forced labor and corporal punishment, and to safeguard Africans' religious and social freedom.

BLAISE DIAGNE of SENEGAL, the first African to serve in the French Chamber of Deputies, delivered the keynote speech at the congress, which attracted fifty-seven delegates. Despite the refusal of the United States and GREAT BRITAIN to issue passports to some potential delegates, Americans were the most numerous contingent, with sixteen delegates. Other nations represented were the French West Indies (GUADELOUPE and MARTINIQUE), thirteen; HAITI, seven; FRANCE, seven; LIBERIA, three; and the Spanish colonies, two. There was one delegate each from the Portuguese colonies, SANTO DOMINGO, England, British Africa, French Africa, ALGERIA, EGYPT, the Belgian Congo (now the DEMOCRATIC REPUBLIC OF THE CONGO), and Abyssinia (ETHIOPIA).

Prominent black Americans at the congress included ROBERT R. MOTON, principal of the TUSKEGEE INSTITUTE; his secretary Nathan A. Hunt; and Lester A. Walton, managing editor of the *New York Age*, a weekly black newspaper in New York. White support was welcome; liberal activists such as Charles Edward Russell and William English Walling of the NATIONAL ASSOCIATION FOR THE ADVANCEMENT OF COLORED PEOPLE (NAACP) attended.

To keep African solidarity alive, Du Bois was also instrumental in the convening of several subsequent gatherings. The second Pan-African Congress was held in three sessions in 1921 in London, Brussels, and Paris; a third congress was held in 1923 in London and Lisbon; a fourth in New York City in 1927; and a fifth in Manchester, England, in 1945. In 1974—well after most African countries had achieved independence—the sixth Pan-African Congress was held in DAR ES SALAAM, TANZANIA, and hosted by Tanzanian President JULIUS NYERERE. Attended by delegates from all over the world, including activists Owusu Sadaukai and AMIRI BARAKA, the gathering revealed a growing split between revolutionary Marxists and those delegates who supported African governments already in power. The seventh Pan-African Congress was held in KAMPALA, UGANDA in April 1994.

See also Decolonization in Africa: An Interpretation; Pan-Africanism; Pan-Africanist Congress.

Bibliography

Walters, Ronald W. *Pan Africanism in the African Diaspora.* Wayne State University Press, 1993.

David P. Johnson, Jr.

Pan-Africanism

Wide range of ideologies that are committed to common political or cultural projects for Africans and people of African descent.

In its most straightforward version, Pan-Africanism is the political project calling for the unification of all Africans into a single African state, to which those in the African diaspora can return. In its vaguer, more cultural, forms, Pan-Africanism has pursued literary and artistic projects that bring together people in AFRICA and her diaspora.

Significant Trends

The Pan-Africanist movement began in the nineteenth century among intellectuals of African descent in North America and the Caribbean who thought of themselves as members of a single, "Negro," race. In this they were merely following the mainstream of nineteenth-century thought in North America and EUROPE, which developed an increasingly strong focus on the idea that human beings were divided into races, each of which had its own distinctive spiritual, physical, and cultural character. As a result, the earliest Pan-Africanists often limited their focus to sub-Saharan Africa: to the region, that is, whose population consists mostly of darker-skinned (or, as they would have said, "Negro") peoples. In this way, they intentionally left out lighter-skinned North Africans, including the large majority who speak Arabic as their first language.

In the twentieth century, however, this way of thinking of African identity in racial terms was challenged. In particular, the intellectuals born in Africa who took over the movement's leadership in the period after the World War II developed a more geographical idea of African identity. The founders of the ORGANIZATION OF AFRICAN UNITY (OAU), such as GAMAL ABDEL NASSER of EGYPT and KWAME NKRUMAH of GHANA, for example, had a notion of Africa that was more straightforwardly continental. African unity for them was the unity of those who shared the African continent (though it continued to include, in some unspecified way, those whose ancestors had left the continent in the enforced exile of the slave trade).

Nevertheless, the movement's intellectual roots lie firmly in the racial understanding of Africa in the thought of the African American and Afro-Caribbean intellectuals who founded it. Because Pan-Africanism began as a movement in the New World, among the descendants of slave populations, and then spread back to Africa, it aimed to challenge anti-black racism on two fronts. On the one hand, it opposed racial domination in the diaspora; on the other, it challenged colonial domination, which almost always took a racial form, in Africa itself. The stresses and strains that have sometimes divided the movement have largely occurred where these two rather different goals have pulled it in different directions.

Intellectual Origins

The idea of linking together the whole "Negro" race for political purposes was developed by a wide range of nineteenth-century African American intellectuals. We can still speak of these nineteenth-century thinkers as Pan-Africanist, even though they did not use the term. Like Pan-Slavism in Eastern Europe and the forms of romantic nationalism that created modern GERMANY and ITALY, early Pan-Africanism reflected a philosophical tradition, derived from the German philosopher Johann Gottfried Herder (1744–1803). In Herder's opinion, peoples (or, as they were often called, nations) such as the Slavs, Germans, and Italians, were the central actors of world history. He suggested that their identities were expressed largely in language, in literature, and in folk culture, and he thought that such nations were naturally drawn together by the desire to live together in states, with a shared language, culture, and traditions. The cultural oneness of a nation led naturally, in Herder's view, to political union.

The first black intellectual to apply this theory in a systematic way to people of African descent was W. E. B. DU BOIS (1868–1963). In a lecture on "The Conservation of Races," published by the American Negro Academy in 1897, Du Bois used the word "Pan-Negroism." Du Bois was an African American who had studied as an undergraduate at Harvard with the philosopher William James. But in 1892 Du Bois had gone on to do graduate work at the Friedrich Wilhelm University in Berlin, and was, therefore, thoroughly familiar with the intellectual traditions of modern European nationalism, as well as with the philosophical tradition that began with Herder.

In "The Conservation of Races" Du Bois argued that "the history of the world is the history, not of individuals, but of groups, not of nations, but of races." (But he mentions Slavs, Teutons—that is, Germans—and the Romance race, indicating that, like so many other Western intellectuals of his day, he took real nations to *be* races.) He argued, too, that the differences among races were "spiritual, psychical, differences—undoubtedly based on the physical, but infinitely transcending them." And, finally, he insisted (in a manner strongly reminiscent of Herder) that each race was "striving . . . in its own way, to develop for civilization its particular message."

The problem for Pan-Negroism was how the Negro people were to deliver their message. Du Bois believed that African Americans (whom he called the "advance guard of the Negro people") were to play the leading role in that task. He thought that they were especially well suited for this task because some of them, like Du Bois himself, had been exposed to the best modern educations and the highest forms of knowledge.

Though Du Bois's formulation had roots in the theorists of European nationalism, he was also strongly influenced by a number of earlier African American thinkers, whose work we can understand most easily in the context of the broad nineteenth-century history of antislavery or "abolitionist" thought. The focus of attention for all the major black thinkers in the New World in the early nineteenth century was the abolition of slavery and of the slave trade. Since most people, both black and white, believed that racial hostility between blacks and whites was inevitable (this view was explicitly held, for example, by Presidents Jefferson and Lincoln) one major preoccupation of some abolitionists concerned finding territories that could be inhabited by freed blacks. The colony of SIERRA LEONE was created in the late eighteenth century by British abolitionists, in part as a home for freed blacks and the black poor of England; the AMERICAN COLONIZATION SOCIETY played a similar role in the creation of LIBERIA in the 1820s. But other schemes were proposed to colonize parts of LATIN AMERICA, the Caribbean, and the American western frontier.

All of these schemes, of course, presupposed that Africans (and their descendants in the New World) belonged naturally together in a political community, separated from other peoples. There were significant voices raised in protest against this assumption—notably that of the American ex-slave and abolitionist FREDERICK DOUGLASS—and they were joined by many others after the United States formally recognized the citizenship of people of African descent in the post–Civil War amendments to the U.S. Constitution. But in the first half of the nineteenth century the majority view, among both black and white intellectuals, was that a home was needed for the Negroes if they were to be free.

Perhaps the most important black intellectual forerunners of Pan-Africanism were three men who addressed themselves to this situation: MARTIN R. DELANY (1812–1885), ALEXANDER CRUMMELL (1822–1898), and EDWARD WILMOT BLYDEN (1832–1912). Martin R. Delany was born in the southern United States, but his family moved to Pennsylvania during his youth. He began a medical education at Harvard, but was forced to leave because white students would not work alongside him. Delany's contributions to the prehistory of Pan-Africanism begin with his own sense of a profound connection with Africa. He was proud that he was a "full-blooded Negro" and he named his children for—among others—TOUSSAINT LOUVERTURE (the black leader of the HAITIAN REVOLUTION), Ramses II (the pharaoh of EGYPT), and ALEXANDRE DUMAS (the French novelist, who had African ancestry). But he was also a powerful voice for black emigration from the United States, arguing in his *The Condition, Elevation, Emigration and Destiny of the Colored People of the United States* (1852) that only in a country without white people could black people flourish. In that early work, Delany did not make the obvious suggestion that blacks should "return" to Africa. This was not because he was against the idea but because, along with other leaders of the re-emigration movement, he believed that most African Americans (convinced by anti-Negro propaganda) were likely to see Africa as a very unattractive place to live. In his *Official Report of the Niger Valley Exploration Party* (1861), written after he had been to Africa, he wrote of the continent as "our fatherland" and argued that its regeneration required the development of a "national character." And he proposed the formula, "Africa for the African race and black men to rule them," which is one of the earliest formulations of a Pan-Africanist principle.

Alexander Crummell was born in NEW YORK and studied at Cambridge University in England. He was the first African American to do so and was an ordained Anglican clergyman. He was also the first African American intellectual to spend a significant amount of time in Liberia. (When Delany visited that country in 1859, he met Crummell, who by then had been there for two decades.) In *The Future of Africa* (1862), a collection of essays and lectures written while he was in Liberia, Crummell developed a vision of Africa as the motherland of the Negro race. In "The English Language in Liberia," based on a lecture given on Liberian independence day in 1860, he argued that African Americans who had been "exiled" in slavery to the New World had been given by divine providence "at least this one item of compensation, namely, the possession of the Anglo-Saxon tongue." Similarly he argued for the providential nature of the transmission of CHRISTIANITY to Negro slaves, and that it was the duty of "free colored men" in America to convert their ancestral continent to Christianity.

In the essay "The Relations and Duties of Free Colored Men in America to Africa," he also expressed with great clarity the underlying racial basis of his understanding of Negro identity. There he defined a race as "a compact, homogeneous population of one blood ancestry and lineage," and argued that each race had certain "determinate proclivities," which manifested themselves in the behavior of its members. Crummell was, with

Blyden, one of the founders of Liberia College (later the University of Liberia). Unlike Blyden, however, he did not become a permanent resident of Liberia, returning rather to the United States, where he continued to argue for the importance of an engagement with Africa on the part of blacks in the African diaspora. Crummell was the leading spirit in the foundation of the AMERICAN NEGRO ACADEMY, and was present at the meeting at which Du Bois first read "The Conservation of Races." He was also a significant influence on Du Bois, who included an essay about Crummell in his extremely influential volume *The Souls of Black Folk* (1903).

Edward Blyden was born in the WEST INDIES but traveled to Liberia in 1850, under the auspices of the American Colonization Society, becoming a citizen of that country for the rest of his life. Like Crummell, he was a priest, and, as we have seen, they worked together in the early days of the University of Liberia. Blyden spoke many languages. His essays include quotations in the original languages from Dante and Virgil, and he studied Arabic in order to teach it at Liberia College. Later he became the Liberian Ambassador to Queen Victoria.

In *Christianity, Islam and the Negro Race* (1887) Blyden expressed the conviction that underlies Du Bois's first explicit formulation of Pan-Africanism: "Among the conclusions to which study and research are conducting philosophers, none is clearer than this—that each of the races of mankind has a specific character and specific work." Blyden, like Crummell, had little respect for the traditional cultures of Africa. They shared the view that Christian blacks in the diaspora had a responsibility to convert their African cousins. But Blyden argued explicitly that what he called Africa's current "state of barbarism" did not reflect any innate deficiency in the Negro. "There is not a single mental or moral deficiency now existing among Africans," he said, " . . . to which we cannot find a parallel in the past history of Europe."

Pan-African Congresses

Pan-Africanism as an intellectual movement begins, then, in the work of Du Bois, Delany, Crummell, and Blyden. But its institutional history starts with Henry Sylvester Williams, a London barrister born in Trinidad. He planned to bring together people of the "African race" from around the world in 1897; and in July 1900, after a preliminary conference in 1899, such a gathering took place in London. (The actual word *Pan-Africanism* seems to have been coined either at this Pan-African Conference or at the earlier planning conference.) There were four African representatives—one each from ETHIOPIA, Sierra Leone, Liberia, and the GOLD COAST colony—and a dozen from North America (among them Du Bois); eleven representatives came from the West Indies, five from London.

The conference opened with the clearly stated aim of allowing black people to discuss the condition of the black race around the world. In 1919 Du Bois and others organized the first Pan-African Congress, in Paris, which brought together representatives from the Americas, Europe, and Africa to discuss the plight of Africans living under colonialism. This was followed by the second Pan-African Congress, also organized by Du Bois, which met in three sessions, in London, Brussels, and Paris, this time with representatives from French and Portuguese colonies in Africa as well. They issued a final declaration that insisted on the equality of the races, the diffusion of democracy, and the development of political institutions in the colonies. It also urged the "return" of Negroes to their own countries and urged the League of Nations to pay attention both to race relations in the industrialized world and to the condition of workers in the colonies.

A third Congress occurred in London in 1923 and continued, according to Du Bois, in Lisbon (though this appears to have been little more than an opportunity for Du Bois to talk to some people from the Portuguese colonies on his way from London to Liberia, where he was the official representative of the United States at the installation of the Liberian president). The fourth Pan-African Congress was held in New York City in 1927. The Pan-African Congress movement then effectively disappeared until the fifth Congress in Manchester in 1945, during which the baton was handed from the diaspora to the continent. Du Bois's contribution now lay in the shadow of that of figures such as Kwame Nkrumah, who was to be Ghana's first prime minister. (And, indeed, Du Bois was the only African American present.) The sixth Congress, held in 1974 in DAR ES SALAAM, was presided over by Tanzanian president JULIUS NYERERE.

During the period between World War I and World War II, in the heyday of the Pan-African Congress movement, the sentiment received a substantial practical boost from the growth of the UNIVERSAL NEGRO IMPROVEMENT ASSOCIATION (UNIA). Led by MARCUS GARVEY, a Jamaican immigrant to the United States, the UNIA became the largest black movement in the African diaspora. While the slogan of the movement was "Back to Africa," and Garvey did indeed plan a shipping line for the purpose, relatively few members of the organization actually left the New World for the Old. Nevertheless, Garvey's commitment to racial pride and to the celebration of black historical achievement, and his concern to link the diaspora to the continent, make him an important figure in the movement's history.

One West Indian–born intellectual *did* play an important role in planning the 1945 Congress, namely GEORGE PADMORE (1902–1959). (Padmore was a pseudonym: he was born Malcolm Nurse.) Padmore was a Trinidadian who had spent some time in the United States, studying at Columbia University and at Fisk (a black university that Du Bois had also attended). He worked as a Communist Party organizer among students at HOWARD UNIVERSITY, the black university in WASHINGTON, D.C. Later he spent time in Germany and in Russia, where he became in 1930 the head of the Negro Bureau of the Red International of labor unions. In the next few years he worked for Communist organizations in Austria and Germany, moving to London in 1935. From then until his death in 1959 he was the leading theorist of Pan-Africanism, and was a close friend and adviser of Kwame Nkrumah. His *Pan-Africanism or Communism* (1956) is probably the most important statement of his position.

Pan-Africanism Today

In the period after World War II African intellectuals were preoccupied with the question of independence. Once independence was attained, Pan-Africanism became an ideology through which relations among the newly independent states could be thought about; Pan-Africanist rhetoric continues to be important in the language of the Organization of African Unity, which was founded in 1963.

In that same period, black intellectuals in North America were taken up with questions of civil rights. There were always resonances between these two projects—Du Bois was involved in both throughout his long life, and died a citizen of Ghana; African diplomats sought to have civil rights questions raised in the forum of the United Nations. But Pan-Africanism took philosophical form in the period leading up to Padmore's work, and its major theoretical works are those of Padmore and Du Bois.

See also Abolitionism in the United States; Back to Africa Movement; Christianity: Missionaries in Africa; Colonial Rule; Diaspora and Displacement; Pan-African Congress of 1919; Political Movements in Africa; Race: An Interpretation; Trinidad and Tobago.

Bibliography

Geis, Immanuel. *London: The Pan-African Movement: A History of Pan-Africanism in America, Europe and Africa.* Africana Publishing Company and Methuen, 1974.

Moses, Wilson J. *The Golden Age of Black Nationalism: 1850–1925.* Archon Books, 1978.

Williams, Michael W. *Pan-Africanism: An Annotated Bibliography.* Salem Press, 1992.

Anthony Appiah

Pan-Africanism and Afro–Latin Americans

"No nos vamos a unir por ser personas negras, sino por identificarnos con las obras de personas negras." (We are not going to unite because we are black, but because we identify with legacies of black people.)

Juan de Dios Mosquera, Movimiento Nacional Cimarrón, Colombia

"In cooperation we need to build bridges. We cannot do it alone."

Charles Mohan, employee association delegate, United States

Between 1919 and 1974 Pan-Africanists organized six international congresses. African Americans from the United States had a crucial role in these forums, and English-speaking black people initially appeared in the forefront. African American W. E. B. Du Bois and Jamaican-born Marcus Garvey were Pan-Africanism's two most important figures in the early twentieth century. While Du Bois toiled for self-reliance and integration, Garvey promoted self-determination and separatism. Both struggled for the promotion of black consciousness and dignity; Du Bois was involved in the organization of the Pan-African congresses for over forty years. The first such congress, in Paris in 1919, resulted in the indictment of imperialism and support for self-determination for African nations. At the next three meetings—1921, 1923, and 1927—colonialism in Africa remained the central focus.

The fifth Pan-African Congress, which met in 1945, produced a schism between Garveyites and followers of Du Bois, as new voices from Africa and the Caribbean emerged. While colonialism remained an important issue, Caribbean Pan-Africanists such as C. L. R. James stressed the need for class analysis of racial problems. For the first time, the congress demanded the outright independence of Africa and the rights of all peoples throughout the African diaspora. Between the fifth and the sixth congresses, a host of regional movements, particularly in Africa, the United States, and the Caribbean, gained momentum. By the time of the sixth Pan-African congress, in 1974, regional movements were on the rise in the Americas. Nationalist struggles and civil rights movements had emerged with specific national agendas, not always in step with international Pan-Africanism.

Latin American Pan-Africanists have long recognized Africa as the source of a shared experience and have denounced European and North American imperialism in Africa, condemned racism and prejudice internationally, celebrated heroes of the African diaspora, and forged links with groups and individuals abroad. Yet Afro–Latin American participation in the Pan-Africanist movement has been historically weak. Language barriers have limited the participation of Spanish- and Portuguese-speaking activists, while sociocultural, economic, and political disenfranchisement often prohibited Afro-Latin Americans from creating strong national or international voices.

Language, for example, becomes a barrier when individuals throughout the diaspora are prohibited from meaningful discourse. Afro–Americans all over the continent speak and write in many languages, from patois, Papiamento, and Garífuna to major European languages. Thus, international dialogue is often fractured by language group. In recent years the propagation of English as an unofficial *lingua franca* has facilitated dialogue among people involved in race consciousness and civil rights movements. But many grassroots organizers do not have access to English classes, and many Latin Americans regard the prevalence of English as a form of cultural imperialism. Adoption of Spanish, however, does not solve the problem entirely, particularly, of course, for Brazilians.

While education and interpretation services slowly erode language barriers among Latin American Pan-Africanists, other factors remain endemic. Political, economic, and cultural underdevelopment greatly affects the ability of would-be Pan-Africanists to participate in global forums. Although Afro–Latin Americans' political participation has never been explicitly restricted by race, slavery, disenfranchisement, and economic deprivation have inhibited the growth of a coherent black middle class. Lower-income classes, in general, have less discretionary time to invest in national, much less international, enterprises. Moreover, lack of political access prohibits racial discrimination from becoming an agenda issue in favor of class inequalities.

The politics of racial identity represent the most formidable enemy of Pan-Africanism. In the great majority of countries in Latin America and the Caribbean, *mestizaje* (miscegenation), nationalism, and color codes have inhibited solidarity among people of African descent within individual countries. In many such countries, race is seemingly unimportant, while color has a more significant role in the social hierarchy. This color consciousness, combined with fervent patriotism and nationalism, encourages identification with the nation rather than with extranational entities. The apparently fluid color line and theories of whitening thus together prohibit the development of a strong race consciousness. Yet, despite such difficulties, many Afro–Latin Americans have opposed national and social constructs that seek to make them "invisible."

Although race consciousness heightened in the post–World War II era, the onslaught of military dictatorships in many Latin American countries further exacerbated the possible emergence of black movements in the 1960s and 1970s. With the return to liberal democratic governments in the 1980s and 1990s, however, national movements and organizations have blossomed. As a consequence, the Americas have witnessed an increase in international cooperation among people of the African diaspora, most notably the series of Congresses on Black Culture in the Americas.

Congresses on Black Culture in the Americas

The Congresses on Black Culture in the Americas, organized between 1977 and 1984, represented a rare success in Pan-African organization. While participation came overwhelmingly from artists and intellectuals, the spirit of the conferences reflected a strong desire to forge solidarity among people of African descent throughout the diaspora.

Held in Cali, COLOMBIA, in 1977, and sponsored by the Organization of American States in conjunction with the Fundación Colombiana de Investigaciones Folklóricas, the First Congress took pride in the fact that it represented the first hemispheric reflection on Afro-Americans by Afro-Americans. After an emotional opening, Afro-American delegates divided themselves among several working commissions to discuss political ideas, religions, aesthetics, and morals; socioeconomic structures; art and technologies; and ethnicity, mestizaje, castes, and classes. The commissions were united in their denunciation of all mechanisms of alienation aimed at people of African descent in the Americas. Delegates called for greater unity, while pledging to increase investigations of the historical importance of Africans in the creation of Latin American culture and to support struggles for liberation in Africa.

The second Congress on Black Culture in the Americas, in PANAMA CITY, PANAMA, in 1980, developed the theme of race and class. Delegates discussed issues under the broad theme of "Cultural Identity of Blacks in the Americas." Sponsored by the Instituto Nacional de Cultura de Panama, with the aid of the Centro de Estudios Afro-Panameños and the Patrimonio Histórico, four commissions were convened, along with roundtables to discuss future strategies of cooperation. According to Congress president Gerado Maloney, two major achievements of the conference were the integration and incorporation of Afro-Americans from all regions of the Americas, including the English- and French-speaking Caribbean, and the conviction of all members to acknowledge the inseparable relationship between ethnicity and class.

The third congress, held in São Paulo, BRAZIL, in 1982, under the directorship of the Brazilian political activist ABDIAS DO NASCIMENTO, in conjunction with the Instituto de Pesquisa e Estudos Afro-Brasileiros, was more defiant in tone. The theme of this congress, "African Diaspora: Political Consciousness and African Culture," reflected the growing political consciousness of Afro-American communities. Increased black consciousness and politicization of black movements led to a more forceful condemnation of racist politics around the globe. Delegates declared solidarity with a number of national liberation movements, particularly in Africa and the Middle East. The conference passed motions of support for, and solidarity with, Namibia's SOUTH WEST AFRICA PEOPLE'S ORGANIZATION (SWAPO), South Africa's AFRICAN NATIONAL CONGRESS (ANC), and the Palestine Liberation Organization. The conference also recognized the need to reach out to marginalized Afro-American communities and organizations in countries previously unrepresented in Pan-African work. In particular, it was noted that Afro-Uruguayans were in danger of being further isolated from national life.

The fourth meeting, initially planned for Paris, under the theme "Afro-America and the European Community," instead took place in Quito, ECUADOR, in 1984, focusing on black women in the Americas.

Since 1984 several regional meetings have drawn scholars, intellectuals, and activists from around the hemisphere. The dream of a formal and permanent Pan-African organization, however, is yet to be achieved. Funding and regional and national problems still plague national movements and make international coordination difficult. Besides, such international organizations have historically emphasized scholarship, art, and intellectual concerns, rather than grassroots activities. Nonetheless, pressures of economic and political globalization, and the collapse of Eastern European state socialism, make the need for international communication among African Americans ever more urgent.

First Seminar on Racism and Xenophobia

The uneven development of the various Afro–Latin American movements, especially in regions not usually associated with people of African diaspora populations, such as the Southern Cone and the Andes, has made communication among many Afro-Latin American grassroots movements difficult. With these constraints in mind, Mundo Afro of URUGUAY announced its plans to host in December 1994 the first Seminar on Racism and Xenophobia, in Montevideo.

The Uruguayan conference reflected, on the one hand, the development of Pan-Africanism in the Americas; on the other hand, it illustrated the long and hard work ahead if the dream of an intercontinental organization is to be realized. Unlike previous meetings, Uruguay was largely anti-academic. Indeed, its U.S. coordinator, Michael Franklin, of the Organization of Africans in the Americas, stressed the problem-solving focus. While political awareness and activism have heightened over the years, activists and grassroots organizers see the importance of establishing a rapport with international political and economic institutions, particularly in the United States. Partnerships with such institutions may provide valuable future contacts and access to funds as well as information, not to mention raising their own visibility internationally and thus nationally. Unfortunately grassroots movements representing poor or disenfranchised minority groups often receive national attention only after they have obtained international recognition, particularly from the United States or the European Union.

The Montevideo conference was, however, far more than an exercise in gaining visibility. Organizers and participants searched for a balance between grassroots action and intellectual cooperation, with the long-term goal of educating the public.

For Afro-Uruguayans the conference was a crucial turning point in a long but slow civil rights struggle. Young and old Uruguayans turned out in support of platforms and ideas that would be of central importance to their communities. While participants were expected from all of the cultural and linguistic regions of the Americas, representatives and advocates of Afro-Latin Americans from the United States, Brazil, Uruguay, Argentina, Honduras, the Dominican Republic, Colombia, Peru, and Cuba constituted the majority of the participants. The absence of major leaders from past conferences and community activists from many other Latin American communities was an indication of far-reaching structural problems that limit communication among Latin American nations. Many activists from Brazil, Central America, and the Caribbean were not aware of the conference, for example. Indeed, there is no intercontinental database that registers the major movements or activists from each country, nor are there sufficient resources to ensure contact and follow-up.

Structural and political problems notwithstanding, Montevideo symbolized an important watershed in black consciousness within the region as delegates began to define, in the words of the official agenda, a "Program for the Development of Black Latin America." In addition, major networking took place after the official presentations, in the lobbies, bars, cafés, and restaurants. Personal contacts were made, and discussions held, among union leaders, representatives of women's groups, human rights and development workers, local campaigners and organizers, and other participants.

The Montevideo Conference: Commissions and Outcomes

The five commissions at Montevideo provided important frameworks for future cooperation and consideration. A brief description of the activities of each commission follows.

Education, Culture, and Communication. Delegates in this commission debated issues related to the educational reality and cultural rejuvenation of Afro-Americans, focusing particularly on proposals that would permit advances within black communities. The commission arrived at several long-term goals, including commitment to set up an inter-American communications network using fax and electronic mail. It was agreed that the interhemispheric network should be further divided into the three regions of North America, the Caribbean and Central America, and South America. Other resolutions included the creation of an intercontinental pressure group responsible for responding to events affecting black communities throughout the hemisphere and the promotion of educational programs related to Africans.

Women and Society. Afro-Americans clearly understand the extra pressures that women face in their respective communities. This commission set out to develop economic alternatives to improve family income, to generate work, and to improve the standard of living of black women around the hemisphere, while promoting the most efficient forms of social integration. The historical contributions of black women to American societies were discussed. These contributions, the session unanimously agreed, have been continually minimized and ignored. The illiteracy, pauperization, and hardship that so many Afro-American women experience today is indicative of that neglect. High unemployment and rural-urban migration have led to problems of sexual exploitation, involuntary sterilization, lack of access to education and health services, and a high incidence of acquired immunodeficiency syndrome (AIDS). The lack of role models, multiplication of negative stereotypes, and severe underrepresentation of women in the decision-making processes of nongovernmental and governmental organizations and agencies further compound the problem. The commission agreed to pursue strategies to increase the visibility of Afro-American women and to guarantee their access to credit, education, and health care.

International Cooperation and Alternative Development. This commission listed its main aim as the generation of collective ideas for a quantitative and qualitative advancement of Afro-American communities in the 3rd millennium. Participants also saw their role as helping to create a continental network of cooperation that would facilitate the sustainable development of Afro-American communities. Representatives from Latin America were particularly concerned to promote cooperative relationships with multinational corporations, nongovernmental organizations, and other international institutions; other delegates warned that relations with international organizations should be approached with caution. Most agreed that grassroots movements should under no circumstances relinquish direction and control of their projects and communities to international financial institutions. Likewise, it was argued that cooperation among Latin American countries should take into account the relative development and potential of each national community. A representative from the international financial community warned that Afro-Americans cannot simply shun international lending institutions, because they need to become not just job seekers, but job creators. Two broad goals expressed by this commission, largely in agreement with proposals made by other commissions, were, first, to encourage black organizations to alert financial institutions to their plans for the development of black communities; and, second, to encourage and persuade financial institutions to direct funds toward black communities.

Political Strategies. Mundo Afro's vision of political strategies was decidedly long-term. After centuries of isolation, Afro–Latin Americans were looking at ways to consolidate and augment their political power. Delegates began their discussion with an eye toward stimulating initiatives with governments and private institutions, which would lead to the further integration of black communities into national life. The development of strategies of cooperation, representation, information, promotion, and technical aid for the interchange of information among the countries of Europe, the Americas, and black Africa became the guiding aim. Many political strategies emerged, ranging from the theoretical and long-term to immediate activities for specific groups and communities. One general project united participants, however: the desire to develop an intercontinental network, based on regional commissions, with a continental directory comprising delegates from each Afro–Latin American organization. Such a network could serve as a coordinating body for the future.

Population, Human Rights, Youth, and the Elderly. Human rights specialists and activists structured their discussions around two main goals: first, to promote human rights for young people, children, and the elderly through continual action and the implementation of specific programs of assistance and development; second, to formulate proposals for better management of the natural environment that reflect the black community's knowledge, experience, and needs in relation to nature and natural resources. Participants regarded human rights, care for the elderly, and guidance for the young as fundamental to the preservation of their African American identity.

Conclusions and Future Prospects

The plethora of proposals, suggestions, and resolutions from the five commissions at Montevideo reflected the political, economic, and cultural diversity within the Afro-American community. While race was the major factor around which the delegates of these five commissions converged, many Latin American civil rights activists are first and foremost interested in political commitment. However, it is the sense of commitment itself, an awareness of the necessity for collective struggle, that united participants and opposed them to a more individualistic and assimilationist outlook. As one delegate put it, "We are interested in conscious people. It doesn't matter if you're black or white. But we want a commitment." While race is the indisputable basis of the shared Pan-African experience, the history of mestizaje and the assimilation of Africans make the issue of levels of commitment an important one among Afro–Latin Americans.

By the end of the four-day encounter, the Montevideo conference had arrived at a series of resolutions for the short and the long term. Personal contacts and institutional partnerships had been built. Delegates unanimously supported the creation of an intercontinental network that would first be based on regional integration. On the closing day of the conference, South American delegates agreed on a second meeting, to be held in April 1995, in the southern Brazilian city of Santa Ana do Livramento, to elaborate on the network, its goals, parameters, and methods of working. Delegates from the United States, the Caribbean, and Central America were also to be invited to the meeting as observers.

The U.S. delegation also committed itself to establishing future communications among Afro–Latin Americans and African Americans in the United States. Planned for late 1995 at HOWARD UNIVERSITY, Washington, D.C., the conference, entitled "Race, Institutional Development and Human Rights: The Present Status and Condition of Blacks in Latin America," would, it was hoped, examine issues of race relations in Latin America on a country-by-country basis, as well as the role of African Americans in addressing some of those issues.

Since 1995, a number of regional initiatives have brought black Latin Americans together to discuss important issues relevant to local development and international cooperation. In August 1996, Afro–Latin Americans gathered at San José and Limón, Costa Rica to celebrate what was billed as a "Black Family Reunion." In November of the same year, Claire Nelson of the Inter-American Development Bank in Washington, D.C. helped organize an unprecedented meeting on "Alleviating Poverty for Minority Communities in Latin America," which saw the participation of black academics and writers, in addition to politicians such as BENEDITA DA SILVA, RIO DE JANEIRO's first black congresswoman. The year 1997 saw similar initiatives, as black Latin Americans continued the dialogue among themselves and with blacks in the United States.

Whatever the outcome of the international network, Montevideo arguably represented a turning point for Pan-Africanism in the Americas. Afro–Latin Americans around the continent are increasingly mobilizing and refusing to allow their national governments to ignore them. They are renewing themselves through forms of political and economic organization, building on international links and partnerships. At the end of the conference, participants shared a more hopeful and purposeful vision of the future, and there was a strong sense of being involved in a process that promises to help release Afro-Latin Americans from the burdens of centuries of oppression.

Originally published in "No Longer Invisible: Afro–Latin Americans Today," Minority Rights Group, London.

Darién J. Davis

Pan-Africanist Congress

South African antiapartheid organization and political party.

Founded in 1959 as an offshoot of the AFRICAN NATIONAL CONGRESS, the Pan-Africanist Congress (PAC) has always been the more radical of the two antiapartheid organizations. Explicitly nationalistic and racialist, less committed to nonviolence than the ANC, the PAC has played an important role in South African history while never achieving the membership or international recognition of its parent organization.

Among the PAC's founders were ROBERT SOBUKWE, Potlako Leballo, A. P. Mda, and other former ANC members. They were disappointed by what they saw as the older organization's excessive caution and willingness to compromise in its campaign to overthrow South Africa's APARTHEID regime. In particular, PAC leaders opposed the ANC's multiracialism—it welcomed white and Indian members—and what was seen as the ANC's embrace of communism.

Their objections grew following the ANC's 1956 adoption of the FREEDOM CHARTER, a document calling for multiracial cooperation and communal economic principles. Arguing for "authentic African nationalism," Sobukwe and others tried to take over the local ANC leadership in the TRANSVAAL, which some felt was the region of strongest Pan-Africanist sentiment. Failing that, and after Leballo's expulsion from the ANC, Sobukwe and his fellow dissidents announced the formation in April 1959 of the Pan-Africanist Congress.

As the PAC's first president, Sobukwe delineated the differences between his organization and the ANC. While the ANC, he said, viewed the antiapartheid movement as "a class struggle," for the PAC the fight was "a national struggle." Accordingly, rather than seeking a free South Africa for all, as the ANC did, the PAC would fight for "Africa for Africans." As part of its wish that black South Africans could escape their "slave mentality," the PAC encouraged a "mental revolution" for the country it called "Azania."

Promising complete revolution by 1963, the PAC boasted some 31,000 members soon after its founding. Beyond the Transvaal, however, its organization was weak. The PAC's first major test came in 1960. For years, Africans had been subject to arrest, fines, and imprisonment if they failed to produce their passes—sometimes called registration books—which contained identification, tax, and travel documents. Sobukwe called for a national demonstration on March 21, asking that Africans gather at their local police stations, turn in their passes, and invite arrest. The largest demonstration was in SHARPVILLE, a black township south of JOHANNESBURG. Police opened fire on the unarmed protesters, killing sixty-nine, almost all of whom were shot in the back while trying to flee.

The government reacted to the widespread rioting that followed the massacre by banning both the PAC and the ANC. Operating in exile in Basutoland (now LESOTHO) and led after 1962 by acting president Leballo, the PAC underwent ideological flux and dissension; by the late 1960s the formerly anticommunist organization was avowedly Maoist. In its support for armed resistance, the PAC attracted new followers after the SOWETO uprising of 1976, but it also lost members to splinter groups, including the Azanian People's Revolutionary Party. The PAC put forth candidates in South Africa's first free elections in 1994, winning 243,000 votes and five seats in the National Assembly.

Kate Tuttle

Panama

Republic in Central America that forms a land bridge between North America and South America, and whose Panama Canal provides a waterway connection between the Atlantic and Pacific oceans.

Most Panamanians are of mixed descent, tracing their background to European (mainly Spanish) colonists and Native Americans. Many are descendants of African slaves or of West Indian workers who immigrated into Panama in the nineteenth and twentieth centuries. Despite increasing integration, these groups are still separated by significant social and cultural differences.

Colonial Period

Before the sixteenth century, a number of indigenous groups inhabited the Isthmus of Panama. They were independent of each other, spoke different languages, and lived sedentary, relatively peaceful lives. The largest indigenous groups were the Ngobe-Buglé (formerly known as Guaymí), Kuna, and Chocó peoples, who continue to live in Panama to this day.

The first European to set foot on the isthmus was the Spanish explorer Rodrigo de Bastidas, in 1501. The first stable Spanish settlement was Nombre de Dios, established by Diego de Nicuesa in 1509. Nicuesa's expedition, which came from Santo Domingo (present-day DOMINICAN REPUBLIC) on the island of HISPANIOLA, included twenty persons of African descent brought as slaves. During the early 1500s, Spanish settlers routinely brought enslaved Africans to the isthmus to perform the bulk of demanding manual labor. In 1519 Governor Pedrarias Dávila founded PANAMA CITY, the colony that was then known as Castilla del Oro. Under Dávila's direction, slaves were forced to construct buildings and churches in the newly founded city. (Panama City was rebuilt near its original location after an English expedition destroyed the city in 1671.) Slaves in the colony also worked in agriculture and in domestic service. By 1530 the population of the isthmus included more than 200 African slaves, according to Panamanian historian Luis Diez Castillo. Indigenous peoples were used as slaves after they were conquered in battles, but for the most part, the Spaniards relied on African slaves.

Panama's central location and the access it provided to the Pacific side of the Americas made it a strategic point for trade and transport. Panama City's importance grew following the Spanish conquest of PERU in the 1530s, as the exploitation of Peru's extensive gold and silver deposits led to increased traffic between SPAIN and the western coast of South America. A rapid growth in the population of the city accompanied this commercial activity.

Slave Resistance

By the mid-1500s, discontent among the slaves had become evident. Slave revolts ensued under the leadership of men such as KING BAYANO, Felipillo, Pedro LUIS DE MOZAMBIQUE, and Antón Mandinga. Many black slaves fled to the thick jungles of Panama, establishing small settlements in the wilderness, up on the mountains, and along the rivers near Panama City and Nombre de Dios. These fugitive slaves frequently raided Spanish settlements for provisions, weapons, and merchandise. The Spaniards sent several expeditions to capture the fugitives, who they called *cimarrones,* or maroons, but the escaped slaves met these manhunts with strong resistance. In the San Blas Mountains, Bayano, who was an especially adept maroon leader, frustrated several of these efforts and led many attacks against the Spanish conquistadores. An expedition led by Spanish military leader Francisco Carreño captured Bayano but then released him on his promise to end the attacks. Bayano continued his assaults, however, and he was captured again. Following Bayano's subsequent escape, another military leader, Pedro de Ursúa, offered him a peace treaty, but then seized him during the negotiations. Bayano subsequently died in a Spanish dungeon. Over time the maroons settled in numerous villages in the wilderness, at times cohabiting with indigenous women, as the escaped slaves were mostly men. One of these settlements, Matachín, was established in the late sixteenth century and survived until the Panama Canal was constructed in the early twentieth century. Another, Pacora, was established in the seventeenth century and is still inhabited, located about 72 kilometers (45 miles) southeast of Panama City.

Another constant threat to the Spaniards was the presence of English and French pirates, who sailed the Atlantic coasts and raided vulnerable settlements in search of gold and merchandise. Several English pirates, or buccaneers, quickly learned to make allies of the maroons, relying on them to negotiate the treacherous jungles surrounding the main settlements and offering, in return, a measure of provisions and the promise of an end to the fugitive life. Many of the ensuing raids, such as those in the late 1500s led by buccaneer Sir Francis Drake and maroon leader Diego, were highly successful. The Spanish crown responded to these threats by recruiting blacks and promising them either their liberty (if they were slaves) or financial remuneration for the capture of fugitive slaves. The crown also increased the penalty that could lawfully be inflicted on short-term escapees; if gone more than a week, a slave could receive a brutal punishment of one hundred lashes.

Manumission and Free Blacks

By the early seventeenth century the local population included a number of freedpersons, as the Spanish slave codes permitted manumission (a legal grant of freedom to slaves). In 1610 the population of Panama City included 146 free mulattoes (persons of mixed African and European descent), 148 free blacks, and 3,500 black slaves. The European population of the city comprised 548 men, 303 women, and 156 children. The crown informally discouraged Spanish men in the Americas from engaging in sexual relations with either black or indigenous women, but the relative scarcity of Spanish women made such relations inevitable.

A royal decree in 1789 ordered all owners of slaves to teach Catholicism to their slaves, to provide for a day of rest, and to ensure them proper food, clothing, and shelter. It prohibited slaveholders, under threat of prosecution, from inflicting grave or permanent injuries upon their slaves. The decree also ordered all slaves to show deference to their owners and allowed punishment in response to impudence, at the discretion of the owner. Still, a net outcome of the decree, according to historian Luis Diez Castillo, was the emancipation of many slaves by their owners, who found the costs of legally maintaining a slave to be prohibitive.

End of Colonial Rule

By the early nineteenth century, the independence movement led by SIMÓN BOLÍVAR and others had weakened Spain's political control in the Americas. Panama subsequently lost much of the commercial and trade activity that had made it prosperous in the previous two centuries. Frustrated by its political instability and deteriorating commercial glory, Panamanian revolutionaries declared Panama's independence from Spain on November 28, 1821. Panama immediately joined Gran Colombia, a federation that also included the present-day republics

The Choco, a semi-migratory indigenous people of Panama, live in small one- or two-family groups. They build their shelters along the banks of rivers, which also serve as their highways and provide livelihood. *CORBIS/Danny Lehman*

of COLOMBIA, VENEZUELA, and ECUADOR. Regional rivalries led the latter two countries to separate from the federation by 1830, causing its dissolution, but Panama remained part of Colombia until 1903. Slavery was abolished in 1851.

Panama's location soon led to another economic boom. In 1848 gold was discovered in the unexplored western United States territory of California, causing a population rush to the territory from the settled eastern states. Wary of the treacherous journey across the United States, thousands of Americans instead sailed down to the Atlantic coast of Panama, made their way through the tropical jungle to the Pacific side of the isthmus, and then sailed northward on the Pacific to the coast of California. Spurred by this increased flow of travelers, the Colombian government commissioned three Americans—W. H. Aspinwall, Henry Chauncey, and John Stevens—to build a railroad that spanned the 72 kilometers (45 miles) from coast to coast. For this task, large numbers of Chinese laborers from Hong Kong and California were hired. In addition, thousands of Jamaicans were hired and transported to the isthmus. These laborers cleared the jungle, laid rails, and lifted heavy machinery under the hot tropical sun. The Panama Railroad was completed by 1855, and many of the laborers settled in the area permanently.

Panama Canal and Independence

By 1879 sentiment had been growing to construct a canal linking the Caribbean Sea to the Pacific Ocean across the Isthmus of Panama. In 1879 a French company was founded, headed by the engineer Ferdinand de Lesseps (credited with the construction of the Suez Canal in Egypt), to begin the massive project, under contract with Colombia. The French hired many technicians from their own country and thousands of new laborers from the Caribbean islands of BARBADOS, SAINT LUCIA, MARTINIQUE, and especially JAMAICA. But the French efforts were defeated by yellow fever, malaria, the heat, and the thick jungle. Within eight years, more than 20,000 laborers died of illnesses. Amid corruption and disorganization, the project was abandoned in 1888.

Around the turn of the century, the United States began to develop an interest in building the canal that the French did not complete. The United States entered negotiations with Colombia regarding the use of the Isthmus of Panama. Much to the frustration of Panamanians, who wished to sustain their economic stability, the United States and Colombia had difficulty agreeing on the terms of the project. Colombia wanted greater remuneration, and the United States saw Colombian demands as delays upon the swift construction of the canal.

On November 3, 1903, Panamanian revolutionaries declared Panama an independent republic. This declaration was supported by the United States. Colombia, fearing military conflict with the United States, did not resist the loss of Panamanian territory, though it did not officially recognize the new republic until years later. Days after the declaration of independence, the United States and Panama signed the Hay-Bunau-Varilla Treaty, which granted the United States the right, in perpetuity, to construct a canal. The treaty also allowed the United States to administer the area called the Panama Canal Zone, which extends eight kilometers (five miles) on either side of the canal from coast to coast. In exchange, Panama received an initial payment of $10 million, an additional $250,000 every year, and the protection of Panama's independence.

Construction of the Panama Canal began in 1904. From then until its completion in 1914, the Panama Canal Commission hired roughly 8,000 Spaniards, 2,000 Italians, 1,000 Greeks, 1,500 Colombians, 5,000 Martinicans, 2,000 Guadalupeans, 1,500 Trinidadians, and nearly 20,000 Barbadians, among others. In all, laborers from the WEST INDIES constituted more than two-thirds of the newly hired work force, or more than 30,000 of the total 45,000. In addition, thousands of American skilled laborers and administrators were hired. The work was intensely physical, consisting of ten-hour days of digging ditches, clearing jungle, and handling explosives. Many West Indians also were hired as carpenters, artisans, and water bearers, and a few were hired as mechanics and electricians.

A major concern early in the construction was the possibility that tropical illnesses would debilitate the workforce. But medicine had advanced rapidly since the years of the French construction effort. The United States brought in its Army medical officer, William Gorgas, to ensure the health of the canal employees. Under his direction, funds were allocated for improved health conditions, fumigation of disease-transmitting mosquitoes, and the early treatment of illnesses. Within two years yellow fever and malaria were under control, sparing many lives.

The payroll for canal workers was quickly divided into the notorious "gold" and "silver" rolls. White Americans were paid higher wages in gold coins, while West Indian canal workers were paid in silver coins of much lower value, purportedly scaled to wages for labor in the Caribbean. European workers were paid more than West Indians even when performing the same labor. The gold and silver designations were translated into the social life of the Canal Zone, so that water fountains, public services, trains, post offices, grocery stores, neighborhoods, and social clubs were equally segregated. In addition, only gold-roll workers were guaranteed paid vacations (forty-two days per year) and paid sick leave. Following the canal's completion in 1914, thousands of West Indians returned to the islands or emigrated to other countries. Those who remained raised families in the Zone while working on the general upkeep of the canal and of the U.S. military bases that had been established in the Zone. The tradition of separate and unequal treatment continued in varying forms after the construction of the canal. The system of gold and silver rolls was not abolished until 1948, although other forms of segregation persisted.

In 1977 Panamanian leader General Omar Torrijos and U.S. president Jimmy Carter signed the Torrijos-Carter Treaty, by which the United States agreed to turn over control of the Canal Zone to Panama in phases, slowly relinquishing complete authority. The Panama Canal Authority, a public corporation, took control of the canal from the Panama Canal Commission on December 31, 1999. That day the United States officially transferred the canal to Panama at a ceremony in the Canal Zone

Panama (At a Glance)

OFFICIAL NAME: Republic of Panama

AREA: 78,200 sq km (30,193 sq mi)

LOCATION: Country in Middle America between Colombia and Costa Rica, bordered by the Caribbean Sea and the North Pacific Ocean

CAPITAL: Panama City (population 1,202,000; 2004 estimate)

OTHER MAJOR CITIES: Colón (population 52,286) and David 76,481 (2000 estimates)

POPULATION: 3,120,000 (2004 estimate)

POPULATION DENSITY: 41 persons per sq km (106 per sq mi)

POPULATION BELOW AGE 15: 30.6 percent (male 461,670; female 443,671; 2003 estimate)

POPULATION GROWTH RATE: 1.36 percent (2003 estimate)

TOTAL FERTILITY RATE: 2.53 children born per woman (2003 estimate)

LIFE EXPECTANCY AT BIRTH: Total population: 72.32 years (male 69.97 years; female 74.79 years; 2003 estimate)

INFANT MORTALITY RATE: 21.44 deaths per 1,000 live births (2003 estimate)

LITERACY RATE (AGE 15 AND OVER WHO CAN READ AND WRITE): Total population: 92.6 percent (male 93.2 percent; female 91.9 percent; 2003 estimate)

EDUCATION: Education is free and compulsory for ages six to fifteen. There are several universities in Panama, including the University of Panamá and the University of Santa María la Antigua.

LANGUAGES: Spanish is the official language, with English spoken by 14 percent of the population. Many Panamanians are bilingual.

ETHNIC GROUPS: 70 percent mestizo (mixed Amerindian and white), 14 percent mixed Amerindian and West Indian, 10 percent white, and 6 percent Amerindian

RELIGIONS: 85 percent of Panama's inhabitants are Roman Catholic and 15 percent are Protestant.

CLIMATE: Tropical, with an average annual low temperature of 78° F (26° C) on the coasts. There are three climatic zones based on elevation: a hot zone, below 2,300 feet (700 meters), that encompasses most of the country, and small temperate and cold zones.

LAND, PLANTS, AND ANIMALS: Panama is divided into roughly four quadrants by mountain ranges that run most of the length of the country, and by a central area of lower land, the site of the Panama Canal. An inactive volcano, Barú, forms the country's highest peak. Of the country's more than 1,600 islands, most are located off the Pacific coast, and include the Pearl Island archipelago. Panama's varied landscapes include mountain forests, savannas, tropical rainforests, tidal lands, beaches, and coral reefs. Animals include anteaters, sloths, jaguars, deer, giant sea turtles, and resident and migratory birds.

NATURAL RESOURCES: Copper, mahogany, shrimp, and hydropower

CURRENCY: The balboa (PAB) and the United States dollar (USD)

GROSS DOMESTIC PRODUCT (GDP): $18.06 billion (2002 estimate)

GDP PER CAPITA: $6,200 (2002 estimate)

GDP REAL GROWTH RATE: 0.7 percent (2002 estimate)

PRIMARY ECONOMIC ACTIVITIES: Services, agriculture, and industry

PRIMARY CROPS: Bananas, rice, corn, coffee, sugarcane, vegetables, livestock, and shrimp

INDUSTRIES: Construction, petroleum refining, brewing, cement and other construction materials, and sugar milling

PRIMARY EXPORTS: Bananas, shrimp, sugar, coffee, and clothing

PRIMARY IMPORTS: Capital goods, crude oil, foodstuffs, consumer goods, and chemicals

PRIMARY TRADE PARTNERS: United States, Sweden, Costa Rica, Honduras, Colombia, Japan, and Venezuela

GOVERNMENT: Panama is a constitutional democracy. The chief of state and head of government is President Martin Torrijos Espino (since September 2004; elected by popular vote to serve a five-year term). The legislative branch is the unicameral Legislative Assembly (seventy-one members, popularly elected to serve five-year terms). The judicial branch includes the Supreme Court of Justice (nine judges appointed for ten-year terms), five superior courts, and three courts of appeal.

Shelle Sumners

---

attended by Panamanian president Mireya Elisa Moscoso de Gruber and former U.S. president Carter.

Blacks in Panama and Racial Relations

The status of the descendants of Africans in Panama has been one of gradual, but incomplete, integration. In the first half of the twentieth century, many Panamanians, including dark-skinned descendants of slaves from colonial times, resented the higher wages of West Indians working in the Canal Zone. West Indians were culturally distinct from Panamanians. They tended to speak only English, to practice a Protestant faith, and—in the early decades of the century—to maintain their loyalty to the islands from whence they came, or even to Britain. They

maintained tight-knit communities almost exclusively in or near the Canal Zone. In 1926 several reactionary Panamanian laws limited the immigration of West Indians, Chinese, and others from non–Spanish-speaking countries, and many immigrants were barred from practicing certain professions. Another major setback to improved racial relations occurred with the promulgation of a new constitution in 1941, under President Arnulfo Arias. The constitution denaturalized all descendants of West Indian and Chinese immigrants who did not speak Spanish. Within a few years, however, Arias was overthrown, and the constitution was replaced in 1946.

Thousands of West Indians and their descendants who did not obtain employment in the upkeep of the canal and U.S. military bases after 1914 settled in large, extremely poor neighborhoods of Panama City and Colón. Many of these neighborhoods continue to be populated predominantly by West Indians, who constitute a distinct minority in Panama because of their cultural differences. Racial categories are neither rigid nor typically employed, and the descendants of Africans who had lived in Panama as slaves are not a distinct group. The state does not include racial categories in its census-taking. Still, discrimination toward West Indians (derogatorily labeled *chombos*) and subtle preferences toward lighter skin and straight hair persist. Clubs and restaurants frequently discriminate against West Indians, although such practices are illegal. In 1999, Panamanian students staged demonstrations outside some of Panama City's most popular nightclubs to protest racial discrimination. That same year the legislature failed to pass a bill that would have amended the country's constitution by prescribing penalties for racial discrimination.

At the same time, many West Indians and their descendants have attained positions of prominence in the intellectual and cultural life of the nation in the twentieth century. Journalist Sydney Young worked on several major newspapers and in 1928 founded the *Panama Tribune*, which championed the rights of West Indians in the Canal Zone. Economist and historian Armando Fortune produced numerous monographs on the history and social status of persons of African ancestry in the country, as well as treatises on diverse topics such as Panamanian oligarchy, racial prejudice, German philosopher Friedrich Nietzsche, and HAITI. Journalist George Westerman wrote extensively on the social conditions of West Indians in Panama, producing the first serious body of work on the subject. Other intellectual activists who continue to champion West Indian rights in Panama are Melva Goodin, Gerardo Maloney, and GRACIELA DIXON.

In 1980 the Museo Afro-Antillano de Panamá (MAAP; Spanish for Panamanian West Indian Museum) was founded. The museum serves as a cultural repository of the West Indian tradition. In 1981 the philanthropic Sociedad de Amigos del MAAP (Society of Friends of MAAP), or SAMAAP, was founded. This organization has served as a cultural, educational, and political leader of the West Indian community and as a defender of its rights. Each successive generation of West Indians is increasingly integrated, at least culturally and politically, into mainstream Panamanian life. That is, they are more likely to speak Spanish, to adopt a Spanish name, and to attend schools with Panamanian children not of West Indian descent. As the United States relinquishes authority over the canal and abandons its military bases, many West Indians are forced to seek employment elsewhere. It remains to be seen to what extent they will be able to find economic sustenance and political involvement in the life of the nation. Panama will face this challenge for many years to come.

See also Colonial Latin America and the Caribbean; Colonial Rule; Maroonage in the Americas; Punishment of Slaves in Colonial Latin America and the Caribbean; Slave Laws in Colonial Spanish America; Slave Rebellions in Latin America and the Caribbean; Slavery in Latin America and the Caribbean.

Panama City, Panama

Capital of Panama, located in the central region of the country on the shores of the gulf of the same name.

The city of Panama is an industrial, commercial, and cultural center. The products most important for its economy are footwear, textile goods, garments from its clothing industry, refined petroleum, and processed foods. Maintenance of the Panama Canal and management of its traffic are important sources of income for the city's economy, as are financial institutions and tourism. The fishing harbor of Balboa and the Tocumen international airport make Panama well linked within the region.

The Universidad de Panama (University of Panama, 1935) and the Universidad de Santa María la Antigua (1965) stand out among the city's institutions of higher learning. The city also boasts conservatories, schools for the plastic arts, schools of dance and theater, and institutes of aeronautics and of maritime navigation. Other cultural institutions include the Museo de Ciencias Naturales (Natural History Museum), the Museo de Historia de Panama (Museum of Panamanian History), the Museo de Arte, which collects colonial religious art, the Museo del Hombre (Museum of Man), and various national institutes of music and culture. Its cathedral, under construction from 1673 to 1760, is one of the city's emblematic buildings.

Founded in 1519 by Pedrarias Dávila, administrator of the then Spanish colony, the city took shape as a shipping and commercial center. Welsh corsair Henry John Morgan destroyed the settlement in 1671, but three years later Spanish colonists reestablished the city some eight kilometers (five miles) west of the original site. In 1717–1718, the city was incorporated into of the viceroyalty of Nueva Granada, and in 1903 became the capital of the independent nation of PANAMA. The construction of the trans-Panamanian railroad, between 1848 and 1855, and of the Panama Canal (1904–1914) contributed enormously to the growth of the city. Population 1,202,000 (2004 estimate).

See also Colonial Latin America and the Caribbean.

Pande

Ethnic group of west Central Africa; also known as Pende.

The Pande are scattered across the western CENTRAL AFRICAN REPUBLIC, western DEMOCRATIC REPUBLIC OF THE CONGO, and northeastern ANGOLA. They speak a Bantu language. Approximately 500,000 people consider themselves Pande.

See also Bantu: Dispersion and Settlement; Ethnicity and Identity in Africa: An Interpretation; Languages, African: An Overview.

Pandeiro, Jackson do

1919–1982

Black musician who popularized the Afro-Brazilian folk styles of Brazil's urban northeast.

Born José Gomes Filho, Jackson do Pandeiro grew up in a poor family in the coastal towns of BRAZIL's *Nordeste* (northeast). His mother was a professional singer, and Jackson performed with her from an early age. Legend has it that he had wanted to play the accordion like his hero LUÍZ GONZAGA, but his family could only afford to buy him a *pandeiro* (tambourine). Besides music, the young Jackson's other great love was American Western films. His nickname, "Jackson," came from his resemblance to the American actor Jack Perry.

At the age of eighteen, Jackson became a professional musician and moved to Recife. There he worked for local radio stations, performing northeastern genres such as *coco*, FORRÓ, and *embolada*. He also recorded his first hit songs, including "Sebastiana" and "Forró em Limoeiro." During this time Jackson met Almira Castilhos de Albuquerque, his first wife and singing partner.

In 1956 Jackson moved to RIO DE JANEIRO, where he combined SAMBA with traditional folk styles, and adopted the stage image of a Rio *malandro* (hustler). His hits included "O Canto da Ema," "Um a Um," and "Xote de Copacabana."

Jackson's music influenced many of Brazil's most popular musicians. Perhaps the most internationally known is GILBERTO GIL, who recorded Jackson's "Chiclete com Banana" ("Bubblegum with Banana"), a wry critique of North American influence on Brazilian culture. Jackson died in July 1982 from medical complications caused by diabetes.

See also Music, Afro-Caribbean Secular.

Bibliography

McGowan, Chris, and Ricardo Pessanha. *The Brazilian Sound: Samba, Bossa Nova, and the Popular Music of Brazil.* 2nd edition. Temple University Press, 1998.

Ben Penglase

Pantoja, Antonia

1921–2002

Afro–Puerto Rican educator, social worker, and activist.

Antonia Pantoja was born in San Juan, PUERTO RICO. She became a teacher in Puerto Rico and then moved to NEW YORK, NEW YORK, where she earned a bachelor's degree from Hunter College and a master's degree in social work from Columbia University.

After graduating, Pantoja founded the organization now known as the National Puerto Rican Forum to develop programs to improve the economic and social circumstances of Puerto Ricans. In and around New York City, she worked with organizations that help minority populations build stronger communities. In 1961 she founded Aspira (from the Spanish word *aspirar*, which means "to aspire to something greater") to address the problem of the high dropout rate of Puerto Rican high-school students in New York City. Since then the organization has been involved in many of the causes of the Puerto Rican and Latino communities, including bilingual education, leadership development, health improvement, and youth empowerment. The organization now has offices in six states and Puerto Rico that offer career and college counseling, financial aid, and other support services to young Latinos. A 1972 lawsuit against the city by Aspira forced New York to establish bilingual classes in English and Spanish. Pantoja later taught at the San Diego State University School of Social Work. After 1984 she spent considerable time developing economic-assistance programs in Puerto Rico.

Pantoja received numerous awards, including the Presidential Medal of Freedom in 1996 (the highest civilian honor in the United States), the Martin Luther King Award of the Kennedy Library for the Minorities, and the Ellis Island Medal of Liberty. Her autobiography, titled *Memoir of a Visionary*, was published shortly after her death in 2002.

Papaya

Common name for a small family of soft-wooded, sparsely branched trees found in tropical West Africa and in other tropical regions of the world.

Papaya is also the name for the representative genus. Four genera and about thirty species are placed in this family of dicots. They share these characteristics: palmately lobed or compound leaves; small, unisexual flowers; and separate male and female plants (dioecious). All parts of the plants contain milky latex in special latex-producing cells.

The common papaya, also called papaw or pawpaw, is native to the Americas, but its exact origin is unknown. It may be a chance hybridization between two other species of the representative genus. It is now widely cultivated in tropical parts of the world, and many varieties have been developed. In the wild, the tree grows to about two meters (about six feet) high, but cultivated trees may be about eight meters (about twenty-five feet) high. The fruits, which vary in shape from spherical to elongated, may weigh as much as nine kilograms (twenty pounds). They are eaten fresh as breakfast fruit or in salads and desserts. Papaya is also exploited for its latex, which contains papain, a proteolytic (protein-digesting) enzyme used in meat tenderizers. Other species of the representative genus are eaten locally in the tropics.

Scientific classification: Papaya is the common name for the family Caricaceae. The representative genus is *Carica*. The common papaya is classified as *Carica papaya*.

See also Plants in Africa.

Papyrus

Common name for a plant of the sedge family; also paper reed.

The papyrus plant grows about one to three meters (about three to ten feet) high and has a woody, aromatic, creeping rhizome (root stalk). The leaves are long and sharp-keeled, and the upright flowering stems are naked, soft, and triangular in shape. The lower part of the stem is as thick as a human arm, and at the top is a compound umbel (flower cluster) of numerous drooping spikelets, with a whorl of eight leaves. Papyrus grows in EGYPT, in ETHIOPIA, in the Jordan River valley, and in Sicily.

Various parts of the plant were used in antiquity for a variety of purposes, including wreaths, sandals, boxes, boats, and rope. The roots were dried and made into fuel. The pith of the stem was sometimes boiled and eaten, but it was used mainly in making papyrus, the type of paper most common in the classical world.

The papyrus of the Egyptians was made of slices of the cellular pith laid lengthwise, with other layers laid crosswise on it. The whole was then moistened with water, pressed and dried, and rubbed smooth with ivory or a smooth shell. The sheets of papyrus, varying from about 12.5 by 22.5 centimeters (about five by nine inches) to about 22.5 by 37.5 centimeters (about nine by fifteen inches), were made into rolls, probably some six to nine meters (about twenty to thirty feet) in length. The Egyptians wrote on papyrus in regular columns, which in literary prose rarely exceeded 7.6 centimeters (three inches) in width; in poetry the columns were often wider to accommodate the length of the verse.

The Greeks seem to have known papyrus as early as the beginning of the fifth century B.C.E., but the earliest extant Greek papyrus is believed to be the *Persae* of the poet Timotheus, who lived during the fifth and early fourth century B.C.E. The use of papyrus for literary works continued among the Greeks and the Romans to the fourth century C.E., when it was superseded by parchment. It was still used for official and private documents until the eighth or ninth century.

Scientific classification: Papyrus belongs to the family Cyperaceae. It is classified as *Cyperus papyrus*.

See also Plants in Africa.

Paraguay

Landlocked country of South America, bordered to the north by Bolivia, to the northeast and east by Brazil, and to the south and southwest by Argentina.

Paraguay has been described as the most homogeneous society in all of South America. The mixing of Guaraní Indian and Spanish created a largely *mestizo* (of indigenous and European ancestry) society that prides itself on its Guaraní descent. What is often overlooked is that people of African descent were also part of the racial and cultural mix since early colonial times. The country's long history of reenslavement under the *amparo* system, and its claim to being the last former Spanish South American territory to emancipate its slaves, have gained little notice. Considering their history and their contributions to the country's development, Afro-Paraguayans deserve more than the brief mention they have traditionally received.

Colonial Paraguay

Long before the Spaniards arrived, seminomadic and warlike tribes of Guaraní speakers settled mostly in the southern part of the region that is now Paraguay. Spanish explorers arrived in the area in 1524 and established colonies in 1536. In 1537 the Fort of Nuestra Señora de la Asunción was founded at the site of the present-day capital of Paraguay. A city council, established there in 1541, became the political center for the province of Paraguay. Eventually Paraguay became the center of Spanish power in the southeastern section of the continent.

A small number of Africans was first introduced into the region in the early 1520s, when the first explorers entered Paraguay searching for gold and other riches. Large-scale importation did not occur in Paraguay as compared to other territories in the southern region of South America because the country lacked significant exploitable resources and had a large Indian population to fulfill its labor needs. The labor that black slaves initially performed in Paraguay was no different than that performed by Indians: cattle ranching, agricultural tasks, and domestic servitude. Only later would blacks be placed in more specialized fields such as iron smelting and road repair.

African slaves were imported to the region through the ports of Buenos Aires and Montevideo. Like most Africans who passed through these ports, most of these slaves were from ANGOLA, taken from the Guinea and CONGO RIVER Stations on the western coast of Africa. Many slaves in Paraguay were of the same cultural group, but there is no indication that they formed ethnic communities once in Paraguay. The number of blacks in Paraguay increased mainly from racial intermixing, not additional importations of African slaves. Estimates of the Afro-Paraguayan population in the colonial period are incomplete as a result of inconsistent records and the misleading observations of record keepers. In 1570, for example, 3,000 mulattoes (of African and European descent) and mestizos were counted together, with no mention of other black groups. Despite the limitations in the available data, evidence indicates a subsequent growth in the Afro-Paraguayan population. The next available records, from 1650, indicate that people of African descent numbered 15,000 in a total population of 250,000. Another jump to 1782, however, shows a population decline to approximately 10,840, which included both free and enslaved Afro-Paraguayans.

Amparo System

Unique to Paraguay was a system of the late sixteenth century called *amparo* ("shelter" or "protection"), in which a manumitted slave who could not pay tribute to the Crown was placed in the protective custody of religious orders or local government officials. In what was essentially a form of *encomienda* (agrarian land grant) for people of African descent, newly "freed" slaves were collected into segregated black towns and forced to work for their custodians in conditions reminiscent of slavery. The amparo system was also used as a form of social control in that it kept blacks under the watchful eye of colonial authorities. Even fugitive slaves from BRAZIL and URUGUAY wanting political asylum became amparos. Instead of returning the fugitives to their owner, Paraguayan officials declared them free upon their entering the territory, then placed them in government custody to become workers on farms or in national factories.

Most Afro-Paraguayan amparos were moved to towns established by religious orders such as the Franciscans, the Jesuits, and the Dominicans. Areguá (Arequi) and Tabapí (Tobapy) were two such towns controlled by these groups. Other settlements were established by the colonial government as military outposts to protect Paraguayan territory. The town of Emboscada, for example, was formed in 1740 when several hundred Afro-Paraguayans under the amparo system were relocated by the government. These blacks lived free but served as soldiers when they were needed to fight the Mbayá (Albayas) Indians. Emboscada was the first of many towns created on the frontier to maintain the country's boundaries.

Perhaps because of the tight control held by the colonial administration under the amparo system, Paraguayan historical records suggest that there were no *cimarrones* (runaway slaves) or even significant SLAVE REBELLIONS. Brief mention is made of an 1838 slave revolt on a farm, but no additional information is available. Considering the long history of slavery in the country, it is surprising that there is no record of major revolts or of a significant number of fugitives. In fact, historical text suggests that it was common practice for a slave to return voluntarily to the owner a few days after escaping. A fugitive's decision to return was influenced by fear of the ire and punishment of the master and the fact that Paraguay's boundaries had become increasingly difficult to escape.

Since Independence

Paraguay lost most of its power and prestige after 1776, when it became part of the viceroyalty of Río de La Plata, administered from Buenos Aires. The leaders of Paraguay increasingly

Paraguay (At a Glance)

Official Name: Republic of Paraguay

Area: 406,750 sq km (157,047 sq mi)

Location: Northeast of Argentina in central South America

Capital: Asunción (1,302,000 population; 2004 estimate)

Other Major Cities: Ciudad del Este (population 133,893), Encarnación (population 58,261), Concepción (population 35,276) (2000 estimates)

Population: 5,878,000 (2004 estimate)

Population Density: 15 persons per sq km (38 per sq mi)

Population Below Age 15: 38.4 percent (male 1,179,084; female 1,141,420; 2003 estimate)

Population Growth Rate: 2.54 percent (2003 estimate)

Total Fertility Rate: 4.02 children born per woman (2003 estimate)

Life Expectancy at Birth: Total population: 74.4 years (male 71.89 years; female 77.03 years; 2003 estimate)

Infant Mortality Rate: 27.71 deaths per 1,000 live births (2003 estimate)

Literacy Rate (age 15 and over who can read and write): Total population: 94 percent (male 94.9 percent; female 93 percent; 2003 estimate)

Education: Education is free and compulsory for ages seven to thirteen, but there is a high dropout rate. The public National University of Asunción offers free higher education. Women account for about half of all university graduates.

Languages: The official languages of Paraguay are Spanish and Guarani.

Ethnic Groups: 95 percent mestizo (mixed Spanish and Amerindian)

Religions: 90 percent of Paraguayans are Roman Catholic, with some Mennonites and other Protestant groups

Climate: A mix of subtropical and tropical, depending on proximity to the Tropic of Capricorn. Summer temperatures range from 77° F to 104° F (25° C to 40° C), and winter temperatures range from 61° F to 73° F (16° C to 23° C). Rainfall is heaviest from October to April. Floods and droughts have been known to affect all of Paraguay on occasion, with attendant agricultural losses.

Land, Plants, and Animals: Paraguay is divided into two regions, the Región Oriental (Eastern Region) and the Región Occidental (Western Region), by the north-south running Paraguay River. The highest mountain peak, in the Cordillera de San Rafael in southeastern Paraguay, is Mount San Rafael (2,789 feet, or 850 meters). A tropical portion of the Región Occidental known as the Chaco Boreal covers about two-thirds of the country and extends into Argentina and Bolivia. Deforestation of Paraguay since the 1970s has been rapid and may result in a total loss of forests in the next fifty years if left unchecked. Paraguay has more than 500 species of hardwoods, including the urunday, curupay, and many varieties of palm. There are cacti and medicinal plants. Animals include monkeys, marsh deer, otters, ocelots, bats, and aquatic rodents. Some of the many birds are ibises, herons, parakeets, eagles, toucans, and doves. Illegal trade threatens macaws and parrots. Among insects there are locusts, mosquitoes, and tarantula spiders. Fish include the piranha.

Natural Resources: Hydropower, timber, iron ore, manganese, and limestone

Currency: guarani (PYG)

Gross Domestic Product (GDP): $25.19 billion (2002 estimate)

GDP per Capita: $4,300 (2002 estimate)

GDP Real Growth Rate: −2.7 percent (2002 estimate)

Primary Economic Activities: Agriculture

Primary Crops: Cotton, sugarcane, soybeans, corn, wheat, tobacco, cassava (tapioca), fruits, vegetables, beef, pork, eggs, milk, and timber

Industries: Sugar, cement, textiles, beverages, and wood products

Primary Exports: Soybeans, feed, cotton, meat, edible oils, and electricity

Primary Imports: Road vehicles, consumer goods, tobacco, petroleum products, and electrical machinery

Primary Trade Partners: Brazil, Argentina, Chile, Bermuda, United States, and China (Hong Kong)

Government: Paraguay is a constitutional republic. The chief of state and head of government is President Nicanor Duarte Frutos (since August 2003; popularly elected to serve a five-year term). The legislative branch is the bicameral Congress, which consists of the forty-five-member Chamber of Senators and the eighty-member Chamber of Deputies (members of both bodies elected by popular vote to serve five-year terms). The judicial branch is headed by the Supreme Court of Justice.

Shelle Sumners

Paraguay

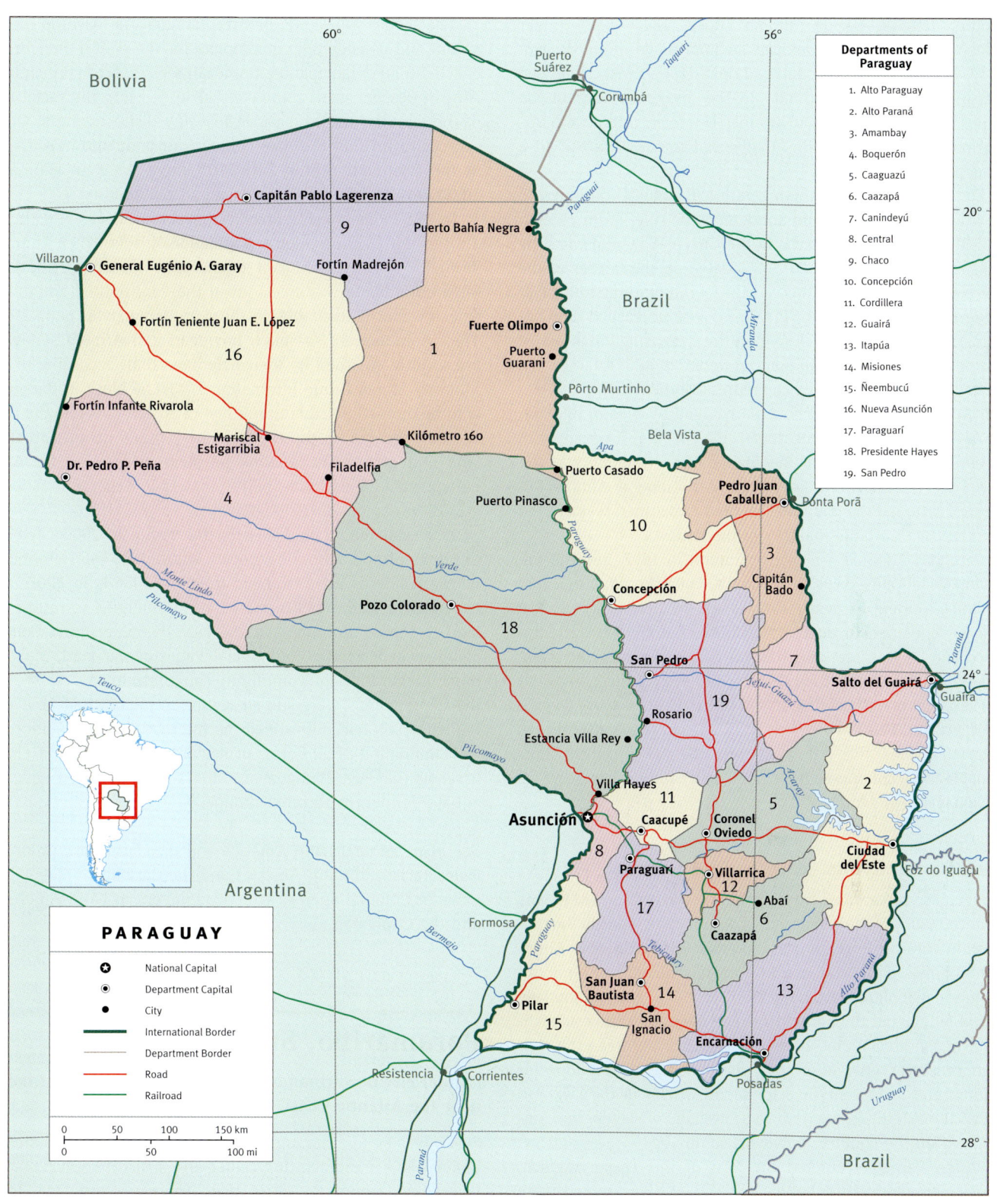

resented their province's loss of status. A new challenge emerged in 1810, when ARGENTINA declared independence from SPAIN and sought to extend its influence over the entire area of the former viceroyalty of Río de La Plata. An Argentine army under General Manuel Belgrano was sent to force Paraguayan acceptance of Buenos Aires's declaration. However, Paraguayan forces repelled Belgrano's army, and Paraguay declared its own independence on May 14, 1811. The new republic developed under the dictatorship of José Gaspar Rodríguez de Francia, who ruled until his death in 1840. Francia was succeeded by another dictator, Carlos Antonio López (1844–1862), under whose rule Paraguay developed an impressive military capability. His son, Francisco Solano López (1862–1870), followed him and involved the country in the disastrous War of the Triple Alliance (1864–1870) against Uruguay, Brazil, and Argentina, a territorial conflict that cost Paraguay more than a third of its population.

For much of the twentieth century, Paraguay continued to be wracked by warfare and antidemocratic rule. From 1932 to 1935 Paraguay fought BOLIVIA in the Chaco War, motivated by a dispute over the Chaco region located on the border of the two countries. Paraguay succeeded in winning three-fourths of the territory in dispute, but the Chaco War unleashed new political demands, particularly within the increasingly nationalist and politically dominant military. A period of authoritarian rule ensued, notably marked by the repressive dictatorship of General Alfredo Stroessner, who was installed by a coup in 1954. Thirty-five years later, Stroessner's rule ended as it began, with a coup. In 1989, however, the change of government was followed by free elections later that year. General Andres Rodriguez, who led the coup that toppled Stroessner, was elected president with a large majority of the vote.

Paraguay adopted a new constitution in 1992, and the following year Juan Carlos Wasmosy became the country's first civilian president in nearly forty years. In 1996 army general Lino Oviedo tried to depose Wasmosy, but Oviedo's attempt failed and he was later jailed for his part in planning the coup. Oviedo's political ally Raul Cubas Grau was elected president in 1998, and one of his first acts in office was to release Oviedo from prison. This move eventually caused the legislature to impeach Cubas the following year. Senate president Luis Gonzalez Macchi succeeded Cubas and continues to serve as Paraguay's president.

Afro-Paraguayans since Independence

Paraguay's separation from Spanish power in 1811 was achieved without the enlistment of Afro-Paraguayans in the military. In contrast to the process in other former Spanish American colonies, independence in Paraguay did not bring about the gradual abolition of slavery there. Afro-Paraguayan bondage continued, as did the amparo system, even with the establishment of the Free Womb Law in 1842. This law freed the children of slaves only after they reached age twenty-four for women and age twenty-five for men. Articles in the law also ended the external slave trade. The systems of slavery and amparo within the country, however, continued.

When Paraguay entered the War of the Triple Alliance, slaves were required for battle. A year later, slave owners were given the option of selling their slaves to the military as soldiers. By 1867 the government had required that all free blacks and slaves enlist in the army. A third of the population, including most Afro-Paraguayans, had been killed by the time Paraguay lost the war. In 1869 the newly elected government ordered the complete abolition of slavery, which took effect in the 1870 constitution.

The historical records of Afro-Paraguayans become inconsistent and considerably incomplete for the period after Brazil enacted total emancipation. Some sources report that people of African descent were completely absorbed into the racial mix of the country and as a result lost any distinctiveness. Other sources claim that the Afro-Paraguayan population flourished in the twentieth century. By 1925 there were an estimated 10,000 to 31,500 Afro-Paraguayans in the country.

In the 1990s some sources claimed that blacks constituted 3.5 percent of the nation's population, placing their number around 156,000. It is difficult to determine the accuracy of these often contradictory sources, given the very limited amount of research that is available on the Afro-Paraguayan population. Their numbers are so small, however, and Afro-Paraguayans are so little regarded by their neighbors that, according to the Minority Rights Group International, "To be black in Paraguay is to be almost invisible to the rest of society." While the constitution recognizes the rights of indigenous peoples to their land and culture, it contains no such recognition for Afro-Paraguayans. This "invisibility" makes it easier for majority groups to exploit Afro-Paraguayans.

A special report published by the group in 2000 cited the example of the Afro-Paraguayan community of Cambucuá, whose residents were expelled from their lands in 1967. The government in the 1990s passed a law intended to return the land to the community, but the current owner must first be compensated for the commercial value of the land, a figure much higher than the community can afford to pay. As of 2003 the Cambucuáns were still struggling to regain their land and Paraguay still had not ratified the International Convention on the Elimination of all Forms of Racial Discrimination (ICERD). It seems that Afro-Paraguayans still face an uphill struggle for equal treatment with other groups.

See also Colonial Latin America and the Caribbean; Colonial Rule; Racism in Latin America and the Caribbean; Slave Laws in Colonial Spanish America; Slavery in Latin America and the Caribbean.

Rob Garrison

Paramaribo, Suriname

Capital city of Suriname, located on the Suriname River near the Atlantic Coast.

SURINAME's largest city and chief seaport, Paramaribo is a commercial and manufacturing center and a distribution point for bauxite and alumina, timber, rice, sugarcane, and citrus fruit. Major products include lumber and processed food. Paramaribo is the site of the University of Suriname (1968); the Suriname Museum (1954), with archaeological, cultural, and natural-history exhibits; the Suriname Cultural Center (1947); and an institute concerned with tropical research. The architecture and canals of the city give it a Dutch aspect. It is served by an airport at Zanderij.

Originally settled by French colonists in the early 1640s on the site of a Native American village, the town was made the capital of a newly established British dependency in the 1650s. The Dutch gained control of the area in the 1660s. Paramaribo became the capital of the newly independent republic of Suriname in 1975. With a racially diverse population that includes people of European, Asian, and African descent, the city is known for its racial tolerance. Population 217,300 (2003 estimate).

See also Colonial Latin America and the Caribbean.

Pare

Ethnic group of Tanzania.

Numbering approximately 300,000, the Pare regard as home the steep craggy Pare Mountains that rise suddenly from the thorn-scrub plains of northeastern Tanzania. The mountains form three distinct clusters: North Pare consists of a wide, fertile, and densely populated plateau; Middle Pare is low, dry, and sparsely populated; and South Pare has long, discrete ridges, small plateaus, and the highest peak, Mt. Shengena (8,080 ft. above sea level), a sacred site and apex of a complex irrigation canal system that twists and turns across and down the mountain slopes.

Composed of alluvial, postvolcanic sediments, gneissic rocks and nonlaterized and laterized soils, the mountains provide important resources such as sandstone, shale, and limestone for construction; clay for brick making and pottery; gemstones for sale; forests for firewood and furniture; and rich arable land for smallholder agriculture, the backbone of the Pare economy.

Pare men, women, and children cultivate small plots at different altitudes across agro-ecological zones and grow several varieties of bananas, maize, beans, sweet potato, cassava, yams, sugarcane, pumpkins, tobacco, and coffee, cardamom, rice, and bananas for sale in local markets and at government cooperatives. Complementing the two rain-fed growing seasons with a third season using traditional irrigation enables farmers to increase the subsistence food supply and the surplus available for sale. Pare also raise domesticated animals, such as chickens, pigs, sheep, goats, and cattle. The last three have symbolic significance in rituals of healing, legitimating marriage, and creating relations of clientage and debt.

To raise money for taxes, school fees, supplies, and medicines, many people also work for wages. In the mountains, people work as teachers, nurses, hospital technicians, craftsmen, kiosk operators, or in a range of day labor activities on farms, as firewood or water collectors, or as domestic workers. Able-bodied men from North and Middle Pare often migrate to urban centers for employment; fewer people migrate from South Pare. Most maintain strong ties to home, usually sending portions of their wages. All Pare regard the mountains as their home and most return to establish a claim, build a house, raise a family, and eventually to die and be buried.

Ties of patrilineal descent and patrilocal marriage bind and persuade. The Pare gain access to and rights over land, irrigated water, trees, and other property through lineage membership. The youngest son is expected to care for parents in their old age (ultimogeniture), although daughters also play important roles as caregivers and providers. Households tend to be nuclear, or extended by one generation. Pare cherish children, who make the life cycle complete and who reconnect the generations when they assume the names of grandparents first on the father's side, then on the mother's. As workers, care providers, and companions, children prove critical in linking Pare households to the wider political economy of the twentieth and twenty-first centuries.

The SWAHILI and Arab slavers and traders who penetrated the Pare hinterland in the 1860s seized children and adults, expanded legitimate exchange, and exacerbated rivalry among Pare chiefs and political aspirants. Under German colonialism (1885–1919), education was compulsory for children, and Christianity, cash crop production, and forced labor were introduced. The Germans appointed official Pare chiefs in order to consolidate leadership, made Pare build schools and churches and plant coffee, and outlawed many customary practices, such as initiation rituals and divination ordeals.

The Chasu language (a Bantu tongue in the Niger-Kordofan family), spoken in parts of North, Middle, and South Pare and widely used in trade and ritual life during the precolonial period, was chosen by German missionaries in the nineteenth century to be the language of Bible translation and school primers. Chasu became the official Pare language under British colonial rule (1919–1961), and chiefdoms were shaped into nine distinct units. Today Pare country is divided into two administrative districts, Mwanga (North) and Same (Middle and South) and most also speak KiSwahili, a coastal language widely used as a lingua franca and now the Republic of Tanzania's official language.

The Pare are well-represented in national politics as exemplified by Cleopa David Msuya, who served both as finance minister and prime minister in the national government. Pare of both districts avidly pursue education and numerous primary and secondary schools throughout each region have been built by parents and community members through self-help (*mtharagambo*) activities.

Mwanga District's infrastructure is more developed than that of Same District because it provides tarmac mountain roads, household electricity and piped water, telephone service, and vocational schools. Government and nongovernment organizations from Scandinavian countries, China, Japan, and elsewhere have been active in both districts in development aid projects to plant trees, raise bees, build school dormitories, rehabilitate traditional irrigation systems, raise heifers, construct fishponds, build a pottery factory, promote women's economic position, and improve health care.

See also Colonial Rule.

Karen A. Porter

Paris-Dakar Rally

Largest and most challenging annual motor vehicle rally in Africa.

The annual Paris-Dakar rally has become a major international motor sports event in North and West Africa, attracting hundreds of teams from around the world. Begun in 1979 by French professional rally driver Thierry Sabine, the rally begins each January in Paris with amateurs and professionals driving cars, motorcycles, and trucks, and ends three weeks later in DAKAR, SENEGAL. (Occasionally the course varies: in 1992 the rally began in LIBYA and ended in CAPE TOWN, SOUTH AFRICA; in 2003 it started in Marseille, FRANCE, and ended in EGYPT.) The sand and heat of the SAHARA are hard on vehicles and drivers alike, and many drivers become lost and must be rescued by the race organizers' helicopters and planes. Thieves and TUAREG rebels have kidnapped teams and confiscated vehicles. Accidents in the rally have claimed dozens of lives.

The race route varies and has passed through many African countries, including ALGERIA, BURKINA FASO, MALI, MAURITANIA, MOROCCO, and SENEGAL. The local economies benefit from the money spent by the racing teams as well as by the organizers, support crews, and journalists. At the end of the race, teams often donate their trucks to regional nongovernmental organizations, and some have used their vehicles to deliver medicines, water pumps, and other goods. But there are also costs, including numerous bystander casualties, extensive environmental damage, and the blight of abandoned vehicles and trash left in the desert. Critics contend that the more than $100 million spent annually on advertising and sponsorships would be better spent on development projects in Africa.

Eric Young

Saxophonist Charlie Parker rehearses in his dressing room before performing at the International Jazz Festival in Paris in 1949. *Bettmann/CORBIS*

Parker, Charlie

1920–1955

Masterful African American alto saxophonist, who along with Dizzy Gillespie founded bebop or modern jazz.

Together with trumpeter DIZZY GILLESPIE, Charlie Parker was the primary creator of BEBOP. His musical innovations profoundly influenced other alto saxophonists, as is evident in the playing of CANNONBALL ADDERLEY, ERIC DOLPHY, Lou Donaldson, Charles McPherson, and Frank Morgan. Indeed, Parker's influence extended well beyond JAZZ to popular music and film and television scores. Despite his musical brilliance, however, Parker led a troubled life that included the use of heroin at an early age, an addiction that contributed to his death and was deeply intertwined with his musical mystique.

Born Charles Christopher Parker in Kansas City, Kansas, he acquired the nickname "Yardbird" (usually shortened to "Bird") as a young man. His father, Charles Parker Sr., was a singer and dancer from Mississippi and Tennessee who abandoned the family when his son was about eleven years old. His mother, Adelaide Bailey Parker, was originally from Oklahoma. In 1927 Parker's family moved across the Kaw River to KANSAS CITY, MISSOURI, an important center of jazz music.

Under the corrupt reign of Democratic boss Thomas Pendergast, Kansas City was a wide-open town, and its bars, honkytonks, and nightclubs remained open until dawn, featuring live music and often no-holds-barred jam sessions. Kansas City gave birth to a freewheeling, stripped-down form of SWING music that was deeply grounded in the BLUES and was epitomized by the COUNT BASIE band. Parker soon developed an interest in music. Lawrence Keyes, a musician and friend of Parker's at Lincoln High School, remarked, "If he had been as conscientious about his school work as he was about music, he would have become a professor, but he was a terrible truant."

During 1935 and 1936, when Parker was about fifteen, his life changed dramatically. He dropped out of school, married Rebecca Ruffin, began playing with the Deans of Swing, a band led by Keyes, and had his first experience with heroin. Within a year he was addicted. Periodically throughout his life Parker would try to limit his heroin use, generally by substituting large quantities of alcohol, which was no less debilitating. In 1938 his first son, Francis Leon Parker, was born. Over the next few years, Parker concentrated on his music and learned from older musicians in Kansas City and at resorts in the Ozarks. In 1939

Parker decided to travel to NEW YORK CITY, the nation's jazz center. There he took part in jam sessions, most notably at two HARLEM nightspots, Clark Monroe's Uptown House and Dan Wall's Chili House.

While jamming at the Chili House one night in December 1939, Parker had a profound musical breakthrough. He recalled: "I'd been getting bored with the stereotyped changes that were being used at the time, and I kept thinking there's bound to be something else. I could hear it sometimes, but I couldn't play it. Well, that night I was working over 'Cherokee,' and as I did I found that by using the higher intervals of a chord as a melody line and backing them with appropriately related changes, I could play the thing I heard. I came alive." Although it took Parker several years to consolidate the full implications of this discovery, his achievement heralded a new era in jazz.

In early 1940, however, Parker left New York for Kansas City to join Jay McShann's big band. Parker would stay with McShann about two and a half years. During the swing era, big bands provided the majority of job opportunities for jazz musicians, but players such as Parker and Gillespie, who was then part of CAB CALLOWAY's orchestra, rankled at their lack of artistic freedom. Parker's job with McShann brought him back to New York City in late 1941 or 1942. Soon he began collaborating with Gillespie, who had independently achieved comparable harmonic breakthroughs.

The musical sparks Parker and Gillespie struck while playing together created modern jazz, initially known as bebop or simply bop. Parker clearly recognized the musical symbiosis between the two and regarded Gillespie as "the other half of my heartbeat." They worked together during 1943 and 1944 in EARL HINES's big band, an important bebop incubator. But they perfected their music in jam sessions, especially at Monroe's Uptown House and Minton's. The new music offered richer harmonic textures, with more varied tempos—much faster on up-tempo songs and much slower on ballads than typical swing-era jazz—and a subtler rhythmic pulse.

Besides his advanced harmonic approach, Parker attained a previously unheard of rhythmic subtlety with his elliptical and fluid melodic lines. His technical mastery allowed him continuously to reinvent melodies, including rapid double-time passages, over the chord sequence of a given song. He was also at ease playing in every key, at a time when many jazz musicians were far more limited.

In 1943, while in WASHINGTON, D.C., with the Hines band, Parker married Geraldine Scott without bothering to divorce his first wife. Parker's heroin habit worsened, and fellow musicians pressured him to quit hard drugs. Instead Parker quit the band and returned to Kansas City, ending his relationship with Scott. The Hines band broke up soon after, and a number of its more modernist players regrouped around a new leader, singer BILLY ECKSTINE, with Gillespie as musical director. The Eckstine band was the first bebop big band and included, besides Gillespie, drummer ART BLAKEY, vocalist SARAH VAUGHAN, and eventually Parker. Yet once again Parker quickly left an environment he found stifling. With few exceptions, the rest of his career involved playing in small groups.

Parker's first significant recording sessions came in late 1944 and 1945, for Savoy and, under Gillespie's leadership, for Musicraft. The latter produced a number of particularly fine recordings, including "Salt Peanuts" and "Shaw 'Nuff." Gillespie and Parker also played an extended gig at the Three Deuces in New York City, which Gillespie later described as the "height of perfection of our music." But Parker's subsequent career was increasingly erratic. Gillespie asked Parker to join him on a trip to California to play at Billy Berg's, a LOS ANGELES nightclub. For Parker, the decision to go was fateful.

In California, Parker made his first classic Dial recordings, including "Moose the Mooche," "Yardbird Suite," and "Ornithology." Yet the arrest of his drug dealer, Emery "Moose the Mooche" Byrd, resulted in Parker's having a nervous breakdown on July 29, 1946, while recording "Lover Man." Parker spent several months in Camarillo State Hospital, and Ross Russell, the owner of Dial Records, released "Lover Man." Although the record was acclaimed by Parker's many followers, Parker insisted that it was "a horrible thing that should never have been released."

Beginning in 1947 Parker made New York City his home base. There he formed his quintet, which included trumpet player MILES DAVIS and drummer MAX ROACH, and recorded a number of sessions for Dial, highlighted by the superb ballads "My Old Flame," "Embraceable You," and "Don't Blame Me." In 1948 Parker began recording with Norman Granz's Verve label, including groundbreaking sessions with strings. However, the greatest moments of his later career took place in concert. Two of these were recorded, a 1949 appearance at Carnegie Hall and a 1953 reunion with Gillespie at Toronto's Massey Hall. During these years, Parker regularly won the *Downbeat* magazine readers' poll for best alto player, and his fame extended to EUROPE, taking him to France in 1949 and to Scandinavia the following year.

But Parker's personal life became increasingly troubled. In 1948 he married his third wife, Doris Sydnor, but left her two years later to enter a relationship with Chan Richardson, with whom he had a daughter, Pree, and a son, Baird. Because of a drug conviction, he lost his cabaret card, required of all musicians playing in New York City nightclubs, which limited his ability to work.

The physical toll of Parker's heroin and alcohol abuse was mounting. Besides making his performances increasingly erratic, it gave him stomach ulcers, liver problems, and at least one heart attack. When he died in 1955, the attending physician estimated Parker's age between fifty and sixty years. In fact, he was only thirty-four. Yet despite his early death, Parker's uncompromising and innovative musicianship have assured his immortality. Indeed, soon after his funeral, graffiti began appearing around New York City proclaiming "Bird Lives!"

See also Music, African American.

Bibliography

Russell, Ross. *Bird Lives: The High Life and Hard Times of Charlie (Yardbird) Parker.* Charterhouse, 1973.

Woidek, Carl. *Charlie Parker: His Music and Life.* University of Michigan Press, 1996.

James Sellman

Parker, John P.

1827–1900

African American abolitionist and entrepreneur.

John P. Parker was born in Norfolk, Virginia, the son of a slave mother and white father, whose names are unknown. At the age of eight, Parker was sold as a slave to an agent in RICHMOND, where he in turn was purchased by a physician from Mobile, Alabama. While employed as a house servant for the physician, Parker learned to read and write. In Mobile he was apprenticed to work in furnaces and iron manufactures as well as for a plasterer. Beaten by the plasterer, Parker attempted to escape, only to be captured aboard a northbound riverboat.

From 1843 to 1845 Parker was hired out as an iron moulder and stevedore in the Mobile area. He proved to be an extraordinarily skilled moulder, which enabled him to earn enough money to purchase his freedom for $1,800 at the end of the two-year period. Obtaining a pass for Indiana, Parker moved to the CINCINNATI area after a freeman requested his assistance in aiding escaped slaves from Kentucky. Thus began his career as a "conductor" on the UNDERGROUND RAILROAD.

In 1848 Parker married Miranda Boulden, a Cincinnati native. They had eight children, a number of whom became teachers. That same year he left Cincinnati, where he had worked as a moulder, to open a general store at Beechwood Factory, Ohio. In 1850 Parker moved to Ripley, Ohio, on the Ohio River across from Mason County, Kentucky, which was the home of the Reverend John Rankin, a Presbyterian clergyman who was also an abolitionist and operator on the Underground Railroad. Parker worked separately from Rankin, believing it not proper "to ask white men how to abduct slaves from Kentucky," and held that the organized church was not sympathetic to the plight of the slave. He assisted fugitives by sending associates to meet them by night and conduct them on rowboats across the Ohio River. Once in Ohio the runaways were escorted by guides to safe havens. During the decade before the EMANCIPATION PROCLAMATION, Parker reputedly assisted more than 1,000 slaves escape to freedom.

Concurrent with his abolitionist activities, Parker established a small foundry in 1854 that produced special and general castings. His employees included white Kentuckians such as James Shrofe, whose family owned slaves that Parker hid and sent northward to Canada.

During the CIVIL WAR, Parker recruited volunteers for the Twenty-seventh Regiment, U.S. Colored Troops, one of two such Ohio units. He was largely responsible for recruiting Kentuckians to the regiment. Meanwhile, his foundry furnished castings for the Union cause.

Parker's entrepreneurial and inventive skills blossomed after the Civil War. His firm, which came to be known as the Ripley Foundry and Machine Company, manufactured slide-valve engines and reapers. At its peak in the 1880s the company employed twenty-five men. A century later the company was still in operation although no longer under family ownership. As the operator of a company of that size, Parker was a wealthy African American by the standards of his day. Perhaps Parker's greatest claim to recognition was as an inventor. He was one the few African Americans who obtained patents before 1900. He patented a screw for tobacco presses in September 1884 and one for a similar device the following year. He is credited with the invention of the "Parker Pulverizer," a type of harrow.

In his later years Parker recounted his life story to Frank M. Gregg, an Ohio newspaperman and the author of several historical studies. Historian Louis Weeks's evaluation best captures John Parker's contributions, naming him "an important, yet unheralded, participant in the UNDERGROUND RAILROAD . . . a successful inventor and businessman . . . and . . . an independent, militant black man in an essentially white power structure." Parker's significance has been obscured by the tendency of most standard works on the Underground Railroad to emphasize the role of white abolitionists and overlook African American involvement, and also because he often worked independently from white abolitionists and received less recognition in the abolitionist press. Parker died in Ripley.

Bibliography

The "Autobiography of a Slave, John Parker, Brown County, Ohio, Circa 1800," is a typescript located in the Flowers Collection of Southern Americana at the Duke University Library. It offers the most complete account of Parker's life.

Baker, Henry Edwin. *The Colored Inventor: A Record of Fifty Years.* 1913.

Obituary, *Cincinnati Commercial Tribune,* February 8, 1900.

Siebert, Wilbur H. *The Mysteries of Ohio's Underground Railroads.* 1951.

Weeks, Louis. "John P. Parker: Black Abolitionist Entrepreneur, 1827–1900." *Ohio History* (Spring 1971): 155–62.

From *American National Biography*. John A. Garraty and Mark C. Carnes, eds. Oxford University Press, 1999. Reprinted by permission of the American Council of Learned Societies.

Frank R. Levstik

Parker, Lawrence Kris

See KRS-One.

Parks, Gordon, Jr.

1934–1979

American filmmaker who inaugurated the blaxploitation film genre.

The son of Sally Alvis and director, writer, and photographer GORDON PARKS SR., Gordon Parks Jr. worked to define his own creative expression independently of his famous father. He even used the name Gordon Rogers early in his career to forge his own identity. After spending his early years at the American School in Paris, Parks graduated from White Plains High School in 1952, worked in NEW YORK CITY's garment district, and joined the army in 1956. In the 1960s, he began his career in entertainment as a café folksinger in New York's Greenwich Village.

Parks entered the field of cinematography as a cameraman on his father's film *The Learning Tree* (1969) and as a still photographer for *Burn* (1969) and *The Godfather* (1972). In 1972 Parks took the director's chair with *Super Fly*, which has often been cited as the defining example of a new genre of African American film: blaxploitation. Set in a dense urban landscape, the film chronicles a conflict between a black criminal and the white organized crime establishment, a symbolic representation of African American male self-determination in the face of an oppressive system. Enhancing this new cinematic form was CURTIS MAYFIELD's memorable score. Despite controversy sparked by its uncritical depiction of a "heroic" drug dealer, *Superfly* was remarkably popular among black audiences hungry for powerful black images in film, and grossed over $24.8 million. Parks quickly followed *Superfly*'s success with three new feature films: *Thomasine and Bushrod* (1974), the action film *Three the Hard Way* (1974), and the teen love story *Aaron Loves Angela* (1975).

Parks moved to KENYA in 1979, where he started the Africa International Productions/Panther Film Company. He died in a plane crash in NAIROBI a short time later.

See also Blaxploitation Films; Film, Blacks in American.

Bibliography

Bogle, Donald. "Gordon Parks, Jr." In *Blacks in American Films and Television: An Encyclopedia.* Garland, 1988.

Marian Aguiar

Parks, Gordon, Sr.

1912–

American photographer famous for his portrait photography, and the first African American director of a major Hollywood motion picture.

Gordon Parks was born in Fort Scott, Kansas, the son of a dirt farmer and the youngest of fifteen children. He left home when he was fifteen, shortly after his mother's death. After an unhappy attempt to move in with a married sister in Minneapolis, Minnesota, Parks ended up spending a frigid winter homeless, an experience that sensitized him to the plight of the poor and that he would draw on in later photography and films. At the time, his hunger and loneliness nearly led him to a life of crime; however, he managed to struggle through high school for a while, working odd jobs herding cattle, carrying bricks, and even touring with a semiprofessional basketball team.

Working as a waiter on the Northern Pacific Railroad, Parks saw magazine photos produced by the Farm Security Administration, a federally funded project that chronicled the GREAT DEPRESSION in rural and urban America. He began taking his own photographs while still working for the railroad. Later, after watching a World War II newsreel by documentary filmmaker Norman Alley, Parks resolved to focus on documentary photography.

In 1937 the self-taught Parks established a photography studio in Saint Paul, Minnesota. He immediately showed an original eye for his subjects, although at first he lacked the technical training to capture them flawlessly. Once, after finally getting the big break of a fashion shoot, he double-exposed all but one photo. Yet even the results of these mishaps captivated his viewers, and Parks soon established himself as a much-in-demand fashion photographer in Saint Paul. His work eventually was discovered by Marva Louis, the wife of boxer JOE LOUIS. Marva helped Parks set up shop as a fashion photographer in the bigger market of CHICAGO, ILLINOIS.

In his spare time, Parks turned his camera from the fantasy world of fashion to the destitute streets of Chicago's South Side. These pictures, exhibited at the South Side Community Art Center, won him a Julius Rosenwald Fellowship in 1941 and an opportunity to work at the Farm Security Administration, where he took on the assignment of showing the "face of America." Under the tutelage of Roy Stryker, the director of the staff photographers, Parks found that he could express himself more powerfully with the camera than with words. "I learned that photography would enable me to show what was right and wrong about America, the world and life," he said.

With the closing of the Farm Security Administration, Parks went to work at the Office of War Information in 1943, then for the Standard Oil Company of New Jersey as a documentary photographer. Continuing his work in fashion photography, he published two books, *Flash Photography* (1947) and *Camera Portraits: The Techniques and Principles of Documentary Portraiture* (1948). In 1948 Parks was hired by *Life* magazine, then one of America's leading pictorial publications, and spent two years based in Paris, France. His work in the United States in the 1950s and early 1960s and a highly acclaimed series on the slums of RIO DE JANEIRO, BRAZIL, won Parks international recognition as a photojournalist. His photographs in the United States dealt with many arenas, from politics to entertainment to the daily routines of ordinary men and women. Particularly noteworthy were his chronicles of the political activities of African Americans: the CIVIL RIGHTS MOVEMENT (later collected into the 1971 anthology *Born Black*), BLACK POWER IN THE UNITED STATES, and the growth of the NATION OF ISLAM.

With photographs driven by a strong sense of narrative, it is no surprise that Parks found another calling in writing. In 1963 he published *The Learning Tree,* the saga of a 1920s farm family very much like Parks's own. *The Learning Tree* was the first in a trilogy of autobiographical novels that was completed by *A Choice of Weapons* (1966) and *To Smile in Autumn: A Memoir* (1979). Parks combined his literary and visual talents in a 1969 movie version of *The Learning Tree,* becoming the first African American director of a major Hollywood movie. His hit movie *Shaft,* often cited as a forerunner of the BLAXPLOITATION FILM genre, was released in 1971, followed by *Leadbelly* (1976) and *The Odyssey of Solomon Northup* (1984), the story of a free black person sold into slavery. Parks was also a poet and composer, and he wrote the music for a ballet about the life of MARTIN LUTHER KING, JR.

Parks received the Spingarn Medal from the NATIONAL ASSOCIATION FOR THE ADVANCEMENT OF COLORED PEOPLE (NAACP) in 1972 and a National Medal of Arts in 1986. In 2002 he was inducted into the International Photography Hall of Fame and received the JACKIE ROBINSON Foundation Lifetime Achievement Award. He is the father of the late filmmaker GORDON PARKS, JR., whose credits include *Super Fly* (1972).

See also Film, Blacks in American.

Marian Aguiar

Parks, Rosa Louise McCauley

1913–

African American civil rights activist, who is often called the Mother of the Civil Rights Movement.

On December 1, 1955, in Montgomery, Alabama, Rosa Parks was arrested for disregarding an order to surrender her bus seat to a white passenger. Her protest galvanized a growing movement to desegregate public transportation and marked a historic turning point in the African American battle for civil rights. Parks was much more than an accidental symbol, however. It is sometimes overlooked that at the time of her arrest, she was no ordinary bus rider; she was an experienced activist with strong beliefs.

Rosa Louise McCauley was born in Tuskegee, Alabama. She was the granddaughter of former slaves and the daughter of James McCauley, a carpenter, and Leona McCauley, a rural schoolteacher. The future civil rights leader grew up in Montgomery, Alabama, where she attended the all-black Alabama State College. In 1932 she married Raymond Parks, a barber, with whom she became active in Montgomery's chapter of the NATIONAL ASSOCIATION FOR THE ADVANCEMENT OF COLORED PEOPLE (NAACP).

Raymond Parks's volunteer efforts went toward helping free the defendants in the famous SCOTTSBORO CASE, in which nine young black men were accused of raping two white women. Rosa Parks worked as the NAACP chapter's youth adviser. In 1943, when Rosa Parks actually joined the NAACP, her involvement with the organization became even greater. She worked with the organization's state president, EDGAR DANIEL NIXON, to mobilize a voter registration drive in Montgomery. That same year, Parks was elected secretary of the Montgomery branch.

In the early 1950s Parks found work as a tailor's assistant at a department store, Montgomery Fair. She also had a part-time job as a seamstress for Virginia and Clifford Durr, a white liberal couple; they encouraged Parks in her civil rights work. Six months before her famous protest, Parks received a scholarship to attend a workshop on school integration for community leaders held at the HIGHLANDER FOLK SCHOOL in Monteagle, Tennessee.

The segregated seating policies on public buses had long been a source of resentment within the black community in Montgomery and in other cities throughout the Deep South. African Americans were required to pay their fares at the front of the bus and then to reboard through the back door. The white bus drivers, who were invested with police powers, frequently harassed blacks, sometimes driving away before African American passengers were able to get back on the bus. During peak hours, the drivers pushed back the boundary markers that segregated the bus, crowding those in the "colored section" to provide more whites with seats.

On December 1, 1955, Parks took her seat in the front of the "colored section" of a Montgomery bus. The driver asked Parks and three other black riders to relinquish their seats to whites, but Parks refused (the others complied). The driver called the police, and Parks was arrested. She was released later that night after Nixon and the Durrs posted a $100 bond.

Although three black women had been arrested earlier that year for similar acts of defiance, and Parks herself had been thrown off a bus by the same driver twelve years before, this time the opponents of segregation were prepared to mount a counterattack. The Supreme Court had ruled against segregated interstate bus travel in 1946, after Irene Morgan, an African American woman, refused to give up her bus seat to a white couple. The Montgomery chapter of the NAACP had been looking for a test case to challenge the legality of segregated seating on city buses and to woo public opinion with a series of protests. The morning after her arrest, Parks agreed to let the NAACP take on her case. Another organization, the Women's Political Council (WPC), led by JOANN ROBINSON, initiated the idea of a one-day bus boycott. Within twenty-four hours of Parks's defiance, the WPC had distributed more than 52,000 fliers announcing the bus boycott, which was to take place the day of Parks's trial. On December 5, as buses went through their routes almost empty, Parks was convicted by the local court. She refused to pay the fine of $14, and with the help of her lawyer, Ed D. Gray, she appealed to the circuit court.

On the evening of December 5, several thousand protesters crowded into the Holt Street Baptist Church to create the MONTGOMERY IMPROVEMENT ASSOCIATION (MIA). They rallied behind its new president, MARTIN LUTHER KING, JR., who had just moved to Montgomery as the new pastor at the Dexter Avenue Baptist Church. What was planned as a daylong bus boycott swelled to 381 days, during which time 42,000 protesters walked, carpooled, or took taxis rather than ride the segregated city buses of Montgomery. In a move designed to reverse the segregation laws on public transportation, King and the MIA filed a separate case in a U. S. district court. The district court ruled for the plaintiffs, declaring segregated seating on buses unconstitutional. The decision was later upheld by the Supreme Court of the United States.

Parks was widely known as the Mother of the Civil Rights Movement, but her iconic stature afforded her little financial security. She lost her job as a seamstress at Montgomery Fair and was unable to find other work in Montgomery. Parks and her husband relocated to Detroit, Michigan, in 1957, where they struggled financially for the next eight years. Parks's fortunes improved somewhat in 1965, when U.S. congressional representative JOHN F. CONYERS, JR. hired her as an administrative assistant, a position she held until 1988.

Parks has remained a committed activist. In the 1980s she worked in support of the South African ANTIAPARTHEID MOVEMENT, and in Detroit in 1987 she founded the Rosa and Raymond Parks Institute for Self-Development, a career counseling center for black youth.

Parks has received numerous awards and tributes, including the NAACP's highest honor, the Spingarn Medal, in 1970 and the prestigious Martin Luther King, Jr. Award in 1980. Cleveland Avenue in the city of Montgomery was renamed Rosa Parks Boulevard in 1965. In 1996 U.S. president Bill Clinton awarded her the Presidential Medal of Freedom, the highest honor that the U.S. government can give to a civilian. Parks received an NAACP image award in 2000 for her appearance in the television drama series *Touched by an Angel*.

A friend once described Parks as someone who, as a rule, did not defy authority, but once determined on a course of action, refused to back down: "She might ignore you, go around you, but never retreat."

See also Civil Rights Movement; Montgomery Bus Boycott.

Marian Aguiar

Parks, Suzan-Lori

1963–

Pulitzer Prize–winning playwright and novelist.

Suzan-Lori Parks is one of a small handful of African American women, among them LORRAINE HANSBERRY and NTOZAKE SHANGE, who have achieved professional success as playwrights in American theater. She was born in Fort Knox, Kentucky, but because her father was a colonel in the U.S. Army, she lived in several states and attended junior high school in Germany. Parks began writing at an early age, with little thought to becoming a playwright. During her undergraduate studies at Mount Holyoke College in South Hadley, Massachusetts, Parks

Novelist and playwright Suzan-Lori Parks was the first African American woman to receive a Pulitzer Prize for Drama, which she won in 2003 for *Topdog/Underdog*. Jamie Painter Young/Corbis

took a creative writing class taught by African American novelist JAMES BALDWIN. She read her character-laden stories aloud in his class with a theatricality that prompted Baldwin to suggest that she try writing for the theater. In describing her creative potential, he called Parks "an utterly astounding and beautiful creature who may become one of the most valuable artists of our time."

Parks's plays include *Imperceptible Mutabilities in the Third Kingdom* (1989), *Death of the Last Black Man in the Whole Entire World* (1990), *The America Play* (1993), *Venus* (1996), and *In the Blood* (1999). In 2002 she received the Pulitzer Prize for Drama for *Topdog/Underdog*. It is the Cain and Abel story of two brothers: Lincoln, a former three-card-monte hustler who now works more honestly as an Abraham Lincoln impersonator in an amusement park, and Booth, a shoplifter who wants to improve his own economic situation by learning his brother's former hustle. The men, abandoned as children, share a squalid apartment where they dream of a better existence made unlikely by their lack of education and opportunity. Parks weaves humor and optimism into the tragic undercurrent of the story.

Although her works illuminate the hardships and often brutal history of the African American experience, Parks denies writing with a specific social agenda. Of *Topdog/Underdog*, she says, "What I love . . . is that for all the pain and sadness and desperation and bleakness, it gives two African American actors the opportunity to come together and work with a director, and embrace this play and it's a beautiful thing, even though it's a painful thing. . . . I just want to give actors, people, a place to be, the characters have a place to be. And people, folk from the community have a place to go to experience the energy of those characters."

Parks's first novel, *Getting Mother's Body,* was published in 2003. She calls it "a deep and reverent bow" to William Faulkner's masterpiece *As I Lay Dying.* Parks admits to an admiration also for the writings of Virginia Woolf and James Joyce, and like their works, hers are known for their dazzlingly playful, dense, theatrical language. One actress has said, "She does the same thing with her work that Shakespeare does with his text. You can't have a lazy tongue. You have to open your mouth, you have to articulate . . . you have to be melodic, you have to have colors and levels and intonations, and she allows you to use your entire instrument."

Parks is a Phi Beta Kappa graduate of Mount Holyoke College in 1985 and holds a degree from the Yale School of Drama, where she is currently an associate artist. In 2001 Parks was the recipient of a $500,000 MacArthur Foundation Fellowship. She teaches playwriting at the California Institute of Arts.

Shelle Sumners

Parliament (musical group)

See Clinton, George.

Parsons, Lucy

1853–1942

African American socialist and anarchist whose work as a journalist and organizer during the late nineteenth and early twentieth centuries made her a prominent figure in American radical politics.

Lucy Parsons has often been portrayed as merely an assistant to her famous anarchist husband, Albert Parsons. Although the couple worked together on many issues, Parsons was herself a leading political figure in American radical social movements. A woman whose alliances shifted over the years from SOCIALISM to anarchism and finally to communism, Parsons was distinctive as a nineteenth-century woman who called for poor people to seize power—by force if necessary.

Accounts differ as to Parsons's racial origins and the extent to which she passed. At one point, she claimed to be the daughter of a Mexican and a Creek Native American, but some historians have pointed to the possibility that she was born a slave in Texas and was partially African American. Her marriage to Albert Parsons, a former Confederate soldier turned Radical Republican, was viewed as interracial. Later in her life, many identified Parsons as black, and her son's race was registered as Negro when he was born.

Shortly after their 1871 marriage, Lucy and Albert Parsons left Waco, Texas, for CHICAGO, ILLINOIS, then a center of labor unrest and radical political movements. After Albert was blacklisted from the printing trade, Lucy supported the family as a dressmaker. The couple became heavily involved in the socialist labor movement, including the Workingmen's Party and the Social Democratic Party. Around 1879 she began writing for journals such as the *Socialist* and *Scribner's Magazine,* arguing the traditional Marxist view that the interests of labor and capital were inherently at odds. During this time, she also actively organized with the Working Women's Union for wageless working women, such as housewives.

As her political thought and work became more radical, Parsons joined the Socialist Revolutionary Club, which advocated military organization and the study of revolutionary tactics. In 1883 she helped found an early American anarchist organization, the International Working People's Association (IWPA). A year later, Parsons published her famous article "To Tramps: The Unemployed, the Disinherited, and Miserable" in the *Alarm,* a socialist journal. In her article, she addressed the 35,000 unemployed in Chicago. She saw them as victims of capitalist overproduction who "received only enough of [their] labor product to furnish [themselves] the bare, coarse necessaries of life."

It was her vision of the dispossessed as potential saboteurs and her closing admonition to "Learn the use of explosives!" that earned Parsons her reputation as "the goddess of Anarchy and would-be destroyer of all existing forms and institutions of government," to use the words of one nineteenth-century journalist. Parsons advocated "propaganda by the deed," a stance argued in her article "Dynamite! The Only Voice the Oppressors of the People Can Understand." She led demonstrations of the unemployed, sometimes with her two children, Lulu and Alfred, in tow.

Some critics have accused Parsons of subordinating issues of race to those of class, pointing to her article "The Negro: Let Him Leave Politics to the Politicians and Prayers to the Preacher," published in 1886 in response to LYNCHINGS of blacks in Carrollton, Mississippi. In this article, she claimed that African Americans were victims of injustices because, as a class, they were poor and economically dependent, but she acknowledged the divisions forced by racism and sexism that were exploited by employers to create cheap labor. Despite the fact that Parsons consistently wrote about racial injustices throughout her life, she maintained the traditional Marxist view that economics are the root of oppression. In this way, she was in her work a forerunner of many of the socialist black thinkers, such as W. E. B. DU BOIS, who would grapple with the intersecting issues of race and class in the American context.

Parsons's commitment to class struggle brought her to the front lines of the 1886 movement for the eight-hour workday. Shortly after a general strike began in Chicago, her husband was arrested after protesters threw a bomb at police during a demonstration in Haymarket Square. Albert Parsons and seven other radical organizers were accused of instigating the bombing through political writings and were sentenced to death. Lucy Parsons turned her energies to a lecture tour, where she spoke of the Haymarket incident and attempted, unsuccessfully, to get her husband's sentence commuted. After the execution of her husband, Parsons traveled widely, speaking on anarchism and the Haymarket incident. She became an icon of free speech for the radical left after being arrested in March 1887 in Columbus, Ohio, before a lecture.

In 1891 Parsons began to edit *Freedom, A Revolutionary Anarchist-Communist Monthly*. In this journal, she denounced racial violence in the South, where "women are stripped to the skin in the presence of leering white-skinned, black-hearted brutes and lashed into insensibility and strangled to death from the limbs of trees."

When the Industrial Workers of the World (IWW) was formed in 1905, Parsons was the second woman (after Mother Jones) to sign up. In 1914 and 1915 she commanded headlines in the mainstream press by leading two mass hunger demonstrations of homeless and unemployed people in SAN FRANCISCO, CALIFORNIA, and in Chicago. Parsons, by then in her sixties, was arrested for her role. She also joined the International Labor Defense (ILD) to fight for the release of "class war prisoners," such as Tom Mooney, and incarcerated African Americans, including the nine boys from Scottsboro, Alabama, accused of rape and Angelo Herndon, a black Communist who led a protest by unemployed workers in Atlanta, Georgia. Late in her life, Parsons's political orientation within the radical movement shifted again, this time toward communism. At the age of eighty-six, she joined the Communist Party.

Following her death in a fire in Chicago, police seized Parsons's books and personal papers, leaving few permanent records of her life and writings.

See also Labor Leaders; Scottsboro Case.

Bibliography
Ashbaugh, Carolyn. *Lucy Parsons: American Revolutionary*. Published for the Illinois Labor History Society by Charles H. Kerr, 1976.

Marian Aguiar

Partido Independiente de Color

Black political party organized in 1908 by Afro-Cuban activists, many of whom were veterans of the War of Independence.

Two years after it was founded, the Partido Independiente de Color was banned, accused of being divisive for CUBA, where, its critics alleged, special political organizations for Afro-Cubans were unnecessary. In 1912 members of the outlawed party organized an insurrection—the Guerrita de Mayo (Little War of May)—which was met with harsh state repression against party members and other Afro-Cubans, leaving from 2,000 to as many as 6,000 people dead.

See also Afro-Cuban Political Mobilization: An Interpretation; Afro-Cubans, Revolts, and Wars for Independence; Cuban Politics Before the Race War of 1912; Cuban War of Independence.

Pascal-Trouillot, Ertha

1943–

Haitian lawyer and temporary president.

Ertha Pascal-Trouillot, one of the first women lawyers in the Caribbean island nation of HAITI, became the first woman to serve on the country's Supreme Court. She also served as the provisional president of Haiti from March 13, 1990, to February 7, 1991.

Born in Petionville, Pascal was the ninth of ten children. Her father died while she was young, and the family had to survive on the money earned by her mother and siblings. In 1971 Pascal graduated from the École de Droit (law school) in GONAÏVES. Soon afterward she married Ernst Trouillot, a lawyer and history teacher who had tutored her. Pascal-Trouillot became an active lawyer, working on cases of labor conflict and family rights at a time when most Haitian women who had completed law school were only assistants in law firms. In January 1979 Pascal-Trouillot was the first woman to be appointed judge of a civil court. Six years later she was the first woman ever to sit on the court of appeals, and in 1988 she was named the first woman justice to sit on Haiti's Cour de Cassation (Supreme Court).

On March 12, 1990, General Prosper Avril, who had ruled Haiti since 1988, was forced from power. As the constitution required, and at the urging of a group of opposition leaders, Haiti's council of state sought a provisional, or temporary, president from the Cour de Cassation to hold office until elections could be held. After two of her senior colleagues refused, Pascal-Trouillot agreed to take the position. Her main task was to share power with the council of state and hold the general elections that Avril had promised before his departure. Pascal-Trouillot's eleven-month presidency was turbulent. In the weeks after her inauguration ten people were killed in riots, and some Haitians accused her government of corruption. At least seventy-six people were killed in an unsuccessful attempt to overthrow her government on January 6, 1991. Pascal-Trouillot stepped down from office a month later, handing over power to JEAN-BERTRAND ARISTIDE. Aristide had Pascal-Trouillot arrested on charges that she had willfully participated in the coup, which she forcefully denied.

Passing in the United States

Phenomenon of African Americans, who approach the "white" racial type in physical appearance, choosing to live and identify themselves, whether temporarily or permanently, as white.

See also Race: An Interpretation.

Pass Laws

South African legislation controlling the movements of blacks and coloureds under the system of apartheid, or racial segregation.

The earliest pass controls were developed in the eighteenth century by the whites in South Africa in order to control black labor and to keep blacks and coloureds (people of mixed racial descent) in inferior positions. A regulation of 1760 passed in the CAPE COLONY (what is now western SOUTH AFRICA) required slaves moving between town and country to carry passes signed by their owners authorizing their journeys. When the British purchased the Cape Colony from the Dutch in 1814, a system of passes already existed for coloureds and blacks. Beginning in 1809, pass laws were introduced and amended frequently across South Africa. The purpose of these laws was to control the movement of blacks and to obtain their labor in both rural and urban areas. The mining industry became a major force behind demands for pass law controls.

Beginning in 1923, pass regulations were constantly tightened and amended. Between 1939 and 1941 as many as 273,790 people were convicted of pass law offenses in the TRANSVAAL alone. Major unrest from 1944 to 1946 in opposition to the pass laws led the government to tighten them still further. By 1948, 265 urban areas had been proclaimed, which meant that black movement was rigidly controlled. In 1952, the Natives (Abolition of Passes and Coordination of Documents) Act substituted a single reference book for eleven existing pass laws. It was a crime for black men and women from the age of sixteen upward to be without their books, which gave their personal information and also their employment record. At the same time an amendment to the Natives (Urban Areas) Act applied strict regulations to all urban areas; a black person entering such an area had only seventy-two hours to find employment before being subject to arrest. Amendments to the laws in 1955, 1957, and 1964 made it increasingly difficult for blacks to qualify for permanent residence in any urban area. The aim was to control the population in such a way that only single male contract laborers could go to work in urban areas, and they could work for no more than a year before returning to the rural areas. What became known as "endorsing out" took place, which meant that Africans without work in an urban area had their passes stamped to show that they had to return to the rural areas.

Many demonstrations, acts of passive resistance, and uprisings were directed at the pass system. In 1930, for example, the Communist Party organized a mass burning of passes on Dingane's Day, a day celebrated in honor of the ZULU chief DINGANE. A major antipass campaign was mounted in 1944. In March 1960 countrywide demonstrations against the pass laws culminated in the SHARPEVILLE MASSACRE of March 21, when the police fired on a crowd of demonstrators, killing sixty-nine blacks. Between 1952 and 1986 millions of blacks were punished by the courts for failing to carry their passes, and by the early 1970s about one million blacks were arrested every year under the pass laws. The pass laws and influx control were finally abolished in 1986 when the process of dismantling the APARTHEID system began.

See also Minerals and Mining in Africa.

Pastinha, Vicente Ferreira

See Mestre Pastinha.

Pastoralism

Livelihood based on the care of domesticated livestock and widely practiced in Africa.

Africa's pastoral populations live primarily in arid and semi-arid regions. Unlike members of many agrarian societies, which combine cultivation with raising livestock, pastoralists depend critically on their animals' milk, meat, hides, and blood, as well as on the sales of yearling livestock to purchase grain and other necessities.

The breeding of domesticated livestock was practiced in combination with farming as early as 11,000 years ago in the MIDDLE EAST and shortly afterward in North Africa. Pure pastoralism (with no farming) emerged as a means of livelihood as early as 4,000 years ago in the Middle East and 3,000 years ago in North Africa. In AFRICA, the principal types of livestock are sheep and goats, dromedaries (single-hump CAMELS), horses, donkeys, and several types of bovine animals, including cattle, zebus, and yaks.

Pastoralists necessarily invest much labor and thought in caring for their herds: They protect livestock from predators, help them find pasture, assist in calving and foaling, and attend to sick animals. In turn, the animals supply milk and meat for nourishment, and their hides provide clothing, storage bags for grain and household goods, water buckets, and in some societies, material to make tents. Additionally, cow dung is used as fuel for kitchen fires. Because pastoral groups are attuned to the biological needs of their herds and faced with the challenges of coping in often marginal environments, they tend to move their herds seasonally. Pastoral division of labor, organization of daily work, economic customs, political alliances, family celebrations, and public rituals all reflect a preoccupation with herding.

The work of pastoral life is divided into herding and watering routines usually performed by men, and milking and food-processing tasks done mostly by women. In most pastoral societies even children work, tending young animals and doing household chores. In some societies, labor is further divided between social classes: A dependent or vassal class cares for most of the livestock, including the herds of a smaller warrior aristocracy, whose men take responsibility for group defense and leadership. This division of labor is seen among groups such as the TUAREG camel herders of the central SAHARA in NIGER and MALI.

A farmer tends his livestock in the Ngundu region of Tanzania. *CORBIS/Paul Almasy*

Pastoralists may be transhumants, part of a basically sedentary group that moves its flocks from summer pastures to winter pastures or from a warm valley in the winter to a cool mountainside in the summer. Other pastoralists, especially those who inhabit the Sahara and other desert areas, are nomadic, following annual migrations in search of pasture in regions where rainfall is erratic and sparse. Pastoral nomads circulate slowly in a "home-well area" during the dry months, relying on a particular well for water and on dried grasses and ACACIA trees for fodder. They then move through a transhumance zone during the wet season, when rainfall creates rich pastures in a river basin or watershed area.

Ritual and family celebrations become most important during the season of abundant pastures, when families and larger social groups congregate to take advantage of the rich vegetation in watershed areas and river valleys. There are frequent parties, musical gatherings, and initiation rituals; young people engage in courting behavior and celebrate weddings at this time. FULANI cattle herders in Niger, for example, celebrate the rainy season with *gereol* dances, in which the men apply colorful makeup to their faces and dance with movements suggestive of camels.

Livestock is also the basis for economic exchange and can be used to create and maintain family and political alliances. In wedding ceremonies of the TURKANA of KENYA, for example, camels are an important part of the bride-wealth. Traditionally, camels were ridden in warfare, and groups such as the Tuarags and Tubus of Nigeria continue to ride camels.

Saharan pastoralists such as Tuaregs, Moors, and Bedouin Arabs specialize in camel and goat herding. These animals are browsers, able to reach or climb the side of acacia trees to eat leaves when no other vegetation is available, giving them an adaptive advantage over cows and sheep in a desert climate. The pastoralists of the SAHEL, such as the Fulani, and those of East and South Africa, such as the MAASAI, Turkana, and Barabaig (to name only a few), mainly raise cattle, grazers that depend on ground-level vegetation.

Today, pure pastoralism is becoming increasingly rare as many young men—traditionally herders—migrate into cities to seek wage labor. Pastoralism also fits uneasily into the national boundaries and politics of contemporary Africa because nomadic herders are remote from government centers and difficult to tax, educate, and control. As they tend to produce only sufficient food to feed themselves, pastoralists are perceived to contribute little to national economic growth. Furthermore, the nomadic existence is generally regarded as primitive and occupies the lowest priority for development funds in many countries. Prevented by national legislation from migrating across administrative borders to distant pastures to save their herds during times of drought, pastoralists in the Sahara, the Sahel, and the Horn of Africa have suffered enormous livestock losses over the past forty years. Many pastoral groups, particularly those in desert environments or in countries undergoing ethnic conflict, suffer from food shortages and lack of adequate medical care. Some pastoral groups, including the SAHRAWI of WESTERN SAHARA, the Moors of MAURITANIA, the Tubus of CHAD and Niger, and the Fulanis and Tuaregs of Niger and Mali, have initiated separatist movements or participated in insurrections to protest unequal treatment by national governments.

See also Animals in Africa; Dance in Sub-Saharan Africa; Rites of Passage and Transition.

Bibliography

Barfield, Thomas J. *The Nomadic Alternative*. Prentice Hall, 1993.

Konczacki, Z. A. *The Economics of Pastoralism: A Case-Study of Sub-Saharan Africa*. F. Cass, 1978.

Barbara Worley

Patassé, Ange-Félix

1937?–

Former president of the Central African Republic.

Ange-Félix Patassé was born in Paoua, in the northwestern CENTRAL AFRICAN REPUBLIC, and studied at the Higher School of Tropical Agriculture in suburban Paris, France. He worked for the Central African Republic's department of agriculture from 1959 to 1965 and held many agriculture and development ministerial positions for the next ten years. President JEAN-BÉDEL BOKASSA appointed him prime minister in September 1976, but two months later, Bokassa dissolved the government and declared himself emperor. Patassé was incarcerated briefly in 1979 before Bokassa was overthrown by DAVID DACKO in a coup d'état backed by the French government. As leader of the opposition, Patassé narrowly lost the 1981 presidential election to Dacko. After Dacko was overthrown later that year by André Kolingba, Patassé was accused of leading an unsuccessful coup in March 1982, and he fled to TOGO. Exiled for ten years, Patassé returned to the Central African Republic when Kolingba was forced to hold multiparty elections in 1992. The Supreme Court ruled the 1992 elections invalid, and the elections were rescheduled for September 1993. Patassé defeated both Kolingba and Dacko in the presidential elections, which were fraught with problems but certified by a delegation of international observers.

Patassé spent most of 1994 trying to reestablish the Central African Republic's close ties with France, which had been weakened during Bokassa's erratic presidency. However, relations further deteriorated after a banking scandal in which a French associate of Patassé was arrested and charged with involvement in the disappearance of 75 million francs in African loan guarantees. Although Patassé met with French president François Mitterrand in 1994, Patassé's diplomatic efforts were undermined by a string of mutinies and civil servant strikes in the Central African Republic from late 1995 until early in 1997. The groups claimed that Patassé had not kept his campaign promise to pay them current wages and owed back wages. These strikes culminated on April 19, 1996, when a group of renegade soldiers from the Central African Republic Army, led by Sergeant Cyriaque Souke, rebelled against Patassé and demanded that he resign from the presidency. About 400 people took part in the first attack, freeing prisoners and looting the capital city of BANGUI. French troops intervened on behalf of Patassé and finally quelled the mutinies. After the mutiny was over, Patassé signed an accord pledging to bring more opposition members into his government. This mutiny, however, was just the first in a series that continued throughout 1996 and into early 1997. In each instance the French Army had to intervene to stop the rebel troops. By the middle of 1997, Patassé had lost public confidence, and state officials threatened to overthrow him and hold new elections. Nevertheless, Patassé was reelected in the 1999 presidential election despite claims from the opposition that voting was rigged. He was deposed in a coup in March 2003.

Elizabeth Heath

Pate Island

Island in Kenya's Lamu archipelago, once the home of one of the most prominent towns on the Swahili Coast.

Pate is the name of both a town and an island. Along with the neighboring Swahili island towns of Faza, Siyu, and Shanga, it once played an important role in Indian Ocean trade, exporting ivory, gold, slaves, and mangrove poles, and importing such luxury items as cloth, beads, and firearms. Pate's early history remains sketchy because the primary written account of Pate's ruling dynasty, *The Pate Chronicle,* is considered inaccurate in places. But scholars have pieced together a rough outline of Pate's history from *The Pate Chronicle,* other written sources, and the archaeological records.

Scholars believe that Pate Town was founded approximately 1300 C.E., after Shanga had already emerged as a power among the Swahili city-states. Pate Town eventually eclipsed Shanga, and by 1500 its trade wealth roughly equaled that of LAMU. Prosperity on the Swahili Coast, however, did not mean political supremacy. Large parts of the coastline were controlled by foreign powers, beginning with the Portuguese in 1498.

Pate's history under foreign occupation was one of repeated rebellion and rapidly shifting political alliances. When the Portuguese established a customs house on Pate Island and imposed a tax on trade, the residents rebelled, first briefly in 1637, and then again in 1660, 1678, 1680, and 1687. Each uprising proved more difficult for the weakening Portuguese to quell. Combined forces from Pate and Oman finally drove the Portuguese off the East African coast in 1698, after a three-year siege of their stronghold on MOMBASA, Fort Jesus.

Another influential power in Pate's history was the Mazrui clan. Although they claimed that their ancestors came from Oman, the Mazrui did not recognize the imam of Oman's claims to the coast. They claimed Mombasa in the late seventeenth century, and for the next hundred years controlled much of the coast, including Pate. Mazrui hegemony lasted until approximately 1810, when forces from Lamu defeated forces from the now-allied Pate and Mombasa. The Mazrui were replaced by the Imam of Oman, SAYYID SA'ID IBN SULTAN, a feat made easier as factions in Pate disputed dynastic succession. Sa'id soon revived the Indian Ocean trade along the coast, which had long been in decline. The sultan's son Majid ibn Sa'id captured Pate in the mid-nineteenth century. The British declared the East African coast a protectorate in 1895 and Pate was eventually made part of colonial KENYA.

Modern Pate has received none of the migrations of upcountry Kenyans that have swelled the larger cities of the Swahili Coast, such as Malindi and Mombasa, nor much of the tourism that has transformed Lamu. Traditional Swahili architecture—coral houses with Arab influences—still predominates in Pate Town. Mangrove swamps ring the island, and almost completely surround the towns of Faza and Siyu. Many coconut plantations exist, although tobacco is the island's principal export crop. Since 2002 United States leaders have taken an increasing interest in Pate Island, which they believe was home to several leading terrorists. The U.S. military has spent nearly $500,000 on projects to improve economic and medical conditions on the island, and to increase its surveillance of the area.

See also Gold Trade; Indian Ocean Slave Trade; Islam in Africa; Ivory Trade; Swahili Coast; Swahili People.

Bibliography

Middleton, John. *The World of the Swahili: An African Mercantile Civilization.* Yale University Press, 1992.

Tolmacheva, Marina. *The Pate Chronicle.* Edited and translated from MSS 177, 321, 344, and 358 of the Library of the University of Dar es Salaam. Michigan State University Press, 1993.

Robert Fay

Paton, Alan Stewart

1903–1988

South African writer and founder of the Liberal Party, best known for his novel *Cry, the Beloved Country*, which explored the human cost of racial division.

A white South African of British descent, Alan Stewart Paton wrote what is considered one of the great African novels in English. His mother was a teacher and his father was a civil servant, and after growing up in Pietermaritzburg he attended the University of Natal. Paton taught school for a decade, then switched careers in 1935 to head JOHANNESBURG's Diepkloof Reformatory, home to 650 black youths who had been labeled "delinquent" by the authorities. As principal he liberalized the reformatory's regulations, giving inmates greater freedom and respect. His interest in social work stemmed in part from his conversion to the Anglican faith and his growing interest in racial justice. When his first novel, *Cry, the Beloved Country*, was published in 1948, the reviews hailed it as "beautiful and profoundly moving . . . steeped in sadness and grief but radiant with hope and compassion."

The book's protagonist is Stephen Kumalo, a ZULU priest who travels to Johannesburg from the countryside in search of his sister and his son. When he arrives, he discovers that his sister has been forced into prostitution and his son has fled after being involved in the murder of a white man. In the book's most famous passage, Paton warns of the specter of large-scale racial violence: "Cry, the beloved country, for the unborn child that is the inheritor of our fear." Not a simple political allegory, Paton's novel contains layers of social and spiritual complexity and ends with the hope of reconciliation between black and white South Africans.

By the end of the twentieth century, *Cry, the Beloved Country* had been translated into twenty languages and had sold more than fifteen million copies. It was adapted into a 1949 play, *Lost in the Stars* (with songs by the composer Kurt Weill), and filmed in 1951 and with JAMES EARL JONES as Kumalo in 1995. In 2003 television talk-show host OPRAH WINFREY selected *Cry, the Beloved Country* for her book club, returning the novel to the best-seller lists.

Paton, who eventually left his job to write full time, also became a political activist. In 1953 he helped found the Liberal Party, of which he was the first president. The party, which advocated universal voting rights and nonviolence, was banned in 1968 when the South African government prohibited all multiracial parties. For most of the 1960s Paton was forbidden to leave the country, but he continued to write, producing a second novel, seven works of nonfiction, and a play. None, however, is as well known as *Cry, the Beloved Country*, which he said was written "to influence my fellow whites." Toward the end of his life, Paton faced significant criticism for opposing economic sanctions against SOUTH AFRICA's APARTHEID regime, which he believed would harm poor blacks.

See also Fiction, English-Language, in Africa.

Bibliography

Alexander, Peter F. *Alan Paton: a Biography.* Oxford University Press, 1994.

Kate Tuttle

Patrocínio, José Carlos do

1853–1905

One of Brazil's most influential abolitionists and journalists of African descent.

The son of a white Catholic priest and a free black fruit vendor, José Carlos do Patrocínio grew up on his father's plantation in Campos, RIO DE JANEIRO, BRAZIL, where he was exposed to the brutalities of slavery. In 1868 he left home to begin an apprenticeship at Misericórdia Hospital in Rio de Janeiro. With the financial assistance of his father and a beneficent society, he went on to complete the pharmacy course. Unable to secure work as a pharmacist, he accepted an offer to live with and tutor the children of a wealthy realtor, whose daughter he later married.

Patrocínio first established himself as an opponent of slavery through the press. In 1877 he joined the staff of the *Gazeta de Notícias,* Rio's daily newspaper. His editorials and poetry won him recognition as a leading abolitionist. In 1881, with the financial support of his father-in-law, Patrocínio bought and took over the *Gazeta de Tarde,* turning it into BRAZIL's most influential abolitionist newspaper. In 1887 he established the equally authoritative abolitionist journal *A Cidade do Rio.* In his lifetime, he published hundreds of articles opposing slavery.

Patrocínio helped coordinate and unite Brazil's abolition movement. In the early 1880s, he became the main figure behind the Associação Central Emancipadora (Central Emancipation Association) and helped compose the manifesto of the Confederação Abolicionista (Abolitionist Confederation). Patrocínio promoted local abolition movements in Ceará, Santos, and his hometown of Campos, and traveled to EUROPE to gather support for the abolitionist movement.

Patrocínio was an inspirational orator, earning the epithet "The Tiger of Abolitionism." In the words of abolitionist Carolina Nabuco, Patrocínio "did not deliver his speeches. He acted them out with extraordinary power . . . they possessed a communicative ardor and a vibrant spontaneity." Patrocínio customarily addressed free black and mulatto (of African and European descent) audiences with fiery rhetoric, hoping to rouse them to participate in the abolition movement. His speeches were sometimes interrupted by whites shouting racial slurs; on one such occasion, he retorted: "God gave me the color of Othello so that I would be the envy of my country."

Patrocínio was instrumental in persuading Princess Isabela, who was acting as regent, to sign the Lei Áurea (Golden Law), which on May 13, 1888, freed all of Brazil's slaves. After abolition, Patrocínio sought to defend the princess from a growing Republican movement and facilitate her ascension to the throne by forming a black militant association called Guarda Negra (Black Guard). But a military revolt in 1889 established the Republic of Brazil, leading to Patrocínio's exile to Amazonas and the suspension of his newspaper. He eventually resumed his journalistic activities, and continued writing until his death in 1905.

See also Anti-Slavery Movement in Latin America; Brazil, Blacks and Politics in: An Interpretation; Slavery in Latin America and the Caribbean.

Bibliography

Magalhães, R., Jr. *A Vida Turbulenta de José do Patrocínio*. Livros Irradiantes, 1972.

Toplin, Robert Brent. *The Abolition of Slavery in Brazil*. Atheneum, 1972.

Aaron Myers

Patronato

System of apprenticeship that required freed slaves to continue working for their masters for a determined period of time; the system was often instituted in Latin America and the Caribbean to circumvent laws that freed slaves.

See also Role of Slaves in Abolition and Emancipation in Latin America and the Caribbean.

Patterson, Floyd

1935–

American professional boxer, an Olympic gold medalist and the first to lose and then regain the heavyweight championship title.

Born in Waco, North Carolina, Floyd Patterson moved with his family to Brooklyn, New York, as a young boy. He experienced a difficult childhood, and was sent to the Wiltwyck School, where he learned BOXING. When he returned to New York City, he entered Golden Gloves competitions, winning national titles in 1951 and 1952 as a middleweight. At the 1952 Summer Olympic Games in Helsinki, Finland, he won all of his fights and the gold medal. After the games, he turned professional.

In his first thirty-six professional fights Patterson lost only once, and in 1956 he beat Archie Moore for the heavyweight title. Patterson became the youngest heavyweight champion and the first Olympic gold medalist to hold the title. He made four successful title defenses before losing to Sweden's Ingemar Johansson in 1959. Johansson knocked Patterson down seven times before the fight was stopped. A year later Patterson knocked out Johansson in the fifth round and became the first boxer to regain the heavyweight title. Patterson defended his title successfully until losing to SONNY LISTON in 1962. Patterson continued to fight but never won another title. In his last fight, in 1972, he was knocked out by Muhammad Ali. Patterson was appointed to the New York State Athletic Commission in 1995, where he served as chairman. He resigned from this post in 1998 because of problems with memory loss.

Jalane Schmidt

Patterson, Percival James

1935–

Jamaican political leader.

Percival James Patterson was the first black prime minister in the Caribbean island nation of JAMAICA. After serving as deputy prime minister and finance minister, Patterson replaced prime minister MICHAEL MANLEY when Manley resigned in 1992. As head of the People's National Party (PNP), Patterson remained prime minister when that party held a majority of seats in the nation's House of Representatives in 1993. Since that time the PNP has retained a majority of House seats. As the leader of the controlling party, Patterson has remained the nation's prime minister.

Patterson, William

1891–1980

American attorney, civil rights activist and Communist Party leader who publicly charged the United States with genocide against African Americans.

Born and raised in the SAN FRANCISCO area, William L. Patterson attended local public schools and later abandoned studies in engineering at the University of California at Berkeley to pursue a J.D. at the Hastings College of Law in San Francisco. At Hastings Patterson began a lifelong involvement in political issues, protesting racism and arguing against African American participation in the "white man's" World War I. Earning his law degree in 1919, Patterson moved to NEW YORK CITY and established a legal practice in HARLEM with two colleagues. His years in New York coincided with the height of the HARLEM RENAISSANCE, and Patterson developed relationships with PAUL

Robeson, W. E. B. Du Bois, and other prominent African American activists. He began to work increasingly with left-wing causes, and was active in the ultimately fruitless campaign to free Nicola Sacco and Bartolomeo Vanzetti, immigrant Italian anarchists who were convicted of murder and executed in 1927.

Convinced that African American oppression was caused by capitalism and economic exploitation, Patterson devoted himself to anticapitalist activities, joining the Communist Party, U.S.A., in 1927 (one of the few African Americans to do so) and studying for three years at the University of the Toiling People of the Far East in Moscow. After returning from the Soviet Union in 1930, Patterson continued his leftist political activities: in 1932 he was elected to the Central Committee of the Communist Party and was the Communist candidate in the New York City mayoral election. Putting his electoral ambitions on hold after failing to win public office, from 1932 to 1946 Patterson focused on legal work as executive director of the Communist-influenced International Labor Defense, helping to plan the legal strategy for the Scottsboro Case defendants.

After moving to Chicago in 1938, Patterson became a community organizer on Chicago's South Side and a writer and editor for Communist newspapers such as the *Daily Record* and the *Daily Worker*. He also worked to safeguard the rights of African Americans and radical activists as the executive director of the Civil Rights Congress, a post he held from 1946 to 1956.

In 1951, Patterson edited *We Charge Genocide: The Crime of Government Against the Negro People,* and joined Paul Robeson in submitting a petition to the United Nations that accused the United States of genocide against African Americans. A year earlier, the U.S. Congress's House Committee on Un-American Activities (HUAC) had demanded that Patterson testify about his Communist associations, and in 1954, he was found in contempt for his refusal to answer HUAC's questions. After three months in prison, he was released upon successful appeal of the contempt citation.

Patterson published his autobiography, *The Man Who Cried Genocide,* in 1971. Though Patterson's political activities had raised the ire of the U.S. government, they earned him the praise of many Communist countries: in 1978, he was awarded the Paul Robeson Memorial Medal by East Germany's Academy of Arts.

Jalane Schmidt

Patton, Charley

1887–1934

American blues guitarist and vocalist, and a key figure in the development of the Mississippi Delta blues style.

Charley Patton was born in Edwards, Mississippi. Although he possessed a strong, deep voice, he was of small stature and too frail to perform the difficult labor on the farms of the Mississippi Delta region, where he lived his entire life. Instead, Patton—whose inability to read, rough personality, and womanizing epitomized the bluesman—learned to play the guitar and compose his own songs. By his early teenage years, he began playing local gigs, performing in Jackson and Yazoo City at parties, work camps, jook joints, and picnics.

After his family's 1912 move to Will Dockery's Plantation near Cleveland, Mississippi, Patton began performing with Willie Brown, Dick Bangston, and Tommy Johnson. He is considered a creator of the Delta blues, the most primitive blues genre, which is characterized by uneven rhyming, spoken—as opposed to sung—lyrics, including shouts, gutteral groans, and haunting moans, and a bottleneck guitar technique in which melodic phrases are often blurred and repeated. Patton's lyrics often recounted the events of his life and those of his friends. His innovative playing style included thumping, and at times talking to his guitar, which created a musical tension and dynamism often imitated by later blues musicians.

Patton made many recordings between 1929 and 1934, including ragtime, folk songs, white rural music, adaptations of popular tunes, religious songs, and of course, blues. Through these recordings, he became one of the first Delta blues performers to emerge from anonymity and achieve broader musical influence.

See also Music, African American.

Jalane Schmidt

Paul, Nathaniel

?–1839

African American abolitionist and minister.

Nathaniel Paul was born in New Hampshire, probably in Exeter, Rockingham County, to unidentified parents. His brother, Thomas Paul, became a minister and community leader in Boston, Massachusetts. The Free Will Baptist Church educated both black and white youths, and Paul may have been a student with his brother at its academy in Hollis, New Hampshire. In 1820 Nathaniel Paul became pastor of the First African Baptist Church in Albany, New York. Influenced by evangelicals and reformers, northern New York was a hotbed of abolitionist activity, with both blacks and whites participating. New York had extirpated slavery gradually—first, in 1799, legislating that all blacks born to slave mothers on or after July 4, 1799 would be indentured servants and then, in 1817, declaring that all slaves born before July 4, 1799 would be freed on July 4, 1827.

In an address of 1827 Paul criticized the slave trade and slavery, celebrated the 1817 law, and named all ninety-five elected New York State officials who had voted for the emancipation act. Like many African Americans in the 1820s, he supported the resettlement of free blacks when it seemed likely to foster social and economic progress, but he opposed the American Colonization Society (ACS), which promoted the expatriation of manumitted slaves to Liberia—an action that most abolitionists believed fortified American slavery. In 1824 Thomas Paul visited Haiti, which was then being touted as a place African Americans might relocate, but he returned to Boston. In 1830 Nathaniel Paul, with his brother Benjamin, resettled in a free black community, Wilberforce, being constructed in Lucan, Ontario, Canada. In 1832 he began a speaking tour of England, Ireland, and Scotland, seeking funds for a manual labor academy at Wilberforce and countering propaganda spread by Elliott Cresson, an ACS agent. Cresson was exaggerating the antislavery thrust of the ACS as he sought to gain support for colonization in British abolitionist and political circles.

Paul cooperated with the noted abolitionist William Lloyd Garrison, another opponent of the ACS, in touring Britain, but a rift between the two men occurred when Paul provided funds for Garrison's journey home to the United States. Paul considered the money a personal loan, while Garrison insisted that it was an expense of their joint abolitionist activities. Paul remained in Britain until 1836, marrying an Englishwoman in 1833 and meeting the most prominent figures in British abolitionism. On returning to Wilberforce, at the request of its leader, Austin Steward, Paul revealed that although he had collected more than $8,000 in British donations, he had nothing to remit, since his expenses of $7,000 and his $50 monthly salary totaled over $9,000. In 1836 Paul returned to Albany, where he became pastor of the Hamilton Street Baptist Church. Poverty marked the last three years of his life.

Several addresses and letters written by Paul survive. His *Address, Delivered on the Celebration of the Abolition of Slavery, in the State of New-York* (1827) noted the oppression and the pernicious influence on society of slaveholding. Paul denounced the persistence of slavery in a republican nation that had been forged in revolution. He praised the American revolutionaries, arguing that slavery was a legacy of colonialism that had improperly survived in the new nation. Addresses, letters, and reports recounting his experience in Britain suggest that he was a gifted author and dynamic orator who effectively countered ACS propaganda as well as soliciting donations for what seemed to be the benefit of African Americans. He proved to be a popular lecturer, and he claimed to prefer English to American life. In this he was not alone, for Henry Nell, the African Canadian sent from Wilberforce by Steward to demand Paul's return, did not himself leave England after accomplishing his errand. Moreover, Paul was in England during parliamentary discussion of West Indian emancipation and the enactment of the Emancipation Act of 1833; his letters to American abolitionists provided information about these momentous events.

Although he was a celebrated figure in the transatlantic abolitionist movement, Paul was also a citizen of Wilberforce and should be viewed in its context. In 1829 black residents of Cincinnati, Ohio, began plans for a mass exodus to Canada. Discriminatory state laws and antiblack riots in 1829 had made many of them pessimistic about their future in the United States. Ohio and Indiana Quakers donated funds for the purchase of land, and the first settlers arrived in Wilberforce in October 1829, followed by members of the Paul family in 1830. Although the settlement was praised at a distance by leading abolitionists, it probably never held more than two hundred inhabitants (one thousand blacks left Cincinnati in 1829–1830, but many settled instead in nearby towns), and it seemed a failure to most sympathetic people who visited it.

Expectations of settlers and abolitionists alike were high, but Wilberforce itself faltered. Schools were open only irregularly. Emigrants from the city of Cincinnati proved unable to farm productively. The officials of the settlement continually bickered over allegations of misuse of funds, questions of representation of the settlers for the purpose of fund-raising, and accusations of moral improprieties. By the 1850s Wilberforce was home to only about fifty people. The lack of a monetary return from Paul's tour and his retreat to Albany in 1836 were symptomatic of the larger problems of resettling people who had been harassed from their homes and of securing competent leadership for a community attempting to reconstitute itself as it fled from racism, inequality, and violence. Paul was a gifted man who fought racism and slavery but who was unable to square his self-interest and the needs of the black community that employed him.

Transcriptions of Nathaniel Paul's speeches and his letters from Britain, in which he relayed information about his speaking tour, appeared in the *Liberator* (1831–1865), William Lloyd Garrison's abolitionist newspaper, published in Boston. His speeches and letters have been reprinted in *The Black Abolitionist Papers, Volume 1: The British Isles, 1830–1865*, ed. C. Peter Ripley et al. (1985): 42–59.

Bibliography

Mitchell, J. Marcus. "The Paul Family" in *Old-Time New England* (1973): 73–77.

Pease, William H., and Jane H. Pease. *Black Utopia: Negro Communal Experiments in America* (1963): 46–62.

Taylor, Nikki. "Reconsidering the 'Forced' Exodus of 1829: Free Black Emigration from Cincinnati, Ohio, to Wilberforce, Canada," in *The Journal of African American History* 87 (Summer 2002): 283–302.

John Saillant

Payne, Christopher H(arrison)

1848–1925

Clergyman, editor, and government official who helped obtain passage of state legislation for the West Virginia Colored Institute.

Christopher Harrison Payne was born of free parents near Red Sulphur Springs, Monroe County, Virginia (now West Virginia). His mother was the slave daughter of James Ellison, who instructed her and set her free. When Christopher was two years old, his father, Thomas Payne, a cattle drover, was stricken with smallpox, and he died while taking a herd over the mountains to market. Payne's mother taught him to read so early that he could not remember when he had not read. By the age of ten, Payne had read through the New Testament.

During the AMERICAN CIVIL WAR (1861–1865) Payne was compelled to serve in the Confederate Army as a valet, but in 1864 he returned to Monroe County to work on a farm. In 1866 Payne married Delilah Ann Hargrove (also given as Hargo), by whom he had six children. He worked on an Ohio River steamboat, settled in Charleston, West Virginia, and went to school at night, beginning an intensive career of work and study that made him the leading African American figure in the state. By 1868 he had gained his teaching certificate and had gone to teach school in the mountains, farming during the summer months. In 1875 he was converted, and the next year he was licensed to preach. In 1877 he was ordained for full work in the ministry and entered the senior class of the Preparatory Department of Richmond Institute (later Virginia Union University) in Virginia. Payne preached in West Virginia from 1878 to 1880, returned to RICHMOND, pastored the Moore Street Baptist Church, and studied at Richmond Institute for three years while working to support his wife, children, and mother. He graduated in 1883 from the academy and the Theological Department of Richmond Institute.

A man of dignity, Payne impressed those he met with his earnestness and competence. He was appointed by the American Baptist Publications Society as a Sunday school missionary and traveled for it from Norfolk, Virginia, where for a while he held a pastorate, through West Virginia. He later estimated that as a minister he had delivered some 1,500 sermons, converted 500 people, and founded nine churches and two Sunday schools while aiding dozens of others. Ill health forced him to give up evangelizing in 1884 and to assume duties as pastor of the First Baptist Church of Coal Valley, West Virginia, but he had established a reputation impressive to white and African American leaders alike. It enabled him to wield influence throughout the area.

Payne edited several weekly newspapers intended to strengthen the African American community and to neutralize prejudice among its foes. The *West Virginia Enterprise,* the *Pioneer,* and *Mountain Eagle* reflected his clear, forceful writing and speech; in addition he provided correspondence for the *Virginia Star* and the *Richmond Planet.* Payne emphasized education for his people: One of his projects was for a school with an industrial department.

Payne entered vigorously into politics. In 1884 he was an alternate delegate to the Republican National Convention. Four years later he represented the Third Congressional District of West Virginia at the convention that nominated Benjamin Harrison for president. Leaders of his state credited Payne's influence among the African American voters with their having won their state campaign, and they endorsed him for minister to LIBERIA in 1889. That year, however, he was appointed deputy collector of internal revenue at Charleston. In 1891 his efforts for improved educational opportunities for youth helped obtain passage of state legislation for a land-grant college, West Virginia Colored Institute (later West Virginia State College) at Farm, thirteen kilometers (eight miles) northwest of Charleston.

Payne had turned to the study of law and in 1896 was admitted to practice in West Virginia. That year he was the first African American to become a member of the state legislature. In 1903 he was appointed U.S. consul to Saint Thomas, Danish West Indies (now the U.S. VIRGIN ISLANDS). When the United States purchased these islands in 1917, Payne's services as consul ended. After the death of his first wife, he remarried and stayed on with his second wife, A. G. Viney of Gallipolis, Ohio, practicing law and acting as prosecuting attorney and police judge until his death in Saint Thomas on December 5, 1925.

Payne was not a spectacular figure, and he did not attain national prominence, but his career was significant in West Virginia. Garland Penn saw him as "unquestionably, the most representative [N]egro in the state of West Virginia, both in religion and politics" (*The Afro-American Press and Its Editors,* 1891, p. 565). Information about Payne's early life is based primarily on the sketch, probably autobiographical, in William J. Simmons's *Men of Mark; Eminent, Progressive and Rising* (1887, pp. 368–73). He was listed in *Who's Who in America* (1916–1917). There are a few additional details in the article by Harrison G. Villard in *Dictionary of American Biography* ([1934] 1962, 7, Part 2:324–25). The dates for his graduation from Richmond Institute are in the *General Catalog* (pp. 20, 21). The obituary, probably written by Carter G. Woodson, in the *Journal of Negro History* (January 1926, pp. 225–27) described him as "this useful man."

From *Dictionary of American Negro Biography* by Rayford W. Logan and Michael R. Winston, editors. Copyright © 1982 by Rayford W. Logan and Michael R. Winston. Reprinted by permission of W. W. Norton & Company, Inc.

See also Clergy in Politics; Saint Thomas and Prince Islands.

Louis Filler

Payne, Daniel Alexander

1811–1893

African American bishop in the African Methodist Episcopal Church who helped establish Wilberforce University for the education of blacks.

Daniel Alexander Payne was born in CHARLESTON, SOUTH CAROLINA, to London Payne, who was of mixed British and African descent, and Martha Payne, who was of mixed Native American and African descent. Both were free blacks, and they placed great importance on Payne's early education. They died before he was ten years old, leaving him to the care of relatives. He continued his education at a school for free blacks in Charleston and thereafter on his own while apprenticed to artisans in several different fields. He later received private tutoring in Greek and Latin.

At the age of seventeen, Payne opened his own school in Charleston with a handful of students. The school grew quickly, and in addition to the daytime curriculum, he taught slaves at night. But in 1834 South Carolina outlawed the education of African Americans and Payne was forced to close the school. The next year he moved to the North, pursuing his own studies at the Lutheran Seminary in Gettysburg, Pennsylvania. His eyesight worsened during his studies and in 1837 his disability forced him to leave the school.

Payne nonetheless received a license to preach, and in 1839 the Franckean Synod of the Lutheran Church ordained him its first African American minister. After a short tenure at a Presbyterian church in New York, Payne established a school in PHILADELPHIA, PENNSYLVANIA in 1840. Denied a Lutheran parish, he joined the AFRICAN METHODIST EPISCOPAL CHURCH (AME) in 1841. At first Payne was reluctant to join the church, wary of the AME's known opposition to educated clergy and its reliance on emotional worship services. Once inside the church, however, Payne worked to institutionalize his formal style and to advance the cause of an educated ministry. Supporters said Payne raised the standards of the AME Church; critics claimed he denigrated African and folk traditions to imitate white respectability.

Payne was soon appointed to the AME's traveling ministry, a role that took him across the Northeast to found schools and build churches. In 1845 he moved to BALTIMORE, MARYLAND where he ministered at the Bethel Church. After coming into conflict with Baltimore blacks over his liturgical style of worship, Payne sought permission from the AME to write a history of the church, which he hoped would create interest in educated, standardized methods of preaching. The writing of the *History of the African Methodist Episcopal Church* (1891) took more than four decades and proved a valuable resource for later historians.

In 1852 Payne was elected a bishop of the church. His travels now extended throughout the country, for the organization of congregations, the creation of schools, and the promotion of informal education among those—such as women and slaves—who could not attend schools. On several occasions his presence in the South drew threats.

In 1863 Payne secured funds to buy WILBERFORCE UNIVERSITY, a school in Xenia, Ohio, that was then owned by the METHODIST EPISCOPAL CHURCH. Payne turned the school over to the AME and became the first black president of the first black-controlled college in the United States. The work to get the struggling college on its feet was formidable. He raised funds to make the college solvent and then more funds to rebuild after a devastating fire in 1865. He also attracted high-caliber teachers and students through his emphasis on discipline and morality. By the early post–Civil War (1861–1865) era, Wilberforce was on solid financial and academic ground. While president, he continued his AME duties, traveling as far as EUROPE. In 1876, however, he resigned from the presidency but remained active in the school as chancellor.

In the last years of his life, Payne devoted increasing amounts of time to his writings. In 1885 he published *Treatise on Domestic Education*, in which he summarized his experiences in schooling. He followed in 1888 with a widely read autobiography, *Recollections of Seventy Years*.

See also Free Blacks in the United States.

Payne, Donald

1934–

Democratic member of the United States House of Representatives from New Jersey, the first black member of Congress from New Jersey.

Donald Payne was born in NEWARK, NEW JERSEY, and received a bachelor's degree from Seton Hall University in 1957. He was a community affairs executive at the Prudential Insurance Company, and he served as national president of the Young Men's Christian Association (YMCA) in 1970. From 1972 to 1978, Payne was a member of the Essex County Board of Freeholders. He became vice president of Urban Data Systems Incorporated in 1975, and served on the Newark Municipal Council from 1982 to 1988.

Payne made two unsuccessful bids for Congress against incumbent Democrat Peter Rodino in 1980 and 1986. When Rodino retired in 1988, Payne easily won the seat representing New Jersey's Tenth Congressional District. A member of the CONGRESSIONAL BLACK CAUCUS, he was reelected to an eighth term in 2002. In 2003 he was appointed a Congressional delegate to the United Nations.

See also Democratic Party.

P'Bitek, Okot

1931–1982

Ugandan poet, novelist, and social anthropologist, who dedicated his life to preserving his country's traditional literature and culture; he wrote in both English and Acholi and is generally regarded as the finest East African poet of the twentieth century.

Born in Gulu, in northern UGANDA, Okot p'Bitek received his early education locally and went on to the prestigious King's College Budo in Uganda. At age twenty-two he wrote his first book, *Lak tar miyo kinyero wi lobo* (1953; translated as *White Teeth*, 1989). This ACHOLI-language novel reflected his strong interests in music, song, literature, and traditional culture—concerns that surfaced in all his subsequent writing.

In the mid-1950s p'Bitek went to GREAT BRITAIN as a member of Uganda's national SOCCER team and stayed on to continue his education. He attended Bristol University, where he earned a diploma in education, and then the University of Oxford, where he earned a B.Litt. (bachelor of letters) degree in social anthropology. Returning to Uganda, he taught at Makerere University in the mid-1960s, then in the late 1960s at the University of Nairobi in KENYA, and again at Makerere University in the late 1970s. He later served as visiting professor or writer in residence at other universities in AFRICA and the United States.

P'Bitek produced his most important works in the mid and late 1960s, beginning with *Song of Lawino, A Lament* (1966;

published in the original Acholi as *Wer pa Lawino,* 1969), the finest of his narrative poems. Drawing on the form and content of traditional Acholi songs of abuse and praise, the poem is a song sung by an illiterate wife who complains about her relationship with her educated husband. Her persistent questioning of why she is abused simply for being African results in a sharp satire of Africans' superficial acceptance of European culture. The husband then states his case in *Song of Ocul* (1970), but his own words condemn him.

P'Bitek also published several books that directly reflect his Acholi background. They include the poetry volume *The Horn of My Love* (1974), the folktale collection *Hare and the Hornbill* (1978), and such nonfiction works as *Religion of the Central Luo* (1971) and *Africa's Cultural Revolution* (1973). The emphasis in all his work, both scholarly and creative, is on the idea that literature is a living social art that must be understood within the context of the culture in which it is produced and enjoyed.

See also Languages, African: An Overview; Poetry, African.

Peake, George

1722–1827

African American soldier, pioneer, and inventor of an agricultural hand mill.

George Peake, whose name was variably spelled Peek and Peak, was a native of Maryland. After living in Pennsylvania, he became the first permanent black settler in Cleveland, Ohio. He was a British soldier in the French and Indian War (1752–1763) and served at the battle of Québec under General James Wolfe. He was later reported to be a deserter from the British army with money entrusted to him to pay the soldiers.

Peake's residence in Cleveland dates from 1809 when he arrived with his family. He bought a forty-hectare (100-acre) farm on the western outskirts of the city. Along with his four sons, he was remembered for giving to the community a highly prized, labor-saving device: a new type of hand mill that he invented. Prior to this mill, grain was processed with a rather crude instrument called a stump mortar and spring pestle, which the pioneer settlers adapted from NATIVE AMERICANS. Peake's mill was also superior to the Native American device because it produced a better quality of ground meal by the use of stones forty-five to fifty centimeters (eighteen to twenty inches) in diameter.

Peake's wife was evidently a woman of some means, for she was reputed to have possession of a half bushel of silver dollars, a mark of distinction when the commercial medium was barter and trade. Peake's ability to purchase a forty-hectare tract of land was evidence that he compared favorably with other pioneers.

Peake died in September 1827 at the patriarchal age of 105; the place of his interment is unknown.

The major source is Russell H. Davis's *Black Americans in Cleveland* (1972). Gertrude V. R. Wickham's *Memorial to Pioneer Women of the Western Reserve* (1896) is the principal source for information about Peake's wife. Earlier sources are John D. Taylor's *History of Rockport, Ohio* (1858) and the *Cleveland Leader* (November 8, 1858). No patent for his hand mill was recorded (Davis to Rayford W. Logan, October 10, 1974).

From *Dictionary of American Negro Biography* by Rayford W. Logan and Michael R. Winston, editors. Copyright © 1982 by Rayford W. Logan and Michael R. Winston. Reprinted by permission of W. W. Norton & Company, Inc.

See also Inventors, African American.

Russell H. Davis

Peake, Mary S(mith)

1823–1862

African American pioneer schoolteacher who was the first teacher in the first school sponsored by the American Missionary Association.

Born free in Norfolk County, Virginia, Mary Smith Peake lived for several years with her aunt in Alexandria, where she acquired a good education. After the District of Columbia returned Alexandria to Virginia in 1846, Alexandria's schools were closed to blacks; Peake moved to Norfolk with her mother. A period of religious mysticism, stemming perhaps from her vision of service to the poor, led her to participate actively in aiding the poor, assisted by the First Baptist Church of Norfolk. After her mother married Thompson Walker, the family moved to Hampton. There, Peake founded the Daughters of Zion to look after the ill and the needy, as well as to teach children and adults in her home. In 1851 she married Thomas D. Peake, who had been freed from slavery some years before, had served in the MEXICAN WAR (1846–1848), and had gone to sea. Their daughter Daisy was born some five years later. On the night of August 7, 1861, during the CIVIL WAR, Confederates burned the town of Hampton. The Peakes escaped to Brown Cottage on the grounds of Chesapeake Female College, downstream and across the Hampton River. On September 17, 1861, Peake opened—on the first floor of Brown Cottage—the first school sponsored by the American Missionary Association. Already in the terminal stages of tuberculosis, she died not long thereafter.

Peake is frequently referred to as the "first Negro teacher in a day school after the beginning of the Civil War." In fact, others had preceded her in teaching in the settlements under Union control. She was, however, the first to teach in a school sponsored by the American Missionary Association. Besides this, "she was the first of the teachers who brought to her work manifest excellence along with dedication, and whose school served as an inspired example for those who followed her."

Most accounts of Peake's life are based on Lewis C. Lockwood's *Mary S. Peake, the Colored Teacher at Fortress Monroe* (1862). He had talked with Peake, her mother, and her contemporaries. Edward Graham of Hampton Institute obtained information about her family in an interview (September 7, 1967) with Gertrude Peake Anderson, daughter of Thomas D. Peake by his second marriage.

From *Dictionary of American Negro Biography* by Rayford W. Logan and Michael R. Winston, editors. Copyright © 1982 by Rayford W. Logan and Michael R. Winston. Reprinted by permission of W. W. Norton & Company, Inc.

Rayford W. Logan

Pedi

Ethnic group of South Africa; also known as Bapedi.

The Pedi primarily inhabit Northern Province, SOUTH AFRICA. Some live in neighboring SWAZILAND. They speak a Bantu language, and are closely related to the SOTHO people. Over 500,000 people consider themselves Pedi.

See also Bantu: Dispersion and Settlement; Ethnicity and Identity in Africa: An Interpretation; Languages, African: An Overview.

Pedroso, Regino

1898–1983

Afro-Chinese politically committed poet also known for his contribution to Négritude poetry.

Described by some scholars as a NÉGRITUDE poet, Regino Pedroso preferred to be identified as a humanist social poet. The many layers of his identity provided much inspiration for his work. As a Marxist and a member of the working class, he spoke for the exploited worker. As a Cuban growing up in a time when politics and racism in the United States had infiltrated his country after the Spanish-Cuban-American War (1895–1898), he cried out against imperialism. As a man of Afro-Chinese descent raised in a society where blackness was depreciated, he condemned racial discrimination and called for revolutionary action. Through his work, Pedroso was able to reach a variety of people and discussed issues like humanism and related themes on which other poets of the time did not focus.

Since Pedroso's heritage was African and Chinese, identity was an issue of central importance to him. Although at one point he declared himself to be predominantly Chinese because of his father's strong influence, Pedroso also acknowledged his African ancestry. Of all his poems, "Hermano Negro" (Black Brother), which addresses the SCOTTSBORO CASE, best illustrates his connection with the plight of people of African descent in CUBA from the late 1920s to the early 1930s. The poem has been interpreted as dealing with basic human struggle instead of a specifically black struggle, yet the imagery is all too revealing. Though Pedroso was well aware of the history of oppression against blacks in Cuba, he was often uninspired by the vision of the Cuban NEGRISTA POETS (such as Zacarías Tallet and Emilio Ballagas), who saw black culture in an exotic, animalistic, and often erotic manner. Like many Afro-Cubans, he avoided the stereotypical images embraced by these poets and focused instead on mobilizing blacks for social protest. In his work, Pedroso applied a variation of the exotic image of blacks and added concrete examples of social injustice against people of African descent to create poetry that gained international recognition.

Credited by his contemporaries in 1927 with being Cuba's first social poet for his work "Salutación fraterna al taller mecánico" (A Fraternal Salute to the Factory), Regino Pedroso paid homage to the community of which he was a part. The support and financial contributions of fellow artists and the working class community enabled him to publish his first book of poetry, *Nosotros* (Us), in 1933. Six years later, he was awarded the National Literary Prize of Cuba for the poem "Más allá canta el mar" (Beyond There Sings the Sea). His work was praised by famous scholars and contemporaries, like the anthropologist FERNANDO ORTIZ (1881–1969), who appreciated the power of "Hermano Negro," and the poet NICOLÁS GUILLÉN (1902–1989), who understood Pedroso's artistic inspirations. Guillén thought of Pedroso as three distinct beings: the avant-garde poet, the social poet, and the Chinese poet. All three came together to create one lyrically pure, true poet who lived the experiences of which he wrote. As a significant contributor to the world of literature, Pedroso remains relatively unstudied. He died in 1983 in HAVANA, but left behind a legacy ripe for exploration.

See also Literature, Black, in Spanish America; Poetry, Caribbean.

Pelé

1940–

Afro-Brazilian soccer player, considered by many to be the greatest in the history of the game.

Born Edson Arantes do Nascimento in Tres Corações, BRAZIL, the son of a semiprofessional SOCCER player, Pelé spent his younger years in the city of Bauru. There he occasionally attended school and performed odd jobs until, while still an adolescent, he began to play for the local youth soccer team. It was at this time that he acquired the nickname "Pelé," by which he is now known throughout the world.

At fifteen, Pelé was transferred to Santos, a team in the much larger port city with the same name. Pelé would play for Santos for most of his career, and he would forever become associated with its white Number 10 shirt—along with the yellow shirt of the Brazilian national team.

In the eighteen years that Pelé played at Santos, the club team won numerous state and national championships in Brazil

Brazilian forward Pelé dribbles the ball past a defender in a 1960 match. *AFP/Getty Images*

and two world club championships, in 1962 and 1963. During what has been called Pelé's reign (in Brazil he is referred to as "King Pelé"), Santos frequently toured throughout the world and enormous crowds gathered wherever they played.

In Asia, Africa, and Europe, fans paid homage to this black Brazilian. Concerned that such devotion might result in offers for Pelé to play for teams in wealthier countries, the Brazilian Congress declared, in 1962, that the twenty-two-year-old was a "non-exportable national treasure." In an often quoted story, a visit to NIGERIA by Pelé's Santos in 1969 caused the warring factions in a civil war to agree to a temporary truce lasting the duration of the Brazilians' stay.

With the Brazilian national team, Pelé played in four World Cups, figuring in Brazil's unprecedented three victories between 1958 and 1970. In 1970 Brazil's military dictatorship claimed the team's victory as its own in an attempt to associate itself with the triumphant soccer team. General Médici hosted the team's players and his military government used an image of Pelé celebrating a goal as part of its propaganda, fueling years of debate concerning Pelé's possible complicity with the authoritarian regime. The song *"Pra frente Brasil"* (Forward, Brazil), composed for the 1970 team, was also appropriated by the government for its propaganda.

Pelé retired from Santos in 1974, and it is rumored that even the president of Brazil attempted, unsuccessfully, to convince him to continue playing. In 1975, however, a multimillion-dollar offer lured him back into the game to play for the New York Cosmos as a North American league attempted to spread soccer to the United States. His second and final retirement came in October of 1977.

Pelé is considered by many to have been the most complete player in the history of soccer and has been repeatedly chosen as the most outstanding athlete of the century. He scored his 1,000th goal in 1969 playing for Santos in RIO DE JANEIRO's famous Maracana Stadium—a goal he dedicated to the "children of Brazil." Pelé would ultimately score a total of 1,279 goals in 1,362 games, only fifty fewer than fellow Brazilian ARTHUR FRIEDENREICH, whose reported 1,329 goals were scored in an earlier time when games generally had higher scores.

Pelé's importance in Brazil is of such magnitude that some have claimed that he would be elected president if he ever chose to be a candidate, despite the country's history of favoring light-skinned leaders. In 1993, in a move widely praised, President Fernando Henrique Cardoso appointed Pelé to the position of minister of Sports. Yet Pelé's fame reaches far beyond the confines of Brazil and sports. He was the first black man to be on the cover of *Life* Magazine, for instance. He received an International Peace award in 1978 and a World Health Organization (WHO) medal in 1989. In 1993 he was inducted into the U.S. National Soccer Hall of Fame, and in 1999 he was named an Athlete of the Century by the U.S. National Olympic Committee.

Marcos Natalí

Peña Gómez, José Francisco

1937–1998

Afro-Dominican politician who was the secretary general of the Dominican Revolutionary Party, president of the Socialist International's Latin American section, and an eloquent spokesman for and defender of political, social, and racial equality.

José Francisco Peña Gómez was born into a poor black family in 1937 in Loma de El Flaco, a village in the mountains bordering HAITI. On October 3 of that same year, the dictator RAFAEL TRUJILLO, motivated by intense nationalism and racist doctrines, ordered his army to kill all Haitians living within the borders of the DOMINICAN REPUBLIC. Fearing that they would be confused with Haitians because the military were killing indiscriminately, Peña Gómez's parents fled to Haiti, to avoid the massacre that took the lives of as many as 20,000 black Dominicans and Haitians. The couple left their children behind in hopes that they would survive under the protection of neighbors. Peña Gómez was adopted by Regino Peña and Fermina Gómez, a *mestizo* (of indigenous and European descent) Dominican peasant couple who brought him up as their own child.

From an early age, Peña Gómez distinguished himself as a brilliant student. At fifteen, he became an instructor in a literacy program for poor children. Later he worked as a teacher in rural and night schools. A wealthy family, whom Peña Gómez had assisted during the literacy campaigns they had sponsored, supported him so that he could continue his studies. He entered law school in 1957 at the Universidad Autónoma de Santo Domingo. During his university studies, he worked as a sports announcer and began to participate in politics.

In 1961 Peña Gómez became an important political figure during the presidential campaign of his political mentor, Dominican Revolutionary Party (Partido Revolucionario Domicano, PRD) leader Juan Bosch. Bosch became the first democratically elected president of the country in 1962, after many years of dictatorship. Seven months later, Bosch's government was overthrown by a military coup, forcing Bosch into exile and thrusting Peña Gómez into leadership of the PRD. In 1965 Peña Gómez successfully led a civil-military revolt demanding Bosch's return. Thousands of United States Marines arrived four days later to stop the upheaval. JOAQUÍN BALAGUER, a former president under Trujillo's dictatorship, became president in 1966 after new (and, some critics say, fraudulent) elections were held. Though Peña Gómez was able to complete his law degree during these years, he was forced into exile by Balaguer's repression against political opponents.

During his years abroad, Peña Gómez attended courses in political science and law at Harvard, Michigan State University, and the University of Paris. After returning to the Dominican Republic, he was credited as the driving force behind PRD victories. In 1978 he was instrumental in the PRD victory that led Antonio Guzmán to the presidency of the Dominican Republic. The PRD won the presidency again in 1982, with Salvador Jorge Blanco as its candidate. Peña Gómez won the election for mayor of SANTO DOMINGO in 1982, and thus became a strong contender for the presidential elections of 1986. However, when the time came to launch his candidacy, leaders of the PRD fought his nomination, arguing that a black man with family links to Haiti would be unable to defeat the opposition candidate Balaguer. Although it presented a white candidate, the PRD lost to Balaguer anyway.

After many years of accepting positions of lesser political importance because of racism, Peña Gómez was nominated for the PRD presidential candidacy in 1990. He and Juan Bosch, now a candidate for the Dominican Liberation Party (Partido de la Liberación Dominicana, PLD), were defeated by the powerful Balaguer, whose political campaign employed racist images to instill the specter of a historically feared Haitian takeover.

In 1994 Peña Gómez lost again to Balaguer in the presidential election, this time by a very narrow margin. The PRD claimed that the elections were fraudulent and marred by yet another racist campaign. After much domestic and international protest, Balaguer was forced to shorten his four-year term to two years and was barred from running for office again.

Peña Gómez ran for president of his country for the last time in 1996 against Leonel Fernández Reyna, a light-skinned mulatto (of African and European descent) candidate who had grown up in New York and was running for the PLD. Peña Gómez won the first round of the presidential elections, receiving 47 percent of the votes compared with Fernández's 39 percent. Fearing a defeat for the second round, in which only the two top candidates from the first round compete, Fernández took advantage of Balaguer's public endorsement in his favor and successfully created yet another racist and xenophobic campaign against his opponent. Peña Gómez was depicted through toy monkeys and gorillas and was charged of being a VODOU practitioner who wanted to annex the Dominican Republic to Haiti. He lost the election by a narrow margin.

Peña Gómez died on May 10, 1998, of pancreatic cancer, less than a week before elections in which he was the favorite candidate for mayor of Santo Domingo.

See also Dominican-Haitian Relations; Racism in Latin America and the Caribbean.

Liliana Obregón

Penn, I(rvine) Garland

1867–1930

African American teacher, editor, and author.

Irvine Garland Penn was born in New Glasgow, a small village in Amherst County, Virginia. When he was five years old he moved with his parents, Isham and Maria Penn, to Lynchburg, Virginia, where there were better schools. In 1882 he entered the junior class of the high school. Needing funds, he taught in a school in Bedford County for one year and graduated from the Lynchburg high school in 1886. From 1886 to 1887 he was superintendent of a school in Amherst County. In 1887 he became a teacher in the Lynchburg public schools and rose to the position of principal.

Meanwhile, Penn had already begun his career as an editor. Before his graduation from high school, he was on the editorial staff of the *Lynchburg Laborer*. His discussion of the material, intellectual, moral, and religious welfare of blacks and of Virginia won the praise of the editors of the white newspapers, the *Spirit of the Valley* and the *Lynchburg Daily Advance*.

Lack of support, however, soon forced the *Laborer* to suspend publication. He then wrote for the *Richmond Planet*, published by John R. Mitchell Jr., and the *Virginia Lancet*. In 1889 he was a correspondent for the *Knoxville Negro World* and the *New York Age*. Daniel B. Williams, who was on the faculty of Virginia Normal and Collegiate Institute, Ettrick, Virginia, mentioned among Penn's more important public speeches an address in 1889 at the annual conference of the black METHODIST EPISCOPAL CHURCH in Charlottesville. The speech advocated the establishment of a theological and normal school in Virginia. Penn was twice appointed commissioner at Lynchburg for the Petersburg Industrial Association, and he was secretary of the Board of Directors of the Lynchburg Real Estate Loan and Trust Company.

Penn is best known for his work *The Afro-American Press and Its Editors,* published by Willey & Co., Springfield, Massachusetts, in 1891. The title page lists contributions by twenty well-known black men and one woman, GERTRUDE BUSTILL MOSSELL. Part One, consisting of seventeen chapters and 105 pages, gives brief accounts of newspapers and magazines published and edited by blacks, from FREEDOM'S JOURNAL and *Rights of All* in 1827 through 1891. Part Two devotes 199 pages to short biographical sketches of seventy-four editors. Most of the sketches are shorter, for example, than those in *Men of Mark; Eminent, Progressive and Rising* (1887) by WILLIAM J. SIMMONS. Like those in Simmons's book, the biographies are usually laudatory. Penn did, however, mention about twenty significant individuals not included in *Men of Mark,* notably JOHN B. RUSSWURM, NATHANIEL PAUL, Thomas Paul, Charles Ray, DAVID RUGGLES, and T. MCCANTS STEWART. Among those to whom Penn expressed appreciation for assistance for loans of books and information were RICHARD T. GREENER, T. THOMAS FORTUNE, ALEXANDER CRUMMELL, FREDERICK DOUGLASS, and BENJAMIN W. ARNETT.

The Afro-American Press and Its Editors has served as a valuable point of departure for later relevant works.

In 1893 Penn wrote an eighty-one-page brochure, *The Reasons Why the Colored Man Is Not in the World's Columbian Exposition, The Afro-American's Contribution to Columbian Literature,* with an introduction by reformer Frederick Douglass. He was head of black exhibits at the Cotton States and International Exposition in ATLANTA on September 18, 1895, and he is said to have asked black leader BOOKER T. WASHINGTON to speak.

Penn was a joint editor with Henry Davenport Northrop and contributor to *The College Life; Or Practical Self-Educator; a Manual of Self-Improvement for the Colored Race . . . Giving Examples and Achievements of Successful Men and Women of the Race . . . Including Afro-American Progress.* Published in 1895, this little-known volume of almost 700 pages and "hundreds of superb engravings" typified the attempt to counter white supremacist sentiment near the end of the nineteenth century. In 1902 Penn was coeditor, along with JOHN WESLEY EDWARD BOWEN, of a somewhat similar volume of 600 pages, *The United Negro: His Problems and His Progress, Containing the Addresses and Proceedings* (of) *The Young People's Christian and Educational Congress, held* (in Atlanta, Georgia,) *August 6, 1902* (reprinted 1969).

From 1897 until 1912 Penn was assistant general secretary of the Methodist Episcopal Church. In 1912 he was elected corresponding secretary of the Methodist Episcopal Board of Education for Negroes. He held the position until 1925, when he became secretary of endowments and field activities in the same department. He was a trustee of many educational institutions and a member of the Joint Commission on Unification of the Methodist Episcopal Church.

Penn's wife predeceased him on June 19, 1930. At the time of her death, they had been married for forty-one years. Penn died on July 22, 1930.

Much of the factual information about Penn is in his work *The Afro-American Press and Its Editors* (1891), with an introduction by Daniel D. Williams. For his career after that date, see THE CRISIS (February 1931, p. 56). See *The Booker T. Washington Papers,* edited by Louis R. Harlan and others, vol. 3, *1889–1895* (1974).

From *Dictionary of American Negro Biography* by Rayford W. Logan and Michael R. Winston, editors. Copyright © 1982 by Rayford W. Logan and Michael R. Winston. Reprinted by permission of W. W. Norton & Company, Inc.

See also Magazines, Newspapers, and Journals; Press, Black, in the United States.

Rayford W. Logan

Penniman, Richard

See Little Richard.

Pentecostalism

Worldwide charismatic Christian movement that originated in the United States at the beginning of the twentieth century.

Pentecostalism emphasizes the believer's baptism in the Holy Spirit and speaking in tongues as central to the Christian experience. Its theological basis is found in the New Testament of the Bible. Chapter two of the Book of Acts recounts how Jesus' disciples were "baptized in the Holy Spirit" while meeting for the Jewish observance of Shabuoth (*Pentecost* in Greek). Glossolalia, or speaking in tongues, was the sign of the baptism. The modern focus on Spirit-baptism has its origins in two main strains of religious experience in America: the Holiness Movement and African American CHRISTIANITY.

The nineteenth-century Holiness Movement influenced a major segment of American Protestantism, particularly the Methodists. The origin of the movement was probably the Methodist belief in perfectionism. These Protestants formed the interdenominational National Holiness Association, from 1867 to 1887. They promoted the idea that once a person had accepted Christ, or experienced justification, he or she would move toward a second state of perfect love known as sanctification, which was to be brought on by a spiritual baptism. The Holiness Movement had both black and white adherents, and it exists today in different forms throughout the United States and elsewhere.

By the 1890s the Holiness Movement had fragmented, and new doctrines were spreading. In 1901 Charles Parham, a white Holiness minister, asserted that instead of sanctification being the final result of Spirit-baptism, it was the glossolalia described in Acts 2 that announced the Spirit's descent upon the human body. Rife with millennialism, the announcement was seen as the harbinger of the Second Coming of Christ.

This Pentecostal idea was preached first in the Midwest, but it soon spread to small circles throughout the South. In 1905 an African American Holiness minister named WILLIAM J. SEYMOUR attended Parham's Bethel Bible School in HOUSTON, TEXAS, where he was forced to listen from outside the lecture room because of Parham's policy of segregation. Nonetheless, Seymour assimilated Parham's teachings into what was already a strong foundation for the belief in Pentecostalism. In 1906 Seymour went to LOS ANGELES, CALIFORNIA, where one of his flock of Evening Light Saints experienced speaking in tongues. This act sparked the Azusa Street Revival, the seminal movement in what is now termed Pentecostalism.

The second strain that gave rise to Pentecostalism was the nature of Christianity practiced by Africans enslaved in the Americas. Merging the teachings of the Bible with styles of worship that had antecedents in traditional African religions, communities of black people produced a new version of Christianity. This synthesis was immediately recognizable in the Azusa Street Revival. Salient features included holy dancing, singing, a trancelike Spirit possession, a focus on testimony and testifying, and the immediate experience of the divine presence in the worship service.

Seymour's Azusa Street Revival was characterized by the participation of people of every race and ethnicity. Native-born and newly immigrated whites, Mexican Americans, Asian Americans, and African Americans gathered to experience the glossolalia Spirit-baptism that they had not found in the churches of other denominations. However, the idea of interracial worship was repugnant to many whites, including the KU KLUX KLAN, who harassed the new Pentecostals. Still, from 1906 until 1914 Seymour's movement attracted Christians from all over the United States who, according to one white parishioner, saw "the color line washed away in the blood [of Jesus Christ]."

Seymour published a journal entitled *Apostolic Faith*, which made explicit his belief that baptism in the Holy Spirit was capable not only of elevating the individual soul, but also of ameliorating the rampant racial hostility of the day. The multitudes in America who adopted Pentecostalism, including a large portion of those involved in the Holiness Movement, were joined by believers around the world who were being evangelized by missionaries. By 1908 Pentecostal missionaries were working in fifty countries.

Seymour had early success at holding together a multiracial ensemble of believers in this new Pentecost experience. However, in 1914 the Assemblies of God was established by whites who desired segregated churches. Around the same time, black Pentecostals removed themselves from bodies such as the Pentecostal Holiness Church. This sparked a pattern of churches separated by race, spawning numerous conferences and associations made up of one racial group or another. Nonetheless, many Pentecostals remained in interracial churches and organizations, including the CHURCH OF GOD IN CHRIST (COGIC) and Pentecostal Assemblies of the World.

Historically, the structure of Pentecostal churches and denominations has differed from that of other Protestant groups in that doctrine and liturgy have not always been determined by a central governing body. Thus, individual pastors have had a significant role in shaping the character of their own congregations. The malleable structure of Pentecostal churches has allowed for significant adaptability across cultures and regions. Since the mid-1970s Pentecostalism has found bases in mainline African American denominations, including several AFRICAN METHODIST EPISCOPAL churches and Baptist churches, where the emotional exuberance of Pentecostal worship had previously been avoided.

Currently, more than 450 million people worldwide—one out of every four Christians—are Pentecostals. According to theologian Harvey Cox, "Pentecostalism is not a denomination or a creed but a movement, a cluster of religious practices and attitudes that transcends ecclesiastical boundaries." Its converts throughout the world are of all races and classes, yet as with its original adherents, Pentecostalism finds its greatest reception from women, the poor, and the oppressed groups of the world. Throughout the African diaspora and within AFRICA itself, millions of people have been drawn to Pentecostalism's empowering beliefs and practices. In LATIN AMERICA—BRAZIL in particular—Pentecostal churches are now competing with the once-dominant Roman Catholic Church for adherents. Beginning in 1910 with Luigi Francescon's Christian Congregations of Brazil, Pentecostalism has emerged as a powerful force in Brazil because of its emphasis on exuberant personal religious experience unmediated by authoritarian leadership. This experience is grounded in the well-being of a community of believers whose goal of communion with the Holy Spirit is seen as leading to Christ's Second Coming.

In Africa, Pentecostalism is the fastest spreading religious movement on the continent, largely as a result of the compatibility of traditional indigenous religions and the doctrines of the movement. Christian churches, independent of non-African rule, have arisen throughout Africa. These churches include the Church of the Lord Jesus Christ on Earth, founded by the prophet SIMON KIMBANGU in 1921, and the Apostolic Church, founded by the prophet John Maranke in 1932. Thousands of new denominations have assimilated indigenous beliefs and practices, including ancestral veneration, spirit possession, and most importantly, healing, into the idiom of Christian baptism and salvation. The remarkable growth of Pentecostalism throughout the world bespeaks a common need for spiritual transcendence and emotional attachment to community.

See also Baptists; Christianity: Independent and Charismatic Churches in Africa; Holy Spirit Movement; Religions, African and Afro-Caribbean, in the United States; Segregation in the United States.

Bibliography

Cox, Harvey. *Fire from Heaven: The Rise of Pentecostal Spirituality and the Reshaping of Religion in the Twenty-First Century.* Addison-Wesley Publishing, 1995.

MacRobert, Iain. *The Black Roots and White Racism of Early Pentecostalism in the U.S.A.* St. Martin's Press, 1988.

Péralte, Charlemagne Masséna

1885–1919

Leader of the so-called Caco rebellion against the first United States occupation of Haiti, which lasted from 1915 to 1934.

Charlemagne Masséna Péralte was born in the rural town of Hinche in central HAITI, and grew up in a prominent middle-class family. While still very young, he entered politics and served in a few minor official roles. When his brother-in-law Oreste Zamor became president in 1914, Péralte was made military commander of the town of Port-de-Paix.

In 1915, at the beginning of the U.S. occupation, Péralte was the military commander of the southern town of Léogane, near PORT-AU-PRINCE. He refused to surrender his command to the American troops, and as a result was fired by the recently "elected" puppet government of President Sudre Dartiguenave. Péralte then withdrew to his estates near Hinche. On October 11, 1917 he was arrested along with his brother Saul, allegedly for plotting against the American invasion. He was sentenced to five years of hard labor in prison, and shortly thereafter his brother Saul was killed in an alleged escape attempt.

Péralte served a year of his prison sentence at CAP-HAÏTIEN. He escaped in September 1918 and returned to the central plateau to launch a liberation war against the U.S. Army. Péralte founded a local peasant army with several thousand supporters, declared the provisional independence of the north, and appointed himself the head of its government.

Péralte's troops attacked local military establishments, and in October 1919 marched on Port-au-Prince itself but were driven back. As the American troops could not defeat him in an open battle because he was using hit-and-run guerrilla tactics, they decided to get rid of him by all necessary means.

Sergeant Herman H. Hanneken, U.S.M.C., soon came up with a plan to reveal Charlemagne's whereabouts. The Americans hired J. B. Conze, whom they groomed as a rebel leader who was supposed to offer his alliance to Péralte. The scheme worked perfectly, and Conze revealed Péralte's plans to the Americans. During an attack on the town of Grande Rivière du Nord, the Americans discovered Charlemagne's headquarters and shot him dead.

Péralte's body was brought to Cap-Haïtien and exposed in the yard of the military barracks, crucified on a door with the Haitian flag around his head. The body was buried secretly by the Americans at the Chabert internment camp. In October 1934, after the departure of the Americans, Péralte was exhumed and reburied, with great pomp, in a Cap-Haïtien cemetery. Péralte has since become a prime symbol of Haitian nationalism.

See also Cacos; Nationalism in Latin America and the Caribbean.

Georges Michel

Percussion Instruments of the Caribbean

Various types of African-derived percussion instruments that are used in Afro-Caribbean music.

The music of the Caribbean reflects its mixed historical legacy, combining elements of African, European, and, to a much lesser extent, Native American cultures. Afro-Caribbean music employs both African-derived musical instruments and those of European derivation that have been creolized or culturally adapted. But arguably the instruments that most characterize and are most important in shaping Caribbean music are African-derived percussion instruments.

New York Times music critic Jon Pareles observed that in African music, "rhythm rules." The musical culture of LATIN AMERICA clearly reflects this African-derived primacy of rhythm. "Life is periodicity and repetition, the cycles of nature," Brazilian songwriter GILBERTO GIL explained, "and rhythm is fundamental." Afro-Caribbean music creates rhythms with a wide range of drums as well as with various other percussion instruments. Although these musical instruments are found throughout the Caribbean, the key areas for a regional overview are CUBA, HAITI, and Trinidad.

It is equally important to understand the cultural setting or context in which an instrument is played, in particular whether it is used for secular or sacred purposes. In Latin America, drums are not played simply for musical entertainment. They often fill roles of a distinctly religious nature. Drums figure prominently in numerous African-derived religious practices that are often syncretized with Roman Catholicism or other institutional religions.

Cuban Drums

African-derived drums constitute the most significant class of Afro-Caribbean instruments. African slaves introduced a wide range of drums of different shapes, sizes, and modes of construction. Most drums are made of wood with a playing surface of tightened leather. They are often played with the bare hands. As Cuban percussionist MONGO SANTAMARÍA declared, the most important rhythms were produced by "skin on skin."

The conga drum is one of the most widespread of these drums and is a variant of the Central African tall drum. The conga drum and closely related variants are common through much of Latin America, from PERU to MEXICO and from BRAZIL to Cuba. The conga drum has a head approximately twenty-five to thirty-eight centimeters (ten to fifteen inches) in diameter, and it stands about one meter (three feet) tall. The conga drummer plays the drum while carrying it by means of a strap over one shoulder or, more commonly, with the drum sitting upright on the ground or mounted on a stand.

Drummers often play two instruments of slightly different diameters, providing two distinct base pitches. They alter the drum's pitch and tone by their manner of striking the drumhead and by pressing and tightening the drumhead with one hand or elbow while striking the surface with the other hand.

Conga drums came to the attention of the wider world in conjunction with the popularity of Latin music during the 1930s and 1940s. Afro-Cuban jazz musicians CHANO POZO and Santamaría are two of the most important conga drummers. In 1940 Cuban composer and bandleader ARSENIO RODRÍGUEZ created the *conjunto* ensemble form by adding a conga drummer, a second trumpeter, and a pianist to his traditional small group. The conjunto played an important role in popularizing the conga drum in Cuban music. Today congas are used widely in JAZZ, rock, and FUNK.

The *bembé* is another tubular drum, typically smaller than the conga drum. This Yoruban-derived instrument is used for secular music and is constructed from a hollowed tree trunk with a skin on one end. The musician tightens the skin by holding it close to a fire. Although bembé drums occasionally are as large as one meter (thirty-nine inches), their average height is .5 meter (nineteen inches).

Even smaller than the bembés are the bongo drums. Like the conga drum, the bongos are played with the hands. Bongos mount together two drums of different diameters, which are approximately twenty to thirty centimeters (eight to twelve inches) in height. They are much less resonant than the conga drum and offer a narrower range of pitch and tone.

A third common drum in Cuban and Puerto Rican percussion sections is the *timbales*. The timbales make use of two relatively short or shallow but deep-toned drums, mounted side by side. The timbales are larger in diameter than a conga drum; each is a different diameter, providing two different pitches. The *timbalero* plays the drums using drumsticks or mallets. The best-known timbalero is Puerto Rican bandleader TITO PUENTE, a skilled timbales player. The *tumbadora* is a larger drum common to Cuba and PUERTO RICO.

Drums are used in a number of African-derived religions found in the Caribbean. Conga drums, for example, are central to practices of the Cuban ABAKUÁS, all-male secret societies created by slaves brought from the Calabar region of southwestern NIGERIA. Cuban SANTERÍA rituals, derived from the religious practices of the YORUBA, include the *batá*, a set of three hourglass-shaped drums, which followers regard as sacred objects.

The largest of the batá, and the lowest in pitch, is the *iyá*, which in Yoruba means "mother." The *itóteles* is a smaller drum, and the *okónkolo* the smallest.

Haitian Drums

Haitian VODOU makes use of *rada* drums, which, like the batá, are a set of three drums of different sizes: the *manman* (mother drum), *segon* (second drum), and the *boula* (the smallest drum and the highest in pitch). Rada drums are typically played with sticks. Unlike the Cuban batá drummers, who play while seated, Haitian rada drummers play while standing up, holding their tall drums upright, at an angle.

There are a wide variety of Haitian drums, ranging in size from the small *tanbou kout,* which is about the size of a single bongo drum, to the *asotò* drum, which stands about three meters (ten feet) tall. Other Haitian drums are the *tambouren*, a short, heavy drum with a large circumference, resembling the smaller tambourine; and the *tanbou a liny*, a drum with skin heads on both ends that are tightened by a rope laced in a zigzag between the heads. The tanbou a liny is used in the *Rara* bands that parade throughout the country during Lent in festivities that climax with Easter. The player carries this drum slung over the shoulder so that it hangs horizontally. Rara bands also employ the *kès,* a sort of snare drum.

Tamboo Bamboos and Steel-Drum Bands

The music of Trinidad once featured two remarkably different kinds of drumlike instruments that were fashioned variously from bamboo tubes, metal pans, and oil drums—some of the few materials that were available as a result of various restrictions imposed by the island's colonial authorities. During the nineteenth century the French and, later, the British colonial administrations—concerned that Trinidad's Carnival sanctioned disorder and lawlessness—attempted to restrain the festivities by prohibiting the use of traditional skin drums that provided vernacular Carnival music.

Although the laws were unevenly enforced, they resulted by the 1880s in the development of bamboo instruments as legal replacements for skin drums. Musicians played bamboo tubes of various lengths by hitting them on the side or striking them upright against the ground. There were numerous bamboo orchestras, also known as tamboo bamboos, but in the twentieth century they gradually fell out of favor. During the 1930s Trinidadian percussionists made increasing use of arrangements of different sorts of metal pans, including wastebaskets and cookie tins, which were struck with mallets. The resulting pan bands replaced the tamboo bamboos.

During the 1940s the steel drum (known in Trinidad as a pan) emerged as the island's most important musical instrument. By the 1940s Trinidad's expanding petroleum industry had strewn the island with abandoned oil drums, and enterprising musicians discovered that the end of the oil drum could be worked and fashioned so as to produce several different tones, even a musical scale.

When the British lifted their wartime prohibition on Carnival at the end of World War II, musicians quickly organized steel-drum Carnival bands, composed of various types of steel drums, including lead pans and tenor pans. In a sense, the steel drum, a mallet-played instrument that produces a series of musical tones, is less a traditional drum than a distant relative of another class of African-derived instruments, the best known of which is the *marimba*.

Other Percussion Instruments

The marimba is one of a class of instruments that are struck with mallets and that produce a greater number of musical tones than a drum. The marimba is fashioned from a series of wooden slats mounted on a frame and arranged so that the slats produce a tonal sequence or scale when struck. It functions as a melody instrument as well as a percussion instrument.

The similarly named but very different *marímbula* is a large relative of the African kalimba or thumb piano. Its low-pitched tones provided a rhythmic and harmonic base for Cuban vernacular music, but it has largely been displaced by the double bass. The young Arsenio Rodríguez played the marimbula before taking up the tres, which became his primary instrument.

The *claves* have had particularly great musical importance in Cuba, where they provide the name for the clave beat, the loping, off-balance beat that characterizes much Cuban music. The instrument itself sets the clave beat. It consists of two fifteen- to twenty-centimeter- (six- to eight-inch-) long wooden cylinders, often made of rosewood because of its resonant quality. The musician plays the claves by cupping one clave in one hand and using the other clave to strike it, producing a sharp tone that is high-pitched and ringing but of short duration.

The *maracas* are one of the best-known percussion instruments used by Afro-Caribbeans. The maracas consist of a pair of shakers and were originally made from small hollowed gourds. The gourds are filled with small pellets and make a distinctive rattle when shaken.

A number of smaller instruments are used in Cuban Santería rituals, including the *güiros* or gourds, known as *abwes* or *chequerés*. The abwe, of Yoruban origin, is a set of three gourds of different sizes. The gourds are dried, hollowed out, and wrapped with a netting that is strung with hard seeds or beads. The musician plays the gourd by shaking it, causing the seeds to rattle against the gourd's surface. The güiro is also widely used in secular music.

The people of both Cuba and Haiti commonly use iron hoe blades as percussion instruments. The musician holds the hoe blade in one hand and strikes it with a length of metal held in the other hand. The cowbell represents another important metal percussion instrument.

Another widely used percussion instrument is the tambourine. The tambourine is a wooden hoop, usually from thirty to fifty centimeters (twelve to twenty inches) in diameter, with metal discs attached so that they ring when the tambourine is shaken. Usually, the tambourine also has a skin attached to one end, which can be struck for a drumlike effect.

In Cuba and throughout the region, ensembles rarely make use of a single type of percussion instrument. Afro-Caribbean percussion sections typically combine a variety of different instruments. A conjunto's rhythm section can include as many as five people, for example, playing conga drum, bongos, maracas, guiro, and cowbell. The variety of percussion instruments in an ensemble significantly increases its rhythmic and textural complexity.

See also Carnivals in Latin America and the Caribbean; Creolized Musical Instruments of the Caribbean; Jazz, Afro-Latin; Music, Afro-Caribbean Religious; Music, Afro-Caribbean Secular; Music, Afro-Cuban; Son; Transatlantic Slave Trade; Trinidad and Tobago.

James Sellman

Pereira, Aristides

1924–

First president of the Republic of Cape Verde.

Aristides Pereira grew up on the island of Boa Vista in CAPE VERDE. After completing school, he trained to become a radio-telegraph technician. By the late 1950s he had moved up to the position of chief of telecommunications in GUINEA-BISSAU, another Portuguese colony. He was also increasingly involved in the labor movement, and was one of the key organizers of the 1959 Pijiguiti strike. The strike, during which Portuguese forces fired on demonstrators, killing at least fifty and wounding more than a hundred others, was a turning point in the growing nationalist movement led by AMÍLCAR CABRAL and the Partido Africano da Independencia da Guine e Cabo Verde (PAIGC). Pereira joined the struggle, and became a member of the PAIGC's Central Committee.

For the next fourteen years Pereira dedicated himself to the fight for Cape Verdean independence, and gradually rose through the ranks of the PAIGC leadership. When Cabral was assassinated in January 1973, Pereira assumed leadership of the PAIGC.

Cape Verde won independence on July 5, 1975. Pereira became the new republic's first president, promising that "Our state will be profoundly democratic and will guarantee the participation of all without distinction of color, religion, or sex in the conduct of the affairs of the states." With PEDRO PIRES as his prime minister, Pereira was part of the PAIGC's victorious joint rule over Cape Verde and Guinea-Bissau. A 1980 coup overthrowing Guinea-Bissau president LUÍS CABRAL ended this affiliation, and Pereira responded to perceived threats to his own government by arresting potential opponents. The crackdown on dissent undermined his promise of democratic rule and added to the grievances of a citizenry already struggling with near-chronic food shortages.

At a time when many newly independent African nations were allying themselves with one or the other of the Cold War superpowers, Pereira advocated nonalignment as well as economic independence for the Cape Verde islands. Toward the latter goal, he promoted Marxist programs of land reform and nationalization. In foreign relations, the administration cultivated controversial relationships with Palestinians as well as with China and Libya, and openly criticized both South African apartheid and foreign intervention in Africa.

From the early 1980s onward, the PAIGC's economic programs as well as its single-party rule met with increasing opposition. Finally, in 1991, Pereira agreed to allow multiparty elections. The PAIGC was defeated by the Movimento para a Democracia (MpD), and Pereira gave up his presidential seat to António Monteiro. Now in semiretirement, he occasionally comments publicly on African affairs.

Marian Aguiar

Pérez Prado, Dámaso

1916–1983

Afro-Cuban pianist and bandleader who was one of the foremost popularizers of the mambo.

In the early 1940s, Dámaso Pérez Prado played piano with the Cuban orchestra Casino de la Playa, but in 1948 he moved to Mexico, which thereafter became his principal base. In 1948, he began recording instrumental mambos with an ensemble inspired by American jazz big bands, using large trumpet, trombone, and saxophone sections. Cuban music was then typically played by smaller, seven-to-ten-member *septetos* and *conjuntos*. RCA Records marketed these mambos for a Latin audience in the United States. In the late 1940s an American Federation of Musicians' strike and recording ban sharply reduced the number of American record releases, and Pérez Prado's recordings gained considerable success in the U.S., although the bandleader did not tour that country until 1951.

Pérez Prado did not play a major role in the Afro-Latin jazz movement epitomized by bandleaders Machito and Tito Puente, but he did feature talented jazz musicians, including such white non-Latinos as trumpeters Pete Candoli (part of Pérez Prado's 1951 U.S. touring band), Shorty Rogers, Maynard Ferguson, and Rolf Erickson. In hiring musicians without regard to race, Pérez Prado actively challenged the Jim Crow practices that were commonplace in American entertainment.

Over the years, Pérez Prado featured numerous Latin American musicians who would later become leaders themselves, including Cuban conga drummer Mongo Santamaría, Cuban singer and guitarist Beny Moré, and future Fania Records founder Johnny Pacheco, who was Dominican. Critics are divided in their assessments of Pérez Prado's musical accomplishments. Latin music scholar John Storm Roberts regarded "Moliendo Café" and other popular Pérez Prado recordings as "among the most awful works of their time," characterizing them as "banal, and worse than banal." On the other hand, Hernando Calvo Ospina credited Pérez Prado with being the "first person to adapt North American jazz bands to Cuban traditions." Most critics, including Roberts, agree that Pérez Prado played a central role in the popularizing of mambo music.

See also Music, Afro-Cuban; Son.

James Sellman

Perry, Lincoln Theodore Monroe

See Fetchit, Stepin.

Perry, Ruth

1939?–

Former transitional president of Liberia, the first woman head of state in modern Africa.

Ruth Perry served as a senator from Grand Cape Mount County, in northern Liberia, before being named chairwoman of Liberia's transitional Council of State in September 1996. Her appointment came at the hands of the factional leaders whose fighting had thrust Liberia into a seven-year-long civil war, but Perry, a widowed grandmother of fifty-seven, dealt firmly with the rival warlords, overseeing a mostly successful disarmament and free elections in July 1997.

Perry, the mother of seven children, first became involved in politics when she finished her husband's term as senator after his death. In the 1980s, she attracted attention for her public opposition to then president Samuel K. Doe's efforts to legalize polygamy. After Charles Taylor's National Patriotic Front of Liberia began to take control of the Liberian countryside in 1989, the country's government collapsed and Perry returned to her home, where she helped shelter refugees. A series of transitional governments were appointed throughout the 1990s, but none held much real power. In 1996 at Abuja, Nigeria, the Economic Community of West African States (ECWAS) brought together the most powerful of the factional leaders to draft a disarmament plan and name a new head of state.

Analysts reported surprise at the choice of Perry, but she quickly warned Taylor and the other warlords that she would "treat them like a mother and, if necessary, that means discipline." Lacking money and political power, Perry used her largely symbolic position to try to educate Liberians about their basic political rights. After nearly a year in office, Perry oversaw the July 1997 elections, widely considered fair, in which Charles Taylor was elected president.

Kate Tuttle

Persian Gulf Wars

America's military confrontations with Iraq in 1991 and 2003, in which African Americans made up a quarter of all U.S. forces in the war zone.

On August 2, 1990, a force of 120,000 Iraqi troops, spearheaded by 850 tanks, invaded and occupied the small nation of Kuwait, sparking an international crisis that culminated in the Persian Gulf War. Although African Americans made up only 12 percent of America's military-age population, they accounted for 26 percent of American military manpower in the Gulf. This overrepresentation of blacks in the American military reflected the military's success in addressing racial prejudice as well as the relative lack of employment opportunities for African Americans.

During the earlier Gulf crisis, two African American officers in particular personified the opportunities available to blacks in the armed services, General COLIN L. POWELL, chairman of the Joint Chiefs of Staff, and Lieutenant General Cal Waller, second in command of U.S. operations in the Gulf. The invasion of Kuwait was significant in that it was America's first foreign policy crisis in the post–Cold War era, as well as the nation's greatest overseas commitment of military power since the VIETNAM WAR. Recalling the domestic unrest and opposition created by the Vietnam War, Powell argued against committing American military forces without first clearly informing and securing the support of the American public.

Moreover, unlike past American interventions, such as the invasions of GRENADA and PANAMA and the Vietnam War itself, the United States did not act unilaterally in the first Persian Gulf War. President George H. W. Bush orchestrated a thirty-eight-nation coalition to oppose Iraq's invasion, which included the former Soviet Union working alongside the United States in an armed conflict. Moreover, U.S. policy employed military intervention only after diplomatic overtures and economic sanctions failed to affect Iraqi leader Saddam Hussein. Nonetheless, some blacks—such as Mark Harrison, the national organizer of the African-American Network Against U.S. Intervention in the Gulf—opposed the military buildup. In general, however, African Americans supported U.S. policy. A Gallop Poll in 1991 found that 59 percent of blacks favored action against Iraq.

Powell and his military planners made a successful effort to concentrate allied forces in the Gulf region well before the start of a military conflict. Two weeks after the Iraqi invasion, Bush ordered U.S. forces to the Gulf to defend Saudi Arabia, an oil-rich U.S. ally, from a possible Iraqi attack—an operation that the Pentagon designated Desert Shield. By mid-October, some 230,000 American troops had arrived in the Persian Gulf, and by January 1991, the troop level reached 580,000, a greater number of troops than the maximum U.S. commitment during the Vietnam War.

When a last-minute United Nations (UN) peace mission to Iraq failed to achieve a resolution, Bush announced the start of allied offensive operations on January 16, 1991, which the Pentagon dubbed "Desert Storm." After more than five weeks of intensive bombing, American and allied forces launched a ground offensive on February 24, 1991. The war ended just five days later, resulting in the deaths of an estimated 100,000 Iraqis. Confounding predictions that African Americans would bear the brunt of American casualties, only 15 percent of the 184 U.S. fatalities were black. Although Hussein's army had been thoroughly defeated, the Iraqi leader remained in power.

U.S.-Iraq relations remained tense throughout the 1990s. Tensions further escalated following the 2000 election of Bush's son George W. Bush to the American presidency and the terrorist attacks in NEW YORK and WASHINGTON D.C. on September 11, 2001. George W. Bush labeled Hussein's regime a threat to U.S. security and accused the dictator of hiding weapons of mass destruction from UN inspectors. In September 2002, Condoleeza Rice, the president's national security advisor, claimed that Iraq had assisted al-Qaeda, the terrorist group responsible

Fleeing their homes for the safety of the mountains, Kurdish refugees cross the Hizel River in 1991 to escape Saddam Hussein's attacks on their villages. *AFP*

Iraqi man celebrates the capture of Saddam Hussein in December 2003. *Alexander Demianchuk/Reuters New Media Inc./Corbis*

for the 9/11 attacks. In December, Colin Powell, then the secretary of state, warned that Iraq would face war if it did not fully comply with UN disarmament resolutions. The U.S. and GREAT BRITAIN increased their military presence in the Persian Gulf region in the early months of 2003. FRANCE, GERMANY, and Russia were among the nations that opposed military action against Iraq. UN weapons inspector Hans Blix believed that, with more time, inspections could prevent war. In early March the UN Security Council indicated that it would not approve a U.S.-backed resolution calling for military action against Iraq. Powell responded that America would lead a coalition to disarm Iraq even without UN authorization.

On March 19, 2003, the U.S. initiated Operation Iraqi Freedom by launching a wave of cruise missiles against targets in Baghdad. Ground combat began hours later when U.S. and British army units invaded southern Iraq. A Gallup Poll taken soon after the fighting began found that less than one-third of African Americans supported the war. In contrast, three-quarters of white Americans supported the military strike. The war was unpopular in many other nations; protesters in major cities around the world held antiwar demonstrations.

U.S. and British forces took less than a month to defeat Iraq's regular army. American troops occupied Baghdad and the British captured Basra by the end of the first week of April. A few days later Kurdish and American forces captured Mosul, Iraq's third largest city. On May 1, President Bush declared that combat operations had ended and that Iraq had been "liberated." Iraqi suicide bombers and paramilitary fighters, however, continued to inflict casualties in the following months. In December 2003 U.S. troops captured Hussein, dashing the hopes of his supporters that he would someday return to power.

As in 1991, African Americans played a significant role in the second Persian Gulf War. In 2003 blacks accounted for 23 percent of American military forces, including 11 percent of the Army's enlisted combat infantry personnel. As of January 2004, 20 percent of the troops killed in the Iraq war were African American.

See also Military, Blacks in the American.

Bibliography

Hiro, Dilip. *Desert Shield to Desert Storm: The Second Gulf War.* Routledge, 1992.
Lanning, Lt. Col. (Ret.) Michael Lee. *The African-American Soldier: From Crispus Attucks to Colin Powell.* Birch Lane Press, 1997.
Powell, Gen. Colin L. *My American Journey.* Random House, 1995.
Roth, David. *Sacred Honor: A Biography of Colin Powell.* Harper, 1993.

Peru

Country in South America, bounded on the north by Ecuador and Colombia, on the east by Brazil and Bolivia, on the south by Chile, and on the west by the Pacific Ocean.

Peru has long been known for the powerful and sophisticated civilization of the Incas, who built their cities high in the mineral-rich Andes Mountains. It is also famous for the Spanish conquistadores who vanquished the enormous Inca Empire in a matter of months, and for the thousands of tons of gold and silver that SPAIN extracted from the region over the next several centuries. Less well known is that the conquest, the extraction, and indeed much of contemporary Peruvian culture was the result of the labor and input of African slaves and their descendants.

Blacks in the Conquest and Colonial Peru

Indigenous peoples, originally migrants from North and Central America, have lived in Peru since at least the ninth millennium B.C.E. As early as 1200 C.E., a Quechua-speaking people known as the Inca began subduing their neighbors, eventually controlling the entire region of the Andes, some 3,000 kilometers (2,000 miles) in length.

In 1524 the Spanish explorer Francisco Pizarro, in the company of Diego de Almagro, entered ECUADOR and Peru searching for the Inca Empire, where there were rumored gold and silver deposits. African slaves were among the members of the earliest such expeditions, serving as both sailors and soldiers. When the Spanish established contact with Indian groups, they assigned some of the slaves the duty of interpreting, based on the dubious belief that Africans, being "primitive" themselves, would better understand the Indians.

Peru

When Pizarro captured and executed the Inca leader Atahualpa in 1532, and when he defeated and plundered the Inca stronghold of Cuzco the following year, African soldiers were among his ranks. Perhaps the most notable of the early black conquistadores of Peru was a slave named JUAN VALIENTE. In 1534 Valiente obtained permission from his owner to join Pedro de Alvarado's army on its passage from GUATEMALA to Peru. Valiente fought fiercely in Peru in 1535 against the remnants of the Incas, then moved on to CHILE, where he gained fame for his fighting against the Araucanian Indians. In the mid-1540s he was rewarded with an estate near Santiago and received an *encomienda,* a group of tribute-paying Indians—probably the first instance in which an African was given an encomienda. Valiente remained, nonetheless, a slave. While negotiations for his freedom were pending with his master (who wanted Valiente returned, along with all the property he had amassed), Valiente was killed by Araucanians at Tucapel.

The wealth of Peru's gold and silver lodes, tucked high in the Andes Mountains, matched the expectations of the Spaniards. In the early years of the colonies, however, the Spaniards used Indians as the main workers of the deep-shaft mines. Not only was Indian labor abundant (originally, at least), but the Spaniards also believed that Africans were ill suited to the cold alpine climate and the dank mines.

Instead, the life of the early Afro-Peruvian slave revolved around the coastal capital of Lima (founded by Pizarro in 1535) and former Inca cities like Cuzco, which were being transformed into Hispanic cities. Afro-Peruvians performed much of the land clearing, road building, and construction to erect these cities. In Lima, slaves were also prominent among the dockworkers and mule drivers who greased the gears of the rapidly growing export of gold and silver and import of food and other goods. Female slaves also performed highly valued domestic tasks like cooking and laundering.

In order to become less dependent on imported food, Peruvian settlers fanned out across the narrow coastal plain and settled at the few well-watered sites. There they established plantations on land cleared and worked by slaves. (Indians were used initially, but most of the coastal Indians had fled to the mountains or had been killed by disease and warfare.) For the most part the crops grown were for the internal use of the colony; little was exported. In some places, cotton production created a viable textile industry in Lima, where slaves worked in the factories. Later, enough sugarcane was grown to export it to Europe. Most haciendas were small, their size dictated by the sparseness of the land. Thus, even the largest of the farms had only a few dozen workers.

The slave trade itself was a costly endeavor since slaves had to journey on a several-month voyage from Africa to the Americas (usually PANAMA). They then traveled overland for several weeks to the Pacific Ocean and were further transported by boat to Lima; many died en route. Slaves were valued for their physical labor. In addition, many of the arriving slaves had worked farms in African climates not unlike that of Peru. Thus they contributed precious expertise about growing crops in a dry land. Other slaves, skilled in crafts and metals before their capture, would continue to work in artisan trades as slaves, in both the city and the country.

By the end of the sixteenth century Peru also had a substantial number of free blacks. Perhaps one-fourth to one-third of Afro-Peruvians had bought their freedom under Spanish laws, had arrived free, or had been granted their freedom for fighting in the conquest with Pizarro. Most of the free blacks, known as *libertos,* shunned the agricultural regions for the cities, particularly Lima, where they worked as low- to mid-wage laborers, maids, and the like. Their actions were rigidly circumscribed: in 1577, for example, the viceroy of Peru banned any black person from owning a weapon. Throughout colonial times blacks were barred as a matter of course from many of the skilled trades.

Although Spanish law allowed any slave to buy his or her freedom, slaves' activities were closely monitored. According to historian Frederick Bowser, the vast majority of slaves who were manumitted between 1580 and 1650 in Lima were women and children, particularly female children—considered the least valuable slaves. Only 4 percent of slaves freed in Lima during that time period were between the ages of sixteen and twenty-five—for a master, the most profitable years of a slave's life. Apparently slaveholders had informal means of keeping their most valuable slaves closely tethered. It is little wonder, then, that when a male liberto obtained his freedom he often elected to join the comparatively egalitarian Spanish colonial army in Peru, or left Peru altogether to enlist in another colony's military. At the turn of the sixteenth century black slaves and libertos made up perhaps 10 percent of Peru's population. In the Andes, African slaves and libertos were probably equal in number to Spaniards until as late as 1640.

Despite the high cost of slaves, demand for imports grew well into the seventeenth century. Occasionally, a few African slaves were bought and/or captured by Indians. With greater frequency, Spanish colonists sent incoming African slaves to work alongside Incas in the gold- and silver-mining gangs of the Andes. In the deep-shaft mines, brutal labor, poor ventilation, and cave-ins conspired to keep the life of a worker short and the demand for slaves high.

The demand for slave labor prompted colonists to circumvent Spain's rigid control of the lucrative slave trade, which it monitored in order to tax. Typically, Spain granted the rights to its slave trade to a particular company or companies and forbade Spanish colonists from trading with anyone else. For example, from 1701 to 1713 several French companies held the *asiento* (the right to the slave trade) for Spanish America. During this time, FRANCE exported several thousand blacks to Peru from their stations along Africa's CONGO RIVER—a long voyage with a high cost. If a buyer was willing to deal with smugglers, slaves could be obtained more cheaply from Portuguese BRAZIL or the British and French colonies in the Caribbean.

Spain reluctantly acknowledged its lack of control over the trade in 1740, when it allowed privileged Peruvian colonists to buy *licencias* (licenses), with which they could buy as many slaves as they wanted from any nation not at war with Spain. The licencia system lasted half a century but did little to curb

Peru (At a Glance)

Official Name: Republic of Peru

Area: 1,285,220 sq km (496,226 sq mi)

Location: Western South America, bordered by Chile, Ecuador, Colombia, Brazil, Bolivia, and the South Pacific Ocean

Capital: Lima (population 7,594,000; 2004 estimate)

Other Major Cities: Arequipa (population 710,103), Callao (population 424,294) (2004 estimates)

Population: 27,167,000 (2004 estimate)

Population Density: 21 persons per sq km (55 per sq mi)

Population Below Age 15: 33.5 percent (male 4,828,531; female 4,678,008; 2003 estimate)

Population Growth Rate: 1.61 percent (2003 estimate)

Total Fertility Rate: 2.81 children born per woman (2003 estimate)

Life Expectancy at Birth: Total population: 70.88 years (male 68.45 years; female 73.43 years; 2003 estimate)

Infant Mortality Rate: 36.97 deaths per 1,000 live births (2003 estimate)

Literacy Rate (age 15 and over who can read and write): Total population: 90.9 percent (male 95.2 percent; female 86.8 percent; 2003 estimate)

Education: Education is free and compulsory for ages six to fifteen, but the quality of education is poor because of inadequately trained teachers, large class size, and poorly furnished facilities. Children from the wealthy families usually attend private schools. There are several universities in Peru, among them the Pontifical Catholic University of Peru and the University of Lima.

Languages: Spanish and Quechua are the official languages of Peru. Aymara is also spoken.

Ethnic Groups: 45 percent Amerindian, 37 percent mestizo (mixed Amerindian and white), 15 percent white, and 3 percent black, Japanese, Chinese, and other

Religions: 90 percent of Peruvians are Roman Catholic.

Climate: There are three main climatic and topographic regions of Peru: the Costa, the Sierra, and the Montaña. The desert Costa is one of the driest regions on earth, but it is not hot. Average temperatures range from 66° F (19° C) to 72° F (22° C). Some vegetation is supported by winter fogs. The climate of the Sierra varies with elevation, and is rainy from December to March. There is permanent snow on some mountain peaks. The eastern Peruvian Montaña climate is hot and humid, with heavy average rainfall throughout the year.

Land, Plants, and Animals: The Costa has three distinct regions, based partly on the width of the land between the Andean mountain ranges and the sea. The northern region is twenty to thirty miles wide in most areas. The central region is narrower and hilly, and the southern region is narrow, with land that is rarely level. The Sierra region includes a portion of the Andes Mountains. In nothern Peru the Andes have lower elevations that rarely exceed 16,000 feet (about 5,000 meters). The central Peruvian Andes are higher and create natural barriers to travel. The southern Andes become a high plateau with scattered mountain peaks. Several of Peru's many rivers flow into Lake Titicaca, the highest navigable lake on earth. The tropical lowlands of the Amazon River Basin, known as the Montaña, cover more than three-fifths of Peru. Some grasses grow in the Costa, and animals include sea lions, penguins, pelicans, and gulls. Fish include tuna, swordfish, and anchovies. Vegetation in the Sierra includes grasses and eucalyptus, and animals include the llama and alpaca. The Montaña is home to thousands of varieties of plants, among them coca. Wildlife includes jaguars and monkeys.

Natural Resources: Copper, silver, gold, oil, timber, fish, iron ore, coal, phosphate, potash, hydropower, and natural gas

Currency: nuevo sol (PEN)

Gross Domestic Product (GDP): $138.8 billion (2002 estimate)

GDP per Capita: $5,000 (2002 estimate)

GDP Real Growth Rate: 5.3 percent (2002 estimate)

Primary Economic Activities: Agriculture, mining and quarrying, manufacturing, construction, transport, and services

Primary Crops: Coffee, cotton, sugarcane, rice, wheat, potatoes, corn, plantains, coca, poultry, beef, dairy products, wool, and fish

Industries: Mining of metals, petroleum, fishing, textiles, clothing, food processing, cement, auto assembly, steel, shipbuilding, and metal fabrication

Primary Exports: Fish and fish products, gold, copper, zinc, crude petroleum and byproducts, lead, coffee, sugar, and cotton

Primary Imports: Machinery, transport equipment, foodstuffs, petroleum, iron and steel, chemicals, and pharmaceuticals

Primary Trade Partners: United States, China, United Kingdom, Switzerland, Japan, Chile, Spain, Colombia, Brazil, Venezuela, and Argentina

Government: Peru is a constitutional republic. The chief of state and head of government is President Alejandro Toledo Manrique (since July 2001; popularly elected for a five-year term). The legislative branch is the unicameral Congress of the Republic of Peru (120 members, elected by popular vote to five-year terms). The judicial branch is headed by the Supreme Court of Justice.

Shelle Sumners

smuggling. After 1795 Spain abandoned the system and allowed any Spanish colonist to buy as many slaves as he wanted from any source not at war with Spain.

Cultural Survival and Resistance

Much of the African slaves' cultural and linguistic heritage was lost as a result of the long distance they were forced to travel and the length of time they sometimes spent in other colonies before arriving in Peru. Nonetheless, many slaves kept the drum-saturated music of their homelands alive, which over the centuries they blended with the string-influenced music of the Spanish colonists. African forms of cooking were also preserved, since preparing food was a task that slaves working as domestics often performed both en route and upon arrival in Spanish America.

As most Afro-Peruvians were converted to Catholicism, African religious customs merged with Christianity. The most prominent example of this syncretism surviving today is the ceremony of El Señor de los Milagros, an annual march through the streets of Lima celebrated by tens of thousands. The ceremony originated in the mid-seventeenth century, when blacks, primarily from ANGOLA, organized in *cofradías*, societies of mutual support. Here, they recalled songs of their homeland and applied them to the Catholic reverence for saints and images, as well as to the belief in Christ as a redeemer who would someday free the righteous. The cofradías thus helped to create a ritual and faith that simultaneously preserved African heritage, upheld Hispanic values, and espoused bold ideas of liberation.

Afro-Peruvians rebelled against Spanish oppression in sporadic outbreaks as early as the 1540s. One of the larger revolts took place when the English buccaneer Sir Francis Drake attacked the city of Lima in 1578. Ultimately Drake released the city, and the Afro-Peruvian revolt, like most such rebellions, was quickly put down.

In some instances, however, slaves fled their masters and established *palenques*—remote villages where they were relatively free from harassment. One of the longest enduring palenques was Huachipa, which was established in the central coastal region in the early 1700s under the direction of a slave known as Francisco Congo, also known as Chavelilla. Few records survive about Congo's rule of Huachipa, but he appears to have steered the settlement through a prosperous period of farming, ranching, and occasional raiding. In 1763 and 1764 another group of *cimarrones* (escaped slaves) in the Carabayllo Valley near Lima leveled such a series of attacks against travelers that the colonial government mounted a punitive expedition against the fugitives. A large force under the command of Pablo Sáenz de Bustamonte, including sixty soldiers from the viceroy's personal guard, dealt a decisive blow to the cimarrones in 1764. The accused ringleaders were executed, the rest beaten and reduced to slavery once again.

Free blacks also exerted autonomy when their limited rights were threatened. In 1779 the government tried to levy a special tax on libertos in order to replenish the ailing treasury. Most complied, but libertos in the northern coastal town of Lambayeque refused. The colonial government apparently intended to punish the resisting libertos, but at roughly the same time Indians under Tupac Amarú began a massive rebellion against the government's oppression of Indians. It was one of the most far-reaching and influential uprisings in the history of colonial Spanish America, but the rebellion was ultimately crushed and Tupac Amarú executed in 1780. The insurgent Indians were joined by many blacks, the most powerful of whom were under the leadership of Juan Santos Atahualpa. The Africans added the liberation of slaves to the demands of the Indians—the first insurrection to include such a demand. Peru's outnumbered Spaniards, badly frightened and in need of black and mulatto allies, allowed the libertos in Lambayeque their tax revolt, and did not retaliate. Even after the defeat of Tupac Amarú, the Spaniards made little attempt to enforce the liberto tax. Eventually the colonial government was forced to enact several of the reforms Tupac Amarú had demanded, though freeing slaves was not among these. Still, Lambayeque remains one of the few instances of Afro-Peruvian triumph over the Spanish colonial regime.

Independent Peru

By the late eighteenth century a reform movement with several factions had evolved in Spanish America generally and in Peru in particular. One such movement advocated an end to black slavery; another, more prominent, camp advocated an end to Spanish rule. Eventually the two merged, albeit somewhat uncomfortably. At the time that SIMÓN BOLÍVAR began his war of liberation against Spain in VENEZUELA, Peru had an estimated 90,000 African slaves. In his first two attempts to liberate Venezuela and COLOMBIA, Bolívar rejected the use of black soldiers. However, by 1819, he began to enlist black troops and defeated Spanish troops in Venezuela and Colombia. His success sparked similar revolts in South America. In 1821 Argentine José de San Martín followed Bolívar's example, drafting blacks, mulattoes, and whites, and seized Lima.

In the rebel armies, blacks were generally segregated from whites into their own regiments and battalions. Often these troops were among the worst supplied and worst fed of all soldiers, yet they were required to undertake some of the most dangerous fighting. The South American wars of independence reached a peak in 1824, when rebel forces under Antonio José de Sucre met Loyalists at Ayacucho and Junín in the mineral-rich region of south central Peru. There, the Husare del Peru, a battalion of libertos, slaves, and mestizos, was largely responsible for the decisive rebel victories that secured the liberation of Peru from Spain.

In 1821, during San Martín's brief rule of war-torn Peru, he emancipated children born to slaves after July 28, 1821. Later that year he freed slaves owned by Loyalists, promised emancipation to slaves who fought honorably in the rebel army, and forbade the importation of slaves in the future. It took several years, however—until 1828—before these freedoms were affirmed by a new constitution. Still, all slaves who were born before July 28, 1821, and all who belonged to rebel sympathizers, were still in bondage.

Matters would worsen before they got better for Peru's remaining slaves, as the country dissolved into civil war in the late 1820s. From then until the mid-1830s a string of short-lived dictators tried to ingratiate themselves with wealthy slaveholders by allowing many abuses against free and enslaved blacks—many libertos experienced conditions that were little better than the slavery from which they had been freed. Such abuses culminated in 1835, when General Felipe Salavery declared that Peru was once again open to the slave trade, and in 1839, when Agustín Gamarra took over the country and signed a law that re-enslaved all libertos for the next half century.

In 1848 slaves on plantations near the northern coastal city of Trujillo staged a widespread revolt. They quickly captured the plantations, retaliated against their masters, and proceeded to march on Trujillo. There, with the help of urban slaves, the insurgents stormed the city, attacked many slaveholders, and held others hostage. When it soon became clear the revolt could not be sustained—Peruvian forces laid siege to and eventually took the city—the slaves killed a good number of the hostages. The revolt unnerved much of Peru, but slavery continued, with between 15,000 and 20,000 in servitude.

Emancipation and Beyond

In 1854 Peru fell into another period of civil war. In order to bolster his muster of troops, President José Rufino Echenique declared that all slaves who joined his army for two years would be freed after the fighting. Not to be outdone, Echenique's rival, Ramón Castilla, declared in December 1854 that all slavery was officially abolished—assuming that he and his army (many of whom he expected would be slaves) could seize power. Many slaves joined Castilla, and by January 1855 he was victorious. True to his word, Castilla ended slavery at last. To mollify Peru's powerful former slaveholders, Castilla's government paid them partial compensation for their loss. Slaves received no compensation for their years of servitude.

After the slaves' emancipation, many fled the coastal plantations and Andean mines for the cities. Former slaveholders were thus left with a labor shortage in both the fields and the mines, a problem they solved by importing massive numbers of workers from East Asia. The indentured laborers, mostly Chinese, were treated as slaves in all but name. Some of the former Afro-Peruvian slaves found work overseeing the Asians. The government and others also employed free blacks to quell the not infrequent riots by maltreated Asians. By 1875 Peru's blacks were surpassed in number by perhaps 80,000 Asians. The increased competition from Asians and Indians (many of whom moved from the highlands to the coastal regions in the late 1800s) made it extremely difficult for Afro-Peruvians to find work.

At the turn of the twentieth century and for decades to follow, many Afro-Peruvians remained in poverty, and most of those lived in urban slums—primarily in Lima. By day, those who could find jobs worked as domestic servants, bus drivers, textile laborers, and construction workers; few of these jobs offered hope of advancement. By night, Afro-Peruvians returned home to neighborhoods severely lacking sanitation. Several families often shared a single water faucet, and houses were extremely overcrowded and poorly built. The situation was little better for the fewer Afro-Peruvians who remained in the countryside and in the mountains and worked the same fields and mines their ancestors had worked as slaves.

Because discrimination was persistent throughout Peru, many Afro-Peruvians denied their African ancestry when they could. Afro-Peruvians commonly aspired for their children to marry lighter-skinned people. Still, the influence of Afro-Peruvian culture extended from music to cooking to sports.

After World War II, Peru underwent a gradual but disruptive change from rule by a privileged oligarchy to rule by a more representative democracy, though military leaders still held power. This change yielded new opportunities in schooling and health for the poor and, simultaneously, a massive rural-to-urban migration. These two factors made Peruvian cities vibrant centers of black culture. African dance and theater groups were founded, Afro-Peruvian literature was more widely disseminated, and racial discrimination against blacks and other minorities eased somewhat by the 1950s and 1960s. Influenced by the CIVIL RIGHTS MOVEMENT in the United States during this time, Afro-Peruvians formed several groups to agitate for political reforms to help blacks. Perhaps the most important of these were the Movimiento Negro Francisco Congo (Francisco Congo Black Movement) and the Asociación pro Derechos Humanos del Negro (Association for Black Human Rights).

In the 1970s several private groups supporting Afro-Peruvian advancement came together briefly around the Cultural Association of Black Peruvian Youth. The association taught Afro-Peruvian children about their heritage and encouraged education and political organization of their communities. Although it ultimately splintered, several factions of the movement continued their work in the 1980s and 1990s, contributing to a greater awareness of black history and culture in Peru. For example, Lima's Afro-Peruvian Research Institute continues to serve as a resource for black studies in Peru. In 1992 singer Susana Baca and her husband Ricardo Pereira founded the Instituto Negrocontinuo to celebrate Afro-Peruvian culture. The center collects oral histories of Afro-Peruvians as well as providing books and other materials for students and researchers interested in studying Afro-Peruvian history and culture.

Politically, Peru has made some progress in improving the social standing and treatment of black Peruvians. In 2000 the government made racial discrimination a crime. Anyone convicted under the law must perform at least sixty days of community service and is barred from holding public office for three years. In addition, several members of Peru's congress are black. Some branches of the military, however, still refrain from promoting blacks to the officer corps, and discriminatory practices remain in many areas of employment and social life. As of the early twenty-first century, however, Afro-Peruvians had yet to coalesce behind one or more political parties that would promote an agenda to help blacks—thus leaving a significant challenge for future generations of Afro-Peruvians.

See also Catholic Church in Latin America and the Caribbean; Colonial Latin America and the Caribbean; Colonial Rule; Mining in Latin America and the Caribbean; Racism in Latin America and the Caribbean; Slave Laws in Colonial Spanish America; Slave Rebellions in Colonial Spanish America; Slavery in Latin America and the Caribbean; Transatlantic Slave Trade.

Bibliography

Blanchard, Peter. *Slavery and Abolition in Early Republican Peru.* SR Books, 1992.

Lockhart, James. *Spanish Peru, 1532–1560: A Social History.* University of Wisconsin Press, 1994.

Luz, Maria Martinez Montiel. *Presencia africana en Sudamerica.* Consejo Nacional para la Cultura y las Artes (Mexico), 1995.

Rout, Leslie B., Jr. *The African Experience in Spanish America: 1502 to the Present Day.* Cambridge University Press, 1976.

Peterson, Oscar Emmanuel

1925–

Canadian jazz pianist and composer, known for his technical brilliance as a soloist and for his hard-driving percussive style on the keyboard.

One of the shining lights in the history of JAZZ, pianist Oscar Peterson was born in Montréal, Québec. Encouraged by his father, a railroad porter who saw music as a refuge from poverty, Peterson began piano lessons at the age of six. He started recording while still in high school and was soon playing on a weekly Montréal radio show. In 1949, brought to New York by producer Norman Granz, Peterson played at Carnegie Hall as part of the popular, star-studded touring group Jazz at the Philharmonic.

After touring regularly with the ensemble, he formed the first incarnation of the Oscar Peterson Trio in 1953 with bassist Ray Brown and guitarist Herb Ellis. After drummer Ed Thigpen replaced Ellis in 1958, the trio remained together until Brown left in 1967. Although Peterson also worked as a sideman with a roster of jazz heavyweights including ELLA FITZGERALD, LOUIS ARMSTRONG, BILLIE HOLIDAY, LESTER YOUNG, and COLEMAN HAWKINS, it was primarily with his trio that he earned his reputation as a dazzling improviser.

Since the 1970s his stellar unaccompanied live performances and recordings have, according to one critic, "proved incontestably that he was one of the greatest solo pianists in the history of jazz." Peterson is a prolific composer and recording artist with more than eighty albums under his belt. He has been nominated for eleven Grammy Awards and has won seven. His 1965 *Canadiana Suite* was nominated by the National Academy of Arts and Science as best jazz composition. Peterson's lifelong devotion to jazz, as well as his tireless opposition to racism, prompted Toronto's York University to name him to a three-year term as chancellor in 1991. Also that year, he was honored with a Toronto Arts Award for lifetime achievement. In 2003 he received the President's Award of the International Association for Jazz Education in Toronto.

Bibliography

Lees, Gene. *Oscar Peterson: The Will to Swing.* Prima Pub., 1990.

Lyons, Len. *The Great Jazz Pianists.* Quill, 1983.

Peter Hudson

Pétion, Alexandre

1770–1818

Prominent figure in the Haitian revolution; president of Haiti.

Alexandre Sabès Pétion was the son of a French colonist and a freeborn mulatto (of African and European descent) woman. It is unclear why he used the name Pétion instead of his father's surname, Sabès. The name Pétion was derived from the nickname "Pitchoun" (little lad). Pétion's father did not recognize his son as his own because of the boy's dark skin, but did send Pétion to FRANCE to be educated.

At the age of eighteen Pétion joined the colonial militia, and in 1791, with the outbreak of the HAITIAN REVOLUTION, he joined the rebellion sparked by the slave rebel BOUKMAN. Pétion initially fought under the black forces led by FRANÇOIS DOMINIQUE TOUSSAINT LOUVERTURE, which managed to expel a British invasion of SAINT-DOMINGUE (now HAITI and the DOMINICAN REPUBLIC) and eventually assume complete control over the island. After this victory, however, discord between the black and mulatto officers in Toussaint's company began to emerge. Pétion's allegiance soon shifted to ANDRÉ RIGAUD's mulatto forces, which more closely reflected Pétion's own background and interests. Rigaud was the leader of the *affranchis* party of freeborn mulattoes who were fighting to obtain complete equality with the whites of Saint-Domingue. Rigaud's forces opposed Toussaint in the 1799 civil war that came to be known as the "War of the South." Pétion was sent to the key city of Jacmel, which was besieged by Toussaint's lieutenants, JEAN-JACQUES DESSALINES and HENRI CHRISTOPHE.

In 1800, when Rigaud's forces were defeated by Toussaint and the conflict ended, Pétion left Saint-Domingue for exile in France. In 1802, though, he returned to the island with French forces sent by Napoleon to restore French rule under the command of General Charles-Victor Leclerc. The French beat back the rebel forces and imprisoned Toussaint, and Toussaint's generals joined the French. The French forces were weakened by disease after the battle, however, and fears grew that they were intent on reinstituting slavery. Pétion realized that Leclerc's rule would mean a loss of rights for both mulattoes and blacks, and joined the new rebel group under the leadership of Dessalines.

On January 1, 1804, the French were finally decisively defeated and the country was declared independent and renamed Haiti. Dessalines became Haiti's new ruler, first as governor-general and later as emperor. Together with Dessalines, Pétion is said to have designed the Haitian flag.

Divisions grew between the black forces and the mulattoes (now led by Pétion), though, and this fact sparked a new revolt against Dessalines. On October 17, 1806, Dessalines was ambushed and killed as he attempted to resolve the revolt, and the presidency was offered by the rebels to his principal lieutenant, HENRI CHRISTOPHE. The presidency that Christophe was offered, however, would have lacked real force: Pétion's group sought to retain the most political power in the government they conceived for a mulatto-controlled senate.

Christophe refused the presidency and marched on PORT-AU-PRINCE, but Pétion's troops forced him back to his stronghold in the north. Christophe led an independent kingdom in the north while a mulatto-controlled republic ruled the south, and this schism would divide Haiti for fourteen years. Pétion was secure within his constituency, though, and he was elected president by the senate in 1807 and again in 1811 and 1815. In 1816 he was declared president for life, with the right to choose his successor.

During his rule Pétion fostered the development of southern Haiti as a republic and was the main force behind its first constitution. He also transformed the new country's agricultural system, organizing a massive land distribution that granted small plots of government land to former soldiers. Although he envisioned a Haiti ruled by a mulatto-controlled oligarchy, with large landholdings mainly in mulatto hands, Pétion implemented policies that had an unforeseen effect on the country's agricultural economy. Originally one of the most prosperous plantation-based export economies in the Caribbean, Haiti's agricultural system came to be characterized by small-scale subsistence production.

Though he held absolute power, Pétion exercised moderation and was genuinely popular among the people, who nicknamed him "Papa bon coeur" (Father good heart). He was influential within the region as well, offering crucial early support to the Pan-American movement in 1816 by assisting SIMÓN BOLÍVAR in his landing at VENEZUELA. Citizens wept openly in the streets when Pétion died at the age of forty-eight—the cause is believed to have been an acute attack of MALARIA.

See also Slave Rebellions in Latin America and the Caribbean.

Paulette Poujol-Oriol

Petioni, Charles A(ugustin)

1885–1951

Caribbean-born African American physician, editor, businessman, and spokesman for West Indian independence.

The son of Charles E. and Alicia (Martin) Petioni, Charles Augustin Petioni was born on August 27, 1885, in Trinidad, where he was educated and began a career in business and journalism. In 1913 he married Rosa Alling. They had two daughters, Margaret (who died before 1950) and Muriel. In 1918 the colonial government of Trinidad sent word to him that his outspoken views about local political and economic conditions had permanently damaged future career opportunities for himself and his family. For that reason he departed for NEW YORK, where he worked as a manual laborer during the day and attended the City College of New York at night. Upon completion of the premedical course at City College, he entered HOWARD UNIVERSITY College of Medicine, from which he graduated in 1925. After an internship at St. Agnes Hospital in Raleigh, North Carolina, he returned to New York, where he began medical practice. He devoted much of his later life to many African American and West Indian social, political, economic, and medical organizations.

From 1901 to 1908 Petioni acquired some knowledge of business while working as a clerk and manager of the Trinidad branch of the famous Paris firm, Félix Potin and Company. He gained experience as a journalist by serving as chief reporter and subeditor of newspapers in Trinidad from 1908 to 1918 and as associate editor of the *New Negro* in New York in 1918. He was the Washington representative of *Business World* from 1921 to 1922. Most significant, from 1921 to 1925 he was a student reporter while at Howard University for *Negro World*, the newspaper of black leader MARCUS GARVEY and his UNIVERSAL NEGRO IMPROVEMENT ASSOCIATION (UNIA).

When Petioni began to practice medicine in New York he became part of a complex struggle for better medical conditions for blacks in HARLEM. Though Harlem Hospital served a neighborhood that had become predominantly black, the facility had only recently admitted black doctors to practice. In addition, black graduates of white medical schools were considered to be, and sometimes considered themselves to be, superior to graduates of black medical schools. Petioni fought for equal status for the graduates of Howard and of Meharry Medical College in Nashville, Tennessee. He later helped to unite the warring factions of black physicians when they came together to found the Central Harlem Medical Society. Later, when conditions in public hospitals had not improved satisfactorily, Petioni helped to organize a group that bought Mount Morris Park Hospital as a private institution for blacks.

Petioni's views on the economic development of what he called *our group* required emancipation from "economic slavery and dependence . . . without any assistance on the part of others." To this end he founded the Metropolitan Benefit Insurance Society, Limited, in Trinidad, as well as the Trinidad Co-operative Bank, Limited. In New York City he founded the Trinidad Benevolent Society and the Lupetner Finance Corporation. This experience led the founders of the Carver Federal

Savings and Loan Association to consult him about their proposed institution, and at the time of his death he was vice chairman of the board of that organization.

Petioni's most significant activities sprang from the needs of the West Indian community in Harlem. He also embraced activities of African Americans, West Indians in the Caribbean, and Africans. The Trinidad Benevolent Association, an organization similar to many in New York, provided social and economic support for West Indian immigrants from the respective islands. Petioni's vision, however, was different from that of many of the organizations: it extended beyond a parochial identification with one island.

In 1930 Petioni founded the West India Committee of America, which became the Caribbean Union. The purposes of this organization were to stimulate the development of West Indian business enterprises, give charity to West Indians in need, find employment for immigrants, encourage naturalization, lobby for better treatment of West Indians under British rule, and foster better relations between native and foreign-born blacks in New York. In 1936 the organization raised money and supplies to aid the defense of ETHIOPIA against ITALY and registered strong protests against GREAT BRITAIN's lifting of sanctions against Italy. Later that year Petioni, as president of the Caribbean Union, led a coalition of black groups to Mayor Fiorello LaGuardia to protest general conditions in Harlem. Specifically, the groups protested the policies of the police department and the board of education. This united effort, for which Petioni was the spokesman, included organizations as diverse as the Communist Party, the Urban League, and the Peace Mission Movement, a religious community led by Father Divine.

The activities of the Caribbean Union demonstrate that although Petioni retained a strong identification with the WEST INDIES, he did not believe in divisions among blacks in their struggle against white oppression. In 1936 he wrote an article "The Intra-racial Problem," in which he expressed great concern about a growing rift between native and foreign-born residents of Harlem. He said that whites who sought to control blacks were the only ones who benefited from this division. He also urged support for a resolution of the National Negro Congress in February 1946 to create an International Negro Congress in order to establish better relationships among blacks throughout the world. He also worked with Baptist minister ADAM CLAYTON POWELL JR., in the successful effort to obtain jobs for blacks in white-owned Harlem businesses.

Petioni was actively involved in events that ultimately led to the independence of some of the British West Indies. In the late 1930s a group of West Indians in New York formed the West Indies National Emergency Committee to discuss the implications of World War II and of U.S. interests in the Caribbean on the future of the West Indies. This group became the West Indies National Council of which Petioni was the second president. Through the active financial support of the West Indian community in the United States the council held mass meetings, sought allies among Latin American governments, and established contacts with leaders in the West Indies. The council also attempted to influence the British and United States governments, in order to assert the right of West Indians for self-determination, self-government, and independence. Petioni, as representative of the council, went to the 1945 United Nations San Francisco Conference to lobby for this right. His activities earned him a place on the United States attorney general's subversive list. Petioni died on October 15, 1951.

Some basic facts about Petioni are in *Who's Who in Colored America* (1950). Information can also be found in the manuscripts of the WORKS PROGRESS ADMINISTRATION study "The Negro in New York," located in the SCHOMBURG CENTER FOR RESEARCH IN BLACK CULTURE in New York City.

From *Dictionary of American Negro Biography* by Rayford W. Logan and Michael R. Winston, editors. Copyright © 1982 by Rayford W. Logan and Michael R. Winston. Reprinted by permission of W. W. Norton & Company, Inc.

See also Hospitals, Black; Medical Associations; Nationalism in Latin America and the Caribbean; Trinidad and Tobago.

Robert G. McGuire III

Petry, Ann Lane

1908–1997

American writer of adult novels and children's literature who chronicled the urban black female experience.

Ann Lane Petry was born and raised in the predominantly white, middle-class community of Saybrook, Connecticut. The daughter of a pharmacist, she worked in her father's drugstore as a teenager and went on to major in pharmacology at the University of Connecticut. After graduating, she worked at and managed the family drugstore in Old Saybrook. Her pharmacological endeavors notwithstanding, Petry wrote short stories while working, none of which have been published. After marrying George Petry, a mystery writer, in 1939, she moved to NEW YORK CITY and dropped pharmacy altogether, choosing instead to develop her career as a writer.

Her first job in New York was at a HARLEM newspaper, the *Amsterdam News,* where she worked for four years. Petry moved on to *The Peoples Voice,* where she wrote a column on Harlem society in the women's section of the paper. Her first published work of fiction, a short story entitled "Marie of the Cabin Club," was a romantic drama that she published under a pseudonym, preferring to save her real name for more serious works. In addition to writing, Petry became involved in community issues. Her activities included, among others, the formation of a black woman's consumer advocacy group, and the establishment of a program in a Harlem school to help children living in crime-ridden neighborhoods.

During this period, Petry joined writing workshops and creative writing classes at Columbia University. She wrote a few short stories, one of which, "On Saturday Night, the Sirens Sound," foreshadowed her first novel, *The Street,* which was to become her first literary coup. This short story, and a few more she wrote, ran in the NATIONAL ASSOCIATION FOR THE AD-

VANCEMENT OF COLORED PEOPLE's newspaper, THE CRISIS, where it caught the attention of editors at Houghton Mifflin. Petry was urged to apply for a writer's fellowship awarded by the publishing company. She did, and won a $2,400 grant and a book contract in 1945.

The Street (1946) was a resounding success, eventually selling more than two million copies, the first book by a black woman to do so. An unsentimental tale of a single mother's fruitless efforts to secure a livelihood and shelter her child from the danger that the street represents, the book launched Petry's career as an author of considerable renown. She went on to publish two more novels, *Country Place* in 1947 and *The Narrows* in 1988. Neither work achieved the level of success that *The Street* had enjoyed, but in later years both were acknowledged as works of great literary merit.

In addition to her novels, Petry authored works of adolescent nonfiction chronicling the lives of historical black figures, including *Harriet Tubman: Conductor on the Underground Railroad* (1955) and *Tituba of Salem Village* (1964). She also wrote two children's books, *The Drugstore Cat* (1949) and *Legend of the Saints* (1970), and penned numerous essays on a variety of topics.

Petry received numerous awards and honors in recognition of her contributions to the black literary canon, juvenile and adult. A visionary and pioneer of multiculturalism and black feminism, Ann Petry died on April 28, 1997 in Old Saybrook, Connecticut.

See also Children's Literature, African American; Feminism in the United States; Literature, African American; Women Writers, Black, in the United States.

James Smethurst

Pettiford, Oscar

1922–1960

Jazz bassist, bandleader, and bebop innovator.

Oscar Pettiford helped to invent and popularize the bass solo in JAZZ, significantly expanding the vocabulary and syntax of the language of the bass. Pettiford drew inspiration from the playing style of Jimmy Blanton, a bassist with DUKE ELLINGTON's band. Blanton had emphasized the melodic possibilities of the instrument at a time when the bass was most often relegated to the rhythm section of an ensemble. Pettiford, following Blanton's lead, plucked his strings with the length, rather than the width, of his index finger, thus extending the tonal and temporal possibilities for individual notes. At his best Pettiford produced a melodic clarity and complexity that echoed that of jazz guitar, and this bravura lent itself to a solo playing style. Pettiford was considered one of the top three bassists of his time, rivaling as well as influencing his contemporaries Ray Brown and CHARLES MINGUS.

Born in Okmulgee, Oklahoma, to parents of Choctaw, Cherokee, and African extraction, Pettiford moved with his family to Minneapolis when he was three. Pettiford came from a show-business family, and he contributed to the family's musical act as it toured the Minnesota vaudeville circuit. He demonstrated precocious musicality and by the age of fourteen was devoting almost all of his attention to the string bass.

In 1943, Pettiford joined on with Charlie Barnet's big-band and followed the group to NEW YORK, where he began working with other musicians. During his early New York years Pettiford collaborated with ROY ELDRIDGE, THELONIOUS MONK, and DIZZY GILLESPIE. Pettiford participated in the legendary jam sessions at Minton's Playhouse, helping to establish the roots of BEBOP, a frenetic, hard-driving, and heavily improvisational style of jazz that broke away from the sweetness and set-arrangements of swing. In 1944 Pettiford and Gillespie headed the first working bebop combo, at the Onyx Club on 52nd Street, but the two parted within a year because of personal differences.

After a brief stint with the legendary tenor saxophonist COLEMAN HAWKINS, Pettiford joined his childhood idol, Duke Ellington, with whose band he remained for three years. Despite a long-running alcohol problem, Pettiford continued to be active on the club and concert circuit both in the United States and abroad. In the early 1950s he returned to New York full time to lead the Café Bohemia's house band, and in 1958 Pettiford emigrated to Copenhagen, where he remained until his death in 1960.

In addition to helping invent bebop and elevating the status of the bass in jazz, Pettiford won many music industry awards for his recordings and contributed a number of memorable songs to the jazz repertory, including *Tricrotism, Bohemia After Dark*, and *Swingin' Till the Girls Come Home*.

See also Music, African American.

Eric Bennett

P-Funk

See Clinton, George.

Phal, Louis

1897–1925

Senegalese boxer known as the Battling Siki.

The first African to win a world BOXING title, Louis Phal was a light heavyweight whose 1922 defeat of the French champion Georges Carpentier won him international fame and, later, the status of a legend. French West African–born Phal has been the subject of two novels and one documentary, yet very little is known of his early life. According to the African American cultural critic Gerald Early, the competing strains of myth and fable about Phal are a portrait in contradiction.

By some accounts an orphan adopted by a French soldier, Phal was depicted as an illiterate primitive by most of the Western press. One obituary in the African American newspaper the

CHICAGO DEFENDER, however, claimed he knew seven languages. He certainly spoke French, having moved as a child to FRANCE, where he served with distinction in the French army during World War I. Known as an artless boxer, Phal became an instant celebrity in France following his victory over Carpentier.

After he moved to the United States in 1923, his behavior outside the ring—drinking, brawling, and sporting flamboyant clothes and exotic pets—alternately delighted and appalled Americans. Mainstream white newspapers called him a "natural man," or even an animal—labels that white athletes with similar lifestyles never received, as Early points out. Phal's career declined quickly; by 1925 he had lost several bouts and was rumored to be on the brink of deportation. In December of that year Phal was fatally shot in the back.

See also French West Africa; Senegal.

Bibliography
Chalk, Ocania. *Pioneers of Black Sport*. Dodd, Mead and Co., 1975.

Kate Tuttle

Philadelphia, Pennsylvania

Major port and manufacturing city in Pennsylvania and the fifth-largest city in the United States.

Philadelphia mayor Wilson Goode prepares for a television speech about the MOVE shootout on March 3, 1986. CORBIS

Africans first arrived in Philadelphia in 1684, when the ship *Isabella* brought 150 slaves. By 1720 around 2,500 Africans had been brought to Pennsylvania as slaves. The growing abolitionist movement of the next few decades led to a 1780 law that began to dismantle slavery. The 1790 census confirmed that Philadelphia's free black community, numbering 2,000, was the largest in the United States. The free blacks formed a burial ground in 1786 and a FREE AFRICAN SOCIETY in 1787. Community members included RICHARD ALLEN and ABSALOM JONES, who together pioneered the independent black church movement in the United States. In a little over a quarter of a century, Philadelphia became home to a number of historic black churches. The African Church, founded in about 1787, became the First African Church of Saint Thomas in 1794, with Jones as its pastor. Two years later, Allen became pastor of the Bethel Methodist Church. The First African Baptist Church was founded in 1809, followed in 1811 by the First African Presbyterian Church. In 1816 Allen and others organized the AFRICAN METHODIST EPISCOPAL CHURCH (AME), the first African American denomination. Over the next 180 years the black churches of Philadelphia became powerful and important institutions, sustaining everyone from a distinctive and large black elite to the BLACK PANTHER PARTY. By 1820 slavery had disappeared from Philadelphia, and African Americans flooded into the city. Among the city's 100,622 inhabitants at that time, 12,110 were free blacks.

In the antebellum period, however, African Americans were excluded from the developing industrial economy and grew increasingly poor. As competition for work grew, so did white hostility. Mobs invaded African American homes during numerous race riots in the 1840s. Prohibited from voting by 1838, blacks regained suffrage in 1871, which precipitated more riots and led to the murder of black leader Octavius Catto.

The black community continued to develop. In 1830 it hosted the first National Negro Convention. By the end of the nineteenth century, it had founded schools, orphanages, welfare societies, nursing homes, and the renowned LINCOLN UNIVERSITY in Oxford. The *Philadelphia Tribune*—the oldest black newspaper still publishing—was founded in 1884 and counted Gertrude Bustill Mossell among its contributors. With the development of wealth came a religious, business, and cultural elite that included HENRY OSSAWA TANNER, a leading American painter of the late nineteenth and early twentieth centuries. Octavius Catto and Gilbert "Gil" Ball founded the Equal Rights League in 1864. Novelist FRANCES ELLEN WATKINS HARPER and FRANCES (FANNY) JACKSON COPPIN were celebrated orators on behalf of black civil rights. In 1871 Coppin succeeded Catto as principal of the Institute for Colored Youth (later Cheyney State College, now University). After the turn of the century, Arthur Huff Fauset fought to improve housing for black Philadelphians, while his sister JESSIE REDMON FAUSET wrote critically acclaimed novels and became literary editor of the *THE CRISIS* in the 1920s.

Until World War I (1914–1918) however, most African Americans worked as laborers and domestics—"purveyors to

Neighbors enjoy a block party in an African American neighborhood in Philadelphia. *CORBIS/Ted Spiegel*

the rich," as W. E. B. DU BOIS said in his pioneering study *The Philadelphia Negro* (1899). Political representation, moreover, was limited.

Nonetheless, blacks flocked to Philadelphia from the South. By 1900, the black community in Philadelphia—numbering 62,613—was the largest in the North. This increased size initiated segregation of the black population in North and West Philadelphia and the creation of segregated bars, restaurants, and hotels. A race riot in 1918 followed labor conflicts and increased demands from African Americans for equality. Turning inward, the black community further developed its own business and professional class.

With the devastation of the GREAT DEPRESSION, unemployment reached 46 percent among employable blacks. NEW DEAL work projects for "Negroes" produced a massive political shift to the DEMOCRATIC PARTY. In 1938, Democrat Crystal Bird Fauset became the first black woman in the U.S. to be elected to a state assembly.

The labor demand created by World War II (1939–1945) precipitated a second, massive migration to Philadelphia, increasing the African American community to 379,000—18 percent of the city's population—by 1950. The Educational Equity League and the NATIONAL ASSOCIATION FOR THE ADVANCEMENT OF COLORED PEOPLE (NAACP) led initiatives against inequality in the schools, but 84.8 percent of black schoolchildren attended black-majority schools in 1950. The NAACP was more successful in its efforts to integrate Girard College in North Philadelphia.

Prominent entertainers and musicians, including BILL COSBY and JOHN COLTRANE, emerged from the postwar generation in Philadelphia, but overall conditions in the black community were bleak, given employment discrimination and housing segregation. In the 1960s, activism grew, the Black Panthers mobilized chapters, and race riots followed. The first black mayor of Philadelphia, W. Wilson Goode, was elected in 1983, then reelected in 1987. Goode's political career was adversely affected in 1985 when police bombed the headquarters of the separatist organization MOVE, a group of black nationalists in West Philadelphia. The bomb killed eleven MOVE members, including children, and started a fire that destroyed two city blocks.

The overall income of black Philadelphians rose moderately in the 1990s, but unemployment and a deteriorating educational system remain serious problems for now and the foreseeable future. Even so, some see the landslide reelection of Mayor John F. Street to a second term in 2003 as encouraging evidence that black leaders in Philadelphia are broadening their political base.

Bibliography

Franklin, Vincent P. *The Education of Black Philadelphia: The Social and Educational History of a Minority Community, 1900–1950.* University of Pennsylvania Press, 1979.

Lane, Roger. *Roots of Violence in Black Philadelphia, 1860–1900.* Harvard University Press, 1986.

Nash, Gary. *Forging Freedom: The Formation of Philadelphia's Black Community, 1720–1840.* Harvard University Press, 1988.

Winch, Julie. *Philadelphia's Black Elite: Activism, Accommodation and the Struggle for Autonomy, 1787–1848.* Temple University Press, 1988.

Jim Mendelsohn

Philip, Marlene Nourbese

1947–

Canadian poet, novelist, and essayist known for experimentation with literary form and for her commitment to social justice.

"English/is a foreign anguish," writes Marlene Nourbese Philip in her poem "Discourse on the Logic of Language" from *She Tries her Tongue; Her Silence Softly Breaks* (1989). The poem examines the often brutal encounter of colonial subjects with the English language and its literature. Philips, through exploring what critic Barbara Fister has described as "the conundrum of language in a postcolonial context," works alongside fellow Canadian poets DIONNE BRAND and Claire Harris, and Caribbean writers EDWARD KAMAU BRATHWAITE and Lorna Goodison.

Born in Tobago, Philip moved to Trinidad with her family when she was eight. Because TRINIDAD AND TOBAGO were then under British colonial rule, Philip received a British education that, she later remarked in a *Books in Canada* interview, "almost drowned out any sense of my own culture." After graduating from the University of the West Indies in JAMAICA in 1968, she emigrated to CANADA, where she earned degrees in political science and law. In 1973 she became a practicing lawyer and subsequently worked for seven years at a legal clinic.

Scorned by Canadian publishers because of its formal innovation and political engagement, *She Tries Her Tongue* received the Cuban Casa de Las Americas prize in 1988 while still in manuscript form. The collection was eventually published in Britain. *Salmon Courage* (1983) and *Thorns* (1980) also engage the intersection of politics, language, and literary form, as does *Looking for Livingstone: An Odyssey of Silence* (1991), Philip's narrative of a metaphoric return to Africa.

Philip also writes children's literature and is a prolific essayist. Her novel for young adults, *Harriet's Daughter* (1988), written as a corrective to the absence of black characters in Canadian children's literature, suffered the same fate as *She Tries Her Tongue*. Canadian presses, afraid that a black protagonist would not sell, rejected it before Heinemann published it in England. After its Canadian publication in 1988 the novel was nominated for several awards; it won the Canadian Learning Materials of the Year award in 1990. Philip's articles and essays collected in *Frontiers* (1992) and *Showing Grit* (1993) demonstrate a persistent critique and an impassioned concern for issues of social justice and equity in the arts, prompting Selwyn R. Cudjoe's assertion that Philip "serves as a lightning rod of black cultural defiance of the Canadian mainstream." More to the point is the epigram in *Frontiers* where Philip dedicates the book to Canada, "in the effort of becoming a space of true belonging."

Philip has also written plays, including *Coups and Calypsos*, produced in London, England and in Toronto in 1999, and a stage adaptation of *Harriet's Daughter*. She was a Guggenheim Fellow for poetry in 1990–1991 and received a McDowell Fellowship in 1991. In 1995 she received the Toronto Arts Award for Writing and Publishing. The Elizabeth Fry Society of Toronto awarded Philip its Rebels for a Cause award in 2001, the same year that she received the YWCA Woman of Distinction in the Arts award. She has taught at York University and the University of Toronto.

Bibliography

Williamson, Janice. *Sounding Differences: Conversations with Seventeen Canadian Women Writers.* University of Toronto Press, 1993.

Peter Hudson

Photography, African

History of photographers and photography trends in Africa.

Photography has flourished in AFRICA since 1839, when the vice regent of EGYPT, Khedive Mehmet, experimented with equipment imported from FRANCE, just months after Louis Daguerre publicized the invention of the silver-plate process. As a result of interaction with Europeans in coastal cities, Africans acquired technical skills that led to the development of photographic studios in the 1860s. A wide range of regionally distinctive traditions arose during the twentieth century and African photographers have revealed a unique outlook in photojournalism, portraiture, and artistic expression. Diverse insights into African social and cultural life are shown in the reportage of Peter Magubane and David Goldblatt in SOUTH AFRICA; in the French West African portraiture style of SEYDOU KEITA; and in the art of contemporary African expatriates in the West, such as Touhami Ennadre from MOROCCO and Rotimi Fani-Kayode from NIGERIA. In contrast to the selective depiction of the continent in colonial photographs, the history of African photography presents a more accurate and far-reaching view of modern Africa's self-perceptions.

Colonialism and Photography

The first photographs of sub-Saharan Africa were taken in early 1840 by M. Worhnitz, a French colonist in MAURITIUS. Plates dated to 1857 are attributed to A. Washington, an ex-slave who left the United States to settle in SIERRA LEONE in 1845. Photography was predominantly used in this era to record the activities of European explorers, missionaries, armies, and administrators. Pierre Trémaux, a French architect, documented his 1847–1854 expedition to North Africa and eastern SUDAN. The German missionary Henry Stern introduced the camera to ETHIOPIA in 1859 (and was imprisoned by Emperor Tewardos II for his intrusive conduct). He was followed in 1896 by Edoardo Ximenes, who published war photography in his magazine *Illustrazione Italiana*, providing propagandistic support for ITALY's ultimately unsuccessful attempt to colonize Ethiopia.

French reconnaissance missions undertaken by Gallieni in 1880 and by Borgnis and Desbordes in 1882–1883 produced landscape views of MALI and portrayals of indigenous peoples. In addition to photographs by the Fathers of the Holy Spirit, who settled in Kita in 1888, and surveys of the Upper Senegal railway photographed by civil servant Ernest Portier in the 1880s, postcards of exotic scenery and informal snapshots of French expatriate life during the 1910s and 1920s were produced by Roger Halbwachs and Charles Drenning in Mauritius and by Oscar Lataque in SENEGAL.

During the nineteenth century, photography was valued for its claim to scientific objectivity, although its images of Africa were widely interpreted to justify the "civilizing mission" of imperialism. While postcards stimulated the early tourist industry, the development of photographic anthropometry, which sought to classify phenotypical distinctions by depicting the faces and bodies of colonized subjects against a measured grid, gave credence to biological notions of "race." The visual emphasis on the "primitive" culture of the NUBA of Sudan found in the celebrated works of English photographer George Rodger and the German Leni Riefenstahl, derived from this genre of ethnographic representation.

Conversely, African apprentices, whom early European photographers required for assistance with the bulky thirteen-by-nineteen-inch box-camera apparatus, rapidly learned to master its techniques. For example, before opening his DAKAR studio in the 1930s, Mama Cassett had studied with Oscar Lataque in the 1920s. Such patterns of enterprise had been established during the latter part of the nineteenth century, particularly in cosmopolitan cities where African commerce with Europeans was commonplace.

Early African Photographers

In the 1860s A. C. Gomes was active in the East African city of ZANZIBAR, as was E. C. Dias in the 1890s. In West Africa, N. Walwin Holm established a studio in the GOLD COAST (now GHANA) city of ACCRA in 1883; his son J. C. Holm relocated the studio to LAGOS, NIGERIA, in 1910. George S. A. Da Costa gave up his position as manager of the Church Missionary Society bookstore in Lagos to open a studio in 1895. He was commissioned by London publisher Allister Macmillan, who described him as "the ablest and best-known professional photographer in Nigeria," to contribute group portraits to *The Red Book of West Africa* (1920), an illustrated compendium of social life in colonial Africa. In Sierra Leone, the Lisk-Carew Brothers produced postcards of FREETOWN and sold them to travelers on the Elder Dempster shipping route, while F. R. C. Lutterdot of the Gold Coast traveled to CAMEROON, GABON, and EQUATORIAL GUINEA in the 1890s, covering patterns of intraregional trade and labor migration that persisted even after the end of the colonial period.

Photography supplanted painting in the West by making portraiture more accessible to the urban middle classes. Similarly, in TOGO, Alex Agbaglo Acolatse produced full-length studio portraits of the LOMÉ bourgeoisie. When he portrayed a father and son dressed in traditional cloth, or twin brothers in collars and ties—comfortably composed and set against the trompe l'oeil backdrops, potted plants, and oriental carpets found in pictures of their Edwardian counterparts—Acolatse conveyed the social esteem in which the individuals and families were held, as well as the photographers themselves. In 1897 Walwin Holm was inducted into the Royal Photographic Society in London.

Ramilijoana opened a studio in MADAGASCAR in 1894, while active as a writer and politician. Reflecting French and Southeast Asian influences, he produced sepia-toned portraits of mixed-race MALAGASY women, whose social status is apparent in their relaxed pose, marcel-wave hairstyles, pearl necklaces, and silk parasols. Razakar photographed Madagascar's Indonesian elite, including a trio of naval cadets expressing a self-assured demeanor in a 1916 print inscribed "*Soyons toujours unis!*" (Let us always be united!).

Studio Portraiture

A large number of African photographers emerged between the 1930s and the 1950s, when increasingly accessible camera technology made portraiture more widely available. Itinerant photographers, such as Daniel Attuomo Amichia, Joseph Moise Agbejelou, and Ehouni, traveled across colonial borders. A postcard view from ANGOLA dated January 27, 1939, shows the itinerant studio tradition in action as Antoine Freitas sets up a camera in a rural setting while a group of curious, rather than suspicious, onlookers watch with interest. Itinerant photographers were called upon to produce identification photos for passports. From his Studio du Nord in Korhogo, CÔTE D'IVOIRE, Cornelius Yao August Azaglo surpassed functional requirements by exerting adept control of lighting conditions in an exterior setting. Set against a plain canvas backdrop, his portraits of laborers and market traders are reminiscent of American photographer Irving Penn's *Worlds in a Small Room* (1970).

The Senegalese photographer Meissa Gaye highlights the city-based tradition of studio portraiture. A former civil servant who initially took identification photos, Gaye opened the Tropical Studio in Saint-Louis in 1945. His medium close-ups of besuited men from notable families, of Muslim MARABOUTS in robes, and of elegant women bedecked with jewelry and elaborate coiffures influenced the subsequent doyen of French West African portraiture, Malian Seydou Keita. Like Mama and Salla Cassett, Gaye and Keita worked as self-employed artisans, wielding technical and artistic skills to meet their clients' demands. As their market expanded in the 1940s to include not only the local elite but also salaried city dwellers, their portraits recorded the aspirations as much as the achievements of their sitters. In addition to patterned fabric backdrops, Keita introduced various props, such as a radio or telephone, to enhance the photographer's representation of his client's wishes.

Portraits intended for exchange among family members and social peers provided a mainstay for African photographers during this period, who included Mix Gueye, Adama Sylla, Doro Sy, and Doudou Diop, all based in Saint-Louis, Senegal. In addition, as decolonization approached in the late 1950s, the growth of newspaper publishing and photographic agencies introduced a new set of options for African photographers.

Postcolonial Era

Keita had studied with French expatriate Pierre Garnier, whose Photo Hall Soudanais encouraged the careers of Mountaga Dembélé, Abderamane Sakaly, Félix Diallo, and Malick Sidibé, all of whom contributed to the active studio scene in Mali's capital, BAMAKO. Sidibé's portrayals of youth enjoying picnics and nightlife capture the optimism of the newly independent nations. Like Phillipe Koujina in NIGER and Depara in the DEMOCRATIC REPUBLIC OF THE CONGO (formerly ZAIRE), he updated the itinerant tradition by taking lightweight cameras out into the urban environment, portraying clients in situ in exchange for a modest fee. Representations of African youth in the postindependence era are also reflected in the self-portraits of Samuel Fosso in the CENTRAL AFRICAN REPUBLIC and in the 1970s work of Zaire's Studio 3Z.

Sidibé also worked freelance for the Agence Nationale d'Information Malieen (ANIM), established in 1963. ANIM was funded by the Soviet Union and East Germany, where its fifteen staff photographers, among them Mody Sory Diallo, were trained. Like the Sylie photo agency in SÉKOU TOURÉ'S GUINEA, ANIM provided national newspapers with photographs of public rallies, visiting heads of state, and daily life scenes. Similarly, Peter Obe provided photographs for the *Lagos Weekly Record* in the 1950s. The key region in the burgeoning development of African photojournalism, however, was South Africa.

The weekly *Drum* magazine, edited by Jim Bailey from 1951 to 1984, combined hard-edged reportage on social injustices with lighthearted scenes of everyday life in townships. Its multiracial team of staff photographers included Bob Gosani, Ranjith Kally, G. R. Naidoo, Lionel Ostendorp, Jurgen Schadeberg, and Ian Berry, all of whom combined topical news and entertainment coverage in their respective portfolios.

Like his contemporary Alf Kumalo, who started at *Bantu World*, *Drum* photographer Peter Magubane established a career in photojournalism. Magubane was a foreign correspondent for *Time* magazine between 1978 and 1980, while based at the *Rand Daily Mail*. Although he was arrested and censored in the 1970s, his career has parallels with those of his white South African counterparts David Goldblatt and Cloete Breytenbach. When commercial infrastructure allows a wider degree of specialization, as the Magnum agency did for Robert Capa and Henri Cartier-Bresson in Paris and New York in the 1940s, photographers may establish a signature style whereby their work is valued by galleries and museums for its aesthetic qualities. Goldblatt's *Some Afrikaners Photographed* (1975) revealed hidden aspects of APARTHEID in the hinterland. Peter Magubane, who won the Robert Capa Award in 1986, gave expression to a humanist outlook, in which his unflinching gaze bore witness to South Africa's tumultuous history.

Contemporary Images

African photography has grown increasingly diverse since the 1970s. Regional variations have given rise to distinct repertoires of documentary observation and artistic exploration. Many African-born photographers have taken opportunities to travel abroad and reside in Africa's global diaspora, while others divide their time among multiple places of residence.

South African contexts foreground documentary reportage as social criticism. Santu Mofekeng emphasizes contrasts of shadow and light in depictions of SOWETO interiors. Rashid Lombard, Andrew Tshabangu, and Zwelethu Methetwa similarly explore urban experiences, whereas South Africans Guy Tillim and John Leibenberg have covered the war-torn landscapes of RWANDA and NAMIBIA. Actuality-based pictures by Mohammed Amin and John Kiyaya in TANZANIA and by Khamis Ramadan in KENYA depict social conflict. In MOZAMBIQUE, by contrast, impressions of MAPUTO nightlife by Ricardo Rangel, narratives of peasant labor by Sergio Santimano and Rui Assubuju, and poetic travelogues by Ale Junior, reveal differences between Lusophone and Anglophone approaches to documentary realism.

Pierrot Men of Madagascar and Yves Pitchen of Mauritius pursue a pictorialist approach influenced by the ethnically mixed worlds of their own countries. One aspect of photography from the Arab world embraces a painterly interest in light, tone, and texture. The Algerian poet and novelist MOHAMMED DIB exhibited photographs of his daily surroundings in the 1940s, which complement contemporary North African observations found in the photographs of Tunisian architecture by Jellel Gastelli and portraits of CAIRO shopkeepers by Egyptian Nubril Bortros. Based in Paris since the 1960s, Moroccan Touhami Ennadre has been widely acclaimed for the blend of figurative and abstract elements in works such *A Corps Cri* (1982), which features highly charged fetal images to evoke the cycle of birth and death.

Opportunities for artistic innovation arise with journeys between the homeland and its diasporas. The Nigerian artist Rotimi Fani-Kayode studied in the United States before he settled in GREAT BRITAIN in the 1980s. His tableaux present a synthesis of YORUBA ritual and the Western male nude. Also based in the Nigerian diaspora, Alfred Iyobhebhe, Oladele Ajiboye Bamboye, and Ike Ude exhibit their works internationally, alongside the post-apartheid generation of southern African artists that includes Gordon Bleach from ZIMBABWE, Jenny Gordon from South Africa, and Maria Gertrud Mamundjembo from Namibia.

Diaspora may act as a catalyst for intercultural exchange, which is exemplified in the contemporary French West African photography scene. Such practitioners as Ivoirian Dorris Harron Kasco, Senegalese Moussa Mbaye and Bouna Medoune Seye, Malian Alioune Bâ, and Mauritanian Moctar Kane are frequently resident in France, where they exhibit and publish widely. They simultaneously contribute to initiatives such as the African Photography Festival, held in Bamako in 1994. Keita participated in the first such festival held in December 1974 and Malian-French cooperation has consistently nurtured a receptive environment for African photography. In 1996 Malian Emmanuel Daou formed Djaw, an organization that aims to distribute African news photographs to global media via digital information technologies. Large-scale survey exhibitions in New York (1996) and Paris (1998) have also introduced the art of African photography to wider audiences. These developments have inspired wide-ranging debates on issues of culture, technology, and representation, which the history of African photography has brought to light.

See also Christianity: Missionaries in Africa; Decolonization in Africa: An Interpretation; Explorers in Africa Since 1800; Press, African; Race: An Interpretation.

Kobena Mercer

Photography, African American

History of black photographers and photography trends in America.

The first known African Americans to practice the art and business of photography were Jules Lion, JAMES PRESLEY BALL, John B. Bailey, Augustus Washington, and the Goodridge Brothers, between 1840 and 1850. They worked as daguerreotypists, documentarians, artists, and studio photographers. The larger American public was fascinated with the daguerreotype as soon as Louis Jacques Mandé Daguerre (1787–1851) publicized the process in FRANCE in 1839. The French inventor Nicéphore Niépce (1765–1833) produced the earliest extant photographic image, made by a camera obscura in 1826. After the death of Niépce, Daguerre successfully fixed an image and announced to the Paris press his discovery, which he named after himself, the daguerreotype, in January of 1839.

Newspapers in the spring of 1839 published accounts of Americans experimenting with the daguerreotype process. On August 19, 1839, Daguerre publicly announced the process and published an instruction manual. By late August newspapers in Paris and London described Daguerre's process in detail. The *Great Western,* one of the fastest known transatlantic steamers of the time, which arrived in NEW YORK on September 10, 1839, is noted for carrying aboard the French and English newspapers with descriptions of the daguerreotype process.

Six months after the public announcements of the process in Paris, Jules Lion, a free man of color, lithographer, and portrait painter, exhibited the first successful daguerreotype views. This first publicized exhibition of works by a black photographer, organized and sponsored by the artist, occurred on March 15, 1840, at the St. Charles Museum in NEW ORLEANS. The exhibition was reported to have drawn a large crowd. Despite the condition of African Americans who were still enslaved, there were numerous free black men and women who had established themselves as daguerreotypers, photographers, inventors, celebrities, artists, and artisans who had gained local and national recognition in their respective cities. Portraits of preachers, soldiers, writers, and prominent and lesser-known African Americans were produced regularly in galleries and studios throughout the country. Portraits of prominent African Americans became popular, and photography increasingly was the chosen medium for creating a likeness. Most of the photographs made in the nineteenth century were not intended for publication or public presentation, except for those made of celebrities, lecturers, and other prominent citizens. Some African American families thought it important to have their images preserved for posterity, however.

During most of photography's early history, images produced by African American photographers were idealized glimpses of family members in romanticized or dramatic settings. Many African American photographers sought to integrate elements of romanticism and classicism, modeled after the style of many painters in previous centuries. Most photographs taken in the early years commemorated a special occasion in the sitter's life such as courtship, marriage, birth, death, graduation, confirmation, military service, anniversaries, or a social or political success.

A number of the early photographers recorded celebratory as well as dispiriting moments within their communities. They photographed genre scenes and landscapes, and they created elaborate backdrops for studio portraits. Many owned and operated studios in small towns and major cities, while others worked as itinerants. They photographed the prosperous, the laborers, and the poor, and they documented the activities of nineteenth-century abolitionists and twentieth-century civil rights activists.

In photography's first decade, the 1840s, James Presley Ball (1825–1905) and Augustus Washington (1820–1875) operated successful galleries in Cincinnati, Ohio, and Hartford, Connecticut. Ball and Washington were active abolitionists who often used their photographic skills to expose the inhumane institution of slavery and to promote the activities of the abolitionist movement. Between 1859 and 1899, photography advanced swiftly with the development of the glass-plate negative and the paper-print processes; images were mounted on cabinet cards, *cartes-de-visite,* and stereographs. With these advances, numerous photographers and itinerants flourished in the North, South, and the emerging West. Studios opened for business producing paper prints as well as tintypes, the newer and faster processes of the period.

At the turn of the century, photography expanded in a variety of ways. Newspapers, journals, and books published photographic images. Schools and colleges offered courses in photography, and correspondence courses were available. C. M. BATTEY (1873–1927) was a noted educator in photography and an accomplished portraitist and fine-art photographer. Battey founded the photography division at TUSKEGEE INSTITUTE, Alabama, in 1916. In 1917 *THE CRISIS* magazine highlighted Battey in the "Men of the Month" column as "one of the few colored photographers who has gained real artistic success." The most extensive portraits of African American leaders produced in the nineteenth and early part of the twentieth century were done by Battey. His photographic portraits of JOHN MERCER LANGSTON, FREDERICK DOUGLASS, W. E. B. DU BOIS, BOOKER T. WASHINGTON, and PAUL LAURENCE DUNBAR were sold nationally and produced in two formats: postcard and poster. Black Americans were subjugated in practice and representation by the dominant culture. In order to resist labeling, black photographers continually redefined the image of African Americans within their photography studios.

Between 1900 and 1919, African American photographers flourished in the larger cities. They produced photographs of rural and urban experiences as well as architecture and images of leisure.

ADDISON SCURLOCK (1883–1964), of WASHINGTON, D.C., HOWARD UNIVERSITY's official photographer, opened his studio in 1911, where he worked with his wife and sons, Robert and George, until 1964. In New York City, JAMES VANDERZEE (1886–1983), undoubtedly the best known of black studio photographers, captured the spirit and life of New York's HARLEM for over fifty years.

During the period defined by Howard University professor and philosopher ALAIN LOCKE in 1925 as "THE NEW NEGRO," photographers lived, recorded, and worked in New York City's Harlem and the rural South. The "New Negro" image replaced the prevailing stereotype of blacks as unintelligent, lazy, and without a work ethic. The photographers working during this period made a conscious attempt, as Cheryl Wall notes, to "convert a defensive into an offensive position, a handicap into an incentive." The 1920s and 1930s witnessed the concluding disenfranchisement of African Americans, the GREAT MIGRATION, a literary and an artistic renaissance, the GREAT DEPRESSION, and President Franklin Delano Roosevelt's NEW DEAL programs. Photographers began to exhibit their work widely in their respective communities. The bulk of this work emerged during an era when the overwhelming majority of postcards, lantern slides, and popular cultural artifacts made of African Americans consisted of crude, degrading racial caricatures. The work and vision of the black photographer can be considered a powerful challenge to the blatantly stereotypical cultural products of African Americans sold and produced during this period. The black photographer provided, by contrast, photographs that depicted a sense of self and self-worth. The photographs celebrated achievements within the photographers' communities and in their personal lives. The photographs of the "New Negro" period provided optimistic overviews of the African American experience in both the 1800s and early 1900s. In the 1920s, young black photographers who viewed themselves as artists moved to the larger cities seeking education, patronage, and support for their art. Harlem was a cultural mecca for many of these photographers.

James Latimer Allen (1907–1977) produced genre portraits of African American men, women, and children. He published and exhibited his work in art journals and galleries. He also photographed writers of the period such as Alain Locke, LANGSTON HUGHES, COUNTEE CULLEN, and CLAUDE MCKAY. Photographers active between 1920 and 1940 included students of C. M. Battey's such as P. H. POLK (1898–1985) of Tuskegee, Alabama, who opened his first studio in Tuskegee in 1927. The following year he was appointed to the faculty of Tuskegee Institute's photography department, photographed prominent visitors such as educator MARY MCLEOD BETHUNE and activist-artist PAUL ROBESON, and made extensive portraits of scientist and inventor GEORGE WASHINGTON CARVER. Richard S. Roberts (1881–1936) of Columbia, South Carolina, opened his studio in the early 1920s. He began studying photography through correspondence courses and specialized journals and advertised that his studio took superior photographs by day or night. Morgan Smith (1910–1993) and Marvin Smith (b. 1910), twin brothers, were prolific photographers in Harlem in the 1930s and early 1940s. They photographed members of the community—famous and infamous—and their cameras also captured political rallies, breadlines during the Great Depression, families, and lindy hoppers at the Savoy Ballroom. Also working in Harlem was Winifred Hall Allen. She documented the businesses owned and operated by women in that community.

She Had Her Keys to the Kingdom from *Africa Series* by Carrie Mae Weems; three c-prints with etched glass, 1993. *Courtesy of the artist*

Robert H. McNeill created a comprehensive documentary record of African American life in Washington during the 1930s and 1940s. Frequently working with the black press, including the PITTSBURGH COURIER, Washington Afro-American, and the CHICAGO DEFENDER, McNeill's photographs documented that African Americans living in a segregated city survived—even thrived—by creating their own social and community organizations.

The Farm Security Administration (FSA) began in 1935 as the Resettlement Administration, an independent coordinating agency that inherited rural relief activities and land-use administration from the Department of the Interior, the Federal Emergency Relief Administration, and the Agricultural Adjustment Administration. The FSA photography project generated 270,000 images of rural, urban, and industrial America between 1935 and 1943. Many of the heavily documented activities of the FSA were of black migrant workers in the South. In 1937 GORDON PARKS decided that he wanted to be a photographer after viewing the work of the FSA photographers. He was hired by the FSA in 1941 and during World War II worked as an Office of War Information correspondent. After the war, he was a photographer for the Standard Oil Company. In 1949 he became the first African American photographer to work on the staff of Life magazine.

Roy DeCarava is the link to contemporary street photography. He studied art at Cooper Union in New York City, the Work Progress Administration's Harlem Art Center, and the George Washington Carver Art School. In 1955 DeCarava collaborated with Langston Hughes on a book entitled The Sweet Flypaper of Life, which depicted the life of a black family in Harlem. In 1954 he founded a photography gallery, which became one of the first galleries in the United States devoted to the exhibition and sale of photography as a fine art. Also noted for his JAZZ photography, DeCarava in 1963 founded the Kamoinge Workshop, a workshop of concerned black photographers. Members included artists such as Shawn Walker, Lou Draper, Beuford Smith, Anthony Barboza, and Ming Smith.

Photographers in the 1930s through the 1960s began working as photojournalists for local newspapers and national magazines marketed for African American audiences, such as Our World, EBONY, JET, Sepia, and Flash. (Only a few African American photojournalists, notably Gordon Parks and Roy DeCarava, were employed for the larger picture magazines such as Life and Sports Illustrated.) Most of them learned photography while in the military and studied photography at schools of journalism.

This period also encompassed the beginning of reportage and the documentation of public and political events. In the 1930s, using smaller hand-held cameras and faster films aided photographers in expressing their frustration and discontent with social and political conditions within their communities. The modern CIVIL RIGHTS MOVEMENT activities were well documented by photographers such as Moneta Sleet Jr., in New York and CHICAGO, and Jack T. Franklin, in PHILADELPHIA. During the active years of the Civil Rights and Black Power Movements, the early 1960s through the 1970s, a significant num-

Award-winning photographer Gordon Parks, Sr., was known for his portraits. He photographed this young boy in front of a newsstand in Harlem in 1943. *CORBIS*

Photographed by Addison N. Scurlock (1883–1964), a black family prepares for a ride in a rowboat near Great Falls, Virginia. Scurlock had a successful studio in Washington, D.C. and served as Howard University's official photographer for fifty years. *Wolfgang Kaehler, 1999 Smithsonian Institution, Washington, D.C.*

ber of socially committed men and women became photographers. They set a different standard in documenting the struggles, achievements, and tragedies of the freedom movement. SNCC (STUDENT NONVIOLENT COORDINATING COMMITTEE) photographers Doug Harris, Elaine Tomlin, and Bob Fletcher were in the forefront documenting the voter registration drives in the South; Roland Freeman, Robert Sengstacke, Howard Bingham, Jeffrey Scales, and Brent Jones photographed the activities of the BLACK PANTHER PARTY and desegregation rallies in the North and on the West Coast. Between 1969 and 1986, six African American photographers received the coveted Pulitzer Prize in photography. The first to win the award was MONETA SLEET JR. in 1969, for a photograph of Mrs. CORETTA SCOTT KING and her daughter at the funeral of Dr. MARTIN LUTHER KING JR.

In the l970s universities and art colleges began to offer undergraduate and graduate degrees in photography. African American photographers began studying photography and creating works for exhibition. Outside of the academy, others studied in community centers and workshops. These photographers began to explore and redefine the photographic image. They respected the photograph as a document and simultaneously looked at the photograph as a metaphor. The symbolic and expressive imagery of the works produced in the 1980s and 1990s is concerned with offering sociological and psychological insights into the past. Many of the themes explored by these photographers focused on their own families and communities. They created symbolic works that referred to social issues such as racism, unemployment, child and sexual abuse, and death and dying. Most of the works were informed by personal experience. The viewer becomes a participant; the viewer is asked to contextualize his or her own experiences with the visual references offered by the photographer and in doing so create a personal historical perspective, interpretation, or meaning. Clarissa Sligh, Lorna Simpson, Jeffrey Scales, Dawoud Bey, Coreen Simpson, Albert Chong, Fern Logan, Carrie Mae Weems, Pat Ward Williams, Willie Middlebrook, Roland Charles, Chester Higgins, Stephen Marc, Cynthia Wiggins, Carla Williams, Christian Walker, Lynn Marshall-Linnemeier, and Hank Sloane Thomas are just a small number of the photographers who began creating works in this genre in the 1980s.

All are engaging storytellers and have discovered the intersection of the private and public in art. A number of contemporary photographers challenge current art practices and, as photographer and writer Rick Bolton states, these artists have created "a new social basis for art." The photobiographers who use appropriation, multiple printing, fabric, straight images, and manipulated photographs make compelling visual statements about modern-day culture and create narratives about our collective history in multiethnic America. The contemporary photobiographers employ themes relating to identity, spirituality, gender, family, race, difference, and stereotyping. Some of the artists are concerned with the implications of historical and contemporary references to women and have offered new strategies in incorporating their personal perspectives in the construction of their work. Many of the photographers mentioned in this essay create provocative and sensitive visual references to their African American cultural experience. Some use text to create tension and paradigms of a sort relating to the transformative nature of the medium.

Prentice H. Polk specialized in portraits at Tuskegee Institute, where he photographed *The Boss* (silver gelatin print) in 1932. *The Corcoran Gallery of Art, Washington, D.C. Museum Purchase, Anna E. Clark Fund.*

Albert Chong uses family photographs, religious icons, and animal remains to explore ritual as it is translated into art. He likens his task to that of archaeologists in unearthing the past to explore family history. Chong is strongly conscious of composition and form. The exact placement of cultural objects acts as a signifier and suggests authentication of his cultural roots. Born in JAMAICA of African and Chinese ancestry, Chong produces works imbued with cultural references relating to both cultures, including that of the Caribbean. His photographs are highly individualized, spiritually oriented images. Coreen Simpson makes portraits that speak to us about the experience of young black men and women living in New York City. Many are oversized images that are extremely stylized, as the photographer and her subject create a visually expressive dialogue. Jeffrey Scales records commonplace scenes and occurrences within his community of Harlem (New York City), while simultaneously addressing cultural and sociological issues. His portraits of young and older men depict connections that are embodied in the bonding of male relationships. He is concerned about stereotyping of black men and how black men are perceived in the culture by their peers and others.

Fern Logan reexamines her family relationships in her art. Using the cyanotype, also known as the blueprint, a printing process based on the light sensitivity of iron salts, Logan critiques memories from her past in a warm voice, using old letters and imagined responses. Looking back at old photographs of her son, she draws up provocative issues about their American childhood and the irony of their fate. Her perspective is written on the print as the photograph is submerged. The issues presented are difficult and are intended to evoke a twentieth-century consciousness of MISCEGENATION. Coming to consciousness in the context of the issues presented within her own family, Logan stimulates an open discussion about race, racism, denial, and domination.

Lorna Simpson focuses on the construction of meaning and values by juxtaposing text and image. Her style creates a format for her critical examination of race and gender. She focuses specifically on the notion of invisibility, representing black women as survivors, protagonists, and victims. Simpson's work is rooted in the tradition of African American storytelling and incorporates visual narratives that border on biography.

Family experiences form the core of inspiration for Clarissa Sligh's work, which is layered with political, familial, and racially charged messages. Using family photographs and archival references, she directs her audience's gaze into sociological relationships centered on experiences in African American communities in the nineteenth and twentieth centuries. Sligh is the keeper of her family album of photographs and other memorabilia. She places her family history within the larger picture of American history. In shifting attention away from her personal experiences, she is able to analyze other shared experiences of black children cross-generationally. She is cognizant of the role she plays in preserving her family history. Sligh's work is important not only because she addresses the realities of racism and sexism in a direct yet not confrontational style but also because she is an accomplished storyteller. Photoartist Sligh looks carefully at her own family relationships and examines the lives of men, women, and children in general. Her images incorporate both historical and social perspectives and her work is provocative and historically introspective.

Christian Walker uses the format of the family photo album to "document" a history of the extended or archetypal African American family. He enlarges this form with paint and pigment as well as vintage rephotographed images, a manipulation that emphasizes the artistic rather than the technical aspects of the medium.

Carla Williams's photographs capture the viewer's and the photographer's imagination and fascination with the human body. Williams's subject is her own body, which she has documented continually for over ten years. Her self-portraits are consciously posed as iconic references to the photographic tableaux of the nineteenth century. She also allows the viewer to explore the notion of being desired by photographing her body at different stages in her life cycle. She projects the fragmented and whole body; the physical representation of the body can be viewed as a link to her past and her future. Her body is linked to her culture and she is interested in the experience of the female body as subject and object to be desired.

CARRIE MAE WEEMS creates sequential photographs and insightful text that examine the experiences of women in general, and black women specifically. Her work brings to life the overlapping of fantasy and lived experiences, where gesture is seen as metaphor.

Black American photographers of the nineteenth, twentieth, and twenty-first centuries respond to their own lives and their communities in similar ways. Some evoke in their work an emotional message that goes beyond the self-representation but connects in the recharacterization of the African American experience. Their photographs are fascinating and important because the photographers have coupled the aspirations and dreams of their subjects with their own.

Many of the photographers working today respond to social issues beyond the sometimes insular photographic community. They comment on politics, culture, family, and history from internal and external points of view. The fact that many of these photographers have likely witnessed societal injustice has not clouded their eyes. In interpreting these works, the viewer is open to multiple readings, including satire, humor, parody, and testimony. The issues addressed in contemporary photography and the interpretations implied coalesce to capture an exhilarating visionary biography of African American life.

See also Magazines, Newspapers, and Journals; Press, Black, in the United States; Racial Stereotypes; Smith, Marvin and Morgan.

Deborah Willis

Piar, Manuel

Mulatto general in Venezuela in the nineteenth century.

See also Bolívar, Simón.

Pickens, William

1881–1954

African American educator, field secretary for the NAACP, and civil rights leader.

William Pickens was born in Anderson County, South Carolina, the sixth of ten children of Jacob and Fannie Pickens, both of whom were former slaves. The family of sharecroppers moved frequently—some twenty times by Pickens's estimate—and relocated to Arkansas in 1887. William was raised in a household in which learning was highly valued, and he became valedictorian of his graduating class at Union High School in Little Rock in 1889 and earned a B.A. from Talledega College, a missionary institution in Alabama, in 1892. Pickens earned a second bachelor's degree, in linguistics, from Yale University, in New Haven, Connecticut, where he received the Phi Beta Kappa key in 1904. He later earned an M.A. degree from FISK UNIVERSITY, in Nashville, Tennessee; a doctorate in literature from Selma University (Alabama); and an L.L.D. from Wiley University in Marshall, Texas.

In 1905 Pickens married Minnie Cooper McAlpine, a graduate of Tougaloo College, with whom he had three children: William, Harriet, and Ruby. Pickens possessed diverse talents and authored two autobiographies, *Heir of Slaves* (1911) and *Bursting Bonds* (1923), as well as the short-story collection *Vengeance of the Gods* (1922) and the essay collection *The New Negro* (1916). Between 1904 and 1914 Pickens taught foreign languages at his alma mater, Talladega, before moving to Wiley University to head their Greek and sociology departments. The following year he accepted a position as dean of Morgan College (now Morgan State University) in Baltimore, Maryland.

Although he initially supported BOOKER T. WASHINGTON's more pragmatic approach to race relations, Pickens evolved into a civil rights militant fairly early in his intellectual career. He supported W. E. B. DU BOIS's radical Niagara movement and was a charter member of the NAACP and the ACLU. He was also ecumenical in his organization affiliations, working to some degree with the League for Industrial Democracy, the YMCA, and the Council for Pan-American Democracy. Given his broad education and training, Pickens was something of a maverick. He proposed to the businesswoman MADAME C. J. WALKER that he accompany her on a trip around the world and write a book about her travels, he praised the Communist Party's work in support of the Scottsboro Boys in the midst of open hostility between the Communists and the NAACP, and he flirted with MARCUS GARVEY's Universal Negro Improvement Association while he was still an NAACP employee.

In 1919 Pickens left Morgan College—where he had risen to the vice presidency—to take a position as assistant to JAMES WELDON JOHNSON of the NAACP. As a founding member of the association, Pickens was well connected with its leadership and had also tirelessly recruited members at Talladega, Wiley, and Morgan College. In 1915 he had accompanied the NAACP chairman Joel E. Spingarn on a dangerous fact-finding mission to Oklahoma, to gather information for a test case challenging Jim Crow on the railroads. In 1920 Johnson was appointed the first black executive secretary of the NAACP, and Pickens was subsequently appointed to the post of field secretary.

During his tenure as field secretary, Pickens shepherded the NAACP through a period of fluctuating membership during the 1920s and the Depression, and he helped lay the groundwork for the association's massive increase in resources and membership in the 1940s. His relations within the NAACP, however, were often rocky, especially with WALTER WHITE, who succeeded Johnson as executive secretary in 1930. Pickens's decision to accept a position with the U.S. Department of the Treasury in 1942 probably was motivated, at least in part, by his deteriorating relations with White. He was succeeded as field secretary by the radical grassroots organizer ELLA BAKER.

In 1942 Pickens was cited as a subversive by the House Un-American Activities Committee (HUAC) and its conservative chairman, Martin Dies. In a gesture that eerily presaged Senator Joseph McCarthy's allegations in Wheeling, West Virginia, almost a decade later, Dies, a conservative Texas Democrat, presented the House of Representatives with a list of thirty-nine "subversives" who should be removed from the federal payroll. Of those people, William Pickens was the only one in federal employ at the time. As a director of the War Savings Staff,

Pickens was charged with increasing the number of African Americans purchasing war bonds. In short order, a measure was introduced that held up the federal budget until such time as Pickens's allegiances could be ascertained. Wary of provoking conservative Southern Democrats who had perpetually threatened to hobble Franklin Roosevelt's presidency, Pickens gave a politic response to the charges. "I do not know Mr. Dies," he remarked, "but feel sure from the position he holds that he would not want to speak anything but the truth. Therefore, I conclude that somebody has misled Mr. Dies" (press release, September 18, 1942, Associated Negro Press Papers, Library of Congress).

With the budget hanging in the balance, some members of HUAC were surprised at Pickens's appearance—not knowing that he was African American. Pickens's appearance thus gave the arch-segregationist Dies an opportunity to link subversion and civil rights. Northern Democrats, mindful of the Great Migration and the swelling numbers of black Democratic voters, however, were less than thrilled with the prospect of questioning Pickens. William Dawson, the black freshman representative from Chicago, devoted his maiden speech to Pickens's defense, and Walter White sent a series of letters to members of the House of Representatives protesting the charges against Pickens. Those charges were ultimately dismissed, and Pickens remained in his position at the Treasury Department.

After World War II, Pickens attempted to return to the NAACP but was blocked by Walter White. Shut out of the organization where he had worked for twenty-three years, Pickens remained with the Treasury Department until 1951, when he retired. Pickens's political radicalism diminished somewhat during this period, and strains of his youthful admiration for Booker T. Washington might be seen in his Treasury Department campaigns to educate blacks on economic matters, savings bonds, and thrift. Pickens traveled extensively after his retirement and died during a cruise aboard the SS *Mauritania,* on April 6, 1954, just one month before the U.S. Supreme Court issued its landmark school desegregation ruling in *Brown v. Board of Education.*

Pickens played a significant role in the development of the NAACP. Between 1920 and 1940 he recruited more members and organized more branches than any other officer in the association, and his efforts helped transform the organization from a small civil rights lobby to a mass organization with nationwide influence.

The primary archival collection of William Pickens's papers is housed at the Schomburg Center for Research in Black Culture in New York City. Substantial information regarding his public career, however, can be found in the NAACP collection at the Library of Congress. His obituary appeared in *The New York Times* on April 7, 1954.

Bibliography

Avery, Sheldon. "Up from Washington: William Pickens and the Negro Struggle for Equality, 1900–1954" (1970).
Pickens, William. *Heir of Slaves* (1911).
———. *Bursting Bonds* (1923, 1991).

William J. Cobb

Pickett, Bill

1870?–1932

Cowboy and rodeo star.

Bill Pickett invented and popularized "bulldogging," a method of steer-wrestling inspired by cattle dogs. To bring a bull to the ground, Pickett would leap atop its back, twist its horns with his hands, and bite its upper lip. Pickett initially adopted "bulldogging" working as a ranch hand, but his steer-wrestling skills soon launched him into the RODEO show business of the West.

Pickett was born near Austin, Texas. He quit school after the fifth grade and began working full time as a cowboy, developing his talents in roping and horsemanship. As a teenager he began performing at carnivals, rodeos, and county fairs throughout the southwest. Initially promoters dressed Pickett as a Mexican bullfighter, obscuring his African American descent for commercial reasons. In 1907 Pickett signed on with the Miller Brothers' 101 Ranch Wild West Show, based in Oklahoma's Cherokee Strip. Pickett adopted the name "The Dusky Demon" and soon earned top billing. Pickett and the Miller Brothers toured widely throughout the United States, playing Madison Square Garden and other top venues. They also performed in CANADA, SOUTH AMERICA, and EUROPE, where Pickett unveiled his rodeo tricks for the likes of King George V and Queen Mary of England. Pickett went into partial retirement after 1916, but remained active both as cowboy and performer until 1932, when he died from a kick in the head by a horse.

Bill Pickett was widely admired for his showmanship and bravery. One of his most devoted fans was the comedian Will Rogers, with whom Pickett sometimes performed. In 1971 the National Rodeo Cowboy Hall of Fame inducted Pickett as its first black honoree, and in 1994 he appeared on a commemorative postage stamp.

See also Sports and African Americans.

Eric Bennett

Pickett, Wilson

1941–

African American soul singer.

Known for his dynamic stage presence and hard-rocking hits such as "Mustang Sally," "Land of 1,000 Dances," and "In the Midnight Hour," Wilson Pickett was one of the biggest SOUL MUSIC stars of the 1960s. Influenced by the GOSPEL MUSIC he sang as a child, along with the RHYTHM AND BLUES then in vogue, Pickett began singing with a band, the Falcons, in 1959. Pickett, who had moved to DETROIT, MICHIGAN, at the age of fifteen, also wrote some of their songs, one of which, "I Found a Love," became a Top Ten hit in 1962.

In 1964 Atlantic Records signed Pickett, sending him to MEMPHIS, TENNESSEE to record his first album. Working with Booker

T. and the MG's—the house band from the STAX record label—Pickett produced some of his most popular songs during this era, which lasted until 1967. Pickett's screams, growls, and moans punctuated the funky beat and powerful horn section that characterized these recordings, which not only defined the Southern soul sound but became some of the most-played dance music ever.

Recording both at Stax and Muscle Shoals (the Atlantic studio famous as the birthplace of ARETHA FRANKLIN's most soulful music), Pickett also toured heavily. Billing himself as "Wicked Pickett," he was known as the king of the dance floor, one of soul's most thrilling performers. Throughout the 1970s and 1980s, Pickett played concerts worldwide, though he ceased to produce noteworthy hits after leaving Atlantic in the early 1970s. Though he announced his retirement in 1991, the same year he was elected to the Rock and Roll Hall of Fame, Pickett returned with a comeback album, *It's Harder Now*, in 1999. His anthology recording, *The Essentials*, was released in 2002.

Kate Tuttle

Pidgin Languages

Languages that develop when people without a common language must communicate. Pidgin languages have small vocabularies and minimal grammar. If a pidgin survives several generations, it may develop into a new language, known as a creole.

For information on
Creole languages: *See* Languages, Creole, in the Caribbean.
Pidgin language in the United States: *See* Gullah.
Pidgin languages based on Portuguese: *See* African Linguistic Influences on Brazilian Portuguese; Atlantic Creoles: The Charter Generations; Literature, Portuguese-Language, in Africa.

Pietri, Pedro Juan

1943–2004

Afro–Puerto Rican poet, educator, and playwright who, with authors such as Miguel Algarín, founded the influential Nuyorican poetry movement.

Pedro Juan Pietri's family moved from PUERTO RICO to NEW YORK CITY's Spanish Harlem in 1947 as part of the migration wave following World War II. He attended New York City public schools and, after completing high school, served in the army and fought in the VIETNAM WAR between 1966 and 1968. The war affected him greatly—especially the mistreatment suffered by blacks and Puerto Ricans—and culminated in his renowned collection of poems, *Puerto Rican Obituary* (1971). After returning to the United States, he taught creative writing at the State University of New York at Buffalo. He directed poetry workshops for children from 1970 to 1972.

In 1974 Pietri became a member of a bilingual childhood project directed by the Puerto Rican Association for Community Affairs and also served as a consultant to El Museo del Barrio, New York's museum honoring the contribution of Latinos in the United States. In 1975 he emerged as one of the city's most distinct voices and, together with MIGUEL ALGARÍN, founded the literary movement known as Nuyorican poetry, in which urban Puerto Rican artists affirmed—often through humor and simultaneous puns in Spanish and English—their identities in verse.

Pietri joined the Cultural Council Foundation as a literary artist in 1978. He has received numerous awards, including a grant from the New York State Council of Creative Arts; a Public Service Grant in 1971, 1974, and 1975; a New York Foundation for the Arts award for poetry in 1986; and a Just Buffalo Inc., award in 1986. His published works include *Traffic Violation* (1973), *Invisible Poetry* (1979*)*, *Out of Order* (1980), *Uptown Train* (1980), and a narrative titled *Lost in the Museum of Natural History* (1981). He has authored numerous plays, including *The Livingroom* (1975), *The Masses Are Asses* (1983), and *Mondo Mambo/A Mambo Rap Sodi* (1990), all of which have been publicly performed in New York. His pieces have been included in several anthologies, among them *Nuyorican Poetry: An Anthology of Puerto Rican Words and Feelings* (1975) and *Herejes y Mitificadores: Muestra de Poesía puertorriqueña en los Estados Unidos* (1980). His extensive list of published works has established him as one of the best-known Puerto Rican authors of his genre.

In 2003, after a diagnosis of advanced stomach cancer, Pietri sought alternative treatment in Mexico. He was returning to New York in March 2004 when he suffered renal failure and died.

See also Nuyorican Poets.

Pinchback, P(inckney) B(enton) S(tewart)

1837–1921

America's first black governor; he held more major political positions than any other African American during Reconstruction.

Pinckney Benton Stewart Pinchback was the free-born son of a wealthy white planter, William Pinchback, and his longtime mistress, an emancipated slave named Eliza Steward. William Pinchback's family successfully challenged his will after his death in 1848, leaving Eliza and their five children destitute. Fearing that Pinchback's relatives would attempt to enslave them, Eliza moved the family to Cincinnati, where Pinchback attended Gilmore's High School.

In 1862, after working as a steward on a Mississippi riverboat, Pinchback joined the Union Army in NEW ORLEANS. He recruited and commanded a company of the Corps d'Afrique, a Louisiana cavalry unit. Initially, all of the Corps d'Afrique's officers were black. The black officers learned, however, that their commissions were subject to qualification examinations. All of the black officers, except Pinchback, were replaced by white officers. When authorities repeatedly ignored Pinchback's demands for equal treatment of black officers and troops, he resigned in protest in September 1863.

Pinchback remained in New Orleans after the CIVIL WAR, helping to shape Louisiana's REPUBLICAN PARTY and holding public offices. In 1867, he served as a member of the state's Constitutional Convention, and a year later, he was elected to Louisiana's state senate. He served as president *pro tempore* of the Senate in 1871, and succeeded Oscar J. Dunn as lieutenant governor after Dunn's death in January 1871. When the Louisiana House of Representatives began impeachment proceedings against Governor Henry Clay Warmoth in December 1872, Pinchback became Louisiana's acting governor, serving until January 1873 when W.P. Kellogg succeeded him.

Pinchback's career suffered several political setbacks. He was elected to the U.S. House of Representatives in 1872, but both Pinchback and his opponent, George A. Sheridan, claimed victory. They contested the seat until February 4, 1875, when the House Committee on Elections judged Sheridan the winner. Meanwhile, in January 1873, the Louisiana legislature elected Pinchback to the U.S. Senate, which was also contested by another rival, W.L. McMillen. Though McMillen eventually acknowledged Pinchback's claim to the seat, senators uncovered evidence that Pinchback had paid $10,000 to obtain it. On March 13, 1875, the Senate denied Pinchback his seat by a vote of thirty-two to twenty-nine.

The end of RECONSTRUCTION in 1877 and the restoration of white supremacist rule in the South ended Pinchback's career in public office, although as a wealthy man with considerable political skills he continued to advocate in behalf of American blacks by attempting to slow the momentum of Southern Democrats who were working to disfranchise blacks and enforce the segregation of the races. He also attempted to sway public opinion by publishing a newspaper, the *Louisianan*. In 1875 he became chairman of the Convention of Colored Newspaper Men, which led to the formation of the Associated Negro Press.

Pinchback succeeded in several business ventures throughout his life. He was a cotton dealer, and helped to found the Mississippi River Packet Company. He also profited from his positions in government and the information that they provided. For instance, Pinchback arranged for the New Orleans Park Commission, on which he served, to purchase property he owned for more than its market value. He also profited from bond speculation, stating that "I belonged to the General Assembly, and knew about what it would do. . . . My investments were made accordingly." In 1897, Pinchback and his wife, Nina Hawthorne, moved to WASHINGTON, D.C. where he became a leading member of the city's black social elite until his death in 1921. Among his grandchildren was JEAN TOOMER, the well-known novelist of the HARLEM RENAISSANCE.

See also Military, Blacks in the American; Press, Black, in the United States; United States House of Representatives, African Americans in; United States Senate, African Americans in the.

Robert Fay

Pindling, Lynden O.

1930–2000

First prime minister and first black leader of the Bahamas.

Sir Lynden O. Pindling was one of the most influential Bahamian politicians. Born in the BAHAMAS, the son of a merchant, Pindling was an outstanding student and was accepted to London University, in England, where he studied law. After returning to the Bahamas and being admitted to the bar in 1953, Pindling joined the new Progressive Liberal Party (PLP), the Bahamas' first political party, which was dedicated to the goal of black political representation. Pindling was elected to Parliament as a PLP representative in 1956, and served as leader of the opposition in the House from 1964 to 1967.

One of Pindling's earliest political triumphs came during a Parliamentary debate on April 27, 1965—the date now remembered as "Black Tuesday." While the population of the Bahamas was over eighty percent black, the political districts at the time had been drawn so that white areas were unfairly overrepresented, and the PLP minority were pushing to have the districts redrawn. At the end of that day's debate, Pindling gave a passionate speech in which he declared that he did not want to be a part of a government that did not accurately represent its constituents. He then took the ceremonial wooden mace that had been the symbol of parliamentary authority in the Bahamas since 1799 and threw it out of an open window, declaring that its power actually belonged outside with the people.

The mace broke in half in the middle of the black crowd that had gathered outside, and Pindling's actions were met with shock and horror by white members of Parliament and the local newspaper, but the drama had an effect. Two years later, when the districts were finally redrawn, the PLP won a majority, and as the party's leader, Pindling became premier of the Bahamas. When the country's constitution was changed in 1969 so that its chief executive would be prime minister instead of simply a premier, Pindling became the first prime minister of the Bahamas.

Pindling was not content to stop with that change, however, and instead led the PLP and the rest of the country in pushing for total independence for the Bahamas from Great Britain. The boldness of this move again shocked many Bahamians, but the campaign was successful, and on July 10, 1973, the Bahamas became an independent country, with Pindling as its first leader. As prime minister, Pindling was noted for his extraordinary speaking ability; as one observer noted, "Witty, caustic, full of mockery and mimicry . . . [m]ixing Bahamian English with Standard English at just the right moments, he is a platform master." He was knighted by Queen Elizabeth in 1983.

Pindling's tremendous popularity allowed him to stay in power until 1992. But his reputation was irrevocably damaged by the charges of drug-trade corruption that were leveled at his administration in the mid-1980s. These accusations and a depressed economy allowed the Free National Movement party to win election in 1992, making Hubert Ingraham the new prime minister, and in 1997 Pindling finally resigned as the leader of the PLP after forty-one years at his party's helm. Pindling's bold leadership and willingness to fight for black political equality forever changed the course of the Bahamas' history.

See also Nationalism in Latin America and the Caribbean.

Lisa Clayton Robinson

Piñeiro, Ignacio

1888–1969

Afro-Cuban bass player, composer, and musical director of the legendary Septeto Nacional from 1927 to 1937 and again from 1958 to 1969.

Together with Arsenio Rodríguez and Miguel Matamoros, Ignacio Piñeiro is universally regarded as one of the most influential figures in the development of contemporary Cuban music, particularly of the Afro-Cuban genre son.

See also Music, Afro-Cuban.

Pippen, Scottie

1965–

American professional basketball player, considered one of the most skilled and versatile players in the National Basketball Association.

Scottie Pippen, a basketball forward, is widely admired for the variety of his talents. In the 1990s he consistently ranked among the National Basketball Association (NBA)'s leaders in scoring, rebounding, assists, and steals.

Born in Hamburg, Arkansas, Pippen was slow to develop as a basketball player and did not win a starting position on a team until his senior year in high school. He enrolled at the University of Central Arkansas in 1983 and worked initially as manager of the basketball team. His play rapidly improved, however, and by his senior year he was a starting guard and the team's best player.

The Seattle SuperSonics selected Pippen in the first round of the 1987 NBA draft and immediately traded him to the Chicago Bulls. Pippen earned a spot as a starting forward for the Bulls during his second year, the 1988–1989 season. Pippen and acclaimed guard Michael Jordan helped lead the Bulls to six NBA championship titles (1991–1993 and 1996–1998). In the 1995–1996 season the Bulls also became the first NBA team to win seventy or more games in a season, finishing with seventy-two victories. Pippen was a member of the United States basketball team known as the Dream Team, which won gold medals at the 1992 Olympic Games in Barcelona, Spain, and the 1996 games in Atlanta, Georgia. Pippen played in the NBA All-Star game in 1990 and from 1992 to 1997. He was elected most valuable player (MVP) of the 1994 All-Star game.

Pippen left the Bulls in 1998 to join the Houston Rockets for one season. He has been a member of the Portland Trailblazers since 1999. He was named to the NBA All-Defensive Team every year from 1991 to 2000. The Chicago Bulls signed Pippen as a free agent in 2003.

Pippin, Horace

1888–1946

American painter, who became famous for his nonacademic approach to art and the inclusion of historical events and personal experiences in his work.

Horace Pippin was born in West Chester, Pennsylvania. He was discovered at a time in art history when artists such as Pablo Picasso were breaking away from academic painting standards to define a modern aesthetic. Art critics and dealers had become particularly interested in self-taught artists whose works had not been influenced by traditional approaches to painting. One such artist was Henri Rousseau, a French painter hailed by Picasso for his unorthodox and dreamlike subject matter, his use of strong colors, and his indifference to perspective. Pippin was compared to Rousseau because of his tendency to ignore concepts of realism, such as perspective and shading.

Another aspect of Pippin's work that intrigued art critics and dealers was the way in which he interpreted historical events in terms of his own personal experiences. His painting *Abraham Lincoln and His Father Building Their Cabin on Pigeon Creek,* for example, is from his childhood memories of Goshen, New York, as reflected in the structure and fixtures of the house. The personal dimension in *John Brown Going to His Hanging* stems from Pippin's inclusion of his grandmother, who had actually witnessed the event in 1859. These personal details lend a sense of immediacy and intimacy to Pippin's depictions of historical events.

Art critic and historian Christian Brinton discovered Pippin after seeing *Cabin in the Cotton* on display in a barbershop window in 1936. Brinton sought out Pippin and arranged for ten of his works to be displayed at the West Chester Community Center. Within a year, four of Pippin's works were included in Masters of Popular Painting, an exhibition of self-taught French and American painters at the Museum of Modern Art, in New York City. In 1940 artist-turned-dealer Robert Carlen mounted Pippin's first gallery show in Philadelphia, Pennsylvania. During the 1940s, Pippin's paintings were purchased by several major American museums, and galleries throughout the country mounted exhibitions featuring his works.

Pippin had an interest in drawing from an early age, but began to paint, in part, to rehabilitate his right arm following a

World War I injury. As a boy, he had won a box of crayons and a set of watercolors for his entry in a contest sponsored by an art supply company. Pippin used the crayons and watercolors to decorate doilies, which were sold at a Sunday school festival. During his childhood and early adulthood, he spent much of his free time drawing.

After the United States declared war in 1917, Pippin enlisted and served as a corporal in what would become known as the 369th Colored Infantry Regiment of the United States Army. He continued to sketch while in the service, but he was made to destroy his sketches for security reasons. Only six of the drawings documenting Pippin's war experiences survive. He was honorably discharged in 1918 after a German sniper's bullet seriously wounded his right shoulder. Pippin, who was very proud of his frontline service, received a French Croix de Guerre in 1919 and a Purple Heart, retroactively, in 1945.

After returning to West Chester after the war, Pippin met Jennie Ora Featherstone, a widow with a young son. They married in 1920, but Pippin's disability check was not enough to support the family. He tried his best, with his good left arm, to assist his wife at her laundry service. In 1925 Pippin began to make pictures by burning images onto wood panels with a hot poker. Intended as therapy for his injured arm, the endeavor enabled him to work out the war memories that continued to trouble him.

Pyrography—burning drawings into wood—was a challenging way for Pippin to resume his creative activities. Because pyrography's laborious process precludes erasure, it required that he plan the entire composition in his head before starting it. Toward the end of the 1920s, with his right arm gaining strength, he attempted his first easel painting, supporting his disabled painting arm at the wrist with his left hand. He spent three years painting and repainting his first work in oil, *The End of the War: Starting Home* (1930), which depicts the surrender of German soldiers against a background of violence and chaos. Although his output was slow and exhausting during the early 1930s, Pippin continued to reconstruct his personal past, particularly childhood and war memories, through painting.

Pippin's growing popularity in the 1940s led to some changes in his work. Philadelphia art collector Albert Barnes championed Pippin's work after seeing his solo exhibition. Pippin attended classes at the Barnes Foundation and the two men shared a friendship for several years. Perhaps inspired by the impressionist paintings in the Barnes collection, Pippin brightened his palette and began to create still-life compositions of meticulously rendered flowers. The impact of other artists is also apparent in Pippin's John Brown paintings, a narrative group of works inspired by the Toussaint Louverture series by American artist JACOB LAWRENCE.

Pippin worked with increasing productivity until his death on July 6, 1946. He created more than 75 of his 137 known works in the last six years of his life. Unlike other important self-taught artists who tended to repeat themselves, Pippin explored a variety of subjects—including American history, biblical themes, winter landscapes, portraits, and scenes of everyday black communal life—using a range of mediums, such as fabric, paper, and wood. In attempting to be direct and true to reality as he understood it, Pippin created works with some of modern art's fundamental characteristics—unmodulated, sharply delineated colors and flat, shadowless forms—which makes him one of the twentieth century's most remarkable artists.

See also Brown, John.

Bibliography

Driskell, David. *Hidden Heritage: Afro-American Art, 1800–1950.* The Association, 1985.

Stein, Judith E., et al. *I Tell My Heart: The Art of Horace Pippin.* Pennsylvania Academy of the Fine Arts in association with Universe Publishing, 1993.

Aaron Myers

Pires, Pedro Verona Rodrigues

1934–

Prime minister of the Republic of Cape Verde from 1975 to 1991 and president since 2001.

Pedro Pires was born in a small village on Fogo Island, CAPE VERDE. While studying engineering in Lisbon, PORTUGAL, he encountered a community of Africans hotly debating the issue of Portuguese COLONIAL RULE. In 1959 Pires joined the underground movement for independence.

Fleeing conscription in the Portuguese army, Pires went to GHANA, where GUINEA-BISSAU nationalist leader AMÍLCAR CABRAL and the Partido Africano da Independencia da Guine e Cabo Verde (PAIGC) were based. From there he went to ALGERIA, where he received military training, and then to CUBA, where in 1966 he helped mastermind a PAIGC invasion of Cape Verde. Although the outlawed party ultimately decided against the invasion, Pires continued to play a key role as both a fighter and an administrator, taking charge of the party's health and education departments.

As Cape Verde and Guinea-Bissau neared independence, Pires acted as PAIGC's chief negotiator, leading a 1974 delegation to talks in London and ALGIERS, as well as lobbying the United States Congress for support. Following independence in 1975, the Cape Verde Popular National Assembly chose Pires to be the first prime minister.

Pires worked alongside fellow PAIGC member ARISTIDES PEREIRA, who now served as president. Pursuing a policy of nonalignment, they attempted to position Cape Verde between the Cold War superpowers, and called on African nations to handle their own affairs through the ORGANIZATION OF AFRICAN UNITY, rather than inviting foreign intervention. The outspoken administration also demanded the end of APARTHEID in SOUTH AFRICA, and appealed to its own citizens to conserve the natural resources of their drought-stricken islands.

Following the split with the Guinea-Bissau PAIGC in 1980, Pires created a new, one-nation party—the Partido Africano da

Independencia da Cabo Verde (PAICV)—as well as a one-party nation. He subsequently undertook agrarian reforms and a campaign to nationalize foreign businesses, raising fears among some Cape Verdeans that Pires was courting support from the Soviet Union, and was perhaps planning to allow a Soviet base on the strategically located islands. Fearing a coup, the administration suppressed dissent through arrests and expulsions.

Despite this, during the 1980s Cape Verde received more per capita economic aid than almost any country in the world, most of it from European nations and expatriate Cape Verdeans, who by then were nearly twice as numerous as the resident population. Even though the administration promised to invest in industrialization and urban renewal, opposition groups as well as the international community called for the end to its one-party rule. In 1991 Cape Verde held the first multiparty elections of any former Portuguese colony. The Movimento para a Democracia (MpD) carried the day, and Pires was forced to resign. He retained his position as the head of the PAICV, however, becoming leader the "loyal opposition." In 2001 political momentum in Cape Verde shifted back in Pires's favor. The PAICV captured a majority of the seats in the National Assembly and Pires was elected president.

See also Cold War and Africa; Nationalism in Africa.

Marian Aguiar

Pitanga, Antônio

1939–

Afro-Brazilian actor.

Antônio Pitanga starred in some of the most important films of CINEMA NOVO, or New Cinema, a movement that influenced moviemaking in BRAZIL between about 1960 and 1980. Born Antônio Sampaio, Pitanga made his debut in *Bahia de Todos os Santos* (1960, Bahia of All Saints), directed by Trigueirinho Neto. In that film he played a character named Pitanga, and he adopted the name.

In 1961 Pitanga starred in *Barravento* (The Turning Wind), the first movie directed by Brazilian film critic Glauber Rocha. In 1963 Pitanga appeared in *Ganga Zumba,* a work by filmmaker CARLOS DIEGUES. Twenty years later Pitanga worked with Diegues again in *Quilombo,* a movie that, like *Ganga Zumba,* celebrated PALMARES, a seventeenth-century community of runaway slaves in the state of Pernambuco. In 1977 Pitanga directed the movie *Na boca do mundo* (In the World's Mouth), on the subjects of race, gender, and class. During the 1990s Pitanga appeared in several Brazilian television series and was elected to a seat on RIO DE JANEIRO's city council as a candidate of the Partido dos Trabalhadores (Workers' Party). He continued to perform film roles as well, appearing in *Villa-Lobos— Uma Vida de Paixão* (2000) and *Apolônio Brasil, Campeão da Alegria* (2003).

See also Cinema, Black, in Brazil.

Pitt, David

1913–1994

Physician and one of the first black politicians in Great Britain.

At a time when prejudice and even violence against blacks was common in GREAT BRITAIN, David Thomas Pitt spoke out for the unrepresented black immigrant community. In his obituary for Pitt in the *Guardian* in 1994, black British journalist Mike Phillips wrote: "At that point, Dr. Pitt was the only black person who figured in the public and political life of the country; and as such, if only by default, when he spoke, he spoke for us."

Born on the island of GRENADA in the WEST INDIES, David Pitt attended Grenada Boys' Secondary school and was raised a devout Roman Catholic. In 1932 he won Grenada's only overseas scholarship to attend the prestigious medical school at the University of Edinburgh in Scotland. After graduating with honors, he returned to the West Indies in 1938 and practiced medicine in Saint Vincent and Trinidad. There he met and married Dorothy Alleyne; they had three children.

In 1943 Pitt helped found the West Indian National Party, and he served as its president until 1947. This party was considered radical in its day because it advocated independence for Trinidad within a West Indian federation. He won election to the borough council in San Fernando, Trinidad, where he also served as deputy mayor. In order to lobby the British government for independence, he traveled to Great Britain in 1947. His efforts were unsuccessful, and he grew disillusioned with West Indian politics. He decided to settle in the London district of Euston, where he established a medical practice that he ran for more than thirty years.

In the 1950s, Pitt was one of the few blacks active in defending the growing black population of Great Britain against discrimination and prejudice. In the 1960s and 1970s, he organized to help immigrants and improve race relations. Pitt became the first and only chair of the Campaign Against Racial Discrimination (CARD), an association founded with the encouragement of MARTIN LUTHER KING JR. Pitt believed in fighting racism within the existing power structure. In 1959 Pitt sought to represent London's wealthy Hampstead district in Parliament, becoming the first West Indian black to seek a seat in Parliament. After a campaign plagued by racist insinuations, Pitt lost the election.

In 1961, however, Pitt won election representing the ethnically mixed, working-class Hackney district in London's city government, the London County Council (LCC). In 1964 this body was absorbed by the Greater London Council (GLC). He served as deputy chair of the GLC from 1969 to 1970 and in 1974 became the first black chair, a post he held until 1975. Pitt paved the way for the multiracial politics for which the GLC became known.

In 1970 Pitt ran for Parliament again, this time as a candidate in London's Clapham district, a secure Labour seat that many believed he would win. He lost by an unusually large margin; race undoubtedly played a large role in his defeat. He was bitterly disappointed, and did not attempt to run for Parliament again.

In 1975 Prime Minister Harold Wilson appointed Pitt to the House of Lords as Lord Pitt of Hampstead. According to Pitt himself, however, his most valued honor was his election as president of the British Medical Association from 1985 to 1986, a position few general practitioners achieve. After his death, many lamented that Pitt "should have been the first black Labour Member of Parliament."

See also London, Blacks in: An Interpretation; Nationalist Movements and Blacks in Latin America and the Caribbean; Saint Vincent and the Grenadines; Trinidad and Tobago.

Bibliography

Phillips, Mike. "David Pitt: Speaking up for the Voiceless." *The Guardian,* Dec. 19, 1994.

Leyla Keough

Pitta do Nascimento, Celso Roberto

1946–

First black mayor of São Paulo, the largest city in Brazil.

Celso Roberto Pitta do Nascimento was born in RIO DE JANEIRO, BRAZIL to a middle-class family. His father was a tradesman and his mother a public servant. At the age of sixteen, after his father's death, Pitta took his first job as a clerk at the Ministry of Planning.

He received his first degree in economics in 1968, from the Federal University of Rio de Janeiro, and traveled to England, where he completed a master's degree in transportation economics at Leeds University in 1971. Pitta then studied advanced administration at the Harvard Business School, graduating in 1980. Pitta worked as a consultant in the fields of administration and finance, and worked for several Brazilian businesses, including Estaleiros Mauá and Casa da Moeda do Brasil. Pitta moved to São Paulo in 1986, where he worked for a large private corporation called Eucatex.

In addition to working in business, Pitta has also been active in the public sector and other areas. He participated in the expansion of the Brazilian navy (from 1975 to 1979), took part in the planning of the subway systems of Rio de Janeiro and SÃO PAULO, and was a member of a Brazilian mission to the International Monetary Fund (IMF) in WASHINGTON D.C. in 1984. He was also named honorary consul of LESOTHO.

Pitta began his political career as secretary of Finance, Budget, and Planning for the city of São Paulo under the administration of Mayor Paulo Maluf, which ended in 1996. Around this time Pitta became affiliated with the Partido Progressista Brasileiro (Brazilian Progressive Party, or PPB). In 1996, with support from the PPB, he was elected mayor of São Paulo for a four-year term. Corruption scandals marred his tenure, and he did not run for reelection.

Pittsburgh Courier

One of the most influential African American newspapers of the early twentieth century.

The *Pittsburgh Courier* was founded in the spring of 1910 by EDWIN HARLESTON and a small group of PITTSBURGH blacks that included attorney ROBERT LEE VANN. At the time of the *Courier's* founding, Pittsburgh's white newspapers either ignored African American news or reported it in a separate section, often focusing on crime and other lurid elements. By the fall of 1910 Vann had become editor, treasurer, and legal counsel of the newspaper and was the driving force behind its growth. Through its first troubled decade Vann steered the *Courier* to a small circulation among Pittsburgh's blacks and used its pages to further his legal career (in 1918 he won appointment as a Pittsburgh city solicitor).

By the early 1920s the *Courier's* circulation reached 55,000, and by the mid-1930s it totaled about 150,000. This growth was partly the result of demographics: large numbers of blacks moved from the South to the North as part of the GREAT MIGRATION of the early 1900s. But it was also the result of shrewd management of the *Courier*: popular journalist GEORGE SCHUYLER was hired to write a widely read column; *Courier* journalists were sent on tours of the South to report on JIM CROW and to attract a national audience; and the *Courier* undertook a well-publicized campaign attacking RACIAL STEREOTYPES in the *Amos 'N' Andy* radio program.

In the 1930s and 1940s the newspaper continued to increase its local and national circulation with coverage of boxer JOE LOUIS and calls for fair treatment of BLACKS IN THE AMERICAN MILITARY during World War II. By 1947 circulation reached a peak of more than 350,000, but in the following years the readership and influence of the *Courier,* like that of many black newspapers, declined steadily as white newspapers began to cover the CIVIL RIGHTS MOVEMENT and other black news. In the 1960s the *Courier* was sold and renamed the *New Pittsburgh Courier,* which continues publication today.

See also Magazines, Newspapers, and Journals; Press, Black, in the United States.

Pittsburgh, Pennsylvania

Manufacturing city in western Pennsylvania whose black population countered its marginal economic position by prospering in civic and cultural spheres.

The historian Roy Lubove describes early industrial Pittsburgh as "the 'Smokey City,' America's classic coketown . . . frequently compared to hell . . . an economic rather than civic entity." Indeed, by the turn of the twentieth century, belching smokestacks and polluted waterways encroached on Pittsburgh's river-valley beauty. African Americans, however, had little hand in the desecration. From Pittsburgh's settlement, around 1760, until World War II blacks found few opportunities in the town's industries.

Despite the poverty that plagued African Americans in Pittsburgh until the AMERICAN CIVIL WAR, their numbers grew from 1,000 to 20,000 during RECONSTRUCTION. Flocks of migrants arrived from Virginia to work in Pittsburgh's factories, but few newcomers found well-paying jobs. White employers excluded blacks from Pittsburgh's thriving iron and glass industries, and most of the blacks settled for unskilled domestic work. Even when World War I occasioned a large demand for industrial labor, foremen hired blacks for only the most grueling and low-paid work. A 1918 sociology study revealed that 95 percent of African American factory workers in Pittsburgh held unskilled positions, regardless of education level. The GREAT DEPRESSION made a bad situation worse, as job opportunities dwindled and unfair hiring practices continued. Although World War II created numerous jobs, black people benefited far less than whites, entering the second half of the century with little hope of improvement.

Nevertheless, the richness of black Pittsburgh's cultural history surpassed that of comparably populated cities. Twenty years before the Civil War, the journalist MARTIN ROBISON DELANY was editing the *Mystery,* one of the earliest black newspapers. His small constituency of poor black readers also supported a large array of churches, clubs, and schools as well as other publications. During Reconstruction, African American civic successes kept pace with the growth in population, and literary societies and philanthropic organizations added to the enduring antebellum network of social groups. Between World War I and 1930, the journalist Robert Vann edited the *PITTSBURGH COURIER,* helping the paper to become the most widely read black periodical in the nation. In the 1930s, Pittsburgh's African American baseball teams often topped the Negro League, boosted there by players Leroy Robert ("Satchel") Paige and James "Cool Papa" Bell. At the same time, the city's JAZZ scene boasted such names as vocalist LENA HORNE and trumpeter ROY ELDRIDGE.

After World War II, white citizens of Pittsburgh created urban renewal programs in which old neighborhoods were cleared to make room for new. For African Americans in Pittsburgh's lower-hill district, "renewal" often meant unfair eviction. The programs worsened ghetto conditions by pushing more people into fewer homes. The fact that the city's steep hills divided the black community among several distinct neighborhoods contributed to the difficulty in achieving political unity.

Pittsburgh, however, endured less urban decay than other, similarly constituted industrial towns. Because Pittsburgh blacks faced fewer opportunities to begin with, the decline of industry brought no sudden shock, no skyrocketing crime or drug use. While economic conditions toward the end of the century worsened, Pittsburgh retained some of its vitality in the jazz music of George Benson, Erroll Garner, and Stanley Turrentine, and the novels and plays of JOHN EDGAR WIDEMAN and AUGUST WILSON. In 1990 blacks made up about 25 percent of the city's population.

Bibliography

Wright, Richard R. Jr. *The Negro in Pennsylvania: A Study in Economic History.* Arno Press, 1969.

Eric Bennett

Pixinguinha

1898–1973

Brazilian bandleader, *choro* **musician,** *sambista,* **and composer of more than 600 instrumental pieces, including choros,** *valsas, maxixes,* **and** *sambas.*

Pixinguinha grew up in a large family in the working class district of Catumbi, in north RIO DE JANEIRO. His birth name was Alfredo da Rocha Viana Jr., but his grandparents gave him the nickname Pizinguim, of African origin, meaning "good child." Eventually, it was Brazilianized, becoming Pixinguinha.

The musical genre *choro* (from the word for "cry") emerged in the late nineteenth century. Pixinguinha's father, a telegraph worker by trade, was a flautist and choro musician. At night his home was the meeting place for many neighborhood choro musicians. In this setting Pixinguinha became immersed in the choro tradition. He was playing flute professionally at age fifteen in Choro Carioca, a group led by his teacher, Irineu de Almeida. Before he was out of his teens, he was well regarded in the music circles of northern Rio de Janeiro.

In 1919, together with DONGA, Pixinguinha formed his first group, Oito Batutas (the Eight Lads). The band got their first break playing in the foyer of the Palais cinema; soon after, they began a national tour.

In 1922 Arnaldo Guine, a rich patron, fronted the money for the Oito Batutas to go to Paris, where they played for six months. These appearances met with disapproval among many upper-class *cariocas* (citizens of Rio), who were outraged at the prospect of a black band acting as BRAZIL's first cultural ambassadors to EUROPE. Discriminatory protests in their own country notwithstanding, the Oito Batutas received favorable reviews in Europe. The band's unique blend of SAMBA, choro, and *maxixe* had provided Europe with its first glimpse of Brazil's rich musical culture. Without a doubt, it was this tour that opened the doors for the massive worldwide exportation of Brazilian music that was to follow.

During the 1930s Pixinguinha embarked on one of the most successful periods of his career. A few years earlier, he had written some arrangements for Carmen Miranda's international debut record, thereby becoming one of the recording industry's most sought-after arrangers. His band, Velha Guarda, provided the instrumental accompaniment for numerous recording projects during this period.

Pixinguinha is often credited with helping to invent the samba. Indeed, it was his colleague, Donga, who recorded the first samba, "Pelo Telefone," in 1917. It has recently been suggested, however, that this composition was likely a group effort in which many musicians, possibly including Pixinguinha, took part. At any rate, Pixinguinha is certainly one of samba's most prolific composers, with pieces numbering in the hundreds. Yet during his lifetime, Pixinguinha was known more for his arrangements than his compositions. Often his complex harmonic language and elaborate formal experimentation met with severe criticism; such was the case with his 1926 choro "Lamento." Today, however, Pixinguinha's innovations are considered to have laid the foundations for MPB (Música Popular Brasileira), and many eminent composers, such as Antonio Carlos Jobim, Chico Buarque, and Milton Nacimento, have cited him as a major influence on their work. Pixinguinha has often been hailed as the King of Samba and the Father of MPB.

See also Contemporary Afro-Brazilian Music.

Gordon Root

Plaatje, Solomon Tshekisho

1876–1932

South African writer and journalist and one of the founders of the African National Congress, serving as its first secretary-general.

Although ethnically a TSWANA of the Rolong branch, Solomon Tshekisho Plaatje took the Dutch name *Plaatje* from a nickname used by his father. Following some schooling in the 1880s, Plaatje took a job as a postal clerk at Kimberley, in NORTHERN CAPE Province, SOUTH AFRICA. During the Boer War (1899–1902) he reported the siege of Mafeking (now Mafikeng) and kept a diary of the period. In 1904 he launched the first newspaper in the Tswana language, *Koranta ea Bechuana* (Newspaper of the Tswana) and began opposing white violations of black rights. In 1912 he became the secretary-general of what was at first known as the South African Native National Congress, later the AFRICAN NATIONAL CONGRESS, with JOHN LANGALIBALELE DUBE as president. Plaatje was a fine orator, and in 1913 went with Dube and a delegation to GREAT BRITAIN to oppose the 1913 Natives Land Act, which had drastically curtailed the right of blacks to purchase or own land. He remained in Great Britain during World War I (1914–1918) where he wrote and published several books. In *Native Life in South Africa* (1916) he outlined the reasons for black opposition to the Land Act. At the end of the war he was part of another black delegation that attended the Versailles peace conference but that was not allowed to participate. He also attended the Pan African Congress, which was held in Paris at the same time, and was among the first South African black leaders to make contact with other African black leaders. Plaatje traveled back to Great Britain and went with delegations to see Prime Minister David Lloyd George and the Archbishop of Canterbury, but failed to obtain help for the black cause in South Africa. From there he traveled to CANADA and the United States.

He wrote poetry and translated five of Shakespeare's plays into Tswana. His novel *Mhudi: An Epic of Native Life 100 Years Ago* (1930) was one of the first novels in English by a black African.

See also Fiction, English-Language, in Africa; Pan-African Congress of 1919; Press, African.

Planciancois, Anselmas

1822–1863

African American hero of the American Civil War who was killed while carrying the Union flag in a major battle at Port Hudson, Louisiana.

Anselmas Planciancois was born free in Louisiana. On September 10, 1862, he enlisted in the Ninety-Sixth Regiment, U.S. Colored Infantry, of the Confederate army. Planciancois was assigned, on September 27, to Company E of the First Louisiana Regiment of Native Guards (Free Colored) with the rank of sergeant. The First and Third Louisiana Native Guards, composed of free blacks, had been organized on May 2, 1861, by Confederate governor Thomas Moore, who feared an attack by Union forces and sought to strengthen his military capacity with African Americans. When the anticipated Union attack occurred, during April of 1862, white Confederate soldiers were militarily compelled to evacuate NEW ORLEANS. The Native Guards, however, stayed behind to protect their families and property.

Shortly afterwards, Union Brigadier General Benjamin Butler, and his successor, General Nathaniel P. Banks, commanding the Department of the Gulf, retained the two regiments for service in the Union Army. Banks changed the name of the First Louisiana to the First Infantry Regiment, Corps d'Afrique. Later, when the Bureau of Colored Troops was organized in 1863, the Corps d'Afrique was renamed the Seventy-Third Regiment, U.S. Colored Troops.

In 1863, Planciancois and his regiment were ordered to participate in the attack upon Port Hudson, the last remaining Confederate fortification on the lower Mississippi. Port Hudson was located approximately thirty miles north of Baton Rouge, Louisiana. It had been built by slave labor and presented a formidable military obstacle for Union troops along the river. The fortification stretched over three miles along an eighty-foot bluff. It was protected by twenty mounted siege guns and thirty pieces of field artillery. Port Hudson was further protected on land by a semicircle of chopped and sharpened trees piled in front of ramparts, which were buttressed by a series of rifle pits and outworks.

The Union forces subjected the stronghold to four hours of bombardment and rushed simultaneously all along the assault line. The Native Guards, with 1,080 men, were formed into four lines on the right flank. Captain ANDREÉ CAILLOUX of Company E led his men into battle, with Planciancois carrying the colors. Cailloux was fatally wounded prior to his company reaching a ditch. The men had to swim across portions of the lower Mississippi in order to reach temporary shelter. Disorganized, the regiments eventually reassembled and made a second assault four hours later. Again they were repulsed by the Confederates. Unknown to the Native Guards, they were the only soldiers assaulting Port Hudson and therefore were the singular focus of the rebel artillery. Incredibly, the Union forces in the center and left flank had failed to mount their offensives during the two operations of the Native Guards. Their lack of activity undoubtedly contributed significantly to the casualties sustained by the advancing black soldiers. In addition to the Native Guards, the First Regiment of Louisiana Engineers engaged in combat on the right flank.

In the final assault against Port Hudson on May 27, 1863, Planciancois carried the flag to the front of the enemy's fortifications. He is reported to have said: "I'll bring back the flag or know the reason why." While waving his company forward, the top of his head was lifted off by a six-pound artillery round and he fell with the flag clutched in his hands. Two African American corporals then struggled for possession of the flag in order to have the honor of bearing it in battle. Before the assault was terminated, six men who had carried the flag were killed. Port Hudson was one of the first major battles in which African American regiments participated.

Planciancois was survived by his wife, Margaret Walts, who was born free in 1829. She married Planciancois on July 5, 1851, in New Orleans, Louisiana. Of their three sons—Louis (born April 21, 1851), Joseph (born February 4, 1853), and Anselmo (born June 9, 1863)—the oldest two died relatively young. One son died in 1871, the second died in 1877. Margaret Planciancois, who received a pension for the military service of her husband, lived with her youngest son.

Relatively few records exist pertaining to the career of Anselmas Planciancois. Among the documents are his pension records in the National Archives and the Records of the Army Adjutant General's Office, Record Group 94. Narratives with information concerning his military career and the battle of Port Hudson are contained in Benjamin Quarles's *The Negro in the Civil War* (1953) and the unpublished master's thesis of Mary F. Berry, "The History of the 73rd and 75th United States Colored Infantry Regiments" (Howard University, Washington, D.C., 1962).

From *Dictionary of American Negro Biography* by Rayford W. Logan and Michael R. Winston, editors. Copyright © 1982 by Rayford W. Logan and Michael R. Winston. Reprinted by permission of W.W. Norton & Company, Inc.

See also Civil War, American; Military, Blacks in the American.

Charles Johnson

Plants in Africa

Useful and ornamental flowers, grains, herbs, and trees that grow in Africa.

For information on
Distribution patterns of plants across the continent of Africa: See Biogeography of Africa.
Food plants: See Banana; Cowpea; Date Palm; Food in Africa; Millet; Papaya; Yams.
Plants grown as cash crops: See Cocoa; Food in Africa; Kola.
Medicinal plants: See Aloe; Chemistry; Kola.
Cosmetic plants: See Henna.
Plants used for paper: See Papyrus.
Ornamental plants: See Arctotis; Blue-Eyed African Daisy; Castor Bean; Gladiolus; Lobelia; Lotus.
Trees: See Acacia; Baobob; Candelabra Tree; Date Palm; Kola; Mahogany; Olive; Palm; Papaya; Sausage Tree.

Plato, Ann

1820?–?

American poet and essayist who was the second African American woman to publish a book in the United States.

Although little is known about the life of Ann Plato, her legacy holds an important place in African American literature. Plato's sole book, *Essays: Including Biographies and Miscellaneous Pieces in Prose and Poetry*, published in 1841, represents the only book of essays issued by a black American between 1840 and 1865. Following that of Phillis Wheatley, it was also only the second book published by an African American woman.

Based on information garnered primarily from her writings, scholars have determined that Plato probably was born about 1820. Her poem "The Infant Class," for example, suggests that Plato began to teach young children when she herself was only fifteen years old. Her poem "The Natives of America" links her to her paternal Native American heritage, and another poem, "I Have No Brother," indicates that she had a brother named Henry, who died when she was very young. Plato probably joined the Congregational Church at the age of thirteen. As she was not a slave, her writing provides unusual insight into the life of a mid-nineteenth-century, middle-class free black woman.

The introduction to Plato's book was written by James W. C. Pennington, minister of the Colored Congregational Church in Hartford. Pennington presents Plato's work by emphasizing first her color, then her age and sex, and finally the literary tradition from which she drew. Pennington was reluctant, but felt obliged to stress that Plato was black: "I am not in the habit of introducing myself or others to notice by the adjective 'colored,' . . . but it seems proper that I should . . . say here that my authoress is a colored lady." He also emphasized Plato's "large heart full of chaste and pious affection for those of her own age and sex. . . ." He compares her to Phillis Wheatley, the eighteenth-century black poet: "She, as Phillis Wheatley was, is passionately fond of reading and delights in searching the Holy Scriptures; and is now rapidly improving her knowledge."

In her book, Plato eulogizes four other black women, all of whom died at an early age: Louisa Sebury, Julia Ann Pell, Eliza Loomis Sherman, and Elizabeth Low. Eleven of Plato's twenty published poems have death as their themes, suggesting Plato's concern with the grim lives often led even by free blacks.

Some scholars have criticized Plato's writing, including one who described it as "the pious, moralistic effusions of a Puritan girl." Many of her poems are juvenile, her verse uneven. She almost always wrote in iambic tetrameter, and her language often reflected her puritanical environment. Still, Plato occasionally branches out to topics outside her personal experience, shedding her moral, florid tone in favor of more politically charged themes, as in her poem "To the First of August," in which Plato hailed the end of slavery in the WEST INDIES in 1838.

Most of Plato's works elucidate events and sentiments drawn from her own life. In "Written upon Being Examined in School Studies for the Preparation of a Teacher" she demands, "Learn me the way to teach the word of love/For that's the pure intelligence above." While Plato's contribution to American literature is often regarded as insignificant, the circumstances in which she wrote elevate her achievements and place her at the head of the canon of esteemed African American poets.

See also Free Blacks in the United States; Poetry, Black, in English; Women Writers, Black, in the United States.

Bibliography

Plato, Ann. *Essays: Including Biographies and Miscellaneous Pieces in Prose and Poetry.* Printed for the author, 1841.

Platters, The

Most successful African American vocal group of the 1950s; they played a key role in popularizing the rhythm and blues vocal harmony group style that has since become known as doo-wop.

The Platters were a popular vocal quintet and a consistent hitmaker for Mercury Records. But at the outset Mercury was more interested in acquiring the Penguins, another West Coast vocal group that had scored a major hit with "Earth Angel," recorded for the small Dootone label. The Platters, on the other hand, had found little success after several early releases on Federal Records. Mercury, one of the six major record companies of the day, wanted the Penguins in order to strengthen its RHYTHM AND BLUES (R&B) catalogue and thus gain more of the African American market. But arranger Buck Ram, who served as manager for both groups, insisted that if Mercury wanted the Penguins, it would have to sign the Platters as well.

In late 1954 Mercury reluctantly agreed. Ironically, the Penguins never had another Top Ten hit, whereas the Platters quickly rose to become the most successful vocal group of the decade. Although they recorded numerous up-tempo R&B numbers, the Platters were above all a ballad group. Their most successful recordings featured the smooth and romantic lead of Tony Williams. Williams ranks as one of the greatest lead tenors of the so-called doo-wop era and—along with Sonny Til of The Orioles, Willie Winfield of the Harptones, and Nate Nelson of the Flamingos—one of the great ballad interpreters of the 1950s.

The Platters were a product of the new African American culture created by the GREAT MIGRATION of blacks out of the South—in particular, those who came to LOS ANGELES, a city that had a black community that tripled in size during the 1940s as a result of the booming wartime economy. Los Angeles was home to the Platters, the Penguins, the Hollywood Flames, the Olympic Games, and many other African American vocal groups, whose members had often begun singing together in informal groups while still in high school.

The Platters began as a quartet in 1952, performing at amateur night competitions at Los Angeles's Club Alabam and more informal settings. Herbert Reed, who had sung bass in a gospel group during his stint in the United States Air Force, suggested the name the Platters. "I remember . . . thinking to myself, on the radio they always say, 'Here's the latest platter by so-and-so,'" Reed recalled. The group experienced several changes in membership over its first two years, including the addition of Williams and Zola Taylor, a fourteen-year-old alto, who became known as "the dish of the Platters." In 1954, not long before signing with Mercury, the group coalesced. Between 1955 and 1960, the years of their greatest success, the Platters consisted of Williams (tenor lead), Taylor (alto), David Lynch (tenor), Paul Robi (baritone), and Reed (bass).

The most demanding fans of African American vocal harmony singing dismissed the Platters for taking a simplistic approach to R&B group harmony singing. The Platters displayed little of the sophisticated voicings or complex harmonies found in the ballads performed by the Flamingos or the Harptones. Yet the Platters attained far greater commercial success, in large part because their singing was direct and emotionally engaging but also because they had the backing of a major record company. The group's first Mercury release, the haunting "Only You" (1955), hit the charts and clearly revealed the group's crossover potential, reaching not only number one on the R&B chart, but a striking number five on the white popular music chart.

Six months later, Mercury released "The Great Pretender" (1955), and the Platters became the first African American group to have a number one hit on the white pop charts. Over the next six years, the group enjoyed phenomenal success. During 1956 the Platters were second only to rock-and-roller Elvis Presley in popularity. By 1962 the group had given Mercury Records thirty-five songs on *Billboard* magazine's Pop Hot 100 chart. A number of their hits, including the memorable "Smoke Gets in Your Eyes" (1958) and "Harbor Lights" (1959) actually ranked higher on the white pop charts than on R&B listings.

Success swept up the five African American singers in a whirlwind of travel and performances. The Platters were particularly significant for their crossing of racial barriers in popular music. They performed in Las Vegas, in Paris at the Olympia Theater with bandleader QUINCY JONES, at the Vatican for Pope Pius XII, and in England for Queen Elizabeth II. In 1959 they became the first African American group to appear in the Eastern bloc, serving as goodwill ambassadors and performing in Poland.

The group's fall from success came suddenly. On August 10, 1959, Cincinnati police arrested the four men in the group for allegedly consorting with prostitutes. The case was eventually dismissed, and *Billboard* magazine published a charge that the arrests were a result of racism. But for several months the Platters discovered that their concert dates were canceled and radio disc jockeys refused to give them airplay.

The Platters returned to popularity with "Harbor Lights" (1959), which reached the pop Top Ten, but their success was short-lived. Williams left the group in 1960 to begin what proved to be a rather unsuccessful solo career. Other personnel changes followed, with Herbert Reed, the last of the original group members, departing in 1969. By the mid-1960s the Platters had become less a group than a franchise. During the 1980s and 1990s, as many as ten different groups calling themselves the "Platters" toured and performed throughout the United States, but most had no relationship to the musicians of the original group.

On the other hand, during the years of their greatest successes the Platters had a powerful impact on popular music. Their importance was belatedly acknowledged by the popular music industry in 1990, when the Platters were inducted into the Rock and Roll Hall of Fame. But Reed, one of the original members of the group, was far more eloquent in summing up the Platters' significance. "[B]ecause of our music," he declared, "white kids had a sense of fair play about blacks long before the CIVIL RIGHTS MOVEMENT.... It opened a lot of doors to a better understanding. And it gave us, five kids from Watts, a taste of a better life...."

See also Music, African American.

James Sellman

Player, Gary

1935–

Top professional golfer from South Africa.

Gary Player may be not only the greatest golfer from SOUTH AFRICA but one of the greatest golfers of all time. He has won more than 100 major international titles and is one of only four men to win each of the game's four major professional tournaments. After a difficult childhood—his mother died when he was eight years old, and his father, a gold miner, barely made enough to live on—he learned to play GOLF on a local course and turned professional in 1953. Four years later he entered the United States Professional Golfers' Association (PGA) circuit. Player's long roster of victories includes the British Open (1959, 1968, 1974), the U.S. PGA (1962, 1972), the U.S. Open (1965), and the Masters (1961, 1974, 1978). In addition, he won the South African Open thirteen times and the Australian Open seven times. Player joined the Senior Tour in 1985 and in 1989 won the U.S. Senior Open.

One of golf's biggest money winners, Player has reputedly traveled more miles than any other athlete in history. Preceded by the achievements of South African Bobby Locke, Player's success helped bring attention to other African golfers, including Nick Price (South Africa) and Ernie Els (Zimbabwe). Like many South African athletes, Player, who is of European descent, competed and lived abroad much of his life, due to international athletic sanctions against South Africa's APARTHEID regime.

Player, who in 1990 was named South African Sportsman of the Century, has worked to improve conditions in his native country. In 1983 he established the Player Foundation, which funds medical, educational, and sports programs for low-income children. The NELSON MANDELA Invitational, a charity tournament that Player initiated in 2000, has attracted top golfers and celebrities and has raised more than $700,000 for children's programs.

Bibliography

Player, Gary. *To be the Best: Reflections of a Champion.* Sidgwick and Jackson, 1991.

Kate Tuttle

Pleasant, Mary Ellen ("Mammy")

1814?–1903?

African American businesswoman and financial backer of abolitionist John Brown.

One of SAN FRANCISCO's most colorful and controversial characters in the late nineteenth century was Mary Ellen Pleasant, a former slave who moved to the city in 1849. She began managing a boarding house whose reputation for cards, liquor, and beautiful women—it is likely her services included procuring prostitutes—earned it a devoted following.

No mere businesswoman, Pleasant involved herself in both local and national politics. In 1858, she personally presented abolitionist JOHN BROWN with a $30,000 U.S. Treasury Bond, after which she traveled south to promote his upcoming revolt. When Brown was captured at Harpers Ferry, Pleasant returned to California under an assumed name, where she raised money for the Union cause in the CIVIL WAR, and continued her work for civil rights.

Throughout her life, Pleasant helped escaped and former slaves find work in San Francisco, mostly as domestic servants. Some historians speculate that Pleasant used her informal employment agency to gather information she used either to advance her business dealings or to blackmail the city's rich whites.

Pleasant lived in an ornate mansion she shared with a white former prostitute, whom she had helped to marry a wealthy financier. Though accounts vary, it seems likely that Pleasant owned the property but posed as its housekeeper. What is certain is that she inspired fear and obedience in what was locally called the "House of Mystery" through her real or implied mastery of Vodou.

Despite her scandalous business and personal affairs, her gravestone emphasizes her political contributions. As she had requested, the epitaph reads, "Mother of Civil Rights in California. Friend of John Brown."

See also Abolitionism in the United States.

Bibliography
Holdredge, Helen. *Mammy Pleasant*. Putnam, 1953.
Wheeler, B. Gordon. *Black California: The History of African-Americans in the Golden State*. Hippocrene Books, 1993.

Kate Tuttle

Plena and Bomba

Two of the most important genres of Afro–Puerto Rican music and dance.

Bomba music is a generic term that refers to a variety of rhythms and kinds of dances, such as *calinda, sica, grasima, lero, cuembe, holande, yuba, bambulae,* and *seis bombeao*. By some accounts bomba music and dance arrived in Puerto Rico in the sixteenth century, brought by the Asantes, who had come from the African region of Ghana. While its precise origins are unclear, the bomba and its many variants continued to evolve, particularly among slaves on the sugar plantations. These slaves would hold bomba dances on Sundays and holidays in places outside the plantations themselves. Many slave rebellions were planned during these gatherings.

The instruments used to accompany bomba music are two drums, *cua* (two sticks), and maracas, a Native American instrument originally used by the Taíno Indians. The drums essentially are barrels with heads of goatskin. The *buleador* is a low-pitched drum that is considered the heart of this music. The *primo* is a high-pitched drum that the drummer uses to communicate with the dancer. The primo player needs to be skilled enough to hold the tempo and at the same time improvise over the buleador's strong rhythmic pattern. A third drummer strikes the sides of the buleador with the cua, and a fourth musician plays the maracas. The dancers and vocalists are important elements in bomba. One or more of the dance couples sustain a rhythmical dance conversation with the primo at a specific point. Different variants of bomba can be distinguished by their rhythm, chants, melodic lines, dance forms, and choreographic changes.

An interesting bomba variant is the *lero,* derived from the French "la rose," because the dancers form a rose pattern in the choreography. The yuba is a 6/8-pattern bomba with much energy. The holande is a perfect bomba for celebration. Still another variation, the seis bombeao, is danced mainly in the town of Loiza on the northeastern coast; the other variants of bomba are danced throughout the island.

The rhythmic pattern of the holande is close to the *plena,* a highly important genre of Afro–Puerto Rican music that had become widely popular by the 1930s. Sometimes referred to as a "sung newspaper," the plena served both as entertainment and as a sort of chronicle reflecting day-to-day issues. Using a structure of chorus followed by lines of improvisation by male or female singers, it became a means by which the people could picture their lives, customs, and circumstances.

The plena has a stronger influence of Spanish music than the bomba, but its Afro-Caribbean character is still apparent. By various accounts the plena originated in the nineteenth century, though the circumstances of its inception are still obscure. It is closely associated with Ponce, Puerto Rico's second largest city, and in particular with the largely black neighborhood of San Antón. The first great professional singer of plenas was the Afro–Puerto Rican Joselino "Bumbum" Oppenheimer. Many of Oppenheimer's compositions, from the early twentieth century, remain classics. By the 1930s, the plena had become a widely popular music.

The principal instruments used in plenas are *panderos,* rounded wooden drums with a goatskin head on one side. The *pleneros* (musicians who perform the genre) use a combination of three panderos: the *bajo,* or bass drum; the *banao* or *segunda,* the second drum; and the *quinto,* which has a higher pitch. To make these instruments, musicians replaced the rounded covers from wooden boxes with goatskin. Another type of pandero, made from the body of a banjo, was created by Puerto Rican pleneros who had emigrated to New York. Panderos are also made from metal pots and from plastic or fiberglass tubes and pipes. The other instruments used are the *guiro* (of Native American origin), the guitar (of Arab-Spanish origin), the *acordeon* (of German origin), and the *cuatro,* a Puerto Rican guitarlike variant also of Spanish origin.

A number of groups promote and maintain the bomba and plena in Puerto Rico. Plena Libre is directed by Gary Nuñez, who is responsible for bringing the plena back to the radio charts. ABC Orchestra is directed by Jesús Cepeda, who borrowed the name from a plena group started by his father in the 1930s. Los Guayacanes, from San Antón, directed by Joe Santiago; Atabal, directed by Hector Rodríguez; and Bomplene are among other groups responsible for promoting the plena.

Other plena groups have been established by Puerto Rican immigrants to the United States. Los Pleneros de la 21, from New York (their name is taken from bus stop #21 in Santurce, Puerto Rico), is directed by Juan Gutiérrez. Los Pleneros del Batey, from Philadelphia, is directed by Joaquín Rivera. La Familia Ayala, from Boston (an extension of la Familia Ayala, from Puerto Rico) is directed by Celia and Sixto Ayala. These and other composers and producers carry a tradition established by Don Rafael Cepeda, Don Rafael Cortijo y su Combo, Ismael Rivera, Ramón "Mon" Rivera, Manuel Jímenez (Canario), Toñin Romero, Petra Cepeda, Marcial Reyes, Tomasito Flores, Enrique Soto (Mayagüez), Jacinto Salomón, Toribio Laporte, Vitrín Calderón, Ramón Pedraza, and many others.

See also Dance in Latin America and the Caribbean; Music, Afro-Caribbean Secular; Percussion Instruments of the Caribbean; Slave Rebellions in Latin America and the Caribbean.

Jorge Arce

Plessy v. Ferguson

Landmark case of 1896 in which the United States Supreme Court established the "separate but equal" doctrine that permitted state-imposed racial segregation despite the "equal protection" clause of the Fourteenth Amendment to the U.S. Constitution.

In 1892, thirty-year-old shoemaker Homer Plessy refused to leave his seat on a train in NEW ORLEANS, LOUISIANA, beginning a legal battle that went all the way to the U.S. Supreme Court. The Court's decision in this case, *Plessy v. Ferguson,* four years later permitted states to institute racially separate public accommodations. It would take nearly sixty years for the Court to reverse itself in a series of decisions beginning with BROWN V. BOARD OF EDUCATION (1954) that overturned the judicial precedent for segregation. In *Gayle v. Browder* (1956), the Court specifically declared segregation in public transportation unconstitutional.

The segregated public transportation system that Plessy challenged in 1892 was relatively new to New Orleans. Train cars in New Orleans were first segregated in 1860, just before the Civil War. Those adorned with black stars were meant for black passengers only—a difficult rule to enforce, because of the many mixed-race people in New Orleans. Plessy himself, who was born free in 1862, was fair-skinned enough to pass for white. In 1867 the city removed the black stars from its trains, and the system returned to its earlier, integrated state.

But with the declining support of the Republican-controlled U.S. government, the effort to rebuild the South and bring full political rights to the former slaves after the Civil War faltered. Increasingly, Southern Democrats took back the power they had lost in Louisiana. In 1890 Democratic governor Francis T. Nicholls, who first gained office as part of an 1877 compromise balancing a Republican president with Democratic control of the South, signed a law resegregating Louisiana's railways. The law stated that train companies had to provide "equal but separate" cars for blacks and whites, and that individuals of different races could not ride together without risking a $25 fine or twenty days in jail. The Louisiana Senate passed the law by a vote of twenty-three to six.

African Americans and CREOLES in New Orleans mobilized to fight the law. A columnist for a black-owned newspaper, RODOLPHE DESDUNES of *The Crusader,* proposed that African Americans boycott the train system. He wrote that blacks "can withdraw the patronage from these corporations and travel only by necessity." But his idea did not take hold. Fears of violent white reprisals limited black political activism, and noted African American leaders such as BOOKER T. WASHINGTON preached patience and accommodation.

A Louisiana group calling itself the Citizens' Committee to Test the Constitutionality of the Separate Car Law, known as the Comité des Citoyens, planned to test the law's constitutionality—specifically, to prove that the law violated the FOURTEENTH AMENDMENT, which guarantees all persons "the equal protection of the laws." Made up of prominent New Orleans blacks and whites, including Desdunes and *The Crusader*'s publisher, Louis Martinet, the committee arranged for Plessy to board a whites-only train. By arrangement with contacts in the East Louisiana Railroad Company, a conductor asked Plessy, who was of mixed race, if he was a "colored man." When Plessy said he was, and refused to move, the conductor and a private detective hired by the committee accompanied him to the police station, where he was booked and then released on $500 bond posted by a committee member.

Judge John H. Ferguson, a Massachusetts native, presided over Plessy's arraignment a month later. Ferguson had earlier ruled the Louisiana law unconstitutional when it demanded segregated train cars for travel between states. Martinet had written in *The Crusader* that with this decision, "JIM CROW is dead as a doornail." But in Plessy's case, Ferguson sided with the state, saying that Louisiana, in compelling racial segregation in its in-state train system, had not violated African Americans' constitutional rights.

Louisiana's State Supreme Court agreed with Ferguson, citing a Massachusetts case that predated both the Civil War and the Fourteenth Amendment, *Roberts* v. *City of Boston* (1849), in which the state's chief justice had written that "prejudice, if it exists, is not created by law and cannot be changed by law." In addition, *Roberts* was the source of the phrase "separate but equal." The opinion also quoted a Pennsylvania case whose ruling rested upon the "natural, legal, and customary difference between the black and white races."

Plessy's lawyer, white activist and writer Albion Tourgée, brought the case before the U.S. Supreme Court in 1896. Tourgée's brief argued that the Louisiana law "is obnoxious to the spirit of republican institutions, because it is a legalization of caste," and that it violated both the Thirteenth and Fourteenth amendments in limiting "the natural rights of man."

The Court ruled seven to one (one justice did not participate) that Plessy's constitutional rights had not been violated. Writing for the majority, Justice Henry B. Brown wrote that while the Fourteenth Amendment had "undoubtedly" been meant to enforce "absolute equality" between the races, it did not "abolish distinction based on color." Brown cited many states' laws mandating separate schools and prohibiting interracial marriages—laws that were themselves ruled unconstitutional later. The opinion also said, "Legislation is powerless to eradicate racial instincts or to abolish distinctions."

Justice John Marshall Harlan, a Southerner, wrote a lone but strong dissent. He cited cases in which segregated juries had been found unconstitutional, and went on to say in plain language what Plessy's opponents would not admit: that the separate car law not only separated the races, but did so to accommodate white racial prejudice. "Our Constitution is color blind," Harlan wrote, and legal segregation allowed "the seeds of race hate to be planted under the sanctions of law." He also wrote, "The thin disguise of 'equal' accommodations . . . will not mislead anyone, nor atone for the wrong this day done."

Harlan's words proved prophetic. The SEPARATE BUT EQUAL DOCTRINE relegated African American children to inadequate and unsafe schools, while the South's Jim Crow laws forbade black citizens from participating on an equal footing with white citizens. Not until the Supreme Court reversed itself in 1954, in *Brown v. Board of Education,* would African Americans be able to claim the rights promised in the Constitution.

See also Reconstruction; Segregation in the United States.

Bibliography
Thomas, Brook. *Plessy v. Ferguson: A Brief History with Documents.* Bedford Books, 1997.
Woodward, C. Vann. *The Strange Career of Jim Crow.* Oxford University Press, 1955.

Kate Tuttle

Plymouth, Montserrat

Former capital of the British dependent territory of Montserrat, an island in the West Indies southeast of Puerto Rico.

Plymouth was located on the southwestern coast of the island territory, in the parish of Saint Anthony. The Soufrière Hills volcanic eruptions that began in 1995 and reached their worst level in the summer of 1997 destroyed Plymouth and much of the southern two-thirds of the island. All 3,500 residents of Plymouth were evacuated.

See also Montserrat; West Indies.

Poetry, African

Written or spoken verse created by Africans.

For information on
African poetic forms and style: *See* Literature, French-Language, in Africa; Literature, Portuguese-Language, in Africa; Oral Traditions in Africa; Somali Songs and Poetry.
Algerian poets: *See* Mohammad Dib.
West African poets: *See* Awoonor, Kofi; Okigbo, Christopher; Omotoso, Kole; Soyinka, Wole.
East African poets: *See* Mapanje, Jack; Senghor, Léopold Sédar; Sousa, Noémia de.
Poets from southern Africa: *See* Brutus, Dennis; Neto, Agostinho.

Poetry, Black, in English

Selection of noted black poets from Africa, Europe, and the Americas who wrote primarily in the English language.

For information on
Poets from Africa: *See* Brutus, Dennis; Mapanje, Jack.
Poets in the Caribbean area: *See* Carter, Martin; Mutabaruka; Walcott, Derek.
Poet from Canada: *See* Philip, Marline Nourbese.
Poet from Great Britain: *See* Johnson, Linton Kwesi.
Poets in the United States: *See* Angelou, Maya; Baraka, Amiri; Brooks, Gwendolyn Elizabeth; Cullen, Countee; Dove, Rita; Dunbar, Paul Laurence; Harper, Frances Ellen Watkins; Hayden, Robert Earl; Horton, George Moses; Hughes, Langston; Johnson, Fenton; Johnson, James Weldon; Jordan, June; Literature, African American; Lorde, Audre Geraldine; McKay, Claude; Sanchez, Sonia; Shange, Ntozake; Tolson, Melvin Beaunorus; Walker, Alice; Wheatley, Phillis; Whitfield, James Monroe.

Poetry, Caribbean

Poets and Literatures of the Caribbean.

For information on
Poetry of the Caribbean: *See* Dub Poetry; Literature, Black, in Spanish America; Literature, English-Language, in the Caribbean; Literature, French-Language, in the Caribbean.
Cuban poets: *See* Arozarena, Marcelino; Guillén, Nicolás; Marti, José; Medina y Céspedes, Antonio; Morejón, Nancy; Pedroso, Regino; Saldaña, Excilia; Serra y Montalvo, Rafael; Valdés, Gabriel de la Concepción ("Plácido").
Dominican poets: *See* Cabral, Manuel del; Cartagena Portalatín, Aída; James, Norberto; Jiménez, Blas.
Poet from French Guiana: *See* Damas, Léon-Gontran.
Haitian poets: *See* Castera, Georges; Coicou, Massillon; Damas, Léon-Gontran; Depestre, René; Durand, Oswald; Etienne, Franck; Sylvain, Georges.
Jamaican poets: *See* Mutabaruka.
Martinican poets: *See* Césaire, Aimé; Glissant, Edouard; Maran, René.
Puerto Rican poets: *See* Algarín, Miguel; Burgos, Julia de; Dávila, Angela María; Palés Matos, Luis.

Pogoro

Ethnic group of Tanzania; also known as Chipogolo and Pogolu.

The Pogoro primarily inhabit eastern TANZANIA. They speak a Bantu language. Over 250,000 people consider themselves Pogoro.

See also Bantu: Dispersion and Settlement; Ethnicity and Identity in Africa: An Interpretation; Languages, African: An Overview.

Poindexter, James P.

1819–1907

Clergyman, abolitionist, politician, civil rights advocate, and the first African American elected to the city council of Columbus, Ohio.

James P. Poindexter was born in RICHMOND, VIRGINIA, the son of Evelina Atkinson, a woman of African American and Cherokee descent, and Joseph Poindexter, a white journalist for the *Richmond Enquirer*. Poindexter attended school in Richmond until his tenth year, when he began an apprenticeship as a barber, an occupation he practiced for many years. In 1837 he married Adelia Atkinson. During 1837 the Poindexters moved to Dublin, Ohio, a village sixteen kilometers (ten miles) north of Columbus. Dissatisfied with life in this farming community, they moved to Columbus the following year, residing there for the remainder of their lives.

Soon after settling in Columbus, Poindexter joined Second Baptist Church, where he preached and officiated when there was no regular minister. In 1847 an African American family that had previously owned slaves in Virginia joined the church. Although the family had sold the slaves before leaving for Ohio, forty members of the congregation, led by Poindexter, left Second Baptist to found the Anti-Slavery Baptist Church. This church remained in existence until 1858, when Poindexter returned to Second Baptist Church as the pastor. He remained there until his resignation in 1898.

Poindexter's barber business, meanwhile, served as his livelihood for many years; it was through this work that he came to know the leading statesmen, lawyers, doctors, and educators of Ohio. Acquaintanceship with them served him well in later securing gubernatorial appointments.

Soon after his arrival in Columbus, Poindexter personally put together teams and wagons to transport escaping slaves northward via the UNDERGROUND RAILROAD. His comrades in this work included members of the African American and white communities in Columbus. For nearly three decades he actively agitated against slavery, and in the decades after the CIVIL WAR (1861–1865) he frequently delivered eloquent addresses at August Emancipation Day celebrations in the African American community.

During the Civil War, Poindexter and his wife, who died in November 1876, formed the Colored Soldiers Relief Society in Columbus. The society dispensed material and financial aid to African American soldiers and their families, since the state had failed to appropriate funds for this purpose.

The FIFTEENTH AMENDMENT to the U.S. Constitution—which was declared in effect on March 30, 1870, and guaranteed voting rights to African American men—led to the emergence of Poindexter as a political figure. In January 1871 he helped convene a mass Convention of Colored Men in Columbus to encourage their voting "for securing and maintaining . . . the legitimate benefits resulting from our newly acquired rights under the Constitution." The convention pledged allegiance to the REPUBLICAN PARTY and its candidates. Although Poindexter promoted the Republican Party among African Americans in the state of Ohio, he based his support on issues he believed in and withdrew his support when he felt the party's actions were misguided.

In the summer of 1873, after his nomination by the Republican Central Committee for a seat in the Ohio House of Representatives (the first such nominee), Poindexter was defeated. He was again defeated in the next election. In 1876, however, Poindexter served as an Ohio delegate to the Republican National Convention that nominated Rutherford B. Hayes of Ohio for president. During the winter of 1876 to 1877, while the seating of the president was still in question, Hayes conferred with Poindexter and FREDERICK DOUGLASS in Columbus to address the so-called Southern question. Hayes recorded in his diary for February 18, 1877: "I talked yesterday with Fred Douglass and Mr. Poindexter, both colored on the Southern question. I told them my views. They approved." The approval by Douglass is not in accord with his statements (*Life and Times of Frederick Douglass* [1962], pp. 536–37). For his support and counsel to Hayes during the campaign, Poindexter received consideration for appointment as U.S. minister to HAITI.

Although unsuccessful in his bid for national office, Poindexter was successful on the local and state levels. In 1880 he was elected to the Columbus City Council, the first black man in the city to serve on that body. Poindexter's competence gained him reelection in 1882 and vice presidency and membership on the Poor Committee. The City Infirmary director noted in his annual report for 1882 that Poindexter was the only one who had taken any marked interest in his duties. In December 1884 Poindexter was appointed to the Columbus Board of Education. He was reelected four times and served for ten years. It was during this period that Poindexter had his greatest personal impact on Columbus society. He chaired the following committees: schoolhouse sites, rules and regulations, textbooks and course of study, and discipline. Poindexter also served as a member of eight other board committees. When Roman Catholic school officials requested the use of an unoccupied room in a public school while awaiting the completion of construction on a school of their own, Poindexter gave his support to the use of the quarters and solved a potentially touchy problem. He vigorously continued his twenty-year agitation for integration of the public schools and adequate physical facilities for schools in African American neighborhoods.

Poindexter received his first state appointment in 1880, when Governor Charles Foster named him to the board of trustees of the Ohio School for the Blind. He remained on the board until 1883. Two years later, however, when Democratic governor George Hoadley nominated him to the board of trustees at Ohio University, his appointment was defeated by two votes on the grounds that he was too partisan. Early in 1887 Poindexter was named to the board of directors of the State Forestry Bureau, a position he held for three consecutive terms until the bureau went out of existence in 1900. In April 1896 he was named to the board of trustees at WILBERFORCE UNIVERSITY in Dayton, Ohio.

Poindexter maintained an active interest in other civic affairs. He headed the Columbus Pastors Union, participated in the Columbus and Ohio Centennial Celebration, and served in the Sons of Protection, an African American burial and benefit association. He was an indefatigable letter writer, and the pages of the *Ohio State Journal* often contained the entire texts of his sermons, as well as position statements on public affairs.

On February 7, 1907, Poindexter died following a prolonged bout with pneumonia. During the period of his illness, clergyman Washington Gladden was a daily visitor to his bedside. Poindexter's memorial service was attended by nearly 2,000 mourners, marking it as one of Columbus's largest to that date.

There are few sources on Poindexter. One of the most comprehensive accounts is Richard C. Minor's "James Preston Poindexter, Elder Statesman of Ohio" (*Ohio History*, 1947). Documentation regarding the Hayes meeting is in *Diary and Letters of Rutherford B. Hayes* (1922–1926), edited by Charles R. Williams. Information about Poindexter's local and state posts is in the published annual reports of each governmental agency; information about his theological and political beliefs is in the files of the *Ohio State Journal*, to which he was a frequent contributor.

From *Dictionary of American Negro Biography* by Rayford W. Logan and Michael R. Winston, editors. Copyright © 1982 by Rayford W. Logan and Michael R. Winston. Reprinted by permission of W. W. Norton & Company, Inc.

See also Abolitionism in the United States; Baptists; Clergy in Politics; Festivals in the United States, African American.

Frank R. Levstik

Pointe-à-Pitre

Town in eastern Guadeloupe, on southwestern Grande-Terre Island, in the West Indies.

Situated on an ocean channel that separates Grande-Terre Island and Basse-Terre Island, Pointe-à-Pitre is the largest town, principal seaport, and leading commercial center of GUADELOUPE. It is the seat of the University Center of Antilles-Guyane (1970) and the Pasteur Institute of Guadeloupe (1948), which has medical-research laboratories. The community was settled by the French in the mid-seventeenth century. By 2003 its population was 21,800.

See also Colonial Latin America and the Caribbean; West Indies.

Pointer Sisters, The

African American singing group; gained fame in the 1970s and 1980s with catchy pop songs that successfully spanned the country and rhythm and blues (R&B) genres.

The Pointer Sisters, Ruth (1946–), Anita (1948–), Bonnie (1950–), and June (1954–), were born and raised in OAKLAND, CALIFORNIA. As children the Pointers sang in the choir of the West Oakland Church of God, where their parents were ministers. Although they performed GOSPEL MUSIC, they grew up listening to the broad range of secular music that abounded in the Bay Area in the 1960s—JAZZ, SOUL, country, and everything in between. The Pointers quickly made contacts in the music industry, and by 1969 they were singing backup for several San Francisco–based musicians, including Elvin Bishop, Taj Mahal, Boz Scaggs, and Tower of Power.

The Pointer Sisters' self-titled debut, issued in 1973 on ABC/Blue Thumb Records, drew from BLUES and soul and enjoyed popular success; the single "Yes We Can Can" climbed to number eleven on the Billboard pop chart. Their sudden popularity led to a number of television appearances, in which the sisters were featured wearing their trademark 1940s-style outfits that were reminiscent of the Andrews Sisters.

The Pointers' success continued in 1974 with the release of their second album, *That's A Plenty*, which featured the hit single "Fairytale," a song that garnered the group's first Grammy Award. The quartet was reduced to a trio when Bonnie Pointer embarked on a solo career with MOTOWN in 1977, but the group remained popular, earning acclaim for their versatility. They experimented with rock on 1978's *Energy*, an album that included the hits "Happiness" and "Fire" (a cover of a Bruce Springsteen song). In the 1980s they focused on rhythm and blues, recording such hits as "Slow Hand" (1981), "What a Surprise" (1981), "Excited" (1982), "I Need You" (1983), and the Grammy Award–winning "Jump" (1983) and "Automatic" (1984). The mid-1980s was the group's heyday, but they continued to perform and record into the 1990s, switching to RCA Records in 1985 and to Motown in 1991. They starred in the musical *Ain't Misbehavin'* in 1995.

Though usually regarded as a pop or R&B group, the Pointer Sisters earned some of their highest accolades for their country performances. In 1974 they performed at the legendary Grand Ole Opry in Nashville, Tennessee, the first African American female group to do so, and they were the first black women to grace the top of Billboard's country and western charts. In honor of their country roots, the Pointers collaborated with Clint Black to cover "Chain of Fools" for the *Rhythm, Country and Blues* collection in 1994.

See also Rhythm and Blues.

Aaron Myers

Poitier, Sidney

1927–

African American actor, director, and filmmaker, who became known as a leading post–World War II African American movie star.

Born in Miami, Florida, Sidney Poitier was raised in the BAHAMAS and returned to the United States as a teenager. He served in the U.S. Army during World War II and moved to New York, New York, in 1945 to study acting. At his first audition for the AMERICAN NEGRO THEATER (ANT), Poitier was rejected because of his strong Caribbean accent. After only six months, he had perfected a mainstream American accent by imitating radio announcers and was accepted on his second audition.

Poitier's first film role was in *No Way Out* (1950). Many leading roles followed, and in 1963 he became the first African American to win the Oscar for best actor for his performance in *Lilies of the Field*. Poitier's other films include *Blackboard Jungle* (1955), *The Defiant Ones* (1958), *In the Heat of the Night, To Sir With Love,* and *Guess Who's Coming to Dinner* (all 1967). He originated the role of Walter Lee Younger in the 1959 Broadway production *A Raisin in the Sun* by LORRAINE HANSBERRY.

Poitier was the first African American to become a major Hollywood star with mainstream audiences. In the process, some members of the black community criticized him for portraying stereotypical "noble Negroes." In response, as the 1960s ended, Poitier began to play more diverse roles. He also began to produce and direct films, directing several hit films in the 1970s and 1980s. He received a Life Achievement Award from the American Film Institute in 1992, and in 1993 he won the first THURGOOD MARSHALL Lifetime Achievement Award given by the NATIONAL ASSOCIATION FOR THE ADVANCEMENT OF COLORED PEOPLE (NAACP).

In 2000 Poitier received a Lifetime Achievement Award from the Screen Actors Guild. The following year he earned a Grammy for the best spoken-word album for his recorded version of his book, *The Measure of a Man: A Spiritual Autobiography*. He also received an NAACP Hall of Fame Award in 2001.

See also Film, Blacks in American.

Bibliography

Poitier, Sidney. *This Life*. Knopf, 1980.

Lisa Clayton Robinson

Pokot

Ethnic group of Kenya; also known as Suk.

The Pokot primarily inhabit the highlands of western KENYA. Some also live in eastern UGANDA. They speak a Nilo-Saharan language and are one of the KALENJIN peoples. Over 350,000 people consider themselves Pokot.

See also Ethnicity and Identity in Africa: An Interpretation; Languages, African: An Overview.

Policy Racket

See Numbers Games.

Polisario Front

A politico-military organization that has struggled for more than three decades to gain national independence for Western Sahara

Polisario Front (Frente Popular para la Liberación de Saguia El-Hamra y Río de Oro) was founded on May 10, 1973, at a secret meeting on the border of WESTERN SAHARA and MAURITANIA. Led mainly by some members of the SAHRAWI ethnic group who had attended the university together in MOROCCO, Polisario announced a program of violent resistance to Spanish colonialism. Ten days after its formation, Polisario launched a guerrilla war against Spanish forces. Although the Spanish initially agreed to hold a referendum on independence for Western Sahara, in late 1975 they decided to allow Morocco and Mauritania to partition and occupy the territory, over the objections of most Sahrawis.

Polisario quickly denounced this annexation and declared Western Sahara to be the Sahrawi Arab Democratic Republic (SADR). The organization worked to evacuate as much of the Sahrawi population as possible to a safe haven within ALGERIA. With support from Algeria, Polisario fought to drive out the two occupying armies. Polisario chose to focus first on Mauritania; in 1979 Mauritania was forced to relinquish its claims in Western Sahara and to recognize the SADR.

Polisario's campaign against Morocco continues today, and has been less successful. Though Polisario managed to inflict heavy losses on Moroccan forces during the 1980s, Moroccan military engineers limited Polisario military incursions by encompassing Western Sahara in an earthen wall, which was protected by motion detectors, explosives, and soldiers. Attempts by the ORGANIZATION OF AFRICAN UNITY (OAU) and United Nations (UN) failed to bring a withdrawal by Morocco, which still controls the main urban areas.

Both Polisario and Morocco faced increasing financial difficulties in the 1990s, and in 1991 the UN brokered a cease-fire agreement, pending a referendum. Disagreements between Polisario and the Moroccan government over the eligibility of voters repeatedly postponed the referendum. In 2003 the UN endorsed a plan that called for a five-year transition period in which Morocco and the Polisario Front would share governing responsibilities. Then a referendum would be held to determine Western Sahara's status. The Polisario Front and Algeria accepted the plan but Morocco has rejected it, determinedly maintaining its claims to the region.

See also Nationalism in Africa; United Nations in Africa.

Bibliography

Gupta, Rakesh. *Saharawi Society: Transition, Resistance and Polisario.* Patriot Publishers, 1988.

Mercer, John. *Spanish Sahara.* Allen & Unwin, 1976.

Robert Fay

Political Movements in Africa

Organized efforts by black Africans to foster political equality, social justice, and freedom from discrimination.

For information on

Movements in Africa: *See* African National Congress; Antiapartheid Movement; Black Consciousness in Africa; Decolonization in Africa: An Interpretation; Environmental Movements in Africa; Feminism in Africa: An Interpretation; Feminism in Islamic Africa; Islamic Fundamentalism: An Interpretation; Mau Mau Rebellion; Nationalism in Africa; Négritude; Polisario Front; Rassemblement Démocratique Africain.

Organizations involved in political movements: *See* Front for the Liberation of Mozambique; Holy Spirit Movement; Inkatha Freedom Party; Pan-Africanist Congress; Popular Movement for the Liberation of Angola; South African Communist Party.

Some movement leaders: *See* Biko, Stephen; Buthelezi, Mangosutho Gatsha; Hani, Chris; Kenyatta, Jomo; Maathai, Wangari; Mandela, Nelson Rolihlahla; Nasser, Gamel Abdel; Nkrumah, Kwame; Nyerere, Julius Kambarage; Saro-Wiwa, Kenule Beeson; Senghor, Léopold Sédar; Sisulu, Walter; Sobukwe, Robert Mangaliso; Tambo, Oliver.

Political Movements in Latin America and the Caribbean

Activism by people of African descent in the centuries-old struggle for political equality, social justice, and freedom from discrimination. Unlike uprisings against racial and economic injustice, political movements tend to establish organizations that work within the system.

For information on

Movements throughout Latin America and the Caribbean: *See* Brazil, Blacks and Politics in: An Interpretation; Gay and Lesbian Movements in Latin America and the Caribbean; Liberation Theology in Latin America and the Caribbean; Nationalist Movements and Blacks in Latin America and the Caribbean; Pan-Africanism and Afro–Latin Americans; Political Parties and Black Social Movements in Latin America and the Caribbean; Role of Slaves in Abolition and Emancipation in Latin America and the Caribbean.

Movements focused in the Caribbean: *See* Afro-Cuban Political Mobilization: An Interpretation; Black Power Movement in the Caribbean; Independence Movements in the British Caribbean.

Organizations involved in political movements: *See* Centro de Articulaçãos de Populações Marginalizadas; Cimarrón; Cultural and Political Organizations in Latin America; Frente Negra Brasileira; Movimento Negro Unificado.

Political leaders: *See* Aristide, Jean-Bertrand; James, Cyril Lionel Richard; Nascimento, Abdias do; Silva, Benedita da.

Political Movements in the United States

Efforts organized by African Americans to foster political equality, social justice, and freedom from discrimination.

For information on

Twentieth-century political movements: *See* Antilynching Movement; Black Nationalism in the United States; Black Power in the United States; Civil Rights Movement; Feminism in the United States; Gay and Lesbian Movements in the United States; Mutual Benefit Societies; New York African Society for Mutual Relief; Pan-Africanism.

Organizations involved in political movements: *See* Black Panther Party; Mississippi Freedom Democratic Party; Montgomery Improvement Association; National Association for the Advancement of Colored People; Niagara Movement; Pan-African Congress of 1919; Revolutionary Action Movement; Student Nonviolent Coordinating Committee; Universal Negro Improvement Association.

Leaders of twentieth-century movements: *See* Du Bois, W(illiam) E(dward) B(urghardt); Garvey, Marcus Moziah; Hamer, Fannie Lou; Jackson, Jesse; King, Martin Luther, Jr.; Malcolm X; Patterson, William.

Nineteenth-century abolitionist movements: *See* Abolitionism in the United States; American Anti-Slavery Society; Underground Railroad.

Political Parties and Black Social Movements in Latin America and the Caribbean

Cultural and social movements seeking recognition and civil rights for African-descended populations in the Caribbean and Latin America during the twentieth century.

In the Spanish- and Portuguese-influenced Caribbean and LATIN AMERICA, myths of racial harmony have served to de-emphasize racial difference and identification. Instead, the stories have emphasized one single national identity despite evidence of racial discrimination in the areas of employment and education and in derogatory stereotypes concerning African and African-descended peoples. As a consequence, people of African descent in many Latin American nation-states rarely organize themselves in terms of racial solidarity or common cultural origin.

Ironically, the first black political parties in the hemisphere were founded by people of African descent in Spanish and Portuguese colonies. These were the PARTIDO INDEPENDIENTE DE COLOR of CUBA and the FRENTE NEGRA BRASILEIRA of BRAZIL (founded in 1908 and 1931 respectively). Both parties were ultimately outlawed via legislation that prohibited political organization according to race and equated black political mobilization for equal rights with racial prejudice and chauvinism. The histories of these parties and their repression by Cuban and Brazilian governments underscore how difficult it was for African-descended populations to organize racially specific political parties in the former Spanish and Portuguese colonies. Often, Afro-Latin peoples who have protested and organized against racial discrimination in their countries have been characterized as racist and anti-national.

In the English-speaking Caribbean and Latin America, however, differences in ideology, COLONIAL RULE, and the racial composition of former colonies have made racial difference and inequality important factors in political mobilization. The first difference between the Anglophone societies and others in the Caribbean and Latin America is the length of time that those in each group were subject to colonial rule. By the mid-nineteenth century most Spanish colonies in the New World had obtained independence, Cuba being a notable exception. By contrast, the move toward national independence in the English-speaking Caribbean would begin in earnest only after World War II. The first attempt at political autonomy in the English-speaking Caribbean was undertaken on the initiative of British colonies of the greater ANTILLES. Several colonies attempted to create a West Indian Federation to seek collective independence from GREAT BRITAIN. However, JAMAICA, a critical member of the federation, abandoned the collective cause after three years. Most commentators suggest that Jamaican nationalist leader NORMAN MANLEY, father of future two-time prime minister MICHAEL MANLEY, did not want Jamaica to bear the economic and political cost of the coalition and decided to withdraw his country from the federation. Jamaica formally abandoned the federation initiative in 1961 and achieved independence from Britain on August 6, 1962. Jamaica's departure from the federation had long-term repercussions for independent political mobilization in the region. It effectively ended the prospects for regional consolidation and alliances against the major powers in the post–World War II period.

The processes of decolonization and the formation of nationalist movements after World War II in the English-speaking Caribbean were two factors that influenced the shape of party politics and political participation. In many colonial societies nationalist politics were deeply intertwined with racial politics, as the quest for political sovereignty was often considered parallel with the struggle for the equal rights for black populations. A key difference between such movements in the English-speaking Caribbean and similar movements in North America and the Spanish-speaking Caribbean was the fact that African Americans constituted the overwhelming majority of the population in places like Jamaica, BERMUDA, BARBADOS, GRENADA, and most Anglophone colonies. This was not always the situation in other Caribbean colonies, where African-descended populations were in the numerical or categorical minority, depending on how they were classified. In the Anglophone societies, where citizenship depended upon the racial hierarchies of colonialism, aspirant nationalist parties had to deal directly with matters of race. This was unavoidable because social hierarchies were usually closely correlated to skin color in these societies and the majority of the poor were black. A second difference was that British colonial rule maintained more legally restricted patterns of racial segregation and interaction. (It should be stated that Spanish colonies like Cuba and NICARAGUA, with Afro-Latin populations, had a combination of Spanish and U.S. influences on racial dynamics and patterns due to U.S. occupation of these countries during the first two decades of the twentieth century.) Most English-speaking colonies elected black leaders to presidential and prime ministerial posts soon after the formation of newly independent nation-states. In the Spanish-speaking Caribbean there was mestizo (referring to peoples of mixed descent) political dominance.

In Caribbean societies with multiple nonwhite populations (these are often known as plural societies), racial and ethnic tensions have often determined political allegiances. The former British colonies of TRINIDAD AND TOBAGO and GUYANA (the only English-speaking country of continental South America) have East Indian- and African-descended populations that are roughly equal in size. In Guyana FORBES BURNHAM used politics based upon race and the Cold War to his advantage to limit support for and prospects for coalition with his chief rival, CHEDDI JAGAN, an East Indian Guyanese, in the 1960s. Burnham also neutralized popular support for more radical political programs offered by black intellectuals such as WALTER RODNEY.

Nationalist sentiment in Trinidad and Tobago in the 1950s led to the formation of the black-dominated People's National Movement (PNM), which won the first federal elections in Trinidad in 1958. ERIC WILLIAMS, the dominant political figure of the Trinidadian independence movement and author of *The Negro in the Caribbean and Capitalism and Slavery,* attempted to unify Trinidad under the banner of non-racialism. As chief minister of the PNM he sought to avoid the Cold War isolation that plagued Cuba because of the Cuban Revolution's adoption of socialist principles and its incorporation into the Soviet Bloc. Williams dismissed SOCIALISM because it would have alienated East Indians and Chinese in the rural areas of Trinidad, who were mainly small landholders. The PNM eventually became embroiled in intense political competition with the East Indian–dominated Democratic Labour Party, led by Radaranth Capildeo. Successive elections and periods of rule were marked with intermittent ethnic and racial conflict. This unrest culminated in a general strike in 1970 and a short-lived black power movement that attempted to unite students and East Indian and black working classes in an assault on what black power advocates called "Afro-Saxonism," or black neocolonialism in the country. After Williams's death in 1981 the PNM, led by Williams's successor George Chambers, continued to lead the country until a massive defeat in the 1986 general elections. The PNM was defeated by the National Alliance for Reconstruction (NAF), whose political platform was marked more by a desire to end PNM rule than a unified coalition of diverse ideological interests. The "One Love" campaign of the NAF sought to replace the ethno-political tenor of Trinidadian party politics with a more ideologically based party competition. This attempt foundered by 1990 as the party's leader, A. N. R. Robinson, a former protege of Eric Williams, was accused of black partisanship by East Indian party members. Abu Bakr, an Afro-Trinidadian Muslim, led a coup attempt in 1990, plunging the nation into a six-day crisis. National dissatisfaction with Robinson did not translate into support for Bakr's coup d'état. Like Williams, the PNM, the black power movement, and the NAF, Bakr tried to unify economically disadvantaged blacks and East Indian Muslims, but to no avail. As in Jamaica and Grenada, two other black-dominated societies with a history of multi-party politics, the association of a specific political party or regime with the state itself led to heightened tensions during electoral campaigns that were manifested in mass demonstrations and violence.

In addition to problems of political participation in multi-ethnic and multiracial societies after independence, many Caribbean societies experienced the brunt of economic recession by the late 1970s and 1980s. This financial lull limited the ability of dominant political parties to make good on campaign promises of economic revival and political reform. In Jamaica the charismatic, cerebral Michael Manley was prime minister twice in the 1970s (1972–1977; 1977–1980) and led the People's National Party during this period. Manley's regime represented an alternative path of democratic socialist development, an attempt to create an economy combining state intervention and social welfare policies with socioeconomic growth and industrial development.

By the 1970s Jamaica emerged as a pivotal nation-state within the ambit of Third World politics. Jamaica's status had a profound impact on Afro-diasporic communities in other parts of the Caribbean and AFRICA, as Manley attempted to steer his political party and Jamaica away from the geopolitical imperatives of the United States. Recession, inflation, and Cold War rhetoric proved to be difficult obstacles for the Manley regime and were used to full political advantage by Edward Seaga, of the Jamaican Labour Party (JLP), who was elected prime minister in 1980.

In Grenada the rise of the popular New Jewel Movement and installation via coup d'état of the charismatic MAURICE BISHOP to the position of president in 1979 further complicated Caribbean politics. By the late 1970s Caribbean nations were often forced to align themselves with the U.S. or risk economic and political isolation.

Like Manley, Bishop alienated the U.S. by expressing solidarity with Cuba and the nonaligned movements of Third World peoples, and the Reagan administration was far less tolerant of ideological diversity in the region than the Carter administration had been. Following the triumph of the Nicaraguan Sandinista revolution in March of 1979, both the Carter and Reagan administrations perceived the increasing autonomy of Manley and Bishop as a threat to U.S. dominance and a sign of increasing Soviet influence. The "red scare" would be put to good use by Edward Seaga during the Jamaican national elections of 1980. Seaga's close relations with the Reagan administration guaranteed monetary aid from both the U.S. and international lending sources.

In October 1983 the U.S. Marines invaded the island of Grenada. The invasion was undertaken under the pretext of protecting U.S. citizens, mainly students, against an alleged communist threat. The supposed danger was posed by the presence of Cuban construction workers on the island to assist in the construction of an airport and the assassination of Maurice Bishop after an internal power struggle between Bishop supporters and a more sectarian, Marxist-Leninist faction led by cabinet member Bernard Coard. Construction workers as well as Grenadan citizens were killed during the invasion. The U.S. students, whose lives were never endangered during the entire crisis, were unharmed and evacuated from the island without incident.

In relatively new nation-states such as these, political conflict often threatens not only particular regimes but the nation's ability to govern itself. The vulnerability of Trinidadian and Grenadan governments in times of crisis highlights the precarious position of new governments and civil societies during moments of political turmoil. It is important to recognize, however, that these nation-states are quite young in relation to other nation-states in the Americas and even in EUROPE. When contrasted to the long, often bloody periods of authoritarian rule in Cuba, Salvador, Guatemala, and the DOMINICAN REPUBLIC, black social movements and political parties of these regions have undergone rapid transformations as these countries have moved from colonies to independent states and developing nations in a short period of time. In these and other independent societies of the English-speaking Caribbean who gained independence over the past forty years, however, the political sovereignty of national independence has not been accompanied by economic and geopolitical sovereignty.

See also Black Power Movement in the Caribbean; Nationalism in Latin America and the Caribbean; Racism in Latin America and the Caribbean.

Michael Hanchard

Polk, Prentice Herman

1898–1984

Photographer and documentarian of the Tuskegee Institute community, as well as of scenes of the everyday lives of slaves and sharecroppers.

Prentice Herman Polk became interested in photography at a young age. He began studying through a correspondence course which he paid for with ten dollars he was mistakenly given as change for a candy bar at a local store.

Polk attended TUSKEGEE INSTITUTE from 1916 to 1920, and was appointed to the faculty of the photography department in 1928. He served as department head from 1933 to 1938. From 1933 to 1982 he was the official school photographer, taking pictures of members of the Tuskegee community as well as visitors such as Henry Ford and Eleanor Roosevelt. He also chronicled the experiences of GEORGE WASHINGTON CARVER. Polk retired in 1982.

See also Photography, African American.

Pollard, Frederick Douglass (Fritz)

1894–1986

Pioneer American football player and the first African American coach in the National Football League.

Frederick Douglass "Fritz" Pollard was born and grew up in CHICAGO, ILLINOIS, and inherited a love of sports from his father, a former boxer, and his older brothers, who played football. By the time he graduated from Chicago's Albert G. Lane Technical High School, he was an accomplished baseball player, a star running back and a three-time Cook County track champion. After high school, he briefly attended and played football for Northwestern, Harvard, and Dartmouth before receiving a scholarship from the Rockefeller family to attend Brown University in 1915. Though just five feet, eight inches and 150 pounds and initially ostracized by his teammates, Pollard eventually became a star running back and defensive player for the Brown football team, leading the squad to a 1916 Rose Bowl game against Washington State. He was the first African American ever to play in the Rose Bowl, and the second to be named an All-American in college football.

After leaving Brown, Pollard briefly pursued a degree in dentistry, worked as director of an army YMCA, and coached football at Lincoln University before being signed to play professionally for the Akron Pros in the American Professional Football League (APFA). Leading the Pros to a championship in 1920, Pollard was named head coach in 1921 and continued to play for the Pros as well. The APFA was renamed the NFL in 1922, making Pollard the first African American coach in NFL history. Pollard remained with the Pros until 1926, and went on to coach NFL teams in Indiana and Milwaukee. He remained the only African American to have coached in the NFL until the 1990s.

In the late 1920s and 1930s, Pollard successfully coached African American football teams in Chicago and NEW YORK before retiring from football in 1937 to pursue a career in business.

Though he struggled against harassment and racial discrimination throughout his collegiate and professional careers (hostile players and crowds would often hurl insults and objects at him), Pollard brought spectacular talent and admirable dignity to American football, and helped to create opportunities for later black players and coaches. He was inducted into the National Football Foundation's collegiate Hall of Fame in 1954, and became the first African American inducted into Brown's Football Hall of Fame in 1971.

See also Football, Collegiate; Football, Professional; Sports and African Americans.

Lisa Clayton Robinson

Poor, Salem

1758–?

American soldier who fought in the American Revolution at the Battle of Bunker Hill.

Salem Poor was born free in Massachusetts. Leaving his wife, he enlisted in a Massachusetts militia company under Captain Benjamin Ames. Like black soldier PETER SALEM, he served with valor during the AMERICAN REVOLUTION at the Battle of Bunker Hill (actually fought at Breed's Hill) on June 17, 1775. Similar to Peter Salem, who was credited, perhaps mistakenly, with killing British major John Pitcairn, Poor was perhaps responsible for killing British lieutenant colonel James Abercrombie. Colonel William Prescott and thirteen other officers petitioned the General Court of Massachusetts a few weeks later, suggesting that the Continental Congress itself bestow "The Reward due to so great and Distinguisht a Caracter." The petition read: "The Subscribers begg leave to Report to your Honble. House (Which Wee do in justice to the Caracter of so Brave a Man) that under Our Own observation, Wee declare that A Negro Man Called Salem Poor of Col. Fryes Regiment, Capt. Ames. Company in the late Battle at Charleston, behaved like an Experienced Officer, as Well as an Excellent Soldier, to Set forth Particulars of his Conduct would be Tedious, Wee Would Only begg leave to say in the Person of this sd. Negro Centers a Brave & gallant Soldier—." There is no record, however, that Poor received a reward.

On July 10, 1775 General George Washington issued instructions that no more blacks were to be recruited but that those already serving, such as Salem Poor, could complete their terms. On November 12, 1775 Washington issued orders prohibiting blacks from serving, whether they were new volunteers or those seeking to reenlist. However, Washington learned that on November 7 Virginia governor Lord Dunmore had proclaimed free all blacks who were willing to serve under the British flag. On December 30 Washington ordered recruiting officers to enlist free blacks. On January 16, 1776 the Continental Congress approved the reenlistment of free blacks. Poor served at the Battle of White Plains, New York (October 28, 1776) and at Valley Forge, Pennsylvania (December 1777).

There are brief accounts of Poor's military service in Benjamin Quarles's *The Negro in the American Revolution* (1961,

p. 11) and Sidney Kaplan's *The Black Presence in the Era of the American Revolution, 1770–1800* (1973, pp. 19–20). Both are based on Revolutionary Rolls (Massachusetts Archives, State House, Boston, 180: 241).

From *Dictionary of American Negro Biography* by Rayford W. Logan and Michael R. Winston, editors. Copyright © 1982 by Rayford W. Logan and Michael R. Winston. Reprinted by permission of W. W. Norton & Company, Inc.

See also Colonial America, Blacks in; Military, Blacks in the American.

Rayford W. Logan

Poor People's Washington Campaign

Demonstration in Washington, D.C., organized in 1968 by the Southern Christian Leadership Conference to demand federal legislation ensuring employment, income, and housing for the poor.

On June 19, 1968, over 50,000 people assembled in WASHINGTON, D.C., to voice their support for the Poor People's Campaign for economic justice in America. The day was the highlight of the SOUTHERN CHRISTIAN LEADERSHIP CONFERENCE'S (SCLC) campaign, set in motion by MARTIN LUTHER KING JR., to secure federal legislation guaranteeing employment, income, and housing for the poor. Considered only minimally successful by most historians, the Poor People's Campaign has been called the last effort of the 1960s mass mobilizations of nonviolent resistance.

The Poor People's Campaign marked several important shifts in the orientation of SCLC as a whole, and in the thinking of Martin Luther King Jr., its leader. The SCLC had expanded its operations from a regional base in the South to a national operation by the mid-1960s. In the South, rural blacks had faced debilitating poverty and segregation: a NATIONAL ASSOCIATION FOR THE ADVANCEMENT OF COLORED PEOPLE (NAACP) survey in Mississippi found that blacks there suffered from hunger, malnutrition, and even starvation. In Northern cities such as CHICAGO, the SCLC found an urban crisis of poverty grounded in ingrained racist economic structures. Here, the organization found, the forces of institutionalized racism did not yield to the strategies of resistance used against segregation in the South.

Martin Luther King Jr. became increasingly critical of a federal government and capitalist system that left a large population of African Americans, urban and rural, in poverty. He said: "We are called upon to help the discouraged beggars in life's market place. But one day we must come to see that an edifice which produces beggars needs restructuring." King pointed directly at the "edifice" of the federal government, which he had formerly viewed as a benevolent force that needed only to understand the conditions under which blacks lived in order to join the fight for change. Poverty, King now claimed, was to blame for the urban riots that plagued the country, and capitalism was to blame for poverty: "When you begin to ask why are there forty million poor people in America, you are raising questions about the economic system, about a broader distribution of wealth. When you ask that question, you begin to question the capitalistic economy."

King took up the suggestion of Marian Wright to have the poor demonstrate in Washington, D.C., and if necessary, disrupt the national government. He envisioned a "tent city," with protesters living out of temporary structures on the mall or Capitol Hill. Unlike King's earlier campaigns for African American equality, this movement was to be staged on behalf of a spectrum of peoples, including NATIVE AMERICANS, Mexican Americans, Puerto Ricans, and Appalachian whites.

King began mobilizing the SCLC for a national campaign amidst fears of an increasingly violent turn in the struggle for rights. The campaign moved slowly, in part for this reason, and in part because of financial and organizational difficulties. Civil rights activists, such as BAYARD RUSTIN and NAACP Executive Secretary ROY WILKINS, questioned the wisdom of a mass march on Washington that might lead to violence, while others, namely President Lyndon B. Johnson and the Federal Bureau of Investigation (FBI), waged an outright campaign to derail the organizing process. When a march led by King in MEMPHIS, TENNESSEE, to support striking sanitation workers turned violent, it seemed to be the end of the campaign to march on Washington.

King's assassination on April 4, 1968, turned the tide of support for the march, and within a month, over half a million dollars in donations poured in for King's movement. The new SCLC leader, the Reverend RALPH ABERNATHY, kept the movement going, and former opponents of the march, such as Rustin, now joined in.

On May 13, the first residents of Resurrection City set up house, populating West Potomac Park in tents made from canvas and plywood. By late May, 2,500 people were living there, including groups from Tennessee, New Mexico, Chicago, and the Mississippi Delta. Each day, Resurrection City residents marched to various federal agencies to present demands. They joined over 50,000 others on Solidarity Day, June 19, for a mass demonstration organized by Sterling Tucker and led by Abernathy and CORETTA SCOTT KING. Five days later, 1,500 police arrived, arresting hundreds and destroying Resurrection City.

For some who had been active in the early successes of the SCLC, the Poor People's Campaign was a failure. Many found the protest poorly organized, despite its lucrative funding, and some protesters were critical of SCLC leaders who slept at nights in a motel. For others, who remembered King's prophecy that organizing around the basic rights of jobs and income would prove even more difficult than opposing the VIETNAM WAR, the Poor People's Campaign was a necessary turn from protests against segregation to a larger demand for economic justice.

Marian Aguiar

Popular Movement for the Liberation of Angola

Leading nationalist organization and a major political party in Angola.

According to the movement's official history, two small nationalist groups created the Popular Movement for the Liberation of ANGOLA (Movimento Popular de Libertação de Angola), or MPLA, in 1956. From the outset, the MPLA's support came primarily from urban, educated members of the OVIMBUNDU ethnic group, Portuguese Marxists, and *mestiços* (of indigenous and European descent). Despite heavy repression from the Portuguese colonial authorities' efforts to suppress nationalist activities, the MPLA succeeded in organizing the 1961 attack on the LUANDA prison that the movement came to consider the beginning of the war.

During the war, the MPLA competed for international and national support with the National Front for the Liberation of Angola, or FNLA, and the NATIONAL UNION FOR THE TOTAL INDEPENDENCE OF ANGOLA, or UNITA. Although the MPLA had not achieved military dominance when PORTUGAL withdrew from Angola in 1975, it was able to capture the capital and thereby proclaim victory. The movement's first leader, AGOSTINHO NETO, became president of independent Angola.

The war did not end at independence, and UNITA fought the MPLA government for the next quarter century. In 1977, the MPLA renamed itself the MPLA-Workers Party, or MPLA-PT, officially adopted Marxist-Leninism, and began a program to radically transform the Angolan economy. With Soviet assistance and advice, the MPLA-PT nationalized most industries, especially agriculture and mining, and renegotiated contracts with Western oil companies. President JOSÉ EDUARDO DOS SANTOS and the MPLA ran Angola as a one-party state, though the party was not monolithic as it was divided along ideological, ethnic, racial, and urban-rural lines. In 1990, with the war going poorly, the MPLA leadership ceded to international pressure to introduce a new constitution calling for economic and political liberalization, including a multiparty system. Elections in 1992 gave MPLA candidates a majority of seats in parliaments, but UNITA refused to recognize the results and resumed the war. In early 1997, as the peace process progressed, the MPLA became the majority party in the government of national reconciliation. The next year, however, hostilities again broke out. Fighting continued until 2002, when UNITA and the government agreed to a cease-fire.

See also Nationalism in Africa.

Eric Young

Population Growth in Sub-Saharan Africa

Historical and contemporary trends in fertility, mortality, and population growth rates in Africa

Up until the past century, Africa's population has grown slowly by world standards. Twentieth-century improvements in hygiene and medical care, however, dramatically reduced mortality rates and contributed to a period of extremely rapid growth between the 1950s and the 1980s. According to a 2002 United Nations estimate, the average woman in AFRICA has 4.9 children during her lifetime. (In contrast, women in EUROPE have only 1.4 children on average.) But fertility rates have begun to decline in several African countries, due to a combination of urbanization, education, and increased contraceptive use. If current trends continue, the population in Africa may stabilize shortly after 2050 at just over two billion people.

African Population Growth in History

For most of human history Africa, like other continents, was inhabited by small groups of foragers who had relatively low rates of population growth. Consequently, in Africa as elsewhere, the total population grew slowly until the advent of agriculture, perhaps around 10,000 years ago. Although increased food supplies supported higher fertility rates, mortality rates remained high in Africa, due to the prevalence of tropical disease. Famines brought on by pestilence and periodic droughts also claimed lives. Until relatively recently, then, most of Africa's agrarian societies have lived under conditions of abundant land but scarce labor. These conditions supported cultural norms that valued large families. Having many children ensured an adequate labor supply, even if some children died, and also provided a degree of old-age security for parents.

European contact from the fifteenth century onward brought new diseases to Africa, including smallpox, syphilis, and gonorrhea. Although these diseases claimed many lives in Africa, they were much less devastating than they were to be in the New World. A far more significant demographic consequence of European expansion was the TRANSATLANTIC SLAVE TRADE. Between the sixteenth and nineteenth centuries, perhaps twelve million Africans were taken aboard ships headed for the Americas. Millions more were sold into the INDIAN OCEAN SLAVE TRADE during this period, and countless others died during slave raids or en route to coastal slave forts. In addition, some groups fleeing slave raiders ended up in regions where sleeping sickness and other deadly diseases were endemic.

European colonialism had mixed effects on African population growth. In some regions, especially Central Africa, colonization brought devastating epidemics of foreign diseases such as smallpox. In 1913, for example, a doctor in NYASALAND (present-day MALAWI) estimated that 93 percent of all adults and 63 percent of all children had been infected with smallpox. Tens of thousands of Africans were also killed by accidents, brutal discipline, and disease in mining camps and on railroad projects. In addition, some incidents of European military action against regional uprisings took a huge toll: the German crackdown on the HERERO rebellion in SOUTH-WEST AFRICA (modern-day NAMIBIA) between 1904 and 1907 led to the deaths of 65,000 of the original population of 80,000 Herero. Colonial

Infant Mortality Rate

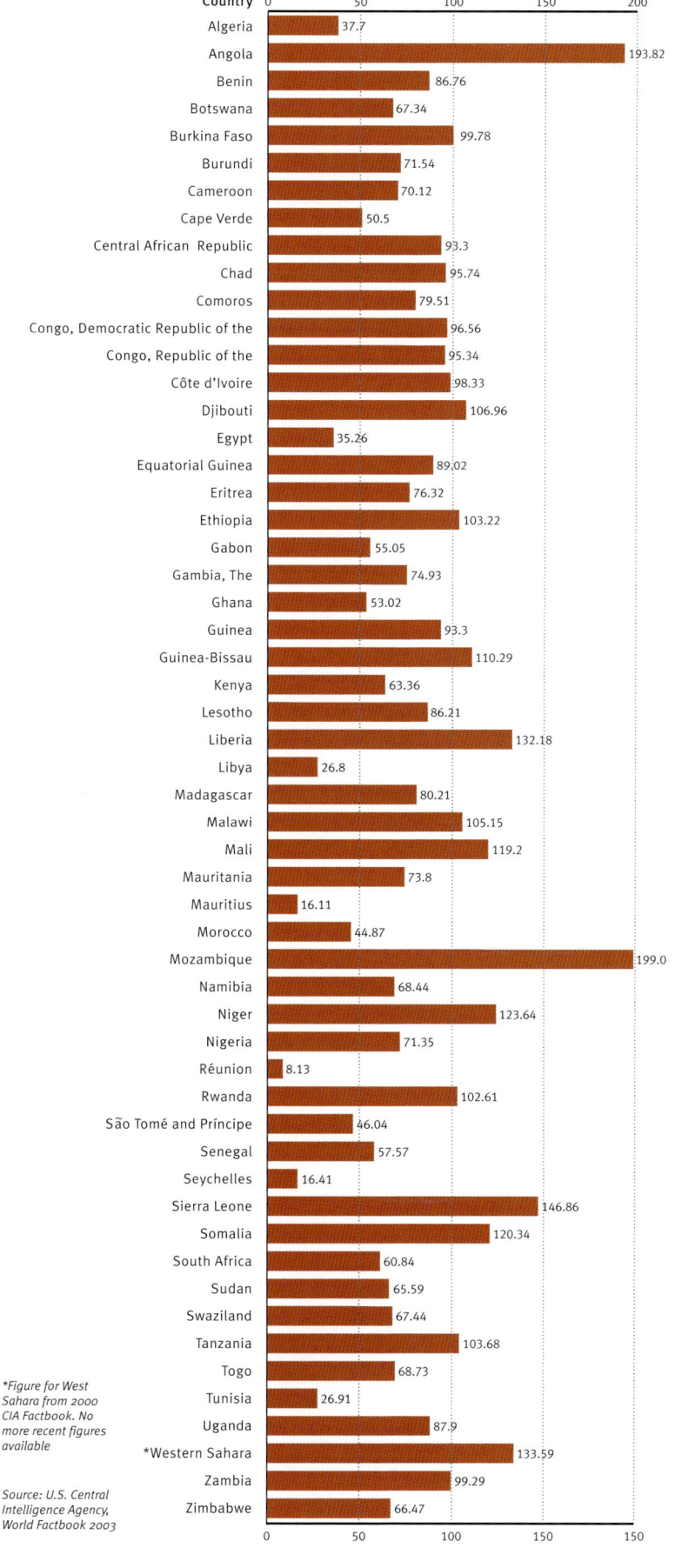

*Figure for West Sahara from 2000 CIA Factbook. No more recent figures available

Source: U.S. Central Intelligence Agency, World Factbook 2003

Population Statistics for Sub-Saharan Africa

Country	Life Expectancy at Birth in Africa		Population Growth in Africa	Population Less Than 15 Years of Age in Africa
	Male	Female	Annual Population Growth Rate 1998	% of Population Under 15 Years Old
Algeria	69.14	72.01	1.65	33
Angola	36.13	37.83	1.97	43
Benin	50.35	51.84	2.95	47
Botswana	32.2	32.32	0.55	39
Burkina Faso	43.02	45.94	2.6	46
Burundi	42.54	43.88	2.18	47
Cameroon	47.15	48.97	2.02	42
Cape Verde	66.53	73.23	0.79	41
Central African Republic	40.18	43.29	1.62	43
Chad	46.97	50.1	3.07	48
Comoros	58.92	63.5	2.96	43
Congo, Democratic Republic of the	46.83	51.09	2.9	48
Congo, Republic of the	49.04	51.02	1.53	38
Côte d'Ivoire	40.34	45.04	2.15	45
Djibouti	41.82	44.48	2.13	43
Egypt	67.94	73.0	1.88	34
Equatorial Guinea	52.63	56.93	2.44	42
Eritrea	51.48	54.92	1.28	45
Ethiopia	40.39	42.11	1.96	45
Gabon	55.45	58.84	2.54	42
Gambia, The	52.39	56.44	3.03	45
Ghana	55.66	57.43	1.45	39
Guinea	48.28	50.83	2.37	44
Guinea-Bissau	45.09	48.91	2.02	42
Kenya	45.02	45.43	1.27	41
Lesotho	36.76	37.13	0.19	38
Liberia	47.03	49.3	1.67	43
Libya	73.91	78.34	2.39	34
Madagascar	53.82	58.53	3.03	45
Malawi	37.57	38.39	2.21	47
Mali	44.7	46.19	2.82	47
Mauritania	49.78	54.13	2.91	46
Mauritius	67.82	75.85	0.84	25
Morocco	67.77	72.41	1.64	33
Mozambique	30.98	31.63	0.82	42
Namibia	44.27	41.22	1.49	42
Niger	42.29	42.12	2.71	48
Nigeria	50.89	51.14	2.53	44
Réunion	70.03	77.0	1.47	31
Rwanda	38.51	40.18	1.84	42
São Tomé and Principe	64.79	67.82	3.18	48
Senegal	54.83	57.95	2.56	44
Seychelles	65.78	76.88	0.46	27
Sierra Leone	40.33	45.42	2.94	45
Somalia	45.67	49.05	3.43	45
South Africa	46.57	46.54	0.01	30
Sudan	56.59	58.93	2.71	44
Swaziland	41.02	37.87	0.83	41

Population Statistics for Sub-Saharan Africa (Continued)

Country	Life Expectancy at Birth in Africa		Population Growth in Africa	Population Less Than 15 Year of Age in Africa
	Male	Female	Annual Population Growth Rate 1998	% of Population Under 15 Years Old
Tanzania	43.33	45.83	1.72	44
Togo	51.47	55.45	2.37	44
Tunisia	72.77	76.15	1.09	27
Uganda	43.42	46.38	2.96	51
Western Sahara*	48.65	51.33	2.29	N/A
Zambia	35.25	35.25	1.52	46
Zimbabwe	40.09	37.89	0.83	40

*Figures for Western Sahara from 2000 CIA Factbook. No more recent figures available.
Source: U.S. Central Intelligence Agency, World Factbook 2003.

land and labor policies that compelled Africans to forgo food-crop cultivation for cash cropping or migrant labor also increased vulnerability to famine in some areas, though famine itself was not a new phenomenon. Parts of UPPER VOLTA (present-day BURKINA FASO) experienced famine in 1931, after a combination of drought and plunging world cotton prices left peasants with neither food nor the money to buy it. Nyasaland also experienced a severe famine in 1949. Finally, venereal diseases (which often led to infertility) and tuberculosis plagued both African and European inhabitants of many colonial-era cities and mining towns.

Nevertheless, colonial public health and sanitation campaigns—aimed partly at improving the health and survival rates of European troops and civil servants stationed in Africa—led to a dramatic drop in mortality rates after World War II (1939–1945). Colonial administrations built hospitals and urban water systems, and undertook smallpox vaccination programs. During the late colonial period, improved access to clean water significantly reduced the incidence of waterborne diseases such as cholera. The development of effective or at least improved treatments for a variety of killers—tuberculosis, syphilis, measles, polio, and MALARIA—also affected mortality rates, as did improved education campaigns on the causes of infant diarrhea. These measures may have contributed to slight increases in fertility rates in some areas, such as the BELGIAN CONGO (present-day DEMOCRATIC REPUBLIC OF THE CONGO). Diseases that caused infertility, such as gonorrhea, had been more rare, while birth spacing, a practice intended to maximize infant survivability, shortened in response to reduced infant mortality.

As a result of these changes, African populations began to increase dramatically in the 1950s. By the 1960s the continent's overall population was growing at approximately 3 percent annually, a rate that remained constant through the 1980s. Many observers in the mid-twentieth century assumed that urbanization and industrialization would lead to a demographic shift toward smaller family size, as had occurred in Europe. But industrialization in Africa has been limited to a few countries, and elsewhere urbanization alone did not, for decades, bring down fertility rates.

Population Growth and Economic Development

African national population growth rates continue to rank among the highest in the world. Except for a few small countries, however—RWANDA, BURUNDI, LESOTHO, and MAURITIUS—population densities remain relatively low. Currently, Africa covers 25 percent of the earth's land surface but contains only about 13 percent of the world's population (about 800 million people). However, by 2050 the population, expected to exceed 1.8 billion, would account for 20 percent of the world's population, and NIGERIA, already Africa's most populous nation, would be the fifth most populous in the world.

Scholars disagree about Africa's capacity to support a much larger population in the future. A great deal will depend not only on how much food Africa will be able to grow for itself—a factor contingent on potential climatic shifts and developments in agricultural technology, among other things—but also on Africa's overall economic prosperity. Currently, the majority of the continent's people depend on land-based livelihoods, but industrialization and increased power on world markets would allow African countries to support potentially much higher population densities.

The more immediate problem for many African countries is that neither government nor the private sector can keep up with the rapidly growing need for housing, education and other social services, and employment. Already, large cities such as JOHANNESBURG and NAIROBI suffer acute shortages of affordable housing, and primary schools across much of the continent are severely overcrowded and underequipped. Some groups, such as Population Action International, argue that population growth rates must decrease—and with them public expenditures on social services—if Africa is ever to achieve sustained economic development. But others argue that fertility rates, and, consequently, population growth rates will fall only if people have access to education, improved medical care, and greater economic security.

Current Demographic Trends

The preference for large families remains widespread in many parts of Africa. Having many children is seen not only as proof of virility, but also as a strategy for increasing the chances that at least some children will be successful and therefore able to provide for the rest of the family. In addition, children's labor is still considered an economic asset, especially in rural areas, but also for the many women and men who make their living in small-scale urban trade and artisanal activities.

But according to the United Nations, fertility rates are declining in several African countries. The fertility rate in KENYA dropped from an estimated 7.5 during the period between 1980 and 1985 to 4.6 between 1995 and 2000. Within the same period, the fertility rate in CÔTE D'IVOIRE decreased from 7.4 to 5.3. The decline is generally linked to family-planning education and families' changing economic demands, among other factors. In North Africa, fertility rates have been declining for several decades, due primarily to women's later marriage ages and the increasing use of contraception. But in sub-Saharan Africa it was not until the 1980s, when contraceptives first became widely available, that fertility rates began to drop. Countries such as MADAGASCAR and TANZANIA have joined Kenya, BOTSWANA, and others in showing a decline in the fertility rate.

The reduction in fertility found in many African countries is probably also a result of the perceived escalating costs of having a large family. A 1991 study in Kenya showed increasing concern about large families among both men and women. School fees are an especially important consideration. In some densely populated rural areas, parents also expressed concern that they would not be able to provide numerous offspring with adequate farmland. Although women in much of Africa have always combined childbearing with work outside the home, at least in some countries there are signs that women are delaying marriage and having fewer children in order to devote more time and energy to their careers.

Demographers and epidemiologists are currently debating how the ongoing acquired immunodeficiency syndrome (AIDS) epidemic will affect population growth in Africa. At the end of 2002, 70 percent of the world's 29.4 million human immunodeficiency virus (HIV) cases occurred in sub-Saharan Africa, and one-quarter of the adult population in Botswana, Namibia, SWAZILAND, and ZIMBABWE was infected with HIV. Between 1985 and 1995 approximately 4.2 million people in Africa died from AIDS. The United Nations Development Program reports that deaths from AIDS have greatly reduced average life expectancies in the twenty-four most severely affected countries. In Botswana, for example, life expectancy at birth has dropped to thirty-five years, its pre-1950 level. If current trends continue, therefore, AIDS is expected to reduce the rate of population growth slightly. But the rise in infant mortality brought on by the epidemic may reverse the demographic shift, as people compensate for the disease by having more children. Precisely how AIDS affects Africa's demographic trends will depend at least in part on whether treatments or preventive vaccines become not only available but affordable in poor countries.

Family-Planning Trends

Initially, most newly independent African governments were reluctant to promote family planning, which was widely viewed as a neocolonial attempt by the West to maintain control over African populations. Kenya became the first African country to actively promote family planning when it began subsidizing contraceptives in 1967; GHANA was next, implementing family-planning policies in 1969. Many African countries have since begun their own programs, and after years of relatively slow progress, some have been fairly successful at promoting contraceptive use. In 1977–1978 only 7 percent of Kenyan couples used contraceptives, for example, but in just fifteen years that number had risen to 33 percent. Similar increases in contraceptive use have occurred in Rwanda and Zimbabwe. Programs geared toward educating women have been credited with the extensive adoption of contraceptives.

Birth control pills are the most widely used method of modern contraception. Depo-Provera injections are commonly used in SOUTH AFRICA, Kenya, and Botswana. In recent years, countries throughout Africa have increasingly promoted condom use as an AIDS prophylactic. In Côte d'Ivoire, for example, condom sales increased from 1.8 million units in 1991 to 12.4 million units in 1996.

But effective family-planning programs in Africa still suffer not only from logistical problems, such as inadequate funding and distribution systems, but also from legal and ideological obstacles. The Catholic Church, which opposes many current family-planning practices, is a powerful lobbying group in many African countries, making governments reluctant to endorse either contraceptive use or abortion. In response, governments of countries where the Catholic Church is influential, such as Kenya, have couched family-planning policies in terms of improving women's health rather than limiting population growth.

See also Acquired Immunodeficiency Syndrome in Africa: An Interpretation; Colonial Rule; Disease and African History; Diseases, Infectious, in Africa; Drought and Desertification; Hunger and Famine; United Nations in Africa; Urbanism and Urbanization in Africa.

Ari Nave

Porgy and Bess

Opera of black life written by white composer George Gershwin, lyricist Ira Gershwin, and novelist DuBose Heyward; premiered on Broadway in 1935 and featured an all-black cast.

Porgy and Bess was based on DuBose Heyward's 1925 novel *Porgy*, as well as on the 1927 dramatization of *Porgy*. Although Heyward originally conceived the musical version as a play with music, George Gershwin insisted that he wanted to write a work that would be sung throughout. Once Heyward agreed, the Gershwins collaborated with him on shaping the play and writing lyrics for the songs.

The Metropolitan Opera in NEW YORK CITY had hoped that *Porgy and Bess* would premiere in their famous OPERA house. Although he was flattered, George Gershwin decided that it would not serve his purposes as well as a production on Broadway. He was concerned about the limited number of performances the opera would receive over several seasons in repertory. He was also adamant that *Porgy and Bess* have a cast of black singers; the Metropolitan had no African American singers in its company. After auditioning hundreds of actors, Gershwin chose the young singers TODD DUNCAN and ANNE BROWN for the roles of Porgy and Bess, and he picked vaudeville star John W. "Bubbles" Sublett (see BUCK AND BUBBLES) for the role of the sharp drug peddler Sportin' Life. Gershwin also hired older performers, including Abbie Mitchell as Clara and J. ROSAMOND JOHNSON as Frazier, whose careers had begun during the first flowering of black musical theater on Broadway. After a two-week run in BOSTON, MASSACHUSETTS, *Porgy and Bess* arrived on October 10, 1935, at Broadway's Alvin Theater, where it had 124 performances. The critics were divided on the merits of the opera. Some thought it contained "some of the loveliest music [Gershwin] has written," while others were disturbed by the "song hits" in the show, which were felt to detract from the musical integrity of the score.

Porgy and Bess, set in the working class black community of Catfish Row in CHARLESTON, SOUTH CAROLINA, tells the story of Porgy, a "crippled Negro beggar," who is in love with Bess. Bess, however, is known along Catfish Row as the woman of another man, Crown. After Crown kills a man during a crap game, he is forced to go into hiding. Porgy takes Bess to his room where, despite her promises to Crown that she would join him when he returned from hiding, she confesses her love for Porgy. When Crown comes back, Porgy confronts him and in their fight strangles Crown to death. Porgy is jailed for a week. On his return he discovers that Bess, fearing that he would be jailed forever, has gone to New York with Sportin' Life. As the opera concludes, Porgy is heading for New York on his goat cart to find his Bess.

Gershwin's score is filled with many songs familiar to audiences today, including "Summertime," "I Got Plenty o' Nuttin'," "Bess You Is My Woman Now," "It Ain't Necessarily So," "There's a Boat Dat's Leavin' Soon for New York," and "Oh, Lawd, I'm on My Way." As the first musical production on Broadway that contained no extended spoken dialogue, *Porgy and Bess* served as a model for later musicals such as Frank Loesser's *The Most Happy Fella* (1956) and Stephen Sondheim's *Passion* (1994).

Heyward's story has been viewed differently in the decades since it first appeared. During the 1920s and 1930s, it was seen as an accurate portrayal of contemporary black life in the South. In the context of the CIVIL RIGHTS MOVEMENT in the 1950s and 1960s, however, the story came to be viewed as burdened by negative stereotyping. In any case, *Porgy and Bess* has become widely accepted as one of the most important American operas.

By Broadway standards, *Porgy and Bess* had only a mildly successful run. By the standards of opera, though, it achieved tremendous success. In 1938 the production toured the West Coast, playing in LOS ANGELES and SAN FRANCISCO, CALIFORNIA. In January 1942 *Porgy and Bess* was revived in a new version. Spoken dialogue replaced most of the recitatives, and many cuts were made to shorten the performance. After playing eight months on Broadway, over twice as long as the original run, *Porgy and Bess* toured twenty-six cities before returning to New York. The shortened version was revived again in New York in 1944. During the 1940s a number of productions were mounted throughout EUROPE. While Brown and Duncan sang in a few of the European performances, most productions employed white singers in blackface. In 1952 a new epoch in the opera's history was marked by a production, supported by the United States Department of State, that toured Europe with many of the cuts restored. This production, which starred African American singers LEONTYNE PRICE and William Warfield, was heard in many European cities, as well as in the MIDDLE EAST and in Central and SOUTH AMERICA. In 1959 Otto Preminger directed a movie version that starred SIDNEY POITIER, DOROTHY DANDRIDGE, SAMMY DAVIS JR., and Brock Peters. The opera continued to be performed frequently through the 1960s and 1970s. In 1985 it finally entered the repertory of the Metropolitan Opera, fifty years after its premiere.

See also Musical Theater in the United States.

Porres, San Martín de

1579–1639

Afro-Peruvian saint canonized in 1962.

Six officially recognized saints lived in colonial PERU during the sixteenth and seventeenth centuries: Toribio de Mogrovejo (1538–1606), second archbishop of Lima and defender of the Indians; Francisco Solano (1549–1619), a Franciscan missionary, musician, and evangelizer of the South; Rosa de Lima (1586–1617), a tertiary of the Order of Preachers, the first native in the New World to be canonized; Juan Macías (1585–1645), a lay brother of the same order, servant of the poor; Ana de los Ángeles Monteagudo (1602–1686), a mystic nun of a cloistered convent in Arequipa; and Martín de Porres. In the context of this generation of saints, Martín is distinctive for being the first mulatto (of African and European descent) ever to be canonized by the Roman Catholic Church.

De Porres was born in Lima on December 9, 1579, the natural son of Juan de Porres, a Spanish nobleman, and Ana Velázquez, a free black woman from PANAMA. His interracial and illegitimate origins were common in Spanish America dur-

Peruvian Martín de Porres became the patron saint of interracial justice.
Oronoz

ing the colonization period. Although his parents never married, his father assumed responsibility for Martín and his sister, and brought them with him to Guayaquil (ECUADOR), where Martín received his elementary schooling. During his childhood and adolescence, he showed signs of a fine sensitivity and a unique generosity for the sick and the poor.

When Martín was twelve, his father brought him back to Lima and left him in the care of his mother, who apprenticed him to a barber-surgeon. Given the important social role that a barber-surgeon had at the time, this was a meaningful mentorship for the young Martín, who quickly gained a reputation as a healer. Three years later, at the age of fifteen, he received the habit of the Third Order of Saint Dominic and entered the Rosary convent of the Friar Priests in Lima, where he spent the next forty-five years.

The Dominican order prohibited black men from receiving the habit. For this reason, Martín de Porres entered the order as a *donate* (servant) for nine years, without being allowed to become a member. However, in 1603, after showing much devotion and dedication to helping the poor and sick, the order made an exception and de Porres was admitted as a lay brother. As an official member of the community, he worked as a barber, healer, and farmer, and allegedly performed miraculous cures on sick people and animals.

Martín based his spiritual life on the strictest practices of prayer and penance, according to the ascetic models of his time. His charity reputedly had no limits both in and out of his convent. He disregarded racial remarks belittling him and tried to aid those who called on him. The future saint was instrumental in the foundation of an orphanage and a foundling hospital in the city of Lima. He also ministered among the African slaves who were brought to Peru. Even animals received the benefit of his generosity.

Martín de Porres was beatified by Pope Gregory XVI in 1837. In 1945 Pius XII proclaimed him the patron of social justice. He was canonized in 1962 by Pope John XXIII, in the context of the preparation for the Second Vatican Council. Martín's fame has transcended the boundaries of Peru and SOUTH AMERICA. For his followers in the five continents, he represents a different paradigm of holiness. As an illegitimate child and a person of color, he was subjected to social and ecclesiastical discrimination, yet he became a symbol of understanding and compassion.

See also Catholic Church in Latin America and the Caribbean; Colonial Latin America and the Caribbean; Racism in Latin America and the Caribbean; Slavery in Latin America and the Caribbean.

Carlos Parra

Port-au-Prince, Haiti

Capital of the Caribbean nation of Haiti.

The city of Port-au-Prince is the national capital of HAITI, which occupies the western third of the Caribbean island of HISPANIOLA. Port-au-Prince is also the capital of the Ouest Department, an administrative division of the country. In 2003 the city's population was estimated at 1,764,000.

Port-au-Prince is Haiti's principal seaport and commercial center. Major manufactures include processed food, beverages, tobacco products, textiles, and building materials. Tourism and construction also contribute to the city's economy. Port-au-Prince is the site of the State University of Haiti (founded in 1920), the National Library, the National Museum, the Archaeological Museum, the Art Center, a technical institute, and a polytechnic college. Other points of interest include the National Palace, the Basilica of Notre Dame, and a stone quay built by the French in 1780. The settlement was laid out by the French in 1749 and served as the capital of the French colony of Saint-Domingue from 1770 to 1804. When Haiti became independent in 1804, the city was chosen as the new nation's capital.

Porter, James Amos

1905–1970

American painter and art historian, instrumental in the development of the scholarly study of African American art.

Born and raised in BALTIMORE, MARYLAND, James Amos Porter studied art as an undergraduate at HOWARD UNIVERSITY, graduating in 1927. He joined the Howard faculty that same year as a drawing and painting instructor and remained a professor there until the end of his life.

The first exhibition of one of Porter's paintings was in 1928. Group and solo exhibitions followed in the United States and abroad. In 1937, already an acknowledged teacher and painter, he earned an M.A. in art history from New York University. In 1935 and 1945 he received Rockefeller Foundation grants, and traveled to EUROPE, HAITI, and CUBA to seek inspiration for his work.

As an artist, Porter was best known for his portraits, including the prize-winning "Woman Holding a Jug" (1933). Several of his paintings are now held by the National Archives in WASHINGTON, D.C., and his portrait of his wife Dorothy Burnett Porter, curator of the Moorland-Spingarn Research Center at Howard University, is in the National Portrait Gallery.

Porter made his most lasting mark, however, as a historian and scholar of African American art. His landmark study, *Modern Negro Art,* published in 1943, remains a foundational text. Porter gave generous attention to his contemporaries in painting and sculpture and helped legitimize their contributions to American art by examining their artistic styles.

See also Art, African American; Historians, African American.

Port Louis, Mauritius

Capital of Mauritius.

Also known as "the star and key to the Indian Ocean," Port Louis played a central role in the Anglo-French struggle for power over the Indian Ocean trade routes to India during the eighteenth and nineteenth centuries. Despite losing its strategic importance when the SUEZ CANAL opened in 1869, Port Louis acted as both a dynamic center for regional trade and as a showcase of development and prosperity in the face of limited natural resources.

Port Louis was home to 176,000 people in 2004. The capital is by far the most densely populated area of MAURITIUS. The city arose around a natural harbor, named Noord-Wester Haven by early Dutch settlers, located on the northwestern shore of the island. When the French took control of Mauritius after 1721, they renamed what was then the undeveloped harbor of Port Louis. The site was chosen for its strategic advantages at a time when naval control of the Indian Ocean seaway was of significant interest to European powers. Ridges with peaks more than 800 meters (2,600 feet) tall surround much of the area, protecting it from land-based attacks. Two forts built by the French—Fort George and Fort William—guard entry to the port.

Within a short period, Port Louis emerged as a major seaport as well as a cosmopolitan town with a diverse population of soldiers, dockworkers, slaves, traders, and colonists of European, African, and Asian descent. A mosque built in 1805 is testament to the diversity of the Mauritian population from an early date. By 1810 the population had reached 24,000. In subsequent years, however, Port Louis was struck by a series of calamities. Cyclones continually damaged the port, sinking ships in the harbor. MALARIA and cholera epidemics in the 1850s and 1860s killed approximately 18,000 people in Port Louis alone (approximately 40,000 people in all), prompting a large number of wealthier residents to flee the urban squalor and head for the highland town of Curepipe. With the opening of the Suez Canal, the importance of Port Louis declined. Despite these setbacks, Port Louis has thrived as an administrative and financial center and remains the country's main port.

While Mauritius is generally characterized by ethnically mixed settlements, some significant residential segregation exists in the observable Chinese, Muslim, and Creole quarters of Port Louis. Events in the capital are a barometer of the country's political and economic climate. As independence approached in the late 1960s, ethnic tensions in the city rose, leading to street clashes between Creole and Muslim groups. British troops quelled the month-long civil disturbance, but only after thirty people died. These incidents, however, have been few and far between.

Today the capital is the only truly urban area of the country. Skyscrapers such as the State Bank sit adjacent to open-air markets. The World Bank provided a loan of $30.5 million in 1995 to improve the port. A large commercial complex, Caudan Waterfront, has been recently constructed, boasting high-end retail shops, restaurants, and a hotel. The city has a markedly bustling atmosphere during the day, particularly as the population swells with the arrival of commuters from the nearby suburban districts. By evening, however, the streets are mostly abandoned as social life takes place mostly within the confines of the city's homes.

See also Creoles; Indian Ocean Slave Trade; Islam in Africa.

Ari Nave

Portocarrero, René

1912–1985

Cuban painter, known around the world for his work about the people, popular festivities, nature, and colors of his country.

René Portocarrero was born in the neighborhood of El Cerro in HAVANA, CUBA, and began painting at an early age. At the age of fourteen, he started formal art studies at the Villarte and San Alejandro academies. Unable to adapt to the teaching environment, he decided to leave school and learn on his own. In 1934, he presented his first exhibition at the Salón de Bellas Artes, in Havana. He taught drawing, painting, and sculpture while continuing to produce his own artistic works, which included murals, ceramics, and theater sets, as well as book and magazine illustrations. His style has been described as "Cuban Baroque."

René Portocarrero maintained that he never planned his work and had no idea what he would paint until his brush was about to strike the canvas. He won many prizes and his works are in the permanent collections of numerous museums throughout the world, including the Museums of Modern Art in San Francisco, New York, São Paulo, Rio de Janeiro, and Paris; the National Gallery in Canada; Bellas Artes in Montevideo and Buenos Aires; and the Instituto de Arte Contemporaneo and Museo Nacional in Havana.

Port-of-Spain, Trinidad and Tobago

Capital of Trinidad and Tobago, a seaport on the northwestern coast of the island of Trinidad, located on the Gulf of Paria.

Port-of-Spain is the commercial center and leading port of TRINIDAD AND TOBAGO. Major manufactures in the area include alcoholic beverages, tobacco products, building materials, processed food, textiles, chemicals, and plastic items. Tourism is also important to the city's economy. Port-of-Spain is the site of the Royal Botanical Gardens; the National Archives; the National Museum and Art Gallery, with a collection of historical and natural history items and fine art; an Anglican cathedral (1816–1823); and a Roman Catholic cathedral (consecrated 1832). In the vicinity of Port-of-Spain are Piarco International Airport and the University of the West Indies (1946).

A Native American village known as Conquerabia occupied the site when the Spanish settled in the area in 1595 and renamed the community Puerto de España. After the British took control of the island in 1797, the settlement's name was Anglicized to Port-of-Spain. The city served as the capital of the Federation of the WEST INDIES from 1958 to 1962, when the grouping was dissolved. In 2004 Port-of-Spain had a population of 54,000.

See also Colonial Latin America and the Caribbean.

Porto-Novo, Benin

Capital and second largest city of the People's Republic of Benin.

The capital of BENIN, Porto-Novo is located on the West African coast, southeast of the port of COTONOU. Originally a village known as Ajase, it was founded during the seventeenth century by an Allada group fleeing conquest by the kingdom of Dahomey. Ajase was conquered by the YORUBA kingdom of OYO in 1730 and became the kingdom's main port.

During the eighteenth century, Ajase served as the Oyos' primary port in the TRANSATLANTIC SLAVE TRADE. Portuguese merchants gained extensive influence in the region, and in 1752 they renamed the port Porto-Novo. In the early nineteenth century, however, the Oyo lost control of the region, and the Portuguese ceded the land to the French. The king of Porto-Novo, fearful of a Dahomean invasion, asked the French for protection; the port was subsequently made a French protectorate. Dahomean attacks on Porto-Novo in the 1880s led to the 1890 and 1892 Franco-Dahomean wars, which in turn led to French colonization in 1894. Porto-Novo became the capital of colonial DAHOMEY in 1900.

Under French COLONIAL RULE, Porto-Novo became the colony's main administrative and economic center. After independence, however, most seafaring commerce moved to the deeper and safer port of neighboring Cotonou. Government followed suit, and by the mid-1970s, Cotonou had essentially become Benin's capital. Consequently, Porto-Novo has few of the modern amenities found in most African capitals; paved roads and reliable phone lines are scarce. Nevertheless, Porto-Novo remains the official capital of Benin and continues to house important cultural centers, such as the National Archives and the National Library, and national treasures, including the recently restored palace of King Toffa, the last king of Porto-Novo. The population is approximately 232,756 (2000 estimate).

See also Dahomey, Early Kingdom of.

Elizabeth Heath

Port Royal Experiment

Series of events that occurred after the United States Navy occupied (1861) South Carolina's Sea Islands, liberating thousands of slaves.

Because it dealt with many of the social, political, and economic questions that would arise in the aftermath of the American CIVIL WAR, the Port Royal Experiment has been called a "rehearsal" for RECONSTRUCTION. The name "Port Royal Experiment" is misleading because it suggests an actual plan or program. This was not the case. The individuals and groups who participated in the Port Royal Experiment—government agents, soldiers, philanthropists, and land speculators among them—converged on this area of the South Carolina coast independently of each other and with their own intentions for the newly liberated blacks. The Port Royal Experiment began on November 6, 1861, when plantation owners on South Carolina's Sea Islands fled the approaching U.S. Navy and abandoned their plantations, leaving behind nearly 10,000 slaves.

Slaves on the Sea Islands had lived far more independently than their counterparts on the mainland. After completing their daily assigned tasks, for example, blacks on the Sea Islands had the remainder of the day for their own activities—hunting, fishing, or cultivating their own gardens. Many blacks had sold their produce and purchased small plots of land for themselves. Freedom for them meant land ownership and subsistence farming, as opposed to working merely to increase someone else's wealth. Soon after the plantation owners fled, blacks on the Sea Islands destroyed the plantation houses and the cotton gins. They claimed the abandoned lands as their own, and began their own independent farms.

News of the federal occupation of the Sea Islands soon reached the North, and many people began to see different possibilities in the situation. A group of philanthropists, called Gideon's Band, traveled south to establish schools to educate the former slaves. Other groups, including U.S. treasury officials, army officers, and speculators, also traveled to the Sea Islands, with fewer altruistic motives, intending to take advantage of the wartime cotton shortage. They planned to purchase the "vacant" plantation lands and to hire the former slaves as cheap labor. In addition to the appeal of potential profits, many whites believed that they could help blacks better adjust to free life by instituting a system of wage labor. While many whites believed that slavery was wrong, they also supposed that slavery had instilled a sense of dependence in blacks. "Giving" blacks the abandoned lands would be equally wrong, they believed, because it would not teach thrift.

Despite protests from blacks, treasury agents sold most of the abandoned land at auction in 1863 and 1864, mostly to government officials, army officers, Northern land speculators, and cotton companies. One Boston company purchased eleven entire plantations. Only by pooling their resources could blacks purchase property; even then, they could only acquire a small percentage of available land.

In January 1865, in the wake of the Emancipation Proclamation, General William T. Sherman issued Special Field Order No. 15, which awarded the remaining unclaimed land on the Sea Islands to freedpeople. Shortly after the end of the Civil War, however, President Andrew Johnson rescinded the order, enabling former plantation owners to reclaim their land and forcing blacks either to work as wage laborers or to leave. Only a few blacks were able to retain the land that they had claimed.

The Port Royal Experiment illustrated the differing, sometimes opposing, conceptions that Northern whites and freedpeople had regarding "freedom" and the government's responsibility toward the former slaves. To former slaves, freedom meant economic independence. To whites, it meant freedom from the master-slave relationship. Many whites considered blacks incapable of living independently—either inherently, or as a result of the debilitations of slavery. The Port Royal Experiment also highlighted how crucial federal support of the freedpeople would be in order for them to succeed in making the transition from slavery to freedom, and it demonstrated, early in the process, how largely indifferent the federal government was to the problems of the former slaves.

See also Emancipation in the United States.

Robert Fay

Portugal

Country in southwestern Europe where blacks have had a presence for centuries.

Black Africans and people of African descent almost certainly came to present-day Portugal with the Romans and Carthaginians toward the end of the first millennium B.C.E., but little record remains of their presence. Likewise, the Muslim occupation (711–1250 C.E.) brought many people of African descent to the region. However, Portugal's modern expansion toward AFRICA dates from the end of the fourteenth century, with the partial occupation of the Canary Islands and the island of Madeira. This expansion had an important sponsor during the fifteenth century in the infante (prince) Dom Henrique (Henry the Navigator). He promoted a number of plunder expeditions led by various noblemen along the western coast of the African continent. In 1444 one of these raids up the SENEGAL RIVER brought a group of black slaves from the area of SENEGAL to Lisbon. As told in Gomes Eanes de Zurara's *History of the Discovery and Conquest of Guinea,* Portugal established a series of outposts, or *feitorías,* both on the coast and the adjacent islands. The first was São Jorge da Mina, later known as Elmina (1482) in present-day GHANA, followed rapidly by Axim (also in Ghana), the CAPE VERDE Islands, and SÃO TOMÉ AND PRÍNCIPE.

The king of Portugal started using the title Lord of Guinea. Arbitration by the pope in 1493 led to a 1494 treaty dividing the world into two spheres of influence: one assigned to SPAIN—which had conquered the Canary Islands—and the other to Portugal. Portugal received all lands east of a north-south line drawn 370 leagues, or roughly 1,790 kilometers (1,110 miles), west of the Cape Verde Islands. This demarcation placed part of BRAZIL and the entire African continent and southern Asia in Portuguese hands. The Portuguese policy of enslavement in Africa was based on the papal bull *Dum diversas* of 1452, which elevated Portuguese raids in West Africa to the equivalent of crusades against infidels and pagans, who could be dispossessed and made perpetual servants of Christian kings. Backed by church policy, the Portuguese exported slaves from Africa, primarily from coastal West Africa, but increasingly also from the coasts of present-day ANGOLA and MOZAMBIQUE. Although most of these slaves were taken to Portuguese colonies in the Atlantic (such as the Cape Verde Islands, São Tomé, or Madeira), or to Brazil, some were brought to Portugal itself.

All sectors of Portuguese society—clergy, nobles, and commoners—owned slaves, though usually only the more affluent could afford them. The nobility used them primarily as domestic servants, and as an external sign of power and prestige, but no group, with the exception of the royal government, possessed large numbers at any point during the fifteenth and sixteenth centuries. At the other end of the spectrum, some black slaves were purchased for employment in undesirable tasks, such as hospital work, then a dangerous occupation due to frequent epidemics.

During the sixteenth century, the Portuguese began to bring enslaved Africans to Portugal in larger numbers. By about 1600, blacks constituted almost 10 percent of the population of Lisbon and parts of the Algarve. There is also abundant evidence of the employment of blacks as crew in ships sailing between Portugal and Africa. Ferrymen carrying passengers across the river Tagus in Lisbon were mostly black. These ferrymen were a source of worry to the authorities, since their control of ferries enabled them to engage in illegal traffic, including the smuggling of escaped slaves.

In Portuguese cities and towns many black slaves—*negros de ganho*—were hired out by their owners to work in agriculture and other industries. In many cases they belonged to noblemen who did not have any means other than the slave labor they hired out. Black slaves who employed themselves outside their masters' homes entered arrangements with their masters to keep part of their earnings and eventually purchase their own freedom, sometimes in installments. Owners often manumitted slaves, especially when slave women bore children fathered by the owner, although former slaves frequently had to serve their owners' families for a set period of time. Several people in a family sometimes inherited a single slave, and this produced the legal case in which an individual was half slave and half free through manumission or self-purchase from one of the owning parties. Clearly, as the Portuguese writer Garcia de Resende put it, a black slave was an excellent investment, since his or her sale in Castile or in the Caribbean islands could double or triple his or her original purchase value.

In the sixteenth century, Portugal was the western European country with the highest percentage of black people, both enslaved and free. Out of a total Portuguese population of slightly over a million, there were around 35,000 blacks by the middle of the sixteenth century, of whom only around 2,000 were free. Migration of whites to India, and also Brazil, made the importation of slave workers a necessity in many cases, but the high prices that African slaves commanded in foreign markets limited their importation to Portugal.

Black Africans in Portugal, both free and enslaved, started organizing church confraternities, such as Our Lady of the Rosary (Nossa Senhora do Rosario) in Lisbon, for mutual help and sometimes to maintain social structures from Africa. These confraternities, or guilds, took part in processions during religious festivals. The processions provided blacks, wearing various forms of African dress, an occasion to show their racial and ethnic pride. The authorities both encouraged and tried to control these organizations, which the rest of the population viewed with suspicion. Black confraternities existed in the main cities: Lisbon, Evora, Elvas, and Lagos. Because of the restrictions blacks faced in Portuguese society, black religious guilds were among the only legal forms of association and organizations to defend the interests of their members.

Religion also created a source of conflict due to the Christian duty to rest on Sundays. Authorities normally made an exception for enslaved blacks, whose domestic work inside their masters' homes was not taken into account. Only their work outside, in which many earned a living for themselves, was subject to the official restrictions. Formal religious life for blacks in Portugal was also beset with difficulties. Black men were barred from the priesthood in general, either because they were slaves or because they were born out of wedlock. The pope granted some exceptions to the second rule, but upon the condition that black priests would limit their activities to other blacks, and mostly outside the Portuguese mainland. In the case of black women, convents only accepted them as slaves to their mistresses, or as lay sisters without the privileges of full vows.

Integration into the larger society was always marred by legal constraints based on principles of *limpeza de sangue,* or blood purity. Free blacks, for instance, were barred from most trades and professions. The guilds of Lisbon and Oporto started passing bans against the admission of blacks, both free and enslaved, as officers in different trades, which consigned them to the trades' lower levels. Black women, on the other hand, had even fewer possibilities for gainful employment, since trade guilds were exclusively male domains. The most lucrative of all forms of self-employment for women was as street vendors, or *regateiras.* Black women sold mostly foodstuffs. They also employed themselves as water sellers, by peddling water in the streets, and as washerwomen, and were considered by the authorities more reliable than free and enslaved Moorish women. Trust in blacks was widespread in general, because their dark skin made it difficult to escape their social condition by flight, a possibility that lay open to lighter-skinned Muslim slaves from North Africa. Nonetheless, records of escapes to Spanish cities such as Seville demonstrate that blacks could find shelter among race brethren in other areas of the Iberian Peninsula. However, the monetary rewards promised by masters for the capture of their escaped slaves made the white population a potential enemy to any escape attempt.

Black slaves fell under court jurisdiction only when their crimes involved people or property outside their masters' household. Punishment for the crime of attempted escape was harsh, including public lashings; the infamous application of the *pingamento* (hot lard poured over the back of the victim), typically reserved for blacks; jail sentences; and sale to a different master or to the king for employment in public works. In most cases, the courts commuted the sentence to lashings or jail in exchange for the payment of a fine by the slave's master. After all, they were dealing with the property of a white Portuguese.

Marriage among blacks in Portugal, although legally possible, was hampered by practical difficulties of all sorts. Interracial marriages were almost impossible, except among free people. More frequent were forced sexual relations between white men and black enslaved women. Most children born to black women in Portugal were extramarital. Few masters owned more than a few slaves, and therefore most slaves lived in separate households belonging to different masters, where they had little opportunity to conclude marriages with other slaves. In some cases the priests themselves were unwilling to perform marriage ceremonies, or the masters themselves were opposed to the union. In any case, the children born to a slave woman always belonged to her master, regardless of the legal status of her husband.

The condition of free blacks in Portugal was in many ways not very different from that of the enslaved ones. Many, after receiving their manumission, still had contractual obligations to their former masters or their families, which they had to fulfill without pay. Finding gainful employment was difficult because of competition from slave laborers and poor whites. Also, prejudice on the part of prospective white employers and numerous legal prohibitions against blacks working in many trades effectively kept almost all blacks on the lowest rungs of the economic ladder.

Portuguese authors like Gil Vicente were the first in Europe to create a stereotype for blacks, both male and female, on stage and in songs and other literary pieces. A stage language called *fala de negro* (black speech) developed and was even exported as a theatrical fashion to neighboring Spain. The practice of staging *entremezes*—one-act intermission pieces between the acts of larger plays—with black comic figures lasted until the end of the nineteenth century. Collections of Renaissance music found in Spain and Portugal also contained many songs that not only reproduced black speech, but clearly reflected the influence of African musical practices, rhythms, and instrumentation. Dances like the *fofa*, developed by blacks in BAHIA in Brazil, became extremely popular in high-society circles during the eighteenth century. AFRO-BRAZILIAN CULTURE was also responsible for the early stages of the *fado*, the national musical composition of Portugal.

In the nineteenth century GREAT BRITAIN pressured Portugal into abolishing the slave trade, and the revolutionary government of 1836 decreed the abolition of the trade in its territories south of the equator. This measure gave rise to an increase in the traffic from coastal West Africa toward Brazil, which had declared independence in 1822. Due to pressure from slave-holding landowners from the Alentejo and Algarve provinces in the south, who succeeded in delaying the measure, the final abolition of slavery in Portugal did not occur until 1877.

In the nineteenth century Portugal had the largest population of African descent in all of Europe, and Lisbon saw the development of a black and mulatto urban population characterized by its economic and social marginalization. They lived mostly in the riverside area, where the men found temporary work as stevedores in the port and in other menial occupations. Meanwhile, black and mulatto women found themselves excluded from attending the fruit and produce markets as vendors, which had been a traditional way of earning their living.

Blacks in Lisbon in the late nineteenth century struggled to preserve traditions of group identity, such as the ritual enthroning of Congo kings and queens, a practice that was still recorded in some white newspapers with a sense of amusement and incomprehension. The revived interest of the Portuguese society and government in the African colonies of Angola and Mozambique relegated the notion of a Portuguese black population to a condition of official nonexistence, especially after the final abolition of slavery on Portuguese territory.

New arrivals of black Africans in Portugal in the twentieth century took place as a result of colonial policies. Immigration of blacks from the African colonies was severely restricted until the 1960s, when international pressure forced the Oliveira Salazar regime to grant the black population of the African colonies equal status with the whites living both in Africa and on the Portuguese mainland. The Portuguese celebrated sports figures such as the soccer superstar Eusebio—originally from Mozambique—who was the star of the Portuguese team in the 1966 World Cup. The new African immigrants living in Portuguese cities faced chronic unemployment and substandard living conditions that the economic crisis of Portugal during the 1970s only worsened. Many of them migrated to other European countries, such as FRANCE, the NETHERLANDS, and even Spain. After the 1974 revolution, provoked by the unresolved colonial war, Portugal granted independence to its African colonies. Since the 1970s Portugal has emulated the model of France and Great Britain in attempting to create a community of Portuguese-speaking peoples, including Brazil and the five new Luso-African republics. Cultural and economic ties between Portugal and its former colonies remain strong.

The flow of migrants from the ex-colonies to Portuguese cities has faced new restrictions with the change in policies after the admission of Portugal to the European Union in 1986. Immigration still continued at this time, however, as Africans from countries other than Portuguese ex-colonies started migrating to the Algarve and Setubal regions, mainly seeking work as agricultural laborers under substandard living conditions. In the 1990s, the Afro-Portuguese population faced an increase in racial violence, including a highly publicized race riot in Lisbon in 1995. Several antiracist organizations mobilized in response to the incidents. In 2000 about 100,000 of Portugal's ten million residents were African immigrants. The lack of economic opportunity for blacks in Portugal has not impeded a high rate of educational achievement, which has increased their social status.

See also Carthage; Dance in Latin America and the Caribbean; Music, African; Transatlantic Slave Trade.

Baltasar Fra-Molinero

Portuguese East Africa

Former name of Mozambique.

See also Mozambique.

Portuguese Guinea

Former name of Guinea-Bissau.

See also Guinea-Bissau.

Portuguese West Africa

Former name of Angola.

See also Angola.

Posey, Cum

1890–1946

African American owner of baseball's Homestead Grays.

Cum Posey was born Cumberland Willis Posey, Jr., in Homestead, Pennsylvania, the son of Cumberland Willis Posey, a businessman, and Anna Stephens, a teacher. The man who made people think about the river town of Homestead for something other than its steel mills and the epic labor confrontation of 1892 was the son of one of black PITTSBURGH's most prominent and wealthy men. Captain Cumberland Posey, Sr., was a riverboat engineer who turned to shipbuilding and later coal mining and real estate. The president of the *Pittsburgh Courier* newspaper, the prestigious Loendi Club, and the Warren Methodist Episcopal Church, the elder Posey bequeathed to his son access to "respectable" black Pittsburgh.

But young Cum gravitated to the sporting scene in the Hill, Pittsburgh's principal ghetto, where he often played for "roughneck" teams against those representing black Pittsburgh's upper crust. After graduating Homestead High School, where he starred in basketball, Cum played at both Holy Ghost College (later renamed Duquesne University) and Penn State. His acceptance was made easier by his light complexion and athletic prowess. At Holy Ghost, he enrolled as Charles W. Cumbert and passed for a white student.

After leaving college, Posey not only joined the Homestead Grays as an outfielder in 1911, but began forming semipro basketball teams. He promoted and starred for the Monticellos and the Loendi Club through the 1920s. Playing both white and black teams from across the nation, Posey's basketball clubs were considered the informal national champions by the black press. *Courier* sportswriter Wendell Smith called the 5'9", 140-pound Posey "the outstanding athlete of the Negro race" during the late 1920s, "perhaps the most colorful figure who has ever raced down the sundown sports trail."

Posey, who married Ethel Truman in 1913 and had five daughters with her, worked as a clerk for the Railway Mail Service until 1920. He divided his time between work and sport, finally opting to focus on sports. By 1917, he was managing and promoting the Homestead Grays. He and Charles Walker were the club's co-owners by the early 1920s, and while Walker handled gate receipts and concessions Posey selected players and booked games. Together they made the club into a profitable business venture by the mid-1920s. Posey recruited some of the best black players in the Americas, including SMOKEY JOE WILLIAMS, Martin Dihigo, Sam Streeter, and Vic Harris, to play alongside the Grays' core of local talent. Posey played for the Grays until 1928 and managed the squad until 1935. Although considered a valuable player, he drew the most praise for his managerial and promotional expertise. Eddie Gottlieb, who owned the Philadelphia Stars of the Negro National League, said: "As a manager and promoter, Cum Posey was one of the greatest baseball men I ever met."

During the 1925 and 1926 seasons, the Grays' record was 232 wins, 29 losses, and 11 ties, with a stretch of 43 consecutive victories. Although most of their games were against white and black semipro teams, the Grays defeated Negro National League clubs as well as teams of white major leaguers in postseason exhibitions.

By 1930, with the addition of future Hall of Famers OSCAR CHARLESTON, Judy Johnson, and JOSH GIBSON, the Grays were considered black baseball's best team. They beat the Lincoln Giants for the Negro championship that fall. But Posey soon lost Gibson, Charleston, Johnson, and other key players to crosstown rival Gus Greenlee, who had made a pro team out of the sandlot Crawfords. The Grays suffered both on the field and at the gate, and Posey turned to Homestead numbers banker Rufus "Sonnyman" Jackson, who helped keep the club afloat financially. The numbers, a lottery in which bettors wager that the three-digit number they select will be the one that "hits" that day, was the largest black-controlled business in the country at that time, and many a Negro League team depended on its revenues to keep afloat.

Posey joined the Negro National League in 1935 and rebuilt the Grays after the Pittsburgh Crawfords' collapse in 1937. With the return of Gibson and the emergence of first baseman Buck Leonard, the Grays had the black equivalents of Babe Ruth and Lou Gehrig. The Grays won an unprecedented nine straight Negro National League pennants from 1937 through 1945 as well as the 1948 Negro World Series, the last ever played.

Posey was widely respected in the sporting world. His players usually accepted a handshake as confirmation of a deal. Former Pittsburgh Steelers' owner Art Rooney, who played against Posey on the sandlots, said that Posey had "a knack of persuasion . . . he always knew when to be hard and when to be compassionate. He was one of the smartest men I knew."

During the late 1930s and WORLD WAR II, Posey booked three games a week for his team at Griffith Stadium in WASHINGTON, D.C., where the Grays frequently outdrew the hapless Senators. Black baseball had become the nation's second largest legal black-owned enterprise, behind only the black insurance companies. While not the wealthiest black owner, Posey was a key figure in league decisions.

Posey wrote a weekly column, "The Sportive Realm," for the *Pittsburgh Courier* in the 1930s and 1940s and used it to critique league policies and attack the influence of white booking agents over black baseball. He also served as the Negro National League secretary and was a member of the Homestead school board.

Although black baseball's prospects seemed bright in the mid-1940s, the postwar integration of the major leagues brought the end of the NEGRO LEAGUES. Posey protested that major league teams were signing his best players, usually without compensation, but he did not live to witness JACKIE ROBINSON's 1947 debut. He died of lung cancer.

Courier writer John L. Clark wrote: "In his death, the race lost one of its most dynamic citizens, baseball lost its best mind . . . Homestead lost its most loyal booster." The Grays played a few more seasons, but folded in 1950. Posey was the principal architect of sport in black Pittsburgh. A fine athlete who starred in basketball and baseball, he transformed a team of steelworkers into black baseball's premier club. Posey not only fielded a team that could contend with white all-star opponents, he put black baseball on a more solid financial and organizational footing.

Bibliography

Peterson, Robert. *Only the Ball Was White*. 1970

Ruck, Rob. *Sandlot Seasons: Sport in Black Pittsburgh*. 1987.

Tygiel, Jules. *Baseball's Great Experiment: Jackie Robinson and His Legacy*. 1983.

From *American National Biography*. John A. Garraty and Mark C. Carnes, eds. Oxford University Press, 1999. Reprinted by permission of the American Council of Learned Societies.

Rob Ruck

Poujol-Oriol, Paulette

1926–

One of the best-known literary personalities in Haiti, who blends the French language with Creole imagery.

Paulette Poujol-Oriol's writing is a testimony to the aspirations and intellectual resiliency of an elite that is often dismissed for its arrogance and condescension toward Haiti's majority peasant class. Her contribution to literary expression lies in connecting the faintly pulsating white roots of the old aristocracy to the rhythm of the black populace through a language of proverbs, folktales, and music. Poujol-Oriol's writing explores potential means by which to effect a cultural reconciliation of Haitian society, which has been historically divided along racial lines.

Born in PORT-AU-PRINCE, HAITI, Poujol-Oriol started her career at the École Normale as a student of literature and business administration. She was the director of studies there for eight years, and taught French literature, history of theater, and dramatic arts. She also founded a theater school for the young. Poujol-Oriol has frequently participated in radio and television projects, while remaining a most active member of the National Society of Dramatic Art. She has contributed to many literary and political magazines. In 1996 she joined the Deschamps Prize jury, and worked for the International Academy for Peace as an advocate for Haitian women's rights.

Poujol-Oriol is active with "La ligue féminine d'action sociale, the first women's organization in Haiti, which has been responsible since l934 for promoting and defending the rights of women of all social strata. Under her direction, its members have labored to enhance women's workplace skills in the fields of education, nursing, and child care.

Poujol-Oriol is best known for her creative literary expression, which she adeptly and subtly manipulates to disseminate important social commentary. In her work she has remained an outspoken voice of opposition against successive dictatorial regimes. In her fiction she denounces governmental abuses and uses her poetic verve to sanction an assassination or to commemorate a notorious death, as, for example, in the poem, "Prières pour deux anges envolés" (Prayers for Two Vanished Angels).

Poujol-Oriol's novels, such as the internationally acclaimed *Le creuset* (The Crucible), for which she received the Henri Deschamps Award in l980, convey a compassionate and moving portrayal of the Haitian search for an ancestral identity built on the power of myths. This novel shows a slice of life in Haiti in which questions are posed in French and answered in CREOLE. *Domestiques,* or maids, share their wisdom with the anguished aristocrats, and past history is relived in the present. Among her other works are the novel *Le Passage* (1996) and such well-known short stories as "La Fleur Rouge" and "Oresca."

Poujol-Oriol's originality stems from an ability to consider, from a position of privilege, the crossing of cultures (*métissage*) that have dissolved themselves in a diasporic blend of Indian, Spanish, French, and African influences. Though a member of the bourgeoisie in a country where the vast majority of the population is illiterate, Poujol-Oriol has kept her writing free of the exotic European wrappings that characterized many other Haitian writers of her generation who had composed abroad.

See also Literature, French-Language, in the Caribbean.

Paulette Smith

Poussaint, Alvin Francis

1934–

American psychiatrist and educator, who does pioneering research on African American–related psychological and social issues.

Alvin Poussaint was born in East HARLEM, New York City, and attended Stuyvesant High School. He received his B.A. from Columbia College in 1956 and an M.D. from Cornell University Medical School in 1960. From 1964 to 1965, he received postgraduate training at the University of California's Neuropsychiatric Institute.

From 1965 to 1967, Poussaint was employed by the Medical Committee for Human Rights in Jackson, Mississippi, where he provided medical care to workers in the CIVIL RIGHTS MOVEMENT and helped desegregate Southern health facilities. He taught at Tufts Medical School from 1965 to 1969 and then at Harvard Medical School. In 1971 he joined the Reverend JESSE JACKSON's OPERATION PUSH (People United to Save Humanity) and served as one of Jackson's advisers in the 1984 presidential campaign. Poussaint was a consultant for *The Cosby Show* from 1984 to 1992 and *A Different World* from 1986 to 1993. He read scripts to ensure that the two television series presented positive images of blacks. Poussaint became a professor of psychiatry and an associate dean at the Harvard Medical School in 1993.

Alvin Poussaint has researched and written about such topics as the psychological and social adjustments of children of interracial marriages and the impact of racism on the psychological development of blacks. He is the author *Why Blacks Kill Blacks* (1972) and the coauthor with James P. Comer of *Raising Black Children* (1992), originally titled *Black Child Care* [1975]). His book *Lay My Burden Down: Unraveling Suicide and the Mental Health Crisis among African Americans* (2000), cowritten with Amy Alexander, addresses the causes and effects of the dramatic increase in suicide rates among black youths since 1980—a rise of 114 percent.

See also Television and African Americans.

Aaron Myers

Poverty in the United States

Strongly correlated with race because of a variety of factors.

See also Work, African Americans and the Changing Nature of, in the Post–World War II Era: An Interpretation.

Powell, Adam Clayton, Jr.

1908–1972

American congressman and minister, one of the most vocal and flamboyant black campaigners for civil rights.

Adam Clayton Powell, Jr., was born in New Haven, Connecticut, and grew up in HARLEM, NEW YORK, where his father was the minister of the Abyssinian Baptist Church, one of the largest congregations in the nation. After a poor academic performance at the City College of New York, Powell attended Colgate University in Hamilton, New York. Light-skinned enough to pass as white, he did so. Upon learning that Powell was black, both the white students among whom Powell had tried to live and the black students whose ethnicity he had rejected were angered.

After graduation, Powell helped in his father's church and briefly attended Union Theological Seminary. He went on to earn a master's degree in religious education from Columbia University and continued to assist his father until 1937, when ADAM CLAYTON POWELL SR. retired and Adam Jr. became pastor of Abyssinian. During this time, Powell maintained a high-profile lifestyle noted for its luxury and associations with the rich and famous.

Asked by the *New York Post* to comment on the HARLEM RIOT OF 1935, he obliged with a scathing attack on discrimination and police brutality. These articles led to a regular "Soap Box" column in the New York AMSTERDAM NEWS and later in the *People's Voice,* which Powell cofounded and published from 1942 to 1946. He also used the pulpit to spur political action. Through marches to city hall and Harlem Hospital, he protested discrimination in hiring and services. He also led the "Don't Buy Where You Can't Work" campaign against NEW YORK's stores; this campaign proved successful in breaking hiring barriers. His pressure on utility companies and a highly effective strike against New York City buses resulted in quotas for the hiring of black employees.

In 1941 Powell won a city council seat as an independent. He continued to challenge discrimination, particularly in New York's public schools, occasionally irritating even reformist mayor Fiorello LaGuardia. In 1943 a new congressional district was established in Harlem that would almost certainly produce the state's first black congressperson. Powell undertook an ambitious campaign for the seat, winning the support of Democrats (on whose ticket he ran), Republicans, and Communists. In 1945 he became the second of the only two black members of Congress.

Adam Clayton Powell speaks at a rally in Harlem in 1963 urging blacks to "work together and fight together." *Bettman/CORBIS*

In his first year, Powell denounced first lady Bess Truman for her affiliation with the Daughters of the American Revolution, which then had racially discriminatory policies. President Harry S. Truman was outraged, and Powell fell out of favor with the White House. Relegated to a marginal role in legislation, Powell pressed his campaign where he could, personally demanding to be served by discriminatory Washington businesses and campaigning to have black journalists admitted to the press galleries. Powell ended segregation in congressional service facilities and challenged congressional representatives who used the word *nigger* on the House floor. He also repeatedly tried to pass what became known as the Powell Amendment, which would have denied funding to institutions that practiced racial discrimination.

In the 1956 presidential election, Powell infuriated his party by supporting Republican Dwight D. Eisenhower, whom he saw as mildly progressive on civil rights. However, in 1960 Powell campaigned ardently for Democrat John F. Kennedy, bringing with him many of the black votes that had gone to Eisenhower in 1956. Kennedy's narrow victory coincided with Powell's rise to the position of chairman of the House Committee on Education and Labor—the first time an African American chaired such a powerful committee. Powell was instrumental in passing much of the progressive legislation enacted in the 1960s, including increases to the minimum wage, protection of civil rights, and the creation of Medicare, Medicaid, and Head Start. A version of the Powell Amendment was finally codified in the landmark Civil Rights Act of 1964.

At the same time that Powell's power was growing, his support was being drained by accusations and scandals. The most serious of these emerged in the early 1950s, when several of Powell's aides were convicted of income tax evasion and rumors circulated that they had also given him kickbacks from their salary. Powell was indicted for tax evasion in 1958, but his trial resulted in a hung jury and the Department of Justice declined to retry him. In 1960 Powell was again embroiled when he accused a constituent of being a "bag woman," someone who carried payoffs to police from illegal gambling rackets. The constituent sued for libel and won a large judgment against Powell, who refused to honor the court's decision and its warrants. The case dragged on for years before Powell agreed to settle. Powell also received negative publicity for his many absences from Congress and for his personal extravagances.

In 1966 a House committee found that Powell had improperly placed his wife on his committee's payroll and vacationed at committee expense in EUROPE and THE BAHAMAS. Powell maintained he was doing neither more nor less than his colleagues and was being held to a racist double standard. In a vote following the November 1966 elections, the House denied to seat Powell. He challenged the vote, and in 1969 the U.S. Supreme Court held that although Congress could expel a member, it could not deny seating someone duly elected. Powell was finally seated after an absence of two years, but without his seniority and with his pay docked to pay for financial abuses. In 1970 CHARLES RANGEL emerged from a field of several Democratic challengers to defeat him.

See also Clergy in Politics; United States House of Representatives, African Americans in the.

Bibliography
Hamilton, Charles V. *Adam Clayton Powell, Jr.: The Political Biography of an American Dilemma.* Atheneum, 1991.

Haygood, Wil. *King of the Cats: The Life and Times of Adam Clayton Powell, Jr.* Houghton Mifflin, 1993.

Powell, Adam Clayton, Sr.
1865–1953

Baptist minister, father of U.S. Representative Adam Clayton Powell, Jr.

Adam Clayton Powell, Sr., worked as a sharecropper and a miner before becoming a Baptist minister in 1892. In 1908, he assumed leadership of the Abyssinian Baptist Church, NEW YORK CITY's oldest black Baptist church. As pastor, Powell expanded both the scope of the church's involvement in the community and the size of its membership. By the time of his retirement in 1937, the congregation was the largest of any Protestant church in the United States. Powell's ministry was succeeded by that of his son, ADAM CLAYTON POWELL, JR., and he spent the rest of his life writing three books and working for civil rights.

See also Baptists.

Lawrie Balfour

Powell, Colin Luther
1937–

United States military leader and secretary of state under President George W. Bush.

When George Walker Herbert Bush was president of the United States, he appointed General Colin Powell chairman of the Joint Chiefs of Staff. Powell's strong leadership role during the Persian Gulf War in 1991 gained him immense popularity.

Military Life

A first-generation American, Colin Powell was born to Jamaican immigrant parents in HARLEM, NEW YORK. The family relocated to the Bronx when Powell was a young child. After graduating from Morris High School in 1954, Powell earned a degree from the City College of New York, where he joined the Reserve Officers Training Corps (ROTC). His academic career was unremarkable, but his experience in the ROTC proved fruitful. He gained the highest rank achievable, cadet colonel, and when he graduated in 1958, he was appointed second lieutenant in the United States Army. Powell received his military training at Fort Benning, Georgia.

His first posting was to West Germany, where he remained for two years, followed by a two-year period in Massachusetts. He met and married Alma Vivian Johnson, a young speech pathologist, in 1962. The couple have three children—Michael, Linda, and Anne Marie. Powell, then a captain, was stationed in Vietnam just months after his marriage. He received the Purple Heart after being injured by a booby trap set by the Viet Cong. Powell returned to the United States in 1963 and moved back to Fort Benning, where he studied and worked as an instructor at the Infantry School.

Moving up through the ranks of the military, Powell became a major in 1966. The highlight of the period was his impressive performance at the United States Army Command and General Staff College, where he distinguished himself by graduating second in his class. He was sent back to Vietnam in 1968 to work under General Charles Gettys. Once again, Powell was wounded, this time in a helicopter accident. Despite his injuries, he saved other servicemen from the burning site of the crash, which earned him his second Purple Heart and a Soldier's Medal.

Political Appointments

On his return from Vietnam in 1969, Powell received a promotion to lieutenant colonel. He earned an M.B.A. degree from George Washington University in 1971. A year later, he received his first political appointment as a White House fellow, assigned to work in the Office of Management and Budget (OMB), under the administration of President Richard Nixon. His tenure at the OMB afforded him the opportunity to work with OMB director Caspar Weinberger and deputy director Frank Carlucci. Both men held Powell in high esteem, and in later years figured prominently in his political advancement.

Capitalizing on Powell's reputation as a troubleshooter, the army assigned him to command an infantry battalion in South Korea, plagued by drug abuse and racial tensions that threatened its effectiveness. The following year he was stationed in the United States, working in the Pentagon. In rapid succession he enrolled in a nine-month program at the National War College, was made a full colonel, and in 1976 was assigned to lead the 2nd Brigade of the 101st Airborne Division at Fort Campbell, Kentucky. Powell returned to the Pentagon in 1977, although not for long. By 1979 he had been promoted to brigadier general and worked briefly as an aide to Charles Duncan, secretary of the Department of Energy.

National Security Council and Joint Chiefs of Staff

Powell's professional rise continued through the 1980s. In 1981 he took on a military assignment, commanding the 4th Infantry Division at Fort Carson, Colorado. Secretary of Defense Caspar Weinberger, Powell's former superior at the OMB, then appointed him senior military assistant. His job was to act as a bridge between the Pentagon and the White House—a role in which he excelled. By mid-1986 Powell had been promoted to lieutenant general, commanding the 5th Corps in Frankfurt, Germany. The Iran-Contra debacle and ensuing restructuring in Washington resulted in Frank Carlucci's appointment as national security adviser. Carlucci requested that Powell be recalled to Washington as his deputy, and although initially hesitant, Powell agreed. Carlucci was appointed secretary of defense in 1987, and Powell received a corresponding promotion to national security adviser. In this position, Powell advocated a strong military budget but opposed the heavy spending on the space-based Strategic Defense Initiative (nicknamed Star Wars). He served as national security adviser until President Ronald Reagan's term ended in January 1989. Three months later Powell became a four-star general.

Powell continued to distinguish himself in diplomatic and military coups, arranging groundbreaking meetings between Reagan and the then leader of the Union of Soviet Socialist Republics (USSR), Mikhail Gorbachev. In recognition of his efforts, President George Herbert Walker Bush appointed Powell chairman of the Joint Chiefs of Staff in 1989. His installation was a double triumph—he was both the youngest person and the first African American appointed to the highest rank in the military.

Early in his term, Powell received President Bush's plan to invade PANAMA and overthrow General Manuel Noriega. Powell reportedly counseled against the invasion, but when Bush chose to proceed, Powell planned the successful assault, which sent 25,000 U.S. troops to Panama in December 1989.

After Iraq invaded Kuwait in August 1990, leading to the outbreak of the PERSIAN GULF WAR (1991), Powell coordinated a successful ground strategy with General Norman Schwarzkopf. The effective military strategy of that campaign gained Powell general approval from the American public. His capable and comforting demeanor proved an added bonus at a time when television was the public's principal source of information on the state of the war. Bush reappointed Powell chairman of the Joint Chiefs of Staff in 1991. During this time, Powell dealt with regional crises in SOMALIA and the former Yugoslavia, but had little success in guiding the administration to a clear policy in either war zone.

In 1992 the American people elected Bill Clinton to be president. Living up to a campaign promise, Clinton explored measures to end the ban on homosexuals in the military. Powell opposed the proposal, and it was largely through his efforts that the watered down "don't ask, don't tell" policy was established, whereby homosexuals were allowed to serve in the armed forces as long as they did not reveal their sexual orientation. Clinton and Powell also disagreed over Clinton's proposal to drastically cut the military budget.

In September of 1993 Colin Powell retired from the military, adding to growing national speculation that he intended to run for president against Clinton in 1996. Powell said little to refute the rumors, concentrating instead on promoting his autobiography, *My American Journey* (1995). At the end of the book tour, Powell announced that he would not seek the presidency, and he retired to private life.

Secretary of State

Powell emerged from retirement after George W. Bush won the presidential election of 2000 and appointed him secretary of state. In that position, Powell has been responsible for overseeing the State Department and for conducting United States foreign policy under the direction of the president. At his confirmation hearing, Powell stated that his policy is guided by the principle that "America stands ready to help any country that wishes to join the democratic world."

Powell's tenure at the State Department has been fraught with serious challenges since the terrorist attacks in New York City and Washington, D.C. on September 11, 2001. Following the attacks, the United States launched air strikes against the al-Qaeda network in Afghanistan. The following year, Powell appeared before the United Nations (UN) to argue the American case for a war against Iraq, which was said to be violating numerous UN resolutions regarding banned weapons. Despite Powell's eloquence, the United States failed to win UN support for a preemptive invasion. The subsequent failure to find weapons of mass destruction diminished international regard for Powell.

In addition to the Iraq War, Colin Powell faced threats that Iran and North Korea had developed the capacity to build nuclear weapons. Continued violence between Palestinians and Israel also remained a matter of serious concern. Despite these challenges, Powell could cite several foreign policy successes, including a global fund to combat HIV/AIDS and the liberation of Afghanistan from Taliban control, as well as improved relations with Russia and China.

See also Military, Blacks in the American; Vietnam War.

Powell, Earl ("Bud")

1924–1966

American jazz pianist, often regarded as the most important bebop pianist of the 1940s.

Born in NEW YORK, NEW YORK, Earl "Bud" Powell began playing at Minton's Playhouse in New York in 1940 and became a student of THELONIUS MONK. From 1942 to 1944 he frequently played with his other mentor, Cootie Williams. Under their guidance he developed his distinctive style and made a significant impact on the piano playing of the emerging BEBOP movement. Mike Baillie has written of Powell that "his total emotional commitment, at times quite ferocious, with an unrelenting sense of urgency . . . comes through on every recording he ever made." Powell, in the trio format, and in other small groups, played with such jazz greats as DIZZY GILLESPIE, CHARLIE PARKER, and MAX ROACH. Among his better known compositions are *Hallucinations,* recorded by MILES DAVIS as *Budo, Dance of the Infidels, Tempus Fugue-it,* and *Bouncing with Bud.*

Powell suffered a head injury in 1945 from a racial incident, after which he experienced several nervous breakdowns. His composition *The Glass Enclosure* is a musical expression of his numerous stays in mental institutions. His playing appearances began to decline in the late 1940s.

In 1959 Powell moved to Paris, where he led a trio with Kenny Clarke until 1962. There he enjoyed a brief renewal of his celebrity status. He returned to America in 1964. After performing a poorly received concert at Carnegie Hall in 1965, he abandoned music altogether.

See also Music, African American.

Pozo y González, Luciano (Chano)

1915–1948

Afro-Cuban conga drummer who helped create Afro-Latin jazz during the 1940s.

Luciano "Chano" Pozo y Gonzales, better known as Chano Pozo, played a seminal role in the founding of AFRO-LATIN JAZZ during the 1940s. Afro-Latin jazz combined Cuban rhythms and song forms with African American JAZZ improvisation and complex, bop-derived harmonies. Cuban jazz trumpeter MARIO BAUZÁ—a pioneering Afro-Latin jazz musician—brought Pozo to NEW YORK in May 1946 and in the following year recommended him to DIZZY GILLESPIE, who wanted a conga drummer for his big band. Pozo had learned to play the conga drum in CUBA through his involvement in an Abakuá secret society. One of his first jazz performances took place at New York City's Carnegie Hall on September 17, 1947, shortly after he joined Gillespie's band.

Pozo was featured on the extended composition "Cubana Be, Cubana Bop," also known as the "Afro-Cuban Suite." Pozo's percussion work was electrifying, and over the succeeding months, Gillespie added more Latin-inspired numbers including "Algo Bueno," also known as "Woody 'n You" (1947), in order to feature his conga drummer. Although Pozo could not read music, he created or co-composed several key examples of Afro-Latin jazz, including "Manteca" (1947), recorded by the Gillespie big-band, and "Tin Tin Deo" (1948), first recorded by a nine-man group under the leadership of saxophonist James Moody.

Pozo's musical career was cut short by his hot temper. Bassist Al McKibbon, who played alongside him in Gillespie's big band, recalled that "Chano was a hoodlum . . . a rough character." He was killed just one month short of his thirty-fourth birthday in the Rio Café, a bar in Spanish Harlem. Nonetheless, his legacy endured in the playing of such Afro-Latin *congeros* as Louis "Sabu" Martinez, his successor in Gillespie's band; MONGO SANTAMARÍA; and Cándido Camero.

See also Abakuás; Music, Afro-Cuban; Percussion Instruments of the Caribbean.

James Sellman

Prata, Luis Sebastiao

See Grande Otelo.

Preciado Bedoya, Antonio

1941–

Afro-Ecuadorian writer.

Antonio Preciado Bedoya was born in the ESMERALDAS, a province on the northern coast of ECUADOR. He grew up with his mother, who was a *lavandera,* a laundrywoman, for other families. Thanks to his academic achievement at school, he was able to finish his high school education and later to graduate from a local university. In addition to his work as a poet, for many years Preciado Bedoya has also been the director of the cultural center and the historical archives of the Banco Central del Ecuador in Esmeraldas, where he also served as the director of the Universidad Luis Vargas Torres.

Preciado Bedoya followed in the footsteps of two other famous Esmeraldian writers, NELSON ESTUPIÑÁN BASS and ADAL-

BERTO ORTIZ. He was influenced by international literary currents of the time, such as AFROCUBANISMO and magical realism, and composed *negrista* poems using black people and Afro-Esmeraldian cultural traditions as his primary material. Many believe that the quality of his poetry has surpassed the composition of his two celebrated predecessors. Preciado's work has been lauded for its use of subtle rhythms in the production of meaning. In "Matábara del hombre malo" (Matábara of the bad man) he writes:

¡Atabé! ¡Atabé! ¡Ururé! ¡Matábara!

Tengo una hoguera de estrellas, de las estrellas más altas, y un lugar en plena luna para que arda. La claridad crece y crece con fuerza de cien mañanas . . . Cátala catún balé, catún balé caté cátala.

("I have a bonfire of stars, of the highest stars and a place in broad moonlight where it can burn.

The brightness grows and grows with the strength of one hundred mornings.")

See also Carpentier, Alejo; Guillén, Nicolás; Negrista Poets.

Bibliography

Hidalgo Alzamora, Laura. "Del ritmo al concepto en la poesía de Preciado." *Cultura, Revista del Banco Central del Ecuador* 3, no.7 (Mayo-Agosto 1980): 102–119.

Jackson, Richard L. *Black Writers in Latin America.* University of New Mexico Press, 1979.

Preciado, Antonio. *Tal como somos.* Ediciones Siglo 20, 1966.

Jean Mutaba Rahier

Présence Africaine

Influential journal produced in Paris after World War II by African intellectuals as part of the movement known as Négritude

Born amid the intellectual tumult shaking post–World War II Paris, *Présence Africaine* has had greater influence on politics and culture than most intellectual journals. It has revolutionized European thought on African culture and helped launch the literary and political careers of several prominent Africans.

After the war a debate emerged in FRANCE over the role of the empire and the fate of the French colonies. In addition, Paris had a sizable population of students and intellectuals from various colonies, including Africans and West Indians, and their opposition to the colonial system had been gaining sympathy among French intellectuals. After the war anticolonial ideas became increasingly mainstream. The wartime experience of Nazi repression had increased the attraction of SOCIALISM and liberalism, and allied opposition to Nazi tyranny made it more difficult for many French to justify undemocratic COLONIAL RULE.

When it first appeared in Paris in 1947, *Présence Africaine* had the effect of a match lit in a room full of gas. *Présence Africaine* changed forever the French and, later, European perception of AFRICA—of its people and culture. It provided intellectual backing for the eventual independence of the former French colonies as well as an influential forum for African writers. It gave a vital boost to French-language African literature.

Senegalese writer ALIOUNE DIOP founded *Présence Africaine* to promote NÉGRITUDE, an intellectual movement that explored the cultural and political ties connecting Africans and people of African descent in the diaspora. Négritude also sought recognition for the achievements of African civilization. The publication did not attack French or European culture per se, but it did challenge the moral and intellectual bases of colonialism and racism. Diop announced three goals for the journal: to publish studies on African culture; to examine ways to integrate Africans into the Western world; and to review art and other topics relevant to Africans and people of African descent. In 1949 Diop founded Présence Africaine Editions, a publishing house for African authors.

Although *Présence Africaine* would remain true to the Pan-Africanist ideal of uniting Africans and their descendants throughout the world, the publication focused primarily on Africa. This choice was partly a response to the newspaper *L'Étudiant Noir*, founded in Paris in the 1930s by the Senegalese LÉOPOLD SÉDAR SENGHOR and AIMÉ CÉSAIRE, from MARTINIQUE, which had adopted a Caribbean focus. Senghor, however, gave his enthusiastic blessing to *Présence Africaine,* calling it "the primary instrument of the Négritude movement." Senghor and Césaire contributed to the 196-page first issue, as did many of the leading French intellectuals of the time, including Jean-Paul Sartre and André Gide. ALBERT CAMUS, who was born and raised in ALGERIA, served on the committee supporting *Présence Africaine.*

Although it began as a monthly, *Présence Africaine* later appeared as a quarterly. Over the years, the journal has tackled topics ranging from France's relationship with its former colonies to the African presence in HAITI and BRAZIL. *Présence Africaine* continues to publish new issues.

See also Decolonization in Africa: An Interpretation; Literature, French-Language, in Africa; Pan-Africanism.

David P. Johnson, Jr.

Press, African

Newspapers and magazines that chronicle events in Africa and are written, edited, and published by Africans.

For information about
African journalism: *See Présence Africaine*; Radio, African.
African journalists: *See* Armah, Ayi Kwei; Azikiwe, Nnamdi; Clark, John Pepper; Diop, Alioune; Hunkanrin, Louis; Plaatje, Solomon Tshekisho.

Press, Black, in Latin America and the Caribbean

Newspapers and magazines that chronicle political, social, and cultural events of communities of people of African descent in Latin America and the Caribbean; also refers to publishers of books, especially poetry collections, by writers of African descent.

The black press did not become established until the early nineteenth century in LATIN AMERICA and the Caribbean. This was due to the oppressive system of slavery and to extremely high illiteracy rates. Indeed, learning to read and write was a punishable offense under some slave codes. Even after abolition, blacks and mulattoes (persons of African and European descent) encountered numerous obstacles to opportunities that involved writing, such as exclusion from higher education. Many of the most celebrated early black poets and journalists were largely self-taught. Those who did publish before the nineteenth century—notably Rosa María Egipcíaca da Vera Cruz in BRAZIL and JOSÉ MANUEL VALDÉS in PERU—were exceptions to the rule.

Materials published by the black community during the nineteenth century included abolitionist pamphlets, chapbooks, newspapers, and periodicals. During most of the century romanticism was the predominant literary ethos, and poetry was the genre of choice in newspapers and magazines. Chapbooks, a type of small, inexpensive book, were used to record improvised verse, such as the *desafios* of Brazil and the *payadas* of ARGENTINA. (Derived from African oral traditions, both are duel-like exchanges that are sung back and forth to guitar accompaniment.) Early black newspapers and periodicals were generally numerous but short-lived. During the twentieth century Pan-African cultural and political movements fueled the publication of periodicals and books directed to a black public. In the French-speaking Caribbean, for instance, tomes of poetry began to be published in the late 1930s as part of the NÉGRITUDE movement, an intellectual and artistic movement that rejected French colonialism and cultural hegemony in favor of a revalorization of the African heritage of Caribbean peoples.

During the nineteenth century many black and mulatto poets earned their living through journalism. Some of the best-known writers, whether poets or journalists or both, often participated in the black press as well as in the broader national or even international presses. Many of these writers, such as Brazilian novelist JOAQUIM MARIA MACHADO DE ASSIS and Brazilian poet AFONSO HENRIQUES DE LIMA BARRETO, did not express a color consciousness or claim any affiliation with a black community, whose cultural expressions lacked literary prestige in the eyes of the white elite. Others, such as Brazilian writer LUÍS GONZAGA PINTO DA GAMA, expressed abolitionist views in both their editorial columns and their poetry. In his social satire poetry, Gama went so far as to criticize his mulatto compatriots for aspiring to European ideals and ignoring their black brethren in bondage.

The indifference to black consciousness on the part of many blacks and mulattos in Latin America and the Caribbean was in many ways a reaction to the rhetoric of WHITENING, or *mestizaje* (whereby racial mixing with whites, it was alleged, would eventually eliminate signs of an African racial heritage in the population). In some Latin American countries, such as Brazil and VENEZUELA, the colonial-era obsession with *castas* (racial groupings based on phenotype, or physical characteristics) translated into immigrant initiatives designed to whiten the population. After the independence struggles of the early nineteenth century in Brazil and the Spanish colonies (except in CUBA and PUERTO RICO, which remained Spanish colonies until 1898), some of the new Latin American nations actively promoted such programs. Despite the overwhelming participation of blacks in military campaigns, the ruling white elite did not consider them an integral part of the new nations.

Afro–Latin Americans often remained unacknowledged as citizens of their respective nations in the mainstream media, which continued to refer to them as either Africans or former slaves. Furthermore, any attempt by Afro–Latin Americans to confront their relative invisibility—that is, the absence of a visible black political, social, and cultural presence in public life—by identifying in print with their African heritage was seen by whites as a denial of nationalistic fervor. To identify with one's African heritage, especially for mulattos, was to reject the social and economic promises of whitening. Given this emphasis on national over racial identity in Latin America and the Caribbean, many people of African descent willingly began to incorporate themselves into a national fabric that did not acknowledge their racial heritage. For this reason, the black press in Latin America and the Caribbean often includes not only material produced by black and mulatto authors that is aimed exclusively at a black audience, but also material intended for the general public.

For purposes of comparison, this overview primarily focuses on the black press in Cuba, Brazil, and ARGENTINA. Cuba had the most extensive black press (including literary, cultural, and political periodicals and pamphlets) in Latin America and the Caribbean during the nineteenth century. An active and diversified black press also existed in Brazil. A large proportion of the populations of these two countries was and continues to be of African descent. By contrast, Argentina is a prime example of a South American country where a thriving black press existed during the nineteenth century but where the black community has since nearly disappeared, due in part to government-sponsored campaigns to promote European immigration.

Black Writers, Abolitionism, and Independence During the Nineteenth Century

Prior to the abolition of SLAVERY IN LATIN AMERICA AND THE CARIBBEAN, black publications were authored and published mainly by free people of color. Free mulattos, especially those of the educated mulatto elite in urban areas, were the most likely to engage in publishing. As a social class, free persons were generally economically weak and politically marginal, though this varied from country to country. The black press was a way for them to establish a means of communication and to assert their own identities. For the most part, however, slaves and free persons respected traditional literary forms and generally referred only euphemistically to their bondage and precarious social positions. In his book *Black Writers in Latin America* (1979), Richard Jackson, a scholar of Afro–Latin American literature, interprets this self-subversion as a way of achieving some distance from the enslaved classes, in keeping with the rhetoric of mestizaje and a strictly European aesthetic perspective.

In Cuba an extensive black press existed during the nineteenth century, both before and after abolition in 1886, and a high degree of black consciousness was evident. Here as elsewhere, the black press was primarily an endeavor of free persons; however, a notable exception was the publication in 1840 of the slave narrative of Juan Francisco Manzano. The narrative, which was the first published autobiographical account of black slavery in Spanish America, was produced at the request of the Cuban literary aficionado Domingo del Monte, who closely guarded its content. The narrative was careful to portray a meek, humble image of a slave, although it was intended for a liberal, white abolitionist audience (its first publication was in English).

Widespread political repression of Afro-Cubans, both free and enslaved, took place after the 1844 Conspiración de la Escalera, in which the Spanish colonial authorities and plantation owners claimed to have discovered a widespread anticolonial and antislavery conspiracy among free persons and slaves. In the aftermath of the alleged conspiracy, harsh punishments and executions decimated the leadership of Cuba's free black population. Among those executed was the free mulatto poet Gabriel de la Concepción Valdés, better known by his pseudonym Plácido, whose protest poetry was perceived as a threat to the ruling order. Despite such adverse circumstances, nearly twenty-five periodicals, mainly literary and political journals, were published from the 1850s to 1900, focusing on issues pertinent to Cuba's black and mulatto communities. These included *La Igualdad* (Equality), published in Havana; *La Voz de la Razón* (Voice of Reason) and *El Progreso* (Progress), both published in Matanzas; and *Patria* (Fatherland) and *El Radical* (The Radical), both published by Cuban exiles in the United States. Many well-known Afro-Cuban writers and political activists first published in these journals.

Martín Morúa Delgado was one of the most prominent Afro-Cuban journalists, publishing widely in Cuba and abroad. Soon after returning to Cuba in 1890, following a political exile, he founded the newspaper *El Tribuno* (The Tribune) as well as the magazine *La Nueva Era* (The New Era) to address the new social situation created in Cuba by the abolition of slavery. Another renowned Afro-Cuban writer and activist was Rafael Serra y Montalvo, who was a close associate of José Martí, Cuba's most famous poet-patriot. Serra established several newspapers and journals, some while he was in exile in New York. After he returned to Cuba in 1902, he published the journal *El Nuevo Criollo* (The New Creole), which criticized discrimination against Afro-Cubans. Along with pro-independence activists Juan Gualberto Gómez, Antonio Maceo y Grajales, and Antonio Medina y Céspedes, many other Afro-Cuban writers were suspected of being revolutionaries. Like Plácido, they were often watched both by local whites—fearful of a full-scale slave insurrection reminiscent of the one that occurred in neighboring Haiti in the late 1700s—and by Spanish authorities who dreaded the possible cooperation of blacks in a movement to gain independence from Spain.

Panama's most notable modernist poet, Gaspar Octavio Hernández, serves as an interesting counterpoint to the strong color consciousness of black and mulatto writers in Cuba. Hernández, a mulatto, obsessively used motifs of whiteness in his poetry and tried to downplay his African heritage; throughout his life he remained aloof from the black community. Largely self-educated, he eventually directed several literary and political newspapers, writing articles that praised Panama's independence from Colombia in 1903 and protested U.S. imperialism when the Panama Canal opened in 1914. Other Afro-Panamanian writers of the late nineteenth and early twentieth centuries included the journalist Edmundo Botello; José Dolores Urriol, famous for his improvisations of satiric verse; Federico Escobar, known as the Black Bard; and modernist poet Cristóbal Martínez, known in literary circles by both his pen name Simón Rivas and his nickname, the "Panamanian Poe."

In Brazil from the late 1700s to the final abolition of slavery in 1888, there were at least half as many free mulattos as there were whites; in fact, they outnumbered whites in some of the northern states. Despite discrimination, free mulattos enjoyed greater economic prosperity and social mobility than did their Cuban counterparts, who tended to align themselves with slave interests. In Brazil they tended to differentiate themselves from both blacks and whites. For the most part they expressed ambivalence toward abolition in print, largely because they depended economically on white slaveholders (some even owned slaves themselves). Because of this tenuous relationship between blacks and mulattos, a vibrant black press like Cuba's did not fully emerge in Brazil until the twentieth century.

Several nineteenth-century Afro-Brazilian poets and journalists argued passionately for the abolition of slavery in such periodicals as *O radical paulistano* (The Radical from São Paulo). In addition to the aforementioned Luís Gonzaga Pinto da Gama, these writers included André Rebouças and José Carlos do Patrocínio. However, most writers involved in the Brazilian abolitionist movement were white, although some free blacks participated in the movement in other capacities. The prevailing inclination among mulatto writers, including one of Brazil's most celebrated novelists, José Maria Machado de Assis, was to refrain from openly addressing the slavery issue in their work.

Argentina also had an active black press in the nineteenth century. Unlike Brazil and Cuba, however, Argentina is known today as a country whose population is mainly of European descent. Buenos Aires was a major slave port in the seventeenth and eighteenth centuries and was home to a sizable black population during this time. By the late 1800s, however, the black press and the community that produced it had largely disappeared in Argentina. Some scholars attribute the community's disappearance to disease, high infant mortality, and participation in the independence wars. After the 1852 exile of Argentine president Juan Manuel Rosas, additional factors that are more difficult to measure gradually diminished the Afro-Argentine presence. The collective desire to *mejorar la sangre* (better one's blood) through whitening and the government's promotion of European immigration altered the face of Argentina. In his book *Afro-Argentine Discourse: Another Dimension of the Black Diaspora* (1996), literary scholar Marvin Lewis maintains that there was "an official, concerted effort to eliminate the blacks from Argentine society." White intellectuals of the time, notably Domingo Faustino Sarmiento, who served as president of Argentina from 1868 to 1874, complemented the government's pro-European immigration policy by advancing theories of so-called scientific racism and, according to Lewis, "downplay[ing] the significance of the black presence in Argentina and . . . eliminat[ing] them as an ethnic component." Since then, blacks have been written out of national and literary histories in Argentina.

According to the 1869 census approximately 80 percent of all Argentines were illiterate. While no literacy figures specifically for Afro-Argentines were recorded, the black periodicals that survive attest to the existence of a literate minority among them. Lewis concludes that "the audience of the black intellectuals was not the illiterate masses, but rather that semiliterate and literate segment of the population which was capable of reading, interpreting, and conveying their message to the less fortunate." Black newspapers of the time attest to the lack of membership in black organizations such as mutual aid societies, not because there were few Afro-Argentines, but because whitening promised economic and social mobility for so many. Although slavery had officially ended in 1853, blacks still suffered racial discrimination and many felt compelled to choose between loyalty to their African heritage and loyalty to their nation. Because so many Afro-Argentines were somewhat indifferent to forming or joining black organizations, the black press became even more important as a means of communicating community issues.

Black periodicals across the country stated that their purpose was to inform, educate, and mobilize Afro-Argentines. Their aim was to improve the economic, social, educational, and cultural status of blacks in Argentina and to combat the official rhetoric that blacks did not exist or were unimportant. The periodicals often published items that focused on color and class. The earliest journals, including *El Proletario* (The Proletariat), date back to the 1850s. Several publications were introduced in the 1870s: *El Unionista* (The Unionist), *La Igualdad* (Equality), *La Juventud* (Youth), and *La Broma* (The Joke). Many publications that subsequently emerged—including *Revista Clarín* (Clarin Magazine), *La Perla* (The Pearl), *El Aspirante* (The Aspirant), *La Raza Africana* (African Race), *La Crónica* (The Chronicle), and *El Artesano* (The Artisan)—were short-lived. However, they attest to a proliferation of black voices in Argentina and to an awareness on the part of Afro-Argentines of a wider black consciousness and of international abolitionist movements.

Social, political, and cultural marginalization had its benefits, however. Ignored for the most part by white Argentines, the black press was able to publish militant poetry long before the advent in the late 1930s of the Négritude Movement. Much like the Afro-Colombian poet CANDELARIO OBESO, who published verse reproducing black speech in 1877, Afro-Argentine Mateo Elejalde published poetry that addressed ethnic identity in *La Broma* (The Joke). Strongly influenced by the romanticist movement, in which poets did not generally touch upon issues of race and ethnicity, Elejalde nonetheless punctuated his poetry with a racial perspective. The better-known HORACIO MENDIZÁBAL, author of *First Verses* (1865) and *Hours of Meditation* (1869), also wrote in the romantic tradition. Still, he was profoundly aware of the status of Argentine blacks, as demonstrated in this excerpt from his poem "My Song," from *Hours of Meditation*:

And we do not have even a homeland, which if it exists
From its bosom knew how to prohibit us;
The burdens may be for the sad man:
And if we have only one right
It has to be the right to die.

Dying for the homeland and enough!
Which is an illegitimate, irrational entity:
For a mulatto of stained caste,
For a vile nigger of a different makeup
Give me a chain and a noose!

Here Mendizábal refers to the overrepresentation of Afro-Argentines among military ranks in fighting that spanned the nineteenth century: the independence wars, civil wars, and border disputes, and the campaigns to exterminate indigenous peoples. Despite such proven national loyalty, Afro-Argentines continued to be marginalized. Afro-Argentine poet and musician CASILDO THOMPSON wrote about a romanticized Africa. He invoked themes of black pride in his most famous poem, "Canto al África" (Song to Africa), which was first published in the journal *La Juventud* in 1877 and then republished in Jorge Miguel Ford's *Bénemeritos de mi estirpe* (Outstanding Members of My Race, 1899), a collection of biographies of outstanding black people in Argentina.

Black Press and Black Consciousness during the Twentieth Century

The black press in Latin America and the Caribbean became even more active during the twentieth century. Ideas sparked by Pan-African Black Consciousness Movements that arose in the late nineteenth century in the Caribbean and the United States rapidly circulated throughout Latin America and took specific national forms. Many journals spearheaded efforts to improve the social, economic, and educational status of blacks. Often these journals were the organs of community ethnic organizations, and reflected differing social and political agendas. Many of them, including *Nuestra Raza* (Our Race) in Uruguay and *O Clarim do Alvorada* (Trumpet of the Dawn) in Brazil, published poetry alongside coverage of local issues and profiles of influential black figures. These journals were key to black literary development in Latin America and the Caribbean, because they provided a forum for the first poems and essays of later well-known writers. Many black and mulatto poets who contributed news articles and editorials as well as poetry to these periodicals, including Nicolás Guillén of Cuba and Aimé Césaire of Martinique, went on to become some of the most renowned writers in Latin America and the Caribbean. Césaire became a leading figure of the Négritude movement and Guillén spearheaded Afrocubanismo, the literary and cultural movement of the late 1920s and early 1930s that sought to reassess the contribution of blacks to Cuban culture.

In the early decades of the twentieth century, African themes were fashionable in international avant-garde art and literary circles as part of the so-called primitivist movement. In Europe the Spanish cubist painter Pablo Picasso drew inspiration from African masks, while in the Caribbean the negrista poets (mostly white and middle-class) imitated and incorporated stereotypical African themes and figures in their work. The audience such work attracted, for the most part, was not black. The literary contributions of black writers such as Guillén stood in sharp contrast to the nostalgic verse of negrista poetry. Guillén's poems were drawn from colloquial black speech and set to the rhythms of son, a traditional form of Afro-Cuban music. His *Motivos de son* (1930) represented a "major turning point for literary blackness," according to Jackson's *Black Writers in Latin America*.

Drawing attention to black contributions as integral to a nation's identity became part of the writer's vocation for many Afro–Latin American and Caribbean writers. In Brazil during the 1930s, the Frente Negra Brasileira (Black Brazilian Front) advocated incorporation into mainstream Brazilian society and avoided, as did many political and social mulatto organizations, a separate black identity. In Uruguay such journals as *Ecos del Porvenir* and *Nuestra Raza* published black viewpoints that were often slightly more radical than those expounded in Brazil, but that clearly reflected national interests. In the Caribbean, Négritude and Rastafarianism tended less toward integration and more toward redefinition of Afro-Caribbean identity. Early journals such as *Trinidad* (founded in 1929) and *The Beacon* (1931) addressed similar issues in Trinidad. Later journals of the region reflect the growth in black consciousness and creativity inspired by the poetry and essays of Césaire. These journals included *Tropiques* (1941) in Martinique, *Bim* (1942) in Barbados, *Focus* (1943) in Jamaica, and *Kyk-Over-Al* (1945) in British Guiana (now Guyana). Many black writers who later attained widespread recognition—including Theodore Wilson Harris, George Lamming, and Derek Walcott—first published in these journals.

In the pages of these journals, some conflicting viewpoints appeared over the issue of identification with the diaspora. One perspective was that some strategic separatism was in order while blacks remained culturally and politically isolated from the ruling elite in their respective nations. In the minds of many, however, to characterize one's poetry or journalism as "black" was to separate oneself from national concerns. Those who expressed solidarity in print with movements like Négritude and Rastafarianism, or who held up the strongly color-conscious work of African American writer Langston Hughes as a model, tended to be educated mulattos. Some periodicals reflected an international awareness and expressed Pan-African solidarity. The Uruguayan journal *Revista Bahía–Hulan Jack,* for example, was named for a predominantly black state of Brazil and for the first black Manhattan borough president, elected in 1953. Black publications with a more national bent, particularly those in Brazil, often focused on African heritage rather than on more immediate concerns, such as the socioeconomic situation of blacks.

Due to the unstable nature of political institutions, long periods of dictatorship in many countries throughout the region, and much ambivalence (even to this day) about color consciousness, black organizations and their journals were never long-lived. *Nuestra Raza,* the longest-running black periodical in Uruguay, was published in Montevideo only from 1933 to 1948. No Latin American or Caribbean organization can claim the historical longevity and relative stability of the National Association for the Advancement of Colored People (NAACP), for example, in the United States. Nor did parallel organizations take root—as historically black churches did in the United States—since organizing along racial lines was discouraged on national levels after independence in Latin America and the Caribbean. In addition, with the advent of Marxism and particularly after the 1959 Cuban Revolution, race and ethnicity in most periodicals and newspapers were overshadowed by class.

In the late 1970s in Brazil, movements advocating black pride and power began to emerge. Organizations such as the Movimento Negro Unificado (Unified Black Movement), the Geledés Black Women's Institute, and the Istituto de Pesquisa da Cultura Negra (Institute for Research on Black Culture) were established and mostly led by middle-class mulattoes and black professionals, and intellectuals. Some like-minded organizations, which numbered approximately 600 by the early 1990s, included Roman Catholic lay brotherhoods, university-based research centers, state-run organizations, political bodies, and informal groups of activists. These groups disseminated scholarly research journals—including *Cadernos Luso-Afro-Brasileiros* (Luso-Afro-Brazilian Notebooks) and *Padê*—and popular publications such as *Raça Brasil* (a Brazilian magazine similar to Ebony) on a much larger scale than the local black periodicals of the nineteenth century.

Black Consciousness Movements have manifested themselves in print in other South American countries as well. The press has been an important medium for what historian Darién Davis describes as a "better organized and more defiant" Black Consciousness Movement, which since the 1980s has openly criticized the rhetoric of whitening for making it difficult to form racial alliances. Many contemporary writers explore national manifestations of "literary blackness," including JORGE ARTEL, ARNOLDO PALACIOS, and MANUEL ZAPATA OLIVELLA in Colombia; JUAN PABLO SOJO in Venezuela; ADALBERTO ORTIZ and NELSON ESTUPIÑÁN BASS in ECUADOR; and QUINCE DUNCAN in COSTA RICA. Like their nineteenth-century predecessors, these Afro–Latin American writers continued the tradition of writing blacks into national and literary histories that have often displaced or co-opted their voices. In the words of Guillén, "*Hay que hacer revolución, pero al mismo tiempo hacer poesía*" ("There has to be revolution, but not without poetry").

See also Abolitionist Novels in Cuba: An Interpretation; African Ethnic Groups in Latin America and the Caribbean; Afro-Cuban Political Mobilization: An Interpretation; Black Church, The; Black Codes in Latin America; Black Consciousness in Brazil; Blackness in Latin America and the Caribbean: An Interpretation; Colonial Latin America and the Caribbean; Education in Latin America and the Caribbean; Haitian Revolution; Literature, Afro-Cuban; Literature, Black, in Brazil; Literature, Black, in Spanish America; Literature, English-Language, in the Caribbean; Literature, French-Language, in the Caribbean; Pan-Africanism and Afro–Latin Americans; Rastafarians; Struggles for Independence in Latin America, Racial Questions during the; Transatlantic Slave Trade; Trinidad and Tobago; White Abolitionists in Brazil; Women Writers of the Caribbean; Women Writers, Black, in Brazil; Women Writers, Black, in Spanish America.

Bibliography

Andrews, George Reid. *The Afro-Argentines of Buenos Aires, 1800–1900.* University of Wisconsin Press, 1980.

Davis, Darién J., ed. *Slavery and Beyond: The African Impact on Latin America and the Caribbean.* Scholarly Resources, 1995.

Jackson, Richard L. *Black Writers in Latin America.* University of New Mexico Press, 1979.

Lewis, Marvin A. *Afro-Argentine Discourse: Another Dimension of the Black Diaspora.* University of Missouri Press, 1996.

Press, Black, in the United States

American newspapers and magazines published by African Americans, focusing on black political, social, and cultural issues.

The black press has represented the spectrum of African American opinion since the nineteenth century. It has enabled African Americans to define their own identity, work for black equality, and present events from a black perspective. In the black press, African Americans have been able to highlight black achievement ignored by the mainstream press and to create a sense of unity by establishing a communication network among literate blacks and sympathetic whites.

The first black newspaper in the United States was *FREEDOM'S JOURNAL*, founded March 16, 1827, in NEW YORK CITY by JOHN B. RUSSWURM and SAMUEL E. CORNISH. Russwurm and Cornish used the paper as a forum to discuss slavery and related issues and to enable blacks in various states to exchange ideas, such as whether blacks should strive for full American citizenship or opt for separation and repatriation to Africa. Cornish, an integrationist, and Russwurm, a separatist, disagreed on that issue; six months after the paper's founding, Cornish left. Russwurm continued to publish *Freedom's Journal* until March 28, 1829, when he moved to LIBERIA, where he lived until his death in 1851.

Cornish began editing PHILIP A. BELL's *Weekly Advocate* in 1837. Later called the *Colored American,* it was published until 1842. The publication was noted for its high editorial quality and its militant call for black unity and full citizenship for black Americans. It also likely was published in New York and PHILADELPHIA; this would have made it the first African American newspaper to operate in more than one city with different editions.

More African Americans began to publish in the mid-nineteenth century. Most publications were in New York City, but several others existed, including Albany's *Elevator,* published by Stephen Myers; Pittsburgh's *Mystery,* published by MARTIN R. DELANY, the first African American graduate of Harvard; and Cleveland's *Alienated American.*

African American newspapers were understandably northern phenomena before the AMERICAN CIVIL WAR. However, in 1856 the *Daily Creole* began publishing in NEW ORLEANS, LOUISIANA, although whites pressured its editors into an antiabolitionist position. The *Daily Creole* was followed by the *New Orleans Tribune,* which appeared in July of 1864 and is considered the first African American daily.

Most newspapers of this era were similar in that they depended on either their publisher's personal resources or contributions from white sympathizers to supplement their small subscription income. Approximately forty newspapers were published before the Civil War, the most important of which was the *North Star,* published by abolitionist and reformer FREDERICK DOUGLASS. Its goal characterized black publishing: "The object of the *North Star* will be to attack slavery in all its forms and aspects; advocate Universal Emancipation; exact the standard of public morality; promote the moral and intellectual improvement of the colored people; and to hasten the day of freedom to our three million enslaved fellow countrymen."

Black publishing proliferated after the Civil War. An estimated 575 black publications began by 1890. Most quickly failed, but many survived, most notably the *Philadelphia Tribune.* Founded in 1884, the *Tribune* continues to be published today, making it the oldest continuously published black newspaper in the United States.

The explosion of black newspapers after the Civil War resulted from increasing literacy and greater mobility among African Americans. These were combined with a further need for advocacy in the battle against segregation, disfranchisement, and LYNCHING. Migrants to the North experienced poor conditions and discrimination that was stifling, if not as debilitating as it was in the South. Thus the black press was still an organ of protest for African Americans. However, as the century ended, protest had to be disguised because of the nation's conservative political shift.

BOOKER T. WASHINGTON, considered the spokesman for black America during this era, wielded great power among the black press by controlling advertisements, loans, and political subsidies. The journalist most closely associated with Washington was T. THOMAS FORTUNE, who was considered the dean of black journalism. Initially employed as a typesetter, Fortune learned the newspaper trade from the ground up. He was one of the only African Americans to write for white dailies such as the *New York Sun* and the *Evening Sun*.

Fortune was committed to racial equality. However, his newspaper, the *New York Age*, experienced the same monetary problems that other black newspapers did. He relied on Washington's financial support and was therefore obligated to write editorials that Washington favored. Some journalists resisted the conservative trend and the muted editorial tones that it demanded from black newspapers. IDA B. WELLS-BARNETT repeatedly risked her life in the South to report atrocities suffered by blacks. WILLIAM MONROE TROTTER, who founded the Boston *Guardian* with George Forbes in 1901, formed the first organized resistance to Washington's ideas. Later, with W. E. B Du BOIS, Trotter founded the NIAGARA MOVEMENT, a forerunner of the NATIONAL ASSOCIATION FOR THE ADVANCEMENT OF COLORED PEOPLE (NAACP).

Black newspapers did not attain commercial success until ROBERT S. ABBOTT founded the *CHICAGO DEFENDER* in 1905. Capitalizing on the sensationalist techniques developed by American publisher William Randolph Hearst, Abbott designed the *Defender* as a paper for the masses. Abbott initially avoided politics, but the paper came into its own when he concentrated on muckraking stories about the black community. By 1920 the *Defender* had a circulation of 283,571.

Another successful paper of the era was the *PITTSBURGH COURIER*, which was founded in 1910 by ROBERT L. VANN. More editorially staid than the *Defender,* the *Courier* nevertheless advocated for the black community, demanding that large industrial firms hire African Americans and European immigrants in the 1920s. One reason the *Courier* succeeded was that it had superior writers, including GEORGE SCHUYLER, a columnist known for his satirical style, and JOEL A. ROGERS, whose "Your History" column told of black achievements that were largely ignored or denied by white society. By 1937 the *Courier*'s weekly circulation exceeded 250,000.

By 1946 the *Courier* produced fourteen local and national editions and had branch offices in twelve cities. It was the most popular black publication even in cities that had their own publications. By May 1947 the *Courier*'s circulation reached 357,212, a record for black newspapers. It declined after 1948 following the death of Vann's successor, Ira Lewis; the paper was eventually purchased by John Sengstacke, Robert Abbott's nephew, who ran the *Defender* after Abbott's death in 1940.

Another modern black national paper was the *Afro-American*. JOHN H. MURPHY, a former slave, created this paper in Baltimore by merging his Sunday-school publication with two others and expanding coverage to include items of general interest. John Murphy died in 1922, and his son, CARL MURPHY, built the *Afro-American* into a national publication. Featuring solid reportage and a moderate editorial point of view, the *Afro-American* nevertheless defended PAUL ROBESON and Du Bois when they were accused of being Communists during the McCarthy era. In addition to the national papers, several successful local papers developed during this era, including the *Amsterdam News,* established in 1909 in New York City; the *Norfolk Journal-Guide,* established in Norfolk, Virginia; and the *Atlanta Daily World*. Established in 1928, the *Atlanta Daily World* is the oldest surviving black daily in the nation and only one of three black dailies to survive into the 2000s.

From 1900 to the CIVIL RIGHTS MOVEMENT of the late 1950s, black papers thrived in almost every city because the mainstream press still either ignored African Americans or portrayed them stereotypically, often as the perpetrators of crimes. So-called black news, if included, appeared in segregated "Afro-American" sections. Even celebrities or sports stars who received mainstream coverage were used to reinforce stereotypes about African Americans.

The discovery by white publications of the drama surrounding the Civil Rights Movement marked a period of decline for the black press. Mainstream newspapers, news magazines, and radio and television networks had greater resources than did the black press and could therefore cover more stories than could black papers. Although the mainstream press began to cover black news, few black journalists were writing the stories. By 1955 only thirty-one African Americans worked on mainstream papers. It was not until 1962, when Mal Goode joined ABC, that a national television network hired its first African American correspondent.

Coverage of black issues didn't change until the late 1960s, after riots in black ghettos forced mainstream editors to reevaluate the role of African Americans in journalism. During the riots, white editors discovered black mistrust for white journalists. They quickly realized that they needed black reporters to get accurate stories regarding black communities. In the early 1970s mainstream newspapers and television began to heavily recruit African American journalists. By the mid-1970s more than 100 African American journalists were working in mainstream publications. By 1990, 4,000 African Americans worked for newspapers.

The mainstream press's coverage of traditionally black issues and recruitment of talented African American journalists devastated the black press. In the 1960s more than 300 black papers were published. By the late 1980s only 170 remained. By 1977 circulation for the *Defender* was 34,000 daily and 38,000 for the weekend edition; the *Pittsburgh New Courier*'s circulation had declined to 30,000 weekly; and the *Afro-American* was at a 34,000 average for two weekday editions (18,500 for its Sunday edition). This decline in readership was paralleled by a drop in quality as talented African American reporters and editors went to mainstream publications.

While black newspapers declined, black magazines thrived. The first black magazine to have a lasting impact was *THE CRI-*

SIS. Created by Du Bois in 1910, the *Crisis* was the official publication of the NAACP. In it Du Bois criticized policies that prevented black progress, and he offered protest techniques. In 1934 Du Bois left after quarreling with the NAACP, and the NAACP continues to publish the *Crisis* today. Other magazines founded on the *Crisis* model include the National Urban League's OPPORTUNITY, which documented the literary and artistic accomplishments of the HARLEM RENAISSANCE, and PHILIP A. RANDOLPH and Chandler Owen's THE MESSENGER.

These magazines paralleled early black newspapers by providing mostly commentary and little news coverage, as well as in their financial dependence on subsidies. Commercially viable black-owned magazines did not exist until the 1940s, when John H. Johnson created *Negro Digest*, the magazine that became the cornerstone of his publishing empire (JOHNSON PUBLISHING COMPANY). Johnson followed *Negro Digest* with EBONY in 1946. In 2002 *Ebony* had a circulation of 1.9 million and JET had a circulation of about one million. Johnson has expanded into radio and television broadcasting and into cosmetics, amassing holdings reportedly worth more than $200 million.

The Civil Rights Movement led to economic improvement for many African Americans, creating a market for magazines aimed at the black middle class, including ESSENCE and *Black Enterprise*. *Essence* was aimed at modern black women, and by 2002 it had achieved a circulation of greater than one million. *Black Enterprise* focused on black entrepreneurs and had a readership of nearly 458,000, by 2002.

African Americans remained underrepresented in journalism. Those who had jobs did not hold decision-making power. A 1985 survey indicated that 95 percent of the journalists at daily newspapers were white, 92 percent of U.S. newspapers had no African Americans in news executive positions, and 54 percent had no African American employees. In 1985 African Americans accounted for more than 11 percent of the U.S. population but only 4 percent of newsroom staff members.

In the late twentieth century, the leading provider of opportunities to African Americans was the Gannett Company, the publisher of *USA Today* and the largest news publisher in the United States. Gannett aggressively recruited and promoted African Americans such as Pam Johnson, who in 1981 became the publisher of the *Ithaca Journal* and the first African American woman to control a mainstream daily. Similarly, Gannett made Robert Maynard publisher of the *Oakland Tribune*, marking the first time an African American published a general-market daily. Maynard eventually purchased the paper.

In the 1990s and early 2000s many African Americans experienced racism at work, received less attractive assignments than their white counterparts, and gained fewer promotions. Compounding these problems was the conservative political and social movement in the United States that began in the early 1980s. This movement challenged AFFIRMATIVE ACTION programs that were designed to encourage African American participation in mainstream professions. African Americans still find themselves largely misrepresented and negatively portrayed by mainstream media. Thus, many of the conditions that prompted African Americans to begin newspapers and magazines in the nineteenth century still exist.

The decline of black newspapers means that a countervailing voice is almost nonexistent. Many African American journalists find themselves walking a fine line between the journalistic ideals of objectivity and advocacy. Faced with isolation in newsrooms, fragmentation, and concerns for their overall effectiveness, black journalists in 1975 founded the NATIONAL ASSOCIATION OF BLACK JOURNALISTS (NABJ) to provide guidance and support. By 2003 the NABJ had 3,300 members working in print and broadcast journalism.

See also Antiabolitionism; Integration: An Interpretation; News Magazines and African Americans; Slavery in the United States.

Robert Fay

Pretoria, South Africa

Administrative capital of South Africa, in the northeastern part of the country in Gauteng province, on the Apies River.

The settlement of Pretoria was established by Marthinus W. Pretorius in 1855 and named in honor of his father, ANDRIES WILHELMUS JACOBUS PRETORIUS, the AFRIKANER (or Boer) soldier and statesman. It became the capital of the South African Republic in 1860, and was the site of clashes between Afrikaners and British during the Boer War. The Peace of Vereeniging, which ended the war, was signed there in 1902. When the Union of South Africa was organized in 1910, Pretoria was designated the seat of its administration, a position it retained after the Republic of South Africa was formed in 1961. Even in the 1990s, Pretoria was the center for the nation's Afrikaner political activities and organizations. Segregated residential areas that grew during the period of APARTHEID divide the city into distinct black, white, Indian, and CAPE COLOURED neighborhoods.

The modern city contains large parks and a number of landmarks. Pretoria is the site of the University of South Africa (founded in 1873), the University of Pretoria (founded as Transvaal University College in 1908; it was renamed in 1930), Vista University (1982), a technical college, the State Library, and government archives. Points of interest include the home of Paul Kruger, president of the South African Republic from 1883 to 1902; the Transvaal Museum, containing natural history displays; the Municipal Art Gallery, featuring South African art; the Pretoria Art Museum, with a collection of seventeenth-century Dutch art; the National Cultural History and Open-Air Museum, with a variety of collections; the Military Museum, which is located in Fort Schanskop (built in 1867); and the National Zoological Gardens.

Pretoria is a major commercial, manufacturing, transportation, and cultural center. Principal products include iron and steel, processed food, ceramics, and chemicals. Population 1,249,700 (2003 estimate).

See also Indian Communities in Africa; South Africa; Transvaal.

Pretorius, Andries Wilhelmus Jacobus

1798–1853

Boer leader and general in nineteenth-century South Africa.

Andries Wilhelmus Jacobus Pretorious grew up in what is now Eastern Cape province and took part in the border war with the Xhosa from 1834 to 1836. He then led a Boer (Afrikaner) exploratory party into Natal in eastern South Africa in 1836. This trip was a prelude to leading a group of Boers called Voortrekkers on a migration called the Great Trek from the Cape Colony into the northern part of South Africa. Following the massacre of another Great Trek leader, Pieter Retief, and his followers by Zulu chief Dingane in February 1838, Pretorius returned to Natal, where he was made commander of a large Afrikaner force of 500 men and fifty-seven wagons. He led them across the mountains into Dingane's territory to avenge Retief by defeating the Zulu warriors at the Battle of Blood River on December 16, 1838. Pretorius then made an alliance with Dingane's brother, Mpande, and together they defeated Dingane's forces.

In 1840 he helped establish the Afrikaner republic of Natalia, which the British seized in 1843. For a time he attempted to work with the British while other Afrikaners moved inland to avoid doing so. He became increasingly disillusioned, however, particularly after Sir Harry Smith, governor of the Cape Colony, annexed the territory between the Orange and Vaal rivers where many Afrikaners had already settled. Pretorius raised an Afrikaner force to fight the British but was defeated by Smith at Boomplaats in August 1848. He fled to the Transvaal in northern South Africa, where he became, with Great Trek leader Hendrik Potgieter, one of the leaders of the Afrikaners. Pretorius was still in favor of negotiating with the British and represented the Afrikaners at the Sand River Convention of 1852 which recognized the independence of the South African Republic in Transvaal. In 1853 Pretorius led several military expeditions against African chiefs. After his death the city of Pretoria was founded and named after him by his son, Marthinus Wessel Pretorius, who later was elected president of the Transvaal.

Price, Florence Beatrice Smith

1887–1953

Composer and pianist who was one of the first African American women to achieve national recognition as a composer.

The third child of Little Rock's first black dentist, Florence Beatrice Smith Price had already published musical compositions as a high school student. She graduated as an organist and teacher from the New England Conservatory of Music in 1906, and in 1912 she married the attorney Thomas J. Price. Florence Price won the Wanamaker Prize in 1932 for her *Symphony in E minor,* which premiered at the 1933 Chicago World's Fair by the Chicago Symphony Orchestra. She thus became the first African American woman to write a score played by a leading American orchestra. Price composed over three hundred works, and her songs and arrangements were performed by some of the most admired voices of her day, including Marian Anderson. Her symphonies and chamber works were famous for incorporating the melodies from Negro spirituals, and her work is considered an important part of the New Negro Arts Movement.

See also Music, African American; Spirituals, African American.

Price, George Cable

1919–

Foremost political leader of Belize in the last half of the twentieth century, and a staunch supporter of independence from Britain, achieved in 1981.

George Cable Price entered politics in 1944, when he ran unsuccessfully for Belize city council. He won a seat on the council three years later. In 1950 he founded the People's United Party (PUP), which sought independence from Great Britain. Price went on to hold a number of leadership positions in the country, including chief minister (1961–1963), premier (1964–1981), and prime minister (1981–1984, 1989–1993). In 2000 he received the Order of National Hero, Belize's highest honor, for his role in the independence movement.

See also British Honduras; Nationalism in Latin America and the Caribbean.

Price, Leontyne

1927–

African American opera singer.

Leontyne Price was the first African American lyric soprano to receive international recognition as an operatic diva. She was especially known for performing the title role of a slave in ancient Egypt in the Italian composer Giuseppe Verdi's *Aïda.*

Mary Violet Leontyne Price was born in Laurel, Mississippi, to James Price, a carpenter, and Katherine Baker Price, both of whom were the children of Methodist ministers. Their church-centered family life focused on religion and work. Price took piano lessons at the age of three, giving her first recital in 1943, and sang in the church choir. At the age of nine she heard African American contralto Marian Anderson in concert and was inspired to live a life of music. The only apparent career path in music for a black woman was teaching music in a segregated public school, so she enrolled in the College of Education and Industrial Arts (now Central State University), a historically black college in Ohio, as a music major. When Price played and sang in several college productions, the faculty recognized her potential as a singer.

After her graduation in 1948, Price was admitted as a voice major to New York's Juilliard School of Music. Performing in a Juilliard production of Verdi's *Falstaff*, she was noticed by American composer Virgil Thomson, who recruited her to make her Broadway debut in a revival of his opera *Four Saints in Three Acts* in 1952. A string of successful performances followed—the role of Bess in a traveling production of George Gershwin's PORGY AND BESS from 1952 to 1954; a recital at New York's Town Hall; and, in 1955, a landmark performance as the first black opera singer on television, in Italian composer Giacomo Puccini's *Tosca*. Price made her opera-house debut in 1957 as Madame Lidoine in *Dialogues des Carmélites* by French composer Francis Poulenc at the San Francisco Opera House. She then began touring the major opera houses of Europe and the United States. From 1952 to 1972 she was married to baritone William Warfield.

Following her triumph in Verdi's *Aïda* at La Scala in Milan, Italy, in 1960, Price became identified as the ideal Aïda. In 1961 she sang for the first time at New York's Metropolitan Opera House as Leonora in Verdi's *Il Trovatore*. Though the Metropolitan had long been resistant to hiring African Americans, Price soon became a fixture there. From 1961 to 1969, she gave 118 Metropolitan Opera performances. She opened the new Metropolitan at Lincoln Center in 1966, in the premiere of American composer Samuel Barber's *Antony and Cleopatra*, an opera written especially for her.

Price concluded her formal career on January 3, 1985, with a final performance of *Aïda*, broadcast on television from the Metropolitan Opera in New York. Recognition of her achievements has come in many forms, including the Presidential Medal of Freedom in 1964, the Spingarn Medal of the NATIONAL ASSOCIATION FOR THE ADVANCEMENT OF COLORED PEOPLE (NAACP) in 1965, and twenty Grammy Awards. Price published a children's book telling the story of *Aïda* in 2000. In September of 2001 she came out of retirement to perform at a concert in honor of the victims of the recent terrorist attacks on New York City and Washington, D.C.

Bibliography

Lyon, Hugh. *Leontyne Price: Highlights of a Prima Donna.* Vantage, 1973.

Price-Mars, Jean

1876–1969

Haitian historian, diplomat, politician, and ethnographer who preceded and influenced the Négritude movement.

Jean Price-Mars was born in Grande Rivière du Nord, HAITI. After studying medicine, anthropology, and political science in Haiti and Paris, he joined the Haitian diplomatic corps. It was through this work that Price-Mars discovered his oratorical skills, giving a great number of lectures on Haitian culture and politics in the 1910s and 1920s that were gathered in his first published works, *La Vocation de l'élite* (1919), *Ainsi parla l'Oncle* (1928), and *Une étape de l'évolution haïtienne* (1929). Price-Mars subsequently split his time between active politics and more intellectual pursuits throughout the rest of his life. During the tumultuous middle of the century, he remained close to Haiti's ever-changing power élite, running twice for president and being appointed ambassador to Paris by FRANÇOIS DUVALIER in 1957.

More significantly, Price-Mars continued to write on the history of Haiti and on the importance of racial and cultural pride in works such as *De Saint-Domingue à Haïti: essai sur la culture, les arts et la littérature* (1959) and *Silhouette de nègres et de négrophiles* (1960). During the humiliating period of the United States occupation of Haiti (1915–1934), Price-Mars strove in his lectures to remind Haitians of their rich cultural heritage.

Although Price-Mars's ideas seem tame by comparison to those of AIMÉ CÉSAIRE and FRANTZ FANON, they were revolutionary in their time and place. LÉOPOLD SÉDAR SENGHOR, for one, acknowledged the debt to Price-Mars, a writer who showed him "the treasures of NÉGRITUDE that he discovered in Haiti, [and] taught me to discover those same riches—albeit in raw and undiluted form—in Africa."

Richard Watts

Pride, Charley Frank

1938–

First African American country music superstar.

Born in Sledge, Mississippi, to a family of sharecroppers, Charley Pride spent his early years surrounded by BLUES music, but chose to pursue country music professionally. Pride began his bid to be the first black to mount the Grand Ole Opry stage (the apex of country music performance) unconventionally—as a BASEBALL player in the late 1950s. Between innings as an outfielder for several NEGRO LEAGUE teams, Pride displayed his sinewy voice and self-taught mastery of the guitar. Eventually, his nightclub singing was noticed and encouraged by Nashville producers. He gave up baseball for music in 1963. The popularity of his first hits, "Snakes Crawl at Night" (1965) and "Just Between You and Me" (1966), earned him invitations to perform at the Opry, the first black country music star to appear there.

Success in music and business followed. He is a superstar singer/composer of over fifty Top Ten hits, winner of three Grammy Awards, *Cash Box* magazine's Top Male Country Singer of the Decade (1970s), and 1971 Country Music Association Entertainer of the Year. He is second only to Elvis Presley in records sold for the RCA label. In addition to other businesses whose profits have made him a multimillionaire, Pride owns First Texas Bank in Dallas, Texas.

While Pride's rise to fame was meteoric, he faced criticism from within the black community, which perceived country music to be a white arena. Also, early in his career, the Nashville music industry hid Pride's race by issuing publicity material without his photo. In order to help others avoid such discrimination, Pride has been active in a new Nashville organization, the Minority Country Music Association. In 2000 Pride became the first African American to be inducted into the Country Music Hall of Fame.

See also Sharecropping.

Prieto Figueroa, Luis Beltrán

1902–1983

Afro-Venezuelan essayist and educator, one of Venezuela's most important politicians during the twentieth century.

In 1941 Luis Beltrán Prieto Figueroa, together with Rómulo Betancourt and other racially mixed politicians, formed the political party Acción Democrática (AD). Emerging from the middle-class student movement, the AD was a social democratic party that wanted to overthrow authoritarian rule and instill democratic reform. The party was successful, coming to power in 1945 under Betancourt, and Prieto Figueroa served briefly as education minister in 1948. In that year a military junta under General Marcos Pérez Jiménez took power. Prieto Figueroa fled the country with other political opposition leaders. The dictatorship lasted until 1958, when democratic reforms were reinstated.

In 1968, after he had returned to VENEZUELA, Prieto Figueroa, who had been a longtime president of the AD, abruptly left the party and formed a rival organization, the People's Electoral Movement. He ran for president unsuccessfully in 1973 and 1978.

Primus, Pearl

1919–1994

Pioneer dancer, choreographer, and teacher who performed, taught, and popularized African American, African, and Caribbean dance styles.

Pearl Primus studied to be a doctor, not a dancer. A biology major at Hunter College in NEW YORK CITY (where her family had emigrated from Trinidad in 1921), then a graduate student of psychology and health education, she was prevented from gaining a laboratory job by racial prejudice. Pressed for money, Primus applied to the National Youth Administration and was placed as an understudy in a dance troupe. Primus's superb athletic ability won her a scholarship to the New Dance Group in 1941. The first black to study and perform there, she began a long career that sought to counteract racism with Afrodiasporic performance culture.

Primus's early work displayed her careful research of traditional African dance styles and her desire to infuse dance with political and social commentary. Her 1943 professional debut, *African Ceremonial,* received such positive reviews that she was able to open on Broadway with her own troupe. Interpreting pieces such as LANGSTON HUGHES's poem *The Negro Speaks of Rivers* (1943) and *Strange Fruit* (1945), the Lewis Allen poem, Primus brought African dance styles to bear on African American racial issues. Her work was recognized by a 1948 Julius Rosenwald Fellowship, which she used to study dance in Central and Western Africa.

While beginning her career, Primus continued her academic work, studying anthropology and education at universities in New York. She met her husband, dancer/choreographer Percival Borde, in Trinidad, while researching folklore there in 1953. She and Borde collaborated until his death in 1979. The couple and their son, Onwin, spent two years in LIBERIA (1959–1961), where Primus directed Liberia's Performing Arts Center.

Throughout the 1960s, Primus focused on teaching. She held numerous academic appointments in anthropology, dance, and ethnic studies in the 1980s and 1990s, after earning her doctorate in education from New York University in 1978. The recipient of many distinguished awards, Primus saw her career capped by the 1991 National Medal of Art, presented to her by the president of the United States, George Bush. Although she stopped performing personally in the 1980s, Primus taught dance until her death in 1994.

See also Dance in Latin America and the Caribbean; Dance in Sub-Saharan Africa; Dance, African American; Trinidad and Tobago.

Prince

1958–

Virtuoso pop musician known for his provocative musical and personal style.

Born Prince Rogers Nelson in Minneapolis, Minnesota, Prince has had many transformations on his journey to pop stardom. Deliberately frustrating efforts to characterize him and his music, he continues to pursue his own artistic path.

Famously private about his personal life, Prince is the biracial son of jazz musicians Mattie Shaw Nelson and John Nelson. Self-taught on the guitar, piano, and drums, he received a recording contract at age twenty. His first album, *For You* (1978), blends FUNK, rock, pop, and JAZZ. Like the albums that followed, it shows the eclectic musical influences of JAMES BROWN, GEORGE CLINTON, JIMI HENDRIX, and the Beatles.

Like his idol, LITTLE RICHARD, Prince is flamboyant in both dress and personality. After *For You,* his next few albums brought him notoriety as a result of their explicitly sexual lyrics and his own provocative androgyny. Neither black nor white, and his music neither rock nor funk, Prince appealed to all, a fact that helped him cross over onto MTV. He created a virtual cult following with the 1982 album *1999*, which went triple platinum, and with *Purple Rain* (1984), which won three Grammy awards. He also starred in and produced a semiautobiographical film, *Purple Rain*, for which he earned an Oscar for best score. Prince's other films include the modestly successful *Under the Cherry Moon* (1986) and *Graffiti Bridge* (1990).

In 1993 Prince retired briefly and was involved in a court battle with his record label, Warner Bros. The dispute prompted him to change his name to an unpronounceable symbol representative of male and female features. He formed his own label in 1996, declaring that he was no longer a "slave" to music industry commercialism or his own former reputation. When the Warner Bros. contract officially ended in 2000, he announced that he was changing his name back to Prince. Among his recent recordings are the albums *###* (2000), *The Very Best of Prince* (2001), and *The Rainbow Children* (2001).

Bibliography

Brown, Geoff. *A Complete Guide to the Music of Prince.* Music Sales, 1995.

Prince, Lucy Terry

1730?–1821

American writer, a pioneering African American poet, known for extraordinary oratorical skills.

Eulogized as one whose "fluidity of . . . speech captured all around her," Lucy Terry Prince is probably the first African American poet. Prince's single surviving poem, "Bars Fight," is the chronicle of a Native American raid on Deerfield, Massachusetts, in 1746. It was not published, however, until 1855 by Josiah Gilbert in his *History of Western Massachusetts*.

Born in West Africa, enslaved, and brought to Rhode Island, Prince was sold at the age of five to a Massachusetts resident, Ebenezer Wells. Baptized soon after, she was taught to read and write, skills that enhanced her poetic ability as well as her later skill at oratorical argument. At age sixteen, she was witness to an Indian raid in a field outside of Deerfield known as "The Bars," and chronicled the experience in a poem that was hailed as an accurate description of the event.

While her reputation as a poet rests on a single poem, Prince's standing as an orator follows from two unusual events. She married Abijah Prince, a free black who purchased her freedom, and moved to Vermont in 1756. They were the parents of six children. When one of her sons was ready to go to college, he was rejected by Williams College because of his race. Incensed by this injustice, Lucy Prince reputedly pleaded her case for three hours in front of the college trustees, quoting both the Bible and the law.

Although unsuccessful with the trustees, a few years later Prince won a case in the United States Circuit Court. When a land dispute between the Princes and their neighbors could not be solved in the local judiciary, it went to the circuit court. Dissatisfied with her lawyer, Isaac Ticknor (later Governor of Vermont), Prince pleaded her own case, earning the praise that she argued "better than [the judge] had heard from any lawyer at the Vermont bar."

See also Free Blacks in the United States; Poetry, Black, in English; Women Writers, Black, in the United States.

Bibliography

Kaplan, Sidney. *The Black Presence in the Era of the American Revolution.* Edited by Sidney Kaplan and Emma Nogrady Kaplan. University of Massachusetts Press, 1989.

Prince, Mary

1788?–1833?

Bermudan slave and first black woman to publish a slave narrative.

The History of Mary Prince, A West Indian Slave, Related by Herself (1831) was the earliest account that gave a firsthand description of the brutality women suffered under slavery. Mary Prince's autobiography became very popular and stirred debate on slavery and the treatment of slaves in the WEST INDIES. Describing the harsh conditions she faced in the West Indies, Prince countered biased white accounts that "slaves don't want to get out of slavery." As she explained, "They [whites] put a cloak about the truth. It is not so. All slaves want to be free. . . . I have been a slave myself—and I know what slaves feel—I can tell by myself what other slaves feel, and by what they have told me." With these words she became the first black woman to challenge the words of whites on behalf of all black people.

Born a slave in BERMUDA around 1788, Prince saw her family members sold to different West Indian plantation owners. Prince herself worked on various estates as a domestic servant and in the fields. Not only did she experience sexual exploitation, but she was left with severe scarring from beatings, and her labor on a salt plantation deformed her feet because of long exposure to the harsh chemicals. Prince married a free black man in 1826, but according to West Indian law she was still the property of her masters, John Wood and his wife, who often beat her in full view of her husband. Rheumatism further disabled Prince, which angered the Woods, who increasingly threatened to evict her. Finally, while traveling in England with the Woods in 1828, Prince escaped.

Having joined the Moravian Church in the West Indies, Prince now sought shelter at the church's branch in London. She obtained financial and legal aid from the British Anti-Slavery Society. One member, Thomas Pringle, hired her, and offered to purchase her freedom from Wood. Wood rebuffed his offer and insisted that she return to the West Indies. Prince refused, even though this meant she would be separated from her husband.

Prince was determined to fight for her freedom in the English courts, parliament, and press. She recounted her slave narrative to a female member of the Anti-Slavery Society; it was then edited by Thomas Pringle, who took pains to keep to the original wording. Despite the publicity she received through the popularity of her book, she seems to have faded from the public imagination soon after, although it is known that she remained legally a slave until 1833, when slavery was abolished in England and its colonies.

See also Slave Laws in Colonial Spanish America; Slave Narratives; Slavery in Latin America and the Caribbean.

Leyla Keough

Prince, Nancy Gardner

1799–1856?

American autobiographer, philanthropist, and chronicler of travels to Russia and Jamaica.

Nancy Gardner Prince's 1850 *Narrative of the Life and Travels of Mrs. Nancy Prince, Written by Herself,* chronicles the antebellum economic conditions of free blacks, her experience in the court of two Russian tsars, and the difficulties of missionary work in politically volatile, newly emancipated JAMAICA. Prince's life, as told in this fascinating volume, reveals the opportunities available to and hindrances suffered by nineteenth-century black women.

Prince's early life as a free black in New England was marked by hunger, hard work, and racism. She endured these harsh conditions by clinging to the dignity of her family history, which included the exploits of an African grandfather who fought in the Revolutionary War, a Native American grandmother once enslaved by the British, and an African stepfather who emancipated himself by jumping off a slave ship. Despite her pride in her heritage, her frustration with the social and economic oppression of free blacks in antebellum America led to her expatriation. After marrying Nero Prince, a former seaman and a servant in the court of Russian tsars Alexander I and Nicholas I, in 1824, she spent the next ten years in EUROPE and Russia. While living in Saint Petersburg, Prince held such diverse positions as director of an orphanage and seamstress to the Empress.

Due to illness, Prince returned to America in 1833 and was soon widowed. In BOSTON, she worked for the AMERICAN ANTI-SLAVERY SOCIETY and set up an orphanage for colored children. Deeply religious, she took two missionary trips to Jamaica in 1841 and 1842 to proselytize blacks emancipated by the British in 1833. In danger from black insurrection and extortion of her limited monetary resources, Prince returned to Boston in 1843 and struggled to support herself. She wrote her autobiography to earn money. The preface to the third edition in 1856 records the author as very ill. Nothing more is known about her life or the conditions of her death.

See also Free Blacks in the United States; Russia and the Former Soviet Union; Women Writers, Black, in the United States.

Prioleau, George W.

1856–1927

African American clergyman and army chaplain.

George W. Prioleau was born in CHARLESTON, SOUTH CAROLINA, to L. S. and Susan Prioleau, who were slaves. He graduated from Claflin College, Orangeburg, South Carolina, in 1875, and taught in the public primary schools of Lyons Township, Orangeburg County. In 1879 he joined the Columbia, South Carolina, Conference of the AFRICAN METHODIST EPISCOPAL CHURCH (AME), of which his father was a pastor at St. Mathews, just north of Orangeburg. His first pastorate was at Double Springs Mission, Laurens County. In 1880 the Columbia Conference sent him to WILBERFORCE UNIVERSITY in Ohio, where he enrolled in the Theological Department. After his 1884 graduation, Prioleau served churches in Hamilton and Troy, Ohio. In 1888 he was appointed professor of theology and homiletics at Wilberforce. After the Theological Department became Payne Theological Seminary, he occupied the chair of historical and pastoral theology (1890–1894). In 1890 he also became presiding elder of the Springfield District of the Northern Ohio Conference. In 1892 Prioleau served as the district's delegate to the General Conference in PHILADELPHIA, PENNSYLVANIA. From that year until 1895 he was also secretary of the Northern Ohio Conference.

In the spring of 1895 Prioleau accepted a commission as chaplain of the Ninth Cavalry, which he joined at Fort Robinson, Nebraska. He contracted MALARIA just prior to departure for the Cuban campaign of the Spanish-American War and spent the summer of 1898 on recruiting duty in his native Charleston. He served two lengthy tours of duty in the Philippines before his transfer to the Tenth Cavalry on the Mexican border in 1915. Two years later, as senior chaplain in the army, Prioleau was promoted to major and was transferred to the Twenty-fifth Infantry at Schofield Barracks near Honolulu, Hawaii. He retired to his home in LOS ANGELES, CALIFORNIA, in 1920 and organized the Bethel AME Church in that city.

Prioleau's first wife, Anna L. Scovell of New Orleans, Louisiana, held two degrees from Wilberforce. She died at the age of forty at Fort Walla Walla, Washington, in February 1903. He married Ethel G. Stafford of Emporia, Kansas, in 1905, while he was stationed at Fort Riley. Prioleau and his second wife had four children: Mary S., Ethel Susanna, George Wesley, and Lois Emma.

Prioleau was a vocal advocate of military careers for African American men. The low military pay still surpassed the income most African Americans could expect, and the army provided some measure of security and dignity. In his only published work, "Is the Chaplain's Work a Necessity?" in Theophilus G. Steward's *Active Service or Religious Work Among the U.S. Soldiers* (1898), he explained his own role as that of a shield against the corrupting influences that abounded in the towns near military posts. His actions suggest a more complex responsibility. In 1917 his efforts to raise funds from Twenty-fifth Infantry soldiers yielded $3,200 for the NATIONAL ASSOCIATION FOR THE ADVANCEMENT OF COLORED PEOPLE (NAACP) and the black victims of the East St. Louis Riot.

After his long ministry in Ohio and tenure at Wilberforce, Prioleau corresponded regularly with the *Cleveland Gazette*. His letters and the news articles in that paper provide substantial information regarding his career. Other biographical data are in Delilah Beasley's *Negro Trail Blazers of California* (1919), in *The Colored American Magazine* (April 1909), and in an article by W. E. B. DU BOIS in THE CRISIS from May 1918.

From *Dictionary of American Negro Biography* by Rayford W. Logan and Michael R. Winston, editors. Copyright © 1982 by Rayford W. Logan and Michael R. Winston. Reprinted by permission of W. W. Norton & Company, Inc.

See also East St. Louis Riot of 1917; Military, Blacks in the American; Spanish-American War, African Americans in the.

Frank N. Schubert

Proctor, Henry Hugh

1868–1933

American Congregational minister, known for establishing community programs within his church.

The child of former slaves, Richard and Hannah (Murray) Proctor, Henry Hugh Proctor attended public school in Fayetteville, Tennessee where, after teaching briefly in Pea Ridge, Tennessee, he became principal. In 1884, Proctor attended Central Tennessee College in Nashville, but soon transferred to nearby FISK UNIVERSITY where he received a B.A. in 1891.

After graduating from Yale Divinity School in 1894, Proctor was ordained as a minister in the Congregational Church. As pastor of the prestigious First Congregational Church in ATLANTA, GEORGIA, from 1894 until 1920, Proctor was instrumental in establishing multifaceted community activity and service programs within his church, while also working with whites to reduce racial strife. He died in 1933 in Brooklyn, New York, where he was pastor of the Nazarene Congregational Church.

Professor Longhair

1918–1980

American rhythm and blues artist, regarded as the progenitor of the post–World War II New Orleans R&B sound.

Henry Byrd was born in Bogalusa, Louisiana, to James L. and Ella Mae Byrd, both musicians, but was reared in NEW ORLEANS solely by his mother. Impoverished, Byrd left school to work on the streets as a musical performer and dancer. At the age of eight, he was working for the CJK Medicine Show as a stunt man, while remaining a street performer.

Despite his learning to play the guitar and the piano, dancing was Byrd's main source of work even into the 1930s, most notably with singer Champion Jack Dupree at the Cotton Club in New Orleans. From 1937 to 1942, Byrd worked mostly outside of entertainment in the Civilian Conservation Corps and as a cook, in addition to gambling professionally throughout Louisiana.

After World War II, Byrd focused on music as his source of livelihood, developing his patented "flamboyant . . . strutting and riffing barrelhouse piano style." Before heading his own band, Professor Longhair and the Four Hairs, in 1949, Byrd played piano with several local bands. Under the names Professor Longhair and his Shuffling Hungarians and Roy Byrd, he recorded several hit records including "Baldhead (a.k.a. 'She Ain't Got No Hair')," "Tipitina," and "Go to the Mardi Gras," known as the "unofficial anthem" of New Orleans. These hits were popular due to Byrd's distinctively hoarse, semi-yodeling singing style, as well as his infectious piano rhythms. From the early 1960s until about 1970 Byrd faded from the musical world, but he regained wide renown after appearing in the 1971 New Orleans Jazz and Heritage Festival.

Professor Longhair's resurgent popularity continued even after his death in 1980; he was posthumously inducted into the Rock and Roll Hall of Fame in 1992. Leaving his mark on pianists from FATS DOMINO and Allen Toussaint to Harry Connick Jr., Professor Longhair according to *Downbeat* magazine, "is the most influential pianist to emerge from the New Orleans milieu since JELLY ROLL MORTON."

See also Music, African American; Rhythm and Blues.

Bibliography

Lichtenstein, Grace, and Laura Dankner. *Musical Gumbo: The Music of New Orleans*. W.W. Norton, 1993.

Prophet, Nancy Elizabeth

1890–1960

American sculptor who was active in the Harlem Renaissance and in Paris through the 1930s.

A classically trained sculptor lauded for her sensitive and dignified busts of people of color, Nancy Elizabeth Prophet was born into humble circumstances in Warwick, Rhode Island. At an early age she was recognized as having unusual artistic skill. Earnings from work as a domestic enabled her to take a degree in painting and portraiture from the Rhode Island School of Design (RISD) in 1918.

A teaching job in HARLEM brought Prophet to NEW YORK during the HARLEM RENAISSANCE. The atmosphere ignited her creativity, and she left New York for Paris's École des Beaux Arts, where she studied from 1922 to 1925. Prophet's next twelve years in Paris were marked by a high level of artistic achievement, during which she produced her well-known sculpture, *Congolaise* (1930). Even though her work was exhibited at Paris salons between 1924 and 1927 and in the United States (at RISD and in BOSTON, 1928), Prophet had great difficulty supporting herself as an artist. In fact, her poverty, malnutrition, and near-starvation were so obvious to other artists in Paris that Henry O. Tanner nominated her for the Harmon Foundation Prize in 1928, hoping to gain her some financial relief. Prophet won the Harmon's Otto Kahn Prize in 1929 for *Head of a Negro* and later won the 1932 Newport Art Association prize for her portrait *Discontent*.

Prophet moved back to the U.S., at the suggestion of her admirer W. E. B. DU BOIS, to take a teaching job at SPELMAN COLLEGE in 1934. With painter Hale Woodruff, she taught art at Atlanta University and Spelman College (1934–1944). Frustrated by a lack of materials, space, and time in which to produce her own art, as well as the prejudices of Atlanta's art community, she returned to Providence in 1944.

Prophet produced little sculpture in her later years, and she was again forced to support herself as a domestic servant. In the last twenty years of her life, she destroyed many of her sculptures and watched her wood and metal artworks rot and rust for lack of money for storage space. Once a producer of "stark, aggressive, naturalistic and non-sentimental" sculpted portraits, she died penniless at the age of seventy.

See also Artists, African American; Sculpture, African American.

Protestant Church in Latin America and the Caribbean

Examines the reasons for Protestantism's appeal among blacks in Latin America and the Caribbean.

Since the nineteenth century, but especially since World War II (1939–1945), Protestant churches in LATIN AMERICA and the Caribbean have been magnets for people of African descent. The reasons are complex. First, in contrast to the Catholic Church, these churches do not carry the stigma of many centuries' complicity with slavery; they offer structures of authority and leadership that are relatively open to people of color; and their doctrine of democratic access to the Holy Spirit is undoubtedly attractive to the socially disempowered.

Historical Protestantism

The first Protestant churches to arrive in the region were noncharismatic BAPTISTS (from the United States) and Methodists (from GREAT BRITAIN). These churches' earliest missionaries strove to attract a mass black audience, but ultimately succeeded only in reaching a small, literate black contingent. In JAMAICA, the Baptist mission was led by George Lisle, a manumitted slave from the American South who arrived in 1783. Although the number of Jamaican slaves converted to Baptism grew to nearly 10,000 on the eve of abolition in the 1830s, and may even have contributed to the slave rebellions of the period, interest in the church declined in the years after emancipation, as it came to be replaced by the indigenous Jamaican religious movements of Native Baptism and Revival Zion. The historical Baptist Church, however, retained the better-educated, urban black elite who did not wish to be mistaken for their proletarian counterparts. Similarly, in BRAZIL, the missionaries of the North American Baptist Church never developed a mass black following. From the start they were associated with the urbanized and educated classes, including better-off mulattos (of African and European descent); this remains the Brazilian Baptists' social base to this day.

The story of the Methodists is similar. Upon arriving in Jamaica from England in the 1780s, they sought to form a cadre of slave ministers. Numerous blacks flocked to the church as a result, but their percentage dwindled in the century following abolition, as nonelite ex-slaves turned to Pentecostal and Rastafarian groups. In Brazil, the Methodists arrived early, in 1836, but directed their attention from the start to the literate mulatto elite, who were happy to find a religion that, unlike the Catholic Church, would not snub them.

The elite people of color who were attracted to the historical Protestant churches found a degree of respect and opportunities for advancement that did not exist for them in the Catholic Church. In Brazil, in addition, the Methodists were innovators in addressing the racial issue. Home to many upwardly mobile mulattos, the Methodist Church became an important location from which to identify and criticize obstacles in the socioeconomic path of people of African descent. As early as the 1950s, the Methodist José da Silva Oliveira preached against white prejudice and sought to promote among blacks an ideology of hard work, literacy, and social uplift. Later, in the 1980s, the Methodists were leaders in founding the national Ministry to Combat Racism. This ministry now has regular meetings at which members examine the teachings of the Bible on racism. The ministry promotes the inclusion in the Protestant liturgy of black music, such as HIP-HOP, REGGAE, RAP, and SAMBA. Despite these efforts, the church, with its emphasis on literacy, cool rationality, and education, continues to appeal primarily to the black elite, not the masses.

Nonorthodox Evangelicalism

No discussion of the participation of the African diaspora in Protestantism would be complete without touching on the powerful nonorthodox Protestant traditions in the Caribbean. In the wake of nineteenth-century revivalist awakenings, religious leaders emerged who articulated powerful Bible-centered visions syncretized with elements of non-Christian and traditional African belief. These include the Spiritual Baptists and Shouters of Trinidad, the Shakers of Saint Vincent, and the Revival Zionists and Rastafarians of Jamaica.

Until the mid-eighteenth century, Protestantism in Jamaica was limited to the Anglicanism of the planter class. In 1783 George Lisle founded the Baptist Church, which eventually led to the emergence of Native Baptists. This group mingled Protestant theology, a strong preoccupation with dreams and visions, and the slave healing cult known as Myal. By the 1860s, more than half the blacks of Kingston were Native Baptists. The 1890s saw the emergence of a major revivalist movement, led by Alexander Bedward, whose preaching united biblical theology with the practice of healing using water from sacred springs. His followers, in turn, divided between the two biblical sects of Pocomania and Revival Zion.

Revival Zion is now, in Jamaica, one of the more popular religious groups among the descendants of slaves. Although staunchly committed to the Bible as its source of inspiration, the religion resembles the non-Christian groups of the hemisphere in its acceptance of possession by entities other than the Holy Spirit. Like the Pentecostals, Revival Zionists seek after the experience of the Holy Ghost; unlike them, they also seek possession by the great prophets and evangelists of the Bible, from Moses, Joshua, and Ezekiel, to the apostles and archangels, to the spirits of the religion's deceased leaders. All these spirits visit the believer, taking him or her through spiritual, shamanlike journeys, and endowing him or her with the ability to heal. This power is also transmitted through drinking water drawn from a sacred spring, thereby bringing the spirits into the bodies of the believers.

Revival Zion has strong Ethiopianist and back-to-Africa dimensions. African ancestors sometimes possess the faithful; the colors of the Ethiopian flag are often present in the ritual center; Ethiopia is regarded as the promised land to which the descendants of slaves would eventually return; and the color of gold, used in the adornment of the central spiritual pole of the cult center, is said to symbolize the lost riches of Africa. The music played during rituals, in contrast to mainstream Protestantism, is self-consciously "African," as it uses traditional drums and percussive rhythms. The ritual itself is strongly reminiscent of the various African-derived cults and is based on the movement of mediums in a counterclockwise direction around a sacred center.

All these elements contributed in the 1930s to the hiving off from Revival Zion of Rastafarianism. Marcus Garvey was very influential among Revival Zionists because of his Ethiopianist views. When Garvey prophesied in 1929 that the Messiah would appear in the form of the Ethiopian emperor, he tapped into the messianism embedded in the Zionist reading of the Bible. Thus when Haile Selassie I was crowned emperor of Ethiopia in 1930, many Revival Zionists took this to be the fulfillment of Garvey's prophecy. Those who accepted the divinity of Selassie and of his power to bring about the long-awaited return of the diaspora to the Zion of Ethiopia began to call themselves by Selassie's pre-imperial name, Ras Tafari. The sect grew quickly in the 1930s, as Ethiopia's Babylonian captivity by the Italian Fascists seemed to many to be the realization of biblical prophecy. The religion fused the notions of sacred nature, healing, and Ethiopianism in the crucible of seething resentment against colonialism and white domination. Between the 1940s and 1960s, the religion thrived in Kingston among the black underclass. In the 1970s the influence of reggae transformed the religion into a worldwide movement. Its roots in Garveyism's Ethiopianism meant that Rasta would become the spiritual and aesthetic heart of the Pan-Africanist movement, from the 1970s to the present. Yet Rastafarianism continues to be a strongly biblical movement, deriving its ideological strength from its reading of the Old Testament.

Pentecostalism

Pentecostalism encompasses the numerous Protestant churches that emphasize the gifts of the Holy Spirit, such as prophecy and speaking in tongues. Pentecostalism is the fastest-growing, most popular form of religiosity in Latin America and the Caribbean today, accounting for up to 85 percent of all Protestants. The religion arrived in Brazil and Jamaica in the second decade of the twentieth century, has grown at breakneck speed since the 1950s, and now boasts more than twenty million faithful in Brazil, as well as half a million in Jamaica. Many of these people are black. While no more than 7 percent of Brazilians identify themselves to census takers as "black," fully 15 percent of Pentecostals do so. And in Jamaica, the majority of Pentecostals are black (rather than mulatto).

The reasons for this growth among blacks are not difficult to determine. In contrast to historical Protestantism, where secular hierarchies are transferred to the church, Pentecostalism makes available the explosive experience of the Holy Spirit, which razes social distinctions. Further, in societies where dark skin tones and nappy hair have low social prestige, people with these features are attracted by Pentecostalism's unequivocal language valuing natural over artificial, and inner over external beauty. Equally important, the building of strong self-esteem offers poor black youth in both societies a powerful alternative to the world of drugs and gangs. And, as is the case for all Pentecostals, irrespective of race, the abandonment of drinking, smoking, adultery, and gambling transforms household relationships, creating greater gender equality and offering couples hope of economic and emotional stability.

Neopentecostalism

Traditional Pentecostal denominations, such as the Assemblies of God, have been slow to tap into the new, emerging groups of young people with hopes for upward mobility. In particular, these churches have been reluctant to incorporate young people's commercial music, dance, and the acceptance of "vanity" (stylish clothing and makeup) into their liturgical forms. Into this gap have moved a number of churches that hived off in the 1970s from the mainstream Pentecostal churches, and now are growing at a rapid clip through television, radio, and spectacular showlike revival meetings. These churches, such as the Universal Church of the Kingdom of God and the Church of

Rebirth, embrace popular music, including traditionally black music, as well as styles of dance and dress that are rejected as too worldly by the older Pentecostals. The churches have a huge youth following, including young people of African descent. Yet because these are young people who can, in general, afford nicer clothes, and who look to religion primarily as a source of sociability rather than survival, they tend to belong to a relatively better-off class segment. The vast majority of poorer blacks continue to participate in the traditional Pentecostal churches. For them, the impact of the Neopentecostals may be felt indirectly, as the older denominations feel obliged to re-think their doctrinal stances on music, dress, and dance. By the end of the twenty-first century, most denominations had internalized the influence of Neopentecostalism.

It has become common in Latin America and the Caribbean for intellectuals who espouse some form of Pan-Africanism or Afrocentrism to criticize both Catholic and Protestant CHRISTIANITY as Eurocentric ideologies imposed on Africans from the outside and having a deracinating influence on them. Without engaging this debate, the foregoing remarks on the Protestant traditions in the region have suggested that these traditions are not inevitably at odds with the development of a strong black racial identity, and that they have even been known at times to contribute to that identity.

See also Afrocentricity; Back to Africa Movement; Catholic Church in Latin America and the Caribbean; Dance in Latin America and the Caribbean; Music, Afro-Caribbean Religious; Pan-Africanism; Rastafarians; Role of Slaves in Abolition and Emancipation in Latin America and the Caribbean.

Bibliography

Austin-Broos, Diane. *Jamaica Genesis: Religion and the Politics of Moral Orders.* University of Chicago Press, 1997.

Bastide, Roger. *The African Religions of Brazil.* Johns Hopkins University Press, 1978.

Glazier, Stephen D. *Marchin' the Pilgrims Home.* Greenwood Press, 1983.

Glazier, Stephen D., ed. *Perspectives on Pentecostalism.* University Press of America, 1980.

Murphy, Joseph M. *Working the Spirit: Ceremonies of the African Diaspora.* Beacon Press, 1994.

John Burdick

Protten, Christian Jacob

1715–1769

Pioneering Christian missionary and educator.

Christian Jacob Protten was born to a Danish soldier and the daughter of a GA chief in Christiansborg, GOLD COAST. He was educated in the Danish school for mulattos (of African and European descent) in Christiansborg Castle, today part of the city of ACCRA in GHANA. In 1726 Protten traveled to Denmark to seek further education. There he caught the notice of King Frederick IV, who became Protten's godfather at his baptism on November 27, 1727.

After meeting the leader of a Christian denomination known as the Moravian Brethren and spending a year at their refuge at Herrnhut, GERMANY, Protten joined the order in 1735. In 1737 he sailed to the Gold Coast (present-day Ghana) to found a Moravian school for Euro-African children at the Dutch post of Elmina. These plans were frustrated by a war between the Dutch and the DAHOMEY Kingdom. Believing him a spy, the Dutch imprisoned Protten. Protten contracted MALARIA and was detained until 1741. He then returned to Herrnhut, and in 1743, he traveled to Saint Thomas as a missionary. He returned to Germany in 1745, and on June 6, 1746, he married a mulatto widow, Rebecca Freundlich.

Protten still harbored the dream of missionary work in the Gold Coast. Moravian leaders, however, would not agree with his wishes. In 1756 he received a commission from the Royal Chartered Danish West India and Guinea Company to teach and preach at the Christiansborg Castle school, which he did until 1761. After a short return to Herrnhut, he traveled once more to the Gold Coast to teach at the Castle mission school. His most lasting accomplishment was a trilingual catechism, written in Danish, Ga, and Twi. This was the first published grammar of a Ghanaian language. In addition, Protten translated Martin Luther's *Smaller Catechism* into Ga and Fante (AKAN).

See also Christianity: Missionaries in Africa; Saint Thomas and Prince Islands.

Robert Fay

Pryor, Richard

1940–

African American comedian known for his free-flowing, uncensored brand of humor.

Considered by many the most influential comedian since 1970, Richard Pryor was born in Peoria, Illinois. His mother, Gertrude Thomas, and his father, Leroy Pryor, met in a brothel managed by Marie Carter, Leroy's mother. Raised in the brothel primarily by Carter, Pryor gravitated to humor early on to cope with his chaotic family life. A disruptive student, Pryor left school at age fourteen and joined a community drama group, which he quit two years later. After serving in the army for two years, Pryor began his stand-up comedy career, performing successfully in Peoria nightclubs and gaining the confidence to go to the more competitive nightclub scene of New York City. Pryor modeled his first performances in New York on the comedy of BILL COSBY and DICK GREGORY.

By the late 1960s, however, Pryor had decided to present "the real side" of himself, replacing a more refined persona with a raw funkiness. His recognition grew as he recorded stand-up routines and appeared in several films, including the drama *Lady Sings the Blues* (1972) and the comedies *Uptown Saturday Night* (1974) and *Silver Streak* (1976). In 1974 Pryor's album *That Nigger's Crazy* became a gold record, and he appeared on the cover of *Rolling Stone* magazine. That same year he won a Writers Guild Award and an American Academy of Humor Award for *Blazing Saddles,* which he cowrote with Mel Brooks. But despite this overwhelming success, Pryor was plagued by drug and money problems. In 1980, at the time of the release of his first self-produced film, *Bustin' Loose,* he had a near-fatal accident freebasing cocaine. Throughout his turbulent life, Pryor retained his sense of humor, as he demonstrated in his biographical film *Jo Jo Dancer, Your Life is Calling* (1986). Despite being diagnosed with multiple sclerosis in 1986, Pryor continued to appear in films, most notably *Harlem Nights* (1989).

Pryor, who has lived in seclusion since the early 1990s, was inducted into the NATIONAL ASSOCIATION FOR THE ADVANCEMENT OF COLORED PEOPLE (NAACP) Hall of Fame in 1996. In 2000 he received the first Mark Twain Award in celebration of American humor.

Public Enemy

One of the premier American rap music groups of the 1980s and 1990s.

Public Enemy infused a FUNK- and SOUL-based sound with sound *samples* (electronic snippets of prerecorded music) and other sound fragments, such as traffic noise and police sirens. A political consciousness pervaded this multilayered sound, through RAP texts and through physical appearance: group members held fake automatic weapons and wore army fatigues and boots, projecting an image of black militancy. Public Enemy's strident lyrics were highly controversial, striking responsive chords with many people while drawing critical responses from many others.

Public Enemy formed in Long Island, New York, in 1987, from the collaborations among lead rappers Chuck D (Carlton Ridenhour) and Flavor Flav (William Drayton), disk jockey (DJ) Terminator X (Norman Rogers), and the group's so-called Minister of Information, Professor Griff (Richard Griffin). The group's producers, Hank Shocklee, Eric "Vietnam" Sadler, and Chuck D, were collectively known as the Bomb Squad. The group took its name from "Public Enemy Number One," a popular rap written by Chuck D along with DJs Hank and Keith Shocklee.

Public Enemy's first release, *Yo! Bum Rush the Show* (1987), relied upon the rhythms of funk music to create an aggressive sound. Their second release, *It Takes Nation of Millions to Hold Us Back* (1988), was layered with additional samples to form a more complex sound. As the group perfected its production and sampling techniques, the content grew more politicized and Public Enemy grew more popular. Chuck D's strong vocals were countered by Flavor Flav's rasping voice, with dance steps by the militaristic quartet known as the S1W (Security of the First World). With this combination, the group advocated black nationalist activism and opposed what it felt was mindless American consumerism. This worldview in combination with Public Enemy's occasional invectives against whites, women, gays, and Jews elicited strong reactions—both positive and negative—from listeners.

In 1989 Public Enemy's song "Fight the Power" was part of the soundtrack for the motion picture *Do the Right Thing,* directed by American filmmaker SPIKE LEE. Shortly thereafter Professor Griff made some anti-Semitic statements to the American press, and the group temporarily disbanded. It soon returned, without Griff, and released the commercially successful and critically acclaimed albums *Fear of a Black Planet* (1990) and *Apocalypse 91 . . . The Enemy Strikes Black* (1991). Other albums by Public Enemy include *Greatest Misses* (1992), *Muse Sick-N-Hour Mess Age* (1994), *He Got Game* (1998), and *The Best of Public Enemy: The Millennium Collection* (2001). Professor Griff, Chuck D, Terminator X, and Flava Flav have also released solo albums.

Public Health

Protection and improvement of the health of entire populations through communitywide action. Public health programs are usually conducted by community groups or by government agencies.

For information on
Primary health care: *See* Health Care in Africa.
Specific public health issues: *See* Acquired Immunodeficiency Syndrome in Africa: An Interpretation; Acquired Immunodeficiency Syndrome in Latin America and the Caribbean; Disease and African History; Diseases, Infectious, in Africa; Female Circumcision in Africa; Guinea Worm; Malaria; Onchocerciasis; Sickle-Cell Anemia; Tsetse Fly.
Public health successes: *See* Diseases, Infectious, in Africa; Eritrea; Hinton, William Augustus; Population Growth in Sub-Saharan Africa.
Public health workers: *See* Drew, Charles Richard; Elders, M. Joycelyn Jones; Hinton, William Augustus; Thoms, Adah B. Samuels; Wright, Louis Tompkins.
Healing practices in folk medicine: *See* Folk Medicine; Traditional Healing in Africa; Traditional Healing in Latin America and the Caribbean.

Public Intellectuals

Academics and writers who have brought their thought and scholarship outside of academic circles and into broader public arena.

For information on
African American intellectuals: *See* American Negro Academy; Appiah, Kwame Anthony; Baldwin, James; Davis, Angela Yvonne; Du Bois, W(illiam) E(dward) B(urghardt); Frazier, Edward Franklin; Gates, Henry

Louis, Jr.; hooks, bell; Johnson, Charles Spurgeon; Jordan, June; Karenga, Maulana Ndabezitha; Locke, Alain Leroy; Lorde, Audre Geraldine; W. E. B. Du Bois: An Interpretation; West, Cornel; Wilson, William Julius; Woodson, Carter G.

African intellectuals: *See* Diop, Alioune; *Présence Africaine*; Senghor, Léopold Sédar; Soyinka, Wole.

Latin American and Caribbean intellectuals: *See* Bellegarde, Dantès; Carneiro, Edison; Dixon, Graciela; Fanon, Frantz; Freyre, Gilberto; Gonzalez, Lélia; Lewis, Arthur; Martí, José; Nascimento, Abdias do; Price-Mars, Jean; Rodney, Walter; Sojo, Juan Pablo; Sylvain, Georges; Williams, Eric; Zapata Olivella, Manuel; Zenón Cruz, Isabelo.

Puello, José Joaquín

1805?–1847

Afro-Dominican military figure and revolutionary.

Little is known about José Joaquín Puello's early life. He was born in Santo Domingo to a family of humble means and at an early age exhibited a keen interest in and talent for handling firearms. His military career began in 1822 when he fought in the Haitian invasion of Santo Domingo under the command of Haitian president Jean-Pierre Boyer. This marked the beginning of a twenty-two-year Haitian occupation of the eastern two-thirds of the island of Hispaniola. For his service in this effort, Puello became captain of one of the Haitian regiments. However, Puello and some of his comrades became dismayed with Haitian policies, which included the imposition of high taxes, confiscation of land, and destruction of the educational system. Puello and others who were disillusioned with Boyer initiated a reform movement that in 1843 resulted in Puello's dismissal from his military post. Puello later protested the formation of a Haiti-Colombia confederation, which threatened to reinstate slavery in Hispaniola.

In order to fight for the creation of a self-governing republic, Puello became active in the Dominican Republic's independence movement. Commanding a large battalion against Haitian forces, he helped the Dominican Republic win its independence from Haiti on February 27, 1844. He was named general and commandant of arms in the capital Santo Domingo and played a significant role in the organization of the *Junta Central Gubernativo* (Central Independent Government).

When the Haitian militia launched a second military campaign against the Dominican Republic on May 10, 1845, Puello and his troops forced them into retreat. Dominican president Pedro Santana recognized Puello's leadership skills and appointed him to a position in the Minsterios de Hacienda y Comercio (Treasury and Commerce Departments). But two years after his appointment, Puello and his brother Gabino were accused of conspiring to overthrow the government through a black insurrection. Although Puello's military record demonstrated his commitment to liberating all peoples, conservatives had earlier accused him of being "anti-white" and of fighting solely in the interests of persons of color on the island. A twenty-five-man commission drawn from the judiciary, legislature, and military condemned Puello and his brother to death. They were executed on December 23, 1847. Despite Puello's role in establishing and maintaining an independent Dominican Republic, he is now a scarcely remembered military hero.

See also Nationalist Movements and Blacks in Latin America and the Caribbean.

Aaron Myers

Puente, Ernesto Antonio (Tito)

1923–2000

Bandleader, composer, multi-instrumentalist—timbales, conga, bongos, vibraphone, piano, and saxophone—and last of the great originators of Afro-Latin jazz.

After the death of Mario Bauzá in 1993, Tito Puente became the last of the early innovators of Afro-Latin jazz to continue to be musically active. Although best known as a bandleader and timbales player, Puente was a multi-instrumentalist, performing on a wide range of percussion instruments as well as on piano and saxophone. For over half a century, he was a dynamic entertainer, emerging in the 1980s as a pop-culture celebrity.

Puente was born in the Spanish Harlem section of New York City. He had hoped to become a dancer, but an ankle injury led him to choose an instrumental career instead. As a youth, he played percussion and piano in the local band Los Happy Boys. He performed with Machito, Fernando Alvarez, and others while still a teenager. He served three years in the United

Tito Puente, composer, bandleader, percussionist, and an originator of Afro-Latin jazz, performs at the Monterey Jazz Festival. *CORBIS/Craig Lovell*

States Navy during World War II, and received his first lessons in composition and orchestration from white bandleader Charlie Spivak aboard the USS *Santee*. Following his discharge in 1945, Puente studied music theory, orchestration, and conducting at the Juilliard School of Music in New York.

During the late 1940s and early 1950s, Puente played a key role in the merging of Latin American rhythms with contemporary JAZZ that produced Afro-Latin jazz. In the late 1940s, he formed The Piccadilly Boys, which later became the Tito Puente Orchestra. The group played a major role in promoting the MAMBO craze of the late 1940s. A decade later, Puente helped popularize the *chachachá* sound. He produced a swinging and danceable style by transforming the music of *charanga* bands—which feature violin and flute—and arranging it for a Latin jazz big band with saxes, trumpets, and trombones. In the 1970s, when SALSA became popular, he gained a new and younger audience.

Puente released over one hundred albums, an accomplishment rivaled by few musicians of any genre. His recording "Abaniquito" (1949) was a hit single and an early crossover success. In the 1970s, Carlos Santana covered two of Puente's compositions: "Para los rumberos" (1956) and a hugely popular rendition of "Oye como va" (1963). Puente's various bands featured many musicians who gained prominence in Afro-Latin jazz, including percussionists RAY BARRETO, MONGO SANTAMARIA, and Willie Bobo; FANIA RECORDS founder JOHNNY PACHECO; and, more recently, saxophonist Mario Rivera, pianist Hilton Ruiz, trumpeter Charlie Sepúlveda, and drummer Ignacio Berroa. Outside of the world of jazz, Puente performed with various Latin music stars, including the Fania All Stars, CELIA CRUZ, and Carlos "Patato" Valdez.

Beginning in the late 1970s, Puente also gained wider exposure in American popular culture. In the 1980s he appeared on *The Cosby Show* and in a stylish and well-received Coca-Cola commercial. He was in Jeremy Marre's made-for-television film *Salsa '79* (1979), and seven years later made his feature film debut with cameos in *Radio Days* (1986) and *Armed and Dangerous* (1986). Puente's most significant film role was in *The Mambo Kings* (1991), playing a Latin jazz bandleader; he also arranged and performed much of the music on the film's soundtrack. He received Grammy Awards for *A Tribute to Benny Moré* (1979), *On Broadway* (1983), *Mambo Diablo* (1985), and *Goza mi timbal* (1989).

Puente continued to record and to perform until the very end of his life. In April 2000, he was declared a Living Legend by the U.S. Library of Congress. He died a month later, just weeks after finishing a series of concerts in Puerto Rico with the Puerto Rico Symphony Orchestra.

James Sellman

Puerto Rico

United States Commonwealth territory and easternmost island of the Greater Antilles.

Puerto Rico exemplifies the complexities of race relations and the use of terminology to describe them. Considered by some as "the whitest of all the Antilles," Puerto Ricans are usually described as mostly Hispanic, a homogeneous race of mixed people. This concept of the Puerto Rican underestimates the African component, one that has had a significant impact on the culture and ethnic composition of Puerto Rico. The African traditions brought to Puerto Rico were syncretized with the Spanish, the Taíno, and, later, the Anglo-American traditions to produce a rich cultural and ethnic amalgam.

The racial mixture of blacks and whites has shaped the concept of race in Puerto Rico. There has been a growing scholarly interest in the Creole blacks and their importance in the formation of the Puerto Rican society, in contrast to the traditional history that has focused on the actions of the ruling white Creole elite. Traditional U.S. conceptions of blackness (anyone with some African blood) and whiteness are of limited use in assessing Puerto Rican conceptions of race. The population's seemingly genial attitude toward race relations in Puerto Rico gives the impression of a society free from racism and prejudice. Yet this idea is proved wrong by the social, political, and economic status of Afro-Puerto Ricans.

Native American Presence

The recorded history of Puerto Rico begins with the arrival of Columbus on November 19, 1493. Puerto Rico was inhabited by the aboriginal Indians named Taínos, who called their island *Boriquén* (or *Borinquén*). Since there is no reliable documentation, estimates regarding the number of Taínos have ranged from the unlikely figure of eight million to the more realistic 30,000. The colonization of San Juan, the name given to the island by the Spanish, began in 1508 when Juan Ponce de León established the first settlement. The Taíno population decreased dramatically during the first period of colonization as a result of the spread of European diseases, various rebellions, and the *encomiendas* system, the regime of forced labor that distributed Taíno Indians among the settlers. Although the Taínos were legally exempted from slavery by royal decree in 1542, rebel Indians were enslaved and exploited by the colonists. By the end of the sixteenth century the Taínos were virtually extinct.

Slavery in Puerto Rico

The first Africans arrived with Columbus in 1493, although the slave trade was not authorized until 1513. Many free blacks, mainly from Seville, emigrated, searching for better opportunities in the New World. They were mainly *ladinos*, or Christianized blacks, who came to serve as domestic servants. In Puerto Rico there were always larger numbers of free blacks than slaves. These free blacks worked in the mines and helped the militia to subjugate the Taínos. They acted individually and moved frequently in search of better work opportunities.

Since the Taíno population was rapidly diminishing, many colonists favored the introduction of black slaves as a substi-

Puerto Rican basketball players celebrate their victory over Canada in the final round of the 2003 FIBA Americas Men's Olympic Qualifying Tournament in San Juan. The team earned a trip to the 2004 Summer Olympics in Athens. CORBIS

tute for the Indian work force. African slaves were initially used to search for gold. Yet during the first half of the sixteenth century the slave population remained relatively small. Only 1,500 enslaved Africans were legally introduced to Puerto Rico from 1536 to 1553. Throughout the seventeenth century the legal trade remained very limited, although an undetermined number of African slaves were introduced as contraband.

In the eighteenth century Puerto Rico's economy remained underdeveloped because SPAIN refused to see the island as anything other than a military outpost. It was not until 1815 that the economic development of Puerto Rico received official support, when Ferdinand VII issued the Real Cédula de Gracias, which liberalized trade, offered incentives for immigrants, and opened Puerto Rican ports to legal commerce. It was also an attempt to "whiten" the island because, at the time, the population was mainly black and mulatto (of African and European descent).

The SUGAR industry became the most important economic activity of Puerto Rico in the nineteenth century. Spain grew more interested in the economic development of the Antilles as a way of regaining control of the mainland. There was a boom in sugar production in CUBA, Spanish Santo Domingo, and Puerto Rico, leading to increased slave importation from West Africa. While information on the slave trade to Puerto Rico is incomplete, the available records indicate that SENEGAL, SUDAN, and GUINEA were major sources. The black population was concentrated in the coastal sugar plantations, in places like Mayagüez, Guayama, and Ponce, in the southern region of the island. The number of black slaves and free *pardos* (mulattos) grew rapidly between 1820 and 1840. For example, from 5,037 slaves in 1765, the number grew to 21,730 in 1821. In the 1830s women constituted almost half of the slave population. They were preferred because they could give birth to more slaves as well as work on the plantations. The forced immigration of Africans reached its peak by the 1840s. The 1845 census shows that there were 216,083 whites, 175,000 free coloreds, and 51,265 slaves in Puerto Rico.

Forced immigration rapidly declined, primarily because of the inability of Puerto Rican plantation owners, or *hacendados,* to compete against the Cuban slave owners in the international slave market. For example, in 1840 the *bozales,* or African-born slaves, constituted 46 percent of the total slave population in Ponce, the city with the largest number of slaves at the time. By 1872 they represented only 18 percent. The last enslaved Africans who came to the island were relatively young and came from NIGERIA, GHANA, and what is now the DEMOCRATIC REPUBLIC OF THE CONGO.

Resistance and the Abolition of Slavery

As in the rest of the Americas, the enslaved population of Puerto Rico resisted the slave system. The first recorded rebellion against European domination in the hemisphere occurred in 1514 and was jointly planned and executed by Taínos and Africans.

Numerous revolts, conspiracies, and individual escapes occurred in different municipalities throughout the island from 1775 to 1873. For example, between 1795 and 1848, twenty-two conspiracies were reported. These acts of resistance occurred mostly in the towns of Guayama and Ponce, where in 1821 the slave Marcos Xiorro revolted without success but achieved legendary status among the slaves. For most slaves, to run away was the only solution to escape from a life of oppressive work and inhumane treatment. For example, slaves were labeled with a red-hot iron called a *carimbo,* used to prevent them from being illegally introduced to the island. They were frequently whipped. Not even pregnant women were exempt; they were forced to lie on the ground with their bellies in a dug-out hole (designed to protect the unborn slave) and were then whipped.

The slaves who successfully escaped to the mountains were called *cimarrones*. In Puerto Rico, there were never enough of them to take over the land or proclaim a war against their oppressors. It was common practice for the cimarrones to set fire to the cane fields as a means of attracting the militia's attention, in order to steal their weapons. Owners controlled and closely watched any slave gatherings. Sometimes the slaves planned conspiracies and revolts when they got together to play and dance *bomba*. They risked being found out by their master/overseer and exposed by other slaves. Colonial authorities encouraged antagonistic relations between slaves by granting liberty to those cimarrones who turned in another escaped slave. They also gave freedom and 500 pesos to blacks who reported any kind of slave conspiracy. Some slaves bought their liberty by paying their owner; however, not many could afford to do this. One slave annually was awarded freedom because of good behavior; some bought their children's freedom when they were baptized. Others escaped bondage by committing suicide. Many of them believed their spirit would return to Africa after they died. Other fugitive slaves escaped to Haiti and Santo Domingo. Given the large free black labor force on the island, some slaves tried to escape their bondage by passing as free workers, moving from town to town until they were discovered.

In 1826 Miguel de la Torre, the governor of Puerto Rico, enacted the first regulation for slave treatment, which was inspired by the increasing number of conspiracies. It required the slave owner to feed slaves properly and provide medical aid in the case of acute illness. Domestic slaves had to convert to Catholicism and remain obedient to authorities and respectful of whites. The regulation imposed harsh penalties for rebellious slaves, including slashing and imprisonment.

In May 1848 Governor Juan Prim adopted the infamous Bando contra la Raza Africana (Proclamation Against the African Race). It was an oppressive ordinance directed against all people of African descent, including free blacks. All blacks were subject to court-martial for any offense. The proclamation also imposed the penalty of "hand cutting" to those free persons of African descent who raised a weapon against whites, even if the aggression was justified. Those slaves found guilty were executed. Harsh prison sentences were imposed on any black who insulted or threatened a white man. The succeeding governor, Juan de la Pezuela, abolished Prim's measures in November of the same year, but rebellions and conspiracies continued.

The system of slavery started to erode in Puerto Rico after the 1850s, with the beginning of Puerto Rico's independence movement. At that time, independence and abolition went hand in hand with political radicalism. Thus the first goal of the independence movement was to end forced labor. The Sociedad Abolicionista Española (Spanish Abolitionist Society) was founded in 1855 by Ramón Emeterio Betances and a group of white Creoles who secretly worked against the institution of slavery. They promised freedom to their slaves if they participated in the revolution. After being exiled in 1867, Betances helped foment the Grito de Lares in 1868, which was the first independence revolt against Spain. Although the Lares revolt failed, it catalyzed the abolition process. Spain was not willing to grant independence to Puerto Rico after Grito de Lares, but it realized that slavery could no longer be maintained in the island. In 1870 the Spanish government passed the Moret Law, which provided for the liberation of children born between 1868

Puerto Rico (At a Glance)

OFFICIAL NAME: Commonwealth of Puerto Rico

AREA: 9,104 sq km (3,515 sq mi)

LOCATION: Island east of the Dominican Republic, between the Caribbean Sea and the North Atlantic Ocean

CAPITAL: San Juan (population 1,221,086; 1996 estimate)

POPULATION: 3,885,877 (2004 estimate)

POPULATION DENSITY: 437 persons per sq km (1,135 per sq mi)

POPULATION BELOW AGE 15: 22.9 percent (male 454,908; female 434,555; 2003 estimate)

POPULATION GROWTH RATE: 0.58 percent (2003 estimate)

TOTAL FERTILITY RATE: 2.02 children born per woman (2003 estimate)

LIFE EXPECTANCY AT BIRTH: Total population: 77.26 years (male 73.27 years; female 81.44 years; 2003 estimate)

INFANT MORTALITY RATE: 9.38 deaths per 1,000 live births (2003 estimate)

LITERACY RATE (AGE 15 AND OVER WHO CAN READ AND WRITE): Total population: 93.8 percent (male 93.7 percent; female 94 percent; 2003 estimate)

EDUCATION: Education is free and compulsory for ages six to sixteen, but there is a high dropout rate. The University of Puerto Rico is the foremost public institution of higher learning on the island. About 25 percent of high school graduates earn a bachelor's degree.

LANGUAGES: Spanish and English

ETHNIC GROUPS: 80.5 percent white (mostly Spanish origin), 8 percent black, 0.4 percent Amerindian, 0.2 percent Asian, and 10.9 percent mixed and other

RELIGIONS: Puerto Ricans are 85 percent Roman Catholic and 15 percent Protestant and other religions.

CLIMATE: Mostly tropical, with some variations depending on elevation and winds. The heaviest rainfall is between May and December. The average lowland temperature is about 78 °F (26 °C), with high humidity that makes the temperature feel higher. Hurricanes are possible between June and November.

LAND, PLANTS, AND ANIMALS: Puerto Rico is mountainous and hilly, with occasional earthquakes. Most people live in the coastal lowlands. Several unnavigable rivers provide hydropower, irrigation, and drinking water. Vegetation includes flowering trees such as the royal poinciana and the African tulip tree. Rare orchids and the Puerto Rican parrot are preserved in the Caribbean National Forest southeast of San Juan. Other animals include lizards, nonpoisonous snakes, mongooses, and many varieties of fish.

NATURAL RESOURCES: Copper, nickel, and potential for onshore and offshore oil

CURRENCY: United States dollar (USD)

GROSS DOMESTIC PRODUCT (GDP): $43.01 billion (2002 estimate)

GDP PER CAPITA: $11,100 (2002 estimate)

GDP REAL GROWTH RATE: −0.2 percent (2002 estimate)

PRIMARY ECONOMIC ACTIVITIES: Agriculture, industry, and services

PRIMARY CROPS: Sugarcane, coffee, pineapples, plantains, bananas, livestock, and chickens

INDUSTRIES: Pharmaceuticals, electronics, apparel, food products, and tourism

PRIMARY EXPORTS: Chemicals, electronics, apparel, canned tuna, rum, beverage concentrates, and medical equipment

PRIMARY IMPORTS: Chemicals, machinery and equipment, clothing, food, fish, and petroleum products

PRIMARY TRADE PARTNERS: United States, United Kingdom, Dominican Republic, Ireland, and Japan

GOVERNMENT: Puerto Rico is a commonwealth associated with the United States. The chief of state is President George W. Bush of the United States (since January 2001). The head of government is Governor Sila M. Calderon (since January 2001; popularly elected to serve a four-year term). The legislative branch is the bicameral Legislative Assembly, consisting of the twenty-eight-member Senate and the fifty-one-member House of Representatives (members of both bodies popularly elected to serve four-year terms). The judicial branch includes the Supreme Court, the Appellate Court, and the Court of First Instance (consisting of two sections: a Superior Court and a Municipal Court).

Shelle Sumners

---

and 1870 and those slaves over 60 years of age. Under this partial abolition statute, about 10,000 slaves were set free in Puerto Rico. More than 90 percent of the slaves at this time were *criollos* (Creoles).

On March 22, 1873 slavery was completely abolished, hastened by the economic situation of the plantation owners. The plantation economy in Puerto Rico had declined after 1850. The slave-owning class had neither the infrastructure nor the cash flow of their Cuban counterparts, and most of them were in debt by the 1860s. Therefore, they were not in an economically viable position to oppose abolition effectively. These factors marked the end of the old plantation system of *haciendas*, characterized by small and midsize plantations owned by white Creoles, and marked the beginning of one of Puerto Rico's worst economic crises. For the former slaves, this period meant the continuation of harsh conditions under an obligatory contract system in which they were paid but had to rely on their owners to survive.

Importance of Free Coloreds on the Island

People of African descent, predominantly free, constituted the majority of the island's inhabitants. The great majority lived restricted lives, with no control over where they lived or worked, no freedom to decide whom to marry, and no access to social institutions. Nevertheless, some managed to secure a rudimentary education; rented or owned land, stores, and houses; and attained important positions. For example, in 1845, reports mentioned Manuel Elías, a free colored silversmith who owned three houses and had three slaves. María Francisca Ferrer owned a house and two male slaves, and saved an impressive amount of money. Also, Micaela Pizarro apparently was in the real estate business and owned slaves. Free people of color used their legal position to acquire some wealth even when they had to deal with racial prejudice. Some inherited property from their masters.

As in the rest of the Spanish America, the free colored men had to serve in the segregated militia. In Puerto Rico, however, they had by royal decree the right to bear arms, even in times of peace, and to protect the island in the event of a slave revolt, an insurrection, or any kind of attack or invasion. These men played a vital role in the defense of the island, especially resisting the English attack of 1797. Apparently, whites were not threatened by the fact that colored men were in charge of defense.

The number of free blacks and pardos increased more rapidly than the number of whites between 1820 and 1840. They suffered more than whites from the consequences of the cholera epidemic that claimed thousands of lives in the second half of the century. They also had to cope, more than whites, with the deterioration of the public health system at the same time. For these reasons, and the fact that the racial classifications changed, the white population in the second half of the century appeared to grow more rapidly. The increasing numbers of those classified as "white" also reflected the fluidity of racial definitions. In a context in which few could claim "purity of blood" and whiteness was the preferred designation, many simply elected to emphasize European ancestry. Under Spanish law, "whiteness" could be purchased, and those who accumulated sufficient wealth paid for an official change in their records.

Free colored people lived in an elaborate caste system, where the degree of whiteness determined their position and possibilities in the colonial society. The stratification of the Puerto Rican society resulting from this system granted superiority to the whites over the pardos and blacks. Mixture between races was associated with illegitimacy and provided whites with another reason for rejecting blacks. Still, limpieza de sangre, or purity (WHITENING) of blood, through marrying a lighter-skinned person, was the way to ascend in the social class structure. Light-skinned people had better economic and social possibilities.

The government always wanted to maintain control over the laboring population, white and black, slave and free. The cholera epidemic also had a great impact on the labor force, and the number of enslaved people declined. Between 1838 and 1868 the government improved the mechanisms of control by implementing mandatory labor laws that affected all laboring sectors, whites as well as blacks and pardos. All men between sixteen and sixty years old who did not own or rent land were called *jornaleros,* or workers who earn a salary. In 1849 Juan de la Pezuela instituted what is known as *la libreta* (the notebook), which stated that every jornalero had to carry a notebook in which the owner made notes on the worker's behavior. Authorities revised la libreta and labeled as "lazy" anyone who was not earning a salary, in which case the worker had to move to another town. This practice often tied the workers to their owner's land and promoted complete dependency.

By the end of the nineteenth century, the majority of blacks in Puerto Rico were "Creole blacks," born and raised on the Island. Creole blacks were better characterized as black Puerto Ricans rather than Africans living in a foreign Caribbean island. While preserving many of the African traditions, blacks adopted much of the Spanish culture and were instrumental in maintaining aspects of the Taíno culture as well. Although Roman Catholicism was the only recognized religion, the vast majority of the population practiced syncretic forms, combining Christian images and traditions with African beliefs. There was a paucity of Roman Catholic clergy and other resources (doctors, etc.), a reflection of Spain's general neglect of Puerto Rico. Thus, lay forms of religion were often the only option for the populace.

Puerto Rico in the Twentieth Century

In 1898, just as Puerto Rico was making progress toward autonomy, it was ceded to the United States under the Treaty of Paris, after the Spanish-American War. The military governed the island for a short time, followed by a civil government outlined in the Foraker Act, which was approved in 1900. U.S. racial attitudes and race issues then began to affect Puerto Rican life, aggravating the already existing racism on the island, in which the definition of a national identity favored the Hispanic heritage over the African. For example, in 1917, with the imminent participation of the United States in World War I, the Jones Act granted American citizenship to Puerto Ricans, many of whom then had to fight in the U.S. military. Since that time, Puerto Ricans have participated in every military conflict in which the United States has been involved. At first, Puerto Rican males were placed in segregated Negro units. Those Puerto Ricans who considered themselves white were offended by this grouping.

Puerto Ricans who migrated to the mainland at the end of the nineteenth century, and especially after World War I and until the 1940s, underwent a similar experience regarding racial classifications. They were confronted with the fact that the way in which they defined themselves differed from the way in which they were perceived on the mainland. The racial prejudice that came from the years of slavery developed into a concept that equated African heritage with a supposed deficiency of performance, both socially and intellectually. This, in turn, clearly affected the development of a national identity on and off the island.

In 1943 Luis Muñoz Marín, who later became the first elected Puerto Rican governor for the Popular Democratic Party when the Commonwealth was established in 1952, passed the first Civil Rights Act of Puerto Rico. Before this legislation, it was common practice to turn away people of color at places that were open to the rest of the public, such as casinos and restaurants. The new act imposed criminal penalties on anyone who denied services to people on the basis of race or color in public places, in businesses, or on public transportation, but the law was not enforced.

The Bill of Rights of Puerto Rico's Constitution was approved in 1952 and included a specific provision prohibiting discrimination on the basis of race, color, or social condition. In 1965 a civil rights commission was created for the purpose of investigating and educating the public and proposing legal reforms on issues of civil rights, including racial discrimination. Under the commonwealth status, the United States Constitution and civil rights laws are fully applicable to Puerto Rico, reinforcing the local laws that existed before federal protections became effective.

Despite these legislative changes, RACISM continued to exist in various forms in the island. For example, in the 1950s the Commission for Civil Rights gathered evidence to prove that Afro–Puerto Rican professors and students were victims of discrimination in the private schools. A correlation exists between race and social class in Puerto Rico. The economic elite in Puerto Rico remains predominantly white, while the Afro–Puerto Rican and mulatto communities are generally associated with substandard conditions and crime. Racial prejudice varies from class to class yet tends to be more evident among members of the upper classes. Such prejudice is also directed against the Dominican undocumented immigrants who come to the island through the Mona Passage, looking for better economic opportunities.

Although the problems of racism are far from being resolved, there is a growing awareness and discussion of the Afro–Puerto Rican situation on both the island and the mainland that have brought many Puerto Ricans of African descent together for the purpose of confronting the issues of discrimination. Scholarly works, such as Isabelo Zenón Cruz's *Narciso descubre su trasero* and José Luis González's *El país de cuatro pisos,* have been essential in rousing awareness. Other important contributions come from Puerto Rican immigrants in the United States who have been deeply influenced by the African American CIVIL RIGHTS MOVEMENT. Organizations, such as the Young Lords, who resemble the BLACK PANTHERS of the 1960s; the Unión de mujeres negras puertorriqueñas (Union of Afro-Puerto Rican Women); and the Concilio puertorriqueño contra el racismo (Puerto Rican Council against Racism), have come forward to take up the cause of Afro–Puerto Ricans.

The 2000 U.S. Census was the first in fifty years to classify Puerto Ricans by race. According to that census, over 80 percent of Puerto Ricans define themselves as white, while about 8 percent identify themselves as black. Although many Puerto Ricans are of mixed ancestry, only 4 percent describe themselves as "mixed-race," and while Puerto Rico is making progress in eliminating racial discrimination, there is still a stigma attached to blackness. For example, one government clerk remarked that when people come to his office to register, "Unless they are really, really black, I put everyone down as white because that helps them later in life."

African heritage is an essential and undeniable part of Puerto Rican culture. It is evident in musical expressions, such as SALSA and the vernacular rhythms of PLENA AND BOMBA, which are also dances; in the language; in the cuisine; and in popular traditions of the island. Afro–Puerto Ricans, such as ROBERTO CLEMENTE, have distinguished themselves in sports. Many political leaders of African descent, such as Pedro Albizu Campos, Ernesto Ramos Antonini, and JOSÉ CELSO BARBOSA, have played important roles in history. In the arts, such musicians as RAFAEL CORTIJO, ISMAEL RIVERA, Rafael Hernández, and WILLIE COLÓN; painters JOSÉ CAMPECHE; and writers JULIA DE BURGOS, Luis Palés Matos, and LUIS RAFEL SÁNCHEZ provide examples of the richness of Afro–Puerto Rican culture.

See also Catholic Church in Latin America and the Caribbean; Colonial Latin America and the Caribbean; Colonial Rule; Racism in Latin America and the Caribbean; Slave Laws in Colonial Spanish America; Slave Rebellions in Colonial Spanish America; Slavery in Latin America and the Caribbean; Transatlantic Slave Trade.

Mayda Grano de Oro

Punishment of Slaves in Colonial Latin America and the Caribbean

Infliction of corporal punishment as corrective and demoralizing penalties for individual slaves and as exemplary measures to control other bonded blacks through terror and fear.

Corporal punishment was designed with various goals in mind. Broadly speaking, one could argue that its purpose was fivefold: (1) deter rebellious behavior; (2) instill fear to prevent defiance from becoming exemplary; (3) inculcate the Roman Catholic religion and prevent the expression of African spiritual practices and other forms of resistance to the colonizers' culture; (4) regulate sexual conduct in order to prevent MISCEGENATION and preserve clear-cut socio-racial hierarchies; and (5) sustain the interests of various corporations or elite groups.

Punishment for slaves in colonial Latin America was of two types: de jure (regulated by law) or de facto (according to the custom and will of the slave owners). De jure punishment was established in *cédulas* (legislation issued by the Spanish king), local edicts and orders (issued by the viceroy), and codes. These laws regulated a variety of corporal punishments for slaves according to the types of crimes and their severity. The punishments escalated from whipping to branding to mutilations to death. The normative structure allowed for masters or government authorities to physically discipline slaves for many actions considered defiant or unruly, such as engaging in religious rites that were not Roman Catholic; gathering in groups; stealing; carrying arms; and talking back to or hitting whites. The most extreme punishment, death, was designated for runaway slaves or for leaders of slave revolts if caught.

Orders and cédulas also set forth punishments for a broad variety of actions and were issued as a direct response to a local offense. For example, as scholar Leslie Rout's research shows, cutting down trees or picking fruit or corn merited 100 floggings for the first offense and the mutilation of the slave's genitals if the action was repeated (PERU, 1537). Male slaves who had sexual relations with Indian women were to be whipped 100 times (CHILE, 1550). Changing the course of an irrigation channel could also merit 100 lashes (Peru, 1537). Slaves who were found to have Indians as their servants would receive 100 whippings for the first offense and have their ears cut off if they were found culpable a second time (Peru, 1551). Playing card games merited 50 to 200 lashes (Chile, 1577). Slaves who worked in the printing business without being under direct control of their master would receive 100 to 200 lashes (MEXICO, 1605).

As if these laws did not allow for severe enough punishment, it has been generally recognized that they were ignored, as local authorities and masters interpreted them to best fit their specific circumstances and cruel creativity. In colonial Latin America, there was a generalized belief that "carelessness, laziness and an aversion to work are natural for the inhabitants of Africa"; therefore slaveholders thought it was necessary to subject them to a harsh regime and to perform exemplifying punishments. Slaves were also believed to be little more than a material good. By holding ownership rights, masters felt they could dispose of the slave according to their own judgment. Compassion was based on limiting damage to the owner's economic investment rather than on humanitarian motives. However, rage against runaways and rebels was particularly vicious because of the challenge they presented to the whole system. Historians have found accounts of escaped or rebellious slaves being roasted to death or hung on the island of HISPANIOLA, fitted with iron collars and thrown to hungry dogs in PANAMA, tortured and beheaded in Mexico, boiled to death in COSTA RICA, dragged through streets and quartered in URUGUAY, and branded with hot irons in BRAZIL.

Epifanio de Moirans, a Spanish priest, described such punishments in his 1682 testimony: "Other [slave owners] will burn [the slaves'] ribs with red hot irons, or apply a knife to their intimate parts; some will cut off pieces of meat or the testicles with a knife; but all of the slaves are jailed with chains, and are made to work this way or with a type of horn made of iron around their neck. Mules and horses are not so ill treated as are Christian slaves by the Catholics of the Indies. . . . The [master's] mistake is to believe that they have ownership over [the slaves] as over pigs; and as such some of the masters and mistresses proceed with furious passion and murder their slaves, drowning them and cutting them up into pieces. . . . Runaways that were captured were beaten until their bones were broken or they were hung by law or they were murdered by their captors . . . In other regions fugitives that were caught received two hundred whippings and had their ears cut off. These are excesses that I have seen and been informed of with all certainty, because I have been able to travel through regions of the Portuguese, Spanish and French, to see the good and bad works of men."

See also Catholic Church in Latin America and the Caribbean; Colonial Latin America and the Caribbean; Slave Laws in Colonial Spanish America; Slave Rebellions in Latin America and the Caribbean; Slavery in Latin America and the Caribbean.

Liliana Obregón

Punt

Mysterious African land that provided ancient Egypt with luxury goods.

Few things are certain about the land of Punt. Scholars have not confidently identified any Puntite artifacts, and they are uncertain of the country's location. In fact, it seems possible that the Egyptians referred to different regions as "Punt" at different times. Egyptians recorded sea journeys to Punt south down the Red Sea, or river journeys via the NILE. Punt may have been in modern-day SUDAN, ETHIOPIA, ERITREA, DJIBOUTI, or SOMALIA—or in more than one of these places at different times. Punt's boundaries could have enclosed coastal areas, inland areas, or both.

Egyptian records document trading expeditions to Punt for more than a thousand years. The Palermo Stone of the Fifth Dynasty first mentions imports from Punt during Sahure's reign (2458–2446 B.C.E.). Most information about Punt comes from reliefs in the temple of the fifteenth-century-B.C.E. female pharaoh Hatshepsut, which tell not only of trade, but also of Puntites and their land. The final Egyptian reference to trade with Punt was during RAMSES III's reign (1194–1163 B.C.E.); however, other sources mention Punt as late as the twenty-sixth Dynasty (672–525 B.C.E.). The Greeks also traded with Punt beginning in the fourth century B.C.E., and Greek geographers wrote of Punt as recently as 100 B.C.E.

Egypt exchanged foods, alcohol, and other goods with Puntites for luxury goods such as myrrh, incense, herbs, electrum, gold, staves, cosmetics, ebony, ivory, monkeys, cattle and hounds, LEOPARD skins, and probably slaves. While the evidence clearly illustrates Egyptian expeditions to Punt, it also appears that the Puntites voyaged to Egypt as traders.

The Egyptian reliefs suggest that Punt was a mostly arid land, rich in minerals and animal life including domestic donkeys, as well as birds, GIRAFFES, ibexes, leopards, ELEPHANTS, and RHINOCEROSES. The people are believed to have been pastoralists who lived in round dwellings on stilts, perhaps to protect the residents from wild animals or to provide shelter for livestock below. The women were mostly slender. The men, clothed in bifurcated kilts, wore their hair both shaved and long, with short, blunt beards, or long beards in the Egyptian style with curled ends.

See also Egypt, Ancient Kingdom of; Gold Trade; Ivory Trade.

Robert Fay

Purvis, Charles Burleigh

1842–1929

African American physician and medical educator.

Charles Burleigh Purvis was born in PHILADELPHIA, PENNSYLVANIA, the son of Robert Purvis, Sr., a well-to-do abolitionist, and Harriet Forten, daughter of James Forten, a prosperous sailmaker and civic leader. Purvis received his early education in QUAKER-administered public schools and then at Oberlin College, 1860–1863. For his medical studies he attended Wooster Medical College, which later was incorporated into Western Reserve University Medical School, in Cleveland, Ohio, graduating with an M.D. in 1865. During the summer of 1864 Purvis served as a military nurse, based at Camp Barker, a contraband hospital in WASHINGTON, D.C., which later formed the foundation of FREEDMEN'S HOSPITAL.

Upon graduating he petitioned to and was accepted by the U.S. Volunteers as an assistant surgeon for the Union army, one of only eight African Americans accepted as surgeons during the war. He held the rank of first lieutenant from 1865 to 1869 and was posted in the Washington, D.C., area. Following the CIVIL WAR the War Department relinquished its control of medical services for African Americans to the Bureau of Refugees, Freedmen, and Abandoned Lands, and like many of the other African American army surgeons, Purvis had his services contracted. The African American population in the capital city had more than doubled between the years of 1860 and 1867, with only six physicians to minister to their needs. With the bureau Purvis served as an assistant surgeon attending patients at an outdoor clinic in Washington, D.C.

In 1869 Purvis was appointed to the medical faculty of HOWARD UNIVERSITY, making him only the second African American to hold such a position at an American university (the first was ALEXANDER T. AUGUSTA). From 1869 to 1873 he lectured on subjects such as materia medica, therapeutics, botany, and medical jurisprudence; during 1871–1872 he held the Thaddeus Stevens Chair; and during 1873–1906 he was professor of obstetrics, gynecology, and diseases of women and children. In 1871 the board of Howard University conferred on him an honorary M.A., and in 1914 he was the recipient of an LL.D. for his service. In 1871 Purvis married Ann Hathaway; they had two children.

In 1873 the entire nation faced a fiscal crisis that prompted the Howard University trustees to ask for the resignations of the entire medical staff. However, the staff was given the option of being reappointed to the faculty on a pro bono basis, a condition that lasted until 1907, when the medical faculty was awarded partial remuneration for its services. Only Doctors Charles Purvis, Alexander Augusta, and Gideon Palmer chose to remain on a "self-supporting" basis, probably because they had income from other sources, including private practices. In an 1873 letter to General O. O. Howard, the university president for whom the institution is named, Purvis wrote, "While I regret the university will not be able to pay me for my services, I feel the importance of every effort being made to carry forward the institution and to make it a success" (Winston, Howard University Archives).

During the crisis Purvis in 1873 assumed the position of secretary pro tempore of the medical department, a position he held until 1896. His leadership and innovative restructuring of the department was instrumental in saving the medical department from demise. Purvis was said to be a hard taskmaster and intolerant of those who failed to keep themselves apprised of the latest medical developments. His determination ensured that all students, and in particular African American and female candidates, continued to be trained as physicians. From 1899 to 1900 he served as president of the faculty and in 1900 was elected to the post of dean, which he declined.

When President James Garfield was wounded in an assassination attempt in 1881 Purvis was one of the consulting physicians, making him the only African American to attend a president of the United States. In acknowledgment of his service, newly elected president Chester A. Arthur appointed him surgeon in chief of Freedmen's Hospital, the teaching facility affiliated with Howard University's medical department. At this time the hospital was administered by the Department of the Interior rather than the War Department, making Purvis the first African American civilian to head a hospital under civilian auspices. He retained the position until 1894. Under his administration the number of patients attended increased greatly, and the care was substantially upgraded.

Purvis, a firm believer in professional development, in 1869 had his name, along with those of Augusta and later A. W. Tucker, all black physicians, forwarded for membership in the Medical Society of the District of Columbia, a branch of the American Medical Association (AMA). Membership in the AMA accorded a physician the latest medical information at lectures and workshops in addition to a level of prestige that could result in increased financial compensation. All three doctors had their applications denied strictly on the basis of race. Despite efforts from a group of local white physicians including Robert Reyburn, Joseph Burrows, and Silas Loomis, and a resolution Senator Charles Sumner of Massachusetts introduced before the U.S. Senate, the drive to have the racist entrance policies of medical societies abolished was defeated.

While residing in Washington, Purvis was also active in civic matters, serving on the board of education and the board of health for the district; the board of medical examiners, 1897–1904; and the board of trade for Washington.

In 1905 he relocated to BOSTON, MASSACHUSETTS, for the remainder of his life and established a general practice. He was admitted to the Massachusetts Medical Society in 1904. However, his affiliation with Howard University continued. He resigned his teaching position in 1907 but was elected in 1908 to the board of trustees, a position he held until 1926. Purvis died in Los Angeles, California.

Bibliography

Cobb, W. Montague. "Original Communications: A Short History of Freedmen's Hospital." *Journal of the National Medical Association* 54, no. 3 (May 1962).

Kaufman, Martin, et al., eds. "Purvis, Charles Burleigh." In *Dictionary of American Medical Biography*. Vol. 2. 1984.

Lamb, Daniel Smith. "Charles Burleigh Purvis, A.M., M.D." In *Howard University Medical Department, A Historical, Biographical and Statistical Souvenir*. 1900; repr. 1971.

Logan, Rayford W. *Howard University: The First Hundred Years 1867–1967*. 1969.

Morais, Herbert M. *The History of the Negro in Medicine*. 1967.

"Purvis, Charles B." *Who Was Who in America with World Notables*. Vol. 4. 1968.

Simmons, William J. "Charles B. Purvis, A.M., M.D." In Simmons's *Men of Mark: Eminent, Progressive and Rising*. 1887; repr. 1968.

From *American National Biography*. John A. Garraty and Mark C. Carnes, eds. Oxford University Press, 1999. Reprinted by permission of the American Council of Learned Societies.

Dalyce Newby

Purvis, Robert

1810–1898

African American abolitionist and reformer.

Robert Purvis was born in Charleston, South Carolina, the son of William Purvis, a naturalized British cotton broker, and Harriet Judah, the free mulatto daughter of a German Jewish flour merchant and an emancipated slave of Moorish extraction. In 1819 the family settled in Philadelphia, and at William's death (1826) Harriet and her three sons came into a substantial fortune. After private schooling, Robert attended Pittsfield and Amherst academies in Massachusetts, leaving the latter in 1829 following a July 4 prank. At age seventeen, inspired by his father's opposition to slavery, he had spoken at an antislavery convention. But in 1830, meeting the abolitionist Benjamin Lundy, whom he would revere all his life, he resolved on a career as a reformer.

A close friend of James Forten, the wealthy black sailmaker, Purvis threw himself into anticolonization activities, denouncing the plan to deport free blacks to colonies outside the United States. He married Forten's daughter, Harriet, in 1831; the couple had eight children. After Harriet's death in 1875, he married Tacy Townsend, a white Quaker. When Lundy's associate, William Lloyd Garrison, looked to publish *The Liberator* (1831) and his hostile *Thoughts on African Colonization* (1832),

Purvis and Forten aided him by gathering subscriptions and raising funds. Both were charter members of the American Anti-Slavery Society formed in Philadelphia in 1833. Following the first annual meeting of the society, Purvis, having obtained a U.S. passport through the intervention of President Andrew Jackson, sailed in 1834 to Great Britain, where for three months he promoted the American antislavery cause and visited relatives. His return voyage provided him with a tale he delighted to tell for the remainder of his life: he had been showered with social courtesies by fellow passengers, notably the racial purist Arthur Peronneau Hayne of South Carolina, all of them miscued by his light complexion, until he disclosed, shortly before landing, that he belonged "to the degraded tribe of Africans."

Back in Philadelphia, Purvis moved his family to a house on 9th and Lombard streets, in the heart of the city's black community. He embraced the free produce movement, which eschewed products of slave labor, such as rice and sugar; joined the black-led American Moral Reform Society, founded to promote "Education, Temperance, Economy, and Universal Liberty," as its corresponding secretary; and journeyed to Harrisburg as a delegate of the Philadelphia City Anti-Slavery Society to launch the Pennsylvania Anti-Slavery Society in 1837. That year, concerned at the abduction of increasing numbers of free blacks by agents sent to apprehend fugitive slaves, Purvis set up a Vigilant Association and, upon its restructuring in 1839 as the Vigilant Committee, was elected president of, in his words, "the first organized society of the Underground Railroad" (Smedley, p. 355). His home served as a haven for fugitive slaves on their way to freedom. He also became prominent as the drafter of *The Appeal of Forty Thousand Citizens, Threatened with Disfranchisement, to the People of Pennsylvania* (1838), a vain attempt to persuade the state electorate not to adopt a new constitution that would wipe away forty-seven years of black voting rights.

In 1842 Philadelphia suffered a race riot, and as in an 1838 riot, Purvis's residence was besieged. This time, abandoning the principle of nonresistance, he was prepared to shoot any intruder. Shaken and indignant, Purvis moved his family to two farms of 140 acres he had bought in Byberry, about fifteen miles away. There he led the life of a gentleman farmer, proud of his prized cattle and horses, blue-ribbon poultry, and orchards. He continued to serve the American Anti-Slavery Society (vice president, 1841–1865; thereafter he was on the Executive Committee) and to uphold radical Garrisonian doctrines, including the dissolution of the political union of the North and South. He was an energetic affiliate of the Bucks County Anti-Slavery Society, the Pennsylvania Anti-Slavery Society (president, 1845–1850), and the Pennsylvania Abolition Society (he was the only nonwhite member from 1840 to 1859). He gave money to the Repeal movement in Ireland, which agitated against the 1800 union of Great Britain and Ireland that had led to a single parliament, championed prison reform as well as temperance (while privately abstaining from liquor and smoking), and advocated women's rights.

The "damnable" Fugitive Slave Act of 1850, with its sweeping and stringent provisions for the restitution of runaway slaves to their masters, galvanized Purvis into publicly advocating violence. Barely one month after the passage of the act, declining reelection as president of the Pennsylvania Abolition Society, which shied away from use of "weapons of death," Purvis declared to its members, "Should any wretch enter my dwelling to execute this . . . law, I'll seek his life. I'll shed his blood, though my own life and that of my family should be sacrificed in consequence" (*The Liberator,* November 1, 1850). Avoiding active participation in the newly formed Philadelphia Vigilance Committee of 1852 due to delicate health, he redoubled his fugitive rescue efforts, his farm having a secret room to hide fugitive slaves until they could be safely spirited away. Although he praised Harriet Beecher Stowe's *Uncle Tom's Cabin* (1852) for its condemnation of "the infernal system" of slavery, he openly deplored its favorable view of black resettlement in LIBERIA, which the state legislature considered endorsing in April.

In 1853 Purvis found himself embroiled in a series of public controversies. In an August issue of his weekly journal, black abolitionist FREDERICK DOUGLASS wounded Purvis deeply by referring to his "blood stained riches," implying that the riches had originated in the production of cotton by slaves. The two men later reconciled, in 1886. In October he was outraged after his son and two women were asked to leave an exhibition at the Franklin Institute in Philadelphia because of their color and after the Poultry Society Fair at the Philadelphia Museum excluded his fowl. The following month he publicized his refusal to pay Byberry's school tax because his children were barred as pupils due to their race. Although he contemplated moving to England or CANADA, he persevered in his commitments. Eventually the Byberry officials, well aware that Purvis was the township's second largest taxpayer, opened school doors to all children. In 1855 ex–fugitive slave and reformer WILLIAM WELLS BROWN asseverated, "There is no colored man in this country to whom the Anti-slavery cause is more indebted than Mr. Purvis" (*The American Fugitive . . . with a Memoir,* p. 312).

The DRED SCOTT decision of March 1857, declaring that Americans of African descent were not U.S. citizens, stirred Purvis's powers of excoriation and hyperbole to increasing frequency. In a fiery speech of May 12 he quoted Justice Roger Taney's opinion that blacks had "no rights which white men are bound to respect." In December 1859 he pronounced JOHN BROWN (1800–1859), who had attempted to incite a slave insurrection at Harpers Ferry that October, the "Jesus Christ of the Nineteenth Century." He claimed in May 1860 that in "this cursed land" with its "hellish laws and precedents" he expected nothing from the new REPUBLICAN PARTY since it supported slavery where it already existed and favored colonization. Five months later, while lambasting slaveholders, he labeled Thomas Jefferson a "scoundrel," although better judgment moved him to omit that epithet in a printed version of his remarks.

Purvis welcomed armed conflict to end slavery, but after the CIVIL WAR began, he criticized the race-related policies of President ABRAHAM LINCOLN, particularly his proposal to deport and colonize freed slaves. He grew to trust the Lincoln administration, however, and took heart from Attorney General Edward Bates's declaration that he believed blacks were citizens, the Dred Scott decision notwithstanding. After the official release of the EMANCIPATION PROCLAMATION, Purvis admitted freely that he was "proud to be an American citizen." When the government began recruiting black troops in 1863, he urged black volunteers to enlist at Camp William Penn near Philadelphia. Joining with others to organize the Pennsylvania Equal Rights League in 1864, he rejoiced at the passage of the FOURTEENTH and FIFTEENTH AMENDMENTS, although he remained a disappointed yet steadfast proponent of woman suffrage.

Greatly respected in the postwar era, Purvis refused an 1867 bid to head the Freedmen's Bureau but served as a commissioner in WASHINGTON, D.C., of the Republican-sponsored FREEDMEN'S BANK (1874–1880). After returning to Philadelphia, he dedicated himself, as an elder statesman of abolitionism, to the defeat of slavery's "twin relic of barbarism, prejudice against color." He supported municipal reform and independent political action to battle race discrimination in city employment, to ameliorate the economic plight of black workers, and to shore up civil rights. In 1881 he backed for mayor Democratic reform candidate Samuel G. King, who after election appointed four black policemen. In 1884, ignoring mounting Republican displeasure because he did not adhere to the party that had freed the slaves, Purvis flirted with the Greenback party. Dissatisfied with the 1887 state civil rights law, he lobbied for more inclusive legislation.

Although increasingly enfeebled by the "weight of years" in later life, Purvis was honored by being named to the Pennsylvania World's Fair Board (1891). He graciously granted interviews on the early days of slave rescues, the last in December 1897; and he enrolled as a founder of the American Negro Historical Society (1897). He died, the last survivor of the American Anti-Slavery Society, in Philadelphia in his home at 16th and Mount Vernon. After his death, books from his large private library, including two bound volumes of *The Liberator* bearing his autograph, were donated to the University of Pennsylvania. The oil portrait of JOSEPH CINQUÉ that he had commissioned by painter Nathaniel Jocelyn to honor the hero of the 1839 Amistad slave ship mutiny was donated to the New Haven Colony Historical Society.

Bibliography

Boromé, Joseph A. "Robert Purvis and His Early Challenge to American Racism." *Negro History Bulletin* 30 (1967): 8–10.

Lane, Roger. *William Dorsey's Philadelphia and Ours: On the Past and Future of the Black City in America.* 1991.

Obituary, *New York Times,* April 16, 1898.

Purvis, John R., comp. *The Purvis Family, 1694–1988.* 1989.

Quarles, Benjamin. *Black Abolitionists.* 1969.

Ripley, C. Peter, ed. *The Black Abolitionist Papers, 1830–1865.* 5 vols. 1985–1992.

Winch, Julie. *Philadelphia's Black Elite: Activism, Accommodation and the Struggle for Autonomy, 1787–1848.* 1988.

From *American National Biography*. John A. Garraty and Mark C. Carnes, eds. Oxford University Press, 1999. Reprinted by permission of the American Council of Learned Societies.

Joseph A. Boromé

Puryear, Martin

1941–

African American sculptor whose works blend African, Asian, and Western artistic traditions.

The work of sculptor Martin Puryear is known for the combination of traditional handicrafts, such as woodworking and basketry, with basic, geometric forms. Puryear's love of both art and handicraft was evident throughout his childhood in WASHINGTON, D.C., where he was fascinated by drawing as well as by the construction of such useful objects as bows, arrows, chairs, canoes, and guitars. Puryear studied biology and art at Catholic University in Washington, graduating with a B.A. degree in 1963. From 1964 to 1966 he served with the Peace Corps in SIERRA LEONE, where he taught biology, French, and English while learning traditional carpentry techniques from local craftspeople. After leaving the Peace Corps, he studied printmaking at the Swedish Royal Academy in Stockholm, but his private studies of woodworking there led him to turn from printmaking to the three-dimensional art of wood sculpture. In 1971 Puryear earned his master's degree in sculpture from Yale University in Connecticut.

By the mid-1970s Puryear began drawing critical and popular attention for sculptures such as *Box and Pole* (1977, Lewiston, New York), an outdoor sculpture that combines a 54-cubic-inch (885-cu cm) wooden cube with a 100-foot (30-m) timber pole. In a time when some artists design but do not actually manufacture the objects they exhibit, Puryear has placed the skills of handicraft at the center of his art. His work often borrows forms and techniques from the architecture and art of nonindustrialized cultures—from Asian yurts (circular huts) to African baskets—adapting them to the more formal and abstract aims of modern art. His sculptures are always finely crafted, although the forms may be rough in appearance. *Lever #2* (1987–1988, Baltimore Museum of Art, Baltimore, Maryland), for example, combines a gangly basket structure with a long, curving tail. *Maroon* (1987–1988, Milwaukee Art Museum, Milwaukee, Wisconsin) is a more compact, earthy form crafted of pine and yellow poplar, as well as steel mesh and tar. Puryear has also created ambitious outdoor installations. One of these, *Bodark Arc* (1982, University Park, Illinois), a vast, curving pathway 392 feet (119 m) in diameter, was influenced by the 1960s earthworks movement, which featured gigantic artworks that became part of the landscape.

Puryear's work has been shown in important group exhibitions such as the Whitney Biennial in 1979, 1981, and 1989 and the Museum of Modern Art's International Survey of Recent Painting and Sculpture in 1984. In 1989 Puryear was the only artist from the United States chosen for the São Paulo Biennial art exhibition in BRAZIL. He won the exhibition's grand prize. That same year Puryear received a prestigious MacArthur Foundation Fellowship. In the early 1990s a major collection of his work toured several American museums. A New York City gallery exhibited four of Puryear's recent pieces in the spring of 2003.

Bibliography

Benezra, Neal. *Martin Puryear*. Thames & Hudson, 1991.

Davies, Hugh M., and Helaine Rosner. *Martin Puryear*. University Gallery, University of Massachusetts at Amherst, 1984.

Pushkin, Aleksandr

1799–1837

Russian poet and author of plays, novels, and short stories, considered the founder of modern Russian literature, whose maternal great-grandfather was African.

Aleksandr Pushkin was of high birth: his father came from a long line of Russian aristocracy, and his mother was the granddaughter of ABRAM HANNIBAL, who proclaimed himself to be an African prince. Sold into slavery in the early eighteenth century, Hannibal became an engineer and major general in the Russian army and was a favorite of Tsar Peter I (Peter the Great).

Enchanted with his African ancestry, Pushkin often employed the subject in his poetry, to the point of exaggeration and obsession, according to his critics. In 1830 Faddey Bulgarin berated Pushkin for bragging about a nobility stemming from a "Negro" who had been "acquired" by a skipper in exchange for a bottle of rum. Pushkin replied sharply to "Figliarin" (which translates roughly into "buffoon") in a poem entitled "My Genealogy":

Postscriptum
Figliarin, snug at home, decided
That my black grandsire, Hannibal,
Was for a bottle of rum acquired
And fell into a skipper's hands.
This skipper was the glorious skipper
Through whom our country was advanced
Who to our native vessel's helm
Gave mightly a sovereign course.
This skipper was accessible
To my grandsire: the blackamoor,
Bought at a bargain, grew up stanch and loyal
The emperor's bosom friend, not slave.

Pushkin was deeply influenced by the Russian folklore and stories his maternal grandmother told him as a child, and he searched out similar stories from Russian villagers throughout his life. Like many Russian aristocrats, he was also well-versed in French language and literature. Educated at the Imperial Lyceum at Tsarskoye Selo, Pushkin demonstrated an early po-

This undated portrait by Vasily Tropinin shows the poet Aleksandr Pushkin, whose work reflected his love of Russian folktales and his fascination with his partially black heritage. Pushkin's great-grandfather, Abram Hannibal, was a slave who became a major general in the Russian army. CORBIS/Bettmann

etic genius in works such as "To My Friend the Poet" (1820), which demonstrated his allegiance to Romantic literary styles.

Pushkin diverged from this style in later works. In *Ruslan and Ludmila* (1820), he espoused a literary manner characterized by ample use of Russian folklore in the form of a narrative poem. Because this work rejected established rules and genres, he was criticized by the main literary schools of the day, Classicism and Sentimentalism. Still, *Ruslan and Ludmila* earned him a reputation as one of Russia's most promising poetic talents.

In 1817 Pushkin accepted a position in the Ministry of Foreign Affairs in St. Petersburg. He participated in the city's social life and belonged to an underground branch of the revolutionary group, Union of Welfare. The radical fervor he expressed through his verse made him an inspiring spokesman for the revolutionaries who fought in the 1825 Decembrist uprising for a constitutional monarchy. They were violently suppressed. It was during this period that Pushkin wrote "Ode to Liberty" (1820), for which he was exiled to the Caucasus.

In works written in exile, called his "southern cycle," Pushkin was clearly influenced by the English poet Lord Byron. He demonstrates the love for liberty typical of his contemporaries in the romantic narrative poems *The Prisoner of the Caucasus* (1822), *The Fountain of Bakhchisarai* (1824), and *The Gypsies* (1824). In 1823 he began *Eugene Onegin* (1931), known to be the first of the great Russian novels (although in verse). Though it is a Byronic love story, in *Eugene Onegin* Pushkin treats the Russian historical setting realistically and the characters objectively.

Pushkin was transferred to Odessa in 1823, but after a series of incidents, including an affair with a superior's wife, he was dismissed from government service in 1824. He was banished to his mother's estate near Pskov, where he wrote *Boris Godunov* (1931), a Russian historical tragedy in the Shakespearean tradition. In *Boris Godunov,* Pushkin emphasizes the moral and political importance of "the judgment of the people" toward their rulers, and proved that he could, as he felt poet-prophets should, "fire the hearts of men with his words."

In 1826 Tsar Nicholas I, recognizing Pushkin's enormous popularity, pardoned him. On his return to the capital, Pushkin continued to evoke Russian nationalist themes in two long poems, *Poltava* (1828) and *The Bronze Horseman* (1833), as well as in his novel of the Pugachev rebellion, *The Captain's Daughter* (1836). He also wrote short stories including *The Queen of Spades* (1834) and a fictionalized biography of his great-grandfather, *The Negro of Peter the Great* (uncompleted version published in 1837). In this biography, Pushkin represented Hannibal in a completely positive manner, making the novel one of the earliest characterizations of the "Negro as hero" in world literature.

Pushkin died tragically February 10, 1837, from wounds that he suffered in a duel he fought in St. Petersburg. Allison Blakely, author of *Russia and the Negro* (1986), argues that Pushkin had been experiencing emotional stress regarding his nominal position at the Court as "Gentlemen of the Chamber," a title usually assigned to aristocratic youths, to which he was appointed primarily because it allowed his beautiful—and notoriously flirtatious—wife to attend social functions. Not only was Pushkin humiliated by his position, but he may have felt insulted by the presence of colorfully attired African slaves at the court. The fateful duel, Blakely asserts, was fought not only on behalf of the Pushkins, but also to defend the honor of his Hannibal ancestry.

See also Russia and the Former Soviet Union.

Bibliography

Blakely, Allison. *Russia and the Negro.* Howard University Press, 1986.

Vickery, Walter N. *Alexander Pushkin.* Twayne Publishers, 1970.

Leyla Keough

Pygmy

People of shorter than average height, who live in the forest of Central Africa; the ethnic groups generally identified as pygmies are the Binga, the Gelli, the Aka, the Twa, and the Mbuti.

The first recorded encounter between so-called pygmies and foreigners occurred in 2500 B.C.E., when Egyptian pharaoh Nefrikare sent an expedition to find the source of the NILE RIVER. The group traveled southward, into the interior of AFRICA, and encountered people of short stature living in the forests. The Egyptians called the people "pygmies" and spread knowledge of them throughout the Mediterranean region. Greek writers Homer and Aristotle both mention pygmies in their writings.

By the thirteenth century, however, the pygmies were widely held to be a myth. Illustrations and descriptions of pygmies depicted them as winged semihuman creatures who lived in treetops, hung from tails, and could make themselves invisible. European contact with pygmies in the sixteenth and seventeenth centuries did little to dispel these myths. In the seventeenth century, English anatomist Edward Tyson published his treatise "The Anatomy of the Pygmie Compared with that of a Monkey, an Ape, and a Man," in which he claimed to scientifically prove, through a comparison of skeletons, that pygmies were actually monkeys. Later it was proven that Tyson's pygmy skeleton was a chimpanzee skeleton.

Although Europeans finally accepted that pygmies were human, they believed them to be racially inferior to other Africans. This idea was promoted by some neighboring groups whom the European explorers and colonialists encountered. Village dwellers such as the Lese tried to "civilize" the neighboring forest dwellers, the Efe. The Lese tried to force the Efe to settle in villages, clear land, and cultivate crops. According to the Lese, however, their attempts failed because the pygmies were of inferior intellect, incapable of reason and foresight, and lazy thieves. These perceptions encouraged Europeans to justify their display of pygmies as exotic oddities in international expositions and fairs, such as the Indian and Colonial Exhibition of 1887 and the Franco-British Exhibition of 1908. Although it is now clear that forest peoples such as the TWA, Mbutis, and Aka have diverse histories and customs, the stereotypes of the pygmy persist to this day.

See also Ethnicity and Identity in Africa: An Interpretation.

Bibliography

Turnbull, Colin M. *The Forest People: A Study of the Pygmies of the Congo.* Simon and Schuster, 1961.

Elizabeth Heath

Qaddafi, Muammar al-

1942–

Head of state in Libya.

Muammar al-Qaddafi (also spelled Moammar Gadhafi, or Mu'ammar al-Qadhdafi) was born to a BEDOUIN family near the town of Surt in LIBYA. The strict Islamic Bedouin way of life profoundly influenced Qaddafi's later asceticism, as well as his political philosophy. As he once noted in an interview, growing up Bedouin helped him discover "the natural laws, natural relationships, life in its true nature, before life knew oppression, coercion and exploitation."

When Qaddafi was a young man, both GAMAL ABDEL NASSER'S nationalist struggle in neighboring EGYPT and the Arab struggle for Palestine drew him to Arab populist politics. In 1961 he entered the Libyan military academy in Benghazi, where he helped found a student military group called the Free Officers Movement and met the men who would eventually plot to overthrow the Libyan monarchy.

In September 1969, at a time when anti-Western Arab nationalist sentiments were running high in Libya, the Free Officers Movement seized power in a two-hour bloodless coup. Some historians have called Qaddafi the engineer of this coup; others have characterized him as simply a participant. Although the new government, known as the Revolutionary Command Council (RCC), was initially headed by former political prisoner Mahmud Sulayman al-Maghrabi, the young Qaddafi rose quickly in the new government's powerful military. At the age of twenty-seven, he had de facto control of Libya. The extent of power sharing during the early period of Qaddafi's rule remains a subject of debate.

Once in control, however, Qaddafi began to overhaul Libyan government and society. He charged many of the nation's former leaders with treason, outlawed the politically influential Islamic Sanusi sect, and weakened tribal affiliations by reorganizing administrative structures. He denounced communism for its atheism, and promoted Muslim asceticism by banning liquor. In 1973 he instituted the so-called People's Committees to enable citizens to directly control local and regional government. The General People's Congress took over as the national representative body from the RCC, and Qaddafi became the general secretariat of the Socialist People's Libyan Arab Jamahiriya (or state of the masses)—thus remaining the nation's ultimate decision maker and military leader. Several years later he created revolutionary committees to guide the People's Committees, and took the title Leader of the Revolution. He also nationalized the oil and banking industries, as well as a large proportion of the retail sector. All these measures were inspired by Qaddafi's vision of populist Arab nationalism, which he described in *The Green Book* (1976).

Not surprisingly, Qaddafi's policies provoked significant opposition. Many of the middle class fled the country. Islamic leaders resented the nationalization of Islamic properties as well as Qaddafi's theological justifications of political policy. Army officers opposed to his reforms staged an unsuccessful coup in 1975 and were subsequently arrested and executed. Qaddafi dealt severely with his challengers and allegedly sponsored the assassination of exiled opposition leaders.

Qaddafi made equally bold moves in foreign policy throughout the 1970s. Intent on creating a powerful pan-Arab state, he negotiated political mergers with Egypt, Syria, TUNISIA, CHAD, MOROCCO, and ALGERIA. Libya was a founding member of—and a militant voice in—the Organization of Petroleum Exporting Countries (OPEC). Qaddafi offered military aid to IDI AMIN'S brutal regime in UGANDA, and then asylum to the dictator after his fall. His public support for and alleged assistance to militant rebels in Chad, the SUDAN, Ireland, the Philippines, and Japan made him an international pariah. In addition, Qaddafi has long been a prominent supporter of an independent Palestine. Throughout the 1970s and 1980s, the United States accused him of supporting anti-Western movements. Following several diplomatic conflicts over the extradition of suspected terrorists, the United States bombed Libya in 1986. Since then tensions between the former trading partners remain high, and the United States has accused Qaddafi of manufacturing chemical weapons. When members of Libya's intelligence forces were implicated in the 1988 bombing of Pan Am flight 103 over Lockerbie, Scotland, and in the 1989 bombing of a French airliner over NIGER, the United Nations and the United States imposed economic and travel sanctions on the country and its government.

Despite this embargo, Libya under Qaddafi is still one of the richest countries in Africa, enjoying high levels of literacy and quality social services. Qaddafi has had little trouble finding European investors or trading partners, and in recent years he has stepped up efforts to cultivate political and economic ties with sub-Saharan African nations. Seemingly secure in his seat of power, Qaddafi continues to pursue ambitious projects, such as the $30 billion Great Man-Made River, touted as the soon-to-be world's largest pipeline, intended to move subterranean water in the southern desert to the heavily populated Mediterranean coast.

By the end of the 1990s, however, Qaddafi appeared eager to take the necessary steps to end sanctions. In 1998 he helped to extradite the Lockerbie suspects, which resulted in a guilty verdict and an agreement that Libya would compensate the families of the victims. In 2000 Qaddafi issued an official declaration announcing the end of Libya's anti-Western policies. Three years later he cooperated with France to negotiate compensation for the families of the 1989 airline bombing, though he has still not admitted responsibility for the attack. According to the British *Daily Telegraph*, Qaddafi has declared that "We are opening a new page in our relations with the West."

See also Islam in Africa; Nationalism in Africa.

Marian Aguiar

Quakers

Religious group that espoused the idea that slavery was morally wrong. In the nineteenth century Quakers promoted manumission and abolition, founded schools for black children and supported their education, and participated in the Underground Railroad.

For information on
Early African American Quakers: *See* Abolitionism in the United States; Cuffe, Paul.
Eighteenth-century Quaker abolitionism: *See* Abolitionism in the United States; At the Heart of Slavery; Free African Society; Manumission Societies; New York Manumission Society.
Eighteenth-century primary school for blacks cofounded by Quakers: *See* African Free School.
Nineteenth-century Quaker school, the Institute for Colored Youth: *See* Bassett, Ebenezer Don Carlos; Bouchet, Edward Alexander; Browne, Hugh M.
The twentieth-century Fellowship of Reconciliation (an interracial, pacifist Quaker organization): *See* Farmer, James; Thurman, Howard.
Black Quakers in the twentieth century: *See* Reid, Ira De A.; Rustin, Bayard.

Quarles, Benjamin

1904–1996

American historian, author, and editor, key figure in emergence of African American history as academic discipline.

Benjamin Quarles was the son of a subway porter. He earned a B.A. in 1931 from Shaw University, an M.A. in 1933, and a Ph.D. in 1940, both from the University of Wisconsin. Quarles taught at Shaw, was the dean of Dillard University in NEW ORLEANS, LOUISIANA, and served as chair of the history department at Morgan State University in BALTIMORE, MARYLAND.

One of the focuses of Quarles's historical research and writing was race relations. His first published journal article was "The Breach Between Douglass and Garrison," which appeared in THE JOURNAL OF NEGRO HISTORY in 1938. Many of his other scholarly articles and monographs have featured the same theme. However, Quarles also focused on the African American contribution during two major American crises in *The Negro in the Civil War* (1953) and *The Negro in the American Revolution* (1961).

Early in his career, two popular misconceptions existed regarding African American history. The first was that African Americans could not write objective history. The second was that few documentary sources existed for research and writing in African American history. Quarles's scholarship did much to dispel these notions. He was the first African American to publish essays in the *Mississippi Valley Historical Review* (now *The Journal of American History*), in 1945 and 1959. He served as a contributing editor to the journal *Phylon* and as an associate editor of *The Journal of Negro History*. Quarles also wrote two textbooks, *The Negro in the Making of America* (1964) and *The Negro American: A Documentary History* (1967, with Leslie H. Fishel Jr.).

See also Historians, African American.

Bibliography

Meier, August. Introduction to *Black Mosaic: Essays in Afro-American History and Historiography,* by Benjamin Quarles. University of Massachusetts Press, 1989.

Robert Fay

Queen Latifah

1970–

African American singer, actress, entertainment executive, and entrepreneur.

Queen Latifah, born Dana Owens in NEWARK, NEW JERSEY, was nicknamed Latifah (which means "delicate" and "sensitive" in Arabic) at the age of eight by a black Muslim cousin. Soon afterward her parents separated, and Latifah moved with her mother, Rita, and older brother, Lance Jr., into a housing project in East Newark. Determined to offer her children a better life, Rita Owens worked two jobs while attending community college. She eventually took a position as an art teacher at Irvington High School, and the family moved to a house on Littleton Avenue in Newark.

In second grade, Latifah was identified as intellectually gifted. Her mother stretched the family finances so that her daughter could attend Saint Anne's School, where Latifah first performed as Dorothy in the school's production of *The Wiz*. In high school, the popular Latifah played power forward on the school's BASKETBALL team. During her sophomore year, she and two friends formed a RAP group called Ladies Fresh. Encouraged by her mother, she began recording and performing, and added "Queen" to her nickname.

Latifah was attending the Borough of Manhattan Community College in NEW YORK CITY when a demo tape featuring her rap "Princess of the Posse" made its way to Tommy Boy Records. The label quickly signed her, and in 1988 she released two singles, "Wrath of My Madness" and "Dance for Me." In 1989 she toured Europe, appeared at the APOLLO THEATER in HARLEM, NEW YORK, and released her first album, *All Hail the Queen*. The album, which earned her the Best New Artist Award for 1990 from the New Music Seminar of Manhattan, went platinum. Its second single, "Ladies First," celebrated black women's contributions to the struggle for black liberation in America, Africa, and throughout the world. It became a rap classic, eventually named as one of the 500 Songs That Shaped Rock 'n' Roll by the Rock and Roll Hall of Fame.

By the time her second album, *Nature of a Sista'*, came out in 1991, Queen Latifah had begun investing in small businesses in her neighborhood. She was also acting in both television and movies, including SPIKE LEE's 1992 film *Jungle Fever*. These successes were marred by contract conflicts that caused her to leave Tommy Boy, and by her brother's tragic death in a motorcycle accident in 1992.

After signing with MOTOWN in 1993, Latifah released her third album, *Black Reign*. The following year she won a Grammy Award for Best Rap Solo Performance for the album's first single, "U.N.I.T.Y.," which denounced sexist attitudes and violence against women. With her newfound clout, Latifah founded Flavor Unit Records and Management, which primarily handles rap and new-style RHYTHM AND BLUES musicians. Latifah also landed a regular spot on the television situation comedy *Living Single*, which lasted five seasons.

Over the next few years Latifah made more movies. Her portrayal of the lesbian bank robber Cleo in *Set It Off* (1996) won praise from movie critics, and her performance as a torch singer in *Living Out Loud* (1998) earned her a nomination for an Image Award from the NATIONAL ASSOCIATION FOR THE ADVANCEMENT OF COLORED PEOPLE (NAACP). Latifah had supporting roles in *The Bone Collector* (1999), *Chicago* (2002), which brought her an Oscar nomination, and *Scary Movie 3* (2003), and she costarred with Steve Martin in the comedy *Bringing Down the House* (2003).

While pursuing her acting career, Latifah has remained involved in music and in other business and community ventures. She has produced and guest-starred in various musical projects, managed Flavor Unit artists, and worked for numerous causes, including antidrug campaigns. In 1997 Queen Latifah received the ARETHA FRANKLIN award for Entertainer of the Year at the SOUL TRAIN Lady of Soul Awards. In 1999 she hosted a television talk show. Latifah released the albums *Order in the Court* in 1998 and *She's a Queen: A Collection of Hits* in 2002. In 2003 she announced plans for a tour, album, and television special for the following year, saying, "For this album, I will choose songs that have shaped me artistically and affected me emotionally."

Marc Mazique

Queen of Sheba

Legendary queen of South Arabia or Ethiopia, credited with marrying King Solomon of Israel and founding Ethiopia's ruling dynasty.

According to the First Book of Kings in the Bible, the Queen of Sheba learned of the wisdom of King Solomon and came to Jerusalem to test him "with hard questions." She arrived in a vast caravan, "with camels that bare spices, and very much gold, and precious stones."

Yemenis and Ethiopians both claim that the Queen of Sheba once ruled in their country. While an ancient kingdom of Saba did flourish in South Arabia (present-day Yemen) some centuries after the reign of Solomon, growing rich from the spice trade, ancient inscriptions reveal that there was also a kingdom in ETHIOPIA known by the dual name Da'amat and Saba. The incense, or spice, that grew in South Arabia also grew on the other side of the Red Sea.

The Ethiopian claim to the Queen of Sheba is detailed in the famous epic *Kebra Nagast* (The Glory of Kings). It is based on the visit described in the Bible but adds that the queen bore a son, Menelik, to King Solomon. When Menelik was grown, he visited his father, who anointed him to rule in AFRICA and sent the sons of his own counselors to help Menelik as king. The young men were unhappy to leave the famous temple in Jerusalem, especially as it contained the Ark of the Covenant, in which the presence of God was believed to dwell. In secret they removed the Ark and took it with them to Ethiopia. For centuries, Ethiopian tradition has maintained that it is still preserved in the cathedral at AKSUM.

The Ethiopian epic seems to have been compiled and recorded in writing during the thirteenth century, but its origin is difficult to determine. It is certainly true that from the restoration of the Solomonic dynasty around 1270 until the death of the last emperor, HAILE SELASSIE I, in 1975, the emperors of Ethiopia claimed descent from Solomon and the Queen of Sheba. The claim was even part of the constitution proclaimed by Selassie in 1955.

Querino, Manoel Raimundo

1851–1923

First Afro-Brazilian historian to document African contributions to Brazil.

During a lifetime that spanned the abolition movement, the emancipation of the slaves, and the beginning of modernization in BRAZIL, Manoel Raimundo Querino distinguished himself as an artist, teacher, social activist, and above all, historian. He was born free one year after the abolition of the slave trade in Brazil. In 1855, a cholera epidemic swept BAHIA claiming the lives of some 30,000 people, including Querino's parents. He was then sent to the state capital, SALVADOR, where Manuel Correira Garcia, a state deputy and a professor in the state teacher training institute, became his guardian. Garcia provided the orphan Querino with an education, which at that time was a privilege enjoyed by few Brazilians—black or white. At the age of seventeen, Querino enlisted in the army and served from 1868 to 1871, during the latter part of the Paraguayan War.

Querino's career as an artist and teacher began in 1871, when he returned to Salvador. There, he continued his studies and began working as a painter and decorator. He became a proponent of the arts in Bahia, helping to found in Salvador a vocational arts school, the Liceu de Artes e Ofícios (1874), and the state's Fine Arts Academy, the Escola de Belas Artes (1877). He studied architecture at the Escola de Belas Artes from 1881 to 1884. In 1885 he began teaching geometric design at the Liceu de Artes e Ofícios, a course he later taught at the Escola de Belas Artes. While in academia, he continued his work as a painter and decorator, earning the credentials that led to his appointment as designer for the Provincial Directory of Public Works (1884–1895). In addition, Querino authored *As Artes na Bahia*, a definitive work on the art, artists, and artisans of Bahia.

Querino became involved in Brazil's labor movement in the mid-1870s. He helped organize *Sociedade Liga Operária Bahiana* (the Bahian Workers Society League) in 1876 and became one of its leading spokespersons. In labor journals such as *A Província* and *O Trabalho*, Querino published articles defending working-class interests. He argued that the government's restrictions on and abuse of labor thwarted the state's prosperity. Querino garnered enough support to win a seat on Salvador's city council in 1889, the year Brazil became a republic. Since 1878, the year Querino joined the Republican Club of Bahia, he had supported the establishment of the republic in hopes that it would redress working-class grievances, but its leaders largely ignored concerns of the working class.

Querino participated in the abolition movement in Brazil during the 1880s, joining the Bahian Liberation Society (est. 1887) and writing a number of articles calling for the "immediate and unconditional freedom" of the slaves. Nevertheless, he did his most important work in connection with Afro-Brazilians after abolition in 1888. While remaining committed to art and the working-class struggle, Querino spent an increasing amount of time researching and writing about Afro-Brazilian culture and history. Until the early twentieth century, books on Brazilian history made little or no mention of the contributions of Africans to the country's development. Querino began documenting and analyzing the history of black Brazilians in order to revise and balance the traditional historiography on Brazil that emphasized European experiences.

Thus, Querino was not only the first Afro-Brazilian historian, but also one of the first Brazilian historians of *any* background to research and document the importance of African culture in Brazil. In highlighting the struggles and achievements of Afro-Brazilians, Querino hoped to combat racism and to imbue Afro-Brazilians with a sense of pride in their past. In works such as "O Colono Prêto como Fator da Civilação Brasileiro" (The African Contribution to Brazilian Civilization), Querino introduced readers to numerous accomplished Afro-Brazilian figures from the past and asserted that, "In truth, it was the black who built Brazil."

Before Querino, no Afro-Brazilian had given his or her perspective on Brazilian history. Querino's perspective was based not only on his own research, but also on his exchanges with the members of the predominantly black neighborhood of Matutú Grande where he lived. For this reason, Arthur Ramos, a leading scholar of Afro-Brazilian history, said, "[Querino] remains one of the most solid sources of honest documentation for the Negro in Brazil."

See also Afro-Brazilian Culture; Art in Latin America and the Caribbean; History, Latin American and Caribbean; Labor Leaders.

Bibliography

Querino, Manuel Raimundo. *The African Contribution to Brazilian Civilization*. Translated by E. Bradford Burns. Arizona State University, 1978.

Querino, Manuel Raimundo. *Costumes africanos no Brasil*. Recife: Fundação Joaquim Nabuco, Editora Massangana, 1988.

Querino, Manuel Raimundo. *A raça africana e os seus costumes*. Progresso, 1955.

Aaron Myers

Quilombhoje

Organization of black writers in Brazil founded in 1980.

Quilombhoje is an Afro-Brazilian literary organization founded by the poet Luiz Silva Cuti. A significant contributor to Brazil's Movimento Negro Unificado (Unified Black Movement), Quilombhoje publishes *Cadernos Negros*, an anthology of black literature established to provide publication opportunities for black writers who had been denied by the commercial and academic presses.

During the late 1970s the black neighborhood of Beixiga, in São Paulo, was an important center for black cultural activity. Beixiga (also known as the Quilombo de Saracura) became home to the famous Vai Vai samba school, the Center for Negro Culture and Art, and later the Federation of Afro-Brazilian Institutes of São Paulo. As a result, Beixiga became a focal point for a group of black writers and poets, many of whom collaborated on Quilombhoje's literary newspaper, *Jornegro*.

In the late 1970s Luiz Silva Cuti and Hugo Ferreira established *Cadernos Negros*, a series that published poetry and short stories by contemporary black writers. In 1980, Cuti decided to formalize the group, which had been meeting routinely for discussions, poetry readings, and debates, and create an Afro-Brazilian literary organization. Quilombhoje was born, and its original members included Oswaldo de Camargo, Abelardo Rodrigues, and the Argentine Paulo Colina.

The group derived its name from the Afro-Brazilian word *quilombo*, an organized settlement to which blacks escaped from enslavement and assimilation and which thus represented a bastion of black resistance. The neologism *Quilombhoje*, which combines the word *quilombo* with *hoje* (today) and *bojo* (a surge, swelling), encompasses the notion of the retaking of the quilombo.

In time the group grew and older members left, making way for a new generation of Quilombhoje, which includes Míriam Álves, Oubí Jnaê Kibuko, Esmeralda Ribeiro, Sônia Fátima de Conceição, and Jamu Minka. Today the group continues to publish the annual anthology *Cadernos Negros* and functions as a nonprofit institution.

See also Literature, Black, in Brazil; Maroonage in the Americas; Samba Schools.

Nicola Cooney

Quilts, African American

Discussion of the influences, traditions, technology, and designs in quilting among African Americans.

Some African American quilts are the visual equivalent of Jazz or Blues, rich with color and symbolism. Characterized by strips, bright colors, large designs, asymmetry, multiple patterns, improvisations, and symbolic forms, these quilts have their roots in African textile techniques and cultural traditions.

Early Influences

Cotton was domesticated along the Niger River in Mali 2,000 years ago for use in making fishnets and woven cloth; however, the actual links between African and African American textile traditions occurred between 1650 and 1850, when Africans were brought to Latin America and the United States. It is possible to trace African textile techniques, aesthetic traditions, and religious symbols that were transformed by the needs and resources of the New World.

Four African civilizations had profound influences on African American folk arts: the Mande-speaking peoples of West Africa (the modern countries of Guinea, Mali, Senegal, and Burkina Faso); Yoruba and Fon peoples from the Republic of Benin and Nigeria; the Ejagham peoples of Nigeria and Cameroon; and the Kongo and Kongo-influenced peoples of Democratic Republic of the Congo and Angola.

African American quilts are unique, resulting from creolizations of various African, American Indian, and European traditions that took place in Brazil, Suriname, Haiti, Cuba, other Caribbean islands, Mexico, and the southern United States. Although men had traditionally been the primary textile artists in Africa, American plantation owners adhered to the European system of labor division, and African women became the principal weavers, seamstresses, and quilters in Southern society.

African American women produced utilitarian and decorative quilts for both African and Anglo households. Many of their quilts were done in what we think of as traditional Anglo-American styles, even though some of these styles may have been adapted from traditional African designs. However, some quilts made for personal, often utilitarian uses were designed and stitched with definite African traditions in mind, passing on African textile traditions from generation to generation over several hundred years.

Because improvisation is basic to many African aesthetic traditions, this African American heritage is not static. Each generation, indeed each quilter, is free to borrow from other traditions and add elements from his or her own cultural history.

Many contemporary African American quilters are unaware of the continuities between African textiles and their quilt designs, but the design and symbolic similarities are so striking as to prompt some historical explanation.

Quilting Techniques

Strips are a construction technique, a dominant design element, and a symbolic form in West African, Caribbean, and African American textiles. Beginning in the eleventh century most cloth in West Africa has been constructed from strips woven on small portable men's looms. These long, narrow strips, once used as a form of currency, are woven plain or with patterns. Some strips are lightly tacked together so as to allow air through while hung up as screens. The TUAREG use such cloths as tent hangings. Woven strips are also sewn together into larger fabrics to be worn as clothing or displayed as wall hangings and banners.

A preference for strip textiles continued in the New World. In Brazil, Mr. Abdias learned to weave on a narrow portable men's loom, which his daughter uses now. In Suriname, on the north coast of SOUTH AMERICA, African women continued African textile ideas when they ran away from plantations to form maroon societies in the Suriname rain forest. Both Djuka and Saramaka women continued to save strips cut from imported commercial cloth until they wanted to make an African style of cape, called *aseésènte,* for their men. The strips were sewn together in an aesthetic fashion, as determined by conversations among various women.

Many strip quilts are made from the smallest usable rectangles of cloth, called "strings." Many African American quilters speak of "strip quilts," "to strip a quilt," and of how vertical strips bring out the design.

While men did most of the weaving in Africa, in all probability it was women who most often created textiles in the New World, and it was women who maintained the strip aesthetic. West African women who came to the United States would have remembered West African cloth made from narrow strips sewn together.

Color and Symbolism

Large shapes and strong contrasting colors, such as the indigo blue and white found in historic and contemporary West African cloth, ensure that a person can recognize a cloth pattern from a distance and in strong sunlight. It can be important to recognize patterns from a distance when one needs to give a proper greeting. Since the most colorful cloth is woven from imported thread, it is expensive, prestigious, and requires a more formal greeting for the wearer.

The tradition of strong colors continued in the New World. In Suriname, maroon women value strong colors in their pieced textiles and say that the colors should "shine" or "burn" and that the color of one piece should "lift up" the one next to it—that is, provide strong contrast.

Many African American quilters, when discussing their use of bright colors, explain that they look for maximum contrast when piecing scraps together. Often scraps are pieced together as they come out of a bag or box; the quilters make last-minute decisions as to whether the pieces show up well next to each other. A Mississippi quilter, Pecolia Warner, speaks of colors that must "hit" each other right, and of "whooping" together contrasting colors.

Blue and white designs, as in the earliest cloths, are still made with domestic cotton dyed blue from a native indigo plant. Later, more colorful fabrics were made by unraveling European cloth and reweaving the bright colors, African-style. Nadsuaso cloth, made by the ASANTE weavers in GHANA, is the best known of the colorful West African textiles. It was once made from silk but has been made with rayon since about 1946.

Most ideas highly valued by cultures are encoded in many forms. Such seems to be the case with African protective religious ideas that have been encoded into visual arts, songs, dance, and black speech in Africa and the New World. All these forms recognize improvisation as a style; and many refer to West African and Central African religious concepts that survive in contemporary African American cultures because they have been encoded in so many ways. The redundancy indicates high value and ensures survivability. The evidence is equally rich, powerful, and eloquent for continuities between African writing and charms traditions in African American architecture, ceramics, painting, sculpture, and environmental arts.

Women's Weave

African women also weave, but on wide stationary looms in their homes. "Women's weave" features wide panels with vertical designs that may look from a distance like the strips of the older "men's weave." While "men's weave" is abundant and sold commercially, "women's weave" is more for personal use.

African wide loom weaving frequently features asymmetrical alignments. Wide loom weaving was also once done by black women in the United States, the same women who made quilts and probably transmitted and preserved certain African textile traditions.

Asymmetry and Improvisation

In West Africa, when woven strips with patterns are sewn together to make a larger fabric, the resulting cloth may have asymmetrical and unpredictable designs. "Offbeat" patterns are one option in West and Central African fabrics. When strips are sewn together, the colored or patterned weft blocks are staggered in relation to those in other strips. Roy Sieber has noted that "the careful matching of the ends of the cloth dispels the impression of an uncalculated overall design."

Asymmetrical arrangements of cloth are a form of improvisation, found in West and Central African textiles. Kongo people praise talented expressions of sound and vision with the phrase *veti dikita,* meaning "the mind plays the pattern strongly." Improvisation, or break-patterning, or flexible patterning, in Kuba raffia cloth and painted Mbute textiles has also been linked to spirit possession. The Kongo scholar Fu-Kiau Bunseki says, "every time there is a break in pattern [it] is the rebirth of [ancestral] power in you."

African American quilters often adapt what we think of as traditional European-American quilt patterns and "African Americanize" them by establishing a pattern in one square and varying it in size, arrangement, and color, in successive squares. Their use of lines, designs, and colors varies with a persistence that goes beyond a possible lack of cloth in any particular size, color, or pattern.

Multiple Patterning

Improvisation, as seen in asymmetrical textiles, shades into multiple patterning, also described as flexible patterning. Improvisation and multiple patterning form an aesthetic tradition shared by the people who made African and Caribbean textiles and African American quilts. Multiple patterns are important in African royal and priestly fabrics, for the number and complexity of patterns in a fabric increase in accordance with the owner's status. Cloth woven for priests and kings may feature various woven patterns within each strip, as well as a variety of strips, each featuring a different pattern. Multiple patterned cloth communicates the prestige, power, and wealth of the wearer, for only the well educated and the wealthy can name the different patterns and afford to pay master weavers.

African cloth thus has social and political significance, for it is worn and displayed as an indicator of wealth, occupation, social status, and history. Robert Farris Thompson has also suggested that certain West African asymmetrical and multiple-patterned strip cloths have more than an aesthetic function; the complex designs serve to keep evil spirits away, because "evil travels in straight lines." If the patterns do not line up easily, the belief is that evil spirits will be confused and slowed down.

Contemporary African American quilts often are made with four different patterns in four large corners. Plummer T. Pettway, of rural Alabama, believes that many different patterns and shapes make the best quilts. "You can't match them. No. It takes all kind of pieces to piece a quilt."

Many contemporary African American quilts may not communicate an owner's status or a religious identification, but they do retain an African aesthetic preference for improvisation, for variations on a theme, and for multiple patterns. Improvisation and multiple patterning are also protective, making copying is impossible. While ostensibly reproducing European-American patterns, many African American quilters maintain African principles of asymmetry, improvisation, multiple patterning, and unpredictable rhythms and tensions similar to those found in other African American arts, such as blues, jazz, AFRICAN AMERICAN VERNACULAR ENGLISH, and dance.

Appliqué

Besides piecing, in which strip patterns may dominate, another basic quilt top construction technique known in EUROPE, Africa, and the United States is appliqué, the art of sewing cut-out shapes onto a larger cloth. While European-American appliqué quilts are primarily decorative, African American appliqué quilts often express stories and ideas in the same manner as in Africa.

With bold appliqué shapes, African cultures recorded court histories, religious values, and personal histories of famous individuals, using designs symbolizing power, skill, leadership, wisdom, courage, balance, composure, and other personal and religious qualities. The best-known African appliqué cloth was made by the Fon people of the Republic of Benin (formerly Dahomey). In the nineteenth century Fon appliqué banners were made by a guild of male artisans to decorate the walls of the royal palace and to depict historic events. The technique was also used to decorate royal umbrellas, flags, costumes, and banners.

Contemporary African American quilters appliqué with shapes drawn from their imagination, from their culture, and from popular American culture shaped by magazines, television, and advertising. Some women cut out magazine illustrations and reproduce them in cloth. Others are inspired by animal pictures and search for appropriate animal-like fuzzy materials; a few make paper templates from dreamed designs; and some, like Pearlie Posey and Sarah Mary Taylor, use people or doll forms, as well as hands.

Continuing Traditions

African American quilt patterns involve aesthetic decisions, but many of those aesthetic choices derive from rich cultural traditions. In their choice of techniques, textiles, forms, design names, and colors, many African American quilters perpetuate African techniques and cloth forms. Strip quilts reflect the strong West African textile traditions that are also evident in African Caribbean fabrics. Many quilt patterns may have been chosen because they awakened a memory of ceremonial textiles.

If only one or two African forms occurred in African American quilts, it could be coincidental. But the numerous instances of similar forms, and sometimes similar meanings, is evidence of a cultural heritage that is stronger than any one lineage.

Like many other African American folk artists, quilters are inspired by dreams. Unlike the dreams of idiosyncratic artists, quilters' dreams, like those of other folk artists, revive visual imagery from the culture of their childhood. Their dreams are culturally conditioned.

African American folk artists have sometimes been labeled idiosyncratic because they don't always know, or care to explain, the African traditions that shape their visions, dreams, and arts. African men and women remembered their artistic techniques and traditions when they came to the New World. They mixed and sorted their own traditions, then combined them with European-American and Native American ideas to create their unique creolized arts. Their combined ideas were passed down from generation to generation, thus preserving many African art traditions.

Some well-known quilt patterns may have been adapted by African Americans because they resemble important ideas in African religions. Some Anglo-American pattern terms such as "Flying Geese," "Rocky Road to California," and "Drunkards Path" are indicative of action; forms such as those found in "Bears Paw" imply action, as in Kongo charms. In Kongo religion, it is important to activate a charm to make it work, and words are often part of the process. Certain "Anglo" patterns may appeal to African American quilters for numerous historic cultural reasons, visual and verbal. Some evoke secret African signs and were used to signal others on the UNDERGROUND RAILROAD.

New Directions

Since the late 1980s African American quilt making has evolved in a new direction. Jesse Lane, FAITH RINGGOLD, Wini McQueen, Joyce Scott, and others have drawn on traditional folk designs for inspiration in creating their fine arts. These trained artists are proud of their mothers' arts and of family heirlooms, and they chose to build on family cultural traditions in creating contemporary arts.

African American folk arts provide evidence that American folk arts are not naive, primitive, or simplistic. African American arts are unique in America, fusing various international traditions to produce new ones. African American artists maintaining this creolized aesthetic demonstrate the power and vision of African cultural traditions in contemporary American society, affirming the extraordinary tenacity of African traditions over hundreds of years.

See also Art, African American; Creolization: An Interpretation; Dance, African American; Maroonage in the Americas.

Maude Wahlman

Quinn, William Paul

1788?–1873

American bishop in the African Methodist Episcopal Church.

Little is known of William Paul Quinn's early life. He was born in a British colony and migrated to Pennsylvania while young, at which time he was introduced to organized religion. An official of the AFRICAN METHODIST EPISCOPAL CHURCH (AME) for over thirty years by 1844, Quinn as an itinerant preacher had organized over 120 AME congregations and 50 Sunday schools in the Midwest, including the slave states of Kentucky and Missouri. In 1849 Quinn was elected the AME church's senior bishop. He settled in Richmond, Indiana, and was active as a pastor and in AME affairs until 1872 when illness forced him into retirement.

In addition to preaching, Quinn also wrote to promote an antislavery agenda. In 1834, Quinn published *The Origins, Horrors and Results of Slavery*, a pamphlet condemning slavery and the South Carolina laws that prohibited education and employment training for African Americans.

See also Abolitionism in the United States.

Bibliography

Payne, Daniel Alexander. *History of the African Methodist Episcopal Church*. 1891. Reprint, with a preface by H.L. Moon. Arno Press, 1969.

Robert Fay

Quirot, Ana Fidelia

1963–

Afro-Cuban track star and Olympic medal winner.

Record-breaking runner Ana Fidelia Quirot won worldwide admiration when, after suffering severe burns to more than a third of her body, made a comeback and won a silver medal at the 1996 Summer Olympic Games.

Quirot was born in Santiago de Cuba, in the eastern province of Oriente on the island of CUBA. At the age of thirteen she gained admittance to one of Cuba's prestigious state-run athletic training schools, where she was able to train as part of her educational curriculum. After completing her studies in the early 1980s, she dedicated much of her time to athletic training. Quirot found her niche in the 400- and 800-meter races. Just as she reached the peak years of her career, however, Cuba boycotted the 1984 and 1988 Summer Olympic Games for political reasons. Quirot, who is strongly patriotic and considers Cuban president Fidel Castro one of her heroes, never expressed regret about the lost opportunities to compete.

Quirot broke from anonymity in international competitions in the late 1980s and early 1990s. At the 1987 Pan American Games, open to amateur athletes from the Americas, she won gold medals in both the 400- and 800-meter races. She was undefeated in the 800-meter race the entire year, with thirty-nine victories, and was named Female Athlete of the Year by the International Amateur Athletic Federation (IAAF), the governing body of international track and field competition. In 1991 the Pan American Games were in HAVANA. Quirot herself had helped to build the stadium, carrying bricks and mortar to the site. She delighted the hometown crowd by taking the gold medal in the 400- and 800-meter events. Known for her physical beauty, she was thereafter a Cuban celebrity and hero, the ideal representative of her nation. In 1992 she participated in her first Olympics, winning the bronze medal in the 800-meter event at the Summer Games in Barcelona.

In January of 1993, Quirot was badly burned in a kitchen fire in her Havana apartment. Because of severe shortages of everyday necessities in Cuba, Quirot had resorted to washing her clothes with water and isopropyl alcohol. Some of the alcohol spilled onto a kerosene stove, causing a flash flame that burned her face, neck, chest, and abdomen. Quirot, who was seven months pregnant, was rushed to a hospital. Because of the trauma, she gave birth prematurely, and the baby died a week later.

Quirot had suffered burns 38 percent of her body. Her doctor told her she probably would not be able to run again and that she would spend a year recovering in the hospital. Quirot started working out in her hospital room just two months into her recovery, riding a stationary bike and running on the hospital stairs. After four months she was out of the hospital and working out on a track, although her training was limited to early morning and nighttime hours, when the sun could not damage her healing skin. She had a brief comeback in November 1993, winning the silver medal in the 800-meter race at the Central American and Caribbean Games in Puerto Rico, but spent 1994 undergoing many plastic surgeries. In 1995 she won the 800-meter gold medal at the world championships in Göteborg, Sweden. The following year, at the Summer Olympics in ATLANTA, GEORGIA, Quirot placed second in the 800-meter race. She then retired from running and became a coach in Cuba's athletic development programs. In 2003 she was elected to Cuba's National Assembly, which includes many nationally known and popular figures.

R

Rabat, Morocco

Capital city of Morocco, located on the Atlantic coast in the northwestern part of the country.

Near Rabat, in the contemporary town of Salé, are the ruins of a Roman settlement said to have originated as a small community of traders. Under Islamic influence after the tenth century, Salé was home to a group of BERBERS from a heretical sect. In 1150 C.E., an ALMOHAD sultan established a rabat, or citadel, for his army near Salé. The position of the fort along the Atlantic ocean and the banks of the Sebou River offered a prime location from which to launch his holy war against SPAIN. By the turn of the century, his son had finished the construction of the city, which came to be known as Rabat al-Fath (autonomous or victorious citadel). Although Rabat flourished first as an imperial city and then as an important military center under the Almohads, only the citadel was left inhabited after that dynasty fell. In the sixteenth century, the historian LEO AFRICANUS described the city as overgrown with vines.

During the early seventeenth century, Rabat's economy benefited from the increased trade, exploration, and piracy in the Atlantic. In the same period Rabat also became home to a large number of Muslim and Jewish refugees from southern Spain following the Christian reconquest. These refugees were a heterogeneous population from different parts of Spain, and they brought the intellectual and cultural influences of Andalusia (southern Spain) and built a new quarter near the citadel. Over the years, these soldiers, merchants, artisans, and seamen transformed the town from a military base into a prosperous port that exported skins, leather, wool, wax, and copper. The city drew a great deal of income from corsair activities, as pirates based out of Rabat plundered ships on the Atlantic and evaded their pursuers in the tricky river channel. In the late seventeenth century, after the sultan successfully suppressed hostile corsairs, the city became a secondary capital for the Alawite Dynasty.

During the late eighteenth and nineteenth centuries, Rabat lost much of its significance as a port of trade, as first the sultan shifted the kingdom's commercial trade to Essaouira and then CASABLANCA outstripped the port in the increasingly European-controlled trade. Conditions further deteriorated as the city faced an earthquake in 1755 followed by a series of plagues, the first of which killed some two-thirds of the population in Rabat and Salé.

Despite its economic decline, Rabat became an important seat of government—the sultan assembled his government there as early as 1768. In 1912 the French made Rabat the administrative capital for the protectorate, and built a modern city for the French expatriate community outside the wall of the medina, or old city, where the Muslims lived. Following independence in 1956, the city became the capital of MOROCCO. The royal residence is located in Rabat as are the government's ministries and embassies. In 1957 the Université Muhammad V was founded as a center for modern education.

The population of Rabat stood at 1,636,600 in 2003. The city's main industries include textiles, fruit and fish processing, and building materials. Artisans continue to produce traditional handicrafts such as worked leather and copper, as well as the famed Rabat carpets.

See also Colonial Rule; Islam in Africa; Judaism in North Africa; North Africa, Roman Rule of.

Marian Aguiar

Rabih al-Zubayr

1845–1900

Slave raider and adventurer who built a nineteenth-century empire that spanned parts of present-day Chad, Central African Republic, Cameroon, Nigeria, and Niger.

Rabih al-Zubayr was born in SUDAN, probably near KHARTOUM, though the details of his early life are uncertain. Some believe that he was originally a slave freed by his master, Zubayr Rahma Mansur, while others think he was born free and joined the Turkic-Egyptian army before working for Zubayr, the largest slave-trader in southern Sudan. He joined Zubayr's company in 1850 and had become a competent military leader by 1875, when the British declared slavery illegal.

When the British forcibly shut down Zubayr's operations four years later, Rabih gathered what was left of Zubayr's slave army and established a raiding stronghold in the AZANDE region to the west. During the 1880s, Rabih and his army attacked and pillaged groups such as the BANDA and SARA. In the early 1890s, Rabih defeated a French expedition and conquered the Bagirmi state in present-day CHAD, from which he staged his conquest of the Bornu Empire to the west. Exploiting divisions among the Bornu rulers, Rabih, in alliance with the ruler of Adamawa in present-day CAMEROON, attacked the empire in 1894. Within three years he had gained control of the entire Bornu Empire, a tract of land stretching from northeastern NIGERIA around LAKE CHAD and into adjacent parts of NIGER and CAMEROON. After securing his new empire, Rabih decided to attack the Damagaram Empire, based in ZINDER, farther west in the area that is now Niger. But the Damagaram resisted his aggression, and French and British efforts to control the region eroded his power. Although he successfully repelled the Europeans for several years, he was killed in battle in 1900, and subsequently his empire was divided between the French and British.

See also Slavery in Africa.

Elizabeth Heath

Race: An Interpretation

Stretch forth! stretch forth! from the south to the north,
From the east to the west—stretch forth! stretch forth!
Strengthen thy stakes and lengthen thy cords—
The world is a tent for the world's true lords!
Break forth and spread over every place
The world is a world for the Saxon race!
Martin Tupper, "The Anglo-Saxon Race"

These famous words were published in 1850 in a new journal called *The Anglo-Saxon*. The publication lasted only a year, but its tone is emblematic of an important development in the way educated Englishmen and women thought of themselves and of what it was that made them English. This development was itself part of a wider movement of ideas in EUROPE and North America. As heirs to the culture of the modern world, a culture so crucially shaped by the ideas that Tupper's poem represents, most twentieth-century readers, not merely in Europe and America but throughout the world, are able to take for granted a set of assumptions about what Tupper means by "race." Those assumptions, which amounted to a new theory of race, inform our modern understanding of literature—indeed of most symbolic culture—in fundamental ways, despite the fact that, as we shall see, many of them have been officially discarded.

That the specific form race theory took was new does not, of course, mean that it had no historical antecedents. Almost as far back as the earliest human writings, we can find more or less well-articulated views about the differences between "our own kind" and the people of other cultures. These doctrines, like modern theories of race, have often placed a central emphasis on physical appearance in defining the "Other," and on common ancestry in explaining why groups of people display differences in their attitudes and aptitudes.

Classical Greeks: Environmentalism

If we call any group of human beings of common descent living together in some sort of association, however loosely structured, a "people," we can say that every human culture that was aware of other peoples seems to have had views about what accounted for the differences—in appearance, in customs, in language—between peoples. This is certainly true of the two main ancient traditions to which Western thinkers look back—those of the classical Greeks and the ancient Hebrews. Thus, we find Hippocrates in the fifth century B.C.E. in Greece seeking to explain the (supposed) superiority of his own people to the peoples of (western) Asia by arguing that the barren soils of Greece had forced the Greeks to become tougher and more independent. Such a view attributes the characteristics of a people to their environment, leaving open the possibility that their descendants could change if they moved to new conditions.

While the general opinion in Greece in the few centuries on either side of the beginning of the common era appears to have been that both the black "Ethiopians" to the south and the blond "Scythians" to the north were inferior to the Hellenes, there was no general assumption that this inferiority was incorrigible. Educated Greeks, after all, knew that in the *Iliad* Homer had described Zeus and other Olympians feasting with the "blameless Ethiopians"; and there are arguments in the works of the pre-Socratic Sophists to the effect that it is individual character and not skin color that determines a person's worth.

Ancient Hebrews and the Old Testament

In the Old Testament, on the other hand, what is thought to be distinctive about peoples is not so much appearance and custom as their relationship, through a common ancestor, to God. Thus, in the book of Genesis, Jehovah says to Abraham: "Go your way out of your country and from your relatives and from the house of your father and to the country that I shall show you; and I shall make a great people of you and I will make your name great" (Genesis 12: 1, 2). And from this founding moment—this covenant or agreement between Abraham and Jehovah—the descendants of Abraham have a special place in history. It is, of course, Abraham's grandson Jacob, who takes the name of Israel: and his descendants thus become the "people of Israel."

The Old Testament is full of names of peoples. Some of them are still familiar—Syrians, Assyrians, and Persians; some of them are less so—Canaanites, Philistines, and Medes. Many of these groups are accounted for in the genealogies of the peoples of the earth and are explicitly seen as descending ultimately not only from the first human couple, Adam and Eve, but more particularly from Noah. Just as the Israelites are "sons of Shem," the children of Ham and of Japheth account for the rest of the human "family."

But while these different peoples are taken to have different specific characteristics and ancestries, the fundamentally theocentric perspective of the Old Testament requires that what *essentially* differentiates them all from the Hebrews is that they do not have the special relationship to Jehovah of the children, the descendants, of Israel. There is very little hint that the early Jewish writers developed any theories about the relative importance of the biological and the cultural inheritances by which God made these different peoples distinct. Indeed, in the theocentric framework it is God's covenant that matters and the very distinction between environmental and inherited characteristics is anachronistic.

Racialists and Concepts of Biological Heredity

Neither the Greeks' environmentalism nor the Hebrews' theocentric notion of the significance of being one people represents ideas that we should naturally apply in understanding Tupper's use of the idea of race. To the extent that we think of Tupper's doggerel as modern, as involving ideas that *we* understand, we will suppose that he believed that the world was "a world for the Saxon race" because of that race's *inherited* capacities. For by Tupper's day a distinctively modern understanding of what it was to be a people—an understanding in terms of our modern notion of race—was beginning to be forged: that notion had at its heart a new scientific conception of biological heredity, even as it carried on some of the roles played in Greek and Hebraic thought by the idea of a people. But it was, also, as we shall see, interwoven with a new understanding of a people as a nation and of the role of culture—and, crucially for our purposes, of literature—in the life of nations.

In short, Tupper, unlike the Greeks and the Hebrews, was what I shall call a *racialist*. He believed, as did most educated Victorians by the midcentury, that we could divide human beings into a small number of groups, called "races," in such a way that all the members of these races shared certain fundamental, biologically heritable, moral, and intellectual characteristics with one another that they did not share with members of any other race. The characteristics that each member of a race was supposed to share with every other were sometimes called the *essence* of that race; they were characteristics that were necessary and sufficient, taken together, for someone to be a member of the race.

Unlike the Greeks and the Hebrews, racialists believed that the racial essence accounted for more than the obvious visible characteristics—skin color, hair—on the basis of which we decide whether people are, say, Asian Americans or Afro-Americans. For a racialist, then, to say someone is "Negro" is not just to say that they have inherited black skin or curly hair: it is to say that their skin color goes along with other important inherited characteristics. By the end of the nineteenth century most Western scientists (indeed, most educated Westerners) believed that racialism was correct and theorists sought to explain many characteristics—including, for example, literary "genius," intelligence, and honesty—by supposing that they were inherited along with (or were in fact part of) a person's racial essence.

Literary Representations of Racial Stereotypes

The twentieth century inherited these conceptions; but it was the nineteenth century that was the heyday of appeals to race in literary study. For by our own day the idea that the concept of race should have any place—let alone an important one—in literary studies has been attacked from a good many directions. Perhaps the most surprising has been an attack in the name of "science." In a society like ours, where most people take their race to be a significant aspect of their identity, it comes as a shock to many to learn that there is a fairly widespread consensus in the sciences of biology and anthropology that the word "race," at least as it is used in most unscientific discussions, refers to nothing that science should recognize as real.

And it is not just the claim that there is a racial essence that can explain a person's moral, intellectual, or literary aptitudes that scientists have rejected. They also believe that such classifications as *Negro, Caucasian,* and *Mongoloid* are of no importance for biological purposes. First, because there are simply too many people who do not fit into any such category; and second, because, even when you succeed in assigning someone to one of these categories—on the basis of skin pigmentation and hair, say—that implies very little about most of their other biological characteristics. Even those scientists who still have a use for the term *race* agree that a good deal of what is popularly believed about races is false—often wildly false.

But, of course, a discussion of some of the literary ramifications of the idea of race can proceed while accepting the essential unreality of races and the falsehood of most of what is believed about them. For, at least in this respect, races are like, for example, witches: however unreal witches are, *belief* in witches, like belief in races, has had—and in many communities continues to have—profound consequences for human social life.

Elizabethan Theater

The racialism we see in Tupper and his contemporaries is real enough to make up for the unreality of races. We can see something of the long process of transition from the views of the ancient world to the racialism we find in Tupper, if we ask how we should interpret the handling of questions of difference between peoples in such plays as Shakespeare's *Othello* (c. 1603) and *The Merchant of Venice* (c. 1597) or in Christopher Marlowe's *The Jew of Malta* (c. 1592).

In each of these plays a central figure—Othello, Shylock, Barabas—plays out a role we can only understand in terms of a stereotype of a people, Moors or Jews, a stereotype we are likely, if we are hasty, to conceive of as simply racialist. So it is important to go carefully. We should begin by recognizing that in Shakespearean England both Jews and Moors were barely an empirical reality. And even though there were small numbers of Jews and black people in England in Shakespeare's day, attitudes to "the Moor" and "the Jew" do not seem to have been based on experience of these people. Furthermore, despite the fact that there was an increasing amount of information available about dark-skinned foreigners in this, the first great period of modern Western exploration, actual reports of black or Jewish foreigners did not play an important part in forming these images, either. Rather, it seems that the stereotypes were based on an essentially theological conception of the status of both Moors and Jews as non-Christians: the former distinguished by their black skin, whose color was associated in Christian iconography with sin and the devil; the latter by their being, as Saint Matthew's account of the Crucifixion suggests, "Christ-killers."

There is good reason, then, to interpret these Elizabethan stereotypes, which *we* might naturally think of as what I have called "racialist," as rooted far less in notions of inherited dispositions and far more in the idea of the Moor and the Jew as infidels; unbelievers whose physical differences are signs (but not causes or effects) of their unbelief. Yet in some ways the most revealing of the plays for the purposes of underscoring the distance that was still to be traveled from Shakespeare's Moor of Venice or Marlowe's Maltese Jew to the imperializing race of Tupper's Anglo-Saxonist vision is a play that does not explicitly invoke either of these the most familiar for us of "racial" stereotypes: and that is Shakespeare's The Tempest.

Metaphor for British Expansion. We are accustomed nowadays to interpretations that cast Caliban as the colonial subject; and that is not anachronistic, given the play's historical context. The Tempest was first performed in 1611 for the court of James I, during an era of extensive overseas expansion. From abundant internal evidence we know that Shakespeare's conception of the "savage and deformed slave" was informed by contemporary pamphlets and speculative essays about the nature of the "native," travelogues describing European encounters with the inhabitants of the New World.

Now Caliban, as Prospero asserts, is "a born devil" (literally, perhaps), "on whose nature / Nurture can never stick" (act 4, scene 1). And if Caliban is the representative colonial, the peculiar brutality of Prospero as colonizer can only be justified by Caliban's incorrigibly devilish nature. For, of course, it is more than just colonialism in general that needs to be justified. What needs to be justified is the especial brutality of the colonization of nonwhite peoples—Africans and Indians. It is only because Caliban is incorrigibly wicked that Prospero can maintain our sympathy while making Caliban's colonization into what is simply a form of slavery. Miranda makes the issue clear the first time she addresses Caliban:

Abhorred slave,
Which any print of goodness wilt not take,
Being capable of all ill! I pitied thee,
Took pains to make thee speak, taught thee each hour one
   thing or other. When thou didst not, savage,
Know thine own meaning, but wouldst gabble like
A thing most brutish, I endowed thy purposes
With words that made them known.
But thy vile race—Though thou didst learn—had that in't
   which good natures
Cannot abide to be with . . . (act 1, scene 2)

Echoes here of the later image of the colonized male subject—ungovernable in his lusts, intractable, learning the colonizer's language in order to articulate his own vile purposes—may lead us to read back into this passage the triumphalist racialism of "The Anglo-Saxon Race." Yet if it is clear enough now how this ideology that will develop into racialism could serve already in the seventeenth century to license the domination of subject peoples, it is important to mark its differences.

The word "race" occurs only in this place in The Tempest, and an unprepared modern reader risks misunderstanding it. For race here in its Elizabethan usage means—as the Oxford English Dictionary tells us—"natural or inherited disposition." Miranda's point in speaking of Caliban's "race" is only to restate her earlier insistence on his individual moral incorrigibility: he will not take any "print of goodness" because it is not in his nature. For Tupper, of course, "race" is also a natural or inherited disposition; but it is, by contrast, one that is shared with a whole people.

Allegory of Colonialism. What is interesting is that the very possibility of reading The Tempest as an allegory of colonialism did not appear to occur to theatrical interpreters of the play until the nineteenth century; while from the mid-nineteenth century on—at the pinnacle of British imperial power—productions of The Tempest in GREAT BRITAIN increasingly reflected ongoing disagreements about the nature of subject peoples and the justice of their colonization. And when a conception of "primitive" peoples became biologized during the later nineteenth century—especially under the influence of Darwin's Origin of Species—we find productions of The Tempest mirrored current speculation. In the age of social Darwinism, Caliban became quite literally the "missing link" of evolutionary theory (the English actor F. R. Benson, who played the part in a touring company all around Britain in the 1890s, spent time observing various apes in the zoo in order to perfect his movements!). If Caliban is the "missing link," his status as a proper object of the colonizer's control is not in doubt. The very fact that by the end of the nineteenth century the character can move back and forth between interpretations as subhuman and as the colonial human subject, shows the tendency of an increasingly biologized idea of race to allow an uneasy oscillation between thinking of the natives as of the same fundamental kind as the ruling race—and thus, both capable of elevation and, at least potentially, *wrongly* subjected—and thinking of them as of a different kind—and thus perpetually its natural subjects.

Victorian Literature

The distance from Shakespeare's understanding of the issue of difference between peoples to the ideas that surrounded Tupper is evidenced in these new Victorian readings of Shakespeare's play. For literary purposes, the developments that begin at the turn of the nineteenth century have another immediate consequence: *race* becomes important as the *theme* of a great body of writing in Europe and North America—and, indeed, in the rest of the world under the influence of "Western" cultures—and the concept often plays a crucial role in structuring plot.

Celebrating the Anglo-Saxon Race. Thus, in *Ivanhoe*, a novel published by the Scottish novelist and poet Sir Walter Scott in 1819, the theme of the story is the hatred between Anglo-Saxons, the "original" inhabitants of Britain, and the Norman rulers imposed upon them by the conquest of England in 1066 by William the Conqueror. The presupposition of the story (which seems to have little historical basis) is that there was a natural antipathy between the Anglo-Saxon race and their French-speaking Norman rulers; and our understanding of the plot depends, in part, on our recognition of the struggle between Anglo-Saxons and Normans not simply as a struggle of the poor and oppressed against their rich oppressors, but as a struggle for Anglo-Saxon national (or, equivalently, racial) autonomy. The racial theme of the book is reinforced by the presence of the character "Isaac the Jew" and his daughter Rebecca; as the Norman aristocracy are stereotyped as lawless and corrupt, and the Anglo-Saxons as noble and downtrodden, Isaac is stereotyped as avaricious, torn between love of his daughter and love of money.

Ideas about race could, in principle, have developed without a commitment to the view that some races were superior to others; but they did not. While the Christian tradition insisted on the common ancestry of all human beings, and the Enlightenment, even when it was critical of official CHRISTIANITY, emphasized the universality of reason, by the middle of the nineteenth century the notion that all races were equal in their capacities was a distinctly minority view. Even those who insisted that all human beings had the same rights largely acknowledged that nonwhite people lacked either the intelligence or the vigor of the white races, among which the highest, it was widely agreed, was the Indo-European stock from which the Germanic peoples emerged. In England and North America, there was a further narrowing of focus: the Anglo-Saxons were the favored offshoot of the Germanic stock.

Indeed, one of the central questions for nineteenth-century race science became the question *why* it was that the white races were superior to the others; and there was an almost equal interest in how the others should be ranked below them. But though there was, therefore, an inevitable element of moral evaluation in most theories of race, it is important to be clear that the racial theme never required a simple identification of one race with evil and another with good. In *Ivanhoe*, our hero—son of Cedric, an *Anglo-Saxon* "nationalist" who wishes to see the reestablishment of the Saxon monarchy—cooperates as a loyal subject with the *Norman* king, Richard the Lionheart, to overthrow the corruption of the Norman nobility that the king has left behind while taking part in the CRUSADES; and, at a crucial point in the plot, Rebecca, Isaac's daughter—despite the essentially anti-Semitic presuppositions of Scott's day—nurses Ivanhoe back to life and falls in love with him. Nevertheless, the book depends not only, as we have seen, on an assumption of the naturalness of racial feeling but also on the maintenance of certain racial boundaries: despite Rebecca's more substantial character, it is Rowena, the Anglo-Saxon heiress, whom Ivanhoe marries, and Rebecca, who is, in a sense, ruled out by race as a spouse, disappears from England with her father at the end of the book.

Forty years after *Ivanhoe*, in *Salammbô*, published in 1862, the French novelist Gustave Flaubert created a similar racial romance, set in ancient CARTHAGE. While the central contrast in the work is between civilized and barbarous peoples—the French word *barbares* (which is both noun and adjective) occurs 238 times, more often than any other noun or adjective—the novel is replete with references to Campanians, Garamantes, Gauls, Greeks, Iberians, Lusitanians, Libyans, Negroes, Numidians, Phoenicians, and Syssites; and these types are often identified with certain physical and moral characteristics.

Ivanhoe and *Salammbô* depend on projecting nineteenth-century racial concerns back into the past. But in the heyday of the European world empires, as the great European powers divided the world between them (and as Americans of European descent conquered Native Americans through their superiority in military technologies) it was common to offer the racial superiority of the "white man" as an explanation for the contemporary successes of imperialism; and these successes became the theme of a substantial body of literature.

Cooper and the American Frontier. In the United States, for example, in James Fenimore Cooper's well-known "Leatherstocking Tales"—from *The Pioneers* (1823) to *The Deerslayer* (1841)—a celebration of the American frontier (itself a substantial literary theme) elicits the overarching theme of the decline of the "red man" and the triumph of the "white man." Cooper's style is in many ways reminiscent of Scott's and, in fact, Cooper could hardly have escaped the influence of Scott's romances: for these were amongst the most widely read and admired works of fiction in the United States in the first half of the nineteenth century. They were adapted over and over again for the American stage, and published in numerous editions (something which was easier in an age before copyright). Scott's interest for Americans must have been in part a consequence of the fact that much of his work, unlike *Ivanhoe*, was devoted to establishing not English but Scottish national feeling. In such adventures as *Rob Roy*, Scott celebrates the people and the life of the Scottish borders; a world whose romantically conceived landscape and rough "manly" manners were easily transferred in imagination to the rigors of North American pioneer life.

Like Scott's representation of the Jew, Cooper's image of the Indian, though stereotyped, was ambivalent—Natty Bumppo, Cooper's hero, distinguishes between "Good Indians"—like Chingachgook, Bumppo's Indian companion, who will fight with the white man against other red men—and

"Bad Indians" who combine the lack of civilization, common to all Indians, with an absence of the natural nobility that Chingachgook displays. In Cooper's racial scheme (unlike Thomas Jefferson's), the Indian is below the "white man" but above the "Negro": Indians in Cooper are sometimes "Nature's gentlemen"; blacks almost always evoke contempt. We could argue that the Negro, in Cooper, plays the same sort of role as the Jew in *Ivanhoe*: the main plot in each case pits one race (Anglo-Saxon, red man) against another (Norman, white man) that dominates it, and the third race (Jew, Negro) provides a point of contrast with each of the others; a point of contrast that allows us to understand the sympathies between the members of the first two races, even though their conflict is at the center of the plot. In this case, then, as I suggested, the hierarchy of races becomes an essential element in structuring the plot.

Race, Nation, and the Idea of Literature

In a world whose politics were so dominated by racialism, it is hardly surprising that races became a central literary theme. What is, perhaps, more puzzling is the fact that many of those works that have been central to our understanding of what literature is are also thematically preoccupied with racial issues. But the reason for this is not far to seek: it lies in the dual connection made in eighteenth- and nineteenth-century thought between, on the one hand, race and nationality, and, on the other, nationality and literature. In short, the nation is the key middle term in understanding the relations between the concept of *race* and the idea of literature.

The first of these linkages, between nation and race, will surely be the less puzzling. In the Old World, where people were the hereditary subjects of monarchies, it was natural that the emergent European nations conceived of themselves in terms of descent. Eighteenth-century theorists of the nation had, of course, to make a sharp distinction between nations and states because in eighteenth-century Europe there was not even an approximate correlation between linguistic and political boundaries. (It is important to remember that the correlation remains in most parts of the world quite rough and ready.) The modern European nationalism, which produced, for example, the German and Italian states, involved trying to create states to correspond to nationalities—nationalities conceived of as sharing a civilization and, more particularly, a language and literature. And because political geography did not correspond to nationalities, eighteenth-century theorists were obliged to draw a distinction between the nation as a natural entity and the state as the product of culture, as a human artifice.

But with the increasing influence of the natural sciences in the nineteenth century, what is natural in human beings—human nature—came increasingly to be thought of in terms of the sciences of biology and anthropology. Inevitably, then, the nation comes more and more to be identified as a biological unit, defined by the shared essence that flows from a common descent.

Roots of Constitutional Monarchy. Yet the increasing identification of race and nation in European—and more particularly in English—thought was a complex process. The Anglo-Saxonism of the nineteenth century in Britain has its roots deep in the soil of historical argument about the English constitution; in the fascinating process through which a rising commercial class transformed the monarchy in Britain from its feudal roots into the "constitutional monarchy" that was established at the Restoration of 1660. In the arguments that surround this development, a mythology took hold in the seventeenth century of a free Anglo-Saxon people, living under parliamentary government in the period before the Norman Conquest of 1066. Increasingly Anglo-Saxon institutions were seen both to account for the Englishman's natural love of freedom and to underlie the immemorial rights of free men against the Crown.

This mythology was counterposed against the mainstream historiography of the Middle Ages, which traced the *History of the Kings of Britain*—as Geoffrey of Monmouth's influential work of 1136 was called—to Brutus, grandson of Aeneas of Troy. It was Geoffrey who established the story of King Arthur, son of Utherpendragon, as forever part of British mythology; and his work played a significant part in providing a framework within which the different cultural streams—Roman, Saxon, Danish, and Norman—that had come together over the first millennium in Britain could be gathered into a single unifying history.

When Richard Verstegen published his influential *Restitution of Decayed Intelligence* in 1605, he claimed that England's Anglo-Saxon past was the past of a Germanic people who shared their language and institutions with the Germanic tribes, whose great courage and fierce independence Tacitus had described many centuries earlier. Verstegen argued that these tribes were also the ancestors of the Danes and the Normans, whose invasions of Britain had thus not essentially disturbed the unity of the English as a Germanic people. The effect of this argument, of course, was to provide for the seventeenth century what the *History of the Kings of England* had provided in the Middle Ages: a framework within which the peoples of England could be conceived as united.

By the eve of the AMERICAN REVOLUTION, Anglo-Saxon historiography and the study of the Anglo-Saxon law, language, and institutions, were established scholarly pursuits; and the notion of a free Anglo-Saxon past, whose reestablishment would be an escape from the monarchy's potential to develop into a tyranny, was one that appealed naturally to such figures as Thomas Jefferson. Anglo-Saxonism spread easily to a United States whose dominant culture imagined itself—even after the Revolution—as British. And when Jefferson, himself no mean Anglo-Saxon scholar, designed a curriculum for the University of Virginia, he included the study of the Anglo-Saxon language, because, as he said, reading the "histories and laws left us in that . . . dialect," students would "imbibe with the language their free principles of government."

Herder and Modern Nationalism. But the deep-rooted character of the second linkage—between nation and literature—will probably be less naturally intelligible. And our starting point for understanding the role of the idea of a national literature in the development of the concept of a national culture must be in the work of the man who developed its first real theoretical articulation: Johann Gottfried Herder.

In his *On the New German Literature: Fragments* of 1767, Herder—who is, in some ways, the first important philosopher of modern nationalism—put forward the notion that language is not just "a tool of the arts and sciences" but "a part of them." Herder's notion of the *Sprachgeist*—literally the "spirit" of the language—embodies the thought that language is not merely the medium through which speakers communicate, but the sacred essence of a nationality. Herder himself identified the highest point of the nation's language in its poetry, both the popular lyrics of the folk song, which he collected, and the work of great poets. The emergence of nationalism, in the eighteenth and early nineteenth centuries, depended upon the imaginative re-creation of a common cultural past that was, in no small part, crafted into a shared tradition by literary scholars like Herder and—to return to an earlier example—Sir Walter Scott, whose *Minstrelsy of the Scottish Border* was intended, as he said in the preface, to "contribute somewhat to the history of my native country; the peculiar features of whose manners and character are daily melting and dissolving into those of her sister and ally" (i.e., England). From its inception, literary history, like the collection of folk culture, served the ends of nation building.

Racial Understandings of Literature in the 1800s. Imposing the post-Herderian identification of the core of the nation with its national literature on top of the racial conception of the nation, we arrive at the racial understanding of literature that flourishes from the mid-nineteenth century in the work of the first modern literary historians. Thomas Carlyle, the great British essayist and man-of-letters, wrote in 1831: "The history of a nation's poetry is the essence of its history." It was only a step from here to the identification of that history with the history of the race. Hippolyte Taine's monumental *History of English Literature,* published in FRANCE in the 1860s—perhaps the first modern literary history of English—begins with the words "History has been transformed, within a hundred years in GERMANY, within sixty in France, and that by the study of their literatures." But he is soon telling us that a race, like the Old Aryans, scattered from the Ganges as far as the Hebrides, settled in every clime, and every stage of civilization, transformed by thirty centuries of revolutions, nevertheless manifests in its languages, religions, literatures, philosophies, the community of blood and of intellect which to this day binds its offshoots together.

What is revealed, in short, by the study of literature that has transformed the discipline of history is the "moral state" of the race whose literature it is. It is because of this conception that Taine finds it proper to start his study of English literature with a chapter on the Saxons; so that chapter 1, book 1 of Taine's *History* begins not in England at all, but in the NETHERLANDS: "As you coast the North Sea from Scheldt to Jutland, you will mark in the first place that the characteristic feature is the want of slope: marsh, waster, shoal; the rivers hardly drag themselves along, swollen and sluggish, with long, black-looking waves . . ." The "Saxons, Angles, Jutes, Frisians . . . [and] Danes" who occupied this region of Holland at the beginning of the first millennium are, according to Taine, the ancestors of the English; but since they, themselves, are of German descent, Taine also refers, in describing this "race" a few pages later, to some of their traits reported in Tacitus.

Anglo-Saxonism and the Literary Canon. It is the conception of the binding core of the English nation as the Anglo-Saxon race that accounts for Taine's decision to identify the origins of English literature, not in its antecedents in the Greek and Roman classics that provided the models and themes of so much of the best-known works of English "poesy"; not in the Italian models that influenced the drama of Marlowe and Shakespeare; but in *Beowulf,* a poem in the Anglo-Saxon tongue, a poem that was unknown to Chaucer and Spenser and Shakespeare, the first poets to write in a version of the English language that we can still almost understand.

Yet this decision was quite representative. When the teaching of English literature was institutionalized in the English universities in the nineteenth century, students were required to learn Anglo-Saxon in order to study *Beowulf*. Anglo-Saxonism thus played a major role in the establishment of the canon of literary works that were to be studied in both British and American colleges; and the teachers who came from these colleges to the high schools brought the Anglo-Saxon canon with them.

American Literature in the 1900s

We must examine one final role for questions of race in literary study, a role that is especially visible in much recent writing about American literature. And that is in understanding how American literature and literary study both reflect the existence of ethnic groups, the very contours of which are, in a certain sense, the product of racism. For, however mythical the notion of race seems to be, we cannot deny the obvious fact that having one set of heritable characteristics—dark skin, say—rather than another—blond hair, for example—can have profound psychological, economic, or other social consequences, especially in societies where many people are not only racialists but racists. Indeed, much of what is said about races nowadays in American social life, while literally false if understood as being about biological races, can be interpreted as reporting truths about social groups—Afro-Americans, Asian Americans, Jewish Americans—whose experience of life and whose political relations are strongly determined by the existence of racist stereotypes.

Afro-American Literary Criticism. The most prominent such reflection of racially understood ethnicity in literary studies in recent years is in the development of Afro-American literary criticism. Anyone who has followed the argument so far will anticipate that the persistent stream of Afro-American nationalist argument (whose beginnings we can trace well before Tupper) has been accompanied by appeals to an African cultural heritage expressed in black folk music, poetry, and song. To the extent that Afro-Americans were thought of as a separate people—and with the rise of racialism, this became increasingly inevitable—nineteenth-century thought proposed nationalism as a reflection of that separate status. Once black nationalism takes on this form, it is equally inevitable that a national literature, consisting of the folk art of the race, should be seen as the highest expression of the black national spirit. Such intellectual pioneers as W. E. B. Du Bois from the latter nineteenth century on attempted to articulate a racial tradition of black letters as a natural expression of the Herderian view of the nation as identified above all else with its expression in "poesy."

But there is another reason why the identification of a history of black literary production has been central not merely to Afro-American literary criticism but to the culture of Afro-Americans: namely, that for almost the whole period in which there have been people of African descent in the New World, a powerful European and American intellectual tradition has consistently denied that black people were capable of contributing to "the arts and letters." Starting before the fixing of *race* as a biological concept, influential figures expressed their doubts about the inherited "capacity of the Negro" to produce literature. Even in the Enlightenment, which emphasized the universality of reason, philosophers such as Voltaire in France, David Hume in Scotland, and Immanuel Kant in Germany, like Jefferson in the New World, denied literary capacity to people of African descent. And, as we have seen, once race was conceptualized in biological terms, such low opinions of black people would lead easily to the belief that these incapacities were part of an inescapable racial essence.

Formation of a Black Canon. In response to this long line of antiblack invective, black writers in the United States since the first major Afro-American poet—Phillis Wheatley, who lived in Boston in the latter part of the eighteenth century—have sought to establish the "capacity of the Negro" by writing and publishing literature. More than this, the major proportion of the published writing of Afro-Americans, even when not directed to countering racist mythology, has been concerned thematically with issues of race, a fact that is hardly surprising in a country where black people were subjected to racial slavery until the mid-nineteenth century and then treated legally as second-class citizens in many places until the 1960s.

The recognition, especially in recent years, of the role of Anglo-Saxonism, in particular, and racism, more generally, in the construction of the canon of literature studied in American university departments of English, has led many scholars to argue for the inclusion of texts by Afro-Americans in that canon, in part because their initial exclusion was an expression of racism. But it has led others to argue for the recognition of an Afro-American tradition of writing, with its own major texts, which can be studied as a canon of their own. Some of those who make such claims—the critics of THE Black Aesthetic movement, for example—have been motivated largely by a black nationalism that is, in part, a response to racism; others have argued for the recognition of a black canon because they have identified formal features in the writings of black authors, which derive from a self-conscious awareness of black literary predecessors and African or Afro-American folk traditions. Though the debates about the Afro-American literary tradition may be couched in terms of the existence of a tradition of aesthetically valuable texts that has been ignored, the issue of an Afro-American is inevitably a political one. The politics of Anglo-Saxonist nationalism *ex*cluded Afro-American culture from the official American canon, and the politics of American race relations inevitably structures discussion of their *in*clusion.

Literature and the Politics of Racial Difference. Differences among peoples, like differences among communities within a single society, play a central role in our thinking about who "we" are; in structuring our values and determining the identities through which we live. In the past century and a half racialism and nationalism, often so bound up together that one can hardly tell them apart, have played a central role in our thinking about these differences, and since one of the contributions of modern nationalism has been to see literature as central to national life, race has been central to literature and to thought about literature throughout this period. The racialism of Tupper's verse now seems merely ridiculous, even though such sentiments went with the reprehensible abuses of British imperialism; but racialism in our own century has produced lynchings in the American South, sustained the racist South African state, and led to the still unthinkable horrors of the Nazi Holocaust. The universal revulsion against these moral disasters does not, unfortunately, mean that racism is over. And so long as it continues it is likely that race will continue to be a preoccupation, not only of the literary history of the nineteenth and twentieth centuries but also of future literary production and literary study.

See also Black Literary and Cultural Movements; Black Nationalism in the United States; Literature, African American; Literature, Black, in Eighteenth-Century Britain and the United States; Racial Stereotypes.

Anthony Appiah

Race and Class in Brazil: An Interpretation

Discussion of the issues of race and class in Brazilian history.

Our understanding of modern-day race relations in Brazil rests primarily on research done between 1945 and 1965. To appreciate the context of that work, we need to look at the history of sociology and anthropology in Brazil. Before 1945 both disciplines were in the early stages of development, centered largely in São Paulo, with clusters of researchers in RIO DE JANEIRO and BAHIA. The 1930s had seen an influx of influential foreign scholars, such as Donald Pierson, Roger Bastide, and Emílio Willems. All played important roles in the development of graduate faculties at the University of São Paulo (USP) and the Escola Livre de Sociologia e Política, both in São Paulo. One of the most significant publications of this era was by the American scholar Donald Pierson, whose *Negroes in Brazil* remains an outstanding research work on Bahia and the Northeast, although its conclusions are now generally rejected.

With the end of World War II, there was a renewed surge of foreign interest that reinforced the efforts of the small community of Brazilian researchers. Prominent among the non-Brazilians were North American anthropologists, especially from Columbia University, and French scholars. Most knowledgeable among the latter was Roger Bastide, who had been in Brazil since 1938 and had already won USP support to begin a large-scale survey research project on race relations of São Paulo. Key Brazilian scholars included FLORESTAN FERNANDES (University of São Paulo) and Thales de Azevedo (Federal University of Bahia). Among those who distinguished themselves in the study of race relations were Charles Wagley, Marvin Harris, Costa Pinto, René Ribeiro, Oracy Nogueira, Fernando Henrique Cardoso, Octávio Ianni, and Arthur Ramos. We largely owe our present knowledge to these researchers and their collaborators.

Several themes have emerged from this body of scholarship. Most relevant for our purposes is the direct, at times explicit, challenge to the long prevailing view of Brazil as a "racial democracy." In its more extreme form, that belief held that race and skin color make virtually no difference in Brazil. Vianna Moog, a prominent Brazilian writer, has stated, "The highest, most significant and most edifying aspect of our culture is racial brotherhood." If there are few dark-skinned Brazilians at the higher levels of society, it simply reflects past disadvantages, poverty and the lack of education that inevitably accompanied slavery. The belief held by the elite was well stated by a former president of the National Congress, "In Brazil, access to society depends upon individual effort, intellectual ability, and merit. . . . We have all inherited common attributes, and what we are building—socially, economically and politically—proves the correctness of our rejection of the myths of racial superiority." This view holds that if race does play a part in stratification, it is a small part. Brazilians may not give the benefit of the doubt to a darker person, but the frequency is not great enough to alter the fact that Brazil is substantially free of racial discrimination.

How did Brazil reach this supposedly harmonious state? The answer, say believers in its racial democracy, is to be found in Brazilian history. Almost in spite of themselves, the Portuguese created a multiracial, slave-based society with a large, free, colored population. Portuguese colonization seemed somehow immune to racial prejudice. In the words of the congressional president, "In our land the three ethnic groups interacted to produce the union of which we are the expression and synthesis." The Portuguese male was crucial in this process. At home he had known the charms of dark-skinned Moorish women, and thus it is not surprising that in the New World he succumbed to the Indian, and later African, women. This trend was reinforced by the absence of women among the Portuguese explorers and colonists. The inevitable outcome was MISCEGENATION.

Most important for future race relations, according to this view, was the fact that Portuguese men had guilty consciences, as well as strong libidos. As a result, they often manumitted the mixed-blood offspring they had sired by their slave women. Affectionate weakness for the illegitimate progeny of miscegenation led directly to the sharp contrast between the fate of people of color in Brazil and the United States. This simplistic idea was well expressed in the 1940s by Waldo Frank, a minor American literary figure who often traveled to LATIN AMERICA: "Why is the difference so great between the exploited Negro of Brazil and the exploited Negro of the United States? Because the latter have known lust and greed of their masters; the former, lust and greed no less, but tenderness also."

The belief in racial democracy, whether it fitted the historical facts or not, has been the operating racial ideal among the Brazilian elite since at least 1920. It accompanies an equally fervent faith in *branqueamento* or "WHITENING," the result of the elite's struggle to reconcile Brazil's actual social relations, the absence of a clear line between white and nonwhite, with the doctrines of scientific racism that had penetrated Brazil from abroad. It also implied that the inexorable process of whitening would produce a white (or light tan?) Brazil. Thus, the legacy of the Portuguese libido would "solve" Brazil's race problem. This remained the elite view through World War II, despite the fact that "scientific racism" had become discredited in academic circles by the 1930s.

Elsewhere, the 1930s saw the application of one of history's most vicious racist dogmas, anti-Semitism. In the aftermath of 1945, Europeans looked abroad for models of interracial peace. Hadn't Brazil for years been disproving the racist shibboleths about miscegenation? In 1950 the United Nations Educational, Scientific, and Cultural Organization (UNESCO) decided to study Brazil's harmonious race relations and share Brazil's secret with the world. International teams of scholars, primarily anthropologists, undertook field research around the country, pursuing common research goals. Such international recognition greatly reinforced the Brazilian elite's belief in their racial democracy. In fact, this and subsequent research raised serious questions about, and partially discredited, this image of Brazilian society.

Other factors were also eroding the image. An important element in the definition of Brazil's racial democracy had always been the contrast with the United States. The phenomena of segregation and racial violence, such as urban riots and LYNCHINGS, were unknown in Brazil. Even if there had once been onerous barriers to black advancement, Brazil had never been infected with the race hatred so evident in the United States. Whatever the precise explanation for the difference, Brazilians could say that their country had the distinction of representing humanity's best future. Hadn't UNESCO said as much?

But the United States was changing. The Supreme Court decision of 1954 in BROWN V. BOARD OF EDUCATION sounded the death knell for racial segregation, and subsequent legislation closed virtually every loophole sought by the die-hard racists. Where once the law had been used to segregate, it was now a force for integration. Both uses assumed a clearly defined biracial society. Both stemmed from the assumption that race is a fundamental, perhaps the most fundamental, characteristic of North Americans.

From the Brazilian viewpoint, it might at first appear that the United States, by finally eliminating legal color bars, was merely catching up to Brazil in the early nineteenth century, when its few color bars, remnants of the colonial era, disappeared. The difference in the United States, however, was the militancy and organization of nonwhites. In the nonviolent resistance movement, led by Southern clergymen such as MARTIN LUTHER KING JR., blacks forcefully claimed their "rights." Brazilian nonwhites had not shown a comparable degree of initiative since final abolition in 1888. United States society, the major point of reference for Brazilians when describing their racial democracy, had changed in a basic way.

Another shift in the Brazilian elite's foreign points of reference occurred in AFRICA. There, as in Asia, World War II brought in its wake a cry for decolonization. The remaining empires of GREAT BRITAIN, FRANCE, HOLLAND, and Belgium were now an unpleasant reminder of the era when white Europeans, using racist language, had taken control of much of today's Third World. In Africa, the departure of the empires and their ruling whites paved the way for the appearance on the world scene of nations totally governed by blacks. This trend contradicted one of the central assumptions of the Brazilian belief in "whitening": the closer to African origins, the less civilized the person of color. Indeed, faith in "whitening" was based on the assumption that the superior racial element, that is, white, was prevailing. Now Africa had, not white, not even mulatto, but black nations. These new peoples wanted no part of "whitening," a doctrine that assumed assimilation, if not extinction, of African identity. As in the case of United States desegregation, history was removing the very landmarks that had helped anchor the Brazilian elite in its racial beliefs.

Brazil's relations with Africa were further complicated by the fact that PORTUGAL was the last European power to relinquish its African colonies. It was a Brazilian, GILBERTO FREYRE, who had spelled out the most ambitious doctrine to justify Portuguese colonialism, "Lusotropicalism." He argued that the Portuguese were the only European colonizers to create a new civilization in the tropics, an accomplishment attributable above all to their racial tolerance. The logical conclusion was that the Lusitanian legacy would spare Portugal the anticolonial violence found elsewhere in Africa. Freyre himself remained a staunch defender of Portuguese COLONIAL RULE.

Because of Antonio Salazar's repressive regime and an enormous per capita investment of resources, the Portuguese government prolonged its rule over ANGOLA and MOZAMBIQUE into the 1970s. By the time the armed struggle began in Africa, Brazil had a military government that was completely committed to the Salazar policy. Freyre, an enthusiastic adherent to the 1964 "revolution" that installed the military, gained increased publicity for his Lusotropical theories. Meanwhile, government censorship prevented an open debate over Brazil's African policy.

As Salazar finally faded from power in the early 1970s, it was his army officers who pushed for withdrawal from Africa. The peoples of Portuguese Africa won independence, and many whites left. After those events were well under way, Brazil also experienced political change. Ernesto Geisel's presidency (1974–1979) brought an "opening" and the possibility for rethinking Brazil's African interests and policies.

One incident shows how this new relationship called into question the Brazilian elite's image of their nation's race relations. In 1978 and 1979, Brazil's leading television network, Rede Globo, broadcast a series for children adapted from stories by Monteiro Lobato. Brazilians generally considered it a high-level effort for the children's hour. Angolan television, which is state controlled, decided to take advantage of this Portuguese-language resource by broadcasting the series in early 1979. This set no precedent, as they had shown Globo's version of JORGE AMADO's *Gabriela, cravo e canela* with no apparent problems. After seven installments, however, the Angolan television abruptly canceled the children's series. It was "racist," they charged, because blacks were depicted only in inferior positions. Most offensive was the role of Tia Nastácia, the sixty-year-old black cook whom the Angolans thought a caricature. Reaction in Brazil was rapid, and many questions arose. Were the Angolans justified? How should blacks be depicted? Had Lobato's characterization been faithfully rendered in the televised script? What was the true meaning of Tia Nastácia's role in the household? Brazil was undoubtedly in for more such surprises in its cultural relations with Africa. It was not the world Freyre had led the Brazilian elite to expect.

These fundamental changes in Brazil's external points of reference in race relations, the United States and Lusophone Africa, did not produce an immediate rethinking of race relations in Brazil; that began only in the late 1970s. There are several reasons for this.

First, the Brazilian elite tenaciously defended their image of Brazil as a racial democracy. They did it in a number of ways. One was to attack as "un-Brazilian" anyone who raised serious questions about race relations in Brazil. Such a tactic was common among politicians, cultural luminaries, and media controllers. The usual argument was, "The only racial 'problems' in Brazil result from the agitation of those who claim there are problems." An interesting case is the reaction to a small "black is beautiful" movement, primarily in Rio de Janeiro. In August 1976, the prominent Rio daily *Jornal do Brasil* ran a feature story of "black Rio," with photographs of young black men wearing Afro hairstyles and platform shoes. This publicity ignited an angry reaction from readers, who denounced the movement and its coverage by the press. Critics implied that reporting on such "un-Brazilian" groups was itself divisive and unpatriotic. As for the movement, it was branded by many whites as a foreign import, illustrating little more than the "cultural alienation" into which Brazilian blacks could slip.

Such vigilance by the elite could not suffice to explain the lack of debate. A second factor was government repression. After 1965, and especially after 1968, successive military governments closely controlled the media and all public events. They justified repression as necessary to meet the threat of "subversion," which in the early 1970s did include a guerrilla movement. But the military branded as "subversive" not only kidnappers with guns but also social scientists with ideas. That was bound to include academics who had raised questions about Brazil's racial democracy.

One of the most dramatic cases in point was the purge of the faculty at the University of São Paulo in 1969. Prominent among those social scientists involuntarily retired were Florestan Fernandes and his colleagues Fernando Henrique Cardoso and Octavio Ianni. Given their well-known, although differing, ideological and political views, it is not surprising that they should be targets for a military concerned with "national security." Could it be coincidental, however, that they were also among the handful of Brazil's researchers into race relations? And that, by their research, writing, and teaching they had raised troubling questions about the realities of Brazilian race relations? The military government frequently intervened to suppress news that contradicted the official image of racial harmony. Under full-scale censorship from 1969 until gradual liberalization began in 1975, television and radio were closely scrutinized. Vigilance was especially intense on the popular television soap operas (*telenovelas*), as well as in SAMBA songs. More often than once, television scripts rejected by the censors touched the subject of race relations.

A similar preoccupation appeared in the censorship of the print media. In 1973 a new journal of opinion, *Argumento*, appeared on the newsstands of São Paulo. It was quickly confiscated by the authorities. On the cover was an African-looking boy and the title of an article comparing postabolition race relations in Brazil and the United States. Although the police gave no explanation, many observers thought the article on race relations had, at least in part, provoked their action. Another example of such moves was the Brazilian government's 1978 decision to bar the Inter-American Foundation from further activity in Brazil. Brazilian authorities believed that this foundation, financed by United States government–originated funds but operating independently from other U.S. agencies, was supporting "subversive" Brazilian organizations. Among the groups receiving financing at that time were three black organizations whose stated purpose of "consciousness raising" undoubtedly displeased Brasília.

A third example of government sensitivity to the issue of race relations came in connection with a scholarly conference on blacks in the Americas, scheduled to be held in Bogotá, COLOMBIA, in August 1977. Countries were invited to send delegations, on the usual assumption that each government would finance their delegates' travel. Not so in Brazil. Brasília dragged its feet on the travel authorization until it was too late, and most of the Brazilian delegates missed the meeting.

Another incident that occurred in the late 1960s was the most revealing of all: the decision to omit race from the census of 1970. Opponents of racial identification argued that the language of racial categories, such as *preto, negro,* and *moreno,* was applied so inconsistently that meaningful data collection would be impossible. No responsible observer would dispute the fact that there is a problem, yet the Census Commission's extreme solution of eliminating race altogether precluded the collection of any data by race whatsoever. Undoubtedly, many commission members who voted for this policy genuinely believed that race could not be studied. In eliminating the category, however, they were reflecting the elite consensus that race was not an independent variable in Brazilian society. Without data, of course, discussion would continue being reduced to the anecdotal level. That is where defenders of Brazil's racial myth have always preferred to operate, dwelling on examples of famous Brazilians whose physical features have borne little relation to their station in life.

There has been another factor responsible for muting Brazilian discussion of race relations: the belief by the Left that race is insignificant. Social class is the most fundamental variable, leftists argue, both for studying society and for changing it. Advocates of this view usually have dismissed race as a "false issue." Because the Left has remained very strong in the university faculties that have produced most Brazilian researchers, its negative attitude toward studying race relations has, ironically, helped contribute to the silence on race sought by the authoritarian government.

In the late 1970s this picture began to change. Attention to race increased, in a small but perceptible fashion. Brazilians of color began to publicly question the myth of racial democracy. With the gradual political opening pursued by the government of Geisel, debate emerged into the open.

Other writers have described in detail the rapid growth of a black movement that contradicts everything the predominant myth would have led us to expect. Brazil now has militant groups that may come to rival their most ambitious counterparts of the Frente Negra era in the 1930s. The *abertura democrática* (transition to democracy) has allowed many taboo topics to surface, with race relations high on the list. Dramatic confirmation of this change came in the decision to include race in the 1980 census. Initially, the census authorities wanted to follow the 1970 precedent of omitting race. That created a strong reaction among the staff and the public and led to reconsideration and a reversal of the decision. The less repressive atmosphere surrounding the 1980 decision facilitated the collection of data that, even if not wholly reliable, are the sine qua non for any informed discussion of race relations.

Before discussing the renewed attention to race in Brazil, it is worth noting that a more traditional area of interest has never lacked attention: Afro-Brazilian religion, folklore, and art. Interest here centered on African origins and African survivals. Most familiar are the religions of CANDOMBLÉ in Bahia and UMBANDA in Rio de Janeiro, both well-known tourist attractions. Included also are the "exotic" costumes and foods identified with Africa. The (adopted) patron saints of this world are

Gilberto Freyre and Jorge Amado, writers who have gained much of their fame by showing the Afro-Brazilian contribution to Brazilian culture and national character. Although undoubtedly important and valuable, the study and preservation of Afro-Brazilian beliefs and customs have been politically very safe. It fits perfectly with the elite view that Brazil's historic links to Africa are now essentially quaint. For this reason, the Sociedade de Estudos da Cultura Negra no Brasil (Society for the Study of Black Culture in Brazil) represented no threat to the government or elite figures. Another example was the Semanas Afro-Brasileiras held at the Museum of Modern Art in Rio de Janeiro in 1974. The emphasis of such groups has allowed them to avoid the thorny questions of present-day race relationships among Brazilians.

A significant change that took place in the late 1970s was the promotion of racial consciousness among Brazilians of color. Although some leading activists were researchers, they did not use questionnaires or interview forms. They believed that they knew what the facts were. As people of color, they passionately believed that Brazil's claim to be a racial democracy was a fraud. They wanted Brazilians to know that their country's race relations bore no relation to the idyllic scene praised by the elite and many foreigners. This activist explosion startled many. Was it possible that a significant "black power" movement was arising in Brazil? The militant tone of these activists was more aggressive than that of any group since the Frente Negra of the 1930s. They repudiated whitening, still Brazil's dominant ideology of race relations, and upheld the virtues of blackness. Most important, they wanted to provoke Afro-Brazilians into racial consciousness. They wanted to act against what they saw as white exploitation, a line of protest that had been forbidden to people of color for forty years.

The new black protest movements could now denounce the conditions that Brazilian scholars had long been documenting. To take one example, Thales de Azevedo, one of the doyens of Brazilian anthropology, attacked the racial democracy myth by publishing a compilation of cases of racial discrimination as reported in the national press. Carlos A. Hasenbalg's important 1979 monograph used similar sources and carried the analysis of discrimination to the most systematic level possible with the limited data then available.

At the end of the twentieth century, major debate continued about the role of race in Brazilian society. Any debate is bounded by the terms by which it is defined. What will be the definitions for the debate on race? What are the questions to be posed? What is the subject to be studied? If it is race relations in the broadest sense, how should we proceed?

Research efforts are needed on all fronts, not least the historical front. Surprising as it might seem, our understanding of the history of Brazilian race relations is extremely uneven. Despite the fame of Gilberto Freyre's writing on Brazil's patriarchal past, and much recent work on slavery by many other scholars, we know all too little about some of the most important features of Brazilian social history. One is the historical experience of free persons of color, both in the colonial era and in the nineteenth century.

In the first half of the 1800s, there was a strong mulatto movement, which even published its own newspapers. An important imperial institution, the Guarda Nacional, had become a vehicle for mulatto mobility. By the 1840s the officer corps included many mulattoes, as they were elected by the predominantly colored ranks. This channel of mobility was abruptly closed in 1850, however, when the Crown made officers appointive. The command soon turned markedly whiter.

The questions are obvious: How extensive was this mulatto movement? What were its relationships to other Brazilians of color, slave and free? Why did the Crown abolish the election of officers? Did the political and social elite see a threat from the mulatto movement? How did they rationalize their actions?

The early decades of the twentieth century provided similar questions. How do we explain the assertion of black and mulatto consciousness in the 1920s and 1930s? Just as they had a century earlier, black newspapers appeared, aggressively promoting the cause of the Brazilian of color. Why did they appear in the 1920s, and not immediately after final abolition in 1888? Were there unusual economic circumstances in the 1920s and 1930s? Were they comparable to those of the early nineteenth century?

This twentieth-century movement was snuffed out by the authoritarian coup of 1937. The disbanding of the black and mulatto organizations was hardly surprising, given the fact that the Estado Nôvo government (1937–1945) was able to repress all opposition groups. But the return of open government in 1945 did not see the reappearance of the movement, and three decades after 1945 it saw nothing comparable to the black and mulatto movements prior to 1937, despite the persistent organizing efforts of a few individuals such as ABDIAS DO NASCIMENTO. That did not come until the late 1970s. Why? Is there a general explanation for the militancy that erupted in the late 1970s, the 1920s to the 1930s, and the 1840s?

Part of the answer lies in a better understanding of the dynamics of Brazilian socioeconomic history. Most important is a deeper understanding of the role of the free person of color before slavery expired in 1888. Some of the most lasting forms of interracial social behavior must have been established in those years. The scholarly consensus has been that Brazil created a multiracial society, as contrasted to the biracial system in the United States. In his extended comparison of the United States and Brazil in *Neither Black nor White* (1971), Carl Degler suggested that the "mulatto escape hatch" was the key to the difference. Yet Degler's book, the most thoughtful and exhaustive comparative analysis of race relations in Brazil and the United States, gives virtually no hard evidence to support his thesis. The reader searches in vain for historical documentation to show that the person of mixed blood got preferential treatment. How do we know that mulattoes enjoyed mobility? What data such as census records, tax records, and court records confirm such mobility? Degler could not provide such information because the necessary research has only recently begun. The escape hatch is a plausible hypothesis, but we await evidence of what actually happened.

One priority area for investigation is relations between whites and persons of color in the labor force. In the southeastern United States, for example, there was a period, roughly 1865 to 1900, when poor whites and newly freed blacks might have made common cause against the old agrarian order. Instead, white politicians successfully got poor whites to focus on the threat of job competition from blacks, rather than the fundamental questions of economic structure. As a result, JIM CROW became fixed in the South and the cause of black progress was set back for decades to come.

There are obvious perils in carrying historical comparison too far. It might well be argued that by the time of the Emancipation Proclamation in the United States there was no possibility for the emergence of a multiracial society. Yet some of the explanations given for the United States case may suggest questions about Brazil. What were the racial attitudes of Brazilian workers? Were they manipulated by employers who used similar techniques to maximize control over the labor force? We know, for example, that racist sentiments helped divide Rio de Janeiro dock workers in the 1910s and 1920s. Did this occur in other sectors? Could such patterns be seen in earlier eras? What effect did these patterns have on subsequent race relations? Such questions are implicit in virtually all our attempts to explain present-day Brazilian race relations.

No amount of subsequent research and documentation, however helpful, will answer all our questions. Just as in the study of race relations in the United States, with its avalanche of monographs, symposia, and syntheses, the questions go too deep and in the end their meaning is too elusive for us to be satisfied with the answers provided by conventional social and economic history. In Brazil, also, we will find ourselves drawn toward examining "mentalities," habits of mind, and social beliefs. What is uniquely Brazilian about Brazilian race relations? Does it have anything to do with the now oft-denigrated idea of Brazilian national character? There has been a long and rich debate over the Brazilian's alleged *cordialidade*. Does that idea furnish any clues in our quest to understand how and why Brazil has created its particular form of multiracial society? What about those qualities that anthropologists, sociologists, and political scientists have explored: patrimonialism, paternalism, and clientelism? However slippery these concepts may be for the historian, we must remind ourselves that the most enduring attempt to explain the United States, that of Alexis de Tocqueville, was built around a discussion of precisely these kinds of collective traits.

Our efforts to understand Brazilian race relations will necessarily carry us into the ongoing debate about the nature of Brazilian society. It will thus parallel and perhaps at times coincide with attention to the history of labor relations in Brazil, also inseparably linked to our views about the essence of Brazilian social relations.

We are, therefore, brought to the elusive relationship between ideas and societies. Seen abstractly, they are socioeconomic structures and ideologies. When viewed historically, they embrace the many realities of human behavior and human thought. We appear to be on the verge of a new burst of inquiry into these realities, and although we may ask new questions and produce new evidence, we will be walking familiar ground.

From "Race and Class in Brazil: Historical Perspectives." *Luso-Brazilian Review,* Vol. 20, No. 1 (Summer 1983) © 1983. Reproduced by permission of the University of Wisconsin Press.

See also Black Consciousness in Brazil; Brazil's Relationship with Africa: An Interpretation; Frente Negra Brasileira; Myth of Racial Democracy in Latin America and the Caribbean; Religions, African, in Brazil; Slavery in Latin America and the Caribbean.

Thomas E. Skidmore

Race and Class Issues in the United States

Interrelated issues that have had a complex effect on African Americans, as made clear in the research of sociologist William Julius Wilson.

See also Wilson, William Julius; Work, African Americans and the Changing Nature of, in the Post–World War II Era: An Interpretation.

Race and the American Presidency

"Our fathers brought forth on this continent," Abraham Lincoln said on a great battlefield of the Civil War, "a new nation, conceived in Liberty, and dedicated to the proposition that all men are created equal." Unfortunately, that proposition remained in doubt for the entire four-score and seven years before Gettysburg, and much of the period since.

Thomas Jefferson's original draft of the nation's founding document, the Declaration of Independence of July 4, 1776, included an assault on slavery that Southerners excised. The Founders who wrote the Constitution included nine specific protections for the South's peculiar institution. It ought not be a surprise that nine of the fifteen commanders-in-chief before Lincoln owned slaves; all five two-term presidents during the years 1789–1861 claimed human property rights; four of the six who did not own slaves were "doughfaces" (Northerners with Southern principles); and the remaining two spoke not a word against slavery during their four-year terms.

A profound ambivalence on questions of race has characterized each of the men who have held the nation's highest office. There have been spectacular exceptions: Lincoln, obviously, and also Lyndon B. Johnson during the great Southern war on JIM CROW in the time of MARTIN LUTHER KING, JR.. But by and large the presidency has been more committed to preserving the nation's original story of white over black. Whether before or after the Civil War, and whether on the issue of slavery, the legal racism that ruled for nearly a century after the RECONSTRUCTION era (1865–1877), or what is often referred to in modern times as institutionalized racism, the White House has acted aggressively in a consistent manner on one lone front: the use of race to organize the voting blocs necessary to carry a presidential candidate to office.

Antebellum White House, 1788–1860

If George Washington fantasized in his private correspondence about freeing the nation's slaves, as president he remained silent when Benjamin Franklin begged his support for a Quaker petition demanding exactly that. The next president, John Adams, questioned the wisdom of emancipation: "Would not the most shiftless among them be in danger of perishing for want . . . work at horrible jobs, become squatters, incorporate with Indians, commit crimes in bands." Such fears immobilized the nation's third president. Jefferson left behind in his writings dozens of assaults on "the malign twins" (the plantation system and slavery), but he saw enough personal utility in the institution to include "25 negroes little and big" in daughter Martha's dowry. James Madison, the fourth president, left the White House obsessed with the threat that he perceived free Southern blacks posed to white women. This was, to say the least, ironic. After Madison died, Daniel Webster, acting out of charity for the widow, Dolly, bought the freedom of his body servant, Paul Jennings. This former slave, now in Madison's class of "vicious free blacks," brought food to the penniless Dolly at Webster's direction. On his own, he gave her money from his pocket.

Jefferson and Madison did oppose the TRANSATLANTIC SLAVE TRADE (though not the interstate slave trade). But that opposition represented the entirety of positive presidential action prior to Lincoln. James Monroe helped form the AMERICAN COLONIZATION SOCIETY. Andrew Jackson denied the growing abolitionist movement the use of the mails and concocted stories if discipline crippled or killed one of his own slaves. "You may say to Dr. Hogg," he wrote to a coconspirator, "that her lament was occasioned by a stroke from Betty [another slave], or jumping over a rope, in which her feet became entangled, and she fell." John Quincy Adams emerged as an abolitionist champion only upon leaving the White House, notably by leading the Gag Rule fight. Martin Van Buren, a New Yorker, conspired with Supreme Court justices in hope of a decision in the AMISTAD case (1841) favorable to the slave interest. Another Northerner, James Buchanan, conspired more successfully in DRED SCOTT V. SANFORD (1857), in which the Supreme Court held that Negroes had "no rights which any white man was bound to respect."

Lincoln would debate *Dred Scott* with Stephen Douglas and help people understand that slavery threatened the dreams and freedoms of white America, too. While Lincoln remained infected with the colonization movement's send-them-back-to-Africa panacea, he believed one thing first and foremost: "If slavery is not wrong, nothing is wrong." More to the point, he was the first chief executive to act his conscience on matters of race. A singular man, he became singularly great in the White House. He made over a war to bring the South back to the Union into a war on slavery, and he did as much as any American at Gettysburg or elsewhere to make over a nation in which Jefferson's proposition was truly the fundamental creed.

From Emancipation to Jim Crow, 1860–1900

Of course, it could not last. Booth's shot and leap at Ford's Theater brought an explicit racist, Andrew Johnson, to the presidency. The Reconstruction wars that Johnson fought with the Radical Republicans in Congress led to the Thirteenth, Fourteenth, and Fifteenth amendments to the Constitution, ending slavery forever. But Reconstruction foundered and died with the Compromise of 1877. At issue were the old questions of using race to organize voting blocs and the fear of race war. The latter proved compelling enough to freeze Ulysses S. Grant in place. Utterly fearless on the Civil War's battlefields, President Grant shook at the thought of sending his armies after the KU KLUX KLAN in Mississippi. Republican pres-

President Lyndon B. Johnson shakes hands with Martin Luther King, Jr., after signing the Civil Rights Act of 1964. *CORBIS/Bettmann*

idents Hayes, Garfield, Arthur, Harrison, and McKinley left the freedpeople's fate within the states of the former Confederacy in the hands of the great white race. Where disenfranchisement and the separate-but-equal doctrine established in the latest Supreme Court case, PLESSY V. FERGUSON (1896), did not suffice, the South relied on lynch-mob terror.

Progressive Era, 1900–1920

Theodore Roosevelt, the first twentieth-century president, also led the Progressive movement (1900–1917), the first of this century's three major periods of liberal reform. Roosevelt's reformist impulse, however, owed a greater debt to *Plessy* than the timeless proposition of Jefferson and Lincoln. This president looked at Klan hoods and ropes in the context of white women raped by Negroes freed too soon. So he supported segregation as a scientific response to problems of racial division. If fully capable of making such a dramatic gesture as inviting BOOKER T. WASHINGTON to dine at the White House, Roosevelt always acted with the politician's eye for votes. Concluding that the key to Republican Party electoral success in this century lay in building up what his successor, William Howard Taft, called "a decent white man's party" below the Mason-Dixon line, he gradually abandoned such gestures. Stumping again for the presidency in 1912 on the Bull Moose ticket, he ran a self-professed "lily white" campaign.

Woodrow Wilson, the next progressive after Roosevelt, already had a decent white man's party in place. So he took a different reformist tack—launching a campaign to institutionalize Jim Crow within the civil service. Wilson also gave a private White House screening of *The Birth of a Nation* (1915), the D. W. Griffith Reconstruction-era epic film that presented the Ku Klux Klan as a heroic force. "History written with lightning," Wilson said. When asked to condemn southern LYNCHING, in contrast, he remained silent. The pressures of World War I, accompanied by a wave of race rioting in Washington, D.C., and elsewhere, did lead him to take a more moderate stance thereafter. But Wilson never abandoned the position he adopted as a young student of history—defending slavery as part of the civilizing process and dismissing Reconstruction as merely "a host of dusky children untimely put out of school."

New Era, 1921–1933

The New Era interlude before the nation's next major reform movement, Franklin D. Roosevelt's NEW DEAL, began with the Warren G. Harding administration's far-ranging search for an indictable offense to hang on MARCUS GARVEY. J. Edgar Hoover, a young Justice Department official who went on to head the Federal Bureau of Investigation, led the charge. The next president, Calvin Coolidge, left town on the day the Ku Klux Klan paraded through the streets of the nation's capital. Herbert Hoover, the third and last New Era chief executive, who had the particular misfortune to preside when the GREAT DEPRESSION arrived, emerged as the most bitter White House enemy of the NATIONAL ASSOCIATION FOR THE ADVANCEMENT OF COLORED PEOPLE (NAACP) in that organization's history. This was the result of the president's nomination of a segregationist, John J. Parker, to the Supreme Court. "Hoover's intransigence," as NAACP executive secretary Walter White said, "permanently alienated Negroes" and thus made the coming political revolution that much more likely.

New Deal, 1933–1945

Such intransigence, combined with New Deal economic reforms, offered African Americans hope enough to cause an exodus from the party of Lincoln to the party of Jefferson Davis. The white South, meanwhile, not only continued to vote Democratic but to enforce Jim Crow by any means necessary. If Franklin Roosevelt so feared alienating those voters that he remained silent even on lynching, he did support anti–poll tax legislation. He also made an occasional symbolic gesture. When the Daughters of the American Revolution refused to allow singer MARIAN ANDERSON to perform in Constitution Hall, Eleanor Roosevelt resigned her DAR membership in protest and her husband approved a free public concert at the Lincoln Memorial. More important, the New Deal established something of a "black brain trust" or "BLACK CABINET" that included MARY MCLEOD BETHUNE and ROBERT WEAVER and approached the ideal of equal treatment for all in several alphabet agencies (notably the Public Works Administration, or PWA).

Roosevelt lacked anything approaching a systematic civil rights program before A. PHILIP RANDOLPH threatened, in the summer before Pearl Harbor, a massive all-black march on Washington to force an executive order creating a FAIR EMPLOYMENT PRACTICE COMMITTEE. Paradoxically, the Roosevelt administration pursued an even more systematic approach on the surveillance front, sending G-men off to spy on the march on Washington and to gather intelligence on the "mood" of Negro communities from HARLEM to Watts. From FDR's election in 1932 to the FBI director's death in 1972 at the end of Richard M. Nixon's first term, J. Edgar Hoover was the first person every chief executive turned to when confronted with any issue along the color line.

Cold War, 1945–1961

Harry S. Truman, who came to the Oval Office at Roosevelt's death in 1945, was an unlikely candidate to make one of the century's most dramatic civil rights gestures. FDR had selected Truman as his vice-presidential candidate in 1944 to appease white Southerners who were alarmed at the left-wing politics of then–vice president Henry Wallace. "Everything is going to be all right," one senator predicted from the funeral train carrying Roosevelt's body. "The new president knows how to handle the niggers." It became clear just how wrong such sentiments were in late 1946 when Truman created a President's Committee on Civil Rights in response to the latest wave of lynching in the Deep South. In 1948 Truman sent civil rights legislation to Congress and issued a stunning executive order ending segregation in the armed forces. If the president's motives were somewhat suspect and he failed to push his own program in Congress, he did create a momentum that helped the modern CIVIL RIGHTS MOVEMENT press forward. Truman did more for racial justice than Franklin Roosevelt or any other predecessor (Lincoln aside)—more, too, than most who would follow.

This post–World War II momentum forced Dwight D. Eisenhower, the first Republican president since Herbert Hoover, to confront his own convictions. Eisenhower was a nineteenth-century man comfortable in the world of *Plessy,* a world that the Supreme Court cracked open in BROWN V. BOARD OF EDUCATION (1954). In 1957 the president sent troops into Arkansas to force state compliance with a federal court order to desegregate Little Rock Central High School. Acting in defense of the federal order (not civil rights), he said the decision to commit the 101st Airborne was the hardest of his presidency because it interfered with his dream to bring the white South over to the GOP. He also had to confront the post-Brown spectacle of black demonstrations and mass protests, notably the MONTGOMERY BUS BOYCOTT, starting in 1955, and the sit-ins of 1960. Coinciding with the rise of television, the new movement strategy pioneered by Martin Luther King, Jr., and others put an incredible amount of pressure on the White House to choose sides in the integrationist/segregationist struggle.

New Frontiers and Great Societies

John F. Kennedy inherited a bewildering array of direct action protest and segregationist violence from the Freedom Rides to the desegregation crisis at the University of Mississippi; from the marches in Bull Connor's Birmingham to a MARCH ON WASHINGTON in 1963 that witnessed Dr. King's "I Have a Dream" speech; from the turn-the-other-cheek rhetoric of Christian churches to the less accommodating rhetoric of MALCOLM X. Intent on keeping both black votes and white Southern votes, Kennedy hoped to wait out the movement. This was not unlike waiting out a snowstorm, as a White House aide noted. By spring 1963 the president finally realized that the movement was not going away and chose sides in his own particular style—sending civil rights legislation to Congress and acquiescing in the decision to place an FBI wiretap on Dr. King's telephone.

By the time John Kennedy died in Dallas and Lyndon B. Johnson took the oath of office, a wave of assassinations in fall 1963 had already shaken the nation. A Ku Klux Klan bomb in the basement of Birmingham's SIXTEENTH STREET BAPTIST CHURCH killed four young girls. In Vietnam, a military coup with at least some CIA assistance toppled and murdered Ngo Dinh Diem. Then, Kennedy's own assassin was gunned down while in police custody and in full view of television cameras. By the time Johnson left office in 1969, assassins would kill Dr. King, Malcolm X, and Robert Kennedy; and the war in Vietnam had become a televised nightmare rivaled only by racial strife at home that set urban America ablaze.

Initially, President Johnson seemed quite determined and capable of putting the fall 1963 violence to rest. In 1964 the Klan rose again, killing three civil rights workers in Neshoba County, Mississippi. But LBJ was already moving his Great Society reforms forward, pushing through Congress the sweeping Civil Rights Act of 1964 and implementing a War on Poverty. In 1965 he responded to Bloody Sunday and other segregationist violence in Selma, Alabama, with the final deathblow for Jim Crow—the VOTING RIGHTS ACT OF 1965. Still, this is where things began coming apart. Rather than celebrate these triumphs, the movement turned leftward with "Black Power," "Off the Pig," and "Burn, Baby, Burn" militancy, and the nation's cities exploded. Watts in 1965 and NEWARK, NEW JERSEY, and DETROIT, MICHIGAN, in 1967 represented only the largest of several hundred riots. Then, when Johnson appointed a presidential commission to investigate the riots, the so-called Kerner Commission identified white racism as the root cause.

John H. Sengstacke presents the Robert S. Abbott award to President Harry S. Truman for his contributions to democracy. Truman had established a President's Committee on Civil Rights in 1946 and had issued an executive order in 1948 ending segregation in the military.
CORBIS/Bettmann

Southern Strategies, 1969–1998

Here, the Republican Party saw an opportunity to fulfill Theodore Roosevelt's dream of building a decent white man's party in the South. In contrast to the Kerner Commission, the GOP's presidential candidate in 1968, Richard Nixon, identified the liberal excesses of John Kennedy's New Frontier and Lyndon Johnson's Great Society as the root cause of racial strife. Nixon also had to counter Alabama Governor George Wallace's third-party appeal for the racist vote. Everything from the fires in Detroit to the new AFFIRMATIVE ACTION bureaucracies and court-ordered busing of schoolchildren made the white South ripe for revolt, and Nixon did not intend to lose those voters to Wallace. Race, to put it another way, was the ultimate wedge issue, a tool to pit black against white generally and the various segments of the old Roosevelt coalition against one another more specifically (e.g., organized labor versus the organized civil rights community). Nixon called this his "Southern strategy," which consisted largely of reminding white voters in the South and white working-class voters in the Midwest that tax-paying white Americans were the victims of a new discrimination created by the Democratic Party.

Southern strategy remained a staple of GOP politics after Watergate. Republican Gerald Ford awkwardly questioned the historic school desegregation case, *Brown v. Board of Education*, and crusaded against court-ordered busing. The next Republican, Ronald Reagan, opened his 1980 campaign against Jimmy Carter at the Neshoba County Fair by telling the crowd that he was a states' righter. The Ku Klux Klansmen who murdered civil rights workers Michael Schwerner, JAMES CHANEY, and Andrew Goodman in Neshoba sixteen years earlier had said they were states' righters, too. Carter's suggestion that the affair demonstrated a racist streak in Reagan merely led to a media debate over whether the charge indicated a mean streak in Jimmy Carter. In 1988 George Bush organized his GOP campaign around the great race taboo, that of a black man who raped a white woman.

Democrat Bill Clinton preempted a repeat of Bush's Willie Horton gambit in the 1992 campaign by baiting JESSE JACKSON (the Sister Souljah affair); by posing with a black chain gang as backdrop for a crime control ad; golfing at a segregated Little Rock club; and presiding over the execution of a black man, Rickey Ray Rector, brain damaged enough to ask the men wielding the needle to save his last meal's dessert pie "for later." In the White House, President Clinton was more aggressive on the subject of racial justice. This was particularly true in the second term, when he offered a mend-it-don't-end-it defense of affirmative action and a Civil Rights Initiative intended to spark a national dialogue on race. The latter also included a pledge in the State of the Union Address of 1998 to accelerate enforcement of current civil rights laws affecting employment, education, housing, and health care.

The United States Supreme Court decided the presidential election of 2000 by employing a southern strategy of its own—namely, a claim in *Bush v. Gore* that the FOURTEENTH AMENDMENT could be used to protect the George W. Bush voter in Florida. The Supreme Court did not reference that amendment on the constitutionality of Republican party efforts, as documented by the U.S. Commission on Civil Rights, to suppress the black vote in Florida during the election and throughout Bush's White House years. Meanwhile, the administration demonstrated a penchant for states' rights rhetoric and the appointment of cabinet officers and federal judges sympathetic to a neo-Confederate cause. Attorney General John Ashcroft, for one, praised the otherwise obscure *Southern Partisan* as a magazine that "helps set the record straight . . . [by] defending Southern patriots like [Gen. Robert E.] Lee, [Gen. Stonewall] Jackson and [Confederate president Jefferson] Davis. Traditionalists must do more. I've got to do more. We've all got to stand up and speak in this respect, or else we'll be taught that these people were giving their lives, subscribing their sacred fortunes and their honor to some perverted agenda." With that comment, the attorney general of the United States—"the peoples' lawyer"—put himself on record in support of the notion that slave owners worked "to further the slaves' peace and happiness." *Southern Partisan* also helped set the record straight by dismissing the Emancipation Proclamation as "sinister" and praising John Wilkes Booth's "behavior" ("not only sane, but sensible").

See also Black Power in the United States; Democratic Party; Fifteenth Amendment; Fourteenth Amendment; Kerner Report; Military, Blacks in the American; Race Riots in the United States; Republican Party; Thirteenth Amendment; Vietnam War.

Kenneth O'Reilly

Race and U.S. Relations with Latin America: An Interpretation

How race has affected the relationship between the U.S. and the countries of Latin America.

For more than 200 years, racial prejudice has poisoned relations between the United States and LATIN AMERICA. For years, the prejudices of the United States led to attempts to dominate the region through military force and economic coercion. United States foreign policy in the region has been shaped by perceptions of Latin Americans as children who are unable to govern themselves properly. U.S.-backed paternalistic policies such as the Monroe Doctrine can be attributed to these flawed racial perceptions. This long history of racism and heavy-handed United States foreign policy has generated widespread animosity toward the United States throughout much of Latin America. From the onset of Latin American independence in the early nineteenth century to the present U.S. antidrug policies, little has changed in the unbalanced relations between the United States and Latin America.

Haiti and Latin America's Push for Independence

On January 1, 1804, the former slave colony of Santo Domingue proclaimed its independence from FRANCE, ending a bloody revolution that began in 1791. The Republic of HAITI became the first free black state, resulting from the first successful slave revolt in Latin America. In addition to undermining slavery as an institution, the HAITIAN REVOLUTION demonstrated that the colonial powers were vulnerable. The Haitian revolution raised fears among plantation owners of the Caribbean basin and Southern United States that relied on slave labor. Plantation owners attempted to keep the rebellion a secret, fearing that their own slaves would follow Haiti's example.

It was from Haiti, in 1816, that Venezuelan general SIMON BOLÍVAR set sail to liberate all areas of Latin America under colonial Spanish rule. With the military and economic support of Haitian president ALEXANDRE PÉTION, Bolivar returned to VENEZUELA, where he began his march to free the Americas. By 1822 Venezuela, COLOMBIA, ECUADOR, PERU, and BOLIVIA had won their independence. In contrast to these new countries, PUERTO RICO and CUBA retained their colonial status and did not seek independence. Fearing that a Haitian-style slave revolt would disrupt their economies, they remained loyal to SPAIN.

Pan-American Conference

United States relations with Latin America had been almost nonexistent during Latin America's struggle for independence. The United States took a position of neutrality during Latin America's many anticolonial wars against Spain. Bolívar unsuccessfully sought aid from the United States to fight against Spain. The United States was uncertain who would win the war and maintained diplomatic relations with both Bolívar and Spain. Unhappy with the U.S. stance, Bolívar scornfully referred to the U.S. position as one of "arithmetic neutrality."

The already tenuous relationship between the United States and Latin America was further damaged in 1823 by the issuing of the Monroe Doctrine. During an annual address to congress, U.S. president James Monroe outlined the doctrine that barred European powers from interfering with the newly independent Spanish American countries. The Monroe Doctrine was a bold, unilateral statement of United States claims to Latin America. While the United States had little real hope of enforcing it against the superior military strength of European powers, the doctrine marked the start of a more aggressive U.S. presence in Latin America.

In 1826, pressed with economic and political problems, Bolívar planned a Pan-American Conference to provide a forum for the newly independent Latin American countries to resolve common problems. The United States Senate narrowly approved participation in the Pan-American Congress and hoped to discuss the future of Haiti and Cuba within a growing U.S. sphere of influence. But the United States did not take the congress seriously, and racial prejudices prevented any real dialogue between the United States and Latin America.

The United States wanted to prevent recognition of Haiti as an independent country. Some senators declined to discuss the issue because they believed that doing so would be "giving Haiti equal rank with communities of men composed of the descendants of the Saxons, the Franks, and ancient Germans." The case of Cuba presented another dilemma. Previous attempts by the United States to purchase Cuba had failed, and the United States wanted Cuba to remain under Spanish rule until it could be incorporated into the United States. The United States feared that Cuba would follow Haiti's example of slave revolt.

Manifest Destiny and Expansion into Mexico

Many white citizens of North America believed their continent had been given to them by God. Accordingly, territorial expansion of the United States became inevitable, and it was viewed by many whites as part of God's master plan. In conquering the continent, they were following manifest destiny, the idea that a Christian God had granted white Americans a right to control North America. In 1803 the United States purchased the Louisiana Territory from France, increasing the area of the United States by approximately 2,100,000 square kilometers (811,000 square miles) of land west of the Mississippi River. Land-hungry white settlers and trappers moved across the Mississippi River into the cotton fields and cattle lands of Louisiana and East Texas. In 1819 Spain ceded Florida to the United States, and in 1821 the United States looked to the northern reaches of MEXICO, recently independent from colonial Spain. Northern Mexico stretched west from what is now Texas to the state of California and north to the Oregon border.

In 1822 the first white settlements were legally established in Texas. Over the next few years there was an influx of immigrants from the southern United States into the Mexican states of Texas and Coahuila. The Southerners continued to rely on slaves as the labor for their agricultural economy. Northern Mexico still belonged to the Mexican Republic, and the sudden influx of United States residents posed a threat to Mexican sovereignty. Fearful of losing its land, Mexico passed a series of laws to discourage further immigration from the United States. In 1829 the Mexican government abolished slavery, and in 1830 it prohibited any further immigration from the United States. Tensions mounted between Mexico and the United States, and fighting erupted on April 21, 1836, in the city of San Jacinto (near present-day Houston). The Battle of San Jacinto ended with the capture of Mexican general Santa Anna, who was forced to recognize Texas's independence and to withdraw his troops to south of the Río Grande. The United States victory ensured that Texas would secede from Mexico.

In 1845 relations between the United States and Mexico grew increasingly worse. A border dispute between the two countries became a catalyst for the MEXICAN WAR. The war lasted from 1846 to 1848, and after many bloody battles it resulted in a decisive U.S. victory that forced Mexico to relinquish claims to its national territory. In 1848 the United States and Mexico signed the Treaty of Guadalupe-Hidalgo, which entitled the United States to the northern half of the Mexican territory.

Some Americans wanted to claim all the land in the vast Mexican Republic. Exactly how much of Mexico the United States would annex presented a dilemma. If the United States annexed the entire Mexican Republic, all Mexican citizens would become U.S. citizens. The words of Florida senator Edward Cabell typified the view of many officials and citizens.

He said that the United States should not convert the "black, white, red, mongrel, miserable population of Mexico—the Mexicans, Indians, Mulattoes, Mestizas [sic], Chinos, Zambos, Quinteros—into free and enlightened American citizens, entitled to all the privileges we enjoy."

Spanish-American War and Expansionist Policies

The United States entered a period of industrial growth during the final decades of the nineteenth century. To compete economically with EUROPE, the country needed trade outlets for its growing industrial and agricultural production. Overseas expansion provided North America with a source for more raw materials, cheap labor, and captive consumers. The United States justified its increasingly aggressive expansionistic behavior in Latin America as complying with its duty to bring civilization to a supposedly latent Latin American culture.

The United States revealed its imperialistic goals when it fought Spain in a war over the Spanish colonies of Cuba, the Philippines, and Puerto Rico. The Spanish-American War lasted almost four months, from April 25 to August 12, 1898. Fighting occurred primarily in or near the Spanish colonies of Cuba and the Philippines. The war provided the United States with an opportunity to acquire an overseas empire and to minimize European influence in Latin America. Spain's defeat guaranteed the independence of Cuba and the transfer of Puerto Rico, the Philippines, and Guam into protectorates of the United States. Puerto Rico was given semicolonial status, while Cuba was granted symbolic independence under close U.S. supervision. Spain's defeat marked the end of the Spanish colonial empire and the rise of the United States as a global power.

In 1901 the United States attached the Platt Amendment to Cuba's new constitution. The amendment justified U.S. intervention in Cuban affairs when the United States deemed such intervention necessary, and it gave the United States the right to build military bases on Cuban soil. The United States also imposed a restrictive democracy on Cuba, denying a large portion of the Cuban population the vote. This became a landmark decision, one that Secretary of State Elihu Root was confident historians would not forget. In 1908 Root declared, "the establishment of popular self-government, based on a limited suffrage, excluding so great a proportion of the elements which have brought ruin to Haiti and San Domingo, will be regarded as an event of first importance."

Big-Stick Policy

Following the Spanish-American War, the United States emerged as the indisputable power in Latin America. An era of Spanish colonialism was replaced by U.S.-backed policies such as the Platt Amendment and the lingering threat of the so-called big stick. "Speak softly and carry a big stick" was the political approach advocated by President Theodore Roosevelt, by which he implied that formal COLONIAL RULE was not necessary for effective control. The big stick of the Roosevelt administration was the threat of war. Although force was rarely used against powerful nations in Europe or Asia, it was used to pressure Latin American countries to comply with the goals of the United States.

United States Intervention in Colombia

In early 1903, the senate of Colombia rejected the Hay-Herrán Treaty. The treaty would have entitled the United States to lease a strip of territory across the Isthmus of Panama to build a canal linking the Atlantic and Pacific oceans. Infuriated by Colombia's lack of cooperation, Roosevelt supported secessionist plans proposed by lobbyists from the Panama Canal Company and the Panamanian elite. On November 3, 1903, the secessionists declared the Isthmus of Panama independent from Colombia. The independence of PANAMA made the construction of the canal possible. The United States immediately recognized the new republic, and the Panamanians signed the Hay-Bunau-Varilla Treaty. The new treaty gave the United States the right to build and operate the Panama Canal, to control a special Canal Zone as if it were U.S. territory, and to annex more land for canal operations and defense. This episode demonstrated that the United States was willing to undermine and subvert democracy in Latin America when sufficient geopolitical interests were at stake.

Roosevelt Corollary

In 1902 Venezuela defaulted on its loan repayments to its European creditors, and the United States acknowledged the rights of GERMANY and GREAT BRITAIN to impose a naval blockade to collect repayment. Roosevelt said that if a Latin American country misbehaved in its dealings with Europe, the United States would "let the European country spank it." Roosevelt soon realized the error of this policy. To keep European influence out of Latin America, the United States needed the ability to intervene in Latin American affairs whenever national interest was at stake. In 1904 President Roosevelt signed the Roosevelt Corollary to the Monroe Doctrine. While the Monroe Doctrine was ostensibly designed to shield Latin America from European influence, the Roosevelt Corollary gave the United States the right to intervene in Latin America when U.S. interests were threatened. Most Latin Americans viewed Roosevelt's policy as a form of racist imperialism. The policy revealed that Roosevelt, like Monroe, was willing to dictate policies affecting the internal affairs of Latin American countries.

United States Intervention in the Dominican Republic and Haiti

In 1907 Roosevelt applied his corollary to the DOMINICAN REPUBLIC. Like Venezuela, the Dominican Republic had an enormous debt, and payment to its European creditors seemed impossible. Roosevelt feared that a European power would physically occupy the Dominican Republic to force repayment. The United States deemed it necessary to directly intervene and occupy the Dominican Republic. The U.S. military operated the Dominican custom receivership service for two years, using money collected to repay the nation's debts. The measure initially aimed at helping the Dominican Republic pay its foreign creditors later expanded into other sectors of Dominican life. From 1916 to 1924 the country was placed under the political administration of the U.S. Marine Corps. Financial supervision continued until 1941.

In 1915 Haiti suffered a similar fate when U.S. admiral William Banks Caperton placed it under the administrative control of the United States and abolished all forms of local government. The United States feared that French and German influences in Haiti posed a threat to security of the Panama Canal. U.S. Marines secured the Haitian countryside and built the institutions needed to govern a modern nation. The United States collected tariffs, paid foreign debts, restructured the government and military, and constructed new roads. The U.S. military occupation of Haiti ended on August 15, 1934. Reforms imposed by the United States did not last, and Haiti fell prey to dictators and disorganization for the next several decades. Although Haiti was left with a much better economic and financial infrastructure, the U.S. occupation failed in one of its primary objectives—establishing a stable democracy. Rather than admit its own failure to build institutions rooted in Haitian society, the United States explained this failure by citing the supposed inferiority of the Haitian people.

Almost fifty years of U.S. intervention in Latin America failed to bring either democracy or a dramatic improvement in the quality of life. In 1908 Cuba's former governor, Charles Magoon, predicted Latin America's inability to move forward. According to Magoon, the region was inhabited by a race that was "hot blooded, high strung, nervous, excitable and pessimistic," as well as "suspicious of everyone." He added that these characteristics would remain despite U.S. occupation "for two or twenty years," emphasizing that Latin Americans would never "be changed by a military occupation."

Cold War (1945–1989)

By the end of World War II in 1945, little had changed in relations between the United States and Latin America. Latin America was regarded as unable to govern itself correctly and as therefore dependent on the United States for political and cultural guidance. The aggressive and paternalistic U.S. policies aimed at preventing Latin America from being swayed to communism reflected this attitude. The United States believed intervention was necessary because of a lack of maturity of the Latin American countries. Secretary of State Allan Dulles warned the U.S. National Security Council that "unlike ourselves, many of the Latin American states are leaping ahead to irresponsible self-government directly out of a semi-colonial status. This presents the communist with an ideal situation to exploit." In short, Dulles argued, Latin America needed U.S. guidance to confront communism.

Guatemala and the United Fruit Company

The 1951 election of leftist Jacobo Arbenz to the presidency of GUATEMALA marked a shift in the Latin American political landscape. Arbenz considered Guatemala too dependent on external forces, especially the United States, and launched a badly needed agrarian reform program. Land was reclaimed from foreign investors and the Creole elite, then redistributed widely among the people of Guatemala. The hardest hit by this policy was the United Fruit Company, a U.S. company that owned large tracts of Guatemalan land. The United Fruit Company also controlled the majority of the country's ports, railroads, roads, and other infrastructure. Threatened by Arbenz's actions, the company accused his administration of being a beachhead for communism. Following intense lobbying by the United Fruit Company, the U.S. State Department and the Central Intelligence Agency also read Arbenz's policies as communist. The United States feared that if one Latin American country became communist, the rest of the region would fall to communism as well. With covert support from the United States, Colonel Carlos Castillo Armas ousted President Arbenz and installed an anticommunist government that supported U.S. interests.

Fidel Castro and Cuba's Defiance of the United States

On January 1, 1959, FIDEL CASTRO overthrew the Cuban dictatorship of FULGENCIO BATISTA and ushered in a new era of United States–Cuban relations. Despite U.S. attempts to keep communism out of Latin America, Castro installed a communist government in Cuba. By establishing a communist regime approximately a hundred miles from the United States, Castro created a major irritant to U.S. control of the area. Castro's radical, defiant policies did not sit well with President John F. Kennedy and his administration. Shortly after taking power, for example, Castro implemented a nationalization policy that directly affected many foreign-owned industries. The U.S.-run sugar industry was nationalized and placed under Cuban control. In response to such actions, the United States broke diplomatic ties with Cuba in 1961.

The United States perceived the emergence of communism in Cuba as evidence of a lack of maturity in the Cuban mentality. To combat the growing threat of communism, Kennedy planned a covert invasion of Cuba in 1961 at the Bay of Pigs. This attempt by the United States to overthrow Castro failed, giving the dictator renewed confidence that pushed him further into the Soviet sphere of influence. The Kennedy administration responded to the communist threat with a threefold strategy. First, the United States trained Latin American military personnel to fight communism in military schools backed by the United States. Second, convinced that social inequality and poverty were the causes of communism, the Kennedy administration launched the Alliance for Progress, a program for technical and financial development among nations friendly to the United States. Finally, the United States ordered an economic blockade of Cuba aimed at destroying the island's SUGAR economy. Kennedy's policies failed to remove Castro, however, and Castro remained a thorn in the side of the United States in following decades.

Carter Administration

With the election of President Jimmy Carter in 1977, the United States reevaluated its foreign policy toward Latin America. The Carter administration sought to promote improved relations and to dismantle old prejudices held both in the United States and in Latin America. Carter denied aid to Latin American dictators based on their human rights violations. He treated Latin Americans with respect, which helped mend the wounds left by previous administrations. In 1977 Carter reached an agreement with Panamanian president Omar Torrijos for the return of the Panama Canal to Panama. After left-wing Sandinistas overthrew Nicaraguan dictator Anastasio Somoza Debayle, Carter engaged the new government in dialogue instead of fighting it. From 1979 until the end of his term in 1981, Carter provided the Sandinista government with financial assistance.

Reagan Years

President Ronald Reagan's election to office in 1981 marked a return to earlier paternalistic policies based on prejudices against Latin America. The Reagan administration believed the United States to be culturally and politically superior to Latin America. Because of this belief, the administration saw it as the duty of the United States to guide Latin America away from the communist threat and safely into democracy. Reagan perceived former president Carter's Latin American policies as weak. Reagan continued to fight what he regarded as the continued advancement of communism in CENTRAL AMERICA, and he denied any further aid to the Nicaraguan Sandinistas. He focused on arming and training counterinsurgency groups to halt the spread of Communism in Latin America. By covertly supporting the Salvadoran army and the Nicaraguan Contra insurgents, Reagan perpetuated bloody and prolonged civil wars in Central America. Determined to gain peace for Central America through personal diplomacy, Costa Rican president Oscar Arias Sánchez called upon EL SALVADOR, Guatemala, HONDURAS, and NICARAGUA to renew the peace process. Civil wars in the region and the tensions between Nicaragua's Sandinista government and the United States stalled all peace talks. In August 1987 the presidents of all five Central American nations signed a peace agreement temporarily halting the bloodshed. President Regan opposed the peace plan and continued to provide military support to right-wing dictatorships.

Post–Cold War Relations and the War on Drugs

The end of the Cold War in 1989 once again changed the dynamics of the relations between the United States and Latin America. Communism no longer seemed to threaten Latin America, since it had for the most part crumbled along with the 1989 fall of the Berlin Wall in Germany. The United States needed a new adversary. The War on Drugs, a policy that portrayed drugs as another destabilizing menace that originated in Latin America, shifted the focus of U.S. foreign policy in the region. According to the United States, the War on Drugs had to be fought in the countries that produced and supplied the drugs. The U.S. militarily intervened in countries such as Colombia, Peru, and Mexico, which were pinpointed as the sources of drug production. Latin American leaders demanded that the problem be treated at an international level, not unilaterally, but they were ignored by the administrations of Ronald Reagan and George Bush. Under both presidents, the United States conditioned economic aid on compliance with its antidrug policies.

The U.S. War on Drugs in Latin America continued during the administrations of Bill Clinton and George W. Bush. Critics reviled the ongoing campaign as a continuation of oppressive American imperialism. In the 2000s, the U.S. pressured BOLIVIA to reduce its coca (the raw material for cocaine) output. Cultivating coca leaves is a centuries old pursuit that has great cultural significance among Bolivia's Indians. American policy created unrest in Bolivia that helped lead to the overthrow of the country's pro-U.S. president, Gonzalo Sánchez de Lozada. Defiance of Washington has spread to other Latin American nations during the Bush administration. In 2003, for example, Mexico and Chile did not support the U.S. efforts to gain United Nations approval for a military action against Iraq.

See also Colonial Latin America and the Caribbean; Human Rights in Latin America and the Caribbean; Independence Movements in the British Caribbean; Latin America and the Caribbean, Blacks in; Slavery in Latin America and the Caribbean; Spanish-American War, African Americans in the.

Race in Latin America

Racial issues and race relations in Latin America.

Millions of Africans of different ethnic groupings were shipped halfway across the world to labor the SUGAR, coffee, tobacco, and rice plantations and the mines of the New World. They brought with them their religions, their languages, their dance, their music, and their instruments. European colonial masters did their utmost to strip these Africans of their freedom, their dignity, and their culture, but culture was perhaps the easiest of the three for peoples of African descent to continue to subvert.

From the United States South and the MEXICAN altiplano in the north, to the Peruvian coastal lowlands and the Argentine pampas down south, the rhythms of AFRICA continued to beat. The SAMBA and CANDOMBLÉ of BRAZIL; the SON and SANTERÍA of CUBA; the street Carnivals of Salvador de Bahia, RIO DE JANEIRO, and a host of other towns and cities; the *merengue* of the DOMINICAN REPUBLIC and VENEZUELA; modern-day SALSA; the very ingredients of the languages spoken and the foods eaten; family, community, and other organizational forms: in all lie manifestations of the strivings of Afro–Latin Americans to create a viable reality in which life could then, and can now, be lived with dignity.

Colonial and postcolonial society partitioned off people, classifying and categorizing skin pigmentation with a bewildering array of legal codes and linguistic terms (170 such terms exist in Brazil alone). In this context, bettering or WHITENING the race denoted upward social mobility, while blackening was equated with backwardness, poverty, and underdevelopment. The exceptions to racial hostility and oppression are pitifully thin at the national level and testify to the stigma of a perverse colonial legacy.

In many countries in LATIN AMERICA and the Caribbean, people of African descent have constituted a majority of the population, and the race issue has been uppermost. But the prevailing currents of the region's history, dominated by a sense of "Europeanness," have repeatedly undermined and denied awareness of the African heritage, forcing Afro–Latin Americans to rediscover their ancestry and culture and renew the struggle for their rights.

Variants in Race Relations

A key variant in race relations in Latin America and the Caribbean occurs between the relatively fluid race relations of, for example, Brazil and Cuba and the more bipolar situation in the United States and the non-Hispanic Caribbean. This has been explained in two ways: in terms of colonial cultures, and in terms of stages of development. One side of the argument is that the reason for the difference is not economic but cultural. Iberians (or people from PORTUGAL and SPAIN), it is claimed, instituted a more benign form of slavery than northern Europeans, because of the strong Moorish influences on, and the nature of feudalism and Catholicism in, the Iberian Peninsula. The counterargument is that there are powerful underlying economic explanations for racism tied to the growth of the plantation economy in the Americas. Thus, it makes little sense to compare nineteenth-century Cuba, a booming slave plantation economy, and nineteenth-century PUERTO RICO, which was an imperial backwater with no significant development of plantation slavery.

Both the "imperial cultures" and the economic materialism approaches tend to focus on power structures and official thinking. A third argument highlights the extent to which people have been active agents in shaping their own history, building and abolishing slavery, erecting and transgressing the intricacies of color and class codes. A distinction has been made between public and private, between the rules of behavior regulating contact between racial groups and actual intimate personal relations. According to this view, Iberian differed from non-Iberian America far more in the public than in the private.

No part of the world, it has been claimed, ever witnessed such a gigantic mixing of races as what took place in Latin America and the Caribbean. It is useful, however, to think of the region in terms of a threefold division within Afro–Latin America, comprising the Caribbean (WEST INDIES) and northeast Brazil; Euro–Latin America, made up of ARGENTINA, URUGUAY, southern CHILE, and south Brazil, which received great waves of European immigrants over the past 100 years; and *mestizo* America, where there are scattered enclaves of indigenous populations such as Mexico, GUATEMALA, the Andes, and the Amazon Basin.

The extent of race mixing in Latin America might have engendered hopes of a new cosmic race, but it also meant that there has been no generally agreed-upon racial classification, and racial distinctions are necessarily vague. What is considered black in one context might be white in another. This depends, to a large extent, on the tensions between prevailing definitions of race—as phenotype, or physical characteristics, and as genotype, or heredity—and on how far there has been cultural as well as biological mixing.

Throughout Latin America, after plantation slavery, a general hardening of race prejudice occurred, incorporating nineteenth-century European pseudoscientific eugenicist notions. These ideas sat uneasily with Latin American intellectual thinking, which romanticized indigenism and Africanism, and celebrated *mestizaje* (or race mixture) as the new symbiosis. As a result, notions of mestizaje were also permeated with ideas about the superiority of whitening. Hence, the contradiction between the myth of racial democracy and the prevalence of discrimination and prejudice against indigenous peoples, blacks, and mulattoes.

Africa and the Atlantic World

Essential to a contemporary understanding of the Afro–Latin American reality is the legacy of almost 400 years of plantation slavery and what is today recognized to have been the largest forced migrations in modern history. Between ten and fifty million Africans were shipped to Brazil, Cuba, the Caribbean, and the United States. Several countries in the region not usually thought of as associated with the traffic also had a substantial African presence, such as Mexico, which received an estimated half-million black captives.

Two aspects of this process have been much debated. The first is the commodity-driven nature of New World slavery, in contrast to Old World slave-based civilizations. The second is the deculturation of Africans in the trauma of THE MIDDLE PASSAGE and what followed. Deculturation, or the loss of African-derived culture by slaves in the Americas, was seen as an inherent consequence of every form of colonial or neocolonial exploitation. It was usual for the dominant class to protect and even stimulate isolated cultural values of the dominated class, but only insofar as those values helped reinforce the desired social structure. The dominated class was forced to seek refuge in its culture as a means of surviving and preserving its identity.

The vast and tortured movement of African peoples across the Atlantic was a major turning point in world history, facilitating the beginnings of the modern world capitalist economy and the emergence of empires spanning oceans. In the field of

Atlantic studies, a key unresolved question is the extent to which both Eurocentric and Afrocentric approaches converge in depicting Africa and Africans as passive victims. How active a partner were Africa's political and economic elite in trade involvement with EUROPE? How far did African slaves accommodate to or resist slavery in the Americas? How strong was African culture in the re-creation of Afro–Latin American societies?

To understand the Africa of Latin America therefore requires more than a retracing of African footsteps. We must grasp how African—along with European, indigenous, and Asian—social groups created new and complex societies that differed from their component parts. After independence and the abolition of slavery, a racist idea gained currency in Latin America, whereby the chaotic situation was explained in terms of, among other things, blacks being the obstacle to the development of Latin American societies. Blaming the victim—perhaps the most damning outcome of the denial of the African past—made subsequent reevaluations of the African contribution to the development of Latin America imperative. This has proven no mean task when racial values were constantly being socially reworked and codified, re-created, and reproduced.

The legal end of slavery, which came last to Cuba (1886) and Brazil (1888), did not end its legacy, and in the struggle over land and labor the process of emancipation proved as varied, long, and bloodied as abolition. Its impact wrought major changes in the nineteenth-century Latin American and world economy, including the collapse of older production centers. It ushered in waves of indentured Asian and immigrant European labor, and massive out-migrations of Afro–Latin Americans from poor and marginal lands to cities and overseas.

From slavery to the present, the predominant—though far from universal—experience for Afro–Latin Americans has been of oppression and inferiorization. There have, however, been times when they have demonstrated great individual and collective achievement, awareness, and organization in challenging their oppression, eliciting official concern and recognition, gaining in political power, and establishing themselves as an accepted part of the culture and national self-identity.

Black Self-Liberation

An important lesson of history is that political leadership matters. Race and ethnicity hold strategic, not inherent or absolute, value. Ethnic and racial identity take on different meanings in different contexts, depending on who uses them and for what purposes. They are relative, situational categories. Competition and conflict between racial and ethnic groups may occur but need not necessarily do so, and may or may not be institutionalized in the political system at a societal level. Political systems may generate heightened racial or ethnic sentiments, but they can also channel negotiations and cross-cutting alliances, allowing scope for individual and collective action.

In the context of Latin America, we can distinguish among three forms of political systems. First are those where one dominant segment of the population claimed that its racial or ethnic identity was the only legitimate one in the nation. Second are the political systems where newly empowered elite sought legitimacy by promoting a synthetic national culture, discouraging racial or ethnic thinking that might separate citizens from the nation. Third are those systems where groups shared more equally in the political life of the nation in proportion to their population, and where citizenship encompassed different yet compatible ethnic identities together constituting the nation.

The first was more likely to occur when a relatively large settler group from the colonizing power attained independence without a social revolution—the U.S. model but one that, to a lesser degree, might be applied to Puerto Rico, the Dominican Republic, Mexico, and South American Andean countries. The second has been perhaps the most common, certainly in Brazil, Cuba, COLOMBIA, and Venezuela, with their evidently significant numbers of African-descended peoples. Central and South American countries, with their smaller Afro-Caribbean and Afro–Latin American enclaves, would fall somewhere between the two. The third case, harboring what might be the closest approximation to racial democracy in the region, is arguably only attributable in part to BELIZE.

Any meaningful notion of racial democracy must encompass black self-liberation. Studies of Afro–Latin America continue to reflect the racist denigration of blacks as primitive, backward, anti-intellectual beings. Antislavery continues to be seen more as a transatlantic than a regional phenomenon, with its own philosophical and ideological underpinnings, involving localized resistance and awareness. Yet black-led antislavery movements represented a critical element at the core of transatlantic abolitionism and might be seen as the first international political movement of modern times.

In the context of the modern-day black Atlantic, African-descended identities and cultures jostle between asserting an absolutist sense of difference and recognizing an awareness of the double consciousness of trying to face (at least) two ways at once, between closure and openness in what have been called cultures of mediation.

Race and Gender

The gender parameters of cultures of mediation, as well as the Afro–Latin American presence, are still to be explored in full. The slaves brought over from Africa were predominantly male and hence skewed the population. As the model transformed into one that was slave-reproducing rather than slave-importing, this was also a highly gendered process. Later Afro-Caribbean migrant workers on the Panama Canal and on Costa Rican and Cuban plantations were also mainly male. Conversely, the more recent Puerto Rican out-migration into the New York garment industry was significantly Afro-female-led.

Moreover, family and kinship patterns, and accompanying value systems, linked with pronatalist (or antinatalist) state policies, have all been crucial in shaping the emergent societies. A modern-day example of this was Puerto Rico's Operation Bootstrap, which was accompanied by a drastic sterilization program that targeted poor and black women.

Prevailing ideas on gender differ markedly in Latin America and the Caribbean, especially where the family and sexuality are concerned, and largely along race lines. The polarized stereotypes are of the white Ibero-American patriarch (with repressed, controlled female) and the black Afro-Caribbean matriarch (with marginal, emasculated male). These are issues that continue to command attention.

See also Afro–Latin American and Afro-Caribbean Identity: An Interpretation; Carnivals in Latin America and the Caribbean; Complexities of Ethnic and Racial Terminology in Latin America and the Caribbean; Cultural Politics of Blackness in Latin America and the Caribbean; Eugenics; Merengue: Music, Race and Nation in the Dominican Republic; Myth of Racial Democracy in Latin America and the Caribbean; Négritude; Race and Class in Brazil: An Interpretation; Race: An Interpretation; Slavery in Latin America and the Caribbean; Transatlantic Slave Trade; Transculturation, Mestizaje, and the Cosmic Race: An Interpretation.

Pedro Pérez-Sarduy
Jean Stubbs

Race Riots in the United States

Events of mass urban violence that have been both a means of white repression of blacks and an expression of black frustration at that repression.

The term *race riot* has been used to describe a variety of acts of collective racial violence in American history. Not all episodes of mass urban violence have been racial in character; such violence has also been driven by antagonisms between workers and employers and by religious animosity. Most riots in the United States, however, have had their roots in racial division.

Antebellum Period and Civil War

During the antebellum period and the AMERICAN CIVIL WAR (1861–1865), race riots erupted in numerous Northern cities. Antiblack and antiabolitionist riots took place in cities such as CINCINNATI, OHIO, and Utica, New York. Racial hostilities sharpened with an influx of European immigrants, who displaced blacks from a variety of skilled and semiskilled labor trades. But white workers were not the only rioters in the North. Members of the propertied classes, whose sympathies with the slaveholding South were fostered by trade, took part as well.

The high-water mark of racial conflict in the nineteenth-century North was the NEW YORK CITY DRAFT RIOT OF 1863. Outraged by the institution of a draft that permitted those who were wealthy enough to hire a substitute to serve in their place when they were summoned into the Union Army, white mobs rioted for several days. Because of longstanding animosities from labor competition and because they saw blacks and abolitionists as the cause of the war, the rioters directed their fury especially at blacks. The violence was not brought to an end until federal troops who had just triumphed over the Confederates at Gettysburg, Pennsylvania, were sent to NEW YORK. The riot resulted in the deaths of scores of people and the destruction of millions of dollars worth of property.

Reconstruction and Jim Crow

Racial rioting during the RECONSTRUCTION era (1865–1877) was shaped by the refusal of much of the white South to accept the Union victory in the Civil War and the subsequent extension of constitutional rights to blacks. A variety of terrorist organizations, most notably the KU KLUX KLAN, resorted to LYNCHING, the assassination of radical officeholders, and the torching of schools to destabilize the Reconstruction governments. In 1866 major riots occurred in cities such as NEW ORLEANS, LOUISIANA, and MEMPHIS, TENNESSEE. The violence in Memphis was stimulated by an influx of black servicemen into the city, which whites saw as a threat to white supremacy. Police played a major role in the violence, and prominent whites constituted some of the mob. By the time order was restored, forty-six blacks had been killed. At the heart of the New Orleans violence was a mob assault upon a Republican-dominated, interracial state constitutional convention that was likely to extend the franchise (the right to vote) to blacks. As the convention assembled, a mob including many of the city's police attacked. Both the Memphis and New Orleans episodes drew wide public attention to the failure of the administration of President Andrew Johnson to protect the safety of Southern blacks and their white Republican allies.

Altogether, according to American historian Melinda Meek Hennessey, thirty-three urban race riots took place during the Reconstruction era. Another major riot took place in New Orleans in 1868, and in 1876 a riot occurred in CHARLESTON, SOUTH CAROLINA, in which the city's blacks held their ground in the fighting with whites. In a number of Reconstruction-era riots, United States Army troops were within close reach of the places where outbreaks occurred but obeyed orders not to interfere in matters supposedly beyond the scope of federal authority. Although racist writers have claimed that in the nineteenth century, Southern race riots were caused by the alleged need to protect white women from black assault, Hennessey's careful analysis of the Reconstruction riots indicates that the dominant activating factor was the desire of whites to maintain political, economic, and social control. The evidence also shows that African Americans did not respond passively to white aggression; Hennessey writes that blacks usually fought back until overwhelmed by superior numbers and firepower.

Major race riots at the turn of the century, particularly the WILMINGTON RIOT OF 1898, and the ATLANTA RIOT OF 1906, aided the triumph of segregation and black disfranchisement. The riot in Wilmington, North Carolina, targeted the threat of an interracial coalition between Republicans and Populists. White Democrats followed their victory in the state election with an armed assault against the city's black community, and they forced local Republican officeholders to resign. The Wilmington riot demonstrated the unwillingness of the national Republican administration to act against even the most flagrant lawlessness, and the basis was laid for new state legislation effectively denying voting rights to blacks. In the Atlanta riot, incited by the racist local press and white politicians seeking to gain office by creating hysteria about the supposed threat of black criminality, white mobs roamed through black neighborhoods and made frenzied attacks on blacks in the city's downtown. The Atlanta violence, taking place in what was said to be the center of progress in the South, evoked wide national attention. Federal authorities once more did nothing.

In the early years of the twentieth century, race riots also spread to the North, making clear that the race question had national scope. In August 1900 mobs attacked blacks in New York City, with the police encouraging the violence. In August 1908 a white mob, incited by false reports that a white woman had been assaulted by a black man in her home, set afire the homes of many blacks in Springfield, Illinois. The Springfield violence was the key event that led to the formation of the NATIONAL ASSOCIATION FOR THE ADVANCEMENT OF COLORED PEOPLE (NAACP), which brought together black activists led by W. E. B. DU BOIS and numerous white liberals and socialists.

Migration and World Wars

The period of World War I (1914–1918), with its large-scale influx of blacks into the North as part of the GREAT MIGRATION, brought a wave of racial rioting as well. In one major instance, violence erupted in the EAST ST. LOUIS RIOT OF 1917. A local packing plant in East St. Louis, Illinois, recruited black strikebreakers, and in response, on July 2, numerous blacks were stoned, kicked, stabbed, and hanged. Some blacks were burned in their homes.

Race riots erupted in American cities during what became known as the Red Summer of 1919. From WASHINGTON, D.C., to Knoxville, Tennessee, and Omaha, Nebraska, white mobs attempted to ensure that the opportunities blacks had gained during the war did not alter the prevailing system of racial subordination. Particularly large and violent were the ELAINE, ARKANSAS, RIOT OF 1919 and the CHICAGO RIOT OF 1919. The violence of that summer was followed by the TULSA RIOT OF 1921, in which rumor of an alleged sexual assault touched off a mob attack on the city's black community. The violence took place in a city in which the Ku Klux Klan had become a powerful force. Many black lives were lost and much property destroyed, but the Tulsa riot was also marked by intense black resistance.

The riots of the 1930s and 1940s marked a shift in the American race riot. After this point, the typical urban rioters changed from white mobs assaulting blacks to blacks expressing mass rage against racial repression. The HARLEM RIOT OF 1935 and the HARLEM RIOT OF 1943 were essentially black rebellions against inequitable conditions and police brutality. The DETROIT RIOT OF 1943 started with a black protest evoked by rumors that a black mother and her child had been killed in the city's Belle Isle Park. The violence quickly turned into an assault by police and white mobs; all of the seventeen people killed by the police were black. The white media and local, state, and federal officials did little to address the legitimate grievances voiced by African Americans in the 1943 events. President Franklin Roosevelt would not agree to an NAACP request that he speak out against racial violence and hatred.

Civil Rights Era and Beyond

Riots in numerous American cities took place during the 1960s, even as victories were won against legal segregation and disfranchisement in the South. The CIVIL RIGHTS MOVEMENT had raised hopes for further progress toward racial equality, but as blacks in Northern cities saw their hopes frustrated, the setting was established for large-scale disorder in cities such as NEWARK, NEW JERSEY; Rochester, New York; Cleveland, Ohio; Cincinnati, Ohio; and CHICAGO. Most significant were the HARLEM RIOT OF 1964, the WATTS RIOT OF 1965, and the DETROIT RIOT OF 1967. Despite the recommendations of riot commissions about the social causes of these disturbances, as in the KERNER REPORT (1968), the government emphasized the use of force to contain the disorders.

The passing of the 1960s did not bring racial tensions to an end, and in 1992 such tensions exploded in the massive LOS ANGELES RIOT OF 1992 that followed the acquittal of four police officers in the beating of Rodney King, an African American motorist. The riots of the late 1960s and early 1990s reflected the lack of governmental attention to the grievances about police brutality and social injustice voiced by African Americans. Such riots have allowed people of other nations to measure American claims to world leadership against the persistence of racial violence within the United States.

See also Antiabolitionism; Segregation in the United States.

Bibliography

Bernstein, Iver. *The New York City Draft Riots: Their Significance for American Society and Politics in the Age of the Civil War.* Oxford University Press, 1990.

Fine, Sidney. *Violence in the Model City: The Cavanagh Administration, Race Relations, and the Detroit Riot of 1967.* University of Michigan Press, 1989.

Hofstadter, Richard, and Michael Wallace, eds. *American Violence: A Documentary History.* Knopf, 1970.

Kerner Commission. *The Kerner Report: The 1968 Report of the National Advisory Commission on Civil Disorders.* Dutton, 1968. Reprint, Pantheon, 1988.

Platt, Anthony, ed. *The Politics of Riot Commissions, 1917–1970.* Macmillan, 1971.

Richards, Leonard L. *Gentlemen of Property and Standing: Anti-Abolition Mobs in Jacksonian America.* Oxford University Press, 1970.

Shapiro, Herbert. *White Violence and Black Response: From Reconstruction to Montgomery.* University of Massachusetts Press, 1988.

Waskow, Arthur I. *From Race Riot to Sit-In, 1919 and the 1960s: A Study in the Connections between Conflict and Violence.* Doubleday, 1966.

Race Riots of 1919

Violence by whites against blacks in the United States after World War I, climaxing during the so-called Red Summer of 1919 with riots in more than twenty-five cities.

For information on

Causes of the riots: *See* Civil Rights Movement; Great Migration; Labor Unions in the United States; Race Riots in the United States.

Riots in Chicago, Illinois: *See* Binga, Jesse; Chicago Riot of 1919; Chicago, Illinois.

Riot in Arkansas: *See* Elaine, Arkansas, Race Riot of 1919; Jones, Scipio A(fricanus).

Reactions to the riots: *See* African Blood Brotherhood; Bruce, John Edward; Great Migration: An Interpretation; Johnson, Charles Spurgeon.

Race War of 1912

Conflict that arose in Cuba in 1912 when an insurrection was mounted to protest the outlawing of the Partido Independiente de Color, an Afro-Cuban political party.

The uprising that sparked the Race War of 1912 was met with harsh repression by the government and armed civilians, which left over 3,000 Afro-Cubans dead. The conflict is also known as the Little War of 1912 or the Little War of May.

See also Afro-Cuban Political Mobilization: An Interpretation; Cuba; Cuban Politics before the Race War of 1912; Partido Independiente de Color.

Racial Consciousness in Africa

See Black Consciousness in Africa.

Racial Consciousness in Brazil

See Black Consciousness in Brazil.

Racial Consciousness in Latin America and the Caribbean

See Black Theology in Latin America and the Caribbean: An Interpretation; Blackness in Latin America and the Caribbean: An Interpretation.

Racial Consciousness in the United States

See Black Consciousness in the United States.

Racial Discrimination in Latin America and the Caribbean

See Myth of Racial Democracy in Latin America and the Caribbean: An Interpretation.

Racial Labels in Latin America and the Caribbean

See Complexities of Ethnic and Racial Terminology in Latin America and the Caribbean.

Racial Mixing in Latin America and the Caribbean

Intermixing among people of Native American, European, and African descent since colonial times.

For information on

Identity questions: *See* Afro–Latin America, Research on; Afro–Latin American and Afro-Caribbean Identity: An Interpretation; Complexities of Ethnic and Racial Terminology in Latin America and the Caribbean.

Social classifications of mixed-race people in Latin America and the Caribbean: *See* Colonial Latin America and the Caribbean; Image of the Mulatta in Latin America and the Caribbean; Latin America, Blacks and Indians in: An Interpretation; Myth of Racial Democracy in Latin America and the Caribbean: An Interpretation; Race in Latin America; Transculturation, Mestizaje, and the Cosmic Race: An Interpretation; Whitening.

Racial mixing in specific Latin American and Caribbean countries: *See* Aruba; Brazil; Garinagu; Puerto Rico; Venezuela.

Reaction of individual Latin Americans to the concept of racial mixing: *See* Estupiñán Bass, Nelson; Freyre, Gilberto; Gratiant, Gilbert.

Racial Stereotypes

Discussion of the issues surrounding racially-based generalizations.

Sticks and stones will break my bones, but names will never hurt me. Our era has moved beyond this proverb, which parents teach vulnerable children. Forget sticks—we worry now about deadly weapons. Forget names—we all have to deal with racial and ethnic stereotypes. Stereotypes are proverbial generalizations broadcast by the powerful media of the modern era. Their racial dimensions are what concern us here, but first let's look at the broad issues stereotypes provoke and the history of the term.

The term *stereotype,* now used with reference to our society's old problem with nasty names, was developed when, at the outset of the modern industrial age in 1798, two European printers invented a new way to reproduce images that would fix them permanently. The image-setting process was called *stereotyping,* and in time the word *stereotype* came to apply to the fixing of intellectual, as opposed to printed, images. One's stereotype of a jet, for instance, wipes away the marks of specific makes in order to stand in for all jets. One's stereotype of a ballet dancer may not be male or female and may not have a realized face; thus the image can represent all ballet dancers. Stereotypes simplify real images in order to make a generalization. All peoples produce stereotyped ideas in order to create a shorthand form of communication among themselves.

All peoples also produce racial stereotypes about themselves and others. That is, people simplify the intellectual images they maintain of specific ethnic groups, including their own, often in cruel or damaging ways. Poor white Southerners ("crackers") are said to be slow, red-necked, and fat. Immigrant Italians ("wops") are said to be short, oily, and hot-tempered. Upper-class whites ("WASPs") are said to be greedy, emotionally cold, and haughty. Negroes ("niggers") are said to be stupid, promiscuous, and happy. These generalizations are not accurate, but they are spread widely—not only by word of mouth but also through images in television, movies, newspapers, music, comic books, talk shows, pseudo-scientific research, and even textbooks. These media make stereotypes, whose dissemination was once confined to oral transmission from one person to another, seem more like factual knowledge than personal opinion.

Perhaps the most chilling aspect of racial stereotyping is that members of groups being characterized sometimes come to believe the generalizations' damaging simplifications. Members of target groups may even try to fulfill the stereotypes. The media regularly depicts people of African descent as drug dealers and teen mothers, and so it is not surprising when young black artists also adopt the roles of thugs and "bitches 'n 'ho's." Even stereotypes that include positive human attributes can warp people. For instance, if the dominant culture emphasizes that men of African descent are excellent athletes or entertainers, the glamour associated with these professions may influence the youth of that group. They may try to fulfill a simplified stereotype of their potential rather than develop other traits. That is the force of stereotypes.

Racial stereotypes reflect and are facilitated by power relations in a society. Stereotypes of a demeaned group are frequently accepted as the truth and are not understood as problematic until the group can manifest its fully human condition. As the group's relative power grows, it can sometimes stop the public proliferation of blatant stereotypes about it. That's what happened in the 1950s when the NATIONAL ASSOCIATION FOR THE ADVANCEMENT OF COLORED PEOPLE (NAACP) made concerted complaints about minstrel shows. The NAACP effectively stopped the practice of white Americans blacking up to represent black people in ragged, ignorant, and grotesque stereotypes. (Isolated examples of whites mounting minstrel shows continued in backwaters of the North and South in the United States into the 1980s. "Darkie Days" survived in England, as in Padstow, Cornwall, into the twentieth-first century, despite complaints from a member of Parliament. Blacks in England remain much less empowered than those in the U.S.)

The many paradoxes in stereotypes are analytically useful. When one group creates stereotypes to manage its thoughts about others, dispassionate observers gain access to the compact assumptions controlling that group's thought. Created in moments and locations of stress and anxiety, stereotypes satisfy various functions for their creators. One group will create stereotypes about another group in order to control them (or fight back against control) or to justify their power over that group (or to strike back against that power). By classifying the target group as subhuman or grotesque, stereotypes are likely to minimize their creators' misgivings about participating in uneven power relations. A stereotype always isolates one perhaps imagined aspect of the target group and substitutes it for the whole. Because it denies the complex humanity of the demeaned target, every racial stereotype says much more about the creators' needs than about the target's nature. Because they always display their creators' dread of the target group, racial stereotypes eventually subvert their makers' cruel intentions. For instance, a cultural group that classifies women of another culture exclusively as mammies displays alarm about its own nurturing capacity. A people that stereotypes others as greedy money-changers betrays its own concern for prosperity.

Studying stereotypes reveals both their present power and their historical flow. Despite their power to disturb us in the present, stereotypes turn in cycles. Their meanings can change dramatically over time. The JIM CROW figure, which rapidly became a stereotype standing for U.S. racism, began (and persists) as a figure of black folklore. Poor white actors and workers who identified with the suffering of black slaves in the early 1800s copied their gestures to speak out against employers. But their opponents, in turn, used the image of this Jim Crow mimicry to mock the alliance between blacks and their sympathizers. It was a full century before the NAACP could gain some control over the stereotype. The evolutionary nature of stereotypes shows that they are anything but permanent. Indeed, they may help change social attitudes over time. Many sensitive artists of every hue have known how to turn stereotypes inside out. They push them hard enough so that audiences see both the stereotypes' cruelty and their makers' weakness.

See also Film, Blacks in American; Minstrelsy; Race: An Interpretation; Radio and African Americans; Television and African Americans.

W. T. Lhamon, Jr.

Racism in Latin America and the Caribbean

See Myth of Racial Democracy in Latin America and the Caribbean: An Interpretation.

Radama I

1793?–1828?

Ruler of the Merina Empire of Madagascar from 1810 to 1828.

The son of ANDRIANAMPOINIMERINA, Radama I distinguished himself at a young age, leading two military operations against the BETSILEO and the Boina when he was only fifteen years old. Upon his father's death in 1810, Radama took the reins of power and continued the campaign to extend the Merina Empire over all of MADAGASCAR, conquering the Toamansing in 1817. Mistakenly predicting that the seventeen-year-old king would be unable to retain control of his father's extended domain, the Bezanozano and Betsileo peoples rebelled. But with a clear military superiority over all other MALAGASY kingdoms, Radama's army quickly quelled the uprisings.

Shortly after England took control of MAURITIUS in 1810, the newly assigned governor, Robert Townsend Farquhar, established diplomatic relations with Radama. The English crown sought to eliminate the slave trade in Mauritius, for which Madagascar was the primary supplier, as well as to limit French influence in the Indian Ocean. To this end, Farquhar's agents entered into a formal alliance with Radama, sealed by an oath of blood that recognized Ramada as the sole king of Madagascar. In exchange for ending the slave trade, Radama received compensation for lost revenue and his troops were trained and armed by British military advisers, enabling him to vastly expand his political domain.

The treaty established by Radama and Farquhar brought agents of the London Missionary Society to Madagascar to set up schools and proselytize the Christian faith, particularly among the MERINA. Radama also sent his two younger brothers, Ratàfika and Rahòvy, to Mauritius for education in 1816, accompanied by several dignitaries. The two princes lived in Farquhar's house while being tutored. Radama's embrace of European technology and culture would eventually lead to a reactionary backlash when his wife RANAVALONA I became queen.

By 1820 Radama had a well-trained and well-armed standing professional army of 13,000 troops. Determined to maintain influence in Madagascar, FRANCE forged alliances with several peripheral kingdoms resistant to Merina rule. However, Radama defeated revolts by the Antankàrana, TSIMIHETY, and SIHANAKA, and came to a diplomatic settlement with the SAKALAVA. By the time of his death, Radama had vastly expanded his empire to include two-thirds of the island.

See also Christianity: Missionaries in Africa; Indian Ocean Slave Trade.

Bibliography

Allen, Philip. M. *Madagascar: Conflicts of Authority in the Great Island.* Westview Press, 1995.

Brown, Mervyn. *Madagascar Rediscovered.* Damien Tunnacliffe, 1978.

Covell, Maureen. *Historical Dictionary of Madagascar.* Scarecrow Press, 1995.

Ari Nave

Radama II

1829?–1863?

King of the Merina Empire of Madagascar from 1861 to 1863.

Radama II was born with the name Rokoto (or Rakotond-Radama), son of King RADAMA I and QUEEN RANAVALONA I of the Merina Empire. However, the actual father of the prince was probably Andriamihaja, the queen's lover, for Rokoto was born eighteen months after the death of Radama.

Prince Rokoto received a Western education despite his mother's anti-European policies and her sometimes brutal determination to preserve traditional MALAGASY culture. Rokoto was particularly influenced by French entrepreneur Jean Lambert, who, along with Rokoto's uncles Raombàna and Rahaniraka, oversaw his education and instilled in him European values.

In response to his mother's injustice and brutality, Rokoto, along with Lambert and other pro-European agents, plotted to overthrow Ranavalona. The commander-in-chief of the armed forces, Raharo, postponed the planned coup by claiming that the palace guards could not be counted on for support. Shortly thereafter the queen learned of the plot, expelled the foreigners involved, and executed all implicated Malagasy. Her son, however, escaped retribution. With Ranavalona's death in 1861, Rokoto took the throne as Radama II, inviting Lambert and other foreigners to return.

Radama II embraced European beliefs and outlawed many of the Malagasy customs his mother had struggled to retain, including circumcision and *famadihana,* or "turning of the dead" (a custom of reclothing bones of ancestors stored in sacred tombs). Radama II also instituted significant pro-Western economic and political reforms. In 1855 he signed the Lambert Charter, a document granting his long-time friend 10 percent of the profits from all industries he developed. These measures alienated him from the core of MERINA aristocrats and Hova commoners in ANTANANARIVO, MADAGASCAR, who had traditionally supported the monarchy. Only two years after taking the throne, Radama II was assassinated.

See also Madagascar.

Bibliography

Brown, Mervyn. *A History of Madagascar.* Damien Tunnacliffe, 1978.

Covell, Maureen. *Historical Dictionary of Madagascar.* Scarecrow Press, 1995.

Ari Nave

Radio, African

Most widespread and influential form of mass media in Africa.

Since the first radio stations began broadcasting in AFRICA during the colonial period, radio has been the continent's most important form of mass media. As more countries gained independence, the medium of radio progressively reached more people. Radio ownership in Africa increased about five times between 1965 and 1984 (from 3 to 16 percent). Between 1960 and 1987, the number of radio transmitters in Africa quadrupled from 252 to 1059. The battery-powered radio is an especially crucial source of information in rural areas, where literacy rates are low, electricity for television is often unavailable, and regular newspaper deliveries are impractical.

Radio broadcasts began in SOUTH AFRICA in 1923. Colonial KENYA began airing British Broadcasting Corporation (BBC) programs in 1927. Colonial governments owned the radio stations, and typically used them to entertain white settlers and broadcast messages intended to discourage Africans from political participation. After World War II, British colonies in West Africa began to train Africans as broadcasters, station managers, and technicians. In addition, the British encouraged programming in indigenous languages. By contrast, FRANCE saw radio as a medium for promoting French language and culture in its own colonies. The French introduced African language broadcasting near the end of the colonial period, both to compete with the British and to reach Africans with pro-French broadcasting more effectively.

After decolonization, African governments used state-owned radio to promote their own economic and political agendas. Besides the usual news and music, some broadcasting was devoted to straightforward public service messages, such as notices about vaccination campaigns. In Upper Volta (now BURKINA FASO), during years of particularly harsh drought, the government used radio to urge people in the worst-stricken northern provinces to migrate south, where more arable land was available. But some of independent Africa's early leaders as GHANA's KWAME NKRUMAH, WILLIAM TUBMAN of LIBERIA, and JOMO KENYATTA of Kenya also used radio to consolidate their own political power. Governments quashed dissent by closing competing stations, or by staffing the stations with political cronies.

Free Speech, Hate Speech, and Censorship

Short-wave radio has traditionally provided an alternative to state radio. The BBC, Voice of America, French National Radio, German and Russian radio outlets, and even the Vatican spend millions of dollars every year to broadcast to Africa in numerous languages. Short-wave radios are more expensive than conventional ones, and they consume batteries at a higher rate. But for years many Africans saw them as the only viable alternative to state-run broadcasts.

The end of the Cold War brought increased pressure on African governments to allow more free speech over the airwaves. Donor nations and agencies began to attach "good government" clauses as conditions for further economic aid, which often included the loosening of state controls over broadcasting.

Not all privately run radio has proven enlightening. In the early 1990s, Radio des Milles Collines, a private Hutu-run radio station in RWANDA, was widely blamed for helping to incite the 1994 genocide of an estimated one million Tutsi and Hutu moderates. Broadcasts encouraged Hutus to take their "spears, clubs, guns, swords, stones, everything, sharpen them, jack them, those enemies, those cockroaches." In SOUTH AFRICA a private AFRIKANER station, Radio Pretoria, issues what has been described by some as neo-Nazi, proAPARTHEID propaganda. Such "hate radio" has come under scrutiny by the United Nations.

But private radio is increasingly diverse, and in some cases remarkably bold. In 1995 in BURUNDI, a country with a history of genocidal conflict similar to neighboring Rwanda, *Studio Ijambo* (Ijambo means "wise words" in Kirundi) produced programs that combined "culture, politics, music, and social issues," with the larger aim of promoting Hutu-Tutsi reconciliation. The nongovernmental organization that founded Studio Ijambo, Search for Common Ground, also operated in Liberia and South Africa. South Africa's Bush Radio aired "In the Pink," a show aimed at the gay and lesbian community. Africa No. 1, a commercially successful private station in GABON, combines popular programming. This has included "Baobab," which features African musicians in Paris; educational programming, such as "Wake Up," a morning show for women; "Dr. Africa," which answers listeners' questions about AIDS and other health issues; and "Africa Noon," which provides midday news.

Yet even though private stations have become much more common in Africa in the past two decades, free speech has not always been assured. In many countries, concentration of ownership, official policies limiting broadcast content, or the unofficial threat of government harassment of journalists have all effectively limited the range of opinions expressed over the airwaves. MALI, where more than forty stations began broadcasting between 1991 and 1996, has become a noted exception.

Technological Trends

Radio's future in Africa will be greatly affected by technological advances. Today battery-powered radios are the most common by far, but electric and solar-powered radios are also available. In about 1994, the South African company BayGen Power Manufacturing developed a wind-up radio, which works like a clock. Listeners crank the radio for thirty seconds, generating enough energy to run the radio for one hour. Cheap energy is only one challenge, however, and much of Africa still receives only minimal radio programming, because of the lack of transmitters and the relatively short transmission range of FM stations. WorldSpace, founded in 1990 by Ethiopian lawyer Noah Samara, launched a satellite named Afristar in October 1998, which provides ninety-six channels of digital radio signals to Africa. In addition to the standard news, sports, and entertainment, WorldSpace features a women's channel, one dedicated to children's issues, and another for health education. Realizing that as much as 75 percent of its potential listeners had no access to electricity, WorldSpace purchased 10 percent of BayGen Manufacturing, and distributed thousands of wind-up radios.

See also Decolonization in Africa: An Interpretation; Hutu and Tutsi; United Nations in Africa.

Robert Fay

Radio and African Americans

History of African Americans on radio from its early days to the present, covering music, comedy, drama, disk jockeys (DJs), managers, owners, and listeners.

Radio has been an important medium in the lives of African Americans. Over time, radio's role in black life and culture has changed from a medium in which African Americans were hired primarily to entertain whites to one that provides news, sports, public affairs programs, music, and other forms of entertainment primarily to African Americans. Moreover, African Americans perform a variety of jobs and duties in today's radio stations and are not limited to announcing or acting positions.

Radio's role in black life and history differs from the roles of television, newspapers, and motion pictures. For example, although African American filmmakers made motion pictures for black audiences during film's nascent years, the majority of African Americans were unfamiliar with these filmmakers and their work. By contrast, African American musicians and singers on early radio were popular artists, and they sold records to black record buyers. Furthermore, radio has played a significant role in popularizing AFRICAN AMERICAN MUSIC, particularly GOSPEL MUSIC, RAP, HIP-HOP, and RHYTHM AND BLUES. Neither film nor television has figured prominently in popularizing black cultural creations in the way that radio has with black music.

Black newspapers have showcased the writing talents of African American poets and writers. Nevertheless, black newspapers have not enjoyed the mass popularity that radio has, mainly because of the latter's engagement with oral traditions, a common feature of African American culture. Since radio extends the human voice and allows African Americans to maintain oral cultural traditions in language arts, black musical forms, and storytelling, the medium holds special meaning for blacks.

Early Radio

During radio's early years, following the first commercial broadcast on KDKA in PITTSBURGH, PENNSYLVANIA, in 1920, African Americans participated in the medium's development as musicians, singers, and actors. African American ownership or management, however, was virtually nonexistent.

Jack Leroy Cooper was the first African American to have a commercially sustained radio program. Cooper's career began at WCAP in WASHINGTON, D.C., in 1925. Later, he moved to WSBC in CHICAGO, ILLINOIS, where he launched the *All-Negro Hour* in 1929. Cooper succeeded in hiring many African Americans to work for him as announcers and salespeople. Additionally, Cooper introduced several programming innovations such as gospel music, a missing persons program created to assist individuals in finding relatives and friends, newscasts, and sports programming. In 1937 Cooper and Richard Stams, another black disc jockey, began broadcasts of the games of the Chicago American Giants in baseball's NEGRO LEAGUES.

As network radio expanded its programming to include more comedy and variety programs in the 1920s and 1930s, black characters were given stereotypical roles. On some programs, African Americans portrayed themselves in this manner. In other shows, such as *AMOS 'N' ANDY* and *Fibber McGee and Molly* (in the part of the maid Beulah), whites portrayed African Americans. The American MINSTRELSY and vaudeville traditions supplied radio with its characterizations of African Americans, as actors playing black roles were asked to speak using heavy Southern accents and dialects that whites believed all African Americans used.

One of the most popular radio comedies in the history of the medium was *Amos 'n' Andy*, a program about a black-owned taxicab company in HARLEM, NEW YORK. The show ran from 1928 to 1960, making it the longest-running series in American radio history. Two white men, Charles Correll and Freeman Gosden, played the parts of Amos and Andy. Other characters, such as Kingfish, the Judge, Ruby, the Widow, Bailiff, and Lightnin', were also played by whites. African Americans had little to do with the show's production. Many African Americans considered *Amos 'n' Andy* to be a degrading and racist depiction of black life and culture. In 1931 the *PITTSBURGH COURIER* newspaper protested the show and called for its cancellation. Twenty years later, a similar protest by the NATIONAL ASSOCIATION FOR THE ADVANCEMENT OF COLORED PEOPLE (NAACP) was mounted against the television version of the series.

Radio-set ownership among African Americans in the 1920s and 1930s reflected their economic status. Approximately 14 percent of urban blacks owned radio sets in 1930, but less than 1 percent of rural farm blacks did. In the South, where most African Americans lived, radio-set ownership rates were lowest. Nevertheless, for special broadcasts of BOXING prizefights and other occasions, groups of African Americans gathered around radios at the corner store, the local barbershop, or a neighbor's home to listen.

Black Music. Most African Americans during the early years of radio wanted to hear the new sounds in JAZZ and the BLUES, two black musical forms. Radio stations were reluctant to play the blues, since white programmers and some African Americans considered this music to be lower class and uncultured. Jazz music, however, did receive considerable airplay. KMBC in KANSAS CITY broadcast Bennie Moten's Radio Orchestra, featuring on some occasions COUNT BASIE. Network radio and some local radio stations made regular broadcasts of black jazz bands. Bandleaders FATS WALLER, CAB CALLOWAY, DUKE ELLINGTON, Erskine Hawkins, JIMMIE LUNCEFORD, Andy Kirk, and Chick Webb made frequent radio broadcasts during the 1930s. Meanwhile, the orchestra led by white bandleader Paul Whiteman gained a huge following by popularizing jazz through his radio shows and recordings. Like *Amos 'n' Andy,* Whiteman's band exploited black culture for economic gain, while at the same time excluding African Americans from his productions and from any revenue generated from their own culture.

African American vocalists, such as MARIAN ANDERSON, ROLAND HAYES, Muriel Rahn, and PAUL ROBESON, sang on early radio broadcasts. Black college and university choirs often made regular singing broadcasts on network radio as well. WILLIAM GRANT STILL, a black classical composer, wrote music that was performed on network radio in the 1930s. On at least one occasion, Still served as conductor for a white orchestra, Willard Robinson's Deep River Orchestra, which appeared on the National Broadcasting Corporation (NBC) network.

Comedy and Drama. In 1937 EDDIE ANDERSON became the first African American actor featured regularly on a network radio program. Anderson portrayed Rochester (a comedic character on the *Jack Benny Show*), who became one of the most popular characters on radio. Rochester was negatively stereotyped, however. He was a character right out of the minstrel tradition, in which black men were characterized as lazy, shiftless womanizers who spent their time lying, drinking, and gambling. To his credit, Anderson nevertheless managed to expand his role as Rochester to the point where some of the negative personality traits associated with African American men were diminished in his character.

Most African American comedians on early radio took on similar stereotypical roles in order to find work. Eddie Green and Ernie Whitman were cast as "coons," following the lower-class stereotype of the minstrel shows, in a 1930s radio production of the musical *Showboat*. At the same time, HATTIE McDANIEL had "mammy" roles in the *Optimistic Doughnut Hour* and in the *Showboat* radio series. In the 1940s most radio roles for African American women were as maids and cooks. African Americans made radio appearances in dramatic presentations as well in the 1930s. The Columbia Broadcasting System (CBS), for example, cast Juano Hernandez in the title role in *John Henry, Black River Giant* (1933). New York City radio stations WMCA and WJZ broadcast weekly black dramas, often employing an African American cast, during the 1930s.

Public Affairs and Wartime Programming. During its early years, radio public affairs programs targeted to African American audiences focused on farming techniques, education, the black family, and, on occasion, racial matters. Public affairs programs in the 1940s, such as NBC's *Freedom's People,* Roy Ottley's *New World a Comin',* and Richard Durham's *Destination Freedom,* provided more positive and historically accurate portrayals of African American achievers and societal concerns. Local radio stations broadcast Ottley and Durham's programs, as network radio avoided controversial shows that dealt with the "race problem." Additionally, radio contributed to religious practices through broadcasts of church services. Radio stations aired gospel music and the singing of church and school choirs, and by 1949 most cities in the United States had at least one African American radio preacher.

During World War II, the U.S. Department of War sponsored *America's Negro Soldiers,* which was broadcast on NBC's Blue Network in 1941. The program included music, singing, and tap dancing as well as sketches and patriotic vignettes that highlighted the historical contributions black soldiers had made in the U.S. Army. The program largely ignored the racism and segregation in American society. While this blindered approach characterized most other wartime propaganda programs created for African Americans, CBS did produce *An Open Letter on Race Hatred,* which focused on the causes and consequences of the DETROIT RIOT OF 1943.

Rise of the Black Radio Market

Radio began to appeal directly to African Americans in the late 1940s. Two factors contributed to this effort. The first factor was that national advertisers realized the economic power of black consumers. In large and small cities, companies that produced staples such as flour, lard, and canned milk came to the realization that if they advertised directly to African American consumers, they could sell their products to them.

At the same time, national network radio began losing audience share, advertising revenue, and top-name performers to the new medium of television. Most of the top stars on network radio chose to move over to television because of the lucrative contracts being offered. The *Amos 'n' Andy* program followed this trend, and black actors replaced white performers for the televised version of this show.

Radio station owners responded to this crisis situation by focusing on local markets, including local black markets. Many stations hired African American DJs to increase the number of listeners and changed their formats to feature rhythm and blues, jazz, gospel, blues, and rock-and-roll music to appeal directly to African Americans.

Radio station WDIA, in MEMPHIS, TENNESSEE, broadcast its first show aimed at a black audience, hosted by pioneer black DJ Nat D. Williams, in 1948. The station devoted its entire schedule to all-black programming soon after. Before that time there were few sustained "black appeal" programs on radio, with the notable exceptions of Cooper's *All Negro Hour* and fellow Chicago DJ Al Benson's shows. WDIA, which promoted itself as the "Mid-South Giant," provided a mix of music and information to African Americans living in Tennessee, Mississippi, and Arkansas. The station became well known for its public affairs and public service activities as well.

Radio stations across the country in the 1950s hired black DJs such as Martha Jean "The Queen" Steinberg and Jack Walker "The Pear-Shaped Talker," who brought their oratorical skills, unique on-air personalities, and knowledge of black music to radio. In addition to playing music, these DJs offered advice on where to shop, how to avoid being robbed, and other public services to assist their listeners in their daily lives. Many African American DJs became cultural heroes, and white DJs imitated their style. For instance, African American DJs invented the concept of "riding gain," which occurs when announcers turn up the volume to emphasize certain parts of a record. They also devised the concept of "talking through" records, which happens when announcers speak over the record as it is played.

Through their programs these disc jockeys introduced features of African American culture to all Americans and influenced the kinds of music that record companies produced. Future cultural icons such as Elvis Presley and singers such as Pat Boone and Carl Perkins listened to black music on the radio and later presented their own versions of it to white audiences. Many white artists "covered" black songs and sold millions of records to white consumers. In this way, black musical forms became ever more popular, as audiences also longed for the authentic versions of these songs.

The black-appeal formats also created opportunities for African American news reporters and public affairs announcers. These individuals, the best known of whom included Roy Woods and Eddie Castleberry, made commercials and announced news, sports, and weather reports. In addition, religious music and broadcasts of Sunday-morning church services appealed to black listeners' need for spiritual guidance.

The CIVIL RIGHTS MOVEMENT benefited from radio's coverage of important leaders and newsworthy events. Radio brought national attention to racial and economic disparities in American society, highlighting issues such as voting rights and the violence and brutality directed at African Americans as they attempted to desegregate public accommodations, schools, and residential neighborhoods. Radio broadcast the sermons of civil rights leader MARTIN LUTHER KING, JR., and message music from black recording artists, and thus the medium gave voice to the countless thousands who had no voice on issues affecting their lives.

Black Ownership and Urban Radio

African American ownership and licensing of radio stations has been low or nonexistent. During the early years of radio, only a handful of African Americans gained access to enough capital to buy a radio station. J. B. Blayton, the first African American to own a commercial radio station in the United States, bought WERD in ATLANTA, GEORGIA, in 1948.

By 1970 African Americans owned only sixteen radio stations out of more than 7,000 commercially operated facilities broadcasting at that time. The decade of the 1970s, however, witnessed strong growth in black radio station ownership. As a result, by 1980 African Americans owned 140 radio stations. By 1996 the number of black-owned radio stations had increased to 170.

The urban contemporary format, which includes rhythm and blues, urban contemporary, urban gospel, and urban rap music forms, is the most popular preference for black radio stations. Fifty-seven percent of all African Americans ages twelve and above listen to this format. Black radio today no longer appeals strictly to blacks, as it did in its infancy; it is popular among Asians, whites, and Hispanics as well. Still, the majority of those listening are African Americans. Ninety percent of the listeners to black-formatted radio stations and 82 percent of listeners to the urban contemporary format are minorities. By contrast, general-market programming only attracts a 21 percent minority audience.

Minority employees are still underrepresented in the radio industry. Although minorities account for 30 percent of the U.S. population, they compose less than 20 percent of all full-time employees at commercial radio stations in the nation.

Finally, the recent movement toward media concentration and consolidation in the radio industry has negatively impacted black station ownership. As consolidation and mergers occur, fewer radio stations owned by individuals or small companies remain. Conglomerates buy additional stations in the same market and are able to reduce expenses by spreading costs across several stations, making it difficult for black-owned stations to compete, since most African American owners have only one station. Consolidation in local radio markets also allows conglomerates to control advertising dollars. These factors have forced many African Americans to sell their radio stations, further reducing the already low numbers of black-owned radio stations.

See also Film, Blacks in American; Press, Black, in the United States; Racial Stereotypes; Television and African Americans; World War II and African Americans.

Bibliography

Cantor, Louis. *Wheelin' on Beale: How WDIA-Memphis Became the Nation's First All-Black Radio Station and Created the Sound that Changed America.* Pharos, 1992.

Fink, Michael. *Inside the Music Industry: Creativity, Process, and Business.* Schirmer, 1996.

George, Nelson. *Hip Hop America.* Viking, 1998.

Lewis, Tom. *Empire of the Air: The Men Who Made Radio.* Burlingame, 1991.

McDonald, J. Fred. *Don't Touch that Dial! Radio Programming in American Life, 1920–1960.* Nelson, 1979.

McDonald, J. Fred, ed. *Richard Durham's Destination Freedom: Scripts from Radio's Black Legacy, 1948–1950.* Praeger, 1989.

Newman, Mark. *Entrepreneurs of Profit and Pride: From Black-Appeal to Radio Soul.* Praeger, 1988.

Ward, Brian. *Just My Soul Responding: Rhythm and Blues, Black Consciousness, and Race Relations.* University of California Press, 1998.

Williams, Gilbert A. *Legendary Pioneers of Black Radio.* Praeger, 1998.

Gilbert A. Williams

Ragtime

African American musical genre of the late nineteenth century that strongly influenced an emerging American popular music and provided a major impetus in the development of jazz.

Although the term *ragtime* has come to connote a particular form of piano music associated with composer SCOTT JOPLIN, it originally applied to a larger body of instrumental music and song. Ragtime emerged in the 1890s and thrived for two decades, as millions of middle-class whites bought sheet music, pianos, and piano rolls. Through its immense commercial success, ragtime gave birth to the American music industry; through its rhythmic and melodic innovations, it signaled the end of America's dependency on Western European music. Ragtime ushered in a new style of concert music that built upon Afro-diasporic musical traditions.

Because ragtime emerged from African American folk music, its precise origins remain undocumented and obscure. Yet the roots of ragtime undoubtedly lie in the music of itinerant black pianists who played in bordellos and saloons. Ironically, ragtime owes its quick acceptance in part to the tradition of MINSTRELSY, which portrayed African Americans as exotic, lazy, and funny. Primed by these stereotypes as well as bastardized versions of black songs, middle-class audiences readily accepted real AFRICAN AMERICAN MUSIC.

The origin of the name *ragtime* also remains obscure. Some historians suspect it derives from the so-called ragged, or syncopated, playing style that characterized black music in the late nineteenth century. Others cite the use of *rag* as a name for a short African American folk tune. Evidence such as an early piece by Joplin, "Original Rags," suggests that ragtime piano originally anthologized folk melodies. Bordello pianists probably collected and blended familiar strains. Nevertheless, the word *rag* soon came to designate the larger structure instead of the fragments of which it was composed.

Joplin, along with black composer James Scott and white composer Joseph Lamb, established the conventions of ragtime piano and influenced a generation of black composers. These composers included Arthur Marshall, Louis Chauvin, and Artie Matthews, all of whom, like Joplin and Scott, came from Missouri. Joplin, Scott, and Lamb also influenced white composers such as Paul Pratt and J. Russell Robinson.

Classic ragtime followed a number of formal conventions. First, it combined marchlike bass notes with a heavily syncopated melody. Second, it comprised self-contained sections of sixteen bars that each repeated once before giving way to a change; a typical pattern was *aa bb a cc dd,* with each letter representing a separate sixteen-measure section. Finally, it usually employed Western European harmonies, beginning and ending on a tonic key while changing in the middle to the subdominant. For instance, a piece that began in C would alternate to F and return to conclude in C.

Joplin and Scott had defined these elements by 1897, just as sales of ragtime sheet music began to boom. Later innovations such as shifted accents and dotted rhythms added to the body of hot, or syncopated, ragtime sounds, but they were not actually syncopated. Ragtime also influenced other African American styles, such as BLUES and JAZZ. In fact, jazz probably grew out of ragtime, a lineage apparent in the career of the great musician and composer JELLY ROLL MORTON.

White bandleader William Krell published the first ragtime piano music, a piece called "Mississippi Rag," in 1897. Between 1897 and 1899 more than 150 "rags," written by both blacks and whites, supplied popular demand. Joplin's "Maple Leaf Rag," released in 1899, sold a million copies in sheet music alone. Ragtime sold so well that New York music companies hurried to mass-produce it, slapping the name *ragtime* on a wide range of music. Hack writers churned out what they called ragtime vocal music, which often contained little or no syncopation at all.

Although many listeners considered Irving Berlin's 1911 hit "Alexander's Ragtime Band" the crowning accomplishment of the ragtime era, the majority of innovations and the best composition had occurred ten years before. Nevertheless, public enthusiasm continued until the late 1910s, reflected in high piano and sheet music sales and the sheer volume of mediocre ragtime-style songs produced by New York's Tin Pan Alley.

The popularity of ragtime provoked much criticism, both from musical conservatives and from moral conservatives. Because ragtime's new rhythms inspired lively dancing, many older people found it threatening, and its syncopation sometimes caused musicians trained in simple European rhythms to find it cacophonous. The controversy reflected ragtime's revolutionary significance. By ushering in the Jazz Age and establishing African American rhythms as viable roots for classical music, ragtime challenged the old order, socially as well as musically. J. B. Priestly wrote, "Out of this ragtime came the fragmentary outlines of the menace to old EUROPE, the domination of America, the emergence of AFRICA, the end of confidence and any feeling of security, the nervous excitement, the feeling of modern times."

See also Dance, African American; Racial Stereotypes.

Bibliography

Blesh, Rudi, and Harriet Janis. *They All Played Ragtime.* 4th ed. Oak Publications, 1971.

Jansen, David A., and Trebor Jay Tichenor. *Rags and Ragtime: A Musical History.* Seabury Press, 1989.

Eric Bennett

Rainey, Joseph Hayne

1832–1887

African American politician.

Joseph Hayne Rainey was born a slave in Georgetown, South Carolina, the son of Edward L. Rainey and Gracia C. (maiden name unknown). The elder Rainey purchased his family's freedom and moved with them in about 1846 (the exact date is unknown) to CHARLESTON where he was employed as a barber at the exclusive Mills House hotel. He prospered and purchased two male slaves in the 1850s. Joseph Rainey received a modest education and was trained by his father as a barber. In 1859 he traveled to PHILADELPHIA and married Susan E. (maiden name unknown). As a result of the intervention of several friends, the couple managed to circumvent the state prohibition against free people of color entering or returning to South Carolina, and they moved to Charleston. After the CIVIL WAR began, Rainey was conscripted to serve as a steward on a Confederate blockade-runner. He was later compelled to work in the construction of Confederate fortifications around Charleston. He escaped with his wife to BERMUDA on a blockade-runner. They settled first in St. George and then in Hamilton. He resumed barbering, and his wife worked as a dressmaker. They returned to Charleston in 1865, shortly after the war ended.

Rainey and his older brother Edward participated in the 1865 Colored Peoples' Convention in Charleston, and Joseph served as a vice president. The convention endorsed legal and political rights for black men and condemned the recently passed black code, which largely restricted black men and women to agricultural and domestic work, defined a master and servant relationship between white employers and black employees, and severely limited the legal and civil rights of black people. In 1867 Congress passed RECONSTRUCTION legislation that divided the South into five military districts, authorized the reestablishment of southern state governments, provided for universal manhood suffrage and black officeholding, and disfranchised those who had supported the Confederacy.

In 1867 Rainey and his wife relocated to Georgetown, where he was elected to the constitutional convention in 1868. Later that year he was elected as a REPUBLICAN to represent Georgetown County in the state senate, and in 1870 he was elected to the U.S. House of Representatives. He filled the unexpired term of white Republican Benjamin F. Whittemore, whose seat had been declared vacant by the House after allegations were made that Whittemore sold appointments to the U.S. Military Academy and U.S. Naval Academy.

Rainey was the first black man to serve in the U.S. Congress. He was reelected four times, serving from 1870 to 1879. In 1878, as white Democrats regained political power in South Carolina, he lost his bid for a sixth term. He was a cautious, conservative, and conciliatory political leader. In the constitutional convention he supported an unsuccessful measure to permit creditors to collect debts owed for the purchase of slaves before the Civil War. He was among the minority who favored the imposition of a one-dollar poll tax with the stipulation that the proceeds be devoted to public education, though the measure would disfranchise impoverished freedmen.

In Congress, Rainey supported the passage in 1872 of the KU KLUX KLAN Act, legislation intended to outlaw the intimidation and violent repression of black people through the enforcement of the FOURTEENTH and FIFTEENTH AMENDMENTS. He also favored a general amnesty to remove remaining disabilities on former Confederates if the civil rights bill prohibiting racial discrimination in public facilities proposed by Senator Charles Sumner was passed. Rainey spoke passionately for both measures on the House floor: "It is not the disposition of my constituents that these disabilities should longer be retained. We are desirous of being magnanimous; it may be that we are so to a fault. Nevertheless we have open and frank hearts towards those who were our former oppressors and taskmasters. We foster no enmity now, and we desire to foster none . . . I implore you, give support to the Civil-rights Bill." Rainey delivered one of the eulogies following Sumner's death in 1874. The amnesty bill passed immediately, but Sumner's civil rights measure was not enacted until 1875.

Though committed to equal treatment in public facilities, Rainey opposed legislation supporting social equality or interracial marriages. As a black man with a fair complexion, he was ridiculed by a black political opponent in an 1868 campaign appearance in Georgetown and accused of having attempted to act white while attending the National Negro Laborers Convention in WASHINGTON, D.C., the previous year. Rainey won the election.

Rainey was a director of the Enterprise Railroad Company, a black-owned Charleston business created in 1870 by several prominent politicians to haul freight by horse-drawn streetcars from the city wharves on the Cooper River to the South Carolina Railroad terminal. The Enterprise did not thrive, and it was taken over by white businessmen in 1873. Rainey also owned stock in the Greenville & Columbia Railroad Company.

Rainey served as an Internal Revenue Service agent in South Carolina from 1879 to 1881. In 1881 he unsuccessfully sought appointment as clerk of the U.S. House of Representatives. His attempt to operate a brokerage and banking business in Washington failed. In poor health and with his finances depleted, he returned in 1887 to Georgetown where he died.

Joseph H. Rainey pursued moderation during Reconstruction. He was determined to protect and to enlarge the civil and political rights of his black constituents while not alienating or offending white citizens.

Bibliography

There are two small collections of Rainey papers and materials in the South Caroliniana Library at the University of South Carolina and in the Duke University Library.

Christopher, Maurine. *America's Black Congressmen.* 1971.
Holt, Thomas. *Black over White: Negro Political Leadership in South Carolina during Reconstruction.* 1977.

Packwood, Cyril Outerbridge. *Detour—Bermuda, Destination—U.S. House of Representatives: The Life of Joseph Hayne Rainey*. 1977.

Rogers, George C., Jr. *The History of Georgetown County, South Carolina*. 1970.

Williamson, Joel. *After Slavery: The Negro in South Carolina during Reconstruction, 1861–1877*. 1965.

From *American National Biography*. John A. Garraty and Mark C. Carnes, eds. Oxford University Press, 1999. Reprinted by permission of the American Council of Learned Societies.

William C. Hine

Rainey, Ma

1886–1939

American classic blues singer and vaudeville performer.

Born in Columbus, Georgia, to minstrelists Thomas and Ella Pridgett, Gertrude Pridgett entered show business at fourteen as a member of the traveling stage show "The Bunch of Blackberries." In 1904 she married showman William "Pa" Rainey, and they formed a song and dance act called "Rainey and Rainey: The Assassinators of the Blues" that lasted until 1916. While touring mostly in the South during that period, and subsequently as a soloist with the Rabbit Foot Minstrels on the Theater Owners' Booking Association (TOBA) circuit, Ma Rainey developed her "classic BLUES" style of rough-edged reality moans and humorous shouts.

In 1923 Ma Rainey began a brief but prolific recording career with CHICAGO-based Paramount Records with "Moonshine Blues." By 1928, she had recorded ninety-three songs, many of which she wrote herself. As a result of the wide circulation of these records, Rainey gained enormous popularity with African Americans. Her contract was rescinded by Paramount, however, because it was felt that her style could not compete with the new male acts such as BIG BILL BROONZY and LEADBELLY, nor with her friend BESSIE SMITH's growing status and stature. Rainey's once appealing raw style was believed to be out of vogue with the African American record-buying public.

Ma Rainey maintained a loyal fan base, however, and continued to perform throughout the country until 1935, when both her sister Malissa and her mother died. Returning to her home in Columbus, she owned and managed two theaters until her death four years later. Rainey's significance within African American popular culture is exemplified not only by her impact on musical heirs such as singer KOKO TAYLOR, but also by her appearance in the writing of poet STERLING BROWN ("Ma Rainey") and playwright AUGUST WILSON ("Ma Rainey's Black Bottom"). In 1990, Ma Rainey was inducted into the Rock and Roll Hall of Fame.

See also Minstrelsy; Music, African American; Musical Theater in the United States.

Bibliography

Lieb, Sandra. *Mother of the Blues: A Study of Ma Rainey*. University of Massachusetts Press, 1981.

Stewart-Baxter, Derrick. *Ma Rainey and the Classic Blues Singers*. Stein and Day, 1970.

Ramgoolam, Seewoosagur

1900–1985

Leader of the Mauritius Labour Party and prime minister of Mauritius from 1968 to 1982.

Born in Bois d'Oiseaux, MAURITIUS, Seewoosagur Ramgoolam grew up in the small village of Belle Rive. An Anglophile and ardent student even as a boy, he left home to attend Royal College of Curepipe, a prestigious Mauritian public secondary school, and then traveled to GREAT BRITAIN for medical school. While in England, Ramgoolam met with Indian nationalist leader Mahatma Gandhi, joined the Fabian Society (a political group committed to SOCIALISM and nonviolence), and became secretary of the local Indian National Congress chapter. Upon returning to Mauritius in 1935, Ramgoolam joined a vanguard of Indo-Mauritian intellectuals and founded a newspaper, the *Advance*.

In 1940 Ramgoolam was nominated to the Council of Government as a representative of Hindu interests. With the extension of suffrage to all literate adults in 1948, Ramgoolam gained a seat in the Legislative Council. He was reelected in 1953 and joined the Mauritian Labour Party (MLP). As party leader, he successfully steered the MLP to victory in the 1959 elections, becoming chief minister in 1961 and premier in 1965. In the interests of political and economic stability, Ramgoolam sought to promote the rights of workers without alienating the island's landed aristocracy. For example, he advocated free market economic policies and abandoned MLP proposals to nationalize SUGAR estates. At the same time, he promised working-class Mauritians a welfare state. Despite opposition from groups fearful of a Hindu-dominated government, Ramgoolam was elected prime minister of newly independent Mauritius in 1968.

His early years in office were tumultuous as a weak economy and high rates of unemployment contributed to widespread discontent. Confronted by labor strikes organized by the Marxist Mouvement Militant Mauricien (MMM), Ramgoolam's government postponed the scheduled 1972 election and declared a state of emergency. MMM leaders were imprisoned without charges, strikes were outlawed, and the press was censored, effectively banning political opposition. Fortunately, world sugar prices rose dramatically during the early 1970s, and a newly created Industrial Export Processing Zone brought in foreign investment and created jobs. Although Ramgoolam's oppressive political measures hurt his party's popularity, he managed to retain his position in the 1976 elections.

But the economy remained a liability. In 1979, with unemployment rates running at 21 percent and inflation at 30 per-

Ramos, Arthur de Araójo Pereira

1903–1949

Prominent Brazilian physician who also dedicated his career to the anthropological study of the influence of Africa on the culture and folklore of Brazil.

Arthur de Araójo Pereira Ramos is considered one of the most prestigious disciples of RAIMUNDO NINA RODRIGUES. Ramos represents the renaissance of Afro-Brazilian studies, which had been dormant for years after the death of Nina Rodrigues. He dedicated himself to rescuing and reediting the work of Nina Rodrigues, by directing the Biblioteca de Divulgação Científica in the 1930s.

Arthur Ramos was born in the northeastern state of Alagoas, and did his secondary studies at the Colégio São João and the Liceu Alagoano in Maceió, the capital of the state of Alagoas. He then moved to BAHIA in order to attend the Medical School of Bahia. He graduated from medical school in 1926, and his interest in psychiatry took him to the Hospital São João de Deus in the city of Salvador the following year. He also worked at the Instituto Nina Rodrigues as a forensic doctor and at the Psychiatric Clinic of the Medical School of Bahia. In 1935 Ramos became a professor of social psychology at the University of the Federal District, and then in 1946 a professor of cultural anthropology at the University of Brazil. He founded the Brazilian Society of Anthropology and Ethnography and directed the department of social sciences at UNESCO, in Paris, where he died in 1949.

Arthur Ramos' written work is extensive. Among his published works are the following: *O negro brasileiro* (1934), *O folclore negro do Brasil* (1935), and *As culturas negras no Brasil* (1936). As one of the distinguished participants of the first and second Afro-Brazilian Congresses, Ramos wrote the articles "*Os mitos de Xangô e sua degradação no* Brasil," "*Culturas negras: Problemas de aculturação no Brasil,*" and "*Nina Rodrigues e os estudos negros.*"

Ramos Antonini, Ernesto

1898–1963

Black Puerto Rican labor leader and politician, the first Speaker of the House of Representatives under the Commonwealth of Puerto Rico.

Ernesto Ramos Antonini was born in Mayaguez, PUERTO RICO. He started his public career as a labor lawyer defending the rights of Puerto Rican workers. In the early 1940s, he successfully represented the General Confederation of Workers of Puerto Rico (GCW), the union that represented the SUGAR workers in important labor cases, and lobbied for the approval of labor-relations laws. He later became secretary of foreign relations for the GCW and established ties with other labor organizations in the United States and abroad. He was a relentless advocate of the unification of the Puerto Rican labor movement, which at the time was badly fragmented.

As a politician, Antonini stood out for his superb public speaking and principled public service. One of the founders and leaders of the Popular Democratic Party, he worked side by side with the first elected governor of Puerto Rico, Luis Muñoz Marín, in the economic development program known as Operation Bootstrap. For fifteen years (1948–1963), he was Speaker of the House of Representatives of Puerto Rico. He was also a delegate in the constituent assembly (1951–1952), which drafted the constitution of the Commonwealth of Puerto Rico.

The son of the renowned pianist and composer Federico Ramos Buensont, Antonini is also remembered for having fostered the formal study of music in Puerto Rico. A talented pianist himself, Antonini authored legislation that established the first publicly funded schools of music, the first conservatory of music, and the Symphony Orchestra of Puerto Rico.

See also Labor Leaders.

Carlos Dalmau

Ramses III

1194–1163 B.C.E.

Egyptian king of the twentieth dynasty, a great military leader who repeatedly saved the country from invasion.

In the fifth year of his reign, Ramses III defeated an attack by the Libyans from the west, and two years later he routed invaders known as the Sea Peoples. In his eleventh year, he again repelled an attempted Libyan invasion. Ramses was also a builder of temples and palaces in the tradition of his nineteenth-dynasty predecessor, Ramses II. His victories are depicted on the walls of his mortuary temple at Medinet Habu, near Luxor. Egyptian records tell of a strike by workers at Ramses's burial site and of a plot against the king near the end of his reign. Ramses III was the last of the great rulers of ancient Egypt. His death was followed by centuries of weakness and foreign domination.

See also Egypt, Ancient Kingdom of.

Ranavalona I, Queen

1790?–1861

Queen of the Merina Empire from 1828 to 1861.

Ranavalona was born with the name Ramavo. Upon the death of her husband and cousin RADAMA I in 1828, Ramavo took the throne as queen of the Merina Empire, a kingdom that extended over most of MADAGASCAR and was recognized by the British as the island's sovereign authority.

During Radama I's tenure, the MERINA court had incorporated English beliefs and values along with their military and financial support. Missionaries had established schools, printed Bibles, and transcribed the MALAGASY language. Many Merina aristocrats and Hova, middle-caste commoners, resented the imposition of British culture and Christian values. Even before coming to power, Ramavo cultivated their support. Upon the death of her husband, she immediately laid claim to the throne, changed her name to Ranavalona ("the lady who has been folded," a reference to her aristocratic attire), and executed all her potential rivals, including Radama's mother, daughter, and nephew. She then began to retract the pro-European policies of her deceased husband, declaring all previously negotiated treaties null and void in 1828 (although she later renegotiated most of them).

Although Ranavalona associated CHRISTIANITY with European hegemony, she initially allowed missionaries to remain in Madagascar because they taught her subjects useful skills, including literacy, carpentry, and metalworking. In 1831 Ranavalona even agreed to let Malagasy be baptized but then quickly reversed her decision when she saw the large number of converts undergoing the religious rite. By 1835 missionaries were banned from proselytizing and Christianity was outlawed. Several converted Malagasy were executed for refusing to denounce their Christian beliefs. Unable to preach, most missionaries left the island.

Although Ranavalona was insistent on retaining Malagasy culture and sovereignty, she was not averse to doing business with Europeans. Notably, Frenchman Napoléon de Lastelle ran coffee and COCOA plantations that became the loci of the island's import-export trade, particularly with FRANCE. Likewise, an adventurer named Jean Laborde ran a SUGAR plantation and oversaw a large complex employing more than 1,200 workers in the manufacture of arms, ammunition, porcelain, and other products. Although known as "the queen's foreigner," Laborde also influenced Ranavalona's son, RADAMA II, who ultimately reversed most of her policies.

In 1845 Ranavalona pronounced that Europeans would be subject to traditional Malagasy law, which included multiple forms of capital and corporal punishment, such as the use of hot irons. The resident foreigners appealed to their governments for protection. After boarding French and British ships, the European traders saw their homes looted, and in response, the ships opened fire on the port of Tamatave. Once news of the event reached Ranavalona, she banned all trade with the British and French except for de Lastelle and Laborde. Although trade relations were ultimately restored, Ranavalona's rash actions weakened her support among the Hova families who had profited from the trade.

French and British agents continued to wrestle for influence in the Merina court. For example, Joseph Lambert, a French entrepreneur, convinced Ranavalona's son to sign the Lambert Charter, a document conceding enormous land and mineral rights once he came to the throne. In 1857 Ranavalona discovered a planned coup d'état, authored in part by Laborde, Lambert, and her son. Laborde and Lambert were promptly expelled, and thousands of others were enslaved for allegedly colluding with the plotters. She spared her son, however, and he succeeded her to the throne.

On Ranavalona's death in 1861, Madagascar reentered relations with EUROPE. While often portrayed simply as a cruel and backward leader, Ranavalona was in fact an astute politician interested in preserving Malagasy sovereignty while retaining profitable economic relations with foreign powers. Her name was frequently evoked by nationalists during French COLONIAL RULE as that of a Malagasy leader who asserted the legitimacy of Malagasy culture.

See also Christianity: Missionaries in Africa; Nationalism in Africa.

Bibliography

Brown, Mervyn. *Madagascar Rediscovered*. Damien Tunnacliffe, 1978.
Covell, Maureen. *Historical Dictionary of Madagascar*. Scarecrow Press, 1995.
Sweetman, David. *Women Leaders in African History*. Heinemann, 1984.

Ari Nave

Randall, Dudley Felker

1914–2000

American poet and publisher who was instrumental in promoting poetry of the Black Arts Movement.

Born in WASHINGTON, D.C., Dudley Felker Randall was the son of a teacher, Ada Viola Bradley Randall, and a Congregational minister, Arthur George Clyde Randall. In 1923 the family moved from Washington, D.C., to DETROIT, MICHIGAN, where Randall spent most of his life.

After completing high school, Randall worked for the Ford Motor Company and served in the army during World War II. He was unable to attend college until his early thirties. In 1949 Randall received a B.A. degree in English from Wayne University (now Wayne State University). He then earned a master of library science degree from the University of Michigan in 1951, providing him with credentials to work as a reference librarian at several colleges, including Morgan State College (now University), and the University of Detroit. In addition, he taught poetry at the University of Michigan and was poet-in-residence at the University of Detroit from 1969 to 1977.

In 1965 Randall established Broadside Press. He published his own poems and other important works by such writers as GWENDOLYN BROOKS, SONIA SANCHEZ, Haki Madhubuti (Don L. Lee), and AUDRE LORDE. These artists viewed African American creativity as the essence of their culture and contributed to the BLACK ARTS MOVEMENT of the late 1960s and early 1970s. Randall's poetry collections include *Cities Burning* (1968), *Love You* (1970), and *A Litany of Friends: New and Selected Poems* (1981).

Randall's major contribution to AFRICAN AMERICAN LITERATURE has been to offer access to a liberating voice in print, where one had not existed on a mass scale since the HARLEM RENAISSANCE. According to poet Addison Gayle, Randall "bridged the gap between poets of the '20s and those of the '60s and '70s."

See also Poetry, Black, in English.

Bibliography
Randall, Dudley. *More to Remember: Poems of Four Decades.* Third World Press, 1971.

Randolph, A(sa) Philip

1889–1979

Founder and president of the Brotherhood of Sleeping Car Porters (BSCP), editor of the *Messenger*, and architect of the March on Washington Movement that led to the establishment of the Fair Employment Practices Committee (FEPC) and the 1963 March on Washington.

Although many civil rights leaders focused on voting, education, and other governmental functions, Asa Philip Randolph spent his long career as a labor leader working to bring more and better jobs to African Americans. After a long, successful battle to win representation for the nation's Pullman car train porters, Randolph was instrumental in the formation of the FAIR EMPLOYMENT PRACTICES COMMITTEE (FEPC), which protected African Americans against job discrimination in the defense industries. In addition, Randolph cofounded and edited THE MESSENGER, a socialist black magazine.

The son of a minister, Randolph was born in Crescent City, Florida, on April 15, 1889. He grew up in Jacksonville, Florida, and graduated from the Cookman Institute in Daytona Beach, Florida, in 1907. A lack of economic opportunity for blacks led Randolph, the class valedictorian, into a series of menial jobs until 1911, when he moved to NEW YORK CITY. Working as an elevator operator and living in HARLEM, NEW YORK, Randolph took classes at the City College of New York and New York University, acted in amateur theatricals, and eventually took a job with a Harlem employment agency.

Labor leader and civil rights activist A. Philip Randolph fought for equality for African Americans throughout his life and with much success. *Bettmann/CORBIS*

In 1914 Randolph met Chandler Owen, whose progressive politics and interest in SOCIALISM matched his own. In 1917 the two founded *The Messenger*. The magazine's editorials strongly opposed the entry of the United States into World War I, saying that "no intelligent Negro is willing to lay down his life for the United States as it now exists." Although the magazine was never profitable, it was influential, offering a more radical voice than that of W. E. B. DU BOIS's *THE CRISIS* or the even more conventional *New York Age*. *The Messenger*, with its advocacy of labor unions, was especially popular among Pullman porters—all of whom were black—who served white railroad passengers in luxurious sleeping cars. Founded just after the Civil War (1861–1865), the Pullman company had by the 1920s become the nation's single largest employer of African Americans. Many of the Pullman porters were college graduates who enjoyed great respect within their communities; however, at work they were subjected to unfair and discriminatory practices.

In 1925, with Randolph at the helm, the BROTHERHOOD OF SLEEPING CAR PORTERS began organizing the nearly 10,000 porters. For ten years Randolph kept the members unified and inspired, often in the face of intimidation and firings, while he negotiated with the president and Congress to amend the Railway Labor Act. Finally, in a hard-won victory hailed by African

Americans and progressives nationwide, the company recognized the union in 1935.

Randolph continued to fight for racial and economic justice in the late 1930s as president of the National Negro Congress before resigning in protest over its increasing domination by Communists. In 1940 he returned to the issue of jobs, joining NATIONAL ASSOCIATION FOR THE ADVANCEMENT OF COLORED PEOPLE (NAACP) secretary WALTER FRANCIS WHITE and T. Arnold Hill of the NATIONAL URBAN LEAGUE in urging U.S. president Franklin D. Roosevelt to desegregate the military and defense industries before World War II. After an unsatisfactory resolution to a meeting with the president, Randolph began planning a march on WASHINGTON, D.C., by the BSCP and others to demand "the right to work and fight for our country." The date for at least 10,000 African Americans to demonstrate before the Lincoln Memorial was set for July 1, 1941. Despite the president's wish to avoid a mass demonstration, Randolph refused to call off the march unless Roosevelt banned discrimination in the burgeoning defense industries. Following another meeting with Randolph and White, the president at last issued EXECUTIVE ORDER 8802, which not only outlawed such discrimination but also established the Fair Employment Practices Committee (FEPC) to investigate breaches of the order.

Although the FEPC operated only from 1941 to 1946, Randolph continued to push for his other goal: desegregation of the U.S. armed forces. When President Harry S. Truman instituted a peacetime draft, Randolph told him "this time Negroes will not take a JIM CROW draft lying down." In July 1948 Truman signed Executive Order 9981, finally ending the segregation of African American soldiers.

Throughout the 1950s, Randolph worked with the NAACP and other civil rights leaders. He helped plan and spoke at Pilgrimage Day, a 1957 prayer meeting in Washington, D.C. He met with President Dwight D. Eisenhower to push for faster school integration in the wake of the BROWN V. BOARD OF EDUCATION Supreme Court decision. He planned a 1958 Youth March for Integrated Schools. He also continued his union work and served as vice president of the newly consolidated AMERICAN FEDERATION OF LABOR AND CONGRESS OF INDUSTRIAL ORGANIZATIONS (AFL-CIO) from 1955 to 1968.

Randolph's brainchild, the March on Washington Movement, bore new fruit in 1963 with the help of civil rights leaders BAYARD RUSTIN and MARTIN LUTHER KING, JR., who along with Randolph mobilized the largest demonstration of the CIVIL RIGHTS MOVEMENT. Speaking before King, the seventy-four-year-old Randolph exhorted the crowd of 250,000 to take part in a "revolution for jobs and freedom." The next year, President Lyndon B. Johnson signed the Civil Rights Act of 1964 and awarded Randolph the Presidential Medal of Freedom. In his final years, Randolph established the A. Philip Randolph Institute, a job skills and training bureau in Harlem. Upon Randolph's death on May 16, 1979, in New York City, Rustin said of his late colleague, "No individual did more to help the poor, the dispossessed and the working class . . . than A. Philip Randolph."

See also Desegregation in the United States; Labor Leaders; Labor Unions in the United States; March on Washington, 1941; March on Washington, 1963; Military, Blacks in the American.

Bibliography

Anderson, Jervis, A. *A. Philip Randolph: A Biographical Portrait.* Harcourt Brace Jovanovich, 1973.

Harris, William Hamilton. *Keeping the Faith: A. Philip Randolph, Milton P. Webster, and the Brotherhood of Sleeping Car Porters, 1925–37.* University of Illinois Press, 1977.

Kate Tuttle

Rangel, Charles Bernard

1930–

Democratic member of the United States House of Representatives from New York.

Charles Rangel was born in HARLEM, NEW YORK. Raised by his mother and grandmother after his parents separated, he dropped out of high school and held several jobs until joining the army in 1948. He served until 1952 and saw action in South Korea, for which he received a Bronze Star and a Purple Heart.

Rangel returned to New York and resumed his high school studies, obtaining his diploma in 1953. He earned a B.S. from the New York School of Commerce in 1957 and a law degree from St. John's Law School in 1960. Rangel held various positions before entering politics. Directly after graduating from law school, he served as an attorney for civil rights activists. In 1961 he was appointed assistant district attorney for the Southern District of New York. Rangel then turned his attention to politics, serving as legal council for the New York City Housing and Redevelopment Board, as legal assistant to then speaker of the New York State Assembly, Judge James L. Watson. In addition, with close friend Percy Sutton, Rangel helped to found the John F. Kennedy Democratic Club in Harlem (later named the REV. MARTIN LUTHER KING, JR., Democratic Club). Rangel's first political office was as the representative from central Harlem to the New York State Assembly, elected by voters in 1966.

Charles Rangel's congressional career began when he unseated Harlem Democratic political stalwart ADAM CLAYTON POWELL, JR., in the closely contested 1970 primary election. Rangel won the general election and became the representative for New York's 15th Congressional District. During Rangel's lengthy legislative career, he distinguished himself as one of the most liberal members of the House. He consistently supported a woman's right to abortion, voted for busing to desegregate public schools, opposed the VIETNAM WAR, and opposed the illegal drug trade. In 1974 he served on the House Judiciary Committee during its hearings on the impeachment of President Richard Nixon. In 1997 Rangel cosponsored the African Growth and Opportunities Act, which was designed to promote economic investment in Africa. In addition, Rangel helped found the CONGRESSIONAL BLACK CAUCUS. In 2002 he was reelected to his seventeenth term in Congress.

See also Democratic Party; Korean War.

Robert Fay

Ranger, Joseph

1760?–?

African American revolutionary war seaman.

Joseph Ranger was born probably in Northumberland County, Virginia, to unknown parents. Ranger was a free African American, or perhaps a runaway slave, who probably worked as a seaman in Northumberland County and Elizabeth City County before the Revolutionary War. In the early eighteenth century, Virginia's waters were sailed extensively by free African Americans and slaves who also worked in the colony's two shipyards. Despite long-standing concern among the elite in the South about arming even free African Americans for fear of inciting slave revolt, the maritime experiences of Virginia's African Americans made them prime candidates for enlistment in the state navy (just as many African American seamen served in the Continental navy).

Joseph Ranger enlisted in the Virginia navy in 1776, one of many African Americans who served on racially mixed naval crews. Ranger served in the Virginia navy for eleven years, the longest recorded term of service of any African American sailor. The Virginia navy was composed of a motley assortment of forty vessels, from barges to ships, which were designed to support the cobbled-together navy created by the Continental Congress in 1775 and to protect the exposed Virginia coastline from British invasion. Ranger's home county of Northumberland provided at least six African American seamen to Virginia's navy.

It was usual for sailors to transfer frequently between ships, and Ranger served aboard four naval vessels, the largest recorded total number of any African American sailor. Ranger first served for three months aboard the ship *Hero*, one of the ships with the largest number of African American crew members. For the next four years he served aboard the *Dragon* as one of five African Americans in a crew of 104. Aboard the *Dragon*, Ranger and the other African American crew members were recorded as receiving full rations of pork, flour, and liquor.

After the *Dragon* was converted into a fire ship in 1780, Ranger transferred to the *Jefferson*, where he served for one year, until it was blown up by the British as it sailed on the James River. After the explosion Ranger was assigned to serve aboard the *Patriot* for approximately six months. Shortly before Cornwallis's surrender at Yorktown on October 19, 1781, Ranger was taken prisoner by the British along with the rest of the *Patriot*'s crew. (He was probably released soon after the surrender.)

The British naval threat to Virginia did not end with the formal cessation of Revolutionary War hostilities, and the Continental Congress granted Virginia the right to maintain two armed ships, the *Liberty* and the *Patriot*, after the war ended. Ranger served aboard both of these ships until Virginia's navy was finally disbanded in 1787.

Ranger had been paid for his service in the navy. He was recorded in the Virginia State Auditors' records as having received two pounds, ten shillings, for one month's service in 1786 and five pounds, seven shillings, for two months' service in 1787. Not much is known of Ranger's life or how he earned a living after the disassembly of the Virginia navy, but he may have continued to work as a sailor.

Within a few years after the end of the Revolutionary War, Ranger received a land grant from the state of Virginia as a reward for his military service. His grant of 100 acres, located in Virginia's western Kentucky and Ohio territories, represented the usual grant received by Virginia's African American privates. Ranger probably never occupied his land but more likely sold it to one of many land speculators who bought up soldiers' bounties for a fraction of their worth.

In addition to his land grant from the state of Virginia, Ranger also qualified for a federal Revolutionary War pension under the congressional acts of 1818, 1820, and 1832. At least twenty-one African Americans in Virginia qualified for veterans' pensions. Joseph Ranger received $96 a year after he swore out a deposition in a local Virginia court attesting to his wartime naval service.

It is unknown when and where Joseph Ranger died. His Revolutionary War service in the Virginia navy exemplifies the importance of African Americans to American military forces, even in states such as Virginia with extremely restrictive slave systems. Ranger's long maritime service shows how African Americans were able to capitalize on their seafaring experience to gain economic status and even freedom. Ranger, like other African American sailors, was rewarded by his state and his country for his patriotic service.

Bibliography

Jackson, L. P. "Virginia Negro Soldiers and Seamen in the American Revolution." *Journal of Negro History* 27 (1942): 247–85.

From *American National Biography*. John A. Garraty and Mark C. Carnes, eds. Oxford University Press, 1999. Reprinted by permission of the American Council of Learned Societies.

Sarah J. Purcell

Rangi

Ethnic group of Tanzania; also known as Irangi and Rongo.

The Rangi primarily inhabit central TANZANIA around the town of Dodoma. They speak a Bantu language. Approximately 400,000 people consider themselves Rangi.

See also Bantu: Dispersion and Settlement; Ethnicity and Identity in Africa: An Interpretation; Languages, African: An Overview.

Ransier, Alonzo Jacob

1834–1882

African American politician.

Alonzo Jacob Ransier was born in CHARLESTON, SOUTH CAROLINA, to free parents. Contemporary accounts described his education as "limited." In the 1850s he secured a position as a shipping clerk with a prominent commercial firm in Charleston. In 1856 he married Louisa Ann Carroll, and they were the parents of eleven children. Carroll died in 1875, and he married Mary Louisa McKinlay in 1876.

Ransier was a leading figure in RECONSTRUCTION and REPUBLICAN politics in South Carolina. He participated in the 1865 Colored Peoples' Convention in Charleston that urged the state's white leaders to enfranchise black men and abolish the black code, a series of measures designed to limit the rights of black people and to confine them to menial and agricultural labor. In 1867 Congress passed a series of Reconstruction laws that provided for the reorganization of the Southern states, the enfranchisement of black men, and the disfranchisement of Southerners who had supported the Confederacy. Ransier subsequently represented Charleston in the 1868 constitutional convention. He served as vice president of the State Republican Executive Committee and then as president from 1868 to 1872, following the assassination of Benjamin F. Randolph. He was elected to the state house of representatives in 1868 and was Charleston County auditor from 1868 to 1870. In the state house in 1870 he sponsored a measure that, while not explicitly guaranteeing civil rights for blacks, provided blacks with the same legal right to pursue judicial remedies available to whites. He was a director and secretary of the Enterprise Railroad Company, a corporation organized in 1870 by black political leaders to operate a horse-drawn streetcar line to haul freight between the South Carolina Railroad terminal and the Cooper River wharves. It did not survive as a black-owned business, and by 1873 a group of white businessmen led by S. S. Solomon had taken over the railroad. Ransier joined with several other black political leaders, including Benjamin A. Boseman, ROBERT SMALLS, ROBERT B. ELLIOTT, and Beverly Nash, in forming the South Carolina Phosphate & Phosphatic River & Mining Company.

Described in 1870 by the *Charleston News and Courier* as exercising "considerable influence," Ransier reached the pinnacle of his political power in the early 1870s. In 1870 he was elected South Carolina's first black lieutenant governor on a ticket headed by incumbent Robert K. Scott. In 1872 he was elected to represent South Carolina's second district in the Forty-Third Congress (1873–1875). From 1875 to 1877 he was the collector for the Internal Revenue Service for South Carolina's second district.

Though Ransier was often regarded as timid and reticent, he was frequently willing to take a bold stand on controversial issues. He joined black delegate WILLIAM WHIPPER in speaking out strongly in the constitutional convention in opposition to legalizing the collection of debts incurred in the purchase of slaves prior to the CIVIL WAR. In doing so, they opposed three formidable black leaders, FRANCIS L. CARDOZO, JOSEPH RAINEY, and William McKinlay, who favored payment. Ransier also joined two other Charleston black leaders, RICHARD H. CAIN and ROBERT C. DELARGE, in opposing a literacy requirement for voting, which was easily defeated. Ransier consistently supported woman suffrage and attended an 1870 woman suffrage convention in Columbia. He urged rigid safeguards to protect black voting rights, insisting that voting "is our chief means for self-defense." He opposed segregation in public education so strongly that he abstained from voting on the 1875 Civil Rights Bill in Congress because provisions prohibiting discrimination in education had been deleted from the measure.

Ransier was deeply involved in the struggles of the Republican Party. In 1872 as a delegate to the Republican National Convention and to a black convention in NEW ORLEANS, Ransier supported Ulysses S. Grant for reelection and would not join reformers who backed Horace Greeley. As a member of the "Charleston Ring," one of the factions that thrived in a divided Republican Party in Charleston, Ransier attacked fellow Republicans for their inept leadership of the public schools. In 1871 he cited the bitter conflicts over patronage among Republicans as the cause of the DEMOCRATIC victory in the municipal election. Yet he was willing to embrace patronage in 1876 when his tenure as Internal Revenue Service collector was about to expire. He pleaded with Governor Daniel Chamberlain for help in securing nomination to office: "I have a large family and no means for their support and would be greatly obliged if my friends will take me into consideration in connection with such a position on the state ticket as they may think me qualified for." He was not nominated, and by 1879 he had been reduced to working as a night watchman at the Charleston Customs House for $1.50 per day. He was later employed at the Pacific Guano works and as a street laborer. When he died in obscurity in Charleston, the *News and Courier* did not note his passing.

Though he was one of South Carolina's prominent political figures by the early 1870s, Alonzo Ransier's influence and reputation faded quickly. Having served as a party leader, lieutenant governor, and congressman, he was not able to sustain that leadership until Reconstruction's end in 1877 when white South Carolinians regained political power.

Bibliography

There are a few letters from Ransier in the Governors' Papers of the South Carolina Department of Archives and History.

Christopher, Maurine. *America's Black Congressmen*. 1971.
Holt, Thomas. *Black over White: Negro Political Leadership in South Carolina during Reconstruction*. 1977.

Williamson, Joel. *After Slavery: The Negro in South Carolina during Reconstruction, 1861–1877*. 1965.

From *American National Biography*. John A. Garraty and Mark C. Carnes, eds. Oxford University Press, 1999. Reprinted by permission of the American Council of Learned Societies.

William C. Hine

Ransom, Reverdy Cassius

1861–1959

African Methodist Episcopal (AME) bishop and civil rights leader.

Reverdy Cassius Ransom was born in Flushing, Ohio, the son of Harriet Johnson, a domestic worker. He never knew the identity of his father. In 1865 his mother married George Ransom, gave her son his surname, and moved to Washington, Ohio. There he began school in the local AFRICAN METHODIST EPISCOPAL CHURCH (AME). At eight, Ransom moved with his family to Cambridge, Ohio, where he attended school with African American youth. In addition to his formal schooling, Ransom worked in a local bank and was tutored by family members of his mother's white employers. In 1881 Ransom married Leanna Watkins of Cambridge, Ohio, and entered WILBERFORCE UNIVERSITY. He transferred to Oberlin College at the end of his first year, but, when he challenged racial discrimination at the liberal white institution, he lost his scholarship. He returned to Wilberforce in 1883, graduating in 1886. Despite the birth of a son, he and his first wife divorced that same year.

Licensed to preach in the AME church in 1883, Ransom was ordained a deacon in 1886 and an elder in 1888. He married Emma Sarah Conner of Salem, Ohio, in 1886. They became the parents of one son. From 1886 to 1888 Ransom served small AME congregations in Altoona and Hollidaysburg, Pennsylvania, and from 1888 to 1890 he pastored a church in Allegheny City, Pennsylvania. Ransom then moved to Ohio, serving at North Street AME Church in Springfield from 1890 to 1893 and at St. John's AME Church in Cleveland from 1893 to 1896. In 1896 Ransom moved to CHICAGO, where he served as pastor of Bethel AME Church from 1896 to 1900. At Bethel he organized a men's Sunday club for the discussion of cultural, moral, and social issues. As early as 1899, Ransom ardently disagreed with BOOKER T. WASHINGTON's accommodationist approach to race relations and the Tuskegeean's forceful determination to control the Afro-American Council.

As Ransom observed the needs of black migrants from the South, he bristled at the constraints of a traditional congregation. Influenced by the work of Jane Addams at Hull-House, he left Bethel in 1900 to organize the Institutional Church and Social Settlement. The building included a large auditorium, a kitchen, a dining room, a gymnasium, and eight other rooms for a nursery, a kindergarten, and boys' and girls' club meetings. It offered concerts, an employment bureau, lecture series, a print shop, and classes in cooking, music, and sewing. A year later, when Ransom attacked the policy rackets in Chicago, the building was bombed. Yet his social ministry at Institutional Church and Social Settlement survived for another three years.

In 1904 Ransom moved to AME congregations in New Bedford and BOSTON, MASSACHUSETTS. As pastor of Boston's Charles Street AME Church, he paid tribute to the spirit of the abolitionists and joined W. E. B. DU BOIS's NIAGARA MOVEMENT to demand social justice for African Americans. In 1906 Ransom addressed the movement's annual meeting at Harpers Ferry, West Virginia, speaking on "The Spirit of John Brown." Ransom moved to NEW YORK's Bethel AME Church in 1907. While there, he helped to organize the NATIONAL ASSOCIATION FOR THE ADVANCEMENT OF COLORED PEOPLE (NAACP). In 1912 Ransom was elected editor of the *A.M.E. Church Review,* the denomination's literary and theological journal. For twelve years he directed the publication of articles on a wide range of issues. At heart, however, Ransom was a pastor on a social mission, and consequently he established a mission to black Manhattan in 1913: The Church of Simon of Cyrene, which ministered to destitute African Americans in New York's "Black Tenderloin." In 1918 the United Civic League of New York sought to place Ransom's name on the ballot as a candidate for Congress from Manhattan's Twenty-first District. Dropped from the ballot because of a discrepancy in his filing petition, Ransom lost an uphill battle as a write-in candidate.

Ransom had represented the AME church at conferences of world Methodism in London (1901 and 1921) and Toronto (1911), and in 1924, at the age of sixty-three, he was already an elder statesman in the AME denomination when he was elected one of its bishops. It is unclear what role his early divorce and rumors of his alcoholism, which were circulated by Booker T. Washington's associates and conservatives within his denomination, may have played in delaying Ransom's elevation to the episcopacy. As a bishop, however, he made his home at Wilberforce University and served as president of the board of trustees from 1932 to 1948. Then, in 1934, Ransom helped to organize the Fraternal Council of Negro Churches and was elected its first president. He was the first African American to serve as a commissioner of Ohio's Board of Pardon and Parole, a position he held from 1936 to 1940, and in 1941 President Franklin D. Roosevelt appointed Ransom as a member of the Volunteer Participation Committee in the Office of Civil Defense. After his wife of fifty-five years died in 1941, Ransom married Georgia Myrtle Teal Hayes of Wilberforce in 1943. A graduate of Cheyney Training School (now Cheyney State University) and Cornell University, she was dean of women at Wilberforce from 1934 to 1943 and an officer of the AME missionary society from 1943 to 1956. In 1952 Ransom retired from the active episcopacy. He died at his home, "Tawawa Chimney Corner," at Wilberforce.

Ransom was his era's foremost advocate of the social gospel in the African American community. He developed institutional church models for urban black communities and was an important radical ally of Du Bois in the struggles with Booker T. Washington that led to the founding of the NAACP. Later, as a bishop and elder statesman in his denomination, he also made advances in African American ecumenism.

Bibliography

The papers of Reverdy Cassius Ransom are in collections at Wilberforce University and at Payne Theological Seminary near Xenia, Ohio.

Luker, Ralph E. *The Social Gospel in Black and White: American Racial Reform, 1885–1912.* 1991.

Morris, Calvin S. *Reverdy C. Ransom: Black Advocate of the Social Gospel.* 1990.

Ransom, Reverdy Cassius. *The Pilgrimage of Harriet Ransom's Son.* 1949.

The Booker T. Washington Papers. Edited by Louis R. Harlan, et al. 1972–1989.

Wills, David. "Reverdy C. Ransom, The Making of an A.M.E. Bishop." In *Black Apostles: Afro-American Clergy Confront the Twentieth Century,* edited by Randall K. Burkett and Richard Newman. 1978.

Wright, Richard R. *The Bishops of the African American Episcopal Church.* 1963.

From *American National Biography*. John A. Garraty and Mark C. Carnes, eds. Oxford University Press, 1999. Reprinted by permission of the American Council of Learned Societies.

Ralph E. Luker

Rap

Urban music that emerged in the 1970s from the hip-hop movement of the South Bronx, New York, and still thrives today.

Rap music combines rhythmic instrumental tracks created by a disc jockey, or DJ, with the spoken, rhyming bravura of a master of ceremonies, or MC. DJs often "sample" pieces of other recorded music in the creation of songs. MCs frequently rap about politics, sexual exploits, the conditions of daily life, and their own (sometimes exaggerated) personal attributes. MCs and DJs appropriate pop culture through lyrical allusions as well as rhythmic sound bites, leading many critics to consider rap the preeminent example of postmodern music. Writer Jon Pareles suggests, "In its structure and its content rap is the music of the television age, and the first truly popular music to adapt the fast, fractured rhythms, the bizarre juxtapositions, and the ceaseless self-promotion that are as much a part of television as logos and laugh tracks."

Unlike television, however, rap gives some African Americans a powerful voice. Its esoteric lyrical form provides ample space for political dissent, and the fact that rap music seems recondite and frightening to some white listeners adds to rap's political sting. In a talk-show discussion, rap activist Harry Allen argued that "black people are attempting to compensate for their lack of power under white supremacy, and it comes out in our art, it comes out in our music. They're trying to make up for what's missing. What's missing is order. What's missing is power." The eager embrace of rap by young whites, however, complicates the dynamic. Rap reflects racial confusion as well as cultural innovation in an age of cable television, digital technology, and marked class stratification.

Forerunners of Rap

The thematic content of many rap songs—egoistic self-assertion, and playful attack on one's competitor—follows traditions of African and African American "toasting" and "signifying." The value that some African tribes assign to oral humor, confidence, and derision has its analog on North American streets. Writer Khephra Burns compares rap music with the "pattin' juba" of the 1850s, in which African Americans joined in "trading tall tales, handing out verbal abuse in rhymes, and providing [their] own rhythmic, chest-whacking, thigh slapping accompaniment."

More immediately, rap draws from the conventions of urban street jive, a form of speech that developed in the black community in CHICAGO, ILLINOIS, in the 1920s. Jive speakers subverted standard usage, adopted metaphorical replacements for common words, and valued wit and innovation. Popular substitutions included "cat" for man, "chick" for woman, "crib" for home, "axe" for instrument, and "bad" for good. HENRY LOUIS GATES JR. suggests that such substitutions "have enabled many blacks to share messages only the initiated understand." This form of linguistic encoding was a ubiquitous survival tool for African Americans in times of slavery.

While derivative of jive in a broad sense, rap lyrics descend directly from a few specific cultural figures of the twentieth century. Black radio DJs from the 1950s (Holmes "Daddy-O" Daylie and Al Benson in Chicago) through the 1970s (DJ Hollywood in NEW YORK) spoke witty, jive-based talk. Heavyweight champion boxer MUHAMMAD ALI showcased the craft of clever rhymes and cocky toasts. H. "RAP" BROWN, a black nationalist who was active in the 1960s, gave both his name and his oratory style to rap music. In the late 1960s, the Watts Prophets of LOS ANGELES and the LAST POETS of HARLEM pioneered a kind of proto-rap by setting Brown's speaking style to rhythmic, musical accompaniments.

The musical roots of rap stretch equally far back in history, drawing upon African and Afro-Caribbean and African American rhythmic styles. In contrast to Western European music, which emphasizes harmonic progression and a sense of linear, forward motion, African music often marks time, emphasizes cycles, incorporates polyrhythmic figures, and includes non-harmonic percussive sounds.

Rap originally took its rhythms from the soul and FUNK of JAMES BROWN, GEORGE CLINTON, and others who had emerged from the RHYTHM AND BLUES (R&B) tradition. As rap developed, other kinds of music were sampled and imitated. In the 1990s, WU TANG CLAN borrowed orchestral excerpts, and SEAN "P. DIDDY" COMBS achieved popularity by rapping to the rhythm track of "Every Breath You Take," a song by the British rock band The Police.

In the Beginning

Popular lore attributes the birth of rap to Jamaican immigrant Clive Campbell, who performed under the name DJ Kool Herc. In JAMAICA, Herc had frequented backyard dance parties that were hosted by sound-systems operator King George, powered by booming speakers, and attended by working-class youth. When Herc DJed his first dance party in New York City in 1973, he joined the Bronx tradition of "mobile DJs," mixing up the music of James Brown, SLY AND THE FAMILY STONE, and Rare Earth for kids on the street. In addition, however, Herc introduced the art of Jamaican toasting, in which DJs speak with humor and syncopation over remixed instrumental versions of records. Herc and other Bronx DJs combined old songs into new danceable collages that contained "break beats"—the rhythmic figures that gave rise to BREAK DANCING.

Herc's popularity grew rapidly and inspired others to imitate his act. Soon a few popular DJs divided the Bronx into competing territories. Friendly rivalries arose between Herc in the west, Afrika Bambaataa in the east, Breakout in the north, and Grandmaster Flash in the south and central Bronx. Competition spawned innovation. Grandmaster Flash invented backspinning, in which he played one record while turning a second one backward, repeating phrases and beats in a stuttering, rhythmic manner. Grandwizard Theodore invented scratching, a technique in which he shimmied a record back and forth beneath the needle of a turntable. Other DJs soon adopted these innovations, which became standards of the rap sound.

DJs first gained popularity by providing a soundtrack for other facets of the HIP-HOP movement, namely dance, GRAFFITI ART, and fashion. By the late 1970s, however, artful mixing became a spectacle unto itself, and crowds ceased dancing in order to watch DJs spin. To keep people on the move, DJs recruited "MCs," who led call-and-response sessions and fired up the crowd with shouts of "get up," and "jam to the beat," in the fashion of James Brown. Such oratory had precedent in GOSPEL MUSIC, the covert rituals of slave religion, and the traditions of West Africa. Grandmaster Flash's MCs, the Furious Five—Melle Mel, Cowboy, Raheim, Kid Creole, and Mr. Ness—completed the genesis of rap when they began speaking to the rhythm of the music, trading rhymes in synch with each other and the DJ.

Rappers often tried to out-rhyme each other, and watching MCs became a major pastime. Independent labels such as Enjoy, Winley, and Sugar Hill Records began to record rap, and the music soon spread to other parts of New York City. In the fall of 1979 a group of rappers from Brooklyn called the SUGARHILL GANG released the hit single "Rapper's Delight." Because it came from Brooklyn, many Bronx residents flouted it as derivative. The song, however, catapulted rap into the public eye, topping the R&B charts and reaching Number Thirty-six on *Billboard*'s Top Forty.

Commercialization of a Genre

In 1980 rapper Kurtis Blow scored two hit singles, "Christmas Rappin'" and "The Breaks," both of which went gold. The same year, Blow played Madison Square Garden with BOB MARLEY and the Commodores. Meanwhile, Bronx hip-hop musicians began to perform in Manhattan's downtown clubs, importing rap to the hub of urban white culture.

In 1981 The Funky Four + 1 More appeared on *Saturday Night Live*, while the *Village Voice* and *20/20* gave coverage to break dancing and rap. In 1983 *Style Wars* took rap to the movies, and a PBS documentary brought it to the attention of suburbanites.

Innovation accompanied acclaim. In the early 1980s, Afrika Bambaataa popularized the use of drum machines and synthesizers, creating the new sound of "techno-pop." Techno-pop, in turn, led to the digital manipulation of samples (pieces of other recorded music), placing rap on the cutting edge of music technology. Rappers who preceded Bambaataa's innovations earned the title of "old school" rappers and included the Fat Boys, Whodini, Kool Moe Dee, and Melle Mel. The "new school" included those who incorporated Bambaataa's digital approach. A feud, originating between Kool Moe Dee and new school rapper LL COOL J (short for Ladies Love Cool James), further characterized the split. New school rappers included QUEEN LATIFAH, DJ Jazzy Jeff & The Fresh Prince, Tone Loc, ICE-T, and ICE CUBE. In addition to New York musicians,

Sean "P Diddy" Combs talks with reporters after receiving a Grammy in 2004 for "Shake Ya Tailfeather." *Mike Blake/Reuters/CORBIS*

Los Angeles–based rappers began developing new styles of their own. Eventually scenes in Houston, Atlanta, and Chicago each produced new hip-hop artists.

Despite the depressed economic conditions under which rap developed, early rappers seldom wrote socially conscious lyrics. As rappers attracted larger audiences in the early 1980s, however, they began to address ghetto conditions and economic inequalities of the United States under President Ronald Reagan. "The Message" (1981) by Grandmaster Flash and the Furious Five marked the advent of political rap, inspiring KRS-One (short for Knowledge Reigns Supreme-Over nearly everyone), Sister Souljah, Public Enemy, and Arrested Development.

Rap's Golden Age

When rap group Run-DMC fused rap and hard rock on their eponymous album in 1984, rap completed its break into the mainstream. The album sold more than 500,000 copies, becoming the first rap L.P. to go gold. Run-DMC's label, Def Jam Records, became the most successful independent record company in the business. Def Jam released hit music by rap star LL Cool J and, in 1985, signed a major distribution agreement with Columbia Records. Run-DMC's success among white audiences as well as their contract with a white-owned label reflected the mainstream appropriation of the new black form.

This appropriation prompted many to speculate about underlying issues of race. To some black critics, white listeners appeared to be seeking thrills from racially motivated fantasies. Writer David Samuels suggests that "the ways in which rap has been consumed and popularized speak not of crosscultural understanding, musical or otherwise, but of a voyeurism and tolerance of racism in which blacks and whites are both complicit."

Throughout the 1980s and 1990s, however, the popularity of white rappers like Vanilla Ice, the Beastie Boys, Third Bass, and House of Pain demonstrated that more than race was at play. Latino rappers began performing in Spanish (Mellow Man Ace, Kid Frost, and Gerardo), while Cypress Hill, with its mixed black and Hispanic membership, suggested that the integration of rap was happening at all levels.

Although rap began as a predominantly male activity, a number of successful female performers punctuated its history. Hit acts included MC Lyte, the Real Roxanne, Roxanne Shante, and Yo-Yo. In the 1990s women rappers often followed the male model, however, portraying men in the same derogatory way that men portrayed women. Sister Souljah broke this limited mold by addressing drug abuse, black-on-black violence, and national politics, while Queen Latifah and Salt-N-Pepa both addressed female self-empowerment. The successful rap arranger, writer, and producer Missy "Misdemeanor" Elliott gained fame as a performer with the 1997 release of her solo debut album, *Supa Dupa Fly*.

Gangsta Rap and Its Alternatives

In the late 1980s, a more brutal brand of rap developed, which described drugs, sex, and violence in detail. Tremendous white consumption of such music made the grim, lurid, and angry lyrics profitable. "Gangsta" rap, as performed by the Geto Boys, N.W.A., Ice Cube, Ice-T, and Too Short, supplied this demand. David Samuels writes that "rap's appeal to whites rested in its evocation of an age-old image of blackness: a foreign, sexually charged and criminal underworld against which the norms of white society are defined . . ."

The glorification of misogyny and violence had ardent critics among both the black and white establishment. In 1990 a Florida district court declared the album "Nasty as They Wanna Be," recorded by the Miami group 2 Live Crew, to be legally obscene—a ruling which outlawed the sale of the record. When Ice-T released "Cop-Killer" in 1991, policemen organized a boycott against Time Warner, the company that distributed the album. In addition, police started blaming crimes on rap songs, as criminals cited the influence of gangsta rap as part of their defense.

Many black critics declared white anger hypocritical, however, by pointing to the uncensored obscenity of popular white comedian Andrew Dice Clay as well as antipolice messages in songs by Eric Clapton, Bob Dylan, and Woody Guthrie. Commenting on "Nasty as They Wanna Be," Henry Louis Gates Jr.

Rapper MC Lyte arrives for the 2003 Soul Train Music Awards. *Seth Joel/CORBIS*

likened the ribaldry of 2 Live Crew to the street tradition of playing the DOZENS: "In the face of racist stereotypes about black sexuality, you can do two things: you can disavow them or explode them with exaggeration. 2 Live Crew, like many hip-hop groups, is engaged in sexual Carnivalesque. Parody reigns supreme . . . their off-color nursery rhymes are part of a venerable Western tradition."

Other African American leaders, however, dissented. Although most opposition reflected nothing more than a generation gap—parents scorning rap as their parents had scorned R&B—some of the criticism was grounded in ethical and political concern. On a talk show in 1993 the Rev. JESSE JACKSON railed against the rhetoric of gangsta rap. In the same year the Rev. CALVIN O. BUTTS III held a rally in New York to run over certain rap albums with a steamroller. Both men thought that the hyperbolic language of gangsta rappers and groups like 2 Live Crew only hurt African Americans in their struggle against racism. Some events in the 1990s led critics to question the lifestyle of gangsta rappers as well as the culpability of the media in celebrity-related crime. These events included the death of rapper Eazy-E from AIDS, and the murders of East Coast–West Coast rivals Chris Wallace (known as Biggie Smalls and The NOTORIOUS B.I.G.) and TUPAC SHAKUR (also known as 2PAC).

An increasingly popular and gentrified form of rap developed concurrently with gangsta rap. In the late 1980s light-hearted songs, more in the spirit of early Bronx rap, garnered popularity. Performers such as Young MC, MC Rob Base & DJ EZ Rock, and DJ Jazzy Jeff & the Fresh Prince recorded clean hits filled with playful braggadocio. Rap-based Saturday morning cartoons appeared in the wake of such songs. In 1990, rap reached prime-time television in the form of "The Fresh Prince of Bel-Air," a situation comedy. Even the more serious rappers often found themselves in the thick of popular culture. L.L. Cool J. landed a sitcom, while Tone Loc, Ice-T, Ice Cube, and Queen Latifah appeared in Hollywood films. WILL SMITH, a.k.a. the Fresh Prince, went furthest in this direction, starring in several blockbuster films including *Independence Day* (1996) and *Men in Black* (1997).

Meanwhile, however, most rappers neither perpetrated gangsta lyrics nor appeared in cartoons. Rappers who were dubbed "alternative" disavowed rap's violence while trying to preserve its edge. They included Me Phi Me, Disposable Heroes of Hiphoprisy, and Arrested Development. KRS-One of Boogie Down Productions initiated the "Stop the Violence" movement and the West Coast Rap All-Starts began the "Human Education against Lies" (H.E.A.L.) program, both of which pitted rap's influence against social ills. More bohemian acts, such as A TRIBE CALLED QUEST and DE LA SOUL, concentrated on musical innovations, developing the art, rather than the politics, of rap.

In the late 1990s, the widespread popularity of the Fugees reflected the new, international direction of rap. The Fugees addressed problems both within and outside of the United States, and one of their members, Haitian Wyclef Jean, released material performed in Creole. Wu Tang Clan, a group of nine rappers from the East Coast, rejected R&B influences, adhering instead to global sensibilities and trends. At the end of the century, rap scenes were burgeoning in most major European cities; MC Solaar of FRANCE drew an international following while Japanese youth began to emulate the rap culture of the West.

Rap's popularity has remained strong into the new century. Since 2000 rap albums have continued to reach multiplatinum status. The two best-selling albums of 2002 were rap recordings: *The Eminem Show* by Eminem, and *Nellyville* by Nelly. A year later the music industry's top-selling album was rapper 50 Cent's *Get Rich or Die Tryin'*, which sold more than 6.5 million copies.

Rap had begun as a homemade music, and its commercialization did not steal it from the streets. In the late 1990s and early 2000s, amateurs across the U.S. and the world continued to create innovative hip-hop sounds, generating a culture far larger than that reflected by the recording industry. "Famous" rap became famous by virtue of mainstream listeners and media, while fresher sounds often remained local and undiscovered. Such new rap continues to prosper as a living art, always outdistancing its commercialized, pop-chart predecessors.

See also Black Nationalism in the United States; Dance, African American; Grandmaster Flash, Melle Mel, and the Furious Five; Film, Blacks in American; Music, African American; Snoop Doggy Dogg; Soul Music; Television and African Americans.

Bibliography

Baker, Houston A. *Black Studies, Rap, and the Academy.* University of Chicago, 1993.

Chuck D. with Yusaf Jah. *Fight the Power: Rap, Race, and Reality.* Delacorte, 1997.

Rose, Tricia. *Black Noise: Rap Music and Black Culture in Contemporary America.* University Press of New England, 1994.

Eric Bennett

Rapier, James Thomas

1837–1883

African American congressman from Alabama.

James Thomas Rapier was born of free parents in Florence, Alabama, the son of John H. Rapier, a barber, and Susan (maiden name unknown). As a youngster, he was sent to live with his father's mother, Sally Thomas, and his father's half-brother, James Thomas, after whom Rapier was named, and to attend school in Nashville, Tennessee. Sally and James Thomas, although legally slaves, hired their own time and lived autonomous lives. Young Rapier thrived under their care and learned to read and write.

At the age of nineteen Rapier was sent by his father to Buxton, Canada West, an all-black settlement, to continue his education. At a school founded by the Presbyterian minister

William King, he studied Latin, Greek, mathematics, and the Bible. He also underwent a religious conversion and later taught school in the settlement. "My coming to Canada is worth all the world to me," he wrote in 1862. "I have a tolerable good education and I am at peace with my Savior."

Returning to the South in 1864, he went to Nashville, and later to Maury County, Tennessee. In 1865 he entered the political arena by delivering a keynote address at the Tennessee Negro Suffrage Convention in Nashville. When former Confederates returned to power during Tennessee's first postwar elections in 1865–1866, Rapier returned home to Florence. With the assistance of his father he rented a farm on Seven Mile Island in the Tennessee River, hired black tenant farmers, and raised a cotton crop.

Following the passage of the Congressional RECONSTRUCTION Acts in 1867, which enfranchised freedmen and provided for new state governments in the South, Rapier again turned to politics. He won a seat at Alabama's first REPUBLICAN convention in Montgomery and helped draft the new party platform calling for free speech, free press, and free schools. But he knew the fragility of the new coalition of blacks and pro-Union whites and asked fellow Republicans to proceed with "calmness, moderation and intelligence." In November 1867 Rapier attended the Alabama Constitutional Convention, supporting a civil rights plank and a moderate franchise clause that would exclude from the vote only those disenfranchised by acts of Congress.

Despite his advocacy of moderation, however, during the tumultuous months preceding the 1868 presidential election, Rapier was driven from his home in Lauderdale County by the KU KLUX KLAN. Barely escaping with his life (several fellow blacks were hanged from a bridge near Florence), he fled to Montgomery, where he spent almost a year in seclusion. In 1869 he attended the National Negro Labor Union convention in WASHINGTON, D.C. (he also attended two subsequent conventions), and in 1871 he founded the Alabama Negro Labor Union in an effort to improve working conditions for laborers and tenant farmers.

In 1870 Rapier became his party's nominee for secretary of state. Despite a vigorous campaign and publishing a newspaper, the *Republican Sentinel,* he went down to defeat largely because of violence and opposition from white Republicans to any black candidate. But at the national level, as a reward for his party loyalty, he was appointed assessor of internal revenue for the Montgomery district in 1871, the first black to attain such a high patronage position in the state.

Using his Montgomery office, in the heart of the Black Belt, he mounted a campaign for the Second District congressional seat, received the nomination, and during a period of calm following the passage of the Enforcement Acts, which provided for federal suppression of the KKK, defeated the popular one-armed Confederate veteran William Oates by a vote of 19,000–16,000. Before taking his seat in Congress, he represented Alabama at the Fifth International Exhibition in Vienna, Austria, reporting on the state's exhibits. During his congressional term (1873–1875), Rapier pushed through a bill to make Montgomery a port of delivery, making federal funds available to assist in dredging the Alabama River as far inland as Montgomery. He also supported legislation to improve education in the South, arguing that federal funds be used to support public schools, and spoke on behalf of Charles Sumner's civil rights bill, which became law in 1875.

Seeking a second term, Rapier launched a campaign in 1874, but renewed violence, intimidation, and voter fraud led to his defeat. Two years later, in the newly gerrymandered Fourth Congressional District, which included Lowndes County where Rapier rented several cotton plantations, he tried again, but fraud and the entry of JEREMIAH HARALSON, a black man from Selma, into the 1876 race resulted in a second defeat. The differences between himself and Haralson were hard to pinpoint—both men advocated civil rights, voter protection, and leadership roles for blacks. In large measure their difference was a matter of style. Haralson was young, brash, outspoken, and rhetorical; Rapier was older, prudent, diplomatic, and his speeches, while forceful (he was an outstanding orator) and well organized, had few rhetorical flourishes.

With the "redemption" of the state by conservatives, Rapier turned his attention to the emigration movement. Appointed collector of internal revenue for the Second Alabama District in 1877, he used the office to urge former slaves to leave Alabama and settle in the West. The black man, he asserted, would never be accorded equal rights or economic opportunity in the South. He traveled several times to Kansas, purchased land for a settlement in Wabaunsee County along the route of the Kansas-Pacific Railway, gave pro-emigration speeches in Alabama, and testified in Washington, D.C., before a Senate committee on emigration.

During the early 1880s, as his health began to decline, Rapier slowed his activity. He had never married, and despite the hectic pace of his career, he was a lonely man who admitted he had few real friends.

By the end of his life, Rapier had come full circle. From seeking to work within the system to gain equal rights for blacks in the South, he now advocated that former slaves and their children should abandon the land of their birth. His efforts, however, were cut short. Rapier died in Lowndes County, Alabama, of pulmonary tuberculosis.

Bibliography

Rapier correspondence can be found in the Rapier-Thomas Papers, Moorland-Spingarn Collection, Howard University, Washington, D.C.

Feldman, Eugene. *Black Power in Old Alabama: The Life and Stirring Times of James T. Rapier.* 1968.

Foner, Eric. *Freedom's Lawmakers: A Directory of Black Office Holders during Reconstruction.* 1993.

Schweninger, Loren. *James T. Rapier and Reconstruction.* 1978.

From *American National Biography.* John A. Garraty and Mark C. Carnes, eds. Oxford University Press, 1999. Reprinted by permission of the American Council of Learned Societies.

Loren Schweninger

Ras Dashen

Mountain in northern Ethiopia, the highest peak in Ethiopia and fourth highest in Africa.

Towering over the Ethiopian Plateau at 4,620 meters (15,157 feet) above sea level, Ras Dashen is part of the Simien Mountains, a volcanic range of jagged peaks. Adjacent to the mountain is the 179-square-kilometer (69-square-mile) Simien Mountains National Park, which was designated a World Heritage Site in 1978 by the United Nations Educational, Scientific and Cultural Organization (UNESCO). UNESCO's World Heritage list recognizes the world's unique natural and cultural places. Three animals unique to ETHIOPIA are found in the area: the Walia ibex, the Simien jackal, and the gelada baboon. The mountain is also the home of the lammergeyer, a vulture with a 2.4-meter (8-foot) wingspan, known as the "bone-breaker" for its habit of breaking its prey's bones by dropping them on rocks. The area's native juniper and olive forests and numerous plants, such as Saint John's wort and heath, have been depleted by cultivation and grazing.

Rassemblement Démocratique Africain

Alliance of nationalist political parties in the French colonies of West and Central Africa.

The Rassemblement Démocratique Africain (RDA) was one of the driving forces of decolonization in several of FRANCE's African colonies. It was founded by African deputies to the French National Assembly at a congress held in 1946 in BAMAKO, the colonial capital of French Sudan (now MALI). The RDA's leading spokesperson in the French assembly was FÉLIX HOUPHOUËT-BOIGNY, the future president of CÔTE D'IVOIRE. The RDA's initial demand was full French citizenship for Africans in France's colonies. Later, the RDA played an important role in debates over the conditions of independence for the French colonies.

In its early years the RDA was allied with the French Communist Party, the only major party in France that supported the RDA's goals. The French government of Charles de Gaulle viewed the RDA as a threat, and the government often arrested RDA activists and banned their meetings. In the early 1950s, the RDA broke with the French Communists and formed closer ties with de Gaulle's government. In AFRICA, the RDA drew its membership primarily from urban areas; trade unions were a particularly strong source of support for the RDA branches in CAMEROON and GUINEA.

By the late 1950s, French military defeats in the French colonies of Indochina and ALGERIA had convinced the French government to accept African demands for decolonization. The RDA favored France's offer to grant its colonies internal self-rule within a "French Community" under the executive control of the French president. For many RDA leaders, this proposal appeared to offer the colonies an opportunity to gain greater autonomy without losing the benefits of French citizenship and economic support. Only SÉKOU TOURÉ of Guinea, the leader of an RDA affiliate, the Parti Démocratique de Guinée, called for complete independence. In 1958 there was a referendum in which African colonies controlled by France were given the option of independence or of retaining ties with France through a federation. Only Guinea voted to reject federation in favor of complete independence. France itself, however, soon abandoned its support for the proposed federation. Within a few years, candidates of RDA-affiliated parties were elected to lead some of the first independent governments of French-speaking Africa. Leaders who began their careers with the RDA included Félix Houphouët-Boigny in Côte d'Ivoire (who had long since abandoned the RDA's initial leftist positions), Sékou Touré in Guinea, MODIBO KEITA in Mali, and HAMANI DIORI in NIGER. After independence the RDA's international influence faded, although many of the leaders it fostered remained in office for years.

See also Decolonization in Africa: An Interpretation; Nationalism in Africa.

Elizabeth Heath

Rastafarians

Members of a social movement, established in Jamaica around 1930, that combines elements of religious prophecy, specifically the idea of a black God and Messiah; the Pan-Africanist philosophy of Marcus Garvey; the ideas of Black Power Movement leader Walter Rodney; and the defiance of reggae music.

Religion has been the principal form of resistance in JAMAICA since colonial times. As one scholar of Rastafarianism, Barry Chevannes, affirms: "Whether resistance through the use of force, or resistance through symbolic forms such as language, folk-tales and proverbs . . . religion was the main driving force among the Jamaican peasants." During the early twentieth century, resistance in JAMAICA reached its pinnacle with the birth of Rastafarianism, as much an Afrocentric worldview and form of black nationalism as it was a new religion, inspired by the independent, anticolonial Christian tradition of the ETHIOPIAN ORTHODOX CHURCH. As Horace Campell notes, "Rastafari culture combines the histories of the children of slaves in different societies. Within it are both the negative and the positive—the idealist and the ideological—responses of an exploited and racially humiliated people."

Rastafari Movement

The roots of Rastafarianism can be traced back to Jamaica's earliest freedom fighters against colonialism. According to Leonard E. Barrett Sr., author of *The Rastafarians*, Jamaica's African population "suffered the most frustrating and oppres-

With his dreadlocks wrapped in a Rasta-colored headdress, a Jamaican flute player performs at an outdoor concert. *Macintyre/Hutchinson*

sive slavery ever experienced in a British colony . . . Under such complete domination two reactions were provoked: fight and flight." The Jamaican maroons—African slaves, who, following the British defeat of the Spaniards in 1655, escaped to the mountains—waged guerrilla warfare against the British colonizers. In 1738 the British were compelled to grant them a limited freedom: although the maroons were allowed their own lands and leaders, they were also required to police the plantation slaves, a duty which they accepted. Henceforth, the maroons were loyal to the Crown. The freedom movement was taken up by plantation slaves. Indeed, in 1831, under the leadership of the slave and Baptist religious leader Samuel Sharpe, Jamaica's slaves waged a mass rebellion against the planters. Like Sharpe, many Jamaican slaves believed that God was calling on them to fight for their freedom—a messianic vision partly influenced by Baptist and Methodist missionaries, who, during the mid-eighteenth century, established churches in Jamaica and contributed to a SYNCRETISM of CHRISTIANITY and the island's African religions. Although the rebellion was violently suppressed by the British authorities in Jamaica, it was one of the key factors in the British Parliament's decision to abolish slavery with a law that went into effect on August 1, 1834.

In 1865 the MORANT BAY REBELLION, another large-scale uprising of Jamaica's rural blacks against the colonial elite, forced political and economic reforms that diminished the power and privileges of Jamaica's ruling, white planter class. Jamaica became a Crown colony. The British drew up a new constitution that removed direct rule from the hands of the local elite and gave decision-making power to an appointed British governor, who presided over a legislative council. Yet the reforms only went so far; the overwhelming majority of council members, nominated by the governor himself, were white, and the gulf that existed between Jamaica's poor blacks (a significant majority of the island's population) and middle-class whites and mulattoes continued to widen.

Jamaica's black population was systematically repressed until 1962, the year British COLONIAL RULE came to an end. Indeed, Jamaican blacks did not have the freedom to assemble or organize trade unions; abysmal working conditions led many to seek employment abroad. In 1914 the Jamaican worker MARCUS GARVEY founded the UNIVERSAL NEGRO IMPROVEMENT ASSOCIATION (UNIA). Garvey's Pan-Africanist philosophy, which established a sense of national identity based on race, instilled in many blacks worldwide the belief that their economic and political liberation could ultimately be found in a strong and unified AFRICA. After spending a decade in GREAT BRITAIN and the United States, in 1927 Garvey returned to Jamaica, where he spread his political views among black workers and farmers. He told blacks to "look to Africa for the crowning of a king to know that your redemption is nigh."

In 1930 Prince Tafari Makonnen was crowned the new emperor of ETHIOPIA, HAILE SELASSIE I ("Power of the Trinity," his baptismal name), a monumental event that many blacks in Africa and the Americas saw as the fulfillment of Garvey's prophecy. Since the Middle Ages, a part of Ethiopia's nobility, including the Makonnens, had perceived themselves as descendants of King Solomon of Judah and the Queen of Sheba. This was a belief stemming from biblical prophecies, including the Song of Solomon 1:5–6, which states: "I am Black, but comely, O ye daughters of Jersusalem, as the tents of Kedar, as the curtains of Solomon." As Chevannes points out, "if Solomon was Black, so was the Christ. Both were descendants of David. Redemption of the African race was therefore at hand." The prophecy was further reinforced by Emperor Haile Selassie himself, who appropriated the titles "King of Kings" and "Conquering Lion of the Tribe of Judah."

The name Rastafari is taken from *Ras*, meaning "prince" in the Amharic language, and *Tafari*, the name of the emperor of Ethiopia. The earliest preachers of the Rastafarian worldview were the Jamaican workers Leonard Howell, Archibald Dunkley, and Joseph Hibbert. They asserted the idea of a black God, who physically lived on the earth; proclaimed that the African peoples shared in this divinity; and equated the liberation of blacks with their repatriation to Africa. Indeed, on three separate occasions (1934, 1956, and 1959) Jamaica's Rastafarian leaders attempted (unsuccessfully, due to a lack of governmental and organizational support) to repatriate brethren to their homeland. Howell also called for "death to Black and White oppressors," an approach that ignited considerable hostility among Jamaica's elite; both Howell and Dunkley were imprisoned on several occasions and Howell was branded "insane."

In 1935 the Italian army invaded Ethiopia, an event that drew attention to the incompetence of the Selassie regime, which had left Ethiopia's peasantry impoverished, uneducated, and untrained in military service and thus entirely unprepared for war. Moreover, Jamaica's economic crisis continued to worsen. Black workers, plagued by malnutrition and low wages, turned to practical action instead of religion as a form of resistance. Spurred on by these developments, the Rastafarian movement became increasingly politicized. During the 1940s and 1950s, leaders intensified their opposition to the colonial state by defying the police and organizing illegal street marches.

During the late 1950s, Claudius Henry, head of a Rastafarian meeting house in KINGSTON, set up a guerrilla training camp and in 1959 unsuccessfully tried to repatriate a group of Jamaican Rastas to Africa. Soon after, the police invaded Henry's headquarters, where they found a supply of arms and a letter inviting the Cuban leader FIDEL CASTRO to take over Jamaica. Henry was arrested and tried on charges of treason. Throughout the 1960s, Rastafarian demonstrations against segregation and black poverty were violently repressed by the Jamaican police and military. While several Rastafari were killed in such clashes, hundreds more were arrested and humiliated by being forced to have their dreadlocks cut off.

Philosophically opposed to a culture of violence, many Rastafari soon turned to more peaceful means of resistance—a goal considerably aided by the visit of Haile Selassie to Jamaica in 1966. As Horace Campbell notes, "state officials had to take a back seat while the mass of the black populace thrust forward to pay homage to the Ethiopian monarch. So profound was the popular feeling expressed for Africa that the Jamaican ruling class realized that it could not simply write off Rastafari." Rastafarian culture was explored and promoted in a plethora of academic studies in Jamaica and abroad, while the Ethiopian Orthodox Church was recognized as an institution worthy of respect. Rastafarianism also gained a new measure of credibility among Jamaica's middle-class blacks and mulattoes who, during the late 1960s, formed their own Rastafarian group, the Twelve Tribes of Israel.

In 1968, Jamaican university lecturer WALTER RODNEY started the Black Power Movement, which significantly influenced the development of Rastafarianism in the Caribbean. Black Power was a call to blacks to overthrow the capitalist order that ensured white dominion, and to reconstruct their societies in the image of blacks. In DOMINICA, GRENADA, and Trinidad, Rastafarians played a central role in radical left-wing politics. In Jamaica, Rastafarian resistance was expressed through cultural forms, particularly REGGAE music. Popular reggae singers, such as BOB MARLEY and PETER TOSH, expressed Rastafarian ideas and social criticism in their song lyrics. During the 1970s, they significantly contributed to the growth of the Rastafarian movement throughout the Caribbean, the United States, England, CANADA, EUROPE, Australia, New Zealand, and parts of LATIN AMERICA.

Rituals and Practices

The rituals and practices central to Rastafarianism developed during the late 1930s and 1940s. Of particular importance are "reasonings" and "binghi." At reasonings, Rastafari members gather informally to offer prayers and smoke ganja, or marijuana, considered a holy weed; it is passed around in a water pipe, which some Rastafari have likened to the Christian communion cup in its symbolic significance. Binghi are all-night celebrations that feature dancing accompanied by the distinctive rhythms of Rasta drums; they are held to mark special occasions throughout the year, such as the coronation of Haile Selassie I, Marcus Garvey's birthday, and the emancipation from slavery. Other significant practices include the wearing of facial hair by adult males (Ras Tafari was pictured with a full beard) and dreadlocks, or long matted hair. According to Chevannes, dreadlocks originated among a group of Rastas known as the Youth Black Faith, who adopted the hairstyle as a symbol of their radically defiant views in a society in which blacks were made to feel ashamed of their skin color and hair texture.

Since the 1980s, the Rastafarian movement has become increasingly secular. Many of the movement's symbols have lost their religious and ideological significance and the influence of Rastafari ideology on Jamaica's urban youth has considerably declined. The Rasta colors (red, green, and gold), in which all Rasta banners and artifacts are painted, have been largely shorn of their ideological meaning and are now worn by all. Dreadlocks too are sported as a trendy hairstyle by both blacks and whites in Jamaica and abroad. The loosening of Rastafari ideology has also led women to become increasingly outspoken within the movement. Women traditionally had been forbidden to play an important role in rituals; they were also expected to show complete deference to males. During the last two decades, however, some women have protested against and defied the movement's patriarchal beliefs and conventions.

The Rastafarian movement in Jamaica remains fragmented and unorganized; brethren adhere to the Rastafarian worldview through inner conviction, and generally prefer autonomy to cohesive organizational structures and rules. Nonetheless, two highly organized Rastafari groups exist in Jamaica: the Bobos and the Twelve Tribes of Israel. The Bobos maintain a communal life on the fringes of Kingston, where they earn a living producing and selling brooms. The Twelve Tribes, on the other hand, is a predominantly middle-class group, led by Prophet Gad. Members of the Twelve Tribes accept the authority of designated group members, pay dues, and hold regular meetings and events. In addition, there is the House of Nyabinghi, a loosely organized assembly of Rasta elders, who settle disputes between brethren and organize events. "Beyond the Assembly of Elders," notes Chevannes, "there is no membership, as such. All are free to come or stay away, to participate or remain silent, to contribute or withhold financial dues . . . the openness of this sort of structure permits a great measure of democracy, in which all are equal, regardless of age, ability or function."

Rastafarianism remains a culture of resistance in many parts of the world. Although the Rastafarian movement has experienced a turbulent social history in Jamaica, it retains significant moral authority there, and its influence is increasingly felt beyond Jamaica. Indeed, it was one of the first full-fledged movements to confront issues of racial identity and prejudice, and to incite Jamaica's middle-class blacks to reflect on the importance of their African heritage.

See also Black Power Movement in the Caribbean; Early Rastafarian Leaders; Maroonage in the Americas; Nationalist Movements and Blacks in Latin America and the Caribbean; Pan-Africanism; Religions, African, in Latin America and the

Caribbean; Slavery in Latin America and the Caribbean; Trinidad and Tobago.

Roanne Edwards

Ratsiraka, Didier

1936–

Former president of Madagascar.

Born in Vatomandry, MADAGASCAR, Didier Ratsiraka was the son of a founding member of the Parti des Déshérités de Madagascar, a pro-Western political party. Taught by Jesuits as a child, Ratsiraka obtained an engineering degree from the French Naval Academy in Brest. After graduating, he joined the Malagasy navy and was posted to the Embassy of Madagascar in France until ailing president PHILIBERT TSIRANANA was ousted during the May 1972 Revolution, when 100,000 protesters marched on the presidential palace. Tsiranana's successor, army chief of staff General Gabriel Ramanatsoa, asked Ratsiraka to return to Madagascar to serve as minister of foreign affairs. An attempted coup d'état resulted in the removal of Ramanatsoa and a power struggle between Ratsiraka and Richard Ratsimandrava, an army colonel. Ratsimandrava became president in 1975, but he was assassinated only six days later. Ratsiraka served on the military council that took control and subsequently named him president of the Second Republic. Ratsiraka was defeated by ALBERT ZAFY in presidential elections between 1992 and 1993. Ratsiraka remained a strong political force, however, eventually beating Zafy in 1996 presidential elections to reclaim the office in 1997.

In the 2001 presidential election, however, businessman Marc Ravalomanana challenged Ratsiraka. In the hotly contested election, Ravalomanana claimed victory and installed himself as head of state, while Ratsiraka, also claiming victory, retreated to Toamasina, where he set up a rival government. This action nearly led to the breakup of the country until the High Constitutional Court of Madagascar confirmed the legitimacy of Ravolomanana's election.

Bibliography

Allen, Philip M. *Madagascar: Conflicts of Authority in the Great Island.* Westview Press, 1995.

Deleris, Ferdinand. *Ratsiraka: Socialism et misère à Madagascar.* L'Harmattan, 1985.

Ratsiraka, Didier. *Charte de la révolution socialiste malagasy.* Imprimerie d'Ouvages Éducatifs, 1975.

Ari Nave

Rawlings, Jerry

1947–

Military officer who twice overthrew the government of Ghana and became president.

Although he came to power as a Marxist populist, Jerry John Rawlings has since successfully instituted free market reforms to revive Ghana's faltering economy. He is often seen as an enigma, however, because of his shifting rhetoric and changing policies.

Born in ACCRA, GHANA, Rawlings is the son of a Scottish pharmacist and a woman of the EWE people, one of Ghana's largest ethnic groups. Politically, Ewe have been among his staunchest supporters. He attended Achimota Secondary School and Ghana Military Academy in Teshie. In 1969 Rawlings became an air force pilot and in 1978 was promoted to flight lieutenant.

Rawlings became politically active in the late 1970s. He blamed government corruption and mismanagement for the food shortages, inflation, and economic stagnation in the country. In 1979, when authorities lifted the ban on political parties, the charismatic Rawlings spoke out against the government and endorsed measures to help the poor. He quickly won wide public support. Rawlings and other junior officers were arrested and imprisoned during an attempted coup in May 1979. A second attempt succeeded a month later, and coup organizers promptly freed Rawlings.

Rawlings became head of the Armed Forces Revolutionary Council (AFRC), which took charge of government with a goal of bringing the previous military regime to justice. During the 112 days the AFRC held power, it tried a number of former officials and military leaders on corruption charges. Akwasi Afrifa, General I. K. Acheampong, and General F. W. K. Akuffo were among the eight former officials executed. In July of that year, the AFRC held previously scheduled elections, which resulted in Hilla Limann's victory as president. Rawlings handed over power to Limann in September. Limann retired Rawlings from the air force, and failed to revitalize Ghana's deteriorating economy. With the country crippled by a staggering foreign debt and an annual inflation rate of over 140 percent, public discontent soared.

In December 1981, Rawlings staged another coup and became head of state as chairman of the Provisional National Defense Council (PNDC). At first the PNDC implemented such Marxist-inspired measures as the creation of worker councils to monitor factory output and Workers' Defense Committees in each neighborhood. Rawlings also sought support from the former Soviet Union and such anti-Western states as LIBYA.

By 1983, however, these measures had clearly failed to reverse the country's economic decline, and Rawlings turned to free-market reforms. Over the next several years, the Rawlings administration devalued Ghana's currency, froze the hiring of public employees, and privatized state-owned enterprises, including several potentially lucrative coffee and cocoa plantations. His austerity measures won approval from Western governments and international organizations, such as the International Monetary Fund, but fostered unhappiness at home. Although Rawlings faced coup attempts each year between 1983 and 1987, he maintained tight control over Ghana's political life. His government jailed opponents and executed at least one person implicated in a coup attempt. Human rights groups, such as Amnesty International, condemned his regime for human rights abuses.

By the early 1990s, the government's reforms had led the country to partial economic recovery. Rawlings remained sufficiently popular to win election in 1992 with 58 percent of the vote. He won reelection to another four-year term in 1996. Foreign observers judged the elections reasonably free and fair. Having announced that he would step down after the December 2000 election, Rawlings ceded office to the newly elected John Kufour, who pledged during his campaign to bring about national reconciliation. To this end, Kufour took steps in 2001 to open investigations into the executions that occurred during the Rawlings regime.

David P. Johnson, Jr.

Rawls, Lou

1936–

American fusion singer and a founder of the Lou Rawls Parade of Stars in support of the United Negro College Fund.

Louis Allen Rawls was born and raised by his grandmother in Chicago, Illinois. Rawls began singing in his church choir at the age of seven. In the mid-1950s, Rawls and his friend SAM COOKE joined two other vocalists to form the Pilgrim Travelers, a GOSPEL group. After the group disbanded in 1959, Rawls sang in BLUES clubs and cafés around LOS ANGELES. At one show, a producer from Capitol Records asked him to submit an audition tape. He soon released his debut album, *Stormy Monday* (1962). *Lou Rawls Live* followed in 1966, achieving gold status on the strength of its single "Love Is a Hurtin' Thing," which reached number one on the RHYTHM-AND-BLUES (R&B) charts. In 1967 Rawls won his first Grammy for Best Male R&B Vocals for the song "Dead End Street." He won again in 1971 for "A Natural Man." Rawls's success continued with his first platinum album, *All Things in Time* (1977), and the Grammy award–winning album *Unmistakably Lou* (1977).

In 1979 Rawls and Anheuser-Busch founded the Lou Rawls Parade of Stars, an annual telethon for the UNITED NEGRO COLLEGE FUND (UNCF). By 1998 Rawls's telethon had raised an estimated $175 million for the UNCF and featured entertainers such as BILL COSBY, WHOOPI GOLDBERG, and STEVIE WONDER. Rawls released two albums in 1993: *Portrait of the Blues* and *Christmas Is the Time*. He has also acted in television and film, from the show *77 Sunset Strip* (in the late 1950s) to the film *Leaving Las Vegas* (1995).

After leaving the Blue Note record label in 1995, Rawls and his associate David Brokaw founded Rawls and Brokaw Records in Los Angeles. Among his releases under his own label was *Seasons 4 U* (1998).

Razaf, Andy

1895–1973

American popular song lyricist.

Andy Razaf had his greatest success writing for HARLEM stage shows of the 1920s, collaborating with greats like WILLIE "THE LION" SMITH, EUBIE BLAKE, and James P. Johnson. His most lasting work, however, was with THOMAS "FATS" WALLER. The two produced many of the era's most popular songs such as "Honeysuckle Rose," "Ain't Misbehavin'," and "The Joint Is Jumpin'." When Harlem stage shows became less popular, Razaf's career declined. He retired after 1940 and died in relative obscurity of kidney failure. He married four times, once to Jean Blackwell, who was the curator of the SCHOMBURG CENTER FOR RESEARCH IN BLACK CULTURE of the New York Public Library.

See also Musical Theater in the United States.

Bibliography

Singer, Barry. *Black and Blue: The Life and Lyrics of Andy Razaf*. Schirmer Books, 1992.

Robert Fay

Reason, Patrick Henry

1816–1898

African American engraver, lithographer, abolitionist, and leader of a fraternal order.

Patrick Henry Reason was born in New York City, one of four children of Michel and Elizabeth Melville Reason. He was baptized on April 17, 1816, as Patrice Rison. His father, Michel Rison, was from Sainte-Anne, Guadeloupe, and his mother, Elizabeth Melville, was from Santo Domingo (in what is now the DOMINICAN REPUBLIC). Patrick's young sister, Policarpe, died in 1818 at age four. His brother Elver (or Elwer) did not attain the prominence that Patrick or his brother Charles Lewis did. All three brothers received their early education at the New York AFRICAN FREE SCHOOL, established on Mulberry Street by the NEW YORK MANUMISSION SOCIETY. Patrick Reason's skill as an engraver was recognized at age thirteen when he made an engraving of the African Free School that was printed as a frontispiece of Charles C. Andrews's *History of the New York African Free Schools . . .* (1830).

In 1833 Patrick Reason, with the consent of his mother (his father having died), was apprenticed for four years to Stephen Henry Gimber "to learn the art, trade and mystery of an engraver." Gimber was to pay Patrick's mother $3 a week. Two years later Patrick designed a stipple engraving of a kneeling slave in an attitude of prayer with chains hanging from her wrists and the inscription "Am I not a woman and a sister?" It was widely used by abolitionists as frontispieces to their publications, on antislavery broadsides, stationery, and commemorative coins. This design was not originally from Reason. A figure of a chained kneeling slave, in similar position and attitude with the motto "Am I not a man and a brother?" was designed in October 1787 for a seal used by the British Committee for the Abolition of the Slave Trade. It was influential in kindling antislavery sentiment in Great Britain, and with its direct and pathetic appeal was no less an inspiration to American abolitionists.

Reason's interest in portraiture began in 1835 when he made a stipple engraving of the likeness of GRANVILLE SHARP that was printed as a frontispiece for *A Memoir of Granville Sharp* (1836) by Charles Stuart. Reason based his engraving on an engraved portrait of Sharp by T. B. Lord of London, England.

For the next fifteen years Reason's portraits and designs appeared as frontispieces in slave narratives, in books such as *The Fountain for Everyday in the Year* (1836) by Lydia M. Child and *Thoughts on Slavery Written in 1774* by John Wesley (reprinted in 1839 by the American Anti-Slavery Society), and in periodicals. An excellent engraving of a slave, James Williams, was published in 1838. On April 12 of that year Reason's business card in the *Colored American* advertised that he was a "portrait and landscape Engraver, Draughtsman and lithographer." The *U.S. Magazine and Democratic Review* printed three excellent engravings by Reason to accompany biographies in the periodical. One, his well-executed portrait of Benjamin Tappan, an antislavery Ohio senator, appeared in the issue of June 1840. The editor noted that it was "a faithful representation of the strongly marked and intellectual countenance of one who has been styled by a contemporary—'the venerable patriarch of the Ohio democracy.' It presents him to the eye as he now daily appears amid the exciting scenes of the American Senate, calm, collected and attentive with the apparent self-possession of one not unconscious of superior strength." Reason had used a painting of Tappan by Washington Blanchard as a model. A copy was published in the *Dictionary of American Portraits* (1967). Reason engraved another portrait of a younger Benjamin Tappan, made from a daguerreotype. Lewis Tappan, a New York businessman and abolitionist, paid Reason $70 to make a steel engraving of his brother Benjamin, and on July 11, 1840, Tappan wrote to Reason that the Tappan family was pleased with the portrait and that the "anti-slavery cause would be advanced if it were known that a Negro was capable of such craftsmanship." He added that "perhaps it will be best to wait until you have engraved two or three more before the secret is out."

Reason's line and stipple engraving of prominent lawyer and diplomat George Mifflin Dallas appeared in the February 1842 issue of the *U.S. Magazine and Democratic Review.* Since no statement indicates it was engraved after a portrait, Reason may have both drawn and engraved it. Another portrait by Reason published in the June 1844 issue contained an engraving of Robert Adrian, the mathematician, after a painting by Charles Cromwell Ingham. It carried the statement that it was engraved by Patrick Henry Reason and signed by Adrian.

Other engravings by Reason include a portrait of Peter Williams, Jr., rector of St. Phillips Church in New York City, deposited for copyright on August 28, 1841.

While he lived in New York, Reason completed a line and stipple engraving of clergyman Baptist Noel, member of the London Emancipation Society, and of clergyman Thomas Baldwin made for the *Baptist Memorial;* the portrait of HENRY BIBB used as a frontispiece for the *Narrative of the Life and Adventure of Henry Bibb* (1850); and the engraved copper nameplate for the coffin of famous orator Daniel Webster, who died on October 24, 1852.

Reason's treatment of groups is seen in his copperplate engraving of a certificate of membership in the Masonic order; an original conception of the Faith, Hope, and Charity composition showing Charity surrounded by her children; and a certificate of membership in the Grand United Order of Odd Fellows. The New York Public Library also has a copperplate engraving of a mountainous landscape after a drawing by W. H. Bartlett, supposed to represent Spanish explorer Vasco Nuñez de Balboa ascending the mountains. Art historian James A. Porter stated that this "meticulous work shows Patrick Henry Reason attained great skill in representation of minute gradations of value" (unpublished notes).

During the NEW YORK CITY DRAFT RIOT OF 1863 the merchants organized a committee for the relief of black victims. HENRY HIGHLAND GARNET, an African American minister who had been asked to aid in the work, wrote an "address to the Executive Committee of merchants for the Relief of Colored People," which was presented to them on August 22, 1863. This acknowledgment was "elaborately engrossed on parchment and tastefully framed by Patrick Reason, one of their own people."

At one time Reason worked for the New York publisher Harpers as an engraver preparing map plates and for a New York firm as engraver of plates for printing banknotes. According to black author and abolitionist MARTIN R. DELANY, he also frequently did government engraving.

Because white engravers refused to work with him, firms often rejected his applications for employment. Reason's name appeared in the New York City directories from 1846 to 1866 as a "col'd" engraver.

Reason married Esther Cunningham of Leeds, England, on June 22, 1862. In 1869 he left New York with his wife and young son, Charles, and went to Cleveland, Ohio, where he had been invited to work as an engraver with several firms. For more than fifteen years Reason worked with the jewelry firm of Sylvester Hogan, a wholesale and retail dealer in fine jewelry and silver plate. The Cleveland Directories listed Reason as an engraver until 1899.

Reason was a member of the New York Philomathean Society, organized in 1830 for literary improvement and social pleasure. He, James Fields, and other members, feeling the need of an organization for mutual protection in case of sickness and death, decided to form their society into an Odd Fellows Lodge. They petitioned the International Order of Odd Fellows for a dispensation on behalf of the Philomathean Society, but their application was refused. They were, however, granted a dispensation from Victoria Lodge No. 448 in Liverpool of which Peter Ogden, a black New Yorker, was a past grand master, and on March 1, 1843, it became Philomathean Lodge No. 646, New York. On February 29, 1844, Philomathean Lodge No. 646 was formally authorized to institute Hamilton Lodge No. 710, New York, with which Reason was affiliated. He designed and engraved the first certificate of membership for the Odd Fellows.

Reason was the composer of the Ruth degree, the first "degree to be conferred under certain conditions on Females" by Hamilton Lodge No. 710, New York, and he was the first person invested with this honor. A subcommittee conferred the degree on him as the founder on August 23, 1858. Reason did much to develop the secret ritual of the order, devising a better system of signs, grips, and words. As past grand master he was the orator at some of the order's annual meetings. At the meeting of September 4, 1856, in Broadway Tabernacle, New York, his speech was said to have been the finest given up to that time.

The souvenir program and Jubilee Celebration Booklet contain facsimile reproductions from the minutes of Hamilton Lodge No. 710; dated February 25, 1847, and March 9, 1848, they are all in the painstaking and beautiful handwriting of Patrick Reason, whose name appears subscribed as permanent secretary.

Reason was also active in the New York Masons. He was grand master from 1862 to 1868 and grand secretary from 1859 to 1860. In 1862 Baron de Bulow of France on his visit to the United States conferred the Thirty-third Degree of Masonry on Reason. On Bulow's second visit to America in 1864 he organized a Supreme Council of Colored Americans whom he had earlier created Thirty-third Degree Masons under a commission as sovereign grand inspector general of the Supreme Council of France. On learning that black brothers were refused recognition by the white brothers, he obtained a special patent and organized a Supreme Council for the States, Territories, and Dependencies with Reason, then most worshipful grand master of Masons for the state of New York, as the presiding officer. Reason was grand master in New York from 1861 to 1867.

As a youth Reason was interested in the educational, social, and economic situation of African Americans. He was an intelligent and able lecturer on behalf of his people. At the age of twenty-two Reason, as president of the Phoenixian Literary Society of New York City, addressed its anniversary meeting on "The Philosophy of the Fine Arts" (July 4, 1837). His speech was reported in newspapers "as well-delivered and showing a talent and research and a thorough knowledge of the subjects full of sound reasoning and historical references." In the fall of the same year he was an active member of a committee appointed to arrange a public meeting to honor influential educator James McCune Smith on his return from a successful educational trip in Europe. During this time Reason also gave evening instruction to individuals and groups in "scientific methods of drawing." In 1838 he was awarded the first premium (prize) for India ink drawing at the Mechanics Institute Fair. At the annual meeting of the AMERICAN ANTI-SLAVERY SOCIETY in 1839, Reason signed a protest "against the principle, assumed by a majority of persons representing said Society at its present meeting that women have the right of originating, debating and voting on questions that come before said Society and are eligible to its various officers."

Interested in education, Reason served as secretary of the New York Society for the Promotion of Education among Colored Children, organized and incorporated on December 7, 1847, because separate black schools were neglected and in some instances closed. Subject to the supervision of the city's board of education, the society had authority to open and manage nonsectarian schools for African American children; two were opened in 1848. Reason participated in the Albany Convention of Colored Citizens in 1840, serving on six important committees. On perhaps one of the most important, he served with abolitionist minister Charles B. Ray, educator James McCune Smith, reformer Theodore S. Wright, and editor Phillip Bell to draft a reply to derogatory remarks concerning blacks made by Secretary of State John C. Calhoun to the British minister to the United States in April 1844 relative to the revolt of slaves on board the *Creole*. At a mass meeting in New York, African Americans empowered a committee to draft a reply, which was written by Smith and forwarded as a memorial to the U.S. Senate.

Patrick Henry Reason died in Cleveland on August 12, 1898, after a long illness. Funeral services were held at his home, 162 Dunbam Street, with burial at Lakeview Cemetery, Cleveland. His wife, Esther, and a son, Charles L. Reason, survived him.

The most useful sources about Patrick Reason are "Indenture, Patrick Reason" (1833); Charles C. Andrews's *History of the New York African Free Schools in the City of New York* (1830); Charles Brooks's *Official History and Manual of the Grand United Order of Odd Fellows in America* (1893); the Cleveland City Directories (1869–1898); New York City Directories (1846–1866); Henry Highland Garnet's *Memorial Discourse Delivered in the Hall of the House of Representatives* (1865, p. 59); William H. Grimshaw's *Official History of Masonry among the Colored People of America* (1903, pp. 130, 348); James A. Porter's *Modern Negro Art* (1943, pp. 35–38, 156, 175); *The Colored American* (April 12, 1838, p. 47; September 22, 1838, p. 123); and *Emancipator* (May 23, 1839, p. 14; September 26, 1839, p. 87). Reason's indenture is in the Moorland-Spingarn Research Center, Howard University, and the record from Register of Baptism and Record of Marriages, Church of St. Peter, New York, is in the Schomburg Center for Research in Black Culture, New York City.

From *Dictionary of American Negro Biography* by Rayford W. Logan and Michael R. Winston, editors. Copyright © 1982 by Rayford W. Logan and Michael R. Winston. Reprinted by permission of W. W. Norton & Company, Inc.

Dorothy B. Porter

Rebouças, André

1838–1898

Afro-Brazilian abolitionist, engineer, and teacher who campaigned for land reform in Brazil's abolitionist movement of the 1880s.

The son of national deputy Antônio Pereira Rebouças, André Rebouças was born in Cachoeira, BAHIA. After studying math and engineering at RIO DE JANEIRO's military school, he traveled and studied in EUROPE. Upon returning to BRAZIL, he became an adviser and strategist during the Paraguayan War (1864–1870). Rebouças then supervised several engineering projects, including the construction of railroads and docks in Rio de Janeiro. Rebouças's engineering achievements won him the respect of the royal family. He later became a professor of botany and math at the city's Polytechnic School, where he established an abolitionist society in 1883.

Rebouças conducted most of his abolitionist work behind the scenes, rarely addressing audiences. He organized abolitionist meetings and associations, and inspired readers with his antislavery literature and propaganda. Rebouças cofounded the *Sociedade brasileira contra a escravidão* (Brazilian Antislavery Society) in Rio de Janeiro in 1880 and became its first treasurer. He was a frequent contributor to the famous abolitionist newspaper *Gazeta da Tarde,* and cowrote the 1883 manifesto for the Rio de Janeiro–based *Confederação abolicionista* (Abolitionist Confederation). In all, Rebouças authored more than 120 antislavery articles as well as numerous essays analyzing Brazil's social and economic problems.

Unlike many other abolitionists, Rebouças realized that emancipation alone, without wider reforms, would likely do little to improve the living standards and opportunities of black Brazilians. For this reason his abolitionist agenda included expanding access to education, which had long been denied to almost all Brazilian slaves. The educational program he envisioned, but never saw realized, called for establishing at least one school in every village in Brazil to educate all segments of the population.

Both during and after the abolition movement, Rebouças distinguished himself as an advocate of land reform. He believed that small-scale farming was the key to Brazil's agricultural progress, and that given a small plot of land and the necessary equipment, ex-slaves and their families would become productive citizens. In his 1883 treatise *Agricultura nacional,* he proposed a program of "rural democracy" that would subdivide large estates for distribution to ex-slaves, immigrants, and the rural poor. As part of this effort, he attempted to set up a government-sponsored Territorial Association to break up plantations that had fallen into debt. Furthermore, Rebouças's abolitionist society proposed that taxes be levied on all uncultivated land located within twenty kilometers of lines of communication.

The Republic of Brazil was established in 1889. Subsequently Rebouças, devoted to the monarchy because it had abolished slavery, accompanied the imperial family into exile. He spent the rest of his life in Europe and AFRICA, and on the island of Madeira, where he died mysteriously exactly ten years after slavery in Brazil ended. Although Rebouças had greater renown in Brazil as an engineer, abolitionist JOAQUIM NABUCO affirmed his importance to abolitionism, saying, "Rebouças incarnated like no one else the antislavery spirit."

See also Anti-Slavery Movement in Latin America.

Bibliography

Santos, Sydney M. G. dos. *André Rebouças e seu tempo.* Petrópolis, 1985.

Veríssimo, Inácio José. *André Rebouças através de sua autobiografia.* J. Olympio, 1939.

Aaron Myers

Reconstruction

Period immediately following the Civil War, during which the United States sought to rebuild the South physically, politically, socially, and economically.

Reconstruction, also called the Second American Revolution, is an often misunderstood era of United States history. For decades, historians presented Reconstruction as a time when the South was a region besieged by a punitive North. According to this view, President ABRAHAM LINCOLN initially offered reasonable terms to the rebellious Southern states to speed reunion; but Radical Republicans, the liberal wing of the REPUBLICAN PARTY, instituted a period of "Negro rule" in which blacks, incompetent to govern, mismanaged the South. In this interpretation, conscientious whites "redeemed" the South by using secret patriotic organizations such as the KU KLUX KLAN to depose black rule. Only during the Second Reconstruction, as the CIVIL RIGHTS MOVEMENT is sometimes called, did most historians begin to reevaluate conclusions about Reconstruction. Concurring with African American intellectual W. E. B. DU BOIS, most scholars now agree that Reconstruction was a period of progressive politics in which newly emancipated blacks, with the help of the federal government and sympathetic whites in the South, helped build a more democratic society.

Role of the Federal Government

Most historians consider Reconstruction to encompass the years from 1865 to 1877. But the course Reconstruction would take, and the questions associated with it, were the subjects of national debate even before the end of the AMERICAN CIVIL WAR. Who should be punished for inciting secession and the war? How would the Southern states be readmitted to the Union? What penalties would apply? What was the federal government's responsibility to the freed slaves? Should the government extend rights to former slaves, and, if so, which rights? How would the Southern economy replace slave labor with free labor? Finally, and perhaps most important to the federal government, who was responsible for implementing Reconstruction policy—the president or the Congress of the United States? Although Lincoln had been granted far-reaching powers during the war, Congress could not allow the president such latitude in peacetime.

By issuing the Emancipation Proclamation on January 1, 1863, Lincoln committed the United States to abolishing slavery. Because slavery had been part of the American social fabric from the nation's beginning, its abolition would fundamentally alter the nation. Combined with this drastic social and political change was the need to rebuild the war-torn South. Many Southern cities lay in ruins. In addition, the loss of farmland and animals, as well as human labor—not only black slaves but whites killed or disabled in the war—jeopardized its agrarian economy.

Presidential Reconstruction

In December 1863 Lincoln introduced the first Reconstruction scheme, the Ten Percent Plan, thus beginning the period known as Presidential Reconstruction. The plan decreed that when one-tenth of a state's prewar voters had taken an oath of loyalty to the U.S. Constitution, its citizens could elect a new state government and apply for readmission to the Union. In addition, Lincoln promised to pardon all but a few high-ranking Confederates if they would take this oath and accept abolition. The plan also required that states amend their constitutions to abolish slavery. Conspicuous in this plan was the stipulation that only whites could vote or hold office. Despite the objections of Northern abolitionists, Lincoln began to implement the plan in Louisiana, which the Union Army had occupied since 1862. In a private meeting at the White House, a group of highly accomplished free blacks from NEW ORLEANS objected to their unequal status. Spurred by this protest, Lincoln unsuccessfully urged Louisiana's governor to allow the state's qualified free blacks to vote.

Congress, believing that Lincoln's Reconstruction plan was too permissive, took a series of steps to counteract it. In late 1864 Congress passed the Wade-Davis Bill, which contained more stringent readmission policies. It required that 50 percent of a state's voters declare loyalty to the Constitution before the state could create a new government, and also that these new governments recognize freedpeople as equal before the law. In

The political cartoon shows a drowning white Southerner refusing help from a black man. President Ulysses S. Grant stands on the shore urging the desperate man to accept whatever help is offered. *CORBIS*

addition, in January 1865 Congress approved the Thirteenth Amendment, which constitutionally ended slavery. It was ratified in December of that year, and in March 1865, Congress established the BUREAU OF REFUGEES, FREEDMEN, AND ABANDONED LANDS, or Freedmen's Bureau, a relief agency for needy refugees. Although the agency represented both black and white refugees, it was primarily intended to aid blacks in the transition from slavery to freedom.

Lincoln indirectly vetoed Wade-Davis by leaving it unsigned until Congress adjourned in late March 1865. He considered the Ten Percent Plan experimental, however, and in his final speech indicated that at least some blacks should vote. Because of this, many historians believe he might have adapted his Ten Percent Plan had he not been assassinated. It was obvious, however, that Lincoln and Congress disagreed on the basic nature of Reconstruction policy. When the war ended and Reconstruction began in earnest, the federal government had no solid plan for its direction.

Congress had adjourned by the end of the war and did not reconvene until December. With Lincoln's assassination in early April 1865, Vice President Andrew Johnson became president, controlling Reconstruction policy at its crucial beginning. Johnson, a poor white from Tennessee, harbored disdain for both the Southern planter aristocracy and blacks. In May 1865 he began issuing proclamations that were even more lenient to the South than Lincoln's.

Johnson pardoned all Southern whites except for Confederate leaders and persons whose wealth exceeded $20,000. They would have to apply personally for Johnson's pardon. Johnson appointed provisional governors and required that, in order to rejoin the Union, the states need only abolish slavery and repudiate both secession and the Confederate war debt. After the rebellious states met these requirements, they were considered "reconstructed." In addition, Johnson ordered that abandoned plantations be returned to their former owners. Although representatives from the Freedmen's Bureau initially refused to follow Johnson's directive, he ultimately sent federal troops to force the return of these lands.

Southern states, encouraged by Johnson's leniency, began to return the old elites to power. In addition, Southern state governments issued Black Codes, laws that aimed to limit black mobility and economic options, and virtually to reinstate the plantation system. Under the Black Codes, interracial marriages were banned and blacks could be forced to sign yearly labor contracts. They could also be declared vagrants for not having a certain (typically unreasonable) amount of money on their person and be sentenced to labor on a white-owned plantation. In addition, these laws limited the types of occupations and property blacks could hold. Other laws sought forcibly to apprentice black children. As a result, freedpeople existed somewhere between freedom and slavery.

Congress had observed these events during its adjournment and, upon returning to WASHINGTON, D.C., in December 1865, sought to alter Johnson's policies. When the newly elected Southern representatives arrived, and Northern congressmen discovered that many of them were former Confederate cabinet members, congressmen, and generals who had won congressional seats in the state governments restored under Johnson, Congress refused to seat them. Many congressional Republicans, especially Radical Republicans such as Thaddeus Stevens in the House of Representatives and Charles Sumner in the Senate, believed that the Johnson state governments should be dissolved and Reconstruction begun again, this time based on equality under law and universal male suffrage. Moderate members of the party, however, attempted to work with Johnson and convince him to modify his policies.

In early 1866 Congress sought to advance Reconstruction by passage of the Freedmen's Bureau Act and the Civil Rights Act. The Freedmen's Bureau Act extended the agency's life for another year. The Civil Rights Act defined people born in the United States as national citizens and stated explicitly what rights they were entitled to regardless of race. Johnson vetoed both bills, insisting that they violated states' rights. Congress quickly overrode Johnson's vetoes. Shortly thereafter, Congress approved the FOURTEENTH AMENDMENT, which was ratified in 1868. Designed to protect the rights of freedpeople and to restrict the political power of former Confederates, the Fourteenth Amendment defined U.S. citizenship much like the Civil Rights Act did and prohibited states from abridging the "privileges or immunities" of citizens without due process. Rather than prohibit states from restricting suffrage, it encouraged Southern states to allow black suffrage by reducing representation in states that disfranchised any male citizens.

Johnson's Reconstruction program became the decisive issue in the 1866 congressional elections. Although Johnson had toured the North to win support for candidates sympathetic to his program, his efforts were mostly unsuccessful. His rhetoric was more influential in the South: all of the former confederate states, except Tennessee, rejected the Fourteenth Amendment, which Johnson had publicly disavowed. By 1867 moderate and radical Republicans in Congress, tired of Johnson's obstruction to their more ambitious Reconstruction plan, began to take advantage of the president's waning power to forge an era of Congressional Reconstruction.

Congressional Reconstruction

After a series of compromises, Congress decided upon a Reconstruction plan that was far broader in range than Johnson's. Between March 1867 and March 1868 Congress passed the Reconstruction Acts, which divided the ten unreconstructed states (except Tennessee, which had already ratified the Fourteenth Amendment) into five military districts. Each district was headed by a commander whose responsibilities included overseeing the writing of new constitutions that provided for enfranchisement of all adult males.

Only after ratifying the new state constitution and the Fourteenth Amendment would a state be considered reconstructed and readmitted to the Union. In addition, Congress passed several laws to restrict Johnson's power to undermine congressional policy. In response, Johnson removed military officers who were enforcing the Reconstruction Act and fired his secretary of war. Shortly thereafter, Congress began impeachment proceedings against Johnson, ultimately coming within one vote of conviction.

In 1869 Congress passed the FIFTEENTH AMENDMENT, which broadened the Fourteenth Amendment's protection of black voting rights, stating that no citizen could be denied the vote on the basis of race, color, or "previous condition of servitude." It was ratified in 1870. In addition, Congress passed the Civil Rights Act of 1875, which barred discrimination by hotels, theaters, and railroads. The act, however, was rarely enforced.

Supreme Court and Reconstruction

The Supreme Court, which had been largely silent during the war years, became active during Reconstruction, helping the retreat from Reconstruction by overturning many Congressional measures. In *Bradwell v. Illinois* (1873), the Court ruled against a female attorney who claimed that in prohibiting her from practicing law because of her gender, Illinois had violated the "privileges and immunities" clause of the Fourteenth Amendment.

The following day, the Court further narrowed the Fourteenth Amendment's scope in the *Slaughterhouse* cases (1873), in which the Court rejected the argument that the Fourteenth Amendment had transformed citizenship by making it the federal government's responsibility. In *United States v. Cruikshank* (1876), the Court ruled that the duty to protect citizens' rights rested with the states. In *United States v. Reese* (1876), the Court ruled that the Fifteenth Amendment did not guarantee citizens the right to vote but rather listed the grounds on which denying the vote was impermissible. Southern states now had a clear path toward the disfranchisement of black voters.

Freedpeople during Reconstruction

For former slaves, their first decision was often whether to stay on the plantation or to move. In general, the choice depended on the disposition of the former master: if a master had been mean or violent, few of his former slaves were likely to remain; if the master had been fair, however, former slaves did often stay. Southern whites exaggerated the number of blacks who refused to work after emancipation as a supporting argument for black inferiority, but these numbers were in fact low. Many freedwomen, however, refused to work in the fields any longer after emancipation, choosing instead to remain at home with their children.

To some freedpeople, emancipation meant the freedom to move about, either because it had been prohibited or because they wished to search for family members who had been sold away during slavery. The Reconstruction era produced many touching stories of ex-slaves who traveled thousands of miles, with very little information to go on, to reunite with family members. Others, sadly, found no success in their searches.

Blacks, denied literacy during slavery, also sought education, often paying for it themselves. By 1877 more than 600,000 African Americans had enrolled in elementary schools through-

Hiram Rhoades Revels (1822–1901) was the son of former slaves. He became a Methodist minister, an educator, and the first African American in the United States Senate. *CORBIS/Nik Wheeler*

out the South. The Freedmen's Bureau founded more than 4,000 schools, including HOWARD UNIVERSITY in Washington, D.C., and many benevolent organizations, black and white, offered education. The American Missionary Association founded seven colleges, including FISK UNIVERSITY in Nashville, Tennessee, and Atlanta University in Georgia.

Freedpeople established other black institutions, especially churches, that profoundly affected African American history. As slaves, blacks had been forced to worship in their masters' churches. After emancipation, freedpeople founded their own churches or moved to black denominations, which served as social and political centers in the black community. Ministers often became community leaders, a practice that continues to this day.

Freedpeople also knew that land meant independence and that they were entitled to some of the lands of their former owners. Early in the war, as the United States Navy approached South Carolina, Confederates abandoned their lands on the Sea Islands, off the South Carolina coast. Freedpeople immediately lobbied for ownership of the land, insisting that the land was rightfully theirs after generations of forced servitude. Instead, the U.S. government implemented the PORT ROYAL EXPERIMENT, in which freedpeople labored in the abandoned sea islands as wageworkers. Eventually, General William T. Sherman issued Special Field Order No. 15, which gave the land to the freedpeople. President Johnson, however, rescinded the order, and the land reverted to its original owners. One of Reconstruction's great failings is that the U.S. government did not effectively redistribute land after the Civil War.

Most freedpeople were unable to buy land and instead rented it for farming from former slave owners. Freedmen's Bureau agents, many of whom wanted to change the Southern economy by introducing Northern concepts such as wage labor, needed to retain enough of the old system to ensure stability. To do this efficiently, Freedmen's Bureau agents developed work contracts, which, in the cash-poor South, promised farm laborers a certain wage in exchange for crops. Although intended to mediate disputes, bureau agents often sided with the former masters. The Freedmen's Bureau grew less active after 1866, leaving tenants and planters to find their own way. Thus contracts between former slaves and masters were not enforced, and freedpeople often had to depend on the goodwill of their former owners.

Freedpeople also took advantage of the franchise, voting almost unanimously for Republican candidates in the 1866 Congressional elections. Freedpeople also joined governments. Largely because of strong black turnout and because Congress banned many former Confederates from politics, the Republican Party won control of many Southern constitutional conventions. Of the 1,000 Republican delegates to constitutional conventions throughout the South, 265 were black.

Participation in government among blacks was greatest in state and local governments, where many attained high rank. FRANCIS CARDOZO was a member of South Carolina's constitutional convention and later served as state secretary of the treasury and as South Carolina's secretary of state. In Louisiana, P. B. S. PINCHBACK became the first black governor in U.S. history. He also served as lieutenant governor, and he was elected to both the U.S. Senate and the U.S. House of Representatives. BLANCHE K. BRUCE was a U.S. senator from Mississippi, as was HIRAM REVELS. In all, sixteen blacks served in the U.S. Congress during Reconstruction.

Although whites who sought to disfranchise blacks justified their actions by claiming that they had been subjected to incompetent "Negro rule," blacks were the majority in only two state conventions, and only in South Carolina's lower house were black representatives a majority. In many ways, the biracial coalitions of which most Republican governments were composed made progressive changes, such as creating state-funded public schools and a fairer tax system, outlawing discrimination in public transportation, and ending the death penalty.

Opposition to Reconstruction

As Reconstruction was implemented, a struggle began in the South over the new social order. On one side were the freedpeople and their allies, who wanted to participate in free society. On the other side were white elites and their followers, who wanted to restore the old order. Many whites—even those who had not owned slaves before the Civil War—found imagining a society in which blacks had the same rights as they did difficult.

Reconstruction inspired deep resentment among Southern whites. Former Confederates were bitter about losing the war and facing their new prospects. They believed that white Republicans were race traitors and objected to the high taxes that Republicans imposed to pay for Reconstruction. Many believed that Reconstruction politics and the politicians who practiced them were corrupt. Although Southerners did not have a defined course, to restore white rule meant white unity. In states with white majorities, convincing white Democrats to vote Democratic was enough to eliminate Republican rule, and by 1871 Democrats had taken back Tennessee, North Carolina, Virginia, and Georgia.

In other states, however, where Republican rule depended on interracial coalitions, white Democrats were determined to convince some people not to vote, often through the violence and intimidation of such terrorist organizations as the Ku Klux Klan, which was founded in 1869. Often led by the most prominent whites in a community, Klan members concealed themselves in white robes and hoods and usually acted at night, beating, LYNCHING, burning, or threatening African Americans and whites who supported the African American cause.

Problems existed between the elite planters, who were almost unanimously Democrats, and the Republicans, who were from three main groups: freedpeople, CARPETBAGGERS (as Northern Republicans were called, supposedly because they had come South with all their possessions in carpetbags), and scalawags (white Southerners who supported Reconstruction). Wherever possible, white Southerners reasserted themselves and their control; forcing blacks to stop voting was their primary tool to regain control of the South. In addition, whites still exercised a great deal of economic control over blacks, who usually had to work for whites. During this period, many blacks were told explicitly, "If you vote, don't come back to work."

Another method of increasing the dependence of blacks on whites was through SHARECROPPING, in which a farmer provided a tenant land and materials in exchange for a share of the crop. Although sharecropping began as a way to maximize land under cultivation and extend credit in a credit-poor region, it relegated many freedpeople and poor whites to a state of virtual peonage. Sometimes the conditions in which peonage and sharecropping put blacks were even worse materially than the conditions of slavery.

Reconstruction Ends

The country had been in an economic depression since around 1873, and white Northern attention turned from the plight of black people in the South to the national economy. State by state, Southern Democrats began to take control of local governments, working to reinstate the conditions of the antebellum South. Southern white supremacists believed, correctly, that Northern whites would no longer enforce Reconstruction policy. They began to subjugate blacks again, reinstating the Black Codes. Many Southern states began to pass segregation, or JIM CROW, laws.

For many, the Compromise of 1877 marks the end of Reconstruction. In the presidential election of 1876, Republican Rutherford B. Hayes and Democrat Samuel J. Tilden were virtually deadlocked. Tilden won the popular vote, but Republicans had control of South Carolina, Florida, and Louisiana, thus giving them control of the electoral college. Because each party in those three states had competing electors, however, Congress needed to decide the election. Hayes, the incumbent, appointed an electoral commission, which, with one more Republican than Democrat, declared him the winner.

The Democrats and the Republicans had made a deal, however, in which the Democrats conceded the White House in exchange for home rule in the remaining three states. In a meeting that, ironically, took place in the black-owned Wormly House Hotel, the Republicans agreed. The remaining military presence in those states departed and Republican rule crumbled: the Democrats had won back the South. Although it would take until the 1890s for them to finish the job, the white supremacists were well on their way to what Southerners referred to as REDEMPTION.

Historians have presented differing interpretations regarding the legacy of Reconstruction. Many historians now argue that Reconstruction fundamentally changed how the United States defines citizenship, as well as the way in which U.S. citizens perceive the power and role of the federal government. The Bill of Rights, for instance, was created to prevent the federal government from infringing on the rights of the people. The Thirteenth, Fourteenth, and Fifteenth amendments, however, placed the federal government in the role of protector of citizens' rights. This new concept of federal power and responsibility provided a framework for the CIVIL RIGHTS MOVEMENT, which, a century later, finally realized what Reconstruction had begun.

See also Black Codes in the United States; Congress, African Americans in; Democratic Party; Electoral Commission of 1877; Emancipation Proclamation and the Thirteenth Amendment; Free Blacks in the United States; Slavery in the United States.

Bibliography

Du Bois, W. E. B. *Black Reconstruction in America.* Russell & Russell, 1935. Reprint, Atheneum, 1992.

Foner, Eric. *Freedom's Lawmakers: A Directory of Black Officeholders during Reconstruction.* Rev. ed. Louisiana State University Press, 1996.

Foner, Eric. *Reconstruction: America's Unfinished Revolution, 1863–1877.* Harper & Row, 1988.

Foner, Eric. *A Short History of Reconstruction.* Harper & Row, 1990.

Jaynes, Gerald D. *Branches Without Roots: Genesis of the Black Working Class in the American South, 1862–1882.* Oxford University Press, 1986.

Litwack, Leon F. *Been in the Storm So Long: The Aftermath of Slavery.* Knopf, 1979.

Olsen, Otto H. *Reconstruction and Redemption in the South.* Louisiana State University Press, 1980.

Rable, George C. *But There Was No Peace: The Role of Violence in the Politics of Reconstruction.* University of Georgia Press, 1984.

Robert Fay

Redding, Jay Saunders

1906–1988

American writer, social critic, and educator.

Jay Saunders Redding grew up in a middle-class family in Wilmington, Delaware. He received his Ph.B. in 1928 and his M.A. in 1932 from Brown University. Redding taught English at a number of colleges and universities, including MOREHOUSE COLLEGE (1928–1931), Louisville Municipal College (1934–1936), and Southern University in Louisiana (1936–1938), where he was department chair.

In 1939, Redding published his first book, *To Make a Poet Black,* in which he trained a critical eye on AFRICAN AMERICAN LITERATURE and produced a unique study. As a result of this scholarship he received a fellowship from the Rockefeller Foundation to study the life of blacks in the South. The product of his study was the semiautobiographical book *No Day of Triumph* (1942). After publishing this book, Redding gained a reputation as a scholar of and spokesperson for both the accomplishments and tribulations of African Americans. In addition to this landmark work, he wrote several other studies including, *They Came in Chains: Americans from Africa* (1950) and *The Negro* (1967).

Redding returned to teaching in 1943, taking a professorship at the Hampton Institute, where he remained until 1966. He also taught at George Washington University (1968–1970) and Cornell University (1970–1975). Besides his scholarly work, Redding wrote for many national publications, including the *Atlantic Monthly* and the *Saturday Review.* He received many awards, including two Guggenheim fellowships and a Ford Foundation fellowship, and numerous honorary degrees.

Bibliography

Gates, Henry Louis, Jr., ed. *Bearing Witness: Selections from African-American Autobiography in the Twentieth Century.* Pantheon Books, 1991.

Redding, Otis

1941–1967

African American singer and songwriter who played a key role in the rise of soul music during the 1960s, but who attained his greatest success only after his premature death.

Otis Redding's life is the stuff of pop-music tragedy. He was born in Dawson, Georgia. From an early age, he clearly had musical talent, first as a drummer, then as a singer. But his family was poor, and he had to endure a series of odd jobs and struggle to make ends meet before he got his big break in 1963, an opportunity to record for MEMPHIS, TENNESSEE–based STAX RECORDS. His career unfolded in a steep upward arc, culminating with a triumphant performance at the 1967 Monterrey Pop Festival. Then—in an instant—it was over. Redding died in December of that year when his chartered plane crashed near Madison, Wisconsin. Since his death, Redding has been hailed as perhaps the quintessential male soul singer. But fame proved far more elusive during his lifetime.

Redding was born to a poor Georgia family and learned to play drums in school. On Sundays he played behind the various gospel groups that performed on local radio station WIBB. In 1957 he dropped out of high school in order to support his family, taking a variety of menial jobs and occasional gigs as a musician. He began to concentrate on his singing and entered a number of local amateur contests. Redding's early singing style was in the tradition of such rock-and-roll shouters as LITTLE RICHARD. In 1961 he made his recording debut, on a small Macon, Georgia, label.

But his big break did not come until two years later, when he was working in the band of guitarist Johnny Jenkins—and serving as the band's chauffeur. During a recording session at Stax Records he had the chance to record a featured vocal, the ballad "These Arms of Mine," which became a RHYTHM AND BLUES (R&B) hit and earned Redding a Stax recording contract. Redding's vocals matured from his earlier shouting style to one that conveyed the emotion behind his lyrics by means of an expressive, hoarse singing voice that was grounded in gospel sonorities.

To black listeners, Redding was one of the definitive examples of the Memphis Soul sound. His live performances were legendary for their intensity and emotional fervor. During 1965 and 1966 Redding scored several R&B hits—including "Mr. Pitiful," "I've Been Loving You Too Long," a version of the Rolling Stones' hit "(I Can't Get No) Satisfaction," and his now-famous rendition of "Try a Little Tenderness"—but none "crossed over" to the white popular-music charts. According to Norm N. Nite's *Rock On Almanac* (1989), Redding only appeared on the American pop charts once in his lifetime—in October 1966, with his now little-remembered recording "Fa-Fa-Fa-Fa-Fa (Sad Song)."

In 1967, however, Redding's incandescent appearance at the Monterrey Pop Festival put him on a trajectory for pop-music stardom. His musical promise is evident in many of his compositions—including "Respect," which became a much bigger hit in the hands of ARETHA FRANKLIN, and "(Sittin' on) The Dock of the Bay," which he recorded just three days before his death at twenty-six. Four members of the Bar-Kays, Redding's back-up band, also died in the crash. With the posthumous release of "(Sittin' on) The Dock of the Bay," Redding charted his first number-one pop single.

See also Gospel Music; Music, African American; Soul Music.

Redemption

Term used by the planter class of Southern whites to describe their campaign to duplicate antebellum social and political conditions in the South following the Civil War and Reconstruction.

After the AMERICAN CIVIL WAR ended in 1865, the United States struggled to define the role that blacks would play in society, especially in the South. During the later stages of RECONSTRUCTION, Northern Republicans in the Congress of the United States sought to secure the citizenship rights for newly emancipated blacks by passing the FOURTEENTH AMENDMENT and the FIFTEENTH AMENDMENT to the U.S. Constitution, the Reconstruction Acts of 1867 and 1868, and the Civil Rights Act of 1875. These measures threatened the nature of Southern society, and some whites in the region undertook a campaign to preserve their way of life. This campaign became known as Redemption. Southern whites, led by those in the planter class, attempted to "redeem" the South by depriving blacks of their political and economic rights through violence, intimidation, and discriminatory laws.

By 1877 many people in the nation believed that Northern Republicans had lost interest in ensuring the rights of blacks in the South. This belief was confirmed by the Compromise of 1877, in which the Republican administration agreed to withdraw federal troops from three Southern states—South Carolina, Florida, and Louisiana—in exchange for those states' electoral votes in the contested 1876 presidential election. The removal of these troops meant that Democrats, or Southern conservatives, would soon oust Republican state governments. The region would be left completely in the control of whites, undermining black gains.

Following the resumption of Democratic rule, Southern legislatures began passing Black Codes—laws that restricted the freedoms and economic options of blacks and sought to reinstate the plantation system. Under the Black Codes, interracial marriages were banned and blacks could be forced to sign yearly labor contracts. They could also be declared vagrants for not having a certain (usually unreasonable) amount of money on their person and sentenced to labor on a white-owned plantation. In addition, these laws limited the types of occupations and property blacks could hold. Black Codes forced black workers out of higher-paying skilled trade and relegated them to low-paying, unskilled positions. Many blacks were kept economically dependent on whites through SHARECROPPING.

White governments in Southern states also imposed racial segregation. Through centuries of slavery, separation of the races had been customary. Beginning with Tennessee in 1875, white governments passed laws that made segregation official, further limiting the freedoms of blacks. By 1890 other Southern states had passed similar laws. Schools, hospitals, restaurants, waiting rooms, and public transportation became segregated. For blacks, violating segregation laws, also known as JIM CROW laws, or even seeking to vote brought punitive retribution through the courts or mob violence and intimidation. LYNCHING became one of the most terrifying ways whites controlled blacks in the South. The illegal practice reached its peak between 1889 and 1899, when an average of 187 lynchings occurred each year, 80 percent of them in the South.

Another favored tool for subordinating blacks was disfranchisement. Southern whites recognized that blacks were certain to vote against conservative Democrats, and throughout the 1870s and 1880s many whites used violence and intimidation to discourage black electoral participation. In the 1890s the Populist Party sought, with black support, to challenge the Southern planter elite, further alarming whites. Beginning with Mississippi in 1890, Southern states amended their constitutions to exclude most blacks and many poor whites from voting, although the laws contained loopholes that allowed well-connected individuals to vote. A side effect of disfranchisement was the exclusion of blacks from full participation in the legal system. Jury pools were selected based on voter registration records and were therefore effectively open only to whites. As a result, blacks faced a hostile justice system in which the only part they played consistently was that of defendant. Because of obstacles such as the poll tax, literacy, and property requirements, black voting fell by 62 percent, and white voting by 37 percent. By the turn of the century, the South had become a one-party region.

The Supreme Court of the United States, which had been largely silent during the Civil War, found its voice during Reconstruction. In a series of decisions over the course of two decades, the Court demonstrated its sympathy for Southern white supremacists. *United States v. Cruishank* (1876) weakened the Fourteenth Amendment, and the *Civil Rights Cases* of 1883 voided the Civil Rights Act of 1875. The final blow to black hopes for equality came in 1896 with the Court's ruling in PLESSY V. FERGUSON, in which the SEPARATE BUT EQUAL DOCTRINE that upheld segregation was articulated. Blacks would not win the right to participate fully in Southern society until the 1960s, with the gains made during the CIVIL RIGHTS MOVEMENT.

See also Black Codes in the United States; Segregation in United States.

Bibliography
Foner, Eric. *Reconstruction: America's Unfinished Revolution, 1863–1877.* Harper & Row, 1988.
Woodward, C. Vann. *Origins of the New South, 1877–1913.* Louisiana State University Press, 1951.

Robert Fay

Reed, Ishmael
1938–

African American novelist, journalist, poet, satirist of Western culture and critic of Eurocentrism.

Born in Chattanooga, Tennessee, Ishmael Reed was raised and educated in Buffalo, New York, where he attended the University of Buffalo from 1956 to 1960. He began his studies in the night school division, but was persuaded to switch to the day school when an English teacher saw talent in his short satirical story "Something Pure."

After moving to the Lower East Side of New York in 1962, Reed began to write professionally. As a journalist he wrote for the *Empire Star Weekly* and later edited the weekly *Advance*. Reed was also involved in the creation of the *East Village Other*, a prototype of modern underground newspapers. In 1967 he published his first novel, *The Free-Lance Pallbearers*, a parody of RALPH ELLISON's bestseller *Invisible Man*. That same year he moved to California's San Francisco Bay area, whose cultural diversity has greatly influenced his writing. With his 1972 novel *Mumbo Jumbo* he presented a counter-mythology, dubbed "HooDooism," which challenges the myth that Western culture must be glorified at the expense of all other cultures. He used satire and parody to emphasize and advocate multiculturalism, or the importance of all cultures, rather than the hegemony of one. His other novels include *Reckless Eyeballing* (1986) and *Japanese by Spring* (1993).

Reed has also furthered the cause of multiculturalism through the Before Columbus Foundation, of which he is a founding member. The organization seeks to publish and promote literature by diverse writers outside the literary canon. Since 1976 the foundation has sponsored the American Book Awards.

Reed has also written poetry and essays. Among his recent nonfiction books is *Another Day at the Front: Dispatches from the Race War* (2003). He has edited critical works, including *From Totems to Hip-Hop* (2003), and has also written *Blues City: A Walk in Oakland* (2003), a personal account of Oakland, California. His writing and satire form a compelling critique of Eurocentrism, and in his multicultural beliefs, he encourages creativity and freedom, not confinement. He teaches in the Department of English at the University of California–Berkeley.

Bibliography
Boyer, Jay. *Ishmael Reed.* Boise State University, 1993.
Martin, Reginald. *Ishmael Reed and the New Black Aesthetic Critics.* Macmillan, 1988.

Reeves, Martha
See Martha and the Vandellas.

Reggae

Style of music that originated in the musically diverse and politically charged climate of Jamaica during the late 1960s.

Reggae combined the Zionistic beliefs of RASTAFARIANS with loping rhythms and rich melodic textures. Reggae's freshness appealed to both casual listeners and dedicated ideologues worldwide, generating a fan base that included Indonesians and Moroccans, Parisians and Brazilians, Irish schoolchildren and American teens. MICHAEL MANLEY, the former prime minister of JAMAICA, favored a political explanation of reggae's appeal: "Among other things, reggae is the spontaneous sound of a local revolutionary impulse. But revolution is a universal category. It is this, possibly, which sets reggae apart, even to the international ear."

Since the "discovery" of Jamaica by Christopher Columbus in 1494, a range of foreign influences—African, European, and American—have defined the culture and ethnic composition of the island. Reggae's forefathers spoke in numerous musical dialects, including Caribbean CALYPSO, English balladic form, and African rhythms. While Jamaica's history led to reggae's musical synthesis, it also provided reggae with its content; the new music often protested the colonialism and exploitation that characterized the last 500 years of the island's history.

Reggae grew most directly from the RHYTHM AND BLUES (R&B) music of the United States. In the 1950s, Jamaicans often listened to R&B songs that were broadcast from Miami, Florida. Local musicians soon covered songs by acts such as FATS DOMINO and Louis Jordan and wrote new tunes in a similar style. The fusion of R&B with Jamaican music, or *mento,* yielded a new form called SKA. Jamaican promoters such as Duke Reid and Clement Dodd recorded local acts, broadcasting ska over large sound systems at outdoor dance parties. Unlike R&B, which emphasized the first and third beats of a measure, ska hit the second and fourth, or "back" beats. In the early 1960s ska evolved into ROCK STEADY, a slower, more bass-driven form.

Amid a quickly changing Jamaican political climate, rock steady soon developed into reggae. During the 1950s and 1960s many Jamaicans migrated to the cities—especially KINGSTON, the capital—in search of better jobs. The demographic shift contributed to the proliferation of Rastafarianism. Inspired by the black nationalist philosophy of MARCUS GARVEY, the Rastafarian movement began in Jamaica early in the twentieth century as a way to cope with the oppressive conditions of colonial Jamaica. Rastafarians adopted the Bible as a sacred text but rejected Christ, couching their faith in the divinity of AFRICA, the homeland. A return to ETHIOPIA—whether spiritual or actual—became the highest goal, and Rastafarians considered Ethiopian king HAILE SELASSIE a messiah.

The apocalyptic vision of Rastafarians appealed to disillusioned immigrants, who had not found the bounty they expected in Kingston. Rural newcomers adopted the religion; the religion, in turn, adopted rock steady as a voice. Since many of the rural immigrants introduced African musical traditions that had survived in the countryside—and since rock steady, like ska, invited musical experimentation—reggae soon emerged. The importation of new recording technology from England, as well as increased overcrowding in the ghettoes of Kingston, also contributed to the synthesis of reggae. In 1968 a band called Toots and the Maytals recorded "Do the Reggay," giving name to the emerging style.

Reggae slowed rock steady as rock steady had slowed ska. The languorous new form included a more robust and driving bass sound that gave the drummer freedom to "play around the beat." In reggae, pianists and guitarists often emphasized beats in unison, producing sparser melodies but richer tones and rhythms. And in reggae the lyrical message had changed. Rock steady's romantic lyrics, which often derived from local proverbs, gave way to frontal descriptions of ghetto life and biting indictments of economic and political oppression. Reggae retained some of rock steady's romance, however. In addition to singing about street toughs or "rude boys," reggae artists described Rastafarian religious rapture and earthly despair in a manner analogous to American BLUES and spirituals.

Jamaican disc jockeys quickly adopted the new music, blasting local recordings over impressive sound systems at outdoor dances. By separating parts of the recorded mix, adding echo effects, and speaking, or *toasting,* along with the music, DJs assumed an active role in the development of reggae's sound. Toasting became a reggae convention that pointed toward the advent of RAP in the United States.

In the 1970s reggae garnered international attention, largely due to the stirring riffs, powerful lyrics, and riveting performances of BOB MARLEY and the Wailers. In the eyes of many, Marley became emblem of reggae and its Rastafarian influences. A 1972 film about the reggae lifestyle, *The Harder They Come,* added to reggae's popularity. *The Harder They Come* starred musician JIMMY CLIFF as an outlaw and pop star and featured a driving reggae soundtrack. After the film was released in the United States in 1973, it became a mainstay of bohemian movie theaters, adding vibrant visuals to the captivating aural picture that Bob Marley created through his music.

Like rock and roll and rap, reggae was soon appropriated by white musicians and adored by white fans. In the mid-1970s its influence appeared in the songs of Paul Simon and Eric Clapton; in the late 1970s and early 1980s it flavored new wave and punk. Rastafarianism's apocalyptic ideology attracted punk rockers, who adopted the rhythmic emphasis of ska-based music in many of their frenzied compositions.

Meanwhile, African American fans of reggae—many of whom came from the WEST INDIES themselves—took the music in other directions. DJs toasted faster and faster until the resulting DANCEHALL reggae seemed an analog of rap. Reggae fans soon globalized a provincial sound, and in the 1980s and 1990s, the international music of "world beat" followed the formula of reggae's wide success.

Since the genesis of reggae was grounded so thoroughly in the Rastafarian movement—and since its portrayal of alienation captivated white Americans during the presidency of Richard Nixon—the music's relevance lessened with the passing of time. While reggae continues to influence the vocabulary of other musical styles, its politico-religious aspect, as epitomized by Bob Marley, has become a historical—rather than living—form. Many fans, however, celebrate this history, and laud the staying power of reggae's message. Writers Steven Davis and Peter Simon proclaim: "Reggae is a philosophy that heals. The mini-trance produced by good roots reggae is Jamaican psychic hygiene for our apocalyptic era."

See also Music, Caribbean; World Music, World Beat, and the Re-Africanization of Latin American Popular Music.

Bibliography

Davis, Stephen, and Peter Simon, eds. *Reggae International.* Thames and Hudson, 1983.

Eric Bennett

Regla de Palo

African-derived Cuban religion that was originally practiced by Bantu-speaking slaves in Cuba's eastern Oriente province and that has gained popularity with many throughout the island.

Along with the YORUBA-derived religion of *Regla de Ocha* or *Lucumí* (more commonly known as SANTERÍA), Palo is the second most popular African-derived religious system in CUBA. Unlike Santería, which has been studied much more extensively, Palo does not feature orisha worship, an alter, or characteristic colors, clothing, or stylized dances dedicated to particular spirits. Both religions feature drumming, music, possession trance, and animal sacrifice as well as systems of divination. Palo divination is ordinarily conducted with an *npaca menzo*, an ox horn mounted with a mirror on its blunt end, used in conjunction with white plates and candle wax, or with *chamalongos,* seven pieces of dried coconut shell that are thrown on the ground. (Multiples of seven hold an important place in Palo numerology.)

The word *palo* means "sticks," or "branches of trees," which adherents (known as *paleros*) believe to hold magical powers. *Monte* means "forest," and trees are important elements believed to possess an animating spirit.

Bantu Origins

The TRANSATLANTIC SLAVE TRADE of the sixteenth through the nineteenth century brought primarily Yoruba- and Bantu-speaking Africans to Cuba. These major African groups, known respectively in Cuba as the Lucumí and the KONGO, have had an enormous influence on Cuban culture as a whole. The term "Bantu" does not refer to a single ethnic group, but to a rather extensive linguistic grouping of sub-Saharan African peoples. Bantu-speaking Africans who were enslaved and brought to Cuba are thought to have resided primarily in the areas of present-day ANGOLA, DEMOCRATIC REPUBLIC OF THE CONGO, and NAMIBIA. It is believed that before their enslavement, these particular Bantu-speaking Africans did not have contact with the Yorubas, who are a linguistically and culturally separate group of people living farther north in present-day NIGERIA. The Bantus brought to Cuba as slaves were predominantly from Angola and the ancient Kingdom of Kongo. At least twenty-seven different Bantu-speaking ethnic groups in Cuba have been identified, including the Quicongos, Quimbandeiros, and Nganguleros from the inner area of the Congo basin. During the initial period of Spanish colonization, most slaves brought to Cuba, particularly to eastern Cuba, were Bantu-speaking. The Yorubas generally came to Cuba later, in the early nineteenth century, after the fall of the city-state Kingdom of Oyo had left them vulnerable to slave traders.

Nzambi and the *Muertos*

Cuban paleros believe that the power of Nzambi, a creator god, resides in all natural elements of the world (such as rocks, trees, and people) and within the spirits of the ancestors, the *nfumbi* and the *npungo,* who served Nzambi during their earthly lives. The nfumbi are the spirits of recent generations of deceased ancestors, who, as a result of their more recent lives, are believed to be in closer proximity to their human descendants. The npungo are ancestors of long ago who are believed to be unified now with the primordial forces that birthed them: namely, the forces of nature—Nzambi himself.

The spirits of Palo are more closely identified with forces of nature, as opposed to the ORISHAS of Santería, who for the most part were at one time archetypal human beings, and thus have comparatively more stable personalities and characteristics that can be directed. In contrast, the spirits of Palo are perceived to be more chaotic and relatively difficult to control, although a talented Palo priest is able to corral them. During Palo rituals, which include polyrhythmic drumming, music, and dances, adherents can become possessed by natural forces and by the *muertos* (spirits of dead ancestors). Such possession is not considered to be worship of these elements but rather worship of Nzambi, the creator who animates everything and mediates all relationships.

Nganga

The goal of Palo is to control events by corralling the forces of nature. This is accomplished by concentrating the powers of Nzambi within the magical center of the religion's rituals, the *nganga.* The nganga is a clay pot or iron cauldron often placed in the home of the palero. It contains many things: earth taken from sites of social and natural significance, such as a courthouse, a graveyard, or a volcano; objects of nature, such as sticks and stones; animal and human bones, the latter often acquired from deceased paleros; and, in the center, a *matari,* or stone. Sometimes a crucifix is included, and such ngangas are termed "Christian." Since Nzambi is believed to animate all elements of the natural order, these objects must be present in the nganga in order for Nzambi to reside there. It is common for Palo ceremonies to begin with a greeting to the nganga, which is considered central to religious ceremonies. The nganga is a Cuban innovation necessitated by the conditions of slavery, which did not allow enslaved paleros sufficient mobility: in Africa, religious practitioners simply visited specific trees or stones believed to be manifestations of Nzambi. It is believed that the nganga must be "fed" with the blood of live animals, which are ritually sacrificed over the nganga by the *tata nganga*, a priest of Palo.

Initiation

Initiation is necessitated not by enthusiasm or desire on the part of the *ngayu* (a potential Palo initiate), but rather by the need to solve a particular problem in the ngayu's life. During an initiation process, the *padrino* (godfather) diagnoses the ngayu through divination and brings the ngayu before the nganga, where promises are made. The ceremony of *rayamiento en palo* is then performed, in which the ngayu may be marked with three small vertical incisions on the tongue, and over each breast or shoulder. At the conclusion of this initiation ceremony, during which the ngayu is said to be "born of the nganga," the tata nganga gives the new palero his own nganga and reveals to him the secrets of Palo, which are well guarded. The new palero must observe certain rules during a period of apprenticeship. When it is determined that the new palero has kept his promise and grown in the religion, he is considered a full member.

Paleros have a different relationship to their spirits than do the adherents of Santería, who must appeal to the sometimes-fickle orishas, submit to their discretion, and await their appearance and assistance, which may or may not be tendered. By contrast, it is the paleros who are masters of the nganga, which is sometimes referred to as the palero's "dog" or "slave." For this reason, it is often said in Cuba that if you don't mind waiting for results, consult with the Roman Catholic Church or with the orishas; if you want immediate results, go to a palero. During palo rituals, paleros command spirits to be manifest in the nganga and to perform requested deeds. A reciprocal bargaining then takes place between the palero and the nganga: if the spirits are to follow the palero's wishes, the palero must "feed" the spirits (through the nganga) according to the pact that has been made between them. Without such a pact, it is believed, the spirit will not act to change events as the palero requests.

The Palo religious community is not as central to the religion as is the "family" of Santería adherents. Although Palo has an extensive set of *reglas,* or rules, the religion is considered to be more flexible regarding the needs of its adherents.

See also African Ethnic Groups in Latin America and the Caribbean; Bantu: Dispersion and Settlement; Oyo, Early Kingdom of; Religions, African, in Latin America and the Caribbean.

Jalane Schmidt

Reid, Ira De A.
1901–1968

American sociologist who contributed to an understanding of race relations, labor, and immigration in America.

As a student, Ira De A. Reid earned degrees from three institutions: a B.A. from MOREHOUSE COLLEGE (1922), an M.A. at the University of Pittsburgh (1925), and a Ph.D. in sociology from Columbia University (1929).

In his role as a sociologist, Reid contributed to an understanding of race relations, adult education, southern SHARECROPPING, and immigration. Among his six books are *Negro Membership in American Labor Unions* (1930), *Adult Education among Negroes* (1936), *Sharecroppers All* (coauthored with Arthur Raper, 1941), and *The Negro Immigrant,* posthumously published in 1969. He lectured and advised the U.S. government and such social service agencies as the American Friends Service Committee on education, human resources, youth services, and social security.

In his academic appointments as a professor of sociology, Reid was a forerunner in the desegregation of the faculties in Northern higher education by scholars from historically black colleges in the South. At Atlanta University, Reid served as professor of sociology (1934–1946) and department chair (1944–1946). Working under his mentor, W. E. B. DU BOIS, Reid was managing editor (1940–1944) and, later, editor of *Phylon,* the scholarly journal on race and culture published by African American scholars. He also produced adult-education radio programs for working-class listeners in ATLANTA. Following a visiting professorship sponsored by the American Friends Service Committee at Haverford College (1946–1947), Reid returned to Haverford as professor and chair of the sociology department (1948–1966), becoming the college's first African American professor.

During the McCarthy era, Reid was erroneously labeled a Communist by a Pennsylvania politician in 1949, leading to a seizure of his passport by the U.S. State Department. Reid joined the Society of Friends (QUAKERS) in 1950. In honor of his scholarship, teaching, and contributions to peace and justice in the U.S. and abroad, Reid received honorary doctorates from Haverford and Morehouse. He died of cancer on August 15, 1968.

See also Colleges and Universities, Historically Black, in the United States.

Bibliography
Reid, Ira de Augustine. *The Negro Immigrant: His Background, Characteristics, and Social Adjustment, 1899–1937.* Columbia University Press, 1939.

Harold Weaver

Reid, V. S.
1913–1987

Jamaican novelist, short story writer, and journalist, known for his use of Jamaican history and dialect in his fiction.

Victor Stafford Reid (often called V. S. or Vic) is one of the pioneering figures in the Anglo-Caribbean literary tradition. Reid was born in Kingston, Jamaica. His father was in the shipping business, and Reid was educated by private tutors and at Kingston Technical High School. He worked as a farm overseer, an advertising executive, and a newspaper and magazine reporter and editor all before beginning his career as a writer. Reid worked as a journalist throughout much of his writing career, and was widely respected as editor of the newspaper *Daily Gleaner,* the political-cultural journal *Public Opinion,* and the newsmagazine *Spotlight.* But he is still best remembered for his historically based fiction, particularly his influential first novel, *New Day* (1949).

New Day is the story of Johnny Campbell, the oldest member of a Jamaican family that closely resembles the Manleys, prominent Jamaican politicians. *New Day* is often praised for being the first West Indian novel to attempt to re-create an authentic West Indian dialect, which has since become a major feature of Caribbean literature. But it is also significant for its use of Caribbean history. As Johnny thinks back over events in his long life, the novel becomes a first-person retelling of Jamaican history, from the 1865 Morant Bay rebellion to a new constitution in 1944. As it explores Jamaican history and culture, the novel celebrates Jamaicans' struggles for independence, and *New Day* is recognized as the first nationalistic Jamaican novel.

Reid's second novel, *The Leopard* (1958), was another historical reconstruction—this time set in Kenya during the Mau Mau rebellion, and portraying the negative consequences of colonialism for one multiracial family. In his later novels, Reid returned to Jamaican history for his subject: *The Jamaicans* (1976), about a pre-maroon-guerrilla group, and *Nanny-Town* (1983), about a famous maroon leader. Reid also wrote a biography of prime minister Norman Manley, *The Horses of Morning,* and a history of Jamaican architecture. In addition to these works, he wrote three historical novels for children: *Sixty-Five* (1960), again about the Morant Bay rebellion; *The Young Warriors* (1967), again about the Maroons; and *Peter of Mount Ephraim* (1971), about the 1831 Samuel Sharpe slave uprising.

Reid once claimed that his work "is necessarily for the next generation." This belief explains his commitment to creating a Jamaican history and national legacy in all of his writings. While Reid was eventually overshadowed by other Caribbean writers, his accomplishments were well recognized during his lifetime. In 1959, he became the first Jamaican to win a Guggenheim Fellowship. He was also awarded the Institute of Jamaica's Silver and Gold Musgrave Medals (1955, 1978), the Order of Jamaica (1980), and the Norman Manley Award for Excellence in Literature (1981). At the time of his death, Reid had just published the first section of a projected three-volume "bio-poem," *The Kingston Chronicles.* Reid's legacy stands as a significant contribution to West Indian literature in general and to Jamaican literature in particular.

See also Jamaica; Literature, English-Language, in the Caribbean; Manley, Michael; Maroonage in the Americas; Slave Rebellions in Latin America and the Caribbean.

Lisa Clayton Robinson

Religions, African

Belief systems created by Africans and people of African descent; some exist only in Africa; others are practiced around the world.

For information on

African religions and religious practices: *See* African Religions: An Interpretation; Bwiti; Golden Stool, The; Rites of Passage and Transition.

Practice of African religions outside of Africa: *See* Magic, Sorcery, and Witchcraft in Africa; Magic, Sorcery, and Witchcraft in the Americas; Religions, African and Afro-Caribbean, in the United States; Religions, African, in Brazil; Religions, African, in Latin America and the Caribbean; Slave Religion.

Specific religious groups: *See* Candomblé; Ifa; Orishas; Rastafarians; Santería; Shango; Vodou; Umbanda; Venezuelan Religion, African Elements in.

Religions, African, in Brazil

Religions that initially arose and developed during the more than 350 years of official and unofficial intensive importation of what were classified as "Sudanese" and "Bantu" African slaves to Brazil.

Practiced by millions of Brazilians, African religions in Brazil are all spirit possession or mediumistic religions. They are found in the capital cities and ports along Brazil's extensive Atlantic coast as well as throughout its vast interior backcountry, towns, and villages.

Brazil's Sudanese slaves came from north of the equator, primarily from West Africa. The Bantu came from south of the equator, primarily from Angola, the Congo, and to a lesser degree, Mozambique. Early evidence of their practices in Brazil includes references by the seventeenth-century Bahian poet Gregório de Mattos to *calundus* (a generic term for African ritual dances) in Salvador, the current capital of the state of Bahia. There are also descriptions in eighteenth-century Inquisition records discovered by anthropologist Luiz Mott of a religious sect of African slaves called *Acotundá,* which flourished in a rural mining district in the state of Minas Gerais in the 1740s.

Today Brazil boasts an enormous variety of African-derived or African-influenced religions, with literally millions of followers (Candomblé and Umbanda). In each, adepts believe in a pantheon of gods or spirits that are summoned in ritual contexts, very often by drums and chanting, and that possess those who are mediums. The possessing gods or spirits then dance or communicate verbally to the community through the entranced mediums, teaching and resolving individual and community problems. The leader of the religious group may also invoke the gods or spirits for private divination consultations. Here, an adept's or client's spiritual development or problems of health, family, finances, and social relations are diagnosed. This can lead either to initiation and religious involvement or to the performance of healing and sorcery rites. Some of the religions also have complex devotional practices informed by rich African mythologies.

All these religions, having descended from the African slaves in Brazil, reflect varying degrees of faithfulness to the original African models. Some are remarkably faithful. But all are also constituted of varying degrees of SYNCRETISM (a mixing, merging, or integrating of religious elements). It is the syncretism of diverse African but also Native Amerindian tribal sources, as well as popular Roman Catholic beliefs and practices—especially concerning the saints, as in what has been called the "cult of the saints" (*see*, for example, NOSSA SENHORA DO ROSÁRIO).

In addition, in the late nineteenth century another influence on some African-Brazilian religions emerged in the two major Brazilian metropolises, RIO DE JANEIRO and São Paulo. This was a European form of Spiritualism, a mediumistic religion originating in America, which revolved around séances and communication with the dead. In Brazil it was called *Espiritísmo*

(Spiritualism) or *Kardecismo* (Kardec-ism) after its French reformer, Allan Kardec (the alias of Hippolyte Léon Rivail). Kardec integrated Spiritualism and spirit-communicated doctrines with Eastern ideas of reincarnation, Swedenborgian philosophy, Christian moral principles, and social-evolutionary dogma. *Kardecismo* was quickly adopted by Brazil's wealthy and intellectual elite. By the 1920s and 1930s, however, *Kardecismo* had also impacted and was impacted by the pariah class African-Brazilian sects of *Macumba* in Rio and São Paulo. The result was a new, class-synthesizing or -mediating continuum of religious forms in these cities, which are referred to under the one umbrella term *Umbanda*.

Syncretic Character and Geography

Viewed broadly in terms of their historical perspective and geographic distribution, we may distinguish three complex syncretic groupings of the African-Brazilian religions. The first consists of the most African or African-influenced religions, what I will call here the "African religions of Brazil," though they are also shaped by non-African influences. These developed in the coastal port cities. In contrast, the second grouping consists of the most Amerindian or Amerindian-influenced and Indio-Catholic of the mediumistic religions, the so-called "Caboclo religions," though they also manifest African influences to varying degrees. These religions originated in the rural backcountry and villages. The third complex refers to the syncretic wedding of the two, what I call the "African-Caboclo religions." These are centered in urban areas that include both the coastal cities and the larger rural towns. The African-Caboclo religions bridge the ideological and ritual characters of the coastal and rural backcountry traditions, and are the fastest growing of the African-Brazilian religions. All the religions of these three broad groupings have evolved and maintained their areas of prevalence for centuries, but have also spread to other regions. The emergence and spread of the Umbandas is another important new development. But let us turn first to each of the three groupings.

Religions from Africa

The African religions of Brazil developed in the major urban centers of the African slave trade along the Brazilian coast (e.g., São Luís in the state of Maranhão, Recife in Pernambuco, Salvador in Bahia, Rio in the state of Rio de Janeiro, and Porto Alegre in Rio Grande do Sul). These cities maintained the largest concentrations of African slaves. Originally there were more than thirty different tribal sources for the African religions of Brazil, and as many distinct religions corresponding to each source. Though elements of many of these persist today, the most readily distinguishable influences are those of the Sudanese-speaking FON and YORUBA of old DAHOMEY (present-day BENIN) and NIGERIA, respectively, and the Bantu-speaking Bakongo, Ambundo, and other ethnic groups from Angola, the REPUBLIC OF THE CONGO (formerly ZAIRE), and Mozambique. In Salvador, Bahia, alone there are more than a thousand practicing centers of the Candomblé religion, which derives from these African tribal and intertribal sources, and more than 2,000 when the syncretic variants of the Candomblés are taken into account. The Candomblés are distinguished according to *nação* (nation, in the sense of ethnic group), such as the *Nagô*, *Kétu*, and *Ijexá Candomblés* (from the Yoruba); *Jêjê Candomblé* (from the Fon); and the *Angola* and *Congo Candomblés* (from BaKongo, Ambundo, and other Bantu groups of Angola and the Republic of the Congo). The liturgical languages spoken and sung in the Candomblés are also called *Nagô* (a Brazilianized Yoruba dialect); *Jêjê* (a Brazilianized dialect of EWE); and *Angola* (a mixture of Bantu-derived dialects and Portuguese). Their gods are referred to as ORISHAS (pronounced *oh-ree-shahs*) in *Nagô*; *voduns* (pronounced *vo-dunes*) in *Jêjê*; and *inquices* (or *een-kee-sees*) in *Angola*. In addition, there is a secret, Yoruba-derived, all-male society devoted to the ancestors called the *Culto aos Eguns* (Cultus to the Ancestors). Its traditional centers are located on the island of Itaparica, near Salvador.

Other African religions in Brazil include the *Tambor de Mina* (Drums of Mina) in the far north (the city of São Luís, Maranhão). This religion takes two forms. The first, a *Mina-Jêjê* form, as in the *Casa das Minas* (House of Minas), is notably of Fon derivation. The second, a *Mina-Nagô* form, as in the *Casa de Nagô* (House of Nagô), syncretizes Fon and Yoruba elements. Also of rich African tradition are the XANGÔ and *Xambá* of the northeast (the city of Recife, Pernambuco), which are of Yoruba derivation. The old *Cabula* (or *Batuque*) of Rio de Janeiro in the southeast was originally of Bantu origin but is now extinct. It was probably the source of the current *Macumba* sects in both Rio and São Paulo. Finally, *Pará* in the far south (the city of Porto Alegre, Rio Grande do Sul) is Yoruba-based, though there are strong Dahoman influences in a variant of *Pará* (which is also called *Batuque* by outsiders, a common name for African practices in Brazil).

These religions are all still remarkably very African, emphasizing African languages and deities, possession-trance dances, and divination procedures that in many cases are guided by a substantial corpus of African myths. The rituals include complex devotions to the gods and their fetish objects and intensive initiations and animal sacrifices, all accompanied by the intricacies of African drumming. However, again, within the group of African religions and across each group's internal variations, they have maintained their original African source traditions in these and other features to varying degrees. The Nagô Candomblé and the Culto aos Eguns of Bahia are considered the most African of the African religions of Brazil.

Caboclo Religions

In contrast, the Caboclo religions of the vast Brazilian hinterland are more predominantly influenced or inspired by Amerindian and Indio-Catholic elements. But it is important to note that in many areas their adherents are not only *mamelucos* (people with white and Indian ancestry), but also black, sometimes predominantly black, African descendants, or *cafu-*

sos (people of black and Indian descent). They are called Caboclo religions because practitioners believe in a pantheon of actual Amerindian spirits or spirits which are stereotypical images of Indians, both of which are called Caboclos. "Caboclo" also refers to the spirits of rural "natives," people born in the Brazilian *sertão* (backcountry), who, like the Indians, are intimately tied to the land, such as the *boiadeiros* (cattle drovers). In some groups, "Caboclo" is also applied to a host of other spirits, including rural African "masters" ("experts") of healing and sorcery. Many other features, such as the healing rites, trance experiences, and music, are also inspired by Amerindian traditions.

At the same time, vestiges of African mythology appear in their conceptualization of the "Caboclo" spirits and of the folk Catholic saints, which are also foundational to the pantheons of Caboclo religions. Moreover, African terms and principles are often found in the ritual practices of Caboclo religions, as we will see. But again the degree of these Amerindian, Indio-Catholic, and African influences varies across regions and particular religious traditions.

Scanning regionally from north to south, the strongest Amerindian influences in the Caboclo religions are found in *Pajelança,* a primarily healing cult of the northern states of Amazonas, Pará, Maranhão, and northern Piauí. Amerindian elements include, for instance, the extensive ritual use of tobacco smoke and hallucinogenic roots, both considered sacred and therapeutic; the use of gourd rattles (*maracás*) and feathers (of the *arara,* a macaw, from the parrot family) to summon familiar spirits, instead of drums; the religious experiences of "trance voyages" (akin to shamanic trance) in addition to spirit possession; and the typical Amerindian healing procedure, in which disease-carrying "objects," such as invisible darts, are sucked out of patients by the leader, or *pajé* (shaman). Finally, the pantheons include not only Caboclos of characteristically Amerindian spirits, but also Amerindian-derived animal and underwater spirits called *companheiros* (companions) or *encantados* (enchanted ones) and the folk Catholic saints.

African influence varies across Pajelança sects, which Mario Andrade distinguishes, broadly, as "Indian" and "Negro" Pajelanças. Pantheons of the latter, for instance, in the state of Maranhão, include simplified versions of the Dahoman Fon gods. But even in the Indian Pajelanças there is an African structure to the ritual possession dances, and many adepts may become mediums, as in African traditions, instead of just the shamanic leader alone.

As one moves south through the rural interior of Brazil, the Amerindian influence decreases and manifests in different ways or with different emphases. An example is the *Catimbó* religion, which is widely practiced in the northeastern states of Rio Grande do Norte, Paraiba, Pernambuco, Ceará, and Southern Piauí. Catimbó is composed of some of the Amerindian characteristics of the Pajelança but with a strong measure of European black and white magic. Thus, like Pajelança, Catimbó also emphasizes *curandeirismo* (healing), and leaders draw from a copious Amerindian herbal pharmacopeia. Also, tobacco and hallucinogenic roots such as the *jurema* (*Mimosa hostilis*) are used ritually, as are maracás and arara feathers to invoke spirits. But Catimbó is also dedicated to *feitiçaria* (sorcery), which derives from medieval European spells and rituals. Further, Catimbó practitioners believe in a different kind of pantheon than in Pajelança. For, in addition to Caboclos and saints, adherents believe in spirits called *mestres* (masters). These are the spirits of deceased Catimbó leaders who are well known for their knowledge of healing and sorcery. They include rural *mestiços* (people of indigenous and European descent) such as Mestre Carlos (Master Carlos), *Índios* (Indians) such as Mestre Itapuã (the name of the Tupi Indian sun god), and *africanos* (Africans) such as Pai Joaquim (Father Joaquim), a wise old African master. In many Catimbós there is also devotion to and possession by gods with Yoruba names such as Xangó and Ogum. These, too, are called *mestres,* and adepts refer to them and the spirits who are stereotypical images of Africans as the African line of the Catimbó. Hence, overall, Amerindian influence is smaller in the Catimbó than in the Pajelança, while European and other sources are stronger.

Passing by the state of Bahia, for a moment, we continue south through the *sertão,* or rural backlands, to the southeastern region of Minas Gerais, Espírito Santo, Rio de Janeiro state, and São Paulo state. Here we encounter the Caboclo religions of the least direct Amerindian influences and greatest African-inspired beliefs and practices. These are the *Canjerês, Cabulas,* and rural *Macumbas*. All appear to have derived from very early Bantu religious sects with Angolese and Congolese gods. But today, they are Caboclo religions dominated by Caboclo spirits and the saints, though their pantheons also include some of the previous Bantu or Bantu-inspired gods, and there is Bantu influence in their ritual vocabulary and drumming. The Caboclo spirits of these religions also now reflect exclusively stereotypical images of the Indian and rural cowboy heroes, rather than actual Amerindian-derived spirits. One such Caboclo is a chief called by the name of a whole tribe, *Tupinambá*. And there are also spirits of deceased folkloric figures, including white leaders (Dom Pedro II, the last emperor of Brazil) as well as wise old Africans, such as the *tias africanas* (African aunts) and Catimbó's Pai Joaquim. Of course, vestiges of Amerindian practices, such as the use of tobacco smoke and the suction of disease-causing objects, are valued in their healing rites. But as in Catimbó, European magic informs other aspects, as it does their sorcery. And adding to the mix, practitioners of these Caboclo religions frequently invoke their own, demonized form of the Yoruba trickster god, Exú, to cause harm and mischief in the lives of others.

Finally, in the state of Bahia, which is sandwiched geographically between the Caboclo religions to the north (the Pajelanças and Catimbós) and to the south (the Canjerês, Cabulas, and rural Macumbas), are Bahia's own *cultos aos caboclos* (Caboclo cults), such as *Piji, Jarê,* and *Bembé*. Like the groups to the north, these religions were influenced by local Amerindian groups, particularly the Kiriri Indians in the case of Piji, and by the regional Cult of the Saints. From the Kiriri Indians, Piji inherited, for example, the ritual use of the hallucinogenic root *jurema* (*Mimosa hostilis*), and added the Kiriri *toré* thump dance to ceremonies. Also, as elsewhere in the sertão, devotees of Piji make frequent pilgrimages to local shrines of the saints and to charismatic miracle-healers in the region who are believed to be "living saints." Paradoxically, Piji leaders emulate both these virtuous living saints and the powerful sorcerers of their local myths in a fusion that attracts messianic followers.

Yet at the same time, Piji is the most African of the Caboclo religions and in that sense resembles the Caboclo sects to the south. Such features as Bantu drumming, African liturgical terms, particular details of animal sacrifices, and initiatory rites that reproduce the preliminary initiatory rites of the African religion of Candomblé characterize many Pijis. Moreover, in addition to the prominent Caboclo spirits, saints, mestres (masters), and encantados (enchanted nature spirits) of their pantheon, many groups worship serpent spirits. These recall the famous serpent deity *Dā* of the Fon-derived Jêjê Candomblés.

That there is a stronger African influence in the Piji than in the other Caboclo religions is not surprising, since both Sudanese Fon and Bantu slaves were sent to work in the mines of the Chapada Diamantina region of rural Bahia, where Piji and Jarê are prevalent. In fact, today, there are still several former *quilombo* communities in the region. The quilombos were hidden enclaves of fugitive African slaves. And, though Piji and Jarê are Caboclo religions with prominent Amerindian-inspired and Indio-Catholic features, they are nevertheless devoutly practiced in these *quilombos remanescentes* (remaining quilombos) and were uniquely influenced by them.

African-Caboclo Religions

This third grouping consists of religious forms that directly combine or integrate the beliefs and practices of the coastal African religions and the hinterland Caboclo religions. Some of these religions actually compartmentalize in parallel fashion the foundations of an African tradition in Brazil, on the one hand, and a rural Caboclo religion, on the other. In one moment they appear to be exemplars of the African tradition and in another moment or in a different ritual, of a Caboclo tradition. In such cases the gods of an African religion and its chants and drumming, its ritual devotional requisites, and possession experiences, for instance, are juxtaposed to a pantheon of Caboclo spirits, saints, and Caboclo-related devotions, healing practices, and other ritual attributes of a Caboclo religion. But still other African-Caboclo religions do not so compartmentalize, and rather integrate African and Caboclo beliefs and practices in unique ways. Often, some of each of these occurs in some of the religions.

For example, the *Candomblé de Caboclo* (Caboclo Candomblé) of Bahia's coastal cities and large rural towns strongly resembles, in part, the regional African religion of Candomblé, and in part the rural Bahian Caboclo religions, such as Piji, though each is simplified and reconciled to the whole. In the Amazonian city of Belém and nearby towns, the religion called *Batuque* both combines and integrates the Caboclo religion of rural Pajelança, such as its central healing beliefs and practices and pantheon of Caboclos and Encantados, with significant features of the regional African religion of Tambor de Mina. Mythologies from each are intertwined, for instance, and gods and spirits manifest as African-Caboclo composites.

These "in between" magico-religious forms, the African-Caboclo religions, are estimated to be the most numerous of the African-Brazilian religions and are rapidly spreading. As a general principle, they occur in urban areas, which include virtually all of the coastal area cities, and are increasingly developing in the large rural towns of their respective states. From north to south and indexed by region and the principal cities where they are prevalent, they include the Batuque, mentioned above, *Babassuê* (*Batuque-de-Santa Barbara*), and *Encanteria* of the northern coastal cities of Belém and São Luís, and inland, Teresinha, respectively; the *Jurema, Xangô de Caboclo*, and *Toré* cults of the northeastern coastal capitals of Fortaleza, Natal, and João Pessoa (for *jurema*), and Recife and Maceió (for both *Xangô de Caboclo* and *Toré*); the Candomblé de Caboclo in Salvador, discussed above; and the urban Macumba of Rio de Janeiro and São Paulo. The Umbandas of these same megametropolises constitute a special form of the African-Caboclo religions known as Umbanda. They are variants of the urban Macumbas, where the African, Caboclo, and folk Catholic elements of the Macumbas syncretize with a strong foundation of Kardecian Spiritualism. Finally, many Umbandas (like most of the Caboclo and African-Caboclo religions) include a negative side, dominated by evil spirits and black magic, which also takes the form of an independent cult called *Quimbanda*.

Dispersion of the African-Brazilian Religions

In all cases these various African-Brazilian religions have spread to regions outside their originating sites and areas of prevalence, often forming other local syncretic combinations. For instance, the Candomblés of Salvador, Bahia, hold tremendous prestige in southern Brazil in cities like Rio, São Paulo, and Porto Alegre. Their popular representation as more mystical and/or truly African encouraged many hundreds of Bahian practitioners of one or another variant of the Candomblés to take advantage of that fame by relocating to these other major metropolitan urban centers. There they founded new and successful *terreiros* (centers), syncretizing with the local religions to varying degrees. And this is true of the other African religions of the coastal cities, such as the Xangôs of Recife and the Tambor de Mina of São Luís, which with their variants have spread to other cities north, south, and inland of their original centers. Of the other religions, most notable is the spread of the Umbandas. Though concentrated in Rio and São Paulo, they have also fanned out to the towns in the rural interior and to the metropolitan urban centers of other regions.

In sum, these three loose categories of the African religions, Caboclo religions, and the African-Caboclo religions serve the purpose of a general description of the African-derived or African-influenced religions in Brazil. The African religions are best represented in the literature, but the Caboclo and African-Caboclo religions (with the exception of the Umbandas) have been given far less attention, as evidenced in Carlos Moura's periodically updated bibliographies on the African-Brazilian religions. For the student of religion, the study of these traditions is in one breath the study of cultural survival under extraordinarily adverse circumstances. And in another breath, it is the study of cultural change, adaptation, and compromise, resulting in the formation of truly Brazilian religions. The study of the tremendous variation not only between but also within each of them has important implications for our understanding of the origins and character of religion, and for our understanding of cultural change, human creativity, and religiosity.

See also African Ethnic Groups in Latin America and the Caribbean; Afro-Brazilian Culture; Bantu: Dispersion and Settlement; Maroonage in the Americas; Orishas; Transatlantic Slave Trade.

Patric V. Giesler

Religions, African, in Latin America and the Caribbean

Examination of how African spiritual roots and New World experiences shaped Vodou, Santería, and Umbanda.

The African-derived religions of Latin American and Caribbean slaves and their descendants are marked by a dual heritage. While deeply rooted in African spiritual traditions, these religions have also been indelibly shaped by the history of New World enslavement, exploitation, and racism. From SHANGO in Trinidad to Cumina in JAMAICA, from Kele in SAINT LUCIA to Batuque in BRAZIL, the story is similar: molded by and resonant with Old World African worldviews, these ritual systems also always express and reflect the wrenching experience of diaspora. This essay explores how three religions, Haitian VODOU, Cuban SANTERÍA, and Brazilian *Umbanda*, illustrate this duality.

Haitian Vodou

In the French colony of SAINT-DOMINGUE (present-day HAITI), where a large number of slaves were from the African kingdom of DAHOMEY, slavery destroyed traditional African priesthoods and secret societies. Still, the great Dahoman deities, known now as *lwa,* came to be worshiped in secret ceremonies administered by religious leaders (*houngans*) who regulated the descent of the lwa into mediums (*ounsis*). The bitter experience of enslavement led to the division of the lwas into *Rada* and *Petro* versions. The Rada version of the lwa is regarded as rooted in AFRICA and tends to be characterized by tranquility and generosity ("Rada" derives from Arada, a kingdom in Dahomey during Haiti's colonial period). The Petro version of the lwa, meanwhile, is rooted in the New World and is characterized by impatience and anger. ("Petro" derives from a certain Dom Pedro, who is supposed to have led a rebellion of runaway slaves in the eighteenth century.) Legba, for example, as a Rada spirit, is the guardian of destiny and preserves the West African notion that the place of each person is established at birth. This Legba is a positive force, representing fecundity and the continuity of generations. As a Petro spirit, in contrast, Legba reflects the deep antagonisms of slave society. He arranges unexpected accidents, works at night, and commits acts of sorcery. In a fit of vindictiveness he can unleash people-eating werewolves, who, like slave catchers, roam the countryside at night to steal people or their possessions.

The Petro versions of two other spirits are particularly important for practitioners of Vodou. Gede, while inheriting his name from Dahomey, is a distinctively New World phenomenon, serving the need of slaves and their descendants to find hope in the midst of oppression. Gede embodies the fact that within every episode of destruction there is the promise of a new beginning. Master of cemeteries and night, Gede is also master of the moon, and carefully watches over the rebirth of the dead. When he possesses a medium, his lifeless, petrified arms and feet recall the maiming and chaining of slavery. Yet far from being defeated by these occurrences, he expresses himself through humor and satire. He mocks pretension, parodies Roman Catholic priests, and sings about the secret foibles of his devotees. He personifies the power of humans to transcend adversity through comic self-awareness.

Another important lwa is Ogou. In Dahomey, Ogou was the god of iron and war. In Saint-Domingue, Ogou gave spiritual sustenance to runaway slave communities, as well as to the great HAITIAN REVOLUTION, which led to the overthrow of slavery and the eventual independence of Haiti from FRANCE. It is believed that the slaves' trust in the powers of Ogou were important to the slave Macandal, who led a major uprising in the 1750s. Legend also has it that BOUKMAN, one of the early leaders of the Haitian Revolution, was a houngan. When in 1791 he assembled his followers, he declared that Ogou had ordered vengeance and would assist the slaves in their task. To this day Ogou is associated in Vodou with these episodes. Boukman's assembly is reenacted annually in Vodou ceremonies, and Ogou sometimes takes on the persona of FRANÇOIS DOMINIQUE TOUSSAINT LOUVERTURE, one of the leaders of the Haitian Revolution. The revolutionary phrase *Vive la liberté* occurs regularly in Ogou's rites; in one, the lwa appears dressed as a guerrilla warrior and reenacts the victory over the French, played by devotees who come attired in eighteenth-century French military uniforms.

After the revolution, the ex-slaves of Haiti had the experience, virtually unique in the hemisphere, of avoiding the return to the plantation. Instead, large numbers of them became small landholders. Like their forebears in Africa, but in contrast to others in the diaspora who never became landowners, Haitians strengthened and renewed their spiritual bond with the land by developing an elaborate system of burying the dead. To this day death provides practitioners of Vodou the occasion to close the circle of history and make sense of diaspora by drawing upon the power of Africa to help fulfill and realize life in the New World. Vodou practitioners believe that upon death the soul migrates back to *Ginen* (Guinea, or Africa), imagined to be a watery depth below the surface of the earth. Going to Africa, the soul finally achieves true freedom and becomes able to return to Haiti. A year and a day after the person's death, a special Vodou ritual calls the spirit back, reclaiming the soul from the waters of Ginen, so that it might help nurture its New World descendants.

Cuban Santería

In contrast to Haitian Vodou, but like CANDOMBLÉ in Brazil and *Shango* in Trinidad, Cuban Santería is based on the YORUBA pantheon of deities, or ORISHAS. A large proportion of the 700,000 Africans brought to CUBA were Yorubas, including numerous priests and priestesses. As in Brazil and Trinidad, enslaved religious leaders established followings in Catholic religious brotherhoods, then moved out of them to create a religion that was both a continuation of traditional African practices and an adaptation to the new needs and experiences of the present. Santería is now practiced in the residences of priests or priestesses who act as godfathers or godmothers to families of mediums. These fictive kin groups, which may include as few as six, and as many as thirty or forty, people, are structured by seniority of initiation into mediumship. Mediums become possessed by one or more of the orishas.

The orishas of Santería are selective reinterpretations of the Yoruba pantheon. Among the Yoruba, Eleguá is an erotic, phallic god invoked in rituals of fertility. In Cuba, in the form of Eleguá, the god has lost these associations, for slaves had little incentive to encourage their own fertility. He has become more sinister, for he may now help to kill and poison enemies and masters. As the gatekeeper to the other gods, he has come to be associated in Cuba with Saint Peter, the Catholic saint who holds the keys to heaven. In Cuba, too, as in Haiti, Ogun is associated with resistance; but unlike in Haiti, where resistance became revolution, the Cuban Ogun avoids overt rebellion. Ogun's traditional connection with warfare became transmuted in Cuba into the sentiments of passive resistance and a burning thirst for justice. His rituals include, symbolically, the chains of enslavement and torture, and the machetes and picks of slave labor. His Catholic counterpart became Saint John the Baptist, in part because this figure wished to bring about a revolution without being able fully to do so himself.

There are a number of Yoruba divinities that govern water, whether the ocean or rivers; these goddesses tend to have strongly sexual overtones and to be associated with the celebration of fertility, large families, and many descendants. In Cuba, too, there is Yemayá, the spirit of the ocean and salt water, and OSHÚN, the spirit of rivers and sweet water. Here, however, these figures are not about creating and celebrating large families. Yemayá exemplifies the sober virtues of motherhood—caretaking, wisdom, nurturance—and is associated with the Virgin Mary. Oshún has become a goddess of youthful beauty and coquetry. Hers is not a sexuality that aims to create large families but rather to remind devotees of the limits of vanity. She too is associated with one of the advocations of Mary.

Of special importance in Cuba is the spirit of Babalú-Ayé. In Africa this is a minor, secondary divinity, but in Cuba, where death and disease under slavery became rampant, this healing god became prominent. Not surprisingly, he became identified with Saint Lazarus, the Catholic saint who is the patron of skin diseases. Thus in the end, the pantheon of African deities that once existed to express and celebrate the intense joys and hopes of life have become in Santería expressions of the longing to overcome oppression and reminders of the limits of human power, desire, and bodies.

Brazilian Umbanda

Umbanda, fast becoming one of the most widely practiced religions in Brazil, emerged in the 1930s as a SYNCRETISM (or fusion) of Yoruba-based Candomblé religion, Catholicism, and European spiritism. It has been suggested that Umbanda reflects the special aptitude for syncretism of the descendants of Bantu and Angolan slaves. Whether or not this is the case, it is clear that in Umbanda, in contrast to the Yoruba-derived religion of Candomblé, the orishas have been relegated to a distant spiritual plane. In their place, three main types of spirits descend to earth and possess mediums. These are the *caboclos,* spirits of people who once walked upon Brazilian ground and breathed Brazilian air, and now, in death, perform works of charity through their intermediaries, the mediums who belong to cult centers.

Caboclos are the spirits of deceased indigenous people. They are admired for their skill in hunting and warfare and their knowledge of the forest. Above all, they are respected as proud

With head shaved and wearing body paint, a man participates in a Candomblé ritual. *Barnabas Bosshart/CORBIS*

and courageous for having resisted slavery. When they possess mediums, their demeanor is haughty, even arrogant. They perform magical healing and offer advice and assistance for the unemployed and people battling the bureaucracy. *Pretos velhos* ("old blacks") are old Brazilian men and women who died while still enslaved. They are characterized not by the fearsome might of the orishas, or even the pride of the caboclos; they are, rather, humble, loving, gentle, and patient. They walk slowly and hunchbacked, sit down in order to consult with their petitioners, speak in soft, stereotyped slave Portuguese, and puff on pipes. Their specialty is offering warm advice to people faced with domestic conflict. The third main category of Umbanda spirits are the *exús*. These are spirits of people, above all, slaves and marginalized blacks, who died unresigned to their lot. They were petty thieves and tricksters who now, in death, make trouble on command and set obstacles in the paths of their petitioners' enemies. They are inherently untrustworthy, often charging handsomely for their knavery. They refuse to conform to the ideal of the subordinate black. As Roger Bastide, a French expert on Afro-Brazilian religion, put it, "this 'bad Negro' is nothing other than the image of the runaway slave."

This pantheon has tended to be interpreted by scholars as embodying racist stereotypes of blacks: the good black is the docile, submissive one; the bad black is the rebellious one; the dignified caboclo Indian is the one who preferred death to enslavement. These may well be the meanings attributed to the caboclo and preto velho spirits by the religion's lighter-skinned practitioners. There is evidence, however, that black practitioners interpret the pantheon differently. In particular, some black mediums have developed relationships with the spirit of ZUMBI, the great seventeenth-century leader of runaway slaves. For them, Zumbi is both an EXÚ and a preto velho. He appears in their cult centers and teaches the pretos velhos the "true" history of slavery in Brazil: how, for instance, the emancipation of slaves did not occur through the good will of the white ruling class, as is taught in Brazilian grade schools, but rather through the struggles and resistance of slaves themselves. These mediums say they know that the pretos velhos suffered under slavery and never felt resigned to it. "They never accepted it," said one medium, "but what could they do? They just nodded and said 'Yes, sir.' But in their hearts they did not accept it." Zumbi's mentorship of the pretos velhos, and his own dual identity as exú and preto velho, reveal that for black adherents of Umbanda, the pretos velhos always retain, just below the surface, the potential to rebel.

The examples of Vodou, Santería, and Umbanda show that the religious traditions of Africa were not transferred to the New World in static form. Rather, slaves and their descendants in Latin America and the Caribbean selected from and reshaped the meanings of the old beliefs to make sense of, and to cope with, the devastation and exploitation of New World slavery and racism. The spirit of the Old World helped them, in the end, to discover, develop bonds with, and, to a certain extent, be healed by the spirits of the New.

See also Catholic Church in Latin America and the Caribbean; Diaspora and Displacement; Religions, African, in Brazil; Slave Rebellions in Latin America and the Caribbean; Slave Religions; Slavery in Latin America and the Caribbean.

John Burdick

Religions, African and Afro-Caribbean, in the United States

Practice and influence of African religions in America.

The Africans bound for the plantations, mines, and workshops of the New World embarked primarily from the coast of western AFRICA between present-day SENEGAL and ANGOLA, and in smaller numbers from what is now MOZAMBIQUE. Among the ten million or so who reached the Western Hemisphere, some began their odyssey as Christians and many more as Muslims. Many of the latter were, unlike their masters, literate. In the United States and BRAZIL, for example, literate Muslim slaves left us with scores of documents in Arabic, while some North American captives even transcribed AFRICAN AMERICAN VERNACULAR ENGLISH in Arabic script. The majority of involuntary migrants, however, had worshiped local gods and ancestors, and more than a few practiced hybrids of local religion and Islam or CHRISTIANITY. These migrants and their American cultural descendants contributed to a complex legacy: various self-described "African" religions came to be practiced by more than a single race, and the practices of many Christians of all colors appear to reflect African influence as well.

The first Africans to reach England's mainland North American colonies arrived at Jamestown in 1619. From then until the end of the slave trade to North America in 1808, as few as 74,000 kidnapped Africans and as many as 400,000 entered this region. One in seven captives embarked from the Senegambian coast, an important supplier for North America during the first century of the trade. Ultimately, a little over a third of arrivals in North America embarked from the Bantu-speaking interior of the Congo-Angola coast in west Central Africa. A bit less than a third, from groups such as the IGBO and IBIBIO, embarked from the West African BIGHT OF BENIN. Though captives taken from the Senegambian coast predominated during the first century of the trade, they constituted only about one out of seven Africans imported before the end of the trade.

There is little documentation of the North American slaves' religious lives during the first century of slavery. What is well known is the enduring white resistance to missionizing them. Some white colonists feared that slaves' conversion would require their owners to emancipate them, that the Africans were too brutish to benefit from Christianity, or that conversion would inspire insubordination or revolt. Moreover, the scarcity of missionaries affected not only blacks but whites as well. Therefore, Albert J. Raboteau, the leading expert on slave religion, concludes, "During the first 120 years of black slavery in British North America, Christianity made little headway in the slave population."

The first large-scale conversion of slaves coincided with the Great Awakening, an unprecedented phenomenon in which a series of religious revivals swept the colonies beginning in the 1740s. From a twentieth-century viewpoint, what is most striking about the eighteenth-century revivals and churches is their interracial character. The "emotionalism" and trancelike behaviors that we now tend to associate specifically with black churches not only were highly developed during this period but were the common property of black and white worshipers. Though the revivals and churches of the Second Great Awakening in the late 1820s and 1830s were less racially integrated, they featured an increasing number of black preachers exhorting and evangelizing white audiences.

Observers of the revivals reported ecstatic shouting, laughing, falling down, jerking, barking and dancing, faith healing, and appeals to dreams and visions, which numerous scholars have attributed to the African cultural influences conveyed by the slaves. Of course, it must be borne in mind that not all African religion is ecstatic. West and Central African religions range from textually oriented Islam and IFA divination to highly dramatic possession religions, few of which involve the sort of verbal and corporal abandon found in Western revivalism. On the other hand, there are significant precedents for these ecstatic behaviors in the early Christian Church. English QUAKERS and other spiritualists held dramatic rituals in resistance to religious institutionalism in the mid-seventeenth century. Indeed, the followers of George Fox (1624–1691), who founded the Society of Friends, were called Quakers precisely because they trembled when under the "leading" of the Holy Spirit. At a later date, English Methodism also came to be characterized by similarly enthusiastic manifestations of the Holy Spirit, which may be one reason for African Americans' strong attraction to this denomination in late-eighteenth- and early-nineteenth-century America. African Americans were also strongly attracted to the BAPTISTS, who like the Methodists at least temporarily condemned slavery, readily ordained black ministers, and allowed the autonomy of black congregations.

Autonomy was an important issue for black Christians, for interracial fellowship in churches was regularly predicated upon the subordination of black rights and interests. Though they remained few until the demise of slavery, separate black churches had emerged by the 1760s. For example, the First African Baptist Church of Savannah, Georgia, was founded in 1788 and boasted 2,417 members, free and slave, by 1830. A former slave and licensed Methodist preacher named RICHARD ALLEN founded Philadelphia's Bethel Church in 1794. He had previously been a member of the predominantly white Saint George Methodist Episcopal Church, but one day he and his companions were dragged from their knees while praying in a part of the church where their race was not allowed. In 1816 Allen founded a distinct denomination called the AFRICAN METHODIST EPISCOPAL CHURCH. The Union Church of Africans in Wilmington, Delaware, was formed in 1815, and the AFRICAN METHODIST EPISCOPAL ZION CHURCH was founded in New York in 1821, having seceded from a mixed-race church in which blacks could take the sacrament only after all the whites had been served. The self-description of these sizable churches as "African" concerned neither their geographical location nor a modern conception of their cultural roots. Indeed, Bishop Daniel Alexander Payne of the African Methodist Church tried to stamp out the famous "ring shout" on the grounds that it was "heathenish." This Southern form of worshipful singing and dancing rhythmically in a counterclockwise circle is often invoked as one of the most telling contributions of African culture to African American Christianity.

Africanness

The Africanness of these denominations, from the perspective of their leadership, lay mainly in their distinctive social status and in their unique responsibility to other Africans and African Americans. The highly literate and scripturally educated leadership of these churches fought for the abolition of slavery and sent missions both to the South and to Africa. Their concern was not to immortalize the so-called heathen past but to redeem their brethren from oppression and ignorance. Despite its distance from the major sources of the slave trade, the biblical "Ethiopia" became for African American Christians a source of hope, a beacon of black dignity and historical centrality within the Christian tradition. This politically Pan-Africanist missionary vision remained alive in the twentieth century and reached its crescendo in the BACK TO AFRICA MOVEMENT of MARCUS GARVEY in the first and second decades of the twentieth century. Garvey led the largest mass organization in African American history, the UNIVERSAL NEGRO IMPROVEMENT ASSOCIATION, which embraced no single denomination but declared the responsibility of African American Christians to missionize and build the African homeland. Garvey's redemptive PAN-AFRICANISM finds prominent successors not only in secular African American fashion and politics but in religious movements like the NATION OF ISLAM.

For many African American Christians and Muslims, identification with Africa implies no correlation between their religions and nonscriptural African ones. Indeed, until recently most African Americans consciously sought to downplay their cultural and hereditary connections to Africa. However, early in the century historian CARTER G. WOODSON, sociologist W. E. B. DU BOIS, and anthropologist Melville J. Herskovits articulated dignified, scholarly visions of Africa, emphasizing its relevance to African American culture and progress. Herskovits, in particular, tried to show that African American culture and, to a lesser extent, Euro-American culture, were replete with "Africanisms," or cultural conventions that derive from Africa. Among these he included the importance of worshipers' being "filled with the Holy Spirit," sacred dance, and musical performance in the church. Similarly classified were certain magical practices of the South, called hoodoo, vodou, and conjure. Herskovits shows that parallel features of African and European cultures are the ones most likely to occasion the continuation of African practices. For example, the prominence of baptism in Christianity allowed Africans to continue practices associated with the widespread worship of river spirits in western Africa. As noted above, subsequent writers have taken the ring shout, most pronounced among the GULLAH of the Georgia Sea Coast Islands, as further evidence of the African connection.

Religion and Voluntary Immigration

Since around 1860, tens of thousands of Portuguese Creole-speaking Cape Verdeans have migrated voluntarily to the United States. Since 1965 they have been joined by tens of thousands of mainland African immigrants from NIGERIA, GHANA, ETHIOPIA, and so forth. A disproportionate number of these are probably Christian: Cape Verdean Catholics, Ethiopian Copts, Nigerian and Ghanaian Anglicans, Baptists, Methodists, and Pentecostals. European-based denominations in Africa underwent a range of adaptations in order to appeal to local populations. They translated their hymnals and the Bible into local languages, incorporated local forms of celebratory dance, and incorporated the sort of age- and gender-based clubs that are common in African societies. They often resisted African beliefs in polygamy, in the cure of ailments attributed to witchcraft, and, above all, in indigenous leadership. African objections resulted in the foundation of numerous so-called African independent churches, which have become much more popular than the mission churches in most African countries. Members of these churches are also well represented among migrants to the United States.

African-Inspired Religions

One reason that many scholars have found it difficult to believe that black North Americans' religious life is devoid of African inspiration is that Africa so obviously contributed to a range of Caribbean and South American religions. These include CANDOMBLÉ and UMBANDA in Brazil, SANTERÍA in CUBA, SHANGO in Trinidad, Obeah and Myalism in JAMAICA, and VODOU in HAITI. What distinguishes religions in these countries from religions in the United States is the high ratio of black to white inhabitants in the Caribbean and South America. Moreover, the religions that are most easily identified with West African sources are practiced in countries that received sizable numbers of enslaved Africans until far later than did the United States. Those countries also have Roman Catholic majorities. The late importation of captives allowed the continual reinforcement of African forms of knowledge in the corresponding African American community, and the prevalence of Roman Catholicism reinforced parallels between the Catholic saints and the multiple gods of, especially, the YORUBA (ORISHAS).

Since the late 1950s, emigration from Caribbean countries has not only established a whole new range of African-inspired religions in the United States but has reshaped the Pan-Africanist impulse among native-born black Americans. An increasing number of African Americans have joined or borrowed practices from Afro-Caribbean traditions in order to realize their own Africanness.

Santería. Of all the New World societies, Cuba received captives from the greatest mix of African origins. The slaves embarked in significant numbers from all parts of the west Central African coast (i.e., between modern EQUATORIAL GUINEA and Angola), from the southeastern coast (Mozambique), and from nearly every part of the West African coast (between Senegambia and CAMEROON). Only the area of modern Ghana failed to supply a major contingent. Between 500,000 and 700,000 African captives reached Cuba over the course of the slave trade, a vast proportion of them arriving in the nineteenth century. These figures for tiny Cuba dwarf reliable estimates of the number of captives entering the whole territory of the modern United States. The high mortality rates of slaves in the Cuban SUGAR industry required the constant importation of replacements.

The size, diversity, and continual replenishment of Cuba's African population allowed a rich array of African-inspired religions to flourish there, even beyond the end of the slave trade. To this day the Abakuá secret society features a dancing masquerade similar to ones found among the EFIK of eastern Nigeria; the Palo Mayombe initiation society identifies its liturgical language and ritual practices with Central African sources; and the worshipers of the orishas identify their gods by easily recognizable Yoruba names. Outsiders call Cuban orisha worship Santería, on the grounds that worshipers tend to regard the Yoruba gods and the Roman Catholic saints as either equivalent or closely linked beings.

Some of these orisha worshipers are diviners called *babalawos*. They cast palm nuts or metal chains to determine the spiritual causes of supplicants' personal problems. They then provide solutions ranging from cleansing fumigations and herb baths to investiture with bead necklaces marking the supplicant's protection by particular gods to full initiation, which prepares the supplicant to be possessed, or better, "mounted," by one of the gods. A person so initiated is called a *santero* or *santera*. He or she makes a commitment to offer regular sacrifices to his or her protector gods, who are represented by stones, shells, and other emblems inside lidded calabashes, bowls, jars, cauldrons, or soup tureens. In exchange, he or she receives the gods' special protection and the right to cast the shells in divinatory readings. Among the gods is Shangó, who rules fire and/or lightning; he is identified with Saint Barbara, whose pagan father killed her for converting to Christianity. In turn, God killed St. Barbara's father with a bolt of lightning. OGUN is the lord of iron and technology; he is often identified, or "syncretized," with Saint George. Yemayá, goddess of the sea, of salt water, and of motherhood, is syncretized with Our Lady of Regla. The trickster god of roads, crossroads, and entrances, Eleguá, is often syncretized with the Holy Child of Atocha. Each orisha carries his or her own food prohibitions and characteristic myths, colors, numbers, animal sacrifices, foods, dances, and drum rhythms.

Every year, the anniversary of a santero or santera's initiation occasions not only sacrifices to his or her gods but visits from friends and godchildren, that is, the people whom he or she has initiated. Diviners may also determine that a santero or santera is obligated to hold annual festivities, called *tam-*

bores or *bembes,* for any god. These are usually held on or close to the day that the Roman Catholic Church consecrates to the corresponding saint.

Vodou in Haiti. Before the revolution that began in 1791, the island of SAINT-DOMINGUE, of which Haiti now occupies the western third, was the most valuable possession in the French colonial empire. Though smaller than Cuba, this island had already received considerably more African captives than Cuba or the United States would receive throughout their participation in the trade. Nearly half of these captives had arrived from west Central Africa and nearly a quarter were from the Bight of Benin, home to such groups as the Yoruba, the FON, and the EWE. Under the ruthless exploitation of 30,000 white settlers, 500,000 African slaves produced the sugar that filled EUROPE'S sugar bowls and FRANCE'S state treasury. The HAITIAN REVOLUTION cut off the influx of African captives, but, fearing Haiti's potential influence on black slaves elsewhere, the European powers and the white-dominated American republics imposed a long-term economic and cultural isolation on the country. Even the Roman Catholic Church withdrew its priests from Haiti until 1860. This left the country's rural citizenry to develop one of the most elaborate African-inspired religions in the Americas.

The isolation of the rural peasantry has created much diversity within Vodou, or Haitian religion. In rural peasant compounds called *lakous,* worshipers take care of a combination of communal ancestors, spirits called *pwen,* which serve for individual advancement, and multipurpose magical objects called *wanga* and *gad*. This religious practice also involves memberships in secret societies and the worship of gods called *lwa* or *misté*. Each lwa is identified with one of several so-called nations, some of which are identifiably African in name, including Nago (Yoruba), Igbo (Ibo), Wangol (Angola), and Siniga (Senegal). The two most inclusive "nations" are called Rada and Petwo. The word *Rada* makes an apparent reference to the town of Allada, or Ardra, the legendary origin of Fon-speaking ancient DAHOMEY's ruling dynasty. In the eighteenth century, Europeans used the town's name to refer to all Dahoman subjects. The origin of *Petwo,* though, is unclear.

Among the Rada spirits are Damballah, Agwe, Aizan, Sogbo, and Legba (who have obvious Dahoman counterparts), Changó and Ogou (who have Yoruba counterparts), Simbi (with its KONGO counterpart), and the prominent lines, or families of associated spirits led by Ezili, Gede, Azaka, and Sirèn (who have no obvious African counterparts). Each god has its own characteristic domain, symbols, and foods. For example, the snake god Damballah is associated with age, purity, the color white, and the ritual consumption of whole eggs. Ogou is the red-clad god of war. His main symbol is the sword. Gede is the Carnivaleque spirit of love and death, while Azaka is the deceivingly simple peasant farmer. Some of the lwa are descendants of Rada gods with distinctive surnames, like Damballah Flangbo, to identify their "hot," or vengeful and fast-acting, character; others have their own separate names, such as Agirualinsu. The lwa are worshiped semipublicly in sanctuaries called *hunfo,* which the gods are said to enter through a center post called the *poto mitan*. Around the post, offerings are made in the form of animal sacrifices and elaborate cornmeal drawings called *vèvè*.

Sudden, wild possession experiences or persistent misfortune may be interpreted as callings to initiation in Vodou. Initiation, or *Kanzo,* regularizes the link between god and devotee, thereby affording greater protection from persecution by sorcerors or offended gods. Initiation also generally prepares believers for properly controlled possession by the lwa. A series of further rites over the years confers higher degrees of knowledge and status within the religion, which are acknowledged in the elaborate dances of greeting between priests. Senior priests are called *hungan* (male) or *mambo* (female). As in Santería, drumming and dance are important in the calling and adoration of the gods in Vodou. On the other hand, divination in Vodou usually takes the form of European-style card reading, and the reading of the shells, common in Santería, has become uncommon in the Haitian religion. Most Haitians participate in Vodou as a family obligation. The protection of the family and the commemoration of its ancestors are often performed through Vodou rituals. Many others serve as professional or semiprofessional priests and healers for a largely non-kin clientele, particularly in PORT-AU-PRINCE or other large towns. There are also many Haitians, especially among the fast-growing population of Pentecostals, who adamantly refuse to participate in Vodou.

Jamaican Revivalism. Like mainland black North American Christianity, Jamaican Revivalism is much more likely to be described as "African" by outsiders than by insiders. The religion's Africanness is inferred from ethnographically observed parallels between Revivalist and West African practices. Some descriptions of Revivalism as "African," however, seem to reflect less about the speakers' information concerning Africa than about the contempt they feel for non-European cultures and nonelite classes generally.

The vast majority of Jamaicans' ancestors clearly came from Africa. Of the 750,000 or so African captives who entered Jamaica, over one-third embarked from the Bight of Biafra (including Igbo, Ibibio, IJAW, and Efik), and less than one-third came from the region of present-day Ghana (Ewe, ASANTE, FANTE, GA, DAGOMBA, etc.). Smaller proportions were from west Central Africa (Kongo, Pende, LUBA, etc.), the Bight of Benin (Yoruba, Fon, GOUN, etc.), and the coast of present-day SIERRA LEONE, LIBERIA, and CÔTE D'IVOIRE (MENDE, SHERBRO, VAI, BAULE, etc.).

Ever since the late eighteenth century, some of these Africans and their Jamaican descendants have been noted for their practice of obeah, a body of herbal and spiritual practices used to cure personal ailments and to harm one's enemies. Obeah men were believed capable of poisoning people and of dominating them by catching their shadows, or *duppies*. From the mid-nineteenth century onward, the British promulgated a series of acts outlawing obeah. Equally well known in the first half of the nineteenth century was an initiatory society called

Myal, devoted to protecting its members from obeah and other sources of harm. Initiation involved swallowing one herbal solution that would induce a deathlike state and another that would wake the initiate. Myalist meetings involved singing, dancing in a circle under one leader's direction, and, most importantly, filling with the Holy Spirit.

Though Jamaica was a British colony, the Church of England denied membership to Afro-Jamaicans until 1834. Afro-Jamaicans often found other religions more supportive of their interests. For example, the leaders of Myalism seem to have played a major role in slave revolts such as Tacky's Rebellion in 1760. Methodists too seemed to champion the cause of the slaves, leading many Myalmen later to become Methodists as well. An epoch-making event occurred in 1783, when the African American Baptist missionary George Lisle left Georgia for KINGSTON. The congregation he led grew into a sizable proportion of Jamaica's nineteenth-century Christians, who came to be called the Native Baptists. English missionary observers noted the centrality of dreams and visions in Native Baptist worship and attributed the religion's distinctiveness to the influence of Africa and of Myalism.

Inspired by religious developments in England, the Great Revival swept Jamaica from 1860–1862. It reshaped Myalism itself into two variants, Zion and Pukumina, which its detractors call Pocomania. Today Zion and Pukumina are both called Revivalism. In Revivalism, worship usually takes place in the yard of the leader's house. A flagpole identifies the ground as sacred and is intended to attract passing spirits. The Zionist variant deals primarily with the triune Christian God, archangels, angels, saints, apostles, and prophets. Zion believers condemn as evil the spirits on whom Pukumina followers focus their attention—fallen angels and the human dead. In Revivalism, generally, each spirit except God is believed to prefer specific foods, colors, and music. Spirits act as personal guides to the worshipers they choose. In exchange for the constant availability of the spirit's protection and advice, the worshiper agrees to feed the spirit regularly.

During certain meetings, members of the congregation, or "bands" (always in the collective plural), seek to be possessed by these supernatural powers. They induce possession through ring dances that resemble those described by observers of nineteenth-century Myalism. The leader coordinates the rhythmic dancing and breathing that lead to trance, to collective travel in the spirit world, and to speaking or singing songs in a nonlexical language. The songs' melodies are then interpreted as either propitious or ominous. Some bands also use marijuana and rum to induce trance. There is an elaborate hierarchy in any given bands, each level of which is responsible for a particular task during journeys through the spirit world. The leader is called the Captain, Shepherd, or Mother. There are also the Cutter, the Hunter, the Sawyer, the Planner, the Nurse, the River Maid, the Bellringer, and so forth. When, in their spirit travels, the bands must cross a river, the River Maid mimes the motions of a swimmer; when the bands enter a church, the Bellringer must mime the action and sound of ringing a bell. Those members with a spirit guide have the knowledge to carry out both beneficent and vengeful tasks through their access to the spirit world.

Jamaican Rastafarianism. The most famous Afro-Jamaican religion is undoubtedly Rastafarianism, which combines the inspirational (as opposed to scriptural) nature of Jamaican folk Christianity with the Pan-Africanist sentiments inspired by Marcus Garvey's Universal Negro Improvement Association and Ethiopianist readings of the Old Testament. Beginning in 1932, the founding figures of Rastafarianism proclaimed the divinity of the new Ethiopian emperor, HAILE SELASSIE, whose titles included Ras Tafari (Prince or Duke of the Tafari royal family) and Conquering Lion of the Tribe of Judah. The Rastafarian hairstyle, characterized by dreadlocks, therefore commemorates the lion's mane as well as the strength of Samson. Some RASTAFARIANS believe that African warriors wore a similar style. Followers interpret the Old Testament as the history of the black people and, under an inspiration they uniquely are believed to possess, as a prophetic but fallible key to understanding events in the contemporary world. Rastafarians believe that marijuana consumption, besides bringing divine inspiration, cures diseases and enhances one's strength. Garvey's dream of a return to Africa became their dream, and some have indeed resettled in Ethiopia, Ghana, and the DEMOCRATIC REPUBLIC OF THE CONGO.

Euro-African Continuum

The religions described here share a range of qualities, each to a greater or lesser extent. The practitioners of some identify strongly and consciously with Africa, while the practitioners of others do not. The strength of such identification may correspond to the degree of the religion's ethnographically identifiable similarity to indigenously African religions, as in the case of Santería, or it may not, as in the case of Ethiopianist Christianity in Jamaica and the United States. All of these religions posit a belief in God but emphasize, to a greater or lesser extent, the preeminence in earthly life of multiple spirit beings. Like many African religions, most of these African American (in the broad sense of the Americas) religions involve sacred dance and endorse its role in inducing immediate contact, which might loosely be called possession, between worshipers and divine beings. Many of these religions involve animal sacrifice, percussive music, and obligatory food offerings to the spirit, as well as the imagery of marriage to one's ruling spirits, which indeed have greater precedents in West African religions than in European Christianity. Yet almost all of them incorporate Christian hymns, prayers, scriptures, and/or icons. Africa has contributed much to the religious life and healing practices of both black and white Americans. But in the context of New World slavery and racism, "Africa" has often been used as a metaphor for low or rebellious social status. For many blacks in the New World, it has also long been a symbol of hope, dignity, and humanity.

See also Abakuás; Catholic Church in Latin America and the Caribbean; Christianity, African: An Overview; Christianity:

Independent and Charismatic Churches in Africa; Christianity: Missionaries in Africa; Early Rastafarian Leaders; Islam and African Americans; Protestant Church in Latin America and the Caribbean; Religions, African, in Latin America and the Caribbean; Transatlantic Slave Trade.

J. Matory

Religious Brotherhoods in Latin America

Secular groups centered around the adoration of particular Catholic saints such as Nossa Senhora do Rosário.

Black religious brotherhoods (*cofradía, cabildo* in Spanish America; *irmandade* in Brazil) were often organized along ethnic lines, and were one of the main institutions which preserved African culture in LATIN AMERICA and the Caribbean.

See also Catholic Church in Latin America and the Caribbean; Nossa Senhora do Rosário.

Remond, Charles Lenox

1810–1873

African American abolitionist who advocated integration and equality.

Charles Lenox Remond was born into a family of abolitionists and activists. His mother helped found the Salem Female Anti-Slavery Society and his father was a lifetime member of the AMERICAN ANTI-SLAVERY SOCIETY (AASS). Like himself, his younger sister, SARAH PARKER REMOND, was a respected abolitionist speaker.

Charles Remond was involved with the AASS nearly from its beginning. Philosophically, he concurred with WILLIAM LLOYD GARRISON's doctrines of nonresistance and moral persuasion. In 1838 the Massachusetts Anti-Slavery Society named him its first full-time black lecturer. In a tour of the British Isles he pressed the cause of abolition, although this was not the sole focus of his advocacy. When the 1840 World's Anti-Slavery Convention, meeting in London, refused to seat women delegates, he spoke against the policy and left the meeting. After returning to the United States he traveled through the Midwest on a speaking tour with FREDERICK DOUGLASS.

Remond's sympathies moved away from nonresistance as federal laws and court rulings of the 1850s soured him on the possibility of ending slavery through moral persuasion. By the late 1850s he came to argue in defense of slave revolts and warned of a violent end to Southern slavery. Despite this turn toward more active resistance, Remond always firmly believed in integration. He sought to make racial justice, not simply emancipation, the cause of the AASS. Remond retired from public life in 1867 and during his last years worked as a clerk in the Boston Customs House.

See also Abolitionism in the United States; Slave Rebellions in the United States.

Remond, Sarah Parker

1826–1894

American abolitionist, rights activist, and physician.

The daughter of a free black immigrant and granddaughter of a black veteran of the AMERICAN REVOLUTION, Sarah Parker Remond was born into a family that would not tolerate the injustices of slavery and inequality. When Salem's high school would not admit Sarah, the family moved to Newport, Rhode Island, until her graduation. Dedicated to education and political activism for both sexes, her mother, Nancy Remond, was a founder of the Salem Female Anti-Slavery Society.

In July of 1842, at the age of sixteen, Sarah joined her brother CHARLES LENOX REMOND on the antislavery lecture circuit. She not only spoke out against slavery, but also challenged segregation in churches, theaters, and other public places. In 1856 she began touring the Midwest as a lecturer with the AMERICAN ANTI-SLAVERY SOCIETY and won acclaim as a persuasive speaker. Also concerned with the rights of women, Remond was a member of the platform group at the 1858 National Women's Rights Convention. From 1859 to 1861 Remond toured England and Ireland with her brother, continuing to rally support for the American antislavery cause. She stayed on in England during the AMERICAN CIVIL WAR, returning to the United States in 1866 to lobby for universal suffrage at the New York Constitutional Convention, an effort that proved unsuccessful.

Remond returned to EUROPE in 1866. In 1868, having studied in Florence, ITALY, Remond received her diploma for "Professional Medical Practice." She married Lorenzo Pintor in 1877 and lived out the rest of her life in Italy.

See also Abolitionism in the United States.

Bibliography
Venet, Wendy Hammond. *Neither Ballots nor Bullets: Women Abolitionists and the Civil War.* University Press of Virginia, 1991.

René, Albert

1935–

Politician and president of the Seychelles.

Born in the Farquhar Islands, SEYCHELLES, Albert René spent his youth on a plantation that his father managed. He attended Saint Louis College, in Victoria on the island of Mahé, and later a school in Saint Moritz, Switzerland. After abandoning plans to become a priest, he studied law in England at Saint Mary's

College, King's College, and the London School of Economics (1962–1964), where he became active in the British Labour Party. Returning home in 1964, he founded the Seychelles People's United Party (SPUP), as well as the nation's first labor union. Elected to the legislative assembly in 1965, René vocally attacked British COLONIAL RULE and opposed plans endorsed by James Mancham, leader of the rival Seychelles Democratic Party (SDP), to integrate the Seychelles into the British Commonwealth. Upon independence, in 1976, René became prime minister in a coalition government headed by Mancham, who became president. In June 1977 SPUP supporters staged an armed coup while Mancham was abroad and installed René, who claimed ignorance of the coup plot, as president.

René initially ruled by decree but, after introducing a new constitution in 1979, the legislative assembly was reinstated. Shortly after the reformulated SPUP, renamed the Seychelles People's Progressive Front (SPPF), became the only legal party in 1979, René, the sole candidate, won election to a five-year term as president and was reelected in 1984 and 1989. A series of attempted coups involving foreign mercenaries in the late 1970s and 1980s made René's rule increasingly autocratic, but in the face of pressure from dissenters at home and international donors in the early 1990s, he endorsed a return to multiparty democracy and a shift toward a free-market economy. In 1993, following the adoption of a new constitution, René won reelection as president. Under René the economy of the Seychelles grew steadily in the early and mid-1990s. He was reelected again in 1998 and in 2001.

Reparations

Government-administered funding and social programs intended to compensate African Americans for the past injustices of slavery and discrimination.

In 1988 the United States government issued a national apology to Japanese Americans who had been placed in American internment camps during World War II and paid $20,000 to each victim. This prompted many African Americans to press for similar reparations. Some also cited as grounds for reparations the unfulfilled Civil War promise that each slave would receive FORTY ACRES AND A MULE; the millions of dollars of German aid to Jews following the Holocaust; and the U.S. Marshall Plan, which rebuilt EUROPE after World War II.

Advocates of reparations have proposed packages that range from $700 billion to $4 trillion. Most favor investing the money in education and economic development for the African American community. This proposed use of reparations contrasts with that of some earlier reparation movements, which sought to found an independent black state (in Africa or in the Southern United States) or secure pensions for ex-slaves and their descendants.

Some opponents of reparations believe that reparations cannot truly make up for past injustices. JESSE JACKSON's aide Frank Watkins made the analogy that, "If you have two people running in a mile race around a track and one has a ball and chain tied around his leg for three laps, you can't take the ball and chain off for the final lap and still expect him to win." Although the U.S. government has not yet awarded reparations to African Americans or made a formal apology for nearly 250 years of slavery, many African Americans continue to demand that the nation officially confront and redress its past injustices.

See also Slavery in the United States.

Bibliography

Munford, Clarence. *Race and Reparations: A Black Perspective for the Twenty-first Century.* Africa World Press, 1996.

Aaron Myers

Representations of Afro-Diasporic Religions in Cinema

Overview of how religions of the African diaspora have been portrayed on film.

Within the discourse of American popular culture, African-based religions have long evoked suggestions of primitivism, superstition, and fear. Widely used terms like "voodoo economics" imply that such practices are a sham, and the popular press more often than not focuses on SANTERÍA's ritual killing of animals than on its ancient traditions. Around every representation lurks a sense of danger: people casting spells, humans growing weaker as someone sticks pins into a doll, and those who have devilish powers not to be tampered with.

A full accounting of world cinema's varied and various dramatizations of African diasporan religions would require an encyclopedia in and of itself. This article offers first a general overview of how American cinema has portrayed such belief systems, and then contrasts the mainstream commercial product with films made in countries where African religions have persisted and are more familiar to the general population.

Because of its power, worldwide influence, and ubiquitousness, Hollywood, from at least the start of its "classical period" in the 1930s and continuing until today, provides a logical starting point. This bastion of escapist cinema stood for the antithesis of everything that avant-garde and revolutionary Third World directors wanted to avoid. Within Hollywood cinema, we find two historical strains. The first and earliest representations centered on the Black Christian church, with particular emphasis on how it is different from its white counterpart. Hollywood consistently zoomed in on distinguishing characteristics: "getting the spirit" (a transformation and continuation of the trance in more traditional African sects); the abundance of movement and music; and a joyful abandonment to the Lord not found in white churches until relatively recently with the advent of charismatic preachers. Films like King Vidor's *Hallelujah* (1929) and Vincent Minnelli's *Cabin in the Sky* (1943), with its god-fearing heroine, "sinful" husband, and final melodramatic battle for the man's soul, set up religion as the marker for "good" versus "unruly" blacks. Despite the fact that these films are anchored in CHRISTIANITY, they dramatize a simple idea of faith that seems quasi-superstitious rather than scripturally knowledgeable.

The second type of representation has aspects in common with both the horror genre and, in its later incarnations, with film noir. These films suggest a literal "journey into darkness," often by a white protagonist who comes face to face with "bizarre rituals" beyond his or her comprehension. Structuring the narrative in this fashion practically ensures identification with the outsider, whose alienated point of view organizes the story; shadowy mise-en-scènes predominate, with natural environments that contrast with the civilized, modern city. Jacques Tourneur's *I Walked with a Zombie* (1943), a sort of prequel to *Jane Eyre*, links a European woman's madness to the nightly "voodoo" rituals on the island where she lives. Pounding drums dominate the soundtrack, suggesting ever-encroaching danger; "natives" don't speak but slink snakelike and dancelike through trees, invariably appearing unexpectedly to startle someone.

Several films from the 1980s, such as Alan Parker's *Angel Heart* (1987) and Jim McBride's *The Big Easy* (1986), continue and develop this trend. *The Big Easy*, for example, raises "voodoo" as a specter, almost symbolic of the relaxed approach to law and order in NEW ORLEANS. VODOU serves as the racially scary underside of the town's more appealing black culture, like JAZZ and Mardi Gras. *The Serpent and the Rainbow* (1987), directed by Wes Craven, combines horror and a variant on the "detective" genre. The hero, a doctor searching for the powder responsible for zombieism, employs many of the strategies of an investigator. "Based on a true story," the film constantly condemns Duvalier's rule in HAITI, and carves Vodou into "positive" and "negative" poles, the former exemplified by the poor who practice the rites collectively, and the latter embodied by a power-hungry police chief who works alone, collecting souls to further his own evil schemes. Within the film, zombieism stands as a metaphor for people who are forced to submit to the control of a tyrant; not surprisingly, their freedom coincides with Duvalier's departure from the island.

And in the paranoid, New Age 1990s, popular television shows like *The X-Files* follow a similar strategy, with the addition of a "politically correct" twist. While acknowledging the United States's participation in propping up Haiti's violent dictatorship, and abuses by the U.S. Army, an episode entitled "Fresh Bones," set in a refugee camp, ultimately elicits shivers from Vodou's painted *vevers* (written symbolic figures), hallucinations that lead to self-destructive behavior, and images of death. Though the activity is ultimately attributed to a white army commander who has appropriated the religion's secrets, Vodou itself is still portrayed from a distant and terror-filled vantage point.

Two American-made films, both directed by women, that incorporate black religion suggest respectful ways to depict ritual. Maya Deren's project on Voudou, *Divine Horsemen* (shot between 1947 and 1951), raises issues of documentary, anthropology, and cinematic techniques. JULIE DASH's *Daughters of the Dust* (1992) presents a unique look at the persistence of various African religions in an isolated area of the United States.

When Deren set out to film Haitian culture, her initial idea concerned only "a carefully conceived plan in which Haitian dance, *as purely a dance form,* would be combined . . . with various non-Haitian elements" (emphasis added). But she soon realized that recording merely the dance would divorce it from the context that gave it meaning: the complete Vodou ritual. Although she did not finish the film (editor Cheril Ito put together sections of the raw footage), some of Deren's cinematic choices still stand out very clearly and raise issues about representation and avant-garde strategies. *Divine Horsemen* features a camera that follows Deren's subjects closely and stays strategically inside the circle where the gods "mount" the mediums; the perspective never transfers to a distant, coolly observant outsider's gaze. And, just as the Vodou ceremony itself cannot focus on a single person, since the gods come and go at will, the camera follows the unpredictably shifting centers of attention as first one person, then another, goes into trance. Furthermore, the film's narration, taken from Deren's book about her experiences in Haiti (where she herself participated in rituals and went into trance), does not posit a gap between Deren and the Haitians: the language never assumes a "they" who accept tenets clearly different from those of the author. No omniscient voice-over states that "the Haitians think" or "those who practice Vodou believe . . . ," phrases suggesting that the person speaking does not accept the truth of this theology. Rather, the narration supplies helpful information about the gods, the ceremonial proceedings, and ritual meaning. One might argue with some of Deren's shooting choices, such as using slow-motion to film a medium possessed by the powerful, fiery *loa* Ogun, but the film shows unprecedented respect for the religion.

Julie Dash's *Daughters of the Dust* resuscitates forgotten memories of GULLAH culture in the isolated islands off the Carolinas, where African traditions remained strong. *Daughters* emphasizes theme more than narrative, as seen in Dash's use of music, choreography that evokes trance dance, and characters as important for the segments of African American society they represent as for their psychology. While she does not fully stage a religious ritual, her film subtly and richly incorporates references to Yoruban gods (a song to Ogun, the orisha associated with iron, plays during a scene in a forge), as well as to Islam, which had spread throughout the African continent. These touches permeate the atmosphere, though they are never referred to directly in speech. An elegiac quality suffuses both these cultural artifacts and the characters themselves, who that very day will leave the island for the mainland, where they will become absorbed into a more mainstream and less culturally isolated lifestyle.

In CUBA and BRAZIL, African religions such as *Santería* and CANDOMBLÉ flourished, and maintained a loyal following. The highly politicized directors who argued for transformative Third World cinema aesthetics reveal a range of attitudes toward and interpretations of the phenomenon, especially in this cinematic movement's early days. Caught between a Marxist notion of religion as "opiate of the people" and the knowledge that these religions had survived despite periods of extreme repression, filmmakers such as Sara Gómez, Tomás Gutiérrez Alea, Manuel Octavio Gómez, Nelson Pereira dos Santos, Glauber Rocha, and Carlos Diegues all either focused on disasporan religion or alluded to it in a telling manner. Cuban director Sara Gómez's *De cierta manera* (*One Way or Another*, 1974–1978) displayed the most negative image: the film constantly juxtaposes documentary footage of rebuilding HAVANA with the fictional tale of two characters struggling to redefine both their relationship and their duties to this newly revolutionary state. In this context, the black religion of *Abakuá* or *Ñañigo*, shown only in the nonfiction sequences, symbolizes a male-only enclave and a stubborn clinging to the past; a mocking voice-over savages the cult.

By the 1980s and 1990s, works such as Octavio Gómez's *Patakin* (shot in the early 1980s) presented a more positive view. *Patakin*, Cuba's first musical film, resembles *One Way or Another* thematically, as it dramatizes its protagonists' efforts to come to terms with one another and their society. But each one bears the name and attributes of a Santería god, perhaps slyly suggesting that each Cuban has connections with a particular *santo*. And because of the generic requirements, the inclusion of plentiful music and dance performed in a mixture of Cuban and African American styles, including jazz, the film blends its political critique with ample pleasure. Tomás Gutiérrez Alea's final two films, codirected with Juan Carlos Taibo, *Fresas y chocolate* (*Strawberry and Chocolate*, 1993) and *Guantanamera* (1994) similarly endorse Santería. The former film's gay character, though white, has religious items in his home and explains their place in Cuban history. The latter contains a brief but infinitely touching voice-over that relates a story of Changó and Yansa and captures the narrative's mixture of death, transcendence, and comedy. A similar shift in attitudes occurred in Brazil's Cinema Novo, as Glauber Rocha's ambivalent *Barravento* (*The Turning Wind*, 1962) gave way to Nelson Pereira dos Santos's more celebratory *Tenda dos milagres* (*Tent of Miracles*, 1977) and *Amuleto de Ogum* (*Amulet of Ogum*, 1975).

Also worth noting are the many documentaries, especially from Brazil and often made by women directors such as Raquel Gerber. These films not only examine the rituals of Candomblé but also widen the area of study to encompass feminist and gay issues.

See also Abakuás; Religions, African, in Latin America and the Caribbean; Religions, African and Afro-Caribbean, in the United States; Yoruba (religion).

Karen Backstein

Representations of Blacks in Golden Age Spain

Depictions of blacks in literature, painting, and theater in sixteenth- and seventeenth-century Spain.

The Golden Age in Spain is generally believed by scholars to have lasted about two centuries, from the early sixteenth to the late seventeenth century. During this period, the Iberian Peninsula, which covers what is today SPAIN and PORTUGAL, experienced an artistic and literary renaissance. Throughout the literature and drama of this era blacks were portrayed negatively, due to their slave status in Spanish society. Spain had recently emerged from a period of Islamic rule by the Moors that had lasted almost 800 years. The Moors, a people from the northern regions of AFRICA, crossed the Strait of Gibraltar in the early eighth century to conquer the Iberian Peninsula. The Moors remained in control of Spain until the late fifteenth century.

In 1492 Ferdinand and Isabella reclaimed Spain in the name of CHRISTIANITY. Their victory concluded the reconquest, the battle between the Catholic and Islamic faiths, of the Iberian Peninsula. Spain's Catholic kings had methodically pushed the Moors south from their northern outposts in Spain. The Catholic victory in 1492 resulted in the expulsion of the Moors and Jews from Spain, unless they converted to the Catholic faith. The Spanish perceived this action as divine retribution for eight centuries of Moorish and Islamic domination. The scars between the Moors and Christians ran deep and influenced political, religious, and racial attitudes toward the vanquished.

The black presence in Spain can be traced back to the era of Moorish rule on the Iberian Peninsula. In the early tenth century black slaves arrived in the city of Córdoba, serving as guardians of the Moorish royalty. Due to their slave status, blacks were referred to as *abid*, the plural form of *abd*, meaning slave, or as *sudán*, referring to their origin in the SUDAN. Soon blacks appeared more prominently in many facets of court and military life.

Traces of black characters in Golden Age Spain appeared in literature and paintings around the fourteenth century. Blacks were rarely portrayed positively. They were often depicted as lazy or idle, and they played the role of comic relief. Examples of these stereotypes were perpetuated in the literature, poetry, and drama of the era.

Depictions in Literature

Toward the end of the fifteenth century, poet Rodrigo Reinosa composed a poem that mocked the speech patterns of blacks. Set in Seville, a hub of slave trade activity, the poem was intended to insult and poke fun at blacks. Reinosa's interpretation of black speech influenced further attacks and lampoons of blacks in the works of other Golden Age authors.

The representation of blacks in Golden Age literature is reflected in the principal novels of the time. *Lazarillo de Tormes* (1554; *Lazaro of Tormes*), an anonymously written novel, tells the tale of a narrow-minded rogue and his misadventures in Golden Age society. The novel launched a new realist genre called the picaresque. In a time when novels primarily dealt with themes of chivalry and courtly love, Lazarillo provided a gritty, almost realistic, portrait of everyday life. The character of Lazarillo served as a mirror to his time, reflecting the prejudices and social structure of Golden Age Spain.

In *Lazarillo de Tormes* the reader is introduced to the black character of Zaide, Lazarillo's stepfather, who works as a shepherd, guarding the livestock of a knight. Zaide and Lazarillo's mother have a child, a *negrito* (a little black one), who is frightened upon the first sight of his black father and begins to cry. Lazarillo feels dishonored by his mother who fell in love with a black slave and leaves home. Lazarillo's fear of being dishonored can be interpreted as comical, since he too is regarded as an undesirable of Spanish society.

In a seventeenth-century novella by María de Zayas entitled *El prevenido engañado* (1637), blacks are portrayed as animalistic creatures. The novella tells the story of a black slave who became the object of a Spanish dame's desires. The affair ends with the slave lying lifeless on the bed, murdered by the Spanish dame after a passionate tryst. De Zayas' story perpetuated the stereotype of blacks as savages who possessed little civility or restraint.

Blacks and Paintings

Juan de Pareja was the black slave of Diego Velázquez, a great Spanish painter. As a slave, de Pareja prepared Veláquez's canvases and mixed his paint, De Pareja honed his artistic skill by watching Velázquez as he painted. After he witnessed the artistic talent of de Pareja, Spain's King Phillip IV suggested that Velázquez give de Pareja his freedom. Velázquez complied and set de Pareja free, but he and his family remained in the painter's service. De Pareja's paintings, which depict religious subject matter, are currently displayed at the Museo del Prado in Madrid, Spain.

Blacks and Theater

In Golden Age theater, black characters were presented as comic relief and reflected the stereotypes of the day. However, exceptions to this practice occur in some plays by Spanish dramatist Lope de Vega. In many of de Vega's plays blacks become integral characters, shedding the image of happy-go-lucky servant or slave. De Vega is one of the few playwrights who represented the black race positively in his plays. To his credit, de Vega composed the couplet "*aunque negros gente son*," which translates as "even Negroes people are." By emphasizing the word *people*, de Vega suggested that he regarded blacks as people, not just slaves.

The real-life story of slave and humanist Juan Latino also presented many Golden Age dramatists with fodder for the role of a positive black character. The character of Latino has appeared in many Golden Age plays, including a comedy by Diego Jiménez entitled *Juan Latino* (1652). Juan Latino was born in ETHIOPIA, traded as a slave, and ended up in the city of Córdoba where he served the duke of Sesa, Gonzalo Fernandez. Throughout his years of service to the duke of Sesa, Latino acquired a solid humanistic training with a strong foundation in Latin. After Latino was released from the duke's service, he served as a Latin teacher at the Cathedral de Granada. Latino married Doña Ana de Carlobal, with whom he had four children. During his life, Latino wrote various books in Latin, including *Epigrammatum liber* (1573; Book of Epigrams), considered to be the first book published by a black man.

See also Racial Stereotypes.

Republican Party

One of the two major political parties in the United States; formed in part to oppose slavery, it has since lost the support of most black Americans.

The Republican Party was formed in 1854 to oppose the westward expansion of SLAVERY IN THE UNITED STATES. Earlier that year, Midwesterners had organized en masse to protest the Kansas-Nebraska Act, which allowed slavery in those territories, and within months the new antislavery party was formed.

By the time of the 1860 election of President ABRAHAM LINCOLN, the Republican Party had toned down its rhetoric concerning the slavery issue. However, the AMERICAN CIVIL WAR established the party as the liberator of slaves and won it the allegiance of the overwhelming majority of black Americans. Lincoln, who issued the Emancipation Proclamation as a war measure and who said that he would retain slavery if it would save the Union, still earned the reputation as a great rescuer of African Americans. Republicans backed the Emancipation Proclamation and authored the Thirteenth, Fourteenth, and Fifteenth amendments to the Constitution. They also encouraged black participation in Republican politics during RECONSTRUCTION.

The liberal wing of the party, the Radical Republicans, largely shaped Reconstruction policy; their primary goal was to secure equal civil and political rights for blacks. Blacks gained voting and citizenship rights, and they played prominent roles in Reconstruction governments in the South as lieutenant governors, members of state legislatures, speakers of state houses of representatives, and secretaries of state. Between 1869 and 1901, twenty black Republicans from the South were elected to the U.S. House of Representatives, and two were elected to the U.S. Senate.

In the Compromise of 1877, Republicans agreed to withdraw federal involvement in the government of Southern states. In exchange, they received enough Southern electoral votes to retain a Republican presidency. The compromise ended Reconstruction. With the Republican presence effectively eliminated from the South, white Southern Democrats worked to disfranchise black voters and to enforce segregation. Between 1877 and 1901, white Democrats "redeemed" the South, a euphemism for eliminating black political and civil rights using various methods, including intimidation and violence. Black appeals to the Republican Party went largely unanswered.

President William McKinley was committed to sectional reconciliation, and he ignored the disfranchisement, segregation, LYNCHING, and poverty suffered by blacks. In 1901 Theodore Roosevelt became president, bringing together the progressive cause and the Republican Party. Roosevelt appointed blacks to federal positions, relied on black conservative educator Booker T. Washington as an adviser on racial issues, and publicly opposed lynching. However, Roosevelt alienated blacks during his second term by summarily discharging three companies of black soldiers; the soldiers had been accused of refusing to inform on fellow soldiers who were charged with terrorizing the town of Brownsville, Texas. Roosevelt's successor, President William Howard Taft, was less committed to the progressive cause. Courting the support of Southern whites, Taft did not appoint any blacks to federal offices in the South. This rendered unsuccessful his attempts to appeal to blacks by appointing them to diplomatic and consular offices.

A split between progressive and conservative Republicans occurred during the early 1900s, and throughout the 1920s antilabor Republicans in Congress and the White House worked to strengthen ties with Southern whites. Presidents Warren Harding and Calvin Coolidge appointed few blacks to federal posts; they also failed to reverse the policy of segregation in the civil service that had been initiated by President Woodrow Wilson, a Democrat. Despite increasing racial violence in the South, neither Harding nor Coolidge supported federal antilynching legislation.

The administration of President Herbert Hoover in the 1930s also sought white support at the expense of blacks. Hoover ignored racial violence and disfranchisement and appointed no more blacks to federal positions than had his predecessors. He further alienated blacks by appointing antiblack whites to federal positions. Hoover also insulted black Americans with his decision to segregate African Americans on a government-sponsored trip to the graves of American soldiers in Europe.

By the time of the Great Depression in the 1930s, African Americans were ready to switch allegiance to Democratic candidate Franklin Delano Roosevelt. Roosevelt's New Deal policies offered tangible economic benefits to blacks. His appointees included numerous blacks who served as racial advisers and who worked against discrimination in federal hiring practices and the distribution of relief benefits. First Lady Eleanor Roosevelt garnered considerable black support for Roosevelt. She supported racial equality and joined interracial organizations such as the Southern Conference for Human Welfare, which worked to organize unions in the South and to replace reactionary Southern politicians. In the 1936 election, 71 percent of black voters supported Roosevelt.

Although they favored Democratic policies, most blacks remained registered as Republicans until the 1940s and 1950s, with the administration of Harry S. Truman. Truman's Fair Deal attempted to continue the social programs of the New Deal. Although the Republican Party enjoyed a brief resurgence of black support during Dwight D. Eisenhower's presidential administration, achieving 39 percent of the black vote in 1952, the civil rights records of Democratic presidents John F. Kennedy and Lyndon B. Johnson won nearly unanimous black support. Furthermore, 1964 Republican presidential candidate Barry Goldwater's position against civil rights positions reduced black membership in the Republican Party to 8 percent, its lowest point ever.

In the following decades Republicans made little progress in attracting black voters. From 1968 through 1980 only 12 to 15 percent of blacks voted Republican. Efforts by Presidents Ronald Reagan and George H. W. Bush to promote black conservatives had little impact on black Republican representation in elected office, but it did result in Bush's nomination of Clarence Thomas to the Supreme Court. By 1992 fewer than 1 percent of blacks serving in elective office were registered Republicans. In the 2000 presidential election, Republican George W. Bush received only 9 percent of the African American vote.

See also Black Cabinet; Brownsville, Texas, Affair; Democratic Party; Emancipation Proclamation and the Thirteenth Amendment; Fifteenth Amendment; Fourteenth Amendment; Redemption; Segregation in the United States; Slavery in the United States; United States House of Representatives, African Americans in the; United States Senate, African Americans in the.

Bibliography

Kousser, J. Morgan. *The Shaping of Southern Politics: Suffrage Restriction and the Establishment of the One-Party South, 1880–1910.* Yale University Press, 1974.

Kurian, George Thomas. *The Encyclopedia of the Republican Party; The Encyclopedia of the Democratic Party.* 4 vols. Sharpe, 1996.

Rutland, Robert. *The Republicans: From Lincoln to Bush.* University of Missouri Press, 1996.

Weiss, Nancy J. *Farewell to the Party of Lincoln: Black Politics in the Age of FDR.* Princeton University Press, 1983.

Robert Fay

Republic of New Africa

African American organization devoted to the establishment of an autonomous black nation in the Southern United States.

At the height of the Black Power Movement in the late 1960s, members of the Republic of New Africa (RNA) called for the creation of an independent black nation spanning the states of Louisiana, Mississippi, Alabama, Georgia, and South Carolina. They advocated cooperative economics and community self-sufficiency. At the same time, members of the RNA aimed to limit political rights and freedom of the press, prohibit unions, make military service mandatory, and legalize polygamy. Their manifesto demanded that the U.S. government cede the five proposed states to the Republic of New Africa and pay $400 billion in reparations to African Americans for the injustices of slavery and segregation.

In 1968, attorney Milton Henry and his brother Richard, former acquaintances of Malcolm X who renamed themselves Gaidi Obadele and Imari Abubakari Obadele, respectively, convened a group of militant black nationalists in Detroit, Michi-

GAN, to discuss the creation of a black nation within the United States. Conference members established the Republic of New Africa and declared their allegiance to the provisional government. They elected Imari Obadele as provisional president.

The Republic of New Africa quickly became a target of the U.S. Federal Bureau of Investigation (FBI), which conducted raids on their meetings. These confrontations were violent and led to the repeated imprisonment of RNA leaders for assault and sedition. Following his 1980 release from prison, Imari Obadele attended Temple University and earned a Ph.D. in political science. While teaching at various universities, he published books and articles upholding the RNA's principles of reparations, acquisition of land, and establishment of an autonomous black nation. Based in WASHINGTON, D.C., with a membership of almost 10,000, the Republic of New Africa continues to promote the formation of a black nation.

See also Black Power in the United States; Black Nationalism in the United States; Segregation in the United States; Slavery in the United States.

Bibliography

Van DeBurg, William L. *New Day in Babylon: The Black Power Movement and American Culture.* University of Chicago Press, 1992.

Aaron Myers

Research about Africans and People of African Descent

Academic fields and research projects dedicated to the study of Africans and people of the African diaspora.

For information on

Research and study projects about people of African descent throughout the world: *See* Moorland-Spingarn Research Collection; Schomburg Center for Research in Black Culture; UNESCO Race Relations Project.

Projects and approaches about Africans: *See* African Studies in the United States: An Interpretation; Afrocentricity; Anthropology in Africa; Black Athena.

Research and study projects about African Americans, *See* An American Dilemma: The Negro Problem and Modern Democracy; Association for the Study of Afro-American Life and History; Collectors of African American Books; Institute of the Black World; Joint Center for Political and Economic Studies; *Journal of Negro History, The.*

Research and study projects about Afro-Latin America, *See* Afro-Latin America, Research on.

Reshewa

Ethnic group of Nigeria; also known as Bareshe, Gungawa, Reshawa, Reshiat, and Tsureshe.

The Reshewa primarily inhabit the banks of the NIGER RIVER in northwestern NIGERIA. They speak a Niger-Congo language. More than 100,000 people consider themselves Reshawa.

See also Languages, African: An Overview.

Rethinking Palmares: Slave Resistance in Colonial Brazil

Colonial BRAZIL, based as it was on the coerced labor of Indians and Africans, was continually threatened by various forms of resistance to the fundamental institution of slavery. Throughout the Americas, wherever slavery was a basic institution, slave resistance, the fear of slave revolt, and the problem of fugitive slaves plagued colonists and colonial administrators. This resistance took a number of forms and was expressed in a variety of ways. Day-to-day recalcitrance, slowdowns, and sabotage were probably the most common forms of resistance, while self-destruction through suicide, infanticide, or overt attempts at vengeance were the most extreme in a personal sense.

In Brazil, the most dramatic examples of collective action were a number of slave revolts that took place in BAHIA in the early nineteenth century, but actions like the MALÊ rebellion of 1835 were truly extraordinary events. By far the most common form of slave resistance in colonial Brazil was flight, and a characteristic problem of the Brazilian slave regime was the continual and widespread existence of fugitive communities called variously *mocambos*, *ladeiras*, *magotes*, or *quilombos*.

In many ways, the topic of slave flight and resistance in Brazil has been treated as a deceptively simple one, and analyses of it have often been based on a limited set of questions to which commonsense answers have been made: Why did slaves flee? To escape slavery. Where were runaway communities located? Far from possible white retaliation. Why did fugitives attack white society? To liberate their fellows and because they hated slavery. Was there class solidarity among slaves? Of course. What kind of societies did fugitives create? More or less egalitarian ones based on African traditions. Noticeably missing from the study of maroonage in Brazil has been concern with some of the issues that have preoccupied students of this phenomenon in other American slave societies or solid evidence that would illuminate some of the more intractable questions about ethnic solidarities, political goals, and strategies, as well as variations in form. Except for the case of Palmares, maroon intentions have not been extensively studied. To what extent did escaped slaves organize a resistance that consciously aimed at overthrowing or at least attacking slave society rather than seeking their personal freedom? This is a question that has remained without answer in Brazil, even though such an answer would provide a measure of the "revolutionary" nature of escaped slave communities. To some extent these questions are difficult to answer because of a lack of appropriate documentation, but a close reading of local sources and the use of ethno-historical techniques may begin to offer a few tentative answers to some of the central questions of fugitive communities in Brazilian slave society.

I will examine aspects of fugitive communities in three major areas of colonial Brazil: the plantation zone of Bahia; the mining district of MINAS GERAIS; and the inaccessible frontier of Alagoas, site of Palmares, the largest fugitive community. The goal of this essay is to find patterns in the origins, creation, internal organization, and destruction of these fugitive communities in order to better understand the slave regime and the way in which Africans and Afro-Brazilians responded to it.

Runaway communities flourished in almost all areas of the captaincy of Bahia, although in some regions the problem was unusually acute. The geography and ecology of much of the Bahian littoral aided escape, and the result was a large number of fugitives and mocambos. A report by an unnamed Jesuit written in 1619 outlined the problem and its perception by white society:

This people has the custom of fleeing to the woods and joining in hideouts where they live by attacks on the settlers, stealing livestock and ruining crops and cane fields which results in much damage and many losses beyond that of loosing [sic] their daily labor. And many of these [escapees] live for many years in the forest never returning and living in these mocambos which are places or villages that they have made deep in the forest. And from here they set out to make their assaults, robbing and stealing and often killing many, and in these attacks they seek to carry off their male and female relatives to live with them like gentiles.

Certain characteristics of the captaincy of Bahia contributed to slave flight and the formation of runaway communities. A major terminus of the TRANSATLANTIC SLAVE TRADE and a major plantation zone throughout its history, Bahia had always maintained a large servile population, which by the end of the colonial era constituted about one-third of the total population. In plantation zones, however, slaves often made up over 60 percent of the inhabitants. Conditions on the *engenhos* (or sugar plantations) were physically exhausting, and treatment in terms of food and housing was poor. Sometimes slaves had to deal with particularly cruel or sadistic masters, but even beyond these the general concept of slave management disregarded the long-term benefits of "good" treatment and emphasized the extraction of as much labor with as little cost as possible. Slaves also lived with limited familial opportunities. Patterns in the transatlantic slave trade and a planter preference for young adult males over women resulted in a chronic gender imbalance. These problems made for a population that had less to lose by flight or other forms of resistance, at least in the view of observers in nineteenth-century Brazil who advocated stable families and a balanced gender ratio among the slaves shared by the slave owners of colonial Bahia. Flight and mocambos remained a feature of Bahian slavery throughout its history.

While the sugar-growing parishes of the Bahian Recôncavo area contained the largest number and highest percentage of slaves, the areas of Bahia experiencing the greatest incidence of mocambo formation were the southern towns of Cairú, Camamú, and Ilhéus. These towns and their surrounding districts were devoted for the most part to the production of manioc, the basic subsistence crop of Brazil. The work requirements were less than those of the sugar plantations, and slaves lived in smaller units in this region. While the predominance of slaves in the population found in the sugar-growing areas was absent, the proportion of slaves in the population of this southern zone still reached between 40 and 60 percent. Relatively good conditions in terms of work requirements, diet, and physical wellbeing as well as a large proportion of slaves in the population have been postulated in other situations as factors that stimulated slave resistance. In this case, however, the frontier nature of this region and its unstable military conditions was the most important contributing factor to successful slave escapes. Cairú and Camamú were constantly threatened by attack from hostile Aimoré Indians. This fact and the distance from military aid coming from Salvador made suppression of slave mocambos difficult. Attacks by Indians, or *gentio barbaro* (savage gentiles), and mocambo raids were linked in the minds of the colonists, and various measures were taken to suppress both. Black and mulatto freedmen, "tame" Indians, and black militia units from Bahia were all used in expeditions to suppress the quilombos, but a major innovation was the use of Indian fighters and backwoodsmen (*bandeirantes*) from São Paulo. This tactic had some success, and "Paulista" contingents were subsequently employed elsewhere in the Northeast for similar operations, the most notable being the destruction of the great quilombo of Palmares in 1684–1685.

While the mocambos of southern Bahia never reached the size or extent of Palmares, the threat they posed was no less real. One mocambo was reported in 1723 to have over 400 inhabitants, but size alone was not the sole determinant of mocambo danger in this region. In another instance, in 1692, a group of fugitives led by five mulatto "captains" began to sack the farmlands near Camamú and threatened to seize the town itself. Not only was southern Bahia disrupted, but the Recôncavo was also thrown into turmoil as word of these events reached the slave quarters of the engenhos and planters feared a similar outbreak. A Portuguese military expedition in 1692 finally destroyed this mocambo by laying siege to the stockaded village. The final battle cry of the defenders: "Death to the whites and long live liberty."

The fear that towns like Cairú and Camamú, far from the centers of governmental authority, might actually be seized was not wholly exaggerated. In 1767 the interim captain of Sergipe de El-Rey reported continual attacks by armed bands of fugitives, adding that in the time of his predecessor an armed band of escaped slaves had marched into town at nine in the morning with flags, drums, and crowns on their heads and demanded that the royal official grant them letters of manumission. The official had sounded the alarm but the absence of troops allowed the fugitives to escape unharmed.

Such audacity also underlined a basic reality. The majority of Bahian mocambos were located relatively close to population centers or to the surrounding plantations. Whereas Palmares flourished in the remote interior of Alagoas and other fugitive communities also existed in remote regions, the vast majority of the Bahian mocambos and those elsewhere in Brazil remained close to towns and farms, although often in inaccessible locations. In fact, some of the towns within the present-day urban network of Salvador originated as runaway communities.

The reasons for this pattern of fugitive settlement are varied. Certainly, until the eighteenth century, hostile Indians constituted an effective barrier to black as well as white penetration of many regions. Most importantly, the internal economy of the mocambos made proximity to settled areas a prerequisite for success. Rather than a return to African pastoral or agricultural pursuits, mocambo economies were often parasitic, based on highway theft, cattle rustling, raiding, and extortion. These activities might be combined with agriculture as well, but rarely did mocambos become wholly self-sufficient and completely isolated from the colonial society that generated and at the same time feared them.

The attacks by escaped slaves led colonial officials to consider mocambo fugitives to be common criminals, thus subject to regular criminal penalties. However, the actions of fugitive slaves were more than simple crimes because they implied, and were sometimes overtly directed as, an attack on the existing social order. In a very real sense mocambo raids foreshadowed the social banditry, or *cangaço,* of postcolonial Brazil. The mocambo represented an expression of social protest in a slave society.

Anti-Mocambo Measures

Colonists and royal officials developed a number of measures to deal with mocambo formation and activity. One tactic was to apprehend fugitives before they could join together in bands. As early as 1612, Alexandre de Moura, captain of Pernambuco, petitioned the Crown for the creation of a *capitão de campo* (bush captain) in each of the eight parishes of that captaincy, who, with the aid of twenty Indians, would hunt down escaped slaves. It is uncertain exactly when these officers were introduced to Bahia, but by 1625 the town council of Salvador had set the scale of rewards for these slave hunters. The capitão de campo, or *capitão do mato* as the office came to be called, worked on a commission basis, receiving a reward for each fugitive captured. This system was the price of reward in accordance with the distance involved. By 1637 these rewards were extended to anyone capturing a fugitive, not just to the bush captains. As we shall see, a similar system was adopted in Minas Gerais and elsewhere in Brazil. The bush captain became a ubiquitous aspect of rural Brazil.

The system was fraught with difficulties. To claim the prescribed rewards, overzealous bush captains were not above arresting slaves who were merely on errands. Slave owners sometimes showed a marked reluctance to pay the fee for old or infirm slaves who were no longer useful. On a number of occasions, a backlog of elderly unclaimed fugitives in the municipal jail of Salvador forced the town council to auction the prisoners to the public in order to pay for expenses. The position of bush captain often attracted somewhat marginal individuals, former slaves and colored freedmen, who were resented by the slave owners and hated by the slaves. Still, the bush captains provided a relatively effective means of apprehending individual fugitives, although controlling the problems of slave revolt or the activities of already-formed mocambos was usually beyond their capacities.

A second and still unstudied method of slave control and capture in Brazil was the calculated use of Indians as slave catchers and as a counterforce to mocambos and possible slave revolts. In the sixteenth century, sugar planters and absentee recipients of donations sought to bring Indians from the interior to serve as a defense force against possible slave uprisings as well as a buffer against still unreduced tribes of the backlands. In the seventeenth century, colonists in Bahia tried unsuccessfully to have Indian villages located near their farms. The Jesuits objected, fearing colonist exploitation of Indians as laborers; the clerics, however, recognized that Indian allies were the "walls and bulwarks" of the colony. As early as 1614, Indians from the Jesuit mission village of São João were used to destroy a mocambo.

Indian irregulars led by Portuguese officers or captains were consistently and successfully employed against mocambos throughout colonial Brazil. The destruction of virtually every mocambo from Palmares to the much smaller hideouts of Bahia, Rio de Janeiro, and Goiás depended to a large extent on Indian troops and auxiliaries.

Paradoxically, there are also many references to the incorporation of African and Afro-Brazilian slaves into Indian villages and of Indian inhabitants in fugitive communities. Portuguese authorities feared the disruptive and potentially dangerous nature of such contacts. In 1706 the Crown ordered that blacks, mixed bloods, and slaves be prevented from penetrating the interior, where they might join with hostile Indian groups. Despite such measures, Afro-Indian cooperation against both the Portuguese and the Dutch in Brazil was common. In Bahia, a famous example of Afro-Indian collaboration is provided by the long-lived syncretic messianic religion called *Santidade,* which flourished in the southern areas of the captaincy in the late sixteenth century among Indian groups. By 1613 it was reported that escaped slaves had joined the movement and were participating in its raids and even stealing slaves from Salvador. As late as 1627, despite punitive expeditions, Santidade adherents were still launching attacks.

This leads us to the still ignored problem of Afro-Indian contacts and social relations. Despite Portuguese attempts to turn the Indians into allies against potential slave resistance, a number of factors drew African slaves and Indians together. For the runaways and unreduced Indian tribes there was the common goal of opposition to the European-imposed slave regime. Within captivity, too, Indians and Africans were often in intimate and common contact. Indians continued to comprise a large, although decreasing, percentage of the plantation labor force in the period 1580–1650, and marriages between blacks and Indians were not uncommon. Indians remained throughout the colonial era both the best potential allies and the most effective opponents of slave fugitives.

The primary tactic employed against mocambos was simply to destroy them and to kill or reenslave their inhabitants. Portuguese opposition to the fugitive communities can be easily explained. Mocambo raids and thefts endangered towns, disrupted production, and cut lines of communication and travel. Moreover, a mocambo either by its raids or by its attraction drew other slaves from captivity. Many observers noted the effects of mocambos on the slave quarters, and one report of 1692 noted that "no settler will have his slaves secure" so long as mocambos persisted. Mocambos posed a threat to the economic and social fabric of this slave regime.

For most colonial officials accommodation with mocambos and white inhabitants was simply unthinkable. Unlike in JAMAICA, where a treaty was finally concluded with the runaway maroons, similar tactics were harshly rebuked when suggested in Brazil. In 1640 Viceroy Jorge de Mascarenhas, marquis of Montalvão, suggested as a wartime measure that a peace mission of a Jesuit linguist and HENRIQUE DIAS, leader of a pro-Portuguese black regiment, be sent to a certain mocambo. The mission offered freedom to runaways if they would serve in the black regiment and if they agreed to harbor no new fugitives. His suggestion met with a stern rebuff from the planter-dominated *câmara* (town council) of Salvador, which stated: "Under no circumstances is it proper to attempt reconciliation nor to give way to slaves who might be conciliated in this matter. That which is proper is only to extinguish them and to conquer them so that those who are still domesticated will not join them and those who are in rebellion will not aspire to greater misdeeds."

The extermination of mocambos was usually carried out by military expeditions conducted by private individuals with local backing or by government troops. Private contracts were sometimes made with backwoodsmen with stipulated rewards for each slave captured. Bush captains, Indian auxiliaries, government-sponsored military columns—all were designed to confront the threat of the fugitive communities to the slave regime.

Mocambo Ethnography: Buraco de Tatú

The varied and disparate documents that mention the activities of escaped slaves in Brazil reveal little about the social and political organization within the fugitive communities. For this reason the documents pertaining to the destruction of the quilombo known as the Buraco de Tatú (Armadillo's Hole) are of singular importance; for although by no means complete they do provide a glimpse into what may have been the history of a typical Bahian mocambo.

In 1763 a Portuguese-led military expedition destroyed the Buraco de Tatú, located just east-northeast of the city of Salvador, near the present-day bathing beaches of Itapoam. Responding to complaints and disturbed by mocambo activities, Dom Marcos de Noronha, count of Arcos and viceroy of Brazil, began in 1760 a campaign to eliminate fugitive communities. In that year, he appointed Joaquim da Costa Cardoso as "captain major of the conquest of savage gentiles" and apparently entrusted him with mounting a punitive expedition. Although Costa Cardoso's commission indicated that hostile Indians were his main objective, he also displayed considerable interest in destroying "various quilombos of Negroes in the outskirts of the city." Neither their numbers nor their location at the time can be determined, but in addition to Itapoam there were also mocambos in Cairú and Ipitanga.

The Buraco de Tatú had existed for twenty years. Like most Bahian mocambos its economy was basically parasitic, based on theft, extortion, and sporadic raiding. The principal victims, however, were not white sugar planters, but rather the blacks who "came every day to the city [Salvador] to sell the food-stuffs they grow on their plots." The most attractive women were also taken back to the mocambo. The chronic lack of women in the Brazilian slave force was reproduced and exacerbated in the mocambos. Fugitives preferred to take black or mulatto women, and there are few references to the abduction of European women. No such charge was made against the inhabitants of the Buraco de Tatú.

Despite the actions of the fugitives, there were freedmen and slaves who out of necessity or sympathy cooperated with the Buraco de Tatú. João Baptista, a mulatto farmer, worked with the runaways and supplied them with firewood. He was apparently not alone in his practices. Blacks in the city of Salvador aided the quilombo by helping the fugitives to enter the city by night in order to buy powder and shot. Such contact was unsettling to slave owners and royal officials, who feared increased escapes or a general uprising. As in other instances, whites also cooperated with the quilombo—in their case to avoid harm to life or property.

The actions taken against nonquilombo blacks and the cooperation between whites and the escaped slaves, although coerced, indicates that the Buraco de Tatú fugitives had no intention of a total war of liberation against all the slave-owning segments of the population. Quilombos, in fact, might provide focal points in more general slave rebellions as they did in Bahia in the early nineteenth century, but in general, the goals of the fugitive communities seem to have been the more immediate and practical ones of survival beyond the control of white society. Slave resistance in all its forms may have been a threat to the slave system, but despite the implications of quilombo existence for the slave "class," planters and colonial officials perceived enough divisions among the slaves to risk arming engenho slaves in order to combat fugitives, as the Count of Ponte suggested in 1807.

The Buraco de Tatú was destroyed on September 2, 1763, and from the military descriptions of that action and a plan drawn by the attackers to illustrate those reports, it is possible to infer much about the internal life of this community. The quilombo was a well-organized village laid out in a rectilinear pattern of six rows of houses bisected by a large central street. There were thirty-two rectangular residence units and since there were approximately sixty-five adults in the quilombo, we can assume that these units represent houses rather than compounds. The close correlation of two adults per house suggests a monogamous pattern, but the evidence is unclear since the accompanying documents make no mention of children. When children born in a quilombo were captured, they often became the property of the expedition's leader, and this may explain their absence from the judicial records. Taken as a whole, the monogamous marital pattern, the rectangular house shape, and the even rows of houses suggest a reproduction of a plantation *senzala* (slave quarters) rather than any specific African pattern. Conversely, the large central street equally dividing the rectangular houses and the existence of what may have been a ceremonial, or a "palaver," house in front of a plaza are all elements found among northwest Bantu groups such as the Koko, Teke (Anzico), and Mabea. The surviving documents, in fact, give little indication of the ethnic origins of the inhabitants of the Buraco de Tatú. At least one inhabitant was a *crioulo* (or Brazil-born black). Another was referred to as a *mandingueiro,* a term that in the mid-eighteenth century simply meant "sorcerer," but could also suggest Mandinga origins for at least this fugitive. The most reasonable assumption is that no one African group inhabited this mocambo.

Like many fugitive communities in Brazil, the Buraco de Tatú was cleverly fortified. Entry into the mocambo was made difficult by an extensive defensive network. A swampy dike about the height of a human protected the rear. The three sides of the village were protected by a maze of sharpened stakes driven into the ground and covered to prevent detection by an unsuspecting intruder. This defense was augmented by a series of twenty-one pits filled with sharpened spikes and disguised by brush and grass. Leading into the mocambo was a false road especially well protected by spikes and camouflaged traps. Only when the watchman placed planks over some of the obstacles did entry and exit become possible. It was a defense quite unlike that of the palisaded Angolan quilombo described by Father Antonio Cavazzi in 1680. Still, covered traps and sharpened stakes were used for village protection in Africa from NIGERIA southward to the Old Kingdom of Kongo and were also used at Palmares and by other fugitive communities.

In the predatory economy of the Buraco de Tatú, agriculture was not a major activity. The plan does show a trellis of *maracuja,* a Brazilian fruit, and a number of small gardens perhaps equivalent to the dawn gardens of the KONGO, but these seem to be devoted to herbs rather than staple crops. No *roças* or farmlands are indicated in the area around the mocambo. These fugitives probably exacted foodstuffs as tribute from their neighbors and may have supplemented their diet with fish since the village was located near the coast. A few aspects of the quilombo's internal life can be gleaned from the report of its destruction. Politically, the Buraco de Tatú had two chieftains or captains. Antonio de Sousa was a war-captain, and a second leader, Theodoro, controlled the quilombo itself. Each leader had a consort who was called a queen. Nine houses were separated from the main village. This separation may simply indicate latecomers or the divided political leadership, or may even suggest the possibility that this was the residence of a lineage unable to live in the main village or even an age group of young males required to live apart. This latter possibility is doubtful, however, since the Portuguese would have found this situation notable enough to mention and the records are silent. The religion of the inhabitants is unknown. Two individuals were mentioned as sorcerers, one of them an old woman. Women are traditionally the leaders in the Yoruba cults still practiced in Bahia, but the dates of this mocambo (1743–1763) precede the large-scale importation of YORUBA slaves in Brazil.

The Buraco de Tatú was destroyed on September 2, 1763. Under the leadership of Joaquim da Costa Cardoso, a force of 200 men, including a troop of grenadiers, but made up mostly of Indian auxiliary militia and Indians from a village in Jaguaripe, carried out the attack. Their battle orders were to remain in the field until "the quilombo has been destroyed, the blacks captured, the resisters killed, the woods searched, the huts and defenses burned, and the trenches filled in." Indian guides were used to scout the quilombo's defenses before the assault was launched. The attack probably came from the unprotected coastal side of the village. Surprise worked to the attackers' advantage until an old woman raised the alarm. The defenders, some of whom were armed with bows, were greatly outnumbered and overwhelmed. The hero for the defense was José Lopes, who fired two shots at the attackers and who shouted defiantly that it would take more than 200 men to capture him. He was mistaken. Four fugitives were killed and sixty-one taken prisoner. No casualties were reported among the expeditionary troops.

Upon their capture the fugitives were incarcerated in Salvador. Thirty-one, whose only crime was to escape slavery, were, in accordance with a Royal Order of March 3, 1741, branded with the letter *f* (*fugido,* or escaped). After their masters paid the costs of capture to the royal treasury, the slaves were returned to captivity. Some were singled out for exemplary punishment. Antonio de Sousa, captain of the quilombo, was sentenced to public flogging and life in the galleys. His friend Miguel Cosme, "reported to be a great thief," received a sentence of flogging and six years at the oars. Theodoro and José Lopes were both whipped in public and sent to the galleys for ten years. João Baptista, the mulatto farmer and accomplice of the fugitives, was sentenced to five years of penal exile and a stiff fine. The two queens received relatively light sentences.

The Buraco de Tatú provides an example that recapitulates many aspects of the history of fugitive communities in Brazil. Relatively small in size (less than 100 inhabitants) and located close to centers of population, these communities developed syncretic traditions fusing Brazilian and African elements. Their inhabitants seem also to have been of various origins, Brazilian-born and Africans of different ethnic backgrounds. Although they stole from slaves and free people of color as well as whites, some freedmen willingly cooperated with the fugitives. The punitive military expedition and the use of Indians within it represented the usual colonial response to the mocambos. Living by their wits and daring, the fugitives of the Buraco de Tatú maintained their independence for twenty years until their actions and the threat of their very existence caused the colonial authorities to exterminate their community. In many ways, the history of the Buraco de Tatú seems to be typical of the history of fugitive communities in Brazil.

Mining Economy of Minas Gerais

The patterns of quilombo formation and the responses of colonial society that we have examined thus far in the case of Bahia were to a large extent reproduced in the mining areas of south central Brazil, although with certain differences, as might be expected given the different social and economic formation of the region. The discovery of rich deposits of gold in the mountainous region that came to be known as Minas Gerais and the subsequent development there of a society based on slave labor created conditions that particularly favored slave runaways and the formation of mocambos. Slaves made up between one-third and one-half of the total population of the captaincy during most of the eighteenth century and free people of color constituted by 1821 another 40 percent of the total. Together, then, the Afro-Brazilian population—slave and free—eventually made up about three-quarters of the inhabitants. Slaves performed virtually every task, but above all they did most of the mining. They were expensive and highly valued. So long as they were productive and turned over to their masters the gold they found, slaves often had considerable autonomy of movement in the mining district. The large sea of slaves and free coloreds provided a potentially friendly environment for runaways. The discontinuous nature of settlement and the mountainous topography provided large inaccessible tracts for hideouts and even in the many urban concentrations, the large free population of color made the detection of fugitives difficult. Moreover, because fugitive slaves could often provide gold that they had stolen or found, some whites were willing to cooperate with the mocambos or to protect fugitives. Finally, in the lawless and restive conditions of early Minas Gerais, slaves were often armed by their owners and participated in the various antigovernment movements and in the civil disturbances of the War of the Emboabas.

All of these conditions contributed to an unstable situation of slave control as well as feelings of insecurity and fear among royal officials, municipal councils, and the white population in general. Rumors of planned slave revolts circulated in the 1700s, but the main problem continued to be mocambos. Throughout the eighteenth century, governors, miners, royal officials, and town councils complained of thefts, murders, abductions, and other crimes committed by *calhambolas,* the inhabitants of mocambos. The response in Minas replicated that of the coastal plantation zones. In Minas, as in Bahia, attempts to use free Indians as slave catchers and the deployment of Indian villages and later of royal troops for this purpose had little impact. Moreover, Minas had distinct problems. Its free population was generally unruly. In the early years of settlement the area experienced a short civil war and a number of antigovernment tax riots. The miners at first also refused to pay a tax for fugitive control. Not until 1744 were royal judges in Minas Gerais authorized to raise money (up to 300 *oitavas* of gold) to pay for antiquilombo operations.

The activist and racist Conde de Assumar (1717–1721) made mocambo control a central concern of his governorship. Like his predecessor, he suggested the arming of Indians and their use as slave catchers. In 1717 he suggested the creation of capitães do mato and by 1722 these posts had been established and a set of standing orders had been issued with a sliding scale of rewards for the return of fugitives depending on the distance the captain had to travel. A modern study of local sources was able to identify 117 quilombos in the region before 1800 and appointments of almost 500 slave catchers during the eighteenth century.

Assumar and various municipal councils in Minas Gerais were so preoccupied with the problem of slave control and mocambos that they were willing to suggest or try a variety of stringent and extraordinary measures aimed not only at the fugitives but also at the attempt to limit the number of manumissions in the region, claiming that the grants of liberty led to slave thefts and prostitution. He also suggested that the large number of free coloreds who controlled property in the area threatened the social hierarchy, and he ordered that free colored residents be prohibited from owning slaves and that no free black could serve as a godparent for a slave. These measures were impossible to enforce but they demonstrated Assumar's fear of a social order in which the lines of race and class had become blurred. For the threat of mocambos, he had other remedies. Unlike Bahia, where antiquilombo operations were left to bush captains or to officially sponsored expeditions, under Assumar anyone wishing to attack a quilombo could do so and carry whatever arms were necessary.

Such measures indicate a level of insecurity and fear in the mining zones seemingly exceeding that of the plantation areas. Assumar was perhaps an extreme example of such concern, but he was not alone. Local town councils in Minas also attempted to come to grips with threats to the social order by various ordinances aimed at controlling the free colored population and by actions against fugitives. A number of antimocambo operations were organized by town councils. In 1735 the câmara of Vila Rica called for the cutting off of a hand as a punishment for fugitive slaves. Perhaps the most infamous action was the barbarous suggestion of the town council of Mariana that fugitives when caught have their Achilles tendon severed, allowing them to hobble to work, but making flight almost impossible.

These attitudes and fears sometimes had dire consequences. In 1716 a quilombo with eighty to one hundred blacks who were raiding the roads near Vila Real and Vila Nova da Rainha was unsuccessfully attacked by a punitive expedition. The two towns organized a second force of 150 men, destroying the quilombo and killing a number of the defenders in a rage after they had surrendered. For the most part quilombos and fugitive slaves were seen as beyond the norms of civil society. In 1738 a petition from residents of Vila Rica to be exempted from prosecution for the death of calhambolas met with a favorable response from the governor.

All of the traditional methods of mocambo and fugitive control were tried in Minas Gerais, along with a few that were extraordinary. The large population of free coloreds in the captaincy and the many poor "vagrants" presented in themselves a threat to the social order, but one that might be effectively mobilized against the quilombos. Efforts to enlist them in anti-quilombo activities were made on various occasions. But these efforts did little to stem the problem. The free poor and the fugitive slaves were both manifestations of the inherent conditions of this society.

Quilombos, then, were an endemic problem in Minas Gerais. They were numerous and sometimes attained large size, although here too it is difficult to know much about their internal organization since we must depend on the descriptions of quilombo destruction. An account of an expedition that rescued some white children from a quilombo, for example, noted that the "mulatto entitled king, a concubine, and four slaves remained at large." Governor Gomes Freire de Andrada described an attack against a "small" quilombo of over 100 blacks made in 1746. This "small" quilombo must have contained between 100 and 200 people. The two largest quilombos of Minas—that of Ambrósio, destroyed in 1746, and the Quilombo Grande, attacked and eliminated in 1759—held large numbers of fugitives, the latter perhaps containing over 1,000 inhabitants. These, however, were exceptionally large in size.

Minas Gerais, therefore, despite its differing economic basis and social and racial configuration, reproduced and intensified many of the conditions that led to mocambo formation in the zones of export agriculture. The early frontier conditions, the considerable freedom of movement allowed to slaves in mining, the urban network, and the racial composition of the region all contributed to the formation of fugitive communities in the region. The response of colonial government to this problem in Minas Gerais and the techniques used to combat it were similar to those applied elsewhere in the colony. It is striking that the term *quilombo* was far more frequently used in Minas Gerais than in Bahia, where *mocambo* was preferred, although by the mid-eighteenth century both terms were in use. The term *quilombo,* in fact, came to mean an encampment of any group of outlaws. However, the term was used primarily to describe fugitive slave communities; and it has become a symbol of slave resistance in Brazil and, in more modern times, of a movement for equality for blacks in Brazil.

The linguistic difference between Bahia and Minas Gerais is to some extent chronological and it is related to the history of the great fugitive community of Palmares, which for almost a century had resisted all efforts to destroy it. Palmares became a symbol for royal administrators of how any fugitive community might become a real threat to civil society in a society so based on slavery. When the Count of Assumar wrote in 1719 "the blacks (of Minas) may be tempted to repeat the acts of the Palmares of Pernambuco, emboldened by their multitude," he was voicing a real fear. While Palmares was atypical in its size and its duration, its history cannot be separated from that of the other fugitive communities, if only because of its influence on how slave owners and royal officials viewed the problem. Moreover, because of its longevity and size and the long contact of colonial society with it, Palmares offers some opportunities to penetrate the internal dynamic of a fugitive community.

Rethinking Palmares

In dealing with the question of fugitive communities in Brazil it is necessary to keep the quilombo of Palmares in mind. Palmares, located in the interior of Alagoas, was by far the longest-lived and largest fugitive community. For almost the whole seventeenth century (1605?–1694) it persisted despite determined attempts to eliminate it by the Dutch and Portuguese colonial governments and by local residents of the neighboring captaincies. Because of its reputed size (over 20,000 inhabitants), longevity, and the continual colonial contact with it, we know more about its internal structure than we do about most of the mocambos. Still, the documentation on Palmares is not extensive and it tends to concentrate on the last decade of its existence and its final destruction. Therefore much remains unknown about it. That fact has not deterred authors from attempting to write its history or for romanticizing it into a "Black Troy," or a "republic." More recently, it has taken on a symbolic importance for Afro-Brazilians in their struggle for racial and social equality.

It has long been recognized that Palmares was based on a number of traditional African forms of political and social organization, although like most fugitive communities it combined these with aspects of European culture and specifically local adaptations. Palmares was not a single community but a number of mocambos united to form a neo-African kingdom. Various eyewitness accounts reveal much about Palmares's internal organization, although we must recognize that Palmares also had a history, and the organization and institutions noted at the end of the seventeenth century were not necessarily those of the earlier period. Moreover, the size of Palmares also changed over time. A mid-seventeenth-century account described Palmares as divided into two main settlements with many smaller ones, placing the population of the various settlements in Palmares at about 11,000. A later and often repeated estimate raised that figure to 20,000. This latter number seems exaggerated. During most of the seventeenth century Pernambuco and its adjacent captaincies had about 200 engenhos with an average of 100 slaves per mill. In other words, the estimate for Palmares of 20,000 inhabitants would equal the number of all slaves in the sugar economy of the region. Although this number seems unlikely, Palmares was undoubtedly the largest fugitive community to have existed in Brazil.

During its long history, Palmares was constantly under attack. The Dutch mounted three expeditions against it and after Portugal regained control of the Northeast in 1654, the war continued. Between 1672 and 1680 there was a military expedition almost every year. The fugitives resisted valiantly, but this constant pressure caused them to sue for peace with a recently arrived governor of Pernambuco in 1678. The "king" of Palmares, GANGA ZUMBA, had in fact tried this policy whenever a new governor arrived. Like the maroons of Jamaica, he had promised loyalty to the Portuguese Crown and return of any new fugitives in exchange for recognition of the quilombo's freedom. The Portuguese accepted these terms but soon violated them, and in Palmares itself a revolt took place in which the accommodationist Ganga Zumba was overthrown and killed by his nephew ZUMBI. The war continued. Expeditions occurred almost annually against the fugitives in the 1680s but with little success. The defenders of Palmares became masters of guerrilla warfare, adept at the use of camouflage and ambush. Frustrated, Portuguese colonial administrators adopted a new tactic. Hardened Indian fighters and slavers from São Paulo who had been used in Bahia to open the interior were now contracted to eliminate Palmares. Their assault began in 1692, and for two years with the aid of local troops and the indispensable Indian allies, they slowly reduced the perimeter of the main mocambo's defenses. The final battle was fought in February 1694. Two hundred fugitives were killed, 500 captured, and another 200 reportedly committed suicide rather than surrender. Zumbi, wounded and in flight, was betrayed, captured, and decapitated. Palmares was no more, but as late as 1746, slaves were still fleeing to the site of Palmares and once again forming into fugitive groups.

European observers did not always understand what they saw, but from their descriptions it is clear that Palmares was an organized state under the control of a king with subordinate chiefs in outlying settlements. While some accounts speak of an election process, the leadership of one village by Ganga Zumba's mother and the succession of Zumbi, Ganga Zumba's nephew, to the throne suggests the existence of a royal lineage. The ceremonial postures and demonstrations of obedience required in the king's presence all point to forms of African kingship. The Palmares fugitives lived by agriculture, although like other mocambos they also traded for arms and other commodities with those whites who lived on the borders. Like most of the mocambos they also raided for women, cattle, and food. As in many African societies, slavery existed in Palmares. Those who came to Palmares by choice were considered free, but those taken in raids were enslaved. The villages of Palmares were protected by palisades, walls, or by a network of hidden traps much like those of the Bahian mocambo of Buraco de Tatú. Religion in the encampments was a fusion of Christian and African elements, although here too there may have been far more African features than observers realized.

In many ways Palmares seems to have been an adaptation of African cultural forms to the Brazilian colonial situation in which slaves of various origins, African and *crioulo,* came together in their common opposition to slavery. Within Palmares, people called each other *malungo,* or comrade, a term of adoptive kinship also used among slaves who had arrived together on the same slave ship.

In Palmares we can see the attempt to form a community out of peoples of disparate origins. Such an attempt had to be made by all fugitive communities, but in the case of Palmares there are some specific features that help to explain its particular history as well as the history of slave resistance in colonial Brazil as a whole. The search for "African" elements at Palmares and in the cultural "survivals" of slaves or fugitives as a whole has too often focused on specific cultural or ethnic identities. In fact, much of what passed for African "ethnicity" in Brazil were colonial creations. Categories or groupings such as "Congo" or "Angola" had no ethnic content in themselves and often combined peoples drawn from broad areas of Africa who before enslavement had shared little sense of relationship or identity. That these categories were sometimes adopted by the slaves themselves indicates not only the slaves' adaptability but also the fact that African societies had considerable experience with, and a variety of institutions for, the integration of disparate peoples and the creation of solidarities across ethnic lines.

There is, I believe, a deeper story in Palmares and one with broad implications for the subsequent history of slave resistance in Brazil. A key to the problem lies in the etymology of the word *quilombo.* This term came to mean in Brazil any community of escaped slaves, and its usual meaning and origin is given as the MBUNDU word for war-camp. By the eighteenth century, the term was in general use in Brazil, but it always remained secondary to the older word *mocambo,* a Mbundu word meaning hideout. In fact, the word *quilombo* does not appear in any contemporaneous document until the end of the seventeenth century except for its midcentury use by the poet Gregório de Mattos, who employed it with the meaning of any place where blacks congregated. The first document I have seen with the term *quilombo* used for a fugitive community is dated 1691 and it deals specifically with Palmares. The chronology and the connection with Palmares are not accidental. Within the term *quilombo* is encoded an unwritten history that only now, because of recent research in African history, can be at least partially understood.

While Palmares combined a number of African cultural traditions and included among its inhabitants crioulos, mulattoes, Indians, and even some renegade whites, or *mestiços,* as well as Africans, clearly the traditions of Angola predominated. Its residents referred to Palmares as *angola janga* (little Angola) in recognition of that fact, and in a complaint of 1672 the municipal council of Salvador referred to the "oppression we all suffer from the gentiles of Angola who live in Palmares." But, within the context of Angolan history, what is the significance of that connection for the history of Palmares?

The kingdom of Ndongo, which the Portuguese came to call ANGOLA in the late sixteenth century, was a land in turmoil, invaded from the coast by the Portuguese and from the interior by bands of marauding warriors from central Africa. The dissolution of the Old Kingdom of Kongo and the LUNDA state in Kitanga created a period of military struggle and disruption that destroyed villages and uprooted peoples. Powerful groups of uprooted warriors, calling themselves IMBANGALA or Yaka (called JAGA by the Portuguese), swept into present-day Angola, disrupting existing states and eventually creating a series of new polities.

The precise origins and cultural traditions of the Imbangala and even the relationship of the designations Jaga, Imbangala, and Yaka have been a matter of debate among Africanists for some time, but some aspects of Imbangala/Jaga society were noted by contemporary observers and are of direct interest to historians of slave resistance in Brazil, and especially to those interested in Palmares. First, the Imbangala raiders lived on a permanent war footing. Reportedly, they killed the babies born to their women, but they integrated adopted children into their ranks so that over time they came to be a composite force of large numbers of people of various ethnic backgrounds united by an organized military structure. That organization and a reputed military ferocity made them the scourge of the region, highly effective and greatly feared. Imbangala-Portuguese relations were alternately hostile and friendly. Between 1611 and 1619, Imbangala lords served as mercenaries for the Portuguese governors and supplied a flow of captives to the slave traders at Luanda. New states were formed by an Imbangala fusion with the indigenous lineages as the Imbangala conquered or created a number of kingdoms among the Mbundu peoples of the Congo-Angola region. Two of these states were the kingdom of Kasange and the kingdom of Matamba, ruled by Queen NZINGA, with whom the Portuguese first fought until the mid-seventeenth century, when an alliance was formed. These states battled each other for control of the Kwango River basin, a struggle that opened up this region to increased slaving.

As the Imbangala moved southward into Angola in the early seventeenth century, they encountered among the Mbundu people an institution that they adapted to their purposes. This was the *ki-lombo,* a male initiation society or circumcision camp where young men were prepared for adulthood and warrior status. The Imbangala molded this institution to their own purposes. Torn from ancestral lands and gods, sharing no common lineage, living by conquest, and—according to European observers—rejecting agriculture, the traditional basis of societies in this region, the Imbangala needed an institution that provided cohesion to the disparate ethnic elements comprising their bands. The ki-lombo, a military society to which any man by training and initiation could belong, served that purpose. Designed for war, this institution created a powerful warrior cult by incorporating large numbers of strangers who lacked a common ancestry. The Imbangala ki-lombo was distinctive because of its ritual laws. Lineage and kinship, so important to the other basically matrilineal peoples of the region, were denied within its confines, and although European observers spoke of infanticide, women could leave the confines of the ki-lombo itself to bear their children. What was prohibited was a legal matrilineal link within the ki-lombo that might challenge the concept of a society structured by initiation rather than by kinship. Historian Joseph Miller believes that the Imbangala killing of their own children was a metaphor for the ceremonial elimination of kinship ties and their replacement with the rules and proscriptions of the ki-lombo.

The creation of a social organization based on association created risks. The inhabitants of the ki-lombo stood in a special spiritual danger since they lacked the normal lineage ancestors who might intercede with the gods on their behalf. Thus a chief figure in the ki-lombo was the *nganga a nzumbi,* a priest whose responsibility was to deal with the spirits of the dead. The Ganga Zumba of Palmares was probably the holder of this office, which was in effect not a personal name but a title. There are other echoes from the descriptions of Angola that seem suggestive. In the Imbangala, quilombo leadership depended on some kind of popular acclaim or election just as some of the Brazilian accounts suggest. Most curious is the observation of Andrew Battell, who lived among the Imbangala and who noted that their chief luxury was palm wine and that their routes and camps were influenced by the availability of palm trees. His comment makes the association of the maroon community with a region of Palmares (the word means palm trees) seem more than coincidental.

If the founders of Palmares had used the Imbangala ki-lombo as the basis for their society, their version of it was incomplete or at least a variation on the basic model. A number of features associated with the Imbangala ki-lombos had no parallel in Brazil. The Imbangala were always referred to as cannibals who practiced cannibalism and human sacrifice to terrorize their enemies. These practices were strictly controlled, as was the preparation of *magi a samba,* a paste made from human fat and other substances that supposedly made the ki-lombo warriors invincible. A strict set of ritual laws (*kijila*) surrounded the ki-lombo. Women were prohibited from the interior compound of the ki-lombo and there were strict ritual proscriptions against menstruating women. None of these customs is mentioned in the surviving documentation on Palmares.

The use of the term *quilombo* in reference to Palmares does not necessarily mean that all the ritual aspects of that institution as they were practiced in Angola were present in Brazil or that the founders or the subsequent leaders of Palmares were necessarily Imbangala. Many aspects of the Imbangala ki-lombo could be found in other Central African institutions like the *kimpasi,* secret initiation camps of the Kongo, which also created new social bonds by association. Much of what was inherent in the ki-lombo would have been understood by non-Imbangala. As noted, Imbangala dynasties and institutions were incorporated in a number of Mbundu states, and the quilombo came to symbolize the sovereignty of these states. Our best source in this regard is Antônio de Oliveira de Cadornega, the principal chronicler of seventeenth-century Angola. Cadornega used the term *quilombo* not only to describe Jaga troops but also as a descriptive term for the kingdoms of Matamba and Kasange. The use of the phrase *kingdom and quilombo* of Matamba was a general descriptive use of *quilombo* that referred to these Imbangala-influenced polities but did not necessarily suggest the full existence of the original institution nor its ritual practices. *Quilombo* was becoming a synonym for a kingdom of a particular type in Angola.

Given the poor documentary record of Palmares, much of the above hypothesis is admittedly tenuous, but I believe there is enough evidence to suggest that the introduction of the term *quilombo* into Brazil in the late seventeenth century was not accidental and that it represented more than simply a linguistic borrowing. If true, then we must deal with the African aspects of Palmares not as "survivals" disembodied from their original cultural milieu, but a far more dynamic and perhaps intentional use of an African institution that had been specifically designed to create a community among peoples of disparate origins and to provide an effective military organization. Surely, the fugitive slaves of Brazil fitted such a description, and the attacks made upon them by colonial governments made the military organization of the quilombo essential for survival. The success of quilombos varied as greatly as the quilombos themselves in size, leadership, longevity, and internal organization. Taken together, Palmares and the smaller fugitive communities represented a continuous commentary on the Brazilian slave regime.

From *Slaves, Peasants, and Rebels: Reconsidering Brazilian Slavery*. University of Illinois Press, 1992. Used with permission.

See also Candomblé; Maroonage in the Americas; Palmares: An African State in Brazil; Slave Rebellions in Latin America and the Caribbean; Syncretism.

Stuart Schwartz

Réunion

Island territory of France located in the Indian Ocean 680 kilometers (420 miles) east of Madagascar.

Although the vast majority of France's overseas possessions are now independent, Réunion has remained a French *département d'outre mer,* an overseas department intricately tied to the political economy of France. The island's demography reflects its history of colonization, slavery, and indentured labor. Creoles (people of mixed African descent) constitute the largest group, followed by people whose descent can be traced directly to France. Réunion is also home to a significant Indian population, mostly Hindu Tamils but also some Catholics and Muslims, as well as Chinese and East African communities. French culture has had a strong influence: the majority of the people speak French and/or Creole and practice Roman Catholicism, and many combine the worship of Catholic saints with popular beliefs in magic and sorcery.

Precolonial and Colonial History

Most accounts of precolonial Réunion claim that the Portuguese explorer Pedro de Mascarenhas discovered the uninhabited volcanic island on February 9, Saint Apolline's Day, during his 1512–1514 voyage to India, after which he named it Saint Appollina. Other sources suggest that another Portuguese explorer, Tristan da Cunha, discovered the island in 1507. Still others have claimed that the Phoenicians, Indians, and Arabs knew of the island much earlier. The first known inclusion of the island on a map occurred in 1518, on a map of the region by the Portuguese cartographer Pedro Reinel. During the early seventeenth century, the French cardinal Armand Jean du Plessis Richelieu sent a ship to take possession of the island under the name Mascarin Island, in honor of its presumed discoverer.

Recognizing the island's strategic location along sea routes to India, France claimed ownership of it in 1638 and renamed it Ile Bourbon. French soldiers expelled from Fort Dauphin, Madagascar, on charges of mutiny moved there in 1662, but it was only formally settled in 1665 by the French East India Company. In 1669 the company's settlement was moved from Saint Paul's Bay to Saint Denis, a harbor on the northern coast. France showed little interest in the small colony until Fort Dauphin was attacked by Malagasy in 1674, after which the French survivors relocated to Bourbon. The island then took center stage in the French *campagnie des Indes* and as the principal port of call between the Cape of Good Hope and French outposts in Pondicherry, India. The early settlement grew very slowly, with only 316 inhabitants (113 of them slaves) in 1698. By 1710 the population had grown to approximately 1,000, but after the French East India Company introduced coffee in 1715, the population grew rapidly, particularly the number of slaves. The company required that all settlers grow the crop, and by 1744 the colony was exporting more than 1,000 tons of coffee each year.

By 1724 the population of the island had grown to 12,500. But France was already turning its attention to nearby Mauritius, abandoned by the Dutch in 1715. Attracted by its excellent natural harbor, the French quickly claimed and began to settle Mauritius under the name Ile de France. Between 1727 and 1735 Bourbon remained the administrative capital, under the governorship of Pierre-Benoît Dunmas, but when Bertrand Francois Mahé de Labourdonnais took over in 1735, he moved the seat of government to Ile de France. The Bourbon economy stagnated during much of the eighteenth century. Coffee harvests were small, and due to increasing production from the West Indies, world coffee prices were low. In response, the settlers began to cultivate alternative crops, including cotton and tobacco. Although the French East India Company introduced spice crops such as cloves, vanilla, and nutmeg, the island's economy came to be centered on the production of food crops for Ile de France.

Ownership of Bourbon, along with Ile de France, transferred from the French East India Company to the French Crown in 1767. After the French Revolution, Bourbon became known as Ile de la Réunion, and a local, elected assembly began to govern the colony. The settlers gained more local autonomy, but the abolition of slavery within the French Empire threatened to undermine their heavily slave-based economy. In the face of settler opposition in Réunion, Ile de France, and elsewhere, France revoked the ban on slavery in 1802, but also resumed direct control over all the island colonies.

France and Great Britain had been competing for hegemony in the Indian Ocean since the War of Austrian Succession (1740–1748). Conflicts continued throughout the eighteenth and nineteenth centuries during the Seven Years' War (1756–1763), the War of American Independence (1775–1783), and finally the Napoleonic Wars (1793–1815). In 1810 the British captured Réunion and Ile de France, renaming them Bourbon and Mauritius, respectively, and firmly establishing British dominance in the Indian Ocean. Because Bourbon's poor harbor minimized its strategic importance and value to Britain, it was returned to France in 1814 under the Treaty of Paris.

The only remaining French possession in the Indian Ocean, Bourbon reoriented agricultural production to prioritize SUGAR, which France had previously imported from Mauritius. Bourbon's annual sugar exports increased from twenty-one tons in 1815 to 74,000 tons in 1860. Meanwhile, because Bourbon was no longer forced to supply food to Mauritius, production of foodstuffs plummeted, and the island became a net food importer by the 1840s.

The year 1848 saw the creation of the Second Republic in France and brought major social reforms. Universal suffrage was instituted and slavery once again abolished in both France and its possessions, including the again-renamed Ile de la Réunion. Once again an economic crisis loomed, as sugar cultivation required a large labor force. Many freed slaves, no longer wishing to work on the large sugar plantations but unable to grow sugar efficiently on the small plots that remained, moved to towns or to the less densely populated highland areas, where they became subsistence horticulturists.

Large numbers of Indians, primarily from Pondicherry, emigrated to Réunion as indentured laborers. The French were permitted to recruit workers from British-controlled India with the stipulation that workers be repatriated upon the completion of their contract, if they so desired. Many did in fact return to India after a stint in Réunion. But the British officially prohibited Réunion's recruitment of Indian labor in 1885, leaving the island's plantation owners more dependent on labor recruited from Malaysia, China, East Africa, and the Annamite Mountains in Vietnam.

Réunion lost much of its strategic significance after the opening of the SUEZ CANAL in 1869. Although some farmers began to diversify into crops used in the production of perfume oils, such as geraniums, vanilla, and vetiver, the economy remained heavily dependent on sugar, and thus vulnerable to fluctuations in world market prices. Nonetheless, the second half of the nineteenth century saw the construction of an artificial port and a railway that spanned the island. These projects helped Réunion increase sugar exports during World War I, but the resulting economic recovery was short-lived. By the end of World War II, Réunion's economy had again deteriorated, leaving much of the population desperately poor. Long relegated to the periphery of French concerns, the troubled island became a département d'outre mer in 1946.

Postcolonial Developments

As a département, Réunion gained representation in the French senate as well as access to government funds for much-needed infrastructure improvements. The island experienced a massive influx of money to improve transportation, communications, and agricultural productivity. Complete political-economic integration with France also meant that Réunionais were eligible for the same government programs, such as social security benefits, free education, and public health care, that were available to other French citizens. These and other social reforms helped build the island's middle class, while protective trade barriers and the establishment of media ties to the *métropole* (continental France) fostered the dominance of French culture, as did the influx of large numbers of Parisian bureaucrats.

In 1973 the French established a military base on the island with 4,000 troops. The following year, Réunion became a region of France, similar in status to the twenty-two other regions of metropolitan France. In the 1980s Réunion's status was once again redefined, this time as a *collectivité territoriale*, which granted the island's residents greater autonomy over internal affairs. Although occasionally certain groups, such as the French Communist Party in 1959 and the ORGANIZATION OF AFRICAN UNITY (OAU) in 1978, have called for the island's independence, the proposals have generally received little support from a population well aware of the economic security gained through territorial ties to France.

Indeed, Réunion's economic improvements since the 1950s have been fueled more by the steady flow of funds from France than by productivity on the island itself. Sugar still dominates the economy, accounting for 60 percent of export earnings, although the industry employs only 9.7 percent of the population. Approximately three-quarters of all employment is within the service sector, especially TOURISM. But large numbers of people are chronically unemployed and dependent upon social security, and a full three-quarters of the population receives social security benefits. Public opinion in France tends to view Réunion as a financial liability. In turn, many Réunionais resent the obvious disparity in wealth between themselves and tourists, the vast majority of whom are French. The average Réunionais earns a gross disposable income only 57 percent that of the typical person in metropolitan France, despite the recent increase in the minimum wage to a level on par with the métropole. The large wealth gap between well-off Réunionais and the many poor residents of the island is also a constant source of tensions that erupted into severe rioting in 1991. Whites and Indians fare better than other groups, whose level of unemployment and poverty are similar to poorer African nations.

See also Colonial Rule; Indian Ocean Slave Trade.

Ari Nave

Revels, Hiram Rhoades

1822–1901

American minister and university president; first African American to serve in the U.S. Senate.

Hiram Revels, the son of former slaves, was born in Fayetteville, North Carolina. He studied at several seminaries in Indiana and Ohio before becoming a minister in the AFRICAN METHODIST EPISCOPAL CHURCH (AME). During the AMERICAN CIVIL WAR, Revels helped to organize African American regiments in Maryland and Mississippi. After the Civil War he moved to Mississippi and became active in REPUBLICAN PARTY politics. He was selected to complete Jefferson Davis's unexpired term in the U.S. Senate. After leaving the Senate, Revels served as the president of Alcorn University.

Bibliography

Litvin, Martin. *Hiram Revels in Illinois: A Biographical Novel about a Lost Chapter in the Life of America's First Black U.S. Senator.* Log City Books, 1974.

Robert Fay

Reverend Ike

1935–

American minister whose teachings emphasize that happiness and fulfillment come from financial prosperity and self-confidence.

Frederick Eikerenkoetter, known familiarly as Reverend Ike, earned a B.A. in theology from the American Bible College in Chicago in 1955. In 1962 he established the United Christian Evangelistic Association (UCEA). For donations, he sent Blessing Plans which he claimed would provide the framework for success.

Eminently successful himself, he became the first African American minister with a television show. By 1972 Reverend Ike claimed over 1,000,000 followers by 1972, and over 7,000,000 ten years later. Critics called him a con artist, and many argued that his belief in personal success undermined African American community advancement and distorted the Christian message. Though less visible today, the UCEA still operates internationally.

Robert Fay

Revolutionary Action Movement

African American nationalist organization, in operation between 1963 and 1968, that advocated violence to achieve black empowerment.

During the 1960s, some African Americans, frustrated by the government's lack of responsiveness to problems in the black community such as unemployment, overcrowded housing, and police brutality, formulated and organized radical ways of effecting political and social change. This large-scale effort became known, overall, as the BLACK POWER MOVEMENT. The Revolutionary Action Movement (RAM), one of the earliest Black Nationalist organizations of the 1960s, asserted that violence was the only way to alter fundamentally the structure of American society.

Through grassroots organizing that included African American history classes, RAM built up a liberation army in PHILADELPHIA, PENNSYLVANIA, and NEW YORK, NEW YORK. The organization also published a bimonthly magazine, *Black America,* and a free weekly, *RAM Speaks.* Its several hundred members included teachers, students, and businesspeople. ROBERT FRANKLIN WILLIAMS, a former leader of a North Carolina branch of the NATIONAL ASSOCIATION FOR THE ADVANCEMENT OF COLORED PEOPLE (NAACP), served as RAM's president while in self-imposed exile, first in CUBA, then in China.

Because of RAM's militant ideology and grassroots activism, the U.S. Federal Bureau of Investigation (FBI) attempted to destroy it. Two 1967 FBI raids of RAM headquarters in New York City led to twenty-four arrests and the seizure of over 130 weapons. Nine RAM members were convicted and imprisoned for conspiring to poison the police force, blow up city hall, and/or murder local and national leaders, including leaders of the NAACP and the NATIONAL URBAN LEAGUE. RAM leaders not imprisoned either left the country or were placed under surveillance. This resulted in the collapse of the organization in 1968. Many former RAM members went on to contribute to the formation of other black nationalist organizations, such as the REPUBLIC OF NEW AFRICA.

See also Black Nationalism in the United States.

Bibliography

Bracey, John H., comp. *Black Nationalism in America.* Edited by John H. Bracey, Jr., August Meier, and Elliott Rudwick. Bobbs-Merrill, 1970.

Brisbane, Robert. *Black Activism: Racial Revolution in the U.S., 1954–1970.* Judson Press, 1974.

Aaron Myers

Rhinoceros

Second largest land mammal after the elephant.

Two species of rhinoceros are found in Africa. The larger of the African species, the white rhinoceros (*Ceratotherium simum*), grows to 1.8 m (6 feet) at the shoulder and weighs up to 2,300 kg (5,000 lb). The black rhinoceros (*Diceros bicornis*) grows to 1.7 m (5.5 ft) and weighs up to 1,100 kg (2,500 lb). Both species possess two horns, the longer of which can grow to over 1 m (3 ft).

The rhinoceros, a nearsighted herbivore, is generally peaceful, becoming aggressive only when its territory is disturbed. Both African species are endangered and are officially protected, although they are still illegally killed because their horns are highly valued as ingredients in traditional Asian medicine and as dagger handles in Yemen. In 1994 naturalists estimated that a total of 2,000 black rhinoceroses and 5,000 white rhinoceroses remain scattered throughout sub-Saharan Africa. This number increased to a total of 13,109 in 1999 and 14,770 in 2003.

Bibliography

Cunningham, Carol, and Joel Berger. *Horn of Darkness: Rhinos on the Edge.* Oxford University Press, 1997.

Robert Fay

Rhodes, Cecil

1853–1902

British colonial statesman and financier; one of the main promoters of British rule in southern Africa.

Cecil Rhodes was born on July 5, 1853, in Bishop's Stortford, England. At the age of seventeen he was sent from his home in England to live with his brother in what is now SOUTH AFRICA. Diamond fields had been discovered at Kimberley in Cape Colony that year, and Rhodes became a diamond prospector. By the time he was nineteen years old he had accumulated a large fortune. At the age of twenty he returned to England to study at the University of Oxford, and for the next eight years he divided his time between the university and the diamond fields. During this period he consolidated the Cape Colony's diamond-mining claims to form De Beers Mining Company.

Rhodes's control over this important industry earned him an audience in the colonial Parliament, where he advocated the use of military might to secure a cheap African labor force. He also expressed his views on race. In a speech before Parliament in 1877 he said, "These are my politics on native affairs, and these are the politics of South Africa. Treat the natives as subject people as long as they continue in a state of barbarism and communal tenure; be the lords over them, and let them be a subject race, and keep the liquor from them."

In 1881 Rhodes entered the Cape Colony Parliament, where he served for the remainder of his life. He was largely responsible for the annexation to the British Empire of Bechuanaland (now BOTSWANA) in 1885. In 1888, with the founding of De Beers Consolidated Mines, Rhodes monopolized the diamond production of Kimberley. That same year he wrested exclusive mining rights from Lobengula, the ruler of Matabeleland (now in ZIMBABWE). In 1889 Rhodes was granted a charter to incorporate the British South Africa Company. It controlled what are now Zimbabwe and ZAMBIA—the area was named Rhodesia in 1894 in honor of Rhodes—until 1923.

In 1890 Rhodes was made prime minister of Cape Colony. Five years later he supported a conspiracy by British settlers in the South African Republic, in what is now northeastern South Africa, to overthrow the government of the republic, which was dominated by AFRIKANER, or Boer, members. The revolt was to be backed by a British South Africa Company force led by Sir Leander Starr Jameson, British administrator of the lands that make up present-day Zimbabwe. On December 29, 1895, Jameson prematurely and unsuccessfully invaded the South African Republic. Rhodes was acquitted of responsibility for the invasion, known as Jameson's Raid, but was censured for his role in the plot against the government of the South African Republic and forced to resign his premiership the following month. After his resignation, he devoted himself to the development of Rhodesia. During the Boer War (1899–1902) he was prominent in the defense of Kimberley. He died on March 26, 1902, in Cape Town, South Africa. In his will, Rhodes left most of his fortune to the establishment of the Rhodes scholarships.

Bibliography

Samkange, Stanlake. *What Rhodes Really Said about Africans.* Harare Publishing House, 1982.

Alonford James Robinson

Rhodesia

Former name of Zimbabwe and Zambia.

Prior to 1964, Rhodesia was a British colony that included the regions of Northern Rhodesia (now ZAMBIA) and Southern Rhodesia (now ZIMBABWE). In 1964 Northern Rhodesia declared its independence, becoming Zambia. After Northern Rhodesia's independence, Southern Rhodesia was commonly referred to as simply Rhodesia. This name became official within the country in 1966, with the approval of a new constitution. This constitution did not receive international recognition, however, because it resulted from the Unilateral Declaration of Independence from Britain by the repressive white-minority government led by IAN DOUGLAS SMITH. In 1980 white rule was toppled, and the newly independent Rhodesia adopted the name Zimbabwe.

Rhodesia, Northern

Former name of Zambia.

See also Zambia.

Rhys, Jean

1890–1979

Novelist and short-story writer.

For many readers, Jean Rhys is best remembered as the English author of the novel *Wide Sargasso Sea* (1966), whose plot is a "prequel" to Charlotte Brontë's novel *Jane Eyre* (1847). For critics of Caribbean literature, however, Rhys poses the provocative question of how one defines a Caribbean writer. Rhys was born in Roseau, Dominica, to a Welsh father and a white Dominican Creole mother, but after moving to England at age sixteen, she never lived in the Caribbean again. Writer and scholar EDWARD KAMAU BRATHWAITE spoke for many West Indians when he argued that "white Creoles in the English and French West Indies have separated themselves by too wide a gulf and have contributed too little culturally as a group" for Rhys and those like her to be considered Caribbean writers. But the influences and impressions of Rhys's Dominican childhood are woven throughout all of her fiction and are essential to *Wide Sargasso Sea,* which is considered one of the best depictions of West Indian Creole society and an important postcolonial Caribbean novel.

Wide Sargasso Sea was written when Rhys was seventy-six years old, and it marked a renaissance in her writing career. As a young woman, Rhys attended drama school in London and then joined a traveling drama troupe for several years. She lived in cities throughout Europe during the 1920s with the first of her three husbands, and began her writing career while living in Paris. Her friends there included writers James Joyce, Ernest Hemingway, and Ford Madox Ford. With their encouragement she published *Left Bank,* her first collection of short stories, in 1927, and her first novel, *Postures*—based on Rhys's affair with Ford and his mistress—in 1928 (it was rereleased the following year as *Quartet*). Three more novels followed in the early 1930s, and while these stories and novels all have European settings, several of their characters have West Indian pasts similar to Rhys's own.

After this productive period, however, her writing slowed, and for most of the 1940s and 1950s she lived in England in relative obscurity. But in 1957, a BBC radio adaptation of her 1934 novel *Good Morning, Midnight* brought Rhys to the attention of critic Francis Wyndham, who encouraged her to rework the old draft that became *Wide Sargasso Sea.* The novel tells the story of *Jane Eyre*'s "madwoman in the attic," a character that Rhys creates as Antoinette Cosway, Mr. Rochester's West Indian first wife. Like Rhys, Antoinette is a white Creole, and through Antoinette's relationship with her black nursemaid Christophine and the other black West Indians around her, Rhys paints a compelling portrait of the complicated, and often incestuous, racial tensions in West Indian society just after emancipation. It is this exploration of race and class that has made *Wide Sargasso Sea* such an important postcolonial Caribbean novel.

Rhys's last collection of stories, *Sleep It Off Lady* (1976), is also set largely in the Caribbean. But it is *Wide Sargasso Sea* that is most often discussed in West Indian journals and included in anthologies of Caribbean literature, and while some critics still question this inclusion, others see it as completely natural. Rhys has been compared to Caribbean writers such as V. S. Naipaul, Paule Marshall, and Michelle Cliff, who also spent most of their lives elsewhere, but whose work nevertheless is identified with the Caribbean literary tradition. Rhys is included in the *Dictionary of Literary Biography* in both volume 36, *British Novelists, 1890–1929: Modernists,* and volume 117, *Twentieth-Century Caribbean and Black African Writers.* The entry in volume 117 asserts that "[t]he themes of alienation, exile, and displacement that are central in her work are also central to Caribbean writing as a whole . . . No one who knows the Caribbean well could deny that Rhys's work is grounded in a Caribbean consciousness."

See also Literature, English-Language, in the Caribbean.

Bibliography

Angier, Carole. *Jean Rhys: Life and Work.* Little, Brown, 1990.

Emery, Mary Lou. *Jean Rhys at "World's End": Novels of Colonial and Sexual Exile.* University of Texas Press, 1990.

Howells, Carol Ann. *Jean Rhys.* St. Martin's Press, 1991.

Lisa Clayton Robinson

Rhythm and Blues

African American musical style developed after World War II that reflected the growing confidence of African Americans and introduced a greater emotional depth to American popular music.

Rhythm and blues (R&B) is the general term for African American popular music since World War II. R&B melded the earlier musical styles of BLUES, JAZZ, BOOGIE-WOOGIE, and GOSPEL MUSIC. It matured in the late 1940s, and between 1954 and 1960 broke through racial barriers and achieved unprecedented visibility in white-oriented popular music. Ultimately, however, this development took control of African Americans' own music away from them, as white performers—backed by major record companies and playing watered-down versions of R&B—in effect hijacked the form.

R&B thus reflects complex relationships between the races as well as the constraints placed on black cultural expression. Yet despite these constraints, R&B transformed American popular culture. It challenged the vapidity of white pop music, and its propulsive beat and sexual overtones catalyzed the development of rock and roll. Most significantly, however, R&B expressed the pride and vitality of a new urban black culture that emerged as a product of the GREAT MIGRATION out of the rural South.

Musical Origins of R&B

R&B developed out of various earlier styles of black music, especially blues, jazz, and gospel and harmony singing. Chicago blues, epitomized by the searing electric guitar of MUDDY WATERS and the raspy, acid-etched singing of HOWLIN' WOLF, emerged almost simultaneously with R&B and was a major component of the R&B sound. Southwestern blues shouters such as Big Joe Turner were also important. The driving, eight-beats-to-the-bar rhythm of boogie-woogie also influenced many piano players, including Amos Milburn and LITTLE RICHARD and provided the underlying rhythm that characterized much R&B.

Jazz contributed to R&B through jump bands like Louis Jordan and his Tympany Five. Jordan's rhythmic approach, using a heavy backbeat that placed the stress on the second and fourth beats of each measure, was particularly important. R&B's gruff, blustery tenor saxophones drew inspiration from jazz players Illinois Jacquet and Arnett Cobb. Indeed, many jazz musicians played in R&B recording sessions or toured in R&B bands, as did JOHN COLTRANE and CLIFFORD BROWN.

Harmony singing contributed the last key ingredient in R&B. African Americans have a tradition of *a cappella* group singing that reaches back at least to the RAGTIME quartets of the late nineteenth century. Many R&B vocal groups began by modeling themselves on such popular singing groups of the 1930s as the MILLS BROTHERS and the INK SPOTS. Even more important was the influence of gospel music. GOSPEL QUARTETS, from the jazzed-up harmonies of the Golden Gate Quartet to the more soulful approach of the SOUL STIRRERS and the Dixie Hum-

African Americans in the Rock and Roll Hall of Fame

Year	Inductee	Category
1986	Robert Johnson	Early Influences
	Jimmy Yancey	Early Influences
	Chuck Berry	Artists
	James Brown	Artists
	Ray Charles	Artists
	Sam Cooke	Artists
	Fats Domino	Artists
	Little Richard	Artists
1987	Louis Jordan	Early Influences
	T-Bone Walker	Early Influences
	Bo Diddley	Artists
	The Coasters	Artists
	Aretha Franklin	Artists
	Marvin Gaye	Artists
	B.B. King	Artists
	Clyde McPhatter	Artists
	Smokey Robinson	Artists
	Big Joe Turner	Artists
	Muddy Waters	Artists
	Jackie Wilson	Artists
1988	Berry Gordy Jr.	Nonperforming
	Leadbelly	Early Influences
	The Drifters	Artists
	The Supremes	Artists
1989	The Ink Spots	Early Influences
	Bessie Smith	Early Influences
	The Soul Stirrers	Early Influences
	Otis Redding	Artists
	The Temptations	Artists
	Stevie Wonder	Artists
1990	Lamont Dozier, Brian Holland & Eddie Holland	Nonperforming
	Louis Armstrong	Early Influences
	Hank Ballard	Artists
	The Platters	Artists
1991	Dave Bartholomew	Nonperforming
	Howlin' Wolf	Early Influences
	La Vern Baker	Artists
	John Lee Hooker	Artists
	The Impressions	Artists
	Wilson Pickett	Artists
	Jimmy Reed	Artists
	Ike and Tina Turner	Artists
1992	Elmore James	Early Influences
	Professor Longhair	Early Influences
	Bobby "Blue" Bland	Artists
	Booker T. and the MGs	Artists
	The Jimi Hendrix Experience	Artists
	The Isley Brothers	Artists
	Sam and Dave	Artists
1993	Dinah Washington	Early Influences
	Ruth Brown	Artists
	Etta James	Artists
	Frankie Lymon & the Teenagers	Artists
	Sly & the Family Stone	Artists
1994	Willie Dixon	Early Influences
	Bob Marley	Artists
1995	The Orioles	Early Influences
	Al Green	Artists
	Martha and the Vandellas	Artists
1996	Gladys Knight and the Pips	Artists
	Little Willie John	Artists
	The Shirelles	Artists
1997	Mahalia Jackson	Early Influences
	The Jackson Five	Artists
	Parliament-Funkadelic	Artists
1998	Allen Toussaint	Nonperforming
	Jelly Roll Morton	Early Influences
	Lloyd Price	Artists
1999	Charles Brown	Early Influences
	Curtis Mayfield	Artists
	The Staple Singers	Artists
2000	Nat "King" Cole	Early Influences
	Billie Holiday	Early Influences
	Earth, Wind & Fire	Artists
	The Moonglows	Artists
	King Curtis	Sidemen
	James Jamerson	Sidemen
	Earl Palmer	Sidemen
2001	Solomon Burke	Artists
	The Flamingos	Artists
	Michael Jackson	Artists
	Johnnie Johnson	Sidemen
2002	Isaac Hayes	Artists
2003	Benny Benjamin	Sidemen
2004	The Dells	Artists
	Prince	Artists

mingbirds, gained popularity in the 1930s and 1940s and offered encouragement to many later R&B singers.

An equally strong influence came from the singing in non-denominational, sanctified churches, with their fervent and freewheeling vocal approach. This style of singing uses complex improvised embellishment (*melisma*), including dips, slides, and *blue notes* (notes that bridge the relationship between the major and minor modes), as seen in the singing of

Clyde McPhatter, Jerry Butler, and OTIS REDDING. The greatest exemplar of the secularized gospel sound, however, was pianist and singer RAY CHARLES.

Cultural Milieu

R&B was above all an urban music, emerging in various black communities that burgeoned during the Great Migration, including Los Angeles's Central Avenue, Chicago's South Side, and HARLEM, NEW YORK. R&B performers perfected their music at Harlem's APOLLO THEATER and in countless nightclubs, cabarets, and after-hours spots that were urban manifestations of the jook joints found throughout the South. Singer Jimmy Witherspoon fondly recalled the many after-hours spots in Los Angeles, including "Alex Lovejoy's Big Legged Chicken, Brother's, Stuff Crouch's Back Stage, [and] Black Dot McGee's."

This new music voiced the pride of a new generation of African Americans. Numerous songs paid tribute to a lively black conviviality, including Milburn's "Chicken Shack Boogie" (1947), Louis Jordan's "Saturday Night Fish Fry" (1949), and the Robins' "Smokey Joe's Café" (1955). R&B also expressed black pride in its masculine braggadocio, which particularly challenged the white practice of referring to black men as "boys." Songs like WILLIE DIXON's "Hoochie Coochie Man" (recorded by Muddy Waters in 1954) and BO DIDDLEY's "I'm a Man" (1955) announced in no uncertain terms that black men's patience was at an end. Initially, however, it remained unclear whether anyone besides African Americans would hear this music, for popular music was as segregated as any other aspect of American life was.

Legacy in American Popular Culture

In the years following World War II, major recording studios concentrated on producing bland music for a white market, virtually ignoring black listeners. A few black performers, such as NAT "KING" COLE, managed to cross over to the white pop music charts. R&B, however, was the domain of small independent record companies, known as indies, that appeared in every U.S. city with a sizable black population. The indies themselves, with the exceptions of Exclusive/Excelsior in Los Angeles, VEE JAY RECORDS in Chicago, and Peacock Records in Houston, Texas, were white-owned.

Although initially meant for blacks, R&B ultimately transformed all of American popular culture by delivering vitality in a bland era. Compared with staid white singers such as Perry Como and Doris Day, the popular R&B acts of AARON ("T-BONE") WALKER, WILLIE MAE ("BIG MAMA") THORNTON, "Screamin'" Jay Hawkins, Clarence "Gatemouth" Brown, and "Bull Moose" Jackson offered raw energy and uninhibited music. R&B lyrics likewise conveyed greater emotional intensity than anything found in white pop music. Where Como crooned lines such as "We can wink at the moon as we hold each other tight," R&B offered earthiness and deep feeling. For example, in "He May Be Your Man" (1945), Helen Humes exclaimed: "Yes, that man rocks me, he rocks me with one steady roll, And he rocks me, Lord, he satisfies my soul."

Similarly, in "I Got a Woman" (1954), Charles sang, "She saves her lovin', early in the mornin', just for me." As was often the case in R&B, his delivery was as important as the song's lyrics. With the horns acting as an amen chorus, he surged through the verses, stoking the emotional fires and at times letting his voice soar into a transcendent falsetto.

Longtime Apollo Theater emcee Ralph Cooper recalled that—long before Elvis Presley made his appearance—such singing drove young audiences wild: "Singers became idols . . . [a]nd when they grabbed a mike, cocked their hips, and swaggered to the backbeat, [the fans'] screaming was the sound of uncontrolled excitement. With all that sexuality letting loose, things got downright hysterical." The growth of R&B also offered young African Americans new avenues for success, symbolized by the dream of winning a major talent contest, such as Amateur Night in Harlem, and finding fame and fortune through music.

Countless vocal groups practiced on street corners, in private homes, and in schoolyards of black neighborhoods hoping for a recording contract. Yet in all but a few cases, music industry gatekeepers, record-company owners, booking agents, and disc jockeys (DJs) were white, and black performers discovered that they had little control over their own music. Even the phrase *R&B* was of white origin, introduced by Jerry Wexler, a reporter for *Billboard* magazine and future head of Atlantic Records, as a euphemism for "race records," the term then in use. On June 25, 1949, *Billboard* renamed its black music chart, and—in the eyes of the music industry—the R&B era officially began.

R&B and Rock and Roll

R&B was music of transgression, challenging the boundaries of segregation. In the mid-1950s, many black R&B performers adopted a harder beat and ascended the pop charts as increasing numbers of white teenagers discovered the more visceral R&B sound. Many first heard this music in the broadcasts of black-format radio stations, such as WDIA in Memphis, Tennessee, or in the broadcasts of the rare white R&B DJs, such as Alan Freed. Historian Robert Pruter noted that package tours of leading R&B acts were also "instrumental in helping break rhythm and blues into the white market as rock 'n' roll music." In 1952 Freed began hosting racially integrated R&B concerts, and in Los Angeles concerts produced by R&B performer Johnny Otis brought together blacks, whites, and Mexican Americans.

Older whites responded by condemning R&B, allegedly on musical grounds but also because it violated racial boundaries. Some blacks, especially those who identified with middle-class values, criticized the music because it was rough and did not project what they considered to be a suitable image of the race. In 1953 the entertainment magazine *Variety* concluded that "100 percent rhythm and blues platters sell only in the colored market, although diluted interpretations have been seeping into the pop field with increasing frequency."

In 1954, however, Cole found his crossover success challenged by such rowdy R&B acts as RUTH BROWN, Ray Charles, RILEY B. ("B.B.") KING, Big Joe Turner, Muddy Waters, the Clovers, and Hank Ballard and the Midnighters. In the following year, CHARLES EDWARD ANDERSON (CHUCK) BERRY, Little Richard, ETTA JAMES, and Bo Diddley all made their recording debuts. The mid-1950s were also the golden era of R&B vocal groups. Some of these groups, like the Clovers, Hank Ballard and the Midnighters, and the Robins (who gave rise to the COASTERS), took a raucous and bluesy approach. Other groups—including the Moonglows, the Harptones, the Orioles, and the Flamingos—emphasized complex vocal constructions and greater interplay between the lead singer and the rest of the group, in a style that the *Chicago Defender*, an African American newspaper, labeled "doo-wop."

For the first time, R&B performers began charting among the year's Top Ten singles, including THE PLATTERS with "My Prayer" in 1956; SAM COOKE with "You Send Me" in 1957; Wilbert Harrison with "Kansas City," The Platters with "Smoke Gets in Your Eyes," and Lloyd Price with "Stagger Lee," all in 1959; and THE DRIFTERS with "Save the Last Dance for Me" and CHUBBY CHECKER with "The Twist" in 1960. The major record companies responded by turning to "covers," recordings made by white groups of black songs with the intention of preempting the hit songs of black performers.

Since the major labels had far greater resources behind their versions, covers often crowded out the black originals. For example, the hit songs of two black groups—"Sh-Boom" (1954), a novelty number by the Chords, and "A Story Untold" (1955), a ballad by the Nutmegs—were successfully covered by Mercury's slick white group, the Crewcuts. On the other hand, the McGuire Sisters' cover of the Moonglows' "Sincerely" (1954) could not keep the original out of the Top Twenty. In the mid-1950s, Elvis Presley launched his career through covers of R&B hits such as Roy Brown's "Good Rockin' Tonight" (1948) and Big Mama Thornton's "Hound Dog" (1953).

End of an Era

By the early 1960s the R&B era was over. Indeed, on November 30, 1963, *Billboard* stopped publishing a separate R&B chart, because the music had effectively been absorbed into the pop music mainstream. African American performers either adapted to fit prevailing white tastes or created new musical forms that were more expressly grounded in black culture. These contrasting approaches were exemplified in the 1960s in the smooth pop stylings of MOTOWN versus the harder edge of SOUL MUSIC, and during the 1970s in the wide appeal of disco versus FUNK music's largely black audience.

Although in later years *Billboard* reintroduced an R&B chart, it has generally served as a residual category for black music that is not RAP, REGGAE, or blues—in a sense, black middle-of-the-road music. In its golden age, however, R&B was by no means a middle-of-the-road musical style. It broke down racial barriers that had long divided American music, furthering a process of cross-fertilization that reaches from the FISK JUBILEE SINGERS, through jazz artists such as LOUIS ("SATCHMO") ARMSTRONG, CABELL (CAB) CALLOWAY, and EDWARD KENNEDY ("DUKE") ELLINGTON, up to the present. In its heyday, R&B offered a high-spirited affirmation of black life. Most of all, it was the musical voice of a generation of African Americans who would no longer tolerate second-class citizenship or balcony seat tickets to the American dream.

See also Jook Joint, The.

Bibliography

Cooper, Ralph, with Steve Dougherty. *Amateur Night at the Apollo.* HarperCollins, 1990.

Groia, Philip. *They All Sang on the Corner: New York City's Rhythm and Blues Vocal Groups of the 1950s.* Edmond Publishing, 1973.

Otis, Johnny. *Upside Your Head!: Rhythm and Blues on Central Avenue.* Wesleyan University Press/University Press of New England, 1993.

Pruter, Robert. *Doo Wop: The Chicago Scene.* University of Illinois Press, 1996.

Redd, Lawrence N. *Rock Is Rhythm and Blues: The Impact of Mass Media.* Michigan State University Press, 1974.

Shaw, Arnold. *Honkers and Shouters: The Golden Years of Rhythm and Blues.* Collier Books, 1978.

James Sellman

Rice, Condoleezza

1954–

First female national security advisor in the United States government

In January of 2001, soon after President George W. Bush took office, he named Condoleezza Rice as his national security advisor. In this role, Rice has had significant influence in shaping the Bush administration's policies toward other international affairs. Her appointment followed several decades of study, research, and activity in the field of foreign policy, with special focus on Russia (the former Soviet Union) and Europe.

Condoleezza Rice was born in 1954 in BIRMINGHAM, ALABAMA. Her father was a college administrator. Her mother was a music teacher who chose her daughter's name—a musical term that means "play with sweetness"—and Condoleezza displayed her own musical talent by becoming a skilled pianist at an early age. She grew up during a difficult era for blacks in the American South. The CIVIL RIGHTS MOVEMENT had not yet eliminated SEGREGATION IN THE UNITED STATES, and Birmingham experienced some of the worst racial violence of that period. Through it all, Rice's parents gave their daughter confidence and a sense of purpose. "My parents had me absolutely convinced," she has said, "that, well, you may not be able to have a hamburger at Woolworth's, but you can be president of the United States."

When Rice was thirteen, her family moved to Denver, Colorado. Two years later, she entered the University of Denver, planning a career as a pianist. But a course in international relations sparked her interest in that subject and she graduated at nineteen with a B.A. degree in political science. She then earned an M.A. from the University of Notre Dame (1975) and a Ph.D. from the Graduate School of International Studies at the University of Denver (1981). Rice has also received honorary doctoral degrees from MOREHOUSE COLLEGE, the University of Alabama, Notre Dame, and the Mississippi College School of Law.

In 1980 Rice began teaching political science at California's Stanford University. During the 1980s she gained recognition as an expert on the Soviet Union, long regarded as the greatest challenge faced by the United States in the realm of international politics. In 1984 she published *Uncertain Allegiance: The Soviet Union and the Czechoslovak Army,* and she cowrote *The Gorbachev Era* (1989), about Soviet leader Mikhail Gorbachev. From 1989 through 1991, during the collapse of the Soviet government and its empire, Rice served as director of Soviet and East European Affairs in the National Security Council in the first Bush administration, that of President George H. W. Bush.

From 1993 to 1999, Rice was Stanford University's provost, a senior official with financial and administrative responsibilities. She was not only the first woman and the first African American to hold that position, but also the youngest. Rice continued to pursue her scholarly and political careers, cowriting *Germany Unified and Europe Transformed* (1995) and advising the federal government on gender issues in military training.

As national security advisor, Rice currently coordinates White House research in international affairs. Along with other administration officials, such as Secretary of State Colin Powell and Vice President Dick Cheney, she contributes information and advice to the president on international matters. Rice's approach to foreign policy favors protecting U.S. interests over building international consensus. For example, one of her concerns has been the 1972 Anti-Ballistic Missile treaty, in which the United States and the Soviet Union agreed not to develop antimissile programs. Rice has said that the treaty should be waived so that the United States can develop such a system, despite criticism of that prospect from other nations.

Rebecca Stefoff

Rice Cultivation in Africa and the Americas

See Agriculture, African, in the Americas: An Interpretation.

Richards, Fannie Moore

1841–1922

African American pioneer teacher and civil rights activist who became the first black public school teacher in Detroit, Michigan.

Fannie Moore Richards was born on October 1, 1841, to a family of prosperous free blacks in Fredericksburg, Virginia. Her father, Adolph Richards, was a man of mixed ancestry from Guadeloupe, Mexico, who had been educated in London, England. He operated a carpentry shop in Fredericksburg. Her mother, Marie Louise Moore, a native of Fredericksburg, was the daughter of Edwin Moore, a Scotsman, and his wife, a free black woman from Toronto, Ontario, Canada. Richards's earliest education was most likely received in the clandestine school maintained by free blacks and taught by a Scots-Irishman in the home of Richard De Baptise, who would later become a prominent Baptist minister.

When Richards's father died in 1851, her mother sold the family property and moved to DETROIT, MICHIGAN, where other free Virginia families such as the De Baptistes and the Pelhams congregated. Richards studied English, history, drawing, and needlework in Toronto, where her sister and brother-in-law lived. Then she attended the Teachers Training School in Detroit.

After operating a private school for three years, Richards was appointed the teacher at Colored School No. 2 in September 1865, becoming Detroit's first black public school teacher. In 1867 she joined forces with relatives, including her brother John D. Richards, a businessman and Republican politician, to lead the fight against the segregated Detroit public schools. The schools provided twelve years of education for whites but only six for blacks. In 1870, after organized black political agitation had led to two acts of the state legislature and a decision by the state supreme court, the school board reluctantly abolished the separate schools for blacks.

Richards was then assigned to the Everett School, where she remained until her retirement on June 6, 1915. During her fifty years of teaching, she became widely esteemed for her continuous study of modern teaching methods, her high standard of scholarship, her knowledge of literature, and especially her sympathy with children of all races. Most of her students were of German, Jewish, or black heritage. They were accustomed to surrounding and clinging to her as she walked to and from school. She visited the homes of her pupils and invited them to her home. In 1872 she was selected to inaugurate the first kindergarten in Detroit. She was honored in 1910 by the daily papers that published the testimonials of influential white citizens.

Although she was the sole black teacher in a predominantly white school, Richards stated that she had never "felt the least discrimination" from either teachers or pupils. She accompanied other teachers on their annual excursions to WASHINGTON, D.C., "just to lend a little color," as she put it. She was devoted to her race and considered her career an example of what blacks could accomplish, given the opportunity. She wrote that "no race has advanced more rapidly than ours, and Negroes have not shown all they can do yet." A close associate of black leader BOOKER TALIAFERRO WASHINGTON, she believed that it was through education that blacks were "going to make their mark."

Richards was a faithful member of the Second Baptist Church, Detroit's oldest black congregation, where she taught

Sunday school for over fifty years. She saved nearly half her meager salary and used the money to found the Phillis Wheatley Home for aged black women on November 12, 1897. Richards served as its first president, and after its incorporation in 1901, as chairman of the board of trustees. When the Freedmen's Progress Commission was organized by the state legislature on April 21, 1915, she was chosen as an honorary vice president. She died on February 13, 1922.

Richards was honored by the city of Detroit in December 1970 when her portrait was placed in the Detroit Historical Museum.

See W. B. Hartgrove's "The Story of Marie Louise Moore and Fannie M. Richards" (*Journal of Negro History,* January 1916), Harvey C. Jackson's "Pioneers and Builders in Michigan: Fannie M. Richards" (*Negro History Bulletin,* May 1942), and "Tea at Museum Honors First Negro Teacher" (*Detroit Historical Society Bulletin,* January 1971).

From *Dictionary of American Negro Biography* by Rayford W. Logan and Michael R. Winston, editors. Copyright © 1982 by Rayford W. Logan and Michael R. Winston. Reprinted by permission of W. W. Norton & Company, Inc.

See also Wheatley, Phillis.

J. Carleton Hayden

Richards, Lloyd George

1919–

Afro-Canadian theater director and educator who directed the award-winning play *A Raisin in the Sun.*

Lloyd Richards was born in Canada to Jamaican immigrants Albert and Rose Richards. His father died when he was young and the family moved to DETROIT, MICHIGAN. Richards graduated from Wayne State University in 1943 and served in the U.S. Air Force as a pilot during World War II. After the war ended in 1945, Richards returned to Detroit and began working in theater and radio drama. In the 1950s he moved to NEW YORK, NEW YORK, where he studied with Paul Mann, a teacher of the Stanislavsky acting method.

Richards's career, however, took him into directing rather than acting. His first major directorial assignment was LORRAINE HANSBERRY's play *A Raisin in the Sun,* which won the 1959 New York Critics Circle Award. Following this success, Richards directed four other Broadway productions during the 1960s. Beginning in the mid-1960s, he also held teaching positions at the New York University School of Arts, the Eugene O'Neill Theater Center, Hunter College, and the Yale School of Drama, where he was appointed dean in 1979. He retired from that position in 1991 and continued to write and direct.

Richards is also known for his collaborations with playwright AUGUST WILSON, starting with a 1982 production of *Ma Rainey's Black Bottom.* Richards directed all of Wilson's plays and received a Tony Award in 1986 for his direction of Wilson's *Fences.* The following year, Richards received the Pioneer Award, the Frederick Douglass Award, and the Golden Plate Award for his accomplishments in drama.

Bibliography
Nadel, Alan, ed. *May All of Your Fences Have Gates: Essays on the Drama of August Wilson.* University of Iowa Press, 1994.

Aaron Myers

Richardson, Gloria St. Clair Hayes

1922–

Leader of the struggle for desegregation in Cambridge, Maryland.

As cochair of the Cambridge Nonviolent Action Committee, Gloria Richardson initiated a series of demonstrations against segregation and the economic oppression of blacks in Cambridge, Maryland. She was among the eighty protesters arrested and fined one cent each in the widely publicized "Penny Trials" of May 1963. After several weeks of violence and the imposition of martial law, Richardson, along with other black leaders and Cambridge officials, signed the Treaty of Cambridge on June 23, 1963. Although criticized for her direct-action tactics at the time, Richardson has since been credited with making desegregation possible in Cambridge. In 1964, she moved to NEW YORK CITY, to work for the Department for the Aging.

Lawrie Balfour

Richmond, Virginia

Center of slave trade, capital of the Confederacy, and cradle of a cohesive African American community.

Only thirty years after its establishment in 1637, a tiny James River trading post on the future site of Richmond was already doing a brisk business in the sale of slaves. The fertile Virginia soil supported a thriving tobacco trade that created a demand for cheap labor. Despite Virginia's manumission laws, which granted freedom to the children of slaves, and an antislavery organization run by QUAKERS, Richmond's slave trade prospered before the Revolutionary War.

The central location of Richmond endowed it with political as well as economic significance, leading to its designation as state capital. As Richmond grew in size and importance, slaves, who constituted half the population and a majority of the work force, actually constructed much of the city. During the American Revolution, slaves worked on public projects, assisted the military, and repaired arms. Two African Americans from Richmond even served in the colonial army, and one spied for the Americans to win his freedom.

Agriculture expanded and thrived around Richmond until the early nineteenth century, when the soil began to show signs of overuse. As tobacco farming declined, so did the demand for slaves. The resulting economic lull led many white citizens of Richmond to talk favorably of abolition. NAT TURNER'S REBELLION, however, in which a band of fugitive slaves killed fifty-seven whites, caused widespread paranoia among slaveholders and undermined the abolitionist movement in Virginia. Meanwhile, the growth of new industries led to new demands for cheap labor and a revitalized slave trade.

Until the AMERICAN CIVIL WAR, African Americans supplied the tobacco and iron industries of Richmond with the majority of their work force. Although still legally enslaved, factory workers enjoyed greater freedom than plantation slaves. They often took responsibility for their own housing, earned bonuses and "board" money, and were allowed considerable physical mobility. These freedoms, and the accompanying discretionary income, enabled factory workers to support a separate economy of craftsmen and business owners that served the black community. Slaves now ran their own boardinghouses and barbershops, and fixed their own shoes. However, Richmond's slave trade continued to prosper, as surplus slaves left over from the tobacco heyday were sold to regions farther south.

African American Richmonders served both the Union and the Confederacy during the Civil War. After Richmond became the capital of the Confederacy in 1861, some slaves were forced to lay new railroads and help reinforce the city's fortifications. Others served alongside free blacks and Union soldiers in undercover operations against the Confederates. Appropriately, black troops led the Union Army into a surrendering Richmond, signaling the end of slavery and the war.

During RECONSTRUCTION the community networks that black factory workers had created became the center of African American economic and social life. "Secret societies" proliferated, and freedpeople met the challenges of emancipation with the help of fraternal orders and churches. This strong social network also enabled the founding of the Richmond Theological Seminary (later Virginia Union University) and newspapers such as the *Richmond Planet*. Experience in earlier mutual-aid organizations facilitated political involvement, and by the 1880s, new movements, such as the Knights of Labor, served working-class blacks as they strove for justice and empowerment. The Knights of Labor included whites as well as blacks and during the early 1880s, class cooperation mitigated the racial divide. Together workers campaigned for better working conditions and higher wages. By 1886, however, the union dissolved, in part from racial tensions. African Americans once again had to work alone.

By 1900 the white establishment of Richmond had instigated an effective counterattack against the gains blacks had won. For the next fifty years, the African American community fought the discriminatory practices of the white elite, in both the public and private sectors. The Richmond Theater and local hotels adopted the JIM CROW system, and whites pushed blacks out of housing and jobs. While black people won some voting rights and founded banks upon previous financial networks, whites enforced segregation in an increasing number of spheres.

World War II marked the end of the most pernicious discrimination. In the early postwar years, African Americans gained access to the Richmond Public Library, found employment with the police and fire departments, and benefited tangibly from the U.S. Supreme Court's *BROWN V. BOARD OF EDUCATION* (1954) ruling, which led to the desegregation of public schools. Richmond's blacks played a significant role in the CIVIL RIGHTS MOVEMENT of the 1950s and 1960s, holding boycotts, fighting poll taxes, and hosting the SOUTHERN CHRISTIAN LEADERSHIP CONFERENCE's convention in 1963.

Like other major U.S. cities in the 1960s and 1970s, Richmond experienced a white evacuation to the suburbs, leaving the city with a black majority. Unfortunately, Richmond also suffered the problems of unemployment and urban decay that the weakening tax-base of white flight caused. Furthermore, white politicians aggravated the problem with efforts to redraw electoral lines to benefit white suburbanites. After seven years of deadlock and court deliberation, the African American community expunged the white-dominated electoral system under the Voting Rights Act, winning control of the local government. Despite the 1977 election of an African American mayor, Henry Marsh III, and the 1989 gubernatorial victory of black candidate LAWRENCE DOUGLAS WILDER, Richmond continued to suffer from crime, violence, drugs, and indigence.

However, under the administration of city manager Calvin D. Jamison, who was appointed in 1998, the city began to rebound. Jamison brought more than $2 billion in new investment to the city and pushed such projects as a new convention center, a biotech research park, high-speed rail transit for downtown neighborhoods, and public safety initiatives.

See also Free Blacks in the United States.

Bibliography

Buni, Andrew. *The Negro in Virginia Politics, 1902–1965.* University Press of Virginia, 1967.
Dabney, Virginius. *Richmond: The Story of a City.* University Press of Virginia, 1976.

Eric Bennett

Rif Republic

Independent Moroccan state from 1921 until 1925.

In 1921 the BERBER inhabitants of the mountainous coastal region of northeast MOROCCO that is known as the Rif created an independent republic. A native to the region, Abd el-Krim, organized this remarkable state that for five years withstood the onslaught of two colonial governments.

Abd el-Krim grew up in a scholarly family in a region near SPAIN's Moroccan possessions, where most people worked as small-scale farmers or herders. He completed both a Muslim education in FÈS and a Spanish education, and worked first for the Spanish colonial Bureau of Native Affairs and then as a Muslim judge in Melilla. By 1915 he opposed the Spanish presence in Morocco; he was imprisoned after making anticolonial statements. After two years he was released and reinstated.

In 1919 Abd el-Krim returned to Ait Waryaghar, his home region in the Rif. Working alongside his brother, he organized a rebellion against the Spanish. The timing was key, since Spain was moving to unite its two existing enclaves by occupying the Rif. In an aggressive campaign during 1921, the forces of Abd el-Krim killed or captured more than half the Spanish forces sent from the Spanish coastal enclave of Melilla, and drove the remainder back.

In 1921 Abd el-Krim established the Republic of Confederated Tribes of the Rif. The state opposed both Spanish and French colonialism in Morocco. President Abd el-Krim led a government modeled on traditional Berber political institutions. Though he instituted *shari'a,* or Islamic law, throughout the region, Abd el-Krim sought to build a modern reformist state. To this end, he outlawed blood feuds and mandated the training of *qadis,* or judges.

Abd el-Krim's firm opposition to foreign rule brought him into fateful conflict with the French. In 1925 he attacked French-held territory and nearly reached the city of Fés. The French retaliated against the growing anticolonialist revolt. France and Spain bolstered their troops to a combined total of 425,000, and they united against their common enemy, the Rif Republic, in a joint attack from two sides. Abd el-Krim surrendered in 1926, and was sent into exile on the Indian Ocean island of RÉUNION.

From 1957 to 1959 the Rif was the site of another secessionist movement, this time against the postcolonial Kingdom of Morocco. Facing regional governmental corruption, unemployment, and trouble along the Algerian border, the Berbers of the Rif invoked the legacy of Abd el-Krim's state. In fact, they called upon the legendary leader himself, who was by then living in EGYPT. The aging Abd el-Krim offered support, possibly encouraging Egypt to supply arms to the rebels. The Moroccan government harshly repressed the uprising.

See also France; Islam in Africa.

Bibliography

Woolman, David S. *Rebels in the Rif: Abd el Krim and the Rif Rebellion.* Stanford University Press, 1968.

Marian Aguiar

Rift Valley

One of the world's most impressive physical features; the defining feature of the East African landscape and site of some of the world's oldest fossil hominids; also known as Great Rift Valley.

The Great Rift Valley was formed about twenty million years ago when two parallel fault lines pulled apart, forcing the land in between to move down. A massive depression resulted, which stretches through East Africa from the Jordan River Valley of the Red Sea to central MOZAMBIQUE. The Rift Valley extends 4,830 km (3,000 mi) and ranges from 40 to 60 km wide (about 25 to 37 mi), varying in depth from a few meters (about 10 ft) to 2,000 m (about 6,600 ft). The Rift Valley actually consists of two valleys, the Eastern and the Western (or Gregory Rift Zone). The Eastern Rift runs from central ETHIOPIA to central KENYA, while the Western Rift runs from north of LAKE VICTORIA to central Mozambique.

Volcanic activity along either side of the rift produced spectacular mountains, most notably Mount KILIMANJARO, Africa's highest peak, and MOUNT KENYA. The Western Rift left a series of depressions that became East Africa's deepest lakes, including LAKE TANGANYIKA, LAKE MALAWI, and LAKE TURKANA. Because the rift lakes have no outlet to the sea, their evaporation often results in high concentrations of minerals in their waters. Although Lake Turkana contains water fresh enough to support fish and wildlife, Lake Magadi, Lake Nakuru, and Lake Elementita are heavily alkaline. Discoveries of fossilized remains of human ancestors, as well as tools and weapons at sites around Lake Turkana in Kenya and in Olduvai Gorge in TANZANIA, provide strong evidence that Africa is the cradle of human evolution.

See map overleaf.

Bibliography

Johns, Chris. *Valley of Life: Africa's Great Rift.* Thomasson-Grant, 1991.

Robert Fay

Rigaud, André

Late 1700s and early 1800s

Military leader of mulatto forces during the Haitian Revolution.

At a young age, André Rigaud went to FRANCE and trained as a soldier in the French army. He was one of many Haitians who fought under French commanders against the British in the AMERICAN REVOLUTION (1775–1783). After returning to HAITI, Rigaud worked as a goldsmith until the outbreak of the HAITIAN REVOLUTION in 1791. He emerged as leader of the mulatto (mixed African and European descent) forces and instigated an insurrection against black military commander FRANÇOIS DOMINIQUE TOUSSAINT LOUVERTURE in 1799. This led to a civil war between the mulatto and black forces that were fighting against French colonial rule. The insurrection failed, leaving about 10,000 of Rigaud's supporters dead, and he fled to France in 1801. The emperor of France, Napoleon Bonaparte I, deported Rigaud to Madagascar.

Riggs, Marlon Troy

1957–1994

Documentary filmmaker and educator who used video to oppose racism and homophobia.

Reflecting on the death of Marlon Troy Riggs from acquired immunodeficiency syndrome (AIDS), cultural theorist Kobena

Mercer observed, "Independent cinema lost the voice and vision of an important artist at the very moment that he was coming into his own." At the time of his death, Riggs was at work on *Black Is & Black Ain't*. This feature-length film, complete by Riggs's collaborators in 1995, chronicled the variety of American identities seen as black.

Born in Fort Worth, Texas, Riggs grew up in a military family, moving from Texas to Georgia to Germany before returning to the United States to attend Harvard University. As an undergraduate he began to explore connections between black and gay identities. His studies led to a senior thesis on the treatment of male homosexuality in literature. After graduating magna cum laude in 1978, Riggs worked briefly at a Texas television station before moving to the San Francisco Bay area of California. He received a master's degree from the Graduate School of Journalism at University of California at Berkeley in 1981 and joined the Berkeley faculty six years later.

Ethnic Notions (1986), the first film Riggs wrote, directed, and produced, won an Emmy Award in 1988 for its investigation of RACIAL STEREOTYPES in American society. That same year, Riggs began work on his most famous film, *Tongues Untied* (1989). A work that interweaves poetry, personal reflections, and scenes from the lives of black gay men, *Tongues Untied* challenged the black community's attitudes toward black homosexuality. It also inspired outraged attacks from conservatives such as North Carolina senator Jesse Helms and religious fundamentalist Patrick Buchanan, who included footage from the film in his 1992 presidential campaign.

Despite deteriorating health, Riggs remained active as a lecturer, teacher, and filmmaker until his death. *Anthem* (1990) and *Non, je ne regrette rien/No Regret* (1991) continued the work of *Tongues Untied* in examining black gay men's experiences. *Color Adjustment* (1991), which earned him a Peabody Award, documented the representation of African Americans on television.

See also Acquired Immunodeficiency Syndrome in the United States; Television and African Americans.

Bibliography

Hemphill, Essex, ed. *Brother to Brother: New Writings by Black Gay Men.* Alyson Publications, 1991.

Lawrie Balfour

Rillieux, Norbert

1806–1894

American inventor and engineer whose patented inventions revolutionized the sugar-refining industry.

Norbert Rillieux was born in NEW ORLEANS, LOUISIANA, to an African American mother and a French father who was an engineer and a plantation owner. After studying engineering at L'École Centrale in Paris, France, Rillieux became the school's youngest instructor in the department of applied mechanics. At L'École Centrale, he published many papers on steam technology.

Rillieux returned to Louisiana in 1840. In 1843, he patented the multiple-effect vacuum pan evaporator. This device heated sugar cane juice in a partial vacuum, which reduced its boiling point, thus allowing a much greater fuel efficiency. This innovation, widely adopted in the sugar refining industry, escalated the rate of production and reduced the price of sugar, thus transforming it from a luxury commodity into a household item. Similar technology was subsequently developed for the production of soap, gelatin, and glue. Some have called Rillieux's evaporator the greatest invention in the history of American chemical engineering.

When post-RECONSTRUCTION conditions proved oppressive in Louisiana for African Americans, Rillieux returned to Paris, serving as headmaster at L'École Centrale. He began to study Egyptology and helped decipher hieroglyphics.

Ringgold, Faith

1934–

African American artist, activist, and author of children's books.

Painter and sculptor Faith Ringgold has spent her artistic career breaking boundaries and opening opportunities for African American creativity, especially that of women. Born in NEW YORK CITY and raised in HARLEM, Ringgold earned a bachelor's degree in art and education in 1955 and a master's of fine arts degree in 1959 from The City College of New York. Dissatisfied with the traditional art training she received in New York and later in Europe, Ringgold studied African art, reading the work of BLACK ARTS MOVEMENT authors and participating in the CIVIL RIGHTS MOVEMENT. Paintings from this period—including *The Flag Is Bleeding* (1967), *US Postage Stamp Commemorating the Advent of Black Power* (1967) and *Die* (1967)—blend the geometric shapes and flat perspective of African-inspired artistic traditions with powerful political and social protest.

Ringgold has been an outspoken critic of racial and gender prejudice in the art world. In the early 1970s she organized protests against the Whitney Museum of American Art and other major museums for excluding the works of blacks and women. In response to the museum world's exclusionary policies, Ringgold and other black women artists formed a collective and organized an exhibit of their own whose title, *Where We At,* announced their visibility. Ringgold's art focuses on black women and black women's issues. Works such as a mural in the Women's House of Detention in Riker's Island, New York (1971–1972), and a performance piece using soft cloth sculptures, *The Wake and Resurrection of the Bicentennial Negro* (1976), focused on women's ability to heal and brought her work to a wider audience.

Since the 1970s, she has documented her local community and national events in life-size soft sculptures, representing everyone from ordinary Harlem denizens to MARTIN LUTHER

KING, JR., and the young victims of the Atlanta child murders (in 1979–1980). She has made much use of fabric, traditionally associated with women, as a medium for artistic creation. Her expression of black women's experience is perhaps best captured in her "storyquilts." These pieces combine quilting and narrative text in works such as *Who's Afraid of Aunt Jemima?* (1982) and the series *Women on a Bridge* (1988), which tell stories of pain and survival in a medium that Ringgold finds essentially female and empowering. She exhibited a series called *The French* Collection in 1990 and followed it with *The American Collection* (1997) and *Coming to Jones Road* (1999–2000), which consists of quilts that show slaves arriving at freedom.

Ringgold adapted one of her quilts into a children's book, *Tar Beach,* which won the 1992 Caldecott Honor Book Award and the Coretta Scott King award. Since that time she has written and illustrated a number of other children's books, including *My Dream of Martin Luther King* (1998), *If a Bus Could Talk: The Story of Rosa Parks* (1999), *The Unvisible Princess* (2001), and *Cassie's Word Quilt* (2002).

Bibliography

Flomenhaft, Eleanor. *Faith Ringgold: A Twenty-five-Year Survey.* The Museum, 1990.

Ringgold, Faith. *We Flew over the Bridge: The Memoirs of Faith Ringgold.* Little, Brown, 1995.

Ring Shout

See Dance, African American.

Rio de Janeiro, Brazil

Second largest city in Brazil and capital of the country from 1763 to 1960; currently the capital of the state of Rio de Janeiro.

Located on the southeastern coast of BRAZIL, Rio de Janeiro's name comes from Portuguese and means "river of January," a reference to its location near the entrance to Gaunabara Bay. Sixteenth-century Portuguese explorers believed the bay to be a large estuary, a water passage where the tide meets a river current. Today Rio de Janeiro is informally divided into four distinct areas. The downtown, which includes the port, is the center of commerce. The South Zone, south of downtown, includes the largely middle- and upper-class beachside neighborhoods of Copacabana, Leblon, and Ipanema as well as middle-class neighborhoods closer to downtown. Hillside favelas (squatter settlements or shantytowns) in the South Zone, such as Rocinha, the largest favela in Brazil, give poor and working-class residents easy access to work in nearby middle-class neighborhoods and tourist districts. The North Zone is the site of most of the city's industrial production. It includes the middle-class neighborhood of Tijuca and numerous poor and working-class neighborhoods and suburbs. The West Zone, stretching from north to south on the western side of the coastal mountains, consists of the wealthy neighborhood of Barra da Tijuca, as well as poor neighborhoods and suburbs. In 1996 the urban agglomeration centered on Rio included 10.3 million residents. Approximately 57 percent of these *cariocas* (residents of Rio) were white, and 42 percent were Afro-Brazilian.

Rio de Janeiro in the Colonial Period

In the first half of the sixteenth century, the coast along Guanabara Bay, an area rich in brazilwood, became the source of conflict between France and Portugal. In March 1565 Estácio de Sá, the nephew of Brazil's governor-general Mem de Sá, established a fort, which eventually developed into the city of Rio de Janeiro. Two years later the Portuguese successfully evicted the French from the region.

Rio remained a relatively unimportant Portuguese outpost, relying on small-scale cultivation of brazilwood and sugar throughout the late sixteenth and seventeenth centuries. By the late 1500s, early Portuguese settlers had mounted expeditions to enslave the indigenous Tupi in the region. Tupi slaves were gradually replaced by Africans as the need for labor increased, although records indicate that enslaved Native Americans were brought to Rio after being captured in wars in Brazil's inland frontiers well into the nineteenth century. In 1585 there were 3,850 households along Guanabara Bay, and the population included only 100 blacks.

The economic and political significance of the city irrevocably changed in the 1690s when gold and diamonds were discovered in the area of the present-day state of MINAS GERAIS, which borders Rio de Janeiro state to the west. The discoveries fostered massive immigration by prospectors and greatly increased the demand for slaves, who were brought through the port of Rio to work in the mines. The boom in mining occurred at a time when the sugar economy in the northeastern captaincies (colonial administrative units) of Pernambuco and BAHIA was in decline, a factor that further shifted the economic center of the colony to Rio. This process culminated in the transfer of the colonial capital from Salvador, Bahia, to Rio in 1763. During this period the city became the most important port of entrance of slaves to Brazil. Between 1723 and 1771, about half the slaves shipped to Brazil from Angola, at the time the main source for slaves to the colony, went through Rio. By 1799 the city had a total population of 43,376, of whom 19,578 (45 percent) were white; 19,571 (45 percent) were black; and 4,227 (9 percent) were mulatto (of African and European descent).

Slave Trade in Rio

From the mid-seventeenth century until the nineteenth century, Rio was the most important port in Brazil's slave trade. Coffee cultivation developed in the late eighteenth and the nineteenth centuries, particularly in the Paraiba Valley, in the interior of Rio de Janeiro province. The cultivation of coffee increased Rio's economic significance as a port as well as the demand for slaves. In 1769 the Marquis of Lavradio, the viceroy of Brazil, designated the Valongo area north of the central square as the marketplace for slaves in the city, and establishments for displaying and auctioning slaves multiplied. In the first decade of the nineteenth century, about 10,000 slaves were imported through Rio each year. In 1808 King João VI transferred the Portuguese court from Lisbon to Rio in order to escape Napoleon's invading forces. He returned to Portugal in 1821, but his son Pedro I chose to stay. Pedro declared Brazil an independent empire and himself king the following year. The transfer of the court to Rio again magnified the city's political and economic significance as well as its importance in the slave trade. Foreign visitors consistently noted Rio's enormous population of black slaves and free blacks.

Most of the slaves in the city came from the West African regions of ANGOLA and CONGO. In the nineteenth century, however, many slaves were brought from East Africa, particularly Mozambique, as traders avoided British efforts to stop the slave trade, efforts that were concentrated in West Africa. Between 1800 and 1850 about 1 million slaves entered the port of Rio.

Slave Life in Rio

Most of the slaves who arrived in Rio were transported to the mines or plantations in the country's interior. However, many remained in the city to work as skilled and unskilled laborers, craftspeople, artisans, and domestic servants. Many were employed in the port, in small-scale agriculture, and in the city's few factories, most of which processed raw materials such as tobacco or iron. Both men and women were expected to work in these occupations. A large number of women worked as domestic servants or as street vendors, selling food or other goods, and slave owners forced many women and girls to earn money as prostitutes.

Some slaves were contracted out by their owners and were permitted to keep a small amount of their earnings, which many saved in the hope of purchasing their freedom. Many slaves aspired to manumission, or the legal concession of freedom, although few were actually manumitted during most of the period of slavery. In 1849 only 10,732 freedpeople lived in the city. The number increased after midcentury; in the 1860s almost 13,000 slaves were manumitted.

Slaves and free people of color developed a rich cultural and associational life. Since colonial times, religious brotherhoods, such as NOSSA SENHORA DO ROSÁRIO dos Homens Pretos (Our Lady of the Rosary of Black Men), were integrated into the Catholic Church. These religious associations doubled as mutual aid societies. Members sometimes pooled their funds toward the purchase of manumission. Blacks in Rio also sustained a number of African and syncretic religions. These religious practices became the object of official censure, and practitioners faced police persecution until the mid-twentieth century.

Rio also became known for CAPOEIRA, an Afro-Brazilian tradition that is simultaneously a form of dance and fighting. *Capoeiristas,* or those who practice Capoeira, formed associations known as *maltas,* which sometimes gathered hundreds of men. Throughout the nineteenth century, imperial authorities and slave owners suspected them of fomenting revolt, and maltas often faced police repression. This continued even after the abolition of slavery in 1888 and into the early twentieth century, as authorities stereotyped capoeiristas as criminals.

Slaves resisted oppression in Rio as they did elsewhere in the Americas. Forms of resistance ranged from individual acts of disobedience, violence, or suicide to revolt or escape. While some small-scale slave uprisings occurred, the city did not experience large-scale slave rebellions, such as those that occurred in Salvador. This was due, in part, to the city's mountainous and forested terrain, which made escape a more attractive option.

Runaway slaves, or maroons, sought refuge in the lushly forested mountains in and around the city. Many established small *quilombos* (maroon communities) and subsisted through small-scale agriculture, trade with slaves or free persons, and robbery. Quilombos were particularly concentrated in three areas: on Corcovado Mountain, today a tourist attraction famous for the statue of Christ that sits atop it; on Desterro Hill, the neighborhood of Santa Teresa, near the downtown area; and in the forested hills north of the city in the area of the present-day neighborhood of Tijuca. In 1826 alone, 426 runaway slaves were arrested in Rio and its suburbs.

Brazil formally abolished its international slave trade in 1831, although it did not enforce the ban until another, stricter law was passed in 1850 under British pressure. The effective abolition of the trade contributed to the relative decline of the slave population in Rio in the second half of the nineteenth century. In 1870 about 50,000 slaves lived in the city.

This period also saw an increase in the influx of Afro-Brazilians from the northeastern provinces, particularly Bahia. Some arrived as slaves, whose masters sold them in Rio, taking advantage of higher market prices after the international trade was abolished. Others arrived as freedpersons, looking for economic opportunity in the capital, a trend that increased after abolition.

Brazil was the last country in the Western Hemisphere to abolish slavery, in 1888. A number of Afro-Brazilians, such as ANDRÉ REBOUÇAS and JOSÉ CARLOS DO PATROCÍNIO, made significant contributions to the political battles that took place in the capital city of Rio leading up to abolition. The following year, the monarchy was replaced by a republican government, marking a new era in Brazil.

Blacks in Rio after Emancipation

At the turn of the twentieth century, Rio's black population was heavily concentrated in the downtown area of the city, stretching from the Conceição Hill to the vast area known as Cidade Nova and forming what came to be known as "Little Africa." This area was the site of tremendous cultural ferment. For instance, it was the birthplace of the popular musical genre SAMBA. Samba developed in social gatherings at the homes of Bahian women, such as TIA CIATA, which early samba musicians, like DONGA and PIXINGUINHA, attended. Later, the area became known for its popular CARNIVAL celebration. Music continues to be a significant form of both political and cultural expression for Afro-Brazilian residents of Rio, perhaps most represented in the 1990s by the funk movement that drew a large following among Afro-Brazilian youth.

Beginning in the late nineteenth century, the liberated slaves faced increasing competition in the labor market from a growing influx of European immigrants. Government subsidies encouraged European immigration, displacing the recently freed black labor force. By 1890 immigrants constituted almost half the population, and blacks were relegated mainly to low-paying sectors of the economy. According to the 1890 census, of the economically active black population in the city, 48 percent were domestic workers, 17 percent worked in industry, and 9 percent worked in agriculture or raised livestock. Following emancipation, many blacks continued to work at the city's port, where some significant workers' organizations arose. One of these, the Resistance Society of Pier Coffee Workers, previously called the Black Company, was probably the first labor organization in Rio to include a majority of blacks in both its ranks and its leadership.

The government's immigration policies reflected a broader ideology of WHITENING, which sought to make the city (and the rest of the country) whiter both demographically and culturally. This ideology was also embodied in massive reconstruction projects of the city's downtown in an attempt to remake the city in Europe's image, from the 1890s into the first decades of the twentieth century. City planners built broad avenues and adopted the art-nouveau style popular in Europe for the new buildings.

These construction projects displaced thousands of Afro-Brazilians who resided in the downtown area. Construction of the city's Central Avenue, for instance, required the destruction of more than 500 buildings in the working-class area. In just one nine-month period, more than 900 houses were demolished. In 1893 officials destroyed the downtown area known as Cabeça do Porco, displacing 2,000 residents. Many of the displaced residents moved either to suburbs in the outskirts of town or to the hillsides interspersed in the city, establishing favelas.

The prototype for contemporary favelas already existed before abolition, as slaves who worked in the city for their owners often built shanties on hillsides. However, the first settlement that came to be known as a favela was established in 1897 on Providencia Hill, later known as Favela Hill. This favela was established by veterans returning home from the military campaign against the messianic leader Antônio Conselheiros, in Bahia. It is likely that these veterans coined the name favela after Favela Hill, which was significant in that campaign. The size and number of these favelas grew precipitously after the GREAT DEPRESSION in the 1930s. This growth was fostered by the massive migration of people from rural areas in the northeast. The residents' position has historically been precarious because they lack title to the land. Under the Brazilian military regime, for instance, government programs displaced residents of Rio's favelas, relocating them to distant government housing, hours from downtown Rio and available jobs. After populist leader Leonel Brizola was elected as mayor of the city in 1982, programs were implemented to provide basic urban services such as running water to favelas and, in some cases, to grant titles to land. These political developments paralleled the growing mobilization of favela residents. The Federation of Favela Associations of the State of Rio de Janeiro (FAFERJ), established in 1975, became increasingly active in the 1980s in voicing the demands of residents for basic services. Of the 5.9 million cariocas who live in the city of Rio de Janeiro (excluding the metropolitan area), approximately one million people live in favelas.

In 1960 the national capital was moved from Rio to the newly constructed city of Brasilia, in the center of the country. This reduction in Rio's political importance paralleled its displacement by São Paulo, to the south, as the country's largest city and most significant industrial center.

Blacks in Rio continue to face discrimination, although the problem is often not acknowledged because of the persistent myth that Brazil is a "racial democracy." Afro-Brazilians still earn less than whites, face discrimination in hiring, and suffer disproportionately from police abuse. Black political and cultural movements emerged throughout the twentieth century to address these realities, including the TEATRO EXPERIMENTAL DO NEGRO (Black Experimental Theater), which was established in Rio in the 1940s by black activist ABDIAS DO NASCIMENTO. A number of organizations emerged in Rio beginning in the 1970s, including the Research Institute for Black Culture (IPCN), the Palmares Foundation, a branch of the MOVIMENTO NEGRO UNIFICADO (Unified Black Movement), and the CENTRO DE ARTICULAÇÃO DE POPULAÇÕES MARGINALIZADAS (Center for the Mobilization of Marginalized Populations). Black leaders such as Nascimento, elected a senator in 1990, and BENEDITA DA SILVA, who in 1998 was elected the first black vice governor of the state of Rio de Janeiro, have also made inroads into the political sphere.

See also Contemporary Afro-Brazilian Music; Human Rights in Latin America and the Caribbean; Mining in Latin America and the Caribbean; Muslim Uprisings in Bahia, Brazil; Myth of Racial Democracy in Latin America and the Caribbean; Religions, African, in Brazil; Rethinking Palmares: Slave Resistance in Colonial Brazil; Role of Slaves in Abolition and Emancipation in Latin America and the Caribbean; White Abolitionists in Brazil.

Bibliography

Karasch, Mary. *Slave Life in Rio de Janeiro, 1808–1850.* Princeton University Press, 1987.

Lopes, Nei. *O Negro no Rio de Janeiro e sua tradição musical: Partido alto, calango, chula e outras cantorias.* Pallas, 1992.

Mattoso de Queirós, Kátia. *To Be a Slave in Brazil: 1550–1888.* Rutgers University Press, 1991.

Moura, Roberto. *Tia Ciata e a pequena África no Rio de Janeiro.* 2nd ed. Secretaria Municipal de Cultura,

Departamento Geral de Documentos e Informação Cultural, Divisão de Editoração, 1995.

Paes de Carvalho, Cyntia, coord. *Favelas e as organizações comunitárias.* Vozes, 1993.

Michelle Gueraldi

Rites of Passage and Transition

Cultural feature of many African societies.

Scholars such as Charles-Arnold Van Gennep have noted that virtually all human societies use ceremonial rites to mark significant transitions in the social status of individuals. These rites highlight and validate changes in a person's status, particularly on the occasion of such life-transforming events as birth, puberty, marriage, parenthood, and death, but also may occur upon taking a political office or joining a secret society.

Comparing the structure of such rituals in diverse cultures, Van Gennep discovered that rites of passage often share similar features, including a period of segregation from everyday life, a liminal state of transition from one status to the next, and a process of reintroduction to the social order with a new standing. Given these similarities, he coined the term "rites of passage" as an analytical concept, though others prefer the term "transition rites." Scholars often draw analogies between rites of passage and the human life cycle. In these rites, individuals are symbolically killed, reborn, and nurtured as they take on new social statuses, and are then reborn into society as new and different persons. Portals often feature prominently in rites of passage, symbolizing the crossing of a threshold into a new social world.

During segregation, the common beginning stage of rites of passage, initiates undergo rituals meant to strip them of their identities and separate them from their previous social statuses. They may be forcibly moved geographically, or made to strip themselves of clothing, hair, or other physical markings of their previous selves. For example, young women's heads are shaved and eyebrows removed on the first day of the *koroseek* initiation ceremony among the Okiek of KENYA. Initiates often undergo rituals and ordeals designed to redefine their social standings. For example they may endure a variety of body modification procedures, including haircuts, tattoos, and scarification. Male circumcision and female excision also commonly mark rites of passage. The LUO of Kenya remove initiates' lower front incisors during initiation rites. Clothing and ornaments may also signify the loss of their previous status.

These rituals are often trials in which pain demarcates boundaries between the old and the new. During the Poro secret society initiation rite of the MENDE in SIERRA LEONE, boys first face circumcision (if they are not already circumcised). Those conducting the rites then force the boys onto the ground and cut their backs with razors while forcing their heads into a hole. The resulting scars signify the teeth marks of the Poro spirit that consumes the boys. Having "died," the initiates will then reemerge from the bush reborn with a new social status.

In many rites of passage, participants next enter a liminal, or transitional, state. Communities often consider initiates exceptionally vulnerable and/or dangerous at this time because they have become socially ambiguous. Anthropologist Victor Turner wrote: "Liminal entities are neither here nor there; they are betwixt and between the positions assigned and arrayed by law, custom, convention, and ceremonial. As such, their ambiguous and intermediate attributes are expressed by a rich variety of symbols in many societies that ritualize social and cultural transitions. Thus, liminality is frequently likened to death, to being in the womb, to invisibility, to darkness, to bisexuality, to the wilderness, and to an eclipse of the sun or moon."

Among the Mende, Poro initiates undergo training periods during which they are considered dangerous. They play pipes and yell warning cries to prevent passersby from coming into contact with them. Poro initiates undergo ordeals—a common feature of rites of passage, particularly initiation rites—during this liminal state. They are deprived of sleep, forced to labor, exposed to the elements, forced to seek their own nourishment in the bush, and instructed in Poro law.

The initiates then reemerge, often through formal ritual procedures, to the normal social fabric with a newly defined identity and a changed social status. Van Gennep coined a term to describe this process: aggregation. The Mende Poro ceremony of rebirth, for example, makes the reluctant Poro spirit give birth to the initiates it has devoured. Using a rope, a female officiator pulls the initiates out of the Poro spirit's womb.

Ceremonies marking initiation into adulthood are the most common rites of passage. They often include trials of pain and stamina, periods of introspection, the teaching of sacred and secret stories, and the use of symbolic representations, including dances and masks, as a means of reshaping individuals' identities. Initiations may take weeks or months, during which the initiates often live together in distinct and segregated houses. While other rites of passage commonly fall into the three phases Van Gennep described, they do not necessarily entail the ordeals associated with initiation rites.

Van Gennep viewed rites of passage as an essential ingredient in the rejuvenation of society. He and other social scientists generally believe that rites of passage serve to preserve social stability by easing the transition of cohorts of individuals into new status and prestige roles; in part, they are a social acknowledgement of aging. As individuals are born and age, their positions in society change. In the absence of rites of passage, society would be fraught with conflict as individuals either struggled to assert new social statuses or resisted these statuses. Some African societies maintain a structure of age-grades, groups of individuals who share similar social status by virtue of their similar age. The NUER of southern SUDAN, for example, are grouped into graduated age-grades, each lasting about ten years. Cohorts who share the same age-grades throughout their lives are called an age set. Ceremonial rites of passage, including ordeals for the earlier age-grades, mark the age set's movement from one grade to another. By institutionalizing the transitions in social status, rites of passage help to eliminate the friction that would otherwise accompany the frequent renegotiations of relative status between individuals and groups within a society.

Some anthropologists, such as Bronislaw Malinowski, have sought to explain the prevalence of rites of passage by noting their psychotherapeutic quality. Such rituals give individuals social support in confronting the anxiety they may feel facing new social roles or major life changes, such as parenthood or the death of loved ones. Funeral rites, for instance, help those who are grieving by ritually introducing the deceased into the world of the afterlife. Mourning rituals, in particular, provide the bereaved with structure at a time when their most fundamental social relations have changed. This structure helps them to face the loss of the deceased.

Others see these rites as a means of creating emotional bonds that maintain social order. The rites use symbolism to reinforce social statuses, norms, and values, and they increase group solidarity by promoting empathy. Individuals who undergo a rite of passage together, such as members of the same age set, often develop strong personal bonds and form a community of equals within the larger community. These horizontal bonds are thought to strengthen the social fabric, particularly since they tend to cross-cut other social categories, such as membership in different lineages.

Although many societies maintain rites of passage, and while these rites often share structural similarities, their cultural content varies widely. Many rites of passage, for example, recognize an individual's entry into adulthood, a status based on age. Yet the meaning of adulthood, and the age at which it begins, varies from culture to culture, ranging from eight years of age among the Gussi of Kenya to between fifteen and eighteen years among the Maasai. The specific symbolism and meaning attached to rites of passage also varies widely. Moreover, the significance of rituals often changes over time within a society. The scholar Maurice Block has shown, for example, that male circumcision rituals among the Merina of Madagascar have been employed to express changing political beliefs. So, while rites of passage may aid in maintaining stability, they also express cultural and social dynamics, and are therefore constantly evolving.

See also Female Circumcision in Africa.

Bibliography

Goldschmidt, Walter. *The Human Career: The Self in the Symbolic World.* Blackwell, 1990.

Kratz, Corinne. *Affecting Performance: Meaning, Movement, and Experience in Okiek Women's Initiation.* Smithsonian Institute Press, 1993.

Turner, Victor. *Celebration: Studies in Festivity and Ritual.* Smithsonian Institution Press, 1982.

Turner, Victor. *Ritual Process.* Aldine, 1969.

Van Gennep, Arnold. *The Rites of Passage.* Translated by Monika B. Vizedom and Gabrielle L. Caffee. University of Chicago Press, 1960.

Ari Nave

Rivera, Ismael

1931–1987

Afro–Puerto Rican singer, musician, bandleader, and composer; also known as El Sonero Mayor.

In 1954 Ismael Rivera and Rafael Cortijo formed the musical group Cortijo y Su Combo, which played Afro–Puerto Rican rhythms such as plena and bomba. The group was based in Santurce, Puerto Rico, and powerfully influenced the development of Caribbean musical styles during the 1950s and 1960s. Rivera's singing style was unmistakable and innovative, oscillating between the harsh urban sound of the new salsa rhythms and the sweet musicality of the old Cuban son. Indeed, Afro-Cuban singer and bandleader Beny Moré called Rivera "El Sonero Mayor" ("the Greatest Son Singer"). In 1971 Rivera started his own group, called Ismael Rivera y Sus Cachimbos. Rivera also studied and promoted black culture in Puerto Rico by advocating the creation of a museum of Afro–Puerto Rican culture in San Juan.

Rivera, Louis Reyes

1945–

Puerto Rican poet, teacher, social worker, and publisher.

Louis Reyes Rivera, born in New York, New York, was deeply influenced by the Black Power Movement in the Caribbean and by Black Power in the United States. His poems have been published in several collections of work by many artists, including *Aloud: Voices from the Nuyoricans Poets Café* (1994), edited by Miguel Algarín and Bob Holman. Rivera has also published *Who Pays the Cost* (1977), *This One for You* (1983), and *Scattered Scripture* (1996).

See also Afro-Latino Cultures in the United States.

Roach, Maxwell Lemuel (Max)

1924–

African American drummer.

Maxwell Lemuel Roach was born in New Land, North Carolina, and grew up in Brooklyn, New York. At the age of ten he began playing the drums in gospel music groups. He graduated from high school in 1941 and in the early 1950s studied at the Manhattan School of Music. By that time he was already part of the world of jazz music.

Roach began performing in 1942 with Charlie Parker and Thelonius Monk at Clark Monroe's Uptown House in Harlem, New York. During the 1940s and 1950s he performed and recorded with other jazz greats, including Duke Ellington, Coleman Hawkins, Dizzy Gillespie, and Clifford Brown. In 1960, Roach recorded *We Insist: Freedom Now Suite,* an album which explores the theme of racial oppression in America and SOUTH AFRICA. In 1970, he created the all-percussion ensemble M'Boom and continued to write, record, and perform music throughout the 1980s and beyond. In 2001 he was one of many jazz musicians who performed at the "Great Night in Harlem" concert in New York City, held to raise funds for the Jazz Foundation of America.

Roach was a part of a small circle of musicians that helped pioneer a form of jazz called BEBOP. Along with Kenny Clarke, Roach redefined jazz drumming by keeping time on the cymbal and using the drums for rhythmic accents. He received an Obie Award in 1985 and a MacArthur Prize in 1988. Roach set a new standard in jazz music not only in terms of the rhythmic complexity and creativity he engineered but also in terms of his political emphasis on racial justice.

Bibliography
Gabbard, Krin, ed. *Representing Jazz.* Duke University Press, 1995.

Aaron Myers

Robben Island

South African island prison, notorious for its brutal treatment of political prisoners.

When NELSON ROLIHLAHLA MANDELA, future president of SOUTH AFRICA, was convicted of treason in 1964 for his work with the AFRICAN NATIONAL CONGRESS (ANC), he was sent to Robben Island to serve out his life sentence. In his autobiography, Mandela described Robben Island, the place where he spent eighteen years before being transferred to other facilities, as "without question the harshest, most iron-fisted outpost in the South African penal system."

Robben Island is situated in the Atlantic Ocean, five miles off the South African coast and ten miles north of CAPE TOWN. The island was used as a prison as early as the seventeenth century. It also housed an army base, leper colony, and insane asylum, but it was not until the 1960s that Robben Island became the country's primary location for incarcerating political prisoners. Such prisoners, often convicted of treason for their association with such ANTIAPARTHEID MOVEMENT groups as the ANC, the PAN-AFRICANIST CONGRESS, or the Communist Party, were kept separately from the other prisoners. Robben Island's political prisoners left their cells, which measured just more than 2 m sq (about seven by seven ft) and lacked heat or plumbing, only to work breaking rocks in the island's limestone quarries. As in everyday South African life, strict racial divisions applied: Indian and "coloured" (the racial category encompassing people of mixed racial descent) prisoners were allowed to wear long pants, socks, and shoes; while blacks like Mandela wore shorts and sandals, even in the wintertime.

Worse, perhaps, than the physical deprivations on Robben Island were the measures designed to isolate political prisoners. The one letter they were allowed to receive each month often arrived cut to pieces by censors. Reading newspapers was strictly forbidden. Yet the prisoners still managed to obtain news from the outside world; they bribed wardens for newspapers, for instance, which they would then copy and share in coded notes. In hushed conversations in the quarry, Mandela, WALTER SISULU, and others transmitted the history of the ANC to new prisoners, leading Robben Island to become known among antiapartheid activists as "the University." Since 1997 Robben Island has been a museum to which government-chartered boats take tourists to see the site of their president's long imprisonment.

Bibliography
Deacon, Harriet. *The Island: A History of Robben Island, 1488–1990.* Mayibuye Books, 1996.

Mandela, Nelson. *Long Walk to Freedom.* Little, Brown, 1994.

Kate Tuttle

Roberts, Charles Luckeyeth (Luckey)

1887–1968

American jazz pianist, composer, bandleader, and stride piano pioneer.

Born in PHILADELPHIA, PENNSYLVANIA, Luckey Roberts had a varied career that reflected the breadth of his musical talent. As a composer, he authored fourteen scores for stage musicals. His popular songs included "Junk Man Rag," "Pork and Beans," and "Mo'lasses," and he composed concert-length works, most notably, *Whistlin' Pete—Miniature Syncopated Rhapsody.* He led his own band from the 1920s through the 1940s. From 1940 to 1954, he owned and operated the Rendezvous Club in HARLEM, NEW YORK, performing nightly piano solos.

Roberts was considered a gifted stride pianist whose elegance and fluent imagination won him the esteem of colleagues, such as James P. Johnson and WILLIE ("THE LION") SMITH.

See also JAZZ.

Robert Fay

Roberts, Frederick Madison

1880–1952

African American newspaper publisher and California state legislator.

Although Frederick Madison Roberts is principally known for his long service as the first black state legislator in California, less well known is the fact that he was the great-grandson of SALLY HEMINGS, President Thomas Jefferson's alleged mistress. One of her sons, Madison Hemings, born on January 19, 1805, moved to Ohio. Madison's youngest daughter, Ellen Wayles Hemings, was the mother of Frederick Madison Roberts.

Roberts was born in Chilicothe, Ohio, in 1880 and was taken at the age of six to LOS ANGELES, CALIFORNIA, where his father was a pioneer undertaker. He graduated from Los Angeles High School, attended the University of Southern California, then worked his way through Colorado College in Colorado Springs and a school of mortuary science. In 1910 he was deputy assessor of El Paso County, Colorado. He edited the weekly *Colorado Springs Light* from 1908 to around 1912. After returning to Los Angeles, Roberts began his long career as a mortician and purchased the *New Age*, a weekly that he edited from around 1912 to 1948. He was for several years principal of the public schools in the all-black town of MOUND BAYOU, Mississippi, after which he returned to Los Angeles and resumed his editorship of the *New Age* and his undertaking business.

In 1918 Roberts was elected on the REPUBLICAN PARTY ticket to the California state legislature from the 74th District (later the 62nd). In that district, two-thirds of the voters were white, although the proportionate number of blacks was increasing. Roberts was repeatedly reelected. In his campaigns and legislative service he was noted as emphasizing Republicanism rather than race. As a result of U.S. president Franklin D. Roosevelt's post-Depression New Deal surge, however, Roberts was defeated in 1934 by Augustus F. Hawkins, a black Democrat. He continued a strong interest in politics, and in 1946 he was a Republican candidate for the House from the 14th Congressional District but was defeated by Helen Gahagan Douglas.

Roberts had just returned from the Republican National Convention of 1952 when he was mortally injured in an automobile accident and died on July 19. He was survived by his widow, Pearl, and two daughters, Gloria and Patricia.

An obituary in the *Los Angeles Times* (July 20, 1952) gives the main facts of Roberts's life. Details of his life through 1918 appear in Delilah L. Beasley's work *The Negro Trail Blazers of California* (1919). The *California Blue Books* and W. N. Davis, Jr., Chief of Archives, furnished further information.

From *Dictionary of American Negro Biography* by Rayford W. Logan and Michael R. Winston, editors. Copyright © 1982 by Rayford W. Logan and Michael R. Winston. Reprinted by permission of W. W. Norton & Company, Inc.

Kenneth Wiggins Porter

Robertson, Oscar

1938–

African Amerian basketball star.

Known during his playing years as "The Big O," Oscar Robertson is considered by many sports critics to be one of the finest all-around players to ever grace a basketball court. He was also a pioneer in integrating the sport. Robertson was the first African American BASKETBALL player at the University of Cincinnati, cocaptain of the 1960 United States Olympic basketball team, and one of the greatest players in the history of the National Basketball Association (NBA).

During his fourteen-season professional career, Robertson helped his team win the NBA championship and scored 26,710 points. He averaged 25.7 points, 9.5 assists, and 7.5 rebounds per game. Robertson won the NBA Most Valuable Player Award in 1964. He is the only player in NBA history to average a triple double (double figures in points, rebounds, and assists) for an entire season. In 1979 Robertson was inducted into the basketball Hall of Fame, and he was chosen in 1997 as one of the NBA's fifty best players of all time.

Born in Charlotte, Tennessee, Robertson grew up in segregated Indianapolis, Indiana, and became a local basketball star at Crispus Attucks High School, an all-black school against which white schools had previously refused to compete. Led by Robertson, Attucks won Indiana state basketball championships in 1955 and 1956. Although Crispus Attucks High School had brought Indianapolis its first state basketball title, city leaders ordered the team outside the city limits for its post-championship celebration. As Robertson recalled, "They said the blacks are gonna tear up downtown."

Robertson was the first African American player at the University of Cincinnati, Ohio, where he often experienced racial prejudice. He was frequently denied hotel accommodations on road trips. Despite such obstacles, Robertson excelled at Cincinnati, averaging 33.8 points per game for the Bearcats and leading the nation in scoring. In addition, he was named All-American and College Player of the Year three times. He led the Bearcats to two Final Four appearances in the National Collegiate Athletic Association tournament and set fourteen collegiate records. Rounding out his amateur career, Robertson was cocaptain of the 1960 United States Olympic basketball team, which captured the gold medal at the games in Rome, Italy.

In the first round of the 1960 NBA draft, Robertson was selected by the Cincinnati Royals. His impact was immediate. In his rookie season Robertson averaged 30.5 points, 9.7 assists, and 10.1 rebounds per game, earning him the Rookie of the Year award. Robertson played with Cincinnati until the end of the 1969–70 season, when he was traded to the Milwaukee Bucks. In Milwaukee, Robertson teamed with the Bucks' new center, KAREEM ABDUL JABBAR (then Lew Alcindor), to help win the NBA championship in 1971. He stayed with the Bucks until his retirement in 1974.

Robertson's impact on professional basketball was not limited to his leadership and athletic accomplishments on the court. As president of the NBA Player's Association from 1965 to 1972 Robertson helped create new economic opportunities for future players. In 1970 he filed an antitrust lawsuit against the NBA on behalf of the Player's Association. The lawsuit challenged the proposed NBA–American Basketball Association merger and the college draft. It also contested the NBA's reserve clause, which prevented players from becoming free agents. In 1976, six years after the suit was filed (and two years after Robertson's retirement), the league settled the case, and the lawsuit eventually led to higher player salaries. Since his playing days, Robertson has worked as a sports analyst for ABC radio and has been involved in numerous business ventures and civic activities.

Robeson, Eslanda Cardozo Goode

1896–1965

American activist and writer who advocated African independence and managed the singing and acting career of her husband, Paul Robeson.

Eslanda Robeson's father died when she was six, and the family moved from her native WASHINGTON, D.C., to NEW YORK CITY. In 1921, she married singer and actor PAUL ROBESON. Eslanda Robeson received a B.S. in chemistry from Columbia University and, in 1945, a Ph.D. in anthropology from the Hartford Seminary Foundation. She cofounded the Council for African Affairs in 1941, and participated in many leftwing causes. She wrote two books: *Paul Robeson, Negro* (1930) and *African Journey* (1945).

Aaron Myers

Robeson, Paul

1898–1976

African American dramatic actor, singer of spirituals, civil rights activist, and political radical.

Paul Robeson was one of the most gifted men of the twentieth century. His resonant bass and commanding presence made him a world-renowned singer and actor and proved equally valuable when he spoke out against bigotry and injustice. By the 1930s Robeson was active in a wide range of causes, but his radicalism led to a long period of political harassment that culminated in his blacklisting during anti-Communist campaigns in the 1950s. Although he resumed performing in the late 1950s, his return to public life was brief. In the 1960s serious health problems sidelined him for good.

Family Background and Education

Robeson's father, William Drew Robeson, was a North Carolina slave who escaped to freedom at age fifteen, graduated from college, and entered the ministry. Robeson's mother was Maria Louisa Bustill, a teacher and a member of a leading black family in PHILADELPHIA, PENNSYLVANIA. The youngest of five children, Robeson was born in Princeton, New Jersey, and was only six years old when his mother died. His father set high expectations for his children and sent them to high school in the neighboring town of Somerville because Princeton's segregated system offered no secondary education for blacks.

In 1915 Robeson won a scholarship to Rutgers College, where he excelled academically. He was elected to Phi Beta Kappa during his junior year, became a champion debater, and was class valedictorian. He was equally triumphant on the athletic field, where his imposing 6-ft 2-in (188-cm), 190-lb (90-kg) frame served him well. Twice named an All-American in football, Robeson also lettered in baseball, basketball, and track. He graduated in 1919. Two years later, while a student at Columbia University Law School, he married Eslanda Goode. Paul and Essie Robeson's relationship was a rocky one, but her assertiveness and gift for organization proved vital to his career. Their only son, Paul Robeson, Jr., was born in 1927. In 1923, after earning his law degree and joining an otherwise all-white firm, Robeson decided to leave the legal profession. He had found his true calling as a performing artist.

Stage, Concert, and Film Career

While in law school, Robeson had occasionally taken parts in amateur theatrical productions, leading in 1922 to his first professional roles—a lead in the short-lived Broadway play *Taboo* and as a replacement cast member in the pioneering all-black musical SHUFFLE ALONG, created by composers JAMES HUBERT ("EUBIE") BLAKE and NOBLE SISSLE. Robeson's career-making opportunity came when he was asked to join the Provincetown

In 1949 African American singer and actor Paul Robeson spoke in Moscow during a celebration of the 150th anniversary of the birth of Russian poet Aleksandr Pushkin. *CORBIS/Bettmann*

Players, an influential Greenwich Village theater company that included playwright Eugene O'Neill among its three associate directors. In 1924 Robeson appeared in a revival of O'Neill's *The Emperor Jones* and premiered in the playwright's *All God's Chillun Got Wings*. In reviewing the latter, drama critic George Jean Nathan praised Robeson as "one of the most thoroughly eloquent, impressive, and convincing actors that I have looked at and listened to in almost twenty years of professional theatergoing." Soon Robeson was offered other roles. Most notably he performed in a 1930 London production of *Othello* opposite actress Peggy Ashcroft; a 1932 Broadway revival of Oscar Hammerstein II and Jerome Kern's musical, *Showboat,* which featured Robeson's dramatic rendition of "Ol' Man River"; and a long-running, critically acclaimed 1943 production of *Othello* on Broadway.

Equally significant were Robeson's musical contributions. Robeson and his longtime pianist and arranger, Lawrence Brown, played a pivotal role in bringing AFRICAN AMERICAN SPIRITUALS into the classical music repertory. A Robeson recital in 1925 at the Greenwich Village Theater was the first in which a black soloist sang an entire program of spirituals. The concert garnered superlative reviews, propelling Robeson into a new career as a concert singer and inspiring similar recitals by other black artists. Robeson also signed a recording contract with the Victor Talking Machine Company, which released his first recorded spirituals later that same year. Although Robeson would sing a wide range of material—including sentimental popular tunes, work songs, political ballads, and folk music from many different lands—he made his mark as an interpreter of spirituals.

During the 1930s Robeson also emerged as a film star. His first role was in *Body and Soul* (1924) by black director OSCAR MICHEAUX, but he was most active on the screen between 1933 and 1942. During this period he was prominently featured in Hollywood versions of *The Emperor Jones* (1933), *Show Boat* (1936), *Tales of Manhattan* (1942), and several British films. Robeson, however, was dissatisfied with his work in motion pictures. He came to believe that—with the exception of *Song of Freedom* (1936) and *The Proud Valley* (1940)—his characters reflected RACIAL STEREOTYPES, or what Robeson derided as "'Stepin Fetchit' comics and savages with leopard skin and spear." Working in films like *Sanders of the River* (1935), which sang the praises of British imperialism, became particularly distasteful to Robeson as he explored his African heritage.

Finding Africa

During the 1930s Robeson made London his primary residence, and "it was there," he recalled, "that I 'discovered' Africa." In 1933 he undertook the study of several African languages at the University of London. He also took part in activities sponsored by the West African Students Union and became acquainted with future African leaders JOMO KENYATTA of KENYA and NNAMDI AZIKIWE of NIGERIA. Robeson began to stress the positive aspects of African life. African culture, he argued, was more spiritual and more grounded in community than that of Europe or white America. Long before the BLACK POWER MOVEMENT, he stressed the need to be "proud of being black . . . For no one respects a man who does not respect himself."

Unlike many American blacks, who saw their role as one of helping to uplift and modernize the African people, Robeson thought it imperative that American-born blacks regain their African roots. He rejected the assimilationism then prevalent among the black elite, insisting that "in every black man flows the rhythm of Africa." At one point, he wrote, "I came to consider that I was an African." Yet Robeson clearly saw this "return to Africa" as a spiritual, rather than a literal, journey. He rejected separatism no less than assimilationism and never abandoned his vision of an integrated society. Instead he fashioned a worldview that anchored cultural diversity in universal values, among which the most important was a faith in human solidarity that lay at the heart of his encounter with SOCIALISM.

Socialism and Political Activism

During the 1930s Robeson began reading about socialism and taking part in political discussions with various activists and scholars, including CYRIL LIONEL ROBERT JAMES, a radical Caribbean theorist; WILLIAM PATTERSON, a black Communist and American trade unionist; and American anarchist Emma Goldman. In 1934 Robeson made the first of many visits to the Union of Soviet Socialist Republics (USSR). He was impressed by the seeming lack of racial prejudice in the USSR and by the Soviet Constitution, which guaranteed citizens equality, "irrespective of their nationality or race." About the same time, Robeson became active in various radical causes. In England he took part in labor and peace rallies and meetings to protest British colonialism in JAMAICA. He spoke at a London rally for Indian nationalist Jawaharlal Nehru, performed at benefit concerts for the Spanish Republic, and in 1938 traveled to Spain to sing for republican troops.

In 1939, Paul and Essie Robeson returned to the United States, where he continued to be politically active. Robeson sang the egalitarian "Ballad for Americans" over national radio late that year and recorded a best-selling version of the song for Victor. He supported the United Auto Workers and other unions of the Congress of Industrial Organizations (CIO). He served on the board of the new Negro Playwrights' Company, and he became chairman of the Council on African Affairs, an American-based organization that provided information on African struggles for freedom and lobbied African concerns. During World War II (1941–1945), Robeson committed his prodigious energies in support of the Allied war effort and in protests against the poll tax, the segregation of America's armed forces, and the segregated venues for some of his own concerts. After the war, Robeson, W(ILLIAM) E(DWARD) B(URGHARDT) DU BOIS, and Bartley Crum, a liberal white lawyer, called for a national conference to secure a federal antilynching law. Robeson also protested the antilabor Taft-Hartley Act and campaigned for the Progressive Party in the 1948 election. Robeson highlighted the black struggle for equality in all his campaign speeches, even those he delivered—at considerable risk—in the Deep South.

Difficulties during the Cold War Era

As the United States entered the Cold War, however, Robeson found himself increasingly isolated. Although he was not a member of the Communist Party, he had close ties to many in the party's leadership. Robeson staunchly defended the Communist Soviet Union despite its 1939 pact with Nazi Germany and despite Soviet leader Nikita Khrushchev's revelations in 1956 about purges by his predecessor, Josef Stalin, during the 1930s. The Federal Bureau of Investigation (FBI) placed Robeson under surveillance as early as 1941 and compiled a massive dossier on his activities. Yet it seems clear that he was targeted as much for his militancy on civil rights issues as for his alleged Communism. The real turning point for Robeson came in 1949 when the Associated Press, in reporting his criticisms of the United States at a peace conference in Paris, France, quoted him as saying: "It is unthinkable that American Negroes would go to war on behalf of those who have oppressed us for generations against a country [the Soviet Union] which in one generation has raised our people to the full dignity of mankind."

Most Americans were outraged. The House Committee on Un-American Activities (HUAC) announced that it would hold hearings to investigate Robeson and the loyalty of black Americans. White liberals and the black establishment, offended by his growing stridency and fearful of the taint of Communism, distanced themselves from him. Even one-time friends, such as WALTER FRANCIS WHITE, executive director of the NATIONAL ASSOCIATION FOR THE ADVANCEMENT OF COLORED PEOPLE (NAACP), and Max Yergan, former executive director of the Council on African Affairs, denounced his remarks.

Later that year, a mob of young white men disrupted an outdoor Robeson concert near Peekskill, New York, attacking concertgoers and sending a dozen to the hospital. Robeson himself narrowly escaped injury. A rescheduled concert, guarded by members of several left-wing CIO unions, came off without incident, but at its conclusion the audience found itself facing a gauntlet of enraged, rock-throwing locals. State and local police did little to restrain the attackers; in fact many joined the mob. A grand jury investigation wrote off the violence as having been provoked by Robeson's previous unpatriotic remarks.

Ultimately, Robeson was silenced, but doing so required the combined efforts of the black establishment—including leaders of the fledgling CIVIL RIGHTS MOVEMENT—white liberals, the entertainment industry, and the government. In 1950, the State Department rescinded Robeson's passport, preventing him from performing or traveling abroad. At home he found himself blacklisted by Broadway and Hollywood, by concert halls and record companies, radio, and television. His only opportunities to perform were at small affairs organized by a dwindling core of radicals and at a few black churches such as Harlem's Mother AFRICAN METHODIST EPISCOPAL ZION CHURCH, whose pastor was Robeson's brother, Rev. Benjamin C. Robeson. Denied a public voice, Robeson struggled mightily to vindicate himself and win back his freedom of travel. In 1956 Robeson testified before HUAC, offering a powerful indictment of America's continuing racial injustice. Robeson also steadfastly refused to condemn the Soviet Union, to provide the names of American Communists, or to answer whether he was a party member, a question which he viewed as a violation of his constitutional rights. In 1957, after a seven-year delay, the State Department finally granted him a hearing on the revocation of his passport. The result was a six-hour grilling, but no change in the government's policy.

Final Years

Robeson fought his lonely battle at great personal cost. In 1955, he began to show the first clear signs of the emotional difficulties that would eventually halt his public activities. It is ironic that he should pay so dearly for his alleged Communism. In truth, what lay at the heart of Robeson's political convictions was not Marxism so much as an empathy for African culture and an identification with common people, the poor, and the oppressed.

By the end of the decade, the worst years of the Cold War had passed, and Robeson's troubles began to ease. In 1958 he gave his first commercial concerts in several years, appearing in Chicago, Illinois; Portland, Oregon; and several California cities. He published *Here I Stand,* a trenchant autobiography written with Lloyd Brown. And a Supreme Court decision permitted him to travel abroad once again. The next few years were busy ones, with American concerts and recording sessions for Vanguard; concert tours of Europe, Australia, and New Zealand; visits to the Soviet Union; and in 1959 another London production of *Othello*. But on March 27, 1961, Robeson suffered a nervous breakdown and attempted suicide. For the rest of his life, he would struggle with severe depression, and his public appearances would be extremely rare. Robeson dropped out of public view and was largely ignored by the leadership of the Civil Rights Movement, except for the militant young leaders of the STUDENT NOVIOLENT COORDINATING COMMITTEE (SNCC). At a gala celebration for his sixty-seventh birthday, Robeson was deeply moved when keynote speaker JOHN LEWIS, then the chairman of SNCC, proclaimed, "We of SNCC are Paul Robeson's spiritual children. We too have rejected gradualism and moderation." Yet beneath Robeson's militancy—and intertwined with it—was a profound compassion and a deep bond with Africa best seen in a passage he wrote in 1936:

"I am a singer and an actor. I am primarily an artist. Had I been born in Africa, I would have belonged, I hope, to that family which sings and chants the glories and legends of the tribe. I would have liked in my mature years to have been a wise elder, for I worship wisdom and knowledge of the ways of men." Paul Robeson's final public appearance was at a benefit dinner for SNCC in 1966.

See also Film, Blacks in American; Integration: An Interpretation; Labor Unions in the United States; Robeson, Eslanda Cardozo Goode

Bibliography

Duberman, Martin Bauml. *Paul Robeson: A Biography.* Knopf, 1989.

Robeson, Paul, with Lloyd Brown. *Here I Stand.* Othello Associates, 1958.

Robeson, Susan. *The Whole World in His Hands: A Pictorial Biography of Paul Robeson.* Citadel Press, 1981.

James Sellman

Robinson, Bill ("Bojangles")

1878–1949

American vaudeville performer, tap dancer, and movie star, considered the most famous African American entertainer of the early twentieth century.

Bill "Bojangles" Robinson was born Luther Robinson, the son of Maxwell Robinson, a machinist, and Maria Robinson, a singer. Robinson and his brother Bill, whose name he would later appropriate, were orphaned when their parents died in 1885. The brothers then lived with their paternal grandmother, Bedilia Robinson, and Robinson worked as a bootblack and danced on street corners for money. He began to use the nickname "Bojangles," which was possibly derived from "jangle," a slang term for fighting, and supposedly invented the expression "Everything's copasetic," which meant "life is great." At age twelve Robinson ran away to WASHINGTON, D.C., where he worked as a street dancer and at a racetrack.

His first professional job came in 1892 as a member of the "pickaninny" chorus—a group of African American children who sang backup for the main performer—in the revue *The South before the War.* After a two-year stint in the army, Robinson moved to NEW YORK, NEW YORK, in 1900, where he emerged as one of the first black stars of vaudeville. At the time, black roles normally were performed by whites in blackface, but from 1902 to 1914, Robinson toured the vaudeville circuit as the partner of the black comedian George W. Cooper. Cooper played the straight man to Robinson's clown. Although the duo had not been a dance team, when it broke up Robinson persuaded his manager, Marty Forkins, to book him performances as a solo dancer. In 1917 Robinson performed for American serviceman ordered to Europe to fight in World War I, and in 1918 he premiered at New York's legendary Palace Theater, where he first performed his trademark "stair dance," a rapid TAP DANCE up and down a five-step staircase, to a standing ovation. Robinson was one of the first black performers to star at the Palace, where audiences were amazed by his dancing. His footwork was complex, graceful, and often improvised. Often bedecked in tails and a top hat tilted to one side, Robinson charmed audiences with his irresistible smile. His career as a vaudeville star culminated in a European tour in 1926.

Robinson became one of the first black Broadway stars, debuting as the lead in the all-black revue, *Blackbirds of 1928.* Newspaper reviews hailed him as the best tap dancer ever. Robinson's other notable Broadway starring appearances include *Brown Buddies* (1930), *Blackbirds of 1933*, *The Hot Mikado* (1939), *All in Fun* (1940), and *Memphis Bound* (1945) Because of his Broadway success, Robinson was crowned the honorary "Mayor of Harlem" in 1933.

Robinson began to make Hollywood films in the 1930s, at a time when the industry offered few opportunities to blacks. His films include *Dixiana* (1930), *Harlem Is Heaven* (1933), and *Hooray for Love* (1935). The films that were most popular, however, were the four he made with white child star Shirley Temple: *The Littlest Colonel* (1935), *The Littlest Rebel* (1935), *Just around the Corner* (1938), and *Rebecca of Sunnybrook Farm* (1938).

Throughout his career Robinson donated money and benefit performances for many causes, including the NATIONAL ASSOCIATION FOR THE ADVANCEMENT OF COLORED PEOPLE (NAACP). In recognition for his achievements and philanthropy, the Negro Actors Guild named Robinson its honorary president in 1937.

Robinson was married three times. In 1907 he married Lena Chase, a relationship that ended in 1922. He next married his business manager Fannie Clay, divorcing her in 1943. He married the dancer Elaine Paines in 1944.

Robinson performed ceaselessly, keeping a hectic dancing schedule well into his sixties. His show business career spanned fifty years. He died of a heart attack backstage after performing with Milton Berle a month before his seventieth birthday. Robinson is remembered as one of the greatest entertainers of the twentieth century. Dance historian Rusty E. Frank wrote of him, "They said that Bill Robinson could do the easiest routine in the world and get away with it because of his charm and charisma. They said that he could drive a dancer crazy with the complexity of a step that looked so easy. But when tap dancers talk about Bill Robinson, they talk about the greatest tap dancer of all time."

See also Films, Blacks in American.

Bibliography

Frank, Rusty E. *Tap!: The Greatest Tap Dance Stars and Their Stories.* CITY, 1990.

Haskins, James, and N. R. Mitgang. *Mr. Bojangles: The Biography of Bill Robinson.* William Morrow, 1988.

Robinson, Eddie

1919–

African American college football coach.

Eddie Robinson may be less well known than coaches at better known universities, but no football coach has led his teams to more victories. Over his fifty-six-year career as coach of the Grambling State University football team, Coach Rob, as he was known, became the first coach of either college or professional football to claim 400 victories.

Born Edward Gay Robinson in Jackson, Louisiana, Robinson became a standout college athlete as the quarterback for

Leland College in Baker, Louisiana. He served as an assistant coach during his final two years there. In 1941, a year after graduating from Leland, Robinson became the head coach at Grambling (then called the Louisiana Negro Normal and Industrial Institute), a historically black college in Grambling, Louisiana.

Lack of funds forced Robinson into more roles than just coach. "Come the day of the game," Robinson told the *New York Times* in 1985, "I marked the field, taped the kids, and drilled the drill squad at halftime. And after the game, I'd write the story." His teams achieved amazing success. In his first year the team won three games and lost five, but the following year it was undefeated, for a perfect 9-0 season. During his career, Robinson compiled a record of 408 wins, 165 losses, and 15 ties, including two more undefeated seasons. Under Robinson, Grambling captured eight National Black College Championships and won or shared in seventeen Southwestern Athletic Conference championships.

Robinson saw more than 200 of his former players become professional players in the National Football League, including Pro Football Hall-of-Famers Willie Davis, Willie Brown, and Buck Buchanan, and standouts Everson Walls and Doug Williams. Beginning in the early 1970s, widespread recruitment of African American athletes by wealthier universities meant that fewer top-quality African American athletes attended historically black colleges, such as Grambling. Still, even with this talent drain, Robinson had only two losing seasons between 1970 and his retirement in 1997. The Football Writers of America Association has commemorated Robinson's contributions to the sport with the Eddie Robinson Award, presented annually to the coach of the year. Robinson and his family have established the Eddie Robinson Foundation to aid high-school seniors who excel in sports.

See also Football, Collegiate; Football, Professional.

Bibliography

Davis, O. K. *Grambling's Gridiron Glory*. O. K. Davis, 1983.

Robinson, Frank

1935–

African American Hall of Fame baseball player who became the first black manager in the major leagues.

Born in Beaumont, Texas, the youngest of ten children, Frank Robinson came onto the major league baseball scene in 1956 as an outfielder with the Cincinnati Reds. He immediately made his presence felt. Robinson captured the National League Rookie of the Year award, hitting .290 and slamming thirty-eight home runs. His home-runs record as a rookie tied a major league record. Robinson maintained his extraordinary play over many years. In 1961 he led the Reds to the National League pennant and earned the league's Most Valuable Player (MVP) award. After the 1965 season, Robinson was traded to the Baltimore Orioles.

Robinson's first season with the Orioles was extraordinary. He hit for a .316 average, hit 49 home runs, drove in 122 runs (RBI), and scored 122 runs—leading the American League in all four major offensive statistical categories. He also led his team to a World Series championship and won baseball's Triple Crown. For his efforts, he was named both World Series and American League MVP. Robinson was the first player to win the MVP award in both leagues.

Robinson also helped the Orioles win another World Series in 1970. He remained with the Orioles until 1971, then played for a succession of teams, including the Los Angeles Dodgers in 1972, the California Angels from 1973 to 1974, and the Cleveland Indians from 1975 to 1976. By the time he retired from playing in 1976, after twenty years of big league play, Robinson had a lifetime batting average of .294. He had also hit 586 home runs, fourth on the all-time list behind HANK AARON, Babe Ruth, and WILLIE MAYS. Robinson also appeared in eleven All-Star Games and was named the MVP of the 1971 game.

Robinson's baseball career did not end after his playing days. In 1975, while still playing with the Indians, Robinson was hired as the club's manager. The appointment made Robinson the first African American to manage a major league baseball team. From 1981 to 1984, he managed the San Francisco Giants. Robinson won the National League Manager of the Year award in 1982, the same year he was inducted into the National Baseball Hall of Fame. In 1988 he returned to Baltimore to manage the Orioles, staying until 1991. Over the course of his career as a manager, Robinson amassed 680 wins and 751 losses. He worked in the Oriole's front office as assistant general manager until 1995. In 1997 Major League Baseball named Robinson director of baseball operations for the Arizona Fall League and consultant to the commissioner for special projects.

Robinson, Jackie

1919–1972

American baseball player and civil rights activist, and the first African American to play major league baseball in modern times.

Born in Cairo, Georgia, to sharecroppers Jerry and Mallie Robinson, Jack Roosevelt Robinson was raised in Pasadena, California, primarily by his mother, who worked as a domestic servant after moving the family from Georgia. Taught by his mother to confront racism by showing his talent, Robinson turned to athletics as a way to compete with the white children who would shout racist epithets at him and his siblings.

At Pasadena's John Muir High School, Robinson starred on several of the school's athletic teams. In 1938 he entered Pasadena Junior College, where he also excelled in sports. In 1940 Robinson transferred to the University of California–Los Angeles (UCLA), where he was the first man in the school's history to earn varsity letters in four sports. An All-America running back in football, he also competed in track and field— breaking his older brother's national record in the broad jump—

Jackie Robinson crosses home plate after hitting his first home run as a Brooklyn Dodger and receives a congratulatory handshake from teammate Tommy Tatum. *Bettmann/CORBIS*

and led the Pacific Coast Conference in scoring while on the basketball team. Ironically, baseball was not Robinson's best sport, nor the one he most enjoyed.

Robinson left UCLA in 1941 before graduating, to become the assistant athletic director of the National Youth Administration Camp in Atascadero, California. During that year he also played semiprofessional football for the Honolulu Bears. With the onset of World War II (1939–1945), Robinson was drafted into the United States Army in 1942. His army experience sharpened his sense of racial injustice. Only after boxer JOE LOUIS intervened with officials in Washington, D.C., on Robinson's behalf did Robinson become an officer at Fort Riley, Kansas. Transferred to Fort Hood, Texas, after protesting the mistreatment of his fellow African American soldiers, Robinson was court-martialed for refusing to sit in the back of an army bus. He was soon reinstated, but was discharged from the army in 1944.

In 1945 Jackie Robinson began his professional baseball career by joining the Kansas City Monarchs of the Negro American League with a salary of $400 per month. Robinson was not accustomed to the difficult schedule and travel of the Negro League, and he was disturbed by the oppressive treatment of black ballplayers throughout the country. He excelled, nonetheless, batting .345 and proving himself to be an all-around talent.

Meanwhile, Branch Rickey, the general manager of the Brooklyn Dodgers, quietly began to search for the best candidate to break the color barrier in major league baseball. The time was right for Rickey's project. In 1944 Commissioner Kenesaw Mountain Landis, who had upheld the so-called gentlemen's agreement to keep the major leagues white only, had died. African American sacrifices during World War II engendered hope and support for their fuller participation in all facets of American society, thus leading to a burgeoning CIVIL RIGHTS MOVEMENT. In a secret vote held by the office of new commissioner Albert "Happy" Chandler, all of the major league executives rejected the idea of integrating baseball, except for Rickey. On October 23, 1945, he defied the executives' vote and signed the college-educated army officer Robinson to a contract with the minor league Montreal Royals, the top team in the Dodgers' farm system.

After playing in Venezuela during the winter, Robinson joined the Royals in Florida for the 1946 spring training season. Robinson's venture into white organized baseball was opposed from the start by coaches, teammates, other teams, and many white fans. Facing racist taunts and segregated living conditions, Robinson managed to lead the Class AAA International League in batting (.349) and runs scored (113), and helped bring his team to the league championship.

In the spring of 1947, Robinson joined the Brooklyn Dodgers in CUBA for spring training. Several Dodgers circulated a petition to exclude Robinson. Dodger manager Leo Durocher told the protesters they could leave if they wanted. Nobody left and Robinson began "baseball's great experiment" in April 1947, becoming the first African American in the major leagues since Moses Fleetwood Walker had played in 1885. He set the league on fire, earning rookie of the year honors with a .297 batting average and a league-leading twenty-nine stolen bases. During his ten seasons with the Dodgers, Robinson batted .311, led the team to six pennants and one World Series Championship, won the 1949 National League most valuable player award, and paved the way for African American players in all professional team sports. Robinson proved himself on and off the field to be an exemplar of character and grace. With the help of his wife Rachel, Robinson heroically upheld his promise to Rickey not to retaliate against racist insults. In 1962, he was inducted into the National Baseball Hall of Fame.

After his baseball career Robinson was vocal in the struggle for integration and black self-improvement, supporting conservative means for improving the conditions of African Americans. He refused to attend games or play in old-timers games because of the dearth of blacks in nonplaying roles. By 1972, however, he celebrated the twenty-fifth anniversary of his debut, throwing out the first pitch in the World Series. He died nine days later, having proved the equality of African Americans in one sphere that also had profound effects on the rest of American society.

See also Baseball in the United States; Negro Leagues.

Bibliography

Robinson, Jackie, with Alfred Duckett. *I Never Had It Made.* Putnam, 1972.

Tygiel, Jules. *Baseball's Great Experiment: Jackie Robinson and His Legacy.* Oxford University Press, 1997.

Robinson, JoAnn Gibson

1912–

African American civil rights activist who was a leader in the Montgomery Bus Boycott.

JoAnn Gibson Robinson was born in Culloden, Georgia. She attended Fort Valley State College and earned an M.A. degree in English from Atlanta University in 1948. Afterward, while teaching at Alabama State College in Montgomery, she became active in the CIVIL RIGHTS MOVEMENT.

Robinson became president of the Women's Political Council (WPC), an organization composed of mainly middle-class black women who were committed to increasing African American participation in civic affairs. The WPC challenged Montgomery's policy of segregated seating on public transportation by organizing the MONTGOMERY BUS BOYCOTT after ROSA PARKS was arrested for violating segregation laws in 1955. The bus boycott's challenge of the policy was successful.

Robinson left Alabama State College in 1960 and taught English in Los Angeles, California, until retiring in 1976. Her 1987 memoir *The Montgomery Bus Boycott and the Women Who Started It* was awarded special acclaim by the Southern Association for Women's Historians. It emphasized the important role women played in the daily organization and the planned activities of the Civil Rights Movement.

Bibliography

Robinson, Jo Ann. *The Montgomery Bus Boycott and the Women Who Started It: The Memoir of Jo Ann Robinson.* University of Tennessee Press, 1987.

Alonford James Robinson

Robinson, Randall

See TransAfrica.

Robinson, Ruby Doris Smith

1942–1967

American civil rights activist and a founder of the Student Nonviolent Coordinating Committee.

Ruby Smith Robinson was inspired as a teenager by media images of the 1950s MONTGOMERY BUS BOYCOTT in Alabama. After joining the CIVIL RIGHTS MOVEMENT, Robinson was arrested for the first time as part of a lunch counter desegregation SIT-IN in 1959, while she was a sophomore at SPELMAN COLLEGE in Atlanta. In 1960 she became one of the founding members of the STUDENT NONVIOLENT COORDINATING COMMITTEE (SNCC).

One of the original Freedom Riders, Robinson helped to create SNCC's "jail, no bail" policy, a strategy to fill Southern jails with protesters and thus keep public attention on the movement. In 1966 Robinson became SNCC's first (and only) female executive secretary. She left SNCC in early 1967, and died of leukemia that October.

See also Freedom Rides.

Bibliography

Hardy, Gayle J. *American Women Civil Rights Activists: Biobibliographies of Sixty-eight Leaders, 1825–1992.* University of Tennessee Press, 1993.

Lisa Clayton Robinson

Robinson, Sugar Ray

1921–1989

One of the great boxers of modern history, noted for lightning speed and impressive power.

Sugar Ray Robinson was born Walker Smith, Jr., in DETROIT, MICHIGAN. He became interested in BOXING early in life, idolizing heavyweight champion JOE LOUIS, who also came from Detroit. To compete in tournaments at a young age, Robinson borrowed the amateur certificate of another fighter, whose name, Ray Robinson, stuck. After an astonishing string of amateur victories in the welterweight division, he won Golden Gloves titles in 1939 and 1940. His style, combining graceful movement with brute power, was described by one of his handlers as "sweet as sugar."

Robinson turned professional in 1940 and won forty straight fights—more than twenty by knockout—until Jake LaMotta beat him by decision in 1943. In World War II, Robinson entered the United States Army and performed in exhibitions for soldiers on the same bill as his hero Louis. He also protested racial segregation in the armed forces, once even fighting a military policeman who harassed Louis for using a whites-only phone. After the war, in December 1946, Robinson captured the welterweight title by defeating Tommy Bell. Defending the title in 1947, he delivered fatal blows to challenger Jimmy Doyle. A reporter asked if Robinson had meant to get Doyle in trouble, and Robinson is said to have replied, "Mister, it's my business to get him into trouble."

Later that year Robinson moved up to the middleweight division. In 1951 he again met LaMotta, now the world middleweight champion, in a fight that reporters called the St. Valentine's Day Massacre. Robinson emerged from the savage contest the winner. Losing his title to Englishman Randy Turpin in July 1951, Robinson won it back in a rematch two months later. In 1952 Robinson went after Joey Maxim, the light heavyweight champion, at New York's Yankee Stadium. Although he outboxed Maxim, Robinson was overwhelmed by the heat and forced to call the fight in the thirteenth round—the only defeat by knockout in his career.

After the fight, Robinson surprised the boxing world by retiring and working for two years as a tap dancer. In 1955, however, he returned to the ring, taking back his middleweight title with a second-round knockout of Bobo Olson. Twice more Robinson lost and regained the title, holding it a record five times. He permanently lost the title to Paul Pender on January 22, 1960. Although his friends encouraged the thirty-eight-year-old Robinson to retire, he continued to fight until 1965, in part to maintain his income. In his later years, he established the Sugar Ray Robinson Youth Foundation for children in LOS ANGELES, CALIFORNIA.

See also Tap Dance; World War II and African Americans.

Bibliography

Robinson, Sugar Ray, and Dave Anderson. *Sugar Ray.* Viking Press, 1970.

Robinson, William ("Smokey")

1940–

African American singer and songwriter.

Known for his romantic lyrics and his passionate, high-ranging voice, RHYTHM AND BLUES (R&B) star Smokey Robinson was the leading member of the MOTOWN group the Miracles from 1958 to 1971. He was one of the most influential singers and songwriters in popular music during the 1960s and 1970s.

William "Smokey" Robinson was born in DETROIT, MICHIGAN. At the age of eighteen, he formed the vocal group later, known as the Miracles, with high-school friends Ronnie White, Pete Moore, Bobby Rogers, and Rogers's sister Claudette, whom Robinson later married. The group impressed Motown owner Berry Gordy, who signed it to a recording contract in 1960.

The Miracles' first hit record was "Shop Around" (1961), an R&B song recorded for Tamla, one of the Motown Record Company labels. It was a phenomenal success, reaching number one on the *Billboard* magazine R&B charts and number two on its pop music charts. The hit helped launch Gordy's young music studio. In the decade that followed, the Miracles produced a highly popular body of work, including the song "You Really Got a Hold on Me" (1962); hard-edged dance tunes such as "Mickey's Monkey" (1963) and "Going to Go-Go" (1965); and the dreamy songs "More Love" (1967) and "I Second That Emotion" (1967). Perhaps even more enduring are the ballads "Ooo Baby Baby" (1965), "The Tracks of My Tears" (1965), and "Baby, Baby Don't Cry" (1969). In 1967 the group became known as Smokey Robinson and the Miracles.

During the 1960s Robinson also wrote and produced classics for other Motown artists. "My Girl" was written for the vocal group the TEMPTATIONS. Robinson wrote classics of SOUL MUSIC for Mary Wells in "You Beat Me to the Punch" (1962) and "My Guy" (1964) and for MARVIN GAYE in "Ain't That Peculiar" (1965). Many popular musicians, including folk-rock artist Bob Dylan, admired Robinson's songwriting skills, and his songs have endured, later recorded by many artists, including the Beatles, ARETHA FRANKLIN, and Luther Vandross, and popular singers Linda Ronstadt and Kim Carnes.

Robinson left the Miracles in 1972 to pursue a solo music career. He released the highly regarded album *Quiet Storm* in 1975 and went on to produce a stream of dreamy romantic songs, including "Cruisin'" (1979), written with longtime collaborator and guitarist Marv Tarplin. Robinson's other notable hits include "Being with You" (1981) and "Just to See Her" (1987; Grammy Award, 1988). Robinson was inducted into the Rock and Roll Hall of Fame in 1987 and won a Grammy Legends Award in 1990. His work was collected on the albums *The Ultimate Collection* (1998) and *Ooo Baby Baby: The Anthology* (2002). Robinson continues to perform, at such venues as the 2003 New Orleans Jazz and Heritage Festival.

Robert Fay

Rock Art, African

Paintings and engravings on rock, found in most regions of Africa, dating from prehistoric times to the twentieth century.

African rock art comprises a variety of painting styles as well as stone tool engravings. Carbon dating suggests that African rock art may have begun as many as 60,000 years ago, but due to erosion and other natural factors, the oldest remaining examples date to 25500 B.C.E.

Rock paintings range from simple outlines of motionless animals and abstract compositions to complex, multicolored scenes of human communities, herds of animals in motion, and expressive characters. Four chronological painting styles mark this development from simplicity to greater complexity. The oldest (4000 B.C.E. to 1 C.E.) uses simple outlines and silhouettes and only one color for each figure. The next (1 to 1000 C.E.) employs the same simple forms, but with the addition of motion. The third style was used during the shortest period

(1000 to 1100 C.E.); artists abandoned the traditional silhouette and focused on realism in outline drawing. Finally, the fourth style (1100 to 1800 C.E.) introduces polychrome paintings of figures and animals in motion and engaged with one another, often superimposed over older paintings. Scholar C. K. Cooke has given these periods approximate dates, but debate has continued about their accuracy. Some research suggests that African artists used these styles concurrently to some degree.

African rock paintings are usually found under rock outcroppings and in the entrances to shallow caves. Paints were made from natural pigments with animal fat, saps, or gums as binders. Rock engravings, or petroglyphs, are less common. The petroglyphs are usually found on the tops of small hills, where they were carved into exposed, rather than sheltered, stone. Typically depicting animals, the carvings are of two kinds: engraved images and pecked images made by chipping at the surface of the stone. Petroglyphs are thought to have taken days to complete, and were probably done by hunters in their spare time as they kept watch for prey.

Rock art exists in North, West, East and southern Africa. In North Africa, the Grande Kabylie region, spanning 7,000 square miles across ALGERIA and TUNISIA, contains one of the continent's richest and most remote concentrations of ancient rock painting and engraving. The paintings were executed on sandstone sites, which may then have served either as places of worship or, as some observers have suggested, as hunters' lucky amulets, intended to draw animals near. Most of the Grand Kabylie paintings are conventionalized representations of humans and animals or abstract "dots and dash" designs, which are common in African rock art. The abstract patterns may be related to the representational paintings, or they may be unrelated practical markings, such as a system for tallying the number of animals killed in a hunt.

Another major site of paintings in North Africa is in the Tassili n'Ajjer, a plateau region in what is now southeastern Algeria. These works may date from as early as 3080 B.C.E. and depict an environment much less arid than the present one. It is suspected that the Tassili n'Ajjer once contained flourishing oases, which disappeared as the Saharan climate grew drier. Three distinct phases have been found in Saharan painting. The first phase(1000 B.C.E. to 100 C.E.) is typified by the "disk-headed" man, a representation of a large-headed person with few, if any, facial features, but given clothing and intricate hair style and accompanied by regional animals. During the "pastoralist" period (100 to 1250 C.E.) depictions of horse-drawn chariots and domesticated animals such as cattle and sheep appear. Finally the "cameline" period marks the introduction of the CAMEL to the SAHARA, and stretches from roughly 1200 C.E. until the twentieth century. Most of the more recent paintings in the Tassili n'Ajjer were created by the TUAREG, and typically portray the horses and nomadic lives of their people.

In East Africa, cave paintings are more abundant than engravings. Sites in KENYA and UGANDA have not yet been well explored or catalogued, but it is known that sites in ETHIOPIA and TANZANIA contain art similar in style and subject to Saharan rock art. Two important series of paintings are found in Ethiopia: one at Genda Bifton, which includes at least 1,000 figures painted as a mural measuring 50 meters long, and the other, dating from at latest 2000 B.C.E., at the Cave of the Wild Boar near Dire Dawa, depicting large groups of herdsmen. In Tanzania, significant sites include Kisana, on the eastern rim of the Iramba plateau, and Ilongero, where thousands of images of wild animals cover a frieze 3 m (9 ft) high and 20 m (70 ft) long.

In southern Africa, MALAWI and ZAMBIA are both rich in painting sites, though many have been continuously inhabited by local populations and therefore are inaccessible and subject to extensive rubbing and erosion. As in other regions, a few sites in Malawi and Zambia have been repeatedly painted over as the older paintings fade. Artists may have maintained these sites to highlight their significance, or the painters may have believed that repainting replenished the energy and authority of the works. Most of the paintings found in this area are abstract compositions of "dot and dash" designs, ladders, "gridirons," spirals, circles, ovals, parallel lines, and hand prints. Possibly the largest abstract rock painting in Africa has been found near Mpunzi Mountain. The painting is 2.5 m (8 ft) long and densely packed with markings; different methods have assigned it dates ranging from 5590 to 2880 B.C.E.

Of all the rock art in Africa, the most well-explored and carefully protected collection is in ZIMBABWE. The rocky Matopos Hills near BULAWAYO are the foremost gallery of southern African rock art. Their abundant, protected overhangs and lush vegetation attracted animals and with them, hunter-painters. These artists used almost every painting style and engraving technique here to depict a wide range of animal, human, and mythological subjects. The large mural near Diana's Vow Farm in Rusape is one of Africa's most remarkable rock art sites. It depicts a sorcerer wearing a jackal mask and ritualistic hair ornaments, men dancing over animals, and some of the most explicitly mythological figures found in rock painting, such as crocodile-men and other half-human, half-animal creatures. While some paintings in Zimbabwe were done as recently as 20 B.C.E., most date from 7450 to 2350 B.C.E.

More contemporary examples of African rock art can be found on a 1,000 km (600 mi) stretch of plateau alongside the Drakensberg mountains in SOUTH AFRICA and LESOTHO. For centuries, KHOIKHOI hunters tracked game on this plateau, and recorded their hunts on rock spires and crags. As other peoples settled in South Africa, the Khoikhoi depicted their arrival and the subsequent struggles over territory. Khoikhoi paintings fall into four historical periods. Pre-1620 paintings include simple representations of human figures and animals. Art from the second period, to about 1800, shows people engaged in peaceful activities and multicolored animals, with attention to shading. Paintings dated to between 1800 and 1830 are also colorful but less carefully defined, and document the arrival of the NGUNI people. Finally, paintings dating from the 1870s depict huge processions of red-coated British troops and cavalry marching through the mountains. These paintings mark the imminent end of the Khoikhoi's freedom to live and hunt in the Drakensberg, and thus the end of the art form as well.

Bibliography

Ritchie, Carson. *Rock Art of Africa*. A. S. Barnes, 1979.

Christopher Tiné

Rock, John Sweat

1825–1866

African American abolitionist, doctor, and the first black lawyer allowed to practice before the Supreme Court of the United States.

John Sweat Rock, the son of free blacks, was born in Salem, New Jersey. He attended common schools in his hometown until the age of nineteen, when he was given the opportunity to study medicine with two white physicians in the area. After being trained by a white dentist, Rock earned his medical degree in 1852 from the American Medical College in PHILADELPHIA, PENNSYLVANIA.

By 1855 Rock relocated to Massachusetts, where he became one of the first African American members of the Massachusetts Medical Society. While in Boston, Rock supported the abolitionist movement, providing medical treatment to FUGITIVE SLAVES. He was a participant in the 1855 abolitionist campaign to desegregate the city's public schools and spoke at the 1858 Faneuil Hall commemoration of CRISPUS ATTUCKS Day.

Rock later earned a law degree and was admitted to the Massachusetts Bar on September 14, 1861. As an active leader in the abolitionist movement, during the AMERICAN CIVIL WAR Rock recruited black soldiers for the Fifty-Fourth and Fifty-Fifth Massachusetts Infantry Regiments. He was the first to speak during the celebration of the Emancipation Proclamation at the Tremont Temple meeting house in Boston on January 1, 1863.

Rock is perhaps best remembered as the first African American to be allowed to argue before the U.S. Supreme Court. This 1865 victory was largely ceremonial, as Rock's health prevented him from actually arguing before the Court.

See also Abolitionism in the United States; Emancipation Proclamation and the Thirteenth Amendment; Fifty-Fourth Massachusetts Volunteer Infantry Regiment; Free Blacks in the United States.

Bibliography

Quarles, Benjamin. *Black Abolitionists*. Oxford University Press, 1969.

Alonford James Robinson

Rock Steady

Musical form that flourished in Jamaica from 1966 to 1968, providing the transition from ska to reggae.

Although the heyday of rock steady lasted for only two years, it brought critical and thematic innovations that strongly influenced the course of Jamaican music. By the mid-1960s, it was evident to working- and lower-class Jamaicans that JAMAICA's 1962 independence from GREAT BRITAIN brought about no substantial improvement in living conditions. British rule was substituted for economic dependence on the United States and jobs were equally difficult to find.

The upbeat shuffle of SKA, reflective of Jamaica's early optimism, was gradually replaced by a sinister, less hurried, and "cooler" sound. An increase in musical stylization accompanied this decrease in tempo. The characteristic trombone solos of ska gave way to instrumental songs with added emphasis on the bass and drum. Instead of playing the bass guitar on the beat, a lagging syncopation became common in rock steady. Influential guitarist Lynn Tait began playing bass lines on his guitar in tandem with the bassist and these changes transformed ska into what became known as rock steady. The new form further distinguished itself from ska because it took as its target audience the rough-and-tumble streetwise youth known as the "rude boy."

"Rock steady" originally referred to the dance steps the form inspired, but the name quickly spread to the music as well. In 1966 rock steady mainstay Alton Ellis released *Rock Steady*, the genre's first full-length album. Ellis was among many top rock steady performers who worked with producer Duke Reid and his seminal Treasure Isle record label.

Rock steady developed in tandem with the "rude boy" culture of KINGSTON, JAMAICA. Rude boys were young city men, many of whom had recently emigrated from rural villages and were unable to make a decent living in the impoverished neighborhoods of West Kingston. Rude boys took to the streets, hustling, stealing, and living with consummate "cool" style. Short pants, slim suits, dark sunglasses, and chrome-covered motorcycles became the rage, although these angry young rebels carried German ratchet knives and guns under their veneer of stylish cool. The Wailers' 1966 hit "Rude Boy" sparked widespread romanticization of the rude boy image. That same year Prince Buster released "Judge Dread," the most famous condemnation of the rude boy. Although "Judge Dread" suggested that rude boy crime was self-destructive to the black community, the song nevertheless met with countless rebuffs in the years to come.

The avalanche of pro–rude boy tunes emphasized its macho vogue with lines such as "Rudies don't fear/Rougher than rougher/Tougher than tough/Strong like iron . . ." While Prince Buster was too comic to deliver truly trenchant political messages, the Ethiopian Judge Dread character in his song was meant to appeal to Jamaicans as a strong symbol of authority, in anticipation of the interest in Rastafarianism which would fuel rock steady's further slowing down into the "dread" rhythms of roots REGGAE in the late 1960s.

Alongside lyrics of rude boy aggression and cool, elements of Rastafarianism began to appear in rock steady's repertoire, especially by the Wailers. The resulting blend of socially conscious lyrics, emphasis on the newly available electric bass guitar, slower tempos, and syncopated melodic accompaniment set the stage for the next development in Jamaican musical evolution, reggae.

See also Marley, Bob; Rastafarians.

Jace Clayton

Rodeo

American sport that combines cowboy skills with Wild West mythologizing.

Charles Sampson, national bull-riding champion in 1982, grew up in the Watts section of Los Angeles, California, and he is African American. In a sport built on the overwhelmingly white mythology of the American Wild West, Sampson's success may seem surprising, but as he points out, there is historical precedent for his career. "Some people still don't realize," Sampson told the *New York Times*, "that something like a quarter of all the cowboys back in the old West were black."

Rodeo grew out of the games and competitions devised by cowboys. Whether along the trail during the great cattle drives or during the twice-yearly round-ups, whenever cowboys gathered together they would compete. As the ranching industry grew, round-ups became festivals where cowboys could drink, gamble, and show off their riding and roping skills. The word rodeo derives from these round-ups, by way of the Spanish "rodear," for encircle or surround.

Despite the end of large-scale cattle drives around 1890, rodeo-based western shows, such as those staged by William "Buffalo Bill" Cody, were popular well into the 1930s. One of the era's most renowned stars was Bill Pickett, a black cowboy known as "the bulldogger" for chasing a steer on horseback, then jumping down and wrestling the steer to the ground without using his hands. His trick, inspired by watching dogs subdue bulls in his native Texas, was to clench the bull's lip between his teeth. Though later a star performer on the rodeo circuit, Pickett had to dress as a Mexican toreador in his early years to evade rules barring blacks from rodeos. Now called steer-wrestling, Pickett's specialty is the only one of rodeo's seven main events to have been invented by an individual.

Gradually, the big western shows headlined by Pickett and colleagues such as Will Rogers and Tom Mix died out. Today's rodeos, no longer produced by local livestock companies, have become big business, with corporate sponsorship from the tobacco, liquor, and clothing industries. Recently the sport has faced charges of animal cruelty by the Humane Society and other groups. Bulldogging a steer in the way Bill Pickett did is no longer legal.

Although black membership in the Professional Rodeo Cowboys Association (PRCA) remains low, the modern era has seen several successful African American riders. Sampson's mentor, Myrtis Dightman, reached the national finals in bull-riding several times in the late 1960s. In 1991 Texan Fred Whitfield became the first black cowboy to win the world tie-down roping (formerly known as calf-roping) title. He has since garnered five more tie-down world titles and one world all-around championship. In 2004 he was inducted into the PRCA ProRodeo Hall of Fame. Events such as the National Black Invitational Rodeo and the Bill Pickett Invitational Rodeo suggest that African American presence in the Wild West sport will continue to grow.

See also Black Cowboys; Sports and African Americans.

Bibliography

Lawrence, Elizabeth A. *Rodeo: An Anthropologist Looks at the Wild and the Tame.* University of Tennessee Press, 1982.

Johnson, Cecil. *Guts: Legendary Black Rodeo Cowboy Bill Pickett.* Summit Group, 1994.

Kate Tuttle

Rodney, Walter

1942–1980

Afro-Guyanese scholar, activist, and author.

Walter Rodney was an outspoken author, scholar, and activist who championed the rights of the working class around the world. He was born in Georgetown, Guyana, in 1942. Rodney excelled academically, displaying a strong command of history and social theory. He graduated from the University of the West Indies in Jamaica and from London University's prestigious School of Oriental and African Studies (SOAS). At the age of twenty-four he was awarded a Ph.D. in history by SOAS.

Rodney's voice was powerful and articulate as he spoke out against colonialism and worked to develop a political consciousness among the Caribbean working class. As a professor, Rodney had a profound impact on students and workers at the University of the West Indies. His immense popularity with young radicals and organized labor threatened the Jamaican government. In 1968, while he was attending a meeting of the Montreal Congress of Black Writers, he was banished from Jamaica. Among the many influential books that Rodney wrote, perhaps the best known is *How Europe Underdeveloped Africa* (1981). In it, he discussed how the colonization of Africa undermined its potential for autonomous development.

Throughout the early 1970s Rodney taught at colleges and universities in Africa, Germany, and Great Britain. In 1973 he returned to his home in Guyana and became a leading figure in Guyanese organized labor. Rodney helped to establish the Working People's Alliance (WPA) in 1973, a multiracial organization that became a vocal opposition political party in 1979. Members of the WPA pushed for economic and political reforms, and they openly criticized Prime Minister Linden Forbes Sampson Burnham.

Under Rodney's leadership, the WPA became one of the leading opposition parties in postindependence Guyana. His activities caught the attention of Prime Minister Burnham, and when Rodney was appointed chair of the history department at the University of the West Indies, Burnham blocked the appointment.

When a suspicious fire in 1979 destroyed the headquarters of the ruling People's National Congress (PNC), Burnham charged Rodney and two other opposition leaders with arson. Although Rodney was never convicted, he was followed and harassed by government officials. After returning from a trip to Africa, Rodney was killed on June 13, 1980, when a bomb ripped through his car. Much to the outrage of Rodney's family and supporters, his brother, Donald, who was injured in the blast, was implicated in the death when he was charged with the illegal possession of explosive materials.

It is widely believed that Burnham, along with members of the PNC, were participants in a plot to kill Rodney. Burnham died in office in 1985, but Rodney's family continued to call for an official investigation. Rodney's eldest son, Shaka, waged a hunger strike in 1995 to force then prime minister CHEDDI JAGAN to conduct an official investigation. Under the leadership of the Netherlands-based International Court of Justice, Guyana reopened the files on Rodney's death.

In 1996 the government brought formal criminal charges in the death of Rodney against former army sergeant Gregory Smith, also known as Cyril Johnson, who was hiding in FRENCH GUIANA. The government also posthumously awarded Rodney the country's highest distinction, the Order of Excellence.

Alonford James Robinson

Rodríguez, Arsenio

1911–1970

Afro-Cuban bandleader and *tres* player who created the medium-sized Cuban *conjunto* ensemble and who played a key role in popularizing the mambo.

Arsenio Rodríguez, also known as the *ciego maravilloso* (the marvelous blind man), was born in Matanzas Province, CUBA. He was one of Cuba's most important musical innovators. He experimented with new ensembles and musical forms, most notably the MAMBO, and in the process laid the foundations for the style known as SALSA MUSIC. His greatest contribution was successfully introducing Afro-Cuban elements into mainstream popular music.

Rodríguez was a third-generation descendant of African slaves, who were taken from the Congo region. He lost his sight at age seven after being kicked by a horse; he commenced his musical career about a year later. Initially he played an African-derived bass instrument, the conga drum, and other percussion instruments. But street *soneros*, musicians who performed the Cuban song form known as SON, introduced Rodríguez to the tres, a six- or nine-stringed instrument in the guitar family, which he quickly mastered. He began composing music while still a teenager, and in his lifetime wrote nearly 200 songs.

In 1940 Rodríguez transformed the typical *septeto* ensemble of trumpet, guitar, tres, maracas, bass, claves, and bongo, by adding a second (and sometimes a third) trumpet, piano, and, most significantly, the conga drum. Before Rodríguez formed his conjunto, a nine-to-eleven-member expansion of the traditional Cuban septeto, most Cuban popular musicians had avoided the conga drum because of its strong association with Africa. With a trumpet section and a deep-toned conga drum, Rodríguez's conjunto played rhythmically driving and eminently danceable music. The conjunto format quickly caught on; its lineal descendant is the contemporary salsa conjunto.

During the 1940s Rodríguez introduced a new son form known as the *son montuno*, which included an extended passage in which the vocalist, and instrumentalists in AFRO-LATIN JAZZ, improvised while the rest of the group played a repeating vamp figure. In formulating the son montuno, he was influenced by the flute riffs of Antonio Arcaño, leader of Arcaño y Sus Maravillas. Along with DÁMASO PÉREZ PRADO, the brothers Orestes and ISRAEL ("CACHAO") LÓPEZ, and Arcaño, Rodríguez also played a key role in originating and popularizing the mambo, which not only inspired a worldwide dance fad but also provided the underlying musical form for much Afro-Latin jazz of the 1940s and 1950s. Moreover, the conjunto format, the son montuno, and the mambo rhythm became three of the key elements in the musical style known as salsa, which rose to worldwide popularity in the 1970s.

Rodríguez visited New York City during the 1940s, where he took part in a historic 1947 recording session that brought together several leading figures in Afro-Latin jazz, including Afro-Cuban conga drummer LUCIANO (CHANO) POZO Y GONZÁLEZ, Puerto Rican vocalist Tito Rodríguez, and MACHITO's orchestra. In the early 1950s Arsenio Rodríguez left Cuba and settled in New York City, where he organized a band that included his brothers, percussionist and vocalist Raúl "Caesar" Travieso and percussionist Israel Moises "Quinque" Travieso. During the 1960s *típico* revival, a "back to the roots" movement within Latin music, Rodríguez gained new recognition as Latin musicians returned to traditional ensembles and performance styles. Yet he himself was never a musical purist or stylistic conservator.

During the 1960s Rodríguez continued to experiment with new instrumental combinations and approaches. At times he replaced one or more of the conjunto's trumpets with saxophones, and he introduced a musical fusion that he called *quindembo*, which he described as a Congolese word for a mixture of many disparate elements. Since his death, Rodríguez has continued to exert a strong influence in Latin music. His compositions, including "Hay fuego en el veinte y tres" and "Bruca manigua," continue to be mainstays in the repertoires of many salsa bands.

See also Percussion Instruments of the Caribbean.

Bibliography

Manuel, Peter, with Kenneth Bilby and Michael Largey. *Caribbean Currents: Caribbean Music from Rumba to Reggae.* Temple University Press, 1995.

Roberts, John Storm. *The Latin Tinge: The Impact of Latin American Music on the United States.* Oxford University Press, 1979.

James Sellman

Rodríguez, Evangelina

1879–1947

Afro-Dominican woman who became the first female physician in the Dominican Republic.

Though harassed throughout her life because she was a black woman working in a male-dominated profession, Evangelina Rodríguez bravely used her scientific knowledge and feminist principles to advocate for social health care as well as equality and education for poor Dominicans, especially women and children.

Ana Evangelina Rodríguez Perozo was born in 1879 as the illegitimate child of Ramón Rodríguez and Felipa Perozo, a poor, illiterate woman who worked as a servant in the homes of wealthy Dominicans. Ramón Rodríguez abandoned the family, and Evangelina's mother died when Evangelina was six years old. The young girl's maternal grandmother, Tomasina, took over the child's care and moved with her to the city of San Pedro de Macorís.

There the family met the poet Rafael Deligne (1863–1902), who was impressed with Evangelina's intelligence and urged Tomasina to send her granddaughter to school. Deligne thus became a father figure and mentor to Rodríguez. With his support she finished her primary studies at the top of her class and went on to become a schoolteacher.

After teaching for a few years Rodríguez decided that she wanted to become a doctor. In 1903 she became the first woman to be accepted to a school of medicine in the DOMINICAN REPUBLIC. Rodríguez finished her studies and dissertation while also working as the headmaster of a girls school. In 1911 she was the first woman to graduate from medical school in her country.

Rodríguez dreamed of pursuing a medical specialization in FRANCE. In 1915 she wrote a book, *Granos de polen,* with the main purpose of raising money for her graduate studies. The book, which outlines her views about health care, was so badly edited and published that it produced more losses than gains. Rodríguez persisted, however, and by 1921, with savings and donations from friends, was able to begin her studies at the Sorbonne University in Paris. In 1925 she became the first black Dominican woman to graduate as a specialist in gynecology and pediatrics from the well-known French university.

On her return to the Dominican Republic, Rodríguez defied conservative church and government policies by working in areas of health care where no other Dominican doctors dared to venture. With a feminist perspective, she actively promoted family planning and education for prostitutes and poor women in order to combat venereal disease. She also founded a health center for people suffering from leprosy and tuberculosis, opened a night school to educate illiterate peasants, founded a maternity and children's hospital, and did charity work for the poorest in her society. Many of these activities scandalized the Catholic Church and the Dominican upper class, who criticized her work. However, Rodríguez found refuge and support in two other black schoolteachers, Altagracia Domínguez and Petronila Angélica Gómez. Together the three women founded *Fémina,* a magazine advocating women's rights.

Immediately after the dictator General RAFAEL TRUJILLO took power in 1930, Rodríguez became an outspoken opponent of his authoritarian regime. Her political standing not only scared many of her paying middle-class patients away but also isolated her from the general medical community. As a result, her mental health began to deteriorate. By 1946, Rodríguez's friends and family had deserted her. Poor, abandoned, and sick, Rodríguez would walk aimlessly around the countryside. Her biographer claims that on one of these walks she was brutally hit and tortured by Trujillo's men and left to die on an abandoned road. She partially recovered from this incident, but in January 1947 she was found dying from hunger and thirst when it was too late to save her.

Although Rodríguez was a very prominent Afro-Dominican woman, her name and her struggle are not included in most Dominican history books. Today, however, two Dominican health facilities have been named in her honor: a sexual and reproductive health clinic for the poorest and most populated sectors of SANTO DOMINGO and a health center in San Rafael del Yuma. Both tributes recognize the significance of Rodríguez's contributions to Dominican medicine.

Liliana Obregón

Rogers, Elymas Payson

1815–1861

African American clergyman, poet, and missionary.

Elymas Payson Rogers was born in Madison, Connecticut, the son of Abel Rogers and Chloe Ladue, farmers. His father, the son of an African slave who had survived a shipwreck off the coast of Connecticut, was raised as family by the Reverend Jonathan Todd, from whom he eventually inherited the farmland on which he made his living. In the early 1830s, Rogers left for Hartford, Connecticut, where he attended school and worked for his board in the home of a Major Caldwell. His first formal church affiliation was established in 1833 as a communicant of the Hartford Talcott Street congregation.

In 1835 Rogers went to Peterboro, New York, to study for the ministry at a school established by the philanthropist-reformer Gerrit Smith. The following year, to pay for his studies, he began teaching at the recommendation of Smith in a public school for black children in Rochester, New York, where he continued for five years. In the spring of 1837 he enrolled at Oneida Institute in Whitesboro, New York, while continuing to teach. Jermain Wesley Loguen, one of Rogers's students, who also went on to study at Oneida, became a prominent abolitionist and AFRICAN METHODIST EPISCOPAL bishop. Rogers later wrote a poem, "Loguen's Position," which denounces the evils of slavery and affirms the legitimacy of Loguen's angry abolitionist stance.

Immediately after his graduation from Oneida in 1841, Rogers became principal of the Trenton, New Jersey, public school for black children. That year he married Harriet E. Sherman, and they settled in Trenton where Rogers pursued his career by teaching and studying theology. On 7 February 1844, he was licensed by the New Brunswick Presbytery and received full ordination to the ministry one year later. His first ministerial position was as pastor of the Witherspoon Street Church in Princeton, New Jersey, where he served for two years.

Rogers sought and obtained membership in the Newark Presbytery on 20 October 1846, when he accepted the pastorate at the Plane Street Church in NEWARK, NEW JERSEY. The next fourteen years were among the most fruitful of his career. By 1857, the church had grown from 23 to 140 communicants and 130 Sabbath scholars. It was one of only two churches described as "prosperous" in the minutes of the 1957 denominational meeting. Rogers served as moderator of the 1856 Presbyterian and Congregational Convention; the following year in PHILADELPHIA, he delivered the opening sermon of the denominational meeting in Philadelphia, which passed a resolution denouncing the DRED SCOTT decision and praising the two dissenting Supreme Court justices.

Rogers's abolitionist fervor is reflected in two published satires: "A Poem on the Fugitive Slave Law" (1855) and "The Repeal of the Missouri Compromise Considered" (1856). The former is an erudite exposition on law written in octosyllabic couplets. It argues that a higher law should take precedence over man-made rules advocated by such men as Blackstone, Witherspoon, and Cicero, when such rules violate human rights. The latter, a longer 925-line poem, also in octosyllabic couplets, is a dialogue between "Freedom" and "Slavery." In it he argues that national greed and expedience had motivated both legislation and popular opinion regarding slavery. Rogers's satires are unusual in antebellum black poetry for their erudition, wit, and courageous expression of moral indignation.

Rogers's active membership in the African Civilization Society led eventually to the fulfillment, albeit brief, of his dream to be a missionary in Africa. On November 5, 1860, he sailed from NEW YORK to FREETOWN, SIERRA LEONE. He visited MONROVIA, BASSA, Sinoe, and Cape Palmas, where he died of fever and heart disease. His early death cut short a career that he had hoped would extend both the gospel of Christ and civilized life to much of Africa.

Bibliography

Rogers's letters are held in the American Missionary Association Archives at the Amistad Research Center, New Orleans, La.

Brown, William Wells. *The Black Man, His Antecedents, His Genius, and His Achievements*. 1863.

Sherman, Joan R. *Afro-Americans of the Nineteenth Century*. 1974.

From *American National Biography*. John A. Garraty and Mark C. Carnes, eds. Oxford University Press, 1999. Reprinted by permission of the American Council of Learned Societies.

Marilyn Demarest Button

Rogers, J(oel) A(ugustus)

1883–1965

Jamaican-born African American historian and journalist.

Joel Rogers was born in JAMAICA on September 6, 1883, the son of Samuel and Emily (Johnstone) Rogers. After serving four years in the Royal Army, Royal Garrison, Heavy Artillery, Rogers came to the United States in 1906 and was naturalized in 1917. For the most part self-educated, he mastered several foreign languages, traveled extensively in Europe and Africa, and became one of the most prolific writers of his time. In 1930 he attended the coronation of Emperor HAILE SELASSIE I of Abyssinia, and after the Italian invasion of ETHIOPIA he covered the conflict from 1935 to 1936 for the *Pittsburgh Courier*. For many years he lived at 37 Morningside Avenue in the heart of HARLEM, NEW YORK, where he had a voluminous library and entertained interested and interesting guests. Most of his books were published by J. A. Rogers Publications.

Rogers contributed articles to the *Journal of Negro History*, THE CRISIS, THE MESSENGER, *Survey Graphic*, and *American Mercury*, and he was for many years writer of an illustrated feature, "Your History," for the *Pittsburgh Courier*. In 1917 his first book, *From "Superman" to Man*, was published by M. A. Donohue & Company in Chicago. Later, Rogers had difficulty in securing publication of his historical books because he lacked formal education and challenged generally accepted views about race and the identity of blacks. On the other hand, Rogers possessed a knowledge of Spanish, French, Portuguese, and German; he also did research in European and African libraries and museums.

An evaluation of Rogers's books is difficult. *From Superman to Man* was first published in 1917, and the fifth edition was published by Rogers around 1941. Concerning that book, critic W. E. B. DU BOIS, quoted on the jacket of Rogers's *Sex and Race* (3 vols., 1940–1944), wrote: "The person who wants in small compass in good English and in attractive form the arguments for the present Negro position should buy and read and recommend to his friends 'From Superman to Man.'" Another significant comment on the inside jacket of *Sex and Race* was that of the Catholic Board for Mission Work among the Colored People, New York City: "There are more objections against the colored race answered in this book more satisfactorily and convincingly than in any book we have read upon the question." A short book of some fifty pages, illustrated by Rogers, is *100 Amazing Facts about the Negro, with Complete Proof; a Short Cut to the World History of the Negro*. First published around 1934, it reached its twenty-fourth revised edition in 1963. The third and enlarged illustrated work, *The Real Facts about Ethiopia*, was published around 1936.

Sex and Race is the most comprehensive of Rogers's books. It includes much of the material in his earlier books, as well as in his *World's Great Men of Color*. In the foreword of volume one, published in 1940, Rogers wrote, "This book is dedicated to a better understanding among all the varieties of the human race." He added in chapter one, "We shall show in these pages that sex relations between so-called whites and blacks go back to prehistoric times on all the continents." All three volumes contain many photographs, footnotes, and appendices.

Whether or not one agrees with some of Rogers's conclusions about The Oldest Race or his racial identification of individuals, the reader must bear the burden to prove the contrary. To be sure, the controversy concerning the first *Homo sapiens* continues. On the basis of knowledge available from 1940 to 1944, Rogers presented conclusions difficult to deny. His documented accounts of *les amours* of well-known personalities—from ancient times through Shakespeare and Baudelaire to the early 1940s—shocked readers.

On a different level, his paragraphs about an October 1928 speech by Universal Negro Improvement Association (UNIA) founder MARCUS MOZIAH GARVEY in Paris, France, are all the more valuable because this period of Garvey's life is relatively unknown.

It was part two of volume two, "Anglo-Saxon America," that probably led some historians and other writers to label Rogers a propagandist. This section, however, is as well documented and in most instances as cautious in its conclusions as are the other sections of the three volumes. Rogers was one of the very few historians of his period who mentioned, for example, businesswoman ELLEANOR ELDRIDGE or slave SALLY HEMINGS.

In addition to his major works, some of Rogers's other books were *As Nature Leads* (1919), *The Ku Klux Spirit* (1923), *World's Greatest Men of African Descent* (1936), *World's Greatest Men and Women of African Descent* (1936), *The Real Facts about Ethiopia* (1936), *Nature Knows No Color Line* (1952), and *Africa's Gift to America* (1951).

It is perhaps not surprising that no institution of higher learning in the United States conferred an honorary degree upon Rogers. In 1930, however, Rogers was elected to membership in the Paris Society of Anthropology. In the same year he was one of the speakers at the International Congress of Anthropology, which was opened by Paul Doumer, president of France. Rogers was also a member of the American Geographical Society and the Academy of Political Science.

Probably no competent critic of Rogers gave a more accurate evaluation than did Du Bois in *The World and Africa* (1947, p. xi): "I have learned much from James [i.e., Joel] A. Rogers. Rogers is an untrained American Negro writer who has done his work under great difficulty without funds and at much personal sacrifice. But no man living has revealed as many important facts about the Negro race as has Rogers. His mistakes are many and his background narrow but he is a true historical student." Rogers, a "proud West Indian," was read more widely than either Du Bois or historian Carter G. Woodson, for many barbershops and other popular places provided his books for customers.

Rogers died at St. Clare's Hospital, New York City, on March 26, 1965, after a few days' illness following a stroke. His funeral was kept secret at his request. He was survived by his widow, Helga Bresenthal Rogers; a half brother, Jan H. Rogers; and a half sister, Constance Hall (*The Crisis*, April 1966, p. 201).

The sparse facts in *Who's Who in Colored America* (1950) are inadequate. Rogers was, for example, one of the few columnists who publicly defended Du Bois when he was indicted (1951) for "failure to register as agent for a foreign principal." A good brief study is W. Burghardt Turner's "Joel Augustus Rogers: An Afro-American Historian" (*Negro History Bulletin*, January 1972, pp. 34–38); it has a photograph and a comprehensive bibliography.

The full text of Rogers's first book, *From "Superman" to Man*, is in the Library of Black America.

From *Dictionary of American Negro Biography* by Rayford W. Logan and Michael R. Winston, editors. Copyright © 1982 by Rayford W. Logan and Michael R. Winston. Reprinted by permission of W. W. Norton & Company, Inc.

Rayford W. Logan
Lisa Clayton Robinson

Rolando, Gloria

1953–

Afro-Cuban director of documentary films.

Gloria Rolando is one of CUBA's leading producers of documentary films on Afro-Cuban culture and history. She believes these subjects hold "legends and universal values that explain the world." In a speech at the conference "Black Women Writers and the Future" in NEW YORK, NEW YORK, in October 1997, Rolando said that her motivation for creating documentary films about Cuba's African heritage was to transform "the tears held back by our ancestors" into life-affirming "tears of joy."

Rolando was born in Havana. In 1976, after completing university studies in music, literature, and art history, she took a job at the Instituto Cubano de Artes e Industrias Cinematograficas (Cuban Institute of Art and Film Industry) in HAVANA. She specialized in documentary films, and after many years as a scriptwriter, narrator, and assistant director, she directed three documentaries, all of which have English-language versions. *Oggún: The Eternal Present* (1991), the first of a projected series on Afro-Cuban traditions, portrays the YORUBA singing tradition, with special focus on LÁZARO RÓS, a well-known Afro-Cuban *akpwon* (Yoruba singer). *Oggún* also explores the SANTERÍA religion and its primary deity, Oggún, the god of metal and warfare. *My Footsteps in Baragua* (1996) studies the cultural effects of the presence in Cuba of immigrants from British Caribbean islands. *Eyes of the Rainbow* (1997) profiles ASSATA SHAKUR, the BLACK PANTHER and Black Liberation Army leader who fled the United States and settled in Cuba. Rolando plans a documentary on the life of Afro-Cuban film director SARA GÓMEZ, who participated in the Cuban revolution and died of asthma at the age of thirty-one. In the early 2000s, Rolando was interviewed for the PBS television series *Adventure Divas*, which included several episodes on Cuba and its history and culture.

Roanne Edwards

Roldán, Amadeo

1900–1939

Afro-Cuban composer, conductor, and violinist, one of the first composers to combine Afro-Cuban folk music with the stylistic traits and forms of European classical music.

During the 1920s, Amadeo Roldán, along with ALEJANDRO GARCÍA CATURLA, was CUBA's leading musical representative of AFROCUBANISMO, an artistic and literary movement that looked to Cuba's urban black culture, folklore, and music as a basis for new art and literary forms. In his compositions, Roldán employed Afro-Cuban folklore and ritual music, as well as the rhythms of Afro-Cuban dances such as the RUMBA, conga, danzón, and son afro cubano. His African-derived works also became central to Cuba's national identity, inciting the slogan, "Down with the lyre, up with the bongo," allegedly coined by the Cuban writer and ethnomusicologist ALEJO CARPENTIER.

Born in Paris, FRANCE, of Cuban parents, Roldán studied music at SPAIN's Madrid Conservatory, where he pursued a classical European education and won the Sarasate violin prize. In 1919 he settled in HAVANA, CUBA. He continued his musical studies with Pedro Sanjuán while playing violin in a local cabaret to support himself. In 1924 he became concertmaster of the Havana Philharmonic Orchestra. Promoted to the position of conductor in 1932, he transformed the orchestra into one of the most distinguished instrumental groups in Latin America and introduced a wealth of contemporary music to the Havana public.

In 1925 Roldán premiered his *Obertura sobre temas cubanos*, the first major symphonic work by a Cuban composer to employ Afro-Cuban elements and musical instruments. His most celebrated work, the ballet *La rebambaramba*, is based on a story by Alejo Carpentier and endeavors to evoke Kings' Day (January 6) celebrations in Havana. The first of its kind in Cuba, the ballet featured black cooks, calash (carriage) drivers, Spanish soldiers and processional groups—a colorful representation of popular life in Cuba during the colonial era.

During the 1930s, the work of two eminent Cubans exerted a decisive influence on Roldán: the Afro-Cuban poet NICOLÁS GUILLÉN and the Cuban ethnomusicologist FERNANDO ORTÍZ. Guillén developed a poetic language based on the SON, an Afro-Cuban musical form, which inspired Roldán to further consolidate an African-derived musical language in such compositions as *Tres toques* (1931–1932) and *Motivos de son* (1934). Through the work of Ortiz, Roldán came to appreciate the highly varied rhythmic patterns of African music. He worked with an *abakuá* drummer and had African drums made for use in performances of his works. Indeed, he scored his *Rítmicas No. 5 and 6* for percussion instruments only, including the *quijada del burro* (donkey's jawbone), a typical African instrument used in Cuba, PERU, and MEXICO.

Although Roldán met an early death in Havana in 1939, he gave formal shape to a distinctive Afro-Cuban musical style, thus profoundly influencing both art music and JAZZ in Cuba up to the present time. Moreover, he mastered prevailing European techniques, employing the most advanced harmony and orchestration. Music scholar Gerard Behague wrote that both Roldan and Carturla "raised the level of musical professionalism in Cuba and opened the way to international music circles for the following generation of Cuban composers."

See also Abakuás; Music, Classical, in Latin America and the Caribbean.

Roanne Edwards

Role of Slaves in Abolition and Emancipation in Latin America and the Caribbean

In light of the complex process of deferral, legal disregard, and noncompliance with international treaties that characterized the abolition movement, slaves' own pursuit of emancipation became decisive. In other words, slave resistance, in the context of the abolitionist phenomenon, developed into the principal means by which the abolition of slavery would be hastened, bit by bit, from the bottom up. The cases of BRAZIL, CUBA, HAITI and JAMAICA are perhaps the most representative. Violent protests and revolts, collective escapes, individual reactions, presumed submission, destruction of property, cane fields set alight: all figure among the actions slaves took to gain their freedom.

In this sense, enslaved men and women cannot be said to have been simple spectators or passive subjects who would leave the determination of their freedom in the hands of the slaveholding elite. To imagine, for instance, that the news, laws, incidents, and arguments common to an evolving abolitionist sentiment did not reach slaves' ears is not to acknowledge reality. Sooner or later, whether through public channels or through the passing whispers of group conversation, slaves would get news of the tortuous juridical/political, military, and economic course of abolition. Among the slave huts, on the plantation, in the house in the city, on the country estate, in the mines—in all these places bands of workers traded views on the HAITIAN REVOLUTION, the debates in the Assembly of Cádiz or in the British Parliament. Thus stirred by the rumors of abolitionism, there were few slaves who did not sense in these events that liberty lay close by, a fact that not only exposed slavery as an anachronistic institution but that also aggravated the tense relationship between masters and slaves.

The slave uprising on the island of Santo Domingo in 1791 is considered one of the most representative incidents in a chain of events leading to abolition and emancipation. Events such as the defeat dealt to the Spanish and English by Dominican blacks, and the triumph of the black and mulatto rebellion against the French that brought about the first black republic in Haiti, decided the course of a history that would soon lead to the abolition of slavery. Yet these events have not always been recognized or legitimized as manifestations of how slaves could gain liberty acting by and for themselves, outside the operations of metropolitan ideology or the political ideas of whites and CREOLES.

From the Haitian Revolution onward, though in earlier periods as well, slave resistance revealed itself to be the bluntest demonstration of the system of slavery's delegitimization. Massive waves of black and mulatto resistance in Haiti provoked the French National Convention, an outgrowth of the French Revolution, to declare the abolition of slavery throughout the French colonies in 1794. The political and military effectiveness of black leader TOUSSAINT LOUVERTURE played an essential role in this decision. In his negotiations with the British and the French, Toussaint reminded them that he knew how to fight just as well as the maroons in the forests of Jamaica, thereby bringing to light the networks of information that escaped slaves had maintained in certain areas of the Caribbean islands since the end of the seventeenth century.

When Napoleon rose to power in FRANCE he not only restored slavery in 1802 but launched a massive invasion in an attempt to quell the rebellion in Haiti. On the island of GUADALOUPE, a French colony, blacks and mulattos rose up against slavery's reinstatement but were defeated by an invasion of French troops. Meanwhile, in Haiti, Toussaint's mistakes and indecision when faced with the extraordinary French invasion force—some 20,000 troops in the first phase alone—prompted a change in the leadership of the Negro uprising, with JEAN-JACQUES DESSALINES, a black military officer, taking command. A regrouping of rebel forces, the knowledge of the restoration of slavery in MARTINIQUE and Guadeloupe, and the participation of the mulatto general, ALEXANDRE PÉTION, were determining factors in the defeat of an invading army of more than 60,000 men and the subsequent declaration of Haitian independence on December 31, 1803. Some twelve years later, SIMÓN BOLÍVAR, seeking political and logistical support, turned to Pétion, promising the abolition of slavery in return.

English abolitionists were alarmed by the slave revolution in Santo Domingo and Haiti and mindful of the abolition of slavery in French colonies by the National Convention of 1794, when they ruled out any action, whether in recognition or favor of the slave revolt, which might have served as a means to apply the definitive pressure needed to achieve the abolition of slavery. They preferred to maintain a passive and distant attitude toward the slaves, believing instead that the abolitionist process should adapt itself to the exclusive procedures of empire.

The slaves in the British West Indies did not, of course, share the same view. There, the tendency to react, to flee, to rebel, began to rise from the outset of the nineteenth century, especially among Creoles, born on colonial soil. Jamaica's case is perhaps the most famous. More and more slaves began to reject the harsh and inhuman work conditions on plantations and fled as often as they could, establishing communities of escaped slaves, or *palenques*, in the inhospitable forests and rural surroundings. The spirit of defiance came to a head in 1831, when the Jamaican maroons revolted en masse. Although the rebellion was put down four months later, it precipitated the British Parliament's drafting a law for the abolition of slavery in colonies throughout the British Empire.

Underlying the movements for emancipation and abolition was the matter of the social conditions and treatment of slaves. "The whip," said a powerful Jamaican slaveholder in 1834, "is the great symbol of slavery in the West Indies," adding that slaves would consider its abolition "the abolition of slavery itself." This statement indicates to what degree the repressive, inhumane treatment of slaves, and the more general social conditions of the slaves' existence, were central to the pursuit of the abolition of slavery. For the most part, slaveholders in the colonies resisted abiding by the standards issued by the metropolis, which were designed to better slaves' day-to-day existence. The BLACK CODE, or laws governing slavery, meant to be applied in Spanish colonies in 1789 as a mechanism for improving the slaves' conditions, brought such opposition from slaveholders, who saw their interests, property rights, and relations with slaves jeopardized, that application of the black code came to be viewed as dangerous. The measure never took effect.

A direct relationship existed between increased production in the colonies and the decline in slaves' social conditions. In Cuba during the first half of the nineteenth century, economic exploitation of the slave population increased, largely because of a notable increase in sugar production. This led to more frequent slave rebellions in the provinces of Havana (1809), MATANZAS (1825), and Güira (1826). In addition, there were major uprisings in many sugar refineries between 1842 and 1843. All these movements were brutally suppressed. Fear of reprisals drove many of the Matanzas slaves to suicide between 1843 and 1844. Nevertheless, such rebellion demonstrated not only the slaves' resolve but also the participation and collaboration of sectors of the free population, especially blacks, mulattos, mestizos, and some whites.

Colonial slaveholders' opposition to measures that sought a partial improvement of the conditions in slave communities corresponded to a fear of emancipatory reactions among slaves, who for their part interpreted these attitudes as owners' betrayal of regulations issued by the metropolitan powers. This standoff intensified the crisis that would ultimately delegitimize slavery as an institution and social practice. For similar reasons, slave owners historically violated the regulations referring to the slaves' evangelization. Undoubtedly, the crisis of slavery was accompanied by theological processes and juridical conversations that no longer guaranteed, nor convincingly justified, whites' and colonists' right to keep fellow human beings in the condition of slavery. With increasing frequency, slaves expressed their opinion in a number of ways, thereby openly defying the legality of slavery. As a New Grenadine (COLOMBIA) slave from Mompós put it: "There are enslaved men only in the legal codes."

Slaves' resistance to, and adaptive capacity within, the slavery dynamic rendered groundless the racist nineteenth-century images of the unproductive slave and of the slave as lacking in social and economic personality. Not only did the "unproductiveness" of slaves arise from, among other things, acts of resistance such as disobedience or destruction of economic goods, but slaves had also been able to consolidate their "own" economy as cultivators of their goods and merchants of their agricultural products in regional markets. Thus, slaves began to participate actively in various economic dynamics through sheer initiative.

In slave societies throughout the Americas, the reactions of the elite to slave revolts, to slaves' emancipatory ideas, and to the proposed abolition of slavery were expressed through the mechanisms of gradual abolition. This process strove to protect slaveholders' property rights above all, while at the same time safeguarding their investments in the buying and selling of slaves. But such an attitude was, for many owners, also due to a pathetic phenomenon, central to slavery in the Americas: whites' disdainful attitudes toward work and their economic dependence on slaves. Furthermore, the gradual emancipation of slaves itself was conceived on the basis of eminently racist assumptions, whose common basis was a belief in the slaves' inability to adapt to living free in society, given their supposed social and cultural inferiority. Gradual abolition, then, produced a group of regulations concerning rights of free birth and slave owner compensation, the creation of the Juntas de Manumisión (Manumission Committees), and the mechanisms that regulated systems of *coartización,* an arrangement by which slaves could purchase their freedom through apprenticeship and *patronato.* Each was a new form of labor control, which tied slaves in the process of emancipation to centers of economic production. In reality, what this meant for those concerned was the prolonged development of a "second horizon of slavery," that is, the setting in motion of a process of reenslavement.

It was to be expected, then, that this would constitute another point of resistance for many slaves, since they watched as the liberty they so ardently pursued was postponed in order to protect their masters' interests. In fact, beginning in the second decade of the nineteenth century in Spanish colonies, and the third decade in the French and British colonies, slaveholders made manifest that they would grant liberty to slaves only if they were compensated for doing so, and/or if it was legislated that slaves were to remain under their control as apprentices or *coartados* (slaves working to buy their freedom) during a period that could span five to twenty years. In the new Hispanic republics, particularly VENEZUELA, ECUADOR, PERU, and Colombia, regulations concerning the laws of free birth instituted both slaveholder compensation and the requirement that slaves remain in the direct service of their masters.

The slaves in the British colonies most actively rejected this system of compulsory labor; they protested measures to such a degree that by 1838, obligatory apprenticeship and patronato ceased to be enforced. A decade later, France and HOLLAND suspended the implementation of coartización, thanks mostly to slave opposition. In 1863 the Dutch colony of SURINAME encountered a similar environment of slave opposition, rendering impossible the application of controls limiting recently liberated slaves' movement between territories. In Spain and Cuba, promulgation in 1870 of the Moret Law, which regulated the gradual abolition of slavery, could not contain an insurrection of Creoles, slaves, and freedpeople that would escalate into the TEN YEARS' WAR of 1868–1878.

Brazil offers perhaps the best example of an important, widespread social movement fiercely opposed to the procedures of the gradual abolition of slavery. Portuguese America's independence in 1822 gave birth to a period of radical confrontation between slavery and the monarchy over slave revolts tied to abolitionist movements and separatist regional forces. Between 1820 and 1850, actions by the monarchic state and the plantation owners were able to neutralize, at least temporarily, the development of armed rebellions. However, during the middle of the nineteenth century, abolitionist activity again intensified in the face of war with PARAGUAY, which laid bare the state's weaknesses. As a result, slaves renewed their acts of disobedience, escape campaigns, and attacks against the agents of slavery (masters, overseers, and so on). In 1871, Brazilian abolitionism gained its first triumph, albeit partial, with the enactment of the Rio Branco Law, or Law of Free Birth. Slaveholders capitalized on its effects, spurred by a rally in coffee production and the consequent climb in the price of slaves.

In the 1880s, slaves in Brazil began to mount increasingly collective escape campaigns, often shielded in their flight by free men and women. At the same time, JOAQUIM NABUCO, RUI BARBOSA and others applied political pressure to end slavery tied to owner compensation. The province of Ceará resolved to abolish slavery, adding momentum to the abolitionist movement in the national arena. Under these circumstances, networks of political agitation linked to illegal action arose, sanctioning the flight of slaves and the burning of the cane fields. A few years before slavery would be entirely abolished, a substantial contingent of men and women prevented the military breakup of Jabaguara's *quilombo* (maroon community) in Santos. By the beginning of 1888, Brazilian slavery faced outright and irreversible collapse, which materialized on May 13, 1888, with the declaration of the abolition of slavery without the possibility of slaveholder compensation. This final resolution in the last country in the Americas to uphold the institution of slavery was made possible only through the combined action of slave revolts and abolitionist organizations.

While slaves held firmly to their decision to advance toward liberty, even risking their lives, white Western society and its offshoots in the American colonies demonstrated not only tremendous fear at the thought of liberating those whom they had enslaved, but also a growing political and social incapacity to coexist with the newly liberated men and women in a society free of slaves. Such incapacity arose from the high degree of dependence on slaves to which masters had grown accustomed. Slaveholders' political power was undoubtedly a factor that reduced the abolitionist movement's potential in the major cities.

In 1776 David Hartley was one of the first in the British House of Commons to condemn the TRANSATLANTIC SLAVE TRADE. Quakers and other abolitionists, including GRANVILLE SHARP and Thomas Clarkson, founded the Abolitionist Society in 1787, with the support of William Wilberforce, who would from then on distinguish himself as a spokesperson for English abolitionism. At the outset, abolitionists mistakenly believed it unnecessary for their campaign to consider the ideas and perceptions about abolition held by the slaves themselves. Because of this, and due to white colonists' harsh opposition to prohibition of the trade, the society decided in 1788 that it would not fight for the abolition of slavery. Abolitionists also struggled against an English monarchy and aristocracy that had strong economic ties to the slave trade, a fact that would delay its prohibition in England for some twenty years. Given these conditions, it is hardly unexpected that it would take a long and tortuous century for England to eliminate slavery. From the end of the eighteenth century and into the nineteenth, the idea advanced by English, French, and Spanish colonists—that the normal and growing supply of slaves was vital for the colonial economies and that an abrupt elimination of slavery would shatter the peaceful existence of colonial societies—remained constant. Proslavery ideas and fear gained momentum in light of the slave uprisings on the island of Santo Domingo, which made it difficult for those who advocated the declaration of the slave trade's illegality. Staring in 1804, abolitionist activity was renewed, by virtue of the notable upturn in sugar production and its consequent increase in the supply of slaves, the subsequent saturation of British sugar market, and the overproduction of sugar. Faced with these excesses, slaveholders in the British colonies became disposed to the abolition of the slave trade, at least for a time, to stem the flow of slaves to other sugar-producing areas such as Cuba and Brazil.

British colonists and slaveholders feared that their economy teetered on the brink of bankruptcy. In 1806 the rise of a new British government—a coalition of Grenville and his Foxite allies—more inclined to the abolition of the slave trade, resulted in an 1807 declaration that it would henceforth be prohibited to off-load slaves in the British colonies. In January of 1808, the U.S. Congress outlawed the importation of slaves in a motion passed in such a way that Southern slaveholders and other sectors of U.S. society with strong interests in the transatlantic slave trade would remain relatively unaware of the change.

As a result of the ban, Jamaican landowners stepped up their opposition to the final elimination of the slave trade. In fact, from 1808 on, the relations between colony and metropolis became increasingly strained as London continued to demand improvements in the situation of slave society as a whole.

After the legal suspension of the slave trade had been achieved, the British Abolitionist Society, with Wilberforce at its head, reiterated its decision not to count the abrogation of slavery among its objectives. Instead, it dedicated its efforts to the resolution of the problem of slaves smuggled aboard British ships flying other nations' flags. The illegal traffic in slaves, by no means a novel practice on the Atlantic, swelled to a grand scale through schemes, shared among English, Portuguese, Spanish, and French traffickers and colonists, which were designed to outmaneuver the new regulations. In 1811 smuggling was classified as a crime and would later be considered piracy. However, the rules against smuggling promoted the illegality of slave commerce by failing to consider fraudulent the trading of slaves among colonies. In an attempt to remedy the situation, a procedure was implemented to register periodically the number of slaves per owner and per hacienda. Once again, this became the object of systematic abuses, permitted by, if not perpetrated by, slaveholders and functionaries. In Trinidad, for instance, of the 25,000 slaves registered in 1812, about 5,000 had been registered fraudulently.

In 1817 British and American members of the industrial and financial classes who were heavily invested in sugar, coffee, and cotton interests in Cuba, Brazil, and the United States began to withdraw their support for measures against the slave trade, because they wanted to maintain the supply of slaves in their colonial economies. Thus, the North American, Brazilian, and Cuban economies emerged as the leaders of the illegal market in slaves. Moreover, the United States would remain reluctant to allow the registry of its ships by the British. Around 1830 a great number of slave ships sailed under the American flag.

Even while international legislation that restricted the commercialization of slaves may have regularly diminished the volume of trade, it was no less true that the flow of slaves into slaveholding colonies remained active, especially until the middle of the nineteenth century. Spain, for example, having decreed in 1820 the slave trade's illegality, made little effort to follow through on the agreement, since Cuba was continuously supplied with an ample number of slaves until 1860. The same situation held true in Brazil, where plantation owners continued to import slaves even though the slave trade had been declared illegal in 1831. Between 1800 and 1855, even under the sway of abolitionism, approximately 1,250,000 slaves embarked for Brazilian shores.

Ultimately, a number of consequences and effects of the antislavery movement turned out to be historically negative and damaging for the African continent, since the abolition of slavery in Latin America and the Caribbean resulted in the commencement of another period of slavery and colonial domination throughout Africa. European colonialists in Africa at the end of the nineteenth century, even imbued with an abolitionist spirit, began to doubt as never before the Africans' capacity to govern themselves. European abolitionist ideology extended its collaboration to the foundation of a new colonialist ideology brought to bear on the "Black Continent."

See also Colonial Rule; Maroonage in the Americas; Transatlantic Slave Trade Database; Slavery in Latin America and the Caribbean.

Rafael Diaz-Diaz

Rollins, Theodore ("Sonny")

1930–

African American jazz tenor saxophonist and composer.

Theodore Rollins, known as "Sonny," influenced JAZZ during the 1950s with his new approaches to musical form and style, then continued to explore new musical frontiers. Born in NEW YORK, NEW YORK, Rollins began making music at age nine, playing the piano and alto saxophone. Picking up the tenor saxophone in 1948, he led a group that included Jackie McLean, Kenny Drew, and Art Taylor. In 1949 Rollins made his first recording with pianist BUD POWELL. For the next six years, Rollins played professionally alongside Powell and other famous jazz artists such as CHARLIE PARKER, FATS NAVARRO, MAX ROACH, and ART BLAKEY. He played most frequently with MILES DAVIS. "Airegin," "Doxy," and "Oleo," songs that Rollins composed and then recorded with Davis in 1954, have become jazz standards.

Rollins joined the Max Roach–Clifford Brown quintet in 1955, working in the RHYTHM AND BLUES–influenced tradition of "hard bop." He made the landmark recording "Valse Hot" in 1956. With "Saxophone Colossus" and "Tenor Madness," recorded with JOHN COLTRANE, Rollins developed a form of jazz "thematic improvisation" form. He led his own group after 1957, fusing jazz with CALYPSO patterns in works such as "St Thomas."

By the late 1950s, Rollins was well established as a gifted and innovative saxophone player. The 1958 recording "Freedom Suite" marked the beginning of a period during which Rollins sometimes withdrew from the public, although he was sometimes seen practicing on New York's Williamsburg Bridge. Rollins returned to public life in 1961, experimenting with free jazz and later recording the score for the film *Alfie* (1966). He left the music scene again in 1968 to follow a spiritual path to India.

In 1971 Rollins once again began recording and performing, producing such works as "G-Man" (1987) and *The Solo Album* (1985). More recent releases include *Saxophone Colossus* and *Way Out West* (both in 1991) and *The Bridge* (2003). He continues to perform at clubs in New York City and elsewhere.

Bibliography

Blancq, Charles. *Sonny Rollins: The Journey of a Jazzman.* Twayne, 1983.

Marian Aguiar

Roman, Charles Victor

1864–1934

African American physician and medical educator.

Roman Charles Victor was born in Williamsport, Pennsylvania, the son of James William Roman, a former slave, and Anna Walker McGuinn, the child of a former slave. Roman's parents met in CANADA, where his father had fled about twenty years before the CIVIL WAR. After the EMANCIPATION PROCLAMATION, a year and a half before Charles's birth, they had moved back to the United States, but making a living there was difficult, and by the time Charles was six, the family returned to Ontario where his father worked as a broom maker. From an early age Charles knew he wanted to be a physician. Soon after the move to Canada, he apprenticed himself to a local herbalist, possibly his grandmother. His practice ended when one of his patients' parents became nervous about the treatment Roman had administered and called in the local doctor, who pronounced the child cured and predicted that one day the young herbalist would become a physician himself.

At the age of twelve Roman moved with his family to Dundas, Ontario, and started working in a cotton mill to supplement the family's meager income. He continued this grueling work until an accident left him lame for life. He entered the Hamilton Collegiate Institute as its first black student and supported himself by selling small items. Despite these obstacles, he took only two years to finish a course of studies that usually took four. Later in life he would describe himself as "a factory boy—the product of the night school and public library, a triumph of democracy and a justification of its creed" (Cobb, p. 301). After graduating from the Canadian school, he wanted to attend McGill University's School of Medicine, but he did not have the money to pay tuition. At the advice of one of his teachers, he headed south and started teaching school.

After five months teaching first grade in Trigg County, Kentucky, Roman decided to spend another year teaching in the South. He still planned to return to Canada one day for medical school, but he happened to board with a physician who was an alumnus of Meharry Medical College. This doctor persuaded Roman to apply to his alma mater in Nashville, Tennessee, and in 1887 Roman entered Meharry. An able and popular teacher, he continued teaching during the day to fund his night medical classes. The Nashville Board of Education required its applicants for teaching jobs to take a competitive examination, and Roman finished first among one hundred white and seventy black teachers who took the test. After apprenticing with a local physician in his third year of medical school, he decided to give up teaching and pursue a career in medicine. He set to work completing a required graduate thesis on prophylaxis, or preventive medicine.

In 1890 Roman received his medical degree from Meharry and moved to Clarksville, Tennessee, where he opened a medical practice. In 1891 he married Margaret Voorhees, a Tennessee native, with whom he later had one child. The young couple moved to Dallas in 1893, and Roman practiced there. Like many physicians of that time, after a few years in practice, Roman decided he needed additional training. In 1899 he went to CHICAGO for a year of postgraduate study, and in 1904 he traveled to England's Royal Ophthalmic Hospital and the Central London Ear, Nose, and Throat Hospital for specialty training in ophthalmology and otolaryngology.

When Roman returned from abroad he contemplated opening a private practice specializing in diseases of the eye, ear, nose, and throat, but George Hubbard, dean of Meharry Medical College, made him a more attractive offer. While in Chicago, Roman had encountered the noted African American physician DANIEL HALE WILLIAMS, who had written to his good friend Hubbard of the younger physician's great promise. When the National Medical Association, the professional society for black physicians, gathered in Nashville in 1903, Hubbard met with Roman and tried to woo him back to Meharry. The following year Roman accepted Hubbard's offer and came to Meharry as the first chair of the ophthalmology and otolaryngology department, a post he retained until 1931.

At Meharry Roman lobbied for the construction of a teaching hospital attached to the university. Meharry used Mercy Hospital as a teaching hospital, but it was becoming increasingly crowded, and the school had no control over its operation. The faculty had long planned to build a hospital to honor Hubbard while he was still alive but had been uncertain where to start construction and how to fund the project. Roman presented a definitive schedule for construction. When the doors of Hubbard Hospital opened in 1912, he was considered one of the key forces behind its rapid completion. His influence in medical circles in Nashville extended beyond Meharry. From 1904 to 1933 he served as director of health at FISK UNIVERSITY, and he started and for a while conducted medical inspections in the city's black public schools.

Throughout his career Roman played an active role in the National Medical Association, founded in 1895. He served a year as its president, but perhaps his greatest contribution was founding and for ten years editing its journal, the *Journal of the National Medical Association*. His leadership role in the national organization of black medical professionals attests directly to the respect he was accorded within this community—respect that was well earned. In 1904, the year of his presidency, the association had only 250 members; four years later Roman proposed that the group start the journal to help raise professional standards and attract more members, and by 1912 membership exceeded 500. Roman described the group in a 1908 speech: "Conceived in no spirit of racial exclusiveness, fostering no ethnic antagonisms, but born of the exigencies of the American environment, the National Medical Association has for its object binding together for mutual cooperation and helpfulness the men and women of African descent who are legally and honorably engaged in the cognate professions of medicine, surgery, pharmacy, and dentistry."

Roman did not restrict his activities to medicine; in the later years of his life he became increasingly involved with the humanities and the state of blacks in America. During WORLD WAR I, for instance, he lectured to black troops about social hygiene. Over the course of his life he wrote more than forty journal articles and two books, which cemented his intellectual reputation among both blacks and whites. After he stepped down as chair of the medical department in 1934, he became professor of medical history and ethics at Meharry.

Roman wrote a number of pamphlets and papers on health, race, and Christian ethics. In 1921 he published a book, *American Civilization and the Negro: The Afro-American in Relation to National Progress*. In this well-received work he discussed the nature of race relations in the United States and the place of blacks in American society. In the introduction he summarized his point of view, saying, "The writer of this volume believes that the differences in mankind are the differences between charcoal and diamonds—differences of condition and not of composition."

Roman, a resonant orator, did not confine his opinions to the printed page. His 1913 speech before the Southern Sociological Congress was described in one local newspaper as the "most significant utterance on the race question" of that year. A devout member of the AFRICAN METHODIST EPISCOPAL CHURCH (AME) for his entire life, he was one of the pillars of Nashville's St. Paul A. M. E. Church community. He taught an adult Sunday school class that was so popular that the pastor invited him to address the entire congregation. Roman's lay sermons, as they came to be called, were imitated in other congregations throughout the country.

Throughout his life Roman enjoyed the respect of his peers, black and white, physicians and humanists. In a world rarely sympathetic to black men, he managed without compromising his ideals to pursue the work that interested him and to help others. He was aware, however, that few black men shared his experiences. In *A History of Meharry Medical College,* published in the year of his death, he wrote, "The young professional man of my race needs to be learned in the lore of the past and wholeheartedly committed to the principles of noblesse oblige. Without these virtues, scientific knowledge will become an individual delusion and a group danger—apples of Sodom that will turn to ashes in the hour of need." Roman continued writing and speaking until his death in Nashville.

Bibliography

Cobb, William Montague. "Medical History." *Journal of the National Medical Association* 45 (1953): 301–304.

Mather, Frank Lincoln, ed. *Who's Who of the Colored Race*. 1915; repr. 1976.

Morais, Herbert M. *The History of the Negro in Medicine*. 1967.

Obituary, *Journal of the National Medical Association* 26 (1934): 174–175.

Roman, Charles Victor. *A History of Meharry Medical College*. 1934.

Summerville, James. *Educating Black Doctors: A History of Meharry Medical College*. 1983.

From *American National Biography*. John A. Garraty and Mark C. Carnes, eds. Oxford University Press, 1999. Reprinted by permission of the American Council of Learned Societies.

Shari Rudavsky

Roman Africa: An Interpretation

Discussion of the Roman presence in North Africa, including the Roman province of Africa, incorporating present-day Tunisia and eastern Algeria.

Roman Africa never constituted a large part of the enormous continent of Africa. Only in EGYPT did Roman control extend deep into the continent along the valley of the NILE RIVER; elsewhere it consisted of a narrow strip of land, sometimes only a few miles in width, between the desert and the sea. At Cyrene, in present-day LIBYA, and at New Carthage, the city erected by the Romans in present-day TUNISIA to replace the one they had destroyed, the climate permitted intensive agriculture and Roman control reached farther inland. Those places, however, were the exception.

But if Roman Africa was never an important part of Africa, it was for 500 years an important part of Rome. The history of this region of the world is vastly complex and, in some respects, still relatively unknown. This article deals with only a few isolated events and the influence of a few men, which, however, was very great and continues until the present day.

Achievements of Caesar Augustus

When Antony and CLEOPATRA lost the naval battle of Actium to the young Octavian, later known as Caesar Augustus, on September 2, 31 B.C.E., their fate was sealed. They escaped and returned to ALEXANDRIA, but it was only a question of time before Octavian would gather his forces and overwhelm them in Egypt. The end came in August of the next year when Cleopatra, recognizing their inevitable defeat, sent a false message to Antony that she had killed herself. He committed suicide. Later, she too died by her own hand. Her death ended the 300-year rule of the Greek Ptolemies over Egypt from their capital in Alexandria.

Octavian, now the unchallenged ruler of the Roman world, immediately set about creating a new kind of government that would, first, be (or seem to be) constitutional, and second, be both effective and enduring. The task was daunting, and perhaps no other man could have accomplished it.

The Roman Republic was in ruins, as everyone knew; it could not be revived. Most men had lost the dignified old Roman sense of moral and political responsibility; luxury and corruption had taken its place, together with a despairing fatalism that vitiated all hope for the future. Caesar Augustus gave them hope again. He established rules of conduct and had laws passed that set strict limits on behavior, both public and private; he returned formal control of legal affairs to the Senate, but gave it no real power; and he claimed no title for himself, not even that of consul, accepting no more than the role of first tribune (or representative) of the people. In time he gave up even that, calling himself only "first citizen," or *princeps,* with the result that the government began to be (and was for 200 years) called a principate. These actions won him great popularity among rich and poor alike; but they did not mean that he gave up any power whatsoever. As time went on, it became very evident that he personally controlled everything and made every important decision: political, economic, even cultural. His will was the will of all, and it could almost be said of him what Dante has Piccarda say of God in *The Divine Comedy*: "Nella sua voluntade è nostra pace" ("In His will is our peace").

Pax Romana

The peace established by Augustus was enjoyed by all Romans, most Italians, and many prominent citizens of the far-flung provinces of the empire—but not by all. Twice during his reign, Augustus, accompanied by great ceremony, opened the doors of the temple of Januarius, symbolizing that the nation was at peace. But on each of those occasions, without ceremony, he closed them again, and they remained closed throughout most of the next 500 years. These wars, however, were not civil strife; they were fought against peoples and tribes on the outskirts of the empire who were either rebelling against Rome or resisting being absorbed by it. Sometimes, of course, these distant conflicts, in Gaul, in Spain, in the East, and in Africa, were accompanied by terrible misery for the conquered victims. The historian Tacitus quotes a Roman officer who, aware of the suffering his men were causing, remarked: "Faciunt solitudinem et pacem appellant" ("They make a wilderness and call it peace"). But it would be merely cynical to affirm that this was always true. In no part of the empire, perhaps, was it less true than along the shore of Africa.

Egypt, in the east, was an ancient civilization that had learned how to govern itself 2,000 years before the Romans came. From Cyrene all the way to the Atlantic a narrow strip of fertile land had been inhabited by independent bands of Berbers,

The ancient theater at Leptis Magna (present-day Tripoli) in Libya, a city believed to have been founded by the Carthaginians as early as 600 B.C.E. *Fundação Pierre Verger* the aboriginal peoples of northern Africa. Over many centuries they had learned to live in diverse ways, as nomads, as hunters and gatherers, as agriculturists. But they had not learned to live with one another without the threat, and the practice, of almost constant warfare. The land was rich, or could be with irrigation; the people were energetic and could be hard working; their immemorial contacts with that other Africa south of the desert offered untold possibilities of trade and gain. For a while, two centuries before, the Carthaginians had kept the Berbers' aggression in check, but without any real attempt to create a political society based on law. This, of course, was what the Romans knew how to do better than anybody. It was natural, therefore, that they brought law, and with law peace, and with peace prosperity to the MAGHREB (stretching from present-day Libya to MOROCCO) during the five centuries from about 100 B.C.E. to about 400 C.E.

The Romans also founded cities, which had been rarities in Africa before their coming. There had been Carthage and a few Phoenician and Greek settlements, but the Romans had obliterated Carthage and paid little attention to the other possibilities of Africa. Now, under the Pax Romana, they paid much attention. A military career, with its promise of steady income and advancement, was a potent attraction for young Berbers. In the area south of Cyrene there was ample water for irrigation, which Roman engineers exploited, thereby helping to found a thriving agriculture; within a few decades Cyrenaica (in present-day eastern Libya) was the main source of grain for southern Italy, including the city of Rome itself. Alexandria, of course, was a world-renowned center of scholarship and literature; but it did not command a monopoly of art and learning, which spread slowly westward along the Mediterranean coastline as new cities were established, as trade and therefore wealth increased, and as perpetual peace came to be an expectation instead of an impossible dream.

Septimius Severus

Two cities of the ancient African coast deserve mention, if only because of their most famous citizens. One of these was Septimius Severus. After the assassination of Emperor Commodus in 192 C.E., a furious power struggle ensued, with the proclamation of four different emperors in the space of a few months. Each was a general with an army faithful to him, and none had any political experience. As much by luck as by skill, Septimius Severus emerged victorious and ruled for eighteen years.

His reign coincides with the effective end of the empire as a constitutional monarchy and its beginning as a military dictatorship, which lasted until it was destroyed by the barbarians in the fifth century. This was probably not Septimius's fault. It had been a long time since Romans had had any sense whatever of ruling themselves according to law; they had been cared for by an absolute executive bureaucracy that had left no opening for political entrepreneurism or innovation. Perhaps, too, by the time Septimius became emperor there was no longer any other way to rule the enormous, sprawling, and unruly world that was Rome. Romans had shown themselves to be brilliant innovators in law, government, and politics, but they were not up to the challenge of creating a polity like the British Empire, for instance, which endured as a workable constitutional monarchy for centuries. In any event, Septimius inaugurated a rigid, despotic tyranny that was markedly different from what had gone before.

Septimius was also the first emperor to have been born in Africa. His birth occurred in Leptis Magna, the site of which is near present-day TRIPOLI in Libya. Founded by the Carthaginians as early as 600 B.C.E., it was a major center for trade with the African interior. It later became the capital of Numidia, after that the seat of government of a Roman province. Already prosperous when Septimius was born there in 146 C.E., Leptis Magna enjoyed a major resurgence as he constructed a series of magnificent buildings to honor his birthplace. Today, their ruins are among the outstanding Roman monuments remaining in the Mediterranean world.

Augustine

Edward Gibbon, in the notorious closing chapters of his great work, *The Decline and Fall of the Roman Empire* (first published in the pregnant year 1776), was so unguarded as to conclude that there were two causes of the decline, not just one: barbarism and religion. The association of the two terms produced much distress in his time, but there is no denying that there is at least some truth in his thesis.

Jesus of Nazareth was born about 6 B.C.E., that is, during the later years of the reign of Augustus. His disciples and followers soon began to create commotions, first in Palestine, then in Rome. The emperors, for both state and private reasons, were resolute pagans. Paganism, after all, was the official religion and many persons had an interest in keeping it that way. In addition, most of the emperors, including Augustus, were worshiped as gods of the Roman pantheon. As a consequence, for 300 years after Christ's birth Christians experienced either persecution or contempt. But they also endured numerous episodes of internal strife based on differences of belief, many of which occasioned charges of heresy.

Africa, perhaps because of its distance from Rome, fostered a number of Christian cults as well as a striking intensity of religious beliefs. Alexandria, in particular, saw several great heresies rise and fall. Arius, for example, the founder (or instigator) of Arianism, which flourished in the fourth century, was an Alexandrian. The Donatist heresy originated in Carthage, also in the fourth century. And Egyptian Christians, who continued to speak Coptic, the final form of the ancient Egyptian language, formed their own church, which today is one of the Eastern or Orthodox Churches. Even if Africa saw the rise of heresy and schism, however, it was also the source of fanatic Christian piety and asceticism in such persons as (for just one example) St. Anthony of Egypt, the founder of Western monasticism, whose temptations by the Devil, in numerous disguises, are the subject of innumerable works of art.

Hippo Regius, another important city of the ancient African littoral that was probably founded by Carthaginians around 400

B.C.E., later became the capital of the Numidian monarchy, and was absorbed by Rome after the defeat of Carthage. Today it is the city of Annaba in ALGERIA. By the time its most famous citizen was born it was officially a Roman *colonia,* which meant that its inhabitants were Roman citizens.

Aurelius Augustinus, whom we know as Augustine, was born at Tagaste, near Hippo, on November 13, 354 C.E., to middle-class parents who soon recognized the intellectual promise of their son and devoted all their resources to his education. At nineteen he was sent to Carthage, where he worked for ten years as a freelance tutor. While there he read Cicero, who introduced him to the seductions of philosophy, and he later became a disciple of the Manichaeans, a religious sect popular in the western empire. His Manichaean teachers proving unable to answer his hard questions, he went to Rome in search of better pupils as well as better teachers. He found neither, but he did discover the works of Plotinus, the Greek pagan Neoplatonist philosopher who opened his mind, he thought, to the belief he was seeking.

Augustine's mother, Monica (now St. Monica in large part because she *was* his mother), was a devout Christian. Her husband was a pagan, and this distressed her; but a greater torture was the fact that her brilliant son, if not a pagan, was not a Christian either. She followed him to Rome and then to Milan, where he had gone to meet the famous Ambrose, bishop of that city. Augustine went to hear Ambrose preach, but, although moved, was not convinced. Monica also visited St. Ambrose and fell to her knees, pleading for him to help convert her son. Gently he raised her, blessed her, and promised: "The son of these tears shall not perish."

As a young man Augustine had formed a relationship with a woman, said to have been "of low birth," who bore him a son whom he called Adeonatus. (There is apparently no record of her name.) The sexual tie between the man and woman was strong, and as time went on he grew to feel that this more than anything stood between him and his elevation to a higher plane of moral and religious existence. He found it hard to break the tie and prayed, as he tells us in his *Confessions,* "Give me chastity, but not yet." The unforgettable honesty of his plea was rewarded in the late summer of 386 C.E., when, sitting in a garden in Milan, he heard some children crying out "tolle lege, tolle lege" ("Take up and read"). He thought at first that they were playing a game, but he could remember no game with those words; then he looked down at the Bible in his lap and opened it at random to these words from Paul's Epistle to the Romans: "Put on the Lord Jesus Christ, and make no provision for the flesh, to gratify its desires" (Rom. 13:14). From that moment he was a Christian.

Augustine was baptized by Ambrose in the spring of 387 C.E., whereupon he determined to return with his mother to Africa. At Ostia, near Rome, his mother fell ill, and he sat with her as she expressed her joy at his newfound freedom. He helped her as they went to the window, where both he and she had a mystical experience that is described in moving terms in the *Confessions.* She died shortly after, and he returned to Hippo alone. Becoming a priest, he was shortly afterward called to serve as bishop of the place. He died there on August 28, 430 C.E.; as he lay near death he heard a clamor of cries and weeping. Asking what had occurred, he was informed that the barbarians were at the gate.

For forty-three years he had served the people of Hippo as pastor, teacher, and judge; but he had served a wider pastorate as well. By the time of his death he was the best known Christian philosopher and theologian in the world, recognized not only for his writings, including especially *The City of God,* but also for his unremitting struggle against heresies that still afflicted the Catholic Church, despite its adoption as the official state religion by the emperor Constantine a century before. One of his last works was the so-called *Rule of St. Augustine,* a prescription for a Christian life that was adopted by several monastic orders and is still followed today. His influence on the culture and self-image of the West is not now as great as it once was, but for at least 1,000 years after his death he perhaps better than any other man defined the Western conception of the history and the destiny of mankind.

End of Roman Africa

The barbarians at Hippo's gate were Vandals, a name that comes down to us as a synonym for willful destructiveness. They were a Germanic tribe that, fleeing the Huns, ranged westward into SPAIN and then eastward again along the African coast of the Mediterranean. Subduing Hippo and the region around it by 435 C.E., they remained the lords of the region for a century, until they were subdued in turn by the Byzantine general Belisarius, after which they disappear from history.

The Vandals may have been vandals, but they were also Romans and Christians to boot. The problem was, they were Arians and believed that Jesus, the Son of God, was only *like* God and was not *of one substance* with God. This distinction was of great importance in the fifth century. The belief survives even today, however, for example among the Jehovah's Witnesses, who assert that Arius was an ancestor of their founder, Charles Taze Russell.

All such distinctions became moot, at least in Africa, within a century or two after the defeat of the Vandals, when the irresistible force of Islam poured out of Arabia first into Persia and Syria, then into Egypt, and then westward across the Maghreb and then into Spain. By 700 C.E. or a few years afterward, Muslims controlled all of North Africa; and the Roman Empire, which by that time had retreated to Byzantium, ceased to exist upon the continent.

See also Berber; Islam in Africa.

Charles Van Doren

Ronga

Ethnic group of Mozambique; also known as Baronga, Rhonga, and Rsonga.

The Ronga primarily inhabit southern MOZAMBIQUE in and around MAPUTO. They speak a Bantu language and are closely related to the TONGA people. Approximately 500,000 people consider themselves Ronga.

See also Bantu: Dispersion and Settlement.

Roots

See Haley, Alexander.

Roper, Dee Dee "Spinderella"

See Salt-N-Pepa.

Ros, Lázaro

1925–

World-famous Cuban *akpuon*, or singer of Lucumí religious folk music, and cofounder of the Conjunto Folklórico Nacional.

Lázaro Ros was born to a poor family in HAVANA in 1925. Even as a child, he was known to have a beautiful voice and he learned ancient songs of the YORUBA from Eugenio de la Rosa, a master singer.

In 1950 Ros was initiated into the Regla de Osha (Rule of Osha)—the system of beliefs and rituals practiced by the Lucumí (Yoruba for "friends"), the descendants of the Nigerian Yoruba people in CUBA, for the worship of ORISHAS, or deities. The Lucumí religion is also known as SANTERÍA, or cult of the saints, because to preserve their religious practices Cuban slaves were forced to meld their orishas with the identities of Roman Catholic saints, whom they ostensibly worshiped for the benefit of white slave owners. Lázaro Ros' particular orisha is Oggun, the warrior spirit who represents, among other things, metal and civilization. In the early 1960s Ros cofounded the Conjunto Folklórico Nacional (National Folkoric Ensemble of Cuba), with which he still performs the rhythmically complex call-and-response devotional Lucumí music.

In 1963 Ros shared a San Francisco stage with Carlos Santana. He has subsequently collaborated with the National Ballet of Cuba and has worked with the contemporary Cuban bands Síntesis and Mezcla, as well as with composer and saxophonist Lucia Hergo. Ros has performed internationally and released several recordings, among them *Olorún* (1994), *Asoyi Cantos Arará* (1995), and *Songs for Eleguá* (2000). He has also composed music for theater and film, including the award-winning *María Antonia*.

Ros and his orisha, Oggun, are the subjects of a documentary, *Oggun: The Eternal Presence,* by film director Gloria Rolando.

Shelle Sumners

Rose, Edward

?–1833?

Mountain man and Indian interpreter.

Edward Rose may have been born in Kentucky, near Louisville, most likely of African, Indian, and white ancestry. The date of his birth remains unknown, as do the names and occupations of his parents. It is possible that Rose was born a slave. The details of Rose's life have been gleaned from the narratives and records of others, including Washington Irving, who claimed that after leaving home as a teenager, Rose became a kind of roving bandit, "one of the gangs of pirates who infested the islands of the Mississippi, plundering boats as they went up and down the river . . . waylaying travelers as they returned by land from New Orleans . . . plundering them of their money and effects, and often perpetuating the most atrocious murders." It appears that Rose left New Orleans after the police broke up his gang, eventually settling in St. Louis, where, in the spring of 1806, the local newspaper described him as big, strong, and hot-tempered, with a swarthy, fierce-looking face.

That same year Rose traveled up the Osage River with a group of hunters, after which he must have returned to St. Louis, because in the spring of 1807 he left from there with Manuel Lisa's fur-trading expedition up the Missouri River, the first major expedition organized after Lewis and Clark's return to St. Louis. Led by Lisa, a St. Louis businessman, the party traveled north, up the Missouri River through present-day North and South Dakota, and then southwest, along the Yellowstone River to the mouth of the Big Horn River, where they established the first trading post on the upper river, Fort Manuel (also called Fort Lisa), in what became Montana. After trading jewelry, tobacco, liquor, weapons, and blankets for pelts with the local Crow Indians (Absaroke or Sparrowhawk people), Lisa and his men returned to St. Louis. Rose, however, chose to remain behind. Living with the Crow in what is now southern Montana and northern Wyoming, Rose learned their culture and language. Because of his appearance, Rose was known as Nez Coupe ("Scarred Nose") and later, after a particularly fierce battle, as Five Scalps.

It has been suggested that during this time Rose partnered with the French frontiersman and husband of Sacagawea, Toussaint Charbonneau, in escorting Arapaho women captured by Snake Indians to European trappers willing to pay for Indian women. In any event, in spring 1809 Rose joined an expedition organized for the purpose of escorting Sheheke (also known, by whites, as Big White), the principal chief of Matootonha, a lower Mandan village, through hostile territory back to his tribe. In 1806 Sheheke, along with his wife and children, had accompanied Lewis and Clark to St. Louis and Washington, D.C., via Monticello, where they met Thomas Jefferson. The first attempt to return Sheheke in 1807, led by Nathaniel Pryor, had failed because of resistance from the Sioux and Arikara. Two years later, with a contract for seven thousand dollars paid to the Missouri Fur Company by the U.S. government, twenty men, including Rose, spent three months traveling with the chief and his family northwest, up the Missouri River to Matootonch, in present-day North Dakota. On the way back to St. Louis, Rose elected to rejoin the Crow.

In 1811 Rose was hired by the "Astorians"—John Jacob Astor's Pacific Fur Company—as a guide for the first expedition to the Pacific Ocean since Lewis and Clark had returned six years earlier. Led by Wilson Price Hunt, a merchant from New Jersey with no experience as a hunter or trapper, the party included sixty-four men and eighty-four horses. Rose joined the party on the plains near the Arikara villages just north of the present-day border between North and South Dakota and guided the expedition through Crow territory. Suspicious of his loyalty to the Crow, Hunt never trusted Rose. Predisposed to believe reports that Rose was organizing a mutiny, Hunt fired him as soon as the party reached the Black Hills of South Dakota, an error in judgment that contributed to many of the expedition's failures. Immediately after dispatching Rose, in an indication of what lay ahead, Hunt and his group became lost as they tried to pass through mountains. A few days later Rose returned with several Crow and helped the party find a pass.

Washington Irving's description of Rose in his 1836 book *Astoria; or, Anecdotes of an Enterprise beyond the Rocky Mountains* must have been typical of attitudes toward Rose, whom he describes as "one of those anomalous beings found on the frontier, who seem to have neither kin nor country . . . and was, withal, a dogged, sullen, silent fellow, with a sinister aspect, and more of the savage than the civilized man in his appearance." Irving continues "This fellow it appears was one of those desperadoes of the frontiers, outlawed by their crimes, who combine the vices of civilized and savage life, and are ten times more barbarous than the Indians with whom they consort."

A year later, in 1812, Manuel Lisa found Rose living with the Arikaras and hired him as a scout. Rose, however, never made it to their meeting place in New Orleans, having attached himself to an Omaha Indian woman, with whom he remained in her tribe until he was arrested for drinking and fighting and taken to St. Louis. Records show that Rose was released in 1813 by the Superintendent of Indian Affairs William Clark, in exchange for Rose's promise to stay out of Indian territory.

Historians are unsure of Rose's activities in the following decade, until March 10, 1823, when he left St. Louis with one hundred men on the ill-fated trapping expedition of William Henry Ashley and Andrew Henry, owners of the Rocky Mountain Fur Company. From the outset Ashley dismissed Rose's counsel against bartering for horses with the Arikara and against mooring company boats on the same side of the river as the tribe. More disastrously, Ashley ignored Rose's warning of an impeding Arikara attack, and when the ambush came, the company's losses were heavy. Attacks on the traders continued until Colonel Henry Leavenworth arrived from Fort Atkinson with two hundred fur traders, frontiersmen, and Lakota and Tankton warriors organized into a frontier militia, the Missouri Legion. Rose was made an ensign, and the militia attacked the Arikara villages in August 1823. In his official report submitted to General Henry Atkinson and dated October 20, 1823, Leavenworth singled out Rose: "I had not found anyone willing to go into those villages, except a man by the name of Rose . . . He appeared to be a brave and enterprising man, and was well acquainted with those Indians . . . He was with General Ashley when he was attacked. The Indians at that time called to him to take care of himself, before they fired upon General Ashley's party."

Trying to salvage the expedition, Ashley assembled a small party of men, described by Harrison Clifford Dale in the *Ashley-Smith Explorations* (1941) as "the most significant group of continental explorers ever brought together." This group included Rose and other such noted frontiersmen as James Clyman, David Jackson, William Sublette, Jim Bridger, Hugh Glass, and Thomas Fitzpatrick. Led by Jedediah Smith, the party traveled up the Grand River and through the Black Hills to the Rockies. From Clyman's diary we learn that Rose's familiarity with the Indian language and customs saved the party from disaster.

Rose served with Smith for the next two years, leaving in May 1825 to join a large treaty-making expedition up the Missouri under the command of General Atkinson and Major Benjamin O'Fallon. Forty men on horseback, under the command of a Lieutenant Armstrong, went with Rose by land; the rest traveled up the river in nine boats. The Yellowstone expedition, as it came to be known, succeeded in signing peace treaties with all the tribes of the river except the Blackfoot. Reports of the expedition by several authors delight in recounting Rose's mythmaking adventures. A clerk whose expedition journal was published in 1929 in the *North Dakota Historical Society Quarterly* documented one oft-repeated tale of Rose's heroics and skill: "Thursday 30 June. Rose, an interpreter, one of the party, we understand, covered himself with bushes and crawled into the gang of 11 Bulls [buffalo] and shot down 6 on the same ground before the others ran off."

Much of the information we know about Rose comes from a biographical sketch of him that Captain Ruben Holmes, a member of the Atkinson-O'Fallon expedition, published in the *St. Louis Beacon* in 1828 (reprinted in the *St. Louis Reveille* in 1848). In "The Five Scalps" (1848), Holmes describes Rose's confrontation with a band of six hundred hostile Crow warriors: "One foot was on the pile of muskets, to prevent the Indians from taking any from it . . . his eye gleamed with triumphant satisfaction. There was an expression about his mouth, slightly curved and compressed, and a little smiling at the curves, indicative of a delirium of delight—his eye, his mouth, the position of his head, and scars on his forehead and nose all united in forming a general expression, that, of itself, seemed to paralyze the nerves of every Indian before him."

Rose apparently rejoined the Crow after the 1825 expedition, and nine years later he rode alongside them in their battles with the Blackfoot. "The old Negro," Zenas Leonard wrote in his autobiography, *Adventures of Zenas Leonard, Fur Trader* (1839), "told them that if the red man was afraid to go among his enemy, he would show them that a black man was not." Rose was one of first black frontiersmen to earn a wide reputation, preceding JIM BECKWOURTH, who was born around 1800, by a generation. Indeed, Beckwourth, who, in his autobiography, *The Life and Times of James P. Beckwourth* (1856), called Rose "one of the best interpreters ever known in the whole Indian country," may have claimed some of the older man's exploits for himself.

When and how Rose—whom Harold Felton describes as "a mountain man's mountain man, a trail blazer's trail blazer"—died remains unknown. Legend has it that Rose, Hugh Glass, and a third mountain man named Menard were killed and scalped on the frozen Yellowstone River in the winter of 1832–1833 by a band of Arikaras hostile to the Crow. A site called Rose's Grave is located at the junction of the Milt and Missouri rivers, on the Milk River near the Yellowstone River.

Bibliography

Burton, Art T. *Black, Buckskin, and Blue: African American Scouts and Soldiers on the Western Frontier* (1999).

Felton, Harold W. *Edward Rose: Negro Trail Blazer* (1967).

Irving, Washington. *Astoria; or, Anecdotes of an Enterprise beyond the Rocky Mountains* (1836).

Lisa Rivo

Roseau, Dominica

Formerly Charlotte Town, capital of the island nation of Dominica, in the West Indies.

Roseau, in southwestern Dominica, is situated at the mouth of the Roseau River. The town is a port that serves as Dominica's main commercial and transportation center. Tourism is also important to the community's economy. A Roman Catholic cathedral built in the eighteenth century and botanical gardens grace the city, and the twin waterfalls at Trafalgar, a popular tourist attraction, are nearby. Population is 16,000 (2003 estimate).

Rosewood Case

One of the worst race riots in American history, in which hundreds of angry whites killed an undetermined number of blacks and burnt down their Florida community.

In 1922 Rosewood, Florida, was a small, predominantly black town. During the winter of 1922, two events in the vicinity of Rosewood aggravated local race relations: the murder of a white schoolteacher in nearby Perry, which led to the murder of three blacks, and a KU KLUX KLAN rally in Gainesville on New Year's Eve.

On New Year's Day of 1923, Fannie Taylor, a young white woman living in Sumner, claimed that a black man sexually assaulted her in her home. A small group of whites began searching for a recently escaped black convict named Jesse Hunter, whom they believed to be responsible. They arrested one suspected accomplice, Aaron Carrier, and lynched another, Sam Carter. The men then targeted Aaron's cousin Sylvester Carrier, a fur trapper and private music instructor, who was rumored to be harboring Jesse Hunter.

A group of twenty to thirty white men went to Sylvester Carrier's house to confront him. They shot his dog, and when his mother stepped outside to talk with the men, they shot her. Sylvester killed two men and wounded four in the shoot-out that ensued. After the men left, the women and children, who had gathered in Carrier's house for protection, fled to the swamp where the majority of Rosewood's residents had already sought refuge.

The white men returned to Carrier's house the following evening. After a brief exchange of gunfire, they entered the house, found the bodies of Sarah Carrier and a black man whom they believed to be Sylvester Carrier, and set the residence on fire. The men then proceeded to rampage through Rosewood, torching other buildings and slaughtering animals. They were joined by a mob of about 200 whites who converged on Rosewood after finding out that a black man had killed two whites.

That night two local white train conductors, John and William Bryce, who knew all of Rosewood's residents, picked up the black women and children and took them to Gainesville. John Wright, a white general store owner who hid a number of black women and children in his home during the riot, planned and helped carry out this evacuation effort. The African Americans who escaped by foot headed for Gainesville or for other cities in the Northern United States.

By the end of the weekend all of Rosewood had been leveled, with the exception of the Wright house and the general store. Although the state of Florida claimed that only eight people had died in the Rosewood riot—two whites and six blacks—testimonies by survivors suggest that more African Americans had perished. No one was charged with the Rosewood murders. After the riot, the town was deserted and even blacks living in surrounding communities had moved out of the area.

It is unclear what became of Jesse Hunter. Residents of nearby Cedar Key claimed that he was captured and killed after the massacre. The descendants of the Carrier family contend that Jesse Hunter was not the man who had attacked Taylor. Philomena Carrier, who had been working with her grandmother Sarah Carrier at Fannie Taylor's house at the time of the alleged sexual assault, claimed that the man responsible was a white railroad engineer. She says that the man had come to see Taylor the morning of January 1 after her husband left for work. After an argument erupted between Taylor and the man, Philomena witnessed the man exit the back door and jog down the road toward Rosewood.

The Carriers' descendants maintain that the man was a Mason and that he persuaded Aaron Carrier, a member of Rosewood's black Masonic lodge, to help him escape by appealing to the society's code requiring members to help one another regardless of race. Carrier in turn persuaded another black Mason, Sam Carter—one of the few men in Rosewood with a wagon—to pick up the white man at Carrier's house and drop him off in the swamp. From there the man disappeared without a trace.

Although the Rosewood riot received national coverage in the *New York Times* and the *Washington Post* as it unfolded, historians generally ignored it and few survivors came forward to tell their story, perhaps for fear of recriminations. In 1993 the Florida Department of Law Enforcement conducted an investigation into the case, which eventually led to the drafting of a bill to compensate the survivors of the massacre.

After an extended debate and several hearings, the Rosewood Bill, which awarded $150,000 to each of the riot's nine eligible black survivors, was passed in April 1994. Despite the state's financial compensation, the survivors remained frightened.

Film director John Singleton, best known for the motion picture *Boyz N the Hood* (1991), released a fictionalized account of the massacre called *Rosewood* in 1997. The film is based on the testimony of survivors of the events in Rosewood.

Bibliography

D'Orso, Michael. *Like Judgement Day: The Ruin and Redemption of a Town Called Rosewood.* G. P. Putnam's Sons, 1996.

Aaron Myers

Ross, Diana

1944–

African American singer and actress.

Diana Ross became famous as the lead singer of the popular MOTOWN music group the SUPREMES. Her songs topped the *Billboard* magazine charts throughout the 1960s, 1970s, and 1980s. She was born Diane Ross in DETROIT, MICHIGAN, the second of six children born to Fred and Ernestine Ross. Ross, who grew up in a poor section of the city, sang with her siblings and parents in the choir at the Olivet Baptist Church and collaborated with neighborhood friends on renditions of the most popular songs of the day. Ross showcased her talent by performing on street corners, in school talent shows, and at dances. In 1959, while still in high school, she joined Mary Wilson, Florence Ballard, and Betty McGlown in a vocal group called the Primettes, the sister group for a group of male singers that later became the TEMPTATIONS. In 1961, after McGlown and her replacement Barbara Martin had left the group, the Primettes signed a recording contract with Motown Record Company as a trio and changed their name to the Supremes.

The Supremes did not have immediate recognition and success. Initially, they sang as backup vocalists or served as hand clappers for other Motown acts, including Mary Wells, MARVIN GAYE, and the Shirelles. In 1964, after three years as a group, the Supremes had their first hit single with "Where Did Our Love Go," their ninth release. A string of hit recordings followed—"Baby Love" (1964), "Come See about Me" (1964), "Stop! In the Name of Love" (1965), and "Back in My Arms Again" (1965). In 1967 Cindy Birdsong replaced Florence Ballard, and the group changed its name to Diana Ross and the Supremes. Shortly after the group's last hit—"Someday We'll Be Together" (1969)—Ross left the Supremes to pursue a solo career in singing and acting. A series of female singers replaced Ross as lead vocalist of the Supremes before the group broke up in 1977.

Ross launched her career as a soloist with the hit single "Ain't No Mountain High Enough" (1970). She then turned her attention to motion pictures. She earned an Academy Award nomination for her 1972 portrayal of JAZZ singer BILLIE HOLLIDAY in *Lady Sings the Blues*, in which she costarred with actor BILLY DEE WILLIAMS. Ross starred in *Mahogany* (1975), singing the hit theme song "Do You Know Where You're Going To?" In 1978 she starred in *The Wiz*. After recording two disco sensations, "Love Hangover" (1976) and "Upside Down" (1980), Ross collaborated with singer Lionel Richie on the ballad "Endless Love" (1981). Ross left Motown Records in 1981 but returned in 1989 to work as a recording artist, an equity partner, and a director of the company.

The Supremes were inducted into the Rock and Roll Hall of Fame in 1988, confirming their status as one of the most famous black performing groups and the most famous female recording group in American music history. As the lead vocalist for the Supremes, Ross had twelve hit singles and sold more than fifty million records. Between 1970 and 1984 she recorded thirty-one albums and more than fifty singles, six of which reached the top spot on the *Billboard* chart. Ross is considered one of the most influential and versatile recording artists of the twentieth century. Collections of her songs, both with the Supremes and as a solo artist, were released on the Motown albums *Diana Ross and the Supremes: The Ultimate Collection* (1997) and *Diana* (2003).

Aaron Myers

Ross-Barnett, Marguerite

1942–1992

American educator who wrote about negative black imagery.

Marguerite Ross-Barnett graduated from Antioch College and earned a doctorate in political science from the University of Chicago. She focused her early work on Indian and African American studies. She taught at Princeton University, HOWARD UNIVERSITY, and Columbia University before being appointed vice chancellor for academic affairs at City University of New York (CUNY) in 1983.

In 1985 Ross-Barnett published *Images of Blacks in Popular Culture: 1865–1955*, a controversial study of negative black stereotypes, based in part on her own collection. A year later she was appointed chancellor of the University of Missouri at St. Louis. She became president of the University of Houston in 1990, where she served until her death of cancer two years later at the age of fifty.

See also Racial Stereotypes.

Marian Aguiar

Rouche, Jean

1917–

French ethnographer and filmmaker.

As a pioneer of ethnographic filmmaking, which documents the lives, customs, and cultures of ethnic groups, Jean Rouche developed styles and techniques that influenced a generation of African moviemakers. Rouche's mother was a painter and his father was a naval explorer. Born in Paris, Rouche trained to be an engineer. He graduated from a prestigious Parisian engineering college in 1941 and immediately left Nazi-occupied FRANCE for the freer West African colony of NIGER.

Rouche was hired to oversee the construction of a road, but lack of equipment halted the project. The engineer, however, had taken an interest in aspects of SONGHAI culture, including spirit possession ceremonies conducted by African workers he had befriended. Fascinated by the rites and curious to learn more, Rouche returned to France, where he enrolled in a doctoral program in anthropology and studied with the famous ethnographer Marcel Griaule. Taking a break from his studies in 1946, he returned to Niger and spent a year exploring the NIGER RIVER. Rouche took a camera on this voyage, and when a group of MANDINKA hunters on Lake Debo encouraged him to film their HIPPOPOTAMUS hunt, his life in cinematography began.

Over the next fifty years, Rouche made more than seventy films and wrote almost twenty books about West Africa and the Songhai. Some scholars still regard him as the foremost authority on the Songhai ethnic group. His early work focused primarily on Songhai rites and rituals and resulted in several well-known films such as *Les Magiciens de Wanzerbé, Les Maîtres fous, Jaguar,* and *Les Tambours d'avant*. In producing these films, Rouche worked in the style called cinéma vérité, a type of documentary filmmaking that stresses "unbiased" realism. He also initiated what he called participatory anthropology, showing the Songhai the films he had made about them in order to have their critical comments and advice. During the 1960s Rouche decided to concentrate solely on ethnographic film, expanding his work to encompass his experiences in West Africa.

During his many travels and film tours, Rouche continually sought out promising young filmmakers. Some of those he hired to work on his projects, such as MOUSTAPHA ALASSANE and SAFI FAYE, eventually became well known for their own work. Rouche's ability to work with minimal equipment and a small film crew earned him the reputation of a versatile and efficient filmmaker. In 1975 the newly independent country of MOZAMBIQUE asked for Rouche's help in building a state film industry, although the country later rejected his efforts.

Although Rouche's filmmaking slowed after the early 1980s, he continued to teach seminars at Paris's anthropological museum, the Musée de l'Homme. His achievements were celebrated in a retrospective of his work in NIAMEY (1986–1987) entitled *Jean Rouche: Seventy Years/Seventy Films*. Despite his popularity, in recent years he has also been the subject of controversy. Some people, like filmmaker OUSMANE SEMBÈNE of SENEGAL, consider Rouche's work a mere continuation of the colonial legacy in African film, viewing cultures as exotic commodities. Others, however, argue that Rouche's films and techniques, regardless of their subject, inspired a generation of African filmmakers, whose work might have otherwise been lost.

See also Cinema, African.

Elizabeth Heath

Roudanez, Louis Charles

1823–1890

African American physician, newspaper proprietor, and Republican Party activist.

Louis Charles Roudanez was born in St. James Parish, Louisiana, the son of Louis Roudanez, a wealthy French merchant, and Aimée Potens, a free woman of color. Roudanez was raised in NEW ORLEANS as a member of the city's free black elite, but in 1844 he left to pursue a professional education in France. In 1853 the faculty of medicine at the University of Paris awarded him a degree in medicine. He graduated with a second medical degree from Dartmouth College in 1857, and soon after he returned to New Orleans to open his own office. In the same year he married Louisa Celie Seulay, and their union produced eight children.

Roudanez continued to build his medical practice during the CIVIL WAR and RECONSTRUCTION, but, like other free men of color in New Orleans, upon federal occupation of south Louisiana in the spring of 1862 he became deeply interested in the issues of Reconstruction in his state. He was one in a group of investors who made possible the creation of the *New Orleans Union,* the wartime political voice of the city's French-speaking free black elite. The paper proved short-lived, and just weeks after its failure in July 1864 Roudanez and his brother Jean-Baptiste Roudanez founded the *New Orleans Tribune*. A bilingual publication, the *Tribune* sought to bring together former slaves and free black people in the cause of racial equality. This first black daily newspaper in the nation reported primarily on politics, and the reform program it promoted bore the ideological imprints of Roudanez and the paper's chief editor, white Belgian radical Jean-Charles Houzeau. It called for universal suffrage, officeholding rights for black men, the right of jury duty, and economic independence for former slaves through a federally sponsored division of plantations. Roudanez also used the paper to aid in the 1869 campaign to end discrimination in public accommodations in New Orleans. The *Tribune* served as the official organ of Louisiana's REPUBLICAN PARTY, although it was at times highly critical of both the state and national party. The paper rejected the 1864 state constitution because it did not extend suffrage to black men, and it was at odds with Andrew Johnson's administration over its lenient Southern policy. Eventually it was Roudanez's opposition to the selection of Henry Clay Warmoth as the Republican gubernatorial candidate in 1868 and Roudanez's role in the nomination of a more radical splinter ticket that caused the party to cut its ties to the *Tribune.* His bolt from the party did much to sully his reputation among many of the black and white activists whom he previously had helped to establish the state party. His insistence on a competing ticket also prompted Houzeau to resign his post, a move which helped to undermine the already financially strapped newspaper. Consequently, it ceased publication in April 1868, although Roudanez's continuing opposition to Governor Warmoth led him to resurrect it the following year for a brief period.

Roudanez disappeared from the public spotlight until 1873, when he and other propertied New Orleanians began a political reform movement under the banner "Unification." Motivated by the perceived deleterious effect of political instability on the city's businesses, this group advocated honest government, racial cooperation in politics and government and an end to political violence, equal civil and political rights for all citizens, desegregation on public conveyances, and an equal distribution of public offices between the races. Roudanez was on the "Committee of One Hundred" that drew up the movement's platform in June of that year. Unification ultimately failed as a movement because it did not garner significant support in Louisiana's country parishes, and, ironically, because of persistent mistrust between white and black participants within the movement itself.

In addition to his activity in politics and journalism, Roudanez was involved in black community affairs. He had a well-earned reputation for philanthropy. In 1865, for example, he donated some of the funds for the building of the Providence Asylum, an institution that was operated by the Louisiana Association for the Benefit of Colored Orphans. He also strongly supported higher education, and he served for a time on the Examining Committee of Straight (now Dillard) University.

Despite his activity in the public realm, his primary professional commitment throughout his life remained in the field of medicine. In the 1870s and 1880s Roudanez ran a large and prosperous practice, reportedly treating both black and white patients. He devoted his final years to maintaining his practice. Roudanez died in New Orleans.

Roudanez's public life was brief, but it had a significant impact on the course of Reconstruction in Louisiana. His newspaper was instrumental in the formation and growth of the Republican Party in the state. Its editorials undoubtedly helped to focus attention on the critical issues of Reconstruction, though its position on some matters proved too extreme for most policymakers. Roudanez himself exemplified the intense interest of black men in postbellum politics and the hopes that free men and freedmen alike invested in the Reconstruction experiment. Moreover, his conflicts with other activists highlighted the problem of disunity that plagued Reconstruction leaders in his and in other Southern states and that contributed to their demise.

Bibliography

Valuable information on Roudanez can be found in manuscript collections at Louisiana State University, Baton Rouge; the Roman Catholic Diocese of Baton Rouge; the University of New Orleans; the Amistad Research Center; the Louisiana Collection at Tulane University; and the Louisiana Division of the New Orleans Public Library.

Blassingame, John W. *Black New Orleans, 1860–1880.* 1973.

Connor, William P. "Reconstruction Rebels: The New Orleans Tribune in Post-War Louisiana." *Louisiana History* 21 (spring 1980): 159–81.

Desdunes, Rodolphe Lucien. *Our People and Our History.* 1973.

Houzeau, Jean-Charles. *My Passage at the "New Orleans Tribune."* 1984.

Obituaries: *New Orleans Picayune,* March 12, 1890; *New Orleans Abeille,* March 13, 1890; and *New Orleans Daily Crusader,* March 22, 1890.

Rankin, David C. "The Origins of Black Leadership in New Orleans during Reconstruction." *Journal of Southern History* 40 (August 1974): 417–40.

Vincent, Charles. *Black Legislators in Louisiana during Reconstruction.* 1976.

From *American National Biography.* John A. Garraty and Mark C. Carnes, eds. Oxford University Press, 1999. Reprinted by permission of the American Council of Learned Societies.

Connie Meale

Roumain, Jacques

1907–1944

Haitian writer, ethnographer, and political dissident whose novel *Gouverneurs de la rosée* is a classic of Haitian literature.

Born in PORT-AU-PRINCE, HAITI, to upper-middle-class mixed-race parents, Roumain attended excellent schools in both HAITI and Europe, where he acquired remarkable language skills (he spoke English, German, and Spanish, in addition to French and Creole) and a profound understanding of European cultures. At a young age, he rejected his parents' cosmopolitanism, returning to Haiti from Paris in 1927 to help found *La Revue Indigène.* This journal, which was instrumental in the development of a specifically Haitian literary aesthetic rooted in traditional peasant life, published many of Roumain's early poems. Roumain wrote prodigiously and fearlessly during this period, publishing two collections of novellas in 1931 (*La Proie et l'ombre* and *Les Fantoches*) that denounced the greed of Haiti's ruling class.

In 1934 Roumain was elected secretary-general of the Haitian Communist Party, which he had helped establish. That same year, Haitian president Sténio Vincent, alarmed by the forceful criticism in Roumain's political writings, ordered him arrested. As a result of international pressure on the Haitian government, Roumain spent only two years in jail. Following his release, Roumain left for FRANCE where he became involved with the Popular Front, an association that would lead him to fight among the antifascists in the Spanish Civil War (the poem "Madrid," recounting this experience, was published in a French journal in 1937). In 1939 Roumain, who found himself once again in France, published an article entitled "Les griefs de l'homme noir" (The Grievances of the Black Man), which attracted both the attention and the ire of the French public.

Roumain published several literary and ethnographic works between 1939 and his death in 1944, but it is *Gouverneurs de la rosée* (1944; *Masters of the Dew*, 1947), published just weeks after he died, that endures as Roumain's most important work. The story of a Haitian peasant who brings two warring factions in a village together in the name of a common cause, the novel is a celebration of the collective potential of the Haitian peasantry. But the lasting appeal of this novel stems from Roumain's ability to express political didacticism in artful language, a lyrical French inflected by Creole words and rhythms. Roumain's successful integration of politics and art is his legacy and continues to serve as a model for many Francophone writers of the Caribbean.

See also Literature, French-Language, in the Caribbean.

Richard Watts

Rowan, Carl Thomas

1925–2000

American journalist, head of United States Information Agency.

Carl Thomas Rowan was born in Ravenscroft, Tennessee. After serving as an officer in the U.S. Navy, which was segregated at the time, Rowan began a career as a newspaper journalist at the white-owned *Minneapolis Tribune*. One of the first African American reporters for a large urban daily newspaper, Rowan captured the racial struggles of the 1950s with a series on discrimination in the South and an article on the landmark segregation case before the U.S. Supreme Court—BROWN V. BOARD OF EDUCATION.

In 1961 Rowan entered government service as deputy assistant secretary of state to President John F. Kennedy. Appointed ambassador to Finland in 1963, he was one of the first African Americans diplomats to serve in a predominantly white nation. That same year he became head of the United States Information Agency (USIA), the highest post in the government's executive branch that an African American had yet held. Rowan remained visible with a nationally syndicated newspaper column, which he continued to write until a few days before his death, as well as radio and television broadcasts. Rowan, whose writings tend to support mainstream liberal politics, drew criticism from both conservatives and radical black nationalists. In 1987 Rowan founded Project Excellence, a program to raise scholarship money for black students around the nation's capital.

Marian Aguiar

Ruanda-Urundi

Former Belgian mandate incorporating present-day Rwanda and Burundi.

See also Burundi; Rwanda.

Rudd, Daniel A.

1854–1933

Catholic layman who organized the first black Catholic congress.

The child of Roman Catholic slaves, Daniel Rudd founded the first African American Catholic newspaper, the *Ohio State Tribune*, in 1886. The newspaper, later called *American Catholic Tribune*, promoted the Catholic Church as an institution recognizing all people as equals. In 1889, Rudd organized the first National Conference of African American Catholics to address such issues as equal access for African Americans to employment, housing, and Catholic schooling. The conference received Pope Leo XIII's blessing and was followed by a visit to President Grover Cleveland. Rudd continued to participate actively in the church, including the first lay Catholic congress, until his death in 1933.

Marian Aguiar

Ruddock, Osbourne

See Tubby, King.

Rudolph, Wilma Glodean

1940–1994

Sprinter and first American woman to win three Olympic gold medals.

Wilma Rudolph was born in Bethlehem, Tennessee. As a child she had suffered from scarlet fever, double pneumonia, and polio, leaving her without the use of her left leg. She wore a brace until age nine, but by age twelve she was the fastest runner in her school. At Burt High School she starred in both track and BASKETBALL. At a track meet at Tuskegee, Alabama, Rudolph impressed coach Ed Temple, who invited her to a summer track camp in Nashville, Tennessee. This led to a place on the 1956 U.S. Olympic 4 × 100-meter relay team in Melbourne, which won the bronze medal. In the 1960 Olympic Games in Rome, Rudolph won gold medals in the 100- and 200-meter dashes and the 4 × 100-meter relay. She held the world record in all three events when she retired from amateur competition in 1962.

After graduating from Tennessee State University in 1963, Rudolph dedicated her professional life to youth programs and education. She worked with the Job Corps in St. Louis and Boston, and the Watts Community Action Committee in Los Angeles, California. Rudolph was inducted to the Black Sports Hall of Fame in 1973, the Women's Sports Hall of Fame in 1980, and the U.S. Olympic Hall of Fame in 1983. In 1981, she founded the Wilma Rudolph Foundation, a nonprofit organization focused on developing young athletic talent. In 1977, she published her autobiography, *Wilma: The Story of Wilma Rudolph*.

See also Olympics, African Americans and the; Track and Field in the United States.

Robert Fay

Ruffin, Josephine Saint Pierre

1842–1924

American journalist, clubwoman, civil rights activist, and suffragist.

Born in BOSTON, MASSACHUSETTS, Josephine Ruffin embarked on her long career of humanitarian work during the AMERICAN CIVIL WAR, when she and her husband George recruited soldiers for the Fifty-Fourth and Fifty-Fifth Massachusetts Volunteer Infantry Regiments. She was active in integrated and African American women's clubs and charitable organizations, including the Associated Charities of Boston and the Massachusetts State Federation of Women's Clubs. In 1893, she founded and was president of the Women's Era Club (WEC), and edited its newspaper, *The Women's Era*, the first newspaper to be owned, managed, and published by African American women.

In 1895, in response to a Missouri editor's assertions that African American women were without virtue, Ruffin organized a national convention of African American women's clubs. Twenty clubs met and formed the NATIONAL FEDERATION OF AFRO-AMERICAN WOMEN. In 1896 they merged with the National League of Colored Women to form the NATIONAL ASSOCIATION OF COLORED WOMEN.

Resistance to integrated clubs led to the "Ruffin Incident" in 1900 at the General Federation of Women's Clubs' biennial meeting in Milwaukee. When the executive board learned that the WEC's members were African Americans, it refused to seat Ruffin, who then refused to leave. Although Northern and Midwestern delegates backed Ruffin, the Southern contingent successfully blocked her participation.

After the WEC disbanded in 1903, Ruffin helped found the Association for the Promotion of Child Training in the South, and the first branch of the NATIONAL ASSOCIATION FOR THE ADVANCEMENT OF COLORED PEOPLE (NAACP) in Boston.

See also Fifty-Fourth Massachusetts Volunteer Infantry Regiment.

Robert Fay

Ruggles, David

1810–1849

Orator, journalist, and militant abolitionist who said "The pleas of crying soft and sparing never answered the purpose of a reform, and never will."

At age twenty, David Ruggles, child of free parents in Connecticut, penned a letter to the Marquis de Lafayette asking for his support for the abolition of slavery. It was the beginning of a prominent public life of lectures and letters for the self-educated Ruggles. Three years later, in 1833, Ruggles traveled as an agent for New York's antislavery newspaper the *Emancipator*, inspiring audiences with news of the growing abolitionist movement.

Ruggles used the written word as well as the orator's platform to describe the horrors of slavery. In 1834, he opened in NEW YORK, NEW YORK, the first known African American bookshop. Such pamphlets as *Extinguisher, Extinguished . . . or David M. Reese, M.D. "Used Up"* (1834) and *The Abrogation of the Seventh Commandment by the American Churches* (1835) were distributed in contemporary slavery debates taking place around the issues of colonization and the women's movement. Expanding his antislavery forum, Ruggles published the first African American weekly magazine, *Mirror of Liberty*, in 1838.

As founder and head of the New York Vigilance Committee, Ruggles risked his own personal safety to protect endangered African Americans. He confronted slavecatchers personally, and published a New York *Slaveholders Directory* (1839) to expose whites thought to own free people. He is remembered for assisting FREDERICK DOUGLASS and over a thousand slaves through the UNDERGROUND RAILROAD.

By 1842 Ruggles was nearly blind and financially ruined after being imprisoned for helping an accused thief. He found support from Lydia Maria Child in Northampton, Massachusetts, and spent his last seven years there building a successful hydropathy, or "water cure," practice.

See also Abolitionism in the United States.

Marian Aguiar

Ruiz Belvis, Segundo

1829–1867

Puerto Rican abolitionist.

Segundo Ruiz Belvis liberated his slaves in PUERTO RICO and founded an abolitionist society with RAMÓN EMETERIO BETANCES. In 1867, he petitioned SPAIN to abolish slavery. He died in CHILE later that year.

Rumba

Secular Afro-Cuban performance ritual synthesizing dance, song, and music.

During the eighteenth century, large numbers of slaves of YORUBA, Calabar, and KONGO descent were brought to CUBA to work in the SUGAR-producing region of MATANZAS. Following the abolition of slavery in 1886, these and other liberated blacks headed to Cuba's urban centers in search of employment and settled on the outskirts of the cities. The rumba was born out of festive social gatherings in the suburban environment of Matanzas during the late nineteenth and early twentieth centuries. Rumba synthesizes African-derived rhythms, songs, and dances, in particular those of Bantu origin. Rumba soon spread to HAVANA and other parts of Cuba and, after World War II, was exported to Europe and the United States, where it was modified into a type of ballroom dance. This article focuses on the original form of rumba, as performed in contemporary Afro-Cuban communities.

A number of percussive instruments accompany the rumba. Originally, empty drawers turned upside down, empty bottles, frying pans, and spoons were used to make music for the rumba. Subsequently, rumba musicians replaced these instruments with wooden boxes, in particular those used to package salted cod and candles. Although wooden boxes are still occasionally incorporated, today rumba instrumentation usually features three conga drums, which are collectively referred to as the *tambores*. These include the bass *tumbador*, the middle-range *tres dos*, and the high-pitched *quinto*. Generally, the tumbador and the tres dos play constant rhythms, while the quinto improvises. Other instruments in the rumba repertoire are the *cata* or *guagua* (a wooden tube played with sticks), the *guiro* (a serrated wooden cylinder played with a metal pick-like object), and either the *maruga* (an iron shaker) or the *maracas*. The *claves* (two hardwood sticks) are struck together to produce a syncopated beat of the same name (*clave*), which provides a distinctive ground rhythm for the other instruments.

There are three types of rumba: yambú, guaguanco, and columbia, each with its own unique rhythms, song format, and dance steps. Of these, the guaguanco is the most popular. It is faster than the yambú, but slower than the columbia.

The music for guaguanco has the following structure: After the claves have set the tempo for the song, the drums and the other instruments gradually join in, and the singer enters with the *diana*, a short string of melodic syllables. The singer, who is usually a man, then proceeds to sing an extended, lyrical solo or duet, known in Spanish as the *canto*, which often recalls and comments upon a certain person or event. The singer eventually indicates a phrase in the song that will be used as the chorus. The dancers usually enter after the chorus has started. An animated call-response section begins in which the singer begins to improvise lines which alternate with the chorus. This exchange may continue for several minutes before the song ends.

In the guaguanco, a male dancer tries to attract the female dancer, but she flirtatiously avoids his advances. While circling around her, the male dancer intermittently makes a quick gesture with his hand or leg that symbolizes an attempt to "possess" the female dancer, who responds by quickly covering her pelvic region with her hands or crossed arms. The ultimate possessive gesture is a pelvic thrust by the male called the *vacunao*. The dance ends when the male has successfully caught the female off-guard with the vacunao or when the female dancer proves herself to be impervious to the male dancer's efforts to possess her.

The yambú is a slower dance in which a male and female performers dance as if they were elderly. The male does not do the vacunao in this dance. The yambú is the least-frequently performed type of rumba.

The columbia is the fastest and most acrobatic of the three types of rumba. Its rhythmic patterns are short and sharp, and it is done by a solo male dancer. Some of the steps are closely related to those performed by members of all-male secret societies known as ABAKUÁS. In the columbia, the dancer and the player of the quinto engage in a competitive dialogue in which the dancer attempts to match through dance steps the rhythmic improvisations of the quinto. Unlike the other two forms of rumba, columbia's lyrics sometimes include words and phrases in African languages, in particular Yoruba.

Rumba continues to be a vital tradition at the grassroots level, especially in and around Matanzas and Havana. During the course of rumba's development, neighborhood-based rumba groups known as *bandos* and *coros de rumba* emerged, mounting performances and hosting parties. Such ensembles as AfroCuba and LOS MUÑEQUITOS DE MATANZAS, whose members span three generations, have achieved international renown.

See also Percussion Instruments of the Caribbean; Son.

Aaron Myers

Run-DMC

Early and influential rap music group from New York City.

The group was known during the 1980s for its aggressive *raps* (spoken rhymes) on top of strong beats. Run-DMC further distinguished its sound by incorporating elements of rock music, specifically heavy-metal guitar, which helped popularize black RAP among many white listeners. By bringing the HIP-HOP street look to the stage, Run-DMC also changed the image of rap, wearing black leather in winter, athletic warm-up suits in summer, and always wearing their signature Adidas sneakers. The first rap group to be regularly broadcast on MTV (Music Television), Run-DMC in 1985 also became the first rap group to appear on the television program "American Bandstand," hosted by media personality Dick Clark.

Run-DMC was formed in 1983 by three friends from NEW YORK CITY's borough of Queens. Rapper Joseph "Run" Simmons recorded as a solo artist in 1982 for his older brother, rap producer Russell "Rush" Simmons, before teaming with rapper Darryl "D.M.C." McDaniels to record two minor singles. The two then brought in disc jockey (DJ) Jason "Jam Master Jay" Mizell and the trio soon became known as Run-DMC. The group released its first album in 1984, *Run-DMC*. On the strength of one song, "Sucker M.C.'s," the record became the best-selling rap album to that time. The album gained attention for its tough-sounding lyrics and its spare, clean sound; the group used only a drum machine and scratchy turntable noises for accompaniment. Another single from the album, "Rock Box," was one of the first rap pieces to include tracks of heavy-metal electric guitar, and was also distributed as a video.

In 1985 Run-DMC released its second album, *King of Rock*, and acted and performed in the motion picture *Krush Groove*, a fictionalized account of Run-DMC and the development of rap-music record label Def Jam. Also in 1985, a number of violent incidents at rap concerts caused the national media to focus on rap as a reflection of violence and drug abuse among young black males. Run-DMC and other rap groups found themselves caught between this negative image and the acceptance of rap by MTV and "American Bandstand."

The group's third album, *Raising Hell* (1986), featured a remake of "Walk This Way," a song first performed by the rock group Aerosmith in 1976. The remake, which included new performances by Aerosmith members Steven Tyler and Joe Perry, was a popular success and was hailed by critics as a breakthrough that masterfully fused white rock music with black rap. In 1988 the group starred in *Tougher Than Leather*, a film produced by Def Jam's Rick Rubin. Other albums from Run-DMC include *Back from Hell* (1990), *Down with the King* (1993), and *Crown Royal* (2001). In 2002 Jason Mizell was shot and killed at a recording studio in Queens.

See also Music, African American.

Runaway Slaves in the United States

See Fugitive Slaves.

RuPaul, Andre Charles

1960–

African American singer, entertainer, actor, and the first openly gay cross-dresser to become a supermodel and mainstream celebrity.

Since the release of his 1992 debut album *Supermodel of the World*, RuPaul has become a nationally recognized celebrity. Although best known as a drag queen, he also enjoys surprising audiences by appearing as a man. "Drag queens are like the shamans of our society, reminding people of what's funny and what's a stereotype," he told *People Weekly* writer Tim Allis in 1993. "I feel very powerful when I'm in drag, and when I'm out of drag I observe our culture." Six feet, seven inches tall in heels, RuPaul is painfully aware of the contradictions of being a black man who wears a platinum wig and platform heels. "When I'm dressed up as this goddess," he told Allis, "people trip over themselves to give me things. But as an African American male, I can walk into an elevator and have people clutch their handbags."

Born RuPaul Andre Charles in New Orleans, Louisiana, RuPaul grew up in San Diego, California, one of four children of Irving Charles, the operator of a beauty supply store, and Ernestine Charles, a college clerk. His parents divorced when he was six. At the age of fifteen he and his sister Renetta moved to ATLANTA, GEORGIA, where he studied at the Northside High School of the Performing Arts. "In school I was kind of alien to every group," he told Guy Trebay of *The New Yorker*. "I was perpetually an outsider . . . until the day I decided to get into drag." Inspired by images of DIANA ROSS, he began performing at Atlanta cabarets and comedy clubs in wigs and high heels. He also sang in various rock groups, including RuPaul and the U-Hauls.

In 1987 he moved to NEW YORK, NEW YORK, where he sang with the band Now Explosion at the Pyramid, a popular gay club. In 1991 he received a contract with Tommy Boy Records. Three songs from *Supermodel of the World* reached number one on the *Billboard* magazine chart, making RuPaul a celebrity. Since then he has contributed to Elton John's *Duets* album, released a Christmas single, "The Little Drummer Boy," and recorded a second album, *Foxy Lady* (1996). In 1995 he won a contract with M.A.C. Cosmetics and was made co-chair of the company's ACQUIRED IMMUNODEFICIENCY SYNDROME (AIDS) fund.

In 1996 RuPaul began hosting a television talk show, with guests such as Dennis Rodman, WHOOPI GOLDBERG, and Cher. He has appeared in numerous films, including SPIKE LEE's *Crooklyn* (1994) and Wayne Wang's *Blue in the Face* (1995). In 2000 he narrated the documentary film *The Eyes of Tammy Faye*, about the life and career of televangelist Tammy Faye Bakker. RuPaul has also appeared in advertisements and fashion shows.

Roanne Edwards

Rush, Bobby

1946–

Democratic member of the United States House of Representatives from Illinois.

Bobby Lee Rush was born in Albany, Georgia, and grew up in CHICAGO, ILLINOIS. He joined the army in 1963, and in 1966 he became active in the CIVIL RIGHTS MOVEMENT in the South. Rush was honorably discharged from the army in 1968, and that same year he helped to found the Illinois BLACK PANTHER PARTY.

During his time with the Black Panthers, Rush also managed a medical clinic that developed the nation's first mass testing program for SICKLE-CELL ANEMIA, a disease that occurs in the United States primarily among blacks. Rush received a bachelor's degree from Roosevelt University in 1974, a master's degree from the University of Illinois in 1994, and a master's degree from the McCormick Theological Seminary in 1998. He is an ordained minister.

Elected a city alderman in Chicago in 1983, Rush served in that position for nearly ten years. In the 1992 Democratic primary for the First Congressional District seat for Illinois, Rush defeated the incumbent representative by a slim margin, then won the general election with 83 percent of the vote. In subsequent elections, voters returned him to congressional office, although in 1999 he made an unsuccessful attempt to be elected mayor of Chicago. Rush is a member of the CONGRESSIONAL BLACK CAUCUS.

Rushing, Jimmy

1903–1972

American jazz vocalist.

Born in Oklahoma City, Oklahoma, Jimmy Rushing was reared in a musical family, and studied piano, violin, and voice from childhood. In 1927, he began his singing career with Walter Page's Blue Devils, moving to BENJAMIN (BENNIE) MOTEN's Kansas City Orchestra two years later. Rushing's career predated the microphone, and his rich and bellowing tenor voice carried over the sound of the band without mechanical amplification. Rushing performed as a vocalist with the WILLIAM JAMES ("COUNT") BASIE Orchestra from 1935 to 1950, producing such songs as "Goin' to Chicago," "How Long, How Long," and the self-descriptive "Mr. Five by Five."

See also Jazz.

Russell, Nipsey

1924–

African American entertainer and the first African American to host a national television show.

Nipsey Russell was born in ATLANTA, GEORGIA. He launched his career in entertainment in 1948 when he moved to NEW YORK, NEW YORK, to try his hand at stand-up comedy. Russell, who did not use black slang or racial references, moved from nightclubs in HARLEM, such as the APOLLO THEATER, Smalls Paradise, and the Baby Grand, to mainstream clubs and television appearances. He was one of the first African Americans to appear on talk shows, frequently seen as a guest of Jack Paar on *The Tonight Show*. He had a serial role on the television comedy *Car 54 Where Are You?* and received good reviews as the Tin Man in the movie *The Wiz*.

Russell, William Fenton (Bill)

1934–

African American basketball player.

BASKETBALL star William Fenton Russell, called Bill, led the Boston Celtics to eleven National Basketball Association (NBA) championship titles. In 1980 sportswriters voted him "Greatest Player in the History of the NBA."

Russell was born in Monroe, Louisiana. By the time he graduated from McClymonds High School in Oakland, California, in 1952, he had already reached the height of six feet, ten inches, at which he later entered the NBA. Russell won an athletic scholarship to the University of San Francisco (USF) and led his college team to National Collegiate Athletic Association (NCAA) championships in 1955 and 1956. Russell was part of the United States basketball team that won the gold medal at the 1956 Olympic Games in Melbourne, Australia.

As a professional player, Russell was a member of the Boston Celtics from 1957 to 1969. Admired as the league's best rebounder and defensive player, he was named the NBA's Most Valuable Player five times and played in twelve All-Star games. In 1966, while still an active player, Russell began coaching the Celtics, becoming the first African American coach in the NBA. As player-coach he led the Celtics to two NBA championships. From 1973 to 1977 he coached the fledgling Seattle SuperSonics, and briefly the Sacramento Kings. He was inducted to the Basketball Hall of Fame in 1975.

A leader off the court as well as on it, Russell was a keen defender of equal rights for African American athletes. In 1966, at the height of his career, Russell voiced a powerful assertion of black pride and protest with his autobiography, *Go Up For Glory*.

Russia and the Former Soviet Union

World's largest country, extending from eastern Europe into northern Asia, which has hosted a black population for centuries.

From the eighteenth century, when Peter the Great first recruited black servants, until the post-Soviet present, black people have been rare in the lands that once comprised the Russian empire and, later, the Soviet Union. Except for tiny black enclaves in the Caucasus, blacks have always been outsiders in this part of the world. As early as 1858, the celebrated black Shakespearean actor IRA ALDRIDGE beguiled Russian audiences with the power of his performances, while his presence sparked heated discussions on racial issues in the Russian press. In the decades preceding the 1917 Bolshevik Revolution, a number of American blacks went to Russia, where they pursued successful careers as businessmen and diplomats.

The heyday for blacks in Russia occurred between the 1917 revolution and the 1960s. Communist leaders, eager to present their country as a place of racial equality, gave visiting black artists, intellectuals, and political figures privileges that the average Soviet citizen could only dream of—albeit not without motives informed by Soviet ideology and international politics. Although blacks encountered racial prejudice in the former Soviet Union, the general reaction to them was one of curiosity more than hostility. Writer LANGSTON HUGHES wrote of his 1932 experience in Russia, "What few Negroes there were in Moscow, of course, were conspicuous wherever they went, attracting friendly curiosity if very dark, and sometimes startling a peasant fresh from the country who had never seen a black face before."

Black Population of the Caucasus

In 1913 Russian naturalist V. P. Vradii published a report on an unusual discovery he had made while visiting the western Caucasus Mountains. He revealed that several hundred blacks were living in small, isolated farming settlements around two Black Sea towns, Batumi and Sukhumi, in what is now the republic of Georgia. Most of the blacks were Muslims and spoke the Abkhazian language. Vradii's testimony was confirmed in the following decades by several journalists and scholars who traveled to the remote region.

The origins of these black inhabitants are not entirely clear. Many were brought from Africa as slaves for local Turkish and Abkhazian rulers between the sixteenth and nineteenth centuries. It is likely, however, that small communities of blacks have lived in the region for much longer. The ancient Greeks established slave-trading colonies on the Black Sea coast, as did the Romans, Arabs, Genoese, and Turks in later centuries. Moreover, the region that is now Georgia was called Colchis by the ancient Greeks, and the Greek historian Herodotus, writing in the fifth century B.C.E., stated that the Colchians had black skin and woolly hair, and that they wove linen in the same manner as the Egyptians. Recent scholars have pointed out a likeness between many Abkhazian and Egyptian place-names, family names, and names of similar customs.

Little is known about the Caucasus blacks. Two who rose to prominence in the early years of the Soviet Union were Shaaban Abash and Bashir Shambe. After the Russian Revolution, Abash, a shepherd, joined the forces supporting the Bolsheviks, and was subsequently elected to the Central Executive Committee of the Abkhazian *Soviet* (city council), the highest local executive authority. Shambe also enlisted in the Red Army and later joined both the Georgian Communist Party and Tbilisi Soviet.

Opinions differ on the current situation of the Caucasus blacks. It is thought that over the years, many have intermarried and assimilated into Abkhazian or wider Soviet society. In 1992, however, the black Russian journalist Yelena Khanga reported that her mother Lily Golden-Hanga visited some of the black villages in the 1960s and discovered that the inhabitants were living in poverty, isolated from other local peoples. Golden-Hanga reported her findings to her longtime friend Svetlana Allilueva, Joseph Stalin's daughter, who defected to the West in 1966 and was at the time writing a book on Russia. Allilueva included Golden-Hanga's findings in her book *Only One Year,* published in the United States in 1969. Her account suggests that some of the Abkhazian blacks had been forcibly relocated by the Soviet authorities—a common fate of other Caucasian peoples, such as the Kabardians and the Chechen-Ingush. In the Soviet edition of Allilueva's book, however, censors removed all references to the plight of the Abkhazian blacks.

Black Servants in Imperial Russia

Beginning with the reign of Peter the Great (1682–1725), blacks were brought to Russia to work as slaves or servants. In the eighteenth and early nineteenth centuries, it was fashionable in Russia, as in the rest of Europe, for wealthy aristocratic families to employ one or two black servants. The tsars also maintained a staff of between ten and twenty blacks. Until the nineteenth century, blacks were acquired as slaves; on arrival in Russia they were given their freedom in exchange for lifelong service. Some are portrayed, with their employers, in paintings by the nineteenth-century artists Karl Briullov and Konstantin Makovskii.

Although most of these blacks came from Africa, some came from the United States. A black man named Nelson accompanied the family of John Quincy Adams to Russia in 1809, when Adams was appointed minister to Russia, and remained after joining the tsar's service. Moreover, most of the ships that sailed to Russia from major U.S. ports in the nineteenth century contained black crewmen, some of whom stayed.

One of those who remained was Nero Prince, a cook and prominent freemason from Boston, who first sailed to Russia in 1810 and settled there to work as a butler for a noble family. When Prince brought his second wife, Nancy, to Russia in 1824, she was presented at court to Tsar Alexander I. Nancy Prince set up a sewing shop, became active in the Russian Bible Society, and helped establish an orphanage in Saint Petersburg. She left firsthand accounts of the great flood of Saint Petersburg of 1824 and the bloody suppression of the Decembrist Revolt in 1825.

The most famous black servant in Russia was ABRAM HANNIBAL, the great-grandfather of one of Russia's best-loved writers, ALEKSANDR PUSHKIN. Hannibal, whose parents were probably from ETHIOPIA, arrived in Russia around 1700 as a servant to Peter the Great and ended his life as a military general and prominent landowner. In 1716 Hannibal was sent by the tsar to Paris for higher education in military engineering. At this time, Peter was in the midst of his lifelong struggle to transform Russia into a major European land power with a large, well-organized army and well-fortified defenses, and many Russians were sent to Western Europe for training in modern military techniques.

Hannibal returned to Russia in 1723 and began working on military engineering projects. After Peter's death, he spent three years designing fortifications in Siberia. In 1730 he was promoted to captain and assigned to Pernau, a fortress in Western Russia on the shores of the Baltic Sea. His carreer flourished under Empress Elizabeth; he was promoted to major general in 1742 and served as commandant of the city of Reval from 1743 to 1751. Hannibal retired in 1762 to one of the many estates he had been given by the empress, and lived there until his death in his early nineties. He is considered Russia's first outstanding modern engineer, an expert in canal and fortress construction, and one of the most highly educated Russians of his time.

In the 1820s, Aleksandr Pushkin wrote a fictionalized biography of Hannibal called *The Negro of Peter the Great,* which, according to Russia scholar Allison Blakely, "represented one of the earliest characterizations of the Negro as hero in world literature." Pushkin often referred in his poetry to his African heritage, which he valued highly and considered a mark of distinction. During the twentieth century, the Russian poets Vladimir Mayakovsky and Marina Tsvetaeva wrote verse extolling Pushkin's black ancestry.

Black Immigrants and Visitors in Russia before 1917

During the late nineteenth century, a number of blacks immigrated to Russia voluntarily in order to improve their economic lot. Exact numbers and other details are difficult to obtain, but studies indicate that most of these immigrants came from the United States. Many of those who became financially successful later left Russia to escape the Bolshevik regime, which considered wealthy people to be enemies of the working class.

George Thomas, an African American, moved to Saint Petersburg in 1890 and adopted the Russian name Fyodor. During the next twenty-five years he became a highly successful businessman, owning a large amusement complex in Moscow called the Aquarium. He is said to have become a close confidant of Tsar Nicholas II. The jockey Jimmy Winkfield, who had twice won the Kentucky Derby, moved to Russia in 1904 to ride horses for wealthy noblemen. He married an aristocratic Russian woman, and at the height of his career in 1916, he is said to have earned $100,000 a year. Other black immigrants found jobs as traveling circus performers and singers.

Three notable black visitors to Russia before 1917 were the Shakespearean actor Ira Aldridge, the philanthropist T. Morris Chester, and the diplomat Richard T. Greener. All three were African American, and all found greater acceptance in Russia than they had experienced at home. Of the three, Aldridge had the greatest impact on Russian society and culture. He left the United States in 1824 to make his career in Europe, and first visited Russia in 1858. He made several tours of Russia between 1861 and 1866, giving Russians a memorable first experience of Shakespeare, even though his performances in English were largely incomprehensible to his audiences. He received an honorary membership in the Imperial Academy of Fine Arts, and became a friend of the famous Ukrainian poet Taras Shevchenko.

Given that Aldridge was the first black person to make a major impression in Russian intellectual circles, his visits stimulated considerable discussion on racial issues in the Russian press and among the public. Although some critics were initially outraged that a black actor would perform Shakespeare, they were soon swept away by Aldridge's talent and humanity. The power of his performances is reflected in a Russian reviewer's assessment of his performance at the time, as cited in Allison Blakely's *Russia and the Negro* (1986): "Look at Aldridge . . . an African, with a swarthy face, dark skin, kinky hair, dilated nostrils, guttural speech. He does not attract us with any exquisite form, such as we are accustomed to, but such is the power of his soul, such is the majesty of his art that you understand everything he says . . . you seem to hear the beating of his heart, you are following a magician through all the gamut of human emotions."

Aldridge's visits came at a time of intense debate surrounding Tsar Alexander II's emancipation of Russia's huge population of serfs, which occurred in 1861. Aldridge's artistic genius served as an example of what an oppressed people could achieve if given the right opportunities; he was often cited by the liberal intelligentsia who were becoming increasingly critical of the autocratic Russian state. During the 1860s, as Russia became more restrictive of radical opinion, Aldridge was forbidden to perform *Macbeth* or *King Lear*, in which a king is killed or goes mad, respectively, apparently because the works offended the tsar. In 1864 he was officially banned from Saint Petersburg.

T. Morris Chester, the leader of the Garnet League—a philanthropic society that provided aid to freed slaves in the United States—visited Russia in the winter of 1866–1867 and was welcomed by Tsar Alexander II. He published an appeal for donations in the daily newspaper *Golos* (The Voice). Among the responses he received was a letter from a Russian peasant landholder and former serf, who wrote that he considered America's freed slaves as "brothers, not merely on account of the principle that all men are brethren, but by the force of those feelings which must unite the freedpeople of one land to those of another." After returning to the United States, Chester became an important state and federal official, and frequently gave public speeches and interviews. Through his visit, many American blacks came to see Russia as a racially tolerant land.

Richard T. Greener, a lawyer and diplomat, and the first African American graduate of Harvard College, served from 1898 to 1905 as the United States commercial agent in Vladivostok, Russia's major Pacific port. While in Russia he wrote many reports for the U.S. government on the economic potential of Siberia and its importance for the United States. Greener made suggestions to local officials for public improvements, and in return was elected to the Statistical Society of Amur and Primorsky provinces, an honor reserved for leading officials and businessmen. When the Russo-Japanese War (1904–1905) broke out, Greener was charged by the U.S. government with protecting Japanese interests in Siberia, and he was forced to leave Russia in 1905. Like Chester, Greener returned to the United States, where he spoke widely to both black and white audiences about his experiences in Russia and the economic opportunities there.

Black Immigrants and Visitors to the Soviet Union

The Soviet Union, the new country formed in 1922 out of the Russian Empire, was a highly attractive destination for many black people. It was, after all, the first country founded on the principles of racial equality, world peace, anticolonialism, and economic advancement of the working class. It seemed to offer an ideal society to those suffering under COLONIAL RULE in Africa, or racism and economic depression in the United States. As a result, many blacks traveled to the Soviet Union, and a number settled there.

The Soviet authorities had many reasons for encouraging blacks to come to their country. They believed that blacks, as members of an oppressed social group, would be key participants in the Communist revolution that would topple colonial and capitalist regimes around the world, and they wanted to ensure that potential revolutionary leaders were firmly under the control of Moscow. Giving blacks free education in Soviet universities was a means to that end. Also, by demonstrating the Soviet Union's own racial tolerance and progressive thinking, Soviet leaders were enhancing their country's appeal to liberal-minded white and black intellectuals around the world, thus securing sympathy for the Communist cause.

Black Students in the Soviet Union before World War II

In 1920, during the Second Congress of the Communist International—the Comintern, the organization formed to spread world revolution—the white American Communist John Reed passed a note to Lenin asking "Should I say something about the Negroes in America?" Lenin wrote back "*Yes. Absolutely necessary.*" After a discussion of the situation of black Americans, the Comintern proposed to invite blacks to study in Russia.

Between 1925 and 1938, several dozen African and West Indian blacks and between sixty and ninety American blacks were invited to study at the Comintern-controlled Stalin Communist University of the Toilers of the East (KUTV) in Moscow. Most completed a fourteen-month program, which principally dealt with Marxist-Leninist theory, although training was also provided in espionage, guerrilla warfare, secret codes, and techniques of underground political work.

The blacks, like all foreign students, were treated as honored guests, receiving free room and board, clothing and travel allowances, special tutors, paid vacations in the Soviet Union and at home, and access to high officials. At that time, no other country offered blacks such opportunities. Yet some blacks encountered racism from both local people and Communist party workers. In his study on blacks in Comintern schools, Woodford McClellan noted that "the Russian-Ukrainian national experiences did not embrace racism . . . on the British, Spanish, or American model, but discrimination directed against minority peoples—Tartars and other Orientals, Turkic peoples, Jews—stained the record of the East Slavs, and black visitors inevitably felt its blows." Indeed, one black student, Pierre Kalmek, reported that he encountered "greater chauvinism here than in capitalist countries. . . . People have spat on me three or four times."

Because the Soviet authorities often suppressed news of racial incidents, it is unclear the extent to which black students experienced racism at KUTV. Like the general public, university teachers were expected to adhere to Communist principles and to suppress racial prejudice. According to McClellan, it was foreign whites, in particular the Americans, British, and Canadians, who were usually responsible for racial provocations in the Comintern schools. In 1932 black students formally complained about racism to the Comintern, which eventually set up an investigative commission. As a result, two whites and one black were expelled from KUTV.

KUTV students also voiced outrage at the abandonment of the film BLACK AND WHITE, which was to have depicted racial and labor conflicts in BIRMINGHAM, ALABAMA. In 1932, twenty-one African Americans, including the writer Langston Hughes, were invited to the Soviet Union to participate in the film project. The Soviets apparently canceled the film, already in progress, at the insistence of Colonel Hugh L. Cooper, the white American supervising the construction of the Dneprostroi hydroelectric power station, who threatened construction delays if the film went ahead. Many black students saw the cancellation of the film as the sacrifice of Communist ideals to economic expediency.

Political, Literary, and Artistic Visitors

Many famous black political activists as well as literary and artistic figures visited the Soviet Union, drawn by its reputed racial tolerance and by its attempt to put Marxist ideas into practice. While some were committed Communists, others were artists or writers who upheld the aims of the Russian Revolution, but had no formal ties to any Communist party.

One of the most important black visitors in the period between the two world wars was Jamaican-born poet CLAUDE MCKAY, who stayed from 1922 to 1923 and wrote about his trip for the American press. Received warmly by such Soviet leaders as Trotsky, Zinoviev, and Bukharin, he was the first black, along with Otto Huiswood, to discuss the American race problem before a Russian audience, at the Fourth Congress of the Comintern (1922). He also became a literary celebrity and was handsomely paid for the publication in the U.S.S.R. of poems, articles, and a Soviet-commissioned book entitled *The Negroes in America* (1923)—a propagandistic discussion of the plight of blacks in America as a key component of the class struggle.

Although McKay was interested in Communist party politics, he saw himself as an independent-minded poet, devoted first and foremost to his art. Reflecting on his experience in Russia, he wrote, "The fact is that I spent most of my leisure time in non-partisan and anti-Bolshevist circles . . . I grew tired to death of meeting the proletarian ambassadors from foreign lands, some of whom bore themselves as if they were the holy messengers of Jesus, Prince of Heaven, instead of working-class representatives." He did, however, enjoy the respect he received in Russia, saying "never in my life did I feel prouder of being an African, a black, and no mistake about it."

The African American lawyer and Communist WILLIAM L. PATTERSON lived in Russia from 1927 to 1930, and married a Russian, with whom he later had two daughters. In Russia he experienced an exhilarating lack of racism: "It is as if one had suffered with a painful affliction for many years and had suddenly awakened to discover that the pain had gone." The African American brothers Otto and Haywood Hall, who became Communists after the 1917 revolution, went to the Soviet Union in the mid-1920s. Like Patterson, Haywood Hall married a Russian. He visited Stalin at the Kremlin in 1927 and became vice-chairman of the Negro subcommittee of the Comintern. He returned to the United States in 1930 to continue his Communist organizational work. Both Patterson and the Hall brothers studied at KUTV.

In 1929 GEORGE PADMORE, a Trinidadian Communist, abandoned his wife and university studies in the United States to travel to Russia. He became an important figure in Profintern, the Comintern's trade union organization. He also lectured at KUTV, had an office in the Kremlin, and was given a special place on the reviewing stand in Red Square for the 1930 May Day parade. In 1930 he was transferred to Vienna to continue his work in the black labor movement. He and fellow African American JAMES FORD were crucial in establishing the International Trade Union Committee of Negro Workers, which was the most important organization in promoting black revolutions around the world. Like many Communist Party Loyalists, Padmore was discredited and expelled from the party in 1934 during Stalin's purges, but he remained devoted to the Soviet system.

Langston Hughes, who traveled to Moscow in 1932 as a consultant on the doomed *Black and White* film project, provided a humorous account of his Soviet experience in his autobiography *I Wonder As I Wander*. In one lively passage he described how Sylvia, one of the actors in the film, also sang African American SPIRITUALS on Radio Moscow. Because all mention of God or Jesus was forbidden, Sylvia chose to spell "God" backward, and sang "Rise, shine, and give Dog the glory!" He also wrote of Emma Harris, a sixty-year-old African American woman, originally from the American South, who had been living in Moscow since before the revolution. According to Hughes, "Everybody in Moscow knew Emma, and Emma knew everybody. Stalin, I am sure, was aware of her presence in the capital." Formerly an actress, Harris joked frequently about the Soviet dictator, saying "anything she wanted to say" in an era when freedom of speech was nonexistent.

The great African American intellectual W. E. B. DU BOIS visited the Soviet Union four times, in 1926, 1936, 1949, and 1958 to 1959. In his autobiography, published in 1968, he said that he felt more comfortable and inconspicuous in Russia than in any other country. During his 1958 visit, Du Bois, accompanied by his wife SHIRLEY GRAHAM DU BOIS, attended a New Year's banquet at the Kremlin. They were joined by the African American singer and actor PAUL ROBESON, who sang "The Song of the Plains" to the accompaniment of a Russian chorus. The following January, the Du Boises met with Soviet leader Nikita Khrushchev. They proposed the creation of an Institute of African Studies, which was founded that same year under the directorship of a friend, Ivan Potekhin, one of the coeditors of the 1954 ethnographic survey *Narody Afriki* (Peoples of Africa). In 1959 W. E. B. Du Bois was awarded the International Lenin Peace Prize.

Paul Robeson, the black artist who has arguably had the greatest influence on Soviet culture, first visited the U.S.S.R. in 1934 at the invitation of the Soviet filmmaker Sergei Eisenstein, who later became a close friend. Robeson and his wife Eslanda traveled to Moscow by train, and had a one-day layover in Berlin, where Adolf Hitler's Nazi Party had come to power the previous year. The contrast between the Berlin train station, where fascist storm troopers and passersby alike glared at the black couple like "wolves waiting to spring," and the welcoming attitude of Soviet officials, who were impressed with Robeson's fluent Russian, left an indelible impression on the American singer. For the next two weeks the Robesons were treated like visiting dignitaries.

Robeson returned to the Soviet Union at least seven times between 1936 and 1961. His concerts included performances of African American spirituals, American labor songs (such as "Joe Hill"), and especially Russian folk and patriotic songs, which endeared him to Russian audiences. He was given the highest honors—the Stalin Peace Prize in 1952, which carried a $25,000 award; a mountain in Central Asia was named after him; he appeared on television; and his songs were played repeatedly on Soviet radio.

Although not a registered Communist, Robeson remained committed to the socialist ideal throughout his life. Long after most American blacks had distanced themselves from Soviet Communism, he continued to feel immense gratitude for the warm welcome he had received in the U.S.S.R. In a 1957 interview with a Soviet newspaper, Robeson explained, "In the Soviet Union I felt like a person for the first time . . . I visited many schools, watched the pupils and saw in their eyes that the children . . . are taught a very important thing: that it is necessary to treat people equally, regardless of their skin color."

JAZZ has been a major vehicle for black cultural influence in Russia. Russians were first introduced to black music by the African American dancer Ida Forsyne, who performed the CAKEWALK in Moscow in 1911. Beginning in the 1920s, numerous black jazz musicians visited the Soviet Union, including the Leland and Drayton revue, Benny Peyton's New Orleans jazz band (with saxophonist SIDNEY BECHET), EARL "FATHA" HINES, the Charles Lloyd Quartet, DUKE ELLINGTON, and B. B. KING.

Cotton Farmers

One of the most striking examples of African American emigration to the Soviet Union is the story of the cotton farmers. In 1931 Oliver Golden, an agricultural specialist who had studied at TUSKEGEE INSTITUTE, organized a group of sixteen black Americans of various professional backgrounds to travel to

Uzbekistan in Soviet Central Asia to develop an experimental cotton plantation. The men were paid the equivalent of several hundred dollars a month, a fortune during the years of the GREAT DEPRESSION. They also enjoyed a month's free vacation every year in elite Crimean resorts. The group spent three years crossing Uzbek seeds with American seeds and finally produced a new strain of cotton that took 25 percent less time to mature than cotton in the American South.

At the time, even the Uzbek capital, Tashkent, was economically primitive, with few cars, telephones, or other conveniences. Donkeys were the chief mode of transportation. In the village of Yangiyul, where the group was sent, women wore veils; polygamy and harems were common; and few, if any, people spoke English. The farmers encountered very little racism during their stay, and being from the rural South, were delighted at the absence of segregation. Joseph Roane, who spent six years in the U.S.S.R., recalled only one racial incident. When he and another black man entered a hotel barber's shop in Moscow and asked for a haircut, two white Americans who were having their hair cut said, "What are you niggers doing here? Get out." When Roane explained the situation to the Russian barbers, they expelled the white men from the shop with lather still on their faces.

The Yangiyul group's initial contract expired in 1934. All the farmers signed up for another three years, but many were sent away from Yangiyul because their skills were needed elsewhere. Roane went to Georgia to help operate a tomato-canning plant. George "Whirlwind" Tynes, formerly a Pittsburgh football star, worked as a poultry breeder, and John Sutton developed a new type of rope, using a fiber derived from rice as a substitute for jute. Both Sutton and Tynes married Russian women.

By 1937 Stalin's purges were in full swing. Anyone suspected of being remotely hostile to Stalin was arrested and interned in labor and death camps, and suspicion of foreigners intensified. Under these conditions, all the Yangiyul members of the group were ordered to adopt Soviet citizenship immediately. Those who did not were expelled from the country. Oliver Golden, the leader of the group, stayed, becoming a popular and innovative professor at the Institute of Irrigation and Mechanization in Tashkent, where he taught until his death in 1940. Thousands of people attended his funeral. He had brought his Polish Jewish wife Bertha with him to Uzbekistan, and they had a daughter, Lily, who later married the Zanzibari leader Abdullah Hanga. In 1988 Lily's daughter Yelena Khanga, who was raised as a black Russian, became the first black commentator on Soviet television—a result of Mikhail Gorbachev's *glasnost* policy that encouraged Soviets to openly voice their opinions on controversial topics.

Other Black Immigrants

Many other blacks came individually as immigrants to the Soviet Union in the 1930s. Robert Robinson, an engineer from Detroit, went to the Soviet Union in 1930. He became a leading inventor and senior engineer at the state ball-bearing plant in Moscow. As with Joseph Roane, the only racism that Robinson is known to have experienced in the Soviet Union was from American visitors. In the early 1930s, he was assigned to a tractor plant in Stalingrad where 300 American engineers worked. When two white Americans ordered him out of the mess hall because of his color, they were arrested, convicted of "white chauvinism," and expelled from the Soviet Union.

In 1932 Homer Smith, a postal worker from Minneapolis, came to work for the Moscow Post Office for a salary higher than his previous wage. He also became the Moscow correspondent for the African American press. He reported that he and other blacks were treated well by the Russians, and were often allowed to go to the front of long lines of people waiting to buy food. He married a Russian woman and remained in the country until after World War II.

The African American actor Wayland Rudd emigrated to Moscow in 1932 after realizing that in the United States his race would restrict him to minor acting roles. He remained in the Soviet Union until his death in 1952, participating in the experimental movements in Russian theater and becoming the first black actor to play the role of Othello in Russian. He stated that the liberated atmosphere of the Russian stage was the most thrilling experience of his life.

Lloyd Patterson, an African American artist, came to the Soviet Union with the 1932 film project. He stayed, married a Russian woman, and worked in the Meyerhold Theatre, then as a journalist, and finally served in World War II, where he died in action. His son James Patterson became a well-known poet, drawing extensively on his dual Russian and African American identity.

Soviet Policy Regarding American Blacks

As has been discussed, the Soviet Union was eager to encourage blacks in the United States to rise up against capitalist society. The Comintern struggled with the issue of how best to motivate the black masses. Marxist-Leninist theory subordinated all differences among people, including racial differences, to the struggle between the ruling class and the workers. Correspondingly, early Soviet doctrine held that racism was an artificial distraction created by the ruling classes in order to divide the workers and distract them from revolution. Feelings of racial or national pride were considered harmful.

By the Sixth Congress of the Comintern in 1928, it became evident that the issue of racial feeling was far more important than had first been thought. James Ford, an African American delegate, criticized the official position and argued that it must be altered if the Communist movement were to attract discontented blacks. As a result, the Comintern redefined the status of American blacks as an oppressed people, much like an African colony, and advocated the creation of an independent black republic in the Southern United States. This remained the official Communist Party stance until 1959, despite the fact that it was highly unsatisfactory to many African American leaders (the NATIONAL ASSOCIATION FOR THE ADVANCEMENT OF COLORED PEOPLE characterized it as "Red segregation"). The policy was abandoned in an effort to improve relations with the United States.

Although the Soviets were able to offer few solutions for American blacks, they succeeded in drawing international attention to the plight of African Americans. From the 1950s onward, Soviet propaganda drew heavily on the sufferings of African Americans. In one of countless Soviet cartoons, two images of the Statue of Liberty are juxtaposed: a conventional view from New York Harbor, and a close-up of the statue's terror-stricken face, with the rays emanating from her head shown to be hooded Klansmen brandishing clubs and guns. Such propaganda disappeared during the Gorbachev era of the late 1980s.

Russian and Soviet Relations with Black Africa

Unlike the European colonial powers, Russia was never significantly involved in the TRANSATLANTIC SLAVE TRADE. Russia laid claim to an enormous portion of land in the American far north, yet most of this land was unexplored and unsuitable for the development of a plantation economy. Moreover, Russia had a long history of enslaving its own people: serf populations, consisting of Russian peasants, provided an abundant supply of indigenous labor until their emancipation in 1861. Although the Russian government acquired a small number of black slaves, they were viewed less as an important labor source than as exotic embellishments to aristocratic households. In 1818 representatives of the tsar called for the abolition of the African slave trade, though their motivation for doing so remains unclear, given that Russia maintained the institution of serfdom for an additional forty-three years.

Before the revolution, the main area of Russia's interest in Africa was the independent kingdom of Ethiopia. Like Russia, Ethiopia was an Orthodox Christian nation. It was also of key geopolitical importance, given its location at the mouth of the Red Sea (the SUEZ CANAL had opened in 1869) and its potential as a base for Russian control of the western Indian Ocean, a goal dear to Russian leaders past and present. Beginning in the mid-1800s, contacts with Ethiopia were developed. Explorers visited, and Russian diplomats sought to forge a military alliance with Ethiopia against the Turkish Ottoman Empire.

The Soviet leaders had specific aims in Africa. As with black America, they hoped to train revolutionaries and to exploit African nationalist feelings in order to encourage anticolonialism and to weaken the capitalist powers. But Soviet policy toward Africa changed dramatically during the 1930s, when the Soviet Union allied itself with GREAT BRITAIN and FRANCE against the growing power of Nazi Germany. This required the Soviets to moderate their anticolonialist stance. In an act that deeply disappointed many blacks, the Soviet Union sold fuel to fascist Italy despite Italy's invasion of Ethiopia. Moreover, the Soviets were secretly discussing with Nazi Germany a partitioning of Africa into colonial-style "spheres of influence," in which Germany would control Central Africa, Italy the north and northeast, and the Soviet Union the eastern coast.

During the 1940s the Soviet Union was engaged in World War II and the mass repression of dissenters within its borders. It was not until the 1950s that the Soviet government once again turned its attention to Africa. Nation-building went into full swing, and new African countries emerged from colonial rule every year. The Soviet Union eagerly provided technical, economic, and military assistance to these new states in order to secure them as allies.

In 1960 Soviet leader Nikita Khrushchev and his advisers strongly believed that the new states of Africa, many of them headed by strong, socialist-oriented leaders such as KWAME NKRUMAH in GHANA, SÉKOU TOURÉ in GUINEA, and MODIBO KEITA in MALI, would bypass capitalism and develop a specifically African version of SOCIALISM. Moreover, the Soviets were hoping that not only these three countries, but also many more would become strong Soviet allies. From the perspective of many African nations, however, the U.S.S.R. was just another northern industrial power seeking to dominate and exploit them.

By the end of the 1960s, after the break with Guinea and the collapse of Nkrumah's and Keita's regimes, the U.S.S.R. had tempered its aspirations in Africa to the provision of limited technical and military advice to many of its governments and the training in the Soviet Union of civil servants and administrators. PATRICE LUMUMBA University, founded in Moscow in 1961, offered a four-year program with courses in a wide range of topics, and free tuition, housing, medical care, and travel. This and similar programs became extremely popular, and by 1966 there were approximately 4,000 African students in the Soviet Union.

Given the larger number of black students than in the 1920s and 1930s, racial incidents surfaced more frequently. Of particular importance was the demonstration held by 500 African students in Red Square in the winter of 1963 to protest the death of a Ghanaian student. Soviet authorities claimed that he had been drinking and had frozen to death. The students argued that he had been murdered by Russians because of his plans to marry a Russian woman.

Some African students felt they were being manipulated by the Soviets for propaganda purposes. As Everest Mulekezi, a Ugandan who came to Moscow University in the late 1950s, described at one gathering of Ugandans: "In our name a stranger called for a vote on a resolution demanding immediate independence for UGANDA . . . Before we could open our mouths, a roar of approval went up. Cameras snapped as the Russian actors gathered around to congratulate us on our 'action.' Tape recordings were made for broadcasts to be beamed back home. Suddenly it was over, and we Ugandans were left dumbfounded and angry."

In the early 1970s, as the U.S.S.R. focused on improving relations with the United States, Soviet involvement in Africa became a lower priority. Beginning in 1975, however, the U.S.S.R. began its most intense period ever of involvement in Africa, intervening militarily in ANGOLA and in the Horn of Africa. The Soviets were able to accomplish this partly due to the unwillingness of the United States to involve itself in foreign conflicts following its defeat in the VIETNAM WAR.

In 1974 PORTUGAL granted independence to Angola, and a bloody civil war broke out among the three principal factions of the Angolan independence movement. By the time Angola became independent in November 1975, the Soviet-backed MOVIMENTO POPULAR DE LIBERTAÇÃO DE ANGOLA, or MPLA (Popular Movement for the Liberation of Angola), was strong enough to form a government. In response, SOUTH AFRICA and the United States began to ship arms to MPLA's opponents, especially to the NATIONAL UNION FOR THE TOTAL INDEPENDENCE OF ANGOLA (UNITA) movement led by JONAS SAVIMBI. The U.S.S.R. now began massive shipments of arms and of Cuban military personnel to the Angolan government. This support from both superpowers fueled a conflict that would devastate Angola for years to come.

Until 1974 Ethiopia had been aligned militarily and economically with the West. The Soviets had supported Ethiopia's long-time enemy SOMALIA, which had embraced socialism with the 1969 arrival in power of General MOHAMMED SIAD BARRE, who had been trained in the Soviet army. During the early 1970s the U.S.S.R. built Somalia's army into one of the strongest in the region. However, by 1974 Siad Barre was moving openly toward alignment with the Arab world, specifically the anti-Soviet regime of Saudi Arabia. In the same year, a Marxist-oriented military council overthrew the regime of HAILE SELASSIE in Ethiopia. Over the next few years, the U.S.S.R. provided large-scale military assistance to Ethiopia, enabling it to win against Somalia in the Ogaden War in 1978. Ethiopia, the largest country in the Horn of Africa, became a Soviet bridgehead in the key strategic region of the Red Sea, a major triumph of Soviet foreign policy.

With the Soviet invasion of Afghanistan in 1979 and the escalation of Soviet-American rivalry in CENTRAL AMERICA during the 1980s, Soviet attentions again turned away from Africa. The arrival of Gorbachev in 1985 caused a gradual withdrawal of the U.S.S.R. from involvement in the Third World, as relations with the West improved and Soviet policymakers focused attention on internal economic and social problems.

Contemporary Problems Facing Black Russians

Since the publication of Allison Blakely's comprehensive study *Russia and the Negro* in 1986, few scholarly accounts have been issued on the contemporary experiences of blacks in Russia or in Central Asia. Since the breakup of the Soviet Union in 1991, however, journalists and human rights activists have observed a sharpening of ethnic and racial strife throughout the region. With the collapse of communism as a unifying ideology, a variety of ethnic and nationalist movements have gained momentum. Moreover, the former Soviet republics have faced continuing economic hardships. Such developments have incited deep-seated racial prejudices and hostilities. Indeed, the majority of nationalist agendas offer a stark contrast to the racial idealism that the Soviet government espoused for so many decades.

Black Russians and visitors to the country report widespread racism, discrimination, and even racially motivated violence.

In a 2002 survey of black residents in Moscow, over half of the respondents described race relations in Russia as "very tense," and remarked that they felt "very uncomfortable" as a black person in Russia. Only 3 percent said they felt that people in shops and offices treated them with respect as Africans; two-thirds said they felt this way only some of the time, while one-third felt they were never treated with respect. Racist comments are a daily fact of life for black Russians, and such comments come from police and other state officials, as well as from ordinary Russians. Of the 180 people surveyed, 66 percent said they had been physically assaulted because of their race. Only two of the 204 attacks reported by survey respondents resulted in the conviction of the attacker.

Much of the violence toward blacks in Russia is perpetrated by "skinheads" and neo-Nazi groups that have flourished since the collapse of the Soviet Union. While most of this violence is directed toward ordinary citizens, diplomats from MADAGASCAR and KENYA have also been assaulted, as has the wife of a South African ambassador. According to many Russian blacks, the police do little to stop such violence, and in many cases the police themselves harass and intimidate blacks. Half of the respondents in the Moscow survey described relations between police and Africans in Moscow as "very tense." Over one-quarter reported being physically assaulted by police. Even when police do take action against racial violence they rarely report the incidents as hate crimes.

Anti-black prejudice is not limited to street encounters between blacks and white Russians. Some blacks accuse the state of institutionalized racism. For example, an immigrant from CAMEROON studying aviation in Moscow complained of a "glass ceiling" for blacks in Russia. "Segregation happens because black people don't have Russian citizenship," he claimed, "So you get so far and then you can't get any further."

On the positive side, nearly half of the blacks surveyed in Moscow said they never hear racist comments from their employers or teachers. Some blacks, trading on both talent and the clear differences between themselves as "ordinary" Russians, have even become prominent media celebrities. An employee for a Russian refugee organization explains that "blacks have an exotic value in Russian advertising, fashion, and media." But, she also cautions, "Audiences lap up the TV shows, but would probably beat up a black celebrity if he or she moved in next door."

Roanne Edwards

Russwurm, John Brown

1799–1851

American publisher of first black newspaper, emigrationist, and Liberian government official.

Born John Brown to a slave mother and a white American merchant father in JAMAICA, he became John Russwurm when his stepmother demanded that his father acknowledge by name his paternity. Sent to Quebec for schooling, Russwurm was taken by his father to Portland, Maine, in 1812. He attended Hebron Academy in Hebron, Maine, and graduated in 1826 from Bowdoin College, one of the first black graduates of an American college. In his graduation speech he advocated the resettlement of American blacks to HAITI.

Moving to NEW YORK, NEW YORK, in 1827, Russwurm helped found FREEDOM'S JOURNAL with SAMUEL E(LI) CORNISH. It was the first black-owned and black-printed newspaper in the United States. The paper employed itinerant black abolitionists and urged an end to Southern slavery and Northern inequality. In February of 1829, he stopped publishing the paper and accepted a position as the superintendent of education in LIBERIA. He left for Liberia having given up hope that African Americans would have any future equality or prosperity in the United States.

In Liberia, in addition to his government position, he edited the *Liberia Herald* and served as a Liberian agent, recruiting American blacks to return to Africa. Russwurm became the first black governor of the Maryland area of Liberia in 1836, and worked to enhance the country's economic and diplomatic position.

Rustin, Bayard

1910–1987

African American civil rights leader and political organizer.

Bayard Rustin was born in West Chester, Pennsylvania, into a Quaker family, and the pacifism he learned from the Society of Friends remained with him his entire life. After a comfortable childhood in West Chester, he studied at West Chester State College. Before graduating, he moved to HARLEM, NEW YORK, during the 1930s and began studying at City College, while singing in local clubs with African American folk artists Josh White and Huddie Ledbetter. Attracted to the Young Communist League's stance on race issues, Rustin joined the group in 1936 and worked as an organizer until 1941, when he quit the party.

His resistance to the government, however, continued throughout 1941 when Rustin was asked by African American civil rights leader A. PHILIP RANDOLPH to help plan a 1941 march on WASHINGTON, D.C., to protest discrimination in defense industries. The march was called off when President Roosevelt made concessions. During World War II (1939–1945), Rustin traveled to California to help interned Japanese Americans protect their property. As a pacifist, Rustin spent two and a half years in prison for refusing to serve in the military.

Rustin's involvement in the Fellowship of Reconciliation (FOR), a radical pacifist movement, connected him to the establishment of the New York branch of the CONGRESS OF RACIAL EQUALITY (CORE). Throughout the 1940s and 1950s he led weekend seminars on nonviolent action for both groups. Rustin helped organize the MONTGOMERY BUS BOYCOTT in 1955, and he was also involved in the formation of the SOUTHERN CHRISTIAN LEADERSHIP CONFERENCE (SCLC). He served as the coordinator of the MARCH ON WASHINGTON, 1963, an event attended by 200,000 people. Rustin was arrested twenty-three times, but he continued to believe that racial equality should be pursued through nonviolent means.

See also Leadbelly; Quakers; World War II and African Americans.

Bibliography
Anderson, Jervis. *Bayard Rustin: Troubles I've Seen, a Biography.* HarperCollins Publishers, 1997.

Rwagasore, Prince Louis

1930–1961

Prince and popular nationalist leader who was elected prime minister on the eve of Burundian independence, but then was assassinated before taking office.

Louis Rwagasore is perhaps the most prominent personification of national reconciliation as well as the tragedy of BURUNDI. His legitimacy as a nationalist leader representing all Burundians was well-founded. The eldest son of King MWAMBUTSA IV, Rwagasore belonged to the Batare dynasty of the predominantly Tutsi *ganwa,* the aristocracy that had historically dominated Burundi's social hierarchy. But his father's clan, the Bambutsa, had remained outside colonial-era disputes between the Batare and the Bezi, and Rwagasore was equally uninterested in provincial rivalries. In the 1950s he studied politics and administration at the Institut Universitaire des Territories d'Outre-Mer in Antwerp, Belgium, and when he returned to Burundi, his father gave him a chiefdom in the Butanyerera district to administer. Ambitious, he became active in advising UPRONA, the leading nationalist party of Urundi, at its inception. His royal lineage also gave legitimacy to UPRONA and he pushed the party to demand independence. In 1959 he married Marie-Rose Ntamikevyo, a Hutu, thus spreading his appeal among Urundi's Hutu majority. Many Burundians believed that Rwagasore's physical features, more typically associated with Hutu than Tutsi, also helped him build transethnic support for the nationalist cause.

Appearances and family ties aside, Rwagasore was a charismatic and inspiring speaker. Belgian colonial officials nicknamed him "the Red Prince" after he appealed to all Burundians to "shake off foreign domination and end slavery." Concerned not only about the prince's obvious popularity but also about his apparent communist leanings, the colonial administration placed Rwagasore under house arrest in late 1960. With independence inevitable, however, the Belgians released Rwagasore. In the September 1961 general elections, UPRONA won overwhelmingly, and the prince became the prime minister-designate. But on October 13 a Greek gunman hired by leaders of the opposition party, who represented the Bezi clan, assassinated Rwagasore, who was dining at the Bon Accueil restaurant on banks of LAKE TANGANYIKA. (In a bizarre twist of events, Rwagasore's father, the king, unknowingly gave a ride to the assassin, whose car had broken down as he fled the scene.) In Burundi, Rwagasore has become a martyr of national reconciliation, and is still considered the one person who could have prevented Burundi's descent into decades of violence.

See also Hutu and Tutsi.

Eric Young

Rwanda

Central African country bordered by Uganda, Tanzania, Burundi, and the Democratic Republic of Congo.

Known as "the land of a thousand hills," Rwanda is one of Africa's smallest and most densely populated countries. Located in a region of fertile land and ample rainfall, precolonial Rwandan society was—according to early European visitors—prosperous and orderly; but it was also extremely hierarchical. A centuries-old TUTSI monarchy ruled over a bureaucracy of chiefs, who in turn collected tribute from HUTU commoners. Under German and then Belgian COLONIAL RULE, stratification in Rwanda grew wider and more rigid, with disastrous consequences. Since that time, social, political, and cultural divisions between Tutsis and Hutus have produced a series of revolutions and civil wars that have killed and displaced millions of Rwandans. Conflict within Rwanda has fueled—and been fueled by—conflicts elsewhere in the Great Lakes region, which includes BURUNDI, UGANDA, and the DEMOCRATIC REPUBLIC OF THE CONGO. Meanwhile, Rwanda faces severe land shortages, poverty, and public health problems.

Early Rwandan Society

The earliest inhabitants of the Great Lakes region were the ancestors of the present-day TWA people (once referred to as the PYGMY by Europeans), who now account for about 1 percent of Rwanda's population. Probably around 1000 B.C.E., BANTU-speaking people from Central Africa began to settle in the fertile highlands that define the landscape of Rwanda and Burundi. Slowly in the course of a long process of political centralization, these people became identified as Hutu; this identity group now constitutes cultivators (although they also raise cattle) as well as the majority of Rwanda's population.

Around the end of the fourteenth century, the region's existing population was joined by new cultural groups who sometimes became identified as Tutsi. Contemporary events have made this period of Rwandan history a subject of great dispute, but at least a few sources indicate that the Tutsi pastoralists coexisted peacefully with the cultivators, at least initially. They intermarried, and came to share the same language—Kinyarwanda—and many of the same social and religious customs, including participation in the *kubandwa* possession cult.

Over the course of several centuries a kingdom gradually emerged in the area of Lake Muhazi. Through a process of conquest and assimilation, this kingdom eventually encompassed about half the area of present-day Rwanda by the end of the nineteenth century. The king, or *mwami*, was considered the physical personification of the land itself. He presided over a large court—many Twa served as court storytellers, dancers, and guards—and an elaborate bureaucracy of chiefs. Each province was administered by chiefs who had three types of responsibilities: administration of agricultural lands, supervision of grazing lands and cattle, and recruitment of soldiers for the king's army. In some areas these administrative responsibilities were divided and carried out by separate individuals, particularly in the central regions of the kingdom. Elsewhere the roles were combined under the authority of a single chief. Where separate chiefs existed for the administration of agricultural lands, these were sometimes Hutu; but Tutsi typically occupied most positions of high political authority.

As the monarchy expanded, it promoted a series of clientship relations, which bound people of different social status in relations of mutual obligation. Under the form of clientship known as *ubuhake,* for example, clients received cattle and protection from a patron, and in return owed the patron their loyalty and service. The patron was also supposed to provide land (though ironically, this land might actually have been expropriated from the client's family or neighbors). From the early nineteenth century, ubuhake spread in association with increased control over land by political authorities. A patron (*shebuja*) was typically Tutsi, but the client (*umugaragu*) could be a Tutsi or a Hutu. A Hutu who gained significant wealth and married a Tutsi woman might, over time, come to be regarded as Tutsi—a process (popularly referred to as *kwiihutura*) that might take a couple of generations and was not available to most people. Conversely, a Tutsi family that fell on hard times and lost its cattle might come to be regarded as "Hutu" over time. Thus, Hutu and Tutsi identity was not defined only by birth; nor were all Tutsi wealthy and powerful. However, high status and political power remained firmly associated with Tutsi identity.

Rwanda under Colonial Rule

As European powers moved to colonize Africa in the late nineteenth century, the Great Lakes region became one of the most contested parts of the continent, in part because the European powers—Great Britain especially—sought control over the source of the NILE RIVER. At the 1884–1886 BERLIN CONFERENCE, GREAT BRITAIN and GERMANY agreed to split the region. Great Britain took the kingdom of BUGANDA and surrounding areas (now known as Uganda), while Germany took Rwanda and the neighboring kingdom of Burundi. The territory of "Ruanda-Urundi," along with the vast territory now known as mainland TANZANIA, together became part of GERMAN EAST AFRICA.

Over the next several years the Berlin agreement meant little in Rwanda, except that a few German explorers passed through. In 1895, however, the death of King Kigeli Rwabugiri led to a violent struggle over succession, the Coup of Rucunshu. This important event pitted members of the powerful

Abega clan (one of four clans that provided queen mothers for successive Rwandan monarchs) against members of the royal Abanyiginya clan. Kanjogera, an Abega clan member and one of Rwabugiri's wives, had been appointed adoptive queen mother of Rutarindwa, the son of Rwabugiri and legitimate heir to the throne. But after Rwabugiri's death, Kanjogera plotted with her brothers to overthrow Rutarindwa. After several bloody battles the Abega emerged victorious; Rutarindwa and his key supporters and ritual specialists were killed, and the Abega proceeded to purge Abanyiginya political authorities and their associates. Kanjogera and her brothers then enthroned Kanjogera's own son Musinga. He was a young boy at the time, so during the early years of German rule it was Musinga's mother and maternal uncles who wielded power at court. They developed a modus vivendi with German-led troops, who, they hoped, would help them extend and consolidate the kingdom.

French as well as German Roman Catholic missionaries also arrived around the turn of the century. Like the colonial administrators, they took the Tutsi's political dominance—as well as their typically tall, thin stature—as an indication of Tutsi racial superiority. Missionaries, in fact, were among the proponents of the now-discredited Hamitic theory, which held that the Tutsi were "caucasoids" from a faraway land (though it was never clear exactly where).

For the Germans, the presence of the Rwandan monarchy eased their own task of colonial rule, even as the presence of the Germans helped the Rwandan royal court to expand its territorial control. In some areas Tutsi political authorities took advantage of German military backing to increase demands on the population for labor, services, and tributes of various kinds. These demands fell particularly heavily on Hutu, creating intense resentment among the rural population. In the north, a region that had never been under firm control of the royal court, efforts by the court to impose Tutsi authorities from central Rwanda met with stiff resistance. In 1911 a Hutu revolt in the region was quashed by Tutsi troops, with help from German military force. This defeat fueled lasting anti-Tutsi sentiment in the north, which later became a stronghold of Hutu nationalism.

Unlike the intense exploitation which took place in German colonies such as German South-West Africa (now NAMIBIA) and Kamerun (now CAMEROON), the German colonial presence in Ruanda-Burundi was hardly visible, except for the experimental attempts at growing export crops undertaken on the region's sloping farmlands. Germany's presence was also short-lived: Germany lost all its African colonies after World War I. Belgium, already the ruler of the massive Belgian Congo, took over control of Ruanda-Urundi.

Like Germany, Belgium adopted a policy of indirect rule, which meant it relied heavily on the monarchy to collect taxes, recruit labor, and maintain social order. For these purposes, the ubuhake system was preserved, but the demands made on the Hutu peasants were greatly intensified. They were required to perform forced labor and pay steep taxes, and if they failed to do so they risked losing their land. In addition, the system of provincial administration with competing authorities, which had traditionally helped to prevent abuses of power in some areas, was replaced by a system in which a single Tutsi chief, according to scholar René Lemarchand, exercised "unfettered control over his people." The resulting exploitation left much of the Hutu population dangerously vulnerable to famine during poor harvest years. Irregular rainfall also hurt yields of coffee—the colony's main export crop, and one that Hutu farmers were required to cultivate.

The rigid ethnic categories implicit in the colonial era hierarchy became official in 1933, when the Belgian administration began requiring all colonial subjects to carry passes identifying themselves as either Tutsi, Hutu, or Twa. No longer could wealthy Hutu become Tutsified—now ethnic identity became absolute and permanent. It also became a means of defining access to education, which for much of the colonial period was provided primarily by the Roman Catholic missions. Children of the Tutsi elite more easily found places in primary schools,

Years of ethnic conflict forced many Rwandans to seek shelter in neighboring countries. Refugee children are shown here in 1994 lining up for food. *Davis Turnley/CORBIS*

and were offered a separate, more challenging curriculum than that of Hutu children. Although few Rwandans had access to secondary schools, of those who did, a larger proportion of Tutsi than Hutu were able to complete primary school and continue beyond it. Indeed, until the early 1950s the elite government-sponsored secondary school in Butare (then called Astrida) retained a minimum height requirement for admission, which effectively excluded students shorter than the prototypically tall Tutsi. Hutu boys were generally only able to pursue further studies in the Roman Catholic seminaries, which were designed to encourage young men to enter the priesthood. The favored treatment of Tutsi in the school system was in part intended to ensure that the elite associated with the monarchy and the colonial civil service shared the values and Christian beliefs of their colonizers.

The Belgians went to considerable lengths to ensure that Tutsi authorities would adopt Christianity. In 1931 they deposed Musinga for recalcitrance and refusal to abandon "pagan" practices. Musinga's son Rudahigwa, who was installed by the Belgians as the new king, embraced Roman Catholicism and cultivated good relations with the Roman Catholic Church as well as the Belgian administration.

In 1945 Ruanda-Urundi became a United Nations (UN) Trust Territory, still under Belgian control. The postwar period, however, saw dramatic pressures for change. From 1947, regular visits to Rwanda by a Visiting Mission of the United Nations Trusteeship Council subjected Belgian policies to outside scrutiny and provided a forum for the expression of discontent by Rwandans. For the first time, in the early 1950s the glaring inequalities in Rwandan society began to receive public attention. Rural dwellers were restive, chafing under heavy labor demands, burdensome rules associated with coffee cultivation (often enforced in abusive fashion), insecure access to land, and the exploitative practices of Tutsi authorities and their henchmen. A new generation of European missionaries showed sympathy for the plight of the Hutu, and provided encouragement to a small core of Hutu leaders who had been educated in Roman Catholic seminaries. During the 1950s a Kinyarwanda-language newspaper, *Kinyamateka*, began to serve as a forum for political debate. Critiques by Hutu activists

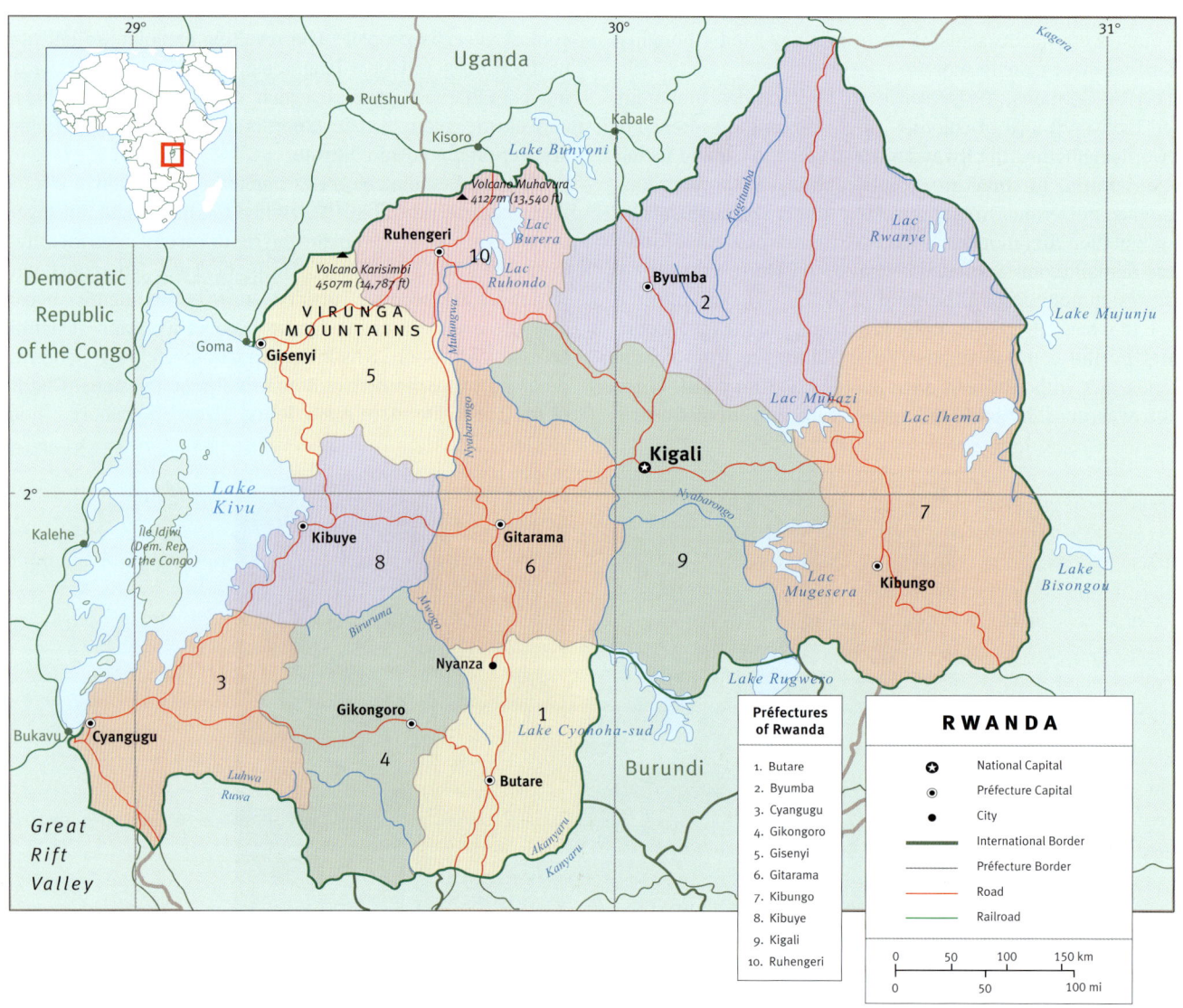

drew attention to inequalities between Hutu and Tutsi and deplored indignities experienced by Hutu at the hands of Tutsi political authorities. These critics also identified conflicts over land as a key issue.

Aware of pressures for change, the Belgian administration introduced indirect elections for local councils, held in 1953 and 1957. These elections provoked anxiety among Tutsi authorities, as the implications of potential ethnic voting blocks became clear. The final years of the decade were marked by a complicated contest over how and when decolonization should occur. In the 1957 Bahutu Manifesto, a Hutu counter-elite challenged the monopoly of power held by Tutsi authorities, and called for reforms to remove the discrimination experienced by Hutu throughout the colonial period. In response, conservative elders at the royal court asserted publicly that Hutu had no right to claim a role in governance. In this charged political atmosphere, hard-liners associated with the royal court began to demand immediate independence from Belgium. Hutu activists countered that independence should wait until the state had been democratized, so as to provide opportunities for Hutu to participate politically.

These positions divided the two main political parties which emerged in Rwanda during this period: the Rwandan National Union (UNAR), a monarchist party with its main following among Tutsi, and the Party for the Emancipation of the Hutu (PARMEHUTU), a pro-Hutu party militating for the interests of Hutu. Another party, Association for the Social Promotion of the Masses (APROSOMA), aimed initially to mobilize all poor people, but appealed mainly to Hutu, while the Democratic Rwandan Assembly was a party of moderate Tutsi, supported by the Belgian administration, who favored political reforms and a constitutional monarchy.

Revolution, Independence, and Republic

The Bahutu Manifesto provided ideological justification for the Rwandan Revolution, which began in central Rwanda in November 1959 as a rural revolt. Triggered by an assault on a Hutu subchief by a group of Tutsi youths, the violence quickly spread to the northwest areas of the country, and, later, to other regions as well. Gangs of Hutu moved from hill to hill, attacking Tutsi authorities and wealthy Tutsi, forcing them to flee, and burning their homes. Belgium attempted to reestablish order by bringing in troops from the Belgian Congo, and appointing Colonel Guy Logiest as military head of the administration in Rwanda. Finding it impossible to continue relying on Tutsi chiefs because of rural resistance, Logiest openly supported PARMEHUTU and assisted in ousting Tutsi authorities, replacing them with Hutu. In September 1961 Rwandans voted in UN-supervised elections to abolish the monarchy and elect Grégoire Kayibanda as president. Meanwhile, more than 100,000 Rwandans, most of them Tutsi, had fled into neighboring countries by the time Rwanda became independent on July 1, 1962.

Under President Kayibanda, the First Republic (1962–1973) was led by Hutu, mostly from southern and central Rwanda. It began and ended with violence. In 1963 a group of armed Rwandan Tutsi exiles invaded Rwanda from Burundi; though the attack was repulsed, the invaders came within about eight kilometers (five miles) of the capital, Kigali. Frightened by this threat, Kayibanda's government allowed (or ordered) the massacre of an estimated 10,000 Tutsi living within the country, thus making the internal population scapegoats for the activities of Tutsi exiles. Ten years later, after Burundi's Tutsi-dominated government and military massacred an estimated 250,000 Hutu, Kayibanda's regime retaliated against Rwandan Tutsi. As the violence increased, a group of northern Hutu, led by General Juvénal Habyarimana, seized power and proclaimed the Second Republic in July 1973.

Calling for national unity while executing ministers from the First Republic, President Habyarimana surrounded himself with a close-knit group of supporters, many of whom were his relatives. A new constitution, instituted in 1975, established the National Revolutionary Movement for Development (MRND) as the only legal political party, and Habyarimana was easily reelected three times over the next fourteen years. Reinforcing a regime that was actually more authoritarian than was the case under Kayibanda, Habyarimana significantly extended the reach of the central government into local communities. His stance toward the Tutsi, however, was more moderate than Kayibanda's. Until the late 1980s the main axes of conflict in Rwanda under Habyarimana were less ethnicity than region and class. Higher status jobs, scholarships, and funds for development went disproportionately to the president's home region in the north, and the gap between a tiny wealthy minority (connected to the government) and the majority of the population became ever wider.

In 1976 Rwanda joined with Burundi and Zaire to form the Economic Community of the Great Lakes Countries (CEPGL). But efforts to coordinate economic development in the region were undermined by ongoing civil conflicts. Refugees from these conflicts were often resented abroad, and many joined their host countries' rebel movements. Many Tutsi refugees in Uganda, for example, helped that country's rebels (among them future Ugandan president YOWERI MUSEVENI) overthrow first IDI AMIN in the 1979 and then MILTON OBOTE in 1985. These Tutsi fighters formed the core of the Rwandan Patriotic Front (RPF), a group determined to win the right to return to their country. In addition, they claimed to want democratic reforms in Rwanda, including the end of one-party rule.

Turmoil and Genocide

Armed and supported financially by Museveni, the RPF's 6,000 troops entered Rwanda from the north in October 1990. They were met by not only the relatively small Rwandan army, but also forces sent by Zaire's President MOBUTU SESE SEKO and paratroopers provided by France, all of whom preferred to maintain Rwanda's status quo. The Habyarimana regime's immediate response to the RPF threat was to jail thousands of suspected sympathizers.

By June 1991, however, in response to pressures for reform from internal groups and foreign donors, Habyarimana had

Rwanda (At a Glance)

Official Name: Rwandese Republic

Area: 26,338 sq km (10,169 sq mi)

Location: Central Africa; borders Burundi, Tanzania, Uganda, the Democratic Republic of the Congo (formerly Zaire)

Capital: Kigali (population 232,733); 1991 estimate

Other Major Cities: Butare (population 28,645); 1991 estimate

Population: 7,810,056 (2003 estimate); genocide and civil war in 1994 killed more than one million Rwandans and forced more than two million to flee to neighboring countries.

Population Density: 296 persons per sq km (about 768 persons per sq mi); 2003 estimate

Population Below Age 15: Total population: 42.5 percent (male 1,667,128; female 1,651,422); 2003 estimate

Population Growth Rate: 1.84 percent (2003 estimate)

Total Fertility Rate: 5.6 children born per woman (2003 estimate)

Life Expectancy at Birth: Total population: 39.33 years (male 38.51 years; female 40.18 years); 2003 estimate

Infant Mortality Rate: 102.61 deaths per 1,000 live births (2003 estimate)

Literacy Rate (age 15 and over can read and write): Total population: 70.4 percent (male 76.3 percent; female 64.7 percent); 2003 estimate

Education: Compulsory in principle for children aged 7 through 15. In the early 1990s primary school enrollment in Rwanda was about 1.1 million, and secondary and technical schools had about 70,000 students.

Languages: The official languages are Kinyarwanda (a Bantu language), French, and English. Kiswahili is also used in commercial centers.

Ethnic Groups: Rwanda is composed of three principle ethnic groups. The Hutu constitute about 84 percent of the total population; the Tutsi, about 15 percent; and the Twa, 1 percent. The Twa are thought to be the original inhabitants of the region.

Religions: About 56.5 percent of the population is Catholic, about 11 percent is Adventist, about 4.6 percent is Muslim, and some 26 percent is Protestant.

Climate: Rwanda is temperate. It has two rainy seasons (from February to April and November to January). Weather is mild in the mountains with frost and snow possible. The average yearly rainfall is 787 mm (31 in) and is heaviest in the western and northwestern mountain regions. Wide temperature variations occur because of elevation differences. The average daily temperature in the Lake Kivu area is 22.8° C (73° F). In the mountains in the northwest, frost occurs at night.

Land, Plants, and Animals: The central portion of Rwanda is dominated by a hilly plateau averaging about 1,700 m (about 5,600 ft) in elevation. On the western side of the plateau is a mountain system averaging about 2,740 m (about 9,000 ft), forming the watershed between the Nile and Congo river systems. The Virunga Mountains, a volcanic range that forms the northern reaches of this system, include Volcan Karisimbi (4,507 m/14,787 ft), Rwanda's highest peak. Forests containing eucalyptus, acacia, and oil palms are concentrated in the western mountains and the Lake Kivu area. Wildlife includes elephants, hippopotamuses, crocodiles, wild boars, leopards, antelope, and lemurs. The Virunga Mountains in northern Rwanda are home to what is estimated to be half of the world's remaining mountain gorillas.

Natural Resources: Gold, cassiterite (tin ore), wolframite (tungsten ore), natural gas, hydropower

Currency: The Rwandan franc

Gross Domestic Product (GDP): $9 billion (2002 estimate)

GDP per Capita: $1,200 (2002 estimate)

GDP Real Growth Rate: 4 percent (2002 estimate)

Primary Economic Activities: Agriculture (45 percent of GDP, 90 percent of work force), industry (20 percent of GDP), services (35 percent of GDP); 2002 estimates

Primary Crops: Coffee, tea, pyrethrum (insecticide made from chrysanthemums), bananas, beans, sorghum, potatoes, livestock

Industries: Cement, agricultural processing, beverages, light consumer goods

Primary Exports: Coffee, tea, hides, cassiterite

Primary Imports: Foodstuffs, machines and equipment, capital goods, steel, petroleum products, cement, construction material

Primary Trade Partners: Germany, Belgium, Italy, Uganda, United Kingdom, France, United States, Kenya, Japan

Government: A constitution, promulgated in 1991 and adopted in 1995, provides for a multiparty democracy with a limited presidential term and independent executive, legislative, and judicial branches. In April 2000 Paul Kagame was elected as president for a five-year term. Bernard Makuza has served as prime minister since March, 2000. The Transitional National Assembly, a unicameral legislature with seventy seats, was established in 1994 and expanded by four seats in 2001. Under the Arusha peace agreement, the number of seats in the assembly was divided among nine political parties. In 2003, Kagame was reelected in the country's first multiparty legislative elections.

agreed to end one-party rule and allow opposition parties to form. Months later, representatives from the former ruling party and the four main opposition parties were included in a coalition government with Habyarimana. Several new parties sprang up, including the multiethnic Liberal Party. Habyarimana also agreed to negotiate with the RPF and the opposition parties. At the same time, however, hard-line Hutu nationalists in Habyarimana's party and the equally hard-line Coalition for the Defense of the Republic (CDR) were recruiting militia troops. The yearlong negotiations, held in ARUSHA, TANZANIA, in 1992–1993, led to a cease-fire between the government and the RPF, as well as an agreement to form a power-sharing transitional government. The hard-line groups, who were left out of the talks and adamantly opposed the results, retaliated by killing Tutsi civilians, including some 300 in one attack in Gisenyi.

Into this already turbulent atmosphere came the voice of an increasingly virulent media. The monthly magazine *Kangura* had in 1990 published its "Call to the Conscience of the Bahutu Peoples," which proclaimed that "Hutu should stop feeling pity for the Tutsi," and that they should "regard as a traitor every Hutu" who did not join in the anti-Tutsi movement. By 1993 the independent radio station Mille Collines (Thousand Hills)—owned by close associates of Habyiramana—urged Hutu to kill the *inyenzi*, or cockroaches, as it called Uganda-born Tutsi. "The grave is only half full," Mille Collines broadcasts blared, asking, "Who will help us fill it?" Such propaganda cast all Tutsi, not just the RPF, as the enemy.

The "enemy" in these broadcasts was presented as an economic as well as political threat—in particular, as a potential thief of Hutu land. Given that the land was already scarce in Rwanda, this was an incendiary charge. Rwanda's economy was in particularly poor shape due to declining world coffee prices, and the Tutsi became a convenient scapegoat for all the country's ills.

In October 1993 the assassination of Burundi's Hutu president Melchior Ndadaye by Tutsi elements in the Burundi army further inflamed tensions in Rwanda. These finally exploded after a plane carrying both Hamyarimana and Burundi's new president, Cyprien Ntariyamira, was shot down over Kigali on April 6, 1994. Although responsibility for the fatal crash remained unclear years later, Hutu hard-liners in the late president's party immediately blamed the RPF.

Just hours after the crash, the Hutu militia (known as *interahamwe*, meaning "those who stand together") began killing both Hutu and Tutsi leaders of the moderate political parties, including members of the transitional government. All of the victims had been identified on a list circulated even before the plane's downing. In the following weeks and months the killing escalated at a horrific rate. The militias set up roadblocks and killed all those with Tutsi identity cards. Some people whose cards identified them as Hutu were also killed, if they were suspected of Tutsi sympathies or if they appeared more Tutsi than Hutu. In addition, militia members searched each hillside to meet the deadline set by Mille Collines radio broadcasts, which stated that "by 5 May, the country must be completely cleansed of Tutsi." The churches offered no sanctuary; some were forcibly invaded, and others were run by priests and nuns who collaborated with the militia. These churches became sites of some of the worst massacres in the genocide.

According to the medical aid group Médecins Sans Frontières, by the end of April an estimated 100,000 people had been killed, mostly by such weapons as machetes and spiked wooden clubs. Rapes were also common. By July, the genocide had claimed more than one-half million victims, and an estimated two million refugees had fled into Burundi, TANZANIA, and Zaire (present-day Democratic Republic of the Congo. The killers included not only interahamwe troops, but also villagers who received orders to kill. Although some Hutu families sheltered Tutsi friends and relatives, they did so at risk to their own lives.

International Response and Aftermath

Although the UN had established an assistance mission to Rwanda (UNAMIR) in October 1993, it did virtually nothing to stop the killings. In fact, the UN Security Council reduced the mission's troops from 2,500 to 270 soon after the genocide started. According to many observers, the UN's hands were tied in part by the United States which, after its highly unpopular participation in an earlier UN peacekeeping mission in SOMALIA, refused to support another intervention in a dangerous and strategically insignificant African country.

Among non-African countries, France alone responded to the Rwandan crisis, securing a large portion of southwestern Rwanda in its Operation Turquoise. The security zone undoubtedly saved some lives, but it also allowed leaders of the hard-line Hutu groups an escape route to the west. Later, in the postgenocide period, elements from the former Rwandan army and from militia groups used refugee camps in neighboring eastern Zaire as a base for incursions into western Rwanda. This created a dilemma for international humanitarian agencies; in providing food, shelter, and medical care to the refugees, most of whom were women and children, they were also aiding militia members, who were visibly indistinguishable from other camp residents.

Throughout the genocide, RPF troops had been advancing on Kigali. They finally took control of the capital on July 4, 1994, and proclaimed a new multiparty government. Both the appointed president, Pasteur Bizimungu, and the prime minister, Faustin Twagiramungu, were Hutu, but most observers agree that from the beginning the government's real leader was Vice President and Defense Minister General PAUL KAGAME, a long-time RPF member. Many of the cabinet and military posts were held by fellow Tutsi from Uganda or other neighboring countries.

The government promised that the genocide's perpetrators would receive swift justice, and by late 1995 an estimated 80,000 Hutu suspects had been arrested. Many died of disease in desperately overcrowded jails while awaiting trial. Rwanda's barely functioning justice system was incapable of trying so many people, and has since proven unable to protect Rwandans in their own villages, where not only the militia but also the army have killed suspected foes. The return of hundreds of thousands of exiled Tutsi after the RPF took power also led to local-level conflicts over property; many Hutu were removed from their homes by force. In addition, clashes between the militia and the army have continued.

In November 1994 the UN Security Council established the International Criminal Tribunal for Rwanda in Arusha, Tanzania. Charged with "prosecuting persons responsible for genocide and other serious violations of international humanitarian law," the tribunal initially moved extremely slowly. Delays were caused by everything from frequent power outages to difficulty bringing to trial the leading suspects, many of whom had fled abroad. Rwanda itself, which lacked trained personnel and had rejected offers from other countries to provide judges and lawyers, began trials only in 1997. In early 1998 the Rwandan government began carrying out death sentences against convicted *genocidaires*.

In the late 1990s Rwanda was plagued not only by internal violence but also by severe economic and public health problems, and by the destabilizing effect of conflict elsewhere in the Great Lakes region. The production of coffee—still the country's main export—had suffered from years of rural dislocation and insecurity, as had food crop production. A $600 million aid package from the European Community in the mid-1990s was expected to help restore the nation's economy, but, in the face of a serious shortage of arable land, farming remained an impoverished livelihood for most of Rwanda's overwhelmingly rural population. In addition, much of the Kagera National Park, home to some of the greatest diversity of animal life in Africa, has reportedly been taken over by cattle herders displaced by war.

With an average fertility rate of six children per woman, Rwanda has one of the highest population growth rates in Africa. Close ties between the Roman Catholic Church and health services have traditionally helped keep family planning programs to a minimum, and some reports suggest birth rates actually rose after the genocide, as many woman tried to rebuild destroyed families. Rwanda also has one of the highest rates of ACQUIRED IMMUNODEFICIENCY SYNDROME (AIDS) infection in Africa, as well as high rates of malnutrition, MALARIA, and tuberculosis.

Even after reported HUMAN RIGHTS abuses, Rwanda's government in the late 1990s continued to enjoy strong support from the United States and Europe, where Kagame was seen to belong to a "new generation" of pragmatic, competent African leaders. Regional instability, however, continued to threaten Rwanda's recovery, as demonstrated by the renewed fighting along the Democratic Republic of the Congo border in mid-1998. Many Tutsi on both sides of the border helped Laurent-Désiré Kabila topple then-Zaire's President Mobutu. But Kabila, facing pressure within his own country, purged his military of Rwandan and Congolese Tutsi in 1997. This breach of trust, combined with the continuing agitation of Hutu refugees in Congo, led Rwanda's government to back an armed rebellion against Kabila's government in the Democratic Republic of the Congo during 1998.

See also Ethnicity in Rwanda; Scramble for Africa; Population Growth in Sub-Saharan Africa; Radio, African; United Nations in Africa.

Kate Tuttle

S

Saar, Betye Irene

1926–

African American artist best known for three-dimensional explorations of history, memory, cultural identity, and spirituality.

Born Betye Brown in LOS ANGELES, CALIFORNIA, Betye Saar (pronounced Say-er) is the daughter of Jefferson and Beatrice Brown. She married artist Richard Saar shortly after earning a B.A. degree in design from the University of California at Los Angeles (UCLA) in 1949. Saar pursued graduate studies at California State University at Long Beach, the University of Southern California, and California State University at Northridge. She has taught at UCLA and at the Parsons-Otis Institute.

Although Saar began as a printmaker and graphic designer, she later made a transition to three-dimensional work. The work that marked this turning point was *Black Girl's Window* (1969), in which Saar placed a print of an African American girl into a segmented window frame with existing objects. She gradually replaced prints in her assemblages with existing objects. She has increased the scale of her work to include room-sized installations, in which she explores ritual and mysticism. In *Mojotech* (1988), an installation created for the Massachusetts Institute of Technology, Saar investigates the relation between technology and magic by creating altars that juxtapose high-tech objects, such as circuit boards, with traditional religious items.

Saar has had solo shows at California State University, Los Angeles and the Museum of Contemporary Art, also in Los Angeles, as well as the Whitney Museum of American Art, New York. Her work is in the permanent collections of the Philadelphia Museum of Art and the Smith College Museum of Art. She was one of two artists who represented the United States in the 1994 São Paulo Biennial in Brazil. One of her most famous pieces is *The Liberation of Aunt Jemima* (1972), which depicts the "mammy" figure, Aunt Jemima, conventionally valued for her reassuring gentleness, as an armed warrior. Along with the mop in her right hand, she holds a gun in her left. This is an expression of Saar's political outlook, which was shaped by the civil rights movement of the 1960s.

See also Artists, African American

Robert Fay

Sab

Ethnic group of Somalia.

The Sab primarily inhabit southern SOMALIA. They speak SOMALI, an Afro-Asiatic language, although they are believed to be partly of Bantu origin. They are sometimes considered a low-status subgroup of the Somali people, and some people called Sab find the label derogatory. The group numbers roughly 500,000.

See also Bantu: Dispersion and Settlement; Languages, African: An Overview.

Saco, José Antonio

1797–1879

White Cuban intellectual who wrote one of the first extensive histories of slavery in Spanish America and promoted abolition in order to decrease the number of blacks in Cuba.

José Antonio Saco received what was a typical education for Catholic boys in early-nineteenth-century CUBA. He first studied in a small schoolhouse next to his home and later transferred to a Catholic school in Santiago de Cuba. Saco continued higher-level education in modern philosophy at the San Carlos seminar in HAVANA. Under the tutelage of Father Félix Varela y Morales, one of the most influential professors and prominent intellectuals of his time, Saco studied with a group of young men who were to become representatives of the urban bourgeoisie that promoted the independence of Cuba from

SPAIN. In his autobiography Saco claims that these early years with Varela, who provided guidance and friendship and whom Saco considered the "most virtuous man" he ever met, were definitive in the formation of his thinking and ideology.

In 1821 Varela asked Saco to take over his seminar in philosophy. This initiated Saco's academic work as a lecturer in philosophy, physics, and chemistry. Later in his life Saco promoted education as a political tool that should adapt to the needs of the country. He felt that without education there would be no progress and advocated that schooling be both free and mandatory. Saco was in favor of education for women, as was his mentor Varela. This seemingly progressive perspective, however, did not include black Cubans as equal members of society.

In 1828 Saco traveled to NEW YORK, NEW YORK and founded *El Mensajero Quincenal* (The Quarterly Messenger), a liberal publication that discussed the problems of continuing with the illegal slave trade to Cuba. In 1830 Saco wrote *Memoria sobre la vagancia* (Memoir on Vagrancy), in which he describes the causes of Cuba's backwardness and gives possible solutions. One of the chapters, entitled "People of Color in the Arts" suggests that certain trades were no longer honorable in Cuba because blacks had become highly involved in them. In 1834 Saco was forced into exile in Trinidad for writing an article that identified him as a significant political critic and leader.

Toward the end of the nineteenth century a massive number of black slaves was imported to Cuba to support the growing SUGAR industry. This increase in the black population and the potential for uprisings (real and imagined) was a cause of great concern among members of the white privileged class of Cuba, who were beginning to conceive a Cuban identity that did not include blacks. Saco became a spokesman for the white middle classes, promoting abolition with the goal of diminishing the role and influence of black people in Cuba. He thought that by encouraging white immigration and miscegenation the island could counterbalance the demographic effects of the slave trade and become a modern and democratic society.

Saco lived almost half of his life—from 1834 to 1879—in exile and wrote prolifically while abroad. It was in exile that Saco wrote his greatest work: the five-volume *Historia de la esclavitud* (History of Slavery; 1875–1879). The introduction to *History of Slavery* calls for the immigration of workers "white and free, from all parts of the world, all races, provided they have a white face and can do honest labor." Saco explicitly expressed his purpose in advocating abolition as well, stating: "I can not deny . . . that I ardently wish, not through violent means, but through pacific ones, the decrease, and if possible, the total extinction of the black race; and I wish it because at our current political state, they can be the most powerful instrument to destroy our island."

As a militant nationalist, Saco clashed with Spanish authorities and opposed the annexation of Cuba to the United States. His works were influential in the independence movement of the time and in the formation of a national identity based on a segregationist idea of society.

See also Conspiración de la Escalera; Cuban War of Independence; Education in Latin America and the Caribbean; Trinidad and Tobago.

Liliana Obregón

Sadat, Anwar al-

1918–1981

President of Egypt, winner of the 1978 Nobel Peace Prize, and the first Arab leader to recognize the state of Israel.

The son of a hospital clerk, Anwar Sadat was born in Mit Abu al-Kawm, a village on the Nile delta. He was part of the first generation of Egyptian soldiers recruited from the middle class rather than the elite, and graduated from Cairo Military Academy in 1938. During World War II (1939–1945), Sadat was twice arrested for conspiring with the Germans' campaign to drive the British from EGYPT. In 1950 he joined the Free Officers Committee Organization, chaired by GAMAL ABDEL NASSER. In 1952 he participated in Nasser's overthrow of the Egyptian monarchy.

After Nasser was elected president of Egypt in 1956, Sadat held various offices in the government, including two terms as vice president (1964–1966 and 1969–1970). After Nasser's death in September 1970, Sadat became president. Although his political opponents considered him an interim leader, he was elected president less than a month later. Sadat moved quickly to consolidate his support, loosening state control over the economy and relaxing restrictions on political activity. In addition, shortly after taking office, Sadat began to strengthen the Egyptian military, which had been soundly defeated by Israel in the 1967 Six-Day War.

Sadat's tenure was marked by an emphasis on foreign policy. In 1972 he expelled Soviet military advisers, signaling an end to Egypt's close ties with the Eastern Bloc. On October 6, 1973, Egypt and Syria attacked Israel, launching the Yom Kippur War. After Egypt's initial successes, Israel took the offensive. Although Egypt did not win the war, it achieved his primary goal—to improve Egypt's negotiating position with Israel. In addition, as the first Arab military leader to reclaim land from Israel, Sadat earned enhanced prestige in the Arab world.

Sadat's lasting legacy was his peace settlement with Israel. In November 1977 he visited Jerusalem and presented his peace plan to the Israeli Knesset (Parliament). Despite widespread criticism from the Arab world, Sadat held a series of diplomatic meetings with Israel, culminating in the Camp David Accords in 1979, in which Egypt normalized relations with Israel. In response, the Arab League promptly expelled Egypt and severed economic ties with the country. (Egypt was readmitted to the Arab League in 1987.) For his efforts to bring peace to the Middle East, Sadat was awarded the 1978 Nobel Peace Prize, which he shared with Israeli prime minister Menachem Begin.

On October 6, 1981, the anniversary of the Yom Kippur War, Sadat presided over a military parade in CAIRO. During the parade, a military vehicle stopped abruptly, and five soldiers who were later linked to an Islamic protest group leapt out and began firing machine guns and throwing hand grenades at the president. Sadat and six others were killed. He was succeeded by his vice president, HOSNI MUBARAK.

Robert Fay

Sade

1959–

Afro-British singer and songwriter known for her smooth and sultry voice.

Sade (pronounced Shar-day) was born Helen Folasade Adu in IBADAN, NIGERIA to a Nigerian economist and a British nurse. In 1963 her parents divorced and she, her brother, and her mother moved to GREAT BRITAIN. In her youth, Sade frequented dance clubs and developed a passion for JAZZ, FUNK, and SOUL MUSIC.

Sade did not at first consider a musical career, though she devoted all of her free time to music. She studied fashion in London and for a few years ran her own design business and supplemented her income by modeling. The manager of Pride, a London funk group, noticed her sensuous good looks and encouraged her to audition as a backup singer for the band, which she joined in the early 1980s.

London clubgoers loved Sade's subtle, restrained style. She developed a substantial following when she and Pride saxophonist Stuart Mathewman began writing songs and playing them between Pride sets. She soon left Pride and signed with Epic, which released her first album, *Diamond Life*, in 1984.

With the popularity of songs such as "Your Love Is King" and "Smooth Operator," *Diamond Life* soared to the top of the music charts in Great Britain and received rave reviews in America. It became the best-selling album by a British woman singer in history and won Sade the Grammy Award for best new artist. In 1985 Epic released the follow-up album, *Promise*, featuring the hit "Sweetest Taboo." *Stronger than Pride* (1988) went platinum within just two weeks of being on the music charts, and the song "No Ordinary Love" from the *Love Deluxe* album, released in 1992, won a Grammy for best rhythm and blues duo or group performance.

Sade values her privacy and seldom gives interviews. She was married briefly to filmmaker Carlos Scola, from 1989 to 1990. In 1995 she moved to JAMAICA to have a child with her partner, Bob Morgan, a record producer.

The Best of Sade, released in 2001, contains sixteen of the singer-songwriter's outstanding performances. Writing in the *New York Times*, Stephen Holden has said, "In a pop climate obsessed with changing sounds and the language of the street, Sade has shown herself to be a pop classicist . . . her best songs find fresh images for expressing time-honored sentiments . . . with a special intensity."

Bibliography

Bego, Mark. *Sade!* Paperjacks, 1986.

Leyla Keough

Safari Hunting

Organized big-game hunting by foreigners in Africa.

Safari, the Swahili term for an expedition, stems from the Arabic *safar*, "to journey." European explorers first used the word to refer to their treks inland from places such as ZANZIBAR. Colonists later adopted the term to describe their organized hunting expeditions, which began in the late nineteenth century.

Initially, European settlers hunted primarily for subsistence. A few colonists, however, became professional hunters. Roualeyn Gordon-Cumming was one such Englishman. During the 1850s his widely read books described his exploits in southern Africa, where he felled countless numbers of GIRAFFE and LION. Likewise, between 1894 and 1896 the Englishman Arthur H. Newman was reportedly the most successful elephant hunter on the continent.

By the turn of the century, however, the age of the "great white hunter" had already passed. The impact of hunting began to raise concerns about the possible extinction of many species. Hunting laws came into effect under the tenets of the 1890 Convention for the Preservation of Wild Animals, Birds, and Fish in Africa. This Anglo-German treaty set aside game reserves to protect species such as the white rhinoceros. Despite these efforts, however, hunting continued, and by 1910 an estimated two-thirds of Africa's three million elephants had been killed. These reserves were also meant to preserve only specific, highly prized species, such as the rhino. Professional full-time hunters continued to engage in "game control," the wholesale slaughter of unwanted species, primarily to clear areas for British settlers to establish farms.

The turn of the twentieth century also saw the rise of commercial safari expeditions that catered to the sport hunter. By this time, British East Africa's transportation infrastructure, including railroads, had developed sufficiently to attract affluent gentleman adventure-travelers eager to bag a lion or elephant and carry home the mane or tusks. Despite the high cost, hunters from Europe and North America traveled two to four weeks by ship to MOMBASA, KENYA. From there they continued by rail to NAIROBI. Although the conductor often stopped the train to allow sportsmen to shoot at elephants or giraffes, others simply took potshots from the moving train.

By the time Theodore Roosevelt visited the region in 1909, the word *safari* generally referred to "shooting expeditions." Safari hunts often involved large numbers of people. An entourage of MAASAI trackers and game drivers and KIKUYU cooks and porters would accompany a party of white hunters, usually on horseback. Roosevelt's unusually large safari included 265 porters and occupied sixty-four tents.

World War I temporarily dampened the growing safari industry. The British acquisition of Tanganyika (part of present-day TANZANIA), however, offered new challenges to wealthy sportsmen seeking "real adventure" who felt that KENYA had become too luxurious and commercial. World War II brought the wholesale slaughter of game by troops with automatic weapons, a trend that continued after the war. Worried about the rapidly diminishing amount of game, the colonial administrations in the late 1940s formed national parks such as SERENGETI NATIONAL PARK in East Africa and began enforcing hunting restrictions. By the 1950s, safari clients were mainly affluent North Americans who, inspired by Hollywood films, went to Kenya hoping to shoot a lion. But fewer and fewer of these hunters were licensed to hunt the Big Five: lion, elephant, leopard, rhino, and buffalo. Rather, photography became the main activity of safari participants. In the 1970s, Tanzania and Kenya banned safari hunting altogether.

See also Rhinoceros; Wildlife Management in Africa.

Ari Nave

Safari Rally

Automobile race held annually in Kenya.

Originally planned as a celebration of the coronation of Queen Elizabeth II in 1953, the Safari Rally has become one of the top events in professional rally racing. In this form of automobile racing, a driver and a navigator attempt to drive a course laid out on public roads within a specified period of time. The inaugural event, called the Coronation Safari, featured amateur drivers—farmers, businessmen, and garage owners—in unmodified cars racing through KENYA, UGANDA, and Tanganyika (now part of TANZANIA), which were then British colonies. By 1962 the rally developed into the East African Safari. It began attracting auto manufacturers and professional drivers from many countries, though Kenyans dominated it historically. Today, the race route is restricted to Kenya and is held under the jurisdiction of the Fédération Internationale de l'Automobile (FIA), a Paris-based international racing body that governs the world rallying circuit.

The course, which organizers constantly change to test the drivers, starts in Kenya's capital, NAIROBI, and may take the teams through the RIFT VALLEYS, past LAKE VICTORIA and LAKE TURKANA, and through coastal areas, including the city of MOMBASA. The race takes place each year around the Christian Easter holiday, and seasonal rains often leave unpaved portions of the course a treacherous series of mud and water holes. Drivers must fight through normal traffic on the paved portions of the road. Mechanical failure or accidents usually prevent more than two-thirds of the starters from finishing. The Safari Rally is rally racing's longest race: a four-day, 4000-km (about 2500-mi) event in which professional drivers, representing teams assembled by automobile manufacturers, compete for the trophy. Many consider it the most prestigious rally race in the world, as well as one of racing's most picturesque and unpredictable events.

Bibliography

Campbell, David. *Rallying: 21 Years of World Championships.* Weidenfeld & Nicolson, 1995.

Radosta, John S. *The New York Times Complete Guide to Auto Racing.* Quadrangle Books, 1971.

Robert Fay

Safwa

Ethnic group of Tanzania.

The Safwa primarily inhabit southwestern TANZANIA. They speak a Bantu language. Approximately 300,000 people consider themselves Safwa.

See also Bantu: Dispersion and Settlement.

Sahara

Largest desert in the world.

The Sahara covers the area between the ATLAS MOUNTAINS to the north, the semiarid SAHEL region to the south, the Red Sea to the east, and the Atlantic Ocean to the west. Although its boundaries have always been unstable, the desert currently stretches about 5,150 km (about 3,200 mi) from east to west and about 1,610 km (about 1,000 mi) from north to south, covering a total land area of about 9.1 million sq km (about 3.5 million sq mi). It comprises three distinct areas: the western Sahara (or Sahara Proper), the Libyan Desert, and the central Ahaggar Mountains and the Tibesti massif, a plateau. In total, the Sahara covers part or all of eleven countries: ALGERIA, CHAD, EGYPT, LIBYA, MALI, MAURITANIA, MOROCCO, NIGER, SUDAN, and TUNISIA. It also covers parts of WESTERN SAHARA, a disputed territory.

Because of ongoing climatic change, the Sahara has not always been a desert. Ten thousand years ago, relatively humid conditions supported a wide variety of savanna flora and fauna, as well as human activities such as agriculture, hunting, and fishing. Much evidence of this activity remains in the forms of rock paintings and tools. Since approximately 5,000 years ago, however, the Sahara's climate has been much less hospitable. Twenty percent of the desert is sand; the rest is predominantly rock and gravel. Average daily temperatures range from 0 degrees Celsius (32 degrees Fahrenheit) to 54.4 degrees Celsius (130 degrees Fahrenheit). Rainfall is minimal and erratic, but at times intense, creating occasional flash floods. In addition, several underground rivers originating in the mountains support lush, tree-lined oases, and the NILE RIVER runs through a portion of the eastern Sahara, leaving the surrounding valley fertile and habitable.

Despite the desert's extreme environment, it is home to nearly 2.5 million humans and many animal species, including gazelles, ANTELOPE, jackals, foxes, badgers, and HYENA. Most of the permanent human settlements are clustered in oases, in the mountain highlands, or at the desert's edges. Three main groups inhabit the desert, but after centuries of interaction, the most clear-cut distinctions among them are linguistic. Arabic-speaking groups, such as the BEDOUIN and the CHAMBA, live on the northern edge. BERBER peoples live on the northern and western edge and include the Shluh or Tashelhayt, and the TUAREG. The Teda (Tubu) live mostly in the eastern part of the desert.

PASTORALISM and trade have long provided the economic basis for survival as well as state-building in the Sahara. The introduction of the CAMEL to the Sahara from Egypt in the early centuries B.C.E. enabled merchant caravans to reach the trading capitals of the early sub-Saharan kingdoms, such as ancient Ghana, which built its wealth partly through control of Saharan salt mines. In addition to salt, many other goods were exchanged: gold, slaves, spices, and leather traveled north, while weapons, horses, textiles, and paper traveled south. Desert peoples not only participated in this trade but also collected tolls and protection money from the caravans. Although trans-Saharan trade diminished as West African trade with Europeans increased, nomadic peoples such as the Tuareg continue to trade Saharan salt for food and other supplies with the communities who live on the desert edges or around the oases. Oasis settlements also support themselves through date production and garden agriculture.

In addition to petroleum deposits in Algeria and Libya, the discovery of minerals such as uranium, iron, bauxite, and phosphate has once again made mining one of the most important sources of revenue for Africa's Saharan states. Most of the desert's nomadic peoples, however, have benefited little from the region's subterranean wealth. With their customary migratory routes and grazing grounds now crossed by national boundaries, many nomadic groups are either neglected or viewed with suspicion by national governments, and the loss of traditional sources of income has made them more vulnerable to the ravages of the desert's recurring droughts.

See also Climate of Africa; Ghana, Early Kingdom of; Minerals and Mining in Africa; Rock Art, African; Salt Trade.

Robert Fay

Sahel

Transition zone between the Sahara and the southern subtropical zone in West Africa.

Named after the Arabic word for shore or border, *sahil,* the Sahel is a hot, semiarid region characterized by sparse savanna vegetation and shrubbery. It covers an area south of the SAHARA approximately 200 to 400 km (about 125 to 250 mi) wide, extending across the African continent from the Atlantic Ocean to the Red Sea and covering at least part of ten countries—SENEGAL, GAMBIA, MAURITANIA, MALI, BURKINA FASO, NIGER, NIGERIA, CHAD, CAMEROON, and SUDAN.

A land of extreme conditions, the Sahel experiences two hot seasons—from approximately February to April and September to October—punctuated by a short rainy season between May and August. During December and January the Harmattan, a wind from the desert, brings cooler weather and thick dust.

Annual rainfall in the Sahel is notoriously variable and unpredictable, but in recent years has averaged between 100 and 200 mm (4 to 8 in) a year. Since the late 1960s rainfall has been gradually declining, but whether this trend indicates that the Sahel is undergoing desertification remains a subject of scientific debate.

Despite its harsh climate, the Sahel has long been home to nomadic pastoralists such as the TUAREG and the FULANI as well as to cities established by the precolonial states of the SONGHAI, the HAUSA, and the SOKOTO CALIPHATE. Food supplies for Sahelian cities such as BAMAKO, OUAGADOUGOU, NIAMEY, and KANO have depended historically on a combination of rainy-season agriculture, irrigation from year-round water sources such as the NIGER RIVER and LAKE CHAD, and trade. Recent experiences of severe drought, however, have caused many to wonder how long the Sahel can continue to support its inhabitants, the majority of whom still rely on land-based livelihoods.

Although periodic droughts have long afflicted the Sahel, environmental, economic, and political changes have recently combined to make many of the region's inhabitants more vulnerable to drought-related deprivation. Severe droughts during 1968–1973 and 1984–1985, for example, led to famine in many rural areas of the Sahel, afflicting millions of people. Many of the victims were pastoralists who, restricted by international borders from migrating to their traditional watering holes, lost or were forced to sell most of their livestock. Others were small farmers too poor to buy food when their own crops failed, and too remotely located to access urban-based food aid. Rural poverty was compounded in many areas by the interrelated problems of soil erosion and deforestation, which reduced the already fragile land's food-producing capacity.

Since the 1980s, numerous international, regional, and local organizations have launched environmental restoration campaigns in the Sahel. Several Sahelian nations have formed the Interstate Committee for Drought Control in the Sahel (CILSS), which coordinates many of the region's research and aid projects. Although much of the funding for forestry and land conservation projects comes from abroad, some of the most successful efforts have been planned and carried out at the village level. But most observers agree that over the long term, reducing vulnerability to drought will depend on improving the region's national economies, which remain some of the poorest and least industrialized in the world.

See also Climate of Africa; Drought and Desertification; Forestry, Participation, and Representation in Africa: An Interpretation; Pastoralism.

Elizabeth Heath

Sahrawi

Ethnic group in Western Sahara, Morocco, and Algeria.

BERBER peoples initially settled in WESTERN SAHARA by the first millennium B.C.E. By the sixth century B.C.E. the Berbers separated into several groups, the most prominent of which were the Sanhadja, the Zenata, the Lemtuna, and the Messoufa.

BEDOUIN Arabs known as the Beni Hassan, originally from Yemen, began settling in the area around the thirteenth century C.E. The Beni Hassan slowly came to dominate the Berber tribes. They intermarried with Sanhadja leaders or subdued them militarily. The conquering Beni Hassan forced the Berbers to pay tribute. Some Berber tribes, therefore, were relegated to an inferior status that did not change until well into the twentieth century. Other Sanhadja, however, declared themselves "people of the book," a term describing followers of the religious teachings of Judaism, Christianity, or Islam; as a result, their status rose to just below that of the Beni Hassan.

Composed of twenty autonomous tribal groups, the Sahrawi did not form an especially cohesive ethnic group in precolonial times. They did, however, share a similar social organization, common mores and customs, and the same religion (Islam) and language (Hassaniya Arabic), as well as intermarriage and alliances. Traditionally, the Sahrawi practiced a mixed economy, one suited to the extreme conditions of the desert. The majority were pastoralists who kept camels, sheep, and goats and migrated seasonally with their animals in search of water and grazing. Camels had multiple purposes: they served as pack animals, a form of exchange, and an instrument of war, and their milk formed the foundation of the Sahrawi diet. Other Sahrawi practiced agriculture, while some of the poorer tribes fished. In addition, the Sahrawi engaged in some trading of animals, wool, skin, salt (their main export), tea, SUGAR, firearms, rugs, and pots.

By 1884 the SCRAMBLE FOR AFRICA was in full swing and the Spanish declared Western Sahara a protectorate. SPAIN exerted control only over an extremely limited area and its hold on the Sahrawi was tenuous at best. The Sahrawi repeatedly attacked Spanish holdings. It was not until 1934 that a combined Spanish and French military effort finally subdued the Sahrawi.

Nevertheless, the Sahrawi continued to practice their traditional way of life. Starting in 1959 the region underwent a prolonged drought, which roughly coincided with the Spanish discovery of phosphate deposits. During this period many Sahrawis gave up their nomadic existence to move to the major population centers in Western Sahara. The Sahrawi formed the POLISARIO FRONT to take up armed struggle against Spanish colonial rule. Upon Spain's pullout from Western Sahara in 1975, the land was occupied by MOROCCO and MAURITANIA. The Sahrawi declared Western Sahara an independent country, and many evacuated to the Tindouf region in ALGERIA. The armed struggle continued, now directed at Mauritania (which recognized the SADR and Western Sahara in 1984) and Morocco.

The United Nations (UN) became involved in the conflict beginning in late 1985. A UN-brokered agreement between Polisario and the government of Morocco was to have resulted in a referendum among the citizens of Western Sahara to determine their future—either as an independent Western Sahara or as part of Morocco. Disagreements between the two governments regarding who should be allowed to vote, however, continued to delay the referendum. By the early 2000s the matter had still not been resolved, and many Sahrawi remained in exile in the Tindouf region in Algeria.

See also Camel; Pastoralism; Salt Trade.

Robert Fay

Saint-Denis, Réunion

Capital city of the French overseas department Réunion, located in the southwestern Indian Ocean.

In 1665, the French East Indian Company commissioned Captain Etienne Regnault to bring the first twenty settlers to RÉUNION. Four years after landing on the island, Regnault established the town of Saint-Denis, named after his boat. The town was built alongside a river bearing the same name. A fort was built in 1671, confirming the importance of the location. By 1735, the population of Saint-Denis had grown to 358 people.

Saint-Denis became the capital of Réunion in 1738 when the new governor, Bertrand-François Mahé de La Bourdonnais, decided the town was more strategically protected against attack than the settlement of Saint Paul. With its coastal location surrounded by steep mountains, Saint-Denis was also better positioned to serve as the island's first port. A 1742 map of the town shows that Saint-Denis had the gridlike structure characteristic of planned cities of the eighteenth century. The first church was constructed in 1743, and the first major marketplace in 1816. The Palace of the Colonial Council was erected in 1834, followed by the City Hall (or Hôtel de Ville) in 1853. During the 1880s an artificial port, known simply as Le Port, was constructed to the northwest, because the natural harbor at Saint-Denis was subject to strong tides and high winds.

Réunion was formally declared an overseas department of FRANCE in 1946. Along with improved infrastructure, augmented social services, and an increasingly service based economy came a population explosion; infant mortality rates plummeted and extended life span increased. Combined with rural-urban migration, this made the number of inhabitants rise from 33,900 in 1946 to 85,444 by 1967, as the city expanded rapidly to the east and south. Saint-Denis also became increasingly marked by class stratification as bureaucrats from *métropole* France arrived to institute new social programs.

Tourism has become increasingly important to the Réunion economy in recent years. Approximately 400,000 visitors, mostly from *métropole* France, visit the island each year. Given the lack of natural resources and the large numbers of visitors, Réunion must import over 2.4 million tons of freight annually. To meet these demands, in 1986 the port of Saint-Denis was significantly extended and a second facility was constructed to the east of the town. Population 145,200 (2004 estimate).

Ari Nave

Saint Domingue

Colonial name of present-day Haiti, on the western third of the island of Hispaniola, ceded to the French in 1697 under the Treaty of Ryswick.

See also Haiti.

Saint-Georges, Chevalier de

1745–1799

Afro-French composer, violinist, conductor, one of the first black composers to make a notable contribution to the European classical music tradition.

A singular figure on the musical landscape of pre-Revolutionary FRANCE, the Chevalier de Saint-Georges gained renown as a composer and violinist. Influenced by the French classical tradition, he wrote in a variety of forms: concertos for violin and orchestra, symphonies, string quartets, operas, sonatas for keyboard and violin, and *simphonies concertantes,* the popular French form of concerto that featured two or more soloists and an orchestra. He was also recognized throughout Europe as one of the outstanding swordsmen of his time, and in 1792 became colonel of his own regiment in France's National Guard. In 1838 he was the subject of a four-volume adventure novel by Roger de Beauvoir.

The Chevalier de Saint-Georges, born Joseph de Boulogne near BASSE-TERRE, GUADELOUPE, West Indies, was the son of an African slave woman and an aristocratic French plantation owner, from whom he inherited his name and title. At the age of ten, he moved with his father to Paris. A student of the great fencing master La Boëssière, Saint-Georges revealed a remarkable strength and speed with the sword, inspiring La Böessière's son to call him "perhaps the most extraordinary man to appear in the history of fencing." In 1787 Saint-Georges took part in a London fencing exhibition with the notorious crossdresser, Chevalier d'Éon—a fight immortalized in a painting by Robineau that depicts d'Éon, in full silk dress and lace bonnet, opposite the dashing figure of Saint-Georges.

Although little is known about his early musical studies, as a young man Saint-Georges studied composition with the French composer François Joseph Gossec, who in 1773 appointed him director of the *Concert des Amateurs,* a newly established public concert series in Paris. Saint-Georges also performed his own violin concertos, which, according to music editor Gabriel Banat, became "a bridge, connecting the violin technique of the violinist-composers of the late baroque . . . to the technique of the nineteenth-century romantics." In 1776 Saint-Georges was invited to become director of the Paris Opéra, an offer withdrawn when political intrigues and racial prejudice incited company members to protest his appointment. He continued to compose and perform and in 1779 was appointed musical director of the distinguished private orchestra of Madame de Montesson.

In the early 1780s Saint-Georges became affiliated with the Freemasons after the "Loge Olympique," a Masonic Lodge in Paris, rescued the Concert des Amateurs from bankruptcy and relocated his orchestra to the Palais Royal. In 1785 the Palais Royal's owner, Duke Philippe Égalité, turned the grounds into a safe enclave for artists and revolutionaries, where class and social distinctions were disregarded. Saint-Georges became a regular performer at the Palais Royal. In addition to his orchestral concerts, he composed and produced several operas. He also developed a close friendship with the duke that involved him in revolutionary politics and led to his arrest and imprisonment in 1793 by the French Revolutionary Tribunal, presided over by Robespierre.

Released from prison in July 1794, Saint-Georges spent two years in Saint-Domingue, the French Caribbean colony where black slaves were in revolt against France. Music historian Eileen Southern wrote that "he fought in the uprisings there against Spain and the slaveholding colonists." On his return to Paris in 1797, he resumed his musical career but died of a gangrenous leg ulcer two years later, at the age of fifty-four.

Roanne Edwards

Saint Kitts and Nevis

Country in the Lesser Antilles, located south of Anguilla and southeast of Puerto Rico in the Caribbean Sea.

Few of the nearly 85,000 tourists who flock to the beaches of Saint Kitts and Nevis each year probably know that the country has been at the forefront of so many different trends in Caribbean history. For example, Saint Kitts was the first settled British colony, Nevis was once universally regarded as the "Queen of the Caribbees" for its success at SUGAR cultivation, and Saint Kitts's workers helped begin the labor movements that eventually brought self-government to the black majorities across the Caribbean. Although it is a small state, Saint Kitts and Nevis has taken the lead in some of the most important movements in the region.

Colonial History

As with most of the Caribbean, Saint Kitts and Nevis's original inhabitants were Arawak and Carib Indians, who migrated from South America to settle in the islands between 5,000 and 7,000 years ago. The Caribs named Saint Kitts Liamuiga, meaning "fertile land," because its volcanic soil was so ideal for agriculture. On November 12, 1493, Christopher Columbus discovered the islands during his second exploratory trip to the Caribbean, an encounter that changed their names and histories forever.

The name Saint Kitts comes from English sailors' slang for St. Christopher, the full legal name of the island. While there is a persistent myth that Columbus himself chose the name San

Residents buy produce at the port of Nevis. Sugar production is a major industry in Saint Kitts and Nevis and has been since the 1700s. *Eye Ubiquitous*

Cristóbal in his own honor, the name was actually given to the island by Spanish sailors, who also named Nevis. Columbus had intended to call that island Saint Martin, because he first sighted it on Saint Martin's feast day. But the sailors began calling it *Nuestra Señora del las Nieves,* or "Our Lady of the Snows," because of the white clouds that permanently surround the island's central peak. The Spanish chose not to establish a permanent settlement on either island, and so the islands of Saint Kitts and Nevis were granted a reprieve from colonization for another hundred years. But by the end of the sixteenth century, both the English and the French used Saint Kitts as a source for salt and building timber. In 1623 GREAT BRITAIN established its first permanent settlement in the WEST INDIES when Thomas Warner led a group of sixteen settlers to what is now Old Road Bay off Saint Kitts.

Two years later they were joined by the first French settlers, when a group led by Pierre Belain d'Esnambue were forced to seek refuge on Saint Kitts after losing a fight to a Spanish galleon. The two colonies' first cooperative effort was to join forces to attack the islands' indigenous inhabitants: most of the remaining Carib Indians were killed during the 1626 massacre at Bloody Point. As the colonies grew, however, their coexistence became more uneasy. The English and French fought over Saint Kitts and Nevis several times over the next 150 years before the islands finally became a single British colony in 1783.

Both the English and French initially used Saint Kitts as a strategic base for colonizing nearby islands—Tortola, MONTSERRAT, and ANTIGUA AND BARBUDA for the English; MARTINIQUE, GUADELOUPE, Saint Martin, Saint Barts, La Désirade, and Les Saintes for the French. It was from this colonization that Saint Kitts became known as the "mother colony of the West Indies." Nevis, on the other hand, was used primarily for agriculture. The first planters grew tobacco, cotton, ginger, and indigo. But when sugar was first introduced to Nevis in 1640, it was immediately apparent that the planters had found the crop that was going to make Nevis the "Queen of the Caribbee." It was also apparent that sugar plantations would require an enormous amount of inexpensive labor to reach their maximum profit potential—and so began the widespread importation of African slaves to Saint Kitts and Nevis.

By the 1660s Saint Kitts had approximately 6,000 inhabitants, roughly one-half of whom were black. One hundred years later, blacks outnumbered whites on the island by ten to one—with 20,000 blacks (most of them still slaves) and 2,000 whites. For white residents of Saint Kitts and Nevis, the eighteenth century was a time of unparalleled prosperity. On Saint Kitts, sugar production rose from 1,000 tons in 1710 to 10,000 tons by 1770, and the figures were even better in Nevis. Nevis's natural hot springs also enabled that island to become the Caribbean's first spa resort. For much of the 1700s European tourists flocked to the lavish Bath Hotel and the other estates that had been built on the island. However, these enormous profits and pleasures came at a cost that was borne by the people who were forced to do the labor.

The *Prince of Orange* tragedy is just one example of the horror that accompanied slavery in the islands. In March 1737 the ship *Prince of Orange* docked at Basseterre, Saint Kitts, with several hundred slaves from Africa's Guinea Coast on board. As was typical, the slaves were kept on the ship for several days to recuperate from the crossing in order that they might look healthy enough to get a better price at auction. The ship's captain recorded in his log that during that time he noticed "a great deal of discontent among the slaves." Both the slave traders on board and those waiting on land were utterly unprepared for the afternoon of March 16, 1737, when more than a hundred slaves jumped overboard together in an attempted mass suicide. Thirty-three slaves drowned, and many more were forcibly rescued but died onshore over the next few days. For those who survived, life on the Saint Kitts and Nevis sugar plantations was arduous, with harsh treatment compounded by difficult work. Many of the plantation owners were absentee landlords, and estates were run by agents or managers whose

Saint Kitts and Nevis (At a Glance)

OFFICIAL NAME: Federation of Saint Kitts and Nevis

FORMER NAME: Saint Christopher; Liamuiga

AREA: 261 sq km (101 sq mi)

LOCATION: Islands in the Caribbean Sea about one-third of the way from Puerto Rico to Trinidad and Tobago

CAPITAL: Basseterre (population 12,000; 2004 estimate)

POPULATION: 39,000 (2004 estimate)

POPULATION DENSITY: 148 persons per sq km (385 per sq mi)

POPULATION BELOW AGE 15: 29 percent (male 5,754; female 5,499; 2003 estimate)

POPULATION GROWTH RATE: 0.13 percent (2003 estimate)

TOTAL FERTILITY RATE: 2.37 children born per woman (2003 estimate)

LIFE EXPECTANCY AT BIRTH: Total population: 71.57 years (male 68.76 years; female 74.56 years; 2003 estimate)

INFANT MORTALITY RATE: 15.39 deaths per 1,000 live births (2003 estimate)

LITERACY RATE (AGE 15 AND OVER WHO HAVE EVER ATTENDED SCHOOL): Total population: 97 percent (male 97 percent; female 98 percent; 2003 estimate)

EDUCATION: Education is free and compulsory for ages five to sixteen.

LANGUAGES: English

ETHNIC GROUPS: Mostly black, with some British, Portuguese, and Lebanese

RELIGIONS: Anglican, other Protestant, and Roman Catholic

CLIMATE: Tropical, cool, and pleasant, with an average annual temperature of 80° F (27° C).

LAND, PLANTS, AND ANIMALS: Saint Kitts is an oval-shaped island with a volcanic ridge down the center. There is black volcanic sand on the beaches. The island of Nevis is circle-shaped and mostly consists of a mountain, Nevis Peak. Vegetation includes the coconut palm, bamboo trees, hibiscus, and hog plums. Animals include hawks and bananaquits (small birds), monkeys, bats, sea turtles, and donkeys.

NATURAL RESOURCES: Arable land

CURRENCY: East Caribbean dollar (XCD)

GROSS DOMESTIC PRODUCT (GDP): $339 million (2002 estimate)

GDP PER CAPITA: $8,800 (2002 estimate)

GDP REAL GROWTH RATE: −1.9 percent (2002 estimate)

PRIMARY ECONOMIC ACTIVITIES: Tourism, export-oriented manufacturing, offshore banking, and agriculture

PRIMARY CROPS: Sugarcane, rice, yams, vegetables, bananas, and fish

INDUSTRIES: Sugar processing, tourism, cotton, salt, copra, clothing, footwear, and beverages

PRIMARY EXPORTS: Machinery, food, electronics, beverages, and tobacco

PRIMARY IMPORTS: Machinery, manufactures, food, and fuels

PRIMARY TRADE PARTNERS: United States, United Kingdom, Canada, Portugal, Trinidad and Tobago, and Japan

GOVERNMENT: The government of Saint Kitts and Nevis is a constitutional monarchy with a Westminster-style parliament. The chief of state is Queen Elizabeth II, represented by Governor-General Cuthbert Montraville Sebastian (since January 1996; appointed by the monarch). The head of government is Prime Minister Dr. Denzil Douglas (since July 1995; the prime minister is usually the leader of the majority party, appointed after legislative elections by the governor-general). The legislative branch is the fourteen-member unicameral National Assembly (three members appointed and eleven elected to serve five-year terms). The judicial branch is the Eastern Caribbean Supreme Court (based on Saint Lucia, with one judge residing in Saint Kitts and Nevis).

Shelle Sumners

---

only concern was making the highest profit possible. Life expectancy for slaves in Saint Kitts and Nevis barely reached double digits.

Emancipation and Emigration

In 1834 slavery was finally abolished in all English colonies. At the end of a four-year "apprenticeship" program, during which former slaves were obligated to work for their former masters in exchange for a small salary, the black inhabitants of Saint Kitts and Nevis were finally free. But for all practical purposes, freedom brought the same economic and employment constraints that slavery had.

Sugar remained the only real industry on the islands, and most of the viable land already belonged to planters who were not interested in redistributing it among the former slaves. As a result, many black Kittitians and Nevisians continued to work in the sugar fields well into the twentieth century, often forced to rent land and housing on the same estates where they had once been slaves. White planters also continued to strictly regulate their employees' working hours, sick days, and physical mobility. A series of natural disasters in the second half of the nineteenth century—the great earthquake of 1843, the cholera epidemic of 1854, the great fire of 1867, and the great flood of 1880—compounded the already miserable living and working conditions on the islands. By the turn of the twentieth century the black majority on Saint Kitts and Nevis were ready for real change.

One way they found it was through emigration. Between 1900 and 1930, approximately 10,000 Kittitians and Nevisians moved to the United States, CUBA, the DOMINICAN REPUBLIC, PANAMA, or neighboring islands in search of better jobs—or at the very least, better treatment. For those who chose to stay, change came through unionizing and fighting for political power. After the collapse of sugar prices during the GREAT DEPRESSION hurt the islands' economy yet again, many planters announced that they would be attempting to salvage their losses by cutting workers' wages and bonuses. This time, the workers decided to fight.

Saint Kitts was at the forefront of the labor movements that swept across the Caribbean in the 1930s. As one historian put it, it was the "Saint Kitts human chain [that] link[ed] the West Indian working class." In 1932 Robert Bradshaw organized the Workers League, Saint Kitts's first union. Black workers also turned to supplementary methods of protest against unfair conditions, most notably the general strikes and riots that occurred in 1935 and 1936. In each case, laborers wanted to create better workplaces. But they were also determined to create a better and fairer political system. The traditional government, which consisted solely of political appointees who were all members of the wealthy white "plantocracy," was long outmoded.

In 1937 the British governor in Saint Kitts and Nevis finally allowed five seats on the legislature to be chosen by popular election. Voting rights were still limited by property and income qualifications, so most of the black majority were still ineligible, but they strategized together to take advantage of the small influence they did have. In 1940 the Workers League became the Saint Kitts and Nevis Trades and Labour Union. It soon established a new political wing, the Saint Kitts and Nevis Labour Party, led by Bradshaw. Bradshaw was elected to the Legislative Council in 1946, marking the beginning of the Labour Party's thirty-year reign in Saint Kitts and Nevis politics.

Enfranchisement and Independence

Universal suffrage was finally granted to all citizens in 1952, along with a legislature consisting of a majority of elected members. The Labour Party easily won all of the available seats in the next elections, and for the first time in its 330-year history as a British Crown colony, Saint Kitts and Nevis was ruled by the majority of its people. In 1967 the country took an important step toward full independence when Saint Kitts, Nevis, and the island of ANGUILLA became a single British state instead of a colony. Anguilla, which had been administered jointly with Saint Kitts and Nevis, opposed the new arrangement, and in 1971 it returned to being a crown colony. Some Nevisians considered following Anguilla's lead, because they were also apprehensive that permanent affiliation with Saint Kitts would threaten Nevis's autonomy. But the British government strongly encouraged Saint Kitts and Nevis to remain together. Despite Nevisian dissent, on September 19, 1983, St. Kitts and Nevis became independent as a single nation.

The Labour Party continued to control the government until 1980, with Bradshaw, who had become the country's first premier in 1967, leading the country until his death in 1978. By the 1970s, however, there were two common complaints about the government: it had assumed too much state control and it had done too little to diversify the economy, which remained one of the Caribbean's last sugar monocultures. The People's Action Movement (PAM), led by Kennedy Simmonds, came to power in 1980 and stayed there until 1995. Under the PAM government Saint Kitts and Nevis successfully increased tourism, providing much-needed new industries for the country. But a 1994 drug trafficking scandal led to the resignation of the deputy prime minister, the arrest of two of his sons, the murder of a third, and the call for new elections three years ahead of schedule. The elections were marred by protests and violence. In July 1995 the Labour Party was returned to power, with Denzil Douglass as the new prime minister. The Labour Party also triumphed in the 2000 elections, winning eight of the eleven seats in parliament. The Nevis-based Concerned Citizen's Movement (CCM), led by Vance Armory, placed second with two seats.

One of the central domestic issues for the federation in recent years has been the status of Nevis. The constitution allows the island to secede from the federation under certain conditions. In 1996, Armory led a group called the Nevis Island Administration that announced that it intended to press for the secession of Nevis from the federation, but the measure was blocked in parliament by the Nevis Reformation Party. A referendum on Nevisian independence two years later also failed. However, the rise of Armory's CCM as the federation's major opposition party makes it likely that secession will remain an important issue for the foreseeable future.

Today, the island nation of Saint Kitts and Nevis has returned to the task of setting the country's course for the twenty-first century. In several areas the islands are at a crossroads. There is of course the disagreement on whether or not Saint Kitts and Nevis should remain a single country. In both islands, tourism increased rapidly during the 1990s, but declined after hurricanes stuck the island in 1998 and 1999. Sugar production remains a key part of the economy. Some of the country's culture remains undeniably British—for example, the government system, the language, and the national passion for cricket—but many more traditions reflect the population's African and Caribbean heritage. Carnival is celebrated grandly every year between Christmas and New Year's, as it is across the Caribbean. The new annual Saint Kitts Music Festival, which began in 1996, gives another indication of the country's diasporic heritage: the five-day festival features SALSA, SOUL, SOCA, SAMBA, REGGAE, and JAZZ and concludes with a GOSPEL revival. These apparent contradictions are characteristic of the entire Caribbean, however, and they are part of what makes Saint Kitts and Nevis a vibrant and vital modern nation.

See also Afro-Caribbean Migrations to the United States; Carnivals in Latin America and the Caribbean; Colonial Latin America and the Caribbean; Colonial Rule; Slave Laws in

Colonial Spanish America; Slavery in Latin America and the Caribbean; Transatlantic Slave Trade.

Lisa Clayton Robinson

Saint Lucia

Island nation in the Caribbean Sea, located south of Martinique and north of Saint Vincent.

As its nickname "The Helen of the West Indies" suggests, Saint Lucia is considered one of the most beautiful islands in the Caribbean. Its beauty is in large measure due to the fact that it has more forests and more indigenous flora and fauna than many Caribbean islands. Saint Lucia was first inhabited by the Arawak Indians, who migrated to the island around 200 C.E. The Carib Indians replaced the Arawaks by about six centuries later. The original Native American name for the island was *Iouanalao,* meaning "the place where the iguana is found."

Some question exists over when Europeans first sighted Saint Lucia. Tradition holds that Christopher Columbus himself discovered the island on Saint Lucy's feast day, December 13, 1502. What is certain, however, is that Carib resistance to European settlement on the island was fierce, and Saint Lucian Caribs were able to resist European colonization until the mid-seventeenth century.

Once colonization began, there was new competition over which European colonial power would control Saint Lucia. Although Spanish explorers had claimed the island first, Spanish colonists never made a serious attempt to settle it, and the real battle for Saint Lucia was fought between the French and the British. Both held other islands close to Saint Lucia, and both coveted the excellent natural harbor at CASTRIES, which is considered one of the best harbors in the WEST INDIES. The British and French struggle for Saint Lucia lasted until 1814, with the island changing hands seven times. The constant political instability meant that neither country was able to develop the permanent plantation economy on Saint Lucia that they had created on other islands.

This was the fortunate development that left much of Saint Lucia's land untouched—land that might otherwise have been covered in SUGAR or coffee plantations by the end of the eighteenth century. But some colonists were able to establish plantations on Saint Lucia and, like plantation owners across the Americas, they turned to Africa for the cheap labor they needed to run their estates. The first African slaves arrived in Saint Lucia around 1763, brought by French planters who had purchased them from the slave traders who abducted them from their West African homes. It was during slavery that the distinctive patois still spoken today developed—a combination of French and several African languages.

The fact that most Saint Lucian blacks spoke French patois put them at a disadvantage when the country permanently became a British territory in 1814, and this linguistic difference is one of the factors that continues to contribute to the island's high illiteracy rate. In 1834 slavery was abolished in all British

Men play dominoes outside a house in Saint Lucia. *CORBIS/Tony Arruza*

territories, making the 13,291 Saint Lucian slaves free. At the time of emancipation Saint Lucia already had more small estates than any of the other Windward Islands, and this number grew as newly emancipated slaves fled their former owners and established their own farms. This left white planters with a labor shortage, and in response they introduced a sharecropping system in 1838. But this system left much to be desired for its black workers, and poverty, smallpox and yellow fever, and other ills plagued both black and white Saint Lucians for much of the nineteenth century.

The introduction of the coal industry in 1883 brought relief for a short time, as did the transfer of a British military base to Saint Lucia from BARBADOS during the same period. But for the most part, Saint Lucia was regarded as a poor, undeveloped nation, even by its Caribbean neighbors. By the middle of the twentieth century, even the sugar industry that had been the backbone of much of the Caribbean economy was in decline. The growth of the BANANA industry in the 1950s finally brought a period of relative prosperity to Saint Lucia, and for the first time the island was able to concentrate on bringing roads, electricity, and a fresh water supply to its large rural population.

Welcome political changes soon followed the economic ones. During its first century of British authority Saint Lucia had been ruled by crown colony government, under which all political decisions regarding the island were made by a council appointed by the British Crown. Representative government was introduced in 1924, but it remained limited to the predominantly white elite, and it was not until 1951 that universal adult suffrage was established. For the first time, black Saint Lucians—who had been the majority on the island since the late eighteenth century—were able to have their say in the country's government.

The first political party to rise to prominence under the new system was the Saint Lucia Labour Party (SLP), which was an

Saint Lucia

Saint Lucia (At a Glance)

OFFICIAL NAME: Saint Lucia

AREA: 616 sq km (238 sq mi)

LOCATION: Island north of Trinidad and Tobago, between the Caribbean Sea and the North Atlantic Ocean

CAPITAL: Castries (population 57,000; 2004 estimate)

POPULATION: 149,000 (2004 estimate)

POPULATION DENSITY: 243 persons per sq km (632 per sq mi)

POPULATION BELOW AGE 15: 31.1 percent (male 25,883; female 24,569; 2003 estimate)

POPULATION GROWTH RATE: 1.25 percent (2003 estimate)

TOTAL FERTILITY RATE: 2.29 children born per woman (2003 estimate)

LIFE EXPECTANCY AT BIRTH: Total population: 73.08 years (male 69.52 years; female 76.9 years; 2003 estimate)

INFANT MORTALITY RATE: 14.37 deaths per 1,000 live births (2003 estimate)

LITERACY RATE (AGE 15 AND OVER WHO HAVE EVER ATTENDED SCHOOL): Total population: 67 percent (male 65 percent; female 69 percent; 1980 estimate)

EDUCATION: Education is free and compulsory, with many Roman Catholic parochial schools. At Castries, students attend a branch of the University of the West Indies.

LANGUAGES: English is the official language of Saint Lucia. French patois is also spoken.

ETHNIC GROUPS: 90 percent black, 6 percent mixed, 3 percent East Indian, and 1 percent white

RELIGIONS: 90 percent of Saint Lucia's inhabitants are Roman Catholic, 3 percent are Anglican, and 7 percent follow other Protestant religions

CLIMATE: Tropical maritime, with temperature and rainfall variations depending on elevation. The average temperature is 80° F (27° C). The rainy season is May to November.

LAND, PLANTS, AND ANIMALS: Saint Lucia is of volcanic origin, and mountainous. Mount Gimie is the highest point, at 3,145 feet (958.6 meters). The sulfur springs of Soufrière attract many tourists. Orchids and birds, including parrots, black finches, and orioles thrive on the island.

NATURAL RESOURCES: Timber, pumice, mineral springs, and geothermal areas

CURRENCY: East Caribbean dollar (XCD)

GROSS DOMESTIC PRODUCT (GDP): $866 million (2002 estimate)

GDP PER CAPITA: $5,400 (2002 estimate)

GDP REAL GROWTH RATE: 3.3 percent (2002 estimate)

PRIMARY ECONOMIC ACTIVITIES: Agriculture, services, industry, commerce, and manufacturing

PRIMARY CROPS: Bananas, coconuts, vegetables, citrus, root crops, and cacao

INDUSTRIES: Clothing, assembly of electronic components, beverages, corrugated cardboard boxes, tourism, lime processing, and coconut processing

PRIMARY EXPORTS: Bananas, clothing, cocoa, vegetables, fruits, and coconut oil

PRIMARY IMPORTS: Food, manufactured goods, machinery and transportation equipment, chemicals, and fuels

PRIMARY TRADE PARTNERS: United Kingdom, United States, Barbados, Brazil, and Trinidad and Tobago

GOVERNMENT: The government of Saint Lucia is a parliamentary democracy. The chief of state is Queen Elizabeth II, represented by Governor-General Dr. Perlette Louisy (since September 1997; appointed by the monarch). The head of government is Prime Minister Kenneth Davis Anthony (since May 1997); the prime minister is usually the leader of the majority party, appointed by the governor-general following legislative elections. The legislative branch is the bicameral Parliament, consisting of the eleven-member Senate and the seventeen-member House of Assembly. The judicial branch is the Eastern Caribbean Supreme Court, with jurisdiction also in Anguilla, Antigua and Barbuda, the British Virgin Islands, Dominica, Grenada, Montserrat, Saint Kitts and Nevis, and Saint Vincent and the Grenadines.

Shelle Sumners

---

offshoot of the St. Lucia Workers Union. In 1961 a faction of younger, university-educated members of the Labour Party broke off to found the United Workers Party (UWP). When the UWP won its first election in 1964, leader John Compton became chief minister of Saint Lucia. Compton led the country's government from 1964 to 1979. After being voted out of office in the 1979 elections, he returned in 1982 for another six years. Compton presided over one of the most important developments in the island's history—its transition to independent statehood within the British Commonwealth on February 22, 1979. Compton resigned as prime minister in 1996 and was replaced by Dr. Vaughn Lewis. The following year the SLP regained power, winning sixteen of seventeen seats in the parliament. Dr. Kenneth Anthony became the new prime minister, a post he retained after another SLP victory in the 2001 elections.

Since independence, the country has been relatively prosperous, particularly as tourism experienced strong growth in the 1990s. The terrorist attacks on the United States of September 11, 2001 brought a steep decline in tourism and the closing of several hotels. In addition, droughts and the changes in the European market, which have threatened the banana industry in the last several years, serve as reminders of the country's need to continue diversifying its economic base. The need for improvements in education also remains a national priority, especially changes that will help the patois-speaking population prosper in the official English society.

Saint Lucia is already celebrated as the home of the Caribbean's two Nobel laureates, economist Sir Arthur Lewis and poet and playwright Derek Walcott. Prominent novelists such as Garth St. Omer also add to the island's reputation. Finally, tourist literature about Saint Lucia is quick to celebrate the island's multicultural African, French, and British heritage as one of its greatest assets. Saint Lucia is already a favorite site for visitors from around the world, and Saint Lucians remain optimistic that their country will continue prospering into the next century.

See also Colonial Rule; Languages, Creole, in the Caribbean; Slavery in Latin America and the Caribbean; Transatlantic Slave Trade

Lisa Clayton Robinson

Saint Thomas and Prince Islands

Former name of São Tomé and Príncipe.

See also São Tomé and Príncipe.

Saint Vincent and the Grenadines

Country consisting of a chain of islands in the Caribbean Sea, with Grenada to the south and Saint Lucia to the north; the southern end of the Grenadines Islands chain is administered with Grenada.

The Carib Indians who inhabited Saint Vincent at the time of Christopher Columbus's 1498 arrival called their island *Youlou* or *Hairoun*, meaning "home of the blessed." Indeed, for centuries before the European invasion of the Caribbean, the hilly, dramatic islands now known as Saint Vincent and the Grenadines were home to several indigenous groups, and they fought to preserve their islands after the colonists arrived. The first inhabitants of these islands were probably Ciboney Indians who arrived around 4300 B.C.E., followed by the Arawaks and then the Caribs. Although Columbus landed on Saint Vincent on the feast day of Saint Vincent, January 22, 1498, the Caribs successfully resisted any permanent European colonization on the island until the early 1700s.

The first outsiders whom the Caribs allowed to settle in Saint Vincent were not Europeans but Africans. In 1675 a Dutch slave ship sank off the coast of Bequia, one of the nearby Grenadine Islands. None of the whites on board survived, but a group of Africans made it to shore. They subsequently migrated to Saint Vincent where they were assimilated into the Carib community. These Africans and their descendants were called Black Caribs, distinguishing them from the indigenous Yellow Caribs. Saint Vincent's reputation as a Carib stronghold quickly spread, and escaped slaves from nearby Saint Lucia and Barbados soon joined Saint Vincent's Black Carib community.

When the Caribs signed a treaty with the Europeans in the early 1700s, allowing European settlement, Saint Vincent's transition to a slave society began. The first European settlers were French, and because they initially held only small farms that could be worked by small numbers of slaves, they coexisted with the Caribs for several years. But as the British also began to occupy the island, and both the British and the French grew interested in spreading out and establishing larger plantations, conflicts arose.

The French took advantage of their better relationship with the Caribs by encouraging them to attack British settlements. After a 1795 revolt, however, in which the Black Caribs seized much of Saint Vincent, the British captured 5,080 Caribs and deported them to British Honduras (present-day Belize). With much of the island's free black leadership now gone, most blacks remaining in Saint Vincent and the Grenadines were slaves.

In 1812 a volcanic eruption on Saint Vincent destroyed many of the island's coffee plants and cacao trees, making conditions even worse for all of the island's residents. All that remained were the sugar plantations, which were not sufficient to support the population. In 1834 slavery was abolished in all British territories, and many former slaves chose to leave the plantations and try to make their own living through subsistence farming. British landowners were forced to turn to East Indian and Portuguese indentured servants to help supply the labor on the sugar plantations. The sugar industry became less profitable as the century went on, however, and an 1877 report found that Saint Vincent was already among the poorest territories in the Caribbean.

The government sought to improve conditions by turning over more land to small farmers. But even blacks who owned their own farms found that they were still largely engaged in subsistence farming and were not able to produce crops for profit. An 1898 hurricane and another volcanic eruption in 1902 destroyed farms throughout the islands, making the precarious economic situation in Saint Vincent and the Grenadines even worse. By the turn of the twentieth century some new crops had been introduced, such as cotton, arrowroot, and coconuts, and by the 1950s bananas would become the most successful crop. The fact that the islands' economy has always been dependent upon agriculture, however, has made it very vulnerable to natural disasters and diseases, and has meant that the majority of the population is employed as agricultural laborers.

It was the demand for better working conditions for these laborers that prompted political reforms. Throughout the nineteenth century and much of the twentieth century, the government of Saint Vincent and the Grenadines was controlled by the islands' elite white minority. In the 1930s George McIntosh organized the Workingmen's Association, the first organization to push for both better working conditions and in-

Saint Vincent and the Grenadines

Saint Vincent and the Grenadines (At a Glance)

Official Name: Saint Vincent and the Grenadines

Area: 389 sq km (150 sq mi)

Location: Islands between the Caribbean Sea and North Atlantic Ocean, north of Trinidad and Tobago

Capital: Kingstown (population 28,000; 2004 estimate)

Population: 120,000 (2004 estimate)

Population Density: 353 persons per sq km (917 per sq mi)

Population Below Age 15: 28.2 percent (male 16,755; female 16,163; 2003 estimate)

Population Growth Rate: 0.34 percent (2003 estimate)

Total Fertility Rate: 1.95 children born per woman (2003 estimate)

Life Expectancy at Birth: Total population: 73.08 years (male 71.3 years; female 74.92 years; 2003 estimate)

Infant Mortality Rate: 15.7 deaths per 1,000 live births (2003 estimate)

Literacy Rate (age 15 and over who have ever attended school): Total population: 96 percent (male 96 percent; female 96 percent; 1970 estimate)

Education: Free but noncompulsory primary education is offered. Schools run by religious organizations provide secondary education.

Languages: English and French patois

Ethnic Groups: 66 percent black, 19 percent mixed-race, 6 percent East Indian, 2 percent Carib Amerindian, and 7 percent other ethnicities

Religions: The population is 47 percent Anglican, 28 percent Methodist, and 13 percent Roman Catholic; also some practice Hinduism, and some are Seventh-Day Adventists and other types of Protestant.

Climate: Tropical maritime, with temperatures that range between 64° and 90° F (18° and 32° C). Precipitation and temperature vary according to elevation. The rainy season is June through December, with possible hurricanes.

Land, Plants, and Animals: Saint Vincent is an island of volcanic mountains covered by lush forests and small streams. The volcano Soufrière became active in 1979, resulting in evacuation of the island and much agricultural damage. Some Grenadine islands are hilly and have coral reefs. Vegetation includes palm trees and flowering cactus, and there are many species of birds on the islands.

Natural Resources: Hydropower and cropland

Currency: East Caribbean dollar (XCD)

Gross Domestic Product (GDP): $339 million (2002 estimate)

GDP per Capita: $2,900 (2002 estimate)

GDP Real Growth Rate: −0.5 percent (2002 estimate)

Primary Economic Activities: Services, agriculture, and industry

Primary Crops: Bananas, coconuts, sweet potatoes, spices, small numbers of cattle, sheep, pigs, goats, and fish

Industries: Food processing, cement, furniture, clothing, and starch

Primary Exports: Bananas, eddoes and dasheen (taro), arrowroot starch, and tennis racquets

Primary Imports: Foodstuffs, machinery and equipment, chemicals and fertilizers, and minerals and fuels

Primary Trade Partners: France, Greece, Spain, United Kingdom, United States, Trinidad and Tobago, and Singapore

Government: Saint Vincent and the Grenadines is a parliamentary democracy. The chief of state is Queen Elizabeth II, represented by Governor-General Sir Frederick Nathaniel Ballantyne (since September 2002; appointed by the monarch). The head of government is Prime Minister Ralph E. Gonsalves (since March 2001; the leader of the majority party is appointed prime minister by the governor-general following legislative elections). The legislative branch is the twenty-one-member unicameral House of Assembly (six appointed senators and fifteen popularly elected representatives who serve five-year terms). The judicial branch is the Eastern Caribbean Supreme Court, based on Saint Lucia, with one judge residing in Saint Vincent and the Grenadines.

Shelle Sumners

---

creased political power for the island's working-class black majority. Similar organizations soon followed, and in the face of these increasingly vocal demands, the first elections that allowed universal adult suffrage were held in 1952.

Ebenezer Joshua, one of the labor leaders elected to the legislature that year, became the founder of Saint Vincent and the Grenadines' first political party, the People's Political Party (PPP). When ministerial government was established in 1957, Joshua became the country's first chief minister, and he remained in control of the government until 1967. In 1969, under new chief minister James Mitchell, Saint Vincent and the Grenadines was granted associated statehood, bringing it even more internal autonomy. But the largest political change came when Saint Vincent and the Grenadines achieved independence on October 27, 1979, becoming an independent state within the British Commonwealth.

With an aim toward improving the country's economy, residents are urged to increase local production and rely less on imported items. *Tim Thompson/Corbis*

Aside from a brief 1980 uprising in which student leaders from Union Island tried to secede from the rest of the state, Saint Vincent and the Grenadines has enjoyed political stability. "Son" Mitchell, the prime minister from 1984 to 2001, followed his father James Mitchell into politics. The 1980 uprising called attention to the fact that residents of the Grenadines often felt unfairly treated by Saint Vincent, which accounts for 90 percent of the country's land and population, and there have been attempts to address these inequities. In recent years tourism has become an important source of revenue for the country, and Saint Vincent and the Grenadines is often regarded as a private playground for the rich and famous.

But for most of the population, the standard of living remains tied to the agricultural industry, primarily single-crop production. Indeed, bananas alone constitute about 50 percent of the country's exports and involve about 60 percent of the workforce. But the agriculture sector is vulnerable to natural disasters—especially hurricanes, which devastated crops in 1994, 1995, and 2002—and as a result unemployment in the 1990s sometimes climbed as high as 40 percent. The country, often considered the second poorest in the Caribbean after Haiti, was by the early 2000s a significant grower of marijuana and a major drug transshipment point.

Discussions in the late 1990s about the possibility of unifying Saint Vincent and the Grenadines with Saint Lucia, Grenada, and Dominica into a single state received support from Prime Minister Mitchell, but were later abandoned. When Mitchell's party lost favor in the 2001 election, Ralph E. Gonsalves became prime minister. Saint Vincent and the Grenadines is a member of the Caribbean Community (CARICOM) and maintains close ties with many western hemisphere nations, including Cuba. It also maintains close ties with the United States, Canada, and Britain.

See also Colonial Latin America and the Caribbean; Slavery in Latin America and the Caribbean.

Lisa Clayton Robinson

Sakalava

Ethnic group of Madagascar.

The Sakalava primarily inhabit western Madagascar. They speak Malagasy, a Malayo-Polynesian language. Over one million people consider themselves Sakalava.

See also Madagascar, Ethnicity in.

Saldanha, José da Natividade

1795–1830

Afro-Brazilian poet, lawyer, fervent nationalist, and political revolutionary.

The illegitimate son of a Portuguese priest and a mulatto woman, José da Natividade Saldanha was born in Santo Amaro de Jaboatão, Pernambuco, Brazil. He went to Portugal, the colonial power, to study law at Coimbra University. While in law school Saldanha wrote and published his first collection of poems, *Poemas dedicadas aos amigos e amantes do Brasil* (Poems Dedicated to the Friends and Lovers of Brazil, 1822).

As a poet marked by Arcadianism, the influential neoclassical movement prevailing in some circles in Portugal and Brazil, Saldanha emphasized national and liberal ideologies that included the idea of a Brazilian republic and the abolition of slavery. Upon returning to Brazil the poet joined the secessionist movements brewing in Pernambuco and became a member of the junta that declared the independence of the Republic of Ecuador from Portugal in 1824. Condemned to death after the failure of this movement, Saldanha fled to the United States and from there to ENGLAND, FRANCE, VENEZUELA, and finally COLOMBIA, where he lived out the rest of his days in poverty. Saldanha died in Bogotá in 1830. During the course of his exile much of his work was lost, and that which remained was collected posthumously in *Poesia de Natividade Saldanha* (Natividade Saldanha's Poetry, 1875).

Saldanha has been called "the singer of the movement of independence." His verse reveals a deep patriotism interlaced with aesthetic sensibility.

See also Brazil, Blacks and Politics in: An Interpretation; Slavery in Latin America and the Caribbean.

Nicola Cooney

Saldaña, Excilia

1946–1999

Poet, essayist, translator, writer, and editor of children's stories whose works integrate her Hispanic poetic heritage with the religious and cultural heritage of the African diaspora.

Born into a middle-class Cuban family, Excilia Saldaña responded with fervor to the social and political changes that occurred in CUBA after the triumph of the 1959 revolution led by FIDEL CASTRO. During her college years, she became fully acquainted with Afro-Cuban culture through the ethnographic work of LYDIA CABRERA and FERNANDO ORTIZ.

Saldaña, like her poetic mentor and Cuba's poet laureate NICOLÁS GUILLÉN, celebrates her African ancestry by populating her poems with the gods and goddesses and flora and fauna symbolically drawn from the Afro-Cuban religion. Saldaña is indebted to Guillén for his integration of African and Hispanic cultural traditions in poetry, but she brings to the forefront the force of the feminine heritage in the Caribbean.

Saldaña's lengthy elegy, *My Name (A Family Anti-Elegy)*, published in 1991 by Ediciones Unión, bears a dedication to both Guillén and her grandmother, Ana Excilia Bregante. While establishing a direct link with Nicolás Guillén's "The Last Name: A Family Elegy" (1951), this poem constitutes an act of poetic self-definition that rejects the male tradition, instead asserting a female tradition inherited from her grandmother. Saldaña repeatedly appeals to the domestic yet mythical figure of her grandmother. Under the guise of rescuing her grandmother's forgotten and unusual name, Excilia, Saldaña establishes her name as the ultimate source of life for her poetry. Like Walt Whitman in "Song of Myself," the poet sets out to create the world of the Caribbean basin by the persistent invocation of her name.

Recreating the grandmother's voice and silences in the written poetic word, Saldaña has published a series of children's books that have been awarded literary prizes in Cuba. The two that have received the most acclaim are *Kele Kele* (1987) and *La Noche* (Night; 1989). The first, a book of prose poems dedicated to young adults, recreates five YORUBA legends based on the rhythm of the "romance," the traditional Spanish verse composed of eight syllables rhyming on every even line on the accented vowels. The second consists of poetic conversations between an inquiring child-self and the grandmother whose wise aphorisms instruct the granddaughter. In her own poetic terms, Saldaña defines for all Cubans their European and African heritage within the context of a feminine voice.

She has written over twenty books, including children's poems and legends, a feminist rewriting of the classics from the Greeks on, two autobiographical epic poems, erotic letters, and a poetic novel. Excilia Saldaña was a visiting professor at the Félix Varela Teaching Institute in Santa Clara and worked as an editor at the children's press Gente Nueva, in Havana. She died in 1999.

Flora González

Salem, Peter

1750–1816

Revolutionary War soldier who played a decisive role in the Battle of Bunker Hill.

Freed from slavery by his owner in order to fight in the Continental Army, Peter Salem was one of about 500 African Americans who served in the Revolutionary War. Along with Salem Poor, Peter Salem fought bravely in early pivotal battles in Massachusetts, including Concord in April 1775 and Bunker (Breed's) Hill in June 1775. Some contemporary eyewitnesses credited Salem with firing the decisive shot that killed British Major John Pitcairn at Bunker Hill. Artist John Trumbull is said to have depicted Salem in his 1786 painting "The Battle of Bunker's Hill," which shows a black soldier holding a musket. Serving bravely until the end of the war, Salem died in poverty in his hometown of Framingham, Massachusetts, after a career as a cane weaver. In 1882, a monument was erected to his memory in Framingham.

See also American Revolution.

Salisbury

Former name of Harare, Zimbabwe.

See also Harare, Zimbabwe; Zimbzabwe.

Salomon, Lysius Félicité

1815–1888

Black Haitian politician who challenged the racial aristocracy imposed by Haiti's mulatto bourgeoisie, eventually becoming president from 1879 to 1888.

Born to a black family of southern landowners in HAITI, Salomon was involved at an early age in social and political activities. In 1843 he became a spokesperson for black peasants of Les Cayes who were rebelling against the mulatto-led Liberal Party. Salomon's participation, which began after the government suppressed the formation of small landholdings in the interest of larger estates, made him a legendary figure. A senator in his early thirties, he went on to hold the influential post of minister of finance for eleven years under FAUSTIN ELIE SOULOUQUE, a national president who later declared himself emperor.

After a coup overthrew Soulouque, Salomon lived in exile in JAMAICA and EUROPE for more than twenty years. During Salomon's period of exile the Haitian elite was divided into various competing groups, and Salomon's family became deeply involved in the ensuing political struggle, which would cost the lives of Salomon's two brothers, two uncles, a brother-in-law, and his adoptive son.

Salomon attempted to return to his homeland in 1876 and 1878, but it was only during the 1879 elections that he returned as a presidential candidate for the black-dominated National Party, and defeated the Liberals by a landslide. As president, Salomon instituted numerous economic and educational reforms, including the creation of the National Bank, the selling off of public lands to poor peasants, and the development of rural schools.

In 1886 Salomon had the 1879 Constitution revised so that he could be reelected president for seven more years. His opponents, fearing that Salomon would establish himself as president for life, conducted a successful insurrection two years later, in 1888. Forced to retire, and ailing, Salomon left for FRANCE, where he died that same year.

Martine Fernandes

Salsa Music

Popular music of Latin America and the Caribbean that incorporates characteristics of rhythm and blues, jazz, and rock.

It is difficult to define exactly what salsa music is or what music falls into the category, or, indeed, if there is a significant difference between the salsa of the 1970s and older Cuban music. What nobody denies is that this commercial label has much to do with the boom in musical production by Cubans, Puerto Ricans, Nuyoricans (New York Puerto Ricans), and other Caribbean communities in the late 1960s and early 1970s. Literally, *salsa* means sauce, a semiliquid combination of ingredients and spices; and some critics affirm that the term accurately describes the particular spicy taste (*sabor*) of this music and its free combination of Afro-Caribbean rhythms. But others state that salsa is only an adulterated form of the Cuban SON and insist that its short period of innovation and experimentation can ultimately be defined by its continuity with Cuban music. Nevertheless, almost everybody recognizes that salsa is the commercial label that names the Afro-Cuban music produced by Spanish-speaking Caribbean communities both in New York and in their homelands since the late 1960s.

Salsa comes from the Afro-Cuban religious and secular music of the slaves. Like in Cuban *son*, the heart of salsa is the clave, a three-two or two-three beat spanning two measures, which creates the syncopated foundation sustaining the lyrics and instrumentation. Salsa groups generally consist of drums, bass, piano, a brass section, and vocals. Like the Cuban *son*, salsa's structure consists of an instrumental introduction, followed by short and simple lyrics, another instrumental section, and the chorus, which includes some lyrical improvisations by the lead singer. There are exceptions to this general form. The call-and-response section between singer and chorus as well as the syncopated beat of the clave are among the musical elements traceable to African musical styles.

The word *salsa* came into use in the late 1960s as a commercial label to identify the music produced principally by FANIA RECORDS, by then emerging as the strongest "Latin" music industry in New York City. Some scholars argue that this new commercial label underscores the differences between the new groups promoted by Fania and the music of the Latin big bands that were extremely popular in New York during the 1950s. They maintain that salsa expresses the "soul" of the Latin (mainly Puerto Rican and Caribbean) neighborhoods of New York, drawing on Cuban music for its rhythmic core but also incorporating some influences from other Afro-Caribbean musical genres as well as from African American music. For them, salsa is an expression of the multicultural experience of the New York ghettos, which combines Cuban and other Afro-Caribbean rhythms with the influence of rock and roll, SOUL, and JAZZ. Salsa is thus not so much a rhythm as a musical style distinguished by its free combination of rhythms, innovation, and experimentation. Critics of this definition argue that whatever the innovation and experimentation, what is called salsa is in fact strongly rooted in such Cuban rhythms as son, *guaracha*, and RUMBA, not to mention MAMBO, which already drew heavily on American jazz.

Whether a new musical phenomenon or an adulteration of Cuban *son*, salsa is strongly linked to the history of the Puerto Rican and Cuban immigration to New York. These communities have influenced the music of their homelands as well as the United States with the growth of the record industry and the radio since the 1920s. During the 1940s and 1950s, Cuban big bands were very popular in New York and other big cities, as well as in Hollywood films. Key among these was the Afro-Cuban band started by Frank Grillo ("MACHITO") and his brother-in-law MARIO BAUZÁ. In the 1950s, Machito's band was a featured attraction at the Palladium Ballroom, the epicenter of the New York Latin scene, along with two bands led by Puerto Rican musicians ERNESTO ANTONIO (TITO) PUENTE and Pablo "Tito" Rodriguez.

During these years, Puerto Rican immigration to the United States increased dramatically to form what was by the early 2000s a population of 2.7 million, over one million of whom live in New York City. This community became the main market for Cuban big-bands, almost all of which contained Puerto Rican musicians.

The 1960s were years of change and commotion. For Puerto Rican and Cuban musicians in New York and PUERTO RICO, the Cuban revolution and subsequent U.S. blockade marked a rupture in communication with CUBA. It was also becoming difficult economically to sustain a big band. New, smaller groups emerged, which required changes in instrumentation, particularly a reduction in the brass section and the number of singers. The big dance halls were also closing, replaced by smaller venues. The new bands needed not only to be smaller but also to include instruments that were easier to carry, such as the electric bass and electric piano.

Four key features, then, can be said to distinguish salsa from other types of Latin music. First, because many salsa music groups were integrated by second rather than first-generation immigrants, New York represented their life experience. This meant that their musical formation not only came from their Afro-Cuban and Puerto Rican heritage but also from greater contact with other American communities, particularly with African Americans. Second, the closing of the big dancing halls put the musicians literally on the streets. Playing on the street and in smaller and cheaper clubs, these musicians formed a somewhat closer tie with the community than had the big bands. Third, the introduction of the electric bass and electric piano changed how the music was played, producing a louder sound closer to that of rock and roll. Fourth, many of the new songs chronicled Nuyorican everyday life, immediately appealing to this community. All these factors were expressed in an aggressive and loudly daring sound, which strongly emphasized improvisations and the free combination of rhythms.

This new genre or style was represented by Fania Records, which effectively and aggressively recruited well-known musicians and bands. JOHNNY PACHECO, the founder of Fania, CELIA CRUZ, and Ray Barreto, as well as the newer bands of Larry Harlow, Bobby Valentín, and WILLIE COLÓN were among the talents working with Fania.

Marked by the New York experience, these young musicians experimented with many rhythms and musical genres. Before salsa, they created the BOOGALOO, a genre closer to soul. The boogaloo in part represented an attempt by Latin musicians to appeal to a non-Latin audience. Boogaloos were often in English and fused elements not only of soul but of RHYTHM AND BLUES. Joe Cuba, Joe Bataan, The Lebron Brothers, and Johnny Colon were among the noted contributors to this genre. Fania, in its early days, recorded Cuban music and boogaloo in almost equal numbers, the latter gaining popularity among the Spanish-speaking community as well among non-Latin audiences. There is no answer that completely explains the boogaloo's demise by the early 1970s. A number of its creators attribute its demise to the politics of the Latin music industry, suggesting that they were shut out of radio and recording after a group of them sought a more independent path for the genre. Perhaps salsa, more strongly rooted in its Afro-Cuban heritage, signified stronger community identity and resistance.

Fania Records continued promoting the new salsa groups, whose sounds and Spanish lyrics made it easier to corner the market in Puerto Rico and other Spanish-speaking Caribbean countries. Indeed, during the 1970s the popularity of salsa spread throughout Latin America but particularly to Caribbean countries. In COLOMBIA, for instance, groups such as Fruko y Los Tesos sowed the seeds for what is now a national industry, producing some of the world's best-known salsa bands (Grupo Niche, Orquesta Guayacán). Venezuela's Oscar d'Leon and Panamanian singer RUBÉN BLADES also became giants on the international stage.

For the Nuyorican community, however, salsa is the music of its people. It expresses their experience, their identity with Afro- and Spanish-Caribbean roots and culture, and the free combination of these with African American musical genres. The adoption of the term *salsa* is said by some to have originated with the Venezuelan radio program "Echale Salsita" (Put on the Sauce), widely broadcast throughout the Caribbean. But the term is also linked with Fania Records, which commercially promoted the genre under the new name.

The commercial promotion also reflects the tensions between autonomous community expression and commercial appropriation. This relation can be seen in the two movies produced by Fania. The first, *Our Latin Thing,* strongly relates salsa to the everyday life of the Nuyorican community; the second, *Salsa,* erases these community signs, replacing them with more homogeneous and ambiguous signs common to a broader Afro-Caribbean tradition.

This process of homogenization of salsa developed into what in the 1980s became known as romantic or erotic salsa, which simplified salsa lyrics into love songs—often based on old romantic ballads. Other musicians, however, continue the innovative lyrics and instrumental experimentation that characterized the genre in the 1970s. In particular, a new generation of Cuban talent has emerged on the international stage. Groups such as Los Van Van and NG La Banda continue to create new musical hybrids, drawing not only on Cuban music but on other musical expressions of the diaspora.

See also Music, Afro-Caribbean Religious; Music, Afro-Caribbean Secular; Nuyorican Poets.

Juan Otero-Garabis

Salt-N-Pepa

The first female rap group to have an album achieve platinum status.

Cheryl "Salt" James, Sandi "Pepa" Denton, and Dee Dee "Spinderella" Roper make up the female RAP trio Salt-N-Pepa. Since their first hit in 1985, these three single mothers have released five award-winning albums (one gold, two platinum, and one triple platinum), and earned the honor of being the first female RAP group to have an album sell over one million copies. Despite the male-dominated rap music industry, Salt-N-Pepa has sold more than four million records and released eight singles that reached *Billboard's* Top Forty, two of which climbed to the number three and four positions on Billboard's Top Ten.

Cheryl James and Sandi Denton first met in the mid-1980s when both were attending nursing school at Queensborough Community College in Queens, New York. While working part-time at a Sears department store, James and Denton met Hurby Azor, who had just finished composing a song entitled "The Showstopper," a lyrical response to the 1985 hit "The Show," released by rappers Doug E. Fresh and Slick Rick. James and Denton performed "Showstopper" later that year.

Taking the name "Super Nature," James and Denton then caught the eye of Next Plateau Records, which quickly signed them. After fans picked up on a line in "Showstopper" in which James and Denton refer to themselves as "the salt and pepa MCs," the duo became known as Salt-N-Pepa. In 1986 they officially changed their name, just in time for the release of their second single, "I'll Take Your Man." That year the group also released its first album, *Hot, Cool, and Vicious*. Featuring such hits as "Tramp," "Beauty and the Beat," and "Push It," *Hot, Cool, and Vicious* was an instant success and sold more than one million copies, earning the group its first platinum album.

In 1987, the group replaced DJ Latoya Hanson with Dee Dee "Spinderella" Roper. With Hurby Azor as its producer, Salt-N-Pepa released its second album, *A Salt with a Deadly Pepa*. Filled with contemporary remixes of ISLEY BROTHERS classics, including "Twist and Shout" and "It's Your Thang," the album received a mixed reaction. It sold 500,000 copies before the group announced plans for its next album.

In 1990 Salt-N-Pepa assumed greater control of the writing, composing, and production of their work and released *Blacks' Magic*. Such hits as "Expression," "Independent," and "Push It" encouraged listeners not to follow the crowd and reminded young women to stand tall and proud. Their message and hard work were rewarded when the album went platinum. A single from the album, "Let's Talk About Sex," captured the attention of ABC News journalist Peter Jennings, who asked Salt-N-Pepa to rewrite the song for a public service announcement about ACQUIRED IMMUNODEFICIENCY SYNDROME (AIDS). The new song, entitled "Let's Talk About AIDS," was released in 1992 and earned the group national acclaim.

Salt-N-Pepa delivered its fourth album, *Very Necessary,* a year later. With top ten hits such as "Shoop" and "Whatta Man," the album went triple platinum. The single "None of Your Business" earned the group a Grammy Award in 1994 for Best Rap Vocal by a Group or Duo. At the height of their career, Salt-N-Pepa's singers have toured the world, promoting female pride and social consciousness. They have won three MTV Video Music Awards, produced an all-female charity album called *Ain't Nuthin' But A She Thang,* and performed the song "Freedom" for the movie *Panther*. In 1995, Salt-N-Pepa signed a multimillion-dollar contract with MCA Records and in 1997 they released their fifth album, *Brand New,* blending thought-provoking lyrics with upbeat HIP-HOP tempos. Salt-N-Pepa remains at the forefront of rap music. *Best of Salt-N-Pepa* was released in 2000. "People who come in contact with us feel the realness and it's not a front with us," says Pepa (Denton). "We are still humbled by our success. We give thanks to God."

See also Feminism in the United States; Music, African American; Womanism.

Alonford James Robinson

Salt Trade

Exchange of salt for commodities such as gold and slaves, particularly in West Africa.

Salt was probably one of the earliest goods traded over long distances in Africa. While the vital mineral was scarce in the savanna and forest regions of Africa, large deposits of salt occurred in the SAHARA. Those who controlled these deposits traded salt for slaves, gold, ivory, craft goods, malaguetta pepper, KOLA nuts, and foodstuffs from the forest and savanna zones. In turn, trans-Saharan traders purchased some of these goods, especially gold, ivory, slaves, and kola nuts, and carried them to North Africa. In exchange for these goods, caravans transported horses and Mediterranean craft goods, such as glass, south across the Sahara.

The accumulation of goods exchanged for salt, including slaves and gold, promoted social stratification in the SAHEL. The trade thus contributed to the rise of empires such as the Ghana, the Mali, and the Songhai, though internal developments also played a role—as did horses, which were obtained in North Africa and increased the military strength of these expansionist kingdoms.

Salt mines in the Sahara produced large slabs of salt, weighing as much as 100 kg (220 lb), which porters transported by CAMEL to central markets in cities such as TOMBOUCTOU, MALI. Slaves working in the enormous salt mines at Taghaza lived in houses and prayed in mosques constructed out of salt slabs. Another source of salt was the SONGHAI EMPIRE, in present-day MALI, where salt functioned as currency. The kingdom's rulers kept the location of salt deposits secret and heavily guarded. Canoes carried large quantities of cake salt from Gao up and down the NIGER RIVER and from river ports throughout West Africa. The mines of the Sahara were not the only source of salt. Kisama in LUANDA, ANGOLA, also produced significant amounts of salt. The IJAW evaporated the seawater of the Niger Delta to produce salt in significant quantities. The kingdom of Bornu also exported salt that was produced by evaporating the saline waters of LAKE CHAD. Customers apparently preferred the taste of the lake salt, heavy in sodium carbonate, rather than pure rock salt for their MILLET porridge.

While plentiful in the Sahara, salt was a scarce and expensive substance in the interior forest and savanna regions. Some sources even suggest that gold-producing peoples exchanged salt in equal weight for gold. Coastal peoples, who could evaporate sea salt, apparently preferred the taste of pure rock salt from the desert. Thus the value of gold depended, to an extent, on the value of salt in the markets of West Africa.

The salt trade helped to promote the spread of Islam, since Muslim traders carrying salt also brought their religion to the people of the south. While the ancient kingdom of Ghana dominated the gold trade during the second half of the first millennium B.C.E., for example, the kingdom depended upon the salt of Aoudaghost to the north. By the twelfth century the rulers of Ghana had converted to Islam.

See also Ghana, Early Kingdom of; Gold Trade; Islam in Africa; Ivory Trade; Kanuri; Mali Empire.

Bibliography

Adshead, S.A.M. *Salt and Civilization*. St. Martin's Press, 1992.

Gray, Richard, and David Birmingham, eds. *Pre-Colonial African Trade: Essays on Trade in Central and Eastern Africa Before 1900*. Oxford University Press, 1970.

Lovejoy, Paul E. *Salt and the Desert Sun: A History of Salt Production and Trade in Central Sudan*. Cambridge University Press, 1986.

Ari Nave

Salvador, Brazil

City in the Brazilian state of Bahia.

See also Bahia; Brazil.

Samba

Brazil's most famous musical genre and dance, created by Brazilians of African descent living in Rio de Janeiro during the late 1800s.

To Brazilians, samba is many different things: abandon and solace, celebration and exuberance, national identity and pride. Though samba is most closely associated with the pre-Lent festivities known as Carnival, there are several forms of samba that are played year-round in various contexts. Percussive instruments dominate samba and give it a highly syncopated, layered sound. Technically, a 2/4 meter with the heaviest accent on the second beat and a stanza-and-refrain structure characterize samba.

Samba is rooted in the music and dance traditions of ANGOLA, the African kingdom (now country) that was home for many of the slaves brought to BRAZIL. The word samba is believed to have derived from the Kimbundu word *semba*, a circle dance that features a navel-touching dance step. Many historians trace the musical roots of samba to the *lundu* music tradition brought to Brazil by slaves from Angola. This African dance and form of music are two of the numerous elements that were fused to create samba in RIO DE JANEIRO during the late 1800s.

Following the abolishment of slavery in 1888 and the subsequent decline of the plantation economy, a large number of ex-slaves living in the northern region of Brazil migrated south to Rio de Janeiro in search of opportunity. Some settled on the steep hillsides surrounding the city, the *morros*, while others settled in a central part of the city in the neighborhood of Estácio near Praça Onze (Plaza Eleven). Praça Onze and the houses of prominent black women known as *tias* (aunts), who sold African food and led services for the worship of African gods, became meeting places for black musicians. The music they played—lundu, polka, and *habanera* as well as *marcha* and *maxixe*, two popular types of Brazilian music—factored in the creation of samba music.

Pioneering musicians such as Ismael Silva distinguished samba from marcha and maxixe by slowing the tempo, and adding longer notes and two-bar phrasing. In 1917 a musician named Donga recorded "Pelo Telefone" (On the Telephone), a song widely regarded as the first samba composition. The traditional form of samba is played on a four-stringed, ukulele-like instrument called *cavaquinho*; a shallow, covered drumhead with jingling disks called the *pandeiro*; and its smaller, cymbal-less counterpart the *tamborim*, which is played with a stick. This form of samba later became known as the *samba de morro*.

Numerous forms of samba developed out of the traditional samba de morro. One of the earliest was *samba de breque*, a style developed during the 1930s by singer Moreira da Silva. In songs such as "Acertei no Milhar" (I Hit Upon Thousands, 1938), Silva would periodically stop the song in order to dramatize the situation he was singing about through improvised dialogues. It was also during the 1930s that numerous white Brazilians began to compose samba songs that popularized samba with the light-skinned middle class. According to historians Chris McGowan and Ricardo Pessanha, these musicians and singers downplayed the rhythm in favor of melody and wrote more complex and often sentimental lyrics.

This form of samba became known as *samba-canção* and is associated with composers such as Noel Rosa and Ary Barroso. Barroso spawned yet another form of samba in 1939 when he recorded one of the most famous Brazilian songs of all time, "Aquarela do Brasil" (Watercolor of Brazil). This song launched a new category of samba called *samba-exaltação* (samba of praise) that celebrated the natural wonders of Brazil.

The national and international popularity of these emerging forms of samba endured through the 1940s and overshadowed the traditional samba de morro. Despite this trend, and the growing tendency of some musicians to fuse samba with other popular styles of music, black Brazilians living on the outskirts of Rio and around Praça Onze preserved and embellished the rhythm of samba de morro. In the 1950s they reasserted the importance of samba de morro during their Carnival celebrations.

In the 1970s several musicians living in Ramos, a suburb of Rio, espoused a form of samba known as *samba-pagode*. They incorporated a type of drum called the *tan-tan*, exchanged the cavaquinho for a banjo, and sang about daily life in a colloquial language that gave their music an unpolished, down-to-earth quality. While the samba-pagode was initially limited to informal settings such as parties, singer Beth Carvalho popularized the form through her 1983 album *Beth Carvalho no Pagode*. Numerous other forms of samba thrive in Brazil today, including *samba de gafieira, samba de roda,* and *samba-reggae.*

See also Carnivals in Latin America and the Caribbean.

Aaron Myers

Samba, Candomblé, and Quilombo in Brazilian Cinema: An Interpretation

> Blackness is like a vibrant and luminous combustible which supplies a kind of telluric energy for a humanity more and more in need of it.
>
> *Gilberto Gil*

For many Americans, the phrase "Brazilian Cinema" instantly elicits the memory of what was in fact a French film—Marcel Camus's *Black Orpheus*. More than any other film, *Black Orpheus* created in the international consciousness a powerful association among three related concepts: Brazilianness, Blackness, and Carnival. North American critics raved about "intoxicating samba music, frenzied dancing and violent costumes" (Bosley Crowther, *New York Times*). In his filmic adaptation of the Vinícius de Moraes source play, the French director combined actual Carnival footage from the 1958 Rio Carnival with staged footage in which thousands of Brazilians, generally for no pay, played at Carnival for the cameras. While in many ways offering a French touristic view of Carnival, *Black Orpheus* did at least have the virtue of foregrounding black talent and black performance. With the exception of Marpessa Dawn as Eurydice, all of the major roles were played by Afro-Brazilian actors and actresses. Although a *New Yorker* reviewer attributed the "seduction" of the film to "its naive quality, emanating from its untrained negro actors . . ." in fact most of the leading actors and actresses were professional performers, many of them from Abdias do Nascimento's Teatro Experimental do Negro.

Black Orpheus called attention to a highly Africanized cultural phenomenon—Carnival—combining ecstatic polyrhythmic percussion with the elaborate folk opera of the samba school pageants. The problem with the seductive imagery, when seen out of context, is the danger of taking the festive part for the social whole. In this sense, *Black Orpheus* advances a romantic and mystical vision of Carnival and Brazil. The film suggests a primitive capacity on the part of the happy black Brazilians to enjoy life no matter how devastating the conditions. As a kind of Brazilian *West Side Story*, *Black Orpheus* prettifies the favelas of Rio and isolates Carnival from its social context. Authentic Carnival offers a dialectical critique of the injustices of everyday life, not a metaphysical transcendence against a postcard backdrop. *Black Orpheus* enlists all the elements of Carnival—dance, rhythm, music, color, laughter—but ultimately in the service of a stereotypical vision.

Sociological Preamble

Because of the danger that a celebration of the Afro-Brazilian cultural contribution to Brazilian cinema might appear to imply an endorsement of Brazil's putative "racial democracy" it is important to provide a modicum of historical and sociological background. Brazil is the largest black nation outside of Africa, with at least 70 million citizens who descend, to one degree or another, from the slaves brought from Africa.

Without developing a thoroughgoing analysis of the racial situation in Brazil, we can posit some initial points as a backdrop for our discussion. First, blacks and mulattos represent the marginalized majority of Brazilian citizens. Second, Brazil is, in structural terms, a racist society. Although Brazilian history is not marked by virulent racism or by racial ghettos and segregation, Afro-Brazilians remain economically, politically, and socially oppressed. Blacks and mulattos are excluded from positions of influence, while they are overrepresented in the favelas, in the prisons, and in the ranks of the underemployed. Brazilian racism is subtle, less a matter of malignant hatred than of paternalist condescension. It consists not in a binary white-over-black but rather in the superimposition of an official integrationist ideology ("racial democracy") on a reality pervaded by a subtle prejudice that white is better.

One striking feature that separates Brazilian from mainstream North American culture is the extent to which the former is highly and consciously Africanized (I emphasize "consciously" because white North America has yet to become fully aware of the ways in which it too has been changed and enriched by the cultural contribution of Afro-Americans). When one speaks of black performance in Brazil, one is also talking about Brazilian performance in general, in the sense that the Brazilian manner, the *jeito*, the way of walking and talking and touching, are thoroughly inflected by African-derived cultural patterns. The flexibility and gregariousness of Brazilian life, the capacity for collective enthusiasm, can be seen, in some measure, as an African inheritance. Even the expansive orality of the culture is marked by Africanism.

My purpose in this essay is to explore the filmic presence of Afro-Brazilian culture and performance in relation to three broad themes: 1) the presence of Afro-Brazilian music and of Brazil's Africanized Carnival; 2) the manifestations of Afro-Brazilian religious forms such as Candomblé, *Macumba*, and Umbanda; and 3) the representation of Afro-Brazilian political struggle, which can also be seen as a kind of performance, this time on the world-historical stage. Brazilian cinema has privileged all these themes, and without them, and without black performance, Brazilian cinema would be immeasurably impoverished. What, then, has been the contribution of Afro-Brazilian culture, specifically in the form of Afro-Brazilian music, Afro-Brazilian religion, and Afro-Brazilian political resistance, within Brazilian cinema?

Afro-Brazilian Music and the Cinema

Brazilian cinema, throughout its history, has been closely linked to Brazilian music, and Brazilian music has always been closely linked to Africa. The African presence marks both erudite music and, more obviously, the popular music of such Afro-Brazilian or Afro-influenced composers and singers as GILBERTO GIL, Jorge Ben, Martinho da Vila, MILTON NASCIMENTO, D. Ivone Lara, Moraes Moreira, Luiz Melodia, CLEMENTINA DE JESUS, Beth Carvalho, Caetano Veloso, and DJAVAN. Africa provided many of the instruments featured in Brazilian music—the *cuica*, the *agogô*, the *berimbau*—and, more important, it provided the cardinal aesthetic principles on which Brazilian music in general, and samba in particular, are built. Contemporary Brazilian popular music is not only dominated by Afro-Brazilian or Afro-influenced composers and singers but it also increasingly addresses, in its lyrics, Afro-Brazilian themes and preoccupations.

Apart from the participation of Afro-Brazilian musicians in composing the musical tracks of Brazilian films—Jorge Ben (*Xica da Silva*), Milton Nascimento (*The Fall*), Gilberto Gil (*Tent of Miracles, Quilombo*)—the Afro-Brazilian musical presence enters the cinema in another form, through the energizing presence of Carnival. While Carnival admittedly has European antecedents, Carnival in Brazil is a highly Africanized phenomenon. The African presence is clearly marked in the central role of polymetric music and dance, of parades and exuberant costume. It is also Afro-Brazilians who give a critical edge to the utopian impulses of Carnival. Since it is they who most obviously suffer the dystopia of unemployment and marginality, it is naturally they who have the greatest investment in the liberatory mechanisms of Carnival. In an atmosphere of gestural freedom and fantasy, revelers play out imaginary roles corresponding to their fondest desires. Poor blacks and mulattos appear as aristocrats in wigs and regal costumes, thus symbolically affirming their nobility within an ephemeral utopia characterized by dignity, abundance, and commonality.

Countless Brazilian films have documented the reality of Carnival. The documentary shorts devoted to Rio's Carnival in the first decades of the twentieth century featured the Afro-Brazilian revelers who then constituted the majority of Rio's population. Although blacks were largely excluded from the symbolically "white" cinema of the silent period, black culture was implicitly present in the frequent representation of Carnival. The very word "Carnival" figures prominently in the titles of a disproportionate number of Brazilian films, ranging from the first "views" through the series of remakes of *O Carnaval Cantado* (The Singing Carnival), first produced in 1919, through sound-era *chanchadas* such as *Alô, Alô Carnaval* (1936) to post–CINEMA NOVO productions such as *Quando o Carnaval Chegar* (When Carnival Comes, 1971). The chanchadas popular through the 1930s, 1940s, and 1950s, in fact, were designated, as if in anticipation of a Bakhtinian analysis, "*filmes carnavalescos*" (Carnivalesque films).

The advent of sound brought the thorough musicalization of Brazilian cinema and with it a strong Afro-Brazilian influence, even if Afro-Brazilians themselves seldom appeared on the screen. In the chanchadas—Rio-based comedies featuring musical numbers and Carnival themes—blacks and mulattos tended to be featured only in minor or background roles. Despite occasional exceptions—Humberto Mauro's *Favela dos Meus Amores* (Favela of my Loves, 1935) features the musicians and dancers of the Portela Samba School—most chanchadas use blacks merely as backdrop for the love intrigues of white stars like Carmen Miranda, Eliane Macedo, or Cyl Farney. Since the chanchadas were partially modeled on the Hollywood musical, a genre not known generally (if one excepts "all-black musicals" like *Hallelujah* and *Cabin in the Sky*) for any exaltation of black culture, they tended to downplay blackness. Although samba was largely an Afro-Brazilian contribution, film after film gave the impression that samba was a white cultural product.

An exception to this rule, ironically, came from a North American director. In 1942, Orson Welles went to Brazil to film two episodes of the never-to-be finished *It's All True*, a semi-documentary aimed at fostering the Good Neighbor policy and countering Nazi propaganda in Latin America. Welles, a jazz lover who had produced an all-black *Macbeth* for the Federal Theatre, went to Brazil already attuned, in a certain measure, to black performance. His guide in Rio was Vinícius de Moraes, author of the source play for *Black Orpheus*, and who later referred to himself as "*o branco mais preto do Brasil*" (the blackest white man in Brazil). Welles became a samba and Carnival enthusiast, to the point that he reconceptualized *It's All True*, originally intended to be a pan-American epic, so as to privilege Brazil. He organized the film around two central characters, a five-year-old boy and a samba school leader (played by Luis Sebastião Prata, commonly known as GRANDE OTELO) desperate over the destruction of Praça Onze, the Rio square through which the samba of the *morros* traditionally enters the city.

Welles dispatched second units to film the *desfiles* of Praça Onze and a *frevo* group from Recife; at the same time he rented the Cinedia studios in Rio to supplement the more authentic footage. Originally planned to emphasize Carnival itself, the Rio episode was transformed into the story of the samba when Welles resolved to explain the origins of a musical-dance form, which Welles had come to see as the Brazilian equivalent of jazz. The key structural idea was to trace the itinerary of the samba from the favelas to its climactic explosion in Carnival in the center of the city. Welles also planned to interweave sequences of Macumba with the sequences of Carnival. From the production stills and existing footage of *It's All True* it is obvious that the film would have revealed a Carnival that was overwhelmingly black. According to Brazilian film critic Paulo Emilio Salles Gomes, Welles saw the film as a hymn of solidarity with the blacks of Rio and with their culture. In fact, this sense of solidarity was not always appreciated. One member of the production crew complained in writing to RKO executives that Welles was overemphasizing the black element and showing too much "ordinary social intercourse" between blacks and whites in Carnival, a feature that would doubtless offend some North American viewers.

One Brazilian director who has repeatedly turned to Afro-Brazilian themes is Nelson Pereira dos Santos. While most directors treated black characters and themes with paternalistic condescension, Pereira dos Santos has consistently accorded blackness respect and pride of place. His *Rio Zona Norte* (Rio Northern Zone, 1957) focuses on the samba composer Espírito da Luz Doares, incarnated brilliantly by Grande Otelo, and on Doares's exploitation. The title refers to the urban topography of Rio de Janeiro, which is divided into the *zona sul* (southern zone), the wealthier (and whiter) area of Rio embracing the beautiful beaches and lovely residential neighborhoods of Copacabana, Ipanema, Leblon, and Lagoa; and the *zona norte* (northern zone), the location of the "*subúrbios,*" that is, the poorer (and blacker) neighborhoods of lower-class working people and *favelados*. Rio, an agreeable city for the residents of the zona sul, can be a hell for the inhabitants of the zona norte, where even the pollution seems to discriminate. (It is no accident that the black movement in music, largely inspired by North American soul and black power influences, emerged from the northern zone). *Rio Zona Norte* shows the world of the samba as experienced by one of the many composers who used to sell their sambas for virtually nothing in the hopes of one day hearing them played on the radio or during Carnival. The history of Brazilian music, like that of North American music, is replete with stories of these struggling and often anonymous musical poets. While the film is not racially schematic, we notice that Espírito's exploiters tend to be white. Maurício (Jece Valedão) pretends to be a friend and collaborator of Espírito's, but in fact he steals his sambas and sells them to the highest bidder. We see a kind of "cordial" Brazilian racism at work, in which embraces and warm words serve as camouflage for a relationship of exploitation. Espírito is manipulated because of his inexperience and his faith that other human beings are as uncalculating and honest as he is; he learns quickly, however, and comes to insist on his right to share in the profits and determine the musical quality of the final product.

The treatment of Espírito in *Rio Zona Norte* clearly contrasts with that given Orpheus in the Marcel Camus film. Orpheus is the "universal" mythic figure, here transported to Brazil, who knows how to make the sun rise; he is largely stripped of all social specificity. Espírito, on the other hand, is rooted in a specific time, place, culture, and even neighborhood. His exploitation, too, is specific; he is exploited by his "partners," by disc jockeys, and by record company managers. *Rio Zona Norte* exposes the process by which samba composers lost financial and artistic control of their own musical production, whether through the crudest kind of exploitation or through a more subtle process of erudite thievery of musical ideas. (A talentless and frustrated middle-class composer speaks of writing a ballet based on Espírito's music.) *Rio Zona Norte* registers the circular process whereby samba originates in the *bactucadas* of the favelas, and then moves to nightclubs and radio, gaining a layer of sophistication with every step, and finally returns to the favelas. Although those who hear Espírito's music on the radio are unaware of his existence, his fellow favelados remember: "The favelas don't forget you," goes one of his sambas, "for the *morro,* the samba didn't die . . ." The samba of the final sequence sets up a series of equations: the morro (the hillside or favela) is the samba and the samba is Brazil: "It's my samba/and Brazil's too." Espírito's sambas speak of the people's suffering as well as their joy. They speak of favela shacks collapsing, of daily humiliations, of wells running dry; they contrast existing social imperfections with an implied utopia. And like the sambas, which speak of sorrow and misery yet communicate an immense capacity for happiness, *Rio Zona Norte* itself creates a dialectical tension between social commentary and sensual pleasure, the tragic and the comic, the bitter and the sweet.

In the wake of Nelson Pereira dos Santos's pioneering efforts, the Cinema Novo directors of the 1960s searched out the dimly illuminated corners of Brazilian life—and especially favela and *sertão* (dry hinterland in the northeast)—creating a cinema in which black Brazilians had a crucial role. The new role for blacks, unfortunately, continued to be a reductive one; blacks came to be seen as the most obvious victims of an oppression that afflicted the majority of Brazilians. Racial categories were subsumed under social and economic ones. Eager to avoid the picturesque and stereotypical vision of Brazil as the land of Carnival and samba, the Cinema Novo directors tended to downplay the specifically cultural contribution of Afro-Brazilians. Carlos Diegues's short film *Escola de Samba, Alegria de Viver* (Samba School Joy of Living), subsequently incorporated into the collective film *Cinco Vezes Favela* (Five Times Favela, 1962), for example, makes the didactic point that the favelados should abandon the escapism of samba for serious political organizing. Designed to illustrate the progressive ideas of white middle-class intellectuals, the films generally failed to confront the racial dimension of oppression or to acknowledge the rich cultural contribution of Afro-Brazilians.

This is not to say that Afro-Brazilian music and culture were entirely absent from the films of the early phases of Cinema Novo. Apart from films specifically dedicated to an Afro-Brazilian theme, such as *O Pagador de Promessas* (The Given Word, 1962) and *Barravento* (1962)—to be discussed subsequently—many Brazilian films evoke political and social conflict through the manipulation of cultural expression, and Afro-Brazilian music is crucial in this regard. *The Given Word,* for example, sets in motion a cultural battle between the African-derived berimbau and church bell, synecdochically encapsulating the larger struggle of Candomblé and Catholicism. Glauber Rocha's *Terra em Transe* (Land in Anguish, 1967) exemplifies a film featuring few Afro-Brazilian actors but in which Afro-Brazilian music and culture play a primordial role. The English title misses the clear reference to the "*transe*" of Candomblé, a reference that structures the entire film and even organizes a montage that periodically goes in and out of "trance." The reference is reinforced by the Candomblé music heard during the credit sequence of the film, superimposed with aerial shots of the coast of Brazil, as if to say: this is the land of Candomblé. The Afro-Brazilian music in the film stands in, as it were, for the people, while Rocha associates each of the representatives of the white political elite with a distinct kind of music. The Mexican rightist Porfirio Diaz is linked to the operas of Verdi and to his Brazilian imitator Carlos Gomes, while the left-intellectual protagonist Paulo Martins is associated with the music of Villa-Lobos, who, like the protagonist and like Rocha himself, is the erudite elaborator of popular themes.

The 1970s witnessed the "re-Carnivalization" of Brazilian cinema, not only as a key trope orienting the filmmakers' productions but also as a concrete presence in the films themselves. The incorporation of Afro-Brazilian music was motivated by a changed attitude as well as a desire to renew contact with the Brazilian audience. Carnival is a literal presence in such films as Carlos Diegues's *Quando O Carnaval Chegar* (When Carnival Comes, 1969), Walter Lima, Jr.'s *Lira do Delírio* (Delirious Lyre, 1978), and Vera Fequeireido's *Samba da Criação do Mundo* (Samba of the Creation of the World, 1979), based on a pageant performed by the Beija Flor Samba School. This same period witnesses a proliferation of documentary tributes to Afro-Brazilian music and musicians: João Carlos Horta's *Pixinguinha* (1969), Carlos Tourinho's *Escola de Samba* (1978), Reinaldo Cozer's *Pérola Negra* (Luiz Melodia, 1979), and Tuna Espinheira's *Samba Não se Aprende na Escola* (One Doesn't Learn Samba at School, 1979).

In other films, Carnival in Brazilian films forms part of the wider circulation of popular and erudite culture. The stories of Diegues's *Xica da Silva* (1976) and Walter Lima, Jr.'s *Chico Rei* (1982), for example, were first presented as samba school pageants for Rio's Carnival. Indeed, Carlos Diegues has said that he conceived both *Xica da Silva* and his most recent *Quilombo* (1984) as "*samba enredos*" (samba plots), that is, as films analogous to the collection of songs, dances, costumes, and lyrics that form part of that popular narrative form called a samba school presentation. The favelados of Fernando Cony Campos's *Ladrões de Cinema* (Cinema Thieves, 1977) steal filmmaking equipment from American tourists visiting Rio for Carnival, and conceive the film they plan to make with the stolen equipment as a kind of samba school narration of a famous episode in Brazilian history—the Minas revolt against Portuguese colonialism in the eighteenth century.

Afro-Brazilian Religion and the Cinema

It is impossible to discuss the Africanization of Brazilian culture without reference to the ongoing and vital role of Afro-Brazilian religions. These religions are extremely diverse; some are of Yoruba origin, others of Kongo; some practice the cult of dead ancestors (*Egungun*), others do not; some are relatively "pure" in the sense of preserving African roots, while others, such as Umbanda, are highly syncretic. Our purpose here is not to analyze these religions but rather to point out their central importance and their relevance to black performance and to Brazilian cinema. The Occidental vice of hierarchizing religions into the "real" religions of the sacred texts—Judaism, Christianity, and to a lesser extent Islam—and the pseudoreligions called "cults," regarded as inferior and superstitious, has blinded many Western people to the beauty and profundity of what Maya Deren called, in reference to Haitian voodoo, religions of "major stature, rare poetic vision and artistic expression."

The gregarious mysticism of Afro-Brazilian religious expression is strongly linked both to Carnival and to black performance. In a participatory religion in which soul claps its hands and sings, the practitioners of Afro-Brazilian religion perform; they dance and sing, the mediums above all, but also the witnesses for whose collective benefit the ritual is performed. Like Carnival, Candomblé is a kind of *festa* performed in an atmosphere of collective enthusiasm. In Bahia, there even exist "play Candomblés," in which mysticism is absent, where people go specifically to dance and sing. But authentic candomblé groups also participate in Carnival in the form of AFOXÉS in BAHIA and *maracatus* in Recife. Apart from these concrete links to Carnival, there is a deeper connection through analogy. In Carnival, individuals play at being another. Candomblé, for its part, can be seen as a form of divinely inspired roleplaying. Both Carnival and Candomblé set in motion a complex play of identities, a creative dialectic of self and other. Just as Carnival transforms a favelado into aristocrat, a spirit possession turns a cook or a maid into the ruler of sea or storm, into IEMANJÁ or IANSAN.

It was only in the 1960s that Brazilian cinema began to speak seriously of Candomblé, and even then with a highly ambiguous attitude. The Cinema Novo directors of the early 1960s, when they did not ignore Afro-Brazilian religion completely, tended to regard it as alienated and marginal, something to be tolerated or reformed by well-meaning leftists. A partial exception to this rule can be found in the films of what has been called the "Bahian Renaissance," the cinematic rediscovery of the cultural riches of Salvador, Bahia, the Africanized metropolis where Candomblé thrives. Anselmo Duarte's *Pagador de Promessas* (The Given Word, 1962) and Glauber Rocha's *Barravento* (1962) both place Candomblé at the center of their preoccupations. The former film centers on the vow of its protagonist, Zé-of-the-Donkey, to carry a cross into the Church of Saint Barbara in gratitude for the miraculous cure of his donkey. The priest refuses him entrance because the vow was proffered at a Candomblé shrine. When they learn of Zé's plight, the people of Bahia, largely black and mulatto, support Zé's right to enter the church. Anticlerical rather than anti-Christian, Duarte contrasts the naïve Christlike faith of Zé with the petrified attitudes of the priest. The practitioners of Candomblé, meanwhile, are shown as sympathetic but misguided. Duarte repeatedly underlines Zé's separation from Candomblé. In the opening *terreiro* sequence, Zé is alone, kneeling at the altar, while the collectivity sings and dances. In order to emphasize that Zé is "really a Christian at heart," Duarte has him refuse repeated invitations to visit the terreiro in Salvador. The film evokes a kind of revolution by having the people take over an institution, yet the "revolution" succeeds, ultimately, only in gaining entrance to a more ecumenical and tolerant Catholic Church, and not in the endorsement of Candomblé or in a call to political action.

Both *The Given Word* and *Barravento* open with images of *abataques* (drums) in a terreiro, but there the similarities end.

If *The Given Word* condemns Candomblé from the point of view of ecumenical Catholicism, *Barravento* would seem to critique Afro-Brazilian religion from the standpoint of historical materialism. The film shows the oppression inflicted on poor black fishermen and apparently denounces the role of Candomblé in legitimating this oppression. The initial explanatory intertitles inform us that blacks are oppressed and that their "superstitions" keep them in a state of passive acquiescence. The protagonist Firmino, a rebel who has just come back from the city, tells his brothers and sisters to forsake religion to fight oppression.

It would be extremely simplistic, however, to see *Barravento* as a monolithic condemnation of Candomblé. Such an interpretation is based only on certain features of the film—namely the explanatory titles—and on certain affirmations by the protagonist. In fact, the surface condemnation of Candomblé, very much in the spirit of the "progressive" left of the period, is contradicted by the film's deep structural features. First, *Barravento* constitutes an extremely affectionate celebration of the poetic beauty and sensuous mise-en-scène of Candomblé. Second, the film insists on the protagonist's isolation from his fellow villagers. His clothing is urban and inappropriate, and his gestures are inordinately theatrical. Throughout the film he addresses the camera directly, as if he were speaking to us, the middle-class public, and not to the fishermen of Buraquinho. The montage isolates him, alternating shots in which he appears alone with shots in which the community appears together. As for the villagers, the film celebrates their collective life, a life in which religion, music, dance, and work form a harmonious whole. The fishermen, for example, perform a *puxada de rede* (pulling in of the net) in a way that combines singing, dancelike movements, and a hymn of praise of Iemanja. Although they are oppressed by the owner of the net, they partially transcend their oppression by using collective strength and artistry. Rocha does not film the puxada de rede in a neutral way; he emphasizes close shots of bare feet in the sand, of hands on the net, of the batuque, all done in such a way as to picture work as a celebration of communitarian integration. *Barravento* can even be seen as an Afro-Brazilian musical that appropriates songs and dances not to entertain but rather to transform and criticize. The entire film is punctuated with music—the joyous *samba de roda* (a circle dance foregrounding individual creativity and prowess), the combative CAPOEIRA with its *berimbau* accompaniment, and the literally entrancing rhythms of Candomblé. Third, as Ismail Xavier has pointed out, the film's system of explanation is profoundly ambiguous: all the narrative events can be explained either in a materialist manner or as evidence of the truth and efficacy of Afro-Brazilian religion.

Whereas most 1960s Cinema Novo films tend to ignore or question the legitimacy of Afro-Brazilian religion, the films of the 1970s are quite different. Black culture, once considered marginal, becomes the vital source of the originality of Brazilian culture. In the 1960s, Cinema Novo directors working in the favelas barely noticed the presence of macumba shrines; their progressive vision had no place for Afro-Brazilian religion. In the 1970s, in contrast, many films celebrate various forms of Afro-Brazilian religious expression. Nelson Pereira dos Santos, who made no mention of black religion in either *Rio 40°* or *Rio Zona Norte*, in his later *Amuleto de Ogum* (Ogum's Amulet, 1975), highlights the syncretic Afro-Brazilian religion called Umbanda, Brazil's fastest growing religion. Umbanda combines African elements—the *orixas*, the centrality of spirit possession—with Catholicism, Cabala, and the spiritism of Allan Kardec.

The odyssey of the hero of *Amuleto*, Gabriel (played by the director's son, Ney Sant'ana), takes him from the Northeast, where his body has been magically "closed," to the notoriously lawless Rio suburb called Caxias. He gradually absorbs the symbology and the cultural universe of Umbanda. In *Amuleto*, Nelson Pereira dos Santos aims to be "popular" not only in his choice of subject matter but also in perspective, discarding all vestiges of superiority and wholeheartedly affirming the values of the milieu depicted and the spectators to whom he hopes to appeal. The film virtually obliges the spectator to become an *umbandista*, at least for the duration of the film, if only to understand the narrated events. The film simply assumes umbandista values, without explaining them to the uninitiated. A Catholic audience, the director has pointed out, need only see a priest raising the Host to know a mass is being celebrated. An umbandista audience, similarly, recognizes the ceremony that "closes" the protagonist's body and recognizes his protection by Ogum, the "hard" deity of war and iron and justice. It recognizes the voice and limp of the *preto velho* and the provocative manners of the *pomba-gira* (evil in the form of a woman). At the same time, the film does not idealize umbanda: one umbanda priest works for popular liberation; the other is a greedy charlatan and opportunist. Umbanda is shown as a kind of cultural master code in which two opposing discourses, one progressive and the other retrograde, struggle for ascendancy. No longer the opiate of the people, Afro-Brazilian religion has now become the scene of struggle and, potentially, the locus of resistance to cultural hegemony.

The same director's *Tenda dos Milagres* (Tent of Miracles, 1967), based on the novel by JORGE AMADO, also deals with Afro-Brazilian culture. Here the black culture-hero Pedro Archanjo (a composite figure based on a number of self-taught black intellectuals from Bahia) defends the Afro-Brazilian spiritual inheritance first against the fashionably racist Social Darwinist theories of Professor Nilo Argilo and then against the clubs and guns of the police. Deployed across a double time frame—a core story set in the past and presented as a film-within-the-film—and a frame story set in the present, *Tent of Miracles* suggests that the ideologically explicit and politically violent racism of the past has merely transmuted itself into the subtler racism of the contemporary mass media. More interesting for our purposes, however, is the fact that Nelson Pereira dos Santos calls attention to the historical reality of the violent repression of Afro-Brazilian cultural manifestations. The turn-of-the-century press in Bahia frequently denounced the "uncivilized" habits of Bahia's blacks, especially around Carnival time: " . . . the authorities should prohibit these batucadas and candomblés which swarm through the streets during Carnival, creating an enormous din, without tone or sound . . . [A]ll this is incompatible with our state of civilization." During slavery, slaves were often obliged to pretend that they were worshiping Christian saints rather than African orixas. But even after the abolition of slavery, blacks were punished for practicing their religion. It was only in the 1970s that Bahia became the first state to suspend the compulsory registration of Afro-Brazilian religious groups with the police. We see this process of repression in *Tent of Miracles* when the white elite forbids the black afoxé groups to appear during Carnival. Throughout the film the Candomblé practitioners are threatened by a brutal and racist police. At the height of the repression, Pedro Archanjo calls on the orixas for help against the police; they cooperate by putting the police thug Zé into a trance that turns him around so that he attacks the police and thus saves the community.

Tent of Miracles is admittedly not without its problems. While the film exposes the repression of Afro-Brazilian culture and thus discredits the myth of "racial democracy," it also promotes the notion of miscegenation as social panacea. The film's generational progression from Black Pedro to his mulatto son Tadei and his white bride Lou suggests a subtly prejudicial parable of whitening as "progress." Archanjo in reality embodies Jorge Amado's ideal of *mestiçismo*, the idea that the true Brazilian can combine European intellectualism with Afro-Brazilian mysticism and sensuality. As the protagonist himself explains: "Pedro Archanjo Ojuobá, reader of books and conversationalist . . . and *iyalorixa*, two different beings, who knows, perhaps the Black and the White? But make no mistake, professor, I'm a mixture of both, one single mulatto." In name and body, Pedro Archanjo incarnates mestiçismo. In his unshakable dignity, subtle humor, and, above all, in the reciprocated tenderness he bears his community, he is a touching figure. By paying homage to him, and by calling attention both to the repression of Afro-Brazilian culture and to the creativity with which Afro-Brazilians have responded to that repression, Nelson Pereira dos Santos has authored a complex if problematic ode of love to Afro-Brazilian culture.

The 1970s and 1980s offer a proliferation of fiction and documentary films paying tribute to Afro-Brazilian religious expression. José Unberto Dias's *O Anjo Negro* (The Black Angel, 1972) is an homage to the power and charm of Candomblé in Bahia. Ibere Cavalcanti's *A Força de Xango* (The Power of Xango, 1979) interweaves amorous intrigues with the supernatural operations of the orixas. Marco Altberg's *Prova de Fogo* (Test of Fire, 1981), emphasizes the utilitarian and therapeutic value of Umbanda, "the poor man's couch." This same period also yields a growing number of serious, respectful documentary studies of Afro-Brazilian religion: Roberto Moura's *Sai dessa, Exû* (1973), Geraldo Sarno's *Iaô*, Juana Elbein dos Santos's *Arte Sacra Negra I* (Black Sacred Art, Part I, 1978), Raquel Gerber's *Ylê Xoroquê* (1981), and Carlos Blajsblat's *Egungun* (1982).

Quilombo: From Carnival to Revolt

As the example of *Tent of Miracles* shows, black religion and black music often acted in concert with black political resistance and revolt. To close our discussion, therefore, we will examine some of the cinematic manifestations of black Brazilians as embodying a revolutionary impulse of revolt against oppression. Some of the earliest historical reconstruction films interestingly were based on the episode known as the "Revolta da Chibata" (the whip revolt) in which the black sailor JOÃO CANDIDO led a revolt against corporal punishment, generally applied by white officers against black sailors, in the Brazilian navy. The incident inspired both documentaries (*Revolta no Rio,* 1910) and staged reconstructions like Lambertini's *A Vida do Cabo João Candido* (The Life of Commander João Candido, 1910). (The latter film, symptomatically, was the first Brazilian film to receive the ambiguous compliment of official censorship.) Our focus here, however, will be on the filmic reflections of a specific instance of black revolt—the phenomenon of the QUILOMBOS or "liberated zones" founded by fugitive blacks in the days of slavery. The official history books of Brazil, written largely by the "winners" of history, tend to privilege white rather than black revolt.

The most famous of the quilombos was PALMARES, the fugitive slave republic that lasted almost a century, from 1595 to 1695, in the face of repeated assaults by both the Dutch and the Portuguese. Palmares at its height counted 20,000 inhabitants and an area roughly one-third the size of Portugal. Carlos Diegues's first feature, *Ganga Zumba* (1963), celebrates Palmares. Based on João Felício dos Santos's novel of the same title, the film focuses on a fugitive black slave, Antão (Antonio Pitango), who discovers that he is a grandson of the king of Palmares. The film combines a harsh portrait of slavery involving forced labor, constant threats, whippings, rape, and murder (a portrait having little to do with the idealized tableau of a benign humanized Lusitanian servitude) with a brief glimpse of the "utopia" of Palmares. A Fanonian ode to black liberation, here taken as metaphor and inspiration for the broad contemporary struggle against neocolonialism, *Ganga Zumba* adopts a black perspective throughout, showing blacks not as mere victims but as active agents who take their destiny into their own hands.

Two later films returned to the subject of Afro-Brazilian political resistance. Carlos Diegues returned to the subject of his first feature in *Quilombo* (1984), this time with a substantial budget and based on more recent historical research into Palmares by Decio Freitas. In this film, Diegues presented Palmares as the "real foundation of Brazil," in which blacks, Indians, and poor whites created a new civilization with its own language, religion, and culture—the first "great utopia of the Americas." Walter Lima, Jr., meanwhile, released *Chico Rei*, a German-Brazilian coproduction based on the historical truth concerning an African king who was enslaved with his family and sold to a slave-owning gold miner in Minas Gerais. "Francisco," as he was called in Portuguese, managed to liberate himself, his family, and his "tribe." Under his direction, the community purchased a mine, which they worked as collective property according to traditional African communitarian forms of labor. As his power and prestige grew, he became a virtual head of state in the area and was renamed Chico Rei. Although less famous than Zumbi or Xica da Silva, Chico Rei was, in Walter Lima's view, more efficacious. His nonviolent methods, a mixture of black entrepreneurship and African communalism, led to a viable economy and the re-Africanization of one community in Brazil. The film closes with a festive *congada* celebrating Chico's "coronation," by which the former tribal organization is reinstituted.

In the 1980s, more than ever, many Brazilian filmmakers seemed to look to Afro-Brazilian culture as a key to Brazilian nationhood, its differentiating feature from European and North American civilization, the vital source of its energy. The nineteenth-century romantics, such as Gonçalves Dias and José de Alencar, had celebrated the "Indian," the "brave warrior," as spiritual symbol of Brazilian nationality. The Indians themselves, meanwhile, were being subjected to a process of physical and cultural genocide. The exaltation of the "brave warrior," meanwhile, implicitly operated at the expense of blacks. The proud history of black rebellion was ignored; the brave Indian, it was subtly insinuated, resisted slavery, while blacks did not. Films such as *Ganga Zumba, Chico Rei,* and *Quilombo* retroactively correct this historic error by foregrounding the long, valiant, and continuing history of black resistance. Other films discussed in this essay, such as *Amuleto de Ogum, Xica da Silva,* and *Tent of Miracles,* highlight what Gilberto Gil calls the "vibrant," "luminous" energy inherent in Afro-Brazilian culture. All the films contribute, in some measure, to the long overdue recognition of the cultural and political role of black Brazilians. But the danger of a new romanticism, in which the same group being hailed for its cultural importance is simultaneously the victim of the cruelest forms of oppression, is always present as long as symbolic cultural victories are not matched by the acquisition of real political and economic power.

Bibliography

Browning, Barbara. *Samba: Resistance in Motion.* Indiana University Press, 1995.

McGowan, Chris, and Ricardo Pessanha. *The Brazilian Sound: Samba, Bossa Nova, and the Popular Music of Brazil.* Billboard Books, 1991.

Robert Stam

Samba, Chéri

1956–

Painter from the Democratic Republic of the Congo, internationally known for his mixture of vivid images with written text that offers biting social and political commentary.

Originally named David Samba wa Mbimba-N'zinga-Nuni Masi, Chéri Samba was born in the village of Kinto-Mvuila in the southern Belgian Congo (now DEMOCRATIC REPUBLIC OF THE CONGO). Samba moved to the country's capital, KINSHASA, in 1972. He trained as a commercial sign painter and cartoonist, and opened his own studio in Kasa Vabu (a district in the city) in 1975. His distinctive style builds on the techniques of African urban signage—bright colors, bold graphic drawing, and a fusion of image and text. Samba mimics the sign-painting style and combines it with ironic written text, sometimes in the tone of advertising copy. In this manner, the artist uses parody to transform the seemingly ordinary painted sign into a medium for sociopolitical critique, inspired by local news and global travel. The text in his paintings is often written in English, French, Kikongo, and Lingala, appealing to both local and international audiences.

His 1994 triptych (work in three parts) titled *Grand Tort de la Colonisation et Grosse Erreur de L'Afrique Independante* (Great Wrong of Colonization and Large Error of Independent Africa), Collection of J. M. Patras, Paris) illustrates his nationalist criticism of the Belgian colonial government that once ruled the country. One painting shows a figure giving a speech reading "Charte de l'OUA" (OAU Charter), referring to the ORGANIZATION OF AFRICAN UNITY, to an audience marked by a political break—the side of African independence versus that of the colonial legacy. In this way, Samba fuses aesthetics with politics in the guise of popular art. This strategy enables Samba to address a variety of themes, ranging from African democracy to Parisian morality, and to cast them in global terms.

Samba is also famous for his prolific production of self-portraits. These include *The Draughtsman Chéri Samba* (1981, J. M. Patras Collection, Paris) and *Autoportrait* (Self-Portrait, Galerie Nomade, Paris, 1989). In these and other paintings, Samba offers his own image against a backdrop of the rhetoric of demands made by media and market, implying that these are major agents in the construction of his artistic identity. Through his self-portraits, Samba caustically speaks to both the local and international art market. For example, in his 1990 painting *Pourquoi ai-je Signé le Contrat?* (Why Have I Signed the Contract?, private collection), Samba portrays himself with the lock around his leg and a noose around his neck, addressing both the limitations and the legalities of the art market. Samba's body of self-conscious, self-promoting work plays off and subverts the desires of Western art critics and audiences to arrogantly categorize seemingly "authentic" self-taught artists in Africa and elsewhere.

Samba has earned tremendous international success, including major exhibitions in New York and Paris. In 2000, the Provinciaal Museum voor Moderne Kunst (Ostend, Belgium) and the Institute of Contemporary Arts (London, England) jointly gave a restrospective show of his work, emphasizing the ways in which his painting style documents social and political issues in African life.

See also Artists, African; Colonial Rule.

Samba, Martin-Paul

1853–1914

German military officer and nationalist leader in Cameroon.

Like many early African nationalists, Martin-Paul Samba in his relationship with colonial authorities progressed from initial cooperation to determined resistance. Born Mebenga-M'Ebono, he became familiar with German settlers during his childhood in what would soon become the German colony of Kamerun (present day CAMEROON). After serving on an expedition led by German explorer Kurt von Morgan, he traveled to Berlin with von Morgan for education and military training. He ultimately reached the rank of captain in the German Imperial Army. In 1895 Samba returned home, and throughout the next fifteen years participated in several expeditions into the hinterland to further German colonial ambitions.

By 1910 Samba had grown acquainted with early nationalists such as RUDOLPH DOUALA MANGA BELL, and had begun to share their grievances. Two years later Samba became chief of the Ebolowa and the leader and strategist of the local anti-colonial resistance movement. Pretending to be a businessman, Samba clandestinely stockpiled weapons and convinced local chiefs to support a future uprising against the Germans. When World War I broke out, Samba notified the French in BRAZZAVILLE (now capital of the REPUBLIC OF THE CONGO) that he would assist them in military action against the Germans. But his letter was intercepted, and Samba was arrested, charged, and convicted of high treason. He was killed by a German firing squad in 1914.

Bibliography

Azan, Madeleine Mbono Samba. *Martin Samba.* ABC, 1976.
Eyongetah, Tambi, and Robert Brain. *A History of the Cameroon.* Longman Group, 1974.

Eric Young

Samba Schools

Organizations that annually mount elaborate musical parades for the pre-Lent Carnival celebration in Brazil.

In 1928 several musicians from the Estácio neighborhood in RIO DE JANEIRO formed the first SAMBA school, Deixa Falar (Let Them Speak). One of the reasons they created this organization was to parade during Carnival, a celebration from which they had historically been denied participation. Other black musicians followed their lead and came together to found their own samba schools, including Mangueira in 1929 and Portela in 1935. Although Afro-Brazilians had informally paraded through their own neighborhoods during Carnival festivities since the early nineteenth century, the samba schools lent a degree of formality to the Afro-Brazilians' street revelry and allowed them to assert their presence during Carnival. When Getúlio Vargas came into political power in 1930, he put an end to the repression of Afro-Brazilians and their samba schools and gave official recognition to their parades.

The Vargas administration changed Carnival by requiring participating samba schools to have a theme (*enredo*) related to Brazilian culture, history, or politics, and by making it into a competition. This fostered the emergence of new samba schools and of increasingly elaborate presentations, including spectacular costumes and magnificent floats. It also led to the creation of a new category of samba music, *samba-enredo*, which features a lead singer whose lyrics illustrate the group's theme and a booming percussion section, the *bateria*, which may include more than 300 members playing more than a dozen different types of percussion instruments.

Over time, many samba schools have become internally diversified—as reflected in the different *alas*, or wings, of each parade, each with distinct costumes—and larger. Today, Rio de Janeiro's Carnival features some sixty samba schools, each averaging 5,000 members and sixty wings. Members of each school invest an enormous amount of time, year-round, and money—as much as one million dollars—in preparing for Carnival, in hopes of being named the best samba school, a title that carries great prestige as well as a sizable financial award. Some of the more famous samba schools include the aforementioned Portela and Mangueira as well as Império Serrano, Beija-Flor, and Mocidade Independente.

Although many light-skinned Brazilians have joined these and other samba schools, most samba schools are composed of Brazilians of African descent. For these Afro-Brazilians samba schools continue to be important sources of identity and pride. They have also provided Afro-Brazilians, who historically have not had a strong political voice, with a means of protest. This is especially true in Salvador, where AFOXÉS/BLOCOS AFROS—Carnival organizations that also offer a variety of social service—have become a major feature of that city's Carnival.

In 1988 on the hundredth anniversary of the abolition of slavery in Brazil, Mangueira's theme was *100 Anos de Liberdade: Realidade ou Illusão* (100 years of Freedom: Reality or Illusion), which was in part a protest of the enduring poverty of blacks in BRAZIL. While the samba school tradition began in Rio in conjunction with Carnival, samba schools and large-scale Carnival celebrations can be found today throughout Brazil, especially in the northeastern seaboard cities of Recife and SALVADOR.

See also Carnivals in Latin America and the Caribbean.

Aaron Myers

Samburu

Ethnic group of Kenya.

The Samburu share the eastern Nilotic language and many of the cultural practices of the MAASAI. The name Samburu is thought to be a derivation of the Maasai word *samburr*, a leather pouch used for carrying meat and honey, and suggests to some that they were once a hunting and gathering society. The Samburu generally refer to themselves as *L'oikop,* another word of Maasai origin. They are believed to have migrated up the NILE RIVER from SUDAN beginning in the fifteenth century C.E. They now reside in the northern highlands of KENYA's Samburu district.

Like the Maasai, the Samburu have traditionally practiced PASTORALISM; they measure wealth by the size of their cattle herds. Each of the eight Samburu clans has a special brand for their cattle, and each Samburu family slits the ears of their cattle according to a particular pattern, to identify the cattle to other clan members. The Samburu typically do not settle in one place for very long, but rather move with their herds in search of water and pasturage. They survive largely on a diet of milk, drunk fresh or curdled as ghee or yogurt, and blood. Blood is obtained by opening a wound in a cow's jugular vein, extracting two or three liters, and closing the wound.

Similar to the Maasai, traditional Samburu society recognizes a series of age-sets. Both female and male youth are circumcised, after which they pass into "adulthood." Females have two significant life stages, girlhood and womanhood. Males have several life stages: after circumcision (roughly between the ages of fourteen and twenty-five) a boy becomes a junior *moran* or warrior. After a period of approximately fifteen years, the junior moran becomes a senior moran, then a junior elder, and finally a senior elder.

The Samburu, after the imposition of British COLONIAL RULE, were considered residents of the Northern Frontier District (NFD), which was closed to Europeans and Africans who were not citizens of colonial Kenya. In addition, Kenyan citizens needed special permission to enter the NFD. Although this isolation freed the Samburu from the more burdensome demands of the colonial government, independence brought an end to the NFD and an abrupt introduction to the politics and market economy of modern Kenya. While some Samburu have settled in towns in northern Kenya, most continue to live with their herds in rural areas.

See also Female Circumcision in Africa; Rites of Passage and Transition.

Bibliography

Magor, Thomasin. *African Warriors: the Samburu.* H. N. Abrams, 1994.

Pavitt, Nigel. *Samburu.* H. Holt, 1992.

Robert Fay

Samo

Ethnic group of Burkina Faso.

The Samo primarily inhabit northwestern BURKINA FASO. Others live in southern MALI. They speak a MANDE language. Approximately 300,000 people consider themselves Samo.

See also Languages, African: An Overview.

Samory Touré

1830?–1900

West African empire builder and fighter against French colonialism.

Born into the Touré clan in the Beyla region of present-day GUINEA, Samory Touré became a soldier in the local conflicts that ravaged the area around the middle of the nineteenth century, and soon began to exploit the situation to his own ends. By 1870 he had forged a large private army, with which he eventually conquered an area reaching from the FOUTA DJALLON in the west to the ASANTE country of present-day GHANA in the east. Establishing his capital at Bissandougou in what is now CÔTE D'IVOIRE, he tried at first to hold off the encroaching French by diplomacy and negotiations but later waged a brilliant, although ultimately unsuccessful, guerrilla war against them. Captured by the French in 1898, Samory Touré died two years later in exile in GABON. He was the great-grandfather of SÉKOU TOURÉ, the first president of modern Guinea.

San

Southern African Khoisan-speaking societies, historically known as nomadic foragers.

The term *San* refers to several different societies in southern Africa. Among the best known are the Kung, who live in eastern NAMIBIA and western BOTSWANA; the Naron of Botswana; and the Xo and the Gwi, who live in the central region of the KALAHARI DESERT.

KHOISAN-speaking societies have inhabited some parts of southern Africa for at least 2,000 years. Although the region's earliest inhabitants probably lived primarily from gathering and hunting, archaeological evidence indicates that they came into contact with pastoral societies earlier than was once believed. Much of this evidence comes from rock paintings in SOUTH AFRICA's mountain ranges. The San's ancestors traded and engaged in tribute relations with the pastoralists (now usually referred to as the KHOIKHOI or Kxoe) and at least some kept livestock themselves. After the arrival of Bantu-speaking cultivators sometime after 200 C.E., many Khoisan speakers were incorporated into their village communities.

The Dutch settlers who arrived on the Cape of Good Hope in 1652 proved less tolerant of San groups' nomadic ways than had earlier immigrants to the region. Although initial meetings between the San and Europeans were amiable, the settlers' demands for land and supplies soon caused tensions. As more Europeans arrived and began settling the Cape interior, they came to see the foraging societies (whom they called Bosjieman, or BUSHMEN) as "bandits" and "outlaws." The Dutch government subsequently authorized the extermination of the San, subjecting generations of "wild Bushmen" to intentional killings. In the 1770s, for example, AFRIKANER migrants (also known as Boers) traveling across the Sneeuwberg Mountains nearly destroyed the adult San population and enslaved the children. In the mid-nineteenth century, Boer communities near the border of present-day Namibia commonly hired "hunting parties" to track and kill San. During this period some San groups, such as the Xam in the Cape Colony, disappeared completely. Other groups fled into remote areas, and many who had previously lived elsewhere migrated into the Kalahari Desert.

Even while they faced persecution from European settlers, San groups became increasingly integrated into the market economy. During the nineteenth century some groups, such as the Western Kweneng, supplied fur, ostrich feathers, skins, and ivory to Goba and TSWANA traders. Others, such as the Kung San, hired their services out to European hunters. By the end of the century, however, ivory and animal skins had become scarce. Many San sought work as field laborers or cattle herders on Tswana farms, often taking the place of men who had left to work in the South African mines. More recently, the San have accepted positions as trackers for European hunting groups; some were even recruited by the South African Defense Force (SADF) during the 1970s and 1980s. Although the San are still commonly stereotyped as foragers, few contemporary San live solely from foraging.

See also Bantu Migrations in Sub-Saharan Africa; Hunting in Africa; Nguni; Pastoralism; Rock Art, African; Safari Hunting.

Elizabeth Heath

Sánchez, Francisco del Rosario

1817–1861

Afro-Dominican revolutionary and political figure, considered one of the founding fathers of the Dominican Republic.

Francisco del Rosario Sánchez's public life started around 1838, when he entered the secret society "La Trinitaria," which fought for the independence of Spanish Santo Domingo (present-day DOMINICAN REPUBLIC) from HAITI. During this period, he became a political ally of the society's leader, Juan Pablo Duarte. Sánchez played a crucial role in the development of the independence movement, and after Duarte went into exile in 1843, Sánchez assumed leadership. In 1844 he took part in the coup that was launched against the Haitian government.

Sánchez subsequently participated in the provisional governing council established after Haiti's exit in 1844, but he was driven into exile after a coup placed political rival General Pedro Santana in the presidency later that year. Sánchez remained in exile until 1848, when President Manuel Jiménez issued an amnesty allowing his return. Jiménez named Sánchez commander of arms. Sánchez served intermittently in the administrations of President Buenaventura Báez and President Pedro Santana, despite Santana's role in the exile of Sánchez and in the executions of Sánchez's brother and aunt in 1845 on charges of conspiracy. In 1857 an uprising by tobacco workers initiated the usurpation of the government then led by Báez, who had driven the nation into a severe economic crisis. Sánchez renounced his position as commander of arms just days before Báez fled to FRANCE and Santana returned to power.

When Santana returned in 1859, Sánchez was again sent into exile, moving to Saint Thomas, Virgin Islands. Santana feared a renewed Haitian occupation and sought reannexation to SPAIN. In January 1861 Sánchez wrote his *Manifiesto contra el Proyecto de Anexión* (Manifesto against the Project of Annexation), in which he called Dominicans to rise to arms in the name of "liberty and independence" and overthrow Santana. With the announcement of the annexation later that year, Sánchez organized forces and prepared to invade the island, but his attempt was unsuccessful. Wounded and captured, he was subsequently tried and executed.

See also Dominican-Haitian Relations.

Sánchez, Luis Rafael

1936–

One of Puerto Rico's major writers, who has explored different genres, including the short story, novel, play, and essay, with equal success.

Luis Rafael Sánchez grew up in the small town of Humacao, then moved to SAN JUAN, PUERTO RICO as a young man. His student days took him to Madrid, Spain and New York, New York to earn degrees in literature. He has traveled in Europe and Latin America, teaching and working in the theater.

When they were first published, the stories included in Sánchez's *En cuerpo de camisa* (1966), constituted a departure from the more canonical models of Puerto Rican narrative. While sharing with previous writers the desire to explore the social and cultural alienation that Puerto Rico's dependent relation to the United States has created, Sánchez's stories are characterized by a corrosive sense of humor that incorporates the urban vernacular into the texture of the prose.

Sánchez is also an important playwright, and has used different dramatic forms, ranging from traditional realism to the incorporation of Brechtian and absurdist elements. His early plays include *Cuento de la cucarachita viudita* (1960); *Los ángeles se han fatigado* (1961); *La hiel nuestra de cada día* (1961); and *O casi el alma* (1964). His extremely successful *La pasión según Antígona Pérez* (1968), is a rewriting of the classical Greek tragedy set in the context of a modern-day Latin American dictatorship. *Quíntuples* (1985) is a highly satirical exploration of grotesque characters that illustrates different degrees and styles of sociocultural alienation in modern Puerto Rican society.

Sánchez achieved international acclaim with the publication of his highly praised novel *La guaracha del Macho Camacho* (1976), his only work to be translated into English (by Gregory Rabassa in 1980), as *Macho Camacho's Beat*. Influenced by the narrative experiments of the Latin American Boom, this novel offers a devastating, albeit humorous, portrayal of Puerto Rican society suffering from the stagnation of colonial domination, social inequalities, and corruption. *La importancia de llamarse Daniel Santos* (1988) is a more optimistic book in which a legendary bolero singer becomes a symbol of popular culture's constant renewal and self-affirmation, and of the people's resistance to cultural alienation. In these books, Sánchez displays a highly elaborate style, musical and baroque, while remaining close to the inflections of everyday speech.

Sánchez has also written essays for newspapers and magazines, exploring the effects of Puerto Rico's political status, cultural life, and national identity ("La generación o sea," 1972; "El debut en Viena," 1975; and others). In 1994 he published *La guagua aérea,* in which he explores the diasporic migrations of Puerto Ricans between the island and the continental United States.

Still writing and skillfully exploring a variety of genres, Sánchez remains one of the most significant voices in contemporary Caribbean writing. He is a distinguished professor emeritus at the University of Puerto Rico and the City University of New York.

See also Colonial Latin America and the Caribbean.

Victor Figueroa

Sanchez, Sonia

1934–

African American writer, activist, and educator who focuses on black women's struggle with racism.

Born Wilsonia Driver in BIRMINGHAM, ALABAMA, Sonia Sanchez moved with her family to HARLEM, NEW YORK when she was a young girl. Sanchez received a B.A. in 1955 from Hunter College in New York and spent the following year studying poetry at New York University.

An activist associated first with the CONGRESS OF RACIAL EQUALITY (CORE), Sanchez was further radicalized by MALCOLM X and the NATION OF ISLAM. Her first volume of poetry, *Homecoming,* appeared in 1969, after several years of publishing in journals with other Black Nationalist poets such as LARRY NEAL and LeRoi Jones (AMIRI BARAKA). Sanchez's poems from this period were experimental and irreverent in style, content, and presentation. She became famous for bravura spoken-word performances that captured the cadences of African American speech. From 1965 to 1969, she taught in San Francisco and was actively involved in the founding of a controversial Black Studies program at San Francisco State University.

Sanchez left the Nation of Islam in the early 1970s to protest the organization's treatment of women. Her poetry and activism since have highlighted black women's struggle with racism from the dominant culture and within the black community. Her best-known collections of poetry are *A Blues Book for Blue Black Magical Women* (1973), a spiritual autobiography, and *homegirls and handgrenades* (1984), for which she earned an American Book Award in 1985. In addition to being a poet, Sanchez is an accomplished playwright, the author of children's books, and the mother of three. In 1997 she was nominated for the National Book Critics' Circle Award and the NAACP Image Award for *Does Your House Have Lions?,* the story about her brother's battle with AIDS.

From 1977 to 1999, Sanchez taught at Temple University in PHILADELPHIA, PENNSYLVANIA, where she held the Laura Carnell Chair in English, served as the faculty director of the Women's Studies Program, and received the Lindback Award for Distinguished Teaching and an honorary doctorate. MAYA ANGELOU calls her "a lion in literature's forest." When she retired, a symposium at Temple, "Celebrating the Works of Sonia Sanchez," explored her contribution to the BLACK ARTS MOVEMENT of the 1960s and her concern with the struggles and triumphs of people of color.

See also Black Nationalism in the United States; Feminism in the United States; Women Writers, Black, in the United States.

Sancho, Ignatius

1729–1780

Educated African ex-slave in Britain whose published letters were an early and important slave narrative.

Ignatius Sancho was born on a slave ship en route to the WEST INDIES; both of his parents died during the journey, casualties of the MIDDLE PASSAGE. Never having lived in Africa, Sancho was in many ways a product of Western civilization. His letters, written between 1768 and 1780, and published posthumously in 1782, proved to the English public that an African could not only master the language and literature of England but become a discriminating reader and a discerning critic.

Upon arriving in Britain, Sancho was bought by three sisters in Greenwich who treated him poorly and denied him education. But the sisters' neighbors, the Duke and Duchess of Montague, were impressed by Sancho's curiosity about books and his quick mind and secretly lent him materials to read. In 1749, when the sisters threatened to sell him into American slavery, Sancho fled to the Montague household.

The Duke and Duchess died a few years later, leaving an inheritance to Sancho, who soon left Greenwich for the literary and artistic circles of London. There he wrote music and befriended musicians and artists, including the famous actor David Garrick. After a brief period of reckless living and gambling, Sancho returned to serve the new Duke of Montague. But gout and a weight problem led him to retire in 1773, and he subsequently opened his own London grocery store, which became popular less for Sancho's produce than for his counsel. The Duchess of Queensbury sought his help with her favored but troublemaking servant Julius Soubise. Other patrons included the artist Joseph Nollekens and the painter John Hamilton Mortimer, who consulted Sancho's artistic sensibilities.

Sancho proved skillful in cultivating friendship and came to have many correspondents, including English novelist Laurence Sterne. Though Sancho praised Sterne's words against slavery, he wrote little on the subject himself, except to place it within the wider context of the greed for money and lust for power of the Christian East Indian traders. Sancho held a deep faith that the conditions blacks and poor faced in this life would be resolved in "our next habitation," where "there will be no care—love will possess our souls—and praise and harmony—and ever fresh rays of knowledge, wonder, and mutual communication will be our employ." He advocated patience to one black correspondent, and advised him to "tread as cautiously as the strictest rectitude can guide ye—yet must you suffer from this—but armed with truth—honesty—and conscious integrity—you will be sure of the plaudit and countenance of the good." In this conviction, and in his words of affection for his West Indian wife, Anne, and their six children, Sancho's writing displays the Sentimentalism of this era.

Although Sancho supported such liberal causes as a more equitable distribution of wealth, his interests as a businessman lay in the proliferation of commerce, and as a patriot, he denounced radicalism. Unlike black radicals such as OTTOBAH CUGOANO or ROBERT WEDDERBURN, he preferred to use moral persuasion and his own example to convince the English people that Africans deserve equal treatment. Scholar Lloyd Brown explains that Sancho's background as a culturally assimilated outsider "subvert[ed] the standard images of the uncivilized Negro." Although he did not write antislavery appeals, Sancho's published letters testified to the humanity of Africans, thus strengthening the arguments of English abolitionists.

Leyla Keough

Sanctification

See Black Church, The; Church of God in Christ.

Sanders, Betty

See Shabazz, Hajj Bahiyah Betty.

Sanderson, Jeremiah Burke

1821–1875

African American abolitionist, California civil rights leader, educator, and clergyman.

Jeremiah Burke Sanderson was born in New Bedford, Massachusetts on August 10, 1821. His father, Daniel, was of Scottish descent and his mother, Sarah, of African and Gay-Head Indian descent. He attended elementary schools for black children in New Bedford. As a young man, he earned the reputation as one of the best-read blacks in New England. He became a barber and practiced his trade in New Bedford and Wareham, Massachusetts.

During his New England years, he was an active abolitionist. He grew up in an atmosphere dominated by the militant abolitionism of WILLIAM LLOYD GARRISON. He made his first reported public address as an active abolitionist in 1841 in Nantucket, Massachusetts at an antislavery meeting at which activist FREDERICK DOUGLASS also made his debut. Throughout the 1840s, Sanderson lectured in Massachusetts and in upper New York State. In 1853 he became a member of the National Council of the National Colored Convention that met in Rochester, New York. In 1854 Sanderson left for California, leaving behind his wife Catherine and five children. His entire family joined him in California in 1859 after the death of his mother-in-law.

During the growing schism between Garrison and Frederick Douglass in the early 1850s, Sanderson had seemed to avoid taking sides, although there is evidence that he quietly leaned toward Douglass. Douglass spoke and wrote flatteringly of Sanderson. But the infighting between abolitionists was loathsome to the gentle nature of the man. It may have been one of the reasons why he left for California, which had been admitted to the union as a free state in 1850. On November 20, 1855, he was one of the signers of a petition for civil rights, especially the right to give testimony in court.

Sanderson was a secretary and delegate to the 1855 and 1856 Colored Conventions of California. He taught school in Sacramento for several months while attempting to influence the local board of education to grant financial support to a school for black children. In 1859 he took charge of the public school for black children in San Francisco. He remained in this position as a teacher and principal until 1865. During his years as a teacher, he was also a pastor in the AFRICAN METHODIST EPISCOPAL CHURCH (AME). He was the organizer and first president in San Francisco of the Young Men's Union Beneficial Society, a black cultural and self-education organization. He was also one of the organizers of the Franchise League (August 12, 1862) and one of the trustees of the Ladies' Union Beneficial Society and of the Ladies' Pacific Accumulating and Benevolent Association, both of San Francisco. From 1868 to 1874 he was in charge of the Stockton school for black children. It was there that he established his statewide reputation as a fine teacher. With other leading blacks in California, Sanderson organized a statewide conference in 1871 to work for integrated education. Another prominent lobbyist was attorney MIFFLIN W. GIBBS. Sanderson entered the political arena and was elected to the Republican State Judicial Convention in 1873. In 1874 he moved to Oakland, where a rapidly growing black community was emerging. There he assumed pastoral duties and took over the leadership of the Equal Rights League of Oakland. In 1875 he was elected secretary of the state conference of AME Churches of California and the state delegate to the AME national conference in Atlanta, Georgia. He died before he could fulfill this charge. On August 19, 1875, he was killed in a train accident in Oakland.

Sanderson was a staunch anti-emigrationist, and in public matters he stood for civil rights for blacks. His public statements reflect pride in his African ancestry and a deep involvement in his church work.

Rudolph M. Lapp's "Jeremiah B. Sanderson: Early California Leader" (*Journal of Negro History,* October 1968) and references in Delilah Beasley's *Negro Trail Blazers of California . . .* (1919) are principal sources on Sanderson. The latter contains a passage from Sanderson's diary. The papers of the beneficial society are in the California State Archives, Sacramento.

From *Dictionary of American Negro Biography* by Rayford W. Logan and Michael R. Winston, editors. Copyright © 1982 by Rayford W. Logan and Michael R. Winston. Reprinted by permission of W. W. Norton & Company, Inc.

Rudolph M. Lapp

Sandoval, Alonso de

Missionary Jesuit priest who devised a system of classification of African slaves being brought to Cartagena de Indias, Colombia, in the seventeenth century.

See also Cartagena de Indias, Colombia.

Sandoval, Arturo

1949–

Classically trained Cuban jazz trumpeter and flügelhorn player and founder of the Afro-Cuban jazz ensemble Irakere.

Arturo Sandoval is one of the most dynamic Cuban JAZZ musicians. Along with pianists Gonzalo Rubalcaba and CHUCHO VALDÉS, and saxophonist PAQUITO D'RIVERA, he is part of a younger generation of misicians who demonstrate the continuing vitality and creativity of Cuban jazz. Sandoval plays superb bravura trumpet, making particularly effective use of a powerful upper register and excellent articulation. His musical approach places him comfortably within the modern jazz mainstream that grew out of BEBOP in the 1940s. In addition, as jazz critic Leonard Feather observed in the *Los Angeles Times,* Sandoval reveals "exceptional talent as a pianist and could easily make his living at the keyboard." He also performs on *timbales* (small drums) with his working jazz group.

Sandoval, the son of an auto mechanic, was born in 1949 in a small village near HAVANA, CUBA. At the age of 13 he started playing in the village band, and after trying various instruments, he settled on the trumpet and its mellow-toned relative, the flügelhorn. Initially, he had little awareness of jazz; a U.S. embargo on Cuba since 1960 had made American jazz recordings all but unavailable. As Sandoval explained in a 1993 interview in *Downbeat* magazine, "The only thing I used to hear was traditional Cuban music, what we call SON, which was played by a septet with a trumpet and bongos."

In 1964 Sandoval entered the Cuban National School of Arts, and studied classical trumpet for three years. After being drafted in 1971, he played in the Orquesta Cubana de Musica Moderna. He also discovered that his interest in jazz involved personal risk. "While I was in the army," he told Leonard Feather, "they caught me listening to Willis Conover's Voice of America jazz show, accused me of being pro-American, and threw me in jail for three and a half months."

Upon completing his military service in 1973, Sandoval—along with Paquito D'Rivera and Chucho Valdés—founded the groundbreaking Afro-Cuban jazz-rock band IRAKERE. The band quickly became Cuba's most popular musical group. In 1977, Sandoval met and played with trumpeter DIZZY GILLESPIE—whom he regards as a primary influence—when the American jazz innovator visited Cuba. He later recorded the album *To Finland Station* (1982) with Gillespie and in the late 1980s toured widely with Gillespie's United Nation Orchestra, which also included D'Rivera. While appearing with the group in Rome in July 1990, Sandoval entered the United States Embassy and requested political asylum for himself, his wife, and his fifteen-year-old son, who had accompanied him on the tour.

Sandoval's music expresses the stylistic diversity that has characterized Afro-Latin jazz from its beginings. His recordings cross many musical boundaries, including jazz, Cuban dance music, and classical or art music. *I Remember Clifford* (1992), Sandoval's tribute to hard bop trumpeter CLIFFORD BROWN (1930–1956), is a straight-ahead jazz album, featuring pieces closely identified with the influential American trumpeter, including a fiery up-tempo rendition of "Cherokee." Sandoval also regularly returns to his roots in Afro-Cuban music, as in *Danzon* (1993).

Like American jazz trumpeter WYNTON MARSALIS, Sandoval has performed classical music, including appearances with symphony orchestras in London, England and Saint Petersburg, Russia. In 1994, he premiered his first classical composition, "Concerto for Trumpet and Orchestra," with the National Symphony Orchestra under the direction of Luis Haza. Writing in the *Washington Post,* critic Mike Joyce described the three-movement, nineteen-minute-long concerto as being "full of sharp and sometimes sudden contrasts, juxtaposing fiery trumpet flourishes with tender flügelhorn balladry, jazz and folk dance rhythms with orchestral rhapsodies, playful exchanges with bravura solos." Sandoval has thus emerged as more than just a trumpeter of superb range and technical mastery. Equally at home in American jazz or in traditional Cuban music, he exemplifies the richness and excitement of the Afro-Latin fusion.

Although his application for United States citizenship was initially rejected, Sandoval has finally become an American citizen. He remains very concerned, however, about his native Cuba. "Castro always justified every problem with the [American] embargo," he said in an interview. "The main problem is the inefficiency of the system. The system doesn't work and it's been demonstrated in all of the ex-Communist countries of the world."

See also Jazz, Afro-Latin; Music, Afro-Cuban; Music, Classical, in Latin America and the Caribbean.

James Sellman

San Francisco and Oakland, California

Although Mexican and Spanish blacks were in the De Anza expedition that settled San Francisco in 1776, until the California Gold Rush there were only a few Africans and African Americans in the San Francisco/Oakland area. Notable among them was WILLIAM ALEXANDER LEIDESDORFF, a merchant in Mexican San Francisco and later U.S. vice consul to Mexico.

After 1848 a small African American community developed on San Francisco's Telegraph Hill and on the waterfront. Among the blacks of California, who could not testify in court cases until 1863 and could not vote until 1869, were well-educated and prosperous people as well as immigrants from the Caribbean and CAPE VERDE, making the group an unusually diverse one in the United States.

A black community developed in West Oakland when the Western Pacific Railroad established its terminus there in 1869. Attracted by railroad and port jobs, blacks came to Oakland and the city's black population increased sixfold—to 6,000—between 1900 and 1920. Under the guidance of C. V. Dellums a well-organized chapter of the BROTHERHOOD OF SLEEPING CAR PORTERS formed in the 1920s.

From 1940 to 1950 the black population in the Bay Area increased from 16,500 to 147,000, the result of labor demand in the Oakland and San Francisco shipyards. Under political and legal pressure, unions began accepting African Americans. But discrimination existed, especially during the Port Chicago Mutiny incident. An explosion at the Port Chicago naval ammunition base, on the Sacramento River, killed 320 people, including 202 black ammunition loaders. Following the explosion, many black sailors refused to return to work out of concern for their safety. Consequently, 258 black sailors were arrested, and 50 were court-martialed.

Housing discrimination was also rampant. In San Francisco the practice forced almost all African Americans into the Fillmore and Bayview–Hunter's Point sections of the city. The growing West Oakland black community expanded into North and East Oakland, as well as to Richmond. Protest against housing discrimination in 1946 led to the appointment of William McKinley Thomas, an African American, as commissioner of the San Francisco Housing Authority and the election of William Byron Rumsford as the first black state legislator from northern California.

By the 1960s, however, most Bay Area African Americans still lived in substandard housing in virtually segregated communities. The black community organized, and in 1964 elected Terry Francois to the San Francisco Board of Supervisors and WILLIE LEWIS BROWN, JR. to the state assembly. Brown became speaker of the California House of Representatives and, most recently, mayor of San Francisco. In the early 1960s the CONGRESS OF RACIAL EQUALITY (CORE) led the opposition to police brutality and advocated for better job opportunities for African Americans and more effective integration of public schools. The Berkeley Free Speech Movement inspired large-scale civil rights protests in 1964. But de facto segregation continued.

The year 1966 was a landmark in the history of the Bay Area black community. Oakland residents BOBBY SEALE and HUEY P. NEWTON formed the radical BLACK PANTHER PARTY, whose platform was to defend local black communities nationwide against continued racism and economic exploitation. Direct, and sometimes armed, opposition to police brutality, the provision of free breakfast for black schoolchildren, and the construction of a housing center for homeless blacks and a community school were among the actions that brought the Panthers to national prominence. By the end of the 1970s, however, internal fighting as well as intense police and FBI scrutiny led to the dissolution of the party—though not before it helped Lionel Wilson become the first black mayor of Oakland in 1977.

In 1968 the Oakland Black Caucus was formed, and in 1971 Oakland's RONALD V. DELLUMS became the first African American from northern California elected to the U.S. Congress. In 1991 Elihu Harris became the second elected black mayor of Oakland. Beset by urban problems and poverty, the black community became concentrated in the Bayview and Fillmore neighborhoods of East Oakland and San Francisco, respectively.

Although San Francisco's black population declined by 22,000 during the 1990s, mostly because of skyrocketing housing costs, the trend began to reverse itself in the early 2000s. Estimates project a 2.8 increase of African American residents in the San Francisco metropolitan area, which includes counties to the south of the city, by 2005. Many are returning to the historically black neighborhoods of the city.

Bibliography

Broussard, Albert S. *Black San Francisco: The Struggle for Racial Equality in the West, 1900–1954.* University Press of Kansas, 1993.

Daniels, Douglas Henry. *Pioneer Urbanites: A Social and Cultural History of Black San Francisco.* Temple University Press, 1980.

Lapp, Rudolph M. *Blacks in Gold Rush California.* Yale University Press, 1977.

McBroome, Delores Nason. *Parallel Communities: African Americans in California's East Bay, 1850–1963.* Garland, 1993.

Newton, Huey. *To Die for the People: The Writings of Huey Newton.* Random House, 1972.

Jim Mendelsohn

Sangaré, Oumou

1968–

Singer and proponent of women's rights in contemporary Africa whose music fuses contemporary and traditional styles.

Known as the songbird of MALI, Oumou Sangaré uses a mix of traditional and modern instruments, along with her powerful voice, to update Mali's renowned Wassoulou sound. Based on music made by hunters, these old songs asked for protection and good fortune in the densely forested Wassoulou region. Sangaré, who says she sings "for the women," retains much of the original sound—using guitar, kamelen ngoni (a small, harplike stringed instrument), and a variety of percussion instruments. To these she adds lyrics dealing with the status of women in a changing Africa.

"In Africa it's still men who make all the decisions," Sangaré says. "It's time for women to be heard." Accordingly, one song on her third album, *Worotan* (1997), describes the outcast status of childless women, while others deal with domestic abuse and polygamy. She feels very strongly about freedom of choice in marriage, as her father had two wives—"a catastrophe," she says.

Although little else is known of her personal life, Sangaré, who sings in her native language, Bambara, has spoken of her mother as her first music teacher, and of a childhood in which she sang often at parties and family gatherings. Formal training with the Mali National Ensemble led to work with Djolive Percussions, a musical group with whom she first toured Europe in 1986. While singing in Paris, Sangaré first heard the legendary South African singer Miriam Makeba, to whom some critics have compared her rich, passionate vocal style. Sangaré's first album, *Moussolou* became West Africa's best-selling recording in 1991. Two years later she followed with *Ko Sira*, which won an award as Europe's favorite world-music album. Sangaré has sung around the world with the Africa Fête tour, and can be heard on the soundtrack of the movie version of Toni Morrison's *Beloved*.

See also Feminism in Africa: An Interpretation; Womanism.

Kate Tuttle

Sani, Alice

See Women Artists, African: An Interpretation.

San Juan, Puerto Rico

Capital, largest city, and principal seaport of the Commonwealth of Puerto Rico, an island located in the western Atlantic Ocean.

Puerto Rico's first European settlement, called Caparra, was begun in 1508 under the direction of the Spanish explorer Juan Ponce de León. Located west of the present-day city of San Juan, the site was inhabited by Taíno indigenous peoples at the time. In 1521 the original settlement was abandoned and moved to the site of what is now called Old San Juan. Interestingly, the names of the settlement and the island eventually became reversed; the settlement was originally known as Puerto Rico (rich port), whereas the island had been named San Juan Bautista (St. John the Baptist) by Christopher Columbus in 1492. The community was subjected to frequent attacks by Europeans (including Sir Francis Drake in 1595), and several imposing fortifications were built. The city of San Juan remained under Spanish control until 1898, when the island was ceded to the United States at the conclusion of the Spanish-American War. The large-scale expansion of the city limits outward from Old San Juan to the mainland has occurred during the twentieth century.

Old San Juan, the historical heart of the city, lies on a small island connected to the mainland by bridges and a causeway. It is characterized by narrow, crooked streets and a number of buildings dating from the sixteenth and seventeenth centuries. The oldest part remains partly enclosed by massive walls and contains several notable forts, such as El Morro (begun in 1539) and San Cristóbal (1600s), both part of San Juan National Historic Site, and La Fortaleza (begun in 1533), which now serves as the governor's mansion. Also on the island is the Cathedral of San Juan Bautista (begun in the 1520s), a Gothic structure that contains the tomb of Ponce de León. On the mainland just east of Old San Juan is the section known as Condado Beach. High-rise luxury hotels and condominiums prevail in this area, which is the main focus of tourist activity in the city. To the south are two separate business districts, Santurce and Hato Rey, both encompassing tall office buildings. Farther south is the residential area of Río Piedras, which contains the main campus of the University of Puerto Rico, founded in 1903. Also in the San Juan area are the Inter-American University of Puerto Rico (1912), the Sacred Heart University (1976), the Museum of Puerto Rican Art, and the Ponce de León Museum.

Since World War II (1939–1945), San Juan's economy has grown rapidly. Major manufactures include chemicals, pharmaceuticals, rum and other beverages, fertilizer, machine tools, electronic equipment, plastic goods, textiles, clothing, and food products. San Juan has excellent transportation facilities. A network of highways connects the city to the rest of the island, and a busy airport at nearby Isla Verde and San Juan's modern port facilities provide connections to international points. In 1996 a heavy commuter rail line was begun to ease traffic congestion on San Juan's highways. Population 421,958 (2000).

See also Colonial Latin America and the Caribbean.

Sankara, Thomas

1949–1987

Revolutionary leader and former president of Burkina Faso.

On October 15, 1987, Thomas Sankara was assassinated in a coup led by troops loyal to Captain Blaise Compaoré. The Compaoré regime later denounced Sankara, calling him a "traitor" to his own revolution that was begun four years earlier. Yet Sankara, who came to power at the age of thirty-three, was widely credited with initiating reforms that benefited the country's most oppressed groups, namely women and the rural poor. Sankara's radical policies and defiant attitude toward the West proved costly, but his integrity—and the changing of the country's name from Upper Volta to BURKINA FASO, "land of upright people"—instilled in many Burkinabè a lasting sense of national pride.

Born in Yako, Upper Volta, Sankara was the third of ten children of a MOSSI mother and a Peul (FULANI) father who worked for the colonial administration's postal service. Sankara's political views took shape during his years of military schooling in the early 1970s. While attending the Antsirabe military academy in MADAGASCAR, he witnessed the 1972 Communist-led revolution, and he had further exposure to Marxist thought while training as a parachutist in FRANCE. After returning to Upper Volta in 1974, he fought in the border war against MALI, which he called a "pointless and unjust battle." He later joined the National Parachute Regiment, underground revolutionary groups, and trade unions.

In 1978 Sankara met Compaoré during military training in Rabat, MOROCCO. The two officers, later stationed together in Upper Volta, became inseparable friends, and set up a small "popular republic" at their base to discuss their revolutionary ideas. In 1981 Sankara became minister of information under the Saye Zerbo government, but soon resigned in protest over government censorship of the RADIO. This stance won widespread support, and when Saye Zerbo was overthrown in 1982, the new military council appointed Sankara prime minister. He used his position to denounce Western imperialism, a stance that particularly appealed to workers and students.

Sankara's radicalism, however, did not endear him to more conservative members of the council, who had him placed under house arrest in May 1983. Students protested in OUAGADOUGOU, and in August 1983 Compaoré led a military coup that brought Sankara to power as president of the new Conseil National de la Revolution (CNR).

During his tenure as president, Sankara initiated a series of reforms, many of them for the benefit of the rural poor. These included irrigation projects, literacy drives, and mass rural vaccination campaigns. He also set out to cut government spending, setting himself as an example: he paid himself a clerk's salary, turned off the presidential palace air conditioning, and drove a secondhand car. A staunch advocate of sexual equality, he called for "the abolition of the system of slavery to which [Burkinabè women] have been subjected for millennia," and started a national campaign encouraging Burkinabè men to partake in house chores and other family responsibilities. He also appointed five women to ministerial posts, and hired a team of women motorcycle guards to escort him in public. On the international level, Sankara supported and raised funds for national liberation movements worldwide.

Not everybody welcomed Sankara's reforms. The president's efforts to undermine the power of rural chiefs and other traditional authorities by installing revolutionary defense committees in villages and neighborhoods, for example, proved especially unpopular among the Mossi, Burkina Faso's largest ethnic group. While the radical wing of Sankara's government felt his reforms had not gone far enough, many members of the business community resented his government's restrictions on trade. Sankara's tendency to dismiss his political opponents from office also cost him support.

The circumstances surrounding Sankara's death remain unclear. Compaoré has denied any involvement in the assassination, but the mysterious disappearances in 1996 of some alleged members of the hit squad have renewed suspicions that the current president still seeks to silence potential informants. The commoner's grave of Sankara in Ouagadougou, meanwhile, still receives daily visitors. Indeed, as *New York Times* writer Howard W. French noted in March 1997, "Few African leaders have been mourned so deeply at home or as widely on this continent since . . . Africa's early independence days."

Bibliography

Englebert, Pierre. *Burkina Faso: Unsteady Statehood in West Africa.* Westview Press, 1996.

Sankara, Thomas. *Thomas Sankara Speaks: The Burkina Faso Revolution, 1983–1987.* Pathfinder Press, 1988.

Wilkins, Michael. "The Death of Thomas Sankara and the Rectification of the People's Revolution in Burkina Faso." *African Affairs* 88, no. 352 (1989): 375–388.

Roanne Edwards

Santa Cruz, Nicomedes

1925–1992

Afro-Peruvian poet, folklorist, essayist, and one of the most important Afro–Latin American intellectuals of the twentieth century.

Nicomedes Santa Cruz is the author of three major collections of poetry: *Décimas* (first edition, 1960; second edition, 1969); *Cumanana* (1964); and *Canto a mi Perú* (Song to My Peru, 1966). Two anthologies of his work appeared in 1971: *Ritmos negros de Perú* (Black Rhythms of Peru) and *Décimas y poemas: Antología* (Décimas and poems: An Anthology). He also wrote a book of literary history and criticism entitled *La décima en el Perú* (The Décima in Peru, 1982). Santa Cruz recited and sang his poetry and shared his knowledge of Peruvian folklore on television and radio, as well as in live performances. He also made three sound recordings: *Canto negro* (Black Song, 1968), *Cumanana, Antología Afroperuana* (Cumanana: Afro-Peruvian Anthology, 1970), and *Socabón* (1975). An English translation of his works is yet to be published.

Although he employed various poetic forms, he is best known for his cultivation of the traditional popular form called the DÉCIMA, a stanza of ten octosyllabic lines with a particular rhyme scheme. It is often improvised and sung to musical accompaniment, and is sometimes used for poetic duels.

Throughout his youth, Santa Cruz was exposed to classical poetry from SPAIN and the popular poetry of his native land of the Peruvian coast. He soon began to create his own verses, and with the coaching of an older gentleman, he mastered the art of composing *décimas*. In his late twenties, he abandoned the profession of ironworking in order to pursue a literary career.

As a young man, Santa Cruz became aware of the racism that permeated Peruvian society. His father had been a writer, but because he was black he received no attention from leading Peruvian literary critics. Santa Cruz's own family discouraged him from marrying a woman because they wanted him to "improve the race" by marrying someone of lighter skin. During the 1950s Santa Cruz noticed that the religious authorities were slow to make sixteenth-century Afro-Peruvian friar MARTÍN DE PORRES into a saint. Santa Cruz used poetry to speak out against such discrimination, and to heighten awareness of the contributions of black people.

Santa Cruz composed poems on a wide range of topics, but he is most noted for his works about the experience of people of African descent in PERU, the Americas, and around the world. In the collection *Décimas,* for example, one finds poems about how the enslaved Africans resisted oppression through their language, religion, music, and dance, and created enduring cultural forms. Santa Cruz also recorded the achievements and struggles of blacks in areas as diverse as Christianity and sports. One poem, for example, pays homage to great SOCCER players from the poet's home neighborhood of La Victoria, in the Peruvian capital of Lima. The well-known poem "Muerte en el ring" ("Death in the ring," in *Cumanana*) describes the death of Cuban boxer Benny "Kid" Paret as an example of the exploitation of poor blacks in violent sports. "Formigas pretas" ("Black ants") is another poem about exploitation; in this case, Santa Cruz describes the toil of blacks in BRAZIL, where he lived in 1963. Three poems in *Cumanana* express solidarity with the struggles of African peoples against colonialism and racism, namely in THE REPUBLIC OF THE CONGO and SOUTH AFRICA. Throughout his poetic career, Santa Cruz affirmed the positive value of African heritage, and denounced racial and ethnic prejudice.

Santa Cruz was committed to improving the political, social, and economic situations of all oppressed peoples. For example, in "Talara" he urged Peru to resist foreign control of Peruvian natural resources. In another poem, he calls for an end to conflicts and exploitation in large cities. Although Santa Cruz was most familiar with the African-influenced coastal region around Lima, he also reached out to the indigenous peoples of the mountainous regions of Peru: poems like "Indio" and "Agro" show that Santa Cruz sympathized with the struggles of Native American tribes and peasants. Santa Cruz's desire for a more equitable society led him to support the Cuban Revolution and to join a Peruvian political party. However, Santa Cruz became disenchanted with Peruvian politics and society, and in the 1970s he moved to Spain, where he resided until his death.

Nicomedes Santa Cruz is known as the foremost Afro-Peruvian poet. While he did much to expose others to the cultural richness of his people and his region, his work spoke to the whole of human experience.

Marveta Ryan

Santamaría, Ramón ("Mongo")

1922–2003

Afro-Cuban conga and bongo drummer and bandleader who found popular success during the 1960s by incorporating elements of rhythm and blues into Afro-Latin jazz.

For more than thirty years, Cuban-born Mongo Santamaría led one of the top-rated bands in Afro-Latin jazz, yet he remains far less well-known than bandleaders MACHITO and TITO PUENTE, who rose to prominence during the 1940s and 1950s. Many scholars and musicians rank Santamaría as the most influential Cuban percussionist since CHANO POZO. He continued to play—well into his seventies—with remarkable speed and authority, employing complex polyrhythms that invariably swung. During the 1960s he created a distinctive fusion of Latin jazz and SOUL MUSIC—anticipating the funky *bugalú* fad—that brought him considerable crossover success, including a Top Ten hit with "Watermelon Man" (1962).

Although he began by studying violin, Santamaría soon switched to drums, dropping out of school to become a professional conga drummer. In 1948, after having established himself as a performer in Cuba, Santamaría went to Mexico City with his cousin Armando Peraza, who would be the long-time percussionist in Carlos Santana's Latin rock band during the 1970s. In the late 1940s Santamaría traveled to New York, where he performed with the city's first *charanga,* an ensemble featuring flute, violins, a percussion section, and vocals. After a short stint in the big band of DÁMASO PÉREZ PRADO, he joined Tito Puente from 1951 to 1957. In concert and on records, Santamaría and *timbales* player Puente played fiery percussion duels that remain legendary among Afro-Latin jazz musicians.

In 1957 Santamaría and fellow percussionist Willie Bobo left Puente's band after having enraged the bandleader by appearing on an album with Latin-jazz vibraphone player Cal Tjader. Tjader quickly hired both musicians, who remained with Tjader's sextet for four years, adding fire and drive to the leader's otherwise cool music. During the 1950s Santamaría began recording as a leader. His early albums generally feature Afro-Latin jazz, but his first, the notable *Changó* (1955), reissued under the title *Drums and Chants*, explores the roots of Afro-Cuban music and includes Santamaría and fellow Cuban percussionists Silvestre Méndez, Carlos "Patato" Valdez, and Julito Collazo.

In 1960 Santamaría and Bobo traveled to Cuba, where they recorded together with a number of outstanding Cuban musicians, including *tres* player Niño Rivera, pianist Paquito Echavarria, and vocalists MERCEDITAS VALDÉS and Carlos Embales. The resulting album, *Our Man in Havana* (1960), was a direct precursor of the *típico* revival movement that emerged in the 1960s as a predominant force in Latin music. In 1961 Santamaría took over Armando Sánchez's Orquesta Nuevo Ritmo and consistently infused the group's flute and strings *charanga* format with a jazz feeling.

After 1962 Santamaría largely abandoned traditional Cuban ensembles and the *típico* movement in favor of Afro-Latin jazz fusion. The infectious soul jazz tune "Watermelon Man" (1962), written by HERBIE HANCOCK, Santamaría's pianist at the time, became a Top Ten hit with virtually no promotion by the record company, and led to Santamaría signing a contract with Columbia Records for a series of highly commercial albums between 1964 and 1969. "Watermelon Man" effectively defined Santamaría's approach for much of the three decades, resulting in Latin versions of such soul hits as "Proud Mary," made famous by Ike and TINA TURNER, "My Cherie Amour" (by STEVIE WONDER), "Love Child" (by the SUPREMES), and even, rather improbably, the country-pop confection "Little Green Apples."

Santamaría helped develop some leading talents in jazz and Latin music, including Hancock, pianist Chick Corea, tenor saxophonist José "Chombo" Silva, and flutist Hubert Laws. He also composed "Afro-Blue" (1958), which became a jazz standard through tenor saxophonist JOHN COLTRANE's influential 1963 rendition, and also worked its way into DIZZY GILLESPIE's repertoire. Santamaría's major albums include *Changó, Afro-Roots* (1958), *Our Man in Havana* (1960), *Skins* (1962), *Soy Yo* (1987), and *Live at Jazz Alley* (1990). Mongo Santamaria died in 2003 and is buried near Miami, Florida.

See also Jazz, Afro-Latin; Music, Afro-Cuban.

James Sellman

Santería

A syncretized religion derived from African and Roman Catholic religious practices and beliefs that developed in Cuba and later spread to other countries.

Santería originated between the sixteenth and nineteenth centuries, when the Spanish colonizers of CUBA imported hundreds of thousands of slaves from Africa to work on the island's sugar and coffee plantations. The Spanish, who established Roman Catholicism in Cuba, baptized these slaves and forbade them to practice African religions. In these circumstances, slaves preserved elements of their religions by identifying their deities, known as ORISHAS, with Roman Catholic saints. This syncretism enabled slaves to worship the orishas secretly while externally paying homage to the Catholic saints. For this reason, the religion that emerged is known as Santería, meaning "the way of the saints."

Historians have identified slaves from the YORUBA ethnic group of southwestern NIGERIA as the most influential group in the development of Santería. Yoruba slaves believed in one supreme being, Olodumaré (who is equated with the Christian concept of God) and numerous orishas, the children and servants of Olodumaré (who are associated with the Christian saints). While the Yoruba religion includes some 400 to 500 orishas, each of which protects and is worshiped by the inhabitants of a different city, the practitioners of Santería recognize only sixteen orishas. In Cuba, this smaller set of intermediary deities is sometimes termed *Lucumí* (the name originally used by the Spanish to refer to Yoruban slaves) in order to distinguish it from the Yoruban pantheon from which it derives.

Because practitioners of Santería regard Olodumaré as a distant, inaccessible God, they focus their religious activities on the intermediary orishas. To those who worship them, the orishas are divine ancestors, immaterial in form, who control some aspect of nature and some domain of human activity. OGUM, for example, is regarded as the deity of iron and minerals, and he oversees blacksmiths and those who drive vehicles with metal parts.

In Santería, an individual develops a reciprocal relationship with one of the orishas. In exchange for guidance and protection, the worshiper makes offerings (*ebó*) to his or her orisha. Communication with the orishas is established through various forms of divination performed by a Santería priest or priestess and through spirit possession, which takes place during drum and dance ceremonies.

Santería employs three types of divination: *obi, dilloggún,* and a combination of the *opelé* and *tablero de Ifá*. For each type, a priest or priestess tosses and interprets the fall of certain objects—a quartered coconut for obi, sixteen cowry shells for dilloggún, and a necklace with eight evenly spaced disks for opelé. The tablero de Ifá is a wooden tray upon which a priest sprinkles powder and draws configurations based on the heads-or-tails patterns resulting from several throws of the opelé.

The three divination types correspond to various individuals in the Santería priesthood. The opelé and the tablero de Ifá are used exclusively by *babalawos,* the male high priests of Santería. The dilloggún are used only by a *santero* or *santera,* a standard Santería priest or priestess. The obi may be used by them both. Divination is used in the early stages of initiation to determine an individual's personal orisha and thereafter to determine the will of the orisha for that person. According to one scholar, divination is the process through which the orishas diagnose people's problems and recommend solutions.

Practitioners of Santería hold elaborate ceremonies called *bembés* to invoke their orishas. Each orisha has its own drum rhythm, song, and dance step. In performing the music and choreography of a particular orisha, a worshiper tries to persuade the orisha to descend upon the ceremony and possess him or her. An orisha that temporarily takes over the body of a worshiper, an act often described as "mounting," is able to participate in the festivities, accepting food offerings and giving advice. The orisha eventually takes leave of his or her human medium, who then regains consciousness without recalling the possession.

Santería has taken root beyond Cuba, especially in the United States. Hundreds of thousands of Cuban exiles have arrived in the United States since the 1959 revolution in Cuba, bringing Santería with them. Many of these Cubans settled in New York City and southern Florida. Over time, the number of non-Cubans practicing Santería has increased and the religion has become more public, but not without some resistance.

A Santería altar in Havana. The faith, which combines African and Roman Catholic religious practices, developed in Cuba and spread to other countries. CORBIS/Robert van der Hilst

Santería's use of animal sacrifice to symbolically feed the orishas triggered a controversial national debate. In 1987 the city of Hialeah, Florida, responded to this practice by banning animal sacrifice. A Supreme Court ruling in 1993, however, stating that the ban represented unconstitutional infringement on freedom of religion, has allowed Santería to continue to thrive in the United States.

See also African Religions: An Interpretation; Catholic Church in Latin America and the Caribbean; Religions, African and Afro-Caribbean, in the United States; Religions, African, in Latin America and the Caribbean; Slavery in Latin America and the Caribbean.

Aaron Myers

Santo Domingo, Dominican Republic

Formerly Ciudad Trujillo; largest city, chief seaport, and capital of the Dominican Republic.

Located at the point where the Ozama River flows into the Caribbean, Santo Domingo, the capital and chief port of the DOMINICAN REPUBLIC, has a fine artificial harbor accessible to most commercial and passenger ships. It is connected by both ship and air lines with principal points in North and South America and is at the hub of a network of modern roads. Santo Domingo is a tourist, economic, and administrative center. It is a manufacturing site for alcoholic beverages, cement, and textiles and serves as a distribution outlet for SUGAR cane, beef and cattle, and other products of the surrounding region. Points of interest include the Cathedral of Santa Maria la Menor (built 1514–1520), believed to contain the remains of Christopher Columbus; the ruins of the palace of Columbus's brother Diego; sixteenth-century churches, such as San Nicolás and San Francisco; and the fortified walls of the original Spanish town. Educational and cultural institutions include the Autonomous University of Santo Domingo, dating from 1538 and said to be the oldest university in the Americas, and Pedro Henríquez Ureña National University, established in 1966.

Founded in 1496 by Bartholomew Columbus, brother of Christopher Columbus, the city is the oldest European settlement extant in the New World. In 1930 it was heavily damaged by a hurricane but was subsequently rebuilt. In 1936 it was renamed Ciudad Trujillo for the Dominican president RAFAEL TRUJILLO. It became Santo Domingo again in 1961 after the assassination of Trujillo and the subsequent fall of his regime. In 1965 the city was the scene of an uprising against the ruling government of the Dominican Republic. In 1996, the city's population was estimated at about 2,000,000.

See also Colonial Latin America and the Caribbean.

Santo Domingo, Teresa Juliana de

1676?–1748

Roman Catholic nun, mystic, and first African woman poet published in modern history.

Sister Teresa Juliana de Santo Domingo was born in Africa with the name Chicaba. By her own testimony, she was the daughter of a king or a chief from the area of La Mina Baxa del Oro. Spanish geographers applied this name to the region then known in English as the Slave Coast, extending from present-day GHANA to NIGERIA. When the girl was nine years old, a slave ship captured her and took her to the island of SÃO TOMÉ, where she was baptized, and then to SPAIN.

Presented to King Carlos II because of her unusual personality and her claim to be the daughter of royalty, she was given by the Spanish king as a present to the Marquis de Mancera, former viceroy of MEXICO. In the household of the Marquis, she revealed a profound religiosity and a spiritual ascendance over her owner's wife. She succeeded in obtaining her freedom and entering the Convento de la Penitencia of the Dominican Order in Salamanca in 1703. There the African nun met immediate rejection and discrimination by the other nuns. However, her mystical visions and her fame as a performer of miracles signaled her as special. She was also popular among the less wealthy nuns, whom she helped with part of the inheritance she had received from her former masters.

Sister Teresa died renowned for her sanctity, and a process for her beatification was initiated shortly after her death. A hagiography appeared in 1751. Her tomb and personal items became the object of a religious cult in her convent and throughout Salamanca, where her prayers were credited with having saved the population from bombs during the War of the Spanish Succession (1701–1714). After the destruction of the convent house during the Napoleonic Wars (1799–1815), her remains and relics were transferred to the Convento de las Madres Dominicas Dueñas in Salamanca. Two portraits of her exist, one of which is currently exhibited in the main staircase of the Renaissance convent house. The convent also holds an autographed letter and the document she signed with her official religious vows. The hagiography contains several passages transcribed from her autobiography, now lost. Among them is a poem that constitutes the first known published work by an African woman in modern history.

Baltasar Fra-Molinero

São Tomé and Príncipe

Africa's smallest country, consisting of two islands off the coast of Gabon in the Gulf of Guinea.

The tiny island nation of São Tomé and Príncipe has had a different history from that of most other African countries. São Tomé and Príncipe—often referred to simply as São Tomé—are two separate islands. Uninhabited before Portuguese exploration in the fifteenth century, the islands were settled by both Africans and Europeans—most brought against their will. In time, a Creole people, known as the FORROS, emerged. Subsequent waves of involuntary migrants passed through the islands, including hundreds of thousands of African slaves on their way across the Atlantic to the markets in BRAZIL and LATIN AMERICA. Originally a SUGAR-growing economy, São Tomé later produced a large share of the world's coffee and COCOA. It has never escaped the limitations of a plantation economy. Its small size and a shortage of skilled workers force it to rely on imported goods and services. It achieved political independence in 1975 from PORTUGAL, its former colonial master. Its abundant natural beauty has begun to attract TOURISM. However, São Tomé remains heavily dependent on foreign aid and a single plantation crop, cocoa.

Geography and Ecology

São Tomé, the larger of the two islands, lies 290 kilometers (180 miles) off the African coast, due west of GABON. Príncipe is 260 kilometers (160 miles) west of the coast of EQUATORIAL GUINEA and 150 kilometers (95 miles) northeast of São Tomé. São Tomé and Príncipe are part of an archipelago of four islands. The other two, Annobón (or Pagalu) and Bioko (formerly known as Fernando Po) are part of Equatorial Guinea. Together, they are known as the Guinea Islands, and form part of a volcanic mountain chain that also includes CAMEROON MOUNTAIN on the mainland.

Despite their small size—São Tomé is 855 square kilometers (330 square miles) and Príncipe just 306 square kilometers (118 square miles)—the islands' steep and rugged terrain creates several microclimates, each suited to different economic activities. The islands receive abundant rainfall on their windward (southwestern) sides, interrupted by dry seasons from January to February and from May to September. There are also arid and semiarid regions on the eastern and northern sides of both islands, where the islands' steep volcanic mountains create rain shadows. Tropical rain forests originally covered the islands; today they remain on the steeper slopes and the wetter sides of the islands, while the remainder of the land has been cleared for agriculture. The country's highest point, known as Pico de São Tomé, towers 2,024 meters (6,640 feet) above the coastline; four other peaks on São Tomé exceed 5,000 feet. Príncipe's mountains do not reach such heights, but an early visitor described it as "a most beautiful romantic looking island," with its cliffs, ravines, and thick forest.

Sugar and Slaves

Portuguese EXPLORERS probably first sighted the Guinea Islands in 1478. After several years of planning, in 1486 João de Paiva founded the first settlement on São Tomé, but the settlement failed shortly thereafter. Álvaro da Caminha, a Portuguese nobleman, was given control over the island in 1493. He quickly sent hundreds of settlers to his town on the bay of Ana de Chaves. The colonies' first inhabitants included a mixture of African slaves, Portuguese criminals, and Jewish children taken from their parents as part of Portugal's religious persecution. Caminha had a hand in creating the subsequent Creole population by enforcing marriage between slave women and male Portuguese convicts. Following Caminha's lead, other Portuguese aristocratic families acquired land on the islands.

During their first two centuries as Portuguese colonies, the islands specialized in the cultivation of sugarcane. During the very early sixteenth century, in fact, the islands were the leading source of sugar for the European market. The islands' plantation economy provided a model for European sugar-producing colonies in Brazil and the Caribbean. Together with timber exports and trade with the peoples along the Gulf of Guinea coast, sugar production provided the colony with an early prosperity.

During the early sixteenth century vast sugar plantations covered São Tomé and Príncipe. The Portuguese brought thousands of African slaves to the island to carry out the back-

São Tomé and Príncipe

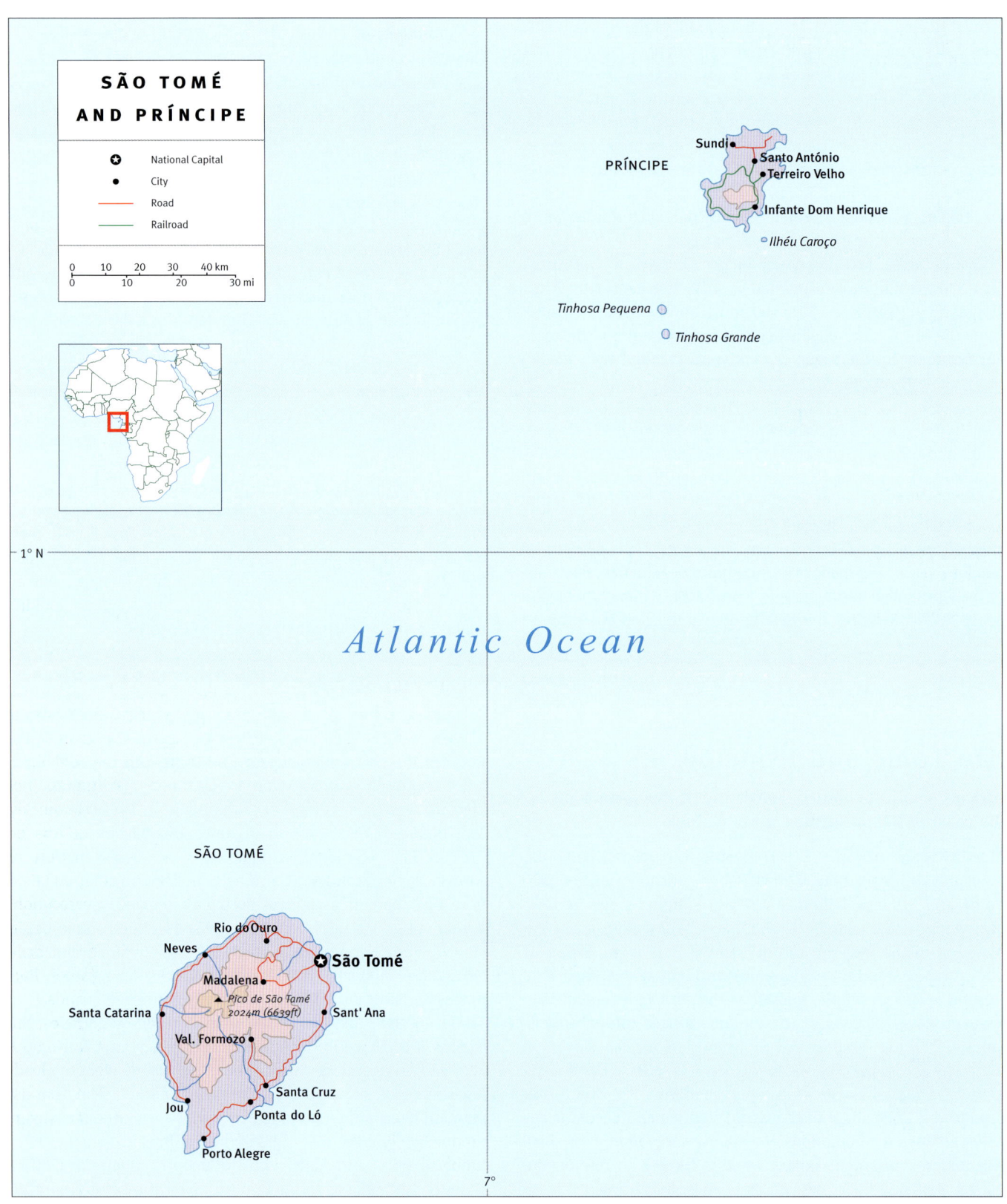

São Tomé and Príncipe (At a Glance)

OFFICIAL NAME: Democratic Republic of São Tomé and Príncipe

AREA: 1,001 sq km (387 sq mi)

LOCATION: In the Gulf of Guinea, along the equator off the western coast of Central Africa

CAPITAL: São Tomé (population 51,886; 2001 estimate)

OTHER MAJOR CITIES: Neves (population 6,650; 2001 estimate)

POPULATION: 175,883 (1998 estimate)

POPULATION DENSITY: 175.7 persons per sq km (about 454 persons per sq mi)

POPULATION BELOW AGE 15: 48 percent (male 42,480; female: 41,411); 2003 estimate

POPULATION GROWTH RATE: 3.2 percent (2003 estimate)

TOTAL FERTILITY RATE: 5.88 children born per woman (2003 estimate)

LIFE EXPECTANCY AT BIRTH: Total population: 66.28 years (male 64.79 years; female 67.82 years); 2003 estimate

INFANT MORTALITY RATE: 46.04 deaths per 1,000 live births (2003 estimate)

LITERACY RATE (AGE 15 AND OVER WHO CAN READ AND WRITE): Total population: 79.3 percent (male 85 percent; female 62 percent); 1991 estimate

EDUCATION: No information available

LANGUAGES: Portuguese is the official language, but most people speak Crioulo, a language combining Portuguese and African elements.

ETHNIC GROUPS: Because it was uninhabited before European colonization in the fifteenth century, much of São Tomé's population consists of the racially mixed descendants of Portuguese settlers and African slaves. Such *mestiços* are also known as *forros,* or *filhos da terra* (children of the earth). In addition, the islands are inhabited by *serviçais* (contract laborers, mostly from the Cape Verde Islands, Angola, and Mozambique), *tongas* (descendants of earlier generations of serviçais), *Angolares* (who take their name from shipwrecked Angolan slaves, though the name now refers to all people of African descent whose livelihood depends not on the plantation economy but on fishing), and Europeans (mostly Portuguese).

RELIGIONS: Christian (Roman Catholic, Evangelical Protestant, Seventh-Day Adventist) about 80 percent.

CLIMATE: Both of the islands that comprise São Tomé and Príncipe share a hot, humid, tropical climate. Temperatures range from an average of 25° C (77° F) in the lower, coastal areas to 18° C (65° F) in the higher elevations. Although there is virtually no seasonal variation in temperature, there is a rainy season from October to May. In addition, rainfall varies greatly, from 5,100 mm (about 200 in) in the southwestern mountains to 1,020 mm (about 40 in) in the lowlands to the northeast.

LAND, PLANTS, AND ANIMALS: São Tomé, the larger of the two islands that make up the Democratic Republic of São Tomé and Príncipe, is home to the country's highest mountain, Pico de São Tomé, with an elevation of 2,024 m (6,640 ft). Both islands are volcanic in origin, with rugged, mountainous interiors. Coastal areas, particularly on the southwestern and northeastern sides, are fertile lowlands. The interior mountains are forested. The islands have few native species of mammals but are home to a great variety of birds.

NATURAL RESOURCES: São Tomé's most important natural resource is its rich soil, which is the basis for its plantation economy.

CURRENCY: The dobra

GROSS DOMESTIC PRODUCT (GDP): $200 million (2002 estimate)

GDP PER CAPITA: $1,200 (2002 estimate)

GDP REAL GROWTH RATE: 4 percent (2002 estimate)

PRIMARY ECONOMIC ACTIVITIES: São Tomé's economy is almost completely dependent on its production and export of cocoa, responsible for about 60 percent of export earnings. Other crops raised include coffee, copra, oil palms, coconuts, bananas, and papayas. A small fishing industry also exists. In recent years the country has attempted to build a tourist industry capitalizing on its great natural beauty.

PRIMARY CROPS: Cocoa, coffee, palm kernels, copra, cinnamon, pepper, coconuts, bananas, papayas, beans, poultry, fish

INDUSTRIES: Light construction, textiles, soap, beer, fish processing, timber

PRIMARY EXPORTS: Cocoa, coffee, copra, and palm oil

PRIMARY IMPORTS: Because of its island location and agricultural specialization, São Tomé imports about 90 percent of its food and nearly all of its consumer goods.

PRIMARY TRADE PARTNERS: Portugal, France, Netherlands, and Germany

GOVERNMENT: São Tomé and Príncipe has been a parliamentary republic since 1990. The country consists of two administrative districts: São Tomé and Príncipe. As of 2001, it was governed by President Fradique de Menezes; Maria das Neves has served as prime minister since 2002. Voters elect a unicameral National Assembly consisting of 55 legislators, which chooses the prime minister and cabinet and appoints justices to the Supreme Court. The dominant party from independence in 1975 into the late 1990s was the Movement for the Liberation of São Tomé and Príncipe (MLSTP). In 2002 the MLSTP won twenty-four seats in the National Assembly, but was strongly challenged by the Force for Change Democratic Movement, which held 23 seats. The Ue-Kedadji coalition controlled the remaining eight seats. São Tomé has universal suffrage for those aged 18 and over.

breaking work of cultivating and harvesting the cane on the plantations, or *roças*. Known for their harsh and unhealthy living conditions, the roças were owned and run by Portuguese landowners; the workers, called *serviçais* or *tongas*, were slaves imported from the African mainland. A growing mixed population, known as *forros* or *filhos da terra*, mostly avoided the roça work that some of their ancestors had done and instead farmed small plots of land and worked as tradesmen.

Sãotoméan sugar, never as high in quality as that exported by Madeira, had difficulty competing with the expanding volume of sugar produced in the Americas. In addition, plant disease and soil exhaustion caused by primitive agricultural practices soon led to lower yields. From a height of 2,800 tons of sugar exported in 1570, by 1600 São Tomé's production had dropped to 857 tons. At the same time, a series of slave uprisings cost the roças a proportion of their labor force when slaves and *Angolares*, supposedly survivors of a wrecked slave ship from ANGOLA, fled to the rain forest. By 1615 the Portuguese had abandoned more than three-quarters of the sugar plantations.

With the collapse of its sugar industry, São Tomé's economy went into a decline. By the late seventeenth century, however, the islands played an increasingly important role in supporting the TRANSATLANTIC SLAVE TRADE. In fact, their strategic position in this trade attracted the interest of the Dutch, who seized the islands for a few years in the 1740s before Portugal managed to reassert control. The islands supported the slave trade in a number of ways. Plantations on the two islands used slave labor to produce food and other supplies for the slave ships. Also, the islands served as a marketplace for slaves brought from the African coast in small vessels. In São Tomé and Príncipe these slaves were sold to traders who loaded them (along with food and supplies) onto larger oceangoing ships for transport to the Americas.

Between 1809 and 1815 about 33,000 slaves entered São Tomé, most of them bound for CUBA or Brazil (then a Portuguese colony). As an important way station between the mainland and the Brazilian slave markets, São Tomé also became a trading center for Brazilian tobacco that was destined for African markets. Because of this, and because of its historic dependence on plantation agriculture, many historians consider São Tomé's history more typical of the WEST INDIES than of Africa.

Coffee and Cocoa

The decline of the slave trade during the early ninettenth century forced São Tomé and Príncipe once again to shift their economic focus. Growing demand for African products, such as ivory and palm oil, allowed São Tomé, with its favorable location and infrastructure, to serve as a market for commodities other than slaves. Meanwhile, the islands' plantations began to cultivate cash crops that were in demand on European markets. Coffee, probably introduced into Príncipe in 1800, became a major cash crop by the 1830s. Cocoa, brought to Príncipe in 1822, was being produced in large amounts by the 1850s. Both industries benefited from a reduction in the export duties charged by Portugal and, more importantly, from the large tracts of land left fallow when the sugar plantations were abandoned. Unlike the earlier sugar boom, the coffee and cocoa boom—at least initially—benefited the forros, São Tomé's local Creole population, many of whom rushed to claim plots of land and farmed them successfully.

It was not long, however, before Portuguese landowners, aided by the Banco Nacional Ultramarino, moved in and foreclosed on many of the Creole small farmers. By the late nineteenth century, the old roça system, first employed in the production of sugar, had been revived, this time to produce cocoa. By this time, however, much had changed. Slavery, which had been made illegal in the Portuguese colonies in 1858, continued under another name. Plantation owners still effectively owned the roça workers, now called *libertos* (freedpeople). Cocoa production boomed, and during the first years of the twentieth century São Tomé and Príncipe were the world's leading producers of cocoa. While the islands continued to produce small amounts of coffee and other cash crops, cocoa came to dominate the islands' economy, as it does to this day.

Press coverage of the importation of slaves from Angola and the bleak conditions of the liberto workers on the roças eventually led to a boycott of São Tomé cocoa by the world's chocolate producers in 1909. Portugal responded by pledging to revamp its recruitment practices. Portugal replaced imported Angolan workers with laborers from MOZAMBIQUE and especially CAPE VERDE. Despite new laws against conscripted labor, it is now clear that Africans were forced to work on the roças until at least World War I. The 1920s saw legislation designed to help workers limit their contracts with the roças and provided for their repatriation. During subsequent decades, plantation owners' exploitation of their lands led to a gradual loss of soil fertility and a decline in cocoa yields.

Independence and Uncertainty

The cocoa plantation economy left a lasting imprint on Sãotoméan society, which, to this day, remains divided along caste and, to a lesser extent, racial lines. The white European planters who owned and ran the roça system depended upon imported African labor. These African laborers, or serviçais, had an abysmally low quality of life, with almost no educational opportunities, no political representation, hard physical labor, and dangerous public health conditions. The Angolares escaped roça work and lived in small fishing villages on the southern coasts. The large Creole population, known as forros, occupied a middle position. A few went abroad, mostly to Portugal, and received a higher education. The majority stayed in São Tomé, where they worked as small farmers or tradesmen. Their culture—in particular, the *tchilolí*, a ritual theatrical dance, along with celebrations of Catholic feast days—has been adopted to some extent by other islanders and provides a basis for a Sãotoméan national identity.

It was the forros who initiated the first protests against the Portuguese since the slave uprisings of the seventeenth century. The forros resented coercive measures, including increased taxes and vagrancy laws, which the Portuguese introduced during the 1930s to force them into roça work. These concerns combined with frustration over the forros' lack of a voice in the islands' government at a time when nationalist movements were taking hold in Africa. In 1953, the tensions boiled over. Following a series of demonstrations by the forros, the roça owners responded with small-scale vigilantism and mobilized armed gangs of serviçais to put down the protest. In doing so, the plantation owners successfully marshaled the historic antipathy between forros and serviçais. An estimated 1,000 forros were killed in the resulting violence.

The event spurred Sãotoméan intellectuals in Portugal and elsewhere to organize a movement to end Portuguese COLONIAL RULE and the oppressive roça system. In 1960 a group of exiled Sãotoméan students formed the Comité de Libertação de São Tomé e Príncipe (CLSTP), which hoped to fight colonial rule by uniting the middle-class forros and the largely disenfranchised serviçais. Among its founders was Manuel Pinto da Costa, who would become the independent country's first president. Taking their message to the world community, the CLSTP won international support, including support at the UNITED NATIONS. But Portuguese repression, including a ban on nationalist literature, kept the budding independence movement from making inroads within São Tomé in the 1960s. Meanwhile, the CLSTP succumbed to internal rivalries and disbanded in the mid-1960s.

The organization that grew in the CLSTP's wake, the Movimento de Libertação de São Tomé e Príncipe (MLSTP) finally won the country's independence. Working with independence armies in Mozambique and GUINEA-BISSAU, the MLSTP forced the Portuguese into a series of concessions, including the right to local self-rule (although Sãotoméans remained subject to colonial authority) in 1974. Pushing for more, the MLSTP—still mostly in exile—inspired local groups to stage massive demonstrations and armed raids against the government. Later that year, at talks in ALGIERS, the Portuguese agreed to grant full independence to São Tomé and Príncipe in July 1975.

At independence, the new government of President Pinto da Costa wrote a constitution establishing São Tomé as a single-party state, led by the Marxist-influenced MLSTP. The party, which demanded of its members a year's training before being named "militants" or full members, exerted increasingly centralized control over the country's political and economic life. Immediately after independence, the government nationalized the cocoa plantations that still formed the basis of the country's economy. This put over 80 percent of the available cropland under central government control. São Tomé initially cultivated close ties with eastern European communist countries and Cuba.

Starting in the mid-1980s, however, economic instability and the need for foreign aid led São Tomé to seek closer ties with the West. In 1987 the country accepted a STRUCTURAL ADJUSTMENT plan sponsored by the International Monetary Fund and the World Bank. A combination of currency devaluation and government budget cuts led to worsening economic conditions initially, and the populace reacted with a series of riots protesting high food costs. Politically, however, the government moved to promote democracy: A new constitution in 1990 allowed for a multiparty system.

Elections in 1991 removed President Pinta da Costa from office. Miguel Trovoada, like Pinto da Costa a prominent forro, assumed the presidency. Trovoada was reelected in 1996 and stepped down in 2001. He was succeeded by Fradique de Menezes, a businessman and former foreign minister. Menezes was toppled by a military coup in July 2003 by officers concerned with "the continuing social and economic decline" of the country. The coup was partly in response to Menezes's frequent changes in the government, which included firing four prime ministers and dissolving parliament during less than two years in office. However, Menezes returned to power less than a week later after striking a deal with the coup leaders. The agreement called for a new government to be formed, with Menezes remaining president in return for pledging to respect the separation of powers between the various branches of government.

Some observers believe that economic factors—in the form of oil reserves off the coast—played a role in the coup. Geological surveys have predicted that the costal waters between São Tomé and Nigeria may hold several billion barrels of oil, leading to questions about who will control and benefit from this potential financial windfall. However, for now the oil exists in theory only; no actual reserves have yet been discovered. Cocoa production continues to be São Tomé's principal economic activity, though state ownership has failed to increase yields. Many believe that tourism will soon become a major income source as well. The country boasts a relatively high literacy rate. However, it continues to depend heavily on foreign aid, and its citizens remain poor. The islands have yet to find a way to move beyond the limits of their plantation economy.

See also Creoles; Nationalism in Africa; Slavery in Africa.

Kate Tuttle

Sara

Name given to a group of peoples living primarily along the Chari and Logone rivers in southern Chad; also refers to the main language of the region; group is also known as Sar.

The people known collectively as the Sara consist of several smaller subgroups that were not always considered a single ethnic group. Among the largest of the subgroups are the Madjingayé, Gambayé, and Goulaye peoples. The estimated 1.5 million people who consider themselves Sara belong to various communities that have different levels of attachment to the group identity. Some groups have considered themselves Sara for many centuries, while others acknowledge a later inclusion. Still others speak the Sara language but consider themselves members of the subgroup only. The Sara language is considered part of the Nilo-Saharan language family, and linguists divided it into five sublanguages.

In addition to language, the Sara peoples share a common traditional lifestyle as village-dwelling fishers and farmers. Their sense of a group identity was forged by the attitude of neighboring Arab groups, who considered the Sara an inferior people. Their northern Arab neighbors raided the Sara for slaves for centuries, and consequently, the Sara initially welcomed the intervention of French colonizers in the early twentieth century. While the French indeed ended the slave trade in CHAD, the lives of many Sara changed drastically under COLONIAL RULE. The French imposed forced labor, especially in railroad construction and other large projects, and established large-scale cotton plantations. In addition, the French selected local chiefs to oversee the village governments, ignoring the political structures traditional in Sara subgroups. Under the influence of the Arabs and Europeans, some Sara converted to Islam or Christianity, although the majority continued to adhere to traditional religious practices.

The Sara were more closely tied to the French colonial government and more Westernized than the population of northern Chad. Thus, the Sara dominated the country's military and civil service, and they gained power as Chad moved toward independence in the 1950s. Chad's first independent leaders eagerly sought Sara approval, and according to some historians, even went so far as to use traditional Sara initiation rituals in governmental functions. Resentment of such attention grew among the peoples of northern Chad and played a part in political disturbances of the 1970s and 1980s.

See also Languages, African: An Overview.

Sarbah, John Mensah

1864–1910

Lawyer and legislator who defended the legal rights of people of the Gold Coast (now Ghana) and who worked to improve the country's educational system.

Born at Cape Coast in 1864, John Mensah Sarbah (also known as Kofi Mensah) was the first son of John and Sarah Sarbah. He attended the Cape Coast Wesleyan School and the Taunton School in England. Sarbah studied law at Lincoln's Inn in London and in 1887 was the first GOLD COAST African admitted to the bar.

Upon his return to Cape Coast, Sarbah established a successful law practice. He considered the traditional political institutions of the Gold Coast basically democratic in nature, and devoted his legal expertise to modernizing these institutions and integrating them into the colony's legal apparatus. At the same time, he fought for laws protecting Africans from colonial oppression and exploitation. Among his many accomplishments, Sarbah, with the help of JOSEPH CASELY-HAYFORD, succeeded in defeating the Lands Bill of 1897, which would have ignored traditional property rights and allowed the British government to dispose of the people's commonly held land without compensation. During the 1890s, he also helped found the Aborigines' Rights Protection Society. In addition, Sarbah established and edited a newspaper, *The Gold Coast People,* and published books and other materials to advance the indigenous cause.

As a legislator, Sarbah served on the Legislative Council of the Gold Coast between 1901 and 1910. As part of a commitment to modernization, Sarbah also worked to improve educational opportunities for Africans. He collected funds and donated money to fund scholarships and to found schools, including the prestigious Mfantsipim School. At times he personally paid teachers' salaries. Sarbah died in 1910, leaving his wife, Ekuah Mariam, and three children.

Robert Fay

Saro-Wiwa, Kenule Beeson

1941–1995

Writer and Ogoni political activist whose campaign against Shell Oil led to his execution by the military government of Nigeria.

Kenule Beeson Saro-Wiwa grew up in a large polygamous Anglican household. A good student, he won a scholarship to study English at Government College in Umauhia. He finished his studies at Ibadan University in 1965, and then worked as a teaching assistant at the University of Nigeria in Nsukka and lectured at Lagos University. Cultivating a taste for pipe-smoking and fine Scotch, he quickly assumed his place among the Nigerian elite, which had assumed power after the British pulled out of NIGERIA in 1960.

During the Biafran Civil War (1967–1970), Saro-Wiwa expressed strong support of the federal government while serving first as administrator of Bonny, and then as a cabinet member in the newly created Rivers State. But political differences with associates caused him to leave the public sector in 1973. Thereafter he devoted himself to his writing career, dabbling in numerous genres and producing many books. By the end of his life he had written four novels, two books of short stories, three books of essays, two volumes of drama, one volume of folklore, and nine children's books. His most famous novel, *Sozaboy: A Novel In Rotten English,* lampooned corruption and power mongering in the military government of Nigeria. Saro-Wiwa also wrote for Nigeria's favorite soap opera and contributed columns to Nigerian as well as English newspapers.

Saro-Wiwa reentered politics in 1987 when President IBRAHIM BABANGIDA appointed him to assist in the proclaimed transition from military to civilian rule. He quit within the year, however, convinced that Babangida's efforts were insincere. Thereafter Saro-Wiwa turned his political energies to human rights and environmental issues in Ogoniland.

The Royal Dutch Shell Company, known as Shell Oil, had been extracting oil from the fertile, swampy lowlands of the Ogonis' 400-sq-mi homeland in southeastern Nigeria since

The Nigerian writer Ken Saro-Wiwa publicized the plight of the Ogoni people, whose land had been seized and polluted by multinational oil companies. His activism on behalf of environmental and human rights led to conflict with the Nigerian government of Sani Abacha, which had Saro-Wiwa executed in 1995. *Reuters/Archive Photos*

1958. The company offered few benefits to local communities, and their sloppy practices contaminated the water and land, reducing fish and crop yields. In 1990 a group of Ogoni traditional leaders formed the Movement for the Survival of the Ogoni People. Listing among their primary goals not only better environmental protection but also Ogoni statehood, the group appointed Saro-Wiwa as spokesman.

Saro-Wiwa joined the movement convinced that success depended on both high-profile protest actions and international support. To the disapproval of the more conservative Ogoni leadership, he supported the sabotage of Shell Oil facilities, carried out by the movement's younger members. Hoping to win the favor of environmentalists in England and the United States, Saro-Wiwa filmed the degradation of Ogoniland and distributed the footage abroad. His efforts caught the attention of environmental groups such as Greenpeace as well as the international media, which further publicized Shell Oil's activities. In 1992 Saro-Wiwa traveled to Geneva, where he addressed the United Nations Working Group on Indigenous Populations; later that year he spoke before a committee of delegates at the United Nations in New York.

Meanwhile, Shell Oil ordered the military government of General SANI ABACHA to protect its operations. Government officials, who profited financially from the company's presence, complied readily by sending troops to Ogoniland. These police efforts were extraordinarily harsh, however, involving the massacre of villages and murder of innocent Ogoni. Shell Oil withdrew from the area in 1993, but the conflict persisted as the federal government maintained operation of the lucrative wells.

On May 21, 1994, Saro-Wiwa was arrested along with fourteen colleagues, allegedly for involvement in the murder of four pro-government Ogoni chiefs. In 1995 the imprisoned Saro-Wiwa won a Goldman Environmental Prize, a prestigious award given annually to one environmental activist on each continent. Despite such publicity and lobbying efforts by numerous foreign parties, however, Saro-Wiwa was hanged on November 10, 1995.

Many Ogoni devotees and foreign activists consider Saro-Wiwa a martyr. Some observers, however, noting his political ambitions and his followers' violent vigilantism, have questioned the purity of his motives. Nonetheless, his imprisonment and execution reflected the injustice and intransigence of the Nigerian military dictatorship.

See also Environmental Movements in Africa.

Eric Bennett

Sasala

Ethnic group of West Africa; also known as Isala, Pisala, and Sissala.

The Sasala primarily inhabit the Upper West Province of northwestern GHANA and neighboring southern BURKINA FASO. They speak a Niger-Congo language and belong to the GRUSI cultural and linguistic group. Approximately 100,000 people consider themselves Sasala.

See also Languages, African: An Overview.

Sassou-Nguesso, Denis

1943–

Army general who served as president of the Republic of the Congo from 1979 to 1992, and again from 1997.

A member of the MBOCHI ethnic group, Denis Sassou-Nguesso was born in Edou, in northern Congo, and began his political career as a soldier. After school he joined the military and trained in FRANCE. In 1963, he returned home to assume command of the airborne infantry, and later took charge of the important BRAZZAVILLE military zone. When northern military officer, MARIEN NGOUABI, came to power in 1968, Sassou-Nguesso became a member of the central committee of the Congolese Workers Party (PCT), the ruling party, and later became the minister of defense. Although it has never been proven, Sassou-Nguesso is a suspect in the plot to assassinate Ngouabi in 1977. Following the assassination, Sassou-Nguesso became vice president of the new PCT military committee.

Two years later, he organized the bloodless overthrow of President Yhombi-Opango and became the country's next leader, elected by the PCT. During the oil boom of the early 1980s, his government dramatically increased spending on public-sector employment and development projects, which helped weaken opposition groups. Sassou-Nguesso targeted his hometown for military recruitment, and brought loyal friends and Mbochi kin into the government. While espousing Marxist-Leninism, Sassou-Nguesso lavishly entertained Western dignitaries, and was known to wear a bulletproof vest under his expensive designer suits. When revenues from oil began to dry up in the mid-1980s, he tried to cut the bloated state bureaucracy, but ran into stiff opposition. Economic decline and widespread protests eventually forced Sassou-Nguesso to make democratic reforms. He placed a distant third in national elections in 1992.

Sassou-Nguesso reappeared on the national political scene in 1997, along with his private militia, the Cobras, and was quickly suspected of plans to disrupt the upcoming presidential elections. Government troops' attempts to arrest Cobra members led to a five-month civil war, which ended in October when Sassou-Nguesso took the capital, Brazzaville, with considerable help from Angolan troops, and reclaimed the presidency. He promised national reconciliation, a return to civilian rule, and a professional military. Sassou-Nguesso's presidency has been marred, however, by violations of the non-aggression pact he signed with LAURENT KABILA, former president of the DEMOCRATIC REPUBLIC OF THE CONGO. Sassou-Nguesso, presidency was confirmed in the 2002 election, although most of the opposition parties had dropped out, citing voting irregularities. That same year, fighting erupted between government troops and a rebel militia led by Frédéric Bintsangou.

Eric Young

Saunders, Prince

?–1839

African American author and colonizationist.

Prince Saunders was born in either Lebanon, Connecticut, or Thetford, Vermont, the son of Cuff Saunders and Phyllis (maiden name unknown). Although the exact date of Prince Saunders's birth remains unknown, he was baptized on July 25, 1784 in Lebanon and received his early schooling in Thetford. He taught at a black school in Colchester, Connecticut, and later studied at Moor's Charity School at Dartmouth College in 1807 and 1808. President John Wheelock (1754–1817) of Dartmouth recommended Saunders as instructor at BOSTON's African School in late 1808. By 1811 Saunders was secretary of the African Masonic Society and had founded the Belles Lettres Society, a literary group. He also taught at the African Baptist Church in Boston, founded by Thomas Paul. He was engaged to one daughter of emigrationist and sea captain PAUL CUFFE. Although the engagement ended for unknown reasons, his acquaintance with Cuffe undoubtedly awakened Saunders to PAN-AFRICANISM and the black colonization movement.

In 1815 Saunders and Thomas Paul traveled to London as delegates to the Masonic Lodge of Africans. Saunders met with many influential British people, including abolitionist leaders William Wilberforce and Thomas Clarkson. As a result of these meetings, Saunders focused his interest on HAITI, the first black republic in the Western Hemisphere. He shared the British abolitionists' desire to anglicize Haiti. In 1816 he made his first visit to Haiti, where King Henri Christophe greeted him enthusiastically. Saunders introduced the concept of vaccination by vaccinating Christophe's children, and he introduced the Lancastrian system of education. Adopted by many schools in the United States, including the AFRICAN FREE SCHOOLS, the system used student monitors to assist teachers and emphasized learning by rote. Saunders then returned to England, where he published his first work, *Haytian Papers* (1816), a collection of Haitian civic laws governing agriculture, commerce, the police, and politics. In December 1816 he traveled again to Haiti. Christophe accused him of publishing *Haytian Papers* without permission and dismissed him as an adviser. Saunders was allowed, however, to continue his work in schools and medicine until 1818, when he sailed to Boston. There he published a second edition of his book.

Living in PHILADELPHIA in 1818, Saunders served as a lay reader for Absalom Jones's St. Thomas's African Episcopal Church. He joined the Pennsylvania Abolition Society and promoted colonization to the Caribbean, especially Haiti. Although it had been supported earlier by black leaders, by 1818 colonization had become intensely unpopular among blacks. JAMES FORTEN and RICHARD ALLEN both denounced colonization as a trick of the newly organized AMERICAN COLONIZATION SOCIETY. Generally, African American and white abolitionists regarded the society as an organization seeking to protect slavery and counteract antislavery. Saunders persisted in his views, however, publishing in 1818 two pamphlets: *An Address Delivered . . . before the Pennsylvania Augustine Society for Education of People of Color* and *A Memoir Presented to the American Convention for Promoting the Abolition of Slavery*.

Saunders settled in Haiti in 1820. He took with him letters from Philadelphia alleging the desire of thousands of free blacks to emigrate to Haiti. Saunders convinced Christophe to supply a ship and $25,000 to initiate colonization. As the agreement neared completion, however, a coup displaced Christophe, who then committed suicide. Saunders was left penniless and friendless. Newly installed President John Pierre Boyer received Saunders politely but refused to guarantee support for the former ally of Christophe. Despite Boyer's expressed desire to promote greater democracy in Haiti, Saunders became disillusioned and feared that Boyer's approach (he abolished universal education, established by Christophe) would cause the downfall of black Haiti. Convinced of Boyer's inability to rule effectively, he lobbied the British and Russian governments to intervene to replace Boyer.

Saunders's disaffection with Haiti's government did not lessen his zeal for emigration to Haiti. It is doubtful that he played a key role in Haitian politics, although a claim has been made that he was Boyer's attorney general. There is no evidence to support this claim in Haitian records, however. Saunders lived in Haiti until his death in PORT-AU-PRINCE.

Saunders's position on colonization continued from the Pan-Africanism of Paul Cuffe and the SIERRA LEONE settlers in the late eighteenth century to the black hostility in the United States toward colonization after 1817. His efforts to create a Pan-African nationalism, of which his involvement with Haitian politics was an exceptional example, became politically unpopular in later years, but he should be recognized for his remarkable abilities as an educator, abolitionist, writer, and public speaker.

Bibliography

Bayard, Franck. "Prince Saunders." In *Dictionary of American Negro Biography*. 1982.

Griggs, Earl Leslie, and Thomas Clarkson, eds. *Henri Christophe and Thomas Clarkson: A Correspondence*. 1952; repr. 1968.

White, Arthur D. "Prince Saunders: An Instance of Social Mobility among Antebellum New England Blacks." *Journal of Negro History* 55 (1975): 526–35.

From *American National Biography*. John A. Garraty and Mark C. Carnes, eds. Oxford University Press, 1999. Reprinted by permission of the American Council of Learned Societies.

Graham Russell Hodges

Sausage Tree

Common name for a type of evergreen tree native to warm, wet grasslands of tropical West Africa.

The sausage tree is grown as an ornamental plant in moist tropical and subtropical areas because of its attractive flowers and unique fruits, which look like giant, dangling sausages. The fruits are not edible, but they are used in traditional African folk medicine to treat abscesses and other skin disorders. The sausage tree may be found at altitudes as high as 1,830 m (6,000 ft). It is typically 4.5 to 7.5 m (15 to 25 ft) tall but may attain heights of 15 m (49 ft). It has a spreading crown that is densely clothed with leaves in summer. The compound leaves (leaves composed of leaflets arranged along a central stem) are paired and opposite one another on the branches. These leaves can grow up to 50 cm (20 in) long. They have seven, nine, or eleven stiff, leathery leaflets, each up to 20 cm (8 in) long and 6 cm (2 in) wide. The flowers are 7.5 to 10 cm (3 to 4 in) long and hang in clusters that grow up to 2 m (6.5 ft) long. The petals of the flowers are fused to form a conspicuous bell-shaped structure that is yellow on the outside and purplish red on the inside. The flowers open at night and close in the morning; they are pollinated by bats attracted by the flowers' scent. The inedible fruit is a woody, gray-brown capsule that hangs from the branch, suspended on a long, ropelike stem. It is 30 to 60 cm (1 to 2 ft) long, about 10 cm (about 4 in) in diameter, and weighs 2 to 5 kg (5 to 12 lb). The fruit takes a year to ripen, has a hard rind and pulp, and contains many seeds.

Scientific classification: The sausage tree belongs to the bignonia family, Bignoniaceae. It is classified as *Kigelia africana* or *Kigelia pinnata*.

Savage, Augusta Christine Fells

1892–1962

American sculptor and arts educator who specialized in portrait sculptures of African American leaders.

The seventh of fourteen children, Augusta Savage began to mold human figures out of clay at age six. She commenced professional art training after moving to NEW YORK City in 1921. Though Savage had briefly studied to be a teacher at the Tallahassee State Normal School (now Florida A&M), she enrolled at Cooper Union to study sculpture.

During the same period, Savage received a commission to sculpt a bust of W. E. B. DU BOIS. Following the success of this work, she sculpted likenesses of other African American leaders including FREDERICK DOUGLASS and MARCUS GARVEY.

Savage continued to create and exhibit portrait sculptures for the next two decades. Many depicted African or African American themes. In 1929, she traveled to Paris to work and study. Returning to America in 1932, she opened the Savage School of Arts and Crafts in HARLEM, where she taught art classes and where her students included JACOB LAWRENCE and Norman Lewis.

In the 1930s, Savage organized black artists to benefit from the NEW DEAL'S WORKS PROGRESS ADMINISTRATION commissions. She opened New York's first gallery devoted to African American art, the short-lived Salon of Contemporary Art, in 1939. Savage also contributed a grand public sculpture, *Lift Every Voice and Sing*, to that year's World's Fair. The plaster sculpture was ultimately demolished when she could not raise the necessary funds to cast it in bronze. Savage retired to Saugerties, New York in the mid-1940s and died there in 1962.

See also Art, African American.

Savary, Joseph

?–1822?

Caribbean-born patriot and soldier of fortune who fought in the Battle of New Orleans during the War of 1812.

Joseph Savary was the close associate of whites and generally referred to as a mulatto Creole of Santo Domingo (now the DOMINICAN REPUBLIC). The names of his parents can only be conjectured. Since he was believed to have been the brother of Belton Savary, another hero of the Battle of NEW ORLEANS, in Louisiana, he was probably the son of Charles Savary and Charlotte Lajoie. Savary was an officer in the Santo Domingan army under the French government and rendered outstanding services to the whites during the 1791 slave uprising. He and his family were among the whites, free people of color, and slaves who fled their native land and finally landed in New Orleans in 1809. When he reached the United States, he brought with him a reputation as an able officer and a man of great courage.

In the meager accounts concerning Savary's early days in Louisiana, he is first mentioned as a member of the privateer-pirate group of French-born Pierre and Jean Lafitte, operating at Barataria Bay in southeastern Louisiana. In fact, Governor William Charles Coles Claiborne had already described the black element of that group as "Santo Domingo negroes of the most desperate character, and no worse than most of their white associates." It was Claiborne who suggested to General Andrew Jackson the enlistment of the Santo Domingans in the American cause during the War of 1812; the general enlisted Savary and his men. Despite the fact that the Santo Domingans were generally admired for their bravery and heroism on the battlefield, they were never fully trusted by the dominant whites.

Historians generally accord to Savary titles such as captain, major, and colonel. In dispatches General Jackson referred to him as "Colonel Savary" and only rarely as "Captain Savary." According to one record, Jackson appointed him again as a major sometime before December 19, 1814. It was before this date, however, that Savary began to organize the Second Battalion of the free men of color. With the exception of a small number of men from Martinique, the Second Battalion was composed almost entirely of Santo Domingans. This group went to Savary's home and was enlisted there, but remained without arms until only a short time before entering the fight.

Savary's Second Battalion of men of color was mustered into service on December 19. The next day Governor Claiborne reported to General Jackson that the battalion was now organized and wished to be put into action. Three days later, having been supplied with repaired muskets that formerly had been regarded as unfit for use, this battalion played a leading role in the battle of the night of December 23. It was in this night's engagement that Savary lifted his voice in Santo Domingan French, translated as "March on! March on, my friends, march on against the enemies of the country!"

On the decisive day of January 8, 1815, both battalions of free colored men were far removed from contact with the British lines. This so-called Line Jackson was where General Jackson himself had taken his stand during the engagement. Yet it was in this area that some of Savary's men made an "unauthorized sortie" in order to reach the British lines where General Sir Edward Pakenham was desperately using his plumed hat to beat his wavering men back into action. Italian-born merchant Vincent Nolté, who was the model for a character in Hervey Allen's original adventure novel *Anthony Adverse*, was a participant in that day's fighting. Famed in the drawing rooms and financial exchanges of two hemispheres, Nolté described the action that followed in a letter to the *Niles Register*: "New Orleans colored regiment were so anxious for glory that they could not be prevented from advancing from over our breast works and exposing themselves." They fought like desperadoes, he added, and deserved distinguished praise.

In this unauthorized sortie, a man whose name went down in army records as Sergeant Belton Savourie returned to Line Jackson in such a wounded condition that he died two days later. All was well, however, with the U.S. forces. General Pakenham had been shot twice, and the utter rout of his forces soon followed. This was probably the day when—according to white tradition—General Jackson, in a moment of wild exultation, hugged Colonel Joseph Savary to his breast on the field of battle. It is a matter of record that Charles Savary, Belton's father, was awarded a sum of money for the death of his son by an act of the Louisiana legislature on February 6, 1815. When Charles died his wife, Charlotte Lajoie, was awarded a pension, on March 22, 1831. Oral traditions among the descendants of the free colored people maintain that it was "Bowie Savourie of Attakapas" who shot General Pakenham, and his name is spelled out *Savourie* in the same erroneous manner as it is entered on army rolls. Years later General Jackson, in describing Pakenham's death in a letter to his former secretary of war, called no name but simply wrote, "I have always believed he fell from the bullet of a free man of color, who was a famous rifle shot and came from the Attakapas region of Louisiana."

The warm admiration that had persisted between General Jackson and Savary suffered a change after hostilities, when Savary apparently defied an order to command his men to march out of the city they had defended. A highly dramatic impact is couched in the general's statement of the refusal of "Captain Savary's corps to march out of the city agreeable to my order." This unrealistic demand that the men should quit the city after hostilities was based on the dominant white group's distrust of armed blacks in its midst. Most of the free men of color who fought in the Battle of New Orleans became disillusioned and regarded themselves as *objets de mépris* (objects of scorn) in the eyes of their former white comrades, a view shared by Savary. Unlike him, one of his closest white associates, Pierre Lafitte, seems to have made no effort to hide his "hatred . . . of the ungrateful Americans." And it was to the warm embrace of the Lafitte brothers at Galveston, Texas that Savary and a large number of his countrymen returned after the Battle of New Orleans.

The Galveston to which Savary returned was the almost undisputed domain of the legendary Lafittes, Pierre and Jean. They and their associates were so involved in international intrigue that it was difficult to unravel the ties of patriotism, smuggling, privateering, filibustering, revolution, and—most probably—outright piracy. Savary had gone to Galveston around August 1816, during the Mexican fight for independence against the Spanish royalists occupying MEXICO. His rendezvous at that time was with Commodore Louis Aury, known as the daring South American naval commander who was then collecting a fleet of vessels to converge at Matagorda, Texas. The number of men he had brought with him is not stated, but it is recorded that some 200 blacks in Aury's little fleet mutinied, took possession of three vessels, and sailed away. Savary then returned to New Orleans, raised forty more blacks, and in company with José Manuel de Herrara, representing the revolutionary Mexican Congress and other soldiers of fortune, landed at Aury's Galveston post and then proceeded to Matagorda.

Both royalists and rebels admired Savary and his Santo Domingans. One royalist writing to the Spanish minister at Philadelphia, Pennsylvania, included "the Santo Domingan free colored people of New Orleans" among those who "will be easily able to ruin the projects that our enemies are forming in the Gulf." General José Alvarez Toledo, the Mexican rebel traitor, in his plan of July 1816 for the suppression of the Mexican Revolution (1810–1820), referred to Colonel Joseph Savary as an intelligence agent to evaluate an alleged offer by Haitian president ALEXANDRE PÉTION to aid Herrara.

More and more, Savary aligned himself with the Mexican insurgents against Spanish rule. By 1816 a group of Mexicans, free blacks, free men of color, whites, and South Americans began to use Galveston, Mexico, Santo Domingo, and HAITI as bases to launch revolutionary activities and privateering expeditions against Spain and Spanish commerce. Savary, Herrara, Alexandre Pétion, Aury, SIMÓN BOLÍVAR, the Lafitte brothers—and even the New Orleans Associates—not only began to threaten but also weakened Spanish rule in South America.

No record has been found of Savary's death. In 1819 he addressed a petition to the Louisiana House of Representatives, requesting a pension for five years. That body reported "the said Joseph Savary deserves a reward for the services by him rendered to this state under command of major general Jackson during the invasion of the British." He was once described as "Colonel Savary, a man in whom Mr. Aury has much confidence." The question naturally arises, then, as to whether he remained with Aury at Galveston and later returned to New Orleans, or whether he continued on to Vera Cruz with Herrara and in a later contact with Pétion agreed to serve as his emissary to the Mexican rebels. Historian Stanley Faye is certain that after Savary left Galveston he returned to New Orleans to live. He offers as proof a brief listing in *Paxton's New Orleans Directory of 1822*.

Some of the principal sources are Roland B. McConnell's *Negro Troops of Antebellum Louisiana: A History of the Battalion of Free Men of Color* (1968) and A. Lacarrière Latour's *Historical Memoirs of the War in West Florida and Louisiana in 1814–1815* (1816). Other principal sources are Harris G. Warren's works "The Firebrand Affair: A Forgotten Incident of the Mexican Revolution" and "Documents Relating to George Graham's Proposal to Jean Lafitte for the Occupation of the Texas Coast" (*Louisiana Historical Quarterly*, vol. 21). See Warren's "Toledo's Reconciliation with Spain" (*Louisiana Historical Quarterly*, vol. 23). See also Stanley Faye's "Privateersmen of the Gulf and Their Prizes" (*Louisiana Historical Quarterly*, vol. 22) and "The Great Stroke of Pierre Lafitte" (*Louisiana Historical Quarterly*, vol. 23).

From *Dictionary of American Negro Biography* by Rayford W. Logan and Michael R. Winston, editors. Copyright © 1982 by Rayford W. Logan and Michael R. Winston. Reprinted by permission of W. W. Norton & Company, Inc.

See also Haitian Revolution.

Marcus B. Christian

Savimbi, Jonas Malheiro

1934–2002

Angolan nationalist politician and leader of the insurgent group National Union for the Total Independence of Angola (UNITA).

Jonas Savimbi was born in Munhango, ANGOLA, then a Portuguese colony. The son of a railway worker, Savimbi attended Protestant mission schools until he won a scholarship to study in PORTUGAL. Already involved in Angolan nationalist politics, Savimbi was detained by Portuguese police three times before he fled to Switzerland, where, in 1965, he graduated from Lausanne University with honors in political and juridical sciences (although he would often refer to himself as a doctor). While he was a university student, Savimbi contacted the MOVIMENTO POPULAR DE LIBERTAÇÃO DE ANGOLA (MPLA), but ultimately decided to join the nationalist Union of Angolan People (UPA), instead. As secretary-general of the UPA, Savimbi worked to gain recognition for the movement and to unite the movement with others, ultimately helping to form the National Front for the Liberation of Angola (FNLA).

Savimbi, a member of the OVIMBUNDU ethnic group, soon became disenchanted with the FNLA's KONGO-dominated leadership and exclusively politico-military strategy, and broke from the party in 1964 to form UNITA two years later. With its base in the south among the Ovimbundu people, and with military assistance from China, UNITA joined the war for independence, launching assaults while also fighting other nationalist groups. Employing Maoist strategies, Savimbi's movement attacked economic targets and sought to politicize the peasantry. After a coup d'état in Portugal in 1974 made Angolan independence inevitable, UNITA struggled to prevail over the other nationalist movements. Despite assistance from SOUTH AFRICA, UNITA failed to gain ascendancy and the MPLA became the dominant political and military force in Angola.

In 1976 Savimbi returned to his base at Huambo, in southern Angola, to fight an insurgency war against the MPLA government that would last more than two decades. In public, Savimbi espoused an ideology that vaguely resembled NÉGRITUDE and claimed to be fighting for a political system in which local ethnic identities and customs would be respected. But it was through charisma and force that Savimbi maintained control of UNITA, and his conservative ideology was probably a product of his sources of international military support. Throughout the 1980s, South Africa, the United States, and western European countries supported Savimbi against the Soviet- and Cuban-backed MPLA government, and it was not until the end of the Cold War that the two sides ended the war. After a peace accord in 1992, UNITA and the MPLA contested the 1994 elections. When it appeared that Angolan president JOSÉ EDUARDO DOS SANTOS would win, Savimbi restarted the war. Two years later, Savimbi took his place at the negotiating table, but peace in Angola remained shaky.

The MPLA and UNITA formed a coalition government in April 1997, but Savimbi refused to leave his stronghold in north central Angola to take part in it. Fighting between UNITA and government forces resumed in 1998. In 2002 Jonas Savimbi was killed in a battle in eastern Angola.

See also Cold War and Africa; Nationalism in Africa; Political Movements in Africa.

Eric Young

Savoy Ballroom

Most famous dance hall in Harlem, New York, and birthplace of the dance style called the Lindy hop; also known as the "Home of the Happy Feet."

Inspired by the success of the segregated Roseland and Arcadia Ballrooms in downtown New York City on Broadway, the white businessmen Moe Gale and Jay Faggen opened a dance hall for African Americans on Lenox Avenue in Harlem. The two white entrepreneurs bought an entire block of property and oversaw the construction of the palatial ballroom, which boasted marble staircases, thick carpets, two bandstands, a soda fountain, and room for 7,000 patrons. Gale and Faggen hired Charles Buchanan, an African American, to manage the Savoy, which he did for the ballroom's thirty-two years of operation. Opening on Friday, March 12, 1926, to the music of Fletcher Henderson's Orchestra, the venture achieved instant success. The Savoy was the first elegant and spacious ballroom in a neighborhood of cramped and poorly ventilated clubs.

During the 1920s and 1930s the Savoy attracted crowds of Harlem residents—as well as white celebrities—to hear the biggest names in big-band music, including DUKE ELLINGTON and LOUIS ARMSTRONG. BENNIE MOTEN's band introduced Kansas City swing to New York at the Savoy in 1932, and the dance hall featured CHICK WEBB's Orchestra, backing ELLA FITZGERALD, from 1932 to 1939. The Savoy also showcased its own house bands, like Fess Williams and his Royal Flush Orchestra, the Charleston Bearcats, and Al Cooper's Savoy Sultans. Arranger and saxophonist Edgar Sampson composed "Stompin' at the Savoy" in 1934, and it became the ballroom's anthem.

White as well as black dancers at the Savoy pioneered the Lindy hop, a fast and free style of swing dancing that broke from conventions of popular dance. Since the crowd at the Savoy placed an unspoken premium on innovative dancing, every dancer tried something new. Each generation of Lindy hoppers kept hopping upwards, and airborne movements in the 1930s superseded the floor steps of the 1920s.

While the harmonious integration of the Savoy was one of its exceptional qualities—black and white bands played, black and white dancers danced—the mingling also caused trouble. Provoked by the written testimony of a white police officer who claimed he had contracted syphilis from an African American prostitute, city officials harassed the Savoy's management and revoked its operating license in April 1943. The ballroom was closed until the following October, a suspension that reflected the heightened racial tension in Harlem during World War II (1939–1945).

After reopening, the ballroom flourished once more, but when rock and roll displaced big-band jazz as America's favorite music, the management found it difficult to book bands. The ballroom closed in 1958 and was demolished to make room for a housing project.

In its thirty-two years of operation, the Savoy Ballroom featured over 250 bands, and many of the biggest names in JAZZ. During those years, the mixed audiences of working class blacks and world-famous white celebrities danced together, peacefully if acrobatically.

Eric Bennett

Sayyid Sa'īd ibn Sultan

1791–1856

African sultan of Oman and founder of the Busaidi dynasty; ruled his empire from the East African island of Zanzibar.

Born in Oman, Sayyid Sa'īd ibn Sultan became the first Omani sultan to formalize control of the East African coastal islands; he began traveling to ZANZIBAR in the early eighteenth century. Recognizing Zanzibar's strategic location for commerce between African, European, and American merchants, Sa'īd took control of the island and surrounding trade routes, including the INDIAN OCEAN SLAVE TRADE. Sa'īd hired traders to bring from the interior caravans of slaves and goods such as ivory and cloth, which he then sold to merchants from Europe. The wealth he accumulated enabled Sa'īd to extend his empire over the coastal region of modern-day TANZANIA. There he allocated part of the revenue from the customs duties and taxes imposed on the local traders to local chiefs of the SWAHILI PEOPLE.

During the 1820s, however, European powers, particularly the British and Germans, stepped up efforts to abolish the profitable Indian Ocean slave trade. Threatening military force, Britain coerced Sa'īd to sign several international treaties, such as the Morseby Treaty, which made it illegal for Sa'īd to sell slaves to Christian merchants, and the Hamerton Treaty, which made the sale of slaves north of MOGADISHU illegal. These treaties effectively destroyed the Zanzibari slave market, forcing Sa'īd to find new uses for the slaves who were still arriving from the African interior. He soon put them to work on the many clove plantations he established around the island. By the time he moved the capital of his empire to Zanzibar in 1840, Zanzibar had become the world's leading exporter of cloves, a title it can still claim today.

After Sa'īd's death in 1856, the Busaidi dynasty split into two factions: the Omani sultans and the Zanzibari sultans. This split was formalized in 1861, when the Sultanate of Zanzibar became a political entity separate from the Omani. Sa'īd's son Majid ibn Sa'īd succeeded him, and the Busaidi family continued to rule the island until Zanzibar's independence in 1963.

Elizabeth Heath

Scarborough, William Sanders

1852-1926

African American classicist, university president, and man of letters. With him begins the first professional work in philology by African Americans.

William Sanders Scarborough was the son of Frances Gwynn (d. 1912) and Jeremiah Scarborough (d.1883). His mother was born in Savannah around 1828, and came to Macon about the age of twenty. Of Yamacraw Indian, Spanish, and African descent, she was the slave of Colonel William De Graffenreid (1821–1873) who was general counsel to the Southwestern and Central railroads in Macon. DeGraffenreid was a descendant of the founder of New Bern, North Carolina, the Swiss Baron Christopher DeGraffenreid (1691–1742). Scarborough's father was born near Augusta around 1822. He had obtained his freedom some time before and was employed by the Georgia Central Railroad in Savannah. DeGraffenreid allowed Frances to marry Jeremiah, and permitted the couple to live in their own home on Cotton Avenue. Scarborough became their sole focus, when his siblings, John Henry and Mary Louisa, died as small children.

He was taught to read and write in secret. For reasons unknown a white man, John C. Thomas (d.1884), a North Carolinian by birth, defied the laws interdicting the education of slaves and tutored the youngster. Before Scarborough was eight, he had mastered the popular textbook Webster's *Blue Backed Speller*. Additional help came later on when Colonel Degraffenreid purchased his college textbooks.

After the Civil War ended, Scarborough attended Lewis High School (also known as Ballard Normal School) in Macon and studied Latin, geometry, and algebra. In the fall of 1869, at age seventeen, he enrolled at Atlanta University, which had been founded by the American Missionary Association two years earlier. He was far ahead of all the other students, and the university catalogue for 1869 lists him as the only member of the senior class. Under the eye of Edmund A. Ware (1837–1885), the university president, and Thomas N. Chase (1838–1912), his professor of Greek, Scarborough finished the college preparatory course in two years, and earned excellent grades in classical languages. He made friends, too. Among them were LUCY LANEY, HENRY FLIPPER, and R. R. Wright, Sr. But his position was singular. All eyes were on him because he was the first student to come through the new university's college preparatory program. Although there was no system of commencement in place and no diplomas were awarded at this time, Scarborough nevertheless felt that he was Atlanta University's first graduate.

Scarborough hoped to continue his studies and wanted to enter Yale University. He had considered a career in law, having been inspired by the dynamic life of JOHN MERCER LANGSTON (1829–1897), but for reasons unknown he matriculated at Oberlin College in 1871 instead. The nineteen-year-old's journey north from Georgia to Ohio was momentous. He settled in at Oberlin after a time, and began to strengthen his command of Greek and Latin under the tutelage of Giles W. Shurtleff (1831–1904) in Latin and William H. Ryder (1842–1918) in Greek. He was a competent enough student to earn extra money tutoring other students in Greek, Latin, and mathematics. He graduated with honors in 1875, and his Class of '75 remained dear to his heart. In later years he traveled back to campus for every reunion he could attend.

After trips to New York City and to Princeton, he returned to Macon. Unable to gain a position at Atlanta University, Scarborough joined the faculty at Lewis High School. About that time he was appointed as a delegate to the Republican state convention in Atlanta and began a lifetime of service to the Republican Party. The situation at Lewis High School was fraught with trouble and erupted in violence during the tumult of the Tilden-Hayes presidential race. In 1876 the school was destroyed by fire—reportedly set by arsonists—and shut down. Friends from his father's A.M.E. church quickly him found another teaching position at Payne Institute in Cokesbury South Carolina, now known as Allen University. However, Ku Klux Klan activities there forced him to quit and he returned to Ohio to study ancient languages at Oberlin Theological Seminary.

A short time later he made a trip to Philadelphia during which he met Daniel Payne (1811–1893), founder of WILBERFORCE UNIVERSITY, and learned from Payne himself that he had been elected to the chair of Greek and Latin at the university. The school, supported by the A.M.E. Church, had an enrollment of less than one hundred at the time. On his arrival he was pleased to find that Sarah Cordelia Bierce (1851–1933), whom he had met at Lewis High School, was also on the faculty. The two were married several years later, on August 2, 1881, in NEW YORK CITY, in a ceremony performed by Bishop William Dickerson and witnessed by Hallie Q. Brown, Bishop Jabez Campbell, and Bishop James Shorter. Scarborough's wife, who was white, had trained to teach at the Oswego Institute in upstate New York. The pair of kindred spirits spent forty-five years at Wilberforce teaching and writing together in their home, Tretton Place.

During the late 1870s and early 1880s, Scarborough worked to establish his reputation as a classical scholar. In 1881, with help from his wife, who worked as his copy editor, and with the encouragement of his friend RICHARD T. GREENER, Scarborough published *First Lessons in Greek*. The book was considered a phenomenon and Scarborough became famous. No person of African descent had ever done such a thing for it was commonly believed that none could master classical languages. The following year he joined the American Philological Association (APA), becoming the organization's third African American member, after Richard T. Greener and EDWARD W. BLYDEN. In 1884 he became the first African American member of the Modern Language Association. Scarborough participated in the activities of these and other learned societies, including the American Negro Academy. He was a lifetime member of the APA, and over twenty summaries of the papers he presented at meetings are recorded in pages of *Transactions of the American Philological Association*.

Challenging JIM CROW with his intellect, he was treated disrespectfully at times and refused access to hotels, trains, and dining rooms. But enthused with the realm of the intellect and the idea of racial uplift, he made the most of his interactions. At an APA meeting in 1892, he presented a paper about Plato in the Rotunda of the University of Virginia, which the white audience received with enthusiasm. The event was unprecedented; no African American had ever lectured in the Rotunda before. In 1907 he was invited to the White House to meet President Theodore Roosevelt, along with members of both the APA and of the Archaeological Institute of America (AIA). In 1921 he joined other APA members in England for the annual meeting of the Classical Association at Cambridge University.

Throughout his life, William Scarborough championed the position of the classically based liberal arts curriculum in a college education. He opposed programs of industrial education that excluded the humanities. Practical skills were necessary, but not sufficient as education. He especially hoped that young African American students would apply their study of Greek and Latin to the examination of African languages. In 1897 Scarborough became vice president of Wilberforce University; he was later elected president, serving from 1908 to 1920. During his presidency he steered the university thorough the vicissitudes of World War I. It was the only African American institution with a nationally supported military department. Scarborough oversaw the management of the Student Army Training Corps (SATC) and later the rehabilitation of returning veterans.

An academic high point for Scarborough was the dedication of the Carnegie Library in 1909. He himself had assembled a large personal library, which he called in ancient Greek his "hospital of the soul." Here he worked on the many essays he published in newspapers, magazines, and scholarly journals, as well as the speeches he was asked to present at college commencements, to literary societies, and at Republican Party events. In 1888 he was the only "man of color" at the first annual Lincoln Day banquet held by the Ohio Republican League in Columbus. He was seated between John Beaver (1837–1914), the governor of Pennsylvania, and John Sherman (1823–1900), with whom he had ridden to the State House. It was a remarkable day for Scarborough; he had heard the guns of William Sherman blasting through Georgia as a teenager, and two decades later, he was dining in public with the general's brother.

The high standards that Scarborough applied to himself, and to his career as a professional intellectual and educator, opened the doors for the next generation of African American students and academics. For over forty years, William Scarborough stood as an exemplary scholar to whites and blacks, both here and abroad.

Bibliography

Ronnick, Michele Valerie. *The First Three African American Members of the American Philological Association*. American Philological Association, 2001.

Weisenburger, Francis P. "Scarborough, William Sanders," in the *Dictionary of American Negro Biography*, Rayford W. Logan and Michael R. Winston, eds. W. W. Norton, 1982.

William S. Scarborough Collection, MIC 179. Ohio Historical Society. Columbus, Ohio.

Michele Valerie Ronnick

Schoelcher, Victor

1804–1893

French abolitionist who played a crucial role in the abolition of slavery in the French colonies in 1848 and who fought tirelessly for the rights of slaves and former slaves throughout his long public career.

Victor Schoelcher was born into a wealthy bourgeois Parisian family, allowing him to undertake the many voyages on which he observed firsthand the terrors of slavery and facilitating his decision to pursue political office.

Schoelcher affirmed his liberal political leanings in the period of the restoration of the French monarchy (1815–1830), and his ideological awakening occurred during a voyage he made in 1829 to MEXICO, the United States, and CUBA, when he was exposed to the harsh reality of slavery. He returned from this trip a fervent abolitionist and joined the Society for the Abolition of Slavery in Paris. In 1833 Schoelcher published his first important work: *De l'esclavage des noirs et de la legislation coloniale* (On the Enslavement of Blacks and Colonial Legislation).

Abolitionist activism in FRANCE increased markedly during the more liberal July Monarchy (1830–1848). The example of Britain, which outlawed slavery in 1834, strengthened the cause of French abolitionists. During this period Schoelcher traveled widely and published influential polemics calling for the immediate suppression of slavery, in opposition to more moderate reformers who argued for the institution's gradual disappearance in order to avoid upsetting colonialist economic productivity. In 1839 Schoelcher visited the French and Danish Antilles, including HAITI, GUADELOUPE, and MARTINIQUE, and after this he published what was perhaps his most influential work: *Des colonies francaises: abolition immediate de l'esclavage* (On the French Colonies: Immediate Abolition of Slavery; 1842). In 1845 Schoelcher traveled throughout the Middle East, observing slavery as it existed in the region. In 1847 he went to SENEGAL to witness the conditions of the capture of African slaves.

In 1848, as undersecretary for the Navy, Schoelcher prepared the decree that abolished slavery in France's colonies. That same year the French republican revolutionary government of February 1848 named Schoelcher undersecretary of state and president of the commission for the abolition of slavery. He remained highly active within the radical left until Napoleon III's coup d'état of December 2, 1851, after which Schoelcher was sent into exile along with other outspoken opponents of the Second Empire (1851–1870) such as Victor Hugo. From Belgium and later England, Schoelcher continued to attack Louis Napoleon's government. With the formation of the Third Republic in 1870 Schoelcher returned to France, where he was elected representative of Martinique and Guiana in the French National Assembly. In 1875 he was named senator for life. During this period Schoelcher fought for obligatory schooling and, as a publicly committed atheist, for the separation of church and state in France. In 1889 Schoelcher published *Vie de Toussaint-Louverture* (Life of TOUSSAINT LOUVERTURE), in which he argues for the contradictory status of Toussaint as both liberator and tyrant of the Haitian people.

From 1848 until well into the twentieth century Schoelcher remained the emblematic figure of liberal thought and practice in the French Antillean colonies. Only after World War II (1939–1945) did Antilleans search for defenders of Antillean autonomy from their own history, such as LOUIS DELGRÈS and JEAN IGNACE. In 1949 the French government placed Schoelcher's ashes in the Pantheon, recognizing and affirming his historical preeminence in the struggle to put into practice and generalize the revolutionary ideals of liberty, equality, and fraternity.

See also Transatlantic Slave Trade.

Nick Nesbitt

Schomburg, Arthur Alfonso

1874–1938

Bibliophile and librarian who collected literature and art of the African diaspora.

Born in San Juan, Puerto Rico, the son of a German father and a West Indian mother, Schomburg spent his childhood in PUERTO RICO. After briefly attending Saint Thomas College in the VIRGIN ISLANDS, he came to the United States in 1891 and began working in a NEW YORK City law office. In New York, Schomburg began to collect literary works and visual art by and about people of African descent. In 1906 Schomburg began working in the mailroom at Bankers Trust Company, where he remained until 1929. He became an active PRINCE HALL Mason, serving as grand secretary of the grand lodge from 1918 to 1926.

In 1911 Schomburg and African American journalist John E. Bruce founded the Negro Society for Historical Research as a base from which to publish articles on black history. In 1922 Schomburg was elected president of the AMERICAN NEGRO ACADEMY. Three years later, his important essay "The Negro Digs Up His Past" appeared in *The New Negro,* edited by African American intellectual ALAIN LOCKE. Schomburg and his collection of books, manuscripts, and artifacts were an invaluable resource and an inspiration to both historians and HARLEM RENAISSANCE artists.

Through his collection of literature and art by people of African descent, Schomburg sought to disprove the pseudoscientific racism of the day.

In 1926 the Carnegie Corporation purchased Schomburg's collection and donated it to the Negro Division of the New York Public Library, the 135th Street branch in HARLEM. Schomburg was hired as curator in 1932, holding the position until his death in 1938. Two years later the library was named the Schomburg Collection of Negro Literature and History, and it has since been renamed the Schomburg Center for Research in Black Culture. It is the largest, most important collection of African and African American cultural materials in the world.

Schomburg Center for Research in Black Culture

Largest collection in the world of materials by and about people of African descent.

In 1925 the New York Public Library opened a Negro Division at its 135th Street branch off Lenox Avenue in HARLEM. The following year, the Carnegie Corporation purchased ARTHUR SCHOMBURG's vast collection of African American books, manuscripts, and art, and donated it to the library. Schomburg, an American who was born in Puerto Rico of mixed-race parentage, had amassed these works in an effort to prove the depth and richness of black history and culture. He became the collection's curator in 1932, a post he held until his death in 1938. The collection has borne his name since 1940.

The collection grew rapidly, and today it houses more than five million items relating to the history and culture of the people of Africa and the African diaspora. In 1972 the New York Public Library transferred the collection from the neighborhood branch system to make it part of their research libraries. Now officially called the Schomburg Center for Research in Black Culture, the collection has five divisions. The art and artifacts division collects objects from the seventeenth century to the present, including masks, weapons, statues, and rare items from such places as the Gold Coast of Africa (present-day GHANA). The general research and reference division possesses flyers, newspapers, magazine clippings, pamphlets, and monographs in English, French, Spanish, Portuguese, German, Russian, and all African languages, as well as indigenous languages such as Creole. The manuscripts, archives, and rare books division houses materials relating to history, literature, politics, and culture. The moving image and recorded sound division features the center's oral history and video documentation programs. The photographs and prints division holds the works of many famous photographers including Gordon Parks, Sr., Coreen Simpson, Aaron Siskind, James VanDerZee, and Carl Van Vechten.

Schomburg Library

See Schomburg Center for Research in Black Culture.

School Desegregation in the United States

Policy of ending racially segregated education by reassigning students from segregated to interracial schools or by operating programs that produce interracial schools by giving students or parents a choice of which desegregated school the student should attend.

Desegregation refers only to the process of bringing students into interracial schools. *Integration*, by comparison, generally refers to the more extensive processes that make schools successfully and equitably interracial. It includes desegregation at the classroom level, fair treatment of students, improved human relations, and a curriculum that reflects and respects the cultures of the various groups of students.

Desegregation in the South

The 1954 decision of the Supreme Court of the United States in Brown v. Board of Education, outlawing legally imposed, or de jure, segregation in Southern schools, set in motion several decades of intense legal and political struggle over the subject of school desegregation. The desegregation struggles eventually spread across the country and came to include Latinos and other groups as well as black students. The contentious process eventually eliminated most aspects of a system that had prohibited blacks from attending white public schools in the South, the part of the country where most blacks lived. The legal principles that came out of this struggle transformed many other aspects of American life and helped trigger the Civil Rights Movement of the 1950s and 1960s.

The Supreme Court's decision in *Brown* found the system of "separate but equal" schools, which operated in seventeen states and the District of Columbia and which had been sanctioned by the Court's earlier decision in Plessy v. Ferguson (1896), to be "inherently unequal." The stage had been set for *Brown* by the decisions in Sweatt v. Painter and *McLaurin v. Oklahoma State Regents* (both 1950), which struck down segregated graduate school arrangements. The Court's unanimous decision in *Brown* solidified this position by holding that the system of racially separated schools for blacks caused profound harm to the excluded, and therefore stigmatized, students.

In a follow-up decree to *Brown* in 1955, the Supreme Court called for the enforcement of desegregation "with all deliberate speed" and relied on the judgment of local federal judges to implement their order. These judges, however, often deferred to local school authorities who refused to comply without a specific court order for their community, so the judicial desegregation effort required hundreds of lawsuits to achieve very modest change. A decade after the Supreme Court's decision, 98 percent of Southern black students were still in completely segregated schools, virtually no whites attended previously black schools, and faculties remained segregated.

School desegregation accelerated only after pressure from the Civil Rights Movement led to the 1964 Civil Rights Act and after the administration of President Lyndon Johnson began to use that law to force very rapid change in schools and other institutions. The law empowered the Justice Department to sue school districts and required the cutoff of federal aid to systems that resisted desegregation.

There was very intense opposition to all desegregation efforts in the South in the decade after *Brown*, but public opinion among both races became much more positive after desegregation was imposed in the late 1960s. After the implementation of the *Brown* decision, survey research showed a dramatic increase in white acceptance of integrated education, while black support for the policy stood at over 90 percent. Acceptance and support for desegregation as a goal for education has remained very high since. Although the South has by far the largest proportion of black students, it had the most desegregated public schools in the United States by 1970 and retained this leadership into the late 1990s.

Busing and Desegregation in the North

In 1971 the Supreme Court expanded on *Brown* when it decided in *Swann v. Board of Education* to require school desegregation in communities such as Charlotte, North Carolina, where residential segregation made it impossible to desegregate using only neighborhood schools. Noting that bus transportation was already an accepted part of the educational system, the Court supported a plan that required the transportation of students of both races to schools in other neighborhoods, a plan that became known as busing. The policy of busing met with overwhelming white opposition (around three-fourths opposed busing in the beginning) and a serious division within the black community. Some critics of busing were opposed to integrated schools in general, while others protested the loss of neighborhood schools. The national administration was hostile as well, as President Richard Nixon directed his officials to stir up white fears about busing for political gains. Nonetheless, busing was rapidly implemented in the South in the early 1970s, and most of the plans lasted into the 1990s, when the Court began reversing its earlier decisions.

In spite of hundreds of demonstrations demanding integrated schools in the North as well as the South, the school desegregation struggle had little impact outside the South for two decades. Northern officials defined their segregation as de facto (occurring even though no law required it) in distinction to the Southern system of de jure segregation. The Supreme Court, however, found evidence of Northern governmental policies of segregation in *Keyes v. Denver School District* (1973), which upheld the right of blacks and Latinos to desegregation in cities outside the South as well. Trials were held in many cities in the North and West. In every major case, plaintiffs succeeded in proving that the segregation was not de facto but was substantially caused by discrimination by educational and housing authorities in locating schools, setting boundaries, assigning teachers, providing courses, and in many other policies. Busing was often a significant element of the plans chosen by the courts to remedy this segregation.

In its 5-4 decision in *Milliken v. Bradley* (1974), however, the Court greatly limited the reach of the *Swann* decision by making it extremely difficult to desegregate across boundary lines separating cities from suburbs; the Court cited the importance of preserving suburban autonomy. Since many Northern cities already had predominantly nonwhite school districts surrounded by predominantly white suburbs, this decision limited the value and durability of desegregation. In his dissent to *Milliken,* Justice THURGOOD MARSHALL held that limiting desegregation in this way would produce unstable and futile desegregation efforts in many big cities with few whites. Experience proved that Marshall was correct. Metropolitan DETROIT, MICHIGAN ended up as the most segregated metropolitan region in the United States, and the major industrial states of the Midwest and the Northeast remained the centers of segregation in the following decades. Meanwhile, the Southern counties where city and suburbs shared a single school district achieved the most extensive and stable desegregation.

Effects of Desegregation

There have been hundreds of studies of the effect of school desegregation. Most show academic achievement gains for black students, probably resulting in large part from the move from the more concentrated poverty of most all-black schools to less impoverished integrated schools. Segregated black and Latino schools are more than fourteen times as likely as segregated white schools to have concentrated poverty among their population. During the desegregation era black high school graduation rates tripled and college enrollment soared. There was also a substantial lowering of the national gaps on standardized tests and college entrance exams, although these gaps began to widen again in the 1990s. While the causes of these changes are complex, the claims made by some critics that the education of blacks was harmed during this period are incorrect.

Desegregation appears to have larger effects on some other aspects of education. Schools not only teach subjects, but they also socialize children, connect them with peer groups and networks, and give them experience in competition and cooperation with other groups. Students from desegregated high schools are more likely to go to college and more likely, once they get to college, to major in scientific and technical subjects and to graduate. These differences persist even among students who have similar test scores, perhaps because the experience of integrated schools prepares nonwhite students for the large white majorities they encounter at most colleges.

School desegregation was put forward by the NATIONAL ASSOCIATION FOR THE ADVANCEMENT OF COLORED PEOPLE (NAACP) and other civil rights organizations as one part of a much larger program of racial change in the United States. From an early period, supporters of school desegregation realized that getting the children into the front doors of interracial schools was only the first step in attaining full access and equal treatment within those schools. Congress recognized this need when it enacted the Emergency School Aid Act, which allocated funds for the particular needs of minority students, at the height of the busing controversy in the South in 1972. That program was repealed, however, in 1981, the first year of the administration of President Ronald Reagan, in spite of studies showing substantial benefits to academics and race relations.

School desegregation was pursued vigorously by Congress and the president for only four years in the mid-1960s. The Supreme Court continued to press the issue only until 1974. The policy proved durable, however, and desegregation actually increased for black students through the 1980s. The reversal of the policy came primarily from an effort by conservative presidents to change the federal courts, which succeeded by the 1990s when the Supreme Court handed down three decisions drastically limiting desegregation.

Segregation, as measured by the percentage of students attending schools in which their own race overwhelmingly predominates, began to increase steadily for black students in the late 1980s, although they remained far less segregated than before the *Brown* decision. By 1996 segregation for blacks had returned to the level of the early 1970s. Many of the largest school districts were ending their desegregation plans. Latinos never experienced significant desegregation, except in parts of Colorado and Texas, and they became increasingly more segregated beginning in the 1960s. By the 1990s, even though they had become the largest minority group of school-age children, they were more segregated than African Americans. Studies of school districts that have returned to segregated neighborhood schools have shown dramatic patterns of inequality among the schools, strongly related to the concentration of poor children only in black and Latino schools under the neighborhood system.

It appears that the early twenty-first century, like the early twentieth century, will be a period in which the United States attempts to achieve "separate but equal" schools. There is no citywide model of success for this effort, however, either in the sixty years between *Plessy* and *Brown* or in recent years, so the issues caused by the segregation of the past are likely to recur.

See also Desegregation in the United States; Integration: An Interpretation; Segregation in the United States; Suburbanization and African Americans.

Bibliography

Dimond, Paul R. *Beyond Busing: Inside the Challenge to Urban Segregation.* University of Michigan Press, l985.

Douglas, Davison M. *Reading, Writing and Race: The Desegregation of the Charlotte Schools.* University of North Carolina Press, 1995.

Greenberg, Jack. *Crusaders in the Courts: How a Dedicated Band of Lawyers Fought for the Civil Rights Revolution.* Basic Books, 1994.

Hawley, Willis D., and others. *Strategies for Effective Desegregation.* Lexington Books, 1983.

Kluger, Richard. *Simple Justice: The History of Brown v. Board of Education and Black America's Struggle for Equality.* Vintage, 1977.

Meier, Kenneth J., Joseph Stewart, Jr., and Robert E. England. *Race, Class and Education: The Politics of Second Generation Discrimination.* University of Wisconsin Press, 1989.

Orfield, Gary, and Susan Eaton. *Dismantling Desegregation: The Quiet Reversal of Brown v. Board of Education.* New Press, 1996.

Gary Orfield

Schreiner, Olive

1855–1920

South African novelist, political activist, and pioneer in her treatment of women in her fiction; well known for her observations on the political future of South Africa, particularly the situation of blacks under apartheid.

Born Olive Emilie Albertina Schreiner in Wittebergen, SOUTH AFRICA (then Cape Colony), she had no formal education but was taught at home by her mother. She began writing two of her novels while supporting herself as a governess from 1874 to 1881, after which she went to England, hoping to study. While in England, Schreiner published *The Story of an African Farm* under the pseudonym Ralph Iron. The story of a young girl growing up on a farm in the grasslands of southern Africa, trying to attain her independence in the face of a rigid, repressive society, the book met with immediate success. In England Schreiner was accepted by literary and political circles and became a supporter of women's rights. She was a friend of Cecil Rhodes, a British statesman and major proponent for British rule in southern Africa, but parted company with him for political reasons. Schreiner caused controversy in relation to Rhodes's activities with her book *Trooper Halkett of Mashonaland* (1897), which criticized the way Rhodesia (which became ZIMBABWE in 1980) was colonized. She returned to South Africa in 1899 and worked on behalf of the Boers, a local, white AFRIKANER group that refused to live under British rule during the Boer War (1899–1902). Schreiner also met and married politician Samuel Cronwright—he changed his name to Cronwright-Schreiner—and they both worked for a variety of political causes. In 1911 she wrote *Women and Labour,* a feminist novel criticizing the relations between men and women. Schreiner spent her last years in England, separated from her husband, but returned to South Africa in 1920, shortly before she died. Her other novels, both with feminist themes, are *From Man to Man* (1927) and *Undine* (1929). They were published posthumously.

Schuyler, George S.

1895–1977

Journalist and novelist known for his conservative political views and the first African American to be recognized primarily as a satirist.

Born in Providence, Rhode Island, Schuyler was raised in Syracuse, New York. He had what he considered an ideal childhood, in which he grew up believing that the United States, even with its considerable racial problems, was the best place for African Americans to live. He dropped out of high school to enlist in the United States Army and spent seven years in the service. During World War I (1914–1918) he served in FRANCE and attained the rank of first lieutenant.

Upon returning to the United States after the war, Schuyler worked in menial jobs and lived with hobos in New York's Bowery before becoming a staff writer in 1923 for the MESSENGER, cofounded and edited by A. PHILIP RANDOLPH. Soon after joining the paper, Schuyler had his own column, "Shafts and Darts: A Page of Calumny and Satire." Later he became the paper's managing editor. Under Schuyler, the publication was considered so inflammatory that Southern members of the United States House of Representatives investigated it.

Schuyler's satire focused on the obsession in the United States with race, a subject he addressed in *Black No More* (1931). In this novel, African Americans are enabled to become white by a surgical process. After their treatment, they disappear from HARLEM and appear as whites in other places. Americans initially believe the race problem is solved. However, the blacks who have received the treatment are discovered to be three shades lighter than the original whites, who then begin adding pigmentation to their skin to differentiate themselves from the new whites, and the race problem begins anew.

Initially *Black No More* was well received. However, critics soon began to pay more attention to African American protest novels, and *Black No More* was eventually forgotten. Adding to this problem was Schuyler's conservatism, which often put him in opposition to his more liberal colleagues and left him alienated from the mainstream African American intelligentsia.

Schuyler continued to publish columns and fiction. In addition to *Black No More,* he wrote *Slaves Today: A Story of Liberia* (1931), which exposed the slave like conditions many laborers experienced in LIBERIA. A third novel, *Black Empire,* which Schuyler wrote under the pen name Samuel I. Brooks, was published posthumously in 1991 and is a compilation of a serial that was published in the PITTSBURGH COURIER from 1936 to 1937.

Schuyler's journalistic contributions were considerable. From 1927 to 1931 Schuyler contributed nine essays to American journalist and essayist H. L. Mencken's *American Mercury.* In addition to his forty-year association with the *Courier,* where he was a columnist and a special correspondent in LATIN AMERICA, the WEST INDIES, and West Africa, he contributed to several white-owned journals, *The Nation, Plain Talk,* and *Common Ground* among them.

Schuyler also published nonfiction, including *Racial Intermarriage in the United States* (1929) and his autobiography *Black and Conservative: The Autobiography of George S. Schuyler,* which was published in 1966.

Schuyler was married to Josephine Cogdell, a white artist who, like her husband, believed that the children of interracial marriages would be genetically superior by virtue of "hybrid vigor" and would thus end racial problems in the United States. They had one daughter, PHILLIPA DUKE SCHUYLER, who became a concert pianist.

Robert Fay

Schuyler, Phillipa Duke

1931–1967

American concert pianist and writer.

Born in New York City, Philippa Schuyler was the only child of the most celebrated interracial marriage of the HARLEM RENAISSANCE—between African American author and journalist GEORGE SCHUYLER and white artist and journalist Josephine Cogdell, from Texas. As a consequence of Cogdell's family farming background, she and Schuyler applied to their daughter the agricultural theory that crossing different genetic strains produced superior offspring possessing "hybrid vigor." The Schuylers were firmly convinced that racial disharmony in the United States could be rectified through creating interracial children, investing all of their hopes for this in their daughter.

As if to materialize her parents' unusual expectations, Philippa Schuyler was in fact a child prodigy whose extraordinary talents were developed by tutors in isolation from her peers. With an IQ of 185, she could read and write at the age of two and a half, and began playing the piano at the age of three. At four, Schuyler was composing, and she performed at the age of five on the radio. By eleven she was touring, and she had over one hundred piano compositions to her credit by the age of thirteen. She scored "Manhattan Nocturne" for one hundred instruments and performed it with the New York Philharmonic in 1944. At the New York World's Fair, New York Mayor Fiorello LaGuardia declared June 19, 1940 "Philippa Duke Schuyler Day."

Despite her abilities, Schuyler's parents shunned the word *prodigy* and attributed her talent to "hybrid genetics, proper nutrition, and intensive education." Her diet consisted exclusively of raw foods as a result of her mother's steadfast belief that cooking destroyed vitamin content. Raised on wheat germ, unpasteurized milk, cod liver oil, mother's milk, fruit, and daily doses of vitamin C, Schuyler also avoided alcohol, tobacco, and sugar—all forbidden in the Schuyler home—for her entire life.

While the country was awed by her genius, Philippa Schuyler's visibility and fame were significantly heightened by her father's media connections as well as his own regular coverage of her exemplary progress in the *PITTSBURGH COURIER*. Moreover, her mother's multiple roles as impresario, relentless business manager, confidante, and best friend guided Schuyler well into adulthood.

For the better part of Schuyler's youth, George Schuyler was away on national and international assignments. A great admirer of her father, she inherited his conservative beliefs in educational advancement, self-help, and introspection. But, despite her proximity to the black intelligentsia, "her precocity was fed on notions and conceits of the white milieu; and her passion for classical music would essentially reflect the same bias."

As a young adult, when white America lost interest in her, Schuyler encountered the race prejudice from which she had previously been shielded as a child curiosity and the daughter of well-to-do parents. Forced to play piano concerts overseas, she traveled to more than eighty countries, giving command performances for ETHIOPIA's Emperor HAILE SELASSIE, Queen Elizabeth of Belgium, and many other international leaders. In spite of her worldwide fame, she was never invited to perform in the United States for comparable leaders.

Spending more than half of the last ten years of her life abroad, Schuyler sought an alternative home where she could find comfort and acceptance: "I had thirty miserable years in the U.S.A. because of having the taint of being a 'strange curiosity' applied to me."

In the late 1950s, Schuyler traveled with a visa from Rome and performed to white audiences in APARTHEID-era SOUTH AFRICA. Shortly after, she briefly toured in Europe as Felipa Monterro, a gifted musician and writer who was no longer identifiable as the daughter of a black journalist. Between 1960 and 1969, she published five books about her life and travels, including one in collaboration with her mother.

In 1963, along with LEONTYNE PRICE and LENA HORNE, Schuyler was honored at the Delta Sigma Theta "We Salute Women of Achievement" awards.

Just before her death, Schuyler had begun a career as a news correspondent, publishing articles in several languages, including French and German. She died at the age of thirty-five in a helicopter crash during the VIETNAM WAR while attempting to rescue Catholic schoolchildren from a war zone in Hue and take them to the shelter of a school in Da Nang.

Schwarz-Bart, Simone

1938–

Afro-Guadeloupean feminist writer, best known for her characterization of strong Caribbean women.

Born in Charente-Maritime, France, Schwarz-Bart returned with her family to GUADELOUPE when she was three years old. She spent her childhood on the island and then left to study in FRANCE, where she met and married novelist André Schwarz-Bart. After traveling widely, the couple settled in GUADELOUPE.

Schwarz-Bart cowrote her first novel, *Un plat de porc aux bananes verts* (1967), with her husband. It tells the story of an old Martinican woman who is spending her last days in an institution for the aged in Paris.

In 1972 she published *Pluie et vent sur Télumée Miracle* (translated as *The Bridge of Beyond*, 1975), a fictional narrative of an old woman recounting the events of her life in a remote, rural region of Guadeloupe. This novel, praised for its portrayal of the black Caribbean experience from a feminine perspective (it engages several generations of women in the narrator's family) and for its masterly use of language, incorporates the rhythms and inflections of the CREOLE language into French.

Schwarz-Bart's third book, *Ti-Jean L'horizon* (1979; translated as *Between Two Worlds: A Novel*, 1981) follows young Ti-Jean, a popular hero of Creole folktales, in a mythical trip from the Caribbean to Africa and back, and tries to capture the different elements that have contributed to the formation of an Afro-Caribbean identity. The author's skillful narration and adept use of language brought her literary recognition and a prize from the French magazine *Elle*. In addition to her novels, Schwarz-Bart also published a play, *Ton Beau Capitaine*, in 1987.

Despite wide praise for her lyrical use of Creole and for her portrayal of Afro-Caribbean identity, some critics have attacked Schwarz-Bart for an excessive use of exoticism. Her work weaves together the real and the magical, along with the Guadaloupean folklore. She is a supporter of NÉGRITUDE, a concept and movement founded by the late Léopold Sédar Senghor, former president of SENEGAL, which seeks to define the collective experience of black people. Most recently, she wrote another book with her husband, *Hommage à la femme noire* (translated as *In Praise of Black Women*, 2001).

See also Creoleness; Francophone Writing; Women Writers of the Caribbean.

Victor Figueroa

Science, Chico

1967–1997

Brazilian bandleader, vocalist, and composer who founded the mangue beat movement.

Chico Science, born Francisco de Assis França, founded the group Chico Science e Nação Zumbi, an innovative multiracial band from Recife that mixes funky bass lines, heavy-metal guitars, and acid jazz ambience with northeast Brazilian rhythms such as the maracatú and the embolada. The group's name, Zumbi Nation, refers to the leader of a seventeenth-century settlement called PALMARES, the largest and longest-lasting community of fugitive slaves in Brazilian history.

The group's 1994 debut, *Da lama ao caos* (From Mud to Chaos), launched mangue beat, a musical movement that includes other bands from Recife such as Mundo Livre S/A and Mestre Ambrósio. The debut album included a manifesto that explains that the *mangue* (the muddy mangrove swamplands that form where rivers meet the ocean) is an ecosystem of enormous fertility and variety that has deteriorated into a site of abject poverty and misery in metropolitan Recife. According to the manifesto, it was necessary to "inject a little energy into the mud and stimulate the fertile potential of the veins of Recife." The symbol of the mangue beat movement was a parabolic antenna stuck in the mud—an image combining a local perspective of urban underdevelopment with global postmodern sensibilities. Chico Science's lyrics mix the poetics of traditional *cordel* literature of the Brazilian northeast with images of urban-industrial society. The group's second album, *Afrociberdélia*, further develops this musical and poetic strategy with more sophisticated production values and extensive sampling of other Brazilian artists. The band has continued to perform despite Chico Science's untimely death in a car accident.

See also Literature, Black, in Brazil.

Christopher Dunn

Scientists and Engineers, African American

African Americans whose careers focused on science and technology—some made contributions to modern life that are used every day; others used their scientific careers as a starting point for careers in other fields. Many overcame tremendous barriers to learning, and some were never fully recognized for their accomplishments.

For information on
Fields in science and technology: *See* Chemistry; Development of Technology, African Americans and the; Inventors, African American.
Physicists: *See* Bouchet, Edward Alexander; Jackson, Shirley Ann; McNair, Ronald.
Chemists: *See* Calloway, Nathaniel Oglesby; Carver, George Washington; Hill, Henry Aaron; Julian, Percy Lavon.
Engineers: *See* Jones, Frederick McKinley; Latimer, Lewis Howard; McCoy, Elijah J.; Rillieux, Norbert; Woods, Granville T.
Biologists: *See* Cobb, Jewel Plummer; Drew, Charles Richard; Just, Ernest Everett; Turner, Charles H.

Scott, Emmett J.

1873–1957

African American secretary of Tuskegee Institute, administrator of the National Negro Business League, and the right-hand man of educator Booker T. Washington.

Emmett Scott was born in Houston, Texas, and worked first as a journalist with the *Houston Post*. In 1894 he founded and edited the weekly *Houston Freeman*. The views therein largely agreed with those of BOOKER T. WASHINGTON, who hired Scott as his personal secretary at the Tuskegee Institute (now TUSKEGEE UNIVERSITY) in 1897. In 1912 he became Tuskegee's secretary, where, as part of the "Tuskegee Machine," he spread Washington's self-help and accommodationist political and social message, which he expounded on in *Tuskegee and Its People* (1910) and *Builder of a Civilization* (1916), a biography of Washington. From 1900 to 1922, Scott served as the chief administrator of Washington's economic self-help organization, the National Negro Business League. Scott left Tuskegee after Washington's death in 1915 and was special assistant to the U.S. secretary of war during WORLD WAR I (1914–1918). From 1919 to 1939, Scott held various positions at HOWARD UNIVERSITY.

Robert Fay

Scott, Hazel

1920–1981

Caribbean American jazz musician and political activist; the first black woman to host her own television show.

Hazel Scott made her debut as a pianist in TRINIDAD at age three. By her eighth birthday, she had performed in NEW YORK City and won a scholarship to the Juilliard School of Music. Scott became a star of radio and Broadway in the 1930s and appeared in several movies in the 1940s. Her marriage in 1945 to HARLEM minister and Congressman ADAM CLAYTON POWELL JR. was one of the year's major social events; they divorced in 1956.

In the late 1940s, Scott became the first black woman to host her own television show, a position which she lost in 1950 when she was accused of being a Communist sympathizer. She refused to perform in segregated theaters and became an outspoken critic of both McCarthyism and racial injustice. After living abroad for five years in the 1960s, she returned to the U.S. and to her television and nightclub career. Called a "musical chameleon" for her ability to shift from JAZZ to CLASSICAL to BLUES, Scott continued to perform until her death.

See also Television and African Americans.

Bibliography

Placksin, Sally. *American Women in Jazz: 1900 to the Present.* Wideview Books, 1982.

Lawrie Balfour

Scott, Robert

1947–

Democratic member of the United States House of Representatives from Virginia

Robert Scott was born in WASHINGTON, D.C., and received a bachelor's degree from Harvard University in 1969. He served in the United States Army Reserves from 1970 to 1974 and in the National Guard from 1974 to 1976. After receiving a law degree from Boston College in 1973, he practiced law until 1991. In 1977 Scott was elected to the Virginia House of Delegates, where he served until 1983. He held a seat in the state senate for the next nine years. In 1992 he was elected as a Democrat to the U.S. House of Representatives from Virginia's Third Congressional District, and was subsequently reelected. He is a member of the CONGRESSIONAL BLACK CAUCUS.

In 2003, Scott urged support for the House Democratic Stimulus Plan, which contained provisions for stimulating the economy and improving jobs. He also proposed the so-called "Scott Amendment," which called for an increase in deployment pay for members of the armed forces while they are not on active duty. The proposal was rejected.

See also Congress, African Americans in.

Scottsboro Case

International cause célèbre during the 1930s, in which nine young black men were accused of raping two white women in Alabama.

The Scottsboro case began in 1931 when two white women, Victoria Bates and Ruby Price, falsely accused nine young African Americans of rape. Throughout the world in the 1930s, the Scottsboro defendants came to symbolize the racism and injustice of the American South. In their initial trials the defendants received what critics described as a "legal lynching." But the assistance of the COMMUNIST PARTY of the United States of America (CPUSA) gave the young men a second chance, and the ensuing struggle became one of the great civil rights cases of the twentieth century.

After several retrials, worldwide protests, massive publicity, and two landmark rulings by the Supreme Court of the United States, only four of the men gained their freedom after spending six years in jail. Full vindication did not come until 1976, when Alabama governor George Wallace pardoned all nine "Scottsboro boys." At that time only one of the defendants, Clarence Norris, was still alive to hear the news.

The incident occurred on March 25, 1931, when several young white men complained that a "bunch of Negroes" had thrown them off a freight train, and a posse in Paint Rock, Alabama searched the train and arrested nine young black men. The posse also discovered two white women wearing men's caps and overalls. Within an hour, the black men and both women were taken to Scottsboro, the seat of Jackson County. The women were examined by two physicians, who found evidence of sexual activity, although probably not within the previous twelve hours, and no signs of rape. The young men—Norris, Olen Montgomery, Haywood Patterson, Ozie Powell, Willie Roberson, Charlie Weems, Eugene Williams, and Andrew and Leroy Wright—were arrested. At twenty years of age, Weems was the oldest; the youngest, Leroy Wright, was thirteen.

Although the women initially denied that any assault had taken place, under the pressure of a lynch mob that filled the

Fearing a mob lynching, Alabama Governor B. M. Miller called the National Guard to the Scottsboro jail to protect the young black men who were accused of raping two white women. From left to right, the accused are: Clarence Norris, Olen Montgomery, Andy Wright, Willie Roberson, Ozie Powell, Eugene Williams, Charlie Weems, Leroy Wright, and Haywood Patterson. *Bettmann/CORBIS*

streets that evening and after repeated goading by a local prosecutor, they conceded that they had been raped by the black youths. Although later investigation revealed that the women were "notorious prostitutes" with prior arrest records on a variety of charges, nothing could shake the Southern ethos that made them symbols of endangered "white Southern womanhood."

During their trials, the nine men received inadequate legal counsel. They were given no witness preparation before entering the courtroom, and in none of the cases did their court-appointed attorneys make closing arguments to the jury. As was customary, each jury was composed of only white men. The trials were concluded in four days with eight guilty verdicts and eight sentences of death. In the case of Leroy Wright, the youngest defendant, the jury could not reach agreement. Jurors had no doubt as to his guilt, but eleven insisted on no penalty less than death, although the state had asked only for life imprisonment. The judge reluctantly declared a mistrial.

Sentencing eight men to death on a single day for the same crime was "without parallel in the history of the nation," the Birmingham *Age-Herald* observed in concluding its trial coverage. But the Scottsboro case was far from over. Even as the trials were under way, the judge received a telegram from the International Labor Defense (ILD), a Communist-front legal organization, demanding a change of venue. The Communist Party decided to take up the young men's defense on the basis of reports from two party representatives, one black and one white, who had been sent to observe the trials. The party's enthusiastic involvement transformed what had essentially been a local matter into a cause of national importance.

In contrast, the NATIONAL ASSOCIATION FOR THE ADVANCEMENT OF COLORED PEOPLE (NAACP) remained aloof. Protective of its reputation, the NAACP was unwilling to aid a group of poor black hoboes unless it was certain of their innocence. Only after the case reached international proportions did the organization offer financial assistance to the ILD. Initially, NAACP representatives had warned the defendants that the Communists were only interested in them for propaganda purposes.

Communist organizing efforts made the Scottsboro case an international cause célèbre, as well as one of the decade's top news stories. The effectiveness of the party's response significantly increased its stature among Depression-era African Americans. Communist-sponsored protests took place in many Northern cities as well as in London, Moscow, and elsewhere around the world. In the process, the CPUSA garnered invaluable publicity for itself, but in the main its efforts drew attention to the plight of the defendants. In so doing, the party challenged the deeper symbolism of the Scottsboro case, in particular, by confronting the virtual equation of "black man" and "rapist."

At the outset, public understanding of the case had been tainted by white visions of black sexual depravity and by a presumption of the defendants' guilt. The party worked to humanize the image of the nine men, especially through rallies and marches that featured their mothers. It inspired sympathetic news stories about the defendants during their lengthy incarceration. As a result of this dogged publicity work, the Scottsboro case came to be seen as a great miscarriage of justice, and its defendants were increasingly regarded as innocent victims of Southern racism. At the same time, the party refused to limit itself to symbolic action; it also mounted an aggressive legal defense.

The ILD provided experienced attorneys to aid in the young men's defense, the most important of whom was distinguished lawyer Samuel Leibowitz. Over the next five years, Leibowitz defended the nine Scottsboro defendants a total of five times. The ILD won the defendants retrials as a result of its successful appeal to the U.S. Supreme Court. The Court ruled in *Powell v. Alabama* (1932) that defendants being tried for capital crimes must receive more than a perfunctory or pro forma defense. Following a change of venue, the trials opened in Decatur, Alabama, before Judge James E. Horton.

In Decatur, Ruby Bates renounced her previous testimony against the nine defendants. Indeed, during 1933 and 1934 she appeared at Communist-organized Scottsboro rallies, posed in photographs with the Scottsboro mothers, and joined 3,000 protesters in a march to the White House seeking the defendants' release from prison. Nonetheless, the first jury, in the trial of Haywood Patterson, again returned a guilty verdict. Personally convinced that Patterson and the other defendants were innocent, Judge Horton set the verdict aside and ordered new trials. As a result, however, Horton was defeated in the May 1934 primary election and replaced by a man far more friendly to the prosecution.

The ILD once more made a successful appeal to the Supreme Court, this time challenging the systematic exclusion of blacks from Alabama jury rolls. In *Norris v. Alabama* (1935), Chief Justice Charles Evans Hughes ruled that the exclusion of African Americans from jury service did in fact deprive black defendants of equal protection under the law, as guaranteed by the FOURTEENTH AMENDMENT. In essence, the Court remanded the case back to the state for retrial. Thus the Scottsboro Nine returned to the courtroom yet again. By this point, a vast amount of testimony had revealed much more than a reasonable doubt as to the young men's guilt.

In 1936, as part of the CPUSA's coalition-oriented Popular Front strategy, the ILD relinquished its primary role in the case in favor of a broader group that included the NAACP, the Socialist Party's League for Industrial Democracy, the American Civil Liberties Union, and the Methodist Federation for Social Service. Although Leibowitz continued as the defendants' counsel, the state of Alabama used the seeming displacement of the Communists as a pretext for seeking a legal compromise.

In the final set of trials that began in 1937, the state dropped all charges against the four youngest defendants—Leroy Wright, Montgomery, Roberson, and Williams. The others were duly convicted, but rather than the death penalty, they received sentences ranging from twenty years to life. Norris, Patterson, Powell, Weems, and Andrew Wright gained their freedom piecemeal between 1943 and 1950. All told, the nine men spent more than one hundred years in the jails and penitentiaries of Alabama.

Bibliography

Carter, Dan T. *Scottsboro: A Tragedy of the American South.* Louisiana State University Press, 1979.

Goodman, James. *Stories of Scottsboro.* Vintage Books, 1994.

James Sellman

Scramble for Africa

Phrase often used to describe the European partition and conquest of Africa in the late nineteenth century.

The *scramble for Africa,* a British term coined in 1884, describes the more than twenty-year period when European powers explored, partitioned, and conquered nearly 90 percent of the African continent. An observer at the time described it as "one of the most remarkable episodes in the history of the world."

Scholars disagree on the exact origins of the scramble. Most date its beginning to the 1870s and its conclusion to 1902, with the British defeat of the Boers (now AFRIKANERS) in SOUTH AFRICA. Explanations for what provoked such rapid conquest fall into two broad categories. The "Eurocentric" explanation contends that European competition for new markets and investments drove imperialist expansion, while the "Afrocentric theory" focuses on the conflicts between African states and peoples. Others contend that it was a combination of the two.

The historical progression of the scramble is clearer. In the mid-1800s European presence on the continent was limited to coastal regions and a few interior areas in the south and east. In 1876, however, Belgium's King LEOPOLD II announced his intent to explore the CONGO region, and in 1879 Leopold sent Sir HENRY MORTON STANLEY to the area. In the same year, the French began building a railway east from DAKAR, hoping to tap potentially huge Sahelian markets. That year FRANCE also joined GREAT BRITAIN in taking financial control of EGYPT.

Tensions between the European powers seeking African spheres of influence increased. In response, Chancellor Otto von Bismarck of Germany convened the BERLIN CONFERENCE OF 1884–1885. The European participants at the conference recognized King Leopold as the legitimate authority in the Congo basin, but, more importantly, it was decided that a European power could only claim an area of Africa that it "effectively occupied." The first phase of the scramble was largely a paper conquest, conducted in the drawing rooms of European capitals. On the continent, explorers and soldiers such as Stanley, PIERRE DE BRAZZA, FREDERICK LUGARD, and CECIL RHODES acted as the agents of European power, conquering weak African chiefs and signing treaties with the powerful ones.

In the early 1890s, treaty making gave way to conquest. Advances in military technology and medicine (especially the discovery of the antimalarial agent quinine) enabled Europeans to send troops into the heart of the continent, where the persistence of inter-African wars facilitated European conquest. Although European firepower crushed most African resistance movements, others, such as those waged by the Boers, NDEBELE, and ZULU in southern Africa, the BAULE in CÔTE D'IVOIRE, and the Mahdi in SUDAN, fought off colonial armies for several years. In ETHIOPIA the Emperor MENELIK II defeated Italian colonization efforts altogether.

In half a generation France, GERMANY, Great Britain, ITALY, PORTUGAL, SPAIN, and King Leopold II of Belgium had acquired thirty new African colonies or protectorates, covering 16 million sq km (6 million sq mi). They had divided a population

of approximately 110 million Africans into forty new political units, with some 30 percent of the borders drawn as straight lines, cutting through villages, ethnic groups, and African kingdoms.

Bibliography

Keltie, Sir Scott. *The Partition of Africa.* Stanford, 1893.
Pakenham, Thomas. *The Scramble for Africa: 1876–1912.* Weidenfeld and Nicolson, 1991.
Robinson, Ronald, and John Gallagher. *Africa and the Victorians: The Official Mind of Imperialism.* Macmillan, 1981.

Eric Young

Sculpture, African American

Three-dimensional artwork in stone, clay, metal, or other durable materials, and the African American artists producing these works.

For information on
Art movements and collections: *See* Art, African American; Harlem Renaissance: The Vogue of the New Negro; Art Collections in the United States.
Sculptors working before 1960: *See* Artis, William Ellisworth; Barthé, Richmond; Catlett, Elizabeth; Fuller, Meta Vaux Warrick; Johnson, Sargent; Lewis, Edmonia; Prophet, Nancy Elizabeth; Savage, Augusta Christine Fells.
Sculptors working since 1960: *See* Chase-Riboud, Barbara Dewayne; Edwards, Melvin; Hammons, David; Mendieta, Ana; Puryear, Martin; Saar, Betye Irene; Wilson, Fred.

Scurlock, Addison

1883–1964

American photographer known for his portraits of African American leaders and of Washington, D.C. luminaries.

The son of George Clay Scurlock, a Washington, D.C. lawyer who had moved his family from Fayetteville, North Carolina, in 1900, Addison Scurlock began his career in photography as an assistant to Moses P. Rice that same year. After four years of apprenticeship, Scurlock started his first studio at home, and in 1911 he opened the Scurlock Studio.

While employed as the official photographer for HOWARD UNIVERSITY, Scurlock produced newsreels in Washington, in addition to a portrait series sponsored by CARTER G. WOODSON for United States schools. Scurlock died at the age of eighty-one, after passing the management of his business on to his son.

See also Photography, African American.

Seacole, Mary

1805–1881

Nurse famous for her courage and honor in serving the British army during the Crimean War (1853–1856).

Unlike her well-known contemporary, Florence Nightingale, Jamaican-born Mary Seacole has been all but forgotten. In 1857, however, one London *Times* reporter noted, "Few names were more familiar to the public during the late [Crimean] war than that of Mrs. Seacole."

The daughter of a Scottish army officer and free black woman in JAMAICA, Mary Seacole was celebrated in GREAT BRITAIN for her work as a nurse in the Crimean War, during which Great Britain and FRANCE aided the Ottoman Empire against Russia. Seacole, who learned FOLK MEDICINE from her mother and became skilled at treating tropical diseases in PANAMA, Jamaica, and COLOMBIA, moved to London in 1854 to enlist in the war effort. Because of racial discrimination, her attempts to join the British army were thwarted. Determined, she made her own way to the Crimea and ran an institution called the British Hotel, which served as a combination of store, dispensary, and hospital for British officers. She also volunteered her services to various military hospitals, and nursed the wounded and dying soldiers on the battlefield.

Seacole recounted her impressions of the war in her autobiography, *The Wonderful Adventures of Mary Seacole in Many Lands* (1857). Her descriptions of the soldiers' injuries and the war are criticized now for their flowery language and excessive sentimentality, but the book was popular at the time for its fervent expression of British patriotism and religiosity. Seacole was the second black woman to publish a book in Great Britain; MARY PRINCE had published her autobiography in 1831.

After the conclusion of the war, the British demonstrated their appreciation of Seacole's service with a four-day benefit festival in her honor at the Royal Surrey Gardens, which was attended by more than 40,000 supporters. She subsisted on the funds that were raised at this event until her death.

Leyla Keough

Seale, Bobby

1936–

Political and social activist in the 1960s, cofounder and chairman of the militant Black Panther Party.

Bobby Seale, the son of George and Thelma Seale, was born in Dallas, Texas and moved to California with his family when he was ten years old. He entered the U.S. Air Force at eighteen and served as an aircraft-sheet mechanic. Three years later, he was dishonorably discharged for insubordination and absence without leave. In 1961 he enrolled at Merritt College in Oakland, California.

While at Merritt, Seale became a member of the Afro-American Association. Through this militant organization, Seale met and befriended fellow student HUEY NEWTON. Together they formed the Soul Students Advisory Committee at the college. In 1966 the two created the BLACK PANTHER PARTY, whose political platform called for equality of opportunity for African Americans and an end to police brutality against black people.

Seale was arrested in 1968 as one of the "Chicago Eight" prosecuted for activities during their participation in demonstrations against the VIETNAM WAR at the Democratic National Convention in CHICAGO, ILLINOIS. He spent two years in jail, and was arrested a second time in 1972, for the murder of a suspected Panther informer, Alex Rackley, but the charges against him were dropped. In 1973 he made an unsuccessful bid for the office of mayor of Oakland, and in 1974 he resigned as chairman of the Black Panther Party. In the 1980s Seale became involved in an organization called Youth Employment Strategies. He published two autobiographies, *Seize the Time: The Story of the Black Panther Party and Huey P. Newton* (1970) and *A Lonely Rage* (1978), as well as *Barbeque'N with Bobby*, intended for sale as a fundraiser for social change.

Bobby Seale currently serves as community liaison with Temple University's Department of African American studies in PHILADELPHIA, PENNSYLVANIA and is the creator-director of R.E.A.C.H! Inc., an organization that promotes "cooperational humanism" throughout the world. He is often invited to speak at colleges and universities. "We must creatively fashion a people's new world order of decent human relationships amongst, between, and around all earth's peoples," he said in a 2001 address in Maryland.

Aaron Myers

Seattle, Washington

American city whose black population long endured mixed messages of racial tolerance in public and private life.

Very few blacks lived in Seattle during the city's first eighty years. African Americans did not arrive in Seattle until 1858, and in 1900, fewer than 400 African Americans lived there. Even by World War II, the black population remained below 4,000. As a result, Seattle whites often took unwarranted pride in their city's racial climate. In an era when other American cities faced massive immigration, racial tension, and ghettoization, Seattle seemed a stable and racially reconciled town.

Although African Americans in Seattle lived where they pleased, voted freely, and shared public transit with whites, they faced persistent economic discrimination. Employment opportunities were few, and whites often presumed that blacks accepted unskilled labor and domestic service jobs because of inbred servility. In truth, the small size of the black community left it powerless to voice dissent, a silence that perpetuated the oppressive stereotypes of white employers.

World War II transformed Seattle. In 1942, the War Manpower Commission and the Civil Service Commission began recruiting African Americans from across the nation to work in the industries of the coastal Northwest. During the war, the black population of Seattle grew from about 4,000 to 16,000. Seattle's shipyards, the Boeing Aircraft Company, and numerous nonmilitary government jobs readily employed newcomers.

Unlike companies that faltered after the wartime boom, Boeing's success continued throughout the century. While Boeing's demand for labor remained high, however, mass immigration exceeded the company's needs, causing poverty, overcrowding, and residential segregation. Seattle's predominantly black Central District grew, schools began to reflect the segregated composition of neighborhoods, and whites elbowed blacks out of white neighborhoods. As a result, African Americans embraced the CIVIL RIGHTS MOVEMENT in the 1960s. Although violent protests did not erupt in Seattle, as they did in other cities, minor skirmishes between activists and police disrupted many businesses in 1967 and 1968.

In the 1970s and 1980s, Seattle's growing financial services and budding computer industry joined Boeing as major employers of blacks. The prospering economy and growing African American population helped to support black politicians, who began to fill public offices. In 1989, Norman Rice was elected the city's first black mayor, with significant support from white voters. At the end of the twentieth century, Seattle began to reflect the kind of tolerance and equality that had falsely characterized the first half of its history.

By 2001 blacks made up 8.4 percent of the city's population, making Seattle's black community the second largest on the west coast, after that of LOS ANGELES, CALIFORNIA. Yet higher costs of living have driven many African Americans into suburban areas. During the 1990s, for the first time since 1930, Seattle's black population declined.

See also World War II and African Americans.

Bibliography
Taylor, Quintard. *The Forging of a Black Community: Seattle's Central District from 1870 through the Civil Rights Era.* University of Washington Press, 1994.

Eric Bennett

Sebei

Ethnic group of Uganda; also known as the Sabaot.

The Sebei mainly live near Mount Elgon in eastern UGANDA. Others live in western KENYA. They speak a Nilo-Saharan language and are one of the KALENJIN peoples. Approximately 100,000 people consider themselves Sebei.

See also Languages, African: An Overview.

Second Great Awakening

Upwelling of religious spirit in the United States, peaking between 1820 and 1840, that particularly affected black people and led to many conversions to Christianity.

For information on
Conversion of slaves: *See* Black Church, The.
Character of religious behavior compared with the first Great Awakening: *See* Religions, African and Afro-Caribbean, in the United States.
Effect on abolition: *See* Abolitionism in the United States.

Secretary Bird

Common name for a large bird of prey found in Africa south of the Sahara.

The secretary bird is more than 1 m (more than 3 ft) in length and has very long legs, a long tail, and a powerful, hooked beak. Many books derive the origin of the bird's name from a fanciful resemblance of its crest of long feathers to a group of quill pens placed behind the ear. The name is actually a mispronunciation of the Arabic name for the species. The general color of the bird is bluish gray; the primaries, thighs, and tail markings are black. The bird feeds on small animals and on reptiles, particularly snakes, generally stalking them. Secretary birds rarely fly. The solitary birds build large, strong nests of twigs in trees or bushes and lay two eggs in a clutch.

Scientific classification: The secretary bird makes up the family Sagittariidae in the order Falconiformes. It is classified as *Sagittarius serpentarius*.

Segogela, Johannes

1936–

South African sculptor who uses traditional woodcarving methods.

Johannes Segogela was born and educated in Sekhukhuneland, located in South Africa's Northern TRANSVAAL region. As a young man, he worked as a boilermaker, and sculpted small wooden figures in his spare time. In 1985 an exhibition of work by little-known contemporary South African artists was organized in JOHANNESBURG, SOUTH AFRICA, and included several of Segogela's figures. The show, called *Tributaries*, helped launch the careers of several participants, Segogela among them.

Segogela's early pieces featured small figures or groups of figures, carved from indigenous wood and decorated with bright enamel paint. Some, such as *Samson and the Lion* (1986), depicted biblical themes, while others portrayed scenes from contemporary urban life. Because these works, which include many elements, are meant to be rearranged, they are never fixed to a base.

Segogela's more recent pieces are highly stylized and somewhat satirical. Biblical lessons remain a common theme, reflecting Segogela's interest in questions of good and evil. *Satan's Fresh Meat Market* (1993), for example, depicts Satan as a butcher surrounded by human body parts. Other sculptures represent current events in South Africa, such as *President Mandela Voting* (1994). Segogela continues to live and work in the Transvaal. In addition to being featured in exhibitions in South Africa, as in the 1999 show *Emergence* in Grahamstown, his work has been shown in galleries and museums throughout Europe, as well as at the 1994 Havana Bienale in CUBA. In 2002 his carved wood sculpture *Burial of Apartheid* accompanied an interview with DESMOND TUTU about forgiveness that appeared in the British journal *Resurgence*.

See also Artists, African.

Bibliography

Ross, D. H. "Masaego Johannes Segogela." In *African Arts* 28, no. 1 (winter 1995): 74–80.

Christopher Tiné

Segregation in the United States

Legal or social practice in the United States of separating people on the basis of their race.

Segregation by law, or de jure segregation, occurred when local, state, or national laws required racial separation, or where the laws explicitly allowed segregation. De jure segregation has been prohibited in the United States since the mid-1960s. De facto segregation, or segregation in fact, occurs when social practices, political acts, economic circumstances, or public policy result in the separation of people by race or ethnicity even though no laws require or authorize their separation. De facto segregation has continued even when state and federal civil rights laws have explicitly prohibited racial segregation.

Segregation by law in the United States dates from the founding of the nation and was particularly widespread in the South for about eighty years, from the 1870s until the courts and the Congress of the United States prohibited legally sanctioned segregation in the 1950s and 1960s. At the end of the twentieth century, de facto segregation remained a problem in many places in the United States. De facto segregation has resulted from residential housing patterns, economic factors, personal choice, "white flight" from central cities, and private and often illegal discrimination by homeowners, real estate agents, and lending institutions. The results are often segregated neighborhoods, and consequently segregated schools, recreational facilities, and other public and private institutions.

Segregation by Law

Although de jure segregation in the United States is most commonly associated with the South, segregation could be found at one time or another in every section of the country. The nation's first legal challenge to segregated schools, *Roberts v. City of Boston* (1849), took place in Massachusetts. A black man named Benjamin F. Roberts sued to force the city of Boston to allow his daughter Sarah to attend the nearest elementary school, and not have to travel across town to a segregated school. Roberts lost his case, but blacks in Massachusetts won a substantial victory when the state legislature prohibited segregation in the public schools in 1855.

The federal government from its inception, meanwhile, created policies that separated blacks from the mainstream of American society. Before the CIVIL WAR (1861–1865), blacks were not allowed to join state militias or the U.S. Army or Navy, and the federal government refused to give passports to free blacks. In *DRED SCOTT V. SANDFORD* (1857), the Supreme Court of the United States declared that blacks could never be citizens of the United States.

At the beginning of the Civil War, the national government refused to allow blacks to fight in the U.S. Army. However, in 1862 the government allowed blacks to enlist in segregated units, led by white officers. By the end of the war, more than 200,000 blacks had served in the U.S. Army and Navy. After the war, the nation adopted three constitutional amendments directed against racial discrimination: the Thirteenth Amendment (1865), ending slavery; the FOURTEENTH AMENDMENT (1868), declaring blacks citizens of the United States and prohibiting state laws that denied any persons within their jurisdiction equal protection under the laws; and the FIFTEENTH AMENDMENT (1870), prohibiting racial discrimination in voting. After the Civil War, most Northern states also prohibited segregation. However, into the 1940s there were pockets of de jure segregation in a few Northern states.

Segregation in the South. After the Civil War, de jure segregation rapidly became the rule in the South. There had been little need for segregation before the war because about 95 percent of all blacks were subject to the racial restrictions of slavery. However, the small free black population in the prewar South had faced segregation or outright exclusion from schools, theaters, taverns, and other public places. Immediately after the war, Southern state legislatures, dominated by former Confederates, passed laws known as BLACK CODES that severely limited the rights of blacks. The codes were slightly different from state to state, but they usually contained limitations on black occupations and ownership of property, and vagrancy laws under which blacks could be forced to work for whites if they were considered unemployed. These codes effectively segregated blacks into the rural areas of the state where they were virtually forced to become farm workers. Laws were also passed that segregated schools, courts, and juries.

In response to these laws, Congress in 1866, led by the Northern-dominated REPUBLICAN PARTY, seized the initiative in remaking the South. Under RECONSTRUCTION, as this process was known, blacks gained the right to vote throughout the former Confederate states and were elected to political offices across the South. By 1868 integrated Southern legislatures had repealed most of the laws that blatantly discriminated against blacks. In 1875 Congress passed a new civil rights act, designed to prohibit segregation in public facilities and accommodations, such as theaters, hotels, and restaurants.

By 1877, however, the DEMOCRATIC PARTY had regained control of the Southern states, ending Reconstruction. The strides that blacks had made—holding political offices, having the right to vote, and participating as equal members of society—were reversed, and the South gradually reimposed racially discriminatory laws. These laws achieved two main goals—disenfranchisement and segregation. In order to take away black political power gained during Reconstruction, the Democratic Party in the South began to disenfranchise blacks (prevent them from voting). There were a variety of methods to stop blacks from voting, including poll taxes, fees that all voters were required to pay and that were too expensive for most blacks; and literacy tests, which required that voters be able to read to vote. Since schooling for blacks had been virtually nonexistent before the Civil War and remained poor after the war, most black adults were illiterate. Literacy tests were often unequally administered, with black voters tested on arcane materials while semiliterate whites were asked only to read their name or some other simple text. The Democrats also began to create a segregated society that separated blacks and whites in almost every sphere of life. They passed laws that created separate schools and separate public facilities.

In addition, the Supreme Court turned its back on racial equality. In *The Civil Rights Cases* (1883), the Court declared that Congress had no power to prevent private acts of discrimination. Writing for the Court, Justice Joseph Bradley declared: "When a man has emerged from slavery, and by the aid of beneficent legislation . . . there must be some stage in the progress of his elevation when he takes the rank of a mere citizen, and ceases to be the special favorite of the laws, and when his rights as a citizen, or a man, are to be protected in the ordinary modes by which other men's rights are protected." Rather than being the "special favorites" of the law, however, blacks were increasingly the special targets of laws that required discrimination and segregation.

The Supreme Court in *PLESSY V. FERGUSON* (1896) upheld the constitutionality of separate railroad cars for blacks and whites. Speaking for the Court, Justice Henry Billings Brown argued that as long as the separate facilities for each race were "equal," they were permitted under the Constitution. In dissent Justice John Marshall Harlan, a Southerner and former slave owner, argued that the "Constitution is colorblind, and neither knows nor tolerates classes among citizens." Justice Harlan pointed out that segregation created a psychological sense of superiority among whites while harming blacks.

After 1900 Southern legislators carried segregation to extremes, solidifying what was known as the JIM CROW system of racial separation. A 1914 Louisiana statute required separate entrances at circuses for blacks and whites; a 1915 Oklahoma law segregated telephone booths; a 1920 Mississippi law made it a crime to advocate or publish "arguments or suggestions in favor of social equality or of intermarriage between whites and

Negroes." Kentucky not only required separate schools, but also provided that no textbook issued to a black would "ever be reissued or redistributed to a white school child" or vice versa. Similarly, Florida required that schoolbooks for blacks be stored separately from those for whites. All Southern states prohibited interracial marriages.

As the United States entered World War II in 1941, the South was a fully segregated society. Every school, restaurant, hotel, train car, waiting room, elevator, public bathroom, college, hospital, cemetery, swimming pool, drinking fountain, prison, and church was either for whites or blacks but never for both. In courtrooms blacks swore on one Bible and whites on another. Throughout the first half of the twentieth century, Southerners were born in segregated hospitals, educated in segregated schools, and buried in segregated graveyards.

Violence and Segregation. Throughout the South, segregation had the support of the legal system and the police. Beyond the law, however, there was always the threat of terrorist violence against blacks who attempted to challenge or even question the established order. During Reconstruction, the KU KLUX KLAN, the Knights of the White Camellia, and other terrorist organizations murdered thousands of blacks and some whites in order to prevent them from voting and participating in public life.

With the demise of Reconstruction in 1877, there was an increase in racial violence as white Southerners tried to reclaim local and state governments and reestablish white domination over blacks. One of the main forms of violence was LYNCHING, when mobs would hang or otherwise execute blacks or others who were presumed to have committed crimes. Between 1884 and 1920 white mobs lynched more than 3,000 blacks in the South. Many were alleged criminals, but blacks were also lynched for any violation of the code of Southern race relations such as talking to a white woman, attempting to vote, or seeming to make trouble.

Opposition before World War II

Violence and the power of state governments made resistance to segregation difficult. Nevertheless, blacks fought segregation at the ballot box, in the courtrooms, and through organizations like the NATIONAL ASSOCIATION FOR THE ADVANCEMENT OF COLORED PEOPLE (NAACP), which was founded in 1909. After the Supreme Court decision in *The Civil Rights Cases* in 1883, blacks throughout the nation held public meetings to discuss and protest the decision, and they organized the Brotherhood of Liberty to plan legal and political action against segregation. The brotherhood commissioned the publication, in 1889, of the first important legal analysis of segregation, in *Justice and Jurisprudence: An Inquiry Concerning the Constitutional Limitations of the Thirteenth, Fourteenth, and Fifteenth Amendments*, a volume of more than 500 pages.

In 1905 a number of black activists, led by W. E. B. DU BOIS, the first black to receive a doctoral degree from Harvard University, met in Niagara Falls to plan strategies to fight for racial equality. By 1909 the NIAGARA MOVEMENT, as the group called itself, led to the formation of the NAACP, a racially integrated organization dedicated to fighting segregation and inequality. Almost immediately, the NAACP began to challenge segregation in the courts. Before World War II started in 1939, there were a few significant victories in the Supreme Court. In *Buchanan v. Warley* (1917), the Court declared unconstitutional a Louisville, Kentucky, law that required that blacks and whites live in certain sections of the city. In *Missouri ex rel. Gaines v. Canada* (1938), the Supreme Court also ruled that Missouri had to open its state-supported law school to blacks, unless it was prepared to build a separate law school for them.

Emergence of the Civil Rights Movement

During and after World War II, challenges to segregation became more common and more successful. Three major factors accounted for this: the GREAT MIGRATION; the changing nature of American politics; and the social and cultural changes connected to the war itself.

The Great Migration. From World War I (1914–1918) through the 1950s, a vast number of blacks migrated from the Southern states to the Northern and Western ones for a number of reasons, including better jobs and schools and a less racist environment. During this time the black population in both the North and South became increasingly urbanized as well. The movement to the cities concentrated blacks in specific neighborhoods, often giving them enough voting power to elect local public officials. Blacks in the North did not face legal barriers to voting, and thus actively participated in the political process. Not surprisingly, white Northern politicians with large black constituencies began to oppose segregation and to support civil rights.

The Great Migration introduced millions of blacks to a world in which formal segregation did not exist and basic facilities, like transportation, restaurants, and public bathrooms, were open to all people. However, the North was not without racism. Blacks could not move to certain neighborhoods, were denied access to many jobs, and were informally segregated. Certain LABOR UNIONS, particularly in the skilled building trades, excluded blacks. But, despite de facto segregation and exclusion by individuals, unions, and employers, blacks who moved to the North were able to live without the degrading oppression of day-to-day segregation. They were thus better able to oppose legalized segregation in the South.

Changes in American Politics. While the Great Migration changed how black Americans lived, the GREAT DEPRESSION of the 1930s and the NEW DEAL, the federal government's response to the Depression, altered American politics by setting a precedent for government activism. The administration of President Franklin Delano Roosevelt assumed a new role of intervening in society to ensure jobs, justice, and the prosperity of the American people, who were severely affected by the economic hardships of the Depression. The president's wife, Eleanor Roosevelt, made clear her hatred for segregation as well. Her most important attack on segregation came in 1939, when the Daughters of the American Revolution (DAR) refused to allow the black opera singer MARIAN ANDERSON to give a concert at Constitution Hall in Washington, D.C. Mrs. Roosevelt publicly resigned from the DAR, while the secretary of the interior, Harold L. Ickes, invited Anderson to give an Easter Sunday concert on the steps of the Lincoln Memorial. This symbolic gesture set a new tone in Washington, one that indicated that the national administration no longer condoned segregation.

By the eve of World War II, black voters regularly elected officials in a number of Northern states, as well as in Kentucky and West Virginia. These newly elected officials actively fought against segregation and racism, although not always successfully. By this time a majority of the members of Congress favored an antilynching bill, but these legislators were never able to overcome Southern filibusters (stalling tactics) in the Senate.

Social and Cultural Changes. World War II was a final impetus to a reinvigorated CIVIL RIGHTS MOVEMENT. The struggle against Nazism forced some Americans to reconsider the legitimacy of racism in the United States. The death of six million Jews in the Holocaust, murdered merely because of their ethnicity, led some Americans to realize that racism could be a threat to democracy itself. Blacks also served in the military in unprecedented numbers. By the end of the war, many blacks had served with whites in integrated units.

Finally, the postwar world forced the national government to face, for the first time, the threat that segregation posed to international relations. After the war, many colonies in Asia and Africa gained their independence from European domination. At the same time, the Cold War struggle with the Communist government of the Union of Soviet Socialist Republics (USSR) forced the United States to court the goodwill of these nations. Segregation undermined the nation's ability to negotiate with these new nations while giving the USSR ammunition in its propaganda war against the United States. Leaders of the American foreign policy establishment urged an end to segregation at home as a way of fighting Communism abroad.

Civil Rights Movement

After the war, the push to end segregation began in earnest, led by NAACP lawyers, veterans, and social activists. Ironically, the first victory came not from lawyers or activists, but from an agreement between a black athlete and a white businessman.

Social Challenges to Segregation. Since the 1880s major league baseball had banned black players. Because of this, black athletes played in the segregated NEGRO LEAGUES. That practice came to an end in 1945 when Branch Rickey, general manager of the Brooklyn Dodgers, signed JACKIE ROBINSON, who two years later entered the major leagues with the Brooklyn Dodgers. During World War II Robinson, a U.S. Army officer, was acquitted in a court-martial for challenging illegal segregation on an army base. Robinson, a brilliant athlete, and many of the black players who followed him—including ROY CAMPANELLA, Don Newcombe, ERNIE BANKS, WILLIE MAYS, and HANK AARON—became stars to white and black fans alike. If the national pastime could be integrated, it seemed only a matter of time before the nation's schools, playgrounds, buses, and restaurants could also be integrated.

Legal Challenges to Segregation. Starting in the 1930s, a group of black attorneys began fighting segregation through the courts. They were led by CHARLES HAMILTON HOUSTON, the vice dean of the law school at HOWARD UNIVERSITY, and his student THURGOOD MARSHALL, who eventually became the first black member of the U.S. Supreme Court. Joining them were other Howard graduates, including Spottswood William Robinson III and Oliver W. Hill. In *Hollins v. Oklahoma* (1935), Houston successfully challenged the exclusion of blacks from juries. In 1939 the NAACP created a separate nonprofit organization called the NAACP LEGAL DEFENSE AND EDUCATIONAL FUND to bring cases that continually challenged segregation and racial discrimination.

After 1942 legal challenges to segregation were more successful; by that year, Franklin Roosevelt's appointments had radically remade the Supreme Court. Between 1946 and 1950, the Court struck down segregation in interstate railroad trains, state-sponsored law schools, and other graduate schools. In *SWEATT V. PAINTER* (1950), the court ordered the University of Texas to integrate its law school.

In the landmark case of *BROWN V. BOARD OF EDUCATION* (1954), the Court declared that "in the field of public education the doctrine of 'separate but equal' has no place." This decision, which was the foundation for SCHOOL DESEGREGATION across the United States, finally tipped the scales against segregation of all kinds. After *Brown*, the court gradually struck down all remaining forms of segregation. In *Gayle v. Browder* (1956), the Supreme Court silently overturned the *Plessy* precedent by holding that segregation was unconstitutional on public buses. This case grew out of the MONTGOMERY BUS BOYCOTT, which began when civil rights activist ROSA PARKS refused to give up her seat to a white passenger. In *Loving v. Virginia* (1967), the court struck down laws banning interracial marriage. By 1968 all forms of de jure segregation had been declared unconstitutional.

Political Challenges to Segregation. During the 1960s demonstrators in the Civil Rights Movement protested segregation throughout the South and in many Northern cities. The protesters held rallies, staged SIT-INS, boycotted segregated businesses, worked to register black voters, and marched to try to end Southern segregation, and they met with often violent resistance from white Southerners. Organizations such as the SOUTHERN CHRISTIAN LEADERSHIP CONFERENCE (SCLC) and the STUDENT NONVIOLENT COORDINATING COMMITTEE (SNCC) were active throughout the South in rallying people to challenge segregation.

In response to the civil rights protests, Congress passed new and stronger civil rights laws in 1964 and 1965. The Civil Rights

Act of 1964 prohibited racial discrimination in public education and public accommodations and by employers or voter registrars. The VOTING RIGHTS ACT OF 1965 suspended the use of voter-qualification tests such as literacy tests, and later amendments to the act banned their use.

By the 1970s violence against civil rights workers had begun to dissipate in the South. Formal segregation was also gone. No level of government maintained separate schools for blacks and whites, and separate facilities such as drinking fountains and restrooms had disappeared. Millions of blacks who had been disenfranchised could vote, and by the 1990s blacks held major public offices in the South, serving as mayors, governors, and state officials. Civil rights spread in the North as well, where blacks served as mayors of the three largest cities and held high office in state and local government. At the national level, blacks served on the Supreme Court, in the House of Representatives and the Senate, in presidential cabinets, and as head of the Joint Chiefs of Staff.

De Facto Segregation

Although de jure segregation was abolished by 1968, de facto segregation was still prevalent in most Northern and Southern cities. Blacks tended to live in all-black neighborhoods, often called ghettos. There were three main reasons for the formation of these neighborhoods. First, real estate agents, banks, and city zoning decisions dictated housing patterns. Often real estate agents would not show blacks homes in white neighborhoods, while banks often refused to loan money to blacks moving into white neighborhoods. City planners often kept neighborhoods segregated through decisions on where to locate streets, interstate highways, access ramps to those highways, and even subway and other rail stations. Such decisions allowed white traffic to bypass black areas and limited black access to white parts of town. Second, while formal segregation in schools disappeared, public officials often created school districts designed to keep blacks and whites separated. Finally, SUBURBANIZATION also increased de facto segregation, as whites increasingly left the cities for suburban communities. In 1968 only two major American cities, WASHINGTON, D.C. and CHARLESTON, SOUTH CAROLINA, had black majorities. By 1990 more than fifteen cities were predominantly black, including Atlanta, Georgia; Baltimore, Maryland; Detroit, Michigan; New Orleans, Louisiana; Newark, New Jersey; and Richmond, Virginia. In addition to these factors, many blacks chose to live in neighborhoods with other blacks, just as whites chose to live with other whites. Blacks who did integrate neighborhoods in both the North and the South often faced violence and intimidation.

Most schools remained segregated, not because the law required it, but because the neighborhoods they served were racially homogenous. In the South, segregation increased when whites removed their children from public schools in response to court-ordered integration. As a result, in Southern communities the public schools were legally integrated, but often only blacks attended them, while whites attended private schools.

Conclusion

In 1903 the black intellectual W. E. B. Du Bois wrote that the single greatest issue of the twentieth century would be the "color line." He was to a great extent correct, both in terms of American domestic politics and of events throughout the world. By the end of the century, de jure segregation in the United States had ended. Racial discrimination was illegal everywhere in the United States. In universities, businesses, the military, and the government, a few blacks were prominent and powerful. Clearly, much had changed in the nation. Blacks remained among the poorest Americans, however, and opportunity seemed unavailable for the majority of young blacks, even as a few were able to achieve great success. And even though the laws no longer permitted discrimination and public policy seemed to favor integration, in the 1990s the nation remained racially polarized and often segregated in fact if not by law.

See also Decolonization in Africa: An Interpretation; Free Blacks in the United States; Military, Blacks in the American; World War II and African Americans.

Paul Finkelman

Séjour, Victor

1817–1874

African American playwright.

Victor Séjour was born in NEW ORLEANS, LOUISIANA, the son of Louis Victor Séjour Marcou, a small businessman, and Eloisa Philippe Ferrand. His father was a black native of the WEST INDIES, and his mother a Creole from New Orleans. Séjour attended an academy in New Orleans for the children of free men of color. As a young man he was an active member of the Artisans, a middle-class Creole society. In 1836 Séjour was sent to Paris to finish his studies. In that same year, his short story "Le Mulâtre" was published in *La Revue des Colonies* (Paris). Another early literary success was a poem, "Le Retour de Napoléon," first published in Paris (Dauvain et Fontaine, 1841), then in New Orleans (H. Lauve et Compagnie, 1845).

Séjour made his playwriting debut at the Théâtre-Français on July 23, 1844 with *Dégarias*. The central character of the play—set in fifteenth-century Spain—is a persecuted Jew who must hide his identity because he married a Christian woman. This was followed by *La Chute de Séjan,* which opened at the same theater on August 21, 1849. During this time, Séjour became involved in Paris literary circles that included Emile Augier, Alexandre Dumas, and Jules Janin. Like certain other Louisiana blacks, he found he could live a life in Paris relatively free of the racial prejudice that would have hounded him in the United States.

Using Shakespeare and Victor Hugo as models, Séjour spent most of his career writing serious plays—some in verse and some in prose—that varied in genre from vast historical dramas to musical melodramas. After his initial successes at the Théâtre-Français, the bulk of his earlier plays were produced at the Porte-Sainte-Martin: *Richard III* (1852), *Les Noces Vénitiennes* (1855), *Le Fils de la Nuit* (1856), *Le Paletot Brun* (1858), *La Tireuse de Cartes* (1859), and *Les Volontaires de 1814* (1862). Like most of Séjour's plays, these often revolve around relationships that are strained by religious, ethnic, or political differences. Two were produced at the Odéon—*André Gérard* (1857) and *Les Grands Vassaux* (1859). *L'Argent du Diable*, a collaboration with Jaime [Adolphe] fils, opened in 1854 at the Théâtre des Variétés. At the Théâtre Impérial du Cirque, Séjour saw two of his major spectacles mounted: *Les Massacres de la Syrie* (1860) and *La Prise de Pekin* (c. 1860).

Séjour's later plays were produced at the "Boulevard Theatres"—the Ambigu-Comique and the Gaîté. The first produced *Le Martyr du Coeur* (1858), a collaboration with Jules Brésil; *Compère Guillery* (1860); *Les Mystères du Temple* (1862); and *Les Fils de Charles-Quint* (1864). At the Gaîté, *Les Aventuriers* (1860) and *Le Marquis Caporal* (1864) were produced, as well as two collaborations with Théodore Barrière—*Les Enfants de la Louve* (1865) and *La Madone des Roses* (1868). At the time of Séjour's death, *Le Vampire* (1874) had been accepted for production at one of the two Boulevard theaters. No matter what the subject matter, the theme of tolerance was always important to Séjour.

The question of Séjour's importance during his lifetime has been debated by scholars. At least one contemporary critic, Théophile Gautier, was fond of him; another, L. Félix Savard, felt his work—violent, unrealistic, and overwritten—exerted a "detestable influence" on the theater of his time (*Chronique Littéraire* 2 [1862]). Séjour's dramatization of the Mortara Case (in which a young Jewish girl had been kidnapped and raised as a Christian)—*La Tireuse de Cartes*—sparked an ongoing controversy as to the political and religious (but not the ethnic) nature of the playwright. Séjour's reply was that he was a Christian who despised intolerance and a man of "sentiment," not of politics.

Several of Séjour's plays were translated and occasionally produced in other countries during the nineteenth century: *Les Noces Vénitiennes* became *The Outlaw of the Adriatic* (London), *André Gérard* was published in Portuguese (Lisbon), and *Le Martyr du Coeur* in Turkish (Constantinople). *La Tireuse de Cartes* was published in Lisbon as *A Mulher Que Deita Cartes* and in Rotterdam as *De Kaartlegster*. *Richard III* was translated into Spanish and produced at the Teatro del Principe in Madrid just months after its Paris opening; two different Spanish versions were published shortly afterward. The play was also produced and published in New Orleans in the original French. Also in New Orleans, *Le Paletot Brun* was produced six months after its run in Paris. In the twentieth century, the play has been translated twice into English: once for publication (1970), and once for a New York production at Circle in the Square (1972).

Jean-François-Constant Mocquard (also known as Moquart)—playwright, Napoleon III's private secretary, and friend to Séjour—arranged for Séjour to write a trio of plays in honor of the monarch. Séjour also wrote *André Gérard* for the great Romantic actor, Frédérick Lemaître. After the play's initial success at the Odéon in 1857, Lemaître revived the title role at the Gaîté in 1861.

Séjour died in Paris of tuberculosis; he was working on a *Cromwell* at the time. Almost twenty years later, the critic Francisque Sarcey was still making references to him in reviews of other plays—as the representative of a style of melodramatic playwriting that the critic abhorred. Minor playwright or not, he was still a reference point for the French audience many years after his death.

Séjour's plays are best remembered for their themes of social protest, especially his concern with anti-Semitism. As well as being one of several playwrights of color in nineteenth-century Paris, such as Dumas, Séjour is now considered part of the growing canon of African American playwrights.

Bibliography

Daley, T. A. "Victor Séjour." *Phylon: The Atlanta University Review of Race and Culture* 4 (1943): 5–17.

Perret, J. John. "Victor Séjour, Black French Playwright from Louisiana." *French Review* 57 (1983): 187–193.

Peterson, Bernard L., Jr. *Early Black American Playwrights and Dramatic Writers*. 1990.

From *American National Biography*. John A. Garraty and Mark C. Carnes, eds. Oxford University Press, 1999. Reprinted by permission of the American Council of Learned Societies.

Nadine D. Pederson

Sekhukhune

1814–1882

Chief of the Pedi people from 1861 to 1879, and the last major African ruler to hold out against European power in the Transvaal of northern South Africa.

On the death of his father, Sekwati, in 1861, Sekhukhune assumed command of the PEDI, although his succession was disputed by his half-brother Mampura. Alarmed by increasing European encroachment in his territory, Sekhukhune became deeply suspicious of the German Lutheran missionaries of the Berlin Missionary Society whom his father had allowed into the kingdom in 1861. He believed that by converting his subjects to CHRISTIANITY, the missionaries were undermining his authority and conspiring against him with the local AFRIKANERS, or Boers. As a result, in 1866 Sekhukhune expelled them and prohibited Christianity. Aware that the Afrikaners would eventually invade his kingdom, he began stockpiling arms. In 1876 the president of the Transvaal Republic, Thomas François Burgers, attacked the Pedi in alliance with Mampura, but Sekhukhune successfully defended the kingdom. In 1877, however, the Transvaal was annexed by Sir Theophilus Shepstone for GREAT BRITAIN, which in 1879 launched its own war against the Pedi. In an uneven struggle, with the Pedi facing two British regiments and 6,000 SWAZI under commander Sir Garnett Wolseley, about 1,000 Pedi were killed and Sekhukhune was captured. He was held prisoner in Pretoria while his half-brother Mampura was installed as chief in his place. In 1881, after the British returned the sovereignty of the TRANSVAAL to the Afrikaners, Sekhukhune was allowed to return to his home. The following year he was assassinated by Mampura, whom the Afrikaners subsequently hanged. This effectively ended the independence of the Pedi.

Selvon, Samuel

1923–1994

Trinidadian novelist, journalist, and dramatist.

Samuel Selvon is often compared to V. S. NAIPAUL. Both writers were born in Trinidad and are considered canonical writers of the WEST INDIES. In addition, both spent much of their careers abroad, and both share the outsider's perspective of having grown up East Indians in predominantly black West Indian society. Despite this outsider status, Selvon strongly identified with his West Indian heritage, and his novels and plays focus on aspects of the West Indian struggle for self-improvement that cut across racial lines. His works often include black characters, and he has been especially praised for his skillful use of Caribbean folk tradition and dialect.

Selvon graduated from Trinidad's Naparima College in 1938 and began writing fiction while serving in the Royal Naval Reserve during World War II (1939–1945). After working as a fiction editor for the *Trinidad Guardian,* Selvon in 1950 emigrated to England, where his first novel, *A Brighter Sun,* was published in 1952. The story of a young Trinidadian Indian trying to establish his identity as he watches his country doing the same, *A Brighter Sun* immediately won Selvon acclaim as part of the rising generation of West Indian writers. The book has been described as having "introduced the great period of Trinidadian novels which continues to this day."

Two years later Selvon won the first of two Guggenheim fellowships. The prolific career that followed produced over a dozen more novels, a collection of prose essays, and an anthology of plays that included the highlights from dramatic works produced on BBC radio. In 1978 Selvon moved from England to CANADA, and many of his later novels focused on the West Indian immigrant experience. Once again Selvon's work featured issues he shared with black West Indians, such as cultural alienation and color prejudice.

Selvon's other honors included a 1969 Hummingbird medal from the government of TRINIDAD AND TOBAGO. He continues to be remembered as a leading figure in the literary tradition of the West Indies.

See also East Indian Communities in the Caribbean; Languages, Creole, in the Caribbean; Literature, English-Language, in the Caribbean; Theater in the Caribbean.

Lisa Clayton Robinson

Sembène, Ousmane

1923–

Senegalese novelist and film director, who is considered one of Africa's leading film directors.

Ousmane Sembène is a pioneer and foundational figure in the history of African cinema. During a career that has spanned fifty years, Ousmane Sembène revolutionized African film through changes in film subject and filmic language. His film style influenced many film directors and has set standards for the premier organization of African film directors: the FÉDÉRATION PANAFRICAINE DES CINÉASTES (FEPACI).

Born in 1923 in the Cassamance region of SENEGAL, Ousmane Sembène received little formal education. He was dismissed from primary school after he struck the headmaster. In 1942 he enlisted in the French colonial army and fought in World War II. His experiences in Europe made him keenly aware of the inequalities of the colonial system, and after returning to Senegal he participated in anticolonial movements, such as the Dakar-Niger railroad strike in 1947. The following year he moved to France.

Sembène first became interested in writing when he realized that there was a lack of literature by African writers available in Europe. His first book, *Le Docker Noir* (1956) describes the difficult life of African dockworkers in France. His next novel *O pays mon beau peuple* (1957) tells of a young man returning to Senegal after living in France for a while. Sembène's next novel, *Les Bouts de bois de Dieu* (God's Bits of Wood, 1960), gained him international fame as one of Africa's most important writers. Sembène returned to Africa soon after its publication, but was struck by how little impact European-language literature had on African people. Believing that film had the potential to reach a wider audience, Sembène enrolled in the Gorki Studio in Moscow in 1961. After he completed his training, he returned to Senegal and began work as a film director.

Ousmane Sembène's first movies, *Barom Sarret* (1963) and *Niaye* (1964), were highly acclaimed by critics and received prizes at film festivals. In 1966 he finished the first feature-length film to be produced in sub-Saharan Africa: *La Noire de. . . .* He soon established his own studio, producing documentaries to provide funding for his own films, which he continued to write and direct. He overcame distribution problems and lack of theaters by initiating film tours that enabled him to travel to the villages in Senegal and show his movies. Lauded by the FEPACI, his methods were soon adopted by other African film directors.

The tours also helped Ousmane Sembène in his efforts to create an African cinematic language. He aspired to develop a filmic language that addressed the problems posed by multiple African languages and dialects. His innovations in this area can clearly be seen in *Le Mandat* (1968) and *Xala* (1974). In *Le Mandat,* Sembène integrated pictures, images, and gestures into the story text. By supplementing the text in this way, he made it possible to communicate the overall plot of the movie, even though the actors speak in WOLOF, one of four major languages in Senegal. In *Xala,* Sembène continued to supplement the narrative, this time with a series of symbols connected to each character to supplement the finer points of the narrative that might be lost among different languages. The approach developed in these films became the model for FEPACI film directors.

Since completing his landmark film *Xala,* Sembène has worked on larger films about historical events in Senegal. *Ceddo* (1977) examines the religious wars in Africa during the seventeenth and eighteenth centuries. *Camp de Thiaroye* (1987) explores the massacre of Senegalese infantrymen, veterans who had served in the French army in World War II, by the French army in Thiaroye. This film won the Jury Special Award at the Venice Film Festival in 1989.

One of Ousmane Sembène's most ambitious films is *Guelwaar,* which addresses the problem of food aid diversion by the government in postcolonial Africa, specifically in Senegal. Although the film was finished in 1994, the Senegalese government has prevented him from releasing and showing *Guelwaar* in Senegal, and the film has had only minor distribution and screening in other areas of the world. Sembène followed this with a comedy, *Faat Kine* (2000), which chronicles the rags-to-riches story of a single mother who rises from gas station attendant in Dakar to manager at a multinational oil company. The story of this liberated woman, born at the same time as Senegalese independence, suggests parallels with the history of Ousmane Sembène's native country.

See also Cinema, African.

Seminole Wars

Nineteenth-century conflict that pitted blacks and Native Americans against the United States Army in Florida.

While some African Americans would later fight against NATIVE AMERICANS on the western frontier, an amalgam of the two groups battled the U.S. Army side by side during the decades-long conflict known as the Seminole Wars. Few Americans realize that the Seminole tribe grew to include blacks as well as Indians, and that the majority of the Seminoles were forced to leave Florida for the West.

Around 1750 a group of Creek Indians left Georgia and established their own community in Florida. They were known as the Seminoles after the Creek word for "runaway." Like some other Indian groups, the Seminoles kept African American slaves. Contemporary accounts show that, unlike white slave owners, the Seminoles allowed their slaves to live freely with their families in exchange for a percentage of their harvests.

At the beginning of the nineteenth century, Florida belonged to the Crown of Spain, which did not recognize the type of slavery practiced by white colonists. Many slaves escaped and fled south to Florida, where the Spanish Crown freed them and gave them land to cultivate. Before long, intermarriage between escaped African Americans—called maroons from the Spanish word for runaways—and the Seminoles and their black slaves became common, and the groups developed kinship bonds.

Seminole Wars

Whites in neighboring states, enraged at the loss of their valuable slaves, pressed the U.S. government for action. Following a series of failed negotiations, in 1816 Congress authorized the use of force. Many black and Indian allies had sought protection in Fort Nichols, an abandoned stronghold on the Apalachicola River in Florida that remained from the WAR OF 1812. The army, coming from both land and sea, attacked the fort in the summer of 1816, killing 270 blacks and 30 Indians.

Those who survived began preparing for war. They harvested and stored their crops, sent the women, children, and livestock deep into the woods, and bought arms and ammunition from Spanish and British traders. On April 19, 1817, General Andrew Jackson—later to become U.S. president—led a charge against the allied black and Indian soldiers.

In May of 1818, after taking the cities of Pensacola and Sewanee, General Jackson wrote to President James Monroe and won permission to end the war. Nearly half his soldiers had died, either from battle wounds or from the indigenous diseases MALARIA and yellow fever. Many of the exiles died as well, but none was captured or re-enslaved.

After the first war came an uneasy peace, interrupted often by white slaveholders and Creek Indians raiding to capture escaped slaves. The existence of FREE BLACKS—in what was at last, following Florida's cessation from Spain in 1819, part of the United States—threatened the institution of slavery, and the Seminoles held valuable land. Once again the government intervened, adopting a policy that relocated the Seminoles, black and Indian, west of the Mississippi, to the Indian Territory in present-day Oklahoma.

While a scouting group traveled west in 1833, government officials broke their agreement and informed the Seminoles they had no choice but to migrate. Angered by yet another broken promise, the Seminoles and maroons again prepared for war. Led by a young, charismatic chief named Osceola, a group of Seminoles waylaid and murdered a local army colonel in 1835. Some accounts suggest that the colonel had earlier jailed Osceola for attempting to protect his wife from being captured as an escaped slave. The army responded with a surprise attack on the Seminoles but was foiled by an advance warning from one of the officer's black slaves.

Fighting continued through 1836 and 1837, with government forces often pinned down and forced to eat their own horses to survive. Meanwhile, the Seminoles refused to sign the treaties the United States offered, because they failed to provide for the freedom of their black allies. Negotiations broke down irretrievably when the army seized the allies' representatives, including Osceola, and had them jailed as prisoners of war. Osceola died in captivity in 1838, the same year nearly 2,000 of his fellow Seminoles were sent west.

By 1842, when the army finally stopped hunting the few remaining Seminoles in Florida, the war had cost the U.S. government more than 1,500 men and $40 million. Experts estimate that about 500 escaped slaves were returned to captivity. It is not known how many blacks and Indians died in their fight to remain free.

After the Wars

Finding their new home—with its sparse game, arid soil, and proximity to both the slaveholding Creeks and the slave state, Arkansas—inhospitable, many Seminoles, black and Indian, moved yet again. Led by an Indian named Wild Cat and a black man named JOHN HORSE, a group of about 300 fled to northern MEXICO, where they tried to resume their peaceful farming life.

Now renowned as great fighters, the Seminoles attracted the attention of Mexico's president, who offered them land in exchange for driving out the Kickapoo Indians. Led by John Kibbits, they did so. In 1870, the U.S. Army, just thirty years after attempting to exterminate the Seminoles, asked for their help in defeating the Plains Indians. In exchange for a promise of land and food, Chief John Horse moved an entire Seminole village to Texas. The outfit, known as the Seminole Negro Indian Scouts, became one of the most decorated U.S. Army units in history. They never lost a man in battle. In a move that would not have surprised their parents, the government failed to keep its promises of land and food to the scouts, leaving them to fend for themselves in often violently racist south Texas. Many black Seminoles, even those who had won Medals of Honor, were denied army pensions.

By the 1960s, only about 1,000 Seminoles still lived in Florida, and perhaps twice that number in Oklahoma, in addition to communities in Mexico. Nearly all can claim both Indian and black ancestors.

See also Maroonage in the Americas.

Kate Tuttle

Sena

Ethnic group of Southern Africa.

The Sena primarily inhabit central MOZAMBIQUE and far southern MALAWI. They speak a Bantu language. Over 1.5 million people consider themselves Sena.

See also Bantu: Dispersion and Settlement.

Senegal

West African country bordered by Mauritania, Mali, Guinea, Guinea-Bissau, and the Atlantic Ocean and nearly surrounding The Gambia, which forms a virtual enclave within Senegal's borders.

Abandoned cannons guard the entrance to the former Portuguese fort on Goreé Island, which later became a French slave trading center and is now a prison. *M & E Bernheim/Woodfin Camp*

Located in the SAHEL region, where kingdoms prospered from trans-Saharan trade in premodern times, Senegal came to serve as the beachhead for France's conquest of a colonial empire in Africa. Senegal's coastal cities were France's first colonial outposts; the country's largest city and capital, DAKAR, served as the capital and the commercial center of colonial FRENCH WEST AFRICA. Citizens of Senegal were the first Africans to gain French citizenship rights, and the African nation has maintained close ties to FRANCE since independence. Members of the French-speaking Senegalese elite occupied administrative posts throughout France's African empire and contributed to the anticolonial struggles of the 1950s.

Senegal's precolonial past, dating back to the eleventh century when the area served as point of entry for ISLAM south of the Sahara, is not as well known as its history under French rule. The TUKULOR and FULANI peoples of interior Senegal helped spread Islam across large areas of West Africa, from MALI to NIGERIA. During the 1990s the Muridiyah, an Islamic brotherhood, remained a powerful force in Senegalese society. Senegal currently faces challenges common to many African countries, including economic stagnation, large income disparities,

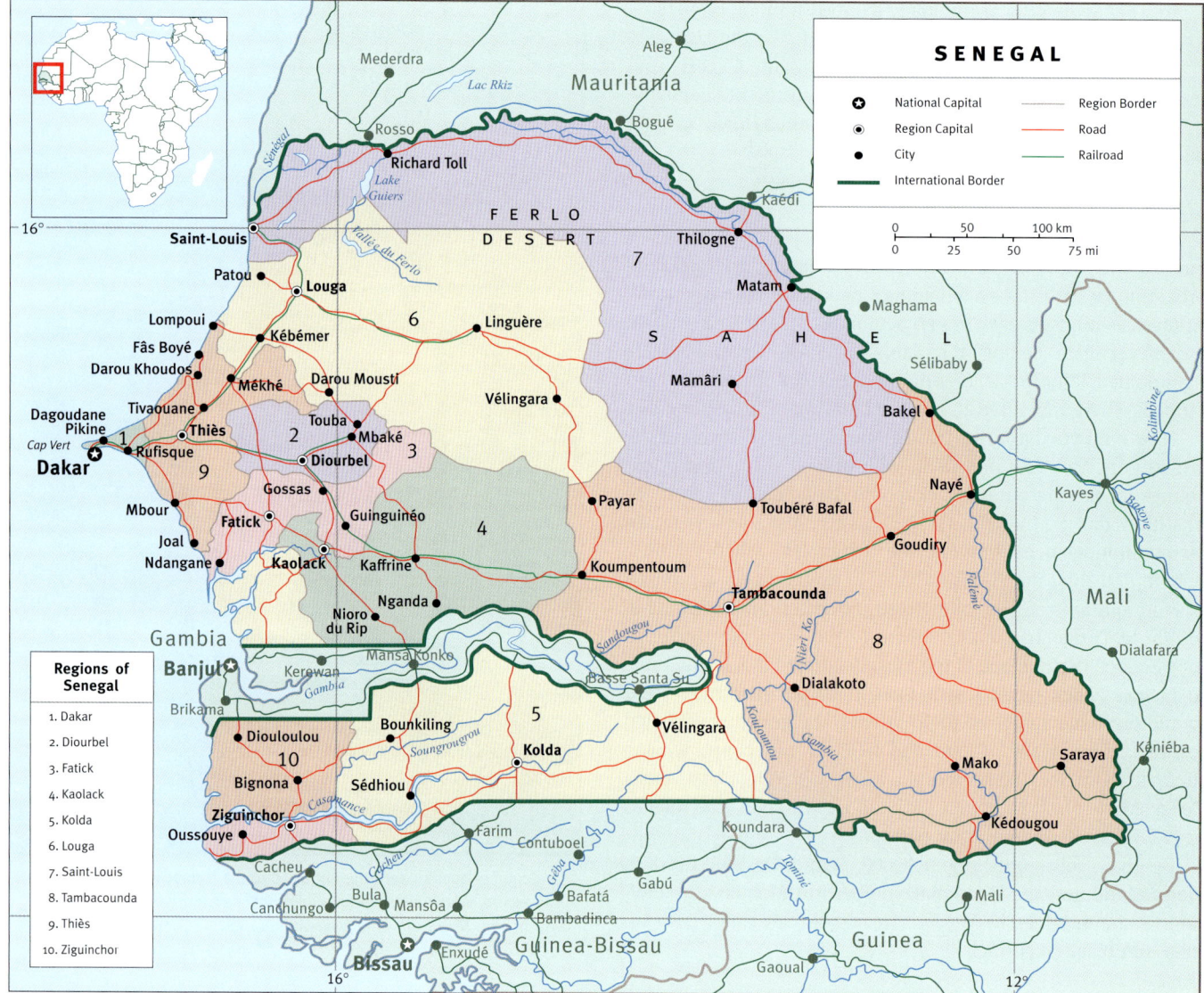

and persistent rebellion by regional separatists in the southern Casamance region. However, Senegal's continued role as an intellectual and cultural center in French-speaking Africa, its relative stability, and its political openness offer the hope that Senegal might once again lead Africa in building a democratic and economically secure society.

Early History

Archaeologists have found stone tools indicating a human presence dating back over 10,000 years in SENEGAMBIA, a region comprising present-day Senegal and THE GAMBIA. They have also found clusters of stone circles, some nearly 2,000 years old, that probably had religious significance. Archaeologists have also found iron-smelting sites dating to the fourth century C.E., indicating the development of metalworking skills among the region's people. By this time speakers of West Atlantic languages (which belong to the larger Niger-Congo family of languages) had probably settled in Senegal. Their descendants include the Fulani, Tukulor, WOLOF, SERER, and JOLA peoples of present-day Senegal.

Scholars disagree on exactly when the ethnic groups living in Senegal today arrived in the region and where they came from. The late Senegalese scholar CHEIKH ANTA DIOP claimed that linguistic and cultural similarities with ancient Egypt indicated that most of Senegal's people had migrated from the NILE RIVER valley. Most linguists and archaeologists, however, doubt the likelihood of such an origin. MANDE-speaking groups such as the MANDINKA doubtless migrated from the NIGER RIVER valley to the east.

The development of metalworking technology by the fourth century C.E. may have contributed to the rise of the region's first centralized state, the Tekrur kingdom in the SENEGAL RIVER valley. This kingdom stretched across the central savanna into the Sahara to the north. Tekrur drew wealth from the lucrative trans-Saharan trade, exchanging gold and slaves from the south

Muslins at prayer during Korite festival. *Sandro Vannini/CORBIS*

for weapons, salt, and luxury goods from the north. Tekrur, dominated by the ancestors of the Tukulor, had extensive contact with peoples from North Africa, including the Zenaga BERBERS. It is from *Zenaga* that the name *Senegal* probably derives.

After their conversion to Islam beginning in the eighth century C.E., Berbers brought Islam to Senegambia. The Zenaga founded a monastery, probably along the Senegal River, around 1040. This hermitage housed an ascetic Islamic sect known as the ALMORAVIDS who swept north and, over the course of the century, conquered MOROCCO and established a Muslim kingdom in SPAIN. The sect's leader, Abd Allah ibn Yasin, converted the Tekrur king, War Jabi, and many of the Tukulor people to Islam.

During the thirteenth century, as Tekrur fell under the dominance of the MALI EMPIRE to the east, the Jolof kingdom arose on the northwestern savanna, conquering the Wolof people. By the end of the century the Jolof had conquered most of the Wolof region, and during the fourteenth century came to dominate the Serer kingdoms of Sine and Saloum as well. Unlike the Tukulor to their east, the Wolof and Serer resisted Islam initially.

Senegal's early history accounts for much of its present cultural diversity. The peoples of the northern grasslands and central savannas, such as the Wolof, Serer, Tukulor, and Fulani, share a tradition of centralized states and social hierarchies based on hereditary castes. They engaged in MILLET and sorghum cultivation and in long-distance trade. The Jola, Bañun (Bainounk), and Manjaco people of the forested southern Casamance region lacked such hierarchical traditions. For most of their history they lived in semiautonomous, relatively egalitarian villages organized by extended family units. They cultivated rice and traded in local markets. These peoples of the forest have generally resisted Islam and maintain their traditional religions to this day.

Arrival of Europeans and Shift to Atlantic Trade

With their exploration of the lower Senegal River in 1444, Portuguese navigators became the first Europeans known to visit Senegambia. The Portuguese soon began to export slaves, and the Wolof and Serer states imported horses, guns, brass, and iron bars. Until the end of the sixteenth century the Senegambian region was the most important source of slaves for the TRANSATLANTIC SLAVE TRADE. During the seventeenth century other European states challenged Portuguese commercial dominance in the region. The Dutch built a series of coastal forts, the most famous of which, on GORÉE ISLAND, quickly developed into a major slave-trading station.

By the late 1600s the strongest European powers on the coast were France and Great Britain, neither of which was strong enough to drive out the other or penetrate the interior, which remained under the control of the indigenous population. In 1659 the French established a slave-trading post on the island of Saint-Louis at the mouth of the Senegal River; they later established a fort there. From Saint-Louis the French moved south. They occupied or destroyed Dutch forts and captured Gorée around 1677. During the eighteenth century Saint-Louis and Gorée developed a French-speaking black and mulatto population of merchants and workers who relied for their livelihoods on the Atlantic trade. The British, meanwhile, established themselves at the mouth of the GAMBIA RIVER in strongholds they would retain for more than 200 years. This division of British and French territory would eventually result in the independent nations of English-speaking The Gambia and French-speaking Senegal.

Slaves were the most profitable commodity in the eighteenth century, and Senegambia exported an average of 2,000 to 3,500 slaves each year. The largest market for slaves in the French empire was the colony of Saint-Domingue (present-day HAITI).

Senegal (At a Glance)

OFFICIAL NAME: Republic of Senegal

AREA: 196,190 sq km (about 74,552 sq mi)

LOCATION: Western Africa; borders the North Atlantic Ocean, Guinea-Bissau, Mali, Guinea, Gambia, and Mauritania

CAPITAL: Dakar (population 2,216,223; 2001 estimate)

OTHER MAJOR CITIES: Thiès (population 273,599), Kaolack (243,209), Ziguinchor (216,971), Rufisque (204,013), and Saint-Louis (154,496); 2001 estimates

POPULATION: 10,580,307 (2003 estimate)

POPULATION DENSITY: 54 persons per sq km (about 142 persons per sq mi)

POPULATION BELOW AGE 15: 43.7 percent (male 2,330,395; female 2,289,706); 2003 estimate

POPULATION GROWTH RATE: 2.56 percent (2003 estimate)

TOTAL FERTILITY RATE: 4.93 children born per woman (2003 estimate)

LIFE EXPECTANCY AT BIRTH: Total population: 56.37 years (male 54.83 years; female 57.95 years); 2003 estimate

INFANT MORTALITY RATE: 57.57 deaths per 1000 live births (2003 estimate)

LITERACY RATE (AGE 15 AND OVER WHO CAN READ AND WRITE): Total population: 40.2 percent (male 50 percent; female 30.7 percent); 2003 estimate

EDUCATION: Education is officially compulsory for all children between the ages of six and twelve, but only 48 percent of primary school–age children attended school in the late 1980s, and only 13 percent of secondary school–age children attended school.

LANGUAGES: French is the official language. Almost half the population also speaks Wolof, the most widely understood of the African languages, but Pulaar, Jola, and Mandinka are also spoken.

ETHNIC GROUPS: 43 percent of the population are Wolof. Other principal ethnic groups are the Pular, Serer, Jola, and Mandinka.

RELIGIONS: About 94 percent of the population are Sunni Muslim. About 5 percent are Christian (mostly Roman Catholic), and 1 percent follow indigenous beliefs.

CLIMATE: Senegal is arid desert in the north and tropical in the south. It has a transitional climate from the dry desert zone in the north to the moist tropical zone in the south. The rainy season lasts from May to November in the north. Average rainfall in the north averages about 350 mm (14 in). In the south the rainy season lasts from June to October, with an average rainfall of about 1,525 mm (about 60 in). Average temperatures on the coast are 22° C (72° F) in January and 28° C (82° F) in July.

LAND, PLANTS, AND ANIMALS: The northern part of Senegal is part of the Sahel, a transition zone between the Sahara Desert on the north and the wetter regions to the south. Vegetation toward the south consists mainly of savanna grass with scattered clumps of trees and spiny shrubs. Farther south, near the Gambia River, trees are more common; in the extreme south there are mangrove swamps and dense forests of oil palms, mahogany, teak, and bamboo. Animals include elephants, lions, cheetahs, and antelope in the less populated eastern half of the country. In the rivers there are hippopotamuses and crocodiles. Senegal also has cobras and boa constrictors.

NATURAL RESOURCES: Mineral resources include phosphates and iron ore. The deposits of iron ore, however, have not been exploited because of their remoteness. Senegal also has reserves of petroleum and natural gas offshore.

CURRENCY: The Communauté Financière Africaine (CFA) franc

GROSS DOMESTIC PRODUCT (GDP): $16.2 billion (2002 estimate)

GDP PER CAPITA: $1,500 (2002 estimate)

GDP REAL GROWTH RATE: 5 percent (2002 estimate)

PRIMARY ECONOMIC ACTIVITIES: Agriculture (employing 78 percent of the labor force), roundwood production, fishing, phosphate mining, and manufacturing

PRIMARY CROPS: Peanuts, millet, corn, sorghum, rice, cotton, tomatoes, green vegetables, and livestock

INDUSTRIES: Agricultural and fish processing, phosphate mining, petroleum refining, and construction materials

PRIMARY EXPORTS: Fish, peanuts, petroleum products, phosphates, and cotton

PRIMARY IMPORTS: Foods and beverages, consumer goods, capital goods, and petroleum

PRIMARY TRADE PARTNERS: European Union (France especially), Nigeria, Côte d'Ivoire, Algeria, China, and Japan

GOVERNMENT: Senegal is a constitutional republic under a multiparty democracy. The executive branch is led by President Abdoulaye Wade, who appointed Prime Minister Idrissa Seck. The prime minister appoints the cabinet, called the Council of Ministers. The legislative branch is the elected, 120-member National Assembly, currently dominated by President Diouf's party, the Socialist Party.

In addition to slaves, major exports included gum arabic, leather, ivory, wax, and gold.

The slave trade and the introduction of modern weaponry disrupted traditional social and political patterns and indirectly fostered the spread of Islam. During the late sixteenth century the Jolof kingdom disintegrated into the rival kingdoms of Jolof, Walo, Cayor, Baol, Sine, and Saloum. Meanwhile, the Tukulor kingdom of Fouta Toro in the northeast and the Mandinka-dominated kingdom of Kaabu in the southeast asserted their independence from the crumbling Mali empire. The competition to supply slaves gave rise to continuous fighting among these states. The emphasis on war reduced food production and caused famine in some areas. Around 1673–1677 Muslim clerics, or MARABOUTS, led an antislavery revolt and tried to topple the slave-trading African aristocracies of the Senegambian states. With French armaments brought from Saint-Louis, the aristocrats were able to crush the revolt. However, the episode doubtless helped spread Islam among the peasantry, who were the main victims of slavery.

French Colony

The spread of Islam and French expansionism occurred simultaneously during the late eighteenth and nineteenth centuries; these two forces shaped modern Senegal. Around 1776 Tukulor marabouts overthrew the Denianké Dynasty that had ruled the state of Fouta Toro for nearly 300 years. The Islamic theocracy they set up in its place sent missionaries throughout the region.

The French slave trade declined after the slave revolt in Saint-Domingue, which began in 1791 and resulted in the independent nation of Haiti. In 1848, France outlawed slavery. The French made several failed attempts to find alternative sources of profit. During the 1830s the French extended their network of trading posts to the southern Casamance region. Finally, during the 1840s, peanuts grown in the central region proved a lucrative export crop.

The lure of the peanut trade spurred the imperialistic government of the French emperor Napoleon III to expand its control over Senegal after 1850. The French wanted to end the economic autonomy of the African states, which controlled inland trading routes and charged tariffs on products crossing their territory. Dakar, which had been a trading post since 1750, was developed as a planned town in 1862 and its port was equipped to handle exports from nearby peanut-growing regions. During the 1850s and 1860s Governor Louis Faidherbe conquered the Wolof and Serer states. These were the first African states to come under direct French control, and their conquest marked the beginning of France's colonial empire in Africa. Faidherbe built a series of forts along the Senegal River and stopped a Muslim advance from the east. About the same time a Tukulor religious leader named UMAR TAL began to attract numerous followers. Starting in 1854 he waged a series of jihads, or "holy wars," in the Senegal and Niger river valleys. The French concluded a treaty with Umar in 1857 in which he agreed to tolerate a French presence in present-day Senegal. During the 1860s, however, African leader Lat Jor Jop began to mount a successful campaign to end French domination in Cayor. In 1871 the French were forced to withdraw from Cayor.

In 1879 the French launched a second campaign of expansion. They built a series of rail lines that facilitated French domination by moving troops inland and bringing peanuts to French-controlled ports. Africa's first railroad connected Dakar to Saint-Louis and to major peanut-growing regions. After three years of fighting to build the railroad through Cayor, the French finally reconquered the state in 1886.

After the defeat of the Wolof rulers, who maintained traditional religious beliefs, many Wolof turned for leadership to a Wolof Muslim cleric, Ahmadu Bamba Mbake. Ahmadu Bamba founded the Muridiyah brotherhood, which converted many Senegalese to Islam and is today the largest and most important Islamic brotherhood in Senegal. Though the French initially feared the authority of Ahmadu Bamba and other powerful marabouts, they eventually sought to cooperate with these leaders, whose doctrines furthered the commercial interests of the French. Ahmadu Bamba and other marabouts urged their rural followers to work hard raising peanuts and to show their devotion by donating their income to the Muridiyah, who steadily gained influence in Senegal's interior.

During the 1890s the French embarked on a campaign of conquest throughout West Africa. Senegal served as a base for this conquest. The campaign included the brutal so-called pacification of the Casamance, which was not fully subjugated until the 1920s. In 1895 the French established the colony of French West Africa, with its capital at Dakar after 1902. Dakar thus became the administrative center for a huge region. Completion of a rail line to BAMAKO in 1923 made Dakar the main port for the vast Niger valley as well.

Senegal was unique among African colonies before World War II in that some of its African residents enjoyed rights as French citizens. In 1890 France extended full citizenship rights to African males living in the Four Communes: Saint-Louis, Dakar, Gorée, and Rufisque. These men had access to a French education and could vote and hold office, provided they were familiar with French language and culture. Dakar, Gorée, and Saint-Louis were France's oldest African possessions, with solid French-speaking African populations. Although these areas contained no more than 5 percent of Senegal's population, the elite society located there would become extremely influential. Senegalese from these towns served as administrators throughout France's African colonies. Senegal thus acquired a leadership role in Francophone Africa far out of proportion to its size.

Peanut production increased from 45,000 to 300,000 tons between 1885 and 1914. The peanut trade made Senegal the richest colony in French West Africa, but mainly benefited the French trading companies and the principal marabouts. Farmers operating on credit often found it hard to pay off debt when peanut prices fell. Farmers often cultivated peanuts at the expense of other food crops, and this increased their dependence on the market for survival.

Recognizing the contribution of the marabouts to Senegal's commerce and its stability as a colony, the French granted them vast tracts of land beginning in the second decade of the twentieth century. The French thus won the marabouts' support for COLONIAL RULE, especially in the interior. In return some Muslim leaders enlisted troops for the French army in World War I to demonstrate their loyalty.

During the mid-twentieth century Senegal assumed a leadership role in French West African politics. In 1914 a French customs officer, BLAISE DIAGNE, became the first African deputy to the French National Assembly. In 1919 he founded the Republican Socialist Party, the first Western-style political party in the region. His leading opponent, LAMINE GUÈYE, Senegal's first black lawyer, took a different path. In 1929 Guèye founded the Senegalese Socialist Party, linked to the French Socialist Party. From 1936 to 1938 the Popular Front, led by the French Socialists, governed France. The Popular Front government eased harsh colonial policies in Africa, restricting the use of forced labor in the colonies, allowing Africans to form trade unions, and making it easier for Africans to become French citizens. Guèye organized Socialist Party chapters around Senegal, and encouraged educated Africans to become politically involved.

A decline in global demand for peanuts in the 1930s caused hardship in Senegal. Living standards declined and debt increased. France provided some relief by providing a guaranteed, protected market for Senegal's products. French banks and export firms, however, gained increased influence over Senegal's economy.

After World War II the French government extended the vote to rural Senegal, which gained a seat in the French assembly alongside that of the communes. Guèye won the election for the urban seat while his protégé, LÉOPOLD SÉDAR SENGHOR, won the rural seat. Senghor later broke with the Socialists and founded his own party, the Senegalese Democratic Bloc (BDS). The Socialists attracted support from the Four Communes and among workers and students, who were becoming increasingly radical. The BDS, on the other hand, received strong support from the newly enfranchised countryside, where the party formed ties with influential marabouts. The BDS gradually became the leading political party in Senegal.

In 1956 France permitted limited self-government within its African colonies. Two years later the Socialists and the BDS merged to form the Senegalese Progressive Union (UPS), which won a strong majority in the 1959 national elections. As demands for independence grew, the UPS negotiated with the French government for independence as part of a Mali Federation, combining present-day Senegal and Mali. On April 4, 1960, the federation became independent. However, rivalry between Senegal and Mali broke up the federation in August, and Senegal became an independent state with Senghor as president.

Independence

From 1960 until 1981 President Senghor dominated Senegalese politics, dispensing patronage with a generous hand to urban elites and rural leaders alike. Under Senghor, Senegal maintained a close relationship to France. Senegal supported the former colonial power's international policies in exchange for economic aid, military support, and a favored position for Senegalese products on the French market.

During the 1960s Senghor advocated African SOCIALISM and instituted a series of Four Year plans. He increased the government's role in the economy by establishing several state-owned firms, including one that controlled peanut prices paid to farmers and handled all peanut exports. The government maintained its alliance with the principal marabouts, who received higher prices for their harvests. Some sources have estimated that at independence, peanuts and their by-products comprised over 80 percent of Senegal's exports. Peanut processing and exporting represented nearly half of Senegal's industrial activity. France bought virtually all of Senegal's peanut production, providing price supports through 1967.

At first Senegal was a multiparty state with competitive elections. However, during a 1962 power struggle with prime minister Mamadou Dia, Senghor had Dia arrested, tried, and imprisoned. Senghor's government banned opposition parties and ran unopposed in subsequent elections. The lack of political debate generated considerable unrest. The government sent in the army to crush student and union strikes in 1968.

The end of French price supports for peanuts in 1967 exposed Senegal to the fluctuations of the global market. In the early 1970s a devastating drought in the Sahel and a rapid rise in the cost of imported oil caused an economic crisis. The World Bank estimated that between 1964 and 1974, Senegal's per capita income had dropped 21 percent in the cities and 3 percent in the countryside. Widespread hardship generated popular discontent.

At the root of the combined economic and political crisis was the fact that Senghor's socialism had failed to address profound structural problems in Senegal's economy. State control over the economy had simply replaced the French colonialists with an African bureaucratic elite rife with nepotism and corruption. During the mid-1970s Senghor and the ruling elite responded to popular discontent by instituting reforms that have been called the "passive revolution," which opened avenues for political opposition. By permitting limited opposition, the elite did not truly give up power; it simply switched tactics, replacing repression and authoritarianism with strategic alliances. In 1976 the government released Dia from prison, and a new constitution permitted three political parties. In 1978 Senghor easily won the first contested presidential election since 1963.

In response to the economic crisis of the 1970s the government promoted other industries, such as fishing and tourism, to reduce reliance on peanuts and phosphates. To fund these programs and pay for oil imports, Senghor's government had to borrow from foreign lenders, who gained increasing control over the Senegalese economy. The economy continued to stagnate, however, and as his popularity declined, Senghor resigned in 1981.

Senghor's protégé, ABDOU DIOUF, took office in 1981 and won every election until 2000. Diouf increased economic and political liberalism. Under pressure from the World Bank, International Monetary Fund, and other aid donors to implement STRUCTURAL ADJUSTMENT, he announced a program in 1985 to privatize state-owned firms, but few firms had actually been sold by the late 1990s. Lower inflation and reduced government spending improved Senegal's financial status in the eyes of the world, but Senegal's rural majority reaped little benefit from these apparent improvements. Meanwhile, the devaluation of Senegal's currency in 1994 by 50 percent caused a substantial jump in the cost of living. Diouf legalized all political parties, regardless of ideology. He included opposition leaders in the government and stressed national reconciliation.

Since Diouf came to power Senegal has had disputes with several of its neighbors. Senegalese troops entered The Gambia in 1981 to put down a coup, and the two governments proclaimed a regional alliance, the SENEGAMBIAN CONFEDERATION. The confederation disbanded in 1989 over Gambian fears of absorption into Senegal. Since then Senegal has accused its neighbor of tolerating massive smuggling. Senegal cut diplomatic relations with MAURITANIA in the late 1980s when a border dispute over grazing rights broke out along the two countries' common border. Bloody massacres occurred in both countries and resulted in the large-scale flight of Senegal's Moorish population to Mauritania, while Mauritania expelled thousands of black farmers to Senegal. Diplomatic relations and communications resumed following the 1991 Islamic Conference.

Around 1984 discontent in the rural Casamance region of Senegal, south of The Gambia, led to the beginning of an internal rebellion by the Movement of Democratic Forces of the Casamance (MFDC). The conflict has several causes. Many Casamance residents blame the region's economic stagnation on neglect by the central government. Although the rebellion is a regional rather than a purely ethnic conflict, religious and cultural differences also foster opposition to the Senegalese government within the region. Unlike other Senegalese, who are overwhelmingly Muslim, residents of the Casamance are largely Christian or adherents of traditional religions. The Catholic priest Diamacoune Senghor, along with Paris-based intellectuals, leads the rebels. Political objections accompany religious ones in this conflict: the Jola and other Casamance peoples resent the Wolof-dominated national government. The discontented region's geographic isolation from the rest of Senegal—it is sandwiched between Guinea-Bissau and The Gambia—has facilitated the rebellion, since it is easy for rebels to withdraw strategically across one of the neighboring borders. Groups such as Amnesty International have accused both the Senegalese government and the MFDC of torture and other human rights violations. The government and rebels have agreed to sporadic truces and negotiations, and France has attempted to mediate, but the rebellion continued in 1998.

The Casamance rebellion has contributed to uneasy relations between Senegal and its southern neighbor, Guinea-Bissau, which Senegal accused of aiding Casamance rebels during the late 1980s. The two countries also disputed offshore fishing and oil-mining rights. In a 1993 agreement Senegal agreed to share fishing and mineral rights with Guinea-Bissau, which in turn agreed to stop providing sanctuary for Casamance fighters. In 1998 forces with purported links to the MFDC mounted an armed rebellion against Guinea-Bissau's government. Senegalese forces intervened in the conflict at the request of Guinea-Bissau's former president Joao Vieira.

In March 2000 Abdoulaye Wade, leader of the Senegalese Democratic Party (PDS), was elected president. Wade came into office promising to solve the Casamance issue within 100 days, but he soon realized the problem was too complicated for a quick solution. He has also failed to significantly improve relations with The Gambia, which refuses to let Senegal build a bridge across Gambian territory to link northern and southern Senegal. Wade favors privatizing much of the economy and pursuing other free-market economic policies. However, Senegal's precarious economy places limits on how much Wade can accomplish, and the country relies heavily on foreign assistance. Although France remained Senegal's most important trading partner and provided about 20 percent of its foreign aid in the late 1990s, the French military and commercial presence in Senegal has diminished in recent decades.

See also Gold Trade; Ivory Trade; Salt Trade; Slavery in Africa

David P. Johnson, Jr.

Senegal River

One of West Africa's longest and most important rivers.

The Senegal River flows for 1,600 km (990 mi), through the countries of MALI, SENEGAL, and MAURITANIA, forming the border between the latter two countries. Its headwaters are located in the FOUTA DJALLON mountains in GUINEA; they meet to form the Senegal River in Bafoulabé, Mali. The river flows northwest, west, and then southwest in a sweeping arc and empties into the Atlantic Ocean near Saint-Louis, Senegal. Boats can navigate the Senegal year-round as far upstream as Podor, Senegal. During the rainy season (roughly July–November), boats reach Kayes, Mali, more than 800 km (500 mi) upstream from the Atlantic.

The Senegal differs from the region's other major rivers in that it flows year-round. In September the river floods, leaving fertile silt as the floodwaters recede. Rice, MILLET, maize, sorghum, tobacco, and sweet potatoes are grown along the Senegal's banks. Local fishermen catch carp, catfish, eel, and bass.

In the early 1970s the governments of Mali, Senegal, and Mauritania formed an international authority to provide for irrigation and hydroelectric power through the construction of the Diama and Manantali dams on the river. The results have been disappointing. Because the dams regulate the river's flow, the annual floods have diminished. This has necessitated the introduction of irrigated agriculture in place of the traditional flood-watered agriculture. Agricultural output decreased after the construction of the dams. The creation of freshwater reservoirs and canals for irrigation agriculture has led to an increase of water-borne diseases, such as MALARIA and schistosomiasis. In addition, the dams' electricity production was disappointing.

See also Diseases, Infectious, in Africa.

Robert Fay

Senegambia, Confederation of

Former federation incorporating both Senegal and The Gambia.

See also Gambia; Senegal.

Senegambia and Niger Territories

Former name of Mali.

See also Mali.

Senga

Ethnic group of Zambia; also known as Nsenga.

The Senga primarily inhabit eastern ZAMBIA. Others live in ZIMBABWE and MOZAMBIQUE. They speak a Bantu language related to that of the neighboring TONGA people. Over 300,000 people consider themselves Senga.

See also Bantu: Dispersion and Settlement.

Senghor, Léopold Sédar

1906–2001

Scholar, poet, philosopher, statesman, founder of the cultural and political movement known as Négritude and the first president of Senegal.

Demonstrating a rare combination of intellectual, artistic, and political skill, Léopold Sédar Senghor towered over modern SENEGAL, unlike any other figure in that country's history. Senghor's quest to find an artistic and political synthesis between African and European ways of life inspired his lifelong record of creative achievement. Although as a youth he immersed himself in French culture, his ultimate inability to become "a black-skinned Frenchman" led him to cultivate his "Africanness." He helped to define two of the key political and intellectual movements of twentieth-century Africa: AFRICAN SOCIALISM and NÉGRITUDE.

Born in Ndjitor, Senegal to a SERER father and a FULANI mother, Senghor strove to represent all of Senegal's peoples in his writing and politics. He attended Roman Catholic mission schools in what was then French West Africa, and in 1922 entered the Collège Libermann, a seminary in DAKAR, where he intended to study for the priesthood. He was forced to leave the seminary after participating in a demonstration against racism. After graduating from secondary school in 1928, Senghor won a scholarship to study in FRANCE.

While at the prestigious École Normale Supérieure in Paris, Senghor studied contemporary French literature, including the work of Charles Baudelaire, the subject of Senghor's thesis. Senghor also studied the intellectual underpinnings of French political thought between the two world wars. Georges Pompidou, who later became the French president, was a classmate and a friend. After some time teaching classics at schools in Tours and Paris, Senghor was drafted into the French Army at the start of World War II (1939–1945),

Outside of class, Senghor absorbed the intellectual ferment of Paris in the 1930s. Black students, writers, and artists from Africa, North America, and the Caribbean were discovering their common roots and defining their identities in opposition to colonial rule. The PAN-AFRICAN CONGRESS OF 1919, the writings of W. E. B. DU BOIS, and the HARLEM RENAISSANCE all recognized and celebrated a growing black confidence and self-awareness, and this intellectual awakening greatly influenced Senghor and his contemporaries. In 1932 Senghor met AIMÉ CÉSAIRE, a writer from MARTINIQUE who would become an influential literary figure. Césaire and Senghor cofounded a newspaper, *L'Étudiant noir* (The Black Student) and promoted a new artistic and intellectual movement, Négritude. The movement went beyond opposition to colonialism to attack white racism. Négritude sought to explore the common experience of peoples of African descent and to formulate a new black identity. Senghor would later say that the philosophy embodies the "sum total of African values of civilization."

The years after World War II were the high point of Senghor's political career. In 1945 and 1946 Senghor, along with his political mentor, LAMINE GUÈYE, was elected to represent Senegal in the French Constituent Assembly (later the National Assembly). He won reelection and served in the National Assembly until 1958. Meanwhile, in 1948, he became a professor at the École Nationale de la France d'Outre Mer.

In 1959 Senghor helped to establish the Mali Federation, an alliance between French Equatorial Africa and French West Africa (present-day Senegal, Mali, Benin, and Burkina Faso), and appealed to French president Charles de Gaulle for independence. Several months later the federation collapsed, and Senghor was elected the first president of the independent republic of Senegal. As a Serer Christian leading a predominantly Muslim and WOLOF country, Senghor's political career itself can be considered an expression of Négritude, in that his African cultural background enabled him to serve and lead his people despite these differences.

Senghor also launched his literary career in earnest in 1945 with the publication of his first book of poetry, *Songs of the Shadow*. Two years later, in collaboration with fellow Senegalese ALIOUNE DIOP, he helped launch the journal *PRÉSENCE AFRICAINE*, which showcased African literature, including Senghor's writing. Torn between two very different worlds, Senghor dramatized the identity crisis of the westernized African. He pushed French poetry past its preoccupation with the exotic, implying a detachment from the other. Instead, Senghor's poetry presents a personal confrontation with Africa past and present. "Black Woman," one of his most famous poems, uses classical Western themes to describe the figure of an African woman and, by extension, black humanity.

Throughout the next two decades, a number of other poetry volumes followed and received critical acclaim both for their vivid language and imagery and for their broader themes. Senghor published less during the years of his presidency. However, he won the Apollinaire Prize for Poetry in 1974, and he published volumes of poetry in 1979 and in 1980.

As Senegalese president during the 1960s and 1970s, Senghor implemented a moderate (pro-Western) form of African socialism, in which the state played a major role in the economy in alliance with the established indigenous elite. He also replaced Senegal's multiparty democracy in the early 1960s with a one-party authoritarian state. In the so-called "passive revolution" of 1976, Senghor responded to economic and political stagnation by introducing greater political and economic freedom. Senegal's economic crisis persisted, however, and bowing to popular discontent, Senghor retired from office in 1981, one of the few African rulers to voluntarily relinquish power. He left a legacy of relative stability and freedom of expression in Senegal. Senghor had monopolized power and discouraged debate and opposition, perhaps contributing to the stagnation of Senegalese politics.

After his retirement, Senghor resettled in Verson, France, his wife's hometown. In 1988 he published a philosophical memoir entitled *Ce que je crois* (What I Believe). During the 1990s he published poetry, and he lived in quiet seclusion until his death in 2001.

See also Pan-Africanism.

David P. Johnson, Jr.

Senufo

Ethnic group of Côte d'Ivoire, Mali, and Burkina Faso; also known as the Siena and Sene.

There are more than three million ethnic Senufo. Many of them live in the Middle Volta valley, between the Bagoe, Bani, and Mouhoun (formerly Black Volta) rivers in West Africa. The Senufo ancestry is not entirely known. Some, at least, are believed to have migrated north from the area around Odienne (in modern-day Côte d'Ivoire) sometime prior to the seventeenth century C.E. As farmers, they adapted techniques for growing corn and MILLET on the region's poor soil.

The peoples now known as the northern, central, and southern Senufo had distinct histories. In the early seventeenth century, DYULA traders migrated from the collapsing SONGHAI empire into the Middle Volta valley and settled among the southern groups. The merchants called their peasant neighbors Senufo, a MANDE term for "those who speak Senari." The Dyula also converted many Senufo chiefs to Islam, and in the eighteenth century the Dyula traders took control of the KONG empire.

Islam made relatively few advances among the northern Senufo (also known as the Supide or the Kenedougou) and central Senufo, at least not until the increased urban migration after WORLD WAR II (1939–1945); traditional Senufo religion has always emphasized the worship of ancestors and earth spirits. The Senufo's secret societies—Lo for men, Sandogo for women—provide for the transmission of ritual knowledge from one generation to the next. Elder Lo members also serve as consultants to village chiefs.

During the colonial era many Senufo migrated to work on cash-cropping schemes in more fertile areas to the south and west; today many Senufo youth still seek wage employment outside their rural homelands. Senufo farmers grow a variety of cash crops, depending on the local ecology. Certain towns in Senufo regions, such as Sikasso, Mali, have become important commercial centers

While the Senufo play relatively minor roles in the national governments of the countries in which they live, they have won international renown for their art. The most spectacular pieces are the sculptures of hornbill birds, which display long beaks and outstretched wings and stand more than four feet high. In recent years many Senufo artisans have begun producing for tourist markets.

See also Rites of Passage and Transition.

Bibliography

Goldwater, Robert. *Senufo Sculpture from West Africa.* New York Graphic Society, 1964.

Imperato, Pascal James. *Historical Dictionary of Mali.* Scarecrow Press, 1996.

Elizabeth Heath

Separate but Equal Doctrine

As stated by the Supreme Court of the United States in *Plessy v. Ferguson* (1896), the idea that providing public and educational facilities to black people separately from the rest of the population adequately fulfills a requirement of equal treatment.

For information on

Court case leading to the "separate but equal" decision: *See* Antoine, Caesar Carpetier; Desdunes, Rodolphe Lucien; *Plessy v. Ferguson*.

Entrenchment of the doctrine in law and custom: *See* Jim Crow; Straker, David Augustus.

Doctrine in operation: *See* Colleges and Universities, Historically Black, in the United States; Segregation in the United States.

Attacks on the doctrine: *See* Houston, Charles Hamilton; NAACP Legal Defense and Educational Fund; *Sweatt v. Painter*.

Defeat of the doctrine: *See* Brown v. Board of Education; Marshall, Thurgood; School Desegregation in the United States.

Serengeti National Park

Park in northern Tanzania.

Established in 1941, Serengeti National Park covers about 14,750 sq km (about 5,700 sq mi) and consists mainly of flat, open grassland, with a few rocky *kopjes* (small hills) and some areas of woodland and bushy savanna in the western part of the park. The Serengeti is the only national park in Africa where seasonal migrations of plains animals take place.

Serengeti National Park is inhabited by more than 200 species of birds and thirty-five species of plains mammals, including CHEETAHS, LEOPARDS, LIONS, and GIRAFFES. ZEBRAS, GNUS (large African antelopes also called wildebeests), gazelles, and elephants did not exist in large numbers in the park until the 1960s, when the rising human population in the region caused a shortage of natural resources and forced many of these animals into the protected area. About 200,000 zebras, two million gnus, one million gazelles, and thousands of elephants now live in the park. The plains of Serengeti National Park are also home to black RHINOCEROSES. During the rainy season, from November to May, millions of animals graze on the park's southeastern plains. This area has few rivers and becomes excessively dry once the rainy season ends, so gnus, gazelles, and zebras migrate to the western savanna and as far north as the grasslands of Masai Mara Game Park, across the KENYA-TANZANIA border, where they spend the dry season.

In 1981 the United Nations Educational, Scientific and Cultural Organization (UNESCO) declared the park a World Heritage Site. Illegal hunting in the park is a serious problem, posing a particular threat to the survival of elephants and rhinoceroses.

Serer

Ethnic group of western Senegal numbering around one million people; also known as Sarer.

The Serer live primarily in SENEGAL and represent one of the largest ethnic affiliations of Senegalese people. Some also live in GUINEA-BISSAU and THE GAMBIA. Their language is part of the Niger-Congo language family. Linguistically and culturally, they are related to the neighboring groups WOLOF, FULANI, and TEMNE. The Serer comprise several smaller subgroups, including the Cangin, which is rapidly becoming assimilated into the larger Wolof community. Most Serer farm MILLET, rice, and peanuts and raise cattle, while others, especially members of the subgroup known as the Nyominka, work as fishers.

Known in the region as being fiercely independent, for many years the Serer fought against outside influence, including that of Islam. Their resistance made them a target of religious warfare in the late nineteenth century, a conflict that ended only when French colonizers gained control of Senegal. Eventually more and more Serer converted to Islam. Serer social structure remains mostly matriarchal, where descent and inheritance are traced through the mother's line. Serer tradition permits polygyny, and in such cases each wife has her own thatched building.

Sermons and Preaching

Grounded in the church and based to a large extent on improvisation, African American speech acts, keyed to the preacher's cadences and rhythms, provided the aesthetic underpinnings for black oral expression. Forced to creatively imagine their face, black people created a mythology to affirm their tradition as valid and meaningful for all people.

The black preacher is the transformational agent who walks the critical tightrope between the sacred and the secular; his speech act (sermon) is the agent for historical location. As the taproot of black American discourse, the sermon historicizes the experiences of blacks in America. The sermon as agent provides a link between generations of black families and makes it possible for the culture of black America to be transmitted over time and for members of the community to adapt to changing external circumstances. In the process, black America's first poet transformed a venerable Western genre and enriched American discourse.

During the largely unrecorded first century and a half of black life in the United States (1619–1770), the African gods were suppressed and forced to adjust to a new reality. In spite of the indifference and antipathy directed at blacks, many of them in the North followed the religious practices of the New Englanders. Led by their priests-turned-preachers, black people in the South began the process of transforming a largely Protestant Christianity that was daily profaned in their midst, and heavily influenced by a staid English tradition, into one that served African functions.

The first Great Awakening, that tumultuous series of outdoor revivals and camp meetings that swept the country around 1740, made the Christian religion reasonably accessible to the black masses. These revivals paved the way for unordained black lay workers to seize the moment in the late eighteenth and early nineteenth centuries for the emergence of the historic black church as "the foundation of Afro-American culture." This independent black tradition was aptly termed "the Invisible Institution" by sociologist E. Franklin Frazier.

Two distinct but overlapping traditions emerged: the slave preachers or "exhorters" who brought color and drama to their imaginative retelling of the trials and triumphs of the Israelites in the Bible, and the learned tradition. The virtuoso style of the slave preacher has been variously described as "old-time Negro Preaching," "spiritual preaching," "whoopology," or "performed" preaching.

Representative figures of these traditions are Harry Hoosier ("Black Harry," d. 1810), who traveled throughout the United

States with Bishop Francis Ashbury, and RICHARD ALLEN (1760–1831). Hoosier, who some claimed to be the greatest orator in America, embodied the tradition of the slave exhorters. He represented the genius of "those black and unknown bards" who burst forth in all of their radiance in the wake of emancipation.

Allen represents those black preachers who preached from a manuscript or notes. Initially they were members of the Methodist Episcopal Church or Baptist Church, before founding their own black churches rather than remaining a segregated church within a church. These became the forerunners for the large urban congregations with a well-connected denominational church hierarchy. They took part in public policy debates at the state and national levels.

With several others in Philadelphia, Allen founded the Free Africa Society in 1787, the first organization for blacks in the United States. It was the institutional forerunner to the black church. Allen and Absalom Jones (1746–1818) founded the Bethel African Methodist Episcopal (AME) Church in 1816, which was the model for the Independent Black Church.

When George Washington (1732–1799) died, the Philadelphia *Gazette* published Richard Allen's Bethel AME Church sermon in which he stressed Washington's belated uneasiness about slavery as a sin. The first appearance of the summarized sermon in the historical record is an anonymous article entitled "Religious Intelligence: An Account of the Baptism of Nine Negroes in Boston, May 26, 1805." From its inception in the second decade of the nineteenth century, the Afro-Protestant press published sermons for distribution as well as news and literature for a community starved to know itself.

Among the early black preachers in America there were such men as David George (c. 1742–1810), preacher of the First Baptist Church at Silver Bluff, South Carolina; GEORGE LIELE (c. 1750–1820) of Burke County, Georgia, an eloquent preacher to blacks and whites; ANDREW BRYAN (1737–1812), founder of the First African Baptist Church of Savannah; the fearless NAT TURNER (1800–1831), who served as a kind of exhorter, preaching on Sundays to slaves and some white people; JOHN CHAVIS (c. 1763–1838) of North Carolina, who was commissioned as a missionary to slaves by the Presbyterians in 1801; and, most rare, LEMUEL HAYNES (1753–1833), a man of learning and eloquence who through all of his life pastored only white Congregational churches in New England.

Haynes, who could have passed for white, did not flaunt his color; he seems to have spoken only once on race and in condemnation of slavery. In "The Nature and Importance of True Republicanism" (1801), he addressed the question of the "pitiful, abject state" of the "poor African among us." In his most famous sermon, "Mystery Developed," Haynes discussed religion, prison conditions, and errant justice. Haynes stood with Jonathan Edwards and George Whitefield with respect to the operations of the Holy Spirit.

Among the earliest black preachers in the Methodist Episcopal Church were ABSALOM JONES, Richard Allen, DANIEL COKER, Abraham Thompson, Morris Brown, James Varick, Christopher Rush, and Henry Evans. FREDERICK DOUGLASS, who was licensed as a local AME Zion Church preacher, was fond of delivering his "Slaveholder's Sermon" to incite to action those who were fence straddlers in the cause of abolition.

The early black preachers shared a commonality of vision with generations of their pulpit brethren; they challenged the church to be relevant and asked the Lord to "give us this day our daily bread" as they created an African American aesthetic that the community recognized and endorsed.

Irrespective of their denominational affiliation, early black preachers were united in their call for freedom, justice, and human dignity. However, their solidarity with the patriarchal system blinded most of them to the injustices of their own practices, even when those practices were similar to what they were trying to escape from in the white church. For example, Richard Allen, the patron saint of the black church, had great difficulty in admitting women to the ministry.

Refusing to be silent in the face of black men taking advantages of their male privilege in relation to black women (which prefigures much of the post–Civil Rights Movement literature by black women writers), black women preachers vigorously critiqued America's shortcomings and black theologies for the apparent lack of black women in a society that tends to devalue both blackness and womanhood. Feeling obliged to proclaim the word, JARENA LEE, one of the most famous "daughters of thunder," issued the first official challenge to the restrictions on women preachers in a black denomination (c. 1811): "If the man may preach, because, the Savior died for him, why not the woman? seeing he died for her also. Is he not a whole Savior, instead of a half one? as those who hold it wrong for a woman to preach, would seem to make it appear" (Bert James Loewenberg and Ruth Bogin, eds., *Black Women in Nineteenth Century American Life*, 1976).

According to C. Eric Lincoln and Lawrence H. Mamiya, in *The Black Church in the African American Experience* (1990), black women were not "officially recognized or ordained as preachers" until the late nineteenth or early twentieth century, though slave women undoubtedly "preached in clandestine services." Unlike their male counterparts, they were required to take "sublimated paths to the ministry" as exhorters, teachers, missionaries, evangelists, religious writers, and wives of clergymen. The AME Zion Church ordained JULIA A. J. FOOTE (1823–1900) as a deacon in 1884 and ordained Mary J. Small as a deacon in 1894. In 1976, PAULI MURRAY (1910–1985) was consecrated and ordained as the first African American female priest of the Episcopal Church at the National Cathedral in Washington, D.C. In 1984 Leontine T. C. Kelly (b. 1930) became the first woman bishop of a major religious denomination in the United States when she was elected head of the United Methodists in the San Francisco area. On February 12, 1989, BARBARA HARRIS (b. 1930), an African American, became the first female Anglican bishop in the world.

Among the earliest black women preachers were Elizabeth, A Colored Preacher of the Gospel (1766–1867), Jarena Lee (1783–185?), *Zilpha Elaw* (c. 1790–184?), *Rebecca Cox Jackson* (1795–1871), and Amanda Berry Smith (1837–1915). Those women who took sublimated paths to the ministry include Maria W. Stewart (1830–1879), HARRIET TUBMAN (1823–1913), and SOJOURNER TRUTH (1797–1883); they were associated with religious abolitionism. Other notable religiously motivated black women became teachers, for example, FANNY JACKSON COPPIN (1836–1913), LUCY CRAFT LANEY (1854–1933), ANNA JULIA COOPER (1858–1964), MARY MCLEOD BETHUNE (1875–1955), and NANNIE HELEN BURROUGHS (1883–1961). Dr. Bethune often preached the required chapel service in the Daytona Normal School, the college she founded, which evolved into the Bethune-Cookman College. Until recently, black women were preachers sans portfolio in the large denominations.

Black religion with its Afro-Christian character surfaced in all of its glory in the wake of the Civil War. Simultaneously, divisions within the church became more pronounced as there was a push for an educated clergy. Preachers came to be defined as progressives as opposed to conservatives, spiritual rather than learned. The spiritual preachers placed a greater emphasis on the experiential dimension of religion, emotional and affective witnessing, and an ideology of blackness, as, for example, Baby Suggs in TONI MORRISON's *Beloved* (1987).

The learned clergy included men such as Peter Williams, Jr. (c. 1780–1840), Episcopal; Daniel A. Payne (1811–1893), AME; William H. Miles (1818–1892), Christian Methodist Episcopal; HENRY HIGHLAND GARNET (1850–1882), Presbyterian; ALEXANDER CRUMMELL (1819–1898), Episcopal; James Augustine Healey (1830–1900), Catholic; Henry McNeal Turner (1834–1915), AME; William Paul Quinn (1788–1873), AME; and FRANCIS J. GRIMKÉ (1850–1937), Presbyterian, described as the last black Puritan. Payne was the arch-antagonist of anti-intellectual tradition within the black church (as was BOOKER T. WASHINGTON, a deeply religious Baptist who often functioned as an unofficial preacher). He epitomized those blacks and whites who strove mightily to stamp out the resurgence of the "African cult," which they perceived as a threat to Western Christianity. Advocates of reparation, Crummell and Turner spent much time in West Africa. They left a diverse body of sermons.

The split in the black church that ensued in the wake of emancipation symbolizes the clash between African and European cultures. This division represents a cultural paradox in the black community: black vernacular tradition rooted in the church transformed American discourse, and its signature performance event was the performed sermon. Nevertheless, the black bourgeoisie who set the social agenda tended to suppress the Afrocentric character of the community. FRANCES ELLEN WATKINS HARPER (1825–1911), an effective orator, ardent social reformer, active figure in the education of blacks, and widely published author, articulated these ideological tensions in her novel of uplift, *Iola Leroy* (1892). The simmering tension provided a dynamic subtext for the HARLEM RENAISSANCE debate on the authenticity of black culture in the 1920s, which flared anew with the cultural nationalism of the BLACK ARTS MOVEMENT in the 1960s.

In spite of black America's move to assimilate, the end of the nineteenth century was dominated by the flamboyant JOHN JASPER (1812–1901), who was steeped in the tradition of the "classic" folk preacher. This Richmond-based Baptist preacher's most famous sermon was "The Sun Do Move." In 1908 William E. Hatcher recorded some of Jasper's sermons and published them under the title *From John Jasper*. Perhaps the first widely available collection of black sermons may have been the book *Elder Cotney's Sermons, Gullah Negro Sermons*, edited by John G. Williams (1895).

The self-consciousness of the sermon as art form marked the beginning of the twentieth century. W. E. B. DU BOIS in *The Souls of Black Folk* (1903) and JAMES WELDON JOHNSON in *God's Trombones: Seven Negro Sermons in Verse* (1927) freed the depiction of the black folk preacher from the constraints of dialect under which CHARLES WADDELL CHESNUTT (1858–1932) and PAUL LAURENCE DUNBAR (1872–1906) chafed, and made him palatable to a growing black middle class ambivalent about its place in American society. As sturdy black cultural bridges, Du Bois and Johnson showed a budding generation of black writers that the black sermon supplied the mythic frame through which the community viewed life in the United States from SPIRITUALS, slave seculars, and SLAVE NARRATIVES to BLUES, JAZZ, poetry, prose fiction, drama, and, later, RAP MUSIC. Their sage observations on black American religious life marked an important milestone in American cultural studies as they revealed the preacher as both a product and a producer of an aesthetic tradition.

Structurally, Du Bois's *Souls*, a mixture of theory, history, and sociology, soars with the rhetoric of the black preacher. Replete with words and imagery straight from the black pulpit, Du Bois's language took on the same biblical flavor black Americans used in the campaign to abolish slavery and to end the nightmare of Reconstruction—the South as Egypt, the promised land, and Canaan. Finally, Du Bois's incisive commentary in "Of the Faith of the Fathers" set the tone for American scholarship on the black church.

With the echo of Jasper's "whooped" sermon at his back, James Weldon Johnson in *God's Trombones* captured the essence of the classic black preacher. Johnson wrote these seven literary sermons "after the manner" of the preacher who is the master of metaphor, triumphant, transcendent, and moving in concert with the community. Johnson, as he notes in his preface, draws on a repertory of classic black sermons that includes the "Valley of the Dry Bones," the "Train Sermon," the "Heavenly March," and the "Creation."

The art and imagination of the black preacher informs the work of numerous Harlem Renaissance figures, such as JEAN TOOMER, LANGSTON HUGHES, COUNTEE CULLEN, and ZORA NEALE HURSTON. The preacher as archetypal performer is the transitional figure in Toomer's modernist text *Cane* (1923). Toomer structures much of his text around the dialogic call-and-response that is a staple of black religious discourse. Hughes devotes a section of his first poetry collection, *The Weary Blues* (1926), as well as a section of his *Selected Poems* (1959), to poems shaped by the sermon. The textual richness of the symbolic universe of the black preacher informs *Not Without Laughter* (1930), "Thank You M'am" (1934), and *Tambourines to Glory* (1958).

Cullen was the adopted son of the Reverend Frederick A. Cullen of Harlem's fashionable Salem Methodist Episcopal

Church; his poetic imagination was governed by an abiding Christian view of the world, as is evident in *The Black Christ and Other Poems* (1929). Much of his religious poetry is filtered through the lens of a vibrant black preaching tradition.

In her 1935 collection of folklore, *Mules and Men,* Hurston included an excerpt from a folk sermon. The sermon is the organizing principle in *Jonah's Gourd Vine* (1934) and *Their Eyes Were Watching God* (1937). Deeply influenced by the power of language and myth in and out of the homiletical mode, *Their Eyes Were Watching God* focuses on the emergence of a female self in a male-dominated world. Hurston also brought a theoretical bent to the Black Aesthetic tradition in her essays published as *The Sanctified Church* (1983).

In addition, Hurston, along with John and Alan Lomax, recorded authentic sermons in the 1930s for the Library of Congress's Archive of Folk Song. In 1941 the black folk sermon formally entered the academy with the publication of the landmark anthology *The Negro Caravan*, edited by STERLING A. BROWN, Arthur P. Davis, and Ulysses Lee. Sermons now appear in most anthologies of American and African American literature.

Other archival work on the black sermon includes nine sermons recorded by sociologist Charles S. Johnson for FISK UNIVERSITY and John Henry Faulk's two-year study on black sermons in Texas, sponsored by the Julius Rosenwald Fund. They formed the core of Faulk's 1941 University of Texas M.A. thesis, "Quickened by de Spurit." Alice Jones's 1942 M.A. thesis for Fisk University was entitled "The Negro Folk Sermon: A Study in the Sociology of Folk Culture." Perceptive studies of African American sermonry include William H. Pipes, *Say Amen Brother!* (1951); J. Mason Brewer, *The Word on the Brazos: Negro Preacher Tales from the Brazos Bottoms of Texas* (1953); Bruce Rosenburg, *Can Those Bones Live?: The Art of the American Folk Preacher* (1970); Henry H. Mitchell, *Black Preaching* (1970); Hortense J. Spillers, "Fabrics of History: Essays on the Black Sermon" (Ph.D. diss., Brandeis University, 1974); Gerald L. Davis, *I Got the Word in Me and I Can Sing It, You Know: A Study of the Performed African-American Sermon* (1985); and Dolan Hubbard, *The Sermon and the African American Literary Imagination* (1994).

The archival collections of African Americana held in the libraries of Fisk, HOWARD UNIVERSITY, the Atlanta University Center, other African American institutions, Boston University, the Library of Congress, and other municipal and university libraries around the nation include a number of significant and historically important sermons "published" by African American preachers or their congregations. For example, the MOORLAND-SPINGARN RESEARCH COLLECTION at Howard University is the repository for the sermons of Francis J. Grimké, BENJAMIN E. MAYS, and HOWARD THURMAN.

The GREAT MIGRATION coincided with the emerging cultural industry in the United States. "Race records" were located at the juncture between black transition from peasant culture to denizens of the city with its emergent jazz aesthetics. They presented black America with an alternative venue to the mainstream commercial recording firms. One of the foremost preaching stars of the "race records" was the Reverend J. M. Gates, whose sermon records in the 1920s were exceeded in the "race record" market only by BESSIE SMITH'S blues. Among those preachers that he influenced was Clarence LaVaughn Franklin (1915–1984), who shaped the religious imagination of the generation of preachers who came of age during the CIVIL RIGHTS MOVEMENT.

The classic novels of the Great Migration introduce the notion of history as a sermon. In *Native Son* (1940) by RICHARD WRIGHT, in *Go Tell It on the Mountain* (1953) by JAMES BALDWIN (as well as his play *The Amen Corner*, 1968), and in INVISIBLE MAN (1952) by RALPH ELLISON, the storefront (sanctified) church is the site where blacks contest modernity and its implications for a people trapped in a perpetual present, acutely aware of their liminal status. Wright subverts the sermon, placing it in the mouth of attorney Boris Max and his passionate defense of Bigger Thomas as if to indict America for its failure to deal affirmatively with the problem of black suffering; Ellison uses sermonic rhetoric to enable his nameless narrator trapped outside of history to structure "the blackness of blackness"; and Baldwin, whose *Go Tell It* represents the apotheosis of the sermon in African American literature, reconstructs the corporate biography to tell how the community "looks back and wonders how we got ovah." This is the autobiographical impulse that drives black American religious discourse.

The civil rights movement presented black America as one nation under a sermon. Echoing the sentiments of anonymous black folk preachers, MARTIN LUTHER KING, JR., invited the nation to step out on space and time and join his downtrodden community in making a more humane world. He called on Americans to adhere to the primary written cultural text (minus the discourse of racism) to which each American pledges allegiance. In his most famous sermon, "I Have a Dream" (1963), King captures the national community's sense of metaphysical possibility when he says, as James Weldon Johnson's preacher does in *God's Trombones*, "Ill make me a world." At that moment he gave the nation a breathtaking vision of the Heavenly City. The essential writings of King are contained in *A Testament of Hope* (1987).

The hegemonic rhetoric of the sermon enabled people, regardless of their ideological orientation, to talk across socioeconomic lines as well as to demand full participation in the American dream. As a consciousness-raising activity, the civil rights movement spawned a call for a black nationalism (SNCC, Black Panthers, MALCOLM X), a black theology (James A. Cone), and a womanist theology (Alice Walker). These diverse voices disturbed the popular imagination when they suggested that we are not one nation under a sermon. Cultural nationalists whose work was influenced by the sermon include AMIRI BARAKA, Haki R. Madhubuti, SONIA SANCHEZ, and Carolyn M. Rodgers.

While King was calling on the republic to end its legacy of racism, black women, who were the backbone of the civil rights movement, were calling on the male-dominated pulpit fraternity to end its legacy of sexism. Alice Walker painted in broad brush strokes the outlines for WOMANISM in *In Search of Our Mothers' Gardens* (1983). It embraces the elements of tradition, community, self, and a critique of white feminist thought. The term was first used in print in Delores S. Williams's 1987 article "Womanist Theology: Black Women's Voices." Womanist theology signals black women's move from the pew to the pulpit. The essential challenge, however, remains to bring the word.

The cultural logic of the sermon infuses the fictive world of diverse African American women writers such as Alice Walker, Toni Morrison, GLORIA NAYLOR, and NTOZAKE SHANGE. In *for colored girls who have considered suicide / when the rainbow is enuf* (1975), Shange captures the temper of a woman-centered discourse when the seven sisters in this choreopoem join hands at its conclusion and chant, "i found god in myself & i loved her." Using sermonic rhetoric as an entrée, black women writers interrogate the ideological, cultural, and sexual politics that take place under the cover of a male-dominated racial mountain. The self-voicing that emerges out of their work evinces a concern for nurturing and female independence.

Perhaps the most imitated preacher of his era, the incomparable C. L. Franklin (1915–1984), described as "the high priest of soul preaching," influenced a generation of black preachers who came of age during the civil rights movement. Franklin, paster of Detroit's New Bethel Baptist Church, was a master of orality and technology. The recorded sermons of this Mississippian swept through a segregated black America like fire shut up in their bones. Among the preachers he influenced were Jasper Williams, Gardener Taylor, Martin Luther King, Jr., Clay Evans, C. L. Moore, Caesar Clark, Donald Parsons, and Jesse L. Jackson. Twenty of Franklin's best sermons have been published as *Give Me This Mountain* (1989). One of his best known sermons is "The Eagle Stirreth Her Nest."

Other outstanding black preachers of the second half of the twentieth century include: Howard Thurman, Benjamin E. Mays, ADAM CLAYTON POWELL, JR., Manuel L. Scott, William Holmes Borders, Wyatt T. Walker, Malcolm X, Samuel D. Proctor, Ozro T. Jones, Jr., CALVIN BUTTS, and Frank Madison Reid III. Notable sermon collections include William M. Philpot's *Best Black Sermons* (1972) and Samuel D. Proctor and William D. Watley's *Sermons from the Black Pulpit* (1984).

The triumph of the sermon in the black American literary imagination is the triumph of aesthetics. It issued directly out of the ethos of the slave community. African American writers transformed the responsive mythology of African American expressive culture, rooted in music and religion, into arresting artistic statements. Their resulting novels, poems, plays, autobiographies, and rap music, those polyvocal jeremiads, interact with each other in complex ways to constitute a specifically African American literary tradition. Their artistic statements speak to African Americans of history in their own words and rhythms and radiate the promise of the future. The preacher, as a sign of black people's subjugation and affirmation, represents the opaque community's historic struggle over language and, consequently, for self-definition. Through speech acts (sermons), the preacher provides the vehicle by which the entire community of faith may participate in shaping its own history and restructuring cultural memory.

Like preachers, black writers unite in their interrogation of what it means to be black in the United States, accenting the connections of their sermons with blacks' varied selves and with both historical and current social conditions. They transform historical consciousness into art, use it as a strategy for representation, and merge it with the political as they present the emergence of a self. The preachers preach beyond the ending of their earthly situation, while the writers write beyond the frame of their time-bound text. The preacher's voice and the writer's pen are the metonymically displaced voice of the community. The black sermon is the mother's milk of African American discourse.

See also Black Church, The.

Bibliography

Hamilton, Charles V. *The Black Preacher in America*, 1972.

Hubbard, Doland. *The Sermon and the African American Literary Imagination*, 1994.

Mitchell, Henry H. *Black Preaching*, 1970.

Overton, Betty J. "Black Women Preachers: A Literary Overview," *Southern Quarterly* 23.3 (Spring 1985); 157–166.

Southern, Eileen, and Josephine Wright. Introduction to *African American Traditions in Song, Sermon, Tale, and Dance 1600s–1920*, 1990.

Washington, James Melvin. *Conversations with God: Two Centuries of Prayers by African Americans*, 1994.

Dolan Hubbard

Serra y Montalvo, Rafael

1858–1909

Cuban poet, journalist, exile, independence leader, and close friend and collaborator of José Martí.

At age thirteen, after finishing primary school, Rafael Serra y Montalvo became a tobacco apprentice. *Tabaqueros* (tobacco workers) were known as the aristocrats of the working class, in part because they were generally well paid but also because of their expensive tastes. Serra was largely self-educated and developed a special affinity for literature. As a young man, he founded primary schools in CUBA that were free of charge, both in HAVANA and in MATANZAS. In 1879 he also established La Armonía (Harmony), a hybrid social welfare and political organization, and began to publish a pro-independence political weekly by the same name. He gradually established himself as a young firebrand, gaining popularity and political prestige.

By 1880, under pressure by a high-ranking colonel to join the military—perhaps to silence his journalistic voice—Serra instead accompanied MARTÍN MORÚA DELGADO, an Afro-Cuban who had been organizing workers at the time, to Key West, Florida, where they lived in exile. There, they reignited cries for Cuban independence that had been squelched by the Zanjón Pact of 1878 (the treaty that ended the TEN YEARS' WAR, a failed war to win independence). He continued to lead and organize political and welfare organizations, and integrated his literary and political interests through poetry readings and through directing the San Carlos Center, where Cuban exiles met for cultural expression and political organization.

Yet Serra's stay in Key West was relatively brief. He soon joined other exiles in NEW YORK who organized resistance to the colonial regime and published Spanish-language newspapers stateside. In 1885 he published his first book, *Ecos del alma* (Echoes of the Soul), in JAMAICA. During this period he helped plan and participated in the Cuban invasion of the same year masterminded by Máximo Gómez and ANTONIO MACEO. When the attempt to secure independence failed, its organizers scattered across the continent. Serra fled to PANAMA and then to Kingston, Jamaica, where he compiled poetry and published *Ideas y pensamientos, album poético, político y literario* (Ideas and Thoughts, Poetic Album, Political and Literary) in 1886.

In 1887 Serra returned once again to New York, where he submitted letters and articles to periodicals in Havana, Matanzas, and New York in support of the independence movement. Active in a number of political and social organizations, he served as secretary for the club Los Independientes and participated in the Cuerpo de Consejo de New York. In 1892 Serra published his first prose book, *Ensayos políticos* (Political Essays), and, in 1894, a short-lived illustrated political and literary journal called *La Verdad* (Truth). With José Martí, Cuba's most famous poet-patriot, he was a founder of the Partido Revolucionario Cubano, the political party organized to fight for Cuban independence, and its newspaper, *Patria* (Fatherland). In 1890 he had established La Liga, a school for Afro-Cubans and Afro–Puerto Ricans living in New York, whose aim was to spread the anticolonial message. La Liga opened branches in Tampa, Florida; Havana; and Santiago de Cuba. These two organizations, the party and the school, influenced many to take up the cause of independence. On February 24, 1895, the CUBAN WAR OF INDEPENDENCE began.

That same year, Martí was killed in battle. In 1896 Serra and the Revolutionary Party published a key illustrated periodical entitled *La Dóctrina de Martí* (Martí's Doctrine). This newspaper repeatedly highlighted the need to address racial discrimination and social reform after independence, neither of which could be taken for granted with the end of colonialism. Also in 1896 he published the second volume of *Ensayos políticos*. It included further articles and letters to him from eminent patriots, including Pedro Betancourt, JUAN GUALBERTO GÓMEZ, José Martí, and others. These documents acknowledged the important role Serra played in the independence movement, from organizing exiles in the United States to laying some of the intellectual foundation for the rebellion. In 1902 Serra returned to Cuba, where he published another journal, *El Nuevo Criollo* (The New Creole). The journal criticized the continued discrimination that Afro-Cubans faced in employment and in social venues as well as government efforts to encourage European immigration so as to "whiten" the country. Serra published two more books before his death: *Para blancos y negros* (For Blacks and Whites) in 1907 and *La república posible* (The Possible Republic) in 1909, which further developed some of his ideas about a multiracial Cuba and the ideological contours of an independent Cuba, first put forth in *Nuevo Criollo*. Martí best summed up Serra's contributions when he characterized him as an "indefatigable worker for our independence."

See also Whitening.

Joy Elizondo

Serval

Long-legged wildcat native to grasslands and brush country of Algeria, Morocco, and sub-Saharan Africa.

The serval is buff-colored, with black spots in rows sometimes merging into stripes down its back and legs. It has a slender body 0.67 to 1 m (2.2 to 3 ft) long and 54 to 62 cm (21 to 24 in) high at the shoulder and a small head with long, rounded ears; it weighs 8.7 to 18 kg (19 to 40 lb). The serval feeds mostly on small mammals, lizards, and birds, although it is powerful enough to kill young ANTELOPE. It hunts by speed and climbs trees well. When captured young, servals can be tamed, but they are difficult to raise.

Scientific classification: The serval belongs to the family Felidae. It is classified as *Felis serval*.

Seven-Seven, Twins

1944–

Nigerian painter, musician, politician, and businessman.

The only survivor in a line of seven sets of twins, Twins Seven-Seven, who was born Taiwo Olaniyi Salan in Ogidi, NIGERIA, named himself to honor this unusual lineage. He began his career as a musician and dancer, and has several records and tours to his credit. Twins Seven-Seven first discovered painting and the graphic arts when he encountered the Mbari Mbayo Club by chance in 1964. The group eventually evolved into the Oshobgo School, a well-known community of Nigerian artists. Ulli Beier, a member of the group, and Seven-Seven wrote a book about Twins's work called *A Dreaming Life*.

Initially, Twins Seven-Seven focused on drawing. His early work demonstrates an attention to fine detail—he would fill the entire visual field with lines and patterns. When Twins Seven-Seven began to paint, he worked on flat sheets of plywood that he pieced together and layered to create a collage effect. His images draw on the YORUBA religion and folklore of central Nigeria, and his themes explore connections between the spiritual and earthly worlds.

During his career, Seven-Seven has been honored with several chieftaincy titles. He currently lives in the United States and exhibits his work in galleries and museums throughout the world. In 2000 his paintings were shown at the National Gallery of African Art in Washington, D.C., in a show called *Oshogbo:*

The Early Years. The Maryland Museum of Art gave him a one-man show, and the Indianapolis Museum of Art featured his work in its Contemporary African Art wing. In 2002 the University of California at Santa Cruz included some of his pieces in the Santa Cruz festival of Global African Music.

See also Artists, African.

Christopher Tiné

Seychelles

African country located in the Indian Ocean and consisting of over one hundred islands.

Strung out along 115 islands and coral atolls in the Indian Ocean, Seychelles is one of the smallest countries in the world, 455 square kilometers (174 square miles) of land scattered across 1.35 million square kilometers (500,000 square miles) of ocean. The vast majority of its 82,800 inhabitants (2004 estimate) live on the largest islands, Mahé, Praslin, and La Digue. Unlike other Indian Ocean island nations, such as MAURITIUS, Seychelles is marked by a relatively homogenous population of mixed African and European descent, except for small Indian, Chinese, and European communities. Despite nearly 200 years of British rule, French cultural influences such as the Catholic Church are still evident, as are African religious practices. Given the islands' small size and poor soil, the inhabitants of the Seychelles have long depended on passersby to sustain their economy. Once a base for pirates and then a supply post for Indian Ocean merchant ships, Seychelles now draws large numbers of beach-loving tourists as well as entrepreneurs attracted to its relatively open investment policies.

Precolonial History

Located 1,600 kilometers (1,000 miles) from the nearest mainland shore, the scattered archipelago was uninhabited by humans until relatively recently. The Seychelles broke away from the African continental plate about fifty million years ago, carrying away fauna and flora that evolved in isolation into unique endemic species found nowhere else. The large double coconuts of the coco-de-mer, for example, would wash up along the shores of the Maldives, another archipelago located south of India. The once rare and mysterious fruit, thought to be an aphrodisiac, was highly prized until specimens were discovered growing in the Seychelles and subsequently exported en masse.

Evidence suggests that early Arab and SWAHILI explorers knew about the Seychelles. An Arabic manuscript written in 810 C.E. describes a place that is probably the Seychelles, as do accounts written by the Arab geographer al-Husayn al-Mas'udi in 915 C.E. Maps associated with these texts denote the Rukh Islands, the word *Rukh* probably being derived from the Divehi word for palm tree, *ruka*, suggesting that inhabitants of the Maldives had knowledge of the "palm tree islands." En route to India, Portuguese explorers spotted the islands in 1501 and named the largest of them the Seven Sisters. For several decades the Portuguese, most notably VASCO DA GAMA, explored the many small islets and reportedly established a small and ultimately unsuccessful settlement in 1598. Employees of the British East India Company explored the islands in 1609. During 1742 and 1743 a French expedition from Mauritius mapped the islands, naming them Ile de la Bourdonnais (after Mauritian governor Mahé de la Bourdonnais). By the time the French crown laid claim to the islands in 1756, they were again uninhabited, with the exception of transient pirates. The French explorer Mahé Morphy renamed the islands Séchelles, honoring the French controller general of finance Vicomte Morceau des Séchelles.

The first settlement was established in 1771 when Captain Lécore of the French ship *Thélémaque* dropped off fifteen French, seven slaves, five South Indians, and a black woman. The islands were considered a dependency of the larger colony Ile de France (Mauritius), from which most settlers originated.

A Seychelles baker removes freshly baked bread from an oven. *CORBIS/Zen Icknow*

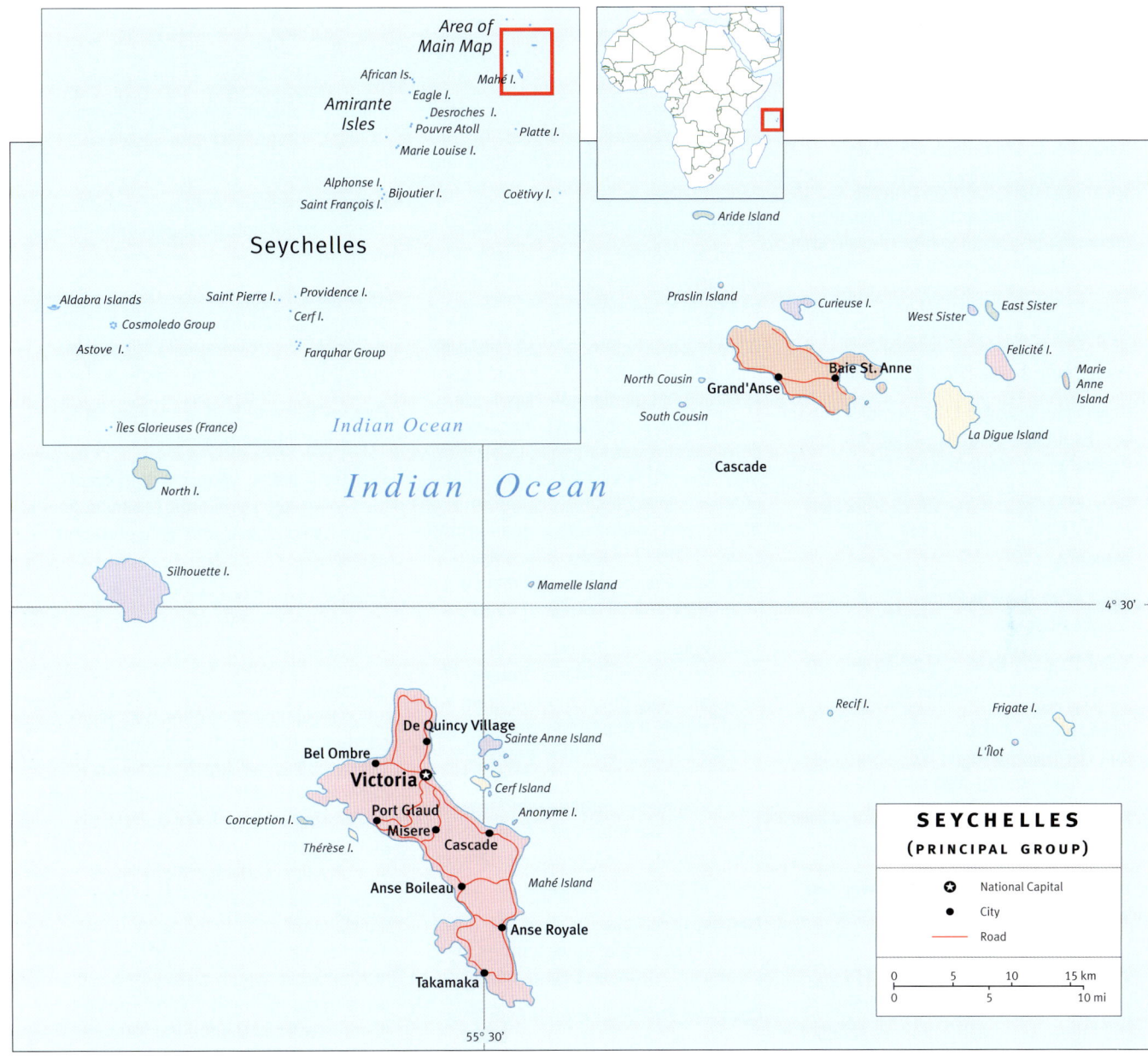

Although they introduced spices such as nutmeg, cloves, and cinnamon, the colonists primarily provided supplies and maintenance for passing ships. Settlers were quick to exploit the existing natural resources, stripping the forests to build and repair ships and harvesting more than 13,000 giant tortoises by 1789. By this time the population had grown to 591, of which 487 were slaves. Hearing of the French Revolution, the colonists claimed independence the following year, although France quickly reestablished sovereignty.

Colonial Period

One of the primary reasons the French laid claim to the Seychelles was to maintain secure sea-lanes. United States merchant ships had been purchasing stolen goods from pirates such as the American captain Nemesis, who commanded a fleet of fifteen vessels with which he raided British and French ships. The infamous French pirate Oliver le Vasseur, known as the Buzzard, also operated from the Seychelles. Legend holds that just before being hanged from the gallows in France, le Vasseur threw his treasure map to the crowd. Based upon this map, a large expedition exhaustively searched what appeared to be human-made tunnels on Mahé from 1948 until 1970 but failed to turn up any valuables.

Tired of pirates preying on its ships, GREAT BRITAIN took control of the Seychelles in 1794, although possession of the islands alternated between the British and the French in the late eighteenth and early nineteenth centuries. In this period of British-French hostility in the Indian Ocean, the governor, Chevalier Queau de Quinssay, hoisted a different flag depend-

Seychelles (At a Glance)

OFFICIAL NAME: Republic of Seychelles

AREA: 455 sq km (about 174 sq mi)

LOCATION: Eastern Africa; a group of 115 islands scattered across the western Indian Ocean, northeast of the island of Madagascar

CAPITAL: Victoria (population 23,200; 2004 estimate)

POPULATION: 82,800 (2004 estimate)

POPULATION DENSITY: 172.8 persons per sq km (about 452 persons per sq mi); concentrated on Mahé Island

POPULATION BELOW AGE 15: 27.3 percent (male 11,116; female 10,844); 2003 estimate

POPULATION GROWTH RATE: 0.46 percent (2003 estimate)

TOTAL FERTILITY RATE: 1.79 children born per woman (2003 estimate)

LIFE EXPECTANCY AT BIRTH: Total population: 71.25 years (male 65.78 years; female 76.88 years); 2003 estimate

INFANT MORTALITY RATE: 16.41 deaths per 1,000 live births (1998 estimate)

LITERACY RATE (AGE 15 AND OVER WHO CAN READ AND WRITE): Total population: 58 percent (1996 estimate)

EDUCATION: Education is officially compulsory for children aged 6 to 15. In 1993 there were 9,873 primary school students, and 763 enrolled in secondary education. One year of National Youth Service is mandatory for higher education.

LANGUAGES: Creole, English, and French are all official languages.

ETHNIC GROUPS: Most Seychellois are of mixed African and French descent; Indian, Chinese, and Arab minorities are also present.

RELIGIONS: About 87 percent of the population are Roman Catholic, about 7 percent are Anglican, and about 6 percent belong to other religions.

CLIMATE: The climate is tropical and humid, with a slighty cooler season during southeast monsoon (late May to September) and a slightly warmer season during northwest monsoon (March to May). For the most part, however, temperatures are roughly constant throughout the year, with average temperatures of 25° C (78° F) in both January and July. Average rainfall is 400 mm (16 in) in January and 50 mm (2 in) in July.

LAND, PLANTS, AND ANIMALS: Of the 115 islands, the 32 in the Mahé Group are rocky and hilly. All of the country's principal islands belong to this group; they include Mahé Island (the largest), Praslin, Silhouette, and La Digue. The 83 coral islands are largely without water resources, and most are uninhabited. Only 18 percent of the islands' land is used for permanent crops.

NATURAL RESOURCES: Guano is the only mineral product; other resources include fish, copra, and cinnamon trees.

CURRENCY: The Seychelles rupee

GROSS DOMESTIC PRODUCT (GDP): $626 million (2002 estimate)

GDP PER CAPITA: $7,800 (2002 estimate)

GDP REAL GROWTH RATE: 1.5% (2002 estimate)

PRIMARY ECONOMIC ACTIVITIES: Tourism, farming, fishing, and small-scale manufacturing

PRIMARY CROPS: Coconuts, cinnamon, vanilla, sweet potatoes, cassava (tapioca), and bananas

INDUSTRIES: Tourism, coconut and vanilla processing, fishing, coir (coconut fiber) rope processing, boatbuilding, printing, furniture, and beverage production

PRIMARY EXPORTS: Fish, cinnamon bark, copra, petroleum products (re-exports)

PRIMARY IMPORTS: Manufactured goods, food, petroleum products, tobacco, beverages, machinery, and transportation equipment

PRIMARY TRADE PARTNERS: France, the United Kingdom, Singapore, Bahrain, and South Africa

GOVERNMENT: The Seychelles is a constitutional republic that gained its independence from the United Kingdom in 1976. It is divided into 23 administrative districts. The executive branch was led by President Albert René and his appointed Council of Ministers 1977–2004. Vice President James Michel was sworn in as president in April 2004. The legislative branch is the thirty-four-member National Assembly (Assemblée Nationale), in which twenty-five seats are elected by popular vote. The remainder are distributed proportionally among political parties that receive at least 10 percent of the popular vote. The assembly is currently dominated by the Seychelles People's Progressive Front (SPPF). The Seychelles National Party (SNP) holds the remaining seats.

---

ing upon which nation's ships were sailing into the harbor, a practice that kept the Seychelles out of the conflict. In the 1814 Treaty of Paris, FRANCE formally ceded Mauritius and the Seychelles, with the latter remaining a dependency of the former.

The British abolished slavery in 1834, although the 9,000 ex-slaves (90 percent of the population) had to endure an additional five years of forced labor "apprenticeship" in the colony's cotton and SUGAR fields. Upon gaining their freedom, the vast majority abandoned the plantations, and harvests dropped dramatically. Plantation owners were able to temporarily replace a portion of the lost labor force by taking on Africans "rescued" from Arab dhow sailing ships engaged in the newly illegal INDIAN OCEAN SLAVE TRADE. These "liberated Africans" were likewise forced to work five-year "apprenticeships" but afterward also quit the plantation fields to work as artisans, fishers, and independent farmers. Strapped for labor, colonists shifted to less labor-intensive crops, such as coconuts, and introduced sharecropping. Since the 1840s coconuts have been the dominant export product, in the form of oil and later as copra (the white meat of the seed), though for a short time during the late nineteenth century exports of vanilla were also important.

During the twentieth century the Seychelles gradually gained autonomy. A governor was assigned in 1897 and suffrage slightly extended. In 1903 the Seychelles became a separate crown colony despite the protest of prominent Seychellois, who preferred the more protected status as a dependency of Mauritius. By 1948, four of the twenty-four seats on the Legislative Council were allocated to elected officials, all of whom represented the Seychelles Taxpayers and Producers Association (STPA). The number of political parties and trade unions grew in the 1950s and 1960s. Among the most prominent were the liberal Seychelles Democratic Party (SDP), led by James Mancham, who preferred to maintain ties to Britain, and the socialist Seychelles People's United Party (SPUP), headed by ALBERT RENÉ, who called for complete independence. In 1967 Britain declared universal suffrage in the Seychelles and doubled the number of elected seats in the Legislative Council. The SDP won four seats and the SPUP won three. Recognizing that independence was inevitable, the British detached several islands from the Seychelles and Mauritius, including Diego Garcia, creating the British Indian Ocean Territory (BIOT) in order to retain a military presence in the area. In return, they built an international airport on Mahé, enabling TOURISM to become a major industry.

Postcolonial Development and Nationhood

Following a constitutional conference held in London, England, in 1970, the Legislative Council became a fully elected Legislative Assembly, dominated by the SDP, with Mancham as chief minister. On June 29, 1976, the islands became the independent Republic of Seychelles, with Mancham as president and René as prime minister. The BIOT islands were returned to Seychelles, although the Mauritian island of Diego Garcia remained under British control.

Less than one year later, on June 5, 1977, René led a coup d'état, ousting Mancham while he was away at a Commonwealth conference in London. SPUP supporters resented Mancham's extravagant lifestyle and economic policies that prioritized tourism and banking over agriculture and fishing. René created a one-party state, declared himself president, party chief, and leader of the armed forces, and renamed the SPUP the Seychelles People's Progressive Front (SPPF). René's socialist policies, such as the formation of state-run farms and the elimination of elite private schools, won little support among the middle and upper classes.

Several times during his first years in office, René claimed to have uncovered coup plots. He temporarily detained individuals under the Public Security Regulations and authorized his government to detain and monitor the mail of suspect individuals under the Post Office Act. In 1981 the then sixty-two-year-old Irishman Mad Mike Hoare flew into Seychelles along with fellow mercenaries from SOUTH AFRICA in an attempt to overthrow René. After a confrontation at the airport, all but six of the mercenaries hijacked an Air India plane and flew back to South Africa, only to be arrested there. At René's request, TANZANIA sent 400 troops to ensure stability; a year later they helped defeat an army mutiny. Some implicated the United States and South Africa, citing those countries' interest in removing a socialist political leader who had pursued a nonaligned foreign policy and advocated a nuclear-free Indian Ocean. René blamed the political unrest on Mancham, who was leading the Mouvement pour le Résistance while exiled in London. Mancham denied any involvement.

The political intrigue continued when Mancham's successor as head of the Mouvement pour le Résistance, Gerard Hoareau, was assassinated in London and it was subsequently discovered that his telephone had been tapped. Hoareau allegedly had been supported by businesspeople interested in creating an offshore banking system to launder money procured through drug trafficking. In 1986 a second reported coup attempt failed, this time led by defense minister Ogilvy Berlouis, who had secretly visited the U.S. Department of Defense in 1985.

Contemporary Events

Despite recurrent coup plots, René was elected to a third term in 1989. In 1991 five of the exiled opposition parties established a coalition, the United Democratic Movement (UDM), led by Dr. Maxime Ferrari. Pressured by the international community and aid donors, particularly France and England, René began to institute democratic reforms, including the reintroduction of a multiparty political system. Opposition leaders, including Ferrari, returned to Seychelles, as did Mancham, who headed the newly formed National Democratic Party (NDP). The SPPF dominated the 1992 elections, which were held to form an assembly and draw up a new constitution. Disagreements over proposed constitutional reforms eventually led Mancham's party to withdraw its representatives in protest. A second assembly was formed in January 1993, producing a constitution that was ratified by a popular referendum in June. René and his party triumphed in the next elections. In 2004 René stepped down and was succeeded by Vice President James Michel.

After the 1993 election, René implemented a number of free-market reforms, promoting the islands as a center for offshore banking. Several national industries, including the port, were privatized. In 1995 the Seychelles raised international concern by announcing the Economic Development Act, which assured any individual who invested a minimum of $10 million against extradition or having assets seized. Under pressure from the United States and other countries, René amended the act to include provisions to prevent money laundering.

Today, most Seychellois work in the service sector, especially the tourist industry. Industrial fishing, particularly for tuna, has become an increasing important sector of the economy in recent years, and in 2000 fishing passed tourism as the country's leading source of foreign exchange. Other industries, however, are struggling. Despite increasing privatization, agriculture has shrunk to only about 3 percent of Seychelles's gross domestic product (GDP), and hopes of finding exploitable petroleum resources have faded. Heavily dependent upon imported food, fuel, and other commodities, the economy faces a near-chronic foreign exchange crisis. In response the government has redoubled efforts to attract foreign investors, creating a tax-free business park in the early 1990s, known as the Seychelles International Trade Zone (SITZ).

See also Colonial Rule; Socialism in Africa.

Bibliography

Benedict, Burton. *People of the Seychelles*. Her Majesty's Stationery Office, 1966.

Franda, M. *The Seychelles: Unquiet Island*. Westview Press, 1982.

Kaplinsky, Raphale. "Prospering at the Periphery: A Special Case—The Seychelles." In *African Islands and Enclaves*. Edited by Robin Cohen. Sage Publications, 1983.

Lionnet, Guy. *The Seychelles*. David and Charles, 1972.

Mancham, James R. *Paradise Raped: Life, Love, and Power in the Seychelles*. Methuen, 1983.

Ari Nave

Seymour, William Joseph

1870–1922

American minister and leader of the Azusa Street Revival in 1906, which marked the birth of the modern Pentecostal movement.

The self-taught son of former slaves, William Joseph Seymour was the first leader of Pentecostalism, a religious movement that has swept the United States, Africa, Latin America, and the rest of the world, acquiring millions of adherents and often described as the religious phenomenon of the twentieth century.

Seymour's religious journey to the Azusa Street Pentecostal Mission in Los Angeles, California began with his experiences growing up as a Baptist and a young adulthood spent in Methodist churches. A follower of the Holiness Movement, a perfectionist group growing out of Methodism, Seymour believed that the achievement of grace was a two-step process. After conversion, God "sanctified" the believer with a "sign." Seymour saw his sign after a bout of smallpox in Cincinnati, Ohio, the result of which was the loss of the use of his left eye.

Then an evangelist, Seymour went to Houston, Texas in 1903 and attended classes offered by Charles F. Parham, a leading white Holiness minister. Since segregation laws prohibited him from sitting with the white students, Seymour listened to lectures in the hallway. Parham taught that speaking in tongues, or glossolalia, was further proof of God's grace, a principle that Seymour came to believe was a third and final step in the achievement of purity.

Arriving in Los Angeles, California in 1906, Seymour preached the doctrine of speaking in tongues, igniting an international religious revival known as Pentecostalism, and named for the religious enthusiasm experienced by Jesus' disciples and described in the Book of Acts. In its early years, the Pentecostal movement under Seymour was unique; despite the racism and sexism of American society at large, the church was integrated and men and women were church officers and preachers. As the movement spread nationally and internationally, much as a result of Seymour's newsletter, *The Apostolic Faith*, it was unable to maintain such policies. The church split into white and black groups by 1915, and Seymour preached to a largely black Azusa Street congregation until his death in 1922.

Shabazz, Hajj Bahiyah Betty

1936–1997

Educator and widow of black leader Malcolm X who became an international black cultural icon symbolizing the growing influence of Malcolm's name and nationalist message.

There is some uncertainty about Betty Shabazz's origins and early life. Reportedly the daughter of Shelman Sandlin and a woman named Sanders, she was born Betty Sanders and grew up as a foster child in the Detroit, Michigan, home of a black family named Malloy. As a youth she was active in her local African Methodist Episcopal Church. She briefly attended Tuskegee Institute (now Tuskegee University) in Alabama but moved to New York City to escape Southern racism and to study at the Brooklyn State Hospital School of Nursing. During her junior year, she attended the Nation of Islam's Temple No. 7 in Harlem. There she taught a women's health and hygiene class and was noticed by Malcolm X, who was a minister at the temple. He proposed to her by telephone from Detroit, and they were married in 1958.

Shabazz converted to Islam and became a dutiful Muslim wife. She left Malcolm temporarily on several occasions, however, presumably over disagreements caused by his extensive travel schedule as a spokesman for the Nation of Islam. They became the parents of six daughters, Attallah, Qubilah, Ilyasah, Gamilah, Malaak, and Malikah. Shabazz was pregnant with the twins Malaak and Malikah when Malcolm was assassinated in the Audubon Ballroom in New York City on February 21, 1965, an event she and her other children witnessed.

After Malcolm's death, Shabazz raised her children and continued her education, which culminated in a Ph.D. degree in educational administration from the University of Massachusetts in 1975. She taught health sciences and then became head of public relations at Medgar Evers College in Brooklyn. She left the Nation of Islam after Malcolm's death, but performed the *hajj*, the sacred Islamic pilgrimage to Mecca, in Saudi Arabia, and considered herself a Sunni Muslim. She believed that Malcolm had been murdered by the Nation of Islam and said so in interviews until 1995, when she had a public reconciliation with LOUIS FARRAKHAN, the head of the Nation of Islam and a rival of Malcolm's at the time of his assassination.

Her reconciliation with Farrakhan helped to establish his legitimacy in the black community, but Shabazz's presence aided even more in the rehabilitation of Malcolm's reputation. During the CIVIL RIGHTS MOVEMENT, Malcolm was considered by many blacks and whites to be a nationalist, a separatist, and even a racist. After his death, however, Malcolm's ideas took on increasing authority as integration failed to solve the crisis of the black urban underclass. Betty Shabazz helped keep Malcolm's name and message fresh, although she personally espoused the more accommodationist self-help doctrine of BOOKER T. WASHINGTON, founder of Tuskegee Institute. She was also active in black social organizations, such as the Links, Delta Sigma Theta, and JACK AND JILL OF AMERICA.

On June 1, 1997, Betty Shabazz's only grandson, twelve-year-old Malcolm Shabazz, set fire to her apartment in Yonkers, New York. A troubled child, he was staying with his grandmother because his own mother, Qubilah, had problems of her own, including substance abuse and involvement in a plot to kill Farrakhan. In the fire, Shabazz received third-degree burns over 95 percent of her body, and she died three weeks later. Shabazz was widely honored at her death, especially by black women, in part because the once-reviled Malcolm X had now become a cultural hero, but primarily because her own life had come to exemplify extraordinary courage and perseverance in the face of great difficulties.

Shaka

1787–1828

Warrior chief who set in motion the far-reaching changes of the *mfecane*, a period of warfare and forced migrations among southern African peoples.

The son of the ZULU chieftain but born of a repudiated wife in what is present-day KwaZulu-Natal, SOUTH AFRICA, Shaka spent his childhood and youth in exile, stigmatized and humiliated. In his twenties he distinguished himself for six years as a warrior in the service of Chief Dingiswayo of the Mthethwa. When Shaka's father died in 1816, Dingiswayo sent Shaka to rule the Zulu. He immediately reorganized the Zulu fighting force and, with innovations in tactics and weaponry, shaped it into a formidable military machine geared to total warfare. Within a year, Shaka had quadrupled the number of his subjects and army members by absorbing conquered groups into his Zulu nation.

By the time his overlord, Dingiswayo, was killed in 1817, Shaka was ready to take on all other groups in the area. This he did in annual campaigns during the next ten years. The result was a wave of migrations by uprooted peoples as far north as modern TANZANIA and as far south as the Cape Colony (later Cape Province). At the same time, the Zulu grew by the addition of other groups, all of which were politically integrated and culturally assimilated. A decade of warfare, however, had taken a heavy toll on the Zulu. Psychologically disturbed throughout his life, and obsessively fearful of being supplanted by an heir, Shaka became clearly deranged by the death of his mother in 1828. Later that year, he was killed by his half-brother, DINGANE, who succeeded him as ruler.

Shakur, Assata

1947–

African American advocate of black revolution in America who was convicted of murdering a New Jersey state trooper in 1973.

Born JoAnne Deborah Byron in the New York City borough of Queens, Assata Shakur spent her early years alternating between living with her mother in New York and with her grandparents in Wilmington, North Carolina. As an adolescent, she ran away from home and lived among strangers until she was taken in by her aunt, Evelyn Williams, a lawyer who later represented Shakur in court. With her aunt's help, Shakur earned her general equivalency diploma (GED) and attended college, first at Manhattan Community College and then at the City College of New York.

In college Shakur became active in student politics, participating in protests and SIT-INS. She was married briefly, becoming JoAnne Chesimard, then changed her name to reflect her African heritage: Assata (meaning "she who struggles") Olugbala ("love for the people") Shakur ("the thankful"). During a stay in OAKLAND, CALIFORNIA, around 1970, she met several members of the BLACK PANTHER PARTY, and on her return east became a leading member of the party's HARLEM, NEW YORK branch. There she coordinated a breakfast program for schoolchildren. Later in 1970, she left the party for the Black Liberation Army (BLA), a small, loosely organized national group that sought to create an armed uprising among blacks.

Between 1971 and 1973, the BLA was believed to have robbed several banks, kidnapped enemies, and attempted to murder several police officers in different cities. Shakur was personally charged with several crimes, including bank robbery, murder of a drug dealer, and attempted murder of police officers. She was also targeted by the Counterintelligence Program (COINTELPRO) of the Federal Bureau of Investigation (FBI), which believed she was a BLA leader. In fact, it is likely that the group had little formal hierarchy, and it is unclear whether COINTELPRO began to track Shakur before or after she joined the BLA.

On May 2, 1973, state troopers stopped Shakur and two other activists, Malik Zayad Shakur and Sundiata Acoli, for a minor traffic violation on the New Jersey Turnpike. A shoot-out ensued, leaving state trooper Werner Foerster and Malik Shakur dead and Assata Shakur severely wounded. The details of the gunfire exchange have never been settled. Shakur was treated for her wounds, but there is evidence that her medical care during her pretrial detention was substandard. She was also subjected to long periods of solitary confinement, and she claimed she was beaten. While awaiting trial for murder, Shakur faced the other charges pending against her. She was acquitted of one bank robbery and one kidnapping. The remaining charges were dropped for lack of evidence and, in one case, due to a hung jury. During this time, Shakur gave birth to a daughter, Kakuya, who had been conceived with a codefendant.

At the murder trial, Shakur proclaimed her innocence, argued that she was being prosecuted for her politics, and offered the testimony of medical experts who claimed that her wounds would have prevented her from firing the fatal bullet. In 1977 she was found guilty of murder and assault and sentenced to life plus twenty-six to thirty-three years in prison. Many American leftists and black activists viewed her as a political prisoner. On November 2, 1979, three visitors to the Correctional Facility for Women in Clinton, New Jersey pulled guns on guards and forced them to release Shakur. The group fled and Shakur was not heard from again until the publication of her autobiography, *Assata Shakur: An Autobiography,* in 1987. The book established her whereabouts in CUBA, where she had been granted political asylum.

In the book, Shakur describes her upbringing and her reasons for becoming a revolutionary, and includes several of her poems. "It is our duty to fight for our freedom . . . We have nothing to lose but our chains," she writes in one poem to Sundiata Acoli. Although she still resides in Cuba, Assata Shakur continues to be an active voice for equal rights in America.

Shakur, Tupac

1971–1996

African American rap star, praised for his thought-provoking lyrics and criticized for his violent lifestyle; one of the most popular rap artists in the world when he was shot and killed at the age of twenty-five.

Tupac Shakur was one of the most influential and controversial voices to emerge from HIP-HOP's much maligned club of so-called gangster rappers. Criticized for their violent lyrics and misogynistic claims, gangster rappers became symbols of the best and worst of American musical creativity. Over a six-year period in the early 1990s Shakur became the voice for a generation of young, often frustrated, African Americans.

Through his music and his life Shakur embodied many of the harsh realities of "ghetto life." His raps addressed the difficulties of being young, black, and poor in the United States, and as a promising actor he captured those realities on the screen. True to the thuggish lifestyle that he rapped about, Shakur was arrested and served time in jail on more than one occasion, and often foreshadowed his own death in his songs and videos. Shakur's predictions of his violent death came true in September 1996, when he was murdered shortly after attending a professional boxing match in Las Vegas, Nevada.

Shakur was born in New York City on June 16, 1971 to black activists Afeni Shakur and Billy Garland. Garland interacted infrequently with his son, but Afeni Shakur exposed the young Shakur to many of the activities and philosophies of the BLACK PANTHER PARTY. At times destitute, Shakur and his mother moved often between apartments in New York City. As a young teenager in HARLEM, he explored his desire to act by joining the 127th Street Ensemble theater group, and was cast as Travis in LORRAINE HANSBERRY's play *A Raisin in the Sun.*

By 1988 the Shakurs had moved several times, finally settling in Marin, California. While in Marin Shakur pursued his interest in music, leaving home in 1988 to join the RAP group Strictly Dope. Three years later he left Strictly Dope and joined forces with friends from Oakland, California, who had formed the successful rap group Digital Underground. Shakur initially served as a background dancer for the group, but he was given an opportunity to rap on the group's 1991 single, "Same Song." His powerful delivery and stage charisma made an immediate impression, and friends were soon urging him to go solo.

In late 1991 Shakur released his first solo album, *2Pacalypse Now,* which sold more than 500,000 copies and featured the acclaimed hit "Brenda's Got a Baby." Heralded for its compelling portrayals of the hardships faced by single black mothers, and rebuked for its vivid depictions of violence, *2Pacalypse Now* marked powerful contradictions within Shakur's music and life. These contradictions would also be manifest on the silver screen.

Shakur's portrayal of the aggressive, unbalanced character Bishop in the movie *Juice* (1992) and his role as Lucky in the film *Poetic Justice* (1993) mirrored many of the problems in his private life. In 1993 Shakur was arrested for using drugs, and he was later sentenced to ten days in jail for brutally beating another rapper with a baseball bat. In October 1993 Shakur was once again arrested for allegedly shooting two off-duty Atlanta police officers. Although the charges were later dropped, Shakur's failure to draw a distinction between his public and private personas earned him public criticism.

Among those to criticize Shakur's music and behavior was C. Delores Tucker, chair of the National Political Congress of Black Women. Tucker objected to Shakur's glorification of what he referred to as "thug life" and urged him to use his podium in more positive ways. Shakur's response to Tucker and other critics was often hostile and bitter. Shakur claimed that in his music he was reflecting a lifestyle inspired by a poverty and despair that many Americans preferred to ignore. He argued that his music represented the voices of those in America's most marginalized communities, and to vilify his music simply vilified the realities facing those communities.

By 1994 Shakur's life was a blurred reflection of his art. In March of that year, Shakur lost his temper when he was cut from a film and was arrested when he assaulted the film's director, Allen Hughes. After spending fifteen days in jail, Shakur's career received a boost when his third film, *Above the Rim,* was released. But eight months later Shakur was back in court defending himself against charges of sexual assault by a nineteen-year-old woman.

Shakur's troubles climaxed in 1995 when he was robbed and shot five times in the lobby of a recording studio in New York City. Like many of the characters in his movies and songs, Shakur managed to defy death. Although it is unclear who was involved in the attempt on Shakur's life, he blamed the shooting on rival rappers from New York, the NOTORIOUS B.I.G. (also known as Biggie Smalls) and SEAN "P. DIDDY" COMBS. At the time, Shakur and Biggie Smalls were leading figures in a fierce rivalry between West Coast and East Coast rappers. When Shakur emerged from the hospital, a jury convicted him of sexual abuse and sentenced him to four and a half years in prison.

While in prison Shakur released his third album, *Me Against the World*, which debuted at number one on the Billboard charts and earned him a Grammy award nomination for Best Rap Album. *Me Against the World* went on to sell more than two million copies in seven months. On the album Shakur talked about his own mortality in the songs "If I Die 2Nite" and "Death Around the Corner," two of many songs that foreshadowed his violent death. Also featured on the album is the song "Dear Mama," which earned Shakur a second Grammy nomination for Best Rap Solo Performance.

After eight months in prison Shakur was released when Suge Knight, head of Death Row Records, paid his one-million-dollar bail. Shakur joined Knight's recording label, and in 1996 he released the double album *All Eyez on Me*. The album has sold five million copies and contains Shakur's biggest hit to date, "California Love." While at Death Row Shakur was part of a team that featured many of the most prominent rappers/producers on the West Coast, including Dr. Dre and SNOOP DOGGY DOGG. By all accounts, Shakur's future seemed very promising.

But that promise ended on September 13, 1996, when Shakur was cut down in a barrage of bullets. Shakur and Knight were in Las Vegas, Nevada, attending the championship fight of boxer MIKE TYSON. After the fight Shakur and Knight were driving along the Las Vegas strip when a car pulled up next to theirs and unloaded several rounds. While attempting to flee into the car's backseat, Shakur was shot several times. Knight sustained minor injuries, but Shakur was placed in intensive care. He was pronounced dead six days later.

After his death, Shakur's estate was plagued by lawsuits, including one by C. Delores Tucker, who claimed that Shakur's derogatory references to her in several of his songs caused damage to her marriage. Lawsuits by Shakur's biological father, and by a fan injured during a rap concert where Shakur allegedly taunted the crowd into rioting, were also filed. In addition, Shakur's mother filed a lawsuit against Death Row Records for control of her son's unreleased songs.

Shakur's final video, filmed a month before his death, depicts his violent demise. Entitled "I Aint Mad At Cha'" the video and song aired publicly just a few days after his death. Altogether, Shakur starred in six movies (three of which—*Bullet*, *Gridlock'd*, and *Gang-Related*—were released in 1997, after Shakur's death) and released six albums, two posthumously. He earned two Grammy award nominations and sold millions of albums around the world. Shakur's voice echoed the concerns and the rage of many young African Americans who are left to face the challenges of the ghetto alone. But his music also spoke to young adults—many of them middle-class blacks and whites—who understood and valued Shakur's ability to bring the hardships of the marginalized to the surface of American culture.

Alonford James Robinson

Shambaa

Ethnic group of Tanzania; also known as Shamba, Sambaa, and Shambala.

The Shambaa primarily inhabit coastal plains of northeastern Tanzania. They speak a Bantu language and form a cultural and linguistic cluster together with the BONDEI and PARE. About 500,000 people consider themselves Shambaa.

See also Bantu: Dispersion and Settlement.

Shangaan

Ethnic group of Mozambique; also known as Changane, Shangana, and Shangane.

The Shangaan primarily inhabit southern MOZAMBIQUE. Others live in SOUTH AFRICA and SWAZILAND. They speak a Bantu language and are closely related to the TONGA people. Approximately 1.5 million people identify themselves as Shangaan.

See also Bantu: Dispersion and Settlement.

Shange, Ntozake

1948–

American writer known for her innovative, experimental drama, poetry, and fiction.

As prolific as she is provocative, Ntozake Shange pushes the limits of literary form as she questions the social and political limitations imposed on people of color, especially women and children. Inventing her own dramatic medium, Shange created the choreopoem, a combination of narrative text, dance, and music. While abandoning conventions of plot and character development, her work explores the diverse experiences of the oppressed.

Born Paulette Williams, the daughter of a surgeon and a psychiatric social worker, Ntozake Shange spent her early years in Trenton, New Jersey, in privileged circumstances. Her parents' friends, including JOSEPHINE BAKER, MILES DAVIS, and W. E. B. DU BOIS, provided a culturally affirming black atmosphere. The family moved to Saint Louis, Missouri, when Shange was eight, and where she was one of the first students to integrate her school.

Depressed by a failed teenage marriage and the limitations she encountered as a talented black woman, Shange attempted suicide several times during her years at Barnard College (1966–1970). She began a new chapter of her life during graduate study at the University of Southern California (USC) in 1973, where she earned an M.A. and changed her name to Ntozake (meaning "she who comes with her own things") and Shange, ("who walks like a lion"). Shange then moved to the San Francisco Bay Area, where she taught women's studies and writing at area colleges and universities, while performing her own poetry and dance. Her best known work, *for colored girls who have considered suicide/when the rainbow is enuf,* originated in poems from this period.

A move to New York, in 1975, provided an opportunity for Shange to have *for colored girls* produced, marking the beginning her success. The production brought Shange an Obie Award (1977), as well as Tony, Emmy, and Grammy nominations. Her other plays include *Mother Courage and Her Children* (1980), an adaptation of the Bertolt Brecht play, featuring a black family in the time of the American Civil War; *Three Pieces* (1981); and *Nomathemba* (1996), a collaboration with the South African a cappella group LADYSMITH BLACK MAMBAZO. She has also published poetry collections, such as *Nappy Edges* (1978), the novel *Sassafras, Cypress and Indigo* (1982), the autobiographical *Betsy Brown* (1985), and *Liliane: Resurrection of the Daughter* (1994).

Shange married jazz musician David Murray in 1977, and they have a daughter, Savannah. She has taught at Villanova University and currently lives in Houston, Texas.

See also Integration: An Interpretation; Women Writers, Black, in the United States.

Shango

African-derived religion practiced in Trinidad that developed during the nineteenth century; also the name of a Yoruba deity worshiped in African-derived religions such as Candomblé and Santería.

There are several dozen Shango centers in TRINIDAD, with thousands of regular devotees and an additional number of less consistent participants and clients. Reflecting its origins among the YORUBA, who were brought to Trinidad as slaves or who arrived there from other islands in the WEST INDIES, the people who practice Shango call themselves "Yoruba people" and call the religion "Yoruba work." Practitioners of Shango often attend Catholic, Protestant, and Shouter (also known as Spiritual Baptist) churches as well.

Shango, CUBA's SANTERÍA, and BRAZIL's CANDOMBLÉ share many elements, because of their common Yoruba origins. All of these religions feature the worship of a pantheon of deities (called ORISHAS in Santería and Candomblé, *orisas* in Yoruba, and *powers* in Shango) and the ritual use of drumming, dance, and singing. In all cases, these Yoruba deities manifest themselves when they possess their devotees during specific rituals, and they are appeased and worshiped through dance, song, and sacrifice. (Though Shango takes its name from one particular deity—Shango, the god of thunder—the religion involves the worship of several other deities.) In the Yoruba religion from which the Shango, Candomblé, and Santería religions derive, each orisha was worshiped in a distinct temple, and was associated with particular geographical features and historically specific lineages. The deities of the three derived religions, however, are worshiped in one common center and are seen as the embodiment of less specific forces of nature. Practitioners of these three religions are also believed to "belong" to particular "powers," who control their fate and who must be appeased through worship and the observance of particular ritual requirements and proscriptions. All three religions are also largely devoted to invoking the blessing and assistance of the orishas in order to solve the problems faced by their devotees in this life, and are less concerned with the issues of sin and absolution, and life after death, that are such central features of Christian religions.

Shango, Candomblé, and Santería have all used elements of Roman Catholicism. Most prominently, the symbols, statues, and iconography of particular Roman Catholic saints have been used to stand for Yoruba deities with whom they share similarities. For example, in Shango, the deity Shango himself is often represented by statues of Saint John the Baptist, while Abatala is symbolized by Saint Benedict, and Ogun by Saint Michael (these correspondences vary within particular Shango temples and are not consistent between Candomblé, Santería, and Shango).

Because its history differs, Shango differs from Candomblé and Santería in other essential respects as well. Reflecting its development in Trinidad, a former British colony, Shango has been more deeply influenced by Protestant Christian religions, not just by Roman Catholicism. According to the scholar George Eaton Simpson, Shango has thus become a more syncretized, or hybrid, religion. For example, in contrast with practices in VODOU shrines in HAITI and Candomblé centers in Brazil, the African symbols used in Shango are not kept in a separate room from the Christian ones. Recently, Shango has been increasingly influenced by the Shouter religion, with which it shares certain similarities, such as the high value placed on the direct experience of the divine.

Each Shango center holds one big annual meeting in addition to the smaller rituals held for particular powers, which are performed three or four times a year. The Shango cult center consists of a shrine area with five or more shrines for the most important powers; a *chapelle,* or small cult house; and a *palais,* where healing ceremonies are held. Shango involves the worship of some non-Yoruba powers as well, like Mama Latay and Gabriel. These powers have certain characteristics that define their personalities and the objects and colors they use. For example, the colors of the deity Shango are red or yellow and red; he dances in the fire and carries a whip (i.e., when his devotees are possessed by him they carry his iconic whip). He receives bulls, rams, red or white cocks, and white pigeons as sacrifices, and is said to be quiet, peaceful, and charitable. Other powers are Ogun (Saint Michael), Oshun, (Saint Philomena or

Saint Anne), Shakpana (Saint Francis, Moses, or Saint Jerome), and Emanja (Saint Anne or Saint Catherine).

In Trinidad, someone becomes a devotee of a certain deity when he or she is possessed by it in a ceremony; when that power assists someone with an illness or a problem; or when it is a family tradition to worship that power. Nevertheless, there is no direct relationship between the deity's personality and the devotee's character. The same deity can even provoke different reactions in the same devotee. The powers punish their followers for behavior they do not like, and they reveal their will in dreams or through the interpretations of Shango priests and priestesses.

The Shango center's large annual ceremony begins on Tuesday night with a prayer meeting. Eshu, the trickster, who is the divine messenger among the deities, is always invoked first and appeased, then dismissed lest he cause too much trouble. Then other male and female powers are invited to appear at the ritual in turn, beginning with Ogun. From time to time, rum or water is poured in the four corners of the palais by a ceremonial assistant or a possessed person. Each person who is possessed by a particular power gets the ritual paraphernalia associated with the deity from the chapelle and comes back to dance near the shrine of the deity. Drumming, dancing, and possessions last all night. People identify the powers through the rhythms played by the drums and from the songs the possessed people sing, the objects they bring back from the chapelle, and the way they behave. The most important stimuli for the possessions is the different beats played on the drums.

In addition to Shango worship in Trinidad, there is also a religion in Grenada called Shango that features the worship of Yoruba deities. The Xangô religion in northeastern Brazil is also Yoruba-derived and broadly similar. Overall, the worship of Shango in Trinidad, as well as in other parts of Latin America and the Caribbean, is one of the more lasting religious legacies of Africa in the New World and is testament to the deep religious conviction and perseverance of generations of Afro-Caribbeans and Latin Americans.

See also Catholic Church in Latin America and the Caribbean; Protestant Church in Latin America and the Caribbean; Religions, African, in Brazil.

Mayda Grano de Oro

Sharecropping

Agriculturally based economic system in which farmers receive a share in the profits from the crops they produce in exchange for working an owner's land.

The African American intellectual W. E. B. DU BOIS once wrote that "[t]he slave went free; stood for a brief moment in the sun; then moved back again toward slavery." Indeed, in the century between emancipation and such CIVIL RIGHTS MOVEMENT victories as the 1964 Civil Rights Act and VOTING RIGHTS ACT OF 1965, several factors conspired to keep former slaves in an inferior position in American society. Disfranchisement, discriminatory JIM CROW laws, segregated schools, and LYNCHING reinforced the political, legal, educational, and social inequality that African Americans faced. But the picture of racial injustice would not be complete without including economic factors—ranging from official and unofficial job discrimination to exclusion from white LABOR UNIONS—that kept African Americans separate and unequal.

Chief among these unequal financial arrangements for rural Southern blacks was sharecropping. Although the details varied throughout time and place, sharecropping was—and is, in the less developed nations that still use it widely—a system in which landlords lease the use of their farmland to tenants, or sharecroppers, in exchange for a percentage of the crop yield. Sharecropping and its variants have existed for many centuries; historians have studied sharecropping systems in ancient Greece, India, China, France, Italy, and parts of Africa. The patronage relationship seen in precolonial RWANDA is one example of a sharecropping system.

In countries that once relied upon slave labor, some form of sharecropping often emerged in the wake of emancipation. This was the case not only in the United States, but also in BRAZIL, parts of the British WEST INDIES, and MEXICO. Nations whose histories did not include slavery nevertheless often went through periods in which sharecropping was the dominant agricultural system, either as a descendent of feudalism or—as seen in SOUTH AFRICA during the early twentieth century—as a capitalist byproduct of COLONIAL RULE.

At the end of the CIVIL WAR (1861–1865) in the United States the American agricultural economy was in a shambles, particularly in the South, which had relied on plantation farming for the production of crops such as rice, sugar, tobacco, and cotton. Former slaves had been freed through the EMANCIPATION PROCLAMATION AND THE THIRTEENTH AMENDMENT to the U. S. Constitution, but the overwhelming majority—most of whom had been agricultural workers—lacked the financial means to acquire land. Despite the mythical RECONSTRUCTION promise of FORTY ACRES AND A MULE for former slaves, the FREEDMEN'S BUREAU controlled at most only about one million acres of Southern farmland; Du Bois and others estimated that equitable land redistribution, even if it had not been politically impossible to accomplish, would have required twenty-five to fifty million acres and the complete overthrow of the white planter aristocracy.

Scholars have offered differing interpretations of the emergence of sharecropping in the American South, but most agree that it was originally a compromise between former slave owners and former slaves. Lacking the capital to pay wages for agricultural work, landowners offered the use of land in exchange. Under Reconstruction, the first sharecropping contracts included provisions protecting sharecroppers by offering them the first lien, or legal ownership, of the crop. While they did not prosper under this system, poor black farmers in the first decade after the Civil War often enjoyed more independence and autonomy—and bargaining power against their landlords—than they did later.

With the collapse of Reconstruction in the late 1870s, however, most sharecropping contracts became more overtly unequal in nature. Landowners used crop-lien laws and high-interest-rate credit at company stores to keep sharecroppers in a state of perpetual debt. Since most sharecroppers raised only one crop—typically cotton—the increasingly depleted soil could not provide them the livestock feed, fruits, and vegetables for their families that subsistence farming would have supplied. By mortgaging next year's crop to pay for this year's food, clothing, and other necessities, many black sharecroppers entered a state of bondage nearly as complete as the one that they had endured under slavery; meanwhile, landowners faced lower financial risk and reduced responsibility for the people who farmed their land. Records show that in 1876 approximately 95 percent of Southern black farmers owned no land at all.

Poor white farmers suffered similar poverty, although they were less likely to be sharecroppers on the former plantations and more likely to work as tenant farmers, a position in which they enjoyed greater autonomy but often faced greater risk. Competition for land—especially land rich in topsoil, such as that in the Mississippi Delta region—further strained race relations that were still poisoned by centuries of slavery. This racial antipathy was often encouraged by more powerful whites, thus helping to create an atmosphere in which lynching and other racist violence kept African Americans from attempting to increase their economic, political, or legal power, or even exercising the rights granted in the Constitution.

As late as the 1920s, studies by the U. S. Department of Agriculture showed that life on a cotton plantation differed little from slavery days, with multiple black workers (including children) supervised by white overseers. Laws regulating the treatment of sharecropper debt in many cases echoed those governing the treatment of slaves: a sharecropper attempting to leave a plantation had to first pay his debt, and could be beaten and arrested if he refused. Landowners could pay off the debt of another landowner's field hand, in effect purchasing the person. Such forced labor, known as peonage, reached its peak under the convict lease system, in which some landowners farmed with chain gangs of convicted criminals in exchange for housing and guarding the prisoners, most of whom were black men.

Shifts in the international cotton market (the United States had provided 80 percent of the world's cotton in 1880, a figure that fell to 40 percent by the late 1930s), mechanization of agriculture, crop devastation by the BOLL WEEVIL and other pests, the GREAT DEPRESSION of the 1930s, and growing migration from the rural South to the urban North were all factors in the decline of sharecropping. In addition, groups like the Southern Tenant Farmers' Union, formed in 1934, advocated for better working conditions and more equitable pay. But the system remained a way of life as late as the 1960s for many African Americans, some of whom still lived in dismal conditions two decades after the application of NEW DEAL programs to the problem of rural poverty. With the rise of urbanization, both within and outside of the South, fewer African Americans worked the fields as their ancestors had done; in many cases they were replaced by migrant farm workers—usually people of color—who faced similar issues of debt, forced labor, and powerlessness.

See also Emancipation in the United States; Migration, Black, in the United States.

Sharif, Omar

1932–

Egyptian actor and champion bridge player.

Born in ALEXANDRIA, EGYPT, then under British COLONIAL RULE, Michel Shahoub was the son of a successful timber merchant. He attended private English schools in EGYPT and then graduated from Cairo's Victoria College. He converted to Islam, changed his name to Omar Sharif, and embarked on an acting career. Sharif achieved stardom in Egypt with *Sina Fil Wadi* (*The Blazing Sun*, 1954), which also starred Faten Hamama, whom he married. They had one child, a son named Tarek.

Sharif's work caught the notice of English director David Lean, who cast him as Sherif Ali ibn el Kharish in *Lawrence of Arabia* (1962). The role earned him an Academy Award nomination, and catapulted him into international stardom. His smoldering romantic presence captivated audiences and made him one of the most successful stars of the 1960s. In 1965 Sharif again teamed up with Lean, this time for the title role in the screen adaptation of Boris Pasternak's novel, *Dr. Zhivago* (1965), another film that achieved both commercial and critical success. He also starred with Barbra Streisand in *Funny Girl* (1968), and appeared in numerous other films.

Sharif was controversial in Egypt and elsewhere in the Arab world. Because of increasing tensions between Arab states and Israel, many considered him a traitor for working with Jewish filmmakers. During the Six-Day Arab-Israeli War, Middle Eastern newspapers published photos of Sharif kissing the Jewish Streisand during rehearsals for *Funny Girl*. Fearing for his safety, he left Egypt with his family shortly thereafter.

The film industry's preference for younger stars set Sharif's career back in the early 1970s. He continued to act in movies, although filmmakers no longer cast him as the leading man. Beginning in the early 1980s, he shifted mainly to television movies and miniseries. Sharif has insisted, however, that his consuming passion is bridge. He is a world-class player with an international tournament named in his honor, and for many years he wrote an internationally syndicated newspaper column on the game. In 1996, after successful heart bypass surgery, Sharif returned to Cairo to live, seeking to "be with friends, and own a home." He nonetheless continues to act. His film career now spans more than five decades. Sharif was widely praised for his lead role performance in *Monsieur Ibrahim et les fleurs du Coran* (2003), a major hit at international film festivals. He received a Golden Lion award for lifetime achievement at the 2003 Vienna Film Festival.

See also Islam in Africa.

Robert Fay

Sharp, Granville

1735–1813

White British abolitionist.

Granville Sharp was a leader of the abolitionist legal battle in GREAT BRITAIN. He assisted lawyers in their efforts to prove that existing British court decisions that condoned slavery and the slave trade were not only inhumane but illegal, according to British law. A contemporary of his once suggested that it was obvious that Sharp was not trained as a lawyer, because he was less interested in the law as it was than in the law as it should be.

Described by scholar Gretchen Gerzina as a man with an "unflinching moral sense," Sharp came from a religious family in Durham, England. His formal education ended when he was fourteen years old. After several apprenticeships, Sharp became a clerk at the ordinance office in London at age twenty-two. He drew most of his satisfaction in life, however, by gathering with his numerous brothers and sisters, all of whom lived in England, to play music together.

In 1765 Sharp had an encounter in his brother's medical office with a severely wounded runaway slave named Jonathan Strong. This was Sharp's introduction to the horrifying conditions of slavery. The Sharp brothers helped Strong until he was healed, and then they found him employment. Three years later, Strong's former owner kidnapped him in order to sell him back into slavery, and Strong asked Granville Sharp for legal assistance. Sharp argued Strong's case successfully and Strong was freed. However, Strong's former owner threatened to sue Sharp for damages. As a result, and in an attempt to intimidate the former owner, Sharp wrote his most famous abolitionist tract, *A Representation of the Injustice and Dangerous Tendency of Tolerating Slavery; or of Admitting the Least Claim of Private Property in the Persons of Men, in England.*

In the memorandum, Sharp reiterated Justice John Holt's 1706 comments that English air was "too pure" for slaves to breathe, or that England was not and should not be a setting conducive to slavery. He showed that several English cases upheld this precedent, despite the 1729 YORKE AND TALBOT OPINION that slaves could be held by West Indian masters while in England. Sharp claimed that only with a preexisting written contract could a master legally keep a person in slavery when traveling to England. Furthermore, he argued, nobody could obtain such a document because no person would freely enter into a contract that submitted him or her to slavery. Sharp rejected the notion that a person could be considered private property and he claimed that when anyone—black or white—entered

English abolitionist Granville Sharp wrote "A toleration of slavery is, in effect, a toleration of inhumanity." Beginning with the case of Jonathon Strong in 1765, Sharp spent decades working to free escaped slaves and to end the institution of slavery in England. *Getty Images*

England, they became a subject of the king. The tract warned Strong's former owners that they could be penalized for defying the 1679 Habeas Corpus Act, which protected the liberty and human rights of British subjects from unjust imprisonment and expatriation. He ended by claiming that "A toleration of Slavery, is, in effect, a toleration of inhumanity." Sharp sent the tract to several British judges, including William Blackstone, who had mentioned Holt's comments in his famous *Commentaries on the Laws of England*, and who warned Sharp of the difficulties ahead—that "it would be uphill work in the Court of King's Bench"—to bring forth such abolitionist claims.

Despite the difficulties, Sharp did not waver from the task. He continued to help kidnapped slaves gain legal rights. In one instance, he assisted the defense for John and Mary Hylas in late 1768, a case in which John Hylas sued his wife's former master for forcibly selling her back into West Indian slavery. Mary Hylas was allowed to return to her husband, but the case did not determine rights of slaves in Britain; according to the court, she was only entitled to her freedom because her husband was free. Then, in 1771 Sharp defended Thomas Lewis, who had been kidnapped and held by his former owner Robert Stapylton. Justice William Mansfield presided over the case. Reluctant to rule on the issue of whether a master had such a right over a slave, Mansfield freed Lewis on the technicality that there was no evidence of Stapylton ever having purchased

Lewis. The judge stated that he hoped the issue of slavery would never be finally discussed. This angered Sharp, who accused Mansfield of "open contempt of the principle of the constitution."

In the case of JAMES SOMERSET a year later, Mansfield could no longer avoid the issue. He ruled that the forcible repatriation of blacks into slavery was illegal. Though Sharp did not attend the Somerset hearings, his support of the defense was invaluable. His active publicizing of the issues surrounding the case greatly influenced the outcome.

After the Somerset case, Sharp continued to be called upon to help former slaves and others who constituted the black poor community in London. Several years before the government funded a plan to resettle the black population in SIERRA LEONE for profit, Sharp had proposed a similar scheme, although his intentions were humanitarian. He envisioned the blacks living in an idealized moral community with a consensual government.

Granville Town, as the settlement was called, was never fully realized, but Sharp continued as a valued member of the Society for the Abolition of the Slave Trade until his death in 1813. Although he did not live to see the results of his work, his tireless efforts on behalf of abolition in Great Britain helped to outlaw the slave trade there in 1833 and to emancipate British slaves in 1838.

See also Holt Decision; Jonathan Strong Case; London's Black Poor and the Sierra Leone Settlement Plan.

Leyla Keough

Sharpe, Samuel

?–1832

Jamaican slave and religious leader, the principal organizer of the 1831 slave rebellion in Jamaica known as the Baptist War, or Christmas Rebellion.

Samuel Sharpe was born a slave in JAMAICA, probably in the northwestern parish of Saint James. Sharpe worked as a domestic slave in Montego Bay, the island's second largest town after Kingston. Literate and intelligent, he was also a passionate and charismatic speaker. He gained prominence working in the Montego Bay Baptist Church, run by British missionaries, where his duties included helping missionary Thomas Burchell with the supervision of membership classes. At the same time, Sharpe preached at the independent black-led Native Baptist Church, where he gained the titles "Daddy" or "Ruler." The Native Baptist movement was established in the late 1700s by blacks who came to Jamaica from the United States.

Sharpe drew upon the Bible to argue that slavery was morally wrong. He also helped spread the widely held view among slaves, who overheard planters' frequent complaints about the abolitionist movement in Britain, that the British Parliament had already abolished slavery and that the local whites were withholding that freedom. On this basis, Sharpe planned a campaign of passive resistance for late 1831, just after Christmas. According to his plan, the slaves would simply cease to work until their owners paid them wages and thereby conceded that the slaves were free. Sharpe developed an alternative strategy of armed rebellion in case the first approach of passive resistance failed. His chief allies included other elite slaves (skilled and domestic workers), many of whom were also Baptists and Native Baptists.

Sharpe used the structure of these churches to help organize the rebellion, spreading the word through nighttime church meetings. He also made use of oaths to exact loyalty from his associates. At one meeting before the rebellion, Sharpe asserted that if the whites would pay them, they would work as before; but if any attempts were made to force them to work as slaves, then they would fight for their freedom. The oath was taken on a Bible.

The rebellion began on December 27. The initial plan of a labor strike soon gave way to an armed revolt. It involved around 20,000 slaves and extended over 1,950 sq km (750 sq mi) in the western part of the island. Although the slaves enjoyed some initial successes, the rebellion was quickly and ferociously suppressed. At least 540 slaves were killed, and fourteen whites lost their lives. By the end of January 1832 Sharpe was in custody. He was tried on April 19 and sentenced to death. On May 23 he was hanged in a public execution in Morant Bay.

Henry Bleby, a missionary who interviewed Sharpe in jail, described him as "certainly the most intelligent and most remarkable slave I ever met with." Before his death, Sharpe declared to Bleby that he "would rather die upon yonder gallows than live in slavery."

Although Sharpe did not live to see the end of slavery, the rebellion he organized helped promote the emancipation cause. One week after Sharpe's execution, the House of Commons (the legislative branch of the British Parliament) established a committee to look into the best means of abolishing slavery. On August 1, 1834, the legislation Sharpe had been seeking went into effect.

See also Protestant Church in Latin America and the Caribbean; Role of Slaves in Abolition and Emancipation in Latin America and the Caribbean; Slave Rebellions in Latin America and the Caribbean.

Bibliography

Bleby, Henry. *Death Struggles of Slavery: Being a Narrative of Facts and Incidents, which Occurred in a British Colony, During the Two Years Immediately Preceding Negro Emancipation.* Hamilton, Adams, 1853.

Heuman, Gad. *"The Killing Time": The Morant Bay Rebellion in Jamaica.* University of Tennessee Press, 1994.

Turner, Mary. *Slaves and Missionaries: The Disintegration of Jamaican Slave Society, 1787–1834.* University of Illinois Press, 1982.

Sharpeville Massacre

See Sharpeville, South Africa.

Sharpeville, South Africa

Black township in South Africa where protesting residents were massacred by police in 1960.

On March 21, 1960, police in SOUTH AFRICA fired upon a group of demonstrators in the black township of Sharpeville, killing at least 69 and injuring nearly 200. The incident sparked both internal turmoil and international outrage against the country's oppressive APARTHEID regime.

Sharpeville, situated south of JOHANNESBURG in South Africa's TRANSVAAL region, was created in 1942. Like other black, "coloured," and Asian townships, Sharpeville was home to people forced to move there in accordance with South Africa's racial segregation laws. Early laws, such as the 1913 Natives Land Act, aimed to keep Africans in rural areas, but rapid industrialization in the 1940s increased demand for cheap labor in the cities. The Urban Areas Acts of the 1940s allowed for greater numbers of "non-whites" to live legally in urban areas, but only in designated townships.

When the AFRIKANER-dominated NATIONAL PARTY came to power in 1948, the government imposed a new and more drastic system of racial control, known as apartheid. In addition to urban residential segregation, the National Government assigned Africans to rural "Bantu Homelands" according to what "tribe" they belonged to. The government also increased enforcement of the PASS LAWS, which forced blacks to carry with them at all times documents such as work permits, tax receipts, and identification information and produce them whenever asked. Anyone who refused could be fined or imprisoned.

By 1960 pass-law protests already had a long history in South Africa, but the protest on March 21 of that year marked a tragic turning point. ROBERT MANGALISO SOBUKWE, leader of the PAN-AFRICANIST CONGRESS (PAC), called for all black South Africans to defy the pass laws by staying home from work so that they could hand in their passes (now called "reference books") at their local police stations.

Starting at about eight in the morning, many gathered at the Sharpeville police station; a similar demonstration unfolded in Langa, a township near CAPE TOWN. Photographic evidence shows that the crowd in Sharpeville was unarmed, peaceful, and significantly smaller than the police report had claimed (about 5,000 people, including numerous children). At the scene, the police—whose ranks soon swelled to 300 officers—neither asked them to disperse, nor warned them of any consequences if they did not. Sometime after half past one, the police opened fire. Of the sixty-nine killed, ten were children; another nineteen children were wounded.

Despite the medical examiner's report, which confirmed witness testimony that most victims were shot in the back while trying to escape the gunfire, the police were never sanctioned for their actions. The massacre, which was widely reported in the international press, led to worldwide criticism and continuing demonstrations throughout South Africa. The South African government subsequently banned the AFRICAN NATIONAL CONGRESS and the PAC (many of the leaders of these two anti-apartheid groups had already fled or been imprisoned). Although the declaration of a state of emergency eventually stifled the protests, Sharpeville was again the site of violence in 1984, when demonstrators against rent increases allegedly killed one of the township's councillors.

Kate Tuttle

Sharpton, Alfred (Al), Jr.

1954–

Pentecostal minister, political and civil rights activist, and the first African American candidate for the New York State Senate.

Alfred Sharpton, Jr., has made a career of placing himself at the front line of the struggle by lower and middle-income African Americans against injustice. Born in Brooklyn, New York, Sharpton began preaching at the age of four and spent his early years as a "wonder boy" sensation on the Pentecostal preaching circuit. In 1964, when he was only ten years old, Sharpton was ordained as a minister and set out on a preaching tour with famed gospel music performer MAHALIA JACKSON. But the divorce of his parents, also occurring that year, propelled Sharpton from middle-class comfort in Queens to public welfare and a housing project in Brooklyn. Having lived in better circumstances, he knew that black poverty was not inevitable and he vowed to fight for improved living and working conditions for African Americans.

In 1969 civil rights leader JESSE JACKSON appointed Sharpton as youth director for OPERATION BREADBASKET, a campaign that boycotted and demonstrated against businesses that failed to hire blacks. In 1971, after high school and a few years at Brooklyn College, Sharpton founded his own organization, the National Youth Movement. After meeting soul singer JAMES BROWN in 1973, Sharpton became his touring manager until the early 1980s, while continuing his political activism at the same time.

Al Sharpton entered politics in 1978 as the first African American to run for a seat in the New York State Senate. In the 1980s Sharpton became involved in a series of racial incidents that occurred in various NEW YORK neighborhoods. In 1986 he organized demonstrations and called for a special prosecutor in the aftermath of a racially motivated incident in Howard Beach, in which a crowd of whites chased Michael Griffiths, a black man, onto a highway, where he was struck and killed by a passing vehicle. Two years later Sharpton served as an adviser to Tawana Brawley, a black teenager who claimed she had been abducted and raped by a gang of whites. Sharpton's credibility came into question when a grand jury found no evidence of any crime against Brawley. Sharpton also played a prominent role in the protests that followed the 1989 shooting death of Yusuf Hawkins, a black youth who was attacked by a white mob in the Bensonhurst section of Brooklyn. In January 1991 Sharpton was preparing to lead a protest march in Bensonhurst when a drunken white man stabbed him in the chest. After recovering from the attack, Sharpton refined and toned down his controversial public image.

In 1991 Sharpton founded the National Action Network, a civil rights organization that seeks economic justice and political empowerment for the disenfranchised. Continuing to pursue a career in politics, Sharpton ran unsuccessfully in the 1992 and 1994 Democratic primaries for the U.S. Senate from New York. Meanwhile, in 1993 he served a well-publicized forty-five-day jail sentence resulting from a 1987 protest march that shut down the Brooklyn Bridge. In 1997 Sharpton made an impressive showing in the city's Democratic mayoral primary, winning 32 percent of the vote. More recently, Sharpton led large demonstrations against brutality in the New York Police Department following the police torture of Haitian immigrant Abner Louima in 1997 and the shooting of unarmed Ghanaian immigrant Amadou Diallo by four New York City policemen in 1999.

In 2003 Sharpton announced his candidacy for the Democratic Party nomination for president in the 2004 election. Although his campaign attracted a certain amount of interest, Sharpton struggled to build a national following strong enough to challenge the Democratic front-runners.

See also Civil Rights Movement; Democratic Party; Pentecostalism.

Kate Tuttle

Shashi

Ethnic group of Tanzania.

The Shashi primarily inhabit TANZANIA just southeast of LAKE VICTORIA. They speak a Bantu language and are closely related to the neighboring SUKUMA people. Over 100,000 people consider themselves Shashi.

See also Bantu: Dispersion and Settlement.

Sheldon, May French

1847–1936

American traveler and best-selling author who was one of the first white women to visit parts of eastern and Central Africa.

May French was born in Beaver, Pennsylvania. After finishing school, she worked in the publishing business in London, England. In 1876 she married American businessman Eli Lemon Sheldon.

Inspired by the writings of her friend, Anglo-American explorer and journalist SIR HENRY MORTON STANLEY, Sheldon set out for MOMBASA, a city on the coast of present-day KENYA, in 1891. Financed by her husband, she was accompanied by more than one hundred porters, servants, and guides. After British authorities in Mombasa refused to help with her travel plans, Sheldon went to nearby ZANZIBAR, where the sultan of Zanzibar gave her porters and a letter of safe conduct for her journey into the interior of what is now TANZANIA. Sheldon first visited the area around KILIMANJARO, Africa's highest peak. Then, accompanied by a British official, she ventured into the surrounding territory and became one of the first white people to explore Lake Chala, which sits inside a steep volcanic cone. Sheldon next ascended about one-quarter of the way up Kilimanjaro to visit another settlement and meet with the local sultan. Her expedition was cut short when she suffered injuries in a fall. She received medical aid and then returned to Mombasa, where she sailed home to England. Sheldon wrote of her travels in *Sultan to Sultan* (1892), in which she described her contact with more than thirty-five different tribes of Central and East Africa. The book became a best-seller in England and the United States.

Sheldon made her second trip to Africa in 1903, visiting what is now the DEMOCRATIC REPUBLIC OF THE CONGO. During World War I (1914–1918), Sheldon raised money for the Belgian Red Cross by giving lectures on her travels in Africa. After the war the Belgian government honored Sheldon by awarding her the Chevalier de l'Ordre de la Couronne.

Shell, Arthur

1946–

A member of the Pro Football Hall of Fame, Shell was the second African American to be named head coach in the National Football League.

Arthur Shell, the oldest of five children, was born in 1946 in the Daniel Jenkins Housing Project in CHARLESTON, SOUTH CAROLINA. When he was fifteen years old, his mother had a fatal heart attack. To help raise his siblings, he went to work with his father at a local paper mill. Shell was a star athlete—in both football and basketball—at Bonds-Wilson High School in North Charleston. Shell's size (6 ft, 5 in) and athletic talent earned him a scholarship in 1963 to attend Maryland State (now Maryland–Eastern Shore), where he played both offense and defense on the school's football team.

In 1968 the Oakland Raiders drafted Shell in the third round. In fifteen seasons with the Raiders, Shell played in 207 regular season and 24 postseason games. He was an eight-time All-Pro, and a member of the Raiders' championship teams in Super Bowl XI and XV. After the 1982 season, Shell retired from professional football and a year later he became an assistant coach with the newly relocated Los Angeles Raiders. In 1989 Shell was inducted into the Professional Football Hall of Fame and named head coach of the Raiders, the first of a small handful of African American coaches to be given that opportunity in the 1990s. FRITZ POLLARD, who retired in 1937, had been the only African American head coach in the NFL prior to Shell's hiring. Shell left the Raiders in 1994, becoming an assistant coach of the Kansas City Chiefs (1995–1996). He was then an assistant coach with the Atlanta Falcons until 2000. Shell is currently a consultant for the NFL and a writer for NFL.com.

See also Football, Collegiate; Football, Professional; Sports and African Americans.

Sherbro

Ethnic group of Sierra Leone.

The Sherbro primarily inhabit coastal southern Sierra Leone, including Sherbro Island. They speak a Niger-Congo language and are related to the TEMNE people. In recent years they have increasingly assimilated to the neighboring MENDE people. Approximately 200,000 people consider themselves Sherbro.

See also Languages, African: An Overview.

Sherrod, Charles

1937–

American civil rights activist, field secretary of the Student Nonviolent Coordinating Committee from 1961 to 1966.

After putting himself through Virginia Union University, where he received a B.A. in 1958 and a B.D. in 1961, Charles Sherrod joined the STUDENT NONVIOLENT COORDINATING COMMITTEE (SNCC) in its struggle against racial discrimination. With the dual aim of helping to achieve desegregation and increased voter registration, Sherrod settled in Georgia, where he and other SNCC members united with local leaders of the African American community to defeat racist laws and practices. Sherrod broke with SNCC in 1966, largely because of his support of white inclusion in the organization. Subsequently, he organized the Southwest Georgia Independent Voters Project, which he directed until 1987, and he worked toward creating agricultural cooperatives in the area. In 1976 he was elected city commissioner in Albany, Georgia, the site of his early work with SNCC. He remained at that position until 1990. In 1996 Sherrod ran unsuccessfully for the Georgia State Senate. He continues to speak about civil rights issues and is currently a chaplain at the Georgia State Prison in Homerville.

See also Civil Rights Movement; Desegregation in the United States.

Shilluk

Ethnic group of Sudan; also known as the Collo.

The Shilluk primarily inhabit the basin of the White Nile in south-central Sudan. They speak a Nilo-Saharan language. Over 150,000 people consider themselves Shilluk.

See also Languages, African: An Overview.

Shirazi

Ethnic group of East Africa and the Indian Ocean islands; also known as Mbwera.

According to oral tradition, beginning in the tenth century immigrants from the Shiraz region of Persia (now Iran) settled the islands and mainland ports of coastal East Africa, from MOGADISHU, SOMALIA in the north to the Sofala coast of MOZAMBIQUE in the south. Many scholars, however, believe that the Shirazi actually began their settlement of the East African coast in the twelfth century and that they originated in Somalia. Shirazi settlers established themselves on the following islands: LAMU, KENYA; Pemba, ZANZIBAR, Mafia, and Kilwa Kisiwani, all in TANZANIA; and the COMOROS. Most likely, the Shirazi combined African, Arab, and Persian elements to form a unique ethnic identity. They contributed to the development of the SWAHILI LANGUAGE and the spread of this language and ISLAM in East Africa.

Known for their mercantile skills, the Shirazi asserted themselves as ruling elites as early as the twelfth century on the islands that were their base. Trade in gold, ivory, and slaves brought prosperity to the Shirazi, who probably commissioned the Husuni Kubwa palace of Kilwa during the thirteenth and fourteenth centuries. Shirazi traders regularly traveled as far as the Arabian Peninsula, Persia, and the Indian subcontinent. The Shirazi never created a single, centralized empire. Several sultanates competed for power as political and economic fortunes waxed and waned. For example, the Shirazi sultanate of Kilwa declined in importance after the fifteenth century, while the Shirazi of coastal Kenya prospered, particularly at Malindi.

Today the Shirazi number over 300,000 and are members of three major subgroups: the Hadimu, the Tumbatu, and the Pemba. The Shirazi distinguish themselves from other SWAHILI PEOPLES. They are particularly concentrated on the island of Zanzibar.

See also Gold Trade; Ivory Trade; Transatlantic Slave Trade.

Ari Nave

Shona

Ethnolinguistic group of southeastern Africa.

The history and culture of the Shona people is contested and complex. Those who call themselves Shona and speak a Shona dialect inhabit present-day ZIMBABWE, southern ZAMBIA, and west-central MOZAMBIQUE. The exact origin of the Shona is unknown: linguists generally contend that the diversity of dialects indicates a first-millennium arrival, while historians usually date the arrival of Shona speakers to the Iron Age. It is agreed that the Shona were most likely the first Bantu-speaking people in the area, displacing the KHOIKHOI and possibly some central Sudanic inhabitants. By the tenth century, Shona speakers had become the most numerous people between the ZAMBEZI and Limpopo rivers, though they were by no means the only inhabitants. The Shona comprised a mosaic of disparate chieftainships, similar in their languages and livelihoods—based on a combination of agriculture and animal husbandry—but with a diversity of religious beliefs and customs. Although all were patrilineal, their political organization and means of succession varied considerably. Familial and dynastic competition was common, though there were no standing armies and major conflicts were few.

After 1000 C.E., centralized states began to emerge among the Shona. It was not until the fourteenth century, however, that these empires became distinguishable, as they competed for trade in GOLD and IVORY with Arab and, later, Portuguese merchants. The first major empire was based at GREAT ZIMBABWE from the twelfth to the fifteenth century, to be succeeded by the Torwa empire based at Khame to the west. At about the same time came the emergence of the Mhonomotapa and the Mutapa state to the northeast, an expansionist gold-producing and trading state. The last great Shona empire was that of Changamire, and those who became known as the Rozvi, a confederation of tribute-paying chieftainships in the southwest. This empire also disintegrated in the mid-1800s, due to the NGUNI invasion resulting from the MFECANE, or violent upheavals in SOUTH AFRICA.

Nineteenth-century NDEBELE invasions and British intrusions led disparate groups, concerned to protect their own interests, to take on Shona as a common identity. Unlike many ethnic groups in Africa, the Shona retain strong beliefs in totems and have never had a myth of the origin of humanity. They believe in a high god, the most prominent and powerful being the *Mwari* of the Changamire, and ancestral spirits, or *mudzimu*. Despite the similarities, the diverse clusters of dialects that roughly correspond to ethnic groups have become increasingly politicized. These include the Korekore in the north of Zimbabwe, the Zezuru in the center, Karanga in the south, Kalanga farther west, Manyika in the east, and the Ndau in the southeast and in west-central Mozambique. In modern Zimbabwean politics the Shona hold most important political positions and are, after whites, the captains of industry. Among the Shona the Zezuru are the predominant group. In Mozambique the Shona-speaking Ndau were prominent as the leadership of the opposition group MOZAMBICAN NATIONAL RESISTANCE (RENAMO). In addition, the Shona, with their contested history and varied past, have also adapted to popular culture; Shona stone sculpture produced by contemporary Shona artists, for example, has gained international recognition as a fine art form.

Bibliography
Beach, David. *The Shona and Their Neighbors.* Blackwell, 1994.
Bourdillon M.F.C. *The Shona Peoples.* Mambo Press, 1976.

Eric Young

Shope

Ethnic group of Mozambique; also known as Chope, Chopi, and Vachopi.

The Shope primarily inhabit southern MOZAMBIQUE. Others live in SOUTH AFRICA. They speak a Bantu language. Approximately 400,000 people consider themselves Shope.

See also Bantu: Dispersion and Settlement.

Shorey, William T.
1859–1919

Barbadian-born African American whaling master, who became the only black captain of major vessels on the West Coast in the late 1880s.

The *San Francisco Chronicle* described William Shorey in 1907 as "the only colored captain on the Pacific Coast." He was born on the island of BARBADOS in 1859 and spent his childhood there. His father was a Scottish sugar planter on the Caribbean island, and his mother, Rosa Frazier, was a native Barbadian.

As the oldest of his mother's eight children it was necessary for Shorey to begin working at an early age. Although slavery had been abolished in Barbados several decades earlier, in 1834, opportunities for a young man like Shorey were still quite limited. He was apprenticed in his early teens to a plumber, but he found the drudgery of this job uncongenial. Strongly attracted to the sea, as were many young men raised on the island, Shorey said goodbye to his family in 1875 and shipped on a British vessel bound for Boston, Massachusetts. The English captain of the ship took a fancy to the alert young crewmember and taught Shorey the rudiments of navigation. Shorey continued to study the vital subject under Captain Whiffer D. Leach, a noted whaling captain of Provincetown, Massachusetts.

E. Keble Chatterton states in *Whalers and Whaling* (1926) that the whaler had a difficult life. This kind of life "was likely to appeal only to three classes of men: those who had been compelled to leave the land to avoid jail or starvation, those who thought they were going to see the world and gain adventures, and those who were determined to work their way up until they owned a whaling ship of their own." All three factors were true in Shorey's case. First, because he was a black man in an age in which racial discrimination was prevalent, the number of jobs in which he might hope to find acceptance and success was limited. However, there had always been a rough sort of democracy on board a whaling ship, where a man was accepted for what he could do, rather than for his race or nationality. Second, for a young man who had grown up in the confines of the island of Barbados, the chance to travel widely must have had a strong appeal. Third, Shorey had a determination to work his way up, and in this he was highly successful.

Shorey shipped on his first whaling voyage in 1876 from Provincetown. He sailed as a *greenhand* but returned as a *boat steerer,* a considerably more important member of the crew. On one of his early voyages, Shorey almost lost his life while pursuing a sperm whale. "Evidently enraged," he related years later, "the whale attacked first one boat, smashing it, and then a second one, and then attacked the one I was in. By good fortune we were able to fire a bomb into him, which, exploding, killed him and saved us."

Undaunted by such harrowing experiences at sea, Shorey diligently pursued his career in whaling. His rise through the ranks was rapid, attesting to his intelligence, skill, and determination. After having spent only four years on whaling ships, he had become an officer by 1880. He sailed from Boston in November 1880 as third mate on the *Emma F. Herriman* on a trip that took him around the world. By the end of the exciting three-year voyage, he had been promoted to first officer. This particular voyage was memorable for another reason. It took him to San Francisco, California, which became his homeport for the rest of his long career.

Shorey shipped again on the *Herriman* in 1884 and 1885, sailing as second and then as first officer on ten-month voyages, which were typical of West Coast whaling. Then, in 1886, only a decade after beginning his whaling career, he gained the coveted position of command, thus becoming the only black captain of major vessels on the West Coast. This was a great tribute to Shorey's ability and stature among his fellow seamen, for the whaling captain had to be a man of varied talents. He had to be an experienced and skilled sailor, an excellent navigator, a shrewd trader, an intelligent and forceful leader, and a person able to assume all kinds of responsibility. "During the course of an average voyage," Elmo Hohman wrote in *The American Whaleman* (1928), the whaling master "was almost certain to act as physician, surgeon, lawyer, diplomat, financial agent, entrepreneur, judge, and peacemaker." Shorey had all the needed qualifications. He was to prove himself one of the most able practitioners of this demanding profession.

In 1887 Shorey married Julia Ann Shelton, the talented daughter of one of the leading black families of San Francisco. They cruised to the Hawaiian Islands aboard the *Herriman* on their honeymoon. Two years later, in 1889, Shorey took command of the recently built brig *Alexander*. He made two successful voyages as captain of the *Alexander* in 1889 and 1890, but disaster struck in 1891. The *Alexander* sank in the Arctic ice pack in the Bering Sea. However, Shorey's skill, courage, and resourcefulness managed to save the entire crew. The loss of the *Alexander* did not affect his career adversely. Upon his return to San Francisco, he was immediately placed in command of another vessel, the *Andrew Hicks*. The *Hicks* was already an old vessel when Shorey took command and had been described by her previous captain as "mighty shaky." It is a further tribute to Shorey's skillful seamanship that he completed eight successful voyages with the *Hicks* between 1892 and 1902.

After serving as captain of the *Hicks* and *Gay Head*—one of the most famous of the San Francisco whalers—Shorey took command of his last vessel, the *John and Winthrop*. Built in Bath, Maine, in 1876—the year Shorey began his whaling career—this sturdy bark sailed under Shorey on five whaling expeditions between 1903 and 1908, with the most exciting voyage occurring in 1907. While in the Sea of Okhotsk off the coast of eastern Russia, the ship experienced two fierce typhoons that badly damaged the vessel. The typhoons carried away several of the ship's longboats and all of the sails, threatening to sink the vessel. Upon returning to port the crew testified that "nothing but Captain Shorey's coolness and clever seamanship saved a wreck."

By the end of the first decade of the twentieth century the whaling bark had become an anachronism, and whaling had become a moribund industry in the United States. Shorey accordingly retired in 1908 and spent the remaining decade of his life ashore in Oakland, California. There, he was a respected member of the community, much sought after as a raconteur of thrilling tales of his exciting profession. He died and was buried there in 1919.

One work devoted to Shorey is E. Berkeley Tompkins's "Black Ahab: William T. Shorey, Whaling Master" (*California Historical Quarterly,* Spring 1972). The work contains extensive footnote references to a variety of unusual sources, including a number of personal interviews with Shorey's daughter, Victoria G. Francis of Berkeley, California. See also Delilah Beasley's work *The Negro Trail Blazers of California* (1919).

From *Dictionary of American Negro Biography* by Rayford W. Logan and Michael R. Winston, editors. Copyright © 1982 by Rayford W. Logan and Michael R. Winston. Reprinted by permission of W. W. Norton & Company, Inc.

E. Berkeley Tompkins

Short, Bobby

1924–

American cabaret singer and pianist, known for suave nightclub performances.

Bobby Short became a recognized talent on the New York cabaret scene as early as 1937, the year he was acclaimed in *Variety* magazine. He toured the United States during the 1940s and 1950s, establishing himself as a premier nightclub act with his elegant stage personality and singing style. Short then settled in NEW YORK CITY, where he played in several Broadway shows and at well-known "café society" nightclubs. Dividing his time between France and the United States, Short has performed four months out of the year at Cafe Carlyle in New York City since 1968. He also continues to record. Short's recent albums include *How's Your Romance* (1999) and *Piano* (2001).

See also Music, African American.

Shuffle Along

All-black musical that brought black entertainers back to Broadway after an absence of almost a decade.

When *Shuffle Along* opened at the 63rd Street Theater in New York City on May 23, 1921, after three months of performances on the road, there was little reason to believe that it would fare any better on Broadway than had previous black musicals. These earlier shows, such as *In Dahomey* (1903), which starred the team of Bert Williams and George Walker, and *The Red Moon* (1909), with Bob Cole and J. Rosamond Johnson, had played brief Broadway runs and then toured for several years. *Shuffle Along* began its New York run $18,000 in debt, with used costumes and minimal sets, and at a theater on the northern end of Broadway.

In creating *Shuffle Along*, composers Eubie Blake and Noble Sissle teamed up with the well-known comic team of Flournoy Miller and Aubrey Lyles, who had performed together since 1907. Miller and Lyles wrote the script, which incorporated some of their earlier vaudeville sketches, while Sissle and Blake provided up-to-date music and song lyrics. The thin plot of the show concerns the escapades of two crooked grocery store owners, Steve Jenkins (played by Miller) and Sam Peck (played by Lyles), each of whom wants to become mayor of Jimtown. When Jenkins wins a rigged election, he and Peck fight one another. A reform candidate, Harry Walton, pushes for a new election, unseats Jenkins, and restores calm to Jimtown. The name of the town evokes the stereotypes and segregation of the Jim Crow system, and the use of black dialect, malapropisms, and characters such as "Strutt, Jimtown Swell" and "Tom Sharper, Political Boss," points to the script's heavy debt to the traditions of minstrelsy. This debt was reinforced by Miller and Lyles's use of blackface and exaggerated stereotypical costumes. Sissle and Blake's score, on the other hand, was innovative in its combination of ragtime, European operetta, sentimental ballads, the blues, and jazz.

Despite its remote location on upper Broadway, *Shuffle Along* attracted mostly white audiences after a few weeks. Most of the Broadway critics wrote favorable reviews, and many compared the show to its white competition. As one critic wrote, using the stereotyped language of the era, "*Shuffle Along* is a darky show that has lost most of its darkiness. It is a semi-darky show that emulates the 'white' performance and—goes it one better." Critics and the public were enthusiastic about the exuberant singing and jazz dancing, as well as the high quality of the young stars. At one time or another during the show's run, the cast included Paul Robeson, Florence Mills, Fredi Washington, Lottie Gee, Gertrude Saunders, Hall Johnson, and Josephine Baker.

Shuffle Along played on Broadway for over a year, giving 504 performances. Its popularity was such that three road companies toured the country, bringing to a nationwide audience hit songs such as "I'm Just Wild About Harry," "Gypsy Blues," "Love Will Find a Way," "I'm Craving for That Kind of Love," and "Everything Reminds Me of You." The success of the show provided a new impetus, at the start of the Harlem Renaissance, to the presentation of many black musicals downtown. During the next ten years, close to fifty black musicals were presented in Broadway houses. Few of them became as successful as *Shuffle Along*, but they did provide more employment for black entertainers. At the same time, they introduced to white society black dances such as the Charleston and the black bottom during the "Roaring Twenties."

See also Dance, African American.

Bibliography

Kimball, Robert, and William Bolcom. *Reminiscing with Sissle and Blake.* Viking, 1973.

Shuttlesworth, Fred L.

1922–

American Baptist minister and civil rights leader who was a founding member and secretary of the Southern Christian Leadership Conference.

Fred Shuttlesworth was born in Mugler, Alabama. After receiving a B.A. from Selma University in Alabama in 1951 and a B.S. from Alabama State Teachers College in 1952, he became pastor first of Bethel Baptist Church, and then of the First Baptist Church in Birmingham, Alabama.

He formed the Alabama Christian Movement for Human Rights (ACMHR) in 1956. As ACMHR's president, from its inception until 1969, Shuttlesworth led Birmingham's integration movement. He was also the secretary of the Southern Christian Leadership Conference (SCLC), founded in 1958. Under the leadership of Martin Luther King, Jr., Shuttlesworth was instrumental in uniting the two organizations in a desegregation campaign, a joining of forces that led to the Birmingham demonstration in the spring of 1963. Shuttlesworth continued to organize demonstrations and marches, and finished his term as secretary of the SCLC in 1970. In 1999 Andrew M. Manis published the biography, *A Fire You Can't Put Out: The Civil Rights Life of Birmingham's Reverend Fred Shuttlesworth.* Fred Shuttlesworth is currently pastor of Greater New Light Baptist Church in Cincinnati, Ohio. He continues to lecture on issues of social justice.

See also Desegregation in the United States; Integration: An Interpretation.

Sia

Ethnic group of West Africa; also known as the Sya.

The Sia primarily inhabit western Burkina Faso and neighboring Mali. They speak a Mande language. Over 100,000 people consider themselves Sia.

Siad Barre, Mohamed

1916–1995

President and military dictator of Somalia from 1969 to 1991.

Mohamed Siad Barre was born in the city of Ganane into a family of nomadic herders in what was then Italian Somaliland. He belonged to the Marehan, a subgroup of the large SOMALI Daarood clan. In 1941, after part of Somalia fell under British control, Siad Barre joined the police force. In 1950 he attended a military academy in Italy, returning home when Somalia achieved independence in 1960.

Siad Barre rose quickly through the ranks of the Somali National Army, reaching the position of major general and commander in chief by 1966. After the assassination of President Abdel-Rashid Ali Shermarke and a military coup d'état in October 1969, Siad Barre took power as head of the Supreme Revolutionary Council.

Barre's promise to end tribalism and forge a modern socialist state won him early support from urban intellectuals and professionals as well as the military. Although he officially banned clan loyalties, he himself depended on clan elders to keep order in rural areas. At the same time, he increased the power of the Supreme Revolutionary Council, censored the press, and banned labor unions. In keeping with his official ideology of "scientific socialism," he also placed a large part of the economy under state control. Some historians have argued that this centralization of power and money in the traditionally dispersed nomadic economy was one of the leading causes of later violence. His successful literacy campaign in the early 1970s included the controversial decision to institutionalize Latin rather than Arabic characters in the long-planned written Somali language.

Known as a chain-smoking insomniac who called journalists for interviews in the middle of the night, Siad Barre's main preoccupation was security. He spared no expense to make the Somali military one of the most powerful armies in Sub-Saharan Africa: by the early 1980s, approximately three-quarters of the state budget went to the military. He bought weapons from both the East and the West during the Cold War, as well as from LIBYA, SOUTH AFRICA, China, and several Middle Eastern countries.

In 1977 Siad Barre used the army to seize the long-disputed territory of OGADEN from ETHIOPIA. When the Soviet-backed Ethiopians reclaimed the territory the following year, Siad Barre appealed to the United States for military and economic aid. He received $100 million a year in exchange for the United States' use of formerly Soviet-occupied Red Sea military facilities.

Siad Barre also used the armed forces against his own people. In addition to many individual cases of torture and assassination, whole clans were subject to mass execution, systematic rape, and village bombardment by military aircraft. The army also destroyed the grazing lands and water reservoirs of rural clans, leading to mass starvation and death by thirst. Between 1978 and 1988, Siad Barre's regime is thought to have killed at least 20,000 Somalis.

Siad Barre was the sole candidate in the 1986 presidential election, assuring him another seven years in office. By 1990, however, international as well as internal pressure had forced him to promise reforms allowing for a multiparty system, legalizing the narcotic Qaat, revoking equal inheritance for women, and liberalizing the economy. By January 1991 it was clear that reforms would not suffice. The paramilitary United Somali Congress took MOGADISHU, and Siad Barre fled to KENYA. After the Kenyan parliament denied him refuge, he went to NIGERIA.

See also African Socialism.

Marian Aguiar

Sickle-Cell Anemia

Genetically inherited condition of the red blood cells that causes chronic anemia, episodes of pain, and eventually death, mainly affecting people of African descent.

According to the National Institutes of Health, sickle-cell disease, often referred to as sickle-cell anemia, affects 72,000 people in the United States, most of whom are African Americans. One out of every 500 African American babies born each year has the disease. Some two million Americans—one out of every twelve African Americans—carry the genetic trait associated with the disease. The prevalence of the disease has produced both a federal and local call for development of appropriate testing of individuals at risk, effective treatments to reduce the debilitating symptoms and irreversible damage to major body systems, genetic screening of fetuses, and remedies for the psychosocial effects on ill individuals and their families.

The sickle-cell disorder is caused by a defective gene. The defect causes the body to produce abnormal red blood cells. The mutation originated in West Africa thousands of years ago, where it served as a survival advantage to West African populations plagued by a deadly form of MALARIA. Individuals who inherited the sickle-cell gene did not contract malaria. In fact, today in areas where malaria is prevalent, such as Equatorial Africa, more deaths result from malaria than from sickle-cell disease.

The sickle-cell gene tells the body to produce an abnormal form of the chemical compound in hemoglobin responsible for bringing oxygen into the red blood cells. Low levels of blood oxygen cause the blood cells to polymerize, or become jagged and tough, taking on a sickle shape, instead of assuming their usual soft round shape. The irregular, hard edges of sickle-shaped red blood cells cause them to get caught and collect in narrow blood vessels, causing restricted blood flow. This restriction causes the so-called pain episode, which can occur unpredictably and for a period of several hours to several days. The sickled cells have a much shorter life span than ordinary cells, causing the blood to be chronically short of red blood cells, which causes anemia in affected individuals. The complications of sickle-cell disease include stroke, osteomyelitis (an inflammatory disease of the bone leading to destruction of bone tissue), priapism (painful and persistent penile erection), and dactylitis (swollen fingers and toes, usually in babies). As the affected individual ages, other complications may arise, including blindness, heart and lung conditions, kidney failure, and damage to the spleen and liver.

Individuals who carry the sickle-cell genetic *trait* do not have the sickle-cell *disease*. Individuals who inherit the sickle-cell gene from only one parent (heterozygous form) have the sickle-cell trait (which has no disease symptoms). Such a person can transmit the sickle-cell gene to future generations, but will not contract the illness. Sickle-cell disease results when an individual inherits the defective gene from both parents (homozygous form).

Contrary to popular conception, sickle-cell disease does not affect only African Americans. In fact, sickle-cell disease can be genetically transmitted across populations to the offspring of any two parents who carry the sickle-cell gene. While a large percentage of the cases in the United States have been among African Americans, the disease has also been found in Burma, Greece, India, Turkey, and Yemen and is not limited to any one social group. The highest incidence of the disease, however, affecting 20 percent of the population, has been found in Central Africa near the equator, where malaria is prevalent.

Testing for sickle-cell disease has improved greatly over the past two decades. In the 1970s the solubility test that was used did not distinguish between people who merely had the heterozygous genetic trait (not diseased) and those who were homozygous for sickled blood cells (diseased). Consequently, the results indicated that a large number of African Americans had the disease. In the black community, a number of concerned leaders and organizations, including the Black Panthers, pressed for increased testing of African Americans, unaware of the deficiency in the testing procedures and the difficulties the test results could pose for their constituents.

In CHICAGO, ILLINOIS, alone, the exaggerated test results of 5,000 black public school children led to the incorrect statistic that one out of every ten children had sickle-cell disease. The resulting overstated claims by the Heart and Lung Institute, an otherwise reputable source, that a significant percentage of the African American population was affected by sickle-cell disease, negatively affected the entire African American community. They were then subject to routine screening for jobs and dramatic increases in insurance rates.

Pressure from the black community and local politicians has led to legislation in twelve states concerning mandatory screening, limited mainly to blacks, for sickle-cell disease. In 1972 Congress passed the National Sickle-Cell Anemia Control Act, which was expanded in 1976 and amended in 1978. The misinformation from the problematic 1970s testing and other popular misunderstandings informed such legislation and led to the government's desire to control the disease, even though it had been demonstrated to be genetically transmitted, not contagious. (The TUSKEGEE SYPHILIS EXPERIMENT was a more sinister example of the U.S. government's intervention in disease "control" among blacks.) Finally, however, federal support of community sickle-cell programs led to the establishment of Comprehensive Sickle Cell Centers, which offered testing, education, and counseling. The centers continued research to develop more sophisticated and more reliable testing procedures, including electrophoresis techniques.

At present, treatment for sickle-cell anemia is aimed at the early detection of the disease so that affected individuals may begin treatment before they manifest debilitating symptoms. Babies who are homozygous for sickle-cell disease can be protected against infections by being given penicillin orally at about four months of age. Patients who have begun to display advanced symptoms are provided with various forms of supportive management, including psychological counseling for the pain and discomfort associated with the disease.

The death rate from sickle-cell disease is decreasing steadily due to improved therapies. Exchange transfusion therapy, which temporarily reduces the number of sickled cells in the blood, is used to manage advanced chronic pain and acute conditions such as stroke. Two experimental drugs were developed in the late 1980s: erythropoietin, a hormone that helps increase the production of red blood cells, and hydroxyurea. Both these medications, when given to sickle-cell disease patients, help promote the synthesis of normal fetal hemoglobin, which replaces some of the sickled blood cells in the individual. Bone marrow transplants have been used to cure children with sickle-cell disease, but the risk of death is as great as 50 percent, and the cost is prohibitive for most families. Gene therapy, in which normal genes are transferred into certain marrow cells, is possibly the future cure for sickle-cell disease, but it is still at an experimental stage.

See also Black Panther Party; Disease and African History; Disease, Medicine, and Health.

Barbara Worley

Sidamo

Ethnic group of Ethiopia; also known as Sidama or Sadama.

According to Sidamo oral tradition, the Sidamo peoples migrated southward from northern ETHIOPIA starting sometime in the sixteenth century. They settled in a region of southwestern Ethiopia that offers a varied landscape where the different Sidamo subgroups cultivate corn, enset (a fruit related to the banana), wheat, and barley. In addition, some Sidamo raise cattle.

Of the approximately three million people who consider themselves Sidamo, most also consider themselves members of one of the many Sidamo subgroups. The largest subgroups are the Yamarico and Aleta. All Sidamo speak the same language, one that belongs to the Eastern Cushitic language family. About 10 percent of Sidamo practice Islam, but the vast majority adhere to traditional religious beliefs, which include worship of a single deity called Magano, a creator figure who is thought to live in the sky.

Sidamo social structures revolve around patrilineal kinship, or descent through the male line. Families so related live together in villages, which are linked in a larger network of regional affiliations. The architecture of Sidamo villages, some of which are heavily walled and fortified, reflects a history of warfare in an often-contested region. Councils of elders generally make group decisions.

Sierra Leone

Country on the Atlantic coast of West Africa, bordered by Liberia and Guinea.

War-torn and impoverished today, Sierra Leone played a role in Africa's colonial history far out of proportion to its size. (It is one of the smallest West African countries, and has a population of 5.7 million.) Abolitionists founded the Sierra Leone Colony at the end of the eighteenth century as a refuge for freed slaves. As Great Britain's first real colony on African soil, Sierra Leone served as a testing ground for subsequent colonial efforts elsewhere on the continent. The colony's mixed population of freed slaves, Europeans, and indigenous Africans gave rise to the unique KRIO culture, which blends Western and indigenous features. As the first group of Africans exposed to British cultural and administrative practices, Sierra Leoneans served in the British colonial administration throughout West Africa. During most of the twentieth century, Sierra Leone provided leaders for West African nationalism. Though Sierra Leone is rich in valuable mineral deposits and agricultural potential, regional resentments and governmental corruption steadily undermined the country's economy in the years after independence and left it vulnerable to military adventurers. Intermittent warfare and civil strife since 1991 have exposed Sierra Leoneans to a nightmare of violence and economic devastation. Partly as a consequence, Sierra Leone is today one of the poorest nations on earth. The return of a civilian government to power in 1998, however, raised hopes that Sierra Leone's fortunes would improve.

Early History

Archaeologists have shown that human beings have inhabited the area now called Sierra Leone since at least 2500 B.C.E. The region's inhabitants were working iron by 600 C.E. During the fifteenth and sixteenth centuries, MANDE-speaking peoples migrated or invaded from the east. They intermarried with the ancestors of the modern Bullom, Kissi, and Krim peoples, who had occupied the country for centuries. The mixture produced such present-day peoples as the MENDE, Loko, and Vai.

In precolonial times people reared cattle in the northern grasslands and savanna, and cultivated plants across the region including rice, MILLET, yams, and vegetables. Women collected and extracted palm oil, which they used for food and soap production. Coastal peoples relied on fish as a major source of protein, and traded sea salt with interior peoples. In the northeast part of the region inhabitants mined iron. Yalunka and Koranko blacksmiths controlled the iron trade and were known as skilled workers. The region's people collected gold, mostly by panning, for trade, religious rituals, and ornaments. Cotton grown and woven in Mendeland and the northeast was an important trade item often used as a currency.

No single state dominated Sierra Leone in the precolonial period. Even the large ethnic groups like the Mende and TEMNE remained divided among smaller chieftaincies that traded and fought with their neighbors. Secret societies such as Poro and Sande, however, cut across these political and ethnic divisions and united men and women throughout the region in networks of trade, mutual assistance, education, and spiritual practice.

Portuguese explorers first anchored off the mountainous Sierra Leone Peninsula in the fifteenth century. They gave the peninsula its name, meaning "lion mountain," which has come to refer to the entire country.

The region's small, militarized political formations profited from the slave trade, which was well established in the region by the sixteenth century. Chiefs along the coast leased land to European slave traders without relinquishing their sovereignty. Local groups exported slaves both directly to Europeans on the coast and, by the eighteenth century, to the FULANI, who led them to FOUTA DJALLON and even Hausaland to the east.

Colonial Era

While British slave traders had traded on the coast for over a century, it was the abolitionist movement that spurred the initial colonization of Sierra Leone. British abolitionists founded the colony to create a community of free blacks. There they hoped to resettle ex-slaves from London, many of whom were legally free but unemployed, poor, and ineligible for the relief provided to white Englishmen. The first attempt at colonization in 1787 failed primarily because of poor weather; poor relations with the local Temne, who inhabited the Sierra Leone peninsula at the time; and the attractive work that nearby African and Afro-European slave traders offered to the literate, English-speaking free black settlers. A second, more successful attempt to settle ex-slaves from Nova Scotia followed in 1792. The settlement was named FREETOWN. Eight years later, the British settled another contingent, consisting of escaped slaves from JAMAICA. The colony, however, soon faced resistance from the local Temne. Although the British had secured treaties from the Temne, transferring much of the peninsula to the new colony, the Temne assumed that the treaties, like those they had concluded with Europeans for generations, merely involved a lease. When the British rejected Temne claims of territorial sovereignty, the Temne declared war and attacked the colony. In response, the British expelled the Temne from the peninsula.

The British declared Freetown, the peninsula, and its environs a Crown Colony in 1808. They established a naval base at Freetown, from which they policed the African coast in an effort to enforce the 1807 British law banning the slave trade. British authorities freed thousands of Africans from slave traders and settled them in the colony between 1808 and 1860. The colony became a magnet for Africans in the region looking for work, trade opportunities, or an escape from their own leaders or owners. Freetown became a major center for the ex-

Sierra Leone

Regional wars and political chaos have displaced thousands of Sierra Leoneans, including these children in a refugee camp near Freetown in 1996. CORBIS/Jon Spaull

ternal trade of the entire region, including the hinterlands that at first remained outside British rule.

The new colony, however, encompassed only Freetown and its immediate environs on the peninsula. The vast majority of present-day Sierra Leone remained in the hands of its indigenous peoples through most of the nineteenth century. Although abolitionists had founded the colony and enforced a ban on the coastal slave trade throughout the region, Fulani traders continued to export slaves to the interior, and the Mende, Temne, and other groups continued to hold slaves. With the abolition of the coastal slave trade, inhabitants focused on the production of other goods for trade with the British. The most important of these was palm oil, although local people traded lumber, ivory, gold, and other products for Western manufactures.

During the nineteenth century the British sought to control the lucrative trade routes emanating from the colony to its hinterlands. A series of wars in the interior, then called "tribal wars" but now more accurately termed "trade wars," frustrated British attempts to assert control. Toward the end of the century, during the SCRAMBLE FOR AFRICA, the British authorities entered a four-sided contest with SAMORY TOURÉ, the French, and Touré's Sikasso enemies (in present-day COTE D'IVOIRE) for Touré's extensive commercial empire, including parts of modern Cote d'Ivoire, GUINEA, and Sierra Leone.

The frontier police posted by the British to guard trade routes after 1890, however, were insufficient for the task. Following a skirmish with the French in 1893, the British abandoned their effort to take control of Touré's eastern holdings, which now fell into French hands. The British declared a protectorate in 1896 over the more immediate hinterland of the Sierra Leone Colony. While the British ruled the colony directly, with a governor and legislative council based in Freetown, in the much larger protectorate they introduced a policy of indirect rule, relying on indigenous chiefs to carry out local administration. The peoples of the protectorate resisted British attempts to assert control, and particularly their imposition of a hut tax, in the Hut Tax War and Mende Rising of 1898.

Ironically, while the British founded the Sierra Leone Colony as a focal point of their campaign against slavery, official British collusion with slavery lasted longer in the protectorate than in any other African territory. Colonial rule served to strengthen the chiefs allied with the British, many of whom relied on slaves to grow and harvest palm oil and other agricultural products. The British allowed this slave economy to persist until 1928, when they finally banned slavery in the protectorate.

The different administrative statuses of the colony and protectorate paralleled differences in wealth, educational resources, and political power. The colony, and especially Freetown, continued to be an important trading center. Syrian traders and large European companies ended Krio domination of the export trade after the late nineteenth century. With their gradual displacement from commerce, however, members of this group, who enjoyed privileged access to Western education, took up important roles as colonial civil servants, not only in Sierra Leone, but in other British colonies as well. Meanwhile, colonial authorities established the protectorate as a source of cash crops and minerals for export. One of the main purposes of the hut tax was to force the region's inhabitants to participate in the cash economy as wage laborers or producers of cash crops. In 1916 the British completed a rail line to the rich agricultural lands of the southeast, where, after the 1920s, COCOA and coffee became important cash crops.

After 1930 diamond and iron mining became an important part of the country's economy. By 1961 over 80 percent of export income came from mining. This mining boom led to rapid urbanization in the 1950s, which aggravated inflation. Increasing political discontent, fueled by high food prices, was expressed most sharply in riots in 1955 and 1956.

Sierra Leoneans were among the earliest modern nationalists in Africa, and many played prominent roles in the National Congress of British West Africa in the 1920s. The process of democratic reforms, which led to independence far more quickly than the British had intended, began after World War II (1939–1945) with the establishment of an assembly for the protectorate. Chiefs dominated this body, which met for the first time in 1946.

Sierra Leone (At a Glance)

OFFICIAL NAME: Sierra Leone

AREA: 71,740 sq km (27,699 sq mi)

LOCATION: Western Africa; borders the North Atlantic Ocean, Guinea, and Liberia

CAPITAL: Freetown (population 1,051,000; 2003 estimate)

OTHER MAJOR CITIES: Koidu (population 113,700) and Makeni (110,700) (2003 estimates)

POPULATION: 5,732,681 (2003 estimate)

POPULATION DENSITY: 80 persons per sq km (207 sq mi)

POPULATION BELOW AGE 15: 44.8 percent (male 1,259,421; female 1,1310,516; 2003 estimate)

POPULATION GROWTH RATE: 2.94 percent (2003 estimate)

TOTAL FERTILITY RATE: 5.86 children born per woman (2003 estimate)

LIFE EXPECTANCY AT BIRTH: Total population: 42.84 years (male 40.33 years; female 45.42 years; 2003 estimate)

INFANT MORTALITY RATE: 146.86 deaths per 1000 live births (2003 estimate)

LITERACY RATE (AGE 15 AND OVER WHO CAN READ AND WRITE): Total population: 31.4 percent (male 45.4 percent; female 18.2 percent; 1995 estimate)

EDUCATION: In 2003 approximately 37 percent of eligible children attended primary school.

LANGUAGES: English is the official language, although its regular use is limited to a literate minority (less than 20 percent of the adult population is literate). About twenty African languages are spoken in Sierra Leone. Mende is the principal language of the south, and Temne is the principal language of the north. Another common language is Krio, a Creole language derived from English and various African languages.

ETHNIC GROUPS: There are thirteen different ethnic groups in the Sierra Leone population. The largest groups are the Mende in the south, who account for nearly 30 percent of the population, and the Temne in the north, who account for nearly 30 percent of the population. Creoles, descendants of freed slaves returned from the Americas, are an important minority in the Freetown area, where small numbers of Lebanese, Indians, and Europeans also reside.

RELIGIONS: About 60 percent of the population is Muslim. About 30 percent adheres to indigenous beliefs, and 10 percent is Christian.

CLIMATE: Tropical. Hot and humid with a rainy season between May and October. The mean temperature in Freetown is 27° C (about 80° F) in January and 26° C (78° F) in July. Annual rainfall averages more than 3800 mm (150 in) along the coast and 2030 mm (about 80 in) in the northern interior.

LAND, PLANTS, AND ANIMALS: Sierra Leone's geography ranges from coastal mangrove swamps to grassy savanna in the north, and mountains in the east. There are dense forests in the southeast that contain varieties of palm, mahogany, and teak trees. Animals include bush pigs, chimpanzees, monkeys, and porcupines. Crocodiles and hippopotamuses are found in the rivers.

NATURAL RESOURCES: Mineral resources include diamonds, bauxite, and rutile. Production, however, has been hampered by civil war and—in the case of diamonds—by overmining and smuggling. Even so, diamond mining continues to be the primary source of hard currency. It is hoped that political stability will allow the reopening of bauxite and rutile mines that closed during the civil war.

CURRENCY: Leones issued by the Bank of Sierra Leone.

GROSS DOMESTIC PRODUCT (GDP): $2.8 billion (2002 estimate)

GDP REAL GROWTH RATE: 5 percent (2002 estimate)

GDP PER CAPITA: $580 (2002 estimate)

EXTERNAL DEBT: $1.5 billion (2002 estimate)

PRIMARY ECONOMIC ACTIVITIES: Agriculture (employing 65 percent of the population), industry, and services

PRIMARY CROPS: Rice, coffee, cocoa, palm kernels, palm oil, peanuts, and livestock

INDUSTRIES: Mining (diamonds, bauxite, and rutile), small-scale manufacturing (textiles, beverages, cigarettes, and footwear), petroleum refining

PRIMARY EXPORTS: Rutile, diamonds, coffee, cocoa, and fish

PRIMARY IMPORTS: Foodstuffs, machinery and equipment, fuels and lubricants, and chemicals

PRIMARY TRADE PARTNERS: United States, United Kingdom, Belgium, Netherlands, Greece, and Germany

GOVERNMENT: Constitutional multiparty democracy. The executive branch is led by President Ahmad Tejan Kabbah, who was elected to a second term in 2002. The president appoints the Ministers of State. The legislative branch is the elected, 105-member House of Representatives.

Elizabeth Heath

The new constitution in 1947 provided for ten elected representatives from the protectorate and did not require that these representatives be literate. The members of the Krio elite feared poor government and a loss of authority if "tribal Africans" gained power. They formed an alliance with conservative chiefs in the Sierra Leone People's Party (SLPP), led by Sir Milton A.S. Margai, a former medical officer and member of the Mende ethnic group. The SLPP won the 1951 election, and the process of constitutional change continued. In 1957 SIAKA STEVENS led a group that broke away from the SLPP to form the People's National Party, and in 1960 he founded the All People's Congress (APC). The SLPP drew most of its support from the Mende south, while the APC dominated the primarily Temne north. In 1958 the SLPP won an electoral victory under a constitution that gave them greater powers. The popular Margai was able to withstand allegations that his administration was tribalist and to fend off demands for another general election before independence in 1961.

Independence

Sierra Leone gained independence on April 27, 1961. In 1964 Albert Margai (who was knighted the following year) succeeded his brother Milton as prime minister. Albert Margai unsuccessfully proposed a one-party government in 1966. He did adopt measures to replace Krio officials in the government's administration. The Krio voters largely shifted their allegiance to the northern-based APC in the 1967 election, and the APC won. The military intervened, ruled for one year, and handed over power to Stevens in 1968.

Sierra Leone has continued to concentrate on the export economy that was established during the colonial period. The country was nonaligned during the Cold War but remained one of the more conservative West African countries, allied with the capitalist West. A development policy passed in 1960 aimed to encourage domestic industrial production.

Stevens's government adopted a more left-wing orientation in the early 1970s. His administration acquired a 52 percent stake in the diamond industry and he developed a closer relationships with the countries of Eastern Europe. However, all of these measures had more to do with an assertive nationalism than communism, and his government retained its close connections with the West. In 1971 a new constitution mandated a strong presidency.

The 1973–1974 oil crisis precipitated a serious economic decline from which Sierra Leone has not yet recovered. The increase in oil prices coincided with a decrease in export earnings. The country's iron ore reserves were depleted, and smugglers increasingly commandeered the country's diamond production and thus deprived the government of vital revenue. Meanwhile, government corruption became pervasive. Beginning in the mid-1970s, the Stevens government faced growing opposition, notably from professionals and the trade unions. Stevens adopted an increasingly autocratic stance, and in 1978 he declared the country a one-party state. However, popular opposition forced Stevens to resign in 1985. His hand-picked successor, Major General Joseph Momoh, went on to win the presidential election that year as the sole legal candidate. Momoh accepted an IMF-supported structural adjustment program beginning in 1986, but this collapsed in 1988 because of debt repayment difficulties. The government accepted a new structural adjustment program in 1989 that involved a range of neoliberal measures, including large cuts in government staffing levels and extensive privatization. Momoh moved to reinstate multiparty democracy. Voters approved a new, more liberal constitution in 1991, and elections were scheduled for later that year.

In the same year, however, the civil war in LIBERIA spilled over into Sierra Leone. Supporters of Liberian rebel leader CHARLES TAYLOR invaded Sierra Leone, and fighting quickly engulfed about one-third of the country. Warfare ravaged the country's already faltering economy. Invaders disrupted agricultural activity and seized control of the lucrative diamond business, which financed continued fighting. Dissatisfaction in the military with Momoh's response to the invasion prompted the 1992 coup led by Captain Valentine Strasser. Strasser continued with the structural adjustment program and attempted to reduce government spending. By 1994 a rebel army, the Revolutionary United Front (RUF), a growing number of predatory "warlords," and Taylor's forces together had reduced much of the countryside to a state of violence and chaos.

Attempts to find a peace included elections in March 1996, in which Alhaji Ahmad Tejan Kabbah of the SLPP won the presidency. Kabbah continued efforts toward peace until junior army officers within the so-called Armed Forces Revolutionary Council, supported by many RUF soldiers, overthrew him in 1997. This coup returned Sierra Leone to a state of violence, political chaos, and economic ruin. Troops from NIGERIA, acting as part of ECOMOG, the joint West African security force, occupied Freetown in early 1998, deposed the military junta, and continued to fight the RUF. The Kamajors, armies of young men who take inspiration from traditional religion and are proud of their hunting prowess, have remained loyal to Kabbah, but are still armed and represent a disruptive influence in parts of the countryside.

By the end of the twentieth century Sierra Leone's economy and infrastructure were shattered from years of civil war. The country's agriculture and rural areas were particularly devastated, and thousands of refugees had fled to Freetown and other overwhelmed urban areas. In 1997 government revenues collapsed almost completely. The formal economy was ruined, and only a limited informal and black-market economy remained.

Under the protection of ECOMOG, President Kabbah was able to return and reestablish his government in 1998. The civil war continued, however, with the RUF reportedly controlling about half of the country's territory. In July 1999 Kabbah and RUF leader Foday Sankoh signed a peace accord that would give the RUF a role in government. Later that year the United Nations established a peacekeeping mission to help monitor the agreement and oversee the disarmament and demobilization of RUF forces. The peace agreement collapsed in the spring of 2000 when RUF rebels clashed with UN forces. The government and the RUF signed another cease-fire in November 2000, allowing UN peacekeepers to disarm tens of thousands of RUF fighters. The disarmament program was declared a success in January 2002. In peaceful elections held in May, Kabbah won a second term as president, and the SLPP won a majority of seats in the legislature.

The civil war, which included some of the worst human rights abuses in modern times, displaced an estimated two million refugees—more than a third of Sierra Leone's population—and impoverished the country. The new government is focusing on disarmament, political stability, and economic recovery.

See also London's Black Poor and the Sierra Leone Settlement Plan; Nationalism in Africa; Slavery in Africa; Structural Adjustment in Africa.

Alistair Chisholm

Signifying

Form of verbal play—centering primarily on the insult—common in African American communities.

Roger Abrahams's early study *Deep Down in the Jungle: Negro Narrative Folklore from the Streets of Philadelphia* (1963, 1970) defines signifying as a verbal mechanism by which anger and aggression may be channeled into relatively harmless form. This form of play offers speakers the opportunity to demonstrate their improvisational mastery of rhyme and rhythm, as well as their capacity to improvise on the verbal play of others. Signifying implies the art of expressing ideas, opinions, feelings, and so forth, by indirection and is, therefore, a culturally specific form of irony. One who signifies says without explicitly saying, criticizes without actually criticizing, insults without really insulting. Abrahams interprets signifying as a fundamentally male ritual, whereby African American men reestablish their sense of manhood so often diminished by the psychological weight of oppression. In its various forms ("rifting," "the dozens," "specifying"), signifying substitutes verbal power for political or economic power.

While Abrahams identifies signifying as a gender-specific practice, others (Mitchell-Kernan, Smitherman, et al.) see this display of verbal expertise within a broader social framework. Smitherman, for instance, identifies signifying's ritualistic quality (as does Abrahams) but further sees this verbal practice as using humor in the service of a "nonmalicious and principled criticism." The rhetoric of signifying, therefore, aims at the formation of community rather than at the expression of dominance.

Recently signifying has developed as a prominent term of art in the realm of literary and cultural criticism. As popularized by HENRY LOUIS GATES, JR., in *The Signifying Monkey: A Theory of Afro-American Literature* (1988), signifying indicates a form of intertextual revision, by which texts establish their relation to other texts, and authors to other authors. The force of this revision is to establish a critical relation to previous discursive statements. In this sense, one signifies on a particular work, author, form, or tradition, by copying central elements or practices, even while revising those in some significant way. The repetition implicit in this form of signifying criticizes or extends the previous and frequently (though not exclusively) white literary or cultural source by setting it within the context of African American expressive culture. FREDERICK DOUGLASS signifies on the autobiography in writing his *Narrative of the Life of Frederick Douglass* (1845); CHARLES WADDELL CHESNUTT signifies on the plantation tradition in *The Conjure Woman* (1899); and RALPH ELLISON signifies on the bildungsroman in *Invisible Man* (1952). Examples of intramural signifying include HARRIET A. JACOBS's revision of Douglass in her *Incidents in the Life of a Slave Girl* (1861), JAMES WELDON JOHNSON's troping of W. E. B. DU BOIS *The Souls of Black Folk* (1903) in *The Autobiography of an Ex-Colored Man* (1912), or TONI MORRISON's reconstruction of the SLAVE NARRATIVE in *Beloved* (1987). In each of these examples, the antecedent text, author, and form are revisited and, hence, reworked. This version of signifying, consequently, offers a theory of how a literary or expressive cultural tradition is built, a theory based on a mode of verbal play deeply embedded in the African American vernacular.

Bibliography

Abrahams, Roger. *Talking Black,* 1976.
Baker, Houston. *Modernism and the Harlem Renaissance,* 1987.
Major, Clarence. *Juba to Jive: A Dictionary of African-American Slang,* 1970; rpt. 1994.
Mitchell-Kernan, Claudia. *Language Behavior in a Black Urban Community,* 1971.
Smitherman, Geneva. *Black Talk: Words and Phrases from the Hood to the Amen Corner,* 1994.

Theodore O. Mason, Jr.

Sihanaka

Ethnic group of Madagascar; also known as Antisihanaka.

The Sihanaka primarily inhabit eastern MADAGASCAR. They speak MALAGASY, a Malyo-Polynesian language. Over 200,000 people consider themselves Sihanaka.

See also Madagascar, Ethnicity in.

Silva, Benedita da

1943–

Afro-Brazilian politician and social activist, the first black woman to enter the Brazilian Congress, and the first woman from the *favelas* to become a major political figure in Brazil.

Benedita da Silva—the "voice of the favelas"—is shown here with U.S. civil rights activist Jesse Jackson, who had come to Brazil in 2002 to urge voters to support Workers Party candidates. *Reuters/CORBIS*

Known affectionately as Bené, Benedita da Silva is one of BRAZIL's foremost political figures. Born and raised in Brazil's FAVELAS, or squatter settlements, she became a leading community organizer. In 1980 she helped found the leftist Partido dos Trabalhadores (the Workers' Party, or PT), a broad-based coalition of workers, grassroots organizers, and intellectuals. Six years later she became the first black woman to enter the Brazilian Congress, where she was one of only 26 women and seven blacks among 559 deputies. Silva has consistently fought to prioritize racial, class, and gender issues within both the PT and Brazil's political institutions, and has strongly opposed discrimination against women and blacks. Indeed, in her opening speech before Congress in 1986, she stated: "If our opinion is not taken into account and we women are not guaranteed equality, we won't feel obligated to respect your laws. We are going to start a rebellion and hundreds of us will occupy the space now taken by insensitive people like you."

The youngest of thirteen children, Silva grew up in RIO DE JANEIRO, in the favela of Chapéu Mangueira. Her father was a construction worker, and her mother earned a living as a washerwoman and midwife. At the age of seven, Silva began supplementing the family income by selling candy and fruit on the street. "My experience growing up on the streets was difficult but it was also a . . . school of life where you learn everything," she noted in her autobiography. Unlike most favelas, Chapéu Mangueira had an elementary school, and at an early age Silva learned to read and write. After the death of her mother in 1957, she began working with the progressive wing of the Catholic Church, which organized literacy and health programs in the favelas.

At the age of sixteen, Silva married a handyman, and during the next four years gave birth to four children—two of whom died shortly after they were born. "I saw my first child buried like a pauper," she wrote in her autobiography. "The image of my baby inside that little box will always be etched in my memory." Silva worked as a housemaid and street vendor, but her family nevertheless lived in poverty and often had to eat from restaurant trash cans to survive. Moreover, during the late 1950s, the government attempted to control the favelas by establishing government-run neighborhood associations that undermined the organizing work of community leaders. In 1964, after the Brazilian military assumed power in a coup, repression of independent organizations increased as did pressures to eradicate and relocate the favelas. Residents of favelas who opposed eviction were often targeted: "We were exiled in our own country," wrote Silva. "We weren't allowed to sing our religious hymns or celebrate our festivals. We dug holes in our houses to hide our books and notepads. We couldn't keep minutes of our meetings because it was considered subversive to demand better living conditions like electricity, plumbing or paved roads."

In 1969 Silva joined the Assembly of God, an Evangelical Protestant Church. "I was going through an extremely difficult period in my life," she said. "I was feeling overwhelmed by poverty and hunger." Silva found emotional and spiritual support in the predominantly conservative Evangelical community—a development that baffled many of her political colleagues, who perceived her religious affiliation to be incompatible with her radical political views. Indeed, Latin American Evangelicals have often aligned themselves with repressive governments. Yet Silva has always maintained her political independence, and sees the church as a place where she can reaffirm and strengthen her faith.

Despite prolonged government repression, Silva played a central role in building the local women's movement. In 1978, with the support of women activists, she was elected president of the Chapéu Mangueira neighborhood association. She continued to work while preparing for the high school equivalency exam. After receiving her high school diploma in 1980, she enrolled in college to study social work, and in 1982 successfully campaigned for the city council. She became the first PT representative in Rio de Janeiro and the first black city councilwoman in Brazil. In 1986 she was elected a federal deputy for the National Assembly; four years later, she was reelected.

In 1992 Silva ran for mayor of Rio de Janeiro. Although she was ahead of her opponent in the polls, the conservative elite launched a bitter campaign in the media to discredit her, and she lost the elections by a narrow margin. Two years later, however, she became the first black woman elected to the Brazilian Senate.

Silva's support base consists of the people she most often represented during her political career: women, blacks, the poor, churchgoers, workers, and social activists. Still, according to Medea Benjamin and Maisa Mendonça, social activists who have followed Silva's career, "Bené moves in and out of the most diverse circles imaginable. In a gathering of blacks or whites, men or women, rich or poor, Bené holds her ground with great dignity. In the Senate, she is mostly surrounded by rich, white men. Although she fights them tooth and nail on economic policies, she greets them with a broad smile."

Silva's political position differs from those of many Brazilian leftist politicians, who typically prioritize class issues over racial ones. As an Afro-Brazilian, she has been subjected to humiliating racial slurs all her life, by both the Brazilian public and the conservative political elite. "Blacks suffer because they are poor, but they are poor precisely because they are black," she argues. "And when blacks do manage to move up the social and economic ladder, they still can't escape racism." At the same time, she believes that the reluctance of Brazilian blacks to embrace their own identity has precluded a "strong, cohesive national movement that can really influence policy." She advocates "a version of socialism that is not imported or top-down, but [one] that respects our culture and works from the bottom up." Central to her vision is agrarian reform. Silva has proposed that land be distributed to the landless, so that they would not have to migrate to the cities to find sustenance, and that people living in the favelas receive legal title to the land on which they already live. "My aim," notes Silva, "is to help gain access to power for groups that have traditionally been locked out." In this vein, she successfully campaigned for an affirmative action policy within the PT that guarantees that at least thirty percent of the party's deputies are women.

Although during her tenure in the senate Silva had to move to Brasília, the capital, she remained an active participant in the community affairs of Chapéu Mangueira, which she still considers her home. Her many years of community work have helped to transform her neighborhood into a model favela—a strong, well-organized community that maintains its own health and educational facilities. In 1998 she was elected deputy governor of the state of Rio de Janeiro. In 2002 Silva took over as governor, finishing the term of Anthony Garotinho, who stepped down to run for president. She currently serves in the Brazilian cabinet as minister of Social Assistance and Promotion.

See also Catholic Church in Latin American and the Caribbean; Protestant Church in Latin American and the Caribbean.

Bibliography

Benjamin, Medea, and Maria Luisa Mendonça. "Benedita da Silva: Community activist and senator, Brazil." *NACLA Report on the Americas* 31, no. 1 (Jul.–Aug. 1997).

Silva, Benedita da (as told to Medea Benjamin and Maisa Mendonça). *Benedita da Silva: An Afro-Brazilian Woman's Story of Politics and Love*. Food First Books, 1997.

Roanne Edwards

Silva, Ismael

1905–1978

Afro-Brazilian musician, composer, and founder of one of Brazil's earliest samba schools.

Ismael Silva was born in Niterói, a city across Guanabara Bay from RIO DE JANEIRO. An early *sambista* (samba musician), Silva was instrumental in the founding of Deixa Falar, one of the first SAMBA SCHOOLS in BRAZIL. Together with other samba artists—Bide, Nilton Bastos, and Armando Marcal—he helped plant the seed for Brazil's fledgling *Escola de Samba* (samba school) system. These four legendary musicians are often referred to as the *Turma do Estácio* (the Estácio Gang), Estácio being a neighborhhood in Rio de Janeiro. Originally, their "school" was more of a music-making club than place of instruction. In fact, it was called a school only because it happened to be situated across the street from a neighborhood grammar school.

In 1929, Ismael Silva and the other members of Deixa Falar were among the first blacks to formally participate in CARNIVAL. Previously, it had been illegal to do so, and was still strongly discouraged by the authorities for years afterward. As a result of the efforts of these early sambistas, more and more blacks began to participate in the parades each year. Many founded their own samba schools, which led to the creation of the thousands of organizations that now comprise Brazil's samba-school system.

Ismael Silva is now considered the most important composer from the Turma do Estácio. His innovations, such as consistent two-bar phrasing and slowing the tempo of samba, helped to differentiate the fledgling genre from its faster-paced nineteenth-century cousins, the *maxixe* and the *marcha*. In fact, according to author Chris McGowan there was a debate for many years over who created the first samba, DONGA or Silva. Ismael insisted that Donga's 1917 success *"Pelo Telephone"* was not a samba at all, but a maxixe. When Donga tauntingly asked, "What, then is a samba?" Silva confidently cited *"Se você jurar,"* his own composition.

Bibliography

McGowan, Chris. *The Brazilian Sound*. Temple University Press, 1988.

Schreiner, Claus. *Música Brasileira: A History of Popular Music and the People of Brazil*. Marion Boyars, 1993.

Silva, Xica da

1734?–?

Afro-Brazilian woman who challenged the aristocracy of colonial Brazil.

In every version of her life story, Francisca "Xica" da Silva is described as a slave who was freed by João Fernandes de Oliveira around 1760. Fernandes was a *contratador*, or a vassal of the Portuguese Crown, sent to the province of MINAS GERAIS in colonial BRAZIL to explore the soil for diamonds and gold. Da Silva lived and worked as a slave until she was purchased by Oliveira, who lived with da Silva as her husband despite the racial prejudice that existed at that time in Brazil.

Instead of sending the mineral riches he discovered to Portugal, Oliveira kept them for himself and became a very rich man. He and da Silva lived a luxurious life in Arraial do Tijuco, a small village in Minas Gerais. He built a palace; imported gifts for da Silva from all over the world, including gold and diamonds; and built her a ship to sail on a nearby river. Xica da Silva came to be known as the unofficial empress of Brazil.

The story of her life was filmed by the noted Brazilian director CARLOS DIEGUES, who called her the Brazilian Joan of Arc. In Diegues's 1976 movie, the Portuguese Crown sends an officer to investigate complaints of irregularities concerning Oliveira's activities. Oliveira ends up returning to Portugal, leaving da Silva and his fortune behind. Without Oliveira's protection and facing the contempt of the local society, da Silva supposedly rescued herself by retreating to a monastery for blacks built under Oliveira's command. Other versions of Xica da Silva's life state that Oliveira never went back to Portugal and that they married, raised a large family, and lived together until their death.

The details of Xica da Silva's biography remain unclear. It is possible that she was a daughter of the slave Silvana Oliveira da Silva, and that she was born a slave in 1734 on the farm of the priest José da Silva e Oliveira Rolim in Minas Gerais. She is also described as being the daughter of a Portuguese father or of an indigenous Brazilian and an Afro-Brazilian slave. Plays, romances, and other sources that tell the story of Xica da Silva repeatedly show signs of white society's hostility to her, including her exclusion from the local Catholic church. Da Silva, however, is generally shown as an astute woman who struggled to overcome the racial and social prejudices of her time.

In 1962 Xica da Silva was the Carnival theme of the Salgueiro SAMBA SCHOOL in RIO DE JANEIRO, and in 1997 a soap opera based on her life was broadcast on Brazil's TV Manchete.

See also Carnivals in Latin America and the Caribbean; Catholic Church in Latin America and the Caribbean; Cinema Novo.

Michelle Gueraldi

Silver, Horace

1928–

African American jazz pianist, band leader, and one of the most important composers for small groups in the history of jazz.

Born Horace Ward Martin Tavares Silver in Norwalk, Connecticut, Silver played tenor saxophone and piano during his high school years, giving up the sax after a short time. He began playing jazz on the piano and was influenced by pianists Earl Hines, Eddie Heywood, and Teddy Wilson, and later by BEBOP pianists BUD POWELL and THELONIOUS MONK. In 1950 he and his trio performed with tenor saxophonist Stan Getz in a Hartford, Connecticut, club. This initial encounter led to a yearlong engagement with Getz, during which time Silver made his first recordings. In 1951 he moved to New York City and worked with tenor saxophonist LESTER YOUNG, trumpeter MILES DAVIS, and other top players. From 1953 to 1956 he worked with the Jazz Messengers, a quintet led by ART BLAKEY. He then formed his own quintet. Along with Blakey, Silver became known as one of the pioneers of the raw-edged, dynamic hard bop sound.

In the 1980s he formed his own record company, Silveto, and confined his quintet's performance tours to two or three months per year. In the 1990s he led larger groups on several tours before returning to the quintet format. Over the years his sidemen have included well-known players such as trumpeters Randy Brecker, Donald Byrd, Art Farmer, Tom Harrell, Blue Mitchell, and Woody Shaw; tenor saxophonists Joe Henderson, Red Holloway, Clifford Jordan, Hank Mobley, and Ralph Moore; bassists Ron Carter and Bob Cranshaw; drummers Carl Burnett, Billy Cobham, Louis Hayes, and Mickey Roker; and vocalist Andy Bey.

Silver's mature piano style is an amalgam of bebop, boogie-woogie, and gospel elements that some writers term "funky." He is fond of inserting melodic quotations into his solo improvisations, and in fast pieces often punctuates his melodies with low-register tone clusters in the left hand. His accompaniments for his wind players are energetic and filled with riffs.

Silver recorded his first compositions in 1951, and after forming his own group he devoted his performances and recordings almost exclusively to his own compositions. Many of these, including "Nica's Dream" (1956), "Señor Blues" (1956), "Peace" (1959), "Sister Sadie" (1959), "Strollin'" (1960), "Filthy McNasty" (1961), "Silver's Serenade" (1963), "Song for My Father" (1964), and "Gregory Is Here" (1972) have become jazz standards.

Bibliography

Lyons, Len. *The Great Jazz Pianists: Speaking of their Lives and Music.* Morrow, 1983.

Ullman, Michael. *Jazz Lives: Portraits in Words and Pictures.* New Republic, 1980.

Silvera, Makeda

1955?–

Jamaican-Canadian editor and writer

Born in KINGSTON, JAMAICA, Makeda Silvera immigrated to Toronto, CANADA in the late 1960s. A lesbian with working-class immigrant roots, Silvera cofounded Sister Vision Press in 1985. Under her editorial direction, Sister Vision has brought discussions of class, gender, and sexuality to the forefront of Canadian literature and redressed the absence of writing by lesbians and women of color in mainstream presses. Silvera has written two collections of short fiction, *Remembering G* (1991) and *Her Head a Village* (1993), as well as a collection of oral testimonies by West Indian domestic workers, *Silenced* (1983). In 2002 she published her first novel, *The Heart Does Not Bend*.

See also Women Writers of the Caribbean.

Bibliography

Silvera, Makeda, ed. *The Other Woman: Women of Colour in Contemporary Canadian Literature.* Sister Vision, 1994.

Peter Hudson

Simkins, Mary Modjeska Monteith

1899–1992

American civil rights activist known for her lifetime commitment to progressive causes.

The child of prosperous parents, Henry Clarence Monteith and Rachel Evelyn Hull Monteith, Modjeska was instilled early on with a sense of both gentility and the duty to fight for equality. After graduating from Benedict College in 1921 with a B.A., she remained at the school until she was hired by the Booker T. Washington School in Columbia, South Carolina a year later. When she married Andrew Whitfield Simkins in 1929, Modjeska was required to leave her job due to the city policy that married women could not teach in public schools.

In 1931, Simkins began working for the South Carolina Tuberculosis Association as Director of Negro Work, establishing clinics and educating the population about the disease. In addition to organizing for several alternative political parties, she was one of the founding members of the South Carolina Conference of Branches of the NATIONAL ASSOCIATION FOR THE ADVANCEMENT OF COLORED PEOPLE (NAACP). In 1942, due to her civil rights activities, she was fired from her job with the Tuberculosis Association.

Elected as state secretary of the NAACP the same year, she led victorious fights for equalizing the pay for African American public school teachers and countermanding the segregated primary elections in South Carolina. Simkins and the NAACP helped to desegregate the South Carolina public schools by filing *Briggs v. Elliot* in 1951, paving the way for BROWN V. BOARD OF EDUCATION in 1954, which ended legal segregation in public schools. Despite her many successful projects, she was not re-elected to her post as state secretary due to her affiliation with the Communist Party. Turning her focus on issues of community development, Simkins worked for the African American–owned Victory Savings Bank in Columbia until her retirement.

Simmons, William James

1849–1890

African American Baptist leader, educator, and race advocate.

William James Simmons was born in CHARLESTON, SOUTH CAROLINA, the son of enslaved parents, Edward Simmons and Esther (maiden name unknown). During his youth Simmons, his mother, and two of his siblings escaped from slavery, relocating in PHILADELPHIA, PENNSYLVANIA. Simmons's uncle, Alexander Tardieu (or Tardiff), a shoemaker, became a father for the children, as well as protector and provider for the fugitive slave family. He moved them from city to city—Philadelphia, Roxbury (Massachusetts), and Chester (Pennsylvania)—to elude persistent slave catchers, before permanently settling in Bordentown, New Jersey. While Simmons never received formal elementary or secondary school education, his uncle made a point of teaching the children to read and write. As a youth Simmons served as an assistant to a white dentist in Bordentown. At the age of fifteen he joined the Union army, participating in a number of major battles in Virginia, ending up in at Appomattox in 1865. After the war, Simmons once again worked briefly as a dental assistant. He converted and affiliated with the white BAPTIST church in Bordentown in 1867, announced his call to the ministry, and enrolled in college with the financial support of church friends.

William Simmons attended Madison (later Colgate) University in 1868. He later attended HOWARD UNIVERSITY in WASHINGTON, D. C., earning B.A. and M.A. degrees in 1873 and 1881, respectively.

To secure additional funds for living expenses while pursuing his education, Simmons taught school in Washington, D. C., serving for a time as principal of Hillsdale Public School. In August 1874 he married Josephine A. Silence of Washington, a union that produced seven children.

For five years the family lived in Florida, where Simmons, after attempting a living from investments in lands and orange farming, returned to teaching, becoming principal of Howard Academy. He also pastored a church and became deputy county clerk and county commissioner. After returning to Washington for several years of teaching, the young Baptist relocated once again in 1879, this time to Lexington, Kentucky, to pastor the First African Baptist Church. In 1880 the fledgling Normal and Theological Institution chose Simmons as its president, and under his leadership the school attained university status in 1884. The name of the institution was changed to State University of Louisville, Kentucky, and in 1918 was changed once again to Simmons University. The school offered the only college education for blacks in the state after the Kentucky legislature outlawed integrated education at Berea College in 1905, and was the only African American institution of higher learning offering undergraduate, law, and medical degrees. Prizing vocational training as well as classical education, Simmons established the Eckstein Norton Institute in Cane Spring, Kentucky, in 1890.

Simmons played major roles in a number of black Baptist conventions, including the Baptist Foreign Mission Convention, established in 1880 to pursue African missions. His role in the formation and presidency of the American National Baptist Convention (ANBC) in 1886 laid the foundation for the emergence in 1895 of the enduring National Baptist Convention, which resulted from a merger of the ANBC and two other groups. Appointed missionary to the South by the predominantly white, northern-based American Baptist Home Mission Society in 1887, Simmons organized churches and advocated black Baptist unity.

Simmons participated in several black state conventions, assemblies of race leaders to deal with critical issues facing African Americans. Simmons remained vigorously opposed to and outspoken about JIM CROW segregation and all forms of racial discrimination, especially as exercised by state and local governments. While essentially a Republican, he called for blacks to place their interests above any particular political party. In the 1880s he predicted that the state governments, not the federal government, were increasingly the places to work for racial progress.

While many Baptist leaders strongly opposed the organization of women's conventions, Simmons heartily encouraged and supported such groups, opening the organizing session of Kentucky women that led eventually to the establishment of the Baptist Women's Educational Convention of Kentucky. In 1882 the Baptist leader founded the *American Baptist* newspaper, in which, as editor, he called for racial and denominational unity. In addition, Simmons established a publication, *Our Women and Children,* calling for racial equality and reform, particularly for women and youth. Significantly, Simmons opened the pages of the magazine to an ecumenical array of women writers who published articles dealing with domestic issues. Simmons achieved lasting fame for his *Men of Mark,* published in 1887, showcasing the accomplishments of black men, most of whom had surmounted the horrors of childhood enslavement. It was his intention to end the generally accepted notion of black inferiority and of promoting a thirst for education among black youth. Interestingly, Simmons planned a sequel outlining the achievements of prominent women, but his premature death interrupted those plans. He died in Cane Spring.

With his contributions regarding denominational unity and missions, racial unity and progress, gender equity, journalism, and politics, Simmons, despite his relatively short life span, emerged as one of the major American leaders of the nineteenth century.

Bibliography

Fitts, Leroy. *A History of Black Baptists*. 1985.

Higginbotham, Evelyn Brooks. *Righteous Discontent: The Women's Movement in the Black Baptist Church, 1880–1920*. 1993.

Martin, Sandy D. *Black Baptists and African Missions*. 1989.

Obituaries: *Louisville Courier-Journal,* October 31 and November 3, 1890; and *New York Age,* November 8, 1890.

Simmons, William J. *Men of Mark*. 1887; repr. 1968.

———. "The Lord's Supper." In *The Negro Baptist Pulpit: A Collection of Sermons and Papers by Colored Baptist Ministers,* edited by Edward M. Brawley. 1890; repr. 1971.

Washington, James M. *Frustrated Fellowship: The Black Baptist Quest for Social Power*. 1986.

From *American National Biography*. John A. Garraty and Mark C. Carnes, eds. Oxford University Press, 1999. Reprinted by permission of the American Council of Learned Societies.

Sandy Dwayne Martin

Simms, Willie

1870–1927

African American jockey and trainer.

William Simms (better known as Willie) was born in Augusta, Georgia, the son of former slaves. Enticed by racing silks as a boy, he ran away from home to become a jockey. He worked for C. H. Pettingill's stable in New York for two years, until trainer Con Leighton "discovered" him riding in Clifton, New Jersey, in 1887.

For Simms's first important race, Leighton assigned him to ride the two-year-old Banquet, a 20-1 underdog, in the 1889 Expectation Stakes. Banquet defeated both the favorite, Bellisarius, ridden by Edward "Snapper" Garrison, and Banquet's preferred stablemate, Chaos. Later, at Monmouth Park in New Jersey, Simms guided Chaos, now a 30-1 underdog, to victory over favored Banquet. Freelancing in 1891, Simms enjoyed great success at Saratoga. In 1892 P. J. Dwyer hired Simms, who won the Champion Stakes aboard Lamplighter. After signing with the Rancocas Stable later in 1892, Simms rode Dobbins in the famous 1893 dead-heat match race with the record money-earner Domino.

In 1895 Simms signed with M. F. Dwyer, who sent him to England for four months. Simms's "American" riding style, which featured extremely short stirrups, a whip, and spurs, was different from that of the English jockeys. The English ridiculed him and his high seat as "the monkey on a stick." In April he became the first American riding an American-owned and -trained horse to win an English race when he finished first in the Crawford Plate at Newmarket on Richard Croker's Eau Gallie. He later had an easy win riding Banquet at Newmarket.

Although Simms achieved some success, English jockeys did not initially copy his more efficient riding style. Two years later, after Tod Sloan won twenty races in England riding in the same fashion, the English switched to the more efficient style.

Simms won the Kentucky Derby on Ben Brush (1896) and Plaudit (1898), the Preakness on Sly Fox (1898), and the Belmont Stakes on Comanche (1893) and Henry of Navarre (1894). His other major stakes wins included the 1895 Champagne Stakes and the 1897 Suburban Handicap on Ben Brush, the 1893 Ladies' Handicap on Naptha, and the Lawrence Realization on Daily America (1893) and Dobbins (1894). Simms earned $20,000 in 1895 and, investing it well, became one of America's wealthiest jockeys. In his career in the United States, he rode 1,173 winners (25 percent) in 4,701 races, placed second 951 times, and finished third 763 times. On three different occasions he won five out of six races in a day. After retiring as a rider in 1902, he trained horses until 1924.

Simms, a bachelor, died of pneumonia in Asbury Park, New Jersey. Characterized in the *Thoroughbred Record* as one of the best jockeys in America in 1895, he was known for his "most excellent judgement, especially on horses that require a lot of coaxing and placing. He had beautiful hands and is especially quick and clever in an emergency." In 1977 he was inducted into the National Museum of Racing Hall of Fame.

Bibliography

Davis, John P. *The American Negro Reference Book*. 1966.
Illustrated Sporting News, May 23, 1908, p. 7.
Lambton, George. *Men and Horses I Have Known*. 1924.
Obituary, *New York Times,* March 1, 1927.
Obituary, *Thoroughbred Record,* March 5, 1927.
The Blood Horse 103 (August 8, 1977): 3,548.

From *American National Biography*. John A. Garraty and Mark C. Carnes, eds. Oxford University Press, 1999. Reprinted by permission of the American Council of Learned Societies.

Steven P. Savage

Simone, Nina

1933–2003

African American vocalist known for her musical versatility and emotionally charged singing.

Nina Simone was widely known as "the high priestess of soul"—less for her interpretation of SOUL MUSIC than for the soulful intensity she brought to her highly eclectic repertoire. From the late 1950s, Simone recorded extensively in the JAZZ, BLUES, SOUL, GOSPEL, and pop idioms, interpreting both standard and original songs. During the 1960s her vocal career took on a powerfully political dimension. Indeed, "more than any other popular performer of the day, she has captured the essence of the black revolution and sings of it without biting her tongue," noted *Ebony* magazine in 1969.

The *All Music Guide to Jazz* (1996) describes Simone's voice as "moody-yet-elegant . . . presenting a fiercely independent soul who harbors enormous (if somewhat hard-bitten) tenderness." The quotation also reflects her struggle to succeed as a black female musician. She had originally dreamed of becoming a classical pianist and, during the 1950s, studied at New York's prestigious Juilliard School of Music. Yet black musicians met with considerable discrimination in the mostly white and exclusive realm of classical music, and Simone soon found herself performing at an Atlantic City nightclub. Asked to sing in addition to play piano, she began her career as a jazz vocalist. In 1959 she achieved a top-twenty hit single with her recording of George Gershwin's "I Love You Porgy."

Simone recorded more than forty albums. Her songs range from ballad interpretations of BILLIE HOLIDAY and Jacques Brel to her own fiercely political pieces, "Old Jim Crow" and "Mississippi Goddam"—responses to the burgeoning violence committed against American blacks during the early 1960s. During the 1970s and 1980s she recorded rarely, but experienced a career comeback in the United States with her 1993 album, *A Single Woman*. In 1999 she received a Lifetime Achievement in Music Award in Dublin. A year later the Association of African American Music presented her with the Diamond Award for Excellence in Music. Nina Simone died in 2003, at her home in France, after a lengthy illness.

See also Music, African American.

Roanne Edwards

Simpson, O. J.

1947–

African American athlete, one of the greatest running backs in the history of American football; defendant in two sensational trials concerning the murder of his ex-wife and her friend.

O.J. Simpson was born in a poor neighborhood of SAN FRANCISCO, CALIFORNIA, the third of four children. His father left the family when Simpson was a child. At a young age Simpson wore leg braces to correct weakness in his legs, but as a teenager at Galileo High School, he was a star athlete, participating in baseball, track, and football. At the same time Simpson received several suspensions from school for misbehavior. He graduated from Galileo in 1965, but his grades kept him from attending a major university. Instead, he enrolled at City College in San Francisco, where he had a remarkable first season of football and was offered several athletic scholarships. He remained another year at City College before meeting the admissions standards for the University of Southern California (USC), which he entered in 1967. That same year, he married his first wife, Marguerite.

Football Career

Standing 6 feet, 1 inch, and weighing 205 pounds, Simpson was big for a running back, but he had tremendous speed—a combination that made him one of the best runners in collegiate history. Over two seasons, he rushed for 3,295 yards, leading USC to a Rose Bowl victory and a national championship in 1967, and earning All-American status for himself that year and the next. In 1968 he won the Heisman Trophy as college football's best player. Simpson also ran track for USC and was a member of a world record–setting 440-yard relay team.

In the 1969 American Football League (AFL) draft, the Buffalo Bills chose Simpson first overall. They used him sparingly during his first three seasons, and he rushed for less than 2,000 total yards, but in 1972, the Bills built their offense around him. The "Juice," as he was called, produced a league-leading 1,251 yards. By this time the AFL had merged with the National Football League (NFL). In 1973 Simpson became the first NFL player to rush for more than 2,000 yards, gaining 2,003. He led the league in rushing again in 1975 and 1976 and was a member of the Pro Bowl team each year from 1972 to 1976. Although the Bills never reached the Super Bowl, Simpson's exciting play drew large crowds. After suffering knee injuries in the mid-1970s, he was traded to the San Francisco 49ers in 1978. At the time of his retirement in 1979, his 11,236 total yards gained was second only to Jim Brown's 12,312 career yards. In 1985 Simpson was elected to the Pro Football Hall of Fame.

Simpson parlayed his fame and good looks into a motion picture and television acting career, including appearances in *The Towering Inferno* (1974), *Roots* (1977), and three *Naked Gun* films (1988, 1991, and 1994). He also endorsed products in television advertisements and was a commentator for televised sports. Having divorced his first wife, he married Nicole Brown in 1985. They had two children before she filed for and received a divorce in 1992. She accused him of physical abuse and womanizing, which he denied.

Simpson Trials

On June 12, 1994, Nicole Brown Simpson and Ronald Goldman, a friend, were found murdered in front of her townhouse in Brentwood, California. She had been stabbed numerous times and her throat was slashed; he had been stabbed seventeen times. Both victims were white. Five days later, Simpson was charged with the killings. Simpson resisted arrest and, with a friend driving his car, led police on a slow-speed chase through greater LOS ANGELES for several hours. As airborne television crews broadcast the pursuit worldwide, Simpson held a gun to his head, threatening to kill himself. He eventually surrendered to police.

Simpson hired a team of prominent defense lawyers and pleaded "100 percent not guilty." By the time the protracted jury selection process began in late September, the case had attracted the attention of millions. Opening arguments began on January 24, 1995, and several television stations and networks broadcast the entire proceedings. Lacking an eyewitness to the crime, the prosecution introduced experts who testified that DNA in blood samples gathered as evidence at the crime scene matched Simpson's, and that DNA in blood found in Simpson's truck and home matched that of the victims. Other items, such as shoe prints and bloody gloves—one of each at the crime scene and at Simpson's home—were introduced in evidence. Although Simpson claimed to have been at home on the night of the killings, a limousine driver testified to the contrary. The prosecution also revealed Simpson's history of spouse abuse, including a 1989 conviction for battery.

The defense argued that the police had obtained much of the evidence illegally, and then handled these items negligently. Experts testified that the laboratory of the Los Angeles Police Department was incompetent and that the blood samples might have been contaminated. The defense also revealed that Detective Mark Fuhrman, a leading investigator in the case, once told a writer he had previously planted evidence against black defendants. The defense also revealed that Fuhrman had used derogatory terms for blacks, contradicting testimony he had given the court. Prosecutors also inadvertently helped the defense team when they asked Simpson to try on one of the bloody gloves: It appeared to be too small for him. In one of the climactic moments of the trial, defense attorney Johnnie Cochran urged the jury, made up of nine blacks, two whites, and one Latino, to send a message about racism and incompetence to the police by acquitting Simpson.

On October 3, 1995, after less than four hours of deliberation, the jury acquitted Simpson of all charges, as hundreds of millions of people watched on television. According to several public opinion polls, a vast majority of blacks agreed with the verdict, while a large majority of whites opposed it. This striking disparity drew attention to the different ways blacks and whites viewed the police, courts, and the prevalence of racism.

After the criminal proceedings, Simpson faced a civil suit, brought by the Goldman family and the estate of Nicole Simpson, for the wrongful deaths of the murder victims. In a civil suit, less proof is needed to find a defendant guilty, and the jury need not reach a unanimous verdict. The trial began on October 23, 1996, and, like the criminal trial, it attracted international attention. On February 4, 1997, a jury of nine whites, one black, one Latino, and one person of mixed black and Asian ancestry found Simpson responsible for the deaths of both Goldman and Nicole Simpson, and awarded $8.5 million in damages to the plaintiffs. Simpson appealed the verdict. Again, opinion polls showed large numbers of whites agreed with the verdict, while large numbers of blacks believed he was not guilty.

Simpson is the author of *I Want to Tell You* (1995), which he wrote while detained during the criminal trial. He continues to maintain his innocence, though admitted in 2003 that if he had not had the money to hire a "dream team" of defense lawyers, he might have been convicted of the murder charges.

See also Criminal Justice System and African Americans; Football, Collegiate; Football, Professional; Film, Blacks in American; Sports and African Americans; Television and African Americans; Track and Field in the United States.

Bibliography
Toobin, Jeffrey. *The Run of His Life: The People v. O.J. Simpson.* Random House, 1996.

Sinatoa, Pama

See Women Artists, African: An Interpretation.

Singer-Songwriters

Professional singers who compose some or all of their own material.

For information on
African singer-songwriters: *See* Kuti, Fela Anikulapo; Makeba, Miriam Zenzi; Youssou N'Dour.

American singer-songwriters: *See* Berry, Charles Edward Anderson (Chuck); Bland, Bobby ("Blue"); Chapman, Tracy; Cooke, Sam; Dixon, Willie; Domino, Fats; Gaye, Marvin; Hill, Lauryn; Leadbelly; Mayfield, Curtis; McDaniel, Hattie; Redding, Otis; Robinson, William ("Smokey"); Thornton, Willie Mae ("Big Mama"); Wilson, Cassandra; Wonder, Stevie.

Latin American and Caribbean singer-songwriters: *See* Blades, Rubén; Bola de Nieve; Caymmi, Dorival; Gil, Gilberto; Gonzaga, Luis; Guerra, Juan Luis; Marley, Bob; Milanés, Pablo; Nascimento, Milton; Tosh, Peter.

British singer-songwriters: *See* Sade.

Singleton, Arthur James ("Zutty")

1898–1975

African American musician and bandleader responsible for innovations in jazz percussion accompaniment.

Born in Bunkie, Louisiana, and raised in NEW ORLEANS, "Zutty" Singleton began his professional musical career at age fifteen as a drummer for silent-film theater orchestras. He served in the U.S. Navy during WORLD WAR I (1914–1918). Returning to New Orleans, he worked as a freelance drummer with several popular local bands, including Papa Celestin's, Louis "Big Eye" Nelson's, and Luis Russell's, in addition to forming his own band around 1920.

In 1924, Singleton recorded his first song, "Frankie and Johnny," with the Fate Marable riverboat band, with which he had performed since 1921. After playing in St. Louis, Missouri with Charlie Creath in 1925, Singleton became an integral part of the burgeoning Chicago School of jazz, which placed soloists such as LOUIS ARMSTRONG in the spotlight. However, he continued to play long stints in other cities, including New York and Los Angeles from the 1930s to the 1950s.

Singleton's use of sock cymbals and wire brushes, along with new accenting techniques, secured his place as an accompanist for such musical giants as Louis Armstrong, "JELLY ROLL" MORTON, "FATS" WALLER, "DIZZY" GILLESPIE, and CHARLIE PARKER, as well as appearances on television and in films. Spanning several decades, Singleton's career was marked by an ability to play flexibly with all types of jazz. In 1953 he settled in New York, while continuing to tour internationally. In 1963 he accepted a permanent position at Jimmy Ryan's, the jazz club on West 57th Street in New York. A stroke forced Singleton to retire in 1970, and he died in New York City five years later.

Singleton, Benjamin ("Pap")

1809–1892

Early advocate of American western migration and Black Nationalism.

As a young man, "Pap" Singleton escaped slavery in Nashville, where he was born and raised. Originally fleeing to Canada, he settled in DETROIT, MICHIGAN, where he harbored FUGITIVE SLAVES until the CIVIL WAR (1861–1865) ended. Believing himself divinely chosen, he returned to Tennessee to begin his lifetime work of establishing an independent black society composed of the new freed people.

Singleton counseled ex-slaves to buy land in rural sections of Tennessee. Rebuffed by white landowners and officials, Singleton worked with W. A. Sizemore and Columbus Johnson, both former slaves, to promote migration west to Kansas. Beginning in the early 1870s, several African American families, led by Singleton, settled there. Historian JOHN HOPE FRANKLIN has noted that when Singleton circulated such fliers as "The Advantage of Living in a Free State" throughout the American South, whites enacted laws and practices to restrict African American movement.

From 1877 to 1879, several hundred Tennessee families migrated to Singleton's new black colonies. In 1879, two years after RECONSTRUCTION ended, over 20,000 African Americans migrated from Southern states to Kansas, earning the name EXODUSTERS. In 1880, the U.S. Senate held an inquiry into this unprecedented movement. Singleton's direct influence remains unclear, yet in his testimony before the Senate he took sole responsibility for the migration, calling himself "the Moses of the colored exodus." Later that year Singleton, the "Father of the Exodus," attempted to ally with the white Greenbacker political party to form a cooperative economy, but by 1883 he organized the Chief League (later Trans-Atlantic Society) to promote black emigration first to Cyprus, then to Africa.

Sinhô

1888–1930

José Barbosa da Silva was the most popular of the early samba composers in Rio de Janeiro, Brazil. His string of Carnival hits during the 1920s earned him the title "King of the Samba."

See also Samba.

Sissle, Noble

1889–1975

American musician and composer who participated in *Shuffle Along*, the most successful musical comedy created by African Americans.

Noble Sissle first sang in his father's Methodist Church, and he was a soloist in his Cleveland, Ohio, high school's glee club. After serving in WORLD WAR I (1914–1918) as a drum major, Sissle had enormous success in the vaudeville theater, teaming up with "EUBIE" BLAKE as the Dixie Duo. In 1921 they created *Shuffle Along*, starring FLORENCE MILLS. *Shuffle Along* changed Broadway musical theater by introducing a JAZZ dancing chorus line and the vitality and style of African American music to a more "refined" mainstream theater. Sissle and Blake wrote songs, including the well-known "I'm Just Wild About Harry." They also produced *Runnin' Wild* (1924) and *Chocolate Dandies* (1924). In 1937 Sissle was the cofounder and first president of the Negro Actors' Guild. In 1945 and 1946, Sissle toured Europe with a USO show, performing a re-staged *Shuffle Along*.

Sisson, Jack

1743?–1821

African American soldier.

Jack Sisson was also known as Tack Sisson, Guy Watson, or Prince. He was one of those African American patriots whose lives were allowed by their contemporaries to become shrouded in obscurity. Little record exists of his whereabouts, activities, or circumstances before or after the exploit for which he is noted—the July 1777 abduction of Brigadier General Richard Prescott, commander of the redcoat garrison at Newport, Rhode Island. Sisson was among the forty volunteers Lieutenant Colonel William Barton raised from his regiment with the intention of seizing a British officer of sufficient rank that he might be exchanged for the captured American general Charles Lee. Some accounts suggest Sisson was Barton's servant. Sisson steered one of the whaleboats that made their way with muffled oars from Tiverton, Rhode Island, toward Prescott's lodgings at the Overing House near Newport. Escaping the attention of British ships, the force landed on the night of 9-10 July and overpowered a sentry outside Prescott's quarters. Finding the door to the British general's room locked, the short but powerfully built Sisson, it was said, butted it twice with his head, breaking open a panel and allowing the latch to be lifted from the inside. Prescott, dressed in not much more than his nightshirt, was spirited away without anyone being killed or even a shot fired. His capture led eventually to the release of General Lee.

The American press celebrated the exploit, one of the solitary bits of good news that patriots received in those dismal months. A ballad circulated at the time placed Sisson at the center of events, though it did not accord him the respect his contribution merited or even call him by his proper name:

A tawney son of Afric's race
Them through the ravine led,
And entering then the Overing house,
They found him in his bed

But to get in they had no means
Except poor Cuffee's head,
Who beat the door down, then rushed in
And seized him in his bed.

Stop, let me put my breeches on,
The general then did pray.
Your breeches, massa, I will take,
For dress we cannot stay.

It is unclear to what extent the emphasis on Sisson's use of his skull as a battering ram partook of a longstanding penchant among many white Americans for making lame jests about the imagined hardness of black people's heads.

In the wake of Prescott's capture, Barton was promoted to colonel, while Sisson enlisted in the Rhode Island First Regiment, which recruited approximately 200 black soldiers, both slave and free. What Sisson did after the war is unclear, but he reportedly celebrated holidays by appearing on parade grounds in his old uniform. Some sources describe him as unhappy that his role in the capture of Prescott was not better known. On November 3, 1821 the *Providence Gazette* reported the death of Sisson, "aged about 78 years," in Plymouth, Massachusetts. Even though he has become an elusive figure, Sisson stands as an emblem of black people's contributions to American freedom through those long decades during which few of them could partake fully of its benefits or could even win from many of their white contemporaries a decent respect for their efforts.

Bibliography

Falkner, Leonard. "Captor of the Barefoot General." *American Heritage* 11 (Aug. 1960): 29–31, 98–100.

Kaplan, Sidney, and Emma Nogrady Kaplan. *The Black Presence in the Era of the American Revolution*, rev. ed. 1989.

Quarles, Benjamin. *The Negro in the American Revolution*. 1961.

Williams, Catharine. *Biography of Revolutionary Heroes*. 1839.

From *American National Biography*. John A. Garraty and Mark C. Carnes, eds. Oxford University Press, 1999. Reprinted by permission of the American Council of Learned Societies.

Patrick G. Williams

Sistren Collective

Women's theater collective founded in Jamaica in 1977 by Honor Ford-Smith. The Sistren Collective creates plays representing Caribbean women's issues, and uses workshops and improvisation to address community concerns.

See also Theater in the Caribbean.

Sisulu, Walter

1912–2003

Former deputy president of the African National Congress and a key figure in South Africa's antiapartheid movement.

Walter Sisulu, known for his commitment to studying and teaching while imprisoned on ROBBEN ISLAND with NELSON MAN-

DELA, was called by one of his AFRICAN NATIONAL CONGRESS (ANC) colleagues "the organization's encyclopedia in prison." A mentor to younger members, such as Mandela and OLIVER TAMBO, Sisulu joined the ANC in 1940, after his impoverished JOHANNESBURG childhood and his work in the country's gold mines had introduced him to the injustices that black South Africans faced.

In addition to helping Mandela and Tambo complete their law studies, Sisulu also joined the two in the newly formed ANC Youth League, planning strategy and serving as its treasurer. Elected ANC secretary general in 1949, Sisulu played a key role in coordinating activities with other antiapartheid groups, including the Communist Party of South Africa (later renamed the SOUTH AFRICAN COMMUNIST PARTY, or SACP) and the South African Indian Congress. This work, he said, influenced his commitment to a multiracial antiapartheid movement. The South African government convicted Sisulu under its Suppression of Communism Act in 1952. Although his sentence was suspended, he was banned from participating in political activity and forced to resign from his ANC position (like other banned leaders, Sisulu continued to work in secret).

Along with Mandela, Walter Sisulu was one of 156 antiapartheid activists charged with treason in 1956. After their 1961 acquittal, Sisulu was among the founders of Umkhonto we Sizwe (Spear of the Nation), the armed paramilitary wing jointly supported by the ANC and the SACP. In 1964, after fleeing house arrest and working underground, Sisulu and six others were captured, convicted of treason, and sentenced to life in prison on Robben Island, SOUTH AFRICA'S notoriously brutal penitentiary for political prisoners. While there, Sisulu read widely and wrote a history of the ANC. After his 1989 release (which came as South Africa began to loosen its apartheid system in the face of international pressure) he told reporters that "it was not possible to despair" while in prison, "because the spirit of the people outside was too great." Elected ANC deputy president in 1991, Sisulu resigned from that position in 1994 at the age of eighty-two. He died in May 2003, two weeks before his ninety-first birthday.

See also Antiapartheid Movement.

Kate Tuttle

Sit-In

African American student protest movement in 1960 in which black students occupied "white-only" lunch counters and other segregated public institutions throughout the South to protest segregated seating.

On February 1, 1960, four black college students sat down at a "white-only" Woolworth's department store lunch counter in Greensboro, North Carolina. Woolworth's counter was one of the many segregated public facilities in the South where African Americans were prohibited from activities such as eating, swimming, and drinking by whites who not only opposed equal treatment of the races but feared any possibility of bodily contact. When the restaurant refused these students service, they remained seated until the store closed for the evening. The students returned each morning for the next five days to occupy the lunch counter, joined by a group of protesters that grew to the hundreds. Faced by a mob of angry white residents and management that refused to serve them a cup of coffee, the students maintained their protest until they forced the store to close its doors.

The protest by Joseph McNeil, Ezell Blair Jr., Franklin McCain, and David Richmand marked the beginning of a grassroots sit-in movement led by African American students against the segregated public spaces of the South. Black or racially integrated groups of students would sit down in white-only spaces and refuse to move until they were served or forcibly removed. By the end of 1960, about 70,000 black students had participated in a sit-in or marched in support of the demonstrators.

Although there had been a few sit-in protests before 1960, including two in 1943, the mass mobilization of 1960 was new. Few in the economically struggling black community of the South had been willing to undertake these types of direct action protests, since they would be in danger of losing their jobs after an arrest. Black students generally had fewer financial responsibilities than their older counterparts, and they were interested in forcing change more immediate than that promised by the legal reform advocated by the NATIONAL ASSOCIATION FOR THE ADVANCEMENT OF COLORED PEOPLE (NAACP).

In 1960, as African American students entered the political arena in large numbers for the first time, the character of civil rights protesting began to change. Influenced by the successful protests led by Mohandas K. Gandhi in India's Independence Movement, black students saw the potential for using nonviolent resistance to undermine the system and segregation. Nonviolence was not just a strategy, although it did garner sympathy from many whites and the national press; it was a moral and revolutionary philosophy. Proponents such as JAMES LAWSON saw nonviolence as an "invincible instrument of war," imbued with "soul force" and moral integrity, that used the mass organization of bodies to strike at the heart of the morally unsound system of segregation.

The pivotal demonstration was the Greensboro sit-in. But students had already begun organizing elsewhere. Shortly after the Greensboro protest, Lawson and the Nashville Student Movement launched a well-organized and orchestrated campaign to integrate the lunch counters of Nashville, Tennessee. In less than a month, Nashville yielded to the pressure of the protests. The success of these original protests inspired other black students throughout the South, who organized sit-ins to force the desegregation of public places.

During 1960 sit-ins began to break down the segregation of the upper South, and lunch counters were integrated in cities in Texas, North Carolina, and Tennessee. The reasons for integration were economic as well as moral. Boycotters, both black and white, supported the protesters, and many merchants did not want to lose the revenue of customers.

However, in the Deep South, including Louisiana, Mississippi, Alabama, Georgia, and South Carolina, white supremacy was more entrenched in the community and local government. Montgomery, Alabama outlawed the demonstrations, and white storeowners refused to serve blacks under the rationale that they could make the rules on their own private property.

Throughout the South, protesters faced not only arrest but vigilante violence as police and the KU KLUX KLAN worked hand in hand to suppress the protests. By the end of 1960, 36,000 students had been arrested and thousands were expelled from college.

With support from African American activist ELLA BAKER of the SOUTHERN CHRISTIAN LEADERSHIP CONFERENCE (SCLC), students formed the STUDENT NONVIOLENT COORDINATING COMMITTEE (SNCC) as a permanent organization in April 1960. SNCC maintained the autonomy of the grassroots students' movement and facilitated training in nonviolent resistance. The strategy of occupying a place as a means of nonviolent protest gained currency in the CIVIL RIGHTS MOVEMENT. Sit-ins at lunch counters inspired similar forms of protest at other types of segregated facilities, such as wade-ins at swimming places.

The efficacy of nonviolent resistance was one of the most important legacies of the 1960 sit-in protests. Segregation was seen to be a moral as well as a legal issue, and the dignity of blacks in the face of white supremacist rage went far to win white and black support for the movement. In the words of the founding members of SNCC, "By appealing to conscience and standing on the moral nature of human existence, nonviolence nurtures the atmosphere in which reconciliation and justice become actual possibilities."

See also Integration: An Interpretation.

Marian Aguiar

Sixteenth Street Baptist Church

Center for civil rights in Birmingham, Alabama, that was the site of a 1963 bombing that killed four African American girls.

On September 15, 1963, four young black girls were killed and twenty other people wounded when a bomb planted by KU KLUX KLAN members exploded at the Sixteenth Street Baptist Church in Birmingham, Alabama. The terrorist attack revealed the growing hostility of segregationists toward the CIVIL RIGHTS MOVEMENT as it was making inroads in the Deep South. At the time of the bombing, Birmingham was in a battle over the desegregation of schools; only weeks before, the National Guard had been called in to protect black students. For civil rights leaders, the bombing, which took place less than three weeks after the euphoria of the 1963 March on Washington, was a reminder of the long struggle that remained.

The Sixteenth Street Baptist Church was a center for the Civil Rights Movement in Birmingham. Leaders such as MARTIN LUTHER KING, JR., FRED L. SHUTTLESWORTH, ANDREW YOUNG, JAMES BEVEL, DICK GREGORY, and RALPH ABERNATHY all regularly took the pulpit at mass rallies of Birmingham's black community, such as the one following King's April 1963 arrest. The church had been the headquarters for a number of desegregation protests, including the May 1963 SOUTHERN CHRISTIAN LEADERSHIP CONFERENCE (SCLC) rally in which more than 2,000 black youths marched from the church through Birmingham.

The Ku Klux Klan targeted the church on the annual Youth Sunday. Eleven-year-old Denise McNair was with Cynthia Wesley, Carole Robertson, and Addie Mae Collins, all aged fourteen, in the basement of the church. They were preparing to take their special roles as ushers when the bomb exploded, killing them and burying them in rubble. Twenty others, including many children, were injured by the blast. In the day of increased tension that followed, two other black youths were killed. A thirteen-year-old black youth was shot by two Eagle Scouts who were on their way home from a white supremacist rally. That evening, a sixteen-year-old black boy was shot by one of the 300 state troopers ordered into the city by Governor George C. Wallace to preserve the peace in Birmingham.

As black and white youths battled in the streets of Birmingham the night of the bombing, many white residents wavered between fear of anti-white violence and feelings of guilt. In the words of white lawyer Charles Morgan the next day, "We all did it . . . every person in this community who has in any way contributed . . . to the popularity of hatred is at least as guilty . . . as the demented fool who threw that bomb." Many in the community, and indeed the nation, struggled with a new awareness of the brutal underside of what had been characterized as simply the Southern way of life.

Connie Lynch articulated the white supremacist reaction. Rallying the Klan shortly after the bombing, Lynch said the victims "weren't children. Children are little people, little human beings, and that means white people . . . They're just little niggers, and if there's four less niggers tonight, then I say, 'Good for whoever planted the bomb!'"

Eight thousand people attended a joint funeral for three of the girls. Martin Luther King, Jr. gave the eulogy to a community that, having witnessed seven bombings within the previous six months, was torn between rage and exhaustion.

An eyewitness reported seeing four men plant the bomb. Police arrested Robert Edward Chambliss after the bombing, but they let him go shortly after. In 1977 Alabama Attorney General William Baxley reopened the case, and Chambliss was tried and convicted for first-degree murder. In 2001 Thomas E. Blanton Jr., a former Ku Klux Klan member, was convicted of murder for his role in the bombing.

Bibliography

Branch, Taylor. *Parting the Waters: America in the King Years, 1954–1963.* Simon and Schuster, 1988.

Marian Aguiar

Ska

Form of Jamaican music that fuses elements of black American music, especially rhythm and blues (R&B), with mento, the island's folk music.

Ska is the product of the encounter of two different black musical traditions, one indigenous to JAMAICA and the other transmitted from the United States to Jamaica via radio in the 1950s. Ska's unique sound derives from its emphasis on the second and fourth beats, a rhythmic characteristic found in other forms of Jamaican music that developed out of ska: ROCK STEADY, REGGAE, DUB, DANCEHALL, and, less prominently, in RHYTHM AND BLUES. In ska, the offbeat, or "drop" as it is sometimes called, is created by the guitar and drums and is sometimes accentuated by the brass section.

During the World War II (1939–1945) era, technological advances made radio broadcasting more extensive and radios more receptive to distant signals, enabling Jamaica to tune in to radio stations based in the Southern United States. Many Jamaicans became infatuated with the sounds of JAZZ and rhythm and blues. Since radios were not readily available or affordable in Jamaica at that time, musical entrepreneurs such as Clement "Sir Coxsone Downbeat" Dodd and Duke "The Trojan" Reid assembled sound systems, mobile audio units consisting of a radio, turntable(s), and speakers, in order to bring black American music to Jamaican audiences.

In the late 1950s, however, rock and roll emerged as the new popular American music, and R&B was less often heard on the airwaves. Jamaicans largely rejected rock and roll, which they found less danceable. In response to this predicament, Dodd began to advocate the creation of a new form of popular music in Jamaica based on swing, R&B, and BOOGIE-WOOGIE as well as MENTO, which previously had been the most popular Jamaican music. One of the first groups to rise to the challenge was Clue J and the Blues Blasters. Although bassist Clue J, who often greeted friends with the buzzword "Skavoovie," inspired the name of this new form of music, ska, a band by the name of the Skatellites defined its sound.

In 1967 a heat wave came over the WEST INDIES that many historians have cited as the cause for ska's transformation into rock steady. Compared to ska, rock steady has a slower tempo, lighter horns, and a heavier bass. Desmond Dekker was one of the early popular rock steady artists. In 1967 his "007 Shanty Town" reached number eleven on the British pop charts, and in 1969 his "Israelites" climbed to the number one spot. The advent of rock steady in the late 1960s marked the end of ska's first phase in Jamaica.

Although ska had largely faded from the Jamaican music scene, British youth who had become infatuated with the music of Jamaican artists such as Dekker revived ska one decade later, around 1979. That same year Jerry Dammers, a member of what would become one of Great Britain's premier ska bands, the Specials (originally the Special A.K.A.), founded the 2 Tone record label, whose name became synonymous with the ska movement in Britain. At a time when police brutality against Jamaican immigrants was on the rise and race riots broke out with increasing frequency, 2 Tone sought to promote racial harmony and unity in Great Britian. This was reflected in the composition of ska bands, the majority of which were racially integrated, and in their aesthetic, which featured black and white clothing combinations and black and white checkered accessories. They adopted as their icon Walt Jabsco, a man in a black suit, white shirt, black tie, white socks, black loafers, sunglasses, and a pork-pie hat. This was essentially a British rehashing of the Jamaican rudeboy often referred to in Jamaican ska, a transformation in which the menacing gangster became a happy, dancing figure.

After affiliating itself with Chrysalis Records around 1980, the 2 Tone label issued a string of hits. Each of the seven singles pressed by 2 Tone at this time sold at least a quarter of a million copies. The label's primary group, the Specials, repeatedly topped the British pop charts with such songs as "Too Much Too Young," "A Message to Rudy," and "Ghost Town." Other groups that enjoyed success recording on the 2 Tone label included the Selecter, Madness, and the (English) Beat. Encouraged by the success of 2 Tone Records, several other ska bands and ska record labels emerged. At ska shows, however, violence frequently erupted between the neatly dressed rudeboys and the poorer skinheads. This made British music venues reluctant to book ska bands and ultimately contributed to the demise of ska in the United Kingdom. The dissolution of the 2 Tone label around 1985 signaled the end of the British ska craze.

In spite of ska's short-lived popularity in Britain, such British artists as Elvis Costello and Madness, who had launched their careers on the 2 Tone label, preserved elements of ska in their music and became well-known in the United States, where ska's third wave began in 1983. That year, ska bands by the names of Not Bob Marley, which later became known as the Toasters, and Bim Skala Bim formed in New York City and Boston, Massachusetts, respectively. In the mid-1980s, each of these groups established their own record labels for the production and distribution of ska music: Moon Records in New York City and Fonograff Records in Boston. As had been the case in Jamaica with Dodd's Studio One and in Britain with Dammers's 2 Tone label, these independent record labels enabled ska to flourish.

Unlike the 2 Tone movement, which attempted to recapture the classic 1960s style of Jamaican ska and its accompanying dress code, the new popularity of ska in the United States witnessed the blending of ska with several different music styles, including hardcore punk, FUNK, and Latin. In the mid- to late 1980s, groups such as the Mighty Mighty Bosstones and Operation Ivy incorporated ska into their hardcore songs. At about the same time, a band called Fishbone created a style of music based on ska and funk. More recently, such groups as Jump With Joey and Babaloo have successfully merged ska with Latin rhythms. Such ska acts as the Allstonians and Skavoovie and the Epitones, however, have attempted to preserve the late 1960s Jamaican ska sound. Most of these bands continue to play and still draw large audiences. The undisputed kings of today's ska scene are the Skatellites, who reunited in 1983 to tour worldwide.

Bibliography

Davis, Stephen, and Peter Simon. *Reggae International.* Thames and Hudson, 1983.

Potash, Chris, ed. *Reggae, Rasta, Revolution.* Schirmer Books, 1997.

Aaron Myers

Slaughter, Henry Proctor

1871–1958

African American typographer, journalist, leader of fraternal organizations, and book collector.

Henry Proctor Slaughter was born in Louisville, Kentucky, the son of Sarah Jane Smith and Charles Henry Slaughter. When he was six years old his father died, leaving his mother with two boys and a girl. He sold newspapers to help support his mother, and as he worked his way through school he became the main support of his family. After graduating as salutatorian from Central High School, he served his apprenticeship as a printer on the *Louisville Champion.* There he became associate editor with Horace Morris, who in 1894 was deputy grand master of the Prince Hall Masons of Kentucky. Slaughter also began to write feature articles for local daily newspapers.

By 1893 Slaughter was foreman of Champion Publishing Company, and in 1894 he became associate editor of the *Lexington Standard.* Shortly afterward, as manager of the *Standard,* he was described as making "logical speeches, having a trenchant pen and strong hand at the helm of the *Standard.*" He studied at Livingstone College in Salisbury, North Carolina, an educational institution affiliated with the AFRICAN METHODIST EPISCOPAL ZION CHURCH (AME). At Livingstone, Slaughter instructed a printing class and became manager-foreman of the AME Zion Publishing House. George W. Clinton, a pastor and editor of the *Star of Zion,* praised Slaughter for his "excellent contributions" during Clinton's absence.

The only African American who took the examination for position of compositor at the Government Printing Office, in 1896 Slaughter accepted an appointment there, which he held until 1937. While employed in the printing trade he served as proofreader, monotypist, linotype operator, compositor, and machinist. Slaughter received his bachelor of laws degree in 1899 and his master of laws degree in 1900 from HOWARD UNIVERSITY, but he never practiced law.

Slaughter's interest in the Independent Order of the Odd Fellows, a fraternal benefit society, developed early. For many years he served as a member of the board of directors, as well as presiding officer, of the lodge of the Grand United Order of Odd Fellows. He was a Thirty-third Degree Mason and editor of the *Odd Fellows Journal* from 1910 until it discontinued publication in 1937. Slaughter served as permanent secretary of the Corinthian Lodge 3859 of Odd Fellows. For a number of years he was a member of the Jonathan Davis Consistory No. 1, Prince Hall Masonry; the Past Grand Master's Conference No. 4, Odd Fellows; and Eudora Household of Ruth No. 1267, Odd Fellows. For several years at the annual meetings of the stockholders of the Odd Fellows Hall Association in Washington, D.C., he was elected to the board of directors. He was also at one time director of the Odd Fellows Hall Association, as well as of the Peoples Savings Bank at Staunton, Virginia.

Slaughter took pride in his membership in the AMERICAN NEGRO ACADEMY, an association of African American intellectuals. He prepared elaborate suppers and luncheons for the members when they met in Washington. He was known to them—and to members of the Mu-So-Lit Club, the Labor Day Bunch, and the Pen and Pencil Club—as a gourmet and one of Washington's most liberal entertainers and hosts.

Slaughter had a long interest in politics. He was a committeeman at the inauguration of presidents William McKinley, Theodore Roosevelt, William Howard Taft, and Woodrow Wilson. For several years Slaughter was secretary of the Kentucky Republican Club in Washington. He also served as staff correspondent of the *Kentucky Standard* in Louisville and special contributor to the *Philadelphia Tribune,* the *American Baptist,* and the *A.M.E. Church Review.* Slaughter was for many years superintendent of St. Luke's Episcopal Sunday School in Washington, D.C., and vestryman of the church. He also served as secretary of the St. Luke's chapter of the Brotherhood of St. Andrew.

In any area where he thought he could be useful, Slaughter associated with men of both races—bishops, ministers, and political figures. He was one of the pallbearers at the funeral of P. B. S. Pinchback of Louisiana, who died on December 20, 1921. Slaughter was reliable, tactful, and made friends easily. His relations with whites were unusual for his times. He was the only African American elected as chairman of a "Chapel," one of the sections of the Typographical Union of the Government Printing Office. At that time the Union had 1,600 members, of whom about twenty were black. At age eighty-six Henry Slaughter was honored as the Sixty-Year Man in the Typographical Union.

Slaughter's lifelong hobby was collecting books, pamphlets, music, photographs, prints, and manuscripts relating to the history of African Americans. He became a well-known authority on the subject. His ten-room residence contained more than 10,000 volumes, many of them rare. "My books are my best friends and I would rather furnish a house with books than with furniture," he often said. In addition to his books he had a file of around 100,000 newspaper clippings concerning important events and persons. He attempted to collect books of all types and on every phase of the slavery question, the Civil War, and the African background. He also aimed to acquire all works by individual black authors. He took great pride in his collection of autograph signatures of the men in Abraham Lincoln's cabinet, the presidents of the United States, and well-known African Americans, and in his rare engravings, broadsides, manuscript letters, slave papers, and a few museum pieces. Slaughter purchased many of his books from the valuable William Carl Bolivar collection in Philadelphia, Pennsylvania; from firms in England and Ireland; and from auction houses in Philadelphia and New York City. In 1946 Atlanta University Center purchased his private library.

In 1904 Slaughter married Ella M. Russell of Jonesboro, Tennessee. She died in 1914, and in 1925 he married Alma R. Level of Chicago, Illinois. They later divorced. After a brief illness, Slaughter died in Washington, D.C., on February 14, 1958. Slaughter was survived by a sister, Ida S. Gray of Louisville, and three nephews: Frank H. Gray of Louisville, Columbus Gray of Philadelphia, and Charles R. Gray of Washington, D.C.

From the time he was a newspaper boy Slaughter learned to save a part of every dollar he earned. His prudent handling of his finances enabled him to build one of the nation's finest private collections of books on black history and culture. His lifelong motto was "learn to know the value of socks and you will learn the value of stocks."

There is no biography of Slaughter. His views are best found in the *Odd Fellows Journal* (1910–1937). The *Journal* has biographical information in the issues from January 5, 1922; January 1, 1925; March 5, 1925; and December 3, 1925. Other biographical information can be found in *Colored American* (May 10, 1902); *Pen and Pencil Club Program, Commemoration of the 85th Anniversary of Birth of Frederick Douglass* (February 14, 1902, and 1903); *Pen and Pencil Pointers* (February 14, 1907); *Who's Who of the Colored Race* (1915, pp. 245–46); the *Washington Times* (May 30, 1936); the *Afro-American* (July 8, 1939); and Slaughter's obituary in the *Washington Afro-American* (February 22, 1958).

From *Dictionary of American Negro Biography* by Rayford W. Logan and Michael R. Winston, editors. Copyright © 1982 by Rayford W. Logan and Michael R. Winston. Reprinted by permission of W. W. Norton & Company, Inc.

Dorothy B. Porter

Slave Laws in Colonial Spanish America

Laws that until the late seventeenth century were issued to control the slave population in Spain's New World colonies.

Slaves of various races and all sorts of physical traits were a source of labor to peoples on the five continents for thousands of years before the conquest and colonization of the Americas. Justifications for the enslavement of human beings in either moral or legal terms have varied. In some societies individuals were enslaved when they committed crimes; when they were born into a social class of slaves; or when out of poverty or extreme indebtedness they had to sell themselves, or were sold by their creditors, into slavery. Other groups enslaved those captured in "just" (properly declared) wars when they considered the enemy inferior or "barbarian" for expressing a different culture, language, or religion. In many cases, slaves could not be differentiated in physical appearance from their masters.

During the middle ages, the greatest proportion of slaves in Western Europe came from the non-Christian, light-skinned central and east European people known as the Saqaliba (or Slavs). As early as the twelfth century, the word for *slave* in all western European languages derived from the word "Slav" (*esclave, esclavo, escravo, schiavo, sklave*). From the eleventh to the late thirteenth centuries, western Europeans embarked on the CRUSADES, which led to an expansion of commercial activity and the capturing of slaves who were Jews, Moors, Turks (Egyptians, Syrians, and Lebanese), white Christians (Sardinians, Greeks, and Russians), and *guanches* (Canary Islanders). During this period, the use of ancient Roman law spread and was assimilated throughout legal systems in Europe.

In the kingdom of Castile and León (SPAIN), King Alfonso X the Wise (1221–1284) commissioned a group of jurists to unify and universalize the norms and legal dispositions of the lands over which he was sovereign. The Siete Partidas (Seven Part Code) was issued as a comprehensive legislation to replace the diverse, confusing, and often contradictory local laws (known as *fueros*), which carried the influence of Roman law. Additionally, the Roman civil code known as Justinian's Corpus Juris Civilis was used as a main source of the Partidas.

In 1493, after Columbus's first trip to America, Pope Alexander VI issued four papal bulls that granted "to the present and future sovereigns of Castile the lands discovered and to be discovered by their envoys and not previously possessed by any Christian owner." The New World, or what Spain called the "Indies," became part of the Crown of Castile. Following from this belief, Castile enjoyed exclusive rights to the New World and reserved the privilege of immigration for Castilian subjects or those authorized by Castile. In theory, the laws and institutions of Castile became the basis of government in Spanish America.

Because the slave population was not characterized by one predominant race before the conquest of the Americas, the laws derived from the Romans, which were used to control the small number of domestic slaves in present-day Spain, were not racially defined. Hence, the norms in the Siete Partidas, which addressed slavery and manumission in Spain at the time of the conquest, were largely the same as those rules that regulated the ancient political and social institution of slavery in Rome. Spanish slave laws, like those in Rome, allowed for various forms of manumission and limitations to punishments, and they did not permit slaves to have legal representation, to be party to a civil law action, or to act as witnesses in matters of great importance. Slavery, and thus the laws regulating the institution, took on a specifically racial character only in the sixteenth century, when the demand for slaves increased with the conquest and colonization of the Americas and when Africa became the largest source of forced labor.

In 1517, Charles I, the king who united the thrones of Castile and Aragón into the Spanish state, issued a decree allowing the direct shipment of blacks from Africa to the Spanish colonies. Hispanicized slaves (who were called *ladinos*) and others brought from Europe were not only more expensive and scarce than Africans, but they were also thought to be responsible for inciting slaves in the Americas to rebel, as happened in HISPANIOLA (in the present-day DOMINICAN REPUBLIC and HAITI) in 1522. Therefore, two final decrees in 1530 and 1532 prohibited the dispatch of any white Moorish, Jewish, or ladino slave to the Indies. From then on, only African-born slaves, who were considered "peaceful and obedient," could be legally shipped to the Indies. *Cédulas* (or royal laws) and slave contracts for the next sixty years continued to insist on the Africanness of slaves, as indicated by their darker skin color, so that they would not be replaced with the sometimes lighter-skinned ladinos, or white pagan slaves. The economic incentives of the African slave trade further contributed to changes in the imagery of slavery, so that the term *esclavos* (slaves) came to be synonymous with *negros* (blacks).

Strict implementation of many of the principles and norms offered by the Siete Partidas were inapplicable to the New World context for a variety of reasons. These included the racial factor; the economic and religious motives that informed the colonizing enterprise; the relation with the indigenous people; the slave trade; and the administrative challenges. From as early as 1526, royal cédulas were created in order to justify and regulate circumstances that were not foreseen by the Siete Partidas or were not harmonious with the new Spanish policies. For example, many of the first slaves brought to the New World from Spain took advantage of the Partidas norm that allowed a slave to marry a free person and therefore become free himself. Cédulas in 1526 and 1538 prohibited further manumission through marriage.

In 1680 the Spanish king issued a compilation summarizing the local legislation in order for the laws to be applied in all of the colonies (known as the *Recopilación de leyes de los Reynos de las Indias*). Colonial officials (such as viceroys and town councillors) issued additional legislation in the form of local ordinances (*ordenanzas*) that regulated slave relations in a particular location. With the need to subjugate the increasing number of slaves and free blacks, the language of the local statutes became racially principled, and the statutes themselves became far more brutal and less permissive than those found in the Siete Partidas or the royal cédulas. The ordinances could be raised to the status of royal cédula by a royal confirmation (*real confirmación*), though this approval could take decades. In the meantime, the local orders regulated punishment and all aspects of social, economic, religious, sexual, and labor relations of slaves. By doing so, they equated "blacks" with the characteristics given generally to slaves since antiquity in order to justify human bondage. Cruel and demeaning punishment could be justified if slaves were objectified as property or chattel in the law. The local laws also constructed a sociocultural idea of blacks as inferior humans. Many norms referred to slaves and free blacks as being sexually deviant, lazy, rebellious, heretic, festive, childlike, and intellectually inferior, among other traits considered negative by the ruling elites.

By 1685 the slave population in the American colonies had become so large that the French king issued the first comprehensive black code (or Code Noir) for France's Caribbean colonies. The Spanish Crown followed with its codification almost a century later by taking into account the French Code Noir, the Siete Partidas, and the legislation that had been produced specifically for the colonies in the past 250 years.

In sum, the treatment of slaves during the colonial era in Spanish America was regulated by several legal sources, often contradictory in nature and purpose and seldom respected. Today, however, we can still view these written laws as embodiments of the ideas then held about black people in the Americas, and can see their persistence in current manifestations of racism, discrimination, and general human rights violations.

See also Black Codes in Latin America; Human Rights in Latin America and the Caribbean; Punishment of Slaves in Colonial Latin America and the Caribbean; Slavery in Africa; Transatlantic Slave Trade.

Liliana Obregón

Slave Narratives

Written autobiographies and oral testimonies by escaped or freed slaves.

At the conclusion of her Pulitzer Prize–winning novel *Beloved* (1987), TONI MORRISON sums up her retelling of one slave family's experience: "It was not a story to pass on." There are certainly logical reasons why the story of SLAVERY might never have been passed on. One, the reason Morrison suggests, was its sheer horror and trauma—those who lived through it may not have wanted to remember their experiences. A second is more practical: it was illegal to teach slaves to read and write, which meant that the act of putting a story on paper was generally prohibited to them. But neither of these reasons kept former slaves from passing on their stories and leaving a record about what living as a piece of property had been like. These slave narratives set the standard for a tradition of African American autobiography that continues today.

Although slave narratives were written in several parts of the African diaspora and in a variety of languages, the majority of published narratives by African slaves and their descendants were written in English in what is now the United States. Black literary scholar HENRY LOUIS GATES, JR. argues that African American slaves were unique in the history of world slavery because they were the only enslaved people to produce a body of writing that testified to their experiences.

For many of these authors, writing narratives served a dual purpose: it was a way of publicizing the horrors they had gone through, and it was also a method of proving their humanity. One of the common arguments in support of race-based slavery was that blacks were simply an inferior species, incapable of thinking and feeling in the ways whites did. Slave authors were able to display their emotions and their intellects through their narratives.

Historians estimate that approximately 6,000 published narratives were written by African American slaves. This number includes both book-length autobiographies and shorter ac-

Frederick Douglass wrote three memoirs, including this one. Although he was born into slavery and self-educated, he was a superb stylist who avoided the ornate tendencies of his time. *CORBIS/Bettmann*

counts published in newspapers or transcribed from interviews, and it spans 170 years' worth of testimonies from ex-slaves. Most of these narratives were actually published or collected after slavery was abolished in 1865, as emancipated slaves looked back on their experiences. The most famous slave narratives, however, are autobiographies by FUGITIVE SLAVES that were published before 1865.

During this period, ex-slaves' narratives were a powerful tool in the fight against slavery. Many abolitionist groups correctly guessed that first-person accounts of the horrors of slavery would be the most effective means of explaining slavery's evils to a wide audience, and they often helped black authors to find publishers and audiences for their work. Approximately seventy slave narratives were published in the United States in book or pamphlet form before the end of the Civil War (1861–1865), and hundreds more appeared in American and British periodicals. Slave narratives often went through multiple editions and sometimes sold thousands of copies in the United States and throughout Europe.

The best-known slave narrative is FREDERICK DOUGLASS's *Narrative of the Life of Frederick Douglass, An American Slave, Written by Himself* (1845). In it, Douglass describes his childhood separation from his mother, his struggle to teach himself to read and write, the brutal whippings he witnessed and received, and his determination to be free—all the while stressing his own humanity and the inhumanity of the system that kept him a slave. Douglass's autobiography was an international bestseller. After its publication, Douglass traveled the world as a lecturer, implicitly providing a model for just how "civilized" blacks could be, and went on to become the most famous and respected black person of the nineteenth century. His narrative's patterns and images were repeated not only in many later slave narratives but also in diverse works of African American literature such as ZORA NEALE HURSTON's *Their Eyes Were Watching God* (1937) and RALPH ELLISON's *Invisible Man* (1952).

Other famous slave narrators from this period include WILLIAM WELLS BROWN, OLAUDAH EQUIANO, and HARRIET JACOBS. Brown was one of the earliest African American novelists. Equiano's narrative, which recounts his memories of life in Africa, his capture, and the MIDDLE PASSAGE, is one of the rare autobiographies in English by a slave who was born in Africa. Jacobs, whose *Incidents in the Life of a Slave Girl* is the best example of a woman's slave narrative, discusses the sexual intimidation and abuse and the agony of being a slave mother that made slavery a different experience for women than for men.

Authors such as HENRY "BOX" BROWN and WILLIAM AND ELLEN CRAFT were memorable for their novel methods of escape from slavery. "Box" Brown's narrative recounts how he was packed into a crate and shipped to the free North as freight. The Crafts tell about traveling disguised as a dark-skinned Spanish gentleman and his black servant. Throughout this period, narrators worked both to give credible accounts of their own individual experiences in slavery and to argue that their experiences were representative and that thousands of others still suffered just as they had. They strove to convince readers that all of the slaves must be freed. And indeed, the narratives did help make the end of American slavery a reality.

After EMANCIPATION, the tone of many slave narratives changed. Authors continued to portray their experiences as slaves, but many had a new purpose in writing. They aimed to prove that slavery had been a testing ground from which African Americans had successfully emerged, ready to participate in the larger American society. BOOKER T. WASHINGTON's 1901 autobiography *Up From Slavery* is the best-known example of this new type of slave narrative. Washington uses many of the same conventions found in Douglass's slave narrative, but he turns them around so that in his autobiography, slavery becomes the foundation for a classic rags-to-riches American success story.

The last documents classified as slave narratives are the transcriptions of interviews with ex-slaves conducted in the first several decades of the twentieth century. The largest collection of these was compiled by interviewers with the federally funded FEDERAL WRITERS' PROJECT in the 1930s, which gathered testimonies from 2,500 ex-slaves in seventeen states.

In the late twentieth century, the slave narratives' presence is still felt throughout African American literature in both form and function. Many authors have written contemporary retellings of slave narratives, in books as varied as Morrison's lyrical *Beloved* (1987), OCTAVIA BUTLER's science fiction novel *Kindred* (1979), and ISHMAEL REED's parody *Flight to Canada* (1976). Other novels, such as *Invisible Man*, use the narratives' themes and structure with very different subject matter. And throughout the history of African American literature, autobiography has remained a dominant genre. Many African Americans still identify with the need to write about themselves as a means of sharing their common humanity. LANGSTON HUGHES, Zora Neale Hurston, RICHARD WRIGHT, MALCOLM X, and MAYA ANGELOU are among the black writers who continued this tradition of using the written word to pass their stories on.

See also Literature, African American.

Bibliography

Andrews, William L. *To Tell a Free Story: The First Century of Afro-American Autobiography, 1760–1865.* University of Illinois Press, 1986.

Davis, Charles T., and Henry Louis Gates, Jr. *The Slave's Narrative.* Oxford University Press, 1985.

Lisa Clayton Robinson

Slave Rebellions in Latin America and the Caribbean

Resistance to slavery by slaves of full or partial African descent, at times joined by freed people and escaped slaves (commonly called maroons).

The struggle against slavery throughout the Americas involved different forms of rebellion. Many slaves escaped; some merged with the urban free black and colored population, while others became maroons and set up their own communities in the backlands, often in cooperation with indigenous peoples. Slaves who remained within the system worked to undermine it, through sabotage of production. At the same time they found ways of using their owners' dependence on their labor to influence their terms of work. And from time to time these slave workers, sometimes in alliance with freed people, erupted in rebellion in an effort to destroy slavery outright.

Maroonage as a Form of Rebellion

Maroonage was the most important single method of mainland slave rebellion until emancipation, and it helped limit the expansion of slavery throughout the continent. Maroon communities (called *palenques* or *cumbes* in Spanish America and *quilombos* or *macombos* in BRAZIL) challenged the slave system and the power of the state because they incited other slaves to join them. In addition to escape, maroon communities made possible other forms of resistance that threatened the colonial order, such as plantation raids and illegal trade. Overall, efforts to suppress them were unsuccessful throughout mainland LATIN AMERICA. Although colonial forces at times destroyed or dispersed maroon communities, the settlements frequently reformed. Many survived long enough to establish an agricultural base for food and their own weapons manufacture, and some were officially granted autonomy. However, autonomy often came with the condition that the maroons halt their illicit activities, recognize colonial authority, and even aid colonial forces in the capture of escaped slaves and in the suppression of slave revolts.

Rebellions before the Haitian Revolution

Where European colonizers consolidated their power, rebellion by escape became increasingly dangerous. Slaves who were caught in flight were severely punished by mutilating, branding, and whipping to death. In the nineteenth century, they also were transported for sale elsewhere in the Americas as a form of exile. Consequently, slaves developed many alternative forms of resistance. Slave workers preserved and developed their own subculture of language, religious beliefs, family, and village organization. They devised day-to-day methods of resistance. Among other forms of sabotage, they worked slowly and inefficiently, made themselves absent, malingered, stole and destroyed property, burned crops, and incapacitated animals and machinery. Most importantly, when plantation work and punishment regimes became intolerable, they engaged in labor bargaining.

Labor bargaining was practiced throughout the Americas, particularly by slaves engaged in large-scale staple crop production. They used their labor as a bargaining tool to protest their terms of work: excessive punishment, increased or excessive work loads and work hours, inadequate food and clothing supplies, and forced removal from one property to another. The bargaining process began with verbal protests; the slaves sent delegates to carry their grievances—bypassing overseers (under-managers) at risk of flogging—directly to owners, attorneys, neighboring planters, or officials. If they failed to act, the whole work force went on strike to demand mediation. Such tactics were often successful, particularly when labor was in short supply, or during harvest time because the owners needed, first and foremost, to get the slaves back to work. Mediation often led, consequently, to some of the changes the slaves demanded, and overseers who provoked strikes were often fired. Strike leaders also risked punishment, often on some other pretext.

The slaves' resistance could not always be expressed by flight, labor bargaining, or covert and cultural methods. Localized revolts sparked by specific grievances and sometimes encouraged by neighboring maroons flared up in slave societies throughout the Americas. They were prompted by bad work conditions and tyrannical overseers; the failure of labor bargaining and the inefficiency of mediation procedures; opportunities created by reductions in local garrisons; and hopes stirred by metropolitan, or local, abolition movements. Large-scale rebellions that aimed to oust settlers and control the entire colony were relatively rare. Such enterprises required careful planning and organization and were usually revealed to the authorities during the planning stage by slaves or free black or colored people who either feared the consequences of rebellion or sought rewards (money or manumission). Four large-scale rebellions nevertheless developed in the eighteenth century: the first in the VIRGIN ISLANDS, the second in JAMAICA, the third in present-day GUYANA, and the last, and largest, in HAITI. These rebellions occurred in Caribbean societies that had an overwhelming majority of slaves, including young Africans trained as fighters, in addition to weak colonial garrisons and divisions in the ruling class. Furthermore, the geographic locations favored guerrilla warfare.

The small, newly settled, and poorly defended Danish colony of Saint John was taken over by slaves in November 1733. They took control of the only fort on the island, killed the twenty-five soldiers in the garrison, and sparked rebellion among the island's 1,087 slaves, most of whom were AKAN people from West Africa. They controlled the island for several months and resisted several attempts by Europeans to reconquer them. Few of the island's 208 resident whites escaped. When a French expedition from Martinique recaptured the island in June 1734, the defiant slave survivors committed mass suicide.

An ambitious attempt also was made to take over the well-developed and well-populated British island of Jamaica, where authorities had negotiated a peace treaty with the maroons in 1739 and believed that they enjoyed internal security. But on Easter Sunday, April 7, 1760, a slave rebellion described by a scholar of the time as "more formidable than any hitherto known in the WEST INDIES" broke out. Britain's Seven Years' War (1756–1763) against France and Spain had depleted the island garrisons, and the slaves, incited by short wartime rations and harsh management, seized their moment. Revolt began among estate slaves, many of them Akan, in the lightly settled northeastern parish of Saint Mary. They invaded Port Maria, captured the fort, and collected guns. Led by a slave called Tacky, who worked in African-style alliance with OBEAH men (the slaves' religious leaders), they raised rebellion among African and Creole slaves throughout the 120-mile-long island. For eighteen months they held the island ransom. The British regained their hold only because the maroons, fulfilling the terms of their peace treaty, gave crucial military assistance.

In 1763 slaves took over the extensive, sparsely populated Dutch mainland colony of Berbice (part of present-day Guyana) and held it for nearly ten months. Although previous slave revolts (in 1733, 1749, 1752, and 1762) had been quickly suppressed, this time the slaves were more united and better organized. Under the leadership of Kofi (also Cuffy), an Akan artisan, about 3,000 slaves from interior plantations drove the few hundred resident whites and their military forces to the coast and took the military garrison of Fort Nassau. Kofi planned to take over the colony and set up an independent African federation, and he began negotiations with the governor through letters. Dutch military reinforcements arrived, however, and Kofi prudently reduced the rebels' claim, to half of Berbice. However, his tactic was rejected by other rebel leaders who were prepared to risk everything for a complete victory: control over the entire colony. The division fragmented the rebellion into opposing factions, allowing the Dutch to win. Kofi committed suicide, and 120 rebels were executed.

These defeats in Jamaica and Berbice were subsequently overshadowed by the Haitian Revolution, which began in 1791 as a slave revolt in the French colony of Saint-Domingue (present-day Haiti). The rebellion was touched off by the 1789 French Revolution and its promise of "Liberty, Equality, and Fraternity" for all its citizens. It soon escalated to include not only slaves, who numbered a half-million in the colony, but also free blacks and people of color. In a desperate effort to end the large-scale rebellion, white officials in the local government emancipated all slaves in the colony in 1793. Upon hearing this news the Republican French National Convention formally abolished slavery in Saint-Domingue and all other French domains in February 1794. However, Napoleon Bonaparte revoked this in 1802, precipitating further rebellion. The revolution did not end until 1804, when the insurgents overthrew French colonial rule and established the independent black-led republic of Haiti.

Impact of the Haitian Revolution

The Haitian Revolution lit a beacon of hope for slaves throughout the continent. The names and deeds of its heroes, commemorated by children's names and on medallions, circulated from the hemisphere's ports to the interior. By intertwining liberty for slaves with anticolonial struggles for independence, it made slavery an international issue and precipitated efforts to outlaw the Atlantic slave trade. It also inspired a number of slave uprisings throughout the Americas, as word of the revolution spread among slaves.

A series of slave revolts took place in the 1790s in the Caribbean. The most impressive and sustained of these occurred in the Windward Islands of GRENADA and SAINT VINCENT, which had passed from French to British control in the 1760s. In Grenada, slaves and freed people formed an alliance led by a mixed-race planter, Julien Fédon. Proclaiming "Liberty, Equality, or Death"—an adaptation of the French revolutionary slogan—they rose in rebellion in March 1795. They quickly established a strong base in the interior, and by February 1796 they dominated the whole island after hard-fought battles against the British. They succumbed only to large-scale invasion later that year. During this same period, slaves were liberated on the nearby island of Saint Vincent by a combined force of the GARINAGU, a people of mixed Caribbean and African descent led by Chief Joseph Chatoyer, and French Republican forces. These events stirred a maroon rebellion on the barely settled island of DOMINICA.

In the Leeward Islands, the slaves of GUADELOUPE (a French colony), who were emancipated by the French Republican government, freed the slaves in SAINT LUCIA in a revolt that lasted from 1794 to 1796. In August 1795 about fifty slaves in one plantation in western Curaçao (NETHERLANDS ANTILLES) refused to continue working, under the claim that a new union between France and the Batavian Republic (the name for the Netherlands from 1795 to 1806) had set them free. They marched to neighboring plantations, and within a few days the island's entire slave population of 1,000 rose up, stormed the prison, and released the prisoners. Several years later in Cuba, JOSÉ ANTONIO APONTE, a free black carpenter, solicited the help of Haitian general Jean-François to organize a large-scale revolt in 1812.

On the Spanish American mainland, the Haitian Revolution inspired slaves in northwestern VENEZUELA. In May 1795 JOSÉ LEONARDO CHIRINOS, a slave of mixed African and indigenous descent, led slaves engaged with free blacks and people of color in cash-crop production near Coro to demand freedom from slavery and new land taxes. The Chirinos-led insurrection raised a band of some 300 rebels who were rapidly suppressed and savagely punished: 170 were executed, including Chirinos. In the Brazilian state of BAHIA in 1798, free people of color allied with slaves in the Revolução dos Sastres (Portuguese for "Tailors' Conspiracy") to claim the equality of all races and a democratic independent government, but they were arrested at the planning stage.

The colonial powers rallied their forces to prevent the revolution that was occurring in Saint-Domingue from spreading throughout the Caribbean. Britain, engaged in a war against France beginning in 1793, sent troops to attack the island of Saint-Domingue from 1794 to 1798 and occupied other French colonies, including Martinique (from 1794 to 1802) and briefly Guadeloupe (1794–1795). In Jamaica, British authorities launched a preemptive attack in 1795 against the Leeward Maroons. After a heroic guerrilla struggle, the maroons accepted amnesty in 1796, only to be treacherously deported first to Nova Scotia, in what later became Canada, and subsequently to SIERRA LEONE, in West Africa. The Spanish placated potentially troublesome maroons in eastern Cuba by recognizing their free status and land claims in 1801. The Dutch meanwhile initiated prolonged campaigns against the maroons in Dutch Guiana (present-day SURINAME) and eventually forced them to retreat farther inland in 1810.

On the Spanish American mainland, the consequences of the Haitian Revolution preoccupied white Creoles as much as, if not more than, European-born whites. Simón Bolívar, one of the preeminent Spanish American independence leaders, received arms and ammunition from Haiti in 1816 on the condition that independence would end slavery. Bolívar's pledge was repeated in countless political manifestos. Although slaves comprised a significant proportion of the independence armies and often fought on the promise of individual freedom, most white Creoles were reluctant to endorse abolition and blocked any legislation. During the confused wartime conditions of the independence struggles from 1810 to 1825, slave uprisings multiplied, and maroonage and flight to towns increased. By 1824, when Spain was conclusively defeated, slave numbers had been significantly reduced.

Slave Rebellions and Abolitionism

The Haitian Revolution underscored the dangers inherent in sustaining slavery by importing Africans, and many countries took steps to outlaw the slave trade. Denmark set the precedent in 1803, followed by Britain and the United States in 1807 and by Spain, Portugal, and Brazil later in the nineteenth century. The revolutionary principles of the French Declaration of the Rights of Man and of the Citizen, such as the premise all people are created equal, and the conviction that wage workers were more productive and less dangerous than slave workers, encouraged campaigns—most notably in Britain—to speed up the process. These circumstances influenced the aims and timing of many nineteenth-century slave rebellions.

Throughout the British Caribbean, rumors about abolition, combined with local hardships, promoted rebellions. Three major slave rebellions took place between the end of Britain's slave trade in 1807 and complete emancipation in 1838. In Barbados, the first slave revolt since 1649 erupted on April 14, 1816, and came to be known as BUSSA'S REBELLION (after its slave leader, Bussa) or the Easter Rebellion. Slaves set sugar estates on fire and seized arms, but the insurrection was suppressed in a matter of days. In 1823 plans to change the slave laws provoked a tremor of revolts and conspiracies throughout the British Caribbean. On August 17 in the British-controlled colony of Demerara (a section of present-day Guyana), blacks led by Quamina and other elite slaves (a class of slaves, often artisans and domestic servants, who achieved a higher social standing than most slaves) burned plantations and imprisoned whites. And in Jamaica, slave SAMUEL SHARPE led slaves in the western parishes—whose membership of mission churches and connections with independent religious sects provided a wide recruiting network—to rebel at sugar harvest time, in December 1831, in what became known as the Baptist War. More than 20,000 armed slaves combined revolt with labor strikes to demand their right to freedom and wages. Within weeks the rebellion was suppressed, but it provided convincing propaganda for the final stages of the British campaign to abolish slavery throughout the British Empire.

On the island of Martinique, in 1848, news of the politically progressive revolution in France and the hope of abolition prompted the slaves to rebel to claim the freedom they expected. Also that year, blacks on the island of Saint Croix, Virgin Islands, hastened their emancipation (in 1847 Danish colonial authorities had promised this would occur in 1859) by staging a massive, well-planned uprising. Led by the young slave Moses Gottlieb, armed columns of slaves, thousands strong, converged on the capital, attacked official residences, and prompted the governor to declare immediate abolition. Although many rebels were severely punished in the aftermath, abolition remained the law.

In Spanish CUBA and on a smaller scale in PUERTO RICO, slavery continued to expand, fed by demand in the sugar industry for illegally imported slaves. Multiple localized uprisings occurred yearly. In 1843 in Cuba, where slaves comprised 70 percent of the population in the sugar provinces, rebel activity intensified on the estates, compounded by urban revolts by free and enslaved Afro-Cubans. An investigation ordered by the Cuban government in 1844 revealed a widespread black conspiracy inspired by the black revolution in Haiti, the Spanish American wars for independence, and British abolitionism. The suppression of the conspiracy unleashed torture and hanging of slaves on a massive scale. As in Spanish America, many individual slaves won their freedom in Cuba by participating in the Ten Years' War (1868–1878), an unsuccessful war for independence from Spain. However, slavery was not fully abolished in Cuba until 1886.

In 1821 Brazil became independent from Portugal without the social dislocation of liberation wars. Its new constitution, dedicated in principle to freedom and equality, prompted two massive demonstrations by some 18,000 slaves in the state of MINAS GERAIS who believed freedom had been granted. The rapidly increasing number of newly imported slave workers to coffee plantations in the south prompted numerous localized rebellions protesting work conditions. But it was Bahia, the cradle of Afro-Brazilian culture, where in 1835 the most serious slave uprising of the century took place. On that occasion some 600 rebels fought the police in the city of Salvador. At least seventy died, four more were executed, and hundreds were harshly punished. Brazil's slave trade did not effectively end until 1850, and abolition was not approved until 1888. Until then flight remained the main form of overt resistance.

Conclusion

Resistance to slavery shaped the slaves' daily lives, and rebellion proclaimed their political goals. Slaves aimed to achieve freedom and independence by escaping the system, or by ending it. Their struggles, which involved alliances with freed persons and Creole nationalists, and the support of international abolitionist movements, were eventually successful. The slaves established a tradition of resistance to oppression for black communities throughout the Americas.

See also Berbice Slave Rebellion; Conspiración de la Escalera; Haitian Revolution; Maroonage in the Americas; Muslim Uprisings in Bahia, Brazil; Palmares: An African State in Brazil; Punishment of Slaves in Colonial Latin America and the Caribbean; Role of Slaves in Abolition and Emancipation in Latin America and the Caribbean; Struggles of Independence in Latin America, Racial Question during; Suriname and French Guiana, Maroon Communities in.

Bibliography

Costa, Emilia Viotti da. *Crowns of Glory, Tears of Blood: The Demerara Slave Rebellion of 1823.* Oxford University Press, 1994.

Craton, Michael. *Testing the Chains: Resistance to Slavery in the British West Indies.* Cornell University Press, 1982.

Klein, Herbert S. *African Slavery in Latin America and the Caribbean.* Oxford University Press, 1986.

Price, Richard, ed. *Maroon Societies: Rebel Slave Communities in the Americas.* Johns Hopkins University Press, 1996.

Reis, João José. *Slave Rebellion in Brazil: The Muslim Uprising of 1835 in Bahia.* Johns Hopkins University Press, 1993.

Judith Morrison

Slave Rebellions in the United States

Collective revolts and conspiracies by slaves and their allies with the aim of violently resisting their enslavement.

The standard work on SLAVERY IN THE UNITED STATES, until the late 1930s, was American historian U. B. Phillips's *American Negro Slavery* (1918). Phillips tells his readers that African American slaves were "impulsive and inconstant, sociable and amorous, voluble, dilatory and negligent, but robust, amiable, obedient and contented; they have been the world's premium slaves." Contrary to this racist mythology, the African American people sought to escape their bondage in myriad ways during the centuries of their enslavement. These ways included ever recurring flight, purchasing freedom (where allowed), self-inflicted wounds, suicide, infanticide (especially of female children), using arson and poison against their owners, and assassinating owners and especially overseers. The highest forms of resistance were conspiracy to rebel and actual rebellion. Akin to rebelling was the phenomenon of maroon communities—groups of fugitive slaves who survived on the outskirts of plantation communities and whose independence constantly threatened plantation stability. These maroon groups sometimes grew to such dimensions that major force was used against them, including U.S. troops.

Conspiracy to rebel and actual rebellion frequently recurred among slaves despite the slave owners' elaborate system of military control and espionage. Slave owners and overseers were armed; regular local patrols monitored slave activity; volunteer military companies and state militias stood ready; and the bulk of federal troops were stationed in the South, especially in Virginia, North Carolina, and Louisiana. Slave owners suppressed revolts and conspiracies mercilessly. Torture of suspects was the rule, and punishments were public and horrendous.

Colonial and Revolutionary Eras

The violent resistance of slaves to their bondage in North America began as soon as African slavery was introduced into the region. The very first attempt to bring African slaves into the territory that would become the United States was in the failed settlement of Spaniards along the South Carolina coast in 1526. This attempt was met with rebellion. Several African slaves revolted, killing a number of their masters and fleeing to nearby Native American settlements.

When the rest of the colony, beset by illness and the hostility of the Native Americans, embarked for Haiti soon after, the escaped Africans were left behind. They became perhaps the first non–Native Americans to settle permanently in North America. As slavery continued to expand in the American colonies, slave revolts continued as well. Two significant revolts were the NEW YORK SLAVE REBELLION OF 1712, which resulted in at least twenty black and Native American conspirators being executed and in stricter slave codes in the Northern colonies, and the STONO REBELLION in South Carolina in 1739, in which more than twenty whites and over twice that many blacks were killed.

While such group unrest was constant throughout the era of slavery, there were periods when particularly intense slave discontent erupted, often in response to specific stimuli. At the end of the eighteenth century, American slaves were inspired with the possibility of revolutionary freedom by the American and French revolutions and particularly by the HAITIAN REVOLUTION (1791–1804), in which a slave revolt led to a civil war and ultimately an independent black nation. In the most significant rebel movement of the era, the GABRIEL PROSSER CONSPIRACY of 1800, the slave Gabriel claimed the inspiration of all three national revolutions for his plan to attack Richmond, Virginia, with a force of hundreds of slaves. His plan was foiled by hurricane floods and betrayal. That these slaves were suppressed by men who were themselves revolutionaries carried a marked irony. James Monroe, governor of Virginia, wrote to Thomas Jefferson, just elected president of the United States, of the fortitude of Gabriel's rebels and asked what to do with these prisoners seeking freedom. The author of the Declaration of Independence advised Monroe to execute as few as necessary and sell the rest to the WEST INDIES.

Late Antebellum Period

In the 1820s and 1830s, rebellions were encouraged by the intense national debates about slavery's extension to new states in the West in 1820 and by the pressures of the economic depression that hit the South from the 1820s to 1832. In 1822, in the DENMARK VESEY CONSPIRACY, Vesey, a free black and a prosperous artisan, organized thousands of blacks and made thorough preparations for an armed attack on CHARLESTON, SOUTH CAROLINA, before his plot was revealed and suppressed. The revelation of Vesey's vast organization disturbed white slave owners, but its impact on the mind of the South was dwarfed by that of the most important slave rebellion in United States history, the revolt of Nat Turner in Southampton, Virginia in 1831. Turner's plot, unlike those of Gabriel and Vesey, involved a limited number of rebels in the beginning—as few as five or six—but the number grew to perhaps sixty or seventy as the effort unfolded. His band killed at least fifty-seven whites and resisted the local militia for three days.

The slavery controversy reclaimed the nation's imagination in the 1850s, and its renewal was accompanied by widespread slave unrest. In 1859 the slave resistance in the South and the abolitionist movement in the North came together when white abolitionist JOHN BROWN and his small force of white and black men attacked the federal armory in Harpers Ferry, Virginia (now West Virginia). Brown had hoped that his raid would provoke a slave rebellion throughout the region. He failed in that goal and was captured and executed, but his subsequent martyrdom made his name a rallying cry for the Union forces in the American CIVIL WAR (1861–1865). Once the Civil War began, the increased possibility of escape made resort to uprisings less necessary, but instances of massive slave unrest in the South occurred during the war, especially collective arson. In 1861 a significant slave conspiracy to rebel was uncovered in Mississippi, resulting in numerous executions—at least forty slaves in and around Natchez suffered this fate.

Rebel Character

Although few of the direct words of the rebels have been passed down through history, the spirit of many of them emerges from reports of the slave owners. Thus, Nat Turner, wounded, in chains, and facing imminent execution, challenged his court-appointed interrogator: "Was not Christ crucified?" Peter Poyas, a fellow rebel with Denmark Vesey, while himself enduring torment, screamed to a comrade who was about to give names to the torturers, "Die silent as you shall see me do." And there is the unnamed rebel in Tennessee, telling his captors to keep up with their beating, for "Frémont hears my screams," referring to John Frémont, the presidential candidate of the new antislavery REPUBLICAN PARTY in 1856.

A marked feature of the slave conspiracies and uprisings was the evidence of sympathy for the rebels coming from some white people. In 1811 a white man, Joseph Wood, was hanged in Louisiana for sympathizing with slave rebels. In the aftermath of Vesey's plot, four white men were convicted and jailed for sympathizing with the rebels. Their crime consisted of telling the slaves, as one of the men put it in the court record, that "they had as much right to fight for their liberty as the white people." Such cross-racial solidarity was often returned, as in the case of SHIELDS GREEN, recently escaped from slavery, who accompanied the abolitionist and former slave FREDERICK DOUGLASS on a visit to John Brown shortly before his raid on Harpers Ferry. As Douglass turned to leave, Green tarried. Douglass said to him, "Shields, are you coming?" "No," said Green, "I believe I'll go with the old man." He did go with Brown, and he died with him.

Not all slave resistance to owners took the form of armed, organized rebellion. In his *Slave Laws in Virginia* (1996), American historian Philip J. Schwarz presents data on the large number of slaves prosecuted in Virginia for their attempts to poison their owners and their families, as well as those tried for conspiracy and insurrection. Incomplete records show that 635 slaves were hanged in Virginia from the end of the American Revolution through the Civil War; Schwarz thinks the correct number was about 945. At times so-called intractable slaves were sold to the West Indies rather than being executed. Available records show that from 1800 to 1865, when slavery was outlawed, 935 Virginia slaves suffered the punishment of transportation, rather than execution; it is questionable which fate was preferable.

The reality of slave rebellions in the United States decidedly negates Phillips's racist concoction of slavery's idyllic nature in the United States and of the slaves' contentment with their condition. Exactly the contrary is the truth: slavery was a hellish system of exploitation in the United States, and those enslaved resisted their condition in every possible way, including conspiracy and rebellion.

See also Abolitionism in the United States; Maroonage in the Americas; Missouri Compromise; Nat Turner's Rebellion.

Herbert Aptheker

Slave Religion

Religious beliefs and practices of African American slaves in North America.

In a system where mobility, marriage, employment, housing, food, and clothing were all regulated by slave owners, religion was the slaves' only form of expression that was not totally under white control. Consequently, religion played a central role in the lives of slaves. Slave congregations became new versions of the African village, with the slave preacher serving as chief, GRIOT, and even doctor. Religious meetings provided important ritual communal opportunities for African American slaves to worship in ways that connected them to African traditions, while also creating, over time, a new belief system adapted to their lives in the Americas. Religion gave individual slaves a sense of their place in the world, a sense of their worth, and a life-sustaining faith in a better future.

Some masters organized mandatory Christian church services, in the hope Christian slaves would be more docile. Some allowed slaves to hold their own services. Many others, however, did not allow their slaves to attend church at all, either because they felt threatened by any such communal gatherings or because they disliked the suggestion that slaves might have souls to be saved. But even on plantations where religious gatherings were forbidden, slaves held secret meetings at night in secluded outdoor sanctuaries—often bush arbors that slaves nicknamed "hush harbors."

Many facts about slaves' religious practices went unrecorded, but it is known that slave religion combined elements of traditional African religions and American evangelical Protestant Christianity. African influences were present in many of the slaves' ceremonies. For example, in the ring shout, a common form of worship, believers formed a circle and moved counterclockwise, shouting and professing their faith, while others stood outside the circle and sang. The call-and-response worship pattern, in which the preacher's sermon was interspersed with responses from members of the audience, also had African roots and is still a common characteristic of African American preaching and music.

Slave theology was predominantly Christian, but slaves appropriated from the Christian Bible only what they found most useful. A common complaint about the sermons preached by white ministers in the slave quarters was that nearly all relied on only one verse: "Slaves, obey your masters." But as slaves learned more about the Bible, they were able to decide what other messages it held for them. Consequently, they identified with the God who favored the poor and meek over the wealthy and strong, the God who praised little David over mighty Goliath, and, above all, the God who freed the Hebrew slaves from their Egyptian captors. In this way, slaves were able to see themselves not as property but as people created in God's image, important in his eyes, and people who would have deliverance and justice in the days to come.

Religious meetings offered benefits beyond the spiritual. Regarded as a democratic space where all were welcome to speak if they felt the spirit, they provided essentially the slaves' only opportunity for public speaking. Consequently, religious meetings provided a rare forum for leadership to emerge, and slave preachers were generally respected as the speakers and leaders of the entire community. NAT TURNER and GABRIEL PROSSER, two famous slave rebellion leaders, both began as religious leaders.

The most common forms of religious expression were SPIRITUALS, songs with a rich double purpose. Slave masters often encouraged this music because they saw the spirituals as simple hymns and thought that singing kept slaves content as they worked. Spirituals also played a key role in teaching the Bible to slaves who were not literate, because the lyrics of common spirituals retell biblical narrative from Creation to Revelation. But many of these lyrics also had a secret meaning. It was common knowledge among the slaves who sang spirituals that "Steal Away" did not only mean to Jesus, and "I Am Bound for the Promised Land" did not only mean heaven. In fact, spirituals offered a method of secretly communicating plans and directions for escape from the plantation.

For all these reasons, slave religion played a crucial part in life. It provided the basis for a cohesive community where slaves were able to communicate more openly and express themselves more freely than in any other context. Through this community, with its shared rituals, beliefs, and songs, slaves could find the spiritual validation and hope for the future that many relied upon to sustain them through their trials. An enslaved woman named Polly summed up one view of the slaves' religious faith: "We poor creatures have need to believe in God, for if God Almighty will not be good to us some day, why were we born? When I heard of his delivering his people from bondage I know it means the poor African."

See also Religions, African.

Bibliography

Hopkins, Dwight N., et al. *Cut Loose Your Stammering Tongue: Black Theology in the Slave Narratives*. Orbis Books, 1991.

Raboteau, Albert J. *Slave Religion: The "Invisible Institution" in the Antebellum South.* Oxford University Press, 1980.

Lisa Clayton Robinson

Slavery and Law in North America

Relationship between criminal, civil, and constitutional law and the development, maintenance, and defense of the institution of North American slavery.

Slavery was unknown in the British Isles when the first English colonists arrived in North America in the late 1500s. Moreover, the very idea of slavery was contrary to English law. Thus, although slavery could be found throughout the Spanish and Portuguese settlements of the Americas, the English did not adopt the institution immediately.

Early Slavery in Virginia

In the early years of the English colonies, the landowning and elite English colonists in Virginia, Maryland, and elsewhere relied on indentured servants, who contracted their services for a limited term of years, for their labor supply. In 1619 the first Africans arrived in Virginia aboard a Dutch ship. The Virginia colonists treated these Africans as indentured servants, and some eventually gained their freedom. Throughout the 1620s the legal system in Virginia seems not to have discriminated against blacks. For example, a record from 1624 notes that "John Phillip, A Negro" was allowed to testify in a lawsuit involving two whites, a right that would later be rescinded for blacks.

By 1640, however, the legal system had begun to single out Africans for distinctly different treatment. In that year a Virginia court sentenced a black indentured servant named John Punch to "serve his said master or his assigns for the time of his natural Life here or elsewhere." No white indentured servant in Virginia ever received such a sentence. At about this time court records and wills indicate that other blacks were being treated as slaves.

The legal system was not uniformly hostile to blacks in the seventeenth century. For example, as late as 1672 a Virginia court freed Edward Mozingo, ruling that he had been brought to the colony as an indentured servant, had served his full term of years, and was entitled to his freedom. A year later the court ruled in favor of a freedom claim by "Andrew Moore, A Servant Negro."

However, Mozingo and Moore were the exceptions to the growing support for slavery by the Virginia courts and legislature. In 1659 and 1660 the Virginia legislature recognized the existence of slaves in the colony by providing an import tax for "foreigners [who] shall import negro slaves." Two years later the legislature provided that if white servants ran away with slaves, the whites would have to serve extra time to make up for the time that the slaves were absent because the slaves could not have any more time added to their service. This law had the practical effect of separating white indentured servants (who still made up the majority of agricultural workers in the English colonies) from black slaves. White workers, who frequently ran away, could no longer afford to share their plans or their hopes of liberty with their black coworkers. This was the beginning of a conscious attempt by the leaders of Virginia and other colonies to drive a wedge between black and white workers.

In 1662 the Virginia legislature passed its most important early statute on slavery. This act declared that "all children born in this country shall be held bond or free only according to the condition of the mother." This legal rule, known as *partus sequitur ventrem* (the offspring follows the mother), was based on Roman law and was a complete reversal of existing English common law. In England the status of a child, even an illegitimate child, was based on the status of the father. But under this rule children in Virginia would follow the status of the mother. Every other English colony in North America eventually adopted this rule.

This law had two practical results. First, it meant that the children of black women throughout the American South would usually be slaves, even if their fathers were free. Second, this law facilitated sexual relations between male owners and female slaves. At this time in the colonies, fathers of children born outside of marriage were frequently prosecuted, both to bring public shame on them and to ensure their support for their children. However, this law took away any fear of such prosecution for sex with slaves. Any children born of such a relationship would be slaves, owned by the owner of the slave mother. The state would have no interest in investigating who the father was, because the master would happily pay for the costs of raising another slave. Thus this law encouraged the sexual exploitation of slave women.

In 1669 the Virginia legislature declared that masters or overseers would not be criminally liable if a slave died while being punished. In 1680 the legislature further declared that any white could kill a slave believed to be a fugitive. The same law provided the severe penalty of 30 lashes for any slave who "shall presume to lift up his hand in opposition" to any white. A 1691 law directed sheriffs to "kill and destroy" slaves hiding out in the woods and further guaranteed that the colony would recompense a master for the value of the dead slave. This law put the military force and the economic power of the colony behind the emerging institution of slavery.

By 1700 slavery was an integral and significant part of the Virginia economy. White indentured servants still outnumbered slaves, but indentured servitude was clearly being eclipsed by slavery. In 1705 Virginia enacted its first comprehensive statute on slavery, "An Act Concerning Servants and Slaves." Combining many earlier acts, the law required that slaves be taxed as property and registered by their owners, explained when runaways or rebellious slaves "may be killed," and described what other punishments might be inflicted on slaves. The law made clear that blacks were a pariah race whose members could not marry whites or associate with them. The law equated blacks with slaves, although in fact hundreds of blacks in the colony were free.

In the South and in the North

By 1750 all of the Southern colonies and most of the Northern ones had adopted slave codes similar to those of Virginia. In the process they managed to create an entirely new area of law, unknown in England, to support slavery in the colonies. While colonial legislatures tinkered with these codes, they remained basically the same until the AMERICAN REVOLUTION (1775–1783).

Slavery was particularly important in the Southern colonies because they relied on large-scale agriculture, although Rhode Island, New York, New Jersey, and Pennsylvania all had significant numbers of slaves as well. The laws of all the colonies were similar. Slaves had virtually no legal rights. They could be executed in most places for numerous crimes that were not capital offenses for whites. Their testimony was restricted in legal cases and could not be used for or against whites. Trials of slaves were usually by special courts. They could not own property, could not possess guns or dogs, could not move about without the consent of their owner, and could not be legally married. Throughout the South, killing a slave was not murder; it was usually considered simply a destruction of property. It was not considered a crime to kill a slave who was resisting white authority, rebelling, or even, in some circumstances, running away. In Virginia, the colony with the largest slave population, and elsewhere in the South, it was even illegal for a master to manumit (voluntarily free) a slave.

Slavery and the Revolution

Slavery was legal in all of the thirteen colonies that revolted against GREAT BRITAIN in the American Revolution. It was also legal in CANADA, where, with the exception of Upper Canada (present-day Ontario), it remained legal until Britain abolished slavery throughout its remaining colonies in 1834. Thereafter Canada generally served as a safe haven for runaway slaves from the United States, who fled by means of the UNDERGROUND RAILROAD.

The American Revolution, however, undermined the basis of slavery through the articulation of the principle "all men are created equal" in the Declaration of Independence. During and after the war Northern patriots took seriously this new ideology and took steps to end slavery. Massachusetts (1780) and New Hampshire (1784), ended slavery outright in their new state constitutions. Vermont had abolished slavery in its 1777 constitution, which was officially recognized when it became the fourteenth state in 1791. Pennsylvania (1780), Connecticut (1784), Rhode Island (1784), New York (1799), and New Jersey (1804) adopted "gradual emancipation statutes," which provided that the children of all slave women would be born free (although subject to indentured service until adulthood), and that no new slaves could be brought in from other states. Upper Canada adopted a similar law in 1793. New York accelerated this process by ending all slavery on July 4, 1827. By the 1840s Pennsylvania and Connecticut had also eliminated the last vestiges of slavery.

The Revolution also had some effect on slavery in the South. For example, in 1791 North Carolina made it a capital offense to murder a slave. The preamble to this statute, which was later declared unenforceable for technical reasons, acknowledged the ideological changes brought about by the Revolution. In 1782 Virginia allowed for the voluntary manumission of slaves by masters. As a result, the free black population of the state grew from about 2,000 to about 30,000 between 1782 and 1806, when Virginia modified the law by requiring newly freed slaves to leave the state. Other Southern states eased restrictions on voluntary manumission. However, none of the Southern states considered actually ending slavery. On the contrary, most Southerners assumed that one of the benefits of the Revolution was the new states' increased right to pass laws that strengthened slavery within their territory.

Slavery and the Constitutional Convention

From the first day of substantive debate at the Constitutional Convention in 1787 until the final signing of the finished Constitution, slavery was a central issue. On the first day of debate the issue of slavery nearly derailed the convention as the delegates considered a proposal to have representation based on population. The discussion had hardly begun when the question of counting or not counting slaves for purposes of representation led to bitter debate. Despite this controversy, the finished Constitution protected slavery in a variety of ways.

The three-fifths clause (Article I, Section 2, Paragraph 3) provided for counting three-fifths of all "other Persons"—slaves—for purposes of representation in Congress, although such people of course could not vote. At the end of the convention Elbridge Gerry of Massachusetts refused to sign the Constitution, at least in part because the three-fifths clause gave the South increased representation and political power because of its slaves.

The slave trade clause (Article I, Section 9, Paragraph 1) prohibited Congress from banning the "Migration or Importation of such Persons as any of the States now existing shall think proper to admit" before the year 1808. Awkwardly phrased and designed to confuse readers, this clause prevented Congress from ending the African slave trade before 1808 but did not require Congress to ban the trade after that date. The clause was a significant exception to the general power granted to Congress to regulate all commerce.

The Electoral College clause (Article II, Section 1, Paragraph 2) provided for the indirect election of the president through an electoral college based on congressional representation. This provision incorporated the three-fifths clause into the Electoral College, giving whites in slave states a disproportionate influence in the election of the president. In 1800 the electoral votes based on slaves provided the margin of victory for the slaveholding candidate, Thomas Jefferson, over John Adams, who had never owned a slave.

The fugitive slave clause (Article IV, Section 2, Paragraph 3) prohibited the states from emancipating a "Person held to Service or Labour in one State . . . and escaping into another"—

a fugitive slave—and required that runaways be returned to their owners if claimed. Oddly, no Northerners commented on this clause during the debates over ratification. By the 1830s, however, it had emerged as the most controversial clause connected to slavery.

Finally, the structure for changing the Constitution provided enormous protection for slavery. Ratification of constitutional amendments required the approval of three-fourths of all the states, so a small minority of the states could block any constitutional change. Only the Northern victory in the AMERICAN CIVIL WAR (1861–1865) finally allowed for the voting bloc of slave states to be overturned. As a condition for the states of the Confederacy to be readmitted into the Union, they were required to approve the Thirteenth Amendment (1865), which abolished slavery.

Southerners left the Constitutional Convention pleased with the result. South Carolina delegate General Charles Cotesworth Pinckney told his state's house of representatives, "We have a security that the general government can never emancipate [the slaves], for no such authority is granted." "In short," Pinckney bragged, "considering all circumstances, we have made the best terms for the security of this species of property it was in our power to make."

Slave Law in the Nineteenth Century

By the early 1800s the Southern states began to move further away from ideas of liberty and equality when it came to slaves. The law of the South after this period usually strengthened slavery as an institution and supported the interests of the master class.

One way of strengthening slavery was to make it less harsh. This would make slave rebellions less likely and undercut abolitionist critiques of the institution. Thus, for example, in the 1820s South Carolina prohibited branding, dismemberment, castration, and other barbaric forms of punishment that had been legal in the colonial period. Similarly, by 1860 all Southern states recognized that no one, not even a master, could murder a slave in cold blood. In *State* v. *Hoover* (1839) the North Carolina Supreme Court upheld the death sentence for a master who tortured his slave to death. Shortly before the Civil War a few Southern states made rape of a slave a crime, although no white was ever prosecuted for such a crime.

Along the same lines, Southern states provided some due process protections for slaves accused of crimes. Courts throughout the South overturned convictions of slaves who were denied a lawyer, coerced into giving confessions, improperly prohibited from calling witnesses, or incorrectly charged. In *Dick v. Mississippi* (1856), for example, the Mississippi court reversed the conviction of a slave for raping a white woman because the indictment described the defendant as "a negro man slave" when in fact "the prisoner was a mulatto slave."

These procedural victories, however, helped few slaves charged with crimes. Most slaves accused of criminal offenses were given quick trials and harsh punishments. Slaves were at all times made subordinate to whites, and the Southern legislatures and courts readily accepted and supported this idea. A few Southern courts held that a slave could resist a white in order to save his or her life, but this was the only exception to the general rule that masters must be obeyed at all times. In *State v. Mann* (1829), the most famous case involving the criminal law of slavery, Chief Judge Thomas Ruffin of the North Carolina Supreme Court reversed the conviction of a man who had shot and wounded a rented slave. Ruffin declared, "The slave, to remain a slave, must be made sensible, that there is no appeal from his master; that his power is in no instance usurped, but is conferred by the laws of man at least, if not by the law of God."

Although restrictions on manumission had been eased in the Southern states during the Revolutionary War period, by 1860 almost all of the states that would join the Confederacy either prohibited manumission or made it extremely difficult. Most slave states made it a crime to teach a slave to read. It was a crime in most of the South to circulate literature critical of slavery, and in the 1850s Harriet Beecher Stowe's antislavery bestseller UNCLE TOM'S CABIN was banned throughout most of the region. Slaves could often not even organize their own worship services without whites being present. Many of these restrictive laws were also applied to the more than a quarter of a million free blacks who lived in the South by 1860. Free blacks from the North or other countries who entered Southern states as merchant seamen were routinely incarcerated while their ships were docked. By 1860 most of the slave South was a closed society in which neither whites nor blacks were allowed to question the value of slavery.

By 1830 slavery had completely disappeared in most of the North, and although a few aging slaves could be found in Pennsylvania, New Jersey, Connecticut, and Illinois, the system itself was dead. In the three decades before the Civil War Northerners passed laws to protect their free black neighbors from kidnapping. Gradually, although grudgingly, Northern whites also offered free blacks some social, political, and economic rights. Blacks could vote in all the New England states except Connecticut, and in New York free blacks who owned property could vote. In the 1850s, blacks held elective or appointive office in Ohio, Massachusetts, and Rhode Island.

Most Northern states passed personal liberty laws designed to frustrate, where possible, attempts by Southerners to reclaim fugitive slaves. Northern states also moved to free the slaves taken into their states by visiting masters. In *Somerset v. Stewart* (1772) the Court of Kings Bench in London had ruled that if a master brought a slave to England, the slave instantly became free. This ruling was part of the common law of the colonies at the time of the Revolution. Despite this precedent, most Northern states at first allowed masters to retain ownership of slaves brought into their states for a short time. However, starting with *Commonwealth v. Aves* (1836) in Massachusetts, the free states began to free slaves the moment they were brought into the North. Before the 1830s about half the slave states recognized the freedom of slaves who had lived in the North, but by 1860 most refused to uphold freedom gained in free states. In *Mitchell v. Wells* (1859) Mississippi even rejected the freedom of a slave whose owner had brought her to Ohio and voluntarily manumitted her there.

Slavery and National Law

After the adoption of the Constitution, Congress and the Supreme Court generally supported slavery. In 1793 Congress passed the first fugitive slave law to help masters recover runaway slaves. An amendment to that law, known as the Fugitive Slave Law of 1850, provided federal help to masters and harsh penalties for anyone interfering with the return of runaway slaves. Throughout the period, the Supreme Court interpreted such laws to benefit masters.

In 1808 Congress banned the importation of slaves. This was not necessarily an antislavery measure, however, as many slave owners in Virginia and Maryland favored such a ban because it would increase the value of their slaves. And Congress and the executive branch effectively did not enforce the ban until the Civil War. Meanwhile, in *The Antelope* (1825) and other cases, the Supreme Court upheld the legality of the international slave trade. In *United States v. Amistad* (1841) the Supreme Court ordered that African slaves who had taken control of their Spanish slave ship and landed on American shores should be set free, but only because they had been illegally imported to Cuba in the first place. Had they been legally held as slaves in Cuba, the Court was prepared to return them to their owners.

In the Northwest Ordinance (1787) Congress banned slavery in the Northwest Territory (the present-day states of Ohio, Indiana, Illinois, Michigan, Wisconsin, and eastern Minnesota). Congress never implemented this part of the law, however, and in Illinois some blacks were held as slaves, or indentured servants for life, until the 1840s. In the MISSOURI COMPROMISE (1820) Congress banned slavery in the territories north and west of the southern boundary of Missouri. In the COMPROMISE OF 1850 Congress modified the ban further to allow slavery in most of the territories ceded to the United States after the Mexican War. And in the Kansas-Nebraska Act (1854) Congress opened up most of the West to slavery.

In DRED SCOTT V. SANDFORD (1857) the Supreme Court ruled that all bans on slavery in the territories were unconstitutional because Southerners had a constitutional right to take their slaves into any federal territories. The Court also ruled that blacks had no legal rights under the Constitution and that they could never be citizens of the United States. The *Dred Scott* decision led to an extraordinary backlash in the North. Abraham Lincoln's sharp critique of the decision helped propel him to the Republican nomination for president in 1860.

The nation effectively overruled *Dred Scott* during and after the Civil War. During the war Congress banned slavery in the territories and in the District of Columbia and, with the enlistment of black troops starting in 1862, acknowledged that African Americans could indeed be part of the United States citizenry. Lincoln's EMANCIPATION PROCLAMATION (1863) declared an end to slavery in all Confederate territory not then under the control of the Union Army, although this could not be enforced while the Confederacy still controlled those areas. The final reversal of *Dred Scott* came with the adoption of the Thirteenth Amendment, which ended slavery everywhere in the United States, and the FOURTEENTH AMENDMENT (1868), which declared that all people born in the United States were citizens of the nation and of the state in which they lived.

See also Abolitionism in the United States; Amistad Mutiny; *Antelope* Case; Criminal Justice System and African Americans; Free Blacks in the United States; Fugitive Slave Laws; Fugitive Slaves; Slave Laws in Colonial Spanish America; Slave Religion; Slavery in the United States; Slavery in Latin America and the Caribbean; Transatlantic Slave Trade.

Bibliography

Fehrenbacher, Don E. *The Dred Scott Case: Its Significance in American Law and Politics.* Oxford University Press, 1978.

Finkelman, Paul. *Dred Scott v. Sandford: A Brief History with Documents.* Bedford, 1997.

Finkelman, Paul. *An Imperfect Union: Slavery, Federalism, and Comity.* University of North Carolina Press, 1981.

Finkelman, Paul. *Slavery and the Founders: Race and Liberty in the Age of Jefferson.* Sharpe, 1996.

Higginbotham, A. Leon, Jr. *In the Matter of Color: Race and the American Legal Process: The Colonial Period.* Oxford University Press, 1978.

Morris, Thomas D. *Free Men All: The Personal Liberty Laws of the North, 1780–1861.* Johns Hopkins University Press, 1974.

Morris, Thomas D. *Southern Slavery and the Law, 1619–1860.* University of North Carolina Press, 1996.

Robinson, Donald L. *Slavery in the Structure of American Politics, 1765–1820.* Harcourt Brace Jovanovich, 1971.

Paul Finkelman

Slavery in Africa

Discussion of the history and practices of slavery in Africa.

Too often, observers have treated Africa as a region in isolation. The history of slavery, in contrast, shows the significance of Africa's socioeconomic connections to other world regions. The very distinctiveness of African society and African slavery results in large part from local responses to global connections.

This essay focuses on three historical points. First, slavery existed and sometimes flourished in Africa before the TRANSATLANTIC SLAVE TRADE, but neither the African continent nor persons of African origin were as prominent in the world of slaveholding as they would later become. Second, the capture and sale of slaves across the Atlantic between 1450 and 1850 encouraged expansion and repeated transformation of slavery

Slaves belonging to the pasha of Taoudenni, in Mali, stack blocks of salt in the 1950s.
CORBIS/Hulton-Deutsch Collection

within Africa, to the point that systems of slavery became central to societies all across the continent. Third, even after the abolition of the transatlantic slave trade (largely accomplished by 1850) and the European conquest of Africa (mostly by 1900), millions of persons remained in slavery in Africa as late as 1930.

The three sections of the essay address each of these points, giving particular attention to the last two. While the argument reviews the rise and decline of export slave trades—across the Atlantic, THE SAHARA, the Red Sea, and the Indian Ocean—it focuses on the nature and extent of slavery within sub-Saharan Africa.

Before the Transatlantic Slave Trade

In ancient EGYPT and NUBIA slavery existed but not as a dominant institution. The enslavement of the Hebrews in Egypt and Babylonia was a significant exception. In classical times, the commercial North African state of Carthage as well as the Greek states and Rome all relied on slave labor in galleys and in agriculture, and acquired some of their slaves through trade with sub-Saharan Africa.

The rise of Islam in the seventh century brought a set of rules that provided protection for those in slave status, but in so doing reinforced the institution of slavery. In Africa, Islam took root first in North Africa, then later in West Africa and along the eastern coast. A large proportion of slaves in Islamic society served as domestics, but slaves also worked as farm laborers and porters. Elite corps of slaves entered the military and government.

Among pre-1500 sub-Saharan states, traces of slavery are only occasionally clear. Evidence of slavery in AKSUM and the Christian kingdoms of Nubia, for example, is scarce. For the ancient West African empires of GHANA and MALI, the written record makes only an occasional reference to slave status. For the Islamic empire of SONGHAI, on the other hand, there are clearer indications of significant numbers of persons held in slave status by the monarchy and by lords of the realm. To the east of Songhai, the kingdom of Kanem-Bornu may also have had substantial numbers of slaves. In East Africa, slaves were important to the labor of the Islamic SWAHILI states along the coast as well as to the greater Indian Ocean regional economy. In the states of Ife, OYO, and BENIN in West Africa, KONGO in Central Africa, and Munhumutapa in what is now ZIMBABWE, slave populations took form around powerful monarchs.

It is difficult to assess the extent of slavery outside of these major states prior to 1500 because of the lack of data. But the earliest written reports by visitors from Europe and North Africa and the later anthropological records suggest that various kinds of slavery existed in smaller as in larger polities.

It is also difficult to assess the *nature* of servility during this era, and to know whether it was equivalent to chattel slavery. By the beginning of the twentieth century, according to the descriptions of European writers, African societies had developed many different types of servitude. But some of this variation may have developed over time, in response to the imposition of chattel slavery in the plantations and mines of the Americas.

During the Transatlantic Slave Trade

Portuguese and Spanish holdings of African slaves expanded with the maritime voyages of the fifteenth century, then grew moderately until, after 1650, the transatlantic trade exceeded the slave trade across the Sahara and Red Sea. Portuguese and then Dutch purchasers focused in SENEGAMBIA, Kongo, ANGOLA, and SIERRA LEONE. Africans' willingness to participate in the export of slaves varied. The kingdom of Benin, for example, eventually withdrew from the slave trade, but in Kongo and Senegambia those willing to profit from capture and export of

A soldier guards slaves linked together by chains, around 1896. *Getty Images*

slaves became dominant. These and then other African societies developed the means to capture, feed, finance, and transport captives for sale to European buyers.

As the trade expanded, Europeans developed a preference for males and were willing to pay more for them. Africans, in contrast, paid higher prices for female slaves, who were preferred because they could be used as domestic and agricultural laborers, as concubines, and as bearers of children. They were also considered easier to control than men. As prices diverged, the European and African markets for slaves grew in tandem. Their parallel expansion meant that, from the seventeenth century, the number of persons in slavery in Africa roughly equaled the number in the Americas.

Between 1700 and 1800, for the western coast of Africa from Senegal to Angola, the export of massive numbers of primarily male slaves led to both overall population decline and the dramatic increase in female slavery. Thus the transatlantic slave trade had not only demographic consequences for African societies but also economic and social ones.

At the turn of the eighteenth century the BIGHT OF BENIN was the principal region of slave supply. Wars among competing coastal states supplied as many as 15,000 slaves per year for export. Many of these slaves spoke the Gbe language and practiced the religion of Vodun (a predecessor of Haitian VODOU). But as 5 percent of the population were exported each year in chains, the population declined and captives became more expensive to collect and deliver. As a result, prices of slaves in the Bight of Benin rose dramatically between 1690 and 1730. As population declined and prices rose in one area, other areas were drawn into the slave trade: the Bight of Biafra (southern NIGERIA), Sierra Leone, the Gold Coast (now GHANA), the REPUBLIC OF THE CONGO, and Angola. As traders all along Africa's west coast began to deliver captives, the excess of males delivered across the Atlantic led to a changed population structure in the homeland. Women exceeded men by a substantial proportion in West and Central Africa, with an average of one hundred adult females for every seventy adult males. In areas such as Angola and the Bight of Benin, the ratio reached two adult women for every man.

Most captive women were sold into slavery and kept by families. A huge system of female-dominated family slavery arose all along the African coast during the eighteenth century. It expanded as long as demand for slaves in the Americas expanded—that is, until the end of the eighteenth century. Women worked as servants or in the fields. They were without family except for their owners and their children, and the children were property of their owners. This century of numerical dominance but social inferiority for women had a lasting influence on the institution of marriage and on the sexual division of labor in societies along Africa's west coast.

Between 1800 and 1850 two distinct but related developments led to both an increase in the number of persons held in slavery in Africa and the overall transformation of Africa systems of slavery. The first development was the growing demand for slaves in the Muslim Mediterranean and the lands bordering the Indian Ocean, beginning in the late eighteenth century. Perhaps this demand reflected the general growth in commercial activity; perhaps it reflected simply the spread of the system of slave labor from the Atlantic Basin. It remained primarily a demand for female slaves, who served largely as domestics. Societies of the northern savanna and the Horn of Africa, therefore, had populations with an excess of males, in contrast to the excess of females in societies along the Atlantic.

The second development occurred along the west coast of Africa, where the decline of slave exports after the gradual abolition of the transatlantic trade led to expansion and transformation of the African system of slavery. African sex ratios tended to equalize as the proportion of exiled males declined. Slaves were now both male and female, and they lived not in the households of their masters but in separate villages. For the continent as a whole, the expansion of this new system of slavery coincided with ongoing population decline. The number of captives exported from West Africa declined, but exports remained high in the Republic of the Congo and Angola, and exports actually rose along the Sahara fringe as well as along the Horn and the east coast of Africa. As population declined and levels of enslavement rose, plantation slavery and slave villages became more common in many areas in Africa. In southern Africa, slavery declined under British COLONIAL RULE in the west but expanded in the east, where slaves were captured for export to lands around the Indian Ocean.

After the Abolition of the Slave Trade

Slave trade across the Atlantic had virtually halted by 1850. But the various regions of the African continent continued to feel heavily the impact of enslavement and slavery for most of the next century. The result was that Africa in the late nineteenth century had more people in slavery than at any previous time. The final great emancipation of the Americas—the United States in 1865, Cuba in 1886, and Brazil in 1888—left Africa, and especially the SOKOTO CALIPHATE in northern Nigeria, holding the world's principal enslaved populations.

Slave exports across the Indian Ocean, the Sahara, and the Red Sea reached their peak in about 1850, then declined at varying rates until the end of the century. During this time, some enslaved Africans were carried across the Red Sea to build an expanded pilgrimage site at Mecca, in Saudi Arabia; others were carried on steamers through the Suez Canal, bound for Istanbul and Izmir.

In coastal West Africa, slavery expanded on plantations producing export commodities such as palm oil. The result was social turmoil, as slaves revolted in several regions from Calabar to DAHOMEY during the 1850s. Although the revolts were suppressed, they also set new limits on the exploitation of slaves. In the Republic of the Congo and Angola, exports finally halted around 1850, though enslavement for local purposes continued. In the northern savanna, exports of slaves peaked in the mid-nineteenth century, but the number of captives exceeded what could be explained as a by-product of export trade. In regions of the upper Niger Valley, there were repeated reports that the majority of the region's population was in slavery, and that the slaves were principally female: they produced grains and textiles for the domestic market and leather goods for export. Captive workers in the Sahara mined salt and produced dates and grains in oases. Slave labor forces in Senegal produced peanuts for export.

In the Horn of Africa, the continued export of slaves to Arabia left large holdings of slaves within Africa. Exports of slaves and a population decline also continued in East Africa, where European purchasers, based in MADAGASCAR and the Mascarene Islands, maintained a high demand for slaves into the 1880s.

In short, the world markets for slave labor and for the goods produced by slaves remained strong in the middle and late nineteenth century, and these markets supported slavery and slave trading in Africa. The European powers poised to invade the continent pointed to the persistence of African slavery to justify colonization. Thus the BERLIN CONFERENCE OF 1884–1885, convened as an antislavery meeting, in fact set the rules for the European conquest of Africa.

Between 1890 and 1940 the European colonial powers strengthened their grip on African lands and African societies and preached a doctrine of antislavery. The result was not, however, immediate emancipation. Large-scale slave raiding came to an end because the European powers had monopolized the use of armed force. But slavery itself continued for millions of Africans until the eve of World War II.

The European conquest of Africa took place, in large measure, between 1880 and 1900. By 1900 African armies had been routed and European hegemony was established nearly everywhere except ETHIOPIA, LIBERIA, MOROCCO, and parts of the Sahara. Great numbers of slaves took their liberty with the change in power, and European authorities decreed, for the most part, that slave raiding was henceforth prohibited. Yet only infrequently were African slaves emancipated. The slaves of Madagascar were liberated after the 1897–1898 French conquest, but British conquests during those same years did not lead to the emancipation of slaves in either SUDAN or the Sokoto caliphate.

With the establishment of colonial rule, slavery was reformed but not abolished. Slave owners, no longer able to hope for new captives, put higher value on infant and child slaves; both the prices and the level of nourishment of children increased. Workloads for adult slaves decreased accordingly, as their survival now became more important. In Ethiopia, for instance, the abolition of slave trade during World War I (when Ethiopia sought European approbation of its regime in order to avoid conquest) brought a rapid rise in prices of child slaves. The accounts of colonial ethnographers who visited African societies after 1900 describe systems that protected the rights of slaves; these rights had been expanded just as slave raiding had ended. The colonial-era African system of slavery without slave raiding corresponded in many ways to antebellum slavery in the United States.

Instead of emancipation, European rulers in Africa resorted to gradual and indirect means to end slavery. One was through the courts: slaves who claimed mistreatment could appeal for redress or emancipation in colonial courts. Slaves could purchase their own freedom. In British colonies, the administration tended to declare that the state no longer recognized the institution of slavery. This approach, first implemented in British India in 1843, prevented slave owners from appealing to the state to retrieve escaped slaves; it also prevented slaves from challenging their condition, since the state argued that slavery no longer existed. Still another device was the legislation of the emancipation of infants born after a given date; in Sierra Leone, for example, the date was 1928. Further, as Paul Lovejoy and Jan Hogendorn have shown, the institution of concubinage continued beyond the era of slavery. Northern Nigerian landowners continued to pressure poor families to provide young women for their harems.

The distinction between slave and master in Africa was not, as in the Americas, typically based on a distinction in race. But indicators such as name, language, scarification, dress, and manners all distinguished the identity and social status of slaves from those of their masters. Thus, while the heritage of slavery was kept alive in the Americas through discrimination by race, the heritage of slavery remained alive in Africa through discrimination by class. African countries, though millions of their inhabitants are descendants of slaves, have no holiday to celebrate the emancipation of slaves. The lack of a clear act of emancipation helped to propagate relations of servility into the middle and late twentieth century.

See also Scramble for Africa; Slavery in Latin America and the Caribbean.

Bibliography

Lovejoy, Paul, and Jan Hogendorn. *Slow Death for Slavery: The Course of Abolition in Northern Nigeria, 1897–1936.* Cambridge University Press, 1993.

Manning, Patrick. *Slavery and African Life.* Cambridge University Press, 1990.

Meillassoux, Claude. *The Anthropology of Slavery: The Womb of Iron and Gold.* Athlone, 1991.

Miers, Suzanne, and Igor Kopytoff, eds. *Slavery in Africa: Historical and Anthropological Perspectives.* University of Wisconsin, 1977.

Patrick Manning

Slavery in Latin America and the Caribbean

Discussion of the origins, history, and practices of slavery in Latin America and the Caribbean.

Slaves have existed on every populated continent since well before the opening up of the Western Hemisphere to European colonization. In fact the modern word "slave" comes from the identification of slaves with Slavic peoples in the Muslim societies of the MIDDLE EAST. There were still Muslim, Christian, and Jewish slaves in Europe and the Middle East in 1492. Most of these slaves were tied to their masters' households and did not produce the basic food or manufactured products in these societies. This was usually done by free urban and peasant labor. In a few societies, however, slaves did make up the primary labor force in agriculture and industry. This type of slavery, sometimes referred to as "industrial slavery," was developed in classical Greece and Rome, and it would become the type of slavery adopted in most of the American colonies.

Why Africans Were Imported

The Spanish and Portuguese conquest of the American hemisphere created a new demand for African slave labor. America was abundant in land but not in labor. Despite the availability of at least twenty to twenty-five million American Indians in 1500, labor was still a high-cost item for the Spanish and the Portuguese. With more opportunities and wealth available through Spanish and Portuguese expansion in Europe, Asia, and Africa, the small populations of the Iberian Peninsula were reluctant to migrate to the New World. Wages necessary to entice European workers to America were too high to make colonization profitable. Moreover, the use of Muslim slaves from North Africa and the Middle East was coming to an end, and the Roman Catholic Church pushed hard to end European enslavement of any Christian peoples. Thus by 1500 most slaves held in Europe were Africans.

Queen Isabel rejected Columbus's proposal that Indians be enslaved. It was held that AMERICAN INDIANS were free subjects and should be enslaved only if they waged war against the Spaniards. Even this "just war" reasoning for enslaving some of the frontier Indians was finally rejected by the Crown in the middle of the sixteenth century. Portuguese colonizers, on the other hand, enslaved Indians from the beginning of their settlement of BRAZIL well into the eighteenth century. But even though Indian slaves in Brazil or Indian peasants in Mexico and Peru were quickly mobilized for the labor needs of the European colonists, there still existed a labor shortage in America due to the decimation of American Indian populations by new European diseases. Indian populations declined in the fifteenth and sixteenth centuries, often to 20 percent or less of their preconquest levels.

In this context importing labor became a necessity. Given the reluctance of poor Europeans to migrate, Africans were seen as an unlimited labor supply that could be brought to America. The institution of slavery, moreover, offered additional advantages to European colonizers. As slaves Africans were completely mobile and could be put to any labor that their masters demanded, without restrictions. Furthermore, because enslavement was usually for life, slaves could not compete with their masters, whereas contract or indentured servants could do so after completing their term of service.

For centuries prior to European penetration, slaves had been exported via the East African ports and by caravans overland to North Africa. Africa was opened to direct European seaborne trade by Portuguese explorers in the early fifteenth century. In 1444 Europeans first shipped African slaves, along with gold and ivory, off the SENEGAMBIA coast, in West Africa. Thereafter a steady trade developed with Africa. A small number of African slaves were thus diverted into the transatlantic slave trade even before Columbus's first voyage. They soon became the most numerous of the slaves in SPAIN and PORTUGAL. Also Portugal began to use African slaves for sugar production in the African coastal islands of CAPE VERDE and SÃO TOMÉ. Thus when the New World was finally opened to European settlement, a steady supply of West African slaves was available to the Europeans, who were accustomed to using them in commercial export agriculture—above all to produce SUGAR.

Slavery in Mexico and Peru

The Spanish conquistadores, enriched by mining in the Caribbean islands, MEXICO, and the Andes, were the first colonists able to pay for the importation of African slaves. By 1650 some 200,000 Africans had been imported to these main-

In his *Voyage pittoresque dans le Brésil* (1835), Johann Moritz Rugendas depicted the daily life of Afro-Brazilian slaves, such as this couple who are plantation workers. *Houghton Library, Harvard University*

land and island regions of Spain. Spaniards found their need for slaves constantly increasing, especially in those lowland regions where European disease had decimated the Indian population. PERU took the most African slaves, because it was initially richer and had a smaller Indian population base than Mexico. There were 3,000 African slaves in the viceroyalty of Peru by the 1550s, half of whom lived in the capital city of Lima. This pattern of slave settlement, with approximately half of the African slaves residing in the cities and working at skilled and unskilled urban occupations, became the norm in the Spanish American colonies. Some slaves were used on small farms to produce fruits and vegetables for city markets; others produced sugar on plantations, though primarily for local rather than European consumption. But the majority of agricultural goods were produced by Indian peasants working either on their own lands in communal villages or as landless workers on the estates of the Spaniards, and all mining was done with free Indian wage laborers or forced Indian contract workers.

But in the cities of Spanish America, African slaves and their descendants played a vital role in the economy. Urban slavery involved both skilled and unskilled labor, and African and Indian artisans were the dominant labor force throughout urban Spanish America. Though they were underrepresented in the elite group of skilled master craftworkers, African and African American (or Creole) slaves and freed people were well represented in the beginning apprenticeship and journeyman levels of the skilled crafts by the middle of the seventeenth century. Sometimes white and even Indian opposition to blacks in the professions was quite bitter, but the lack of a powerful American guild organization permitted blacks, both free and slave, to exercise most crafts, even at the master level. So important were these slave and free colored skilled, semiskilled, and unskilled workers in the continental and island colonies of Spain and Portugal that in all the major ports and cities of Latin America they made up close to half of the population by the eighteenth century. In fact, both Portuguese and Spanish America were far more urbanized than any other American zones in this period, with twenty-one cities having a population of 50,000 to 100,000 persons.

It was common for urban slaves to live on their own and to rent themselves out or make contracts for work as semi-autonomous artisans, and often both groups paid their masters a given weekly or monthly sum. Others lived in their master's house to be fed and controlled by their owners. Relative to rural slaves, therefore, those residing in urban centers had more options available in their economic and social activities. It was also among these slaves that the common-law practice of self-purchase (called either *coartación* in Spanish, or *coartação* in Portuguese) developed. This practice allowed slaves to take their masters to court and force them to sell the slaves to themselves in installments over a fixed period of time. During this period when the slaves were purchasing their freedom, the masters could not sell them to a third party. The whole process was a very expensive undertaking and was usually used by only a minority of skilled slaves who had the ability to accumulate savings.

After Peru, the viceroyalty of New Spain (or Mexico) was the most important region for importing slaves into Spanish America. By the seventeenth century, they also numbered close to the total white colonist population in most of Mexico's cities and were as heavily urban as in Spanish South America. As in Peru, Afro-American (used here to refer to people of African descent in the Americas) slaves in this region were also used in sugar production for the local and regional markets on relatively small estates with no more than forty slaves per unit. As elsewhere in continental Spanish America, the Afro-American slaves in the rural areas worked primarily in mixed farming enterprises rather than on the type of commercial plantations that exported to Europe, prevalent in Brazil and the WEST INDIES. African slaves could also be found alongside free Indian workers weaving and doing other tasks in the local textile factories (*obrajes*). In northern Mexico, there was even an early attempt to use slaves in silver mining, though free Indian workers quickly replaced them. Ultimately, urban slavery was less important in Mexico, due to the larger presence of Indians in all the leading towns.

Given its much larger Indian population, Mexico ended up with a smaller African slave population than Peru. By 1646 Mexico's slave population peaked at 35,000, while by this time Peru had some 100,000 Afro-Americans. Moreover, Mexico progressively freed most of its slave population and stopped importing Africans on a major scale. By the 1790s it had only

6,000 Afro-American slaves left, while Peru still had some 90,000.

Slavery in Colonial Brazil

In the 1530s Portugal finally began the systematic exploitation of Brazil. Although both Indian and Afro-American slaves were initially used on the plantations (*fazendas*), by 1600 Africans and their descendants dominated the slave labor force, producing sugar for the European market. Brazil became the model for all other major slave plantations in the Caribbean and North America. Although the Brazilians exploited American Indian slave labor with an intensity and profitability no other European power developed in America, Brazilian Indians, like their counterparts throughout the Americas, suffered terrible devastation from previously unknown diseases. Thus after 1600 Africans replaced Indians on the Brazilian sugar estate, and only when African slave markets were closed to them in the middle decades of the seventeenth century did the Brazilians temporarily return to Indian labor.

The revolt of the Dutch provinces of Spain in 1584 would set the stage for the expansion of the sugar plantation model to the Caribbean. In 1621 the Dutch West Indies Company was established to compete with the Portuguese in Africa and America. Eventually the Dutch took Pernambuco, Brazil's premier sugar province. The company then denied Portuguese access to its sources of African slaves. It seized both the Gold Coast (El Mina) and most of Angola in the late 1630s and early 1640s. The impact of this Dutch colonization in Brazil was profound. For the Portuguese it meant that Bahia replaced Pernambuco as the leading sugar province, and it encouraged the temporary reemergence of Indian slavery until the Portuguese African ports could be recaptured. The ensuing interior Indian slave trade led by the residents of São Paulo opened up additional regions to Portuguese settlement and ultimately to a major new use of slave labor in the newly discovered interior gold and diamond fields of Minas Gerais and Mato Grosso in the eighteenth century.

Caribbean Colonies

For the rest of America, Dutch Brazil would become the source for the tools, techniques, credit, and slaves that would carry the sugar revolution into the West Indies. Because fighting between the Dutch and Portuguese in the interior reduced Pernambuco's role as the region's leading sugar producer, the Dutch began to bring slaves and the latest milling equipment to the British and French settlers in the Caribbean, whose sugar they transported and sold on the European market. It was thus the Dutch from Brazil who brought the sugar technology, machinery, and even slaves to the struggling English island of Barbados and the French islands of Martinique and Guadeloupe.

These islands of the Lesser Antilles were first settled by the English and French in the 1620s. Indentured European workers composed the labor force until an export crop was developed that could pay for the importation of African slaves. After experimenting with tobacco, indigo, and other crops, colonizers finally settled on sugar, and it was the Dutch from Brazil who were crucial in opening up the sugar industries. The success of sugar transformed these islands. From largely white populations living on small farms with relatively few slaves, the islands were dominated by the 1680s and 1690s by African slaves, and most of the land was owned by a few whites controlling very large estates. In the 1650s the English seized Jamaica from the Spanish; then came the French settlement of Saint-Domingue on the western half of the island of Hispaniola, in the 1660s. These two colonies by the late eighteenth century would be the premier sugar-producing zone in the Americas. Thus by the end of the seventeenth century, the French and English had established thriving sugar colonies in both the Greater and Lesser Antilles, and these islands had already absorbed over 450,000 African slaves. This figure compares with the 500,000 to one million African slaves who arrived in Brazil and with the 350,000 to 400,000 who arrived in Spanish America before 1700. The French and English colonies on the North American continent were primarily small free farmer agricultural colonies except in the region from the Chesapeake Bay to the south, and those colonies that used slaves brought in fewer than 30,000 Africans in this same period.

The West Indian sugar plantation colonies of France and England were unique by American standards. Whereas in Brazil and eventually the United States slaves represented only about a third of the population, in the West Indies African slaves were three-quarters or more of the population. In contrast to the continental slave plantation, the typical plantation on these islands was double the norm in terms of slaves and usually held around 200 slaves per unit. In most of the British and French islands, blacks dominated the population by a ratio of ten to one. Moreover, 95 percent of the slaves were found in the rural areas and 75 percent were involved in sugar. Urban slavery of the kind developed in Spanish and Portuguese America was of minor importance in a society where the leading towns held less than 15,000 persons. Also, diversified commercial foodstuffs production for local consumption, which was a major occupation of Peruvian blacks, hardly existed in societies that were so dependent on foreign imports, or slave subsistence plot production, for all their basic food supplies.

Haitian Revolution Affects Slavery

The dominant West Indian colony was French Saint-Domingue. By the 1780s it had 460,000 slaves, though, unlike the British islands, it also had an important free colored class of some 13,000 persons, many of whom were slave and plantation owners, a group unique in the Americas. In fact it was the conflict between the white and mulatto plantation owners in this wealthiest of West Indian colonies that opened the way for a successful slave rebellion in 1791. After years of bitter fighting and the defeat of several invading armies, the end result was the liberation of the slaves and the creation of the independent government of Haiti in 1804. The fighting and the abolition of slave labor combined to destroy first the sugar production in this, the world's leading sugar producer, and then its major coffee output as well.

The result of the HAITIAN REVOLUTION was a profound change in the relative importance of American slave plantation agriculture. The elimination of sugar exports and the progressive decline of coffee from this French island permitted all the competing plantation areas to expand production. By the fourth and fifth decades of the nineteenth century, CUBA would emerge as the world's leading sugarcane producer, and Brazil would become the leading producer of coffee. But everywhere in the New World slave plantation agriculture surged, both because of the elimination of Saint-Domingue's production and because of a rapid expansion of the sugar, coffee, and cotton market in Europe.

The Haitian slave revolution also had an impact on the treatment of slaves and free colored persons in all the major slave societies of America. Fearful of a possible slave rebellion in their own societies, other colonies and republics repressed free blacks, made manumission more difficult, and passed harsher slave codes. In the case of Cuba, PUERTO RICO, and Brazil it led to a reluctance of the planter and master class to support independence movements or regional rebellions. Although manumission and full rights were restored in most Latin American areas, in the United States the role of free blacks only worsened in the course of the nineteenth century.

Cuba in the 1800s

The leading slave society in the West Indies in the nineteenth century was the Spanish-controlled island of Cuba. Neglected for most of the colonial period by the Spanish Crown, the island exported free labor and produced tobacco. It was also used as a provisioning center for the colonial fleets. But the Crown finally promoted sugar plantations and slavery on the island just before the Haitian rebellion and in 1789 permitted the free importation of slaves by any foreign merchants. The result was a spectacular growth of sugar production. By the 1830s, Cuba's sugar output equaled that of Jamaica, and a decade later it became the world's leading producer of sugar. Coffee, brought by migrating French planters, also became a major plantation crop, and by the late 1830s, the island's coffee plantations numbered just over 2,000 units and employed some 50,000 slaves, a number equal to those employed in sugar. Nineteenth-century Cuba followed the eighteenth-century Caribbean model in basic organization of plantations and slaves. But it resembled more the rest of Latin America in the size and growth of both its free colored and white populations and the relative importance of its urban centers. Cuban towns (defined as over 1,000 persons) contained over half a million persons by the 1860s, only 76,000 of whom were slaves. Though slaves increased to 370,000 by the 1860s, there were now 233,000 free colored, and whites still accounted for well over half the island's population of 1.4 million persons.

Given the dynamism of the expanding sugar economy and the dependence on slaves, the Cuban planters and the Spanish government fought against the abolition of the transatlantic slave trade. But in the early 1860s this ended for Cuba, the last slave-importing region in America, and the Cuban planters decided to experiment with forced labor of Mayan Indians brought from Yucatan and indentured Chinese servants, all of whom worked alongside the African and American-born black slaves. By the early 1860s over 100,000 Chinese were working in the Cuban sugar fields. There was also a major revival of sugar production after the Napoleonic Wars (1799–1815) in the remaining French West Indian colonies of Martinique and Guadeloupe. By the early decades of the nineteenth century, these two islands held 160,000 slaves and were also beginning to supplement this sugar plantation labor force with indentured workers from Africa and other regions.

Slavery in Brazil

The discovery of gold in central Brazil in the late 1690s opened up an entirely new activity for slave usage. The gold mines of Minas Gerais were the wealthiest in the world in the eighteenth century, and they were worked exclusively by African slave labor. Later, diamond deposits were discovered in the same region, and those industries together employed some 225,000 slaves by the late eighteenth century. This expansion of slave labor in the interior provinces was matched by the growth of traditional and new plantation agriculture along the coast.

The Haitian collapse revived the sugar industry in the older northeastern plantations and the sugar fields in RIO DE JANEIRO. But even more important was the expansion of Brazilian coffee production. Although coffee was grown in Brazil as early as the eighteenth century, the introduction of the latest West Indian technology created a new opportunity for expansion. By 1831 the value of coffee exports surpassed the value of sugar exports, and by the middle of the decade Brazil was the world's largest producer, shipping double the combined output of Cuba and Puerto Rico, previously the major coffee producers in the Americas. Coffee was a slave crop. It was produced primarily in three states in central Brazil: Rio de Janeiro, São Paulo, and the old mining state of Minas Gerais. Slaves were imported into Brazil until the 1860s when the British finally forced the Brazilians to end their slave trade. Thereafter an internal slave trade developed that moved Brazilian slaves in ever larger numbers into coffee.

Nevertheless, although the coffee plantations increased the number of slave workers to 284,000, by 1883 the majority of Brazil's slaves did not work in the coffee fields of the central-south zone. By 1872 some 563,000 rural slaves worked both in other plantation crops such as sugar and in a host of other rural occupations, including cattle raising. The remaining 690,000 of the economically active slaves not directly engaged in agriculture in 1872 were often closely allied with plantation life. The most obvious example was the 95,000 slaves listed as day laborers, many of whom were employed in the fazendas alongside the resident slave forces. Some of the 7,000 artisans listed as working in wood and metal crafts, especially carpenters and blacksmiths, may also have been employed on plantations. But as the example of Minas Gerais reveals, there was also within the vast slave labor force of 1.5 million slaves a significant proportion who were not directly related to export agriculture yet still played a significant economic role in the economy. Many of Brazil's 1.5 million slaves also lived in the cities, composing 15 percent of the urban population in towns of 20,000 or more. But it was the recently freed slaves and their descendants, some 4.2 million persons, who made up most of the country's urban population and were a major presence in all the rural areas.

Freed People under Slavery

The process and rate of manumission in Latin America represents a major difference among slave systems in the Americas. Unlike in the United States, Latin American governments recognized the right to manumission of all slaves. In Latin America manumission was both voluntary and involuntary on the part of the master class and involved a complex pattern of passive and active intervention by the slaves themselves. Close to half of the manumitted slaves purchased their freedom, two-thirds tended to be women, and most were manumitted at less than forty-five years of age. These demographic factors help explain the very rapid growth of free black populations through both new manumissions and children born to free black women. More urban slaves had access to manumission than did rural ones, but in no area was manumission ever stopped.

Although manumission had occurred from the beginning of colonization, its pace increased in the eighteenth and nineteenth centuries. This led to a major growth of free colored populations everywhere in the Latin American world. By 1800 there were more free colored persons than there were slaves in continental Spanish America. In the region of northeastern South America known as the viceroyalty of New Granada and encompassing the future republics of COLOMBIA and ECUADOR, there were 420,000 free colored persons as compared to 80,000 slaves. In VENEZUELA there were 198,000 free colored persons and about 64,000 slaves despite a thriving slave plantation zone producing cacao beans. The Mexican viceroyalty had about 70,000 free colored persons and 10,000 slaves by 1810. In all the colonies of Spain on the continent, there were a total of 650,000 free persons of color and 271,000 slaves. With the exception of Cuba Spain's island possessions were little different. Puerto Rico in 1820 had 104,000 free persons of color and 22,000 slaves, whereas Cuba by 1861 contained 232,000 free colored and 371,000 African slaves. Brazil had an even more dynamic growth of the free colored population in the nineteenth century, well before final abolition of slavery occurred in 1888. At the time of the first imperial census of 1872 there were 4.2 million free colored persons in Brazil compared to 1.5 million slaves and 3.8 million whites.

In contrast to the rest of Latin America, the population of free blacks relative to the number of slaves remained small in both the French West Indies and the English colonies. In the 1780s, just prior to the French Revolution, the major French colonies had 30,000 free colored persons and 575,000 slaves. Unlike the British islands, however, these free blacks played a far more important role in their local economies, many being major slaveholders and plantation owners in their own right.

This difference in the importance of the free colored classes, in each of the major regions of the Americas, was due to many factors. The most important was the willingness of the Spanish and Portuguese colonies and republics to accept normal market and religious forces that produced a large number of manumitted ex-slaves. Though all slave societies in the Americas began with a fairly steady process of manumission, most of the Anglo-Saxon and French colonies slowly closed down this process. In the Latin American context, this process was never stopped, and in fact increased in intensity over time. Thus the free colored, even before the end of slavery, played a major economic role within their local societies. This does not mean they faced any lesser opposition from whites or that racism and exclusion did not operate. All slave societies in the Americas eventually became intensely racist over time. It does mean, however, that whites were unable or unwilling to use these beliefs to deny access of the free colored to some level of social and economic mobility. The creation of active and large free colored populations in all these societies also helped prepare the transition for all slaves to roles of citizens and economically participatory members of the post-abolition societies.

Freed people, whatever their relative economic position in the colonial societies, all played a crucial role in the polities in which they entered. They formed their own important militia companies in both Spanish and Portuguese America and were a crucial element in the defense establishments of these colonies well into the nineteenth century. Moreover there was not a major social or political movement in the nineteenth century in which these free persons did not participate, from the wars of independence to the establishment of revolutionary regimes. They also had their own religious confraternities or brotherhoods in the Catholic Church that were important social institutions that often helped maintain the survival of African religious practices and ideas. These fraternal organizations, which often built their own churches and acted as burial societies as well, helped people to maintain friendships and create group identities. They were found in every city in Latin America that had a substantial free black population.

Conclusion

The end of slavery in Latin America varied from region to region. In the continental colonies, the wars of independence from 1808 to 1825 led to freeing of large numbers of slaves by both republicans and royalists, so that even before final emancipation slaves were a reduced element among the colored population. CHILE was the first to free its 4,000 slaves unconditionally, in 1823, and MEXICO freed the 3,000 slaves remaining in the 1830s. Most of the other new republics did not finally liberate all remaining slaves until the 1850s, though most adopted early laws declaring freedom for all children born of slaves. In the French colonies of America, some 177,500 were finally liberated in 1848, but the islands of Cuba and Puerto Rico and the major slave system of Brazil were not destroyed until the 1880s. In 1871 Brazil finally adopted a law of free birth, as did Spain for Cuba and Puerto Rico in 1868. Final emancipation for all slaves came to the Spanish Caribbean islands in 1886 and to Brazil in 1888.

See also Andes, Blacks During Colonial Times in the; Catholic Church in Latin America and the Caribbean; Colonial Latin America and the Caribbean; Mining in Latin America and the Caribbean; Role of Slaves in Abolition and Emancipation in Latin America and the Caribbean.

Slavery in the United States

Discussion of the origins, history, and practices of slavery in the United States.

Slavery has appeared in many forms throughout its long history. Slaves have served in capacities as diverse as concubines, warriors, servants, craftsmen, tutors, and victims of ritual sacrifice. In the New World (the Americas), however, slavery emerged as a system of forced labor designed to facilitate the production of staple crops. Depending on location, these crops included SUGAR, tobacco, coffee, and cotton; in the Southern United States, by far the most important staples were tobacco and cotton. A stark racial component distinguished this modern Western slavery from the slavery that existed in other times and places: the vast majority of slaves consisted of Africans and their descendants, whereas the vast majority of masters consisted of Europeans and their descendants.

Slavery has played a central role in the history of the United States. It existed in all the English mainland colonies and came to dominate productive relations from Maryland south. Most of the Founding Fathers were large-scale slaveholders, as were eight of the first twelve presidents of the United States. Debate over slavery increasingly dominated American politics, leading eventually to the nation's only civil war, which in turn finally brought slavery to an end. After emancipation, overcoming slavery's legacy remained a crucial issue in American history, from RECONSTRUCTION following the CIVIL WAR to the CIVIL RIGHTS MOVEMENT a century later.

Introduction of Slavery

There was nothing inevitable about the use of black slaves. Although Dutch traders brought twenty Africans to Jamestown, Virginia, as early as 1619, throughout most of the seventeenth century the number of Africans in the English mainland colonies grew very slowly. During those years colonists experimented with two other sources of unfree labor: Native American slaves and European indentured servants.

Although some Native American slaves existed in every colony, the number was limited. Indian men balked at performing agricultural labor, which they regarded as women's work, and colonists complained that they were "haughty" and made poor slaves. Even more important, the settlers found it more convenient to sell NATIVE AMERICANS captured in war to planters in the Caribbean than to turn them into slaves on their own terrain, where escape was relatively easy and violent resistance a constant threat. Ultimately, the policy of killing Indians or driving them away from white settlements proved incompatible with their widespread employment as slaves.

Far more important as a form of labor than Indian slavery was white indentured servitude. Most indentured servants consisted of poor Europeans who, desiring to escape harsh condi-

A plaque identifies a block on a street in Fredericksburg, Virginia, where slaves were sold at auction. *CORBIS/Bettmann*

tions and take advantage of fabled opportunities in America, traded three to seven years of their labor in exchange for the transatlantic passage. At first predominantly English but later increasingly Irish, Welsh, and German, servants consisted primarily (although not exclusively) of young males. Once in the colonies, they were essentially temporary slaves; most served as agricultural workers although some, especially in the North, were taught skilled trades. During the seventeenth century, they performed most of heavy labor in the Southern colonies and also provided the bulk of immigrants to those colonies.

For a variety of reasons, foremost among them improved conditions in England, the number of persons willing to sell themselves into indentured servitude declined sharply toward the end of the seventeenth century. Since the labor needs of the rapidly growing colonies were increasing, this decline in servant migration produced a labor crisis. To meet the need, landowners turned to African slaves, who from the 1680s began to supplant the labor of indentured servants; in Virginia, for example, blacks (the great majority of whom were slaves) increased from about 7 percent of the population in 1680 to more than 40 percent by the middle of the eighteenth century. During the first two-thirds of the seventeenth century Holland and PORTUGAL had dominated the African slave trade, and the number of Africans available to English colonists was limited. During the late seventeenth and eighteenth centuries, by contrast, naval superiority gave England a dominant position in the slave trade, and English traders (some of whom lived in English America) transported millions of Africans across the Atlantic.

The TRANSATLANTIC SLAVE TRADE produced one of the largest forced migrations in history. From the early sixteenth century to the mid-nineteenth century, between ten and eleven million Africans were torn from their homes, herded onto ships where they were sometimes so tightly packed that they could barely move, and deposited in a strange new land. (Since others died in transit, Africa's loss of population was greater still.) By far the largest importers of slaves were BRAZIL and the Caribbean sugar colonies; together, they received well over three-quarters of all Africans brought to the New World. About 6 percent of the total (600,000 to 650,000 persons) came to the area of the present United States.

During the Colonial Era

Slavery spread quickly in the American colonies. At first the legal status of Africans in America was poorly defined, and some—like European indentured servants—managed to become free after several years of service. From the 1660s, however, the colonies began enacting laws that defined and regulated slave relations; central to these laws was the provision that black slaves, and the children of slave women, would serve for life. By the eve of the AMERICAN REVOLUTION, slaves constituted about 40 percent of the population of the southern mainland colonies, with the highest concentration in South Carolina, where well over half the population were slaves.

Slaves performed numerous tasks, from clearing the forest to serving as guides, trappers, craftsmen, nurses, and house servants, but they were most essential as agricultural laborers and most numerous where landowners sought to grow staple crops for market. The most important of these crops were tobacco in the upper South (Maryland, Virginia, North Carolina) and rice in the lower South (South Carolina and Georgia); farther south still, on Caribbean islands such as BARBADOS, JAMAICA, and SAINT-DOMINGUE, sugar was an even more valuable slave-grown commodity. Slaves also worked on large wheat-producing estates in New York and on horse-breeding farms in Rhode Island, but climate and soil restricted the development of commercial agriculture in the Northern colonies, and slavery never became as economically central as in the South. Slaves in the North were typically held in small numbers, and most served as domestic servants; only in New York, with its Dutch legacy, did they form more than 10 percent of the population, and in the North as a whole less than 5 percent of the inhabitants were slaves.

By the mid-eighteenth century American slavery had acquired a number of distinctive features. Well over 90 percent of American slaves lived in the South, where demographic conditions contrasted sharply with those to both the south and the north. In Caribbean colonies such as Jamaica and Saint-Domingue, blacks outnumbered whites by more than ten to one and slaves often lived on huge estates whose inhabitants numbered in the hundreds; in the Northern colonies, blacks were few and slaves were typically held in small groups of less than five. The South, by contrast, was neither overwhelmingly white nor overwhelmingly black: slaves formed a large minority of the population (in some areas, of course, they formed the majority), and despite regional variations, most slaves lived on small and medium-sized holdings containing between five and fifty slaves.

A second distinctive feature was the rapid "Americanization" of both masters and slaves. English colonists quickly came to feel "at home" on their American holdings. Few sought to make quick killings on their planting ventures and then retire to a life of leisure in England, and the kind of absentee ownership common in much of the Caribbean was relatively rare in the American South; instead, masters typically took an active role in running their farms and plantations. Equally significant was the shift from an African to an African American slave population. By the eve of the American Revolution, only about 20 percent of American slaves were African-born (although the concentration of Africans remained higher in South Carolina and Georgia), and after the outlawing of new slave imports in 1808, the proportion of African-born slaves became tiny. The emergence of a native-born slave population had numerous important consequences. To take one example, among African-born slaves (imported primarily for their ability to perform physical labor) there were few children and men outnumbered women by about two to one; American-born slaves, by contrast, began their slave careers as children and included approximately even numbers of males and females.

This shift from African to African American was closely related to a third distinctive characteristic of American slavery that was in many ways the most important of all: in contrast to most other slaves in the New World, those in the United States experienced what demographers refer to as "natural population growth." Elsewhere, in regions as diverse as Brazil, Jamaica, Saint-Domingue, and CUBA, slave mortality rates exceeded birth rates, and growth of the slave population depended on the importation of new slaves from Africa; as soon as that importation ended, the slave population began to decline. At first, deaths among slaves also exceeded births in the American colonies, but in the eighteenth century those colonies experienced a demographic transition as birth rates rose, mortality rates fell, and the slave population became self-reproducing. This transition, which occurred earlier in the upper than in the lower South, meant that even after the outlawing of slave imports in 1808, the number of slaves would continue to grow rapidly; during the next half century the slave population of the United States more than tripled, from about 1.2 million to almost 4 million in 1860. The natural growth of the slave population shaped a distinctive slavery in the American South and hastened the transition among slaves from African to African American.

Revolutionary Challenges

Throughout most of the colonial period, opposition to slavery among white Americans was virtually nonexistent. Settlers in the seventeenth and early eighteenth centuries came from a sharply stratified society in which the upper classes savagely exploited members of the "lower orders"; lacking a later generation's belief in natural human equality, they saw little reason to question the enslavement of Africans. As they sought to mold a docile labor force, these planters resorted to harshly repressive measures that included liberal use of whippings and brandings.

Gradually, as slavery became more entrenched, changes occurred in the way masters looked on their slaves (and themselves). Many second-generation masters, who unlike their parents had grown up with slaves, came to regard them as inferior members of their extended families, and to look upon themselves as kindly patriarchs who, like benevolent despots, ruled their "people" firmly but fairly and looked after their needs. Such slave owners continued to rely heavily on the lash (and other forms of punishment) for discipline, and few slaves saw their owners as the kindly guardians that they proclaimed themselves to be. Still, the most extreme forms of physical abuse became less common over the course the eighteenth century, at the same time that many slave owners accepted the idea that they should treat their slaves humanely.

Some slave owners went further. The last third of the eighteenth century saw the first widespread questioning of slavery by white Americans. This questioning was boosted by the American Revolution, which sparked a sharp increase in egalitarian thinking. Many of the Founding Fathers, including George Washington and Thomas Jefferson, while slaveholders, were profoundly troubled by slavery; leery of rash actions, they initiated a series of cautious acts that they thought would lead to slavery's gradual abolition.

These acts included measures in all states north of Delaware to abolish slavery. A few states did away with slavery immediately. More typical were gradual emancipation acts such as that passed by Pennsylvania in 1780, whereby all children born to slaves in the future would be freed at age twenty-eight. Two significant measures dating from 1787 included the Northwest Ordinance, which barred slavery from the Northwest Territory (which included much of what is now the upper Midwest), and a compromise reached at the Constitutional Convention that would allow Congress to outlaw the importation of slaves in 1808. Meanwhile, a number of states passed acts to ease the freeing of slaves by individuals, hundreds of whom—especially in the upper South—set some or all of their slaves free. In addition, tens of thousands of slaves acted on their own, taking advantage of wartime disruption to escape from their masters. As a result, the number of free blacks, which had been tiny before the Revolution, surged during the last quarter of the eighteenth century.

Nevertheless, the Revolutionary-era challenge to slavery proved successful only in the North, where the investment in slaves was small. The antislavery movement never made much headway in Georgia and South Carolina, where labor-hungry planters rushed to import tens of thousands of Africans before the 1808 cutoff. In the upper South, Revolution-inspired egalitarianism withered in the 1790s and 1800s. And because the American slave population was self-reproducing, the end of slave imports did not undermine slavery as it did elsewhere, or as many of the Founding Fathers expected. The ultimate result of the first antislavery movement was to leave slavery a newly sectional institution, on the road to abolition throughout the North but largely unscathed in the South.

During the Antebellum Era

During the antebellum (pre–Civil War) years slavery expanded aggressively along with the United States. Fueled by a surging world demand for cotton, slavery spread quickly into the new states of the Southwest; by the 1830s Alabama, Mississippi, and Louisiana formed the heart of a new "cotton kingdom," together producing more than half of the nation's supply of the crop. The great bulk of this cotton was cultivated by slaves. Between 1790 and 1860 about one million slaves (almost twice the number of Africans shipped to the United States during the whole period of the transatlantic slave trade) moved west, some together with their masters and others as part of a new domestic trade in which owners from the seaboard states provided "surplus" slaves to planters in the Southwest.

As slavery grew, so too did its diversity. Slavery varied according to region, crops, and size of holdings. On farms and small plantations most slaves came in frequent contact with their owners, but on very large plantations, where slave owners often employed overseers, slaves might rarely see their masters. Some owners left their holdings entirely in the care of subordinates, usually hired white overseers but sometimes slaves. A few slave owners were even black themselves: a small percentage of free blacks owned slaves, in some cases essentially as a fiction so that they could protect family members, but more often to profit, like other slaveholders, from unfree labor. Most slaves on large holdings worked in gangs, under the supervision of overseers and (slave) drivers. Some, however, especially in the coastal region of South Carolina and Georgia, labored under the task system: assigned a certain amount of work to complete in a day, they received less supervision than gang laborers and were free to use their time as they wished once they had completed their daily assignments. In addition to performing fieldwork, slaves served as house servants, nurses, midwives, carpenters, blacksmiths, drivers, preachers, gardeners, and handymen.

Despite such variations, there were a number of dominant trends. First, slavery was overwhelmingly rural: in 1860 only about 5 percent of all slaves lived in towns of at least 2,500 persons. Second, although some slaves lived on giant estates and others on small farms, the norm was in between: in 1860 about one-half of all slaves lived on holdings of ten to forty-nine, with one-quarter on smaller and one-quarter on larger units. (Holdings tended to be bigger in the Deep South than in the upper South.) Third, most slaves lived with resident masters; owner absenteeism was most prevalent in the South Carolina and Georgia low country, but in the South as a whole it was less common than in the Caribbean. Fourth, most able-bodied adult slaves engaged in fieldwork. Owners relied heavily on children, the elderly, and the infirm for so-called nonproductive work (such as house service); only the largest plantations could spare healthy adults for exclusive assignment to specialized occupations. The main business of Southern farms and plantations—and of the slaves who supported them—was to grow cotton, tobacco, rice, corn, wheat, hemp, and sugar.

Southern slaveholders took an active role in managing their human property. Viewing themselves as the slaves' guardians, they stressed the degree to which they cared for their "people." The character of such care varied, but in purely material terms—food, clothing, housing, medical attention—it was generally better in the antebellum than in the colonial period and (judging by measurable criteria such as slave height and life expectancy) better in the American South than in the Caribbean or Brazil. Although young children were often malnourished, most working slaves received a steady supply of pork and corn which, if lacking in nutritional balance (about which antebellum Americans knew nothing), provided sufficient calories to fuel their labor, especially when supplemented with produce that slaves raised on the garden plots that they were often allotted. Clothing and housing were crude but functional: slaves typically received four coarse "suits" per year (pants and shirts for men, dresses for women, long shirts for children) and lived in small wooden cabins, one to a family. Wealthy slave owners often sent for physicians to treat slaves who became ill; given the state of medical knowledge, however, such treatment—which could range from providing various concoctions to "bleeding" a patient—often did as much harm as good.

Masters intervened continuously in the lives of their slaves, from directing their labor to approving (and disapproving) marriages. Some masters made elaborate written rules and most engaged in constant meddling—directing, nagging, threatening, and punishing. Many took advantage of their position to exploit slave women sexually. What slaves hated most about slavery was not the hard work to which they were subjected (most people in the rural United States expected to engage in hard physical labor), but the lack of control over their lives—their lack of freedom. Masters may have prided themselves on the care they provided for their "people"; the slaves, however, had a different idea of that care. They resented the constant interference in their lives and struggled to achieve whatever autonomy they could.

Slave Life and Slave Resistance

Such autonomy was not totally lacking. In the quarters—the collection of slave cabins that on large plantations resembled a miniature village—slaves developed their own way of life. The degree of social independence available to slaves was not constant: throughout the South, a continuing power struggle raged in which slaves strove to increase and masters strove to limit this independence. The character and resolution of this struggle in turn depended on a host of factors, from size of holdings and organization of production to residence and disposition of masters. Masters were rarely able, however, to shape the lives of their slaves as fully as they wanted.

Away from the view of owners and overseers, slaves lived their own lives. They made friends and made love, played and prayed, sang, told stories, cooked, joked, quarreled, and engaged in the necessary chores of day-to-day living, from cleaning house, cooking, and sewing to working on their garden plots. Especially important as anchors of the slaves' lives were their families and their religion.

Throughout the South, the family defined the actual living arrangements of slaves: most slaves lived together in nuclear families—mother, father, children. The security and stability of these families faced severe challenges: no state law recognized marriage among slaves, masters rather than parents had legal authority over slave children, and the possibility of forced separation, through sale, hung over every family. (Such separations were especially frequent in the slave-exporting states of the upper South.) Still, despite their tenuous status, families served as the slaves' most basic refuge, the center of private lives that owners could never fully control.

Religion served as a second refuge. Although African slaves usually clung to their native religions, and many slave owners in the early colonial period were leery of those who sought to convert their slaves to Christianity (in part because of fears that converted slaves would have to be freed), during the antebellum years Christianity was increasingly central to the slaves' cultural life. Many slaves were converted during the religious revivals that swept the South in the late eighteenth and early nineteenth centuries. Slaves typically belonged to the same denominations as white Southerners—Baptists and Methodists were the largest groups—and some masters encouraged their "people" to come to the white church, where they usually sat in a special slave gallery and received advice about being obedient to their masters. In the quarters, however, there developed a parallel (invisible) church controlled by the slaves themselves, who listened to sermons delivered by their own preachers. Not all slaves had access to these preachers and not all accepted their message, but for many, religion served as a great comfort in a hostile world.

If their families and religion helped slaves to avoid total control by their owners, slaves also more directly challenged that control through active resistance. The limits of such resistance must be kept in mind. Unlike slaves in Saint-Domingue, who rose up against their French masters in bloody rebellion and established the black republic of HAITI in 1804, American slaves faced a balance of power that discouraged armed resistance. When it occurred, such resistance was always quickly suppressed and followed by harsh repression designed to discourage repetition. Aside from conspiracies aborted before any actual outbreak of violence in New York (1741), Virginia (1800), and South Carolina (1822), the most noted uprisings included the STONO REBELLION near CHARLESTON, SOUTH CAROLINA (1739), an attempted attack on NEW ORLEANS, LOUISIANA (1811), and the NAT TURNER insurrection that rocked Southampton County, Virginia, in 1831. The Turner insurrection, which at its peak included sixty to eighty rebels, resulted in the deaths of about sixty whites; the number of blacks killed during the uprising and executed or lynched afterward may have reached one hundred. But the rebellion lasted less than two days and was easily suppressed by local residents. Like other slave uprisings in the United States, it caused enormous fear among whites but did not seriously threaten the slave regime.

Lower-level resistance was both more widespread and more successful. This included silent sabotage, or foot dragging, by slaves who pretended to be sick, feigned difficulty understanding instructions, and "accidentally" misused tools and animals. It also included small-scale resistance by individuals who fought back physically—at times successfully—against what they regarded as unjust treatment. But the most common form of resistance was flight. About 1,000 slaves per year managed to escape to the North during the late antebellum period (most from the upper South), but this represented only the tip of the iceberg, since for every slave who made it to freedom, several more tried. Other fugitives remained within the South, heading for cities or swamps, or hiding out near their plantations for days or weeks before either returning voluntarily or being tracked down and captured. On a continuing basis, slaves "voted with their feet" against slavery.

Like all people, slaves felt diverse, overlapping attachments. They identified as members of families, parishioners of churches, residents of particular farms and plantations, and members of an exploited class, the fruits of whose labor were appropriated by their owners. They also identified as African Americans and saw themselves as an oppressed people. Because the vast majority of blacks in the antebellum South were slaves, the line separating black from white approximated that separating slave from free, and the class exploitation of slave by master often appeared indistinguishable from the racial oppression of black by white. Racial identification drew support not only from common African origins and the close ties that often existed between slaves and free blacks but also from the virulent racism of many non-slaveholding whites that made it easy for slaves to look upon whites in general as their oppressors. Early African American cultural identity was forged in the crucible of slavery.

Sectional Tensions over Slavery

Slavery was an increasingly Southern institution. Abolition of slavery in the North, begun in the Revolutionary era and largely complete by the 1830s, divided the United States into the slave South and the free North. As this happened, slavery came—both to Northerners and Southerners—to define the essence of the South: to defend slavery was to be pro-Southern, whereas opposition to slavery was anti-Southern. Although most Southern whites did not own slaves (the proportion of white families that owned slaves declined from 35 percent to 26 percent between 1830 and 1860), slavery more and more set the South off from the rest of the country—and the Western world. If at one time slavery had been common in much of the New World, by the middle of the nineteenth century it remained only in Brazil, Cuba, PUERTO RICO, and the southern United States. In an era that celebrated "liberty" and "equality," the slave South came to seem backward and repressive, associated in many people's minds with that other bastion of reaction, serfholding Russia.

In fact, the slave economy grew rapidly, enriched by the spectacular increase of cotton cultivation to meet the burgeoning demand of Northern and European textile manufacturers. But Southern economic growth was based largely on putting more acreage under cultivation; the South did not undergo the kind of industrial revolution that was beginning to transform the North, and the South remained almost entirely rural. In 1860 there were only five Southern cities with more than 50,000 inhabitants (only one of which, New Orleans, was in the Deep South); less than 10 percent of Southerners lived in towns of at least 2,500 persons, compared to more than 25 percent of Northerners. The South also increasingly lagged in other indices of modernization, from railroad construction to literacy and public education.

But the biggest gap between North and South was ideological. As Northern states abolished slavery and then saw the growth of a small but articulate abolitionist movement, Southern white spokesmen—from politicians to ministers, newspaper editors, and authors—rallied around slavery as the bedrock of Southern society. Defenders of slavery developed a wide range of arguments to buttress their cause, from those that stressed the institution's practical necessity to those that depicted it as a positive good. They made heavy use of religious themes, pointing to the biblical curse of Ham to explain the origins of black bondage and portraying slavery as part of God's plan for civilizing a primitive, heathen people.

Racial justifications were especially prevalent among proslavery arguments, in part because of the widespread racism that united most white Americans and in part because such arguments were especially effective in appealing to the majority of Southern whites who did *not* own slaves. The extreme—so-called scientific—version of these arguments purported to prove that blacks were so physiologically different from whites that they amounted to a different species (or, in the reformulation of some theoreticians, were the products of a separate creation). Such an approach violated the Christian sensibilities of too many Southern whites, however, to become a central staple of proslavery propaganda. Far more common were brief, unscientific, and vaguely supported assertions that blacks were by nature different, inferior, and therefore unsuited for freedom. Hardworking, loyal, and productive under loving but firm direction (i.e., slavery), they supposedly lacked the intellectual capacity for independent existence and in freedom would quickly degenerate, perhaps even fall into extinction.

During the 1840s and 1850s Southern spokesmen increasingly based their case for slavery on social arguments that contrasted the harmonious, orderly, religious, and conservative society that supposedly existed in the South with the tumultuous, heretical, and mercenary ways of a North torn apart by radical reform, individualism, class conflict, and—worst of all—abolitionism. Insisting that Southern slaves were treated far better than Northern wage laborers, proslavery ideologues developed a biting critique of free-labor capitalism (wage-slavery) as cruel, exploitative, and selfish, and pointed to the degraded condition of supposedly free British paupers and Irish peasants. This defense in many ways represented the mirror image of the free-labor argument increasingly prevalent in the North: as free-labor spokesmen argued that slavery kept the South backward, poor, inefficient, and degraded, proslavery advocates retorted that only slavery could save the South (and the world) from the evils of modernity run wild.

From the mid-1840s the struggle over slavery became more and more central to American politics. Northerners committed to free soil (the idea that new, western territories should be reserved exclusively for free white settlers) clashed repeatedly with Southern spokesmen who insisted that any limitation on slavery's expansion represented unconstitutional meddling with the Southern order and a grave affront to Southern honor. In 1860 the election of Abraham Lincoln as president on a free-soil platform set off a major political and constitutional crisis, as seven states in the Deep South seceded from the United States and formed the Confederate States of America; the start of hostilities between the United States and the rebel Confederates in April 1861 led to the additional secession of four states in the upper South. (Four other slave states—Maryland, Delaware, Kentucky, and Missouri—remained in the Union, as did the new state of West Virginia, which split off from Virginia.)

Emancipation—and After

Ironically, although Southern politicians supported secession in order to preserve slavery, their action led instead to slavery's death. As the war dragged on, Northern war aims gradually shifted from preserving the Union to abolishing slavery and *remaking* the Union. Two especially important catalysts of this shift included (1) the wartime behavior of Southern blacks, who under conditions of weakened authority at home increasingly refused to behave like slaves; and (2) the changing views of Northern whites, a growing number of whom accepted the Radical Republican position that the war provided an ideal opportunity to overthrow slavery and institute a sweeping transformation of the Southern social order.

Slavery ended for hundreds of thousands of Southern blacks well before the Confederate surrender, as Union troops occupied larger and larger areas of the South and as increasing numbers of slaves fled from their owners and sought refuge within Union lines. In Union-occupied areas of the South, blacks experienced a rehearsal for Reconstruction, as federal officials experimented with various forms of free and semi-free labor and as Northern missionaries established schools to help turn slaves into citizens. The freed people's enthusiasm for education, in turn, created a powerful impression among Northern whites and contributed to their growing determination that the war must yield what President Lincoln termed "a new birth of freedom."

This goal received symbolic recognition with the Emancipation Proclamation that Lincoln issued on January 1, 1863. Although the proclamation applied only to areas under rebel control, and did not end slavery in the United States, it marked a clear turning point in the struggle against the "peculiar institution": a war for union had become a war for freedom, and henceforth everyone recognized that a federal victory would mean the death of slavery. During the second half of the war, as slavery crumbled in much of the South, more than 188,000 African Americans, both Southern and Northern, served in the Union's armed forces, fighting to hasten that death. The Thirteenth Amendment to the Constitution, passed by Congress in January and ratified by the states in December 1865, completed the process, outlawing slavery everywhere in the United States.

Despite the overthrow of slavery, at war's end the future status of the former slaves remained unclear and resolving that status remained at the center of the nation's political agenda. An intense struggle ensued, as freed people strove for economic security, social autonomy, and civil rights; former slave owners sought to preserve their old prerogatives; and Northern politicians divided among themselves over the proper course of Reconstruction. The compromise that resulted from this struggle yielded an unprecedented—although temporary—national commitment to turn former slaves into citizens, anchored by the FOURTEENTH and FIFTEENTH AMENDMENTS to the Constitution and the Reconstruction Acts of 1867 and 1868. Together, these measures provided basic civil rights to former slaves, enfranchised black males, and imposed a largely self-administered democratization process on the former Confederate states, under federal supervision.

Emancipation brought many tangible rewards. Among the most obvious was a significant increase in personal freedom that came with no longer being someone else's property: whatever hardships they faced, free blacks could not be forcibly sold away from their loved ones. But emancipation did not bring full equality, and many of the most striking gains of Reconstruction—including the substantial political power that African Americans were briefly able to exercise—were soon lost. In the decades after Reconstruction African Americans experienced continued poverty and exploitation and a rising tide of violence at the hands of whites determined to reimpose black subordination. They also experienced new forms of discrimination, spearheaded by a variety of state laws that instituted rigid racial segregation in virtually all areas of life and that (in violation of the Fourteenth and Fifteenth Amendments) effectively disfranchised black voters. The struggle to overcome the bitter legacy of slavery would be long and arduous.

See also Abolitionism in the United States; Cotton Production in the United States; Emancipation Proclamation and the Thirteenth Amendment; Race and the American Presidency.

Bibliography

Blassingame, John W. *The Slave Community: Plantation Life in the Antebellum South.* Oxford University Press, 1979.

Fogel, Robert W. *Without Consent or Contract: The Rise and Fall of American Slavery.* Norton, 1989.

Genovese, Eugene D. *Roll, Jordan, Roll: The World the Slaves Made.* Pantheon Books, 1974.

Goodheart, Lawrence B., et al., eds. *Slavery in American Society.* D.C. Heath, 1993.

Kolchin, Peter. *American Slavery, 1619–1877.* Hill and Wang, 1993.

Morgan, Philip D. *Slave Counterpoint: Black Culture in the Eighteenth-Century Chesapeake and Lowcountry.* Published for the Omohundro Institute of Early American History and Culture by the University of North Carolina Press, 1998.

Rose, Willie Lee, ed. *A Documentary History of Slavery in North America.* Oxford University Press, 1976.

Stampp, Kenneth M. *The Peculiar Institution: Slavery in the Ante-Bellum South.* Knopf, 1956.

Peter Kolchin

Sleet, Moneta J., Jr.

1926–1996

Photojournalist whose work chronicled pivotal moments in contemporary black history, such as the 1968 funeral of Martin Luther King, Jr. and Ghana's independence in 1957. He was the first African American man to win a Pulitzer Prize.

Moneta Sleet, Jr. was born in Owensboro, Kentucky. Wanting to be a photographer since early childhood, he studied photography and business at Kentucky State College. In 1955 he became a staff photographer for *Ebony* magazine. On assignment, he met Martin Luther King, Jr. in 1956 and the two remained friends until King's assassination. Sleet received the Pulitzer Prize in 1969 for his photograph of King's widow, Coretta Scott King, and daughter in mourning at King's funeral. During this period Sleet photographed the marches and rallies of the Civil Rights Movement and won critical acclaim for his sensitive and vivid photos of both famous and ordinary people.

See also Photography, African American.

Slinger, Francisco

See Mighty Sparrow.

Slovo, Joe

1926–1995

Lawyer, antiapartheid activist, and general secretary of the South African Communist Party.

Lithuanian-born Joe Slovo moved to South Africa at the age of nine and grew up in a working-class Jewish neighborhood in Johannesburg. In 1942 he joined the Communist Party of South Africa (later renamed the South African Communist Party) and, shortly thereafter, the South African Army, with which he fought in World War II (1939–1945). After the war he studied law at the University of Witwatersrand, where he befriended Nelson Mandela, who was then the university's only black student. When Mandela and others formed the African National Congress (ANC) Youth League in 1944, Slovo argued for the multiracial cooperation that became an ANC trademark.

Slovo acted as Mandela's lawyer in his first trial for treason in 1956, a trial in which Slovo was also a defendant. In the early 1960s he helped found Umkhonto we Sizwe, the ANC's covert military wing, and served for a time as its commander in chief. After the government raided Umkhonto's headquarters, Slovo was forced into twenty-seven years of exile—years that Slovo spent working against Apartheid from London, Zambia, and Mozambique. In 1982 his wife Ruth First, also an antiapartheid activist, was assassinated.

Known for his quick wit and gentle humor (in his first public speech after the ANC ban was lifted in 1990, he began, "As I was saying before I was so rudely interrupted . . . "), Slovo helped negotiate the transition to democratic government that culminated in South Africa's first free elections in 1994. He served as the minister of housing for Nelson Mandela, South Africa's first black president, allocating $500 million in government loans for black township residents to buy their own homes. Ten years after becoming the first white person elected to the ANC Executive Committee, Slovo died in 1995 after a long battle with cancer.

Bibliography

Slovo, Joe. *Slovo: The Unfinished Autobiography.* Hodder & Stoughton, 1995.

Kate Tuttle

Slowe, Lucy Diggs

1883–1937

African American educator, feminist, and tennis player.

Lucy Diggs Slowe was born in Berryville, Virginia, a farming community in Clark County. Following the premature deaths of her parents, Henry Slowe and Fannie Potter, the owners of the only hotel in Berryville, young Lucy joined the home of Martha Slowe Price, her paternal aunt in Lexington, Virginia. A few years later she and the Price family moved to BALTIMORE, MARYLAND, to improve their economic and educational opportunities. Looking back on her childhood, Lucy noted that her aunt had very pronounced ideas on dignity, morality, and religion, which she did not fail to impress upon Lucy and her cousin.

Always an excellent student, Lucy was salutatorian of her 1904 class at Baltimore Colored High School and the first female graduate of her high school to receive a college scholarship to HOWARD UNIVERSITY. At Howard University she was active in numerous literary, social, musical, and athletic pursuits. In her senior year, she served as president of the women's tennis club and vice president of the Alpha Phi Literary Society, and was a chaperone for female underclass students. She graduated in 1908 as class valedictorian. Her involvement with cocurricular life at Howard sparked her interest in a career in education.

In 1908, while still an undergraduate at Howard, Slowe was a charter member of Alpha Kappa Alpha Sorority, Inc. She drafted its first constitution and was the first vice president. Slowe's relationship with Howard administrators is cited as a major reason why the constitution of Alpha Kappa Alpha Sorority Inc., was approved. Slowe's values and aspirations helped shape the mission and traditions of America's first Greek letter organization for black women. New pledges of Alpha Kappa Alpha worldwide annually memorize her name as one of their sorority's founders.

At Howard, Slowe developed a love for the game of tennis. For many years she was considered one of the three top black female tennis players in America. In the summer of 1910 she, along with other male and female black tennis players, conducted one of the first recorded black traveling tours to introduce tennis to black communities across the nation. In 1917 she won the singles title at the first national tournament of the, American Tennis Association (ATA), an organization founded to promote black tennis. She was one of the founding members of the ATA, and by virtue of winning its first national tournament, she became the first female black national champion in any sport. Slowe continued to play tennis well into her adult years and to encourage black children to play the game.

After graduation Slowe returned to Baltimore in September 1908 to teach English at her high school. During summers and extended school breaks she pursued a master's degree at Teachers College, Columbia University, in what is now known as educational administration. She completed her master's studies in 1916, developing lifetime relationships with faculty members at Teachers College. She was a frequent visitor there, giving lectures and engaging her peers in the study of student personnel issues. Slowe attributed much of her success to her ongoing research in this field.

In 1916 Slowe was invited to return to WASHINGTON, D.C., to teach English at Armstrong High School and serve as "lady principal," or dean of girls. After three years at Armstrong High School, she was selected to organize Shaw Junior High School, Washington's first junior high for blacks. In 1920 she established an extension center of Columbia University at Shaw, which trained hundreds of black teachers. Many Washingtonians questioned the need for a black junior high school, but Slowe silenced her critics by creating a model school.

Slowe was appointed dean of women and associate professor of English at Howard University in June 1922. In an era when the enrollment of black women at colleges was on the rise, she shaped a new vision of what a college education could do for African American women. She developed a progressive student-life program for women, focusing on housing, health, social life, community service, and educational and vocational guidance. Slowe emphasized the need for women to be prepared for independent life and to take advantage of any and all professional opportunities. Moreover, she used Howard as a laboratory to train black female educators across the country. When Slowe assumed her position, she was the first female dean of women at Howard and the first formally trained student personnel dean on a black college campus.

At Howard, Slowe implemented a series of programs designed to provide a more equitable campus experience. She created a Women's Student League to provide a platform for leadership and self-governance, with mandatory membership for all female students. Slowe created cultural and social events that were previously unavailable to women at Howard University. She elevated the role of female staff under her supervision by teaching them how to counsel and mentor, rather than matron and monitor. Numerous Howard traditions were launched during the Slowe era, including the Christmas vespers service, a concert-lecture series, teas, coffee hours, current-events discussions, volunteer activities in the community, and book clubs. She also established an annual fund, raising money for needy women students. Her most lasting legacy was the creation of the Fourth Street campus, designed for women.

Slowe understood the importance of organizations. She founded or was active in many organizations dedicated to the problems of African Americans. In 1935 Slowe was one of the founders of the National Council of Negro Women and served as its first secretary. She was also the leading force behind the creation of the National Association of Deans of Women and

Advisors of Girls in Negro Schools, serving as president for many years. She served on numerous boards in and around Washington, D.C., and worked with the National Young Women's Christian Association and the Women's International League for Peace and Freedom. These organizations were an integral part of her efforts to improve the treatment and condition of black women college students.

The JIM CROW society of her day did not dampen her belief in the benefits of an integrated society for blacks and whites. Slowe worked for social justice and integration. Her lifelong association with educators at Columbia's Teachers College provided her with opportunities to influence predominantly white institutions. Slowe once advised Boston College not to house black students in segregated housing, reflecting her belief that a college campus ought to be a place where people of different races learned from each other. She was an adviser to the Race Relations Group of the North American Home Missions of the National Student Council and thought that communication between racial groups was very important, both on and off the campus.

Not all of Slowe's ideas were readily accepted. Her work with the National Association of College Women was largely directed toward establishing higher academic standards for women, to steer them as much toward political science and natural sciences as education and home economics. Her belief that rules governing women at Howard ought to be reduced to a minimum and personal honor and responsibility increased to a maximum conflicted with the prevailing paternalist philosophy of the day. She unnerved some in the black community by challenging them to see their daughters as professionals and leaders, not just teachers and socialites. Her little-known "memorandum on the sexual harassment of black women" was considered a betrayal by some and suicidal by others. Often at odds with male leadership in the black community, Slowe noted, in a letter dated May 22, 1928, "I have had the courage of my convictions even though sometimes I have had to suffer personal discomfort for standing up for them."

Following an extended illness caused by influenza and kidney disease, Slowe died at the age of fifty-three in Washington, D.C. In recognition of her life, the District of Columbia Public Schools named an elementary school in her honor. Howard University named a dormitory for her, and a window at the university's Andrew Rankin Chapel also honors her. Beyond these tributes to a life serving others, Slowe deserves scholarly recognition from professionals in student personnel work as well as from feminists and historians of education. Her enlightened practices in student personnel work and her forward-looking attitudes about women and their place in both the university and society mark her as an activist and a thinker well ahead of her time.

In the introduction to *Ain't I a Woman: Black Women and Feminism,* bell hooks writes: "At a time in American history when black women in every area of the country might have joined together to demand social equality for women and a recognition of the impact of sexism on our social status, we were by and large silent." Lucy Diggs Slowe was not silent. She devoted her life to joining with other women, black and white, to advance the educational, cultural, and social opportunities for women in general and black women in particular. She practiced, published, and preached her ideas, leaving a human and ideological legacy that helped open closed doors of education for all.

The Moorland Spingarn Collection at Howard University contains the personal papers of Lucy Diggs Slowe and the majority of the available biographical materials on her.

Bibliography
Ransom, Joanna Houston. "Innovations Introduced into the Women's Program at Howard University by the Late Dean Lucy D. Slowe," *Journal of the National Association of College Women* 14 (1937).
Turner, Geneva C. "Slowe School." *Negro History Bulletin* (January 1955).

Leroy Nesbitt Jr.
Desmond Wolfe

Sly and the Family Stone

Interracial musical group formed in the late 1960s by African American singer Sly Stone, Sly and the Family Stone, together with singer James Brown, helped create the funk music style.

Sly and the Family Stone played a key role in the genesis of FUNK, a musical fusion combining GOSPEL-inspired SOUL MUSIC with the guitar-driven sound and performance style of 1960s psychedelic rock. Sly Stone was born Sylvester Stewart in 1944 and moved in the 1950s with his family from Texas to SAN FRANCISCO. After playing in several area bands, he became a RHYTHM AND BLUES (R&B) disc jockey for stations KSOL and later KDIA. As a record producer for Autumn Records, he recorded such local bands as the Beau Brummels and the Mojo Men. In 1967 he organized Sly and the Family Stone, which was unique among 1960s rock or funk bands for including both blacks and whites, and women as well as men.

The group featured punchy horn riffs and wild guitar solos played over a deep funk rhythm. It soon had two hits, "Everyday People" (1968) and "Hot Fun in the Summertime" (1969), and appeared at the 1969 Woodstock Festival. The group's songs often displayed a racial militancy reminiscent of the Black Power movement, as in "Don't Call Me Nigger, Whitey" (1969). The album *There's a Riot Going On* (1971) combined social commentary with highly danceable music that set the pattern for funk music in the 1970s.

By the early 1970s, Sly and the Family Stone's music had turned darkly pessimistic as Stone began to fall apart. He became addicted to narcotics and acquired a reputation for unreliability after repeated no-shows at concerts. Sly and the Family Stone produced one more exceptional album, *Fresh* (1973), but the public's changing musical tastes and Stone's mounting personal problems ended the group's national visibility.

In the early 1980s, Stone joined GEORGE CLINTON on Funkadelic's *The Electric Spanking of War Babies* (1981) and toured with the P-Funk All-Stars. During the 1980s, Stone was repeatedly in trouble with the law and spent time in prison for cocaine possession.

In 1993, the year that he was inducted into the Rock and Roll Hall of Fame, Stone was reportedly living in a sheltered-housing complex. In the summer of 2003, eighteen months after receiving an R&B Foundation Pioneer Award, five of the original members of the Family Stone reunited to record a new album. Sly Stone, however, was unable to join them due to his continuing drug, legal, and medical problems. Despite his difficulties, Stone made a lasting contribution to modern music. The urban soul, funk, and RAP styles all reveal a debt to the music of Sly and the Family Stone.

See also Black Power in the United States; Brown, James; Gospel Music; Music, African American.

James Sellman

Smalls, Robert

1839–1915

Civil War pilot and U.S. congressman, who achieved fame by sailing the Confederate steamship *Planter* to the Union side.

Born into slavery in Beaufort, South Carolina, Robert Smalls later moved to CHARLESTON, SOUTH CAROLINA, and learned navigation. As a slave, he was permitted to hire himself out as a boatman. During the CIVIL WAR (1861–1865), he was made a wheelman (the title "pilot" being reserved for whites) of the steamboat *Planter,* because of his familiarity with local waterways. On May 12, 1862, with the white crewmembers on the shore, Smalls stowed his family and several other slaves on board, and piloted the ship across Union lines. The *Planter* was a 300-ton armed vessel that Smalls presented to the United States Army; he also provided useful intelligence about Confederate operations. The story of the incident was wildly popular throughout the North, and Smalls was awarded $1,500 and made a second lieutenant in the Union's Colored Troops. The *Planter* became a Union transport ship, and Smalls was made its pilot. In 1863, when the ship was refitted as a gunboat, Smalls became its captain.

Smalls learned to read and write during the war. When he returned to Beaufort during RECONSTRUCTION he became active in the REPUBLICAN PARTY and embarked on a political career. He also joined the state militia, achieving the rank of brigadier general. Smalls had attended the 1864 Republican National Convention, and was elected to South Carolina's Constitutional Convention of 1868, where he helped rewrite the state's constitution. From 1868 to 1874 he was a member of the state legislature.

In 1874 Smalls was elected to the first of five terms in the United States House of Representatives. A loyal Republican, he fought for free compulsory public education, health care, and civil rights for African Americans. Smalls was also influential in the business community, investing in South Carolina real estate and companies. He was defeated for reelection to Congress in 1886, when the influence of Reconstruction and its reforms subsided. From 1890 to 1913 Smalls was the customs collector for the port of Beaufort. He remained active in the Republican Party until his death in 1915.

Smith, Ada "Bricktop"

1894–1984

Singer and nightclub owner whose Parisian café attracted a wealthy and famous international clientele in the 1920s and 1930s.

A performer throughout her childhood, Ada Smith left school at age sixteen to begin her career as a singer and dancer in minstrel and vaudeville shows. Her bright red hair earned her the nickname "Bricktop." She performed extensively in NEW YORK, LOS ANGELES, and CHICAGO. In 1924 she began singing at Paris's Le Grand Duc, a nightclub favored by the Parisian elite and community of black expatriates, where she became acquainted with Cole Porter, JOSEPHINE BAKER, and Pablo Picasso, among others. In 1927 she bought the club and renamed it Bricktop's; it became one of Paris's most popular nightclubs in the 1930s. Smith left Paris in 1939 because of WORLD WAR II. A string of nightclubs she opened in the 1940s and 1950s failed, and Smith retired from the business in 1964, except for occasional singing engagements in the 1970s.

See also Minstrelsy.

Bibliography

Bricktop, with James Haskins. *Bricktop.* Atheneum, 1983.

Smith, Albert Alexander

1896–1940

American painter, illustrator, and jazz musician whose work emphasized African American daily life.

Albert Smith was born in NEW YORK, NEW YORK. He was trained in piano and guitar at the Ethical Culture High School in New York, and later studied at the National Academy of Design in Belgium, where he twice won the Suyden Bronze Medal. After serving in a military band during WORLD WAR I, he settled in Paris in the 1920s, where his art was frequently exhibited. He gained international fame as an artist having exhibitions in Brussels and New York. He worked often as an illustrator for the magazines *THE CRISIS* and *OPPORTUNITY.* Creating daily scenes from African American life, Smith wanted to enforce positive images of black folk through art. He supported himself playing banjo in Paris cabarets.

Smith, Anna Deveare

1950–

American actor, playwright, and educator.

Born in BALTIMORE, MARYLAND, Anna Deveare Smith was the oldest of Deveare and Anna Smith's five children. Her father owned a coffee and tea business, while her mother was an elementary school principal. In 1971, after receiving a bachelor's degree in linguistics from Beaver College (now Arcadia University), Smith left for SAN FRANCISCO, CALIFORNIA, where her acting talent earned her a place at the American Conservatory Theater and enabled her to work as an actor and director. She received a Master of Fine Arts degree in 1976, and left for NEW YORK CITY in the same year. There, Smith played minor roles in soap operas and worked for KLM Airlines before becoming a drama teacher at Carnegie-Mellon University in PITTSBURGH, PENNSYLVANIA.

Though a casting agent had once told her she was too pale to convincingly portray black characters, Smith launched a one-woman performance, *On the Road: A Search for American Character* (1983), beginning a quest to dramatically represent America's multiple voices and identities. In 1992 Smith produced the twenty-six character, one-woman performance, *Fires in the Mirror*, which dealt with the riots that erupted in Crown Heights, a section of Brooklyn, after an African American child was accidentally killed by a Jewish motorist, and a Jewish scholar was stabbed in apparent retaliation. Based on interviews with more than fifty people connected to the riots, Smith described the performance as an exploration of the causes and impact of the incident, and of "the place where language fails, where people have to struggle to find words."

Fires in the Mirror received an Obie Award, a Drama Desk Award, the Lucille Lortel Award, the $10,000 Kesselring Prize, and the George and Elizabeth Marton Award, and was runner-up for a Pulitzer Prize. This success led directly to a commission that created *Twilight: Los Angeles 1992,* a performance that similarly examined the five days of rioting in LOS ANGELES that followed the acquittal of four policeman accused of severely beating a black motorist, Rodney King. *Twilight* opened in 1993 in L.A., then moved to New York City, where it was the first nonmusical show by a black woman to open on Broadway in ten years. *Twilight* won two Tony Award nominations, an Obie Award, A Drama Desk Award, and an Outer Circle Critics Special Achievement Award. Because *Twilight*, like *Fires*, was dependent on Smith's verbatim portrayals of the people she interviewed (a work of "documentary" rather than a work of "theater"), the Pulitzer board decided to withdraw her nomination for the prize.

Other works by Smith include the plays *A Birthday Card and Aunt Julia's Shoes* (1983), *Aye, Aye, Aye, I'm Integrated* (1984), and *House Arrest* (2000). She appeared in the motion pictures *Dave* (1993), *Philadelphia* (1993), *The American President* (1995), and *The Human Stain* (2003), and had recurring roles in the popular television shows *The Practice* and *The West Wing.* In 2000 Smith published *Talk To Me: Travels in Media and Politics,* a probing look at the role of the presidency in American society that features more than 400 interviews. She continues to appear in television, motion picture, and stage productions.

Smith has taught at Yale University, the University of Southern California at Los Angeles, and Stanford University. She is currently a professor at the Tisch School of the Arts at New York University.

See also Film, Blacks in American; Los Angeles Riot of 1992; Television and African Americans.

Bibliography

Laurino, Maria. "Sensitivity Comes From 'The Soles of the Feet.'" *Newsday,* Feb. 23, 1994.

Smith, Anna Deavere. *Fires in the Mirror: Crown Heights, Brooklyn and Other Identities.* Anchor Books/Doubleday, 1993.

Smith, Arthur Lee, Jr.

See Asante, Molefi Kete.

Smith, Bessie

1894–1937

African American singer who was the greatest blues vocalist of the 1920s.

Bessie Smith was the greatest of the classic BLUES singers of the 1920s, laying the foundation for subsequent female blues and JAZZ performers. Her singing combined an array of vocal embellishments, including scoops, slides, and so-called blue notes (tones that bridge the musical relationship between the major and minor modes), with a rhythmic freedom that heightened the emotional effect of her lyrics. African American audiences loved her, especially in the South and in those regions of the North where recent Southern migrants settled. These fans appreciated her rough, down-home style. "She could bring about mass hypnotism," NEW ORLEANS guitarist Danny Barker recalled. "When she was performing you could hear a pin drop." This was in part because of her musical artistry and showmanship; it was also because many identified with her success. Smith had risen from poverty to comparative wealth on her own terms and by her own talent. Many African Americans also admired her attitude toward white people—Smith made no effort to befriend whites and never altered her performing style to appeal to them.

Bessie Smith was born in 1894, in a poor section of Chattanooga, Tennessee. One of seven children who were orphaned at a young age, she was singing on street corners by the time she was nine. She grew into a tall woman with a powerful and expressive voice. In 1912, while she was still a teenager, Smith joined a traveling vaudeville show. Surprisingly, she was hired as a dancer rather than as a singer, joining her dancer and comedian brother Clarence, who was already in the show. The troupe also included blues singer MA RAINEY, who reportedly took Smith under her wing.

Smith settled in ATLANTA, GEORGIA, where she performed regularly at the 81 Theater, part of the black nationwide Theater Owners' Booking Association (TOBA) circuit. She began touring on the TOBA circuit, performing in the North as well as in the Southeast, and by the end of WORLD WAR I (1914–1918), she was its star attraction. During these years Smith also had a brief marriage to Jack Gee and began a lifetime of hard drinking. She entered a recording studio for the first time when she was nearly thirty years old and a fully formed artist.

With the phenomenal success of "Crazy Blues," recorded in 1920 by Mamie Smith (no relation), record companies began to produce "race records" for African American listeners and to seek black talent. At least two companies rejected Smith before Columbia Record Company brought her to its NEW YORK studios in 1923. Unlike many classic blues vocalists whose singing backgrounds were in vaudeville or popular music, Smith was primarily grounded in the blues. Consequently, as pianist Clarence Williams later explained, a number of record companies "said that her voice was too rough."

African American listeners did not agree. In less than six months her first recording—"Down Hearted Blues"—sold an astonishing 780,000 copies. In fact, Smith played a direct role in rescuing Columbia, nearly in receivership at the time, and helping to put the company on a firm financial base. Columbia proclaimed its new star the Empress of the Blues, but Smith received no royalties, only a flat fee for each recording. During the 1920s she recorded prolifically with a wide range of accompanists, including cornetist LOUIS ARMSTRONG, clarinet player SIDNEY BECHET, pianist FLETCHER HENDERSON, and her two favorite musicians, trumpet player Joe Smith and trombone player Charlie Green.

In addressing what made Smith "such a superior singer," musicologist Gunther Schuller emphasized the importance of her "remarkable ear for and control of intonation . . . [her] perfectly centered, naturally produced voice . . . [her] extreme sensitivity to word meaning and the sensory, almost physical, feeling of a word; and related to this, superb diction and what singers call projection."

Among her important recordings are "Jailhouse Blues," recorded in 1923; "Cold in Hand Blues," "J. C. Holmes Blues," and "You've Been a Good Old Wagon," recorded in 1925; "Gin House Blues" and "Young Woman's Blues," recorded in 1926; and "Nobody Knows You When You're Down and Out," recorded in 1929. Throughout her career, she also recorded popular songs and standards that were not blues-based, including "After You've Gone" (1927) and "Gimme a Pigfoot" (1933).

Smith toured extensively. During the winter she appeared at black theaters and occasionally at whites-only venues, such as Nashville's Orpheum Theater. In warm weather she headlined her own big-tent variety show, with the entire cast traveling from one performance to the next in her private Pullman car. In 1924 she made her first radio broadcast on WMC in MEMPHIS, TENNESSEE, singing a set that included "Mistreatin' Papa" and "Chicago Bound." Five years later she starred in a black-and-white short, *St. Louis Blues,* singing the title song; it is the only film footage of Smith performing. Although her Northern audiences declined when the blues craze passed in the late 1920s, Smith remained popular throughout the South, where the blues was indigenous. After the GREAT DEPRESSION put an end to her recording career in 1933, she continued performing before appreciative Southern audiences.

During the 1930s Smith made the transition from a heavier blues style to the more lightly swinging jazz of the swing era. She was featured at the renowned APOLLO THEATER in HARLEM in 1935 and a short time later substituted for BILLIE HOLIDAY in the Broadway show *Stars over Broadway.* Smith appeared to be on the verge of a comeback when she was killed in an automobile accident in 1937. Record producer John Hammond, writing in *Downbeat* magazine five years after her death, and playwright Edward Albee, in *The Death of Bessie Smith* (1960), popularized the notion that the singer died because a whites-only hospital refused to admit her. However, her biographer Chris Albertson concluded that Smith died at the scene of the accident and, given the extent of her injuries, could not have been saved.

Bibliography

Albertson, Chris. *Bessie.* Stein and Day, 1972.
Schuller, Gunther. *Early Jazz: Its Roots and Musical Development.* Oxford University Press, 1968.

James Sellman

Smith, Clara

1894?–1935

American blues singer and pianist during the 1920s.

Born in Spartanburg, South Carolina, Clara Smith began performing around 1910, working the Southern black vaudeville circuit. By 1918 she was a star in the Theater Owners' Booking Association (TOBA), which managed acts for black theater. Smith settled in HARLEM in 1923, where she played in cellar clubs, speakeasies, and revues.

One of Smith's biggest recorded hits was "Every Woman's Blues" (1923). On her recordings, Smith performed with FLETCHER HENDERSON, LOUIS ARMSTRONG, and Don Redman, and sang duets with BESSIE SMITH (no relation). Known as "Queen of the Moaners," she had a style that was both dramatic and comic. She is best remembered for expressive performances of songs like "Whip It to a Jelly" that played with sexual double entendres. Smith also managed her own revues, including the Clara Smith Theatrical Club.

See also Blues.

Marian Aguiar

Smith, Clarence ("Pine Top")

1904–1929

American jazz pianist who originated the boogie-woogie style.

Born in Troy, Alabama, Clarence "Pine Top" Smith began to play piano professionally in 1918, working at clubs in Birmingham before touring on the vaudeville and black Theater Owners' Booking Association (TOBA) circuit. He was discovered by Charles "Cow Cow" Davenport in the mid-1920s, and began recording in 1928. With "Pine Top's Boogie Woogie" (1928) he coined the term BOOGIE-WOOGIE. The style, marked by lively improvised melodies on the right hand and rolling eight-to-the-bar figures on the left, developed as one of the most important strains of JAZZ piano. Smith recorded twenty songs in all, including "Pine Top's Blues." He died at twenty-five during a brawl in a CHICAGO dance hall.

Marian Aguiar

Smith, Ian Douglas

1919–

Prime minister of Southern Rhodesia and leading politician in Zimbabwe.

Throughout his life, Ian Smith has been a conservative rebel. For years he was one of the most ardent proponents of white settler society in southern Africa, and he has since become one of the most vociferous critics of independent rule in ZIMBABWE.

Born and raised in colonial SOUTHERN RHODESIA, Smith joined the British Royal Air Force in 1939. After serving as a combat pilot in World War II, Smith attended Rhodes University in SOUTH AFRICA and after graduation returned to Southern Rhodesia to work on his large cattle ranch. Smith was elected to the Legislative Assembly of the British colony as a member of the Liberal Party in 1948, only to switch five years later to the more conservative United (Federal) Party. He later became chief whip but left the party in 1961 to help form the Rhodesian Front, a party opposed to making concessions to Africans. There he served as deputy prime minister until a right-wing revolt propelled him into the leadership position.

Smith became prime minister in April 1964, vowing to proclaim white-ruled Rhodesia's independence from GREAT BRITAIN. He called for an all-white referendum and with overwhelming support made his Unilateral Declaration of Independence in November 1965, putting Southern Rhodesia on a collision course with rising African nationalism. Despite the imposition of severe international sanctions, Smith remained intransigent for several years, promising the white community that the government would fight "communist terrorism" (i.e. African nationalists of ZANU and ZAPU) to the end, and that Rhodesia would remain a settler state as long as he lived. Meanwhile, he remained a centrist in Rhodesian politics, purging the leadership of right-wing elements. Representing whites of the small town and farm communities, Smith and his "cowboy cabinet" were disliked by the Rhodesian business community, but it was ultimately the financial strength of this community that sustained the economy throughout fifteen years of war.

As the war expanded and South African pressure increased, Smith gradually became more amenable to African demands and four years later recognized the possibility of independence. A long series of negotiations culminated in the "internal settlement" with conservative nationalists, wherein Smith would be a member of a rotating chairmanship. Most African Zimbabweans, the main nationalist groups, and the international community, however, did not recognize the internal settlement, and Smith was forced to sue for peace.

When Zimbabwean independence occurred in 1980, Smith remained in the parliament as head of the opposition all-white Republican Front (the new Rhodesian Front), later known as the Conservative Alliance of Zimbabwe. As one of the government's most vocal critics, Smith was suspended from parliament in 1987 because of his outspoken moral support for South Africa. Soon thereafter he formally retired from politics after serving four decades in parliament. In retirement, Smith continued to lambaste Zimbabwe's economic policies, even as other whites disavowed him and sought to work with the government. He has retained a significant following throughout Zimbabwe, among both white and black, who see him as a symbol of the country's lost prosperity. Smith has published *The Great Betrayal: The Memoirs of Ian Douglas Smith* (1997) and *Bitter Harvest* (2002), in which he blames Great Britain and ROBERT MUGABE for Zimbabwe's current problems.

See also Colonial Rule; Nationalism in Africa; Political Movements in Africa.

Bibliography

Joyce, Peter. *Anatomy of a Rebel: Smith of Rhodesia: A Biography.* Graham Publishing, 1974.

Smith, Ian Douglas. *The Great Betrayal: The Memoirs of Ian Douglas Smith.* Blake Publishing, 1997.

Eric Young

Smith, James Todd

See LL Cool J.

Smith, Joshua Bowen

1813–1879

African American abolitionist.

Joshua Bowen Smith was born in Coatesville, Pennsylvania. Little is known of his childhood except that he obtained an education in the local public schools through the influence and financial support of a wealthy QUAKER woman.

Smith moved to BOSTON in 1836 and found employment as a headwaiter at the Mount Washington House. Over the following decade, while serving tables, he made the acquaintance of Francis G. Shaw, Charles Sumner, and other notable whites on the periphery of the antislavery movement. Many of these men became his lifelong friends. Smith also worked briefly as a personal servant for the Shaw family, then joined the staff of Henry L. W. Thacker, a local black caterer. In 1849 Smith opened his own catering establishment. Over the next twenty-five years he developed a successful business and gained a sizable personal fortune by serving gatherings of the local elite, as well as catering various functions at Harvard College, antislavery bazaars, and commemorations of the EMANCIPATION PROCLAMATION. He gained a reputation among Bostonians as "the prince of caterers."

In the 1840s Smith emerged as an important figure in the local abolitionist crusade. Through his friendships with Shaw and Sumner he became a close acquaintance and ally of WILLIAM LLOYD GARRISON, George Luther Stearns, Theodore Parker, and other prominent abolitionists; he remained a devoted follower of Garrison for nearly three decades. He regularly attended and sometimes chaired antislavery gatherings in Boston's African American community. And he actively participated in the struggle to end segregation in the city's public school system. But Smith expended the bulk of his energies in aiding and protecting FUGITIVE SLAVES who reached Boston. After the arrest in 1842 of George Latimer, a slave from Virginia, Smith helped found and served as vice president of the New England Freedom Association, an all-black organization devoted to providing runaway slaves with food, clothing, shelter, transportation, and legal aid. Some of the actions taken by the Freedom Association were not only illegal but occasionally violent; nevertheless, Smith viewed them as legitimate antislavery work. When the interracial Boston Committee of Vigilance was formed in 1846, he became a vocal member of its executive committee. He served briefly as the committee's agent, interviewing and arranging assistance for fugitives who came to the members' attention.

After passage of the FUGITIVE SLAVE Act of 1850, which created a federal apparatus for the capture and return of runaway bondsmen, Smith encouraged Boston's blacks to resist the efforts of slave hunters and federal agents to enforce the law. He urged slaves in the city to purchase revolvers and, if necessary, to use them to prevent their recapture. He pressed local free blacks to protect the fugitives in their midst. At one antislavery gathering, speaking from the pulpit of Boston's African Meeting House, he brandished a bowie knife and a pistol, declared his intent to wield them to protect runaways, and demonstrated the proper method for their use. Smith became an active member of the newly created Boston Vigilance Committee (the successor to the Committee of Vigilance in 1850), personally feeding, clothing, and transporting to Canada several slaves who reached Boston. He even used his catering business to further these efforts. While catering he could keep a watchful eye on the movements of slave hunters in the city, and he could also provide temporary employment to a number of runaways. Smith refused to cater an affair for Senator Daniel Webster of Massachusetts, protesting Webster's vocal support of the act.

Smith welcomed the coming of the CIVIL WAR, seeing in it an opportunity to overthrow the institution of slavery. In 1861 Governor John Andrew selected him as the caterer for the 12th Massachusetts Regiment, the first volunteer unit raised in the state during the war. Because of his devotion to the Union cause in the conflict, he agreed to perform the task for a lower price than that charged by other Boston caterers. During the ninety-three days the regiment trained in Boston prior to leaving for the South, he furnished daily rations for the officers and enlisted men. His expenditures amounted to $40,378. This proved to be Smith's financial undoing. The governor initially refused to pay the bill, citing inadequate legislative appropriations for the purpose. Although the catering bills of all other units were paid by the state, Smith received only $23,760.80, and then only after the federal government made funds available to the state for that purpose. He petitioned the state for payment of the balance several times before his death, but the debt remained unpaid. Despite personal frugality and keen business skills, he never recovered his lost fortune.

Even with his precarious finances, Smith remained an important figure in Boston's African American community after the war. Well respected by local whites, he was selected in 1867 as the first black member of St. Andrew's Lodge of Freemasons of Massachusetts. A REPUBLICAN PARTY stalwart, he represented Cambridge in the Massachusetts Senate in 1873 and 1874 and was one of the few blacks to attend national party conventions during that time. Smith died at his Cambridgeport residence after an illness of several months. He was survived by his wife, Emiline (maiden name unknown); their only child, a daughter, had preceded him in death. Hundreds of leading Bostonians turned out to pay their respects at his funeral. At his death his generosity became even more apparent: he left debts some thirty times greater than the value of his estate, in large part on account of his unpaid expenditures for the Twelfth Massachusetts Regiment and decades of contributions to the abolitionist cause.

Bibliography

Bartlett, Irving H. "Abolitionists, Fugitives, and Imposters in Boston, 1846–1847." *New England Quarterly* 55 (1982): 97–110.

Horton, James Oliver, and Lois E. Horton. *Black Bostonians: Family Life and Community Struggle in the Antebellum North*. 1979.

Obituaries: *Boston Evening Transcript,* July 7 and July 8, 1879, and *Boston Evening Traveler,* July 8, 1879.

Ripley, C. Peter, et al., eds. *The Black Abolitionist Papers*. Vol. 3. 1991.

From *American National Biography*. John A. Garraty and Mark C. Carnes, eds. Oxford University Press, 1999. Reprinted by permission of the American Council of Learned Societies.

Roy E. Finkenbine

Smith, Mamie

1883–1946

First African American female singer to record the blues.

Born in Cincinnati, Ohio, Mamie Smith began performing in vaudeville shows at the age of ten and came to New York in 1913 with the Smart Set Revue. After she appeared in Perry Bradford's musical *Made in Harlem* (1920), Bradford helped her get a recording contract at Okeh Records for "That Thing Called Love" (1920) and "You Can't Keep a Good Man Down" (1920). Later that year she recorded "Crazy Blues" with a backup band including Willie ("the Lion") Smith. "Crazy Blues" sold close to a million copies. Its success energized the "race music" industry, which marketed blues and jazz recordings specifically to an African American audience. Smith continued to tour as a singer and actress throughout the 1930s and 1940s, appearing in films such as *Paradise in Harlem* (1939), and on stage with Billie Holiday.

Marian Aguiar

Smith, Marvin and Morgan

Marvin 1910– / Morgan 1910–1993

American photographers who depicted Harlem during the Great Depression.

The twin sons of tenant farmers, Marvin and Morgan Smith grew up in Lexington, Kentucky, where they began painting and drawing. After moving to New York, they studied art under Augusta Savage and painted murals with the Works Progress Administration (WPA), a federal employment assistance program during the Great Depression. The Smiths realistically captured Harlem in the 1930s on film, with photographs of Savoy Ballroom lindy hoppers, street corner preachers, and breadlines. In 1937, they were hired by New York's Amsterdam News as staff photographers. After a brief period in France, the Smiths opened their M&M studio near the Apollo Theater. Their photographs continued to appear in prominent African American newspapers and magazines such as *Ebony*, *The Crisis*, and the *Pittsburgh Courier*. In 1997, four years after Morgan's death, the University of Kentucky Press published *Harlem: The Vision of Morgan and Marvin Smith,* featuring more than 150 of their photographs. Marvin continues to reside in Harlem.

See also Photography, African American.

Marian Aguiar

Smith, Stephen

1795?–1873

African American businessman and minister.

Stephen Smith was born near Harrisburg, Dauphin County, Pennsylvania, the son of an unknown father and Nancy Smith (maiden name unknown), a Cochran family servant. On July 10, 1801 Thomas Boude, a former revolutionary war officer from Columbia, Lancaster County, Pennsylvania, purchased the boy's indenture. As Smith grew to manhood, he proved so able that Boude eventually made him manager of his entire lumber business.

On January 3, 1816 Smith borrowed $50 to purchase his freedom from Boude. Later that year Smith married Harriet Lee, a domestic servant in the Jonathan Mifflin home. They had no children. Free of his indenture, Smith entered the lumber business for himself, while his wife ran an oyster house. In 1820 his one-and-a-half lots were valued at $300. Thirteen years later, he owned six houses and lots worth $3,000, stocks and bonds of equal value, "a pleasure carriage," a horse, and a cow. His lumberyard became one of the largest on the Susquehanna River. This success aroused the envy of some whites; an anonymous hate letter in 1835 accused him of inflating property prices with his excessive bids.

When the race riots of 1834–1835 broke out in Columbia, Smith's place of business was a target. Windows were broken, his desk rifled, and papers scattered. His property and life in jeopardy, Smith offered his holdings for sale, but after six months with no takers, he withdrew his offer. His financial strength enabled him to weather the 1837 bank panic. With his business partner, William Whipper, a relative and an equally astute merchant, Smith's Columbia investments included $9,000 in a bridge company and $18,000 in a bank. Moving to Philadelphia in 1842, he increased his holdings of houses, lots, stocks, and bonds and expanded his lumber and coal business. By 1849 Smith and Whipper had an inventory of "several thousand bushels of coal," over two million feet of lumber, "and twenty-two of the finest merchantmen cars running on the railroad from Columbia to Philadelphia and Baltimore" (Worner, p. 185). When his partnership with Whipper ended, his wife's nephew, Ulysses B. Vidal, joined him in the coal business.

Smith's business dealings were not his sole occupation. In 1832 he purchased a church building in Columbia and founded the Mount Zion African Methodist Episcopal Church (AME). Six years later he was ordained an AME minister.

Early on, Smith turned his talents to race rights and reform. He was a well-known participant in the Underground Railroad; Whipper told William Still that it was known "far down in the slave region, that Smith & Whipper, the negro lumber merchants, were engaged in secreting fugitive slaves" (Still, p. 739). Smith opposed the colonization movement and supported the early strivings of Whipper's American Moral Reform Society in 1834–1835. A frequent but not addicted conventiongoer and mass-meeting participant, he fought for the abolition of slavery, the removal of "white" from the state constitution, and the integration of Philadelphia's railway cars. Smith supported the temperance movement and was an officer in a number of black organizations, including the Odd Fellows, Social, Civil, and Statistical Association; the Grand Tabernacle of the Independent Order of Brothers and Sisters of Love and Charity; and the

Union League Association. He hosted JOHN BROWN for a week in 1858 and, along with JAMES WORMLEY and HENRY HIGHLAND GARNET, had a leadership role in the movement to erect a Lincoln memorial monument.

An occasional victim of white persecution, he had also earned the respect of many whites and worked with them in his business and charitable endeavors. His race views were unequivocal but moderate. In 1855 he was aware "that the colored people of the city of Philadelphia could not obtain [an] opportunity to learn mechanical trades. But," he added, "wherever a colored man understood a trade, he was sustained in Philadelphia" (Foner and Lewis, vol. 1, p. 262). As time went on, Smith became more pessimistic. He discouraged black attempts to integrate the Philadelphia railway cars because he doubted such attempts would receive the support of the city's white citizens.

During the CIVIL WAR, though a member of Bethel AME Church, Smith served for a year or so as pastor in charge of the Zion AME Mission Church. He worked with Bethel's committee to collect food, clothing, and money for contrabands in WASHINGTON, D.C. He helped to organize one meeting and chaired a second at which FREDERICK DOUGLASS spoke, urging black recruits for the army and equal rights for all men and women. A short-term trustee of WILBERFORCE UNIVERSITY, he headed a committee to raise funds for that institution.

After Appomattox, Smith continued his business and church activities. Not assigned a parish, he occasionally preached and frequently spoke ("in his usual animated and forcible style") in and around the city. He and his wife regularly summered in Cape May. His major charitable interest centered on a home for the elderly and the Olive Cemetery. He bought the cemetery at a forced auction for payment of debts and rejoiced when in 1863 the state supreme court resolved a seven-year-old management dispute in his favor. The next year Smith and some white QUAKERS established the Philadelphia Home for the Aged and Infirm. In 1870 a new building was dedicated, a gift of Stephen and Harriet Smith. By bequest the Smiths endowed the home with almost $250,000.

Beyond this, his denomination, including Bethel Church, benefited from his continuing generosity and special gifts. He built the Zion AME Mission church in 1857 and contributed to the establishment of an AME church in Cape May. With nine others, Smith put up $1,000 to buy the vacated Institute for Colored Youth building and convert it into a meeting hall with stores for black retailers.

As an individual, Smith was quiet but stubborn. In 1856 he chastised the *Christian Recorder* editor, Jabez Campbell, for criticizing an AME General Conference ruling, asserting that the editor should "vindicate her [the church's] acts, defend her organization, discipline and laws." Be patient, he urged; "try them, and if they do not suit, repeal them" (*Christian Recorder,* March 4, 1856). Five years later, the AME district conference settled another dispute between the two men in Smith's favor. At the 1864 general conference, some Bethel members protested his seat for unstated reasons, but their claim was denied. Early in 1873 Wilberforce University's president, Bishop DANIEL PAYNE, stung by rumors of Smith's lack of confidence in him, published an offer to resign if Smith would endow the institution with a $100,000 gift. Smith's terse response praised Payne "as a man of learning and a Christian gentleman," but questioned his abilities to manage finances (*Christian Recorder,* March 6, 1873).

This was probably Smith's last public statement before illness incapacitated him. After his death in Philadelphia, Pennsylvania, he was praised as "the ablest financier and the wealthiest man among the colored people," and "one of the best-known colored citizens of Philadelphia." Smith's life was a rags-to-riches saga, unique in the nineteenth-century black community. He tried to live his Christian creed, courageously patient under persecution, moderate in materialism, and sensitive to the less fortunate.

Bibliography

Foner, Philip S., and Ronald L. Lewis. *The Black Worker to 1869*. Vol. 1. 1978.

Foner, Philip S., and George Walker, eds. *Proceedings of the Black State Conventions, 1840–1865*. Vol. 1. 1979.

Obituaries: *New National Era,* December 4, 1873, *Philadelphia Public Ledger,* November 15, 1873, and *Philadelphia Inquirer,* November 19, 1873.

Quarles, Benjamin. *Black Abolitionists*. 1969.

Still, William. *The Underground Rail Road*. 1872.

The Christian Recorder, 1854–1856, 1861–1873.

Worner, William F. "The Columbia Race Riots." *Lancaster County Historical Society Papers* 26, no. 8 (October 1922): 175–187.

From *American National Biography*. John A. Garraty and Mark C. Carnes, eds. Oxford University Press, 1999. Reprinted by permission of the American Council of Learned Societies.

Leslie H. Fishel

Smith, Venture

1729?–1805

Slave, entrepreneur, and autobiographer.

Venture Smith, also known as Broteer Venture, was born in Dukandarra, GUINEA, the eldest child of Saungm Furro, a prince. His mother, whose name is unknown, was the first of his polygynist father's three wives. She took five-year-old Broteer and her two younger children when she left her husband to protest his marrying the third wife without her consent. After traveling for five days over about 140 miles, she left Broteer with a farmer before returning to the country where she was born. The farmer treated Broteer like a son, employing him for a year as a shepherd, until the boy's father sent for him. Returning to Dukandarra, Broteer found that his mother and father had reconciled.

This domestic peace was soon interrupted, however, by the sudden invasion of a hostile army, instigated and equipped by

Europeans. Although Broteer's father paid tribute, the entire community was forced to flee for their safety. The family's hiding place was soon discovered, and Broteer watched as his father fought and eventually was tortured to death. Broteer and his other family members were taken captive. Young Broteer worked as a servant to the leader of the army's scouting party, carrying his gun, as well as food, cooking supplies, and a 25-pound stone for grinding corn. He also participated in raids on other African nations as the army made its way to Africa's west coast. Taken prisoner yet again when another army defeated his captors, Broteer and his companions were offered in sale to a slave ship from Rhode Island, commanded by Captain Collingwood and his first mate, Thomas Mumford. Broteer was purchased for four gallons of rum and a piece of calico by the ship's steward, Robertson Mumford. Mumford called him "Venture," the latter recalls in his autobiography, *A Narrative of the Life and Adventures of Venture* (1798), "on account of his having purchased me with his own private venture." The ship sailed first to BARBADOS. Of the slaves who survived a devastating shipboard smallpox epidemic, all but four were sold there. Venture was among those who sailed on to Rhode Island, where he began life as an American slave at eight years of age.

Venture worked as a household servant at his master's residence on Fishers Island, carding wool and pounding corn under the constant threat of punishment. His master was often away from home, and Venture frequently was subject to the whims of Mumford's son James, who once hung Venture on a cattle gallows for an hour. At age twenty-two Venture married Margaret ("Meg," maiden name unknown), also the slave of his master, with whom he would eventually have four children. After participating in an abortive escape attempt and returning to his master, Venture was sold to Thomas Stanton and moved to Stonington Point, Connecticut. Stanton bought Venture's wife and baby daughter a year and a half later. After repeated beatings by Stanton and his family, Venture was first pawned to Daniel Edwards, Esq., as a cupbearer and waiter and then sold to Colonel Smith at age thirty-one. Having saved a substantial sum of money by shining shoes, fishing, raising and selling vegetables, and doing other odd jobs, Venture purchased his freedom from Smith and adopted the latter's surname as his own.

By the time he was forty-six years old, Smith had purchased his entire family. As a free man he engaged in numerous business ventures, from selling watermelon to cutting wood to running a shipping business. In his memoir he claims to have repeatedly loaned money to both blacks and whites, only to be defaulted on by those who took "advantage of my ignorance of numbers." At age forty-seven Smith moved with his family to East Haddam, Connecticut. He composed and published his memoirs at age sixty-nine with an anonymous amanuensis-editor, and amassed 100 acres of land and three houses. He died in East Haddam or Haddam Neck, Connecticut.

Venture Smith is best known for his Narrative, which was reprinted at least three times in the century after his death. Smith's classic slave narrative provides a rare glimpse of the African component of the slave trade and a critical look at slavery in the eighteenth century. Perhaps most important is Smith's portrait of himself as an African American self-made man. In it he records not only his participation in but also his disillusionment with the American Dream.

Bibliography

Andrews, William L. *To Tell a Free Story: The First Century of Afro-American Autobiography, 1760–1865*. 1986.

Starling, Marion Wilson. *The Slave Narrative: Its Place in American History*. 2d ed. 1988.

From *American National Biography*. John A. Garraty and Mark C. Carnes, eds. Oxford University Press, 1999. Reprinted by permission of the American Council of Learned Societies.

Jeannine Delombard

Smith, Will

1968–

American recording artist and motion-picture actor, known for his crossover rap hits and his relaxed, affable screen presence; also known as the Fresh Prince.

Will Smith was born Willard Christopher Smith Jr. in PHILADELPHIA, PENNSYLVANIA. While still in high school, he began performing with partner Jeff Townes as DJ Jazzy Jeff & the Fresh Prince, and the two became favorites in the Philadelphia area. Based on this local success, Smith rejected a scholarship from the Massachusetts Institute of Technology, opting instead for a show business career. By 1988, driven by the hit song "Parents Just Don't Understand," which earned the duo the first Grammy ever given for best RAP performance, their album *He's the DJ, I'm the Rapper* reached double-platinum status—one of the first HIP-HOP albums to do so. A later record, *Homebase* (1991), yielded the smash "Summertime," for which they received a second Grammy for best rap performance.

Smith's recording success led to his transition to television. He was tapped to star in the situation comedy *The Fresh Prince of Bel Air*, which ran from 1990 to 1996. And his success on the small screen led Smith to motion pictures, beginning with a drama about teen runaways, *Where the Day Takes You* (1992). His first high-profile dramatic role came in *Six Degrees of Separation* (1993), in which Smith played a gay con man who claims to be the son of American actor SIDNEY POITIER, a role for which he received critical praise.

Tall, wholesomely handsome, and easygoing, Smith had earned a wide-ranging audience among music and film fans by the late 1990s. His 1997 musical release *Big Willie Style* spawned multiple hit songs, including "Gettin' Jiggy Wit It," which won Smith his first solo Grammy, "Miami," and "Just the Two of Us." The latter song celebrates Smith's first son, Willard C. "Trey" Smith III, the child of his first marriage, to Sheree Zampino. Smith became a movie star based on the popularity of such hits as *Bad Boys* (1995), *Independence Day* (1996), and

Men in Black (1997). He followed these with starring roles in films such as *Enemy of the State* (1998) and *The Legend of Bagger Vance* (2000). His performance as boxer MUHAMMAD ALI in *Ali* (2001) earned him an Academy Award nomination for best actor. Smith is currently one of Hollywood's most sought-after and highly paid leading men. He earned twenty million dollars apiece, plus a percentage of the gross, for *Men in Black II* (2002), and *Bad Boys II* (2003). Smith, who continues to record, released the album *Born to Reign* in 2002. Smith's second wife is actress Jada Pinkett Smith, with whom he has a son, Jaden, and a daughter, Willow.

See also Film, Blacks in American; Music, African American.

Smith, William Gardner

1927–1974

American novelist whose work affirms a uniquely black artistry within the larger community.

William Gardner Smith spent much of his adult life as an exile, living in Paris and, for a time, in GHANA. While writing for black periodicals in the United States and FRANCE, he wrote *Return to Black America* (1970), and four novels, *Last of the Conquerors* (1948), *Anger at Innocence* (1950); *South Street* (1954); and *The Stone Face* (1963), all of which attempt to resolve the tensions between African Americans and a hostile larger society. Smith's project for himself and other black writers was twofold: to harness deep empathy for suffering in the service of expressing profound truth, but to resist a persistent artistic victimization of blacks, which ended only in artistic ineffectiveness. Smith's work resembles that of other black writers of the 1940s and 1950s, including RICHARD WRIGHT, JAMES BALDWIN, and ANN PETRY, who depicted the conflicts between the artist and his or her society, and specifically between the black artist trying to establish a name in a largely white society unwilling to recognize black artistic achievements. Although his own work found only a relatively small audience, Smith's concerns anticipate more recent developments in AFRICAN AMERICAN LITERATURE.

Bibliography

Hodges, Leroy S. *Portrait of an Expatriate: William Gardner Smith.* Greenwood Press, 1985.

Robert Fay

Smith, Willie ("the Lion")

1897–1973

African American jazz pianist and composer.

Born in Goshen, New York, Willie "the Lion" Smith was raised in NEWARK, NEW JERSEY, by his mother and his stepfather. By age fifteen he was playing the piano professionally in local clubs and parties. Smith was an innovator in the "stride" style of JAZZ piano, which features a strong pumping line in the left hand.

As early as 1921 Smith was making records, having performed in the backup band for MAMIE SMITH's "Crazy Blues." Although less well known than his contemporaries JAMES P. JOHNSON and FATS WALLER, Smith influenced musicians, most notably DUKE ELLINGTON. Smith's career surged in the 1950s and 1960s, and he recorded extensively. He published his autobiography, *Music on My Mind,* in 1964.

Bibliography

O'Meally, Robert. *The Jazz Cadence of American Culture.* Columbia University Press, 1998.

Robert Fay

Smith, Willie Mae Ford

1906?–1994

American gospel singer and preacher who contributed to the organized growth and development of gospel music.

Willie Mae Ford Smith's involvement with the world of GOSPEL MUSIC started early; the daughter of the deacon of a Baptist Church, she sang in church as a child. As a teen she was the lead vocalist in a gospel quartet she formed with her sisters. The group performed to great acclaim at the National Baptist Convention of 1922.

Smith was ordained as a minister in 1926, but as a woman was forbidden to preach in the BAPTIST CHURCH, an edict that prompted her departure from that church in later years. In 1932, along with THOMAS A. DORSEY and SALLIE MARTIN, Smith formed the National Convention of Gospel Choirs and Choruses, an establishment credited with the nationwide popularization and development of gospel music. She then took on a post as the director of the National Convention Soloists Bureau, where she was charged with teaching and mentoring young gospel singers.

Departing from the Baptist Church in 1939, Smith joined the Holiness Church of God Apostolic, and began to make fewer stage performances, focusing instead on singing principally at religious gatherings. It was at these performances where Smith's trademark "sermonette," a short, spoken statement preceding the song, gained fame.

In spite of the fact that she never focused on developing a professional recording career, Smith's impact on the world of gospel music remains unparalleled. Her protégés include MAHALIA JACKSON, the O'Neal twins, Martha Bass, and Delois Barret Campbell. The documentary *Say Amen, Somebody* celebrated Smith's life and contributions to gospel music. On February 4, 1994, Willie Mae Ford Smith died in St. Louis.

Aaron Myers

Snaër, Samuel, Jr.

1835–1900?

African American musician, composer, and orchestra conductor.

Samuel Snaër was born in NEW ORLEANS, LOUISIANA. His father was an organist in one of the white churches of the city; the younger Snaër served in a similar position as organist for Saint Mary's Italian Church for many years. A teacher of violin and piano, he played with talent a dozen different musical instruments, among them the violin, violoncello, piano, and organ. He was unsurpassed as a violoncellist. According to historian RODOLPHE DESDUNES, Snaër "was perhaps a greater musical savant than was Macarty," one of his leading contemporaries.

Snaër, like many men of genius, had a rather contradictory nature, and for this reason he confused many who witnessed his actions in different situations. He was of an easygoing, amiable disposition, careless with his manuscripts, not very energetic in seeking publishers for his music, and those manuscripts that were returned to him after careless hand-to-hand journeys among friends were later consigned to the bottom of his trunk, to oblivion and insects. Both of his biographers, JAMES MONROE TROTTER and Desdunes, bemoaned his extreme modesty and his lack of caution in lending his manuscripts. Desdunes, however, while admitting his musical genius, says that he never became prominent in his profession, and that long before his death his indolence made him forgotten as the musical genius that he really was. On the other hand, Trotter, who wrote while Snaër was still living, spoke of him as a brilliant pianist, a skillful performer on the violin and violoncello, and an esteemed teacher of violin and piano. Both of these biographers, however, seemed to sense the fact that racial difficulties had hurt this man who had a beautiful tenor voice but would not sing and who was too indifferent to court the attention of music publishers. His very environment produced in him a resignation to apathy and indifference during his later years.

In 1853, when only eighteen years of age, Snaër composed his "Sous sa Fenêtre, paroles de L. P. Canonge," published by Louis Grunewald in 1866. During that same year Grunewald also published his "Le Chant du Départ, paroles de A. Garreau," of which two editions were issued. His "Rappele-Toi, paroles de A. Musset," was published by Grunewald in 1865. The words to all of these songs seem to have been written by white men. Canonge was a prominent theatrical manager of his day, and Armand Garreau was a prominent writer and beloved tutor of many young black people. Then followed *Grazielle* (unpublished manuscript), for full orchestra, "Le Bohémien" (1877?), and "Le Chant des Canotiers" (unpublished manuscript)—the last probably of folk origin. These compositions were followed by a large number of polkas, mazurkas, quadrilles, and waltzes. Like most composers' popular compositions of that day, Snaër's were based on love, Carnival, and other romantic themes, but his close connection as church organist introduced the more solemn note found in many of his masses. Lengthy excerpts from his *Gloria* (unpublished manuscript) and *Agnus Dei* (unpublished manuscript), each composed for three voices, are reproduced in Trotter's *Music and Some Highly Musical People* (1878).

Despite his timidity and retiring disposition, Snaër sometimes blazed forth like a star of the first magnitude. One of these occasions was during a benefit concert for Louise De Mortié's orphanage, when he led his own orchestra in the opening number on the program, an overture that he had composed. Some of the finest free blacks that the city had produced were in attendance. The Orleans Theater was filled and a group of prominent white Northern "adventurers" were present in imposing array. On this night of May 10, 1865, before a vast audience, Snaër returned to the stage to conduct his orchestra in Edmond Dédé's *Quasimodo* Symphony (1865). It was a galaxy of musical stars: when VICTOR-EUGÈNE MACARTY appeared at the piano it was later described as a musical triumph. When it was Basile Barès's turn to take the stage he "held the house in rapture" with the playing of two of his own compositions: "The Magic Belles" (1865?) and "The Fusées Musicales" (1865?). In 1877, on the night of October 14 when a "Grand Vocal and Instrumental Concert" was presented at the Masonic Hall, St. Peter and St. Claude Streets, Snaër's "Le Bohémien" was included in the program. Said Trotter: "'Le Bohémien' is one of several of Professor Snaër's pieces that show him to be a writer of fine abilities." Snaër's facility in composing was matched by his facility in remembering his scores. Twenty-six years after he had composed "Sous sa Fenêtre," and without having seen the score for many years, he could sit down and write it out, note for note. He could recall equally well each of his compositions, even those of an elaborate and difficult character. He once wrote from memory a great solemn mass that he had composed several years earlier. In later years he became interested in chess playing and left a reputation as a player of merit.

From *Dictionary of American Negro Biography* by Rayford W. Logan and Michael R. Winston, editors. Copyright © 1982 by Rayford W. Logan and Michael R. Winston. Reprinted by permission of W. W. Norton & Company, Inc.

Marcus B. Christian

Snipes, Wesley

1962–

African American actor known for his versatility, Wesley Snipes has appeared in a wide range of film genres, including drama, comedy, sport, and action.

Born in Orlando, Florida, Snipes grew up in the Bronx, New York. He began acting early, appearing in his first off-Broadway stage production, *The Me Nobody Knows*, at the age of twelve. Deciding on a career in show business, he studied dance, singing, and drama at the High School of the Performing Arts in New York until 1977, when his family returned to Orlando. Continuing to study DRAMA, Snipes earned a scholarship to the State University of New York at Purchase and graduated in 1984 with a B.A. degree in theater arts. After appearing in the Broadway show *The Boys of Winter* (1985), he soon moved to on-screen roles.

Since his transition from stage to film, Snipes has played a wide range of characters, but he remains most well known for his roles in comedy and action films. Snipes gained early celebrity by playing a high school football player in *Wildcats* (1986) and the fleet-footed Willie Mays Hayes in *Major League* (1989). His widest early exposure, however, was in his role as a street tough in Michael Jackson's 1987 music video "Bad." Roles in the comedy *White Men Can't Jump* (1992) and the action-adventure film *Passenger 57* (1992), both box office hits, propelled Snipes into bona fide Hollywood stardom. He then played a wide variety of characters, including a Los Angeles police officer investigating a Japanese corporation in *Rising Sun* (1993), drag queen Noxeema Jackson in *To Wong Foo, Thanks for Everything, Julie Newmar* (1995), and a human-vampire hybrid in the live-action version of the comic book *Blade* (1998). Other action films Snipes starred in include *Demolition Man* (1993), *Drop Zone* (1994), and *Murder at 1600* (1997).

Snipes's work in popular action and comedy films has obscured his work in more dramatic fare. He received critical acclaim for roles in *King of New York* (1990) and *New Jack City* (1991), as well as in two films by actor-director SPIKE LEE—*Mo' Better Blues* (1990) and *Jungle Fever* (1991). Snipes also appeared in some lesser-known but well-respected dramas, such as *The Waterdance* (1992). In addition, he received a CableACE award for his portrayal of a soldier in the HBO series *Vietnam War Story* (1988).

In 1996 Snipes moved behind the scenes when he founded the Amen Ra production company. One of the company's first efforts was the documentary *John Henrik Clarke: A Great and Mighty Walk* (1996), about the African American writer and educator. Amen Ra also produced the directorial debut of writer MAYA ANGELOU, *Down in the Delta* (1998), and the science-fiction film *Futuresport* (1998), which was made for television.

Snipes is divorced and has a son, Jelani, born in 1988. Snipes is an avid student of martial arts, especially the Brazilian fight and dance form known as CAPOEIRA. He remains one of Hollywood's top leading men. His recent films include the *Blade* sequels, *Blade II* (2002) and *Blade: Trinity* (2004).

See also Film, Blacks in American; Jackson, Michael, and the Jackson Family.

Snoop Doggy Dogg

1972–

The best-known figure in gangsta rap, a genre that chronicles in explicit detail life in and around the gangs of urban America.

Born Calvin Broadus in LOS ANGELES, CALIFORNIA, Snoop Doggy Dogg's career began suddenly, when Dr. Dre, recently retired from NIGGAZ WITH ATTITUDE (N.W.A.), asked Snoop to RAP on the title song from the soundtrack to the film *Deep Cover*. The track, which described the murder of an undercover cop, was an underground hit, and Snoop joined the roster of Dre's Death Row Records.

In 1992, Dr. Dre released his solo debut, *The Chronic*, which featured Snoop's slow, nasal drawl on tracks like "Nuthin' but a 'G' Thang." *The Chronic* album achieved multi-platinum success, and Snoop capitalized on his sudden fame with *Doggystyle* (1993)—the most highly anticipated debut in HIP-HOP history. Tracks like "Doggy Dogg World" and "Gin and Juice" exemplified the feel-good side of Snoop's "Long Beach Sound," while "Murder Was the Case" prefigured Snoop's subsequent trial (and acquittal) in a murder case.

In 1996 Dr. Dre quit Death Row, leaving Marion "Suge" Knight to run the label. Snoop appeared on tracks by label mates Tha Dogg Pound and TUPAC SHAKUR, but the absence of his mentor, Dr. Dre, was sorely felt. *Tha Doggfather* (1996), Snoop's sophomore effort, garnered respectable sales but negative reviews. On the eve of the album's release, Shakur was murdered; a few months later, Knight was indicted for probation violations. With Death Row in disarray, Snoop made an acrimonious public split. He has since recorded with the New Orleans–based No Limit Records and with Priority Records, his current label. His recent albums include *Top Dogg* (1999), *The Last Meal* (2000), and *Paid Tha Cost to Be Da Boss* (2002). Snoop Dogg, as he is now called, has also worked onscreen. He has been a guest cohost on the television show *Jimmy Kimmel Live*, and appeared in the film *Starsky & Hutch* (2004).

See also Film, Blacks in American; Music, African American; Television and African Americans.

Andrew Du Bois

Sobhuza II

1899–1982

Ngwenyama **(paramount chief or king) of Swaziland (1921–1982).**

Following the death in 1899 of his father, King Bhunu, Sobhuza II was named heir to the throne when only six months old. Labotsibeni, his grandmother, ruled on his behalf until he was twenty-two. Studying first under a South African tutor, Sobhuza completed secondary education at the National School at Zombodze, which was built by his grandmother so that Sobhuza would not be forced to attend missionary schools. Shortly after his formal induction as ngwenyama in December 1921, Sobhuza petitioned King George V of GREAT BRITAIN for the return of Swazi lands that had been allocated to British settlers in the 1907 Partitions Proclamation. When diplomatic efforts failed he initiated legal proceedings, which were also unsuccessful. During WORLD WAR II (1939–1945) he managed to gain some land concessions from the British in exchange for Swazi support for the British war effort. When negotiations with the British for independence began in 1964, Sobhuza founded the Imbokodvo National Movement (INM), a traditionalist political party that swept parliamentary elections in 1964. The INM convinced the British to redraft a Swazi constitution vesting executive power in the ngwenyama. Following independence in September 1968 the INM continued to dominate the legislature. Sobhuza suspended the constitution in 1973, replacing it in

1978 with a new constitution. The new constitution consolidated his powers and replaced the legislative council with the Libandla, an advisory body without legislative powers and composed of members nominated by local councils. An economic modernizer, Sobhuza exploited Swaziland's mineral and forest resources, encouraged tourism, and established the nation as an important regional power. Resisting democracy as "un-Swazi," he was an extremely popular autocrat. Sobhuza died in 1982 after ruling for sixty-one years, making him the longest-reigning monarch in the world. He left more than 100 wives and 200 children, and was succeeded by his second-youngest son, MSWATI III.

Sobukwe, Robert Mangaliso

1924–1978

South African nationalist leader and a founder of the Pan-Africanist Congress (PAC).

Robert Mangaliso Sobukwe joined the Youth League of the AFRICAN NATIONAL CONGRESS (ANC) while still a student at the University of Fort Hare, in Alice, in what is now EASTERN CAPE province. In 1952, when teaching in Standerton in present-day MPUMALANGA province, he was dismissed for his participation in the ANC's Defiance Campaign against APARTHEID, the South African government's system of racial separation. He then obtained a post at the University of Witwatersrand in JOHANNESBURG, teaching in the Bantu studies department.

Sobukwe became increasingly politically militant and broke with the ANC in 1958. In 1959 he was one of the founders of the PAN-AFRICANIST CONGRESS (PAC), and he served as its first president. He argued that blacks should not rely upon white allies. The PAC appealed to black nationalism, and, in contrast to the ANC, it saw the future SOUTH AFRICA as a black rather than a multiracial state.

Sobukwe organized nationwide demonstrations against the restrictive PASS LAWS on March 21, 1960. During the demonstration in the township of SHARPEVILLE, police panicked and fired on the demonstrators, killing sixty-nine blacks. Sobukwe and other leaders were arrested, the PAC and the ANC were banned, and Sobukwe was sentenced to three years in jail. At the end of his three-year term he was not released but was transferred to the maximum-security prison at ROBBEN ISLAND. The government was so fearful of his influence that a special legal amendment known as the "Sobukwe clause" was passed in order to make it possible to jail him indefinitely without trial, which the government did for the next six years. There were widespread international protests at this treatment. In 1969 Sobukwe was released but was put under a banning order, meaning he was restricted to his home area of Kimberley, in what is now NORTHERN CAPE province. He was not allowed to attend meetings, and he could not be quoted anywhere in South Africa. Sobukwe spent his last years practicing law in Kimberley.

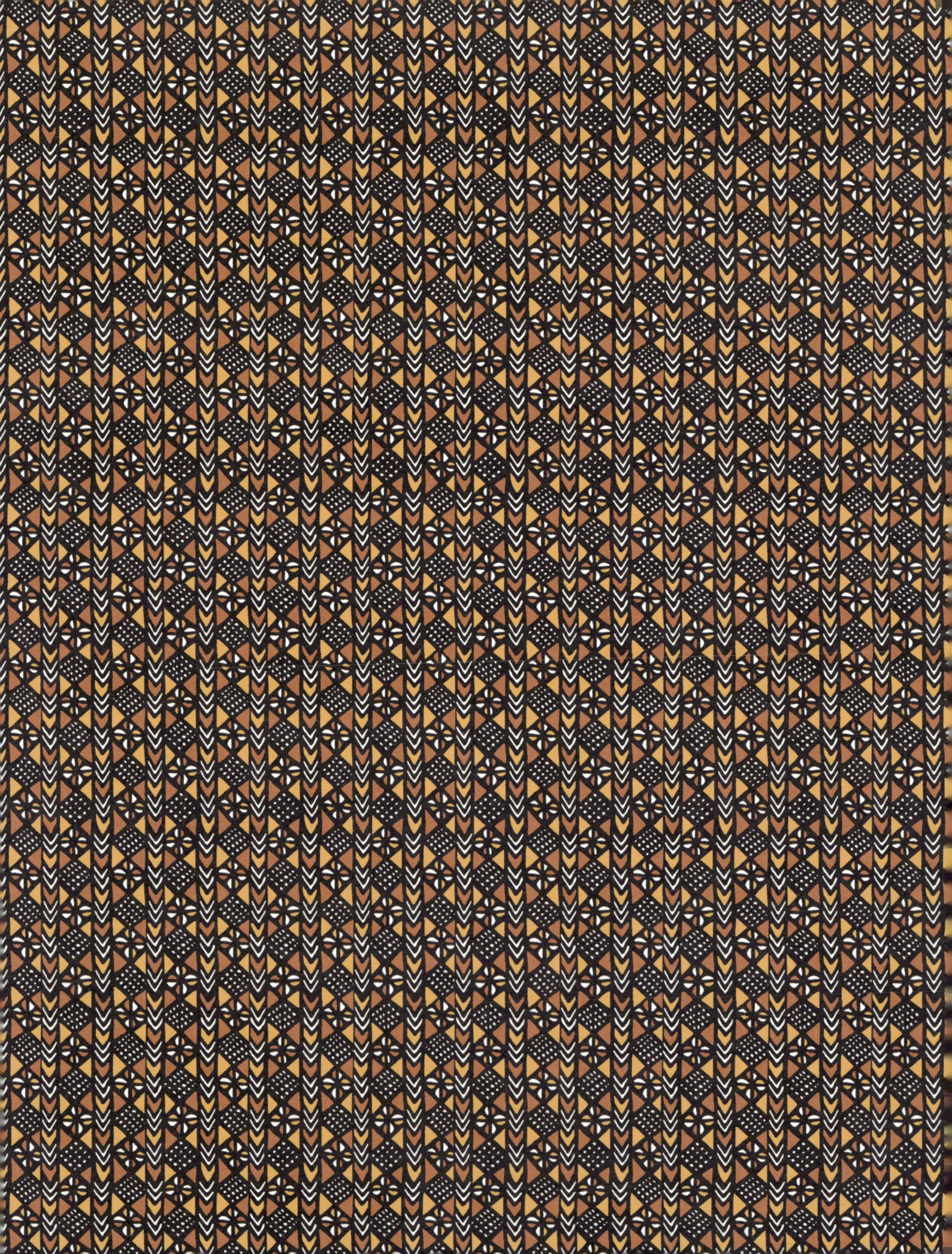